Official 2013
National Football League
Record
& Fact Book

NATIONAL FOOTBALL LEAGUE
345 Park Avenue, New York, N.Y. 10154 (212) 450-2000. NFL Internet Address: http://www.NFL.com

Printed in the United States of America.

A National Football League Book.

Compiled by the NFL Communications Department and Seymour Siwoff, Elias Sports Bureau.
Statistics by Elias Sports Bureau.

Edited by Jon Zimmer, NFL Communications Department, and Matt Marini. Layout by William Tham.
Cover photo: Super Bowl Most Valuable Player Joe Flacco of the Super Bowl XLVII champion Baltimore Ravens.
Cover photography by David Stluka, AP Images. Design by NFL Creative.

Time Home Entertainment Inc.
1271 Avenue of the Americas, New York, N.Y. 10020
Manufactured in the United States of America.
First printing, July 2013.
10 9 8 7 6 5 4 3 2 1

TABLE OF CONTENTS

2013 SCHEDULE AND NOTE CALENDAR

All times local. Dates and times subject to change.
Nationally televised games indicated by network in parentheses.

Sunday, August 4	Hall of Fame Game at Canton, Ohio	
	Dallas _____ vs. Miami _____	(NBC) 8:00

PRESEASON/WEEK 1

Thursday, August 8	Cincinnati_____ at Atlanta_____	(ESPN) 8:00
	Baltimore _____ at Tampa Bay _____	7:30
	St. Louis _____ at Cleveland _____	8:00
	Washington _____ at Tennessee _____	7:00
	Denver _____ at San Francisco _____	6:00
	Seattle _____ at San Diego _____	7:00
Friday, August 9	New York Jets _____ at Detroit _____	7:30
	Miami _____ at Jacksonville _____	7:30
	New England _____ at Philadelphia _____	7:30
	Chicago _____ at Carolina_____	8:00
	Arizona _____ at Green Bay _____	7:00
	Houston _____ at Minnesota _____	7:00
	Kansas City _____ at New Orleans _____	7:00
	Dallas _____ at Oakland _____	7:00
Saturday, August 10	New York Giants _____ at Pittsburgh _____	7:30
Sunday, August 11	Buffalo _____ at Indianapolis _____	1:30

PRESEASON/WEEK 2

Thursday, August 15	San Diego _____ at Chicago _____	(ESPN) 7:00
	Carolina _____ at Philadelphia _____	7:30
	Atlanta _____ at Baltimore _____	7:30
	Detroit _____ at Cleveland _____	7:30
Friday, August 16	Tampa Bay _____ at New England _____	(FOX) 8:00
	Minnesota _____ at Buffalo _____	7:00
	San Francisco _____ at Kansas City _____	7:00
	Oakland _____ at New Orleans _____	7:00
Saturday, August 17	Dallas _____ at Arizona _____	1:30
	Tennessee _____ at Cincinnati _____	7:00
	Jacksonville _____ at New York Jets _____	7:30
	Miami _____ at Houston _____	7:00
	Green Bay _____ at St. Louis _____	7:00
	Denver _____ at Seattle _____	7:00
Sunday, August 18	Indianapolis _____ at New York Giants _____	(FOX) 7:00
Monday, August 19	Pittsburgh _____ at Washington _____	(ESPN) 8:00

PRESEASON/WEEK 3

Thursday, August 22	Carolina _____ at Baltimore _____	(ESPN) 8:00
	New England _____ at Detroit _____	7:30
Friday, August 23	Seattle _____ at Green Bay _____	(CBS) 7:00
	Chicago _____ at Oakland _____	7:00
Saturday, August 24	St. Louis _____ at Denver _____	(CBS) 6:00
	Buffalo _____ at Washington _____	4:30
	Cleveland _____ at Indianapolis _____	7:00
	New York Jets _____ at New York Giants _____	7:00
	Philadelphia _____ at Jacksonville _____	7:30
	Tampa Bay _____ at Miami _____	7:30
	Kansas City _____ at Pittsburgh _____	7:30
	Cincinnati _____ at Dallas _____	7:00
	Atlanta _____ at Tennessee _____	7:00
	San Diego _____ at Arizona _____	7:00
Sunday, August 25	New Orleans _____ at Houston _____	(FOX) 3:00
	Minnesota _____ at San Francisco _____	(NBC) 5:00

PRESEASON/WEEK 4

Thursday, August 29	Detroit _____ at Buffalo _____	7:00
	Indianapolis _____ at Cincinnati _____	7:00
	Philadelphia _____ at New York Jets _____	7:00
	Jacksonville _____ at Atlanta _____	7:30
	Pittsburgh _____ at Carolina _____	7:30
	New Orleans _____ at Miami _____	7:30
	New York Giants _____ at New England _____	7:30
	Washington _____ at Tampa Bay _____	7:30
	Cleveland _____ at Chicago _____	7:00
	Houston _____ at Dallas _____	7:00
	Tennessee _____ at Minnesota _____	7:00
	Green Bay _____ at Kansas City _____	7:00
	Baltimore _____ at St. Louis _____	7:00
	Arizona _____ at Denver _____	7:00
	San Francisco _____ at San Diego _____	7:00
	Oakland _____ at Seattle _____	7:00

KICKOFF 2013

KICKOFF WEEKEND

Thursday, September 5	Baltimore _____ at Denver _____	(NBC) 6:30
Sunday, September 8	New England _____ at Buffalo _____	1:00
FOX-TV National Weekend	Seattle _____ at Carolina _____	1:00
	Cincinnati _____ at Chicago _____	12:00
	Miami _____ at Cleveland _____	1:00
	Minnesota _____ at Detroit _____	1:00
	Oakland _____ at Indianapolis _____	1:00
	Kansas City _____ at Jacksonville _____	1:00
	Atlanta _____ at New Orleans _____	12:00
	Tampa Bay _____ at New York Jets _____	1:00
	Tennessee _____ at Pittsburgh _____	1:00
	Arizona _____ at St. Louis _____	3:25
	Green Bay _____ at San Francisco _____	1:25
	New York Giants _____ at Dallas _____	(NBC) 7:30
Monday, September 9	Philadelphia _____ at Washington _____	(ESPN) 7:10
	Houston _____ at San Diego _____	(ESPN) 7:20

SECOND WEEK

Thursday, September 12	New York Jets _____ at New England _____	(NFLN) 8:25
Sunday, September 15	St. Louis _____ at Atlanta _____	1:00
CBS-TV National Weekend	Cleveland _____ at Baltimore _____	1:00
	Carolina _____ at Buffalo _____	1:00
	Minnesota _____ at Chicago _____	12:00
	Washington _____ at Green Bay _____	12:00
	Tennessee _____ at Houston _____	12:00
	Miami _____ at Indianapolis _____	1:00
	Dallas _____ at Kansas City _____	12:00
	San Diego _____ at Philadelphia _____	1:00
	Detroit _____ at Arizona _____	1:05
	New Orleans _____ at Tampa Bay _____	4:05
	Denver _____ at New York Giants _____	4:25
	Jacksonville _____ at Oakland _____	1:25
	San Francisco _____ at Seattle _____	(NBC) 5:30
Monday, September 16	Pittsburgh _____ at Cincinnati _____	(ESPN) 8:40

THIRD WEEK

Thursday, September 19	Kansas City _____ at Philadelphia _____	(NFLN) 8:25
Sunday, September 22	Houston _____ at Baltimore _____	1:00
CBS-TV National Weekend	Green Bay _____ at Cincinnati _____	1:00
	New York Giants _____ at Carolina _____	1:00
	St. Louis _____ at Dallas _____	12:00
	Cleveland _____ at Minnesota _____	12:00
	Tampa Bay _____ at New England _____	1:00
	Arizona _____ at New Orleans _____	12:00
	San Diego _____ at Tennessee _____	12:00
	Detroit _____ at Washington _____	1:00
	Atlanta _____ at Miami _____	4:05
	Buffalo _____ at New York Jets _____	4:25
	Indianapolis _____ at San Francisco _____	1:25
	Jacksonville _____ at Seattle _____	1:25
	Chicago _____ at Pittsburgh _____	(NBC) 8:30
Monday, September 23	Oakland _____ at Denver _____	(ESPN) 6:40

FOURTH WEEK

INTERNATIONAL
SERIES 2013

Open Date: Carolina, Green Bay

Thursday, September 26	San Francisco _____ at St. Louis _____	(NFLN) 7:25
Sunday, September 29	Baltimore _____ at Buffalo _____	1:00
FOX-TV National Weekend	Cincinnati _____ at Cleveland _____	1:00
	Chicago _____ at Detroit _____	1:00
	Seattle _____ at Houston _____	12:00
	Indianapolis _____ at Jacksonville _____	1:00
	New York Giants _____ at Kansas City _____	12:00
	Pittsburgh _____ at Minnesota (London) _____	6:00
	Arizona _____ at Tampa Bay _____	1:00
	New York Jets _____ at Tennessee _____	3:05
	Philadelphia _____ at Denver _____	2:25
	Washington _____ at Oakland _____	1:25
	Dallas _____ at San Diego _____	1:25
	New England _____ at Atlanta _____	(NBC) 8:30
Monday, September 30	Miami _____ at New Orleans _____	(ESPN) 7:40

FIFTH WEEK

Open Date: Minnesota, Pittsburgh, Tampa Bay, Washington

Thursday, October 3	Buffalo _____ at Cleveland _____	(NFLN) 8:25
Sunday, October 6	New Orleans _____ at Chicago _____	12:00
CBS-TV National Weekend	New England _____ at Cincinnati _____	1:00
	Detroit _____ at Green Bay _____	12:00
	Seattle _____ at Indianapolis _____	1:00
	Baltimore _____ at Miami _____	1:00
	Philadelphia _____ at New York Giants _____	1:00
	Jacksonville _____ at St. Louis _____	12:00
	Kansas City _____ at Tennessee _____	12:00
	Carolina _____ at Arizona _____	1:05
	Denver _____ at Dallas _____	3:25
	San Diego _____ at Oakland _____	1:25
	Houston _____ at San Francisco _____	(NBC) 5:30
Monday, October 7	New York Jets _____ at Atlanta _____	(ESPN) 8:40

SIXTH WEEK

Open Date: Atlanta, Miami

Thursday, October 10	New York Giants _____ at Chicago _____	(NFLN) 7:25
Sunday, October 13	Green Bay _____ at Baltimore _____	1:00
FOX-TV National Weekend	Cincinnati _____ at Buffalo _____	1:00
	Detroit _____ at Cleveland _____	1:00
	St. Louis _____ at Houston _____	12:00
	Oakland _____ at Kansas City _____	12:00
	Carolina _____ at Minnesota _____	12:00
	Pittsburgh _____ at New York Jets _____	1:00
	Philadelphia _____ at Tampa Bay _____	1:00
	Jacksonville _____ at Denver _____	2:05
	Tennessee _____ at Seattle _____	1:05
	New Orleans _____ at New England _____	4:25
	Arizona _____ at San Francisco _____	1:25
	Washington _____ at Dallas _____	(NBC) 7:30
Monday, October 14	Indianapolis _____ at San Diego _____	(ESPN) 5:40

SEVENTH WEEK

Open Date: New Orleans, Oakland

Thursday, October 17	Seattle _____ at Arizona _____	(NFLN) 5:25
Sunday, October 20	Tampa Bay _____ at Atlanta _____	1:00
CBS-TV National Weekend	St. Louis _____ at Carolina _____	1:00
	Cincinnati _____ at Detroit _____	1:00
	San Diego _____ at Jacksonville _____	1:00
	Houston _____ at Kansas City _____	12:00
	Buffalo _____ at Miami _____	1:00
	New England _____ at New York Jets _____	1:00
	Dallas _____ at Philadelphia _____	1:00
	Chicago _____ at Washington _____	1:00
	San Francisco _____ at Tennessee _____	3:05
	Cleveland _____ at Green Bay _____	3:25
	Baltimore _____ at Pittsburgh _____	4:25
	Denver _____ at Indianapolis _____	(NBC) 8:30
Monday, October 21	Minnesota _____ at New York Giants _____	(ESPN) 8:40

EIGHTH WEEK

Open Date: Baltimore, Chicago, Houston, Indianapolis, San Diego, Tennessee

Thursday, October 24	Carolina _____ at Tampa Bay _____	(NFLN) 8:25
Sunday, October 27	Dallas _____ at Detroit _____	1:00
FOX-TV National Weekend	San Francisco _____ at Jacksonville (London) _____	5:00
	Cleveland _____ at Kansas City _____	12:00
	Miami _____ at New England _____	1:00
	Buffalo _____ at New Orleans _____	12:00
	New York Giants _____ at Philadelphia _____	1:00
	Pittsburgh _____ at Oakland _____	1:05
	New York Jets _____ at Cincinnati _____	4:05
	Atlanta _____ at Arizona _____	1:25
	Washington _____ at Denver _____	2:25
	Green Bay _____ at Minnesota _____	(NBC) 7:30
Monday, October 28	Seattle _____ at St. Louis _____	(ESPN) 7:40

NINTH WEEK

Open Date: Arizona, Denver, Detroit, Jacksonville, New York Giants, San Francisco

Thursday, October 31	Cincinnati _____ at Miami _____	(NFLN) 8:25
Sunday, November 3	Kansas City _____ at Buffalo _____	1:00
CBS-TV National Weekend	Atlanta _____ at Carolina _____	1:00
	Minnesota _____ at Dallas _____	12:00
	New Orleans _____ at New York Jets _____	1:00
	Tennessee _____ at St. Louis _____	12:00
	San Diego _____ at Washington _____	1:00
	Philadelphia _____ at Oakland _____	1:05
	Tampa Bay _____ at Seattle _____	1:05
	Baltimore _____ at Cleveland _____	4:25
	Pittsburgh _____ at New England _____	4:25
	Indianapolis _____ at Houston _____	(NBC) 7:30
Monday, November 4	Chicago _____ at Green Bay _____	(ESPN) 7:40

TENTH WEEK

Open Date: Cleveland, Kansas City, New England, New York Jets

Thursday, November 7	Washington _____ at Minnesota _____	(NFLN) 7:25
Sunday, November 10	Seattle _____ at Atlanta _____	1:00
FOX-TV National Weekend	Cincinnati _____ at Baltimore _____	1:00
	Detroit _____ at Chicago _____	12:00
	Philadelphia _____ at Green Bay _____	12:00
	St. Louis _____ at Indianapolis _____	1:00
	Oakland _____ at New York Giants _____	1:00
	Buffalo _____ at Pittsburgh _____	1:00
	Jacksonville _____ at Tennessee _____	12:00
	Carolina _____ at San Francisco _____	1:05
	Houston _____ at Arizona _____	2:25
	Denver _____ at San Diego _____	1:25
	Dallas _____ at New Orleans _____	(NBC) 7:30
Monday, November 11	Miami _____ at Tampa Bay _____	(ESPN) 8:40

ELEVENTH WEEK

Open Date: Dallas, St. Louis

Thursday, November 14	Indianapolis _____ at Tennessee _____	(NFLN) 7:25
Sunday, November 17	New York Jets _____ at Buffalo _____	1:00
CBS-TV National Weekend	Baltimore _____ at Chicago _____	12:00
	Cleveland _____ at Cincinnati _____	1:00
	Oakland _____ at Houston _____	12:00
	Arizona _____ at Jacksonville _____	1:00
	San Diego _____ at Miami _____	1:00
	Washington _____ at Philadelphia _____	1:00
	Detroit _____ at Pittsburgh _____	1:00
	Atlanta _____ at Tampa Bay _____	1:00
	Kansas City _____ at Denver _____	2:05
	San Francisco _____ at New Orleans _____	3:25
	Minnesota _____ at Seattle _____	1:25
	Green Bay _____ at New York Giants * _____	(NBC) 8:30
Monday, November 18	New England _____ at Carolina _____	(ESPN) 8:40

Sunday Night Games In Weeks 11-16 Subject to Change

TWELFTH WEEK
Open Date: Buffalo, Cincinnati,
Philadelphia, Seattle

Thursday, November 21	New Orleans _____ at Atlanta _____	(NFLN) 8:25
Sunday, November 24	New York Jets _____ at Baltimore _____	1:00
FOX-TV National Weekend	Pittsburgh _____ at Cleveland _____	1:00
	Tampa Bay _____ at Detroit _____	1:00
	Minnesota _____ at Green Bay _____	12:00
	Jacksonville _____ at Houston _____	12:00
	San Diego _____ at Kansas City _____	12:00
	Carolina _____ at Miami _____	1:00
	Chicago _____ at St. Louis _____	12:00
	Indianapolis _____ at Arizona _____	2:05
	Tennessee _____ at Oakland _____	1:05
	Dallas _____ at New York Giants _____	4:25
	Denver _____ at New England * _____	(NBC) 8:30
Monday, November 25	San Francisco _____ at Washington _____	(ESPN) 8:40

Sunday Night Games In Weeks 11-16 Subject to Change

THIRTEENTH WEEK

NFL THANKSGIVING 2013

Thursday, November 28	Green Bay _____ at Detroit _____	(FOX) 12:30
	Oakland _____ at Dallas _____	(CBS) 3:30
	Pittsburgh _____ at Baltimore _____	(NBC) 8:30
Sunday, December 1	Tampa Bay _____ at Carolina _____	1:00
CBS-TV National Weekend	Jacksonville _____ at Cleveland _____	1:00
	Tennessee _____ at Indianapolis _____	1:00
	Denver _____ at Kansas City _____	12:00
	Chicago _____ at Minnesota _____	12:00
	Miami _____ at New York Jets _____	1:00
	Arizona _____ at Philadelphia _____	1:00
	Atlanta _____ at Buffalo (Toronto) _____	4:05
	St. Louis _____ at San Francisco _____	1:05
	New England _____ at Houston _____	3:25
	Cincinnati _____ at San Diego _____	1:25
	New York Giants _____ at Washington * _____	(NBC) 8:30
Monday, December 2	New Orleans _____ at Seattle _____	(ESPN) 5:40

Sunday Night Games In Weeks 11-16 Subject to Change

FOURTEENTH WEEK

Thursday, December 5	Houston _____ at Jacksonville _____	(NFLN) 8:25
Sunday, December 8	Minnesota _____ at Baltimore _____	1:00
FOX-TV National Weekend	Indianapolis _____ at Cincinnati _____	1:00
	Cleveland _____ at New England _____	1:00
	Oakland _____ at New York Jets _____	1:00
	Carolina _____ at New Orleans _____	12:00
	Detroit _____ at Philadelphia _____	1:00
	Miami _____ at Pittsburgh _____	1:00
	Buffalo _____ at Tampa Bay _____	1:00
	Kansas City _____ at Washington _____	1:00
	Tennessee _____ at Denver _____	2:05
	St. Louis _____ at Arizona _____	2:25
	New York Giants _____ at San Diego _____	1:25
	Seattle _____ at San Francisco _____	1:25
	Atlanta _____ at Green Bay * _____	(NBC) 7:30
Monday, December 9	Dallas _____ at Chicago _____	(ESPN) 7:40

Sunday Night Games In Weeks 11-16 Subject to Change

FIFTEENTH WEEK

Thursday, December 12 San Diego _____ at Denver _____	(NFLN) 6:25
Sunday, December 15 Washington _____ at Atlanta _____	1:00
CBS-TV National Weekend Chicago _____ at Cleveland _____	1:00
Houston _____ at Indianapolis _____	1:00
Buffalo _____ at Jacksonville _____	1:00
New England _____ at Miami _____	1:00
Philadelphia _____ at Minnesota _____	12:00
Seattle _____ at New York Giants _____	1:00
New Orleans _____ at St. Louis _____	12:00
San Francisco _____ at Tampa Bay _____	1:00
Arizona _____ at Tennessee _____	12:00
New York Jets _____ at Carolina _____	4:05
Kansas City _____ at Oakland _____	1:05
Green Bay _____ at Dallas _____	3:25
Cincinnati _____ at Pittsburgh * _____	(NBC) 8:30
Monday, December 16 Baltimore _____ at Detroit _____	(ESPN) 8:40

Sunday Night Games In Weeks 11-16 Subject to Change

SIXTEENTH WEEK

Sunday, December 22 Miami _____ at Buffalo _____	1:00
FOX-TV National Weekend New Orleans _____ at Carolina _____	1:00
Minnesota _____ at Cincinnati _____	1:00
Denver _____ at Houston _____	12:00
Tennessee _____ at Jacksonville _____	1:00
Indianapolis _____ at Kansas City _____	12:00
Cleveland _____ at New York Jets _____	1:00
Chicago _____ at Philadelphia _____	1:00
Tampa Bay _____ at St. Louis _____	12:00
Dallas _____ at Washington _____	1:00
New York Giants _____ at Detroit _____	4:05
Arizona _____ at Seattle _____	1:05
Pittsburgh _____ at Green Bay _____	3:25
Oakland _____ at San Diego _____	1:25
New England _____ at Baltimore* _____	(NBC) 8:30
Monday, December 23 Atlanta _____ at San Francisco _____	(ESPN) 5:40

Sunday Night Games In Weeks 11-16 Subject to Change

SEVENTEENTH WEEK

Sunday, December 29 Carolina _____ at Atlanta _____	1:00
CBS-TV and FOX-TV National Weekend Green Bay _____ at Chicago _____	12:00
Baltimore _____ at Cincinnati _____	1:00
Philadelphia _____ at Dallas _____	12:00
Jacksonville _____ at Indianapolis _____	1:00
New York Jets _____ at Miami _____	1:00
Detroit _____ at Minnesota _____	12:00
Buffalo _____ at New England _____	1:00
Tampa Bay _____ at New Orleans _____	12:00
Washington _____ at New York Giants _____	1:00
Cleveland _____ at Pittsburgh _____	1:00
Houston _____ at Tennessee _____	12:00
San Francisco _____ at Arizona _____	2:25
Denver _____ at Oakland _____	1:25
Kansas City _____ at San Diego _____	1:25
St. Louis _____ at Seattle _____	1:25

Sunday Night Game In Week 17 TBD

PLAYOFFS

Wild Card Playoff Games
Site Priorities

Two Wild Card teams (division non-champions with best two records) from each conference and the division champions with the third and fourth-best record in each conference will enter the first round of the playoffs. The division champion with the third-best record will play host to the Wild Card team with the second-best record. The division champion with the fourth-best record will play host to the Wild Card team with the best record. There are no restrictions on intra-division games.

Saturday, January 4, 2014   American Football Conference

_____ at _____ (NBC)

National Football Conference

_____ at _____ (NBC)

Sunday, January 5, 2014   American Football Conference

_____ at _____ (CBS)

National Football Conference

_____ at _____ (FOX)

Divisional Playoff Games
Site Priorities

In each conference, the two division champions with the highest won-lost-tied percentage during the regular season will play host to the Wild Card winners. The division champion with the best record in each conference is assured of playing the lowest seeded Wild Card survivor. There are no restrictions on intra-division games.

Saturday, January 11, 2014   American Football Conference

_____ at _____ (CBS)

National Football Conference

_____ at _____ (FOX)

Sunday, January 12, 2014   American Football Conference

_____ at _____ (CBS)

National Football Conference

_____ at _____ (FOX)

Championship Games
Site Priorities for
Championship Games

The home teams will be the surviving playoff winners with the highest seeds. A Wild Card team cannot play host unless two Wild Card teams are in the game, in which case the Wild Card team that was seeded highest in the first round of the playoffs will be the home team.

Sunday, January 19, 2014   American Football Conference

_____ at _____ (CBS)

National Football Conference

_____ at _____ (FOX)

Pro Bowl

Sunday, January 26, 2014   Pro Bowl at Aloha Stadium, Honolulu, Hawaii

_____ vs. _____ (NBC)

Super Bowl XLVIII

Sunday, February 2, 2014   Super Bowl XLVIII at MetLife Stadium, New York/New Jersey

_____ vs. _____ (FOX)

2013 NATIONALLY TELEVISED GAMES
All times ET

Thursday, Sept. 5	Baltimore at Denver (NBC)	8:30
Sunday, Sept. 8	N.Y. Giants at Dallas (NBC)	8:30
Monday, Sept. 9	Philadelphia at Washington (ESPN)	7:10
	Houston at San Diego (ESPN)	10:20
Thursday, Sept. 12	N.Y. Jets at New England (NFL Network)	8:25
Sunday, Sept. 15	San Francisco at Seattle (NBC)	8:30
Monday, Sept. 16	Pittsburgh at Cincinnati (ESPN)	8:40
Thursday, Sept. 19	Kansas City at Philadelphia (NFL Network)	8:25
Sunday, Sept. 22	Chicago at Pittsburgh (NBC)	8:30
Monday, Sept. 23	Oakland at Denver (ESPN)	8:40
Thursday, Sept. 26	San Francisco at St. Louis (NFL Network)	8:25
Sunday, Sept. 29	New England at Atlanta (NBC)	8:30
Monday, Sept. 30	Miami at New Orleans (ESPN)	8:40
Thursday, Oct. 3	Buffalo at Cleveland (NFL Network)	8:25
Sunday, Oct. 6	Houston at San Francisco (NBC)	8:30
Monday, Oct. 7	N.Y. Jets at Atlanta (ESPN)	8:40
Thursday, Oct. 10	N.Y. Giants at Chicago (NFL Network)	8:25
Sunday, Oct. 13	Washington at Dallas (NBC)	8:30
Monday, Oct. 14	Indianapolis at San Diego (ESPN)	8:40
Thursday, Oct. 17	Seattle at Arizona (NFL Network)	8:25
Sunday, Oct. 20	Denver at Indianapolis (NBC)	8:30
Monday, Oct. 21	Minnesota at N.Y. Giants (ESPN)	8:40
Thursday, Oct. 24	Carolina at Tampa Bay (NFL Network)	8:25
Sunday, Oct. 27	Green Bay at Minnesota (NBC)	8:30
Monday, Oct. 28	Seattle at St. Louis (ESPN)	8:40
Thursday, Oct. 31	Cincinnati at Miami (NFL Network)	8:25
Sunday, Nov. 3	Indianapolis at Houston (NBC)	8:30
Monday, Nov. 4	Chicago at Green Bay (ESPN)	8:40
Thursday, Nov. 7	Washington at Minnesota (NFL Network)	8:25
Sunday, Nov. 10	Dallas at New Orleans (NBC)	8:30
Monday, Nov. 11	Miami at Tampa Bay (ESPN)	8:40
Thursday, Nov. 14	Indianapolis at Tennessee (NFL Network)	8:25
Sunday, Nov. 17	Green Bay at N.Y. Giants (NBC)*	8:30
Monday, Nov. 18	New England at Carolina (ESPN)	8:40
Thursday, Nov. 21	New Orleans at Atlanta (NFL Network)	8:25
Sunday, Nov. 24	Denver at New England (NBC)*	8:30
Monday, Nov. 25	San Francisco at Washington (ESPN)	8:40
Thursday, Nov. 28	Green Bay at Detroit (CBS)	12:30
	Oakland at Dallas (FOX)	4:30
	Pittsburgh at Baltimore (NBC)	8:30
Sunday, Dec. 1	N.Y. Giants at Washington (NBC)*	8:30
Monday, Dec. 2	New Orleans at Seattle (ESPN)	8:40
Thursday, Dec. 5	Houston at Jacksonville (NFL Network)	8:25
Sunday, Dec. 8	Atlanta at Green Bay (NBC)*	8:30
Monday, Dec. 9	Dallas at Chicago (ESPN)	8:40
Thursday, Dec. 12	San Diego at Denver (NFL Network)	8:25
Sunday, Dec. 15	Cincinnati at Pittsburgh (NBC)*	8:30
Monday, Dec. 16	Baltimore at Detroit (ESPN)	8:40
Sunday, Dec. 22	New England at Baltimore (NBC)*	8:30
Monday, Dec. 23	Atlanta at San Francisco (ESPN)	8:40
Sunday, Dec. 29	To be determined (NBC)*	8:30

PLAYOFFS

POSTSEASON GAMES

Saturday, January 4	AFC and NFC Wild Card Playoffs (NBC)	
Sunday, January 5	AFC and NFC Wild Card Playoffs (CBS and FOX)	
Saturday, January 11	AFC and NFC Divisional Playoffs (CBS and FOX)	
Sunday, January 12	AFC and NFC Divisional Playoffs (CBS and FOX)	
Sunday, January 19	AFC and NFC Championship Games (CBS and FOX)	
Sunday, January 26	Pro Bowl (NBC) in Honolulu, Hawaii	
Sunday, February 2	Super Bowl XLVIII in New York/New Jersey (FOX)	

The NFL again will utilize "flexible scheduling" in 2013.

Flexible scheduling moves will be announced at least 12 days before games in Weeks 11-16. In Week 17, the flexible scheduling move will be announced at least six days before the game. Flexible scheduling will ensure quality matchups on Sunday night in those weeks and give "surprise" teams a chance to play their way on to primetime.

2013

Mid-July — Preseason training camps open. Clubs not permitted to open official preseason camp earlier than July 5. Veteran players cannot be required to report earlier than 15 days prior to club's first preseason game.

July 15 — Deadline at 4 P.M., New York time, for any club that designated a Franchise Player to sign such player to a multi-year contract or extension. After this date, the player may sign only a one-year contract with the designating club for the 2013 season, and such contract cannot be extended until after the Club's last regular season game.

July 22 — Signing period ends at 4 P.M., New York time, for Transition Players with outstanding tenders. After this date and through 4 P.M., New York time, on the Tuesday after the 10th regular season weekend, Old Club has exclusive negotiating rights to these players.

July 22# — Signing period ends at 4 P.M., New York time, for Unrestricted Free Agents to whom a June 1 tender was made by Old Club. After this date and through 4 P.M., New York time, on the Tuesday after the 10th regular season weekend, Old Club has exclusive negotiating rights to these players.

#or the first scheduled day of the first NFL training camp, whichever is later.

August 2-4 — Hall of Fame Weekend.

August 5 — Pro Football Hall of Fame Game, Canton, Ohio: Dallas vs. Miami

August 6 — Deadline for players under contract to report to earn a season of free-agency credit.

August 6 — If a Drafted Rookie has not signed with his club by this date, he may not be traded to any other club in 2013.

August 8-11 — First Preseason Weekend.

August 10-14 — Deadline for club to provide written notice to certain unsigned players and the NFLPA of its intent to place them on the Exempt List if they fail to report no later than one day prior to the club's second preseason game. Any player who fails to report prior to the deadline will be ineligible to play or receive compensation for at least three games (preseason or regular season) from the time that he reports.

August 27 — Roster cut-down to maximum of 75 players on Active List by 4 P.M., New York time.

August 28 — All tryouts on this date and for the remainder of the season must be reported to the League office.

August 31 — Roster cut-down to maximum of 53 players on Active/Inactive List by 6 P.M., New York time. Clubs may dress minimum of 43 and maximum of 46 players for each regular-season and postseason game.

August 31 — Simultaneously with the cut-down to 53, clubs that have players in the categories of Active/Physically Unable to Perform or Active/Non-Football Injury or Illness must take one of the following options: Place player on Reserve/Physically Unable to Perform or Reserve/Non-Football Injury or Illness, whichever is applicable; ask waivers; terminate; trade; or continue to count him on Active List.

September 1 — After 12 noon, New York time, clubs may establish a Practice Squad of eight players by signing free agents who do not have an accrued season of free-agency credit or who were on the 46-player Active List for less than nine regular-season games during their only Accrued Season(s). A player cannot participate on the Practice Squad for more than three seasons.

September 4 — All clubs are required to file a personnel (injury) report with their conference information manager by 4:00 P.M., New York time. Reports are to be filed every Wednesday, Thursday and Friday before a regular-season game by 4:00 P.M., New York time (or as soon as possible after the completion of practice). An update must also be reported if there is any change in a player's condition after Friday.

September 5, 8-9 — Regular Season opens.

September 6, 9-10 — Beginning on these dates vested veterans terminated from the Active List or Inactive List (and from Reserve/Injured if the player is placed on Reserve/Injured after the beginning of the regular season) are entitled to receive, after the end of the regular-season schedule, Termination Pay pursuant to the terms of the CBA.

September 24 — Priority on multiple waiver claims is now based on the current season's standing.

October 15 — Beginning the day after the conclusion of the sixth regular-season weekend and continuing through the day after the conclusion of the eleventh regular-season weekend, clubs are permitted to begin practicing players on Reserve/Physically Unable to Perform and Reserve/Non-Football Injury or Illness for a period not to exceed 21 days. Players may be activated during the 21-day practice period or until 4 P.M., New York time, on the day after the conclusion of the 21-day period.

October 29 — All trading ends at 4 P.M., New York time.

October 30 — Players with at least four previous pension-credited seasons are subject to the waiver system for the remainder of the regular season and postseason.

November 12	Signing period ends at 4 P.M., New York time, for Franchise Players who are eligible to receive Offer Sheets.
November 12	Deadline for clubs to sign by 4 P.M., New York time, their unsigned Franchise and Transition Players, including Franchise Players who were eligible to receive Offer Sheets until this date. If still unsigned after this date, such players are prohibited from playing in NFL in 2013.
November 12	Deadline for clubs to sign by 4 P.M., New York time, their Unrestricted Free Agents to whom June 1 tender was made. If still unsigned after this date, such players are prohibited from playing in NFL in 2013.
November 12	Deadline for clubs to sign by 4 P.M., New York time, their Restricted Free Agents to whom June 1 tender was made. If such players remain unsigned, they are prohibited from playing in NFL in 2013.
November 12	Deadline for clubs to sign Drafted players by 4 P.M., New York time. If such players remain unsigned, they are prohibited from playing in NFL in 2013.
November 29	Deadline for reinstatement of players in Reserve List categories of Retired, Did Not Report, and Exclusive Rights, and of players who were placed on Reserve/Left Squad in a previous season.
December 27	Deadline for waiver requests in 2013, except for "special waiver requests," which have a 10-day claiming period, with termination or assignment delayed until after the Super Bowl.
December 30	Clubs may begin signing free-agent players for the 2014 season.

2014

January 4-5	Wild Card Playoff Games.
January 11-12	Divisional Playoff Games.
January 19	AFC and NFC Championship Games.
January 26	Pro Bowl, Honolulu, Hawaii.
February 2	Super Bowl XLVIII, MetLife Stadium, New York-New Jersey.

2015

February 1	Super Bowl XLIX, University of Phoenix Stadium, Glendale, Arizona.

2016

February 7*	Super Bowl L, Levi's Stadium, San Francisco.

2017

February 5*	Super Bowl LI, Reliant Stadium, Houston.

Tentative date

The NFL is online to provide fans and media quick and easy access to all the latest professional football information.

NFL.COM—(http://NFL.com)

NFL.com, the league's year-round home page on the Internet, provides NFL information during the regular season, postseason, and offseason, including:

NEWS/STATS: Up-to-the-minute NFL news and analysis, plus game previews, injury reports, and player and team stats.

GAMEDAY COVERAGE: Live game coverage with instant highlights, play-by-play, scores, and statistics, including graphical drive charts and comprehensive scoreboard that reloads automatically with the latest information.

VIDEO HIGHLIGHTS: The site showcases instant game highlights, NFL Films video highlights of the previous week's games as well as upcoming matchups. Video also supports feature stories and team highlight clips from every game last season. In addition, exclusive NFL Network programming is featured as well as original video content.

SUBSCRIPTION PRODUCTS: Three premium video products, NFL Preseason Live, NFL Game Rewind & NFL Game Pass, that enable fans in the United States and around the world to watch games online, on demand and in HD with DVR controls.

NFL MOBILE PRODUCTS: A suite of mobile products including the premium product "NFL Mobile only from Verizon" that delivers live NFL Network *Thursday Night Football*, NBC's *Sunday Night Football*, ESPN's *Monday Night Football* and NFL RedZone to fans on the go.

NFL.COM/ESPANOL—(http://NFL.com/ESPANOL)

The official Spanish-language site of the NFL provides in depth information on teams and players, and offers highlights of every NFL game in Spanish. The site includes Hispanic player diaries, live radio broadcasts, up-to-date stats, fantasy football, and more.

NFLEVOLUTION.COM—(http://nflevolution.com)

The site outlines the ways the NFL is addressing player health and safety issues. It houses information on the partnerships, programs and initiatives the NFL supports to protect the health of current and former NFL players and to promote safe play and healthy lifestyles at all levels of football and other sports. The site provides information to promote health and safety at all playing levels, including partnerships with USA Football and the Centers for Disease Control and Prevention.

NFLFLAG.COM—(http://nflflag.com)

NFLFLAG.com focuses on the NFL FLAG Program, which is also part of NFL PLAY 60. Boys and girls ages 5-17 nationwide have the opportunity to display their skills in a non-contact environment by playing against their peers in five-on-five flag football games. Our website is a resource for league organizers, coaches, parents and youth organizations who want to start or find a local NFL FLAG league in their area as well as promote a positive experience for their youth participants.

NFLRUSH.COM—(http://www.NFLRUSH.com)

NFLRUSH.com, which is targeted to kids 6-15, is the official kids' website of the National Football League, offering unique customizable content, games, fantasy football for kids, contests, videos, fun daily features on NFL players and information on the NFL's Youth Football programs. NFLRUSH.com also features fun and interactive fitness information as part of the NFL PLAY 60 campaign, which encourages kids to be active for 60 minutes a day. The NFLRUSH ZONE, a role playing game on NFLRUSH.com, is an immersive virtual world where kids are able to create avatars, join their favorite team, play games, chat, watch the NFL RUSH ZONE animated series and compete with friends in safe and fun environment.

USAFOOTBALL.COM—(http://usafootball.com)

USA Football is an independent, non-profit organization which is leading the growth and development of youth, high school and international amateur football. USA Football helps youth and amateur football organizations keep the sport fun, safe, and accessible by offering resources focused on coaching education, league enhancement, officiating development and health and safety awareness. The organization also serves as the designated United States representatives to the International Federation of American Football. Based Indianapolis, USA Football was endowed by the NFL and NFLPA in 2002.

NFL.COM/COMMUNITY—(http://www.nfl.com/community)

This site is dedicated to the community service initiatives of the National Football League and the 32 member clubs. It provides news, history and informative links relating to the NFL's three primary service themes: reversing childhood obesity trends (NFL PLAY 60), the global fight against breast cancer (A Crucial Catch), and honoring the Veterans and men and women of the US Armed Forces (Salute to Service). The NFL also takes pride in recognizing the philanthropic efforts of its players, coaches and staff through the annual presentations of the Walter Payton NFL Man of the Year, Salute to Service, and NFL Teacher of the Year awards.

PROFOOTBALLHOF.COM—(http://profootballhof.com)

Profootballhof.com is the official site of the Pro Football Hall of Fame in Canton, Ohio. In addition to a complete visitor's guide to the Hall, the site features bios, stories and Q & A's with Hall of Fame inductees, a detailed archive of football history, and information on appearances by members of the Hall.

OFFICIAL NFL TEAM SITES

In addition to a dedicated area on NFL.com, all 32 teams have their own Websites, which have separate URLs, and are linked from NFL.com.

Arizona Cardinals (www.azcardinals.com)
Atlanta Falcons (www.atlantafalcons.com)
Baltimore Ravens (www.baltimoreravens.com)
Buffalo Bills (www.buffalobills.com)
Carolina Panthers (www.panthers.com)
Chicago Bears (www.chicagobears.com)
Cincinnati Bengals (www.bengals.com)
Cleveland Browns (www.clevelandbrowns.com)
Dallas Cowboys (www.dallascowboys.com)
Denver Broncos (www.denverbroncos.com)
Detroit Lions (www.detroitlions.com)
Green Bay Packers (www.packers.com)
Houston Texans (www.houstontexans.com)
Indianapolis Colts (www.colts.com)
Jacksonville Jaguars (www.jaguars.com)
Kansas City Chiefs (www.kcchiefs.com)
Miami Dolphins (www.miamidolphins.com)
Minnesota Vikings (www.vikings.com)
New England Patriots (www.patriots.com)
New Orleans Saints (www.neworleanssaints.com)
New York Giants (www.giants.com)
New York Jets (www.newyorkjets.com)
Oakland Raiders (www.raiders.com)
Philadelphia Eagles (www.philadelphiaeagles.com)
Pittsburgh Steelers (www.steelers.com)
St. Louis Rams (www.stlouisrams.com)
San Diego Chargers (www.chargers.com)
San Francisco 49ers (www.49ers.com)
Seattle Seahawks (www.seahawks.com)
Tampa Bay Buccaneers (www.buccaneers.com)
Tennessee Titans (www.titansonline.com)
Washington Redskins (www.redskins.com)

NFL Network provides fans with a network to call their own. Seven days a week, 24 hours a day, 365 days a year, fans turn to NFL Network to receive information and insight straight from the field, team headquarters, league offices and everywhere the NFL is making news.

NFL Network gives fans unprecedented year-round inside access to all NFL events, including the Super Bowl, Playoffs, regular season, preseason, Pro Bowl, Pro Football Hall of Fame induction weekend, NFL Draft, Scouting Combine, Senior Bowl, league meetings, minicamps and training camps.

The 13-game *Thursday Night Football* schedule on NFL Network kicks off Week 2 with the New England Patriots hosting the New York Jets. Emmy-nominated analyst Mike Mayock joins play-by-play announcer Brad Nessler and sideline reporter Alex Flanagan for every *Thursday Night Football* game.

In addition, NFL Network is the only place on television for fans to view NFL games outside their initial live airings. From original broadcast versions of past Super Bowls, in-week replays of current games, original network telecasts of classic NFL regular season and postseason games, to every preseason game — NFL Network is truly the year-round destination for football fans. NFL Network is currently in more than 72 million homes and has carriage agreements with each of the country's largest television providers. If your provider doesn't currently offer NFL Network, please call (866) NFL-NETWORK.

NFL.com and NFL Mobile offer written content, exclusive video features, live streaming of NFL Network on NFL Mobile from Verizon, and much more, ensuring that the football fan is never far away from the NFL.

KEY PROGRAMMING

EXCLUSIVE LIVE PRIMETIME GAMES
NFL Network's expanded 13-game, regular-season Thursday Night primetime schedule kicks off in high definition on September 12. Each game, at 8:00 PM ET, will be preceded by a two-hour pregame show and followed by a live post-game show.

NFL TOTAL ACCESS
NFL Network's signature show is the football show of record. *NFL Total Access* is uniquely structured to see the game through the participants' eyes, airing at 7:00 PM ET Monday through Saturday. Covering all 32 teams, *NFL Total Access* features interviews with players, coaches and other key league personnel.

NFL AM
Wake up to the NFL on NFL Network with *NFL AM* Monday through Friday at 6:00 AM ET. The four-hour show discusses and debates all of the NFL news, and features guests from around the league.

FIRST ON THE FIELD
First on the Field returns this season, kicking off at 7:00 AM ET each Sunday, providing the first look at the day's NFL action.

NFL GAMEDAY MORNING
NFL GameDay Morning is the most comprehensive pregame show on the air Sundays at 9:00 AM ET during the regular season and playoffs, providing fans with the news and notes, as well as live reports from around the league.

NFL GAMEDAY SCOREBOARD
After Sunday's early games conclude, *NFL GameDay Scoreboard* takes viewers around the league for post-game press conferences and game highlights. *NFL GameDay Scoreboard* airs at 4:00 PM ET on Sundays and continues through the Sunday afternoon games.

NFL GAMEDAY HIGHLIGHTS
Following the late afternoon games, *NFL GameDay Highlights* analyzes the events of the day with highlights from all completed games, expert commentary, on-field interviews and postgame press conferences.

NFL GAMEDAY FINAL
After each Sunday's final game, *NFL GameDay Final* delivers comprehensive coverage of the day's action at 11:30 PM ET. The 90-minute show features highlights, post-game press conferences, on-field interviews, analysis and more in wrapping up each NFL Sunday.

NFL REPLAY
NFL games will be re-aired with the original television announcers and cameras. This offering features the most exciting games each week in an abbreviated format (eliminating halftime and other non-critical elements), and includes enhancements to each broadcast such as additional camera angles, sideline sound and postgame interviews.

PLAYBOOK
NFL Network uses the "all 22" game film watched each week by coaches and players to present football's ultimate chalkboard show. *Playbook*, produced at NFL Films, offers 60-minute strategy sessions with NFL Network analysts, who focus on each week's key matchups and discuss technique and game planning with coaches and players.

THE TOP 100: PLAYERS OF 2013
The Top 100 is the annual series which sparks wide debate each offseason on NFL Network. Current players vote for their peers to compile a list of the top 100 playmakers today, counting down from 100 to 1 with 10 players featured in each episode.

AMERICA'S GAME
The Emmy Award-winning original series continues its profiles of Super Bowl champions with the 2012 Baltimore Ravens.

A FOOTBALL LIFE
The two-time Emmy-nominated *A Football Life* biography series returns for a third season on NFL Network. The NFL Films-produced series offers a look inside the untold stories of NFL icons.

NFL's TOP 10
Putting a fresh twist on the countdown genre, *NFL's Top 10* is a fast-paced series that provides an irreverent look at some of the most intriguing subjects in the NFL, creating and debating a top ten list for each category. Each 60-minute episode counts down from No. 10 to the top ranking in each category.

SOUND FX
The sounds of the game that only NFL Films can capture – with exclusive on-field and sideline microphone access – will be featured on the Emmy award-winning *Sound FX*.

PRESEASON GAMES
NFL Network is the only place on television where fans can view all 65 NFL preseason games in high-definition.

Log on to www.NFL.com/NFLnetwork for more information on NFL Network.

SCHEDULING FORMULA

The NFL expanded to 32 teams in 2002 with the addition of the Houston Texans. In addition, the NFL realigned for the first time since 1970—into eight divisions of four teams each—and the scheduling formula that was introduced guarantees for the first time that all teams play each other on a regular, rotating basis. Although the number of teams has increased to 32, the number of playoff teams remains the same at 12.

Under the NFL scheduling formula, every team within a division plays 16 games as follows:

- Home and away against its three division opponents (6 games).
- The four teams from another division within its conference on a rotating three-year cycle (4 games).
- The four teams from a division in the other conference on a rotating four-year cycle (4 games).
- Two intraconference games based on the prior year's standings (2 games). These games will match a first-place team against the first-place teams in the two same-conference divisions the team is not scheduled to play that season. The second-place, third-place, and fourth-place teams in a conference will be matched in the same way each year.

The schedule format takes each team through a cycle of games—home and away—against every other team in the league. From 2002-2009, every team played every other team at least twice—once home and once away. After the 2008 season, a decision was made to continue with the same rotation in 2010 and beyond.

In determining how to begin the divisional rotation in 2002, the displacement of teams from their old divisions in the new alignment was taken into account. Preference was given to scheduling games with former division rivals and other regional opponents for clubs realigned from otherwise intact divisions.

FUTURE SCHEDULING ROTATION

		2013	2014
AFC EAST	Intraconference	AFCN	AFCW
	Interconference	NFCS	NFCN
AFC NORTH	Intraconference	AFCE	AFCS
	Interconference	NFCN	NFCS
AFC SOUTH	Intraconference	AFCW	AFCN
	Interconference	NFCW	NFCE
AFC WEST	Intraconference	AFCS	AFCE
	Interconference	NFCE	NFCW
NFC EAST	Intraconference	NFCN	NFCW
	Interconference	AFCW	AFCS
NFC NORTH	Intraconference	NFCE	NFCS
	Interconference	AFCN	AFCE
NFC SOUTH	Intraconference	NFCW	NFCN
	Interconference	AFCE	AFCS
NFC WEST	Intraconference	NFCS	NFCE
	Interconference	AFCS	AFCW

AFC EAST NON-DIVISIONAL OPPONENTS 2013

	BUFFALO		MIAMI		NEW ENGLAND		N.Y. JETS	
	Home	Away	Home	Away	Home	Away	Home	Away
IIntraconference by Division	BALT	CLE	BALT	CLE	CLE	BALT	CLE	BALT
	CIN	PITT	CIN	PITT	PITT	CIN	PITT	CIN
Interconference by Division	ATL	NO	ATL	NO	NO	ATL	NO	ATL
	CAR	TB	CAR	TB	TB	CAR	TB	CAR
Intraconference by Position	AFCW	AFCS	AFCW	AFCS	AFCW	AFCS	AFCW	AFCS

AFC EAST NON-DIVISIONAL OPPONENTS 2014

	BUFFALO		MIAMI		NEW ENGLAND		N.Y. JETS	
	Home	Away	Home	Away	Home	Away	Home	Away
Intraconference by Division	KC	DEN	KC	DEN	DEN	KC	DEN	KC
	SD	OAK	SD	OAK	OAK	SD	OAK	SD
Interconference by Division	GB	CHI	GB	CHI	CHI	GB	CHI	GB
	MINN	DET	MINN	DET	DET	MINN	DET	MINN
Intraconference by Position	AFCN	AFCS	AFCN	AFCS	AFCN	AFCS	AFCN	AFCS

AFC NORTH NON-DIVISIONAL OPPONENTS 2013

	BALTIMORE		CINCINNATI		CLEVELAND		PITTSBURGH	
	Home	Away	Home	Away	Home	Away	Home	Away
Intraconference by Division	NE	BUFF	NE	BUFF	BUFF	NE	BUFF	NE
	NYJ	MIA	NYJ	MIA	MIA	NYJ	MIA	NYJ
Interconference by Division	GB	CHI	GB	CHI	CHI	GB	CHI	GB
	MINN	DET	MINN	DET	DET	MINN	DET	MINN
Intraconference by Position	AFCS	AFCW	AFCS	AFCW	AFCS	AFCW	AFCS	AFCW

AFC NORTH NON-DIVISIONAL OPPONENTS 2014

	BALTIMORE		CINCINNATI		CLEVELAND		PITTSBURGH	
	Home	Away	Home	Away	Home	Away	Home	Away
Intraconference by Division	JAX	HOU	JAX	HOU	HOU	JAX	HOU	JAX
	TENN	IND	TENN	IND	IND	TENN	IND	TENN
Interconference by Division	ATL	NO	ATL	NO	NO	ATL	NO	ATL
	CAR	TB	CAR	TB	TB	CAR	TB	CAR
Intraconference by Position	AFCW	AFCE	AFCW	AFCE	AFCW	AFCE	AFCW	AFCE

AFC SOUTH NON-DIVISIONAL OPPONENTS 2013

	HOUSTON		INDIANAPOLIS		JACKSONVILLE		TENNESSEE	
	Home	Away	Home	Away	Home	Away	Home	Away
Intraconference by Division	DEN	KC	DEN	KC	KC	DEN	KC	DEN
	OAK	SD	OAK	SD	SD	OAK	SD	OAK
Interconference by Division	STL	ARIZ	STL	ARIZ	ARIZ	STL	ARIZ	STL
	SEA	SF	SEA	SF	SF	SEA	SF	SEA
Intraconference by Position	AFCE	AFCN	AFCE	AFCN	AFCE	AFCN	AFCE	AFCN

AFC SOUTH NON-DIVISIONAL OPPONENTS 2014

	HOUSTON		INDIANAPOLIS		JACKSONVILLE		TENNESSEE	
	Home	Away	Home	Away	Home	Away	Home	Away
Intraconference by Division	BALT	CLE	BALT	CLE	CLE	BALT	CLE	BALT
	CIN	PITT	CIN	PITT	PITT	CIN	PITT	CIN
Interconference by Division	PHIL	DALL	PHIL	DALL	DALL	PHIL	DALL	PHIL
	WASH	NYG	WASH	NYG	NYG	WASH	NYG	WASH
Intraconference by Position	AFCE	AFCW	AFCE	AFCW	AFCE	AFCW	AFCE	AFCW

AFC WEST NON-DIVISIONAL OPPONENTS 2013

	DENVER		KANSAS CITY		OAKLAND		SAN DIEGO	
	Home	Away	Home	Away	Home	Away	Home	Away
Intraconference by Division	JAX	HOU	HOU	JAX	JAX	HOU	HOU	JAX
	TENN	IND	IND	TENN	TENN	IND	IND	TENN
Interconference by Division	PHIL	DALL	DALL	PHIL	PHIL	DALL	DALL	PHIL
	WASH	NYG	NYG	WASH	WASH	NYG	NYG	WASH
Intraconference by Position	AFCN	AFCE	AFCN	AFCE	AFCN	AFCE	AFCN	AFCE

AFC WEST NON-DIVISIONAL OPPONENTS 2014

	DENVER		KANSAS CITY		OAKLAND		SAN DIEGO	
	Home	Away	Home	Away	Home	Away	Home	Away
Intraconference by Division	BUFF	NE	NE	BUFF	BUFF	NE	NE	BUFF
	MIA	NYJ	NYJ	MIA	MIA	NYJ	NYJ	MIA
Interconference by Division	ARIZ	STL	STL	ARIZ	ARIZ	STL	STL	ARIZ
	SF	SEA	SEA	SF	SF	SEA	SEA	SF
Intraconference by Position	AFCS	AFCN	AFCS	AFCN	AFCS	AFCN	AFCS	AFCN

NFC EAST NON-DIVISIONAL OPPONENTS 2013

	DALLAS		N.Y. GIANTS		PHILADELPHIA		WASHINGTON	
	Home	Away	Home	Away	Home	Away	Home	Away
Intraconference by Division	GB	CHI	GB	CHI	CHI	GB	CHI	GB
	MINN	DET	MINN	DET	DET	MINN	DET	MINN
Interconference by Division	DEN	KC	DEN	KC	KC	DEN	KC	DEN
	OAK	SD	OAK	SD	SD	OAK	SD	OAK
Intraconference by Position	NFCW	NFCS	NFCW	NFCS	NFCW	NFCS	NFCW	NFCS

NFC EAST NON-DIVISIONAL OPPONENTS 2014

	DALLAS		N.Y. GIANTS		PHILADELPHIA		WASHINGTON	
	Home	Away	Home	Away	Home	Away	Home	Away
Intraconference by Division	ARIZ	STL	ARIZ	STL	STL	ARIZ	STL	ARIZ
	SF	SEA	SF	SEA	SEA	SF	SEA	SF
Interconference by Division	HOU	JAX	HOU	JAX	JAX	HOU	JAX	HOU
	IND	TENN	IND	TENN	TENN	IND	TENN	IND
Intraconference by Position	NFCS	NFCN	NFCS	NFCN	NFCS	NFCN	NFCS	NFCN

NFC NORTH NON-DIVISIONAL OPPONENTS 2013

	CHICAGO		DETROIT		GREEN BAY		MINNESOTA	
	Home	Away	Home	Away	Home	Away	Home	Away
Intraconference by Division	DALL	PHIL	DALL	PHIL	PHIL	DALL	PHIL	DALL
	NYG	WASH	NYG	WASH	WASH	NYG	WASH	NYG
Interconference by Division	BALT	CLE	BALT	CLE	CLE	BALT	CLE	BALT
	CIN	PITT	CIN	PITT	PITT	CIN	PITT	CIN
Intraconference by Position	NFCS	NFCW	NFCS	NFCW	NFCS	NFCW	NFCS	NFCW

NFC NORTH NON-DIVISIONAL OPPONENTS 2014

	CHICAGO		DETROIT		GREEN BAY		MINNESOTA	
	Home	Away	Home	Away	Home	Away	Home	Away
Intraconference by Division	NO	ATL	NO	ATL	ATL	NO	ATL	NO
	TB	CAR	TB	CAR	CAR	TB	CAR	TB
Interconference by Division	BUFF	NE	BUFF	NE	NE	BUFF	NE	BUFF
	MIA	NYJ	MIA	NYJ	NYJ	MIA	NYJ	MIA
Intraconference by Position	NFCE	NFCW	NFCE	NFCW	NFCE	NFCW	NFCE	NFCW

NFC SOUTH NON-DIVISIONAL OPPONENTS 2013

	ATLANTA		CAROLINA		NEW ORLEANS		TAMPA BAY	
	Home	Away	Home	Away	Home	Away	Home	Away
Intraconference by Division	STL	ARIZ	STL	ARIZ	ARIZ	STL	ARIZ	STL
	SEA	SF	SEA	SF	SF	SEA	SF	SEA
Interconference by Division	NE	BUFF	NE	BUFF	BUFF	NE	BUFF	NE
	NYJ	MIA	NYJ	MIA	MIA	NYJ	MIA	NYJ
Intraconference by Position	NFCE	NFCN	NFCE	NFCN	NFCE	NFCN	NFCE	NFCN

NFC SOUTH NON-DIVISIONAL OPPONENTS 2014

	ATLANTA		CAROLINA		NEW ORLEANS		TAMPA BAY	
	Home	Away	Home	Away	Home	Away	Home	Away
Intraconference by Division	CHI	GB	CHI	GB	GB	CHI	GB	CHI
	DET	MINN	DET	MINN	MINN	DET	MINN	DET
Interconference by Division	CLE	BALT	CLE	BALT	BALT	CLE	BALT	CLE
	PITT	CIN	PITT	CIN	CIN	PITT	CIN	PITT
Intraconference by Position	NFCW	NFCE	NFCW	NFCE	NFCW	NFCE	NFCW	NFCE

NFC WEST NON-DIVISIONAL OPPONENTS 2013

	ARIZONA		ST. LOUIS		SAN FRANCISCO		SEATTLE	
	Home	Away	Home	Away	Home	Away	Home	Away
Intraconference by Division	ATL	NO	NO	ATL	ATL	NO	NO	ATL
	CAR	TB	TB	CAR	CAR	TB	TB	CAR
Interconference by Division	HOU	JAX	JAX	HOU	HOU	JAX	JAX	HOU
	IND	TENN	TENN	IND	IND	TENN	TENN	IND
Intraconference by Position	NFCN	NFCE	NFCN	NFCE	NFCN	NFCE	NFCN	NFCE

NFC WEST NON-DIVISIONAL OPPONENTS 2014

	ARIZONA		ST. LOUIS		SAN FRANCISCO		SEATTLE	
	Home	Away	Home	Away	Home	Away	Home	Away
Intraconference by Division	PHIL	DALL	DALL	PHIL	PHIL	DALL	DALL	PHIL
	WASH	NYG	NYG	WASH	WASH	NYG	NYG	WASH
Interconference by Division	KC	DEN	DEN	KC	KC	DEN	DEN	KC
	SD	OAK	OAK	SD	SD	OAK	OAK	SD
Intraconference by Position	NFCN	NFCS	NFCN	NFCS	NFCN	NFCS	NFCN	NFCS

TOP ACTIVE PASSERS
1,000 or more attempts

		Yrs.	Att.	Comp.	Pct. Comp.	Yards	TD	Pct. TD	Had Int.	Pct. Int.	Ratings Pts.
1.	Aaron Rodgers	8	2,665	1,752	65.7	21,661	171	6.4	46	1.7	104.9
2.	Tom Brady	13	5,958	3,798	63.7	44,806	334	5.6	123	2.1	96.6
3.	Peyton Manning	15	7,793	5,082	65.2	59,487	436	5.6	209	2.7	95.7
4.	Tony Romo	9	3,240	2,097	64.7	25,737	177	5.5	91	2.8	95.6
5.	Philip Rivers	9	3,564	2,268	63.6	27,891	189	5.3	93	2.6	94.5
6.	Drew Brees	12	6,149	4,035	65.6	45,919	324	5.3	165	2.7	94.3
7.	Ben Roethlisberger	9	3,762	2,374	63.1	29,844	191	5.1	108	2.9	92.7
8.	Matt Schaub	9	2,823	1,816	64.3	21,944	120	4.3	70	2.5	91.9
9.	Matt Ryan	5	2,637	1,654	62.7	18,957	127	4.8	60	2.3	90.9
10.	Joe Flacco	5	2,489	1,507	60.5	17,633	102	4.1	56	2.2	86.3
11.	Carson Palmer	9	4,110	2,568	62.5	29,465	189	4.6	130	3.2	86.2
12.	Cam Newton	2	1,002	590	58.9	7,920	40	4.0	29	2.9	85.3
13.	Jay Cutler	7	2,955	1,796	60.8	21,316	136	4.6	100	3.4	84.0
14.	Andy Dalton	2	1,044	629	60.2	7,067	47	4.5	29	2.8	83.9
15.	Matthew Stafford	4	1,863	1,114	59.8	12,807	80	4.3	54	2.9	82.8
16.	Eli Manning	9	4,457	2,612	58.6	31,527	211	4.7	144	3.2	82.7
17.	Jason Campbell	7	2,182	1,328	60.9	14,682	76	3.5	52	2.4	82.5
18.	Matt Hasselbeck	14	5,018	3,029	60.4	34,517	201	4.0	147	2.9	82.2
19.	Michael Vick	10	2,889	1,626	56.3	20,274	123	4.3	82	2.8	80.6
20.	Matt Cassel	8	2,044	1,203	58.9	13,495	82	4.0	57	2.8	80.4
21.	Josh Freeman	4	1,873	1,101	58.8	12,963	78	4.2	63	3.4	79.8
22.	Kyle Orton	7	2,214	1,293	58.4	14,621	81	3.7	57	2.6	79.7
23.	Alex Smith	7	2,177	1,290	59.3	14,280	81	3.7	63	2.9	79.1
24.	Byron Leftwich	9	1,605	930	57.9	10,532	58	3.6	42	2.6	78.9
25.	Tarvaris Jackson	7	1,053	625	59.4	7,075	38	3.6	35	3.3	77.7

TOP ACTIVE SCORERS
(number in parentheses represents 2-point conversions scored)

		Yrs.	TD	FG	PAT	TP
1.	Adam Vinatieri	17	0	413	626(1)	1,867
2.	Ryan Longwell	16	0	361	604	1,687
3.	David Akers	15	0	367	521	1,622
4.	Olindo Mare	16	0	356	487	1,555
5.	Sebastian Janikowski	13	0	324	417	1,389
6.	Jay Feely	12	1	299	407	1,310
7.	Phil Dawson	14	1	305	350	1,271
8.	Rian Lindell	13	0	283	401	1,250
9.	Shayne Graham	12	0	245	368	1,103
10.	Matt Bryant	11	0	233	324	1,023
11.	Josh Brown	10	0	231	310	1,003
12.	Randy Moss	14	157	0	0(4)	950
13.	Lawrence Tynes	9	0	190	357	927
14.	Rob Bironas	8	0	214	274	916
15.	Robbie Gould	8	0	208	278	902
16.	Nate Kaeding	9	0	181	352	895
17.	Stephen Gostkowski	7	0	170	355	865
18.	Josh Scobee	9	0	192	272	848
19.	Mason Crosby	6	0	152	306	762
20.	Shaun Suisham	8	0	152	190	646
21.	Nick Folk	6	0	134	242	644
22.	Billy Cundiff	9	0	139	217	634
23.	Tony Gonzalez	16	103	0	0(3)	624
24.	Mike Nugent	8	0	146	182	620
25.	Matt Prater	6	0	117	185	536

TOP ACTIVE SCORERS (TOUCHDOWNS)

		Yrs.	Rush	Rec.	Ret.	Tot.
1.	Randy Moss	14	0	156	1	157
2.	Tony Gonzalez	16	0	103	0	103
3.	Antonio Gates	10	0	83	0	83
4.	Adrian Peterson	6	76	4	0	80
5.	Reggie Wayne	12	0	78	0	78
6.	Larry Fitzgerald	9	0	77	0	77
7.	Maurice Jones-Drew	7	63	11	2	76
8.	Steve Smith	12	2	63	6	71
9.	Willis McGahee	9	63	5	0	68
10.	Santana Moss	12	0	64	3	67
	Michael Turner	9	66	1	0	67
12.	Plaxico Burress	12	0	64	0	64
	Steven Jackson	9	56	8	0	64
14.	Donald Driver	14	1	61	0	62
	Frank Gore	8	51	10	1	62
16.	Brandon Jacobs	8	56	4	0	60
17.	Anquan Boldin	10	1	58	0	59
18.	Marques Colston	7	0	58	0	58
19.	Andre Johnson	10	0	56	0	56
20.	Calvin Johnson	6	1	54	0	55
21.	Greg Jennings	7	0	53	0	53
22.	Roddy White	8	0	52	0	52
23.	Dallas Clark	10	0	50	0	50
	Arian Foster	4	44	6	0	50
25.	Marshawn Lynch	6	46	3	0	49
	DeAngelo Williams	7	43	6	0	49

TOP ACTIVE RUSHERS

		Yrs.	Att.	Yards	TD
1.	Steven Jackson	9	2,395	10,135	56
2.	Adrian Peterson	6	1,754	8,849	76
3.	Frank Gore	8	1,911	8,839	51
4.	Willis McGahee	9	1,957	8,097	63
5.	Michael Turner	9	1,639	7,338	66
6.	Maurice Jones-Drew	7	1,570	7,268	63
7.	Chris Johnson	5	1,463	6,888	44
8.	Marshawn Lynch	6	1,452	6,132	46
9.	Cedric Benson	8	1,600	6,017	32
10.	DeAngelo Williams	7	1,169	5,784	43
11.	Michael Vick	10	791	5,551	34
12.	Ray Rice	5	1,216	5,520	33
13.	Matt Forté	5	1,262	5,327	26
14.	Ronnie Brown	8	1,216	5,171	37
15.	Brandon Jacobs	8	1,083	4,856	56
16.	Jamaal Charles	5	784	4,536	17
17.	Arian Foster	4	1,010	4,521	44
18.	Ahmad Bradshaw	6	921	4,232	32
19.	Fred Jackson	6	932	4,231	19
20.	Reggie Bush	7	967	4,162	29
21.	Ryan Grant	6	956	4,148	27
22.	LeSean McCoy	4	835	3,866	30
23.	Jonathan Stewart	5	818	3,836	27
24.	Rashard Mendenhall	5	864	3,549	29
25.	Shonn Greene	4	822	3,423	18

TOP ACTIVE SCRIMMAGE YARDS LEADERS

		Yrs.	Rush	Rec	Total	TD
1.	Randy Moss	14	159	15,292	15,451	156
2.	Tony Gonzalez	16	14	14,268	14,282	103
3.	Steven Jackson	13	10,135	3,324	13,459	64
4.	Reggie Wayne	12	5	13,063	13,058	78
5.	Steve Smith	12	387	11,452	11,839	65
6.	Frank Gore	8	8,839	2,631	11,470	61
7.	Andre Johnson	10	54	11,254	11,308	56
8.	Larry Fitzgerald	9	55	10,413	10,468	77
9.	Anquan Boldin	10	214	10,165	10,379	59
10.	Adrian Peterson	6	8,849	1,526	10,375	80
11.	Donald Driver	14	217	10,137	10,354	62
12.	Santana Moss	12	262	9,715	9,977	64
13.	Maurice Jones-Drew	7	7,268	2,559	9,827	74
14.	Willis McGahee	9	8,097	1,319	9,416	68
15.	Jason Witten	10	0	8,948	8,948	44
16.	Roddy White	8	19	8,725	8,744	52
17.	Wes Welker	9	151	8,580	8,731	38
18.	Chris Johnson	5	6,888	1,658	8,546	48
19.	Plaxico Burress	11	7	8,499	8,492	64
20.	Antonio Gates	10	0	8,321	8,321	83
21.	Ray Rice	5	5,520	2,713	8,233	39
22.	Calvin Johnson	6	167	7,836	8,003	55
23.	Brandon Marshall	7	118	7,755	7,873	45
24.	Michael Turner	9	7,338	528	7,866	67
25.	Matt Forté	5	5,327	2,325	7,652	35

TOP ACTIVE PASS RECEIVERS

		Yrs.	No.	Yards	TD
1.	Tony Gonzalez	16	1,242	14,268	103
2.	Randy Moss	14	982	15,292	156
3.	Reggie Wayne	12	968	13,063	78
4.	Andre Johnson	10	818	11,254	56
5.	Jason Witten	10	806	8,948	44
6.	Anquan Boldin	10	772	10,165	58
	Steve Smith	12	772	11,452	63
8.	Wes Welker	9	768	8,580	38
9.	Larry Fitzgerald	9	764	10,413	77
10.	Donald Driver	14	743	10,137	61
11.	Santana Moss	12	680	9,715	64
12.	Antonio Gates	10	642	8,321	83
13.	Roddy White	8	622	8,725	52
14.	Brandon Marshall	7	612	7,755	45
15.	Plaxico Burress	11	553	8,499	64
16.	Marques Colston	7	532	7,394	58
17.	Deion Branch	11	518	6,644	39
18.	Calvin Johnson	6	488	7,836	54
19.	Dallas Clark	10	474	5,322	50
20.	Chris Cooley	9	429	4,711	33
21.	Randy McMichael	11	426	4,539	24
22.	Greg Jennings	7	425	6,537	53
23.	Nate Burleson	10	418	5,169	38
24.	Dwayne Bowe	6	415	5,728	39
25.	Heath Miller	8	408	4,680	39

TOP ACTIVE INTERCEPTORS

		Yrs.	No.	Yards	TD
1.	Ed Reed	11	61	1,541	7
2.	Charles Woodson	15	55	896	11
3.	Champ Bailey	14	52	464	4
4.	Asante Samuel	10	50	727	6
5.	DeAngelo Hall	9	39	789	3
6.	Nate Clements	12	36	508	5
7.	Terence Newman	10	34	345	3
8.	Charles Tillman	10	33	606	8
9.	Rashean Mathis	10	30	512	3
	Troy Polamalu	10	30	362	2
11.	Chris Gamble	9	27	326	2
	Adrian Wilson	12	27	508	2
	Antoine Winfield	14	27	259	2
14.	Sheldon Brown	11	26	419	4
15.	Antonio Cromartie	7	25	460	3
16.	London Fletcher	15	23	168	2
	Kerry Rhodes	8	23	402	0
18.	Leon Hall	6	22	245	2
	Brian Urlacher	13	22	324	2
	Tramon Williams	6	22	411	1
21.	Michael Griffin	6	21	287	1
	Quentin Jammer	11	21	210	1
	Marcus Trufant	10	21	370	2
24.	Chris Hope	11	20	367	1
	Johnathan Joseph	7	20	356	4
	Corey Webster	8	20	226	1

TOP ACTIVE PUNT RETURNERS
40 or more punt returns

	Yrs.	No.	Yards	Avg.	TD
1. Julian Edelman	4	72	943	13.1	3
2. Devin Hester	7	246	2,985	12.1	12
3. Patrick Peterson	2	95	1,125	11.8	4
4. Roscoe Parrish	8	165	1,920	11.6	3
5. Santana Moss	12	112	1,268	11.3	3
6. Marc Mariani	3	73	819	11.2	2
7. Eddie Royal	5	93	1,031	11.1	2
8. Josh Cribbs	8	195	2,154	11.0	3
9. Ted Ginn	6	130	1,425	11.0	3
10. Jeremy Kerley	2	48	525	10.9	1
11. Domenik Hixon	6	56	597	10.7	1
12. Danny Amendola	4	89	934	10.5	0
13. DeSean Jackson	5	117	1,223	10.5	4
14. Eric Weems	6	78	815	10.4	1
15. Davone Bess	5	115	1,196	10.4	0
16. Adam Jones	6	117	1,208	10.3	5
17. Randall Cobb	2	57	587	10.3	2
18. Darius Reynaud	4	84	850	10.1	2
19. Brandon Tate	4	73	734	10.1	1
20. Wes Welker	9	241	2,417	10.0	0
21. Trindon Holliday	2	48	481	10.0	1
22. Jacoby Jones	6	216	2,161	10.0	4
23. Nate Clements	12	82	816	10.0	2
24. Leon Washington	7	168	1,668	9.9	0
25. Micheal Spurlock	6	58	573	9.9	2

TOP ACTIVE KICKOFF RETURNERS
40 or more kickoff returns

	Yrs.	No.	Yards	Avg.	TD
1. Joe McKnight	3	76	2,205	29.0	2
2. Percy Harvin	4	114	3,183	27.9	5
3. Richard Goodman	3	52	1,433	27.6	1
4. Johnny Knox	4	55	1,506	27.4	1
5. David Wilson	1	57	1,533	26.9	1
6. Danieal Manning	7	115	3,085	26.8	1
7. Randall Cobb	2	72	1,905	26.5	1
8. Leodis McKelvin	5	91	2,407	26.5	1
9. Terrence McGee	10	207	5,450	26.3	5
10. Jacoby Jones	6	102	2,657	26.0	3
11. Quintin Demps	5	63	1,638	26.0	1
Maurice Jones-Drew	7	79	2,054	26.0	2
13. Deji Karim	3	86	2,228	25.9	1
14. Leon Washington	7	244	6,315	25.9	8
15. Josh Cribbs	8	387	10,015	25.9	8
16. Antonio Brown	3	44	1,134	25.8	1
17. Brad Smith	7	107	2,746	25.7	4
18. Darren Sproles	7	316	8,041	25.4	2
19. Stefan Logan	4	171	4,343	25.4	1
20. Jacoby Ford	3	64	1,621	25.3	4
21. Michael Turner	9	44	1,111	25.3	0
22. Jalen Parmele	4	43	1,078	25.1	0
23. LaRod Stephens-Howling	4	163	4,067	25.0	3
24. Adam Jones	6	80	1,989	24.9	0
25. Courtney Roby	7	121	3,007	24.9	1

TOP ACTIVE PUNTERS
50 or more punts

	Yrs.	No.	Avg.	LG
1. Bryan Anger	1	91	47.8	73
2. Shane Lechler	13	1,014	47.5	80
3. Thomas Morstead	4	235	47.1	70
4. Brandon Fields	6	451	46.4	71
5. Britton Colquitt	8	254	46.2	67
6. Andy Lee	9	790	45.9	82
7. Johnny Hekker	1	82	45.8	68
8. Donnie Jones	9	736	45.6	80
9. Pat McAfee	4	290	45.5	66
10. Mat McBriar	9	549	45.4	75
11. Mike Scifres	10	573	45.3	71
12. Brett Kern	5	354	45.1	71
13. Jon Ryan	7	548	45.0	77
14. Matt Bosher	2	130	44.9	63
15. Dustin Colquitt	8	657	44.7	81
16. Sam Koch	7	558	44.6	74
17. Chris Kluwe	8	623	44.4	70
18. Robert Malone	3	141	44.3	64
19. Zoltan Mesko	3	175	44.2	65
20. Tim Masthay	3	196	44.2	71
21. Kevin Huber	4	324	44.0	72
22. Shawn Powell	1	65	44.0	62
23. Chas Henry	2	82	44.0	62
24. Brian Moorman	12	918	44.0	84
25. Steve Weatherford	7	503	43.9	68

TOP ACTIVE QUARTERBACK SACKERS

	Yrs.	No.
1. John Abraham	13	122.0
2. Jared Allen	9	117.0
3. Julius Peppers	11	111.5
4. DeMarcus Ware	8	111.0
5. Dwight Freeney	11	107.5
6. Robert Mathis	10	91.5
7. Terrell Suggs	10	84.5
8. Andre Carter	12	78.5
9. Justin Smith	12	75.5
10. Osi Umenyiora	9	75.0
11. Trent Cole	8	71.0
12. Shaun Phillips	9	69.5
13. Will Smith	9	67.5
14. James Harrison	10	64.0
15. Elvis Dumervil	6	63.5
Mario Williams	7	63.5
17. Tamba Hali	13	62.5
Vonnie Holliday	15	62.5
19. Kyle Vanden Bosch	11	58.0
20. Richard Seymour	12	57.5
21. Kevin Williams	10	56.5
22. Jason Babin	9	55.0
23. Chris Clemons	8	53.5
24. LaMarr Woodley	6	52.0
25. Justin Tuck	8	49.5

The **Green Bay Packers** need 10 regular-season victories to become the second team in NFL history with 700 regular-season victories. The Packers (690-530-36) would join Chicago (722-526-42) as the only teams to accomplish the feat.

The **Pittsburgh Steelers** need one victory to become the first AFC team in history with 600 total victories. Pittsburgh's all-time record is 599-546-21.

Pittsburgh can become the third team to lead the league in fewest net yards allowed for three consecutive seasons. Boston/Washington (1935-37) and Chicago (1984-86) are the only teams to accomplish the feat. The Steelers have led the league in fewest net yards allowed in 10 different seasons, the most of any team in NFL history.

The **San Francisco 49ers** need five regular-season victories to reach 500 regular-season victories. San Francisco's all-time regular season record is 495-413-14.

The **San Diego Chargers** need one regular-season victory to reach 400 regular-season victories. San Diego's all-time regular-season record is 399-394-11.

The **Tennessee Titans** need eight regular-season victories to reach 400 regular-season victories. Tennessee's all-time regular-season record is 392-406-6.

Bill Belichick, New England, needs five victories to surpass Chuck Noll (209) for fifth place all-time in career victories. In 18 seasons, Belichick has 205 career victories.

Mike Shanahan, Washington, needs nine victories to surpass Bill Parcells (183) for 10th place all-time in career victories. In 19 seasons, Shanahan has 175 career victories.

Andy Reid, Kansas City, needs 10 victories to become the 21st coach in NFL history to win 150 games. In 14 seasons, Reid has 140 career victories.

Peyton Manning, Denver, needs 4,000 passing yards to become the first player in NFL history with 13 4,000-yard seasons. Manning is the only quarterback to accomplish the feat in 12 seasons.

Manning needs 566 pass attempts and 1,875 passing yards to surpass Dan Marino (8,358 attempts; 61,361 yards) for second place all-time in each category. In 15 seasons, Manning has 7,793 pass attempts and 59,487 passing yards.

Manning has 22 games with four or more touchdown passes and needs two such games to surpass Brett Favre (23) for the most games with four touchdown passes in NFL history (see Brees note).

Manning can increase his NFL record total of 300-yard passing games. In 15 seasons, Manning has 72 300-yard passing games (see Brees note).

Manning has led the league in touchdown passes three times in his career and can tie Drew Brees, Len Dawson, Brett Favre, Johnny Unitas and Steve Young (4) for the most seasons leading the league in touchdown passes (see Brady and Brees notes).

Drew Brees, New Orleans, needs 4,000 passing yards to join Peyton Manning (12) as the only players in NFL history with at least eight 4,000-yard passing seasons. In 12 seasons, Brees has seven 4,000-yard seasons.

Brees needs 30 touchdown passes to become the first player to pass for at least 30 touchdowns in six consecutive seasons. Brees has accomplished the feat in each of the past five seasons, tied with Brett Favre for the longest streak in NFL history.

Brees has 20 games with four or more touchdown passes and needs four such games to surpass Peyton Manning (22) and Brett Favre (23) for the most games with four touchdown passes in NFL history (see Manning note).

Brees needs to pass for 300 yards in six games to surpass Peyton Manning (72) for the most 300-yard passing games in NFL history (see Manning note). In 12 seasons, Brees has 67 300-yard passing games.

Brees needs 19 touchdown passes to surpass Tom Brady (334) and Fran Tarkenton (342) for fourth place all-time (see

Brady note). In 12 seasons, Brees has 324 touchdown passes.

Brees needs 89 completions to surpass John Elway (4,123) for fourth place all-time. In 12 seasons, Brees has 4,035 completions.

Brees needs 3,407 passing yards to surpass Vinny Testaverde (46,233), Fran Tarkenton (47,003) and Warren Moon (49,325) for fifth place all-time (see Brady note). In 12 seasons, Brees has 45,919 passing yards.

Brees can become the first player to lead the league in touchdown passes five times in his career. Brees is currently tied with Len Dawson, Brett Favre, Johnny Unitas and Steve Young (4) for the most such seasons in NFL history.

Brees has led the league in passing yards four times in his career and can tie Sonny Jurgensen and Dan Marino (5) for the most seasons leading the league in passing yards.

Tom Brady, New England, needs to throw a touchdown pass in each of his next seven games to surpass Drew Brees (54) for the most consecutive games with a touchdown pass in NFL history. Brady has thrown a touchdown pass in each of his past 48 games.

Brady has led the league in touchdown passes three times in his career and can tie Drew Brees, Len Dawson, Brett Favre, Johnny Unitas and Steve Young (4) for the most seasons leading the league in touchdown passes (see Brees and Manning notes).

Brady needs nine touchdown passes to surpass Fran Tarkenton (342) for fourth place all-time. In 13 seasons, Brady has 334 touchdown passes (see Brees note).

Brady needs 4,520 passing yards to surpass Drew Brees (45,919), Vinny Testaverde (46,233), Fran Tarkenton (47,003) and Warren Moon (49,325) for fifth place all-time (see Brees note). In 13 seasons, Brady has 44,806 passing yards.

Brady needs 4,000 passing yards to join Brett Favre (6), Dan Marino (6), Drew Brees (7) and Peyton Manning (12) as the only players in NFL history with at least six 4,000-yard passing seasons. In 13 seasons, Brady has five 4,000-yard passing seasons.

Aaron Rodgers, Green Bay, has led the league in passer rating in each of the past two seasons and can join Peyton Manning (3) and Steve Young (4) as the only players to do so in three consecutive seasons.

Rodgers has posted a 100+ passer rating in each of the past two seasons and can tie Steve Young (3) for the most such consecutive seasons in NFL history.

Philip Rivers, San Diego, has led the league in average yards per pass three times in his career and can join Steve Young (5) and Sid Luckman (7) as the only players in NFL history to do so in at least four seasons.

Andrew Luck, Indianapolis, needs 4,000 passing yards to become the first player in NFL history to pass for 4,000 yards in consecutive seasons to begin his career. Luck passed for an NFL rookie-record 4,374 yards in 2012.

Adrian Peterson, Minnesota, needs 10 rushing touchdowns to join Emmitt Smith (8) and LaDainian Tomlinson (9) as the only players in NFL history to rush for 10 touchdowns in at least seven different seasons.

Peterson has four 200-yard rushing games in his career. Peterson needs two 200-yard games to surpass Tiki Barber (5) and tie O.J. Simpson (6) for the most all-time.

Steven Jackson, Atlanta, needs 1,000 rushing yards to join Curtis Martin (10), Barry Sanders (10) and Emmitt Smith (11) as the only players in NFL history to rush for 1,000 yards in nine consecutive seasons. Jackson has rushed for 1,000 yards in each of the past eight seasons.

Ray Rice, Baltimore, can join Marshall Faulk (4) as the only players in NFL history to record at least 1,000 rushing yards and 700 receiving yards in three different seasons. In five seasons, Rice has accomplished the feat twice.

Tony Gonzalez, Atlanta, needs 58 receptions to join Jerry Rice

(1,549) as the only players in NFL history with 1,300 career catches. In 16 seasons, Gonzalez has 1,242 receptions – the most ever by a tight end.

Gonzalez needs a reception in each of his next five games to join Jerry Rice (274) as the only players with a reception in at least 200 consecutive games. Gonzalez has a reception in each of his past 195 games.

Gonzalez needs 50 receptions to join Jerry Rice (17) as the only players in NFL history with 16 50-reception seasons. Gonzalez is the only player in NFL history with 15 consecutive 50-reception seasons.

Gonzalez needs 1,025 receiving yards to surpass Marvin Harrison (14,580), Tim Brown (14,934), Isaac Bruce (15,208) and Randy Moss (15,292) for third place all-time. In 16 seasons, Gonzalez has 14,268 receiving yards – the most ever by a tight end.

Gonzalez needs seven touchdowns to surpass Don Hutson (105), Tim Brown (105) and Barry Sanders (109) for 15th on the all-time list. In 16 seasons, Gonzalez has 103 touchdowns – the most ever by a tight end.

Calvin Johnson, Detroit, needs two 200-yard receiving games to surpass Lance Alworth (5) for the most all-time. In six seasons, Johnson has four career 200-yard games.

Johnson needs 1,500 receiving yards to join Andre Johnson (3), Marvin Harrison (3) and Jerry Rice (4) as the only players with at least three such seasons in NFL history (see A. Johnson note). In six seasons, Johnson has two 1,500-yard receiving seasons.

Wes Welker, Denver, needs 100 receptions to become the first player in NFL history with six 100-catch seasons. Welker is the only player with five 100-reception seasons.

Welker has led the league in receptions three times and can join Lionel Taylor (5) and Don Hutson (8) as the only players to lead the league in receptions at least four times.

Andre Johnson, Houston, needs 1,500 receiving yards to join Jerry Rice (4) as the only players with four 1,500-yard seasons. In 10 seasons, Johnson has three 1,500-yard receiving seasons.

Johnson needs 100 receptions to join Wes Welker as the only players in NFL history with five 100-catch seasons (see Marshall, Wayne and Welker notes). In 10 seasons, Johnson has four 100-catch seasons.

Brandon Marshall, Chicago, needs 100 receptions to join Wes Welker as the only players in NFL history with five 100-catch seasons (see A. Johnson, Wayne and Welker notes). In seven seasons, Marshall has four 100-catch seasons.

Reggie Wayne, Indianapolis, needs 100 receptions to join Wes Welker as the only players in NFL history with five 100-catch seasons (see A. Johnson, Marshall and Welker notes). In 12 seasons, Wayne has four 100-catch seasons.

Wayne needs 1,000 receiving yards to join Terrell Owens (9), Jimmy Smith (9), Tim Brown (9), Randy Moss (10) and Jerry Rice (14) as the only players in NFL history with at least nine 1,000-yard receiving seasons. In 12 seasons, Wayne has eight 1,000-yard receiving seasons.

Rob Gronkowski, New England, needs 10 touchdown catches to become the first tight end in NFL history with at least 10 touchdown catches in four consecutive seasons. Gronkowski is the only tight end in history to accomplish the feat in three consecutive seasons.

Ed Reed, Houston, is the all-time leader in interception-return yards and can add to his NFL record. In 11 seasons, Reed has 1,541 interception-return yards.

Reed is tied with Everson Walls (3) for the most seasons leading the league in interceptions and can become the first player in NFL history to lead the league in interceptions four times.

Reed needs eight interceptions to surpass Dick LeBeau (62), Dave Brown (62), Darren Sharper (63), Ronnie Lott (63), Ken Riley (65) and Dick "Night Train" Lane (68) for fourth place all-time. In 11 seasons, Reed has 61 interceptions.

Charles Woodson, Oakland, needs two interception-return touchdowns to surpass Rod Woodson (12) for the most all-time. In 15 seasons, Woodson has 11 interception-return touchdowns.

Jared Allen, Minnesota, has led the league in sacks twice in his career and can become the first player to lead the league three times since the sack became an official statistic in 1982 (see Ware note).

DeMarcus Ware, Dallas, has led the league in sacks twice in his career and can become the first player to lead the league three times since the sack became an official statistic in 1982 (see Allen note).

Ware needs 10 sacks to join John Randle (8) and Reggie White (9) as the only players with 10 sacks in at least eight consecutive seasons since 1982. Ware has accomplished the feat in each of the past seven seasons.

Devin Hester, Chicago, needs two return touchdowns to surpass Deion Sanders (19) for the most all-time. In seven seasons, Hester has 18 return touchdowns (12 punt return, five kickoff return and one missed field goal return).

Joshua Cribbs, Oakland, is tied with Leon Washington (8) for the most kickoff-return touchdowns in NFL history and needs one to attain sole possession of first place (see Washington note).

Cribbs needs 236 kick-return yards to surpass Dante Hall (10,136) and Mel Gray (10,250) for third place all-time. In eight seasons, Cribbs has 10,015 kick-return yards.

Leon Washington, New England, is tied with Joshua Cribbs (8) for the most kickoff-return touchdowns in NFL history and needs one to attain sole possession of first place (see Cribbs note).

Adam Vinatieri, Indianapolis, needs 138 points to surpass John Kasay (1,970), Jason Elam (1,983), George Blanda (2,002) and Matt Stover (2,004) for fifth place all-time. In 17 seasons, Vinatieri has 1,867 points.

Vinatieri needs 100 points to join Jason Elam (16) as the only players in NFL history to score 100 points in 16 different seasons. In 17 seasons, Vinatieri has accomplished the feat 15 times.

David Akers, Detroit, needs to convert a field-goal attempt in each of his next six games to surpass Matt Stover (38) for the most consecutive games with a field goal in NFL history. Akers has kicked a field goal in each of his past 33 games.

COACHES RECORDS

ACTIVE COACHES' CAREER RECORDS (Order Based on Career Victories)
Start of 2013 Season

Coach	Team(s)	Regular Season					Postseason			Career			
		Yrs.	Won	Lost	Tied	Pct.	Won	Lost	Pct.	Won	Lost	Tied	Pct.
Bill Belichick	Cleveland Browns, New England Patriots	18	187	101	0	.649	18	8	.692	205	109	0	.653
Mike Shanahan	Los Angeles Raiders, Denver Broncos, Washington Redskins	19	167	125	0	.572	8	6	.571	175	131	0	.572
Tom Coughlin	Jacksonville Jaguars, New York Giants	17	151	121	0	.555	12	7	.632	163	128	0	.560
Jeff Fisher	Houston/Tennessee Oilers, Tennessee Titans, St. Louis Rams	18	149	128	1	.538	5	6	.455	154	134	1	.535
Andy Reid	Philadelphia Eagles, Kansas City Chiefs	14	130	93	1	.583	10	9	.526	140	102	1	.578
John Fox	Carolina Panthers, Denver Broncos	11	94	82	0	.534	6	5	.545	100	87	0	.535
Mike McCarthy	Green Bay Packers	7	74	38	0	.661	6	4	.600	80	42	0	.656
Marvin Lewis	Cincinnati Bengals	10	79	80	1	.497	0	4	.000	79	84	1	.485
Mike Tomlin	Pittsburgh Steelers	6	63	33	0	.656	5	3	.625	68	36	0	.654
Sean Payton	New Orleans Saints	7	62	34	0	.646	5	3	.625	67	37	0	.644
John Harbaugh	Baltimore Ravens	5	54	26	0	.675	9	4	.692	63	30	0	.677
Pete Carroll	New York Jets, New England Patriots, Seattle Seahawks	7	58	54	0	.518	3	4	.429	61	58	0	.513
Gary Kubiak	Houston Texans	7	59	53	0	.527	2	2	.500	61	55	0	.526
Mike Smith	Atlanta Falcons	5	56	24	0	.700	1	4	.200	57	28	0	.671
Rex Ryan	New York Jets	4	34	30	0	.531	4	2	.667	38	32	0	.543
Jim Harbaugh	San Francisco 49ers	2	24	7	1	.766	3	2	.600	27	9	1	.743
Jim Schwartz	Detroit Lions	4	22	42	0	.344	0	1	.000	22	43	0	.338
Jason Garrett	Dallas Cowboys	3	21	19	0	.525	0	0	---	21	19	0	.525
Leslie Frazier	Minnesota Vikings	3	16	22	0	.421	0	1	.000	16	23	0	.410
Mike Munchak	Tennessee Titans	2	15	17	0	.469	0	0	---	15	17	0	.469
Ron Rivera	Carolina Panthers	2	13	19	0	.406	0	0	---	13	19	0	.406
Chuck Pagano	Indianapolis Colts	1	11	5	0	.688	0	1	.000	11	6	0	.647
Joe Philbin	Miami Dolphins	1	7	9	0	.438	0	0	---	7	9	0	.438
Greg Schiano	Tampa Bay Buccaneers	1	7	9	0	.438	0	0	---	7	9	0	.438
Dennis Allen	Oakland Raiders	1	4	12	0	.250	0	0	---	4	12	0	.250
Bruce Arians	Arizona Cardinals	0	0	0	0	---	0	0	---	0	0	0	---
Gus Bradley	Jacksonville Jaguars	0	0	0	0	---	0	0	---	0	0	0	---
Rob Chudzinski	Cleveland Browns	0	0	0	0	---	0	0	---	0	0	0	---
Chip Kelly	Philadelphia Eagles	0	0	0	0	---	0	0	---	0	0	0	---
Doug Marrone	Buffalo Bills	0	0	0	0	---	0	0	---	0	0	0	---
Mike McCoy	San Diego Chargers	0	0	0	0	---	0	0	---	0	0	0	---
Marc Trestman	Chicago Bears	0	0	0	0	---	0	0	---	0	0	0	---

COACHES WITH 100 CAREER VICTORIES (Order Based on Career Victories)
Start of 2013 Season

			Regular Season				Postseason			Career			
Coach	Team(s)	Yrs.	Won	Lost	Tied	Pct.	Won	Lost	Pct.	Won	Lost	Tied	Pct.
1. Don Shula	Baltimore Colts, Miami Dolphins	33	328	156	6	.677	19	17	.528	347	173	6	.666
2. George Halas	Chicago Bears	40	318	148	31	.682	6	3	.667	324	151	31	.682
3. Tom Landry	Dallas Cowboys	29	250	162	6	.607	20	16	.556	270	178	6	.603
4. Earl (Curly) Lambeau	Green Bay Packers, Chicago Cardinals, Washington Redskins	33	226	132	22	.631	3	2	.600	229	134	22	.631
5. Chuck Noll	Pittsburgh Steelers	23	193	148	1	.566	16	8	.667	209	156	1	.572
6. **Bill Belichick**	Cleveland Browns, New England Patriots	18	187	101	0	.649	18	8	.692	205	109	0	.653
Marty Schottenheimer	Cleveland Browns, Kansas City Chiefs, Washington Redskins, San Diego Chargers	21	200	126	1	.613	5	13	.278	205	139	1	.596
8. Dan Reeves	Denver Broncos, New York Giants, Atlanta Falcons	23	190	165	2	.535	11	9	.550	201	174	2	.536
9. Chuck Knox	Los Angeles Rams, Buffalo Bills, Seattle Seahawks	22	186	147	1	.558	7	11	.389	193	158	1	.550
10. Bill Parcells	New York Giants, New England Patriots, New York Jets, Dallas Cowboys	19	172	130	1	.569	11	8	.579	183	138	1	.570
11. **Mike Shanahan**	Los Angeles Raiders, Denver Broncos, Washington Redskins	19	167	125	0	.572	8	6	.571	175	131	0	.572
12. Mike Holmgren	Green Bay Packers, Seattle Seahawks	17	161	111	0	.592	13	11	.542	174	122	0	.588
13. Joe Gibbs	Washington Redskins	16	154	94	0	.621	17	7	.708	171	101	0	.629
14. Paul Brown	Cleveland Browns, Cincinnati Bengals	21	166	100	6	.624	4	8	.333	170	108	6	.612
15. Bud Grant	Minnesota Vikings	18	158	96	5	.621	10	12	.455	168	108	5	.608
16. **Tom Coughlin**	Jacksonville Jaguars, New York Giants	17	151	121	0	.555	12	7	.632	163	128	0	.560
17. Bill Cowher	Pittsburgh Steelers	15	149	90	1	.623	12	9	.571	161	99	1	.619
18. Marv Levy	Kansas City Chiefs, Buffalo Bills	17	143	112	0	.561	11	8	.579	154	120	0	.562
Jeff Fisher	Houston/Tennessee Oilers, Tennessee Titans, St. Louis Rams	18	149	128	1	.538	5	6	.455	154	134	1	.535
20. Steve Owen	New York Giants	23	151	100	17	.602	2	8	.200	153	108	17	.586
21. Tony Dungy	Tampa Bay Buccaneers, Indianapolis Colts	13	139	69	0	.668	9	10	.474	148	79	0	.652
22. **Andy Reid**	Philadelphia Eagles, Kansas City Chiefs	14	130	93	1	.583	10	9	.526	140	102	1	.578
23. Hank Stram	Kansas City Chiefs, New Orleans Saints	17	131	97	10	.574	5	3	.625	136	100	10	.576
24. Weeb Ewbank	Baltimore Colts, New York Jets	20	130	129	7	.502	4	1	.800	134	130	7	.508
25. Mike Ditka	Chicago Bears, New Orleans Saints	14	121	95	0	.560	6	6	.500	127	101	0	.557
26. Dick Vermeil	Philadelphia Eagles, St. Louis Rams, Kansas City Chiefs	15	120	109	0	.524	6	5	.545	126	114	0	.525
27. Jim Mora	New Orleans Saints, Indianapolis Colts	15	125	106	0	.541	0	6	.000	125	112	0	.527
28. George Seifert	San Francisco 49ers, Carolina Panthers	11	114	62	0	.648	10	5	.667	124	67	0	.649
29. Sid Gillman	Los Angeles Rams, Los Angeles-San Diego Chargers, Houston Oilers	18	122	99	7	.552	1	5	.167	123	104	7	.542
30. George Allen	Los Angeles Rams, Washington Redskins	12	116	47	5	.712	2	7	.222	118	54	5	.686
Norv Turner	Washington Redskins, Oakland Raiders, San Diego Chargers	15	114	122	1	.483	4	4	.500	118	126	1	.484
32. Dennis Green	Minnesota Vikings, Arizona Cardinals	13	113	94	0	.546	4	8	.333	117	102	0	.534
33. Don Coryell	St. Louis Cardinals, San Diego Chargers	14	111	83	1	.572	3	6	.333	114	89	1	.561
34. John Madden	Oakland Raiders	10	103	32	7	.759	9	7	.563	112	39	7	.739
35. Ray (Buddy) Parker	Chicago Cardinals, Detroit Lions, Pittsburgh Steelers	15	104	75	9	.581	3	1	.750	107	76	9	.585
36. Vince Lombardi	Green Bay Packers, Washington Redskins	10	96	34	6	.739	9	1	.900	105	35	6	.750
Tom Flores	Oakland-Los Angeles Raiders, Seattle Seahawks	12	97	87	0	.527	8	3	.727	105	90	0	.538
38. Bill Walsh	San Francisco 49ers	10	92	59	1	.609	10	4	.714	102	63	1	.617
39. Jon Gruden	Oakland Raiders, Tampa Bay Buccaneers	11	95	81	0	.540	5	4	.556	100	85	0	.541
John Fox	Carolina Panthers, Denver Broncos	11	94	82	0	.534	6	5	.545	100	87	0	.535

Active coaches in bold.
From 1920-71, tie games were not included in winning percentage.

78th Annual NFL Draft, April 25-27, 2013
+Denotes Compensatory Selection
#Denotes Underclassman Selection

ARIZONA CARDINALS
1. Jonathan Cooper—7, G, North Carolina
2.# Kevin Minter—45, LB, Louisiana State
3.# Tyrann Mathieu—69, DB, Louisiana State
4. Alex Okafor—103, LB, Texas
   Earl Watford—116, G, James Madison, from
       NEW YORK GIANTS
5. Stepfan Taylor—140, RB, Stanford
6. Ryan Swope—174, WR, Texas A&M
   Andre Ellington—187, RB, Clemson, from
       NEW YORK GIANTS
7. D.C. Jefferson—219, TE, Rutgers

ATLANTA FALCONS
1. Desmond Trufant—22, DB, Washington
2. Robert Alford—60, DB, Southeastern Louisiana
4. Malliciah Goodman—127, DE, Clemson
+ Levine Toilolo—133, TE, Stanford
5.# Stansly Maponga—153, DE, Texas Christian
7.+ Kemal Ishmael—243, DB, Central Florida
 + Zeke Motta—244, DB, Notre Dame
 + Sean Renfree—249, QB, Duke

BALTIMORE RAVENS
1.# Matt Elam—32, DB, Florida
2. Arthur Brown—56, LB, Kansas State, from SEATTLE
3. Brandon Williams—94, DT, Missouri Southern
4. John Simon—129, LB, Ohio State
 + Kyle Juszczyk—130, RB, Harvard
5.+ Ricky Wagner—168, G, Wisconsin
6. Kapron Lewis-Moore—200, DE, Notre Dame
 + Ryan Jensen—203, C, Colorado State-Pueblo
7. Aaron Mellette—238, WR, Elon
 + Marc Anthony—247, DB, California

BUFFALO BILLS
1. E.J. Manuel—16, QB, Florida State, from ST. LOUIS
2.# Robert Woods—41, WR, Southern California
   Kiko Alonso—46, LB, Oregon, from ST. LOUIS
3. Marquise Goodwin—78, WR, Texas, from ST. LOUIS
4. Duke Williams—105, DB, Nevada
5. Jonathan Meeks—143, DB, Clemson
6. Dustin Hopkins—177, K, Florida State
7. Chris Gragg—222, TE, Arkansas

CAROLINA PANTHERS
1. Star Lotulelei—14, DT, Utah
2. Kawann Short—44, DT, Purdue
4. Edmund Kugbila—108, G, Valdosta State
5. A.J. Klein—148, LB, Iowa State
6. Kenjon Barner—182, RB, Oregon

CHICAGO BEARS
1. Kyle Long—20, G, Oregon
2. Jon Bostic—50, LB, Florida
4. Khaseem Greene—117, LB, Rutgers
5. Jordan Mills—163, T, Louisiana Tech, from ATLANTA
6. Cornelius Washington—188, DE, Georgia
7.# Marquess Wilson—236, WR, Washington State,
       from ATLANTA

CINCINNATI BENGALS
1. Tyler Eifert—21, TE, Notre Dame
2.# Giovani Bernard—37, RB, North Carolina, from OAKLAND
   Margus Hunt—53, DE, Southern Methodist
3. Shawn Williams—84, DB, Georgia
4. Sean Porter—118, LB, Texas A&M
5. Tanner Hawkinson—156, G, Kansas
6. Rex Burkhead—190, RB, Nebraska
   Cobi Hamilton—197, WR, Arkansas, from NEW ENGLAND
7.+ Reid Fragel—240, T, Ohio State
 + T.J. Johnson—251, C, South Carolina

CLEVELAND BROWNS
1.# Barkevious Mingo—6, DE, Louisiana State
2. Choice Exercised in 2012 Supplemental Draft
       for Josh Gordon, WR, Baylor
3. Leon McFadden—68, DB, San Diego State
6. Jamoris Slaughter—175, DB, Notre Dame
7. Armonty Bryant—217, DE, East Central, from MIAMI
   Garrett Gilkey—227, T, Chadron State,
       from CINCINNATI through SAN FRANCISCO

DALLAS COWBOYS
1.# Travis Frederick—31, C, Wisconsin, from SAN FRANCISCO
2.# Gavin Escobar—47, TE, San Diego State
3. Terrance Williams—74, WR, Baylor,
       from CAROLINA through SAN FRANCISCO
   J.J. Wilcox—80, DB, Georgia Southern
4. B.W. Webb—114, DB, William & Mary
5.# Joseph Randle—151, RB, Oklahoma State
6. DeVonte Holloman—185, LB, South Carolina

DENVER BRONCOS
1. Sylvester Williams—28, DT, North Carolina
2. Montee Ball—58, RB, Wisconsin
3. Kayvon Webster—90, DB, South Florida
5. Quanterus Smith—146, DE, Western Kentucky,
       from MIAMI through GREEN BAY
   Tavarres King—161, WR, Georgia
6. Vinston Painter—173, T, Virginia Tech,
       from PHILADELPHIA through CLEVELAND,
       SAN FRANCISCO and GREEN BAY
7. Zac Dysert—234, QB, Miami (Ohio)

DETROIT LIONS
1. Ezekiel Ansah—5, DE, Brigham Young
2. Darius Slay—36, DB, Mississippi State
3. Larry Warford—65, G, Kentucky
4.+ Devin Taylor—132, DE, South Carolina
5. Sam Martin—165, P, Appalachian State,
       from BALTIMORE through SEATTLE
6. Corey Fuller—171, WR, Virginia Tech
   Theo Riddick—199, RB, Notre Dame,
       from SAN FRANCISCO through
       BALTIMORE and SEATTLE
7. Michael Williams—211, TE, Alabama
 + Brandon Hepburn—245, LB, Florida A&M

GREEN BAY PACKERS

1. Datone Jones—26, DE, UCLA
2.# Eddie Lacy—61, RB, Alabama, from SAN FRANCISCO
4.# David Bakhitari—109, T, Colorado,
      from NEW ORLEANS through MIAMI
    J.C. Tretter—122, T, Cornell
    Johnathan Franklin—125, RB, UCLA, from DENVER
5. Micah Hyde—159, DB, Iowa
 + Josh Boyd—167, DE, Mississippi State
6. Nate Palmer—193, LB, Illinois State
7. Charles Johnson—216, WR, Grand Valley State,
      from TENNESSEE through SAN FRANCISCO
    Kevin Dorsey—224, WR, Maryland,
      from DALLAS through MIAMI
    Sam Barrington—232, LB, South Florida

HOUSTON TEXANS

1.# DeAndre Hopkins—27, WR, Clemson
2. D.J. Swearinger—57, DB, South Carolina
3. Brennan Williams—89, T, North Carolina
#+ Sam Montgomery—95, DE, Louisiana State
4. Trevardo Williams—124, LB, Connecticut
6. David Quessenberry—176, T, San Jose State,
      from TENNESSEE through MINNESOTA,
      ARIZONA and OAKLAND
    Alan Bonner—195, WR, Jacksonville State
    Chris Jones—198, DT, Bowling Green,
      from ATLANTA through ST. LOUIS
 + Ryan Griffin—201, TE, Connecticut

INDIANAPOLIS COLTS

1.# Bjoern Werner—24, DE, Florida State
3. Hugh Thornton—86, G, Illinois
4. Khaled Holmes—121, C, Southern California
5. Montori Hughes—139, DT, Tennessee-Martin,
      from CLEVELAND
6. John Boyett—192, DB, Oregon
7. Kerwynn Williams—230, RB, Utah State
 + Justice Cunningham—254, TE, South Carolina

JACKSONVILLE JAGUARS

1.# Luke Joeckel—2, T, Texas A&M
2. Johnathan Cyprien—33, DB, Florida International
3. Dwayne Gratz—64, DB, Connecticut
4.# Ace Sanders—101, WR, South Carolina,
      from PHILADELPHIA
5. Denard Robinson—135, RB, Michigan
6. Josh Evans—169, DB, Florida
7. Jeremy Harris—208, DB, New Mexico State
    Demetrius McCray—210, DB, Appalachian State,
      from PHILADELPHIA

KANSAS CITY CHIEFS

1. Eric Fisher—1, T, Central Michigan
3. Travis Kelce—63, TE, Cincinnati
+# Knile Davis—96, RB, Arkansas
4. Nico Johnson—99, LB, Alabama
5. Sanders Commings—134, DB, Georgia
6. Eric Kush—170, C, California (Pa.)
 + Braden Wilson—204, RB, Kansas State
7. Mike Catapano—207, LB, Princeton

MIAMI DOLPHINS

1. Dion Jordan—3, DE, Oregon, from OAKLAND
2. Jamar Taylor—54, DB, Boise State, from INDIANAPOLIS
3. Dallas Thomas—77, T, Tennessee
    Will Davis—93, DB, Utah State,
      from SAN FRANCISCO through GREEN BAY
4.# Jelani Jenkins—104, LB, Florida, from CLEVELAND
 # Dion Sims—106, TE, Michigan State,
      from NEW YORK JETS through NEW ORLEANS
5. Mike Gillislee—164, RB, Florida,
      from SAN FRANCISCO through CLEVELAND
 + Caleb Sturgis—166, K, Florida
7.+ Don Jones—250, DB, Arkansas State

MINNESOTA VIKINGS

1.# Sharrif Floyd—23, DT, Florida
 # Xavier Rhodes—25, DB, Florida State, from SEATTLE
 # Cordarrelle Patterson—29, WR, Tennessee,
      from NEW ENGLAND
4. Gerald Hodges—120, LB, Penn State
5. Jeff Locke—155, P, UCLA
6. Jeff Baca—196, G, UCLA, from DENVER through
      PHILADELPHIA and TAMPA BAY
7. Michael Mauti—213, LB, Penn State, from ARIZONA
    Travis Bond—214, G, North Carolina,
      from BUFFALO through SEATTLE
    Everett Dawkins—229, DT, Florida State,
      reacquired through NEW ENGLAND
      and TAMPA BAY

NEW ENGLAND PATRIOTS

2. Jamie Collins—52, LB, Southern Mississippi,
      from MINNESOTA
    Aaron Dobson—59, WR, Marshall
3.# Logan Ryan—83, DB, Rutgers, from MINNESOTA
    Duron Harmon—91, DB, Rutgers
4. Josh Boyce—102, WR, Texas Christian,
      from DETROIT through MINNESOTA
7. Michael Buchanan—226, DE, Illinois,
      from CHICAGO and TAMPA BAY
    Steve Beauharnais—235, LB, Rutgers

NEW ORLEANS SAINTS

1. Kenny Vaccaro—15, DB, Texas
3. Terron Armstead—75, T, Arkansas-Pine Bluff
    John Jenkins—82, NT, Georgia,
      from CHICAGO through MIAMI
5.# Kenny Stills—144, WR, Oklahoma
6. Rufus Johnson—183, LB, Tarleton State

NEW YORK GIANTS

1. Justin Pugh—19, T, Syracuse
2.# Johnathan Hankins—49, DT, Ohio State
3.# Damontre Moore—81, DE, Texas A&M
4. Ryan Nassib—110, QB, Syracuse,
      from SAN DIEGO through ARIZONA
5. Cooper Taylor—152, DB, Richmond
7. Eric Herman—225, G, Ohio
 + Michael Cox—253, RB, Massachusetts

NEW YORK JETS

1.# Dee Milliner—9, DB, Alabama
 # Sheldon Richardson—13, DT, Missouri, from TAMPA BAY
2. Geno Smith—39, QB, West Virginia
3. Brian Winters—72, T, Kent State
5. Oday Aboushi—141, T, Virginia
6. William Campbell—178, G, Michigan
7. Tommy Bohanon—215, RB, Wake Forest

OAKLAND RAIDERS

1. D.J. Hayden—12, DB, Houston, from MIAMI
2.# Menelik Watson—42, T, Florida State, from MIAMI
3. Sio Moore—66, LB, Connecticut
4. Tyler Wilson—112, QB, Arkansas, from TAMPA BAY
6. Nick Kasa—172, TE, Colorado
 Latavius Murray—181, RB, Central Florida,
  from TAMPA BAY
 Mychal Rivera—184, TE, Tennessee,
  from ST. LOUIS through HOUSTON
 + Stacy McGee—205, DT, Oklahoma
7. Brice Butler—209, WR, San Diego State
 David Bass—233, DE, Missouri Western, from HOUSTON

PHILADELPHIA EAGLES

1. Lane Johnson—4, T, Oklahoma
2.# Zach Ertz—35, TE, Stanford
3.# Bennie Logan—67, DT, Louisiana State
4. Matt Barkley—98, QB, Southern California,
  from JACKSONVILLE
5. Earl Wolff—136, DB, North Carolina State
7.# Joe Kruger—212, DE, Utah, from CLEVELAND
 Jordan Poyer—218, DB, Oregon State, from TAMPA BAY
 + David King—239, DE, Oklahoma

PITTSBURGH STEELERS

1.# Jarvis Jones—17, LB, Georgia
2.# Le'Veon Bell—48, RB, Michigan State
3. Markus Wheaton—79, WR, Oregon State
4. Shamarko Thomas—111, DB, Syracuse,
  from MIAMI through CLEVELAND
 Landry Jones—115, QB, Oklahoma
5. Terry Hawthorne—150, DB, Illinois
6. Justin Brown—186, WR, Oklahoma
 + Vince Williams—206, LB, Florida State
7. Nicholas Williams—223, DE, Samford

ST. LOUIS RAMS

1. Tavon Austin—8, WR, West Virginia, from BUFFALO
 # Alec Ogletree—30, LB, Georgia, from ATLANTA
3. T.J. McDonald—71, DB, Southern California, from BUFFALO
 # Stedman Bailey—92, WR, West Virginia, from ATLANTA
4. Barrett Jones—113, C, Alabama
5. Brandon McGee—149, DB, Miami
 Zac Stacy—160, RB, Vanderbilt, from HOUSTON

SAN DIEGO CHARGERS

1. D.J. Fluker—11, T, Alabama
2. Manti Te'o—38, LB, Notre Dame, from ARIZONA
3.# Keenan Allen—76, WR, California
5.# Steve Williams—145, DB, California
6. Tourek Williams—179, LB, Florida International
7. Brad Sorensen—221, QB, Southern Utah

SAN FRANCISCO 49ERS

1.# Eric Reid—18, DB, Louisiana State, from DALLAS
2. Cornellius Carradine—40, DE, Florida State,
  from TENNESSEE
 Vance McDonald—55, TE, Rice, from GREEN BAY
3.# Corey Lemonier—88, LB, Auburn, from GREEN BAY
4. Quinton Patton—128, WR, Louisiana Tech
 + # Marcus Lattimore—131, RB, South Carolina
5. Quinton Dial—157, DT, Alabama, from INDIANAPOLIS
6. Nick Moody—180, LB, Florida State, from MIAMI
7. B.J. Daniels—237, QB, South Florida
 + Carter Bykowski—246, T, Iowa State
 + Marcus Cooper—252, DB, Rutgers

SEATTLE SEAHAWKS

2. Christine Michael—62, RB, Texas A&M, from BALTIMORE
3. Jordan Hill—87, DT, Penn State
4. Chris Harper—123, WR, Kansas State
5. Jesse Williams—137, DT, Alabama, from DETROIT
 # Tharold Simon—138, DB, Louisiana State, from OAKLAND
 Luke Willson—158, TE, Rice
6.# Spencer Ware—194, RB, Louisiana State
7. Ryan Seymour—220, G, Vanderbilt, from NEW ORLEANS
 Ty Powell—231, LB, Harding
 + Jared Smith—241, G, New Hampshire
 + Michael Bowie—242, T, Northeastern State (Okla.)

TAMPA BAY BUCCANEERS

2. Johnthan Banks—43, DB, Mississippi State
3. Mike Glennon—73, QB, North Carolina State
4.# Akeem Spence—100, DT, Illinois, from OAKLAND
 # William Gholston—126, DE, Michigan State,
  from NEW ENGLAND
5. Steven Means—147, DE, Buffalo
6. Mike James—189, RB, Miami, from MINNESOTA

TENNESSEE TITANS

1. Chance Warmack—10, G, Alabama
2.# Justin Hunter—34, WR, Tennessee,
  from KANSAS CITY through SAN FRANCISCO
3. Blidi Wreh-Wilson—70, DB, Connecticut
 + Zaviar Gooden—97, LB, Missouri
4. Brian Schwenke—107, C, California
5. Lavar Edwards—142, DE, Louisiana State
6.+ Khalid Wooten—202, DB, Nevada
7.+ Daimion Stafford—248, DB, Nebraska

WASHINGTON REDSKINS

2.# David Amerson—51, DB, North Carolina State
3.# Jordan Reed—85, TE, Florida
4. Phillip Thomas—119, DB, Fresno State
5. Chris Thompson—154, RB, Florida State
 Brandon Jenkins—162, LB, Florida State,
  from NEW ENGLAND
6. Bacarri Rambo—191, DB, Georgia
7.# Jawan Jamison—228, RB, Rutgers

NUMBER OF PLAYERS DRAFTED— 2013

BY POSITION:

Defensive Backs	52
Linebackers	33
Running Backs	27
Wide Receivers	27
Defensive Ends	25
Tackles	20
Defensive Tackles	16
Tight Ends	16
Guards	15
Quarterbacks	11
Centers	7
Kicker	2
Punters	2
Nose Tackle	1

BY COLLEGE:

Florida State	11
Alabama	9
Louisiana State	9
Florida	8
Georgia	8
Rutgers	7
South Carolina	7
Notre Dame	6
Oklahoma	6
Connecticut	5
North Carolina	5
Oregon	5
Texas A&M	5
Arkansas	4
California	4
Clemson	4
Illinois	4
Southern California	4
Tennessee	4
UCLA	4
Kansas State	3
Michigan State	3
Mississippi State	3
North Carolina State	3
Ohio State	3
Penn State	3
San Diego State	3
South Florida	3
Stanford	3
Syracuse	3
Texas	3
West Virginia	3
Wisconsin	3
Appalachian State	2
Central Florida	2
Colorado	2
Florida International	2
Iowa State	2
Louisiana Tech	2
Miami	2
Michigan	2
Missouri	2
Nebraska	2
Nevada	2
Oregon State	2
Rice	2
Texas Christian	2
Utah	2
Utah State	2
Vanderbilt	2
Virginia Tech	2

Arkansas-Pine Bluff	1
Arkansas State	1
Auburn	1
Baylor	1
Boise State	1
Bowling Green	1
Brigham Young	1
Buffalo	1
California (Pa.)	1
Central Michigan	1
Chadron State	1
Cincinnati	1
Colorado State-Pueblo	1
Cornell	1
Duke	1
East Central	1
Elon	1
Florida A&M	1
Fresno State	1
Georgia Southern	1
Grand Valley State	1
Harding	1
Harvard	1
Houston	1
Illinois State	1
Iowa	1
Jacksonville State	1
James Madison	1
Kansas	1
Kent State	1
Kentucky	1
Marshall	1
Maryland	1
Massachusetts	1
Miami (Ohio)	1
Missouri Southern	1
Missouri Western	1
New Hampshire	1
New Mexico State	1
Northeastern State (Okla.)	1
Ohio	1
Oklahoma State	1
Princeton	1
Purdue	1
Richmond	1
Samford	1
San Jose State	1
Southeastern Louisiana	1
Southern Methodist	1
Southern Mississippi	1
Southern Utah	1
Tarleton State	1
Tennessee-Martin	1
Valdosta State	1
Virginia	1
Wake Forest	1
Washington	1
Washington State	1
Western Kentucky	1
William & Mary	1

BY CONFERENCE:

Southeastern	63
Atlantic Coast	31
Pacific 12	28
Big 12	22
Big Ten	22
Big East	19
Conference USA	8
Independent	7
Mid-American	7
Mountain West	7
Western Athletic	6
Southern	5
Colonial Athletic	4
Sun Belt	4
Ivy	3
Mid-America Intercollegiate Athletic	3
Great American	2
Ohio Valley	2
Rocky Mountain Athletic	2
Big Sky	1
Great Lakes Intercollegiate Athletic	1
Gulf South	1
Lone Star	1
Mid-Eastern Athletic	1
Missouri Valley Football	1
Pennsylvania State Athletic	1
Southland	1
Southwestern Athletic	1

UNDERCLASSMEN IN THE DRAFT

Year	D1-FBS	Drafted	In Top 10
1990	28	18	5
1991	23	19	1
1992	30	21	5
1993	34	24	5
1994	31	25	6
1995	33	22	2
1996	24	16	4
1997	34	25	6
1998	32	19	3
1999	31	22	5
2000	26	20	4
2001	35	27	5
2002	38	26	2
2003	47	32	5
2004	43	35	5
2005	51	37	4
2006	52	33	6
2007	40	29	5
2008	53	39	4
2009	46	41	5
2010	53	46	5
2011	56	43	8
2012	65	44	8
2013	73	52	3

The NFL uses a system of Referee Replay Review to aid officiating. The following procedures will be used:

Reviews by Referee: All Replay Reviews will be conducted by the Referee on a field-level monitor after consultation with the other covering official(s), prior to review. A decision will be reversed only when the Referee has indisputable visual evidence available to him that warrants the change.

Coaches' Challenge: In each game, a team will be permitted two challenges that will initiate Instant Replay reviews except for plays when the on-field ruling is a score for either team, an interception, a fumble or backward pass that is recovered by an opponent or goes out of bounds through an opponent's end zone, or a muffed scrimmage kick recovered by the kicking team. A team is also prohibited from challenging any ruling after the two-minute warning of each half, and throughout any overtime period. Each challenge will require the use of a team time out. If a challenge is upheld, the time out will be restored to the challenging team. If both challenges are upheld, a third challenge will be awarded to the challenging team. No challenges will be recognized from a team that has exhausted its time outs.

Replay Official's Request for Review: After all scoring plays, interceptions, fumbles and backward passes that are recovered by an opponent or go out of bounds through an opponent's end zone, muffed scrimmage kicks recovered by the kicking team, and after the two-minute warning of each half throughout any overtime period, any Replay Review will be initiated by a Replay Official from a Replay Booth comparable to the location of the coaches' booth or Press Box. There is no limit to the number of Replay Reviews that may be initiated by the Replay Official. His ability to initiate a review will be unrelated to the number of time outs that either team has remaining, and no time out will be charged for any review initiated by the Replay Official.

Time Limit: Each review will be a maximum of 60 seconds in length, timed from when the Referee begins his review of the replay at the field-level monitor.

Reviewable Plays: The Replay System will cover the following play situations only:

A. Plays governed by Sideline, Goal Line, End Zone, and End Line:
   1. Scoring plays, including a runner breaking the plane of the goal line.
   2. Pass complete/incomplete/intercepted at sideline, goal line, end zone, and end line.
   3. Runner/receiver in or out of bounds.
   4. Recovery of loose ball in or out of bounds.

B. Passing Plays:
   1. Pass ruled complete/incomplete/intercepted in the field of play.
   2. Touching of a forward pass by an ineligible receiver.
   3. Touching of a forward pass by a defensive player.
   4. Quarterback (Passer) forward pass or fumble.
   5. Illegal forward pass beyond the line of scrimmage.
   6. Illegal forward pass after change of possession.
   7. Forward or backward pass thrown from behind the line of scrimmage.

C. Other Reviewable Plays:
   1. Runner not ruled down by defensive contact.
   2. Runner ruled down by defensive contact when the recovery of a fumble by an opponent or a teammate occurs in the action that happens following the fumble.
   3. Runner ruled out of bounds when the recovery of a fumble by an opponent or a teammate occurs in the action that happens following the fumble.
   4. Ruling of incomplete pass when the recovery of a passer's fumble, or the recovery of a backward pass, by an opponent or a teammate occurs in the action following the fumble or backward pass.
   5. Ruling of a loose ball out of bounds when it is recovered in the field of play by an opponent or a teammate in the action after the ball hits the ground.

Note 1: If the ruling of down by contact or incomplete pass is changed, the ball belongs to the recovering player at the spot of the recovery of the fumble, and any advance is nullified. If the ball goes out of bounds in an end zone, the result of the play will be either a touchback or a safety.

Note 2: If the Referee does not have indisputable visual evidence as to which player recovered the loose ball, the ruling on the field will stand.

Note 3: This does not apply to complete/incomplete passes, or the ruling of forward progress.

   6. Forward progress with respect to a first down.
   7. Touching of a kick.
   8. A field goal or Try attempt that crosses below or above the crossbar, inside or outside the uprights when it is lower than the top of the uprights, or touches anything.
   9. Number of players on the field at the snap.
   10. Illegal forward handoff.
   11. A loose ball in play striking a video board, guide wire, sky cam, or any other object.

Non-reviewable plays include, but are not limited to:
1. Status of the clock.
2. Proper down.
3. Penalty administration.
4. Runner ruled down by defensive contact (not involving fumbles).
5. Forward progress not relating to first down or goal line.
6. Recovery of a loose ball that does not involve a boundary line or the end zone.
7. Field goal or try attempts that cross above either upright without touching anything.
8. Inadvertent whistle.

INSTANT REPLAY HISTORY

From 1986-1991, a limited system of Instant Replay was used on a year-by-year basis. Replay also was experimented with during the 1996 and 1998 preseasons. For the 1999 season, the NFL introduced a system of Referee Replay Review to aid officiating. That system was extended on a one-year basis for the 2000 season and then approved for the next three years through 2003. The system was extended on a five-year basis in March 2004 and was later installed permanently in March 2007.

Following are the results of the different systems:

REGULAR SEASON, 1986-1991

Year	Games	Plays Closely Reviewed	Reversals
1986	224	374	38
1987	210	490	57
1988	224	537	53
1989	224	492	65
1990	224	504	73
1991	224	570	90
TOTAL	1,330	2,967	376

PRESEASON, 1996, 1998

Year	Games	Challenges	Reversals
1996	10	13	3
1998	10	10	3
TOTAL	20	23	6

REGULAR SEASON, 1999-2012

Year	Games	Total Replay Reviews	Challenges	Reversals
1999	248	195	133	57
2000	248	247	179	84
2001	248	258	191	89
2002	256	294	208	94
2003	256	255	184	66
2004	256	283	233	88
2005	256	295	223	92
2006	256	311	237	107
2007	256	327	250	122
2008	256	315	229	117
2009	256	328	228	126
2010	256	361	252	133
2011	256	390	209	172
2012	256	435	157	170
TOTAL	3,560	4,294	2,913	1,517

TIE-BREAKING PROCEDURES

The following procedures will be used to break standings ties for postseason playoffs and to determine regular-season schedules. Note: Tie games count as one-half win and one-half loss for both clubs.

TO BREAK A TIE WITHIN A DIVISION

If, at the end of the regular season, two or more clubs in the same division finish with the best won-lost-tied percentage, the following steps will be taken until a champion is determined:

TWO CLUBS

1. Head-to-head (best won-lost-tied percentage in games between the clubs.)

2. Best won-lost-tied percentage in games played within the division.

3. Best won-lost-tied percentage in common games.

4. Best won-lost-tied percentage in games played within the conference.

5. Strength of victory in all games.

6. Strength of schedule in all games.

7. Best combined ranking among conference teams in points scored and points allowed in all games.

8. Best combined ranking among all teams in points scored and points allowed in all games.

9. Best net points in common games.

10. Best net points in all games.

11. Best net touchdowns in all games.

12. Coin toss.

THREE OR MORE CLUBS

(Note: If two clubs remain tied after one or more clubs are eliminated during any step, tie-breaker re-starts at Step One of two-club format. If three clubs remain tied after a fourth club is eliminated during any step, tie-breaker re-starts at Step One of three-club format.)

1. Head-to-head (best won-lost-tied percentage in games among the clubs.)

2. Best won-lost-tied percentage in games played within the division.

3. Best won-lost-tied percentage in common games.

4. Best won-lost-tied percentage in games played within the conference.

5. Strength of victory in all games.

6. Strength of schedule in all games.

7. Best combined ranking among conference teams in points scored and points allowed in all games.

8. Best combined ranking among all teams in points scored and points allowed in all games.

9. Best net points in common games.

10. Best net points in all games.

11. Best net touchdowns in all games.

12. Coin toss.

TO BREAK A TIE FOR THE WILD-CARD TEAM

If necessary to break ties to determine the two Wild Card clubs from each conference, the following steps will be taken:

A. If all the tied clubs are from the same division, apply division tie-breaker.

B. If the tied clubs are from different divisions, apply the following steps:

TWO CLUBS

1. Head-to-head, if applicable.

2. Best won-lost-tied percentage in the games played within the conference.

3. Best won-lost-tied percentage in common games, minimum of four.

4. Strength of victory in all games.

5. Strength of schedule in all games.

6. Best combined ranking among conference teams in points scored and points allowed in all games.

7. Best combined ranking among all teams in points scored and points allowed in all games.

8. Best net points in conference games.

9. Best net points in all games.

10. Best net touchdowns in all games.

11. Coin toss.

THREE OR MORE CLUBS

(Note: If two clubs remain tied after one or more clubs are eliminated during any step, tie-breaker re-starts at Step One of two-club format. If three clubs remain tied after a fourth club is eliminated during any step, tie-breaker re-starts at Step Two of three-club format.)

1. Apply division tie-breaker to eliminate all but highest ranked club in each division prior to proceeding to step two. The original seeding within a division upon application of the division tie-breaker remains the same for all subsequent applications of the procedure that are necessary to identify the two Wild Card participants.

2. Head-to-head sweep (apply only if one has defeated each of the others or one club has lost to each of the others.)

3. Best won-lost-tied percentage in games played within the conference.

4. Best won-lost-tied percentage in common games, minimum of four.

5. Strength of victory in all games.

6. Strength of schedule in all games.

7. Best combined ranking among conference teams in points scored and points allowed in all games.

8. Best combined ranking among all teams in points scored and points allowed in all games.

9. Best net points in conference games.

10. Best net points in all games.

11. Best net touchdowns in all games.

12. Coin toss.

When the first Wild Card Team has been identified, the procedure is repeated to name the second Wild Card (i.e., eliminate all but the highest ranked club in each division prior to proceeding to step two). In situations where three teams from the same division are involved in the procedure, the original seeding of the teams remains the same for subsequent applications of the tie-breaker if the top-ranked team in that division qualifies for a Wild Card berth.

OTHER TIE-BREAKING PROCEDURES

1. Only one club advances to the playoffs in any tie-breaking step. Remaining tied clubs revert to the first step of the applicable division or Wild Card tie-breakers. As an example, if two clubs remain tied in any tie-breaker step after all other clubs have been eliminated, the procedure reverts to Step 1 of the two-club format to determine the winner. When one club wins the tie-breaker, all other clubs revert to Step 1 of the applicable two-club or three-club format.

2. In comparing records against common opponents among tied teams, the best won-lost-tied percentage is the deciding factor since teams may have played an unequal number of games.

3. To determine home-field priority among division-titlists, apply Wild Card tie-breakers.

4. To determine home-field priority for Wild Card qualifiers, apply division tie-breakers (if teams are from the same division) or Wild Card tie-breakers (if teams are from different divisions).

5. To determine the best combined ranking among conference teams in points scored and points allowed, add a team's position in the two categories, and the lowest score wins. For example, if Team A is first in points scored and second in points allowed, its combined ranking is "3." If Team B is third in points scored and first in points allowed, its combined ranking is "4." Team A then wins the tiebreaker. If two teams are tied for a position, both teams are awarded the ranking as if they held it solely. For example, if Team A and Team B are tied for first in points scored, each team is assigned a ranking of "1" in that category, and if Team C is third, its ranking will still be "3."

TIE-BREAKING PROCEDURE FOR SELECTION MEETING

1. Clubs not participating in the playoffs shall select in the first through 20th positions in reverse standings order.

2. The Super Bowl winner is last and Super Bowl loser is next-to-last.

3. The losers of the Conference Championship games shall select 29th and 30th based on won-lost-tied percentage.

4. The losers of the Divisional playoff games shall select 25th through 28th based on won-lost-tied percentage.

5. The losers of the Wild Card games shall select 21st through 24th based on won-lost-tied percentage.

If ties exist in any grouping except (2) above, such ties shall be broken by strength-of-schedule. If any ties cannot be broken by strength-of-schedule, the divisional or conference tie-breakers, if applicable, shall be applied. Any ties that still exist shall be broken by a coin flip.

WAIVERS

The waiver system is a procedure by which player contracts or NFL rights to players are made available by a club to other clubs in the League. During the procedure, the 31 other clubs either file claims to obtain the players or waive the opportunity to do so—thus the term "waiver." Claiming clubs are assigned players on a priority based on the inverse of won-and-lost standing. The claiming period is 24 hours from the first business day after the Super Bowl through the conclusion of the regular season. If a player passes through waivers unclaimed, he becomes a free agent. All waivers are no recall and no withdrawal. Under the Collective Bargaining Agreement, from the beginning of the waiver system each year through the trading deadline, any veteran who has acquired four years of pension credit is not subject to the waiver system if the club desires to release him. After the trading deadline, such players are subject to the waiver system.

ACTIVE/INACTIVE LIST

The Active/Inactive List is the principal status for players participating for a club. It consists of all players under contract who are eligible for preseason, regular-season, and postseason games. Teams are permitted to open training camp with no more than 90 players under contract and thereafter must meet two mandatory roster reductions prior to the season opener. Teams will be permitted an Active List of 46 players and an Inactive List of seven players for each regular-season and postseason game. Teams also are permitted to establish Practice Squads of up to eight players who are eligible to participate in practice, but these players remain free agents and are eligible to sign with any other team in the league.

August 27.....................Roster reduction to 75 players
August 31.....................Roster reduction to 53 players
September 1.................Teams establish a Practice Squad of
 up to eight players

In addition to the squad limits described above, the overall roster limit of 90 players remains in effect throughout the regular season and postseason. The overall limit is applicable to players on a team's Active, Inactive, and certain Exempt Lists, players on the Practice Squad, and players on the Reserve List as Injured, Physically Unable to Perform, Non-Football Illness/Injury, and Suspended by Club.

RESERVE LIST

The Reserve List is a status for players who, for reasons of injury, retirement, military service, or other circumstances, are not immediately available for participation with a club. Players on Reserve/Injured are not eligible to practice or return to the Active/Inactive List in the same season that they are placed on Reserve. Players in the category of Reserve/Retired, Reserve/Did Not Report, Reserve/Exclusive Rights, and players who were placed in the category of Reserve/Left Squad in a previous season may not be reinstated during the period from 30 days before the end of the regular season through the postseason.

ANNUAL ACTIVE PLAYER LIMITS

NFL

Year(s)	Limit
2011-13	46
1991-2010	45**
1985-90	45
1983-84	49
1982	45†-49
1978-81	45
1975-77	43
1974	47
1964-73	40
1963	37
1961-62	36
1960	38
1959	36
1957-58	35
1951-56	33
1949-50	32
1948	35
1947	35*-34
1945-46	33
1943-44	28
1940-42	33
1938-39	30
1936-37	25
1935	24
1930-34	20
1926-29	18
1925	16

** 45 plus a third quarterback
† 45 for first two games
* 35 for first three games

AFL

Year(s)	Limit
1966-69	40
1965	38
1964	34
1962-63	33
1960-61	35

NFL FREE AGENCY MOVEMENT

The following chart details veteran free agents who signed with new teams:

	Unrestricted	Restricted	Transition	Franchise	TOTALS
1993	108	8	4	1	121
1994	121	7	4	0	132
1995	171	6	2	0	179
1996	100	4	2	0	106
1997	86	2	2	0	90
1998	112	4	1	2	119
1999	115	2	1	0	118
2000	107	4	0	0	111
2001	93	4	0	0	97
2002	130	1	0	0	131
2003	111	5	1	0	117
2004	124	1	1	0	126
2005	104	3	0	0	107
2006	149	4	1	0	154
2007	126	4	0	0	130
2008	132	3	0	0	135
2009	128	0	0	0	128
2010	51	1	0	0	52
2011	163	0	0	0	163
2012	143	0	0	0	143

The AFC

**American Football Conference
North Division**
Team Colors: Black, Purple, and Metallic
Gold
1 Winning Drive
Owings Mills, Maryland 21117
Telephone: (410) 701-4000

2013 SCHEDULE
PRESEASON
Aug. 8	at Tampa Bay	7:30
Aug. 15	**Atlanta**	7:30
Aug. 22	**Carolina**	8:00
Aug. 29	at St. Louis	8:00

REGULAR SEASON
Sep. 5	at Denver (Thurs)	8:30
Sep. 15	**Cleveland**	1:00
Sep. 22	**Houston**	1:00
Sep. 29	at Buffalo	1:00
Oct. 6	at Miami	1:00
Oct. 13	**Green Bay**	1:00
Oct. 20	at Pittsburgh	4:25
Oct. 27	BYE	
Nov. 3	at Cleveland	4:25
Nov. 10	**Cincinnati**	1:00
Nov. 17	at Chicago	1:00
Nov. 24	**New York Jets**	1:00
Nov. 28	**Pittsburgh** (Thurs)	8:30
Dec. 8	**Minnesota**	1:00
Dec. 16	at Detroit (Mon)	8:40
Dec. 22	**New England**	*8:30
Dec. 29	at Cincinnati	1:00

*All times ET; Sunday night games in
Weeks 11-16 subject to change

Stadium: M&T Bank Stadium
(opened in 1998)
• **Capacity:** 71,008
1101 Russell Street
Baltimore, Maryland 21230
Playing Surface: Sportexe Momentum
Training Camp: 1 Winning Drive
Owings Mills, MD 21117

M&T BANK STADIUM

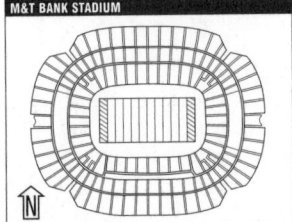

CLUB OFFICIALS
Owner: Steve Bisciotti
President: Dick Cass
Executive Vice President/General
Manager: Ozzie Newsome
Senior Vice President/Public and
Community Relations: Kevin Byrne
Senior Vice President of Football
Administration: Pat Moriarty
Assistant General Manager: Eric DeCosta
Vice President and Chief Financial
Officer: Jeff Goering
Vice President, Corporate Sales
and Business Development:
Kevin Rochlitz
Vice President, Strategic Partnerships
and Sales: Ed Burchell
Vice President, Marketing: Gabrielle Dow
Vice President, Operations: Bob Eller
Vice President, Information Technology:
Bill Jankowski
Vice President, Ticket Sales and
Operations: Baker Koppelman
Vice President, Broadcasting:
Larry Rosen
Vice President, Stadium Operations:
Roy Sommerhof
Vice President of Digital Media:
Michelle Andres
Director of College Scouting: Joe Hortiz
Director of Pro Personnel:
Vincent Newsome
Senior Personnel Assistant:
George Kokinis
Assistant Director of Pro Personnel:
Chad Alexander
Senior Advisor of Player Development:
O.J. Brigance
Director of Player Development:
Harry Swayne
Director of Football Analytics: Sandy Weil
National Scout: Joe Douglas
Scouts: Mark Azevedo, David Blackburn,
Jack Glowik, Milt Hendrickson,
Andrew Weidl, Lonnie Young
Equipment Manager: William Sheridan
Head Athletic Trainer: Mark Smith
Director of Football Video Operations:
Jon Dubé
Assistant Director of Football Video
Operations: Mark Bienvenu
Senior Director, Fields & Grounds/Head
Groundskeeper: Don Follett
Senior Director of Premium
Services/Suites: Theresa Abato
Controller: Jim Coller
Director of Media Relations: Chad Steele
Assistant Director of Public Relations:
Patrick Gleason
Director, Broadcasting Administration:
Don DiRaddo
Director, Information Technology:
Nick Fusee
Director, Human Resources:
Elizabeth Jackson
Director, Security: Darren Sanders
Director of Marketing: Brad Downs
Director of Sales: Keith Weldon
Director of Community Relations:
Heather Darney

COACHING HISTORY
(164-128-1)
Records include postseason games
1996-98	Ted Marchibroda	16-31-1
1999-2007	Brian Billick	85-67-0
2008-2012	John Harbaugh	63-30-0

PAID ATTENDANCE
Home 557,835   Away 520,171
Total 1,078,006
Single-game home record,
71,547 (1/15/12)
Single-season home record, 557,835
(2012)

2013 DRAFT CHOICES
Round	Name	Pos.	College
1	Matt Elam	DB	Florida
2	Arthur Brown	LB	Kansas State
3	Brandon Williams	DT	Missouri Southern
4	John Simon	LB	Ohio State
	Kyle Juszczyk	RB	Harvard
5	Ricky Wagner	G	Wisconsin
6	Kapron Lewis-Moore	DE	Notre Dame
	Ryan Jensen	C	Colorado St.-Pueblo
7	Aaron Mellette	WR	Elon
	Marc Anthony	DB	California

2012 TEAM RECORD
PRESEASON (2-2)

Date	Result	Opponent
08/09	W 31-17	at Atlanta
08/17	L 12-27	Detroit
08/23	W 48-17	Jacksonville
08/30	L 17-31	at St. Louis

REGULAR SEASON (10-6)

Date	Result	Opponent
09/10	W 44-13	Cincinnati
09/16	L 23-24	at Philadelphia
09/23	W 31-30	New England
09/27	W 23-16	Cleveland
10/07	W 9-6	at Kansas City
10/14	W 31-29	Dallas
10/21	L 13-43	at Houston
11/04	W 25-15	at Cleveland
11/11	W 55-20	Oakland
11/18	W 13-10	at Pittsburgh
11/25	W 16-13	at San Diego (OT)
12/02	L 20-23	Pittsburgh
12/09	L 28-31	at Washington (OT)
12/16	L 17-34	Denver
12/23	W 33-14	New York Giants
12/30	L 17-23	at Cincinnati

POSTSEASON (4-0)

Date	Result	Opponent
01/06	W 24-9	Indianapolis
01/12	W 38-35	at Denver (2OT)
01/20	W 28-13	at New England
02/03	W 34-31	vs San Francisco
		at New Orleans

(OT) Overtime

SCORE BY PERIODS

Ravens	88	108	98	101	3 —	398
Opponents	70	103	86	82	3 —	344

2012 TEAM STATISTICS

	Ravens	Opp.
Total First Downs	314	326
Rushing	98	105
Passing	182	187
Penalty	34	34
3rd Down: Made/Att	80/217	83/232
3rd Down Pct.	36.9	35.8
4th Down: Made/Att	6/14	6/12
4th Down Pct.	42.9	50.0
Possession Avg.	28:09	31:51
Total Net Yards	5640	5615
Avg. Per Game	352.5	350.9
Total Plays	1042	1086
Avg. Per Play	5.4	5.2
Net Yards Rushing	1901	1965
Avg. Per Game	118.8	122.8
Total Rushes	444	492
Net Yards Passing	3739	3650
Avg. Per Game	233.7	228.1
Sacked/Yards Lost	38/257	37/250
Gross Yards	3996	3900
Att./Completions	560/334	557/335
Completion Pct.	59.6	60.1
Had Intercepted	11	13
Punts/Average	83/47.1	89/46.2
Net Punting Avg.	83/40.8	89/41.2
Penalties/Yards	121/1127	107/929
Fumbles/Ball Lost	14/5	23/12
Touchdowns	44	33
Rushing	17	15
Passing	22	15
Returns	5	3

2012 INDIVIDUAL STATISTICS

PASSING

	Att.	Comp.	Yds.	Pct.	TD	Int.	Tkld.	Rate
Flacco	531	317	3817	59.7	22	10	35/227	87.7
Taylor	29	17	179	58.6	0	1	3/30	62.3
Ravens	560	334	3996	59.6	22	11	38/257	86.4
Opponents	557	335	3900	60.1	15	13	37/250	80.6

SCORING

	TD R	TD P	TD Rt	PAT	FG	Saf	PTS
Tucker	0	0	0	42/42	30/33	0	132
Rice	9	1	0	0/0	0/0	0	60
T. Smith	0	8	0	0/0	0/0	0	48
Pitta	0	7	0	0/0	0/0	0	42
Boldin	0	4	0	0/0	0/0	0	26
J. Jones	0	1	3	0/0	0/0	0	24
Flacco	3	0	0	0/0	0/0	0	18
Allen	1	0	0	0/0	0/0	0	6
Doss	0	1	0	0/0	0/0	0	6
Koch	1	0	0	0/0	0/0	0	6
Leach	1	0	0	0/0	0/0	0	6
Pierce	1	0	0	0/0	0/0	0	6
E. Reed	0	0	1	0/0	0/0	0	6
Taylor	1	0	0	0/0	0/0	0	6
C. Williams	0	0	1	0/0	0/0	0	6
Ravens	17	22	5	42/42	30/33	0	398
Opponents	15	15	3	31/31	37/39	1	344

2-Pt Conversions: Boldin, Ravens 1-2, Opponents 1-2

RUSHING

	No.	Yds	Avg	LG	TD
Rice	257	1143	4.4	46	9
Pierce	108	532	4.9	78	1
Taylor	14	73	5.2	28	1
Allen	16	61	3.8	20	1
Leach	9	32	3.6	6	1
Flacco	32	22	0.7	16	3
Koch	2	17	8.5	10	1
T. Smith	3	9	3.0	13	0
J. Jones	1	6	6.0	6	0
Boldin	1	3	3.0	3	0
Considine	1	3	3.0	3	0
Ravens	444	1901	4.3	78	17
Opponents	492	1965	4.0	31t	15

RECEIVING

	No.	Yds	Avg	LG	TD
Boldin	65	921	14.2	43	4
Pitta	61	669	11.0	61t	7
Rice	61	478	7.8	43	1
T. Smith	49	855	17.4	54	8
J. Jones	30	406	13.5	47	1
Dickson	21	225	10.7	40	0
Leach	21	143	6.8	18	0
Doss	7	123	17.6	39	1
Pierce	7	47	6.7	11	0
D. Reed	5	66	13.2	23	0
D. Thompson	5	51	10.2	25	0
Allen	2	12	6.0	7	0
Ravens	334	3996	12.0	61t	22
Opponents	335	3900	11.6	59	15

INTERCEPTIONS

	No.	Yds	Avg	LG	TD
C. Williams	4	90	22.5	63t	1
E. Reed	4	78	19.5	34t	1
Graham	2	20	10.0	20	0
Webb	1	8	8.0	8	0
Kruger	1	0	0.0	0	0
Pollard	1	0	0.0	0	0
Ravens	13	196	15.1	63t	2
Opponents	11	231	21.0	98t	3

PUNTING

	No.	Yds.	Avg.	In 20	LG
Koch	83	3911	47.1	28	60
Ravens	83	3911	47.1	28	60
Opponents	89	4113	46.2	32	63

PUNT RETURNS

	Ret	FC	Yds	Avg	LG	TD
J. Jones	37	16	341	9.2	63t	1
Doss	4	4	53	13.3	40	0
E. Reed	1	1	1	1.0	1	0
Webb	1	5	9	9.0	9	0
Ravens	43	26	404	9.4	63t	1
Opponents	49	13	383	7.8	64	0

KICKOFF RETURNS

	No.	Yds	Avg	LG	TD
J. Jones	38	1167	30.7	108t	2
D. Thompson	15	389	25.9	49	0
Allen	3	56	18.7	20	0
Gradkowski	1	12	12.0	12	0
Graham	1	7	7.0	7	0
L. Williams	1	5	5.0	5	0
Pitta	1	0	0.0	0	0
Ravens	60	1636	27.3	108t	2
Opponents	37	859	23.2	42	0

FIELD GOALS

	1-19	20-29	30-39	40-49	50+
Tucker	0/0	8/8	8/8	10/13	4/4
Ravens	0/0	8/8	8/8	10/13	4/4
Opponents	1/1	7/7	14/14	12/13	3/4

SACKS

	No.
Kruger	9.0
Ngata	5.0
Ellerbe	4.5
A. Jones	4.5
Pollard	2.0
Suggs	2.0
McPhee	1.5
Upshaw	1.5
Ayanbadejo	1.0
O. Brown	1.0
Ihedigbo	1.0
Kemoeatu	1.0
Lewis	1.0
McClellan	1.0
C. Williams	1.0
Ravens	37.0
Opponents	38.0

RECORD HOLDERS
INDIVIDUAL RECORDS—CAREER

Category	Name	Performance
Rushing (Yds.)	Jamal Lewis, 2000-06	7,801
Passing (Yds.)	Joe Flacco, 2008-2012	17,633
Passing (TDs)	Joe Flacco, 2008-2012	102
Receiving (No.)	Derrick Mason, 2005-2010	471
Receiving (Yds.)	Derrick Mason, 2005-2010	5,777
Interceptions	Ed Reed, 2002-2012	61
Punting (Avg.)	Sam Koch, 2006-2012	44.6
Punt Return (Avg.)	Jermaine Lewis, 1996-2001	11.8
Kickoff Return (Avg.)	Corey Harris, 1998-2001	24.0
Field Goals	Matt Stover, 1996-2008	354
Touchdowns (Tot.)	Jamal Lewis, 2000-06	47
Points	Matt Stover, 1996-2008	1,464
*Sacks	Terrell Suggs, 2003-2012	84.5

INDIVIDUAL RECORDS—SINGLE SEASON

Category	Name	Performance
Rushing (Yds.)	Jamal Lewis, 2003	2,066
Passing (Yds.)	Vinny Testaverde, 1996	4,177
Passing (TDs)	Vinny Testaverde, 1996	33
Receiving (No.)	Derrick Mason, 2007	103
Receiving (Yds.)	Michael Jackson, 1996	1,201
Interceptions	Ed Reed, 2004, 2008	9
Punting (Avg.)	Sam Koch, 2012	47.1
Punt Return (Avg.)	Jermaine Lewis, 2000	16.1
Kickoff Return (Avg.)	Jacoby Jones, 2012	30.7
Field Goals	Matt Stover, 2000	35
Touchdowns (Tot.)	Ray Rice, 2011	15
Points	Matt Stover, 2000	135
*Sacks	Peter Boulware, 2001	15.0

INDIVIDUAL RECORDS—SINGLE GAME

Category	Name	Performance
Rushing (Yds.)	Jamal Lewis, 9-14-03	295
Passing (Yds.)	Vinny Testaverde, 10-27-96	429
Passing (TDs)	Tony Banks, 9-10-00	5
Receiving (No.)	Priest Holmes, 10-11-98	13
Receiving (Yds.)	Qadry Ismail, 12-12-99	268
Interceptions	Many times	2
	Last time by Ed Reed, 9-11-11	
Field Goals	Matt Stover, 9-21-97, 12-26-99, 10-28-00, 10-14-07	5
	Billy Cundiff, 11-22-09, 10-16-11	5
Touchdowns (Tot.)	Marcus Robinson, 11-23-03	4
Points	Marcus Robinson, 11-23-03	24
*Sacks	Michael McCrary, 11-8-98	4.0
	Peter Boulware, 1-7-02	4.0

Sacks became an official statistic in 1982.

2013 VETERAN ROSTER

No.	Name	Pos.	Ht.	Wt.	Birthdate	NFL Exp.	College	Hometown	How Acq.	'12 Games/ Starts
	Adkins, Spencer	OLB	5-11	236	5/16/87	4	Miami	Naples, Fla.	FA-'13	0*
35	Allen, Anthony	RB	6-1	223	8/6/88	3	Georgia Tech	Tampa, Fla.	D7-'11	16/0
86	#Bajema, Billy	TE	6-4	259	10/31/82	9	Oklahoma State	Oklahoma City, Okla.	UFA(StL)-'12	8/1
28	Berry, Damien	RB	5-10	223	10/21/88	2	Miami	Belle Glade, Fla.	FA-'11	0*
23	Brown, Chykie	CB	5-11	190	12/26/86	3	Texas	Houston, Texas	D5a-'11	16/1
38	e Brown, Omar	S	5-11	195	6/6/88	2	Marshall	Moncks Corner, S.C.	FA-'12	3/0
47	#Brown, Ricky	LB	6-2	235	12/27/83	8	Boston College	Cincinnati, Ohio	FA-'12	0*
56	Bynes, Josh	LB	6-1	240	8/24/89	2	Auburn	Lauderdale Lakes, Fla.	FA-'11	10/3
99	Canty, Chris	DL	6-7	317	11/10/82	9	Virginia	Charlotte, N.C.	UFA(NYG)-'13	9/9*
62	Cody, Terrence	NT	6-4	341	6/28/88	4	Alabama	Fort Myers, Fla.	D2b-'10	15/3
	#Considine, Sean	S	6-0	212	12/17/82	9	Iowa	Byron, Ill.	UFA(Ariz)-'12	16/0
46	Cox, Morgan	LS	6-4	241	4/26/86	4	Tennessee	Collierville, Tenn.	FA-'10	16/0
84	+Dickson, Ed	TE	6-4	255	7/25/87	4	Oregon	Bellflower, Calif.	D3-'10	13/11
17	Doss, Tandon	WR	6-2	207	9/22/89	3	Indiana	Indianapolis, Ind.	D4-'11	14/0
58	Dumervil, Elvis	OLB	5-11	260	1/19/84	8	Louisville	Miami, Fla.	FA-'13	16/16*
5	Flacco, Joe	QB	6-6	245	1/16/85	6	Delaware	Audubon, N.J.	D1-'08	16/16
66	Gradkowski, Gino	G/C	6-3	300	11/5/88	2	Delaware	Pittsburgh, Pa.	D4a-'12	16/0
24	Graham, Corey	CB	6-0	196	7/25/85	7	New Hampshire	Buffalo, N.Y.	UFA(Chi)-'12	16/8
95	Hall, Bryan	DL/LB	6-0	291	9/12/88	2	Arkansas State	Paducah, Ky.	FA-'11	5/0
54	Hamilton, Adrian	LB	6-3	251	11/29/87	2	Prairie View A&M	Dallas, Texas	FA-'12	2/0
8	Hanie, Caleb	QB	6-2	222	9/11/85	6	Colorado State	Forney, Texas	FA-'13	0*
70	Harewood, Ramon	G/T	6-6	334	2/3/87	4	Morehouse	St. Michael, Barbados	D6-'10	6/5
29	Huff, Michael	S	6-0	211	3/6/83	8	Texas	Irving, Texas	FA-'13	16/16*
32	Ihedigbo, James	S	6-1	214	12/3/83	7	Massachusetts	Amherst, Mass.	FA-'12	16/3
25	Jackson, Asa	CB/RS	5-10	190	12/2/89	2	Cal Poly	Sacramento, Calif.	D5-'12	3/0
37	Johnson, Chris	CB	6-1	200	9/25/79	10	Louisville	Longview, Texas	FA-'12	4/1
97	Jones, Arthur	DE	6-3	315	6/3/86	4	Syracuse	Endicott, N.Y.	D5b-'10	16/6
12	Jones, Jacoby	WR/RS	6-2	220	7/11/84	7	Lane	New Orleans, La.	FA-'12	16/3
	#Kemoeatu, Ma'ake	NT	6-5	345	1/10/79	11	Utah	Tonga	FA-'12	15/13
4	Koch, Sam	P	6-1	218	8/13/82	8	Nebraska	Seward, Neb.	D6a-'06	16/0
44	Leach, Vonta	FB	6-0	260	11/6/81	10	East Carolina	Rowland, N.C.	UFA(Hou)-'11	16/13
41	e Levine, Anthony	DB	5-11	203	3/27/87	2	Tennessee State	Winston Salem, N.C.	FA-'12	2/0
94	McAdoo, Michael	OLB	6-7	245	7/9/90	3	North Carolina	Antioch, Tenn.	FA-'11	0*
98	#McBean, Ryan	DT	6-5	305	4/23/84	6	Oklahoma State	Euless, Texas	FA-'12	0*
53	McClain, Jameel	ILB	6-1	245	7/25/85	6	Syracuse	Philadelphia, Pa.	FA-'08	13/13
50	McClellan, Albert	LB	6-2	245	6/4/86	3	Marshall	Lakeland, Fla.	FA-'10	14/12
78	McKinnie, Bryant	T	6-8	354	9/23/79	12	Miami	Woodbury, N.J.	FA-'11	16/0
90	McPhee, Pernell	DE	6-3	280	12/17/88	3	Mississippi State	Pahokee, Fla.	D5b-'11	12/6
92	Ngata, Haloti	DT	6-4	340	1/21/84	8	Oregon	Salt Lake City, Utah	D1-'06	14/14
74	Oher, Michael	T	6-4	315	5/27/82	5	Mississippi	Memphis, Tenn.	D1-'09	16/16
72	Osemele, Kelechi	G/T	6-5	335	6/24/89	2	Iowa State	Houston, Texas	D2b-'12	16/16
30	Pierce, Bernard	RB	6-0	218	5/10/90	2	Temple	Ardmore, Pa.	D3-'13	16/0
88	Pitta, Dennis	TE	6-4	245	6/29/85	4	Brigham Young	Moorpark, Calif.	D4-'10	16/5
34	e Rainey, Bobby	RB	5-8	212	10/16/87	2	Western Kentucky	Griffin, Ga.	FA-'12	0*
16	Reed, David	WR/RS	6-0	190	3/22/87	4	Utah	New Britain, Conn.	D5a-'10	5/0
76	Reid, Jah	G/T	6-7	340	7/21/88	3	Central Florida	Haines City, Fla.	D3-'11	9/7
27	Rice, Ray	RB	5-8	212	1/22/87	6	Rutgers	New Rochelle, N.Y.	D2-'08	16/16
68	t- Shipley, A.Q.	C	6-1	309	6/25/86	2	Penn State	Moon Township, Pa.	T(Ind)-'13	14/5*
22	Smith, Jimmy	CB	6-2	205	7/26/88	3	Colorado	Colton, Calif.	D1-'11	11/2
82	Smith, Torrey	WR	6-0	205	1/26/89	3	Maryland	Falmouth, Va.	D2-'11	16/16
96	Spears, Marcus	DT	6-4	315	3/8/83	9	Louisiana State	Baton Rouge, La.	FA-'13	15/6*
11	Streeter, Tommy	WR	6-5	220	10/7/89	2	Miami	Miami, Fla.	D6-'12	0*
55	Suggs, Terrell	OLB	6-3	260	10/11/82	11	Arizona State	Chandler, Ariz.	D1a-'03	8/8
2	Taylor, Tyrod	QB	6-1	215	8/3/89	3	Virginia Tech	Hampton, Va.	D6-'11	7/0
33	Thompson, Christian	S	6-0	211	6/14/90	2	South Carolina State	North Lauderdale, Fla.	D4b-'12	7/0
83	Thompson, Deonte	WR/RS	6-0	203	2/14/89	2	Florida	Belle Glade, Fla.	FA-'12	6/0
9	Tucker, Justin	K	6-0	180	11/21/89	2	Texas	Austin, Texas	FA-'12	16/0
93	Tyson, DeAngelo	DE	6-2	310	4/12/89	2	Georgia	Statesboro, Ga.	D7-'12	10/2
91	Upshaw, Courtney	OLB	6-2	272	12/13/89	2	Alabama	Eufaula, Ala.	D2a-'12	16/9
21	Webb, Lardarius	CB/RS	5-10	182	10/12/85	5	Nicholls State	Opelika, Ala.	D3-'09	6/6
15	Williams, LaQuan	WR	6-0	195	6/27/88	3	Maryland	Baltimore, Md.	FA-'11	11/0
73	Yanda, Marshal	G/T	6-3	315	9/15/84	7	Iowa	Anamosa, Iowa	D3b-'07	14/14

* Adkins last active with Atlanta in '11; Berry missed '12 season because of injury; R. Brown missed '12 season because of injury; Canty played nine games with the New York Giants in '12; Dumervil played 16 games with Denver; Hanie inactive for 15 games with Denver; Huff played 16 games with Oakland; McAdoo missed '12 season because of injury; McBean missed '12 season because of injury; Rainey inactive for three games; Shipley played 14 games with Indianapolis; Spears played 15 games with Dallas; Streeter missed '12 season because of injury.

t- Ravens traded for Shipley (Ind).

\# Unrestriced Free Agent; subject to developments.

\+ Restricted Free Agent; subject to developments.

e   Exclusive rights; subject to developments.

Traded—WR Anquan Boldin (15 games in '12) to San Francisco.

Players lost through free agency (4): ILB Dannell Ellerbe (Mia; 13); OLB Paul Kruger (Cle; 15); S Ed Reed (Hou; 16); CB Cary Williams (Phil; 16).

Also played with Ravens in '12—LB Brendon Ayanbadejo (16 games), C Matt Birk (16), S Emanuel Cook (5), OLB Sergio Kindle (1), LB Ray Lewis (6), S Bernard Pollard (13), G Bobbie Williams (13).

FIRST-YEAR ROSTER

Name	Pos.	Ht.	Wt.	Birthdate	College	Hometown	How Acq.
Anthony, Marc	CB	5-11	196	11/14/89	California	Chandler, Ariz.	D7b
Brown, Arthur	LB	6-0	242	6/17/90	Kansas State	Wichita, Kan.	D2
Brown, Marlon	WR	6-5	216	4/22/91	Georgia	Memphis, Tenn.	FA
Bryant, D.J. (1)	LB	6-3	248	3/3/89	James Madison	Baltimore, Md.	FA-'12
Carr, Nigel (1)	LB	6-2	247	1/22/90	Alabama State	Jacksonville, Fla.	FA-'12
Carter, Rashaad	WR	6-3	205	10/18/89	Tusculum	Stone Mountain, Ga.	FA
Copeland, Brandon	LB	6-3	260	7/2/91	Pennsylvania	Baltimore, Md.	FA
Cornell, Jack (1)	G/T	6-6	320	6/4/89	Illinois	Quincy, Ill.	FA-'12
Crist, Dayne	QB	6-4	235	10/9/89	Kansas State	Sherman Oaks, Calif.	FA
Devey, Jordan	T	6-6	317	1/11/88	Memphis	American Fork, Utah	FA
Elam, Matt	S	5-10	210	9/21/91	Florida	West Palm Beach, Fla.	D1
Furstenburg, Matt	TE	6-3	244	6/19/89	Maryland	Flemington, N.J.	FA
Gaines, Rogers	T	6-6	334	10/28/89	Tennessee State	Nashville, Tenn.	FA
Gurley, Tori (1)	WR	6-4	232	11/22/87	South Carolina	Rock Hill, S.C.	FA
Hines, Omarius	WR	6-0	215	12/18/89	Florida	Corsicana, Texas	FA
Jensen, Ryan	C	6-4	304	5/27/91	Colorado State-Pueblo	Fort Morgan, Colo.	D6b
Juszczyk, Kyle	FB	6-1	248	4/23/91	Harvard	Medina, Ohio	D4b
Lee, Mo	CB	6-1	191	8/10/89	Utah	Miami, Fla.	FA
Lewis-Moore, Kapron	DE	6-4	300	1/24/90	Notre Dame	Weatherford, Texas	D6a
McClain, Antoine (1)	G	6-5	336	12/6/89	Clemson	Anniston, Ala.	FA-'12
Mellette, Aaron	WR	6-2	217	12/28/89	Elon	Sanford, N.C.	D7a
Miller, Lonyae (1)	RB	6-0	216	4/29/88	Fresno State	Fontana, Calif.	FA-'12
Mims, David (1)	T	6-8	335	5/18/88	Virginia Union	Charlotte, N.C.	FA
Pericak, Will	DE	6-3	296	12/30/89	Colorado	Boulder, Colo.	FA
Silvestro, Alex (1)	TE	6-3	260	11/15/88	Rutgers	Gibbstown, N.J.	FA-'12
Simon, John	OLB	6-1	257	10/14/90	Ohio State	Youngstown, Ohio	D4a
Stephens, Reggie (1)	C	6-3	325	8/28/87	Iowa State	Rowlett, Texas	FA-'12
Trawick, Brynden	S	6-2	215	10/23/89	Troy	Marietta, Ga.	FA
Unga, J.J.	T	6-5	320	1/5/87	Midwestern State	Rochester, Calif.	FA
Walker, Gary	S	6-0	200	5/10/91	Idaho	Rialto, Calif.	FA
Watson Jr., Steve	TE/FB	6-4	268	5/5/88	Michigan	Denver, Colo.	FA
Williams, Brandon	DT	6-1	335	2/21/89	Missouri Southern State	Kirkwood, Mo.	D3
Williams, Meshak	OLB	6-3	245	6/3/91	Kansas State	Sylvester, Ga.	FA

The term NFL Rookie is defined as a player who is in his first season of professional football and has not been on the roster of another professional football team for any regular-season or postseason games. A Rookie is designated by an "R" on NFL rosters. Players who have been active in another professional football league or players who have NFL experience, including either preseason training camp or being on an Active List or Inactive List, or on Reserve/Injured or Reserve/Physically Unable to Perform for fewer than six regular-season games, are termed NFL First-Year Players. An NFL First-Year Player is designated by a "1" on NFL rosters. Thereafter, a player is credited with an additional year of experience for each season in which he accumulates six games on the Active List or Inactive List, or on Reserve/Injured or Reserve/Physically Unable to Perform.

Log on to www.baltimoreravens.com for an up-to-date roster.

COACHING STAFF

Head Coach,
John Harbaugh

Pro Career: John Harbaugh was hired as the third head coach in Baltimore Ravens history on January 19, 2008. In each of his five seasons (2008-2012), the Ravens have earned a playoff berth, with Baltimore becoming the only NFL team to reach the postseason every year during that span. Impressively, Harbaugh is also the only head coach in NFL history (since 1970 merger) to win a playoff game in each of his first five years. In 2012, Baltimore won the AFC North for the second straight season and capped the season by capturing the franchise's second Super Bowl title. The Ravens topped the Colts at home in the Wild Card round and followed that up by earning a Divisional Round victory at top-seeded Denver before advancing to Super Bowl XLVII by winning at New England in the AFC Championship Game. In the Super Bowl in New Orleans, the Ravens bested the NFC champion San Francisco 49ers 34-31. In 2008, his initial campaign with the team, Baltimore set an NFL record that season for most total wins (13) by a team with both a rookie head coach and a rookie starting quarterback (Joe Flacco). Harbaugh spent his first 10 NFL seasons (1998-2007) with Philadelphia. He was the Eagles' secondary coach in 2007, after nine seasons as its special teams coordinator. He was voted the 2001 NFL's Special Teams Coach of the Year by his coaching peers. Career record: 63-30.

Background: Played defensive back at Miami (Ohio) from 1980-83, earned degree in political science. Coached collegiately at Western Michigan (1984-86), Pittsburgh (1987), Morehead State (1988), Cincinnati (1989-1996), and Indiana (1997).

Personal: Born in Perrysburg, Ohio on September 23, 1962, Harbaugh and his wife, Ingrid, have a daughter, Alison. Son of longtime college coach Jack, and his brother, Jim, the current 49ers head coach, played for the Ravens in 1998. John's brother-in-law, Tom Crean, Indiana University's basketball coach, is married to his sister, Joani.

ASSISTANT COACHES

Teryl Austin, secondary; born March 3, 1965, Sharon, Pa. Defensive back Pittsburgh 1984-87. Pro defensive back Montreal Machine (WLAF) 1991. College coach: Penn State 1991-92, Wake Forest 1993-95, Syracuse 1996-98, Michigan 1999-2002, Florida 2010. Pro coach: Seattle Seahawks 2003-06, Arizona Cardinals 2007-09, joined Ravens in 2011.

Juney Barnett, asst. strength and conditioning; born January 11, 1979, Philadelphia. Defensive back Bloomsburg 1997-2000. No pro playing experience. College coach: Bloomsburg 2001, Army 2005, Kansas 2012. Pro coach: Baltimore Ravens 2003-05, Minnesota Vikings, 2006-2011, re-joined Ravens in 2012.

Clarence Brooks, defensive line; born May 20, 1951, New York, N.Y. Guard Massachusetts 1970-73. No pro playing experience. College coach: Massachusetts 1976-1980, Syracuse 1981-89, Arizona 1990-92. Pro coach: Chicago Bears 1993-98, Cleveland Browns 1999, Miami Dolphins 2000-04, joined Ravens in 2005.

Randy Brown, kicking consultant; born July 30, 1967, Marlton, N.J. Kicker Catawba 1985-88. No pro playing experience. College coach: Catawba 1989, Tennessee-Chattanooga 2003. Pro coach: Chicago Bears 1998-2000, Philadelphia Eagles 2004-05, joined Ravens in 2008.

Jim Caldwell, offensive coordinator; born January 16, 1955, Beloit, Wisc. Defensive back Iowa 1973-76. No pro playing experience. College coach: Iowa 1997, Southern Illinois 1978-1980, Northwestern 1981, Colorado 1982-84, Louisville 1985, Penn State 1986-1992, Wake Forest 1993-2000 (head coach). Pro coach: Tampa Bay Buccaneers 2001, Indianapolis Colts 2002-2011 (head coach 2008-2011), joined Ravens in 2012.

Juan Castillo, run game coordinator; born October 8, 1959, Port Isabel, Texas. Linebacker Texas A&I 1978-1980. No pro playing experience. College coach: Texas A&M-Kingsville 1982-85, 1990-94. Pro coach: Philadelphia Eagles: 1995-2012, joined Ravens in 2013.

Wade Harman, tight ends; born October 1, 1963, Corydon, Iowa. Linebacker Drake 1985, Utah State 1986. No pro playing experience. College coach: Utah State 1987-1991, Pacific 1992-95, Morningside 1996. Pro coach: Minnesota Vikings 1997-98, joined Ravens in 1999.

Chris Hewitt, asst. special teams; born July 22, 1974, Kingston, Jamaica. Defensive back Cincinnati 1993-96. Pro defensive back New Orleans Saints 1997-99. College coach: Notre Dame 2003, Rutgers 2004-2011. Pro coach: Joined Ravens in 2012.

Jim Hostler, wide receivers; born November 11, 1966, Pittsburgh, Pa. Defensive back Indiana (Pa.) 1986-89. No pro playing experience. College coach: Indiana (Pa.) 1990-92, 1994-99, Juniata (Pa.) 1993. Pro coach: Kansas City Chiefs 2000, New Orleans Saints 2001-02, New York Jets 2003-04, San Francisco 49ers 2005-07, joined Ravens in 2008.

Don Martindale, inside linebackers; born May 19, 1963, Dayton, Ohio. Linebacker Defiance College 1981-84. College coach: Defiance 1986-87, Notre Dame 1994-95, Cincinnati 1996-98, Western Illinois 1999, Western Kentucky 2001-03. Pro coach: Oakland Raiders 2004-08, Denver Broncos 2009-2010, joined Ravens in 2012.

Andy Moeller, offensive line; June 15, 1964, Grand Rapids, Mich. Linebacker Michigan 1983-86. No pro playing experience. College coach: Indiana 1987, Army 1988-1993, Missouri 1994-99, Michigan 2000-07. Pro coach: Joined Ravens in 2008.

Ted Monachino, linebackers; born October 15, 1966, Council Bluffs, Iowa. Defensive lineman Missouri 1988-1990. No pro playing experience. College coach: Texas Christian 1996-97, James Madison 1998, Southwest Missouri State 1999, Boise State 2000, Arizona State 2001-05. Pro coach: Jacksonville Jaguars 2006-09, joined Ravens in 2010.

Wilbert Montgomery, running backs; born September 16, 1954, Greenville, Miss. Running back Abilene Christian 1973-76. Pro running back Philadelphia Eagles 1977-1984, Detroit Lions 1985. Pro Coach: St. Louis Rams 1997-2005, Detroit Lions 2006-07, joined Ravens in 2008.

Dean Pees, defensive coordinator; born September 4, 1949, Dunkirk, Ohio. Attended Bowling Green State. No college or pro playing experience. College coach: Findlay 1979-1982, Miami (Ohio) 1983-86, Naval Academy 1987-89, Toledo 1990-93, Notre Dame 1994, Michigan State 1995-97, Kent State 1998-2003. Pro coach: New England Patriots 2004-09, joined Ravens in 2010.

Bob Rogucki, strength and conditioning; born September 27, 1953, Clarksburg, W.Va. No college or pro playing experience. College coach: Penn State 1981, Weber State 1982, Army 1983-89. Pro coach: Arizona Cardinals 1990-2003, Jacksonville Jaguars 2004, Philadelphia Eagles 2006-07, joined Ravens in 2008.

Jerry Rosburg, special teams coordinator/asst. head coach; born November 24, 1955, Fairmont, Minn. Linebacker North Dakota State 1974-77. No pro playing experience. College coach: Northern Michigan 1981-86, Western Michigan 1987-1991, Cincinnati 1992-95, Minnesota 1996, Boston College 1997-98, Notre Dame 1999-2000. Pro coach: Cleveland Browns 2001-06, Atlanta Falcons 2007, joined Ravens in 2008.

Steve Spagnuolo, senior defensive assistant; born December 21, 1959, Whitinsville, Mass. Wide Receiver Springfield College 1978-1981. No pro playing experience. College coach: Massachusetts 1982-83, Lafayette (Pa.) 1984-86, Connecticut 1987-1991, Maine 1993-94, Rutgers 1994-95, Bowling Green 1996-97. Pro coach: Barcelona Dragons (WLAF) 1992, Frankfurt Galaxy (NFL Europe) 1998, Philadelphia Eagles 1999-2006, New York Giants 2007-08, St. Louis Rams 2009-2011 (head coach), New Orleans Saints 2012, joined Ravens in 2013.

Craig Ver Steeg, senior offensive assistant; born September 11, 1960, Inglewood, Calif. No college or pro playing experience. College coach: Southern California 1984-85, Utah 1986-89, Cincinnati 1990-93, Harvard 1994-95, Illinois 1999, Utah 2001-02, Rutgers 2003-07. Pro coach: Chicago Bears 1996-97, joined Ravens in 2008.

Todd Washington, asst. offensive line; born July 19, 1976, Nassawadox, Va. Guard/center Virginia Tech 1993-97. Pro guard/center Tampa Bay 1998-2002, Houston 2003-05. College coach: San Diego 2007-09. Pro coach: Hartford Colonials (UFL) 2010, joined Ravens in 2011.

Matt Weiss, defensive assistant; born March 1, 1983, New Haven, Conn. Punter Vanderbilt 2001-02. No pro playing experience. College coach: Stanford 2008. Pro coach: Joined Ravens in 2009.

American Football Conference
East Division
Team Colors: Royal, Red, White and
Navy
One Bills Drive
Orchard Park, New York 14127-2296
Telephone: (716) 648-1800

2013 SCHEDULE
PRESEASON
Aug. 11 at Indianapolis 1:30
Aug. 16 **Minnesota** 7:00
Aug. 24 at Washington 4:30
Aug. 29 **Detroit** 7:00

REGULAR SEASON
Sep. 8 **New England** 1:00p
Sep. 15 **Carolina** 1:00p
Sep. 22 at New York Jets...............4:25p
Sep. 29 **Baltimore** 1:00p
Oct. 3 at Cleveland (Thurs) 8:25p
Oct. 13 **Cincinnati** 1:00p
Oct. 20 at Miami 1:00p
Oct. 27 at New Orleans 1:00p
Nov. 3 **Kansas City** 1:00p
Nov. 10 at Pittsburgh 1:00p
Nov. 17 **New York Jets**.................1:00p
Nov. 24 BYE
Dec. 1 **Atlanta** (Toronto) 4:05p
Dec. 8 at Tampa Bay 1:00p
Dec. 15 at Jacksonville 1:00p
Dec. 22 **Miami** 1:00p
Dec. 29 at New England 1:00p
All times ET

Stadium: Ralph Wilson Stadium
(opened in 1973)
•**Capacity:** 72,498
One Bills Drive
Orchard Park, New York
14127-2296
Playing Surface: A-Turf Titan
Training Camp: St. John Fisher College
Rochester, N.Y. 14618

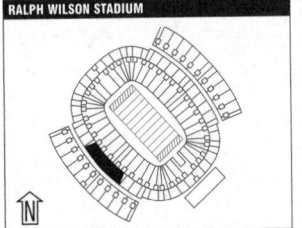
RALPH WILSON STADIUM

CLUB OFFICIALS
Owner: Ralph C. Wilson, Jr.
President and Chief Executive Officer:
Russ Brandon
Chief Financial Officer:
Jeffrey C. Littmann
General Manager: Doug Whaley
Special Assistant: Buddy Nix
Executive Vice President of Strategic
Planning: Mary Owen
Senior Vice President of
Communications: Scott Berchtold
Senior Vice President of Marketing and
Broadcasting: Marc Honan
Senior Vice President of Government
Relations and External Affairs:
Bill Munson
Senior Vice President of Football
Administration: Jim Overdorf
Senior Vice President of Business
Development: Bruce Popko
Senior Vice President of Business
Operations: Dave Wheat
Vice President of Community Relations:
Gretchen Geitter
Vice President of Information
Technology: Dan Evans
Vice President Event Operations and
Guest Experience: Andy Major
Consultant: Christy Wilson Hofmann
Director of Player Personnel Jim Monos
Director of Pro Personnel: Tom Gibbons
Director of College Scouting:
Kelvin Fisher
Senior Director of Security: Chris Clark
Senior Director of Stadium Operations:
Matt Hunter
Director of Marketing Programs and
Merchandise: Tim Kehoe
Director of Player Programs:
Paul Lancaster
Controller: Frank Wojnicki
Director of Equipment Operations:
Jeff Mazurek
Assistant Equipment Managers:
Randy Ribbeck, Spencer Haws
Head Certified Athletic Trainer:
Bud Carpenter
Certified Athletic Trainers: Chris Fischetti,
Shone Gipson, Greg McMillen
Video Director: Greg Estes
Assistant Video Director: Wes Burnard
Video Assistant: Dexter Carlo
Coordinator of College Scouting and
National Cross Checker: Doug Majeski
Scouts: Chuck Cook, Brian Fisher,
Brad Forsyth, Matt Hand,
Pete Harris (BLESTO), Shawn Heinlen,
CJ Leak, Darrell Moody, Tom Roth,
(emeritus) David G. Smith,
(emeritus) David W. Smith,
Theo Young

COACHING HISTORY
(384-441-8)
Records include postseason games

1960-61	Buster Ramsey	11-16-1
1962-65	Lou Saban	38-18-3
1966-68	Joe Collier*	13-17-1
1968	Harvey Johnson	1-10-1
1969-1970	John Rauch	7-20-1
1971	Harvey Johnson	1-13-0
1972-76	Lou Saban**	32-29-1
1976-77	Jim Ringo	3-20-0
1978-1982	Chuck Knox	38-38-0
1983-85	Kay Stephenson***	10-26-0
1985-86	Hank Bullough****	4-17-0
1986-1997	Marv Levy	123-78-0
1998-2000	Wade Phillips	29-21-0
2001-03	Gregg Williams	17-31-0
2004-05	Mike Mularkey	14-18-0
2006-09	Dick Jauron#	24-33-0
2009	Perry Fewell	3-4-0
2010-12	Chan Gailey	16-32-0

*Released after two games in 1968
**Resigned after five games in 1976
***Released after four games in 1985
****Released after nine games in 1986
#Released after nine games in 2009

PAID ATTENDANCE
Home 478,457   Away 518,945
Total 997,402
Single-game home record,
80,368 (10/4/92)
Single-season home record,
635,889 (1991)

2013 DRAFT CHOICES
Round	Name	Pos.	College
1	E.J. Manuel	QB	Florida St.
2	Robert Woods	WR	Southern California
	Kiko Alonso	LB	Oregon
3	Marquise Goodwin	WR	Texas
4	Duke Williams	DB	Nevada
5	Jonathan Meeks	DB	Clemson
6	Dustin Hopkins	K	Florida St.
7	Chris Gragg	TE	Arkansas

2012 TEAM RECORD
PRESEASON (0-4)

Date	Result		Opponent
08/09	L	6-7	Washington
08/17	L	14-36	at Minnesota
08/25	L	7-38	Pittsburgh
08/30	L	32-38	at Detroit

REGULAR SEASON (6-10)

Date	Result		Opponent
09/09	L	28-48	at New York Jets
09/16	W	35-17	Kansas City
09/23	W	24-14	at Cleveland
09/30	L	28-52	New England
10/07	L	3-45	at San Francisco
10/14	W	19-16	at Arizona (OT)
10/21	L	34-35	Tennessee
11/04	L	9-21	at Houston
11/11	L	31-37	at New England
11/15	W	19-14	Miami
11/25	L	13-20	at Indianapolis
12/02	W	34-18	Jacksonville
12/09	L	12-15	St. Louis
12/16	L	17-50	Seattle
12/23	L	10-24	at Miami
12/30	W	28-9	New York Jets

(OT) Overtime

SCORE BY PERIODS

Bills	84	109	78	70	3	—	344
Opponents	89	115	109	122	0	—	435

2012 TEAM STATISTICS

	Bills	Opp.
Total First Downs	301	349
Rushing	103	136
Passing	176	182
Penalty	22	31
3rd Down: Made/Att	77/198	92/209
3rd Down Pct.	38.9	44.0
4th Down: Made/Att	5/8	6/12
4th Down Pct.	62.5	50.0
Possession Avg.	30:04	29:56
Total Net Yards	5486	5806
Avg. Per Game	342.9	362.9
Total Plays	983	1042
Avg. Per Play	5.6	5.6
Net Yards Rushing	2217	2333
Avg. Per Game	138.6	145.8
Total Rushes	442	470
Net Yards Passing	3269	3473
Avg. Per Game	204.3	217.1
Sacked/Yards Lost	30/161	36/196
Gross Yards	3430	3669
Att./Completions	511/309	536/306
Completion Pct.	60.5	57.1
Had Intercepted	17	12
Punts/Average	80/44.3	72/44.6
Net Punting Avg.	80/37.1	72/36.2
Penalties/Yards	104/871	80/693
Fumbles/Ball Lost	23/17	26/9
Touchdowns	40	53
Rushing	12	23
Passing	24	25
Returns	4	5

2012 INDIVIDUAL STATISTICS

PASSING

	Att.	Comp.	Yds.	Pct.	TD	Int.	Tkld.	Rate
Fitzpatrick	505	306	3400	60.6	24	16	30/161	83.3
Thigpen	5	3	30	60.0	0	0	0/0	77.1
Bra. Smith	1	0	0	0.0	0	1	0/0	0.0
Bills	511	309	3430	60.5	24	17	30/161	82.2
Opponents	536	306	3669	57.1	25	12	36/196	84.4

SCORING

	TD R	TD P	TD Rt	PAT	FG	Saf	PTS
Lindell	0	0	0	39/39	21/24	0	102
Spiller	6	2	0	0/0	0/0	0	48
Chandler	0	6	0	0/0	0/0	0	36
St. Johnson	0	6	0	0/0	0/0	0	36
F. Jackson	3	1	0	0/0	0/0	0	24
Jones	0	4	0	0/0	0/0	0	24
Bra. Smith	1	2	1	0/0	0/0	0	24
McKelvin	0	0	2	0/0	0/0	0	12
L. Smith	0	2	0	0/0	0/0	0	12
Choice	1	0	0	0/0	0/0	0	6
Fitzpatrick	1	0	0	0/0	0/0	0	6
Graham	0	1	0	0/0	0/0	0	6
B. Scott	0	0	1	0/0	0/0	0	6
Kelsay	0	0	0	0/0	0/0	1	2
Bills	12	24	4	39/39	21/24	1	344
Opponents	23	25	5	50/51	21/28	0	435

2-Pt Conversions: Bills 0-1, Opponents 2-2

RUSHING

	No.	Yds	Avg	LG	TD
Spiller	207	1244	6.0	62	6
F. Jackson	115	437	3.8	15	3
Fitzpatrick	48	197	4.1	20	1
Choice	47	193	4.1	22	1
Bra. Smith	14	116	8.3	35	1
J. White	8	34	4.3	9	0
Graham	1	5	5.0	5	0
Thigpen	1	-1	-1.0	-1	0
Dickerson	1	-8	-8.0	-8	0
Bills	442	2217	5.0	62	12
Opponents	470	2333	5.0	83t	23

RECEIVING

	No.	Yds	Avg	LG	TD
St. Johnson	79	1046	13.2	63	6
Chandler	43	571	13.3	43	6
Spiller	43	459	10.7	66t	2
Jones	41	443	10.8	68t	4
F. Jackson	34	217	6.4	34	1
Graham	31	322	10.4	51	1
Bra. Smith	14	152	10.9	35t	2
Dickerson	9	117	13.0	24	0
Martin	4	41	10.3	16	0
L. Smith	4	13	3.3	5	2
Choice	4	9	2.3	5	0
Nelson	2	31	15.5	21	0
McIntyre	1	9	9.0	9	0
Bills	309	3430	11.1	68t	24
Opponents	306	3669	12.0	53	25

INTERCEPTIONS

	No.	Yds	Avg	LG	TD
Byrd	5	81	16.2	45	0
B. Scott	4	66	16.5	32	1
Gilmore	1	23	23.0	23	0
McKelvin	1	9	9.0	9	0
Rogers	1	-1	-1.0	-1	0
Bills	12	178	14.8	45	1
Opponents	17	256	15.1	57t	2

PUNTING

	No.	Yds.	Avg.	In 20	LG
Powell	65	2860	44	23	62
Moorman	15	682	45.5	2	66
Bills	80	3542	44.3	25	66
Opponents	72	3210	44.6	27	66

PUNT RETURNS

	Ret	FC	Yds	Avg	LG	TD
McKelvin	23	14	431	18.7	88t	2
Rogers	3	4	14	4.7	14	0
Byrd	0	3	0	—	—	0
Bills	26	21	445	17.1	88t	2
Opponents	35	14	517	14.8	75t	2

KICKOFF RETURNS

	No.	Yds	Avg	LG	TD
McKelvin	18	510	28.3	59	0
Bra. Smith	18	496	27.6	89t	1
Easley	2	75	37.5	55	0
Rogers	2	55	27.5	28	0
Carrington	1	0	0.0	0	0
L. Smith	1	0	0.0	0	0
Bills	42	1136	27.0	89t	1
Opponents	51	1144	22.4	96t	1

FIELD GOALS

	1-19	20-29	30-39	40-49	50+
Lindell	1/1	3/3	10/11	6/7	1/2
Bills	1/1	3/3	10/11	6/7	1/2
Opponents	3/3	6/6	5/7	6/10	1/2

SACKS

	No.
M. Williams	10.5
Dareus	5.5
Ky. Williams	5.0
Moore	3.0
Barnett	2.0
Carrington	2.0
Sp. Johnson	2.0
Kelsay	2.0
Sheppard	2.0
Anderson	1.0
Merriman	1.0
Bills	36.0
Opponents	30.0

RECORD HOLDERS
INDIVIDUAL RECORDS—CAREER

Category	Name	Performance
Rushing (Yds.)	Thurman Thomas, 1988-1999	11,938
Passing (Yds.)	Jim Kelly, 1986-1996	35,467
Passing (TDs)	Jim Kelly, 1986-1996	237
Receiving (No.)	Andre Reed, 1985-1999	941
Receiving (Yds.)	Andre Reed, 1985-1999	13,095
Interceptions	George (Butch) Byrd, 1964-1970	40
Punting (Avg.)	Brian Moorman, 2001-2012	43.9
Punt Return (Avg.)	Leodis McKelvin, 2008-2012	16.3
Kickoff Return (Avg.)	O.J. Simpson, 1969-1977	30.0
Field Goals	Steve Christie, 1992-2000	234
Touchdowns (Tot.)	Andre Reed, 1985-1999	87
	Thurman Thomas, 1988-1999	87
Points	Steve Christie, 1992-2000	1,011
*Sacks	Bruce Smith, 1985-1999	**171.0

INDIVIDUAL RECORDS—SINGLE SEASON

Category	Name	Performance
Rushing (Yds.)	O.J. Simpson, 1973	2,003
Passing (Yds.)	Drew Bledsoe, 2002	4,359
Passing (TDs)	Jim Kelly, 1991	33
Receiving (No.)	Eric Moulds, 2002	100
Receiving (Yds.)	Eric Moulds, 1998	1,368
Interceptions	Billy Atkins, 1961	10
	Tom Janik, 1967	10
Punting (Avg.)	Brian Moorman, 2011	48.2
Punt Return (Avg.)	Leodis McKelvin, 2012	18.7
Kickoff Return (Avg.)	Terrence McGee, 2005	30.2
Field Goals	Steve Christie, 1998	33
Touchdowns (Tot.)	O.J. Simpson, 1975	23
Points	Steve Christie, 1998	140
*Sacks	Bruce Smith, 1990	19.0

INDIVIDUAL RECORDS—SINGLE GAME

Category	Name	Performance
Rushing (Yds.)	O.J. Simpson, 11-25-76	273
Passing (Yds.)	Drew Bledsoe, 9-15-02	463
Passing (TDs)	Jim Kelly, 9-8-91	6
Receiving (No.)	Andre Reed, 11-20-94	15
Receiving (Yds.)	Lee Evans, 11-19-06	265
Interceptions	Many times	3
	Last time by Nate Clements, 10-20-02	
Field Goals	Steve Christie, 10-20-96	6
Touchdowns (Tot.)	Cookie Gilchrist, 12-8-63	5
Points	Cookie Gilchrist, 12-8-63	30
*Sacks	Cornelius Bennett, 12-27-87	4.0
	Bruce Smith, 12-9-90, 9-18-94	4.0

*Sacks became an official statistic in 1982.
**NFL Record

2013 VETERAN ROSTER

No.	Name	Pos.	Ht.	Wt.	Birthdate	NFL Exp.	College	Hometown	How Acq.	'12 Games/ Starts
93	Anderson, Mark	DE	6-4	255	5/26/83	8	Alabama	Tulsa, Okla.	UFA(NE)-'12	5/4
53	Bradham, Nigel	OLB	6-2	241	9/4/89	2	Florida State	Crawfordville, Fla.	D4a-'12	16/11
90	Branch, Alan	DT	6-6	325	12/29/84	7	Michigan	Rio Rancho, N.M.	UFA(Sea)-'13	16/16*
33	Brooks, Ron	DB	5-10	190	10/16/88	2	Louisiana State	Irving, Texas	D4b-'12	9/2
74	Brown, Colin	C	6-7	326	8/29/85	2	Missouri	Braymer, Mo.	FA-'10	1/1
29	Butler, Crezdon	CB	6-1	191	5/26/87	3	Clemson	Asheville, N.C.	FA-'12	6/0*
31	Byrd, Jairus	FS	5-10	203	10/7/86	5	Oregon	Clayton, Mo.	D2a-'09	16/16
92	Carrington, Alex	DT	6-5	301	6/19/87	4	Arkansas State	Tupelo, Miss.	D3-'10	16/0
80	Caussin, Mike	TE	6-5	243	2/26/87	2	James Madison	Springfield, Va.	FA-'10	0*
84	Chandler, Scott	TE	6-7	260	7/23/85	7	Iowa	Bedford, Texas	FA-'10	15/13
20	Choice, Tashard	RB	5-10	210	11/20/84	5	Georgia Tech	Hampton, Ga.	FA-'11	11/0
99	Dareus, Marcell	DT	6-3	331	3/13/90	3	Alabama	Huffman, Ala.	D1-'11	16/16
82	Dickerson, Dorin	WR	6-1	226	3/31/88	3	Pittsburgh	Imperial, Pa.	FA-'12	11/0
54	Dowtin, Marcus	LB	6-2	226	1/22/89	2	North Alabama	Upper Marlboro, Md.	FA-'13	3/0*
81	Easley, Marcus	WR	6-2	217	11/2/87	2	Connecticut	Stratford, Conn.	D4-'10	3/0
18	Elliott, Kevin	WR	6-3	205	12/21/88	2	Florida A&M	Orlando, Fla.	FA-'12	13/1*
96	Gilbert, Jarron	DT	6-5	289	9/30/86	2	San Jose State	Chino, Calif.	FA-'11	0*
24	Gilmore, Stephon	CB	6-1	190	9/19/90	2	South Carolina	Rock Hill, S.C.	D1-'12	16/16
77	Glenn, Cordy	LT	6-6	345	9/18/89	2	Georgia	Riverdale, Ga.	D2-'12	13/13
11	Graham, T.J.	WR	5-11	188	7/27/89	2	North Carolina State	Raleigh, N.C.	D3-'12	15/11
75	Hairston, Chris	RT	6-6	330	4/26/89	3	Clemson	Winston-Salem, N.C.	D4b-'11	12/8
44	Heath, T.J.	CB	6-1	184	9/11/87	2	Jacksonville State	Alexandria, Ala.	FA-'12	0*
55 t-	Hughes, Jerry	LB	6-2	254	8/13/88	4	Texas Christian	Sugar Land, Texas	T(Ind)-'13	16/6*
22	Jackson, Fred	RB	6-1	216	2/20/81	7	Coe College	Fort Worth, Texas	FA-'06	10/8
7	Jackson, Tarvaris	QB	6-2	225	4/21/83	8	Alabama State	Montgomery, Ala.	T(Sea)-'12	0*
13	Johnson, Stevie	WR	6-2	207	7/22/86	6	Kentucky	San Francisco, Calif.	D7b-'08	16/16
4	Kolb, Kevin	QB	6-3	218	8/24/84	7	Houston	Stephenville, Texas	FA-'13	6/5*
91	Lawson, Manny	LB	6-5	240	7/3/84	8	North Carolina State	Goldsboro, N.C.	UFA(Cin)-'13	16/10*
9	Lindell, Rian	K	6-3	227	1/20/77	14	Washington State	Vancouver, Wash.	FA-'03	16/0
21	McKelvin, Leodis	CB	5-10	185	9/4/85	6	Troy	Waycross, Ga.	D1-'08	13/4
52	Moats, Arthur	OLB	6-2	250	3/14/88	4	James Madison	Portsmouth, Va.	D6a-'10	14/4
79	Pears, Erik	RT	6-8	316	6/25/82	8	Colorado State	Price, Utah	FA-'10	7/7
6	Powell, Shawn	P	6-4	243	11/29/88	2	Florida State	Rome, Ga.	FA-'12	13/0
26	Rogers, Justin	CB	5-11	181	1/16/88	3	Richmond	Baton Rouge, La.	D7a-'11	16/1
65	Sanborn, Garrison	LS	6-1	240	7/31/85	5	Florida State	Tampa, Fla.	FA-'09	16/0
43	Scott, Bryan	OLB	6-1	220	4/13/81	11	Penn State	Doylestown, Pa.	FA-'07	16/1
25	Searcy, Da'Norris	SS	5-11	216	11/16/88	3	North Carolina	Decatur, Ga.	D4a-'11	15/0
87	Shuler, Mickey	TE	6-4	247	10/9/86	2	Penn State	Lido Beach, N.Y.	FA-'13	0*
30	Silva, Mana	DB	6-0	206	8/17/88	2	Hawaii	Hilo, Hawaii	FA-'12	10/0*
16	Smith, Brad	WR	6-2	213	12/12/83	8	Missouri	Youngstown, Ohio	FA-'11	15/2
85	Smith, Lee	TE	6-6	265	11/21/87	3	Marshall	Powell, Tenn.	FA-'11	16/6
61	Snow, David	G/C	6-4	303	11/9/89	2	Texas	Gilmer, Texas	UFA-'12	5/2
28	Spiller, C.J.	RB	5-11	200	8/5/87	4	Clemson	Lake Butler, Fla.	D1-'10	16/9
98	Troup, Torell	DT	6-3	327	6/23/88	4	Central Florida	Conyers, Ga.	D2-'10	0*
60	Urbik, Kraig	G/C	6-5	324	9/23/85	5	Wisconsin	Hudson, Wisc.	FA-'10	13/13
66	Welch, Thomas	OT	6-7	310	6/19/87	3	Vanderbilt	Brentwood, Tenn.	FA-'12	3/0
51	White, Chris	OLB	6-3	238	1/15/89	3	Mississippi State	Vancleave, Miss.	D6-'11	15/0
23	Williams, Aaron	DB	6-0	199	4/23/90	3	Texas	Round Rock, Texas	D2-'11	11/10
95	Williams, Kyle	DT	6-1	303	6/10/83	8	Louisiana State	Ruston, La.	D5a-'06	16/16
94	Williams, Mario	DE	6-6	292	1/31/85	8	North Carolina State	Richlands, N.C.	UFA(Hou)-'12	16/16
70	Wood, Eric	C	6-4	310	3/18/86	5	Louisville	Cincinnati, Ohio	D1b-'09	14/14
71	Young, Sam	RT	6-8	316	6/24/87	4	Notre Dame	Coral Springs, Fla.	FA-'11	12/4

*   Branch played 16 games with Seattle in '12; Butler played one game with Arizona, two with Washington and six with Buffalo; Caussin missed '12 season because of injury; Dowtin played three games with the New York Jets; Elliott played 13 games with Jacksonville; Gilbert last active with New York Jets in '10; Heath did not play in two games; Hughes played 16 games with Indianapolis; T. Jackson inactive for 16 games; Kolb played six games with Arizona; Lawson played 16 games with Cincinnati; Shuler last active with Miami in '10; Silva played three games with Dallas and seven with Buffalo; Troup missed '12 season because of injury.

t-   Bills traded for Hughes (Ind).

Traded—LB Kelvin Sheppard (16 games in '12) to Indianapolis.

Players lost through free agency (3): G Andy Levitre (Tenn; 16 games in '12), DE Kyle Moore (Chi; 12), G Chad Rinehart (SD; 7).

Also played with Bills in '12—LB Nick Barnett (16 games), QB Ryan Fitzpatrick (16), DB Delano Howell (1), DE Spencer Johnson (14), WR Donald Jones (12), DE Chris Kelsay (9), WR Ruvell Martin (14), DE Shawne Merriman (10), CB Terrence McGee (7), FB Corey McIntyre (16), P Brian Moorman (3), LB Kirk Morrison (2), WR David Nelson (1), K John Potter (6), QB Tyler Thigpen (4), RB Johnny White (3), SS George Wilson (16).

FIRST-YEAR ROSTER

Name	Pos.	Ht.	Wt.	Birthdate	College	Hometown	How Acq.
Alonso, Kiko	LB	6-3	238	8/14/90	Oregon	Los Gatos, Calif.	D2b
Blatnick, Jamie	DE	6-3	253	6/24/89	Oklahoma State	Celina, Texas	FA
Brown, Kourtnei (1)	LB	6-4	253	4/17/88	Clemson	Charlotte, N.C.	FA
Brown, Zach (1)	RB	5-10	220	2/6/89	Pittsburgh	Royal Palm Beach, Fla.	FA-'12
Bryant, Corbin (1)	DE	6-4	300	1/4/88	Northwestern	Chicago, Ill.	FA-'12
Chibane, Zack	G	6-5	293	1/28/91	Syracuse	Paramus, N.J.	FA
Cross, Izaan	DE	6-4	300	5/1/91	Georgia Tech	Flowery Branch, Ga.	FA
Dangerfield, Jordan	DB	5-11	200	12/25/90	Towson	Royal Palm Beach, Fla.	FA
Eckerson, Hutch (1)	T	6-6	310	2/19/88	South Carolina	Lumberton, N.C.	FA
Edwards, Kip	CB	6-1	200	12/4/89	Missouri	Arlington, Texas	FA
Ellis, Dominique (1)	DB	5-11	195	8/25/89	South Carolina State	Union, Ga.	FA
Gaskins, Kendall	RB	6-1	238	11/4/90	Richmond	Burlington, N.J.	FA
Goodwin, Marquise	WR	5-9	179	11/19/90	Texas	Garland, Texas	D3
Gragg, Chris	TE	6-3	244	6/30/90	Arkansas	Warren, Ark.	D7
Hogan, Chris (1)	WR	6-1	220	10/24/88	Monmouth	Ramapo, N.J.	FA-'12
Hopkins, Dustin	K	6-2	193	10/1/90	Florida State	Houston, Texas	D6
Kaufman, Brandon	WR	6-5	215	10/26/90	Eastern Washington	Denver, Co.	FA
Kearney, Vernon	CB	6-2	185	1/31/89	Lane	Bradenton, Fla.	FA
Lloyd, Greg (1)	LB	6-1	247	2/10/89	Connecticut	Clermont, Fla.	FA-'12
Manuel, EJ	QB	6-4	237	3/19/90	Florida State	Virginia Beach, Va.	D1
Meeks, Jonathan	DB	6-0	209	11/8/89	Clemson	Rock Hill, S.C.	D5
Pough, Keith	LB	6-3	225	2/5/90	Howard	Orangeburg, S.C.	FA
Robey, Nickell	CB	5-8	165	1/17/92	Southern California	Frostproof, Fla.	FA
Rogers, Da'Rick	WR	6-3	205	6/18/91	Tennessee Tech	Calhoun, Ga.	FA
Rolle, Jumal	CB	6-0	185	5/28/90	Catawba	Wilson, N.C.	FA-'12
Ross, Jay (1)	DT	6-3	319	10/3/87	East Carolina	Dayton, Ohio	D5a-'12
Sanders, Zebrie (1)	T	6-6	320	12/4/89	Florida State	Riverdale, Ga.	FA-'12
Scott, Chris (1)	T	6-4	360	8/4/87	Tennessee	Overland Park, Kan.	FA-'12
Smith, Brian (1)	LB	6-3	240	1/8/89	Notre Dame	Schenectady, N.Y.	FA
Smith, Drew	FB	6-2	225	4/12/90	Albany	Solana Beach, Calif.	FA
Stahovich, Brian (1)	P	5-11	197	4/14/90	San Diego State	Oakland, Calif.	FA
Summers, Frank (1)	RB	5-9	248	9/6/85	Nevada-Las Vegas	Honolulu, Hawaii	FA
Tipoti, Aaron	DT	6-2	280	1/4/90	California	Fresno, Calif.	FA
Tuel, Jeff	QB	6-3	221	2/12/91	Washington State	Hopewell, Pa.	FA
Turnley, Ryan	C	6-6	320	5/1/90	Pittsburgh	Reno, Nev.	D4
Williams, Duke	DB	5-11	201	10/5/90	Nevada	Florissant, Mo.	FA-'12
Williams, Keith (1)	G	6-5	330	4/8/88	Nebraska	Carson, Calif.	D2a
Woods, Robert	WR	6-0	190	4/10/92	Southern California		

The term NFL Rookie is defined as a player who is in his first season of professional football and has not been on the roster of another professional football team for any regular-season or postseason games. A Rookie is designated by an "R" on NFL rosters. Players who have been active in another professional football league or players who have NFL experience, including either preseason training camp or being on an Active List or Inactive List, or on Reserve/Injured or Reserve/Physically Unable to Perform for fewer than six regular-season games, are termed NFL First-Year Players. An NFL First-Year Player is designated by a "1" on NFL rosters. Thereafter, a player is credited with an additional year of experience for each season in which he accumulates six games on the Active List or Inactive List, or on Reserve/Injured or Reserve/Physically Unable to Perform.

Log on to www.buffalobills.com for an up-to-date roster.

COACHING STAFF

Head Coach,
Doug Marrone

Pro Career: Marrone was named Buffalo's 16th head coach on January 7, 2013. He enters his eighth season in the NFL coaching ranks and first as a head coach. Marrone spent the previous four years as the head coach of his alma mater's football program at Syracuse University from 2009-2012. Prior to his Syracuse tenure, Marrone spent seven years in the NFL. From 2006-08 he served as the offensive coordinator of the New Orleans Saints. From 2002-05 he was the offensive line coach of the New York Jets. Before arriving in New York, Marrone coached the tight ends and tackles at Tennessee in 2001. He spent the 2000 season at Georgia as the program's offensive line coach after spending the previous five years at Georgia Tech. In 1995, Marrone was the director of football operations before coaching the tight ends in 1996 and offensive line from 1997-99. Marrone's coaching career began in 1992 at Cortland (N.Y.) State as the school's tight ends coach before stints as the offensive line coach at the U.S. Coast Guard Academy (1993) and Northeastern University in 1994. He was drafted in the sixth round of the 1986 NFL draft by the Los Angeles Raiders and played two years in the NFL, first with the Miami Dolphins in 1987 and with the Saints in 1989. He also had playing stints with Pittsburgh, Dallas and Minnesota before closing his career with the NFLE London Monarchs (1991-92). Career record: 0-0.

Background: Marrone was a three-year letterman (1983-85) at Syracuse as an offensive lineman. He earned a degree in liberal arts from Syracuse in 1991.

Personal: Born July 25, 1964, Bronx, N.Y. He and wife, Helen, have two daughters, Madeline and Anne, and a son, Mack.

ASSISTANT COACHES

Greg Adkins, tight ends; born March 25, 1968, Cross Lanes, W. Va. Offensive line Marshall 1986-89. No pro playing experience. College coach: Marshall 1991-95, Georgia 1996-2000, Troy 2001-02, Tennessee 2003-08, Syracuse 2009-2012. Pro coach: Joined Bills in 2013.

Kurt Anderson, offensive quality control; born August 8, 1978, Glenview, Ill. Offensive line Michigan 1997-2001. No pro playing experience. College coach: Indiana State 2005, Michigan 2006-07, Eastern Michigan 2008-2012. Pro coach: Joined Bills in 2013.

John Anselmo, special teams assistant; born September 23, 1949, Freeport, N.Y. Quarterback Cortland State 1968-1970. No pro playing experience. College coach: Nassau (N.Y.) C.C. 1977-1994, 1999-2008, Georgia Tech 1995-98, Syracuse 2009-2012. Pro coach: Joined Bills in 2013.

Samson Brown, asst. defensive backs; born January 11, 1980, Bronx, N.Y. Free safety Albany 1999-2002. No pro playing experience. College coach: Siena 2003, RPI 2004-05, Hofstra 2006, Albany 2007-09. Pro coach: New York Jets 2010-11, joined Bills in 2013.

Stephen Brown, asst. to the head coach; born May 3, 1987, Charlotte, N.C. Attended Tennessee. No college or pro playing experience. College coach: Syracuse 2009-2012. Pro coach: joined Bills in 2013.

Eric Ciano, head strength and conditioning; born August 8, 1973, Waltham, Mass. Offensive line Springfield (Mass.) College 1993-97. No pro playing experience. College coach: Tennessee 1997-99, Louisiana Tech 2000-02, Tennessee 2002-04, Georgia Tech 2005-09. Pro coach: Joined Bills in 2010.

Danny Crossman, special teams coordinator; born January 17, 1967, El Paso, Texas. Defensive back Pittsburgh Kansas 1985, Pittsburgh 1987-89. Pro defensive back Washington Redskins 1990, Detroit Lions 1991-92. College coach: U.S. Coast Guard Academy 1993, Western Kentucky 1994-96, Central Florida 1997-98, Georgia Tech 1999-2001, Michigan State 2002. Pro coach: Carolina Panthers 2003-09, Detroit Lions 2010-12, joined Bills in 2013.

Chuck Driesbach, linebackers; born August 9, 1952, Philadelphia, Pa. Wide receiver Villanova 1972-74. No pro playing experience. College coach: Kansas State 1976-1983, Wake Forest 1984-86, East Carolina 1987-88, Mississippi 1989, Cornell 1990-92, Pittsburgh 1993-96, Western Michigan 1997-2000, Texas Christian 2001, Mississippi 2002-04, Michigan State 2005-06, Rice 2007-2011. Pro coach: Joined Bills in 2013.

Brian Fleury, defensive quality control; born January 22, 1980, Germantown, Md. Quarterback Maryland 1998, Towson 1999-2002. No pro playing experience. College coach: Maryland 2003-04, Sacred Heart 2005-08, Towson 2009-2012. Pro coach: Joined Bills in 2013.

Nathaniel Hackett, offensive coordinator/quarterbacks; born December 19, 1979, Fullerton, Calif. Linebacker/long snapper U.C. Davis 1999-2002. No pro playing experience. College coach: U.C. Davis 2003, Stanford 2003-05, Syracuse 2010-12. Pro coach: Tampa Bay Buccaneers 2006-07, Buffalo Bills 2008-09, re-joined Bills in 2013.

Donnie Henderson, defensive backs; born May 17, 1957, Baltimore, Md. Defensive back Utah State 1978-79. No pro playing experience. College coach: Utah State 1983-88, Idaho 1989, California 1990-91, Arizona State 1992-97, Houston 1998, Southern 2011, Syracuse 2012. Pro coach: Baltimore Ravens 1999-2003, New York Jets 2004-05, Detroit Lions 2006, Jacksonville Jaguars 2008, California Redwoods (UFL) 2009, Arizona Cardinals 2010, joined Bills in 2013.

Ike Hilliard, wide receivers; born April 5, 1976, Patterson, La. Wide receiver Florida 1994-96. Pro wide receiver New York Giants 1997-2004, Tampa Bay Buccaneers 2005-08. Pro coach: Florida Tuskers (UFL) 2009-2010, Miami Dolphins 2011, Washington Redskins 2012, joined Bills in 2013.

Hal Luther, asst. strength and conditioning; born March 24, 1974, Dolgeville, N.Y. Quarterback Springfield (Mass.) College 1992-95. No pro playing experience. College coach: Western Michigan 1996, Wisconsin-LaCrosse 1996-97, North Carolina State 1998-2000, Syracuse 2000-2012. Pro coach: Joined Bills in 2013.

Pat Morris, offensive line; born April 7, 1954, Cleveland, Ohio. Offensive lineman Southern California 1972-75. No pro playing experience. College coach: Southern California 1976-77, 1983-86, Northern Arizona 1978, Minnesota 1979-1982, Michigan State 1987-1994, Stanford 1995-96. Pro coach: San Francisco 49ers 1997-2003, Detroit Lions 2004-05, Minnesota Vikings 2006-2010, Tampa Bay Buccaneers 2011, joined Bills in 2013.

Jim O'Neil, linebackers; born August 26, 1978, Philadelphia, Pa. Defensive end Towson 1997-2000. No pro playing experience. College coach: Albany 2001, Pennsylvania 2002, Northwestern 2003-04, Towson 2005, Eastern Michigan 2006-08. Pro coach: New York Jets 2009-2012, joined Bills in 2013.

Mike Pettine, defensive coordinator; born September 25, 1966, Doylestown, Pa. Safety Virginia 1984-87. No pro playing experience. College coach: Pittsburgh 1993-94. Pro coach: Baltimore Ravens 2002-08, New York Jets 2009-2012, joined Bills in 2013.

Jason Rebrovich, defensive quality control; born March 15, 1978, Clarence, N.Y. Defensive line Alfred State 1996-97, Cortland 1998-99. No pro playing experience. College coach: Cortland 2001-04, 2008-2010, Ferris State 2005-07, Syracuse 2011-12. Pro coach: Joined Bills in 2013.

Jason Vrable, offensive quality control; born January 23, 1985, South Park, Pa. Quarterback Marietta College 2004-06. No pro playing experience. College coach: Marietta 2007, Robert Morris 2008, Syracuse 2009-2010, Charleston 2011-12. Pro coach: Joined Bills in 2013.

Anthony Weaver, defensive line; born July 28, 1980, Saratoga Springs, N.Y. Defensive end Notre Dame 1998-2001. Pro defensive line Baltimore Ravens 2002-05, Houston Texans 2006-08. College coach: Florida 2010, North Texas 2011. Pro coach: New York Jets 2012, joined Bills in 2013.

Tyrone Wheatley, running backs; born January 19, 1972, Inkster, Mich. Running back Michigan 1991-94. Pro running back New York Giants 1995-98, Oakland Raiders 1999-2004. College coach: Ohio Northern 2008, Eastern Michigan 2009, Syracuse 2010-12. Pro coach: Joined Bills in 2013.

American Football Conference
North Division
Team Colors: Black, Orange, and White
One Paul Brown Stadium
Cincinnati, Ohio 45202-3492
Telephone: (513) 621-3550
Ticket Office (513) 621-TDTD (8383)

2013 SCHEDULE
PRESEASON
Aug. 8   at Atlanta............................8:00
Aug. 17   **Tennessee** 7:00
Aug. 24   at Dallas.............................8:00
Aug. 29   **Indianapolis**.......................7:00

REGULAR SEASON
Sep. 8   at Chicago 1:00
Sep. 16   **Pittsburgh** (Mon) 8:40
Sep. 22   **Green Bay** 1:00
Sep. 29   at Cleveland 1:00
Oct. 6   **New England** 1:00
Oct. 13   at Buffalo 1:00
Oct. 20   at Detroit 1:00
Oct. 27   **New York Jets** 4:05
Oct. 31   at Miami (Thurs) 8:25
Nov. 10   at Baltimore 1:00
Nov. 17   **Cleveland** 1:00
Nov. 24   BYE
Dec. 1   at San Diego 4:25
Dec. 8   **Indianapolis** 1:00
Dec. 15   at Pittsburgh *8:30
Dec. 22   **Minnesota** 1:00
Dec. 29   **Baltimore** 1:00
All times ET

Stadium: Paul Brown Stadium
           (opened in 2000)
           •**Capacity:** 65,515
           One Paul Brown Stadium
           Cincinnati, Ohio 45202-3492
Playing Surface: Synthetic
Training Camp: Paul Brown Stadium
                Cincinnati, Ohio 45202

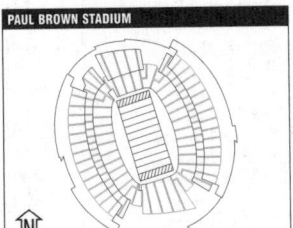

PAUL BROWN STADIUM

CLUB OFFICIALS
President: Mike Brown
Senior Vice President: Pete Brown
Executive Vice President: Katie Blackburn
Vice President: Paul Brown
Vice President: Troy Blackburn
Business Manager: Bill Connelly
Chief Financial Officer: Bill Scanlon
Director of Business Development:
   Bob Bedinghaus
Managing Director of Paul Brown
   Stadium: Eric Brown
Directors of Technology: Michael Kayes,
   Jo Ann Ralstin
Bengals.com Editor: Geoff Hobson
Director of Security: Rusty Guy
Director of Sales and Public Affairs:
   Jeff Berding
Director of Corporate Sales, Marketing
   and Broadcasting: Brian Sells
Ticket Manager: Tim Kelly
Director of Player Relations: Eric Ball
Director of Player Personnel: Duke Tobin
Public Relations Director: Jack Brennan
Athletic Trainer: Paul Sparling
Equipment Manager: Jeff Brickner
Video Director: Travis Brammer

COACHING HISTORY
(310-396-2)
Records include postseason games
1968-1975	Paul Brown	55-59-1
1976-78	Bill Johnson*	18-15-0
1978-79	Homer Rice	8-19-0
1980-83	Forrest Gregg	34-27-0
1984-1991	Sam Wyche	64-68-0
1992-96	Dave Shula**	19-52-0
1996-2000	Bruce Coslet***	21-39-0
2000-02	Dick LeBeau	12-33-0
2003-2012	Marvin Lewis	79-84-1

  * Resigned after five games in 1978
 ** Released after seven games in 1996
*** Resigned after three games in 2000

PAID ATTENDANCE
Home 466,774   Away 498,130
Total 964,904
Single-game home record,
   66,188 (10/28/07)
Single-season home record, 516,154
   (2006)

2013 DRAFT CHOICES
Round	Name	Pos.	College
1	Tyler Eifert	TE	Notre Dame
2	Giovani Bernard	RB	North Carolina
	Margus Hunt	DE	Southern Methodist
3	Shawn Williams	DB	Georgia
4	Sean Porter	LB	Texas A&M
5	Tanner Hawkinson	G	Kansas
6	Rex Burkhead	RB	Nebraska
	Cobi Hamilton	WR	Arkansas
7	Reid Fragel	T	Ohio St.
	T.J. Johnson	C	South Carolina

CINCINNATI BENGALS

2012 TEAM RECORD

PRESEASON (2-2)

Date	Result	Opponent
08/10	W 17-6	New York Jets
08/16	W 24-19	at Atlanta
08/23	L 13-27	Green Bay
08/30	L 16-20	at Indianapolis

REGULAR SEASON (10-6)

Date	Result	Opponent
09/10	L 13-44	at Baltimore
09/16	W 34-27	Cleveland
09/23	W 38-31	at Washington
09/30	W 27-10	at Jacksonville
10/07	L 13-17	Miami
10/14	L 24-34	at Cleveland
10/21	L 17-24	Pittsburgh
11/04	L 23-31	Denver
11/11	W 31-13	New York Giants
11/18	W 28-6	at Kansas City
11/25	W 34-10	Oakland
12/02	W 20-13	at San Diego
12/09	L 19-20	Dallas
12/13	W 34-13	at Philadelphia
12/23	W 13-10	at Pittsburgh
12/30	W 23-17	Baltimore

POSTSEASON (0-1)

Date	Result	Opponent
01/05	L 13-19	at Houston

SCORE BY PERIODS

Bengals	113	104	63	111	0	—	391
Opponents	42	102	80	96	0	—	320

2012 TEAM STATISTICS

	Bengals	Opp.
Total First Downs	292	307
Rushing	95	99
Passing	173	183
Penalty	24	25
3rd Down: Made/Att	74/217	79/219
3rd Down Pct.	34.1	36.1
4th Down: Made/Att	11/16	5/12
4th Down Pct.	68.8	41.7
Possession Avg.	30:26	29:34
Total Net Yards	5323	5115
Avg. Per Game	332.7	319.7
Total Plays	1016	1034
Avg. Per Play	5.2	4.9
Net Yards Rushing	1745	1715
Avg. Per Game	109.1	107.2
Total Rushes	430	423
Net Yards Passing	3578	3400
Avg. Per Game	223.6	212.5
Sacked/Yards Lost	46/229	51/361
Gross Yards	3807	3761
Att./Completions	540/335	560/346
Completion Pct.	62.0	61.8
Had Intercepted	16	14
Punts/Average	76/46.6	86/44.4
Net Punting Avg.	76/42.0	86/36.8
Penalties/Yards	99/857	90/779
Fumbles/Ball Lost	19/10	26/16
Touchdowns	43	34
Rushing	11	13
Passing	28	16
Returns	4	5

2012 INDIVIDUAL STATISTICS

PASSING

	Att.	Comp.	Yds.	Pct.	TD	Int.	Tkld.	Rate
Dalton	528	329	3669	62.3	27	16	46/229	87.4
Gradkowski	11	5	65	45.5	0	0	0/0	64.6
Sanu	1	1	73	100.0	1	0	0/0	158.3
Bengals	540	335	3807	62.0	28	16	46/229	88.1
Opponents	560	346	3761	61.8	16	14	51/361	80.7

SCORING

	TD R	TD P	TD Rt	PAT	FG	Saf	PTS
Nugent	0	0	0	35/35	19/23	0	92
Green	0	11	0	0/0	0/0	0	66
Brown	0	0	0	8/8	11/12	0	41
Green-Ellis	6	0	0	0/0	0/0	0	36
Gresham	0	5	0	0/0	0/0	0	30
Dalton	4	0	0	0/0	0/0	0	24
Hawkins	0	4	0	0/0	0/0	0	24
Sanu	0	4	0	0/0	0/0	0	24
Binns	0	1	0	0/0	0/0	0	6
Dunlap	0	0	1	0/0	0/0	0	6
Gilberry	0	0	1	0/0	0/0	0	6
Hall	0	0	1	0/0	0/0	0	6
A. Jones	0	0	1	0/0	0/0	0	6
M. Jones	0	1	0	0/0	0/0	0	6
Peerman	1	0	0	0/0	0/0	0	6
Pressley	0	1	0	0/0	0/0	0	6
Tate	0	1	0	0/0	0/0	0	6
Bengals	11	28	4	43/43	30/35	0	391
Opponents	13	16	5	33/33	27/32	0	320

2-Pt Conversions: Bengals 0-0, Opponents 1-1

RUSHING

	No.	Yds	Avg	LG	TD
Green-Ellis	278	1094	3.9	48	6
Peerman	36	258	7.2	48	1
Dalton	47	120	2.6	17	4
Leonard	33	106	3.2	11	0
M. Jones	3	47	15.7	37	0
Green	4	38	9.5	20	0
Scott	8	35	4.4	29	0
Hawkins	6	30	5.0	11	0
Sanu	5	15	3.0	7	0
Herron	4	5	1.3	6	0
Tate	1	0	0.0	0	0
Huber	1	-1	-1.0	-1	0
Gradkowski	4	-2	-0.5	0	0
Bengals	430	1745	4.1	48	11
Opponents	423	1715	4.1	32t	13

RECEIVING

	No.	Yds	Avg	LG	TD
Green	97	1350	13.9	73t	11
Gresham	64	737	11.5	55t	5
Hawkins	51	533	10.5	59t	4
Green-Ellis	22	104	4.7	13	0
Binns	18	210	11.7	48t	1
M. Jones	18	201	11.2	23	1
Sanu	16	154	9.6	34	4
Tate	13	211	16.2	44t	1
Leonard	11	67	6.1	16	0
Peerman	9	85	9.4	16	0
Charles	8	101	12.6	25	0
Whalen	7	53	7.6	10	0
Pressley	1	1	1.0	1t	1
Bengals	335	3807	11.4	73t	28
Opponents	346	3761	10.9	71t	16

INTERCEPTIONS

	No.	Yds	Avg	LG	TD
Crocker	3	52	17.3	29	0
Nelson	3	10	3.3	10	0
Hall	2	61	30.5	44	1
Newman	2	0	0.0	0	0
Clements	1	21	21.0	21	0
Dunlap	1	14	14.0	14t	1
Johnson	1	3	3.0	3	0
Sims	1	3	3.0	3	0
Bengals	14	164	11.7	44	2
Opponents	16	187	11.7	37	4

PUNTING

	No.	Yds.	Avg.	In 20	LG
Huber	76	3540	46.6	33	69
Bengals	76	3540	46.6	33	69
Opponents	86	3816	44.4	22	68

PUNT RETURNS

	Ret	FC	Yds	Avg	LG	TD
A. Jones	26	0	301	11.6	81t	1
Tate	21	11	187	8.9	32	0
Bengals	47	11	488	10.4	81t	1
Opponents	27	14	210	7.8	60	0

KICKOFF RETURNS

	No.	Yds	Avg	LG	TD
Tate	32	795	24.8	45	0
A. Jones	3	64	21.3	31	0
Peerman	2	37	18.5	19	0
Charles	2	17	8.5	10	0
Pressley	2	15	7.5	8	0
Bengals	41	928	22.6	45	0
Opponents	60	1468	24.5	105t	1

FIELD GOALS

	1-19	20-29	30-39	40-49	50+
Nugent	2/2	5/5	5/5	6/9	1/2
Brown	0/0	3/3	4/4	3/3	1/2
Bengals	2/2	8/8	9/9	9/12	2/4
Opponents	1/1	6/7	7/7	11/12	2/5

SACKS

	No.
Atkins	12.5
Johnson	11.5
Gilberry	6.5
Dunlap	6.0
Geathers	3.0
Lawson	2.0
Peko	2.0
Burfict	1.0
Howard	1.0
A. Jones	1.0
Maualuga	1.0
Nelson	1.0
Rey	1.0
(group)	1.0
Still	0.5
Bengals	51.0
Opponents	46.0

RECORD HOLDERS
INDIVIDUAL RECORDS—CAREER

Category	Name	Performance
Rushing (Yds.)	Corey Dillon, 1997-2003	8,061
Passing (Yds.)	Ken Anderson, 1971-1986	32,838
Passing (TDs)	Ken Anderson, 1971-1986	197
Receiving (No.)	Chad Johnson, 2001-2010	751
Receiving (Yds.)	Chad Johnson, 2001-2010	10,783
Interceptions	Ken Riley, 1969-1983	65
Punting (Avg.)	Kevin Huber, 2009-2012	44.0
Punt Return (Avg.)	Brandon Tate, 2011-12	10.1
Kickoff Return (Avg.)	Lemar Parrish, 1970-77	24.7
Field Goals	Jim Breech, 1980-1992	225
Touchdowns (Tot.)	Pete Johnson, 1977-1983	70
Points	Jim Breech, 1980-1992	1,151
*Sacks	Eddie Edwards, 1977-1988	47.5

INDIVIDUAL RECORDS—SINGLE SEASON

Category	Name	Performance
Rushing (Yds.)	Rudi Johnson, 2005	1,458
Passing (Yds.)	Carson Palmer, 2007	4,131
Passing (TDs)	Carson Palmer, 2005	32
Receiving (No.)	T.J. Houshmandzadeh, 2007	112
Receiving (Yds.)	Chad Johnson, 2007	1,440
Interceptions	Deltha O'Neal, 2005	10
Punting (Avg.)	Kevin Huber, 2012	46.6
Punt Return (Avg.)	Lemar Parrish, 1974	18.8
Kickoff Return (Avg.)	Tremain Mack, 1999	27.1
Field Goals	Mike Nugent, 2011	33
Touchdowns (Tot.)	Carl Pickens, 1995	17
Points	Mike Nugent, 2011	132
*Sacks	Eddie Edwards, 1983	13.0

INDIVIDUAL RECORDS—SINGLE GAME

Category	Name	Performance
Rushing (Yds.)	Corey Dillon, 10-22-00	278
Passing (Yds.)	Boomer Esiason, 10-7-90	490
Passing (TDs)	Carson Palmer, 9-16-07	6
Receiving (No.)	Carl Pickens, 10-11-98	13
Receiving (Yds.)	Chad Johnson, 11-12-06	260
Interceptions	Many times	3
	Last time by Leon Hall, 12-21-08	
Field Goals	Shayne Graham, 11-11-07	7
Touchdowns (Tot.)	Larry Kinnebrew, 10-28-84	4
	Corey Dillon, 12-4-97	4
Points	Larry Kinnebrew, 10-28-84	24
	Corey Dillon, 12-4-97	24
*Sacks	Antwan Odom, 9-20-09	5.0

Sacks became an official statistic in 1982.

2013 VETERAN ROSTER

No.	Name	Pos.	Ht.	Wt.	Birthdate	NFL Exp.	College	Hometown	How Acq.	'12 Games/ Starts
92	Anderson, Jamaal	DE	6-6	280	2/6/86	7	Arkansas	Little Rock, Ark.	UFA(Ind)-'12	2/0
97	Atkins, Geno	DT	6-1	300	3/28/88	4	Georgia	Pembroke Pines, Fla.	D4a-'10	16/16
65	Boling, Clint	G	6-5	311	5/9/89	3	Georgia	Alpharetta, Ga.	D4-'11	16/16
55	Burfict, Vontaze	LB	6-1	245	9/24/90	2	Arizona State	Corona, Calif.	FA-'12	16/14
80	Charles, Orson	TE	6-3	250	1/27/91	2	Georgia	Tampa, Fla.	D4-'12	16/6
22	# Clements, Nate	S/CB	6-0	205	12/12/79	13	Ohio State	Shaker Heights, Ohio	FA-'11	15/9
73	Collins, Anthony	T	6-5	315	11/2/85	6	Kansas	Beaumont, Texas	D4-'08	5/0
32	Conner, John	FB	5-11	245	6/8/87	4	Kentucky	West Chester, Ohio	FA-'12	2/0
64	Cook, Kyle	C	6-3	315	7/25/83	6	Michigan State	Macomb, Mich.	FA-'07	4/2
33	# Crocker, Chris	S	5-11	197	3/9/80	11	Marshall	Chesapeake, Va.	FA-'12	13/9
14	Dalton, Andy	QB	6-2	220	10/29/87	3	Texas Christian	Katy, Texas	D2-'11	16/16
96	Dunlap, Carlos	DE	6-6	280	2/28/89	4	Florida	North Charleston, S.C.	D2-'10	14/1
44	Dye, Tony	S	5-10	200	2/11/90	2	UCLA	Corona, Calif.	FA-'12	0*
91	Geathers, Robert	DE	6-3	280	8/11/83	10	Georgia	Georgetown, S.C.	D4b-'04	16/16
21	Ghee, Brandon	CB	6-0	193	6/6/87	4	Wake Forest	Fayetteville, N.C.	D3b-'10	0*
95	Gilberry, Wallace	DE	6-2	275	12/5/84	6	Alabama	Bay Minette, Ala.	FA-'12	14/0
18	Green, A.J.	WR	6-4	207	7/31/88	3	Georgia	Summerville, S.C.	D1-'11	16/16
42	Green-Ellis, BenJarvus	HB	5-11	220	7/2/85	6	Mississippi	New Orleans, La.	UFA(NE)-'12	15/15
84	Gresham, Jermaine	TE	6-5	260	6/16/88	4	Oklahoma	Ardmore, Okla.	D1-'10	16/15
29	Hall, Leon	CB	5-11	195	12/9/84	7	Michigan	Vista, Calif.	D1-'07	14/14
46	Harris, Clark	LS	6-5	255	7/10/84	5	Rutgers	Manahawkin, N.J.	FA-'09	16/0
16	Hawkins, Andrew	WR	5-7	180	3/10/86	3	Toledo	Johnstown, Pa.	W(StL)-'11	14/2
53	# Howard, Thomas	LB	6-3	245	7/14/83	8	Texas-El Paso	Lubbock, Texas	UFA(Oak)-'11	1/1
10	Huber, Kevin	P	6-1	212	7/16/85	5	Cincinnati	Cincinnati, Ohio	D5-'09	16/0
43	Iloka, George	S	6-4	225	6/20/90	2	Boise State	Houston, Texas	D5c-'12	7/0
8	Johnson, Josh	QB	6-3	205	5/15/86	5	San Diego	Oakland, Calif.	UFA(Cle)-'13	1/0*
93	Johnson, Michael	DE	6-7	270	2/7/87	5	Georgia Tech	Selma, Ala.	D3a-'09	16/15
24	Jones, Adam	CB	5-10	185	9/30/83	7	West Virginia	Atlanta, Ga.	FA-'10	16/5
82	Jones, Marvin	WR	6-2	195	3/12/90	2	California	Fontana, Calif.	D5b-'12	11/5
27	Kirkpatrick, Dre	CB	6-2	190	10/26/89	2	Alabama	Gadsden, Ala.	D1a-'12	5/0
59	Lamur, Emmanuel	LB	6-4	232	6/8/89	2	Kansas State	West Palm Beach, Fla.	FA-'12	9/0
58	Maualuga, Rey	LB	6-2	250	1/20/87	5	Southern California	Eureka, Calif.	D2-'09	16/16
51	Maybin, Aaron	LB	6-4	240	4/6/88	5	Penn State	Baltimore, Md.	FA-'13	8/0*
26	Mays, Taylor	S	6-3	230	2/7/88	4	Southern California	Seattle, Wash.	T(SF)-'11	16/3
45	Miles, Jeromy	S	6-2	210	7/20/87	4	Massachusetts	Sicklerville, N.J.	FA-'10	16/1
52	Moch, Dontay	LB	6-2	255	7/19/88	2	Nevada	Phoenix, Ariz.	D3-'11	1/0
20	Nelson, Reggie	S	5-11	210	9/21/83	7	Florida	Melbourne, Fla.	T(Jax)-'10	14/14
23	Newman, Terence	CB	5-10	192	9/4/78	11	Kansas State	Salina, Kan.	FA-'12	15/15
2	Nugent, Mike	K	5-10	190	3/2/82	9	Ohio State	Centerville, Ohio	FA-'10	12/0
30	Peerman, Cedric	HB	5-10	211	10/10/86	4	Virginia	Gladys, Va.	W(Det)-'10	14/1
94	Peko, Domata	DT	6-3	322	11/27/84	8	Michigan State	Pago Pago (American Samoa)	D4-'06	16/16
	Pollak, Mike	G	6-3	300	1/5/00	6	Arizona State	Tempe, Ariz.	UFA(Car)-'13	1/0*
38	Prater, Shaun	CB	5-10	190	10/27/89	2	Iowa	Omaha, Neb.	D5a-'12	0*
36	Pressley, Chris	FB	5-11	260	8/8/86	5	Wisconsin	Woodbury, N.J.	FA-'10	14/7
89	Quinn, Richard	TE	6-4	264	9/6/86	5	North Carolina	Maple Heights, Ohio	FA-'12	0*
57	Rey, Vincent	LB	6-2	250	9/6/87	3	Duke	Far Rockaway, N.Y.	FA-'10	16/1
66	Robinson, Trevor	C/G	6-5	305	5/16/90	2	Notre Dame	Elkhorn, Neb.	FA-'12	13/7
5	Robinson, Zac	QB	6-3	215	9/29/86	2	Oklahoma State	Littleton, Colo.	FA-'11	0*
83	Rogers, Taveon	WR	5-11	190	8/17/90	2	New Mexico State	Lancaster, Calif.	FA-'12	0*
74	Roland, Dennis	T/G	6-9	322	3/10/83	6	Georgia	Bolivar, Mo.	FA-'08	16/2
31	Sands, Robert	S	6-4	215	11/3/89	3	West Virginia	Carol City, Fla.	D5-'11	0*
12	Sanu, Mohamed	WR	6-2	210	8/22/89	2	Rutgers	South Brunswick, N.J.	D3a-'12	9/3
11	Sanzenbacher, Dane	WR	5-11	180	13/13/88	3	Ohio State	Toledo, Ohio	W(Chi)-'12	5/0*
28	Scott, Bernard	HB	5-10	198	2/10/84	5	Abilene Christian	Vernon, Texas	D6b-'09	2/0
9	Skelton, John	QB	6-6	244	3/17/88	4	Fordham	El Paso, Texas	W(Ariz)-'13	7/6*
81	Smith, Alex	TE	6-4	258	5/22/82	9	Stanford	Denver, Colo.	UFA(Cle)-'13	12/2*
71	# Smith, Andre	T	6-4	335	1/25/87	5	Alabama	Birmingham, Ala.	D1-'09	16/16
75	Still, Devon	DT	6-5	305	7/11/89	2	Penn State	Wilmington, Del.	D2-'12	8/0
19	Tate, Brandon	WR	6-1	200	10/5/87	5	North Carolina	Burlington, N.C.	W(NE)-'11	16/3
79	Thompson, Brandon	DT	6-2	320	10/19/89	2	Clemson	Thomasville, Ga.	D3b-'12	3/0
88	Whalen, Ryan	WR	6-1	200	7/26/89	3	Stanford	Alamo, Calif.	D6-'11	9/0
70	Wharton, Travelle	G	6-4	320	5/19/81	10	South Carolina	Fountain Inn, S.C.	FA-'12	0*
77	Whitworth, Andrew	T	6-7	330	12/12/81	8	Louisiana State	West Monroe, La.	D2-'06	16/16
68	Zeitler, Kevin	G	6-4	315	3/8/90	2	Wisconsin	Waukesha, Wis.	D1b-'12	16/16

*   Dye missed '12 season because of injury; Ghee missed '12 season because of injury; J. Johnson played one game with Cleveland in '12; Maybin played eight games with the New York Jets; Pollak played one game with Carolina; Prater missed '12 season because of injury; Quinn inactive for 15 games; Z. Robinson last active with Patriots in '10; Rogers missed '12 season because of injury; Sands missed '12 season because of injury: Sanzenbacher played five games with Chicago, inactive for one game with Cincinnati; Skelton played seven games with Arizona; Alex Smith played 12 games with Cleveland; Wharton missed '12 season because of injury.

\#   Unrestricted Free Agent; subject to developments.

Players lost through free agency (6): K Josh Brown (NYG; 4 games), QB Bruce Gradkowski (Pitt; 2), LB Manny Lawson (Buff; 16), HB Brian Leonard (TB; 15), DT Pat Sims (Oak.; 8); LB Dan Skuta (SF; 16).

Also played with Bengals in '12—CB Jason Allen (4 games), WR Armon Binns (8), C Jeff Faine (8), LB Roddrick Muckelroy (5).

FIRST-YEAR ROSTER

Name	Pos.	Ht.	Wt.	Birthdate	College	Hometown	How Acq.
Bernard, Giovani	HB	5-9	202	11/22/91	North Carolina	Boca Raton, Fla.	D2a
Black, Larry	DT	6-2	302	12/1/89	Indiana	Cincinnati, Ohio	FA
Brown, Terrence	CB	5-11	176	3/4/91	Stanford	Torrance, Calif.	FA
Burkhead, Rex	HB	5-10	214	7/2/90	Nebraska	Plano, Texas	D6a
Chappelear, Travis	DT	6-5	263	4/3/89	Northwest Missouri State	Urbana, Mo.	FA
Davis, Bryce (1)	TE/LS	6-3	245	6/16/89	Central Oklahoma	Duncan, Okla.	FA-'12
DiManche, Jayson	LB	6-1	232	9/22/90	Southern Illinois	Hamilton, N.J.	FA
Eifert, Tyler	TE	6-6	250	9/8/90	Notre Dame	Fort Wayne, Ind.	D1
Evans, DeQuin (1)	DE	6-2	265	5/17/87	Kentucky	Long Beach, Calif.	FA
Fragel, Reid	T	6-8	308	2/22/91	Ohio State	Grosse Pointe Farms, Mich.	D7a
Goard, Tyrone	WR	6-4	205	4/30/89	Eastern Kentucky	Charleston, W. Va.	FA
Hamilton, Cobi	WR	6-2	212	11/13/90	Arkansas	Texarkana, Texas	D6b
Hawkinson, Tanner	G	6-5	300	5/14/90	Kansas	McPherson, Kansas	D5
Herron, Daniel (1)	HB	5-10	215	3/21/89	Ohio State	Warren, Ohio	D6-'12
Hunt, Margus	DE	6-8	277	7/14/87	Southern Methodist	Karksi-Nuia (Estonia)	D2b
Johnson, T.J.	C	6-4	310	7/17/90	South Carolina	Aynor, S.C.	D7b
Joiner, Brandon (1)	LB	6-3	245	4/27/89	Arkansas State	Killeen, Texas	FA-'12
Lewis-Harris, Chris (1)	CB	5-10	180	2/11/89	Tennessee-Chattanooga	Smyrna, Ga.	FA-'12
McCalebb, Onterio	CB	5-10	170	8/10/89	Auburn	Fort Meade, Fla.	FA
Porter, Sean	LB	6-1	230	1/12/91	Texas A&M	Schertz, Texas	D4
Roundtree, Roy	WR	6-1	180	3/7/89	Michigan	Trotwood, Ohio	FA
Schaffer, J.K. (1).	LB	6-0	232	6/10/90	Cincinnati	Cincinnati, Ohio	FA-'12
Sharp, Quinn	K/P	6-1	189	11/12/89	Oklahoma State	Mansfield, Texas	FA
Stephens, Terrence	DT	6-1	307	1/7/91	Stanford	Germantown, Md.	FA
Stoudermire, Troy	CB	5-10	199	7/1/90	Minnesota	Dallas, Texas	FA
Sullen, John	G	6-6	332	12/31/90	Auburn	Auburn, Ala.	FA
Taylor, Bruce	LB	6-1	237	12/31/89	Virginia Tech	Riceboro, Ga.	FA
Williams, Shawn	S	6-0	213	5/13/91	Georgia	Damascus, Ga.	D3

The term NFL Rookie is defined as a player who is in his first season of professional football and has not been on the roster of another professional football team for any regular-season or postseason games. A Rookie is designated by an "R" on NFL rosters. Players who have been active in another professional football league or players who have NFL experience, including either preseason training camp or being on an Active List or Inactive List, or on Reserve/Injured or Reserve/Physically Unable to Perform for fewer than six regular-season games, are termed NFL First-Year Players. An NFL First-Year Player is designated by a "1" on NFL rosters. Thereafter, a player is credited with an additional year of experience for each season in which he accumulates six games on the Active List or Inactive List, or on Reserve/Injured or Reserve/Physically Unable to Perform.

Log on to www.bengals.com for an up-to-date roster.

CINCINNATI BENGALS

COACHING STAFF

Head Coach,
Marvin Lewis

Pro Career: Marvin Lewis in 2013 extends his Bengals-record head coaching tenure to 11 seasons. He has led his team to the postseason in three of the last four years, making the Bengals one of only seven teams to make three or more playoff trips in that span. Lewis opens 2013 with 79 career victories, 15 more than any other Bengals' coach (Sam Wyche 64). The Bengals went 10-6 in the 2012 regular season. Cincinnati was a Wild Card playoff entry for the second straight year, rocketing into the playoffs with a 7-1 record in the season's second half, tying the 1981 Super Bowl team for the best second-half by a Cincinnati team in a 16-game season. The 2012 Bengals achieved a rare NFL feat, becoming only the ninth of 131 teams since 1990 to rise from a 3-5 start to the playoffs. In 2011, Lewis guided a young squad with new stars that posted a 9-7 mark to reach the playoffs. He was the consensus choice as NFL Coach of the Year in 2009, when the Bengals won the AFC North title while sweeping all six division games. The Bengals were AFC North champions under Lewis also in 2005. Lewis was named the ninth head coach in Bengals history on January 14, 2003. In 2002, Lewis was Washington Redskins defensive coordinator and assistant head coach. He spent six seasons (1996-2001) as defensive coordinator with the Baltimore Ravens, a tenure that included a Super Bowl victory in the 2000 season. In 2000, Lewis' defense set the NFL record for fewest points allowed in a 16-game campaign (165), and the unit has been widely considered as one of the best NFL defenses of all time. Prior to Baltimore, Lewis spent four seasons (1992-95) with the Pittsburgh Steelers as linebackers coach. Career record: 79-84-1.

Background: Earned All-Big Sky Conference honors as a linebacker at Idaho State (1978-1980), and saw action at quarterback and free safety. Received his bachelor's degree in physical education and Master's degree in athletic administration. Inducted into Idaho State's Hall of Fame in 2001. Began his coaching career at Idaho State (1981-84), winning an NCAA Division I-AA championship in 1981. Was also the linebackers coach at Long Beach State (1985-86), New Mexico (1987-89), and Pittsburgh (1990-91).

Personal: Born September 23, 1958, McDonald, Pa. Lewis and his wife, Peggy, have two children—Whitney and Marcus.

ASSISTANT COACHES

Paul Alexander, asst. head coach/offensive line; born February 12, 1960, Rochester, N.Y. Tackle Cortland State 1979-1981. No pro playing experience. College coach: Penn State 1982-84, Michigan 1985-86, Central Michigan

1987-1991. Pro coach: New York Jets 1992-93, joined Bengals in 1994.

Mark Carrier, defensive backs; born April 28, 1968, Lake Charles, La. Defensive back Southern California 1987-89. Pro defensive back Chicago Bears 1990-96, Detroit Lions 1997-99, Washington Redskins 2000. College coach: Arizona State 2004-05. Pro coach: Baltimore Ravens 2006-09, New York Jets 2010-11, joined Bengals in 2012.

Kyle Caskey, asst. offensive line/quality control; born Dec. 7, 1978, Daingerfield, Texas. Tight end Texas A&M 1997-98. No pro playing experience. College coach: Louisiana-Monroe 2004-05, Indiana State 2006-08, Mississippi 2009. Pro coach: Joined Bengals in 2010.

Brayden Coombs, asst. special teams/quality control; born Oct. 24, 1986, Cincinnati, Ohio. Wide receiver-defensive back Miami (Ohio) 2005-09. No pro playing experience. Pro coach: Joined Bengals in 2012.

Jeff Friday, asst. strength and conditioning; born Oct. 11, 1966, Milwaukee, Wisc. Attended Wisconsin-Milwaukee. No college or pro playing experience. College coach: Illinois State 1990-91, Northwestern 1992-95. Pro coach: Minnesota Vikings 1996-98, Baltimore Ravens 1999-2007, joined Bengals in 2010.

Jay Gruden, offensive coordinator; born March 4, 1967, Tiffin, Ohio. Quarterback Louisville 1985-88. Pro quarterback Barcelona Dragons (WLAF) 1990, Sacramento Surge (WLAF) 1990, Tampa Bay Storm (AFL) 1991-96, Orlando Predators (AFL) 2002-03. Pro coach: Nashville Katz (AFL) 1997, Orlando Predators (AFL) 1998-2001 (head coach) and 2004-08 (head coach), Tampa Bay Buccaneers 2002-08, Florida Tuskers (UFL) 2009-10 (head coach 2010), joined Bengals in 2011.

Paul Guenther, linebackers; born Nov. 22, 1971, Richboro, Pa. Linebacker Ursinus College 1990-93. No pro playing experience. College coach: Western Maryland 1994-95, Ursinus College 1996, 1997-2001 (head coach 1997-2001), Jacksonville 1997. Pro coach: Washington Redskins 2002-03, joined Bengals in 2005.

Jay Hayes, defensive line; born March 3, 1960, South Fayette, Pa. Defensive end Idaho 1978-1981. Pro defensive end/linebacker Michigan Panthers (USFL) 1984, Memphis Showboats (USFL) 1985. College coach: Notre Dame 1988-1991, California 1992-94, Wisconsin 1995-98. Pro coach: Pittsburgh Steelers 1999-2001, Minnesota Vikings 2002, joined Bengals in 2003.

Jonathan Hayes, tight ends; born Aug. 11, 1962, South Fayette, Pa. Linebacker/tight end Iowa 1981-84. Pro tight end Kansas City Chiefs 1985-1993, Pittsburgh Steelers 1994-96. College coach: Oklahoma 1999-2002. Pro coach:

Joined Bengals in 2003.

Hue Jackson, special assistant to head coach/running backs; born Oct. 22, 1965, Los Angeles, Calif. Quarterback Pacific 1985-86. No pro playing experience. College coach: Pacific 1987-89, Cal State-Fullerton 1990-91, Arizona State 1992-95, California 1996, Southern California 1997-2000. Pro coach: London Monarchs (WLAF) 1991, Washington Redskins 2001-03, Cincinnati Bengals 2004-06, Atlanta Falcons 2007, Baltimore Ravens 2008-09, Oakland Raiders 2010-11 (head coach 2011), re-joined Bengals in 2012.

David Lippincott, asst. linebackers/quality control; born July 6, 1977, Cincinnati, Ohio. Attended Dayton. No college or pro playing experience. College coach: Bluffton 2000-02, Minnesota 2003-04, Richmond 2005-07. Pro coach: Joined Bengals in 2011.

Chip Morton, strength and conditioning; born November 27, 1962, Hamden, Conn. Attended North Carolina. No college or pro playing experience. College coach: Ohio State 1985-86, Penn State 1987-1991. Pro coach: San Diego Chargers 1992-94, Carolina Panthers 1995-98, Baltimore Ravens 1999-2001, Washington Redskins 2002, joined Bengals in 2003.

Darrin Simmons, special teams coordinator; born April 9, 1973, Elkhart, Kan. Punter Kansas 1993-95. No pro playing experience. College coach: Kansas 1996, Minnesota 1997. Pro coach: Baltimore Ravens 1998, Carolina Panthers 1999-2002, joined Bengals in 2003.

James Urban, wide receivers; born Dec. 1, 1973, Mechanicsburg, Pa. Wide receiver Washington and Lee 1993-96. No pro playing experience. College coach: Clarion 1997-98, Pennsylvania 1999-2003: Pro coach: Philadelphia Eagles 2004-10, joined Bengals in 2011.

Ken Zampese, quarterbacks; born July 19, 1967, Santa Maria, Calif. Wide receiver San Diego 1985-88. No pro playing experience. College coach: San Diego 1989, Southern California 1990-91, Northern Arizona 1992-95, Miami (Ohio) 1996-97. Pro coach: Philadelphia Eagles 1998, Green Bay Packers 1999, St. Louis Rams 2000-02, joined Bengals in 2003.

Adam Zimmer, asst. defensive backs; born January 13, 1984, Ogden, Utah. Defensive back Trinity (Texas) 2002-05. No pro playing experience. Pro coach: New Orleans Saints 2006-09, Kansas City Chiefs 2010-12, joined Bengals in 2013.

Mike Zimmer, defensive coordinator; born June 5, 1956, Peoria, Ill. Quarterback/linebacker Illinois State 1974-76. No pro playing experience. College coach: Missouri 1979-1980, Weber State 1981-88, Washington State 1989-1993. Pro coach: Dallas Cowboys 1994-2006, Atlanta Falcons 2007, joined Bengals in 2008.

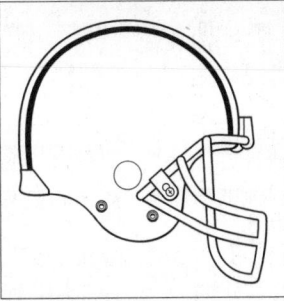

American Football Conference
North Division
Team Colors: Brown, Orange, and White
76 Lou Groza Blvd.
Berea, Ohio 44017
Telephone: (440) 891-5000

2013 SCHEDULE
PRESEASON
Aug. 8	**St. Louis**	8:00
Aug. 15	**Detroit**	7:30
Aug. 24	at Indianapolis	7:00
Aug. 29	at Chicago	8:00

REGULAR SEASON
Sep. 8	**Miami**	1:00
Sep. 15	at Baltimore	1:00
Sep. 22	at Minnesota	1:00
Sep. 29	**Cincinnati**	1:00
Oct. 3	**Buffalo** (Thurs)	8:25
Oct. 13	**Detroit**	1:00
Oct. 20	at Green Bay	4:25
Oct. 27	at Kansas City	1:00
Nov. 3	**Baltimore**	4:25
Nov. 10	BYE	
Nov. 17	at Cincinnati	1:00
Nov. 24	**Pittsburgh**	1:00
Dec. 1	**Jacksonville**	1:00
Dec. 8	at New England	1:00
Dec. 15	**Chicago**	1:00
Dec. 22	at New York Jets	1:00
Dec. 29	at Pittsburgh	1:00

All times ET
Stadium: FirstEnergy Stadium (opened in 1999)
  •**Capacity:** 73,300
  100 Alfred Lerner Way
  Cleveland, Ohio 44114
Playing Surface: Grass
Headquarters/Training Camp:
    76 Lou Groza Boulevard
    Berea, Ohio 44017

FIRSTENERGY STADIUM

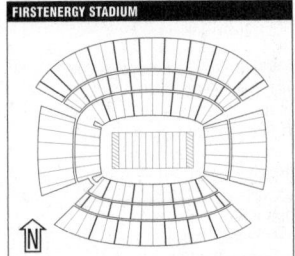

CLUB OFFICIALS
Owner: Jimmy Haslam
Chief Executive Officer: Joe Banner
President: Alec Scheiner
Head Coach: Rob Chudzinski
General Manager: Michael Lombardi
Assistant General Manager: Ray Farmer
Executive Vice President, General
  Counsel: Sashi Brown
Executive Vice President, Chief Revenue
  Officer: Brent Stehlik
Executive Vice President, Strategic
  Initiatives: Bryan Wiedmeier
Chief Financial Officer: David A. Jenkins
Senior Advisor and Special Counsel:
  Fred Nance
Vice President, Ticket Sales and Service:
  John Davis
Vice President, Corporate Partnerships:
  Matt Goodman
Vice President, Fan Experience &
  Marketing: Kevin Griffin
Vice President, Media Relations:
  Neal Gulkis
Vice President, Community Outreach:
  Renee Harvey
Vice President, Security: Carl Meyer
Vice President, Marketing: Brett Reynolds
Director, Stadium Operations:
  Todd Argust
Director, Content & Production:
  Reagan Berube
Director, Video: Chad Bogard
Director, Corporate Partnerships:
  Seamus Carr
Director, Operations: Phil Dangerfield
Director, Information Technology:
  Brandon Covert
Director, Premium & Suite Sales and
  Service: Nick Frasco
Director, Football Research and Player
  Personnel Assistant: Ken Kovash
Director, Suite Sales & Service:
  Paul Mocho
Director, Creative Services:
  George Muller
Director, Administration: Mike Nikolaus
Director, Partnership Service and
  Activation: Nicole Peters
Director, Legal Affairs: Megan Rogers
Director, Finance: Gregory Rush
Director, Player Personnel: Jon Sandusky
Director, Ticket Operations: John Schulze
Director, Player Engagement: Aaron Shea
Director, Season and Group Ticket Sales:
  Bob Sivik
Director, Community Relations:
  Jenner Tekancic
Director, Guest Relations:
  Lauren Voorhies
Head Athletic Trainer: Joe Sheehan
Head Equipment Manager: Brad Melland
Head Groundskeeper: Chris Powell
Senior Editor: Vic Carucci

COACHING HISTORY
(458-437-10)
Records include postseason games
1950-1962	Paul Brown	115-49-5
1963-1970	Blanton Collier	79-38-2
1971-74	Nick Skorich	30-26-2
1975-77	Forrest Gregg*	18-23-0
1977	Dick Modzelewski	0-1-0
1978-1984	Sam Rutigliano**	47-52-0
1984-88	Marty Schottenheimer	46-31-0
1989-1990	Bud Carson***	12-14-1
1990	Jim Shofner	1-6-0
1991-95	Bill Belichick	37-45-0
1999-2000	Chris Palmer	5-27-0
2001-04	Butch Davis****	24-36-0
2004	Terry Robiskie	1-4-0
2005-08	Romeo Crennel	24-40-0
2009-2010	Eric Mangini	10-22-0
2011-12	Pat Shurmur	9-23-0

*Resigned after 13 games in 1977
**Released after eight games in 1984
***Released after nine games in 1990
****Resigned after 11 games in 2004

PAID ATTENDANCE
Home 533,415   Away 523,330
Total 1,056,745
Single-game home record,
  85,073 (9/21/70)
Single-season home record, 620,496
  (1980)

2013 DRAFT CHOICES
Round	Name	Pos.	College
1	Barkevious Mingo	DE	Louisiana St.
3	Leon McFadden	DB	San Diego St.
6	Jamoris Slaughter	DB	Notre Dame
7	Armonty Bryant	DE	East Central
	Garrett Gilkey	T	Chadron St.

2012 TEAM RECORD
PRESEASON (2-2)

Date	Result		Opponent
808/10	W	19-17	at Detroit
08/16	W	35-10	at Green Bay
08/24	L	10-27	Philadelphia
08/30	L	20-28	Chicago

REGULAR SEASON (5-11)

Date	Result		Opponent
09/09	L	16-17	Philadelphia
09/16	L	27-34	at Cincinnati
09/23	L	14-24	Buffalo
09/27	L	16-23	at Baltimore
10/07	L	27-41	at New York Giants
10/14	W	34-24	Cincinnati
10/21	L	13-17	at Indianapolis
10/28	W	7-6	San Diego
11/04	L	15-25	Baltimore
11/18	L	20-23	at Dallas (OT)
11/25	W	20-14	Pittsburgh
12/02	W	20-17	at Oakland
12/09	W	30-7	Kansas City
12/16	L	21-38	Washington
12/23	L	12-34	at Denver
12/30	L	10-24	at Pittsburgh

(OT) Overtime

SCORE BY PERIODS

Browns	50	89	69	94	0	—	302
Opponents	84	96	75	110	3	—	368

2012 TEAM STATISTICS

	Browns	Opp.
Total First Downs	279	345
Rushing	71	104
Passing	185	203
Penalty	23	38
3rd Down: Made/Att	67/218	85/223
3rd Down Pct.	30.7	38.1
4th Down: Made/Att	7/16	7/11
4th Down Pct.	43.8	63.6
Possession Avg.	27:59	32:01
Total Net Yards	5028	5821
Avg. Per Game	314.3	363.8
Total Plays	998	1095
Avg. Per Play	5.0	5.3
Net Yards Rushing	1593	1898
Avg. Per Game	99.6	118.6
Total Rushes	396	457
Net Yards Passing	3435	3923
Avg. Per Game	214.7	245.2
Sacked/Yards Lost	36/233	38/233
Gross Yards	3668	4156
Att./Completions	566/328	600/378
Completion Pct.	58.0	63.0
Had Intercepted	18	17
Punts/Average	90/41.8	88/46.0
Net Punting Avg.	90/37.1	88/37.0
Penalties/Yards	113/1005	120/1008
Fumbles/Ball Lost	22/8	25/12
Touchdowns	31	44
Rushing	12	14
Passing	16	27
Returns	3	3

2012 INDIVIDUAL STATISTICS

PASSING	Att.	Comp.	Yds.	Pct.	TD	Int.	Tkld.	Rate
Weeden	517	297	3385	57.4	14	17	28/186	72.6
Lewis	32	22	204	68.8	1	1	3/14	83.3
McCoy	17	9	79	52.9	1	0	4/25	85.2
Jo. Johnson	0	0	0	—	0	0	1/8	—
Browns	566	328	3668	58.0	16	18	36/233	73.5
Opponents	600	378	4156	63.0	27	17	38/233	86.6

SCORING	TD R	TD P	TD Rt	PAT	FG	Saf	PTS
Dawson	0	0	0	29/29	29/31	0	116
Richardson	11	1	0	0/0	0/0	0	72
Gordon	0	5	0	0/0	0/0	0	30
Little	0	4	0	0/0	0/0	0	24
Benjamin	0	2	1	0/0	0/0	0	18
Watson	0	3	0	0/0	0/0	0	18
S. Brown	0	0	1	0/0	0/0	0	6
J. Cameron	0	1	0	0/0	0/0	0	6
Hardesty	1	0	0	0/0	0/0	0	6
D. Jackson	0	0	1	0/0	0/0	0	6
Browns	12	16	3	29/29	29/31	0	302
Opponents	14	27	3	42/42	20/24	0	368

2-Pt Conversions: Browns 0-2, Opponents 1-2

RUSHING	No.	Yds	Avg	LG	TD
Richardson	267	950	3.6	32t	11
Hardesty	65	271	4.2	25	1
Weeden	27	111	4.1	25	0
Benjamin	6	66	11.0	35	0
B. Jackson	8	54	6.8	25	0
Cribbs	6	42	7.0	16	0
Ventrone	1	35	35.0	35	0
Ogbonnaya	8	30	3.8	9	0
Little	2	15	7.5	17	0
McCoy	4	15	3.8	15	0
Lewis	1	3	3.0	3	0
Norwood	1	1	1.0	1	0
Browns	396	1593	4.0	35	12
Opponents	457	1898	4.2	80t	14

RECEIVING	No.	Yds	Avg	LG	TD
Little	53	647	12.2	43	4
Richardson	51	367	7.2	27	1
Gordon	50	805	16.1	71t	5
Watson	49	501	10.2	27	3
Ogbonnaya	24	187	7.8	38	0
J. Cameron	20	226	11.3	28	1
Benjamin	18	298	16.6	69t	2
Massaquoi	17	254	14.9	54	0
Norwood	13	137	10.5	27	0
Smith	13	47	3.6	17	0
Cooper	8	106	13.3	28	0
Cribbs	7	63	9.0	24	0
B. Jackson	2	20	10.0	14	0
Hardesty	2	16	8.0	9	0
Smelley	1	3	3.0	3	0
Weeden	0	-9	—	-9	0
Browns	328	3668	11.2	71t	16
Opponents	378	4156	11.0	64t	27

INTERCEPTIONS	No.	Yds	Avg	LG	TD
Haden	3	64	21.3	50	0
U. Young	3	44	14.7	44	0
S. Brown	3	20	6.7	19t	1
D. Jackson	2	31	15.5	27t	1
Robertson	2	1	0.5	1	0
Ward	1	37	37.0	37	0
Gipson	1	23	23.0	23	0
Fort	1	10	10.0	10	0
Winn	1	0	0.0	0	0
Browns	17	230	13.5	50	2
Opponents	18	296	16.4	63t	2

PUNTING	No.	Yds.	Avg.	In 20	LG
Hodges	90	3766	41.8	29	58
Browns	90	3766	41.8	29	58
Opponents	88	4044	46	27	66

PUNT RETURNS	Ret	FC	Yds	Avg	LG	TD
Cribbs	38	8	457	12.0	60	0
Benjamin	3	1	149	49.7	93t	1
Browns	41	9	606	14.8	93t	1
Opponents	34	26	343	10.1	81t	1

KICKOFF RETURNS	No.	Yds	Avg	LG	TD
Cribbs	43	1178	27.4	74	0
Benjamin	3	76	25.3	29	0
Hagg	2	8	4.0	5	0
Stephens	1	7	7.0	7	0
Ja. Johnson	1	0	0.0	0	0
Browns	50	1269	25.4	74	0
Opponents	43	853	19.8	34	0

FIELD GOALS	1-19	20-29	30-39	40-49	50+
Dawson	0/0	8/9	8/9	6/6	7/7
Browns	0/0	8/9	8/9	6/6	7/7
Opponents	0/0	2/3	7/7	10/12	1/2

SACKS	No.
Sheard	7.0
Parker	6.0
Rucker	4.0
D. Jackson	3.5
Hughes	3.0
Maiava	2.0
Rubin	2.0
U. Young	1.5
S. Brown	1.0
Fort	1.0
Fujita	1.0
Robertson	1.0
Stephens	1.0
Taylor	1.0
Ward	1.0
Winn	1.0
(group)	1.0
Browns	38.0
Opponents	36.0

RECORD HOLDERS
INDIVIDUAL RECORDS—CAREER

Category	Name	Performance
Rushing (Yds.)	Jim Brown, 1957-1965	12,312
Passing (Yds.)	Brian Sipe, 1974-1983	23,713
Passing (TDs)	Brian Sipe, 1974-1983	154
Receiving (No.)	Ozzie Newsome, 1978-1990	662
Receiving (Yds.)	Ozzie Newsome, 1978-1990	7,980
Interceptions	Thom Darden, 1972-74, 1976-1981	45
Punting (Avg.)	Dave Zastudil, 2006-2010	44.1
Punt Return (Avg.)	Greg Pruitt, 1973-1981	11.8
Kickoff Return (Avg.)	Greg Pruitt, 1973-1981	26.3
Field Goals	Phil Dawson, 1999-2012	305
Touchdowns (Tot.)	Jim Brown, 1957-1965	126
Points	Lou Groza, 1950-59, 1961-67	1,349
*Sacks	Clay Matthews, 1978-1993	62.0

INDIVIDUAL RECORDS—SINGLE SEASON

Category	Name	Performance
Rushing (Yds.)	Jim Brown, 1963	1,863
Passing (Yds.)	Brian Sipe, 1980	4,132
Passing (TDs)	Brian Sipe, 1980	30
Receiving (No.)	Ozzie Newsome, 1983	89
	Ozzie Newsome, 1984	89
	Kellen Winslow, 2006	89
Receiving (Yds.)	Braylon Edwards, 2007	1,289
Interceptions	Thom Darden, 1978	10
	Anthony Henry, 2001	10
Punting (Avg.)	Gary Collins, 1965	46.7
Punt Return (Avg.)	Leroy Kelly, 1965	15.6
Kickoff Return (Avg.)	Billy Lefear, 1975	31.7
Field Goals	Phil Dawson, 2008	30
Touchdowns (Tot.)	Jim Brown, 1965	21
Points	Jim Brown, 1965	126
*Sacks	Reggie Camp, 1984	14.0

INDIVIDUAL RECORDS—SINGLE GAME

Category	Name	Performance
Rushing (Yds.)	Jerome Harrison, 12-20-09	286
Passing (Yds.)	Brian Sipe, 10-25-81	444
Passing (TDs)	Frank Ryan, 12-12-64	5
	Bill Nelsen, 11-2-69	5
	Brian Sipe, 10-7-79	5
	Kelly Holcomb, 11-28-04	5
	Derek Anderson, 9-16-07	5
Receiving (No.)	Ozzie Newsome, 10-14-84	14
Receiving (Yds.)	Ozzie Newsome, 10-14-84	191
Interceptions	Many times	3
	Last time by Anthony Henry, 11-18-01	
Field Goals	Phil Dawson, 11-5-06	6
Touchdowns (Tot.)	Dub Jones, 11-25-51	**6
Points	Dub Jones, 11-25-51	36
*Sacks	Andra Davis, 11-9-03	4.0

*Sacks became an official statistic in 1982.
**NFL Record

2013 VETERAN ROSTER

No.	Name	Pos.	Ht.	Wt.	Birthdate	NFL Exp.	College	Hometown	How Acq.	'12 Games/ Starts
24	Bademosi, Johnson	DB	6-0	200	7/23/90	2	Stanford	Silver Springs, Md.	FA-'12	16/0
34	Barnes, Kevin	DB	6-1	190	9/15/86	4	Maryland	Glen Burnie, Md.	FA-'13	2/0*
82	Barnidge, Gary	TE	6-5	250	9/22/85	6	Louisville	Middleburg, Fla.	UFA(Car)-'13	16/5*
80	Benjamin, Travis	WR	5-10	175	12/29/89	2	Miami	Belle Glade, Fla.	D4a-'12	14/3
18 t-	Bess, Davone	WR	5-10	195	9/13/85	6	Hawai'i	Oakland, Calif.	T(Mia)-'13	13/13*
#	Brown, Sheldon	DB	5-10	200	3/19/79	12	South Carolina	Fort Lawn, S.C.	T(Phil)-'10	15/14
92	Bryant, Desmond	DL	6-6	310	12/15/85	5	Harvard	Elizabethtown, N.C.	UFA(Oak)-'13	16/8*
79	Butler, Rashad	OL	6-4	310	2/10/83	8	Miami	Palm Beach Gardens, Fla.	UFA(Hou)-'13	0*
84	Cameron, Jordan	TE	6-5	245	8/7/88	3	Southern California	Newbury Park, Calif.	D4a-'11	14/6
17	Campbell, Jason	QB	6-5	230	12/31/81	9	Auburn	Laurel, Miss.	UFA(Chi)-'13	6/1*
94	Carder, Tank	LB	6-2	235	1/18/89	2	Texas Christian	Sweeny, Texas	W(Buff)-'12	15/1
2	Conley, T.J.	P	6-1	215	8/29/85	2	Idaho	Walla Walla, Wash.	FA-'13	0*
88	Cooper, Josh	WR	5-10	190	1/8/89	2	Oklahoma State	Mustang, Okla.	FA-'12	6/1
75	Cousins, Oniel	OL	6-4	315	6/29/84	6	Texas-El Paso	Fullerton, Calif.	W(Balt)-'11	13/0
81	Davis, Kellen	TE	6-7	265	11/11/85	6	Michigan State	Adrian, Mich.	FA-'13	16/15*
58	Fort, L.J.	LB	6-0	230	1/3/90	2	Northern Iowa	Waynesville, Mo.	FA-'12	16/1
39	Gipson, Tashaun	DB	5-11	205	8/7/90	2	Wyoming	Dallas, Texas	FA-'12	10/3
13	Gordon, Josh	WR	6-3	225	4/13/91	2	Baylor	Houston, Texas	SD2-'12	16/13
7	Graham, Shayne	K	6-0	210	12/9/77	12	Virginia Tech	Radford, Va.	UFA(Hou)-'13	16/0*
77	Greco, John	OL	6-4	315	3/24/85	6	Toledo	Youngstown, Ohio	T(StL)-'11	14/10
87	Gronkowski, Dan	TE	6-5	255	1/21/85	3	Maryland	Williamsville, N.Y.	FA-'13	0*
54	Groves, Quentin	LB	6-3	265	7/5/84	6	Auburn	Greenville, Miss.	UFA(Ariz)-'13	16/7*
23	Haden, Joe	DB	5-11	190	4/14/89	4	Florida	Fort Washington, Md.	D1-'10	11/11
27	Hagg, Eric	DB	6-1	205	9/15/89	3	Nebraska	Peoria, Ariz.	D7-'11	11/4
20	Hardesty, Montario	RB	6-0	225	2/1/87	4	Tennessee	New Bern, N.C.	D2b-'10	11/1
#	Hodges, Reggie	P	6-0	220	1/26/82	7	Ball State	Champaign, Ill	FA-'09	16/0
93	Hughes, John	DL	6-2	320	4/27/88	2	Cincinnati	Gahanna, Ohio	D3-'12	16/2
#	Jackson, Brandon	RB	5-10	216	10/2/85	7	Nebraska	Horn Lake, Miss.	UFA (GB)-'11	2/0
52	Jackson, D'Qwell	LB	6-0	240	9/26/83	8	Maryland	Largo, Fla.	D2-'06	16/16
50	Johnson, James-Michael	LB	6-1	240	8/20/89	2	Nevada	Las Vegas, Nev.	D4b-'12	10/8
67	Kitchen, Ishmaa'ily	DL	6-1	330	8/24/88	2	Kent State	Youngstown, Ohio	W(Balt)-'12	15/0
99	Kruger, Paul	LB	6-4	270	2/15/86	5	Utah	Orem, Utah	UFA(Balt)-'13	15/6*
66	Lauvao, Shawn	OL	6-3	315	10/26/87	4	Arizona State	Honolulu, Hawaii	D3b-'10	16/16
28 t-	Lewis, Dion	RB	5-8	195	9/27/90	3	Pittsburgh	Albany, N.Y.	T(Phil)-'13	9/0*
9	Lewis, Thaddeus	QB	6-2	210	11/19/87	3	Duke	Opa-Locka, Fla.	W(StL)-'11	1/1
15	Little, Greg	WR	6-2	220	5/30/89	3	North Carolina	Durham, N.C.	D2b-'11	16/16
55	Mack, Alex	OL	6-4	311	11/19/85	5	California	Santa Barbara, Calif.	D1-'09	16/16
48	Marecic, Owen	FB	6-0	245	10/4/88	3	Stanford	Portland, Ore.	D4b-'11	10/2
31	Miller, Prince	DB	5-9	210	1/14/88	2	Georgia	Duncan, S.C.	FA-'12	2/0
60	Miller, Ryan	OL	6-7	320	7/6/89	2	Colorado	Littleton, Colo.	D5-'12	8/0
56	Moten, Adrian	LB	6-2	230	4/22/88	2	Maryland	Suitland, Md.	FA-'12	1/0*
11	Nelson, David	WR	6-5	215	11/7/86	4	Florida	Wichita Falls, Texas	FA-'13	1/1*
10	Norwood, Jordan	WR	5-11	180	9/29/86	3	Penn State	State College, Pa.	FA-'10	2/0
25	Ogbonnaya, Chris	RB	6-0	225	5/5/86	4	Texas	Houston, Texas	FA-'11	15/1
21	Owens, Chris	DB	5-9	180	12/1/86	5	San Jose State	Los Angeles, Calif.	UFA(Atl)-'13	13/1*
#	Parker, Juqua	DL	6-2	250	5/15/78	13	Oklahoma State	Houston, Texas	UFA(Phil)-'12	16/0
62	Pinkston, Jason	OL	6-4	305	9/5/87	3	Pittsburgh	Pittsburgh, Pa.	D5b-'11	6/6
33	Richardson, Trent	RB	5-9	230	7/10/90	2	Alabama	Pensacola, Fla.	D1a-'12	15/15
53	Robertson, Craig	LB	6-1	229	2/11/88	2	North Texas	Stafford, Texas	FA-'11	16/3
71	Rubin, Ahtyba	DL	6-2	330	7/25/86	6	Iowa State	Pensacola, Fla.	D6a-'08	13/13
70	Sanford, Brian	DL	6-2	280	9/12/87	3	Temple	Hartford, Conn.	FA-'11	1/0
72	Schwartz, Mitchell	OL	6-5	320	6/8/89	2	California	Pacific Palisades, Calif.	D2-'12	16/16
74	Shaw, Jarrod	OL	6-3	316	1/7/88	2	Tennessee	Lafayette, La.	FA-'11	0*
97	Sheard, Jabaal	LB	6-2	255	5/10/89	3	Pittsburgh	Hollywood, Hills, Fla.	D2a-'11	16/16
22	Skrine, Buster	DB	5-9	185	4/26/89	3	Chattanooga	Woodstock, Ga.	D5a-'11	16/6
98	Taylor, Phil	DL	6-3	335	4/7/88	3	Baylor	Clinton, Md.	D1-'11	8/7
73	Thomas, Joe	OL	6-6	312	12/4/84	7	Wisconsin	Brookfield, Wis.	D1a-'07	16/16
#	Ventrone, Ray	DB	5-10	200	10/21/82	8	Villanova	Pittsburgh, Pa.	FA-'09	12/0
26	Wade, Trevin	DB	5-10	190	8/1/89	2	Arizona	Austin, Texas	D7a-'12	13/0
43	Ward, T.J.	DB	5-10	200	12/12/86	4	Oregon	San Francisco, Calif.	D2a-'10	14/14
3	Weeden, Brandon	QB	6-3	220	10/14/83	2	Oklahoma State	Edmond, Okla.	D1b-'12	15/15
90	Winn, Billy	DL	6-4	295	4/15/89	2	Boise State	Las Vegas, Nev.	D6b-'12	16/10
57	Yount, Christian	LS	6-1	256	7/8/88	3	UCLA	Coto de Caza, Calif.	FA-'11	16/0

* Barnes played two games with Detroit in '12; Barnidge played 16 games with Carolina; Bess played 13 games with Miami; Bryant played 16 games with Oakland; Butler missed '12 season because of injury with Houston; Campbell played six games with Chicago; Conley last active with New York Jets in '11; Davis played 16 games with Chicago; Graham played 16 games with Houston; Gronkowski last active with Cleveland in '11; Groves played 16 games with Arizona; Kruger played 15 games with Baltimore; Lewis played nine games with Philadelphia; Moten played one game with Philadelphia; Nelson played one game with Buffalo; Owens played 13 games with Atlanta; Shaw inactive for eight games.

t- Browns traded for Bess (Mia), Lewis (Phil).

#Unrestricted Free Agent; subject to developments.

Traded—QB Colt McCoy (3 games in '12) to San Francisco.

Retired—Scott Fujita, 11-year linebacker, 4 games in '12.

Players lost through free agency (7): WR Joshua Cribbs (Oak; 16 games), K Phil Dawson (SF; 16), QB Josh Johnson (Cin; 1), LB Kaluka Maiava (Oak; 16), WR Mohamed Massaquoi (Jax; 9), TE Alex Smith (Cin; 12), TE Benjamin Watson (NO; 16).

Also played with Browns in '12—DB Dimitri Patterson (7 games), DL Frostee Rucker (16), DL Emmanuel Stephens (8), DB Usama Young (13).

FIRST-YEAR ROSTER

Name	Pos.	Ht.	Wt.	Birthdate	College	Hometown	How Acq.
Adams, Aaron	OL	6-5	305	5/16/89	Eastern Kentucky	Lake Worth, Fla.	FA
Adams, Kendrick (1)	DL	6-5	250	11/3/88	Louisiana State	Enterprise, Ala.	FA-'12
Alford, Dominic (1)	OL	6-3	320	2/22/88	Minnesota	Cleveland, Ohio	FA
Ashford, Perez	WR	5-11	190	3/2/91	Northern Illinois	Shaker Heights, Ohio	FA
Aubrey, Josh	DB	5-10	200	4/9/91	Stephen F. Austin	Tyler, Texas	FA
Auguste, Akeem	DB	5-10	185	10/10/89	South Carolina	Hollywood, Fla.	FA
Bogotay, Brandon	K	6-3	207	5/8/89	Georgia	San Diego, Calif.	FA
Bryant, Armonty	DL	6-4	265	5/5/90	East Central	Wichita Falls, Texas	D7a
Cave, Braxston	OL	6-3	305	7/29/89	Notre Dame	Granger, Ind.	FA
Cook, Jamaine	RB	5-9	210	8/19/91	Youngstown State	Middleburg Heights, Ohio	FA
Croom, Dominique	WR	6-2	190	4/26/91	Central Arkansas	Cherokee, Ala.	FA
Davis, Hall (1)	DL	6-4	270	3/2/87	Louisiana-Lafayette	Baton Rouge, La.	FA-'12
Davis, Keenan	WR	6-2	220	1/30/91	Iowa	Cedar Rapids, Iowa	FA
Faulk, Chris	OL	6-6	330	1/1/90	Louisiana State	Slidell, La.	FA
Gilkey, Garrett	OL	6-6	320	7/7/90	Chadron State	Sandwich, Ill.	D7b
Hauptmann, Caylin	OL	6-3	300	7/10/91	Florida International	Los Angeles, Calif.	FA
Hoskins, Garrett	TE	6-2	250	8/5/91	Eastern Michigan	Grand Rapids, Mich.	FA
Jean-Baptiste, Nicolas (1)	DL	6-1	330	3/8/89	Baylor	Houston, Texas	FA
Kanneh, Abdul	DB	5-10	185	9/9/90	New Mexico Highlands	London, England	FA
Kruger, Dave	DL	6-5	285	5/17/90	Utah	Orem, Utah	FA
Lanning, Spencer (1)	P	5-11	200	5/21/88	South Carolina	Rock Hill, S.C.	FA
McFadden, Leon	DB	5-9	195	10/26/90	San Diego State	Bellflower, Calif.	D3
Mingo, Barkevious	LB	6-4	240	10/4/90	Louisiana State	West Monroe, La.	D1
Rau, Ryan (1)	LB	6-1	230	7/30/90	Portland State	Folsom, Calif.	W(Phil)
Richardson, Kent (1)	DB	5-11	200	4/21/87	West Virginia	Tallahassee, Fla.	FA
Roberson, Cordell	WR	6-4	205	12/3/90	Stephen F. Austin	Jefferson, Texas	FA
Rouse, Robbie	RB	5-6	190	2/5/91	Fresno State	San Diego, Calif.	FA
Slaughter, Jamoris	DB	6-0	195	12/22/89	Notre Dame	Stone Mountain, Ga.	D6
Smelley, Brad (1)	TE	6-2	235	4/20/89	Alabama	Tuscaloosa, Ala.	D7b-'12
Staples, Justin	DL	6-4	245	12/10/89	Illinois	Lakewood, Ohio	FA
Tannahill, Travis	TE	6-4	255	2/8/90	Kansas State	Overland Park, Kansas	FA
Walcott, Ausar	DL	6-2	230	1/1/90	Virginia	Hackensack, N.J.	FA
Wallace, Martin	OL	6-6	305	4/22/90	Temple	New York, N.Y.	FA

The term NFL Rookie is defined as a player who is in his first season of professional football and has not been on the roster of another professional football team for any regular-season or postseason games. A Rookie is designated by an "R" on NFL rosters. Players who have been active in another professional football league or players who have NFL experience, including either preseason training camp or being on an Active List or Inactive List, or on Reserve/Injured or Reserve/Physically Unable to Perform for fewer than six regular-season games, are termed NFL First-Year Players. An NFL First-Year Player is designated by a "1" on NFL rosters. Thereafter, a player is credited with an additional year of experience for each season in which he accumulates six games on the Active List or Inactive List, or on Reserve/Injured or Reserve/Physically Unable to Perform.

Log on to www.clevelandbrowns.com for an up-to-date roster.

COACHING STAFF
Head Coach,
Rob Chudzinski
Pro Career: Rob Chudzinski was named the 14th full-time head coach in Browns history on January 10, 2013. Chudzinski comes to the team after spending the past two seasons as the Carolina Panthers' offensive coordinator. Chudzinski re-joins the Browns organization, where he spent the 2004 season as tight ends coach and 2007-08 as offensive coordinator. In 2007, he orchestrated Cleveland's best offense in terms of total yards (5,621), passing yards (3,726) and points scored (402) since the club's return in 1999. With the Panthers in 2011 Chudzinski tutored Cam Newton, who became the first rookie in NFL history to throw for 4,000 yards. The Panthers also became the first team in league history with three 700-yard rushers in DeAngelo Williams (836), Jonathan Stewart (761) and Newton (706). Prior to Carolina, Chudzinski had two stints with the San Diego Chargers (2005-06 and 2009-10). From 1994-2003, Chudzinski coached at the University of Miami. During his three seasons as offensive coordinator (2001-03), the Hurricanes played in a BCS Bowl game each year, including two National Championship appearances. Career record: 0-0.
Background: Chudzinski played tight end at Miami from 1986-1990, was a three-year starter and a member of two national championship teams (1987 and 1989). He graduated with a B.A. in business administration in 1990 and went on to earn his MBA in 1996.
Personal: Born May 12, 1968, Toledo, Ohio. He and his wife, Sheila, have two sons, Kaelan and Rian, and one daughter, Margaret.

ASSISTANT COACHES
Bobby Babich, asst. defensive back; born July 30, 1983, Tulsa, Okla. Cornerback North Dakota State 2002-05. No pro playing experience. College coach: Kent State 2006, Eastern Illinois 2007-2010. Pro coach: Carolina Panthers 2011-12, joined Browns in 2013.
Brian Baker, outside linebackers; born June 20, 1962, Baltimore, Md. Linebacker Maryland 1981-83. No pro playing experience. College coach: Maryland 1984-85, Army 1986, Georgia Tech 1987-1995. Pro coach: San Diego Chargers 1996, Detroit Lions 1997-2000, Minnesota Vikings 2001-05, St. Louis Rams 2006-2008, Carolina Panthers 2009-2010, Dallas Cowboys 2011-12, joined Browns in 2013.
Louie Cioffi, defensive backs; born September 21, 1973, Greenlawn, N.Y. Attended SUNY-Stony Brook. No college or pro playing experience. College coach: C.W. Post 1995-96. Pro coach: New York Jets 1993-94, Cincinnati Bengals 1997-2010, Arizona Cardinals 2011-12, joined Browns in 2013.
Joe Cullen, defensive line; born December 15, 1967, Quincy, Mass. Nose guard Massachusetts 1986-89. No pro playing experience. College coach: Massachusetts 1990-91, Richmond 1992-98, 2000, Louisiana State 1999, Memphis 2001, Indiana 2002-04, Illinois 2005, Idaho State 2009. Pro coach:

Detroit Lions 2006-08, Jacksonville Jaguars 2010-12, joined Browns in 2013.
Chris DiSanto, asst. strength and conditioning; born July 3, 1977, Holland, Pa. Defensive lineman West Chester (Pa.). No pro playing experience. College coach: California 2012. Pro coach: Philadelphia 2000-01, Minnesota Vikings 2007, Oakland Raiders 2008-2011, joined Browns in 2013.
Jon Embree, tight ends, born October 15, 1965, Englewood, Colo. Tight end Colorado 1983-1986. Pro tight end Los Angeles Rams 1987-88, Seattle Seahawks 1989. College coach: Colorado 1991, 1993-2002, 2011-12 (head coach 2011-12), UCLA 2003-05. Pro coach: Kansas City Chiefs 2006-08, Washington Redskins 2010, joined Browns in 2013.
Ken Flajole, inside linebackers; born October 4, 1954, Seattle, Wash. Linebacker Wenatchee Valley (Wash.) C.C. 1972-73, Pacific Lutheran 1974-75. No pro playing experience. College coach: Pacific Lutheran 1977-78, Washington 1979, Montana 1980-85, Texas El-Paso 1986-88, Missouri 1989-1993, Richmond 1994, Hawaii 1995, Nevada 1996-97. Pro coach: Green Bay Packers 1998, Seattle Seahawks 1999-2002, Carolina Panthers 2003-08, St. Louis Rams 2009-2011, New Orleans Saints 2012, joined Browns in 2013.
Steve Gara, special assistant to the head coach; born July 26, 1978, St. Louis, Mo. No college or pro playing experience. Pro coach: San Diego Chargers 2007-2012, joined Browns in 2013.
Ray Horton, defensive coordinator; born April 12, 1960, Tacoma, Wash. Cornerback Washington 1979-1982. Pro cornerback Cincinnati Bengals 1983-88, Dallas Cowboys 1989-1992. Pro coach: Washington Redskins 1994-96, Cincinnati Bengals 1997-2001, Detroit Lions 2002-03, Pittsburgh Steelers 2004-2010, Arizona Cardinals 2011-12, joined Browns in 2013.
Derik Keyes, asst. strength and conditioning; born September 29, 1985, Laurel, Miss. Safety Louisiana-Lafayette 2005-08. No pro playing experience. College coach Louisiana-Lafayette 2009, 2011, South Alabama 2010. Pro coach: Houston Texans 2012, joined Browns in 2013.
Shawn Mennenga, special teams assistant; born January 8, 1971, Melbourne, Iowa. Defensive back Missouri 1992. No pro playing experience. College coach: Southwest Baptist 1994-96, Western Kentucky 1997, Hutchinson (Kan.) C.C. 1998-2000, Culver-Stockton 2001-04 (head coach 2002-04), Fort Hays State 2005-08, South Dakota State 2009-10. Pro coach: Joined Browns in 2013.
Daron Roberts, defensive quality control; born November 29, 1978, Mt. Pleasant, Texas. No college or pro playing experience. College coach: West Virginia 2011-12. Pro coach: Kansas City Chiefs 2007-08, Detroit Lions 2009-10, joined Browns in 2013.
Brad Roll, strength and conditioning; born July 4, 1958, Houston, Texas. Center Blinn (Texas) J.C. 1977, Stephen F. Austin State 1978-1980. No pro playing experience. College coach: Stephen F. Austin State 1980, Louisiana-Lafayette 1981-86, Kansas 1987-88, Miami

1989-1992, Southern California 2012. Pro coach: Tampa Bay Buccaneers 1993-95, Miami Dolphins 1996-2003, Buffalo Bills 2004-05, St. Louis Rams 2006-07, Oakland Raiders 2008-2011, joined Browns in 2013.
John Settle, running backs; born June 2, 1965, Reidsville, N.C. Running back Appalachian State 1983-86. Pro running back Atlanta Falcons 1987-1990, Washington Redskins 1991-92. College coach: Appalachian State 1994, Fresno State 1998-2005, Wisconsin 2006-2010. Pro coach: Cleveland Browns 1995, Baltimore Ravens 1996-97, Carolina Panthers 2011-12, re-joined Browns in 2013.
Shane Steichen, offensive quality control; born May 11, 1985, Sacramento, Calif. Quarterback Nevada-Las Vegas 2003-06. No pro playing experience. College coach: Nevada-Las Vegas 2007-09, Louisville 2010. Pro coach: San Diego Chargers 2011-12, joined Browns in 2013.
Mike Sullivan, offensive line; born December 22, 1967, Chicago, Ill. Offensive lineman Miami 1986-1990. Pro offensive lineman Dallas Cowboys 1991, Tampa Bay Buccaneers 1992-95. College coach: Miami 2000, Western Michigan 2005-06. Pro coach: Cleveland Browns 2001-04, 2007-08, San Diego Chargers 2009-2012, re-joined Browns in 2013.
Chris Tabor, special teams coordinator; born March 4, 1971, St. Joseph, Mo. Quarterback Benedictine College 1989-1992. No pro playing experience. College coach: Hutchinson (Kan.) C.C. 1994, Central Methodist College 1995-96, Missouri 1997-2000, Culver-Stockton College 2001 (head coach), Utah State 2002-05, Western Michigan 2006-07. Pro coach: Chicago Bears 2008-2010, joined Browns in 2011.
Norv Turner, offensive coordinator, born May 17, 1952, LeJeune, N.C. Quarterback Oregon 1971-74. No pro playing experience. College coach: Oregon 1975, Southern California 1976-1984. Pro coach: Los Angeles Rams 1985-1990, Dallas Cowboys 1991-93, Washington Redskins 1994-2000 (head coach), San Diego Chargers 2001, 2007-2012 (head coach 2007-2012), Miami Dolphins 2002-03, Oakland Raiders 2004-05, San Francisco 49ers 2006, joined Browns in 2013.
Scott Turner, wide receivers; born August 7, 1982, Englewood, Calif. Quarterback Nevada-Las Vegas 2002-04. No pro playing experience. College coach: Oregon State 2005, Pittsburgh 2008-2010. Pro coach: Carolina Panthers 2011-12, joined Browns in 2013.
George Warhop, offensive line; born September 19, 1961, Riverside, Calif. Guard/center Mt. San Jacinto (Calif.) J.C. 1979-1980, Cincinnati 1981-82. No pro playing experience. College coach: Cincinnati 1983, Kansas 1984-86, Vanderbilt 1987-89, New Mexico 1990, Southern Methodist 1993, Boston College 1994-95. Pro coach: London Monarchs (World League) 1991-92, St. Louis Rams 1996-97, Arizona Cardinals 1998-2002, Dallas Cowboys 2003-04, San Francisco 49ers 2005-08, joined Browns in 2009.

American Football Conference
West Division
Team Colors: Orange, Broncos Navy
Blue, and White
13655 Broncos Parkway
Englewood, Colorado 80112
Telephone: (303) 649-9000

2013 SCHEDULE
PRESEASON
Aug. 8   at San Francisco 7:00
Aug. 17 at Seattle.........................8:00
Aug. 24 **St. Louis**.......................6:00
Aug. 29 **Arizona** 7:00

REGULAR SEASON
Sep. 5   **Baltimore** (Thurs) 6:30
Sep. 15 at New York Giants........2:25
Sep. 23 **Oakland** (Mon).............6:40
Sep. 29 **Philadelphia** 2:25
Oct. 6   at Dallas 2:25
Oct. 13 **Jacksonville** 2:05
Oct. 20 at Indianapolis 6:30
Oct. 27 **Washington** 2:25
Nov. 3   BYE
Nov. 10 at San Diego 2:25
Nov. 17 **Kansas City** 2:05
Nov. 24 at New England *6:30
Dec. 1   at Kansas City 11:00a
Dec. 8   **Tennessee** 2:05
Dec. 12 **San Diego** (Thurs) 6:25
Dec. 22 at Houston 11:00a
Dec. 29 at Oakland 2:25
*All times MT; Sunday night games in
   Weeks 11-16 subject to change
Stadium: Sports Authority Field at Mile
   High (opened in 2001)
   •**Capacity:** 76,125
   1701 Bryant Street
   Denver, Colorado 80204
Playing Surface: DD Grassmaster
Training Camp: 13655 Broncos Parkway
             Englewood, Colorado
             80112

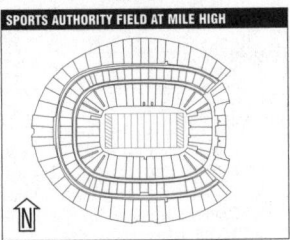

SPORTS AUTHORITY FIELD AT MILE HIGH

CLUB OFFICIALS
Owner and CEO: Pat Bowlen
President: Joe Ellis
Executive VP of Football Operations:
   John Elway
Head Coach: John Fox
FOOTBALL STAFF
Director of Player Personnel: Matt Russell
Director of Pro Personnel: Tom Heckert
Director of Football Administration:
   Mike Sullivan
Head Athletic Trainer: Steve Antonopulos
BUSINESS STAFF
General Counsel/Executive Vice
   President: Rich Slivka
Senior Vice President of Business
   Development: Mac Freeman
CFO: Justin Webster
Vice President of Operations:
   Chip Conway
Vice President of Community
   Development: Cindy Kellogg
Executive Director of Media Relations:
   Patrick Smyth
Executive Director of Ticket Operations
   and Administration: Kirk Dyer
STADIUM MANAGEMENT COMPANY
Stadium General Manager: Andy Gorchov

COACHING HISTORY
(437-392-10)
Records include postseason games
1960-61   Frank Filchock..............7-20-1
1962-64   Jack Faulkner* 9-22-1
1964-66   Mac Speedie** 6-19-1
1966   Ray Malavasi 4-8-0
1967-1971 Lou Saban*** 20-42-3
1971   Jerry Smith 2-3-0
1972-76   John Ralston...............34-33-3
1977-1980 Robert (Red) Miller......42-25-0
1981-1992 Dan Reeves...............117-79-1
1993-94   Wade Phillips 16-17-0
1995-2008 Mike Shanahan 146-91-0
2009-2010 Josh McDaniels**** ..11-17-0
2010   Eric Studesville................1-3-0
2011-12   John Fox....................22-13-0
      *Released after four games in 1964
      **Resigned after two games in 1966
   ***Resigned after nine games in 1971
****Released after 12 games in 2010

PAID ATTENDANCE
Home 601,635   Away 530,435
Total 1,132,070
Single-game home record,
   76,716 (11/9/09)
Single-season home record, 601,635
   (2012)

2013 DRAFT CHOICES
Round	Name	Pos.	College
1	Sylvester Williams	DT	North Carolina
2	Montee Ball	RB	Wisconsin
3	Kayvon Webster	DB	South Florida
5	Quanterus Smith	DE	Western Kentucky
	Tavarres King	WR	Georgia
6	Vinston Painter	T	Virginia Tech
7	Zac Dysert	QB	Miami (Ohio)

2012 TEAM RECORD
PRESEASON (2-2)

Date	Result		Opponent
08/09	W	31-3	at Chicago
08/18	L	10-30	Seattle
08/26	L	24-29	San Francisco
08/30	W	16-13	at Arizona

REGULAR SEASON (13-3)

Date	Result		Opponent
09/09	W	31-19	Pittsburgh
09/17	L	21-27	at Atlanta
09/23	L	25-31	Houston
09/30	W	37-6	Oakland
10/07	L	21-31	at New England
10/15	W	35-24	at San Diego
10/28	W	34-14	New Orleans
11/04	W	31-23	at Cincinnati
11/11	W	36-14	at Carolina
11/18	W	30-23	San Diego
11/25	W	17-9	at Kansas City
12/02	W	31-23	Tampa Bay
12/06	W	26-13	at Oakland
12/16	W	34-17	at Baltimore
12/23	W	34-12	Cleveland
12/30	W	38-3	Kansas City

POSTSEASON (0-1)

Date	Result		Opponent
01/12	L	35-38	Baltimore (2OT)

(OT) Overtime

SCORE BY PERIODS

Broncos	66	116	153	146	0 —	481
Opponents	70	81	62	76	0 —	289

2012 TEAM STATISTICS

	Broncos	Opp.
Total First Downs	380	287
Rushing	112	73
Passing	232	183
Penalty	36	31
3rd Down: Made/Att	96/213	66/216
3rd Down Pct.	45.1	30.6
4th Down: Made/Att	3/5	7/18
4th Down Pct.	60.0	38.9
Possession Avg.	31:16	28:44
Total Net Yards	6366	4652
Avg. Per Game	397.9	290.8
Total Plays	1090	1015
Avg. Per Play	5.8	4.6
Net Yards Rushing	1832	1458
Avg. Per Game	114.5	91.1
Total Rushes	481	404
Net Yards Passing	4534	3194
Avg. Per Game	283.4	199.6
Sacked/Yards Lost	21/137	52/364
Gross Yards	4671	3558
Att./Completions	588/402	559/321
Completion Pct.	68.4	57.4
Had Intercepted	11	16
Punts/Average	67/46.3	94/48.1
Net Punting Avg.	67/42.1	94/41.9
Penalties/Yards	100/805	123/951
Fumbles/Ball Lost	22/14	23/8
Touchdowns	57	32
Rushing	12	5
Passing	37	25
Returns	8	2

2012 INDIVIDUAL STATISTICS

PASSING

	Att.	Comp.	Yds.	Pct.	TD	Int.	Tkld.	Rate
Manning	583	400	4659	68.6	37	11	21/137	105.8
Osweiler	4	2	12	50.0	0	0	0/0	56.3
Prater	1	0	0	0.0	0	0	0/0	39.6
Broncos	588	402	4671	68.4	37	11	21/137	105.3
Opponents	559	321	3558	57.4	25	16	52/364	79.4

SCORING

	TD R	TD P	TD Rt	PAT	FG	Saf	PTS
Prater	0	0	0	55/55	26/32	0	133
Decker	0	13	0	0/0	0/0	0	78
D. Thomas	0	10	0	0/0	0/0	0	60
Dreessen	0	5	0	0/0	0/0	0	30
Stokley	0	5	0	0/0	0/0	0	30
McGahee	4	0	0	0/0	0/0	0	26
Moreno	4	0	0	0/0	0/0	0	24
Ball	1	1	0	0/0	0/0	0	12
T. Carter	0	0	2	0/0	0/0	0	12
Harris	0	0	2	0/0	0/0	0	12
Hester	2	0	0	0/0	0/0	0	12
Holliday	0	0	2	0/0	0/0	0	12
Tamme	0	2	0	0/0	0/0	0	12
Hillman	1	0	0	0/0	0/0	0	6
Miller	0	0	1	0/0	0/0	0	6
Porter	0	0	1	0/0	0/0	0	6
Unrein	0	1	0	0/0	0/0	0	6
Adams	0	0	0	0/0	0/0	1	2
Dumervil	0	0	0	0/0	0/0	1	2
Broncos	12	37	8	55/55	26/32	2	481
Opponents	5	25	2	29/29	22/25	1	289

2-Pt Conversions: McGahee, Broncos 1-2, Opponents 0-3

RUSHING

	No.	Yds	Avg	LG	TD
McGahee	167	731	4.4	31	4
Moreno	138	525	3.8	20	4
Hillman	85	330	3.9	31	1
Ball	42	158	3.8	22	1
Hester	17	81	4.8	18	2
Caldwell	1	14	14.0	14	0
Manning	23	6	0.3	10	0
Osweiler	8	-13	-1.6	-1	0
Broncos	481	1832	3.8	31	12
Opponents	404	1458	3.6	36	5

RECEIVING

	No.	Yds	Avg	LG	TD
D. Thomas	94	1434	15.3	71t	10
Decker	85	1064	12.5	55	13
Tamme	52	555	10.7	36	2
Stokley	45	544	12.1	38t	5
Dreessen	41	356	8.7	30	5
McGahee	26	221	8.5	31	0
Moreno	21	167	8.0	26	0
Willis	10	90	9.0	19	0
Hillman	10	62	6.2	29	0
Ball	7	61	8.7	17	1
Green	5	63	12.6	28	0
Holliday	2	17	8.5	15	0
Caldwell	1	18	18.0	18	0
Gronkowski	1	11	11.0	11	0
Hester	1	7	7.0	7	0
Unrein	1	1	1.0	1t	1
Broncos	402	4671	11.6	71t	37
Opponents	321	3558	11.1	61t	25

INTERCEPTIONS

	No.	Yds	Avg	LG	TD
Harris	3	144	48.0	98t	2
Woodyard	3	40	13.3	25	0
T. Carter	2	55	27.5	40t	1
Bailey	2	18	9.0	18	0
Leonhard	2	0	0.0	0	0
Porter	1	43	43.0	43t	1
Miller	1	26	26.0	26t	1
Moore	1	23	23.0	23	0
Bruton	1	-2	-2.0	-2	0
Broncos	16	347	21.7	98t	5
Opponents	11	218	19.8	80t	2

PUNTING

	No.	Yds.	Avg.	In 20	LG
Colquitt	67	3105	46.3	27	67
Broncos	67	3105	46.3	27	67
Opponents	94	4524	48.1	35	68

PUNT RETURNS

	Ret	FC	Yds	Avg	LG	TD
Holliday	31	4	334	10.8	76t	1
Leonhard	15	16	89	5.9	16	0
Decker	2	0	22	11.0	13	0
Broncos	48	20	445	9.3	76t	1
Opponents	33	17	203	6.2	40	0

KICKOFF RETURNS

	No.	Yds	Avg	LG	TD
Bolden	14	270	19.3	33	0
Holliday	11	358	32.5	105t	1
Leonhard	1	18	18.0	18	0
Ball	1	0	0.0	0	0
Gronkowski	1	0	0.0	0	0
Broncos	28	646	23.1	105t	1
Opponents	34	751	22.1	50	0

FIELD GOALS

	1-19	20-29	30-39	40-49	50+
Prater	1/1	7/7	10/11	5/9	3/4
Broncos	1/1	7/7	10/11	5/9	3/4
Opponents	0/0	7/7	6/7	6/8	3/3

SACKS

	No.
Miller	18.5
Dumervil	11.0
Wolfe	6.0
Woodyard	5.5
Harris	2.5
Ayers	2.0
Vickerson	2.0
Adams	1.0
Brooking	1.0
Moore	1.0
Trevathan	1.0
Mays	0.5
Broncos	52.0
Opponents	21.0

RECORD HOLDERS
INDIVIDUAL RECORDS—CAREER

Category	Name	Performance
Rushing (Yds.)	Terrell Davis, 1995-2002	7,607
Passing (Yds.)	John Elway, 1983-1998	51,475
Passing (TDs)	John Elway, 1983-1998	300
Receiving (No.)	Rod Smith, 1995-2007	849
Receiving (Yds.)	Rod Smith, 1995-2007	11,389
Interceptions	Steve Foley, 1976-1986	44
Punting (Avg.)	Britton Colquitt, 2009-2012	46.2
Punt Return (Avg.)	Darrien Gordon, 1997-98	12.5
Kickoff Return (Avg.)	Abner Haynes, 1965-66	26.3
Field Goals	Jason Elam, 1993-2007	395
Touchdowns (Tot.)	Rod Smith, 1995-2007	71
Points	Jason Elam, 1993-2007	1,786
*Sacks	Simon Fletcher, 1985-1995	97.5

INDIVIDUAL RECORDS—SINGLE SEASON

Category	Name	Performance
Rushing (Yds.)	Terrell Davis, 1998	2,008
Passing (Yds.)	Peyton Manning, 2012	4,659
Passing (TDs)	Peyton Manning, 2012	37
Receiving (No.)	Rod Smith, 2001	113
Receiving (Yds.)	Rod Smith, 2000	1,602
Interceptions	Goose Gonsoulin, 1960	11
Punting (Avg.)	Britton Colquitt, 2011	47.4
Punt Return (Avg.)	Floyd Little, 1967	16.9
Kickoff Return (Avg.)	Bill Thompson, 1969	28.5
Field Goals	Jason Elam, 1995, 2001	31
Touchdowns (Tot.)	Terrell Davis, 1998	23
Points	Terrell Davis, 1998	138
*Sacks	Von Miller, 2012	18.5

INDIVIDUAL RECORDS—SINGLE GAME

Category	Name	Performance
Rushing (Yds.)	Mike Anderson, 12-3-00	251
Passing (Yds.)	Jake Plummer, 10-31-04	499
Passing (TDs)	Frank Tripucka, 10-28-62	5
	John Elway, 11-18-84	5
	Gus Frerotte, 11-19-00	5
Receiving (No.)	Brandon Marshall, 12-13-09	**21
Receiving (Yds.)	Shannon Sharpe, 10-20-02	214
Interceptions	Goose Gonsoulin, 9-18-60	**4
	Willie Brown, 11-15-64	**4
	Deltha O'Neal, 10-7-01	**4
Field Goals	Gene Mingo, 10-6-63	5
	Rich Karlis, 11-20-83	5
	Jason Elam, 9-3-95, 10-13-02	5
Touchdowns (Tot.)	Clinton Portis, 12-7-03	5
Points	Clinton Portis, 12-7-03	30
*Sacks	Karl Mecklenburg, 9-15-85, 12-1-85	4.0
	Simon Fletcher, 11-4-90	4.0
	Elvis Dumervil, 9-20-09	4.0

*Sacks became an official statistic in 1982.
**NFL Record

2013 VETERAN ROSTER

No.	Name	Pos.	Ht.	Wt.	Birthdate	NFL Exp.	College	Hometown	How Acq.	'12 Games/ Starts
20	Adams, Mike	SS	5-11	200	3/24/81	10	Delaware	Wayne, N.J.	UFA(Cle)-'12	16/16
91	Ayers, Robert	DE	6-3	274	9/6/85	5	Tennessee	Bennettsville, S.C.	D1b-'09	15/0
24	Bailey, Champ	CB	6-0	192	6/22/78	15	Georgia	Folkston, Ga.	T(Wash)-'04	16/15
35	Ball, Lance	RB	5-9	215	6/2/85	5	Maryland	Teaneck, N.J.	FA-'10	15/0
68	Beadles, Zane	G	6-4	305	11/19/86	4	Utah	Sandy, Utah	D2-'10	16/16
93	Beal, Jeremy	DE	6-3	276	12/2/87	2	Oklahoma	Carrollton, Texas	D7b-'11	0*
64	Blake, Philip	G/C	6-3	320	11/27/85	2	Baylor	Lennoxville, Quebec	D4b-'12	0*
31	Bolden, Omar	CB	5-10	195	12/20/88	2	Arizona State	Ontario, Calif.	D4a-'12	16/0
55	Bradley, Stewart	LB	6-4	258	11/2/83	6	Nebraska	Salt Lake City, Utah	FA-'13	16/0*
46	Brewer, Aaron	LS	6-5	225	7/5/90	2	San Diego State	Fullerton, Calif.	FA-'12	16/0*
30	Bruton, David	SS	6-2	217	7/23/87	5	Notre Dame	Miamisburg, Ohio	D4a-'09	16/0
29	Butler, Mario	CB	6-1	187	10/20/88	2	Georgia Tech	Ponte Vedra, Fla.	FA-'12	1/0*
17	Caldwell, Andre	WR	6-0	190	4/15/85	6	Florida	Tampa, Fla.	UFA(Cin)-'12	8/0
28	Carter, Quinton	SS	6-1	200	7/20/88	3	Oklahoma	Las Vegas, Nev.	D4a-'11	3/0
32	Carter, Tony	CB	5-9	175	5/24/86	5	Florida State	Jacksonville, Fla.	FA-'11	15/0
78	Clady, Ryan	T	6-6	315	9/6/86	6	Boise State	Rialto, Calif.	D1-'08	16/16
75	Clark, Chris	T	6-5	305	10/1/85	5	Southern Mississippi	New Orleans, La.	W(Minn)-'10	16/0
4	Colquitt, Britton	P	6-3	205	3/20/85	5	Tennessee	Knoxville, Tenn.	FA-'09	16/0
54	Davis, C.J.	C/G	6-2	308	2/2/87	4	Pittsburgh	Imperial, Pa.	FA-'12	7/0
87	Decker, Eric	WR	6-3	218	3/15/87	4	Minnesota	Cold Spring, Minn.	D3b-'10	16/15
81	Dreessen, Joel	TE	6-4	245	7/26/82	8	Colorado State	Fort Morgan, Colo.	UFA(Hou)-'12	16/15
42	Fannin, Mario	RB	5-11	224	12/4/87	3	Auburn	Hampton, Ga.	FA-'11	0*
74	Franklin, Orlando	T	6-7	330	12/16/87	3	Miami	Delray Beach, Fla.	D2b-'11	16/16
85	Green, Virgil	TE	6-5	252	8/3/88	3	Nevada	Tulare, Calif.	D7a-'11	12/2
25	Harris, Chris	CB	5-10	190	6/18/89	3	Kansas	Bixby, Okla.	FA-'11	15/12
40	Hester, Jacob	FB	5-11	235	5/8/85	6	Louisiana State	Shreveport, La.	FA-'12	3/0
21	Hillman, Ronnie	RB	5-10	190	9/14/91	2	San Diego State	La Habra, Calif.	D3-'12	13/0
11	Holliday, Trindon	WR	5-5	170	4/27/86	4	Louisiana State	Zachary, La.	FA-'12	15/0
33	Ihenacho, Duke	SS	6-1	205	6/16/89	2	San Jose State	San Mateo, Calif.	FA-'12	2/0
56	Irving, Nate	SLB	6-1	240	7/12/88	3	North Carolina State	Wallace, N.C.	D3-'11	15/0
70	Jackson, Malik	DL	6-5	270	1/11/90	2	Tennessee	Van Nuys, Calif.	D5-'12	14/0
37	Johnson, Jeremiah	RB	5-9	200	2/15/87	4	Oregon	Los Angeles, Calif.	FA-'10	0*
53	Johnson, Steven	MLB	6-1	237	3/28/88	2	Kansas	Wallingford, Pa.	FA-'12	11/0
94	Knighton, Terrance	DT	6-3	330	7/4/86	5	Temple	Windsor, Conn.	UFA(Jax)-'13	16/4*
73	Kuper, Chris	G	6-4	303	12/19/82	8	North Dakota	Anchorage, Alaska	D5-'06	7/5
18	Manning, Peyton	QB	6-5	230	3/24/76	16	Tennessee	New Orleans, La.	FA-'12	16/16
51	Mays, Joe	MLB	5-11	250	7/6/85	6	North Dakota State	Chicago, Ill.	T(Phil)-'10	6/4
23	McGahee, Willis	RB	6-0	235	10/20/81	11	Miami	Miami, Fla.	FA-'11	10/9
58	Miller, Von	SLB	6-3	237	3/26/89	3	Texas A&M	DeSoto, Texas	D1-'11	16/16
26	Moore, Rahim	FS	6-1	196	2/11/90	3	UCLA	Los Angeles, Calif.	D2a-'11	16/15
27	Moreno, Knowshon	RB	5-11	200	7/16/87	5	Georgia	Middletown, N.J.	D1a-'09	8/6
6	Osweiler, Brock	QB	6-8	240	11/22/90	2	Arizona State	Kalispell, Mont.	D2b-'12	5/0
90	Phillips, Shaun	SLB	6-3	250	5/13/81	10	Purdue	Willingboro, N.J.	UFA(SD)-'13	16/16*
5	Prater, Matt	K	5-10	195	8/10/84	7	Central Florida	Estero, Fla.	PS(Mia)-'07	16/0
65	Ramirez, Manny	G	6-3	313	2/13/83	7	Texas Tech	Houston, Texas	FA-'11	15/11
45	Rodgers-Cromartie, Dominique	CB	6-2	182	4/7/86	6	Tennessee State	Bradenton, Fla.	UFA(Phil)-'13	16/16*
98	Siliga, Sealver	NT	6-2	307	4/26/90	2	Utah	West Jordan, Utah	FA-'11	1/0
84	Tamme, Jacob	TE	6-3	236	3/15/85	6	Kentucky	Danville, Ky.	UFA(Ind)-'12	16/8
88	Thomas, Demaryius	WR	6-3	229	12/25/87	4	Georgia Tech	Montrose, Ga.	D1a-'10	16/16
80	Thomas, Julius	TE	6-5	255	6/27/88	3	Portland State	Stockton, Calif.	D4b-'11	4/0
59	Trevathan, Danny	WLB	6-1	232	3/24/90	2	Kentucky	Leesburg, Fla.	D6-'12	16/0
96	Unrein, Mitch	NT	6-4	291	3/25/87	3	Wyoming	Eaton, Colo.	FA-'10	16/2
65	Vasquez, Louis	G	6-5	335	4/11/87	5	Texas Tech	Corsicana, Texas	UFA(SD)-'13	16/16*
99	Vickerson, Kevin	DT	6-5	290	1/8/83	8	Michigan State	Detroit, Mich.	FA-'10	16/14
50	Walton, J.D.	C	6-3	305	3/24/87	4	Baylor	Allen, Texas	D3a-'10	4/4
83	Welker, Wes	WR	5-9	185	5/1/81	10	Texas Tech	Oklahoma City, Okla.	UFA(NE)-'13	16/12*
95	Wolfe, Derek	DE	6-5	300	2/24/90	2	Cincinnati	Lisbon, Ohio	D2a-'12	16/16
52	Woodyard, Wesley	WLB	6-0	229	7/21/86	6	Kentucky	LaGrange, Ga.	FA-'08	15/14

* Beal missed '12 season due to injury; Blake missed '12 season due to injury; Bradley played 16 games with Arizona; Butler played one game with Dallas; Fannin missed '12 season due to injury; J. Johnson last active with Denver in '11; Knighton played 16 games with Jacksonville; Phillips played 16 games with San Diego; Rodgers-Cromartie played 16 games with Philadelphia; Vasquez played 16 games with San Diego; Welker played 16 games with New England.

Players lost through free agency (3): DE Jason Hunter (Oak; 0 games in '12), S Jim Leonhard (NO; 16), CB Tracy Porter (Oak; 6).

Also played with Broncos in '12—DT Justin Bannon (16 games), LB Keith Brooking (16), DE Elvis Dumervil (16), RB Chris Gronkowski (14), C Dan Koppen (15), S Jim Leonhard (16), CB Tracy Porter (6), WR Brandon Stokley (15), DT Ty Warren (1), WR Matt Willis (15).

FIRST-YEAR ROSTER

Name	Pos.	Ht.	Wt.	Birthdate	College	Hometown	How Acq.
Anderson, C.J.	RB	5-8	224	2/10/91	California	Vallejo, Calif.	FA
Ball, Montee	RB	5-10	217	12/5/90	Wisconsin	Wentzville, Mo.	D2
Bateman, Kemonte'	WR	6-1	185	2/22/90	New Mexico State	Los Angeles, Calif.	FA
Boren, Justin (1)	G	6-2	215	4/28/88	Ohio State	Pickerington, Ohio	FA
Cornick, Paul (1)	T	6-6	310	3/15/89	North Dakota State	Orono, Minn.	FA-'12
Doerr, Ryan	P	6-3	189	6/19/89	Kansas State	Katy, Texas	FA
Dysert, Zac	QB	6-3	231	2/8/90	Miami-Ohio	Ada, Ohio	D7
Foketi, Manase	G	6-5	325	9/18/90	Kansas State	Hesperia, Calif.	FA
Fuga, Romney	DT	6-2	318	5/25/88	Brigham Young	Huntington Beach, Calif.	FA
Garland, Ben (1)	G	6-5	275	4/6/88	Air Force	Grand Junction, Colo.	FA-'10
Gideon, Blake (1)	S	6-1	205	7/25/89	Texas	Leander, Texas	FA-'12
Hester, Aaron	CB	6-1	207	3/1/90	UCLA	Compton, Calif.	FA
Holmes, Damien	LB	6-2	250	10/12/90	UCLA	Colton, Calif.	FA
Kaveinga, Uona	LB	5-11	243	2/2/90	Brigham Young	Lawndale, Calif.	FA
King, Tavarres	WR	6-0	189	7/14/90	Georgia	Mt. Airy, Ga.	D5b
McCray, Lerentee	LB	6-3	249	8/26/90	Florida	Dunnellon, Fla.	FA
McDuffie, Quincy	WR	5-10	178	9/24/90	Central Florida	Orlando, Fla.	FA
Orton, Greg (1)	WR	6-3	199	12/17/86	Purdue	Dayton, Ohio	FA-'11
Painter, Vinston	T	6-6	309	10/11/89	Virginia Tech	Norfolk, Va.	D6
Rasner, Ross	S	6-0	212	4/18/91	Arkansas	Waco, Texas	FA
Reed, Lucas	TE	6-6	250	1/29/89	New Mexico	Tucson, Ariz.	FA
Robinson, Gerell (1)	WR	6-4	222	10/13/89	Arizona State	Chandler, Ariz.	FA-'12
Saulsberry, Quentin (1)	C	6-3	305	10/14/88	Mississippi State	Coldwater, Miss.	FA-'12
Smith, Quanterus	DE	6-5	250	11/26/89	Western Kentucky	Loganville, Ga.	D5a
Tanyi, Lanston	DE	6-2	250	10/20.90	Colorado State	Shelby, N.C.	FA
Webster, Kayvon	CB	5-11	198	2/1/91	South Florida	Opa-Locka, Fla.	D3
Williams, Sylvester	DT	6-2	313	11/21/88	North Carolina	Jefferson City, Mo.	D1
Youboty, John	DE	6-4	252	2/25/90	Temple	Houston, Texas	FA

The term NFL Rookie is defined as a player who is in his first season of professional football and has not been on the roster of another professional football team for any regular-season or postseason games. A Rookie is designated by an "R" on NFL rosters. Players who have been active in another professional football league or players who have NFL experience, including either preseason training camp or being on an Active List or Inactive List, or on Reserve/Injured or Reserve/Physically Unable to Perform for fewer than six regular-season games, are termed NFL First-Year Players. An NFL First-Year Player is designated by a "1" on NFL rosters. Thereafter, a player is credited with an additional year of experience for each season in which he accumulates six games on the Active List or Inactive List, or on Reserve/Injured or Reserve/Physically Unable to Perform.

Log on to www.denverbroncos.com for an up-to-date roster.

COACHING STAFF

Head Coach,
John Fox

Pro Career: John Fox was named the 14th head coach in Denver Broncos history on January 13, 2011. He joined the Broncos after spending the previous nine seasons (2002-2010) as the head coach of the Carolina Panthers. In 24 NFL seasons, he has appeared in two Super Bowls and three conference championship games as a head coach or coordinator. He compiled a 73-71 (.507) regular-season record with the Panthers that included three 11-win campaigns, two NFC South titles and three playoff appearances. Carolina went 5-3 in the postseason under Fox, appearing in two NFC Championship Games and one Super Bowl (XXXVIII in 2003). Has registered four postseason road victories. Prior to coaching the Panthers, Fox was the defensive coordinator for the N.Y. Giants (1997-2001). In 2000, Fox helped the Giants reach Super Bowl XXXV, including posting the first shutout in a conference title game since 1986. Before joining the Giants, was a consultant for the Rams (1996), defensive coordinator for the Raiders (1994-95), defensive backs coach for the Chargers (1992-93) and Steelers (1989-1991), and secondary coach for the USFL's Los Angeles Express (1985). Career record: 100-87.

Background: Defensive back at San Diego State (1976-77). Coached at San Diego State (1978), U.S. International (1979) Boise State (1980), Long Beach State (1981), Utah (1982), Kansas (1983), Iowa State (1984), and Pittsburgh (1986-88). Received bachelor's degree in physical education and earned a teaching credential from San Diego State.

Personal: Born February 8, 1955, in Virginia Beach, Va. He and his wife, Robin, have four children—Mathew, Mark, Cody, and Halle.

ASSISTANT COACHES

Clancy Barone, tight ends; born July 26, 1963, San Andreas, Calif. Offensive lineman Cal State-Sacramento 1981-82, Nevada 1985-86. No pro playing experience. College coach: American River (Calif.) J.C. 1987-89, Cal State-Sacramento 1990-92, Texas A&M 1993, Eastern Illinois 1994-96, Wyoming 1997-99, Houston 2000-02, Texas State 2003. Pro coach: Atlanta Falcons 2004-06, San Diego Chargers 2007-08, joined Broncos in 2009.

Chris Beake, quality control defense; born September 10, 1972, Kansas City, Mo. Quarterback Air Force 1991-92. No pro playing experience. College coach Air Force 1994. Pro coach San Francisco 49ers 1999-2003, 2010, Atlanta Falcons 2004-06, Seattle Seahawks 2008-09, Cleveland Browns 2011-12, joined Broncos in 2013.

Brian Callahan, offensive assistant; born June 10, 1984, Champaign, Ill. Quarterback UCLA 2002-06. No pro playing experience. College coach: UCLA 2006-07. Pro coach: Joined Broncos in 2010.

Jim Bob Cooter, offensive assistant; born July 3, 1984, Huntsville, Ala. Quarterback Tennessee 2002-06. No pro playing experience. College coach: Tennessee 2007-08. Pro coach Indianapolis Colts 2009-11, Kansas City Chiefs 2012, joined Broncos in 2013.

Jack Del Rio, defensive coordinator; born April 4, 1963, Castro Valley, Calif. Linebacker Southern California 1981-84. Pro linebacker New Orleans Saints 1985-86, Kansas City Chiefs 1987-88, Dallas Cowboys 1989-1991, Minnesota Vikings 1992-95. Pro coach: New Orleans Saints 1997-98, Baltimore Ravens 1999-2001, Carolina Panthers 2002, Jacksonville Jaguars 2003-2011 (head coach), joined Broncos in 2012.

Mike Eubanks, asst. strength and conditioning; born December 31, 1980, Kansas City, Kan. Defensive back Wisconsin-Eau Claire. No pro playing experience. Pro coach: Jacksonville 2009-2011, joined Broncos in 2012.

Sam Garnes, asst. secondary; born July 12, 1974, Bronx, N.Y. Safety Cincinnati 1992-96. Pro safety N.Y. Giants 1997-2001, N.Y. Jets 2002-03. Pro coach: Cologne Centurions (NFL Europe) 2006, Las Vegas Locomotives (UFL) 2009, Carolina Panthers 2010, joined Broncos in 2011.

Adam Gase, offensive coordinator; born March 29, 1978, Ypsilanti, Mich. Attended Michigan State. No college or pro playing experience. College coach: Louisiana State 2000-02. Pro coach: Detroit Lions 2003-07, San Francisco 49ers 2008, joined Broncos in 2009.

Jason George, asst. strength and conditioning; born October 3, 1968, Winnipeg, Manitoba, Canada. Safety Manitoba 1991-92. No pro playing experience. College coach: Kansas 1997-98, Fordham 1998-2008. Pro coach: Jacksonville 2009-2011, joined Broncos in 2012.

Greg Knapp, quarterbacks; born March 3, 1963, Seal Beach, Calif. Quarterback Sacramento State 1982-85. No pro playing experience. College coach: Sacramento State 1986-1994. Pro coach: San Francisco 49ers 1995-2003, Atlanta Falcons 2004-06, Oakland Raiders 2007-08, Seattle Seahawks 2009, Houston Texans 2010-11, Oakland Raiders 2012, joined Broncos in 2013.

Anthony Lomando, asst. strength and conditioning; born October 4, 1982, Katy, Tex. Cal Poly State University-San Louis Obispo. No college or pro playing experience. Pro coach: Jacksonville 2009-2011; joined Broncos in 2012.

Dave Magazu, offensive line; born June 10, 1957, Taunton, Mass. Defensive tackle Springfield College 1976-79. No pro playing experience. College coach: Ithaca 1980, Western Michigan 1981, Eastern Michigan 1982, Michigan 1983, Northern Illinois 1984, Ball State 1985-86, Navy 1987-89, Indiana State 1990-91, Colorado State 1992-94, Kentucky 1995-96, Memphis

1997-98, Boston College 1999-2002. Pro coach: Carolina Panthers 2003-10, joined Broncos in 2011.

Luke Richesson, strength and conditioning; born April 29, 1974, Kansas City, Mo. Defensive back Kansas 1992-96. No pro playing experience. College coach: Wyoming 1998, Arizona State 1999-2000. Pro coach: Jacksonville 2009-2011, joined Broncos in 2012.

Jay Rodgers, defensive line; born August 29, 1976, St. Paul, Minn. Quarterback Indiana 1996-98, Missouri State 1999. No pro playing experience. College coach: Missouri State 2004, Stephen F. Austin 2005-06, Iowa State 2007-08. Pro coach: Joined Broncos in 2009.

Jeff Rodgers, special teams coordinator; born January 12, 1978, St. Paul, Minn. Linebacker North Texas 1996-99. College coach: Arizona 2001-02, Kansas State 2008. Pro coach: San Francisco 49ers 2003-07, Carolina Panthers 2009-2010, joined Broncos in 2011.

Richard Smith, linebackers; born October 17, 1955, Los Angeles, Calif. Offensive lineman Rio Hondo (Calif.) J.C. 1975-76, Fresno State 1977-78. College coach: Rio Hondo (Calif.) J.C. 1979-1980, Cal State-Fullerton 1981-83, California 1984-86, Arizona 1987. Pro coach: Houston Oilers 1988-1992, Denver Broncos 1993-96, San Francisco 49ers 1997-2002, Detroit Lions 2003-04, Miami Dolphins 2005, Houston Texans 2006-08, Carolina Panthers 2009-2010, re-joined Broncos 2011.

Eric Studesville, running backs; born May 29, 1967, Madison, Wisc. Defensive back Wisconsin-Whitewater 1985-88. No pro playing experience. College coach: Wingate 1994, Kent State 1995-96. Pro coach: Chicago Bears 1997-2000, New York Giants 2001-03, Buffalo Bills 2004-2009, joined Broncos in 2010 (interim head coach, four games in 2010).

Derius Swinton, asst. special teams; born April 26, 1985, Newport News, VA. Safety Hampton 2003-06. No pro playing experience. College coach: Tennessee 2007-08. Pro coach: St. Louis Rams 2009-2011, Kansas City Chiefs 2012, joined Broncos in 2013.

Tyke Tolbert, wide receivers; born September 15, 1967, Conroe, Texas. Wide receiver Louisiana State 1988-1990. No pro playing experience. College coach: Louisiana State 1994, Ohio 1995, Northeast Louisiana 1996-97, Auburn 1998, Louisiana-Lafayette 1999-2001, Florida 2002. Pro coach: Arizona Cardinals 2003, Buffalo Bills 2004-09, Carolina Panthers 2010, joined Broncos in 2011.

Corey Undlin, secondary; born June 29, 1971, St. Cloud, Minn. Defensive back California Lutheran 1990-94. No pro playing experience. College coach: California Lutheran 1998-2001, Fresno State 2002-03. Pro coach: New England Patriots 2004, Cleveland Browns 2005-08, Jacksonville Jaguars 2009-2011, joined Broncos in 2012.

American Football Conference
South Division
Team Colors: Deep Steel Blue, Battle
Red, and Liberty White
Two Reliant Park
Houston, Texas 77054
Telephone: (832) 667-2000

2013 SCHEDULE
PRESEASON
Aug. 9   at Minnesota 7:00
Aug. 17 **Miami** 7:00
Aug. 25 **New Orleans**.....................3:00
Aug. 29 at Dallas.............................7:00

REGULAR SEASON
Sep. 9   at San Diego (Mon) 9:20
Sep. 15 **Tennessee** 12:00
Sep. 22 at Baltimore 12:00
Sep. 29 **Seattle** 12:00
Oct. 6   at San Francisco 7:30
Oct. 13 **St. Louis** 12:00
Oct. 20 at Kansas City 12:00
Oct. 27 BYE
Nov. 3   **Indianapolis** 7:30
Nov. 10 at Arizona 3:25
Nov. 17 **Oakland** 12:00
Nov. 24 **Jacksonville** 12:00
Dec. 1   **New England** 3:25
Dec. 5   at Jacksonville (Thurs) 7:25
Dec. 15 at Indianapolis 12:00
Dec. 22 **Denver** 12:00
Dec. 29 at Tennessee 12:00
All times CT

Stadium: Reliant Stadium
(opened in 2002)
•**Capacity:** 71,054
Houston, Texas 77054
Playing Surface: Grass
Training Camp: Methodist Training
Center

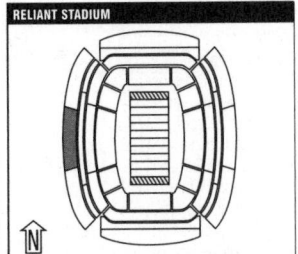

RELIANT STADIUM

CLUB OFFICIALS
Chairman and CEO: Robert C. McNair
Vice Chairman: Philip Burguières
Vice Chairman and COO: D. Cal McNair
General Manager/Executive Vice
President of Football Operations:
Rick Smith
President: Jamey Rootes
Senior Vice President, Treasurer and
CFO: Scott Schwinger
Executive Vice President, General
Counsel and CAO: Suzie Thomas
Senior Vice President, Ticketing and
Event Management: John Schriever
Vice President, Corporate Development:
Greg Grissom
Vice President and Chief Accounting
Officer: Marilan Logan
Vice President, Football Administration:
Chris Olsen
Vice President, Finance: Greg Watson
Vice President, Information Technology:
Jeff Schmitz
Director of Football Operations: Doug West
Director of Security: Emmett Baylor
Director of Football Information Systems:
Russell Joyner
Director of Player Engagement:
Sean Washington
Director of College Scouting:
Mike Maccagnan
Director of Pro Personnel: Brian Gardner
Senior Personnel Advisor: Bobby Grier
Pro Scouts: Kevin Murphy, Larry Wright
National College Scouts: Jon Carr,
Ed Lambert
College Scouts: Bob Beers,
Ryan Cavanaugh, Rob Kisiel,
Mike Martin, Bob Merritt, Nathan Trott
Player Personnel Scout: Mozique McCurtis
Director of Sports Medicine/Head Athletic
Trainer: Geoff Kaplan
Coordinator of Rehabilitation/Assistant
Athletic Trainer: Roland Ramirez
Assistant Athletic Trainer:
A.J. Van Valkenburgh
Director of Equipment Services:
Jay Brunetti
Equipment Services Assistants:
Mike Parson, Christian Snell
Director of Video Operations: Joe Malota
Assistant Director of Video Operations:
Tim Brog
Video Operations Asst.: Gresham Oliver
Sr. Director of Communications:
Kevin Cooper
Controller and Sr. Director of Risk
Management: Jan Kelly
Associate General Counsel and Sr.
Director: Greg Kondritz
Sr. Director of Treasury: Jon Southern
Sr. Director of Human Resources:
Glenda Morrison
Sr. Director of Even Operations and Guest
Services: Diane Crossey
Sr. Director of Marketing:
Jennifer Davenport
Director of Premium Seating:
Brian Varnadoe
Director of Ticketing and Event Sales:
Derek Beeman
Director of Luxury Suite Service:
Shari Rainey
Director of Accounting: Tamala Croasmun

COACHING HISTORY
(79-101-0)
2002-05   Dom Capers.................18-46-0
2006-2012 Gary Kubiak 61-55-0

PAID ATTENDANCE
Home 560,395   Away 521,451
Total 1,081,846
Single-game home record,
71,7238 (1/5/13)
Single-season home record,
560,395 (2012)

2013 DRAFT CHOICES

Round	Name	Pos.	College
1	DeAndre Hopkins	WR	Clemson
2	D.J. Swearinger	DB	South Carolina
3	Brennan Williams	T	North Carolina
	Sam Montgomery	LB	Louisiana St.
4	Trevardo Williams	LB	Connecticut
6	David Quessenberry	T	San Jose St.
	Alan Bonner	WR	Jacksonville St.
	Chris Jones	DT	Bowling Green
	Ryan Griffin	TE	Connecticut

2012 TEAM RECORD
PRESEASON (3-1)

Date	Result	Opponent
08/11	W 26-13	at Carolina
08/18	W 20-9	San Francisco
08/25	L 27-34	at New Orleans
08/30	W 28-24	Minnesota

REGULAR SEASON (12-4)

Date	Result	Opponent
09/09	W 30-10	Miami
09/16	W 27-7	at Jacksonville
09/23	W 31-25	at Denver
09/30	W 38-14	Tennessee
10/08	W 23-17	at New York Jets
10/14	L 24-42	Green Bay
10/21	W 43-13	Baltimore
11/04	W 21-9	Buffalo
11/11	W 13-6	at Chicago
11/18	W 43-37	Jacksonville (OT)
11/22	W 34-31	at Detroit (OT)
12/02	W 24-10	at Tennessee
12/10	L 14-42	at New England
12/16	W 29-17	Indianapolis
12/23	L 6-23	Minnesota
12/30	L 16-28	at Indianapolis

(OT) Overtime

POSTSEASON (1-1)

Date	Result	Opponent
01/05	W 19-13	Cincinnati
01/13	L 28-41	at New England

SCORE BY PERIODS

Texans	94	136	100	74	12	—	416
Opponents	77	83	85	83	3	—	331

2012 TEAM STATISTICS

	Texans	Opp.
Total First Downs	341	292
Rushing	114	94
Passing	205	167
Penalty	22	31
3rd Down: Made/Att	83/221	71/215
3rd Down Pct.	37.6	33.0
4th Down: Made/Att	4/7	5/16
4th Down Pct.	57.1	31.3
Possession Avg.	32:53	27:07
Total Net Yards	5953	5172
Avg. Per Game	372.1	323.3
Total Plays	1090	1015
Avg. Per Play	5.5	5.1
Net Yards Rushing	2123	1560
Avg. Per Game	132.7	97.5
Total Rushes	508	390
Net Yards Passing	3830	3612
Avg. Per Game	239.4	225.8
Sacked/Yards Lost	28/216	44/269
Gross Yards	4046	3881
Att./Completions	554/354	581/308
Completion Pct.	63.9	53.0
Had Intercepted	13	15
Punts/Average	88/47.2	92/45.4
Net Punting Avg.	88/40.5	92/40.0
Penalties/Yards	108/873	90/863
Fumbles/Ball Lost	12/4	23/14
Touchdowns	46	38
Rushing	19	5
Passing	22	29
Returns	5	4

2012 INDIVIDUAL STATISTICS

PASSING	Att.	Comp.	Yds.	Pct.	TD	Int.	Tkld.	Rate
Schaub	544	350	4008	64.3	22	12	27/216	90.7
Yates	10	4	38	40.0	0	1	1/0	11.7
Texans	554	354	4046	63.9	22	13	28/216	89.2
Opponents	581	308	3881	53.0	29	15	44/269	80.0

SCORING	TD R	TD P	TD Rt	PAT	FG	Saf	PTS
S. Graham	0	0	0	45/45	31/38	0	138
Foster	15	2	0	0/0	0/0	0	102
Daniels	0	6	0	0/0	0/0	0	36
A. Johnson	0	4	0	0/0	0/0	0	24
Casey	0	3	0	0/0	0/0	0	18
G. Graham	0	3	0	0/0	0/0	0	18
Tate	2	0	0	0/0	0/0	0	12
Walter	0	2	0	0/0	0/0	0	12
Braman	0	0	1	0/0	0/0	0	6
Forsett	1	0	0	0/0	0/0	0	6
Jackson	0	0	1	0/0	0/0	0	6
Jean	0	1	0	0/0	0/0	0	6
Joseph	0	0	1	0/0	0/0	0	6
Manning	0	0	1	0/0	0/0	0	6
Martin	0	1	0	0/0	0/0	0	6
Posey	0	0	1	0/0	0/0	0	6
Yates	1	0	0	0/0	0/0	0	6
Barwin	0	0	0	0/0	0/0	1	2
Texans	19	22	5	45/45	31/38	1	416
Opponents	5	29	4	38/38	21/24	1	331

2-Pt Conversions: Texans 0-0, Opponents 0-0

RUSHING	No.	Yds	Avg	LG	TD
Foster	351	1424	4.1	46	15
Forsett	63	374	5.9	81t	1
Tate	65	279	4.3	25	2
Martin	4	53	13.3	21	0
Casey	1	6	6.0	6	0
Yates	2	-1	-0.5	1t	1
Posey	1	-3	-3.0	-3	0
Schaub	21	-9	-0.4	8	0
Texans	508	2123	4.2	81t	19
Opponents	390	1560	4.0	29	5

RECEIVING	No.	Yds	Avg	LG	TD
A. Johnson	112	1598	14.3	60t	4
Daniels	62	716	11.5	39t	6
Walter	41	518	12.6	52t	2
Foster	40	217	5.4	23	2
Casey	34	330	9.7	30	3
G. Graham	28	263	9.4	30	3
Tate	11	49	4.5	11	0
Martin	10	85	8.5	18	1
Jean	6	151	25.2	54t	1
Posey	6	87	14.5	36	0
Forsett	3	38	12.7	18	0
Schaub	1	-6	-6.0	-6	0
Texans	354	4046	11.4	60t	22
Opponents	308	3881	12.6	81t	29

INTERCEPTIONS	No.	Yds	Avg	LG	TD
Jackson	4	71	17.8	63t	1
Joseph	2	88	44.0	52t	1
Manning	2	59	29.5	55t	1
Quin	2	22	11.0	22	0
McCain	1	86	86.0	86	0
Dobbins	1	7	7.0	7	0
Cushing	1	1	1.0	1	0
Keo	1	1	1.0	1	0
Sharpton	1	-2	-2.0	-2	0
Texans	15	333	22.2	86	3
Opponents	13	136	10.5	26	0

PUNTING	No.	Yds.	Avg.	In 20	LG
Do. Jones	88	4150	47.2	28	66
Texans	88	4150	47.2	28	66
Opponents	92	4176	45.4	35	70

PUNT RETURNS	Ret	FC	Yds	Avg	LG	TD
Martin	22	10	267	12.1	71	0
Holliday	16	6	147	9.2	36	0
Texans	38	16	414	10.9	71	0
Opponents	48	15	483	10.1	72t	1

KICKOFF RETURNS	No.	Yds	Avg	LG	TD
Martin	31	741	23.9	54	0
Holliday	10	194	19.4	30	0
Manning	1	18	18.0	18	0
Casey	1	0	0.0	0	0
Keo	1	0	0.0	0	0
Texans	44	953	21.7	54	0
Opponents	62	1595	25.7	101t	2

FIELD GOALS	1-19	20-29	30-39	40-49	50+
S. Graham	1/1	8/8	11/11	7/9	4/9
Texans	1/1	8/8	11/11	7/9	4/9
Opponents	0/0	5/5	7/8	4/6	5/5

SACKS	No.
Watt	20.5
A. Smith	7.0
Mercilus	6.0
Barwin	3.0
Reed	2.5
Jamison	1.0
Manning	1.0
Quin	1.0
Ruud	1.0
James	0.5
McCain	0.5
Texans	44.0
Opponents	28.0

RECORD HOLDERS
INDIVIDUAL RECORDS—CAREER

Category	Name	Performance
Rushing (Yds.)	Arian Foster, 2009-2012	4,521
Passing (Yds.)	Matt Schaub, 2007-2012	20,911
Passing (TDs)	Matt Schaub, 2007-2012	114
Receiving (No.)	Andre Johnson, 2003-2012	818
Receiving (Yds.)	Andre Johnson, 2003-2012	11,254
Interceptions	Dunta Robinson, 2004-09	13
Punting (Avg.)	Matt Turk, 2007-2011	42.3
Punt Return (Avg.)	Jacoby Jones, 2007-2011	10.2
Kickoff Return (Avg.)	André Davis, 2007-09	25.4
Field Goals	Kris Brown, 2002-09	172
Touchdowns (Tot.)	Andre Johnson, 2003-2012	56
Points	Kris Brown, 2002-09	767
*Sacks	Mario Williams, 2006-2011	53.0

INDIVIDUAL RECORDS—SINGLE SEASON

Category	Name	Performance
Rushing (Yds.)	Arian Foster, 2010	1,616
Passing (Yds.)	Matt Schaub, 2009	4,770
Passing (TDs)	Matt Schaub, 2009	29
Receiving (No.)	Andre Johnson, 2008	115
Receiving (Yds.)	Andre Johnson, 2012	1,598
Interceptions	Marcus Coleman, 2003	7
Punting (Avg.)	Donnie Jones, 2012	47.2
Punt Return (Avg.)	Keshawn Martin, 2012	12.1
Kickoff Return (Avg.)	André Davis, 2007	30.3
Field Goals	Neil Rackers, 2011	32
Touchdowns (Tot.)	Arian Foster, 2010	18
Points	Shayne Graham, 2012	138
*Sacks	J.J. Watt, 2012	20.5

INDIVIDUAL RECORDS—SINGLE GAME

Category	Name	Performance
Rushing (Yds.)	Arian Foster, 9-12-10	231
Passing (Yds.)	Matt Schaub, 11-18-12	527
Passing (TDs)	Matt Schaub, 11-18-12	5
Receiving (No.)	Andre Johnson, 11-18-12	14
Receiving (Yds.)	Andre Johnson, 11-18-12	273
Interceptions	Glover Quin, 10-28-10	3
Field Goals	Kris Brown, 9-7-03, 12-4-05, 10-7-07	5
Touchdowns (Tot.)	Ryan Moats, 11-1-09	3
	Arian Foster, 9-12-10, 10-23-11	3
Points	Ryan Moats, 11-1-09	18
	Arian Foster, 9-12-10, 10-23-11	18
*Sacks	Connor Barwin, 11-27-11	4.0

Sacks became an official statistic in 1982.

2013 VETERAN ROSTER

No.	Name	Pos.	Ht.	Wt.	Birthdate	NFL Exp.	College	Hometown	How Acq.	'12 Games/ Starts
50	Braman, Bryan	OLB	6-5	251	5/4/87	3	West Texas A&M	Spokane, Wash.	FA-'11	14/0
79	Brooks, Brandon	G	6-5	340	8/19/89	2	Miami (Ohio)	Milwaukee, Wisc.	D3b-'12	6/0
76	Brown, Duane	T	6-4	320	8/30/85	5	Virginia Tech	Richmond, Va.	D1-'08	16/16
4	Bullock, Randy	K	5-9	208	12/16/89	2	Texas A&M	Klein, Texas	D5-'12	0*
62	#Caldwell, Antoine	G	6-3	315	4/19/86	5	Alabama	Montgomery, Ala.	D3-'09	11/6
22	Carmichael, Roc	CB	5-10	195	9/9/88	3	Virginia Tech	Clinton, Md.	D4-'11	6/0
40	Clutts, Tyler	FB	6-2	260	11/9/84	3	Fresno State	Clovis, Calif.	T(Chi)-'12	16/0
95	#Cody, Shaun	NT	6-4	307	1/22/83	9	Southern California	Hacienda Heights, Calif.	UFA(Det)-'09	13/12
93	Crick, Jared	DE	6-4	287	8/21/89	2	Nebraska	Cozad, Neb.	FA-'12	15/0
56	Cushing, Brian	ILB	6-3	255	1/24/87	5	Southern California	Park Ridge, N.J.	D1-'09	5/5
81	Daniels, Owen	TE	6-3	249	11/9/82	8	Wisconsin	Naperville, Ill.	D4-'06	15/14
27	#Demps, Quintin	SS	5-11	208	6/29/85	6	Texas-El Paso	San Antonio, Texas	FA-'10	12/0
52	Dobbins, Tim	ILB	6-1	236	12/10/82	8	Iowa State	Nashville, Tenn.	FA-'11	14/6
23	Foster, Arian	RB	6-1	228	8/24/86	5	Tennessee	San Diego, Calif.	FA-'09	16/16
45	#Fox, Keyaron	ILB	6-3	228	1/24/82	10	Georgia Tech	Atlanta, Ga.	FA-'12	0*
66	Gardner, Andrew	T	6-6	309	4/4/86	4	Georgia Tech	Tyrone, Ga.	FA-'11	3/0
88	Graham, Garrett	TE	6-3	244	8/4/86	4	Wisconsin	Brick, N.J.	D4b-'10	15/9
26	Harris, Brandon	CB	5-10	194	1/24/90	3	Miami	Miami, Fla.	D2b-'11	8/0
91	Harris, Ra'Shon	NT	6-5	301	8/26/86	2	Oregon	Pensacola, Fla.	FA-'11	0*
68	Harris, Ryan	T	6-5	300	3/11/85	6	Notre Dame	Minneapolis, Minn.	FA-'12	16/2
72	Hunter, David	DE	6-2	303	9/19/89	2	Houston	Houston, Texas	FA-'12	0*
25	Jackson, Kareem	CB	5-10	192	4/10/88	4	Alabama	Macon, Ga.	D1-'10	16/15
53	#James, Bradie	ILB	6-2	240	1/17/81	11	Louisiana State	Monroe, La.	UFA(Dall)-'12	15/15
96	Jamison, Tim	DE	6-3	285	2/26/86	5	Michigan	Harvey, Ill.	FA-'09	6/0
18	Jean, Lestar	WR	6-3	212	2/5/88	3	Florida Atlantic	Miami, Fla.	FA-'11	14/1
80	Johnson, Andre	WR	6-3	230	7/11/81	11	Miami	Miami, Fla.	D1-'03	16/16
60	Jones, Ben	G/C	6-3	303	7/2/89	2	Georgia	Centreville, Ala.	D4a-'12	16/10
33	Jones, Greg	FB	6-1	265	5/9/81	10	Florida State	Columbia, S.C.	UFA(Jax)-'13	12/4*
24	Joseph, Johnathan	CB	5-11	189	4/16/84	8	South Carolina	Rock Hill, S.C.	UFA(Cin)-'11	14/14
39	Karim, Deji	RB	5-8	209	11/18/86	4	Southern Illinois	Oklahoma City, Okla.	FA-'13	3/0*
31	Keo, Shiloh	FS	5-11	202	12/17/87	3	Idaho	Everett, Wash.	D5-'11	16/0
9	Lechler, Shane	P	6-2	230	8/7/76	14	Texas A&M	East Bernard, Texas	UFA(Oak)-'13	16/0*
38	Manning, Danieal	FS	5-11	210	8/9/82	8	Abilene Christian	Corsicana, Texas	UFA(Chi)-'11	16/16
82	Martin, Keshawn	WR	5-11	190	3/15/90	2	Michigan State	Inkster, Mich.	D4b-'12	16/1
21	McCain, Brice	CB	5-9	185	12/10/86	5	Utah	Terrell, Texas	D6-'09	12/2
97	McClain, Terrell	NT	6-2	300	7/20/88	3	South Florida	Pensacola, Fla.	FA-'12	4/0*
3	McGee, Stephen	QB	6-3	225	9/27/85	2	Texas A&M	Round Rock, Texas	FA-'13	0*
59	Mercilus, Whitney	OLB	6-4	257	7/21/90	2	Illinois	Akron, Ohio	D1-'12	16/4
92	Mitchell, Earl	NT	6-3	300	9/25/87	4	Arizona	Galena Park, Texas	D3-'10	16/3
53	Mohamed, Mike	ILB	6-3	245	3/11/88	2	California	Brawley, Calif.	FA-'13	1/0*
55	Myers, Chris	C	6-4	288	9/15/81	9	Miami	Miami, Fla.	T(Den)-'08	16/16
57	#Nading, Jesse	OLB	6-5	257	7/3/85	5	Colorado State	Highlands Ranch, Colo.	FA-'08	16/0
75	Newton, Derek	T	6-6	318	11/16/87	3	Arkansas State	Utica, Miss.	D7a-'11	14/14
11	Posey, DeVier	WR	6-1	206	3/15/90	2	Ohio State	Cincinnati, Ohio	D3a-'12	11/1
58	Reed, Brooks	OLB	6-3	257	2/28/87	3	Arizona	Tucson, Ariz.	D2a-'11	12/12
20	Reed, Ed	FS	5-11	205	9/11/78	12	Miami	St. Rose, La.	UFA(Balt)-'13	16/16*
30	#Routt, Stanford	CB	6-1	195	7/26/83	9	Houston	Austin, Texas	FA-'12	9/7*
54	#Ruud, Barrett	ILB	6-2	241	5/20/83	9	Nebraska	Lincoln, Neb.	FA-'12	12/1*
8	Schaub, Matt	QB	6-5	239	6/25/81	10	Virginia	West Chester, Pa.	T(Atl)-'07	16/16
51	Sharpton, Darryl	ILB	5-11	234	1/1/88	4	Miami	Coral Gables, Fla.	D4a-'10	7/5
94	Smith, Antonio	DE	6-4	284	10/21/81	9	Oklahoma State	Oklahoma City, Okla.	UFA(Ariz)-'09	16/16
74	Smith, Wade	G	6-4	307	4/26/81	11	Memphis	Dallas, Texas	UFA(KC)-'10	16/16
44	Tate, Ben	RB	5-11	215	8/21/88	4	Auburn	Salisbury, Md.	FA-'07	11/0
99	Watt, J.J.	DE	6-5	295	3/22/89	3	Wisconsin	Pewaukee, Wisc.	D1-'11	16/16
46	Weeks, Jon	LS	5-10	248	2/17/86	4	Baylor	Bethpage, N.Y.	FA-'11	16/0
67	White, Cody	G	6-3	301	7/1/88	2	Illinois State	Columbus, Ohio	FA-'12	0*
13	Yates, T.J.	QB	6-4	219	5/28/87	3	North Carolina	Marietta, Ga.	D5b-'11	4/0

* Bullock missed '12 season because of injury; Butler missed '12 season because of injury; Fox missed '12 season because of injury; Ra'Shon Harris missed the '12 season because of injury; Hunter inactive for 1 game; G. Jones played 12 games with Jacksonville; Karim played 3 games with Indianapolis; Lechler played 16 games for Oakland; McClain played one game for New England and three games with Houston; McGee last active with Dallas in '11; Mohamed played one game with Denver; E. Reed played 16 games with Baltimore; Routt played 7 games with Kansas City and played two games for Houston; Ruud played three games with New Orleans and nine games with Houston; White inactive in 11 games.

\# Unrestriced Free Agent; subject to developments.

Players lost through free agency (8): CB Alan Ball (Jax; 11 games in '12), OLB Connor Barwin (Phil; 16), T Rashad Butler (Cle; 0), FB James Casey (Phil; 16), RB Justin Forsett (Jax; 16), K Shayne Graham (Cle; 16), P Donnie Jones (Phil; 16), FS Glover Quin (Det; 16).

Also played with Texans in '12—ILB Mister Alexander (6 games), RB Jonathan Grimes (6), WR Trindon Holliday (5), S Troy Nolan (4), SS Eddie Pleasant (2).

FIRST-YEAR ROSTER

Name	Pos.	Ht.	Wt.	Birthdate	College	Hometown	How Acq.
Adams, Johnny	CB	5-10	175	6/9/89	Michigan State	Akron, Ohio	FA
Bonner, Alan	WR	5-10	190	11/5/90	Jacksonville State	Newnan, Ga.	D6b
Boren, Zach	FB	6-0	255	5/13/91	Ohio State	Pickerington, Ohio	FA
Bouye, A.J.	CB	6-0	183	8/16/91	Central Florida	Tucker, Ga.	FA
Browner, Keith (1)	DE	6-4	288	4/7/88	California	Los Angeles, Calif.	FA-'12
Byrne, Jake (1)	TE	6-4	258	1/24/90	Wisconsin	Rogers, Ark.	FA-'12
Collins, Bryan	G	6-3	303	11/7/90	Southern Methodist	Keller, Texas	FA
Collins, Cameron (1)	ILB	6-2	246	9/29/89	Oregon State	Santa Monica, Calif.	FA-'12
Cruse, Andy	WR	6-3	216	1/13/90	Miami (Ohio)	Cincinnati, Ohio	FA
Davis, Ja'Gared	ILB	6-0	245	9/11/90	Southern Methodist	Crockett, Texas	FA
Frierson, Evan	ILB	6-2	234	5/24/90	Illinois State	Washington, D.C.	FA
Graham, Ray	RB	5-9	193	9/18/90	Pittsburgh	Elizabeth, N.J.	FA
Griffin, Ryan	TE	6-6	256	1/11/90	Connecticut	Londonderry, N.H.	D6d
Hopkins, DeAndre	WR	6-1	207	6/6/92	Clemson	Central, S.C.	D1
Horn, Tyler (1)	C	6-4	305	3/1/89	Miami	Memphis, Tenn.	FA
Howard, Travis	CB	6-1	197	11/24/89	Ohio State	Miami, Fla.	FA
Jefferson, Willie	OLB	6-5	233	1/31/91	Stephen F. Austin	Beaumont, Texas	FA
Johnson, Delano (1)	DE	6-4	290	1/13/88	Bowie State	Baltimore, Md.	FA-'12
Johnson, Dennis	RB	5-7	193	2/24/90	Arkansas	Texarkana, Ark.	FA
Johnson, Orhian	S	6-3	211	10/9/89	Ohio State	St. Petersburg, Fla.	FA
Jones, Chris	NT	6-2	306	7/12/90	Bowling Green	Brownsburg, Ind.	D6c
Keenum, Case (1)	QB	6-1	206	2/17/88	Houston	Abilene, Texas	FA-'12
Kupper, Alex	G	6-3	305	2/14/90	Louisville	Louisville, Ky.	FA
Lemon, Alec	WR	6-1	207	7/1/91	Syracuse	Crofton, Md.	FA
Maehl, Jeff (1)	WR	6-0	184	3/16/89	Oregon	Paradise, Calif.	FA-'11
Mondek, Nick (1)	T	6-5	308	11/3/88	Purdue	Naperville, Ill.	D6-'12
Montgomery, Sam	OLB	6-3	262	5/25/90	Louisiana State	Greenwood, S.C.	D3b
Nwachukwu, EZ	WR	5-11	196	12/15/90	Texas A&M	Allen, Texas	FA
Okine, Earl	DE	6-6	286	1/4/90	Florida	Gainesville, Fla.	FA
Pleasant, Eddie (1)	SS	5-10	202	12/17/88	Oregon	Compton, Calif.	FA-'12
Quessenberry, David	T	6-5	307	8/24/90	San Jose State	La Jolla, Calif.	D6a
Shapiro, Andrew	P	6-0	203	9/4/90	Fresno State	Walnut Creek, Calif.	FA
Smith, Mike	WR	6-0	201	8/22/90	Connecticut	Houston, Texas	FA
Starling, Jawanza	S	6-0	206	6/21/91	Southern California	Tallahassee, Fla.	FA
Supernaw, Phillip (1)	TE	6-5	248	1/30/90	Ouachita Baptist	Katy, Texas	FA-'12
Swearinger, D.J.	SS	5-10	207	9/1/91	South Carolina	Greenwood, S.C.	D2
Tuggle, Justin	OLB	6-3	247	1/4/90	Kansas State	Alpharetta, Ga.	FA
Williams, Brennan	T	6-6	314	2/5/91	North Carolina	West Roxbury, Mass	D3a
Williams, Trevardo	OLB	6-1	237	12/31/90	Connecticut	Bridgeport, Conn.	D4
Wood, Cierre	RB	5-11	205	2/21/91	Notre Dame	Oxnard, Calif.	FA

The term NFL Rookie is defined as a player who is in his first season of professional football and has not been on the roster of another professional football team for any regular-season or postseason games. A Rookie is designated by an "R" on NFL rosters. Players who have been active in another professional football league or players who have NFL experience, including either preseason training camp or being on an Active List or Inactive List, or on Reserve/Injured or Reserve/Physically Unable to Perform for fewer than six regular-season games, are termed NFL First-Year Players. An NFL First-Year Player is designated by a "1" on NFL rosters. Thereafter, a player is credited with an additional year of experience for each season in which he accumulates six games on the Active List or Inactive List, or on Reserve/Injured or Reserve/Physically Unable to Perform.

Log on to www.houstontexans.com for an up-to-date roster.

COACHING STAFF
Head Coach,
Gary Kubiak

Pro Career: Gary Kubiak is in his eighth season as head coach of the Houston Texans and is the winningest coach in franchise history. Kubiak has led the Texans to back-to-back AFC South titles and the first two playoff appearances in franchise history in 2011 and 2012. Houston set a franchise record with a 12-4 record and advanced to the Divisional round of the playoffs for the second consecutive season in 2012. In 2011, the Texans finished 10-6, won their first division title, advanced to the playoffs for the first time and won their first ever playoff game. Kubiak has led the Texans to the five best seasons in franchise history, producing the first winning season in 2009 at 9-7. The Texans are the only team in the NFL to produce a rushing, receiving, passing yardage and sack leader since Kubiak became head coach. Prior to joining the Texans, Kubiak spent 20 of the previous 23 years in Denver, including 11 years (1995-2005) as Denver's offensive coordinator, helping guide the Broncos to back-to-back titles in Super Bowls XXXII and XXXIII. Kubiak tutored QB John Elway from 1995-98. Kubiak began his coaching career as Texas A&M's running backs coach (1992-93). Kubiak was the San Francisco 49ers quarterbacks coach in 1994, winning Super Bowl XXIX. He is a veteran of six Super Bowls—three as a player and three as a coach. Career record: 61-55.

Background: Kubiak starred at quarterback for Texas A&M (1979-1982), earning all-Southwest Conference honors as a senior. He played for the Broncos (1983-1991) as Elway's backup. Kubiak played in 119 career games, threw 14 touchdowns, and was a part of three teams that reached the Super Bowl.

Personal: Born August 15, 1961 in Houston, Texas. He and his wife, Rhonda, have three sons—Klint, Klay, and Klein.

ASSISTANT COACHES

John Benton, offensive line; born December 13, 1963, Los Angeles, Calif. Offensive lineman Colorado State 1986-1990. No pro playing experience. College coach: California University (Pa.) 1990-94, Colorado State 1996-2003. Pro coach: St. Louis Rams 2004-05, joined Texans in 2006.

Perry Carter, asst. defensive backs; born August 15, 1971, McComb, Miss. Defensive back Southern Mississippi 1989-1993. Pro defensive back Arizona Cardinals 1994, Kansas City Chiefs 1995, Oakland Raiders 1996-98, Edmonton Eskimos (CFL) 2000-01, Montreal Alouettes (CFL) 2002, British Columbia Lions (CFL) 2003-04. College coach: Texas A&M-Commerce 2004. Pro coach: Hamburg Sea Devils (NFLEL) 2006, joined Texans in 2006.

Rick Dennison, offensive coordinator; born June 22, 1958, Kalispell, Mont. Tight end Colorado State 1976-79. Pro linebacker Denver Broncos 1982-1990. Pro coach: Denver Broncos 1995-2009, joined Texans in 2010.

Karl Dorrell, quarterbacks; born December 18, 1968, Alameda, Calif. Wide receiver UCLA 1982-86. No pro playing experience. College coach: UCLA 1988, 2003-07 (head coach 2003-07), Central Florida 1989, Northern Arizona 1990-91, Colorado 1992-93, 1995-98, Arizona State 1994, Washington 1999. Pro coach: Denver Broncos 2000-02, Miami Dolphins 2008-2011, joined Texans in 2012.

Dan Hammerschmidt, offensive assistant; born May 20, 1964, Pomona, Calif. Safety Colorado State 1982-85. No pro playing experience. College coach: Colorado State 1986, 1996-2007, 2010-11, Texas Christian 1987, Duke 1988-1994, Virginia Military Institute 1995, Rice 2008, Wyoming 2009. Pro coach: Joined Texans in 2012.

Chick Harris, running backs; born September 21, 1945, Durham, N.C. Running back Northern Arizona 1966-69. No pro playing experience. College coach: Colorado State 1970-71, Long Beach State 1972-73, Washington 1975-1980. Pro coach: Detroit Wheels (WFL) 1974, Buffalo Bills 1981-82, Seattle Seahawks 1983-1991, Los Angeles Rams 1992-94, Carolina Panthers 1995-2001, joined Texans in 2002.

Reggie Herring, linebackers; born July 3, 1959, Myrtle Beach, S.C. Linebacker Florida State 1978-1980. No pro playing experience. College coach: Oklahoma State 1981-85, Auburn 1986-1991, Texas Christian 1992-93, Clemson 1994-2001, North Carolina State 2004, Arkansas 2005-07 (interim head coach 2007). Pro coach: Houston Texans 2002-03, Dallas Cowboys 2008-2010, re-joined Texans in 2011.

Vance Joseph, defensive backs; born September 20, 1972, Marrero, La. Defensive back Colorado 1990-94. Pro defensive back New York Jets 1995, Indianapolis Colts 1996. College coach: Colorado 1999-2001, 2002-03, Wyoming 2002, Bowling Green State 2004. Pro coach: San Francisco 49ers 2005-2010, joined Texans in 2011.

Bobby King, asst. linebackers; born June 29, 1978, Louisville, Ky. Defensive line Texas El-Paso 1998-2000. No pro playing experience. College coach: Texas El-Paso 2002-03, West Texas A&M 2005, 2008-09, Baylor 2006-07. Pro coach: Dallas Cowboys 2010, joined Texans in 2011.

Larry Kirksey, wide receivers; born January 6, 1951, Harlan, Ky. Wide receiver Eastern Kentucky 1970-73. No pro playing experience. College coach: Miami (Ohio) 1974-76, Kentucky 1977-1981, Kansas 1982, Kentucky State 1983 (head coach), Florida 1984-88, Pittsburgh 1989, Alabama 1990-93, Texas A&M 2000, Middle Tennessee State 2006. Pro coach: San Francisco 49ers 1994-99, Detroit Lions 2001-02, Jacksonville Jaguars 2003, Denver Broncos 2004, joined Texans in 2007.

Bill Kollar, asst. head coach/defensive line; born November 27, 1952, Warren, Ohio. Defensive end Montana State 1971-73. Pro defensive end Cincinnati Bengals 1974-76, Tampa Bay Buccaneers 1977-1981. College coach: Illinois 1985-87, Purdue 1988-89. Pro coach: Tampa Bay Buccaneers 1984, Atlanta Falcons 1990-2000, St. Louis Rams 2001-05, Buffalo Bills 2006-08, joined Texans in 2009.

Bob Ligashesky, asst. special teams; born June 2, 1962, Pittsburgh, Pa. Defensive back Indiana (Pa.) 1982-84. No pro playing experience. Pro coach: Jacksonville Jaguars 2004, St. Louis Rams 2005-06, Pittsburgh Steelers 2007-09, Denver Broncos 2010, Oakland Raiders 2011, Tampa Bay Buccaneers 2012, joined Texans in 2013.

Marc Lubick, asst. wide receivers; born November 13, 1977, Bozeman, Mont. Defensive back Montana State 1996-99. No pro playing experience. College coach: Colorado State 2000-02, 2005-09. Pro coach: St. Louis Rams 2003-04 (scout), joined Texans in 2010.

Joe Marciano, special teams coordinator; born February 10, 1954, Dunmore, Pa. Quarterback Temple 1972-75. No pro playing experience. College coach: East Stroudsburg State 1977, Rhode Island 1978-79, Villanova 1980, Penn State 1981, Temple 1982. Pro coach: Philadelphia/Baltimore Stars (USFL) 1983-85, New Orleans Saints 1986-1995, Tampa Bay Buccaneers 1996-2001, joined Texans in 2002.

Brian Pariani, tight ends; born July 2, 1965, San Francisco, Calif. No college or pro playing experience. College coach: UCLA 1989, Syracuse 2005. Pro coach: San Francisco 49ers 1991-94, Denver Broncos 1994-2004, joined Texans in 2006.

Wade Phillips, defensive coordinator; born June 21, 1947, Orange, Texas. Linebacker Houston 1966-68. No pro playing experience. College coach: Houston 1969, Oklahoma State 1973-74, Kansas 1975. Pro coach: Houston Oilers 1976-1980, New Orleans Saints 1981-85 (interim head coach for four games 1985), Philadelphia Eagles 1986-88, Denver Broncos 1989-1994 (head coach 1993-94), Buffalo Bills 1995-2000 (head coach 1998-2000), Atlanta Falcons 2002-03 (interim head coach for three games in 2003), San Diego Chargers 2004-06, Dallas Cowboys 2007-10 (head coach), joined Texans in 2011.

Jim Ryan, asst. offensive line; born May 18, 1957, Bellmawr, N.J. Linebacker William & Mary 1974-78. Linebacker Denver Broncos 1979-1988. Pro coach: Denver Broncos 2005-08, Omaha Nighthawks (UFL) 2010, joined Texans in 2011.

Jeff Zgonina, asst. defensive line; born May 24, 1970, Chicago, Ill. Defensive tackle Purdue 1989-1992. Pro defensive tackle Pittsburgh Steelers 1993-1994, Carolina Panthers 1995, Atlanta Falcons 1996, St. Louis Rams 1997, 1999-2002, Indianapolis Colts 1998, Miami Dolphins 2003-2006, Houston Texans 2007-09. Pro coach: Joined Texans in 2013.

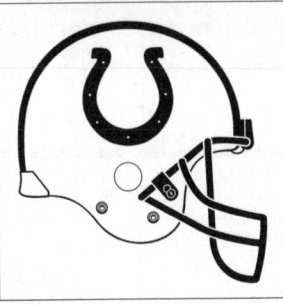

**American Football Conference
South Division
Team Colors:** Royal Blue and White
**P.O. Box 535000
Indianapolis, Indiana 46253
Telephone:** (317) 297-2658

2013 SCHEDULE
PRESEASON
Aug. 11   Buffalo 1:30
Aug. 18   at New York Giants 7:00
Aug. 24   Cleveland 7:00
Aug. 29   at Cincinnati 7:00

REGULAR SEASON
Sep. 8   Oakland 1:00
Sep. 15   Miami 1:00
Sep. 22   at San Francisco 4:25
Sep. 29   at Jacksonville 1:00
Oct. 6   Seattle 1:00
Oct. 14   at San Diego (Mon) 8:40
Oct. 20   Denver 8:30
Oct. 27   BYE
Nov. 3   at Houston 8:30
Nov. 10   St. Louis 1:00
Nov. 14   at Tennessee (Thurs).........8:25
Nov. 24   at Arizona 4:05
Dec. 1   Tennessee 1:00
Dec. 8   at Cincinnati 1:00
Dec. 15   Houston 1:00
Dec. 22   at Kansas City 1:00
Dec. 29   Jacksonville 1:00
*All times ET

Stadium: Lucas Oil Stadium (opened in
2008) •**Capacity:** 63,000
500 South Capitol Avenue
Indianapolis, Indiana 46225
Playing Surface: FieldTurf
Training Camp: Anderson University
1100 East Fifth Street
Anderson, IN 46012

LUCAS OIL STADIUM

CLUB OFFICIALS
Owner and CEO: James Irsay
Vice Chairman/Owner:
   Carlie Irsay-Gordon
Vice Chairman/Owner: Casey Foyt
Vice Chairman/Owner: Kalen Irsay
General Manager: Ryan Grigson
Head Coach: Chuck Pagano
Chief Operating Officer: Pete Ward
Senior Vice President of Sponsorship
   Sales: Jay Souers
Vice President-Finance: Kurt Humphrey
Vice President-Ticket Operations/Guest
   Services: Larry Hall
Senior Director of Communications:
   Avis Roper
Vice President of Sponsorship Sales:
   Matt Godbout
Vice President of Premium Seating and
   Ticket Sales: Greg Hylton
Vice President and General Counsel:
   Dan Emerson
Vice President of Football Operations:
   Jimmy Raye
Director of Football Administration:
   Mike Bluem
Associate Director of Pro Personnel:
   Kevin Rogers
Vice President of Equipment Operations:
   Jon Scott
Video Director: Erik Kunttu
Head Athletic Trainer: Dave Hammer
Director of Rehabilitation: Erin Barill
Assistant Equipment Managers:
   Mike Mays, Sean Sullivan,
   Brian Seabrooks
Assistant Trainers: Dave Walston,
   Kyle Davis
Assistant Video Director: John Starliper

COACHING HISTORY
**Baltimore 1953-1983
(483-436-7)**
Records include postseason games
1953   Keith Molesworth 3-9-0
1954-1962   Weeb Ewbank 61-52-1
1963-69   Don Shula 73-26-4
1970-72   Don McCafferty* 26-11-1
1972   John Sandusky 4-5-0
1973-74   Howard Schnellenberger**..4-13-0
1974   Joe Thomas 2-9-0
1975-79   Ted Marchibroda 41-36-0
1980-81   Mike McCormack...........9-23-0
1982-84   Frank Kush*** 11-28-1
1984   Hal Hunter.......................0-1-0
1985-86   Rod Dowhower**** 5-24-0
1986-1991   Ron Meyer# 36-36-0
1991   Rick Venturi 1-10-0
1992-95   Ted Marchibroda 32-35-0
1996-97   Lindy Infante 12-21-0
1998-2001   Jim Mora 32-34-0
2002-08   Tony Dungy..................92-33-0
2009-2011   Jim Caldwell 28-24-0
2012   Chuck Pagano................11-6-0
   *Released after five games in 1972
   **Released after three games in 1974
   ***Resigned after 15 games in 1984
****Released after 13 games in 1986
   #Released after five games in 1991

PAID ATTENDANCE
Home 505,819   Away 515,516
Total 1,021,335
Single-game home record,
   67,650 (1/24/10)
Single-season home record,
   520,687 (2010)

2013 DRAFT CHOICES
Round	Name	Pos.	College
1	Bjoern Werner	LB	Florida St.
3	Hugh Thornton	G	Illinois
4	Khaled Holmes	C/G	Southern California
5	Montori Hughes	DT	UT Martin
6	John Boyett	S	Oregon
7	Kerwynn Williams	RB	Utah St.
	Justice Cunningham	TE	South Carolina

2012 TEAM RECORD
PRESEASON (2-2)

Date	Result		Opponent
08/12	W	38-3	St. Louis
08/19	L	24-26	at Pittsburgh
08/25	L	17-30	at Washington
08/30	W	20-16	Cincinnati

REGULAR SEASON (11-5)

Date	Result		Opponent
09/09	L	21-41	at Chicago
09/16	W	23-20	Minnesota
09/23	L	17-22	Jacksonville
10/07	W	30-27	Green Bay
10/14	L	9-35	at New York Jets
10/21	W	17-13	Cleveland
10/28	W	19-13	at Tennessee (OT)
11/04	W	23-20	Miami
11/08	W	27-10	at Jacksonville
11/18	L	24-59	at New England
11/25	W	20-13	Buffalo
12/02	W	35-33	at Detroit
12/09	W	27-23	Tennessee
12/16	L	17-29	at Houston
12/23	W	20-13	at Kansas City
12/30	W	28-16	Houston

POSTSEASON (0-1)

Date	Result		Opponent
01/06	L	9-24	at Baltimore

(OT) Overtime

SCORE BY PERIODS

Colts	93	96	81	81	6	—	357
Opponents	69	144	78	96	0	—	387

2012 TEAM STATISTICS

	Colts	Opp.
Total First Downs	360	325
Rushing	110	102
Passing	208	190
Penalty	42	33
3rd Down: Made/Att	98/229	75/197
3rd Down Pct.	42.8	38.1
4th Down: Made/Att	7/8	3/7
4th Down Pct.	87.5	42.9
Possession Avg.	30:36	29:24
Total Net Yards	5799	5988
Avg. Per Game	362.4	374.3
Total Plays	1109	995
Avg. Per Play	5.2	6.0
Net Yards Rushing	1671	2200
Avg. Per Game	104.4	137.5
Total Rushes	440	428
Net Yards Passing	4128	3788
Avg. Per Game	258.0	236.8
Sacked/Yards Lost	41/246	32/189
Gross Yards	4374	3977
Att./Completions	628/339	535/334
Completion Pct.	54.0	62.4
Had Intercepted	18	12
Punts/Average	74/47.6	71/47.0
Net Punting Avg.	74/40.3	71/41.2
Penalties/Yards	94/801	128/1208
Fumbles/Ball Lost	21/9	11/3
Touchdowns	40	42
Rushing	11	14
Passing	23	23
Returns	6	5

2012 INDIVIDUAL STATISTICS

PASSING	Att.	Comp.	Yds.	Pct.	TD	Int.	Tkld.	Rate
Luck	627	339	4374	54.1	23	18	41/246	76.5
Hilton	1	0	0	0.0	0	0	0/0	39.6
Colts	628	339	4374	54.0	23	18	41/246	76.4
Opponents	535	334	3977	62.4	23	12	32/189	90.1

SCORING	TD R	TD P	TD Rt	PAT	FG	Saf	PTS
Vinatieri	0	0	0	37/37	26/33	0	115
Hilton	0	7	1	0/0	0/0	0	48
Luck	5	0	0	0/0	0/0	0	30
Wayne	0	5	0	0/0	0/0	0	30
Allen	0	3	0	0/0	0/0	0	18
Avery	0	3	0	0/0	0/0	0	18
Ballard	2	1	0	0/0	0/0	0	18
Carter	3	0	0	0/0	0/0	0	18
Butler	0	0	2	0/0	0/0	0	12
Fleener	0	2	0	0/0	0/0	0	12
D. Brown	1	0	0	0/0	0/0	0	8
Brazill	0	1	0	0/0	0/0	0	6
Freeman	0	0	1	0/0	0/0	0	6
Karim	0	0	1	0/0	0/0	0	6
M. Moore	0	1	0	0/0	0/0	0	6
Vaughn	0	0	1	0/0	0/0	0	6
Colts	11	23	6	37/37	26/33	0	357
Opponents	14	23	5	39/39	32/41	0	387

2-Pt Conversions: D. Brown, Colts 1-2, Opponents 0-3

RUSHING	No.	Yds	Avg	LG	TD
Ballard	211	814	3.9	26	2
D. Brown	108	417	3.9	19	1
Luck	62	255	4.1	19	5
Carter	32	122	3.8	20	3
Hilton	5	29	5.8	19	0
M. Moore	13	20	1.5	6	0
Avery	4	9	2.3	7	0
Allen	3	5	1.7	3	0
R. Hughes	1	5	5.0	5	0
Wayne	1	-5	-5.0	-5	0
Colts	440	1671	3.8	26	11
Opponents	428	2200	5.1	86t	14

RECEIVING	No.	Yds	Avg	LG	TD
Wayne	106	1355	12.8	33	5
Avery	60	781	13.0	48	3
Hilton	50	861	17.2	70t	7
Allen	45	521	11.6	40	3
Fleener	26	281	10.8	26t	2
Ballard	17	152	8.9	19	1
Brazill	11	186	16.9	42t	1
D. Brown	9	93	10.3	39	0
M. Moore	6	77	12.8	32	1
Adams	2	26	13.0	13	0
Saunders	2	15	7.5	11	0
Carter	1	13	13.0	13	0
Jones	1	8	8.0	8	0
Collie	1	6	6.0	6	0
R. Hughes	1	3	3.0	3	0
Palmer	1	-4	-4.0	-4	0
Colts	339	4374	12.9	70t	23
Opponents	334	3977	11.9	80t	23

INTERCEPTIONS	No.	Yds	Avg	LG	TD
Butler	4	101	25.3	51	2
Davis	3	26	8.7	26	0
Zbikowski	1	20	20.0	20	0
Freeman	1	4	4.0	4t	1
Vaughn	1	3	3.0	3t	1
Mathis	1	1	1.0	1	0
Powers	1	0	0.0	0	0
Colts	12	155	12.9	51	4
Opponents	18	406	22.6	87t	3

PUNTING	No.	Yds.	Avg.	In 20	LG
McAfee	73	3520	48.2	26	64
Colts	74	3520	47.6	26	64
Opponents	71	3340	47	24	66

PUNT RETURNS	Ret	FC	Yds	Avg	LG	TD
Hilton	26	18	300	11.5	75t	1
Brazill	2	1	12	6.0	8	0
Zbikowski	0	1	0	—	—	0
Colts	28	20	312	11.1	75t	1
Opponents	32	14	375	11.7	68t	1

KICKOFF RETURNS	No.	Yds	Avg	LG	TD
Vaughn	10	209	20.9	40	0
Karim	9	328	36.4	101t	1
Hilton	7	118	16.9	26	0
Zbikowski	6	123	20.5	34	0
Lefeged	4	68	17.0	19	0
Brazill	3	50	16.7	20	0
M. Moore	3	50	16.7	24	0
Sowell	1	11	11.0	11	0
Colts	43	957	22.3	101t	1
Opponents	34	841	24.7	50	0

FIELD GOALS	1-19	20-29	30-39	40-49	50+
Vinatieri	1/1	8/8	4/7	9/10	4/7
Colts	1/1	8/8	4/7	9/10	4/7
Opponents	0/0	6/6	15/16	8/11	3/8

SACKS	No.
Mathis	8.0
Freeney	5.0
J. Hughes	4.0
Bethea	2.0
Freeman	2.0
Redding	2.0
Conner	1.0
Davis	1.0
Fokou	1.0
Geathers	1.0
Gordy	1.0
Guy	1.0
Nevis	1.0
Westerman	1.0
Zbikowski	1.0
Colts	32.0
Opponents	41.0

RECORD HOLDERS
INDIVIDUAL RECORDS—CAREER

Category	Name	Performance
Rushing (Yds.)	Edgerrin James, 1999-2005	9,226
Passing (Yds.)	Peyton Manning, 1998-2010	54,828
Passing (TDs)	Peyton Manning, 1998-2010	399
Receiving (No.)	Marvin Harrison, 1996-2008	1,102
Receiving (Yds.)	Marvin Harrison, 1996-2008	14,580
Interceptions	Bob Boyd, 1960-68	57
Punting (Avg.)	Pat McAfee, 2009-2012	45.5
Punt Return (Avg.)	Ron Gardin, 1970-71	13.5
Kickoff Return (Avg.)	Jim Duncan, 1969-1971	32.6
Field Goals	Mike Vanderjagt, 1998-2005	217
Touchdowns (Tot.)	Marvin Harrison, 1996-2008	128
Points	Mike Vanderjagt, 1998-2005	995
*Sacks	Dwight Freeney, 2002-2012	107.5

INDIVIDUAL RECORDS—SINGLE SEASON

Category	Name	Performance
Rushing (Yds.)	Edgerrin James, 2000	1,709
Passing (Yds.)	Peyton Manning, 2010	4,700
Passing (TDs)	Peyton Manning, 2004	49
Receiving (No.)	Marvin Harrison, 2002	**143
Receiving (Yds.)	Marvin Harrison, 2002	1,722
Interceptions	Tom Keane, 1953	11
Punting (Avg.)	Pat McAfee, 2012	48.2
Punt Return (Avg.)	T.J. Rushing, 2007	13.1
Kickoff Return (Avg.)	Jim Duncan, 1970	35.4
Field Goals	Mike Vanderjagt, 2003	37
Touchdowns (Tot.)	Lenny Moore, 1964	20
Points	Mike Vanderjagt, 2003	157
*Sacks	Dwight Freeney, 2004	16.0

INDIVIDUAL RECORDS—SINGLE GAME

Category	Name	Performance
Rushing (Yds.)	Edgerrin James, 10-15-00	219
Passing (Yds.)	Peyton Manning, 10-31-04	472
Passing (TDs)	Peyton Manning, 9-28-03, 11-25-04	6
Receiving (No.)	Reggie Wayne, 10-3-10	15
Receiving (Yds.)	Raymond Berry, 11-10-57	224
Interceptions	Many times Last time by Mike Prior, 12-20-92	3
Field Goals	Many times Last time by Mike Vanderjagt, 12-7-03	5
Touchdowns (Tot.)	Many times Last time by Joseph Addai, 11-26-06	4
Points	Many times Last time by Joseph Addai, 11-26-06	24
*Sacks	Johnie Cooks, 11-25-84	4.5

*Sacks became an official statistic in 1982.
**NFL Record

2013 VETERAN ROSTER

No.	Name	Pos.	Ht.	Wt.	Birthdate	NFL Exp.	College	Hometown	How Acq.	'12 Games/ Starts
83	Allen, Dwayne	TE	6-3	255	2/24/90	2	Clemson	Fayetteville, N.C.	D3-'12	16/16
79	Anderson, Justin	G	6-5	342	4/15/88	2	Georgia	Ocilla, Ga.	D7-'12	0*
51	Angerer, Pat	ILB	6-0	236	1/31/87	4	Iowa	Bettendorf, Iowa	D2-'10	11/3
36	Asante, Larry	S	6-0	210	3/7/88	2	Nebraska	Alexandria, Va.	FA-'13	0*
33	Ballard, Vick	RB	5-10	217	7/16/90	2	Mississippi State	Pascagoula, Miss.	D5-'12	16/12
41	Bethea, Antoine	S	5-11	196	7/27/84	8	Howard	Newport News, Va.	D6-'06	16/16
15	Brazill, LaVon	WR	5-11	191	3/15/89	2	Ohio	Lantana, Fla.	D6-'12	15/0
31	Brown, Donald	RB	5-10	210	4/11/87	5	Connecticut	Atlantic Highlands, N.J.	D1-'09	10/4
38	Brown, Sergio	S	6-2	210	5/22/88	4	Notre Dame	Maywood, Ill.	W(NE)-'12	16/0
20	Butler, Darius	CB	5-10	185	3/18/86	5	Connecticut	Tamarac, Fla.	FA-'12	11/4
34	Carter, Delone	RB	5-9	238	6/22/87	3	Syracuse	Copley, Ohio	D4-'11	10/0
74	Castonzo, Anthony	T	6-7	315	8/9/88	3	Boston College	Hawthorn Woods, Ill.	D1-'11	16/16
61	Chapman, Josh	NT	6-0	316	6/10/90	2	Alabama	Hoover, Ala.	D5-'12	0*
78	Cherilus, Gosder	T	6-7	325	6/28/84	6	Boston College	Somerville, Mass.	UFA(Det)-'13	16/16*
53	Conner, Kavell	ILB	6-0	243	2/23/87	4	Clemson	Richmond, Va.	D7-'10	14/12
23	Davis, Vontae	CB	5-11	205	5/27/88	5	Illinois	Washington, D.C.	T(Mia)-'12	10/10
80	Fleener, Coby	TE	6-6	252	9/20/88	2	Stanford	Lemont, Ill.	D2-'12	12/10
97	Franklin, Aubrayo	DT	6-1	315	8/27/80	11	Tennessee	Johnson City, Tenn.	UFA(SD)-'13	12/9*
50	Freeman, Jerrell	ILB	6-0	234	5/1/86	2	Mary Hardin-Baylor	Waco, Texas	FA-'12	16/16
27	Gordy, Josh	CB	5-11	195	2/9/87	3	Central Michigan	Warthen, Ga.	T(StL)-'12	15/1
25	Green, Marshay	CB	5-10	175	1/14/86	2	Mississippi	Bastrop, La.	FA-'12	1/0
67	Guy, Lawrence	DE	6-4	300	3/17/90	3	Arizona State	Las Vegas, Nev.	FA-'12	9/2
54	Harvey, Mario	ILB	6-0	264	8/10/87	2	Marshall	Forsyth, Ga.	FA-'12	13/0
8	Hasselbeck, Matt	QB	6-4	225	9/25/75	15	Boston College	Norfolk, Mass.	FA-'13	8/5*
39 t-	Havili, Stanley	FB	6-0	245	11/14/87	3	Southern California	Salt Lake City, Utah	T(Phil)-'13	15/2*
65	Heard, Kellen	DT	6-6	339	10/17/85	3	Memphis	Wharton, Texas	FA-'12	11/0
81	Heyward-Bey, Darrius	WR	6-2	216	2/26/87	5	Maryland	Silver Springs, Md.	FA-'13	15/14*
55	Hickman, Justin	OLB	6-2	258	7/20/85	2	UCLA	Glendale, Ariz.	FA-'12	12/0
13	Hilton, T.Y.	WR	5-9	183	11/14/89	2	Florida International	Miami, Fla.	D3-'12	15/1
26	Howell, Delano	S	5-11	201	11/17/89	2	Stanford	Newhall, Calif.	FA-'12	6/0
71	Ijalana, Ben	G	6-4	337	8/6/89	3	Villanova	Hainesport, N.J.	D2-'11	0*
99	Jean Francois, Ricky	DT	6-3	295	11/23/86	5	Louisiana State	Miami, Fla.	UFA(SF)-'13	16/3*
46	Jones, Dominique	TE	6-3	255	8/15/87	2	Shepherd	San Diego, Calif.	FA-'12	4/1
30	Landry, LaRon	S	6-0	220	10/14/84	7	Louisiana State	Metairie, La.	UFA(NYJ)-'13	16/15*
35	Lefeged, Joe	S	6-0	205	6/2/88	3	Rutgers	Germantown, Md.	FA-'11	16/4
72	Linkenbach, Jeff	T	6-6	323	6/9/87	4	Cincinnati	Sandusky, Ohio	FA-'10	16/8
12	Luck, Andrew	QB	6-4	234	9/12/89	2	Stanford	Houston, Texas	D1-'12	16/16
56	Lutrus, Scott	ILB	6-3	247	4/23/88	2	Connecticut	Brookfield, Conn.	FA-'11	0*
91	Mathews, Ricardo	DT	6-3	300	7/30/87	4	Cincinnati	Jacksonville, Fla.	D7-'10	16/5
98	Mathis, Robert	OLB	6-2	245	2/26/81	11	Alabama A&M	Atlanta, Ga.	D5-'03	12/12
1	McAfee, Pat	P	6-1	220	5/2/87	5	West Virginia	Plum, Pa.	D7-'09	16/0
75	McGlynn, Mike	G/C	6-4	327	3/8/85	6	Pittsburgh	Austintown, Ohio	UFA(Cin)-'12	16/16
96	McKinney, Brandon	NT	6-2	345	8/24/83	8	Michigan State	Dayton, Ohio	UFA(Balt)-'12	0*
95	Moala, Fili	DE	6-4	310	6/23/85	5	Southern California	Buena Park, Calif.	D2-'09	8/8
94	Nevis, Drake	DT	6-1	310	5/8/89	3	Louisiana State	Harvey, La.	D3-'11	9/3
45	Overton, Matt	LS	6-0	254	7/6/85	2	Western Washington	Tracy, Calif.	FA-'12	16/0
10	Palmer, Nathan	WR	5-11	195	4/14/89	2	Northern Illinois	Elkhart, Ind.	FA-'12	5/0
90	Redding, Cory	DE	6-4	315	11/15/80	11	Texas	Houston, Texas	UFA(Balt)-'12	14/14
76	Reitz, Joe	G	6-7	322	8/24/85	3	Western Michigan	Fishers, Ind.	FA-'10	9/8
64	Satele, Samson	C	6-3	299	11/29/84	7	Hawaii	Kailua, Hawaii	UFA(Oak)-'12	11/11
85	Saunders, Weslye	TE	6-5	270	1/16/89	3	South Carolina	Durham, N.C.	FA-'12	11/4
59 t-	Sheppard, Kelvin	LB	6-2	244	1/2/88	3	Louisiana State	Stone Mountain, Ga.	T(Buff)-'13	16/15*
52	Sidbury, Lawrence	OLB	6-3	261	2/6/86	5	Richmond	Cheltenham, Md.	UFA(Atl)-'13	10/0*
60	Sowell, Bradley	T	6-7	320	6/6/89	2	Mississippi	Hernando, Miss.	FA-'12	10/0
58	Spears, Quinton	LB	6-4	234	5/11/88	2	Prairie View A&M	Huntsville, Texas	FA-'13	0*
68	Tevaseu, Martin	NT	6-2	325	10/7/87	3	Nevada-Las Vegas	Booneville, Calif.	W(NYJ)-'12	13/2
66	Thomas, Donald	G	6-4	305	9/25/85	6	Connecticut	West Haven, Conn.	UFA(NE)-'13	16/7*
28	Toler, Greg	CB	6-0	192	1/2/85	5	St. Paul's	Washington, D.C.	UFA(Ariz)-'13	11/2*
32	Vaughn, Cassius	CB	5-11	195	11/3/87	4	Mississippi	Memphis, Tenn.	T(Den)-'12	16/11
4	Vinatieri, Adam	K	6-0	206	12/28/72	18	South Dakota State	Rapid City, S.D.	UFA(NE)-'06	16/0
93	Walden, Erik	OLB	6-2	250	8/21/85	6	Middle Tennessee St.	Dublin, Ga.	UFA(GB)-'13	15/9*
87	Wayne, Reggie	WR	6-0	198	11/17/78	13	Miami	New Orleans, La.	D1-'01	16/15
17	Whalen, Griff	WR	5-11	185	3/1/90	2	Stanford	Sylvania, Ohio	FA-'12	0*
21	Williams, Teddy	CB	6-1	201	7/3/88	2	Texas-San Antonio	Tyler, Texas	FA-'12	7/0
63	Ziemba, Lee	T	6-6	320	3/29/89	3	Auburn	Rogers, Ark.	FA-'12	0*

* Anderson spent 10 games on the reserve/physically unable to perform list; Asante last active with Tampa Bay in '11; Chapman inactive for two games; Cherilus played 16 games with Detroit in '12; Franklin played 12 games with San Diego; Hasselbeck played 8 games with Tennessee; Havili played 15 games with Philadelphia; Heyward-Bey played 15 games with Oakland; Ijalana missed '12 season because of injury; Jean Francois played 16 games with San Francisco; Landry played 16 games with the New York Jets; Lutrus missed '12 season because of injury; McKinney missed '12 season because of injury; Sheppard played 16 games with Buffalo; Sidbury played 10 games with Atlanta; Spears last active with Cleveland in '11; Thomas played 16 games with New England; Toler played 11 games with Arizona; Walden played 15 games with Green Bay; Whalen missed '12 season because of injury; Ziemba missed '12 season because of injury with Carolina.

t- Colts traded for Havili (Phil), Sheppard (Buff).

Traded—DE Clifton Geathers (8 games in '12) to Philadelphia, LB Jerry Hughes (16 games) to Buffalo, C A.Q. Shipley (14 games) to Baltimore.

Players lost through free agency (5): WR Donnie Avery (KC; 16 games), ILB Moise Fokou (Tenn; 16), NT Antonio Johnson (Tenn; 14), CB Jerraud Powers (Ariz; 8), QB Drew Stanton (Ariz; 0).

Also played with Colts in '12—OLB Mario Addison (3 games), LB Jerry Brown (1), WR Austin Collie (1), DT Antonio Dixon (2), G Trai Essex (2), OLB Dwight Freeney (14), T Tony Hills (6), T Winston Justice (12), RB Deji Karim (3), CB Justin King (3), TE Kyle Miller (1), RB Mewelde Moore (9), G Seth Olsen (5), LB Jamaal Westerman (9), S Tom Zbikowski (11).

FIRST-YEAR ROSTER

Name	Pos.	Ht.	Wt.	Birthdate	College	Hometown	How Acq.
Boyett, John	S	5-10	204	12/20/89	Oregon	Napa, Calif.	D6
Chapman, Allen	CB	5-11	176	7/23/91	Kansas State	San Francisco, Calif.	FA
Cleary, Emmett	T	6-7	313	4/27/90	Boston College	Arlington Heights, Ill.	D7
Cunningham, Justice	TE	6-3	258	1/14/91	South Carolina	Pageland, S.C.	FA
Griffin, Robert (1)	T	6-6	330	11/22/89	Baylor	Euless, Texas	FA
Harnish, Chandler (1)	QB	6-2	220	7/28/88	Northern Illinois	Bluffton, Ind.	FA-'12
Holmes, Khaled	C/G	6-3	302	1/19/90	Southern California	Santa Ana, Calif.	D4
Hughes, Montori	DT	6-4	329	8/25/90	Tennessee-Martin	Murfreesboro, Tenn.	D5
Kelley, Jeremy	WR	6-6	225	6/9/88	Maine	West Seneca, N.Y.	FA
Killeen, Jake	OLB	6-4	240	2/15/86	Charleston Southern	Reno, Nev.	FA
McManus, Brandon	K/P	6-3	201	7/25/91	Temple	Hatfield, Pa.	FA
McNary, Josh	LB	6-0	251	4/10/88	Army	Houston, Texas	FA
Meggett, Davin (1)	RB	5-8	215	3/22/90	Maryland	Clinton, Md.	FA-'12
Moore, Dan	RB	5-11	235	2/1/90	Montana	Tucson, Ariz.	FA
O'Bryant, Denodus	RB	5-9	194	9/17/89	Lindenwood	Washington, Mo.	FA
Price, Sheldon	CB	6-2	180	3/26/91	UCLA	Chino Hills, Calif.	FA
Prime, C.O.	LB	6-1	255	10/29/89	Wagner	Laval, Quebec	FA
Rumble, Rodrick	WR	6-2	209	5/2/90	Idaho State	Oak Harbor, Wash.	FA
Sambrano, Jabin (1)	WR	5-11	175	3/12/90	Montana	Temecula, Calif.	FA
Sampson, Lanear	WR	5-11	205	7/17/90	Baylor	Mesquite, Texas	FA
Schmeig, Rick	C	6-3	305	4/6/90	Purdue	Cincinnati, Ohio	FA
Simmons, Monte (1)	LB	6-3	226	1/29/89	Kent State	Swissvale, Pa.	FA-'12
Swanson, Daxton	CB	5-11	185	3/21/91	Sam Houston State	Waco, Texas	FA
Thornton, Hugh	G	6-3	320	6/28/91	Illinois	Oberlin, Ohio	D3
Werner, Bjoern	OLB	6-3	266	8/30/90	Florida State	Berlin, Germany	D1
Williams, Kerwynn	RB	5-8	195	6/9/91	Utah State	Las Vegas, Nev.	D7

The term NFL Rookie is defined as a player who is in his first season of professional football and has not been on the roster of another professional football team for any regular-season or postseason games. A Rookie is designated by an "R" on NFL rosters. Players who have been active in another professional football league or players who have NFL experience, including either preseason training camp or being on an Active List or Inactive List, or on Reserve/Injured or Reserve/Physically Unable to Perform for fewer than six regular-season games, are termed NFL First-Year Players. An NFL First-Year Player is designated by a "1" on NFL rosters. Thereafter, a player is credited with an additional year of experience for each season in which he accumulates six games on the Active List or Inactive List, or on Reserve/Injured or Reserve/Physically Unable to Perform.

Log on to www.colts.com for an up-to-date roster.

COACHING STAFF
Head Coach,
Chuck Pagano
Pro Career: Chuck Pagano's 2012 season proved to be one of the most inspirational stories in NFL history. Named head coach of the Indianapolis Colts on January 25, 2012, Pagano was forced to take a leave of absence just three games into the season after being diagnosed with acute promyelocytic leukemia, a curable form of the disease, which is a cancer of the blood and bone marrow cells. Offensive Coordinator Bruce Arians assumed the role of the team's interim head coach and led the Colts to a 9-3 record in Pagano's absence. During that timeframe, Indianapolis secured a playoff berth and accomplished one of their primary goals—extending the season for Pagano. From his hospital bed, Pagano was in constant communication with the coaching staff and players. He analyzed practices, while continuing game-planning schemes. Pagano returned to the team for the regular season finale with a playoff berth already intact, and defeated Houston 28-16. In AFC Wild Card Game, the Colts fell to Pagano's former team and eventual Super Bowl XLVII champion Baltimore Ravens. Prior to joining the Colts, he spent four seasons with the Baltimore Ravens and the last (2011) as the team's defensive coordinator. Pagano also served as the defensive backs coach of the Oakland Raiders (2005-06) and the secondary coach of the Cleveland Browns (2001-04). Career record: 11-6.
Background: Pagano was a safety at Wyoming from 1980-83. No pro playing experience. Coached collegiately at Southern California (1984-85), Miami (1986), Boise State (1987-88), East Carolina (1989), Nevada-Las Vegas (1990-91), East Carolina (1992-94), Miami (1995-2000), North Carolina (2007).
Personal: Born in Boulder, Colo. on October 2, 1960. He and his wife, Tina, have three daughters: Tara, Taylor and Tori. His brother, John, is the defensive coordinator of the San Diego Chargers.

ASSISTANT COACHES
Roy Anderson, safeties; born October 5, 1979, Tallahassee, Fla. Quarterback Howard 1997-2001. No pro playing experience. Pro coach: Baltimore Ravens 2009-2011, joined Colts in 2012.
Tim Berbenich, offensive assistant; born December 19, 1979, Huntington, N.Y. Wide receiver Hamilton College 1999-2002. No pro playing experience. Pro coach: New York Jets 2002-2005, Tampa Bay Buccaneers 2006-2011, joined Colts in 2013.
Brant Boyer, asst. special teams; born June 27, 1971, Ogden, Utah. Linebacker Arizona 1992-94. Pro linebacker Miami Dolphins 1994, Jacksonville Jaguars 1995-2000, Cleveland Browns 2001-03. Pro coach: Joined Colts in 2012.
Clyde Christensen, quarterbacks; born January 28, 1956, Covina, Calif.

Quarterback Fresno City College 1975, North Carolina 1976-78. No pro playing experience. College coach: Mississippi 1979, East Tennessee State 1980-82, Temple 1983-85, East Carolina 1986-88, Holy Cross 1989-1990, South Carolina 1991, Maryland 1992-93, Clemson 1994-95. Pro coach: Tampa Bay Buccaneers 1996-2001, joined Colts in 2002.
Gary Emanuel, defensive line; born October 30, 1958, New London, Conn. Offensive lineman Westchester (N.Y.) C.C. 1976-78, Plymouth State 1979-1980. No pro playing experience. College coach: Plymouth State 1981-84, West Chester 1985-86, Massachusetts 1986-88, Dartmouth 1988-1990, Syracuse 1991-93, Washington State 1994-96, Purdue 1997-2004, San Jose State 2007, Rutgers 2008-09, Purdue 2010-11. Pro coach: San Francisco 49ers 2005-06, joined Colts in 2012.
Jeff FitzGerald, linebackers; born April 18, 1960, Burbank, Calif. Linebacker Oregon State 1980. No pro playing experience. College coach: Cincinnati 1985, Alabama 1986-89, San Diego State 1994-97. Pro coach: Tampa Bay Buccaneers 1990-93, Washington Redskins 1998-99, Arizona Cardinals 2000-03, Baltimore Ravens 2004-07, Cincinnati Bengals 2008-2011, joined Colts in 2012.
Joe Gilbert, offensive line; born January 22, 1965, Horseheads, N.Y. Offensive lineman Hamilton University 1984-87. No pro playing experience. College coach: Albany 1987-88, Pennsylvania 1989-1990, Northeastern 1991-93, Maine 1994-99, Mansfield 2000 (head coach), Toledo 2001-03, Central Florida 2004-06, Toledo 2007, Houston 2008, Illinois 2009-2011. Pro coach: Joined Colts in 2012.
Mike Gillhamer, secondary; born February 20, 1956, Oakland, Calif. Defensive back Carroll College 1972, Wenatchee (Wash.) J.C. 1973, Humboldt State 1974-75. No pro playing experience. College coach: College of the Sequoias 1979-1983, Weber State 1984, Utah 1985-1989, San Jose State 1990-93, Nevada 1994-95, Oregon 2001-02, Louisville 2003, Illinois 2011. Pro coach: New York Giants 1997-2000, Carolina Panthers 2004-2010, joined Colts in 2012.
Frank Giufre, offensive quality control; born April 5, 1977, Canastota, N.Y. Offensive lineman Syracuse 1995-99. No pro playing experience. College coach: Miami 2001-03, Sacred Heart 2004-06, Maine 2007-2011. Pro coach: Joined Colts in 2012.
Pep Hamilton, offensive coordinator; born September 19, 1974, Charlotte, N.C. Quarterback Howard 1993-1996. No pro playing experience. College coach: Howard 1997-2001, Stanford 2010-2012. Pro coach: Kansas City Chiefs 2000, Washington Redskins 2001, Baltimore Ravens 2002, New York Jets 2003-2005, San Francisco 49ers 2006, Chicago Bears 2007-2009, joined Colts in 2013.
Richard Howell, asst. strength & condition

ing; born February 19, 1972, Bladenboro, N.C. Quarterback Davidson 1990-93. No pro playing experience. College coach: Davidson 1994-98, North Carolina 1998-99. Pro coach: Barcelona Dragons (NFLE) 1999, joined Colts in 2000.
Hal Hunter, asst. offensive line; born July 8, 1959, Canonsburg, Pa. Linebacker Northwestern 1978. No pro playing experience. College coach: William & Mary 1982, Pittsburgh 1983-1984, Columbia 1985, Indiana (Pa.) 1986, Akron 1987-1990, Vanderbilt 1991-1994, Louisiana State 1995-1999, Indiana 2000-2001, North Carolina 2002-05. Pro coach: San Diego Chargers 2006-2012, joined Colts in 2013.
Greg Manusky, defensive coordinator; born August 12, 1966, Wilkes-Barre, Pa. Linebacker Colgate 1983-87. Pro linebacker Washington Redskins 1988-1990, Minnesota Vikings 1991-93, Kansas City Chiefs 1994-99. Pro coach: Washington Redskins 2001, San Diego Chargers 2002-06, San Francisco 49ers 2007-2010, San Diego Chargers 2011, joined Colts in 2012.
Roger Marandino, strength & conditioning; born February 19, 1971, Elmer, N.J. No college or pro playing experience. College coach: Connecticut 1993-95, Brown 1995-2011. Pro coach: Philadelphia Eagles 2011, joined Colts in 2012.
Tom McMahon, special teams coordinator; Helena, Mont. Carroll College 1988-1991. No pro playing experience. College coach: Carroll College 1992, 1994, Utah State 1995-2005, Louisville 2006. Pro coach: Atlanta Falcons 2007-2008, St. Louis Rams 2009-2011, Kansas City Chiefs 2012, joined Colts in 2013.
Alfredo Roberts, tight ends; born March 17, 1965, Fort Lauderdale, Fla. Tight end Miami 1983-87. Pro tight end Kansas City Chiefs 1988-1990, Dallas Cowboys 1991-93. College coach: Florida Atlantic 1999-2002. Pro coach: Jacksonville Jaguars 2003-06, Cleveland Browns 2007-08, Tampa Bay Buccaneers 2009-2011, joined Colts in 2012.
David Walker, running backs; born December 4, 1969, Rochester, N.Y. Running back Syracuse 1989-1992. No pro playing experience. College coach: Syracuse 1995-2004, Pittsburgh 2005-2010. Pro coach: Joined Colts in 2011.
Brad White, defensive quality control; born August 13, 1982, Concord, Mass. Linebacker Georgia 2000, Wake Forest 2002-04. No pro playing experience. College coach: Wake Forest 2007-08, Murray State 2009, Air Force 2010-11. Pro coach: Joined Colts in 2012.
Charlie Williams, wide receivers; born January 31, 1958, Torrance, Calif. Defensive back Colorado State 1978-79. No pro playing experience. College coach: Long Beach City College 1984, New Mexico 1986-87, Texas Christian 1988-1991, Minnesota 1992, Miami 1993-95, South Carolina 2003, Arizona 2004-06, North Carolina 2007-2011. Pro coach: Tampa Bay Buccaneers 1996-2001, joined Colts in 2012.

American Football Conference
South Division
Team Colors: Teal, Black, and Gold
EverBank Field
One EverBank Field Drive
Jacksonville, Florida 32202
Telephone: (904) 633-6000

2013 SCHEDULE
PRESEASON
Aug. 9	**Miami**	7:30
Aug. 17	at New York Jets	7:30
Aug. 24	**Philadelphia**	7:30
Aug. 29	at Atlanta	7:30

REGULAR SEASON
Sep. 8	**Kansas City**	1:00
Sep. 15	at Oakland	4:25
Sep. 22	at Seattle	4:25
Sep. 29	**Indianapolis**	1:00
Oct. 6	at St. Louis	1:00
Oct. 13	at Denver	4:05
Oct. 20	**San Diego**	1:00
Oct. 27	**San Francisco** (London)	1:00
Nov. 3	BYE	
Nov. 10	at Tennessee	1:00
Nov. 17	**Arizona**	1:00
Nov. 24	at Houston	1:00
Dec. 1	at Cleveland	1:00
Dec. 5	**Houston** (Thurs)	8:25
Dec. 15	**Buffalo**	1:00
Dec. 22	**Tennessee**	1:00
Dec. 29	at Indianapolis	1:00

All times ET
Stadium: EverBank Field
(opened in 1995)
• **Capacity:** 67,246
One EverBank Field Drive
Jacksonville, Florida 32202
Playing Surface: Grass
Training Camp: EverBank Field
One EverBank Field Drive
Jacksonville, Florida 32202

EVERBANK FIELD

CLUB OFFICIALS
Owner: Shahid Khan
President: Mark Lamping
General Manager: David Caldwell
Senior Vice President, Communications:
Dan Edwards
Senior Vice President, Fan Engagement:
Hussain Naqi
Senior Vice President, Corporate
Partnerships: Scott Massey
Senior Vice President, Ticket Sales:
Chad Johnson
Vice President and General Counsel:
Megha Parekh
Vice President, Finance and Planning;
Kelly Flanagan
President, Jaguars Foundation:
Peter Racine

Assistant Director, Player Personnel:
Andy Dengler
Director, College Scouting: Kyle O'Brien
Assistant Director, College Scouting:
Paul Roell
Eastern Regional Scout: Mark Ellenz
College Scouts: Jason DesJarlais,
Jarrod Highberger, Marty Miller,
Tim Mingey, Brian Simmons
BLESTO Scout: Jared Kirksey
Director of Pro Personnel: Chris Polian
Pro Scout: Chris Driggers
Executive Assistant, Player Personnel:
Dana DesJarlais

Senior Vice President, Football
Technology & Analytics: Tony Khan
Director, Football Research: Daniel Adler
Director, Team Security: Skip Richardson
Director, Football Administration:
Tim Walsh
Director, Player Development:
Marcus Pollard
Head Athletic Trainer: Michael Ryan
Director, Football Technology:
Mike Perkins
Equipment Manager: Jimmy Luck

Director, Public Relations: Ryan Robinson
Communications Coordinator:
Tad Dickman
Community Relations Coordinator:
Renzo Sheppard
Executive Assistant to SVP,
Communications: Katie Vaughn

COACHING HISTORY
(145-154-0)
Records include postseason games
1995-2002	Tom Coughlin	72-64-0
2003-2011	Jack Del Rio*	69-73-0
2011	Mel Tucker	2-3-0
2012	Mike Mularkey	2-14-0

*Released after 11 games in 2011

PAID ATTENDANCE
Home 443,498   Away 477,813
Total 921,311
Single-game home record,
74,143 (12/28/98)
Single-season home record,
561,472 (1998)

2013 DRAFT CHOICES
Round	Name	Pos.	College
1	Luke Joeckel	T	Texas A&M
2	Johnathan Cyprien	DB	Florida International
3	Dwayne Gratz	DB	Connecticut
4	Ace Sanders	WR	South Carolina
5	Denard Robinson	RB	Michigan
6	Josh Evans	DB	Florida
7	Jeremy Harris	DB	New Mexico St.
	Demetrius McCray	DB	Appalachian St.

2012 TEAM RECORD
PRESEASON (3-1)

Date	Result	Opponent
08/10	W 32-31	New York Giants
08/17	W 27-24	at New Orleans
08/23	L 17-48	at Baltimore
08/30	W 24-14	Atlanta

REGULAR SEASON (2-14)

Date	Result	Opponent
09/09	L 23-26	at Minnesota (OT)
09/16	L 7-27	Houston
09/23	W 22-17	at Indianapolis
09/30	L 10-27	Cincinnati
10/07	L 3-41	Chicago
10/21	L 23-26	at Oakland (OT)
10/28	L 15-24	at Green Bay
11/04	L 14-31	Detroit
11/08	L 10-27	Indianapolis
11/18	L 37-43	at Houston (OT)
11/25	W 24-19	Tennessee
12/02	L 18-34	at Buffalo
12/09	L 10-17	New York Jets
12/16	L 3-24	at Miami
12/23	L 16-23	New England
12/30	L 20-38	at Tennessee

(OT) Overtime

SCORE BY PERIODS

Jaguars	50	71	43	88	3 —	255
Opponents	66	134	87	142	15 —	444

2012 TEAM STATISTICS

	Jaguars	Opp.
Total First Downs	269	364
Rushing	76	133
Passing	157	194
Penalty	36	37
3rd Down: Made/Att	64/216	89/215
3rd Down Pct.	29.6	41.4
4th Down: Made/Att	8/26	4/9
4th Down Pct.	30.8	44.4
Possession Avg.	27:29	32:31
Total Net Yards	4788	6088
Avg. Per Game	299.3	380.5
Total Plays	994	1100
Avg. Per Play	4.8	5.5
Net Yards Rushing	1369	2256
Avg. Per Game	85.6	141.0
Total Rushes	358	545
Net Yards Passing	3419	3832
Avg. Per Game	213.7	239.5
Sacked/Yards Lost	50/327	20/128
Gross Yards	3746	3960
Att./Completions	586/328	535/341
Completion Pct.	56.0	63.7
Had Intercepted	17	12
Punts/Average	92/47.3	68/46.0
Net Punting Avg.	92/40.8	68/40.3
Penalties/Yards	101/955	101/820
Fumbles/Ball Lost	20/9	17/11
Touchdowns	26	48
Rushing	5	19
Passing	20	21
Returns	1	8

2012 INDIVIDUAL STATISTICS

PASSING

	Att.	Comp.	Yds.	Pct.	TD	Int.	Tkld.	Rate
Henne	308	166	2084	53.9	11	11	28/169	72.2
Gabbert	278	162	1662	58.3	9	6	22/158	77.4
Jaguars	586	328	3746	56.0	20	17	50/327	74.7
Opponents	535	341	3960	63.7	21	12	20/128	89.8

SCORING

	TD R	TD P	TD Rt	PAT	FG	Saf	PTS
Scobee	0	0	0	18/19	25/28	0	93
Shorts	0	7	0	0/0	0/0	0	42
Blackmon	0	5	0	0/0	0/0	0	32
Lewis	0	4	0	0/0	0/0	0	24
Jennings	2	0	0	0/0	0/0	0	14
Jones-Drew	1	1	0	0/0	0/0	0	12
Owens	1	0	0	0/0	0/0	0	8
M. Harris	0	0	1	0/0	0/0	0	6
Henne	1	0	0	0/0	0/0	0	6
Shipley	0	1	0	0/0	0/0	0	6
Spurlock	0	1	0	0/0	0/0	0	6
Whimper	0	1	0	0/0	0/0	0	6
Jaguars	5	20	1	18/19	25/28	0	255
Opponents	19	21	8	46/46	36/43	0	444

2-Pt Conversions: Blackmon, Jennings,
Jaguars 3-7, Opponents 1-1

RUSHING

	No.	Yds	Avg	LG	TD
Jones-Drew	86	414	4.8	59t	1
Jennings	101	283	2.8	21	2
Owens	42	209	5.0	32t	1
Parmele	40	143	3.6	28	0
Murphy	23	92	4.0	14	0
Toston	17	74	4.4	14	0
Henne	19	64	3.4	15	1
Gabbert	18	56	3.1	10	0
Blackmon	2	23	11.5	12	0
Greg B. Jones	5	8	1.6	4	0
Todman	3	8	2.7	6	0
Thomas	1	-1	-1.0	-1	0
Shorts	1	-4	-4.0	-4	0
Jaguars	358	1369	3.8	59t	5
Opponents	545	2256	4.1	53	19

RECEIVING

	No.	Yds	Avg	LG	TD
Blackmon	64	865	13.5	81t	5
Shorts	55	979	17.8	80t	7
Lewis	52	540	10.4	26	4
Robinson	24	252	10.5	32	0
Shipley	23	244	10.6	36	1
Jennings	19	130	6.8	26	0
Spurlock	14	121	8.6	22	1
Jones-Drew	14	86	6.1	13	1
Thomas	13	80	6.2	12	0
Greg B. Jones	11	64	5.8	10	0
Elliott	10	108	10.8	22	0
Owens	8	113	14.1	53	0
Parmele	7	60	8.6	26	0
Clemons	3	41	13.7	17	0
Toston	3	41	13.7	21	0
Whimper	2	11	5.5	10	1
Potter	2	6	3.0	4	0
Stanback	1	6	6.0	6	0
Ta'ufo'ou	1	5	5.0	5	0
Todman	1	0	0.0	0	0
Henne	1	-6	-6.0	-6	0
Jaguars	328	3746	11.4	81t	20
Opponents	341	3960	11.6	59	21

PUNTING

	No.	Yds.	Avg.	In 20	LG
Anger	91	4353	47.8	31	73
Jaguars	92	4353	47.3	31	73
Opponents	68	3131	46	20	65

INTERCEPTIONS

	No.	Yds	Avg	LG	TD
Cox	4	18	4.5	16	0
Posluszny	3	20	6.7	13	0
Landry	1	47	47.0	21	0
Lowery	1	21	21.0	21	0
Bosworth	1	10	10.0	10	0
Prosinski	1	6	6.0	4	0
M. Harris	1	0	0.0	0	0
Jaguars	12	122	10.2	23	0
Opponents	17	400	23.5	79t	5

PUNT RETURNS

	Ret	FC	Yds	Avg	LG	TD
Shipley	10	1	75	7.5	15	0
Thomas	8	1	56	7.0	18	0
Spurlock	6	4	51	8.5	28	0
Cosby	5	4	46	9.2	15	0
Ross	3	3	16	5.3	6	0
Jones-Drew	2	0	4	2.0	4	0
Jaguars	34	13	248	7.3	28	0
Opponents	40	29	495	12.4	81t	2

KICKOFF RETURNS

	No.	Yds	Avg	LG	TD
Jennings	10	241	24.1	29	0
Parmele	10	233	23.3	38	0
Spurlock	6	118	19.7	24	0
Shipley	6	117	19.5	24	0
Murphy	5	118	23.6	32	0
Cosby	5	99	19.8	32	0
Todman	4	78	19.5	24	0
Toston	3	65	21.7	25	0
Thomas	2	34	17.0	20	0
Potter	1	11	11.0	11	0
Selvie	1	0	0.0	0	0
Jaguars	53	1114	21.0	38	0
Opponents	39	1009	25.9	55	0

FIELD GOALS

	1-19	20-29	30-39	40-49	50+
Scobee	1/1	4/4	8/8	11/13	1/2
Jaguars	1/1	4/4	8/8	11/13	1/2
Opponents	0/0	7/7	17/19	9/12	3/5

SACKS

	No.
Alualu	3.5
Mincey	3.0
Mosley	2.5
Knighton	2.0
Lane	2.0
Posluszny	2.0
Babin	1.5
Branch	1.0
M. Harris	1.0
Selvie	1.0
Allen	0.5
Jaguars	20.0
Opponents	50.0

RECORD HOLDERS
INDIVIDUAL RECORDS—CAREER

Category	Name	Performance
Rushing (Yds.)	Fred Taylor, 1998-2008	11,271
Passing (Yds.)	Mark Brunell, 1995-2003	25,698
Passing (TDs)	Mark Brunell, 1995-2003	144
Receiving (No.)	Jimmy Smith, 1995-2005	862
Receiving (Yds.)	Jimmy Smith, 1995-2005	12,287
Interceptions	Rashean Mathis, 2003-2012	30
Punting (Avg.)	Bryan Anger, 2012	47.8
Punt Return (Avg.)	Bobby Shaw, 2002	12.4
Kickoff Return (Avg.)	Maurice Jones-Drew, 2006-2012	26.0
Field Goals	Mike Hollis, 1995-2001	175
Touchdowns (Tot.)	Maurice Jones-Drew, 2006-2012	76
Points	Mike Hollis, 1995-2001	764
*Sacks	Tony Brackens, 1996-2003	55.0

INDIVIDUAL RECORDS—SINGLE SEASON

Category	Name	Performance
Rushing (Yds.)	Maurice Jones-Drew, 2011	1,606
Passing (Yds.)	Mark Brunell, 1996	4,367
Passing (TDs)	David Garrard, 2010	23
Receiving (No.)	Jimmy Smith, 1999	116
Receiving (Yds.)	Jimmy Smith, 1999	1,636
Interceptions	Rashean Mathis, 2006	8
Punting (Avg.)	Bryan Anger, 2012	47.8
Punt Return (Avg.)	Reggie Barlow, 1998	12.9
Kickoff Return (Avg.)	Maurice Jones-Drew, 2006	27.7
Field Goals	Mike Hollis, 1997, 1999	31
Touchdowns (Tot.)	Fred Taylor, 1998	17
Points	Mike Hollis, 1997	134
*Sacks	Tony Brackens, 1999	12.0

INDIVIDUAL RECORDS—SINGLE GAME

Category	Name	Performance
Rushing (Yds.)	Fred Taylor, 11-19-00	234
Passing (Yds.)	Mark Brunell, 9-22-96	432
Passing (TDs)	Mark Brunell, 11-29-98	4
	Quinn Gray, 12-30-07	4
	David Garrard, 10-31-10	4
	Chad Henne, 11-18-12	4
Receiving (No.)	Keenan McCardell, 10-20-96	16
Receiving (Yds.)	Jimmy Smith, 9-10-00	291
Interceptions	Many times	2
	Last time by Derek Cox, 10-31-10	
Field Goals	Mike Hollis, 12-1-96, 11-30-97, 9-10-00	5
	Josh Scobee, 11-25-07, 10-10-10	5
Touchdowns (Tot.)	James Stewart, 10-12-97	5
Points	James Stewart, 10-12-97	30
*Sacks	Kelvin Pritchett, 10-5-97	3.0
	John Henderson, 10-6-02	3.0
	Paul Spicer, 9-25-05	3.0

*Sacks became an official statistic in 1982.

2013 VETERAN ROSTER

No.	Name	Pos.	Ht.	Wt.	Birthdate	NFL Exp.	College	Hometown	How Acq.	'12 Games/ Starts
50	Allen, Russell	LB	6-3	238	5/5/86	5	San Diego State	Oceanside, Calif.	FA-'09	16/16
93	Alualu, Tyson	DT	6-3	295	5/12/87	4	California	Honolulu, Hawaii	D1-'10	16/16
19	Anger, Bryan	P	6-3	202	10/6/88	2	California	Camarillo, Calif.	D3-'12	16/0
72	Asper, Mark	OL	6-7	325	11/8/85	2	Oregon	Rexburg, Idaho	W(Minn)-'12	1/0
58	Babin, Jason	DE	6-3	267	5/24/80	10	Western Michigan	Paw Paw, Mich.	W(Phil)-'12	16/16*
23	Ball, Alan	CB	6-2	197	3/29/85	6	Illinois	Detroit, Mich.	UFA(Hou)-'13	11/0*
14	Blackmon, Justin	WR	6-1	210	1/9/90	2	Oklahoma State	Ardmore, Okla.	D1-'12	16/15
38	Blake, Antwon	DB	5-9	198	8/8/90	2	Texas-El Paso	Houston, Texas	FA-'12	16/0
47	Brackett, Brett	TE	6-5	246	12/13/87	2	Penn State	Lawrence, N.J.	W(Phil)-'12	0*
78	Bradfield, Cameron	OL	6-4	308	9/14/87	3	Grand Valley State	Grand Rapids, Mich.	FA-'11	14/12
90	Branch, Andre	DE	6-5	265	7/14/89	2	Clemson	Richmond, Va.	D2-'12	13/3
60	Brewster, Mike	G/C	6-4	305	7/27/89	2	Ohio State	Orlando, Fla.	FA-'12	12/7
48	Cain, Jeremy	LS	6-1	245	3/24/80	7	Massachusetts	Fort Lauderdale, Fla.	W(Wash)-'09	16/0
68	Deaderick, Brandon	DE	6-4	305	8/19/87	4	Alabama	Elizabethtown, Ky.	W(NE)-'13	14/5*
96	Egboh, Pannel	DE	6-6	277	3/23/86	2	Stanford	Mesquite, Texas	FA-'12	12/0*
21	Forsett, Justin	RB	5-8	194	10/14/85	6	California	Lakeland, Fla.	UFA(Hou)-'13	16/0*
11	Gabbert, Blaine	QB	6-4	235	10/15/89	3	Missouri	Ballwin, Mo.	D1-'11	10/10
43	Grimes, Jonathan	RB	5-10	209	12/21/89	2	William & Mary	Fairfax, Va.	W(Hou)-'12	9/0*
20	Harris, Mike	CB	5-10	188	1/5/89	2	Florida State	Miami, Fla.	D6-'12	15/5
55	Hayes, Geno	LB	6-1	226	8/10/87	6	Florida State	Greenville, Fla.	UFA(Chi)-'13	15/3*
7	Henne, Chad	QB	6-3	230	7/2/85	6	Michigan	Wyomissing, Pa.	UFA(Mia)-'12	10/6
32	Jones-Drew, Maurice	RB	5-7	210	3/23/85	8	UCLA	Antioch, Calif.	D2-'06	6/5
92	Lane, Austen	DE	6-6	265	11/9/87	4	Murray State	Iola, Wis.	D5b-'10	11/7
89	Lewis, Marcedes	TE	6-6	272	5/19/84	8	UCLA	Long Beach, Calif.	D1-'06	16/15
25	Lowery, Dwight	DB	5-11	212	1/23/86	6	San Jose State	Santa Cruz, Calif.	T(NYJ)-'11	9/9
99	Marks, Sen'Derrick	DT	6-2	294	2/23/87	5	Auburn	Mobile, Ala.	UFA(Tenn)-'13	14/14*
53	Marshall, Brandon	LB	6-1	238	9/10/89	2	Nevada	North Las Vegas, Nev.	D5-'12	5/0
13	Massaquoi, Mohamed	WR	6-2	207	11/24/86	5	Georgia	Charlotte, N.C.	UFA(Cle)-'13	9/5*
63	Meester, Brad	C	6-3	292	3/23/77	14	Northern Iowa	Parkersburg, Iowa	D2-'00	16/16
97	Miller, Roy	DT	6-2	310	7/9/87	5	Texas	Killeen, Texas	UFA(TB)-'13	15/14*
94	Mincey, Jeremy	DL	6-4	265	12/14/83	6	Florida	Statesboro, Ga.	FA-'10	16/16
75	Monroe, Eugene	T	6-5	306	4/18/87	5	Virginia	Plainfield, N.J.	D1-'09	16/16
64	Nowak, Drew	G	6-3	300	3/7/90	2	Western Michigan	Green Bay, Wisc.	FA-'12	0*
77	Nwaneri, Uche	G	6-3	310	3/20/84	7	Purdue	Garland, Texas	D5a-'07	15/15
24	Owens, Montell	RB	5-10	225	5/4/84	8	Maine	Wilmington, Del.	FA-'06	13/4
98	Pendleton, Jeris	DT	6-2	315	11/7/83	2	Ashland	Chicago, Ill.	D7-'12	4/0
51	Posluszny, Paul	LB	6-2	242	10/10/84	7	Penn State	Aliquippa, Pa.	UFA(Buff)-'11	16/16
15	Price, Taylor	WR	6-1	195	10/8/87	4	Ohio	Hilliard, Ohio	W(NE)-'11	0*
42	Prosinski, Chris	S	6-1	208	4/28/87	3	Wyoming	Buffalo, Wyo.	D4b-'11	16/7
65	Rackley, Will	G/C	6-3	310	10/11/89	3	Lehigh	Riverdale, Ga.	D3-'11	0*
87	Reisner, Allen	TE	6-3	225	9/29/88	2	Iowa	Marion, Iowa	W(Minn)-'12	0*
22	Rutland, Kevin	CB	6-0	193	4/2/88	3	Missouri	Houston, Texas	FA-'12	13/1
10	Scobee, Josh	K	6-1	210	6/23/82	10	Louisiana Tech	Longview, Texas	D5a-'04	16/0
16	Shipley, Jordan	WR	6-0	188	12/23/85	4	Texas	Burnet, Texas	FA-'12	6/2
84	Shorts III, Cecil	WR	6-0	202	12/22/87	3	Mount Union	Cleveland, Ohio	D4a-'11	14/9
95	Smith, D'Anthony	DT	6-2	300	6/9/88	4	Louisiana Tech	Pickering, La.	D3-'10	8/0
66	Spitz, Jason	G/C	6-3	298	12/19/82	8	Louisville	Jacksonville, Fla.	UFA(GB)-'11	0*
86	Stanback, Isaiah	TE	6-2	228	8/16/84	4	Washington	Seattle, Wash.	FA-'12	2/0
57	Stanford, Julian	LB	6-1	230	9/2/90	2	Wagner	Bloomfield, Conn.	FA-'12	16/6
45	Ta'ufo'ou, Will	FB	5-11	247	6/19/86	2	California	San Carlos, Calif.	FA-'12	6/1
36	Trufant, Marcus	CB	5-11	187	12/25/80	11	Washington State	Tacoma, Wash.	UFA(Sea)-'13	12/2*
85	Veldman, Matt	TE	6-7	255	8/12/88	2	North Dakota State	Becker, Minn.	FA-'12	0*

* Babin played 11 games with Houston, five games with Jacksonville in '12; Ball played 11 games with Houston; Brackett missed '12 season because of injury; Deaderick played 14 games with New England; Egboh played 12 games with Tennessee; Forsett played 16 games with Houston; Grimes three games with the New York Jets, six games with Houston, and did not play for one game with Jacksonville; Hayes played 15 games with Chicago; Marks played 14 games with Tennessee; Massaquoi played nine games with Cleveland; Miller played 15 games with Tampa Bay; Nowak missed '12 season because of injury; Price missed '12 season because of injury; Rackley missed '12 season because of injury; Reisner inactive one game; Spitz missed '12 season because of injury; Trufant played 12 games with Seattle; Veldman missed '12 season because of injury.

Traded—WR Mike Thomas (7 games in '12) to Detroit.

Players lost through free agency (5): OL Eben Britton (Chi; 11 games in '12), CB Derek Cox (SD; 12), RB Rashad Jennings (Oak; 10), FB Greg Jones (Hou; 12), DT Terrance Knighton (Den; 16).

Also played with Jaguars in '12—OL Daniel Baldridge (1 game), FB Brock Bolen (IR), LB Kyle Bosworth (16), DE John Chick (8), TE Colin Cloherty (1), WR Quan Cosby (2), WR Kevin Elliott (13), S Chris Harris (5), LB Greg Jones (6), S Dawan Landry (16), CB Rashean Mathis (12), CB William Middleton (10), DE Aaron Morgan (4), DT C.J. Mosley (16), CB Antwaun Molden (3), RB Richards Murphy (5), RB Jalen Parmele (11), TE Zach Potter (16), WR Laurent Robinson (7), CB Aaron Ross (14), DE George Selvie (9), LB Daryl Smith (2), TE Stephen Spach (1), WR/KR Micheal Spurlock (6), TE Maurice Stovall (10), OL Herb Taylor (2), RB Keith Toston (4), C/G Steve Vallos (2), T Guy Whimper (16).

FIRST-YEAR ROSTER

Name	Pos.	Ht.	Wt.	Birthdate	College	Hometown	How Acq.
Banjo, Chris	S	5-10	204	2/26/90	Southern Methodist	Sugar Land, Texas	FA
Barnes, T.J.	DT	6-7	364	6/14/90	Georgia Tech	Enterprise, Ala.	FA
Bomar, Maalik	LB	6-0	232	8/1/90	Cincinnati	Cincinnati, Ohio	FA
Brown, Mike (1)	WR	5-10	200	2/9/89	Liberty	Charlottesville, Va.	FA-'12
Burley, Marcus	CB	5-10	185	7/16/90	Delaware	Richmond, Va.	FA
Clemons, Toney (1)	WR	6-2	210	10/11/88	Colorado	New Kensington, Pa.	PS(Pitt)-'12
Cyprien, Johnathan	S	6-0	217	1/1/90	Florida International	N. Miami Beach, Fla.	D2
Davis, Ryan (1)	DE	6-2	260	2/24/89	Bethune-Cookman	Tampa, Fla.	FA-'12
Dill, R.J.	OT	6-6	316	7/26/90	Rutgers	Mechanicsburg, Penn.	FA
Eskridge, De'Leon	RB	5-11	215	12/19/89	San Jose State	San Francisco, Calif.	FA
Evans, Josh	S	6-0	205	6/5/91	Florida	Irvington, N.J.	D6
Gerberry, Dan (1)	C	6-3	302	11/10/85	Ball State	Youngstown, Ohio	FA
Gratz, Dwayne	CB	5-11	201	3/8/90	Connecticut	Piscataway, N.J.	D3
Green, Jeremiah	LB	6-1	245	5/8/90	Nevada	Tulare, Calif.	FA
Griggs, J.D.	DE	6-5	244	11/5/90	Akron	Piscataway, N.J.	FA
Harris, Jeremy	CB	6-2	185	4/26/91	New Mexico State	Dorsey, Calif.	D7a
Hazel, Paul	DE	6-5	227	5/4/90	Western Michigan	Miami, Fla.	FA
Joeckel, Luke	OT	6-6	306	11/6/91	Texas A&M	Arlington, Texas	D1
Jones, Abry	DT	6-4	312	9/8/91	Georgia	Warner Robins, Ga.	FA
McCray, Demetrius	CB	6-0	185	5/11/91	Appalachian State	Covington, Ga.	D7b
Miles, Jamal	WR	5-9	188	2/28/91	Arizona State	Peoria, Arizona	FA
Milhim, Stephane	G	6-4	300	11/20/90	Massachusetts	Pembroke Pines, Fla.	FA
Otten, Ryan	TE	6-6	241	4/7/90	San Jose State	Loomis, Calif.	FA
Palmer, Tobais	WR	5-11	178	2/20/90	North Carolina State	Pittsboro, N.C.	FA
Pasztor, Austin (1)	G	6-7	308	11/26/90	Virginia	Tillsonburg, Ontario	FA-'12
Pryor, Lonnie	FB	6-0	224	2/22/90	Florida State	Okeechobee, Fla.	FA
Reed, Kyler	TE	6-3	225	4/14/90	Nebraska	Shawnee, Kan.	FA
Reynolds, LaRoy	LB	6-1	243	11/3/90	Virginia	Norfolk, Va.	FA
Robinson, Denard	RB	6-0	197	9/22/90	Michigan	Deerfield Beach, Fla.	D5
Rodgers, Jordan	QB	6-1	212	8/30/88	Vanderbilt	Chico, Calif.	FA
Sanders, Ace	WR/PR	5-7	178	11/11/91	South Carolina	Bradenton, Fla.	D4
Scott, Matt	QB	6-3	212	11/9/90	Arizona	Corona, Calif.	FA
Terrell, Steven	S	5-10	197	9/21/90	Texas A&M	Allen, Texas	FA
Tinker, Carson	LS	6-0	233	11/15/89	Alabama	Murfreesboro, Tenn.	FA
Todman, Jordan (1)	RB	5-10	198	2/24/90	Connecticut	North Dartmouth, Mass.	PS(Minn)-'12
Tomlin, Roderick	OT	6-5	312	12/10/90	Murray State	Jackson, Tenn.	FA
Wilson, Trey	CB	6-0	193	11/11/90	Vanderbilt	Shreveport, La.	FA
Zimmer, Michael	LB	6-1	235	9/23/90	Illinois State	Wheeling, Ill.	FA

The term NFL Rookie is defined as a player who is in his first season of professional football and has not been on the roster of another professional football team for any regular-season or postseason games. A Rookie is designated by an "R" on NFL rosters. Players who have been active in another professional football league or players who have NFL experience, including either preseason training camp or being on an Active List or Inactive List, or on Reserve/Injured or Reserve/Physically Unable to Perform for fewer than six regular-season games, are termed NFL First-Year Players. An NFL First-Year Player is designated by a "1" on NFL rosters. Thereafter, a player is credited with an additional year of experience for each season in which he accumulates six games on the Active List or Inactive List, or on Reserve/Injured or Reserve/Physically Unable to Perform.

Log on to www.jaguars.com for an up-to-date roster.

COACHING STAFF
Head Coach,
Gus Bradley

Pro Career: Gus Bradley was named the fifth head coach in Jacksonville Jaguars history on January 17, 2013. Bradley spent the last four seasons (2009-12) with the Seattle Seahawks as defensive coordinator and played an important role in the club advancing to the postseason twice. Under Bradley's direction in 2012, the Seahawks led the NFL by allowing a franchise-record low 15.3 points per game despite playing with the third-youngest defensive starting unit in the league. He joined Seattle after spending three years (2006-08) with the Tampa Bay Buccaneers, serving the last two as linebackers coach after one season as their defensive quality control coach. Prior to Tampa Bay, Bradley spent 10 seasons (1996-2005) as an assistant coach at North Dakota State. He was the head coach at Fort Lewis College for four months (December 1995-March 1996) and was defensive coordinator/linebackers coach at Fort Lewis for four seasons (1992-1995). Prior to Fort Lewis, he was a graduate assistant coach at NDSU for two seasons (1990-1991). Career record: 0-0.

Background: Four-year letterman at North Dakota State (1984-1988), where he was a free safety and punter, a four-time academic All-North Central Conference selection and a member of the 1988 national championship football team. He earned his bachelor's degrees in business administration (1989) and physical education (1990) from North Dakota State as well as a master's degree in athletic administration in 1992.

Personal: Born July 5, 1966 in Zumbrota, Minnesota. He and his wife, Michaela, have four children, Carter, Anna, Eli and Ella.

ASSISTANT COACHES

Bob Babich, defensive coordinator; born February 20, 1961, Aliquippa, Pa. Linebacker Mesa (Colo.) C.C. 1979-1980, Tulsa 1981-82. No pro playing experience. College coach: Tulsa 1984-87, 1990, Wisconsin 1988-89, Bowling Green 1991, East Carolina 1992-93, Pittsburgh 1994-96, North Dakota State 1997-2002 (head coach). Pro coach: St. Louis Rams 2003, Chicago Bears 2004-2012, joined Jaguars in 2013.

Brandon Blaney, defensive assistant; born November 3, 1975, Joplin, Mo. Attended Youngstown State. No college or pro playing experience. College coach: Youngstown State 1995-98, Oklahoma 1999-2000, Ohio State 2001, Kansas 2002-09. Pro coach: Joined Jaguars in 2011.

Luke Butkus, asst. offensive line coach; born June 26, 1979, Steger, Ill. Center Illinois 1998-2001. Pro center Chicago Bears 2002, San Diego Chargers 2002, Rhein Fire (NFL Europe) 2003, Cologne Centurions (NFL Europe) 2004. College coach: Oregon 2005-06, Illinois 2012. Pro coach: Chicago Bears 2007-09, Seattle Seahawks 2010-11, joined Jaguars in 2013.

Mark Duffner, linebackers; born July 19, 1953, Annandale, Va. Defensive lineman William & Mary 1972-74. No pro playing experience. College coach: Ohio State 1975-76, Cincinnati 1977-1980, Holy Cross 1981-1991 (head coach 1986-1991), Maryland 1992-1996 (head coach). Pro coach: Cincinnati Bengals 1997-2002, Green Bay Packers 2003-05, joined Jaguars in 2006.

Jedd Fisch, offensive coordinator; born May 5, 1976, Livingston, N.J. No college or pro playing experience. College coach: Florida 1999-2000, Minnesota 2009, Miami 2011-12. Pro coach: New Jersey Red Dogs (Arena League) 1998, Houston Texans 2001-03, Baltimore Ravens 2004-07, Denver Broncos 2008, Seattle Seahawks 2010, joined Jaguars in 2013.

Alex Hampton, strength assistant; born March 23, 1989, Hobart, Tasmania, Australia. Attended Deakin University. No college or pro playing experience. College coach: Florida State 2012. Pro coach: Joined Jaguars in 2013.

Jess Langvardt, strength assistant; born September 28, 1982, North Platte, Neb. No pro playing experience. College coach: Sterling College 2005-09, 2012, Memphis 2009-2011, Tulane 2012. Pro coach: Joined Jaguars in 2013.

Mike Mallory, special teams coordinator; born Nov. 16, 1962, Bowling Green, Ohio. Linebacker Michigan 1982-85. No pro playing experience. College coach: Indiana 1986-87, Kent State 1988-1990, Eastern Illinois 1991-92, Rhode Island 1993-95, Northern Illinois 1996-99, Maryland 2000, Illinois 2001-05, Kansas 2006, Louisville 2007. Pro coach: New Orleans Saints 2008-2012, joined Jaguars in 2013.

Ron Middleton, tight ends/asst. special teams; born July 17, 1965, Atmore, Ala. Tight end Auburn 1982-85. Pro tight end Atlanta Falcons 1986-87, Washington Redskins 1988, 1990-93, Cleveland Browns 1989, Los Angeles Rams 1994, San Diego Chargers 1995. College coach: Troy 1997-98, Mississippi 1999-2003, Alabama 2007, Duke 2008-2012. Pro coach: Tampa Bay Buccaneers 2004-06, joined Jaguars in 2013.

Tom Myslinski, strength and conditioning; born December 7, 1968, Rome, N.Y. Guard Tennessee 1989-1991. Pro guard Washington Redskins 1992, Buffalo Bills 1993, Chicago Bears 1993-94, Jacksonville Jaguars 1995, Pittsburgh Steelers 1996-97, 2000, Indianapolis Colts 1998, Dallas Cowboys 1999. College coach: Robert Morris 2005-06, Memphis 2010, North Carolina 2011. Pro coach: Cleveland Browns 2003-04, 2007-09, joined Jaguars in 2012.

Terry Richardson, running backs; born October 8, 1971, Ft. Lauderdale, Fla. Running back Syracuse 1990-93. Pro running back Cincinnati Bengals 1994, Philadelphia Eagles 1995, Kansas City Chiefs 1996, Pittsburgh Steelers 1996-97. College coach: Connecticut 1999-2010, Miami 2011-12. Pro coach: Joined Jaguars in 2013.

Mike Rutenberg, asst. defensive backs; born October 29, 1981, Washington, D.C. Attended Cornell. No college or pro playing experience. College coach: UCLA 2006-08, New Mexico State 2009-2012. Pro coach: Washington Redskins 2003-05, joined Jaguars in 2013.

Frank Scelfo, quarterbacks; born February 9, 1959, Abbeville, La. Attended Northeast Louisiana. No college or pro playing experience. College coach: Tulane 1996-2006, Louisiana Tech 2007-09, Arizona 2010-11. Pro coach: Joined Jaguars in 2013.

Cedric Scott, asst. strength and conditioning; born October 19, 1977, Gulfport, Miss. Defensive end Southern Mississippi 1997-2000. Pro defensive end New York Giants 2001, Cleveland Browns 2002. College coach: Southern Mississippi 2009-2011. Pro coach: Joined Jaguars in 2012.

Matthew Smiley, asst. special teams; born October 2, 1978, Danville, Ill. Wide receiver Illinois 1997-98. No pro playing experience. College coach: Dartmouth 2005-06, Eureka College 2007-08 (interim head coach 2008), Eastern Illinois 2009-2011, Charleston Southern 2012. Pro coach: Joined Jaguars in 2013.

Tony Sorrentino, offensive quality control; born June 28, 1983, Belleville, N.J. Wide receiver The College of New Jersey 2001-04. No pro playing experience. College coach: The College of New Jersey 2006-07, 2012, Minnesota 2009-2010, Miami 2011. Pro coach: Joined Jaguars in 2013.

Jerry Sullivan, wide receivers; born July 13, 1944, Miami, Fla. Quarterback Florida State 1963-64. No pro playing experience. College coach: Kansas State 1971-72, Texas Tech 1973-75, South Carolina 1976-1982, Indiana 1983, Louisiana State 1984-1990, Ohio State 1991. Pro coach: San Diego Chargers 1992-96, Detroit Lions 1997-2000, Arizona Cardinals 2001-03, Miami Dolphins 2004, San Francisco 49ers 2005-2010, joined Jaguars in 2012.

DeWayne Walker, defensive backs; born December 3, 1960, Los Angeles, Calif. Defensive back Pasadena City (Calif.) C.C. 1978-79, Minnesota 1980-81. Pro defensive back Edmonton Eskimos (CFL) 1982, Arizona Outlaws (USFL) 1983, Oakland Invaders (USFL) 1984. College coach: Mt. San Antonio (Calif.) J.C. 1988-1992, Utah State 1993, Brigham Young 1994, Oklahoma State 1995, California 1996-97, Southern California 2001, UCLA 2006-08, New Mexico State 2009-2012 (head coach). Pro coach: New England Patriots 1998-2000, New York Giants 2002-03, Washington Redskins 2004-05, joined Jaguars in 2013.

Todd Wash, defensive line; born July 19, 1968, Miles City, Mont. Linebacker North Dakota State 1988-1991. No pro playing experience. College coach: Fort Lewis College 1996-99 (head coach 1997-99), Nebraska-Kearney 2000-01, North Dakota State 2002-03, 2005-06, Missouri Southern State 2004. Pro coach: Tampa Bay Buccaneers 2006-2010, Seattle Seahawks 2011-12, joined Jaguars in 2013.

George Yarno, offensive line; born August 12, 1957, Spokane, Wash. Offensive line Washington State 1975-78. Pro offensive line Tampa Bay Buccaneers 1979-1983, 1985-87, Denver Gold (USFL) 1984-85, Atlanta Falcons 1988, Houston Oilers 1989, Green Bay Packers 1990. College coach: Louisiana State 2001-02, Washington State 2003-07. Pro coach: Tampa Bay Buccaneers 2008, Detroit Lions 2009-12, joined Jaguars in 2013.

American Football Conference
West Division
Team Colors: Red, Gold, and White
One Arrowhead Drive
Kansas City, Missouri 64129
Telephone: (816) 920-9300

2013 SCHEDULE
PRESEASON
Aug. 9   at New Orleans..................7:00
Aug. 16 San Francisco 7:00
Aug. 24 at Pittsburgh......................6:30
Aug. 29 Green Bay..........................7:00

REGULAR SEASON
Sep. 8   at Jacksonville 12:00
Sep. 15 Dallas 12:00
Sep. 19 at Philadelphia (Thurs).......7:25
Sep. 29 New York Giants 12:00
Oct. 6   at Tennessee 12:00
Oct. 13 Oakland 12:00
Oct. 20 Houston 12:00
Oct. 27 Cleveland 12:00
Nov. 3   at Buffalo 12:00
Nov. 10 BYE
Nov. 17 at Denver 3:05
Nov. 24 San Diego 12:00
Dec. 1   Denver 12:00
Dec. 8   at Washington 12:00
Dec. 15 at Oakland 3:05
Dec. 22 Indianapolis 12:00
Dec. 29 at San Diego 3:25
All times CT

Stadium: Arrowhead Stadium
            (opened in 1972,
            fully renovated in 2010)
            •**Capacity:** 76,416
            One Arrowhead Drive
            Kansas City, Missouri 64129
Playing Surface: Grass
Training Camp: Missouri Western St. Univ.
            St. Joseph, Missouri 64507

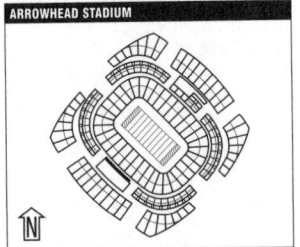

ARROWHEAD STADIUM

CLUB OFFICIALS
Chairman & CEO: Clark Hunt
Head Coach: Andy Reid
General Manager: John Dorsey
President: Mark Donovan
Director of Pro Personnel: Chris Ballard
Director of Pro Scouting: Will Lewis
Director of College Scouting:
    Marvin Allen
Director of Football Administration:
    Trip MacCracken
Senior Vice President of Business
    Operations: Bill Chapin
Chief Financial Officer: Dan Crumb
Vice President of Communications:
    Ted Crews
Vice President of Stadium Operations:
    David Young
Vice President of Human Resources and
    Administration: Kirsten Krug
Director of Facilities: Brandon Hamilton
Director of Special Events: Gary Spani
Director of Information Technology:
    Bob Stirton
Director of Marketing and Event
    Acquisition: Jeremy Slavens
Director of Fan Experience: Jayne Martin
Director of Ticket Sales: Tyler Kirby
Director of Ticket Operations:
    Dave Felsen
Director of Event Operations:
    Luke Hyvonen
Director of Sales: Shawn Long
Equipment Manager: Allen Wright
Assistant Equipment Managers:
    Chris Shropshire, Kyle Crumbaugh,
    Jimmy White
Head Athletic Trainer: Rick Burkholder
Assistant Athletic Trainers: Aaron
    Borgmann, David Glover, Nick Potter
Director of Video Operations: Pat Brazil
Assistant Director of Video Operations:
    Ken Radino
Video Assistants: Colin Clark,
    Josh Schmidt

COACHING HISTORY
Dallas Texans 1960-62
(412-402-12)
Records include postseason games
1960-1974	Hank Stram	129-79-10
1975-77	Paul Wiggin*	11-24-0
1977	Tom Bettis	1-6-0
1978-1982	Marv Levy	31-42-0
1983-86	John Mackovic	30-35-0
1987-88	Frank Gansz	8-22-1
1989-1998	Marty Schottenheimer	104-65-1
1999-2000	Gunther Cunningham	16-16-0
2001-05	Dick Vermeil	44-37-0
2006-08	Herm Edwards	15-34-0
2009-2011	Todd Haley**	19-26-0
2011-12	Romeo Crennel	4-15-0

*Released after seven games in 1977
**Released after 13 games in 2011

PAID ATTENDANCE
Home 520,214   Away 483,447
Total 1,003,661
Single-game home record,
    *82,893 (10/2/00)
Single-season home record,
    629,569 (1999)
*Arrowhead Stadium attendance: 78,502
Kauffman Stadium attendance: 4,391

2013 DRAFT CHOICES
Round	Name	Pos.	College
1	Eric Fisher	T	Central Michigan
3	Travis Kelce	TE	Cincinnati
	Knile Davis	RB	Arkansas
4	Nico Johnson	LB	Alabama
5	Sanders Commings	DB	Georgia
6	Eric Kush	OL	California (Pa.)
	Braden Wilson	FB	Kansas St.
7	Mike Catapano	LB	Princeton

2012 TEAM RECORD

PRESEASON (1-3)

Date	Result	Opponent
08/10	W 27-17	Arizona
08/18	L 17-31	at St. Louis
08/24	L 14-44	Seattle
08/30	L 3-24	at Green Bay

REGULAR SEASON (2-14)

Date	Result	Opponent
09/09	L 24-40	Atlanta
09/16	L 17-35	at Buffalo
09/23	W 27-24	at New Orleans (OT)
09/30	L 20-37	San Diego
10/07	L 6-9	Baltimore
10/14	L 10-38	at Tampa Bay
10/28	L 16-26	Oakland
11/01	L 13-31	at San Diego
11/12	L 13-16	at Pittsburgh (OT)
11/18	L 6-28	Cincinnati
11/25	L 9-17	Denver
12/02	W 27-21	Carolina
12/09	L 7-30	at Cleveland
12/16	L 0-15	at Oakland
12/23	L 13-20	Indianapolis
12/30	L 3-38	at Denver

(OT) Overtime

SCORE BY PERIODS

Chiefs	42	54	43	69	3	—	211
Opponents	95	121	106	100	3	—	425

2012 TEAM STATISTICS

	Chiefs	Opp.
Total First Downs	286	301
Rushing	118	106
Passing	144	176
Penalty	24	19
3rd Down: Made/Att	70/212	79/202
3rd Down Pct.	33.0	39.1
4th Down: Made/Att	7/15	3/4
4th Down Pct.	46.7	75.0
Possession Avg.	30:02	29:58
Total Net Yards	5108	5704
Avg. Per Game	319.3	356.5
Total Plays	1015	973
Avg. Per Play	5.0	5.9
Net Yards Rushing	2395	2171
Avg. Per Game	149.7	135.7
Total Rushes	500	482
Net Yards Passing	2713	3533
Avg. Per Game	169.6	220.8
Sacked/Yards Lost	40/224	27/161
Gross Yards	2937	3694
Att./Completions	475/273	464/279
Completion Pct.	57.5	60.1
Had Intercepted	20	7
Punts/Average	83/46.8	74/46.8
Net Punting Avg.	83/40.8	74/39.5
Penalties/Yards	92/733	81/670
Fumbles/Ball Lost	26/17	19/6
Touchdowns	18	47
Rushing	9	11
Passing	8	29
Returns	1	7

2012 INDIVIDUAL STATISTICS

PASSING

	Att.	Comp.	Yds.	Pct.	TD	Int.	Tkld.	Rate
Cassel	277	161	1796	58.1	6	12	19/101	66.7
Quinn	197	112	1141	56.9	2	8	21/123	60.1
Hillis	1	0	0	0.0	0	0	0/0	39.6
Chiefs	475	273	2937	57.5	8	20	40/224	63.8
Opponents	464	279	3694	60.1	29	7	27/161	99.9

SCORING

	TD R	TD P	TD Rt	PAT	FG	Saf	PTS
Succop	0	0	0	17/17	28/34	0	101
Charles	5	1	0	0/0	0/0	0	36
Bowe	0	3	0	0/0	0/0	0	18
Draughn	2	0	0	0/0	0/0	0	12
Baldwin	0	1	0	0/0	0/0	0	6
Boss	0	1	0	0/0	0/0	0	6
Cassel	1	0	0	0/0	0/0	0	6
Hillis	1	0	0	0/0	0/0	0	6
Jones	0	0	1	0/0	0/0	0	6
McCluster	0	1	0	0/0	0/0	0	6
Moeaki	0	1	0	0/0	0/0	0	6
Houston	0	0	0	0/0	0/0	1	2
Chiefs	9	8	1	17/17	28/34	1	211
Opponents	11	29	7	47/47	32/38	0	425

2-Pt Conversions: Chiefs 0-1, Opponents 0-0

RUSHING

	No.	Yds	Avg	LG	TD
Charles	285	1509	5.3	91t	5
Hillis	85	309	3.6	18	1
Draughn	59	233	3.9	25	2
Cassel	27	145	5.4	21	1
McCluster	12	70	5.8	19	0
Quinn	19	66	3.5	12	0
Gray	7	44	6.3	15	0
Eachus	5	18	3.6	7	0
Copper	1	1	1.0	1	0
Chiefs	500	2395	4.8	91t	9
Opponents	482	2171	4.5	47	11

RECEIVING

	No.	Yds	Avg	LG	TD
Bowe	59	801	13.6	47	3
McCluster	52	452	8.7	31	1
Charles	35	236	6.7	22	1
Moeaki	33	453	13.7	38	1
Draughn	24	158	6.6	23	0
Baldwin	20	325	16.3	57	1
Hillis	10	62	6.2	15	0
Copper	8	79	9.9	17	0
Breaston	7	74	10.6	24	0
Wylie	6	53	8.8	16	0
Newsome	5	73	14.6	28	0
Maneri	5	51	10.2	19	0
Boss	3	65	21.7	29	1
O'Connell	3	18	6.0	11	0
Gray	2	18	9.0	12	0
Eachus	1	19	19.0	19	0
Chiefs	273	2937	10.8	57	8
Opponents	279	3694	13.2	62t	29

INTERCEPTIONS

	No.	Yds	Avg	LG	TD
Flowers	3	28	9.3	29	0
Routt	2	49	24.5	32	0
Houston	1	32	32.0	32	0
Berry	1	0	0.0	0	0
Elam	0	10	—	10	0
Chiefs	7	119	17.0	32	0
Opponents	20	368	18.4	78t	4

PUNTING

	No.	Yds.	Avg.	In 20	LG
Colquitt	83	3887	46.8	45	71
Chiefs	83	3887	46.8	45	71
Opponents	74	3466	46.8	17	70

PUNT RETURNS

	Ret	FC	Yds	Avg	LG	TD
Arenas	34	4	303	8.9	27	0
Wylie	5	2	26	5.2	13	0
McCluster	2	2	6	3.0	6	0
Breaston	1	0	21	21.0	21	0
Copper	1	0	25	25.0	25	0
Chiefs	43	8	381	8.9	27	0
Opponents	27	22	362	13.4	93t	2

KICKOFF RETURNS

	No.	Yds	Avg	LG	TD
Draughn	23	537	23.3	41	0
Wylie	9	191	21.2	26	0
Arenas	9	177	19.7	27	0
Bellamy	5	101	20.2	27	0
Gray	1	33	33.0	33	0
Copper	1	16	16.0	16	0
Toribio	1	4	4.0	4	0
Chiefs	49	1059	21.6	41	0
Opponents	27	690	25.6	77	0

FIELD GOALS

	1-19	20-29	30-39	40-49	50+
Succop	0/0	4/5	12/15	10/12	2/2
Chiefs	0/0	4/5	12/15	10/12	2/2
Opponents	0/0	11/11	12/14	7/8	2/5

SACKS

	No.
Houston	10.0
Hali	9.0
Jackson	3.0
Johnson	2.0
Pitoitua	2.0
Flowers	1.0
Chiefs	27.0
Opponents	40.0

RECORD HOLDERS
INDIVIDUAL RECORDS—CAREER

Category	Name	Performance
Rushing (Yds.)	Priest Holmes, 2001-07	6,070
Passing (Yds.)	Len Dawson, 1962-1975	28,507
Passing (TDs)	Len Dawson, 1962-1975	237
Receiving (No.)	Tony Gonzalez, 1997-2008	916
Receiving (Yds.)	Tony Gonzalez, 1997-2008	10,940
Interceptions	Emmitt Thomas, 1966-1978	58
Punting (Avg.)	Dustin Colquitt, 2005-2012	44.7
Punt Return (Avg.)	Noland Smith, 1967-69	11.1
Kickoff Return (Avg.)	Noland Smith, 1967-69	26.8
Field Goals	Nick Lowery, 1980-1993	329
Touchdowns (Tot.)	Priest Holmes, 2001-07	83
Points	Nick Lowery, 1980-1993	1,466
*Sacks	Derrick Thomas, 1989-1999	126.5

INDIVIDUAL RECORDS—SINGLE SEASON

Category	Name	Performance
Rushing (Yds.)	Larry Johnson, 2006	1,789
Passing (Yds.)	Trent Green, 2004	4,591
Passing (TDs)	Len Dawson, 1964	30
Receiving (No.)	Tony Gonzalez, 2004	102
Receiving (Yds.)	Derrick Alexander, 2000	1,391
Interceptions	Emmitt Thomas, 1974	12
Punting (Avg.)	Dustin Colquitt, 2012	46.8
Punt Return (Avg.)	Dante Hall, 2003	16.3
Kickoff Return (Avg.)	Dave Grayson, 1962	29.7
Field Goals	Nick Lowery, 1990	34
Touchdowns (Tot.)	Priest Holmes, 2003	27
Points	Priest Holmes, 2003	162
*Sacks	Derrick Thomas, 1990	20.0

INDIVIDUAL RECORDS—SINGLE GAME

Category	Name	Performance
Rushing (Yds.)	Jamaal Charles, 1-3-10	259
Passing (Yds.)	Elvis Grbac, 11-5-00	504
Passing (TDs)	Len Dawson, 11-1-64	6
Receiving (No.)	Tony Gonzalez, 1-2-05	14
Receiving (Yds.)	Stephone Paige, 12-22-85	309
Interceptions	Bobby Ply, 12-16-62	**4
	Bobby Hunt, 10-4-64	**4
	Deron Cherry, 9-29-85	**4
Field Goals	Ryan Succop, 9-23-12	6
Touchdowns (Tot.)	Abner Haynes, 11-26-61	5
Points	Abner Haynes, 11-26-61	30
*Sacks	Derrick Thomas, 11-11-90	**7.0

*Sacks became an official statistic in 1982.
**NFL Record

2013 VETERAN ROSTER

No.	Name	Pos.	Ht.	Wt.	Birthdate	NFL Exp.	College	Hometown	How Acq.	'12 Games/ Starts
39	Abdullah, Husain	S	6-0	204	7/27/85	5	Washington State	Pomona, Calif.	FA-'13	0*
76	Albert, Branden	T	6-5	316	11/4/84	6	Virginia	Glen Burnie, Md.	D1b-'08	13/11
71	Allen, Jeff	OL	6-4	306	1/8/90	2	Illinois	Chicago, Ill.	D2-'12	16/13
73	Asamoah, Jon	G	6-4	305	7/21/88	4	Illinois	Park Forest, Ill.	D3a-'10	15/15
17	Avery, Donnie	WR	5-11	200	6/12/84	5	Houston	Houston, Texas	UFA(Ind)-'13	16/15*
97	Bailey, Allen	DL	6-3	288	3/25/89	3	Miami	Sapelo Island, Ga.	D3b-'11	10/1
89	Baldwin, Jonathan	WR	6-4	230	8/10/89	3	Pittsburgh	Aliquippa, Pa.	D1-'11	15/7
29	Berry, Eric	S	6-0	211	12/29/88	4	Tennessee	Fairburn, Ga.	D1-'10	16/16
82	Bowe, Dwayne	WR	6-2	221	9/21/84	7	Louisiana State	Miami, Fla.	D1-'07	13/12
30	Brown, Jalil	DB	6-1	204	10/14/87	3	Colorado	Phoenix, Ariz.	D4-'11	15/2
25	Charles, Jamaal	RB	5-11	199	12/27/86	6	Texas	Port Arthur, Texas	D3a-'08	16/15
2	Colquitt, Dustin	P	6-3	210	5/6/82	9	Tennessee	Knoxville, Tenn.	D3-'05	16/0
15	Copper, Terrance	WR	6-0	207	3/12/82	10	East Carolina	Washington, N.C.	FA-'11	15/0
10	Daniel, Chase	QB	6-0	225	10/7/86	4	Missouri	Southlake, Texas	UFA(NO)-'13	16/0
34	# Daniels, Travis	DB	6-1	195	9/8/82	9	Louisiana State	Hollywood, Fla.	FA-'12	15/0
70	DeVito, Mike	DL	6-3	305	6/10/84	7	Maine	Wellfleet, Mass.	UFA(NYJ)-'13	16/15*
54	Diles, Zac	LB	6-2	245	6/11/85	7	Kansas State	Abilene, Texas	UFA(Tenn)-'13	6/1*
96	Dixon, Marcus	DL	6-4	295	9/16/84	3	Hampton	Rome, Ga.	FA-'13	3/0*
20	Draughn, Shaun	RB	6-0	205	12/7/87	2	North Carolina	Tarboro, N.C.	FA-'11	16/0
75	Durand, Ryan	OL	6-5	301	11/17/85	2	Syracuse	Fitchburg, Mass.	FA-'13	0*
27	# Elam, Abram	S	6-0	207	10/15/81	8	Kent State	Riviera Beach, Fla.	UFA(Dall)-'12	12/7
80	Fasano, Anthony	TE	6-4	255	4/20/84	8	Notre Dame	Verona, N.J.	UFA(Mia)-'13	16/16*
24	Flowers, Brandon	CB	5-9	187	2/18/86	6	Virginia Tech	Delray Beach, Fla.	D2-'08	15/15
43	Gafford, Thomas	LS	6-2	250	1/29/83	6	Houston	Friendswood, Texas	FA-'09	16/0
13	Gilyard, Mardy	WR	6-1	187	12/2/86	2	Cincinnati	Daytona Beach, Fla.	FA-'13	8/0*
32	Gray, Cyrus	RB	5-10	206	11/18/89	2	Texas A&M	DeSoto, Texas	D6-'12	10/0
91	Hali, Tamba	LB	6-3	275	11/3/83	8	Penn State	Teaneck, N.J.	D1-'06	15/15
31	Hartman, Tysyn	DB	6-3	206	8/9/89	2	Kansas State	Wichita, Kan.	FA-'12	11/2
40	# Hillis, Peyton	RB	6-2	250	1/21/86	6	Arkansas	Conway, Ark.	FA-'12	13/2
66	# Hochstein, Russ	G	6-4	305	10/7/77	11	Nebraska	Hartington, Neb.	FA-'12	11/1
50	Houston, Justin	LB	6-3	258	1/12/89	3	Georgia	Statesboro, Ga.	D3a-'11	16/16
61	Hudson, Rodney	OL	6-2	299	7/12/89	3	Florida State	Mobile, Ala.	D2-'11	3/3
94	Jackson, Tyson	DE	6-4	296	6/6/86	5	Louisiana State	Edgard, La.	D1-'09	15/15
56	Johnson, Derrick	LB	6-3	242	11/22/82	9	Texas	Waco, Texas	D1-'05	16/16
99	Jones, Edgar	LB	6-3	262	12/1/84	6	Southeast Missouri	Rayville, La.	UFA(Balt)-'12	16/0
55	Jordan, Akeem	LB	6-1	230	8/17/85	7	James Madison	Harrisonburg, Va.	FA-'13	14/7*
52	Lemon, Orie	LB	6-1	242	9/9/87	2	Oklahoma State	Houston, Texas	FA-'13	5/0*
23	Lewis, Kendrick	S	6-0	198	6/16/88	3	Mississippi	New Orleans, La.	D5a-'10	9/9
65	# Lilja, Ryan	G	6-2	290	10/15/81	10	Kansas State	Shawnee, Kan.	FA-'10	15/15
22	McCluster, Dexter	RB	5-8	170	8/25/88	3	Mississippi	Largo, Fla.	D2a-'10	16/6
81	Moeaki, Tony	TE	6-3	252	6/8/87	4	Iowa	Wheaton, Ill.	D3b-'10	15/14
90	Muir, Daniel	DT	6-2	322	9/12/83	5	Kent State	Lanham, Md.	FA-'13	3/0*
84	Newsome, Jamar	WR	6-1	201	11/5/87	2	Central Florida	Boca Ciega, Fla.	FA-'12	6/2
85	# O'Connell, Jake	TE	6-3	250	11/6/85	5	Miami (Ohio)	Naples, Fla.	D7b-'09	8/0
92	Poe, Dontari	DT	6-3	346	8/18/90	2	Memphis	Memphis, Tenn.	D1-'12	16/16
95	Powe, Jerrell	DL	6-2	331	3/15/87	3	Mississippi	Waynesboro, Miss.	D6-'11	9/0
21	Robinson, Dunta	CB	5-10	183	4/11/82	10	South Carolina	Athens, Ga.	FA-'13	16/16*
74	Schwartz, Geoff	OL	6-6	340	7/11/86	4	Oregon	Pacific Palisades, Calif.	UFA(Minn)-'13	13/0*
42	t-Sherman, Anthony	FB	5-10	242	12/11/88	3	Connecticut	North Attleboro, Mass.	T(Ariz)-'12	13/4*
52	# Siler, Brandon	LB	6-2	239	12/5/85	7	Florida	Orlando, Fla.	UFA(SD)-'11	16/4
11	t-Smith, Alex	QB	6-4	217	5/7/84	8	Utah	La Mesa, Calif.	T(SF)-'13	10/9*
27	Smith, Sean	CB	6-3	218	7/14/87	5	Utah	Pasadena, Calif.	UFA(Mia)-'13	16/16*
90	# Smith, Shaun	DE	6-2	325	8/19/81	10	South Carolina	Brooklyn, N.Y.	FA-'12	8/0
12	Stanzi, Ricky	QB	6-4	228	9/3/87	2	Iowa	Mentor, Ohio	D5a-'11	0
79	Stephenson, Donald	OL	6-6	312	9/30/88	2	Oklahoma	Blue Springs, Mo.	D3-'12	16/7
6	Succop, Ryan	K	6-2	218	9/19/86	5	South Carolina	Hickory, N.C.	D7c-'09	16/0
38	Thorpe, Neiko	DB	6-2	185	2/1/90	2	Auburn	Tucker, Ga.	FA-'12	9/0
98	Toribio, Anthony	DL	6-1	315	3/1/85	3	Carson-Newman	Miami, Fla.	FA-'12	11/0
56	# Williams, Leon	LB	6-3	248	7/30/83	6	Miami	Brooklyn, N.Y.	FA-'12	4/0
19	Wylie, Devon	WR	5-9	187	9/2/88	2	Fresno State	Roseville, Calif.	D4-'12	6/1
51	Zombo, Frank	LB	6-3	254	3/5/87	4	Central Michigan	Sterling Heights, Mich.	FA-'12	7/0*

* Abdullah last active with Minnesota in '11; Avery played 16 games with Indianapolis in '12; DeVito played 16 games with New York Jets; Diles played six games with Tennessee; Dixon played three games with New York Jets; Durand last active with Tennessee in '10; Fasano played 16 games with Miami; Gilyard played six games with Philadelphia and two with the New York Jets; Jordan played 14 games with Philadelphia; Lemon played five games with Dallas; Muir played three games with New York Jets; Robinson played 16 games with Atlanta; Schwartz played 13 games with Detroit; Sherman played 13 games with Arizona; A. Smith played 10 games with San Francisco; Se. Smith played 16 games with Miami; Zombo played seven games with Green Bay.

\# Unrestriced Free Agent; subject to developments.

t- Traded for Anthony Sherman (Ariz), Alex Smith (SF).

Traded—CB Javier Arenas (16 games in '12) to Arizona.

Players lost through free agency (3): DE Glenn Dorsey (SF; 4 games in '12), DE Ropati Pitoitua (Tenn; 15), QB Brady Quinn (Sea; 10).

Also played with Chiefs in '12—LB Jovan Belcher (11 games), WR Josh Bellamy (3), TE Kevin Boss (2), WR Steve Breaston (10), QB Matt Cassel (9), RB Nate Eachus (11), LB Corey Greenwood (16), LB Bryan Kehl (3), TE Steve Maneri (13), DE Bryan Mattison (4), DE Ropati Pitoitua (15), CB Jacques Reeves (2), CB Stanford Routt (7), LB Cameron Sheffield (2), LB Andy Studebaker (16), LB Leon Williams (4), T Eric Winston (16).

FIRST-YEAR ROSTER

Name	Pos.	Ht.	Wt.	Birthdate	College	Hometown	How Acq.
Baker, Steven	T	6-8	310	11/24/88	East Carolina	Tarboro, N.C.	FA
Bellamy, Josh (1)	WR	6-0	206	5/18/89	Louisville	St. Petersburg, Fla.	FA-'12
Bray, Tyler	QB	6-4	215	12/27/91	Tennessee	Kingsburg, Calif.	FA
Brock, Kevin (1)	TE	6-5	249	4/9/86	Rutgers	Hackensack, N.J.	FA
Broussard, Risean	DL	6-2	276	9/8/91	Hinds (Miss.) C.C.	Lake Charles, La.	FA
Castillo, Greg	S	5-11	187	5/3/90	Iowa	Mount Laurel, N.J.	FA
Catapano, Mike	LB	6-4	270	8/17/90	Princeton	Bayville, N.Y.	D7
Chavis, Miguel (1)	DE	6-5	285	10/26/88	Clemson	Fayetteville, N.C.	FA
Commings, Sanders	DB	6-0	223	3/8/90	Georgia	Augusta, Ga.	D5
Davis, Knile	RB	5-10	227	10/5/91	Arkansas	Missouri City, Texas	D3b
Draheim, Tommie (1)	OL	6-4	309	12/23/88	San Diego State	Lakeside, Calif.	FA
Drakeford, Darin	LB	6-1	240	7/5/91	Maryland	Washington, D.C.	FA
Fisher, Eric	T	6-7	306	1/5/91	Central Michigan	Rochester, Mich.	D1
Foster, Otha	DB	6-0	204	9/27/88	West Alabama	Angie, La.	FA
Glenn, Justin	S	5-11	214	12/22/89	Washington	Mukilteo, Wash.	FA
Hammond, Frankie	WR	6-1	184	2/17/90	Florida	Hallandale Beach, Fla.	FA
Harris, Demetrius	TE	6-7	230	7/29/91	Wisconsin-Milwaukee	Jacksonville, Ark.	FA
Hawkins, A.J.	OL	6-1	310	5/26/90	Mississippi	Lithonia, Ga.	FA
Hemingway, Junior (1)	WR	6-1	225	12/27/88	Michigan	Conway, S.C.	D7b-'12
Jackson, Buddy (1)	CB	6-1	180	3/3/89	Pittsburgh	Plantation, Fla.	FA
Johnson, Nico	LB	6-2	249	6/19/90	Alabama	Andalusia, Ala.	D4
Kelce, Travis	TE	6-5	260	10/5/89	Cincinnati	Cleveland Heights, Ohio	D3a
Kelly, Colin	OL	6-5	298	12/29/89	Oregon State	Kelso, Wash.	FA
Kilgore, Chad (1)	LB	6-1	230	8/8/89	Northwest Missouri State	Orrick, Mo.	FA
Kush, Eric	OL	6-4	313	9/9/89	California (Pa.)	Bridgeville, Pa.	D6a
Lohr, Rob	DE	6-4	290	3/1/90	Vanderbilt	Phoenixville, Pa.	FA
Madison, Brad	DL	6-4	265	11/4/89	Missouri	Bethany, Mo.	FA
Martin, Josh	LB/DE	6-3	245	11/7/91	Columbia	Aurora, Colo.	FA
McDougald, Brad	S	6-1	209	11/15/90	Kansas	Columbus, Ohio	FA
Patterson, Lucas (1)	OL	6-4	295	9/19/87	Texas A&M	Kingsville, Texas	FA-'12
Reynolds, Matt	T	6-4	310	5/31/86	Brigham Young	Provo, Utah	FA
Richardson, Rico	WR	6-1	185	7/1/91	Jackson State	Natchez, Miss.	FA
Roberts, Jordan	RB	5-10	222	5/29/90	Charleston	Madison, W. Va.	FA
Rogers, James	CB	6-1	188	5/27/89	Michigan	Madison Heights, Mich.	FA
Shoemaker, Tyler (1)	WR	6-1	213	9/14/88	Boise State	Meridian, Idaho	FA
Waldron, Dustin (1)	TE	6-5	310	5/24/90	Portland State	Pleasant Hill, Ore.	FA-'12
Wilson, Braden	FB	6-4	254	10/9/89	Kansas State	Smith Center, Kan.	D6b
Wilson, Ridge	LB/DE	6-4	256	2/7/91	West Alabama	Louisville, Ky.	FA

The term NFL Rookie is defined as a player who is in his first season of professional football and has not been on the roster of another professional football team for any regular-season or postseason games. A Rookie is designated by an "R" on NFL rosters. Players who have been active in another professional football league or players who have NFL experience, including either preseason training camp or being on an Active List or Inactive List, or on Reserve/Injured or Reserve/Physically Unable to Perform for fewer than six regular-season games, are termed NFL First-Year Players. An NFL First-Year Player is designated by a "1" on NFL rosters. Thereafter, a player is credited with an additional year of experience for each season in which he accumulates six games on the Active List or Inactive List, or on Reserve/Injured or Reserve/Physically Unable to Perform.

Log on to www.kcchiefs.com for an up-to-date roster.

COACHING STAFF

Head Coach,
Andy Reid

Pro Career: Andy Reid was named the 13th head coach in Kansas City Chiefs history on January 7, 2013. Prior to joining the Chiefs, Reid served as the head coach of the Philadelphia Eagles for 14 years (1999-2012), earning NFL Coach of the Year honors three times. Reid compiled the best win total (140) and playoff victory total (10) in Philadelphia Eagles history. He captured six division titles and five trips to the NFC Championship Game. During his tenure in Philadelphia, only New England (9) earned more divisional playoff round appearances than Philadelphia (7). In his 21-year NFL coaching career, Reid's teams have made the playoffs 15 times (19-14 record). He has coached in the Super Bowl three times and the NFC Championship game nine times. Reid was an assistant coach with Green Bay (1992-98). With Green Bay, Reid helped the Packers earn a Super Bowl XXXI victory over New England. Career record: 140-102-1.

Background: Coached at Brigham Young (1982), San Francisco State (1983-85) Northern Arizona (1986), Texas-El Paso (1987-88) and Missouri (1989-1991). Reid was an offensive tackle and guard on three Cougar Holiday Bowl teams. Reid graduated with a bachelor's degree in physical education. He also received a master's degree in professional leadership in physical education and athletics.

Personal: Born in Los Angeles, Calif. On March 19, 1958, Reid and his wife Tammy have five children—the late Garrett, Britt, Crosby, Drew Ann, and Spencer.

ASSISTANT COACHES

Eric Bieniemy, running backs; born August 15, 1969, New Orleans, La. Running back Colorado 1987-1990. Pro running back San Diego 1991-94, Cincinnati Bengals 1995-98, Philadelphia Eagles 1999. College coach: Colorado 2001-02, UCLA 2003-05, Colorado 2009-2012. Pro coach: Minnesota Vikings 2006-2010, joined Chiefs in 2013.

Tommy Brasher, defensive line; born Dec. 30, 1940, El Dorado, Ark. Linebacker Arkansas 1962-63. No pro playing experience. College coach: Arkansas 1970, Virginia Tech 1971, Northeast Louisiana 1974, 1976, Southern Methodist 1977-1981. Pro coach: Shreveport Steamer (WFL) 1975, New England Patriots 1982-84, Philadelphia Eagles 1985, Atlanta Falcons 1986-89, Tampa Bay Buccaneers 1990, Seattle Seahawks 1992-98, Philadelphia Eagles 1999-2005, 2012, joined Chiefs in 2013.

Brad Childress, spread game analyst/special projects; born June 27, 1956, Aurora, Ill. Quarterback/wide receiver Eastern Illinois 1975. No pro playing experience. College coach: Illinois 1978-1984, Northern Arizona 1986-89, Utah 1990, Wisconsin 1991-98. Pro coach: Indianapolis Colts 1985, Philadelphia Eagles 1999-2005, Minnesota Vikings 2006-2010 (head coach), Cleveland Browns 2012, joined Chiefs in 2013.

Eugene Chung, asst. offensive line; born June 14, 1969, Prince George's County, Md. Offensive lineman Virginia Tech 1988-1991. Pro offensive lineman New England Patriots 1992-94, Jacksonville Jaguars 1995, Indianapolis Colts 1997. Pro coach: Philadelphia Eagles 2010-12, joined Chiefs in 2013.

Travis Crittenden, asst. strength and conditioning; born April 6, 1981, Wichita Falls, Texas. Tackle Fork Union Military Academy 1999, Virginia Military Institute 2000-03. No pro playing experience. Pro coach: Philadelphia Eagles 2012, joined Chiefs in 2013.

David Culley, asst. head coach/wide receivers; born September 17, 1955, Sparta, Tenn. Quarterback Vanderbilt 1973-77. No pro playing experience. College coach: Austin Peay 1978, Vanderbilt 1979-1981, Middle Tennessee State 1982, Tennessee-Chattanooga 1983, Western Kentucky 1984, Southwestern Louisiana 1985-88, Texas-El Paso 1989-1990, Texas A&M 1991-93. Pro coach: Tampa Bay Buccaneers 1994-95, Pittsburgh Steelers 1996-98, Philadelphia Eagles 1999-2012, joined Chiefs in 2013.

Mark DeLeone, quality control; born June 30, 1987, Syracuse, N.Y. Attended Iowa. No college or pro playing experience. College coach: Florida 2010, Temple 2011. Pro coach: New York Jets 2012, joined Chiefs in 2013.

Gary Gibbs, linebackers; born August 13, 1952, Beaumont, Texas. Linebacker Oklahoma 1972-74. No pro playing experience. College coach: Oklahoma 1975-1994 (head coach 1989-1994), Georgia 2000, Louisiana State 2001. Pro coach: Dallas Cowboys 2002-04, New Orleans Saints 2006-08, joined Chiefs in 2009.

Al Harris, defensive assistant/secondary; born December 7, 1974, Pompano Beach, Fla. Cornerback Trinity Valley (Texas) C.C. 1993-94, Texas A&M-Kingsville 1995-96. Pro cornerback Tampa Bay Buccaneers 1997, Philadelphia Eagles 1998-2002, Green Bay Packers 2003-09, Miami Dolphins 2010, St. Louis Rams 2011. Pro coach: Miami Dolphins 2012, joined Chiefs in 2013.

Andy Heck, offensive line; born January 1, 1967, Fargo, N.D. Tackle Notre Dame 1985-88. Pro tackle Seattle Seahawks 1989-1993, Chicago Bears 1994-98, Washington Redskins 1999-2000. College coach: Virginia 2001-03. Pro coach: Jacksonville Jaguars 2004-12, joined Chiefs in 2013.

Corey Matthaei, quality control; born February 1, 1985, Fircrest, Wash. Offensive lineman Willamette 2003-06. No pro playing experience. College coach: Willamette 2007. Pro coach: Philadelphia Eagles 2008-2012, joined Chiefs in 2013.

Tom Melvin, tight ends; born October 1, 1961, Redwood City, Calif. Offensive lineman San Francisco State 1982-83. No pro playing experience. College coach: San Francisco State 1984-85, Northern Arizona 1986-87, California-Santa Barbara 1988-1990, Occidental College 1991-98. Pro coach: Philadelphia Eagles 1999-2012, joined Chiefs in 2013.

Matt Nagy, quarterbacks; born April 24, 1978, Plainfield, N.J. Quarterback Delaware 1996-2000. Pro quarterback New York Dragons (AFL) 2002, Carolina Cobras (AFL) 2004, Georgia

Force (AFL) 2005-06, Columbus Destroyers (AFL) 2007-08. Pro coach: Philadelphia Eagles 2011-12, joined Chiefs in 2013.

Kevin O'Dea, asst. special teams; born June 9, 1960, Williamsport, Pa. Wide receiver/defensive back Lock Haven 1984-85. No pro playing experience. College coach: Lock Haven 1986, Cornell 1987, Virginia 1988-1990, Penn State 1991-93. Pro coach: San Diego Chargers 1994-95, Tampa Bay Buccaneers 1996-2001, Detroit Lions 2002-03, Arizona Cardinals 2004-05, Chicago Bears 2006-07, New York Jets 2008-09, Chicago Bears 2011-12, joined Chiefs in 2013.

Doug Pederson, offensive coordinator; born January 31, 1968, Bellingham, Wash. Quarterback Louisiana-Monroe 1987-1990. Pro quarterback Miami Dolphins 1993-95, Green Bay Packers 1995-98, 2001-04, Philadelphia Eagles 1999, Cleveland Browns 2000. Pro coach: Philadelphia Eagles 2009-2012, joined Chiefs in 2013.

Britt Reid, quality control; born April 28, 1985, San Francisco, Calif. Attended Temple. No college or pro playing experience. College coach: Temple 2012. Pro coach: Joined Chiefs in 2013.

Barry Rubin, strength and conditioning; born June 25, 1957, Monroe, La. Running back/punter Louisiana State 1976-77, tight end/punter Northwestern (La.) State 1978-1980. No pro playing experience. College coach: Northeast Louisiana 1981-83, 1987-1990, 1994, Louisiana State 1984-85. Pro coach: Green Bay Packers 1995-2005, Philadelphia Eagles 2008-2012, joined Chiefs in 2013.

Brent Salazar, asst. strength and conditioning; born May 22, 1980, Denver, Colo. Attended New Mexico. No college or pro playing experience. College coach: New Mexico 2002-03, Nevada-Las Vegas 2005, Pacific 2006. Pro coach: Joined Chiefs in 2007.

Bob Sutton, defensive coordinator; born January 28, 1951, Ypsilanti, Mich. Attended Eastern Michigan. No college or pro playing experience. College coach: Michigan 1972-73, Syracuse 1974, Western Michigan 1975-76, 1980-81, Illinois 1977-79, North Carolina State 1982, Army 1983-1999 (head coach 1991-99). Pro coach: New York Jets 2000-2012, joined Chiefs in 2013.

Emmitt Thomas, defensive backs; born June 3, 1943, Angleton, Texas. Quarterback/wide receiver Bishop (Texas) College 1963-65. Pro defensive back Kansas City Chiefs 1966-1978. Inducted into Pro Football Hall of Fame 2008. College coach: Central Missouri State 1979-1980. Pro coach: St. Louis Cardinals 1981-85, Washington Redskins 1986-1994, Philadelphia Eagles 1995-98, Green Bay Packers 1999, Minnesota Vikings 2000-01, Atlanta Falcons 2002-09 (interim head coach 2007), re-joined Chiefs in 2010.

Dave Toub, special teams coordinator; born June 1, 1962, Ossining, N.Y. Offensive lineman Springfield College 1980-81, Texas-El Paso 1983-84. No pro playing experience. College coach: Texas El-Paso 1987-89, Missouri 1989-2000. Pro coach: Philadelphia Eagles 2001-03, Chicago Bears 2004-2012, joined Chiefs in 2013.

**American Football Conference
East Division**
Team Colors: Aqua, Coral, Blue, and
White
**7500 S.W. 30th Street
Davie, Florida 33314**
Telephone: (954) 452-7000

2013 SCHEDULE
PRESEASON
Aug. 4   vs. Dallas, at Canton, OH....8:00
Aug. 9   at Jacksonville.....................7:30
Aug. 17   at Houston..........................8:00
Aug. 24   **Tampa Bay**.........................7:30
Aug. 29   **New Orleans**.......................7:30

REGULAR SEASON
Sep. 8   at Cleveland 1:00
Sep. 15   at Indianapolis 1:00
Sep. 22   **Atlanta** 4:05
Sep. 30   at New Orleans (Mon) 8:40
Oct. 6   **Baltimore** 1:00
Oct. 13   BYE
Oct. 20   **Buffalo** 1:00
Oct. 27   at New England 1:00
Oct. 31   **Cincinnati** (Thurs)...............8:25
Nov. 11   at Tampa Bay (Mon)...........8:40
Nov. 17   **San Diego** 1:00
Nov. 24   **Carolina** 1:00
Dec. 1   at New York Jets 1:00
Dec. 8   at Pittsburgh 1:00
Dec. 15   **New England** 1:00
Dec. 22   at Buffalo 1:00
Dec. 29   **New York Jets** 1:00
All times ET
Stadium: Sun Life Stadium
(opened in 1987)
 •**Capacity:** 75,192
2269 Dan Marino Blvd.
Miami Gardens, Florida 33056
Playing Surface: Grass (PAT)
Training Camp: Nova Southeastern Univ.
7500 S.W. 30th Street
Davie, Florida 33314

SUN LIFE STADIUM

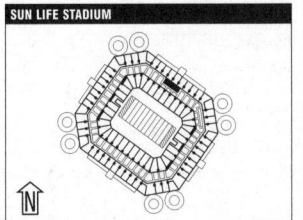

CLUB OFFICIALS
Chairman of the Board/Managing General
Partner: Stephen M. Ross
Chief Executive Officer: Mike Dee
General Manager: Jeff Ireland
Executive Vice President of Football
Administration: Dawn Aponte
Senior Vice President of Operations-Sun
Life Stadium: Todd Boyan
Senior Vice President/Chief Financial and
Administrative Officer:
Mark Brockelman
Senior Vice President of Operations-
Davie: Bill Galante
Senior Vice President of Media Relations:
Harvey Greene
Senior Vice President-Chief Technology
Officer: Tery Howard
Senior Vice President-Chief Marketing
Officer: Claudia Lezcano
Senior Vice President/Special Advisor:
Nat Moore
Senior Vice President-Chief Revenue
Officer: Jim Rushton
Vice President of Corporate Partnerships
and Integrated Media Group Sales:
Bob Lynch
Vice President of Ticket Sales and
Retention: George Torres
General Counsel: Adam Zissman
Assistant General Manager: Brian Gaine
Director of College Scouting: Chris Grier
Assistant Director of Pro Scouting:
Chris Shea
Head Athletic Trainer: Kevin O'Neill
Equipment Manager: Joe Cimino
Video Director: Bob Hack
Director of Player Development:
Kaleb Thornhill
Senior Director of Internet and
Publications: Scott Stone
Senior Director of Media Relations:
Jason Jenkins
Director of Communications: Fitz Ollison
Senior Director of Programming and
Production: Jeff Griffith
Senior Director of Cheerleaders and
Entertainment: Dorie Grogan
Cheerleader Manager: Emily Snow
Senior Director of Community Relations:
Ilona Wolpin
Director of Youth Programs: Twan Russell
Senior Group Director Marketing and
Content: Wayne Partello
Director of Security: Stuart Weinstein

COACHING HISTORY
(427-329-4)
Records include postseason games
1966-69   George Wilson.............15-39-2
1970-1995 Don Shula 274-147-2
1996-99   Jimmy Johnson...........38-31-0
2000-04   Dave Wannstedt* 43-33-0
2004   Jim Bates....................3-4-0
2005-06   Nick Saban.................15-17-0
2007   Cam Cameron 1-15-0
2008-2011 Tony Sparano** 29-33-0
2011   Todd Bowles 2-1-0
2012   Joe Philbin 7-9-0
*Resigned after nine games in 2004
**Released after 13 games in 2011

PAID ATTENDANCE
Home 455,711   Away 526,909
Total 982,620
Single-game home record,
75,283 (10/27/96)
Single-season home record, 592,161
(1999)

2013 DRAFT CHOICES

Round	Name	Pos.	College
1	Dion Jordan	DE	Oregon
2	Jamar Taylor	DB	Boise St.
3	Dallas Thomas	T	Tennessee
	Will Davis	DB	Utah St.
4	Jelani Jenkins	LB	Florida
	Dion Sims	TE	Michigan St.
5	Mike Gillislee	RB	Florida
	Caleb Sturgis	K	Florida
7	Don Jones	DB	Arkansas St.

2012 TEAM RECORD
PRESEASON (0-4)

Date	Result		Opponent
08/10	L	7-20	Tampa Bay
08/17	L	17-23	at Carolina
08/24	L	6-23	Atlanta
08/29	L	13-30	at Dallas

REGULAR SEASON (7-9)

Date	Result		Opponent
09/09	L	10-30	at Houston
09/16	W	35-13	Oakland
09/23	L	20-23	New York Jets (OT)
09/30	L	21-24	at Arizona (OT)
10/07	W	17-13	at Cincinnati
10/14	W	17-14	St. Louis
10/28	W	30-9	at New York Jets
11/04	L	20-23	at Indianapolis
11/11	L	3-37	Tennessee
11/15	L	14-19	at Buffalo
11/25	W	24-21	Seattle
12/02	L	16-23	New England
12/09	L	13-27	at San Francisco
12/16	W	24-3	Jacksonville
12/23	W	24-10	Buffalo
12/30	L	0-28	at New England

(OT) Overtime

SCORE BY PERIODS

Dolphins	50	91	71	76	0	—	288
Opponents	70	92	48	101	6	—	317

2012 TEAM STATISTICS

	Dolphins	Opp.
Total First Downs	288	320
Rushing	93	79
Passing	158	215
Penalty	37	26
3rd Down: Made/Att	78/207	87/238
3rd Down Pct.	37.7	36.6
4th Down: Made/Att	5/15	12/17
4th Down Pct.	33.3	70.6
Possession Avg.	28:32	31:28
Total Net Yards	4984	5708
Avg. Per Game	311.5	356.8
Total Plays	981	1073
Avg. Per Play	5.1	5.3
Net Yards Rushing	1802	1734
Avg. Per Game	112.6	108.4
Total Rushes	440	431
Net Yards Passing	3182	3974
Avg. Per Game	198.9	248.4
Sacked/Yards Lost	37/243	42/242
Gross Yards	3425	4216
Att./Completions	504/293	600/353
Completion Pct.	58.1	58.8
Had Intercepted	13	10
Punts/Average	76/49.7	86/44.4
Net Punting Avg.	76/40.7	86/39.4
Penalties/Yards	82/724	121/1045
Fumbles/Ball Lost	25/13	23/6
Touchdowns	31	32
Rushing	15	10
Passing	13	18
Returns	3	4

2012 INDIVIDUAL STATISTICS

PASSING	Att.	Comp.	Yds.	Pct.	TD	Int.	Tkld.	Rate
Tannehill	484	282	3294	58.3	12	13	35/234	76.1
Mat. Moore	19	11	131	57.9	1	0	2/9	96.6
Fields	1	0	0	0.0	0	0	0/0	39.6
Dolphins	504	293	3425	58.1	13	13	37/243	76.7
Opponents	600	353	4216	58.8	18	10	42/242	83.4

SCORING	TD R	TD P	TD Rt	PAT	FG	Saf	PTS
Carpenter	0	0	0	26/26	22/27	0	92
Bush	6	2	0	0/0	0/0	0	48
Kaeding	0	0	0	3/3	1/3	0	6
Fasano	0	5	0	0/0	0/0	0	32
Thomas	4	0	0	0/0	0/0	0	24
Lane	2	1	0	0/0	0/0	0	20
Clay	0	2	0	0/0	0/0	0	12
Tannehill	2	0	0	0/0	0/0	0	12
Thigpen	0	0	2	0/0	0/0	0	12
Bess	0	1	0	0/0	0/0	0	6
Hartline	0	1	0	0/0	0/0	0	6
L. Miller	1	0	0	0/0	0/0	0	6
Mar. Moore	0	1	0	0/0	0/0	0	6
Vernon	0	0	1	0/0	0/0	0	6
Dolphins	15	13	3	29/29	23/30	0	288
Opponents	10	18	4	30/30	31/40	0	317

2-Pt Conversions: Fasano, Lane, Dolphins 2-2, Opponents 1-2

RUSHING	No.	Yds	Avg	LG	TD
Bush	227	986	4.3	65t	6
Thomas	91	325	3.6	20	4
L. Miller	51	250	4.9	28	1
Tannehill	49	211	4.3	31	2
Lane	13	13	1.0	4	2
Mar. Moore	1	9	9.0	9	0
Thigpen	1	8	8.0	8	0
Clemons	1	3	3.0	3	0
Fields	1	0	0.0	0	0
Mat. Moore	5	-3	-0.6	1	0
Dolphins	440	1802	4.1	65t	15
Opponents	431	1734	4.0	62	10

RECEIVING	No.	Yds	Avg	LG	TD
Hartline	74	1083	14.6	80t	1
Bess	61	778	12.8	39	1
Fasano	41	332	8.1	22	5
Bush	35	292	8.3	25	2
Clay	18	212	11.8	31t	2
Thomas	15	156	10.4	32	0
Matthews	11	151	13.7	30	0
Lane	11	79	7.2	24	1
Mar. Moore	6	116	19.3	37	1
Binns	6	67	11.2	21	0
L. Miller	6	45	7.5	12	0
Gaffney	4	68	17.0	30	0
Armstrong	3	12	4.0	9	0
Naanee	1	19	19.0	19	0
Thigpen	1	15	15.0	15	0
Dolphins	293	3425	11.7	80t	13
Opponents	353	4216	11.9	66	18

INTERCEPTIONS	No.	Yds	Avg	LG	TD
R. Jones	4	28	7.0	15	0
Smith	2	31	15.5	31	0
Clemons	2	29	14.5	29	0
Marshall	1	7	7.0	7	0
Starks	1	4	4.0	4	0
Dolphins	10	99	9.9	31	0
Opponents	13	198	15.2	49t	2

PUNTING	No.	Yds.	Avg.	In 20	LG
Fields	74	3715	50.2	29	67
Carpenter	1	29	29	1	29
Kaeding	1	35	35	0	35
Dolphins	76	3779	49.7	30	67
Opponents	86	3815	44.4	36	71

PUNT RETURNS	Ret	FC	Yds	Avg	LG	TD
Thigpen	26	6	316	12.2	72t	1
Bess	4	18	30	7.5	11	0
R. Jones	1	0	0	0.0	0	0
Matthews	0	1	0	—	—	0
Dolphins	31	25	346	11.2	72t	1
Opponents	43	11	484	11.3	79t	1

KICKOFF RETURNS	No.	Yds	Avg	LG	TD
Thigpen	38	1040	27.4	96t	1
Lane	2	42	21.0	24	0
Dolphins	40	1082	27.1	96t	1
Opponents	35	868	24.8	98t	1

FIELD GOALS	1-19	20-29	30-39	40-49	50+
Carpenter	0/0	3/3	9/9	8/10	2/5
Kaeding	0/0	0/0	0/0	1/3	0/0
Dolphins	0/0	3/3	9/9	9/13	2/5
Opponents	2/2	6/6	13/15	9/12	1/5

SACKS	No.
Wake	15.0
Odrick	5.0
Starks	4.5
Misi	3.5
Vernon	3.5
Burnett	2.5
Wilson	2.0
Soliai	1.5
Carroll	1.0
Dansby	1.0
R. Jones	1.0
McCann	1.0
McDaniel	0.5
Dolphins	42.0
Opponents	37.0

RECORD HOLDERS
INDIVIDUAL RECORDS—CAREER

Category	Name	Performance
Rushing (Yds.)	Larry Csonka, 1968-1974, 1979	6,737
Passing (Yds.)	Dan Marino, 1983-1999	61,361
Passing (TDs)	Dan Marino, 1983-1999	420
Receiving (No.)	Mark Clayton, 1983-1992	550
Receiving (Yds.)	Mark Duper, 1982-1992	8,869
Interceptions	Jake Scott, 1970-75	35
Punting (Avg.)	Brandon Fields, 2007-2012	46.4
Punt Return (Avg.)	Jeff Ogden, 2000-01	13.7
Kickoff Return (Avg.)	Mercury Morris, 1969-1975	26.5
Field Goals	Olindo Mare, 1997-2006	245
Touchdowns (Tot.)	Mark Clayton, 1983-1992	82
Points	Olindo Mare, 1997-2006	1,048
*Sacks	Jason Taylor, 1997-2007, 2009, 2011	131.0

INDIVIDUAL RECORDS—SINGLE SEASON

Category	Name	Performance
Rushing (Yds.)	Ricky Williams, 2002	1,853
Passing (Yds.)	Dan Marino, 1984	5,084
Passing (TDs)	Dan Marino, 1984	48
Receiving (No.)	O.J. McDuffie, 1998	90
Receiving (Yds.)	Mark Clayton, 1984	1,389
Interceptions	Dick Westmoreland, 1967	10
Punting (Avg.)	Brandon Fields, 2012	50.2
Punt Return (Avg.)	Jeff Ogden, 2000	17.0
Kickoff Return (Avg.)	Duriel Harris, 1976	32.9
Field Goals	Olindo Mare, 1999	39
Touchdowns (Tot.)	Mark Clayton, 1984	18
Points	Olindo Mare, 1999	144
*Sacks	Jason Taylor, 2002	18.5

INDIVIDUAL RECORDS—SINGLE GAME

Category	Name	Performance
Rushing (Yds.)	Ricky Williams, 12-1-02	228
Passing (Yds.)	Dan Marino, 10-23-88	521
Passing (TDs)	Bob Griese, 11-24-77	6
	Dan Marino, 9-21-86	6
Receiving (No.)	Chris Chambers, 12-4-05	15
Receiving (Yds.)	Brian Hartline, 9-30-12	253
Interceptions	Dick Anderson, 12-3-73	**4
Field Goals	Olindo Mare, 10-17-99	6
Touchdowns (Tot.)	Paul Warfield, 12-15-73	4
	Mark Ingram, 11-27-94	4
	Ronnie Brown, 9-21-08	4
Points	Paul Warfield, 12-15-73	24
	Mark Ingram, 11-27-94	24
	Ronnie Brown, 9-21-08	24
*Sacks	Cameron Wake, 9-30-12	4.5

*Sacks became an official statistic in 1982.
**NFL Record

2013 VETERAN ROSTER

No.	Name	Pos.	Ht.	Wt.	Birthdate	NFL Exp.	College	Hometown	How Acq.	'12 Games/ Starts
19	Binns, Armon	WR	6-3	209	9/8/89	2	Cincinnati	Pasadena, Calif.	W(Cin)-'12	3/0
5	Carpenter, Dan	K	6-2	225	11/25/85	6	Montana	Helena, Mont.	FA-'08	14/0
28	Carroll, Nolan	CB	6-1	205	1/18/87	4	Maryland	Green Grove Spring, Fla.	D5a-'10	14/10
77	Clabo, Tyson	T	6-6	329	10/17/81	9	Wake Forrest	Knoxville, Tenn.	FA-'13	16/16*
42	Clay, Charles	FB/TE	6-3	250	2/13/89	3	Tulsa	Little Rock, Ark.	D6-'11	14/9
30	Clemons, Chris	FS	6-1	214	9/15/85	5	Clemson	Arcadia, Fla.	D5b-'09	16/16
92	Denney, John	LS	6-5	255	12/13/78	9	Brigham Young	Thornton, Colo.	FA-'05	16/0
7	Devlin, Pat	QB	6-3	225	4/12/88	3	Delaware	Exton, Pa.	FA-'11	0*
84	Egnew, Michael	TE	6-5	255	11/1/89	2	Missouri	Plainview, Texas	D3b-'12	2/0
59	Ellerbe, Dannell	LB	6-1	240	11/29/85	5	Georgia	Rockingham, N.C.	UFA(Balt)-'13	13/7*
2	Fields, Brandon	P	6-5	245	5/21/84	7	Michigan State	Toledo, Ohio	D7b-'07	16/0
56	Freeny, Jonathan	LB	6-2	250	6/15/89	2	Rutgers	Margate, Fla.	FA-'12	16/0
75	Garner, Nate	G	6-7	325	1/18/85	6	Arkansas	Roland, Ark.	W(NYJ)-'08	16/4
10	Gibson, Brandon	WR	6-0	205	8/13/87	5	Washington State	Puyallup, Wash.	UFA(StL)-'13	16/13*
21	Grimes, Brent	DB	5-10	183	7/19/83	7	Shippensburg	Philadelphia, Pa.	UFA(Atl)-'13	1/1*
82	Hartline, Brian	WR	6-2	199	11/22/86	5	Ohio St.	North Canton, Ohio	D4-'09	16/15
68	Incognito, Richie	G	6-3	319	7/5/83	9	Nebraska	Englewood, N.J.	UFA(Buff)-'10	16/16
74	Jerry, John	G	6-5	345	6/14/86	4	Mississippi	Batesville, Miss.	D3-'10	16/16
20	Jones, Reshad	S	6-1	210	2/25/88	4	Georgia	Atlanta, Ga.	D5b-'10	16/16
57	Kaddu, Josh	LB	6-3	242	3/12/90	2	Oregon	Vacaville, Calif.	D5-'12	4/0
81	Keller, Dustin	TE	6-2	255	9/25/84	6	Purdue	Lafayette, Ind.	UFA(NYJ)-'13	8/5*
41	Lane, Jorvorskie	FB	5-11	258	2/4/87	2	Texas A&M	Lufkin, Texas	FA-'12	16/5
61	Louis, Lance	G	6-3	320	4/4/85	5	San Diego State	New Orleans, La.	UFA(Chi)-'13	11/11*
31	Marshall, Richard	CB	5-11	198	12/12/84	7	Fresno State	Los Angeles, Calif.	UFA(Ariz)-'12	4/4
71	Martin, Jonathan	T	6-5	312	8/19/89	2	Stanford	North Hollywood, Calif.	D2-'12	16/16
90	Martin, Vaughn	DL	6-4	308	4/18/86	5	Western Ontario	Negril, Jamaica	UFA(SD)-'13	12/12*
18	Matthews, Rishard	WR	6-0	210	10/12/89	2	Nevada	Santa Ana, Calif.	D7b-'12	8/1
37	McCray, Kelcie	S	6-1	200	9/21/88	2	Arkansas State	Columbus, Ga.	FA-'12	0*
86	Miller, Kyle	TE	6-5	260	4/18/88	2	Mount Union	Elida, Ohio	W(Ind)-'12	0*
26	Miller, Lamar	RB	5-10	218	4/25/91	2	Miami	Miami, Fla.	D4-'12	14/1
55	Misi, Koa	LB	6-3	257	1/17/87	4	Utah	Santa Rosa, Calif.	D2-'10	14/14
8	Moore, Matt	QB	6-3	216	8/9/84	7	Oregon State	Newhall, Calif.	UFA(Car)-'11	2/0
98	Odrick, Jared	DE	6-5	302	12/31/87	4	Penn State	Lebanon County, Pa.	D1-'10	16/13
24	Patterson, Dimitri	CB	5-10	200	6/18/83	7	Tuskegee	Orlando, Fla.	W(Cle)-'12	2/2
38	Posey, Julian	CB	5-11	187	7/17/88	2	Ohio	Cincinnati, Ohio	FA-'12	2/0
51	Pouncey, Mike	C	6-5	303	7/24/89	3	Florida	Lakeland, Fla.	D1-'11	16/16
97	Randall, Kheeston	DT	6-5	309	5/7/89	2	Texas	Beaumont, Texas	D7a-'12	12/0
64	Samuda, Josh	G	6-3	315	12/23/88	2	Massachusetts	Hollywood, Fla.	FA-'12	16/0
79	Shelby, Derrick	DE	6-2	270	3/4/89	2	Utah	Houston, Texas	FA-'12	16/0
96	Soliai, Paul	DT	6-4	345	12/30/83	7	Utah	Pago Pago, American Samoa	D4-'07	16/16
53	Spitler, Austin	LB	6-2	250	10/26/86	4	Ohio State	Bellbrook, Ohio	D7b-'10	15/0
25	Stanford, RJ	CB	5-10	185	5/6/88	3	Utah	Chino, Calif.	W(Car)-'12	16/0
94	Starks, Randy	DT	6-3	305	12/14/83	10	Maryland	Waldorf, Md.	UFA(Tenn)-'08	16/16
17	Tannehill, Ryan	QB	6-4	222	7/27/88	2	Texas A&M	Big Spring, Texas	D1-'12	16/16
34	Thigpen, Marcus	RB	5-9	195	5/15/86	2	Indiana	Detroit, Mich.	FA-'12	16/0
33	Thomas, Daniel	RB	6-1	233	10/29/87	3	Kansas State	Hilliard, Fla.	D2-'11	12/0
93	Trusnik, Jason	LB	6-4	252	6/6/84	7	Ohio Northern	Macedonia, Ohio	UFA(Cle)-'11	16/2
50	Vernon, Olivier	DE	6-2	268	10/7/90	2	Miami	Miami, Fla.	D3a-'12	16/0
91	Wake, Cameron	DE	6-3	258	1/30/82	5	Penn State	Hyattsville, Md.	FA-'09	16/16
11	Wallace, Mike	WR	6-0	199	8/1/86	5	Mississippi	New Orleans, La.	UFA(Pitt)-'13	15/14*
52	Wheeler, Philip	LB	6-2	240	12/12/84	6	Georgia Tech	Columbus, Ga.	UFA(Oak)-'13	16/16*
27	Wilson, Jimmy	S	5-11	205	7/30/86	3	Montana	San Diego, Calif.	D7b-'11	15/3
72	Yeatman, Will	T	6-6	270	4/10/88	3	Maryland	San Diego, Calif.	W(NE)-'11	4/0

* Clabo played 16 games with Atlanta in '12; Devlin inactive for 16 games; Ellerbe played 13 games with Baltimore; Gibson played 16 games with St. Louis; Grimes played 1 game for Atlanta; Keller played 8 games with the New York Jets; Louis played 11 games with Chicago; Martin played 12 games with San Diego; McCray missed '12 season because of injury: K. Miller inactive for six games; Wallace played 15 games with Pittsburgh; Wheeler played 16 games with Oakland.

Traded—WR Davone Bess (13 games in '12) to Cleveland.

Players lost through free agency (6): RB Reggie Bush (Det; 16 games in '12), TE Anthony Fasano (KC; 16), K Nate Kaeding (TB: 2), T Jake Long (StL; 12), DT Tony McDaniel (Sea; 11), CB Sean Smith (KC; 16).

Also played with Dolphins in '12—S Jonathan Amaya (12 games), WR Anthony Armstrong (5), DE Ryan Baker (1), LB Kevin Burnett (16), CB Michael Coe (1), S Tyrone Culver (4), LB Karlos Dansby (16), DE Andre Fluellen (2), WR Jabar Gaffney (3), TE Jeron Mastrud (14), CB Bryan McCann (8), WR Marlon Moore (14), WR Legedu Naanee (4), S Troy Nolan (3), LB Mike Rivera (1), S Anderson Russell (3).

FIRST-YEAR ROSTER

Name	Pos.	Ht.	Wt.	Birthdate	College	Hometown	How Acq.
Adams, Jeff	T	6-7	305	9/6/89	Columbia	La Grange, Ill.	FA
Alecxih, Chas	DT	6-3	304	2/10/89	Pittsburgh	Lancaster, Pa.	FA
Barker, Chris	G	6-2	305	8/3/90	Nevada	Fontana, Calif.	FA
Brenner, Sam	C	6-2	301	4/27/90	Utah	Oceanside, Calif.	FA
Bumphis, Chad	WR	5-10	196	10/18/89	Mississippi State	Tupelo, Miss.	FA
Burden, Chandler	G	6-4	313	11/17/89	Kentucky	Hamilton, Ohio	FA
Burnette, Chris	DT	6-2	285	2/15/90	Old Dominion	Baltimore, Md.	FA
Clay, Michael	LB	5-11	230	8/30/91	Oregon	San Jose, Calif.	FA
Collins, Junior	WR	5-10	180	11/28/91	Mt. Union	Geneva, N.Y.	FA
Davis, Will	CB	5-11	186	5/8/90	Utah State	Spokane, Wash.	D3b
Francis, AJ	DT	6-5	309	5/7/90	Maryland	Severn, Md.	FA
Fuller, Jeff	WR	6-4	223	4/20/90	Texas A&M	McKinney, Texas	FA
Gillislee, Mike	RB	5-11	208	11/1/90	Florida	DeLand, Fla.	D5a
Gray, Jonas (1)	RB	5-9	225	6/27/90	Notre Dame	Pontiac, Mich.	FA-'12
Highsmith, Alonzo	LB	6-0	234	11/21/89	Arkansas	Missouri City, Texas	FA
Hines, David	LB	6-0	226	2/25/90	Florida Atlantic	Miami, Fla.	FA
Jenkins, Jelani	LB	6-0	243	3/13/92	Florida	Olney, Md.	D4a
Johnson, Keelan	S	5-11	209	9/26/89	Arizona State	Mesa, Ariz.	FA
Jones, Don	CB	5-11	191	5/14/90	Arkansas State	Town Creek, Ala.	D7
Jordan, Dion	DE	6-6	248	3/5/90	Oregon	Chandler, Ariz.	D1
Kovacs, Jordan	S	5-10	205	6/12/90	Michigan	Curtice, Ohio	FA
Liaina, Ina	FB	5-11	240	1/3/90	San Jose State	Oxnard, Calif.	FA
Marshall, Cameron	RB	5-9	211	10/14/91	Arizona State	San Jose, Calif.	FA
McDonald, Andrew	T	6-4	310	9/8/88	Indiana	Indianapolis, Ind.	FA
Okpalaugo, Tristan	DE	6-4	245	10/10/89	Fresno State	Livermore, Calif.	FA
Onyenekwu, Emeka	DE	6-3	251	3/10/90	Louisiana-Lafayette	New Orleans, La.	FA
Posey, Julian (1)	CB	5-11	187	7/17/88	Ohio	Cincinnati, Ohio	FA-'12
Presley, De'Andre	DB	6-0	185	1/10/90	Appalachian State	Tampa, Fla.	FA
Robinson, Lee	LB	6-2	253	4/23/87	Alcorn State	Gloster, Miss.	FA
Scales, Patrick	LS	6-4	248	2/11/88	Utah State	Pleasant View, Utah	FA
Sims, Dion	TE	6-4	262	2/18/91	Michigan State	Detroit, Mich.	D4b
Sinkfield, Terrell	WR	6-0	198	12/10/90	Northern Iowa	Minnetonka, Minn.	FA
Stockemer, Taylor	WR	6-4	215	10/26/89	Arkansas State	Van Buren, Ark.	FA
Sturgis, Caleb	K	5-9	188	8/9/89	Florida	St. Augustine, Fla.	D5b
Taylor, Jamar	CB	5-10	192	9/29/90	Boise State	San Diego, Calif.	D2
Thomas, Dallas	OL	6-5	306	10/30/89	Tennessee	Baton Rouge, La.	D3a
Tyms, Brian	WR	6-3	210	2/21/89	Florida A&M	Ft. Lauderdale, Fla.	FA
Ward, Patrick	T	6-6	305	1/11/91	Northwestern	Homer Glen, Ill.	FA

The term NFL Rookie is defined as a player who is in his first season of professional football and has not been on the roster of another professional football team for any regular-season or postseason games. A Rookie is designated by an "R" on NFL rosters. Players who have been active in another professional football league or players who have NFL experience, including either preseason training camp or being on an Active List or Inactive List, or on Reserve/Injured or Reserve/Physically Unable to Perform for fewer than six regular-season games, are termed NFL First-Year Players. An NFL First-Year Player is designated by a "1" on NFL rosters. Thereafter, a player is credited with an additional year of experience for each season in which he accumulates six games on the Active List or Inactive List, or on Reserve/Injured or Reserve/Physically Unable to Perform.

Log on to www.miamidolphins.com for an up-to-date roster.

COACHING STAFF
Head Coach,
Joe Philbin
Pro Career: Became the ninth coach in Dolphins history on January 20, 2012. Philbin joined Miami after serving as the offensive coordinator with the Green Bay Packers from 2007-2011. During that era, his offense ranked in the top 10 in points scored and total yards every season. In five seasons at the helm of the Packers' prolific offense, the team scored 2,263 points (third in the NFL during that span). In 2011, the Packers set franchise records for victories (15), points (560), and total yards (6,357). The 560 points ranked second in NFL history. In 2008-09, the Packers became the first team in league annals to have a 4,000-yard passer (Aaron Rodgers), a 1,200-yard rusher (Ryan Grant) and two 1,000-yard receivers (Greg Jennings, Donald Driver) in consecutive seasons. Philbin joined the Packers in 2003 as an assistant offensive line coach. He served as the tight ends/assistant offensive line coach from 2004-05 and offensive line coach in 2006. Career record: 7-9.
Background: Philbin played one year at Washington & Jefferson, where he earned his degree in sociology. He has coached collegiately at Tulane (1984-85), Worcester Polytechnic Institute (1986-87), Allegheny (1990-93), Ohio (1994), Northeastern (1995-96), Harvard (1997-98) and Iowa (1999-2002).
Personal: Born July 2, 1961 in Springfield, Mass. He and his wife Diane have six children Matthew, John, Kevin, Tim, Colleen and a deceased son, Michael.

ASSISTANT COACHES
Blue Adams, asst. defensive backs; born October 15, 1979, Miami, Fla. Defensive back Cincinnati 1998-2003. Pro defensive back New York Giants/Jacksonville Jaguars 2003, Rhein Fire 2004, Tampa Bay Buccaneers 2005-06, Cincinnati Bengals 2007. College coach: Purdue 2010, Northern Iowa 2011. Pro coach: Joined Dolphins in 2012.
Lou Anarumo, defensive backs; born August 18, 1966, Staten Island, N.Y. Attended Wagner. No college or pro playing experience. College coach: U.S. Merchant Marine Academy 1989-1990, 1992-94, Wagner 1990, Syracuse 1990-91, Harvard 1995-2000, Marshall 2001-03, Purdue 2004-2011. Pro coach: Joined Dolphins in 2012.
Charlie Bullen, asst. defensive line; born September 28, 1984, Palatine, Ill. Attended Iowa. No college or pro playing experience. College coach: Iowa 2007-2011. Pro coach: Joined Dolphins in 2012.
Dan Campbell, tight ends; born April 13, 1976, Clifton, Texas. Tight end Texas A&M 1994-98. Pro tight end New York

Giants 1999-2002, Dallas Cowboys 2003-05, Detroit Lions 2006-08, New Orleans Saints 2009. Pro coach: Joined Dolphins in 2010.
David Corrao, asst. linebackers; born June 11, 1974, Mission Viejo, Calif. Running back San Diego 1992. No pro playing experience. College coach: Syracuse 2000-03, Northeastern 2004, Mississippi 2005-07. Pro coach: Joined Dolphins in 2008.
Kevin Coyle, defensive coordinator: born January 14, 1956, Staten Island, N.Y. Defensive back Massachusetts 1975-77. No pro playing experience. College coach: Cincinnati 1978-79, Arkansas 1980, U.S. Merchant Marine Academy 1981, Holy Cross 1982-1990, Syracuse 1991-93, Maryland 1994-96, Fresno State 1997-2000. Pro coach: Cincinnati Bengals 2001-2010. Pro coach: Joined Dolphins in 2012.
George Edwards, linebackers: born January 16, 1967, Siler City, N.C. Linebacker Duke 1985-89. No pro playing experience. College coach: Florida 1990-91, Appalachian State 1992-95, Duke 1996, Georgia 1997. Pro coach: Dallas Cowboys 1998-2001, Washington Redskins 2002-03, Cleveland Browns 2004, Miami Dolphins 2005-09, Buffalo Bills 2010-11, re-joined Dolphins in 2012.
Ben Johnson, asst. quarterbacks; born May 11, 1986, Charleston, S.C. Quarterback North Carolina 2004-08. No pro playing experience. College coach: Boston College 2010-11. Pro coach: Joined Dolphins in 2012.
Darren Krein, head strength & conditioning; born July 7, 1971, Aurora, Colo. Linebacker/defensive end Miami 1989-1993. Pro linebacker San Diego Chargers 1994, Barcelona Dragons (NFLE) 1996. Pro coach: Seattle Seahawks 1997-98, 2002-09, joined Dolphins in 2011.
Marwan Maalouf, asst. special teams; born November 26, 1976, Beirut, Lebanon. Guard Baldwin-Wallace 1997-99. No pro playing experience. College coach: Baldwin-Wallace 2000, Fordham 2001, Rutgers 2002-03. Pro coach: Cleveland Browns 2004-06, Baltimore Ravens 2008-2011, Indianapolis Colts 2012, joined Dolphins in 2013.
Phil McGeoghan, asst. wide receivers; July 8, 1979 in Springfield, Mass. Wide receiver Maine 1998-2000. Pro wide receiver Denver 2001. College coach: Maine 2007, Naval Academy Prep 2008, South Florida 2009-2011. Pro coach: Joined Dolphins in 2012.
Chris Mosley, asst. offensive line, born December 5, 1977, Jacksonville, Fla. Running back Southeast Missouri State 1997-98, Washington & Jefferson 1999-2000. College coach: Washington & Jefferson 2004, Akron 2005, Villanova 2006, Boston College 2007, Princeton 2008, St. Anselm 2011. Pro coach: Tampa Bay Buccaneers 2009-10, joined

Dolphins in 2012.
Jeff Nixon, running backs; born October 16, 1974, Rochester, Pa. Running back West Virginia 1993-94, Penn State 1996. No pro playing experience. College coach: Penn State 1997, Princeton 1998, Shippensburg 1999-2002, Tennessee-Chattanooga 2003-05, Temple 2006. Pro coach: Philadelphia Eagles 2007-2010, joined Dolphins in 2011.
Ken O'Keefe, wide receivers; born August 18, 1953, Milford, Conn. No pro playing experience. College coach: New Haven 1976-77, Allegheny 1986-1997, Fordham 1998, Iowa 1999-2011. Pro coach: Joined Dolphins in 2012.
Dave Puloka, asst. strength and conditioning; born January 12, 1979, Arlington, Mass. Linebacker Holy Cross 1997-2000. No pro playing experience. College coach: Stevens Institute of Technology 2005, Virginia 2006. Pro coach: Atlanta Falcons 2007, joined Dolphins in 2008.
Darren Rizzi, special teams coordinator; born July 21, 1970, Hillsdale, N.J. Tight end Rhode Island 1988-1991. College coach: Rhode Island 1992, Colgate 1993, New Haven 1993-97, Northeastern 1998, New Haven 1999-2001 (head coach), Rutgers 2002-07, Rhode Island 2008 (head coach). Pro coach: Joined Dolphins in 2009.
Kacy Rodgers, defensive line; born June 24, 1969, Humboldt, Tenn. Linebacker/defensive end Tennessee 1988-1991. Pro linebacker Shreveport Pirates (CFL) 1994. College coach: Tennessee-Martin 1994-97, Louisiana-Monroe 1998, Middle Tennessee State 1999-2001, Arkansas 2002. Pro coach: Dallas Cowboys 2003-07, joined Dolphins in 2008.
Mike Sherman, offensive coordinator; born December 19, 1954, Norwood, Mass. Defensive end/offensive tackle Central Connecticut State 1974-77. No pro playing experience. College coach: Pittsburgh 1981-82, Tulane 1983-84, Holy Cross 1985-88, Texas A&M 1989-1993, 95-97, 2008-2011 (head coach 2008-2011), UCLA 1994. Pro coach: Green Bay Packers 2000-05 (head coach 2002-05), Houston Texans 2006-07, joined Dolphins in 2012.
Zac Taylor, quarterbacks; born May 10, 1983, Norman Okla. Quarterback Nebraska 2005-06. Pro quarterback Tampa Bay Buccaneers 2007. College coach: Texas A&M 2011. Pro coach: Joined Dolphins in 2012.
Jim Turner, offensive line; born January 15, 1965, Boston, Mass. Fullback 1983-86. No pro playing experience. College coach: Northeastern 1994-98, Louisiana Tech 1999, Harvard 2000-02, Temple 2003-05, Delaware 2005-06, Texas A&M 2008-2011. Pro coach: Joined Dolphins in 2012.

**American Football Conference
East Division
Team Colors:** Blue, Red, Silver, and White
**Gillette Stadium
One Patriot Place
Foxborough, Massachusetts 02035
Telephone: (508) 543-8200**

2013 SCHEDULE
PRESEASON
Aug. 9	at Philadelphia	7:30
Aug. 16	**Tampa Bay**	8:00
Aug. 22	at Detroit	7:30
Aug. 29	**New York Giants**	7:30

REGULAR SEASON
Sep. 8	at Buffalo	1:00
Sep. 12	**New York Jets** (Thurs)	8:25
Sep. 22	**Tampa Bay**	1:00
Sep. 29	at Atlanta	8:30
Oct. 6	at Cincinnati	1:00
Oct. 13	**New Orleans**	4:25
Oct. 20	at New York Jets	1:00
Oct. 27	**Miami**	1:00
Nov. 3	**Pittsburgh**	4:25
Nov. 10	BYE	
Nov. 18	at Carolina (Mon)	8:40
Nov. 24	**Denver**	*8:30
Dec. 1	at Houston	4:25
Dec. 8	**Cleveland**	1:00
Dec. 15	at Miami	1:00
Dec. 22	at Baltimore	*8:30
Dec. 29	**Buffalo**	1:00

*All times ET; Sunday night games in
Weeks 11-16 subject to change
Stadium: Gillette Stadium
(opened in 2002)
• **Capacity:** 68,756
One Patriot Place
Foxborough, Massachusetts 02035
Playing Surface: FieldTurf
Training Camp: Gillette Stadium
Foxborough, MA 02035

GILLETTE STADIUM

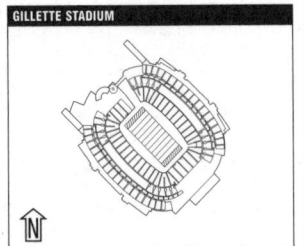

CLUB OFFICIALS
Chairman & CEO: Robert K. Kraft
President: Jonathan A. Kraft
President of New England Patriots
  Charitable Foundation: Josh Kraft
Director of Player Development:
  Kevin Anderson
Vice President of Human Resources:
  Robin Boudreau
Chief Operating Officer of TeamOps
  Security: Mark Briggs
Equipment Manager: Dave Schoenfeld
Director of Player Personnel:
  Nick Caserio
Vice President of Information
  Technology: Pat Curley
Video Director: Jimmy Dee
Senior Vice President of Marketing and
  Brand Development: Jennifer Ferron
Vice President of Customer Marketing
  and Strategy: Jessica Gelman
Vice President, The Kraft Group and Club
  Counsel, the New England Patriots:
  Robyn Glaser
Vice President of Media and Community
  Relations: Stacey James
Publisher and Vice President of Content:
  Fred Kirsch
Vice President of Corporate Sales:
  Murray Kohl
Director of Research: Richard Miller
Vice President of Stadium Business
  Development and External Affairs:
  Dan Murphy
Director of Football / Head Coach
  Administration: Berj Najarian
Senior Vice President of Finance,
  Administration and Operation:
  James Nolan
Vice President of Corporate
  Relationships: David Pearlstein
Senior Football Advisor: Floyd Reese
Senior Executive Producer of Broadcast
  Production: Matt Smith
Director of Cheerleaders: Tracy Sormanti
Executive Director of Community Affairs:
  Andre Tippett
Senior Director of Marketing Services
  and Operations: Gail Titus
Head Athletic Trainer: Jim Whalen
Vice President of Food and Beverage:
  David Wheeler
Vice President of Finance: Jim Wilson
Executive Director of The Hall at Patriot
  Place presented by Raytheon:
  Bryan Morry
Senior Director of Sales: Brian Oates

COACHING HISTORY
**Boston 1960-1970
(450-386-9)**
Records include postseason games
1960-61	Lou Saban*	7-12-0
1961-68	Mike Holovak	53-47-9
1969-1970	Clive Rush**	5-16-0
1970-72	John Mazur***	9-21-0
1972	Phil Bengtson	1-4-0
1973-78	Chuck Fairbanks****	46-41-0
1978	Hank Bullough-Ron Erhardt#	0-1-0
1979-1981	Ron Erhardt	21-27-0
1982-84	Ron Meyer##	18-16-0
1984-89	Raymond Berry	51-41-0
1990	Rod Rust	1-15-0
1991-92	Dick MacPherson	8-24-0
1993-96	Bill Parcells	34-34-0
1997-99	Pete Carroll	28-23-0
2000-2012	Bill Belichick	168-64-0

*Released after five games in 1961
**Released after seven games in 1970
***Resigned after nine games in 1972
****Suspended for final regular-season game in 1978
#Co-coaches
##Released after eight games in 1984

PAID ATTENDANCE
Home 536,452   Away 567,239
Total 1,103,691
Single-game home record,
  71,768 (11/30/08)
Single-season home record,
  579,182 (2007)

2013 DRAFT CHOICES
Round	Name	Pos.	College
2	Jamie Collins	LB	Southern Mississippi
	Aaron Dobson	WR	Marshall
3	Logan Ryan	DB	Rutgers
	Duron Harmon	DB	Rutgers
4	Josh Boyce	WR	Texas Christian
7	Michael Buchanan	DE	Illinois
	Steve Beauharnais	LB	Rutgers

2012 TEAM RECORD
PRESEASON (1-3)

Date	Result	Opponent
08/09	W 7-6	New Orleans
08/20	L 17-27	Philadelphia
08/24	L 28-30	at Tampa Bay
08/29	L 3-6	at New York Giants

REGULAR SEASON (12-4)

Date	Result	Opponent
09/09	W 34-13	at Tennessee
09/16	L 18-20	Arizona
09/23	L 30-31	at Baltimore
09/30	W 52-28	at Buffalo
10/07	W 31-21	Denver
10/14	L 23-24	at Seattle
10/21	W 29-26	New York Jets (OT)
10/28	W 45-7	at St. Louis
11/11	W 37-31	Buffalo
11/18	W 59-24	Indianapolis
11/22	W 49-19	at New York Jets
12/02	W 23-16	at Miami
12/10	W 42-14	Houston
12/16	L 34-41	San Francisco
12/23	W 23-16	at Jacksonville
12/30	W 28-0	Miami

POSTSEASON (1-1)

Date	Result	Opponent
01/13	W 41-28	Houston
01/20	L 13-28	Baltimore
(OT) Overtime		

SCORE BY PERIODS

Patriots	113	177	103	161	3 —	557
Opponents	67	81	75	108	0 —	331

2012 TEAM STATISTICS

	Patriots	Opp.
Total First Downs	444	340
Rushing	151	100
Passing	256	207
Penalty	37	33
3rd Down: Made/Att	110/226	82/205
3rd Down Pct.	48.7	40.0
4th Down: Made/Att	8/12	9/23
4th Down Pct.	66.7	39.1
Possession Avg.	30:41	29:19
Total Net Yards	6846	5972
Avg. Per Game	427.9	373.3
Total Plays	1191	1046
Avg. Per Play	5.7	5.7
Net Yards Rushing	2184	1630
Avg. Per Game	136.5	101.9
Total Rushes	523	415
Net Yards Passing	4662	4342
Avg. Per Game	291.4	271.4
Sacked/Yards Lost	27/182	37/213
Gross Yards	4844	4555
Att./Completions	641/402	594/369
Completion Pct.	62.7	62.1
Had Intercepted	9	20
Punts/Average	61/42.4	67/50.3
Net Punting Avg.	61/37.9	67/41.6
Penalties/Yards	97/840	101/932
Fumbles/Ball Lost	14/7	42/21
Touchdowns	67	38
Rushing	25	10
Passing	34	27
Returns	8	1

2012 INDIVIDUAL STATISTICS

PASSING

	Att.	Comp.	Yds.	Pct.	TD	Int.	Tkld.	Rate
Brady	637	401	4827	63.0	34	8	27/182	98.7
Mallett	4	1	17	25.0	0	1	0/0	5.2
Patriots	641	402	4844	62.7	34	9	27/182	97.7
Opponents	594	369	4555	62.1	27	20	37/213	86.9

SCORING

	TD R	TD P	TD Rt	PAT	FG	Saf	PTS
Gostkowski	0	0	0	66/66	29/35	0	153
Ridley	12	0	0	0/0	0/0	0	72
Gronkowski	0	11	0	0/0	0/0	0	66
Woodhead	4	3	0	0/0	0/0	0	42
Welker	0	6	0	0/0	0/0	0	36
Edelman	0	3	2	0/0	0/0	0	30
Hernandez	0	5	0	0/0	0/0	0	30
Lloyd	0	4	1	0/0	0/0	0	30
Brady	4	0	0	0/0	0/0	0	24
Vereen	3	1	0	0/0	0/0	0	24
Bolden	2	0	0	0/0	0/0	0	12
Dennard	0	0	1	0/0	0/0	0	6
Gregory	0	0	1	0/0	0/0	0	6
Hightower	0	0	1	0/0	0/0	0	6
McCourty	0	0	1	0/0	0/0	0	6
Stallworth	0	1	0	0/0	0/0	0	6
Talib	0	0	1	0/0	0/0	0	6
Patriots	25	34	8	66/66	29/35	1	557
Opponents	10	27	1	38/38	21/25	1	331

2-Pt Conversions: Patriots 0-1, Opponents 0-0

RUSHING

	No.	Yds	Avg	LG	TD
Ridley	290	1263	4.4	41	12
Woodhead	76	301	4.0	19	4
Bolden	56	274	4.9	27	2
Vereen	62	251	4.0	16	3
Edelman	4	45	11.3	47	0
Brady	23	32	1.4	7	4
Welker	2	20	10.0	11	0
Hernandez	1	5	5.0	5	0
Hilliard	1	2	2.0	2	0
Mallett	8	-9	-1.1	-1	0
Patriots	523	2184	4.2	47	25
Opponents	415	1630	3.9	31	10

RECEIVING

	No.	Yds	Avg	LG	TD
Welker	118	1354	11.5	59	6
Lloyd	74	911	12.3	53	4
Gronkowski	55	790	14.4	41	11
Hernandez	51	483	9.5	31	5
Woodhead	40	446	11.2	25	3
Edelman	21	235	11.2	56t	3
Branch	16	145	9.1	25	0
Vereen	8	149	18.6	83t	1
Ridley	6	51	8.5	20	0
Hoomanawanui	5	109	21.8	41	0
Fells	4	85	21.3	35	0
Bolden	2	11	5.5	11	0
Stallworth	1	63	63.0	63t	1
Winslow	1	12	12.0	12	0
Patriots	402	4844	12.0	83t	34
Opponents	369	4555	12.3	68t	27

PUNTING

	No.	Yds.	Avg.	In 20	LG
Mesko	60	2585	43.1	28	62
Patriots	61	2585	42.4	28	62
Opponents	67	3372	50.3	23	66

INTERCEPTIONS

	No.	Yds	Avg	LG	TD
McCourty	5	53	10.6	34	0
Wilson	4	87	21.8	45	0
Dennard	3	95	31.7	87t	1
Gregory	3	50	16.7	36	0
Chung	2	27	13.5	27	0
Talib	1	59	59.0	59t	1
Cole	1	0	0.0	0	0
Mayo	1	0	0.0	0	0
Patriots	20	371	18.6	87t	2
Opponents	9	112	12.4	63	0

PUNT RETURNS

	Ret	FC	Yds	Avg	LG	TD
Welker	25	7	243	9.7	31	0
Edelman	17	1	263	15.5	68t	1
Patriots	42	8	506	12.0	68t	1
Opponents	23	19	154	6.7	25	0

KICKOFF RETURNS

	No.	Yds	Avg	LG	TD
McCourty	27	654	24.2	104t	1
Edelman	3	38	12.7	32	0
Welker	3	33	11.0	17	0
Woodhead	2	43	21.5	23	0
Slater	2	39	19.5	20	0
Gronkowski	1	0	0.0	0	0
Patriots	38	807	21.2	104t	1
Opponents	60	1229	20.5	62	0

FIELD GOALS

	1-19	20-29	30-39	40-49	50+
Gostkowski	0/0	8/8	10/12	9/13	2/2
Patriots	0/0	8/8	10/12	9/13	2/2
Opponents	0/0	6/6	5/6	9/11	1/2

SACKS

	No.
Ninkovich	8.0
Jones	6.0
Hightower	4.0
Francis	3.0
Mayo	3.0
Scott	3.0
Wilfork	3.0
Cunningham	2.5
Love	1.5
Deaderick	1.0
Martin	1.0
Spikes	1.0
Patriots	37.0
Opponents	27.0

RECORD HOLDERS
INDIVIDUAL RECORDS—CAREER

Category	Name	Performance
Rushing (Yds.)	Sam Cunningham, 1973-79, 1981-82	5,453
Passing (Yds.)	Tom Brady, 2000-2012	44,806
Passing (TDs)	Tom Brady, 2000-2012	334
Receiving (No.)	Wes Welker, 2007-2012	672
Receiving (Yds.)	Stanley Morgan, 1977-1989	10,352
Interceptions	Raymond Clayborn, 1977-1989	36
	Ty Law, 1995-2004	36
Punting (Avg.)	Tom Tupa, 1996-98	44.7
Punt Return (Avg.)	Julian Edelman, 2009-2012	13.1
Kickoff Return (Avg.)	Ellis Hobbs, 2005-08	27.7
Field Goals	Adam Vinatieri, 1996-2005	263
Touchdowns (Tot.)	Stanley Morgan, 1977-1989	68
Points	Adam Vinatieri, 1996-2005	1,158
*Sacks	Andre Tippett, 1982-1993	100.0

INDIVIDUAL RECORDS—SINGLE SEASON

Category	Name	Performance
Rushing (Yds.)	Corey Dillon, 2004	1,635
Passing (Yds.)	Tom Brady, 2011	5,235
Passing (TDs)	Tom Brady, 2007	**50
Receiving (No.)	Wes Welker, 2009	123
Receiving (Yds.)	Wes Welker, 2011	1,569
Interceptions	Ron Hall, 1964	11
Punting (Avg.)	Zoltan Mesko, 2011	46.5
Punt Return (Avg.)	Julian Edelman, 2012	15.5
Kickoff Return (Avg.)	Raymond Clayborn, 1977	31.0
Field Goals	Stephen Gostkowski, 2008	36
Touchdowns (Tot.)	Randy Moss, 2007	23
Points	Gino Cappelletti, 1964	155
*Sacks	Andre Tippett, 1984	18.5

INDIVIDUAL RECORDS—SINGLE GAME

Category	Name	Performance
Rushing (Yds.)	Tony Collins, 9-18-83	212
Passing (Yds.)	Tom Brady, 9-12-11	517
Passing (TDs)	Tom Brady, 10-21-07, 10-18-09	6
Receiving (No.)	Troy Brown, 9-22-02	16
	Wes Welker, 9-25-11	16
Receiving (Yds.)	Wes Welker, 9-25-11	217
Interceptions	Many times	3
	Last time by Leigh Bodden 11-22-09	
Field Goals	Gino Cappelletti, 10-4-64	6
Touchdowns (Tot.)	Randy Moss, 11-18-07	4
Points	Gino Cappelletti, 12-18-65	28
*Sacks	Andre Carter, 11-13-11	4.0

*Sacks became an official statistic in 1982.
**NFL Record

2013 VETERAN ROSTER

No.	Name	Pos.	Ht.	Wt.	Birthdate	NFL Exp.	College	Hometown	How Acq.	'12 Games/ Starts
48	Aiken, Danny	LS	6-4	260	8/28/88	3	Virginia	Roanoke, Va.	W(Buff)-'11	16/0
16	Aiken, Kamar	WR	6-2	213	5/30/89	3	Central Florida	Hollywood, Fla.	FA-'12	1/0
26	#Allen, Will	CB	5-10	195	8/5/78	13	Syracuse	Syracuse, N.Y.	UFA(Mia)-'12	0*
	Amendola, Danny	WR	5-11	188	11/2/85	5	Texas Tech	The Woodlands, Texas	UFA(StL)-'13	11/8*
24	Arrington, Kyle	CB	5-10	195	8/12/86	5	Hofstra	Accokeek, Md.	FA-'09	16/12
88	Ballard, Jake	TE	6-6	275	12/21/87	3	Ohio State	Springboro, Ohio	W(NYG)-'12	0*
30	#Barrett, Josh	S	6-2	225	11/22/84	6	Arizona State	Reno, Nev.	W(Den)-'10	0*
	Benard, Marcus	DL	6-2	256	7/26/85	4	Jackson State	Ypsilanti, Mich.	FA-'13	0*
92	Bequette, Jake	DE	6-5	265	2/21/89	2	Arkansas	Little Rock, Ark.	D3-'12	3/0
t-	Blount, LeGarrette	RB	6-0	247	12/5/86	4	Oregon	Perry, Fla.	T(TB)-'13	13/0*
38	Bolden, Brandon	RB	5-11	220	1/26/90	2	Mississippi	Baton Rouge, La.	FA-'12	10/0
12	Brady, Tom	QB	6-4	225	8/3/77	14	Michigan	San Mateo, Calif.	D6b-'00	16/16
84	#Branch, Deion	WR	5-9	195	7/18/79	12	Louisville	Albany, Ga.	FA-'12	10/4
61	Cannon, Marcus	OL	6-5	340	5/6/88	3	Texas Christian	Odessa, Texas	D5a-'11	16/1
23	Cole, Marquice	CB	5-10	195	11/13/83	5	Northwestern	Hazel Crest, Ill.	FA-'12	14/1
63	Connolly, Dan	OL	6-4	310	9/2/82	8	Southeast Missouri St.	St. Louis, Mo.	UFA(Jax)-'08	14/14
96	Cunningham, Jermaine	DE	6-3	255	4/24/88	4	Florida	Stone Mountain, Ga.	D2b-'10	12/3
71	Deaderick, Brandon	DL	6-4	305	8/19/87	4	Alabama	Elizabethtown, Ky.	D7b-'10	14/5
37	Dennard, Alfonzo	CB	5-10	200	9/9/89	2	Nebraska	Rochelle, Ga.	D7a-'12	10/7
21	Dowling, Ras-I	CB	6-1	210	5/9/88	3	Virginia	Chesapeake, Va.	D2a-'11	7/0
43	Ebner, Nate	DB	6-0	210	12/14/88	2	Ohio State	Dublin, Ohio	D6-'12	15/0
11	Edelman, Julian	WR	5-10	200	5/22/86	5	Kent State	Redwood City, Calif.	D7a-'09	9/3
86	Fells, Daniel	TE	6-4	265	9/23/83	7	UC Davis	Fullerton, Calif.	UFA(Den)-'12	13/4
42	Fiammetta, Tony	FB	6-0	250	8/22/86	4	Syracuse	Walkersville, Md.	FA-'12	0*
52	Fletcher, Dane	LB	6-2	245	9/14/86	4	Montana State	Bozeman, Mont.	FA-'10	0*
94	Francis, Justin	DL	6-4	270	2/8/89	2	Rutgers	Opa-Locka, Fla.	FA-'12	10/0
3	Gostkowski, Stephen	K	6-1	215	1/28/84	8	Memphis	Madison, Miss.	D4b-'06	16/0
28	Gregory, Steve	S	5-11	200	1/8/83	8	Syracuse	Staten Island, N.Y.	UFA(SD)-'12	12/12
87	Gronkowski, Rob	TE	6-6	265	5/14/89	4	Arizona	Pittsburgh, Pa.	D2a-'10	11/11
82	Herman, Brad	TE	6-5	255	12/29/89	2	Iowa	Metamora, Ill.	FA-'12	0*
81	Hernandez, Aaron	TE	6-1	245	11/6/89	4	Florida	Bristol, Conn.	D4-'10	10/10
54	Hightower, Dont'a	LB	6-3	270	3/12/90	2	Alabama	Lewisburg, Tenn.	D1b-'12	14/13
13	Holmes, Andre	WR	6-4	223	6/16/88	2	Hillsdale	Elk Grove, Ill.	FA-'12	7/0*
47	+Hoomanawanui, Michael	TE	6-4	263	7/4/88	4	Illinois	Bloomington, Ill.	FA-'12	14/6
	Jenkins, Michael	WR	6-4	214	6/18/82	10	Ohio State	Tampa, Fla.	UFA(Minn)-'13	16/8*
95	Jones, Chandler	DE	6-5	260	2/27/90	2	Syracuse	Endicott, N.Y.	D1a-'12	14/13
	Jones, Donald	WR	6-0	208	12/17/87	4	Youngstown State	Plainfield, N.J.	FA-'13	12/10*
	Kafka, Mike	QB	6-3	225	7/25/87	3	Northwestern	Oak Lawn, Ill.	FA-'13	0*
	Kelly, Thommy	DL	6-6	325	12/27/80	10	Mississippi State	Jackson, Miss.	FA-'13	16/16*
90	Koutouvides, Niko	LB	6-2	245	3/25/81	10	Purdue	New Britain, Conn.	FA-'12	14/0
74	Love, Kyle	DL	6-1	315	11/18/86	4	Mississippi State	Fairburn, Ga.	FA-'10	16/12
15	Mallett, Ryan	QB	6-6	245	6/5/88	3	Arkansas	Texarkana, Texas	D3b-'11	4/0
70	Mankins, Logan	G	6-4	310	3/10/82	9	Fresno State	Catheys Valley, Calif.	D1-'05	10/10
26	#Martin, Derrick	S	5-10	203	5/16/85	8	Wyoming	Denver, Colo.	FA-'12	5/0
51	Mayo, Jerod	LB	6-1	250	2/23/86	6	Tennessee	Hampton, Va.	D1-'08	16/16
32	McCourty, Devin	DB	5-10	195	8/13/87	4	Rutgers	Montvale, N.J.	D1-'10	16/16
65	McDonald, Nick	OL	6-4	305	6/27/87	4	Grand Valley State	Sterling Heights, Mich.	FA-'11	12/1
14	Mesko, Zoltan	P	6-5	230	3/6/86	4	Michigan	Twinsburg, Ohio	D5-'10	16/0
50	Ninkovich, Rob	DL	6-2	260	2/1/84	8	Purdue	Blue Island, Ill.	FA-'09	16/16
71	#Richard, Jamey	OL	6-5	295	10/9/84	6	Buffalo	Weston, Conn.	UFA(Ind)-'12	0*
22	Ridley, Stevan	RB	5-11	220	1/27/89	3	Louisiana State	Natchez, Miss.	D3a-'11	16/12
59	Rivera, Mike	LB	6-2	255	1/10/86	2	Kansas	Shawnee Mission, Kan.	FA-'12	11/1*
99	#Scott, Trevor	DE	6-5	250	8/30/84	6	Buffalo	Potsdam, N.Y.	UFA(Oak)-'12	14/2
18	Slater, Matthew	WR	6-0	210	9/9/85	6	UCLA	Anaheim, Calif.	D5-'08	16/0
77	Solder, Nate	T	6-8	320	4/12/88	3	Colorado	Buena Vista, Colo.	D1-'11	16/16
55	Spikes, Brandon	LB	6-2	255	9/3/87	4	Florida	Shelby, N.C.	D2c-'10	15/14
19	#Stallworth, Donte'	WR	6-0	200	11/10/80	11	Tennessee	Sacramento, Calif.	UFA(Wash)-'12	1/0
	Svitek, Will	T	6-6	308	1/8/82	8	Stanford	Newbury Park, Calif.	FA-'13	0*
31	t Talib, Aqib	CB	6-1	205	2/13/86	6	Kansas	Richardson, Texas	T(TB)-'12	10/9*
53	Tarpinian, Jeff	LB	6-3	240	10/16/87	2	Iowa	Omaha, Neb.	FA-'11	3/0
34	Vereen, Shane	RB	5-9	205	5/2/89	3	California	Valencia, Calif.	D2b-'11	13/1
76	Vollmer, Sebastian	T	6-8	320	7/10/84	5	Houston	Kaarst, Germany	D2d-'09	15/15
	Washington, Leon	RB	5-8	203	8/29/82	8	Florida State	Jacksonville, Fla.	FA-'13	16/0*
62	Wendell, Ryan	OL	6-2	300	3/4/86	5	Fresno State	Diamond Bar, Calif.	FA-'08	16/16
58	#White, Tracy	LB	6-0	235	4/14/81	11	Howard	St. Stephen, S.C.	T(Phil)-'10	11/1
75	Wilfork, Vince	DL	6-2	325	11/4/81	10	Miami	Boynton Beach, Fla.	D1a-'04	16/16
41	Williams, Malcolm	DB	5-11	205	11/22/87	3	Texas Christian	Grand Prairie, Texas	D7-'11	2/0
	Wilson, Adrian	S	6-3	230	10/12/79	13	North Carolina State	High Point, N.C.	D2-'12	15/14

2013 VETERAN ROSTER CONTINUED

No.	Name	Pos.	Ht.	Wt.	Birthdate	NFL Exp.	College	Hometown	How Acq.	'12 Games/ Starts
27	Wilson, Tavon	DB	6-0	210	3/19/90	2	Illinois	Washington, D.C.	FA-'13	16/4
66	Zusevics, Markus	OL	6-5	300	4/25/89	2	Iowa	Arlington Heights, Ill.	FA-'12	0*

* Allen missed '12 season because of injury; Amendola played 11 games with St. Louis in '12; Ballard last active with the New York Giants in '11; Barrett missed '12 season because of injury; Benard missed '12 season because of injury with Cleveland; Fiammetta last active with Dallas in '11; Fletcher missed '12 season because of injury; Herman missed '12 season because of injury; Holmes played seven games with Dallas; Jenkins played 16 games with Detroit; D. Jones played 12 games with Buffalo; Kafka last active with Philadelphia in '11; Kelly played 16 games with Oakland; Richard missed '12 season because of injury; Rivera played one game with Miami and 10 games with New England; Svitek missed '12 season because of injury with Atlanta; Talib played four games with Tampa Bay and six games with New England; Washington played 16 games with Seattle; A. Wilson played 15 games with Arizona; Zusevics did not play in one game, inactive for five games.

\# Unrestricted Free Agent; subject to developments.

t- Patriots traded for Blount (TB).

Traded—RB Jeff Demps (0 games in '12) to Tampa Bay.

Players lost through free agency (4): S Patrick Chung (Phil; 12 games in '12), G Donald Thomas (Ind; 16), WR Wes Welker (Den; 16), RB Danny Woodhead (SD; 16).

Also played with Patriots in '12—DL Ron Brace (10 games), LB Bobby Carpenter (4), S Patrick Chung (12), FB Lex Hilliard (2), WR Brandon Lloyd (16), DL Terrell McClain (1), DB Sterling Moore (8), OL Mitch Petrus (2), WR Greg Salas (1), TE Visanthe Shiancoe (5), TE Kellen Winslow (1).

FIRST-YEAR ROSTER

Name	Pos.	Ht.	Wt.	Birthdate	College	Hometown	How Acq.
Allen, Ryan	P	6-2	215	2/28/90	Louisiana Tech	Salem, Ore.	FA
Armstead, Armond (1)	DL	6-5	298	8/3/90	Southern California	Elk Grove, Calif.	FA
Bartholomew, Ben	FB	6-2	252	7/31/89	Tennessee	Nashville, Tenn.	FA
Beauharnais, Steve	LB	6-2	230	5/2/90	Rutgers	Saddle Brook, N.J.	D7b
Boyce, Josh	WR	5-11	203	5/6/91	Texas Christian	Copperas Cove, Texas	D4
Buchanan, Michael	DL	6-6	250	1/24/91	Illinois	Homewood, Ill.	D7a
Cherrington, Dewayne	DL	6-3	335	8/3/90	Mississippi State	Lawrenceville, Ga.	FA
Collins, Jamie	LB	6-3	250	10/20/89	Southern Mississippi	McCall Creek, Miss.	D2a
Davis, Kanorris	S	5-10	203	1/21/90	Troy	Perry, Ga.	FA
Develin, James (1)	RB	6-3	251	7/23/88	Brown	Dublin, Ohio	FA
Dobson, Aaron	WR	6-3	203	7/23/91	Marshall	Dunbar, W. Va.	D2b
Ebert, Jeremy (1)	WR	6-0	195	4/6/89	Northwestern	Hilliard, Ohio	D7b-'12
Fisher, Elvis	OL	6-5	300	10/25/88	Missouri	St. Petersburg, Fla.	FA
Ford, Brandon	TE	6-3	240	12/31/89	Clemson	Wando, S.C.	FA
Forston, Marcus (1)	DL	6-3	305	9/28/89	Miami	Miami, Fla.	FA
Grissom, Cory	DL	6-2	316	6/9/90	South Florida	LaGrange, Ga.	FA
Harmon, Duron	DB	6-1	200	1/24/91	Rutgers	Magnolia, Del.	D3b
Hines, Quentin	RB	5-11	190	10/8/90	Akron	Detroit, Mich.	FA
Jones, Brandon	CB	6-1	187	11/2/89	Rutgers	Atco, N.J.	FA
Kline, Josh	OL	6-3	310	12/29/89	Kent State	Mason, Ohio	FA
McDonald, Chris	OL	6-5	298	11/13/89	Michigan State	Sterling Heights, Mich.	FA
Moe, TJ	WR	6-0	200	10/14/90	Missouri	O'Fallon, Mo.	FA
Morris, Stephon	CB	5-8	186	1/12/91	Penn State	Greenbelt, Md.	FA
Robertson, Tracy (1)	DL	6-4	280	9/26/89	Baylor	Houston, Texas	FA-'12
Ryan, Logan	CB	5-11	191	2/9/91	Rutgers	Vorhees, N.J.	D3a
Sluss, Ian	LB	6-0	225	1/14/90	Portland State	Vista, Calif.	FA
Stankiewitch, Matt	OL	6-4	290	2/8/90	Penn State	Schuylkill Haven, Pa.	FA
Sudfeld, Zach	TE	6-7	225	4/17/89	Nevada	Modesto, Calif.	FA
Thompkins, Kenbrell	WR	6-1	190	7/29/88	Cincinnati	Miami, Fla.	FA
Vega, Jason (1)	DL	6-4	256	5/30/87	Northeastern	Brockton, Mass.	FA
Vellano, Joe	DL	6-2	285	10/30/88	Maryland	Rexford, N.Y.	FA
Zupancic, Mike	LS	6-5	240	12/14/89	Eastern Michigan	Trabuco, Calif.	FA

The term NFL Rookie is defined as a player who is in his first season of professional football and has not been on the roster of another professional football team for any regular-season or postseason games. A Rookie is designated by an "R" on NFL rosters. Players who have been active in another professional football league or players who have NFL experience, including either preseason training camp or being on an Active List or Inactive List, or on Reserve/Injured or Reserve/Physically Unable to Perform for fewer than six regular-season games, are termed NFL First-Year Players. An NFL First-Year Player is designated by a "1" on NFL rosters. Thereafter, a player is credited with an additional year of experience for each season in which he accumulates six games on the Active List or Inactive List, or on Reserve/Injured or Reserve/Physically Unable to Perform.

Log on to www.patriots.com for an up-to-date roster.

COACHING STAFF
Head Coach,
Bill Belichick

Pro Career: Bill Belichick is in his 39th season as an NFL coach and is the only head coach in NFL history to win three Super Bowl titles in a four-year span. Belichick is currently ranked sixth on the NFL's all-time list with 205 total victories. Hired by Chairman and CEO Robert Kraft on January 27, 2000, Belichick is in his 14th season as New England's head coach. Through 13 seasons, Belichick has delivered three Super Bowl championships, five conference titles, 10 division crowns and 17 playoff victories, while posting an overall record of 168-64. Belichick directed the Patriots to victories in Super Bowls XXXVI (2001), XXXVIII (2003) and XXXIX (2004), and in 2007 he became the first head coach to guide his team to a 16-0 regular season. Only one coach (Pittsburgh's Chuck Noll, 4) has won more Super Bowls than Belichick, and his three Super Bowl titles tie Washington's Joe Gibbs and San Francisco's Bill Walsh for second place on the NFL's all-time list. He has won more regular-season games (126) and more games overall (140) during a 10-year stretch (2003-2012) than any other head coach in NFL history over any decade. Belichick has led the Patriots to a winning record in each of the last 12 seasons, the second longest stretch by a coach with one franchise (Tom Landry, 16 years, Cowboys 1970-1985). In 2012, Belichick guided the Patriots to a 12-4 record, a division title and his seventh AFC Championship game appearance. Belichick helped the Patriots become the first franchise in NFL history to score 500 or more points in four seasons (2007-589, 2010-518, 2011-513 and 2012-557). Belichick is the only head coach in NFL history to win at least 13 regular-season games in five separate seasons. Belichick's Patriots teams own the all-time NFL records for consecutive victories, including the postseason (21 from 2003-04) and consecutive playoff victories (10 from 2001-05). Belichick's 18 postseason wins are third all-time, behind Tom Landry (20) and Don Shula (19). Over a 100-game span from 2003-08, he directed the Patriots to an 82-18 record – the best record for any 100-game span in NFL history. Belichick (.653) has the third highest winning percentage among coaches with at least 150 wins, trailing only Hall of Famers George Halas (.682) and Don Shula (.666). Belichick's recent accomplishments are the latest triumphs in a career during which he has helped produce five Super Bowl titles, eight conference championships and 17 division titles since entering the NFL in 1975. He won his first two Super Bowls as the defensive coordinator for the New York Giants in 1986 and 1990 before claiming three Super Bowl championships with the Patriots. George Seifert is the only other man to have won multiple Super Bowls both as a head coach and as an assistant coach. Belichick launched his coaching career in 1975 with the Baltimore Colts and continued as an assistant coach with Detroit (1976-77), Denver (1978) and the New York Giants (1979-1990). Belichick was named head coach of the Cleveland Browns in 1991, becoming the youngest head coach in the NFL at age 38. By 1994, Belichick's Browns advanced to the second round of the playoffs. In 1996, Belichick joined New England and was a key contributor to the Patriots first division title in 10 years en route to an appearance in Super Bowl XXXI. He then spent three seasons with the New York Jets from 1997 to 1999. Career record: 205-109.

Background: Belichick was a center/tight end at Wesleyan 1971-74.

Personal: Born April 16, 1952, Nashville, Tenn.

ASSISTANT COACHES

Josh Boyer, cornerbacks; born January 21, 1977, Heath, Ohio. Wide receiver/defensive back Muskingum College 1996-99. No pro playing experience. College coach: King's College (Pa.) 2000, Dayton 2001, Kent State 2002-03, Bryant University 2004, South Dakota School of Mines and Technology 2005. Pro coach: Joined Patriots in 2006.

Moses Cabrera, asst. strength and conditioning; born August 20, 1978, Deming, N.M. Oral Roberts 1996-2000. No pro playing experience. College coach: Fresno State 2004-09, Colorado 2010. Pro coach: Joined Patriots in 2010.

Brian Daboll, offensive assistant; born April 4, 1975, Welland, Ont., Canada. Safety Rochester 1995-97. No pro playing experience. College coach: William & Mary 1997, Michigan State 1998-99. Pro coach: New England Patriots 2000-06, New York Jets 2007-08, Cleveland Browns 2009-2010, Miami Dolphins 2011, Kansas City Chiefs 2012, re-joined Patriots in 2013

Ivan Fears, running backs; born November 15, 1954, Portsmouth, Va. Running back William & Mary 1973-75. No pro playing experience. College coach: William & Mary 1977-79, Syracuse 1980-1990. Pro coach: New England Patriots 1991-92, Chicago Bears 1993-98, re-joined Patriots in 1999.

Brian Flores, safeties; born February 24, 1981, Brooklyn, N.Y. Linebacker Boston College 1999-2003. No pro playing experience. Pro coach: Joined Patriots in 2008.

George Godsey, tight ends; born January 1, 1979, Tampa, Fla. Quarterback Georgia Tech 1998-2001. Pro quarterback Tampa Bay Storm (AFL) 2003. College coach: Central Florida 2004-2010. Pro coach: Joined Patriots in 2011.

Patrick Graham, defensive line; born January 24, 1979, Des Plaines, Ill.

Defensive line Yale 1997-2001. College coach: Wagner College 2002-03, Richmond 2004-06, Notre Dame 2007-08. Pro coach: Joined Patriots in 2009.

Pepper Johnson, linebackers; born July 29, 1964, Detroit, Mich. Linebacker Ohio State 1982-85. Pro linebacker New York Giants 1986-1992, Cleveland Browns 1993-95, Detroit Lions 1996, New York Jets 1997-98. Pro coach: Joined Patriots in 2001.

Joe Judge, special teams assistant; born December 31, 1981, Philadelphia, Pa. Running back Mississippi State 2000-04. No pro playing experience. College coach: 2005-07 Mississippi State, Birmingham-Southern 2008, Alabama 2009-11. Pro coach: Joined Patriots in 2011.

Josh McDaniels, offensive coordinator/quarterbacks; born April 22, 1976, Canton, Ohio. No pro playing experience. College coach: Michigan State 1999-2000. Pro coach: New England Patriots 2001-2008, Denver Broncos, 2009-2010 (head coach), St. Louis Rams 2011, re-joined Patriots in 2012.

Harold Nash, strength and conditioning; born May 5, 1970, New Orleans, La. Defensive back Louisiana-Lafayette 1988-1993. Pro defensive back Shreveport Pirates (CFL) 1994-95, Montreal Alouettes (CFL) 1996-99, Winnipeg Blue Bombers (CFL) 1999-2003, Edmonton Eskimos (CFL) 2004. Pro coach: Joined Patriots in 2005.

Scott O'Brien, special teams; born June 25, 1957, Superior, Wisc. Linebacker Wisconsin-Superior 1975-78. No pro playing experience. College coach: Wisconsin-Superior 1980-82, Nevada-Las Vegas 1983-85, Rice 1986, Pittsburgh 1987-1990. Pro coach: Cleveland Browns 1991-95, Baltimore Ravens 1996-98, Carolina Panthers 1999-2004, Miami Dolphins 2005-06, Denver Broncos 2007-08, joined Patriots in 2009.

Chad O'Shea, receivers; born December 18, 1972, Houston, Texas. Quarterback Marshall 1991-93, Houston 1994-95. No pro playing experience. College coach: Houston 1996-99, Southern Mississippi 2000-02. Pro coach: Kansas City Chiefs 2003-05, Minnesota Vikings 2006-08, joined Patriots in 2009.

Matt Patricia, defensive coordinator; born September 13, 1974, Sherrill, N.Y. Center-guard Rensselaer 1992-96. No pro playing experience. College coach: Rensselaer 1996, Amherst 1999-2000, Syracuse 2001-03. Pro coach: Joined Patriots in 2004.

Dante Scarnecchia, asst. head coach/offensive line; born February 15, 1948, Los Angeles, Calif. Center/guard California Western 1968-1970. No pro playing experience. College coach: California Western 1970-72, Iowa State 1973-74, Southern Methodist 1975-76, Pacific 1977-78, Northern Arizona 1979, Southern Methodist 1980-81. Pro coach: New England Patriots 1982-88, Indianapolis Colts 1989-1990, re-joined Patriots in 1991.

American Football Conference
East Division
Team Colors: Green and White
1 Jets Drive
Florham Park, New Jersey 07932
Telephone (973) 549-4800

2013 SCHEDULE
PRESEASON
Aug. 9	at Detroit	7:30
Aug. 17	**Jacksonville**	7:30
Aug. 24	at New York Giants	7:00
Aug. 29	**Philadelphia**	7:00

REGULAR SEASON
Sep. 8	**Tampa Bay**	1:00
Sep. 12	at New England (Thurs)	8:25
Sep. 22	**Buffalo**	4:25
Sep. 29	at Tennessee	4:05
Oct. 7	at Atlanta (Mon)	8:40
Oct. 13	**Pittsburgh**	1:00
Oct. 20	**New England**	1:00
Oct. 27	at Cincinnati	4:05
Nov. 3	**New Orleans**	1:00
Nov. 10	BYE	
Nov. 17	at Buffalo	1:00
Nov. 24	at Baltimore	1:00
Dec. 1	**Miami**	1:00
Dec. 8	**Oakland**	1:00
Dec. 15	at Carolina	4:05
Dec. 22	**Cleveland**	1:00
Dec. 29	at Miami	1:00

All times ET; Sunday night games in Weeks 11-16 subject to change
Stadium: MetLife Stadium
(opened in 2010)
•**Capacity:** 82,500
East Rutherford, New Jersey 07073
Playing Surface: FieldTurf
Training Camp: SUNY Cortland
Cortland, New York 13045

METLIFE STADIUM

CLUB OFFICIALS
Chairman and CEO:
Robert Wood Johnson IV
President, Neil Glat
General Manager: John Idzik
S.V.P., Corporate Sales, Marketing & Stadium Dev.: Marc Riccio
S.V.P., Consumer & Premium Sales and Services: Rob Sullivan
S.V.P., Marketing & Fan Engagement: Seth Rabinowitz
Chief Financial Officer: Brian Friedman
V.P., Business & Legal Affairs: Hymie Elhai
V.P., Corporate Marketing and Business Development: Bob Brennfleck
V.P., IT: Tom Murphy
V.P., Security and Facility Operations: Robert Mastroddi
Senior Executive, College Scouting: Terry Bradway
Director, Pro Personnel: Brendan Prophett
Director, College Scouting: Jeff Bauer
Coordinator, College Scouting: Dan Zbojovsky
Personnel Scouts: Matt Bazirgan, Aaron Glenn, Cole Hufnagel, Jay Mandolesi
Assistant, Pro Personnel: Greg Nejmeh
Assistant, Player Personnel: Kathryn Smith
Manager, Football Administration: Jacqueline Davidson
Senior Director, Athletic Training: John Mellody
Assistant Athletic Trainers: Josh Koch, Dave Zuffelato
Senior Director, New Business Development: Jeff Fernandez
Senior Director, Multimedia & Production: Rich Gentile
Senior Director, Football Operations: Clay Hampton
Senior Director, Ticket Operations: Jeff Hecker
Senior Director, Corporate Partnerships: Jennifer Linn
Senior Director, Events & Game Operations: Brian Mulligan
Senior Director, Merchandise and Concessions: Chris Pierce
Senior Director, Media Relations: Bruce Speight
Director, Equipment: Gus Granneman
Manager, Equipment: Vito Contento
Assistant Manager, Equipment: Jim Gallione
Assistant, Equipment: Brendan Burger
Director, Community Relations: Jesse Linder
Director, Player Development: David Szott
Director, Video: Tim Tubito

COACHING HISTORY
New York Titans 1960-62
(377-444-8)
Records include postseason games
1960-61	Sammy Baugh	14-14-0
1962	Clyde (Bulldog) Turner	5-9-0
1963-1973	Weeb Ewbank	73-78-6
1974-75	Charley Winner*	9-14-0
1975	Ken Shipp	1-4-0
1976	Lou Holtz**	3-10-0
1976	Mike Holovak	0-1-0
1977-1982	Walt Michaels	41-49-1
1983-89	Joe Walton	54-59-1
1990-93	Bruce Coslet	26-39-0
1994	Pete Carroll	6-10-0
1995-96	Rich Kotite	4-28-0
1997-99	Bill Parcells	30-20-0
2000	Al Groh	9-7-0
2001-05	Herman Edwards	41-44-0
2006-08	Eric Mangini	23-26-0
2009-2012	Rex Ryan	38-32-0

*Released after nine games in 1975
**Resigned after 13 games in 1976

PAID ATTENDANCE
Home 600,443   Away 490,110
Total 1,090,553
Single-game home record, 79,572 (11/19/06)
Single-season home record, 628,773 (2002)

2013 DRAFT CHOICES
Round	Name	Pos.	College
1	Dee Milliner	DB	Alabama
	Sheldon Richardson	DT	Missouri
2	Geno Smith	QB	West Virginia
3	Brian Winters	OL	Kent St.
5	Oday Aboushi	OL	Virginia
6	Will Campbell	G	Michigan
7	Tommy Bohanon	FB	Wake Forest

2012 TEAM RECORD
PRESEASON (0-4)

Date	Result	Opponent
08/10	L 6-17	at Cincinnati
08/18	L 3-26	New York Giants
08/26	L 12-17	Carolina
08/30	L 10-28	at Philadelphia

REGULAR SEASON (6-10)

Date	Result	Opponent
09/09	W 48-28	Buffalo
09/16	L 10-27	at Pittsburgh
09/23	W 23-20	at Miami (OT)
09/30	L 0-34	San Francisco
10/08	L 17-23	Houston
10/14	W 35-9	Indianapolis
10/21	L 26-29	at New England (OT)
10/28	L 9-30	Miami
11/11	L 7-28	at Seattle
11/18	W 27-13	at St. Louis
11/22	L 19-49	New England
12/02	W 7-6	Arizona
12/09	W 17-10	at Jacksonville
12/17	L 10-14	at Tennessee
12/23	L 17-27	San Diego
12/30	L 9-28	at Buffalo

(OT) Overtime

SCORE BY PERIODS

Jets	58	69	67	84	3 —	281
Opponents	72	120	69	111	3 —	375

2012 TEAM STATISTICS

	Jets	Opp.
Total First Downs	299	293
Rushing	102	96
Passing	162	161
Penalty	35	36
3rd Down: Made/Att	80/217	84/226
3rd Down Pct.	36.9	37.2
4th Down: Made/Att	7/14	12/15
4th Down Pct.	50.0	80.0
Possession Avg.	29:55	30:05
Total Net Yards	4787	5174
Avg. Per Game	299.2	323.4
Total Plays	1034	1019
Avg. Per Play	4.6	5.1
Net Yards Rushing	1896	2138
Avg. Per Game	118.5	133.6
Total Rushes	494	495
Net Yards Passing	2891	3036
Avg. Per Game	180.7	189.8
Sacked/Yards Lost	47/287	30/170
Gross Yards	3178	3206
Att./Completions	493/272	494/266
Completion Pct.	55.2	53.8
Had Intercepted	19	11
Punts/Average	86/44.7	89/44.3
Net Punting Avg.	86/37.6	89/39.9
Penalties/Yards	83/708	109/805
Fumbles/Ball Lost	32/18	16/12
Touchdowns	31	44
Rushing	12	17
Passing	14	20
Returns	5	7

2012 INDIVIDUAL STATISTICS

PASSING

	Att.	Comp.	Yds.	Pct.	TD	Int.	Tkld.	Rate
Sanchez	453	246	2883	54.3	13	18	34/209	66.9
McElroy	31	19	214	61.3	1	1	11/71	79.2
Tebow	8	6	39	75.0	0	0	2/7	84.9
Kerley	1	1	42	100.0	0	0	0/0	118.8
Jets	493	272	3178	55.2	14	19	47/287	68.3
Opponents	494	266	3206	53.8	20	11	30/170	78.2

SCORING

	TD R	TD P	TD Rt	PAT	FG	Saf	PTS
Folk	0	0	0	30/30	21/27	0	93
Greene	8	0	0	0/0	0/0	0	48
Powell	4	0	0	0/0	0/0	0	24
Cumberland	0	3	0	0/0	0/0	0	18
S. Hill	0	3	0	0/0	0/0	0	18
Kerley	0	2	1	0/0	0/0	0	18
Keller	0	2	0	0/0	0/0	0	12
Schilens	0	2	0	0/0	0/0	0	12
Cromartie	0	0	1	0/0	0/0	0	6
J. Hill	0	1	0	0/0	0/0	0	6
Holmes	0	1	0	0/0	0/0	0	6
Landry	0	0	1	0/0	0/0	0	6
McKnight	0	0	1	0/0	0/0	0	6
Wilkerson	0	0	1	0/0	0/0	0	6
Jets	12	14	5	30/30	21/27	1	281
Opponents	17	20	7	43/43	22/31	1	375

2-Pt Conversions: Jets 0-1, Opponents 0-1

RUSHING

	No.	Yds	Avg	LG	TD
Greene	276	1063	3.9	36	8
Powell	110	437	4.0	18	4
McKnight	30	179	6.0	61	0
Tebow	32	102	3.2	22	0
Hilliard	8	31	3.9	9	0
McElroy	8	30	3.8	15	0
Sanchez	22	28	1.3	8	0
Gates	1	12	12.0	12	0
Kerley	5	8	1.6	5	0
Grimes	2	6	3.0	5	0
Jets	494	1896	3.8	61	12
Opponents	495	2138	4.3	94t	17

RECEIVING

	No.	Yds	Avg	LG	TD
Kerley	56	827	14.8	66	2
Cumberland	29	359	12.4	39	3
Keller	28	317	11.3	32	2
Schilens	28	289	10.3	25t	2
S. Hill	21	252	12.0	33t	3
Holmes	20	272	13.6	38	1
Greene	19	151	7.9	30	0
Powell	17	140	8.2	16	0
Gates	16	224	14.0	42	0
Reuland	11	83	7.5	18	0
Edwards	10	125	12.5	19	0
Hilliard	4	23	5.8	9	0
Gilyard	2	15	7.5	11	0
J. Hill	2	15	7.5	10	1
Grimes	2	7	3.5	4	0
Bellore	1	23	23.0	23	0
McKnight	1	18	18.0	18	0
H. Smith	1	16	16.0	16	0
White	1	13	13.0	13	0
Epps	1	9	9.0	9	0
K. Bell	1	2	2.0	2	0
Cromartie	1	-2	-2.0	-2	0
Jets	272	3178	11.7	66	14
Opponents	266	3206	12.1	83t	20

PUNTING

	No.	Yds.	Avg.	In 20	LG
Malone	84	3848	45.8	27	61
Jets	86	3848	44.7	27	61
Opponents	89	3947	44.3	38	62

INTERCEPTIONS

	No.	Yds	Avg	LG	TD
Cromartie	3	53	17.7	40t	1
Landry	2	42	21.0	24	1
Lankster	2	0	0.0	0	0
Scott	1	11	11.0	11	0
E. Smith	1	5	5.0	5	0
Wilson	1	5	5.0	5	0
Revis	1	1	1.0	1	0
Jets	11	117	10.6	40t	2
Opponents	19	264	13.9	86	1

PUNT RETURNS

	Ret	FC	Yds	Avg	LG	TD
Kerley	19	36	208	10.9	68t	1
Wilson	4	2	30	7.5	19	0
Jets	23	38	238	10.3	68t	1
Opponents	31	24	375	12.1	63t	1

KICKOFF RETURNS

	No.	Yds	Avg	LG	TD
McKnight	39	1072	27.5	100t	1
Gates	5	144	28.8	47	0
Cromartie	2	42	21.0	22	0
E. Smith	1	19	19.0	19	0
Reuland	1	14	14.0	14	0
Wilson	1	9	9.0	9	0
Bellore	1	8	8.0	8	0
Jets	50	1308	26.2	100t	1
Opponents	54	1184	21.9	104t	1

FIELD GOALS

	1-19	20-29	30-39	40-49	50+
Folk	0/0	7/8	6/8	5/7	3/4
Jets	0/0	7/8	6/8	5/7	3/4
Opponents	0/0	5/5	5/6	10/15	2/5

SACKS

	No.
Coples	5.5
Wilkerson	5.0
McIntyre	3.5
Harris	3.0
Pace	3.0
Scott	2.5
Thomas	2.5
Allen	1.0
Y. Bell	1.0
DeVito	1.0
Lankster	1.0
Po'uha	1.0
Jets	30.0
Opponents	47.0

RECORD HOLDERS
INDIVIDUAL RECORDS—CAREER

Category	Name	Performance
Rushing (Yds.)	Curtis Martin, 1998-2005	10,302
Passing (Yds.)	Joe Namath, 1965-1976	27,057
Passing (TDs)	Joe Namath, 1965-1976	170
Receiving (No.)	Don Maynard, 1960-1972	627
Receiving (Yds.)	Don Maynard, 1960-1972	11,732
Interceptions	Bill Baird, 1963-69	34
Punting (Avg.)	Ben Graham, 2005-08	43.7
Punt Return (Avg.)	Dick Christy, 1961-63	16.2
Kickoff Return (Avg.)	Joe McKnight, 2010-12	29.0
Field Goals	Pat Leahy, 1974-1991	304
Touchdowns (Tot.)	Don Maynard, 1960-1972	88
Points	Pat Leahy, 1974-1991	1,470
*Sacks	Mark Gastineau, 1979-1988	74.0

INDIVIDUAL RECORDS—SINGLE SEASON

Category	Name	Performance
Rushing (Yds.)	Curtis Martin, 2004	1,697
Passing (Yds.)	Joe Namath, 1967	4,007
Passing (TDs)	Vinny Testaverde, 1998	29
Receiving (No.)	Al Toon, 1988	93
Receiving (Yds.)	Don Maynard, 1967	1,434
Interceptions	Dainard Paulson, 1964	12
Punting (Avg.)	Robert Malone, 2012	45.8
Punt Return (Avg.)	Dick Christy, 1961	21.3
Kickoff Return (Avg.)	Joe McKnight, 2011	31.6
Field Goals	Jim Turner, 1968	34
Touchdowns (Tot.)	Thomas Jones, 2008	15
Points	Jim Turner, 1968	145
*Sacks	Mark Gastineau, 1984	22.0

INDIVIDUAL RECORDS—SINGLE GAME

Category	Name	Performance
Rushing (Yds.)	Thomas Jones, 10-18-09	210
Passing (Yds.)	Joe Namath, 9-24-72	496
Passing (TDs)	Joe Namath, 9-24-72	6
	Brett Favre, 9-28-08	6
Receiving (No.)	Clark Gaines, 9-21-80	17
Receiving (Yds.)	Don Maynard, 11-17-68	228
Interceptions	Many times	3
	Last time by Ty Law, 1-1-06	
Field Goals	Jim Turner, 11-3-68	6
	Bobby Howfield, 12-3-72	6
Touchdowns (Tot.)	Wesley Walker, 9-21-86	4
Points	Wesley Walker, 9-21-86	24
*Sacks	Mark Gastineau, 11-6-83, 9-2-84	4.0
	John Abraham, 11-4-01	4.0

Sacks became an official statistic in 1982.

2013 VETERAN ROSTER

No.	Name	Pos.	Ht.	Wt.	Birthdate	NFL Exp.	College	Hometown	How Acq.	'12 Games/Starts
38	Adams, Royce	DB	6-0	190	5/3/88	2	Purdue	Cleveland, Ohio	FA-'11	0*
39	Allen, Antonio	S	6-1	210	9/23/88	2	South Carolina	Ocala, Fla.	D7a-'12	7/1
95	Barnes, Antwan	LB	6-1	251	10/19/84	7	Florida International	Miami, Fla.	UFA(SD)-'13	11/0*
54	Bellore, Nick	LB	6-1	250	5/12/89	3	Central Michigan	Whitefish Bay, Wis.	FA-'11	16/0
22	Berry, Aaron	CB	5-11	180	6/25/88	4	Pittsburgh	Harrisburg, Pa.	FA-'12	7/0
32	Bush, Josh	S	5-11	205	3/6/89	2	Wake Forest	Lexington, N.C.	D6-'12	16/0
66	Colon, Willie	OL	6-3	315	4/9/83	8	Hofstra	Bronx, N.Y.	FA-'13	11/11*
98	Coples, Quinton	DE	6-6	290	6/22/90	2	North Carolina	Kinston, N.C.	D1-'12	16/2
31	Cromartie, Antonio	CB	6-2	210	4/15/84	8	Florida State	Tallahassee, Fla.	T(SD)-'10	16/16
87	Cumberland, Jeff	TE	6-4	260	5/2/87	4	Illinois	Columbus, Ohio	FA-'10	15/12
56	Davis, Demario	LB	6-2	239	1/11/89	2	Arkansas State	Brandon, Miss.	D3-'12	16/3
62	Ducasse, Vladimir	OL	6-5	325	10/15/87	4	Massachusetts	Stamford, Conn.	D2-'10	16/0
#Edwards, Braylon		WR	6-3	214	2/23/83	9	Michigan	Detroit, Mich.	W(Sea)-'12	13/4*
93	Ellis, Kenrick	DT	6-4	346	12/10/87	3	Hampton	Greenacres, Fla.	D3-'11	12/2
60	Ferguson, D'Brickashaw	T	6-6	310	12/10/83	8	Virginia	Freeport, N.Y.	D1a-'06	16/16
34	Fletcher, Donnie	CB	6-1	195	5/23/90	2	Boston College	Cleveland, Ohio	FA-'12	3/0
2	Folk, Nick	K	6-1	222	11/5/84	7	Arizona	Hollywood, Calif.	FA-'10	16/0
71	Garay, Antonio	DL	6-4	320	11/30/79	8	Boston College	Rahway, N.J.	FA-'13	8/0*
19	Gates, Clyde	WR	5-11	197	6/13/86	3	Abilene Christian	Vernon, Texas	W(Mia)-'12	11/2
23	Goodson, Mike	RB	6-0	210	5/23/87	5	Texas A&M	Klein, Texas	UFA(Oak)-'13	12/0*
52	Harris, David	LB	6-2	250	1/21/84	7	Michigan	Grand Rapids, Mich.	D2-'07	16/16
94	Harrison, Damon	DL	6-4	350	11/29/88	2	William Penn	Lake Charles, La.	FA-'12	5/0
84	Hill, Stephen	WR	6-4	215	4/25/91	2	Georgia Tech	Lithonia, Ga.	D2-'12	11/8
36	Hilliard, Lex	FB	5-11	235	7/30/84	5	Montana	Kalispell, Mont.	FA-'12	14/9*
10	Holmes, Santonio	WR	5-11	192	3/3/84	8	Ohio State	Belle Glade, Fla.	T(Pitt)-'10	4/4
77	Howard, Austin	T	6-7	333	3/22/87	4	Northern Iowa	Davenport, Iowa	FA-'11	16/16
33 t-	Ivory, Chris	RB	6-0	222	3/22/88	4	Tiffin	Longview, Texas	T(NO)-'13	6/2*
37	Jarrett, Jaiquawn	S	6-0	196	9/21/89	2	Temple	Brooklyn, N.Y.	FA-'12	1/0*
11	Kerley, Jeremy	WR	5-9	188	11/8/88	3	Texas Christian	Hutto, Texas	D5-'11	16/7
26	Landry, Dawan	S	6-1	212	12/30/82	8	Georgia Tech	Ama, La.	FA-'13	16/16*
21	Lankster, Ellis	CB	5-9	190	6/3/86	4	West Virginia	Whistler, Ala.	FA-'10	15/1
47	Lansanah, Danny	LB	6-1	255	8/28/85	2	Connecticut	Harrisburg, Pa.	FA-'12	0*
42	Lockett, Bret	S	6-1	220	10/7/86	4	UCLA	San Dimas, Calif.	FA-'12	0*
3	Malone, Robert	P	6-2	215	2/14/88	3	Fresno State	Orange, Calif.	FA-'12	16/0
74	Mangold, Nick	C	6-4	307	1/13/84	8	Ohio State	Centerville, Ohio	D1b-'06	16/16
53	Mauga, Josh	LB	6-1	245	6/20/87	4	Nevada	Fallon, Nev.	FA-'09	5/0
14	McElroy, Greg	QB	6-2	225	5/10/88	3	Alabama	Southlake, Tex.	D7a-'11	2/1
50	McIntyre, Garrett	LB	6-3	255	11/26/84	3	Fresno State	South Lake Tahoe, Calif.	FA-'11	16/4
25	McKnight, Joe	RB	5-11	205	4/16/88	4	Southern California	River Ridge, La.	D4-'10	15/0
#Moore, Brandon		G	6-3	305	6/3/80	11	Illinois	Gary, Ind.	FA-'02	16/16
97	Pace, Calvin	LB	6-4	265	10/28/80	11	Wake Forest	Douglasville, Ga.	UFA(Ariz)-'08	16/16
64	Peterman, Stephen	G	6-4	323	1/11/82	9	Louisiana State	Waveland, Miss.	FA-'13	16/16*
29	Powell, Bilal	RB	5-10	204	10/27/88	3	Louisville	Lakeland, Fla.	D4-'11	14/2
46	Purdum, Tanner	LS	6-3	270	1/1/86	4	Baker	Enid, Okla.	FA-'10	16/0
88	Reuland, Konrad	TE	6-4	260	4/4/87	2	Stanford	Mission Viejo, Calif.	W(SF)-'12	16/3
6	Sanchez, Mark	QB	6-2	225	11/11/86	5	Southern California	Mission Viejo, Calif.	D1-'09	15/15
55	Sapp, Ricky	LB	6-4	252	11/14/86	3	Clemson	Bamberg, S.C.	FA-'11	4/0
#Schilens, Chaz		WR	6-4	225	11/7/85	6	San Diego State	Mesa, Ariz.	UFA(Oak)-'12	15/6
72	Schlauderaff, Caleb	G	6-4	302	11/7/87	3	Utah	Shelton, Wash.	T(GB)-'11	0*
82	Smith, Hayden	TE	6-6	255	4/10/85	2	Metropolitan State–Denver	Penrith, Australia	FA-'12	5/0
#Thomas, Bryan		LB	6-4	265	6/7/79	12	Alabama-Birmingham	Birmingham, Ala.	D1-'02	12/10
35	Trufant, Isaiah	CB	5-8	170	12/9/82	3	Eastern Washington	Tacoma, Wash.	FA-'11	9/1
30	Walls, Darrin	CB	6-0	190	6/20/88	3	Notre Dame	Pittsburgh, Pa.	FA-'12	6/1
17	White, Jordan	WR	6-0	215	6/4/88	2	Western Michigan	Cleveland, Ohio	D7b-'12	2/0
96	Wilkerson, Muhammad	DL	6-4	315	10/22/89	3	Temple	Linden, N.J.	D1-'11	16/15
20	Wilson, Kyle	CB	5-10	190	5/30/87	4	Boise State	Piscataway, N.J.	D1-'10	16/15

* Adams missed '12 season because of injury; Barnes played 11 games with San Diego in '12; Colon played 11 games with Pittsburgh; Edwards played 10 games with Seattle and 3 games with the New York Jets; Garay played eight games with San Diego; Goodson played 12 games with Oakland; Hilliard played two games with New England and 12 games with the New York Jets; Ivory played six games with New Orleans; Jarrett played one game with Philadelphia; Landry played 16 games with Jacksonville; Lansanah last active with Green Bay '08; Lockett last active with New England '09; Peterman played 16 games with Detroit; Schlauderaff inactive for 14 games.

Unrestricted Free Agent; subject to developments.

t- Jets traded for Ivory (NO).

Traded—CB Darrelle Revis (2 games in '12) to Tampa Bay.

Retired—David Garrard, 9-year quarterback, 0 games in '12.

Players lost through free agency (6): S Yeremiah Bell (Ariz; 16), DE Mike DeVito (KC; 16), RB Shonn Greene (Tenn; 16), TE Dustin Keller (Mia; 8), S LaRon Landry (Ind; 16), G Matt Slauson (Chi; 16).

Also played with Jets in '12—RB Kahlil Bell (3 games), FB John Conner (3), DL Marcus Dixon (3), LB Marcus Dowtin (3), TE Dedrick Epps (3), WR Mardy Gilyard (2), RB John Griffin (1), RB Jonathan Grimes (3), WR Jason Hill (3), LB Aaron Maybin (8), DT Sione Po'uha (12), LB Bart Scott (15), S Eric Smith (12), T Jason Smith (16), QB Tim Tebow (12), WR Patrick Turner (2).

FIRST-YEAR ROSTER

Name	Pos.	Ht.	Wt.	Birthdate	College	Hometown	How Acq.
Aboushi, Oday	OL	6-5	308	6/5/91	Virginia	Brooklyn, N.Y.	D5
Aumavae, Junior (1)	DT	6-2	310	4/29/86	Minnesota State	Palmer, Alaska	FA-'12
Bohanon, Tommy	FB	6-1	247	9/10/90	Wake Forest	North Fort Myers, Fla.	D7
Campbell, Will	G	6-5	308	7/6/91	Michigan	Detroit, Mich.	D6
Coleman, Lanier (1)	DT	6-4	322	12/21/86	Louisiana-Lafayette	New Orleans, La.	FA
Collins, Joseph (1)	WR	6-3	200	1/11/88	Weber State	Seaside, Calif.	FA-'12
Crocker, Eric (1)	CB	6-2	195	5/20/87	Arkansas-Monticello	Stockton, Calif.	FA-'12
Davis, Marcus	WR	6-3	233	12/21/89	Virginia Tech	Virginia Beach, Va.	W(NYG)
Davis, Troy	LB	6-2	251	1/6/91	Central Florida	Queens, N.Y.	FA
Dickson, JoJo (1)	LB	6-1	245	7/13/89	Idaho	Wailuku, Hawaii	FA-'12
Finau, Tevita (1)	DT	6-5	288	1/13/86	Utah	Lahaina, Hawaii	FA-'12
Freeman, Dalton	C	6-5	291	6/18/90	Clemson	Pelion, S.C.	FA
Gilleo, Trey	OL	6-7	309	11/24/89	Northern Arizona	Kingman, Ariz.	FA
Griffin, John (1)	RB	5-11	208	12/17/88	Massachusetts	Westminster, Mass.	FA-'12
Hazelton, Vidal (1)	WR	6-2	209	1/9/88	Cincinnati	Staten Island, N.Y.	FA-'12
Landolt, Dennis (1)	T	6-4	306	11/15/86	Penn State	Burlington, N.J.	FA-'12
Maher, Brett	K	6-0	185	11/21/89	Nebraska	Kearney, Nebr.	FA
Mayo, Thomas (1)	WR	6-2	205	2/13/90	California (Pa.)	Reston, Va.	FA-'12
McDonough, Jake	DL	6-5	305	11/3/89	Iowa State	Urbandale, Iowa	FA
Miles, Rontez	S	6-0	203	11/25/88	California (Pa.)	Braddock, Pa.	FA
Milliner, Dee	CB	6-0	201	9/14/91	Alabama	Millbrook, Ala.	D1a
Pantale, Chris	TE	6-5	254	3/22/90	Boston College	Wayne, N.J.	FA
Popek, Mark	OL	6-7	308	8/31/90	South Florida	Plant City, Fla.	FA
Progar-Jackson, Sean	LB	6-3	250	6/7/90	Northern Illinois	Glenview, Ill.	FA
Quigley, Ryan	P	6-3	188	1/26/90	Boston College	Little River, S.C.	FA
Richardson, Sheldon	DL	6-3	294	11/30/90	Missouri	St. Louis, Mo.	D1b
Rogers, Zach	WR	6-0	172	11/22/90	Tennessee	Nashville, Tenn.	FA
Ryan, Titus (1)	WR	6-0	193	5/19/84	Concordia College	Tuscaloosa, Ala.	FA-'12
Shanahan, Mike	TE	6-4	241	12/28/89	Pittsburgh	North Huntingdon, Pa.	FA
Simms, Matt (1)	QB	6-3	210	9/27/88	Tennessee	Franklin Lakes, N.J.	FA-'12
Smith, Geno	QB	6-3	221	10/10/90	West Virginia	Miami, Fla.	D2
Smith, Jacquies (1)	LB	6-2	260	3/18/90	Missouri	Dallas, Texas	FA-'12
Spadola, Ryan	WR	6-3	200	2/15/91	Lehigh	Howell, N.J.	FA
Stroud, K.J.	WR	6-3	205	12/20/89	Bethune-Cookman	Brooklyn, N.Y.	FA
Tripucka, Travis (1)	LS	6-1	240	5/3/89	Massachusetts	Charlotte, N.C.	FA-'12
Winters, Brian	OL	6-4	320	7/10/91	Kent State	Hudson, Ohio	D3

The term NFL Rookie is defined as a player who is in his first season of professional football and has not been on the roster of another professional football team for any regular-season or postseason games. A Rookie is designated by an "R" on NFL rosters. Players who have been active in another professional football league or players who have NFL experience, including either preseason training camp or being on an Active List or Inactive List, or on Reserve/Injured or Reserve/Physically Unable to Perform for fewer than six regular-season games, are termed NFL First-Year Players. An NFL First-Year Player is designated by a "1" on NFL rosters. Thereafter, a player is credited with an additional year of experience for each season in which he accumulates six games on the Active List or Inactive List, or on Reserve/Injured or Reserve/Physically Unable to Perform.

Log on to www.newyorkjets.com for an up-to-date roster.

COACHING STAFF
Head Coach,
Rex Ryan

Pro Career: Named the 15th full-time head coach of the New York Jets on January 19, 2009. During Ryan's four-year tenure, the Jets have fielded a top five defense three times. Since Ryan became head coach, club ranks second in the NFL in total defense (294.8) and first in passing defense (186.3). In 2010, directed team to 11-5 record and became second coach in NFL history to guide a club to the conference championship game in his first two seasons after inheriting a team that did not reach the playoffs the year prior to him becoming head coach. In 2009, led team to the AFC Championship Game as a first-time head coach. Ryan spent 10 seasons (1999-2008) with the Baltimore Ravens. Ravens allowed fewest points in NFL history for 16-game season (165) in 2000 en route to winning Super Bowl XXXV. Began NFL career with Arizona under his father, Buddy Ryan, as coach for defensive line (1994) and linebackers (1995). Career record: 38-32.

Background: Coached at Eastern Kentucky (1987-88), New Mexico Highlands (1989), Morehead State (1990-93), Cincinnati (1996-97) and Oklahoma (1998). Played defensive end at Southwestern Oklahoma State with his twin brother, Rob, who is the New Orleans defensive coordinator. Earned his bachelor's and master's degree in physical education at Eastern Kentucky.

Personal: Born December 13, 1963, Ardmore, Okla. Ryan and his wife Michelle have two sons, Payton and Seth.

ASSISTANT COACHES

Louie Aguiar, asst. special teams; born June 30, 1966, Livermore, Calif. Punter Chabot (Calif.) College, punter/kicker Utah State 1987-88. Pro punter Barcelona Dragons (WLAF) 1991, New York Jets 1991-93, Kansas City Chiefs 1994-98, Green Bay Packers 1999, Chicago Bears 2000. Pro coach: Joined Jets in 2013.

Bobby April III, quality control/defense; born August 15, 1981, Tucson, Ariz. Attended Louisiana-Lafayette. No college or pro playing experience. College coach: Tulane 2005-06, Portland State 2007-09, Nicholls State 2010. Pro coach: Philadelphia Eagles 2011-12, joined Jets in 2013.

Mike Devlin, offensive line; born November 16, 1969, Blacksburg, Va. Offensive line Iowa 1989-1992. Pro offensive lineman Buffalo Bills 1993-95, Arizona Cardinals 1996-99. College coach: Toledo 2004-05. Pro coach: Arizona Cardinals 2000-03, joined Jets in 2006.

Karl Dunbar, defensive line; born May 18, 1967, Plaisance, La. Defensive lineman Louisiana State 1986-89. Pro defensive lineman Pittsburgh Steelers 1990, New Orleans Saints 1992-93, Arizona

Cardinals 1994-95. College coaching: Nicholls State 1998-99, Louisiana State 2000-01, Oklahoma State 2002-03. Pro coach: Chicago Bears 2004, Louisiana State 2005, Minnesota Vikings 2006-2011, joined Jets in 2012.

Justus Galac, head strength and conditioning; born August 15, 1980, Cattaraugus, N.Y. Nose tackle SUNY Brockport 1998-2001. No pro playing experience. College coach: SUNY Brockport 2002, Dickenson College 2003-04, Villanova 2005-11. Pro coach: Joined Jets in 2012.

Steve Hagen, tight ends; born September 15, 1961, Forest City, Iowa. Wide receiver Cal Lutheran 1979-1983. No pro playing experience. College coach: Illinois 1984, Kansas 1985-86, Northern Arizona 1987-88, Notre Dame 1989-1990, Kent State 1991, Nevada 1992-93, Nevada-Las Vegas 1994-95, Wartburg 1996, San Jose State 1997-98, California 1999-2000, Fresno State 2006, North Carolina 2007-08. Pro coach: Cleveland Browns 2001-04, 2009-12, joined Jets in 2013.

Ron Heller, asst. offensive line; born August 25, 1962, East Meadow, N.Y. Offensive tackle Penn State 1980-83. Pro offensive tackle Tampa Bay Buccaneers 1984-87, Philadelphia Eagles 1988-92, Miami Dolphins 1993-95. Pro coach: Amsterdam Admirals (NFLE) 2004, 2006-07, Toronto Argonauts (CFL) 2009, Jacksonville Jaguars 2010-11, Omaha Knighthawks (UFL) 2012, joined Jets in 2013.

Ben Kotwica, special teams coordinator; born December 8, 1974, Tinley Park, Ill. Linebacker Army 1993-96. No pro playing experience. Pro coach: Joined Jets in 2007.

Sanjay Lal, wide receivers; born July 23, 1969, London, England. Wide receiver UCLA 1989, Washington 1990-93. Pro receiver St. Louis Rams 1998, Scottish Claymores (NFLE) 1999. College coach: Los Medanos (Calif.) College 2003, St. Mary's College 2004, California 2005-06. Pro coach: Oakland Raiders 2007-2011, joined Jets in 2012.

David Lee, quarterbacks; born July 2, 1953, Cape Girardeau, Mo. Quarterback Vanderbilt 1971-74. No pro playing experience. College coach: Tennessee-Martin 1975-1976, Vanderbilt 1977, Mississippi 1978-1982, 2011, New Mexico 1983, Arkansas 1984-88, 2001-02, 2007, Texas-El Paso 1989-1993 (head coach), Rice 1994-2000. Pro coach: Dallas Cowboys 2003-06, Miami Dolphins 2008-2010, Buffalo Bills 2012, joined Jets in 2013.

Anthony Lynn, asst. head coach/running backs; born December 21, 1968, McKinney, Texas. Running back Texas Tech 1987-1991. Pro running back Denver Broncos 1993, 1997-99, San Francisco 49ers 1996. Pro coach: Denver Broncos 2000-02, Jacksonville Jaguars 2003-04, Dallas Cowboys 2005-06, Cleveland Browns 2007-08, joined Jets in 2009.

Tim McDonald, defensive backs; born

January 6, 1965, Fresno, Calif. Defensive back Southern California 1983-86. Pro defensive back St. Louis/Phoenix Cardinals 1987-1992, San Francisco 49ers 1993-99. College coach: Fresno State 2012. Pro coach: Joined Jets in 2013.

Marty Mornhinweg, offensive coordinator; born March 29, 1962, Edmond, Okla. Quarterback Montana 1981-84. Pro quarterback Denver Dynamite (AFL) 1987. College coach: Montana 1985, Texas-El Paso 1986-87, Northern Arizona 1988, 1994, Southeast Missouri State 1989-1990, Missouri 1991-93. Pro coach: Green Bay Packers 1995-96, San Francisco 49ers 1997-2000, Detroit Lions 2001-02 (head coach), Philadelphia Eagles 2003-2012, joined Jets in 2013.

Pierre Ngo, asst. strength and conditioning; born August 19, 1984, Muskogee, Okla. Linebacker Tulsa 2004-05, Oklahoma 2006. No pro playing experience. College coach: Arizona State 2008, 2011-12, Nevada-Las Vegas 2008-09. Pro coach: Joined Jets in 2013.

Paul Ricci, asst. strength and conditioning; born November 15, 1969, Washington Township, N.J. Offensive lineman Penn State 1988-89. No pro playing experience. College coach: Maryland 2008-2010, Texas Tech 2011. Pro coach: Arizona Cardinals 1996-97, Baltimore Ravens 1999-2007, joined Jets in 2012.

Brian Smith, asst. defensive backs; born July 15, 1979, Wilmington, Del. Defensive back Massachusetts 1997-2000. No pro playing experience. College coach: Massachusetts 2004-2006. Pro coach: Joined Jets in 2007.

Dennis Thurman, defensive coordinator; born April 13, 1956, Los Angeles, Calif. Defensive back Southern California 1974-77. Pro defensive back Dallas Cowboys 1978-1985, St. Louis Cardinals 1986. College coach: Southern California 1993-2000. Pro coach: Phoenix Cardinals 1988-89, Ohio Glory (WLAF) 1992, Baltimore Ravens 2002-07, joined Jets in 2009.

Brian VanGorder, linebackers; born April 17, 1959, Jackson, Mich. Linebacker Wayne State 1977-1980. No pro playing experience. College coach: Grand Valley State 1989-1991, Wayne State 1992-94 (head coach), Central Florida 1995-97, Central Michigan 1998-99, Western Illinois 2000, Georgia 2001-04, Georgia Southern 2006 (head coach), Auburn 2012. Pro coach: Jacksonville Jaguars 2005, Atlanta Falcons 2007-2011, joined Jets in 2013.

Jeff Weeks, assistant/linebackers; born May 30, 1962, Denver, Colo. Wide receiver Southwest Oklahoma State 1982-84, Northwest Oklahoma State 1995. No pro playing experience. College coach: Western Kentucky 1987-88, Morehead State 1990-91, Phoenix (Ariz.) C.C. 1996, Oklahoma 1999, Fort Scott (Kan.) C.C. 2001-04, Southeast Oklahoma State 2005, Texas A&M-Kingsville 2006. Pro coach: Oakland Raiders 2008, New York Jets 2009-2011, re-joined Jets in 2013.

American Football Conference
West Division
Team Colors: Silver and Black
1220 Harbor Bay Parkway
Alameda, California 94502
Telephone: (510) 864-5000

2013 SCHEDULE
PRESEASON
Aug. 9	**Dallas**	7:00
Aug. 16	at New Orleans	5:00
Aug. 23	**Chicago**	7:00
Aug. 29	at Seattle	7:00

REGULAR SEASON
Sep. 8	at Indianapolis	10:00a
Sep. 15	**Jacksonville**	1:25
Sep. 23	at Denver (Mon)	5:40
Sep. 29	**Washington**	1:25
Oct. 6	**San Diego**	1:25
Oct. 13	at Kansas City	10:00a
Oct. 20	BYE	
Oct. 27	**Pittsburgh**	1:05
Nov. 3	**Philadelphia**	1:05
Nov. 10	at New York Giants	10:00a
Nov. 17	at Houston	10:00a
Nov. 24	**Tennessee**	1:05
Nov. 28	at Dallas (Thurs)	1:30
Dec. 8	at New York Jets	10:00a
Dec. 15	**Kansas City**	1:05
Dec. 22	at San Diego	1:25
Dec. 29	**Denver**	1:25

All times PT

Stadium: O.co Coliseum
  (opened in 1966)
  •**Capacity:** 53,286
  7000 Coliseum Way
  Oakland, CA 94621-1917
Playing Surface: Grass
Training Camp: Napa Valley Marriott
  Napa, California 94558

O.CO COLISEUM

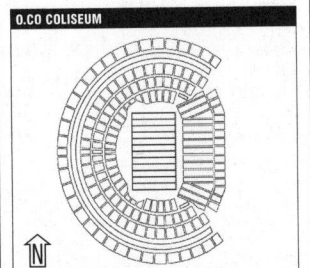

CLUB OFFICIALS
Owner: Mark Davis
General Manager: Reggie McKenzie
Director – Football Administration:
  Tom Delaney
Director – Player Personnel:
  Joey Clinkscales
Director – College Scouting:
  Shaun Herock
Scouting Coordinator: Teddy Atlas
Pro Scouts: Von Hutchins, Larry Marmie,
  Dane Vandernat
College Scouts: Calvin Branch, Zack
  Crockett, Brad Kaplan, Mickey Marvin,
  David McCloughan, Raleigh McKenzie,
  Trey Scott
Head Athletic Trainer: H. Rod Martin
Team Orthopedist: Dr. Warren King
Equipment Manager: Bob Romanski
Video Director: Dave Nash
Assistant to Head Coach: Tom Jones
Director – Media Relations: Zak Gilbert
Director – Player Engagement:
  Lamonte Winston
Director – Team Security: Fred Formosa
Football Operations: Pete Caracciolo
Legal: Jeff Birren, Dan Ventrelle
Finance: Marc Badain, Tom Blanda
Tickets, Suites & Premium Seats:
  Mark Shearer
Youth/Community: Rosie Bone
Sponsorships: Robert Kinnard
Director – Public Affairs: Mike Taylor
Internet: Jerry Knaak
Broadcasting: Vittorio DeBartolo
Technology: Matthew Pasco

COACHING HISTORY
Oakland 1960-1981
Los Angeles 1982-1994
(455-381-11)
Records include postseason games

1960-61	Eddie Erdelatz*	6-10-0
1961-62	Marty Feldman**	2-15-0
1962	Red Conkright	1-8-0
1963-65	Al Davis	23-16-3
1966-68	John Rauch	35-10-1
1969-1978	John Madden	112-39-7
1979-1987	Tom Flores	91-56-0
1988-89	Mike Shanahan***	8-12-0
1989-1994	Art Shell	56-41-0
1995-96	Mike White	15-17-0
1997	Joe Bugel	4-12-0
1998-2001	Jon Gruden	40-28-0
2002-03	Bill Callahan	17-18-0
2004-05	Norv Turner	9-23-0
2006	Art Shell	2-14-0
2007-08	Lane Kiffin****	5-15-0
2008-2010	Tom Cable	17-27-0
2011	Hue Jackson	8-8-0
2012	Dennis Allen	4-12-0

  * Released after two games in 1961
  ** Released after five games in 1962
  *** Released after four games in 1989
  **** Released after four games in 2008

PAID ATTENDANCE
Home 415,571   Away 530,039
Total 945,610
Single-game home record,
  62,660 (11/3/02)
Single-season home record,
  471,151 (2002)

2013 DRAFT CHOICES
Round	Name	Pos.	College
1	D.J. Hayden	DB	Houston
2	Menelik Watson	T	Florida St.
3	Sio Moore	LB	Connecticut
4	Tyler Wilson	QB	Arkansas
6	Nick Kasa	TE	Colorado
	Latavius Murray	RB	Central Florida
	Mychal Rivera	TE	Tennessee
	Stacy McGee	DT	Oklahoma
7	Brice Butler	WR	San Diego St.
	David Bass	DE	Missouri Western

2012 TEAM RECORD

PRESEASON (1-3)

Date	Result		Opponent
08/13	L	0-3	Dallas
08/17	L	27-31	at Arizona
08/25	W	31-20	Detroit
08/30	L	3-21	at Seattle

REGULAR SEASON (4-12)

Date	Result		Opponent
09/10	L	14-22	San Diego
09/16	L	13-35	at Miami
09/23	W	34-31	Pittsburgh
09/30	L	6-37	at Denver
10/14	L	20-23	at Atlanta
10/21	W	26-23	Jacksonville (OT)
10/28	W	26-16	at Kansas City
11/04	L	32-42	Tampa Bay
11/11	L	20-55	at Baltimore
11/18	L	17-38	New Orleans
11/25	L	10-34	at Cincinnati
12/02	L	17-20	Cleveland
12/06	L	13-26	Denver
12/16	W	15-0	Kansas City
12/23	L	6-17	at Carolina
12/30	L	21-24	at San Diego

(OT) Overtime

SCORE BY PERIODS

Raiders	35	89	54	109	3 —	290
Opponents	106	101	146	90	0 —	443

2012 TEAM STATISTICS

	Raiders	Opp.
Total First Downs	300	304
Rushing	72	95
Passing	200	180
Penalty	28	29
3rd Down: Made/Att	77/220	83/212
3rd Down Pct.	35.0	39.2
4th Down: Made/Att	4/16	8/14
4th Down Pct.	25.0	57.1
Possession Avg.	29:27	30:33
Total Net Yards	5504	5672
Avg. Per Game	344.0	354.5
Total Plays	1032	995
Avg. Per Play	5.3	5.7
Net Yards Rushing	1420	1897
Avg. Per Game	88.8	118.6
Total Rushes	376	444
Net Yards Passing	4084	3775
Avg. Per Game	255.3	235.9
Sacked/Yards Lost	27/208	25/185
Gross Yards	4292	3960
Att./Completions	629/376	526/347
Completion Pct.	59.8	66.0
Had Intercepted	16	11
Punts/Average	82/46.7	69/46.0
Net Punting Avg.	82/39.0	69/42.9
Penalties/Yards	108/939	101/925
Fumbles/Ball Lost	22/10	14/8
Touchdowns	28	50
Rushing	4	18
Passing	24	28
Returns	0	4

2012 INDIVIDUAL STATISTICS

PASSING

	Att.	Comp.	Yds.	Pct.	TD	Int.	Tkld.	Rate
Palmer	565	345	4018	61.1	22	14	26/199	85.3
Leinart	33	16	115	48.5	0	1	1/9	44.4
Pryor	30	14	155	46.7	2	1	0/0	70.8
Lechler	1	1	4	100.0	0	0	0/0	83.3
Raiders	629	376	4292	59.8	24	16	27/208	82.4
Opponents	526	347	3960	66.0	28	11	25/185	97.5

SCORING

	TD R	TD P	TD Rt	PAT	FG	Saf	PTS
Janikowski	0	0	0	25/25	31/34	0	118
Moore	0	7	0	0/0	0/0	0	42
Heyward-Bey	0	5	0	0/0	0/0	0	30
Myers	0	4	0	0/0	0/0	0	24
Streater	0	3	0	0/0	0/0	0	20
McFadden	2	1	0	0/0	0/0	0	18
Criner	0	1	0	0/0	0/0	0	8
Goodson	0	1	0	0/0	0/0	0	6
Gordon	0	1	0	0/0	0/0	0	6
Palmer	1	0	0	0/0	0/0	0	6
Pryor	1	0	0	0/0	0/0	0	6
Reece	0	1	0	0/0	0/0	0	6
Raiders	4	24	0	25/25	31/34	0	290
Opponents	18	28	4	50/50	31/37	0	443

2-Pt Conversions: Criner, Streater,
Raiders 2-3, Opponents 0-0

RUSHING

	No.	Yds	Avg	LG	TD
McFadden	216	707	3.3	64t	2
Reece	59	271	4.6	17	0
Goodson	35	221	6.3	43	0
Stewart	25	101	4.0	14	0
Pryor	10	51	5.1	9	1
Palmer	18	36	2.0	9	1
Jones	6	21	3.5	7	0
Heyward-Bey	2	16	8.0	20	0
Schmitt	2	1	0.5	2	0
Lechler	2	0	0.0	0	0
Moore	1	-5	-5.0	-5	0
Raiders	376	1420	3.8	64t	4
Opponents	444	1897	4.3	70t	18

RECEIVING

	No.	Yds	Avg	LG	TD
Myers	79	806	10.2	29	4
Reece	52	496	9.5	56	1
Moore	51	741	14.5	58	7
McFadden	42	258	6.1	20	1
Heyward-Bey	41	606	14.8	59	5
Streater	39	584	15.0	64t	3
Hagan	20	259	13.0	38	0
Goodson	16	195	12.2	64t	1
Criner	16	151	9.4	17	1
Stewart	8	62	7.8	26	0
Ausberry	7	92	13.1	31	0
Jones	2	11	5.5	7	0
Gordon	2	9	4.5	8	1
Pryor	1	22	22.0	22	0
Raiders	376	4292	11.4	64t	24
Opponents	347	3960	11.4	64	28

INTERCEPTIONS

	No.	Yds	Avg	LG	TD
Giordano	2	45	22.5	24	0
Hanson	2	24	12.0	21	0
Adams	2	0	0.0	0	0
Huff	2	0	0.0	0	0
Branch	1	11	11.0	11	0
Burris	1	7	7.0	7	0
Lee	1	4	4.0	4	0
Raiders	11	91	8.3	24	0
Opponents	16	296	18.5	79t	2

PUNTING

	No.	Yds.	Avg.	In 20	LG
Lechler	81	3826	47.2	21	68
Raiders	82	3826	46.7	21	68
Opponents	69	3171	46	26	71

PUNT RETURNS

	Ret	FC	Yds	Avg	LG	TD
Adams	25	9	139	5.6	47	0
Moore	9	4	32	3.6	19	0
Giordano	0	1	0	—	0	0
Mitchell	0	0	2	—	2	0
Raiders	34	14	173	5.1	47	0
Opponents	45	16	450	10.0	28	0

KICKOFF RETURNS

	No.	Yds	Avg	LG	TD
Francies	20	475	23.8	32	0
Goodson	16	359	22.4	51	0
Stewart	3	43	14.3	16	0
Jones	2	22	11.0	16	0
Reece	1	36	36.0	36	0
Raiders	42	935	22.3	51	0
Opponents	30	868	28.9	105t	2

FIELD GOALS

	1-19	20-29	30-39	40-49	50+
Janikowski	1/1	9/9	10/10	5/5	6/9
Raiders	1/1	9/9	10/10	5/5	6/9
Opponents	1/1	6/7	7/8	11/14	6/7

SACKS

	No.
Bryant	4.0
Houston	4.0
Shaughnessy	3.5
Seymour	3.0
Wheeler	3.0
Carter	2.5
Burris	1.5
Kelly	1.0
McClain	1.0
Mitchell	1.0
Tollefson	0.5
Raiders	25.0
Opponents	27.0

RECORD HOLDERS
INDIVIDUAL RECORDS—CAREER

Category	Name	Performance
Rushing (Yds.)	Marcus Allen, 1982-1992	8,545
Passing (Yds.)	Ken Stabler, 1970-79	19,078
Passing (TDs)	Ken Stabler, 1970-79	150
Receiving (No.)	Tim Brown, 1988-2003	1,070
Receiving (Yds.)	Tim Brown, 1988-2003	14,734
Interceptions	Willie Brown, 1967-1978	39
	Lester Hayes, 1977-1986	39
Punting (Avg.)	Shane Lechler, 2000-2012	**47.5
Punt Return (Avg.)	Claude Gibson, 1963-65	12.6
Kickoff Return (Avg.)	Jack Larscheid, 1960-61	28.4
Field Goals	Sebastian Janikowski, 2000-2012	324
Touchdowns (Tot.)	Tim Brown, 1988-2003	104
Points	Sebastian Janikowski, 2000-2012	1,389
*Sacks	Greg Townsend, 1983-1993, 1997	107.5

INDIVIDUAL RECORDS—SINGLE SEASON

Category	Name	Performance
Rushing (Yds.)	Marcus Allen, 1985	1,759
Passing (Yds.)	Rich Gannon, 2002	4,689
Passing (TDs)	Daryle Lamonica, 1969	34
Receiving (No.)	Tim Brown 1997	104
Receiving (Yds.)	Tim Brown, 1997	1,408
Interceptions	Lester Hayes, 1980	13
Punting (Avg.)	Shane Lechler, 2009	51.1
Punt Return (Avg.)	Claude Gibson, 1964	14.4
Kickoff Return (Avg.)	Harold Hart, 1975	30.5
Field Goals	Jeff Jaeger, 1993	35
Touchdowns (Tot.)	Marcus Allen, 1984	18
Points	Sebastian Janikowski, 2010	142
*Sacks	Derrick Burgess, 2005	16.0

INDIVIDUAL RECORDS—SINGLE GAME

Category	Name	Performance
Rushing (Yds.)	Napoleon Kaufman, 10-19-97	227
Passing (Yds.)	Cotton Davidson, 10-25-64	427
Passing (TDs)	Tom Flores, 12-22-63	6
	Daryle Lamonica, 10-19-69	6
Receiving (No.)	Tim Brown, 12-21-97	14
	Brandon Myers, 12-2-12	14
Receiving (Yds.)	Art Powell, 12-22-63	247
Interceptions	Many times	3
	Last time by Rod Woodson, 9-29-02	
Field Goals	Sebastian Janikowski, 11-27-11	6
Touchdowns (Tot.)	Art Powell, 12-22-63	4
	Marcus Allen, 9-24-84	4
	Harvey Williams, 11-16-97	4
	Darren McFadden, 10-24-10	4
Points	Art Powell, 12-22-63	24
	Marcus Allen, 9-24-84	24
	Harvey Williams, 11-16-97	24
	Darren McFadden, 10-24-10	24
*Sacks	Howie Long, 10-2-83	5.0

*Sacks became an official statistic in 1982.
**NFL Record

2013 VETERAN ROSTER

No.	Name	Pos.	Ht.	Wt.	Birthdate	NFL Exp.	College	Hometown	How Acq.	'12 Games/ Starts
28	Adams, Phillip	DB	5-11	195	7/20/88	4	South Carolina State	Rock Hill, S.C.	W(Sea)-'12	14/2
86	Ausberry, David	TE	6-4	258	9/25/87	3	Southern California	Lemoore, Calif.	D7-'11	16/0
75	Bair, Brandon	DL	6-6	285	11/24/84	2	Oregon	St. Anthony, Idaho	FA-'12	0*
69	Barnes, Khalif	T	6-6	321	4/21/82	9	Washington	Spring Valley, Calif.	UFA(Jax)-'09	9/9
77	Barron, Alex	T	6-8	315	9/28/82	8	Florida State	Orangeburg, S.C.	FA-'13	0*
70	Bergstrom, Tony	OL	6-5	310	8/6/86	2	Utah	Salt Lake City, Utah	D3-'12	9/1
96	Bilukidi, Christo	DT	6-5	320	12/13/89	2	Georgia State	Ottawa, Ont.	D6-'12	13/0
33	Branch, Tyvon	S	6-0	210	12/11/86	6	Connecticut	Cicero, N.Y.	D4-'08	14/14
65	Brisiel, Mike	G	6-5	310	3/14/83	6	Colorado State	Fayetteville, Ark.	UFA(Hou)-'12	15/15
95	Burnett, Kaelin	LB	6-4	240	9/6/89	2	Nevada	Lakewood, Calif.	FA-'12	6/0
94	Burnett, Kevin	LB	6-3	230	12/24/82	8	Tennessee	Compton, Calif.	FA-'13	16/16*
56	Burris, Miles	LB	6-2	240	6/27/88	2	San Diego State	Granite Bay, Calif.	D4-'12	16/15
#	Carlisle, Cooper	G	6-5	310	8/11/77	14	Florida	McComb, Miss.	UFA(Den)-'07	16/16
97	Carter, Andre	DE	6-4	260	5/12/79	13	California	San Jose, Calif.	FA-'12	12/0
35	Chekwa, Chimdi	CB	6-0	190	9/7/88	2	Ohio State	Clermont, Fla.	D4-'11	3/0
57	Clayton, Keenan	LB	6-1	230	6/19/87	4	Oklahoma	Sulphur Springs, Texas	W(Phil)-'12	15/0
59	Condo, Jon	LS	6-3	245	8/26/81	7	Maryland	Philipsburg, Pa.	FA-'06	16/0
91	Crawford, Jack	DE	6-5	281	9/7/88	2	Penn State	Longport, N.J.	D5-'12	4/0
	Cribbs, Josh	WR	6-1	192	6/9/83	9	Kent State	Washington, D.C.	UFA(Cle)-'13	16/2*
84	Criner, Juron	WR	6-3	221	12/12/89	2	Arizona	Las Vegas, Nev.	D5-'12	12/0
15	t- Flynn, Matt	QB	6-3	230	6/20/85	6	Louisiana State	Tyler, Texas	T(Sea)-'13	3/0*
12	Ford, Jacoby	WR	5-9	190	7/27/87	4	Clemson	Royal Palm Beach, Fla.	D4-'10	0*
31	Francies, Coye	CB	6-1	185	11/15/86	3	San Jose State	Rancho Cordova, Calif.	FA-'12	15/0
#	Gaither, Omar	LB	6-1	235	3/18/84	8	Tennessee	Charlotte, N.C.	FA-'12	7/5
#	Giordano, Matt	S	5-11	204	10/16/82	9	California	Clovis, Calif.	FA-'11	16/13
50	Goethel, Travis	LB	6-2	255	7/27/87	4	Arizona State	Vista, Calif.	D6-'10	8/0
82	Gordon, Richard	TE	6-4	268	6/7/87	3	Miami	Miami, Fla.	D6-'11	13/1
#	Hagan, Derek	WR	6-2	210	9/21/84	8	Arizona State	Palmdale, Calif.	FA-'12	14/2
23	Hanson, Joselio	CB	5-9	185	8/13/81	9	Texas Tech	Inglewood, Calif.	FA-'12	16/5
	Holmes, Andre	WR	6-4	210	6/16/88	2	Hillsdale	Elk Grove, Ill.	W(NE)-'13	7/0*
99	Houston, Lamarr	DE	6-3	300	6/24/87	4	Texas	Colorado Springs, Colo.	D2-'10	16/16
93	Hunter, Jason	DE	6-4	270	8/28/83	7	Appalachian State	Fayetteville, N.C.	UFA(Den)-'13	0*
11	Janikowski, Sebastian	K	6-1	258	3/2/78	14	Florida State	Daytona Beach, Fla.	D1-'00	16/0
21	Jenkins, Mike	CB	5-10	197	3/22/85	6	South Florida	Bradenton, Fla.	UFA(Dall)-'13	13/2*
27	Jennings, Rashad	RB	6-1	231	3/26/85	5	Liberty	Lynchburg, Va.	UFA(Jax)-'13	10/6*
22	Jones, Taiwan	CB	6-0	197	7/26/88	3	Eastern Washington	Antioch, Calif.	D4-'11	14/0
2	King, Marquette	P	6-0	190	10/26/88	2	Fort Valley State	Macon, Ga.	FA-'12	0*
	Kluwe, Chris	P	6-4	215	12/24/81	9	UCLA	Los Alamitos, Calif.	FA-'13	16/0*
49	Kurn, Mario	LB	6-2	240	7/3/90	2	San Diego	Encinitas, Calif.	FA-'12	0*
#	Leinart, Matt	QB	6-5	225	5/11/83	8	Southern California	Santa Ana, Calif.	UFA(Hou)-'12	2/0
50	Maiava, Kaluka	LB	6-0	230	12/27/86	4	Southern California	Wailuku, Hawaii	UFA(Cle)-'13	16/13*
	Mastrud, Jeron	TE	6-5	255	12/17/87	4	Kansas State	Beaverton, Ore.	FA-'13	14/1*
20	McFadden, Darren	RB	6-1	218	8/27/87	6	Arkansas	North Little Rock, Ark.	D1-'08	12/12
17	Moore, Denarius	WR	6-0	190	12/9/88	3	Tennessee	Tatum, Texas	D5-'11	15/15
76	Nix, Lucas	OL	6-5	320	9/28/89	2	Pittsburgh	Jefferson Hills, Pa.	FA-'12	1/0
49	Olawale, Jamize	FB/RB	6-1	240	4/17/89	2	North Texas	Long Beach, Calif.	FA-'12	3/0
67	Parsons, Alex	C/G	6-4	316	9/14/87	2	Southern California	Irvine, Calif.	FA-'10	16/1
24	Porter, Tracy	CB	5-11	188	8/11/86	6	Indiana	Port Allen, La.	UFA(Den)-'13	6/4*
6	Pryor, Terrelle	QB	6-4	233	6/20/89	3	Ohio State	Jeanette, Pa.	SD3-'11	3/1
45	Reece, Marcel	FB	6-1	255	6/23/85	4	Washington	Inglewood, Calif.	FA-'08	16/14
53	Roach, Nick	LB	6-1	234	6/16/85	7	Northwestern	Milwaukee, Wisc.	UFA(Chi)-'13	16/14*
29	Ross, Brandian	DB	6-1	191	9/28/89	2	Youngstown State	Meadowbrook, Va.	FA-'12	14/1
#	Seymour, Richard	DT	6-6	317	10/6/79	13	Georgia	Gadsden, S.C.	T(NE)-'09	8/8
90	Sims, Pat	DT	6-2	310	11/29/85	5	Auburn	Ft. Lauderdale, Fla.	UFA(Cin)-'13	8/0*
36	Smith, Reggie	S	6-1	192	9/3/86	5	Oklahoma	Edmond, Okla.	FA-'13	0*
79	Smith, Willie	T	6-5	310	11/13/86	3	East Carolina	Kenly, N.C.	W(Wash)-'12	9/7
#	Spencer, Shawntae	CB	6-0	190	2/22/82	10	Pittsburgh	Pittsburgh, Pa.	UFA(SF)-'12	2/2
32	Stewart, Jeremy	RB	5-11	215	2/17/89	2	Stanford	Baton Rouge, La.	FA-'12	4/0
80	Streater, Rod	WR	6-3	200	2/9/88	2	Temple	Burlington, N.J.	FA-'12	16/2
68	Veldheer, Jared	T	6-8	321	6/14/87	4	Hillsdale	Grand Rapids, Mich.	D3-'10	16/16
98	Walker, Vance	DT	6-2	305	4/26/87	4	Georgia Tech	Fort Mill, S.C.	UFA(Atl)-'13	16/9*
61	Wisniewski, Stefen	C/G	6-3	307	3/22/89	3	Penn State	Pittsburgh, Pa.	D2-'11	15/15
	Woodson, Charles	DB	6-1	202	10/7/76	16	Michigan	Fremont Ohio	FA-'13	7/7*
26	Young, Usama	S	6-0	200	5/8/85	7	Kent State	Largo, Md.	FA-'13	13/11*

* Bair inactive for one game; Barron last active with Dallas in '10; Ke. Burnett played 16 games with Miami; Cribbs played 16 games with Cleveland; Flynn played three games with Seattle; Ford missed '12 season because of injury; Holmes played seven games with Dallas; Hunter missed '12 season because of injury; Jenkins played 13 games with Dallas; Jennings played 10 games with Jacksonville; King missed '12 season because of injury; Kluwe played 16 games with Minnesota; Kurn missed '12 season because of injury; Maiava played 16 games with Cleveland; Mastrud played 14 games with Miami; Porter played six games with Denver; Roach played 16 games with Chicago; Sims played eight games with Cincinnati; R. Smith last active with San Francisco in '11; Walker played 16 games with Atlanta; Woodson played seven games with Green Bay; Young played 13 games with Cleveland.

\# Unrestricted Free Agent; subject to developments.

t- Raiders traded for Flynn (Sea).

Traded—QB Carson Palmer (15 games in '12) to Arizona.

Players lost through free agency (7): DT Desmond Bryant (Cle; 16 games), RB Mike Goodson (NYJ; 12), P Shane Lechler (Hou; 16), S Mike Mitchell (Car; 16), TE Brandon Myers (NYG; 16), DE Matt Shaughnessy (Ariz; 16), LB Philip Wheeler (Mia; 16).

Also played with Raiders in '12—CB Ron Bartell (6 games), LB Aaron Curry (2), WR Darrius Heyward-Bey (15), DB Michael Huff (16), DT Tommy Kelly (16), CB Pat Lee (8), FB Owen Schmitt (13), LB Vic So'oto (4), DE David Tollefson (15).

FIRST-YEAR ROSTER

Name	Pos.	Ht.	Wt.	Birthdate	College	Hometown	How Acq.
Bass, David	DE	6-4	256	9/11/90	Missouri Western State	St. Louis, Mo.	D7b
Boyko, Billy	LB	6-2	240	8/3/91	Lehigh	Northampton, Pa.	FA
Butler, Brice	WR	6-3	213	1/29/90	San Diego State	Norcross, Ga.	D7a
Carmona, Eddy (1)	K	5-10	203	9/4/88	Harding	Charleston, Ark.	FA
Casey-Thomas, Chance	CB	5-11	190	3/11/91	Baylor	Crosby, Texas	FA
Cowan, Bobby	P	6-4	220	3/5/90	Idaho	Vancouver, Wash.	FA
Foster, Jason (1)	G	6-3	300	10/21/88	Rhode Island	East Pittsford, Vt.	FA-'12
Harper, Eric	LB	6-3	240	10/29/87	Grambling State	New Orleans, La.	FA
Hayden, DJ	CB	5-11	190	6/27/90	Houston	Houston, Texas	D1
Hoese, Jon (1)	FB	6-2	248	7/4/89	Minnesota	Glencoe, Minn.	FA
Jenkins, Greg	WR	6-1	208	8/23/89	Alabama State	Dade City, Fla.	FA
Johnson, Shelton	S	6-0	197	7/16/90	Wisconsin	Carrollton, Texas	FA
Jones, Johnny (1)	NT	6-4	314	10/19/88	Marshall	Clewiston, Fla.	FA
Kasa, Nick	TE	6-6	265	11/5/90	Colorado	Thornton, Colo.	D6a
Leonhardt, Brian	TE	6-5	255	4/2/90	Bemidji State	Blaine, Minn.	FA
Mady, Lamar	G	6-2	315	12/13/90	Youngstown State	Topeka, Kan.	FA
McGee, Stacy	DT	6-3	310	1/17/90	Oklahoma	Muskogee, Okla.	D6d
McGloin, Matt	QB	6-1	210	12/2/89	Penn State	Scranton, Pa.	FA
McGuffie, Sam	WR	5-10	200	10/16/89	Rice	Cypress, Texas	FA
Moore, Sio	LB	6-1	240	5/2/90	Connecticut	Apex, N.C.	D3
Murray, Latavius	RB	6-3	230	1/18/90	Central Florida	Nedrow, N.Y.	D6b
Nelms, Cory (1)	DB	6-1	191	2/27/88	Miami	Neptune, N.J.	FA-'12
Padron, Kyle	QB	6-3	225	3/27/91	Eastern Washington	Southlake, Texas	FA
Rivera, Mychal	TE	6-3	245	9/8/90	Tennessee	Valencia, Calif.	D6c
Robinson, Ryan	DE	6-4	255	12/9/90	Oklahoma State	Buford, Ga.	FA
Robiskie, Andrew	C	6-1	297	5/18/89	Western Illinois	Chagrin Falls, Ohio	FA
Session, Travionte (1)	WR	6-2	195	7/18/89	Nevada	Long Beach, Calif.	FA-'12
Taufa'asau, Kurt	DT	6-2	300	9/18/90	Wyoming	Pago Pago, American Samoa	FA
Vernon, Conner	WR	6-0	192	8/18/90	Duke	Miami, Fla.	D2
Watson, Menelik	T	6-5	315	12/22/88	Florida State	Manchester, England	D2
Wetzel, John	T	6-7	315	7/18/91	Boston College	Pittsburgh, Pa.	FA
White, Mitchell	CB	5-11	184	3/30/90	Michigan State	Livonia, Mich.	FA
Williams, Deonté	RB	5-10	213	7/9/90	Cal Poly	Oakland, Calif.	FA
Williams, Isaiah (1)	WR	6-2	201	1/30/87	Maryland	Bergen, N.J.	FA
Wilson, Tyler	QB	6-2	215	8/16/89	Arkansas	Greenwood, Ark.	D4

The term NFL Rookie is defined as a player who is in his first season of professional football and has not been on the roster of another professional football team for any regular-season or postseason games. A Rookie is designated by an "R" on NFL rosters. Players who have been active in another professional football league or players who have NFL experience, including either preseason training camp or being on an Active List or Inactive List, or on Reserve/Injured or Reserve/Physically Unable to Perform for fewer than six regular-season games, are termed NFL First-Year Players. An NFL First-Year Player is designated by a "1" on NFL rosters. Thereafter, a player is credited with an additional year of experience for each season in which he accumulates six games on the Active List or Inactive List, or on Reserve/Injured or Reserve/Physically Unable to Perform.

Log on to www.raiders.com for an up-to-date roster.

COACHING STAFF

Head Coach,
Dennis Allen

Pro Career: Allen becomes the 18th head coach in the 52-year history of the Oakland Raiders. At age 40, Allen is the youngest current head coach in the NFL. Allen has 17 years of coaching experience, including 10 as an NFL assistant. He was on the coaching staff of teams that captured the division title four times—Denver, 2011; New Orleans, 2009, 2006; Atlanta, 2004—and qualified for the postseason in two other seasons—2010 and 2002. In 2011, Allen was the NFL's second-youngest defensive coordinator when hired by the Denver Broncos in 2011. He coordinated a defense that helped the Broncos win the AFC West and post a wild card victory. The Broncos improved 12 spots over the previous year in overall defensive ranking (from 32nd to 20th). Allen was an assistant coach for five seasons (2006-2010) with New Orleans. Tutored a secondary that played a key role in helping the Saints to their first Super Bowl victory (XLIV). His unit accounted for an NFL-high six interception returns for touchdowns en route to their championship. First NFL coaching position was as a defensive assistant for Atlanta (2002-05). Career record: 4-12.
Background: Allen played at Texas A&M, where he was a four-year letterman as a safety. Coached with the Aggies (1996-99) and Tulsa (2000-01). Was signed by Buffalo as an undrafted college free agent and spent training camp with the Bills (1996). Father played as a linebacker for the Atlanta Falcons from 1968-1972.
Personal: Born September 22, 1972, in Atlanta, Ga. Allen and his wife, Alisson, have a son, Garrison, and a daughter, Layla.

ASSISTANT COACHES

Bobby April, special teams coordinator; born April 15, 1953, New Orleans, La. Linebacker Nicholls State 1972-76. College coach: Southern Miss 1978, Tulane 1979, Arizona 1980-86, Southern California 1987-1990, Ohio State 1990. Pro coach: Atlanta Falcons 1991-93, Pittsburgh Steelers 1994-95, New Orleans Saints 1996-99, St. Louis Rams 2001-03, Buffalo Bills 2004-09, Philadelphia Eagles 2010-12, joined Raiders in 2013.
Keith Burns, asst. special teams; born September 26, 1960, Hurst, Texas. Safety Arkansas 1980-82. College coach: Arkansas 1984, Pacific 1985-88, Rice 1989-1992, Southern California 1993-97, Arkansas 1998-99, Tulsa 2000-02, San Jose State 2004-09, Kansas State 2010, Mississippi 2011. Pro coach: Joined Raiders in 2012.
John DeFilippo, quarterbacks; born April 12, 1978, Youngstown, Ohio. Quarterback James Madison 1996-1999. College coach: Fordham 2000, Notre Dame 2001-

02, Columbia 2003-04, San Jose State 2010-11. Pro coach: New York Giants 2005-06, Oakland Raiders 2007-08, New York Jets 2009, re-joined Raiders in 2012.
Ted Gilmore, wide receivers; born March 21, 1967, Wichita, Kan. Receiver Butler County (Kan.) Community College 1986-87, Wyoming 1988-89. No pro playing experience. College coach: Wyoming 1994-98, Kansas 1999, Houston 2000, Purdue 2001-02, Colorado 2003-04, Nebraska 2005-10, Southern California 2011. Pro coach: Joined Raiders in 2012.
John Grieco, asst. strength and conditioning; born October 7, 1972, Greensburg, Pa. No pro playing experience. College coach: Florida 1995-2003, East Carolina 2004-05, Nevada-Las Vegas 2006-09, Louisiana-Monroe 2010-11. Pro coach: Joined Raiders in 2012.
Justin Griffith, quality control-offense; born July 21, 1980, Magee, Miss. Running back Mississippi State 1999-2002. Pro running back Atlanta Falcons 2003-06, Oakland Raiders 2007-08, Seattle Seahawks 2009. Pro coach: Seattle Seahawks 2011, joined Raiders in 2012.
Mark Hutson, tight ends; born August 29, 1966, Fort Smith, Ark. Offensive line Oklahoma 1984-87. No pro playing experience. College coach: Oklahoma 1990-92, Murray State 1993-97, Boise State 1997, Arkansas 1998-99, Tulsa 2000-02, Eastern Illinois 2003-2006 (interim head coach 2006), Tulane 2007-2011 (interim head coach 2011). Pro coach: Joined Raiders in 2012.
Clayton Lopez, defensive backs; born May 26, 1970, Los Angeles, Calif. Defensive back Nevada 1991-94. No playing experience. College coach: Nevada 1995-98, Seattle Seahawks 1999-2003, Oakland Raiders 2004-05, Detroit Lions 2006-08, St. Louis Rams 2009-2011, re-joined Raiders in 2012.
Johnnie Lynn, defensive backs; born December 19, 1956, Los Angeles, Calif. Defensive back UCLA 1975-78. Cornerback New York Jets 1979-1986. College coach: Arizona 1987-1993. Pro coach: Tampa Bay Buccaneers 1994-95, San Francisco 49ers 1996, New York Giants 1997-2003, Baltimore Ravens 2004-05, San Francisco 49ers 2006-2010, Philadelphia Eagles 2011, joined Raiders in 2012.
Al Miller, strength and conditioning; born August 29, 1947, El Dorado, Ark. Wide receiver Northeast Louisiana. No pro playing experience. College coach: Mississippi State 1980, Northeast Louisiana 1981, Alabama 1982-85. Pro coach: Denver Broncos 1985-1992, New York Giants 1993-96, Atlanta Falcons 1997-2005, joined Raiders in 2012.
Greg Olson, offensive coordinator; born March 1, 1961, Richland, Wash. Quarterback Spokane Falls (Wash.) J.C. 1981-82, Central Washington 1983-84.

College coach: Washington State 1987-89, Central Washington 1990-93, Idaho 1994-96, Purdue 1997-2000, 2002. Pro coach: San Francisco 49ers 2001, Chicago Bears 2003, Detroit Lions 2004-05, St. Louis Rams 2006-07, Tampa Bay Buccaneers 2008-2011, Jacksonville Jaguars 2012, joined Raiders in 2013.
Bob Sanders, linebackers; born December 5, 1953, Jacksonville, N.C. Defensive player Davidson College 1972-75. College coach: Georgia Tech 1978, East Carolina 1980-82, Richmond 1983-84, Duke 1985-88, Duke 1989, Florida 1990-2000. Pro coach: Miami Dolphins 2001-2004, Green Bay Packers 2005-08, Buffalo Bills 2009-2012, joined Raiders in 2013.
Eric Sanders, quality control-defense; born August 2, 1983, Poughkeepsie, N.Y. No pro playing experience. College coach: UC Davis 2006, 2008-09, Utah State 2007. Pro coach: Joined Raiders in 2010.
Al Saunders, senior offensive assistant; born February 1, 1947, London, England. Defensive back San Jose State 1966-68. No pro playing experience. College coach: Southern California 1970-71, Missouri 1972, Utah State 1973-75, California 1976-1981, Tennessee 1982. Pro coach: San Diego Chargers 1983-88 (head coach 1986-88), Kansas City Chiefs 1989-1998, St. Louis Rams 1999-2000, Kansas City Chiefs 2001-05, Washington Redskins 2006-07, St. Louis Rams 2008, Baltimore Ravens, 2009-2010, joined Raiders in 2011.
Kelly Skipper, running backs; born July 25, 1967, Brawley, Calif. Running back Fresno State 1985-88. No pro playing experience. College coach: Fresno State 1989-1997, UCLA 1998-2002, Washington State 2003-06. Pro coach: Joined Raiders in 2007.
Tony Sparano, asst. head coach/offensive line; born Oct. 7, 1961, West Haven, Conn. Center New Haven 1984-87. College coach: Boston University 1988-1993, New Haven 1994-98. Pro coach: Cleveland Browns 1999-2000, Washington Redskins 2001, Jacksonville Jaguars 2002, Dallas Cowboys 2003-07, Miami Dolphins 2008-2011 (head coach), New York Jets 2012, joined Raiders in 2013.
Jason Tarver, defensive coordinator; born August 28, 1974, Palo Alto, Calif. No pro playing experience. College coach: UCLA 1998-2000, Stanford 2011. Pro coach: San Francisco 49ers 2001-2010, joined Raiders in 2012.
Terrell Williams, defensive line; born June 19, 1974, Los Angeles, Calif. Nose guard East Carolina 1995-96. No pro playing experience. College coach: Fort Scott (Kan.) C.C. 1998, North Carolina A&T 1999-2001, Youngstown State 2002-2003, Akron 2004-2005, Purdue 2006-2009, Texas A&M 2010-11. Pro coach: Joined Raiders in 2012.

American Football Conference
North Division
Team Colors: Black and Gold
3400 South Water Street
Pittsburgh, Pennsylvania 15203
Telephone: (412) 432-7800

2013 SCHEDULE
PRESEASON
Aug. 10	**New York Giants**	7:30
Aug. 19	at Washington	8:00
Aug. 24	**Kansas City**	7:30
Aug. 29	at Carolina	7:30

REGULAR SEASON
Sep. 8	**Tennessee**	1:00
Sep. 16	at Cincinnati (Mon)	8:40
Sep. 22	**Chicago**	8:30
Sep. 29	at Minnesota (London)	1:00
Oct. 6	BYE	
Oct. 13	at New York Jets	1:00
Oct. 20	**Baltimore**	4:25
Oct. 27	at Oakland	4:05
Nov. 3	at New England	4:25
Nov. 10	**Buffalo**	1:00
Nov. 17	**Detroit**	1:00
Nov. 24	at Cleveland	1:00
Nov. 28	at Baltimore (Thurs)	8:30
Dec. 8	**Miami**	1:00
Dec. 15	**Cincinnati**	*8:30
Dec. 22	at Green Bay	4:25
Dec. 29	**Cleveland**	1:00

All times ET; Sunday night games in Weeks 11-16 subject to change
Stadium: Heinz Field (opened in 2001)
• **Capacity:** 65,500
100 Art Rooney Avenue
Pittsburgh, Pennsylvania 15212
Playing Surface: Natural Grass
Training Camp: St. Vincent College
Latrobe, PA 15650

HEINZ FIELD

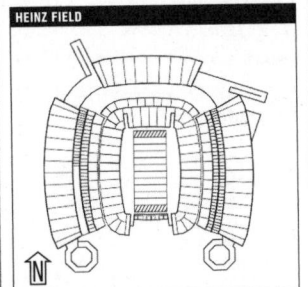

CLUB OFFICIALS
Chairman: Daniel M. Rooney
President: Arthur J. Rooney II
Vice President: Arthur J. Rooney Jr.
Administration Advisor: Charles H. Noll
Director of Planning & Development:
Mark Hart
Director of Finance: Bob Tyler
Director of Football and Business
Administration: Omar Khan
General Manager: Kevin Colbert
College Scouting Coordinator:
Phil Kreidler
Pro Scouting Coordinator: Brandon Hunt
Head Athletic Trainer: John Norwig
Director of Marketing: Tony Quatrini
Communications Coordinator:
Burt Lauten
Director of Stadium Management:
Jim Sacco
Video/Facilities Coordinator:
Bob McCartney
HR Manager: Katrina Smith
Ticket Manager: Ben Lentz

COACHING HISTORY
Pittsburgh Pirates 1933-39
(599-546-21)
Records include postseason games
1933	Forrest (Jap) Douds	3-6-2
1934	Luby DiMelio	2-10-0
1935-36	Joe Bach	10-14-0
1937-39	Johnny (Blood) McNally*	6-19-0
1939-1940	Walt Kiesling	3-13-3
1941	Bert Bell**	0-2-0
	Aldo (Buff) Donelli***	0-5-0
1941-44	Walt Kiesling****	13-20-2
1945	Jim Leonard	2-8-0
1946-47	Jock Sutherland	13-10-1
1948-1951	Johnny Michelosen	20-26-2
1952-53	Joe Bach	11-13-0
1954-56	Walt Kiesling	14-22-0
1957-1964	Raymond (Buddy) Parker	51-47-6
1965	Mike Nixon	2-12-0
1966-68	Bill Austin	11-28-3
1969-1991	Chuck Noll	209-156-1
1992-2006	Bill Cowher	161-99-1
2007-2012	Mike Tomlin	68-36-0

*Released after three games in 1939
**Resigned after two games in 1941
***Released after five games in 1941
****Co-coach with Earle (Greasy) Neale in
Philadelphia-Pittsburgh merger in 1943 and
with Phil Handler in Chicago Cardinals-
Pittsburgh merger in 1944

PAID ATTENDANCE
Home 512,961   Away 572,508
Total 1,085,469
Single-game home record,
66,662 (1/23/11)
Single-season home record,
517,599 (2009)

2013 DRAFT CHOICES
Round	Name	Pos.	College
1	Jarvis Jones	LB	Georgia
2	Le'Veon Bell	RB	Michigan St.
3	Markus Wheaton	WR	Oregon St.
4	Shamarko Thomas	DB	Syracuse
	Landry Jones	QB	Oklahoma
5	Terry Hawthorne	DB	Illinois
6	Justin Brown	WR	Oklahoma
	Vince Williams	LB	Florida St.
7	Nicholas Williams	DE	Samford

PITTSBURGH STEELERS

2012 TEAM RECORD

PRESEASON (3-1)

Date	Result	Opponent
08/09	L 23-24	at Philadelphia
08/19	W 26-24	Indianapolis
08/25	W 38-7	at Buffalo
08/30	W 17-16	Carolina

REGULAR SEASON (8-8)

Date	Result	Opponent
09/09	L 19-31	at Denver
09/16	W 27-10	New York Jets
09/23	L 31-34	at Oakland
10/07	W 16-14	Philadelphia
10/11	L 23-26	at Tennessee
10/21	W 24-17	at Cincinnati
10/28	W 27-12	Washington
11/04	W 24-20	at New York Giants
11/12	W 16-13	Kansas City (OT)
11/18	L 10-13	Baltimore
11/25	L 14-20	at Cleveland
12/02	W 23-20	at Baltimore
12/09	L 24-34	San Diego
12/16	L 24-27	at Dallas (OT)
12/23	L 10-13	Cincinnati
12/30	W 24-10	Cleveland

(OT) Overtime

SCORE BY PERIODS

Steelers	57	114	71	91	3 —	336
Opponents	60	103	78	70	3 —	314

2012 TEAM STATISTICS

	Steelers	Opp.
Total First Downs	307	273
Rushing	80	78
Passing	202	169
Penalty	25	26
3rd Down: Made/Att	94/224	73/206
3rd Down Pct.	42.0	35.4
4th Down: Made/Att	6/13	8/11
4th Down Pct.	46.2	72.7
Possession Avg.	32:07	27:53
Total Net Yards	5324	4413
Avg. Per Game	332.8	275.8
Total Plays	1023	951
Avg. Per Play	5.2	4.6
Net Yards Rushing	1537	1450
Avg. Per Game	96.1	90.6
Total Rushes	412	391
Net Yards Passing	3787	2963
Avg. Per Game	236.7	185.2
Sacked/Yards Lost	37/225	37/196
Gross Yards	4012	3159
Att./Completions	574/354	523/299
Completion Pct.	61.7	57.2
Had Intercepted	14	10
Punts/Average	79/43.0	88/45.2
Net Punting Avg.	79/37.6	88/40.0
Penalties/Yards	92/938	100/882
Fumbles/Ball Lost	33/16	19/10
Touchdowns	36	33
Rushing	8	9
Passing	27	19
Returns	1	5

2012 INDIVIDUAL STATISTICS

PASSING

	Att.	Comp.	Yds.	Pct.	TD	Int.	Tkld.	Rate
Roethlisberger	449	284	3265	63.3	26	8	30/182	97.0
C. Batch	70	45	475	64.3	1	4	3/12	64.9
Leftwich	53	25	272	47.2	0	1	3/24	54.9
A. Brown	2	0	0	0.0	0	1	0/0	0.0
Sanders	0	0	0	—	0	0	1/7	—
Steelers	574	354	4012	61.7	27	14	37/225	88.1
Opponents	523	299	3159	57.2	19	10	37/196	79.0

SCORING

	TD R	TD P	TD Rt	PAT	FG	Saf	PTS
Suisham	0	0	0	34/34	28/31	0	118
Miller	0	8	0	0/0	0/0	0	50
Wallace	0	8	0	0/0	0/0	0	48
A. Brown	0	5	0	0/0	0/0	0	30
Dwyer	2	0	0	0/0	0/0	0	12
Pope	0	2	0	0/0	0/0	0	12
Rainey	2	0	0	0/0	0/0	0	12
Redman	2	0	0	0/0	0/0	0	12
B. Batch	1	0	0	0/0	0/0	0	6
Burress	0	1	0	0/0	0/0	0	6
Will Johnson	0	1	0	0/0	0/0	0	6
Leftwich	1	0	0	0/0	0/0	0	6
Mendenhall	0	1	0	0/0	0/0	0	6
Sanders	0	1	0	0/0	0/0	0	6
Timmons	0	0	1	0/0	0/0	0	6
Steelers	8	27	1	34/34	28/31	0	336
Opponents	9	19	5	30/31	28/33	0	314

2-Pt Conversions: Miller, Steelers 1-2, Opponents 1-2

RUSHING

	No.	Yds	Avg	LG	TD
Dwyer	156	623	4.0	34	2
Redman	110	410	3.7	28	2
Mendenhall	51	182	3.6	20	0
Rainey	26	102	3.9	19	2
Roethlisberger	26	92	3.5	14	0
B. Batch	25	49	2.0	10	1
Leftwich	1	31	31.0	31t	1
A. Brown	7	24	3.4	13	0
Gilreath	1	7	7.0	7	0
Will Johnson	2	7	3.5	5	0
Wallace	5	7	1.4	13	0
Sanders	1	4	4.0	4	0
Suisham	1	-1	-1.0	-1	0
Steelers	412	1537	3.7	34	8
Opponents	391	1450	3.7	64t	9

RECEIVING

	No.	Yds	Avg	LG	TD
Miller	71	816	11.5	43	8
A. Brown	66	787	11.9	60t	5
Wallace	64	836	13.1	82t	8
Sanders	44	626	14.2	37	1
Redman	19	244	12.8	55	0
Dwyer	18	106	5.9	15	0
Cotchery	17	205	12.1	24	0
Will Johnson	15	137	9.1	26	1
Rainey	14	60	4.3	14	0
Mendenhall	9	62	6.9	15	1
Paulson	7	51	7.3	9	0
B. Batch	4	31	7.8	15	0
Burress	3	42	14.0	18	1
Pope	3	9	3.0	7	2
Steelers	354	4012	11.3	82t	27
Opponents	299	3159	10.6	71t	19

INTERCEPTIONS

	No.	Yds	Avg	LG	TD
Timmons	3	80	26.7	53t	1
Clark	2	26	13.0	26	0
C. Allen	2	6	3.0	6	0
Woodley	1	11	11.0	11	0
Taylor	1	3	3.0	3	0
Polamalu	1	1	1.0	1	0
Steelers	10	127	12.7	53t	1
Opponents	14	168	12.0	43t	2

PUNTING

	No.	Yds.	Avg.	In 20	LG
Butler	77	3374	43.8	26	79
Roethlisberger	1	26	26	1	26
Steelers	79	3400	43	27	79
Opponents	88	3979	45.2	35	64

PUNT RETURNS

	Ret	FC	Yds	Avg	LG	TD
A. Brown	27	8	183	6.8	29	0
Sanders	9	9	93	10.3	63	0
Rainey	3	0	16	5.3	13	0
Gilreath	2	2	8	4.0	5	0
Steelers	41	19	300	7.3	63	0
Opponents	30	20	306	10.2	63t	1

KICKOFF RETURNS

	No.	Yds	Avg	LG	TD
Rainey	39	1035	26.5	68	0
Sanders	1	27	27.0	27	0
Paulson	1	16	16.0	16	0
Will Johnson	1	8	8.0	8	0
Pope	1	0	0.0	0	0
Steelers	43	1086	25.3	68	0
Opponents	46	1103	24.0	51	0

FIELD GOALS

	1-19	20-29	30-39	40-49	50+
Suisham	0/0	7/8	8/8	12/12	1/3
Steelers	0/0	7/8	8/8	12/12	1/3
Opponents	0/0	8/8	6/8	10/11	4/6

SACKS

	No.
Harrison	6.0
Timmons	6.0
Worilds	5.0
Keisel	4.5
Foote	4.0
Woodley	4.0
Hood	3.0
McLendon	2.0
Heyward	1.5
Polamalu	1.0
Steelers	37.0
Opponents	37.0

RECORD HOLDERS
INDIVIDUAL RECORDS—CAREER

Category	Name	Performance
Rushing (Yds.)	Franco Harris, 1972-1983	11,950
Passing (Yds.)	Ben Roethlisberger, 2004-2012	29,844
Passing (TDs)	Terry Bradshaw, 1970-1983	212
Receiving (No.)	Hines Ward, 1998-2011	1,000
Receiving (Yds.)	Hines Ward, 1998-2011	12,083
Interceptions	Mel Blount, 1970-1983	57
Punting (Avg.)	Bobby Joe Green, 1960-61	45.7
Punt Return (Avg.)	Bobby Gage, 1949-1950	14.9
Kickoff Return (Avg.)	Lynn Chandnois, 1950-56	29.6
Field Goals	Gary Anderson, 1982-1994	309
Touchdowns (Tot.)	Franco Harris, 1972-1983	100
Points	Gary Anderson, 1982-1994	1,343
*Sacks	Jason Gildon, 1994-2003	77.0

INDIVIDUAL RECORDS—SINGLE SEASON

Category	Name	Performance
Rushing (Yds.)	Barry Foster, 1992	1,690
Passing (Yds.)	Ben Roethlisberger, 2009	4,328
Passing (TDs)	Ben Roethlisberger, 2007	32
Receiving (No.)	Hines Ward, 2002	112
Receiving (Yds.)	Yancey Thigpen, 1997	1,398
Interceptions	Mel Blount, 1975	11
Punting (Avg.)	Bobby Joe Green, 1961	47.0
Punt Return (Avg.)	Bobby Gage, 1949	16.0
Kickoff Return (Avg.)	Lynn Chandnois, 1952	35.2
Field Goals	Norm Johnson, 1995	34
Touchdowns (Tot.)	Willie Parker, 2006	16
Points	Norm Johnson, 1995	141
*Sacks	James Harrison, 2008	16.0

INDIVIDUAL RECORDS—SINGLE GAME

Category	Name	Performance
Rushing (Yds.)	Willie Parker, 12-7-06	223
Passing (Yds.)	Ben Roethlisberger, 12-20-09	503
Passing (TDs)	Terry Bradshaw, 11-15-81	5
	Mark Malone, 9-8-85	5
	Ben Roethlisberger, 11-5-07, 10-9-11	5
Receiving (No.)	Courtney Hawkins, 11-1-98	14
Receiving (Yds.)	Plaxico Burress, 11-10-02	253
Interceptions	Jack Butler, 12-13-53	**4
Field Goals	Gary Anderson, 10-23-88	6
	Jeff Reed, 12-1-02	6
Touchdowns (Tot.)	Ray Mathews, 10-17-54	4
	Roy Jefferson, 11-3-68	4
Points	Ray Mathews, 10-17-54	24
	Roy Jefferson, 11-3-68	24
*Sacks	Chad Brown, 10-13-96	4.5

*Sacks became an official statistic in 1982.
**NFL Record

2013 VETERAN ROSTER

No.	Name	Pos.	Ht.	Wt.	Birthdate	NFL Exp.	College	Hometown	How Acq.	'12 Games/ Starts
76	Adams, Mike	OT	6-7	323	3/10/90	2	Ohio State	Farrell, Pa.	D2-'12	10/6
28	Allen, Cortez	CB	6-1	196	10/29/88	3	The Citadel	Ocala, Fla.	D4-'11	15/3
20	Batch, Baron	RB	5-10	210	12/21/87	3	Texas Tech	Midland, Texas	D7-'11	12/0
16	#Batch, Charlie	QB	6-2	216	12/5/74	16	Eastern Michigan	Homestead, Pa.	FA-'02	2/2
68	Beachum, Kelvin	G	6-3	303	6/8/89	2	Southern Methodist	Mexia, Texas	D7d-'12	7/5
84	Brown, Antonio	WR	5-10	186	7/10/88	4	Central Michigan	Miami, Fla.	D6b-'10	13/10
31	Brown, Curtis	CB	6-0	185	9/24/88	3	Texas	Longview, Texas	D3-'11	15/0
80	Burress, Plaxico	WR	6-5	232	8/12/77	12	Michigan State	Norfolk, Va.	FA-'12	4/3
9	Butler, Drew	P	6-1	204	5/10/89	2	Georgia	Duluth, Ga.	FA-'12	16/0
54	Carter, Chris	LB	6-1	248	4/6/89	3	Fresno State	Fontana, Calif.	D5-'11	8/3
25	Clark, Ryan	S	5-11	205	10/12/79	12	Louisiana State	Marrero, La.	UFA(Wash)-'06	15/15
89	Cotchery, Jerricho	WR	6-1	200	6/16/82	10	North Carolina State	Birmingham, Ala.	FA-'11	14/2
66	DeCastro, David	G	6-5	316	1/11/90	2	Stanford	Bellevue, Wash.	D1-'12	4/3
27	Dwyer, Jonathan	RB	5-11	229	7/26/89	4	Georgia Tech	Marietta, Ga.	D6a-'10	13/6
50	Foote, Larry	LB	6-1	239	6/12/80	12	Michigan	Detroit, Mich.	FA-'10	16/16
73	Foster, Ramon	G	6-6	325	1/7/86	5	Tennessee	Henning, Tenn.	FA-'09	16/16
22	Gay, William	CB	5-10	190	1/1/85	7	Louisville	Tallahassee, Fla.	FA-'13	16/15*
77	Gilbert, Marcus	OT	6-6	330	2/15/88	3	Florida	Fort Lauderdale, Fla.	D2-'11	5/5
18	Gilreath, David	WR	5-10	169	12/11/88	2	Wisconsin	New Hope, Minn.	FA-'12	3/0
21	Golden, Robert	S	5-11	202	9/13/90	2	Arizona	Fresno, Calif.	FA-'12	15/0
5	Gradkowski, Bruce	QB	6-1	220	12/27/83	8	Toledo	Pittsburgh, Pa.	UFA(Cin)-'13	2/0*
98	#Hampton, Casey	NT	6-1	325	9/3/77	13	Texas	Galveston, Texas	D1-'01	16/16
97	Heyward, Cameron	DE	6-5	288	5/6/89	3	Ohio State	Pittsburgh, Pa.	D1-'11	16/0
96	Hood, Ziggy	DE	6-3	300	2/16/87	5	Missouri	Amarillo, Texas	D1-'09	16/16
91	#Johnson, Brandon	LB	6-5	245	4/5/83	8	Louisville	Birmingham, Ala.	FA-'12	14/0
85	Johnson, David	TE	6-2	260	8/26/87	5	Arkansas State	Pine Bluff, Ark.	D7b-'09	0*
46	Johnson, Will	FB	6-2	238	11/14/89	2	West Virginia	Dayton, Ohio	FA-'12	16/7
99	Keisel, Brett	DE	6-5	285	9/19/78	12	Brigham Young	Greybull, Wyo.	D7b-'02	16/16
37	King, Justin	CB	5-11	197	5/11/87	5	Penn State	Pittsburgh, Pa.	FA-'12	3/0*
4	Leftwich, Byron	QB	6-5	250	1/14/80	11	Marshall	Washington, D.C.	T(TB)-'10	2/1
64	#Legursky, Doug	C/G	6-1	315	6/9/86	5	Marshall	Frankfurt, Germany	FA-'08	16/3
62	Malecki, John	G	6-2	298	5/26/88	2	Pittsburgh	Murrysville, Pa.	FA-'11	1/0
90	McLendon, Steve	NT	6-4	280	1/3/86	4	Troy	Ozark, Ala.	FA-'09	16/0
83	Miller, Heath	TE	6-5	256	10/22/82	9	Virginia	Swords Creek, Va.	D1-'05	15/15
8	Moorman, Brian	P	6-0	174	2/5/76	13	Pittsburg State	Sedgwick, Kan.	FA-'13	15/0*
81	Paulson, David	TE	6-4	246	2/22/89	2	Oregon	Auburn, Wash.	D7b-'12	16/5
47	Pianalto, Zack	TE	6-4	250	5/27/89	2	North Carolina	Springdale, Ark.	FA-'13	0*
43	Polamalu, Troy	S	5-10	207	4/19/81	11	Southern California	Santa Ana, Calif.	D1-'03	7/7
45	#Pope, Leonard	TE	6-8	264	9/10/83	8	Georgia	Americus, Ga.	FA-'12	16/2
53	Pouncey, Maurkice	C	6-4	304	7/24/89	4	Florida	Lakeland, Fla.	D1-'10	15/15
33	Redman, Isaac	RB	6-0	230	11/10/84	4	Bowie State	Paulsboro, N.J.	FA-'09	14/5
57	Robinson, Adrian	LB	6-1	250	11/21/89	2	Temple	Harrisburg, Pa.	FA-'12	12/0
7	Roethlisberger, Ben	QB	6-5	241	3/2/82	10	Miami (Ohio)	Cory Rawson, Ohio	D1-'04	13/13
47	Rolle, Brian	LB	5-10	240	11/20/88	2	Ohio State	Immokalee, Fla.	FA-'13	4/0*
88	Sanders, Emmanuel	WR	5-11	180	3/17/87	4	Southern Methodist	Bellville, Texas	D3-'10	16/7
87	Spaeth, Matt	TE	6-7	260	11/24/83	7	Minnesota	St. Michael, Minn.	FA-'13	16/8*
51	Spence, Sean	LB	5-11	231	6/7/90	2	Miami	Miami, Fla.	D3-'12	0*
78	#Starks, Max	OT	6-8	345	1/10/82	10	Florida	Orlando, Fla.	FA-'12	16/16
34	Stephens-Howling, LaRod	RB	5-7	185	4/26/87	5	Pittsburgh	Johnstown, Pa.	UFA(Ariz)-'13	15/4*
6	Suisham, Shaun	K	6-0	200	12/29/81	9	Bowling Green	Wallaceburg, Ont. Canada	FA-'10	16/0
55	Sylvester, Stevenson	LB	6-4	231	7/18/88	4	Utah	Las Vegas, Nev.	D5c-'10	10/0
74	Ta'amu, Alameda	NT	6-3	348	8/23/90	2	Washington	Kent, Wash.	D4-'12	0*
24	Taylor, Ike	CB	6-2	195	5/5/80	11	Louisiana-Lafayette	Gretna, La.	D4-'03	12/12
94	Timmons, Lawrence	LB	6-1	234	5/14/86	7	Florida State	Florence, S.C.	D1-'07	16/16
23	Van Dyke, DeMarcus	CB	6-1	187	1/17/89	3	Miami	Miami, Fla.	FA-'12	9/0
41	Ventrone, Ross	DB	5-8	195	9/27/86	2	Villanova	Pittsburgh, Pa.	FA-'13	0*
60	Warren, Greg	LS	6-3	252	10/18/81	9	North Carolina	Goldsboro, N.C.	FA-'05	16/0
61	Whimper, Guy	T	6-5	315	3/21/83	8	East Carolina	Honolulu, Hawai'i	FA-'13	16/6*
4	Wilson, John Parker	QB	6-2	215	10/17/85	4	Alabama	Hoover, Ala.	W(Jax)-'12	0*
48	Wilson, Kion	LB	6-0	230	10/24/86	4	South Florida	Jacksonville, Fla.	FA-'13	0*
56	Woodley, LaMarr	LB	6-2	265	11/3/84	7	Michigan	Saginaw, Mich.	D2-'07	13/13
65	Woods, Al	DE	6-4	307	3/25/87	4	Louisiana State	Jennings, La.	FA-'11	12/0
93	Worilds, Jason	LB	6-2	262	3/3/88	4	Virginia Tech	Carteret, N.J.	D2-'10	16/3

* Gay played 16 games with Arizona in '12; Gradkowski played two games with Cincinnati in '12; D. Johnson missed '12 season because of injury; King played three games with Indianapolis; Moorman played three games with Buffalo and 12 games with Dallas; Pianalto last active with Tampa Bay in '11; Rolle played four games with Philadelphia in '12; Spaeth played 16 games with Chicago; Spence missed '12 season because of injury; Stephens-Howling played 15 games with Arizona; Ta'amu inactive for seven games; Ventrone last active with New England in '11; Whimper played 16 games with Jacksonville; J.P. Wilson did not play in one game with Jacksonville; K. Wilson last active with Carolina in '11.

\# Unrestriced Free Agent; subject to developments.

Players lost through free agency (5)—S Will Allen (Dall; 16 games), CB Keenan Lewis (NO; 16), RB Rashard Mendenhall (Ariz; 6), S Ryan Mundy (NYG; 16), WR Mike Wallace (Mia; 15).

Also played with Steelers in '12—OL Willie Colon (11 games), LB James Harrison (13), QB Brian Hoyer (2), RB Chris Rainey (16).

FIRST-YEAR ROSTER

Name	Pos.	Ht.	Wt.	Birthdate	College	Hometown	How Acq.
Arnfelt, Brian	DE	6-4	298	10/11/89	Northwestern	Lake Elmo, Minn.	FA
Baxter, Alan	LB	6-0	238	3/28/91	Northern Illinois	Buffalo Grove, Ill.	FA
Bell, Le'Veon	RB	6-1	244	2/18/92	Michigan State	Reynoldsburg, Ohio	D2
Brown, Justin	WR	6-3	209	3/10/91	Oklahoma	Wilmington, Del.	D6a
Cheadle, Justin (1)	G	6-3	305	3/11/89	California	Bakersfield, Calif.	FA-'12
Cromartie-Smith, Damon (1)	S	6-2	203	2/19/87	Texas-El Paso	Riverside, Calif.	FA-'10
Dunn, Reggie	WR	5-9	178	1/5/89	Utah	Compton, Calif.	FA
Embernate, Nik	G	6-4	304	11/3/90	San Diego State	Yucaipa, Calif.	FA
Fangupo, Hebron (1)	DT	6-0	324	7/19/85	Brigham Young	Orange County, Calif.	W(Sea)-'12
Farrell, Mike	OT	6-6	303	8/23/89	Penn State	Pittsburgh, Pa.	FA
Garvin, Terence	LB	6-3	221	1/1/91	West Virginia	Baltimore, Md.	FA
Golic, Jr., Mike	OT	6-4	300	9/28/89	Notre Dame	Voorhees, N.J.	FA
Green, Isaiah (1)	CB	5-10	180	8/10/89	Fresno State	Los Angeles, Calif.	FA-'12
Hagans, Cordian	DE	6-4	299	2/7/89	Louisiana-Lafayette	Long Island, N.Y.	FA
Hawthorne, Terry	CB	6-0	195	1/1/90	Illinois	East St. Louis, Ill.	D5
Hrapmann, Daniel (1)	K	5-9	164	4/21/89	Southern Mississippi	New Orleans, La.	FA
Hubbard, Chris	G	6-4	286	4/23/91	Alabama-Birmingham	Columbus, Ga.	FA
Hunter, Omar	DT	6-0	318	12/27/89	Florida	Buford, Ga.	FA
Ingram, Luke	LS	6-5	258	7/24/90	Hawaii	Mililani, Hawaii	FA
Jones, Jarvis	LB	6-2	245	10/13/89	Georgia	Columbus, Ga.	D1
Jones, Landry	QB	6-3	221	4/4/89	Oklahoma	Artesia, N.M.	D4b
Long, Joe (1)	OT	6-5	304	7/27/89	Wayne State (Mich.)	Lapeer, Mich.	FA-'12
Madsen, Joe	C	6-3	310	9/1/89	West Virginia	Chardon, Ohio	FA
McCoy, Jamie (1)	TE	6-3	240	7/21/87	Texas A&M	Midland, Texas	FA-'12
McFadden, Marshall (1)	LB	6-1	233	8/4/86	South Carolina State	Lamar, S.C.	FA-'12
McNeal, Curtis	RB	5-7	191	12/3/89	Southern California	Los Angeles, Calif.	FA
Moore, Kashif (1)	WR	5-9	180	11/21/88	Connecticut	Burlington, N.J.	FA
Moye, Derek (1)	WR	6-5	210	8/12/88	Penn State	Rochester, Pa.	FA-'12
Thomas, Shamarko	S	5-9	217	2/23/91	Syracuse	Virginia Beach, Va.	D4a
Victorian, Josh (1)	CB	5-10	190	7/10/88	Louisiana Tech	New Orleans, La.	FA-'12
Wheaton, Markus	WR	5-11	182	2/7/91	Oregon State	Chandler, Ariz.	D3
Williams, Nick	DE	6-4	309	2/21/90	Samford	Birmingham, Ala.	D7
Williams, Vince	LB	6-1	250	12/27/89	Florida State	Davenport, Fla.	D6b
Woods, J.D.	WR	6-0	203	2/7/90	West Virginia	Naples, Fla.	FA

The term NFL Rookie is defined as a player who is in his first season of professional football and has not been on the roster of another professional football team for any regular-season or postseason games. A Rookie is designated by an "R" on NFL rosters. Players who have been active in another professional football league or players who have NFL experience, including either preseason training camp or being on an Active List or Inactive List, or on Reserve/Injured or Reserve/Physically Unable to Perform for fewer than six regular-season games, are termed NFL First-Year Players. An NFL First-Year Player is designated by a "1" on NFL rosters. Thereafter, a player is credited with an additional year of experience for each season in which he accumulates six games on the Active List or Inactive List, or on Reserve/Injured or Reserve/Physically Unable to Perform.

Log on to www.steelers.com for an up-to-date roster.

COACHING STAFF
Head Coach,
Mike Tomlin

Pro Career: Named the sixteenth head coach in Steelers history when he replaced Bill Cowher on January 22, 2007. Became the youngest coach (36 years, 323 days) in NFL history to win a Super Bowl when the Steelers defeated the Arizona Cardinals, 27-23, in Super Bowl XLIII on February 1, 2009. Tomlin reached the playoffs four times in his first five seasons and he is the only coach in Steelers' history to win division titles each of his first two seasons. In 2010 Tomlin's club won its third division title in a four-year span. In 2008, Tomlin directed the Steelers to a 12-4 record, winning his second-consecutive AFC North title. That season culminated with a Super Bowl triumph, making Tomlin one of only seven coaches in league history to win a Super Bowl within his first two seasons as an NFL head coach. In his first season, Tomlin guided the Steelers to a 10-6 record and their first AFC North title since 2004. Tomlin was the Minnesota Vikings defensive coordinator in 2006 after spending the previous five seasons (2001-05) as defensive backs coach for the Tampa Bay Buccaneers. Tomlin coached one of the top defensive backfields in the NFL for the Buccaneers, culminating with its performance in Super Bowl XXXVII. The secondary recorded four interceptions, returning two for touchdowns to help Tampa Bay capture the franchise's first Super Bowl title. Tomlin served two seasons as the defensive backs coach at the University of Cincinnati (1999-2000) before going to Tampa Bay. Prior to joining the Cincinnati staff, Tomlin had a short stint on the coaching staff at Tennessee-Martin and then spent two seasons at Arkansas State. He spent the 1996 season as a graduate assistant at Memphis. Tomlin began his coaching career in 1995 as wide receivers coach at Virginia Military Institute. Career record: 68-36.

Background: Was a three-year starter at wide receiver at William & Mary (1990-94) and finished his career with 101 receptions for 2,046 yards and a school-record 20 touchdown receptions. A first-team All-Yankee Conference selection in 1994, he established a school record with a 20.2 yards per catch average. Tomlin was a teammate of current Viking Pro Bowl safety Darren Sharper at William and Mary. Graduated in 1994 with a degree in sociology.

Personal: Born in Hampton, Va., on March 15, 1972. He and his wife, Kiya, have two sons, Dino and Mason, and a daughter Harlyn Quinn.

ASSISTANT COACHES

Jack Bicknell, Jr., offensive line; born February 7, 1963, North Plainfield, N.J. Center Boston College 1981-1985. No pro playing experience. College coach: Boston College 1985-86, 2007-08, New Hampshire 1987-1996, Louisiana Tech 1997-2006. Pro coach: New York Giants 2009-2011, Kansas City Chiefs 2012, joined Steelers in 2013.

Keith Butler, linebackers; born May 16, 1956, Anniston, Ala. Linebacker Memphis 1974-77. Pro linebacker Seattle Seahawks 1978-1987. College coach: Memphis 1990-97, Arkansas State 1998. Pro coach: Cleveland Browns 1999-2002, joined Steelers in 2003.

James Daniel, tight ends; born January 17, 1953, Wetumpka, Ala. Guard Alabama State 1970-73. No pro playing experience. College coach: Auburn 1981-1992. Pro coach: New York Giants 1993-96, Atlanta Falcons 1997-2003, joined Steelers in 2004.

Randy Fichtner, quarterbacks; born November 7, 1963, Cleveland, Ohio. Defensive back Purdue 1982-85. No pro playing experience. College coach: Michigan 1986-87, Southern California 1988, Nevada-Las Vegas 1989, Memphis 1990-93, Purdue 1994-96, Arkansas State 1997-2000, Memphis 2001-06. Pro coach: Joined Steelers in 2007.

Todd Haley, offensive coordinator; February 28, 1967, Atlanta, Ga. No college or pro playing experience. Pro coach: New York Jets 1997-2000, Chicago Bears 2001-03, Dallas Cowboys 2004-06, Arizona Cardinals 2007-08, Kansas City Chiefs 2009-2011, joined Steelers in 2012.

Carnell Lake, defensive backs; born July 15, 1967, Salt Lake City, Utah. Outside linebacker UCLA 1985-1988. Pro defensive back Pittsburgh Steelers 1989-1998, Jacksonville Jaguars 1999-2000, Baltimore Ravens 2001. College coach: UCLA 2009. Pro coach: Joined Steelers in 2011.

Dick LeBeau, defensive coordinator; born September 9, 1937, London, Ohio. Defensive back Ohio State 1955-58. Pro cornerback Detroit Lions 1959-1972. Pro coach: Philadelphia Eagles 1973-75, Green Bay Packers 1976-79, Cincinnati Bengals 1980-1991, 1997-2002 (head coach 2000-02), Pittsburgh Steelers 1992-96, Buffalo Bills 2003, re-joined Steelers in 2004.

Richard Mann, wide receivers; born April 20, 1947, Aliquippa, Pa. Tight end Arizona State 1966-68. No pro playing experience. College coach: Arizona State 1974-79, Louisville 1980-81. Pro coach: Baltimore/Indianapolis Colts 1982-84, Cleveland Browns 1985-1993, New York Jets 1994-1996, Baltimore Ravens 1997-98, Kansas City Chiefs 1999-2000, Washington Redskins 2001, Tampa Bay Buccaneers 2002-09, joined Steelers in 2013.

John Mitchell, asst. head coach/defensive line; born October 14, 1951, Mobile, Ala. Defensive end Eastern Arizona J.C. 1969-1970, Alabama 1971-72. No pro playing experience. College coach: Alabama 1973-76, Arkansas 1977-1982, Temple 1986, Louisiana State 1987-1990. Pro coach: Birmingham Stallions (USFL) 1983-85, Cleveland Browns 1991-93, joined Steelers in 1994.

Danny Smith, special teams; born September 7, 1953, Pittsburgh, Pa. Defensive back Edinboro State 1971-75. No pro playing experience. College coach: Edinboro State 1976, Clemson 1979, William & Mary 1980-83, The Citadel 1984-86, Georgia Tech 1987-1994. Pro coach: Philadelphia Eagles 1995-98, Detroit Lions 1999-2000, Buffalo Bills 2001-03, Washington Redskins 2004-2012, joined Steelers in 2013.

Kirby Wilson, running backs; born August 24, 1961, Los Angeles, Calif. Running back/wide receiver Pasadena (Calif.) C.C. 1979-1980, Illinois 1981-82. Pro cornerback Winnipeg Blue Bombers (CFL) 1983, Toronto Argonauts (CFL) 1984. College coach: Pasadena (Calif.) C.C. 1985, L.A. Southwest (Calif.) J.C. 1989-1990, Southern Illinois 1991-92, Wyoming 1993-94, Iowa State 1995-96, Southern California 2001. Pro coach: New England Patriots 1997-99, Washington Redskins 2000, Tampa Bay Buccaneers 2002-03, Arizona Cardinals 2004-06, joined Steelers in 2007.

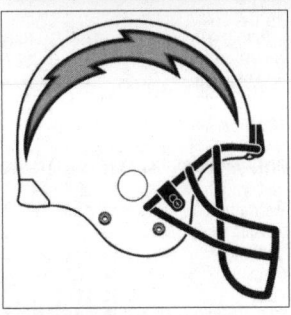

**American Football Conference
West Division**
Team Colors: Navy Blue, Powder Blue,
White, and Gold
P.O. Box 609609
San Diego, California 92160-9609
Telephone: (858) 874-4500

2013 SCHEDULE
PRESEASON
Aug. 8   **Seattle**...............................7:00
Aug. 15 at Chicago..........................5:00
Aug. 24 at Arizona...........................7:00
Aug. 29 **San Francisco** 7:00

REGULAR SEASON
Sep. 9   **Houston** (Mon)...................7:20
Sep. 15 at Philadelphia 10:00a
Sep. 22 at Tennessee 10:00a
Sep. 29 **Dallas** 1:25
Oct. 6   at Oakland 1:25
Oct. 14 **Indianapolis** (Mon) 5:40
Oct. 20 at Jacksonville 10:00a
Oct. 27 BYE
Nov. 3   at Washington 10:00a
Nov. 10 **Denver** 1:25
Nov. 17 at Miami 10:00a
Nov. 24 at Kansas City 10:00a
Dec. 1   **Cincinnati** 1:25
Dec. 8   **New York Giants**................1:25
Dec. 12 at Denver (Thurs) 5:25
Dec. 22 **Oakland** 1:25
Dec. 29 **Kansas City** 1:25
All times PT;

Stadium: Qualcomm Stadium
          (opened in 1967)
          •**Capacity:** 70,000 (app.)
          9449 Friars Road
          San Diego, California 92108
Playing Surface: Grass
Training Camp: Chargers Park
          4020 Murphy Canyon Rd.
          San Diego, CA 92123

QUALCOMM STADIUM

CLUB OFFICIALS
Owner: Alex G. Spanos
Chairman of the Board-President:
    Dean A. Spanos
Executive Vice President:
    Michael A. Spanos
Executive Vice President-Chief Executive
    Officer: A.G. Spanos
General Manager: Tom Telesco
Executive Vice President of Football
    Administration-Player Finance:
    Ed McGuire
Executive Vice President of Football
    Operations: John Spanos
Executive Vice President-Chief Financial
    Officer: Jeanne M. Bonk
Senior Vice President-Chief Marketing
    Officer: Ken Derrett
Director of Player Personnel:
    JoJo Wooden
Director of Pro Scouting:
    Dennis Abraham
Director of College Scouting: Kevin Kelly
Senior Executive: Randy Mueller
Head Athletic Trainer: James Collins
Director of Video Operations:
    Brian Duddy
Equipment Manager: Bob Wick
Director of Player Development:
    Arthur Hightower
Vice President of Marketing Partnerships:
    Dennis O'Leary
Senior Director of Ticket Sales and
    Service: Todd Poulsen
Senior Director Premium Seat Sales:
    Rod Emmons
Director of Business Operations:
    John Hinek
Director of Public Relations: Bill Johnston
Director of Public Affairs &
    Corporate/Community Relations:
    Kimberley Layton
Director of Digital Media: Nicoletta Ruhl
Director of Security: Bill Stetson
Director of Stadium/Game Operations &
    Events: Sean O'Connor
Controller: Marsha Wells
Director of Ticket Operations:
    Michael L. Dougherty

COACHING HISTORY
Los Angeles 1960
(409-410-11)
Records include postseason games
1960-69   Sid Gillman* 83-51-6
1969-1970 Charlie Waller 9-7-3
1971   Sid Gillman** 4-6-0
1971-73   Harland Svare*** 7-17-2
1973   Ron Waller.....................1-5-0
1974-78   Tommy Prothro**** ...21-39-0
1978-1986 Don Coryell# 72-60-0
1986-88   Al Saunders 17-22-0
1989-1991 Dan Henning...............16-32-0
1992-96   Bobby Ross...............50-36-0
1997-98   Kevin Gilbride## 6-16-0
1998   June Jones.....................3-7-0
1999-2001 Mike Riley...................14-34-0
2002-06   Marty Schottenheimer.47-35-0
2007-2012 Norv Turner 59-43-0
          *Retired after nine games in 1969
        **Resigned after 10 games in 1971
      ***Resigned after eight games in 1973
    ****Resigned after four games in 1978
          #Resigned after eight games in 1986
        ##Released after six games in 1998

PAID ATTENDANCE
Home 479,843   Away 524,319
Total 1,004,162
Single-game home record,
    69,288 (11/7/99)
Single-season home record,
    547,937 (2005)

2013 DRAFT CHOICES

Round	Name	Pos.	College
1	D.J. Fluker	T	Alabama
2	Manti Te'o	LB	Notre Dame
3	Keenan Allen	WR	California
5	Steve Williams	DB	California
6	Tourek Williams	LB	Florida International
7	Brad Sorensen	QB	Southern Utah

2012 TEAM RECORD
PRESEASON (3-1)

Date	Result	Opponent
08/09	W 21-13	Green Bay
08/18	W 28-20	Dallas
08/24	W 12-10	at Minnesota
08/30	L 3-35	at San Francisco

REGULAR SEASON (7-9)

Date	Result	Opponent
09/10	W 22-14	at Oakland
09/16	W 38-10	Tennessee
09/23	L 3-27	Atlanta
09/30	W 37-20	at Kansas City
10/07	L 24-31	at New Orleans
10/15	L 24-35	Denver
10/28	L 6-7	at Cleveland
11/01	W 31-13	Kansas City
11/11	L 24-34	at Tampa Bay
11/18	L 23-30	at Denver
11/25	L 13-16	Baltimore (OT)
12/02	L 13-20	Cincinnati
12/09	W 34-24	at Pittsburgh
12/16	L 7-31	Carolina
12/23	W 27-17	at New York Jets
12/30	W 24-21	Oakland

(OT) Overtime

SCORE BY PERIODS

Chargers	99	100	70	81	0 —	350
Opponents	72	79	69	127	3 —	350

2012 TEAM STATISTICS

	Chargers	Opp.
Total First Downs	293	316
Rushing	81	85
Passing	184	201
Penalty	28	30
3rd Down: Made/Att	82/217	90/214
3rd Down Pct.	37.8	42.1
4th Down: Made/Att	6/11	4/10
4th Down Pct.	54.5	40.0
Possession Avg.	31:10	28:50
Total Net Yards	4756	5223
Avg. Per Game	297.3	326.4
Total Plays	988	1012
Avg. Per Play	4.8	5.2
Net Yards Rushing	1461	1542
Avg. Per Game	91.3	96.4
Total Rushes	411	406
Net Yards Passing	3295	3681
Avg. Per Game	205.9	230.1
Sacked/Yards Lost	49/311	38/244
Gross Yards	3606	3925
Att./Completions	528/338	568/347
Completion Pct.	64.0	61.1
Had Intercepted	15	14
Punts/Average	84/46.6	80/45.4
Net Punting Avg.	84/40.6	80/40.2
Penalties/Yards	103/796	102/798
Fumbles/Ball Lost	24/11	29/14
Touchdowns	39	42
Rushing	4	10
Passing	26	28
Returns	9	4

2012 INDIVIDUAL STATISTICS

PASSING

	Att.	Comp.	Yds.	Pct.	TD	Int.	Tkld.	Rate
Rivers	527	338	3606	64.1	26	15	49/311	88.6
Alexander	1	0	0	0.0	0	0	0/0	39.6
Chargers	528	338	3606	64.0	26	15	49/311	88.5
Opponents	568	347	3925	61.1	28	14	38/244	87.9

SCORING

	TD R	TD P	TD Rt	PAT	FG	Saf	PTS
Novak	0	0	0	33/33	18/20	0	87
Alexander	0	7	0	0/0	0/0	0	42
Gates	0	7	0	0/0	0/0	0	42
Floyd	0	5	0	0/0	0/0	0	30
Kaeding	0	0	0	6/6	7/7	0	27
Battle	3	1	0	0/0	0/0	0	24
Rosario	0	3	0	0/0	0/0	0	18
Spurlock	0	0	2	0/0	0/0	0	12
Jammer	0	0	2	0/0	0/0	0	12
Meachem	0	2	0	0/0	0/0	0	12
Williams	0	0	2	0/0	0/0	0	12
Phillips	0	0	1	0/0	0/0	1	8
Butler	0	0	1	0/0	0/0	0	6
Mathews	1	0	0	0/0	0/0	0	6
Royal	0	1	0	0/0	0/0	0	6
Weddle	0	0	1	0/0	0/0	0	6
Scifres	0	0	0	0/0	0/0	0	0
Chargers	4	26	9	39/39	25/27	1	350
Opponents	10	28	4	39/39	19/21	0	350

RUSHING

	No.	Yds	Avg	LG	TD
Mathews	184	707	3.8	31	1
Battle	95	311	3.3	52	3
R. Brown	46	220	4.8	21	0
Brinkley	39	115	2.9	13	0
McClain	14	42	3.0	17	0
Rivers	27	40	1.5	11	0
Royal	3	22	7.3	11	0
Weddle	2	10	5.0	6	0
Meachem	1	-6	-6.0	-6	0
Chargers	411	1461	3.6	52	4
Opponents	406	1542	3.8	41	10

RECEIVING

	No.	Yds	Avg	LG	TD
Floyd	56	814	14.5	39	5
Gates	49	538	11.0	34t	7
R. Brown	49	371	7.6	25	0
Mathews	39	252	6.5	24	0
Alexander	37	658	17.8	80t	7
Royal	23	234	10.2	31	1
Battle	15	108	7.2	18	1
Meachem	14	207	14.8	46	2
Brinkley	12	77	6.4	12	0
Rosario	10	95	9.5	18	3
Spurlock	9	79	8.8	13	0
McMichael	9	51	5.7	13	0
McClain	8	29	3.6	12	0
L. Green	4	56	14.0	31	0
Ajirotutu	3	45	15.0	28	0
Clary	1	-8	-8.0	-8	0
Chargers	338	3606	10.7	80t	26
Opponents	347	3925	11.3	55	28

INTERCEPTIONS

	No.	Yds	Avg	LG	TD
Jammer	3	89	29.7	80t	1
Weddle	3	52	17.3	23t	1
Williams	2	90	45.0	59t	2
Lynch	2	50	25.0	30	0
Cason	2	34	17.0	31	0
Butler	1	21	21.0	21t	1
Bird	1	0	0.0	0	0
Chargers	14	336	24.0	80t	5
Opponents	15	220	14.7	83t	2

PUNTING

	No.	Yds.	Avg.	In 20	LG
Scifres	81	3914	48.3	30	66
Chargers	84	3914	46.6	30	66
Opponents	80	3635	45.4	29	79

PUNT RETURNS

	Ret	FC	Yds	Avg	LG	TD
Spurlock	11	12	188	17.1	63t	1
Royal	12	2	64	5.3	14	0
Weddle	7	1	48	6.9	20	0
Carr	2	5	11	5.5	11	0
Cason	1	2	9	9.0	9	0
Chargers	33	22	320	9.7	63t	1
Opponents	40	15	362	9.1	24	0

KICKOFF RETURNS

	No.	Yds	Avg	LG	TD
Goodman	18	497	27.6	39	0
Spurlock	10	257	25.7	99t	1
Carr	5	102	20.4	26	0
Brinkley	4	86	21.5	28	0
Ingram	2	-1	-0.5	0	0
Cason	1	16	16.0	16	0
Chargers	40	957	23.9	99t	1
Opponents	45	1017	22.6	71	0

FIELD GOALS

	1-19	20-29	30-39	40-49	50+
Novak	1/1	5/5	6/6	4/4	2/4
Kaeding	1/1	3/3	0/0	3/3	0/0
Chargers	2/2	8/8	6/6	7/7	2/4
Opponents	3/3	3/3	5/6	7/7	1/2

SACKS

	No.
Phillips	9.5
Liuget	7.0
Reyes	5.5
Barnes	3.0
Butler	3.0
English	1.5
Johnson	1.5
Gachkar	1.0
Garay	1.0
Gilchrist	1.0
Ingram	1.0
Martin	1.0
Weddle	1.0
Spikes	0.5
Taylor	0.5
Chargers	38.0
Opponents	49.0

RECORD HOLDERS
INDIVIDUAL RECORDS—CAREER

Category	Name	Performance
Rushing (Yds.)	LaDainian Tomlinson, 2001-09	12,490
Passing (Yds.)	Dan Fouts, 1973-1987	43,040
Passing (TDs)	Dan Fouts, 1973-1987	254
Receiving (No.)	Antonio Gates, 2003-2012	642
Receiving (Yds.)	Lance Alworth, 1962-1970	9,584
Interceptions	Gill Byrd, 1983-1992	42
Punting (Avg.)	Mike Scifres, 2003-2012	45.3
Punt Return (Avg.)	Darrien Gordon, 1993-96	13.7
Kickoff Return (Avg.)	Leslie (Speedy) Duncan, 1964-1970	25.3
Field Goals	John Carney, 1990-2000	261
Touchdowns (Tot.)	LaDainian Tomlinson, 2001-09	153
Points	John Carney, 1990-2000	1,076
*Sacks	Leslie O'Neal, 1986-1995	105.5

INDIVIDUAL RECORDS—SINGLE SEASON

Category	Name	Performance
Rushing (Yds.)	LaDainian Tomlinson, 2006	1,815
Passing (Yds.)	Dan Fouts, 1981	4,802
Passing (TDs)	Philip Rivers, 2008	34
Receiving (No.)	LaDainian Tomlinson, 2003	100
Receiving (Yds.)	Lance Alworth, 1965	1,602
Interceptions	Antonio Cromartie, 2007	10
Punting (Avg.)	Mike Scifres, 2012	48.3
Punt Return (Avg.)	Leslie (Speedy) Duncan, 1965	15.5
Kickoff Return (Avg.)	Keith Lincoln, 1962	28.4
Field Goals	John Carney, 1994	34
Touchdowns (Tot.)	LaDainian Tomlinson, 2006	**31
Points	LaDainian Tomlinson, 2006	**186
*Sacks	Leslie O'Neal, 1992	17.0
	Shawne Merriman, 2006	17.0

INDIVIDUAL RECORDS—SINGLE GAME

Category	Name	Performance
Rushing (Yds.)	LaDainian Tomlinson, 12-28-03	243
Passing (Yds.)	Philip Rivers, 9-26-10	455
Passing (TDs)	Dan Fouts, 11-22-81	6
Receiving (No.)	Kellen Winslow, 10-7-84	15
Receiving (Yds.)	Wes Chandler, 12-20-82	260
Interceptions	Many times	3
	Last time by Antonio Cromartie, 11-11-07	
Field Goals	John Carney, 9-5-93, 9-18-93	6
	Greg Davis, 10-5-97	6
Touchdowns (Tot.)	Kellen Winslow, 11-22-81	5
Points	Kellen Winslow, 11-22-81	30
*Sacks	Leslie O'Neal, 11-16-86	5.0

*Sacks became an official statistic in 1982.
**NFL Record

2013 VETERAN ROSTER

No.	Name	Pos.	Ht.	Wt.	Birthdate	NFL Exp.	College	Hometown	How Acq.	'12 Games/ Starts
84	+Alexander, Danario	WR	6-5	217	8/7/88	4	Missouri	Marlin, Texas	FA-'12	10/6
64	Baxter, Colin	C	6-3	310	7/31/87	2	Arizona	Rolling Hills, Calif.	FA-'11	4/0
97	Bird, Bront	ILB	6-4	250	3/17/89	2	Texas Tech	Odessa, Texas	FA-'12	5/0
41	Brown, Cornelius	CB	5-11	198	2/26/88	2	Texas-El Paso	Houston, Texas	FA-'13	0*
30	Brown, Ronnie	RB	6-0	230	12/12/81	9	Auburn	Cartersville, Ga.	UFA(Phil)-'12	14/1
86	Brown, Vincent	WR	5-11	190	1/25/89	3	San Diego State	Rancho Cucamonga, Calif.	D3a-'11	0*
3	Butler, Deon	WR	5-10	182	1/4/86	4	Penn State	Woodbridge, Va.	FA-'13	1/0*
56	Butler, Donald	ILB	6-1	242	10/17/88	4	Washington	Fair Oaks, Calif.	D3-'10	12/12
66	Clary, Jeromey	T	6-6	320	11/5/83	7	Kansas State	Mansfield, Texas	D6a-'06	14/14
22	Cox, Derek	CB	6-1	195	9/22/86	5	William & Mary	Greenville, N.C.	UFA(Jax)-'13	12/12*
50	Dillard, Phillip	LB	6-2	250	12/10/86	2	Nebraska	Jenks, Okla.	FA-'12	0*
62	Dombrowski, Brandyn	G	6-5	323	4/3/85	4	San Diego State	Las Vegas, Nev.	FA-'08	0*
77	Dunlap, King	T	6-9	330	9/14/85	6	Auburn	Brentwood, Tenn.	UFA(Phil)-'13	14/12*
52	English, Larry	OLB	6-2	255	1/22/86	5	Northern Illinois	Aurora, Ill.	D1-'09	14/0
80	Floyd, Malcom	WR	6-5	225	9/8/81	8	Wyoming	Sacramento, Calif.	FA-'04	14/14
59	Gachkar, Andrew	ILB	6-3	240	11/4/88	3	Missouri	Overland Park, Kan.	D7-'11	16/0
85	Gates, Antonio	TE	6-4	255	6/18/80	11	Kent State	Detroit, Mich.	FA-'03	15/15
38	Gilchrist, Marcus	CB	5-10	198	12/8/88	3	Clemson	High Point, N.C.	D2a-'11	16/4
15	Goodman, Richard	WR/KR	6-0	192	4/23/87	3	Florida State	Ft. Lauderdale, Fla.	FA-'10	7/0
89	Green, Ladarius	TE	6-6	240	5/29/90	2	Louisiana-Lafayette	Pensacola, Fla.	D4-'12	4/1
44	Gronkowski, Chris	FB	6-2	245	12/26/86	4	Arizona	Williamsville, N.Y.	FA-'13	14/0*
61	Hardwick, Nick	C	6-4	305	9/2/81	10	Purdue	Indianapolis, Ind.	D3b-'04	16/16
79	Harris, Mike	T	6-5	318	12/5/88	2	UCLA	Duarte, Calif.	FA-'12	15/9
70	Haslam, Kevin	T	6-5	310	11/8/86	4	Rutgers	Mahwah, N.J.	FA-'12	5/3
54	Ingram, Melvin	OLB	6-2	265	4/26/89	2	South Carolina	Rockingham, N.C.	D1-'12	16/2
96	Johnson, Jarret	OLB	6-3	260	8/14/81	11	Alabama	Chiefland, Fla.	UFA(Balt)-'12	15/14
94	Liuget, Corey	DE	6-2	300	3/18/90	3	Illinois	Miami, Fla.	D1-'11	16/16
24	Mathews, Ryan	RB	6-0	220	10/10/87	4	Fresno State	Bakersfield, Calif.	D1-'10	12/9
33	McClain, Le'Ron	FB	6-0	260	12/27/84	7	Alabama	Northport, Ala.	UFA(KC)-'12	16/9
12	Meachem, Robert	WR	6-2	215	9/28/84	7	Tennessee	Tulsa, Okla.	UFA(NO)-'12	15/3
60	Molk, David	C	6-1	300	12/15/88	2	Michigan	Lemont, Ill.	D7a-'12	12/0
57	Mouton, Jonas	ILB	6-2	240	3/17/88	3	Michigan	Los Angeles, Calif.	D2b-'11	3/0
42	Nelson, Kyle	LS	6-2	240	10/3/86	2	New Mexico State	China Springs, Texas	FA-'12	6/0
9	Novak, Nick	K	6-0	198	8/21/81	6	Maryland	Charlottesville, Va.	FA-'12	13/0
74	Ohrnberger, Rich	C-G	6-2	300	2/14/86	5	Penn State	East Meadow, N.Y.	UFA(Ariz)-'13	13/4*
26	Patrick, Johnny	CB	5-11	190	8/17/88	3	Louisville	DeLand, Fla.	W(NO)-'13	15/1*
83	Phillips, John	TE	6-5	251	6/11/87	5	Virginia	Hot Springs, Va.	UFA(Dall)-'13	16/7*
91	Reyes, Kendall	DE	6-4	300	9/26/89	2	Connecticut	Nashua, N.H.	D2-'12	16/4
78	Rinehart, Chad	G	6-5	321	5/4/85	6	Northern Iowa	Boone, Iowa	UFA(Buff)-'13	7/2*
17	Rivers, Philip	QB	6-5	228	12/8/81	10	North Carolina State	Athens, Ala.	T(NYG)-'04	16/16
11	Royal, Eddie	WR/KR	5-10	185	5/21/86	6	Virginia Tech	Chantilly, Va.	UFA(Den)-'12	10/2
72	Schilling, Stephen	G-T	6-5	312	6/21/88	2	Michigan	Bellevue, Wash.	D6b-'11	2/0
5	Scifres, Mike	P	6-2	215	10/8/80	11	Western Illinois	Destrehan, La.	D5-'03	16/0
25	Stuckey, Darrell	S	5-11	208	6/16/87	4	Kansas	Kansas City, Kan.	D4-'10	12/0
28	Taylor, Brandon	SS	5-11	205	1/29/90	2	Louisiana State	Franklinton, La.	D3-'12	4/1
93	Thomas, Cam	DT	6-4	335	12/12/86	4	North Carolina	Robbins, N.C.	D5a-'10	16/3
32	Weddle, Eric	FS	5-11	200	1/4/85	7	Utah	Alta Loma, Calif.	D2-'07	16/16
6	Whitehurst, Charlie	QB	6-5	226	8/6/82	8	Clemson	Alpharetta, Ga.	UFA(Sea)-'12	0*
47	Windt, Mike	LS	6-1	237	5/29/86	4	Cincinnati	Cincinnati, Ohio	FA-'10	10/0
39	Woodhead, Danny	RB	5-8	200	1/25/85	6	Chadron State	North Platte, Neb.	UFA(NE)-'13	16/2*
29	Wright, Shareece	CB	5-11	182	4/8/87	3	Southern California	Colton, Calif.	D3b-'11	10/0
99	Wynn, Jarius	DE	6-3	285	8/29/86	5	Georgia	Lincolnton, Ga.	UFA(Tenn)-'13	7/0*

* C. Brown last active with Indianapolis in '10; V. Brown missed '12 season because of injury; Butler played in one game with Seattle in '12; Cox played 12 games with Jacksonville; Dillard last played with the New York Giants in '10; Dombrowski spent '12 season on Reserve-Non-Football Illness list; Dunlap played 14 games with Philadelphia; Gronkowski played 14 games for Denver in '12; Ohrnberger played 13 games with Arizona; Patrick played 15 games with New Orleans; J. Phillips played 16 games with Dallas; Rinehart played seven games with Buffalo; Whitehurst did not play in 16 games; Woodhead played 16 games with New England; Wynn played seven games with Tennessee.

+ Restricted Free Agent; subject to developments.

Players lost through free agency (6): OLB Antwan Barnes (NYJ; 11 games in '12), CB Antoine Cason (Ariz; 16), DT Aubrayo Franklin (Ind; 12), DE Vaughn Martin (Mia; 12), OLB Shaun Phillips (Den; 6), G Louis Vasquez (Den; 16).

Also played with Chargers in '12—WR Seyi Ajirotutu (3 games), RB Jackie Battle (16), SS Atari Bigby (11), RB Curtis Brinkley (10), CB Chris Carr (9), T Jared Gaither (4), DT Antonio Garay (8), G Tyronne Green (13), OLB Gary Guyton (1), G Rex Hadnot (16), CB Quentin Jammer (16), S Corey Lynch (16), TE Randy McMichael (16), TE Dante Rosario (13), ILB Takeo Spikes (16), WR Michael Spurlock (8), G-T Reggie Wells (2), ILB Demorrio Williams (14).

FIRST-YEAR ROSTER

Name	Pos.	Ht.	Wt.	Birthdate	College	Hometown	How Acq.
Addae, Jahleel	S	5-10	195	1/24/90	Central Michigan	Valrico, Fla.	FA
Allen, Keenan	WR	6-2	211	4/27/92	California	Greensboro, N.C.	D3
Baker, Edwin (1)	RB	5-8	200	6/1/91	Michigan State	Highland Park, Mich.	D7b-'12
Becton, Nick	T	6-6	323	2/11/90	Virginia Tech	Wilmington, N.C.	FA
Beltre, Frank	OLB	6-2	240	1/28/90	Towson	Randolph, N.J.	FA
Brown, Greg	CB	5-10	188	1/21/90	Kansas	Cedar Hill, Tex.	FA
Cattouse, Sean (1)	S	6-2	210	10/4/88	California	Chicago, Ill.	FA-'12
Cotton, Ben	TE	6-5	256	6/13/89	Nebraska	Ames, Iowa	FA
Cromartie, Marcus	CB	6-0	195	12/3/90	Wisconsin	Mansfield, Texas	FA
DePalma, Dan (1)	WR	5-11	192	7/21/89	West Chester (Pa.)	Verona, N.J.	FA
Fluker, D.J.	T	6-5	339	3/13/91	Alabama	Foley, Ala.	D1
Gatson, Greg (1)	CB	5-11	165	3/24/89	Arkansas	Memphis, Tenn.	FA-'12
Geathers, Kwame	DT	6-6	335	10/4/90	Georgia	Georgetown, S.C.	FA
Harrell, Logan (1)	DE	6-2	280	9/25/89	Fresno State	Santa Margarita, Calif.	FA-'12
Hermann, Mike	QB	6-5	250	11/27/89	Rensselaer Polytechnic Institute	Hilton Head, S.C.	FA
Hill, Michael	RB	5-10	209	8/14/89	Missouri Western	St. Joseph, Mo.	FA
Jerideau, Byron	DT	6-1	334	5/38/90	South Carolina	Green Pond, S.C.	FA
Johnson, Josh	CB	5-10	199	9/10/90	Purdue	Dade City, Fla.	FA
Kent, Richard	P	6-1	199	8/17/89	Vanderbilt	Marietta, Ga.	FA
McFarland, Jamarkus	DE	6-2	305	11/26/90	Oklahoma	Lufkin, Texas	FA
Molls, Daniel	ILB	6-0	238	2/12/91	Toledo	North Royalton, Ohio	FA
Moore, Brandon	DE	6-5	317	4/7/91	Texas	Montgomery, Ala.	FA
Okoro, Kenny	CB	6-0	195	10/18/89	Wake Forest	Greensboro, N.C.	FA
Richards, Randy	T	6-3	303	1/24/91	Missouri State	Royal Palm Beach, Fla.	FA
Rolf, David	TE	6-3	257	4/16/90	Utah	Piqua, Ohio	FA
Scafe, Damik (1)	DE	6-2	300	4/26/88	Boston College	Windsor, Conn.	FA-'11
Sorensen, Brad	QB	6-5	230	3/13/88	Southern Utah	Colton, Calif.	D7
Tasker, Luke	WR	5-11	190	1/18/91	Cornell	East Aurora, N.Y.	FA
Te'o, Manti	ILB	6-1	241	1/26/91	Notre Dame	Laie, Hawaii	D2
Troutman, Johnnie (1)	G	6-4	330	11/11/87	Penn State	Brown Mills, N.J.	D5-'12
Walker, Dallas	TE	6-6	235	2/22/88	Western Michigan	Madison, Miss.	FA
Walker, Devan	OLB	6-2	240	3/12/90	Southeastern Louisiana	Baton Rouge, La.	FA
Whittaker, Fozzy (1)	RB	5-10	202	2/2/89	Texas	Houston, Texas	W(Ariz)
Williams, Steve	CB	5-10	185	3/7/91	California	Dallas, Texas	D5
Williams, Tourek	OLB	6-4	262	5/9/91	Florida International	Miami, Fla.	D6
Willie, Mike (1)	WR	6-2	220	6/17/90	Arizona State	Long Beach, Calif.	FA-'12

The term NFL Rookie is defined as a player who is in his first season of professional football and has not been on the roster of another professional football team for any regular-season or postseason games. A Rookie is designated by an "R" on NFL rosters. Players who have been active in another professional football league or players who have NFL experience, including either preseason training camp or being on an Active List or Inactive List, or on Reserve/Injured or Reserve/Physically Unable to Perform for fewer than six regular-season games, are termed NFL First-Year Players. An NFL First-Year Player is designated by a "1" on NFL rosters. Thereafter, a player is credited with an additional year of experience for each season in which he accumulates six games on the Active List or Inactive List, or on Reserve/Injured or Reserve/Physically Unable to Perform.

Log on to www.chargers.com for an up-to-date roster.

COACHING STAFF
Head Coach,
Mike McCoy
Pro Career: On January 15, 2013, Mike McCoy was named the 15th head coach in team history. He came from Denver, where he spent the 2009-2012 seasons. Last season, McCoy was part of a staff that saw the Broncos win the second-most games in franchise history (13). Denver won 11 straight games to end the regular season and entered the playoffs as the No. 1 seed in the AFC. McCoy began his coaching career with Carolina in 2000, joining the Panthers as an offensive assistant before being elevated to quarterbacks coach. He spent a total of nine seasons with the Panthers, serving additionally as wide receivers coach (2001), quarterbacks coach (2002-08) and passing game coordinator (2007-08). The Panthers totaled three playoff appearances, two division titles, two NFC Championship Game appearances and a berth in Super Bowl XXXVIII (2003) during McCoy's tenure on the staff. Career record: 0-0.
Background: McCoy played quarterback at Long Beach State and Utah before signing with the Denver Broncos as an undrafted free agent in 1995. He spent his rookie season on the practice squad in Green Bay and then had stops with NFL Europe's Amsterdam Admirals, his hometown San Francisco 49ers and the Philadelphia Eagles before concluding his playing career with the Canadian Football League's Calgary Stampeders in 1999.
Personal: Born in San Francisco, Ca., April 1, 1972. McCoy and his wife, Kellie, have a daughter, Liv, and a son, Luke.

ASSISTANT COACHES
Craig Aukerman, asst. special teams; born November 22, 1976, McComb, Ohio. Defensive back/wide receiver Findlay 1995-98. No pro playing experience. College coach: Findlay 2000, Miami (Ohio) 2001-02, 2005-08, Western Kentucky 2003-04, Kent State 2009. Pro coach: Denver Broncos 2010, Jacksonville Jaguars 2011-12, joined Chargers in 2013.
Joe Barry, linebackers; born July 5, 1970, Murphysboro, Ill. Linebacker Michigan 1989-1990, Southern California 1991-93. No pro playing experience. College coach: Southern California 1995, 2010-11, Northern Arizona 1996-98, Nevada-Las Vegas 1999. Pro coach: San Francisco 49ers 2000, Tampa Bay Buccaneers 2001-06, 2009, Detroit Lions 2007-08, joined Chargers in 2012.
Joe D'Alessandris, offensive line; born April, 29, 1954, Aliquippa, Pa. Guard Western Carolina 1972-76. No pro playing experience. College coach: Western Carolina 1977-78, Livingston 1979-1983, Memphis 1984-85, Tennessee-Chattanooga 1986-89, Samford 1993, Texas A&M 1994, Pittsburgh 1996, Duke 1997-2001, Georgia Tech 2002-07. Pro coach: Ottawa Rough Riders (CFL) 1990, Birmingham Fire (WLAF) 1991-92, Memphis (AFL) 1995, Kansas City Chiefs 2008-09,

Buffalo Bills 2010-12, joined Chargers in 2013.
Andrew Dees, asst. offensive line; born December 1, 1969, Babylon, N.Y. Offensive line/tight end Syracuse 1988-1991. Pro offensive line Cincinnati Bengals 1992, Seattle Seahawks 1993. College coach: Wagner 1997, Stony Brook 1998-2000, Buffalo 2001-05, Temple 2006-2010, Massachusetts 2011. Pro coach: Buffalo Bills 2012, joined Chargers in 2013.
Fred Graves, wide receivers; born March 2, 1950, Los Angeles, Calif. Halfback/split end Utah 1969-1971. No pro playing experience. College coach: Northeast Missouri State 1975-76, Western Illinois 1977-78, New Mexico State 1979-1981, Utah 1982-2000. Pro coach: Buffalo Bills 2001-03, Cleveland Browns 2004, Detroit Lions 2005, Tennessee Titans 2007-2010, Carolina Panthers 2011-12, joined Chargers in 2013.
Chad Grimm, quality control-defense; born May 18, 1985, Fairfax, Va. Linebacker Virginia Tech 2003-06. No pro playing experience. Pro coach: Arizona 2009-2012, joined Chargers in 2013.
Don Johnson, defensive line; born November 3, 1954, Newark, N.J. Linebacker Jersey City State 1973-76. College coach: Jersey City State 1984-85. Riverside (Calif.) C.C. 1987-1990, Cal State-Fullerton 1991-92, Nevada 1995-98, UCLA 1999-2004. Pro coach: Chicago Bears 2005-06, Oakland Raiders 2007-08, joined Chargers in 2009.
Kent Johnston, strength and conditioning; born February 21, 1966, Mexia, Texas. Defensive back Stephen F. Austin 1974- 77. No pro playing experience. College coach: Northwestern Louisiana 1981, Alabama 1985-86, 2004-05. Pro coach: Tampa Bay Buccaneers 1987-1991, Green Bay Packers 1992-98, Seattle Seahawks 1999-2003, Cleveland Browns 2010-12, joined Chargers in 2013.
Rick Lyle, assistant strength and conditioning; born February 26, 1971, Monroe, La. Defensive lineman Missouri 1989-1993. defensive lineman Cleveland Browns 1994- 95, Baltimore Ravens 1996, New York Jets 1997-2001, New England Patriots 2002-03. Pro coach: New York Jets 2006-08, Cleveland Browns 2009-2012, joined Chargers in 2013.
Jason Michael, tight ends; born October 15, 1978, Portsmouth, Ohio. Quarterback Western Kentucky 1999-2002. No pro playing experience. College coach: Tennessee 2003-04, 2008. Pro coach: Oakland Raiders 2005, New York Jets 2006-07, San Francisco 49ers 2009-2010, joined Chargers in 2011.
Ron Milus, secondary; born November, 25, 1963, Tacoma, Wash. Cornerback Washington 1982-85. College coach: Washington 1991-98, Texas A&M 1999. Pro coach: Denver Broncos 2000-02, 2011-12, Arizona Cardinals 2003, New York Giants 2004-05, St. Louis Rams 2006-08, Carolina Panthers 2009-2010, joined Chargers in 2013.

John Pagano, defensive coordinator; born March 30, 1967, Boulder, Colo. Linebacker Mesa State College 1985-88. No pro playing experience. College coach: Mesa State College 1989, Nevada-Las Vegas 1990-91, Louisiana Tech 1994, Mississippi 1995. Pro coach: New Orleans Saints 1996-97, Indianapolis Colts 1998-2001, joined Chargers in 2002.
Frank Reich, quarterbacks; born December 4, 1961, Freeport, N.Y. Quarterback Maryland 1981-84. Pro quarterback Buffalo Bills 1985-1994, Carolina Panthers 1995, New York Jets 1996, Detroit Lions 1997-98. Pro coach: Indianapolis Colts 2008-2011, Arizona Cardinals 2012, joined Chargers in 2013.
Nick Sirianni, quality control-offense; born June 15, 1981, Jamestown, N.Y. Wide receiver Mount Union 2000-03. No pro playing experience. College coach: Mount Union 2004-05, Indiana (Pa.) 2006-08. Pro coach: Kansas City 2009-2012, joined Chargers in 2013.
Kevin Spencer, special teams coordinator; born November 2, 1953, Queens, N.Y. Outside linebacker Springfield College 1971. No pro playing experience. College coach: SUNY-Cortland 1975-76, Cornell 1979-1980, Ithaca 1981-86, Wesleyan 1987-1991. Pro coach: Cleveland Browns 1991-94, Oakland Raiders 1995-97, Indianapolis Colts 1998-2001, Pittsburgh Steelers 2002-06, Arizona Cardinals 2007-12, joined Chargers in 2013.
Byron Storer, asst. linebackers; born May 1, 1984, Modesto, Calif. Fullback California 2002-06. Pro fullback Tampa Bay Buccaneers 2007-09. Pro coach: Tampa Bay Buccaneers 2009-2011, joined Chargers in 2012.
Ken Whisenhunt, offensive coordinator; born February 28, 1962, Atlanta, Ga. Tight end/H-back Georgia Tech 1980-84. Pro tight end Atlanta Falcons 1985-88, Washington Redskins 1989-1990, New York Jets 1991-93. College coach: Vanderbilt 1995-96. Pro coach: Baltimore Ravens 1997-98, Cleveland Browns 1999, New York Jets 2000, Pittsburgh Steelers 2001-06, Arizona Cardinals 2007-2012 (head coach), joined Chargers in 2013.
Greg Williams, asst. secondary; born March 12, 1976, Chicago, Ill. Wide receiver/defensive back North Carolina 1994-97. Pro defensive back Amsterdam Admirals (NFL Europe) 1999-2000, San Francisco Demons (XFL) 2001, Indiana Firebirds (AFL) 2001-03, Chicago Rush (AFL) 2004. College coach: Arizona State 2003, College of DuPage 2004-05, Arkansas Tech 2006-07, Pittsburgh 2008. Pro coach: Joined Chargers in 2009.
Ollie Wilson, running backs; born March 3, 1951, Worcester, Mass. Wide receiver Springfield 1971-73. No pro playing experience. College coach: Springfield 1975, Northeastern 1976-1982, California 1983-1990. Pro coach: Atlanta Falcons 1991-96, 2002-07, San Diego Chargers 1997-2001, re-joined Chargers in 2008.

American Football Conference
South Division
Team Colors: Navy, Titans Blue, Red, Silver
460 Great Circle Road
Nashville, Tennessee 37228
Telephone: (615) 565-4000

2013 SCHEDULE
PRESEASON
Aug. 8	**Washington**	7:00
Aug. 17	at Cincinnati	6:00
Aug. 24	**Atlanta**	7:00
Aug. 29	at Minnesota	7:00

REGULAR SEASON
Sep. 8	at Pittsburgh	12:00
Sep. 15	at Houston	12:00
Sep. 22	**San Diego**	12:00
Sep. 29	**New York Jets**	3:05
Oct. 6	**Kansas City**	12:00
Oct. 13	at Seattle	3:05
Oct. 20	**San Francisco**	3:05
Oct. 27	BYE	
Nov. 3	at St. Louis	12:00
Nov. 10	**Jacksonville**	12:00
Nov. 14	**Indianapolis** (Thurs)	7:25
Nov. 24	at Oakland	3:05
Dec. 1	at Indianapolis	12:00
Dec. 8	at Denver	3:05
Dec. 15	**Arizona**	12:00
Dec. 22	at Jacksonville	12:00
Dec. 29	**Houston**	12:00

All times CT

Stadium: LP Field (opened in 1999)
 • **Capacity:** 69,143
  One Titans Way
  Nashville, Tennessee 37213
Playing Surface: Natural Grass
Training Camp: Baptist Sports Park
  460 Great Circle Road
  Nashville, TN 37228

LP FIELD

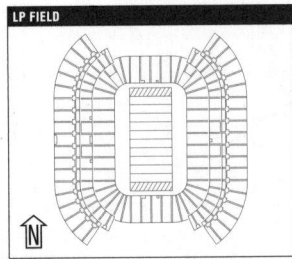

CLUB OFFICIALS
Founder/Owner/Chairman of the Board/CEO/ President:
 K.S. "Bud" Adams, Jr.
Executive V.P. of Administration/Facilities:
 Don MacLachlan
Executive V.P./General Manager:
 Ruston Webster
Senior Vice President/General Counsel:
 Elza Bullock
Vice President/Community Relations:
 Bob Hyde
Vice President/CFO: Jenneen Kaufman
Vice President/Marketing:
 Ralph Ockenfels
Vice President/Business Operations and Sales: Stuart Spears
Vice President/Player Personnel:
 Lake Dawson
Vice President/Football Administration:
 Vincent Marino
Head Coach: Mike Munchak
Director of Player Development:
 Tina Tuggle
Equipment Manager: Paul Noska
Asst. Equipment Manager: Joey Barranco
Video Director: Anthony Pastrana
Asst. Video Director: Craig Patterson
Head Athletic Trainer: Brad Brown
Asst. Athletic Trainers: Don Moseley,
 Casey Carter
Scouting Consultant: C.O. Brocato
Director of College Scouting:
 Blake Beddingfield
College Scouts: Johnny Meads, Phil Neri,
 Jon Salge, Richard Shelton,
 Marvin Sunderland, Brandon Taylor
Pro Personnel Assistants: Trey Koziol,
 Dale Thompson
Operations Manager: Brent Akers
Director of Marketing: Brad McClanahan
Director of Broadcasting: Mike Keith
Director of Information Systems:
 Russ Hudson
Asst. Dir. of Information Systems:
 Craig Pelat
Director of Internet Operations/Publications: Gary Glenn
Internet Coordinator: Jeff Harding
Community Relations Coordinator:
 Jerry Blessing
Asst. General Counsel: Blu Whipple
Director of Security: Jim Arts
Director of Cheerleading: Stacie Kinder
Mascot Coordinator: Pete Nelson
Director of Media Relations:
 Robbie Bohren
Asst. Director of Media Relations:
 Dwight Spradlin
Media Relations Assistant: Jared Puffer
Senior Director of Ticketing:
 Marty Collins
Asst. Dir. Of Ticket Operations:
 Tim Zenner
Asst. Ticket Manager: Josh Ward
Ticketing/Hospitality Club Member Manager: Anthony Hall
Director of Suite Sales and Services:
 Bill Wainwright
General Manager of LP Field:
 Walter Overton
Facilities Manager: Dempsey Henderson
Event and Customer Relations Coordinator: Tracy Holliday
Head Groundskeeper: Terry Porch

COACHING HISTORY
Houston 1960-1996
(406-425-6)
Records include postseason games
1960-61	Lou Rymkus*	12-7-1
1961	Wally Lemm	10-0-0
1962-63	Frank (Pop) Ivy	17-12-0
1964	Sammy Baugh	4-10-0
1965	Hugh Taylor	4-10-0
1966-1970	Wally Lemm	28-40-4
1971	Ed Hughes	4-9-1
1972-73	Bill Peterson**	1-18-0
1973-74	Sid Gillman	8-15-0
1975-1980	O.A. (Bum) Phillips	59-38-0
1981-83	Ed Biles***	8-23-0
1983	Chuck Studley	2-8-0
1984-85	Hugh Campbell****	8-22-0
1985-89	Jerry Glanville	35-35-0
1990-94	Jack Pardee#	44-35-0
1994-2010	Jeff Fisher	147-126-0
2011-12	Mike Munchak	15-17-0

*Released after five games in 1961
**Released after five games in 1973
***Resigned after six games in 1983
****Released after 14 games in 1985
#Released after 10 games in 1994

PAID ATTENDANCE
Home 525,231   Away 487,666
Total 1,012,897
Single-game home record,
 69,149, many times (last: 12/18/05)
Single-season home record,
 553,192 (2005)

2013 DRAFT CHOICES
Round	Name	Pos.	College
1	Chance Warmack	G	Alabama
2	Justin Hunter	WR	Tennessee
3	Blidi Wreh-Wilson	DB	Connecticut
	Zaviar Gooden	LB	Missouri
4	Brian Schwenke	C	California
5	Lavar Edwards	DE	Louisiana St.
6	Khalid Wooten	DB	Nevada
7	Daimion Stafford	DB	Nebraska

2012 TEAM RECORD
PRESEASON (3-1)

Date	Result	Opponent
08/11	L 17-27	at Seattle
08/17	W 30-7	at Tampa Bay
08/23	W 32-27	Arizona
08/30	W 10-6	New Orleans

REGULAR SEASON (6-10)

Date	Result	Opponent
09/09	L 13-34	New England
09/16	L 10-38	at San Diego
09/23	W 44-41	Detroit (OT)
09/30	L 14-38	at Houston
10/07	L 7-30	at Minnesota
10/11	W 26-23	Pittsburgh
10/21	W 35-34	at Buffalo
10/28	L 13-19	Indianapolis (OT)
11/04	L 20-51	Chicago
11/11	W 37-3	at Miami
11/25	L 19-24	at Jacksonville
12/02	L 10-24	Houston
12/09	L 23-27	at Indianapolis
12/17	W 14-10	New York Jets
12/23	L 7-55	at Green Bay
12/30	W 38-20	Jacksonville

(OT) Overtime

SCORE BY PERIODS

Titans	72	94	66	95	3 —	330
Opponents	155	58	116	136	6 —	471

2012 TEAM STATISTICS

	Titans	Opp.
Total First Downs	260	358
Rushing	70	122
Passing	166	210
Penalty	24	26
3rd Down: Made/Att	83/217	85/214
3rd Down Pct.	38.2	39.7
4th Down: Made/Att	5/15	6/14
4th Down Pct.	33.3	42.9
Possession Avg.	27:18	32:42
Total Net Yards	5010	5999
Avg. Per Game	313.1	374.9
Total Plays	957	1086
Avg. Per Play	5.2	5.5
Net Yards Rushing	1687	2035
Avg. Per Game	105.4	127.2
Total Rushes	378	483
Net Yards Passing	3323	3964
Avg. Per Game	207.7	247.8
Sacked/Yards Lost	39/254	39/241
Gross Yards	3577	4205
Att./Completions	540/318	564/374
Completion Pct.	58.9	66.3
Had Intercepted	16	19
Punts/Average	83/46.4	70/44.1
Net Punting Avg.	83/40.4	70/36.1
Penalties/Yards	106/847	86/717
Fumbles/Ball Lost	21/12	15/5
Touchdowns	36	55
Rushing	10	16
Passing	17	31
Returns	9	8

2012 INDIVIDUAL STATISTICS

PASSING

	Att.	Comp.	Yds.	Pct.	TD	Int.	Tkld.	Rate
Locker	314	177	2176	56.4	10	11	25/151	74.0
Hasselbeck	221	138	1367	62.4	7	5	14/103	81.0
Smith	5	3	34	60.0	0	0	0/0	80.4
Titans	540	318	3577	58.9	17	16	39/254	76.9
Opponents	564	374	4205	66.3	31	19	39/241	92.7

SCORING

	TD R	TD P	TD Rt	PAT	FG	Saf	PTS
Bironas	0	0	0	35/35	25/31	0	110
C. Johnson	6	0	0	0/0	0/0	0	36
Britt	0	4	0	0/0	0/0	0	26
Cook	0	4	0	0/0	0/0	0	24
Washington	0	4	0	0/0	0/0	0	24
Wright	0	4	0	0/0	0/0	0	24
Harper	3	0	0	0/0	0/0	0	18
Reynaud	0	0	3	0/0	0/0	0	18
Brown	0	0	2	0/0	0/0	0	12
Campbell	0	0	1	0/0	0/0	0	6
Locker	1	0	0	0/0	0/0	0	6
McCarthy	0	0	1	0/0	0/0	0	6
Stevens	0	1	0	0/0	0/0	0	6
Verner	0	0	1	0/0	0/0	0	6
Witherspoon	0	0	1	0/0	0/0	0	6
Titans	10	17	9	35/35	25/31	1	330
Opponents	16	31	8	52/52	29/31	0	471

2-Pt Conversions: Britt, Titans 1-1, Opponents 1-2

RUSHING

	No.	Yds	Avg	LG	TD
C. Johnson	276	1243	4.5	94t	6
Locker	41	291	7.1	32	1
Hasselbeck	13	38	2.9	16	0
Reynaud	16	33	2.1	11	0
Harper	19	30	1.6	13	3
Mooney	5	19	3.8	8	0
Ringer	2	14	7.0	9	0
Babineaux	1	10	10.0	10	0
Q. Johnson	4	5	1.3	3	0
Wright	1	4	4.0	4	0
Titans	378	1687	4.5	94t	10
Opponents	483	2035	4.2	46	16

RECEIVING

	No.	Yds	Avg	LG	TD
Wright	64	626	9.8	38	4
Washington	46	746	16.2	71t	4
Britt	45	589	13.1	46	4
Cook	44	523	11.9	61t	4
C. Johnson	36	232	6.4	22	0
Williams	30	324	10.8	27	0
Stevens	23	275	12.0	46	1
Thompson	6	46	7.7	12	0
Hawkins	5	62	12.4	42	0
Preston	5	59	11.8	21	0
Q. Johnson	5	40	8.0	17	0
Reynaud	5	35	7.0	9	0
Ringer	3	12	4.0	6	0
Harper	1	8	8.0	8	0
Titans	318	3577	11.2	71t	17
Opponents	374	4205	11.2	82t	31

INTERCEPTIONS

	No.	Yds	Avg	LG	TD
Griffin	4	59	14.8	33	0
McCourty	4	29	7.3	28	0
Brown	3	156	52.0	79t	2
Verner	2	11	5.5	11	0
McCarthy	1	49	49.0	49t	1
Witherspoon	1	40	40.0	40t	1
Babineaux	1	10	10.0	10	0
Ayers	1	2	2.0	2	0
R. Johnson	1	2	2.0	2	0
Afalava	1	0	0.0	0	0
Titans	19	358	18.8	79t	4
Opponents	16	260	16.3	63t	4

PUNTING

	No.	Yds.	Avg.	In 20	LG
Kern	81	3855	47.6	30	71
Titans	83	3855	46.4	30	71
Opponents	70	3084	44.1	29	67

PUNT RETURNS

	Ret	FC	Yds	Avg	LG	TD
Reynaud	31	17	410	13.2	81t	2
Campbell	0	0	65	—	65t	1
Titans	31	17	475	15.3	81t	3
Opponents	39	15	405	10.4	58	0

KICKOFF RETURNS

	No.	Yds	Avg	LG	TD
Reynaud	53	1240	23.4	105t	1
Hawkins	7	205	29.3	71	0
Stevens	1	18	18.0	18	0
McCourty	1	14	14.0	14	0
Witherspoon	1	6	6.0	6	0
Williams	0	6	—	6	0
Titans	63	1489	23.6	105t	1
Opponents	33	860	26.1	89t	1

FIELD GOALS

	1-19	20-29	30-39	40-49	50+
Bironas	0/0	6/6	13/13	5/10	1/2
Titans	0/0	6/6	13/13	5/10	1/2
Opponents	0/0	11/11	5/6	9/9	4/5

SACKS

	No.
Morgan	6.5
Ayers	6.0
Wimbley	6.0
Brown	5.5
Klug	3.5
Casey	3.0
Mi. Martin	3.0
Wynn	2.0
Marks	1.5
Griffin	1.0
Witherspoon	1.0
Titans	39.0
Opponents	39.0

RECORD HOLDERS
INDIVIDUAL RECORDS—CAREER
Category Name Performance

Rushing (Yds.) ....Eddie George, 1996-2003 10,009
Passing (Yds.) ....Warren Moon, 1984-1993...33,685
Passing (TDs) ....Warren Moon, 1984-1993..196
Receiving (No.) ....Ernest Givins, 1986-1994 542
Receiving (Yds.) ....Ernest Givins, 1986-1994 7,935
Interceptions ....Jim Norton, 1960-68 45
Punting (Avg.) ....Brett Kern, 2009-2012 ....44.7
Punt Return (Avg.) ....Billy Johnson, 1974-1980 ....13.2
Kickoff Return (Avg.) ....Bobby Jancik, 1962-67 ....26.5
Field Goals ....Al Del Greco, 1991-2000 246
Touchdowns (Tot.) ....Eddie George, 1996-2003 74
Points...Al Del Greco, 1991-2000 1,060
*Sacks...Ray Childress, 1985-1995 ....75.5

INDIVIDUAL RECORDS—SINGLE SEASON
Category Name Performance

Rushing (Yds.) ....Chris Johnson, 2009 2,006
Passing (Yds.) ....Warren Moon, 1991 4,690
Passing (TDs) ....George Blanda, 1961 36
Receiving (No.) ....Charley Hennigan, 1964 101
Receiving (Yds.) ....Charley Hennigan, 1961 1,746
Interceptions ....Fred Glick, 1963..12
                                            Mike Reinfeldt, 1979 12
Punting (Avg.) ....Brett Kern, 2012...47.6
Punt Return (Avg.) ....Billy Johnson, 1977 ....15.4
Kickoff Return (Avg.) ....Ken Hall, 1960 ....31.3
Field Goals ....Al Del Greco, 1998..36
Touchdowns (Tot.) ....Earl Campbell, 1979 19
Points...Al Del Greco, 1998..136
*Sacks...William Fuller, 1991 ....15.0

INDIVIDUAL RECORDS—SINGLE GAME
Category Name Performance

Rushing (Yds.) ....Chris Johnson, 11-1-09 228
Passing (Yds.) ....Warren Moon, 12-16-90 527
Passing (TDs) ....George Blanda, 11-19-61 ....**7
Receiving (No.) ....Charley Hennigan, 10-13-61 13
                                            Haywood Jeffires, 10-13-91 13
                                            Drew Bennett, 12-19-04 13
Receiving (Yds.) ....Charley Hennigan, 10-13-61 272
Interceptions ....Many times 3
                                            Last time by Keith Bulluck, 9-24-07
Field Goals ....Rob Bironas, 10-21-07 ....**8
Touchdowns (Tot.)..Billy Cannon, 12-10-61 5
Points...Billy Cannon, 12-10-61 30
*Sacks...William Fuller, 11-28-93 ....4.0

*Sacks became an official statistic in 1982.
**NFL Record

2013 VETERAN ROSTER

No.	Name	Pos.	Ht.	Wt.	Birthdate	NFL Exp.	College	Hometown	How Acq.	'12 Games/ Starts
58	# Adibi, Xavier	LB	6-2	242	10/18/84	6	Virginia Tech	Hampton, Va.	FA-'12	6/0
38	Afalava, Al	S	5-11	212	1/20/87	4	Oregon State	Laie, Hawaii	FA-'12	12/2
54	Amano, Eugene	G/C	6-3	300	3/1/82	10	SE Missouri State	San Diego, Calif.	D7-'04	0*
56	Ayers, Akeem	LB	6-3	254	7/10/89	3	UCLA	Los Angeles, Calif.	D2-'11	16/14
57	Bailey, Patrick	LB	6-4	235	11/19/85	6	Duke	Elmendorf, Texas	W(Pitt)-'10	12/0
79	Baldridge, Daniel	T	6-8	308	10/21/85	2	Marshall	Opelousas, La.	FA-'12	0*
98	# Ball, Dave	DE	6-5	255	1/4/81	9	UCLA	Dixon, Calif.	FA-'08	0*
2	Bironas, Rob	K	6-0	210	1/29/78	9	Ga. Southern/Auburn	Louisville, Ky.	FA-'05	16/0
48	Brinkley, Beau	LS	6-4	237	1/25/90	2	Missouri	Kearney, Mo.	FA-'12	16/0
18	Britt, Kenny	WR	6-3	215	9/19/88	5	Rutgers	Bayonne, N.J.	D1-'09	14/11
55	Brown, Zach	LB	6-1	242	10/23/89	2	North Carolina	Estill, S.C.	D2-'12	16/13
37	Campbell, Tommie	CB	6-3	205	9/19/87	3	California (Pa.)	Aliquippa, Pa.	D7b-'11	14/0
99	Casey, Jurrell	DT	6-1	300	12/5/89	3	Southern California	Long Beach, Calif.	D3-'11	16/16
69	Clayton, Zach	DT	6-2	299	1/1/88	2	Auburn	Opelika, Ala.	D7a-'11	0*
75	Dawson, Keyunta	DE	6-3	265	9/13/85	6	Texas Tech	Shreveport, La.	FA-'12	3/0
62	# Devan, Kyle	C/G	6-2	306	2/10/85	4	Oregon State	Sacramento, Calif.	FA-'12	4/1
78	# Douzable, Leger	DE	6-4	284	5/31/86	5	Central Florida	Tampa, Fla.	FA-'12	0*
7	Enderle, Nathan	QB	6-4	240	1/12/88	2	Idaho	North Platte, Neb.	FA-'13	0*
4	Fitzpatrick, Ryan	QB	6-2	225	11/24/82	9	Harvard	Gilbert, Ariz.	FA-'13	16/16*
53	Fokou, Moise	LB	6-1	236	8/28/85	5	Maryland	Cameroon, Africa	UFA(Ind)-'13	16/1*
77	Gibson, Thaddeus	DE	6-2	243	10/21/87	2	Ohio State	Euclid, Ohio	FA-'12	0*
22	Greene, Shonn	RB	5-11	226	8/21/85	5	Iowa	Sicklerville, N.J.	UFA(NYJ)-'13	16/14*
33	Griffin, Michael	S	6-0	203	1/4/85	7	Texas	Austin, Texas	D1-'07	16/16
23	Harper, Jamie	RB	5-11	233	9/11/89	3	Clemson	Jacksonville, Fla.	D4b-'11	10/0
96	Harris, DaJohn	DT	6-3	306	1/24/89	2	Southern California	Inglewood, Calif.	FA-'12	7/0
64	# Harris, Leroy	G/C	6-3	303	6/6/84	7	North Carolina State	Raleigh, N.C.	D4a-'07	8/8
87	Hawkins, Lavelle	WR	5-11	194	7/12/86	6	California	Stockton, Calif.	D4b-'08	7/1
94	Hill, Sammie	DT	6-4	329	11/8/86	5	Stillman	West Blocton, Ala.	UFA(Det)-'13	15/3*
28	Johnson, Chris	RB	5-11	191	9/23/85	6	East Carolina	Orlando, Fla.	D1-'08	16/15
45	Johnson, Quinn	FB	6-1	263	9/30/86	5	Louisiana State	New Orleans, La.	T(GB)-'11	16/8
32	Johnson, Robert	S	6-2	206	2/13/87	3	Utah	Los Angeles, Calif.	D5-'10	12/3
6	Kern, Brett	P	6-2	217	2/17/86	6	Toledo	Grand Island, N.Y.	W(Den)-'09	16/0
97	Klug, Karl	DT	6-3	275	3/31/88	3	Iowa	Caledonia, Minn.	D5-'11	16/1
67	Levitre, Andy	G	6-2	305	5/15/86	5	Oregon State	Felton, Calif.	UFA(Buff)-'13	16/16*
10	Locker, Jake	QB	6-3	234	6/15/88	3	Washington	Ferndale, Wash.	D1-'11	11/11
72	# Lutui, Deuce	G	6-4	338	5/5/83	8	Southern California	Mesa, Ariz.	FA-'12	8/8
83	Mariani, Marc	WR	6-1	190	5/2/87	4	Montana	Havre, Mont.	D7a-'10	0*
26	Martin, Markelle	S	6-0	207	6/20/90	2	Oklahoma State	Wichita Falls, Texas	D6-'12	0*
93	Martin, Mike	DT	6-1	306	9/1/90	2	Michigan	Detroit, Mich.	D3-'12	16/1
60	# Matthews, Kevin	C/G	6-3	302	2/4/87	3	Texas A&M	Houston, Texas	FA-'10	14/2
52	McCarthy, Colin	LB	6-1	238	5/30/88	3	Miami	Tampa, Fla.	D4a-'11	7/7
30	McCourty, Jason	CB	6-0	188	8/13/87	5	Rutgers	Montvale, N.J.	D6a-'09	16/16
51	# McRath, Gerald	LB	6-3	228	6/6/86	5	Southern Mississippi	Powder Springs, Ga.	D4a-'09	0*
91	Morgan, Derrick	DE	6-3	278	1/6/89	4	Georgia Tech	Coatesville, Pa.	D1-'10	16/16
29	# Mouton, Ryan	CB	5-9	184	9/23/86	5	Hawaii	Houston, Texas	D3b-'09	13/2
66	Otto, Mike	T	6-5	310	7/24/83	6	Purdue	Kokomo, Ind.	D7-'07	6/3
92	Pitoitua, Ropati	DE	6-8	315	4/6/85	4	Washington State	Spanaway, Wash.	UFA(KC)-'13	15/10*
31	Pollard, Bernard	S	6-1	225	12/23/84	8	Purdue	Fort Wayne, Ind.	FA-'13	13/13*
25	Reynaud, Darius	RB	5-9	201	12/29/84	5	West Virginia	Luling, La.	FA-'12	16/0
21	# Ringer, Javon	RB	5-9	213	2/2/87	5	Michigan State	Dayton, Ohio	D5-'09	2/0
71	Roos, Michael	T	6-7	306	10/5/82	9	Eastern Washington	Vancouver, Wash.	D2-'05	15/15
24	Sensabaugh, Coty	CB	5-11	189	11/15/88	2	Clemson	Kingsport, Tenn.	D4-'12	16/3
59	Shaw, Tim	LB	6-1	236	3/27/84	6	Penn State	Livonia, Mich.	W(Chi)-'10	16/2
11	Smith, Rusty	QB	6-5	226	1/28/87	4	Florida Atlantic	Jacksonville, Fla.	D6a-'10	1/0
90	Solomon, Scott	DE	6-3	262	11/5/88	2	Rice	San Antonio, Texas	D7-'12	13/0
60	Spencer, Chris	C/G	6-3	309	3/28/82	9	Mississippi	Madison, Miss.	UFA(Chi)-'13	10/5*
88	Stevens, Craig	TE	6-3	268	9/1/84	6	California	San Pedro, Calif.	D3-'08	15/15
76	Stewart, David	T	6-7	315	8/28/82	9	Mississippi State	Moulton, Ala.	D4b-'05	12/12
68	Stingily, Byron	T	6-5	313	9/9/88	3	Louisville	Country Club Hills, Ill.	D6-'11	5/2
64	Studdard, Kasey	G	6-3	304	7/1/84	6	Texas	Denver, Colo.	FA-'13	0*
84	Thompson, Taylor	TE	6-6	268	10/19/89	2	Southern Methodist	Prosper, Texas	D5-'12	16/4
58	Turner, Robert	G/C	6-4	308	8/20/84	6	New Mexico	Austin, Texas	UFA(StL)-'13	16/16*
61	Velasco, Fernando	C/G	6-4	312	2/22/85	4	Georgia	Wrens, Ga.	FA-'08	16/16
20	Verner, Alterraun	CB	5-10	187	12/13/88	4	UCLA	Carson, Calif.	D4-'10	16/16
82	Walker, Delanie	TE	6-0	242	8/12/84	8	Central Missouri State	Pomona, Calif.	UFA(SF)-'13	16/4*
16	Wallace, Roberto	WR	6-4	222	5/10/86	3	San Diego State	Panama City, Fla.	FA-'13	0*

2013 VETERAN ROSTER (CONTINUED)

No.	Name	Pos.	Ht.	Wt.	Birthdate	NFL Exp.	College	Hometown	How Acq.	'12 Games/ Starts
89	Walter, Kevin	WR	6-3	218	8/4/81	11	Eastern Michigan	Vernon Hills, Ill.	FA-'13	16/14*
85	Washington, Nate	WR	6-1	177	8/28/83	9	Tiffin	Toledo, Ohio	UFA(Pitt)-'09	16/14
17	Williams, Damian	WR	6-1	199	5/26/88	4	Southern California	Springdale, Ark.	D3a-'10	13/2
39	Wilson, George	S	6-0	214	3/14/81	8	Arkansas	Paducah, Ky.	FA-'13	16/16*
35	Wilson, Tracy	S	6-2	203	2/27/89	2	Northern Illinois	Harvey, Illinois	FA-'12	9/0
95	Wimbley, Kamerion	DE	6-4	255	10/13/83	8	Florida State	Wichita, Kansas	FA-'12	16/16
92	#Witherspoon, Will	LB	6-1	240	8/19/80	12	Georgia	Panama City, Fla.	FA-'10	14/5
13	Wright, Kendall	WR	5-10	196	11/12/89	2	Baylor	Pittsburg, Texas	D1-'12	15/5

* Amano missed '12 season due to injury; Baldridge played one game with Jacksonville in '12; Ball missed '12 season due to injury; Clayton last active with Tennessee in '11; Douzable missed '12 season because of injury; Enderle last active with Chicago in '11; Fitzpatrick played 16 games with Buffalo; Fokou played 16 games with Indianapolis; Gibson last active with Chicago in '11; Greene played 16 games with the New York Jets; Hill played 15 games with Detroit; Levitre played 16 games with Buffalo; Mariani missed '12 season due to injury; Ma. Martin missed '12 season because of injury; McRath missed '12 season due to injury; Pitoitua played 15 games with Kansas City; Pollard played 13 games with Baltimore; Spencer played 10 games with Chicago; Studdard last active with Houston in '10; Turner played 16 games with St. Louis; Walker played 16 games with San Francisco; Wallace last active with Miami in '11; Walter played 16 games with Houston; G. Wilson played 16 games with Buffalo;

\# Unrestricted Free Agent; subject to developments.

Retired—Steve Hutchinson, 12-year guard, 12 games in '12.

Players lost through free agency (4): TE Jared Cook (StL; 13 games in '12), Zac Diles (KC; 6), Sen'Derrick Marks (Jax; 14), DE Jarius Wynn (SD; 7).

Also played with Titans in '12—Jordan Babineaux (16 games), Brandon Barden (3), Pannel Egboh (6), Darren Evans (1), QB Matt Hasselbeck (8), Troy Kropog (1), Collin Mooney (2), Mitch Petrus (2), Michael Preston (4),

FIRST-YEAR ROSTER

Name	Pos.	Ht.	Wt.	Birthdate	College	Hometown	How Acq.
Atkinson, Eloy	C	6-3	315	1/24/90	Texas-El Paso	Los Fresnos, Texas	FA
Baker, George	CB	5-11	180	12/2/89	South Florida	Miami, Fla.	FA
Barden, Brandon (1)	TE	6-4	251	3/15/89	Vanderbilt	Lincolnton, Ga.	FA-'12
Bonani, Maikon	K	5-10	176	1/29/89	South Florida	Lake Wales, Fla.	FA
Borel, Diondre (1)	WR	6-0	199	12/12/88	Utah State	Oakley, Calif.	FA-'12
Charles, Stefan	DT	6-5	302	6/9/88	Regina	Oshawa, Ontario	FA
Doyle, Jack	TE	6-6	253	5/5/90	Western Kentucky	Indianapolis, Ind.	FA
Edwards, Lavar	DE	6-4	277	4/29/90	Louisiana State	Baton Rouge, La.	D5
Gooden, Zaviar	LB	6-1	234	8/31/90	Missouri	Pflugerville, Texas	D3b
Harvey, Travis	WR	6-2	185	5/18/90	Florida A&M	Inglewood, Calif.	FA
Hunter, Justin	WR	6-4	196	5/20/91	Tennessee	Virginia Tech, Va.	D2
Jefferson, Stefphon	RB	5-11	210	8/14/91	Nevada	Lemoore, Calif.	FA
Johnson, Oscar	G	6-6	330	3/1/90	Louisiana Tech	Crystal Springs, Miss.	FA
Mooney, Collin (1)	FB	5-10	247	4/3/86	Army	Katy, Texas	FA-'12
Nicholas, Nigel	DT	6-3	269	5/3/90	Oklahoma State	Rossville, Ohio	FA
Pierce, Matthew	CB	5-10	194	9/4/90	Valdosta State	New Orleans, La.	FA
Preston, Michael (1)	WR	6-5	206	6/1/89	Heidelberg	Euclid, Ohio	FA-'11
Ross, Rashad	WR	6-0	167	2/2/90	Arizona State	Vallejo, Calif.	FA
Schwenke, Brian	C	6-3	314	3/22/91	California	Oceanside, Calif.	D4
Sewell, Matt	T	6-7	337	1/26/90	McMaster	Milton, Ontario, Canada	FA
Stafford, Daimion	S	6-1	205	2/18/91	Nebraska	Norco, Calif.	D7
Warmack, Chance	G	6-2	317	9/14/91	Alabama	Atlanta, Ga.	D1
Watkins, Dontel	WR	6-2	194	4/4/90	Murray State	Nashville, Tenn.	FA
Webb, Martell (1)	TE	6-3	276	11/10/89	Michigan	Pontiac, Mich.	FA-'12
Willard, Jonathan	LB	6-2	225	1/10/90	Clemson	Loris, S.C.	FA
Wooten, Khalid	CB	5-11	210	2/19/90	Nevada	Rialto, Calif.	D6
Wort, Tom	LB	6-0	235	1/29/91	Oklahoma	New Braunfels, Texas	FA
Wreh-Wilson, Blidi	CB	6-1	195	12/5/89	Connecticut	Edinboro, Pa.	D3a

The term NFL Rookie is defined as a player who is in his first season of professional football and has not been on the roster of another professional football team for any regular-season or postseason games. A Rookie is designated by an "R" on NFL rosters. Players who have been active in another professional football league or players who have NFL experience, including either preseason training camp or being on an Active List or Inactive List, or on Reserve/Injured or Reserve/Physically Unable to Perform for fewer than six regular-season games, are termed NFL First-Year Players. An NFL First-Year Player is designated by a "1" on NFL rosters. Thereafter, a player is credited with an additional year of experience for each season in which he accumulates six games on the Active List or Inactive List, or on Reserve/Injured or Reserve/Physically Unable to Perform.

Log on to www.titansonline.com for an up-to-date roster.

COACHING STAFF

Head Coach,
Mike Munchak

Pro Career: Munchak became the 16th head coach in franchise history on Feb. 7, 2011, after spending the previous 29 seasons with the team as a player and coach. In leading the Titans to a 9-7 record in 2011, he became the sixth Titans/Oilers head coach to reach nine wins in his first season. After his playing career, Munchak spent three seasons as an offensive assistant/quality control coach (1994-96). In 1997, he became the offensive line coach and held that position for 14 years. Four of his offensive linemen totaled 10 Pro Bowl invitations, and his offensive lines paved the way for five different running backs to total 11 1,000-yard rushing seasons. His offensive line allowed the second fewest sacks (28.3 sacks per season) in the NFL since he assumed control of the group in 1997. During a 12-year playing career as a guard for the Houston Oilers (1982-1993), Munchak started 156 games (seventh in franchise history) and earned nine Pro Bowl invitations. He was selected to the NFL's "All-Decade" team for the 1980s. In 1996, his No. 63 jersey was retired by the club, and in 2001, he became the fifth franchise player to be inducted into the Pro Football Hall of Fame. Career record: 15-17.

Background: Played at Penn State (1979-81) for Joe Paterno. Graduated with a degree in business administration. The Oilers made him the eighth overall pick and the first offensive lineman selected in the 1982 NFL Draft.

Personal: Born March 5, 1960, in Scranton, Pa. Munchak and his wife, Marci, have two daughters, Alexandra and Julie.

ASSISTANT COACHES

Steve Brown, asst. secondary; born March 20, 1960, Sacramento, Calif. Defensive back Oregon 1978-1982. Pro cornerback Houston Oilers 1983-1990. College coach: Kentucky 2003-2011. Pro coach: St. Louis Rams 1995-2000, joined Titans in 2012.

Sylvester Croom, running backs; born September 25, 1954, Tuscaloosa, Ala. Linebacker/tight end/center Alabama 1971-74. Pro center New Orleans Saints 1975. College coach: Alabama 1976-1986, Mississippi State 2004-08 (head coach). Pro coach: Tampa Bay Buccaneers 1987-1990, Indianapolis Colts 1991, San Diego Chargers 1992-96, Detroit Lions 1997-2000, Green Bay Packers 2001-03, St. Louis Rams 2009-2011, Jacksonville Jaguars 2012, joined Titans in 2013.

Jonathan Gannon, defensive assistant/quality control; born Jan. 4, 1983, Cleveland. Safety Louisville 2001-02. No pro playing experience. College coach: Louisville 2006. Pro coach: Atlanta Falcons 2007, St. Louis Rams 2009-2011 (scout), joined Titans in 2012.

Jerry Gray, defensive coordinator; born December 16, 1962, Lubbock, Texas. Safety Texas 1981-84. Pro defensive back Los Angeles Rams 1985-1991, Houston Oilers 1992, Tampa Bay Buccaneers 1993. College coach: Southern Methodist 1995-96. Pro coach: Tennessee Titans 1997-2000, Buffalo Bills 2001-05, Washington Redskins 2006-09, Seattle Seahawks 2010, joined Titans in 2011.

George Henshaw, tight ends; born January 22, 1948, Richmond, Va. Defensive tackle West Virginia 1967-69. No pro playing experience. College coach: West Virginia 1970-75, Florida State 1976-1982, Alabama 1983-86, Tulsa 1987 (head coach). Pro coach: Denver Broncos 1988-1992, New York Giants 1993-96, Tennessee Oilers/Titans 1997-2005, New Orleans Saints 2006-07, joined Titans in 2013.

Steve Hoffman, asst. special teams; born September 8, 1958, Camden, N.J. Quarterback/ wide receiver/ running back/ kicker/ punter Dickinson College 1976-79. Pro punter Washington Federals (USFL) 1983. College coach: Miami 1985-88. Pro coach: Dallas Cowboys 1989-2004, Atlanta Falcons 2006, Miami Dolphins 2007-08, Kansas City Chiefs 2009-2011, Oakland Raiders 2012, joined Titans in 2013.

Shawn Jefferson, wide receivers; born February 22, 1969, Jacksonville, Fla. Wide receiver Central Florida 1988-1990. Pro wide receiver San Diego Chargers 1991-95, New England Patriots 1996-99, Atlanta Falcons 2000-02, Detroit Lions 2003. Pro coach: Detroit Lions 2005-2012, joined Titans in 2013.

Nate Kaczor, special teams; born April 8, 1967, Scott City, Kan. Center Utah State 1987-89. No pro playing experience. College coach: Utah State 1991-99, Nebraska- Kearney 2000-03, Idaho 2004-05, Louisiana-Monroe 2006-07. Pro coach: Jacksonville Jaguars 2008-2011, joined Titans in 2012.

Dowell Loggains, offensive coordinator; born October 1, 1980, Newport, Ark. Quarterback Arkansas 2000-04. No pro playing experience. Pro coach: Dallas Cowboys 2005, joined Titans in 2006.

Bruce Matthews, offensive line; born August 8, 1961, Raleigh, N.C. Offensive lineman Southern California 1979-1982. Pro offensive lineman Houston Oilers/Tennessee Titans 1983-2001. Inducted into Pro Football Hall of Fame in 2007. Pro coach: Houston Texans 2009-2010, joined Titans in 2011.

Brett Maxie, secondary; born January 13, 1962, Dallas, Texas. Safety Texas Southern 1982-84. Pro safety New Orleans Saints 1985-1993, Atlanta Falcons 1994, Carolina Panthers 1995-96, San Francisco 49ers 1997. Pro coach: Carolina Panthers 1998, San Francisco 49ers 1999-2003, Miami Dolphins 2007, Dallas Cowboys 2008-2011, joined Titans in 2012.

Keith Millard, defensive assistant/pass rush specialist; born March 18, 1962, Pleasanton, Calif. Defensive lineman Washington State 1980-84. Pro defensive lineman Jacksonville Bulls (USFL) 1985, Minnesota Vikings 1985- 1991, Seattle Seahawks 1992, Green Bay Packers 1992, Philadelphia Eagles 1993. College coach: Fort Lewis 1996, Menlo College 1997-2000. Pro coach: San Francisco Demons (XFL), Denver Broncos 2002-04, Oakland Raiders 2005-08, Tampa Bay Buccaneers 2011, joined Titans in 2012.

Chet Parlavecchio, linebackers; born February 14, 1960, Irvington, N.J. Linebacker Penn State 1978-1981. Pro linebacker Green Bay Packers 1982-83, St. Louis Cardinals 1983. College coach: Temple 1992-93. Pro coach: Joined Titans in 2011.

Dave Ragone, quarterbacks; born October 3, 1979, Middleburg Heights, Ohio. Quarterback Louisville 1999-2002. Pro quarterback Houston Texans 2003-05. Pro coach: Hartford Colonels (UFL) 2010, joined Titans in 2011.

Tracy Rocker, defensive line; born April 9, 1966, Atlanta. Defensive tackle Auburn 1984-88. Pro defensive tackle Washington Redskins 1989-1990, Orlando Thunder (WFL) 1991. College coach: West Alabama 1994-96, Troy 1997-2001, Cincinnati 2002, Arkansas 2003-07, Ole Miss 2008, Auburn 2009-2010. Pro coach: Joined Titans in 2011.

Arthur Smith, offensive line/tight ends assistant; born May 27, 1982, Memphis, Tenn. Offensive lineman North Carolina 2001-05. No pro playing experience. College coach: North Carolina 2006. Pro coach: Washington Redskins 2007-08, joined Titans in 2011.

Steve Watterson, asst. head coach/ strength & conditioning; born November 27, 1956, Newport, R.I. Attended Rhode Island. No college or pro playing experience. Pro coach: Philadelphia Eagles 1984-85, joined Titans/Oilers in 1986.

Gregg Williams, senior assistant/defense; born July 15, 1958, Excelsior Springs, Mo. Quarterback Northeastern Missouri State 1976-79. No pro playing experience. College coach: Houston 1988-89. Pro coach: Houston Oilers/Tennessee Titans 1990-2000, Buffalo Bills 2001-03 (head coach), Washington Redskins 2004-07, Jacksonville Jaguars 2008, New Orleans Saints 2009-2011, joined Titans in 2013.

The NFC

National Football Conference
West Division
Team Colors: Cardinal Red, Black, and
White
8701 S. Hardy Drive
Tempe, Arizona 85284
Telephone: (602) 379-0101

2013 SCHEDULE
PRESEASON
Aug. 9	at Green Bay	5:00
Aug. 17	**Dallas**	1:30
Aug. 24	**San Diego**	7:00
Aug. 29	at Denver	6:00

REGULAR SEASON
Sep. 8	at St. Louis	1:25
Sep. 15	**Detroit**	1:05
Sep. 22	at New Orleans	10:00a
Sep. 29	at Tampa Bay	10:00a
Oct. 6	**Carolina**	1:05
Oct. 13	at San Francisco	1:25
Oct. 17	**Seattle** (Thurs)	5:25
Oct. 27	**Atlanta**	1:25
Nov. 3	BYE	
Nov. 10	**Houston**	2:25
Nov. 17	at Jacksonville	11:00a
Nov. 24	**Indianapolis**	2:05
Dec. 1	at Philadelphia	11:00a
Dec. 8	**St. Louis**	2:25
Dec. 15	at Tennessee	11:00a
Dec. 22	at Seattle	2:05
Dec. 29	**San Francisco**	2:25

*All times MDT/PST

Stadium: University of Phoenix Stadium
(opened in 2006)
• **Capacity:** 65,000
1 Cardinals Drive
Glendale, Arizona 85305
Playing Surface: Grass

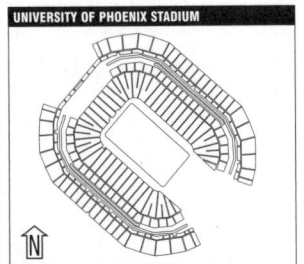
UNIVERSITY OF PHOENIX STADIUM

CLUB OFFICIALS
Owner: William V. Bidwill
President: Michael Bidwill
General Manager: Steve Keim
Executive Vice President/Chief Operating
Officer: Ron Minegar
Vice President, Player Personnel:
Jason Licht
Chief Financial Officer: Greg Lee
General Counsel: David Koeninger
Vice President, Media Relations:
Mark Dalton
Vice President, Marketing: Lisa Manning
Vice President, Business Development:
Steve Ryan
Vice President, Information Technology:
Mark Feller
Vice President, Security: Rick Knight
Vice President, Stadium Operations:
John Drum
Senior Director, Player Programs:
Anthony Edwards
Senior Director, Broadcasting/Executive
Producer: Tim DeLaney
Senior Director, Community Relations:
Luis Zendejas
Senior Director, Ticketing: Steve Bomar
Senior Director, Ticket Sales:
Ron Campbell
Director, Media Relations: Chris Melvin
Director, Pro Scouting: Quentin Harris
Director, College Scouting: Dru Grigson
Director, Football Administration:
Mike Disner
Director, Premium Seat & Guest
Services: Cari Maas
Director, Business Development:
Mike Iaquinta
Director, Corporate Partnership Service &
Activation: Scott Coleman
Director, Cheerleading: Heather Karberg
Website Manager: Darren Urban
Video Director: Rob Brakel
Video Assistant: Jeff Wallo
Head Athletic Trainer: Tom Reed
Assistant Athletic Trainers:
Jim Shearer, Jeff Herndon,
Chad Cook
Equipment Manager: Mark Ahlemeier
Assistant Equipment Manager:
Steve Christensen
Football Operations Coordinator:
Matt Caracciolo

COACHING HISTORY
Chicago 1920-1959, St. Louis 1960-1987
(507-717-39)
Records include postseason games
1920-22	John (Paddy) Driscoll	17-8-4
1923-24	Arnold Horween	13-8-1
1925-26	Norman Barry	16-8-2
1927	Guy Chamberlin	3-7-1
1928	Fred Gillies	1-5-0
1929	Dewey Scanlon	6-6-1
1930	Ernie Nevers	5-6-2
1931	LeRoy Andrews*	0-1-0
1931	Ernie Nevers	5-3-0
1932	Jack Chevigny	2-6-2
1933-34	Paul Schissler	6-15-1
1935-38	Milan Creighton	16-26-4
1939	Ernie Nevers	1-10-0
1940-42	Jimmy Conzelman	8-22-3
1943-45	Phil Handler**	1-29-0
1946-48	Jimmy Conzelman	27-10-0
1949	Phil Handler-Buddy Parker***	2-4-0
1949	Raymond (Buddy) Parker	4-1-1
1950-51	Earl (Curly) Lambeau****	7-15-0
1951	Phil Handler-Cecil Isbell#	1-1-0
1952	Joe Kuharich	4-8-0
1953-54	Joe Stydahar	3-20-1
1955-57	Ray Richards	14-21-1
1958-1961	Frank (Pop) Ivy##	15-31-2
1961	Chuck Drulis-Ray Prochaska-	
	Ray Willsey###	2-0-0
1962-65	Wally Lemm	27-26-3
1966-1970	Charley Winner	35-30-5
1971-72	Bob Hollway	8-18-2
1973-77	Don Coryell	42-29-1
1978-79	Bud Wilkinson####	9-20-0
1979	Larry Wilson	2-1-0
1980-85	Jim Hanifan	39-50-1
1986-89	Gene Stallings@	23-34-1
1989	Hank Kuhlmann	0-5-0
1990-93	Joe Bugel	20-44-0
1994-95	Buddy Ryan	12-20-0
1996-2000	Vince Tobin@@	29-44-0
2000-03	Dave McGinnis	17-40-0
2004-06	Dennis Green	16-32-0
2007-2012	Ken Whisenhunt	49-53-0

    * Resigned after one game in 1931
   ** Co-coach with Walt Kiesling in Chicago
     Cardinals-Pittsburgh merger in 1944
 *** Co-coaches for first six games in 1949
**** Resigned after 10 games in 1951
    # Co-coaches
   ## Resigned after 12 games in 1961
 ### Co-coaches
Released after 13 games in 1979
    @ Released after 11 games in 1989
  @@ Released after seven games in 2000

PAID ATTENDANCE
Home 458,225	Away 523,537

Total 981,762
Single-game home record, 73,025*
(9/19/93)
Single-season home record, 516,646 (2007)
*Team also had attendance of 103,467 for regular-
season home game at Azteca Stadium, Mexico City,
Mexico

2013 DRAFT CHOICES
Round	Name	Pos.	College
1	Jonathan Cooper	G	North Carolina
2	Kevin Minter	LB	Louisiana St.
3	Tyrann Mathieu	DB	Louisiana St.
4	Alex Okafor	LB	Texas
	Earl Watford	G	James Madison
5	Stepfan Taylor	RB	Stanford
6	Ryan Swope	WR	Texas A&M
	Andre Ellington	RB	Clemson
7	D.C. Jefferson	TE	Rutgers

2012 TEAM RECORD
PRESEASON (1-4)

Date	Result	Opponent
08/05	L 10-17	vs. New Orleans (HOF)
08/10	L 17-27	at Kansas City
08/17	W 31-27	Oakland
08/23	L 27-32	at Tennessee
08/30	L 13-16	Denver

REGULAR SEASON (5-11)

Date	Result	Opponent
09/09	W 20-16	Seattle
09/16	W 20-18	at New England
09/23	W 27-6	Philadelphia
09/30	W 24-21	Miami (OT)
10/04	L 3-17	at St. Louis
10/14	L 16-19	Buffalo (OT)
10/21	L 14-21	at Minnesota
10/29	L 3-24	San Francisco
11/04	L 17-31	at Green Bay
11/18	L 19-23	at Atlanta
11/25	L 17-31	St. Louis
12/02	L 6-7	at New York Jets
12/09	L 0-58	at Seattle
12/16	W 38-10	Detroit
12/23	L 13-28	Chicago
12/30	L 13-27	at San Francisco

(OT) Overtime

SCORE BY PERIODS

Cardinals	51	85	36	75	3	—	250
Opponents	60	136	97	61	3	—	357

2012 TEAM STATISTICS

	Cardinals	Opp.
Total First Downs	246	288
Rushing	58	107
Passing	168	160
Penalty	20	21
3rd Down: Made/Att	58/230	73/222
3rd Down Pct.	25.2	32.9
4th Down: Made/Att	10/24	4/9
4th Down Pct.	41.7	44.4
Possession Avg.	29:01	30:59
Total Net Yards	4209	5405
Avg. Per Game	263.1	337.8
Total Plays	1018	1041
Avg. Per Play	4.1	5.2
Net Yards Rushing	1204	2192
Avg. Per Game	75.3	137.0
Total Rushes	352	506
Net Yards Passing	3005	3213
Avg. Per Game	187.8	200.8
Sacked/Yards Lost	58/378	38/228
Gross Yards	3383	3441
Att./Completions	608/337	497/270
Completion Pct.	55.4	54.3
Had Intercepted	21	22
Punts/Average	112/46.5	93/44.8
Net Punting Avg.	112/41.4	93/39.2
Penalties/Yards	102/857	100/810
Fumbles/Ball Lost	25/13	17/11
Touchdowns	25	40
Rushing	10	12
Passing	11	20
Returns	4	8

2012 INDIVIDUAL STATISTICS

PASSING

PASSING	Att.	Comp.	Yds.	Pct.	TD	Int.	Tkld.	Rate
J. Skelton	201	109	1132	54.2	2	9	15/98	55.4
Kolb	183	109	1169	59.6	8	3	27/159	86.1
Lindley	171	89	752	52.0	0	7	12/91	46.7
Hoyer	53	30	330	56.6	1	2	4/30	65.8
Cardinals	608	337	3383	55.4	11	21	58/378	63.1
Opponents	497	270	3441	54.3	20	22	38/228	71.2

SCORING

SCORING	TD R	TD P	TD Rt	PAT	FG	Saf	PTS
Feely	0	0	0	25/25	25/28	0	100
Roberts	0	5	0	0/0	0/0	0	30
Wells	5	0	0	0/0	0/0	0	30
Fitzgerald	0	4	0	0/0	0/0	0	24
Stephens-Howling	4	0	0	0/0	0/0	0	24
Floyd	0	2	0	0/0	0/0	0	12
Bethel	0	0	1	0/0	0/0	0	6
Johnson	0	0	1	0/0	0/0	0	6
Kolb	1	0	0	0/0	0/0	0	6
Sanders	0	0	1	0/0	0/0	0	6
Toler	0	0	1	0/0	0/0	0	6
Cardinals	10	11	4	25/25	25/28	0	250
Opponents	12	20	8	38/38	25/35	1	357

2-Pt Conversions: Cardinals 0-0, Opponents 1-2

RUSHING

RUSHING	No.	Yds	Avg	LG	TD
Stephens-Howling	110	356	3.2	52	4
Wells	88	234	2.7	31t	5
Powell	60	217	3.6	17	0
R. Williams	58	164	2.8	25	0
Kolb	16	100	6.3	22	1
Johnson	2	64	32.0	40	0
Roberts	4	29	7.3	15	0
Peterson	2	13	6.5	17	0
Doucet	2	9	4.5	6	0
Lindley	4	7	1.8	8	0
Hoyer	1	6	6.0	6	0
J. Skelton	4	5	1.3	2	0
Feely	1	0	0.0	1	0
Cardinals	352	1204	3.4	52	10
Opponents	506	2192	4.3	46	12

RECEIVING

RECEIVING	No.	Yds	Avg	LG	TD
Fitzgerald	71	798	11.2	37t	4
Roberts	64	759	11.9	46t	5
Floyd	45	562	12.5	53	2
Housler	45	417	9.3	33	0
Doucet	28	207	7.4	18	0
Powell	19	132	6.9	25	0
King	17	129	7.6	27	0
Stephens-Howling	17	106	6.2	24	0
Heap	8	94	11.8	28	0
R. Williams	7	44	6.3	12	0
Sherman	5	39	7.8	19	0
Peterson	3	11	3.7	7	0
Smith	2	21	10.5	13	0
Dray	2	15	7.5	12	0
Wells	1	24	24.0	24	0
Kelemete	1	10	10.0	10	0
Byrd	1	8	8.0	8	0
Maui'a	1	7	7.0	7	0
Cardinals	337	3383	10.0	53	11
Opponents	270	3441	12.7	80t	20

INTERCEPTIONS

INTERCEPTIONS	No.	Yds	Avg	LG	TD
Peterson	7	64	9.1	31	0
Rhodes	4	39	9.8	30	0
Toler	2	102	51.0	102t	1
Johnson	2	87	43.5	53t	1
Gay	2	7	3.5	6	0
Acho	2	2	1.0	2	0
Washington	1	7	7.0	7	0
Lenon	1	0	0.0	0	0
Wilson	1	-2	-2.0	-2	0
Cardinals	22	306	13.9	102t	2
Opponents	21	379	18.0	45	5

PUNTING

PUNTING	No.	Yds.	Avg.	In 20	LG
Zastudil	112	5209	46.5	46	70
Cardinals	112	5209	46.5	46	70
Opponents	93	4166	44.8	30	68

PUNT RETURNS

PUNT RETURNS	Ret	FC	Yds	Avg	LG	TD
Peterson	51	14	426	8.4	26	0
Roberts	3	0	15	5.0	10	0
Cardinals	54	14	441	8.2	26	0
Opponents	48	36	415	8.6	52	0

KICKOFF RETURNS

KICKOFF RETURNS	No.	Yds	Avg	LG	TD
Powell	21	507	24.1	65	0
Stephens-Howling	18	405	22.5	38	0
Doucet	1	18	18.0	18	0
Cardinals	40	930	23.3	65	0
Opponents	32	846	26.4	83	0

FIELD GOALS

FIELD GOALS	1-19	20-29	30-39	40-49	50+
Feely	0/0	6/6	9/10	8/10	2/2
Cardinals	0/0	6/6	9/10	8/10	2/2
Opponents	1/1	6/7	7/8	7/12	4/7

SACKS

SACKS	No.
Washington	9.0
Campbell	6.5
Acho	4.0
Groves	4.0
Schofield	4.0
Wilson	3.0
Lenon	2.0
Dockett	1.5
Eason	1.0
Gay	1.0
Rhodes	1.0
Talley	1.0
Cardinals	38.0
Opponents	58.0

RECORD HOLDERS
INDIVIDUAL RECORDS—CAREER

Category	Name	Performance
Rushing (Yds.)	Ottis Anderson, 1979-1986	7,999
Passing (Yds.)	Jim Hart, 1966-1983	34,639
Passing (TDs)	Jim Hart, 1966-1983	209
Receiving (No.)	Larry Fitzgerald, 2004-2012	764
Receiving (Yds.)	Larry Fitzgerald, 2004-2012	10,413
Interceptions	Larry Wilson, 1960-1972	52
Punting (Avg.)	Jerry Norton, 1959-1961	44.9
Punt Return (Avg.)	Charley Trippi, 1947-1955	13.7
Kickoff Return (Avg.)	Ollie Matson, 1952, 1954-58	28.5
Field Goals	Jim Bakken, 1962-1978	282
Touchdowns (Tot.)	Larry Fitzgerald, 2004-2012	77
Points	Jim Bakken, 1962-1978	1,380
*Sacks	Freddie Joe Nunn, 1985-1993	66.5

INDIVIDUAL RECORDS—SINGLE SEASON

Category	Name	Performance
Rushing (Yds.)	Ottis Anderson, 1979	1,605
Passing (Yds.)	Neil Lomax, 1984	4,614
Passing (TDs)	Kurt Warner, 2008	30
Receiving (No.)	Larry Fitzgerald, 2005	103
Receiving (Yds.)	David Boston, 2001	1,598
Interceptions	Bob Nussbaumer, 1949	12
Punting (Avg.)	Ben Graham, 2009	47.0
Punt Return (Avg.)	John (Red) Cochran, 1949	20.9
Kickoff Return (Avg.)	Ollie Matson, 1958	35.5
Field Goals	Neil Rackers, 2005	40
Touchdowns (Tot.)	John David Crow, 1962	17
Points	Neil Rackers, 2005	140
*Sacks	Simeon Rice, 1999	16.5

INDIVIDUAL RECORDS—SINGLE GAME

Category	Name	Performance
Rushing (Yds.)	Beanie Wells, 11-27-11	228
Passing (Yds.)	Boomer Esiason, 11-10-96 (OT)	522
Passing (TDs)	Jim Hardy, 10-2-50	6
	Charley Johnson, 9-26-65, 11-2-69	6
Receiving (No.)	Sonny Randle, 11-4-62	16
Receiving (Yds.)	Sonny Randle, 11-4-62	256
Interceptions	Bob Nussbaumer, 11-13-49	**4
	Jerry Norton, 11-20-60, 11-26-61	**4
	Kwamie Lassiter, 12-27-98	**4
Field Goals	Jim Bakken, 9-24-67	7
Touchdowns (Tot.)	Ernie Nevers, 11-28-29	**6
Points	Ernie Nevers, 11-28-29	**40
*Sacks	Curtis Greer, 12-18-83	4.5

*Sacks became an official statistic in 1982.
**NFL Record

2013 VETERAN ROSTER

No.	Name	Pos.	Ht.	Wt.	Birthdate	NFL Exp.	College	Hometown	How Acq.	'12 Games/ Starts
94	Acho, Sam	LB	6-3	257	9/6/88	3	Texas	Dallas, Texas	D4-'11	16/16
97	Alexander, Lorenzo	LB	6-1	244	5/31/83	7	California	Berkeley, Calif.	UFA(Wash)-'13	16/0*
27	Amaya, Jonathon	S	6-2	205	11/25/88	4	Nevada	Diamond Bar, Calif.	FA-'13	12/0*
35 t-	Arenas, Javier	CB	5-9	197	10/28/87	4	Alabama	Tampa, Fla.	T(KC)-'13	16/9*
37	Bell, Yeremiah	S	6-0	205	3/3/78	10	Eastern Kentucky	Winchester, Ky.	UFA(NYJ)-'13	16/16*
31	Bethel, Justin	CB/S	6-0	200	6/17/90	2	Presbyterian	Blythewood, S.C.	D6a-'12	16/0
54	Brinkley, Jasper	LB	6-1	252	7/12/85	5	South Carolina	Thomson, Ga.	UFA(Minn)-'13	16/15*
75	Brown, Levi	T	6-6	324	3/16/84	7	Penn State	Norfolk, Va.	D1-'07	0*
17	Byrd, LaRon	WR	6-4	220	8/18/89	2	Miami	Hahnville, La.	FA-'12	4/0
93	Campbell, Calais	DE	6-8	300	9/1/86	6	Miami	Aurora, Colo.	D2-'08	13/12
79	Carter, David	DT	6-5	300	12/10/87	3	UCLA	Fontana, Calif.	D6b-'11	16/4
20	Cason, Antoine	CB	6-1	195	7/9/86	6	Arizona	Long Beach, Calif.	UFA(SD)-'13	16/16*
71	Colledge, Daryn	G	6-4	308	2/11/82	8	Boise State	North Pole, Alaska	UFA(GB)-'11	16/16
55	Dansby, Karlos	LB	6-4	250	11/3/81	10	Auburn	Birmingham, Ala.	FA-'13	16/16*
16	Dillard, Jarrett	WR	5-11	190	12/21/85	4	Rice	San Antonio, Texas	FA-'13	0*
90	Dockett, Darnell	DT	6-4	290	5/27/81	10	Florida State	Burtonsville, Md.	D3-'04	15/14
81	Dray, Jim	TE	6-5	255	12/31/86	4	Stanford	Paramus, N.J.	D7-'10	13/0
74	Fanaika, Paul	T	6-5	327	4/9/86	4	Arizona State	San Mateo, Calif.	FA-'13	0*
4	Feely, Jay	K	5-10	208	5/23/76	13	Michigan	Tampa, Fla.	UFA(NYJ)-'10	16/0
11	Fitzgerald, Larry	WR	6-3	218	8/31/83	10	Pittsburgh	Minneapolis, Minn.	D1-'04	16/16
23	Fleming, Jamell	CB	5-11	206	5/5/89	2	Oklahoma	Arlington, Texas	D3-'12	15/3
15	Floyd, Michael	WR	6-2	220	11/27/89	2	Notre Dame	St. Paul, Minn.	D1-'12	16/3
69	Gibson, Mike	G/C	6-4	305	11/18/85	6	California	Napa, Calif.	FA-'12	0*
84	Housler, Rob	TE	6-5	250	3/17/88	3	Florida Atlantic	El Paso, Texas	D3-'11	15/9
49	Johnson, Rashad	S	5-11	204	1/2/86	5	Alabama	Sulligent, Ala.	D3-'09	15/3
64	Kelemete, Senio	G	6-3	300	5/10/90	2	Washington	Seattle, Wash.	D5-'12	1/0
87	King, Jeff	TE	6-3	260	2/19/83	8	Virginia Tech	Pulaski, Va.	UFA(Car)-'11	16/12
82	Leach, Mike	LS	6-2	235	10/18/76	14	William & Mary	Jefferson Township, N.J.	FA-'09	16/0
14	Lindley, Ryan	QB	6-3	232	6/22/89	2	San Diego State	Alpine, Calif.	D6b-'12	6/4
95	Lumpkin, Ricky	DT	6-4	306	9/7/88	2	Kentucky	Clarksville, Tenn.	FA-'11	1/0
70	Massie, Bobby	T	6-6	316	8/1/89	2	Mississippi	Lynchburg, Va.	D4-'12	16/16
22	McCann, Bryan	CB	5-11	185	9/29/87	4	Southern Methodist	Oklahoma City, Okla.	FA-'13	8/0*
28	Mendenhall, Rashard	RB	5-10	225	6/19/87	6	Illinois	Skokie, Ill.	UFA(Pitt)-'13	6/4*
59	Nash, Zack	LB	6-4	260	9/23/89	2	Sacramento State	Vacaville, Calif.	FA-'12	8/0
3 t-	Palmer, Carson	QB	6-5	235	12/27/79	11	Southern California	Rancho Santa Margarita, Calif.	T(Oak)-'13	15/15*
21	Peterson, Patrick	CB	6-1	219	7/11/90	3	Louisiana State	Pompano Beach, Fla.	D1-'11	16/16
76	Potter, Nate	T	6-5	295	5/16/88	2	Boise State	Boise, Idaho	D7-'12	8/6
33	Powell, William	RB	5-9	207	3/9/88	2	Kansas State	Duncanville, Texas	FA-'11	13/1
25	Powers, Jerraud	CB	5-10	187	7/19/87	5	Auburn	Decatur, Ala.	UFA(Ind)-'13	8/8*
73	Rachal, Chilo	G	6-5	323	3/15/86	6	Southern California	Compton, Calif.	UFA(Ariz)-'13	9/8*
12	Roberts, Andre	WR	5-11	195	1/9/88	4	The Citadel	Columbia, S.C.	D3-'10	15/15
98	Rucker, Frostee	DE	6-3	280	9/14/83	8	Southern California	Tustin, Calif.	FA-'13	16/16*
50	Schofield, O'Brien	LB	6-3	242	4/3/87	4	Wisconsin	Great Lakes, Ill.	D4-'10	9/9
63	Sendlein, Lyle	C	6-3	308	3/16/84	7	Texas	Scottsdale, Ariz.	FA-'07	11/11
91	Shaughnessy, Matt	DE	6-5	285	9/23/86	5	Wisconsin	Norwich, Conn.	UFA(Oak)-'13	16/16*
29	Smith, Alfonso	RB	6-1	209	1/23/87	4	Kentucky	Louisville, Ky.	FA-'10	11/0
83	Sperry, Kory	TE	6-5	265	4/10/85	5	Colorado State	Pueblo, Colo.	FA-'12	1/0
5	Stanton, Drew	QB	6-3	243	5/7/84	7	Michigan State	Farmington Hills, Mich.	UFA(Ind)-'13	0*
96	Talley, Ronald	DE	6-3	286	2/21/86	3	Delaware	Detroit, Mich.	FA-'12	3/1
26	Taylor, Curtis	S	6-2	212	7/13/85	3	Louisiana State	Franklinton, La.	FA-'12	0*
56	Walker, Reggie	LB	6-0	244	12/15/86	5	Kansas State	Sacramento, Calif.	FA-'09	14/0
58	Washington, Daryl	LB	6-2	238	10/9/86	4	Texas Christian	Irving, Texas	D2-'10	16/16
66	Wedige, Scott	C	6-4	310	11/20/88	2	Northern Illinois	Elkhorn, Wisc.	FA-'12	2/0
92	Williams, Dan	DT	6-3	314	6/1/87	4	Tennessee	Memphis, Tenn.	D1-'10	15/11
34	Williams, Ryan	RB	5-9	207	4/9/90	3	Virginia Tech	Manassas, Va.	D2-'11	5/3
9	Zastudil, Dave	P	6-3	220	10/26/78	12	Ohio	Bay Village, Ohio	FA-'11	16/0

* Alexander played 16 games with Washington in '12; Amaya played 12 games with Miami; Arenas played 16 games with Kansas City; Bell played 16 games with New York Jets; Brinkley played 16 games with Minnesota; Brown missed '12 season because of injury; Cason played 16 games with San Diego; Dansby played 16 games with Miami; Dillard last active with Jacksonville in '11; Fanaika last active with Seattle in '11; Gibson last active with Seattle in '11; McCann played eight games with Oakland; Mendenhall played six games with Pittsburgh; Palmer played 15 games with Oakland; Powers played eight games with Indianapolis; Rachal played nine games with Chicago; Rucker played 16 games with Cleveland; Shaughnessy played 16 games with Oakland; Stanton did not play 16 games with Indianapolis; Taylor last active with San Francisco in '10.

t- Cardinals traded for Arenas (KC), Palmer (Oak).

Players lost through free agency (4): LB Quentin Groves (Cle; 16 games in '12), G Rich Ohrnberger (SD; 13), RB LaRod Stephens-Howling (Pitt; 14), CB Greg Toler (Ind; 11).

Also played with Cardinals in '12—CB Michael Adams (15 games), T D'Anthony Batiste (15), LB Stewart Bradley (16), CB Crezdon Butler (1), WR Early Doucet (12), DT Nick Eason (16), CB William Gay (16), TE Todd Heap (2), DE Vonnie Holliday (16), QB Brian Hoyer (2), QB Kevin Kolb (6), LB Paris Lenon (16), FB Reagan Maui'a (3), G Pat McQuistan (6), S Kerry Rhodes (15), S James Sanders (15), FB Anthony Sherman (13), QB John Skelton (7), G/C Adam Snyder (14), RB Beanie Wells (8), LB Jamaal Westerman (5), S Adrian Wilson (15).

FIRST-YEAR ROSTER

Name	Pos.	Ht.	Wt.	Birthdate	College	Hometown	How Acq.
Auffray, Kyle	TE	6-5	254	12/27/86	New Hampshire	Cornwall, N.Y.	FA
Batson, Will (1)	P	6-3	210	9/8/86	North Alabama	Killen, Ala.	FA
Bice, Adam	C	6-4	302	6/30/89	Akron	Dresden, Ohio	FA
Brown, Jaron	WR	6-2	205	1/8/90	Clemson	Cheraw, S.C.	FA
Buckner, Dan	WR	6-4	215	5/31/90	Arizona	Allen, Texas	FA
Caprioglio, Joe	T	6-6	315	3/12/90	Colorado State	Highlands Ranch, Colo.	FA
Cooper, Jonathan	G	6-2	311	1/19/90	North Carolina	Wilmington, N.C.	D1
Demens, Kenny	LB	6-1	242	2/4/90	Michigan	Oak Park, Mich.	FA
Ellington, Andre	RB	5-9	199	2/3/89	Clemson	Moncks Corner, S.C.	D6b
Fugger, Tim (1)	LB	6-4	248	7/1/89	Vanderbilt	San Diego, Calif.	FA-'12
Gill, Robert	TE	5-10	180	2/27/84	Texas State	San Antonio, Texas	FA
Giordano, Dan	LB	6-4	260	9/17/89	Cincinnati	Frankfort, Ill.	FA
Gottlieb, Alex (1)	TE	6-4	255	7/4/90	William & Mary	Delray Beach, Fla.	FA
Harris, Javon	S	5-11	206	2/7/91	Oklahoma	Lawton, Okla.	FA
Hill, Josh	CB	5-11	203	11/2/89	California	Houston, Texas	FA
Jefferson, D.C.	TE	6-6	255	5/7/89	Rutgers	Winter Haven, Fla.	D7
Jefferson, Tony	S	5-11	212	1/27/92	Oklahoma	Chula Vista, Calif.	FA
Johnson-Webb, Jamaal	T	6-6	306	3/6/90	Alabama A&M	Atlanta, Ga.	FA
Jones, Korey	LB	6-2	233	4/4/89	Wyoming	Fort Collins, Colo.	FA
Lawson, Javone	WR	6-1	183	2/17/90	Louisiana-Lafayette	New Orleans, La.	FA
Mathieu, Tyrann	S	5-9	186	5/13/92	Louisiana State	New Orleans, La.	D3
Minter, Kevin	LB	6-0	246	12/3/90	Louisiana State	Suwanee, Ga.	D2
Okafor, Alex	LB	6-4	261	2/8/91	Texas	Pflugerville, Texas	D4a
Parker, Colin (1)	LB	6-1	223	5/6/89	Arizona State	Chandler, Ariz.	FA-'12
Rios, Michael	WR	6-2	203	6/9/90	Marist	Miami, Fla.	FA
Scott, Padric	DT	6-0	309	1/8/90	Florida A&M	Tallahassee, Fla.	FA
Shaw, Tyler	WR	6-0	180	1/5/90	NW Missouri State	St. Louis, Mo.	FA
Swope, Ryan	WR	6-0	204	9/20/90	Texas A&M	Austin, Texas	D6a
Taylor, Kerry (1)	WR	6-0	200	2/20/89	Arizona State	Chandler, Ariz.	FA
Taylor, Stepfan	RB	5-9	216	6/9/91	Stanford	Mansfield, Texas	D5
TerBush, Caleb	QB	6-5	225	1/5/90	Purdue	Metamora, Ill.	FA
Thompson, Everrette (1)	DE	6-6	272	12/18/89	Washington	Renton, Wash.	FA-'12
Watford, Earl	G	6-3	300	6/24/90	James Madison	Philadelphia, Pa.	D4b
Yell, Ronnie	CB	5-10	188	4/15/91	San Jose State	San Diego, Calif.	FA

The term NFL Rookie is defined as a player who is in his first season of professional football and has not been on the roster of another professional football team for any regular-season or postseason games. A Rookie is designated by an "R" on NFL rosters. Players who have been active in another professional football league or players who have NFL experience, including either preseason training camp or being on an Active List or Inactive List, or on Reserve/Injured or Reserve/Physically Unable to Perform for fewer than six regular-season games, are termed NFL First-Year Players. An NFL First-Year Player is designated by a "1" on NFL rosters. Thereafter, a player is credited with an additional year of experience for each season in which he accumulates six games on the Active List or Inactive List, or on Reserve/Injured or Reserve/Physically Unable to Perform.

Log on to www.azcardinals.com for an up-to-date roster.

COACHING STAFF

Head Coach,
Bruce Arians

Pro Career: Became an NFL head coach for the first time when hired by Arizona on January 17, 2013. Comes to Arizona after working as offensive coordinator for the Indianapolis Colts in 2012, while also serving 12 games as interim head coach during Chuck Pagano's absence while being treated for leukemia. Arians was selected as the 2012 AP NFL Coach of the Year after leading Indianapolis to a 9-3 record and helping the Colts clinch a playoff berth while tying the NFL record for most wins ever by an interim coach. Arians previously coached at the pro level with the Pittsburgh Steelers (offensive coordinator, wide receivers, 2004-2011), Cleveland Browns (offensive coordinator, 2001-03), the Colts (quarterbacks, 1998-2000), the New Orleans Saints (tight ends, 1996) and the Kansas City Chiefs (running backs, 1989-1992). Career record: 0-0.

Background: Arians played quarterback (1972-74) collegiately at Virginia Tech and was voted the team's MVP as a senior. He coached on the collegiate level, including six seasons as head coach at Temple (1983-88). He also coached at Virginia Tech (1977), Mississippi State (1978-1980, 1993-95) and Alabama (1981-82, 1997).

Personal: Born October 3, 1952 in Paterson, N.J., Arians and his wife, Christine, have two children—son, Jake and daughter, Kristi Anne.

ASSISTANT COACHES

Pete Alosi, asst. strength and conditioning; born July 31, 1982, Massapequa, N.Y. Linebacker Salisbury 2000-02. No pro playing experience. Pro coach: Joined Cardinals in 2010.

James Bettcher, outside linebackers; born May 27, 1978, Lakeville, Ind. Offensive lineman St. Francis 1999-2002. No pro playing experience. College coach: St. Francis 2003-05, Bowling Green 2006, North Carolina 2007-09, Ball State 2010, New Hampshire 2011. Pro coach: Indianapolis Colts 2012, joined Cardinals in 2013.

Anthony Blevins, coaching assistant/special teams; born July 23, 1976, Birmingham, Ala. Cornerback Alabama-Birmingham 1995-98. Pro cornerback Birmingham Steeldogs (AFL2) 2000, Birmingham Thunderbolts (XFL) 2000-01. College coach: Tennessee-Martin 2008, Tennessee State 2009-2011, Alabama-Birmingham 2012. Pro coach: Joined Cardinals in 2013.

Todd Bowles, defensive coordinator; born November 18, 1963, Elizabeth, N.J. Defensive back Temple 1982-85. Pro defensive back Washington Redskins 1986-1990, 1992-93, San Francisco 49ers 1991. College coach: Morehouse College 1997, Grambling State 1998-99. Pro coach: New York Jets 2000, Cleveland Browns 2001-04, Dallas Cowboys 2005-07, Miami Dolphins 2008-2011 (interim head coach 2011), Philadelphia Eagles 2012, joined Cardinals in 2013.

Brentson Buckner, defensive line; born September 30, 1971, Charlotte, N.C. Defensive tackle Clemson 1990-93. Pro defensive tackle Pittsburgh Steelers 1994-96, Cincinnati Bengals 1997, San Francisco 49ers 1998-2000, Carolina Panthers 2001-05. Pro coach: Joined Cardinals in 2013.

Mike Caldwell, linebackers; born August 31, 1971, Oak Ridge, Tenn. Linebacker Middle Tennessee State 1989-1992. Pro linebacker Cleveland Browns 1993-95, Baltimore Ravens 1996, Arizona Cardinals 1997, Philadelphia Eagles 1998-2001, Chicago Bears 2002, Carolina Panthers 2003. Pro coach: Philadelphia Eagles 2008-2012, joined Cardinals in 2013.

Rick Christophel, tight ends; born October 27, 1952, Reading, Ohio. Quarterback Austin Peay 1971-74. No pro playing experience. College coach: Austin Peay 1975, 1979-1981, 2007-2012 (head coach 2007-2012), Southern Arkansas State 1982, Cincinnati 1983, Rice 1984-85, Vanderbilt 1986-1990, Mississippi State 1991-94, Alabama-Birmingham 1995-2001, 2004-06. Pro coach: Joined Cardinals in 2013.

Darryl Drake, wide receivers; born December 11, 1956, Louisville, Ky. Wide receiver Western Kentucky 1975-78. Pro wide receiver Ottawa Rough Riders (CFL) 1981. College coach: Western Kentucky 1983-91, Georgia 1992-96, Baylor 1997, Texas 1998-2003. Pro coach: Chicago Bears 2004-2012, joined Cardinals in 2013.

Kevin Garver, offensive assistant; born July 28, 1987, Tuscaloosa, Ala. Attended Alabama. No college or pro playing experience. College coach: Alabama 2007-2012. Pro coach: Joined Cardinals in 2013.

Harold Goodwin, offensive coordinator; born November 14, 1973, Columbia S.C. Offensive lineman Michigan 1992-94. No pro playing experience. College coach: Michigan 1995-97, Eastern Michigan 1998-99, Central Michigan 2000-03. Pro coach: Chicago Bears 2004-06, Pittsburgh Steelers 2007-2011, Indianapolis Colts 2012, joined Cardinals in 2013.

Steve Heiden, asst. special teams/asst. tight ends; born September 21, 1976, Rushford, Minn. Tight end South Dakota State 1995-98. Pro tight end San Diego Chargers 1999-2001, Cleveland Browns 2002-09. College coach: Concordia University 2012. Pro coach: Joined Cardinals in 2013.

Amos Jones, special teams coordinator; born December 31, 1959, Tallahassee, Fla. Safety/running back Alabama 1978-1980. No pro playing experience. College coach: Alabama 1981-82, 1990-91, Temple 1983-88, Pittsburgh 1992, Tulane 1995-96, Cincinnati 1999-2002, James Madison 2003, Mississippi State 2004-06. Pro coach: British Columbia (CFL) 1997, Pittsburgh Steelers 2007-2012, joined Cardinals in 2013.

Freddie Kitchens, quarterbacks; born November 29, 1974, Gadsden, Ala. Quarterback Alabama 1994-97. No pro playing experience. College coach: Glenville State College 1999, Louisiana State 2000, North Texas 2001-03, Mississippi State 2004-05. Pro coach: Dallas Cowboys 2006, joined Cardinals in 2007.

John Lott, strength and conditioning coordinator; born May 9, 1964, Denton, Texas. Offensive lineman North Texas 1983-86. Pro offensive lineman Pittsburgh Steelers 1987. College coach: North Texas 1989-1990, Houston 1991-96. Pro coach: New York Jets 1997-2004, Cleveland Browns 2005-06, joined Cardinals in 2007.

Stump Mitchell, running backs; born March 15, 1959, St. Mary's Ga. Running back The Citadel 1977-1980. Pro running back St. Louis/Phoenix Cardinals 1981-89. College coach: Morgan State 1995-98 (head coach 1996-98), Southern 2010-12. Pro coach: San Antonio Rough Riders (WLAF) 1991, Seattle Seahawks 1999-2007, Washington Redskins 2008-09, joined Cardinals in 2013.

Tom Moore, asst. head coach/offense; born November 7, 1938, Owatonna, Minn. Quarterback Iowa 1957-1960. No pro playing experience. College coach: Iowa 1961-62, Dayton 1965-68, Wake Forest 1969, Georgia Tech 1970-71, Minnesota 1972-73, 1975-76. Pro coach: New York Stars (WFL) 1974, Pittsburgh Steelers 1977-1989, Minnesota Vikings 1990-93, Detroit Lions 1994-96, New Orleans Saints 1997, Indianapolis Colts 1998-2010, joined Cardinals in 2013.

Tom Pratt, pass rush specialist; born June 21, 1935, Edgerton, Wisc. Linebacker Miami 1953-56. No pro playing experience. College coach: Miami 1957-1960, Southern Mississippi 1961-62, U.S. Coast Guard Academy 1997. Pro coach: Kansas City Chiefs 1963-1977, 1989-1994, 2000, New Orleans Saints 1978-1980, Cleveland Browns 1981-88, Tampa Bay Buccaneers 1995, joined Cardinals in 2013.

Nick Rapone, defensive backs; born April 25, 1956, New Castle, Pa. Wide receiver Virginia Tech 1974-77. No pro playing experience. College coach: Pittsburgh 1979-1980, 1989-1992, East Tennessee State 1981-82, Temple 1983-88, 1999-2005, Connecticut 1995-98, Delaware 2006-2012. Pro coach: Joined Cardinals in 2013.

Kevin Ross, cornerbacks; born January 16, 1962, Camden, N.J. Defensive back Temple 1980-83. Pro defensive back Kansas City Chiefs 1984-93, 1997, Atlanta Falcons 1994-95, San Diego Chargers 1996. Pro coach: Minnesota Vikings 2003-05, San Diego Chargers 2007-08, Oakland Raiders 2010-11, joined Cardinals in 2013.

Ryan Slowik, defensive assistant/asst. def. backs; born Dec. 27, 1980, Chicago, Ill. Safety Wisconsin-Oshkosh 2002-03. No pro playing experience. College coach: Wisconsin-Oshkosh 2004. Pro coach: Denver Broncos 2005-08, joined Cardinals in 2009.

Larry Zierlein, asst. offensive line; born July 12, 1945, Norton, Kan. Linebacker/tight end Pratt (Kan.) J.C. 1967-68, linebacker Fort Hays State 1969-1970. No pro playing experience. College coach: Fort Hays State 1970-71, Houston 1978-1986, Tulane 1988-1990, 1995-96, Louisiana State 1993-94, Cincinnati 1997-2000. Pro coach: Washington (AFL) 1987, New York/New Jersey Knights (WLAF) 1991-92, Cleveland Browns 2001-04, Buffalo Bills 2006, Pittsburgh Steelers 2007-09, Hartford Colonials (UFL) 2011, joined Cardinals in 2013.

National Football Conference
South Division
Team Colors: Black, Red, Silver, and White
4400 Falcon Parkway
Flowery Branch, Georgia 30542
Telephone: (770) 965-3115

2013 SCHEDULE
PRESEASON
Aug. 8	**Cincinnati**	8:00
Aug. 15	at Baltimore	7:30
Aug. 24	at Tennessee	8:00
Aug. 29	**Jacksonville**	7:30

REGULAR SEASON
Sep. 8	at New Orleans	1:00
Sep. 15	**St. Louis**	1:00
Sep. 22	at Miami	4:05
Sep. 29	**New England**	8:30
Oct. 7	**New York Jets** (Mon)	8:40
Oct. 13	BYE	
Oct. 20	**Tampa Bay**	1:00
Oct. 27	at Arizona	4:25
Nov. 3	at Carolina	1:00
Nov. 10	**Seattle**	1:00
Nov. 17	at Tampa Bay	1:00
Nov. 21	**New Orleans** (Thurs)	8:25
Dec. 1	at Buffalo (Toronto)	4:05
Dec. 8	at Green Bay	*8:30
Dec. 15	**Washington**	1:00
Dec. 23	at San Francisco (Mon)	8:40
Dec. 29	**Carolina**	1:00

All times ET; Sunday night games in Weeks 11-16 subject to change
Stadium: Georgia Dome
(opened in 1992)
• **Capacity:** 71,228
One Georgia Dome Drive
Atlanta, Georgia 30313
Playing Surface: FieldTurf
Training Camp: Atlanta Falcons
4400 Falcon Parkway
Flowery Branch, GA 30542

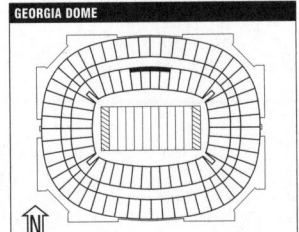

GEORGIA DOME

CLUB OFFICIALS
Owner & Chairman: Arthur M. Blank
President & CEO: Rich McKay
General Manager: Thomas Dimitroff
Head Coach: Mike Smith
Director of Human Resources:
Karen Walters
Executive Vice President of
Administration & CFO: Greg Beadles
Senior Vice President of Sales &
Marketing: Tim Zulawski
Vice President of Community Relations:
Kendyl Baugh Moss
Controller/CFO Retail: Rob Geoffroy
Vice President of Football
Communications: Reggie Roberts
Vice President of Information
Technology: Danny Branch
Chief Marketing Officer: Jim Smith
Senior Director of Media Relations:
Frank Kleha
Senior Director of Player Development:
Kevin Winston
Director of Logistics and Facilities:
Spencer Treadwell
Director of Ticket Operations:
Mike Gilsenan
Director of Event Marketing: Roddy White
Director of Player Personnel: Steve Sabo
Director of Pro Personnel: DeJuan Polk
Director of Football Operations: Nick Polk
Associate Director of Player Personnel:
Lionel Vital
Director of College Scouting: Steve Sabo
Eastern Regional Scout: Marvin Allen
National Scout: Mark Olson
Regional Scout: Shepley Heard
Area Scouts: Anthony Robinson,
Michael Ross, Tokunbo Abanikanda,
Mike Potts, Sae Woon Jo
Pro Scout: Bob Kronenberg
Scouting Assistant: Scott Sika
Director of Sports Medicine &
Performance: Marty Lauzon
Assistant Athletic Trainer: Danny Long
Assistant Athletic Trainer: Eric Avila
Video Director: Mike Crews
Video Assistant: Phil Tieman
Equipment Manager: Brian Boigner
Director of New Media: Dan Levak
Football Communications Coordinator:
Brian Cearns
Football Communications Coordinator:
Matt Haley

COACHING HISTORY
(319-414-6)
Records include postseason games
1966-68	Norb Hecker*	4-26-1
1968-1974	Norm Van Brocklin**	37-49-3
1974-76	Marion Campbell***	6-19-0
1976	Pat Peppler	3-6-0
1977-1982	Leeman Bennett	47-44-0
1983-86	Dan Henning	22-41-1
1987-89	Marion Campbell****	11-32-0
1989	Jim Hanifan	0-4-0
1990-93	Jerry Glanville	28-38-0
1994-96	June Jones	19-30-0
1997-2003	Dan Reeves#	52-61-1
2003	Wade Phillips	2-1-0
2004-06	Jim Mora	27-23-0
2007	Bobby Petrino##	3-10-0
2007	Emmitt Thomas	1-2-0
2008-2012	Mike Smith	57-28-0

*Released after three games in 1968
**Released after eight games in 1974
***Released after five games in 1976
****Retired after 12 games in 1989
#Released after 13 games in 2003
##Resigned after 13 games in 2007

PAID ATTENDANCE
Home 543,702   Away 524,523
Total 1,068,225
Single-game home record,
71,151 (10/22/06)
Single-season home record,
553,979 (1992)

2013 DRAFT CHOICES
Round	Name	Pos.	College
1	Desmond Trufant	DB	Washington
2	Robert Alford	DB	Southeastern Louisiana
4	Malliciah Goodman	DE	Clemson
	Levine Toilolo	TE	Stanford
5	Stansly Maponga	DE	Texas Christian
7	Kemal Ishmael	DB	Central Florida
	Zeke Motta	DB	Notre Dame
	Sean Renfree	QB	Duke

2012 TEAM RECORD
PRESEASON (1-3)

Date	Result	Opponent
08/09	L 17-31	Baltimore
08/16	L 19-24	Cincinnati
08/24	W 23-6	at Miami
08/30	L 14-24	at Jacksonville

REGULAR SEASON (13-3)

Date	Result	Opponent
09/09	W 40-24	at Kansas City
09/17	W 27-21	Denver
09/23	W 27-3	at San Diego
09/30	W 30-28	Carolina
10/07	W 24-17	at Washington
10/14	W 23-20	Oakland
10/28	W 30-17	at Philadelphia
11/04	W 19-13	Dallas
11/11	L 27-31	at New Orleans
11/18	W 23-19	Arizona
11/25	W 24-23	at Tampa Bay
11/29	W 23-13	New Orleans
12/09	L 20-30	at Carolina
12/16	W 34-0	New York Giants
12/22	W 31-18	at Detroit
12/30	L 17-22	Tampa Bay

POSTSEASON (1-1)

Date	Result	Opponent
01/13	W 30-28	Seattle
01/20	L 24-28	San Francisco

SCORE BY PERIODS

Falcons	91	131	68	129	0 —	419
Opponents	59	101	55	84	0 —	299

2012 TEAM STATISTICS

	Falcons	Opp.
Total First Downs	342	298
Rushing	70	99
Passing	246	189
Penalty	26	10
3rd Down: Made/Att	92/204	81/200
3rd Down Pct.	45.1	40.5
4th Down: Made/Att	2/8	6/13
4th Down Pct.	25.0	46.2
Possession Avg.	30:52	29:08
Total Net Yards	5906	5849
Avg. Per Game	369.1	365.6
Total Plays	1021	991
Avg. Per Play	5.8	5.9
Net Yards Rushing	1397	1971
Avg. Per Game	87.3	123.2
Total Rushes	378	411
Net Yards Passing	4509	3878
Avg. Per Game	281.8	242.4
Sacked/Yards Lost	28/210	29/182
Gross Yards	4719	4060
Att./Completions	615/422	551/337
Completion Pct.	68.6	61.2
Had Intercepted	14	20
Punts/Average	62/45.9	64/47.9
Net Punting Avg.	62/40.7	64/42.5
Penalties/Yards	55/415	83/641
Fumbles/Ball Lost	9/4	16/11
Touchdowns	46	31
Rushing	12	16
Passing	32	14
Returns	2	1

2012 INDIVIDUAL STATISTICS

PASSING

	Att.	Comp.	Yds.	Pct.	TD	Int.	Tkld.	Rate
Ryan	615	422	4719	68.6	32	14	28/210	99.1
Falcons	615	422	4719	68.6	32	14	28/210	99.1
Opponents	551	337	4060	61.2	14	20	29/182	77.1

SCORING

	TD R	TD P	TD Rt	PAT	FG	Saf	PTS
Bryant	0	0	0	44/44	33/38	0	143
Turner	10	1	0	0/0	0/0	0	66
Jones	0	10	0	0/0	0/0	0	60
Gonzalez	0	8	0	0/0	0/0	0	48
White	0	7	0	0/0	0/0	0	42
Jac. Rodgers	1	1	0	0/0	0/0	0	12
Babineaux	0	0	1	0/0	0/0	0	6
Dr. Davis	0	1	0	0/0	0/0	0	6
Douglas	0	1	0	0/0	0/0	0	6
M. Johnson	0	1	0	0/0	0/0	0	6
Palmer	0	1	0	0/0	0/0	0	6
Ryan	1	0	0	0/0	0/0	0	6
Samuel	0	0	1	0/0	0/0	0	6
Snelling	0	1	0	0/0	0/0	0	6
Falcons	12	32	2	44/44	33/38	0	419
Opponents	16	14	1	30/30	27/32	1	299

2-Pt Conversions: Falcons 0-2, Opponents 0-1

RUSHING

	No.	Yds	Avg	LG	TD
Turner	222	800	3.6	43	10
Jac. Rodgers	94	362	3.9	43	1
Ryan	34	141	4.1	16	1
Snelling	18	63	3.5	11	0
Jones	6	30	5.0	18	0
Douglas	2	4	2.0	5	0
McCown	2	-3	-1.5	-1	0
Falcons	378	1397	3.7	43	12
Opponents	411	1971	4.8	72t	16

RECEIVING

	No.	Yds	Avg	LG	TD
Gonzalez	93	930	10.0	25	8
White	92	1351	14.7	59	7
Jones	79	1198	15.2	80t	10
Jac. Rodgers	53	402	7.6	32	1
Douglas	38	395	10.4	37	1
Snelling	31	203	6.5	16	1
Turner	19	128	6.7	60t	1
Palmer	6	22	3.7	6	1
Dr. Davis	4	40	10.0	15t	1
Cox	3	22	7.3	11	0
Coffman	1	12	12.0	12	0
Polite	1	8	8.0	8	0
Gallarda	1	7	7.0	7	0
M. Johnson	1	1	1.0	1t	1
Falcons	422	4719	11.2	80t	32
Opponents	337	4060	12.0	77t	14

INTERCEPTIONS

	No.	Yds	Avg	LG	TD
DeCoud	6	42	7.0	24	0
Samuel	5	110	22.0	79t	1
Moore	4	51	12.8	33	0
McClain	1	32	32.0	32	0
Weatherspoon	1	6	6.0	6	0
Robinson	1	4	4.0	4	0
Nicholas	1	3	3.0	3	0
Babineaux	1	-2	-2.0	-2	0
Falcons	20	246	12.3	79t	1
Opponents	14	158	11.3	34	1

PUNTING

	No.	Yds.	Avg.	In 20	LG
Bosher	60	2847	47.5	22	63
Falcons	62	2847	45.9	22	63
Opponents	64	3065	47.9	24	67

PUNT RETURNS

	Ret	FC	Yds	Avg	LG	TD
Franks	21	18	163	7.8	28	0
Douglas	5	1	42	8.4	11	0
Falcons	26	19	205	7.9	28	0
Opponents	26	23	241	9.3	37	0

KICKOFF RETURNS

	No.	Yds	Avg	LG	TD
Jac. Rodgers	23	592	25.7	77	0
Snelling	2	16	8.0	9	0
Polite	1	24	24.0	24	0
Douglas	1	8	8.0	8	0
Falcons	27	640	23.7	77	0
Opponents	48	1065	22.2	65	0

FIELD GOALS

	1-19	20-29	30-39	40-49	50+
Bryant	1/1	8/9	10/11	10/13	4/4
Falcons	1/1	8/9	10/11	10/13	4/4
Opponents	0/0	10/10	8/10	7/8	2/4

SACKS

	No.
Abraham	10.0
Biermann	4.0
Babineaux	3.5
Walker	3.0
Weatherspoon	3.0
Nicholas	2.0
Robinson	1.5
DeCoud	1.0
Moore	1.0
Falcons	29.0
Opponents	28.0

RECORD HOLDERS
INDIVIDUAL RECORDS—CAREER

Category	Name	Performance
Rushing (Yds.)	Gerald Riggs, 1982-88	6,631
Passing (Yds.)	Steve Bartkowski, 1975-1985	23,470
Passing (TDs)	Steve Bartkowski, 1975-1985	154
Receiving (No.)	Roddy White, 2005-2012	622
Receiving (Yds.)	Roddy White, 2005-2012	8,725
Interceptions	Rolland Lawrence, 1973-1980	39
Punting (Avg.)	Matt Bosher, 2011-12	44.9
Punt Return (Avg.)	Darrien Gordon, 2001	14.1
Kickoff Return (Avg.)	Darrick Vaughn, 2000-01	25.7
Field Goals	Morten Andersen, 1995-2000, 2006-07	184
Touchdowns (Tot.)	Michael Turner, 2008-2012	61
Points	Morten Andersen, 1995-2000, 2006-07	806
Sacks*	John Abraham, 2006-2012	68.5

INDIVIDUAL RECORDS—SINGLE SEASON

Category	Name	Performance
Rushing (Yds.)	Jamal Anderson, 1998	1,846
Passing (Yds.)	Matt Ryan, 2012	4,719
Passing (TDs)	Matt Ryan, 2012	32
Receiving (No.)	Roddy White, 2010	115
Receiving (Yds.)	Roddy White, 2010	1,389
Interceptions	Scott Case, 1988	10
Punting (Avg.)	Matt Ryan, 2012	47.5
Punt Return (Avg.)	Darrien Gordon, 2001	14.1
Kickoff Return (Avg.)	Darrick Vaughn, 2000	27.7
Field Goals	Matt Bryant, 2012	33
Touchdowns (Tot.)	Michael Turner, 2008	17
Points	Matt Bryant, 2012	143
Sacks*	John Abraham, 2008	16.5

INDIVIDUAL RECORDS—SINGLE GAME

Category	Name	Performance
Rushing (Yds.)	Michael Turner, 9-7-08	220
Passing (Yds.)	Chris Chandler, 12-23-01	431
Passing (TDs)	Wade Wilson, 12-13-92	5
Receiving (No.)	William Andrews, 11-15-81	15
Receiving (Yds.)	Roddy White, 10-11-09	210
Interceptions	Many times	2
	Last time by William Moore, 11-29-12	
Field Goals	Norm Johnson, 11-13-94	6
Touchdowns (Tot.)	T.J. Duckett, 12-12-04	4
	Michael Turner, 11-23-08	4
Points	T.J. Duckett, 12-12-04	24
	Michael Turner, 11-23-08	24
Sacks*	Chuck Smith, 10-12-97	5.0

Sacks became an official statistic in 1982.

2013 VETERAN ROSTER

No.	Name	Pos.	Ht.	Wt.	Birthdate	NFL Exp.	College	Hometown	How Acq.	'12 Games/ Starts
95	Babineaux, Jonathan	DT	6-2	300	10/12/81	9	Iowa	Port Arthur, Texas	D2-'05	16/16
72	Baker, Sam	OT	6-5	301	5/30/85	6	Southern California	Tustin, Calif.	D1b-'08	16/16
71	Biermann, Kroy	DE	6-3	255	9/12/85	6	Montana	Hardin, Mont.	D5b-'08	16/3
63	Blalock, Justin	OG	6-4	326	12/20/83	7	Texas	Dallas, Texas	D2a-'07	16/16
5	Bosher, Matt	K/P	6-0	208	10/18/87	3	Miami	Jupiter, Fla.	D6-'10	16/0
3	Bryant, Matt	K	5-9	203	5/29/75	12	Baylor	Orange, Texas	FA-'09	16/0
86	Coffman, Chase	TE	6-6	250	11/10/86	4	Missouri	Peculiar, Mo.	FA-'12	5/0
15	Cone, Kevin	WR	6-2	216	3/20/88	3	Georgia Tech	Stone Mountain, Ga.	FA-'11	12/0
4	Davis, Dominique	QB	6-3	210	7/17/89	2	East Carolina	Lakeland, Fla.	FA-'12	0*
19	Davis, Drew	WR	6-1	205	1/4/89	2	Oregon	Denver, Colo.	FA-'12	16/0
28	DeCoud, Thomas	S	6-2	192	3/19/85	6	California	Vallejo, Calif.	D3c-'08	16/16
52	Dent, Akeem	LB	6-1	239	9/27/87	3	Georgia	Atlanta, Ga.	D3-'11	16/13
83	Douglas, Harry	WR	6-0	183	9/16/84	5	Louisville	Jonesboro, Ga.	D3-'08	15/1
34	Ewing, Bradie	FB	5-11	243	12/26/89	2	Wisconsin	Richland Center, Wisc.	D5-'12	0*
24	Franks, Dominique	CB	6-0	197	10/8/87	3	Oklahoma	Tulsa, Okla.	D5a-'10	16/0
87	Gallarda, Tommy	TE	6-5	262	5/8/88	2	Boise State	Brea, Calif.	FA-'11	9/0
88	Gonzalez, Tony	TE	6-5	247	2/27/76	17	California	Torrance, Calif.	T(KC)-'09	16/16
47	Harris, Josh	LS	6-1	224	4/27/89	2	Auburn	Carrollton, Ga.	FA-'12	16/0
61	Hawley, Joe	C	6-3	302	10/22/88	4	Nevada-Las Vegas	Yorba Linda, Calif.	D4-'10	6/0
76	Holmes, Lamar	T	6-6	333	7/8/89	2	Southern Mississippi	Gastonia, N.C.	D3-'12	1/0
39	Jackson, Steven	RB	6-2	240	7/22/83	10	Oregon State	Las Vegas, Nev.	FA-'13	16/16*
51	James, Robert	LB	5-11	224	12/26/83	4	Arizona State	Glendale, Ariz.	FA-'10	16/0
94	Jerry, Peria	DT	6-2	295	8/23/84	4	Mississippi	Batesville, Miss.	D1-'09	14/9
79	Johnson, Mike	OL	6-6	304	4/2/87	3	Alabama	Pensacola, Fla.	D3b-'10	16/1
11	Jones, Julio	WR	6-3	220	2/3/89	3	Alabama	Foley, Ala.	D1-'11	16/15
66	Konz, Peter	G	6-5	317	12/20/89	2	Wisconsin	Neenah, Wisc.	D2-'12	16/10
68	Manley, Phillipkeith	G	6-5	309	5/7/90	2	Toledo	Hamilton, Ohio	FA-'12	0*
96	Massaquoi, Jonathan	DE	6-2	264	5/18/88	2	Troy	Lawrenceville, Ga.	D5b-'12	8/0
98	Matthews, Cliff	DE	6-4	268	8/5/89	3	South Carolina	Cheraw, S.C.	D7b-'11	10/0
27	McClain, Robert	CB	5-9	195	7/22/88	4	Connecticut	Philadelphia, Pa.	FA-'12	15/3
65	McClendon, Jacques	G/C	6-3	324	12/10/87	3	Tennessee	Cleveland, Tenn.	FA-'12	0*
20	Mitchell, Charles	S	5-11	205	9/13/89	2	Mississippi State	Clarksdale, Miss.	D6-'12	10/0
25	Moore, William	S	6-0	221	5/18/85	4	Missouri	Hayti, Mo.	D2-'09	12/12
54	Nicholas, Stephen	LB	6-3	236	5/1/83	7	South Florida	Jacksonville, Fla.	D4a-'07	16/15
91	Peters, Corey	DT	6-3	305	6/8/88	4	Kentucky	Louisville, Ky.	D3a-'10	10/8
75	Reynolds, Garrett	OG	6-7	310	7/1/87	5	North Carolina	Knoxville, Tenn.	D5b-'09	7/6
92	Robertson, Travian	DT	6-4	304	12/9/88	2	South Carolina	Laurinburg, N.C.	D7-'12	7/0
32	Rodgers, Jacquizz	RB	5-6	196	2/6/90	3	Oregon State	Richmond, Texas	D5-'11	16/0
2	Ryan, Matt	QB	6-4	217	5/17/85	6	Boston College	Exton, Pa.	D1a-'08	16/16
22	Samuel, Asante	CB	5-10	185	1/6/81	11	Central Florida	Lauderdale Lakes, Fla.	T(Phil)-'12	15/15
29	Schillinger, Shann	S	6-0	200	5/22/86	4	Montana	Baker, Mont.	D6-'10	0*
35	Smith, Antone	RB	5-9	192	9/17/85	4	Florida State	Pahokee, Fla.	FA-'09	13/0
44	Snelling, Jason	RB	5-11	234	12/29/83	7	Virginia	Chester, Va.	D7-'07	16/2
17	Toone, Tim	WR	5-10	175	2/14/85	2	Weber State	Peoria, Ariz.	FA-'12	0*
90	Umenyiora, Osi	DE	6-3	255	11/16/81	11	Troy	London, England	FA-'13	16/4*
30	Vaughan, Josh	RB	6-0	225	12/3/86	3	Richmond	Richmond, Va.	FA-'12	0*
56	Weatherspoon, Sean	LB	6-2	244	12/29/87	4	Missouri	Jasper, Texas	D1-'10	13/13
84	White, Roddy	WR	6-0	211	11/2/81	9	Alabama-Birmingham	James Island, S.C.	D1-'05	16/15

* Do. Davis inactive for 16 games; Ewing missed '12 season because of injury; Jackson played 16 games with St. Louis in '12; Manley inactive for eight games; McClendon last active with Indianapolis in '10; Schillinger missed '12 season because of injury, Toone inactive for five games, did not play in two games; Umenyiora played 16 games with the New York Giants; Vaughan last active with Carolina in '11.

Players lost through free agency (5): DB Brent Grimes (Mia; 1 game in '12), QB Luke McCown (NO; 2), DB Christopher Owens (Cle; 13), DE Lawrence Sidbury (Ind; 10), DT Vance Walker (Oak; 16).

Also played with Falcons in '12—DE John Abraham (16 games), T Tyson Clabo (16), FB Mike Cox (8), DE Ray Edwards (9), S Chris Hope (16), Terrence Johnson (2), TE Michael Palmer (13), FB Lousaka Polite (6), CB Dunta Robinson (16).

FIRST-YEAR ROSTER

Name	Pos.	Ht.	Wt.	Birthdate	College	Hometown	How Acq.
Alford, Robert	CB	5-10	186	11/1/88	Southeast Louisiana	Hammond, La.	D2
Banks, Brian	LB	6-2	250	7/24/85	Long Beach Poly (HS)	Long Beach, Calif.	FA
Bartu, Joplo	LB	6-2	230	10/3/90	Texas State	Waller, Texas	FA
Campbell, Devonte	FB	6-2	255	6/27/89	Maryland	Forestville, Md.	FA
Clancy, Nick	LB	6-3	232	11/3/89	Boston College	Plainfield, Ill.	FA
Doege, Seth	QB	6-1	197	12/18/88	Texas Tech	Wolfforth, Texas	FA
Evans, Rashad	WR	5-9	187	8/28/90	Fresno State	San Francisco, Calif.	FA
Goggins, Deon	FB	6-1	272	11/3/88	Syracuse	Los Angeles, Calif.	FA
Goins, Theo	G	6-4	317	11/1/88	Central Florida	Houston, Texas	FA
Goodman, Malliciah	DE	6-4	276	1/4/90	Clemson	Florence, S.C.	D4a
Gunn, Harland (1)	G	6-2	310	8/30/89	Miami	Omaha, Neb.	FA-'12
Henderson, Cam	DE	6-5	245	6/20/90	Central Florida	Birmingham, Ala.	FA
Huynh, Neal	DT	6-4	315	6/22/90	Ohio	Altoona, Pa.	FA
Ishmael, Kemal	S	6-0	206	5/6/91	Central Florida	Miami, Fla.	D7a
Jackson, Marcus (1)	WR	6-1	195	5/20/89	Lamar	Tyler, Texas	FA-'12
Johnson, Darius	WR	5-10	175	2/22/91	Southern Methodist	Missouri City, Texas	FA
Jones, Terren	T	6-7	341	11/19/91	Alabama State	Ft. Walton Beach, Fla.	FA
Lee, Saeed	CB	5-10	182	1/20/91	Alabama State	Miami, Fla.	FA
Maponga, Stansly	DE	6-2	265	3/5/91	Texas Christian	Carrollton, Texas	D5
Moore, Martel	WR	6-0	183	11/2/90	Northern Illinois	San Antonio, Texas	FA
Motta, Zeke	S	6-2	215	5/14/90	Notre Dame	Vero Beach, Fla.	D7b
Nissley, Adam	TE	6-6	267	5/6/88	Central Florida	Cumming, Ga.	FA
Regis, Micanor (1)	DT	6-3	305	11/3/89	Miami	Pahokee, Fla.	FA-'12
Renfree, Sean	QB	6-5	225	4/28/90	Duke	Scottsdale, Ariz.	D7c
Replogle, Adam	DT	6-3	294	10/10/90	Indiana	Centerville, Ohio	FA
Rodgers, James (1)	WR	5-7	188	12/20/88	Oregon State	Richmond, Texas	FA-'12
Russell, Donald	RB	5-11	212	8/4/90	Georgia State	West Palm Beach, Fla.	FA
Sanders, Troy	S	6-0	214	1/23/91	Appalachian State	Chester, S.C.	FA
Savoie, Alec	T	6-7	322	9/28/89	McNeese State	Lafayette, La.	FA
Schiller, Pat (1)	LB	6-2	235	11/12/88	Northern Illinois	Geneva, Ill.	FA-'12
Schraeder, Ryan	T	6-7	300	5/4/88	Valdosta State	Wichita, Kan.	FA
Sellwood, Sean	P	6-3	203	7/11/90	Utah	Salt Lake City, Utah	FA
Shelley, Jeremy	K	5-10	165	10/25/90	Alabama	Raleigh, N.C.	FA
Smith, Matt	C	6-4	296	5/1/90	Kentucky	Louisville, Ky.	FA
Szczerba, Andrew (1)	TE	6-6	256	7/16/88	Penn State	Wilmington, Del.	FA-'12
Thompson, Peyton (1)	CB	5-11	180	9/26/90	San Jose State	Granite Bay, Calif.	FA-'12
Thurmond, Brandon	DE	6-2	260	2/15/90	Arkansas-Pine Bluff	Augusta, Ga.	FA
Toilolo, Levine	TE	6-8	265	7/30/91	Stanford	La Mesa, Calif.	D4b
Trufant, Desmond	CB	6-0	190	9/10/90	Washington	Tacoma, Wash.	D1
Wingo, Ronnie	RB	6-0	231	2/18/91	Arkansas	St. Louis, Mo.	FA
Worrilow, Paul	LB	6-0	230	5/1/90	Delaware	Wilmington, Del.	FA

The term NFL Rookie is defined as a player who is in his first season of professional football and has not been on the roster of another professional football team for any regular-season or postseason games. A Rookie is designated by an "R" on NFL rosters. Players who have been active in another professional football league or players who have NFL experience, including either preseason training camp or being on an Active List or Inactive List, or on Reserve/Injured or Reserve/Physically Unable to Perform for fewer than six regular-season games, are termed NFL First-Year Players. An NFL First-Year Player is designated by a "1" on NFL rosters. Thereafter, a player is credited with an additional year of experience for each season in which he accumulates six games on the Active List or Inactive List, or on Reserve/Injured or Reserve/Physically Unable to Perform.

Log on to www.atlantafalcons.com for an up-to-date roster.

COACHING STAFF
Head Coach,
Mike Smith

Pro Career: Mike Smith was named the 14th head coach in Atlanta Falcons franchise history on January 23, 2008. In five seasons with the team, he has compiled a 56-24 regular-season record, three playoff appearances and, for the first time in franchise history, four consecutive winning seasons. His .688 winning percentage is the best in team history over a three-year period. Smith's 33 wins are easily the most victories by a Falcons head coach in his first three years on the job. Smith's club posted the NFC's top record at 13-3 in both 2010 and 2012. When Smith's charges captured the NFC South title in 2010, it was only the fourth Division crown in franchise history (and first since 2004) and the eight consecutive victories in 2010 was the second longest streak ever. In 2008, Smith guided the Falcons to an 11-5 record, marking a seven-win turnaround from the previous season. For his efforts, he was named the Associated Press and *Sporting News* NFL Coach of the Year. From 2003-07, Smith served as the defensive coordinator for the Jacksonville Jaguars following a four-year stint with the Baltimore Ravens from 1999-2002, which included the team's 2000 Super Bowl season. Prior to the NFL, Smith coached at San Diego State (1982-85), Morehead State (1986), and Tennessee Tech (1987-1998). Career record: 57-28.

Background: Played linebacker for the CFL's Winnipeg Blue Bombers (1982). He played at East Tennessee (1977-1981) and named defensive MVP twice at his position. Led team with 186 tackles as a senior.

Personal: Born November 30, 1959 in Chicago, Ill. Native of Daytona Beach, Florida. He and his wife Julie have one daughter, Logan.

ASSISTANT COACHES

Keith Armstrong, special teams coordinator; born December 15, 1963, Levittown, Pa. Running back Temple 1983-86. No pro playing experience. College coach: Temple 1987, Miami 1988, Akron 1989, Oklahoma State 1990-92, Notre Dame 1993. Pro coach: Atlanta Falcons 1994-96, Chicago Bears 1997-2000, Miami Dolphins 2001-2007, re-joined Falcons 2008.

Jonas Beauchemin, strength and conditioning assistant; born October 11, 1984, Burlington, Vt. Attended Keene State. No college or pro playing experience. Pro coach: Joined Falcons in 2009.

Gerald Brown, running backs; born September 4, 1959, Sweetwater, Tenn. Attended Memphis State. No college or pro playing experience. College coach: Tennessee Tech 1991-2000, Indiana 2002-07. Pro coach: Joined Falcons in 2008.

Mark Collins, defensive assistant; born August 30, 1975, Sault Ste. Marie, Mich. Defensive end/outside linebacker East Tennessee State 1995-98. No pro playing experience. College coach: East Tennessee State 1999-2002, Michigan 2003-04, Elon, 2005, Georgia Southern, 2006, Georgia 2007, Louisiana-Monroe 2009. Pro coach: Joined Falcons in 2010.

Joe Danna, defensive backs; born April 3, 1977, Midland, Mich. Attended Central Michigan. No college or pro playing experience. College coach: Michigan 1999-2000, Georgia 2001, Central Michigan 2002-05, Georgia Southern 2006, James Madison 2007. Pro coach: Atlanta Falcons 2008-09, Miami Dolphins 2010-11, re-joined Falcons in 2012.

Paul Dunn, offensive line; born July 7, 1960, Philadelphia, Pa. Offensive lineman Pittsburgh 1978-1982. No pro playing experience. College coach: Pittsburgh 1983, 2005-07, Penn State 1984-85, Edinboro 1986-88, Rutgers 1989, Maine 1990-93, Cincinnati 1994-95, Vanderbilt 1996-97, Kansas State 1998-2002, Kentucky 2003-04. Pro coach: Joined Falcons in 2008.

Ray Hamilton, defensive line; born January 20, 1951, Omaha, Neb. Nose tackle Oklahoma 1969-1972. Pro defensive lineman New England Patriots 1973-1981. College coach: Tennessee 1992. Pro coach: New England Patriots 1985-89, Tampa Bay Buccaneers 1991, Los Angeles Raiders 1993-94, New York Jets 1994-96, 2000, New England Patriots 1997-99, Cleveland Browns 2001-02, Jacksonville Jaguars 2003-07, joined Falcons in 2008.

Pat Hill, offensive line; born December 17, 1951, Los Angeles, Calif. Center UC Riverside 1970-1973. No pro playing experience. College coach: Los Angeles Valley College 1974-76, Utah 1977-1980, Nevada-Las Vegas 1981-82, Fresno State 1984-89, 1997-2011 (head coach 1997-2011), Arizona 1990-91. Pro coach: Calgary Stampeders (CFL) 1983, Cleveland Browns 1992-95, Baltimore Ravens 1996, joined Falcons in 2012.

Dirk Koetter, offensive coordinator; born February 5, 1959, Pocatello, Idaho. Quarterback Idaho State 1978-1981. No pro playing experience. College coach: San Francisco State 1985, Texas El-Paso 1986-88, Missouri 1989-1993, Boston College 1994-95, Oregon 1996-97, Boise State 1998-2000 (head coach), Arizona State 2001-06 (head coach). Pro coach: Jacksonville Jaguars 2007-2011, joined Falcons in 2012.

Tim Lewis, secondary; born December 18, 1961, Quakertown, Pa. Cornerback Pittsburgh 1979-1982. Pro cornerback Green Bay Packers 1983-86. Pro coach: Pittsburgh Steelers 1995-2003, New York Giants 2004-06, Carolina Panthers 2007-08, Seattle Seahawks 2009, joined

Falcons in 2010.

A.J. Neibel, head strength and conditioning; born August 31, 1972, Cupertino, Calif. Attended Long Beach State. No college or pro playing experience. Pro coach: Oakland Raiders 2003-09, joined Falcons in 2011.

Mike Nolan, defensive coordinator; born March 7, 1965, Haverhill, Mass. Safety Oregon 1978-1980. No pro playing experience. College coach: Oregon 1981, Stanford 1982-83, Rice 1984-85, Louisiana State 1986. Pro coach: Denver Broncos 1987-1992, 2009, New York Giants 1993-96, Washington Redskins 1997-99, New York Jets 2000, Baltimore Ravens 2001-04, San Francisco 49ers 2005-08 (head coach), Miami Dolphins 2010-11, joined Falcons in 2012.

Glenn Pires, linebackers; born September 13, 1958, New Bedford, Mass. Offensive lineman Springfield College 1976-79. No pro playing experience. College coach: Dartmouth 1985-88, Syracuse 1989-1994, Michigan State 1995. Pro coach: Arizona Cardinals 1996-2000, Detroit Lions 2001-02, Miami Dolphins 2003-07, joined Falcons in 2008.

Terry Robiskie, wide receivers; born November 12, 1954, New Orleans, La. Running back Louisiana State 1973-76. Pro running back Oakland Raiders 1977-79, Miami Dolphins 1980-81. Pro coach: Los Angeles Raiders 1982-1993, Washington Redskins 1994-2000 (interim head coach 2000), Cleveland Browns 2001-06 (interim head coach 2004), Miami Dolphins 2007, joined Falcons in 2008.

Chris Scelfo, tight ends; born September 30, 1963, New Iberia, La. Center Northeast Louisiana 1981-84. No pro playing experience. College coach: Northeast Louisiana 1986-87, Oklahoma 1988-89, Marshall 1990-95, Georgia 1996-98, Tulane 1998-2006. Pro coach: Joined Falcons in 2008.

Eric Sutulovich, asst. special teams; born February 28, 1974, Kansas City, Kan. Tight end Louisiana Tech 1993-95. No pro playing experience. College coach: Louisiana Tech 1997-99, Pittsburgh 2000, Kansas 2006. Pro coach: Houston Texans 2002-05, Detroit Lions 2008, joined Falcons in 2009.

Glenn Thomas, quarterbacks; born September 22, 1977, Eastland, Texas. Attended Texas Tech. No college or pro playing experience. College coach: Texas Tech 1998-2001, Midwestern State 2001-07. Pro coach: Joined Falcons in 2008.

Andrew Weidinger, offensive assistant; born July 10, 1982, Phoenix, Ariz. Attended Arizona. No college or pro playing experience. Pro coach: Joined Falcons in 2008.

**National Football Conference
South Division**
Team Colors: Black, Panther Blue, and
Silver
800 South Mint Street
Charlotte, North Carolina 28202-1502
Telephone: (704) 358-7000

2013 SCHEDULE
PRESEASON

Aug. 9	**Chicago**	8:00
Aug. 15	at Philadelphia	7:30
Aug. 22	at Baltimore	8:00
Aug. 29	**Pittsburgh**	7:30

REGULAR SEASON

Sep. 8	**Seattle**	1:00
Sep. 15	at Buffalo	1:00
Sep. 22	**New York Giants**	1:00
Sep. 29	BYE	
Oct. 6	at Arizona	4:05
Oct. 13	at Minnesota	1:00
Oct. 20	**St. Louis**	1:00
Oct. 24	at Tampa Bay (Thurs)	8:25
Nov. 3	**Atlanta**	1:00
Nov. 10	at San Francisco	4:05
Nov. 18	**New England** (Mon)	8:40
Nov. 24	at Miami	1:00
Dec. 1	**Tampa Bay**	1:00
Dec. 8	at New Orleans	1:00
Dec. 15	**New York Jets**	4:05
Dec. 22	**New Orleans**	1:00
Dec. 29	at Atlanta	1:00

*All times ET
Stadium: Bank of America Stadium
(opened in 1996)
• **Capacity:** 73,504
Charlotte, North Carolina
28202-1502
Playing Surface: Grass
Training Camp: Wofford College
Spartanburg,
South Carolina 29303

BANK OF AMERICA STADIUM

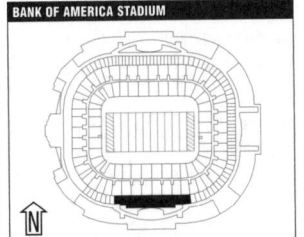

CLUB OFFICIALS
Owner/Founder: Jerry Richardson
President, Panthers Football LLC:
Danny Morrison
General Manager: Dave Gettleman
General Counsel: Richard Thigpen
Chief Financial Officer: Dave Olsen
Controller: Mike Dudan
Director of Human Resources:
Larry Griffin
Director of Pro Scouting: Mark Koncz
Director of College Scouting:
Don Gregory
College Scouts: Matt Allen, Jeff Beathard,
Ryan Cowden, Khary Darlington,
Robert Haines, Jeff Morrow,
John Peterson, Mike Szabo
Director of Communications:
Charlie Dayton
Assistant Director of Communications:
Steven Drummond
Director of Ticket Operations:
Phil Youtsey
Director of Community Relations and
Cheerleader/Mascot Programs:
Riley Fields
Director of Sponsor Sales and Services:
John Berger
Director of Broadcast Administration:
Henry Thomas
Executive Producer-Television:
Greg Brannon
Executive Producer-Radio: David Langton
Director of Team Administration:
Rob Rogers
Director of Team Operations:
Brandon Beane
Video Director: Mark Hobbs
Assistant Video Director: Jeff Mueller
Head Trainer: Ryan Vermillion
Assistant Trainer: Mark Shermansky
Equipment Manager: Jackie Miles
Assistant Equipment Manager: Don Toner
Director of Security: Lance Emory
Stadium Operations Manager: Scott Paul
Director of Entertainment: Tina Becker
Director of PantherVision: Kyle Ritchie
Facility Manager: Matthew Getz
Head Groundskeeper: Tom Vaughan

COACHING HISTORY
(138-160-0)
Records include postseason games

1995-98	Dom Capers	31-35-0
1999-2001	George Seifert	16-32-0
2002-2010	John Fox	78-74-0
2011-12	Ron Rivera	13-19-0

PAID ATTENDANCE
Home 573,102   Away 490,877
Total 1,063,979
Single-game home record,
76,136 (12/10/95)
Single-season home record, 579,192
(2006)

2013 DRAFT CHOICES

Round	Name	Pos.	College
1	Star Lotulelei	DT	Utah
2	Kawann Short	DT	Purdue
4	Edmund Kugbila	G	Valdosta St.
5	A.J. Klein	LB	Iowa St.
6	Kenjon Barner	RB	Oregon

2012 TEAM RECORD

PRESEASON (2-2)

Date	Result	Opponent
08/11	L	13-26 Houston
08/17	W	23-17 Miami
08/26	W	17-12 at New York Jets
08/30	L	16-17 at Pittsburgh

REGULAR SEASON (7-9)

Date	Result	Opponent
09/09	L	10-16 at Tampa Bay
09/16	W	35-27 New Orleans
09/20	L	7-36 New York Giants
09/30	L	28-30 at Atlanta
10/07	L	12-16 Seattle
10/21	L	14-19 Dallas
10/28	L	22-23 at Chicago
11/04	W	21-13 at Washington
11/11	L	14-36 Denver
11/18	L	21-27 Tampa Bay (OT)
11/26	W	30-22 at Philadelphia
12/02	L	21-27 at Kansas City
12/09	W	30-20 Atlanta
12/16	W	31-7 at San Diego
12/23	W	17-6 Oakland
12/30	W	44-38 at New Orleans

(OT) Overtime

SCORE BY PERIODS

Panthers	97	91	76	93	0 —	357
Opponents	80	81	68	128	6 —	363

2012 TEAM STATISTICS

	Panthers	Opp.
Total First Downs	328	325
Rushing	123	98
Passing	171	195
Penalty	34	32
3rd Down: Made/Att	88/204	73/202
3rd Down Pct.	43.1	36.1
4th Down: Made/Att	3/9	10/19
4th Down Pct.	33.3	52.6
Possession Avg.	29:43	30:17
Total Net Yards	5771	5329
Avg. Per Game	360.7	333.1
Total Plays	988	1010
Avg. Per Play	5.8	5.3
Net Yards Rushing	2088	1761
Avg. Per Game	130.5	110.1
Total Rushes	462	416
Net Yards Passing	3683	3568
Avg. Per Game	230.2	223.0
Sacked/Yards Lost	36/244	39/284
Gross Yards	3927	3852
Att./Completions	490/284	555/371
Completion Pct.	58.0	66.8
Had Intercepted	12	11
Punts/Average	77/42.4	67/45.9
Net Punting Avg.	77/36.5	67/40.3
Penalties/Yards	98/835	86/711
Fumbles/Ball Lost	22/10	18/12
Touchdowns	44	37
Rushing	21	11
Passing	19	22
Returns	4	4

2012 INDIVIDUAL STATISTICS

PASSING	Att.	Comp.	Yds.	Pct.	TD	Int.	Tkld.	Rate
Newton	485	280	3869	57.7	19	12	36/244	86.2
D. Anderson	4	4	58	100.0	0	0	0/0	118.8
A. Edwards	1	0	0	0.0	0	0	0/0	39.6
Panthers	490	284	3927	58.0	19	12	36/244	86.5
Opponents	555	371	3852	66.8	22	11	39/284	91.7

SCORING	TD R	TD P	TD Rt	PAT	FG	Saf	PTS
Newton	8	0	0	0/0	0/0	0	48
Gano	0	0	0	20/21	9/11	0	47
Medlock	0	0	0	23/23	7/10	0	44
Tolbert	7	0	0	0/0	0/0	0	42
D. Williams	5	2	0	0/0	0/0	0	42
Olsen	0	5	0	0/0	0/0	0	30
LaFell	0	4	0	0/0	0/0	0	24
S. Smith	0	4	0	0/0	0/0	0	24
Munnerlyn	0	0	2	0/0	0/0	0	12
Murphy	0	1	1	0/0	0/0	0	12
Stewart	1	1	0	0/0	0/0	0	12
Barnidge	0	1	0	0/0	0/0	0	6
Godfrey	0	0	1	0/0	0/0	0	6
Pilares	0	1	0	0/0	0/0	0	6
Onatolu	0	0	0	0/0	0/0	1	2
Panthers	21	19	4	43/44	16/21	1	357
Opponents	11	22	4	32/32	35/37	1	363

2-Pt Conversions: Panthers 0-0, Opponents 1-4

RUSHING	No.	Yds	Avg	LG	TD
Newton	127	741	5.8	72t	8
D. Williams	173	737	4.3	65	5
Stewart	93	336	3.6	21	1
Tolbert	54	183	3.4	13	7
LaFell	3	35	11.7	25	0
S. Smith	3	27	9.0	15	0
Pilares	1	17	17.0	12	0
Joe Adams	3	13	4.3	5	0
Murphy	1	3	3.0	3	0
A. Smith	3	0	0.0	3	0
Nakamura	1	-4	-4.0	—	0
Panthers	462	2088	4.5	72t	21
Opponents	416	1761	4.2	65t	11

RECEIVING	No.	Yds	Avg	LG	TD
S. Smith	73	1174	16.1	66	4
Olsen	69	843	12.2	47t	5
LaFell	44	677	15.4	62	4
Tolbert	27	268	9.9	26	0
Murphy	25	336	13.4	55	1
Stewart	17	157	9.2	30	1
D. Williams	13	187	14.4	53t	2
Barnidge	6	78	13.0	24t	1
A. Edwards	5	121	24.2	82	0
Pilares	2	42	21.0	36t	1
Hartsock	2	30	15.0	25	0
Joe Adams	1	7	7.0	7	0
Newton	0	6	—	6	0
Gross	0	1	—	1	0
Panthers	284	3927	13.8	82	19
Opponents	371	3852	10.4	60t	22

INTERCEPTIONS	No.	Yds	Avg	LG	TD
Munnerlyn	2	107	53.5	74t	2
Nakamura	2	39	19.5	21	0
Kuechly	2	22	11.0	25	0
Godfrey	2	9	4.5	9t	1
Beason	1	2	2.0	2	0
Norman	1	2	2.0	2	0
Davis	1	0	0.0	0	0
Panthers	11	181	16.5	74t	3
Opponents	12	200	16.7	44	3

PUNTING	No.	Yds.	Avg.	In 20	LG
Nortman	76	3267	43.0	20	63
Panthers	77	3267	42.4	20	63
Opponents	67	3073	45.9	31	65

PUNT RETURNS	Ret	FC	Yds	Avg	LG	TD
Munnerlyn	14	5	72	5.1	20	0
Joe Adams	11	11	127	11.5	21	0
A. Edwards	2	2	77	38.5	69	0
Panthers	27	18	276	10.2	69	0
Opponents	37	20	318	8.6	76t	1

KICKOFF RETURNS	No.	Yds	Avg	LG	TD
A. Edwards	12	260	21.7	35	0
Joe Adams	9	208	23.1	31	0
Pilares	9	216	24.0	28	0
A. Smith	6	131	21.8	26	0
Tolbert	1	26	26.0	26	0
Munnerlyn	1	17	17.0	17	0
Fua	1	9	9.0	9	0
Panthers	39	867	22.2	35	0
Opponents	39	739	18.9	45	0

FIELD GOALS	1-19	20-29	30-39	40-49	50+
Gano	0/0	3/3	3/3	2/3	1/2
Medlock	0/0	2/2	3/3	2/4	0/1
Panthers	0/0	5/5	6/6	4/7	1/3
Opponents	1/1	8/8	8/9	13/14	5/5

SACKS	No.
Johnson	12.5
Hardy	11.0
D. Edwards	6.0
Alexander	2.5
Addison	1.0
Applewhite	1.0
R. Edwards	1.0
Kearse	1.0
Kuechly	1.0
(group)	1.0
Keiser	0.5
Neblett	0.5
Panthers	39.0
Opponents	36.0

RECORD HOLDERS
INDIVIDUAL RECORDS—CAREER

Category	Name	Performance
Rushing (Yds.)	DeAngelo Williams, 2006-2012	5,784
Passing (Yds.)	Jake Delhomme, 2003-09	19,258
Passing (TDs)	Jake Delhomme, 2003-09	120
Receiving (No.)	Steve Smith, 2001-2012	772
Receiving (Yds.)	Steve Smith, 2001-2012	11,452
Interceptions	Chris Gamble, 2004-2012	27
Punting (Avg.)	Todd Sauerbrun, 2001-04	45.5
Punt Return (Avg.)	Winslow Oliver, 1996-98	10.7
Kickoff Return (Avg.)	Michael Bates, 1996-2000	25.7
Field Goals	John Kasay, 1995-2010	351
Touchdowns (Tot.)	Steve Smith, 2001-2012	71
Points	John Kasay, 1995-2010	1,482
*Sacks	Julius Peppers, 2002-09	81.0

INDIVIDUAL RECORDS—SINGLE SEASON

Category	Name	Performance
Rushing (Yds.)	DeAngelo Williams, 2008	1,515
Passing (Yds.)	Steve Beuerlein, 1999	4,436
Passing (TDs)	Steve Beuerlein, 1999	36
Receiving (No.)	Steve Smith, 2005	103
Receiving (Yds.)	Steve Smith, 2005	1,563
Interceptions	Doug Evans, 2001	8
Punting (Avg.)	Todd Sauerbrun, 2001	47.5
Punt Return (Avg.)	Winslow Oliver, 1996	11.5
Kickoff Return (Avg.)	Michael Bates, 1996	30.2
Field Goals	John Kasay, 1996	37
Touchdowns (Tot.)	DeAngelo Williams, 2008	20
Points	John Kasay, 1996	145
*Sacks	Kevin Greene, 1998	15.0

INDIVIDUAL RECORDS—SINGLE GAME

Category	Name	Performance
Rushing (Yds.)	DeAngelo Williams, 12-30-12	210
Passing (Yds.)	Cam Newton, 9-18-11	432
Passing (TDs)	Steve Beuerlein, 1-2-00	5
Receiving (No.)	Steve Smith, 11-20-05	14
Receiving (Yds.)	Steve Smith, 10-30-05	201
Interceptions	Deon Grant, 9-22-02	3
Field Goals	John Kasay, 12-5-04	6
Touchdowns (Tot.)	DeAngelo Williams, 11-30-08, 12-21-08	4
Points	DeAngelo Williams, 11-30-08, 12-21-08	24
*Sacks	Charles Johnson, 9-30-12	3.5

*Sacks became an official statistic in 1982.

2013 VETERAN ROSTER

No.	Name	Pos.	Ht.	Wt.	Birthdate	NFL Exp.	College	Hometown	How Acq.	'12 Games/ Starts
15	Adams, Joe	WR	5-11	180	11/22/89	2	Arkansas	Little Rock, Ark.	D4b-'12	9/0
97	Addison, Mario	DE	6-3	260	9/6/87	3	Troy	Tarrant, Ala.	FA-'12	4/1
90	Alexander, Frank	DE	6-4	270	12/17/89	2	Oklahoma	Baton Rouge, La.	D4a-'12	16/3
3	Anderson, Derek	QB	6-6	230	6/15/83	9	Oregon State	Scappoose, Ore	FA-'11	2/0
93	#Applewhite, Antwan	DE	6-3	270	12/31/85	6	San Diego State	Harbor City, Calif.	FA-'11	5/3
71	Austin, Thomas	C/G	6-4	310	11/14/86	3	Clemson	Camden, S.C.	FA-'12	4/1
52	Beason, Jon	LB	6-0	235	1/14/85	7	Miami	Miami, Fla.	D1-'07	4/4
77	Bell, Byron	T	6-5	340	1/17/89	3	New Mexico	Greenville, Texas	FA-'11	15/15
93	Blackburn, Chase	LB	6-3	245	6/10/83	9	Akron	Marysville, Ohio	UFA(NYG)-'13	15/15*
47	Brockel, Richie	TE/FB	6-1	255	7/24/86	3	Boise State	Phoenix, Ariz.	FA-'11	16/0
62	Byers, Jeff	G/C	6-4	310	9/7/85	2	Southern California	Loveland, Colo.	FA-'11	14/7
73	Campbell, Bruce	T	6-6	315	5/25/88	4	Maryland	Hamden, Conn.	T(Oak)-'12	5/0
26	Campbell, D.J.	S	6-0	200	7/24/89	2	California	North Las Vegas, Nev.	D7-'12	5/4
78	Chandler, Nate	DT	6-4	300	6/1/89	2	UCLA	San Diego, Calif.	FA-'12	10/0
7	Clausen, Jimmy	QB	6-2	215	9/21/87	4	Notre Dame	Westlake Village, Calif.	D2-'10	0*
91	Cole, Colin	DT	6-2	330	6/24/80	7	Iowa	Fort Lauderdale, Fla.	FA-'13	0*
58	Davis, Thomas	LB	6-1	235	3/22/83	9	Georgia	Shellman, Ga.	D1-'05	15/12
31	Dockery, James	CB	6-1	185	11/9/88	3	Oregon State	Palm Desert, Calif.	FA-'12	7/2
14	Edwards, Armanti	WR	5-11	190	3/8/88	4	Appalachian State	Greenwood, S.C.	D3b-'10	16/0
92	Edwards, Dwan	DT	6-3	300	5/16/81	10	Oregon State	Columbus, Montana	FA-'12	14/14
29	Florence, Drayton	CB	6-0	195	12/19/80	11	Tuskegee	Ocala, Fla.	UFA(Det)-'13	8/3*
94	Fua, Sione	DT	6-1	310	6/15/88	3	Stanford	Encino, Calif.	D3b-'11	13/1
9	Gano, Graham	K	6-2	195	4/9/87	4	Florida State	Cantonment, Fla.	FA-'12	6/0
12	Gettis, David	WR	6-3	220	8/27/87	4	Baylor	Los Angeles, Calif.	D6b-'10	2/0
19	Ginn Jr., Ted	WR	5-11	180	4/12/85	7	Ohio State	Cleveland, Ohio	UFA(SF)-'13	13/0*
30	Godfrey, Charles	S	5-11	210	11/15/85	6	Iowa	Baytown, Texas	D3a-'08	15/15
69	Gross, Jordan	T	6-4	305	7/20/80	11	Utah	Fruitland, Idaho	D1-'03	16/16
63	Hangartner, Geoff	C/G	6-5	300	4/22/82	9	Texas A&M	New Braunfels, Texas	FA-'11	12/12
76	Hardy, Greg	DE	6-4	290	7/28/88	4	Mississippi	Millington, Tenn.	D6a-'10	15/10
84	Hartsock, Ben	TE	6-4	260	7/5/80	10	Ohio State	Chillicothe, Ohio	FA-'11	15/5
75	Hicks, Hayworth	G	6-3	335	10/3/88	2	Iowa State	Palmdale, Calif.	FA-'12	0*
87	Hixon, Domenik	WR	6-2	195	10/8/84	8	Akron	Columbus, Ohio	UFA(NYG)-'13	13/3*
55	Hogue, Doug	LB	6-2	226	2/1/89	3	Syracuse	Yonkers, N.Y.	W(Det)-'12	9/0
53	Jacobs, Ben	LB	6-4	243	4/17/88	2	Fresno State	Las Vegas, Nev.	FA-'13	0*
44	Jansen, J.J.	LS	6-2	245	1/20/86	6	Notre Dame	Phoenix, Ariz.	T(GB)-'09	16/0
95	Johnson, Charles	DE	6-2	285	7/10/86	7	Georgia	Hawkinsville, Ga.	D3-'07	16/16
42	Jones, Colin	S	6-0	208	10/27/87	3	Texas Christian	Bridgeport, Texas	T(SF)-'12	15/0
67	Kalil, Ryan	C	6-2	295	3/29/85	7	Southern California	Corona, Calif.	D2b-'07	5/5
99	Kearse, Frank	DT	6-5	315	10/28/88	3	Alabama A&M	Savannah, Ga.	FA-'11	8/4
59	Kuechly, Luke	LB	6-3	235	4/20/91	2	Boston College	Cincinnati, Ohio	D1-'12	16/16
11	LaFell, Brandon	WR	6-2	210	11/4/86	4	Louisiana State	Houston, Texas	D3a-'10	14/12
23	#Martin, Sherrod	S	6-1	200	10/12/84	5	Troy	Griffin, Ga.	D2b-'09	12/0
21	Mitchell, Mike	S	6-0	215	6/10/87	5	Ohio	Fort Thomas, Ky.	UFA(Oak)-'13	16/2*
20	Moore, D.J.	CB	5-9	180	3/22/87	5	Vanderbilt	Spartanburg, S.C.	UFA(Chi)-'13	13/2*
41	Munnerlyn, Captain	CB	5-8	190	4/10/88	5	South Carolina	Mobile, Ala.	D7-'09	16/11
43	Nakamura, Haruki	S	5-10	205	4/18/86	6	Cincinnati	Lakewood, Ohio	UFA(Bal)-'12	13/13
1	Newton, Cam	QB	6-5	245	5/11/89	3	Auburn	College Park, Ga.	D1-'11	16/16
24	Norman, Josh	CB	6-0	195	12/15/87	2	Coastal Carolina	Greenwood, S.C.	D5-'12	16/12
8	Nortman, Brad	P	6-2	210	9/12/89	2	Wisconsin	Brookfield, Wisc.	D6-'12	16/0
88	Olsen, Greg	TE	6-5	255	3/11/85	7	Miami	Wayne, N.J.	T(Chi)-'11	16/16
81	Pilares, Kealoha	WR	5-10	200	2/20/88	3	Hawaii	Honolulu, Hawaii	D5-'11	8/0
33	Poole, Tauren	RB	5-10	215	10/19/89	2	Tennessee	Toccoa, Ga.	FA-'12	0*
40	Russell, Anderson	S	6-0	208	5/30/87	3	Ohio State	Atlanta, Ga.	FA '12	3/0
57	Senn, Jordan	LB	5-11	235	6/11/84	6	Portland State	Beaverton, Ore	FA-'09	16/0
61	Silatolu, Amini	G	6-4	315	9/16/88	2	Midwestern State	Tracy, Calif.	D2-'12	15/15
36	Smith, Armond	RB	5-9	190	5/7/86	2	Union College	Stone Mountain, Ga.	FA-'12	4/0
89	Smith, Steve	WR	5-9	185	5/12/79	13	Utah	Los Angeles, Calif.	D3-'01	16/16
28	Stewart, Jonathan	RB	5-10	235	3/21/87	6	Oregon	Lacey, Wash.	D1a-'08	9/6
22	Thomas, Josh	CB	5-11	190	5/3/89	3	Buffalo	Cedar Hills, Texas	W(Dal)-'11	16/4
35	Tolbert, Mike	FB	5-9	245	11/23/85	6	Coastal Carolina	Douglasville, Ga.	UFA(SD)-'12	16/5
34	Williams, DeAngelo	RB	5-9	215	4/25/83	8	Memphis	Wynne, Ark.	D1-'06	16/10
65	Williams, Garry	T	6-3	320	8/20/86	5	Kentucky	Louisville, Ky.	FA-'09	16/9
54	Williams, Jason	LB	6-1	245	4/23/86	5	Western Illinois	Chicago, Ill.	W(Phi)-'12	5/0

* Blackburn played 15 games with the New York Giants in '12; Clausen inactive for 16 games; Cole last active with Seattle in '10; Florence played eight games with Detroit; Ginn, Jr. played 13 games with San Francisco; Hicks inactive five games and did not play in one game with the New York Jets, Kansas City and Carolina; Hixon played 13 games for the New York Giants; Jacobs last active with Cleveland in '11; Mitchell played 16 games with Oakland; Moore played 13 games with Chicago; Poole missed '12 season because of injury.

\# Unrestricted Free Agent; subject to developments.

Players lost through free agency (4): TE Gary Barnidge (Cle; 16 games in '12), WR Louis Murphy (NYG; 16), LB Jason Phillips (Phil; 16), G Mike Pollak (Cin; 1).

Also played with Panthers in '12—LB James Anderson (12 games), OL Jeremy Bridges (2), DT Ron Edwards (11), CB Chris Gamble (4), DE Thomas Keiser (4), K Justin Medlock (10), DT Andre Neblett (11), LB Kenny Onatolu (4), CB Ron Parker (3), G Zack Williams (1).

FIRST-YEAR ROSTER

Name	Pos.	Ht.	Wt.	Birthdate	College	Hometown	How Acq.
Barner, Kenjon	RB	5-9	190	4/28/89	Oregon	Sherman Oaks, Calif.	D6
Bersin, Brenton (1)	WR	6-3	211	5/9/90	Wofford	Charlotte, N.C.	FA
Brock, Logan (1)	TE	6-3	242	10/5/88	Texas Christian	Copperas Cove, Texas	FA
Bryant, Lamont (1)	WR	6-5	225	1/6/88	Morgan State	Newport News, Va.	FA-'12
Cameron, Colby	QB	6-2	210	4/5/90	Louisiana Tech	Newbury Park, Calif.	FA
Folkerts, Brian (1)	C	6-4	303	1/30/90	Washburn	Florissant, Mo.	FA
Gay, Jordan	P	6-1	210	3/29/90	Centre College (Ky.)	Danville, Ky.	FA
Gaydosh, Linden	DT	6-3	314	1/4/91	Calgary	Peace River, Alberta, Canada	FA
Hixson, Nick (1)	CB	6-1	185	1/15/89	Hillsdale College (Mich.)	Remus, Mich.	FA-'12
Horton, Wes	DE	6-5	265	1/18/90	Southern California	Sherman Oaks, Calif.	FA
Ikharo, Taulib (1)	WR	5-10	183	7/27/89	Louisiana Tech	Oakland, Calif.	FA
Jones, Robert	G	6-3	315	4/19/90	East Carolina	Tucker, Ga.	FA
Klein, A.J.	LB	6-1	250	7/30/91	Iowa State	Kimberly, Wisc.	D5
Kugbila, Edmund	G	6-4	315	9/21/90	Valdosta State	Lawrenceville, Ga.	D4
Lester, Robert	S	6-1	210	4/30/88	Alabama	Foley, Ala.	FA
Lineberry, Morgan	K	6-1	195	1/25/91	Abilene Christian	Dallas, Texas	FA
Lotulelei, Star	DT	6-2	310	12/20/89	Utah	South Jordan, Utah	D1
Mobley, Tori	G	6-3	290	10/3/89	Jacksonville State	Columbus, Ga.	FA
Nzegwu, Louis (1)	DE	6-4	255	5/15/89	Wisconsin	Platteville, Wisc.	FA
Roh, Craig	DE	6-4	270	1/25/91	Michigan	Scottsdale, Ariz.	FA
Rosario, Nelson (1)	TE	6-5	225	12/24/89	UCLA	Oceanside, Calif.	FA-'12
Shaw, James (1)	WR	5-11	190	2/27/89	Jacksonville State	Odenville, Ala.	FA
Short, Kawann	DT	6-3	310	2/2/89	Purdue	East Chicago, Ind.	D2
Walker, Casey	DT	6-1	335	12/6/89	Oklahoma	Garland, Texas	FA
Webb, R.J. (1)	WR	6-2	201	8/24/87	Furman	Pickens, S.C.	FA
Wells, Justin (1)	G	6-4	315	1/6/88	St. Augustine's	Baltimore, Md.	FA
White, Melvin	CB	6-1	200	6/26/90	Louisiana Lafayette	Freeport, Texas	FA
Williams, Brandon (1)	TE	6-4	250	10/12/87	Oregon	Blue Island, Ill.	FA
Zordich, Michael	FB	6-1	235	10/29/89	Penn State	Youngstown, Ohio	FA

The term NFL Rookie is defined as a player who is in his first season of professional football and has not been on the roster of another professional football team for any regular-season or postseason games. A Rookie is designated by an "R" on NFL rosters. Players who have been active in another professional football league or players who have NFL experience, including either preseason training camp or being on an Active List or Inactive List, or on Reserve/Injured or Reserve/Physically Unable to Perform for fewer than six regular-season games, are termed NFL First-Year Players. An NFL First-Year Player is designated by a "1" on NFL rosters. Thereafter, a player is credited with an additional year of experience for each season in which he accumulates six games on the Active List or Inactive List, or on Reserve/Injured or Reserve/Physically Unable to Perform.

Log on to www.panthers.com for an up-to-date roster.

COACHING STAFF

Head Coach,
Ron Rivera

Pro Career: Became the fourth coach in Carolina Panthers history on January 11, 2011. In his first season at the helm, the Panthers won four more games than in 2010 on the strength of a prolific offense which improved from last in the NFL in 2010 to seventh in 2011. In 2012, his second season, the Panthers increased their win total to seven games while moving from 28th to 10th in overall defense. Before joining the Panthers, Rivera worked with the San Diego Chargers from 2007-2010, coaching inside linebackers before taking over as defensive coordinator midway through the 2008 season. In 2010, San Diego led the NFL with an average of 271.6 total yards allowed per game and gave up a league-low 177.8 passing yards per game. In 2009, the team ranked 16th in total defense and 11th against the pass. From 2004-06, Rivera oversaw the Chicago Bears defense, guiding the unit to two top-five finishes in the league. In 2006, the Bears defense led the NFL with 44 takeaways and finished fifth in total defense and third in scoring defense, helping propel Chicago to an appearance in Super Bowl XLI. In 2005, Rivera's defensive unit ranked second in the NFL in total defense and first in scoring defense. The Bears went 43 consecutive quarters without allowing more than seven points – the longest streak in the NFL since 1969. Prior to serving as defensive coordinator with the Bears, Rivera was linebackers coach for the Eagles (1999-2003) and defensive quality control coach for the Bears (1997-98). He is just the third Latino head coach in NFL history, joining Tom Flores with the Oakland Raiders (1979-1987) and Seattle Seahawks (1992-94) and Tom Fears with the New Orleans Saints (1967-1970). A second-round draft choice in 1984 by Chicago, Rivera played nine seasons with the Bears. Primarily an outside linebacker, he was a member of the Super Bowl XX championship team in 1985. Career record: 13-19.

Background: Linebacker at California (1980-83).

Personal: Born January 7, 1962 in Fort Ord, Calif. He and his wife, Stephanie, have two children—Christopher and Courtney.

ASSISTANT COACHES

Ray Brown, asst. offensive line; born December 12, 1962, Marion, Ark. Offensive lineman/tight end Arkansas State 1983-85. Pro offensive lineman St. Louis/Phoenix Cardinals 1986-88, Washington Redskins 1989-1995, 2004-05, San Francisco 49ers 1996-2001, Detroit Lions 2002-03. Pro coach: Washington Redskins 2006, Buffalo Bills 2008-09, San Francisco 49ers 2010, joined Panthers in 2011.

Bruce DeHaven, asst. special teams; born

September 6, 1948, Trousdale, Kan. Attended Southwestern (Kan.) College. No college or pro playing experience. College coach: Kansas 1979-1981, New Mexico State 1982. Pro coach: New Jersey Generals (USFL) 1983, Pittsburgh Maulers (USFL) 1984, Orlando Renegades (USFL) 1985, Buffalo Bills 1987-1999, 2010-12, San Francisco 49ers 2000-02, Dallas Cowboys 2003-06, Seattle Seahawks 2007-09, joined Panthers in 2013.

Ken Dorsey, quarterbacks; born April 22, 1981, Orinda, Calif. Quarterback Miami 1999-2002. Pro quarterback San Francisco 49ers 2003-05, Cleveland Browns 2006-08, Toronto Argonauts (CFL) 2010. Pro scout: Carolina Panthers 2011-12. Pro coach: Joined Panthers in 2013.

Pete Hoener, tight ends; born June 14, 1954, Peoria, Ill. Tight end/defensive end Bradley 1969-1970. No pro playing experience. College coach: Missouri 1975-76, Illinois State 1977, Indiana State 1978-1984, Illinois 1987-88, Purdue 1989-1991, Texas Christian 1992-97, Iowa State 1998-99, Texas A&M 2000. Pro coach: St. Louis/Arizona Cardinals 1985-86, 2001-03, Chicago Bears 2004, San Francisco 49ers 2005-2010, joined Panthers in 2011.

Al Holcomb, linebackers; born October 22, 1970, Queens, N.Y. Attended West Virginia. No college or pro playing experience. College coach: Temple 1995-96, Colby College 1997, Bloomsburg 1998-2003, Kutztown 2004-05, Lafayette 2006-08. Pro coach: New York Giants 2009-2012, joined Panthers in 2013.

Joe Kenn, strength and conditioning; born October 13, 1966, Far Rockaway, N.Y. Guard Wake Forest 1987-88. No pro playing experience. College coach: Wake Forest 1991 (winter/spring), Boise State 1991-98, Utah 1999-2000, Arizona State 2001-07, Louisville 2008-09. Pro coach: Joined Panthers in 2011.

John Matsko, offensive line; born February 2, 1951, Cleveland, Ohio. Fullback Kent State 1970-72. No pro playing experience. College coach: Miami (Ohio) 1974-75, 1977, North Carolina 1978-1984, Navy 1985, Arizona 1986, Southern California 1987-1991. Pro coach: Phoenix Cardinals 1992-93, New Orleans Saints 1994-96, New York Giants 1997-98, St. Louis Rams 1999-2005, Kansas City Chiefs 2006-07, Baltimore Ravens 2008-2010, joined Panthers in 2011.

Sean McDermott, defensive coordinator; born March 21, 1974, Omaha, Neb. Safety William & Mary 1994-97. No pro playing experience. College coach: William & Mary 1998. Pro coach: Philadelphia Eagles 1999-2010, joined Panthers in 2011.

Sam Mills III, asst. defensive line; born May 20, 1978, Long Branch, N.J. Defensive back Montclair State 1997-1999. No pro playing experience. Pro coach: Joined Panthers in 2005.

Ricky Proehl, wide receivers; born March

7, 1968, Bronx, N.Y. Wide receiver Wake Forest 1986-89. Pro wide receiver Phoenix/Arizona Cardinals 1990-94, Seattle Seahawks 1995-96, Chicago Bears 1997, St. Louis Rams 1998-2002, Carolina Panthers 2003-05, Indianapolis Colts 2006. Pro coach: Joined Panthers in 2011.

Richard Rogers, special teams coordinator; born October 28, 1961, St. Louis, Mo. Linebacker California 1980-83. No pro playing experience. College coach: Diablo Valley (Calif.) C.C. 1989-94, San Jose State, 1995-1996, Portland State 1997-2000, New Mexico State 2001-2004, Holy Cross 2005-2011. Pro coach: Joined Panthers in 2012.

Mike Shula, offensive coordinator; born June 3, 1965, Baltimore, Md. Quarterback Alabama 1984-86. Pro quarterback Tampa Bay Buccaneers 1987. College coach: Alabama 2003-06 (head coach). Pro coach: Tampa Bay Buccaneers 1988-1990, 1996-99, Miami Dolphins 1991-92, 2000-02, Chicago Bears 1993-95, Jacksonville Jaguars 2007-2010, joined Panthers in 2011.

Jim Skipper, running backs; born January 23, 1949, Breaux Bridge, La. Defensive back Whittier College 1971-72. No pro playing experience. College coach: Cal Poly-Pomona 1974-76, San Jose State 1977-78, Pacific 1979, Oregon 1980-82. Pro coach: Philadelphia/Baltimore Stars (USFL) 1983-85, New Orleans Saints 1986-1995, Arizona Cardinals 1996, New York Giants 1997-2000, San Francisco Demons (XFL) 2001 (head coach), Carolina Panthers 2002-2010, Tennessee Titans 2011-12, re-joined Panthers in 2013.

Lance Taylor, asst. wide receivers; born July 17, 1981, Mobile, Ala. Wide receiver Alabama 2000-2003. No pro playing experience. College coach: Alabama 2008, Appalachian State 2009. Pro coach: New York Jets 2010-12, joined Panthers in 2013.

Eric Washington, defensive line; born October 29, 1969, Shreveport, La. Tight end Grambling State 1989-1990. No pro playing experience. College coach: Texas A&M 1997, Ohio 2001-03, Northwestern 2004-07. Pro coach: Chicago Bears 2008-2010, joined Panthers in 2011.

Steve Wilks, secondary/passing defense coordinator; born August 8, 1969, Charlotte, N.C. Defensive back Appalachian State 1987-1991. No pro playing experience. College coach: Johnson C. Smith 1995-96, Savannah State 1997-1999, Illinois State 2000, Appalachian State 2001, East Tennessee State 2002, Bowling Green State 2003, Notre Dame 2004, Washington 2005. Pro coach: Chicago Bears 2006-2008, San Diego Chargers 2009-2011, joined Panthers in 2012.

**National Football Conference
North Division
Team Colors:** Navy Blue, Orange, and White
**Halas Hall at Conway Park
1920 Football Drive
Lake Forest, Illinois 60045
Telephone:** (847) 295-6600

**2013 SCHEDULE
PRESEASON**
Aug. 9   at Carolina..........................7:00
Aug. 15 **San Diego** 7:00
Aug. 23 at Oakland 9:00
Aug. 29 **Cleveland** 7:00

REGULAR SEASON
Sep. 8   **Cincinnati** 12:00
Sep. 15 **Minnesota** 12:00
Sep. 22 at Pittsburgh 7:30
Sep. 29 at Detroit 12:00
Oct. 6   **New Orleans** 12:00
Oct. 10 **New York Giants** (Thurs)....7:25
Oct. 20 at Washington 12:00
Oct. 27 BYE
Nov. 4   at Green Bay (Mon) 7:40
Nov. 10 **Detroit** 12:00
Nov. 17 **Baltimore** 12:00
Nov. 24 at St. Louis 12:00
Dec. 1   at Minnesota 12:00
Dec. 9   **Dallas** (Mon)....................7:40
Dec. 15 at Cleveland 12:00
Dec. 22 at Philadelphia 12:00
Dec. 29 **Green Bay** 12:00
All times CT

Stadium: Soldier Field
            (opened in 1924)
            •Capacity: 61,500
            1410 S. Museum Campus Dr.
            Chicago, Illinois 60605
Playing Surface: Natural Grass
Training Camp: Olivet-Nazarene Univ.
            Bourbonnais, Illinois
            60901

SOLDIER FIELD

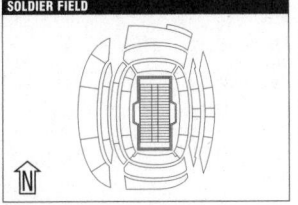

CLUB OFFICIALS
Chairman: George H. McCaskey
Secretary: Virginia H. McCaskey
President and CEO: Ted Phillips
General Manager: Phil Emery
Senior Director of Special Projects: Pat McCaskey
Senior Director of Business Development & Alumni Relations: Brian McCaskey
Vice President of Business Administration: John Bostrom
Vice President of Communications: Scott Hagel
Vice President of Sales & Marketing: Chris Hibbs
Vice President of Football Administration and General Counsel: Cliff Stein
Chief Financial Officer & Treasurer: Karen Murphy
Senior Director of Ticket Operations: Lee Twarling
Director of Player Development: Isaiah Harris
Director of Video Services: Dave Hendrickson
Assistant Video Director: Dean Pope
College Video Coordinator: Dan Tuohy
Video Assistant: Jack Dowling
Head Athletic Trainer: Chris Hanks
Assistant Head Athletic Trainer/Director of Rehabilitation: Bobby Slater
Head Equipment Manager: Tony Medlin
Assistant Equipment Managers: Carl Piekarski, Joseph Shaw, Travis Knoch
Director of Pro Scouting: Kevin Turks
Director of College Scouting: Marty Barrett
Associate Director of Pro Scouting: Dwayne Joseph
Executive Scout/Asst. Director of College Scouting: Jeff Shiver
Senior National Scout: Mark Sadowski
National Scout: Rex Hogan
Area Scouts: Breck Ackley, Jay Muraco, Francis Saint-Paul, Sam Summerville, Zach Truty
Scout/Player Personnel: Ryan Kessenich, David Williams
Scouting Assistants: Bobby Macedo, Andre Odom
Director of Community Relations: Caroline Guip Schrenker
Director of Broadcasting & Scoreboard Operations: Greg Miller
Media Services Manager: Jim Christman
Media Relations Coordinator: Mike Corbo
Media Relations Assistant: Jared Ellerson

COACHING HISTORY
**Decatur Staleys 1920,
Chicago Staleys 1921
(739-544-42)**
Records include postseason games
1920-29	George Halas	84-31-19
1930-32	Ralph Jones	24-10-7
1933-1942	George Halas*	88-24-4
1942-45	Hunk Anderson-Luke Johnsos**	24-12-2
1946-1955	George Halas	76-43-2
1956-57	John (Paddy) Driscoll	14-10-1
1958-1967	George Halas	76-53-6
1968-1971	Jim Dooley	20-36-0
1972-74	Abe Gibron	11-30-1
1975-77	Jack Pardee	20-23-0
1978-1981	Neill Armstrong	30-35-0
1982-1992	Mike Ditka	112-68-0
1993-98	Dave Wannstedt	41-57-0
1999-2003	Dick Jauron	35-46-0
2004-2012	Lovie Smith	.'.............84-66-0

*Retired after five games to enter U.S. Navy
**Co-coaches

PAID ATTENDANCE
Home 483,950   Away 532,526
Total 1,016,476
Single-game home record,
    66,900 (9/5/93)
Single-season home record, 527,769
    (1999)

2013 DRAFT CHOICES
Round	Name	Pos.	College
1	Kyle Long	G	Oregon
2	Jon Bostic	LB	Florida
4	Khaseem Greene	LB	Rutgers
5	Jordan Mills	T	Louisiana Tech
6	Cornelius Washington	DE	Georgia
7	Marquess Wilson	WR	Washington St.

2012 TEAM RECORD
PRESEASON (3-1)

Date	Result		Opponent
08/09	L	3-31	Denver
08/18	W	33-31	Washington
08/24	W	20-17	at New York Giants
08/30	W	28-20	at Cleveland

REGULAR SEASON (10-6)

Date	Result		Opponent
09/09	W	41-21	Indianapolis
09/13	L	10-23	at Green Bay
09/23	W	23-6	St. Louis
10/01	W	34-18	at Dallas
10/07	W	41-3	at Jacksonville
10/22	W	13-7	Detroit
10/28	W	23-22	Carolina
11/04	W	51-20	at Tennessee
11/11	L	6-13	Houston
11/19	L	7-32	at San Francisco
11/25	W	28-10	Minnesota
12/02	L	17-23	Seattle (OT)
12/09	L	14-21	at Minnesota
12/16	L	13-21	Green Bay
12/23	W	28-13	at Arizona
12/30	W	26-24	at Detroit

(OT) Overtime

SCORE BY PERIODS

Bears	92	93	79	111	0	—	375
Opponents	48	97	54	72	6	—	277

2012 TEAM STATISTICS

	Bears	Opp.
Total First Downs	292	286
Rushing	99	75
Passing	163	186
Penalty	30	25
3rd Down: Made/Att	80/219	78/220
3rd Down Pct.	36.5	35.5
4th Down: Made/Att	5/13	10/16
4th Down Pct.	38.5	62.5
Possession Avg.	31:33	28:27
Total Net Yards	4969	5050
Avg. Per Game	310.6	315.6
Total Plays	999	1021
Avg. Per Play	5.0	4.9
Net Yards Rushing	1970	1627
Avg. Per Game	123.1	101.7
Total Rushes	470	388
Net Yards Passing	2999	3423
Avg. Per Game	187.4	213.9
Sacked/Yards Lost	44/299	41/289
Gross Yards	3298	3712
Att./Completions	485/287	592/350
Completion Pct.	59.2	59.1
Had Intercepted	16	24
Punts/Average	81/42.0	89/43.6
Net Punting Avg.	81/39.4	89/38.8
Penalties/Yards	102/811	78/704
Fumbles/Ball Lost	20/8	35/20
Touchdowns	42	29
Rushing	11	6
Passing	21	19
Returns	10	4

2012 INDIVIDUAL STATISTICS

PASSING	Att.	Comp.	Yds.	Pct.	TD	Int.	Tkld.	Rate
Cutler	434	255	3033	58.8	19	14	38/250	81.3
Campbell	51	32	265	62.7	2	2	6/49	72.8
Bears	485	287	3298	59.2	21	16	44/299	80.4
Opponents	592	350	3712	59.1	19	24	41/289	71.3

SCORING	TD R	TD P	TD Rt	PAT	FG	Saf	PTS
Gould	0	0	0	33/33	21/25	0	96
Marshall	0	11	0	0/0	0/0	0	66
Forte	5	1	0	0/0	0/0	0	36
Bush	5	0	0	0/0	0/0	0	30
Mare	0	0	0	7/7	6/8	0	25
Jeffery	0	3	0	0/0	0/0	0	18
Tillman	0	0	3	0/0	0/0	0	18
Bennett	0	2	0	0/0	0/0	0	12
Briggs	0	0	2	0/0	0/0	0	12
Davis	0	2	0	0/0	0/0	0	12
Allen	1	0	0	0/0	0/0	0	6
Bowman	0	0	1	0/0	0/0	0	6
Hester	0	1	0	0/0	0/0	0	6
Jennings	0	0	1	0/0	0/0	0	6
Spaeth	0	1	0	0/0	0/0	0	6
Urlacher	0	0	1	0/0	0/0	0	6
Wootton	0	0	1	0/0	0/0	0	6
Wright	0	0	1	0/0	0/0	0	6
Podlesh	0	0	0	0/0	0/0	0	2
Bears	11	21	10	40/40	27/33	0	375
Opponents	6	19	4	26/26	23/27	2	277

2-Pt Conversions: Podlesh, Bears 1-2, Opponents 2-2

RUSHING	No.	Yds	Avg	LG	TD
Forte	248	1094	4.4	46	5
Bush	114	411	3.6	20	5
Cutler	41	233	5.7	24	0
Allen	27	124	4.6	46t	1
Bell	29	76	2.6	18	0
Campbell	7	28	4.0	13	0
Hester	3	6	2.0	8	0
Marshall	1	-2	-2.0	-2	0
Bears	470	1970	4.2	46t	11
Opponents	388	1627	4.2	80t	6

RECEIVING	No.	Yds	Avg	LG	TD
Marshall	118	1508	12.8	56	11
Forte	44	340	7.7	47	1
Bennett	29	375	12.9	60t	2
Jeffery	24	367	15.3	55	3
Hester	23	242	10.5	39	1
Davis	19	229	12.1	25	2
Bush	9	83	9.2	18	0
Spaeth	6	28	4.7	13t	1
Adams	4	40	10.0	17	0
Rodriguez	4	21	5.3	11	0
Weems	2	27	13.5	18	0
Allen	2	16	8.0	15	0
Bell	1	11	11.0	11	0
Sanzenbacher	1	7	7.0	7	0
Louis	1	4	4.0	4	0
Bears	287	3298	11.5	60t	21
Opponents	350	3712	10.6	62	19

INTERCEPTIONS	No.	Yds	Avg	LG	TD
Jennings	9	105	11.7	31	1
Wright	4	45	11.3	45t	1
Tillman	3	71	23.7	36t	3
Briggs	2	110	55.0	74t	2
Conte	2	70	35.0	35	0
Moore	2	2	1.0	2	0
Urlacher	1	46	46.0	46t	1
Hayden	1	39	39.0	39	0
Bears	24	488	20.3	74t	8
Opponents	16	241	15.1	56t	2

PUNTING	No.	Yds.	Avg.	In 20	LG
Podlesh	81	3399	42	34	64
Bears	81	3399	42	34	64
Opponents	89	3883	43.6	33	65

PUNT RETURNS	Ret	FC	Yds	Avg	LG	TD
Hester	40	6	331	8.3	44	0
Bennett	1	1	2	2.0	2	0
Bowman	1	0	0	0.0	0	0
Moore	1	0	0	0.0	0	0
Weems	1	1	0	0.0	0	0
Bears	44	8	333	7.6	44	0
Opponents	25	25	84	3.4	17	0

KICKOFF RETURNS	No.	Yds	Avg	LG	TD
Hester	24	621	25.9	40	0
Weems	13	231	17.8	27	0
Adams	3	38	12.7	15	0
Bennett	2	24	12.0	18	0
Allen	2	10	5.0	7	0
Wootton	2	0	0.0	0	0
Steltz	1	5	5.0	5	0
Bears	47	929	19.8	40	0
Opponents	37	767	20.7	38	0

FIELD GOALS	1-19	20-29	30-39	40-49	50+
Gould	0/0	7/7	5/7	7/9	2/2
Mare	0/0	2/3	3/3	1/2	0/0
Bears	0/0	9/10	8/10	8/11	2/2
Opponents	0/0	2/2	11/13	8/10	2/2

SACKS	No.
Peppers	11.5
Idonije	7.5
Wootton	7.0
Melton	6.0
McClellin	2.5
Paea	2.5
Briggs	1.5
Roach	1.5
Okoye	1.0
Bears	41.0
Opponents	44.0

RECORD HOLDERS
INDIVIDUAL RECORDS—CAREER

Category	Name	Performance
Rushing (Yds.)	Walter Payton, 1975-1987	16,726
Passing (Yds.)	Sid Luckman, 1939-1950	14,686
Passing (TDs)	Sid Luckman, 1939-1950	137
Receiving (No.)	Walter Payton, 1975-1987	492
Receiving (Yds.)	Johnny Morris, 1958-1967	5,059
Interceptions	Gary Fencik, 1976-1987	38
Punting (Avg.)	George Gulyanics, 1947-1952	44.5
Punt Return (Avg.)	George McAfee, 1940-1950	**12.8
Kickoff Return (Avg.)	Gale Sayers, 1965-1971	**30.6
Field Goals	Kevin Butler, 1985-1995	243
Touchdowns (Tot.)	Walter Payton, 1975-1987	125
Points	Kevin Butler, 1985-1995	1,116
*Sacks	Richard Dent, 1983-1993, 1995	124.5

INDIVIDUAL RECORDS—SINGLE SEASON

Category	Name	Performance
Rushing (Yds.)	Walter Payton, 1977	1,852
Passing (Yds.)	Erik Kramer, 1995	3,838
Passing (TDs)	Erik Kramer, 1995	29
Receiving (No.)	Brandon Marshall, 2012	118
Receiving (Yds.)	Brandon Marshall, 2012	1,508
Interceptions	Mark Carrier, 1990	10
Punting (Avg.)	Bobby Joe Green, 1963	46.5
Punt Return (Avg.)	Devin Hester, 2010	17.1
Kickoff Return (Avg.)	Gale Sayers, 1967	37.7
Field Goals	Robbie Gould, 2006	32
Touchdowns (Tot.)	Gale Sayers, 1965	22
Points	Kevin Butler, 1985	144
*Sacks	Richard Dent, 1984	17.5

INDIVIDUAL RECORDS—SINGLE GAME

Category	Name	Performance
Rushing (Yds.)	Walter Payton, 11-20-77	275
Passing (Yds.)	Johnny Lujack, 12-11-49	468
Passing (TDs)	Sid Luckman, 11-14-43	**7
Receiving (No.)	Jim Keane, 10-23-49	14
Receiving (Yds.)	Harlon Hill, 10-31-54	214
Interceptions	Many times	3
	Last time by Mark Carrier, 12-9-90	
Field Goals	Roger LeClerc, 12-3-61	5
	Mac Percival, 10-20-68	5
Touchdowns (Tot.)	Gale Sayers, 12-12-65	**6
Points	Gale Sayers, 12-12-65	36
*Sacks	Richard Dent, 11-4-84, 12-27-87	4.5

*Sacks became an official statistic in 1982.
**NFL Record

2013 VETERAN ROSTER

No.	Name	Pos.	Ht.	Wt.	Birthdate	NFL Exp.	College	Hometown	How Acq.	'12 Games/ Starts
86	Adams, Kyle	TE	6-4	255	1/19/88	3	Purdue	Austin, Texas	FA-'11	15/2
25	Allen, Armando	RB	5-8	190	4/30/89	2	Notre Dame	Opa Locka, Fla.	FA-'11	15/0
50	Anderson, James	LB	6-2	235	9/26/83	8	Virginia Tech	Roanoke Rapids, N.C.	FA-'13	12/12*
32	#Bell, Kahlil	RB	5-11	219	12/10/86	5	UCLA	San Anselmo, Calif.	FA-'09	4/0
80	Bennett, Earl	WR	6-0	206	3/23/87	6	Vanderbilt	Birmingham, Ala.	D3a-'08	12/4
83	Bennett, Martellus	TE	6-6	265	1/10/87	6	Texas A&M	Alief, Texas	UFA(NYG)-'13	16/16*
38	Bowman, Zackary	CB	6-1	196	11/18/84	6	Nebraska	Anchorage, Alaska	D5a-'08	11/0
55	Briggs, Lance	LB	6-1	244	11/12/80	11	Arizona	Sacramento, Calif.	D3-'03	16/16
62	Britton, Eben	G/T	6-6	308	10/14/87	5	Arizona	Burbank, Calif.	UFA(Jax)-'13	11/5*
78	Brown, James	T/G	6-4	306	11/30/88	2	Troy	Magnolia, Miss.	FA-'12	5/3
29	Bush, Michael	RB	6-1	245	6/16/84	7	Louisville	Louisville, Ky.	UFA(Oak)-'12	13/1
74	Bushrod, Jermon	T	6-5	320	8/19/84	7	Towson	Fredericksburg, Va.	UFA(NO)-'13	16/16*
72	Carimi, Gabe	G/T	6-7	316	6/13/88	3	Wisconsin	Cottage Grove, Wisc.	D1-'11	16/14
93	Collins, Nate	DT	6-2	296	12/14/87	4	Virginia	White Plains, N.Y.	UFA(Jax)-'12	9/0
47	Conte, Chris	S	6-2	203	2/23/89	3	California	Los Angeles, Calif.	D3-'11	15/15
52	Costanzo, Blake	LB	6-1	235	4/14/84	7	Lafayette	Franklin Lakes, N.J.	UFA(SF)-'12	14/1
6	Cutler, Jay	QB	6-3	220	4/29/83	8	Vanderbilt	Santa Claus, Ind.	T(Den)-'09	15/15
88	Eldridge, Brody	TE	6-5	265	3/31/87	3	Oklahoma	La Cygne, Kan.	FA-'12	0*
75	Fluellen, Andre	DT	6-2	302	3/7/85	6	Florida State	Cartersville, Ga.	UFA(Det)-'13	5/1*
22	Forté, Matt	RB	6-2	218	12/10/85	6	Tulane	Slidell, La.	D2-'08	15/15
63	Garza, Roberto	C/G	6-2	310	3/26/79	13	Texas A&M-Kingsville	Rio Hondo, Texas	UFA(Atl)-'05	16/16
9	Gould, Robbie	K	6-0	185	12/30/81	9	Penn State	Lock Haven, Pa.	FA-'05	13/0
35	Hardin, Brandon	S	6-3	217	10/30/89	2	Oregon State	Kealakekua, Hawaii	D3-'12	0*
24	Hayden, Kelvin	CB	6-0	195	7/23/83	9	Illinois	Chicago, Ill.	UFA(Atl)-'12	16/2
23	Hester, Devin	KR/PR	5-11	190	11/4/82	8	Miami	Riviera Beach, Fla.	D2b-'06	15/5
71	#Idonije, Israel	DL	6-6	275	11/17/80	10	Manitoba	Lagos, Nigeria	FA-'03	16/11
79	Irvin, Corvey	DT	6-2	295	5/3/85	3	Georgia	Augusta, Ga.	FA-'13	12/0*
17	Jeffery, Alshon	WR	6-3	216	2/14/90	2	South Carolina	St. Matthews, S.C.	D2-'12	10/6
26	Jennings, Tim	CB	5-8	185	12/24/83	8	Georgia	Orangeburg, S.C.	UFA(Ind)-'10	14/14
87	Maneri, Steve	TE	6-7	280	3/20/88	3	Temple	Saddle Brook, N.J.	FA-'13	13/8*
65	Mannelly, Patrick	LS	6-5	265	4/18/75	16	Duke	Atlanta, Ga.	D6b-'98	16/0
10	#Mare, Olindo	K	5-11	185	6/6/73	16	Syracuse	Hollywood, Fla.	FA-'12	3/0
15	Marshall, Brandon	WR	6-4	230	3/23/84	8	Central Florida	Pittsburgh, Pa.	T(Mia)-'12	16/16
94	McBride, Turk	DE	6-2	278	5/30/85	7	Tennessee	Camden, N.J.	UFA(NO)-'13	7/0*
99	McClellin, Shea	DE	6-3	260	8/1/89	2	Boise State	Caldwell, Idaho	D1-'12	14/0
12	McCown, Josh	QB	6-4	213	7/4/79	11	Sam Houston State	Jacksonville, Texas	FA-'11	0*
27	McManis, Sherrick	CB	6-1	193	12/19/87	4	Northwestern	Peoria, Ill.	T(Hou)-'12	12/0
69	Melton, Henry	DT	6-3	295	10/11/86	5	Texas	Grapevine, Texas	D4a-'09	14/14
85	Miller, Gabe	TE	6-3	257	12/5/87	2	Oregon State	Lake Oswego, Ore.	FA-'12	0*
67	Moore, Kyle	DE	6-6	263	10/25/86	5	Southern California	Kathleen, Ga.	UFA(Buff)-'13	12/7*
46	Nelson, Tom	S	5-11	200	12/4/86	3	Illinois State	Arlington Heights, Ill.	FA-'13	0*
43	#Nolan, Troy	S	6-0	200	9/7/86	5	Arizona State	Los Angeles, Calif.	FA-'12	8/1*
91	#Okoye, Amobi	DT	6-2	292	6/10/87	7	Louisville	Huntsville, Ala.	FA-'12	9/0
84	Onobun, Fendi	TE	6-6	260	11/17/86	3	Houston	Houston, Texas	FA-'13	0*
95	Ozougwu, Cheta	DE	6-2	255	11/18/88	2	Rice	Houston, Texas	FA-'12	2/0
92	Paea, Stephen	DT	6-1	300	5/11/88	3	Oregon State	Vava'u, Tonga	D2-'11	15/14
90	Peppers, Julius	DE	6-7	287	1/18/80	12	North Carolina	Bailey, N.C.	UFA(Car)-'10	16/16
8	Podlesh, Adam	P	5-11	200	8/11/83	7	Maryland	Pittsford, N.Y.	UFA(Jax)-'11	16/0
48	Rodriguez, Evan	FB	6-2	239	9/21/88	2	Temple	North Bergen, N.J.	D4-'12	12/5
79	Scott, Jonathan	T	6-6	318	1/10/83	7	Texas	Dallas, Texas	FA-'12	12/7
68	Slauson, Matt	G	6-5	315	2/18/86	5	Nebraska	Colorado Springs, Colo.	UFA(NYJ)-'13	16/16*
20	Steltz, Craig	S	6-1	210	5/7/86	6	Louisiana State	Metairie, La.	D4-'08	13/0
97	Thomas, J.T.	LB	6-1	236	8/15/88	3	West Virginia	Ft. Lauderdale, Fla.	D6-'11	16/0
33	Tillman, Charles	CB	6-2	198	2/23/81	11	Louisiana-Lafayette	Copperas Cove, Texas	D2-'03	16/16
59	Trahan, Patrick	LB	6-2	236	11/7/86	2	Mississippi	New Orleans, La.	FA-'11	1/0
45	Unga, Harvey	RB	6-0	237	1/18/87	2	Brigham Young	Provo, Utah	S7-'10	0*
54	#Urlacher, Brian	LB	6-4	258	5/25/78	14	New Mexico	Lovington, N.M.	D1-'00	12/12
37	Walters, Anthony	S	6-1	207	9/19/88	3	Delaware	Philadelphia, Pa.	FA-'11	16/1
73	Webb, J'Marcus	T	6-7	333	8/8/88	4	West Texas A&M	Mesquite, Texas	D7-'10	16/16
14	Weems, Eric	WR/KR	5-9	195	7/4/85	7	Bethune-Cookman	Daytona Beach, Fla.	UFA(Atl)-'12	16/1
58	Williams, D.J.	LB	6-1	242	7/20/82	10	Miami	Pittsburg, Calif.	FA-'13	7/1*
70	Williams, Edwin	G/C	6-3	315	12/10/86	4	Maryland	Washington, D.C.	FA-'10	6/2
98	Wootton, Corey	DE	6-6	270	6/22/87	4	Northwestern	Rutherford, N.J.	D4-'10	16/7
21	Wright, Major	S	5-11	204	7/1/88	4	Florida	Miramar, Fla.	D3-'10	16/16
36	Zbikowski, Tom	S	5-11	200	5/22/85	6	Notre Dame	Arlington Heights, Ill.	FA-'13	11/11*

* Anderson played 12 games with Carolina in '12; Bennett played 16 games with the New York Giants; Britton played 11 games with Jacksonville; Bushrod played 16 games with New Orleans; Eldridge inactive 4 games; Fluellen played 3 games with Detroit and 2 with Miami; Hardin missed '12 season because of injury; Irvin played 12 games with Tampa Bay; Maneri played 13 games with Kansas City; McBride played seven games with New Orleans; McCown inactive six games, did not play 1 game; Miller last active with Kansas City in '11; Moore played 12 games with Buffalo; Nelson last active with Philadelphia in '11; Nolan played three games with Miami, four games with Houston, and one game with Chicago; Onobun last active with Jacksonville in '11; Slauson played 16 games with the New York Jets; Unga did not play in one game; D.J. Williams played seven games with Denver; Zbikowski played 16 games with Indianapolis.

\# Unrestricted Free Agent; subject to developments.

Players lost through free agency (7): QB Jason Campbell (Cle; 6 games in '12), LB Geno Hayes (Jax; 15), G Lance Louis (Mia; 11), DB D.J. Moore (Car; 13), G Chilo Rachal (Ariz; 9), OLB Nick Roach (Oak; 16), G Chris Spencer (Tenn; 10).

Also played with Bears in '12—LB Dom DiCicco (4 games), WR Dane Sanzenbacher (5), T Chris Williams (3).

FIRST-YEAR ROSTER

Name	Pos.	Ht.	Wt.	Birthdate	College	Hometown	How Acq.
Anderson, Joe (1)	WR	6-1	196	11/21/88	Texas Southern	Texarkana, Texas	FA-'12
Blanchard, Matt (1)	QB	6-3	225	3/21/89	Wisconsin-Whitewater	Lake Zurich, Ill.	FA-'12
Boggs, Taylor (1)	C	6-3	285	2/20/87	Humboldt State	Pasadena, Calif.	FA
Bostic, Jonathan	LB	6-1	245	5/5/91	Florida	Wellington, Fla.	D2
Brandon, Cory (1)	T	6-7	324	10/5/87	Oklahoma	Corsicana, Texas	FA-'12
Dennis, Derek (1)	OL	6-3	315	7/16/88	Temple	Queens, N.Y.	FA-'12
Fields, Demetrius	WR	6-0	210	7/7/90	Northwestern	Dallas, Texas	FA
Ford, Michael	RB	5-10	216	5/27/90	Louisiana State	Leesville, La.	FA
Franklin, Jerry (1)	LB	6-1	245	1/10/88	Arkansas	Marion, Ark.	FA-'12
Frey, Isaiah (1)	CB	6-0	190	4/6/90	Nevada	Olivehurst, Calif.	FA-'12
Golden, Brittan (1)	WR	5-11	186	7/20/88	West Texas A&M	Denver City, Texas	FA-'12
Greene, Khaseem	LB	6-1	241	2/4/89	Rutgers	Elizabeth, N.J.	D4
Hurst, Demontre	CB	5-10	183	3/24/91	Oklahoma	Lancaster, Texas	FA
Jones, Maurice	CB	5-9	193	7/2/89	Temple	Belleville, N.J.	FA
Lenz, Josh	WR	6-0	194	9/22/90	Iowa State	Dubuque, Iowa	FA
Lonergan, P.J.	C	6-4	305	7/30/90	Louisiana State	New Orleans, La.	FA
Long, Kyle	G	6-6	313	12/5/88	Oregon	Ivy, Va.	D1
Mills, Jordan	T	6-5	316	12/24/90	Louisiana Tech	Thibodaux, La.	D5
Minter, Zach	DT	6-1	297	11/6/90	Montana State	Glendale, Ariz.	FA
Moss, Dale (1)	WR	6-3	213	9/24/88	South Dakota State	Brandon, S.D.	FA-'12
Quarles, Cyhl (1)	S	6-3	212	4/6/89	Wake Forest	Tucker, Ga.	FA
Rucker, Marcus	WR	6-4	185	5/19/90	Memphis	Memphis, Tenn.	FA
Russell, Brent	DT	6-2	300	8/16/89	Georgia Southern	Comer, Ga.	FA
Signor, Austin	K	6-4	230	6/15/87	Eastern Illinois	Urbandale, Iowa	FA
Toliver, Terrence (1)	WR	6-5	204	5/7/88	Louisiana State	Hempstead, Texas	FA
Tupou, Christian	DT	6-2	290	5/7/89	Southern California	Sacramento, Calif.	FA
Washington, Cornelius	DE	6-4	265	9/10/89	Georgia	Hephzibah, Ga.	D6
Way, Tress	P	6-1	215	4/18/90	Oklahoma	Tulsa, Okla.	FA
Whiteside, Aston (1)	DE	6-2	255	5/19/89	Abilene Christian	Vernon, Texas	FA-'12
Wilson, C.J.	CB	5-11	187	11/18/89	North Carolina State	Lincolnton, N.C.	FA
Wilson, Lawrence (1)	LB	6-1	229	11/16/87	Connecticut	Tuscaloosa, Ala.	FA
Wilson, Marquess	WR	6-4	184	9/14/92	Washington State	Hephzibah, Ga.	D7

The term NFL Rookie is defined as a player who is in his first season of professional football and has not been on the roster of another professional football team for any regular-season or postseason games. A Rookie is designated by an "R" on NFL rosters. Players who have been active in another professional football league or players who have NFL experience, including either preseason training camp or being on an Active List or Inactive List, or on Reserve/Injured or Reserve/Physically Unable to Perform for fewer than six regular-season games, are termed NFL First-Year Players. An NFL First-Year Player is designated by a "1" on NFL rosters. Thereafter, a player is credited with an additional year of experience for each season in which he accumulates six games on the Active List or Inactive List, or on Reserve/Injured or Reserve/Physically Unable to Perform.

Log on to www.chicagobears.com for an up-to-date roster.

COACHING STAFF

Head Coach,
Marc Trestman

Pro Career: Named the fourteenth head coach in Chicago Bears history on January 15, 2004. Over the previous five seasons as head coach in the Canadian Football League, Trestman led the Montreal Alouettes to back-to-back Grey Cup championships in 2009 and 2010 and was named the CFL's Coach of the Year in 2009. During his time in Montreal, Trestman compiled a 59-31 (.656) regular season record, which included four East Division titles and a 5-3 (.625) record in the playoffs. Trestman has 17 years of coaching experience in the NFL, including eight as an offensive coordinator and 13 working with quarterbacks. During his time in the NFL, Trestman helped his teams to eight playoff appearances, two conference championship games and a Super Bowl appearance (XXXVII as offensive coordinator of the Raiders). Under Trestman, Raiders quarterback Rich Gannon was named NFL MVP in 2002. Trestman oversaw the NFL's No. 1 scoring offense as offensive coordinator of the San Francisco 49ers in 1995, the No. 2 scoring offense with the Oakland Raiders in 2002 and the No. 3 scoring offense with the 49ers in 1996. Trestman also has NFL coaching experience with the Minnesota Vikings, Cleveland Browns, Detroit Lions, Arizona Cardinals and Miami Dolphins. He was also a consultant to the New Orleans Saints. Collegiately, Trestman has been a part of the coaching staffs of the Miami Hurricanes and North Carolina State. Career record: 0-0.

Background: Quarterback for University of Minnesota and Minnesota State University Moorhead. He was a college coach at Miami (1981-84) and North Carolina State (2005-06).

Personal: Born January 15, 1956 in Minneapolis, Minnesota. Trestman and wife, Cindy, have two daughters-Sarahanne and Chloe.

ASSISTANT COACHES

Jim Arthur, strength and conditioning assistant; born July 12, 1978, Cheshire, Conn. Attended Springfield (Mass.) College. No college or pro playing experience. College coach: Springfield (Mass.) College 2000, Louisiana Tech 2001, Boston College 2002. Pro coach: Joined Bears in 2005.

Andy Bischoff, tight ends; born December 8, 1972, Fargo, N.D. Offensive line South Dakota 1989-1993. No pro playing experience. Pro coach: Montreal Alouettes (CFL) 2008-2012, joined Bears in 2013.

Matt Cavanaugh, quarterbacks; born October 27, 1956, Youngstown, Ohio. Quarterback Pittsburgh 1974-77. Pro quarterback New England Patriots 1978-1982, San Francisco 49ers 1983-85, Philadelphia Eagles 1986-89, New York

Giants 1990-91. College coach: Pittsburgh 1991-93, 2005-08. Pro coach: Arizona Cardinals 1994-95, San Francisco 49ers 1996, Chicago Bears 1997-98, Baltimore Ravens 1999-2004, New York Jets 2009-2012, joined Bears in 2013.

Mike Clark, strength and conditioning; born August 22, 1954, Wichita, Kan. Center Ottawa 1973-76. No pro playing experience. College coach: Kansas 1977-78, 1982, Wyoming 1981, Oregon 1983-87, Southern California 1988-89, Texas A&M 1990-2003. Pro coach: Seattle Seahawks 2004-09, Kansas City Chiefs 2010-12, joined Bears in 2013.

Joe DeCamillis, asst. head coach/special teams coordinator; born June 29, 1965, Arvada, Colo. Attended Wyoming. No college or pro playing experience. Pro coach: Denver Broncos 1988-1992, New York Giants 1993-96, Atlanta Falcons 1997-2006, Jacksonville Jaguars 2007-08, Dallas Cowboys 2009-2012, joined Bears in 2013.

Sean Desai, defensive quality control; born April 21, 1983, Shelton, Conn. Attended Boston University. No college or pro playing experience. College coach: Temple 2007-2010, Miami, 2011, Boston College 2012. Pro coach: Joined Bears in 2013.

Mike Groh, wide receivers; born December 19, 1971, Charlottesville, Va. Quarterback Virginia, 1991-95. Pro Rhein Fire (WLAF) 1997. College coach: Virginia 2001-08, Alabama 2009, 2011-12, Louisville 2010. Pro coach: New York Jets 2000, joined Bears in 2013.

Chris Harris, defensive quality control; born August 6, 1982, Little Rock, Ark. Safety Louisiana Monroe 2001-04. Pro safety Chicago Bears 2005-06, 2010-11, Carolina Panthers 2007-09, Detroit Lions 2011, Jacksonville Jaguars 2012. Pro coach: Joined Bears in 2013.

Jon Hoke, defensive backs; born January 24, 1957, Kettering, Ohio. Defensive back Ball State 1976-79. Pro defensive back Chicago Bears 1980. College coach: Bowling Green 1983-86, San Diego State 1987-88, Kent State 1989-1993, Missouri 1994-98, Florida 1999-2001. Pro coach: Houston Texans 2002-08, joined Bears in 2009.

Aaron Kromer, offensive coordinator/offensive line; born April 30, 1967, Sandusky, Ohio. Tackle Miami (Ohio) 1986-89. No pro playing experience. College coach: Miami (Ohio) 1990-98, Northwestern 1999-2000. Pro coach: Oakland Raiders 2001-04, Tampa Bay Buccaneers 2005-07, New Orleans Saints 2008-2012 (interim head coach first six games 2012), joined Bears in 2013.

Pat Meyer, asst. offensive line; born April 5, 1972, Youngstown, Ohio. Offensive line Colorado State 1991-94. Offensive line St. Louis Stampede (AFL) 1996. College coach: Memphis 1997-1999, North

Carolina State 2000-06, Colorado State 2008-2011. Pro coach: Montreal Alouettes (CFL) 2012, joined Bears in 2013.

Brendan Nugent, offensive quality control; born February 14, 1983, Port Chester, N.Y. Linebacker Catholic University of America 2001-04. No pro playing experience. College coach: Iowa 2005-06, William & Mary 2007-2011. Pro coach: Montreal Alouettes (CFL) 2012, joined Bears in 2013.

Skip Peete, running backs; born January 30, 1963, Mesa, Ariz. Wide receiver Arizona 1981-82, Kansas 1984-85. Pro wide receiver New York Jets 1987. College coach: Pittsburgh 1988-1992, Michigan State 1993-94, Rutgers 1995, UCLA 1996-97. Pro coach: Oakland Raiders 1998-2006, Dallas Cowboys 2007-2012, joined Bears in 2013.

Mike Phair, defensive line; born November 8, 1969, Mesa, Ariz. Linebacker Mesa (Ariz.) C.C. 1988-89, Arizona State 1990-91. No pro playing experience. College coach: Arizona State 1999-2000, Tiffin University 2001. Pro coach: Seattle Seahawks 2008-2010, joined Bears in 2011.

Michael Sinclair, asst. defensive line; born January 31, 1968, Galveston, Tex. Defensive end Eastern New Mexico 1986-1990. Pro defensive end Seattle Seahawks 1991-2001, Philadelphia Eagles 2002. Pro coach: Hamburg Sea Devils (NFL Europe) 2007-08, Montreal Alouettes (CFL) 2008-2012, joined Bears in 2013.

Dwayne Stukes, asst. special teams; born January 24, 1977, Portsmith, Va. Cornerback/safety Virginia 1996-1999. Pro safety Berlin Thunder (NFL Europe) 2001-2002, Colorado Crush (AFL) 2004. Pro coach: Tampa Bay Buccaneers 2006-2011, joined Bears in 2013.

Tim Tibesar, linebackers; born August 27, 1972, St. Paul, Minn. Linebacker North Dakota 1993-96. No pro playing experience. College coach: Grossmont (Calif.) J.C. 1998, California 1999, Cornell 2000, North Dakota 2001-05, Kansas State 2006-08, Purdue 2012. Pro coach: Montreal Alouettes (CFL) 2009-2011, joined Bears in 2013.

Mel Tucker, asst. head coach/defensive coordinator; born January 4, 1972, Cleveland, Ohio. Defensive back Wisconsin 1992-95. No pro playing experience. College coach: Michigan State 1997-98, Miami (Ohio) 1999, Louisiana State 2000, Ohio State 2001-04. Pro coach: Cleveland Browns 2005-08, Jacksonville Jaguars 2009-12 (interim head coach 2011), joined Bears in 2013.

Carson Walch, offensive quality control; born March 6, 1978, Milwaukee, Wisc. Running back/wide receiver Winona State 1996-99. No pro playing experience. College coach: Dakota State 2003-05, St. Thomas (Minn.) 2006, Winona State 2007-09. Pro coach: Montreal Alouettes (CFL) 2010-12, joined Bears in 2013.

National Football Conference
East Division
Team Colors: Royal Blue, Metallic Silver Blue, and White
Cowboys Center, One Cowboys Parkway
Irving, Texas 75063
Telephone: (972) 556-9900

2013 SCHEDULE
PRESEASON
Aug. 4	vs. Miami, at Canton, OH	7:00
Aug. 9	at Oakland	9:00
Aug. 17	at Arizona	3:30
Aug. 24	**Cincinnati**	7:00
Aug. 29	**Houston**	7:00

REGULAR SEASON
Sep. 8	**New York Giants**	7:30
Sep. 15	at Kansas City	12:00
Sep. 22	**St. Louis**	12:00
Sep. 29	at San Diego	3:25
Oct. 6	**Denver**	3:25
Oct. 13	**Washington**	7:30
Oct. 20	at Philadelphia	12:00
Oct. 27	at Detroit	12:00
Nov. 3	**Minnesota**	12:00
Nov. 10	at New Orleans	7:30
Nov. 17	BYE	
Nov. 24	at New York Giants	3:25
Nov. 28	**Oakland** (Thurs)	3:30
Dec. 9	at Chicago (Mon)	7:40
Dec. 15	**Green Bay**	3:25
Dec. 22	at Washington	12:00
Dec. 29	**Philadelphia**	12:00

*All times CT
Stadium: Cowboys Stadium (opened in 2009)
 •**Capacity:** 80,000 (expandable to 100,000 for special events)
 One Legends Way
 Arlington, Texas 76011
Playing Surface: Sportfield Softtop
Training Camp: Marriott Residence Inn Oxnard, California 93030

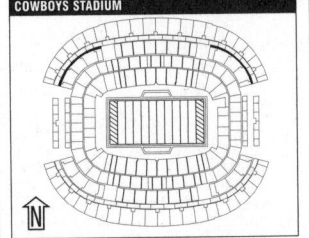

COWBOYS STADIUM

CLUB OFFICIALS
Owner/President/General Manager: Jerry Jones
Chief Operating Officer/Executive Vice President/Director of Player Personnel: Stephen Jones
Executive Vice President/VP of Brand Management/President Charity Foundation: Charlotte Anderson
Executive Vice President/Chief Sales and Marketing Officer: Jerry Jones Jr.
CFO: David Frey
Senior Vice President, Sales and Marketing: Greg McElroy
Vice President Public Relations/ Communications: Rich Dalrymple
Director of Corporate Communications: Brett Daniels
Director of Community Relations and Alumni Affairs: Emily Robbins
Assistant Director of Player Personnel: Tom Ciskowski
Director of Player Development: Bryan Wansley
Director of Information Technology: John Winborn
Director of Broadcasting: Scott Purcel
Internet Director: Derek Eagleton
Director of Ticket Operations: Ann Bihari
Head Athletic Trainer: Jim Maurer
Equipment Manager: Mike McCord
Video Director: Robert Blackwell
Cheerleader Director: Kelli Finglass

COACHING HISTORY
(489-365-6)
Records include postseason games
1960-1988	Tom Landry	270-178-6
1989-1993	Jimmy Johnson	51-37-0
1994-97	Barry Switzer	45-26-0
1998-99	Chan Gailey	18-16-0
2000-02	Dave Campo	15-33-0
2003-06	Bill Parcells	34-32-0
2007-2010	Wade Phillips*	35-24-0
2010-12	Jason Garrett	21-19-0

*Released after eight games in 2010

PAID ATTENDANCE
Home 631,289   Away 561,579
Total 1,192,868
Single-game home record, 105,121 (9/20/09)
Single-season home record, 631,289 (2012)

2013 DRAFT CHOICES
Round	Name	Pos.	College
1	Travis Frederick	C	Wisconsin
2	Gavin Escobar	TE	San Diego St.
3	Terrance Williams	WR	Baylor
	J.J. Wilcox	DB	Georgia Southern
4	B.W. Webb	DB	William & Mary
5	Joseph Randle	RB	Oklahoma St.
6	DeVonte Holloman	LB	South Carolina

2012 TEAM RECORD
PRESEASON (3-1)

Date	Result		Opponent
08/13	W	3-0	at Oakland
08/18	L	20-28	at San Diego
08/25	W	20-19	St. Louis
08/29	W	30-13	Miami

REGULAR SEASON (8-8)

Date	Result		Opponent
09/05	W	24-17	at New York Giants
09/16	L	7-27	at Seattle
09/23	W	16-10	Tampa Bay
10/01	L	18-34	Chicago
10/14	L	29-31	at Baltimore
10/21	W	19-14	at Carolina
10/28	L	24-29	New York Giants
11/04	L	13-19	at Atlanta
11/11	W	38-23	at Philadelphia
11/18	W	23-20	Cleveland (OT)
11/22	L	31-38	Washington
12/02	W	38-33	Philadelphia
12/09	W	20-19	at Cincinnati
12/16	W	27-24	Pittsburgh (OT)
12/23	L	31-34	New Orleans (OT)
12/30	L	18-28	at Washington

(OT) Overtime

SCORE BY PERIODS

Cowboys	36	88	84	162	6 —	376
Opponents	71	127	79	120	3 —	400

2012 TEAM STATISTICS

	Cowboys	Opp.
Total First Downs	338	317
Rushing	76	92
Passing	237	195
Penalty	25	30
3rd Down: Made/Att	93/212	81/202
3rd Down Pct.	43.9	40.1
4th Down: Made/Att	8/11	6/11
4th Down Pct.	72.7	54.5
Possession Avg.	30:33	29:27
Total Net Yards	5994	5687
Avg. Per Game	374.6	355.4
Total Plays	1049	986
Avg. Per Play	5.7	5.8
Net Yards Rushing	1265	2003
Avg. Per Game	79.1	125.2
Total Rushes	355	441
Net Yards Passing	4729	3684
Avg. Per Game	295.6	230.3
Sacked/Yards Lost	36/263	34/211
Gross Yards	4992	3895
Att./Completions	658/434	511/320
Completion Pct.	66.0	62.6
Had Intercepted	19	7
Punts/Average	69/44.0	74/45.4
Net Punting Avg.	69/39.1	74/37.1
Penalties/Yards	117/853	89/726
Fumbles/Ball Lost	20/10	18/9
Touchdowns	41	45
Rushing	8	17
Passing	29	22
Returns	4	6

2012 INDIVIDUAL STATISTICS

PASSING

	Att.	Comp.	Yds.	Pct.	TD	Int.	Tkld.	Rate
Romo	648	425	4903	65.6	28	19	36/263	90.5
Orton	10	9	89	90.0	1	0	0/0	137.1
Cowboys	658	434	4992	66.0	29	19	36/263	91.3
Opponents	511	320	3895	62.6	22	7	34/211	94.7

SCORING

	TD R	TD P	TD Rt	PAT	FG	Saf	PTS
Bailey	0	0	0	37/37	29/31	0	124
Bryant	0	12	0	0/0	0/0	0	74
Austin	0	6	0	0/0	0/0	0	36
F. Jones	3	2	0	0/0	0/0	0	30
Murray	4	0	0	0/0	0/0	0	24
Ogletree	0	4	0	0/0	0/0	0	24
Witten	0	3	0	0/0	0/0	0	18
Harris	0	1	1	0/0	0/0	0	14
Romo	1	0	0	0/0	0/0	0	8
Carr	0	0	1	0/0	0/0	0	6
Claiborne	0	0	1	0/0	0/0	0	6
Hatcher	0	0	1	0/0	0/0	0	6
Phillips	0	1	0	0/0	0/0	0	6
Cowboys	8	29	4	37/37	29/31	0	376
Opponents	17	22	6	43/44	29/33	0	400

2-Pt Conversions: Bryant, Harris, Romo, Cowboys 3-4, Opponents 0-1

RUSHING

	No.	Yds	Avg	LG	TD
Murray	161	663	4.1	48	4
F. Jones	111	402	3.6	22t	3
Dunbar	21	75	3.6	18	0
Tanner	25	61	2.4	9	0
Romo	30	49	1.6	15	1
Vickers	3	11	3.7	13	0
Ogletree	2	9	4.5	5	0
Bryant	2	-5	-2.5	6	0
Cowboys	355	1265	3.6	48	8
Opponents	441	2003	4.5	43	17

RECEIVING

	No.	Yds	Avg	LG	TD
Witten	110	1039	9.4	36	3
Bryant	92	1382	15.0	85t	12
Austin	66	943	14.3	49	6
Murray	35	251	7.2	22	0
Ogletree	32	436	13.6	65	4
F. Jones	25	262	10.5	39	2
Harris	17	222	13.1	36	1
Beasley	15	128	8.5	20	0
Vickers	13	104	8.0	17	0
Hanna	8	86	10.8	29	0
Phillips	8	55	6.9	19	1
Dunbar	6	33	5.5	14	0
Tanner	4	41	10.3	15	0
Holmes	2	11	5.5	7	0
Romo	1	-1	-1.0	-1	0
Cowboys	434	4992	11.5	85t	29
Opponents	320	3895	12.2	68t	22

INTERCEPTIONS

	No.	Yds	Avg	LG	TD
Carr	3	120	40.0	47t	1
Peprah	1	27	27.0	27	0
Claiborne	1	0	0.0	0	0
Lee	1	0	0.0	0	0
McCray	1	0	0.0	0	0
Cowboys	7	147	21.0	47t	1
Opponents	19	340	17.9	74t	3

PUNTING

	No.	Yds.	Avg.	In 20	LG
Moorman	56	2497	44.6	22	64
C. Jones	12	542	45.2	6	60
Cowboys	69	3039	44	28	64
Opponents	74	3362	45.4	25	68

PUNT RETURNS

	Ret	FC	Yds	Avg	LG	TD
Harris	22	11	354	16.1	78t	1
Bryant	12	2	66	5.5	44	0
Cowboys	34	13	420	12.4	78t	1
Opponents	29	15	279	9.6	98t	1

KICKOFF RETURNS

	No.	Yds	Avg	LG	TD
Dunbar	12	261	21.8	44	0
F. Jones	11	236	21.5	29	0
Harris	11	210	19.1	29	0
Phillips	1	20	20.0	20	0
Vickers	1	14	14.0	14	0
Cowboys	36	741	20.6	44	0
Opponents	50	1102	22.0	108t	1

FIELD GOALS

	1-19	20-29	30-39	40-49	50+
Bailey	1/1	5/5	13/13	7/7	3/5
Cowboys	1/1	5/5	13/13	7/7	3/5
Opponents	0/0	9/9	9/12	9/10	2/2

SACKS

	No.
Ware	11.5
Spencer	11.0
Hatcher	4.0
V. Butler	3.0
Brent	1.5
Lissemore	1.0
Sims	1.0
Spears	1.0
Cowboys	34.0
Opponents	36.0

RECORD HOLDERS
INDIVIDUAL RECORDS—CAREER

Category	Name	Performance
Rushing (Yds.)	Emmitt Smith, 1990-2002	**17,162
Passing (Yds.)	Troy Aikman, 1989-2000	32,942
Passing (TDs)	Tony Romo, 2003-2012	177
Receiving (No.)	Jason Witten, 2003-2012	806
Receiving (Yds.)	Michael Irvin, 1988-1999	11,904
Interceptions	Mel Renfro, 1964-1977	52
Punting (Avg.)	Mat McBriar, 2004-2011	45.3
Punt Return (Avg.)	Deion Sanders, 1995-99	13.3
Kickoff Return (Avg.)	Mel Renfro, 1964-1977	26.4
Field Goals	Rafael Septien, 1978-1986	162
Touchdowns (Tot.)	Emmitt Smith, 1990-2002	164
Points	Emmitt Smith, 1990-2002	986
*Sacks	DeMarcus Ware, 2005-2012	111.0

INDIVIDUAL RECORDS—SINGLE SEASON

Category	Name	Performance
Rushing (Yds.)	Emmitt Smith, 1995	1,773
Passing (Yds.)	Tony Romo, 2012	4,903
Passing (TDs)	Tony Romo, 2007	36
Receiving (No.)	Michael Irvin, 1995	111
Receiving (Yds.)	Michael Irvin, 1995	1,603
Interceptions	Everson Walls, 1981	11
Punting (Avg.)	Mat McBriar, 2006	48.2
Punt Return (Avg.)	Bob Hayes, 1968	20.8
Kickoff Return (Avg.)	Mel Renfro, 1965	30.0
Field Goals	Richie Cunningham, 1997	34
Touchdowns (Tot.)	Emmitt Smith, 1995	25
Points	Emmitt Smith, 1995	150
*Sacks	DeMarcus Ware, 2008	20.0

INDIVIDUAL RECORDS—SINGLE GAME

Category	Name	Performance
Rushing (Yds.)	DeMarco Murray, 10-23-11	253
Passing (Yds.)	Don Meredith, 11-10-63	460
Passing (TDs)	Many times	5
	Last time by Tony Romo, 11-23-06	
Receiving (No.)	Jason Witten, 10-28-12	18
Receiving (Yds.)	Miles Austin, 10-11-09	250
Interceptions	Many times	3
	Last time by Terence Newman, 12-14-03	
Field Goals	Chris Boniol, 11-18-96	7
	Billy Cundiff, 9-15-03	7
Touchdowns (Tot.)	Many times	4
	Last time by Terrell Owens, 11-18-07	
Points	Many times	24
	Last time by Terrell Owens, 11-18-07	
*Sacks	Jim Jeffcoat, 11-10-85	5.0

*Sacks became an official statistic in 1982.
**NFL Record

2013 VETERAN ROSTER

No.	Name	Pos.	Ht.	Wt.	Birthdate	NFL Exp.	College	Hometown	How Acq.	'12 Games/ Starts
55	Albright, Alex	LB	6-5	260	1/29/88	3	Boston College	Cincinnati, Ohio	FA-'11	14/2
26	Allen, Will	S	6-1	200	6/17/82	10	Ohio State	Dayton, Ohio	UFA(Pitt)-'13	16/7*
62	Arkin, David	G	6-5	306	10/7/87	2	Missouri State	Wichita, Kan.	D4-'11	0*
13	Armstrong, Anthony	WR	5-11	179	3/29/83	4	West Texas A&M	Carrollton, Texas	FA-'13	6/0*
19	Austin, Miles	WR	6-2	217	6/30/84	8	Monmouth	Garfield, N.J.	FA-'06	16/15
5	Bailey, Dan	K	6-0	189	1/26/88	3	Oklahoma State	Mustang, Okla.	FA-'11	16/0
79	Bass, Ben	DE	6-5	283	10/12/89	2	Texas A&M	Plano, Texas	FA-'12	2/0
11	Beasley, Cole	WR	5-8	177	4/26/89	2	Southern Methodist	Little Elm, Texas	FA-'12	10/0
73	Bernadeau, Mackenzy	G	6-4	320	1/3/86	6	Bentley	Waltham, Ma.	UFA(Car)-'12	16/16
92	Brent, Josh	NT	6-2	320	1/30/88	4	Illinois	Bloomington, Ill.	S7-'10	12/5
88	Bryant, Dez	WR	6-2	220	11/4/88	4	Oklahoma State	Lufkin, Texas	D1-'10	16/14
72	Callaway, Robert	DT	6-5	324	2/14/88	2	Saginaw Valley State	Mt. Morris, Mich.	FA-'11	2/0
39	Carr, Brandon	CB	6-0	210	5/19/86	6	Grand Valley State	Flint, Mich.	UFA(KC)-'12	16/16
54	Carter, Bruce	LB	6-2	240	2/19/88	3	North Carolina	Havelock, N.C.	D2-'11	11/11
42	Church, Barry	S	6-2	218	2/11/88	4	Toledo	Pittsburgh, Pa.	FA-'10	3/3
24	Claiborne, Morris	CB	5-11	185	2/7/90	2	Louisiana State	Shreveport, La.	D1-'12	15/15
86	Cochart, Colin	TE	6-4	258	7/7/87	3	South Dakota State	Kewaunee, Wisc.	FA-'13	0*
63	Cook, Ryan	C/G	6-6	325	5/8/83	8	New Mexico	Albuquerque, N.M.	T(Mia)-'12	13/11
67	Costa, Phil	C	6-3	313	7/11/87	4	Maryland	Moorestown, N.J.	FA-'10	3/3
98	Crawford, Tyrone	DE	6-4	285	11/22/89	2	Boise State	Windsor, Ontario	D3-'12	16/0
25	Dunbar, Lance	RB	5-8	191	1/25/90	2	North Texas	Haltom City, Texas	FA-'12	12/0
52	Durant, Justin	LB	6-1	240	9/21/85	7	Hampton	Florence, S.C.	UFA(Det)-'13	16/14*
68	Free, Doug	T	6-6	325	1/6/84	7	Northern Illinois	Manitowoc, Wisc.	D4b-'07	16/16
84	Hanna, James	TE	6-4	249	7/14/89	2	Oklahoma	Flower Mound, Texas	D6-'12	16/2
17	Harris, Dwayne	WR	5-10	200	9/16/87	3	East Carolina	Stone Mountain, Ga.	D6-'11	16/0
97	Hatcher, Jason	DT	6-6	305	7/13/82	8	Grambling State	Jena, La.	D3b-'06	16/16
96	Hayden, Nick	DT	6-4	300	2/4/86	6	Wisconsin	Hartland, Wisc.	FA-'13	0*
37	Johnson, Matt	S	6-1	215	7/22/89	2	Eastern Washington	Olympia, Wash.	D4b-'12	0*
6	Jones, Chris	P	6-0	208	7/21/89	2	Carson Newman	Rome, Ga.	FA-'11	4/0
60	Kowalski, Kevin	C/G	6-3	304	1/2/89	3	Toledo	Macedonia, Ohio	FA-'11	0*
91	Ladouceur, Louis-Philippe	LS	6-5	255	3/13/81	9	California	Pointe-Claire, Quebec	FA-'05	16/0
50	Lee, Sean	LB	6-2	245	7/22/86	4	Penn State	Pittsburgh, Pa.	D2-'10	6/6
95	Lissemore, Sean	NT	6-3	303	9/11/87	4	William & Mary	Dumont, N.J.	D7-'10	10/6
71	Livings, Nate	G	6-4	320	3/16/82	6	Louisiana State	Lake Charles, La.	UFA(Cin)-'12	16/16
40	McCray, Danny	S	6-1	222	3/10/88	4	Louisiana State	Houston, Texas	FA-'10	15/10
21	Mitchell, Carlton	WR	6-3	215	4/6/88	3	South Florida	Gainesville, Fla.	FA-'13	0*
21	Moore, Sterling	CB	5-10	200	2/3/90	3	Southern Methodist	Antioch, Calif.	PS(NE)-'12	13/0*
29	Murray, DeMarco	RB	6-0	215	2/12/88	3	Oklahoma	Las Vegas, Nev.	D3-'11	10/10
18	Orton, Kyle	QB	6-4	225	11/14/82	9	Purdue	Altoona, Iowa	UFA(KC)-'12	1/0
78	Parnell, Jermey	T	6-6	311	7/20/86	4	Mississippi	Blytheville, Ark.	FA-'10	16/1
90	Ratliff, Jay	DT	6-4	303	8/29/81	9	Auburn	Valdosta, Ga.	D7-'05	6/6
9	Romo, Tony	QB	6-2	230	4/21/80	11	Eastern Illinois	Burlington, Wisc.	FA-'03	16/16
32	Scandrick, Orlando	CB	5-10	191	2/10/87	6	Boise State	Los Alamitos, Calif.	D5-'08	11/3
53	Sheffield, Cameron	DE	6-2	257	2/12/88	3	Troy	Portal, Ga.	FA-'13	1/0*
59	Sims, Ernie	LB	6-0	230	12/23/84	8	Florida State	Tallahassee, Fla.	FA-'12	10/6
77	Smith, Tyron	T	6-5	308	12/12/90	3	Southern California	Moreno Valley, Calif.	D1-'11	15/15
93	Spencer, Anthony	DE	6-3	250	1/23/84	7	Purdue	Fort Wayne, Ind.	D1-'07	14/14
34	Tanner, Phillip	RB	5-10	217	8/8/88	3	Middle Tennessee State	Dallas, Texas	FA-'11	14/0
23	Underwood, Brandon	CB	6-1	197	6/24/86	3	Cincinnati	Hamilton, Ohio	FA-'13	0*
47	Vickers, Lawrence	FB	6-0	250	5/8/83	7	Colorado	Houston, Texas	FA-'12	16/6
94	Ware, DeMarcus	DE	6-4	254	7/31/82	9	Troy	Auburn, Ala.	D1a-'05	16/16
51	Wilber, Kyle	DE	6-4	246	4/26/89	2	Wake Forest	Apopka, Fla.	D4a-'12	10/0
82	Witten, Jason	TE	6-6	261	5/6/82	11	Tennessee	Elizabethton, Tenn.	D3-'03	16/16

* Allen played 16 games with Pittsburgh in '12; Arkin did not play in five games and inactive 11 games; Armstrong played five games with Miami and one game with Dallas; Cochart last active with Cincinnati in '11; Durant played 16 games with Detroit; Hayden last active with Cincinnati in '11; Johnson missed '12 season because of injury; Kowalski did not play in three games and inactive for three games; Mitchell last active with Cleveland in '11; Moore played eight games with New England; Sheffield played one game with Kansas City; Underwood last active with Green Bay in '10.

Players lost through free agency (5): LB Victor Butler (NO; 16 games in '12), DT Kenyon Coleman (NO; 7), CB Mike Jenkins (Oak; 13), WR Kevin Ogletree (TB; 15), TE John Phillips (SD; 16).

Also played with Cowboys in '12—CB Vince Agnew (4 games), CB Mario Butler (1), CB Michael Coe (3), LB Dan Connor (14), G Derrick Dockery (15), S Eric Frampton (13), WR Andre Holmes (7), RB Felix Jones (16), LB Orie Lemon (5), CB LeQuan Lewis (3), P Brian Moorman (12), S Charlie Peprah (5), LB Brady Poppinga (4), DT Brian Schaefering (3), S Gerald Sensabaugh (16), S Mana Silva (3), DT Marcus Spears (15).

FIRST-YEAR ROSTER

Name	Pos.	Ht.	Wt.	Birthdate	College	Hometown	How Acq.
Amos, Anthony	WR	5-11	179	8/2/90	Middle Tennessee State	Fayetteville, N.C.	FA
Benford, Tim (1)	WR	5-11	200	9/7/89	Tennessee Tech	Chattanooga, Tenn.	FA-'12
Benton, Spencer	P	6-1	189	3/20/89	Clemson	Myrtle Beach, S.C.	FA
Brewer, Xavier	CB	5-10	197	1/25/90	Clemson	Jacksonville, Fla.	FA
Coale, Danny (1)	WR	6-0	190	6/27/88	Virginia Tech	Lexington, Va.	D5-'12
Coughman, Edawn (1)	T	6-4	316	7/21/88	Shaw	Atlanta, Ga.	FA
Dominguez, Ray (1)	G	6-4	329	7/12/88	Arkansas	Bainbridge, Ga.	FA
Escobar, Gavin	TE	6-6	251	2/3/91	San Diego State	Orange County, Calif.	D2
Frederick, Travis	C	6-3	317	3/18/91	Wisconsin	Sharon, Wisc.	D1
Freedman, Paul	TE	6-5	273	12/9/90	Virginia	Belleair Beach, Fla.	FA
Green, Jared (1)	WR	6-1	192	4/1/89	Southern University	Vienna, Va.	FA
Hall, D.J. (1)	G	6-1	323	12/24/88	Texas State	Palestine, Texas	FA
Hamilton, Jakar	S	5-11	197	10/2/89	South Carolina State	Johnston, S.C.	FA
Harris, Dustin	CB	5-10	171	1/29/91	Texas A&M	Livingston, Texas	FA
Heath, Jeff	S	6-1	210	5/14/91	Saginaw Valley State	Lake Orion, Mich.	FA
Holloman, DeVonte	LB	6-2	243	2/12/91	South Carolina	Charlotte, N.C.	D6
Hughlett, Charley (1)	LS	6-4	251	5/16/90	Central Florida	Tampa, Fla.	FA
Igbinosun, Ikponmwosa (1)	DT	6-3	289	9/10/90	Southern Connecticut State	Rahway, N.J.	FA-'12
Lacey, Deon	LB	6-1	227	7/18/90	West Alabama	Brighton, Ala.	FA
Lawrence, Cameron	LB	6-2	236	1/20/91	Mississippi State	Coldwater, Miss.	FA
Lawrence, Kendial	K	5-9	196	4/13/91	Missouri	Rockwall, Texas	FA
Leary, Ronald (1)	G	6-3	318	4/29/89	Memphis	Baton Rouge, La.	FA-'12
Magee, Brandon	LB	5-11	225	10/22/90	Arizona State	Corona, Calif.	FA
McSurdy, Caleb (1)	LB	6-1	248	2/24/90	Montana	Boise, Idaho	D7-'11
Pellerin, Micah (1)	S	6-0	202	11/23/88	Hampton	Madison, Miss.	FA-'12
Randle, Joseph	RB	6-0	198	12/29/91	Oklahoma State	Wichita, Kan.	D5
Reed, Taylor	LB	5-11	244	8/7/91	Southern Methodist	Beaumont, Texas	FA
Rogers, Eric	WR	6-3	211	2/12/91	Cal Lutheran	Duarte, Calif.	FA
Smith, Andre (1)	TE	6-5	267	9/26/88	Virginia Tech	Savannah, Ga.	FA-'12
Smith, Devin	CB	5-10	187	8/8/90	Wisconsin	Coppell, Texas	FA
Stephens, Nick (1)	QB	6-3	226	5/19/87	Tarleton State	Flower Mound, Texas	FA-'12
Taylor, Monte (1)	DE	6-4	283	2/10/89	Cincinnati	Los Angeles, Calif.	FA-'12
Webb, B.W.	CB	5-11	180	5/3/90	William & Mary	Newport News, Va.	D4
Weems, Darrion (1)	T	6-5	320	9/4/88	Oregon	Winnetka, Calif.	PS(Den)-'12
Wilcox, J.J.	S	6-0	219	2/14/91	Georgia Southern	Cairo, Ga.	D3b
Williams, Dalton	QB	6-3	217	4/8/90	Akron	Coppell, Texas	FA
Williams, Terrance	WR	6-2	202	9/18/89	Baylor	Dallas, Texas	D3a

The term NFL Rookie is defined as a player who is in his first season of professional football and has not been on the roster of another professional football team for any regular-season or postseason games. A Rookie is designated by an "R" on NFL rosters. Players who have been active in another professional football league or players who have NFL experience, including either preseason training camp or being on an Active List or Inactive List, or on Reserve/Injured or Reserve/Physically Unable to Perform for fewer than six regular-season games, are termed NFL First-Year Players. An NFL First-Year Player is designated by a "1" on NFL rosters. Thereafter, a player is credited with an additional year of experience for each season in which he accumulates six games on the Active List or Inactive List, or on Reserve/Injured or Reserve/Physically Unable to Perform.

Log on to www.dallascowboys.com for an up-to-date roster.

DALLAS COWBOYS

COACHING STAFF
Head Coach,
Jason Garrett
Pro Career: Named the eighth head coach in Dallas Cowboys history on January 5, 2011 and became the first former Cowboys player to become the team's head coach. Named the club's interim head coach at the midpoint of the 2010 season and went on to guide a Dallas team that had started the season with a 1-7 record to a 5-3 mark down the stretch. Since the 2007 season Garrett had been the Cowboys offensive coordinator, and in 2008, he was assigned the additional duties of being the club's assistant head coach. Under Garrett, the Dallas offense finished among the NFL's top-10 four times: 2012 (6th), 2010 (10th), 2009 (2nd), and 2007 (2nd). From the start of the 2007 season, the club's cumulative numbers for total net yards (35,583) and gross passing yards (25,513) represent the best totals over a six-year span in team history. En route to winning the 2009 NFC Eastern Division title, Dallas established club records for total offensive yards (6,390), net passing yards (4,287) and pass completions (347). Dallas won the NFC East in 2007 with a team-record tying 13 victories and finished second in the NFL in scoring. Garrett was named *Pro Football Weekly's* NFL's Assistant Coach of the Year in March of 2008. Career record: 21-19.
Background: Played quarterback at Princeton (1987-88) and was named the Ivy League's Player of the Year and honorable mention All American as a senior. Played professionally in World League and Canadian Football League (both 1991) before joining Dallas (1992-99), Giants (2000-03), Buccaneers (2004) and Dolphins (also 2004). Key reserve on three Super Bowl teams with the Cowboys and one with the Giants. Began his coaching career as quarterbacks coach with Dolphins for Nick Saban.
Personal: Born March 28, 1966, in Abington, Pa. He and his wife Brill reside in Dallas.

ASSISTANT COACHES
Joe Baker, asst. secondary coach; born June 29, 1969, Glen Ridge, N.J. Wide receiver Princeton 1987-1990. No pro playing experience. College coach: East Stroudsburg 1991, Samford 1993, Wisconsin 1999. Pro coach: Birmingham Fire (WFL) 1992, Jacksonville Jaguars 1995-98, New Orleans Saints 2004-05, Green Bay Packers 2005, St. Louis Rams 2006, Denver Broncos 2007-08, Tampa Bay Buccaneers 2009-2011, joined Cowboys in 2012.
Rich Bisaccia, special teams coordinator; born June 3, 1960, Yonkers, N.Y. Defensive back Yankton College 1979-1982. Pro defensive back Philadelphia Stars (USFL) 1983. College coach: Wayne State College 1983-87, South Carolina 1988-1993,

Clemson 1994-98, Mississippi 1999-2001. Pro coach: Tampa Bay Buccaneers 2002-2010, San Diego Chargers 2011-12, joined Cowboys in 2013.
Ben Bloom, defensive quality control/linebackers; born October 17, 1982, Wellesley, Mass. Offensive line Tufts 2001-04. No pro playing experience. College coach: Tufts 2005-07, Harvard 2008. Pro coach: Cleveland Browns 2010, joined Cowboys in 2011.
Chris Boniol, asst. special teams; born December 9, 1971, Alexandria, La. Kicker Louisiana Tech 1990-93. Pro kicker Dallas Cowboys 1994-96, Philadelphia Eagles 1997-98, Chicago Bears 1999. Pro coach: Joined Cowboys in 2010.
Dave Borgonzi, offensive/defensive assistant; born November 19, 1982, Everett, Mass. Linebacker Amherst College 2001-04. No pro playing experience. College coach: Syracuse 2006-07, Harvard 2008-10. Pro coach: Joined Cowboys in 2011.
Gary Brown, running backs; born July 1, 1969, Williamsport, Pa. Running back Penn State 1987-1990. Pro running back Houston Oilers 1991-95, San Diego Chargers 1997, New York Giants 1998-99. College coach: Lycoming 2003-05, Susquehanna 2006-07, Rutgers 2008. Pro coach: Cleveland Browns 2009-2012, joined Cowboys in 2013.
Bill Callahan, offensive coordinator/offensive line; born July 31, 1956, Chicago, Ill. Quarterback Benedictine 1975-77. No pro playing experience. College coach: Illinois 1980-86, Northern Arizona 1987-88, Southern Illinois 1989, Wisconsin 1990-94, Nebraska 2004-07 (head coach). Pro coach: Philadelphia Eagles 1995-97, Oakland Raiders 1998-2003 (head coach 2002-03), New York Jets 2008-2011, joined Cowboys in 2012.
Derek Dooley, wide receivers; born June 10, 1968, Athens, Ga. Wide receiver Virginia 1987-1990. No pro playing experience. College coach: Georgia 1996, Southern Methodist 1997-99, Louisiana State 2000-04, Louisiana Tech 2007-09 (head coach), Tennessee 2010-12 (head coach). Pro coach: Miami Dolphins 2005-06, joined Cowboys in 2013.
Matt Eberflus, linebackers; born May 17, 1970, Toledo, Ohio. Linebacker Toledo 1988-1991. No pro playing experience. College coach: Toledo 1992-2000, Missouri 2001-08. Pro coach: Cleveland Browns 2009-2010, joined Cowboys in 2011.
Jerome Henderson, secondary; born August 8, 1969, Portsmouth, Va. Defensive back Clemson 1987-1990. Pro cornerback New England Patriots 1991-93, 1996, Buffalo Bills 1993-94, Philadelphia Eagles 1995, New York Jets 1997-98. Pro coach: New York Jets 2007-08, Cleveland Browns 2009-2011, joined Cowboys in 2012.
Monte Kiffin, defensive coordinator; born February 29, 1940, Lexington, Neb. Offensive/defensive tackle Nebraska 1959-

1963. Pro defensive end Winnipeg Blue Bombers (CFL) 1965. College coach: Nebraska 1966-1976, Arkansas 1977-79, North Carolina State 1980-82 (head coach), Tennessee 2009, Southern California 2010-12. Pro coach: Green Bay Packers 1983, Buffalo Bills 1984-85, Minnesota Vikings 1986-89, 1991-94, New York Jets 1990, New Orleans Saints 1995, Tampa Buccaneers 1996-2008, joined Cowboys in 2013.
Leon Lett, defensive assistant/defensive line; born October 12, 1968, Mobile, Ala. Defensive tackle Hinds (Miss.) C.C. 1987-88, Emporia State 1989-1990. Pro defensive tackle Dallas Cowboys 1991-2000, Denver Broncos 2001. College coach: Louisiana-Monroe 2009-2010. Pro coach: Joined Cowboys in 2011.
Rod Marinelli, defensive line; born July 13, 1949, Rosemead, Calif. Offensive/defensive tackle Utah 1968, offensive tackle California Lutheran 1970-72. No pro playing experience. College coach: Utah State 1976, California 1983-1991, Arizona State 1992-94, Southern California 1995. Pro coach: Tampa Bay Buccaneers 1996-2005, Detroit Lions 2006-08 (head coach), Chicago Bears 2009-2012, joined Cowboys in 2013.
Keith O'Quinn, offensive quality control/wide receivers; born July 28, 1973, Pensacola, Fla. Safety North Texas 1991-96. No pro playing experience. College coach: Hardin-Simmons 2000-02, Abilene Christian 2003-04. Pro coach: Joined Cowboys in 2011.
Wes Phillips, tight ends; born February 17, 1979, Houston, Texas. Quarterback Texas-El Paso 1997-2001. Pro quarterback San Diego Riptide (AFL2) 2002-03. College coach: Texas-El Paso 2004, West Texas A&M 2004-05, Baylor 2006. Pro coach: Joined Cowboys in 2007.
Frank Pollack, asst. offensive line; born November 5, 1967, Camp Springs, Md. Offensive tackle/offensive guard Northern Arizona 1985-89. Pro tackle, guard San Francisco 49ers 1990-97. College coach: Northern Arizona 2005-06. Pro coach: Houston Texans 2007-2011, Oakland Raiders 2012, joined Cowboys in 2013.
Wade Wilson, quarterbacks; born February 1, 1959, Commerce, Texas. Quarterback East Texas State 1977-1980. Pro quarterback Minnesota Vikings 1981-1991, Atlanta Falcons 1992, New Orleans Saints 1993-94, Dallas Cowboys 1995-97, Oakland Raiders 1998-99. Pro coach: Dallas Cowboys 2000-2003, Chicago Bears 2004-06, re-joined Cowboys in 2007.
Mike Woicik, strength and conditioning; born September 26, 1956, Baltimore. Attended Boston College. No college or pro playing experience. College coach: Springfield College 1978-1980, Syracuse 1980-89. Pro coach: Dallas Cowboys 1990-96, New Orleans Saints 1997-99, New England Patriots 2000-10, re-joined Cowboys in 2011.

National Football Conference
North Division
Team Colors: Honolulu Blue and Silver
222 Republic Drive
Allen Park, Michigan 48101
Telephone: (313) 216-4000

2013 SCHEDULE
PRESEASON
Aug. 9 **New York Jets** 7:30
Aug. 15 at Cleveland 7:30
Aug. 22 **New England** 7:30
Aug. 29 at Buffalo 7:00

REGULAR SEASON
Sep. 8 **Minnesota** 1:00
Sep. 15 at Arizona 4:05
Sep. 22 at Washington 1:00
Sep. 29 **Chicago** 1:00
Oct. 6 at Green Bay 1:00
Oct. 13 at Cleveland 1:00
Oct. 20 **Cincinnati** 1:00
Oct. 27 **Dallas** 1:00
Nov. 3 BYE
Nov. 10 at Chicago 1:00
Nov. 17 at Pittsburgh 1:00
Nov. 24 **Tampa Bay** 1:00
Nov. 28 **Green Bay** (Thurs) 12:30
Dec. 8 at Philadelphia 1:00
Dec. 16 **Baltimore** (Mon) 8:40
Dec. 22 **New York Giants** 4:05
Dec. 29 at Minnesota 1:00
All times ET

Stadium: Ford Field (opened in 2002)
•**Capacity:** 64,500
2000 Brush Street
Detroit, Michigan 48226
Playing Surface: FieldTurf
Training Camp: 222 Republic Drive
Allen Park, Michigan
48101

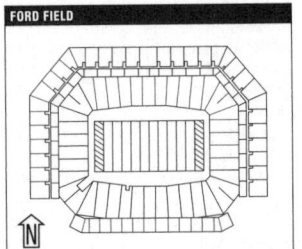

FORD FIELD

CLUB OFFICIALS
Chairman and Owner: William Clay Ford
Vice Chairman: William Clay Ford, Jr.
President: Tom Lewand
Executive Vice President of Football
Operations and General Manager:
Martin Mayhew
Senior Personnel Executive: James Harris
Senior Personnel Executive:
Brian Xanders
Corporate Secretary: Dave Hempstead
Senior Vice President of
Communications: Bill Keenist
Senior Advisor: Tom Lesnau
Senior Vice President, Marketing &
Partnerships: Elizabeth Parkinson
Senior Vice President & CFO: Luis Perez
Senior Advisor: Tom Lesnau
Vice President of Football Operations:
Cedric Saunders
Vice President of Pro Personnel:
Sheldon White
Director of College Scouting:
Scott McEwen
Player Personnel: Cary Conklin,
Chad Henry, Joe Kelleher,
Rob Lohman, Miller McCalmon,
Silas McKinnie, Lance Newmark,
Charlie Sanders, Dave Sears,
Dave Uyrus, Darren Anderson
Director of Community Relations:
Robert Wooley
Director of Media Relations:
Matt Barnhart
Director of Broadcasting and Production:
Bryan Bender
Director of Corporate Communications:
Ben Manges
Director of Ticket Operations:
Mark Graham
Coordinator of Athletic Medicine/Athletic
Training: Dean Kleinschmidt
Equipment Manager: Tim O'Neill
Video Director: Robert Yanagi

COACHING HISTORY
Portsmouth Spartans 1930-33
(517-622-32)
Records include postseason games

Year	Coach	Record
1930	Hal (Tubby) Griffen	5-6-3
1931-36	George (Potsy) Clark	49-20-6
1937-38	Earl (Dutch) Clark	14-8-0
1939	Elmer (Gus) Henderson	6-5-0
1940	George (Potsy) Clark	5-5-1
1941-42	Bill Edwards*	4-9-1
1942	John Karcis	0-8-0
1943-47	Charles (Gus) Dorais	20-31-2
1948-1950	Alvin (Bo) McMillin	12-24-0
1951-56	Raymond (Buddy) Parker	50-24-2
1957-1964	George Wilson	55-45-6
1965-66	Harry Gilmer	10-16-2
1967-1972	Joe Schmidt	43-35-7
1973	Don McCafferty	6-7-1
1974-76	Rick Forzano**	15-17-0
1976-77	Tommy Hudspeth	11-13-0
1978-1984	Monte Clark	43-63-1
1985-88	Darryl Rogers***	18-40-0
1988-1996	Wayne Fontes	67-71-0
1997-2000	Bobby Ross****	27-32-0
2000	Gary Moeller	4-3-0
2001-02	Marty Mornhinweg	5-27-0
2003-05	Steve Mariucci#	15-28-0
2005	Dick Jauron	1-4-0
2006-08	Rod Marinelli	10-38-0
2009-2012	Jim Schwartz	22-43-0

* Released after three games in 1942
** Resigned after four games in 1976
*** Released after 11 games in 1988
**** Resigned after nine games in 2000
\# Released after 11 games in 2005

PAID ATTENDANCE
Home 501,519   Away 501,740
Total 1,003,259
Single-game home record,
80,444 (12/20/81)
Single-season home record, 644,904
(1980)

2013 DRAFT CHOICES
Round	Name	Pos.	College
1	Ezekiel Ansah	DE	Brigham Young
2	Darius Slay	DB	Mississippi St.
3	Larry Warford	G	Kentucky
4	Devin Taylor	DE	South Carolina
5	Sam Martin	P	Appalachian St.
6	Corey Fuller	WR	Virginia Tech
	Theo Riddick	RB	Notre Dame
7	Michael Williams	TE	Alabama
	Brandon Hepburn	LB	Florida A&M

2012 TEAM RECORD
PRESEASON (2-2)

Date	Result	Opponent
08/10	L 17-19	Cleveland
08/17	W 27-12	at Baltimore
08/25	L 20-31	at Oakland
08/30	W 38-32	Buffalo

REGULAR SEASON (4-12)

Date	Result	Opponent
09/09	W 27-23	St. Louis
09/16	L 19-27	at San Francisco
09/23	L 41-44	at Tennessee (OT)
09/30	L 13-20	Minnesota
10/14	W 26-23	at Philadelphia (OT)
10/22	L 7-13	at Chicago
10/28	W 28-24	Seattle
11/04	W 31-14	at Jacksonville
11/11	L 24-34	at Minnesota
11/18	L 20-24	Green Bay
11/22	L 31-34	Houston (OT)
12/02	L 33-35	Indianapolis
12/09	L 20-27	at Green Bay
12/16	L 10-38	at Arizona
12/22	L 18-31	Atlanta
12/30	L 24-26	Chicago

(OT) Overtime

SCORE BY PERIODS

Lions	61	105	57	146	3	—	372
Opponents	77	137	59	158	6	—	437

2012 TEAM STATISTICS

	Lions	Opp.
Total First Downs	382	305
Rushing	84	107
Passing	272	167
Penalty	26	31
3rd Down: Made/Att	97/228	76/208
3rd Down Pct.	42.5	36.5
4th Down: Made/Att	6/15	5/6
4th Down Pct.	40.0	83.3
Possession Avg.	31:16	28:44
Total Net Yards	6540	5458
Avg. Per Game	408.8	341.1
Total Plays	1160	998
Avg. Per Play	5.6	5.5
Net Yards Rushing	1613	1889
Avg. Per Game	100.8	118.1
Total Rushes	391	420
Net Yards Passing	4927	3569
Avg. Per Game	307.9	223.1
Sacked/Yards Lost	29/212	34/237
Gross Yards	5139	3806
Att./Completions	740/445	544/346
Completion Pct.	60.1	63.6
Had Intercepted	17	11
Punts/Average	76/41.4	79/45.9
Net Punting Avg.	76/36.9	79/40.8
Penalties/Yards	103/944	93/789
Fumbles/Ball Lost	24/16	19/6
Touchdowns	39	49
Rushing	17	13
Passing	22	26
Returns	0	10

2012 INDIVIDUAL STATISTICS

PASSING	Att.	Comp.	Yds.	Pct.	TD	Int.	Tkld.	Rate
Stafford	727	435	4967	59.8	20	17	29/212	79.8
Sh. Hill	13	10	172	76.9	2	0	0/0	157.9
Lions	740	445	5139	60.1	22	17	29/212	81.5
Opponents	544	346	3806	63.6	26	11	34/237	91.7

SCORING	TD R	TD P	TD Rt	PAT	FG	Saf	PTS
Hanson	0	0	0	38/38	32/36	0	134
Leshoure	9	0	0	0/0	0/0	0	54
C. Johnson	0	5	0	0/0	0/0	0	30
Stafford	4	0	0	0/0	0/0	0	24
T. Young	0	4	0	0/0	0/0	0	24
Bell	3	0	0	0/0	0/0	0	18
Pettigrew	0	3	0	0/0	0/0	0	18
Burleson	0	2	0	0/0	0/0	0	14
Broyles	0	2	0	0/0	0/0	0	12
K. Smith	1	1	0	0/0	0/0	0	12
Durham	0	1	0	0/0	0/0	0	6
Heller	0	1	0	0/0	0/0	0	6
Robiskie	0	1	0	0/0	0/0	0	6
Scheffler	0	1	0	0/0	0/0	0	6
Thomas	0	1	0	0/0	0/0	0	6
Vanden Bosch	0	0	0	0/0	0/0	1	2
Lions	17	22	0	38/38	32/36	1	372
Opponents	13	26	10	46/46	31/41	0	437

2-Pt Conversions: Burleson, Lions 1-1, Opponents 2-3

RUSHING	No.	Yds	Avg	LG	TD
Leshoure	215	798	3.7	16	9
Bell	82	414	5.0	67	3
K. Smith	37	134	3.6	19	1
Stafford	35	126	3.6	11	4
Thomas	6	58	9.7	22	0
Burleson	8	48	6.0	16	0
Logan	3	17	5.7	13	0
T. Young	2	16	8.0	11	0
K. Williams	2	3	1.5	2	0
Sh. Hill	1	-1	-1.0	-1	0
Lions	391	1613	4.1	67	17
Opponents	420	1889	4.5	81t	13

RECEIVING	No.	Yds	Avg	LG	TD
C. Johnson	122	1964	16.1	53	5
Pettigrew	59	567	9.6	24	3
Bell	52	485	9.3	50	0
Scheffler	42	504	12.0	57	1
Leshoure	34	214	6.3	15	0
T. Young	33	383	11.6	46t	4
Burleson	27	240	8.9	26	2
Broyles	22	310	14.1	40	2
Thomas	5	28	5.6	12	1
Heller	17	150	8.8	19	1
K. Smith	10	79	7.9	13	1
Durham	8	125	15.6	27	1
Logan	6	28	4.7	10	0
Robiskie	4	44	11.0	21	1
K. Williams	2	9	4.5	5	0
Chapas	1	6	6.0	6	0
Stafford	1	3	3.0	3	0
Lions	445	5139	11.5	57	22
Opponents	346	3806	11.0	71t	26

INTERCEPTIONS	No.	Yds	Avg	LG	TD
Carey	2	51	25.5	28	0
Houston	2	2	1.0	2	0
Florence	1	29	29.0	29	0
Silva	1	26	26.0	26	0
J. Green	1	18	18.0	18	0
Lacey	1	10	10.0	10	0
Coleman	1	0	0.0	0	0
Delmas	1	0	0.0	0	0
Levy	1	-1	-1.0	-1	0
Lions	11	135	12.3	29	0
Opponents	17	475	27.9	102t	4

PUNTING	No.	Yds.	Avg.	In 20	LG
Harris	67	2783	41.5	21	58
Graham	6	248	41.3	2	46
Hanson	3	118	39.3	1	46
Lions	76	3149	41.4	24	58
Opponents	79	3626	45.9	34	73

PUNT RETURNS	Ret	FC	Yds	Avg	LG	TD
Logan	33	23	300	9.1	48	0
Thomas	1	3	0	0.0	0	0
A. Smith	1	0	2	2.0	2	0
Lions	35	26	302	8.6	48	0
Opponents	33	26	328	9.9	77t	2

KICKOFF RETURNS	No.	Yds	Avg	LG	TD
Logan	28	597	21.3	40	0
Bell	2	54	27.0	30	0
Thomas	1	12	12.0	12	0
Reiff	1	10	10.0	10	0
Scheffler	1	7	7.0	7	0
Heller	1	1	1.0	1	0
Lions	34	681	20.0	40	0
Opponents	52	1213	23.3	105t	2

FIELD GOALS	1-19	20-29	30-39	40-49	50+
Hanson	1/1	3/3	10/10	16/19	2/3
Lions	1/1	3/3	10/10	16/19	2/3
Opponents	0/0	11/11	9/10	10/15	1/5

SACKS	No.
Avril	9.5
Suh	8.0
Fairley	5.5
Vanden Bosch	3.5
Jackson	2.5
C. Williams	2.0
J. Green	1.0
(group)	1.0
Durant	0.5
Tulloch	0.5
Lions	34.0
Opponents	29.0

RECORD HOLDERS
INDIVIDUAL RECORDS—CAREER

Category	Name	Performance
Rushing (Yds.)	Barry Sanders, 1989-1998	15,269
Passing (Yds.)	Bobby Layne, 1950-58	15,710
Passing (TDs)	Bobby Layne, 1950-58	118
Receiving (No.)	Herman Moore, 1991-2001	670
Receiving (Yds.)	Herman Moore, 1991-2001	9,174
Interceptions	Dick LeBeau, 1959-1972	62
Punting (Avg.)	Yale Lary, 1952-53, 1956-1964	44.3
Punt Return (Avg.)	Jack Christiansen, 1951-58	12.8
Kickoff Return (Avg.)	Pat Studstill, 1961-67	25.7
Field Goals	Jason Hanson, 1992-2012	495
Touchdowns (Tot.)	Barry Sanders, 1989-1998	109
Points	Jason Hanson, 1992-2012	2,150
*Sacks	Robert Porcher, 1992-2003	95.5

INDIVIDUAL RECORDS—SINGLE SEASON

Category	Name	Performance
Rushing (Yds.)	Barry Sanders, 1997	2,053
Passing (Yds.)	Matthew Stafford, 2011	5,038
Passing (TDs)	Matthew Stafford, 2011	41
Receiving (No.)	Herman Moore, 1995	123
Receiving (Yds.)	Calvin Johnson, 2012	**1,964
Interceptions	Don Doll, 1950	12
	Jack Christiansen, 1953	12
Punting (Avg.)	Yale Lary, 1963	48.9
Punt Return (Avg.)	Pat Studstill, 1962	15.8
Kickoff Return (Avg.)	Mel Gray, 1994	28.4
Field Goals	Jason Hanson, 1993	34
Touchdowns (Tot.)	Barry Sanders, 1991	17
Points	Jason Hanson, 2012	134
*Sacks	Robert Porcher, 1999	15.0

INDIVIDUAL RECORDS—SINGLE GAME

Category	Name	Performance
Rushing (Yds.)	Barry Sanders, 11-13-94	237
Passing (Yds.)	Matthew Stafford, 1-1-12	520
Passing (TDs)	Gary Danielson, 12-9-78	5
	Matthew Stafford, 11-9-09, 11-20-11, 1-1-12	5
Receiving (No.)	Herman Moore, 12-4-95	14
Receiving (Yds.)	Cloyce Box, 12-3-50	302
Interceptions	Don Doll, 10-23-49	**4
Field Goals	Garo Yepremian, 11-13-66	6
	Jason Hanson, 10-17-99	6
Touchdowns (Tot.)	Dutch Clark, 10-22-34	4
	Cloyce Box, 12-3-50	4
	Barry Sanders, 11-24-91	4
Points	Dutch Clark, 10-22-34	24
	Cloyce Box, 12-3-50	24
	Barry Sanders, 11-24-91	24
*Sacks	Bill Gay, 9-4-83	5.5

*Sacks became an official statistic in 1982.
**NFL Record

2013 VETERAN ROSTER

No.	Name	Pos.	Ht.	Wt.	Birthdate	NFL Exp.	College	Hometown	How Acq.	'12 Games/ Starts
2	Akers, David	K	5-10	200	12/9/74	16	Louisville	Lexington, Ky.	FA-'13	16/0*
16	Austin, Terrence	WR	5-11	171	8/25/88	3	UCLA	Long Beach, Calif.	FA-'13	0*
31	Bartell, Ron	CB	6-1	210	2/22/82	9	Howard	Detroit, Mich.	FA-'12	1/1
35	Bell, Joique	RB	5-11	220	8/4/86	3	Wayne State	Benton Harbor, Mich.	FA-'11	16/0
28	Bentley, Bill	CB	5-10	176	5/16/89	2	Louisiana-Lafayette	Pahokee, Fla.	D3-'12	4/3
44	Best, Jahvid	RB	5-10	199	1/30/89	4	California	Richmond, Calif.	D1b-'10	0*
84	Broyles, Ryan	WR	5-10	188	4/9/88	2	Oklahoma	Norman, Okla.	D2-'12	10/3
13	Burleson, Nate	WR	6-0	198	8/19/81	11	Nevada	Seattle, Wash.	UFA(Sea)-'10	6/5
21	Bush, Reggie	RB	6-0	203	3/2/85	8	Southern California	Spring Valley, Calif.	UFA(Mia)-'13	16/16*
32	Carey, Don	S	5-11	192	2/14/87	5	Norfolk State	Norfolk, Va.	FA-'12	9/6
49	Curry, Dominique	WR	6-2	223	8/16/87	2	California (Pa)	Philadelphia, Pa.	FA-'13	0*
26	Delmas, Louis	S	5-11	202	4/12/87	5	Western Michigan	North Miami Beach, Fla.	D2-'09	8/8
18	Durham, Kris	WR	6-6	216	3/17/88	3	Georgia	Calhoun, Ga.	FA-'12	4/3
98	Fairley, Nick	DT	6-4	298	1/23/88	3	Auburn	Mobile, Ala.	D1-'11	13/7
70	Fox, Jason	T	6-6	314	5/2/88	4	Miami	Fort Worth, Texas	D4-'10	1/0
65	Gandy, Dylan	C	6-3	295	3/8/82	8	Texas Tech	Harlingen, Texas	FA-'09	16/0
36	Green, Jonté	CB	6-0	184	7/19/89	2	New Mexico State	St. Petersburg, Fla.	D6-'12	15/5
33	Greenwood, Chris	CB	6-1	193	7/10/89	2	Albion College	Detroit, Mich.	D5b-'12	0*
5	#Harris, Nick	P	6-2	218	7/23/78	13	California	Avondale, Ariz.	FA-'12	13/0
36	#Harrison, Jerome	RB	5-9	205	2/26/83	9	Washington State	Kalamazoo, Mich.	UFA(Phil)-'11	0*
89	#Heller, Will	TE	6-6	275	2/28/81	11	Georgia Tech	Dunwoody, Ga.	UFA(Sea)-'09	16/5
14	Hill, Shaun	QB	6-3	220	1/9/80	12	Maryland	Parsons, Kan.	T(SF)-'10	1/0
78	Hilliard, Corey	T	6-6	300	4/26/85	5	Oklahoma State	New Orleans, La.	FA-'09	0*
23	Houston, Chris	CB	5-11	178	10/18/84	7	Arkansas	Austin, Texas	T(Atl)-'10	14/14
81	Johnson, Calvin	WR	6-5	236	9/29/85	7	Georgia Tech	Tyrone, Ga.	D1-'07	16/16
46	Johnson, Domonique	CB	6-1	191	11/7/85	4	Jackson State	La Marque, Texas	FA-'13	7/0*
24	Johnson, Tyrell	S	6-0	207	5/19/85	6	Arkansas State	Rison, Ark.	FA-'12	4/0
91	Jones, Jason	DE	6-5	276	5/23/86	6	Eastern Michigan	Southfield, Mich.	UFA(Sea)-'13	0*
27	#Lee, Pat	CB	6-0	200	2/20/84	6	Auburn	Miami, Fla.	W(Oak)-'12	7/0
25	Leshoure, Mikel	RB	6-0	233	3/30/90	3	Illinois	Champaign, Ill.	D2b-'11	14/14
54	Levy, DeAndre	LB	6-2	238	3/26/87	5	Wisconsin	Milwaukee, Wisc.	D3a-'09	14/13
97	Lewis, Ronnell	DE	6-2	253	9/17/90	2	Oklahoma	Dewar, Okla.	D4-'12	8/0
50	Lewis, Travis	LB	6-2	222	1/15/88	2	Oklahoma	San Antonio, Texas	D7-'12	13/0
11	#Logan, Stefan	RB	5-6	180	6/2/81	5	South Dakota	Miami, Fla.	W(Pitt)-'10	16/0
86	Long, Lance	WR	5-11	186	5/4/86	3	Mississippi State	Shelby Township, Mich.	FA-'13	0*
17	Moore, Kellen	QB	6-0	197	7/12/89	2	Boise State	Prosser, Wash.	FA-'12	0*
	Mosley, C.J.	DT	6-2	310	8/6/83	9	Missouri	Fort Knox, Ky.	FA-'13	16/13*
48	Muhlbach, Don	LS	6-4	265	8/17/81	10	Texas A&M	Lufkin, Texas	FA-'04	16/0
61	Nagy, Bill	G	6-3	308	10/26/87	3	Wisconsin	Hudson, Ohio	FA-'12	0*
95	Nwagbuo, Ogemdi	DT	6-5	312	12/24/85	4	Michigan State	Spring Valley, Calif.	FA-'12	1/0
10	#Osgood, Kassim	WR	6-5	220	5/20/80	11	San Diego State	Salinas, Calif.	FA-'12	16/0
82	Overbay, Nathan	TE	6-5	270	1/4/87	2	Eastern Washington	Lakewood, Wash.	FA-'13	0*
58	Palmer, Ashlee	LB	6-1	236	4/7/86	5	Mississippi	Compton, Calif.	W(Buff)-'10	16/2
87	Pettigrew, Brandon	TE	6-5	265	2/23/85	5	Oklahoma State	Tyler, Texas	D1b-'09	14/11
27	Quin, Glover	S	6-0	209	1/15/86	5	New Mexico	Summit, Miss.	UFA(Hou)-'13	16/16*
51	Raiola, Dominic	C	6-1	295	12/30/78	13	Nebraska	Honolulu, Hawaii	D2a-'01	16/16
71	Reiff, Riley	T	6-6	313	12/1/88	2	Iowa	Parkston, S.D.	D1-'12	16/8
80	Robiskie, Brian	WR	6-4	212	12/3/87	5	Ohio State	Chagrin Falls, Ohio	FA-'12	16/16
63	Saddler-McQueen, Jimmy	DT	6-2	299	8/4/87	2	Texas A&M - Kingsville	Houston, Texas	FA-'12	1/0
85	Scheffler, Tony	TE	6-5	255	2/15/83	8	Western Michigan	Chelsea, Mich.	T(Den)-'10	15/4
39	Silva, Ricardo	S	6-3	225	5/9/88	2	Hampton	Baltimore, Md.	FA-'11	10/6
67	Sims, Rob	G	6-3	312	12/6/83	8	Ohio State	Macedonia, Ohio	T(Sea)-'10	16/16
30	#Smith, Kevin	RB	6-1	217	12/17/86	6	Central Florida	Miami, Fla.	FA-'11	12/2
42	Spievey, Amari	S	5-11	195	4/15/88	4	Iowa	Middleton, Conn.	D3-'10	5/2
9	Stafford, Matthew	QB	6-3	232	2/7/88	5	Georgia	Highland Park, Texas	D1a-'09	16/16
90	Suh, Ndamukong	DT	6-4	307	1/6/87	4	Nebraska	Portland, Ore.	D1a-'10	16/16
11	Thomas, Devin	WR	6-2	221	11/15/86	5	Michigan State	Canton, Mich.	FA-'13	0*
19	t-Thomas, Mike	WR	5-8	198	6/4/87	5	Arizona	DeSoto, Texas	T(Jax)-'12	16/4*
55	Tulloch, Stephen	LB	5-11	240	1/1/85	8	North Carolina State	Miami, Fla.	UFA(Tenn)-'11	16/16
29	Wendling, John	S	6-1	222	6/4/83	7	Wyoming	Rock Springs, Wyo.	FA-'10	16/3
15	West, Chastin	WR	6-1	217	5/1/87	2	Fresno State	Moorpark, Calif.	FA-'13	0*
59	Whitehead, Tahir	LB	6-2	228	4/2/90	2	Temple	Newark, N.J.	D5a-'12	14/0
99	#Williams, Corey	DT	6-4	320	8/17/80	10	Arkansas State	Camden, Ark.	T(Cle)-'10	7/5
79	Young, Willie	DE	6-4	251	9/19/85	4	North Carolina State	Palm Beach Gardens, Fla.	D7a-'10	16/0

* Akers played 16 games with San Francisco in '12; T. Austin last active with Washington in '11; Best missed '12 season because of injury; Bush played 16 games with Miami; Curry last active with St. Louis in '11; Greenwood missed '12 season because of injury; Harrison last active with Detroit in '11; D. Johnson played 7 games with Washington; Jones played 12 games with Seattle; Long inactive for one game; Moore inactive for 16 games; Mosley played 16 games with Jacksonville; Nagy missed '12 season because of injury; Overbay missed '12 season because of injury; Quin played 16 games with Houston; D. Thomas last active with New York Giants in '11; M. Thomas played seven games with Jacksonville and nine games with Detroit; West last active with Jacksonville in '11.

Unrestricted Free Agent; subject to developments.

t- Lions traded for Thomas (Jax).

Retired—Jeff Backus, 12-year tackle, 15 games in '12; Jason Hanson, 21-year kicker, 16 games in '12.

Players lost through free agency (8): DE Cliff Avril (Sea; 16 games), T Gosder Cherilus (Ind; 16), LB Justin Durant (Dall; 16), CB Drayton Florence (Car; 8), DT Andre Fluellen (Chi; 3), DT Sammie Hill (Tenn; 15), DE Lawrence Jackson (Minn; 15), CB Jacob Lacey (Minn; 11).

Also played with Lions in '12—DB Kevin Barnes (2 games), S Erik Coleman (12), P Ben Graham (3), TE Will Heller (16), DB Justin Miller (2), G Stephen Peterman (16), CB Alphonso Smith (4), DE Kyle Vanden Bosch (16), RB Keiland Williams (5), WR Titus Young (10).

FIRST-YEAR ROSTER

Name	Pos.	Ht.	Wt.	Birthdate	College	Hometown	How Acq.
Ansah, Ezekiel	DE	6-5	271	5/29/89	Brigham Young	Accra, Ghana	D1
Austin, Rodney (1)	G	6-4	311	12/4/88	Elon	Charlotte, N.C.	FA-'12
Bishop, Freddie	DE	6-3	251	2/25/90	Western Michigan	Inkster, Mich.	FA
Brooks, Michael	DT	6-3	294	8/28/91	East Carolina	Roxboro, N.C.	FA
Burrell, Troy	WR	5-10	182	7/12/89	Wayne State	Port Huron, Mich.	FA-'12
Carder, Alex	QB	6-2	215	10/22/89	Western Michigan	Shawnee, Kan.	FA
Chapas, Shaun (1)	FB	6-2	244	5/2/88	Georgia	Jacksonville, Fla.	FA-'12
Clingan, Blake	P	6-3	233	12/7/88	Central Florida	Coral Springs, Fla.	FA
Edwards, Patrick	WR	5-9	175	10/25/88	Houston	Hearne, Texas	FA-'12
Elkins, Alex	LB	6-3	230	8/27/90	Oklahoma State	High Point, N.C.	FA
Fauria, Joseph	TE	6-7	255	1/16/90	UCLA	Encino, Calif.	FA
Fuller, Corey	WR	6-2	196	6/23/90	Virginia Tech	Baltimore, Md.	D6
Hepburn, Brandon	LB	6-4	235	12/6/89	Florida A&M	Pomona, N.Y.	D7
Holtz, Austin	T	6-5	301	11/1/89	Ball State	Holt, Mich.	FA
Keyton, Darren	C	6-3	305	6/15/90	Central Michigan	Traverse City, Mich.	FA
Martin, Sam	P	6-1	205	2/27/90	Appalachian State	Fayetteville, Ga.	D5
Menzie, DeQuan (1)	CB	5-11	202	1/11/90	Alabama	Columbus, Ga.	FA
Messina, Carmen (1)	LB	6-2	236	9/8/88	New Mexico	Addison, Ill.	FA-'12
Miller, Steven	RB	5-7	172	3/23/91	Appalachian State	Piscataway, N.J.	FA
Morgan, Jon	LB	6-1	233	12/22/89	Albany	Copiague, N.Y.	FA
Neloms, Martavius	FS	6-0	189	9/4/91	Kentucky	Memphis, Tenn.	FA
Overbay, Nathan	TE	6-5	270	1/4/87	Eastern Washington	Lakewood, Wash.	FA
Riddick, Theo	RB	5-9	200	5/4/91	Notre Dame	Manville, N.J.	D6
Rugland, Håvard	K	6-2	240	10/7/84	Stavanger (Norway)	Aalgaard, Norway	FA
Smith, Lionel (1)	CB	5-11	184	8/18/87	Texas A&M	Bellaire, Texas	FA-'12
Slay, Darius	CB	6-1	192	1/1/91	Mississippi State	Brunswick, Ga.	D2
Taylor, Devin	DE	6-7	276	11/15/89	South Carolina	Beaufort, S.C.	D4
Waddle, LaAdrian	T	6-6	321	7/21/91	Texas Tech	Columbus, Texas	FA
Warford, Larry	G	6-3	333	7/18/91	Kentucky	Richmond, Ky.	D3
Weaver, Ross (1)	CB	6-1	210	1/29/87	Michigan State	Southfield, Mich.	FA-'11
Williams, Michael	TE	6-6	270	9/8/90	Alabama	Reform, Ala.	D7
Wilson, Cody	WR	5-9	191	3/5/91	Central Michigan	Rochester Hills, Mich.	FA

The term NFL Rookie is defined as a player who is in his first season of professional football and has not been on the roster of another professional football team for any regular-season or postseason games. A Rookie is designated by an "R" on NFL rosters. Players who have been active in another professional football league or players who have NFL experience, including either preseason training camp or being on an Active List or Inactive List, or on Reserve/Injured or Reserve/Physically Unable to Perform for fewer than six regular-season games, are termed NFL First-Year Players. An NFL First-Year Player is designated by a "1" on NFL rosters. Thereafter, a player is credited with an additional year of experience for each season in which he accumulates six games on the Active List or Inactive List, or on Reserve/Injured or Reserve/Physically Unable to Perform.

Log on to www.detroitlions.com for an up-to-date roster.

COACHING STAFF

**Head Coach,
Jim Schwartz**

Pro Career: Named Lions' twenty-fifth head coach on January 16, 2009. Schwartz enters his fifth season in Detroit after helping the team to their first playoff appearance since 1999. He came to Detroit following 10 seasons with the Tennessee Titans, including the past eight as defensive coordinator. As the Titans' defensive coordinator since 2001, Schwartz's defensive unit held firm in two major defensive categories that factored significantly in the team's overall success; rushing defense and third-down conversion. From 2001-08, Tennessee ranked fifth in rushing yards allowed per game (103.5) and sixth in third-down conversion percentage (36.1). Before joining the Titans in 1999, he spent three years (1996-98) as a defensive assistant/quality control coach with the Baltimore Ravens. During his tenure in Baltimore, he also coached the team's outside linebackers. After the Cleveland Browns moved to Baltimore following the 1995 season, Schwartz made the transition from player personnel to coaching. From 1993-95, he worked in the Browns' player personnel department, serving as both a college and pro scout. Career record: 22-43.

Background: Schwartz worked on the college level for four years before moving onto the NFL. He began his coaching career as a graduate assistant coach at the University of Maryland, tutoring the Terrapins' linebackers in 1989 and then served as graduate assistant at the University of Minnesota (1990). He became a position coach in the secondary at North Carolina Central (1991) before moving to Colgate (1992) as linebackers coach. Played collegiately at Georgetown University where he lettered four years at linebacker. In 1988 he earned numerous honors that include Division III CoSIDA/GTE Academic All-America, All-America and team captain.

Personal: Born June 2, 1966, in Baltimore, Md. He and his wife, Kathy, have twins Christian and Allison along with a younger daughter Maria. He earned a degree in economics at Georgetown as well as Distinguished Economics Graduate honors.

ASSISTANT COACHES

Jason Arapoff, coordinator of physical development; born July 8, 1965, Weymouth, Mass. Defensive back Springfield College 1985-88. No pro playing experience. Pro coach: Washington Redskins 1992-2000, joined Lions in 2001.

Bradford Banta, asst. linebackers; born December 14, 1979, Baton Rouge, La. Tight end Southern California 1990-93, Pro tight end/long snapper Indianapolis Colts 1993-99, New York Jets 2000, Detroit Lions 2001-03, Buffalo Bills 2004. College coach: Tennessee-Chattanooga 2007. Pro coach: Joined Lions in 2008.

John Bonamego, special teams coordinator; August 14, 1963, Waynesboro, Penn. Wide receiver/safety Central Michigan 1984-87. No pro playing experience. College coach: Maine 1988-1991, Lehigh 1992, Army 1993-98. Pro coach: Green Bay Packers 2003-05, New Orleans Saints 2006-07, Miami Dolphins 2008-2010, New Orleans Saints 2011, Jacksonville Jaguars 2012, joined Lions in 2013.

Matt Burke, linebackers; born March 25, 1976, Hudson, Mass. Safety Dartmouth 1994-97. No pro playing experience. College coach: Boston College 2000-02, Harvard 2003. Pro coach: Tennessee Titans 2006-08, joined Lions in 2009.

Gunther Cunningham, defensive coordinator; born June 19, 1946, Munich, Germany. Linebacker/placekicker Oregon 1966-68. No pro playing experience. College coach: Oregon 1969-1971, Arkansas 1972, Stanford 1973-76, California 1977-1980. Pro coach: Hamilton Tiger-Cats (CFL) 1981, Baltimore/Indianapolis Colts 1982-84, San Diego Chargers 1985-1990, L.A. Raiders 1991-94, Kansas City Chiefs 1995-2000, 2004-08 (head coach 1999-2000), Tennessee Titans 2001-03, joined Lions in 2009.

Todd Downing, quarterbacks; born July 22, 1980, Eden Prairie, Minn. Attended Minnesota. No college or pro playing experience. Pro coach: Minnesota Vikings 2003-05, St. Louis Rams 2006-08, joined Lions in 2009.

Terry Heffernan, asst. offensive line; born October 12, 1980, Arlington Heights, Ill. Center Dayton 2001-03. No pro playing experience. College coach: Cumberland 2003, Louisville 2004, Michigan 2005-06, Wayne State 2007-12. Pro coach: Joined Lions in 2013.

Bobby Johnson, tight ends; born February 28, 1963, Akron, Ohio. Offensive tackle Miami (Ohio) 1992-94. No pro playing experience. College coach: Akron 1995-98, Miami (Ohio) 1999-2004, Indiana 2005-09. Pro coach: Buffalo Bills 2010-11, Jacksonville Jaguars 2012, joined Lions in 2013.

Kris Kocurek, defensive line; born November 15, 1978, Rockdale, Texas. Defensive tackle Texas Tech 1997-2000. Pro defensive tackle Seattle Seahawks 2001, Tennessee Titans 2002. College coach: Texas Tech 2003, Texas A&M-Kingsville 2004-05, Texas A&M-Commerce 2006, West Texas A&M 2007, Stephen F. Austin State 2008. Pro coach: Joined Lions in 2009.

Tim Lappano, wide receivers; born October 14, 1956, Spokane, Wash. Running back Idaho 1978-1981. No pro playing experience. College coach: Idaho 1982-85, Wyoming 1986, Washington State 1987-1991, California 1992-95, Wyoming 1996, Purdue 1997, Oregon State 2000-02, Washington 2005-08. Pro coach: Seattle Seahawks 1998, San Francisco 49ers 2003-04, joined Lions in 2009.

Scott Linehan, offensive coordinator; born September 17, 1963, Sunnyside, Wash. Quarterback Idaho 1982-86. No pro playing experience. College coach: Idaho 1989-1990, 1992-93, Nevada-Las Vegas 1991, Washington 1994-98, Louisville 1999-2001. Pro coach: Minnesota Vikings 2002-04, Miami Dolphins 2005, St Louis Rams 2006-08 (head coach), joined Lions in 2009.

Curtis Modkins, running backs/run game coordinator; born November 15, 1970. Running back Texas Christian 1990-92. No pro playing experience. College coach: Texas Christian 1995-97, New Mexico 1998-2001, Georgia Tech 2002-07. Pro coach: Kansas City Chiefs 2008, Arizona Cardinals 2009, Buffalo Bills 2010-12, joined Lions in 2013.

Ted Rath, asst. strength and conditioning; born November 22, 1983, Monroe, Mich. Linebacker Toledo 2003-06. No pro playing experience. College coach: Toledo 2007-09. Pro coach: Joined Lions in 2009.

Marcus Robertson, secondary; born October 2, 1969, Pasadena, Calif. Defensive back Iowa State 1987-1990. Pro safety Houston Oilers/Tennessee Titans 1991-2000, Seattle Seahawks 2001-02. Pro coach: Tennessee Titans 2007-2011, joined Lions in 2012.

Evan Rothstein, quality control/special teams; born April 20, 1988, Merrick, N.Y. Attended SUNY Cortland. No college or pro playing experience. College coach: SUNY Cortland 2010, Syracuse 2010-11. Pro coach: Joined Lions in 2012.

Kyle Valero, offensive assistant; born April 24, 1986. Attended Florida State. No college or pro playing experience. College coach: Florida State 2008-09. Pro coach: Tampa Bay Buccaneers 2002-03, joined Lions in 2010.

Jeremiah Washburn, offensive line; Guard Arkansas 1998-2000. No pro playing experience. College coach: Arkansas 2000-01. Pro coach: Carolina Panthers 2002, Baltimore Ravens 2003-08, joined Lions in 2009.

Jim Washburn, asst. defensive line/pass rush: born December 2, 1963, Shelby N.C. Defensive line Gardner Webb 1970-73. No pro playing experience. College coach: Southern Methodist 1976, Lees-McRae 1977-78, Livingston 1979, New Mexico 1980-82, South Carolina 1983-1988, Arkansas 1994-1997, Houston 1998. Pro coach: Tennessee Titans 1999-2010, Philadelphia Eagles 2011-12, joined Lions in 2013.

**National Football Conference
North Division
Team Colors:** Dark Green, Gold, and White
Lambeau Field Atrium
1265 Lombardi Avenue
Green Bay, Wisconsin 54304
Telephone: (920) 569-7500

2013 SCHEDULE
PRESEASON

Aug. 9	**Arizona**	7:00
Aug. 17	at St. Louis	7:00
Aug. 23	**Seattle**	7:00
Aug. 29	at Kansas City	7:00

REGULAR SEASON

Sep. 8	at San Francisco	3:25
Sep. 15	**Washington**	12:00
Sep. 22	at Cincinnati	12:00
Sep. 29	BYE	
Oct. 6	**Detroit**	12:00
Oct. 13	at Baltimore	12:00
Oct. 20	**Cleveland**	3:25
Oct. 27	at Minnesota	7:30
Nov. 4	**Chicago** (Mon)	7:40
Nov. 10	**Philadelphia**	12:00
Nov. 17	at New York Giants	*7:30
Nov. 24	**Minnesota**	12:00
Nov. 28	at Detroit (Thurs)	11:30a
Dec. 8	**Atlanta**	*7:30
Dec. 15	at Dallas	3:25
Dec. 22	**Pittsburgh**	3:25
Dec. 29	at Chicago	12:00

*All times CT; Sunday night games in
Weeks 11-16 subject to change
Stadium: Lambeau Field (opened in 1957)
• **Capacity:** 80,750
1265 Lombardi Avenue
Green Bay, Wisconsin 54304
Playing Surface: DD GrassMaster
Training Camp: St. Norbert College
De Pere, Wisconsin 54115

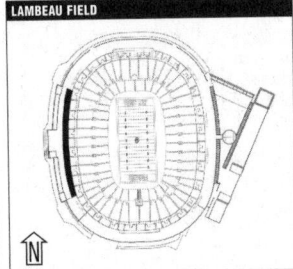

LAMBEAU FIELD

CLUB OFFICIALS

President and Chief Executive Officer:
Mark Murphy
Executive Vice President/General
Manager/Director of Football
Operations: Ted Thompson
Vice President of Football Administration/
Player Finance: Russ Ball
Vice President of Finance and
Administration: Paul Baniel
Vice President of Sales and Marketing:
Tim Connolly
Vice President and General Counsel:
Ed Policy
Director of Pro Personnel: Eliot Wolf
Director of College Scouting:
Brian Gutekunst
Director of Player Development:
Rob Davis
Director of Research and Development:
Mike Eayrs
Director of Public Relations:
Jason Wahlers
Director of Public Affairs:
Aaron Popkey
Assistant Director of Public Relations:
Sarah Quick
Communications Manager: Tom Fanning
Public Relations Coordinator:
Jonathan Butnick
Director of Ticket Operations:
Mark Wagner
Director of Marketing and Corporate
Sales: Craig Benzel
Director of Guest and Stadium
Experience: Jennifer Ark
Director of Human Resources:
Nicole Ledvina
Director of Retail Operations:
Kate Hogan
Director of Information Technology:
Wayne Wichlacz
Director of Facility Operations:
Ted Eisenreich
Director of Security/Risk Management:
Doug Collins
Director of Packers Media Group and
Brand Engagement: Joan Malcheski
Manager of Community Outreach &
Player/Alumni Relations:
Cathy Dworak
Senior Personnel Executive:
Alonzo Highsmith
West Regional Scout: Sam Seale
Assistant Director of Pro Personnel:
Tim Terry
Area Scouts: Lee Gissendaner,
Jon-Eric Sullivan,
John Wojciechowski,
Richmond Williams
Pro Scouts: Chad Brinker, Glenn Cook
College Scouts: Mike Owen,
Alonzo Dotson
College Scouting Coordinator: Danny
Mock
Coaching Administrator: Jason Simmons
Strength and Conditioning Assistants:
Thadeus Jackson, Zac Woodfin
Football Administration Coordinator:
Matt Klein
Video Director: Bob Eckberg
Head Athletic Trainer: Pepper Burruss
Equipment Manager: Gordon (Red) Batty

COACHING HISTORY
(720-548-36)

Records include postseason games

1921-1949	Earl (Curly) Lambeau	.212-106-21
1950-53	Gene Ronzani*	14-31-1
1953	Hugh Devore- Ray (Scooter) McLean**	0-2-0
1954-57	Lisle Blackbourn	17-31-0
1958	Ray (Scooter) McLean	1-10-1
1959-1967	Vince Lombardi	98-30-4
1968-1970	Phil Bengtson	20-21-1
1971-74	Dan Devine	25-28-4
1975-1983	Bart Starr	53-77-3
1984-87	Forrest Gregg	25-37-1
1988-1991	Lindy Infante	24-40-0
1992-98	Mike Holmgren	84-42-0
1999	Ray Rhodes	8-8-0
2000-05	Mike Sherman	59-43-0
2006-2012	Mike McCarthy	80-42-0

*Resigned after 10 games in 1953
**Co-coaches

PAID ATTENDANCE

Home 564,062   Away 532,054
Total 1,096,116
Single-game home record,
71,213 (11/1/09)
Single-season home record,
566,418 (2007)

2013 DRAFT CHOICES

Round	Name	Pos.	College
1	Datone Jones	DE	UCLA
2	Eddie Lacy	RB	Alabama
4	David Bakhtiari	T	Colorado
	JC Tretter	T	Cornell
	Johnathan Franklin	RB	UCLA
5	Micah Hyde	CB	Iowa
	Josh Boyd	DE	Mississippi St.
6	Nate Palmer	LB	Illinois St.
7	Charles Johnson	WR	Grand Valley St.
	Kevin Dorsey	WR	Maryland
	Sam Barrington	LB	South Florida

2012 TEAM RECORD
PRESEASON (2-2)

Date	Result	Opponent
08/09	L 13-21	at San Diego
08/16	L 10-35	Cleveland
08/23	W 27-13	at Cincinnati
08/30	W 24-3	Kansas City

REGULAR SEASON (11-5)

Date	Result	Opponent
09/09	L 22-30	San Francisco
09/13	W 23-10	Chicago
09/24	L 12-14	at Seattle
09/30	W 28-27	New Orleans
10/07	L 27-30	at Indianapolis
10/14	W 42-24	at Houston
10/21	W 30-20	at St. Louis
10/28	W 24-15	Jacksonville
11/04	W 31-17	Arizona
11/18	W 24-20	at Detroit
11/25	L 10-38	at New York Giants
12/02	W 23-14	Minnesota
12/09	W 27-20	Detroit
12/16	W 21-13	at Chicago
12/23	W 55-7	Tennessee
12/30	L 34-37	at Minnesota

POSTSEASON (1-1)

Date	Result	Opponent
01/05	W 24-10	Minnesota
01/12	L 31-45	at San Francisco

SCORE BY PERIODS

Packers	83	126	89	135	0	— 433
Opponents	53	118	80	85	0	— 336

2012 TEAM STATISTICS

	Packers	Opp.
Total First Downs	341	308
Rushing	85	83
Passing	213	191
Penalty	43	34
3rd Down: Made/Att	90/213	83/218
3rd Down Pct.	42.3	38.1
4th Down: Made/Att	7/13	9/23
4th Down Pct.	53.8	39.1
Possession Avg.	30:26	29:34
Total Net Yards	5751	5388
Avg. Per Game	359.4	336.8
Total Plays	1042	1033
Avg. Per Play	5.5	5.2
Net Yards Rushing	1702	1896
Avg. Per Game	106.4	118.5
Total Rushes	433	418
Net Yards Passing	4049	3492
Avg. Per Game	253.1	218.3
Sacked/Yards Lost	51/293	47/309
Gross Yards	4342	3801
Att./Completions	558/374	568/313
Completion Pct.	67.0	55.1
Had Intercepted	8	18
Punts/Average	71/42.9	75/44.7
Net Punting Avg.	71/38.9	75/38.9
Penalties/Yards	103/923	123/1055
Fumbles/Ball Lost	16/8	18/5
Touchdowns	53	37
Rushing	9	12
Passing	40	24
Returns	4	1

2012 INDIVIDUAL STATISTICS

PASSING

	Att.	Comp.	Yds.	Pct.	TD	Int.	Tkld.	Rate
Rodgers	552	371	4295	67.2	39	8	51/293	108.0
Harrell	4	2	20	50.0	0	0	0/0	64.6
Masthay	2	1	27	50.0	1	0	0/0	135.4
Packers	558	374	4342	67.0	40	8	51/293	108.3
Opponents	568	313	3801	55.1	24	18	47/309	76.8

SCORING

	TD R	TD P	TD Rt	PAT	FG	Saf	PTS
Crosby	0	0	0	50/50	21/33	0	113
Ja. Jones	0	14	0	0/0	0/0	0	84
Cobb	0	8	1	0/0	0/0	0	54
Nelson	0	7	0	0/0	0/0	0	44
G. Jennings	0	4	0	0/0	0/0	0	24
Crabtree	0	3	0	0/0	0/0	0	18
Driver	0	2	0	0/0	0/0	0	12
Finley	0	2	0	0/0	0/0	0	12
Grant	2	0	0	0/0	0/0	0	12
Harris	2	0	0	0/0	0/0	0	12
Rodgers	2	0	0	0/0	0/0	0	12
Benson	1	0	0	0/0	0/0	0	6
Daniels	0	0	1	0/0	0/0	0	6
M. Jennings	0	0	1	0/0	0/0	0	6
Kuhn	1	0	0	0/0	0/0	0	6
Moses	0	0	1	0/0	0/0	0	6
Starks	1	0	0	0/0	0/0	0	6
Packers	9	40	4	50/50	21/33	0	433
Opponents	12	24	1	34/34	26/30	0	336

2-Pt Conversions: Nelson, Packers 1-3, Opponents 1-3

RUSHING

	No.	Yds	Avg	LG	TD
Green	135	464	3.4	41	0
Rodgers	54	259	4.8	27t	2
Starks	71	255	3.6	22t	1
Benson	71	248	3.5	11	1
Harris	34	157	4.6	21	2
Cobb	10	132	13.2	28	0
Grant	31	127	4.1	18	2
Kuhn	23	63	2.7	9	1
Harrell	4	-3	-0.8	0	0
Packers	433	1702	3.9	41	9
Opponents	418	1896	4.5	82t	12

RECEIVING

	No.	Yds	Avg	LG	TD
Cobb	80	954	11.9	39t	8
Ja. Jones	64	784	12.3	49	14
Finley	61	667	10.9	40	2
Nelson	49	745	15.2	73	7
G. Jennings	36	366	10.2	45	4
Green	18	125	6.9	19	0
Kuhn	15	148	9.9	32	0
Benson	14	97	6.9	18	0
Crabtree	8	203	25.4	72t	3
Driver	8	77	9.6	26t	2
D. Williams	7	57	8.1	12	0
Boykin	5	27	5.4	9	0
Starks	4	31	7.8	9	0
Harris	2	17	8.5	11	0
Grant	1	34	34.0	34	0
Taylor	1	11	11.0	11	0
Rodgers	1	-1	-1.0	-1	0
Packers	374	4342	11.6	73	40
Opponents	313	3801	12.1	80t	24

INTERCEPTIONS

	No.	Yds	Avg	LG	TD
Hayward	6	81	13.5	24	0
Shields	3	32	10.7	32	0
T. Williams	2	38	19.0	38	0
Walden	2	22	11.0	20	0
Burnett	2	1	0.5	1	0
M. Jennings	1	72	72.0	72t	1
McMillian	1	0	0.0	0	0
Woodson	1	0	0.0	0	0
Packers	18	246	13.7	72t	1
Opponents	8	47	5.9	20	0

PUNTING

	No.	Yds.	Avg.	In 20	LG
Masthay	70	3043	43.5	30	65
Packers	71	3043	42.9	30	65
Opponents	75	3350	44.7	22	73

PUNT RETURNS

	Ret	FC	Yds	Avg	LG	TD
Cobb	31	21	292	9.4	75t	1
J. Ross	4	1	103	25.8	58	0
Shields	1	0	0	0.0	0	0
Packers	36	22	395	11.0	75t	1
Opponents	24	26	179	7.5	25	0

KICKOFF RETURNS

	No.	Yds	Avg	LG	TD
Cobb	38	964	25.4	46	0
J. Ross	3	86	28.7	44	0
D. Williams	2	24	12.0	12	0
Packers	43	1074	25.0	46	0
Opponents	51	1193	23.4	41	0

FIELD GOALS

	1-19	20-29	30-39	40-49	50+
Crosby	0/0	5/5	5/7	9/12	2/9
Packers	0/0	5/5	5/7	9/12	2/9
Opponents	0/0	8/8	7/7	6/8	5/7

SACKS

	No.
Matthews	13.0
Neal	4.5
Moses	4.0
Hawk	3.0
Walden	3.0
Wilson	2.5
Worthy	2.5
Burnett	2.0
Daniels	2.0
B. Jones	2.0
Perry	2.0
Smith	2.0
Woodson	1.5
House	1.0
Shields	1.0
(group)	1.0
Packers	47.0
Opponents	51.0

RECORD HOLDERS
INDIVIDUAL RECORDS—CAREER

Category	Name	Performance
Rushing (Yds.)	Ahman Green, 2000-06, 2009	8,322
Passing (Yds.)	Brett Favre, 1992-2007	**61,655
Passing (TDs)	Brett Favre, 1992-2007	**442
Receiving (No.)	Donald Driver, 1999-2012	743
Receiving (Yds.)	Donald Driver, 1999-2012	10,137
Interceptions	Bobby Dillon, 1952-59	52
Punting (Avg.)	Craig Hentrich, 1994-97	42.8
Punt Return (Avg.)	Desmond Howard, 1996, 1999	13.8
Kickoff Return (Avg.)	Travis Williams, 1967-1970	26.7
Field Goals	Ryan Longwell, 1997-2005	226
Touchdowns (Tot.)	Don Hutson, 1935-1945	105
Points	Ryan Longwell, 1997-2005	1,054
*Sacks	Kabeer Gbaja-Biamila, 2000-08	74.5

INDIVIDUAL RECORDS—SINGLE SEASON

Category	Name	Performance
Rushing (Yds.)	Ahman Green, 2003	1,883
Passing (Yds.)	Aaron Rodgers, 2011	4,643
Passing (TDs)	Aaron Rodgers, 2011	45
Receiving (No.)	Sterling Sharpe, 1993	112
Receiving (Yds.)	Robert Brooks, 1995	1,497
Interceptions	Irv Comp, 1943	10
Punting (Avg.)	Tim Masthay, 2011	45.6
Punt Return (Avg.)	Billy Grimes, 1950	19.1
Kickoff Return (Avg.)	Travis Williams, 1967	**41.1
Field Goals	Chester Marcol, 1972	33
	Ryan Longwell, 2000	33
Touchdowns (Tot.)	Ahman Green, 2003	20
Points	Paul Hornung, 1960	176
*Sacks	Tim Harris, 1989	19.5

INDIVIDUAL RECORDS—SINGLE GAME

Category	Name	Performance
Rushing (Yds.)	Ahman Green, 12-28-03	218
Passing (Yds.)	Matt Flynn, 1-1-12	480
Passing (TDs)	Matt Flynn, 1-1-12	6
	Aaron Rodgers, 10-14-12	6
Receiving (No.)	Don Hutson, 11-22-42	14
Receiving (Yds.)	Billy Howton, 10-21-56	257
Interceptions	Bobby Dillon, 11-26-53	**4
	Willie Buchanon, 9-24-78	**4
Field Goals	Chris Jacke, 11-11-90, 10-14-96	5
	Ryan Longwell, 9-24-00	5
Touchdowns (Tot.)	Paul Hornung, 12-12-65	5
Points	Paul Hornung, 10-8-61	33
*Sacks	Vonnie Holliday, 12-22-02	5.0

Sacks became an official statistic in 1982.
**NFL Record*

2013 VETERAN ROSTER

No.	Name	Pos.	Ht.	Wt.	Birthdate	NFL Exp.	College	Hometown	How Acq.	'12 Games/ Starts
67	Barclay, Don	T/G	6-4	305	4/18/89	2	West Virginia	Harmony, Pa.	FA-'12	16/4
55	Bishop, Desmond	LB	6-2	238	7/24/84	7	California	Fairfield, Calif.	D6b-'07	0*
11	Boykin, Jarrett	WR	6-2	218	11/4/89	2	Virginia Tech	Matthews, N.C.	FA-'12	10/0
75	Bulaga, Bryan	T	6-5	314	3/21/89	4	Iowa	Woodstock, Ill.	D1-'10	9/9
42	Burnett, Morgan	S	6-1	209	1/13/89	4	Georgia Tech	College Park, Ga.	D3-'10	16/16
24	Bush, Jarrett	CB	6-0	200	5/21/84	8	Utah State	Vacaville, Calif.	W(Car)-'06	16/1
18	Cobb, Randall	WR	5-10	192	8/22/90	3	Kentucky	Alcoa, Tenn.	D2-'11	15/8
2	Crosby, Mason	K	6-1	207	9/3/84	7	Colorado	Georgetown, Texas	D6c-'07	16/0
76	Daniels, Mike	DE	6-0	291	5/5/89	2	Iowa	Blackwood, N.J.	D4a-'12	14/0
62	Dietrich-Smith, Evan	C/G	6-2	308	7/19/86	4	Idaho State	Salinas, Calif.	FA-'10	16/6
88	Finley, Jermichael	TE	6-5	247	3/26/87	6	Texas	Diboll, Texas	D3-'08	16/14
49	Francois, Robert	LB	6-2	255	5/14/85	4	Boston College	Byfield, Mass.	FA-'09	16/0
61	Goode, Brett	LS	6-1	255	11/2/84	6	Arkansas	Fort Smith, Ark.	FA-'08	16/0
20	Green, Alex	RB	6-0	225	6/23/88	3	Hawaii	Portland, Ore.	D3-'11	12/4
6	Harrell, Graham	QB	6-2	215	5/22/85	2	Texas Tech	Ennis, Texas	FA-'10	4/0
50	Hawk, A.J.	LB	6-1	247	1/6/84	8	Ohio State	Centerville, Ohio	D1-'06	14/14
29	Hayward, Casey	CB	5-11	192	9/9/89	2	Vanderbilt	Perry, Ga.	D2b-'12	16/7
31	House, Davon	CB	6-0	195	7/10/89	3	New Mexico State	Palmdale, Calif.	D4-'11	9/5
68	Hughes, Kevin	T	6-4	304	8/6/88	2	Southeastern Louisiana	Amite City, La.	FA-'13	0*
43	Jennings, M.D.	S	6-0	187	7/25/88	3	Arkansas State	Calhoun City, Miss.	FA-'11	16/10
97	Jolly, Johnny	DT	6-3	325	2/21/83	5	Texas A&M	Houston, Texas	D6a-'06	0*
59	Jones, Brad	LB	6-3	242	4/1/86	5	Colorado	East Lansing, Mich.	D7-'09	16/10
89	Jones, James	WR	6-1	208	3/31/84	7	San Jose State	San Jose, Calif.	D3a-'07	16/16
30	Kuhn, John	RB	6-0	250	9/9/82	8	Shippensburg	York, Pa.	W(Pitt)-'07	14/3
70	Lang, T.J.	G	6-4	318	9/20/87	5	Eastern Michigan	Birmingham, Mich.	D4-'09	15/15
57	Lattimore, Jamari	LB	6-2	230	10/6/88	3	Middle Tennessee State	Hialeah, Fla.	FA-'11	14/0
56	Manning, Terrell	LB	6-2	237	4/16/90	2	North Carolina State	Laurinburg, N.C.	D5-'12	5/0
8	Masthay, Tim	P	6-1	200	3/16/87	4	Kentucky	Murray, Ky.	FA-'10	16/0
52	Matthews, Clay	LB	6-3	255	5/14/86	5	Southern California	Agoura Hills, Calif.	D1b-'09	12/12
22	McMillian, Jerron	S	5-11	203	4/2/89	2	Maine	Hillside, N.J.	D4b-'12	16/0
54	Moses, Dezman	LB	6-2	249	1/4/89	2	Tulane	Willingboro, N.J.	FA-'12	16/6
85	Mulligan, Matthew	TE	6-4	267	1/18/85	5	Maine	Howland, Maine	FA-'13	16/9*
96	Neal, Mike	DE	6-3	294	6/26/87	4	Purdue	Merrillville, Ind.	D2-'10	11/1
87	Nelson, Jordy	WR	6-3	217	5/31/85	6	Kansas State	Riley, Kan.	D2a-'08	12/10
74	Newhouse, Marshall	T	6-4	319	9/29/88	4	Texas Christian	Dallas, Texas	D5b-'10	16/16
53	Perry, Nick	LB	6-3	265	4/12/90	2	Southern California	Detroit, Mich.	D1-'12	6/5
79	Pickett, Ryan	DT	6-2	340	10/8/79	13	Ohio State	Zephyrhills, Fla.	UFA(StL)-'06	16/16
81	Quarless, Andrew	TE	6-4	252	10/6/88	4	Penn State	Uniondale, N.Y.	D5a-'10	0*
90	Raji, B.J.	DT	6-2	337	7/11/86	5	Boston College	Washington Township, N.J.	D1a-'09	14/14
28	Richardson, Sean	S	6-2	216	1/21/90	2	Vanderbilt	Linden, Ala.	FA-'12	5/0
12	Rodgers, Aaron	QB	6-2	225	12/2/83	9	California	Chico, Calif.	D1-'05	16/16
78	Sherrod, Derek	T/G	6-5	321	4/23/89	3	Mississippi State	Caledonia, Miss.	D1-'11	0*
37	Shields, Sam	CB	5-11	184	12/8/87	4	Miami	Sarasota, Fla.	FA-'10	10/8
71	Sitton, Josh	G	6-3	318	6/6/86	6	Central Florida	Pensacola, Fla.	D4b-'08	16/16
44	Starks, James	RB	6-2	218	2/25/86	4	Buffalo	Niagara Falls, N.Y.	D6-'10	6/2
82	Taylor, Ryan	TE	6-3	254	11/16/87	3	North Carolina	Winston-Salem, N.C.	D7a-'11	16/1
64	Van Roten, Greg	G/C	6-3	303	2/26/90	2	Pennsylvania	Mineola, N.Y.	FA-'12	7/0
84	Williams, D.J.	TE	6-2	245	9/10/88	3	Arkansas	Little Rock, Ark.	D5-'11	13/2
38	Williams, Tramon	CB	5-11	191	3/16/83	7	Louisiana Tech	Napoleonville, La.	FA-'06	16/16
98	Wilson, C.J.	DE	6-3	290	3/30/87	4	East Carolina	Pinetown, N.C.	D7-'10	11/7
99	Worthy, Jerel	DE	6-2	308	4/28/90	2	Michigan State	Huber Heights, Ohio	D2a-'12	14/4

* Bishop missed '12 season because of injury; Hughes last active with St. Louis in '11; Jolly last active with Green Bay in '09; Mulligan played 16 games with St. Louis in '12; Quarless missed '12 season because of injury; Sherrod missed '12 season because of injury.

Players lost through free agency (2): WR Greg Jennings (Minn; 8 games), LB Erik Walden (Ind; 15).

Also played with Packers in '12—RB Cedric Benson (5 games), TE Tom Crabtree (16), WR Donald Driver (13), RB Ryan Grant (4), DE Phillip Merling (3), RB Brandon Saine (6), C Jeff Saturday (14), LB Vic So'oto (1), LB D.J. Smith (6), DB Charles Woodson (7), LB Frank Zombo (7).

FIRST-YEAR ROSTER

Name	Pos.	Ht.	Wt.	Birthdate	College	Hometown	How Acq.
Amosa, Jonathan	FB	5-11	247	10/16/90	Washington	Seattle, Wash.	FA
Bakhtiari, David	T	6-4	300	9/30/91	Colorado	San Mateo, Calif.	D4a
Barrington, Sam	LB	6-1	235	10/5/90	South Florida	Jacksonville, Fla.	D7c
Bostick, Brandon (1)	TE	6-3	250	5/3/89	Newberry	Florence, S.C.	FA-'12
Boyd, Josh	DE	6-3	310	8/3/89	Mississippi State	Philadelphia, Miss.	D5b
Brown, Matt	QB	6-3	225	8/15/90	Illinois State	Marion, Ill.	FA
Coleman, B.J. (1)	QB	6-3	231	9/16/88	Tennessee-Chattanooga	Chattanooga, Tenn.	D7b-'12
Cunningham, Sederrik	WR	5-11	192	7/18/89	Furman	Zephyrhills, Fla.	FA
Datko, Andrew (1)	T	6-6	315	8/15/90	Florida State	Fort Lauderdale, Fla.	D7a-'12
Dorsey, Kevin	WR	6-1	207	2/23/90	Maryland	Forestville, Md.	D7b
Franklin, Johnathan	RB	5-10	205	10/23/89	UCLA	Los Angeles, Calif.	D4c
Gerhart, Garth (1)	C	6-1	310	10/21/88	Arizona State	Norco, Calif.	FA-'12
Harris, DuJuan (1)	RB	5-8	203	9/3/88	Troy	Brooksville, Fla.	FA-'12
Hyde, Micah	CB	6-0	197	12/31/90	Iowa	Fostoria, Ohio	D5a
Johnson, Charles	WR	6-2	215	2/27/89	Grand Valley State	Erlanger, Ky.	D7a
Johnson, Micah (1)	LB	6-2	265	6/22/88	Kentucky	Fort Campbell, Ky.	FA-'12
Jones, Datone	DE	6-4	285	7/24/90	UCLA	Compton, Calif.	D1
Lacy, Eddie	RB	5-11	230	6/2/90	Alabama	Geismar, La.	D2
Lewis, Patrick	C	6-1	311	1/30/91	Texas A&M	Reserve, La.	FA
Means, Loyce (1)	CB	5-10	188	3/31/89	Houston	Houston, Texas	FA
Miller, Jordan (1)	DT	6-1	316	2/1/88	Southern	Largo, Md.	FA-'12
Mulumba, Andy	LB	6-3	260	1/31/90	Eastern Michigan	Montreal	FA
Nixon, James (1)	CB	6-0	186	2/2/88	California (Pa.)	Hamden, Conn.	FA-'12
Palmer, Nate	LB	6-2	248	9/23/89	Illinois State	Chicago, Ill.	D6
Pease, Angelo	RB	5-10	211	8/12/91	Kansas State	Cairo, Ga.	FA
Peña, Gilbert	DT	6-2	330	11/15/86	Mississippi	Yonkers, N.Y.	FA
Powell, Chaz (1)	S	6-0	203	1/1/88	Penn State	Glen Rock, Pa.	FA-'12
Ross, Jeremy (1)	WR	6-0	215	3/16/88	California	Elk Grove, Calif.	FA-'12
Savage, Donte	LB	6-1	252	5/5/89	New Mexico State	Portland, Ore.	FA
Smith, Brandon (1)	CB	6-1	205	2/23/87	Arizona State	Bakersfield, Calif.	FA
Stoneburner, Jake	TE	6-3	249	8/25/89	Ohio State	Dublin, Ohio	FA
Tavecchio, Giorgio (1)	K	5-10	182	7/16/90	California	Moraga, Calif.	FA
Taylor, Lane	G	6-3	324	11/22/89	Oklahoma State	Arlington, Texas	FA
Tretter, JC	T	6-4	307	2/12/91	Cornell	Akron, N.Y.	D4b
Walker, Tyrone	WR	5-10	191	8/25/90	Illinois State	Indianapolis, Ind.	FA
White, Myles	WR	6-0	182	3/30/90	Louisiana Tech	Livonia, Mich.	FA
Wilson, Jarvis	LB	6-1	245	7/12/90	Prairie View A&M	Fort Worth, Texas	FA

The term NFL Rookie is defined as a player who is in his first season of professional football and has not been on the roster of another professional football team for any regular-season or postseason games. A Rookie is designated by an "R" on NFL rosters. Players who have been active in another professional football league or players who have NFL experience, including either preseason training camp or being on an Active List or Inactive List, or on Reserve/Injured or Reserve/Physically Unable to Perform for fewer than six regular-season games, are termed NFL First-Year Players. An NFL First-Year Player is designated by a "1" on NFL rosters. Thereafter, a player is credited with an additional year of experience for each season in which he accumulates six games on the Active List or Inactive List, or on Reserve/Injured or Reserve/Physically Unable to Perform.

Log on to www.packers.com for an up-to-date roster.

COACHING STAFF

Head Coach,
Mike McCarthy

Pro Career: Named the fourteenth head coach in team history January 12, 2006. Joined Vince Lombardi and Mike Holmgren as the only coaches to guide the Packers to a Super Bowl title with a win over Pittsburgh in Super Bowl XLV. Joined Pittsburgh's Bill Cowher (2005) as the only Super Bowl-winning coaches to lead their respective teams to three road wins as the No. 6 seed in the postseason en route to a world title. Has led the Packers to playoff appearances in five of his seven seasons at the helm, and the team's five postseason berths over the past six seasons are the most by an NFC team. Has guided the club to back-to-back NFC North titles, the first time Green Bay has done so since winning three straight division crowns from 2002-04. His .656 winning percentage (including playoffs) ranks No. 3 among active NFL coaches (min. 50 games) entering 2013. Has led the Packers to 47 regular-season wins since 2009, the second most in the NFL over that span and the second most in franchise history over four seasons. Reached 75 wins (including playoffs) in his 114th career game, tied for No. 1 among active coaches with Kansas City's Andy Reid. In 2011, guided the team to a franchise-record 15 wins as well as team marks for points (560), touchdowns (70) and total net yards (6,482) on the way to the NFC North title and the top seed in the conference for the first time since 1996. The offense has ranked in the top 10 in scoring and total yards in six of his seven seasons as head coach. Named Motorola Coach of the Year, matched a then-franchise record with 13 wins, and won NFC North Division title in 2007. Became the first coach since Lombardi to lead Packers to a championship game in his second season. Had returned to Green Bay after serving as the team's quarterbacks coach in 1999. The list of quarterbacks he has coached includes Joe Montana, Elvis Grbac, Rich Gannon, Brett Favre, Matt Flynn, Aaron Rodgers, Matt Hasselbeck, Aaron Brooks, Jake Delhomme, Marc Bulger, Steve Bono, and Jeff Blake—a collection that has combined for 37 career Pro Bowl selections and 10 Super Bowl starts. Career record: 80-42.

Background: Graduated with business administration degree from Baker University. Was an all-conference tight end (1985-86), helping the school to a NAIA Division II runner-up finish as a senior captain. Coached collegiately at Fort Hays State (1987-88) and Pittsburgh (1989-1992), before moving to the NFL with the Chiefs (1993-98), Packers (1999), Saints (2000-04) and 49ers (2005).

Personal: Born November 10, 1963, in Pittsburgh, Pa. Family includes wife Jessica and children Alexandra, Jack, George, Gabrielle and Isabella.

ASSISTANT COACHES

Edgar Bennett, wide receivers; born February 15, 1969, Jacksonville, Fla. Running back Florida State 1987, 1989-1991. Pro running back Green Bay Packers 1992-96, Chicago Bears 1998-99. Pro coach: Joined Packers in 2001.

James Campen, offensive line; born June 11, 1964, Sacramento, Calif. Center Sacramento City (Calif.) J.C. 1982-83, Tulane 1984-85. Pro center New Orleans Saints 1987-88, Green Bay Packers 1989-1993. Pro coach: Joined Packers in 2004.

Dom Capers, defensive coordinator; born August 7, 1950, Cambridge, Ohio. Defensive back Mount Union 1968-1971. No pro playing experience. College coach: Kent State 1972-74, Hawaii 1975-76, San Jose State 1977, California 1978-79, Tennessee 1980-81, Ohio State 1982-83. Pro coach: Philadelphia/Baltimore Stars (USFL) 1984-85, New Orleans Saints 1986-1991, Pittsburgh Steelers 1992-94, Carolina Panthers 1995-98 (head coach), Jacksonville Jaguars 1999-2000, Houston Texans 2001-05 (head coach), Miami Dolphins 2006-07, New England Patriots 2008, joined Packers in 2009.

Tom Clements, offensive coordinator; born June 18, 1953, McKees Rocks, Pa. Quarterback Notre Dame 1972-74. Pro quarterback Ottawa Rough Riders (CFL) 1975-78, Hamilton Tiger-Cats (CFL) 1979, 1981-82, Kansas City Chiefs 1980, Winnipeg Blue Bombers (CFL) 1983-87. College coach: Notre Dame 1992-95. Pro coach: New Orleans Saints 1997-99, Kansas City Chiefs 2000, Pittsburgh Steelers 2001-03, Buffalo Bills 2004-05, joined Packers in 2006.

Jerry Fontenot, tight ends; born November 21, 1966, Lafayette, La. Guard Texas A&M 1985-88. Pro center Chicago Bears 1989-1996, New Orleans Saints 1997-2003, Cincinnati Bengals 2004. Pro coach: Joined Packers in 2006.

Kevin Greene, outside linebackers; born July 31, 1962, Schenectady, N.Y. Linebacker Auburn 1980-85. Pro linebacker Los Angeles Rams 1985-1992, Pittsburgh Steelers 1993-95, Carolina Panthers 1996, San Francisco 49ers 1997, Carolina Panthers 1998-99. Pro coach: Joined Packers in 2009.

Joel Hilgenberg, asst. offensive line; born July 10, 1962, Iowa City, Iowa. Center Iowa 1980-83. Pro center/guard New Orleans Saints 1984-1993. Pro coach: Joined Packers in 2011.

Mark Lovat, strength & conditioning coordinator; born Oct. 9, 1969, Pocatello, Idaho. Attended Butler. No college or pro playing experience. Pro coach: Joined Packers in 1999.

Ben McAdoo, quarterbacks; born July 7, 1977, Homer City, Pa. Attended Indiana University (Pa.). No college or pro playing experience. College coach: Michigan State 2001, Fairfield 2002, Pittsburgh 2003, Akron 2004, Stanford 2005. Pro coach: New Orleans Saints 2004, San Francisco

49ers 2005, joined Packers in 2006.

Scott McCurley, defensive quality control; born August 1, 1980, New Castle, Pa. Linebacker Pittsburgh 1998-2002. No pro playing experience. College coach: Pittsburgh 2003-05. Pro coach: Joined Packers in 2006.

Chad Morton, special teams assistant; born April 4, 1977, Torrance, Calif. Running back Southern California 1995-99. Pro running back New Orleans Saints 2000, N.Y. Jets 2001-02, Washington Redskins 2003-04, New York Giants 2005-06. Pro coach: Joined Packers in 2009.

Winston Moss, asst. head coach/inside linebackers; born December 24, 1965, Miami, Fla. Linebacker Miami 1983-86. Pro linebacker Tampa Bay Buccaneers 1987-1990, Los Angeles Raiders 1991-94, Seattle Seahawks 1995-97. Pro coach: Seattle Seahawks 1998, New Orleans Saints 2000-05, joined Packers in 2006.

Darren Perry, secondary-safeties; born December 29, 1968, Norfolk, Va. Safety Penn State 1989-1991. Pro safety Pittsburgh Steelers 1992-98, San Diego Chargers 1999, New Orleans Saints 2000. Pro coach: Cincinnati Bengals 2002, Pittsburgh Steelers 2003-06, Oakland Raiders 2007-08, joined Packers in 2009.

John Rushing, offensive assistant/special teams; born February 26, 1972, Merced, Calif. Defensive back Washington State 1991-94. No pro playing experience. College coach: Willamette (Ore.) 1996-97, Boise State 1998-99, Montana State 2000-02, Utah State 2003-08. Pro coach: Joined Packers in 2009.

Shawn Slocum, special teams coordinator; born February 21, 1965, Bryan, Texas. Linebacker Texas A&M 1983-84. No pro playing experience. College coach: Texas A&M 1989, 1991-97, 2000-02, Pittsburgh 1990, Southern California 1998-99, Mississippi 2005. Pro coach: Joined Packers in 2006.

Mike Trgovac, defensive line; born February 27, 1959, Youngstown, Ohio. Defensive lineman Michigan 1977-1980. No pro playing experience. College coach: Michigan 1983-85, Ball State 1986-88, Navy 1989, Colorado State 1990-91, Notre Dame 1992-94. Pro coach: Philadelphia Eagles 1995-98, Green Bay Packers 2000-01, Washington Redskins 2000-01, Carolina Panthers 2002-08, re-joined Packers in 2009.

Alex Van Pelt, running backs; born May 1, 1970, Pittsburgh, Pa. Quarterback Pittsburgh 1989-1992. Pro quarterback Buffalo Bills 1995-2003. College coach: Buffalo 2005. Pro coach: Frankfurt Galaxy (NFLE) 2005, Buffalo Bills 2006-09, Tampa Bay Buccaneers 2010-11, joined Packers in 2012.

Joe Whitt Jr., secondary-cornerbacks; born July 19, 1978, Auburn, Ala. Wide receiver Auburn 1997-99. No pro playing experience. College coach: Auburn 2000-01, The Citadel 2002, Louisville 2003-06. Pro coach: Atlanta Falcons 2007, joined Packers in 2008.

National Football Conference
North Division
Team Colors: Purple, Gold, and White
9520 Viking Drive
Eden Prairie, Minnesota 55344
Telephone: (952) 828-6500

2013 SCHEDULE
PRESEASON
Aug. 9	**Houston**	7:00
Aug. 16	at Buffalo	6:00
Aug. 25	at San Francisco	7:00
Aug. 29	**Tennessee**	7:00

REGULAR SEASON
Sep. 8	at Detroit	12:00
Sep. 15	at Chicago	12:00
Sep. 22	**Cleveland**	12:00
Sep. 29	**Pittsburgh** (London)	12:00
Oct. 6	BYE	
Oct. 13	**Carolina**	12:00
Oct. 21	at New York Giants (Mon)	7:40
Oct. 27	**Green Bay**	7:30
Nov. 3	at Dallas	12:00
Nov. 7	**Washington** (Thurs)	7:25
Nov. 17	at Seattle	3:25
Nov. 24	at Green Bay	12:00
Dec. 1	**Chicago**	12:00
Dec. 8	at Baltimore	12:00
Dec. 15	**Philadelphia**	12:00
Dec. 22	at Cincinnati	12:00
Dec. 29	**Detroit**	12:00

All times CT
Stadium: Mall of America Field at
Hubert H. Humphrey Metrodome
(opened in 1982)
• **Capacity:** 63,731
425 Chicago Avenue
Minneapolis, Minnesota 55415
Playing Surface: Sportexe Momentum
Training Camp: Minnesota State-Mankato
Mankato, Minnesota
56001

MALL OF AMERICA FIELD AT HUBERT H. HUMPHREY METRODOME

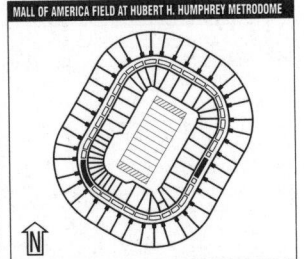

CLUB OFFICIALS
Owner/Chairman: Zygi Wilf
Owner/President: Mark Wilf
Owner/Vice Chairman: Leonard Wilf
Ownership Partners: Reggie Fowler,
Alan Landis, David Mandelbaum
General Manager: Rick Spielman
Vice President of Public Affairs/Stadium
Development: Lester Bagley
Vice President of Football Operations:
Rob Brzezinski
Vice President of Sales and Marketing:
Steve LaCroix
Vice President of Finance: Steve Poppen
Vice President of Operations and Legal
Counsel: Kevin Warren
Vice President of Strategic Planning &
Business Initiatives: Jonathan Wilf
Director of College Scouting:
Scott Studwell
Director of Corporate Communications:
Jeff Anderson
Director of Public Relations: Bob Hagan
Director of Community Relations:
Brad Madson
Director of Operations/Team Travel:
Luther Hippe
Director of Operations & Facilities:
Chad Lundeen
Director of Suites and Premium Seating:
J.P. Paul
Director of Ticketing and Hospitality:
Phil Huebner
Director of Video: Bob Marcus
Executive Director of Player
Development/Legal: Les Pico
Director of Security: Kim Klawiter
Head Athletic Trainer: Eric Sugarman
Equipment Manager: Dennis Ryan
Director of Marketing & Business
Development: Dannon Hulskotter
Director of Corporate Sales: Mike Slates
Director of Human Resources:
Lisa Larson

COACHING HISTORY
(445-382-9)
Records include postseason games
1961-66	Norm Van Brocklin	29-51-4
1967-1983	Bud Grant	161-99-5
1984	Les Steckel	3-13-0
1985	Bud Grant	7-9-0
1986-1991	Jerry Burns	55-46-0
1992-2001	Dennis Green*	101-70-0
2001-05	Mike Tice	33-34-0
2006-2010	Brad Childress**	40-37-0
2010-12	Leslie Frazier	16-23-0

*Resigned after 15 games in 2001
**Released after 10 games in 2010

PAID ATTENDANCE
Home 473,161   Away 513,614
Total 986,775
Single-game home record,
64,482 (11/2/03)
Single-season home record,
510,741 (1998)

2013 DRAFT CHOICES
Round	Name	Pos.	College
1	Sharrif Floyd	DT	Florida
	Xavier Rhodes	DB	Florida St.
	Cordarrelle Patterson	WR	Tennessee
4	Gerald Hodges	LB	Penn St.
5	Jeff Locke	P	UCLA
6	Jeff Baca	G	UCLA
7	Michael Mauti	LB	Penn St.
	Travis Bond	G	North Carolina
	Everett Dawkins	DT	Florida St.

2012 TEAM RECORD
PRESEASON (1-3)

Date	Result		Opponent
08/10	L	6-17	at San Francisco
08/17	W	36-14	Buffalo
08/24	L	10-12	San Diego
08/30	L	24-28	at Houston

REGULAR SEASON (10-6)

Date	Result		Opponent
09/09	W	26-23	Jacksonville (OT)
09/16	L	20-23	at Indianapolis
09/23	W	24-13	San Francisco
09/30	W	20-13	at Detroit
10/07	W	30-7	Tennessee
10/14	L	26-38	at Washington
10/21	W	21-14	Arizona
10/25	L	17-36	Tampa Bay
11/04	L	20-30	at Seattle
11/11	W	34-24	Detroit
11/25	L	10-28	at Chicago
12/02	L	14-23	at Green Bay
12/09	W	21-14	Chicago
12/16	W	36-22	at St. Louis
12/23	W	23-6	at Houston
12/30	W	37-34	Green Bay

(OT) Overtime

POSTSEASON (0-1)

Date	Result	Opponent	Attendance
01/05	L 10-24	at Green Bay	71,548

SCORE BY PERIODS

Vikings	101	112	74	89	3 —	379
Opponents	60	104	77	107	0 —	348

2012 TEAM STATISTICS

	Vikings	Opp.
Total First Downs	306	345
Rushing	113	82
Passing	163	229
Penalty	30	34
3rd Down: Made/Att	78/210	95/230
3rd Down Pct.	37.1	41.3
4th Down: Made/Att	7/11	11/20
4th Down Pct.	63.6	55.0
Possession Avg.	28:36	31:24
Total Net Yards	5385	5600
Avg. Per Game	336.6	350.0
Total Plays	1001	1083
Avg. Per Play	5.4	5.2
Net Yards Rushing	2634	1692
Avg. Per Game	164.6	105.8
Total Rushes	486	427
Net Yards Passing	2751	3908
Avg. Per Game	171.9	244.3
Sacked/Yards Lost	32/184	44/284
Gross Yards	2935	4192
Att./Completions	483/300	612/391
Completion Pct.	62.1	63.9
Had Intercepted	12	10
Punts/Average	72/45.0	76/44.0
Net Punting Avg.	72/39.7	76/40.0
Penalties/Yards	90/830	111/949
Fumbles/Ball Lost	21/11	23/12
Touchdowns	39	39
Rushing	16	10
Passing	18	28
Returns	5	1

2012 INDIVIDUAL STATISTICS

Passing	Att.	Comp.	Yds.	Pct.	TD	Int.	Tkld.	Rate
Ponder	483	300	2935	62.1	18	12	32/184	81.2
Vikings	483	300	2935	62.1	18	12	32/184	81.2
Opponents	612	391	4192	63.9	28	10	44/284	92.3

SCORING	TD R	TD P	TD Rt	PAT	FG	Saf	PTS
Walsh	0	0	0	36/36	35/38	0	141
Peterson	12	1	0	0/0	0/0	0	80
Rudolph	0	9	0	0/0	0/0	0	56
Harvin	1	3	1	0/0	0/0	0	30
Jenkins	0	2	0	0/0	0/0	0	12
Ponder	2	0	0	0/0	0/0	0	12
Smith	0	0	2	0/0	0/0	0	12
Wright	0	2	0	0/0	0/0	0	12
S. Burton	0	1	0	0/0	0/0	0	6
Gerhart	1	0	0	0/0	0/0	0	6
Griffen	0	0	1	0/0	0/0	0	6
Sherels	0	0	1	0/0	0/0	0	6
Vikings	16	18	5	36/36	35/38	0	379
Opponents	10	28	1	33/35	25/30	0	348

2-Pt Conversions: Peterson, Rudolph,
Vikings 2-3, Opponents 3-4

RUSHING	No.	Yds	Avg	LG	TD
Peterson	348	2097	6.0	82t	12
Ponder	60	253	4.2	29	2
Gerhart	50	169	3.4	22	1
Harvin	22	96	4.4	20	1
Wright	2	11	5.5	8	0
Asiata	3	9	3.0	5	0
Webb	1	-1	-1.0	-1	0
Vikings	486	2634	5.4	82t	16
Opponents	427	1692	4.0	76t	10

RECEIVING	No.	Yds	Avg	LG	TD
Harvin	62	677	10.9	45	3
Rudolph	53	493	9.3	29	9
Jenkins	40	449	11.2	32	2
Peterson	40	217	5.4	20	1
Simpson	26	274	10.5	33	0
Wright	22	310	14.1	65	2
Gerhart	20	155	7.8	21	0
Aromashodu	11	182	16.5	31	0
Carlson	8	43	5.4	14	0
Ellison	7	65	9.3	29	0
S. Burton	5	35	7.0	13	1
Felton	3	35	11.7	17	0
Reisner	1	13	13.0	13	0
Asiata	1	2	2.0	2	0
Ponder	1	-15	-15.0	-15	0
Vikings	300	2935	9.8	65	18
Opponents	391	4192	10.7	73	28

INTERCEPTIONS	No.	Yds	Avg	LG	TD
Smith	3	87	29.0	56t	2
Winfield	3	37	12.3	31	0
Robinson	2	68	34.0	44	0
Griffen	1	29	29.0	29t	1
Greenway	1	3	3.0	3	0
Vikings	10	224	22.4	56t	3
Opponents	12	72	6.0	35	1

PUNTING	No.	Yds.	Avg.	In 20	LG
Kluwe	72	3237	45	18	59
Vikings	72	3237	45	18	59
Opponents	76	3344	44	28	65

PUNT RETURNS	Ret	FC	Yds	Avg	LG	TD
Sherels	32	27	287	9.0	77t	1
Vikings	32	27	287	9.0	77t	1
Opponents	41	12	341	8.3	32	0

KICKOFF RETURNS	No.	Yds	Avg	LG	TD
Harvin	16	574	35.9	105t	1
Sherels	16	422	26.4	41	0
Robinson	3	61	20.3	24	0
Asiata	3	55	18.3	22	0
Ballard	2	12	6.0	8	0
Jefferson	1	20	20.0	20	0
Felton	1	16	16.0	16	0
Reed	1	10	10.0	10	0
Rudolph	1	1	1.0	1	0
Vikings	44	1171	26.6	105t	1
Opponents	33	795	24.1	94	0

FIELD GOALS	1-19	20-29	30-39	40-49	50+
Walsh	0/0	10/10	8/9	7/9	10/10
Vikings	0/0	10/10	8/9	7/9	10/10
Opponents	1/1	5/5	5/6	10/12	4/6

SACKS	No.
Allen	12.0
Robison	8.5
Griffen	8.0
Greenway	3.0
Henderson	3.0
Evans	2.0
Guion	2.0
Williams	2.0
Ballard	1.0
Cook	1.0
Smith	1.0
Winfield	0.5
Vikings	44.0
Opponents	32.0

RECORD HOLDERS
INDIVIDUAL RECORDS—CAREER

Category	Name	Performance
Rushing (Yds.)	Adrian Peterson, 2007-2012	8,849
Passing (Yds.)	Fran Tarkenton, 1961-66, 1972-78	33,098
Passing (TDs)	Fran Tarkenton, 1961-66, 1972-78	239
Receiving (No.)	Cris Carter, 1990-2001	1,004
Receiving (Yds.)	Cris Carter, 1990-2001	12,383
Interceptions	Paul Krause, 1968-1979	53
Punting (Avg.)	Chris Kluwe, 2005-2012	44.4
Punt Return (Avg.)	Mewelde Moore, 2004-07	10.4
Kickoff Return (Avg.)	Percy Harvin, 2009-2012	27.9
Field Goals	Fred Cox, 1963-1977	282
Touchdowns (Tot.)	Cris Carter, 1990-2001	110
Points	Fred Cox, 1963-1977	1,365
*Sacks	John Randle, 1990-2000	114.0

INDIVIDUAL RECORDS—SINGLE SEASON

Category	Name	Performance
Rushing (Yds.)	Adrian Peterson, 2012	2,097
Passing (Yds.)	Daunte Culpepper, 2004	4,717
Passing (TDs)	Daunte Culpepper, 2004	39
Receiving (No.)	Cris Carter, 1994, 1995	122
Receiving (Yds.)	Randy Moss, 2003	1,632
Interceptions	Paul Krause, 1975	10
Punting (Avg.)	Chris Kluwe, 2008	47.6
Punt Return (Avg.)	David Palmer, 1995	13.2
Kickoff Return (Avg.)	Percy Harvin, 2012	35.9
Field Goals	Gary Anderson, 1998	35
	Blair Walsh, 2012	35
Touchdowns (Tot.)	Chuck Foreman, 1975	22
Points	Gary Anderson, 1998	164
*Sacks	Jared Allen, 2011	22.0

INDIVIDUAL RECORDS—SINGLE GAME

Category	Name	Performance
Rushing (Yds.)	Adrian Peterson, 11-4-07	**296
Passing (Yds.)	Tommy Kramer, 11-2-86	490
Passing (TDs)	Joe Kapp, 9-28-69	**7
Receiving (No.)	Rickey Young, 12-16-79	15
Receiving (Yds.)	Sammy White, 11-7-76	210
Interceptions	Many Times	3
	Last time by Darren Sharper, 11-13-05	
Field Goals	Rich Karlis, 11-5-89	7
Touchdowns (Tot.)	Chuck Foreman, 12-20-75	4
	Ahmad Rashad, 9-2-79	4
Points	Chuck Foreman, 12-20-75	24
	Ahmad Rashad, 9-2-79	24
*Sacks	Randy Holloway, 9-16-84	5.0

*Sacks became an official statistic in 1982.
**NFL Record

2013 VETERAN ROSTER

No.	Name	Pos.	Ht.	Wt.	Birthdate	NFL Exp.	College	Hometown	How Acq.	'12 Games/ Starts
69	Allen, Jared	DE	6-6	270	4/3/82	10	Idaho State	Los Gatos, Calif.	T(KC)-'08	16/16
44	Asiata, Matt	RB	6-0	234	7/24/87	2	Utah	Santa Ana, Calif.	FA-'11	16/0
99	Ballard, Christian	DT	6-4	283	1/3/89	3	Iowa	Lawrence, Kan.	D4-'11	16/0
61	Berger, Joe	C	6-5	305	5/25/82	8	Michigan Tech	Newaygo, Mich.	FA-'11	16/0
4	Bethel-Thompson, McLeod	QB	6-3	230	9/3/88	2	Sacramento State	San Francisco, Calif.	FA-'12	0*
36	Blanton, Robert	S	6-1	200	9/7/89	2	Notre Dame	Matthews, N.C.	D5-'12	13/0
27	Burton, Brandon	CB	5-11	190	7/31/89	3	Utah	Houston, Texas	D5-'11	4/0
11	Burton, Stephen	WR	6-1	224	12/11/89	3	West Texas A&M	Lakewood, Calif.	D7b-'11	12/1
89	Carlson, John	TE	6-5	248	5/12/84	5	Notre Dame	Litchfield, Minn	UFA(Sea)-'12	14/6
16	Cassel, Matt	QB	6-4	228	5/17/82	9	Southern California	Chatsworth, Calif.	UFA(KC)-'13	9/8*
57	Cole, Audie	LB	6-5	239	6/1/89	2	North Carolina State	Monroe, Mich.	D7a-'12	5/0
20	Cook, Chris	CB	6-2	212	2/15/87	4	Virginia	Lynchburg, Va.	D2a-'10	10/10
51	Dean, Larry	LB	6-0	226	8/7/88	3	Valdosta State	Tifton, Ga.	FA-'11	16/0
40	Ellison, Rhett	FB	6-5	250	10/3/88	2	Southern California	Portola Valley, Calif.	D4b-'12	16/8
90	Evans, Fred	DT	6-4	305	11/6/83	7	Texas St.-San Marcos	Morgan Park, Ill.	FA-'07	16/1
42	Felton, Jerome	FB	6-0	248	7/3/86	6	Furman	Madisonville, Tenn	UFA(Ind)-'12	16/7
63	Fusco, Brandon	G	6-4	306	7/26/88	3	Slippery Rock	Cranberry Township, Pa.	D6c-'11	16/16
32	Gerhart, Toby	RB	6-0	231	3/28/87	4	Stanford	Norco, Calif.	D2b-'10	16/0
52	Greenway, Chad	LB	6-2	242	1/12/83	7	Iowa	Mt. Vernon, S.D.	D1-'06	16/16
97	Griffen, Everson	DE	6-3	273	12/22/87	4	Southern California	Avondale, Ariz.	D4-'10	16/1
98	Guion, Letroy	DT	6-4	303	6/21/87	6	Florida State	Starke, Fla.	D5b-'08	15/15
50	Henderson, Erin	LB	6-3	244	7/1/86	5	Maryland	Aberdeen, Md.	FA-'08	14/10
94	Jackson, Lawrence	DE	6-4	278	8/30/85	6	Southern California	Inglewood, Calif.	UFA(Det)-'13	15/0*
24	Jefferson, A.J.	CB	6-1	190	4/4/88	4	Fresno State	Bakersfield, Calif.	T(Ariz)-'12	15/7
15	Jennings, Greg	WR	6-0	195	9/21/83	8	Western Michigan	Kalamazoo, Mich.	UFA(GB)-'13	8/5*
74	Johnson, Charlie	G	6-4	305	5/2/84	8	Oklahoma State	Sherman, Texas	UFA(Ind)-'11	16/16
92	Johnson, George	DE	6-4	270	12/11/87	4	Rutgers	Glassboro, N.J.	FA-'12	2/0
75	Kalil, Matt	T	6-7	308	7/6/89	2	Southern California	Corona, Calif.	D1a-'12	16/16
79	Keith, Brandon	T	6-5	338	11/21/84	4	Northern Iowa	McAlester, Okla.	FA-'13	0*
78	Kropog, Troy	G	6-6	295	7/31/86	4	Tulane	Metairie, La.	FA-'12	1/0*
26	Lacey, Jacob	CB	5-10	183	5/28/87	5	Oklahoma State	Garland, Texas	UFA(Det)-'13	11/9*
71	Loadholt, Phil	T	6-8	343	1/21/86	5	Oklahoma	Fountain, Colo.	D2-'09	16/16
46	Loeffler, Cullen	LS	6-5	241	1/27/81	10	Texas	Ingram, Texas	FA-'04	16/0
73	Love, DeMarcus	T	6-4	315	3/7/88	2	Arkansas	Lancaster, Texas	D6a-'11	0*
58	McKenzie, Tyrone	LB	6-2	245	12/11/85	3	South Florida	Riverview, Fla.	FA-'11	16/0
55	Mitchell, Marvin	LB	6-3	246	10/21/84	7	Tennessee	Norfolk, Va.	UFA(Mia)-'12	11/1
72	Olsen, Seth	G	6-5	305	12/17/85	4	Iowa	Omaha, Neb.	FA-'13	5/4*
28	Peterson, Adrian	RB	6-1	217	3/21/85	7	Oklahoma	Palestine, Texas	D1-'07	16/16
7	Ponder, Christian	QB	6-2	229	2/25/88	3	Florida State	Colleyville, Texas	D1-'11	16/16
41	Raymond, Mistral	S	6-1	194	9/7/87	3	South Florida	Palmetto, Fla.	D6b-'11	10/3
91	Reed, D'Aundre	DE	6-4	260	1/1/88	2	Arizona	Moreno Valley, Calif.	D7a-'11	6/0
21	Robinson, Josh	CB	5-10	199	1/8/91	2	Central Florida	Sunrise, Fla.	D3-'12	16/6
96	Robison, Brian	DE	6-3	259	4/27/83	7	Texas	Splendora, Texas	D4-'07	15/15
82	Rudolph, Kyle	TE	6-6	258	11/9/89	3	Notre Dame	Cincinnati, Ohio	D2-'11	16/16
33	Sanford, Jamarca	S	5-10	200	8/27/85	5	Mississippi	Batesville, Miss.	D7-'09	16/10
34	Sendejo, Andrew	S	6-1	200	9/9/87	3	Rice	Spring Branch, Texas	FA-'11	13/0
35	Sherels, Marcus	CB	5-10	175	9/30/87	3	Minnesota	Rochester, Minn.	FA-'10	16/0
81	Simpson, Jerome	WR	6-2	189	2/4/86	6	Coastal Carolina	Reidsville, N.C.	UFA(Cin)-'12	12/10
22	Smith, Harrison	S	6-2	214	2/2/89	2	Notre Dame	Knoxville, Tenn.	D1b-'12	16/16
65	Sullivan, John	C	6-4	301	8/8/85	6	Notre Dame	Old Greenwich, Conn.	D6a-'08	16/16
3	Walsh, Blair	K	5-10	192	1/8/90	2	Georgia	Boca Raton, Fla.	D6-'12	16/0
14	Webb, Joe	WR	6-4	220	11/14/86	4	Alabama-Birmingham	Birmingham, Ala.	D6-'10	1/0
93	Williams, Kevin	DT	6-5	311	8/16/80	11	Oklahoma State	Fordyce, Ark.	D1-'03	16/16
17	Wright, Jarius	WR	5-10	180	11/25/89	2	Arkansas	Warren, Ark.	D4a-'12	7/1

* Bethel-Thompson was inactive for 16 games with Minnesota in '12; Cassel played nine games with Kansas City in '12; Jackson played 15 games with Detroit; Jennings played eight games with Green Bay; Keith last active with Arizona in '11; Kropog played one game with Tennessee, inactive for 4 games with Minnesota; Lacey played 11 games with Detroit; Love missed '12 season because of injury; Olsen played 5 games with Indianapolis.

Players lost through free agency (3): LB Jasper Brinkley (Ariz; 16 games), WR Michael Jenkins (NE; 16), G Geoff Schwartz (KC; 13).

Traded—WR Percy Harvin (9 games in '12) to Seattle.

Also played with Vikings in '12—WR Devin Aromashodu (15 games), P Chris Kluwe (16), TE Allen Reisner (4), CB Antoine Winfield (16).

FIRST-YEAR ROSTER

Name	Pos.	Ht.	Wt.	Birthdate	College	Hometown	How Acq.
Anderson, Colin	TE	6-4	240	11/21/89	Furman	St. Louis, Mo.	FA
Baca, Jeff	G	6-3	302	1/10/90	UCLA	Mission Viejo, Calif.	D6
Baker, Chase (1)	DT	6-2	300	5/21/88	Boise State	Rocklin, Calif.	FA-'12
Banyard, Joe (1)	RB	5-10	205	11/12/88	Texas-El Paso	Sweetwater, Texas	FA-'12
Bishop, Brandan	S	6-1	208	1/23/91	NC State	Boca Raton, Fla.	FA
Bond, Travis	G	6-7	330	12/10/90	North Carolina	Windsor, N.C.	D7b
Brown, LaMark (1)	TE	6-4	221	7/5/89	Minn. State-Mankato	Hazelwood, Mo.	FA-'12
Childs, Greg (1)	WR	6-3	217	3/10/90	Arkansas	Warren, Ark.	D4c-'12
Dawkins, Everett	DT	6-2	300	6/13/90	Florida State	Duncan, S.C.	D7c
Eubanks, Darius	S	6-1	215	7/12/91	Georgia Southern	Thomson, Ga.	FA
Felder, Bobby (1)	CB	5-11	200	9/23/90	Nicholls State	McComb, Miss.	FA-'12
Floyd, Sharrif	DT	6-3	305	5/28/91	Florida	Philadelphia, Pa.	D1a
Ford, Chase (1)	TE	6-6	255	7/19/90	Miami	Corrigan, Texas	FA-'12
Highsmith, Erik	WR	6-1	190	11/20/90	North Carolina	Vanceboro, N.C.	FA
Hodges, Gerald	LB	6-2	243	1/17/91	Penn State	Paulsboro, N.J.	D4
Holmes, Tyler (1)	G	6-4	312	7/24/88	Tulsa	Ontario, Canada	FA-'12
Jackson, Mark	T	6-5	332	7/5/88	Glenville State	Columbus, Ohio	FA
Jackson, Marquis	DE	6-4	280	1/11/90	Portland State	Lake Balboa, Calif.	FA
Line, Zach	FB	6-1	233	4/26/90	Southern Methodist	Oxford, Miss.	FA
Locke, Jeff	P	6-0	208	9/27/89	UCLA	Glendale, Ariz.	D5
Mauti, Michael	LB	6-2	240	1/19/90	Penn State	Mandeville, La.	D7a
McCloud, Anthony	DT	6-2	313	8/6/89	Florida State	Thomasville, Ga.	FA
McCoy, Greg (1)	CB	5-9	187	9/8/88	Texas Christian	Dallas, Texas	FA
Murphy, Kevin (1)	T	6-7	305	2/16/90	Harvard	San Clemente, Calif.	W(SF)-'12
Patterson, Cordarrelle	WR	6-2	220	3/17/91	Tennessee	Rock Hill, S.C.	D1c
Randle, Bradley	RB	5-7	193	9/17/90	Nevada-Las Vegas	Murrieta, Calif.	FA
Rhodes, Xavier	CB	6-1	210	6/19/90	Florida State	Miami, Fla.	D1b
Smith, Rodney	WR	6-5	220	3/11/90	Florida State	Miami, Fla.	FA
Summers, Chris (1)	WR	6-5	215	7/10/89	Liberty	Jacksonville, Fla.	FA-'12
Thielen, Adam	WR	6-2	195	8/22/90	Minnesota State-Mankato	Detroit Lakes, Minn.	FA
Ukwu, Collins	DE	6-4	260	1/6/90	Kentucky	La Vergne, Tenn.	FA
Vandenberg, James	QB	6-3	220	11/23/89	Iowa	Keokuk, Iowa	FA
Wentz, Camden	C	6-3	305	11/27/90	NC State	Marietta, Ga.	FA
Williams, Jerodis	RB	5-10	203	3/30/91	Furman	Prattville, Ala.	FA
Williams, Nathan	LB	6-3	245	10/16/89	Ohio State	Columbus, Ohio	FA
Williams, Roderick (1)	CB	5-10	180	5/27/87	Alcorn State	Monroe, Ala.	FA

The term NFL Rookie is defined as a player who is in his first season of professional football and has not been on the roster of another professional football team for any regular-season or postseason games. A Rookie is designated by an "R" on NFL rosters. Players who have been active in another professional football league or players who have NFL experience, including either preseason training camp or being on an Active List or Inactive List, or on Reserve/Injured or Reserve/Physically Unable to Perform for fewer than six regular-season games, are termed NFL First-Year Players. An NFL First-Year Player is designated by a "1" on NFL rosters. Thereafter, a player is credited with an additional year of experience for each season in which he accumulates six games on the Active List or Inactive List, or on Reserve/Injured or Reserve/Physically Unable to Perform.

Log on to www.vikings.com for an up-to-date roster.

COACHING STAFF

Head Coach,
Leslie Frazier

Pro Career: Named the eighth head coach in Vikings' history on January 3, 2011 after serving as the club's interim head coach for the final six games of the 2010 season. Frazier led the 2012 Vikings to the biggest turnaround in franchise history, improving by 7 wins from 2011, and going 10-6 and securing a Wild Card berth in the NFC playoffs. Under Frazier, Adrian Peterson became the team's all-time leading rusher and was named the MVP in 2012 after rushing for 2,097 yards. In Frazier's first game as interim head coach, Nov. 28, 2010, he snapped a nine-game road losing streak by defeating the Washington Redskins 17-13. The Vikings finished the season 3-3, picking up two road victories, despite having to move two home games off-site after the Metrodome roof collapsed due to a major Twin Cities snow storm. Before coming head coach of the Vikings, Frazier led one of the NFL's top defenses from 2007-2010 in Minnesota, and helped the Vikings to NFC North division titles in 2008 and 2009. Frazier won Super Bowl as a player (starting cornerback with 1985 Bears in Super Bowl XX) and coach (Super Bowl XLI as a defensive backs coach with Indianapolis). In his 14 seasons as an NFL coach, and 11 years of collegiate experience prior to that, Frazier has suffered a losing season only three times. He has coached on eight playoff teams in his 14 NFL seasons and been a part of six division championships. Career record: 16-23.

Background: Coached at Trinity (1988-1996) and Illinois (1997-98). Was NFL assistant with the Eagles (1999-2002), Bengals (2003-04), and Colts (2005-06) before joining the Vikings as their assistant head coach/defensive coordinator in 2007. Played defensive back collegiately at Alcorn State (1977-1980) and professionally with the Bears (1981-86).

Personal: Born April 3, 1959 in Columbus, Miss. He and wife Gayle have three children: Kieron, Chantel and Corey, who plays defensive back at Rice. Frazier earned degree in business administration.

ASSISTANT COACHES

Brendan Daly, defensive line; born September 10, 1975, Springfield, Ill. Tight end Drake 1993-96. No pro playing experience. College coach: Drake 1998, Villanova 1999, 2005, Maryland 2000, Oklahoma State 2001-03, Illinois State 2004. Pro coach: Minnesota Vikings 2006-08, St. Louis Rams 2009-2011, joined Vikings in 2012.

Jeff Davidson, offensive line; born October 3, 1967, Akron, Ohio. Offensive line Ohio State 1986-89. Pro offensive lineman Denver Broncos 1990-92, New Orleans Saints 1994. Pro coach: New Orleans Saints 1995-96, New England Patriots 1997-2004, Cleveland Browns 2005-06, Carolina Panthers 2007-10, joined Vikings in 2011.

Ryan Ficken, special teams assistant; born February 20, 1980, Aurora, Colo. Wide receiver Arizona State 1998-99. No pro playing experience. College coach: UCLA 2004-06.

Pro coach: Joined Vikings in 2007.

Jeff Howard, asst. to the head coach; born January 13, 1983, Grand Island, Neb. Linebacker Eastern New Mexico 2001-04. No pro playing experience. College coach: Texas Tech 2011-12. Pro coach: Joined Vikings in 2013.

Jeff Imamura, defensive assistant/secondary; born May 22, 1974, Lubbock, Texas. Attended Texas Christian. No college or pro playing experience. College coach: Texas Christian 1997-99, Northern Arizona 2000-02, Saginaw Valley State 2003. Pro coach: Joined Vikings in 2006.

Craig Johnson, quarterbacks; born March 3, 1960, Rome, N.Y. Quarterback Wyoming 1979-1982. No pro playing experience. College coach: Wyoming 1983, Arkansas 1984, Army 1985, Rutgers 1986-88, Virginia Military Institute 1989-1991, Northwestern 1992-96, Maryland 1997-99. Pro coach: Tennessee Titans 2000-10, joined Vikings in 2011.

Jimmie Johnson, tight ends; born October 6, 1966, Augusta, Ga. Tight end Howard 1985-88. Pro tight end Washington Redskins 1989-1991, Detroit Lions 1992-93, Kansas City Chiefs 1994, Philadelphia Eagles 1995-98. College coach: South Carolina State 2001, Shaw 2002-03, Texas Southern 2004-05. Pro coach: Joined Vikings in 2006.

Tom Kanavy, strength and conditioning; born April 8, 1970, Archibald, Pa. Attended Penn State. No college or pro playing experience. College coach: Miami 1993, Penn State 1993-95. Pro coach: Philadelphia Eagles 1995-2005, joined Vikings in 2006.

Klint Kubiak, offensive quality control/wide receivers; born February 17, 1987, Houston, Texas. Defensive Back Colorado State 2005-09. No pro playing experience. College coach: Texas A&M 2010-13. Pro coach: Joined Vikings in 2013.

Aaron McLaurin, asst. strength and conditioning; born February 27, 1984, Buffalo, N.Y. Attended Hampton University. No college or pro playing experience. College coach: Michigan State 2008-2010, Colgate 2011. Pro coach: Joined Vikings in 2012.

Bill Musgrave, offensive coordinator; born November 11, 1967, Grand Junction, Colo. Quarterback Oregon 1987-1990. Pro quarterback San Francisco 49ers 1991-94, Denver Broncos 1995-96. College coach: Virginia 2001-02. Pro coach: Oakland Raiders 1997, Philadelphia Eagles 1998, Carolina Panthers 1999-2000, Jacksonville Jaguars 2003-04, Washington Redskins 2005, Atlanta Falcons 2006-2010, joined Vikings in 2011.

Fred Pagac, linebackers; born April 26, 1952, Richeyville, Pa. Tight end Ohio State 1971-73. Pro tight end Chicago Bears 1974, Tampa Bay Buccaneers 1976. College coach: Ohio State 1978-2000. Pro coach: Oakland Raiders 2001-03, Kansas City Chiefs 2004-05, joined Vikings in 2006.

Mike Priefer, special teams coordinator; born August 21, 1966, Cleveland, Ohio. Quarterback/wide receiver Navy 1985-88. No pro playing experience. College coach: Navy 1994-96, Youngstown State 1997-98, Virginia Military Institute 1999, Northern Illinois 2000-

01. Pro coach: Jacksonville Jaguars 2002, N.Y. Giants 2003-05, Kansas City Chiefs 2006-08, Denver Broncos 2009-10, joined Vikings in 2011.

Diron Reynolds, asst. defensive line; born February 23, 1971, Aiken, S.C. Linebacker Wake Forest 1990-93. No pro playing experience. College coach: Wake Forest 1997-2000, Indiana 2001. Pro coach: Indianapolis Colts 2002-06, Miami Dolphins 2007, joined Vikings in 2009.

James Saxon, running backs; born March 23, 1966, Beaufort, S.C. Running back American River (Calif.) C.C. 1984-85, San Jose State 1986-87. Pro running back Kansas City Chiefs 1988-1991, Miami Dolphins 1992-94, Philadelphia Eagles 1995. College coach: Rutgers 1997-98, Menlo 1999. Pro coach: Buffalo Bills 2000, Kansas City Chiefs 2001-07, Miami Dolphins 2008-10, joined Vikings in 2011.

Ryan Silverfield, asst. offensive line; born August 4, 1980, Jacksonville, Fla. Attended Hampden-Sydney. No college or pro playing experience. College coach: Hampden-Sydney 2000-03, Jacksonville 2005, Central Florida 2006-07. Pro coach: Joined Vikings in 2008.

Mike Singletary, asst. head coach/linebackers; born October 9, 1958, Houston, Texas. Linebacker Baylor 1977-1980. Pro linebacker Chicago Bears 1981-1992. Pro coach: Baltimore Ravens 2003-04, San Francisco 49ers 2005-2010 (head coach 2008-2010), joined Vikings in 2011.

Kevin Stefanski, asst. quarterbacks; born May 8, 1982, Philadelphia, Pa. Safety Pennsylvania 2000-04. No pro playing experience. College coach: Pennsylvania 2005. Pro coach: Joined Vikings in 2006.

George Stewart, wide receivers; born December 29, 1958, Little Rock, Ark. Guard Arkansas 1977-1980. No pro playing experience. College coach: Minnesota 1984-85, Notre Dame 1986-88. Pro coach: Pittsburgh Steelers 1989-1991, Tampa Bay Buccaneers 1992-95, San Francisco 49ers 1996-2002, Atlanta Falcons 2003-06, joined Vikings in 2007.

Martin Streight, asst. strength and conditioning; born June 20, 1969, Trenton, N.J. Attended Indiana (Penn.). No college or pro playing experience. College coach: Penn State 1994, Princeton 1995-96. Pro coach: Philadelphia Eagles 1995-96, Arizona Cardinals 1997-2003, Scottish Claymores (NFLE) 2003, Berlin Thunder (NFLE) 2004-05, joined Vikings in 2006.

Alan Williams, defensive coordinator; born November 4, 1969, Norfolk, Va. Running back William & Mary 1988-1991. No pro playing experience. College coach: William & Mary 1996-2000. Pro coach: Tampa Bay Buccaneers 2001, Indianapolis Colts 2002-2011, joined Vikings in 2012.

Joe Woods, defensive backs; born June 25, 1970, Natrona Heights, Pa. Safety Illinois State 1988-1991. College coach: Muskingum 1992, Eastern Michigan 1993, Northwestern (La.) State 1994, Grand Valley State 1994-96, Kent State 1997, Hofstra 1998-2000, Western Michigan 2001-03. Pro coach: Tampa Bay Buccaneers 2004-05, joined Vikings in 2006.

**National Football Conference
South Division**
Team Colors: Old Gold, Black, and White
5800 Airline Drive
Metairie, Louisiana 70003
Telephone: (504) 733-0255

2013 SCHEDULE
PRESEASON
Aug. 9   **Kansas City** 7:00
Aug. 16 **Oakland** 7:00
Aug. 25 at Houston 3:00
Aug. 29 at Miami.............................6:30

REGULAR SEASON
Sep. 8   **Atlanta** 12:00
Sep. 15 at Tampa Bay 3:05
Sep. 22 **Arizona** 12:00
Sep. 30 **Miami** (Mon).....................7:40
Oct. 6   at Chicago 12:00
Oct. 13 at New England 3:25
Oct. 20 BYE
Oct. 27 **Buffalo** 12:00
Nov. 3   at New York Jets 12:00
Nov. 10 **Dallas** 7:30
Nov. 17 **San Francisco** 3:25
Nov. 21 at Atlanta (Thurs) 7:25
Dec. 2   at Seattle (Mon) 7:40
Dec. 8   **Carolina** 12:00
Dec. 15 at St. Louis 12:00
Dec. 22 at Carolina 12:00
Dec. 29 **Tampa Bay** 12:00
All times CT

Stadium: Mercedes-Benz Superdome
  (opened in 1975)
  • **Capacity:** 73,000
  1500 Poydras Street
  New Orleans, Louisiana 70112
Playing Surface: UBU Speed Series-S5-M
Training Camp: New Orleans Saints
  Metairie, Louisiana 70003

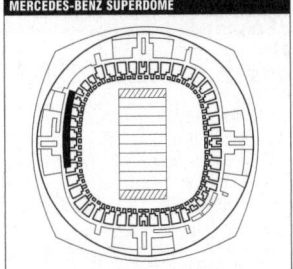

MERCEDES-BENZ SUPERDOME

CLUB OFFICIALS
Owner/Chairman of the Board:
  Tom Benson
Owner/Vice Chairman of the Board:
  Rita Benson LeBlanc
President: Dennis Lauscha
Executive Vice President/General
  Manager: Mickey Loomis
Senior Vice President of
  Communications: Greg Bensel
Senior Vice President of Marketing and
  Business Development: Ben Hales
Senior Vice President/Chief Financial
  Officer: Ed Lang
Senior Vice President/General Counsel:
  Vicky Neumeyer
Senior Vice President of Sales:
  Mike Stanfield
Vice President of Corporate
  Partnerships: Jean-Paul Dardenne
Director of Football Administration:
  Khai Harley
Director of Operations: James Nagaoka
Director of Pro Scouting: Ryan Pace
Pro Scouts: Terry Fontenot, Ryan Powell
Director of College Scouting:
  Rick Reiprish
College Scouting Coordinator:
  Jason Mitchell
Regional Scouts: Josh Lucas,
  Dwaune Jones
Area Scouts: Brian Adams, Mike Baugh,
  Ryan Hollern, Terry Wooden
Combine Scout: Joey Vitt Jr.
Salary Cap Analyst/Player Personnel:
  Joseph Laine
Scouting Assistants: Michael Parenton,
  Casey Talley
Equipment Manager: Dan Simmons
Assistant Equipment Manager:
  John Baumgartner
Equipment Assistant: Corey Gaudet
Head Athletic Trainer: Scottie B. Patton
Assistant Athletic Trainers:
  Duane Brooks, Kevin Mangum
Assistant Athletic Trainer/Physical
  Therapist: Beau Lowery
Video Director: Dave Desposito
Assistant Video Director: Joe Alley
Video Assistants: Paul Zimmer,
  Ryan Murphy
Director of Player Development:
  Fred McAfee
Director of Security: Danny Lawless
Senior Director of Football
  Communications: Doug Miller
Football Communications Manager:
  Justin Macione
Football Communications Assistant:
  Matt Mendelson
Director of Photography:
  Michael C. Hebert
IT Director: Jeff Huffman
Facilities Manager: Terry Ashburn
Administrative Director: Jay Romig

COACHING HISTORY
(312-403-5)
Records include postseason games
1967-70	Tom Fears*	13-34-2
1970-72	J.D. Roberts	7-25-3
1973-75	John North**	11-23-0
1975	Ernie Hefferle	1-7-0
1976-77	Hank Stram	7-21-0
1978-80	Dick Nolan***	15-29-0
1980	Dick Stanfel	1-3-0
1981-85	O.A. (Bum) Phillips****	27-42-0
1985	Wade Phillips	1-3-0
1986-96	Jim Mora#	93-78-0
1996	Rick Venturi	1-7-0
1997-99	Mike Ditka	15-33-0
2000-05	Jim Haslett	46-52-0
2006-2011	Sean Payton	67-37-0
2012	Aaron Kromer##	2-4-0
	Joe Vitt###	5-5-0

  * Released after seven games in 1970
 ** Released after six games in 1975
*** Released after 12 games in 1980
**** Resigned after 12 games in 1985
  \# Resigned after eight games in 1996
 \#\# Interim head coach first six games in 2012
\#\#\# Interim head coach final 10 games in 2012

PAID ATTENDANCE
Home 560,396   Away 560,625
Total 1,121,021
Single-game home record,
  73,085 (12/26/11)
Single-season home record,
  573,876 (2008)

2013 DRAFT CHOICES
Round	Name	Pos.	College
1	Kenny Vaccaro	S	Texas
3	Terron Armstead	T	Arkansas-Pine Bluff
	John Jenkins	DT	Georgia
5	Kenny Stills	WR	Oklahoma
6	Rufus Johnson	LB	Tarleton St.

2012 TEAM RECORD

PRESEASON (2-3)

Date	Result		Opponent
08/05	W	17-10	Arizona
08/09	L	6-7	at New England
08/17	L	24-27	Jacksonville
08/25	W	34-27	Houston
08/30	L	6-10	at Tennessee

REGULAR SEASON (7-9)

Date	Result		Opponent
09/09	L	32-40	Washington
09/16	L	27-35	at Carolina
09/23	L	24-27	Kansas City (OT)
09/30	L	27-28	at Green Bay
10/07	W	31-24	San Diego
10/21	W	35-28	at Tampa Bay
10/28	L	14-34	at Denver
11/05	W	28-13	Philadelphia
11/11	W	31-27	Atlanta
11/18	W	38-17	at Oakland
11/25	L	21-31	San Francisco
11/29	L	13-23	at Atlanta
12/09	L	27-52	at New York Giants
12/16	W	41-0	Tampa Bay
12/23	W	34-31	at Dallas (OT)
12/30	L	38-44	Carolina

(OT) Overtime

SCORE BY PERIODS

Saints	101	154	110	93	3	—	461
Opponents	96	133	96	126	3	—	454

2012 TEAM STATISTICS

	Saints	Opp.
Total First Downs	352	380
Rushing	64	116
Passing	267	236
Penalty	21	28
3rd Down: Made/Att	91/207	80/208
3rd Down Pct.	44.0	38.5
4th Down: Made/Att	8/14	10/19
4th Down Pct.	57.1	52.6
Possession Avg.	28:36	31:24
Total Net Yards	6574	7042
Avg. Per Game	410.9	440.1
Total Plays	1067	1089
Avg. Per Play	6.2	6.5
Net Yards Rushing	1577	2361
Avg. Per Game	98.6	147.6
Total Rushes	370	457
Net Yards Passing	4997	4681
Avg. Per Game	312.3	292.6
Sacked/Yards Lost	26/190	30/194
Gross Yards	5187	4875
Att./Completions	671/423	602/370
Completion Pct.	63.0	61.5
Had Intercepted	19	15
Punts/Average	74/50.1	63/45.7
Net Punting Avg.	74/43.2	63/40.1
Penalties/Yards	104/911	102/835
Fumbles/Ball Lost	13/5	19/11
Touchdowns	58	53
Rushing	10	18
Passing	43	31
Returns	5	4

2012 INDIVIDUAL STATISTICS

PASSING	Att.	Comp.	Yds.	Pct.	TD	Int.	Tkld.	Rate
Brees	670	422	5177	63.0	43	19	26/190	96.3
Daniel	1	1	10	100.0	0	0	0/0	108.3
Saints	671	423	5187	63.0	43	19	26/190	96.4
Opponents	602	370	4875	61.5	31	15	30/194	93.8

SCORING	TD R	TD P	TD Rt	PAT	FG	Saf	PTS
Hartley	0	0	0	57/57	18/22	0	111
Colston	0	10	0	0/0	0/0	0	60
J. Graham	0	9	0	0/0	0/0	0	54
Sproles	1	7	0	0/0	0/0	0	50
Moore	0	6	0	0/0	0/0	0	36
Ingram	5	0	0	0/0	0/0	0	30
D. Thomas	0	4	0	0/0	0/0	0	24
Morgan	0	3	0	0/0	0/0	0	18
Collins	0	2	0	0/0	0/0	0	12
Ivory	2	0	0	0/0	0/0	0	12
Pi. Thomas	1	1	0	0/0	0/0	0	12
Brees	1	0	0	0/0	0/0	0	6
Henderson	0	1	0	0/0	0/0	0	6
Jenkins	0	0	1	0/0	0/0	0	6
Mack	0	0	1	0/0	0/0	0	6
P. Robinson	0	0	1	0/0	0/0	0	6
Roby	0	0	1	0/0	0/0	0	6
Vilma	0	0	1	0/0	0/0	0	6
Saints	10	43	5	57/57	18/22	0	461
Opponents	18	31	4	53/53	27/33	1	454

2-Pt Conversions: Sproles, Saints 1-1,
Opponents 0-0

RUSHING	No.	Yds	Avg	LG	TD
Ingram	156	602	3.9	31	5
Pi. Thomas	105	473	4.5	48	1
Sproles	48	244	5.1	47	1
Ivory	40	217	5.4	56t	2
Daniel	3	17	5.7	19	0
Henderson	1	13	13.0	13	0
Brees	15	5	0.3	11	1
Cadet	1	5	5.0	5	0
Morgan	1	1	1.0	1	0
Saints	370	1577	4.3	56t	10
Opponents	457	2361	5.2	91t	18

RECEIVING	No.	Yds	Avg	LG	TD
J. Graham	85	982	11.6	46	9
Colston	83	1154	13.9	60	10
Sproles	75	667	8.9	44	7
Moore	65	1041	16.0	51	6
Pi. Thomas	39	354	9.1	36	1
Henderson	22	316	14.4	41	1
Collins	14	70	5.0	12	2
D. Thomas	11	86	7.8	20t	4
Morgan	10	379	37.9	80t	3
Ingram	6	29	4.8	16	0
Cadet	5	44	8.8	17	0
Camarillo	4	44	11.0	13	0
Ivory	2	15	7.5	13	0
Roby	1	9	9.0	9	0
Higgins	1	-3	-3.0	-3	0
Saints	423	5187	12.3	80t	43
Opponents	370	4875	13.2	95	31

INTERCEPTIONS	No.	Yds	Avg	LG	TD
P. Robinson	3	99	33.0	99t	1
Greer	3	31	10.3	28	0
Harper	2	41	20.5	41	0
Abdul-Quddus	2	12	6.0	12	0
Mack	1	73	73.0	73t	1
Jenkins	1	55	55.0	55t	1
Bush	1	40	40.0	40	0
Vilma	1	18	18.0	18t	1
White	1	0	0.0	0	0
Saints	15	369	24.6	99t	4
Opponents	19	356	18.7	70	3

PUNTING	No.	Yds.	Avg.	In 20	LG
Morstead	74	3707	50.1	20	70
Saints	74	3707	50.1	20	70
Opponents	63	2876	45.7	23	63

PUNT RETURNS	Ret	FC	Yds	Avg	LG	TD
Sproles	23	14	183	8.0	37	0
Cadet	1	2	2	2.0	2	0
Moore	1	3	5	5.0	5	0
P. Robinson	0	1	0	—	—	0
Saints	25	20	190	7.6	37	0
Opponents	31	12	391	12.6	69	0

KICKOFF RETURNS	No.	Yds	Avg	LG	TD
Cadet	26	690	26.5	75	0
Sproles	18	483	26.8	48	0
Pi. Thomas	5	91	18.2	38	0
Galette	1	2	2.0	2	0
Collins	1	0	0.0	0	0
Saints	51	1266	24.8	75	0
Opponents	42	1049	25.0	97t	1

FIELD GOALS	1-19	20-29	30-39	40-49	50+
Hartley	0/0	9/9	4/6	2/3	3/4
Saints	0/0	9/9	4/6	2/3	3/4
Opponents	0/0	7/7	11/13	8/9	1/4

SACKS	No.
Jordan	8.0
Smith	6.0
Galette	5.0
Wilson	3.0
Bunkley	2.5
T. Johnson	2.0
Lofton	1.0
P. Robinson	1.0
Vilma	1.0
Shanle	0.5
Saints	30.0
Opponents	26.0

RECORD HOLDERS
INDIVIDUAL RECORDS—CAREER

Category	Name	Performance
Rushing (Yds.)	Deuce McAllister, 2001-09	6,096
Passing (Yds.)	Drew Brees, 2006-2012	33,571
Passing (TDs)	Drew Brees, 2006-2012	244
Receiving (No.)	Eric Martin, 1985-1993	532
	Marques Colston, 2006-2012	532
Receiving (Yds.)	Eric Martin, 1985-1993	7,854
Interceptions	Dave Waymer, 1980-89	37
Punting (Avg.)	Thomas Morstead, 2009-2012	47.1
Punt Return (Avg.)	Mel Gray, 1986-88	13.4
Kickoff Return (Avg.)	Walt Roberts, 1967	26.3
Field Goals	Morten Andersen, 1982-1994	302
Touchdowns (Tot.)	Marques Colston, 2006-2012	58
Points	Morten Andersen, 1982-1994	1,318
*Sacks	Rickey Jackson, 1981-1993	115.0

INDIVIDUAL RECORDS—SINGLE SEASON

Category	Name	Performance
Rushing (Yds.)	George Rogers, 1981	1,674
Passing (Yds.)	Drew Brees, 2011	**5,476
Passing (TDs)	Drew Brees, 2011	46
Receiving (No.)	Jimmy Graham, 2011	99
Receiving (Yds.)	Joe Horn, 2004	1,399
Interceptions	Dave Whitsell, 1967	10
Punting (Avg.)	Thomas Morstead, 2012	50.1
Punt Return (Avg.)	Mel Gray, 1987	14.7
Kickoff Return (Avg.)	John Gilliam, 1967	30.1
Field Goals	Morten Andersen, 1985	31
	John Carney, 2002	31
Touchdowns (Tot.)	Dalton Hilliard, 1989	18
Points	John Kasay, 2011	147
*Sacks	Pat Swilling, 1991	17.0
	La'Roi Glover, 2000	17.0

INDIVIDUAL RECORDS—SINGLE GAME

Category	Name	Performance
Rushing (Yds.)	George Rogers, 9-4-83	206
Passing (Yds.)	Drew Brees, 11-19-06	510
Passing (TDs)	Billy Kilmer, 11-2-69	6
	Drew Brees, 9-13-09	6
Receiving (No.)	Tony Galbreath, 9-10-78	14
Receiving (Yds.)	Wes Chandler, 9-2-79	205
Interceptions	Tommy Myers, 9-3-78	3
	Dave Waymer, 10-6-85	3
	Reggie Sutton, 10-18-87	3
	Gene Atkins, 12-22-91	3
	Sammy Knight, 9-9-01	3
Field Goals	Many times	5
	Last time by John Carney, 9-26-04	
Touchdowns (Tot.)	Joe Horn, 12-14-03	4
	Reggie Bush, 12-3-06	4
Points	Joe Horn, 12-14-03	24
	Reggie Bush, 12-3-06	24
*Sacks	Many times	4.0
	Last time by Wayne Martin, 9-21-97	

*Sacks became an official statistic in 1982.
**NFL Record

2013 VETERAN ROSTER

No.	Name	Pos.	Ht.	Wt.	Birthdate	NFL Exp.	College	Hometown	How Acq.	'12 Games/ Starts
42	Abdul-Quddus, Isa	S	6-1	205	8/3/89	3	Fordham	Union, N.J.	FA-'11	15/3
44	Atkins, Baraka	DE	6-4	265	9/28/84	3	Miami	Sarasota, Fla.	FA-'13	0*
9	Brees, Drew	QB	6-0	209	1/15/79	13	Purdue	Austin, Texas	UFA(SD)-'06	16/16
71	Brown, Charles	T	6-5	297	4/10/87	4	Southern California	Chino Hills, Calif.	D2-'10	10/3
77	Bunkley, Brodrick	DT	6-2	306	11/23/83	8	Florida State	Tampa, Fla.	UFA(Den)-'12	15/15
25	Bush, Rafael	S	5-11	200	5/12/87	3	South Carolina State	Williston, S.C.	W(Den)-'12	16/0
90	Butler, Victor	LB	6-2	245	7/29/87	5	Oregon State	Rialto, Calif.	UFA(Dall)-'13	16/1*
39	Cadet, Travaris	RB	6-1	210	2/1/89	2	Appalachian State	Miami, Fla.	FA-'12	13/0
56	Chamberlain, Chris	LB	6-1	238	9/30/85	6	Tulsa	Bethany, Okla.	UFA(StL)-'12	0*
99	Coleman, Kenyon	DE	6-5	293	4/10/79	12	UCLA	Alta Loma, Calif.	UFA(Dall)-'13	7/5*
45	Collins, Jed	FB	6-1	255	3/3/86	3	Washington State	Mission Viejo, Calif.	FA-'10	15/7
12	Colston, Marques	WR	6-4	225	6/5/83	8	Hofstra	Harrisburg, Pa.	D7b-'06	16/13
60	de la Puente, Brian	C	6-3	306	5/13/85	4	California	San Clemente, Calif.	FA-'10	16/16
47	Drescher, Justin	LS	6-1	235	1/1/88	4	Colorado	Southlake, Texas	FA-'10	16/0
73	Evans, Jahri	G	6-4	318	8/22/83	8	Bloomsburg	Philadelphia, Pa.	D4-'06	16/16
93	Galette, Junior	LB	6-2	258	3/27/88	4	Stillman	Montvale, N.J.	FA-'10	12/1
17	Givens, Chris	WR	6-2	203	1/28/89	2	Miami (Ohio)	Chillicothe, Ohio	FA-'12	0*
80	Graham, Jimmy	TE	6-7	265	11/24/86	4	Miami	Goldsboro, N.C.	D3-'10	15/9
33	Greer, Jabari	CB	5-11	180	2/11/82	10	Tennessee	Jackson, Tenn.	UFA(Buff)-'09	14/13
66	Grubbs, Ben	G	6-3	310	3/10/84	7	Auburn	Eclectic, Ala.	UFA(Bal)-'12	16/16
41	Harper, Roman	S	6-1	200	12/11/82	8	Alabama	Prattville, Ala.	D2-'06	16/16
79	Harris, Bryce	T	6-6	300	1/16/89	2	Fresno State	Tulare, Calif.	FA-'12	2/1
5	Hartley, Garrett	K	5-8	195	5/16/86	6	Oklahoma	Southlake, Texas	FA-'08	16/0
57	Hawthorne, David	LB	6-0	246	5/14/85	6	Texas Christian	Corsicana, Texas	UFA(Sea)-'12	11/10
65	Henry, Ricky	G	6-4	310	7/27/87	3	Nebraska	Omaha, Neb.	FA-'12	1/0
54	Herring, Will	LB	6-3	241	8/28/83	6	Auburn	Opelika, Ala.	UFA(Sea)-'11	16/1
76	Hicks, Akiem	DT	6-5	324	11/16/89	2	Regina	Fair Oaks, Calif.	D3-'12	14/0
53	Humber, Ramon	LB	5-11	232	8/10/87	5	North Dakota State	Brooklyn Park, Minn.	FA-'10	13/0
22	Ingram, Mark	RB	5-9	215	12/21/89	3	Alabama	Flint, Mich.	D1b-'11	16/5
27	Jenkins, Malcolm	S	6-0	204	12/20/87	5	Ohio State	Piscataway, N.J.	D1-'09	13/13
96	Johnson, Tom	DT	6-3	288	8/30/84	3	Southern Mississippi	Moss Point, Miss.	FA-'11	15/0
70	Jones, Marcel	T	6-7	320	9/4/88	2	Nebraska	Phoenix, Ariz.	D7-'12	0*
94	Jordan, Cameron	DE	6-4	287	7/10/89	3	California	Chandler, Ariz.	D1a-'11	16/16
36	Leonhard, Jim	S	5-8	188	10/27/82	9	Wisconsin	Tony, Wisc.	UFA(Den)-'13	16/1*
28	Lewis, Keenan	CB	6-1	208	5/17/86	5	Oregon State	New Orleans, La.	UFA(Pitt)-'13	16/16*
50	Lofton, Curtis	LB	6-0	241	6/2/86	6	Oklahoma	Kingfisher, Okla.	UFA(Atl)-'12	16/16
7	McCown, Luke	QB	6-4	217	7/12/81	10	Louisiana Tech	Jacksonville, Texas	UFA(Atl)-'13	2/0*
16	Moore, Lance	WR	5-9	190	8/31/83	8	Toledo	Westerville, Ohio	FA-'05	15/7
13	Morgan, Joseph	WR	6-1	184	3/23/88	3	Walsh	Canton, Ohio	FA-'11	14/5
6	Morstead, Thomas	P	6-4	235	3/8/86	5	Southern Methodist	Pearland, Texas	D5-'09	16/0
69	Olsen, Eric	G	6-3	305	6/16/88	3	Notre Dame	Brooklyn, N.Y.	FA-'11	16/4
87	Parker, Preston	WR	6-0	200	2/13/87	3	North Alabama	Delray Beach, Fla.	FA-'12	2/0*
97	Richardson, Jay	DE	6-6	280	1/27/84	6	Ohio State	Dublin, Ohio	FA-'12	0*
21	Robinson, Patrick	CB	5-11	191	9/7/87	4	Florida State	Miami, Fla.	D1-'10	16/16
15	Roby, Courtney	WR	6-0	189	1/10/83	8	Indiana	Indianapolis, Ind.	FA-'08	13/0
98	Romeus, Greg	DE	6-5	267	4/29/88	3	Pittsburgh	Coral Springs, Fla.	D7a-'11	0*
78	Smith, Jason	T	6-5	310	4/30/86	5	Baylor	Dallas, Texas	FA-'13	16/0*
91	Smith, Will	DE	6-3	282	7/4/81	10	Ohio State	Utica, N.Y.	D1-'04	16/16
43	Sproles, Darren	RB	5-6	190	6/20/83	9	Kansas State	Olathe, Kan.	UFA(SD)-'11	13/6
64	Strief, Zach	T	6-7	320	9/22/83	8	Northwestern	Milford, Ohio	D7a-'06	12/12
23	Thomas, Pierre	RB	5-11	215	12/18/84	7	Illinois	Lansing, Ill.	FA-'07	15/4
67	Tiller, Andrew	G	6-5	326	3/13/89	2	Syracuse	Central Islip, N.Y.	D6-'12	0*
88	Toon, Nick	WR	6-4	218	11/4/88	2	Wisconsin	Middleton, Wisc.	D4-'12	0*
51	Vilma, Jonathan	LB	6-1	230	4/16/82	10	Miami	Coral Gables, Fla.	T(NYJ)-'08	11/10
75	Walker, Tyrunn	DT	6-3	294	3/18/90	2	Tulsa	New Iberia, La.	FA-'12	0*
10	Wallace, Seneca	QB	5-11	205	8/6/80	10	Iowa State	Rancho Cordova, Calif.	FA-'13	0*
82	Watson, Benjamin	TE	6-3	255	12/18/80	10	Georgia	Rock Hill, S.C.	UFA(Cle)-'13	16/14*
24	White, Corey	CB	6-1	205	5/9/90	2	Samford	Dunwoody, Ga.	D5-'12	10/4
95	Wilson, Martez	DE	6-4	252	9/21/88	3	Illinois	Chicago, Ill.	D3a-'11	16/0

* Atkins last active with San Francisco in '09; Butler played 16 games with Dallas in '12; Chamberlain missed '12 season because of injury; Coleman played seven games with Dallas; Givens missed '12 season because of injury; Jones missed '12 season because of injury; Leonhard played 16 games with Denver; Lewis played 16 games with Pittsburgh; McCown played 2 games with Atlanta; Parker played two games with Tampa Bay; Richardson last active with Seattle in '10; Romeus missed '12 season because of injury; J. Smith played 16 games with the New York Jets; Tiller missed '12 season because of injury; Toon missed '12 season because of injury; Walker inactive for 15 games and did not play for 1 game; Wallace last active with Cleveland in '11; Watson played 16 games with Cleveland.

Traded—RB Chris Ivory (6 games in '12) to the New York Jets.

Players lost through free agency (4): T Jermon Bushrod (Chi; 16 games in '12), LB Jonathan Casillas (TB; 14), QB Chase Daniel (KC; 16), DE Turk McBride (Chi; 7).

Also played with Saints in '12—WR Greg Camarillo (5), DT Sedrick Ellis (16), WR Devery Henderson (15 games), CB Elbert Mack (7), DB Jerome Murphy (2), CB Johnny Patrick (15), T William Robinson (6), LB Barrett Ruud (3), LB Scott Shanle (7), TE David Thomas (15).

FIRST-YEAR ROSTER

Name	Pos.	Ht.	Wt.	Birthdate	College	Hometown	How Acq.
Aaitui, Isaako (1)	DT	6-4	315	1/25/87	Nevada-Las Vegas	Pago Pago	FA
Armstead, Terron	T	6-5	304	7/23/91	Arkansas-Pine Bluff	Cahokia, Ill.	D3a
Broughton, Braylon (1)	DE	6-6	272	12/25/87	Texas Christian	Dallas, Texas	FA-'12
Davis, A.J. (1)	CB	6-0	183	7/6/89	Jacksonville State	Pinson, Ala.	FA-'12
Fayson, Jarred (1)	WR	6-0	214	10/13/87	Illinois	Tampa, Fla.	FA-'12
Foster, Glenn	DE	6-4	285	5/31/90	Illinois	Chicago, Ill.	FA
Griffin, Ryan	QB	6-5	206	11/17/89	Tulane	Westlake Village, Calif.	FA
Hakim, Saalim (1)	WR	5-11	188	2/1/90	Tarleton State	Las Vegas, Nev.	FA-'12
Higgins, Michael (1)	TE	6-5	242	12/7/87	Nebraska-Omaha	Beatrice, Neb.	FA-'11
Hill, Josh	TE	6-5	229	5/21/90	Idaho State	Blackfoot, Idaho	FA
Jenkins, John	DT	6-3	359	7/11/89	Georgia	Meriden, Conn.	D3b
Johnson, Austin (1)	FB	6-2	240	6/16/89	Tennessee	Hickory, N.C.	FA-'12
Johnson, Rufus	LB	6-5	272	8/28/90	Tarleton State	Dallas, Texas	D6
Lelito, Tim	G	6-4	315	7/21/89	Grand Valley State	St. Clair, Mich.	FA
Leonard, Brent	WR	6-2	186	5/18/90	Louisiana-Monroe	Keller, Texas	FA
Lindsey, Korey (1)	CB	5-10	194	2/3/89	Southern Illinois	Baton Rouge, La.	FA
Maltos, Jose	K	5-9	201	8/18/91	Nuevo Leon	San Nicolas, Mexico	FA
Martin, Eric	LB	6-2	250	7/21/91	Nebraska	Moreno Valley, Calif.	FA
Mealer, Elliot	C	6-5	308	6/30/89	Michigan	Wauseon, Ohio	FA
Milton, Keavon	TE	6-4	293	6/23/90	Louisiana-Monroe	Canton, Texas	FA
Nelson, Jerico (1)	S	5-10	216	9/19/89	Arkansas	Destrehan, La.	FA-'12
Reddick, Kevin	LB	6-1	246	12/28/89	North Carolina	New Bern, N.C.	FA
Robinson, Khiry	RB	6-0	220	12/28/89	West Texas A&M	Belton, Texas	FA
Shipman, Ray	LB	6-5	242	11/19/89	Central Florida	Miami Gardens, Fla.	FA
Steed, Ryan (1)	CB	5-11	185	7/21/90	Furman	Summerville, S.C.	FA-'12
Stills, Kenny	WR	6-0	190	4/22/92	Oklahoma	Carlsbad, Calif.	D5
Sweeting, Rod	CB	6-0	187	9/28/90	Georgia Tech	Luella, Ga.	FA
Tanner, Andy (1)	WR	6-0	183	5/16/88	Midwestern State	Rockwall, Texas	FA-'10
Thomas, Chase	LB	6-3	241	6/10/89	Stanford	Marietta, Ga.	FA
Turner, Dion (1)	CB	5-11	194	5/23/89	Southern Utah	Hanford, Calif.	FA-'12
Vaccaro, Kenny	S	6-0	214	2/15/91	Texas	Early, Texas	D1
Warren, Jeremiah (1)	G	6-4	320	9/20/87	South Florida	Panama City, Fla.	FA

The term NFL Rookie is defined as a player who is in his first season of professional football and has not been on the roster of another professional football team for any regular-season or postseason games. A Rookie is designated by an "R" on NFL rosters. Players who have been active in another professional football league or players who have NFL experience, including either preseason training camp or being on an Active List or Inactive List, or on Reserve/Injured or Reserve/Physically Unable to Perform for fewer than six regular-season games, are termed NFL First-Year Players. An NFL First-Year Player is designated by a "1" on NFL rosters. Thereafter, a player is credited with an additional year of experience for each season in which he accumulates six games on the Active List or Inactive List, or on Reserve/Injured or Reserve/Physically Unable to Perform.

Log on to www.neworleanssaints.com for an up-to-date roster.

COACHING STAFF

Head Coach,
Sean Payton

Pro Career: Named the fourteenth head coach in Saints history on Jan. 18, 2006 and has led the team to four playoff appearances, three NFC South titles, two NFC Championship berths and the Super Bowl XLIV title. Earned unanimous NFL Coach of the Year honors in his first season in 2006 and received the same honors from some outlets in 2009. Considered one of the NFL's brightest offensive minds, the Saints have ranked among the league's top ten offenses each season since his arrival, including finishing first in the NFL (with a league record 7,474 yards) in 2011, in addition to 2009, 2008 and 2006. With Dallas Cowboys (2003-05), served as the assistant head coach/passing game coordinator in 2005 after spending his first two seasons as assistant head coach/quarterbacks. Coached four years with the New York Giants (1999-2002), the last three seasons as offensive coordinator, and was quarterbacks coach for the Philadelphia Eagles (1997-98). Career record: 67-37.

Background: Earned a degree in communications at Eastern Illinois, where he departed with a school-record 10,665 passing yards, then the third-highest total in NCAA Division I-AA history. A three-time All-American, Payton had brief playing stops with Chicago of the Arena League, the CFL's Ottawa Rough Riders and the Chicago Bears in 1987. Payton coached collegiately at San Diego State (1988-89, 1992-93), Indiana State (1990-91), Miami (Ohio) in 1994-95, and Illinois (1996).

Personal: Born Dec. 29, 1963 in San Mateo, Calif. and raised in Naperville, Ill., Payton has a daughter, Meghan, and a son, Connor.

ASSISTANT COACHES

Charles Byrd, asst. strength and conditioning; born June 24, 1981, Oxford, Ohio. Defensive back Morehead State 2001-04. Pro defensive back Las Vegas Gladiators (AFL) 2006. College coach: Miami (Ohio) 2006-07. Pro coach: Joined Saints in 2008.

Pete Carmichael, offensive coordinator; born October 6, 1971, Framingham, Mass. Attended Boston College. No college or pro playing experience. College coach: New Hampshire 1994, Louisiana Tech 1995-99. Pro coach: Cleveland Browns 2000, Washington Redskins 2001, San Diego Chargers 2002-05, joined Saints in 2006.

Andre Curtis, asst. secondary; born December 8, 1976, Beaverdam, Va. Linebacker Virginia Military Institute 1996-99. No pro playing experience. College coach: Virginia Military Institute 2000-03, Georgia Southern 2004-05. Pro coach: New York Giants 2006-08, St. Louis Rams 2009-2011, joined Saints in 2012.

Dan Dalrymple, head strength and conditioning; born Aug. 26, 1965, Cleveland, Ohio. Offensive lineman Miami (Ohio) 1983-86. No pro playing experience. College coach: Miami (Ohio) 1987-2005. Pro coach: Joined Saints in 2006.

Henry Ellard, wide receivers; born July 21, 1961, Fresno, Calif. Wide receiver Fresno State 1979-1982. Pro wide receiver/punt returner Los Angeles Rams 1983-1993, Washington Redskins 1994-98, New England Patriots 1998. College coach: Fresno State 2000. Pro coach: St. Louis Rams 2001-08, New York Jets 2009-2011, joined Saints in 2012.

Bret Ingalls, offensive line; born Aug. 19, 1960, San Jose, Calif. Running back Wichita State 1979-1981. No pro playing experience. College coach: Idaho 1982-88, San Diego State 1989-1993, Eastern Michigan 1994, Louisville 1995-96, Northern Iowa 1997-99, Idaho 2000-03, Indiana State 2004, Miami (Ohio) 2005, Northwestern 2006-08. Pro coach: Joined Saints in 2009.

Bill Johnson, defensive line; born June 23, 1955, Monroe, La. Defensive lineman Northwestern (La.) State 1976-79. No pro playing experience. College coach: Northwestern (La.) State 1980-84, McNeese State 1985-86, Miami 1987, Louisiana Tech 1988-89, Arkansas 1990-91, 2000, Texas A&M 1992-99. Pro coach: Atlanta Falcons 2001-06, Denver Broncos 2007-08, joined Saints in 2009.

Stan Kwan, asst. special teams; born November 2, 1967, Phoenix. Attended South Mountain (Ariz.) C.C., San Diego State. No college or pro playing experience. Pro coach: San Diego Chargers 1991-96, Detroit Lions 1997-2000, Arizona Cardinals 2001-03, Detroit Lions 2004-09, Buffalo Bills 2010-12, joined Saints in 2013.

Joe Lombardi, quarterbacks; born June 6, 1971, Seattle, Wash. Tight end Air Force 1992-94. No pro playing experience. College coach: Dayton 1996-98, Virginia Military Institute 1999, Bucknell 2000, Mercyhurst 2002-05. Pro coach: New York/New Jersey Hitmen (XFL) 2001, Atlanta Falcons 2006, joined Saints in 2007.

Terry Malone, tight ends; born February 26, 1960, Buffalo, N.Y. Tight end Holy Cross 1978-1982. No pro playing experience. College coach: Arizona 1983-84, Holy Cross 1985, Bowling Green 1986-1995, Boston College 1996, Michigan 1997-2005. Pro coach: Joined Saints in 2006.

Wesley McGriff, secondary; born January 23, 1968, Tifton, Ga. Linebacker Savannah State 1986-89. No pro playing experience. College coach: Savannah State 1990-94, Kentucky State 1995-99, Eastern Kentucky 2000, Kentucky 2001-02, Baylor 2003-06, Miami 2007-2010, Vanderbilt 2011, Mississippi 2012. Pro coach: Joined Saints in 2013.

Greg McMahon, special teams coordinator; born Jan. 2, 1960, Rantoul, Ill. Defensive back Eastern Illinois 1978-1981. No pro playing experience. College coach: Eastern Illinois 1982, Minnesota 1983-84,

North Alabama 1985-87, Southern Illinois 1988, Valdosta State 1989, Nevada Las-Vegas 1990-91, Illinois 1992-2004, East Carolina 2005. Pro coach: Joined Saints in 2006.

Dan Roushar, running backs; born September 27, 1960, Clinton, Iowa. Quarterback Northern Illinois 1982-83. No pro playing experience. College coach: Northern Illinois 1984, Butler 1986-1992, Rhode Island 1993, Ball State 1994, Illinois 1995-96, Northern Illinois 1997-2002, Cincinnati 2003-06, Michigan State 2007-2012. Pro coach: Joined Saints in 2013.

Rob Ryan, defensive coordinator; born December 13, 1962, Ardmore, Okla. Linebacker Oklahoma State 1984, Southwestern Oklahoma State 1985-86. No pro playing experience. College coach: Western Kentucky 1987, Ohio State 1988, Tennessee State 1989-1993, Hutchinson (Kan.) C.C. 1996, Oklahoma State 1997-99. Pro coach: Arizona Cardinals 1994-95, New England Patriots 2000-03, Oakland Raiders 2004-08, Cleveland Browns 2009-10, Dallas Cowboys 2011-12, joined Saints in 2013.

Carter Sheridan, offensive assistant/wide receivers; born Nov. 20, 1977, New Orleans, La. Defensive back Florida A&M 1996-98. No pro playing experience. Pro coach: Joined Saints in 2006.

Frank Smith, offensive assistant/offensive line; born February 21, 1981, Milwaukee, Wisc. Offensive lineman Miami (Ohio) 1999-2003. No pro playing experience. College coach: Miami (Ohio) 2004-05, Butler 2006-09. Pro coach: Joined Saints in 2010.

Marcus Ungaro, defensive assistant; born October 9, 1984, Seattle. Defensive back Southwestern College 2004-05. No pro playing experience. Pro coach: Joined Saints in 2010.

Joe Vitt, asst. head coach/linebackers; born August 23, 1954, Syracuse, N.Y. Linebacker Towson State 1974-78. No pro playing experience. Pro coach: Baltimore Colts 1979-1981, Seattle Seahawks 1982-1991, Los Angeles Rams 1992-94, Philadelphia Eagles 1995-98, Green Bay Packers 1999, Kansas City Chiefs 2000-03, St. Louis Rams 2004-05 (head coach, final 11 games of 2005), joined Saints in 2006 (interim head coach, final 10 games of 2012).

Rob Wenning, strength and conditioning assistant; born December 10, 1984, Coldwater, Ohio. Offensive line/tight end Findlay (Ohio) 2003-06. No pro playing experience. College coach: Ohio State 2007, Louisiana State 2008-2009. Pro Coach: Joined Saints in 2010.

Brian Young, defensive assistant/linebackers; born July 8, 1977, Lawton, Okla. Defensive tackle Texas El-Paso 1996-99. Pro defensive tackle St. Louis Rams 2002, New Orleans Saints 2004-08. Pro coach: Joined Saints in 2009.

National Football Conference
East Division
Team Colors: Blue, Red, and White
Timex Performance Center
1925 Giants Drive
East Rutherford, New Jersey 07073
Telephone: (201) 935-8111

2013 SCHEDULE

PRESEASON

Aug. 10	at Pittsburgh	7:30
Aug. 18	**Indianapolis**	7:00
Aug. 24	**New York Jets**	7:00
Aug. 29	at New England	7:30

REGULAR SEASON

Sep. 8	at Dallas	8:30
Sep. 15	**Denver**	4:25
Sep. 22	at Carolina	1:00
Sep. 29	at Kansas City	1:00
Oct. 6	**Philadelphia**	1:00
Oct. 10	at Chicago (Thurs)	8:25
Oct. 21	**Minnesota** (Mon)	8:40
Oct. 27	at Philadelphia	1:00
Nov. 3	BYE	
Nov. 10	**Oakland**	1:00
Nov. 17	**Green Bay**	*8:30
Nov. 24	**Dallas**	4:25
Dec. 1	at Washington	*8:30
Dec. 8	at San Diego	4:25
Dec. 15	**Seattle**	1:00
Dec. 22	at Detroit	4:05
Dec. 29	**Washington**	1:00

*All times ET; Sunday night games in Weeks 11-16 subject to change
Stadium: MetLife Stadium (opened in 2010)
  • **Capacity:** 82,500
  East Rutherford, New Jersey 07073
Playing Surface: FieldTurf
Training Camp: University at Albany
  1400 Washington Avenue
  Albany, New York 12222

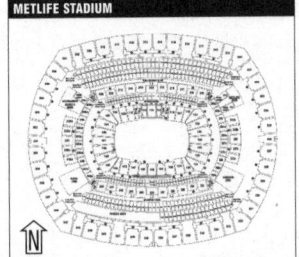

METLIFE STADIUM

CLUB OFFICIALS

President/CEO: John K. Mara
Chairman/EVP: Steve Tisch
Treasurer: Jonathan Tisch
Senior Vice President-General Manager:
  Jerry Reese
Senior Vice President and Chief
  Marketing Officer: Michael Stevens
Senior Vice President and General
  Counsel: William J. Heller, Esq.
Senior Vice President, Player Personnel:
  Chris Mara
Senior Vice President, Medical Services:
  Ronnie Barnes
Senior Vice President and Chief Financial
  Officer: Christine Procops
Senior Vice President, Corporate
  Partnerships: John Maguire
Senior Vice President, Communications:
  Pat Hanlon
Vice President, Communications:
  Peter John-Baptiste
Vice President of Community Relations:
  Frank Mara
Vice President of Marketing:
  Rusty Hawley
Vice President of Media and
  Partnerships: Dan Lynch
Vice President, Giants Entertainment:
  Don Sperling
Vice President, Business Development:
  Doug Smoyer
Vice President of Finance:
  Steven Hamrahi
Assistant General Manager:
  Kevin Abrams
Director of Pro Player Personnel:
  Ken Sternfield
Assistant Director of Pro Player
  Personnel: Matt Shauger
Director of College Scouting: Marc Ross
Director of Player Development:
  Charles Way
Pro Scouts: Patrick Hanscomb,
  Tim McDonnell
College Scouts: Joe Collins,
  Jeremiah Davis, Steve Verderosa,
  Jeremy Breit, Steve Devine,
  Donnie Etheridge, Ryan Jones,
  Steve Malin, Chris Pettit, Chris Watts
Director of Ticketing: John Gorman
Director of Administration: Jim Phelan
Director of Community Relations:
  Allison Stangeby
Director of Creative Services:
  Doug Murphy
Communications Manager:
  DeAndré Phillips
Assistant Head Athletic Trainer:
  Steve Kennelly
Coordinator or Rehabilitation:
  Byron Hansen
Physical Therapist/Assistant Athletic
  Trainer: Leigh Weiss
Equipment/Locker Room Manager:
  Ed Wagner, Jr.
Equipment Director: Joseph Skiba
Assistant Equipment Managers:
  Ed Skiba, Tim Slaman
Video Director: Dave Maltese
Assistant Video Directors:
  Carmen Pizzano, Ed Triggs,
  Steve Venditti
Assistant Director of Community
  Relations: Jen Conley
Directors of Information Technology:
  Julie Glisky, Justin Warren
Director of Client Services:
  Ethan Medley

COACHING HISTORY

(678-562-33)
Records include postseason games

1925	Bob Folwell	8-4-0
1926	Joe Alexander	8-4-1
1927-28	Earl Potteiger	15-8-3
1929-1930	LeRoy Andrews*	24-5-1
1930	Benny Friedman-Steve Owen	2-0-0
1931-1953	Steve Owen	153-108-17
1954-1960	Jim Lee Howell	55-29-4
1961-68	Allie Sherman	57-54-4
1969-1973	Alex Webster	29-40-1
1974-76	Bill Arnsparger**	7-28-0
1976-78	John McVay	14-23-0
1979-1982	Ray Perkins	24-35-0
1983-1990	Bill Parcells	85-52-1
1991-92	Ray Handley	14-18-0
1993-96	Dan Reeves	32-34-0
1997-2003	Jim Fassel	60-56-1
2004-2012	Tom Coughlin	91-64-0

*Released after 15 games in 1930
**Released after seven games in 1976

PAID ATTENDANCE

Home 639,513   Away 554,478
Total 1,193,991
Single-game home record,
  82,287 (1/1/12)
Single-season home record,
  639,513 (2012)

2013 DRAFT CHOICES

Round	Name	Pos.	College
1	Justin Pugh	T	Syracuse
2	Johnathan Hankins	DT	Ohio St.
3	Damontre Moore	DE	Texas A&M
4	Ryan Nassib	QB	Syracuse
5	Cooper Taylor	DB	Richmond
7	Eric Herman	G	Ohio
	Michael Cox	RB	Massachusetts

2012 TEAM RECORD
PRESEASON (2-2)

Date	Result		Opponent
08/10	L	31-32	at Jacksonville
08/18	W	26-3	at New York Jets
08/24	L	17-20	Chicago
08/29	W	6-3	New England

REGULAR SEASON (9-7)

Date	Result		Opponent
09/05	L	17-24	Dallas
09/16	W	41-34	Tampa Bay
09/20	W	36-7	at Carolina
09/30	L	17-19	at Philadelphia
10/07	W	41-27	Cleveland
10/14	W	26-3	at San Francisco
10/21	W	27-23	Washington
10/28	W	29-24	at Dallas
11/04	L	20-24	Pittsburgh
11/11	L	13-31	at Cincinnati
11/25	W	38-10	Green Bay
12/03	L	16-17	at Washington
12/09	W	52-27	New Orleans
12/16	L	0-34	at Atlanta
12/23	L	14-33	at Baltimore
12/30	W	42-7	Philadelphia

SCORE BY PERIODS

Giants	101	138	73	117	0	—	429
Opponents	86	103	84	71	0	—	344

2012 TEAM STATISTICS

	Giants	Opp.
Total First Downs	327	317
Rushing	103	104
Passing	187	196
Penalty	37	17
3rd Down: Made/Att	78/192	84/198
3rd Down Pct.	40.6	42.4
4th Down: Made/Att	5/10	10/21
4th Down Pct.	50.0	47.6
Possession Avg.	29:10	30:50
Total Net Yards	5687	6134
Avg. Per Game	355.4	383.4
Total Plays	968	1016
Avg. Per Play	5.9	6.0
Net Yards Rushing	1862	2066
Avg. Per Game	116.4	129.1
Total Rushes	409	449
Net Yards Passing	3825	4068
Avg. Per Game	239.1	254.3
Sacked/Yards Lost	20/142	33/231
Gross Yards	3967	4299
Att./Completions	539/323	534/341
Completion Pct.	59.9	63.9
Had Intercepted	15	21
Punts/Average	58/47.5	54/44.9
Net Punting Avg.	58/39.4	54/40.8
Penalties/Yards	72/578	102/900
Fumbles/Ball Lost	13/6	25/14
Touchdowns	47	38
Rushing	18	9
Passing	26	26
Returns	3	3

2012 INDIVIDUAL STATISTICS

PASSING	Att.	Comp.	Yds.	Pct.	TD	Int.	Tkld.	Rate
Manning	536	321	3948	59.9	26	15	19/136	87.2
Carr	3	2	19	66.7	0	0		84.0
Giants	539	323	3967	59.9	26	15	20/142	87.2
Opponents	534	341	4299	63.9	26	21	33/231	88.7

SCORING	TD R	TD P	TD Rt	PAT	FG	Saf	PTS
Tynes	0	0	0	46/46	33/39	0	145
Cruz	0	10	0	0/0	0/0	0	60
A. Brown	8	0	0	0/0	0/0	0	50
Bradshaw	6	0	0	0/0	0/0	0	36
Wilson	4	1	1	0/0	0/0	0	36
Bennett	0	5	0	0/0	0/0	0	30
Nicks	0	3	0	0/0	0/0	0	18
Randle	0	3	0	0/0	0/0	0	18
Hixon	0	2	0	0/0	0/0	0	12
Boley	0	0	1	0/0	0/0	0	6
Hynoski	0	1	0	0/0	0/0	0	6
Pascoe	0	1	0	0/0	0/0	0	6
Pierre-Paul	0	0	1	0/0	0/0	0	6
Giants	18	26	3	46/46	33/39	0	429
Opponents	9	26	3	38/38	26/30	0	344

2-Pt Conversions: A. Brown, Giants 1-1, Opponents 0-0

RUSHING	No.	Yds	Avg	LG	TD
Bradshaw	221	1015	4.6	37	6
A. Brown	73	385	5.3	31	8
Wilson	71	358	5.0	52t	4
Lumpkin	9	42	4.7	22	0
Manning	20	30	1.5	13	0
Hynoski	5	20	4.0	5	0
D. Scott	6	9	1.5	5	0
Jernigan	1	6	6.0	6	0
Carr	3	-3	-1.0	-1	0
Giants	409	1862	4.6	52t	18
Opponents	449	2066	4.6	78	9

RECEIVING	No.	Yds	Avg	LG	TD
Cruz	86	1092	12.7	80t	10
Bennett	55	626	11.4	33t	5
Nicks	53	692	13.1	50	3
Hixon	39	567	14.5	41	2
Bradshaw	23	245	10.7	59	0
Randle	19	298	15.7	56	3
Barden	14	220	15.7	31	0
A. Brown	12	86	7.2	17	0
Hynoski	11	50	4.5	8	1
Pascoe	4	35	8.8	16	1
Wilson	4	34	8.5	15t	1
Jernigan	3	22	7.3	9	0
Giants	323	3967	12.3	80t	26
Opponents	341	4299	12.6	62t	26

INTERCEPTIONS	No.	Yds	Avg	LG	TD
S. Brown	8	307	38.4	70	0
Webster	4	45	11.3	38	0
Boley	3	74	24.7	51	0
Rolle	2	42	21.0	22	0
Pierre-Paul	1	28	28.0	28t	1
Amukamara	1	0	0.0	0	0
Blackburn	1	0	0.0	0	0
Hosley	1	0	0.0	0	0
Giants	21	496	23.6	70	1
Opponents	15	288	19.2	73t	2

PUNTING	No.	Yds.	Avg.	In 20	LG
Weatherford	58	2757	47.5	22	68
Giants	58	2757	47.5	22	68
Opponents	54	2426	44.9	19	61

PUNT RETURNS	Ret	FC	Yds	Avg	LG	TD
Randle	15	15	108	7.2	18	0
Hixon	5	4	36	7.2	10	0
Giants	20	19	144	7.2	18	0
Opponents	38	5	353	9.3	68	0

KICKOFF RETURNS	No.	Yds	Avg	LG	TD
Wilson	57	1533	26.9	97t	1
A. Brown	3	42	14.0	22	0
Jernigan	2	60	30.0	60	0
Bennett	1	13	13.0	13	0
Giants	63	1648	26.2	97t	1
Opponents	70	1662	23.7	74	0

FIELD GOALS	1-19	20-29	30-39	40-49	50+
Tynes	0/0	11/11	14/16	7/9	1/3
Giants	0/0	11/11	14/16	7/9	1/3
Opponents	1/1	9/10	8/8	6/7	2/4

SACKS	No.
Pierre-Paul	6.5
Umenyiora	6.0
Joseph	4.0
Tuck	4.0
Blackburn	3.0
Canty	3.0
Kiwanuka	3.0
Bernard	1.0
Tracy	1.0
Williams	1.0
Boley	0.5
Giants	33.0
Opponents	20.0

RECORD HOLDERS
INDIVIDUAL RECORDS—CAREER

Category	Name	Performance
Rushing (Yds.)	Tiki Barber, 1997-2006	10,449
Passing (Yds.)	Phil Simms, 1979-1993	33,462
Passing (TDs)	Eli Manning, 2004-2012	211
Receiving (No.)	Amani Toomer, 1996-2008	668
Receiving (Yds.)	Amani Toomer, 1996-2008	9,497
Interceptions	Emlen Tunnell, 1948-1958	74
Punting (Avg.)	Don Chandler, 1956-1964	43.8
Punt Return (Avg.)	Ward Cuff, 1941-45	12.1
Kickoff Return (Avg.)	Rocky Thompson, 1971-73	27.2
Field Goals	Pete Gogolak, 1966-1974	126
Touchdowns (Tot.)	Frank Gifford, 1952-1964	78
Points	Pete Gogolak, 1966-1974	646
*Sacks	Michael Strahan, 1993-2007	141.5

INDIVIDUAL RECORDS—SINGLE SEASON

Category	Name	Performance
Rushing (Yds.)	Tiki Barber, 2005	1,860
Passing (Yds.)	Eli Manning, 2011	4,933
Passing (TDs)	Y.A. Tittle, 1963	36
Receiving (No.)	Steve Smith, 2009	107
Receiving (Yds.)	Victor Cruz, 2011	1,536
Interceptions	Otto Schnellbacher, 1951	11
	Jim Patton, 1958	11
Punting (Avg.)	Don Chandler, 1959	46.6
Punt Return (Avg.)	Merle Hapes, 1942	15.5
Kickoff Return (Avg.)	John Salscheider, 1949	31.6
Field Goals	Ali Haji-Sheikh, 1983	35
	Jay Feely, 2005	35
	John Carney, 2008	35
Touchdowns (Tot.)	Joe Morris, 1985	21
Points	Jay Feely, 2005	148
*Sacks	Michael Strahan, 2001	**22.5

INDIVIDUAL RECORDS—SINGLE GAME

Category	Name	Performance
Rushing (Yds.)	Tiki Barber, 12-30-06	234
Passing (Yds.)	Phil Simms, 10-13-85	513
Passing (TDs)	Y.A. Tittle, 10-28-62	**7
Receiving (No.)	Tiki Barber, 1-2-00	13
Receiving (Yds.)	Del Shofner, 10-28-62	269
Interceptions	Many times	3
	Last time by Terry Kinard, 9-20-87	
Field Goals	Joe Danelo, 10-18-81	6
Touchdowns (Tot.)	Ron Johnson, 10-2-72	4
	Earnest Gray, 9-7-80	4
	Rodney Hampton, 9-24-95	4
Points	Ron Johnson, 10-2-72	24
	Earnest Gray, 9-7-80	24
	Rodney Hampton, 9-24-95	24
*Sacks	Osi Umenyiora, 9-30-07	6.0

*Sacks became an official statistic in 1982.
**NFL Record

2013 VETERAN ROSTER

No.	Name	Pos.	Ht.	Wt.	Birthdate	NFL Exp.	College	Hometown	How Acq.	'12 Games/ Starts
89	Adams, Kris	WR	6-3	194	9/4/87	2	Texas-El Paso	Everman, Texas	FA-'13	3/0*
20	Amukamara, Prince	CB	6-0	207	6/6/89	3	Nebraska	Glendale, Ariz.	D1-'11	3/11
96	Austin, Marvin	DT	6-2	312	1/1/89	3	North Carolina	Washington, D.C.	D2-'11	8/0
64	Baas, David	C	6-4	312	9/28/81	9	Michigan	Sarasota, Fla.	UFA(SF)-'11	16/16
65	Beatty, Will	T	6-6	319	3/2/85	5	Connecticut	York, Pa.	D2-'09	16/15
77	Boothe, Kevin	G	6-5	320	7/5/83	8	Cornell	Fort Lauderdale, Fla.	W(Oak) -'07	16/16
73	Brewer, James	T	6-6	330	12/23/87	3	Indiana	Indianapolis, Ind.	D4-'11	6/0
3	Brown, Josh	K	6-0	202	4/29/79	11	Nebraska	Foyil, Okla.	UFA(Cin)-'13	4/0*
27	Brown, Stevie	S	5-11	221	7/17/87	4	Michigan	Columbus, Ind.	FA-'12	16/11
35	Brown, Andre	RB	6-0	227	12/15/86	4	North Carolina State	Greenville, N.C.	FA-'11	10/2
19	Buehler, David	K	6-2	230	2/5/87	4	Southern California	Canyon Country, Calif.	FA-'13	0*
46	Caldwell, David	DB	5-11	212	5/19/87	2	William & Mary	Montclair, N.J.	FA-'13	0*
60	Capers, Selvish	OL	6-5	315	11/13/86	2	West Virginia	Kenner, La.	FA-'12	3/0
8	Carr, David	QB	6-3	212	7/21/79	12	Fresno State	Bakersfield, Calif.	FA-'11	2/0
53	Conner, Dan	LB	6-2	241	11/2/85	6	Penn State	Wallingford, Pa.	FA-'13	14/8*
63	Cordle, Jim	C	6-3	320	8/22/87	3	Ohio State	Lancaster, Ohio	FA-'10	15/0
80	+Cruz, Victor	WR	6-0	204	11/11/86	4	Massachusetts	Paterson, N.J.	FA-'10	16/16
59	Curry, Aaron	LB	6-2	255	4/6/86	6	Wake Forest	Fayetteville, N.C.	FA-'13	2/0*
61	DeGeare, Chris	G	6-4	335	2/17/87	2	Wake Forest	Kernersville, N.C.	FA-'13	0*
51	DeOssie, Zak	LS	6-4	249	5/24/84	7	Brown	No. Andover, Mass.	D4-'07	16/0
66	Diehl, David	T	6-5	304	9/15/80	11	Illinois	Oak Lawn, Ill.	D5-'03	13/9
58	Herzlich, Mark	LB	6-4	246	9/1/87	3	Boston College	Berwyn, Pa.	FA-'11	16/2
25	Hill, Will	S	6-1	207	3/7/90	2	Florida	Jersey City, N.J.	FA-'12	12/0
28	Hosley, Jayron	CB	5-10	178	9/18/90	2	Virginia Tech	Delray Beach, Fla.	D3-'12	12/6
45	Hynoski, Henry	FB	6-1	266	12/30/88	3	Pittsburgh	Elysburg, Pa.	FA-'11	16/11
99	Jenkins, Cullen	DT	6-2	305	1/20/81	11	Central Michigan	Detroit, Mich.	FA-'13	16/16*
12	Jernigan, Jerrel	WR	5-8	189	6/14/89	3	Troy	Eufaula, Ala.	D3-'11	9/0
97	Joseph, Linval	DT	6-4	323	10/10/88	4	East Carolina	Gainesville, Fla.	D2-'10	16/16
94	Kiwanuka, Mathias	DE	6-5	267	3/8/83	8	Boston College	Indianapolis, Ind.	D1-'06	16/15
78	Kuhn, Markus	DT	6-4	299	5/6/86	2	NC State	Weinheim, Germany	D7-'12	10/1
10	Manning, Eli	QB	6-4	218	1/3/81	10	Mississippi	New Orleans, La.	T(SD)-'04	16/16
38	McBride, Trumaine	DB	5-9	185	9/24/85	6	Mississippi	Clarkdale, Miss.	FA-'13	0*
21	Mundy, Ryan	S	6-1	209	2/11/85	5	West Virginia	Pittsburgh, Pa.	UFA(Pitt)-'13	16/3*
18	Murphy, Louis	WR	6-2	200	5/11/87	5	Florida	St. Petersburg, Fla.	UFA(Car)-'13	16/5*
83	Myers, Brandon	TE	6-3	256	9/4/85	5	Iowa	Monroe, Iowa	UFA(Oak)-'13	16/16*
88	Nicks, Hakeem	WR	6-1	208	1/14/88	5	North Carolina	Charlotte, N.C.	D1-'09	13/11
71	Ojomo, Adewale	DE	6-4	270	11/14/88	2	Miami	Miami, Fla.	FA-'12	1/0
17	Painter, Curtis	QB	6-4	230	6/24/85	4	Purdue	Vincennes, Ind.	FA-'13	0*
86	Pascoe, Bear	TE	6-5	283	2/23/86	5	Fresno State	Porterville, Calif.	FA-'09	15/3
93	Patterson, Mike	DT	6-1	300	9/1/83	9	Southern California	Los Alamitos, Calif.	FA-'13	5/0*
52	Paysinger, Spencer	LB	6-2	236	6/28/88	3	Oregon	Los Angeles, Calif.	FA-'11	16/3
90	Pierre-Paul, Jason	DE	6-5	278	1/1/89	4	South Florida	Deerfield Beach, Fla.	D1-'10	16/15
82	Randle, Rueben	WR	6-2	208	5/7/91	2	Louisiana State	Bastrop, La.	D2-'12	16/1
55	Rivers, Keith	LB	6-2	235	5/5/86	5	Southern California	Lake Mary, Fla.	T(Cin)-'12	11/6
81	Robinson, Adrien	TE	6-4	264	9/23/88	2	Cincinnati	Indianapolis, Ind.	D4-'12	2/0
95	Rogers, Shaun	DT	6-4	350	3/12/79	13	Texas	La Porte, Texas	FA-'12	0*
26	Rolle, Antrel	S	6-0	206	12/16/82	9	Miami	Homestead, Fla.	FA-'10	16/16
31	Ross, Aaron	CB	6-0	190	9/15/82	7	Texas	Tyler, Texas	FA-'13	14/9*
39	Sash, Tyler	S	6-0	215	5/27/88	3	Iowa	Oskaloosa, Iowa	D6-'11	7/0
33	Scott, Da'Rel	RB	5-11	210	5/26/88	3	Maryland	Conshohocken, Pa.	D7-'11	4/0
76	Snee, Chris	G	6-3	305	1/18/82	10	Boston College	Montrose, Pa.	D2-'04	16/16
24	Thomas, Terrell	CB	6-0	191	1/8/85	6	Southern California	Alto Loma, Calif.	D2-'08	0*
41	Torain, Ryan	RB	6-0	220	8/10/86	5	Arizona State	Shawnee, Kan.	FA-'12	2/0
98	Tracy, Adrian	DE	6-2	245	4/6/87	3	William & Mary	Sterling, Va.	D6-'10	16/0
69	Trattou, Justin	DE	6-4	255	8/28/88	3	Florida	Ramsey, N.J.	FA-'11	0*
91	Tuck, Justin	DE	6-5	268	3/29/83	9	Notre Dame	Kellyton, Ala.	D3-'05	15/14
5	Weatherford, Steve	P	6-2	211	12/17/82	8	Illinois	Terre Haute, Ind.	FA-'11	16/0
23	Webster, Corey	CB	6-0	200	3/2/82	9	Louisiana State	Vacherie, La.	D2-'05	16/16
57	Williams, Jacquian	LB	6-3	224	7/20/88	3	South Florida	Riverview, Fla.	D6-'11	10/6
22	Wilson, David	RB	5-9	205	6/15/91	2	Virginia Tech	Danville, Va.	D1-'12	16/2

* Adams played three games with Indianapolis in '12; J. Brown played four games with Cincinnati in '12; Buehler last active with Dallas in '11; Caldwell last active with Indianapolis in '11; Conner played 14 games with Dallas; Curry played two games with Oakland; DeGeare last active with Minnesota in '10; Jenkins played 16 games with Philadelphia; McBride last active with Jacksonville in '11; Mosley missed '12 season because of injury; Mundy played 16 games with Pittsburgh; Murphy played 16 games with Carolina; Myers played 16 games with Oakland; Painter last active with Indianapolis in '11; Patterson played five games with Philadelphia; Rogers missed '12 season because of injury; Ross played in 14 games with Jacksonville in '12; Thomas missed '12 season because of injury; Trattou missed '12 season because of injury.

+ Restricted Free Agent; subject to developments.

Players lost through free agency (6): TE Marcellus Bennett (Chi; 16), LB Chase Blackburn (Car; 15), DT Chris Canty (Balt; 9), WR Domenik Hixon (Car; 13), S Kenny Phillips (Phil; 7), DE Osi Umenyiora (Atl; 16).

Also played with Giants in '12—WR Ramses Barden (12 games), TE Travis Beckum (4), LB Michael Boley (16), RB Ahmad Bradshaw (14), CB Michael Coe (7), CB Terrence Frederick (2), T Sean Locklear (12), RB Kregg Lumpkin (5), G Mitch Petrus (6), RB Ryan Torain (2), CB Justin Tryon (16), K Lawrence Tynes (16).

FIRST-YEAR ROSTER

Name	Pos.	Ht.	Wt.	Birthdate	College	Hometown	How Acq.
Broha, Matt (1)	DE	6-4	255	6/6/89	Louisiana Tech	Baton Rouge, La.	FA-'12
Childers, Jamie	TE	6-5	250	6/26/88	Coastal Carolina	Mount Pleasant, S.C.	FA
Collins, Brandon	WR	5-11	180	4/21/89	Southeast Louisiana	Brenham, Texas	FA
Cox, Michael	RB	6-0	220	11/14/88	Massachusetts	Avon, Conn.	D7b
Dennard, Antonio	CB	5-11	190	12/20/89	Langston	Frisco, Texas	FA
Frederick, Terrence	CB	5-10	187	2/10/90	Texas A&M	Katy, Texas	FA
Goodin, Stephen	G	6-6	310	8/5/88	Nebraska-Kearney	Hastings, Neb.	FA
Hankins, Johnathan	DT	6-2	320	3/30/92	Ohio State	Detroit, Mich.	D2
Hardy, Kevin	WR	6-0	182	4/27/90	Citadel	Ocala, Fla.	FA
Herman, Eric	G	6-4	320	8/5/89	Ohio	Oregon, Ohio	D7a
James, Charles	CB	5-9	179	5/14/90	Charleston Southern	Jacksonville, Fla.	FA
Jasper, Michael	G	6-4	375	10/8/86	Bethel	Mount Juliet, Tenn.	FA
McCants, Matt	T	6-5	309	8/18/89	Alabama-Birmingham	Mobile, Ala.	FA
Mertile, Junior	CB	6-1	197	10/26/89	Florida International	Miami, Fla.	FA
Moore, Damontre	DE	6-5	250	9/11/92	Texas A&M	Garland, Texas	D3
Mosely, Jordan	C	6-3	290	10/18/90	Johnson C. Smith	Columbia, S.C.	FA
Muasau, Jake	LB	6-1	243	4/15/90	Georgia State	Sierra Vista, Ariz.	FA
Nassib, Ryan	QB	6-2	223	3/10/90	Syracuse	Malvern, Pa.	D4
Pugh, Justin	T	6-4	301	8/15/90	Syracuse	Holland, Pa.	D1
Sabino, Etienne	LB	6-3	237	11/13/90	Ohio State	No. Miami Beach, Fla.	FA
Scott, Laron (1)	DB	5-9	184	7/12/87	Georgia Southern	Warner Robins, Ga.	FA-'12
Stevenson, John	S	5-11	197	9/9/89	Georgia Southern	Stone Mountain, Ga.	FA
Taylor, Cooper	S	6-4	228	4/14/90	Richmond	Atlanta, Ga.	D5
Tweedy, Alonzo	S	6-2	193	7/27/89	Virginia Tech	Richmond, Va.	FA
Wright, Jeremy	RB	5-11	205	1/28/91	Louisville	Clermont, Fla.	FA

The term NFL Rookie is defined as a player who is in his first season of professional football and has not been on the roster of another professional football team for any regular-season or postseason games. A Rookie is designated by an "R" on NFL rosters. Players who have been active in another professional football league or players who have NFL experience, including either preseason training camp or being on an Active List or Inactive List, or on Reserve/Injured or Reserve/Physically Unable to Perform for fewer than six regular-season games, are termed NFL First-Year Players. An NFL First-Year Player is designated by a "1" on NFL rosters. Thereafter, a player is credited with an additional year of experience for each season in which he accumulates six games on the Active List or Inactive List, or on Reserve/Injured or Reserve/Physically Unable to Perform.

Log on to www.giants.com for an up-to-date roster.

COACHING STAFF

Head Coach,
Tom Coughlin

Pro Career: Was named the sixteenth head coach in Giants history on January 6, 2004. This season marks Coughlin's tenth with the Giants and eighteenth as an NFL head coach. In, 2012 Coughlin led the Giants to a 9-7 record and the team's third-straight winning season and eighth consecutive non-losing season. In 2011, he helmed the Giants to their second championship in four seasons with a 21-17 win against the New England Patriots in Super Bowl XLVI. He also guided the team to a 9-7 record, en route to winning an NFC East crown. In 2010, the Giants posted a record of 10-6. The Giants finished the 2009 season with an 8-8 record. In the 2008 season the Giants finished with a 12-4 record, which won the NFC East division. Coughlin directed the Giants 17-14 win over the New England Patriots in Super Bowl XLII on February 3, 2008, the third championship in the team's history. Coached the Giants to an 11-5 record, the NFC East title and the playoffs in 2005-06, his second and third seasons with the team. Coughlin previously spent eight years (1995-2002) with the Jacksonville Jaguars. Under Coughlin, the Jaguars had the most victories of any NFL expansion team in its first seven seasons. They were also the only expansion team in NFL history to advance to the playoffs four times in their first five seasons. Coughlin's team went 9-7 in 1996 and an NFL-best 14-2 in 1999, both times reaching the AFC Championship Game. Coughlin previously coached the Philadelphia Eagles (1984-85), Green Bay Packers (1986-87), and Giants (1988-1990). He was a member of the Giants' Super Bowl XXV champion coaching staff. Career record: 163-128.

Background: Served as head coach at Boston College (1991-93), and coached at Syracuse (1969, 1974-1980), Rochester Institute of Technology 1970-73 (head coach), and Boston College (1981-83). Played wingback for Syracuse (1965-67).

Personal: Born August 31, 1946, Waterloo, N.Y. Tom and his wife Judy have two daughters, Keli and Katie; two son-in-laws named Chris; two sons, Brian and Tim; two daughters-in-law, Andrea (Tim's wife) and Susie (Brian's wife); and 10 grandchildren, Emma Rose, Dylan, Shea, Cooper, Caroline, Marin, Wesley, Brennon, Clara, and Walker.

ASSISTANT COACHES

Joe Danos, asst. strength and conditioning; born Jan. 2, 1981, New Orleans, La. No college or pro playing experience. College coach: Louisiana State 2005-06, Southern Methodist 2007-09, Florida State 2010-12. Pro coach: Joined Giants in 2013.

Perry Fewell, defensive coordinator; born September 7, 1962, Gastonia, N.C. Defensive back Lenoir-Rhyne 1981-84. No pro playing experience. College coach: North Carolina 1985-86, Army 1987, 1992-94, Kent State 1988-1991, Vanderbilt 1995-97. Pro coach: Jacksonville Jaguars 1998-2002, St. Louis Rams 2003-04, Chicago Bears 2005, Buffalo Bills 2006-09, joined Giants in 2010.

Pat Flaherty, offensive line; born April 27, 1956, Hanover, Pa. Center East Stroudsburg 1974-77. No pro playing experience. College coach: East Stroudsburg 1980-81, Penn State 1982-83, Rutgers 1984-1991, East Carolina 1992, Wake Forest 1993-98, Iowa 1999. Pro coach: Washington Redskins 2000, Chicago Bears 2001-03, joined Giants in 2004.

Kevin Gilbride, offensive coordinator; born August 27, 1951, New Haven, Conn. Quarterback/tight end Southern Connecticut State 1971-73. No pro playing experience. College coach: Idaho State 1974-75, Tufts 1976-77, American International 1978-79, Southern Connecticut State 1980-84, East Carolina 1987-88. Pro coach: Ottawa Rough Riders (CFL) 1985-86, Houston Oilers 1989-1994, Jacksonville Jaguars 1995-96, San Diego Chargers 1997-98 (head coach), Pittsburgh Steelers 1999-2000, Buffalo Bills 2002-2003, joined Giants in 2004.

Kevin M. Gilbride, wide receivers; born December 14, 1979, Jacksonville, Fla. Quarterback Hawaii 2000. No pro playing experience. College coach: Syracuse 2004-05, Georgetown 2006, Temple 2007-09. Pro coach: Joined Giants in 2010.

Peter Giunta, secondary/corners; born August 11, 1956, Salem, Mass. Running back/defensive back Northeastern 1974-77. No pro playing experience. College coach: Penn State 1981-83, Brown 1984-87, Lehigh 1988-1990. Pro coach: Philadelphia Eagles 1991-94, N.Y. Jets 1995-96, St. Louis Rams 1997-2000, Kansas City Chiefs 2001-2005, joined Giants in 2006.

Jim Hermann, linebackers; born December 8, 1960, Hollywood, Calif. Linebacker Michigan 1979-1982. No pro playing experience. College coach: Michigan 1983, 1986-2005. Pro coach: New York Jets 2006-2008, joined Giants in 2009.

Jerald Ingram, running backs; born December 24, 1960, Dayton, Ohio. Fullback Michigan 1979-1983. College coach: Michigan 1984, Ball State 1985-1990, Boston College 1991-93. Pro coach: Jacksonville Jaguars 1994-2002, joined Giants in 2004.

Larry Izzo, asst. special teams; born September 26, 1974, Fort Belvoir, Va. Linebacker Rice 1992-95. Pro linebacker/special teamer Miami Dolphins 1996-2000, New England Patriots 2001-08, New York Jets 2009. Pro coach: Joined Giants in 2011.

Robbie Leonard, defensive assistant; born July 14, 1985, Moon Township, Pa., Linebacker Washington & Jefferson College 2004, North Carolina State 2005-08. No pro playing experience College coach: North Carolina State 2010-12. Pro coach: Joined Giants in 2013.

David Merritt Sr., secondary/safeties; born September 8, 1971, Raleigh, N.C. Linebacker North Carolina State 1989-1992. Pro linebacker Miami Dolphins 1993, Arizona Cardinals 1993-96, Rhein Fire (NFLE) 1997. College coach: Chattanooga 1997, Virginia Military Institute 1998-2000. Pro coach: New York Jets 2001-2003, joined Giants in 2004.

Robert Nunn, defensive line; born June 10, 1965, Apache, Okla. Linebacker Oklahoma State 1984-87. No pro playing experience. College coach: Northeastern Oklahoma 1988, Tennessee 1989-1990, Georgia Military 1991-99. Pro coach: Miami Dolphins 2000-02, 2004, Washington Redskins 2003, Green Bay Packers 2005-08, Tampa Bay Buccaneers 2009, joined Giants in 2010.

Jerry Palmieri, strength and conditioning; born October 30, 1958, Englewood, N.J. Attended Montclair State. No college or pro playing experience. College coach: North Carolina 1982-83, Oklahoma State 1984-86, Kansas State 1987-1992, Boston College 1993-94. Pro coach: Jacksonville Jaguars 1995-2002, New Orleans Saints 2003, joined Giants in 2004.

Markus Paul, asst. strength and conditioning; born April 1, 1966, Orlando, Fla. Safety Syracuse 1984-88. Pro safety Chicago Bears 1989-1993, Tampa Bay Buccaneers 1993. Pro coach: New Orleans Saints 1998-99, New England Patriots 2000-04, New York Jets 2005-2006, joined Giants in 2007.

Michael Pope, tight ends; born March 15, 1942, Monroe, N.C. Quarterback Lenoir-Rhyne 1962-64. No pro playing experience. College coach: Florida State 1970-74, Texas Tech 1975-77, Mississippi 1978-1982. Pro coach: New York Giants 1983-1991, Cincinnati Bengals 1992-93, New England Patriots 1994-96, Washington Redskins 1997-99, re-joined Giants in 2000.

Tom Quinn, special teams coordinator; born January 27, 1968, Pasadena, Calif. Linebacker Arizona 1986-1990. No pro playing experience. College coach: Davidson College 1991, James Madison 1992-94, Boston 1995, Holy Cross 1996-98, San Jose State 1999-2001, Stanford 2002-05. Pro coach: Joined Giants in 2006.

Ryan Roeder, offensive assistant; born February 14, 1980, Bethlehem, Pa., Quarterback Albany 1999-2002. No pro playing experience. College coach: Holy Cross 2004, Temple 2006-08, Rhode Island 2009, Princeton 2010-12. Pro coach: Joined Giants in 2013.

Sean Ryan, quarterbacks; born May 1, 1972, Glenn Falls, N.Y. Defensive back Hamilton College 1994. No pro playing experience. College coach: Albany 1998-99, Colgate 2000, Boston College 2001-02, Columbia 2003-04, Harvard 2006. Pro coach: Joined Giants in 2007.

Lunda Wells, asst. offensive line; born February 10, 1983, Baker, Ala. Offensive line Southern 2003-07. No pro playing experience. College coach: Louisiana State 2008-2011. Pro coach: Joined Giants in 2012.

National Football Conference
East Division
Team Colors: Midnight Green, Silver, Black,
and White
NovaCare Complex
One NovaCare Way
Philadelphia, Pennsylvania 19145
Telephone: (215) 463-2500

2013 SCHEDULE
PRESEASON
Aug. 9	**New England**	7:30
Aug. 15	**Carolina**	7:30
Aug. 24	at Jacksonville	7:30
Aug. 29	at New York Jets	7:00

REGULAR SEASON
Sep. 9	at Washington (Mon)	7:10
Sep. 15	**San Diego**	1:00
Sep. 19	**Kansas City** (Thurs)	8:25
Sep. 29	at Denver	4:25
Oct. 6	at New York Giants	1:00
Oct. 13	at Tampa Bay	1:00
Oct. 20	**Dallas**	1:00
Oct. 27	**New York Giants**	1:00
Nov. 3	at Oakland	4:05
Nov. 10	at Green Bay	1:00
Nov. 17	**Washington**	1:00
Nov. 24	BYE	
Dec. 1	**Arizona**	1:00
Dec. 8	**Detroit**	1:00
Dec. 15	at Minnesota	1:00
Dec. 22	**Chicago**	1:00
Dec. 29	at Dallas	1:00

All times ET

Stadium: Lincoln Financial Field
(opened in 2003)
•**Capacity:** 69,144
One Lincoln Financial Field Way
Philadelphia, Pennsylvania 19148
Playing Surface: Natural Grass
Training Camp: Lehigh University
Bethlehem, PA 18015

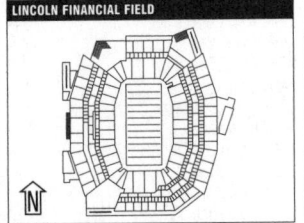

LINCOLN FINANCIAL FIELD

CLUB OFFICIALS
Chairman/Chief Executive Officer:
Jeffrey Lurie
President: Don Smolenski
Head Coach: Chip Kelly
General Manager: Howie Roseman
Chief Financial Officer: Frank Gumienny
Senior Vice President/Business:
Ari Roitman
Executive Director of Eagles Youth
Partnership: Sarah Martinez-Helfman
Vice President of Player Personnel:
Tom Gamble
Director of Football Media Relations:
Derek Boyko
Director of Human Resources:
Kristie Pappal
Manager of Community Relations:
Julie Hirshey
Vice President of Event Operations and
Event Services: Leonard Bonacci
Director of Ticket Operations:
Laini Delawter
Director of Ticket Client Relations:
Leo Carlin
Director of Merchandise:
Brendan McQuillen
Director of Team Security: Dom DiSandro
Head Athletic Trainer: Chris Peduzzi
Assistant Athletic Trainer: Joe O'Pella
Video Director: Stewart Cramer
Head Equipment Manager:
Greg Delimitros

COACHING HISTORY
(540-581-26)
Records include postseason games
1933-35	Lud Wray	9-21-1
1936-1940	Bert Bell	10-44-2
1941-1950	Earle (Greasy) Neale*	66-44-5
1951	Alvin (Bo) McMillin**	2-0-0
1951	Wayne Millner	2-8-0
1952-55	Jim Trimble	25-20-3
1956-57	Hugh Devore	7-16-1
1958-1960	Lawrence (Buck) Shaw	20-16-1
1961-63	Nick Skorich	15-24-3
1964-68	Joe Kuharich	28-41-1
1969-1971	Jerry Williams***	7-22-2
1971-72	Ed Khayat	8-15-2
1973-75	Mike McCormack	16-25-1
1976-1982	Dick Vermeil	57-51-0
1983-85	Marion Campbell****	17-29-1
1985	Fred Bruney	1-0-0
1986-1990	Buddy Ryan	43-38-1
1991-94	Rich Kotite	37-29-0
1995-98	Ray Rhodes	30-36-1
1999-2012	Andy Reid	140-102-1

*Co-coach with Walt Kiesling in Philadelphia-
Pittsburgh merger in 1943
**Retired after two games in 1951
***Released after three games in 1971
****Released after 15 games in 1985

PAID ATTENDANCE
Home 523,444	Away 547,866

Total 1,071,310
Single-game home record,
72,111 (11/1/81)
Single-season home record,
557,325 (1980)

2013 DRAFT CHOICES
Round	Name	Pos.	College
1	Lane Johnson	T	Oklahoma
2	Zach Ertz	TE	Stanford
3	Bennie Logan	DT	Louisiana St.
4	Matt Barkley	QB	Southern California
5	Earl Wolff	DB	North Carolina St.
7	Joe Kruger	DE	Utah
	Jordan Poyer	DB	Oregon St.
	David King	DE	Oklahoma

PHILADELPHIA EAGLES

2012 TEAM RECORD
PRESEASON (4-0)

Date	Result	Opponent
08/09	W 24-23	Pittsburgh
08/20	W 27-17	at New England
08/24	W 27-10	at Cleveland
08/30	W 28-10	New York Jets

REGULAR SEASON (4-12)

Date	Result	Opponent
09/09	W 17-16	at Cleveland
09/16	W 24-23	Baltimore
09/23	L 6-27	at Arizona
09/30	W 19-17	New York Giants
10/07	L 14-16	at Pittsburgh
10/14	L 23-26	Detroit (OT)
10/28	L 17-30	Atlanta
11/05	L 13-28	at New Orleans
11/11	L 23-38	Dallas
11/18	L 6-31	at Washington
11/26	L 22-30	Carolina
12/02	L 33-38	at Dallas
12/09	W 23-21	at Tampa Bay
12/13	L 13-34	Cincinnati
12/23	L 20-27	Washington
12/30	L 7-42	at New York Giants

SCORE BY PERIODS

Eagles	31	92	78	79	0 —	280
Opponents	106	111	83	141	3 —	444

2012 TEAM STATISTICS

	Eagles	Opp.
Total First Downs	332	317
Rushing	111	108
Passing	190	178
Penalty	31	31
3rd Down: Made/Att	83/222	83/203
3rd Down Pct.	37.4	40.9
4th Down: Made/Att	14/24	2/10
4th Down Pct.	58.3	20.0
Possession Avg.	29:36	30:24
Total Net Yards	5665	5491
Avg. Per Game	354.1	343.2
Total Plays	1079	994
Avg. Per Play	5.3	5.5
Net Yards Rushing	1874	2021
Avg. Per Game	117.1	126.3
Total Rushes	413	479
Net Yards Passing	3791	3470
Avg. Per Game	236.9	216.9
Sacked/Yards Lost	48/284	30/198
Gross Yards	4075	3668
Att./Completions	618/367	485/292
Completion Pct.	59.4	60.2
Had Intercepted	15	8
Punts/Average	72/46.3	78/43.7
Net Punting Avg.	72/36.9	78/37.7
Penalties/Yards	98/813	118/996
Fumbles/Ball Lost	37/22	21/5
Touchdowns	29	52
Rushing	10	11
Passing	18	33
Returns	1	8

2012 INDIVIDUAL STATISTICS

PASSING

	Att.	Comp.	Yds.	Pct.	TD	Int.	Tkld.	Rate
Vick	351	204	2362	58.1	12	10	28/153	78.1
Foles	265	161	1699	60.8	6	5	20/131	79.1
Edwards	2	2	14	100.0	0	0	0/0	95.8
Eagles	618	367	4075	59.4	18	15	48/284	78.6
Opponents	485	292	3668	60.2	33	8	30/198	99.6

SCORING

	TD R	TD P	TD Rt	PAT	FG	Saf	PTS
Henery	0	0	0	25/26	27/31	0	106
Maclin	0	7	0	0/0	0/0	0	42
McCoy	2	3	0	0/0	0/0	0	30
Brown	4	0	0	0/0	0/0	0	24
Cooper	0	3	0	0/0	0/0	0	18
Harbor	0	2	0	0/0	0/0	0	12
Jackson	0	2	0	0/0	0/0	0	12
Celek	0	1	0	0/0	0/0	0	6
Foles	1	0	0	0/0	0/0	0	6
Havili	1	0	0	0/0	0/0	0	6
D. Johnson	0	0	1	0/0	0/0	0	6
Lewis	1	0	0	0/0	0/0	0	6
Vick	1	0	0	0/0	0/0	0	6
Eagles	10	18	1	25/26	27/31	0	280
Opponents	11	33	8	51/52	27/29	0	444

2-Pt Conversions: Eagles 0-3, Opponents 0-0

RUSHING

	No.	Yds	Avg	LG	TD
McCoy	200	840	4.2	34	2
Brown	115	564	4.9	65t	4
Vick	62	332	5.4	20	1
Lewis	13	69	5.3	17t	1
Foles	11	42	3.8	14	1
Havili	6	22	3.7	8	1
D. Johnson	3	12	4.0	7	0
Jackson	3	-7	-2.3	5	0
Eagles	413	1874	4.5	65t	10
Opponents	479	2021	4.2	43	11

RECEIVING

	No.	Yds	Avg	LG	TD
Maclin	69	857	12.4	70t	7
Celek	57	684	12.0	34	1
McCoy	54	373	6.9	36	3
Avant	53	648	12.2	39	0
Jackson	45	700	15.6	77t	2
Harbor	25	186	7.4	19	2
Cooper	23	248	10.8	23	3
D. Johnson	19	256	13.5	32	0
Brown	13	56	4.3	11	0
Havili	7	43	6.1	9	0
Lewis	2	24	12.0	28	0
Eagles	367	4075	11.1	77t	18
Opponents	292	3668	12.6	63t	33

PUNTING

	No.	Yds.	Avg.	In 20	LG
McBriar	55	2560	46.5	13	66
Henry	16	776	48.5	2	62
Eagles	72	3336	46.3	15	66
Opponents	78	3410	43.7	22	66

PUNT RETURNS

	Ret	FC	Yds	Avg	LG	TD
D. Johnson	26	23	291	11.2	98t	1
Gilyard	2	3	15	7.5	11	0
Boykin	1	0	7	7.0	7	0
Jackson	1	0	-3	-3.0	-3	0
Eagles	30	26	310	10.3	98t	1
Opponents	40	15	542	13.6	78t	1

INTERCEPTIONS

	No.	Yds	Avg	LG	TD
Rodgers-Cromartie	3	14	4.7	14	0
Coleman	2	13	6.5	7	0
Anderson	1	4	4.0	4	0
Asomugha	1	0	0.0	0	0
Ryans	1	0	0.0	0	0
Eagles	8	31	3.9	14	0
Opponents	15	391	26.1	99t	3

KICKOFF RETURNS

	No.	Yds	Avg	LG	TD
Boykin	45	1037	23.0	44	0
Brown	8	156	19.5	25	0
Havili	2	18	9.0	18	0
Lewis	1	33	33.0	33	0
Cooper	1	14	14.0	14	0
Jordan	1	1	1.0	1	0
Polk	1	0	0.0	0	0
Thornton	1	0	0.0	0	0
Eagles	60	1259	21.0	44	0
Opponents	41	1012	24.7	53	0

FIELD GOALS

	1-19	20-29	30-39	40-49	50+
Henery	0/0	8/9	8/9	11/12	0/1
Eagles	0/0	8/9	8/9	11/12	0/1
Opponents	1/1	8/8	7/7	9/9	2/4

SACKS

	No.
Babin	5.5
Cox	5.5
Graham	5.5
Jenkins	4.0
Cole	3.0
Boykin	1.0
Hunt	1.0
Kendricks	1.0
Patterson	1.0
Ryans	1.0
Thornton	1.0
Tapp	0.5
Eagles	30.0
Opponents	48.0

RECORD HOLDERS
INDIVIDUAL RECORDS—CAREER

Category	Name	Performance
Rushing (Yds.)	Wilbert Montgomery, 1977-1984	6,538
Passing (Yds.)	Donovan McNabb, 1999-2009	32,873
Passing (TDs)	Donovan McNabb, 1999-2009	216
Receiving (No.)	Harold Carmichael, 1971-1983	589
Receiving (Yds.)	Harold Carmichael, 1971-1983	8,978
Interceptions	Bill Bradley, 1969-1976	34
	Eric Allen, 1988-1994	34
	Brian Dawkins, 1996-2008	34
Punting (Avg.)	Joe Muha, 1946-1950	42.9
Punt Return (Avg.)	Ernie Steele, 1942-48	16.8
Kickoff Return (Avg.)	Steve Van Buren, 1944-1951	26.7
Field Goals	David Akers, 1999-2010	294
Touchdowns (Tot.)	Harold Carmichael, 1971-1983	79
Points	David Akers, 1999-2010	1,323
*Sacks	Reggie White, 1985-1992	124.0

INDIVIDUAL RECORDS—SINGLE SEASON

Category	Name	Performance
Rushing (Yds.)	Wilbert Montgomery, 1979	1,512
Passing (Yds.)	Donovan McNabb, 2008	3,916
Passing (TDs)	Sonny Jurgensen, 1961	32
Receiving (No.)	Brian Westbrook, 2007	90
Receiving (Yds.)	Mike Quick, 1983	1,409
Interceptions	Bill Bradley, 1971	11
Punting (Avg.)	Joe Muha, 1948	47.2
Punt Return (Avg.)	Steve Van Buren, 1944	15.3
Kickoff Return (Avg.)	Al Nelson, 1972	29.1
Field Goals	David Akers, 2008	33
Touchdowns (Tot.)	LeSean McCoy, 2011	20
Points	David Akers, 2008	144
*Sacks	Reggie White, 1987	21.0

INDIVIDUAL RECORDS—SINGLE GAME

Category	Name	Performance
Rushing (Yds.)	Steve Van Buren, 11-27-49	205
Passing (Yds.)	Donovan McNabb, 12-5-04	464
Passing (TDs)	Adrian Burk, 10-17-54	**7
Receiving (No.)	Don Looney, 12-1-40	14
	Brian Westbrook, 11-4-07	14
Receiving (Yds.)	Tommy McDonald, 12-10-61	237
Interceptions	Russ Craft, 9-24-50	**4
Field Goals	Tom Dempsey, 11-12-72	6
Touchdowns (Tot.)	Many times	4
	Last time by Brian Westbrook, 11-27-08	
Points	Bobby Walston, 10-17-54	25
*Sacks	Clyde Simmons, 9-15-91	4.5
	Hugh Douglas, 10-18-98	4.5

*Sacks became an official statistic in 1982.
**NFL Record

2013 VETERAN ROSTER

No.	Name	Pos.	Ht.	Wt.	Birthdate	NFL Exp.	College	Hometown	How Acq.	'12 Games/ Starts
29	Allen, Nate	S	6-1	210	11/30/87	4	South Florida	Cape Coral, Fla.	D2-'10	15/13
30	Anderson, Colt	S	5-10	194	10/25/85	4	Montana	Butte, Mont.	UFA(Minn)-'10	14/4
81	Avant, Jason	WR	6-0	212	4/20/83	8	Michigan	Chicago, Ill.	D4b-'06	14/6
76	Barbre, Allen	T	6-4	305	6/22/84	6	Southern Missouri	Neosho, Mo.	FA-'13	0*
98	Barwin, Connor	LB	6-4	260	10/15/86	5	Cincinnati	Detroit, Mich.	UFA(Hou)-'13	16/16*
17	t- Benn, Arrelious	WR	6-2	220	9/8/88	4	Illinois	Washington, D.C.	T(TB)-'13	8/1*
22	Boykin, Brandon	CB	5-10	185	7/13/90	2	Georgia	Fayetteville, Ga.	D4-'12	16/4
34	Brown, Bryce	RB	6-0	223	5/14/91	2	Kansas State	Wichita, Kan.	D7-'12	16/4
57	Brown, Everette	DE	6-1	263	8/7/87	4	Florida State	Stantonsburg, N.C.	FA-'13	0*
85	Casey, James	TE	6-3	240	9/22/84	5	Rice	Azle, Texas	UFA(Hou)-'13	16/9*
87	Celek, Brent	TE	6-4	255	1/25/85	7	Cincinnati	Cincinnati, Ohio	D5b-'07	15/14
51	Chaney, Jamar	LB	6-0	242	10/11/86	4	Mississippi State	St. Lucie, Fla.	D7a-'10	14/5
23	Chung, Patrick	S	5-11	210	8/19/87	5	Oregon	Rancho Cucamonga, Calif.	UFA(NE)-'13	12/8*
58	Cole, Trent	DE	6-3	270	10/5/82	9	Cincinnati	Xenia, Ohio	D5a-'05	16/16
42	Coleman, Kurt	S	5-11	195	7/1/88	4	Ohio State	Clayton, Ohio	D7c-'10	14/14
14	Cooper, Riley	WR	6-3	222	9/9/87	4	Florida	Clearwater, Fla.	D5b-'10	11/5
91	Cox, Fletcher	DT	6-4	300	12/13/90	2	Mississippi State	Yazoo City, Miss.	D1-'12	15/9
75	Curry, Vinny	DE	6-3	266	6/30/88	2	Marshall	Neptune, N.J.	D2b-'12	6/0
90	Dixon, Antonio	DT	6-3	325	7/17/85	4	Miami	Miami, Fla.	W(Wash)-'09	3/0*
3	Dixon, Dennis	QB	6-3	215	1/11/85	5	Oregon	San Leandro, Calif.	FA-'13	0*
46	Dorenbos, Jon	LS	6-0	250	7/21/80	11	Texas-El Paso	Garden Grove, Calif.	FA-'06	16/0
24	Fletcher, Bradley	CB	6-0	200	6/25/86	5	Iowa	Youngstown, Ohio	UFA(StL)-'13	16/4*
9	Foles, Nick	QB	6-6	243	1/20/89	2	Arizona	Austin, Texas	D3-'12	7/6
64	t- Geathers, Clifton	DE	6-7	325	12/11/87	3	South Carolina	Hemingway, S.C.	T(Ind)-'13	8/0*
55	Graham, Brandon	DE	6-2	268	4/3/88	4	Michigan	Detroit, Mich.	D1-'10	16/6
82	Harbor, Clay	TE	6-3	255	7/2/87	4	Missouri State	Dwight, Ill.	D4d-'10	14/9
6	Henery, Alex	K/P	6-1	177	8/18/87	3	Nebraska	Omaha, Neb.	D4b-'11	16/0
79	Herremans, Todd	T	6-6	321	10/13/82	9	Saginaw Valley State	Ravenna, Mich.	D4b-'05	8/8
27	Hughes, Brandon	CB	5-11	185	5/23/86	5	Oregon State	Bloomington, Ill.	UFA(NYG)-'10	16/0
56	Hunt, Phillip	DE	6-1	254	1/10/86	3	Houston	Fort Worth, Texas	FA-'11	13/0
10	Jackson, DeSean	WR	5-10	175	12/1/86	6	California	Long Beach, Calif.	D2b-'08	11/11
13	Johnson, Damaris	WR	5-8	170	11/22/89	2	Tulsa	Destrehan, La.	FA-'12	14/1
8	Jones, Donnie	P	6-2	221	7/5/80	10	Louisiana State	Baton Rouge, La.	UFA(Hou)-'13	16/0*
62	Kelce, Jason	C	6-3	295	11/5/87	3	Cincinnati	Cleveland, Ohio	D6a-'11	2/2
67	Kelly, Dennis	T	6-8	321	1/16/90	2	Purdue	Chicago Heights, Ill.	D5-'12	13/10
95	Kendricks, Mychal	LB	6-0	240	9/28/90	2	California	Fresno, Calif.	D2a-'12	15/14
78	Kopa, Matt	T	6-6	310	2/25/87	2	Stanford	Elk Grove, Calif.	FA-'12	0*
35	Lindley, Trevard	CB	6-0	183	2/2/86	2	Kentucky	Lithia Springs, Ga.	D4a-'10	0*
18	Maclin, Jeremy	WR	6-0	198	5/11/88	5	Missouri	Kirkwood, Mo.	D1-'09	15/15
31	Marsh, Curtis	CB	6-1	197	3/1/88	3	Utah State	Simi Valley, Calif.	D3-'11	15/0
69	Mathis, Evan	G	6-5	302	11/1/81	9	Alabama	Homewood, Ala.	UFA(Cin)-'11	16/16
50	Matthews, Casey	LB	6-1	240	1/16/89	3	Oregon	Westlake Village, Calif.	D4a-'11	16/1
25	McCoy, LeSean	RB	5-11	208	7/12/88	5	Pittsburgh	Harrisburg, Pa.	D2-'09	12/12
74	Menkin, Nate	T/G	6-5	300	10/4/88	2	Mary Hardin-Baylor	Lago Vista, Texas	W(Hou)-'12	0*
16	Miller, Nick	WR	5-9	180	3/29/87	4	Southern Utah	Mesa, Ariz.	FA-'13	0*
86	Moore, Evan	TE	6-6	250	1/3/85	5	Stanford	Brea, Calif.	FA-'13	15/1
71	Peters, Jason	T	6-4	340	1/22/82	10	Arkansas	Queen City, Texas	T(Buff)-'09	0*
52	Phillips, Jason	LB	6-1	240	2/14/86	5	Texas Christian	Waller, Texas	UFA(Car)-'13	16/2*
21	Phillips, Kenny	S	6-2	217	11/24/86	6	Miami	Miami, Fla.	UFA(NYG)-'13	7/6*
32	Polk, Chris	RB	5-11	222	12/16/89	2	Washington	Redlands, Calif.	FA-'12	7/0
66	Reynolds, Dallas	G/C	6-4	320	4/23/84	2	Brigham Young	Provo, Utah	FA-'09	16/14
59	Ryans, DeMeco	LB	6-1	247	7/28/84	8	Alabama	Bessemer, Ala.	T(Hou)-'12	16/16
19	Salas, Greg	WR	6-1	209	8/25/88	3	Hawaii	Chino, Calif.	W(NE)-'12	2/0*
84	Sampson, DeMarco	WR	6-2	204	12/19/85	2	San Diego State	Chula Vista, Calif.	FA-'13	0*
43	Sims, David	S	5-10	210	10/20/86	2	Iowa State	Gainesville, Fla.	T(Cle)-'12	15/1
97	Sopoaga, Isaac	DL	6-2	330	9/4/81	10	Hawaii	Pago Pago, American Samoa	UFA(SF)-'13	15/9*
68	Tennant, Matt	C	6-4	300	3/19/87	4	Boston College	Cincinnati, Ohio	FA-'12	8/0
72	Thornton, Cedric	DT	6-4	309	6/21/88	2	Southern Arkansas	Star City, Ark.	FA-'11	16/0
61	Vandervelde, Julian	G	6-2	300	10/7/87	2	Iowa	Davenport, Iowa	D5b-'11	0*
7	Vick, Michael	QB	6-0	215	6/26/80	12	Virginia Tech	Newport News, Va.	FA-'09	10/10
77	Wang, Ed	T	6-5	315	3/12/87	3	Virginia Tech	Ashburn, Va.	FA-'13	0*
63	Watkins, Danny	G	6-3	310	11/6/84	3	Baylor	Kelowna, B.C., Canada	D1-'11	11/6
26	Williams, Cary	CB	6-1	190	12/23/84	5	Washburn	Hollywood, Fla.	UFA(Balt)-'13	16/16*

* Barbre last active with Seattle in '11; Barwin played 16 games with Houston in '12; Benn played eight games with Tampa Bay; E. Brown last active with San Diego in '11; Casey played 16 games with Houston; Chung played 12 games with New England; A. Dixon played one game with Philadelphia and two games with Indianapolis; D. Dixon last active with Pittsburgh in '10; Fletcher played 16 games with St. Louis; Geathers played eight games with Indianapolis; Jones played 16 games with Houston; Kopa inactive for four games; Lindley last active with Philadelphia in '10; Menkin inactive for 13 games; Miller last active with St. Louis in '11; Moore played one game with Philadelphia and 14 games with Seattle; Peters missed '12 season because of injury; J. Phillips played 16 games with Carolina; K. Phillips played seven games with the New York Giants; Salas played one game with Philadelphia and one game with New England; Sampson last active with Arizona in '11; Sopoaga played 15 games with San Francisco; Vandervelde did not play in one game; Wang last active with Buffalo in '10; Williams played 16 games with Baltimore.

\# Unrestricted Free Agent; subject to developments.

t- Eagles traded for Benn (TB), Geathers (Ind).

Traded—Eagles traded Havili (15 games in '12) to Indianapolis.

Players lost through free agency (4): T King Dunlap (SD; 14 games in '12), DT Derek Landri (TB; 16), CB Dominique Rodgers-Cromartie (Den; 16), DE Darryl Tapp (Wash; 13).

Also played with Eagles in '12—CB Nnamdi Asomugha (16 games), DE Jason Babin (11), QB Trent Edwards (1), WR Mardy Gilyard (6), P Chas Henry (3), S Jaiquawn Jarrett (1), DT Cullen Jenkins (16), LB Akeem Jordan (14), P Mat McBriar (13), LB Adrian Moten (1), DT Mike Patterson (5), LB Ryan Rau (4), LB Brian Rolle (4), G Jake Scott (7), G Steve Vallos (2), LB Jason Williams (2).

FIRST-YEAR ROSTER

Name	Pos.	Ht.	Wt.	Birthdate	College	Hometown	How Acq.
Acho, Emmanuel (1)	LB	6-2	240	11/10/90	Texas	Dallas, Texas	T(Cle)-'13
Barkley, Matt	QB	6-2	227	9/8/90	Southern California	Newport Beach, Calif.	D4
Carrier, Derek (1)	TE	6-4	241	8/25/90	Beloit	Edgerton, Wisc.	FA-'12
Cunningham, B.J. (1)	WR	6-2	215	5/29/89	Michigan State	Columbus, Ohio	FA-'12
Ertz, Zach	TE	6-5	250	11/10/90	Stanford	Orange, Calif.	D2
Igwenagu, Emil (1)	FB	6-2	245	3/27/89	Massachusetts	Raleigh, N.C.	FA-'12
Johnson, Lane	T	6-6	303	5/8/90	Oklahoma	Groveton, Texas	D1
King, David	DE	6-4	285	12/27/89	Oklahoma	Houston, Texas	D7c
Kinne, G.J. (1)	QB	6-2	234	12/1/88	Tulsa	Mesquite, Texas	FA
Knott, Jake	LB	6-3	252	10/24/90	Iowa State	Waukee, Iowa	FA
Kruger, Joe	DE/LB	6-6	269	6/4/92	Utah	Orem, Utah	D7a
Logan, Bennie	DT	6-2	309	12/28/89	Louisiana State	Shreveport, La.	D3
McCoy, Chris (1)	DE/LB	6-3	261	11/26/86	Middle Tennessee State	Villa Rica, Ga.	FA
Momah, Ifeanyi	WR	6-6	229	10/23/89	Boston College	Greenlawn, N.Y.	FA
Murphy, Will	WR	6-2	193	5/15/90	Oregon	Albany, Ore.	FA
Poyer, Jordan	CB	6-0	191	4/25/91	Oregon State	The Dalles, Ore.	D7b
Purcell, Nic	T	6-6	300	9/20/85	Golden West	Auckland, New Zealand	FA
Quinn, Kyle	C	6-3	290	2/9/90	Arizona	Brentwood, Calif.	FA
Remington, Isaac	DE	6-6	305	6/16/89	Oregon	Queen Creek, Ariz.	FA
Shaw, Will	TE	6-3	245	1/5/91	Youngstown State	Baltimore, Md.	FA
Shepard, Russell	WR	6-1	195	11/17/90	Louisiana State	Houston, Texas	FA
Square, Damion	DE	6-3	286	2/6/89	Alabama	Houston, Texas	FA
Tobin, Matt	T	6-6	290	6/5/90	Iowa	Dyersville, Iowa	FA
Tucker, Matthew	RB	6-1	227	5/24/91	Texas Christian	Tyler, Texas	FA
Walker, Daryell	DE	6-6	285	2/4/91	Hampton	Hampton, Va.	FA
Whitley, Eddie (1)	CB	6-0	191	10/26/89	Virginia Tech	Fayetteville, N.C.	FA-'12
Wing, Brad	P	6-3	197	1/27/91	Louisiana State	Melbourne, Australia	FA
Wolff, Earl	S	5-11	209	12/15/89	North Carolina State	Raeford, N.C.	D5

The term NFL Rookie is defined as a player who is in his first season of professional football and has not been on the roster of another professional football team for any regular-season or postseason games. A Rookie is designated by an "R" on NFL rosters. Players who have been active in another professional football league or players who have NFL experience, including either preseason training camp or being on an Active List or Inactive List, or on Reserve/Injured or Reserve/Physically Unable to Perform for fewer than six regular-season games, are termed NFL First-Year Players. An NFL First-Year Player is designated by a "1" on NFL rosters. Thereafter, a player is credited with an additional year of experience for each season in which he accumulates six games on the Active List or Inactive List, or on Reserve/Injured or Reserve/Physically Unable to Perform.

Log on to www.philadelphiaeagles.com for an up-to-date roster.

COACHING STAFF
Head Coach,
Chip Kelly
Pro Career: Chip Kelly became the 21st head coach in franchise history on January 16, 2013. It is his first NFL coaching experience after 23 years of working in the college ranks. One of college football's most successful coaches, Kelly put his stamp on a new generation of offensive schemes during his four years at the helm of the University of Oregon program. In four seasons as the head coach of the Ducks, he compiled a 46-7 overall record and transformed the school into one of the nation's premiere college football destinations. Career record: 0-0.
Background: Attended the University of New Hampshire and earned a bachelor's degree in physical education in 1990. Coached at Columbia (1990-91), New Hampshire (1992, 1994-2006), Johns Hopkins (1993), Oregon (2007-12)
Personal: Born November 25, 1963, Dover, N.H.

ASSISTANT COACHES
Greg Austin, asst. offensive line; born November 19, 1984, Cypress, Texas. Guard Nebraska 2003-06. No pro playing experience. College coach: Oregon 2011-12. Pro coach: Joined Eagles in 2013.
Jerry Azzinaro, defensive line/assistant head coach; born July 11, 1958, Brooklyn, N.Y. Linebacker American International 1978-1981. No pro playing experience. College coach: American International 1982-84, 1987-1991, Westfield 1985, Western New England 1986, Massachusetts 1992-94, 1997, Boston College 1995-96, Maine 1998, Syracuse 1999-2003, Duke 2004-06, New Hampshire 2007, Marshall 2008, Oregon 2009-2012. Pro coach: Joined Eagles in 2013.
Bob Bicknell, wide receivers; November 13, 1969, Holliston, Mass. Tight end Boston College 1989-1991. No pro playing experience. College coach: Boston University 1993-97, Temple 2006. Pro coach: Frankfurt Galaxy 1998-99, Berlin Thunder 2000-03, Cologne Centurions (NFL Europe) 2004-05, Kansas City Chiefs 2007-09, Buffalo Bills 2010-12, joined Eagles in 2013.
Erik Chinander, asst. defensive line; born December 19, 1979. Offensive line Iowa 1998-2002. No pro playing experience. College coach: Ellsworth (Iowa) C.C. 2003, Northern Iowa 2004-09, Oregon 2010-12. Pro coach: Joined Eagles in 2013.
Bill Davis, defensive coordinator; born November 5, 1965, Youngstown, Ohio. Quarterback/wide receiver Cincinnati 1985-88. No pro playing experience. College coach: Michigan State 1990-91. Pro coach: Pittsburgh Steelers 1992-94, Carolina Panthers 1995-98, Cleveland Browns 1999, Green Bay Packers 2000,

Atlanta Falcons 2001-03, New York Giants 2004, San Francisco 49ers 2005-06, Arizona Cardinals 2007-10, Cleveland Browns 2011-12, joined Eagles in 2013.
Mike Dawson, defensive quality control; born November 26, 1974, Secaucus, N.J. Linebacker UMass-Amherst 1994-96. No pro playing experience. College coach: UMass-Lowell 1998, Maine 1998-99, Pittsburgh 1999, New Hampshire 2000-05, Akron 2006-08, Boston College 2009-11. Pro coach: Joined Eagles in 2013.
Dave Fipp, special teams coordinator; born August 8, 1974, Albuquerque, N.M. Safety Arizona 1994-97. No pro playing experience. College coach: Holy Cross 1998-99, Arizona 2000, Cal Poly 2001-03, Nevada 2004, San Jose State 2005-07. Pro coach: San Francisco 49ers 2008-2010, Miami Dolphins 2011-12, joined Eagles in 2013.
Matthew Harper, asst. special teams; born November 26, 1984, Secaucus, N.J. Safety City College of San Francisco 2004-05, Oregon 2006-07. No pro playing experience. College coach: City College of San Francisco 2008, Oregon 2009-2012. Pro coach: Joined Eagles in 2013.
Josh Hingst, strength and conditioning; born December 29, 1978, Fremont, Neb. Attended Nebraska. No college or pro playing experience. College coach: Florida State 2003-07. Pro coach: Jacksonville Jaguars 2012, joined Eagles in 2013.
Bill Lazor, quarterbacks; born June 14, 1972, Scranton, Pa. Quarterback Cornell 1990-93. No pro playing experience. College coach: Cornell 1994-2000, Buffalo 2001-02, Virginia 2010-12. Pro coach: Atlanta Falcons 2003, Washington Redskins 2004-07, Seattle Seahawks 2008-09, joined Eagles in 2013.
John Lovett, defensive backs; born December 1, 1950, Nyack, N.Y. Linebacker C.W. Post 1970-73. No pro playing experience. College coach: Union College 1978-1982, Brown 1983, Maine 1985-88, 1994, Cincinnati 1989-1992, Nevada-Las Vegas 1993, Maine 1994, Ole Miss 1994-98, Auburn 1999-2001, Clemson 2002-04, Bowling Green 2005-06, North Carolina 2007-08, Miami 2009-2010, Texas Tech 2012. Pro coach: New York Jets 1984, joined Eagles in 2013.
Todd Lyght, asst. defensive backs; born February 9, 1969, Kwajalein, Marshall Islands. Cornerback Notre Dame 1987-1990. Pro cornerback Los Angeles/St. Louis Rams 1991-2000, Detroit Lions 2001-02. College coach: Oregon 2011-12. Pro coach: Joined Eagles in 2013.
Bill McGovern, outside linebackers; born December 31, 1962, Teaneck, N.J. Defensive back Holy Cross 1981-84. No pro playing experience. College coach: Pennsylvania 1985, Holy Cross 1986-87, Massachusetts 1988-1990, Holy Cross 1991-92, Massachusetts 1993, Boston

College 1994-96, Pittsburgh 1997-99, Boston College 2000-2012. Pro coach: Joined Eagles in 2013.
Rick Minter, inside linebackers; born October 4, 1954, Nash, Texas. Defensive end Henderson State 1973-76. No pro playing experience. College coach: Henderson State 1977, Arkansas 1978, Louisiana Tech 1979, North Carolina State 1980-82, New Mexico State 1984, Ball State 1985-1991, Notre Dame 1992-93, Cincinnati 1994-2003, South Carolina 2004, Notre Dame 2005-07, Marshall 2008-09, Indiana State 2010, Kentucky 2011-12. Pro coach: Joined Eagles in 2013.
Justin Peelle, asst. tight ends; born March 15, 1979, Fresno, Calif. Tight end Oregon 1997-2001. Pro tight end San Diego Chargers 2002-05, Miami Dolphins 2006-07, Atlanta Falcons 2008-2010, San Francisco 49ers 2011. Pro coach: Joined Eagles in 2013.
Pat Shurmur, offensive coordinator; born April 14, 1965, Dearborn, Mich. Center/linebacker Michigan State 1984-87. No pro playing experience. College coach: Michigan State 1988-1997, Stanford 1998. Pro coach: Philadelphia Eagles 1999-2008, St. Louis Rams 2009-2010, Cleveland Browns 2011-12 (head coach), re-joined Eagles in 2013.
Duce Staley, running backs; born February 27, 1975, Tampa, Fla. Running back South Carolina 1995-96. Pro running back Philadelphia Eagles 1997-2003, Pittsburgh Steelers 2004-06. Pro coach: Joined Eagles in 2011.
Jeff Stoutland, offensive line; born February 10, 1962, New York City, N.Y. Linebacker Southern Connecticut State. No pro playing experience. College coach: Southern Connecticut State 1984-85, 1988-1992, Syracuse 1986-87, 1997-99, Cornell 1993-96, Michigan State 2000-06, Miami 2007-2010, Alabama 2011-12. Pro coach: Joined Eagles in 2013.
Press Taylor, offensive quality control. Quarterback Butler (Kan.) C.C. 2007-08, Marshall 2009-2010. No pro playing experience. College coach: Tulsa 2011-12. Pro coach: Joined Eagles in 2013.
Ted Williams, tight ends; born November 17, 1943, Lyons, Texas. Attended Cal Poly-Pomona. No college or pro playing experience. College coach: UCLA 1980-89, Washington State 1991-93, Arizona 1994. Pro coach: Joined Eagles in 1995.

National Football Conference
West Division
Team Colors: New Century Gold,
Millennium Blue, and White
One Rams Way
St. Louis, Missouri 63045
Telephone: (314) 982-7267

2013 SCHEDULE
PRESEASON
Aug. 8   at Cleveland 7:00
Aug. 17   **Green Bay**........................7:00
Aug. 24   at Denver.............................7:00
Aug. 29   **Baltimore**.........................7:00

REGULAR SEASON
Sep. 8   **Arizona** 3:25
Sep. 15   at Atlanta 12:00
Sep. 22   at Dallas 12:00
Sep. 26   **San Francisco** (Thurs) 7:25
Oct. 6   **Jacksonville** 12:00
Oct. 13   at Houston 12:00
Oct. 20   at Carolina 12:00
Oct. 28   **Seattle** (Mon) 7:40
Nov. 3   **Tennessee** 12:00
Nov. 10   at Indianapolis 12:00
Nov. 17   BYE
Nov. 24   **Chicago** 12:00
Dec. 1   at San Francisco 3:05
Dec. 8   at Arizona 3:25
Dec. 15   **New Orleans** 12:00
Dec. 22   **Tampa Bay** 12:00
Dec. 29   at Seattle 3:25
All times CT

Stadium: Edward Jones Dome
(opened in 1995)
  •Capacity: 66,000
901 N. Broadway
St. Louis, Missouri 63101
Playing Surface: FieldTurf
Training Camp: Russell Training Center
1 Rams Way
St. Louis, Missouri 63045

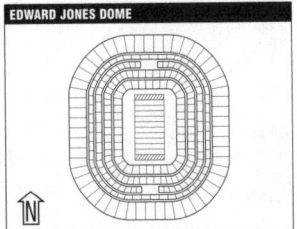

EDWARD JONES DOME

CLUB OFFICIALS
Owner/Chairman: Stan Kroenke
Executive Vice President of Football
  Operations/Chief Operating Officer:
  Kevin Demoff
General Manager: Les Snead
Treasurer: Jeff Brewer
Vice President of Finance:
  Michael T. Naughton
General Counsel: Todd Davis
Executive Vice President/Chief Revenue
  Officer: Bob Reif
Vice President of Broadcasting and
  Creative: Scott Brooks
Vice President of Corporate
  Communications and Civic Affairs:
  Molly Higgins
Vice President of Marketing and Brand
  Strategy: Brian Killingsworth
Vice President/Executive Services,
  Special Projects: Mike Moyneur
Vice President of Sales: Mike O'Keefe
Senior Director of Communications:
  Artis Twyman
VP/ Ticket Sales and Premium Seating:
  Jake Bye
Director of Video Operations:
  Larry Clerico
Director of Information Technology:
  Bill Consoli
Director of Special Events: Keely Fimbres
Director of Player Engagement:
  La'Roi Glover
Director of Internet Services and
  Business Development: Keith Harris
Director of Player Personnel:
  Lawrence McCutcheon
Director of Player Personnel:
  Taylor Morton
Director of Pro Personnel: Ran Carthon
Director of Security: Steve Miller
Director of Partnership Development and
  Administration: Susan Slemmer
Director of Operations: Bruce Warwick
Director of Corporate Sales:
  Chad Watson
Director of Ticket Operations:
  Kanyon West
Head Trainer: Reggie Scott
Assistant Trainers: Byron Cunningham,
  James Lomax, Tyler Williams
Equipment Manager: Jim Lake
Assistant Equipment Managers:
  Matt Taylor, John Welby, Ben Bloomer
Director of College Scouting:
  Brad Holmes
Senior Player Personnel Analyst:
  Rich Snead
Player Personnel Coordinator: JW Jordan
National Scouts: Lawrence McCutcheon,
  Ted Monago
Scouts: Ray Agnew, Evan Ardoin,
  Barto Danton, George Foster,
  Sean Gustus, Brian Heimerdinger,
  Steve Kazor, Brian Shields,
  Will Rodriguez
Scouting Assistant: Brian Hill

COACHING HISTORY
Cleveland 1937-1945,
Los Angeles 1946-1994
(539-538-21)
Records include postseason games
1937-38   Hugo Bezdek*............1-13-0
1938   Art Lewis.....................4-4-0
1939-1942 Earl (Dutch) Clark......16-26-2
1944   Aldo (Buff) Donelli........4-6-0
1945-46   Adam Walsh 16-5-1
1947   Bob Snyder..................6-6-0
1948-49   Clark Shaughnessy 14-8-3
1950-52   Joe Stydahar**...........19-9-0
1952-54   Hamp Pool...............23-11-2
1955-59   Sid Gillman 28-32-1
1960-62   Bob Waterfield*** 9-24-1
1962-65   Harland Svare 14-31-3
1966-1970 George Allen 49-19-4
1971-72   Tommy Prothro 14-12-2
1973-77   Chuck Knox 57-20-1
1978-1982 Ray Malavasi 43-36-0
1983-1991 John Robinson 79-74-0
1992-94   Chuck Knox 15-33-0
1995-96   Rich Brooks 13-19-0
1997-99   Dick Vermeil..............25-26-0
2000-05   Mike Martz****.........56-36-0
2005   Joe Vitt 4-7-0
2006-08   Scott Linehan#.........11-25-0
2008   Jim Haslett...................2-10-0
2009-2011 Steve Spagnuolo 10-38-0
2012   Jeff Fisher.....................7-8-1
      *   Released after three games in 1938
     **   Resigned after one game in 1952
    ***   Resigned after eight games in 1962
   ****   Took medical leave after five games in 2005
      #   Released after four games in 2008

PAID ATTENDANCE
Home 465,157   Away 470,642
Total 935,799
Single-game home record,
  66,273 (12/10/00)
Single-season home record,
  520,926 (1999)

2013 DRAFT CHOICES
Round	Name	Pos.	College
1	Tavon Austin	WR	West Virginia
	Alec Ogletree	LB	Georgia
3	T.J. McDonald	DB	Southern California
	Stedman Bailey	WR	West Virginia
4	Barrett Jones	C	Alabama
5	Brandon McGee	DB	Miami
	Zac Stacy	RB	Vanderbilt

2012 TEAM RECORD
PRESEASON (2-2)

Date	Result	Opponent
08/12	L 3-38	at Indianapolis
08/18	W 31-17	Kansas City
08/25	L 19-20	at Dallas
08/30	W 31-17	Baltimore

REGULAR SEASON (7-8-1)

Date	Result	Opponent
09/09	L 23-27	at Detroit
09/16	W 31-28	Washington
09/23	L 6-23	at Chicago
09/30	W 19-13	Seattle
10/04	W 17-3	Arizona
10/14	L 14-17	at Miami
10/21	L 20-30	Green Bay
10/28	L 7-45	New England
11/11	T 24-24	at San Francisco (OT)
11/18	L 13-27	New York Jets
11/25	W 31-17	at Arizona
12/02	W 16-13	San Francisco (OT)
12/09	W 15-12	at Buffalo
12/16	L 22-36	Minnesota
12/23	W 28-13	at Tampa Bay
12/30	L 13-20	at Seattle

(OT) Overtime

SCORE BY PERIODS

Rams	53	84	56	103	3	—	299
Opponents	74	114	63	97	0	—	348

2012 TEAM STATISTICS

	Rams	Opp.
Total First Downs	287	327
Rushing	79	107
Passing	189	197
Penalty	19	23
3rd Down: Made/Att	67/209	80/213
3rd Down Pct.	32.1	37.6
4th Down: Made/Att	13/24	6/16
4th Down Pct.	54.2	37.5
Possession Avg.	28:54	31:06
Total Net Yards	5264	5482
Avg. Per Game	329.0	342.6
Total Plays	1002	1041
Avg. Per Play	5.3	5.3
Net Yards Rushing	1714	1880
Avg. Per Game	107.1	117.5
Total Rushes	410	442
Net Yards Passing	3550	3602
Avg. Per Game	221.9	225.1
Sacked/Yards Lost	35/233	52/325
Gross Yards	3783	3927
Att./Completions	557/332	547/362
Completion Pct.	59.6	66.2
Had Intercepted	14	17
Punts/Average	82/45.8	73/44.3
Net Punting Avg.	82/39.9	73/39.5
Penalties/Yards	130/978	90/758
Fumbles/Ball Lost	24/8	17/4
Touchdowns	32	37
Rushing	5	18
Passing	22	16
Returns	5	3

2012 INDIVIDUAL STATISTICS

PASSING

	Att.	Comp.	Yds.	Pct.	TD	Int.	Tkld.	Rate
Bradford	551	328	3702	59.5	21	13	35/233	82.6
Clemens	3	1	39	33.3	0	1	0/0	42.4
Hekker	3	3	42	100.0	1	0	0/0	158.3
Rams	557	332	3783	59.6	22	14	35/233	82.7
Opponents	547	362	3927	66.2	16	17	52/325	83.9

SCORING

	TD R	TD P	TD Rt	PAT	FG	Saf	PTS
Zuerlein	0	0	0	26/26	23/31	0	95
Gibson	0	5	0	0/0	0/0	0	30
Jackson	4	0	0	0/0	0/0	0	26
Kendricks	0	4	0	0/0	0/0	0	26
Jenkins	0	0	4	0/0	0/0	0	24
Pettis	0	4	0	0/0	0/0	0	24
Amendola	0	3	0	0/0	0/0	0	20
Givens	0	3	0	0/0	0/0	0	20
Quick	0	2	0	0/0	0/0	0	12
Bradford	1	0	0	0/0	0/0	0	6
Finnegan	0	0	1	0/0	0/0	0	6
Mulligan	0	1	0	0/0	0/0	0	6
D. Richardson	0	0	0	0/0	0/0	0	2
Rams	5	22	5	26/26	23/31	1	299
Opponents	18	16	3	36/36	30/37	0	348

2-Pt Conversions: Amendola, Givens, Kendricks, D. Richardson, Rams 4-6, Opponents 0-1

RUSHING

	No.	Yds	Avg	LG	TD
Jackson	257	1042	4.1	46	4
D. Richardson	98	475	4.8	53	0
Bradford	37	127	3.4	21	1
Pead	10	54	5.4	19	0
Givens	3	12	4.0	14	0
Amendola	2	8	4.0	6	0
Clemens	2	5	2.5	5	0
Hekker	1	-9	-9.0	-9	0
Rams	410	1714	4.2	53	5
Opponents	442	1880	4.3	82t	18

RECEIVING

	No.	Yds	Avg	LG	TD
Amendola	63	666	10.6	56	3
Gibson	51	691	13.5	34t	5
Givens	42	698	16.6	65	3
Kendricks	42	519	12.4	80t	4
Jackson	38	321	8.4	22	0
Pettis	30	261	8.7	36	4
D. Richardson	24	163	6.8	26	0
St. Smith	14	131	9.4	25	0
Quick	11	156	14.2	39	2
Mulligan	8	84	10.5	18	1
McNeill	4	31	7.8	10	0
Pead	3	16	5.3	9	0
Harkey	1	21	21.0	21	0
McLeod	1	21	21.0	21	0
Turner	0	4	—	4	0
Rams	332	3783	11.4	80t	22
Opponents	362	3927	10.8	68t	16

INTERCEPTIONS

	No.	Yds	Avg	LG	TD
Jenkins	4	150	37.5	41t	3
Finnegan	3	68	22.7	32	1
Dunbar	2	63	31.5	42	0
Laurinaitis	2	18	9.0	18	0
Trumaine Johnson	2	4	2.0	4	0
C. Dahl	1	38	38.0	38	0
McIntosh	1	34	34.0	34	0
Sims	1	5	5.0	5	0
Fletcher	1	2	2.0	2	0
Rams	17	382	22.5	42	4
Opponents	14	182	13.0	45t	2

PUNTING

	No.	Yds.	Avg.	In 20	LG
Hekker	82	3756	45.8	22	68
Rams	82	3756	45.8	22	68
Opponents	73	3231	44.3	32	63

PUNT RETURNS

	Ret	FC	Yds	Avg	LG	TD
Amendola	17	10	122	7.2	22	0
Pettis	11	9	77	7.0	23	0
Jenkins	9	1	46	5.1	14	0
Rams	37	20	245	6.6	23	0
Opponents	41	12	402	9.8	26	0

KICKOFF RETURNS

	No.	Yds	Avg	LG	TD
Givens	23	539	23.4	48	0
Pead	10	212	21.2	32	0
Amendola	2	16	8.0	12	0
Miller	1	13	13.0	13	0
Pettis	1	13	13.0	13	0
C. Dahl	1	6	6.0	6	0
Rams	38	799	21.0	48	0
Opponents	30	730	24.3	69	0

FIELD GOALS

	1-19	20-29	30-39	40-49	50+
Zuerlein	1/1	4/4	4/6	7/7	7/3
Rams	1/1	4/4	4/6	7/7	7/3
Opponents	0/0	5/6	9/9	10/13	6/9

SACKS

	No.
Long	11.5
Quinn	10.5
Hayes	7.0
Dunbar	4.5
Brockers	4.0
Mikell	3.0
Sims	3.0
Langford	2.0
Cudjo	1.0
Finnegan	1.0
Fletcher	1.0
Haggan	1.0
McIntosh	1.0
(group)	1.0
Laurinaitis	0.5
Rams	52.0
Opponents	35.0

RECORD HOLDERS
INDIVIDUAL RECORDS—CAREER

Category	Name	Performance
Rushing (Yds.)	Steven Jackson, 2004-2012	10,135
Passing (Yds.)	Jim Everett, 1986-1993	23,758
Passing (TDs)	Roman Gabriel, 1962-1972	154
Receiving (No.)	Isaac Bruce, 1994-2007	942
Receiving (Yds.)	Isaac Bruce, 1994-2007	14,109
Interceptions	Ed Meador, 1959-1970	46
Punting (Avg.)	Danny Villanueva, 1960-64	44.3
Punt Return (Avg.)	Az-Zahir Hakim, 1998-2001	11.4
Kickoff Return (Avg.)	Ron Brown, 1984-89, 1991	26.3
Field Goals	Jeff Wilkins, 1997-2007	265
Touchdowns (Tot.)	Marshall Faulk, 1999-2005	85
Points	Jeff Wilkins, 1997-2007	1,223
*Sacks	Leonard Little, 1998-2008	81.0

INDIVIDUAL RECORDS—SINGLE SEASON

Category	Name	Performance
Rushing (Yds.)	Eric Dickerson, 1984	**2,105
Passing (Yds.)	Kurt Warner, 2001	4,830
Passing (TDs)	Kurt Warner, 1999	41
Receiving (No.)	Isaac Bruce, 1995	119
Receiving (Yds.)	Isaac Bruce, 1995	1,781
Interceptions	Dick (Night Train) Lane, 1952	**14
Punting (Avg.)	Donnie Jones, 2008	50.0
Punt Return (Avg.)	Woodley Lewis, 1952	18.5
Kickoff Return (Avg.)	Verda (Vitamin T) Smith, 1950	33.7
Field Goals	Jeff Wilkins, 2003	39
Touchdowns (Tot.)	Marshall Faulk, 2000	26
Points	Jeff Wilkins, 2003	163
*Sacks	Kevin Carter, 1999	17.0

INDIVIDUAL RECORDS—SINGLE GAME

Category	Name	Performance
Rushing (Yds.)	Willie Ellison, 12-5-71	247
Passing (Yds.)	Norm Van Brocklin, 9-28-51	**554
Passing (TDs)	Many times	5
	Last time by Kurt Warner, 10-10-99	
Receiving (No.)	Tom Fears, 12-3-50	18
Receiving (Yds.)	Willie Anderson, 11-26-89	**336
Interceptions	Many times	3
	Last time by Keith Lyle, 12-15-96	
Field Goals	Bob Waterfield, 12-9-51	5
	Jeff Wilkins, 10-1-00	5
Touchdowns (Tot.)	Many times	4
	Last time by Marshall Faulk, 10-20-02	
Points	Many times	24
	Last time by Marshall Faulk, 10-20-02	
*Sacks	Gary Jeter, 9-18-88	5.0

*Sacks became an official statistic in 1982.
**NFL Record

2013 VETERAN ROSTER

No.	Name	Pos.	Ht.	Wt.	Birthdate	NFL Exp.	College	Hometown	How Acq.	'12 Games/ Starts
68	Barksdale, Joe	T	6-5	329	1/1/88	3	Louisiana State	Detroit, Mich.	W(Oak)-'12	6/2
61	Barnes, Tim	C	6-4	300	5/14/88	2	Missouri	Longwood, Mo.	FA-'11	15/0
8	Bradford, Sam	QB	6-4	224	11/8/87	4	Oklahoma	Oklahoma City, Okla.	D1-'10	16/16
90	Brockers, Michael	DT	6-5	322	12/21/90	2	Louisiana State	Houston, Texas	D1-'12	13/12
57	Brown, Sammy	LB	6-2	242	4/17/90	2	Houston	Wiggins, Miss.	FA-'12	1/0
10	Clemens, Kellen	QB	6-2	200	6/7/83	8	Oregon	Burns, Ore.	W(Hou)-'11	2/0
52	+Cole, Justin	LB	6-3	242	11/22/87	3	San Jose State	Chino Hills, Calif.	FA-'11	16/0
71	Conrath, Matt	DT	6-7	290	8/11/89	2	Virginia	Oak Lawn, Ill.	FA-'12	1/0
89	Cook, Jared	TE	6-5	248	4/7/87	5	South Carolina	Suwanee, Ga.	UFA(Tenn)-'13	13/5*
93	Cudjo, Jermelle	DT	6-2	311	9/28/86	4	Central Oklahoma	Lawton, Okla.	FA-'09	15/4
62	Dahl, Harvey	G	6-5	308	6/24/81	7	Nevada-Reno	Fallon, Nev.	UFA(Atl)-'11	14/14
37	Daniels, Matt	S	6-0	211	9/27/89	2	Duke	Fayetteville, Ga.	FA-'12	4/0
9	Davis, Austin	QB	6-2	221	6/2/89	2	Southern Mississippi	Meridian, Miss.	FA-'12	0*
58	Dunbar, Jo-Lonn	LB	6-0	226	3/13/85	6	Boston College	Syracuse, N.Y.	UFA(NO)-'12	16/16
31	Finnegan, Cortland	CB	5-10	188	2/2/84	8	Samford	Milton, Fla.	UFA(Tenn)-'12	16/15
42	Ganaway, Terrance	RB	6-1	240	10/7/88	2	Baylor	DeKalb, Texas	W(NYJ)-'12	3/0
13	Givens, Chris	WR	6-0	198	12/6/89	2	Wake Forest	Wylie, Texas	D4-'12	15/12
51	#Haggan, Mario	LB	6-3	274	3/30/80	10	Mississippi State	Clarksdale, Miss.	UFA(Den)-'12	11/2
46	Harkey, Cory	TE	6-4	260	6/17/90	2	UCLA	Chino Hills, Calif.	FA-'12	5/0
95	Hayes, William	DE	6-3	272	5/2/85	6	Winston-Salem State	High Point, N.C.	UFA(Tenn)-'12	16/0
6	Hekker, Johnny	P	6-5	227	2/8/90	2	Oregon State	Bothell, Wash.	FA-'12	16/0
56	Hull, Josh	LB	6-3	245	5/21/87	4	Penn State	Millheim, Pa.	D7c-'10	16/1
21	Jenkins, Janoris	CB	5-10	193	10/29/88	2	North Alabama	Pahokee, Fla.	D2b-'12	15/14
22	Johnson, Trumaine	CB	6-2	204	1/1/90	2	Montana	Stockton, Calif.	D3-'12	16/3
88	Kendricks, Lance	TE	6-3	247	1/30/88	3	Wisconsin	Milwaukee, Wisc.	D2-'11	16/14
98	Langford, Kendall	DT	6-6	295	1/27/86	6	Hampton	Petersburg, Va.	UFA(Mia)-'12	16/16
55	Laurinaitis, James	LB	6-2	250	12/3/86	5	Ohio State	Plymouth, Minn.	D2-'09	16/16
91	Long, Chris	DE	6-3	270	3/28/85	6	Virginia	Charlottesville, Va.	D1-'08	16/16
77	Long, Jake	T	6-7	319	5/9/85	6	Michigan	Lapeer, Mich.	UFA(Mia)-'13	12/12*
50	#McIntosh, Rocky	LB	6-2	242	11/15/82	7	Miami	Gaffney, S.C.	UFA(Wash)-'12	16/9
23	McLeod, Rodney	S	5-10	183	6/23/90	2	Virginia	Oxon Hill, Md.	FA-'12	16/0
84	McNeill, Mike	TE	6-4	235	3/7/88	3	Nebraska	St. Louis, Mo.	FA-'11	14/1
44	McQuaide, Jake	LS	6-2	247	12/7/87	3	Ohio State	Cincinnati, Ohio	FA-'11	16/0
24	Pead, Isaiah	RB	5-10	197	12/14/89	2	Cincinnati	Columbus, Ohio	D2c-'12	15/1
18	Pettis, Austin	WR	6-3	207	5/6/88	3	Boise State	Orange, Calif.	D3-'11	14/2
33	Pointer, Quinton	S	5-9	186	4/16/88	2	Nevada-Las Vegas	Ft. Myers, Fla.	FA-'12	6/0
83	Quick, Brian	WR	6-3	220	6/5/89	2	Appalachian State	Columbia, S.C.	D2a-'12	15/1
94	Quinn, Robert	DE	6-4	264	5/18/90	3	North Carolina	Ladson, S.C.	D1-'11	16/14
84	Radway, Raymond	WR	6-3	204	7/5/87	2	Abilene Christian	McKinney, Texas	FA-'12	0*
79	#Richardson, Barry	T	6-6	319	5/15/86	5	Clemson	Mt. Pleasant, S.C.	UFA(KC)-'12	16/16
26	Richardson, Daryl	RB	5-10	196	4/12/90	2	Abilene Christian	Jacksonville, Fla.	D7b-'12	16/0
76	Saffold, Rodger	T	6-5	314	6/6/88	4	Indiana	Bedford, Ohio	D2-'10	10/10
92	Sims, Eugene	DE	6-6	265	3/18/86	4	West Texas A&M	Mt. Olive, Miss.	D6b-'10	13/2
66	Smith, Shelley	G	6-4	297	5/21/87	4	Colorado State	Avondale, Ari.	W(Hou)-'12	11/6
20	Stewart, Darian	S	5-11	214	8/4/88	4	South Carolina	Huntsville, Ala.	FA-'10	12/0
73	Watkins, Rokevious	G	6-3	338	2/24/89	2	South Carolina	Fairburn, Ga.	D5-'12	1/0
63	Wells, Scott	C	6-2	300	1/7/81	10	Tennessee	Brentwood, Tenn.	UFA(GB)-'12	7/7
65	Williams, Chris	G/T	6-6	320	8/26/85	4	Vanderbilt	Baton Rouge, La.	FA-'12	3/0
54	Williams, Jabara	LB	6-2	238	7/6/89	2	Stephen F. Austin	Nacogdoches, Texas	FA-'12	0*
4	Zuerlein, Greg	K	6-0	187	12/27/87	2	Missouri Western	Lincoln, Nebr.	D6-'12	16/0

* Cook played 13 games with Tennessee in '12; Davis did not play in one game, inactive for 15 games; J. Long played 12 games with Miami; Radway missed '11 season with Dallas because of injury; J. Williams last active with Chicago in '11.

\# Unrestricted Free Agent; subject to developments.

Players lost through free agency (7): WR Danny Amendola (NE; 11 games in '12), S Craig Dahl (SF; 16), CB Bradley Fletcher (Phil; 16), WR Brandon Gibson (Mia; 16), RB Steven Jackson (Atl; 16), WR Steve Smith (TB; 9), C/G Robert Turner (Tenn; 16).

Also played with Rams in '12—DT Kellen Heard (8 games), T Wayne Hunter (14), TE Matthew Mulligan (16), S Quintin Mikell (16), FB Brit Miller (9), G Quinn Ojinnaka (6).

FIRST-YEAR ROSTER

Name	Pos.	Ht.	Wt.	Birthdate	College	Hometown	How Acq.
Akins, C.J.	WR	6-1	192	5/10/91	Angelo State	Harker Heights, Texas	FA
Austin, Tavon	WR	5-8	174	3/15/91	West Virginia	Baltimore, Md.	D1a
Baer, Brett	K/P	5-10	194	1/30/90	Louisiana-Lafayette	Brandon, Miss.	FA
Bailey, Steadman	WR	5-10	193	11/11/90	West Virginia	Miami, Fla.	D3b
Bates, Daren	LB	5-11	212	11/27/90	Auburn	Olive Branch, Miss.	FA
Blake, Emory	WR	6-0	196	7/18/91	Auburn	Austin, Tex.	FA
Brodine, Mason (1)	DE	6-7	270	2/18/88	Nebraska-Kearney	Elm Creek, Neb.	FA-'12
Cunningham, Benjamin	RB	5-10	209	7/7/90	Middle Tennessee	Nashville, Tenn.	FA
Davis, Cody	S	6-1	204	6/6/89	Texas Tech	Stephenville, Texas	FA
Goebel, Garrett	DT	6-4	292	3/11/89	Ohio State	Villa Park, Ill.	FA
Graham, Cameron (1)	TE	6-3	244	2/6/89	Louisville	Inglewood, Calif.	FA-'12
Hus, Jorgen	LS	6-1	232	9/12/89	Regina	Saskatoon, Sask.	FA
Johnson, Nick (1)	WR	5-11	187	8/16/89	Henderson State	Santa Cruz, Calif.	FA-'12
Jones, Barrett	C/G	6-4	306	5/25/90	Alabama	Germantown, Tenn.	D4
Lapuaho, Al	DT	6-2	301	8/4/91	Utah State	West Valley City, Utah	FA
Lutzenkirchen, Philip	TE	6-3	258	6/1/91	Auburn	Marietta, Ga.	FA
McDonald, T.J.	S	6-2	219	1/26/91	Southern California	Fresno, Calif.	D3a
McGee, Brandon	CB	5-11	193	12/11/89	Miami	Plantation, Fla.	D5a
Nsekhe, Ty (1)	T	6-8	325	10/27/85	Texas State	Arlington, Texas	W(Ind)-'12
Ogletree, Alec	LB	6-2	242	9/25/91	Georgia	Newnan, Ga.	D1b
Reynolds, Chase (1)	RB	6-0	200	10/22/87	Montana	Drummond, Mont.	FA-'11
Smith, Cannon	S	6-0	205	10/21/90	Memphis	Memphis, Tenn.	FA
Stacy, Zac	RB	5-8	216	4/9/91	Vanderbilt	Centreville, Ga.	D5b
Steeples, Robert	CB	6-1	194	11/27/89	Memphis	St. Louis, Mo.	FA
Stevens, Eric	FB	5-11	240	10/1/89	California	San Pedro, Calif.	FA
Stewart, Jonathan	LB	6-3	242	11/23/90	Texas A&M	Shreveport, La.	FA
Washington, Brandon (1)	G	6-2	320	8/13/88	Miami	Miami, Fla.	FA-'12

The term NFL Rookie is defined as a player who is in his first season of professional football and has not been on the roster of another professional football team for any regular-season or postseason games. A Rookie is designated by an "R" on NFL rosters. Players who have been active in another professional football league or players who have NFL experience, including either preseason training camp or being on an Active List or Inactive List, or on Reserve/Injured or Reserve/Physically Unable to Perform for fewer than six regular-season games, are termed NFL First-Year Players. An NFL First-Year Player is designated by a "1" on NFL rosters. Thereafter, a player is credited with an additional year of experience for each season in which he accumulates six games on the Active List or Inactive List, or on Reserve/Injured or Reserve/Physically Unable to Perform.

Log on to www.stlouisrams.com for an up-to-date roster.

COACHING STAFF
Head Coach,
Jeff Fisher
Pro Career: Named the twenty-sixth head coach in franchise history on January 17, 2012. Fisher ranks tied for 18th on the NFL's career wins list (154, including postseason), and fourth among active coaches. Spent 16 full seasons as head coach of the Tennessee Titans, 11 as executive vice president. Guided the Titans to six playoff appearances, three division titles, two AFC Championship games (1999, 2002) and one Super Bowl appearance (XXXIV). Joined the Oilers'/Titans' coaching staff in 1994. He was elevated to head coach in November 1994, replacing Jack Pardee, for the season's final six games. Previously coached with Philadelphia Eagles (defensive backs, 1986-88), Los Angeles Rams (youngest defensive coordinator in NFL, 1989-1991), and San Francisco 49ers (defensive backs, 1992-93). Played with Chicago Bears (1981-85) as a defensive back and return specialist. Earned a Super Bowl ring following Chicago's Super Bowl XX victory (1985), despite spending the year on injured reserve with an ankle injury that prematurely ended his playing career. Fisher began his post-playing career that season by assisting Buddy Ryan as the Bears' "unofficial" coach. Career record: 154-134-1.
Background: Played defensive back at Southern California.
Personal: Born February 25, 1958 in Woodland Hills, California. Has three children: sons Brandon (age 25) and Trent (age 20), and daughter Tara (age 23).

ASSISTANT COACHES
Adam Bailey, asst. strength coach; born March 30, 1976, Lindale, Texas. No college or pro playing experience. College coach: Texas 1996-97, Louisville 1998-99, Auburn 2000-01, Missouri 2002-03. Pro coach: New Orleans Saints 2004-09, joined Rams in 2010.
Rob Boras, tight ends; born Sept. 30, 1970, Glen Ellyn, Ill. Center De Pauw 1988-1991. No pro playing experience. College coach: DePauw 1992-93, Texas 1994-97, Benedictine 1998 (head coach), Nevada-Las Vegas 1999-2003. Pro coach: Chicago Bears 2004-09, Jacksonville Jaguars 2010-11, joined Rams in 2012.
Paul Boudreau, offensive line; born Dec. 30, 1949, Arlington, Mass. Guard Boston College 1970-73. No pro playing experience. Pro coach: New Orleans Saints 1987-1993, Detroit Lions 1994-96, New England Patriots 1997-98, Miami Dolphins 1999-2000, Carolina Panthers 2001-02, Jacksonville Jaguars 2003-05, St. Louis Rams 2006-07, Atlanta Falcons 2008-2011, re-joined Rams in 2012.
Paul F. Boudreau, asst. special teams; born June 2, 1975, Boston, Mass. No college or pro playing experience. College coach: Northeastern 1997-98, Cincinnati 1998-99, Brown 2000-06, Central Connecticut State 2007-08, Massachusetts Maritime 2010, Widener 2011. Pro coach: Joined Rams in 2012.

Joe Bowden, asst. linebackers; born February 25, 1970, Dallas, Texas. Linebacker Oklahoma 1988-1991. Pro linebacker Houston Oilers/Tennessee Titans 1992-99, Dallas Cowboys 2000. College coach: Central Oklahoma 2006-08. Pro coach: Joined Rams in 2012.
Frank Bush, linebackers; born January 10, 1963, Athens, Ga. Linebacker North Carolina State 1981-1984. Pro linebacker Houston Oilers 1985-86. Pro coach: Houston Oilers 1987-1991 (scout), 1992-94, Denver Broncos 1995-2003, Arizona Cardinals 2004-06, Houston Texans 2007-2010, Tennessee Titans 2011-12, joined Rams in 2013.
Chuck Cecil, secondary; born Nov. 8, 1964, Red Bluff, Calif. Defensive back Arizona 1983-87. Pro safety Green Bay Packers 1988-1992, Phoenix Cardinals 1993, Houston Oilers 1995. Pro coach: Tennessee Titans 2001-2010, joined Rams in 2012.
Frank Cignetti, quarterbacks; born October 4, 1965, Pittsburgh, Pa. Safety Indiana Univ. (Pa.) 1985-88. No pro playing experience. College coach: Pittsburgh 1989, Indiana Univ. (Pa.) 1990-98, Fresno State 2002-05, North Carolina 2006, California 2008, Pittsburgh 2009-2010, Rutgers 2011. Pro coach: Kansas City Chiefs 1999, New Orleans Saints 2000-01, San Francisco 49ers 2007, joined Rams in 2012.
Andy Dickerson, asst. offensive line; born January 29, 1982, Wilmington, Del. Offensive lineman Tufts 1999-2002. No pro playing experience. College coach: Tufts 2003. Pro coach: New York Jets 2006-08, 2011, Cleveland Browns 2009-2010, joined Rams in 2012.
John Fassel, special teams coordinator; born January 10, 1974, Anaheim, Calif. Wide receiver/quarterback Pacific 1994-95, Weber State 1996-98. No pro playing experience. College coach: Bucknell 1999, 2001, Idaho State 2000, New Mexico Highlands 2002-03. Pro coach: Amsterdam Admirals (NFLE) 2000, Baltimore Ravens 2005-07, Oakland Raiders 2008-2011, joined Rams in 2012.
Brandon Fisher, asst. secondary, born June 16, 1987, Franklin, Tenn. Safety/linebacker Montana 2007-09. No pro playing experience. Pro coach: Detroit Lions 2011, joined Rams in 2012.
Rock Gullickson, strength; born April 11, 1955, Moorhead, Minn. Guard Moorhead State 1973-76. No pro playing experience. College coach: Moorhead State 1978, Maryville State (N.D.) 1979-1980, South Dakota State 1981, Montana State 1982-89, Rutgers 1990-92, Texas 1993-97, Louisville 1998-99. Pro coach: New Orleans Saints 2000-05, Green Bay Packers 2006-08, joined Rams in 2009.
Dave McGinnis, asst. head coach; born August 7, 1951, Independence, Kan. Defensive back Texas Christian 1970-73. No pro playing experience. College coach: Texas Christian 1973-74, 1982, Missouri 1975-77, Indiana State 1978, 1980-81, Kansas State 1983-85. Pro coach: Chicago Bears 1986-1995, Arizona Cardinals 1996-2003 (head

coach 2000-03), Tennessee Titans 2004-2011, joined Rams in 2012.
Brian Schottenheimer, offensive coordinator; born October 16, 1973, Denver, Colo. Quarterback Kansas 1992, Florida 1993-96. No pro playing experience. College coach: Syracuse 1999, Southern California 2000. Pro coach: St. Louis Rams 1997, Kansas City Chiefs 1998, Washington Redskins 2001, San Diego Chargers 2002-05, New York Jets 2006-2011, joined Rams in 2012.
Ray Sherman, wide receivers; born Nov. 27, 1951, Berkeley, Calif. Wide receiver/defensive back Fresno State 1971-72. No pro playing experience. College coach: San Jose State 1974, California 1975, 1981, Michigan State 1976-77, Wake Forest 1978-1980, Purdue 1982-85, Georgia 1986-87. Pro coach: Houston Oilers 1988-89, Atlanta Falcons 1990, San Francisco 49ers 1991-93, New York Jets 1994, Minnesota Vikings 1995-97, 1999, Pittsburgh Steelers 1998, Green Bay Packers 2000-04, Tennessee Titans 2005-06, Dallas Cowboys 2007-2010, joined Rams in 2012.
Clyde Simmons, asst. defensive line; born August 4, 1964, Lanes, S.C. Defensive end Western Carolina 1982-85. Pro defensive end Philadelphia Eagles 1986-1993, Arizona Cardinals 1994-95, Jacksonville Jaguars 1996-97, Cincinnati Bengals 1998, Chicago Bears 1999-2000. Pro coach: New York Jets 2010, joined Rams in 2012.
Ben Sirmans, running backs; born October 17, 1970, East Orange, N.J. Running back Maine 1990-93. No pro playing experience. College coach: Maine 1996-99, Kent State 2000-04, Michigan State 2005-06, Boston College 2007-2011. Pro coach: Joined Rams in 2012.
Andy Sugarman, offensive quality control; born May 23, 1972, Lafayette, Calif. No college or pro playing experience. College coach: California 1991-97. Pro coach: San Francisco 49ers 1998-2002, Detroit Lions 2003-05, Atlanta Falcons 2007, joined Rams in 2009.
Tim Walton, defensive coordinator; born March 11, 1971. Defensive back Ohio State 1990-94. No pro playing experience. College coach: Bowling Green 1995-99, Memphis 2000-01, 2008, Syracuse 2002, Louisiana State 2003, Miami 2004-07. Pro coach: Detroit Lions 2009-2012, joined Rams in 2013.
Mike Waufle, defensive line; born June 27, 1954, Hornell, N.Y. U.S. Marines 1972-75. Defensive lineman Bakersfield (Calif.) J.C. 1975-76, Utah State 1977-78. No pro playing experience. College coach: Alfred 1979, Utah State 1980-84, Fresno State 1985-88, UCLA 1989, Oregon State 1990-91, California 1992-97. Pro coach: Oakland Raiders 1998-2003, 2010-11, New York Giants 2004-09, joined Rams in 2012.
Dennard Wilson, defensive quality control; born March 31, 1982, Upper Marlboro, Md. Safety Maryland 2000-03. Pro safety Washington Redskins 2004. College coach: Maryland 2007-08. Pro coach: Joined Rams in 2012.

**National Football Conference
West Division**
Team Colors: 49ers Gold and 49ers Red
4949 Marie P. DeBartolo Way
Santa Clara, California 95054
Telephone: (408) 562-4949

2013 SCHEDULE
PRESEASON
Aug. 8	**Denver**	6:00
Aug. 16	at Kansas City	5:00
Aug. 25	**Minnesota**	5:00
Aug. 29	at San Diego	7:00

REGULAR SEASON
Sep. 8	**Green Bay**	1:25
Sep. 15	at Seattle	5:30
Sep. 22	**Indianapolis**	1:25
Sep. 26	at St. Louis (Thurs)	5:25
Oct. 6	**Houston**	5:30
Oct. 13	**Arizona**	1:25
Oct. 20	at Tennessee	1:05
Oct. 27	at Jacksonville (London)	10:00a
Nov. 3	BYE	
Nov. 10	**Carolina**	1:05
Nov. 17	at New Orleans	1:25
Nov. 25	at Washington (Mon)	5:40
Dec. 1	**St. Louis**	1:05
Dec. 8	**Seattle**	1:25
Dec. 15	at Tampa Bay	10:00a
Dec. 23	**Atlanta** (Mon)	5:40
Dec. 29	at Arizona	1:25

All times PT

Stadium: Candlestick Park
  (opened in 1960)
  •**Capacity:** 69,732
  San Francisco, California 94124
Playing Surface: Natural Grass
Training Camp: SAP Training Center
                4949 Marie P. DeBartolo Way
                Santa Clara, CA 95054

CANDLESTICK PARK

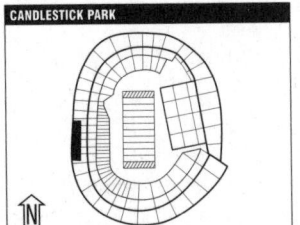

CLUB OFFICIALS
OWNERSHIP
Co-Chairman: Denise DeBartolo York
Co-Chairman: John York
Chief Executive Officer: Jed York
President: Gideon Yu
Ownership: Mark Wan
Ownership: John M. Sobrato
MANAGEMENT
General Manager: Trent Baalke
Chief Operating Officer: Paraag Marathe
Chief Financial Officer: Cipora Herman
Chief Sales Officer: John Vidalin
Chief Technology Officer: Kunal Malik
Executive Vice President: Patty Inglis
Executive Vice President of Development:
  Larry MacNeil
Vice President of Ticketing & Suites:
  Jamie Brandt
Vice President of Corporate Sales:
  Ethan Casson
Vice President of Stadium Operations &
Security: Jim Mercurio
Vice President of Football Affairs:
  Keena Turner
Vice President of Football Operations:
  Jeff Ferguson
Director of Legal Affairs: Hannah Gordon
Director of College Scouting: Joel Patten
Director of Public Relations: Bob Lange
New Stadium Project Executive: Jack Hill
Equipment Manager: Steve Urbaniak
Video Operations Manager: Mike Bracken
Director of Football Administration:
  Brian Hampton
Director of Broadcasting & Corporate
  Sales: Bob Sargent
Director of Marketing: Ali Towle
Director of Stadium Operations:
  Larry Minasian
Director of Engineering Operations:
  Pat Rogan
Director of Finance: Scott Sabatino
Director of Security: Dan Cory
Senior Director, Technology:
  Dan Williams
Director of Technology: Joe Trdinich
Director of Alumni Relations:
  Guy McIntrye
Director of Community Relations/49ers
Foundation: Joanne Pasternack
Director of Facilities: Bill Howell
Head Groundskeeper: Matthew Greiner
Director of Business: Morrie Eisenberg

COACHING HISTORY
(516-423-14)
Records include postseason games
1950-54	Lawrence (Buck) Shaw	33-25-2
1955	Norman (Red) Strader	4-8-0
1956-58	Frankie Albert	19-17-1
1959-1963	Howard (Red) Hickey*	27-27-1
1963-67	Jack Christiansen	26-38-3
1968-1975	Dick Nolan	56-56-5
1976	Monte Clark	8-6-0
1977	Ken Meyer	5-9-0
1978	Pete McCulley**	1-8-0
1978	Fred O'Connor	1-6-0
1979-1988	Bill Walsh	102-63-1
1989-1996	George Seifert	108-35-0
1997-2002	Steve Mariucci	60-43-0
2003-04	Dennis Erickson	9-23-0
2005-08	Mike Nolan***	18-37-0
2008-2010	Mike Singletary****	19-22-0
2010	Jim Tomsula	1-0-0
2011-12	Jim Harbaugh	27-9-1

      * Resigned after three games in 1963
    ** Released after nine games in 1978
  *** Released after seven games in 2008
**** Released after 15 games in 2010

PAID ATTENDANCE
Home 536,047   Away 525,700
Total 1,061,747
Single-game home record,
  69,732 (1/12/13)
Single-season home record,
  544,228 (1999)

2013 DRAFT CHOICES
Round	Name	Pos.	College
1	Eric Reid	DB	Louisiana St.
2	Cornellius Carradine	DE	Florida St.
	Vance McDonald	TE	Rice
3	Corey Lemonier	LB	Auburn
4	Quinton Patton	WR	Louisiana Tech
	Marcus Lattimore	RB	South Carolina
5	Quinton Dial	DT	Alabama
6	Nick Moody	LB	Florida St.
7	B.J. Daniels	QB	South Florida
	Carter Bykowski	T	Iowa St.
	Marcus Cooper	DB	Rutgers

SAN FRANCISCO 49ERS

2012 TEAM RECORD

PRESEASON (3-1)

Date	Result		Opponent
08/10	W	17-6	Minnesota
08/18	L	9-20	at Houston
08/26	W	29-24	at Denver
08/30	W	35-3	San Diego

REGULAR SEASON (11-4-1)

Date	Result		Opponent
09/09	W	30-22	at Green Bay
09/16	W	27-19	Detroit
09/23	L	13-24	at Minnesota
09/30	W	34-0	at New York Jets
10/07	W	45-3	Buffalo
10/14	L	3-26	New York Giants
10/18	W	13-6	Seattle
10/29	W	24-3	at Arizona
11/11	T	24-24	St. Louis (OT)
11/19	W	32-7	Chicago
11/25	W	31-21	at New Orleans
12/02	L	13-16	at St. Louis (OT)
12/09	W	27-13	Miami
12/16	W	41-34	at New England
12/23	L	13-42	at Seattle
12/30	W	27-13	Arizona

POSTSEASON (2-1)

Date	Result		Opponent
01/12	W	45-31	Green Bay
01/20	W	28-24	at Atlanta
02/03	L	31-34	vs Baltimore
			at New Orleans

(OT) Overtime

SCORE BY PERIODS

49ers	57	110	100	130	0	—	397
Opponents	54	63	55	98	3	—	273

2012 TEAM STATISTICS

	49ers	Opp.
Total First Downs	322	284
Rushing	128	72
Passing	172	178
Penalty	22	34
3rd Down: Made/Att	68/194	71/215
3rd Down Pct.	35.1	33.0
4th Down: Made/Att	8/12	14/25
4th Down Pct.	66.7	56.0
Possession Avg.	30:49	29:11
Total Net Yards	5789	4710
Avg. Per Game	361.8	294.4
Total Plays	969	1012
Avg. Per Play	6.0	4.7
Net Yards Rushing	2491	1507
Avg. Per Game	155.7	94.2
Total Rushes	492	407
Net Yards Passing	3298	3203
Avg. Per Game	206.1	200.2
Sacked/Yards Lost	41/253	38/270
Gross Yards	3551	3473
Att./Completions	436/289	567/337
Completion Pct.	66.3	59.4
Had Intercepted	8	14
Punts/Average	67/48.1	79/45.7
Net Punting Avg.	67/43.2	79/39.1
Penalties/Yards	109/960	93/758
Fumbles/Ball Lost	26/8	21/11
Touchdowns	44	29
Rushing	17	7
Passing	23	19
Returns	4	3

2012 INDIVIDUAL STATISTICS

PASSING

	Att.	Comp.	Yds.	Pct.	TD	Int.	Tkld.	Rate
Kaepernick	218	136	1814	62.4	10	3	16/112	98.3
Ale. Smith	218	153	1737	70.2	13	5	24/137	104.1
Hunter	0	0	0	—	0	0	1/4	
49ers	436	289	3551	66.3	23	8	41/253	101.2
Opponents	567	337	3473	59.4	19	14	38/270	78.0

SCORING

	TD R	TD P	TD Rt	PAT	FG	Saf	PTS
Akers	0	0	0	44/44	29/42	0	131
Gore	8	1	1	0/0	0/0	0	60
Crabtree	0	9	0	0/0	0/0	0	54
V. Davis	0	5	0	0/0	0/0	0	30
Kaepernick	5	0	0	0/0	0/0	0	30
Moss	0	3	0	0/0	0/0	0	18
Walker	0	3	0	0/0	0/0	0	18
Dixon	2	0	0	0/0	0/0	0	12
Hunter	2	0	0	0/0	0/0	0	12
Brooks	0	0	1	0/0	0/0	0	6
Manningham	0	1	0	0/0	0/0	0	6
Rogers	0	0	1	0/0	0/0	0	6
Whitner	0	0	1	0/0	0/0	0	6
K. Williams	0	1	0	0/0	0/0	0	6
McDonald	0	0	0	0/0	0/0	1	2
49ers	17	23	4	44/44	29/42	1	397
Opponents	7	19	3	27/27	22/27	1	273

2-Pt Conversions: 49ers 0-0, Opponents 2-2

RUSHING

	No.	Yds	Avg	LG	TD
Gore	258	1214	4.7	37	8
Kaepernick	63	415	6.6	50t	5
Hunter	72	371	5.2	26	2
Ale. Smith	31	132	4.3	24	0
James	27	125	4.6	26	0
Dixon	21	78	3.7	9	2
Manningham	3	64	21.3	29	0
Goldson	1	31	31.0	31	0
K. Williams	4	21	5.3	9	0
Miller	5	18	3.6	9	0
Crabtree	1	8	8.0	8	0
Ginn	1	7	7.0	7	0
Jacobs	5	7	1.4	3	0
49ers	492	2491	5.1	50t	17
Opponents	407	1507	3.7	35	7

RECEIVING

	No.	Yds	Avg	LG	TD
Crabtree	85	1105	13.0	49t	9
Manningham	42	449	10.7	40	1
V. Davis	41	548	13.4	53	5
Moss	28	434	15.5	55	3
Gore	28	234	8.4	26	1
Walker	21	344	16.4	45	3
K. Williams	14	212	15.1	57	1
Miller	12	84	7.0	26	0
Hunter	9	60	6.7	12	0
Celek	4	51	12.8	35	0
James	3	29	9.7	15	0
Ginn	2	1	0.5	1	0
49ers	289	3551	12.3	57	23
Opponents	337	3473	10.3	53	19

INTERCEPTIONS

	No.	Yds	Avg	LG	TD
Goldson	3	21	7.0	20	0
Brown	2	17	8.5	12	0
Culliver	2	4	2.0	4	0
Willis	2	2	1.0	2	0
Rogers	1	63	63.0	63	0
Brooks	1	50	50.0	50t	1
Whitner	1	42	42.0	42t	1
Bowman	1	11	11.0	11	0
Ald. Smith	1	6	6.0	6	0
49ers	14	216	15.4	63	2
Opponents	8	70	8.8	24	0

PUNTING

	No.	Yds.	Avg.	In 20	LG
Lee	67	3226	48.1	36	66
49ers	67	3226	48.1	36	66
Opponents	79	3609	45.7	24	70

PUNT RETURNS

	Ret	FC	Yds	Avg	LG	TD
Ginn	32	12	326	10.2	38	0
K. Williams	4	6	52	13.0	20	0
49ers	36	18	378	10.5	38	0
Opponents	36	18	249	6.9	75t	1

KICKOFF RETURNS

	No.	Yds	Avg	LG	TD
James	14	417	29.8	62	0
K. Williams	13	353	27.2	94	0
Ginn	11	253	23.0	31	0
Hunter	7	165	23.6	31	0
Walker	4	28	7.0	18	0
49ers	49	1216	24.8	94	0
Opponents	48	1289	26.9	66	0

FIELD GOALS

	1-19	20-29	30-39	40-49	50+
Akers	1/1	8/9	11/13	7/13	2/6
49ers	1/1	8/9	11/13	7/13	2/6
Opponents	0/0	4/4	9/9	4/6	5/8

SACKS

	No.
Ald. Smith	19.5
Brooks	6.5
J. Smith	3.0
McDonald	2.5
Bowman	2.0
Jean Francois	2.0
Rogers	1.0
Sopoaga	1.0
Willis	0.5
49ers	38.0
Opponents	41.0

RECORD HOLDERS
INDIVIDUAL RECORDS—CAREER

Category	Name	Performance
Rushing (Yds.)	Frank Gore, 2005-2012	8,839
Passing (Yds.)	Joe Montana, 1979-1992	35,124
Passing (TDs)	Joe Montana, 1979-1992	244
Receiving (No.)	Jerry Rice, 1985-2000	1,281
Receiving (Yds.)	Jerry Rice, 1985-2000	19,247
Interceptions	Ronnie Lott, 1981-1990	51
Punting (Avg.)	Andy Lee, 2004-2012	45.9
Punt Return (Avg.)	Ted Ginn Jr., 2010-12	11.8
Kickoff Return (Avg.)	Abe Woodson, 1958-1964	29.4
Field Goals	Ray Wersching, 1977-1987	190
Touchdowns (Tot.)	Jerry Rice, 1985-2000	187
Points	Jerry Rice, 1985-2000	1,130
*Sacks	Bryant Young, 1994-2007	89.5

INDIVIDUAL RECORDS—SINGLE SEASON

Category	Name	Performance
Rushing (Yds.)	Frank Gore, 2006	1,695
Passing (Yds.)	Jeff Garcia, 2000	4,278
Passing (TDs)	Steve Young, 1998	36
Receiving (No.)	Jerry Rice, 1995	122
Receiving (Yds.)	Jerry Rice, 1995	1,848
Interceptions	Dave Baker, 1960	10
	Ronnie Lott, 1986	10
Punting (Avg.)	Andy Lee, 2011	50.9
Punt Return (Avg.)	Jimmy Williams, 2002	16.8
Kickoff Return (Avg.)	Joe Arenas, 1953	34.4
Field Goals	David Akers, 2011	**44
Touchdowns (Tot.)	Jerry Rice, 1987	23
Points	David Akers, 2011	166
*Sacks	Aldon Smith, 2012	19.5

INDIVIDUAL RECORDS—SINGLE GAME

Category	Name	Performance
Rushing (Yds.)	Frank Gore, 11-19-06	212
Passing (Yds.)	Joe Montana, 10-14-90	476
Passing (TDs)	Joe Montana, 10-14-90	6
Receiving (No.)	Terrell Owens, 12-17-00	20
Receiving (Yds.)	Jerry Rice, 12-18-95	289
Interceptions	Dave Baker, 12-4-60	**4
Field Goals	Ray Wersching, 10-16-83	6
	Jeff Wilkins, 9-29-96	6
Touchdowns (Tot.)	Jerry Rice, 10-14-90	5
Points	Jerry Rice, 10-14-90	30
*Sacks	Fred Dean, 11-13-83	6.0

*Sacks became an official statistic in 1982.
**NFL Record

2013 VETERAN ROSTER

No.	Name	Pos.	Ht.	Wt.	Birthdate	NFL Exp.	College	Hometown	How Acq.	'12 Games/ Starts
24	Asomugha, Nnamdi	CB	6-2	210	7/6/81	11	California	Los Angeles, Calif.	FA-'13	16/16*
81 t-	Boldin, Anquan	WR	6-1	220	10/3/80	11	Florida State	Pahokee, Fla.	T(Balt)-'13	15/15*
75	Boone, Alex	G/T	6-8	300	5/4/87	4	Ohio State	Cleveland, Ohio	FA-'09	16/16
53	Bowman, NaVorro	LB	6-0	242	5/28/88	4	Penn State	Forestville, Md.	D3-'10	16/16
26	Brock, Tramaine	CB	5-10	197	8/20/88	4	Belhaven	Long Beach, Miss.	FA-'10	16/0
55	Brooks, Ahmad	LB	6-3	259	3/14/84	8	Virginia	Woodbridge, Va.	W(Cin)-'08	16/16
25	Brown, Tarell	CB	5-10	193	1/6/85	7	Texas	Mesquite, Texas	D5-'07	16/16
88	Celek, Garrett	TE	6-5	252	5/29/88	2	Michigan State	Cincinnati, Ohio	FA-'12	13/0
20	Cox, Perrish	CB	6-0	190	1/7/87	3	Oklahoma State	Waco, Texas	FA-'12	16/0
15	Crabtree, Michael	WR	6-1	214	9/14/87	5	Texas Tech	Dallas, Texas	D1-'09	16/16
29	Culliver, Chris	CB	6-0	199	8/17/88	3	South Carolina	Garner, N.C.	D3-'11	16/6
43	Dahl, Craig	S	6-1	212	6/17/85	6	North Dakota State	Madison Lake, Minn.	UFA(StL)-'13	16/16*
76	Davis, Anthony	T	6-5	323	10/11/89	4	Rutgers	Piscataway, N.J.	D1a-'10	16/16
85	Davis, Vernon	TE	6-3	250	1/31/84	8	Maryland	Washington, D.C.	D1a-'06	16/16
9	Dawson, Phil	K	5-11	200	1/23/75	15	Texas	Dallas, Texas	UFA(Cle)-'13	16/0*
92	Divens, Lamar	DT	6-3	340	11/12/85	4	Tennessee State	Fayetteville, Tenn.	FA-'12	0*
24	Dixon, Anthony	RB	6-1	233	9/24/87	4	Mississippi State	Terry, Miss.	D6a-'10	16/0
83	Dobbs, Demarcus	DL	6-2	282	11/30/87	3	Georgia	Savannah, Ga.	FA-'11	12/0
90	Dorsey, Glenn	DL	6-1	297	8/1/85	6	Louisiana State	Baton Rouge, La.	UFA(KC)-'13	4/4*
58	Fleming, Darius	LB	6-2	255	7/19/89	2	Notre Dame	Chicago, Ill.	D5-'12	0*
59	Goodwin, Jonathan	C	6-3	318	12/2/78	12	Michigan	Columbia, S.C.	FA-'11	16/16
21	Gore, Frank	RB	5-9	217	5/14/83	9	Miami	Coral Gables, Fla.	D3a-'05	16/16
14	Hall, Chad	WR	5-8	187	5/23/86	4	Air Force	Norcross, Ga.	FA-'12	0*
33	Hampton, Jewel	RB	5-9	210	12/23/89	2	Southern Illinois	Indianapolis, Ind.	FA-'12	0*
98	Haralson, Parys	LB	6-0	255	1/24/84	8	Tennessee	Madison, Miss.	D5-'06	0*
15	Hastings, Joe	WR	6-0	185	5/5/87	2	Washburn	Wichita, Kan.	FA-'13	0*
32	Hunter, Kendall	RB	5-7	199	9/16/88	3	Oklahoma State	Tyler, Texas	D4-'11	11/0
77	Iupati, Mike	G	6-5	331	5/12/87	4	Idaho	Anaheim, Calif.	D1b-'12	16/16
23	James, LaMichael	RB	5-9	195	10/22/89	2	Oregon	Texarkana, Texas	D2-'12	4/0
17	Jenkins, A.J.	WR	6-0	192	9/30/89	2	Illinois	Jacksonville, Fla.	D1-'12	3/0
86	Jennings, Brian	TE/LS	6-5	242	10/14/76	14	Arizona State	Mesa, Ariz.	D7b-'00	16/0
63	Jerod-Eddie, Tony	DT	6-5	301	3/29/90	2	Texas A&M	DeSoto, Texas	FA-'12	1/0
50	Johnson, Cam	LB	6-3	268	5/24/90	2	Virginia	Greenbelt, Md.	D7-'12	2/0
7	Kaepernick, Colin	QB	6-4	230	11/3/87	3	Nevada	Turlock, Calif.	D2-'11	13/7
67	Kilgore, Daniel	G	6-3	308	12/18/87	3	Appalachian State	Kingsport, Tenn.	D5-'11	16/0
4	Lee, Andy	P	6-2	180	8/11/82	10	Pittsburgh	Westminster, S.C.	D6a-'04	16/0
78	Looney, Joe	G	6-3	309	8/31/90	2	Wake Forest	Lake Worth, Fla.	D4-'12	0*
82	Manningham, Mario	WR	6-0	185	5/25/86	6	Michigan	Warren, Ohio	FA-'12	12/10
28	McBath, Darcel	S	6-1	198	10/28/85	5	Texas Tech	Gainesville, Texas	FA-'12	16/0
2 t-	McCoy, Colt	QB	6-1	215	9/5/86	4	Texas	Tuscola, Texas	T(Cle)-'13	3/0*
91	McDonald, Ray	DT	6-3	290	9/2/84	7	Florida	Belle Glade, Fla.	D3b-'07	16/16
49	Miller, Bruce	FB	6-2	248	8/6/87	3	Central Florida	Woodstock, Ga.	D7a-'11	16/13
19	Moore, Marlon	WR	6-0	190	9/3/87	4	Fresno State	Sacramento, Calif.	FA-'13	14/2*
89	Morrah, Cameron	TE	6-3	251	3/18/87	5	California	Claremont, Calif.	FA-'13	0*
30	Robinson, Trenton	S	5-9	193	2/16/90	2	Michigan State	Bay City, Mich.	D6a-'12	3/0
22	Rogers, Carlos	CB	6-0	192	7/2/81	9	Auburn	Augusta, Ga.	FA-'11	16/16
51	Skuta, Dan	LB	6-2	250	4/21/86	5	Grand Valley State	Burton, Mich.	UFA(Cin)-'13	16/0*
99	Smith, Aldon	LB	6-4	258	9/25/89	3	Missouri	Raytown, Mo.	D1-'11	16/16
94	Smith, Justin	DT	6-4	285	9/30/79	13	Missouri	Jefferson City, Mo.	FA-'08	14/14
	Snyder, Adam	G	6-6	325	1/30/82	8	Oregon	Fullerton, Calif.	FA-'13	14/14*
27	Spillman, C.J.	S	6-0	199	5/6/86	5	Marshall	Louisville, Ky.	W(SD)-'10	16/0
74	Staley, Joe	T	6-5	315	8/30/84	7	Central Michigan	Rockford, Mich.	D1b-'07	16/16
3	Tolzien, Scott	QB	6-3	208	9/4/87	3	Wisconsin	Rolling Meadows, Ill.	W(SD)-'11	0*
48	Tukuafu, Will	DL	6-4	293	1/3/84	3	Oregon	Salt Lake City, Utah	FA-'10	14/0
31	Whitner, Donte	S	5-10	208	7/24/85	8	Ohio State	Cleveland, Ohio	FA-'11	16/16
57	Wilhoite, Michael	LB	6-0	240	12/7/86	2	Washburn	Topeka, Kan.	FA-'11	5/0
93	Williams, Ian	NT	6-1	305	8/31/89	3	Notre Dame	Altamonte Springs, Fla.	FA-'11	3/0
10	Williams, Kyle	WR	5-10	186	7/19/88	4	Arizona State	Scottsdale, Ariz.	D6c-'10	11/3
52	Willis, Patrick	LB	6-1	240	1/25/85	7	Mississippi	Bruceton, Tenn.	D1a-'07	16/16

* Asomugha played 16 games with Philadelphia in '12; Boldin played 15 games with Baltimore; Dahl played 16 games with St. Louis; Dawson played 16 games with Cleveland; Divens last active with Baltimore in '10; Dorsey played four games with Kansas City; Fleming missed '12 season because of injury; Hall played in one postseason game; Hampton inactive for five games; Haralson missed '12 season because of injury; Hastings last active with San Francisco in '11; Looney inactive for 16 games; McCoy played three games with Cleveland; Moore played 14 games with Miami; Morrah missed '12 season because of injury; Skuta played 16 games with Cincinnati; Snyder played 14 games with Arizona; Tolzien inactive for 13 games and did not play in three games.

t- 49ers traded for Boldin (Balt) and McCoy (Cle).

Traded—QB Alex Smith (10 games in '12) to Kansas City.

Players lost through free agency (5): WR Ted Ginn Jr. (Car; 13 games), S Dashon Goldson (TB; 16), DT Ricky Jean Francois (Ind; 16), NT Isaac Sopoaga (Phil; 15), TE Delanie Walker (Tenn; 16).

Also played with 49ers in '12—K David Akers (16 games), LB Eric Bakhtiari (5), G Leonard Davis (16), LB Tavares Gooden (15), LB Larry Grant (16), LB Clark Haggans (9), RB Brandon Jacobs (2), WR Randy Moss (16).

FIRST-YEAR ROSTER

Name	Pos.	Ht.	Wt.	Birthdate	College	Hometown	How Acq.
Bykowski, Carter	T	6-7	306	7/25/90	Iowa State	Eden Prairie, Minn.	D7b
Carradine, Cornellius "Tank"	DT	6-4	273	2/18/90	Florida State	Cincinnati, Ohio	D2a
Carter, Sherman	C	6-3	304	9/13/88	Tennessee State	La Vergne, Tenn.	FA
Cooper, Marcus	CB	6-2	192	2/1/90	Rutgers	Hartford, Conn.	D7c
Daniels, B.J.	QB	5-11	217	10/24/89	South Florida	Tallahassee, Fla.	D7a
Debniak, Alex	FB	6-2	240	1/5/90	Stanford	Hudsonville, Mich.	FA
Dial, Quinton	DT	6-5	318	7/21/90	Alabama	Pinson, Ala.	D5
Gray, MarQueis	TE	6-4	250	11/7/89	Minnesota	Indianapolis, Ind.	FA
Harper, D.J.	RB	5-9	211	9/21/89	Boise State	Houston, Texas	FA
Jacobs, Chuck	WR	6-0	178	5/11/90	Utah State	Richmond, Calif.	FA
Lattimore, Marcus	RB	5-11	221	8/9/90	South Carolina	Duncan, S.C.	D4b
Lemonier, Corey	LB	6-3	255	11/19/91	Auburn	Hialeah, Fla.	D3
Lockette, Ricardo (1)	WR	6-2	211	5/21/86	Fort Valley State	Albany, Ga.	FA-'12
Marquardt, Luke	T	6-8	315	3/23/90	Azusa Pacific	Sammamish, Wash.	FA
McDermott, Kevin	LS	6-4	234	1/12/90	UCLA	Nashville, Tenn.	FA
McDonald, Vance	TE	6-4	267	6/13/90	Rice	Winnie, Texas	D2b
Moody, Nick	LB	6-1	236	1/29/90	Florida State	Philadelphia, Pa.	D6
Morris, Darryl	CB	5-10	188	9/4/90	Texas State	San Antonio, Texas	FA
Netter, Al (1)	G	6-6	310	7/21/89	Northwestern	Rohnert Park, Calif.	FA-'12
Okoye, Lawrence	DL	6-6	304	10/6/91	No College	Croydon, Great Britain	FA
Omameh, Patrick	G	6-4	305	12/29/89	Michigan	Columbus, Ohio	FA
Patton, Quinton	WR	6-0	204	10/29/91	Louisiana Tech	Nashville, Tenn.	D4a
Purcell, Mike	NT	6-3	303	4/20/91	Wyoming	Highlands Ranch, Colo.	FA
Reid, Eric	S	6-1	213	12/10/91	Louisiana State	Baton Rouge, La.	D1
Rose, Lowell	CB	6-1	192	3/11/90	Tulsa	Los Angeles, Calif.	FA
Santella, Anthony (1)	P	6-2	190	3/6/88	Illinois	Wauconda, Ill.	FA
Schepler, Jason	RB	6-2	274	2/6/90	Northern Illinois	Woodstock, Ill.	FA
Stupar, Nate (1)	LB	6-2	240	3/14/88	Penn State	State College, Pa.	FA-'12
Thomas, Michael (1)	S	5-11	182	3/17/90	Stanford	Houston, Texas	FA-'12
Tribue, Wayne (1)	G	6-3	329	4/30/90	Temple	Philadelphia, Pa.	FA-'12
Wiggins, Kenny (1)	T	6-6	314	8/8/88	Fresno State	Elk Grove, Calif.	FA-'12

The term NFL Rookie is defined as a player who is in his first season of professional football and has not been on the roster of another professional football team for any regular-season or postseason games. A Rookie is designated by an "R" on NFL rosters. Players who have been active in another professional football league or players who have NFL experience, including either preseason training camp or being on an Active List or Inactive List, or on Reserve/Injured or Reserve/Physically Unable to Perform for fewer than six regular-season games, are termed NFL First-Year Players. An NFL First-Year Player is designated by a "1" on NFL rosters. Thereafter, a player is credited with an additional year of experience for each season in which he accumulates six games on the Active List or Inactive List, or on Reserve/Injured or Reserve/Physically Unable to Perform.

Log on to www.49ers.com for an up-to-date roster.

COACHING STAFF

Head Coach,
Jim Harbaugh

Pro Career: Named the seventeenth head coach in 49ers history on Jan. 7, 2011. In just two seasons, Harbaugh has tallied a 27-9-1 overall record, won two NFC West Division titles and one NFC Championship. He followed a 13-3 rookie campaign, which earned him Associated Press 2011 NFL Coach of the Year honors, with a 13-5-1 mark in 2012. Harbaugh is just the second NFL coach to win consecutive division titles in his first two seasons after inheriting a team with a losing record. His 24 regular season wins are tied for the third most by any coach in NFL history over their first two seasons. Harbaugh was previously the head coach at Stanford (2007-2010), where he led the Cardinal to its first BCS game appearance and victory in the Orange Bowl, in 2010. He was head coach at the University of San Diego (2004-06). Harbaugh started in the NFL as an offensive assistant with the Oakland Raiders (2002-03). His first coaching job came from his father, Jack Harbaugh, at Western Kentucky as a volunteer assistant coach. Played 15 years with the Bears (1987 first-round pick), Colts, Ravens, Chargers and Panthers. He appeared in one Pro Bowl and was placed in the Colts' Ring of Honor in 2005. Career record: 27-9-1.

Background: Harbaugh earned first team All-America and Big Ten Player of the Year honors as a senior at Michigan, finishing third in the Heisman Trophy balloting.

Personal: Born December 23, 1963, Toledo, Ohio. He and his wife, Sarah, have two daughters, Addison and Katherine. He also has three children, Jay, James Jr. and Grace.

ASSISTANT COACHES

Geep Chryst, quarterbacks; born June 25, 1962, Madison, Wisc. Linebacker Princeton 1981-84. Pro linebacker Orlando Thunder (World League) 1992. College coach: Wisconsin-Platteville 1987, Wisconsin 1988, Wyoming 1989-1990. Pro coach: Orlando Thunder (World League) 1991, Chicago Bears 1991-95, Arizona Cardinals 1996-98, San Diego Chargers 1999-2000, Arizona Cardinals 2001-03, Carolina Panthers 2006-2010, joined 49ers in 2011.

Ronald Curry, offensive assistant; born May 28, 1979, Hampton, Va. Wide receiver North Carolina 1998-2001. Pro wide receiver Oakland Raiders 2002-08. Pro coach: Joined 49ers in 2013.

Reggie Davis, tight ends; born September 3, 1976, Long Beach, Calif. Linebacker/tight end Washington 1994-98. Pro tight end San Diego Chargers 1999-2000. College coach: San Diego State 2004, UNLV 2005-07, Oregon State 2008-2010. Pro coach: Joined 49ers in 2011.

Ed Donatell, secondary; born February 4, 1957, Akron, Ohio. Defensive back Glenville (W. Va.) State 1975-78. No pro playing experience. College coach: Kent State 1979-1980, Washington 1981-82, 2008, Pacific

1983-85, Idaho 1986-88, Cal State Fullerton 1989. Pro coach: New York Jets 1990-94, Denver Broncos 1995-99, Green Bay Packers 2000-03, Atlanta Falcons 2004-06, New York Jets 2007, Denver Broncos 2009-2010, joined 49ers in 2011.

Tim Drevno, offensive line; born April 20, 1969, Torrance, Calif. Offensive lineman El Camino (Calif.) J.C. 1987-88, Cal State Fullerton 1989-1991. No pro playing experience. College coach: Cal State Fullerton 1991-92, Montana State 1993-97, UNLV 1998, San Jose State 1999, Idaho 2000-02, San Diego 2003-06, Stanford 2007-2010. Pro coach: Joined 49ers in 2011.

Ejiro Evero, offensive assistant; born January 6, 1981, Colchester, England. Safety California-Davis 2000-03. No pro playing experience. College coach: California-Davis 2005-06, Redlands 2010. Pro coach: Tampa Bay Buccaneers 2007-09, joined 49ers in 2011.

Vic Fangio, defensive coordinator; born August 22, 1958, Dunmore, Pa. Attended East Stroudsburg State. No pro playing experience. College coach: North Carolina 1983, Stanford 2010. Pro coach: Philadelphia/Baltimore Stars (USFL) 1984-85, New Orleans Saints 1986-1994, Carolina Panthers 1995-98, Indianapolis Colts 1999-2001, Houston Texans 2002-05, Baltimore Ravens 2006-09, joined 49ers in 2011.

Peter Hansen, defensive assistant/quality control; born May 30, 1979, Palo Alto, Calif. Tight end/quarterback Arizona 1997-2001. Pro player Cannes Iron Mask (France) 2003. College coach: Stanford 2008-2010. Pro coach: Joined 49ers in 2011.

Greg Jackson, asst. secondary; born August 20, 1966, Hialeah, Fla. College safety Louisiana State 1985-88. Pro safety New York Giants 1989-1993, Philadelphia Eagles 1994-95, New Orleans Saints 1996, San Diego Chargers 1997-2000. College coach: Idaho 2003, Louisiana-Monroe 2004-2006, Tulane 2007-09, Wisconsin 2010. Pro coach: Joined 49ers in 2011.

Jim Leavitt, linebackers; born December 5, 1956, Harlingen, Texas. No college or pro playing experience. College coach: Missouri 1978-79, Dubuque 1980-81, Morning Side 1983-87, Iowa 1988-89, Kansas State 1990-95, South Florida 1995-2009. Pro Coach: Joined 49ers in 2011.

John Morton, wide receivers; born Sept. 24, 1969, Rochester Hills, Mich. Wide receiver Western Michigan 1991-92. Pro wide receiver Toronto Argonauts (CFL) 1995-96, Frankfurt Galaxy (World League) 1997. College coach: San Diego 2005, Southern California 2007-2010. Pro coach: Oakland Raiders 2002-04, New Orleans Saints 2006, joined 49ers in 2011.

Tom Rathman, running backs; born October 7, 1962, Grand Island, Neb. Running back Nebraska 1983-85. Pro running back San Francisco 49ers 1986-1993, Los Angeles Raiders 1994. College coach: Menlo College 1996. Pro coach: San Francisco 1997-2002, Detroit Lions 2003-05, Oakland Raiders 2007-08, re-joined 49ers in 2009.

Greg Roman, offensive coordinator; born August 19, 1972, Atlantic City, N.J. Defensive line/linebacker John Carroll 1990-94. No pro playing experience. College coach: Stanford 2009-2010. Pro coach: Carolina Panthers 1995-2001, Houston Texans 2002-05, Baltimore Ravens 2006-07, joined 49ers in 2011.

Brad Seely, asst. head coach/special teams coordinator; born September 6, 1956, Vinton, Iowa. Offensive lineman South Dakota State 1974-77. No pro playing experience. College coach: South Dakota State 1978, Colorado State 1980, Southern Methodist 1981, North Carolina State 1982, Pacific 1983, Oklahoma State 1984-88. Pro coach: Indianapolis Colts 1989-1993, New York Jets 1994, Carolina Panthers 1995-98, New England Patriots 1999-2008, Cleveland Browns 2009-2010, joined 49ers in 2011.

Tracy Smith, special teams assistant; born February 23, 1982, Beaumont, Texas. No college or pro playing experience. College coach: Utah State 2006-08. Pro coach: Cleveland Browns 2009-10, Seattle Seahawks 2011, joined 49ers in 2012.

Mike Solari, offensive line, born January 16, 1955, Daly City, Calif. Offensive lineman San Diego State 1972-75. No pro playing experience. College coach: Mira Costa (Calif.) J.C. 1978, U.S. International 1979, Boise State 1980, Cincinnati 1981-82, Kansas 1983-85, Pittsburgh 1986, Alabama 1990-91. Pro coach: Dallas Cowboys 1987-88, Phoenix Cardinals 1989, San Francisco 49ers 1992-1996, Kansas City Chiefs 1997-2007, Seattle Seahawks 2008-09, rejoined 49ers in 2010.

Kevin Tolbert, asst. strength and conditioning; born September 11, 1958, St. Albans, N.Y. Fullback Naval Academy 1978-1980. No pro playing experience. College coach: Miami 1998-2000, Michigan 2001-07, Stanford 2009-2010. Pro coach: Philadelphia Eagles 1996-97, Detroit Lions 2008, joined 49ers in 2011.

Jim Tomsula, defensive line; born April 14, 1967, Homestead, Pa. Middle Tennessee State 1985-86, Catawba College 1987-1990. No pro playing experience. College coach: Charleston Southern 1997. Pro coach: London Monarchs (NFLE) 1998, Scottish Claymores (NFLE) 1999-2003, Berlin Thunder (NFLE) 2004-05, Rhein Fire (NFLE) 2006 (head coach), joined 49ers in 2007 (interim head coach, one game, 2010).

Mark Uyeyama, head strength and conditioning; born December 2, 1975, Vancouver, B.C. Nose Guard Butte (Mont.) C.C. 1994-95, Northern State 1996-97. No pro playing experience. College coach: Arizona State 2001-03, Utah State 2004-07. Pro coach: Joined 49ers in 2008.

Paul Wulff, senior offensive assistant; born February 25, 1967, Woodland, Calif. Offensive lineman Washington State 1985-89. Pro offensive lineman New York Jets 1990, Raleigh-Durham Skyhawks (World League) 1991, New York/New Jersey Knights (World League) 1992. College coach: Eastern Washington 1993-2007, Washington State 2008-2011 (head coach). Pro coach: Joined 49ers in 2012.

**National Football Conference
West Division**
Team Colors: Action Green, College Navy,
Wolf Grey
**Virginia Mason Athletic Center
12 Seahawks Way
Renton, Washington 98056
Telephone:** (425) 203-8000

2013 SCHEDULE
PRESEASON

Aug. 8	at San Diego	7:00
Aug. 17	**Denver**	7:00
Aug. 23	at Green Bay	5:00
Aug. 29	**Oakland**	7:00

REGULAR SEASON

Sep. 8	at Carolina	10:00a
Sep. 15	**San Francisco**	5:30
Sep. 22	**Jacksonville**	1:25
Sep. 29	at Houston	10:00a
Oct. 6	at Indianapolis	10:00a
Oct. 13	**Tennessee**	1:05
Oct. 17	at Arizona (Thurs)	5:25
Oct. 28	at St. Louis (Mon)	5:40
Nov. 3	**Tampa Bay**	1:05
Nov. 10	at Atlanta	10:00a
Nov. 17	**Minnesota**	1:25
Nov. 24	BYE	
Dec. 2	**New Orleans** (Mon)	5:40
Dec. 8	at San Francisco	1:25
Dec. 15	at New York Giants	10:00a
Dec. 22	**Arizona**	1:05
Dec. 29	**St. Louis**	1:25

All times PT
Stadium: CenturyLink Field
(opened in 2002)
•Capacity: 67,000
Playing Surface: FieldTurf
Training Camp: VMAC
Renton, WA 98056

CENTURYLINK FIELD

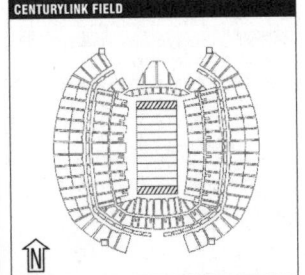

CLUB OFFICIALS
Chairman: Paul Allen
President: Peter McLoughlin
Executive Vice President of Football
Operations & Head Coach: Pete Carroll
General Manager: John Schneider
CFO & VP/Finance: Karen Beckman
Chief Commercial Officer: Eric Mastalir
Senior VP/General Counsel: Lance Lopes
VP/Sales & Marketing: Chuck Arnold
VP/Community Relations: Mike Flood
VP/Human Resources & Administration:
Cindy Kelley
VP/Communications, Broadcasting &
Web Content: Dave Pearson
VP/Technology: Chip Suttles
VP/Football Administration: Matt Thomas
Senior Personnel Executive:
Scot McCloughan
Director of Pro Personnel: Tag Ribary
Director of College Scouting: Scott
Fitterer
Director of Health & Player Performance:
Sam Ramsden
Director of Football Video: Brad Campbell
Equipment Manager: Erik Kennedy
Football Operations Coordinator:
Matt Capurro
Team Travel: Jeremy Young
Director of Finance: Peter Fonfara
Director of Communications:
Lane Gammel
Director of Community Outreach:
Sandy Gregory
Director of Retail Operations: Sue Harris
Director of Corporate Communications:
Suzanne Lavender
Director of Ticket Sales & Service:
Chris Lawrence
Director of I.T.: Sterling Monroe
Director of Digital & Emerging Media:
Kenton Olson
Director of Marketing: Jeff Richards
Managing Director of Suite Sales &
Service: Amy Sprangers
Director of Event Presentation & Fan
Engagement: Mark Tamar
Director of Fields & Facilities:
John Wright
Executive Producer/Seahawks Radio
Network: Matt Johnson

COACHING HISTORY
(289-312-0)
Records include postseason games

1976-1982	Jack Patera*	35-59-0
1982	Mike McCormack	4-3-0
1983-1991	Chuck Knox	83-67-0
1992-94	Tom Flores	14-34-0
1995-98	Dennis Erickson	31-33-0
1999-2008	Mike Holmgren	90-80-0
2009	Jim Mora	5-11-0
2010-12	Pete Carroll	27-25-0

*Released after two games in 1982

PAID ATTENDANCE
Home 530,486   Away 459,378
Total 989,864
Single-game home record,
68,681 (12/16/00)
Single-season home record,
533,657 (2007)

2013 DRAFT CHOICES

Round	Name	Pos.	College
2	Christine Michael	RB	Texas A&M
3	Jordan Hill	DT	Penn St.
4	Chris Harper	WR	Kansas St.
5	Jesse Williams	DT	Alabama
	Tharold Simon	DB	Louisiana St.
	Luke Willson	TE	Rice
6	Spencer Ware	FB	Louisiana St.
7	Ryan Seymour	G	Vanderbilt
	Ty Powell	LB	Harding
	Jared Smith	G	New Hampshire
	Michael Bowie	T	Northeastern St. (OK)

2012 TEAM RECORD

PRESEASON (4-0)

Date	Result	Opponent
08/11	W 27-17	Tennessee
08/18	W 30-10	at Denver
08/24	W 44-14	at Kansas City
08/30	W 21-3	Oakland

REGULAR SEASON (11-5)

Date	Result	Opponent
09/09	L 16-20	at Arizona
09/16	W 27-7	Dallas
09/24	W 14-12	Green Bay
09/30	L 13-19	at St. Louis
10/07	W 16-12	at Carolina
10/14	W 24-23	New England
10/18	L 6-13	at San Francisco
10/28	L 24-28	at Detroit
11/04	W 30-20	Minnesota
11/11	W 28-7	New York Jets
11/25	L 21-24	at Miami
12/02	W 23-17	at Chicago (OT)
12/09	W 58-0	Arizona
12/16	W 50-17	at Buffalo
12/23	W 42-13	San Francisco
12/30	W 20-13	St. Louis

POSTSEASON (1-1)

Date	Result	Opponent
01/06	W 24-14	at Washington
01/13	L 28-30	at Atlanta

(OT) Overtime

SCORE BY PERIODS

Seahawks	98	122	87	99	6 —	412
Opponents	51	84	42	68	0 —	245

2012 TEAM STATISTICS

	Seahawks	Opp.
Total First Downs	311	295
Rushing	129	80
Passing	153	186
Penalty	29	29
3rd Down: Made/Att	80/199	76/198
3rd Down Pct.	40.2	38.4
4th Down: Made/Att	11/18	3/10
4th Down Pct.	61.1	30.0
Possession Avg.	31:36	28:24
Total Net Yards	5610	4899
Avg. Per Game	350.6	306.2
Total Plays	974	968
Avg. Per Play	5.8	5.1
Net Yards Rushing	2579	1649
Avg. Per Game	161.2	103.1
Total Rushes	536	368
Net Yards Passing	3031	3250
Avg. Per Game	189.4	203.1
Sacked/Yards Lost	33/203	36/247
Gross Yards	3234	3497
Att./Completions	405/259	564/327
Completion Pct.	64.0	58.0
Had Intercepted	10	18
Punts/Average	65/45.6	78/45.1
Net Punting Avg.	65/40.8	78/40.0
Penalties/Yards	110/890	102/902
Fumbles/Ball Lost	16/8	27/13
Touchdowns	49	25
Rushing	16	8
Passing	27	15
Returns	6	2

2012 INDIVIDUAL STATISTICS

PASSING

	Att.	Comp.	Yds.	Pct.	TD	Int.	Tkld.	Rate
Wilson	393	252	3118	64.1	26	10	33/203	100.0
Flynn	9	5	68	55.6	0	0	0/0	79.9
Rice	2	1	25	50.0	0	0	0/0	95.8
Tate	1	1	23	100.0	1	0	0/0	158.3
Seahawks	405	259	3234	64.0	27	10	33/203	100.6
Opponents	564	327	3497	58.0	15	18	36/247	71.8

SCORING

	TD R	TD P	TD Rt	PAT	FG	Saf	PTS
Hauschka	0	0	0	46/48	24/27	0	118
Lynch	11	1	0	0/0	0/0	0	72
Rice	0	7	0	0/0	0/0	0	42
Tate	0	7	0	0/0	0/0	0	42
Wilson	4	0	0	0/0	0/0	0	24
Baldwin	0	3	0	0/0	0/0	0	18
McCoy	0	3	0	0/0	0/0	0	18
Z. Miller	0	3	0	0/0	0/0	0	18
Robinson	0	2	0	0/0	0/0	0	12
Sherman	0	0	2	0/0	0/0	0	12
Washington	1	0	1	0/0	0/0	0	12
Edwards	0	1	0	0/0	0/0	0	6
J. Johnson	0	0	1	0/0	0/0	0	6
Smith	0	0	1	0/0	0/0	0	6
Thomas	0	0	1	0/0	0/0	0	6
Seahawks	16	27	6	46/48	24/27	0	412
Opponents	8	15	2	24/24	23/25	1	245

2-Pt Conversions: Seahawks 0-0, Opponents 0-1

RUSHING

	No.	Yds	Avg	LG	TD
Lynch	315	1590	5.0	77t	11
Wilson	94	489	5.2	25t	4
Turbin	80	354	4.4	26	0
Washington	23	83	3.6	14	1
Robinson	12	49	4.1	29	0
Tate	3	20	6.7	13	0
Obomanu	1	11	11.0	11	0
Rice	2	6	3.0	3	0
Flynn	4	-5	-1.3	-1	0
Ryan	2	-18	-9.0	0	0
Seahawks	536	2579	4.8	77t	16
Opponents	368	1649	4.5	74	8

RECEIVING

	No.	Yds	Avg	LG	TD
Rice	50	748	15.0	46t	7
Tate	45	688	15.3	51	7
Z. Miller	38	396	10.4	30	3
Baldwin	29	366	12.6	50	3
Lynch	23	196	8.5	27	1
Turbin	19	181	9.5	20	0
McCoy	18	291	16.2	67	3
Robinson	13	126	9.7	20	2
Edwards	8	74	9.3	16	1
Obomanu	4	58	14.5	36	0
Martin	4	42	10.5	15	0
Washington	4	31	7.8	9	0
Kearse	3	31	10.3	17	0
Moore	1	6	6.0	6	0
Seahawks	259	3234	12.5	67	27
Opponents	327	3497	10.7	56	15

INTERCEPTIONS

	No.	Yds	Avg	LG	TD
Sherman	8	57	7.1	29	1
Thomas	3	80	26.7	57t	1
Wagner	3	55	18.3	45	0
Browner	3	39	13.0	35	0
Wright	1	24	24.0	24	0
Seahawks	18	255	14.2	57t	2
Opponents	10	115	11.5	34	1

PUNTING

	No.	Yds.	Avg.	In 20	LG
Ryan	65	2963	45.6	30	73
Seahawks	65	2963	45.6	30	73
Opponents	78	3515	45.1	30	66

PUNT RETURNS

	Ret	FC	Yds	Avg	LG	TD
Washington	41	17	356	8.7	52	0
Browner	1	0	-1	-1.0	-1	0
Tate	0	1	0	—	—	0
Seahawks	42	18	355	8.5	52	0
Opponents	29	17	252	8.7	38	0

KICKOFF RETURNS

	No.	Yds	Avg	LG	TD
Washington	27	784	29.0	98t	1
Baldwin	1	3	3.0	3	0
Obomanu	1	0	0.0	0	0
Seahawks	29	787	27.1	98t	1
Opponents	50	1147	22.9	40	0

FIELD GOALS

	1-19	20-29	30-39	40-49	50+
Hauschka	1/1	7/7	10/10	5/5	1/4
Seahawks	1/1	7/7	10/10	5/5	1/4
Opponents	0/0	6/7	8/8	5/5	4/5

SACKS

	No.
Clemons	11.5
Irvin	8.0
Jones	3.0
Mebane	3.0
J. Johnson	2.0
Scruggs	2.0
Wagner	2.0
Hill	1.5
Branch	1.0
Sherman	1.0
Wright	1.0
Seahawks	36.0
Opponents	33.0

RECORD HOLDERS
INDIVIDUAL RECORDS—CAREER

Category	Name	Performance
Rushing (Yds.)	Shaun Alexander, 2000-07	9,429
Passing (Yds.)	Matt Hasselbeck, 2001-2010	29,434
Passing (TDs)	Dave Krieg, 1980-1991	195
Receiving (No.)	Steve Largent, 1976-1989	819
Receiving (Yds.)	Steve Largent, 1976-1989	13,089
Interceptions	Dave Brown, 1976-1986	50
Punting (Avg.)	Jon Ryan, 2008-2012	45.0
Punt Return (Avg.)	Charlie Rogers, 1999-2001	12.7
Kickoff Return (Avg.)	Leon Washington, 2010-12	26.2
Field Goals	Norm Johnson, 1982-1990	159
Touchdowns (Tot.)	Shaun Alexander, 2000-07	112
Points	Norm Johnson, 1982-1990	810
*Sacks	Jacob Green, 1980-1991	97.5

INDIVIDUAL RECORDS—SINGLE SEASON

Category	Name	Performance
Rushing (Yds.)	Shaun Alexander, 2005	1,880
Passing (Yds.)	Matt Hasselbeck, 2007	3,966
Passing (TDs)	Dave Krieg, 1984	32
Receiving (No.)	Bobby Engram, 2007	94
Receiving (Yds.)	Steve Largent, 1985	1,287
Interceptions	John Harris, 1981	10
	Kenny Easley, 1984	10
Punting (Avg.)	Jon Ryan, 2011	46.6
Punt Return (Avg.)	Charlie Rogers, 1999	14.5
Kickoff Return (Avg.)	Leon Washington, 2012	29.0
Field Goals	Todd Peterson, 1999	34
Touchdowns (Tot.)	Shaun Alexander, 2005	28
Points	Shaun Alexander, 2005	168
*Sacks	Michael Sinclair, 1998	16.5

INDIVIDUAL RECORDS—SINGLE GAME

Category	Name	Performance
Rushing (Yds.)	Shaun Alexander, 11-11-01	266
Passing (Yds.)	Matt Hasselbeck, 12-29-02	449
Passing (TDs)	Dave Krieg, 12-2-84, 9-15-85, 11-28-88	5
	Warren Moon, 10-26-97	5
	Matt Hasselbeck, 11-23-03, 9-24-06	5
Receiving (No.)	Steve Largent, 10-18-87	15
Receiving (Yds.)	Steve Largent, 10-18-87	261
Interceptions	Kenny Easley, 9-3-84	3
	Eugene Robinson, 12-6-92	3
	Darryl Williams, 9-21-97	3
	Lofa Tatupu, 12-2-07	3
	Marcus Trufant, 12-9-07	3
Field Goals	Norm Johnson, 9-20-87, 12-18-88	5
	Olindo Mare, 10-24-10, 11-14-10	5
	Todd Peterson, 9-26-99	5
	Steven Hauschka, 11-13-11	5
Touchdowns (Tot.)	Shaun Alexander, 9-29-02	5
Points	Shaun Alexander, 9-29-02	30
*Sacks	Many times	4.0
	Last time by Chris Clemons, 9-24-12	

*Sacks became an official statistic in 1982.

2013 VETERAN ROSTER

No.	Name	Pos.	Ht.	Wt.	Birthdate	NFL Exp.	College	Hometown	How Acq.	'12 Games/ Starts
56	Avril, Cliff	DE	6-3	260	4/8/86	6	Purdue	Green Cove Springs, Fla.	UFA(Det)-'13	16/16*
89	Baldwin, Doug	WR	5-10	189	9/21/88	3	Stanford	Gulf Breeze, Fla.	FA-'11	14/4
72	Bennett, Michael	DE	6-4	274	11/13/85	5	Texas A&M	Alief, Texas	UFA(TB)-'13	16/16*
37	Blackmon, Will	CB	6-0	210	10/27/84	7	Boston College	Providence, R.I.	FA-'13	0*
52	Bradford, Allen	LB	5-11	235	8/31/88	3	Southern California	San Bernardino, Calif.	W(TB)-'11	1/0
39	Browner, Brandon	CB	6-4	221	8/2/84	3	Oregon State	Sylmar, Calif.	FA-'11	12/12
79	Bryant, Red	DE	6-4	323	4/18/84	6	Texas A&M	Jasper, Texas	D4-'08	16/16
77	Carpenter, James	G	6-5	321	3/22/89	3	Alabama	Augusta, Ga.	D1-'11	7/7
31	Chancellor, Kam	SS	6-3	232	4/3/88	4	Virginia Tech	Norfolk, Va.	D5-'10	16/16
91	Clemons, Chris	DE	6-3	254	10/30/81	10	Georgia	Griffin, Ga.	T(Phil)-'10	16/16
55	Farwell, Heath	LB	6-0	235	12/31/81	9	San Diego State	Fontana, Calif.	FA-'11	16/0
68	Giacomini, Breno	T	6-7	318	9/27/85	6	Louisville	Cambridge, Mass.	PS(GB)-'10	16/16
49	Gresham, Clint	LS	6-3	240	8/24/86	4	Texas Christian	Corpus Christi, Texas	FA-'10	16/0
27	Guy, Winston	SS	6-1	218	4/23/90	2	Kentucky	Lexington, Ky.	D6b-'12	2/0
11	t- Harvin, Percy	WR	5-11	184	5/28/88	5	Florida	Virginia Beach, Va.	T(Minn)-'13	9/8*
4	Hauschka, Steven	K	6-4	210	6/29/85	6	North Carolina State	Needham, Mass.	W(Den)-'11	16/0
94	Howard, Jaye	DT	6-3	301	12/20/88	2	Florida	Apopka, Fla.	D4b-'12	2/0
51	Irvin, Bruce	DE	6-3	248	11/1/87	2	West Virginia	Atlanta, Ga.	D1-'12	16/0
61	Jeanpierre, Lemuel	G/C	6-3	301	5/19/87	4	South Carolina	Orlando, Fla.	FA-'10	15/0
32	Johnson, Jeron	SS	5-10	212	6/12/88	3	Boise State	Compton, Calif.	FA-'11	16/0
63	Johnson, Rishaw	G	6-3	313	2/23/89	2	California (Pa.)	Hammond, La.	FA-'12	0*
15	Kearse, Jermaine	WR	6-1	209	2/6/90	2	Washington	Lakewood, Wash.	FA-'12	7/1
20	Lane, Jeremy	CB	6-0	190	7/14/90	2	Northwestern St. (La.)	Tyler, Texas	D6a-'12	13/3
24	Lynch, Marshawn	RB	5-11	215	4/22/86	7	California	Oakland, Calif.	T(Buff)-'10	16/16
85	McCoy, Anthony	TE	6-5	259	12/28/87	4	Southern California	Fresno, Calif.	D6-'10	16/5
99	McDaniel, Tony	DT	6-7	305	1/20/85	8	Tennessee	Columbia, S.C.	UFA(Mia)-'13	11/0*
69	McDonald, Clinton	DT	6-2	297	1/6/87	5	Memphis	Jacksonville, Ark.	T(Cin)-'11	14/0
84	McGrath, Sean	TE	6-5	247	12/3/87	2	Henderson State	Chicago, Ill.	FA-'12	2/0
67	McQuistan, Paul	G/T	6-6	315	4/30/83	8	Weber State	San Diego, Calif.	FA-'11	16/16
42	Maragos, Chris	FS	5-10	200	1/6/87	4	Wisconsin	Racine, Wis.	FA-'11	16/0
14	Martin, Charly	WR	6-1	212	3/20/84	5	West Texas A&M	Walla Walla, Wash.	FA-'12	4/1
41	Maxwell, Byron	CB	6-1	207	2/23/88	3	Clemson	Charleston, S.C.	D6-'11	9/0
92	Mebane, Brandon	DT	6-1	311	1/15/85	7	California	Los Angeles, Calif.	D3-'07	16/16
86	Miller, Zach	TE	6-5	255	12/11/85	7	Arizona State	Phoenix, Ariz.	UFA(Oak)-'11	16/15
74	Moffitt, John	G	6-4	319	10/28/86	3	Wisconsin	Guilford, Conn.	D3-'11	8/6
57	Morgan, Mike	LB	6-3	226	1/16/88	3	Southern California	Dallas, Texas	FA-'11	16/1
76	Okung, Russell	T	6-5	310	10/7/87	4	Oklahoma State	Houston, Texas	D1a-'10	15/15
36	Parker, Ron	CB	6-0	206	8/17/87	3	Newberry College	St. Helena Island, S.C.	FA-'12	2/0
75	Person, Mike	T	6-4	299	6/17/88	3	Montana State	Glendive, Mont.	FA-'12	0*
6	Portis, Josh	QB	6-3	211	7/14/87	3	California (Pa.)	Woodland Hills, Calif.	FA-'11	0*
10	Quinn, Brady	QB	6-3	235	10/27/84	7	Notre Dame	Dublin, Ohio	UFA(KC)-'13	10/8*
18	Rice, Sidney	WR	6-4	202	9/1/86	7	South Carolina	Gaffney, S.C.	UFA(Minn)-'11	16/16
26	Robinson, Michael	FB	6-1	240	2/6/83	8	Penn State	Richmond, Va.	FA-'10	16/6
9	Ryan, Jon	P	6-0	217	11/26/81	8	Regina	Regina, Saskatchewan	FA-'08	16/0
98	Scruggs, Greg	DE	6-3	284	8/17/90	2	Louisville	Cincinnati, Ohio	D7b-'12	11/0
35	Shead, DeShawn	CB	6-2	220	6/28/88	2	Portland State	Palmdale, Calif.	FA-'12	0*
25	Sherman, Richard	CB	6-3	195	3/30/88	3	Stanford	Compton, Calif.	D5a-'11	16/16
53	Smith, Malcolm	LB	6-0	226	7/5/89	3	Southern California	Northridge, Calif.	D7b-'11	16/3
16	Swain, Brett	WR	6-0	200	6/21/85	4	San Diego State	Carlsbad, Calif.	FA-'13	0*
64	Sweezy, J.R.	G	6-5	298	4/8/89	2	North Carolina State	Mooresville, N.C.	D7a-'12	13/3
81	Tate, Golden	WR	5-10	202	8/2/88	4	Notre Dame	Hendersonville, Tenn.	D2-'10	15/15
29	Thomas, Earl	FS	5-10	202	5/7/89	4	Texas	Orange, Texas	D1b-'10	16/16
28	Thurmond, Walter	CB	5-11	190	8/12/87	4	Oregon	West Covina, Calif.	D4a-'10	2/1
22	Turbin, Robert	RB	5-10	222	12/2/89	2	Utah State	Fremont, Calif.	D4a-'12	16/0
60	Unger, Max	C	6-5	305	4/14/86	5	Oregon	Kailua-Kona, Hawaii	D2-'09	16/16
54	Wagner, Bobby	LB	6-0	241	6/27/90	2	Utah State	Ontario, Calif.	D2-'12	16/15
19	Walters, Bryan	WR	6-0	190	11/4/87	4	Cornell	Kirkland, Wash.	FA-'12	0*
3	Wilson, Russell	QB	5-11	206	11/29/88	2	Wisconsin	Richmond, Va.	D3-'12	16/16
83	Williams, Stephen	WR	6-5	208	6/29/86	3	Toledo	Levelland, Texas	FA-'13	0*
21	Winfield, Antoine	CB	5-9	180	6/24/77	15	Ohio State	Akron, Ohio	FA-'13	16/15*
50	Wright, K.J.	LB	6-4	246	7/23/89	3	Mississippi State	Olive Branch, Miss.	D4a-'11	15/15

* Avril played 16 games with Detroit in '12; Bennett played 16 games with Tampa Bay; Blackmon last active with N.Y. Giants in '11; Harvin played nine games with Minnesota; R. Johnson inactive for four games; McDaniel played 11 games with Miami; Person inactive for eight games; Portis last active with Seattle in '11; Quinn played 10 games with Kansas City; Shead inactive for four games; Swain last active with San Francisco in '11; Walters last active with San Diego in '11; Williams last active with Arizona in '11; Winfield played 16 games with Minnesota.

t- Seahawks traded for Harvin (Minn).

Traded—QB Matt Flynn (3 games in '12) to Oakland.

Players lost through free agency (3): DT Alan Branch (Buff; 16 games), DE Jason Jones (Det; 12), CB Marcus Trufant (Jax; 12).

Also played with Seahawks in '12—WR Deon Butler (1 game), WR Braylon Edwards (10), DT Hebron Fangupo (1), LB Leroy Hill (13), TE Evan Moore (14), WR Ben Obomanu (8), T Frank Omiyale (16), RB Leon Washington (16).

FIRST-YEAR ROSTER

Name	Pos.	Ht.	Wt.	Birthdate	College	Hometown	How Acq.
Austin, Matt	WR	6-2	202	7/1/88	Utah State	Monrovia, Calif.	FA
Bailey, Alvin	T	6-3	320	8/26/91	Arkansas	Broken Arrow, Okla.	FA
Bates, Phil (1)	WR	6-1	220	9/20/89	Ohio University	Omaha, Neb.	FA-'12
Boatright, Kenneth	DE	6-3	254	3/6/90	Southern Illinois	Bolingbrook, Ill.	FA
Bowie, Michael	T	6-4	332	9/25/91	Northeastern State	Tulsa, Okla.	D7d
Coleman, Derrick (1)	RB	6-0	233	10/18/90	UCLA	West Los Angeles, Calif.	FA-'12
Harper, Chris	WR	6-1	234	9/10/89	Kansas State	Wichita, Kan.	D4
Helfet, Cooper (1)	TE	6-3	239	6/2/89	Duke	Kentfield, Calif.	FA-'12
Hill, Jordan	DT	6-1	303	2/8/91	Penn State	Steelton, Pa.	D3
Johnson, Jerrod	QB	6-5	251	7/27/88	Texas A&M	Houston, Texas	FA
Knox, Kyle (1)	LB	6-1	220	3/10/89	Fresno State	Los Angeles, Calif.	FA-'12
Lotulelei, John	LB	5-11	233	12/4/91	Nevada-Las Vegas	Kihei, Hawaii	FA
Marshall, Victor	TE	6-4	235	6/2/88	British Columbia	Kirkland, Wash.	FA
Mayowa, Benson	DE	6-3	236	8/3/91	Idaho	Inglewood, Calif.	FA
Michael, Christine	RB	5-10	221	11/9/90	Texas A&M	Beaumont, Texas	D2
Polk, Ray	SS	6-1	219	4/22/90	Colorado	Scottsdale, Ariz.	FA
Powell, Ty	LB	6-2	249	4/27/88	Harding (Ark.)	Marina, Calif.	D7b
Roussos, Jordon	G	6-3	307	8/8/91	Bowling Green	Pittsburgh, Pa.	FA
Seymour, Ryan	G	6-4	301	2/7/90	Vanderbilt	Kingsland, Ga.	D7a
Simon, Tharold	CB	6-2	202	3/6/91	Louisiana State	Eunice, La.	D5b
Smith, Jared	G	6-4	302	3/20/90	New Hampshire	Greencastle, Pa.	D7c
Steiner, Adam	LS	6-2	240	5/23/90	Akron	Canton, Ohio	FA
Toomer, Korey (1)	LB	6-2	234	12/9/88	Idaho	Las Vegas, Nev.	D5
Wade, Myles (1)	DT	6-1	300	8/30/89	Portland State	Portland, Ore.	FA-'12
Ware, Spencer	FB	5-10	229	11/23/91	Louisiana State	Cincinnati, Ohio	D6
Wiggs, Carson	K	6-1	222	2/20/90	Purdue	Grand Prairie, Texas	FA
Wilkins, Craig	LB	6-1	243	11/28/89	Old Dominion	Washington, D.C.	FA
Williams, Jesse	DT	6-3	325	11/2/90	Alabama	Brisbane, Australia	D5a
Willson, Luke	TE	6-5	252	1/15/90	Rice	LaSalle, Ontario, Canada	D5c

The term NFL Rookie is defined as a player who is in his first season of professional football and has not been on the roster of another professional football team for any regular-season or postseason games. A Rookie is designated by an "R" on NFL rosters. Players who have been active in another professional football league or players who have NFL experience, including either preseason training camp or being on an Active List or Inactive List, or on Reserve/Injured or Reserve/Physically Unable to Perform for fewer than six regular-season games, are termed NFL First-Year Players. An NFL First-Year Player is designated by a "1" on NFL rosters. Thereafter, a player is credited with an additional year of experience for each season in which he accumulates six games on the Active List or Inactive List, or on Reserve/Injured or Reserve/Physically Unable to Perform.

Log on to www.seahawks.com for an up-to-date roster.

COACHING STAFF

Head Coach,
Pete Carroll

Pro Career: Named as Seattle's eighth head coach on January 11, 2010. Began his NFL career as defensive backs coach for the Buffalo Bills (1984) and Minnesota Vikings (1985-89), before becoming the N.Y. Jets defensive coordinator (1990-93) and head coach (1994). He spent two years as the San Francisco 49ers defensive coordinator (1995-96) before leading the New England Patriots to a 27-21 record and two playoff appearances as head coach (1997-99). He returned to the NFL after spending nine years (2001-09) as head coach at USC, where he won seven consecutive Pac-10 titles (2002-08), two national championships and led the Trojans to a 97-19 record. Career record: 61-58.

Background: Two-time All-Pacific Coast Conference safety at Pacific (1971-72). Earned degree in business administration (1973) and secondary teaching credential and master's degree in physical education (1976) from Pacific. College coach: Pacific 1974-76, 1983, Arkansas 1977, Iowa State 1978, Ohio State 1979, North Carolina State 1980-82, USC 2001-09.

Personal: Born September 15, 1951 in San Francisco, Calif. He and his wife, Glena, have three children: Brennan, Nate, Jaime, and two grandchildren: Dillon and Colbie Jaye.

ASSISTANT COACHES

Darrell Bevell, offensive coordinator; born January 6, 1970, Yuma, Ariz. Quarterback Northern Arizona 1989, Wisconsin 1992-95. No pro playing experience. College coach: Westmar 1996, Iowa State 1997, Connecticut 1998-99. Pro coach: Green Bay Packers 2000-05, Minnesota Vikings 2006-2010, joined Seahawks in 2011.

Kippy Brown, wide receivers; born March 6, 1955, Sweetwater, Tenn. Quarterback Memphis State 1974-77. No pro playing experience. College coach: Memphis State 1978-1980, Louisville 1982, Tennessee 1983-89, 1993-94, 2009. Pro coach: New York Jets 1990-92, Tampa Bay Buccaneers 1995, Miami Dolphins 1996-99, Green Bay Packers 2000, Houston Texans 2002-05, Detroit Lions 2006-08, joined Seahawks in 2010.

Tom Cable, asst. head coach/offensive line; born November 26, 1964, Merced, Calif. Offensive lineman Idaho 1982-86. Pro lineman Indianapolis Colts 1987. College coach: Idaho 1987-88, San Diego State 1989, Cal State-Fullerton 1990, UNLV 1991, California 1992-97, Idaho 2000-03, UCLA 2004-05. Pro coach: Atlanta Falcons 2006, Oakland Raiders 2007-10 (head coach 2008-2010), joined Seahawks in 2011.

Dave Canales, asst. quarterbacks/offensive quality control; born May 7, 1981, Carson, Calif. Wide receiver Azusa Pacific 2000-03. No pro playing experience. College coach: El Camino (Calif.) J.C. 2006-08, Southern California 2009. Pro coach: Joined Seahawks in 2010.

Chris Carlisle, head strength & conditioning; born August 7, 1962, Mason City, Iowa. Offensive lineman North Iowa Area Community College 1980-81, Chadron (Neb.) State College 1982-83. No pro playing experience. College coach: Arkansas 1992-93, Trinity Valley (Texas) C.C. 1997, Tennessee 1998-2000, Southern California 2001-09. Pro coach: Joined Seahawks in 2010.

Nate Carroll, offensive assistant; born March 24, 1987, Edina, Minn. Attended Southern California. No college or pro playing experience. Pro coach: Joined Seahawks in 2010.

Keith Carter, quality control/offense; born July 2, 1982, Downingtown, Pa. Tight end UCLA 2001-04. No pro playing experience. College coach: Wagner College 2006, Redlands 2007-08, University of San Diego 2009-2011. Pro coach: Joined Seahawks in 2011.

Mondray Gee, asst. strength & conditioning; born June 15, 1976, Detroit, Mich. Attended Michigan State. No college or pro playing experience. College coach: Michigan State 2000-01. Pro coach: Detroit Lions 2001-07, Green Bay Packers 2008-09, joined Seahawks in 2010.

Travis Jones, defensive line; born June 6, 1972, Milledgeville, Ga. Linebacker Georgia 1991-94. Pro linebacker Baltimore Stallions (CFL) 1995. College coach: Georgia: 1997, Appalachian State 1998-2000, Kansas 2001-02, Louisiana State 2003-04. Pro coach: Miami Dolphins 2005-07, New Orleans Saints 2008-2012, joined Seahawks in 2012.

Marquand Manuel, defensive assistant; born July 11, 1979, Miami, Fla. Safety Florida 1998-2001. Pro safety Cincinnati Bengals 2002-03, Seattle Seahawks 2004-05, Green Bay Packers 2006, Carolina Panthers 2007, Denver Broncos 2008, Detroit Lions 2009. Pro coach: Joined Seahawks in 2011.

Pat McPherson, tight ends; born April 15, 1969, Santa Clara, Calif. Linebacker Santa Clara 1991-92. No pro playing experience. Pro coach: San Francisco 49ers 1996, Denver Broncos 1998-2008, joined Seahawks in 2011.

Ken Norton, Jr., linebackers; born September 29, 1966, Lincoln, Ill. Linebacker UCLA 1984-87. Pro linebacker Dallas Cowboys 1988-1993, San Francisco 49ers 1994-2000. College coach: Southern California 2004-09. Pro coach: Joined Seahawks in 2010.

Dan Quinn, defensive coordinator; born September 11, 1970, Orange, N.J. Defensive lineman Salisbury State 1990-93. No pro playing experience. College coach: William & Mary 1994, Virginia Military Institute 1995, Hofstra 1997-2000, Florida 2010-11. Pro coach: San Francisco 49ers 2001-04, Miami Dolphins 2005-06, New York Jets 2007-08, Seattle Seahawks 2009-2010, re-joined Seahawks 2013.

Kris Richard, defensive backs/cornerbacks; born October 28, 1978, Carson, Calif. Defensive back Southern California 1998-2001. Pro defensive back Seattle Seahawks 2002-04, San Francisco 49ers

2005. College coach: Southern California 2008-09. Pro coach: Joined Seahawks in 2010.

Pat Ruel, asst. offensive line; born December 5, 1950, Coral Gables, Fla. Offensive lineman Miami 1971-72. No pro playing experience. College coach: Miami 1974-76, Arkansas 1977, Washington State 1978-1981, Texas A&M 1982-84, Northern Illinois 1985-87, Kansas 1988-1996, Michigan State 1998-99, USC 2005-09. Pro coach: Detroit Lions 2000, Green Bay Packers 2001-02, Buffalo Bills 2003, New York Giants 2004, joined Seahawks in 2010.

Robert Saleh, quality control/defense; born January 31, 1979, Dearborn, Mich. Tight end Northern Michigan 1997-2000. No pro playing experience. College coach: Michigan State 2002-03, Central Michigan 2004. Pro coach: Houston Texans 2005-2010, joined Seahawks in 2010.

Brian Schneider, special teams coordinator; born May 16, 1971, San Diego, Calif. Linebacker Colorado State 1989-1993. No pro playing experience. College coach: Colorado State 1994-2002, UCLA 2003-05, Iowa State 2006, Air Force 2007, Southern California 2009. Pro coach: Oakland Raiders 2007-08, joined Seahawks in 2010.

Rocky Seto, asst. defensive backs/safeties; born March 12, 1976, Arcadia, Calif. Linebacker Southern California 1997-98. No pro playing experience. College coach: Southern California 1999-2009. Pro coach: Joined Seahawks in 2010.

Carl Smith, quarterbacks; born April 26, 1948, Wasco, Calif. Quarterback Bakersfield 1966-67, defensive back Cal Poly-San Luis Obispo 1969-1970. No pro playing experience. College coach: Cal Poly-San Luis Obispo 1971, Colorado 1972-73, Southwestern Louisiana 1974-78, Lamar 1979-1981, North Carolina State 1982, Southern California 2004. Pro coach: Philadelphia/Baltimore Stars 1983-85, New Orleans Saints 1986-1996, New England Patriots 1997-99, Cleveland Browns 2001-03, 2009-2010, Jacksonville Jaguars 2005-06, joined Seahawks in 2011.

Sherman Smith, running backs; born November 1, 1954, Youngstown, Ohio. Quarterback Miami (Ohio) 1972-75. Pro running back Seattle Seahawks 1976-1982, San Diego Chargers 1983-84. College coach: Miami (Ohio) 1990-91, Illinois 1992-94. Pro coach: Houston Oilers/Tennessee Titans 1995-2007, Washington Redskins 2008-09, joined Seahawks in 2010.

Nick Sorensen, coaching assistant/special teams; born July 31, 1978, Winter Haven, Fla. Safety Virginia Tech 1997-2000. Pro safety St. Louis Rams 2001-02, Jacksonville Jaguars 2003-06, Cleveland Browns 2007-2010. Pro coach: Joined Seahawks in 2012.

Jamie Yanchar, asst. strength & conditioning, born December 29, 1963, Cleveland, Ohio. Attended Louisville. No college or pro playing experience. College coach: Southern California 1990-2009. Pro coach: Joined Seahawks in 2010.

National Football Conference
South Division
Team Colors: Buccaneer Red, Pewter,
Black, and Orange
One Buccaneer Place
Tampa, Florida 33607
Telephone: (813) 870-2700

2013 SCHEDULE
PRESEASON
Aug. 8	**Baltimore**	7:30
Aug. 16	at New England	8:00
Aug. 24	at Miami	7:30
Aug. 29	**Washington**	7:30

REGULAR SEASON
Sep. 8	at New York Jets	1:00
Sep. 15	**New Orleans**	4:05
Sep. 22	at New England	1:00
Sep. 29	**Arizona**	1:00
Oct. 6	BYE	
Oct. 13	**Philadelphia**	1:00
Oct. 20	at Atlanta	1:00
Oct. 24	**Carolina** (Thurs)	8:25
Nov. 3	at Seattle	4:05
Nov. 11	**Miami** (Mon)	8:40
Nov. 17	**Atlanta**	1:00
Nov. 24	at Detroit	1:00
Dec. 1	at Carolina	1:00
Dec. 8	**Buffalo**	1:00
Dec. 15	**San Francisco**	1:00
Dec. 22	at St. Louis	1:00
Dec. 29	at New Orleans	1:00
All times ET

Stadium: Raymond James Stadium
(opened in 1998)
• **Capacity:** 65,908
Tampa, Florida 33607
Playing Surface: Grass
Training Camp: One Buccaneer Place
Tampa, Florida 33607

RAYMOND JAMES STADIUM

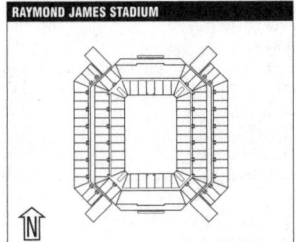

CLUB OFFICIALS
Owner/President: Malcom Glazer
Co-Chairman: Bryan Glazer
Co-Chairman: Joel Glazer
Co-Chairman: Edward Glazer
General Manager: Mark Dominik
Chief Operating Officer: Brian Ford
Director of Player Personnel:
Dennis Hickey
Director of Player Engagement:
Terry Cousin
Director of Football Operations:
Kevin MacConnell
Director of Team Security: Henry Duran
Special Assistant to the Head Coach:
Butch Davis
Coordinator of Pro Scouting:
Shelton Quarles
Coordinator of Football Administration:
Mike Greenberg
Pro Personnel Assistant: Rob McCartney
National Scout: Jim Abrams
College Scouts: Andre Forde,
Briand Hudspeth, Byron Kiefer,
Tony Kinkela, Bill Rees,
Justin Sheridan, Seth Turner,
Mike Yowarsky
Combine Scout: Tony Hardie
Chief Financial Officer: Joe Fada
General Legal Counsel: David Cohen
Chief Marketing Officer: Jason Dial
Chief Partnership Officer: Jim Pyne
Director of Broadcast Operations:
Jeff Ryan
Director of Communications: TBD
Director of Community Relations:
Eileen Sweeney
Director of Corporate Security and
Facilities: Andres Trescastro
Director of Creative Services: Clark Moss
Director of Group Sales: Amy Saxon
Director of Guest/Member Relations: TBD
Director of Human Resources:
Kristin Houston
Director of Information Technology:
Ed Johnston
Director of Sales: Ben Milsom
Director of Special Events and Game
Operations: Connie Mojallal
Director of Sports Medicine and
Performance: Todd Toriscelli
Director of Rehabilitation:
Shannon Merrick
Team Sports Dietitian: Kevin Luhrs
Head Equipment Manager:
James Sorenson
Asst. Equipment Manager: Mike Myrick
Video Director: Dave Levy
Asst. Video Director: Chris Bryan
Cheerleading Manager: Catherine Boyd
Player Benefits and Alumni Program
Manager: Jill Hobbs
Purchasing Manager: Brian Mathiews
Senior Manager of Game Operations and
Special Events: Jim Mackes
Senior Public Relations Manager:
Michael Pehanich
Senior Ticket Operations Manager: TBD
Senior Writer: Scott Smith
Team Operations Manager: Tim Jarocki
Ticket Operations Manager: Amy Weber
Video Production Manager: Ed Bottger

COACHING HISTORY
(235-359-1)
Records include postseason games
1976-1984	John McKay	45-91-1
1985-86	Leeman Bennett	4-28-0
1987-1990	Ray Perkins*	19-41-0
1990-91	Richard Williamson	4-15-0
1992-95	Sam Wyche	23-41-0
1996-2001	Tony Dungy	56-46-0
2002-08	Jon Gruden	60-57-0
2009-2011	Raheem Morris	17-31-0
2012	Greg Schiano	7-9-0

*Released after 13 games in 1990

PAID ATTENDANCE
Home 409,052   Away 541,168
Total 950,220
Single-game home record,
73,523 (12/7/97)
Single-season home record,
545,980 (1979)

2013 DRAFT CHOICES
Round	Name	Pos.	College
2	Johnthan Banks	DB	Mississippi St.
3	Mike Glennon	QB	North Carolina St.
4	Akeem Spence	DT	Illinois
	William Gholston	DE	Michigan St.
5	Steven Means	DE	Buffalo
6	Mike James	RB	Miami

2012 TEAM RECORD

PRESEASON (2-2)

Date	Result		Opponent
08/10	W	20-7	at Miami
08/17	L	7-30	Tennessee
08/24	W	30-28	New England
08/29	L	3-30	at Washington

REGULAR SEASON (7-9)

Date	Result		Opponent
09/09	W	16-10	Carolina
09/16	L	34-41	at New York Giants
09/23	L	10-16	at Dallas
09/30	L	22-24	Washington
10/14	W	38-10	Kansas City
10/21	L	28-35	New Orleans
10/25	W	36-17	at Minnesota
11/04	W	42-32	at Oakland
11/11	W	34-24	San Diego
11/18	W	27-21	at Carolina (OT)
11/25	L	23-24	Atlanta
12/02	L	23-31	at Denver
12/09	L	21-23	Philadelphia
12/16	L	0-41	at New Orleans
12/23	L	13-28	St. Louis
12/30	W	22-17	at Atlanta

SCORE BY PERIODS

Buccaneers	94	77	88	124	6 —	389
Opponents	71	127	73	123	0 —	394

2012 TEAM STATISTICS

	Buccaneers	Opp.
Total First Downs	301	329
Rushing	89	75
Passing	188	226
Penalty	24	28
3rd Down: Made/Att	76/212	88/219
3rd Down Pct.	35.8	40.2
4th Down: Made/Att	7/17	6/14
4th Down Pct.	41.2	42.9
Possession Avg.	30:11	29:49
Total Net Yards	5820	6078
Avg. Per Game	363.8	379.9
Total Plays	1008	1031
Avg. Per Play	5.8	5.9
Net Yards Rushing	1837	1320
Avg. Per Game	114.8	82.5
Total Rushes	416	377
Net Yards Passing	3983	4758
Avg. Per Game	248.9	297.4
Sacked/Yards Lost	26/161	27/193
Gross Yards	4144	4951
Att./Completions	566/311	627/410
Completion Pct.	54.9	65.4
Had Intercepted	17	18
Punts/Average	77/44.7	79/45.1
Net Punting Avg.	77/37.4	79/40.0
Penalties/Yards	101/819	103/851
Fumbles/Ball Lost	16/6	16/8
Touchdowns	44	48
Rushing	13	13
Passing	27	30
Returns	4	5

2012 INDIVIDUAL STATISTICS

PASSING

	Att.	Comp.	Yds.	Pct.	TD	Int.	Tkld.	Rate
Freeman	558	306	4065	54.8	27	17	26/161	81.6
Orlovsky	7	4	51	57.1	0	0	0/0	80.1
Williams	1	1	28	100.0	0	0	0/0	118.8
Buccaneers	566	311	4144	54.9	27	17	26/161	81.8
Opponents	627	410	4951	65.4	30	18	27/193	93.5

SCORING

	TD R	TD P	TD Rt	PAT	FG	Saf	PTS
Barth	0	0	0	39/39	28/33	0	123
Martin	11	1	0	0/0	0/0	0	72
Williams	0	9	0	0/0	0/0	0	54
Jackson	0	8	0	0/0	0/0	0	50
Clark	0	4	0	0/0	0/0	0	24
Blount	2	0	0	0/0	0/0	0	12
Underwood	0	2	0	0/0	0/0	0	12
Barber	0	0	1	0/0	0/0	0	6
Byham	0	1	0	0/0	0/0	0	6
Hayward	0	1	0	0/0	0/0	0	6
L. Johnson	0	0	1	0/0	0/0	0	6
Lorig	0	1	0	0/0	0/0	0	6
Stocker	0	1	0	0/0	0/0	0	6
Wright	0	0	1	0/0	0/0	0	6
Buccaneers	13	27	4	39/39	28/33	0	389
Opponents	13	30	5	45/45	19/28	0	394

2-Pt Conversions: Jackson, Buccaneers 1-4, Opponents 2-3

RUSHING

	No.	Yds	Avg	LG	TD
Martin	319	1454	4.6	70t	11
Blount	41	151	3.7	35	2
Freeman	39	139	3.6	13	0
Ware	11	51	4.6	17	0
Tandy	1	18	18.0	18	0
Benn	3	16	5.3	9	0
Parker	1	7	7.0	7	0
Underwood	1	1	1.0	1	0
Buccaneers	416	1837	4.4	70t	13
Opponents	377	1320	3.5	64t	13

RECEIVING

	No.	Yds	Avg	LG	TD
Jackson	72	1384	19.2	95	8
Williams	63	996	15.8	65	9
Martin	49	472	9.6	64t	1
Clark	47	435	9.3	33	4
Underwood	28	425	15.2	62	2
Stocker	16	165	10.3	33	1
Ware	14	100	7.1	23	0
Lorig	12	83	6.9	16	1
Benn	4	26	6.5	9	0
Byham	3	18	6.0	10	1
C. Owusu	1	24	24.0	24	0
Strouther	1	14	14.0	14	0
Blount	1	2	2.0	2	0
Buccaneers	311	4144	13.3	95	27
Opponents	410	4951	12.1	80t	30

INTERCEPTIONS

	No.	Yds	Avg	LG	TD
Barber	4	160	40.0	78t	1
L. Johnson	3	86	28.7	83t	1
A. Black	2	34	17.0	34	0
Wright	1	60	60.0	60t	1
McDonald	1	40	40.0	40	0
David	1	27	27.0	27	0
Barron	1	12	12.0	12	0
Biggers	1	0	0.0	0	0
Foster	1	0	0.0	0	0
Gorrer	1	0	0.0	0	0
L. Lewis	1	0	0.0	0	0
Talib	1	0	0.0	0	0
Buccaneers	18	419	23.3	83t	3
Opponents	17	269	15.8	74t	3

PUNTING

	No.	Yds.	Avg.	In 20	LG
Koenen	76	3440	45.3	22	64
Buccaneers	77	3440	44.7	22	64
Opponents	79	3563	45.1	21	66

PUNT RETURNS

	Ret	FC	Yds	Avg	LG	TD
Parrish	30	15	298	9.9	39	0
Shipley	3	1	10	3.3	9	0
Strouther	3	3	16	5.3	13	0
Buccaneers	36	19	324	9.0	39	0
Opponents	40	16	440	11.0	45	0

KICKOFF RETURNS

	No.	Yds	Avg	LG	TD
Benn	13	306	23.5	55	0
L. Lewis	5	106	21.2	33	0
Parrish	4	86	21.5	25	0
Smith	3	55	18.3	23	0
Underwood	2	47	23.5	25	0
Ware	2	25	12.5	18	0
A. Black	1	3	3.0	3	0
Jackson	1	2	2.0	2	0
Buccaneers	31	630	20.3	55	0
Opponents	27	680	25.2	44	0

FIELD GOALS

	1-19	20-29	30-39	40-49	50+
Barth	0/0	7/7	3/4	12/13	6/9
Buccaneers	0/0	7/7	3/4	12/13	6/9
Opponents	0/0	9/10	8/10	1/5	1/3

SACKS

	No.
Bennett	9.0
McCoy	5.0
Te'o-Nesheim	4.0
Bowers	3.0
David	2.0
Foster	2.0
Barber	1.0
Biggers	1.0
Buccaneers	27.0
Opponents	26.0

RECORD HOLDERS
INDIVIDUAL RECORDS—CAREER

Category	Name	Performance
Rushing (Yds.)	James Wilder, 1981-89	5,957
Passing (Yds.)	Vinny Testaverde, 1987-1992	14,820
Passing (TDs)	Josh Freeman, 2009-2012	78
Receiving (No.)	James Wilder, 1981-89	430
Receiving (Yds.)	Mark Carrier, 1987-1992	5,018
Interceptions	Ronde Barber, 1997-2012	47
Punting (Avg.)	Michael Koenen, 2011-12	45.2
Punt Return (Avg.)	Clifton Smith, 2008	14.1
Kickoff Return (Avg.)	Aaron Stecker, 2000-03	23.8
Field Goals	Martin Gramatica, 1999-2004	137
Touchdowns (Tot.)	Mike Alstott, 1996-2006	71
Points	Martin Gramatica, 1999-2004	592
*Sacks	Warren Sapp, 1995-2003	77.0

INDIVIDUAL RECORDS—SINGLE SEASON

Category	Name	Performance
Rushing (Yds.)	James Wilder, 1984	1,544
Passing (Yds.)	Josh Freeman, 2012	4,065
Passing (TDs)	Josh Freeman, 2012	27
Receiving (No.)	Keyshawn Johnson, 2001	106
Receiving (Yds.)	Mark Carrier, 1989	1,422
Interceptions	Ronde Barber, 2001	10
Punting (Avg.)	Josh Bidwell, 2005	45.6
Punt Return (Avg.)	Karl Williams, 1996	21.1
Kickoff Return (Avg.)	Sammie Stroughter, 2009	29.5
Field Goals	Martin Gramatica, 2002	32
	Matt Bryant, 2008	32
Touchdowns (Tot.)	James Wilder, 1984	13
Points	Matt Bryant, 2008	131
*Sacks	Warren Sapp, 2000	16.5

INDIVIDUAL RECORDS—SINGLE GAME

Category	Name	Performance
Rushing (Yds.)	Doug Martin, 11-4-12	251
Passing (Yds.)	Doug Williams, 11-16-80	486
Passing (TDs)	Steve DeBerg, 9-13-87	5
	Brad Johnson, 11-3-02	5
	Josh Freeman, 12-26-10	5
Receiving (No.)	James Wilder, 9-15-85	13
	Earnest Graham, 10-21-07	13
Receiving (Yds.)	Vincent Jackson, 10-21-12	216
Interceptions	Ronde Barber, 12-23-01, 12-4-05	3
	Aqib Talib, 9-21-08	3
Field Goals	Martin Gramatica, 12-29-02	5
Touchdowns (Tot.)	Jimmie Giles, 10-20-85	4
	Doug Martin, 11-4-12	4
Points	Jimmie Giles, 10-20-85	24
*Sacks	Marcus Jones, 10-19-00	4.0
	Simeon Rice, 10-12-03	4.0

Sacks became an official statistic in 1982.

2013 VETERAN ROSTER

No.	Name	Pos.	Ht.	Wt.	Birthdate	NFL Exp.	College	Hometown	How Acq.	'12 Games/ Starts
24	Barron, Mark	S	6-2	213	10/27/89	2	Alabama	Mobile, Ala.	D1a-'12	16/16
10	Barth, Connor	K	5-11	200	4/11/86	6	North Carolina	Wilmington, N.C.	FA-'09	15/0
43	Black, Ahmad	S	5-9	184	12/12/89	2	Florida	Lakeland, Fla.	D5-'11	16/1
91	Bowers, Da'Quan	DE	6-4	288	2/23/90	3	Clemson	Bamberg, S.C.	D2-'11	10/0
82	Byham, Nate	TE	6-4	264	6/27/88	4	Pittsburgh	Franklin, Pa.	FA-'12	11/2
52	Casillas, Jonathan	LB	6-1	227	6/3/87	5	Wisconsin	New Brunswick, N.J.	UFA(NO)-'13	14/1*
#Clark, Dallas		TE	6-3	252	6/12/79	11	Iowa	Bode, Iowa	FA-'12	16/7
94	Clayborn, Adrian	DE	6-3	280	7/6/88	3	Iowa	St. Louis, Mo.	D1-'11	3/3
84	Crabtree, Tom	TE	6-4	245	11/4/85	4	Miami (Ohio)	Carroll, Ohio	FA-'13	14/6*
51	Cutrera, Jacob	LB	6-3	238	5/18/88	4	Louisiana State	Lafayette, La.	FA-'11	8/0
54	David, Lavonte	LB	6-1	233	1/23/90	2	Nebraska	Miami, Fla.	D2-'12	16/16
t- Demps, Jeff		RB	5-7	191	1/8/90	2	Florida	Groveland, Fla.	FA-'12	0*
69	Dotson, Demar	T	6-9	315	10/11/85	5	Southern Miss	Alexandria, La.	FA-'09	16/15
89	Douglas, David	WR	6-1	205	6/27/89	2	Arizona	McKinney, Texas	FA-'12	1/0
48	Economos, Andrew	LS	6-1	250	6/24/82	8	Georgia Tech	Atlanta, Ga.	FA-'06	16/0
59	Foster, Mason	LB	6-1	241	3/1/89	3	Washington	Seaside, Calif.	D3-'11	16/16
5	Freeman, Josh	QB	6-6	240	1/13/88	5	Kansas State	Kansas City, Mo.	D1-'09	16/16
26	Gaitor, Anthony	CB	5-10	182	10/9/88	3	Florida International	Miami, Fla.	D7a-'11	4/2
95	Gibson, Gary	DT	6-3	312	5/5/82	8	Rutgers	Lafayette, N.Y.	UFA(StL)-'12	16/1
38	Goldson, Dashon	S	6-2	200	9/18/84	7	Washington	Carson, Calif.	UFA(SF)-'13	16/16*
53	Goode, Najee	LB	6-0	244	6/4/89	2	West Virginia	Cleveland, Ohio	D5-'12	2/0
36	Gorrer, Danny	CB	6-0	180	6/1/86	4	Texas A&M	Port Arthur, Texas	W(Sea)-'12	6/1
35	Grimm, Cody	S	5-11	200	2/26/87	4	Virginia Tech	Fairfax, Va.	D7-'10	9/0
57	Hayward, Adam	LB	6-1	240	6/23/84	7	Portland State	Westminster, Calif.	D6-'07	16/5
8	Henry, Chas	P	6-3	219	1/6/89	2	Florida	Dallas, Ga.	FA-'13	3/0*
83	Jackson, Vincent	WR	6-5	230	1/14/83	9	Northern Colorado	Colorado Springs, Colo.	UFA(SD)-'12	16/16
29	Johnson, Leonard	CB	5-10	200	3/30/90	2	Iowa State	Clearwater, Fla.	FA-'12	16/6
75	Joseph, Davin	G	6-3	313	11/22/83	8	Oklahoma	Hallandale, Fla.	D1-'06	0*
9	Koenen, Michael	P	5-11	198	7/13/82	9	Western Washington	Ferndale, Wash.	UFA(Atl)-'11	16/0
90	Landri, Derek	DT	6-2	290	9/21/83	7	Notre Dame	Concord, Calif.	UFA(Phil)-'13	16/7*
62	Larsen, Ted	C/G	6-2	305	6/13/87	4	North Carolina State	Palm Harbor, Fla.	W(NE)-'10	16/13
30	Leonard, Brian	RB	6-1	225	2/3/84	7	Rutgers	Gouverneur, N.Y.	UFA(Cin)-'13	15/0*
78	Levingston, Lazarius	DT	6-4	292	11/16/87	3	Louisiana State	Ruston, La.	FA-'12	3/0
23	Lewis, Myron	CB	6-2	203	11/24/87	4	Vanderbilt	Pompano Beach, Fla.	D3-'10	9/0
41	Lorig, Erik	FB/TE	6-4	250	11/17/86	4	Stanford	Palos Verdes, Calif.	D7c-'10	16/8
22	Martin, Doug	RB	5-9	215	1/13/89	2	Boise State	Oakland, Calif.	D1b-'12	16/16
97	Masifilo, Matthew	DT	6-3	280	10/1/89	2	Stanford	Ewa Beach, Hawaii	FA-'12	0*
#McDonald, Brandon		CB	5-11	185	8/26/85	7	Memphis	Collins, Miss.	FA-'12	11/0
93	McCoy, Gerald	DT	6-4	300	2/25/88	4	Oklahoma	Oklahoma City, Okla.	D1-'10	16/16
79	Meredith, Jamon	T	6-5	312	5/11/86	5	South Carolina	Simpsonville, S.C.	UFA(Pitt)-'12	14/12
87	Miller, Zach	TE	6-5	236	10/4/84	4	Nebraska-Omaha	Wahoo, Neb.	FA-'13	0*
98	Morgan, Aaron	DE	6-4	250	9/24/88	4	Louisiana-Monroe	Amite, La.	FA-'12	11/0*
77	Nicks, Carl	G	6-5	349	5/14/85	6	Nebraska	Salinas, Calif.	UFA(NO)-'12	7/7
86	Noble, Danny	TE	6-5	248	3/30/89	2	Toledo	Elyria, Ohio	FA-'12	4/0
85	Ogletree, Kevin	WR	6-1	198	8/5/87	5	Virginia	Queens, N.Y.	UFA(Dall)-'13	15/1*
6	Orlovsky, Dan	QB	6-5	230	8/18/83	9	Connecticut	Shelton, Conn.	UFA(Ind)-'12	1/0
80	Owusu, Chris	WR	6-2	200	1/6/90	2	Stanford	Westlake Village, Calif.	FA-'12	5/0
#Parrish, Roscoe		PR/WR	5-9	175	7/16/82	9	Miami	Miami, Fla.	FA-'12	13/0
70	Penn, Donald	T	6-5	340	4/27/83	8	Utah State	Playa Del Rey, Calif.	FA-'06	16/16
t- Revis, Darrelle		CB	5-11	198	7/14/85	7	Pittsburgh	Aliquippa, Pa.	T(NYJ)-'13	2/2*
34	Smith, Michael	RB	5-9	205	8/9/88	2	Utah State	Tucson, Ariz.	FA-'12	1/0
12	Smith, Steve	WR	5-11	195	5/6/85	7	Southern California	Anchorage, Alaska	UFA(StL)-'13	9/2*
88	Stocker, Luke	TE	6-5	253	7/7/88	3	Tennessee	Berea, Ky.	D4-'11	16/10
#Stroughter, Sammie		WR	5-10	189	1/3/86	5	Oregon State	Sacramento, Calif.	D7b-'09	2/0
37	Tandy, Keith	DB	5-10	205	2/12/89	2	West Virginia	Hopkinsville, Ky.	D6-'12	9/0
50	Te'o-Nesheim, Daniel	DE	6-3	263	6/12/87	4	Washington	Kameula, Hawaii	FA-'11	16/13
11	Underwood, Tiquan	WR	6-1	183	2/17/87	5	Rutgers	Lawrenceville, N.J.	FA-'12	15/3
74	Wallace, Cody	C/G	6-4	300	11/26/84	4	Texas A&M	Cuero, Texas	W(Hou)-'12	8/0
56	Watson, Dekoda	LB	6-2	240	3/3/88	4	Florida State	Aiken, S.C.	D7b-'10	16/0
92	White, Markus	DE	6-4	284	11/25/87	3	Florida State	West Palm Beach, Fla.	FA-'12	3/0*
19	Williams, Mike	WR	6-2	212	5/18/87	4	Syracuse	Buffalo, N.Y.	D4-'10	16/16
21	Wright, Eric	CB	5-10	200	7/24/85	7	Nevada-Las Vegas	San Francisco, Calif.	UFA(Det)-'12	10/10
72	Wynn, Desmond	G/T	6-6	303	2/23/89	2	Rutgers	Wilmington, Del.	FA-'12	0*
76	Zuttah, Jeremy	G/C	6-4	308	6/1/86	6	Rutgers	Edison, N.J.	D3-'08	16/16

* Casillas played 14 games with New Orleans in '12; Demps missed '12 season because of injury with New England; Goldson played 16 games with San Francisco; Henry played three games with Philadelphia; Joseph missed '12 season because of injury; Landri played 16 games with Philadelphia; Leonard played 15 games with Cincinnati; Masifilo inactive for seven games; Miller missed '12 season because of injury; Morgan played four games with Jacksonville and seven games with Tampa Bay; Ogletree played 15 games with Dallas; Revis played two games with the New York Jets; S. Smith played nine games with St. Louis; White played one game with Washington; Wynn missed '12 season because of injury.

\# Unrestricted Free Agent; subject to developments.

t- Buccaneers traded for Demps (NE), Revis (NYJ).

Traded—WR Arrelious Benn (8 games in '12) to Philadelphia, RB LeGarrette Blount (13 games) to New England, CB Aqib Talib (4 games) to New England.

Retired—Ronde Barber, 17-year cornerback, 16 games in '12.

Players lost through free agency (4): DE Michael Bennett (Sea; 16 games in '12), CB E.J. Biggers (Wash; 13), DT Roy Miller (Jax; 15), T Jeremy Trueblood (Wash; 9).

Also played with Buccaneers in '12—G Roger Allen (5 games), G/T Derek Hardman (3), WR Corvey Irvin (12), DE George Johnson (5), CB LeQuan Lewis (5), WR Preston Parker (2), WR Jordan Shipley (1).

FIRST-YEAR ROSTER

Name	Pos.	Ht.	Wt.	Birthdate	College	Hometown	How Acq.
Baker, Sean (1)	S	5-11	210	11/6/88	Ball State	Youngstown, Ohio	FA-'12
Banks, Johnthan	CB	6-2	186	10/3/89	Mississippi State	Maben, Miss.	D2
Carr, Deveron	CB	5-11	190	8/10/90	Arizona State	Scottsdale, Ariz.	FA
Clebert, Richard (1)	NT	6-0	303	11/15/85	South Florida	Miami, Fla.	FA
DePaola, Andrew (1)	LS	6-1	216	7/28/87	Rutgers	Parkton, Md.	FA
Dunsmore, Drake (1)	TE	6-3	245	11/4/88	Northwestern	Lenexa, Kan.	D7b-'12
Holland, Joe (1)	LB	6-1	231	8/20/88	Purdue	Indianapolis, Ind.	FA-'12
Gholston, William	DE	6-6	273	7/31/91	Michigan State	Detroit, Mich.	D4b
Glennon, Mike	QB	6-6	222	12/12/89	North Carolina State	Centreville, Va.	D3
James, Mike	RB	5-10	223	4/13/91	Miami	Haines City, Fla.	D6
Johnson, Jerry	WR	6-2	207	8/1/90	UCLA	Los Angeles, Calif.	FA
Landi, Evan	TE	6-3	240	4/15/90	South Florida	Coral Springs, Fla.	FA
Means, Steven	DE	6-4	257	6/16/90	Buffalo	Buffalo, N.Y.	D5
Melvin, Rashaan	CB	6-2	192	10/2/89	Northern Illinois	Waukegan, Ill.	FA
Monroe, D.J.	WR	5-8	175	7/9/89	Texas	Angleton, Texas	FA
Moseley, Willie	LB	6-4	232	5/18/90	Buffalo	Richmond, Va.	FA
Owusu, Ernest (1)	DE	6-4	277	5/26/88	California	Nashville, Tenn.	FA-'12
Page, Eric (1)	WR	5-9	183	9/23/91	Toledo	Toledo, Ohio	FA
Remmers, Mike (1)	T	6-5	300	4/11/89	Oregon State	Portland, Ore.	FA-'12
Rogers, James (1)	CB	6-0	182	5/27/89	Michigan	Detroit, Mich.	FA-'12
Saenz, Nick (1)	DB	6-0	195	2/23/90	Houston	Houston, Texas	FA-'12
Schwab, Brice	T	6-6	303	10/4/89	Arizona State	West Sunbury, Pa.	FA
Shavers, Akeem	RB	5-10	198	1/8/90	Purdue	Texarkana, Texas	FA
Smith, Adam	G	6-5	322	4/9/90	Western Kentucky	Murfreesboro, Tenn.	FA
Smith, Branden	CB	5-11	172	12/19/89	Georgia	Atlanta, Ga.	FA
Speller, Nick	T	6-5	300	9/4/89	Massachusetts	Baltimore, Md.	FA
Spence, Akeem	DT	6-1	306	11/29/91	Illinois	Fort Walton Beach, Fla.	D4a
Jason Weaver	T	6-4	313	4/12/89	Southern Miss	New Orleans, La.	FA
Weber, Adam (1)	QB	6-1	209	8/3/87	Minnesota	Arden Hills, Minn	FA-'12
Wynn, Desmond (1)	G	6-5	313	2/23/89	Rutgers	Wilmington, Del.	FA-'12
Wright, Tim	WR	6-3	219	4/7/90	Rutgers	Wall Township, N.J.	FA

The term NFL Rookie is defined as a player who is in his first season of professional football and has not been on the roster of another professional football team for any regular-season or postseason games. A Rookie is designated by an "R" on NFL rosters. Players who have been active in another professional football league or players who have NFL experience, including either preseason training camp or being on an Active List or Inactive List, or on Reserve/Injured or Reserve/Physically Unable to Perform for fewer than six regular-season games, are termed NFL First-Year Players. An NFL First-Year Player is designated by a "1" on NFL rosters. Thereafter, a player is credited with an additional year of experience for each season in which he accumulates six games on the Active List or Inactive List, or on Reserve/Injured or Reserve/Physically Unable to Perform.

Log on to www.buccaneers.com for an up-to-date roster.

COACHING STAFF

Head Coach,
Greg Schiano

Pro Career: Named the ninth head coach in franchise history on January 27, 2012, Greg Schiano enters his second season at the helm. In his first season leading Tampa Bay, Schiano's impact was evident in all three phases of the game while instilling a culture change within the organization. He transformed a team that had lost its final 10 games of 2011 into a competitive 7-9 club—tied for second place in the NFC South—with seven of those losses being decided by one score or less. Schiano's seven wins in his debut season marked the second-most by a Buccaneers first-year head coach. Prior to his time in Tampa, Schiano spent 21 seasons as a college coach, including 12 seasons as the head coach for Rutgers, leading the Scarlet Knights to unprecedented levels of success. Career record: 7-9.

Background: Played linebacker at Bucknell (1986-88). Coached at Ramapo High School (NJ) in 1988 before serving a season at Rutgers (1989 graduate assistant) followed by six seasons at Penn State (1990 graduate assistant and 1991-95 defensive backfield). After three years with the Chicago Bears, Schiano spent two seasons at Miami as defensive coordinator (1998-99) before becoming the Rutgers head coach (2000-2011).

Personal: Born on June 1, 1966 in Wyckoff, N.J. He and his wife, Christy, have four children: Joey, John, Matt, and Lena Kate.

ASSISTANT COACHES

Brian Angelichio, tight ends; born December 27, 1972, Ilion, N.Y. Linebacker St. Lawrence 1991-95. No pro playing experience. College coach: SUNY-Brockport 1995, Ithaca 1996-2005, Pittsburgh 2006-2010, Rutgers 2011. Pro coach: Joined Buccaneers in 2012.

Bob Bostad, offensive line; born September 7, 1966, Pardeeville, Wisc. Linebacker UW-Stevens Point 1986-89. No pro playing experience. College coach: UW-Stevens Point 1990-91, Minnesota 1992-94, Cal State-Northridge 1995-96, San Jose State 1997-98, New Mexico 1999-2005, Wisconsin 2006-2011. Pro coach: Joined Buccaneers in 2012.

Jay Butler, head strength and conditioning; born September 10, 1969, Hillsborough, N.J. Offensive tackle Bucknell 1988-1991. No pro playing experience. College coach: East Carolina 1992-95, Dartmouth 1996-2000, Rutgers 2001-2011. Pro coach: Joined Buccaneers in 2012.

Earnest Byner, running backs; born September 15, 1962, Milledgeville, Ga. Running back East Carolina 1980-1993. Pro running back Cleveland Browns 1984-88, 1994-95, Washington Redskins 1989-1993, Baltimore Ravens 1996-97. Pro coach: Washington Redskins 2004-07, Tennessee Titans 2008-09, Jacksonville Jaguars 2010-11, joined Buccaneers in 2012.

Bryan Cox, pass rush specialist; born February 17, 1968, East St. Louis, Ill. Linebacker Western Illinois 1987-1990. Pro linebacker Miami Dolphins 1991-95, Chicago Bears 1996-97, New York Jets 1998-2000, New England Patriots 2001, New Orleans Saints 2002. Pro coach: New York Jets 2006-08, Cleveland Browns 2009-2010, Miami Dolphins 2011, joined Buccaneers in 2012.

Bob Fraser, asst. defensive coordinator; born January 18, 1963, Pittsburgh, Pa. Defensive lineman Allegheny 1981-84. No pro playing experience. College coach: Allegheny 1985-86, 1989-1991, 1997-2005, Rutgers 1987-88, 2006-2011, Holy Cross 1992-95, Northeastern 1996. Pro coach: Joined Buccaneers in 2012.

Phil Galiano, asst. special teams; born September 8, 1977, Norristown, Pa. Safety Shippensburg 1997-99. No pro playing experience. College coach: Dickinson 2000, New Haven 2001, Villanova 2002, Rutgers 2003-06, 2010-11, Florida International 2007-09. Pro coach: Joined Buccaneers in 2012.

John Garrett, wide receivers; born March 2, 1965, Danville, Pa. Wide receiver Columbia 1983-85, Princeton 1986-87. Pro wide receiver Cincinnati Bengals 1989, Buffalo Bills 1991, San Antonio Riders (World League) 1991. College coach: Virginia 2004-06. Pro coach: Cincinnati Bengals 1995-98, 2001-02, Arizona Cardinals 1999-2000, Dallas Cowboys 2007-2012, joined Buccaneers in 2013.

Jeff Hafley, secondary-safeties; born April 4, 1979, Montvale, N.J. Wide receiver Siena 1997-2000. No pro playing experience. College coach: Worcester Polytechnic 2001, Albany 2002-05, Pittsburgh 2006-2010, Rutgers 2011. Pro coach: Joined Buccaneers in 2012.

Steve Loney, asst. offensive line; born April 26, 1952, Marshalltown, Iowa. Offensive lineman Iowa State 1970-73. No pro playing experience. College coach: Iowa State 1974, 1995-97, 2000-01, Missouri Western State 1975-76, Morehead State 1979-1983, The Citadel 1984-86, Colorado State 1989-1992, Connecticut 1994, Minnesota 1998-99, Drake 2007. Pro coach: Phoenix Cardinals 1993, Minnesota Vikings 2002-2005, Arizona Cardinals 2006, St. Louis Rams 2008-2011, joined Buccaneers 2012.

Tem Lukabu, defensive assistant; born August 6, 1981, Avenel, N.J. Linebacker Colgate 2002-04. No pro playing experience. College coach: Rhode Island 2008-09, Rutgers 2010-11. Pro coach: Joined Buccaneers in 2012.

Ben McDaniels, offensive assistant; born June 6, 1980, Barberton, Ohio. Quarterback Kent State 1999-2001. No pro playing experience. College coach: Minnesota 2004-05. Pro coach: Denver Broncos 2009-2010, joined Buccaneers 2012.

John McNulty, quarterbacks; born May 29, 1968, Scranton, Pa. Safety Penn State 1988-1990. No pro playing experience. College coach: Michigan 1991-94, Connecticut 1995-97, Rutgers 2004-08. Pro coach: Jacksonville Jaguars 1998-2002, Dallas Cowboys 2003, Arizona Cardinals 2009-2012, joined Buccaneers in 2013.

Randy Melvin, defensive line; born April 3, 1959, Aurora, Ill. Defensive line Eastern Illinois 1978-1981. No pro playing experience. College coach: Eastern Illinois 1988-1994, Wyoming 1995-96, Purdue 1997-99, Rutgers 2002-04, 2010, Temple 2009. Pro coach: New England Patriots 2000-01, Cleveland Browns 2005-08, British Columbia Lions (CFL) 2011, joined Buccaneers in 2012.

Tony Oden, secondary-cornerbacks; born June 30, 1973, Cleveland, Ohio. Linebacker Baldwin-Wallace College 1991-95. No pro playing experience. College coach: Millersville (Pa.) 1996, Boston College 1997, Army 1998-99, East Carolina 2000-02, Eastern Michigan 2003. Pro coach: Houston Texans 2004-05, New Orleans Saints 2006-2011, Jacksonville Jaguars 2012, joined Buccaneers in 2012.

Jimmy Raye, senior offensive assistant; born March 26, 1946, Fayetteville, N.C. Quarterback Michigan State 1965-67. Pro quarterback Philadelphia Eagles 1969. College coach: Michigan State 1971-75, Wyoming 1976. Pro coach: San Francisco 49ers 1977, 2009-2010, Detroit Lions 1978-79, Atlanta Falcons 1980-82, 1987-89, Los Angeles Rams 1983-84, 1991, Tampa Bay Buccaneers 1985-86, New England Patriots 1990, Kansas City Chiefs 1992-2000, Washington Redskins 2001, New York Jets 2002-03, 2006-08, Oakland Raiders 2004-05, re-joined Buccaneers in 2012.

Bill Sheridan, defensive coordinator; born January 27, 1959, Detroit, Mich. Linebacker Grand Valley State 1977-1981. No pro playing experience. College coach: Michigan 1985-86, 2002-04, Maine 1987-88, Cincinnati 1989-1991, Army 1992-97, Michigan State 1998-2000. Pro coach: New York Giants 2005-09, Miami Dolphins 2010-11, joined Buccaneers in 2012.

Robb Smith, linebackers; born May 10, 1975, Pittsburgh, Pa. Safety Allegheny 1993-97. No pro playing experience. College coach: Iowa 1999-2001, Maine 2002-08, Rutgers 2009-2012. Pro coach: Joined Buccaneers in 2012.

Mike Sullivan, offensive coordinator; born January 28, 1967, Santa Maria, Calif. Defensive back Army 1986-89. No pro playing experience. College coach: Humboldt State 1993-94, Army 1995-96, 1999-2000, Youngstown State 1997-98, Ohio 2001. Pro coach: Jacksonville Jaguars 2002-03, New York Giants 2004-2011, joined Buccaneers in 2012.

Joe Vaughn, asst. strength and conditioning; born November 14, 1982, Del City, Okla. Center Northeastern Oklahoma 2001-02, Kansas 2003-04. No pro playing experience. College coach: Kansas 2006, 2007-2011, Oklahoma 2007. Pro coach: Joined Buccaneers in 2012.

Dave Wannstedt, special teams coordinator; born May 21 1952, Baldwin, Pa. Tackle Pittsburgh 1970-73. No pro playing experience. College coach: Pittsburgh 1975-78, 2005-2010 (head coach 2005-2010), Oklahoma State 1979-1982, Southern California 1983-85, Miami 1986-88. Pro coach: Dallas Cowboys 1989-1992, Chicago Bears 1993-98 (head coach), Miami Dolphins 1999-2004 (head coach 2000-04), Buffalo Bills 2011-12, joined Buccaneers in 2013.

**National Football Conference
East Division**
Team Colors: Burgundy and Gold
Redskins Park
21300 Redskins Park Drive
Ashburn, Virginia 20147
Telephone: (703) 726-7000

2013 SCHEDULE
PRESEASON
Aug. 8	at Tennessee	8:00
Aug. 19	**Pittsburgh**	8:00
Aug. 24	**Buffalo**	4:30
Aug. 29	at Tampa Bay	7:30

REGULAR SEASON
Sep. 9	**Philadelphia** (Mon)	7:10
Sep. 15	at Green Bay	1:00
Sep. 22	**Detroit**	1:00
Sep. 29	at Oakland	4:25
Oct. 6	BYE	
Oct. 13	at Dallas	8:30
Oct. 20	**Chicago**	1:00
Oct. 27	at Denver	4:25
Nov. 3	**San Diego**	1:00
Nov. 7	at Minnesota (Thurs)	8:25
Nov. 17	at Philadelphia	1:00
Nov. 25	**San Francisco** (Mon)	8:40
Dec. 1	**New York Giants**	*8:30
Dec. 8	**Kansas City**	1:00
Dec. 15	at Atlanta	1:00
Dec. 22	**Dallas**	1:00
Dec. 29	at New York	1:00

*All times ET; Sunday night games in
Weeks 11-16 subject to change*
Stadium: FedExField (opened in 1997)
  • **Capacity:** 85,000
    1600 FedEx Way
    Landover, Maryland 20785
Playing Surface: Natural Grass
Training Camp: Bon Secours Washington
    Redskins Training Center
    Richmond, Virginia 23220

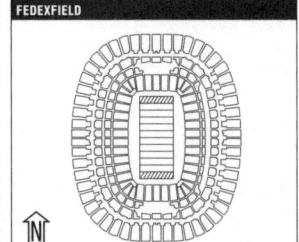

FEDEXFIELD

CLUB OFFICIALS
Owner: Daniel M. Snyder
Executive Vice President/General
  Manager: Bruce Allen
Executive Vice President/Head Coach:
  Mike Shanahan
Chief Marketing Officer: Mitch Gershman
President, Business Operations:
  Dennis Greene
Senior Vice President, Executive
  Producer of Media: Larry Michael
Senior Vice President, Stadium
  Operations: Lon Rosenberg
Senior Vice President, Chief Strategy
  Officer: Shripal Shah
Senior Vice President, Communications:
  Tony Wyllie
Vice President, Football Administration/
  General Counsel: Eric Schaffer
Vice President, Corporate Controller:
  Stephen Choi
Vice President, Sales: Jason Friedman
Vice President, Sales and Marketing:
  Nancy Hubacher
Vice President, Information Technology:
  Asheesh Kinra
Vice President, Sales and Marketing:
  Rod Nenner
Vice President, Ticket Operations:
  Jeff Ritter
Vice President, Business Operations and
  Executive Entertainment:
  John Schlieman
Vice President, Sales, Marketing and
  Strategic Alliances: Scott Shepherd
Vice President, Finance: Joe Smilari
Vice President, Administration:
  Aaron Waller
Director of Player Personnel:
  Scott Campbell
Director of Pro Personnel:
  Morocco Brown
Pro Scouts: Richard Mann II, Alex Santos
College Scouts: Tim Gribble, Kyle Smith,
  Cole Spencer, David Whittington,
  Jim Zeches
BLESTO Scout: Darryl Franklin
Director of Football Operations: Paul Kelly
Senior Executive: A.J. Smith
Director of Player Development:
  Malcolm Blacken
Executive Director, Washington Redskins
  Charitable Foundation: Jane Rodgers
Head Athletic Trainer: Larry Hess
Assistant Athletic Trainers: Elliott Jermyn,
  Eli Bisnett-Cobb, Kyle Blackman
Video Director: Mike Bracken
Video Department: Zachary Kennedy,
  Mike Adams
Equipment Manager: Brad Berlin
Assistant Equipment Manager:
  Anders Beutel, Darwin Beacham
Assistant Director of Communications:
  Daniel Sampson
Communications Manager: Ross Taylor
Corporate Communications:
  Angela Alfano

COACHING HISTORY
Boston 1932-36
(585-551-27)
Records include postseason games
1932	Lud Wray	4-4-2
1933-34	William (Lone Star) Dietz	11-11-2
1935	Eddie Casey	2-8-1
1936-1942	Ray Flaherty	56-23-3
1943	Arthur (Dutch) Bergman	7-4-1
1944-45	Dudley DeGroot	14-6-1
1946-48	Glen (Turk) Edwards	16-18-1
1949	John Whelchel*	3-3-1
1949-1951	Herman Ball**	4-16-0
1951	Dick Todd	5-4-0
1952-53	Earl (Curly) Lambeau	10-13-1
1954-58	Joe Kuharich	26-32-2
1959-1960	Mike Nixon	4-18-2
1961-65	Bill McPeak	21-46-3
1966-68	Otto Graham	17-22-3
1969	Vince Lombardi	7-5-2
1970	Bill Austin	6-8-0
1971-77	George Allen	69-35-1
1978-1980	Jack Pardee	24-24-0
1981-1992	Joe Gibbs	140-65-0
1993	Richie Petitbon	4-12-0
1994-2000	Norv Turner***	50-60-1
2000	Terry Robiskie	1-2-0
2001	Marty Schottenheimer	8-8-0
2002-03	Steve Spurrier	12-20-0
2004-07	Joe Gibbs	31-36-0
2008-09	Jim Zorn	12-20-0
2010-12	Mike Shanahan	21-28-0

*Released after seven games in 1949
**Released after three games in 1951
***Released after 13 games in 2000

PAID ATTENDANCE
Home 571,591   Away 530,615
Total 1,102,206
Single-game home record,
  90,910 (12/30/07)
Single-season home record,
  * 711,471 (2007)
NFL Record

2013 DRAFT CHOICES
Round	Name	Pos.	College
2	David Amerson	DB	North Carolina St.
3	Jordan Reed	TE	Florida
4	Phillip Thomas	DB	Fresno St.
5	Chris Thompson	RB	Florida St.
	Brandon Jenkins	LB	Florida St.
6	Bacarri Rambo	DB	Georgia
7	Jawan Jamison	RB	Rutgers

2012 TEAM RECORD
PRESEASON (3-1)

Date	Result		Opponent
08/09	W	7-6	at Buffalo
08/18	L	31-33	at Chicago
08/25	W	30-17	Indianapolis
08/29	W	30-3	Tampa Bay

REGULAR SEASON (10-6)

Date	Result		Opponent
09/09	W	40-32	at New Orleans
09/16	L	28-31	at St. Louis
09/23	L	31-38	Cincinnati
09/30	W	24-22	at Tampa Bay
10/07	L	17-24	Atlanta
10/14	W	38-26	Minnesota
10/21	L	23-27	at New York Giants
10/28	L	12-27	at Pittsburgh
11/04	L	13-21	Carolina
11/18	W	31-6	Philadelphia
11/22	W	38-31	at Dallas
12/03	W	17-16	New York Giants
12/09	W	31-28	Baltimore (OT)
12/16	W	38-21	at Cleveland
12/23	W	27-20	at Philadelphia
12/30	W	28-18	Dallas

POSTSEASON (0-1)

Date	Result		Opponent
01/06	L	14-24	Seattle

(OT) Overtime

SCORE BY PERIODS

Redskins	79	138	95	121	3 —	436
Opponents	80	114	46	148	0 —	388

2012 TEAM STATISTICS

	Redskins	Opp.
Total First Downs	341	340
Rushing	144	89
Passing	171	223
Penalty	26	28
3rd Down: Made/Att	68/190	95/215
3rd Down Pct.	35.8	44.2
4th Down: Made/Att	12/17	8/14
4th Down Pct.	70.6	57.1
Possession Avg.	31:05	28:55
Total Net Yards	6131	6043
Avg. Per Game	383.2	377.7
Total Plays	994	1031
Avg. Per Play	6.2	5.9
Net Yards Rushing	2709	1532
Avg. Per Game	169.3	95.8
Total Rushes	519	363
Net Yards Passing	3422	4511
Avg. Per Game	213.9	281.9
Sacked/Yards Lost	33/244	32/209
Gross Yards	3666	4720
Att./Completions	442/291	636/393
Completion Pct.	65.8	61.8
Had Intercepted	8	21
Punts/Average	70/42.6	65/46.4
Net Punting Avg.	70/37.2	65/39.4
Penalties/Yards	116/985	100/811
Fumbles/Ball Lost	26/6	17/10
Touchdowns	52	43
Rushing	22	11
Passing	24	31
Returns	6	1

2012 INDIVIDUAL STATISTICS

PASSING

PASSING	Att.	Comp.	Yds.	Pct.	TD	Int.	Tkld.	Rate
Griffin III	393	258	3200	65.6	20	5	30/217	102.4
Cousins	48	33	466	68.8	4	3	3/27	101.6
Morgan	1	0	0	0.0	0	0	0/0	39.6
Redskins	442	291	3666	65.8	24	8	33/244	102.1
Opponents	636	393	4720	61.8	31	21	32/209	87.0

SCORING

SCORING	TD R	TD P	TD Rt	PAT	FG	Saf	PTS
Forbath	0	0	0	33/34	17/18	0	84
A. Morris	13	0	0	0/0	0/0	0	78
Moss	0	8	0	0/0	0/0	0	48
Griffin III	7	0	0	0/0	0/0	0	42
Cundiff	0	0	0	17/17	7/12	0	38
Garcon	0	4	1	0/0	0/0	0	30
Hankerson	0	3	0	0/0	0/0	0	18
Morgan	0	2	1	0/0	0/0	0	18
A. Robinson	0	3	0	0/0	0/0	0	18
Royster	2	0	0	0/0	0/0	0	12
Young	0	2	0	0/0	0/0	0	12
R. Jackson	0	0	1	0/0	0/0	0	6
Kerrigan	0	0	1	0/0	0/0	0	6
Paul	0	1	0	0/0	0/0	0	6
Paulsen	0	1	0	0/0	0/0	0	6
M. Williams	0	0	1	0/0	0/0	0	6
J. Wilson	0	0	1	0/0	0/0	0	6
Cousins	0	0	0	0/0	0/0	0	2
Redskins	22	24	6	50/51	24/30	0	436
Opponents	11	31	1	36/36	28/30	0	388

RUSHING

RUSHING	No.	Yds	Avg	LG	TD
A. Morris	335	1613	4.8	39t	13
Griffin III	120	815	6.8	76t	7
Royster	23	88	3.8	12	2
Young	14	60	4.3	16	0
Banks	7	36	5.1	21	0
Morgan	3	25	8.3	9	0
Cousins	3	22	7.3	17	0
Moss	3	14	4.7	12	0
A. Robinson	1	14	14.0	14	0
Garcon	2	9	4.5	7	0
Grant	1	5	5.0	5	0
Hankerson	2	5	2.5	3	0
Helu	2	2	1.0	1	0
Briscoe	1	1	1.0	1	0
F. Davis	1	1	1.0	1	0
Paul	1	-1	-1.0	-1	0
Redskins	519	2709	5.2	76t	22
Opponents	363	1532	4.2	53	11

RECEIVING

RECEIVING	No.	Yds	Avg	LG	TD
Morgan	48	510	10.6	32	2
Garcon	44	633	14.4	88t	4
Moss	41	573	14.0	77t	0
Hankerson	38	543	14.3	68t	3
Paulsen	25	308	12.3	31	1
F. Davis	24	325	13.5	29	0
Royster	15	109	7.3	25	0
A. Robinson	11	237	21.5	68t	3
A. Morris	11	77	7.0	20	0
Paul	8	152	19.0	37	1
Young	8	109	13.6	28	2
Banks	8	15	1.9	8	0
Helu	7	45	6.4	21	0
Briscoe	2	22	11.0	14	0
Cooley	1	8	8.0	8	0
Redskins	291	3666	12.6	88t	24
Opponents	393	4720	12.0	85t	31

INTERCEPTIONS

INTERCEPTIONS	No.	Yds	Avg	LG	TD
Fletcher	5	29	5.8	10	0
Hall	4	62	15.5	27	0
R. Jackson	4	19	4.8	17	1
J. Wilson	2	8	4.0	7	0
Gomes	1	49	49.0	49	0
Kerrigan	1	28	28.0	28t	1
Meriweather	1	25	25.0	25	0
M. Williams	1	24	24.0	24t	1
Crawford	1	12	12.0	12	0
Doughty	1	1	1.0	1	0
Redskins	21	257	12.2	49	3
Opponents	8	142	17.8	41	0

PUNTING

PUNTING	No.	Yds.	Avg.	In 20	LG
Rocca	68	2984	43.9	22	61
Redskins	70	2984	42.6	22	61
Opponents	65	3018	46.4	23	66

PUNT RETURNS

PUNT RETURNS	Ret	FC	Yds	Avg	LG	TD
Banks	26	5	178	6.8	27	0
Crawford	8	2	156	19.5	64	0
Hall	1	0	0	0.0	0	0
J. Wilson	1	0	1	1.0	1	0
Redskins	36	7	335	9.3	64	0
Opponents	39	19	320	8.2	39	0

KICKOFF RETURNS

KICKOFF RETURNS	No.	Yds	Avg	LG	TD
Banks	22	527	24.0	55	0
Paul	13	283	21.8	48	0
Royster	2	39	19.5	22	0
Hall	1	43	43.0	43	0
Redskins	38	892	23.5	55	0
Opponents	55	1264	23.0	48	0

FIELD GOALS

FIELD GOALS	1-19	20-29	30-39	40-49	50+
Forbath	0/0	3/3	2/3	11/11	1/1
Cundiff	0/0	1/1	3/5	3/4	0/2
Redskins	0/0	4/4	5/8	14/15	1/3
Opponents	0/0	6/6	10/10	8/9	4/5

SACKS

SACKS	No.
Kerrigan	8.5
R. Jackson	4.5
Riley	3.5
Fletcher	3.0
Alexander	2.5
Cofield	2.5
Bowen	1.0
Hall	1.0
Orakpo	1.0
Pugh	1.0
M. Williams	1.0
J. Wilson	1.0
(group)	1.0
C. Wilson	0.5
Redskins	32.0
Opponents	33.0

RECORD HOLDERS
INDIVIDUAL RECORDS—CAREER

Category	Name	Performance
Rushing (Yds.)	John Riggins, 1976-79, 1981-85	7,472
Passing (Yds.)	Joe Theismann, 1974-1985	25,206
Passing (TDs)	Sammy Baugh, 1937-1952	187
Receiving (No.)	Art Monk, 1980-1993	888
Receiving (Yds.)	Art Monk, 1980-1993	12,026
Interceptions	Darrell Green, 1983-2001	54
Punting (Avg.)	Sammy Baugh, 1937-1952	45.1
Punt Return (Avg.)	Johnny Williams, 1952-53	12.8
Kickoff Return (Avg.)	Bobby Mitchell, 1962-68	28.5
Field Goals	Mark Moseley, 1974-1986	263
Touchdowns (Tot.)	Charley Taylor, 1964-1977	90
Points	Mark Moseley, 1974-1986	1,206
*Sacks	Dexter Manley, 1981-89	91.0

INDIVIDUAL RECORDS—SINGLE SEASON

Category	Name	Performance
Rushing (Yds.)	Alfred Morris, 2012	1,613
Passing (Yds.)	Jay Schroeder, 1986	4,109
Passing (TDs)	Sonny Jurgensen, 1967	31
Receiving (No.)	Art Monk, 1984	106
Receiving (Yds.)	Santana Moss, 2005	1,483
Interceptions	Dan Sandifer, 1948	13
Punting (Avg.)	Sammy Baugh, 1940	**51.4
Punt Return (Avg.)	Johnny Williams, 1952	15.3
Kickoff Return (Avg.)	Mike Nelms, 1981	29.7
Field Goals	Mark Moseley, 1983	33
Touchdowns (Tot.)	John Riggins, 1983	24
Points	Mark Moseley, 1983	161
*Sacks	Dexter Manley, 1986	18.5

INDIVIDUAL RECORDS—SINGLE GAME

Category	Name	Performance
Rushing (Yds.)	Gerald Riggs, 9-17-89	221
Passing (Yds.)	Brad Johnson, 12-26-99	471
Passing (TDs)	Sammy Baugh, 10-31-43, 11-23-47	6
	Mark Rypien, 11-10-91	6
Receiving (No.)	Roy Helu, 11-6-11	14
Receiving (Yds.)	Anthony Allen, 10-4-87	255
Interceptions	Sammy Baugh, 11-14-43	**4
	Dan Sandifer, 10-31-48	**4
	DeAngelo Hall, 10-24-10	**4
Field Goals	Many times	5
	Last time by Shaun Suisham, 11-4-07	
Touchdowns (Tot.)	Dick James, 12-17-61	4
	Larry Brown, 12-16-73	4
Points	Dick James, 12-17-61	24
	Larry Brown, 12-16-73	24
*Sacks	Dexter Manley, 10-2-88	4.0
	Ken Harvey, 11-23-97	4.0
	Phillip Daniels, 12-18-05	4.0
	Brian Orakpo, 12-13-09	4.0

*Sacks became an official statistic in 1982.
**NFL Record

2013 VETERAN ROSTER

No.	Name	Pos.	Ht.	Wt.	Birthdate	NFL Exp.	College	Hometown	How Acq.	'12 Games/Starts
92	Baker, Chris	NT	6-2	333	10/8/87	2	Hampton	Windsor, Conn.	FA-'11	14/0
48	Bernstine, Jordan	S	5-11	214	5/31/89	2	Iowa	Des Moines, Iowa	D7b-'12	1/0
30	Biggers, E.J.	CB	6-0	185	6/13/87	5	Western Michigan	North Miami Beach, Fla.	UFA(TB)-'13	13/12*
72	Bowen, Stephen	DE	6-5	310	3/28/84	8	Hofstra	Dix Hills, N.Y.	UFA(Dall)-'11	16/16
45	Boyce, Dorson	FB	6-2	249	6/25/88	2	Washington	Queens, N.Y.	FA-'12	0*
97	Brace, Ron	NT	6-3	330	12/18/86	5	Boston College	Worcester, Mass.	FA-'13	10/0*
19	Briscoe, Dezmon	WR	6-2	210	8/31/89	3	Kansas	Dallas, Texas	W(TB)-'12	7/0
94	Carriker, Adam	DE	6-6	305	5/6/84	7	Nebraska	Kennewick, Wash.	T(StL)-'10	2/2
66	Chester, Chris	G	6-3	309	1/12/83	8	Oklahoma	Tustin, Calif.	UFA(Balt)-'11	16/16
96	Cofield, Barry	NT	6-4	318	3/19/84	8	Northwestern	Cleveland Heights, Ohio	UFA(NYG)-'11	16/16
12	Cousins, Kirk	QB	6-3	209	8/19/88	2	Michigan State	Holland, Mich.	D4a-'12	3/1
20	Crawford, Richard	CB	5-11	188	8/1/90	2	Southern Methodist	Oceanside, Calif.	D7a-'12	10/0
83	Davis, Fred	TE	6-4	247	1/15/86	6	Southern California	Toledo, Ohio	D2b-'08	7/7
38	Davis, Tristan	RB	5-10	211	5/5/86	2	Auburn	East Point, Ga.	FA-'11	0*
37	Doughty, Reed	S	6-1	206	11/4/82	8	Northern Colorado	Johnstown, Colo.	D6-'06	16/10
59	Fletcher, London	LB	5-10	242	5/19/75	16	John Carroll	Cleveland, Ohio	UFA(Buff)-'07	16/16
2	Forbath, Kai	K	5-11	197	9/2/87	2	UCLA	Sherman Oaks, Calif.	FA-'12	11/0
88	Garçon, Pierre	WR	6-0	212	8/8/86	6	Mount Union	Greenacres, Fla.	UFA(Ind)-'12	10/10
73	Gettis, Adam	G	6-2	292	12/9/88	2	Iowa	Frankfort, Ill.	D5-'12	0*
64	Golston, Kedric	DL	6-4	318	5/30/83	8	Georgia	Tyrone, Ga.	D6-'06	16/0
24	Gomes, DeJon	S	6-0	201	11/17/89	3	Nebraska	Union City, Calif.	D5a-'11	15/4
10	Griffin III, Robert	QB	6-2	217	2/12/90	2	Baylor	Copperas Cove, Texas	D1-'12	15/15
8	Grossman, Rex	QB	6-1	225	8/23/80	11	Florida	Bloomington, Ind.	UFA(Hou)-'10	0*
23	Hall, DeAngelo	CB	5-10	193	11/19/83	10	Virginia Tech	Chesapeake, Va.	FA-'08	16/16
85	Hankerson, Leonard	WR	6-2	211	1/30/89	3	Miami	Fort Lauderdale, Fla.	D3-'11	16/6
29	Helu, Jr., Roy	RB	5-11	215	12/7/88	3	Nebraska	Danville, Calif.	D4-'11	3/0
34	Holland, Devin	S	6-0	205	10/18/88	2	McNeese State	Baton Rouge, La.	FA-'12	0*
79	Hurt, Maurice	G/T	6-3	329	11/8/87	3	Florida	Milledgeville, Ga.	D7b-'11	13/1
50	Jackson, Rob	LB	6-4	266	11/3/85	5	Kansas State	West Haven, Conn.	D7b-'08	16/14
99	Jenkins, Jarvis	DE	6-4	315	4/24/88	3	Clemson	Central, S.C.	D2-'11	16/14
53	Kehl, Bryan	LB	6-2	243	6/16/84	6	Brigham Young	Cottonwood Heights, Utah	W(KC)-'12	8/0*
91	Kerrigan, Ryan	LB	6-4	260	8/16/88	3	Purdue	Muncie, Ind.	D1-'11	16/16
67	LeRibeus, Josh	G	6-2	315	7/2/89	2	Southern Methodist	Richardson, Texas	D3-'12	5/0
78	Lichtensteiger, Kory	G	6-2	284	3/22/85	5	Bowling Green	Convoy, Ohio	FA-'10	16/16
72	Matthews, Kevin	C	6-3	302	2/4/87	3	Texas A&M	Sugar Land, Texas	FA-'13	14/2*
31	Meriweather, Brandon	S	5-11	197	1/14/84	7	Miami	Apopka, Fla.	UFA(Chi)-'12	1/1
93	Merling, Phillip	DE	6-5	315	4/19/85	4	Clemson	Fork Union, Va.	FA-'12	3/0*
25	Minnifield, Chase	CB	6-0	186	3/31/89	2	Virginia	Lexington, Ky.	FA-'12	0*
63	Montgomery, Will	OL	6-3	304	2/13/83	8	Virginia Tech	Clifton, Va.	FA-'08	16/16
15	Morgan, Joshua	WR	6-1	220	6/20/85	6	Virginia Tech	Washington, D.C.	UFA(SF)-'12	16/15
46	Morris, Alfred	RB	5-10	218	12/12/88	2	Florida Atlantic	Pensacola, Fla.	D6a-'12	16/16
89	Moss, Santana	WR	5-10	189	6/1/79	13	Miami	Carol City, Fla.	T(NYJ)-'05	16/1
55	Muckelroy, Roddrick	LB	6-2	250	10/27/86	4	Texas	Hallsville, Texas	FA-'12	5/0*
45	Murphy, Jerome	CB	6-0	200	1/13/87	3	South Florida	Elizabeth, N.J.	FA-'12	5/0
95	Neild, Chris	NT	6-2	325	12/1/87	3	West Virginia	Stroudsburg, Pa.	D7d-'11	0*
98	Orakpo, Brian	LB	6-4	257	7/31/86	5	Texas	Houston, Texas	D1-'09	2/2
77	Pashos, Tony	T	6-6	325	8/3/80	10	Illinois	Lockport, Ill.	FA-'13	0*
84	Paul, Niles	TE	6-1	233	8/9/89	3	Nebraska	Omaha, Neb.	D5b-'11	16/4
82	Paulsen, Logan	TE	6-5	261	2/26/87	4	UCLA	West Hills, Calif.	FA-'10	16/10
74	Polumbus, Tyler	T	6-8	305	4/10/85	5	Colorado	Englewood, Colo.	FA-'11	15/15
32	Pugh, Jordan	S	5-11	210	1/29/88	4	Texas A&M	Plano, Texas	FA-'12	13/0
56	Riley, Perry	LB	6-0	238	5/3/88	4	Louisiana State	Stone Mountain, Ga.	D4-'10	16/16
11	Robinson, Aldrick	WR	5-10	181	11/24/88	2	Southern Methodist	Waxahachie, Texas	D6b-'11	15/1
52	Robinson, Keenan	LB	6-3	238	7/7/89	2	Texas	Plano, Texas	D4b-'12	11/0
6	Rocca, Sav	P	6-5	263	11/20/73	7	Lakeside	Reservoir, Australia	UFA(Phil)-'11	16/0
22	Royster, Evan	RB	6-1	216	11/26/87	3	Penn State	Chantilly, Va.	D6a-'11	16/0
58	So'oto, Vic	LB	6-3	263	8/19/87	3	Brigham Young	Carlsbad, Calif.	FA-'12	5/0*
57	Sundberg, Nick	LS	6-0	251	7/29/87	4	California	Phoenix, Ariz.	FA-'10	8/0
54	Tapp, Darryl	LB	6-1	270	9/13/84	8	Virginia Tech	Chesapeake, Va.	UFA(Phil)-'13	13/0*
69	Trueblood, Jeremy	T	6-8	320	5/10/83	8	Boston College	Indianapolis, Ind.	UFA(TB)-'13	9/1*
5	White, Pat	QB	6-0	190	2/25/86	2	West Virginia	Daphne, Ala.	FA-'13	0*
25	Williams, Keiland	RB	5-11	230	8/14/86	4	Louisiana State	Lafayette, La.	FA-'12	14/0*
71	Williams, Trent	T	6-5	325	7/19/88	4	Oklahoma	Longview, Texas	D1-'10	16/16
26	Wilson, Josh	CB	5-9	188	3/11/85	7	Maryland	Upper Marlboro, Md.	UFA(Balt)-'11	16/16
90	Worthington, Doug	DE	6-5	311	8/10/87	2	Ohio State	Athol Springs, N.Y.	W(TB)-'11	6/0
36	Young, Darrel	FB	5-11	251	4/8/87	4	Villanova	Amityville, N.Y.	FA-'10	16/8

* Biggers played 13 games with Tampa Bay in '12; Boyce missed '12 season because of injury; Brace played 10 games with New England; T. Davis missed '12 season because of injury; Gettis inactive for 16 games; Grossman inactive for 14 games, did not play in two games; Holland last active with Tampa Bay in '11; Kehl played three games with Kansas City and five games with Washington; Matthews played 14 games with Tennessee; Merling played three games with Green Bay; Minnifield missed '12 season because of injury; Muckelroy played five games with Cincinnati; Neild missed '12 season because of injury; Pashos last active with Cleveland in '11; So'oto played one game with Green Bay and four games with Oakland; Tapp played 13 games with Philadelphia; Trueblood played nine games with Tampa Bay; White last active with Miami in '09; K. Williams played five games with Detroit and nine games with Washington

Players lost through free agency (1): LB Lorenzo Alexander (Ariz; 16 games in '12).

Also played with Redskins in '12—LB Mario Addison (5 games), WR Brandon Banks (12), T Jordan Black (14), CB Crezdon Butler (2), TE Chris Cooley (9), K Billy Cundiff (5), RB Ryan Grant (1), CB Cedric Griffin (9), CB D.J. Johnson (7), CB David Jones (5), LS Justin Snow (8), LB Markus White (2), S Madieu Williams (16).

FIRST-YEAR ROSTER

Name	Pos.	Ht.	Wt.	Birthdate	College	Hometown	How Acq.
Amerson, David	CB	6-1	205	12/8/91	North Carolina State	Greensboro, N.C.	D2
Anunoby, Chigbo (1)	DL	6-4	324	1/4/89	Morehouse	Jefferson City, Mo.	FA-'12
Ashworth, Jacolby	OL	6-3	300	8/29/90	Houston	Lufkin, Texas	FA
Burdette, Marvin	LB	5-11	230	9/9/90	Alabama-Birmingham	Batesville, Miss.	FA
Compton, Tom (1)	T	6-5	308	5/10/89	South Dakota	Rosemount, Minn.	D6b-'12
Compton, Will	LB	6-2	230	9/19/89	Nebraska	Bonne Terre, Mo.	FA
Dawson, Skye	WR	5-9	183	12/2/90	Texas Christian	Mesquite, Texas	FA
Elmore, Ricky (1)	LB	6-2	255	2/1/88	Arizona	Simi Valley, Calif.	FA-'12
Hamilton, Dominique (1)	DL	6-5	315	1/18/89	Missouri	El Paso, Texas	FA-'12
Jamison, Jawan	RB	5-7	203	11/23/91	Rutgers	Starke, Fla.	D7
Jenkins, Brandon	LB	6-2	251	2/9/90	Florida State	Tallahassee, Fla.	D5b
Kettani, Eric (1)	FB	5-11	240	3/26/87	Navy	Mentor, Ohio	FA-'12
Kimbrough, Jeremy	LB	5-11	240	5/22/91	Appalachian State	Ellenwood, Ga.	FA
Lewis, Lance (1)	WR	6-2	207	11/1/88	East Carolina	Concord, N.C.	FA
Nixon, Xavier	OL	6-6	314	9/17/90	Florida	Fayetteville, N.C.	FA
Ogbuehi, Emmanuel	TE	6-3	235	8/17/90	Georgia State	Hoschton, Ga.	FA
Peterson, Deangelo (1)	TE	6-3	243	1/11/89	Louisiana State	New Orleans, La.	FA-'12
Rambo, Bacarri	S	6-0	215	6/27/90	Georgia	Donalsonville, Ga.	D6
Reed, Jordan	TE	6-3	243	7/3/90	Florida	New London, Conn.	D3
Reeves, Chip	WR	5-10	176	12/24/89	Troy	Stone Mountain, Ga.	FA
Stevens, Tevita	OL	6-1	306	7/4/87	Utah	Hemet, Calif.	FA
Thomas, Phillip	S	6-0	210	3/1/89	Fresno State	Bakersfield, Calif.	D4
Thompson, Chris	RB	5-8	187	10/20/90	Florida State	Madison, Fla.	D5a
Williams, Nick	WR	5-10	184	11/23/90	Connecticut	Princeton, N.J.	FA

The term NFL Rookie is defined as a player who is in his first season of professional football and has not been on the roster of another professional football team for any regular-season or postseason games. A Rookie is designated by an "R" on NFL rosters. Players who have been active in another professional football league or players who have NFL experience, including either preseason training camp or being on an Active List or Inactive List, or on Reserve/Injured or Reserve/Physically Unable to Perform for fewer than six regular-season games, are termed NFL First-Year Players. An NFL First-Year Player is designated by a "1" on NFL rosters. Thereafter, a player is credited with an additional year of experience for each season in which he accumulates six games on the Active List or Inactive List, or on Reserve/Injured or Reserve/Physically Unable to Perform.

Log on to www.redskins.com for an up-to-date roster.

COACHING STAFF
Head Coach,
Mike Shanahan

Pro Career: Became the 28th coach in franchise history when he replaced Jim Zorn on January 6, 2010. Mike Shanahan joined the Redskins after spending 14 seasons as head coach of the Denver Broncos (1995-2008). Shanahan led the Broncos to back-to-back Super Bowl championships in 1997 and 1998, becoming just the fifth head coach to accomplish that feat, and is the only coach to win seven consecutive postseason games in a two-year period. During his NFL career, Shanahan has been a part of teams that have played in nine conference championship games and six Super Bowls. In 32 seasons as a pro and college coach, Shanahan's teams have participated in postseason or bowl games 23 times. Under Shanahan's guidance, Denver set then-NFL records by posting the most victories in both a two-year (33, 1997-98) and three-year (46, 1996-98) span. In 17 years (14 with Denver and three as offensive coordinator with the San Francisco 49ers), Shanahan's offenses finished number one in the NFL four times, second three times and third twice. Shanahan was an assistant with Denver (1984-87, 1989-1991) and San Francisco (1992-94). Returned to Denver as quarterbacks coach on October 6, 1989, after posting 8-12 record as the Los Angeles Raiders' head coach. Career record: 175-131.

Background: Shanahan coached at Oklahoma (1975-76), Northern Arizona (1977), Eastern Illinois (1978), Minnesota (1979), and Florida (1980-83).

Personal: Born in Oak Park, Illinois, on August 24, 1952. He was a wishbone quarterback/defensive back at Eastern Illinois. Mike and his wife, Peggy, have two children—Kyle and Krystal.

ASSISTANT COACHES

Jacob Burney, defensive line; born January 24, 1959, Chattanooga, Tenn. Defensive tackle Tennessee-Chattanooga 1977-1980. No pro playing experience. College coach: New Mexico 1983-86, Tulsa 1987, Mississippi State 1988, Wisconsin 1989, UCLA 1990-92, Tennessee 1993. Pro coach: Cleveland Browns/Baltimore Ravens 1994-98, Carolina Panthers 1999-2001, Denver Broncos 2002-08, joined Redskins 2010.

Keith Burns, special teams; born May 16, 1972, Greeleyville, S.C. Linebacker Oklahoma State 1992-93. Pro linebacker Denver Broncos 1994-98, Chicago Bears 1999, Denver Broncos 2000-03, 2005-06, Tampa Bay Buccaneers 2004. Pro coach: Denver Broncos 2007-2012, joined Redskins in 2013.

Chad Englehart, asst. strength and conditioning; born June 5, 1981, New Orleans, La. Attended Southeastern Louisiana. No college or pro playing experience. College coach: New Orleans 2006. Pro coach: Florida Tuskers (UFL) 2009, joined Redskins in 2010.

Richmond Flowers, coaching assistant; born May 4, 1978, Birmingham, Ala. Wide receiver Duke 1996, 1998-99, Tennessee-Chattanooga 2000. Pro wide receiver Dallas Cowboys 2001, Washington Redskins 2002. Pro coach: joined Redskins in 2010.

Chris Foerster, offensive line; born October 12, 1961, Milwaukee, Wisc. Center Colorado State 1979-1982. No pro playing experience. College coach: Colorado State 1983-87, Stanford 1988-1991, Minnesota 1992. Pro coach: Minnesota Vikings 1993-95, Tampa Bay Buccaneers 1996-2001, Indianapolis Colts 2002-03, Miami Dolphins 2004, Baltimore Ravens 2005-07, San Francisco 49ers 2008-09, joined Redskins in 2010.

Jim Haslett, defensive coordinator; born December 9, 1955, Pittsburgh, Pa. Defensive end Indiana (Pa.) 1975-78. Pro linebacker Buffalo Bills 1979-1986, N.Y. Jets 1987. College coach: Buffalo 1988-1990. Pro coach: Sacramento Surge (NFLE) 1991-92, Los Angeles Raiders 1993-94, New Orleans Saints 1995-96, Pittsburgh Steelers 1997-99, New Orleans Saints 2000-05 (head coach), St. Louis Rams 2006-08 (head coach 2008), Florida Tuskers (UFL head coach 2009), joined Redskins in 2010.

Richard Hightower, asst. defensive backs/asst. special teams; born September 15, 1980, Houston, Texas. Wide receiver/defensive back Texas 1998-2002. No pro playing experience. College coach: Minnesota 2009. Pro coach: Houston Texans 2006-08, joined Redskins in 2010.

Matt LaFleur, quarterbacks; born November 3, 1979, Mt. Pleasant, Mich. Quarterback/wide receiver Western Michigan 1998-99, Saginaw Valley State 2000-02. Pro quarterback Omaha Beef (NIFL) 2002, Billings Outlaws (NIFL) 2002. College coach: Saginaw Valley State 2003, Central Michigan 2004-05, Northern Michigan 2006, Ashland 2007. Pro coach: Houston Texans 2008-09, joined Redskins in 2010.

Mike McDaniel, wide receivers; born March 6, 1983, Greeley, Colo. Wide receiver Yale 2001-04. No pro playing experience. Pro coach: Houston Texans 2006-08, California Redwoods (UFL) 2009, Sacramento Mountain Lions (UFL) 2010, joined Redskins in 2011.

Sean McVay, tight ends; born January 24, 1986, Marietta, Ga. Wide receiver Miami (Ohio) 2004-07. No pro playing experience. Pro coach: Tampa Bay Buccaneers 2008, Florida Tuskers (UFL) 2009, joined Redskins in 2010.

Chris Morgan, asst. offensive line; born September 24, 1976, Killeen, Texas. Offensive lineman Colorado 1996-99. No pro playing experience. College coach: Idaho 2003. Pro coach: Oakland Raiders 2009-2010, joined Redskins in 2011.

Raheem Morris, defensive backs; born September 3, 1976, Irvington, N.J. Safety Hofstra 1994-97. No pro playing experience. College coach: Hofstra 1998, 2000-01, Cornell 1999, Kansas State 2006. Pro coach: Tampa Bay Buccaneers 2002-05, 2007-2011 (head coach 2009-2011), joined Redskins in 2012.

Aubrey Pleasant, offensive assistant; born August 20, 1986; Safety Wisconsin 2005-08. No pro playing experience. College coach: Michigan 2011-12. Pro coach: Joined Redskins in 2013.

Kyle Shanahan, offensive coordinator; born December 14, 1979, Minneapolis,. Minn. Wide receiver Duke 1998-99, Texas 2000-02. No pro playing experience. College coach: UCLA 2003. Pro coach: Tampa Bay Buccaneers 2004-05, Houston Texans 2006-09, joined Redskins in 2010.

Bob Slowik, linebackers; born May 16, 1954, Pittsburgh, Pa. Defensive back Delaware 1973-76. No pro playing experience. College coach: Delaware 1978, Florida 1979-1982, Drake 1983, Rutgers 1984-89, East Carolina 1990-91. Pro coach: Dallas Cowboys 1992, Chicago Bears 1993-98, Cleveland Browns 1999, Green Bay Packers 2000-04, Denver Broncos 2005-2008, joined Redskins 2010.

Bobby Slowik, defensive assistant; born June 7, 1987, Princeton, N.J. Wide receiver Michigan Tech 2005-09. No pro playing experience. Pro coach: Joined Redskins in 2011.

Bobby Turner, asst. head coach/running backs; born May 6, 1949, East Chicago, Ind. Defensive back Indiana State 1968-1971. No pro playing experience. College coach: Indiana State 1975-1982, Fresno State 1983-88, Ohio State 1989-1990, Purdue 1991-94. Pro coach: Denver Broncos 1995-2009, joined Redskins in 2010.

Ray Wright, strength and conditioning; born December 30, 1971, Fort Worth, Texas. Running back/wide receiver Duke 1990-95. No pro playing experience. College coach: Cornell 2000, Maryland 2001. Pro coach: Houston Texans 2002-09, joined Washington in 2010.

2012 Season in Review

2012 TRADES (since May 1)

Tight end **Kellen Winslow** from Tampa Bay to Seattle for an unannounced future selection. (5/22)

Defensive back **Cassius Vaughn** from Denver to Indianapolis for fullback **Chris Gronkowski**. (5/23)

Defensive tackle **Ollie Ogbu** from Indianapolis to Philadelphia for defensive back **Domonique Johnson**. (7/22)

Wide receiver **Louis Murphy** from Oakland to Carolina for an unannounced future selection (#219). (7/24)

Tackle **Jeff Otah** from Carolina to New York Jets for an unannounced future selection. (7/24)

Defensive tackle **Brian Price** from Tampa Bay to Chicago for an unannounced future selection (#226). (7/27)

Linebacker **Moise Fokou** and linebacker **Greg Lloyd** from Philadelphia to Indianapolis for defensive back **Kevin Thomas** and an unannounced future selection. (8/3)

Linebacker **Barrett Ruud** from St. Louis to Indianapolis for an unannounced selection. (8/21)

Defensive back **Josh Gordy** from Seattle to New Orleans for an unannounced selection (G **Ryan Seymour**). (8/22)

Defensive back **Vontae Davis** from Miami to Indianapolis for an unannounced selection. (8/27)

Quarterback **Tarvaris Jackson** from Seattle to Buffalo for an unannounced selection (#214). (8/27)

Defensive back **Kevin Barnes** from Washington to Detroit for an unannounced selection. (8/27)

Tackle **Jason Smith** from St. Louis to New York Jets for tackle **Wayne Hunter**. (8/29)

Center **Ryan Cook** from Miami to Dallas for an unannounced selection. (8/31)

Fullback **Tyler Clutts** from Chicago to Houston for defensive back **Sherrick McManis**. (8/31)

Defensive back **Colin Jones** from San Francisco to Carolina for an unannounced future selection. (8/31)

Defensive back **David Sims** and an unannounced selection from Cleveland to Philadelphia for an unannounced future selection (DE **Joe Kruger**). (8/31)

Defensive back **A.J. Jefferson** and for an unannounced selection from Arizona to Minnesota for an unannounced future selection (LB **Michael Mauti**). (9/1)

Wide receiver **Greg Salas** from St. Louis to New England for an unannounced future selection. (9/1)

Wide receiver **Mike Thomas** from Jacksonville to Detroit for an unannounced future selection. (10/31)

Defensive back **Aqib Talib** and an unannounced selection from Tampa Bay (DE **Michael Buchanan**) to New England for an unannounced future selection (DE **William Gholston**). (11/1)

* Draft choice number is listed if club later traded the pick.

2013 TRADES

Quarterback **Alex Smith** from San Francisco to Kansas City for Chiefs' 2013 second-round selection (#34) and an unannounced selection. (3/12)

Wide receiver **Anquan Boldin** from Baltimore to San Francisco for 49ers' 2013 sixth-round selection (#199). (3/12)

Wide receiver **Percy Harvin** from Minnesota to Seattle for the Seahawks' 2013 first-round selection (DB **Xavier Rhodes**), Bills' 2013 seventh-round selection (G **Travis Bond**), and an unannounced selection. (3/12)

Wide receiver **Arrelious Benn** and the Buccaneers' 2013 seventh-round selection (DB **Jordan Poyer**) from Tampa Bay to Philadelphia for two unannounced selections. (3/16)

Defensive end **Clifton Geathers** from Indianapolis to Philadelphia for running back **Stanley Havili**. (3/28)

Quarterback **Matt Flynn** from Seattle to Oakland for the Raiders' 2013 fifth-round selection (DB **Tharold Simon**) and an unannounced selection. (4/1)

Quarterback **Colt McCoy** and the Eagles' 2013 sixth-round selection from Cleveland to San Francisco for the 49ers' 2013 fifth-round selection (#164) and Bengals' 2013 seventh-round selection (T **Garrett Gilkey**). (4/2)

Quarterback **Carson Palmer** and the Panthers' 2013 seventh-round selection (#219) from Oakland to Arizona for the Titans' 2013 sixth-round selection (#176) and an unannounced selection. (4/2)

Linebacker **Emmanuel Acho** from Cleveland to Philadelphia for running back **Dion Lewis**. (4/11)

Defensive back **Darrelle Revis** from the New York Jets to Tampa Bay for the Buccaneers' 2013 first-round selection (DT **Sheldon Richardson**) and an unannounced selection. (4/22)

Oakland trades Raiders' 2013 first-round selection (DE **Dion Jordan**) from Oakland to Miami for the Dolphins' 2013

first-round selection (DB **D.J. Hayden**) and 2013 second-round selection (T **Menelik Watson**). (4/25)

Buffalo trades Bills' 2013 first-round selection (WR **Tavon Austin**) and 2013 third-round selection (DB **T.J. McDonald**) from Buffalo to St. Louis for the Rams' 2013 first-round selection (QB **E.J. Manuel**), second-round selection (LB **Kiko Alonso**), third-round selection (WR **Marquise Goodwin**), and seventh-round selection (TE **Chris Gragg**). (4/25)

Dallas trades Cowboys' 2013 first-round selection (DB **Eric Reed**) from Dallas to San Francisco for the 49ers' 2013 first-round selection (C **Travis Frederick**) and the Panthers' 2013 third-round selection (WR **Terrance Williams**). (4/25)

St. Louis trades Redskins' 2013 first-round selection (DB **Desmond Trufant**) and Patriots' 2015 seventh-round selection from St. Louis to Atlanta for the Falcons' 2013 first-round selection (LB **Alec Ogletree**), third-round selection (WR **Stedman Bailey**), and sixth-round selection (#198). (4/25)

New England trades Patriots' 2013 first-round selection (WR **Cordarrelle Patterson**) from New England to Minnesota for Vikings' 2013 second-round selection (LB **Jamie Collins**), 2013 third-round selection (DB **Logan Ryan**), Lions' 2013 fourth-round selection (WR **Josh Boyce**), and Vikings' 2013 seventh-round selection (#229). (4/25)

San Francisco trades Chiefs' 2013 second-round selection (WR **Justin Hunter**) from San Francisco to Tennessee for the Titans' 2013 second-round selection (DE **Cornellius Carradine**), 2013 seventh-round selection (#216), and 2014 third-round selection. (4/26)

Arizona trades 2013 second-round selection (LB **Manti Te'o**) from Arizona to San Diego for the Chargers' 2013 second-round selection (LB **Kevin Minter**) and 2013 fourth-round selection (#110). (4/26)

Green Bay trades 2013 second-round selection (TE **Vance McDonald**) from Green Bay to San Francisco for 49ers' 2013 second-round selection (RB **Eddie Lacy**) and Eagles' 2013 sixth-round selection (#173). (4/26)

Seattle trades 2013 second-round selection (LB **Arthur Brown**) from Seattle to Baltimore for Ravens' 2013 second-round selection (running back **Christine Michael**), 2013 fifth-round selection (#165), and 49ers' 2013 sixth-round selection (#199). (4/26)

Miami trades wide receiver **Davone Bess**, Dolphins' 2013 fourth-round selection (#111) and Dolphins' 2013 seventh-round selection (DE **Armonty Bryant**) from Miami to Cleveland for the Browns' 2013 fourth-round selection (LB **Jelani Jenkins**) and 49ers' 2013 fifth-round selection (running back **Mike Gillislee**). (4/26)

Running back **Chris Ivory** from New Orleans to the New York Jets for Jets' 2013 fourth-round selection (#106). (4/26)

Miami trades Bears' 2013 third-round selection (NT **John Jenkins**) from Miami to New Orleans for Jets' 2013 fourth-round selection (TE **Dion Sims**) and Saints' 2013 fourth-round selection (#109).(4/26)

Green Bay trades Packers' 2013 third-round selection (LB **Corey Lemonier**) from Green Bay to San Francisco for 49ers' 2013 third-round selection (#93) and Titans' 2013 seventh-round selection (WR **Charles Johnson**). (4/26)

Green Bay trades 49ers' 2013 third-round selection (DB **Will Davis**) from Green Bay to Miami for Saints' 2013 fourth-round selection (T **David Bakhtiari**), Dolphins' 2013 fifth-round selection (#146), and Cowboys' 2013 seventh-round selection (WR Kevin Dorsey). (4/26)

Jacksonville trades Jaguars' 2013 fourth-round selection (QB **Matt Barkley**) from Jacksonville to Philadelphia for Eagles' 2013 fourth-round selection (WR **Ace Sanders**) and 2013 seventh-round selection (DB **Demetrius McCray**). (4/27)

Oakland trades Raiders' 2013 fourth-round selection (DT **Akeem Spence**) from Oakland to Tampa Bay for Buccaneers' 2013 fourth-round selection (QB **Tyler Wilson**) and 2013 sixth-round selection (running back **Latavius Murray**). (4/27)

Arizona trades Chargers' 2013 fourth-round selection (QB **Ryan Nassib**) from Arizona to the New York Giants for Giants' 2013 fourth-round selection (G **Earl Watford**) and 2013 sixth-round selection (running back **Andre Ellington**). (4/27)

Cleveland trades Dolphins' 2013 fourth-round selection (DB **Shamarko Thomas**) from Cleveland to Pittsburgh for Steelers' 2014 third-round selection. (4/27)

Denver trades Broncos' 2013 fourth-round selection (running back **Johnathan Franklin**) from Denver to Green Bay for Dolphins' 2013 fifth-round selection (DE **Quanterus Smith**) and Eagles' 2013 sixth-round selection (T **Vinston Painter**). (4/27)

Detroit trades Lions' 2013 fifth-round selection (DT **Jesse Williams**) from Detroit to Seattle for Ravens' 2013 fifth-round selection (P **Sam Martin**) and 49ers' 2013 sixth-round selection (running back **Theo Riddick**). (4/27)

Cleveland trades Browns' 2013 fifth-round selection (DT **Montori Hughes**) from Cleveland to Indianapolis for Colts' 2014 fourth-round selection. (4/27)

Chicago trades Bears' 2013 fifth-round selection (DE **Stansly Maponga**) from Chicago to Atlanta for Falcons' 2013 fifth-round selection (T **Jordan Mills**) and 2013 seventh-round selection (WR **Marquess Wilson**). (4/27)

Houston trades Texans' 2013 fifth-round selection (running back **Zac Stacy**) from Houston to St. Louis for Rams' 2013 sixth-round selection (#184) and Falcons' 2013 sixth-round selection (DT **Chris Jones**). (4/27)

Oakland trades Titans' 2013 fifth-round selection (T **David Quessenberry**) from Oakland to Houston for Rams' 2013 sixth-round selection (TE **Mychal Rivera**) and Texans' 2013 seventh-round selection (DE **David Bass**). (4/27)

Running back **LeGarrette Blount** from Tampa Bay to New England for running back **Jeff Demps** and Vikings' 2013 seventh-round selection (#229). (4/27)

Minnesota trades Vikings' 2013 sixth-round selection (running back **Mike James**) from Minnesota to Tampa Bay for Broncos' 2013 sixth-round selection (G **Jeff Baca**) and Vikings' 2013 seventh-round selection (DT **Everett Dawkins**). (4/27)

* Draft choice number is listed if club later traded the pick.

PRESEASON STANDINGS
AMERICAN FOOTBALL CONFERENCE
East Division

	W	L	T	Pct.	Pts.	OP
New England	1	3	0	.250	55	69
Buffalo	0	4	0	.000	59	119
Miami	0	4	0	.000	43	96
New York Jets	0	4	0	.000	31	88

North Division

	W	L	T	Pct.	Pts.	OP
Pittsburgh	3	1	0	.750	104	71
Baltimore	2	2	0	.500	108	92
Cincinnati	2	2	0	.500	70	72
Cleveland	2	2	0	.500	84	82

South Division

	W	L	T	Pct.	Pts.	OP
Houston	3	1	0	.750	101	80
Jacksonville	3	1	0	.750	100	117
Tennessee	3	1	0	.750	89	67
Indianapolis	2	2	0	.500	99	75

West Division

	W	L	T	Pct.	Pts.	OP
San Diego	3	1	0	.750	64	78
Denver	2	2	0	.500	81	75
Kansas City	1	3	0	.250	61	116
Oakland	1	3	0	.250	61	75

AFC PRESEASON RECORDS—TEAM BY TEAM

East Division

BUFFALO (0-4)

6	Washington	7
14	at Minnesota	36
7	Pittsburgh	38
32	at Detroit	38
59		119

MIAMI (0-4)

7	Tampa Bay	20
17	at Carolina	23
6	Atlanta	23
13	at Dallas	30
43		96

NEW ENGLAND (1-3)

7	New Orleans	6
17	Philadelphia	27
28	at Tampa Bay	30
3	at New York Giants	6
55		69

NEW YORK JETS (0-4)

6	at Cincinnati	17
3	New York Giants	26
12	Carolina	17
10	at Philadelphia	28
31		88

North Division

BALTIMORE (2-2)

31	at Atlanta	17
12	Detroit	27
48	Jacksonville	17
17	at St. Louis	31
108		92

CINCINNATI (2-2)

17	New York Jets	6
24	at Atlanta	19
13	Green Bay	27
16	at Indianapolis	20
70		72

CLEVELAND (2-2)

19	at Detroit	17
35	at Green Bay	10
10	Philadelphia	27
20	Chicago	28
84		82

PITTSBURGH (3-1)

23	at Philadelphia	24
26	Indianapolis	24
38	at Buffalo	7
17	Carolina	16
104		71

South Division

HOUSTON (3-1)

26	at Carolina	13
20	San Francisco	9
27	at New Orleans	34
28	Minnesota	24
101		90

INDIANAPOLIS (2-2)

38	St. Louis	3
24	at Pittsburgh	26
17	at Washington	30
20	Cincinnati	16
99		75

JACKSONVILLE (3-1)

32	New York Giants	31
27	at New Orleans	24
17	at Baltimore	48
24	Atlanta	14
100		117

TENNESSEE (3-1)

17	at Seattle	27
30	at Tampa Bay	7
32	Arizona	27
10	New Orleans	6
89		67

West Division

DENVER (2-2)

31	at Chicago	3
10	Seattle	30
24	San Francisco	29
16	at Arizona	13
81		75

KANSAS CITY (1-3)

27	Arizona	17
17	at St. Louis	31
14	Seattle	44
3	at Green Bay	24
61		116

OAKLAND (1-3)

0	Dallas	3
27	at Arizona	31
31	Detroit	20
3	at Seattle	21
61		75

SAN DIEGO (3-1)

21	Green Bay	13
28	Dallas	20
12	at Minnesota	10
3	San Francisco	35
64		78

NFC PRESEASON RECORDS—TEAM BY TEAM

East Division

DALLAS (3-1)

3	at Oakland	0
20	at San Diego	28
20	St. Louis	19
30	Miami	13
73		60

NEW YORK GIANTS (2-2)

31	at Jacksonville	32
26	at New York Jets	3
17	Chicago	20
6	New England	3
80		58

PHILADELPHIA (4-0)

24	Pittsburgh	23
27	at New England	17
27	at Cleveland	10
28	New York Jets	10
106		60

WASHINGTON (3-1)

7	at Buffalo	6
31	at Chicago	33
30	Indianapolis	17
30	Tampa Bay	3
98		59

North Division

CHICAGO (3-1)

3	Denver	31
33	Washington	31
20	at New York Giants	17
28	at Cleveland	20
84		99

DETROIT (2-2)

17	Cleveland	19
27	at Baltimore	12
20	at Oakland	31
38	Buffalo	32
102		94

GREEN BAY (2-2)

13	at San Diego	21
10	Cleveland	35
27	at Cincinnati	13
24	Kansas City	3
74		72

MINNESOTA (1-3)

6	at San Francisco	17
36	Buffalo	14
10	San Diego	12
24	at Houston	28
76		71

South Division

ATLANTA (1-3)

17	Baltimore	31
19	Cincinnati	24
23	at Miami	6
14	at Jacksonville	24
73		85

CAROLINA (2-2)

13	Houston	26
23	Miami	17
17	at New York Jets	12
16	at Pittsburgh	17
69		72

NEW ORLEANS (2-3)

17	vs. Arizona (a)	10
6	at New England	7
24	Jacksonville	27
34	Houston	27
6	at Tennessee	10
87		81

TAMPA BAY (2-2)

20	at Miami	7
7	Tennessee	30
30	New England	28
3	at Washington	30
60		95

West Division

ARIZONA (1-4)

10	vs. New Orleans (a)	17
17	at Kansas City	27
31	Oakland	27
27	at Tennessee	32
13	Denver	16
98		119

ST. LOUIS (2-2)

3	at Indianapolis	38
31	Kansas City	17
19	at Dallas	20
31	Baltimore	17
84		92

SAN FRANCISCO (3-1)

17	Minnesota	6
9	at Houston	20
29	at Denver	24
35	San Diego	3
90		53

SEATTLE (4-0)

27	Tennessee	17
30	at Denver	10
44	at Kansas City	14
21	Oakland	3
122		44

(a) Pro Football Hall of Fame Game, Canton, OH

PRESEASON STANDINGS
NATIONAL FOOTBALL CONFERENCE

East Division

	W	L	T	Pct.	Pts.	OP
Philadelphia	4	0	0	1.000	106	60
Dallas	3	1	0	.750	73	60
Washington	3	1	0	.750	98	59
New York Giants	2	2	0	.500	80	58

North Division

	W	L	T	Pct.	Pts.	OP
Chicago	3	1	0	.750	84	99
Detroit	2	2	0	.500	102	94
Green Bay	2	2	0	.500	74	72
Minnesota	1	3	0	.250	76	71

South Division

	W	L	T	Pct.	Pts.	OP
Carolina	2	2	0	.500	69	72
Tampa Bay	2	2	0	.500	60	95
New Orleans	2	3	0	.400	87	81
Atlanta	1	3	0	.250	73	85

West Division

	W	L	T	Pct.	Pts.	OP
Seattle	4	0	0	1.000	122	44
San Francisco	3	1	0	.750	90	53
St. Louis	2	2	0	.500	84	92
Arizona	1	4	0	.200	98	119

AMERICAN FOOTBALL CONFERENCE

BALTIMORE RAVENS (10-6)
44	Cincinnati	13
23	at Philadelphia	24
31	New England	30
23	Cleveland	16
9	at Kansas City	6
31	Dallas	29
13	at Houston	43
25	at Cleveland	15
55	Oakland	20
13	at Pittsburgh	10
16	at San Diego (OT)	13
20	Pittsburgh	23
28	at Washington (OT)	31
17	Denver	34
33	New York Giants	14
17	at Cincinnati	23
398		**344**

BUFFALO BILLS (6-10)
28	at New York Jets	48
35	Kansas City	17
24	at Cleveland	14
28	New England	52
3	at San Francisco	45
19	at Arizona (OT)	16
34	Tennessee	35
9	at Houston	21
31	at New England	37
19	Miami	14
13	at Indianapolis	20
34	Jacksonville	18
12	St. Louis	15
17	Seattle (Toronto)	50
10	at Miami	24
28	New York Jets	9
344		**435**

CINCINNATI BENGALS (10-6)
13	at Baltimore	44
34	Cleveland	27
38	at Washington	31
27	at Jacksonville	10
13	Miami	17
24	at Cleveland	34
17	Pittsburgh	24
23	Denver	31
31	New York Giants	13
28	at Kansas City	6
34	Oakland	10
20	at San Diego	13
19	Dallas	20
34	at Philadelphia	13
13	at Pittsburgh	10
23	Baltimore	17
391		**320**

CLEVELAND BROWNS (5-11)
16	Philadelphia	17
27	at Cincinnati	34
14	Buffalo	24
16	at Baltimore	23
27	at New York Giants	41
34	Cincinnati	24
13	at Indianapolis	17
7	San Diego	6
15	Baltimore	25
20	at Dallas (OT)	23
20	Pittsburgh	14
20	at Oakland	17
30	Kansas City	7
21	Washington	38
12	at Denver	34
10	at Pittsburgh	24
302		**368**

DENVER BRONCOS (13-3)
31	Pittsburgh	19
21	at Atlanta	27
25	Houston	31
37	Oakland	6
21	at New England	31
35	at San Diego	24
34	New Orleans	14
31	at Cincinnati	23
36	at Carolina	14
30	San Diego	23
17	at Kansas City	9
31	Tampa Bay	23
26	at Oakland	13
34	at Baltimore	17
34	Cleveland	12
38	Kansas City	3
481		**289**

HOUSTON TEXANS (12-4)
30	Miami	10
27	at Jacksonville	7
31	at Denver	25
38	Tennessee	14
23	at New York Jets	17
24	Green Bay	42
43	Baltimore	13
21	Buffalo	9
13	at Chicago	6
43	Jacksonville (OT)	37
34	at Detroit (OT)	31
24	at Tennessee	10
14	at New England	42
29	Indianapolis	17
6	Minnesota	23
16	at Indianapolis	28
416		**331**

INDIANAPOLIS COLTS (11-5)
21	at Chicago	41
23	Minnesota	20
17	Jacksonville	22
30	Green Bay	27
9	at New York Jets	35
17	Cleveland	13
19	at Tennessee (OT)	13
23	Miami	20
27	at Jacksonville	10
24	at New England	59
20	Buffalo	13
35	at Detroit	33
27	Tennessee	23
17	at Houston	29
20	at Kansas City	13
28	Houston	16
357		**387**

JACKSONVILLE JAGUARS (2-14)
23	at Minnesota (OT)	26
7	Houston	27
22	at Indianapolis	17
10	Cincinnati	27
3	Chicago	41
23	at Oakland (OT)	26
15	at Green Bay	24
14	Detroit	31
10	Indianapolis	27
37	at Houston (OT)	43
24	Tennessee	19
18	at Buffalo	34
10	New York Jets	17
3	at Miami	24
16	New England	23
20	at Tennessee	38
255		**444**

KANSAS CITY CHIEFS (2-14)
24	Atlanta	40
17	at Buffalo	35
27	at New Orleans (OT)	24
20	San Diego	37
6	Baltimore	9
10	at Tampa Bay	38
16	Oakland	26
13	at San Diego	31
13	at Pittsburgh (OT)	16
6	Cincinnati	28
9	Denver	17
27	Carolina	21
7	at Cleveland	30
0	at Oakland	15
13	Indianapolis	20
3	at Denver	38
211		**425**

MIAMI DOLPHINS (7-9)
10	at Houston	30
35	Oakland	13
20	New York Jets (OT)	23
21	at Arizona (OT)	24
17	at Cincinnati	13
17	St. Louis	14
30	at New York Jets	9
20	at Indianapolis	23
3	Tennessee	37
14	at Buffalo	19
24	Seattle	21
16	New England	23
13	at San Francisco	27
24	Jacksonville	3
24	Buffalo	10
0	at New England	28
288		**317**

NEW ENGLAND PATRIOTS (12-4)
34	at Tennessee	13
18	Arizona	20
30	at Baltimore	31
52	at Buffalo	28
31	Denver	21
23	at Seattle	24
29	New York Jets (OT)	26
45	at St. Louis (London)	7
37	Buffalo	31
59	Indianapolis	24
49	at New York Jets	19
23	at Miami	16
42	Houston	14
34	San Francisco	41
23	at Jacksonville	16
28	Miami	0
557		**331**

NEW YORK JETS (6-10)
48	Buffalo	28
10	at Pittsburgh	27
23	at Miami (OT)	20
0	San Francisco	34
17	Houston	23
35	Indianapolis	9
26	at New England (OT)	29
9	Miami	30
7	at Seattle	28
27	at St. Louis	13
19	New England	49
7	Arizona	6
17	at Jacksonville	10
10	at Tennessee	14
17	San Diego	27
9	at Buffalo	28
281		**375**

OAKLAND RAIDERS (4-12)
14	San Diego	22
13	at Miami	35
34	Pittsburgh	31
6	at Denver	37
20	at Atlanta	23
26	Jacksonville (OT)	23
26	at Kansas City	16
32	Tampa Bay	42
20	at Baltimore	55
17	New Orleans	38
10	at Cincinnati	34
17	Cleveland	20
13	Denver	26
15	Kansas City	0
6	at Carolina	17
21	at San Diego	24
290		**443**

PITTSBURGH STEELERS (8-8)
19	at Denver	31
27	New York Jets	10
31	at Oakland	34
16	Philadelphia	14
23	at Tennessee	26
24	at Cincinnati	17
27	Washington	12
24	at New York Giants	20
16	Kansas City (OT)	13
10	Baltimore	13
14	at Cleveland	20
23	at Baltimore	20
24	San Diego	34
24	at Dallas (OT)	27
10	Cincinnati	13
24	Cleveland	10
336		**314**

SAN DIEGO CHARGERS (7-9)
22	at Oakland	14
38	Tennessee	10
3	Atlanta	27
37	at Kansas City	20
24	at New Orleans	31
24	Denver	35
6	at Cleveland	7
31	Kansas City	13
24	at Tampa Bay	34
23	at Denver	30
13	Baltimore (OT)	16
13	Cincinnati	20
34	at Pittsburgh	24
7	Carolina	31
27	at New York Jets	17
24	Oakland	21
350		**350**

TENNESSEE TITANS (6-10)
13	New England	34
10	at San Diego	38
44	Detroit (OT)	41
14	at Houston	38
7	at Minnesota	30
26	Pittsburgh	23
35	at Buffalo	34
13	Indianapolis (OT)	19
20	Chicago	51
37	at Miami	3
19	at Jacksonville	24
10	Houston	24
23	at Indianapolis	27
14	New York Jets	10
7	at Green Bay	55
38	Jacksonville	20
330		**471**

NATIONAL FOOTBALL CONFERENCE

ARIZONA CARDINALS (5-11)
20	Seattle	16
20	at New England	18
27	Philadelphia	6
24	Miami (OT)	21
3	at St. Louis	17
16	Buffalo (OT)	19
14	at Minnesota	21
3	San Francisco	24
17	at Green Bay	31
19	at Atlanta	23
17	St. Louis	31
6	at New York Jets	7
0	at Seattle	58
38	Detroit	10
13	Chicago	28
13	at San Francisco	27
250		**357**

ATLANTA FALCONS (13-3)
40	at Kansas City	24
27	Denver	21
27	at San Diego	3
30	Carolina	28
24	at Washington	17
23	Oakland	20
30	at Philadelphia	17
19	Dallas	13
27	at New Orleans	31
23	Arizona	19
24	at Tampa Bay	23
23	New Orleans	13
20	at Carolina	30
34	New York Giants	0
31	at Detroit	18
17	Tampa Bay	22
419		**299**

CAROLINA PANTHERS (7-9)
10	at Tampa Bay	16
35	New Orleans	27
7	New York Giants	36
28	at Atlanta	30
12	Seattle	16
14	Dallas	19
22	at Chicago	23
21	at Washington	13
14	Denver	36
21	Tampa Bay (OT)	27
30	at Philadelphia	22
21	at Kansas City	27
30	Atlanta	20
31	at San Diego	7
17	Oakland	6
44	at New Orleans	38
357		**363**

CHICAGO BEARS (10-6)
41	Indianapolis	21
10	at Green Bay	23
23	St. Louis	6
34	at Dallas	18
41	at Jacksonville	3
13	Detroit	7
23	Carolina	22
51	at Tennessee	20
6	Houston	13
7	at San Francisco	32
28	Minnesota	10
17	Seattle (OT)	23
14	at Minnesota	21
13	Green Bay	21
28	at Arizona	13
26	at Detroit	24
375		**277**

DALLAS COWBOYS (8-8)
24	at New York Giants	17
7	at Seattle	27
16	Tampa Bay	10
18	Chicago	34
29	at Baltimore	31
19	at Carolina	14
24	New York Giants	29
13	at Atlanta	19
38	at Philadelphia	23
23	Cleveland (OT)	20
31	Washington	38
38	Philadelphia	33
20	at Cincinnati	19
27	Pittsburgh (OT)	24
31	New Orleans (OT)	34
18	at Washington	28
376		**400**

DETROIT LIONS (4-12)
27	St. Louis	23
19	at San Francisco	27
41	at Tennessee (OT)	44
13	Minnesota	20
26	at Philadelphia (OT)	23
7	at Chicago	13
28	Seattle	24
31	at Jacksonville	14
24	at Minnesota	34
20	Green Bay	24
31	Houston	34
33	Indianapolis	35
20	at Green Bay	27
10	at Arizona	38
18	Atlanta	31
24	Chicago	26
372		**437**

GREEN BAY PACKERS (11-5)
22	San Francisco	30
23	Chicago	10
12	at Seattle	14
28	New Orleans	27
27	at Indianapolis	30
42	at Houston	24
30	at St. Louis	20
24	Jacksonville	15
31	Arizona	17
24	at Detroit	20
10	at New York Giants	38
23	Minnesota	14
27	Detroit	20
21	at Chicago	13
55	Tennessee	7
34	at Minnesota	37
433		**336**

MINNESOTA VIKINGS (10-6)
26	Jacksonville (OT)	23
20	at Indianapolis	23
24	San Francisco	13
20	at Detroit	13
30	Tennessee	7
26	at Washington	38
21	Arizona	14
17	Tampa Bay	36
20	at Seattle	30
34	Detroit	24
10	at Chicago	28
14	at Green Bay	23
21	Chicago	14
36	at St. Louis	22
23	at Houston	6
37	Green Bay	34
379		**348**

NEW ORLEANS SAINTS (7-9)
32	Washington	40
27	at Carolina	35
24	Kansas City (OT)	27
27	at Green Bay	28
31	San Diego	24
35	at Tampa Bay	28
14	at Denver	34
28	Philadelphia	13
31	Atlanta	27
38	at Oakland	17
21	San Francisco	31
13	at Atlanta	23
27	at New York Giants	52
41	Tampa Bay	0
34	at Dallas (OT)	31
38	Carolina	44
461		**464**

NEW YORK GIANTS (9-7)
17	Dallas	24
41	Tampa Bay	34
36	at Carolina	7
17	at Philadelphia	19
41	Cleveland	27
26	at San Francisco	3
27	Washington	23
29	at Dallas	24
20	Pittsburgh	24
13	at Cincinnati	31
38	Green Bay	10
16	at Washington	17
52	New Orleans	27
0	at Atlanta	34
14	at Baltimore	33
42	Philadelphia	7
429		**344**

PHILADELPHIA EAGLES (4-12)
17	at Cleveland	16
24	Baltimore	23
6	at Arizona	27
19	New York Giants	17
14	at Pittsburgh	16
23	Detroit (OT)	26
17	Atlanta	30
13	at New Orleans	28
23	Dallas	38
6	at Washington	31
22	Carolina	30
33	at Dallas	38
23	at Tampa Bay	21
13	Cincinnati	34
20	Washington	27
7	at New York Giants	42
280		**444**

ST. LOUIS RAMS (7-8-1)
23	at Detroit	27
31	Washington	28
6	at Chicago	23
19	Seattle	13
17	Arizona	3
14	at Miami	17
20	Green Bay	30
7	New England (London)	45
24	at San Francisco (OT)	24
13	New York Jets	27
31	at Arizona	17
16	San Francisco (OT)	13
15	at Buffalo	12
22	Minnesota	36
28	at Tampa Bay	13
13	at Seattle	20
299		**348**

SAN FRANCISCO 49ERS (11-4-1)
30	at Green Bay	22
27	Detroit	19
13	at Minnesota	24
34	at New York Jets	0
45	Buffalo	3
3	New York Giants	26
13	Seattle	6
24	at Arizona	3
24	St. Louis (OT)	24
32	Chicago	7
31	at New Orleans	21
13	at St. Louis (OT)	16
27	Miami	13
41	at New England	34
13	at Seattle	42
27	Arizona	13
397		**273**

SEATTLE SEAHAWKS (11-5)
16	at Arizona	20
27	Dallas	7
14	Green Bay	12
13	at St. Louis	19
16	at Carolina	12
24	New England	23
6	at San Francisco	13
24	at Detroit	28
30	Minnesota	20
28	New York Jets	7
21	at Miami	24
23	at Chicago (OT)	17
58	Arizona	0
50	at Buffalo (Toronto)	17
42	San Francisco	13
20	St. Louis	13
412		**245**

TAMPA BAY BUCCANEERS (7-9)
16	Carolina	10
34	at New York Giants	41
10	at Dallas	16
22	Washington	24
38	Kansas City	10
28	New Orleans	35
36	at Minnesota	17
42	at Oakland	32
34	San Diego	24
27	at Carolina (OT)	21
23	Atlanta	24
23	at Denver	31
21	Philadelphia	23
0	at New Orleans	41
13	St. Louis	28
22	at Atlanta	17
389		**394**

WASHINGTON REDSKINS (10-6)
40	at New Orleans	32
28	at St. Louis	31
31	Cincinnati	38
24	at Tampa Bay	22
17	Atlanta	24
38	Minnesota	26
23	at New York Giants	27
12	at Pittsburgh	27
13	Carolina	21
31	Philadelphia	6
38	at Dallas	31
17	New York Giants	16
31	Baltimore (OT)	28
38	at Cleveland	21
27	at Philadelphia	20
28	Dallas	18
436		**388**

FINAL STANDINGS

AMERICAN FOOTBALL CONFERENCE

East Division	W	L	T	Pct.	Pts.	OP
* New England	12	4	0	.750	557	331
Miami	7	9	0	.438	288	317
New York Jets	6	10	0	.375	281	375
Buffalo	6	10	0	.375	344	435

North Division	W	L	T	Pct.	Pts.	OP
* Baltimore	10	6	0	.625	398	344
# Cincinnati	10	6	0	.625	391	320
Pittsburgh	8	8	0	.500	336	314
Cleveland	5	11	0	.313	302	368

South Division	W	L	T	Pct.	Pts.	OP
* Houston	12	4	0	.750	416	331
# Indianapolis	11	5	0	.688	357	387
Tennessee	6	10	0	.375	330	471
Jacksonville	2	14	0	.125	255	444

West Division	W	L	T	Pct.	Pts.	OP
* Denver	13	3	0	.813	481	289
San Diego	7	9	0	.438	350	350
Oakland	4	12	0	.250	290	443
Kansas City	2	14	0	.125	211	425

NATIONAL FOOTBALL CONFERENCE

East Division	W	L	T	Pct.	Pts.	OP
* Washington	10	6	0	.625	436	388
New York Giants	9	7	0	.563	429	344
Dallas	8	8	0	.500	376	400
Philadelphia	4	12	0	.250	280	444

North Division	W	L	T	Pct.	Pts.	OP
* Green Bay	11	5	0	.688	433	336
# Minnesota	10	6	0	.625	379	348
Chicago	10	6	0	.625	375	277
Detroit	4	12	0	.250	372	437

South Division	W	L	T	Pct.	Pts.	OP
* Atlanta	13	3	0	.813	419	299
Carolina	7	9	0	.438	357	363
New Orleans	7	9	0	.438	461	454
Tampa Bay	7	9	0	.438	389	394

West Division	W	L	T	Pct.	Pts.	OP
* San Francisco	11	4	1	.719	397	273
# Seattle	11	5	0	.688	412	245
St. Louis	7	8	1	.469	299	348
Arizona	5	11	0	.313	250	357

* Division champion
# Wild Card team

New York Jets finished ahead of Buffalo based on better record in common games (5-7 to Bills' 3-9). Baltimore finished ahead of Cincinnati based on better division record (4-2 to Bengals' 3-3). New England finished ahead of Houston based on head-to-head victory. Minnesota finished ahead of Chicago based on better division record (4-2 to Bears' 3-3). Carolina finished ahead of New Orleans and Tampa Bay based on better record against common opponents than Tampa Bay (6-4 to Buccaneers' 5-5) and head-to-head sweep over the Saints. New Orleans finished ahead of Tampa Bay based on head-to-head sweep.

WILD CARD PLAYOFFS

AFC
HOUSTON 19, Cincinnati 13
BALTIMORE 24, Indianapolis 9

NFC
GREEN BAY 24, Minnesota 10
Seattle 24, WASHINGTON 14

DIVISIONAL PLAYOFFS

AFC
NEW ENGLAND 41, Houston 28
Baltimore 38, DENVER 35 (2 OT)

NFC
ATLANTA 30, Seattle 28
SAN FRANCISCO 45, Green Bay 31

CHAMPIONSHIP GAMES

AFC
Baltimore 28, NEW ENGLAND 13

NFC
San Francisco 28, ATLANTA 24

AFC-NFC PRO BOWL

NFC 62, AFC 35
at Aloha Stadium, Honolulu, Hawaii

SUPER BOWL XLVII

Baltimore (AFC) 34, San Francisco (NFC) 31
at Mercedes-Benz Superdome, New Orleans, Louisiana

Home teams in playoff games are indicated in CAPS.

FIRST WEEK STANDINGS

American Football Conference

East Division	W	L	T	Pct.	Pts.	OP
New England	1	0	0	1.000	34	13
New York Jets	1	0	0	1.000	48	28
Buffalo	0	1	0	.000	28	48
Miami	0	1	0	.000	10	30

North Division	W	L	T	Pct.	Pts.	OP
Baltimore	1	0	0	1.000	44	13
Cincinnati	0	1	0	.000	13	44
Cleveland	0	1	0	.000	16	17
Pittsburgh	0	1	0	.000	19	31

South Division	W	L	T	Pct.	Pts.	OP
Houston	1	0	0	1.000	30	10
Indianapolis	0	1	0	.000	21	41
Jacksonville	0	1	0	.000	23	26
Tennessee	0	1	0	.000	13	34

West Division	W	L	T	Pct.	Pts.	OP
Denver	1	0	0	1.000	31	19
San Diego	1	0	0	1.000	22	14
Kansas City	0	1	0	.000	24	40
Oakland	0	1	0	.000	14	22

National Football Conference

East Division	W	L	T	Pct.	Pts.	OP
Dallas	1	0	0	1.000	24	17
Philadelphia	1	0	0	1.000	17	16
Washington	1	0	0	1.000	40	32
New York Giants	0	1	0	.000	17	24

North Division	W	L	T	Pct.	Pts.	OP
Chicago	1	0	0	1.000	41	21
Detroit	1	0	0	1.000	27	23
Minnesota	1	0	0	1.000	26	23
Green Bay	0	1	0	.000	22	30

South Division	W	L	T	Pct.	Pts.	OP
Atlanta	1	0	0	1.000	40	24
Tampa Bay	1	0	0	1.000	16	10
Carolina	0	1	0	.000	10	16
New Orleans	0	1	0	.000	32	40

West Division	W	L	T	Pct.	Pts.	OP
Arizona	1	0	0	1.000	20	16
San Francisco	1	0	0	1.000	30	22
St. Louis	0	1	0	.000	23	27
Seattle	0	1	0	.000	16	20

SECOND WEEK STANDINGS

American Football Conference

East Division	W	L	T	Pct.	Pts.	OP
Buffalo	1	1	0	.500	63	65
Miami	1	1	0	.500	58	55
New England	1	1	0	.500	45	43
New York Jets	1	1	0	.500	52	33

North Division	W	L	T	Pct.	Pts.	OP
Baltimore	1	1	0	.500	67	37
Cincinnati	1	1	0	.500	47	71
Pittsburgh	1	1	0	.500	46	61
Cleveland	0	2	0	.000	43	51

South Division	W	L	T	Pct.	Pts.	OP
Houston	2	0	0	1.000	57	17
Indianapolis	1	1	0	.500	44	61
Jacksonville	0	2	0	.000	30	53
Tennessee	0	2	0	.000	23	72

West Division	W	L	T	Pct.	Pts.	OP
San Diego	2	0	0	1.000	60	24
Denver	1	1	0	.500	52	46
Kansas City	0	2	0	.000	41	75
Oakland	0	2	0	.000	27	57

National Football Conference

East Division	W	L	T	Pct.	Pts.	OP
Philadelphia	2	0	0	1.000	41	39
Dallas	1	1	0	.500	31	44
New York Giants	1	1	0	.500	58	58
Washington	1	1	0	.500	68	63

North Division	W	L	T	Pct.	Pts.	OP
Chicago	1	1	0	.500	51	44
Detroit	1	1	0	.500	46	50
Green Bay	1	1	0	.500	45	40
Minnesota	1	1	0	.500	46	46

South Division	W	L	T	Pct.	Pts.	OP
Atlanta	2	0	0	1.000	67	45
Carolina	1	1	0	.500	45	43
Tampa Bay	1	1	0	.500	50	51
New Orleans	0	2	0	.000	59	75

West Division	W	L	T	Pct.	Pts.	OP
Arizona	2	0	0	1.000	40	34
San Francisco	2	0	0	1.000	57	41
St. Louis	1	1	0	.500	54	55
Seattle	1	1	0	.500	43	27

THIRD WEEK STANDINGS

American Football Conference

East Division	W	L	T	Pct.	Pts.	OP
Buffalo	2	1	0	.667	87	79
New York Jets	2	1	0	.667	81	75
Miami	1	2	0	.333	65	66
New England	1	2	0	.333	82	64

North Division	W	L	T	Pct.	Pts.	OP
Baltimore	2	1	0	.667	98	67
Cincinnati	2	1	0	.667	85	102
Pittsburgh	1	2	0	.333	77	75
Cleveland	0	3	0	.000	57	75

South Division	W	L	T	Pct.	Pts.	OP
Houston	3	0	0	1.000	88	42
Indianapolis	1	2	0	.333	61	83
Jacksonville	1	2	0	.333	52	70
Tennessee	1	2	0	.333	67	113

West Division	W	L	T	Pct.	Pts.	OP
San Diego	2	1	0	.667	63	51
Denver	1	2	0	.333	77	77
Kansas City	1	2	0	.333	68	99
Oakland	1	2	0	.333	61	88

National Football Conference

East Division	W	L	T	Pct.	Pts.	OP
Dallas	2	1	0	.667	47	54
New York Giants	2	1	0	.667	94	65
Philadelphia	2	1	0	.667	47	66
Washington	1	2	0	.333	99	101

North Division	W	L	T	Pct.	Pts.	OP
Chicago	2	1	0	.667	74	50
Minnesota	2	1	0	.667	70	59
Detroit	1	2	0	.333	87	94
Green Bay	1	2	0	.333	57	54

South Division	W	L	T	Pct.	Pts.	OP
Atlanta	3	0	0	1.000	94	48
Carolina	1	2	0	.333	52	79
Tampa Bay	1	2	0	.333	60	67
New Orleans	0	3	0	.000	83	102

West Division	W	L	T	Pct.	Pts.	OP
Arizona	3	0	0	1.000	67	40
San Francisco	2	1	0	.667	70	65
Seattle	2	1	0	.667	57	39
St. Louis	1	2	0	.333	60	78

WEEK 1 RESULTS

Wednesday, September 5
Dallas 24, NEW YORK GIANTS 17

Sunday, September 9
CHICAGO 41, Indianapolis 21
Philadelphia 17, CLEVELAND 16
DETROIT 27, St. Louis 23
HOUSTON 30, Miami 10
Atlanta 40, KANSAS CITY 24
MINNESOTA 26, Jacksonville 23 (OT)
Washington 40, NEW ORLEANS 32
NEW YORK JETS 48, Buffalo 28
New England 34, TENNESSEE 13
ARIZONA 20, Seattle 16
San Francisco 30, GREEN BAY 22
TAMPA BAY 16, Carolina 10
DENVER 31, Pittsburgh 19

Monday, September 10
BALTIMORE 44, Cincinnati 13
San Diego 22, OAKLAND 14

In the 2012 Week By Week section, home teams are indicated by ALL CAPS.

For game recaps, box scores, and video highlights, please visit www.NFL.com/scores.

WEEK 2 RESULTS

Thursday, September 13
GREEN BAY 23, Chicago 10

Sunday, September 16
BUFFALO 35, Kansas City 17
CAROLINA 35, New Orleans 27
CINCINNATI 34, Cleveland 27
INDIANAPOLIS 23, Minnesota 20
Houston 27, JACKSONVILLE 7
MIAMI 35, Oakland 13
Arizona 20, NEW ENGLAND 18
NEW YORK GIANTS 41, Tampa Bay 34
PHILADELPHIA 24, Baltimore 23
ST. LOUIS 31, Washington 28
SEATTLE 27, Dallas 7
PITTSBURGH 27, New York Jets 10
SAN DIEGO 38, Tennessee 10
SAN FRANCISCO 27, Detroit 19

Monday, September 17
ATLANTA 27, Denver 21

WEEK 3 RESULTS

Thursday, September 20
New York Giants 36, CAROLINA 7

Sunday, September 23
CHICAGO 23, St. Louis 6
Buffalo 24, CLEVELAND 14
DALLAS 16, Tampa Bay 10
Jacksonville 22, INDIANAPOLIS 17
New York Jets 23, MIAMI 20 (OT)
MINNESOTA 24, San Francisco 13
Kansas City 27, NEW ORLEANS 24 (OT)
TENNESSEE 44, Detroit 41 (OT)
Cincinnati 38, WASHINGTON 31
ARIZONA 27, Philadelphia 6
Atlanta 27, SAN DIEGO 3
Houston 31, DENVER 25
OAKLAND 34, Pittsburgh 31
BALTIMORE 31, New England 30

Monday, September 24
SEATTLE 14, Green Bay 12

FOURTH WEEK STANDINGS
American Football Conference

East Division	W	L	T	Pct.	Pts.	OP
Buffalo	2	2	0	.500	115	131
New England	2	2	0	.500	134	92
New York Jets	2	2	0	.500	81	109
Miami	1	3	0	.250	86	90
North Division	W	L	T	Pct.	Pts.	OP
Baltimore	3	1	0	.750	121	83
Cincinnati	3	1	0	.750	112	112
Pittsburgh	1	2	0	.333	77	75
Cleveland	0	4	0	.000	73	98
South Division	W	L	T	Pct.	Pts.	OP
Houston	4	0	0	1.000	126	56
Indianapolis	1	2	0	.333	61	83
Jacksonville	1	3	0	.250	62	97
Tennessee	1	3	0	.250	81	151
West Division	W	L	T	Pct.	Pts.	OP
San Diego	3	1	0	.750	100	71
Denver	2	2	0	.500	114	83
Kansas City	1	3	0	.250	88	136
Oakland	1	3	0	.250	67	125

National Football Conference

East Division	W	L	T	Pct.	Pts.	OP
Philadelphia	3	1	0	.750	66	83
Dallas	2	2	0	.500	65	88
New York Giants	2	2	0	.500	111	84
Washington	2	2	0	.500	123	123
North Division	W	L	T	Pct.	Pts.	OP
Chicago	3	1	0	.750	108	68
Minnesota	3	1	0	.750	90	72
Green Bay	2	2	0	.500	85	81
Detroit	1	3	0	.250	100	114
South Division	W	L	T	Pct.	Pts.	OP
Atlanta	4	0	0	1.000	124	76
Carolina	1	3	0	.250	80	109
Tampa Bay	1	3	0	.250	82	91
New Orleans	0	4	0	.000	110	130
West Division	W	L	T	Pct.	Pts.	OP
Arizona	4	0	0	1.000	91	61
San Francisco	3	1	0	.750	104	65
St. Louis	2	2	0	.500	79	91
Seattle	2	2	0	.500	70	58

FIFTH WEEK STANDINGS
American Football Conference

East Division	W	L	T	Pct.	Pts.	OP
New England	3	2	0	.600	165	113
Buffalo	2	3	0	.400	118	176
Miami	2	3	0	.400	103	103
New York Jets	2	3	0	.400	98	132
North Division	W	L	T	Pct.	Pts.	OP
Baltimore	4	1	0	.800	130	89
Cincinnati	3	2	0	.600	125	129
Pittsburgh	2	2	0	.500	93	89
Cleveland	0	5	0	.000	100	139
South Division	W	L	T	Pct.	Pts.	OP
Houston	5	0	0	1.000	149	73
Indianapolis	2	2	0	.500	91	110
Jacksonville	1	4	0	.200	65	138
Tennessee	1	4	0	.200	88	181
West Division	W	L	T	Pct.	Pts.	OP
San Diego	3	2	0	.600	124	102
Denver	2	3	0	.400	135	114
Oakland	1	3	0	.250	67	125
Kansas City	1	4	0	.200	94	145

National Football Conference

East Division	W	L	T	Pct.	Pts.	OP
New York Giants	3	2	0	.600	152	111
Philadelphia	3	2	0	.200	80	99
Dallas	2	2	0	.500	65	88
Washington	2	3	0	.400	140	147
North Division	W	L	T	Pct.	Pts.	OP
Chicago	4	1	0	.800	149	71
Minnesota	4	1	0	.800	120	79
Green Bay	2	3	0	.400	112	111
Detroit	1	3	0	.250	100	114
South Division	W	L	T	Pct.	Pts.	OP
Atlanta	5	0	0	1.000	148	93
Tampa Bay	1	3	0	.250	82	91
Carolina	1	4	0	.200	92	125
New Orleans	1	4	0	.200	141	154
West Division	W	L	T	Pct.	Pts.	OP
Arizona	4	1	0	.800	94	78
San Francisco	4	1	0	.800	149	68
St. Louis	3	2	0	.600	96	94
Seattle	3	2	0	.600	86	70

SIXTH WEEK STANDINGS
American Football Conference

East Division	W	L	T	Pct.	Pts.	OP
Buffalo	3	3	0	.500	137	192
Miami	3	3	0	.500	120	117
New England	3	3	0	.500	188	137
New York Jets	3	3	0	.500	133	141
North Division	W	L	T	Pct.	Pts.	OP
Baltimore	5	1	0	.833	161	118
Cincinnati	3	3	0	.500	149	163
Pittsburgh	2	3	0	.400	116	115
Cleveland	1	5	0	.167	134	163
South Division	W	L	T	Pct.	Pts.	OP
Houston	5	1	0	.833	173	115
Indianapolis	2	3	0	.400	100	145
Tennessee	2	4	0	.333	114	204
Jacksonville	1	4	0	.200	65	138
West Division	W	L	T	Pct.	Pts.	OP
Denver	3	3	0	.500	170	138
San Diego	3	3	0	.500	148	137
Oakland	1	4	0	.200	87	148
Kansas City	1	5	0	.167	104	183

National Football Conference

East Division	W	L	T	Pct.	Pts.	OP
New York Giants	4	2	0	.667	178	114
Philadelphia	3	3	0	.500	103	125
Washington	3	3	0	.500	178	173
Dallas	2	3	0	.400	94	119
North Division	W	L	T	Pct.	Pts.	OP
Chicago	4	1	0	.800	149	71
Minnesota	4	2	0	.667	146	117
Green Bay	3	3	0	.500	154	135
Detroit	2	3	0	.400	126	137
South Division	W	L	T	Pct.	Pts.	OP
Atlanta	6	0	0	1.000	171	113
Tampa Bay	2	3	0	.400	120	101
Carolina	1	4	0	.200	92	125
New Orleans	1	4	0	.200	141	154
West Division	W	L	T	Pct.	Pts.	OP
Arizona	4	2	0	.667	110	97
San Francisco	4	2	0	.667	152	94
Seattle	4	2	0	.667	110	93
St. Louis	3	3	0	.500	110	111

WEEK 4 RESULTS
Thursday, September 27
BALTIMORE 23, Cleveland 16

Sunday, September 30
ATLANTA 30, Carolina 28
New England 52, BUFFALO 28
Minnesota 20, DETROIT 13
HOUSTON 38, Tennessee 14
San Diego 37, KANSAS CITY 20
San Francisco 34, NEW YORK JETS 0
ST. LOUIS 19, Seattle 13
ARIZONA 24, Miami 21 (OT)
Cincinnati 27, JACKSONVILLE 10
DENVER 37, Oakland 6
GREEN BAY 28, New Orleans 27
Washington 24, TAMPA BAY 22
PHILADELPHIA 19, New York Giants 17

Monday, October 1
Chicago 34, DALLAS 18

Byes: Indianapolis, Pittsburgh

WEEK 5 RESULTS
Thursday, October 4
ST. LOUIS 17, Arizona 3

Sunday, October 7
Miami 17, CINCINNATI 13
INDIANAPOLIS 30, Green Bay 27
Baltimore 9, KANSAS CITY 6
MINNESOTA 30, Tennessee 7
NEW YORK GIANTS 41, Cleveland 27
PITTSBURGH 16, Philadelphia 14
Atlanta 24, WASHINGTON 17
Seattle 16, CAROLINA 12
Chicago 41, JACKSONVILLE 3
NEW ENGLAND 31, Denver 21
SAN FRANCISCO 45, Buffalo 3
NEW ORLEANS 31, San Diego 24

Monday, October 8
Houston 23, NEW YORK JETS 17

Byes: Dallas, Detroit,
Oakland, Tampa Bay

WEEK 6 RESULTS
Thursday, October 11
TENNESSEE 26, Pittsburgh 23

Sunday, October 14
ATLANTA 23, Oakland 20
BALTIMORE 31, Dallas 29
CLEVELAND 34, Cincinnati 24
MIAMI 17, St. Louis 14
NEW YORK JETS 35, Indianapolis 9
Detroit 26, PHILADELPHIA 23 (OT)
TAMPA BAY 38, Kansas City 10
Buffalo 19, ARIZONA 16 (OT)
SEATTLE 24, New England 23
New York Giants 26, SAN FRANCISCO 3
WASHINGTON 38, Minnesota 26
Green Bay 42, HOUSTON 24

Monday, October 15
DENVER 35, San Diego 24

Byes: Carolina, Chicago,
Jacksonville, New Orleans

SEVENTH WEEK STANDINGS
American Football Conference

East Division	W	L	T	Pct.	Pts.	OP
New England	4	3	0	.571	217	163
Miami	3	3	0	.500	120	117
Buffalo	3	4	0	.429	171	227
New York Jets	3	4	0	.429	159	170
North Division	W	L	T	Pct.	Pts.	OP
Baltimore	5	2	0	.714	174	161
Pittsburgh	3	3	0	.500	140	132
Cincinnati	3	4	0	.429	166	187
Cleveland	1	6	0	.143	147	180
South Division	W	L	T	Pct.	Pts.	OP
Houston	6	1	0	.857	216	128
Indianapolis	3	3	0	.500	117	158
Tennessee	3	4	0	.429	149	238
Jacksonville	1	5	0	.167	88	164
West Division	W	L	T	Pct.	Pts.	OP
Denver	3	3	0	.500	170	138
San Diego	3	3	0	.500	148	137
Oakland	2	4	0	.333	113	171
Kansas City	1	5	0	.167	104	183

National Football Conference

East Division	W	L	T	Pct.	Pts.	OP
New York Giants	5	2	0	.714	205	137
Dallas	3	3	0	.500	113	133
Philadelphia	3	3	0	.500	103	125
Washington	3	4	0	.429	201	200
North Division	W	L	T	Pct.	Pts.	OP
Chicago	5	1	0	.833	162	78
Minnesota	5	2	0	.714	167	131
Green Bay	4	3	0	.571	184	155
Detroit	2	4	0	.333	133	150
South Division	W	L	T	Pct.	Pts.	OP
Atlanta	6	0	0	1.000	171	113
New Orleans	2	4	0	.333	176	182
Tampa Bay	2	4	0	.333	148	136
Carolina	1	5	0	.167	106	144
West Division	W	L	T	Pct.	Pts.	OP
San Francisco	5	2	0	.714	165	100
Arizona	4	3	0	.571	124	118
Seattle	4	3	0	.571	116	106
St. Louis	3	4	0	.429	130	141

WEEK 7 RESULTS

Thursday, October 18
SAN FRANCISCO 13, Seattle 6

Sunday, October 21
Tennessee 35, BUFFALO 34
Dallas 19, CAROLINA 14
HOUSTON 43, Baltimore 13
INDIANAPOLIS 17, Cleveland 13
MINNESOTA 21, Arizona 14
NEW YORK GIANTS 27, Washington 23
Green Bay 30, ST. LOUIS 20
New Orleans 35, TAMPA BAY 28
NEW ENGLAND 29, New York Jets 26 (OT)
OAKLAND 26, Jacksonville 23 (OT)
Pittsburgh 24, CINCINNATI 17

Monday, October 22
CHICAGO 13, Detroit 7

Byes: Atlanta, Denver, Kansas City, Miami, Philadelphia, San Diego

EIGHTH WEEK STANDINGS
American Football Conference

East Division	W	L	T	Pct.	Pts.	OP
New England	5	3	0	.625	262	170
Miami	4	3	0	.571	150	126
Buffalo	3	4	0	.429	171	227
New York Jets	3	5	0	.375	168	200
North Division	W	L	T	Pct.	Pts.	OP
Baltimore	5	2	0	.714	174	161
Pittsburgh	4	3	0	.571	167	144
Cincinnati	3	4	0	.429	166	187
Cleveland	2	6	0	.250	154	186
South Division	W	L	T	Pct.	Pts.	OP
Houston	6	1	0	.857	216	128
Indianapolis	4	3	0	.571	136	171
Tennessee	3	5	0	.375	162	257
Jacksonville	1	6	0	.143	103	188
West Division	W	L	T	Pct.	Pts.	OP
Denver	4	3	0	.571	204	152
Oakland	3	4	0	.429	139	187
San Diego	3	4	0	.429	154	144
Kansas City	1	6	0	.143	120	209

National Football Conference

East Division	W	L	T	Pct.	Pts.	OP
New York Giants	6	2	0	.750	234	161
Dallas	3	4	0	.429	137	162
Philadelphia	3	4	0	.429	120	155
Washington	3	5	0	.375	213	227
North Division	W	L	T	Pct.	Pts.	OP
Chicago	6	1	0	.857	185	100
Green Bay	5	3	0	.625	208	170
Minnesota	5	3	0	.625	184	167
Detroit	3	4	0	.429	161	174
South Division	W	L	T	Pct.	Pts.	OP
Atlanta	7	0	0	1.000	201	130
Tampa Bay	3	4	0	.429	184	153
New Orleans	2	5	0	.286	190	216
Carolina	1	6	0	.143	128	167
West Division	W	L	T	Pct.	Pts.	OP
San Francisco	6	2	0	.750	189	103
Arizona	4	4	0	.500	127	142
Seattle	4	4	0	.500	140	134
St. Louis	3	5	0	.375	137	186

WEEK 8 RESULTS

Thursday, October 25
Tampa Bay 36, MINNESOTA 17

Sunday, October 28
CHICAGO 23, Carolina 22
CLEVELAND 7, San Diego 6
DETROIT 28, Seattle 24
GREEN BAY 24, Jacksonville 15
Miami 30, NEW YORK JETS 9
Atlanta 30, PHILADELPHIA 17
PITTSBURGH 27, Washington 12
New England 45, ST. LOUIS 7 (London)
Indianapolis 19, TENNESSEE 13 (OT)
Oakland 26, KANSAS CITY 16
New York Giants 29, DALLAS 24
DENVER 34, New Orleans 14

Monday, October 29
San Francisco 24, ARIZONA 3

Byes: Baltimore, Buffalo, Cincinnati, Houston

NINTH WEEK STANDINGS
American Football Conference

East Division	W	L	T	Pct.	Pts.	OP
New England	5	3	0	.625	262	170
Miami	4	4	0	.500	170	149
Buffalo	3	5	0	.375	180	248
New York Jets	3	5	0	.375	168	200
North Division	W	L	T	Pct.	Pts.	OP
Baltimore	6	2	0	.750	199	176
Pittsburgh	5	3	0	.625	191	164
Cincinnati	3	5	0	.375	189	218
Cleveland	2	7	0	.222	169	211
South Division	W	L	T	Pct.	Pts.	OP
Houston	7	1	0	.875	237	137
Indianapolis	5	3	0	.625	159	191
Tennessee	3	6	0	.333	182	308
Jacksonville	1	7	0	.125	117	219
West Division	W	L	T	Pct.	Pts.	OP
Denver	5	3	0	.625	235	175
San Diego	4	4	0	.500	185	157
Oakland	3	5	0	.375	171	229
Kansas City	1	7	0	.125	133	240

National Football Conference

East Division	W	L	T	Pct.	Pts.	OP
New York Giants	6	3	0	.667	254	185
Dallas	3	5	0	.375	150	181
Philadelphia	3	5	0	.375	133	183
Washington	3	6	0	.333	226	248
North Division	W	L	T	Pct.	Pts.	OP
Chicago	7	1	0	.875	236	120
Green Bay	6	3	0	.667	239	187
Minnesota	5	4	0	.556	204	197
Detroit	4	4	0	.500	192	188
South Division	W	L	T	Pct.	Pts.	OP
Atlanta	8	0	0	1.000	220	143
Tampa Bay	4	4	0	.500	226	185
New Orleans	3	5	0	.375	218	229
Carolina	2	6	0	.250	149	180
West Division	W	L	T	Pct.	Pts.	OP
San Francisco	6	2	0	.750	189	103
Seattle	5	4	0	.556	170	154
Arizona	4	5	0	.444	144	173
St. Louis	3	5	0	.375	137	186

WEEK 9 RESULTS

Thursday, November 1
SAN DIEGO 31, Kansas City 13

Sunday, November 4
Denver 31, CINCINNATI 23
Baltimore 25, CLEVELAND 15
GREEN BAY 31, Arizona 17
HOUSTON 21, Buffalo 9
INDIANAPOLIS 23, Miami 20
Detroit 31, JACKSONVILLE 14
Chicago 51, TENNESSEE 20
Carolina 21, WASHINGTON 13
Tampa Bay 42, OAKLAND 32
SEATTLE 30, Minnesota 20
Pittsburgh 24, NEW YORK GIANTS 20
ATLANTA 19, Dallas 13

Monday, November 5
NEW ORLEANS 28, Philadelphia 13

Byes: New England, New York Jets, St. Louis, San Francisco

TENTH WEEK STANDINGS
American Football Conference

East Division	W	L	T	Pct.	Pts.	OP
New England	6	3	0	.667	299	201
Miami	4	5	0	.444	173	186
Buffalo	3	6	0	.333	211	285
New York Jets	3	6	0	.333	175	228
North Division	**W**	**L**	**T**	**Pct.**	**Pts.**	**OP**
Baltimore	7	2	0	.778	254	196
Pittsburgh	6	3	0	.667	207	177
Cincinnati	4	5	0	.444	220	231
Cleveland	2	7	0	.222	169	211
South Division	**W**	**L**	**T**	**Pct.**	**Pts.**	**OP**
Houston	8	1	0	.889	250	143
Indianapolis	6	3	0	.667	186	201
Tennessee	4	6	0	.400	219	311
Jacksonville	1	8	0	.111	127	246
West Division	**W**	**L**	**T**	**Pct.**	**Pts.**	**OP**
Denver	6	3	0	.667	271	189
San Diego	4	5	0	.444	209	191
Oakland	3	6	0	.333	191	284
Kansas City	1	8	0	.111	146	256

National Football Conference

East Division	W	L	T	Pct.	Pts.	OP
New York Giants	6	4	0	.600	267	216
Dallas	4	5	0	.444	188	204
Philadelphia	3	6	0	.333	156	221
Washington	3	6	0	.333	226	248
North Division	**W**	**L**	**T**	**Pct.**	**Pts.**	**OP**
Chicago	7	2	0	.778	242	133
Green Bay	6	3	0	.667	239	187
Minnesota	6	4	0	.600	238	221
Detroit	4	5	0	.444	216	222
South Division	**W**	**L**	**T**	**Pct.**	**Pts.**	**OP**
Atlanta	8	1	0	.889	247	174
Tampa Bay	5	4	0	.556	260	209
New Orleans	4	5	0	.444	249	256
Carolina	2	7	0	.222	163	216
West Division	**W**	**L**	**T**	**Pct.**	**Pts.**	**OP**
San Francisco	6	2	1	.722	213	127
Seattle	6	4	0	.600	198	161
Arizona	4	5	0	.444	144	173
St. Louis	3	5	1	.389	161	210

WEEK 10 RESULTS
Thursday, November 8
Indianapolis 27, JACKSONVILLE 10

Sunday, November 11
BALTIMORE 55, Oakland 20
Denver 36, CAROLINA 14
CINCINNATI 31, New York Giants 13
Tennessee 37, MIAMI 3
MINNESOTA 34, Detroit 24
NEW ENGLAND 37, Buffalo 31
NEW ORLEANS 31, Atlanta 27
TAMPA BAY 34, San Diego 24
SEATTLE 28, New York Jets 7
Dallas 38, PHILADELPHIA 23
St. Louis 24, SAN FRANCISCO 24 (OT-tie)
Houston 13, CHICAGO 6

Monday, November 12
PITTSBURGH 16, Kansas City 13 (OT)

Byes: Arizona, Cleveland, Green Bay, Washington

ELEVENTH WEEK STANDINGS
American Football Conference

East Division	W	L	T	Pct.	Pts.	OP
New England	7	3	0	.700	358	225
Buffalo	4	6	0	.400	230	299
Miami	4	6	0	.400	187	205
New York Jets	4	6	0	.400	201	241
North Division	**W**	**L**	**T**	**Pct.**	**Pts.**	**OP**
Baltimore	8	2	0	.800	267	206
Pittsburgh	6	4	0	.600	217	190
Cincinnati	5	5	0	.500	248	237
Cleveland	2	8	0	.200	189	234
South Division	**W**	**L**	**T**	**Pct.**	**Pts.**	**OP**
Houston	9	1	0	.900	293	180
Indianapolis	6	4	0	.600	210	260
Tennessee	4	6	0	.400	219	311
Jacksonville	1	9	0	.100	164	289
West Division	**W**	**L**	**T**	**Pct.**	**Pts.**	**OP**
Denver	7	3	0	.700	301	212
San Diego	4	6	0	.400	232	221
Oakland	3	7	0	.300	208	322
Kansas City	1	9	0	.100	152	284

National Football Conference

East Division	W	L	T	Pct.	Pts.	OP
New York Giants	6	4	0	.600	267	216
Dallas	5	5	0	.500	211	224
Washington	4	6	0	.400	257	254
Philadelphia	3	7	0	.300	162	252
North Division	**W**	**L**	**T**	**Pct.**	**Pts.**	**OP**
Chicago	7	3	0	.700	249	165
Green Bay	7	3	0	.700	263	207
Minnesota	6	4	0	.600	238	221
Detroit	4	6	0	.400	236	246
South Division	**W**	**L**	**T**	**Pct.**	**Pts.**	**OP**
Atlanta	9	1	0	.900	270	193
Tampa Bay	6	4	0	.600	287	230
New Orleans	5	5	0	.500	287	273
Carolina	2	8	0	.200	184	243
West Division	**W**	**L**	**T**	**Pct.**	**Pts.**	**OP**
San Francisco	7	2	1	.750	245	134
Seattle	6	4	0	.600	198	161
Arizona	4	6	0	.400	163	196
St. Louis	3	6	1	.350	174	237

WEEK 11 RESULTS
Thursday, November 15
BUFFALO 19, Miami 14

Sunday, November 18
ATLANTA 23, Arizona 19
Tampa Bay 27, CAROLINA 21 (OT)
DALLAS 23, Cleveland 20 (OT)
Green Bay 24, DETROIT 20
HOUSTON 43, Jacksonville 37 (OT)
Cincinnati 28, KANSAS CITY 6
New York Jets 27, ST. LOUIS 13
WASHINGTON 31, Philadelphia 6
New Orleans 38, OAKLAND 17
DENVER 30, San Diego 23
NEW ENGLAND 59, Indianapolis 24
Baltimore 13, PITTSBURGH 10

Monday, November 19
SAN FRANCISCO 32, Chicago 7

Byes: Minnesota, New York Giants, Seattle, Tennessee

TWELFTH WEEK STANDINGS
American Football Conference

East Division	W	L	T	Pct.	Pts.	OP
New England	8	3	0	.727	407	244
Miami	5	6	0	.455	211	226
Buffalo	4	7	0	.364	243	319
New York Jets	4	7	0	.364	221	290
North Division	**W**	**L**	**T**	**Pct.**	**Pts.**	**OP**
Baltimore	9	2	0	.818	283	219
Cincinnati	6	5	0	.545	282	247
Pittsburgh	6	5	0	.545	231	210
Cleveland	3	8	0	.273	209	248
South Division	**W**	**L**	**T**	**Pct.**	**Pts.**	**OP**
Houston	10	1	0	.909	327	211
Indianapolis	7	4	0	.636	230	273
Tennessee	4	7	0	.364	238	335
Jacksonville	2	9	0	.182	188	308
West Division	**W**	**L**	**T**	**Pct.**	**Pts.**	**OP**
Denver	8	3	0	.727	318	221
San Diego	4	7	0	.364	245	237
Oakland	3	8	0	.273	218	356
Kansas City	1	10	0	.091	161	301

National Football Conference

East Division	W	L	T	Pct.	Pts.	OP
New York Giants	7	4	0	.636	305	226
Dallas	5	6	0	.455	242	262
Washington	5	6	0	.455	295	285
Philadelphia	3	8	0	.273	184	282
North Division	**W**	**L**	**T**	**Pct.**	**Pts.**	**OP**
Chicago	8	3	0	.727	277	175
Green Bay	7	4	0	.636	273	245
Minnesota	6	5	0	.545	248	249
Detroit	4	7	0	.364	267	280
South Division	**W**	**L**	**T**	**Pct.**	**Pts.**	**OP**
Atlanta	10	1	0	.909	294	216
Tampa Bay	6	5	0	.545	310	254
New Orleans	5	6	0	.455	308	304
Carolina	3	8	0	.273	214	265
West Division	**W**	**L**	**T**	**Pct.**	**Pts.**	**OP**
San Francisco	8	2	1	.773	276	155
Seattle	6	5	0	.545	219	185
St. Louis	4	6	1	.409	205	254
Arizona	4	7	0	.364	180	227

WEEK 12 RESULTS
Thursday, November 22
Houston 34, DETROIT 31 (OT)
Washington 38, DALLAS 31
New England 49, NEW YORK JETS 19

Sunday, November 25
CHICAGO 28, Minnesota 10
CINCINNATI 34, Oakland 10
CLEVELAND 20, Pittsburgh 14
INDIANAPOLIS 20, Buffalo 13
JACKSONVILLE 24, Tennessee 19
Denver 17, KANSAS CITY 9
MIAMI 24, Seattle 21
Atlanta 24, TAMPA BAY 23
St. Louis 31, ARIZONA 17
San Francisco 31, NEW ORLEANS 21
Baltimore 16, SAN DIEGO 13 (OT)
NEW YORK GIANTS 38, Green Bay 10

Monday, November 26
Carolina 30, PHILADELPHIA 22

THIRTEENTH WEEK STANDINGS
American Football Conference

East Division	W	L	T	Pct.	Pts.	OP
New England	9	3	0	.750	430	260
Buffalo	5	7	0	.417	277	337
Miami	5	7	0	.417	227	249
New York Jets	5	7	0	.417	228	296

North Division	W	L	T	Pct.	Pts.	OP
Baltimore	9	3	0	.750	303	242
Cincinnati	7	5	0	.583	302	260
Pittsburgh	7	5	0	.583	254	230
Cleveland	4	8	0	.333	229	265

South Division	W	L	T	Pct.	Pts.	OP
Houston#	11	1	0	.917	351	221
Indianapolis	8	4	0	.667	265	306
Tennessee	4	8	0	.333	248	359
Jacksonville	2	10	0	.167	206	342

West Division	W	L	T	Pct.	Pts.	OP
Denver*	9	3	0	.750	349	244
San Diego	4	8	0	.333	258	257
Oakland	3	9	0	.250	235	376
Kansas City	2	10	0	.167	188	322

National Football Conference

East Division	W	L	T	Pct.	Pts.	OP
New York Giants	7	5	0	.583	321	243
Dallas	6	6	0	.500	280	295
Washington	6	6	0	.500	312	301
Philadelphia	3	9	0	.250	217	320

North Division	W	L	T	Pct.	Pts.	OP
Chicago	8	4	0	.667	294	198
Green Bay	8	4	0	.667	296	259
Minnesota	6	6	0	.500	262	272
Detroit	4	8	0	.333	300	315

South Division	W	L	T	Pct.	Pts.	OP
Atlanta*	11	1	0	.917	317	229
Tampa Bay	6	6	0	.500	333	285
New Orleans	5	7	0	.417	321	327
Carolina	3	9	0	.250	235	292

West Division	W	L	T	Pct.	Pts.	OP
San Francisco	8	3	1	.708	289	171
Seattle	7	5	0	.583	242	202
St. Louis	5	6	1	.458	221	267
Arizona	4	8	0	.333	186	234

*Clinched division title
#Clinched playoff berth

WEEK 13 RESULTS
Thursday, November 29
ATLANTA 23, New Orleans 13

Sunday, December 2
BUFFALO 34, Jacksonville 18
Seattle 23, CHICAGO 17 (OT)
Indianapolis 35, DETROIT 33
GREEN BAY 23, Minnesota 14
KANSAS CITY 27, Carolina 21
New England 23, MIAMI 16
NEW YORK JETS 7, Arizona 6
ST. LOUIS 16, San Francisco 13 (OT)
Houston 24, TENNESSEE 10
DENVER 31, Tampa Bay 23
Pittsburgh 23, BALTIMORE 20
Cleveland 20, OAKLAND 17
Cincinnati 20, SAN DIEGO 13
DALLAS 38, Philadelphia 33

Monday, December 3
WASHINGTON 17, New York Giants 16

FOURTEENTH WEEK STANDINGS
American Football Conference

East Division	W	L	T	Pct.	Pts.	OP
New England*	10	3	0	.769	472	274
New York Jets	6	7	0	.462	245	306
Buffalo	5	8	0	.385	289	352
Miami	5	8	0	.385	240	276

North Division	W	L	T	Pct.	Pts.	OP
Baltimore	9	4	0	.692	331	273
Cincinnati	7	6	0	.538	321	280
Pittsburgh	7	6	0	.538	278	264
Cleveland	5	8	0	.385	259	272

South Division	W	L	T	Pct.	Pts.	OP
Houston#	11	2	0	.846	365	263
Indianapolis	9	4	0	.692	292	329
Tennessee	4	9	0	.308	271	386
Jacksonville	2	11	0	.154	216	359

West Division	W	L	T	Pct.	Pts.	OP
Denver*	10	3	0	.769	375	257
San Diego	5	8	0	.385	292	281
Oakland	3	10	0	.231	248	402
Kansas City	2	11	0	.154	195	352

National Football Conference

East Division	W	L	T	Pct.	Pts.	OP
New York Giants	8	5	0	.615	373	270
Dallas	7	6	0	.538	300	314
Washington	7	6	0	.538	343	329
Philadelphia	4	9	0	.308	240	341

North Division	W	L	T	Pct.	Pts.	OP
Green Bay	9	4	0	.692	323	279
Chicago	8	5	0	.615	308	219
Minnesota	7	6	0	.538	283	286
Detroit	4	9	0	.308	320	342

South Division	W	L	T	Pct.	Pts.	OP
Atlanta*	11	2	0	.846	337	259
Tampa Bay	6	7	0	.462	354	308
New Orleans	5	8	0	.385	348	379
Carolina	4	9	0	.308	265	312

West Division	W	L	T	Pct.	Pts.	OP
San Francisco	9	3	1	.731	316	184
Seattle	8	5	0	.615	300	202
St. Louis	6	6	1	.500	236	279
Arizona	4	9	0	.308	186	292

*Clinched division title
#Clinched playoff berth

WEEK 14 RESULTS
Thursday, December 6
Denver 26, OAKLAND 13

Sunday, December 9
St. Louis 15, BUFFALO 12
CAROLINA 30, Atlanta 20
Dallas 20, CINCINNATI 19
CLEVELAND 30, Kansas City 7
INDIANAPOLIS 27, Tennessee 23
New York Jets 17, JACKSONVILLE 10
MINNESOTA 21, Chicago 14
San Diego 34, PITTSBURGH 24
Philadelphia 23, TAMPA BAY 21
WASHINGTON 31, Baltimore 28 (OT)
NEW YORK GIANTS 52, New Orleans 27
SAN FRANCISCO 27, Miami 13
SEATTLE 58, Arizona 0
GREEN BAY 27, Detroit 20

Monday, December 10
NEW ENGLAND 42, Houston 14

FIFTEENTH WEEK STANDINGS
American Football Conference

East Division	W	L	T	Pct.	Pts.	OP
New England*	10	4	0	.714	506	315
Miami	6	8	0	.429	264	279
New York Jets	6	8	0	.429	255	320
Buffalo	5	9	0	.357	306	402

North Division	W	L	T	Pct.	Pts.	OP
Baltimore#	9	5	0	.643	348	307
Cincinnati	8	6	0	.571	355	293
Pittsburgh	7	7	0	.500	302	291
Cleveland	5	9	0	.357	280	310

South Division	W	L	T	Pct.	Pts.	OP
Houston*	12	2	0	.857	394	280
Indianapolis	9	5	0	.643	309	358
Tennessee	5	9	0	.357	285	396
Jacksonville	2	12	0	.143	219	383

West Division	W	L	T	Pct.	Pts.	OP
Denver*	11	3	0	.786	409	274
San Diego	5	9	0	.357	299	312
Oakland	4	10	0	.286	263	402
Kansas City	2	12	0	.143	195	367

National Football Conference

East Division	W	L	T	Pct.	Pts.	OP
Dallas	8	6	0	.571	327	338
New York Giants	8	6	0	.571	373	304
Washington	8	6	0	.571	381	350
Philadelphia	4	10	0	.286	253	375

North Division	W	L	T	Pct.	Pts.	OP
Green Bay*	10	4	0	.714	344	292
Chicago	8	6	0	.571	321	240
Minnesota	8	6	0	.571	319	308
Detroit	4	10	0	.286	330	380

South Division	W	L	T	Pct.	Pts.	OP
Atlanta*	12	2	0	.857	371	259
New Orleans	6	8	0	.429	389	379
Tampa Bay	6	8	0	.429	354	349
Carolina	5	9	0	.357	296	319

West Division	W	L	T	Pct.	Pts.	OP
San Francisco#	10	3	1	.750	357	218
Seattle	9	5	0	.643	350	219
St. Louis	6	7	1	.464	258	315
Arizona	5	9	0	.357	224	302

*Clinched division title
#Clinched playoff berth

WEEK 15 RESULTS
Thursday, December 13
Cincinnati 34, PHILADELPHIA 13

Sunday, December 16
ATLANTA 34, New York Giants 0
Denver 34, BALTIMORE 17
Green Bay 21, CHICAGO 13
Washington 38, CLEVELAND 21
HOUSTON 29, Indianapolis 17
MIAMI 24, Jacksonville 3
NEW ORLEANS 41, Tampa Bay 0
Minnesota 36, ST. LOUIS 22
ARIZONA 38, Detroit 10
Seattle 50, BUFFALO 17 (Toronto)
Carolina 31, SAN DIEGO 7
DALLAS 27, Pittsburgh 24 (OT)
OAKLAND 15, Kansas City 0
San Francisco 41, NEW ENGLAND 34

Monday, December 17
TENNESSEE 14, New York Jets 10

SIXTEENTH WEEK STANDINGS
American Football Conference

East Division	W	L	T	Pct.	Pts.	OP
New England*	11	4	0	.733	529	331
Miami	7	8	0	.467	288	289
New York Jets	6	9	0	.400	272	347
Buffalo	5	10	0	.333	316	426

North Division	W	L	T	Pct.	Pts.	OP
Baltimore*	10	5	0	.667	381	321
Cincinnati#	9	6	0	.600	368	303
Pittsburgh	7	8	0	.467	312	304
Cleveland	5	10	0	.333	292	344

South Division	W	L	T	Pct.	Pts.	OP
Houston*	12	3	0	.800	400	303
Indianapolis#	10	5	0	.667	329	371
Tennessee	5	10	0	.333	292	451
Jacksonville	2	13	0	.133	235	406

West Division	W	L	T	Pct.	Pts.	OP
Denver*	12	3	0	.800	443	286
San Diego	6	9	0	.400	326	329
Oakland	4	11	0	.267	269	419
Kansas City	2	13	0	.133	208	387

National Football Conference

East Division	W	L	T	Pct.	Pts.	OP
Washington	9	6	0	.600	408	370
Dallas	8	7	0	.533	358	372
New York Giants	8	7	0	.533	387	337
Philadelphia	4	11	0	.267	273	402

North Division	W	L	T	Pct.	Pts.	OP
Green Bay*	11	4	0	.733	399	299
Chicago	9	6	0	.600	349	253
Minnesota	9	6	0	.600	342	314
Detroit	4	11	0	.267	348	411

South Division	W	L	T	Pct.	Pts.	OP
Atlanta*	13	2	0	.867	402	277
New Orleans	7	8	0	.467	423	410
Carolina	6	9	0	.400	313	325
Tampa Bay	6	9	0	.400	367	377

West Division	W	L	T	Pct.	Pts.	OP
San Francisco#	10	4	1	.700	370	260
Seattle#	10	5	0	.667	392	232
St. Louis	7	7	1	.500	286	328
Arizona	5	10	0	.333	237	330

*Clinched division title
#Clinched playoff berth

WEEK 16 RESULTS
Saturday, December 22
Atlanta 31, DETROIT 18

Sunday, December 23
CAROLINA 17, Oakland 6
New Orleans 34, DALLAS 31 (OT)
GREEN BAY 55, Tennessee 7
Minnesota 23, HOUSTON 6
New England 23, JACKSONVILLE 16
Indianapolis 20, KANSAS CITY 13
MIAMI 24, Buffalo 10
San Diego 27, NEW YORK JETS 17
Washington 27, PHILADELPHIA 20
Cincinnati 13, PITTSBURGH 10
St. Louis 28, TAMPA BAY 13
DENVER 34, Cleveland 12
Chicago 28, ARIZONA 13
BALTIMORE 33, New York Giants 14
SEATTLE 42, San Francisco 13

SEVENTEENTH WEEK STANDINGS
American Football Conference

East Division	W	L	T	Pct.	Pts.	OP
New England*	12	4	0	.750	557	331
Miami	7	9	0	.438	288	317
New York Jets	6	10	0	.375	281	375
Buffalo	6	10	0	.375	344	435

North Division	W	L	T	Pct.	Pts.	OP
Baltimore*	10	6	0	.625	398	344
Cincinnati#	10	6	0	.625	391	320
Pittsburgh	8	8	0	.500	336	314
Cleveland	5	11	0	.313	302	368

South Division	W	L	T	Pct.	Pts.	OP
Houston*	12	4	0	.750	416	331
Indianapolis#	11	5	0	.688	357	387
Tennessee	6	10	0	.375	330	471
Jacksonville	2	14	0	.125	255	444

West Division	W	L	T	Pct.	Pts.	OP
Denver*	13	3	0	.813	481	289
San Diego	7	9	0	.438	350	350
Oakland	4	12	0	.250	290	443
Kansas City	2	14	0	.125	211	425

National Football Conference

East Division	W	L	T	Pct.	Pts.	OP
Washington*	10	6	0	.625	436	388
New York Giants	9	7	0	.563	429	344
Dallas	8	8	0	.500	376	400
Philadelphia	4	12	0	.250	280	444

North Division	W	L	T	Pct.	Pts.	OP
Green Bay*	11	5	0	.688	433	336
Minnesota#	10	6	0	.625	379	348
Chicago	10	6	0	.625	375	277
Detroit	4	12	0	.250	372	437

South Division	W	L	T	Pct.	Pts.	OP
Atlanta*	13	3	0	.813	419	299
Carolina	7	9	0	.438	357	363
New Orleans	7	9	0	.438	461	454
Tampa Bay	7	9	0	.438	389	394

West Division	W	L	T	Pct.	Pts.	OP
San Francisco*	11	4	1	.719	397	273
Seattle#	11	5	0	.688	412	245
St. Louis	7	8	1	.469	299	348
Arizona	5	11	0	.313	250	357

*Clinched division title
#Clinched wild-card berth

WEEK 17 RESULTS
Sunday, December 30
Tampa Bay 22, ATLANTA 17
BUFFALO 28, New York Jets 9
CINCINNATI 23, Baltimore 17
Chicago 26, DETROIT 24
INDIANAPOLIS 28, Houston 16
Carolina 44, NEW ORLEANS 38
NEW YORK GIANTS 42, Philadelphia 7
PITTSBURGH 24, Cleveland 10
TENNESSEE 38, Jacksonville 20
DENVER 38, Kansas City 3
MINNESOTA 37, Green Bay 34
NEW ENGLAND 28, Miami 0
SAN DIEGO 24, Oakland 21
SAN FRANCISCO 27, Arizona 13
SEATTLE 20, St. Louis 13
WASHINGTON 28, Dallas 18

2012 NFL PAID ATTENDANCE BREAKDOWN

Games	Attendance	Average
NFL Preseason Total		
65	3,644,321	56,066
NFL Regular-Season Total		
256	16,658,950	65,074
NFL Postseason Total		
12	821,433	66,453
NFL All Games		
333	21,124,704	63,438

1.1-MILLION CLUB
During the 2012 season, six teams drew more than 1.1 million paid attendance home and away during the regular season. The New York Giants led the NFL in regular-season paid attendance (1,193,991). The Giants also led the league in home paid attendance (639,513).

Team	Total Paid Home Attendance	Total Paid Visiting Attendance	Total Paid Cumulative Attendance
New York Giants	639,513	554,478	1,193,991
Dallas	631,289	561,579	1,192,868
Denver	601,635	530,435	1,132,070
New Orleans	560,396	560,625	1,121,021
New England	536,452	567,239	1,103,691
Washington	571,591	530,615	1,102,206

For complete year-by-year attendance records, see pages 537-538.

2012 AFC PLAYERS OF THE WEEK

	Offense	Defense	Special Teams
Week 1	QB Joe Flacco, Baltimore	CB Tracy Porter, Denver	PR-WR Jeremy Kerley, N.Y. Jets
Week 2	RB Reggie Bush, Miami	DE J.J. Watt, Houston	PR-CB Adam Jones, Cincinnati
Week 3	RB Jamaal Charles, Kansas City	DE Michael Johnson, Cincinnati	KR-RB Darius Reynaud, Tennessee
Week 4	QB Tom Brady, New England	LB Donald Butler, San Diego	K Matt Prater, Denver
Week 5	WR Reggie Wayne, Indianapolis	DT Randy Starks, Miami	K Shaun Suisham, Pittsburgh
Week 6	QB Peyton Manning, Denver	S Jairus Byrd, Buffalo	KR-WR Jacoby Jones, Baltimore
Week 7	RB Chris Johnson, Tennessee	DE Lamarr Houston, Oakland	KR-DB Devin McCourty, New England
Week 8	QB Tom Brady, New England	LB Wesley Woodyard, Denver	DE Olivier Vernon, Miami
Week 9	QB Andrew Luck, Indianapolis	CB Ike Taylor, Pittsburgh	KR-WR Trindon Holliday, Denver
Week 10	QB Andy Dalton, Cincinnati	CB Darius Butler, Indianapolis	KR-WR Jacoby Jones, Baltimore
Week 11	QB Matt Schaub, Houston	LB Von Miller, Denver	PR-CB Leodis McKelvin, Buffalo
Week 12	RB Ray Rice, Baltimore	LB D'Qwell Jackson, Cleveland	PR-WR T.Y. Hilton, Indianapolis
Week 13	QB Brady Quinn, Kansas City	DE Carlos Dunlap, Cincinnati	K Shaun Suisham, Pittsburgh
Week 14	QB Tom Brady, New England	CB Cassius Vaughn, Indianapolis	PR-WR Travis Benjamin, Cleveland
Week 15	RB Knowshon Moreno, Denver	DE J.J. Watt, Houston	K Sebastian Janikowski, Oakland
Week 16	RB Ray Rice, Baltimore	DT Geno Atkins, Cincinnati	PR-WR Michael Spurlock, San Diego
Week 17	QB Peyton Manning, Denver	CB Vontae Davis, Indianapolis	PR-RB Darius Reynaud, Tennessee

2012 AFC PLAYERS OF THE MONTH

	Offense	Defense	Special Teams
September	WR A.J. Green, Cincinnati	DE J.J. Watt, Houston	KR-RB Darius Reynaud, Tennessee
October	QB Peyton Manning, Denver	DE Cameron Wake, Miami	K Sebastian Janikowski, Oakland
November	WR Andre Johnson, Houston	LB Von Miller, Denver	KR-WR Jacoby Jones, Baltimore
December	QB Peyton Manning, Denver	DE J.J. Watt, Houston	K Josh Brown, Cincinnati

2012 NFC PLAYERS OF THE WEEK

	Offense	Defense	Special Teams
Week 1	QB Robert Griffin III, Washington	DB Ronde Barber, Tampa Bay	K Blair Walsh, Minnesota
Week 2	WR Hakeem Nicks, N.Y. Giants	DE Calais Campbell, Arizona	P Tim Masthay, Green Bay
Week 3	WR Larry Fitzgerald, Arizona	DE Chris Clemons, Seattle	K Lawrence Tynes, N.Y. Giants
Week 4	QB Aaron Rodgers, Green Bay	LB Patrick Willis, San Francisco	K Greg Zuerlein, St. Louis
Week 5	QB Drew Brees, New Orleans	CB Charles Tillman, Chicago	P Johnny Hekker, St. Louis
Week 6	QB Aaron Rodgers, Green Bay	S Antrel Rolle, N.Y. Giants	K Jason Hanson, Detroit
Week 7	RB Adrian Peterson, Minnesota	CB Charles Tillman, Chicago	P Andy Lee, San Francisco
Week 8	QB Alex Smith, San Francisco	S Stevie Brown, N.Y. Giants	CB Davon House, Green Bay
Week 9	RB Doug Martin, Tampa Bay	LB Brian Urlacher, Chicago	CB Sherrick McManis, Chicago
Week 10	TE Jimmy Graham, New Orleans	CB Richard Sherman, Seattle	PR Dwayne Harris, Dallas
Week 11	QB Robert Griffin III, Washington	LB Aldon Smith, San Francisco	K Dan Bailey, Dallas
Week 12	QB Cam Newton, Carolina	CB Janoris Jenkins, St. Louis	KR-PR Leon Washington, Seattle
Week 13	QB Russell Wilson, Seattle	S William Moore, Atlanta	K Greg Zuerlein, St. Louis
Week 14	RB Adrian Peterson, Minnesota	LB Luke Kuechly, Carolina	KR-RB David Wilson, N.Y. Giants
Week 15	QB Colin Kaepernick, San Francisco	CB Brandon Carr, Dallas	K Blair Walsh, Minnesota
Week 16	QB Matt Ryan, Atlanta	DE Julius Peppers, Chicago	DE Red Bryant, Seattle
Week 17	RB Alfred Morris, Washington	S Stevie Brown, N.Y. Giants	K Blair Walsh, Minnesota

2012 NFC PLAYERS OF THE MONTH

	Offense	Defense	Special Teams
September	QB Matt Ryan, Atlanta	CB Tim Jennings, Chicago	KR-WR Percy Harvin, Minnesota
October	QB Aaron Rodgers, Green Bay	CB Charles Tillman, Chicago	K Lawrence Tynes, N.Y. Giants
November	WR Calvin Johnson, Detroit	LB Aldon Smith, San Francisco	LB Dekoda Watson, Tampa Bay
December	RB Adrian Peterson, Minnesota	LB London Fletcher, Washington	K Blair Walsh, Minnesota

2012 NFL ROOKIES OF THE MONTH

	Offense (College)		Defense (College)	
September	QB	Robert Griffin III, Washington (Baylor)	DE	Chandler Jones, New England (Syracuse)
October	RB	Doug Martin, Tampa Bay (Boise State)	CB	Casey Hayward, Green Bay (Vanderbilt)
November	QB	Robert Griffin III, Washington (Baylor)	LB	Lavonte David, Tampa Bay (Nebraska)
December	QB	Russell Wilson, Seattle (Wisconsin)	LB	Luke Kuechly, Carolina (Boston College)

2012 PRO FOOTBALL AWARDS

ASSOCIATED PRESS

Most Valuable Player	Adrian Peterson
Offensive Player of the Year	Adrian Peterson
Defensive Player of the Year	J.J. Watt
Offensive Rookie of the Year	Robert Griffin III
Defensive Rookie of the Year	Luke Kuechly
Coach of the Year	Bruce Arians
Comeback Player of the Year	Peyton Manning

THE SPORTING NEWS

Offensive Player of the Year	Adrian Peterson
Defensive Player of the Year	J.J. Watt
Rookie of the Year	Robert Griffin III
Coach of the Year	Mike Smith
Coordinator of the Year	Bruce Arians
Executive of the Year	Ryan Grigson
Comeback Player of the Year	Adrian Peterson

PRO FOOTBALL WEEKLY/PFWA

Most Valuable Player	Adrian Peterson
Offensive Player of the Year	Adrian Peterson
Defensive Player of the Year	J.J. Watt
Offensive Rookie of the Year	Robert Griffin III
Defensive Rookie of the Year	Luke Kuechly
Comeback Player of the Year	Adrian Peterson
Most Improved Player	Dez Bryant
Golden Toe	Blair Walsh
Coach of the Year	Bruce Arians
Assistant Coach of the Year	Bruce Arians
Executive of the Year	Ryan Grigson

SPORTS ILLUSTRATED

Most Valuable Player	Adrian Peterson
Offensive Player of the Year	Adrian Peterson
Defensive Player of the Year	J.J. Watt
Offensive Rookie of the Year	Russell Wilson
Defensive Rookie of the Year	Bobby Wagner
Coaches of the Year	Chuck Pagano
	Bruce Arians
Comeback Players of the Year	Peyton Manning
	Adrian Peterson
Executive of the Year	John Schneider

MAXWELL CLUB PLAYER OF THE YEAR

Bert Bell Trophy	Adrian Peterson

WALTER PAYTON/ NFL MAN OF THE YEAR

Man of the Year	Jason Witten
Man of the Year Finalist	Larry Fitzgerald
Man of the Year Finalist	Joe Thomas

SUPER BOWL XLVII MOST VALUABLE PLAYER

Pete Rozelle Trophy	Joe Flacco

AFC-NFC 2013 PRO BOWL MOST VALUABLE PLAYER

Pro Bowl MVP	Kyle Rudolph

FEDEX AIR & GROUND NFL PLAYERS OF THE YEAR

FedEx Air NFL Player of the Year	Peyton Manning
FedEx Ground NFL Player of the Year	Adrian Peterson

PEPSI ROOKIE OF THE YEAR

Rookie of the Year	Russell Wilson

GMC NEVER SAY NEVER MOMENT OF THE YEAR

Moment of the Year Award	Torrey Smith

2012 ALL-PRO TEAMS

2012 PFW/PFWA ALL-PRO TEAM

Selected by *Pro Football Weekly* and the Professional Football Writers of America

Offense:

Peyton Manning, Denver	Quarterback
Adrian Peterson, Minnesota	Running Back
Marshawn Lynch, Seattle	Running Back
Rob Gronkowski, New England	Tight End
Calvin Johnson, Detroit	Wide Receiver
Brandon Marshall, Chicago	Wide Receiver
Duane Brown, Houston	Tackle
Ryan Clady, Denver	Tackle
Mike Iupati, San Francisco	Guard
Marshal Yanda, Baltimore	Guard
John Sullivan, Minnesota	Center

Defense:

J.J. Watt, Houston	End
Cameron Wake, Miami	End
Geno Atkins, Cincinnati	Tackle
Vince Wilfork, New England	Tackle
Von Miller, Denver	Outside Linebacker
Aldon Smith, San Francisco	Outside Linebacker
Patrick Willis, San Francisco	Inside Linebacker
Richard Sherman, Seattle	Cornerback
Charles Tillman, Chicago	Cornerback
Earl Thomas, Seattle	Safety
Eric Weddle, San Diego	Safety

Special Teams:

Blair Walsh, Minnesota	Kicker
Andy Lee, San Francisco	Punter
Jacoby Jones, Baltimore	Kick Returner
Leodis McKelvin, Buffalo	Punt Returner
Matthew Slater, New England	Special Teams Player

2012 ASSOCIATED PRESS ALL-PRO TEAM

Selected by the Associated Press

Offense:

Peyton Manning, Denver	Quarterback
Adrian Peterson, Minnesota	Running Back
Marshawn Lynch, Seattle	Running Back
Vonta Leach, Baltimore	Fullback
Tony Gonzalez, Atlanta	Tight End
Calvin Johnson, Detroit	Wide Receiver
Brandon Marshall, Chicago	Wide Receiver
Duane Brown, Houston	Tackle
Ryan Clady, Denver	Tackle
Jahri Evans, New Orleans	Guard
Mike Iupati, San Francisco	Guard
Max Unger, Seattle	Center

Defense:

J.J. Watt, Houston	End
Cameron Wake, Miami	End
Geno Atkins, Cincinnati	Tackle
Vince Wilfork, New England	Tackle
Von Miller, Denver	Outside Linebacker
Aldon Smith, San Francisco	Outside Linebacker
Patrick Willis, San Francisco	Inside Linebacker
NaVorro Bowman, San Francisco	Inside Linebacker
Richard Sherman, Seattle	Cornerback
Charles Tillman, Chicago	Cornerback
Earl Thomas, Seattle	Safety
Dashon Goldson, San Francisco	Safety

Special Teams:

Blair Walsh, Minnesota	Kicker
Andy Lee, San Francisco	Punter
Jacoby Jones, Baltimore	Kick Returner

2012 ALL-NFL TEAM

Selected by the Associated Press, *Pro Football Weekly,* and the Professional Football Writers of America

Offense:

Peyton Manning, Denver (PFW, AP)	Quarterback
Adrian Peterson, Minnesota (PFW, AP)	Running Back
Marshawn Lynch, Seattle (PFW, AP)	Running Back
Vonta Leach, Baltimore (AP)	Fullback
Rob Gronkowski, New England (PFW)	Tight End
Tony Gonzalez (AP)	Tight End
Calvin Johnson, Detroit (PFW, AP)	Wide Receiver
Brandon Marshall, Chicago (PFW, AP)	Wide Receiver
Duane Brown, Houston (PFW, AP)	Tackle
Ryan Clady, Denver (PFW, AP)	Tackle
Mike Iupati, San Francisco (PFW, AP)	Guard
Marshal Yanda, Baltimore (PFW)	Guard
Jahri Evans, New Orleans (AP)	Guard
John Sullivan, Minnesota (PFW)	Center
Max Unger, Seattle (AP)	Center

Defense:

J.J. Watt, Houston (PFW, AP)	End
Cameron Wake, Miami (PFW, AP)	End
Geno Atkins, Cincinnati (PFW, AP)	Tackle
Vince Wilfork, New England (PFW, AP)	Tackle
Von Miller, Denver (PFW, AP)	Outside Linebacker
Aldon Smith, San Francisco (PFW, AP)	Outside Linebacker
Patrick Willis, San Francisco (PFW, AP)	Inside Linebacker
NaVorro Bowman, San Francisco (AP)	Inside Linebacker
Richard Sherman, Seattle (PFW, AP)	Cornerback
Charles Tillman, Chicago (PFW, AP)	Cornerback
Earl Thomas, Seattle (PFW, AP)	Safety
Eric Weddle, San Diego (PFW)	Safety
Dashon Goldson, San Francisco (AP)	Safety

Special Teams:

Blair Walsh, Minnesota (PFW, AP)	Kicker
Andy Lee, San Francisco (PFW, AP)	Punter
Jacoby Jones, Baltimore (PFW, AP)	Kick Returner
Leodis McKelvin, Buffalo (PFW)	Punt Returner
Matthew Slater, New England (PFW)	Special Teams Player

2012 PFW/PFWA ALL-ROOKIE TEAM

Selected by *Pro Football Weekly* and the Professional Football Writers of America

Offense:

Robert Griffin III, Washington	Quarterback
Alfred Morris, Washington	Running Back
Doug Martin, Tampa Bay	Running Back
Dwayne Allen, Indianapolis	Tight End
T.Y. Hilton, Indianapolis	Wide Receiver
Justin Blackmon, Jacksonville	Wide Receiver
Matt Kalil, Minnesota	Tackle
Mitchell Schwartz, Cleveland	Tackle
Kevin Zeitler, Cincinnati	Guard
Amini Silatolu, Carolina	Guard
None	Center

Defense:

Fletcher Cox, Philadelphia	Defensive Lineman
Chandler Jones, New England	Defensive Lineman
Bruce Irvin, Seattle	Defensive Lineman
Michael Brockers, St. Louis	Defensive Lineman
Bobby Wagner, Seattle	Linebacker
Luke Kuechly, Carolina	Linebacker
Lavonte David, Tampa Bay	Linebacker
Casey Hayward, Green Bay	Cornerback
Janoris Jenkins, St. Louis	Cornerback
Harrison Smith, Minnesota	Safety
Mark Barron, Tampa Bay	Safety

Special Teams:

Blair Walsh, Minnesota	Kicker
Bryan Anger, Jacksonville	Punter
T.Y. Hilton, Indianapolis	Punt Returner
David Wilson, N.Y. Giants	Kick Returner
Johnson Bademosi, Cleveland	Special Teams Player

TEN BEST RUSHING PERFORMANCES, 2012

	Att.	Yards	TD
1. Doug Martin	25	251	4
Tampa Bay vs. Oakland, Nov. 4			
2. Jamaal Charles	33	233	1
Kansas City vs. New Orleans, Sept. 23			
3. Jamaal Charles	22	226	1
Kansas City vs. Indianapolis, Dec. 23			
4. Adrian Peterson	24	212	1
Minnesota vs. St. Louis, Dec. 16			
5. Adrian Peterson	21	210	1
Minnesota vs. Green Bay, Dec. 2			
DeAngelo Williams	21	210	2
Carolina vs. New Orleans, Dec. 30			
7. Alfred Morris	33	200	3
Washington vs. Dallas, Dec. 30			
Ahmad Bradshaw	30	200	1
New York Giants vs. Cleveland, Oct. 7			
9. Adrian Peterson	34	199	1
Minnesota vs. Green Bay, Dec. 30			
10. Chris Johnson	18	195	2
Tennessee vs. Buffalo, Oct. 21			

There were 123 100-yard rushing performances in 2012.

MOST 100-YARD RUSHING PERFORMANCES, 2012

Player, Team	100-Yd. Games
Marshawn Lynch, Seattle	10
Adrian Peterson, Minnesota	10
Jamaal Charles, Kansas City	7
Arian Foster, Houston	7
Alfred Morris, Washington	7
Chris Johnson, Tennessee	5
Doug Martin, Tampa Bay	5
C.J. Spiller, Buffalo	5
Ahmad Bradshaw, New York Giants	4
BenJarvus Green-Ellis, Cincinnati	4
Ray Rice, Baltimore	4
Stevan Ridley, New England	4
Matt Forté, Chicago	3
Frank Gore, San Francisco	3
LeSean McCoy, Philadelphia	3
Darren McFadden, Oakland	3
Willis McGahee, Denver	3
Trent Richardson, Cleveland	3
Bryce Brown, Philadelphia	2
Reggie Bush, Miami	2
Jonathan Dwyer, Pittsburgh	2
Shonn Greene, New York Jets	2
Steven Jackson, St. Louis	2
Knowshon Moreno, Denver	2
LaRod Stephens-Howling, Arizona	2
Michael Turner, Atlanta	2
17 players tied with	1

TEN BEST PASSING PERFORMANCES, 2012

	Att.	Comp.	Yds.	TD
1. Matt Schaub	43	55	527	5
Houston vs. Jacksonville, Nov. 18				
2. Eli Manning	31	51	510	3
New York Giants vs. Tampa Bay, Sept. 16				
3. Drew Brees	37	53	446	3
New Orleans vs. Dallas, Dec. 23				
Drew Brees	35	54	446	3
New Orleans vs. Green Bay, Sept. 30				
5. Matthew Stafford	37	56	443	0
Detroit vs. Atlanta, Dec. 22				
Tom Brady	36	65	443	1
New England vs. San Francisco, Dec. 16				
7. Tony Romo	37	62	441	3
Dallas vs. Washington, Nov. 22				
Matthew Stafford	31	61	441	2
Detroit vs. Houston, Nov. 22				
9. Tony Romo	36	62	437	1
Dallas vs. New York Giants, Oct. 28				
10. Andrew Luck	30	48	433	2
Indianapolis vs. Miami, Nov. 4				

There were 126 300-yard passing performances in 2012.

MOST 300-YARD PASSING PERFORMANCES, 2012

Player, Team	300-Yd. Games
Drew Brees, New Orleans	10
Peyton Manning, Denver	9
Tony Romo, Dallas	9
Tom Brady, New England	8
Matthew Stafford, Detroit	8
Matt Ryan, Atlanta	7
Andrew Luck, Indianapolis	6
Carson Palmer, Oakland	6
Aaron Rodgers, Green Bay	6
Joe Flacco, Baltimore	5
Sam Bradford, St. Louis	3
Andy Dalton, Cincinnati	3
Josh Freeman, Tampa Bay	3
Robert Griffin III, Washington	3
Eli Manning, New York Giants	3
Cam Newton, Carolina	3
Ben Roethlisberger, Pittsburgh	3
Mark Sanchez, New York Jets	3
Michael Vick, Philadelphia	3
Brandon Weeden, Cleveland	3
Ryan Fitzpatrick, Buffalo	2
Nick Foles, Philadelphia	2
Chad Henne, Jacksonville	2
Jake Locker, Tennessee	2
Philip Rivers, San Diego	2
Matt Schaub, Houston	2
10 players tied with 1	1

TEN BEST RECEIVING PERFORMANCES, 2012

	No.	Yards	TD
1. Andre Johnson	14	273	1
Houston vs. Jacksonville, Nov. 18			
2. Brian Hartline	12	253	1
Miami vs. Arizona, Sept. 30			
3. Justin Blackmon	7	236	1
Jacksonville vs. Houston, Nov. 18			
4. Calvin Johnson	11	225	0
Detroit vs. Atlanta, Dec. 22			
5. Dez Bryant	9	224	2
Dallas vs. New Orleans, Dec. 23			
6. Vincent Jackson	7	216	1
Tampa Bay vs. New Orleans, Oct. 21			
7. Reggie Wayne	13	212	1
Indianapolis vs. Green Bay, Oct. 7			
8. Calvin Johnson	12	207	1
Detroit vs. Minnesota, Nov. 11			
9. Hakeem Nicks	10	199	1
New York Giants vs. Tampa Bay, Sept. 16			
10. Brandon Lloyd	10	190	0
New England vs. San Francisco, Dec. 16			

There were 192 100-yard receiving performances in 2012.

MOST 100-YARD RECEIVING PERFORMANCES, 2012

Player, Team	100-Yd. Games
Calvin Johnson, Detroit	11
Brandon Marshall, Chicago	7
Demaryius Thomas, Denver	7
Roddy White, Atlanta	7
Andre Johnson, Houston	6
Dez Bryant, Dallas	5
Victor Cruz, New York Giants	5
A.J. Green, Cincinnati	5
T.Y. Hilton, Indianapolis	5
Vincent Jackson, Tampa Bay	5
Steve Smith, Carolina	5
Wes Welker, New England	5
Michael Crabtree, San Francisco	4
Julio Jones, Atlanta	4
Lance Moore, New Orleans	4
Cecil Shorts, Jacksonville	4
Randall Cobb, Green Bay	3
Marques Colston, New Orleans	3
Rob Gronkowski, New England	3
Brian Hartline, Miami	3
Percy Harvin, Minnesota	3
Steve Johnson, Buffalo	3
Jeremy Maclin, Philadelphia	3
Reggie Wayne, Indianapolis	3
Mike Williams, Tampa Bay	3
Jason Witten, Dallas	3
Danario Alexander, San Diego	2
Danny Amendola, St. Louis	2
Miles Austin, Dallas	2
Donnie Avery, Indianapolis	2
Davone Bess, Miami	2
Dwayne Bowe, Kansas City	2
Eric Decker, Denver	2
Larry Fitzgerald, Arizona	2
Malcom Floyd, San Diego	2
Pierre Garcon, Indianapolis	2
Tony Gonzalez, Atlanta	2
Jimmy Graham, New Orleans	2
DeSean Jackson, Philadelphia	2
Brandon Lloyd, New England	2
Jordy Nelson, Green Bay	2
Andre Roberts, Arizona	2
Torrey Smith, Baltimore	2
Darren Sproles, New Orleans	2
Mike Wallace, Pittsburgh	2
35 players tied with	1

TOP QUARTERBACK SACK PERFORMANCES, 2012

	No.
1. Aldon Smith	5.5
San Francisco vs. Chicago, Nov. 19	
2. Cameron Wake	4.5
Miami vs. Arizona, Sept. 30	
3. Chris Clemons	4.0
Seattle vs. Green Bay, Sept. 24	
4. Kendall Reyes	3.5
San Diego vs. New York Jets, Dec. 23	
Brian Robison	3.5
Minnesota vs. Arizona, Oct. 21	
Charles Johnson	3.5
Carolina vs. Atlanta, Sept. 30	
Clay Matthews	3.5
Green Bay vs. Chicago, Sept. 13	
8. Justin Francis	3.0
New England vs. Miami, Dec. 30	
Everson Griffen	3.0
Minnesota vs. Green Bay, Dec. 30	
Chris Long	3.0
St. Louis vs. Seattle, Dec. 30	
Julius Peppers	3.0
Chicago vs. Arizona, Dec. 23	
J.J. Watt	3.0
Houston vs. Indianapolis, Dec. 16	
Cameron Wake	3.0
Miami vs. San Francisco, Dec. 9	
Mario Williams	3.0
Buffalo vs. Indianapolis, Nov. 25	
J.J. Watt	3.0
Houston vs. Detroit, Nov. 22	
Von Miller	3.0
Denver vs. San Diego, Nov. 18	
Cameron Jordan	3.0
New Orleans vs. Philadelphia, Nov. 5	
Von Miller	3.0
Denver vs. Cincinnati, Nov. 4	
Greg Hardy	3.0
Carolina vs. Chicago, Oct. 28	
John Abraham	3.0
Atlanta vs. Oakland, Oct. 14	
Robert Quinn	3.0
St. Louis vs. Arizona, Oct. 4	
Justin Houston	3.0
Kansas City vs. New Orleans, Sept. 23	
Michael Johnson	3.0
Cincinnati vs. Washington, Sept. 23	
D'Qwell Jackson	3.0
Cleveland vs. Cincinnati, Sept. 16	

There were 243 3.0-plus sack performances in 2012.

MOST 3.0-PLUS SACK PERFORMANCES, 2012

Player, Team	3.0-Sack Games
Von Miller, Denver	2
Cameron Wake, Miami	2
J.J. Watt, Houston	2
18 players tied with	1

For week-by-week listings of top performances from 1970 to the present, please visit www.NFL.com/stats/topperformers.

AMERICAN FOOTBALL CONFERENCE OFFENSE

	Balt.	Buff.	Cin.	Cle.	Den.	Hou.	Ind.	Jax.	KC	Mia.	NE	NYJ	Oak.	Pitt.	SD	Tenn.
First Downs	314	301	292	279	380	341	360	269	286	288	444	299	300	307	293	260
Rushing	98	103	95	71	112	114	110	76	118	93	151	102	72	80	81	70
Passing	182	176	173	185	232	205	208	157	144	158	256	162	200	202	184	166
Penalty	34	22	24	23	36	22	42	36	24	37	37	35	28	25	28	24
Rushes	444	442	430	396	481	508	440	358	500	440	523	494	376	412	411	378
Net Yds. Gained	1901	2217	1745	1593	1832	2123	1671	1369	2395	1802	2184	1896	1420	1537	1461	1687
Avg. Gain	4.3	5.0	4.1	4.0	3.8	4.2	3.8	3.8	4.8	4.1	4.2	3.8	3.8	3.7	3.6	4.5
Avg. Yds. per Game	118.8	138.6	109.1	99.6	114.5	132.7	104.4	85.6	149.7	112.6	136.5	118.5	88.8	96.1	91.3	105.4
Passes Attempted	560	511	540	566	588	554	628	586	475	504	641	493	629	574	528	540
Completed	334	309	335	328	402	354	339	328	273	293	402	272	376	354	338	318
% Completed	59.6	60.5	62.0	58.0	68.4	63.9	54.0	56.0	57.5	58.1	62.7	55.2	59.8	61.7	64.0	58.9
Total Yds. Gained	3996	3430	3807	3668	4671	4046	4374	3746	2937	3425	4844	3178	4292	4012	3606	3577
Times Sacked	38	30	46	36	21	28	41	50	40	37	27	47	27	37	49	39
Yds. Lost	257	161	229	233	137	216	246	327	224	243	182	287	208	225	311	254
Net Yds. Gained	3739	3269	3578	3435	4534	3830	4128	3419	2713	3182	4662	2891	4084	3787	3295	3323
Avg. Yds. per Game	233.7	204.3	223.6	214.7	283.4	239.4	258.0	213.7	169.6	198.9	291.4	180.7	255.3	236.7	205.9	207.7
Net Yds. per Pass Play	6.25	6.04	6.11	5.71	7.44	6.58	6.17	5.38	5.27	5.88	6.98	5.35	6.23	6.20	5.71	5.74
Yds. Gained per Comp.	11.96	11.10	11.36	11.18	11.62	11.43	12.90	11.42	10.76	11.69	12.05	11.68	11.41	11.33	10.67	11.25
Combined Net Yds. Gained	5640	5486	5323	5028	6366	5953	5799	4788	5108	4984	6846	4787	5504	5324	4756	5010
% Total Yds. Rushing	33.7	40.4	32.8	31.7	28.8	35.7	28.8	28.6	46.9	36.2	31.9	39.6	25.8	28.9	30.7	33.7
% Total Yds. Passing	66.3	59.6	67.2	68.3	71.2	64.3	71.2	71.4	53.1	63.8	68.1	60.4	74.2	71.1	69.3	66.3
Avg. Yds. per Game	352.5	342.9	332.7	314.3	397.9	372.1	362.4	299.3	319.3	311.5	427.9	299.2	344.0	332.8	297.3	313.1
Ball Control Plays	1042	983	1016	998	1090	1090	1109	994	1015	981	1191	1034	1032	1023	988	957
Avg. Yds. per Play	5.4	5.6	5.2	5.0	5.8	5.5	5.2	4.8	5.0	5.1	5.7	4.6	5.3	5.2	4.8	5.2
Avg. Time of Poss.	28:09	30:04	30:26	27:59	31:16	32:53	30:36	27:29	30:02	28:32	30:41	29:55	29:27	32:07	31:10	27:18
Third Down Efficiency	36.9	38.9	34.1	30.7	45.1	37.6	42.8	29.6	33.0	37.7	48.7	36.9	35.0	42.0	37.8	38.2
Had Intercepted	11	17	16	18	11	13	18	17	20	13	9	19	16	14	15	16
Yds. Opp Returned	231	256	187	296	218	136	406	400	368	198	112	264	296	168	220	260
Ret. by Opp. for TD	3	2	4	2	2	0	3	5	4	2	0	1	2	2	2	4
Punts	83	80	76	90	67	88	74	92	83	76	61	86	82	79	84	83
Yds. Punted	3911	3542	3540	3766	3105	4150	3520	4353	3887	3779	2585	3848	3826	3400	3914	3855
Avg. Yds. per Punt	47.1	44.3	46.6	41.8	46.3	47.2	47.6	47.3	46.8	49.7	42.4	44.7	46.7	43.0	46.6	46.4
Punt Returns	43	26	47	41	48	38	28	34	43	31	42	23	34	41	33	31
Yds. Returned	404	445	488	606	445	414	312	248	381	346	506	238	173	300	320	475
Avg. Yds. per Return	9.4	17.1	10.4	14.8	9.3	10.9	11.1	7.3	8.9	11.2	12.0	10.3	5.1	7.3	9.7	15.3
Returned for TD	1	2	1	1	1	0	1	0	0	1	1	1	0	0	1	3
Kickoff Returns	60	42	41	50	28	44	43	53	49	40	38	50	42	43	40	63
Yds. Returned	1636	1136	928	1269	646	953	957	1114	1059	1082	807	1308	935	1086	957	1489
Avg. Yds. per Return	27.3	27.0	22.6	25.4	23.1	21.7	22.3	21.0	21.6	27.1	21.2	26.2	22.3	25.3	23.9	23.6
Returned for TD	2	1	0	1	0	0	1	0	0	1	1	1	0	0	1	1
Fumbles	14	23	19	22	22	12	21	20	26	25	14	32	22	33	24	21
Lost	5	17	10	8	14	4	9	9	17	13	7	18	10	16	11	12
Out of Bounds	1	0	1	1	2	1	2	2	1	3	3	1	1	4	2	3
Own Rec. for TD	0	0	0	0	0	0	0	0	0	0	1	0	0	0	0	0
Opp. Rec. by	12	9	16	12	8	14	3	11	6	6	21	12	8	10	14	5
Opp. Rec. for TD	0	0	1	0	1	0	0	0	1	0	3	1	0	0	2	1
Penalties	121	104	99	113	100	108	94	101	92	82	97	83	108	92	103	106
Yds. Penalized	1127	871	857	1005	805	873	801	955	733	724	840	708	939	938	796	847
Total Points Scored	398	344	391	302	481	416	357	255	211	288	557	281	290	336	350	330
Total TDs	44	40	43	31	57	46	40	26	18	31	67	31	28	36	39	36
TDs Rushing	17	12	11	12	12	19	11	5	9	15	25	12	4	8	4	10
TDs Passing	22	24	28	16	37	22	23	20	8	13	34	14	24	27	26	17
TDs on Ret. and Rec.	5	4	4	3	8	5	6	1	1	3	8	5	0	1	9	9
Extra Point Kicks	42	39	43	29	55	45	37	18	17	29	66	30	25	34	39	35
Extra Point Kicks Att.	42	39	43	29	55	45	37	19	17	29	66	30	25	34	39	35
2Pt Conversions	1	0	0	0	1	0	1	3	0	2	0	0	2	1	0	1
2Pt Conversions Att.	2	1	0	2	2	0	2	7	1	2	1	1	3	2	0	1
Safeties	0	1	0	0	2	1	0	0	1	0	1	1	0	0	1	1
Field Goals Made	30	21	30	29	26	31	26	25	28	23	29	21	31	28	25	25
Field Goals Attempted	33	24	35	31	32	38	33	28	34	30	35	27	34	31	27	31
% Successful	90.9	87.5	85.7	93.5	81.3	81.6	78.8	89.3	82.4	76.7	82.9	77.8	91.2	90.3	92.6	80.6

AMERICAN FOOTBALL CONFERENCE DEFENSE

	Balt.	Buff.	Cin.	Cle.	Den.	Hou.	Ind.	Jax.	KC	Mia.	NE	NYJ	Oak.	Pitt.	SD	Tenn.
First Downs	326	349	307	345	287	292	325	364	301	320	340	293	304	273	316	358
Rushing	105	136	99	104	73	94	102	133	106	79	100	96	95	78	85	122
Passing	187	182	183	203	183	167	190	194	176	215	207	161	180	169	201	210
Penalty	34	31	25	38	31	31	33	37	19	26	33	36	29	26	30	26
Rushes	492	470	423	457	404	390	428	545	482	431	415	495	444	391	406	483
Net Yds. Gained	1965	2333	1715	1898	1458	1560	2200	2256	2171	1734	1630	2138	1897	1450	1542	2035
Avg. Gain	4.0	5.0	4.1	4.2	3.6	4.0	5.1	4.1	4.5	4.0	3.9	4.3	4.3	3.7	3.8	4.2
Avg. Yds. per Game	122.8	145.8	107.2	118.6	91.1	97.5	137.5	141.0	135.7	108.4	101.9	133.6	118.6	90.6	96.4	127.2
Passes Attempted	557	536	560	600	559	581	535	535	464	600	594	494	526	523	568	564
Completed	335	306	346	378	321	308	334	341	279	353	369	266	347	299	347	374
% Completed	60.1	57.1	61.8	63.0	57.4	53.0	62.4	63.7	60.1	58.8	62.1	53.8	66.0	57.2	61.1	66.3
Total Yds. Gained	3900	3669	3761	4156	3558	3881	3977	3960	3694	4216	4555	3206	3960	3159	3925	4205
Times Sacked	37	36	51	38	52	44	32	20	27	42	37	30	25	37	38	39
Yds. Lost	250	196	361	233	364	269	189	128	161	242	213	170	185	196	244	241
Net Yds. Gained	3650	3473	3400	3923	3194	3612	3788	3832	3533	3974	4342	3036	3775	2963	3681	3964
Avg. Yds. per Game	228.1	217.1	212.5	245.2	199.6	225.8	236.8	239.5	220.8	248.4	271.4	189.8	235.9	185.2	230.1	247.8
Net Yds. per Pass Play	6.14	6.07	5.56	6.15	5.23	5.78	6.68	6.90	7.20	6.19	6.88	5.79	6.85	5.29	6.07	6.57
Yds. Gained per Comp.	11.64	11.99	10.87	10.99	11.08	12.60	11.91	11.61	13.24	11.94	12.34	12.05	11.41	10.57	11.31	11.24
Combined Net																
Yds. Gained	5615	5806	5115	5821	4652	5172	5988	6088	5704	5708	5972	5174	5672	4413	5223	5999
% Total Yds. Rushing	35.0	40.2	33.5	32.6	31.3	30.2	36.7	37.1	38.1	30.4	27.3	41.3	33.4	32.9	29.5	33.9
% Total Yds. Passing	65.0	59.8	66.5	67.4	68.7	69.8	63.3	62.9	61.9	69.6	72.7	58.7	66.6	67.1	70.5	66.1
Avg. Yds. per Game	350.9	362.9	319.7	363.8	290.8	323.3	374.3	380.5	356.5	356.8	373.3	323.4	354.5	275.8	326.4	374.9
Ball Control Plays	1086	1042	1034	1095	1015	1015	995	1100	973	1073	1046	1019	995	951	1012	1086
Avg. Yds. per Play	5.2	5.6	4.9	5.3	4.6	5.1	6.0	5.5	5.9	5.3	5.7	5.1	5.7	4.6	5.2	5.5
Avg. Time of Poss.	31:51	29:56	29:34	32:01	28:44	27:07	29:24	32:31	29:58	31:28	29:19	30:05	30:33	27:53	28:50	32:42
Third Down Efficiency	35.8	44.0	36.1	38.1	30.6	33.0	38.1	41.4	39.1	36.6	40.0	37.2	39.2	35.4	42.1	39.7
Intercepted By	13	12	14	17	16	15	12	12	7	10	20	11	11	10	14	19
Yds. Returned By	196	178	164	230	347	333	155	122	119	99	371	117	91	127	336	358
Returned for TD	2	1	2	2	5	3	4	0	0	0	2	2	0	1	5	4
Punts	89	72	86	88	94	92	71	68	74	86	67	89	69	88	80	70
Yds. Punted	4113	3210	3816	4044	4524	4176	3340	3131	3466	3815	3372	3947	3171	3979	3635	3084
Avg. Yds. per Punt	46.2	44.6	44.4	46.0	48.1	45.4	47.0	46.0	46.8	44.4	50.3	44.3	46.0	45.2	45.4	44.1
Punt Returns	49	35	27	34	33	48	32	40	27	43	23	31	45	30	40	39
Yds. Returned	383	517	210	343	203	483	375	495	362	484	154	375	450	306	362	405
Avg. Yds. per Return	7.8	14.8	7.8	10.1	6.2	10.1	11.7	12.4	13.4	11.3	6.7	12.1	10.0	10.2	9.1	10.4
Returned for TD	0	2	0	1	0	1	1	2	2	1	0	1	0	1	0	0
Kickoff Returns	37	51	60	43	34	62	34	39	27	35	60	54	30	46	45	33
Yds. Returned	859	1144	1468	853	751	1595	841	1009	690	868	1229	1184	868	1103	1017	860
Avg. Yds. per Return	23.2	22.4	24.5	19.8	22.1	25.7	24.7	25.9	25.6	24.8	20.5	21.9	28.9	24.0	22.6	26.1
Returned for TD	0	1	0	0	0	2	0	0	0	1	0	1	2	0	0	1
Fumbles	23	26	26	25	23	23	11	17	19	23	42	16	14	19	29	15
Lost	12	9	16	12	8	14	3	11	6	6	21	12	8	10	14	5
Out of Bounds	3	3	1	2	0	0	1	1	3	3	3	0	0	1	2	2
Own Rec. for TD	0	0	0	0	0	1	0	0	0	0	1	0	0	0	0	0
Opp. Rec. by	5	17	10	8	14	4	9	9	17	13	7	18	10	16	11	12
Opp. Rec. for TD	0	0	0	0	0	0	0	0	1	0	0	3	0	2	1	1
Penalties	107	80	90	120	123	90	128	101	81	121	101	109	101	100	102	86
Yds. Penalized	929	693	779	1008	951	863	1208	820	670	1045	932	805	925	882	798	717
Total Points Scored	344	435	320	368	289	331	387	444	425	317	331	375	443	314	350	471
Total TDs	33	53	34	44	32	38	42	48	47	32	38	44	50	33	42	55
TDs Rushing	15	23	13	14	5	5	14	19	11	10	10	17	18	9	10	16
TDs Passing	15	25	16	27	25	29	23	21	29	18	27	20	28	19	28	31
TDs on Ret. and Rec.	3	5	5	3	2	4	5	8	7	4	1	7	4	5	4	8
Extra Point Kicks	31	50	33	42	29	38	39	46	47	30	38	43	50	30	39	52
Extra Point Kicks Att.	31	51	33	42	29	38	39	46	47	30	38	43	50	31	39	52
2Pt Conversions	1	2	1	1	0	0	0	1	0	1	0	0	0	1	1	1
2Pt Conversions Att.	2	2	1	2	3	0	3	1	0	2	0	1	0	2	3	2
Safeties	1	0	0	0	1	1	0	0	0	0	1	1	0	0	0	0
Field Goals Made	37	21	27	20	22	21	32	36	32	31	21	22	31	28	19	29
Field Goals Attempted	39	28	32	24	25	24	41	43	38	40	25	31	37	33	21	31
% Successful	94.9	75.0	84.4	83.3	88.0	87.5	78.0	83.7	84.2	77.5	84.0	71.0	83.8	84.8	90.5	93.5

NATIONAL FOOTBALL CONFERENCE OFFENSE

	Ariz.	Atl.	Car.	Chi.	Dall.	Det.	GB	Minn.	NO	NYG	Phil.	StL	SF	Sea.	TB	Wash.
First Downs	246	342	328	292	338	382	341	306	352	327	332	287	322	311	301	341
Rushing	58	70	123	99	76	84	85	113	64	103	111	79	128	129	89	144
Passing	168	246	171	163	237	272	213	163	267	187	190	189	172	153	188	171
Penalty	20	26	34	30	25	26	43	30	21	37	31	19	22	29	24	26
Rushes	352	378	462	470	355	391	433	486	370	409	413	410	492	536	416	519
Net Yds. Gained	1204	1397	2088	1970	1265	1613	1702	2634	1577	1862	1874	1714	2491	2579	1837	2709
Avg. Gain	3.4	3.7	4.5	4.2	3.6	4.1	3.9	5.4	4.3	4.6	4.5	4.2	5.1	4.8	4.4	5.2
Avg. Yds. per Game	75.3	87.3	130.5	123.1	79.1	100.8	106.4	164.6	98.6	116.4	117.1	107.1	155.7	161.2	114.8	169.3
Passes Attempted	608	615	490	485	658	740	558	483	671	539	618	557	436	405	566	442
Completed	337	422	284	287	434	445	374	300	423	323	367	332	289	259	311	291
% Completed	55.4	68.6	58.0	59.2	66.0	60.1	67.0	62.1	63.0	59.9	59.4	59.6	66.3	64.0	54.9	65.8
Total Yds. Gained	3383	4719	3927	3298	4992	5139	4342	2935	5187	3967	4075	3783	3551	3234	4144	3666
Times Sacked	58	28	36	44	36	29	51	32	26	20	48	35	41	33	26	33
Yds. Lost	378	210	244	299	263	212	293	184	190	142	284	233	253	203	161	244
Net Yds. Gained	3005	4509	3683	2999	4729	4927	4049	2751	4997	3825	3791	3550	3298	3031	3983	3422
Avg. Yds. per Game	187.8	281.8	230.2	187.4	295.6	307.9	253.1	171.9	312.3	239.1	236.9	221.9	206.1	189.4	248.9	213.9
Net Yds. per Pass Play	4.51	7.01	7.00	5.67	6.81	6.41	6.65	5.34	7.17	6.84	5.69	6.00	6.91	6.92	6.73	7.20
Yds. Gained per Comp.	10.04	11.18	13.83	11.49	11.50	11.55	11.61	9.78	12.26	12.28	11.10	11.39	12.29	12.49	13.32	12.60
Combined Net Yds. Gained	4209	5906	5771	4969	5994	6540	5751	5385	6574	5687	5665	5264	5789	5610	5820	6131
% Total Yds. Rushing	28.6	23.7	36.2	39.6	21.1	24.7	29.6	48.9	24.0	32.7	33.1	32.6	43.0	46.0	31.6	44.2
% Total Yds. Passing	71.4	76.3	63.8	60.4	78.9	75.3	70.4	51.1	76.0	67.3	66.9	67.4	57.0	54.0	68.4	55.8
Avg. Yds. per Game	263.1	369.1	360.7	310.6	374.6	408.8	359.4	336.6	410.9	355.4	354.1	329.0	361.8	350.6	363.8	383.2
Ball Control Plays	1018	1021	988	999	1049	1160	1042	1001	1067	968	1079	1002	969	974	1008	994
Avg. Yds. per Play	4.1	5.8	5.8	5.0	5.7	5.6	5.5	5.4	6.2	5.9	5.3	5.3	6.0	5.8	5.8	6.2
Avg. Time of Poss.	29:01	30:52	29:43	31:33	30:33	31:16	30:26	28:36	28:36	29:10	29:36	28:54	30:49	31:36	30:11	31:05
Third Down Efficiency	25.2	45.1	43.1	36.5	43.9	42.5	42.3	37.1	44.0	40.6	37.4	32.1	35.1	42.0	35.8	35.8
Had Intercepted	21	14	12	16	19	17	8	12	19	15	15	14	8	10	17	8
Yds. Opp Returned	379	158	200	241	340	475	47	72	356	288	391	182	70	115	269	142
Ret. by Opp. for TD	5	1	3	2	3	4	0	1	3	2	3	2	0	1	3	0
Punts	112	62	77	81	69	76	71	72	74	58	72	82	67	65	77	70
Yds. Punted	5209	2847	3267	3399	3039	3149	3043	3237	3707	2757	3336	3756	3226	2963	3440	2984
Avg. Yds. per Punt	46.5	45.9	42.4	42.0	44.0	41.4	42.9	45.0	50.1	47.5	46.3	45.8	48.1	45.6	44.7	42.6
Punt Returns	54	26	27	44	34	35	36	32	25	20	30	37	36	42	36	36
Yds. Returned	441	205	276	333	420	302	395	287	190	144	310	245	378	355	324	335
Avg. Yds. per Return	8.2	7.9	10.2	7.6	12.4	8.6	11.0	9.0	7.6	7.2	10.3	6.6	10.5	8.5	9.0	9.3
Returned for TD	0	0	0	0	1	0	1	1	0	0	1	0	0	0	0	0
Kickoff Returns	40	27	39	47	36	34	43	44	51	63	60	38	49	29	31	38
Yds. Returned	930	640	867	929	741	681	1074	1171	1266	1648	1259	799	1216	787	630	892
Avg. Yds. per Return	23.3	23.7	22.2	19.8	20.6	20.0	25.0	26.6	24.8	26.2	21.0	21.0	24.8	27.1	20.3	23.5
Returned for TD	0	0	0	0	0	0	0	1	0	1	0	0	0	1	0	0
Fumbles	25	9	22	20	20	24	16	21	13	13	37	24	26	16	16	26
Lost	13	4	10	8	10	16	8	11	5	6	22	8	8	8	6	6
Out of Bounds	2	2	2	0	0	3	0	2	3	0	2	4	3	1	1	3
Own Rec. for TD	0	0	1	0	0	0	0	0	0	0	0	0	1	0	0	2
Opp. Rec. by	11	11	12	20	9	6	5	12	11	14	5	4	11	13	8	9
Opp. Rec. for TD	1	1	0	1	2	0	1	0	0	1	0	1	1	1	0	1
Penalties	102	55	98	102	117	103	103	90	104	72	98	130	109	110	101	116
Yds. Penalized	857	415	835	811	853	944	923	830	911	578	813	978	960	890	819	985
Total Points Scored	250	419	357	375	376	372	433	379	461	429	280	299	397	412	389	436
Total TDs	25	46	44	42	41	39	53	39	58	47	29	32	44	44	44	52
TDs Rushing	10	12	21	11	8	17	9	16	10	18	10	5	17	16	13	22
TDs Passing	11	32	19	21	29	22	40	18	43	26	18	22	23	27	27	24
TDs on Ret. and Rec.	4	2	4	10	4	0	4	5	5	3	1	5	4	6	4	6
Extra Point Kicks	25	44	43	40	37	38	50	36	57	46	25	26	44	46	39	50
Extra Point Kicks Att.	25	44	44	40	37	38	50	36	57	46	26	26	44	48	39	51
2Pt Conversions	0	0	0	1	3	1	1	2	1	1	0	5	0	0	1	1
2Pt Conversions Att.	0	2	0	2	4	1	3	3	1	1	3	6	0	0	4	1
Safeties	0	0	1	0	0	1	0	0	0	0	1	1	0	0	0	0
Field Goals Made	25	33	16	27	29	32	21	35	18	33	27	23	29	24	28	24
Field Goals Attempted	28	38	21	33	31	36	33	38	22	39	31	31	42	27	33	30
% Successful	89.3	86.8	76.2	81.8	93.5	88.9	63.6	92.1	81.8	84.6	87.1	74.2	69.0	88.9	84.8	80.0

NATIONAL FOOTBALL CONFERENCE DEFENSE

	Ariz.	Atl.	Car.	Chi.	Dall.	Det.	GB	Minn.	NO	NYG	Phil.	StL	SF	Sea.	TB	Wash.
First Downs	288	298	325	286	317	305	308	345	380	317	317	327	284	295	329	340
Rushing	107	99	98	75	92	107	83	82	116	104	108	107	72	80	75	89
Passing	160	189	195	186	195	167	191	229	236	196	178	197	178	186	226	223
Penalty	21	10	32	25	30	31	34	34	28	17	31	23	34	29	28	28
Rushes	506	411	416	388	441	420	418	427	457	449	479	442	407	368	377	363
Net Yds. Gained	2192	1971	1761	1627	2003	1889	1896	1692	2361	2066	2021	1880	1507	1649	1320	1532
Avg. Gain	4.3	4.8	4.2	4.2	4.5	4.5	4.5	4.0	5.2	4.6	4.2	4.3	3.7	4.5	3.5	4.2
Avg. Yds. per Game	137.0	123.2	110.1	101.7	125.2	118.1	118.5	105.8	147.6	129.1	126.3	117.5	94.2	103.1	82.5	95.8
Passes Attempted	497	551	555	592	511	544	568	612	602	534	485	547	567	564	627	636
Completed	270	337	371	350	320	346	313	391	370	341	292	362	337	327	410	393
% Completed	54.3	61.2	66.8	59.1	62.6	63.6	55.1	63.9	61.5	63.9	60.2	66.2	59.4	58.0	65.4	61.8
Total Yds. Gained	3441	4060	3852	3712	3895	3806	3801	4192	4875	4299	3668	3927	3473	3497	4951	4720
Times Sacked	38	29	39	41	34	34	47	44	30	33	30	52	38	36	27	32
Yds. Lost	228	182	284	289	211	237	309	284	194	231	198	325	270	247	193	209
Net Yds. Gained	3213	3878	3568	3423	3684	3569	3492	3908	4681	4068	3470	3602	3203	3250	4758	4511
Avg. Yds. per Game	200.8	242.4	223.0	213.9	230.3	223.1	218.3	244.3	292.6	254.3	216.9	225.1	200.2	203.1	297.4	281.9
Net Yds. per Pass Play	6.01	6.69	6.01	5.41	6.76	6.17	5.68	5.96	7.41	7.17	6.74	6.01	5.29	5.42	7.28	6.75
Yds. Gained per Comp.	12.74	12.05	10.38	10.61	12.17	11.00	12.14	10.72	13.18	12.61	12.56	10.85	10.31	10.69	12.08	12.01
Combined Net Yds. Gained	5405	5849	5329	5050	5687	5458	5388	5600	7042	6134	5491	5482	4710	4899	6078	6043
% Total Yds. Rushing	40.6	33.7	33.0	32.2	35.2	34.6	35.2	30.2	33.5	33.7	36.8	34.3	32.0	33.7	21.7	25.4
% Total Yds. Passing	59.4	66.3	67.0	67.8	64.8	65.4	64.8	69.8	66.5	66.3	63.2	65.7	68.0	66.3	78.3	74.6
Avg. Yds. per Game	337.8	365.6	333.1	315.6	355.4	341.1	336.8	350.0	440.1	383.4	343.2	342.6	294.4	306.2	379.9	377.7
Ball Control Plays	1041	991	1010	1021	986	998	1033	1083	1089	1016	994	1041	1012	968	1031	1031
Avg. Yds. per Play	5.2	5.9	5.3	4.9	5.8	5.5	5.2	5.2	6.5	6.0	5.5	5.3	4.7	5.1	5.9	5.9
Avg. Time of Poss.	30:59	29:08	30:17	28:27	29:27	28:44	29:34	31:24	31:24	30:50	30:24	31:06	29:11	28:24	29:49	28:55
Third Down Efficiency	32.9	40.5	36.1	35.5	40.1	36.5	38.1	41.3	38.5	42.4	40.9	37.6	33.0	38.4	40.2	44.2
Intercepted By	22	20	11	24	7	11	18	10	15	21	8	17	14	18	18	21
Yds. Returned By	306	246	181	488	147	135	246	224	369	496	31	382	216	255	419	257
Returned for TD	2	1	3	8	1	0	1	3	4	1	0	4	2	2	3	3
Punts	93	64	67	89	74	79	75	76	63	54	78	73	79	78	79	65
Yds. Punted	4166	3065	3073	3883	3362	3626	3350	3344	2876	2426	3410	3231	3609	3515	3563	3018
Avg. Yds. per Punt	44.8	47.9	45.9	43.6	45.4	45.9	44.7	44.0	45.7	44.9	43.7	44.3	45.7	45.1	45.1	46.4
Punt Returns	48	26	37	25	29	33	24	41	31	38	40	41	36	29	40	39
Yds. Returned	415	241	318	84	279	328	179	341	391	353	542	402	249	252	440	320
Avg. Yds. per Return	8.6	9.3	8.6	3.4	9.6	9.9	7.5	8.3	12.6	9.3	13.6	9.8	6.9	8.7	11.0	8.2
Returned for TD	0	0	1	0	1	2	0	0	0	0	1	0	1	0	0	0
Kickoff Returns	32	48	39	37	50	52	51	33	42	70	41	30	48	50	27	55
Yds. Returned	846	1065	739	767	1102	1213	1193	795	1049	1662	1012	730	1289	1147	680	1264
Avg. Yds. per Return	26.4	22.2	18.9	20.7	22.0	23.3	23.4	24.1	25.0	23.7	24.7	24.3	26.9	22.9	25.2	23.0
Returned for TD	0	0	0	0	1	2	0	0	1	0	0	0	0	0	0	0
Fumbles	17	16	18	35	18	19	18	23	19	25	21	17	21	27	16	17
Lost	11	11	12	20	9	6	5	12	11	14	5	4	11	13	8	10
Out of Bounds	2	2	0	6	1	0	4	4	2	2	2	3	0	1	1	1
Own Rec. for TD	0	0	0	1	0	0	0	0	0	1	0	0	0	0	1	0
Opp. Rec. by	13	4	10	8	10	16	8	11	4	6	22	8	8	8	6	6
Opp. Rec. for TD	3	0	0	0	0	2	0	0	0	0	4	1	1	1	1	0
Penalties	100	83	86	78	89	93	123	111	102	102	118	90	93	102	103	100
Yds. Penalized	810	641	711	704	726	789	1055	949	835	900	996	758	758	902	851	811
Total Points Scored	357	299	363	277	400	437	336	348	454	344	444	348	273	245	394	388
Total TDs	40	31	37	29	45	49	37	39	53	38	52	37	29	25	48	43
TDs Rushing	12	16	11	6	17	13	12	10	18	9	11	18	7	8	13	11
TDs Passing	20	14	22	19	22	26	24	28	31	26	33	16	19	15	30	31
TDs on Ret. and Rec.	8	1	4	4	6	10	1	1	4	3	8	3	3	2	5	1
Extra Point Kicks	38	30	32	26	43	46	34	33	53	38	51	36	27	24	45	36
Extra Point Kicks Att.	38	30	32	26	44	46	34	35	53	38	52	36	27	24	45	36
2Pt Conversions	1	0	1	2	0	2	1	3	0	0	0	0	2	0	2	5
2Pt Conversions Att.	2	1	4	2	1	3	4	4	0	0	0	1	2	1	3	7
Safeties	1	1	1	2	0	0	0	0	1	0	0	0	1	1	0	0
Field Goals Made	25	27	35	23	29	31	26	25	27	26	27	30	22	23	19	28
Field Goals Attempted	35	32	37	27	33	41	30	30	33	30	29	37	27	25	28	30
% Successful	71.4	84.4	94.6	85.2	87.9	75.6	86.7	83.3	81.8	86.7	93.1	81.1	81.5	92.0	67.9	93.3

AFC, NFC, AND NFL SUMMARY

	AFC Offense Total	AFC Offense Average	AFC Defense Total	AFC Defense Average	NFC Offense Total	NFC Offense Average	NFC Defense Total	NFC Defense Average	NFL Total	NFL Average
First Downs	5013	313.3	5100	318.8	5148	321.8	5061	316.3	10161	317.5
Rushing	1546	96.6	1607	100.4	1555	97.2	1494	93.4	3101	96.9
Passing	2990	186.9	3008	188.0	3150	196.9	3132	195.8	6140	191.9
Penalty	477	29.8	485	30.3	443	27.7	435	27.2	920	28.8
Rushes	7033	439.6	7156	447.3	6892	430.8	6769	423.1	13925	435.2
Net Yds. Gained	28833	1802.1	29982	1873.9	30516	1907.3	29367	1835.4	59349	1854.7
Avg. Gain	—	4.1	—	4.2	—	4.4	—	4.3	—	4.3
Avg. Yds. per Game	—	112.6	—	117.1	—	119.2	—	114.7	—	115.9
Passes Attempted	8917	557.3	8796	549.8	8871	554.4	8992	562.0	17788	555.9
Completed	5355	334.7	5303	331.4	5478	342.4	5530	345.6	10833	338.5
% Completed	—	60.1	—	60.3	—	61.8	—	61.5	—	60.9
Total Yds. Gained	61609	3850.6	61782	3861.4	64342	4021.4	64169	4010.6	125951	3936.0
Times Sacked	593	37.1	585	36.6	576	36.0	584	36.5	1169	36.5
Yds. Lost	3740	233.8	3642	227.6	3793	237.1	3891	243.2	7533	235.4
Net Yds. Gained	57869	3616.8	58140	3633.8	60549	3784.3	60278	3767.4	118418	3700.6
Avg. Yds. per Game	—	226.1	—	227.1	—	236.5	—	235.5	—	231.3
Net Yds. per Pass Play	—	6.09	—	6.20	—	6.41	—	6.29	—	6.25
Yds. Gained per Comp.	—	11.50	—	11.65	—	11.75	—	11.60	—	11.63
Combined Net Yds. Gained	86702	5418.9	88122	5507.6	91065	5691.6	89645	5602.8	177767	5555.2
% Total Yds. Rushing	—	33.3	—	34.0	—	33.5	—	32.8	—	33.4
% Total Yds. Passing	—	66.7	—	66.0	—	66.5	—	67.2	—	66.6
Avg. Yds. per Game	—	338.7	—	344.2	—	355.7	—	350.2	—	347.2
Ball Control Plays	16543	1033.9	16537	1033.6	16339	1021.2	16345	1021.6	32882	1027.6
Avg. Yds. per Play	—	5.2	—	5.3	—	5.6	—	5.5	—	5.4
Third Down Efficiency	—	37.8	—	37.8	—	38.5	—	38.5	—	38.2
Interceptions	243	15.2	213	13.3	225	14.1	255	15.9	468	14.6
Yds. Returned	4016	251.0	3343	208.9	3725	232.8	4398	274.9	7741	241.9
Returned for TD	38	2.4	33	2.1	33	2.1	38	2.4	71	2.2
Punts	1284	80.3	1283	80.2	1185	74.1	1186	74.1	2469	77.2
Yds. Punted	58981	3686.3	58823	3676.4	53359	3334.9	53517	3344.8	112340	3510.6
Avg. Yds. per Punt	—	45.9	—	45.8	—	45.0	—	45.1	—	45.5
Punt Returns	583	36.4	576	36.0	550	34.4	557	34.8	1133	35.4
Yds. Returned	6101	381.3	5907	369.2	4940	308.8	5134	320.9	11041	345.0
Avg. Yds. per Return	—	10.5	—	10.3	—	9.0	—	9.2	—	9.7
Returned for TD	14	0.9	12	0.8	4	0.3	6	0.4	18	0.6
Kickoff Returns	726	45.4	690	43.1	669	41.8	705	44.1	1395	43.6
Yds. Returned	17362	1085.1	16339	1021.2	15530	970.6	16553	1034.6	32892	1027.9
Avg. Yds. per Return	—	23.9	—	23.7	—	23.2	—	23.5	—	23.6
Returned for TD	10	0.6	9	0.6	3	0.2	4	0.3	13	0.4
Fumbles	350	21.9	351	21.9	328	20.5	327	20.4	678	21.2
Lost	180	11.3	167	10.4	149	9.3	162	10.1	329	10.3
Out of Bounds	28	1.8	25	1.6	28	1.8	31	1.9	56	1.8
Own Rec. for TD	1	0.1	2	0.1	4	0.3	3	0.2	5	0.2
Opp. Rec.	167	10.4	180	11.3	161	10.1	148	9.3	328	10.3
Opp. Rec. for TD	10	0.6	8	0.5	11	0.7	13	0.8	21	0.7
Penalties	1603	100.2	1640	102.5	1610	100.6	1573	98.3	3213	100.4
Yds. Penalized	13819	863.7	14025	876.6	13402	837.6	13196	824.8	27221	850.7
Total Points Scored	5587	349.2	5944	371.5	6064	379.0	5707	356.7	11651	364.1
Total TDs	613	38.3	665	41.6	684	42.8	632	39.5	1297	40.5
TDs Rushing	186	11.6	209	13.1	215	13.4	192	12.0	401	12.5
TDs Passing	355	22.2	381	23.8	402	25.1	376	23.5	757	23.7
TDs on Ret. and Rec.	72	4.5	75	4.7	67	4.2	64	4.0	139	4.3
Extra Point Kicks	583	36.4	637	39.8	646	40.4	592	37.0	1229	38.4
Extra Point Kicks Att.	584	36.5	639	39.9	651	40.7	596	37.3	1235	38.6
2Pt Conversions	12	0.8	10	0.6	17	1.1	19	1.2	29	0.9
2Pt Conversions Att.	27	1.7	24	1.5	31	1.9	34	2.1	58	1.8
Safeties	9	0.6	5	0.3	4	0.3	8	0.5	13	0.4
Field Goals Made	428	26.8	429	26.8	424	26.5	423	26.4	852	26.6
Field Goals Attempted	503	31.4	512	32.0	513	32.1	504	31.5	1016	31.8
% Successful	—	85.1	—	83.8	—	82.7	—	83.9	—	83.9

CLUB LEADERS

	Offense	Defense
First Downs	New England 444	Pittsburgh 273
Rushing	New England 151	San Francisco 72
Passing	Detroit 272	Arizona 160
Penalty	Green Bay 43	Atlanta 10
Rushes	Seattle 536	Washington 363
Net Yds. Gained	Washington 2709	Tampa Bay 1320
Avg. Gain	Minnesota 5.4	Tampa Bay 3.5
Passes Attempted	Detroit 740	Kansas City 464
Completed	Detroit 445	N.Y. Jets 266
% Completed	Atlanta 68.6	Houston 53.0
Total Yds. Gained	New Orleans 5187	Pittsburgh 3159
Times Sacked	N.Y. Giants 20	Denver & St. Louis 52
Yds. Lost	Denver 137	Denver 364
Net Yds. Gained	New Orleans 4997	Pittsburgh 2963
Net Yds. per Pass Play	Denver 7.4	Denver 5.2
Yds. Gained per Comp.	Carolina 13.8	San Francisco 10.3
Combined Net Yds. Gained	New England 6846	Pittsburgh 4413
% Total Yds. Rushing	Minnesota 48.9	Tampa Bay 21.7
% Total Yds. Passing	Dallas 78.9	N.Y. Jets 58.7
Ball Control Plays	New England 1191	Pittsburgh 951
Avg. Yds. per Play	Washington 6.2	Denver 4.6
Avg. Time of Poss.	Houston 32:53	—
Third Down Efficiency	New England 48.7	Denver 30.6
Interceptions	—	Chicago 24
Yds. Returned	—	N.Y. Giants 496
Returned for TD	—	Chicago 8
Punts	Arizona 112	—
Yds. Punted	Arizona 5209	—
Avg. Yds. per Punt	New Orleans 50.1	—
Punt Returns	Arizona 54	New England 23
Yds. Returned	Cleveland 606	Chicago 84
Avg. Yds. per Return	Buffalo 17.1	Chicago 3.4
Returned for TD	Tennessee 3	—
Kickoff Returns	N.Y. Giants & Tennessee 63	Kansas City & Tampa Bay 27
Yds. Returned	N.Y. Giants 1648	Tampa Bay 680
Avg. Yds. per Return	Baltimore 27.3	Carolina 18.9
Returned for TD	Baltimore 2	—
Total Points Scored	New England 557	Seattle 245
Total TDs	New England 67	Seattle 25
TDs Rushing	New England 25	Denver & Houston 5
TDs Passing	New Orleans 43	Atlanta 14
TDs on Ret. and Rec.	Chicago 10	Atlanta & Green Bay & Minnesota & New England & Washington 1
Extra Point Kicks	New England 66	Seattle 24
2-Point Conversions	St. Louis 5	—
Safeties	Denver 2	—
Field Goals Made	Minnesota 35	San Diego & Tampa Bay 19
Field Goals Attempted	San Francisco 42	San Diego 21
% Successful	Cleveland & Dallas 93.5	Tampa Bay 67.9

NFL CLUB RANKINGS BY YARDS

	Offense			Defense		
	Total	Rush	Pass	Total	Rush	Pass
Arizona	32	32	28	12	28	5
Atlanta	8	29	6	24	21	23
Baltimore	16	11	15	17	20	17
Buffalo	19	6	25	22	31	10
Carolina	12	9	16	10	14	13
Chicago	28	10	29	5	8	8
Cincinnati	22	18	17	6	12	7
Cleveland	25	24	19	23	19	25
Dallas	6	31	3	19	22	19
Denver	4	16	5	2	3	3
Detroit	3	23	2	13	16	14
Green Bay	13	20	9	11	17	11
Houston	7	8	11	7	7	16
Indianapolis	10	22	7	26	29	21
Jacksonville	29	30	21	30	30	22
Kansas City	24	5	32	20	27	12
Miami	27	17	26	21	13	27
Minnesota	20	2	31	16	11	24
New England	*1	7	4	25	9	29
New Orleans	2	25	*1	32	32	31
New York Giants	14	14	12	31	25	28
New York Jets	30	12	30	8	26	2
Oakland	18	28	8	18	18	20
Philadelphia	15	13	13	15	23	9
Pittsburgh	21	26	14	*1	2	*1
St. Louis	23	19	18	14	15	15
San Diego	31	27	24	9	6	18
San Francisco	11	4	23	3	4	4
Seattle	17	3	27	4	10	6
Tampa Bay	9	15	10	29	*1	32
Tennessee	26	21	22	27	24	26
Washington	5	*1	20	28	5	30

T = Tied for position   * = League Leader

AFC TAKEAWAYS/GIVEAWAYS

	Takeaways			Giveaways			Net
	Int	Fum	Total	Int	Fum	Total	Diff.
New England	20	21	41	9	7	16	+25
Houston	15	14	29	13	4	17	+12
Baltimore	13	12	25	11	5	16	+9
Cincinnati	14	16	30	16	10	26	+4
Cleveland	17	12	29	18	8	26	+3
San Diego	14	14	28	15	11	26	+2
Denver	16	8	24	11	14	25	-1
Jacksonville	12	11	23	17	9	26	-3
Tennessee	19	5	24	16	12	28	-4
Oakland	11	8	19	16	10	26	-7
Miami	10	6	16	13	13	26	-10
Pittsburgh	10	10	20	14	16	30	-10
Indianapolis	12	3	15	18	9	27	-12
Buffalo	12	9	21	17	17	34	-13
N.Y. Jets	11	12	23	19	18	37	-14
Kansas City	7	6	13	20	17	37	-24
Totals	213	167	380	243	180	423	-43

NFC TAKEAWAYS/GIVEAWAYS

	Takeaways			Giveaways			Net
	Int	Fum	Total	Int	Fum	Total	Diff.
Chicago	24	20	44	16	8	24	+20
Washington	21	10	31	8	6	14	+17
N.Y. Giants	21	14	35	15	6	21	+14
Atlanta	20	11	31	14	4	18	+13
Seattle	18	13	31	10	8	18	+13
San Francisco	14	11	25	8	8	16	+9
Green Bay	18	5	23	8	8	16	+7
Tampa Bay	18	8	26	17	6	23	+3
New Orleans	15	11	26	19	5	24	+2
Carolina	11	12	23	12	10	22	+1
Arizona	22	11	33	21	13	34	-1
Minnesota	10	12	22	12	11	23	-1
St. Louis	17	4	21	14	8	22	-1
Dallas	7	9	16	19	10	29	-13
Detroit	11	6	17	17	16	33	-16
Philadelphia	8	5	13	15	22	37	-24
Totals	255	162	417	225	149	374	+43

SCORING

POINTS

AFC:	153	Stephen Gostkowski, New England
NFC:	145	Lawrence Tynes, N.Y. Giants

TOUCHDOWNS

AFC:	17	Arian Foster, Houston
NFC:	14	James Jones, Green Bay

EXTRA POINT KICKS

AFC:	66	Stephen Gostkowski, New England
NFC:	57	Garrett Hartley, New Orleans

TWO-POINT EXTRA POINT PLAYS

AFC:	1	*	Justin Blackmon, Jacksonville
	1		Anquan Boldin, Baltimore
	1		Kenny Britt, Tennessee
	1		Donald Brown, Indianapolis
	1	*	Juron Criner, Oakland
	1		Anthony Fasano, Miami
	1		Rashad Jennings, Jacksonville
	1	*	Jorvorskie Lane, Miami
	1		Willis McGahee, Denver
	1		Heath Miller, Pittsburgh
	1		Montell Owens, Jacksonville
	1	*	Rod Streater, Oakland
NFC:	1		Danny Amendola, St. Louis
	1		Andre Brown, N.Y. Giants
	1		Dez Bryant, Dallas
	1		Nate Burleson, Detroit
	1	*	Kirk Cousins, Washington
	1	*	Chris Givens, St. Louis
	1		Dwayne Harris, Dallas
	1		Steven Jackson, St. Louis
	1		Vincent Jackson, Tampa Bay
	1		Lance Kendricks, St. Louis
	1		Jordy Nelson, Green Bay
	1		Adrian Peterson, Minnesota
	1		Adam Podlesh, Chicago
	1	*	Daryl Richardson, St. Louis
	1		Tony Romo, Dallas
	1		Kyle Rudolph, Minnesota
	1		Darren Sproles, New Orleans

FIELD GOALS

NFC:	35	*	Blair Walsh, Minnesota
AFC:	31		Shayne Graham, Houston
	31		Sebastian Janikowski, Oakland

FIELD GOAL ATTEMPTS

NFC:	42	David Akers, San Francisco
AFC:	38	Shayne Graham, Houston

LONGEST FIELD GOAL

NFC:	63	David Akers, San Francisco at Green Bay, September 9
AFC:	57	Sebastian Janikowski, Oakland vs. Kansas City, December 16

MOST POINTS, GAME

NFC:	24	*	Doug Martin, Tampa Bay at Oakland, November 4 (4 TD)
AFC:	19		Ryan Succop, Kansas City at New Orleans, September 23 (6-6 FG, 1-1 PAT) - (OT)

TEAM LEADERS, POINTS

AFC BALTIMORE, 132, *Justin Tucker; BUFFALO, 102, Rian Lindell; CINCINNATI, 92, Mike Nugent; CLEVELAND, 116, Phil Dawson; DENVER, 133, Matt Prater; HOUSTON, 138, Shayne Graham; INDIANAPOLIS, 115, Adam Vinatieri; JACKSONVILLE, 93, Josh Scobee; KANSAS CITY, 101, Ryan Succop; MIAMI, 92, Dan Carpenter; NEW ENGLAND, 153, Stephen Gostkowski; N.Y. JETS, 93, Nick Folk; OAKLAND, 118, Sebastian Janikowski; PITTSBURGH, 118, Shaun Suisham; SAN DIEGO, 87, Nick Novak; TENNESSEE, 110, Rob Bironas

NFC ARIZONA, 100, Jay Feely; ATLANTA, 143, Matt Bryant; CAROLINA, 48, Cam Newton; CHICAGO, 96, Robbie Gould; DALLAS, 124, Dan Bailey; DETROIT, 134, Jason Hanson; GREEN BAY, 113, Mason Crosby; MINNESOTA, 141, *Blair Walsh; NEW ORLEANS, 111, Garrett Hartley; N.Y. GIANTS, 145, Lawrence Tynes; PHILADELPHIA, 106, Alex Henery; ST. LOUIS, 95, *Greg Zuerlein; SAN FRANCISCO, 131, David Akers; SEATTLE, 118, Steven Hauschka; TAMPA BAY, 123, Connor Barth; WASHINGTON, 84, Kai Forbath

TEAM CHAMPION

AFC:	557	New England
NFC:	461	New Orleans

NFL TOP TEN SCORERS—KICKERS

	XP	XPA	FG	FGA	PTS
Gostkowski, Stephen, N.E.	66	66	29	35	153
Tynes, Lawrence, NY-G	46	46	33	39	145
Bryant, Matt, Atl.	44	44	33	38	143
* Walsh, Blair, Min.	36	36	35	38	141
Graham, Shayne, Hou.	45	45	31	38	138
Hanson, Jason, Det.	38	38	32	36	134
Prater, Matt, Den.	55	55	26	32	133
* Tucker, Justin, Bal.	42	42	30	33	132
Akers, David, S.F.	44	44	29	42	131
Bailey, Dan, Dal.	37	37	29	31	124

NFL TOP TEN SCORERS—NONKICKERS

	TD	TDR	TDP	TDM	2-PT.	PTS
Foster, Arian, Hou.	17	15	2	0	0	102
Jones, James, G.B.	14	0	14	0	0	84
Peterson, Adrian, Min.	13	12	1	0	1	80
Decker, Eric, Den.	13	0	13	0	0	78
* Morris, Alfred, Was.	13	13	0	0	0	78
Bryant, Dez, Dal.	12	0	12	0	1	74
Lynch, Marshawn, Sea.	12	11	1	0	0	72
* Martin, Doug, T.B.	12	11	1	0	0	72
* Richardson, Trent, Cle.	12	11	1	0	0	72
Ridley, Stevan, N.E.	12	12	0	0	0	72

AFC—INDIVIDUAL SCORERS

KICKERS

	XP	XPA	FG	FGA	PTS
Gostkowski, Stephen, N.E.	66	66	29	35	153
Graham, Shayne, Hou.	45	45	31	38	138
Prater, Matt, Den.	55	55	26	32	133
* Tucker, Justin, Bal.	42	42	30	33	132
Janikowski, Sebastian, Oak.	25	25	31	34	118
Suisham, Shaun, Pit.	34	34	28	31	118
Dawson, Phil, Cle.	29	29	29	31	116
Vinatieri, Adam, Ind.	37	37	26	33	115
Bironas, Rob, Ten.	35	35	25	31	110
Lindell, Rian, Buf.	39	39	21	24	102
Succop, Ryan, K.C.	17	17	28	34	101
Folk, Nick, NYJ	30	30	21	27	93
Scobee, Josh, Jac.	18	19	25	28	93
Carpenter, Dan, Mia.	26	26	22	27	92
Nugent, Mike, Cin.	35	35	19	23	92
Novak, Nick, S.D.	33	33	18	20	87
Brown, Josh, Cin.	8	8	11	12	41
Kaeding, Nate, S.D.-Mia.	9	9	8	10	33

Player that was a rookie in 2012

NONKICKERS

Player	TD	TDR	TDP	TDM	2-PT.	PTS
Foster, Arian, Hou.	17	15	2	0	0	102
Decker, Eric, Den.	13	0	13	0	0	78
* Richardson, Trent, Cle.	12	11	1	0	0	72
Ridley, Stevan, N.E.	12	12	0	0	0	72
Green, A.J., Cin.	11	0	11	0	0	66
Gronkowski, Rob, N.E.	11	0	11	0	0	66
Rice, Ray, Bal.	10	9	1	0	0	60
Thomas, Demaryius, Den.	10	0	10	0	0	60
Miller, Heath, Pit.	8	0	8	0	1	50
Bush, Reggie, Mia.	8	6	2	0	0	48
Greene, Shonn, NYJ	8	8	0	0	0	48
* Hilton, T.Y., Ind.	8	0	7	1	0	48
Smith, Torrey, Bal.	8	0	8	0	0	48
Spiller, C.J., Buf.	8	6	2	0	0	48
Wallace, Mike, Pit.	8	0	8	0	0	48
Alexander, Danario, S.D.	7	0	7	0	0	42
Gates, Antonio, S.D.	7	0	7	0	0	42
Moore, Denarius, Oak.	7	0	7	0	0	42
Pitta, Dennis, Bal.	7	0	7	0	0	42
Shorts, Cecil, Jac.	7	0	7	0	0	42
Woodhead, Danny, N.E.	7	4	3	0	0	42
Chandler, Scott, Buf.	6	0	6	0	0	36
Charles, Jamaal, K.C.	6	5	1	0	0	36
Daniels, Owen, Hou.	6	0	6	0	0	36
Green-Ellis, BenJarvus, Cin.	6	6	0	0	0	36
Johnson, Chris, Ten.	6	6	0	0	0	36
Johnson, Steve, Buf.	6	0	6	0	0	36
Welker, Wes, N.E.	6	0	6	0	0	36
* Blackmon, Justin, Jac.	5	0	5	0	1	32
Fasano, Anthony, Mia.	5	0	5	0	1	32
Brown, Antonio, Pit.	5	0	5	0	0	30
Dreessen, Joel, Den.	5	0	5	0	0	30
Edelman, Julian, N.E.	5	0	3	2	0	30
Floyd, Malcom, S.D.	5	0	5	0	0	30
* Gordon, Josh, Cle.	5	0	5	0	0	30
Gresham, Jermaine, Cin.	5	0	5	0	0	30
Hernandez, Aaron, N.E.	5	0	5	0	0	30
Heyward-Bey, Darrius, Oak.	5	0	5	0	0	30
Lloyd, Brandon, N.E.	5	0	4	1	0	30
* Luck, Andrew, Ind.	5	5	0	0	0	30
Stokley, Brandon, Den.	5	0	5	0	0	30
Wayne, Reggie, Ind.	5	0	5	0	0	30
Boldin, Anquan, Bal.	4	0	4	0	1	26
Britt, Kenny, Ten.	4	0	4	0	1	26
McGahee, Willis, Den.	4	4	0	0	1	26
Battle, Jackie, S.D.	4	3	1	0	0	24
Brady, Tom, N.E.	4	4	0	0	0	24
Cook, Jared, Ten.	4	0	4	0	0	24
Dalton, Andy, Cin.	4	4	0	0	0	24
Hawkins, Andrew, Cin.	4	0	4	0	0	24
Jackson, Fred, Buf.	4	3	1	0	0	24
Johnson, Andre, Hou.	4	0	4	0	0	24
Jones, Donald, Buf.	4	0	4	0	0	24
Jones, Jacoby, Bal.	4	0	1	3	0	24
Lewis, Marcedes, Jac.	4	0	4	0	0	24
Little, Greg, Cle.	4	0	4	0	0	24
Moreno, Knowshon, Den.	4	4	0	0	0	24
Myers, Brandon, Oak.	4	0	4	0	0	24
Powell, Bilal, NYJ	4	4	0	0	0	24
* Sanu, Mohamed, Cin.	4	0	4	0	0	24
Smith, Brad, Buf.	4	1	2	1	0	24
Thomas, Daniel, Mia.	4	4	0	0	0	24
Vereen, Shane, N.E.	4	3	1	0	0	24
Washington, Nate, Ten.	4	0	4	0	0	24
* Wright, Kendall, Ten.	4	0	4	0	0	24
* Lane, Jorvorskie, Mia.	3	2	1	0	1	20
* Streater, Rod, Oak.	3	0	3	0	1	20
* Allen, Dwayne, Ind.	3	0	3	0	0	18
Avery, Donnie, Ind.	3	0	3	0	0	18
Ballard, Vick, Ind.	3	2	1	0	0	18
* Benjamin, Travis, Cle.	3	0	2	1	0	18
Bowe, Dwayne, K.C.	3	0	3	0	0	18
Carter, Delone, Ind.	3	3	0	0	0	18
Casey, James, Hou.	3	0	3	0	0	18
Cumberland, Jeff, NYJ	3	0	3	0	0	18
Flacco, Joe, Bal.	3	3	0	0	0	18
Graham, Garrett, Hou.	3	0	3	0	0	18
Harper, Jamie, Ten.	3	3	0	0	0	18
* Hill, Stephen, NYJ	3	0	3	0	0	18
Kerley, Jeremy, NYJ	3	0	2	1	0	18
McFadden, Darren, Oak.	3	2	1	0	0	18
Reynaud, Darius, Ten.	3	0	0	3	0	18
Rosario, Dante, S.D.	3	0	3	0	0	18
Spurlock, Micheal, S.D.-Jac.-S.D.	3	0	1	2	0	18
Watson, Benjamin, Cle.	3	0	3	0	0	18
Jennings, Rashad, Jac.	2	2	0	0	1	14
Ball, Lance, Den.	2	1	1	0	0	12
* Bolden, Brandon, N.E.	2	2	0	0	0	12
* Brown, Zach, Ten.	2	2	0	0	0	12
Butler, Darius, Ind.	2	0	0	2	0	12
Carter, Tony, Den.	2	0	0	2	0	12
Clay, Charles, Mia.	2	0	2	0	0	12
Draughn, Shaun, K.C.	2	2	0	0	0	12
Dwyer, Jonathan, Pit.	2	2	0	0	0	12
* Fleener, Coby, Ind.	2	0	2	0	0	12
Harris, Chris, Den.	2	0	0	2	0	12
Hester, Jacob, Den.	2	2	0	0	0	12
Holliday, Trindon, Den.	2	0	0	2	0	12
Jammer, Quentin, S.D.	2	0	0	2	0	12
Jones-Drew, Maurice, Jac.	2	1	1	0	0	12
Keller, Dustin, NYJ	2	0	2	0	0	12
McKelvin, Leodis, Buf.	2	0	0	2	0	12
Meachem, Robert, S.D.	2	0	2	0	0	12
Pope, Leonard, Pit.	2	0	2	0	0	12
* Rainey, Chris, Pit.	2	2	0	0	0	12
Redman, Isaac, Pit.	2	2	0	0	0	12
Schilens, Chaz, NYJ	2	0	2	0	0	12
Smith, Lee, Buf.	2	0	2	0	0	12
Tamme, Jacob, Den.	2	0	2	0	0	12
* Tannehill, Ryan, Mia.	2	2	0	0	0	12
Tate, Ben, Hou.	2	2	0	0	0	12
Thigpen, Marcus, Mia.	2	0	2	0	0	12
Walter, Kevin, Hou.	2	0	2	0	0	12
Williams, Demorrio, S.D.	2	0	0	2	0	12
Brown, Donald, Ind.	1	1	0	0	1	8
* Criner, Juron, Oak.	1	0	1	0	1	8
Owens, Montell, Jac.	1	1	0	0	1	8
Phillips, Shaun, S.D.	1	0	0	1	0	^8
Allen, Anthony, Bal.	1	1	0	0	0	6
Baldwin, Jon, K.C.	1	0	1	0	0	6
Batch, Baron, Pit.	1	0	1	0	0	6
Bess, Davone, Mia.	1	0	1	0	0	6
Binns, Armon, Cin.	1	0	1	0	0	6
Boss, Kevin, K.C.	1	0	1	0	0	6
Braman, Bryan, Hou.	1	0	0	1	0	6
* Brazill, LaVon, Ind.	1	0	1	0	0	6
Brown, Sheldon, Cle.	1	0	0	1	0	6
Burress, Plaxico, Pit.	1	0	1	0	0	6
Butler, Donald, S.D.	1	0	0	1	0	6
Cameron, Jordan, Cle.	1	0	1	0	0	6
Campbell, Tommie, Ten.	1	0	0	1	0	6
Cassel, Matt, K.C.	1	1	0	0	0	6
Choice, Tashard, Buf.	1	0	0	1	0	6
Cromartie, Antonio, NYJ	1	0	0	1	0	6
* Dennard, Alfonzo, N.E.	1	0	0	1	0	6
Doss, Tandon, Bal.	1	0	1	0	0	6
Dunlap, Carlos, Cin.	1	0	0	1	0	6
Fitzpatrick, Ryan, Buf.	1	1	0	0	0	6
Forsett, Justin, Hou.	1	1	0	0	0	6
Freeman, Jerrell, Ind.	1	0	0	1	0	6
Gilberry, Wallace, Cin.	1	0	0	1	0	6
Goodson, Mike, Oak.	1	0	1	0	0	6
Gordon, Richard, Oak.	1	0	1	0	0	6
* Graham, T.J., Buf.	1	0	1	0	0	6
Gregory, Steve, N.E.	1	0	0	1	0	6
Hall, Leon, Cin.	1	0	0	1	0	6
Hardesty, Montario, Cle.	1	1	0	0	0	6
* Harris, Mike, Jac.	1	0	0	1	0	6
Hartline, Brian, Mia.	1	0	1	0	0	6

	TD	TDR	TDP	TDM	2-PT.	PTS
Henne, Chad, Jac.	1	1	0	0	0	6
* Hightower, Dont'a, N.E.	1	0	0	1	0	6
Hill, Jason, NYJ	1	0	1	0	0	6
Hillis, Peyton, K.C.	1	1	0	0	0	6
* Hillman, Ronnie, Den.	1	1	0	0	0	6
Holmes, Santonio, NYJ	1	0	1	0	0	6
Jackson, D'Qwell, Cle.	1	0	0	1	0	6
Jackson, Kareem, Hou.	1	0	0	1	0	6
Jean, Lestar, Hou.	1	0	1	0	0	6
Johnson, Will, Pit.	1	0	1	0	0	6
Jones, Adam, Cin.	1	0	0	1	0	6
Jones, Edgar, K.C.	1	0	1	0	0	6
* Jones, Marvin, Cin.	1	0	1	0	0	6
Joseph, Johnathan, Hou.	1	0	0	1	0	6
Karim, Deji, Ind.	1	0	0	1	0	6
Koch, Sam, Bal.	1	1	0	0	0	6
Landry, LaRon, NYJ	1	0	0	1	0	6
Leach, Vonta, Bal.	1	1	0	0	0	6
Leftwich, Byron, Pit.	1	1	0	0	0	6
Locker, Jake, Ten.	1	1	0	0	0	6
Manning, Danieal, Hou.	1	0	0	1	0	6
* Martin, Keshawn, Hou.	1	0	1	0	0	6
Mathews, Ryan, S.D.	1	1	0	0	0	6
McCarthy, Colin, Ten.	1	0	0	1	0	6
McCluster, Dexter, K.C.	1	0	1	0	0	6
McCourty, Devin, N.E.	1	0	0	1	0	6
McKnight, Joe, NYJ	1	0	0	1	0	6
Mendenhall, Rashard, Pit.	1	0	1	0	0	6
* Miller, Lamar, Mia.	1	1	0	0	0	6
Miller, Von, Den.	1	0	0	1	0	6
Moeaki, Tony, K.C.	1	0	1	0	0	6
Moore, Marlon, Mia.	1	0	1	0	0	6
Moore, Mewelde, Ind.	1	0	1	0	0	6
Palmer, Carson, Oak.	1	1	0	0	0	6
Peerman, Cedric, Cin.	1	1	0	0	0	6
* Pierce, Bernard, Bal.	1	1	0	0	0	6
Porter, Tracy, Den.	1	0	0	1	0	6
* Posey, DeVier, Hou.	1	0	0	1	0	6
Pressley, Chris, Cin.	1	0	1	0	0	6
Pryor, Terrelle, Oak.	1	1	0	0	0	6
Reece, Marcel, Oak.	1	0	1	0	0	6
Reed, Ed, Bal.	1	0	0	1	0	6
Royal, Eddie, S.D.	1	0	1	0	0	6
Sanders, Emmanuel, Pit.	1	0	1	0	0	6
Scott, Bryan, Buf.	1	0	0	1	0	6
Shipley, Jordan, Jac.	1	0	1	0	0	6
Stallworth, Donte', N.E.	1	0	1	0	0	6
Stevens, Craig, Ten.	1	0	1	0	0	6
Talib, Aqib, N.E.	1	0	0	1	0	6
Tate, Brandon, Cin.	1	0	1	0	0	6
Taylor, Tyrod, Bal.	1	1	0	0	0	6
Thomas, Mike, Jac.	1	0	1	0	0	6
Timmons, Lawrence, Pit.	1	0	0	1	0	6
Unrein, Mitch, Den.	1	0	1	0	0	6
Vaughn, Cassius, Ind.	1	0	0	1	0	6
Verner, Alterraun, Ten.	1	0	0	1	0	6
* Vernon, Olivier, Mia.	1	0	0	1	0	6
Weddle, Eric, S.D.	1	0	0	1	0	6
Whimper, Guy, Jac.	1	0	1	0	0	6
Wilkerson, Muhammad, NYJ	1	0	0	1	0	6
Williams, Cary, Bal.	1	0	0	1	0	6
Witherspoon, Will, Ten.	1	0	0	1	0	6
Yates, T.J., Hou.	1	1	0	0	0	6
Adams, Mike, Den.	0	0	0	0	0	^2
Barwin, Connor, Hou.	0	0	0	0	0	^2
Dumervil, Elvis, Den.	0	0	0	0	0	^2
Houston, Justin, K.C.	0	0	0	0	0	^2
Kelsay, Chris, Buf.	0	0	0	0	0	^2

^ *Safety*
Team safety credited to New England, N.Y. Jets, and
   Tennessee.
\# *Scored kicking extra point*

NFC—INDIVIDUAL SCORERS

KICKERS

	XP	XPA	FG	FGA	PTS
Tynes, Lawrence, NY-G	46	46	33	39	145
Bryant, Matt, Atl.	44	44	33	38	143
* Walsh, Blair, Min.	36	36	35	38	141
Hanson, Jason, Det.	38	38	32	36	134
Akers, David, S.F.	44	44	29	42	131
Bailey, Dan, Dal.	37	37	29	31	124
Barth, Connor, T.B.	39	39	28	33	123
Hauschka, Steven, Sea.	46	48	24	27	118
Crosby, Mason, G.B.	50	50	21	33	113
Hartley, Garrett, N.O.	57	57	18	22	111
Henery, Alex, Phi.	25	26	27	31	106
Feely, Jay, Ariz	25	25	25	28	100
Gould, Robbie, Chi.	33	33	21	25	96
* Zuerlein, Greg, St.L	26	26	23	31	95
Forbath, Kai, Was.	33	34	17	18	84
Gano, Graham, Car.	20	21	9	11	47
Medlock, Justin, Car.	23	23	7	10	44
Cundiff, Billy, Was.	17	17	7	12	38
Mare, Olindo, Chi.	7	7	6	8	25

NONKICKERS

	TD	TDR	TDP	TDM	X2G	PTS
Jones, James, G.B.	14	0	14	0	0	84
Peterson, Adrian, Min.	13	12	1	0	1	80
* Morris, Alfred, Was.	13	13	0	0	0	78
Bryant, Dez, Dal.	12	0	12	0	1	74
Lynch, Marshawn, Sea.	12	11	1	0	0	72
* Martin, Doug, T.B.	12	11	1	0	0	72
Marshall, Brandon, Chi.	11	0	11	0	0	66
Turner, Michael, Atl.	11	10	1	0	0	66
Colston, Marques, N.O.	10	0	10	0	0	60
Cruz, Victor, NY-G	10	0	10	0	0	60
Gore, Frank, S.F.	10	8	1	1	0	60
Jones, Julio, Atl.	10	0	10	0	0	60
Rudolph, Kyle, Min.	9	0	9	0	1	56
Cobb, Randall, G.B.	9	0	8	1	0	54
Crabtree, Michael, S.F.	9	0	9	0	0	54
Graham, Jimmy, N.O.	9	0	9	0	0	54
Leshoure, Mikel, Det.	9	9	0	0	0	54
Williams, Mike, T.B.	9	0	9	0	0	54
Brown, Andre, NY-G	8	8	0	0	1	50
Jackson, Vincent, T.B.	8	0	8	0	1	50
Sproles, Darren, N.O.	8	1	7	0	1	50
Gonzalez, Tony, Atl.	8	0	8	0	0	48
Moss, Santana, Was.	8	0	8	0	0	48
Newton, Cam, Car.	8	8	0	0	0	48
Nelson, Jordy, G.B.	7	0	7	0	1	44
* Griffin III, Robert, Was.	7	7	0	0	0	42
Maclin, Jeremy, Phi.	7	0	7	0	0	42
Rice, Sidney, Sea.	7	0	7	0	0	42
Tate, Golden, Sea.	7	0	7	0	0	42
Tolbert, Mike, Car.	7	7	0	0	0	42
White, Roddy, Atl.	7	0	7	0	0	42
Williams, DeAngelo, Car.	7	5	2	0	0	42
Austin, Miles, Dal.	6	0	6	0	0	36
Bradshaw, Ahmad, NY-G	6	6	0	0	0	36
Forté, Matt, Chi.	6	5	1	0	0	36
Moore, Lance, N.O.	6	0	6	0	0	36
* Wilson, David, NY-G	6	4	1	1	0	36
Bennett, Martellus, NY-G	5	0	5	0	0	30
Bush, Michael, Chi.	5	5	0	0	0	30
Davis, Vernon, S.F.	5	0	5	0	0	30
Garcon, Pierre, Was.	5	0	4	1	0	30
Gibson, Brandon, St.L	5	0	5	0	0	30
Harvin, Percy, Min.	5	1	3	1	0	30
Ingram, Mark, N.O.	5	5	0	0	0	30
Johnson, Calvin, Det.	5	0	5	0	0	30
Jones, Felix, Dal.	5	3	2	0	0	30
Kaepernick, Colin, S.F.	5	5	0	0	0	30
McCoy, LeSean, Phi.	5	2	3	0	0	30
Olsen, Greg, Car.	5	0	5	0	0	30
Roberts, Andre, Ariz	5	0	5	0	0	30
Wells, Beanie, Ariz	5	5	0	0	0	30

Player	TD	TDR	TDP	TDM	2-PT.	PTS
Jackson, Steven, St.L	4	4	0	0	1	26
Kendricks, Lance, St.L	4	0	4	0	1	26
* Brown, Bryce, Phi.	4	4	0	0	0	24
Clark, Dallas, T.B.	4	0	4	0	0	24
Fitzgerald, Larry, Ariz	4	0	4	0	0	24
* Jenkins, Janoris, St.L	4	0	0	4	0	24
Jennings, Greg, G.B.	4	0	4	0	0	24
LaFell, Brandon, Car.	4	0	4	0	0	24
Murray, DeMarco, Dal.	4	4	0	0	0	24
Ogletree, Kevin, Dal.	4	0	4	0	0	24
Pettis, Austin, St.L	4	0	4	0	0	24
Smith, Steve, Car.	4	0	4	0	0	24
Stafford, Matthew, Det.	4	4	0	0	0	24
Stephens-Howling, LaRod, Ariz	4	4	0	0	0	24
Thomas, David, N.O.	4	0	4	0	0	24
* Wilson, Russell, Sea.	4	4	0	0	0	24
Young, Titus, Det.	4	0	4	0	0	24
Amendola, Danny, St.L	3	0	3	0	1	20
* Givens, Chris, St.L	3	0	3	0	1	20
Baldwin, Doug, Sea.	3	0	3	0	0	18
Bell, Joique, Det.	3	3	0	0	0	18
Cooper, Riley, Phi.	3	0	3	0	0	18
Crabtree, Tom, G.B.	3	0	3	0	0	18
Hankerson, Leonard, Was.	3	0	3	0	0	18
* Jeffery, Alshon, Chi.	3	0	3	0	0	18
McCoy, Anthony, Sea.	3	0	3	0	0	18
Miller, Zach, Sea.	3	0	3	0	0	18
Morgan, Joe, N.O.	3	0	3	0	0	18
Morgan, Josh, Was.	3	0	2	1	0	18
Moss, Randy, S.F.	3	0	3	0	0	18
Nicks, Hakeem, NY-G	3	0	3	0	0	18
Pettigrew, Brandon, Det.	3	0	3	0	0	18
* Randle, Rueben, NY-G	3	0	3	0	0	18
Robinson, Aldrick, Was.	3	0	3	0	0	18
Tillman, Charles, Chi.	3	0	0	3	0	18
Walker, Delanie, S.F.	3	0	3	0	0	18
Witten, Jason, Dal.	3	0	3	0	0	18
Burleson, Nate, Det.	2	0	2	0	1	14
Harris, Dwayne, Dal.	2	0	1	1	1	14
Bennett, Earl, Chi.	2	0	2	0	0	12
Blount, LeGarrette, T.B.	2	2	0	0	0	12
Briggs, Lance, Chi.	2	0	0	2	0	12
* Broyles, Ryan, Det.	2	0	2	0	0	12
Collins, Jed, N.O.	2	0	2	0	0	12
Davis, Kellen, Chi.	2	0	2	0	0	12
Dixon, Anthony, S.F.	2	2	0	0	0	12
Driver, Donald, G.B.	2	0	2	0	0	12
Finley, Jermichael, G.B.	2	0	2	0	0	12
* Floyd, Michael, Ariz	2	0	2	0	0	12
Grant, Ryan, G.B.	2	2	0	0	0	12
Harbor, Clay, Phi.	2	0	2	0	0	12
Harris, DuJuan, G.B.	2	2	0	0	0	12
Hixon, Domenik, NY-G	2	0	2	0	0	12
Hunter, Kendall, S.F.	2	2	0	0	0	12
Ivory, Chris, N.O.	2	2	0	0	0	12
Jackson, DeSean, Phi.	2	0	2	0	0	12
Jenkins, Michael, Min.	2	0	2	0	0	12
Munnerlyn, Captain, Car.	2	0	0	2	0	12
Murphy, Louis, Car.	2	0	1	1	0	12
Ponder, Christian, Min.	2	2	0	0	0	12
* Quick, Brian, St.L	2	0	2	0	0	12
Robinson, Michael, Sea.	2	0	2	0	0	12
Rodgers, Aaron, G.B.	2	2	0	0	0	12
Rodgers, Jacquizz, Atl.	2	1	1	0	0	12
Royster, Evan, Was.	2	2	0	0	0	12
Sherman, Richard, Sea.	2	0	0	2	0	12
* Smith, Harrison, Min.	2	0	0	2	0	12
Smith, Kevin, Det.	2	1	1	0	0	12
Stewart, Jonathan, Car.	2	1	1	0	0	12
Thomas, Pierre, N.O.	2	1	1	0	0	12
Underwood, Tiquan, T.B.	2	0	2	0	0	12
Washington, Leon, Sea.	2	1	0	1	0	12
* Wright, Jarius, Min.	2	0	2	0	0	12
Young, Darrel, Was.	2	0	2	0	0	12
Romo, Tony, Dal.	1	1	0	0	1	8
Allen, Armando, Chi.	1	1	0	0	0	6
Babineaux, Jonathan, Atl.	1	0	0	1	0	6
Barber, Ronde, T.B.	1	0	0	1	0	6
Barnidge, Gary, Car.	1	0	1	0	0	6
Benson, Cedric, G.B.	1	1	0	0	0	6
* Bethel, Justin, Ariz	1	0	0	1	0	6
Boley, Michael, NY-G	1	0	0	1	0	6
Bowman, Zack, Chi.	1	0	0	1	0	6
Bradford, Sam, St.L	1	1	0	0	0	6
Brees, Drew, N.O.	1	1	0	0	0	6
Brooks, Ahmad, S.F.	1	0	0	1	0	6
Burton, Stephen, Min.	1	0	1	0	0	6
Byham, Nate, T.B.	1	0	1	0	0	6
Carr, Brandon, Dal.	1	0	0	1	0	6
Celek, Brent, Phi.	1	0	1	0	0	6
* Claiborne, Morris, Dal.	1	0	0	1	0	6
* Daniels, Mike, G.B.	1	0	0	1	0	6
Davis, Drew, Atl.	1	0	1	0	0	6
Douglas, Harry, Atl.	1	0	1	0	0	6
Durham, Kris, Det.	1	0	1	0	0	6
Edwards, Braylon, Sea.	1	0	1	0	0	6
Finnegan, Cortland, St.L	1	0	0	1	0	6
* Foles, Nick, Phi.	1	1	0	0	0	6
Gerhart, Toby, Min.	1	1	0	0	0	6
Godfrey, Charles, Car.	1	0	0	1	0	6
Griffen, Everson, Min.	1	0	0	1	0	6
Hatcher, Jason, Dal.	1	0	0	1	0	6
Havili, Stanley, Phi.	1	1	0	0	0	6
Hayward, Adam, T.B.	1	0	0	1	0	6
Heller, Will, Det.	1	0	1	0	0	6
Henderson, Devery, N.O.	1	0	1	0	0	6
Hester, Devin, Chi.	1	0	1	0	0	6
Hynoski, Henry, NY-G	1	0	1	0	0	6
Jackson, Rob, Was.	1	0	0	1	0	6
Jenkins, Malcolm, N.O.	1	0	0	1	0	6
Jennings, M.D., G.B.	1	0	0	1	0	6
Jennings, Tim, Chi.	1	0	0	1	0	6
* Johnson, Damaris, Phi.	1	0	0	1	0	6
Johnson, Jeron, Sea.	1	0	0	1	0	6
Johnson, Rashad, Ariz	1	0	0	1	0	6
* Johnson, Leonard, T.B.	1	0	0	1	0	6
Johnson, Mike, Atl.	1	0	1	0	0	6
Kerrigan, Ryan, Was.	1	0	0	1	0	6
Kolb, Kevin, Ariz	1	1	0	0	0	6
Kuhn, John, G.B.	1	1	0	0	0	6
Lewis, Dion, Phi.	1	1	0	0	0	6
Lorig, Erik, T.B.	1	0	1	0	0	6
Mack, Elbert, N.O.	1	0	0	1	0	6
Manningham, Mario, S.F.	1	0	1	0	0	6
* Moses, Dezman, G.B.	1	0	0	1	0	6
Mulligan, Matthew, St.L	1	0	1	0	0	6
Palmer, Michael, Atl.	1	0	1	0	0	6
Pascoe, Bear, NY-G	1	0	1	0	0	6
Paul, Niles, Was.	1	0	1	0	0	6
Paulsen, Logan, Was.	1	0	1	0	0	6
Phillips, John, Dal.	1	0	1	0	0	6
Pierre-Paul, Jason, NY-G	1	0	0	1	0	6
Pilares, Kealoha, Car.	1	0	0	1	0	6
Robinson, Patrick, N.O.	1	0	0	1	0	6
Robiskie, Brian, Det.	1	0	1	0	0	6
Roby, Courtney, N.O.	1	0	0	1	0	6
Rogers, Carlos, S.F.	1	0	0	1	0	6
Ryan, Matt, Atl.	1	1	0	0	0	6
Samuel, Asante, Atl.	1	0	0	1	0	6
Sanders, James, Ariz	1	0	0	1	0	6
Scheffler, Tony, Det.	1	0	1	0	0	6
Sherels, Marcus, Min.	1	0	0	1	0	6
Smith, Malcolm, Sea.	1	0	0	1	0	6
Snelling, Jason, Atl.	1	0	1	0	0	6
Spaeth, Matt, Chi.	1	0	1	0	0	6
Starks, James, G.B.	1	1	0	0	0	6
Stocker, Luke, T.B.	1	0	1	0	0	6
Thomas, Earl, Sea.	1	0	0	1	0	6
Toler, Greg, Ariz	1	0	0	1	0	6
Urlacher, Brian, Chi.	1	0	0	1	0	6

	TD	TDR	TDP	TDM	2-PT.	PTS		TD	TDR	TDP	TDM	2-PT.	PTS
Vick, Michael, Phi.	1	1	0	0	0	6	McDonald, Ray, S.F.	0	0	0	0	0	^2
Vilma, Jonathan, N.O.	1	0	0	1	0	6	Onatolu, Kenny, Car.	0	0	0	0	0	^2
Whitner, Donte, S.F.	1	0	0	1	0	6	Podlesh, Adam, Chi.	0	0	0	0	1	2
Williams, Kyle, S.F.	1	0	1	0	0	6	* Richardson, Daryl, St.L	0	0	0	0	1	2
Williams, Madieu, Was.	1	0	0	1	0	6	Vanden Bosch, Kyle, Det.	0	0	0	0	0	^2
Wilson, Josh, Was.	1	0	0	1	0	6							
Wootton, Corey, Chi.	1	0	0	1	0	6	^ Safety						
Wright, Eric, T.B.	1	0	0	1	0	6	Team safety credited to St. Louis						
Wright, Major, Chi.	1	0	0	1	0	6	# Scored kicking extra point						
* Cousins, Kirk, Was.	0	0	0	0	1	2							

AMERICAN FOOTBALL CONFERENCE—SCORING

	TD	TDR	TDP	TDM	XKG	XKAtt	X2G	X2Att	FG	FGA	SAF	POINTS
New England	67	25	34	8	66	66	0	1	29	35	1	557
Denver	57	12	37	8	55	55	1	2	26	32	2	481
Houston	46	19	22	5	45	45	0	0	31	38	1	416
Baltimore	44	17	22	5	42	42	1	2	30	33	0	398
Cincinnati	43	11	28	4	43	43	0	0	30	35	0	391
Indianapolis	40	11	23	6	37	37	1	2	26	33	0	357
San Diego	39	4	26	9	39	39	0	0	25	27	1	350
Buffalo	40	12	24	4	39	39	0	1	21	24	1	344
Pittsburgh	36	8	27	1	34	34	1	2	28	31	0	336
Tennessee	36	10	17	9	35	35	1	1	25	31	1	330
Cleveland	31	12	16	3	29	29	0	2	29	31	0	302
Oakland	28	4	24	0	25	25	2	3	31	34	0	290
Miami	31	15	13	3	29	29	2	2	23	30	0	288
N.Y. Jets	31	12	14	5	30	30	0	1	21	27	1	281
Jacksonville	26	5	20	1	18	19	3	7	25	28	0	255
Kansas City	18	9	8	1	17	17	0	1	28	34	1	211
AFC Total	613	186	355	72	583	584	12	27	428	503	9	5587
AFC Average	38.3	11.6	22.2	4.5	36.4	36.5	0.8	1.7	26.8	31.4	0.6	349.2

NATIONAL FOOTBALL CONFERENCE—SCORING

	TD	TDR	TDP	TDM	XKG	XKAtt	X2G	X2Att	FG	FGA	SAF	POINTS
New Orleans	58	10	43	5	57	57	1	1	18	22	0	461
Washington	52	22	24	6	50	51	1	1	24	30	0	436
Green Bay	53	9	40	4	50	50	1	3	21	33	0	433
N.Y. Giants	47	18	26	3	46	46	1	1	33	39	0	429
Atlanta	46	12	32	2	44	44	0	2	33	38	0	419
Seattle	49	16	27	6	46	48	0	0	24	27	0	412
San Francisco	44	17	23	4	44	44	0	0	29	42	1	397
Tampa Bay	44	13	27	4	39	39	1	4	28	33	0	389
Minnesota	39	16	18	5	36	36	2	3	35	38	0	379
Dallas	41	8	29	4	37	37	3	4	29	31	0	376
Chicago	42	11	21	10	40	40	1	2	27	33	0	375
Detroit	39	17	22	0	38	38	1	1	32	36	1	372
Carolina	44	21	19	4	43	44	0	0	16	21	1	357
St. Louis	32	5	22	5	26	26	5	6	23	31	1	299
Philadelphia	29	10	18	1	25	26	0	3	27	31	0	280
Arizona	25	10	11	4	25	25	0	0	25	28	0	250
NFC Total	684	215	402	67	646	651	17	31	424	513	4	6064
NFC Average	42.8	13.4	25.1	4.2	40.4	40.7	1.1	1.9	26.5	32.1	0.3	379.0
NFL Total	1297	401	757	139	1229	1235	29	58	852	1016	13	11651
NFL Average	40.5	12.5	23.7	4.3	38.4	38.6	0.9	1.8	26.6	31.8	0.4	364.1

FIELD GOALS

FIELD GOAL PERCENTAGE
NFC:	.944	Kai Forbath, Washington
AFC:	.935	Phil Dawson, Cleveland

FIELD GOALS
NFC:	35	* Blair Walsh, Minnesota
AFC:	31	Shayne Graham, Houston
	31	Sebastian Janikowski, Oakland

FIELD GOAL ATTEMPTS
NFC:	42	David Akers, San Francisco
AFC:	38	Shayne Graham, Houston

FIELD GOALS, GAME
AFC:	6	Ryan Succop, Kansas City at New Orleans, September 23 (6 attempts) - (OT)
NFC:	5	Lawrence Tynes, N.Y. Giants at Carolina, September 20 (5 attempts)
	5	Justin Medlock, Carolina at Chicago, October 28 (5 attempts)
	5	Lawrence Tynes, N.Y. Giants at Dallas, October 28 (5 attempts)
	5	* Blair Walsh, Minnesota at St. Louis, December 16 (5 attempts)

LONGEST FIELD GOAL
NFC:	63	David Akers, San Francisco at Green Bay, September 9
AFC:	57	Sebastian Janikowski, Oakland vs. Kansas City, December 16

AVERAGE YARDS MADE
NFC:	42.3	* Greg Zuerlein, St. Louis
AFC:	38.7	* Justin Tucker, Baltimore

AMERICAN FOOTBALL CONFERENCE—FIELD GOALS

	FG	FGA	Pct	Long
Cleveland	29	31	.935	53
San Diego	25	27	.926	51
Oakland	31	34	.912	57
Baltimore	30	33	.909	56
Pittsburgh	28	31	.903	52
Jacksonville	25	28	.893	50
Buffalo	21	24	.875	50
Cincinnati	30	35	.857	55
New England	29	35	.829	53
Kansas City	28	34	.824	52
Houston	31	38	.816	51
Denver	26	32	.813	53
Tennessee	25	31	.806	53
Indianapolis	26	33	.788	53
N.Y. Jets	21	27	.778	54
Miami	23	30	.767	53
AFC Total	428	503	—	57
AFC Average	26.8	31.4	.851	—

NATIONAL FOOTBALL CONFERENCE—FIELD GOALS

	FG	FGA	Pct	Long
Dallas	29	31	.935	51
Minnesota	35	38	.921	56
Arizona	25	28	.893	61
Detroit	32	36	.889	53
Seattle	24	27	.889	52
Philadelphia	27	31	.871	49
Atlanta	33	38	.868	55
Tampa Bay	28	33	.848	57
N.Y. Giants	33	39	.846	50
Chicago	27	33	.818	54
New Orleans	18	22	.818	53
Washington	24	30	.800	50
Carolina	16	21	.762	51
St. Louis	23	31	.742	60
San Francisco	29	42	.690	63
Green Bay	21	33	.636	54
NFC Total	424	513	—	63
NFC Average	26.5	32.1	.827	—
League Total	852	1016	—	63
League Average	26.6	31.8	.839	—

AFC—INDIVIDUAL FIELD GOALS

	1-19 Yards	20-29 Yards	30-39 Yards	40-49 Yards	50 or Longer	Totals	Avg Yds Att	Avg Yds Made	Avg Yds Miss	Long
Dawson, Phil, Cle.	0-0 —	8-9 .889	8-9 .889	6-6 1.000	7-7 1.000	29-31 .935	37.2	37.4	33.5	53
Janikowski, Sebastian, Oak.	1-1 1.000	9-9 1.000	10-10 1.000	5-5 1.000	6-9 .667	31-34 .912	37.4	35.3	58.7	57
* Tucker, Justin, Bal.	0-0 —	8-8 1.000	8-8 1.000	10-13 .769	4-4 1.000	30-33 .909	39.2	38.7	44.3	56
Suisham, Shaun, Pit.	0-0 —	7-8 .875	8-8 1.000	12-12 1.000	1-3 .333	28-31 .903	36.9	36.2	43.7	52
Novak, Nick, S.D.	1-1 1.000	5-5 1.000	6-6 1.000	4-4 1.000	2-4 .500	18-20 .900	36.2	34.2	54.5	51
Scobee, Josh, Jac.	1-1 1.000	4-4 1.000	8-8 1.000	11-13 .846	1-2 .500	25-28 .893	37.5	36.3	47.3	50
Lindell, Rian, Buf.	1-1 1.000	3-3 1.000	10-11 .909	6-7 .857	1-2 .500	21-24 .875	36.1	35.0	44.3	50
Gostkowski, Stephen, N.E.	0-0 —	8-8 1.000	10-12 .833	9-13 .692	2-2 1.000	29-35 .829	37.1	35.9	42.8	53
Nugent, Mike, Cin.	2-2 1.000	5-5 1.000	5-5 1.000	6-9 .667	1-2 .500	19-23 .826	37.1	35.2	46.3	55
Succop, Ryan, K.C.	0-0 —	4-5 .800	12-15 .800	10-12 .833	2-2 1.000	28-34 .824	37.3	37.6	35.8	52
Graham, Shayne, Hou.	1-1 1.000	8-8 1.000	11-11 1.000	7-9 .778	4-9 .444	31-38 .816	38.2	35.5	49.7	51
Carpenter, Dan, Mia.	0-0 —	3-3 1.000	9-9 1.000	8-10 .800	2-5 .400	22-27 .815	39.9	37.6	49.8	53
Prater, Matt, Den.	1-1 1.000	7-7 1.000	10-11 .909	5-9 .556	3-4 .750	26-32 .813	36.2	34.2	45.0	53
Bironas, Rob, Ten.	0-0 —	6-6 1.000	13-13 1.000	5-10 .500	1-2 .500	25-31 .806	37.5	35.4	46.5	53
Vinatieri, Adam, Ind.	1-1 1.000	8-8 1.000	4-7 .571	9-10 .900	4-7 .571	26-33 .788	38.9	37.0	46.1	53
Folk, Nick, NYJ	0-0 —	7-8 .875	6-8 .750	5-7 .714	3-4 .750	21-27 .778	36.3	35.5	38.8	54
(Nonqualifiers)										
Brown, Josh, Cin.	0-0 —	3-3 1.000	4-4 1.000	3-3 1.000	1-2 .500	11-12 .917	37.3	35.6	56.0	52
Kaeding, Nate, S.D.-Mia.	1-1 1.000	3-3 1.000	0-0 —	4-6 .667	0-0 —	8-10 .800	35.5	33.5	43.5	45
AFC Totals	10-10 1.000	106-110 .964	142-155 .916	125-158 .791	45-70 .643	428-503 .851	37.4	36.1	45.2	57
NFL Totals	16-16 1.000	215-223 .964	270-303 .891	259-323 .802	92-151 .609	852-1016 .839	37.8	36.4	45.0	63

Leader based on overall percentage, minimum 16 field goals

NFC—INDIVIDUAL FIELD GOALS

	1-19 Yards	20-29 Yards	30-39 Yards	40-49 Yards	50 or Longer	Totals	Avg Yds Att	Avg Yds Made	Avg Yds Miss	Long
Forbath, Kai, Was.	0-0 —	3-3 1.000	2-3 .667	11-11 1.000	1-1 1.000	17-18 .944	40.4	40.6	37.0	50
Bailey, Dan, Dal.	1-1 1.000	5-5 1.000	13-13 1.000	7-7 1.000	3-5 .600	29-31 .935	37.3	36.2	52.5	51
* Walsh, Blair, Min.	0-0 —	10-10 1.000	8-9 .889	7-9 .778	10-10 1.000	35-38 .921	39.3	39.3	39.3	56
Feely, Jay, Ariz	0-0 —	6-6 1.000	9-10 .900	8-10 .800	2-2 1.000	25-28 .893	38.6	38.2	41.7	61
Hanson, Jason, Det.	1-1 1.000	3-3 1.000	10-10 1.000	16-19 .842	2-3 .667	32-36 .889	39.4	38.6	46.3	53
Hauschka, Steven, Sea.	1-1 1.000	7-7 1.000	10-10 1.000	5-5 1.000	1-4 .250	24-27 .889	35.4	33.1	54.0	52
Henery, Alex, Phi.	0-0 —	8-9 .889	8-9 .889	11-12 .917	0-1 .000	27-31 .871	35.5	34.7	40.5	49
Bryant, Matt, Atl.	1-1 1.000	8-9 .889	10-11 .909	10-13 .769	4-4 1.000	33-38 .868	36.6	36.3	38.6	55
Barth, Connor, T.B.	0-0 —	7-7 1.000	3-4 .750	12-13 .923	6-9 .667	28-33 .848	41.3	40.1	48.4	57
Tynes, Lawrence, NY-G	0-0 —	11-11 1.000	14-16 .875	7-9 .778	1-3 .333	33-39 .846	35.2	33.8	42.3	50
Gould, Robbie, Chi.	0-0 —	7-7 1.000	5-7 .714	7-9 .778	2-2 1.000	21-25 .840	36.6	35.6	41.8	54
Hartley, Garrett, N.O.	0-0 —	9-9 1.000	4-6 .667	2-3 .667	3-4 .750	18-22 .818	34.6	32.7	43.5	53
* Zuerlein, Greg, St.L	1-1 1.000	4-4 1.000	4-6 .667	7-7 1.000	7-13 .538	23-31 .742	44.7	42.3	51.8	60
Akers, David, S.F.	1-1 1.000	8-9 .889	11-13 .846	7-13 .538	2-6 .333	29-42 .690	37.5	35.2	42.5	63
Crosby, Mason, G.B.	0-0 —	5-5 1.000	5-7 .714	9-12 .750	2-9 .222	21-33 .636	41.8	38.7	47.4	54
(Nonqualifiers)										
Cundiff, Billy, Was.	0-0 —	1-1 1.000	3-5 .600	3-4 .750	0-2 .000	7-12 .583	40.2	37.1	44.4	45
Gano, Graham, Car.	0-0 —	3-3 1.000	3-3 1.000	2-3 .667	1-2 .500	9-11 .818	36.2	32.9	51.0	51
Medlock, Justin, Car.	0-0 —	2-2 1.000	3-3 1.000	2-4 .500	0-1 .000	7-10 .700	36.1	32.6	44.3	45
Mare, Olindo, Chi.	0-0 —	2-3 .667	3-3 1.000	1-2 .500	0-0 —	6-8 .750	31.5	31.5	31.5	40
NFC Totals	6-6 1.000	109-113 .965	128-148 .865	134-165 .812	47-81 .580	424-513 .827	38.2	36.8	44.7	63
NFL Totals	16-16 1.000	215-223 .964	270-303 .891	259-323 .802	92-151 .609	852-1016 .839	37.8	36.4	45.0	63

Leader based on overall percentage, minimum 16 field goals
* *Player that was a rookie in 2012*

RUSHING

YARDS
NFC: 2097 Adrian Peterson, Minnesota
AFC: 1509 Jamaal Charles, Kansas City

YARDS, GAME
NFC: 251 * Doug Martin, Tampa Bay at Oakland,
November 4 (25 attempts, 4 TD)
AFC: 233 Jamaal Charles, Kansas City at New Orleans,
September 23 (33 attempts, 1 TD) - (OT)

LONGEST
AFC: 94 Chris Johnson, Tennessee vs. N.Y. Jets,
December 17 - TD
NFC: 82 Adrian Peterson, Minnesota at Green Bay,
December 2 - TD
82 Adrian Peterson, Minnesota at St. Louis,
December 16 - TD

ATTEMPTS
AFC: 351 Arian Foster, Houston
NFC: 348 Adrian Peterson, Minnesota

ATTEMPTS, GAME
NFC: 34 Adrian Peterson, Minnesota vs. Green Bay,
December 30 (199 yards, 1 TD)
AFC: 33 Jamaal Charles, Kansas City at New Orleans,
September 23 (233 yards, 1 TD) - (OT)

YARDS PER ATTEMPT
NFC: 6.8* Robert Griffin III, Washington
AFC: 6.0 C.J. Spiller, Buffalo

TOUCHDOWNS
AFC: 15 Arian Foster, Houston
NFC: 13 * Alfred Morris, Washington

TEAM LEADERS, YARDS
AFC: BALTIMORE, 1143, Ray Rice; BUFFALO, 1244, C.J. Spiller; CINCINNATI, 1094, BenJarvus Green-Ellis; CLEVELAND, 950, *Trent Richardson; DENVER, 731, Willis McGahee; HOUSTON, 1424, Arian Foster; INDI-ANAPOLIS, 814, *Vick Ballard; JACKSONVILLE, 414, Maurice Jones-Drew; KANSAS CITY, 1509, Jamaal Charles; MIAMI, 986, Reggie Bush; NEW ENGLAND, 1263, Stevan Ridley; N.Y. JETS, 1063, Shonn Greene; OAKLAND, 707, Darren McFadden; PITTSBURGH, 623, Jonathan Dwyer; SAN DIEGO, 707, Ryan Mathews; TENNESSEE, 1243, Chris Johnson

NFC: ARIZONA, 356, LaRod Stephens-Howling; ATLANTA, 800, Michael Turner; CAROLINA, 741, Cam Newton; CHICAGO, 1094, Matt Forté; DALLAS, 663, DeMarco Murray; DETROIT, 798, Mikel Leshoure; GREEN BAY, 464, Alex Green; MINNESOTA, 2097, Adrian Peterson; NEW ORLEANS, 602, Mark Ingram; N.Y. GIANTS, 1015, Ahmad Bradshaw; PHILADELPHIA, 840, LeSean McCoy; ST. LOUIS, 1042, Steven Jackson; SAN FRANCISCO, 1214, Frank Gore; SEATTLE, 1590, Marshawn Lynch; TAMPA BAY, 1454, *Doug Martin; WASHINGTON, 1613, *Alfred Morris

TEAM CHAMPION
NFC: 2709 Washington
AFC: 2395 Kansas City

Player that was a rookie in 2012

NFL TOP TEN RUSHERS

	Att	Yards	Avg	Long	TD
Peterson, Adrian, Min.	348	2097	6.0	82t	12
* Morris, Alfred, Was.	335	1613	4.8	39t	13
Lynch, Marshawn, Sea.	315	1590	5.0	77t	11
Charles, Jamaal, K.C.	285	1509	5.3	91t	5
* Martin, Doug, T.B.	319	1454	4.6	70t	11
Foster, Arian, Hou.	351	1424	4.1	46	15
Ridley, Stevan, N.E.	290	1263	4.4	41	12
Spiller, C.J., Buf.	207	1244	6.0	62	6
Johnson, Chris, Ten.	276	1243	4.5	94t	6
Gore, Frank, S.F.	258	1214	4.7	37	8

AFC—INDIVIDUAL RUSHERS

	Att	Yards	Avg	Long	TD
Charles, Jamaal, K.C.	285	1509	5.3	91t	5
Foster, Arian, Hou.	351	1424	4.1	46	15
Ridley, Stevan, N.E.	290	1263	4.4	41	12
Spiller, C.J., Buf.	207	1244	6.0	62	6
Johnson, Chris, Ten.	276	1243	4.5	94t	6
Rice, Ray, Bal.	257	1143	4.4	46	9
Green-Ellis, BenJarvus, Cin.	278	1094	3.9	48	6
Greene, Shonn, NYJ	276	1063	3.9	36	8
Bush, Reggie, Mia.	227	986	4.3	65t	6
* Richardson, Trent, Cle.	267	950	3.6	32t	11
* Ballard, Vick, Ind.	211	814	3.9	26	2
McGahee, Willis, Den.	167	731	4.4	31	4
Mathews, Ryan, S.D.	184	707	3.8	31	1
McFadden, Darren, Oak.	216	707	3.3	64t	2
Dwyer, Jonathan, Pit.	156	623	4.0	34	2
* Pierce, Bernard, Bal.	108	532	4.9	78	1
Moreno, Knowshon, Den.	138	525	3.8	20	4
Jackson, Fred, Buf.	115	437	3.8	15	3
Powell, Bilal, NYJ	110	437	4.0	18	4
Brown, Donald, Ind.	108	417	3.9	19	1
Jones-Drew, Maurice, Jac.	86	414	4.8	59t	1
Redman, Isaac, Pit.	110	410	3.7	28	2
Forsett, Justin, Hou.	63	374	5.9	81t	1
* Hillman, Ronnie, Den.	85	330	3.9	31	1
Thomas, Daniel, Mia.	91	325	3.6	20	4
Battle, Jackie, S.D.	95	311	3.3	52	3
Hillis, Peyton, K.C.	85	309	3.6	18	1
Woodhead, Danny, N.E.	76	301	4.0	19	4
Locker, Jake, Ten.	41	291	7.1	32	1
Jennings, Rashad, Jac.	101	283	2.8	21	1
Tate, Ben, Hou.	65	279	4.3	25	2
* Bolden, Brandon, N.E.	56	274	4.9	27	2
Hardesty, Montario, Cle.	65	271	4.2	25	1
Reece, Marcel, Oak.	59	271	4.6	17	0
Peerman, Cedric, Cin.	36	258	7.2	48	1
* Luck, Andrew, Ind.	62	255	4.1	19	5
Vereen, Shane, N.E.	62	251	4.0	16	3
* Miller, Lamar, Mia.	51	250	4.9	28	1
Draughn, Shaun, K.C.	59	233	3.9	25	2
Goodson, Mike, Oak.	35	221	6.3	43	0
Brown, Ronnie, S.D.	46	220	4.8	21	0
* Tannehill, Ryan, Mia.	49	211	4.3	31	2
Owens, Montell, Jac.	42	209	5.0	32t	1
Fitzpatrick, Ryan, Buf.	48	197	4.1	20	1
Choice, Tashard, Buf.	47	193	4.1	22	1
Mendenhall, Rashard, Pit.	51	182	3.6	20	0
McKnight, Joe, NYJ	30	179	6.0	61	0
Ball, Lance, Den.	42	158	3.8	22	1
Cassel, Matt, K.C.	27	145	5.4	21	1
Parmele, Jalen, Jac.	40	143	3.6	28	0
Carter, Delone, Ind.	32	122	3.8	20	3
Dalton, Andy, Cin.	47	120	2.6	17	4
Smith, Brad, Buf.	14	116	8.3	35	1
Brinkley, Curtis, S.D.	39	115	2.9	13	0
* Weeden, Brandon, Cle.	27	111	4.1	25	0

	Att	Yards	Avg	Long	TD
Leonard, Brian, Cin.	33	106	3.2	11	0
* Rainey, Chris, Pit.	26	102	3.9	19	2
Tebow, Tim, NYJ	32	102	3.2	22	0
* Stewart, Jeremy, Oak.	25	101	4.0	14	0
Murphy, Richard, Jac.	23	92	4.0	14	0
Roethlisberger, Ben, Pit.	26	92	3.5	14	0
Hester, Jacob, Den.	17	81	4.8	18	2
Toston, Keith, Jac.	17	74	4.4	14	0
Taylor, Tyrod, Bal.	14	73	5.2	28	1
McCluster, Dexter, K.C.	12	70	5.8	19	0
* Benjamin, Travis, Cle.	6	66	11.0	35	0
Quinn, Brady, K.C.	19	66	3.5	12	0
Henne, Chad, Jac.	19	64	3.4	15	1
Allen, Anthony, Bal.	16	61	3.8	20	1
Gabbert, Blaine, Jac.	18	56	3.1	10	0
Jackson, Brandon, Cle.	8	54	6.8	25	0
* Martin, Keshawn, Hou.	4	53	13.3	21	0
Pryor, Terrelle, Oak.	10	51	5.1	9	1
Batch, Baron, Pit.	25	49	2.0	10	1
* Jones, Marvin, Cin.	3	47	15.7	37	0
Edelman, Julian, N.E.	4	45	11.3	47	0
* Gray, Cyrus, K.C.	7	44	6.3	15	0
Cribbs, Josh, Cle.	6	42	7.0	16	0
McClain, Le'Ron, S.D.	14	42	3.0	17	0
Rivers, Philip, S.D.	27	40	1.5	11	0
Green, A.J., Cin.	4	38	9.5	20	0
Hasselbeck, Matt, Ten.	13	38	2.9	16	0
Palmer, Carson, Oak.	18	36	2.0	9	1
Scott, Bernard, Cin.	8	35	4.4	29	0
Ventrone, Raymond, Cle.	1	35	35.0	35	0
White, Johnny, Buf.	8	34	4.3	9	0
Hilliard, Lex, N.E.-NYJ	9	33	3.7	9	0
Reynaud, Darius, Ten.	16	33	2.1	11	0
Brady, Tom, N.E.	23	32	1.4	7	4
Leach, Vonta, Bal.	9	32	3.6	6	1
Leftwich, Byron, Pit.	1	31	31.0	31t	1
Harper, Jamie, Ten.	19	30	1.6	13	3
Hawkins, Andrew, Cin.	6	30	5.0	11	0
McElroy, Greg, NYJ	8	30	3.8	15	0
Ogbonnaya, Chris, Cle.	8	30	3.8	9	0
* Hilton, T.Y., Ind.	5	29	5.8	19	0
Sanchez, Mark, NYJ	22	28	1.3	8	0
Brown, Antonio, Pit.	7	24	3.4	13	0
* Blackmon, Justin, Jac.	2	23	11.5	12	0
Flacco, Joe, Bal.	32	22	0.7	16	3
Royal, Eddie, S.D.	3	22	7.3	11	0
Jones, Taiwan, Oak.	6	21	3.5	7	0
Moore, Mewelde, Ind.	13	20	1.5	6	0
Welker, Wes, N.E.	2	20	10.0	11	0
* Mooney, Collin, Ten.	5	19	3.8	8	0
* Eachus, Nate, K.C.	5	18	3.6	7	0
Koch, Sam, Bal.	2	17	8.5	10	1
Heyward-Bey, Darrius, Oak.	2	16	8.0	20	0
Little, Greg, Cle.	2	15	7.5	17	0
McCoy, Colt, Cle.	4	15	3.8	15	0
* Sanu, Mohamed, Cin.	5	15	3.0	7	0
Caldwell, Andre, Den.	1	14	14.0	14	0
Ringer, Javon, Ten.	2	14	7.0	9	0
* Lane, Jorvorskie, Mia.	13	13	1.0	4	2
Gates, Clyde, NYJ	1	12	12.0	12	0
Babineaux, Jordan, Ten.	1	10	10.0	10	0
Weddle, Eric, S.D.	2	10	5.0	6	0
Avery, Donnie, Ind.	4	9	2.3	7	0
Moore, Marlon, Mia.	1	9	9.0	9	0
Smith, Torrey, Bal.	3	9	3.0	13	0
Jones, Greg B., Jac.	5	8	1.6	4	0
Kerley, Jeremy, NYJ	5	8	1.6	5	0
Thigpen, Marcus, Mia.	1	8	8.0	8	0
Todman, Jordan, Jac.	3	8	2.7	6	0
Gilreath, David, Pit.	1	7	7.0	7	0
Johnson, Will, Pit.	2	7	3.5	5	0
Wallace, Mike, Pit.	5	7	1.4	13	0
Casey, James, Hou.	1	6	6.0	6	0
* Grimes, Jonathan, NYJ	2	6	3.0	5	0
Jones, Jacoby, Bal.	1	6	6.0	6	0
Manning, Peyton, Den.	23	6	0.3	10	0
* Allen, Dwayne, Ind.	3	5	1.7	3	0
* Graham, T.J., Buf.	1	5	5.0	5	0
Hernandez, Aaron, N.E.	1	5	5.0	5	0
* Herron, Dan, Cin.	4	5	1.3	6	0
Hughes, Robert, Ind.	1	5	5.0	5	0
Johnson, Quinn, Ten.	4	5	1.3	3	0
Sanders, Emmanuel, Pit.	1	4	4.0	4	0
* Wright, Kendall, Ten.	1	4	4.0	4	0
Boldin, Anquan, Bal.	1	3	3.0	3	0
Clemons, Chris, Mia.	1	3	3.0	3	0
Considine, Sean, Bal.	1	3	3.0	3	0
Lewis, Thad, Cle.	1	3	3.0	3	0
Copper, Terrance, K.C.	1	1	1.0	1	0
Norwood, Jordan, Cle.	1	1	1.0	1	0
Schmitt, Owen, Oak.	2	1	0.5	2	0
Fields, Brandon, Mia.	1	0	0.0	0	0
Lechler, Shane, Oak.	2	0	0.0	0	0
Tate, Brandon, Cin.	1	0	0.0	0	0
Huber, Kevin, Cin.	1	-1	-1.0	-1	0
Suisham, Shaun, Pit.	1	-1	-1.0	-1	0
Thigpen, Tyler, Buf.	1	-1	-1.0	-1	0
Yates, T.J., Hou.	2	-1	-0.5	1t	1
Gradkowski, Bruce, Cin.	4	-2	-0.5	0	0
Moore, Matt, Mia.	5	-3	-0.6	1	0
* Posey, DeVier, Hou.	1	-3	-3.0	-3	0
Shorts, Cecil, Jac.	1	-4	-4.0	-4	0
Moore, Denarius, Oak.	1	-5	-5.0	-5	0
Wayne, Reggie, Ind.	1	-5	-5.0	-5	0
Meachem, Robert, S.D.	1	-6	-6.0	-6	0
Dickerson, Dorin, Buf.	1	-8	-8.0	-8	0
Mallett, Ryan, N.E.	8	-9	-1.1	-1	0
Schaub, Matt, Hou.	21	-9	-0.4	8	0
* Osweiler, Brock, Den.	8	-13	-1.6	-1	0

t = Touchdown
Leader based on most yards gained
* Player that was a rookie in 2012

NFC—INDIVIDUAL RUSHERS

	Att	Yards	Avg	Long	TD
Peterson, Adrian, Min.	348	2097	6.0	82t	12
* Morris, Alfred, Was.	335	1613	4.8	39t	13
Lynch, Marshawn, Sea.	315	1590	5.0	77t	11
* Martin, Doug, T.B.	319	1454	4.6	70t	11
Gore, Frank, S.F.	258	1214	4.7	37	8
Forté, Matt, Chi.	248	1094	4.4	46	5
Jackson, Steven, St.L	257	1042	4.1	46	4
Bradshaw, Ahmad, NY-G	221	1015	4.6	37	6
McCoy, LeSean, Phi.	200	840	4.2	34	2
* Griffin III, Robert, Was.	120	815	6.8	76t	7
Turner, Michael, Atl.	222	800	3.6	43	10
Leshoure, Mikel, Det.	215	798	3.7	16	9
Newton, Cam, Car.	127	741	5.8	72t	8
Williams, DeAngelo, Car.	173	737	4.3	65	5
Murray, DeMarco, Dal.	161	663	4.1	48	4
Ingram, Mark, N.O.	156	602	3.9	31	5
* Brown, Bryce, Phi.	115	564	4.9	65t	4
* Wilson, Russell, Sea.	94	489	5.2	25t	4
* Richardson, Daryl, St.L	98	475	4.8	53	0
Thomas, Pierre, N.O.	105	473	4.5	48	1
Green, Alex, G.B.	135	464	3.4	41	0
Kaepernick, Colin, S.F.	63	415	6.6	50t	5

	Att	Yards	Avg	Long	TD		Att	Yards	Avg	Long	TD
Bell, Joique, Det.	82	414	5.0	67	3	Williams, Kyle, S.F.	4	21	5.3	9	0
Bush, Michael, Chi.	114	411	3.6	20	5	Hynoski, Henry, NY-G	5	20	4.0	5	0
Jones, Felix, Dal.	111	402	3.6	22t	3	Tate, Golden, Sea.	3	20	6.7	13	0
Brown, Andre, NY-G	73	385	5.3	31	8	Miller, Bruce, S.F.	5	18	3.6	9	0
Hunter, Kendall, S.F.	72	371	5.2	26	2	* Tandy, Keith, T.B.	1	18	18.0	18	0
Rodgers, Jacquizz, Atl.	94	362	3.9	43	1	Daniel, Chase, N.O.	3	17	5.7	19	0
* Wilson, David, NY-G	71	358	5.0	52t	4	Logan, Stefan, Det.	3	17	5.7	13	0
Stephens-Howling, LaRod, Ariz	110	356	3.2	52	4	Pilares, Kealoha, Car.	1	17	17.0	12	0
* Turbin, Robert, Sea.	80	354	4.4	26	0	Benn, Arrelious, T.B.	3	16	5.3	9	0
Stewart, Jonathan, Car.	93	336	3.6	21	1	Young, Titus, Det.	2	16	8.0	11	0
Vick, Michael, Phi.	62	332	5.4	20	1	Moss, Santana, Was.	3	14	4.7	12	0
Rodgers, Aaron, G.B.	54	259	4.8	27t	2	Robinson, Aldrick, Was.	1	14	14.0	14	0
Starks, James, G.B.	71	255	3.6	22t	1	* Adams, Joe, Car.	3	13	4.3	5	0
Ponder, Christian, Min.	60	253	4.2	29	2	Henderson, Devery, N.O.	1	13	13.0	13	0
Benson, Cedric, G.B.	71	248	3.5	11	1	Peterson, Patrick, Ariz	2	13	6.5	17	0
Sproles, Darren, N.O.	48	244	5.1	47	1	* Givens, Chris, St.L	3	12	4.0	14	0
Wells, Beanie, Ariz	88	234	2.7	31t	5	* Johnson, Damaris, Phi.	3	12	4.0	7	0
Cutler, Jay, Chi.	41	233	5.7	24	0	Obomanu, Ben, Sea.	1	11	11.0	11	0
Ivory, Chris, N.O.	40	217	5.4	56t	1	Vickers, Lawrence, Dal.	3	11	3.7	13	0
Powell, William, Ariz	60	217	3.6	17	0	* Wright, Jarius, Min.	2	11	5.5	8	0
Tolbert, Mike, Car.	54	183	3.4	13	7	Asiata, Matt, Min.	3	9	3.0	5	0
Gerhart, Toby, Min.	50	169	3.4	22	1	Doucet, Early, Ariz	2	9	4.5	6	0
Williams, Ryan, Ariz	58	164	2.8	25	0	Garcon, Pierre, Was.	2	9	4.5	7	0
Harris, DuJuan, G.B.	34	157	4.6	21	2	Ogletree, Kevin, Dal.	2	9	4.5	5	0
Blount, LeGarrette, T.B.	41	151	3.7	35	2	Scott, Da'Rel, NY-G	6	9	1.5	5	0
Ryan, Matt, Atl.	34	141	4.1	16	1	Amendola, Danny, St.L	2	8	4.0	6	0
Freeman, Josh, T.B.	39	139	3.6	13	0	Crabtree, Michael, S.F.	1	8	8.0	8	0
Smith, Kevin, Det.	37	134	3.6	19	1	Ginn, Ted, S.F.	1	7	7.0	7	0
Cobb, Randall, G.B.	10	132	13.2	28	0	Jacobs, Brandon, S.F.	5	7	1.4	3	0
Grant, Ryan, Was.-G.B.	32	132	4.1	18	2	* Lindley, Ryan, Ariz	4	7	1.8	8	0
Smith, Alex, S.F.	31	132	4.3	24	0	Parker, Preston, T.B.	1	7	7.0	7	0
Bradford, Sam, St.L	37	127	3.4	21	1	Hester, Devin, Chi.	3	6	2.0	8	0
Stafford, Matthew, Det.	35	126	3.6	11	4	Hoyer, Brian, Ariz	1	6	6.0	6	0
* James, LaMichael, S.F.	27	125	4.6	26	0	Jernigan, Jerrel, NY-G	1	6	6.0	6	0
Allen, Armando, Chi.	27	124	4.6	46t	1	Rice, Sidney, Sea.	2	6	3.0	3	0
Kolb, Kevin, Ariz	16	100	6.3	22	1	Brees, Drew, N.O.	15	5	0.3	11	1
Harvin, Percy, Min.	22	96	4.4	20	1	* Cadet, Travaris, N.O.	1	5	5.0	5	0
Royster, Evan, Was.	23	88	3.8	12	2	Clemens, Kellen, St.L	2	5	2.5	5	0
Washington, Leon, Sea.	23	83	3.6	14	1	Hankerson, Leonard, Was.	2	5	2.5	3	0
Dixon, Anthony, S.F.	21	78	3.7	9	2	Skelton, John, Ariz	4	5	1.3	2	0
Bell, Kahlil, Chi.	.29	76	2.6	18	0	Douglas, Harry, Atl.	2	4	2.0	5	0
* Dunbar, Lance, Dal.	21	75	3.6	18	0	Murphy, Louis, Car.	1	3	3.0	3	0
Lewis, Dion, Phi.	13	69	5.3	17t	1	Williams, Keiland, Det.	2	3	1.5	2	0
Johnson, Rashad, Ariz	2	64	32.0	40	0	Helu, Roy, Was.	2	2	1.0	1	0
Manningham, Mario, S.F.	3	64	21.3	29	0	Briscoe, Dezmon, Was.	1	1	1.0	1	0
Kuhn, John, G.B.	23	63	2.7	9	1	Davis, Fred, Was.	1	1	1.0	1	0
Snelling, Jason, Atl.	18	63	3.5	11	0	Morgan, Joe, N.O.	1	1	1.0	1	0
Tanner, Phillip, Dal.	25	61	2.4	9	0	Underwood, Tiquan, T.B.	1	1	1.0	1	0
Young, Darrel, Was.	14	60	4.3	16	0	Feely, Jay, Ariz	1	0	0.0	0	0
Thomas, Mike, Jac.-Det.	7	57	8.1	22	0	Smith, Armond, Car.	3	0	0.0	3	0
* Pead, Isaiah, St.L	10	54	5.4	19	0	Hill, Shaun, Det.	1	-1	-1.0	-1	0
Ware, D.J., T.B.	11	51	4.6	17	0	Paul, Niles, Was.	1	-1	-1.0	-1	0
Robinson, Michael, Sea.	12	49	4.1	29	0	Webb, Joe, Min.	1	-1	-1.0	-1	0
Romo, Tony, Dal.	30	49	1.6	15	1	Marshall, Brandon, Chi.	1	-2	-2.0	-2	0
Burleson, Nate, Det.	8	48	6.0	16	0	Carr, David, NY-G	3	-3	-1.0	-1	0
* Foles, Nick, Phi.	11	42	3.8	14	1	Harrell, Graham, G.B.	4	-3	-0.8	0	0
Lumpkin, Kregg, NY-G	9	42	4.7	22	0	McCown, Luke, Atl.	2	-3	-1.5	-1	0
Banks, Brandon, Was.	7	36	5.1	21	0	Nakamura, Haruki, Car.	1	-4	-4.0	-4	0
LaFell, Brandon, Car.	3	35	11.7	25	0	Bryant, Dez, Dal.	2	-5	-2.5	6	0
Goldson, Dashon, S.F.	1	31	31.0	31	0	Flynn, Matt, Sea.	4	-5	-1.3	-1	0
Jones, Julio, Atl.	6	30	5.0	18	0	Jackson, DeSean, Phi.	3	-7	-2.3	5	0
Manning, Eli, NY-G	20	30	1.5	13	0	* Hekker, Johnny, St.L	1	-9	-9.0	-9	0
Roberts, Andre, Ariz	4	29	7.3	15	0	Ryan, Jon, Sea.	2	-18	-9.0	0	0
Campbell, Jason, Chi.	7	28	4.0	13	0						
Smith, Steve, Car.	3	27	9.0	15	0	*t = Touchdown*					
Morgan, Josh, Was.	3	25	8.3	9	0	*Leader based on most yards gained*					
* Cousins, Kirk, Was.	3	22	7.3	17	0	* *Player that was a rookie in 2012*					
Havili, Stanley, Phi.	6	22	3.7	8	1						

AMERICAN FOOTBALL CONFERENCE—RUSHING

	Att	Yards	Avg	Long	TD
Kansas City	500	2395	4.8	91t	9
Buffalo	442	2217	5.0	62	12
New England	523	2184	4.2	47	25
Houston	508	2123	4.2	81t	19
Baltimore	444	1901	4.3	78	17
N.Y. Jets	494	1896	3.8	61	12
Denver	481	1832	3.8	31	12
Miami	440	1802	4.1	65t	15
Cincinnati	430	1745	4.1	48	11
Tennessee	378	1687	4.5	94t	10
Indianapolis	440	1671	3.8	26	11
Cleveland	396	1593	4.0	35	12
Pittsburgh	412	1537	3.7	34	8
San Diego	411	1461	3.6	52	4
Oakland	376	1420	3.8	64t	4
Jacksonville	358	1369	3.8	59t	5
AFC Total	7033	28833	4.1	94t	186
AFC Average	439.6	1802.1	4.1	—	11.6

NATIONAL FOOTBALL CONFERENCE—RUSHING

	Att	Yards	Avg	Long	TD
Washington	519	2709	5.2	76t	22
Minnesota	486	2634	5.4	82t	16
Seattle	536	2579	4.8	77t	16
San Francisco	492	2491	5.1	50t	17
Carolina	462	2088	4.5	72t	21
Chicago	470	1970	4.2	46t	11
Philadelphia	413	1874	4.5	65t	10
N.Y. Giants	409	1862	4.6	52t	18
Tampa Bay	416	1837	4.4	70t	13
St. Louis	410	1714	4.2	53	5
Green Bay	433	1702	3.9	41	9
Detroit	391	1613	4.1	67	17
New Orleans	370	1577	4.3	56t	10
Atlanta	378	1397	3.7	43	12
Dallas	355	1265	3.6	48	8
Arizona	352	1204	3.4	52	10
NFC Total	6892	30516	4.4	82t	215
NFC Average	430.8	1907.3	4.4	—	13.4
League Total	13925	59349	—	94t	401
League Average	435.2	1854.7	4.3	—	12.5

PASSING

HIGHEST RATING
NFC:	108.0	Aaron Rodgers, Green Bay
AFC:	105.8	Peyton Manning, Denver

COMPLETION PERCENTAGE
NFC:	68.6	Matt Ryan, Atlanta
AFC:	68.6	Peyton Manning, Denver

ATTEMPTS
NFC:	727	Matthew Stafford, Detroit
AFC:	637	Tom Brady, New England

COMPLETIONS
NFC:	435	Matthew Stafford, Detroit
AFC:	401	Tom Brady, New England

YARDS
NFC:	5177	Drew Brees, New Orleans
AFC:	4827	Tom Brady, New England

YARDS, GAME
AFC:	527	Matt Schaub, Houston vs. Jacksonville, November 18 (43-55, 5 TD) - (OT)
NFC:	510	Eli Manning, N.Y. Giants vs. Tampa Bay, September 16 (31-51, 3 TD)

LONGEST
NFC:	95	Josh Freeman (to Vincent Jackson) Tampa Bay vs. New Orleans, October 21
AFC:	83	Tom Brady (to Shane Vereen) New England at N.Y. Jets, November 22 - TD

YARDS PER ATTEMPT
NFC:	8.14*	Robert Griffin III, Washington
AFC:	7.99	Peyton Manning, Denver

TOUCHDOWN PASSES
NFC:	43	Drew Brees, New Orleans
AFC:	37	Peyton Manning, Denver

TOUCHDOWN PASSES, GAME
NFC:	6	Aaron Rodgers, Green Bay at Houston, October 14 (24-37, 338 yards)
AFC:	5	Matt Schaub, Houston vs. Jacksonville, November 18 (43-55, 527 yards) - (OT)

LOWEST INTERCEPTION PERCENTAGE
NFC:	1.3 *	Robert Griffin III, Washington
AFC:	1.3	Tom Brady, New England

TEAM CHAMPION (MOST NET YARDS)
NFC:	4997	New Orleans
AFC:	4662	New England

NFL TOP TEN PASSERS

	Att	Comp	Pct Comp	Yds	Avg Gain	TD	Pct TD	Long	Int	Pct Int	Sack	Yds Lost	Rating Points
Rodgers, Aaron, G.B.	552	371	67.2	4295	7.78	39	7.1	73	8	1.4	51	293	108.0
Manning, Peyton, Den.	583	400	68.6	4659	7.99	37	6.3	71t	11	1.9	21	137	105.8
* Griffin III, Robert, Was.	393	258	65.6	3200	8.14	20	5.1	88t	5	1.3	30	217	102.4
* Wilson, Russell, Sea.	393	252	64.1	3118	7.93	26	6.6	67	10	2.5	33	203	100.0
Ryan, Matt, Atl.	615	422	68.6	4719	7.67	32	5.2	80t	14	2.3	28	210	99.1
Brady, Tom, N.E.	637	401	63.0	4827	7.58	34	5.3	83t	8	1.3	27	182	98.7
Roethlisberger, Ben, Pit.	449	284	63.3	3265	7.27	26	5.8	82t	8	1.8	30	182	97.0
Brees, Drew, N.O.	670	422	63.0	5177	7.73	43	6.4	80t	19	2.8	26	190	96.3
Schaub, Matt, Hou.	544	350	64.3	4008	7.37	22	4.0	60t	12	2.2	27	216	90.7
Romo, Tony, Dal.	648	425	65.6	4903	7.57	28	4.3	85t	19	2.9	36	263	90.5

AMERICAN FOOTBALL CONFERENCE—PASSING

	Att	Comp	Pct Comp	Gross Yards	Sacked	Yds Lost	Net Yards	Yds/ Att	Yards/ Comp	TD	Pct TD	Long	Int	Pct Int
New England	641	402	62.7	4844	27	182	4662	7.56	12.05	34	5.30	83t	9	1.4
Denver	588	402	68.4	4671	21	137	4534	7.94	11.62	37	6.29	71t	11	1.9
Indianapolis	628	339	54.0	4374	41	246	4128	6.96	12.90	23	3.66	70t	18	2.9
Oakland	629	376	59.8	4292	27	208	4084	6.82	11.41	24	3.82	64t	16	2.5
Houston	554	354	63.9	4046	28	216	3830	7.30	11.43	22	3.97	60t	13	2.3
Pittsburgh	574	354	61.7	4012	37	225	3787	6.99	11.33	27	4.70	82t	14	2.4
Baltimore	560	334	59.6	3996	38	257	3739	7.14	11.96	22	3.93	61t	11	2.0
Cincinnati	540	335	62.0	3807	46	229	3578	7.05	11.36	28	5.19	73t	16	3.0
Jacksonville	586	328	56.0	3746	50	327	3419	6.39	11.42	20	3.41	81t	17	2.9
Cleveland	566	328	58.0	3668	36	233	3435	6.48	11.18	16	2.83	71t	18	3.2
San Diego	528	338	64.0	3606	49	311	3295	6.83	10.67	26	4.92	80t	15	2.8
Tennessee	540	318	58.9	3577	39	254	3323	6.62	11.25	17	3.15	71t	16	3.0
Buffalo	511	309	60.5	3430	30	161	3269	6.71	11.10	24	4.70	68t	17	3.3
Miami	504	293	58.1	3425	37	243	3182	6.80	11.69	13	2.58	80t	13	2.6
N.Y. Jets	493	272	55.2	3178	47	287	2891	6.45	11.68	14	2.84	66	19	3.9
Kansas City	475	273	57.5	2937	40	224	2713	6.18	10.76	8	1.68	57	20	4.2
AFC Total	8917	5355	—	61609	593	3740	57869	—	—	355	—	83t	243	—
AFC Average	557.3	334.7	60.1	3850.6	37.1	233.8	3616.8	6.91	11.50	22.2	4.0	—	15.2	2.7

NATIONAL FOOTBALL CONFERENCE—PASSING

	Att	Comp	Pct Comp	Gross Yards	Sacked	Yds Lost	Net Yards	Yds/ Att	Yards/ Comp	TD	Pct TD	Long	Int	Pct Int
New Orleans	671	423	63.0	5187	26	190	4997	7.73	12.26	43	6.41	80t	19	2.8
Detroit	740	445	60.1	5139	29	212	4927	6.94	11.55	22	2.97	57	17	2.3
Dallas	658	434	66.0	4992	36	263	4729	7.59	11.50	29	4.41	85t	19	2.9
Atlanta	615	422	68.6	4719	28	210	4509	7.67	11.18	32	5.20	80t	14	2.3
Green Bay	558	374	67.0	4342	51	293	4049	7.78	11.61	40	7.17	73	8	1.4
Tampa Bay	566	311	54.9	4144	26	161	3983	7.32	13.32	27	4.77	77t	15	3.0
Philadelphia	618	367	59.4	4075	48	284	3791	6.59	11.10	18	2.91	77t	15	2.4
N.Y. Giants	539	323	59.9	3967	20	142	3825	7.36	12.28	26	4.82	80t	15	2.8
Carolina	490	284	58.0	3927	36	244	3683	8.01	13.83	19	3.88	82	12	2.4
St. Louis	557	332	59.6	3783	35	233	3550	6.79	11.39	22	3.95	80t	14	2.5
Washington	442	291	65.8	3666	33	244	3422	8.29	12.60	24	5.43	88t	8	1.8
San Francisco	436	289	66.3	3551	41	253	3298	8.14	12.29	23	5.28	57	8	1.8
Arizona	608	337	55.4	3383	58	378	3005	5.56	10.04	11	1.81	53	21	3.5
Chicago	485	287	59.2	3298	44	299	2999	6.80	11.49	21	4.33	60t	16	3.3
Seattle	405	259	64.0	3234	33	203	3031	7.99	12.49	27	6.67	67	10	2.5
Minnesota	483	300	62.1	2935	32	184	2751	6.08	9.78	18	3.73	65	12	2.5
NFC Total	8871	5478	—	64342	576	3793	60549	—	—	402	—	95	225	—
NFC Average	554.4	342.4	61.8	4021.4	36.0	237.1	3784.3	7.25	11.75	25.1	4.5	—	14.1	2.5
League Total	17788	10833	—	125951	1169	7533	118418	—	—	757	—	95	468	—
League Average	555.9	338.5	60.9	3936.0	36.5	235.4	3700.6	7.08	11.63	23.7	4.3	—	14.6	2.6

AFC—INDIVIDUAL PASSERS

	Att	Comp	Pct Comp	Yds	Avg Gain	TD	Pct TD	Long	Int	Pct Int	Sack	Yds Lost	Rating Points
Manning, Peyton, Den.	583	400	68.6	4659	7.99	37	6.3	71t	11	1.9	21	137	105.8
Brady, Tom, N.E.	637	401	63.0	4827	7.58	34	5.3	83t	8	1.3	27	182	98.7
Roethlisberger, Ben, Pit.	449	284	63.3	3265	7.27	26	5.8	82t	8	1.8	30	182	97.0
Schaub, Matt, Hou.	544	350	64.3	4008	7.37	22	4.0	60t	12	2.2	27	216	90.7
Rivers, Philip, S.D.	527	338	64.1	3606	6.84	26	4.9	80t	15	2.8	49	311	88.6
Flacco, Joe, Bal.	531	317	59.7	3817	7.19	22	4.1	61t	10	1.9	35	227	87.7
Dalton, Andy, Cin.	528	329	62.3	3669	6.95	27	5.1	59t	16	3.0	46	229	87.4
Palmer, Carson, Oak.	565	345	61.1	4018	7.11	22	3.9	64t	14	2.5	26	199	85.3
Fitzpatrick, Ryan, Buf.	505	306	60.6	3400	6.73	24	4.8	68t	16	3.2	30	161	83.3
Gabbert, Blaine, Jac.	278	162	58.3	1662	5.98	9	3.2	80t	6	2.2	22	158	77.4
* Luck, Andrew, Ind.	627	339	54.1	4374	6.98	23	3.7	70t	18	2.9	41	246	76.5
* Tannehill, Ryan, Mia.	484	282	58.3	3294	6.81	12	2.5	80t	13	2.7	35	234	76.1
Locker, Jake, Ten.	314	177	56.4	2176	6.93	10	3.2	71t	11	3.5	25	151	74.0
* Weeden, Brandon, Cle.	517	297	57.4	3385	6.55	14	2.7	71t	17	3.3	28	186	72.6
Henne, Chad, Jac.	308	166	53.9	2084	6.77	11	3.6	81t	11	3.6	28	169	72.2
Sanchez, Mark, NYJ	453	246	54.3	2883	6.36	13	2.9	66	18	4.0	34	209	66.9
Cassel, Matt, K.C.	277	161	58.1	1796	6.48	6	2.2	46	12	4.3	19	101	66.7
(Nonqualifiers)													
Moore, Matt, Mia.	19	11	57.9	131	6.89	1	5.3	37	0	0.0	2	9	96.6
McCoy, Colt, Cle.	17	9	52.9	79	4.65	1	5.9	21	0	0.0	4	25	85.2
Lewis, Thad, Cle.	32	22	68.8	204	6.38	1	3.1	23	1	3.1	3	14	83.3
Hasselbeck, Matt, Ten.	221	138	62.4	1367	6.19	7	3.2	37	5	2.3	14	103	81.0
McElroy, Greg, NYJ	31	19	61.3	214	6.90	1	3.2	30	1	3.2	11	71	79.2
Pryor, Terrelle, Oak.	30	14	46.7	155	5.17	2	6.7	38	1	3.3	0	0	70.8
Batch, Charlie, Pit.	70	45	64.3	475	6.79	1	1.4	43	4	5.7	3	12	64.9
Gradkowski, Bruce, Cin.	11	5	45.5	65	5.91	0	0.0	44	0	0.0	0	0	64.6
Taylor, Tyrod, Bal.	29	17	58.6	179	6.17	0	0.0	25	1	3.4	3	30	62.3
Quinn, Brady, K.C.	197	112	56.9	1141	5.79	2	1.0	57	8	4.1	21	123	60.1
Leftwich, Byron, Pit.	53	25	47.2	272	5.13	0	0.0	37	1	1.9	3	24	54.9
Leinart, Matt, Oak.	33	16	48.5	115	3.48	0	0.0	20	1	3.0	1	9	44.4
Yates, T.J., Hou.	10	4	40.0	38	3.80	0	0.0	19	1	10.0	1	0	11.7
(Fewer than Ten Attempts)													
Alexander, Danario, S.D.	1	0	0.0	0	0.00	0	0.0	—	0	0.0	0	0	39.6
Brown, Antonio, Pit.	2	0	0.0	0	0.00	0	0.0	—	1	50.0	0	0	0.0
Fields, Brandon, Mia.	1	0	0.0	0	0.00	0	0.0	—	0	0.0	0	0	39.6
Hillis, Peyton, K.C.	1	0	0.0	0	0.00	0	0.0	—	0	0.0	0	0	39.6
* Hilton, T.Y., Ind.	1	0	0.0	0	0.00	0	0.0	—	0	0.0	0	0	39.6
Johnson, Josh, Cle.	0	0	—	0	—	0	—	—	0	—	1	8	-1.0
Kerley, Jeremy, NYJ	1	1	100.0	42	42.00	0	0.0	42	0	0.0	0	0	118.8
Lechler, Shane, Oak.	1	1	100.0	4	4.00	0	0.0	4	0	0.0	0	0	83.3
Mallett, Ryan, N.E.	4	1	25.0	17	4.25	0	0.0	17	1	25.0	0	0	5.2
* Osweiler, Brock, Den.	4	2	50.0	12	3.00	0	0.0	7	0	0.0	0	0	56.3
Prater, Matt, Den.	1	0	0.0	0	0.00	0	0.0	—	0	0.0	0	0	39.6
Sanders, Emmanuel, Pit.	0	0	—	0	—	0	—	—	0	—	1	7	-1.0
* Sanu, Mohamed, Cin.	1	1	100.0	73	73.00	1	100.0	73t	0	0.0	0	0	158.3
Smith, Brad, Buf.	1	0	0.0	0	0.00	0	0.0	—	1	100.0	0	0	0.0
Smith, Rusty, Ten.	5	3	60.0	34	6.80	0	0.0	17	0	0.0	0	0	80.4
Tebow, Tim, NYJ	8	6	75.0	39	4.88	0	0.0	23	0	0.0	2	7	84.9
Thigpen, Tyler, Buf.	5	3	60.0	30	6.00	0	0.0	12	0	0.0	0	0	77.1

t = Touchdown
Leader based on rating points, minimum 224 attempts
* *Player that was a rookie in 2012*

NFC—INDIVIDUAL PASSERS

	Att	Comp	Pct Comp	Yds	Avg Gain	TD	Pct TD	Long	Int	Pct Int	Sack	Yds Lost	Rating Points
Rodgers, Aaron, G.B.	552	371	67.2	4295	7.78	39	7.1	73	8	1.4	51	293	108.0
* Griffin III, Robert, Was.	393	258	65.6	3200	8.14	20	5.1	88t	5	1.3	30	217	102.4
* Wilson, Russell, Sea.	393	252	64.1	3118	7.93	26	6.6	67	10	2.5	33	203	100.0
Ryan, Matt, Atl.	615	422	68.6	4719	7.67	32	5.2	80t	14	2.3	28	210	99.1
Brees, Drew, N.O.	670	422	63.0	5177	7.73	43	6.4	80t	19	2.8	26	190	96.3
Romo, Tony, Dal.	648	425	65.6	4903	7.57	28	4.3	85t	19	2.9	36	263	90.5
Manning, Eli, NY-G	536	321	59.9	3948	7.37	26	4.9	80t	15	2.8	19	136	87.2
Newton, Cam, Car.	485	280	57.7	3869	7.98	19	3.9	82	12	2.5	36	244	86.2
Bradford, Sam, St.L	551	328	59.5	3702	6.72	21	3.8	80t	13	2.4	35	233	82.6
Freeman, Josh, T.B.	558	306	54.8	4065	7.28	27	4.8	95	17	3.0	26	161	81.6
Cutler, Jay, Chi.	434	255	58.8	3033	6.99	19	4.4	60t	14	3.2	38	250	81.3
Ponder, Christian, Min.	483	300	62.1	2935	6.08	18	3.7	65	12	2.5	32	184	81.2
Stafford, Matthew, Det.	727	435	59.8	4967	6.83	20	2.8	57	17	2.3	29	212	79.8
* Foles, Nick, Phi.	265	161	60.8	1699	6.41	6	2.3	46	5	1.9	20	131	79.1
Vick, Michael, Phi.	351	204	58.1	2362	6.73	12	3.4	77t	10	2.8	28	153	78.1
(Nonqualifiers)													
Hill, Shaun, Det.	13	10	76.9	172	13.23	2	15.4	46t	0	0.0	0	0	157.9
Orton, Kyle, Dal.	10	9	90.0	89	8.90	1	10.0	21	0	0.0	0	0	137.1
Smith, Alex, S.F.	218	153	70.2	1737	7.97	13	6.0	55	5	2.3	24	137	104.1
* Cousins, Kirk, Was.	48	33	68.8	466	9.71	4	8.3	77t	3	6.3	3	27	101.6
Kaepernick, Colin, S.F.	218	136	62.4	1814	8.32	10	4.6	57	3	1.4	16	112	98.3
Kolb, Kevin, Ariz	183	109	59.6	1169	6.39	8	4.4	46t	3	1.6	27	159	86.1
Campbell, Jason, Chi.	51	32	62.7	265	5.20	2	3.9	45	2	3.9	6	49	72.8
Hoyer, Brian, Ariz	53	30	56.6	330	6.23	1	1.9	53	2	3.8	4	30	65.8
Skelton, John, Ariz	201	109	54.2	1132	5.63	2	1.0	40	9	4.5	15	98	55.4
* Lindley, Ryan, Ariz	171	89	52.0	752	4.40	0	0.0	28	7	4.1	12	91	46.7
(Fewer than Ten Attempts)													
Anderson, Derek, Car.	4	4	100.0	58	14.50	0	0.0	23	0	0.0	0	0	118.8
Carr, David, NY-G	3	2	66.7	19	6.33	0	0.0	15	0	0.0	1	6	84.0
Clemens, Kellen, St.L	3	1	33.3	39	13.00	0	0.0	39	1	33.3	0	0	42.4
Daniel, Chase, N.O.	1	1	100.0	10	10.00	0	0.0	10	0	0.0	0	0	108.3
Edwards, Armanti, Car.	1	0	0.0	0	0.00	0	0.0	—	0	0.0	0	0	39.6
Edwards, Trent, Phi.	2	2	100.0	14	7.00	0	0.0	8	0	0.0	0	0	95.8
Flynn, Matt, Sea.	9	5	55.6	68	7.56	0	0.0	27	0	0.0	0	0	79.9
Harrell, Graham, G.B.	4	2	50.0	20	5.00	0	0.0	11	0	0.0	0	0	64.6
* Hekker, Johnny, St.L	3	3	100.0	42	14.00	1	33.3	21	0	0.0	0	0	158.3
Hunter, Kendall, S.F.	0	0	—	0	—	0	—	—	0	—	1	4	-1.0
Masthay, Tim, G.B.	2	1	50.0	27	13.50	1	50.0	27t	0	0.0	0	0	135.4
Morgan, Josh, Was.	1	0	0.0	0	0.00	0	0.0	—	0	0.0	0	0	39.6
Orlovsky, Dan, T.B.	7	4	57.1	51	7.29	0	0.0	24	0	0.0	0	0	80.1
Rice, Sidney, Sea.	2	1	50.0	25	12.50	0	0.0	25	0	0.0	0	0	95.8
Tate, Golden, Sea.	1	1	100.0	23	23.00	1	100.0	23t	0	0.0	0	0	158.3
Williams, Mike, T.B.	1	1	100.0	28	28.00	0	0.0	28	0	0.0	0	0	118.8

t = Touchdown
Leader based on rating points, minimum 224 attempts
* *Player that was a rookie in 2012*

PASS RECEIVING

RECEPTIONS

NFC:	122	Calvin Johnson, Detroit
AFC:	118	Wes Welker, New England

RECEPTIONS, GAME

NFC:	18	Jason Witten, Dallas vs. N.Y. Giants, October 28 (167 yards, 0 TD)
AFC:	14	Andre Johnson, Houston vs. Jacksonville, November 18 (273 yards, 1 TD) - (OT)
	14	Brandon Myers, Oakland vs. Cleveland, December 2 (130 yards, 1 TD)

YARDS

NFC:	1964	Calvin Johnson, Detroit
AFC:	1598	Andre Johnson, Houston

YARDS, GAME

AFC:	273	Andre Johnson, Houston vs. Jacksonville, November 18 (14 receptions, 1 TD) - (OT)
NFC:	225	Calvin Johnson, Detroit vs. Atlanta, December 22 (11 receptions, 0 TD)

LONGEST

NFC:	95	Vincent Jackson (from Josh Freeman) Tampa Bay vs. New Orleans, October 21
AFC:	83	Shane Vereen (from Tom Brady) New England at N.Y. Jets, November 22 - TD

YARDS PER RECEPTION

NFC:	19.2	Vincent Jackson, Tampa Bay
AFC:	17.8	Cecil Shorts, Jacksonville

TOUCHDOWNS

NFC:	14	James Jones, Green Bay
AFC:	13	Eric Decker, Denver

TEAM LEADERS, RECEPTIONS

AFC: BALTIMORE, 65, Anquan Boldin; BUFFALO, 79, Steve Johnson; CINCINNATI, 97, A.J. Green; CLEVELAND, 53, Greg Little; DENVER, 94, Demaryius Thomas; HOUSTON, 112, Andre Johnson; INDIANAPOLIS, 106, Reggie Wayne; JACKSONVILLE, 64, •Justin Blackmon; KANSAS CITY, 59, Dwayne Bowe; MIAMI, 74, Brian Hartline; NEW ENGLAND, 118, Wes Welker; N.Y. JETS, 56, Jeremy Kerley; OAKLAND, 79, Brandon Myers; PITTSBURGH, 71, Heath Miller; SAN DIEGO, 56, Malcom Floyd; TENNESSEE, 64, •Kendall Wright

NFC: ARIZONA, 71, Larry Fitzgerald; ATLANTA, 93, Tony Gonzalez; CAROLINA, 73, Steve Smith; CHICAGO, 118, Brandon Marshall; DALLAS, 110, Jason Witten; DETROIT, 122, Calvin Johnson; GREEN BAY, 80, Randall Cobb; MINNESOTA, 62, Percy Harvin; NEW ORLEANS, 85, Jimmy Graham; N.Y. GIANTS, 86, Victor Cruz; PHILADELPHIA, 69, Jeremy Maclin; ST. LOUIS, 63, Danny Amendola; SAN FRANCISCO, 85, Michael Crabtree; SEATTLE, 50, Sidney Rice; TAMPA BAY, 72, Vincent Jackson; WASHINGTON, 48, Josh Morgan

NFL TOP TEN PASS RECEIVERS

	No	Yards	Avg	Long	TD
Johnson, Calvin, Det.	122	1964	16.1	53	5
Marshall, Brandon, Chi.	118	1508	12.8	56	11
Welker, Wes, N.E.	118	1354	11.5	59	6
Johnson, Andre, Hou.	112	1598	14.3	60t	4
Witten, Jason, Dal.	110	1039	9.4	36	3
Wayne, Reggie, Ind.	106	1355	12.8	33	5
Green, A.J., Cin.	97	1350	13.9	73t	11

	No	Yards	Avg	Long	TD
Thomas, Demaryius, Den.	94	1434	15.3	71t	10
Gonzalez, Tony, Atl.	93	930	10.0	25	8
Bryant, Dez, Dal.	92	1382	15.0	85t	12
White, Roddy, Atl.	92	1351	14.7	59	7

NFL TOP TEN RECEIVERS BY YARDS

	Yards	No	Avg	Long	TD
Johnson, Calvin, Det.	1964	122	16.1	53	5
Johnson, Andre, Hou.	1598	112	14.3	60t	4
Marshall, Brandon, Chi.	1508	118	12.8	56	11
Thomas, Demaryius, Den.	1434	94	15.3	71t	10
Jackson, Vincent, T.B.	1384	72	19.2	95	8
Bryant, Dez, Dal.	1382	92	15.0	85t	12
Wayne, Reggie, Ind.	1355	106	12.8	33	5
Welker, Wes, N.E.	1354	118	11.5	59	6
White, Roddy, Atl.	1351	92	14.7	59	7
Green, A.J., Cin.	1350	97	13.9	73t	11

AFC—INDIVIDUAL RECEIVERS

	No	Yards	Avg	Long	TD
Welker, Wes, N.E.	118	1354	11.5	59	6
Johnson, Andre, Hou.	112	1598	14.3	60t	4
Wayne, Reggie, Ind.	106	1355	12.8	33	5
Green, A.J., Cin.	97	1350	13.9	73t	11
Thomas, Demaryius, Den.	94	1434	15.3	71t	10
Decker, Eric, Den.	85	1064	12.5	55	13
Johnson, Steve, Buf.	79	1046	13.2	63	6
Myers, Brandon, Oak.	79	806	10.2	29	4
Hartline, Brian, Mia.	74	1083	14.6	80t	1
Lloyd, Brandon, N.E.	74	911	12.3	53	4
Miller, Heath, Pit.	71	816	11.5	43	8
Brown, Antonio, Pit.	66	787	11.9	60t	5
Boldin, Anquan, Bal.	65	921	14.2	43	4
* Blackmon, Justin, Jac.	64	865	13.5	81t	5
Wallace, Mike, Pit.	64	836	13.1	82t	8
Gresham, Jermaine, Cin.	64	737	11.5	55t	5
* Wright, Kendall, Ten.	64	626	9.8	38	4
Daniels, Owen, Hou.	62	716	11.5	39t	6
Bess, Davone, Mia.	61	778	12.8	39	1
Pitta, Dennis, Bal.	61	669	11.0	61t	7
Rice, Ray, Bal.	61	478	7.8	43	1
Avery, Donnie, Ind.	60	781	13.0	48	3
Bowe, Dwayne, K.C.	59	801	13.6	47	3
Kerley, Jeremy, NYJ	56	827	14.8	66	2
Floyd, Malcom, S.D.	56	814	14.5	39	5
Shorts, Cecil, Jac.	55	979	17.8	80t	7
Gronkowski, Rob, N.E.	55	790	14.4	41	11
Little, Greg, Cle.	53	647	12.2	43	4
Tamme, Jacob, Den.	52	555	10.7	36	2
Lewis, Marcedes, Jac.	52	540	10.4	26	4
Reece, Marcel, Oak.	52	496	9.5	56	1
McCluster, Dexter, K.C.	52	452	8.7	31	1
Moore, Denarius, Oak.	51	741	14.5	58	7
Hawkins, Andrew, Cin.	51	533	10.5	59t	4
Hernandez, Aaron, N.E.	51	483	9.5	31	5
* Richardson, Trent, Cle.	51	367	7.2	27	1
* Hilton, T.Y., Ind.	50	861	17.2	70t	7
* Gordon, Josh, Cle.	50	805	16.1	71t	5
Smith, Torrey, Bal.	49	855	17.4	54	8
Gates, Antonio, S.D.	49	538	11.0	34t	7
Watson, Benjamin, Cle.	49	501	10.2	27	3
Brown, Ronnie, S.D.	49	371	7.6	25	0
Washington, Nate, Ten.	46	746	16.2	71t	4
Britt, Kenny, Ten.	45	589	13.1	46	4
Stokley, Brandon, Den.	45	544	12.1	38t	5
* Allen, Dwayne, Ind.	45	521	11.6	40	3
Sanders, Emmanuel, Pit.	44	626	14.2	37	1
Cook, Jared, Ten.	44	523	11.9	61t	4
Chandler, Scott, Buf.	43	571	13.3	43	6
Spiller, C.J., Buf.	43	459	10.7	66t	2
McFadden, Darren, Oak.	42	258	6.1	20	1
Heyward-Bey, Darrius, Oak.	41	606	14.8	59	5

2012 INDIVIDUAL STATISTICS—PASS RECEIVING

	No	Yards	Avg	Long	TD
Walter, Kevin, Hou.	41	518	12.6	52t	2
Jones, Donald, Buf.	41	443	10.8	68t	4
Dreessen, Joel, Den.	41	356	8.7	30	5
Fasano, Anthony, Mia.	41	332	8.1	22	5
Woodhead, Danny, N.E.	40	446	11.2	25	3
Foster, Arian, Hou.	40	217	5.4	23	2
* Streater, Rod, Oak.	39	584	15.0	64t	3
Mathews, Ryan, S.D.	39	252	6.5	24	0
Alexander, Danario, S.D.	37	658	17.8	80t	7
Johnson, Chris, Ten.	36	232	6.4	22	0
Bush, Reggie, Mia.	35	292	8.3	25	2
Charles, Jamaal, K.C.	35	236	6.7	22	1
Casey, James, Hou.	34	330	9.7	30	3
Jackson, Fred, Buf.	34	217	6.4	34	1
Moeaki, Tony, K.C.	33	453	13.7	38	1
* Graham, T.J., Buf.	31	322	10.4	51	1
Jones, Jacoby, Bal.	30	406	13.5	47	1
Williams, Damian, Ten.	30	324	10.8	27	0
Cumberland, Jeff, NYJ	29	359	12.4	39	3
Keller, Dustin, NYJ	28	317	11.3	32	2
Schilens, Chaz, NYJ	28	289	10.3	25t	1
Graham, Garrett, Hou.	28	263	9.4	30	3
* Fleener, Coby, Ind.	26	281	10.8	26t	2
McGahee, Willis, Den.	26	221	8.5	31	0
Binns, Armon, Cin.-Mia.	24	277	11.5	48t	1
Robinson, Laurent, Jac.	24	252	10.5	32	0
Ogbonnaya, Chris, Cle.	24	187	7.8	38	0
Draughn, Shaun, K.C.	24	158	6.6	23	0
Stevens, Craig, Ten.	23	275	12.0	46	1
Shipley, Jordan, Jac.	23	244	10.6	36	1
Royal, Eddie, S.D.	23	234	10.2	31	1
Spurlock, Micheal, S.D.-Jac.-S.D.	23	200	8.7	22	1
Green-Ellis, BenJarvus, Cin.	22	104	4.7	13	0
* Hill, Stephen, NYJ	21	252	12.0	33t	3
Edelman, Julian, N.E.	21	235	11.2	56t	3
Dickson, Ed, Bal.	21	225	10.7	40	0
Moreno, Knowshon, Den.	21	167	8.0	26	0
Leach, Vonta, Bal.	21	143	6.8	18	0
Baldwin, Jon, K.C.	20	325	16.3	57	1
Holmes, Santonio, NYJ	20	272	13.6	38	1
Hagan, Derek, Oak.	20	259	13.0	38	0
Cameron, Jordan, Cle.	20	226	11.3	28	1
Redman, Isaac, Pit.	19	244	12.8	55	0
Greene, Shonn, NYJ	19	151	7.9	30	0
Jennings, Rashad, Jac.	19	130	6.8	26	0
* Benjamin, Travis, Cle.	18	298	16.6	69t	2
Clay, Charles, Mia.	18	212	11.8	31t	2
* Jones, Marvin, Cin.	18	201	11.2	23	1
Edwards, Braylon, Sea.-NYJ	18	199	11.1	19	1
Dwyer, Jonathan, Pit.	18	106	5.9	15	0
Massaquoi, Mohamed, Cle.	17	254	14.9	54	0
Cotchery, Jerricho, Pit.	17	205	12.1	24	0
* Ballard, Vick, Ind.	17	152	8.9	19	1
Powell, Bilal, NYJ	17	140	8.2	16	0
Gates, Clyde, NYJ	16	224	14.0	42	0
Goodson, Mike, Oak.	16	195	12.2	64t	1
* Sanu, Mohamed, Cin.	16	154	9.6	34	4
* Criner, Juron, Oak.	16	151	9.4	17	1
Branch, Deion, N.E.	16	145	9.1	25	0
Thomas, Daniel, Mia.	15	156	10.4	32	0
Johnson, Will, Pit.	15	137	9.1	26	1
Battle, Jackie, S.D.	15	108	7.2	18	1
Meachem, Robert, S.D.	14	207	14.8	46	2
Smith, Brad, Buf.	14	152	10.9	35t	2
Jones-Drew, Maurice, Jac.	14	86	6.1	13	1
* Rainey, Chris, Pit.	14	60	4.3	14	0
Tate, Brandon, Cin.	13	211	16.2	44t	1
Norwood, Jordan, Cle.	13	137	10.5	27	0
Smith, Alex, Cle.	13	47	3.6	17	0
Brinkley, Curtis, S.D.	12	77	6.4	12	0
* Brazill, LaVon, Ind.	11	186	16.9	42t	1
* Matthews, Rishard, Mia.	11	151	13.7	30	0

	No	Yards	Avg	Long	TD
Reuland, Konrad, NYJ	11	83	7.5	18	0
* Lane, Jorvorskie, Mia.	11	79	7.2	24	1
Leonard, Brian, Cin.	11	67	6.1	16	0
Jones, Greg B., Jac.	11	64	5.8	10	0
Tate, Ben, Hou.	11	49	4.5	11	0
* Elliott, Kevin, Jac.	10	108	10.8	22	0
Rosario, Dante, S.D.	10	95	9.5	18	3
Willis, Matt, Den.	10	90	9.0	19	0
* Martin, Keshawn, Hou.	10	85	8.5	18	1
Hillis, Peyton, K.C.	10	62	6.2	15	0
* Hillman, Ronnie, Den.	10	62	6.2	29	0
Dickerson, Dorin, Buf.	9	117	13.0	24	0
Brown, Donald, Ind.	9	93	10.3	39	0
Peerman, Cedric, Cin.	9	85	9.4	16	0
Mendenhall, Rashard, Pit.	9	62	6.9	15	1
McMichael, Randy, S.D.	9	51	5.7	13	0
Vereen, Shane, N.E.	8	149	18.6	83t	1
Owens, Montell, Jac.	8	113	14.1	53	0
* Cooper, Josh, Cle.	8	106	13.3	28	0
* Charles, Orson, Cin.	8	101	12.6	25	0
Copper, Terrance, K.C.	8	79	9.9	17	0
* Stewart, Jeremy, Oak.	8	62	7.8	26	0
McClain, Le'Ron, S.D.	8	29	3.6	12	0
Doss, Tandon, Bal.	7	123	17.6	39	1
Ausberry, David, Oak.	7	92	13.1	31	0
Breaston, Steve, K.C.	7	74	10.6	24	0
Cribbs, Josh, Cle.	7	63	9.0	24	0
Ball, Lance, Den.	7	61	8.7	17	1
Parmele, Jalen, Jac.	7	60	8.6	26	0
Whalen, Ryan, Cin.	7	53	7.6	10	0
* Paulson, David, Pit.	7	51	7.3	9	0
* Pierce, Bernard, Bal.	7	47	6.7	11	0
Jean, Lestar, Hou.	6	151	25.2	54t	1
Moore, Marlon, Mia.	6	116	19.3	37	1
* Posey, DeVier, Hou.	6	87	14.5	36	0
Moore, Mewelde, Ind.	6	77	12.8	32	1
* Wylie, Devon, K.C.	6	53	8.8	16	0
Ridley, Stevan, N.E.	6	51	8.5	20	0
* Thompson, Taylor, Ten.	6	46	7.7	12	0
* Miller, Lamar, Mia.	6	45	7.5	12	0
Hoomanawanui, Michael, N.E.	5	109	21.8	41	0
Newsome, Jamar, K.C.	5	73	14.6	28	0
Reed, David, Bal.	5	66	13.2	23	0
Green, Virgil, Den.	5	63	12.6	28	0
Hawkins, Lavelle, Ten.	5	62	12.4	42	0
Preston, Michael, Ten.	5	59	11.8	21	0
Maneri, Steve, K.C.	5	51	10.2	19	0
* Thompson, Deonte, Bal.	5	51	10.2	25	0
Johnson, Quinn, Ten.	5	40	8.0	17	0
Reynaud, Darius, Ten.	5	35	7.0	9	0
Fells, Daniel, N.E.	4	85	21.3	35	0
Gaffney, Jabar, Mia.	4	68	17.0	30	0
* Green, Ladarius, S.D.	4	56	14.0	31	0
Martin, Ruvell, Buf.	4	41	10.3	16	0
Batch, Baron, Pit.	4	31	7.8	15	0
Hilliard, Lex, NYJ	4	23	5.8	9	0
Smith, Lee, Buf.	4	13	3.3	5	2
Choice, Tashard, Buf.	4	9	2.3	5	0
Boss, Kevin, K.C.	3	65	21.7	29	1
Ajirotutu, Seyi, S.D.	3	45	15.0	28	0
Burress, Plaxico, Pit.	3	42	14.0	18	1
* Clemons, Toney, Jac.	3	41	13.7	17	0
Toston, Keith, Jac.	3	41	13.7	21	0
Forsett, Justin, Hou.	3	38	12.7	18	0
O'Connell, Jake, K.C.	3	18	6.0	11	0
Armstrong, Anthony, Mia.	3	12	4.0	9	0
Ringer, Javon, Ten.	3	12	4.0	6	0
Pope, Leonard, Pit.	3	9	3.0	7	2
Nelson, David, Buf.	2	31	15.5	21	0
Adams, Kris, Ind.	2	26	13.0	13	0
Jackson, Brandon, Cle.	2	20	10.0	14	0
* Gray, Cyrus, K.C.	2	18	9.0	12	0

	No	Yards	Avg	Long	TD		No	Yards	Avg	Long	TD
Holliday, Trindon, Hou.-Den.	2	17	8.5	15	0	Moore, Lance, N.O.	65	1041	16.0	51	6
Hardesty, Montario, Cle.	2	16	8.0	9	0	Jones, James, G.B.	64	784	12.3	49	14
Gilyard, Mardy, NYJ	2	15	7.5	11	0	Roberts, Andre, Ariz	64	759	11.9	46t	5
Hill, Jason, NYJ	2	15	7.5	10	1	Williams, Mike, T.B.	63	996	15.8	65	9
Saunders, Weslye, Ind.	2	15	7.5	11	0	Amendola, Danny, St.L	63	666	10.6	56	3
Allen, Anthony, Bal.	2	12	6.0	7	0	Harvin, Percy, Min.	62	677	10.9	45	3
* Bolden, Brandon, N.E.	2	11	5.5	11	0	Finley, Jermichael, G.B.	61	667	10.9	40	2
Holmes, Andre, Dal.-N.E.	2	11	5.5	7	0	Pettigrew, Brandon, Det.	59	567	9.6	24	3
Jones, Taiwan, Oak.	2	11	5.5	7	0	Celek, Brent, Phi.	57	684	12.0	34	1
Whimper, Guy, Jac.	2	11	5.5	10	1	Bennett, Martellus, NY-G	55	626	11.4	33t	5
Gordon, Richard, Oak.	2	9	4.5	8	1	McCoy, LeSean, Phi.	54	373	6.9	36	3
* Grimes, Jonathan, NYJ	2	7	3.5	4	0	Nicks, Hakeem, NY-G	53	692	13.1	50	3
Potter, Zach, Jac.	2	6	3.0	4	0	Avant, Jason, Phi.	53	648	12.2	39	0
Stallworth, Donte', N.E.	1	63	63.0	63t	1	Rudolph, Kyle, Min.	53	493	9.3	29	9
Bellore, Nick, NYJ	1	23	23.0	23	0	Rodgers, Jacquizz, Atl.	53	402	7.6	32	1
Pryor, Terrelle, Oak.	1	22	22.0	22	0	Bell, Joique, Det.	52	485	9.3	50	0
* Eachus, Nate, K.C.	1	19	19.0	19	0	Gibson, Brandon, St.L	51	691	13.5	34t	5
Naanee, Legedu, Mia.	1	19	19.0	19	0	Rice, Sidney, Sea.	50	748	15.0	46t	7
Caldwell, Andre, Den.	1	18	18.0	18	0	Nelson, Jordy, G.B.	49	745	15.2	73	7
McKnight, Joe, NYJ	1	18	18.0	18	0	* Martin, Doug, T.B.	49	472	9.6	64t	1
* Smith, Hayden, NYJ	1	16	16.0	16	0	Morgan, Josh, Was.	48	510	10.6	32	2
Thigpen, Marcus, Mia.	1	15	15.0	15	0	Clark, Dallas, T.B.	47	435	9.3	33	4
Carter, Delone, Ind.	1	13	13.0	13	0	Jackson, DeSean, Phi.	45	700	15.6	77t	2
Reisner, Allen, Min.	1	13	13.0	13	0	Tate, Golden, Sea.	45	688	15.3	51	7
* White, Jordan, NYJ	1	13	13.0	13	0	* Floyd, Michael, Ariz	45	562	12.5	53	2
Winslow, Kellen, N.E.	1	12	12.0	12	0	Housler, Rob, Ariz	45	417	9.3	33	0
Gronkowski, Chris, Den.	1	11	11.0	11	0	LaFell, Brandon, Car.	44	677	15.4	62	4
Epps, Dedrick, NYJ	1	9	9.0	9	0	Garcon, Pierre, Was.	44	633	14.4	88t	4
McIntyre, Corey, Buf.	1	9	9.0	9	0	Forté, Matt, Chi.	44	340	7.7	47	1
Harper, Jamie, Ten.	1	8	8.0	8	0	* Givens, Chris, St.L	42	698	16.6	65	3
* Jones, Dominique, Ind.	1	8	8.0	8	0	Kendricks, Lance, St.L	42	519	12.4	80t	4
Hester, Jacob, Den.	1	7	7.0	7	0	Scheffler, Tony, Det.	42	504	12.0	57	1
Collie, Austin, Ind.	1	6	6.0	6	0	Manningham, Mario, S.F.	42	449	10.7	40	1
Stanback, Isaiah, Jac.	1	6	6.0	6	0	Moss, Santana, Was.	41	573	14.0	77t	8
Ta'ufo'ou, Will, Jac.	1	5	5.0	5	0	Davis, Vernon, S.F.	41	548	13.4	53	5
Hughes, Robert, Ind.	1	3	3.0	3	0	Jenkins, Michael, Min.	40	449	11.2	32	2
* Smelley, Brad, Cle.	1	3	3.0	3	0	Peterson, Adrian, Min.	40	217	5.4	20	1
Pressley, Chris, Cin.	1	1	1.0	1t	1	Hixon, Domenik, NY-G	39	567	14.5	41	2
Unrein, Mitch, Den.	1	1	1.0	1t	1	Thomas, Pierre, N.O.	39	354	9.1	36	1
Todman, Jordan, Jac.	1	0	0.0	0	0	Hankerson, Leonard, Was.	38	543	14.3	68t	3
Cromartie, Antonio, NYJ	1	-2	-2.0	-2	0	Miller, Zach, Sea.	38	396	10.4	30	3
* Palmer, Nathan, S.F.-Ind.	1	-4	-4.0	-4	0	Douglas, Harry, Atl.	38	395	10.4	37	1
Henne, Chad, Jac.	1	-6	-6.0	-6	0	Jackson, Steven, St.L	38	321	8.4	22	0
Schaub, Matt, Hou.	1	-6	-6.0	-6	0	Jennings, Greg, G.B.	36	366	10.2	45	4
Clary, Jeromey, S.D.	1	-8	-8.0	-8	0	Murray, DeMarco, Dal.	35	251	7.2	22	0
* Weeden, Brandon, Cle.	0	-9	—	-9	0	Leshoure, Mikel, Det.	34	214	6.3	15	0
						Young, Titus, Det.	33	383	11.6	46t	4
						Ogletree, Kevin, Dal.	32	436	13.6	65	4
						Snelling, Jason, Atl.	31	203	6.5	16	1
						Pettis, Austin, St.L	30	261	8.7	36	4
						Bennett, Earl, Chi.	29	375	12.9	60t	2
						Baldwin, Doug, Sea.	29	366	12.6	50	3
						Moss, Randy, S.F.	28	434	15.5	55	3
						Underwood, Tiquan, T.B.	28	425	15.2	62	2
						Gore, Frank, S.F.	28	234	8.4	26	1
						Doucet, Early, Ariz	28	207	7.4	18	0
						Tolbert, Mike, Car.	27	268	9.9	26	0
						Burleson, Nate, Det.	27	240	8.9	26	2
						Simpson, Jerome, Min.	26	274	10.5	33	0
						Murphy, Louis, Car.	25	336	13.4	55	1
						Paulsen, Logan, Was.	25	308	12.3	31	1
						Jones, Felix, Dal.	25	262	10.5	39	2
						Harbor, Clay, Phi.	25	186	7.4	19	0
						* Jeffery, Alshon, Chi.	24	367	15.3	55	3
						Davis, Fred, Was.	24	325	13.5	29	0
						* Richardson, Daryl, St.L	24	163	6.8	26	0
						Cooper, Riley, Phi.	23	248	10.8	23	3
						Bradshaw, Ahmad, NY-G	23	245	10.7	59	0
						Hester, Devin, Chi.	23	242	10.5	39	1
						Lynch, Marshawn, Sea.	23	196	8.5	27	1
						Henderson, Devery, N.O.	22	316	14.4	41	1
						* Broyles, Ryan, Det.	22	310	14.1	40	2

t = Touchdown; * Player that was a rookie in 2012
Leader based on receptions

NFC—INDIVIDUAL RECEIVERS

	No	Yards	Avg	Long	TD
Johnson, Calvin, Det.	122	1964	16.1	53	5
Marshall, Brandon, Chi.	118	1508	12.8	56	11
Witten, Jason, Dal.	110	1039	9.4	36	3
Gonzalez, Tony, Atl.	93	930	10.0	25	8
Bryant, Dez, Dal.	92	1382	15.0	85t	12
White, Roddy, Atl.	92	1351	14.7	59	7
Cruz, Victor, NY-G	86	1092	12.7	80t	10
Crabtree, Michael, S.F.	85	1105	13.0	49t	9
Graham, Jimmy, N.O.	85	982	11.6	46	9
Colston, Marques, N.O.	83	1154	13.9	60	10
Cobb, Randall, G.B.	80	954	11.9	39t	8
Jones, Julio, Atl.	79	1198	15.2	80t	10
Sproles, Darren, N.O.	75	667	8.9	44	7
Smith, Steve, Car.	73	1174	16.1	66	4
Jackson, Vincent, T.B.	72	1384	19.2	95	8
Fitzgerald, Larry, Ariz	71	798	11.2	37t	4
Maclin, Jeremy, Phi.	69	857	12.4	70t	7
Olsen, Greg, Car.	69	843	12.2	47t	5
Austin, Miles, Dal.	66	943	14.3	49	6

	No	Yards	Avg	Long	TD
* Wright, Jarius, Min.	22	310	14.1	65	2
Walker, Delanie, S.F.	21	344	16.4	45	3
Gerhart, Toby, Min.	20	155	7.8	21	0
* Randle, Rueben, NY-G	19	298	15.7	56	3
* Johnson, Damaris, Phi.	19	256	13.5	32	0
Davis, Kellen, Chi.	19	229	12.1	25	2
* Turbin, Robert, Sea.	19	181	9.5	20	0
Powell, William, Ariz	19	132	6.9	25	0
Turner, Michael, Atl.	19	128	6.7	60t	1
McCoy, Anthony, Sea.	18	291	16.2	67	3
Green, Alex, G.B.	18	125	6.9	19	0
Thomas, Mike, Jac.-Det.	18	108	6.0	12	1
Harris, Dwayne, Dal.	17	222	13.1	36	1
Stewart, Jonathan, Car.	17	157	9.2	30	1
Heller, Will, Det.	17	150	8.8	19	1
King, Jeff, Ariz	17	129	7.6	27	0
Stephens-Howling, LaRod, Ariz	17	106	6.2	24	0
Stocker, Luke, T.B.	16	165	10.3	33	1
Kuhn, John, G.B.	15	148	9.9	32	0
* Beasley, Cole, Dal.	15	128	8.5	20	0
Royster, Evan, Was.	15	109	7.3	25	0
Barden, Ramses, NY-G	14	220	15.7	31	0
Williams, Kyle, S.F.	14	212	15.1	57	1
Smith, Steve, St.L	14	131	9.4	25	0
Ware, D.J., T.B.	14	100	7.1	23	0
Benson, Cedric, G.B.	14	97	6.9	18	0
Collins, Jed, N.O.	14	70	5.0	12	2
Williams, DeAngelo, Car.	13	187	14.4	53t	2
Robinson, Michael, Sea.	13	126	9.7	20	2
Vickers, Lawrence, Dal.	13	104	8.0	17	0
* Brown, Bryce, Phi.	13	56	4.3	11	0
Brown, Andre, NY-G	12	86	7.2	17	0
Miller, Bruce, S.F.	12	84	7.0	26	0
Lorig, Erik, T.B.	12	83	6.9	16	1
Robinson, Aldrick, Was.	11	237	21.5	68t	3
Aromashodu, Devin, Min.	11	182	16.5	31	0
* Quick, Brian, St.L	11	156	14.2	39	2
Thomas, David, N.O.	11	86	7.8	20t	4
* Morris, Alfred, Was.	11	77	7.0	20	0
Hynoski, Henry, NY-G	11	50	4.5	8	1
Morgan, Joe, N.O.	10	379	37.9	80t	3
Smith, Kevin, Det.	10	79	7.9	13	1
Bush, Michael, Chi.	9	83	9.2	18	0
Hunter, Kendall, S.F.	9	60	6.7	12	0
Crabtree, Tom, G.B.	8	203	25.4	72t	3
Paul, Niles, Was.	8	152	19.0	37	1
Durham, Kris, Det.	8	125	15.6	27	1
Young, Darrel, Was.	8	109	13.6	28	2
Heap, Todd, Ariz	8	94	11.8	28	0
* Hanna, James, Dal.	8	86	10.8	29	0
Mulligan, Matthew, St.L	8	84	10.5	18	1
Driver, Donald, G.B.	8	77	9.6	26t	2
Phillips, John, Dal.	8	55	6.9	19	1
Carlson, John, Min.	8	43	5.4	14	0
Banks, Brandon, Was.	8	15	1.9	8	0
Ellison, Rhett, Min.	7	65	9.3	29	0
Williams, D.J., G.B.	7	57	8.1	12	0
Helu, Roy, Was.	7	45	6.4	21	0
Williams, Ryan, Ariz	7	44	6.3	12	0
Havili, Stanley, Phi.	7	43	6.1	9	0
Barnidge, Gary, Car.	6	78	13.0	24t	1
* Dunbar, Lance, Dal.	6	33	5.5	14	0
Ingram, Mark, N.O.	6	29	4.8	16	0
Logan, Stefan, Det.	6	28	4.7	10	0
Spaeth, Matt, Chi.	6	28	4.7	13t	1
Palmer, Michael, Atl.	6	22	3.7	6	1
Edwards, Armanti, Car.	5	121	24.2	82	0
* Cadet, Travaris, N.O.	5	44	8.8	17	0
Sherman, Anthony, Ariz	5	39	7.8	19	0
Burton, Stephen, Min.	5	35	7.0	13	1
* Boykin, Jarrett, G.B.	5	27	5.4	9	0
Obomanu, Ben, Sea.	4	58	14.5	36	0

	No	Yards	Avg	Long	TD
* Celek, Garrett, S.F.	4	51	12.8	35	0
Camarillo, Greg, N.O.	4	44	11.0	13	0
Robiskie, Brian, Det.	4	44	11.0	21	1
Martin, Charly, Sea.	4	42	10.5	15	0
Tanner, Phillip, Dal.	4	41	10.3	15	0
Adams, Kyle, Chi.	4	40	10.0	17	0
Davis, Drew, Atl.	4	40	10.0	15t	1
Pascoe, Bear, NY-G	4	35	8.8	16	1
* Wilson, David, NY-G	4	34	8.5	15t	1
McNeill, Mike, St.L	4	31	7.8	10	0
Starks, James, G.B.	4	31	7.8	9	0
Washington, Leon, Sea.	4	31	7.8	9	0
Benn, Arrelious, T.B.	4	26	6.5	9	0
* Rodriguez, Evan, Chi.	4	21	5.3	11	0
Felton, Jerome, Min.	3	35	11.7	17	0
* Kearse, Jermaine, Sea.	3	31	10.3	17	0
* James, LaMichael, S.F.	3	29	9.7	15	0
Cox, Mike, Atl.	3	22	7.3	11	0
Jernigan, Jerrel, NY-G	3	22	7.3	9	0
Byham, Nate, T.B.	3	18	6.0	10	1
* Pead, Isaiah, St.L	3	16	5.3	9	0
Peterson, Patrick, Ariz	3	11	3.7	7	0
Pilares, Kealoha, Car.	2	42	21.0	36t	1
Hartsock, Ben, Car.	2	30	15.0	25	0
Weems, Eric, Chi.	2	27	13.5	18	0
Lewis, Dion, Phi.	2	24	12.0	28	0
Briscoe, Dezmon, Was.	2	22	11.0	14	0
Smith, Alfonso, Ariz	2	21	10.5	13	0
Harris, DuJuan, G.B.	2	17	8.5	11	0
Allen, Armando, Chi.	2	16	8.0	15	0
Dray, Jim, Ariz	2	15	7.5	12	0
Ivory, Chris, N.O.	2	15	7.5	13	0
Bell, Kahlil, NYJ-Chi.	2	13	6.5	11	0
Williams, Keiland, Det.	2	9	4.5	5	0
Ginn, Ted, S.F.	2	1	0.5	1	0
Grant, Ryan, G.B.	1	34	34.0	34	0
* Owusu, Chris, T.B.	1	24	24.0	24	0
Wells, Beanie, Ariz	1	24	24.0	24	0
* Harkey, Cory, St.L	1	21	21.0	21	0
* McLeod, Rodney, St.L	1	21	21.0	21	0
Stroughter, Sammie, T.B.	1	14	14.0	14	0
Reisner, Allen, Min.	1	13	13.0	13	0
Coffman, Chase, Atl.	1	12	12.0	12	0
Taylor, Ryan, G.B.	1	11	11.0	11	0
* Kelemete, Senio, Ariz	1	10	10.0	10	0
Roby, Courtney, N.O.	1	9	9.0	9	0
* Byrd, LaRon, Ariz	1	8	8.0	8	0
Cooley, Chris, Was.	1	8	8.0	8	0
Polite, Lousaka, Atl.	1	8	8.0	8	0
* Adams, Joe, Car.	1	7	7.0	7	0
Gallarda, Tommy, Atl.	1	7	7.0	7	0
Maui'a, Reagan, Ariz	1	7	7.0	7	0
Sanzenbacher, Dane, Chi.	1	7	7.0	7	0
Chapas, Shaun, Det.	1	6	6.0	6	0
Moore, Evan, Sea.	1	6	6.0	6	0
Louis, Lance, Chi.	1	4	4.0	4	0
Stafford, Matthew, Det.	1	3	3.0	3	0
Asiata, Matt, Min.	1	2	2.0	2	0
Blount, LeGarrette, T.B.	1	2	2.0	2	0
Johnson, Mike, Atl.	1	1	1.0	1t	1
Rodgers, Aaron, G.B.	1	-1	-1.0	-1	0
Romo, Tony, Dal.	1	-1	-1.0	-1	0
Higgins, Mike, N.O.	1	-3	-3.0	-3	0
Ponder, Christian, Min.	1	-15	-15.0	-15	0
Newton, Cam, Car.	0	6	—	6	0
Turner, Robert, St.L	0	4	—	4	0
Gross, Jordan, Car.	0	1	—	1	0

t = Touchdown; * Player that was a rookie in 2012
Leader based on receptions

INTERCEPTIONS

INTERCEPTIONS
NFC: 9 Tim Jennings, Chicago
AFC: 5 Jairus Byrd, Buffalo
5 Devin McCourty, New England

INTERCEPTIONS, GAME
AFC: 2 Devin McCourty, New England at Buffalo,
September 30 (34 yards, 0 TD)
2 Sean Smith, Miami at Arizona, September 30
(31 yards, 0 TD) - (OT)
2 Jairus Byrd, Buffalo at Arizona,
October 14 (36 yards, 0 TD) - (OT)
2 Chris Harris, Denver at San Diego,
October 15 (46 yards, 1 TD)
2 Terence Newman, Cincinnati vs. Denver,
November 4 (0 yards, 0 TD)
2 Darius Butler, Indianapolis at Jacksonville,
November 8 (62 yards, 1 TD)
2 Michael Griffin, Tennessee vs. N.Y. Jets,
December 17 (26 yards, 0 TD)
2 Jason McCourty, Tennessee vs. N.Y. Jets,
December 17 (29 yards, 0 TD)
2 Cortez Allen, Pittsburgh vs. Cincinnati,
December 23 (6 yards, 0 TD)
2 Patrick Chung, New England at Jacksonville,
December 23 (27 yards, 0 TD)
2 Vontae Davis, Indianapolis vs. Houston,
December 30 (26 yards, 0 TD)
2 * Zach Brown, Tennessee vs. Jacksonville,
December 30 (109 yards, 2 TD)

NFC: 2 Tim Jennings, Chicago vs. Indianapolis,
September 9 (28 yards, 0 TD)
2 Kurt Coleman, Philadelphia at Cleveland,
September 9 (13 yards, 0 TD)
2 Dominique Rodgers-Cromartie,
Philadelphia at Cleveland,
September 9 (0 yards, 0 TD)
2 Tramon Williams, Green Bay vs. Chicago,
September 13 (38 yards, 0 TD)
2 Thomas DeCoud, Atlanta at San Diego,
September 23 (-2 yards, 0 TD)
2 Major Wright, Chicago at Dallas,
October 1 (0 yards, 0 TD)
2 Antrel Rolle, N.Y. Giants at San Francisco,
October 14 (42 yards, 0 TD)
2 * Casey Hayward, Green Bay at Houston,
October 14 (37 yards, 0 TD)
2 Tim Jennings, Chicago vs. Carolina,
October 28 (27 yards, 1 TD)
2 Stevie Brown, N.Y. Giants at Dallas,
October 28 (37 yards, 0 TD)
2 Tim Jennings, Chicago vs. Houston,
November 11 (10 yards, 0 TD)
2 * Janoris Jenkins, St. Louis at Arizona,
November 25 (75 yards, 2 TD)
2 William Moore, Atlanta vs. New Orleans,
November 29 (16 yards, 0 TD)
2 Morgan Burnett, Green Bay vs. Minnesota,
December 2 (1 yard, 0 TD)
2 Kerry Rhodes, Arizona at N.Y. Jets,
December 2 (32 yards, 0 TD)
2 Don Carey, Detroit vs. Indianapolis,
December 2 (51 yards, 0 TD)
2 Stevie Brown, N.Y. Giants vs. New Orleans,
December 9 (91 yards, 0 TD)
2 Richard Sherman, Seattle vs. Arizona,
December 9 (19 yards, 1 TD)

2 * Bobby Wagner, Seattle vs. Arizona,
December 9 (45 yards, 0 TD)
2 Jabari Greer, New Orleans vs. Tampa Bay,
December 16 (3 yards, 0 TD)

YARDS
NFC: 307 Stevie Brown, N.Y. Giants
AFC: 156 * Zach Brown, Tennessee

LONGEST
NFC: 102 Greg Toler, Arizona vs. Detroit,
December 16 - TD
AFC: 98 Chris Harris, Denver at Baltimore,
December 16 - TD

TOUCHDOWNS
NFC: 3 * Janoris Jenkins, St. Louis
3 Charles Tillman, Chicago
AFC: 2 * Zach Brown, Tennessee
2 Darius Butler, Indianapolis
2 Chris Harris, Denver
2 Demorrio Williams, San Diego

TEAM LEADERS, INTERCEPTIONS
AFC: BALTIMORE, 4, Ed Reed, Cary Williams; BUFFALO,
5, Jairus Byrd; CINCINNATI, 3, Chris Crocker,
Reggie Nelson; CLEVELAND, 3, Sheldon Brown,
Joe Haden, Usama Young; DENVER, 3, Chris Harris,
Wesley Woodyard; HOUSTON, 4, Kareem Jackson;
INDIANAPOLIS, 4, Darius Butler; JACKSONVILLE, 4,
Derek Cox; KANSAS CITY, 3, Brandon Flowers;
MIAMI, 4, Reshad Jones; NEW ENGLAND, 5, Devin
McCourty; N.Y. JETS, 3, Antonio Cromartie;
OAKLAND, 2, Phillip Adams, Matt Giordano, Joselio
Hanson, Michael Huff; PITTSBURGH, 3, Lawrence
Timmons; SAN DIEGO, 3, Quentin Jammer, Eric
Weddle; TENNESSEE, 4, Michael Griffin, Jason
McCourty

NFC: ARIZONA, 7, Patrick Peterson; ATLANTA, 6, Thomas
DeCoud; CAROLINA, 2, *Luke Kuechly, Charles
Godfrey, Captain Munnerlyn, Haruki Nakamura;
CHICAGO, 9, Tim Jennings; DALLAS, 3, Brandon
Carr; DETROIT, 2, Don Carey, Chris Houston;
GREEN BAY, 6, *Casey Hayward; MINNESOTA, 3,
*Harrison Smith, Antoine Winfield; NEW ORLEANS,
3, Jabari Greer, Patrick Robinson; N.Y. GIANTS, 8,
Stevie Brown; PHILADELPHIA, 3, Dominique
Rodgers-Cromartie; ST. LOUIS, 4, *Janoris Jenkins;
SAN FRANCISCO, 3, Dashon Goldson; SEATTLE, 8,
Richard Sherman; TAMPA BAY, 4, Ronde Barber;
WASHINGTON, 5, London Fletcher

TEAM CHAMPION
NFC: 24 Chicago
AFC: 20 New England

NFL TOP TEN INTERCEPTORS

	No	Yards	Avg	Long	TD
Jennings, Tim, Chi.	9	105	11.7	31	1
Brown, Stevie, NY-G	8	307	38.4	70	0
Sherman, Richard, Sea.	8	57	7.1	29	1
Peterson, Patrick, Ariz	7	64	9.1	31	0
DeCoud, Thomas, Atl.	6	42	7.0	24	0
* Hayward, Casey, G.B.	6	81	13.5	24	0
Byrd, Jairus, Buf.	5	81	16.2	45	0
Fletcher, London, Was.	5	29	5.8	10	0
McCourty, Devin, N.E.	5	53	10.6	34	0
Samuel, Asante, Atl.	5	110	22.0	79t	1

AFC—INDIVIDUAL INTERCEPTORS

	No	Yards	Avg	Long	TD
Byrd, Jairus, Buf.	5	81	16.2	45	0
McCourty, Devin, N.E.	5	53	10.6	34	0
Butler, Darius, Ind.	4	101	25.3	51	2
Williams, Cary, Bal.	4	90	22.5	63t	1
* Wilson, Tavon, N.E.	4	87	21.8	45	0
Reed, Ed, Bal.	4	78	19.5	34t	1
Jackson, Kareem, Hou.	4	71	17.8	63t	1
Scott, Bryan, Buf.	4	66	16.5	32	1
Griffin, Michael, Ten.	4	59	14.8	33	0
McCourty, Jason, Ten.	4	29	7.3	28	0
Jones, Reshad, Mia.	4	28	7.0	15	0
Cox, Derek, Jac.	4	18	4.5	16	0
* Brown, Zach, Ten.	3	156	52.0	79t	2
Harris, Chris, Den.	3	144	48.0	98t	2
* Dennard, Alfonzo, N.E.	3	95	31.7	87t	1
Jammer, Quentin, S.D.	3	89	29.7	80t	1
Timmons, Lawrence, Pit.	3	80	26.7	53t	1
Haden, Joe, Cle.	3	64	21.3	50	0
Cromartie, Antonio, NYJ	3	53	17.7	40t	1
Crocker, Chris, Cin.	3	52	17.3	29	0
Weddle, Eric, S.D.	3	52	17.3	23t	1
Gregory, Steve, N.E.	3	50	16.7	36	0
Young, Usama, Cle.	3	44	14.7	44	0
Woodyard, Wesley, Den.	3	40	13.3	25	0
Flowers, Brandon, K.C.	3	28	9.3	29	0
Davis, Vontae, Ind.	3	26	8.7	26	0
Brown, Sheldon, Cle.	3	20	6.7	19t	1
Posluszny, Paul, Jac.	3	20	6.7	13	0
Nelson, Reggie, Cin.	3	10	3.3	10	0
Williams, Demorrio, S.D.	2	90	45.0	59t	2
Joseph, Johnathan, Hou.	2	88	44.0	52t	1
Hall, Leon, Cin.	2	61	30.5	44	1
Manning, Danieal, Hou.	2	59	29.5	55t	1
Talib, Aqib, T.B.-N.E.	2	59	29.5	59t	1
Carter, Tony, Den.	2	55	27.5	40t	1
Lynch, Corey, S.D.	2	50	25.0	30	0
Routt, Stanford, K.C.	2	49	24.5	32	0
Giordano, Matt, Oak.	2	45	22.5	24	0
Landry, LaRon, NYJ	2	42	21.0	24	1
Cason, Antoine, S.D.	2	34	17.0	31	0
Jackson, D'Qwell, Cle.	2	31	15.5	27t	1
Smith, Sean, Mia.	2	31	15.5	31	0
Clemons, Chris, Mia.	2	29	14.5	29	0
Chung, Patrick, N.E.	2	27	13.5	27	0
Clark, Ryan, Pit.	2	26	13.0	26	0
Hanson, Joselio, Oak.	2	24	12.0	21	0
Quin, Glover, Hou.	2	22	11.0	22	0
Graham, Corey, Bal.	2	20	10.0	20	0
Bailey, Champ, Den.	2	18	9.0	18	0
Verner, Alterraun, Ten.	2	11	5.5	11	0
Allen, Cortez, Pit.	2	6	3.0	6	0
Robertson, Craig, Cle.	2	1	0.5	1	0
Adams, Phillip, Oak.	2	0	0.0	0	0
Huff, Michael, Oak.	2	0	0.0	0	0
Lankster, Ellis, NYJ	2	0	0.0	0	0
Leonhard, Jim, Den.	2	0	0.0	0	2
Newman, Terence, Cin.	2	0	0.0	0	0
McCain, Brice, Hou.	1	86	86.0	86	0
McCarthy, Colin, Ten.	1	49	49.0	49t	1
Landry, Dawan, Jac.	1	47	47.0	21	0
Porter, Tracy, Den.	1	43	43.0	43t	1
Witherspoon, Will, Ten.	1	40	40.0	40t	1
Ward, T.J., Cle.	1	37	37.0	37	0
Houston, Justin, K.C.	1	32	32.0	32	0
Miller, Von, Den.	1	26	26.0	26t	1
* Gilmore, Stephon, Buf.	1	23	23.0	23	0
* Gipson, Tashaun, Cle.	1	23	23.0	23	0
Moore, Rahim, Den.	1	23	23.0	23	0
Butler, Donald, S.D.	1	21	21.0	21t	1
Clements, Nate, Cin.	1	21	21.0	21	0
Lowery, Dwight, Jac.	1	21	21.0	21	0
Zbikowski, Tom, Ind.	1	20	20.0	20	0
Dunlap, Carlos, Cin.	1	14	14.0	14t	1
Branch, Tyvon, Oak.	1	11	11.0	11	0
Scott, Bart, NYJ	1	11	11.0	11	0
Woodley, LaMarr, Pit.	1	11	11.0	11	0
Babineaux, Jordan, Ten.	1	10	10.0	10	0
Bosworth, Kyle, Jac.	1	10	10.0	10	0
* Fort, L.J., Cle.	1	10	10.0	10	0
McKelvin, Leodis, Buf.	1	9	9.0	9	0
Webb, Lardarius, Bal.	1	8	8.0	8	0
* Burris, Miles, Oak.	1	7	7.0	7	0
Dobbins, Tim, Hou.	1	7	7.0	7	0
Marshall, Richard, Mia.	1	7	7.0	7	0
Prosinski, Chris, Jac.	1	6	6.0	4	0
Smith, Eric, NYJ	1	5	5.0	5	0
Wilson, Kyle, NYJ	1	5	5.0	5	0
Freeman, Jerrell, Ind.	1	4	4.0	4t	1
Lee, Pat, Oak.	1	4	4.0	4	0
Starks, Randy, Mia.	1	4	4.0	4	0
Johnson, Michael, Cin.	1	3	3.0	3	0
Sims, Pat, Cin.	1	3	3.0	3	0
Taylor, Ike, Pit.	1	3	3.0	3	0
Vaughn, Cassius, Ind.	1	3	3.0	3t	1
Ayers, Akeem, Ten.	1	2	2.0	2	0
Johnson, Robert, Ten.	1	2	2.0	2	0
Cushing, Brian, Hou.	1	1	1.0	1	0
Keo, Shiloh, Hou.	1	1	1.0	1	0
Mathis, Robert, Ind.	1	1	1.0	1	0
Polamalu, Troy, Pit.	1	1	1.0	1	0
Revis, Darrelle, NYJ	1	1	1.0	1	0
Afalava, Al, Ten.	1	0	0.0	0	0
Berry, Eric, K.C.	1	0	0.0	0	0
Bird, Bront, S.D.	1	0	0.0	0	0
Cole, Marquice, N.E.	1	0	0.0	0	0
* Harris, Mike, Jac.	1	0	0.0	0	0
Kruger, Paul, Bal.	1	0	0.0	0	0
Mayo, Jerod, N.E.	1	0	0.0	0	0
Pollard, Bernard, Bal.	1	0	0.0	0	0
Powers, Jerraud, Ind.	1	0	0.0	0	0
* Winn, Billy, Cle.	1	0	0.0	0	0
Rogers, Justin, Buf.	1	-1	-1.0	-1	0
Bruton, David, Den.	1	-2	-2.0	-2	0
Sharpton, Darryl, Hou.	1	-2	-2.0	-2	0
Elam, Abram, K.C.	0	10	—	10	0

t = Touchdown; *Player that was a rookie in 2012
Leader based on interceptions

NFC—INDIVIDUAL INTERCEPTORS

	No	Yards	Avg	Long	TD
Jennings, Tim, Chi.	9	105	11.7	31	1
Brown, Stevie, NY-G	8	307	38.4	70	0
Sherman, Richard, Sea.	8	57	7.1	29	1
Peterson, Patrick, Ariz	7	64	9.1	31	0
* Hayward, Casey, G.B.	6	81	13.5	24	0
DeCoud, Thomas, Atl.	6	42	7.0	24	0
Samuel, Asante, Atl.	5	110	22.0	79t	1
Fletcher, London, Was.	5	29	5.8	10	0
Barber, Ronde, T.B.	4	160	40.0	78t	1
* Jenkins, Janoris, St.L	4	150	37.5	41t	3
Hall, DeAngelo, Was.	4	62	15.5	27	0
Moore, William, Atl.	4	51	12.8	33	0
Webster, Corey, NY-G	4	45	11.3	38	0
Wright, Major, Chi.	4	45	11.3	45t	1
Rhodes, Kerry, Ariz	4	39	9.8	30	0
Jackson, Rob, Was.	4	19	4.8	17	1

	No	Yards	Avg	Long	TD
Carr, Brandon, Dal.	3	120	40.0	47t	1
Robinson, Patrick, N.O.	3	99	33.0	99t	1
* Smith, Harrison, Min.	3	87	29.0	56t	2
* Johnson, Leonard, T.B.	3	86	28.7	83t	1
Thomas, Earl, Sea.	3	80	26.7	57t	1
Boley, Michael, NY-G	3	74	24.7	51	0
Tillman, Charles, Chi.	3	71	23.7	36t	3
Finnegan, Cortland, St.L	3	68	22.7	32	1
* Wagner, Bobby, Sea.	3	55	18.3	45	0
Browner, Brandon, Sea.	3	39	13.0	35	0
Winfield, Antoine, Min.	3	37	12.3	31	0
Shields, Sam, G.B.	3	32	10.7	32	0
Greer, Jabari, N.O.	3	31	10.3	28	0
Goldson, Dashon, S.F.	3	21	7.0	20	0
Rodgers-Cromartie, Domin, Phi.	3	14	4.7	14	0
Briggs, Lance, Chi.	2	110	55.0	74t	2
Munnerlyn, Captain, Car.	2	107	53.5	74t	2
Toler, Greg, Ariz	2	102	51.0	102t	1
Johnson, Rashad, Ariz	2	87	43.5	53t	1
Conte, Chris, Chi.	2	70	35.0	35	0
* Robinson, Josh, Min.	2	68	34.0	44	0
Dunbar, Jo-Lonn, St.L	2	63	31.5	42	0
Carey, Don, Det.	2	51	25.5	28	0
Rolle, Antrel, NY-G	2	42	21.0	22	0
Harper, Roman, N.O.	2	41	20.5	41	0
Nakamura, Haruki, Car.	2	39	19.5	21	0
Williams, Tramon, G.B.	2	38	19.0	38	0
Black, Ahmad, T.B.	2	34	17.0	34	0
* Kuechly, Luke, Car.	2	22	11.0	25	0
Walden, Erik, G.B.	2	22	11.0	20	0
Laurinaitis, James, St.L	2	18	9.0	18	0
Brown, Tarell, S.F.	2	17	8.5	12	0
Coleman, Kurt, Phi.	2	13	6.5	7	0
Abdul-Quddus, Isa, N.O.	2	12	6.0	12	0
Godfrey, Charles, Car.	2	9	4.5	9t	1
Wilson, Josh, Was.	2	8	4.0	7	0
Gay, William, Ariz	2	7	3.5	6	0
Culliver, Chris, S.F.	2	4	2.0	4	0
* Johnson, Trumaine, St.L	2	4	2.0	4	0
Acho, Sam, Ariz	2	2	1.0	2	0
Houston, Chris, Det.	2	2	1.0	2	0
Moore, D.J., Chi.	2	2	1.0	2	0
Willis, Patrick, S.F.	2	2	1.0	2	0
Burnett, Morgan, G.B.	2	1	0.5	1	0
Mack, Elbert, N.O.	1	73	73.0	73t	1
Jennings, M.D., G.B.	1	72	72.0	72t	1
Rogers, Carlos, S.F.	1	63	63.0	63	0
Wright, Eric, T.B.	1	60	60.0	60t	1
Jenkins, Malcolm, N.O.	1	55	55.0	55t	1
Brooks, Ahmad, S.F.	1	50	50.0	50t	1
Gomes, DeJon, Was.	1	49	49.0	49	0
Urlacher, Brian, Chi.	1	46	46.0	46t	1
Whitner, Donte, S.F.	1	42	42.0	42t	1
Bush, Rafael, N.O.	1	40	40.0	40	0
McDonald, Brandon, T.B.	1	40	40.0	40	0
Hayden, Kelvin, Chi.	1	39	39.0	39	0
Dahl, Craig, St.L	1	38	38.0	38	0
McIntosh, Rocky, St.L	1	34	34.0	34	0
McClain, Robert, Atl.	1	32	32.0	32	0
Florence, Drayton, Det.	1	29	29.0	29	0
Griffen, Everson, Min.	1	29	29.0	29t	1
Kerrigan, Ryan, Was.	1	28	28.0	28t	1
Pierre-Paul, Jason, NY-G	1	28	28.0	28t	1
* David, Lavonte, T.B.	1	27	27.0	27	0
Peprah, Charlie, Dal.	1	27	27.0	27	0
Silva, Ricardo, Det.	1	26	26.0	26	0
Meriweather, Brandon, Was.	1	25	25.0	25	0
Williams, Madieu, Was.	1	24	24.0	24t	1
Wright, K.J., Sea.	1	24	24.0	24	0

	No	Yards	Avg	Long	TD
* Green, Jonte, Det.	1	18	18.0	18	0
Vilma, Jonathan, N.O.	1	18	18.0	18t	1
* Barron, Mark, T.B.	1	12	12.0	12	0
* Crawford, Richard, Was.	1	12	12.0	12	0
Bowman, NaVorro, S.F.	1	11	11.0	11	0
Lacey, Jacob, Det.	1	10	10.0	10	0
Washington, Daryl, Ariz	1	7	7.0	7	0
Smith, Aldon, S.F.	1	6	6.0	6	0
Weatherspoon, Sean, Atl.	1	6	6.0	6	0
Sims, Eugene, St.L	1	5	5.0	5	0
Anderson, Colt, Phi.	1	4	4.0	4	0
Robinson, Dunta, Atl.	1	4	4.0	4	0
Greenway, Chad, Min.	1	3	3.0	3	0
Nicholas, Stephen, Atl.	1	3	3.0	3	0
Beason, Jon, Car.	1	2	2.0	2	0
Fletcher, Bradley, St.L	1	2	2.0	2	0
* Norman, Josh, Car.	1	2	2.0	2	0
Doughty, Reed, Was.	1	1	1.0	1	0
Amukamara, Prince, NY-G	1	0	0.0	0	0
Asomugha, Nnamdi, Phi.	1	0	0.0	0	0
Biggers, E.J., T.B.	1	0	0.0	0	0
Blackburn, Chase, NY-G	1	0	0.0	0	0
* Claiborne, Morris, Dal.	1	0	0.0	0	0
Coleman, Erik, Det.	1	0	0.0	0	0
Davis, Thomas, Car.	1	0	0.0	0	0
Delmas, Louis, Det.	1	0	0.0	0	0
Foster, Mason, T.B.	1	0	0.0	0	0
Gorrer, Danny, T.B.	1	0	0.0	0	0
* Hosley, Jayron, NY-G	1	0	0.0	0	0
Lee, Sean, Dal.	1	0	0.0	0	0
Lenon, Paris, Ariz	1	0	0.0	0	0
* Lewis, LeQuan, T.B.	1	0	0.0	0	0
McCray, Danny, Dal.	1	0	0.0	0	0
* McMillian, Jerron, G.B.	1	0	0.0	0	0
Ryans, DeMeco, Phi.	1	0	0.0	0	0
* White, Corey, N.O.	1	0	0.0	0	0
Woodson, Charles, G.B.	1	0	0.0	0	0
Levy, DeAndre, Det.	1	-1	-1.0	-1	0
Babineaux, Jonathan, Atl.	1	-2	-2.0	-2	0
Wilson, Adrian, Ariz	1	-2	-2.0	-2	0

t = Touchdown; Leader based on interceptions
* *Player that was a rookie in 2012*

AMERICAN FOOTBALL CONFERENCE—INTERCEPTIONS

	No	Yards	Avg	Long	TD
New England	20	371	18.6	87t	2
Tennessee	19	358	18.8	79t	4
Cleveland	17	230	13.5	50	2
Denver	16	347	21.7	98t	5
Houston	15	333	22.2	86	3
Cincinnati	14	164	11.7	44	2
San Diego	14	336	24.0	80t	5
Baltimore	13	196	15.1	63t	2
Buffalo	12	178	14.8	45	1
Indianapolis	12	155	12.9	51	4
Jacksonville	12	122	10.2	23	0
N.Y. Jets	11	117	10.6	40t	2
Oakland	11	91	8.3	24	0
Miami	10	99	9.9	31	0
Pittsburgh	10	127	12.7	53t	1
Kansas City	7	119	17.0	32	0
AFC Total	213	3343	15.7	98t	33
AFC Average	13.3	208.9	15.7	—	2.1

NATIONAL FOOTBALL CONFERENCE—INTERCEPTIONS

	No	Yards	Avg	Long	TD
Chicago	24	488	20.3	74t	8
Arizona	22	306	13.9	102t	2
N.Y. Giants	21	496	23.6	70	1
Washington	21	257	12.2	49	3
Atlanta	20	246	12.3	79t	1
Green Bay	18	246	13.7	72t	1
Seattle	18	255	14.2	57t	2
Tampa Bay	18	419	23.3	83t	3
St. Louis	17	382	22.5	42	4
New Orleans	15	369	24.6	99t	4
San Francisco	14	216	15.4	63	2
Carolina	11	181	16.5	74t	3
Detroit	11	135	12.3	29	0
Minnesota	10	224	22.4	56t	3
Philadelphia	8	31	3.9	14	0
Dallas	7	147	21.0	47t	1
NFC Total	255	4398	17.2	102t	38
NFC Average	15.9	274.9	17.2	—	2.4
League Total	468	7741	—	102t	71
League Average	14.6	241.9	16.5	—	2.2

KICKOFF RETURNS

YARDS PER RETURN
AFC: 30.7 Jacoby Jones, Baltimore
NFC: 29.0 Leon Washington, Seattle

YARDS
NFC: 1533 * David Wilson, N.Y. Giants
AFC: 1240 Darius Reynaud, Tennessee

YARDS, GAME
NFC: 227 * David Wilson, N.Y. Giants vs. New Orleans, December 9 (4 returns, 1 TD)
AFC: 221 Josh Cribbs, Cleveland at N.Y. Giants, October 7 (6 returns, 0 TD)

LONGEST
AFC: 108 Jacoby Jones, Baltimore vs. Dallas, October 14 - TD
NFC: 105 Percy Harvin, Minnesota at Detroit, September 30 - TD

RETURNS
NFC: 57 * David Wilson, N.Y. Giants
AFC: 53 Darius Reynaud, Tennessee

RETURNS, GAME
AFC: 7 Darius Reynaud, Tennessee vs. Chicago, November 4 (145 yards, 0 TD)
7 Joe McKnight, N.Y. Jets vs. New England, November 22 (168 yards, 0 TD)
7 Josh Cribbs, Cleveland vs. Washington, December 16 (191 yards, 0 TD)
NFC: 7 Arrelious Benn, Tampa Bay at N.Y. Giants, September 16 (180 yards, 0 TD)

TOUCHDOWNS
AFC: 2 Jacoby Jones, Baltimore
NFC: 1 Percy Harvin, Minnesota
1 Leon Washington, Seattle
1 * David Wilson, N.Y. Giants

TEAM CHAMPION
AFC: 27.3 Baltimore
NFC: 27.1 Seattle

NFL TOP TEN KICKOFF RETURNERS

	No	Yards	Avg	Long	TD
Jones, Jacoby, Bal.	38	1167	30.7	108t	2
Washington, Leon, Sea.	27	784	29.0	98t	1
McKnight, Joe, NYJ	39	1072	27.5	100t	1
Cribbs, Josh, Cle.	43	1178	27.4	74	0
Thigpen, Marcus, Mia.	38	1040	27.4	96t	1
* Wilson, David, NY-G	57	1533	26.9	97t	1
* Cadet, Travaris, N.O.	26	690	26.5	75	0
* Rainey, Chris, Pit.	39	1035	26.5	68	0
Holliday, Trindon, Hou.-Den.	21	552	26.3	105t	1
Hester, Devin, Chi.	24	621	25.9	40	0

AFC—INDIVIDUAL KICKOFF RETURNERS

	No	Yards	Avg	Long	TD
Jones, Jacoby, Bal.	38	1167	30.7	108t	2
McKnight, Joe, NYJ	39	1072	27.5	100t	1
Cribbs, Josh, Cle.	43	1178	27.4	74	0
Thigpen, Marcus, Mia.	38	1040	27.4	96t	1
* Rainey, Chris, Pit.	39	1035	26.5	68	0
Holliday, Trindon, Hou.-Den.	21	552	26.3	105t	1
Tate, Brandon, Cin.	32	795	24.8	45	0
McCourty, Devin, N.E.	27	654	24.2	104t	1
* Martin, Keshawn, Hou.	31	741	23.9	54	0
Francies, Coye, Oak.	20	475	23.8	32	0
Reynaud, Darius, Ten.	53	1240	23.4	105t	1
Draughn, Shaun, K.C.	23	537	23.3	41	0
(Nonqualifiers)					
McKelvin, Leodis, Buf.	18	510	28.3	59	0
Goodman, Richard, S.D.	18	497	27.6	39	0
Smith, Brad, Buf.	18	496	27.6	89t	1
Spurlock, Micheal, S.D.-Jac.-S.D.	16	375	23.4	99t	1
Goodson, Mike, Oak.	16	359	22.4	51	0
* Thompson, Deonte, Bal.	15	389	25.9	49	0
* Bolden, Omar, Den.	14	270	19.3	33	0
Jennings, Rashad, Jac.	10	241	24.1	29	0
Parmele, Jalen, Jac.	10	233	23.3	38	0
Vaughn, Cassius, Ind.	10	209	20.9	40	0
Karim, Deji, Ind.	9	328	36.4	101t	1
* Wylie, Devon, K.C.	9	191	21.2	26	0
Arenas, Javier, K.C.	9	177	19.7	27	0
Hawkins, Lavelle, Ten.	7	205	29.3	71	0
* Hilton, T.Y., Ind.	7	118	16.9	26	0
Zbikowski, Tom, Ind.	6	123	20.5	34	0
Shipley, Jordan, Jac.	6	117	19.5	24	0
Gates, Clyde, NYJ	5	144	28.8	47	0
Murphy, Richard, Jac.	5	118	23.6	32	0
Carr, Chris, S.D.	5	102	20.4	26	0
* Bellamy, Josh, K.C.	5	101	20.2	27	0
Cosby, Quan, Jac.	5	99	19.8	32	0
Brinkley, Curtis, S.D.	4	86	21.5	28	0
Todman, Jordan, Jac.	4	78	19.5	24	0
Lefeged, Joe, Ind.	4	68	17.0	19	0
* Benjamin, Travis, Cle.	3	76	25.3	29	0
Toston, Keith, Jac.	3	65	21.7	25	0
Jones, Adam, Cin.	3	64	21.3	31	0
Allen, Anthony, Bal.	3	56	18.7	20	0
* Brazill, LaVon, Ind.	3	50	16.7	20	0
Moore, Mewelde, Ind.	3	50	16.7	24	0
* Stewart, Jeremy, Oak.	3	43	14.3	16	0
Edelman, Julian, N.E.	3	38	12.7	32	0
Welker, Wes, N.E.	3	33	11.0	17	0
Easley, Marcus, Buf.	2	75	37.5	55	0
Rogers, Justin, Buf.	2	55	27.5	28	0
Woodhead, Danny, N.E.	2	43	21.5	23	0
Cromartie, Antonio, NYJ	2	42	21.0	22	0
* Lane, Jorvorskie, Mia.	2	42	21.0	24	0
Slater, Matthew, N.E.	2	39	19.5	20	0
Peerman, Cedric, Cin.	2	37	18.5	19	0
Jones, Taiwan, Oak.	2	22	11.0	16	0
* Charles, Orson, Cin.	2	17	8.5	10	0
Pressley, Chris, Cin.	2	15	7.5	8	0
Hagg, Eric, Cle.	2	8	4.0	5	0
* Ingram, Melvin, S.D.	2	-1	-.5	0	0
Reece, Marcel, Oak.	1	36	36.0	36	0
* Gray, Cyrus, K.C.	1	33	33.0	33	0
Sanders, Emmanuel, Pit.	1	27	27.0	27	0
Smith, Eric, NYJ	1	19	19.0	19	0
Leonhard, Jim, Den.	1	18	18.0	18	0
Manning, Danieal, Hou.	1	18	18.0	18	0
Stevens, Craig, Ten.	1	18	18.0	18	0
Cason, Antoine, S.D.	1	16	16.0	16	0

	No	Yards	Avg	Long	TD
Copper, Terrance, K.C.	1	16	16.0	16	0
* Paulson, David, Pit.	1	16	16.0	16	0
McCourty, Jason, Ten.	1	14	14.0	14	0
Reuland, Konrad, NYJ	1	14	14.0	14	0
* Gradkowski, Gino, Bal.	1	12	12.0	12	0
Potter, Zach, Jac.	1	11	11.0	11	0
* Sowell, Bradley, Ind.	1	11	11.0	11	0
Wilson, Kyle, NYJ	1	9	9.0	9	0
Bellore, Nick, NYJ	1	8	8.0	8	0
Johnson, Will, Pit.	1	8	8.0	8	0
Graham, Corey, Bal.	1	7	7.0	7	0
Stephens, Emmanuel, Cle.	1	7	7.0	7	0
Witherspoon, Will, Ten.	1	6	6.0	6	0
Williams, LaQuan, Bal.	1	5	5.0	5	0
Toribio, Anthony, K.C.	1	4	4.0	4	0
Ball, Lance, Den.	1	0	0.0	0	0
Carrington, Alex, Buf.	1	0	0.0	0	0
Casey, James, Hou.	1	0	0.0	0	0
Gronkowski, Chris, Den.	1	0	0.0	0	0
Gronkowski, Rob, N.E.	1	0	0.0	0	0
* Johnson, James-Michael, Cle.	1	0	0.0	0	0
Keo, Shiloh, Hou.	1	0	0.0	0	0
Pitta, Dennis, Bal.	1	0	0.0	0	0
Pope, Leonard, Pit.	f1	0	0.0	0	0
Selvie, George, Jac.	1	0	0.0	0	0
Smith, Lee, Buf.	1	0	0.0	0	0
Williams, Damian, Ten.	0	6	—	6	0

t = Touchdown; f = Fair Catch
Leader based on average return, minimum 20 returns
* *Player that was a rookie in 2012*

NFC—INDIVIDUAL KICKOFF RETURNERS

	No	Yards	Avg	Long	TD
Washington, Leon, Sea.	27	784	29.0	98t	1
* Wilson, David, NY-G	57	1533	26.9	97t	1
* Cadet, Travaris, N.O.	26	690	26.5	75	0
Hester, Devin, Chi.	24	621	25.9	40	0
Rodgers, Jacquizz, Atl.	23	592	25.7	77	0
Cobb, Randall, G.B.	38	964	25.4	46	0
Powell, William, Ariz	21	507	24.1	65	0
Banks, Brandon, Was.	22	527	24.0	55	0
* Givens, Chris, St.L	23	539	23.4	48	0
* Boykin, Brandon, Phi.	45	1037	23.0	44	0
Logan, Stefan, Det.	28	597	21.3	40	0
(Nonqualifiers)					
Sproles, Darren, N.O.	18	483	26.8	48	0
Stephens-Howling, LaRod, Ariz	18	405	22.5	38	0
Harvin, Percy, Min.	16	574	35.9	105t	1
Sherels, Marcus, Min.	16	422	26.4	41	0
* James, LaMichael, S.F.	14	417	29.8	62	0
Williams, Kyle, S.F.	13	353	27.2	94	0
Benn, Arrelious, T.B.	13	306	23.5	55	0
Paul, Niles, Was.	13	283	21.8	48	0
Weems, Eric, Chi.	13	231	17.8	27	0
* Dunbar, Lance, Dal.	12	261	21.8	44	0
Edwards, Armanti, Car.	12	260	21.7	35	0
Ginn, Ted, S.F.	11	253	23.0	31	0
Jones, Felix, Dal.	11	236	21.5	29	0
Harris, Dwayne, Dal.	11	210	19.1	29	0
* Pead, Isaiah, St.L	10	212	21.2	32	0
Pilares, Kealoha, Car.	9	216	24.0	28	0
* Adams, Joe, Car.	9	208	23.1	31	0
* Brown, Bryce, Phi.	8	156	19.5	25	0
Hunter, Kendall, S.F.	7	165	23.6	31	0
Smith, Armond, Car.	6	131	21.8	26	0
* Lewis, LeQuan, T.B.	5	106	21.2	33	0
Thomas, Pierre, N.O.	5	91	18.2	38	0

	No	Yards	Avg	Long	TD
Parrish, Roscoe, T.B.	4	86	21.5	25	0
Walker, Delanie, S.F.	4	28	7.0	18	0
Ross, Jeremy, G.B.	3	86	28.7	44	0
* Robinson, Josh, Min.	3	61	20.3	24	0
Asiata, Matt, Min.	3	55	18.3	22	0
* Smith, Michael, T.B.	3	55	18.3	23	0
Thomas, Mike, Jac.-Det.	3	46	15.3	20	0
Brown, Andre, NY-G	3	42	14.0	22	0
Adams, Kyle, Chi.	3	38	12.7	15	0
Jernigan, Jerrel, NY-G	2	60	30.0	60	0
Bell, Joique, Det.	2	54	27.0	30	0
Underwood, Tiquan, T.B.	2	47	23.5	25	0
Royster, Evan, Was.	2	39	19.5	22	0
Ware, D.J., T.B.	2	25	12.5	18	0
Bennett, Earl, Chi.	2	24	12.0	18	0
Williams, D.J., G.B.	2	24	12.0	12	0
Havili, Stanley, Phi.	2	18	9.0	18	0
Amendola, Danny, St.L	2	16	8.0	12	0
Snelling, Jason, Atl.	2	16	8.0	9	0
Ballard, Christian, Min.	2	12	6.0	8	0
Allen, Armando, Chi.	2	10	5.0	7	0
Wootton, Corey, Chi.	2	0	0.0	0	0
Hall, DeAngelo, Was.	1	43	43.0	43	0
Lewis, Dion, Phi.	1	33	33.0	33	0
Tolbert, Mike, Car.	1	26	26.0	26	0
Polite, Lousaka, Atl.	1	24	24.0	24	0
Jefferson, A.J., Min.	1	20	20.0	20	0
Phillips, John, Dal.	1	20	20.0	20	0
Doucet, Early, Ariz	1	18	18.0	18	0
Munnerlyn, Captain, Car.	1	17	17.0	17	0
Felton, Jerome, Min.	1	16	16.0	16	0
Cooper, Riley, Phi.	1	14	14.0	14	0
Vickers, Lawrence, Dal.	1	14	14.0	14	0
Bennett, Martellus, NY-G	1	13	13.0	13	0
Miller, Brit, St.L	1	13	13.0	13	0
Pettis, Austin, St.L	1	13	13.0	13	0
Reed, D'Aundre, Min.	1	10	10.0	10	0
* Reiff, Riley, Det.	1	10	10.0	10	0
Fua, Sione, Car.	1	9	9.0	9	0
Douglas, Harry, Atl.	1	8	8.0	8	0
Scheffler, Tony, Det.	1	7	7.0	7	0
Dahl, Craig, St.L	1	6	6.0	6	0
Steltz, Craig, Chi.	1	5	5.0	5	0
Baldwin, Doug, Sea.	1	3	3.0	3	0
Black, Ahmad, T.B.	1	3	3.0	3	0
Galette, Junior, N.O.	1	2	2.0	2	0
Jackson, Vincent, T.B.	1	2	2.0	2	0
Heller, Will, Det.	1	1	1.0	1	0
Jordan, Akeem, Phi.	1	1	1.0	1	0
Rudolph, Kyle, Min.	1	1	1.0	1	0
Collins, Jed, N.O.	1	0	0.0	0	0
Obomanu, Ben, Sea.	1	0	0.0	0	0
* Polk, Chris, Phi.	1	0	0.0	0	0
Thornton, Cedric, Phi.	1	0	0.0	0	0
Ellison, Rhett, Min.	f0	0	—	0	0

t = Touchdown; f = Fair Catch
Leader based on average return, minimum 20 returns
* Player that was a rookie in 2012

AMERICAN FOOTBALL CONFERENCE—KICKOFF RETURNS

	No	Yards	Avg	Long	TD
Baltimore	60	1636	27.3	108t	2
Miami	40	1082	27.1	96t	1
Buffalo	42	1136	27.0	89t	1
N.Y. Jets	50	1308	26.2	100t	1
Cleveland	50	1269	25.4	74	0
Pittsburgh	43	1086	25.3	68	0
San Diego	40	957	23.9	99t	1
Tennessee	63	1489	23.6	105t	1
Denver	28	646	23.1	105t	1
Cincinnati	41	928	22.6	45	0
Oakland	42	935	22.3	51	0
Indianapolis	43	957	22.3	101t	1
Houston	44	953	21.7	54	0
Kansas City	49	1059	21.6	41	0
New England	38	807	21.2	104t	1
Jacksonville	53	1114	21.0	38	0
AFC Total	726	17362	23.9	108t	10
AFC Average		45.4	1085.1	23.9	— 0.6

NATIONAL FOOTBALL CONFERENCE—KICKOFF RETURNS

	No	Yards	Avg	Long	TD
Seattle	29	787	27.1	98t	1
Minnesota	44	1171	26.6	105t	1
N.Y. Giants	63	1648	26.2	97t	1
Green Bay	43	1074	25.0	46	0
New Orleans	51	1266	24.8	75	0
San Francisco	49	1216	24.8	94	0
Atlanta	27	640	23.7	77	0
Washington	38	892	23.5	55	0
Arizona	40	930	23.3	65	0
Carolina	39	867	22.2	35	0
St. Louis	38	799	21.0	48	0
Philadelphia	60	1259	21.0	44	0
Dallas	36	741	20.6	44	0
Tampa Bay	31	630	20.3	55	0
Detroit	34	681	20.0	40	0
Chicago	47	929	19.8	40	0
NFC Total	669	15530	23.2	105t	3
NFC Average		41.8	970.6	23.2	— 0.2
League Total	1395	32892	—	108t	13
League Average		43.6	1027.9	23.6	— 0.4

AVERAGE YARDS PER PUNT
AFC: 50.2 Brandon Fields, Miami
NFC: 50.1 Thomas Morstead, New Orleans

NET AVERAGE YARDS PER PUNT
NFC: 43.2 Andy Lee, San Francisco
AFC: 42.1 Britton Colquitt, Denver

LONGEST
AFC: 79 * Drew Butler, Pittsburgh vs. San Diego,
                December 9
NFC: 73 Jon Ryan, Seattle vs. Green Bay, September
                24

PUNTS
NFC: 112 Dave Zastudil, Arizona
AFC: 91 * Bryan Anger, Jacksonville

PUNTS, GAME
AFC: 10 Reggie Hodges, Cleveland vs. Pittsburgh,
                November 25 (383 yards)
         10 Donnie Jones, Houston at Tennessee,
                December 2 (489 yards)
         10 Brett Kern, Tennessee vs. N.Y. Jets,
                December 17 (391 yards)
NFC: 10 Dave Zastudil, Arizona at N.Y. Jets,
                December 2 (448 yards)
         10 Michael Koenen, Tampa Bay vs. Philadelphia,
                December 9 (424 yards)

TEAM CHAMPION
NFC: 50.1 New Orleans
AFC: 49.7 Miami

AMERICAN FOOTBALL CONFERENCE—PUNTING

	Total Punts	Yards	Long	Avg	TB	Blk	Opp Ret	Return Yards	In 20	Net Avg
Miami	76	3779	67	49.7	10	0	43	484	30	40.7
Indianapolis	74	3520	64	47.6	8	1	32	375	26	40.3
Jacksonville	92	4353	73	47.3	5	1	40	495	31	40.8
Houston	88	4150	66	47.2	5	0	48	483	28	40.5
Baltimore	83	3911	60	47.1	7	0	49	383	28	40.8
Kansas City	83	3887	71	46.8	7	0	27	362	45	40.8
Oakland	82	3826	68	46.7	9	1	45	450	21	39.0
San Diego	84	3914	66	46.6	7	3	40	362	30	40.6
Cincinnati	76	3540	69	46.6	7	0	27	210	33	42.0
Tennessee	83	3855	71	46.4	5	2	39	405	30	40.4
Denver	67	3105	67	46.3	4	0	33	203	27	42.1
N.Y. Jets	86	3848	61	44.7	8	2	31	375	27	38.5
Buffalo	80	3542	66	44.3	3	0	35	517	25	37.1
Pittsburgh	79	3400	79	43.0	6	1	30	306	27	37.6
New England	61	2585	62	42.4	6	1	23	154	28	37.9
Cleveland	90	3766	58	41.8	4	0	34	343	29	37.1
AFC Total	1284	58981	79	——	101	12	576	5907	465	——
AFC Average	80.3	3686.3	--	45.9	6.3	0.8	36.0	369.2	29.1	39.8

NATIONAL FOOTBALL CONFERENCE—PUNTING

	Total Punts	Yards	Long	Avg	TB	Blk	Opp Ret	Return Yards	In 20	Net Avg
New Orleans	74	3707	70	50.1	6	0	31	391	20	43.2
San Francisco	67	3226	66	48.1	4	0	36	249	36	43.2
N.Y. Giants	58	2757	68	47.5	6	0	38	353	22	39.4
Arizona	112	5209	70	46.5	8	0	48	415	46	41.4
Philadelphia	72	3336	66	46.3	7	1	40	542	15	36.9
Atlanta	62	2847	63	45.9	4	2	26	241	22	40.7
St. Louis	82	3756	68	45.8	4	0	41	402	22	39.9
Seattle	65	2963	73	45.6	3	0	29	252	30	40.8
Minnesota	72	3237	59	45.0	2	0	41	341	18	39.7
Tampa Bay	77	3440	64	44.7	6	1	40	440	22	37.4
Dallas	69	3039	64	44.0	3	1	29	279	28	39.1
Green Bay	71	3043	65	42.9	5	1	24	179	30	38.9
Washington	70	2984	61	42.6	3	2	39	320	22	37.2
Carolina	77	3267	63	42.4	7	1	37	318	20	36.5
Chicago	81	3399	64	42.0	6	0	25	84	34	39.4
Detroit	76	3149	58	41.4	1	0	33	328	24	36.9
NFC Total	1185	53359	73	——	75	9	557	5134	411	——
NFC Average	74.1	3334.9	--	45.0	4.7	0.6	34.8	320.9	25.7	39.4
NFL Total	2469	112340	79	——	176	21	1133	11041	876	——
NFL Average	77.2	3510.6	--	45.5	5.5	0.7	35.4	345.0	27.4	39.6

NFL TOP TEN PUNTERS

	No	Yards	Long	Avg	Total Punts	TB	Blk	Opp Ret	Return Yards	In 20	Net Avg
Fields, Brandon, Mia.	74	3715	67	50.2	74	9	0	43	484	29	41.2
Morstead, Thomas, N.O.	74	3707	70	50.1	74	6	0	31	391	20	43.2
Scifres, Mike, S.D.	81	3914	66	48.3	84	7	3	40	362	30	40.6
McAfee, Pat, Ind.	73	3520	64	48.2	74	8	1	32	375	26	40.3
Lee, Andy, S.F.	67	3226	66	48.1	67	4	0	36	249	36	43.2
* Anger, Bryan, Jac.	91	4353	73	47.8	92	5	1	40	495	31	40.8
Kern, Brett, Ten.	81	3855	71	47.6	83	5	2	39	405	30	40.4
Weatherford, Steve, NY-G	58	2757	68	47.5	58	6	0	38	353	22	39.4
Bosher, Matt, Atl.	60	2847	63	47.5	62	4	2	26	241	22	40.7
Lechler, Shane, Oak.	81	3826	68	47.2	82	9	1	45	450	21	39.0

AFC—INDIVIDUAL PUNTERS

	No	Yards	Long	Avg	Total Punts	TB	Blk	Opp Ret	Return Yards	In 20	Net Avg
Fields, Brandon, Mia.	74	3715	67	50.2	74	9	0	43	484	29	41.2
Scifres, Mike, S.D.	81	3914	66	48.3	84	7	3	40	362	30	40.6
McAfee, Pat, Ind.	73	3520	64	48.2	74	8	1	32	375	26	40.3
* Anger, Bryan, Jac.	91	4353	73	47.8	92	5	1	40	495	31	40.8
Kern, Brett, Ten.	81	3855	71	47.6	83	5	2	39	405	30	40.4
Lechler, Shane, Oak.	81	3826	68	47.2	82	9	1	45	450	21	39.0
Jones, Donnie, Hou.	88	4150	66	47.2	88	5	0	48	483	28	40.5
Koch, Sam, Bal.	83	3911	60	47.1	83	7	0	49	383	28	40.8
Colquitt, Dustin, K.C.	83	3887	71	46.8	83	7	0	27	362	45	40.8
Huber, Kevin, Cin.	76	3540	69	46.6	76	7	0	27	210	33	42.0
Colquitt, Britton, Den.	67	3105	67	46.3	67	4	0	33	203	27	42.1
Malone, Robert, NYJ	84	3848	61	45.8	86	8	2	31	375	27	38.5
* Powell, Shawn, Buf.	65	2860	62	44.0	65	2	0	27	345	23	38.1
* Butler, Drew, Pit.	77	3374	79	43.8	78	6	1	30	306	26	37.8
Mesko, Zoltan, N.E.	60	2585	62	43.1	61	6	1	23	154	28	37.9
Hodges, Reggie, Cle.	90	3766	58	41.8	90	4	0	34	343	29	37.1
(Nonqualifiers)											
Kaeding, Nate, Mia.	1	35	35	35.0	1	1	0	0	0	0	15.0
Carpenter, Dan, Mia.	1	29	29	29.0	1	0	0	0	0	1	29.0
Roethlisberger, Ben, Pit.	1	26	26	26.0	1	0	0	0	0	1	26.0

Leader based on average, minimum 40 punts

NFC—INDIVIDUAL PUNTERS

	No	Yards	Long	Avg	Total Punts	TB	Blk	Opp Ret	Return Yards	In 20	Net Avg
Morstead, Thomas, N.O.	74	3707	70	50.1	74	6	0	31	391	20	43.2
Lee, Andy, S.F.	67	3226	66	48.1	67	4	0	36	249	36	43.2
Weatherford, Steve, NY-G	58	2757	68	47.5	58	6	0	38	353	22	39.4
Bosher, Matt, Atl.	60	2847	63	47.5	62	4	2	26	241	22	40.7
McBriar, Mat, Phi.	55	2560	66	46.5	56	7	1	26	378	13	36.5
Zastudil, Dave, Ariz	112	5209	70	46.5	112	8	0	48	415	46	41.4
* Hekker, Johnny, St.L	82	3756	68	45.8	82	4	0	41	402	22	39.9
Ryan, Jon, Sea.	65	2963	73	45.6	65	3	0	29	252	30	40.8
Koenen, Michael, T.B.	76	3440	64	45.3	77	6	1	40	440	22	37.4
Kluwe, Chris, Min.	72	3237	59	45.0	72	2	0	41	341	18	39.7
Moorman, Brian, Buf.-Dal.	71	3179	66	44.8	71	4	0	32	429	24	37.6
Rocca, Sav, Was.	68	2984	61	43.9	70	3	2	39	320	22	37.2
Masthay, Tim, G.B.	70	3043	65	43.5	71	5	1	24	179	30	38.9
* Nortman, Brad, Car.	76	3267	63	43.0	77	7	1	37	318	20	36.5
Podlesh, Adam, Chi.	81	3399	64	42.0	81	6	0	25	84	34	39.4
Harris, Nick, Det.	67	2783	58	41.5	67	1	0	28	241	21	37.6
(Nonqualifiers)											
Henry, Chas, Phi.	16	776	62	48.5	16	0	0	14	164	2	38.3
Jones, Chris, Dal.	12	542	60	45.2	13	0	1	5	22	6	40.0
Graham, Ben, Det.	6	248	46	41.3	6	0	0	3	77	2	28.5
Hanson, Jason, Det.	3	118	46	39.3	3	0	0	2	10	1	36.0

Leader based on average, minimum 40 punts
* Player that was a rookie in 2012

PUNT RETURNS

YARDS PER RETURN
AFC: 18.7 Leodis McKelvin, Buffalo
NFC: 16.1 Dwayne Harris, Dallas

YARDS
AFC: 481 Trindon Holliday, Houston-Denver
NFC: 426 Patrick Peterson, Arizona

YARDS, GAME
AFC: 160 Darius Reynaud, Tennessee vs. Jacksonville,
December 30 (3 returns, 2 TD)
NFC: 104 * Damaris Johnson, Philadelphia at Dallas,
December 2 (2 returns, 1 TD)

LONGEST
NFC: 98 * Damaris Johnson, Philadelphia at Dallas,
December 2 - TD
AFC: 93 * Travis Benjamin, Cleveland vs. Kansas City,
December 9 - TD

RETURNS
NFC: 51 Patrick Peterson, Arizona
AFC: 47 Trindon Holliday, Houston-Denver

RETURNS, GAME
AFC: 8 Trindon Holliday, Denver at Carolina,
November 11 (125 yards, 1 TD)
NFC: 6 * Janoris Jenkins, St. Louis at Miami,
October 14 (21 yards, 0 TD)
6 Stefan Logan, Detroit at Chicago,
October 22 (7 yards, 0 TD)
6 Marcus Sherels, Minnesota at Houston,
December 23 (50 yards, 0 TD)

FAIR CATCHES
AFC: 36 Jeremy Kerley, N.Y. Jets
NFC: 27 Marcus Sherels, Minnesota

TOUCHDOWNS
AFC: 2 Leodis McKelvin, Buffalo
2 Darius Reynaud, Tennessee
NFC: 1 Randall Cobb, Green Bay
1 Dwayne Harris, Dallas
1 * Damaris Johnson, Philadelphia
1 Marcus Sherels, Minnesota

TEAM CHAMPION
AFC: 17.1 Buffalo
NFC: 12.4 Dallas

NFL TOP TEN PUNT RETURNERS

	No	FC	Yards	Avg	Long	TD
McKelvin, Leodis, Buf.	23	14	431	18.7	88t	2
Harris, Dwayne, Dal.	22	11	354	16.1	78t	1
Reynaud, Darius, Ten.	31	17	410	13.2	81t	2
Thigpen, Marcus, Mia.	26	6	316	12.2	72t	1
* Martin, Keshawn, Hou.	22	10	267	12.1	71	0
Cribbs, Josh, Cle.	38	8	457	12.0	60	0
Jones, Adam, Cin.	26	0	301	11.6	81t	1
* Hilton, T.Y., Ind.	26	18	300	11.5	75t	1
* Johnson, Damaris, Phi.	26	23	291	11.2	98t	1
Holliday, Trindon, Hou.-Den.	47	10	481	10.2	76t	1

AFC—INDIVIDUAL PUNT RETURNERS

	No	FC	Yards	Avg	Long	TD
McKelvin, Leodis, Buf.	23	14	431	18.7	88t	2
Reynaud, Darius, Ten.	31	17	410	13.2	81t	2
Thigpen, Marcus, Mia.	26	6	316	12.2	72t	1
* Martin, Keshawn, Hou.	22	10	267	12.1	71	0
Cribbs, Josh, Cle.	38	8	457	12.0	60	0
Jones, Adam, Cin.	26	0	301	11.6	81t	1
* Hilton, T.Y., Ind.	26	18	300	11.5	75t	1
Holliday, Trindon, Hou.-Den.	47	10	481	10.2	76t	1
Welker, Wes, N.E.	25	7	243	9.7	31	0
Jones, Jacoby, Bal.	37	16	341	9.2	63t	1
Arenas, Javier, K.C.	34	4	303	8.9	27	0
Tate, Brandon, Cin.	21	11	187	8.9	32	0
Brown, Antonio, Pit.	27	8	183	6.8	29	0
Adams, Phillip, Oak.	25	9	139	5.6	47	0
(Nonqualifiers)						
Kerley, Jeremy, NYJ	19	36	208	10.9	68t	1
Edelman, Julian, N.E.	17	1	263	15.5	68t	1
Spurlock, Micheal, S.D.-Jac.-S.D.	17	16	239	14.1	63t	1
Leonhard, Jim, Den.	15	16	89	5.9	16	0
Shipley, Jordan, T.B.-Jac.	13	2	85	6.5	15	0
Royal, Eddie, S.D.	12	2	64	5.3	14	0
Sanders, Emmanuel, Pit.	9	9	93	10.3	63	0
Moore, Denarius, Oak.	9	4	32	3.6	19	0
Weddle, Eric, S.D.	7	1	48	6.9	20	0
Cosby, Quan, Jac.	5	4	46	9.2	15	0
* Wylie, Devon, K.C.	5	2	26	5.2	13	0
Doss, Tandon, Bal.	4	4	53	13.3	40	0
Bess, Davone, Mia.	4	18	30	7.5	11	0
Wilson, Kyle, NYJ	4	2	30	7.5	19	0
* Benjamin, Travis, Cle.	3	1	149	49.7	93t	1
* Rainey, Chris, Pit.	3	0	16	5.3	13	0
Ross, Aaron, Jac.	3	3	16	5.3	6	0
Rogers, Justin, Buf.	3	4	14	4.7	14	0
Decker, Eric, Den.	2	0	22	11.0	13	0
* Brazill, LaVon, Ind.	2	1	12	6.0	8	0
Carr, Chris, S.D.	2	5	11	5.5	11	0
Gilreath, David, Pit.	2	2	8	4.0	5	0
McCluster, Dexter, K.C.	2	2	6	3.0	6	0
Jones-Drew, Maurice, Jac.	2	0	4	2.0	4	0
Copper, Terrance, K.C.	1	0	25	25.0	25	0
Breaston, Steve, K.C.	1	0	21	21.0	21	0
Cason, Antoine, S.D.	1	2	9	9.0	9	0
Webb, Lardarius, Bal.	1	5	9	9.0	9	0
Reed, Ed, Bal.	1	1	1	1.0	1	0
Jones, Reshad, Mia.	1	0	0	0.0	0	0
Campbell, Tommie, Ten.	0	0	65	—	65t	1
Mitchell, Mike, Oak.	0	0	2	—	2	0
Byrd, Jairus, Buf.	0	3	0	—	—	0
Giordano, Matt, Oak.	0	1	0	—	—	0
* Matthews, Rishard, Mia.	0	1	0	—	—	0
Zbikowski, Tom, Ind.	0	1	0	—	—	0

t = Touchdown
Leader based on average return, minimum 20 returns
* Player that was a rookie in 2012

NFC—INDIVIDUAL PUNT RETURNERS

	No	FC	Yards	Avg	Long	TD
Harris, Dwayne, Dal.	22	11	354	16.1	78t	1
* Johnson, Damaris, Phi.	26	23	291	11.2	98t	1
Ginn, Ted, S.F.	32	12	326	10.2	38	0
Parrish, Roscoe, T.B.	30	15	298	9.9	39	0
Cobb, Randall, G.B.	31	21	292	9.4	75t	1
Logan, Stefan, Det.	33	23	300	9.1	48	0
Sherels, Marcus, Min.	32	27	287	9.0	77t	1
Washington, Leon, Sea.	41	17	356	8.7	52	0
Peterson, Patrick, Ariz	51	14	426	8.4	26	0
Hester, Devin, Chi.	40	6	331	8.3	44	0
Sproles, Darren, N.O.	23	14	183	8.0	37	0
Franks, Dominique, Atl.	21	18	163	7.8	28	0
Banks, Brandon, Was.	26	5	178	6.8	27	0
(Nonqualifiers)						
Amendola, Danny, St.L	17	10	122	7.2	22	0
* Randle, Rueben, NY-G	15	15	108	7.2	18	0
Munnerlyn, Captain, Car.	14	5	72	5.1	20	0
Bryant, Dez, Dal.	12	2	66	5.5	44	0
* Adams, Joe, Car.	11	11	127	11.5	21	0
Pettis, Austin, St.L	11	9	77	7.0	23	0
Thomas, Mike, Jac.-Det.	9	4	56	6.2	18	0
* Jenkins, Janoris, St.L	9	1	46	5.1	14	0
* Crawford, Richard, Was.	8	2	156	19.5	64	0
Douglas, Harry, Atl.	5	1	42	8.4	11	0
Hixon, Domenik, NY-G	5	4	36	7.2	10	0
Ross, Jeremy, G.B.	4	1	103	25.8	58	0
Williams, Kyle, S.F.	4	6	52	13.0	20	0
Stroughter, Sammie, T.B.	3	3	16	5.3	13	0
Roberts, Andre, Ariz	3	0	15	5.0	10	0
Edwards, Armanti, Car.	2	2	77	38.5	69	0
Gilyard, Mardy, Phi.	2	3	15	7.5	11	0
* Boykin, Brandon, Phi.	1	0	7	7.0	7	0
Moore, Lance, N.O.	1	3	5	5.0	5	0
Bennett, Earl, Chi.	1	1	2	2.0	2	0
* Cadet, Travaris, N.O.	1	2	2	2.0	2	0
Smith, Alphonso, Det.	1	0	2	2.0	2	0
Wilson, Josh, Was.	1	0	1	1.0	1	0
Bowman, Zack, Chi.	1	0	0	0.0	0	0
Hall, DeAngelo, Was.	1	0	0	0.0	0	0
Moore, D.J., Chi.	1	0	0	0.0	0	0
Shields, Sam, G.B.	1	0	0	0.0	0	0
Weems, Eric, Chi.	1	1	0	0.0	0	0
Browner, Brandon, Sea.	1	0	-1	-1.0	-1	0
Jackson, DeSean, Phi.	1	0	-3	-3.0	-3	0
Robinson, Patrick, N.O.	0	1	0	—	—	0
Tate, Golden, Sea.	0	1	0	—	—	0

t = Touchdown
Leader based on average return, minimum 20 returns
* Player that was a rookie in 2012

AMERICAN FOOTBALL CONFERENCE—PUNT RETURNS

	No	FC	Yards	Avg	Long	TD
Buffalo	26	21	445	17.1	88t	2
Tennessee	31	17	475	15.3	81t	3
Cleveland	41	9	606	14.8	93t	1
New England	42	8	506	12.0	68t	1
Miami	31	25	346	11.2	72t	1
Indianapolis	28	20	312	11.1	75t	1
Houston	38	16	414	10.9	71	0
Cincinnati	47	11	488	10.4	81t	1
N.Y. Jets	23	38	238	10.3	68t	1
San Diego	33	22	320	9.7	63t	1
Baltimore	43	26	404	9.4	63t	1
Denver	48	20	445	9.3	76t	1
Kansas City	43	8	381	8.9	27	0
Pittsburgh	41	19	300	7.3	63	0
Jacksonville	34	13	248	7.3	28	0
Oakland	34	14	173	5.1	47	0
AFC Total	583	287	6101	10.5	93t	14
AFC Average	36.4	17.9	381.3	10.5	—	0.9

NATIONAL FOOTBALL CONFERENCE—PUNT RETURNS

	No	FC	Yards	Avg	Long	TD
Dallas	34	13	420	12.4	78t	1
Green Bay	36	22	395	11.0	75t	1
San Francisco	36	18	378	10.5	38	0
Philadelphia	30	26	310	10.3	98t	1
Carolina	27	18	276	10.2	69	0
Washington	36	7	335	9.3	64	0
Tampa Bay	36	19	324	9.0	39	0
Minnesota	32	27	287	9.0	77t	1
Detroit	35	26	302	8.6	48	0
Seattle	42	18	355	8.5	52	0
Arizona	54	14	441	8.2	26	0
Atlanta	26	19	205	7.9	28	0
New Orleans	25	20	190	7.6	37	0
Chicago	44	8	333	7.6	44	0
N.Y. Giants	20	19	144	7.2	18	0
St. Louis	37	20	245	6.6	23	0
NFC Total	550	294	4940	9.0	98t	4
NFC Average	34.4	18.4	308.8	9.0	—	0.3
League Total	1133	581	11041	—	98t	18
League Average	35.4	18.2	345.0	9.7	—	0.6

SACKS

MOST SACKS
AFC: 20.5 J.J. Watt, Houston
NFC: 19.5 Aldon Smith,
San Francisco

MOST SACKS, GAME
NFC: 5.5 Aldon Smith, San
Francisco vs. Chicago,
November 19
AFC: 4.5 Cameron Wake, Miami
at Arizona,
September 30 - (OT)

TEAM LEADERS, SACKS
AFC: BALTIMORE, 9.0, Paul
Kruger; BUFFALO, 10.5,
Mario Williams; CINCINNATI,
12.5, Geno Atkins; CLEVE-
LAND, 7.0, Jabaal Sheard;
DENVER, 18.5, Von Miller;
HOUSTON, 20.5, J.J. Watt;
INDIANAPOLIS, 8.0, Robert
Mathis; JACKSONVILLE, 3.5,
Tyson Alualu; KANSAS CITY,
10.0, Justin Houston; MIAMI,
15.0, Cameron Wake; NEW
ENGLAND, 8.0, Rob
Ninkovich; N.Y. JETS, 5.5,
*Quinton Coples; OAKLAND,
4.0, Desmond Bryant, Lamarr
Houston; PITTSBURGH, 6.0,
James Harrison, Lawrence
Timmons; SAN DIEGO, 9.5,
Shaun Phillips; TENNESSEE,
6.5, Derrick Morgan

NFC: ARIZONA, 9.0, Daryl Wash-
ington; ATLANTA, 10.0, John
Abraham; CAROLINA, 12.5,
Charles Johnson; CHICAGO,
11.5, Julius Peppers; DAL-
LAS, 11.5, DeMarcus Ware;
DETROIT, 9.5, Cliff Avril;
GREEN BAY, 13.0, Clay
Matthews; MINNESOTA,
12.0, Jared Allen; NEW
ORLEANS, 8.0, Cameron Jor-
dan; N.Y. GIANTS, 6.5, Jason
Pierre-Paul; PHILADELPHIA,
5.5, *Fletcher Cox, Jason
Babin, Brandon Graham; ST.
LOUIS, 11.5, Chris Long;
SAN FRANCISCO, 19.5,
Aldon Smith; SEATTLE, 11.5,
Chris Clemons; TAMPA BAY,
9.0, Michael Bennett; WASH-
INGTON, 8.5, Ryan Kerrigan

TEAM CHAMPION
AFC: 52 Denver
NFC: 52 St. Louis

NFL TOP TEN LEADERS—SACKS

	Sacks
Watt, J.J., Hou.	20.5
Smith, Aldon, S.F.	19.5
Miller, Von, Den.	18.5
Wake, Cameron, Mia.	15.0
Matthews, Clay, G.B.	13.0
Atkins, Geno, Cin.	12.5
Johnson, Charles, Car.	12.5
Allen, Jared, Min.	12.0
Clemons, Chris, Sea.	11.5
Johnson, Michael, Cin.	11.5
Long, Chris, St.L	11.5
Peppers, Julius, Chi.	11.5
Ware, DeMarcus, Dal.	11.5

AMERICAN FOOTBALL CONFERENCE—SACKS

	Sacks	Yards
Denver	52	364
Cincinnati	51	361
Houston	44	269
Miami	42	242
Tennessee	39	241
Cleveland	38	233
San Diego	38	244
Baltimore	37	250
New England	37	213
Pittsburgh	37	196
Buffalo	36	196
Indianapolis	32	189
N.Y. Jets	30	170
Kansas City	27	161
Oakland	25	185
Jacksonville	20	128
AFC Total	585	3642
AFC Average	36.5	227.6

NATIONAL FOOTBALL CONFERENCE—SACKS

	Sacks	Yards
St. Louis	52	325
Green Bay	47	309
Minnesota	44	284
Chicago	41	289
Carolina	39	284
Arizona	38	228
San Francisco	38	270
Seattle	36	247
Dallas	34	211
Detroit	34	237
N.Y. Giants	33	231
Washington	32	209
New Orleans	30	194
Philadelphia	30	198
Atlanta	29	182
Tampa Bay	27	193
NFC Total	584	3891
NFC Average	36.5	243.2
League Total	1169	7533
League Average	36.5	235.4

AFC—INDIVIDUAL SACKS

	Sacks
Watt, J.J., Hou.	20.5
Miller, Von, Den.	18.5
Wake, Cameron, Mia.	15.0
Atkins, Geno, Cin.	12.5
Johnson, Michael, Cin.	11.5
Dumervil, Elvis, Den.	11.0
Williams, Mario, Buf.	10.5
Houston, Justin, K.C.	10.0
Phillips, Shaun, S.D.	9.5
Hali, Tamba, K.C.	9.0
Kruger, Paul, Bal.	9.0
Mathis, Robert, Ind.	8.0
Ninkovich, Rob, N.E.	8.0
Babin, Jason, Phi.-Jac.	7.0
Liuget, Corey, S.D.	7.0
Sheard, Jabaal, Cle.	7.0
Smith, Antonio, Hou.	7.0
Gilberry, Wallace, Cin.	6.5
Morgan, Derrick, Ten.	6.5
Ayers, Akeem, Ten.	6.0
Dunlap, Carlos, Cin.	6.0
Harrison, James, Pit.	6.0
* Jones, Chandler, N.E.	6.0
* Mercilus, Whitney, Hou.	6.0
Parker, Juqua, Cle.	6.0
Timmons, Lawrence, Pit.	6.0
Wimbley, Kamerion, Ten.	6.0
* Wolfe, Derek, Den.	6.0
* Brown, Zach, Ten.	5.5
* Coples, Quinton, NYJ	5.5
Dareus, Marcell, Buf.	5.5
* Reyes, Kendall, S.D.	5.5
Woodyard, Wesley, Den.	5.5
Freeney, Dwight, Ind.	5.0
Ngata, Haloti, Bal.	5.0
Odrick, Jared, Mia.	5.0
Wilkerson, Muhammad, NYJ	5.0
Williams, Kyle, Buf.	5.0
Worilds, Jason, Pit.	5.0
Ellerbe, Dannell, Bal.	4.5
Jones, Arthur, Bal.	4.5
Keisel, Brett, Pit.	4.5
Starks, Randy, Mia.	4.5
Bryant, Desmond, Oak.	4.0
Foote, Larry, Pit.	4.0
* Hightower, Dont'a, N.E.	4.0
Houston, Lamarr, Oak.	4.0
Hughes, Jerry, Ind.	4.0
Rucker, Frostee, Cle.	4.0
Woodley, LaMarr, Pit.	4.0
Alualu, Tyson, Jac.	3.5
Jackson, D'Qwell, Cle.	3.5
Klug, Karl, Ten.	3.5
McIntyre, Garrett, NYJ	3.5
Misi, Koa, Mia.	3.5
Shaughnessy, Matt, Oak.	3.5
* Vernon, Olivier, Mia.	3.5
Barnes, Antwan, S.D.	3.0
Barwin, Connor, Hou.	3.0
Butler, Donald, S.D.	3.0
Casey, Jurrell, Ten.	3.0
* Francis, Justin, N.E.	3.0
Geathers, Robert, Cin.	3.0
Harris, David, NYJ	3.0
Hood, Ziggy, Pit.	3.0
* Hughes, John, Cle.	3.0
Jackson, Tyson, K.C.	3.0
* Martin, Mike, Ten.	3.0

	Sacks
Mayo, Jerod, N.E.	3.0
Mincey, Jeremy, Jac.	3.0
Moore, Kyle, Buf.	3.0
Pace, Calvin, NYJ	3.0
Scott, Trevor, N.E.	3.0
Seymour, Richard, Oak.	3.0
Wheeler, Philip, Oak.	3.0
Wilfork, Vince, N.E.	3.0
Burnett, Kevin, Mia.	2.5
Carter, Andre, Oak.	2.5
Cunningham, Jermaine, N.E.	2.5
Harris, Chris, Den.	2.5
Mosley, C.J., Jac.	2.5
Reed, Brooks, Hou.	2.5
Scott, Bart, NYJ	2.5
Thomas, Bryan, NYJ	2.5
Ayers, Robert, Den.	2.0
Barnett, Nick, Buf.	2.0
Bethea, Antoine, Ind.	2.0
Carrington, Alex, Buf.	2.0
Freeman, Jerrell, Ind.	2.0
Johnson, Derrick, K.C.	2.0
Johnson, Spencer, Buf.	2.0
Kelsay, Chris, Buf.	2.0
Knighton, Terrance, Jac.	2.0
Lane, Austen, Jac.	2.0
Lawson, Manny, Cin.	2.0
Maiava, Kaluka, Cle.	2.0
McLendon, Steve, Pit.	2.0
Peko, Domata, Cin.	2.0
Pitoitua, Ropati, K.C.	2.0
Pollard, Bernard, Bal.	2.0
Posluszny, Paul, Jac.	2.0
Redding, Cory, Ind.	2.0
Rubin, Ahtyba, Cle.	2.0
Sheppard, Kelvin, Buf.	2.0
Suggs, Terrell, Bal.	2.0
Vickerson, Kevin, Den.	2.0
Wilson, Jimmy, Mia.	2.0
Wynn, Jarius, Ten.	2.0
* Burris, Miles, Oak.	1.5
English, Larry, S.D.	1.5
Heyward, Cameron, Pit.	1.5
Johnson, Jarret, S.D.	1.5
Love, Kyle, N.E.	1.5
Marks, Sen'Derrick, Ten.	1.5
McPhee, Pernell, Bal.	1.5
Soliai, Paul, Mia.	1.5
* Upshaw, Courtney, Bal.	1.5
Young, Usama, Cle.	1.5
Adams, Mike, Den.	1.0
* Allen, Antonio, NYJ	1.0
Anderson, Mark, Buf.	1.0
Ayanbadejo, Brendon, Bal.	1.0
Bell, Yeremiah, NYJ	1.0
* Branch, Andre, Jac.	1.0
Brooking, Keith, Den.	1.0
* Brown, Omar, Bal.	1.0
Brown, Sheldon, Cle.	1.0
* Burfict, Vontaze, Cin.	1.0
Carroll, Nolan, Mia.	1.0
Conner, Kavell, Ind.	1.0
Dansby, Karlos, Mia.	1.0
Davis, Vontae, Ind.	1.0
Deaderick, Brandon, N.E.	1.0
DeVito, Mike, NYJ	1.0
Flowers, Brandon, K.C.	1.0
Fokou, Moise, Ind.	1.0
* Fort, L.J., Cle.	1.0

	Sacks
Fujita, Scott, Cle.	1.0
Gachkar, Andrew, S.D.	1.0
Garay, Antonio, S.D.	1.0
Geathers, Clifton, Ind.	1.0
Gilchrist, Marcus, S.D.	1.0
Gordy, Josh, Ind.	1.0
Griffin, Michael, Ten.	1.0
Guy, Lawrence, Ind.	1.0
* Harris, Mike, Jac.	1.0
Howard, Thomas, Cin.	1.0
Ihedigbo, James, Bal.	1.0
* Ingram, Melvin, S.D.	1.0
Jamison, Tim, Hou.	1.0
Jones, Adam, Cin.	1.0
Jones, Reshad, Mia.	1.0
Kelly, Tommy, Oak.	1.0
Kemoeatu, Ma'ake, Bal.	1.0
Lankster, Ellis, NYJ	1.0
Lewis, Ray, Bal.	1.0
Manning, Danieal, Hou.	1.0
Martin, Derrick, N.E.	1.0
Martin, Vaughn, S.D.	1.0
Maualuga, Rey, Cin.	1.0
McCann, Bryan, Mia.	1.0
McClain, Rolando, Oak.	1.0
McClellan, Albert, Bal.	1.0
Merriman, Shawne, Buf.	1.0
Mitchell, Mike, Oak.	1.0
Moore, Rahim, Den.	1.0
Nelson, Reggie, Cin.	1.0
Nevis, Drake, Ind.	1.0
Polamalu, Troy, Pit.	1.0
Pouha, Sione, NYJ	1.0
Quin, Glover, Hou.	1.0
Rey, Vincent, Cin.	1.0
Robertson, Craig, Cle.	1.0
Ruud, Barrett, Hou.	1.0
Selvie, George, Jac.	1.0
Spikes, Brandon, N.E.	1.0
Stephens, Emmanuel, Cle.	1.0
Taylor, Phillip, Cle.	1.0
* Trevathan, Danny, Den.	1.0
Ward, T.J., Cle.	1.0
Weddle, Eric, S.D.	1.0
Westerman, Jamaal, Ind.	1.0
Williams, Cary, Bal.	1.0
* Winn, Billy, Cle.	1.0
Witherspoon, Will, Ten.	1.0
Zbikowski, Tom, Ind.	1.0
Allen, Russell, Jac.	0.5
James, Bradie, Hou.	0.5
Mays, Joe, Den.	0.5
McCain, Brice, Hou.	0.5
McDaniel, Tony, Mia.	0.5
Spikes, Takeo, S.D.	0.5
* Still, Devon, Cin.	0.5
* Taylor, Brandon, S.D.	0.5
Tollefson, Dave, Oak.	0.5

* Player that was a rookie in 2012

NFC—INDIVIDUAL SACKS

Player	Sacks
Smith, Aldon, S.F.	19.5
Matthews, Clay, G.B.	13.0
Johnson, Charles, Car.	12.5
Allen, Jared, Min.	12.0
Clemons, Chris, Sea.	11.5
Long, Chris, St.L	11.5
Peppers, Julius, Chi.	11.5
Ware, DeMarcus, Dal.	11.5
Hardy, Greg, Car.	11.0
Spencer, Anthony, Dal.	11.0
Quinn, Robert, St.L	10.5
Abraham, John, Atl.	10.0
Avril, Cliff, Det.	9.5
Bennett, Michael, T.B.	9.0
Washington, Daryl, Ariz	9.0
Kerrigan, Ryan, Was.	8.5
Robison, Brian, Min.	8.5
Griffen, Everson, Min.	8.0
* Irvin, Bruce, Sea.	8.0
Jordan, Cameron, N.O.	8.0
Suh, Ndamukong, Det.	8.0
Idonije, Israel, Chi.	7.5
Hayes, William, St.L	7.0
Wootton, Corey, Chi.	7.0
Brooks, Ahmad, S.F.	6.5
Campbell, Calais, Ariz	6.5
Pierre-Paul, Jason, NY-G	6.5
Edwards, Dwan, Car.	6.0
Melton, Henry, Chi.	6.0
Smith, Will, N.O.	6.0
Umenyiora, Osi, NY-G	6.0
* Cox, Fletcher, Phi.	5.5
Fairley, Nick, Det.	5.5
Graham, Brandon, Phi.	5.5
Galette, Junior, N.O.	5.0
McCoy, Gerald, T.B.	5.0
Dunbar, Jo-Lonn, St.L	4.5
Jackson, Rob, Was.	4.5
Neal, Mike, G.B.	4.5
Acho, Sam, Ariz	4.0
Biermann, Kroy, Atl.	4.0
* Brockers, Michael, St.L	4.0
Groves, Quentin, Ariz	4.0
Hatcher, Jason, Dal.	4.0
Jenkins, Cullen, Phi.	4.0
Joseph, Linval, NY-G	4.0
* Moses, Dezman, G.B.	4.0
Schofield, O'Brien, Ariz	4.0
Te'o-Nesheim, Daniel, T.B.	4.0
Tuck, Justin, NY-G	4.0
Babineaux, Jonathan, Atl.	3.5
Riley, Perry, Was.	3.5
Vanden Bosch, Kyle, Det.	3.5
Blackburn, Chase, NY-G	3.0
Bowers, Da'Quan, T.B.	3.0
Butler, Victor, Dal.	3.0
Canty, Chris, NY-G	3.0
Cole, Trent, Phi.	3.0
Fletcher, London, Was.	3.0
Greenway, Chad, Min.	3.0
Hawk, A.J., G.B.	3.0
Henderson, Erin, Min.	3.0
Jones, Jason, Sea.	3.0
Kiwanuka, Mathias, NY-G	3.0
Mebane, Brandon, Sea.	3.0
Mikell, Quintin, St.L	3.0
Sims, Eugene, St.L	3.0
Smith, Justin, S.F.	3.0

Player	Sacks
Walden, Erik, G.B.	3.0
Walker, Vance, Atl.	3.0
Weatherspoon, Sean, Atl.	3.0
Wilson, Adrian, Ariz	3.0
Wilson, Martez, N.O.	3.0
* Alexander, Frank, Car.	2.5
Alexander, Lorenzo, Was.	2.5
Bunkley, Brodrick, N.O.	2.5
Cofield, Barry, Was.	2.5
Jackson, Lawrence, Det.	2.5
* McClellin, Shea, Chi.	2.5
McDonald, Ray, S.F.	2.5
Paea, Stephen, Chi.	2.5
Wilson, C.J., G.B.	2.5
* Worthy, Jerel, G.B.	2.5
Bowman, NaVorro, S.F.	2.0
Burnett, Morgan, G.B.	2.0
* Daniels, Mike, G.B.	2.0
* David, Lavonte, T.B.	2.0
Evans, Fred, Min.	2.0
Foster, Mason, T.B.	2.0
Guion, Letroy, Min.	2.0
Jean Francois, Ricky, S.F.	2.0
Johnson, Jeron, Sea.	2.0
Johnson, Tom, N.O.	2.0
Jones, Brad, G.B.	2.0
Langford, Kendall, St.L	2.0
Lenon, Paris, Ariz	2.0
Nicholas, Stephen, Atl.	2.0
* Perry, Nick, G.B.	2.0
* Scruggs, Greg, Sea.	2.0
Smith, D.J., G.B.	2.0
* Wagner, Bobby, Sea.	2.0
Williams, Corey, Det.	2.0
Williams, Kevin, Min.	2.0
Brent, Josh, Dal.	1.5
Briggs, Lance, Chi.	1.5
Dockett, Darnell, Ariz	1.5
Hill, Leroy, Sea.	1.5
Roach, Nick, Chi.	1.5
Robinson, Dunta, Atl.	1.5
Woodson, Charles, G.B.	1.5
Addison, Mario, Car.	1.0
Applewhite, Antwan, Car.	1.0
Ballard, Christian, Min.	1.0
Barber, Ronde, T.B.	1.0
Bernard, Rocky, NY-G	1.0
Biggers, E.J., T.B.	1.0
Bowen, Stephen, Was.	1.0
* Boykin, Brandon, Phi.	1.0
Branch, Alan, Sea.	1.0
Cook, Chris, Min.	1.0
Cudjo, Jermelle, St.L	1.0
DeCoud, Thomas, Atl.	1.0
Eason, Nick, Ariz	1.0
Edwards, Ron, Car.	1.0
Finnegan, Cortland, St.L	1.0
Fletcher, Bradley, St.L	1.0
Gay, William, Ariz	1.0
* Green, Jonte, Det.	1.0
Haggan, Mario, St.L	1.0
Hall, DeAngelo, Was.	1.0
House, Davon, G.B.	1.0
Hunt, Phillip, Phi.	1.0
Kearse, Frank, Car.	1.0
* Kendricks, Mychal, Phi.	1.0
* Kuechly, Luke, Car.	1.0
Lissemore, Sean, Dal.	1.0
Lofton, Curtis, N.O.	1.0

Player	Sacks
McIntosh, Rocky, St.L	1.0
Moore, William, Atl.	1.0
Okoye, Amobi, Chi.	1.0
Orakpo, Brian, Was.	1.0
Patterson, Mike, Phi.	1.0
Pugh, Jordan, Was.	1.0
Rhodes, Kerry, Ariz	1.0
Robinson, Patrick, N.O.	1.0
Rogers, Carlos, S.F.	1.0
Ryans, DeMeco, Phi.	1.0
Sherman, Richard, Sea.	1.0
Shields, Sam, G.B.	1.0
Sims, Ernie, Dal.	1.0
* Smith, Harrison, Min.	1.0
Sopoaga, Isaac, S.F.	1.0
Spears, Marcus, Dal.	1.0
Talley, Ronald, Ariz	1.0
Thornton, Cedric, Phi.	1.0
Tracy, Adrian, NY-G	1.0
Vilma, Jonathan, N.O.	1.0
Williams, Jacquian, NY-G	1.0
Williams, Madieu, Was.	1.0
Wilson, Josh, Was.	1.0
Wright, K.J., Sea.	1.0
Boley, Michael, NY-G	0.5
Durant, Justin, Det.	0.5
Keiser, Thomas, Car.	0.5
Laurinaitis, James, St.L	0.5
Neblett, Andre, Car.	0.5
Shanle, Scott, N.O.	0.5
Tapp, Darryl, Phi.	0.5
Tulloch, Stephen, Det.	0.5
Willis, Patrick, S.F.	0.5
Wilson, Chris, Was.	0.5
Winfield, Antoine, Min.	0.5

* Player that was a rookie in 2012

FUMBLES

MOST FUMBLES

AFC:	15	Philip Rivers, San Diego
NFC:	12	* Robert Griffin III, Washington

MOST FUMBLES, GAME

AFC:	4	Philip Rivers, San Diego vs. Carolina, December 16
NFC:	4	Colin Kaepernick, San Francisco at New England, December 16

OWN FUMBLES RECOVERED

NFC:	4	Frank Gore, San Francisco
	4	* Robert Griffin III, Washington
	4	Patrick Peterson, Arizona
AFC:	3	Shonn Greene, N.Y. Jets
	3	* Trent Richardson, Cleveland
	3	Ben Roethlisberger, Pittsburgh
	3	Mark Sanchez, N.Y. Jets

OWN FUMBLES RECOVERED, GAME

NFC:	3	Patrick Peterson, Arizona vs. Miami, September 30 (0 yards, 0 TD) - (OT)
AFC:	2	Shonn Greene, N.Y. Jets vs. Buffalo, September 9 (0 yards, 0 TD)
	2	Randy McMichael, San Diego vs. Tennessee, September 16 (0 yards, 0 TD)
	2	Chad Henne, Jacksonville at Miami, December 16 (0 yards, 0 TD)

OPPONENTS' FUMBLES RECOVERED

AFC:	4	Tim Dobbins, Houston
	4	Rob Ninkovich, New England
	4	Vince Wilfork, New England
NFC:	4	Kelvin Hayden, Chicago
	4	Julius Peppers, Chicago

OPPONENTS' FUMBLES RECOVERED, GAME

AFC:	2	Larry Foote, Pittsburgh vs. Philadelphia, October 7 (0 yards, 0 TD)
	2	Steve Gregory, New England at N.Y. Jets, November 22 (30 yards, 1 TD)
	2	Reshad Jones, Miami vs. Buffalo, December 23 (24 yards, 0 TD)
NFC:	2	Carlos Rogers, San Francisco at N.Y. Jets, September 30 (52 yards, 1 TD)
	2	Kelvin Hayden, Chicago at Tennessee, November 4 (15 yards, 0 TD)

YARDS

NFC:	93	James Sanders, Arizona
AFC:	72	Alterraun Verner, Tennessee

LONGEST

NFC:	93	James Sanders, Arizona vs. Philadelphia, September 23 - TD
AFC:	72	Alterraun Verner, Tennessee vs. Detroit, September 23 - TD - (OT)

AFC—TOUCHDOWNS ON FUMBLE RECOVERIES

Carter, Tony, Den.	1
Edelman, Julian, N.E.	1
Gilberry, Wallace, Cin.	1
Gregory, Steve, N.E.	1
* Hightower, Dont'a, N.E.	1
Jammer, Quentin, S.D.	1
Jones, Edgar, K.C.	1
Lloyd, Brandon, N.E.	1
Phillips, Shaun, S.D.	1
Verner, Alterraun, Ten.	1
Wilkerson, Muhammad, NYJ	1

NFC—TOUCHDOWNS ON FUMBLE RECOVERIES

Babineaux, Jonathan, Atl.	1
Boley, Michael, NY-G	1
Bowman, Zack, Chi.	1
* Claiborne, Morris, Dal.	1
* Daniels, Mike, G.B.	1
Garcon, Pierre, Was.	1
Gore, Frank, S.F.	1
Hatcher, Jason, Dal.	1
* Jenkins, Janoris, St.L	1
Morgan, Josh, Was.	1
Murphy, Louis, Car.	1
Rogers, Carlos, S.F.	1
Sanders, James, Ariz	1
Smith, Malcolm, Sea.	1
Wilson, Josh, Was.	1

AFC FUMBLES—INDIVIDUAL

	Fum	Own Rec	Opp Rec	Yards	Tot Rec
Adams, Mike, Den.	0	0	2	0	2
Adams, Phillip, Oak.	2	0	0	0	0
* Allen, Antonio, NYJ	0	0	1	0	1
Allen, Cortez, Pit.	0	0	1	21	1
* Allen, Dwayne, Ind.	1	2	0	0	2
Allen, Russell, Jac.	0	0	1	0	1
Alualu, Tyson, Jac.	0	0	1	0	1
Arenas, Javier, K.C.	2	1	0	0	1
Arrington, Kyle, N.E.	0	0	1	0	1
Ausberry, David, Oak.	0	1	0	0	1
Avery, Donnie, Ind.	1	0	0	0	0
Ayanbadejo, Brendon, Bal.	0	0	1	0	1
Babin, Jason, Jac.	0	0	1	0	1
Bailey, Allen, K.C.	0	0	1	1	1
Ball, Lance, Den.	1	1	1	0	2
* Ballard, Vick, Ind.	3	2	0	0	2
Bannan, Justin, Den.	0	0	1	0	1
Barnes, Antwan, S.D.	0	0	2	1	2
Barwin, Connor, Hou.	0	0	1	0	1
Batch, Charlie, Pit.	1	1	0	0	1
Bell, Kahlil, NYJ	1	0	0	0	0
Bell, Yeremiah, NYJ	0	0	3	18	3
Bellore, Nick, NYJ	1	1	0	0	1
* Benjamin, Travis, Cle.	1	1	0	0	1
Bess, Davone, Mia.	1	0	0	0	0
Bigby, Atari, S.D.	0	0	1	0	1
Binns, Armon, Cin.	1	0	0	0	0
Birk, Matt, Bal.	0	1	0	0	1
* Blackmon, Justin, Jac.	1	1	0	0	1
* Blake, Antwon, Jac.	0	0	1	0	1
* Bolden, Omar, Den.	1	0	0	0	0
Boldin, Anquan, Bal.	0	1	0	0	1
Bosworth, Kyle, Jac.	1	0	0	0	0
Bowe, Dwayne, K.C.	1	0	0	0	0
* Bradham, Nigel, Buf.	0	0	1	0	1
Brady, Tom, N.E.	2	1	0	-3	1
* Branch, Andre, Jac.	0	0	1	0	1
* Brazill, LaVon, Ind.	1	0	0	0	0
Breaston, Steve, K.C.	1	1	0	0	1
Brinkley, Curtis, S.D.	1	1	0	0	1
Britt, Kenny, Ten.	2	2	0	-2	2
Britton, Eben, Jac.	0	1	0	0	1
Brown, Antonio, Pit.	4	2	0	0	2
* Brown, Omar, Bal.	0	1	0	12	1
Brown, Ronnie, S.D.	0	1	0	0	1
Brown, Sheldon, Cle.	0	0	2	0	2
* Brown, Zach, Ten.	1	0	2	6	2
* Burfict, Vontaze, Cin.	0	0	2	0	2
Bush, Reggie, Mia.	4	0	0	0	0
Butler, Darius, Ind.	0	0	1	0	1

	Fum	Own Rec	Opp Rec	Yards	Tot Rec
Byrd, Jairus, Buf.	0	0	2	0	2
Campbell, Tommie, Ten.	0	1	0	0	1
Carter, Delone, Ind.	1	0	0	0	0
Carter, Tony, Den.	0	1	1	65	2
Cassel, Matt, K.C.	9	1	0	-8	1
Castonzo, Anthony, Ind.	0	1	0	0	1
Chandler, Scott, Buf.	2	1	0	0	1
Charles, Jamaal, K.C.	5	0	0	0	0
Chick, John, Jac.	0	0	1	0	1
Clark, Ryan, Pit.	0	0	1	2	1
Clemons, Chris, Mia.	0	0	1	-3	1
Colon, Willie, Pit.	0	1	0	0	1
Condo, Jon, Oak.	0	0	1	3	1
Cook, Jared, Ten.	1	0	0	0	0
Cribbs, Josh, Cle.	6	2	0	-18	2
* Criner, Juron, Oak.	1	1	0	0	1
Crocker, Chris, Cin.	0	0	1	12	1
Cunningham, Jermaine, N.E.	0	0	2	0	2
Dalton, Andy, Cin.	4	0	0	0	0
Dareus, Marcell, Buf.	0	0	1	0	1
* Davis, DeMario, NYJ	0	0	1	-4	1
* DeCastro, David, Pit.	0	1	0	0	1
Demps, Quintin, Hou.	0	0	1	0	1
Dickerson, Dorin, Buf.	1	0	0	0	0
Dobbins, Tim, Hou.	0	0	4	32	4
Draughn, Shaun, K.C.	2	1	0	0	1
Dunlap, Carlos, Cin.	0	0	3	2	3
Dwyer, Jonathan, Pit.	2	0	0	0	0
Edelman, Julian, N.E.	1	0	1	22	1
English, Larry, S.D.	0	0	1	0	1
Epps, Dedrick, NYJ	1	0	0	0	0
Fields, Brandon, Mia.	1	1	0	-10	1
Fitzpatrick, Ryan, Buf.	8	2	0	0	2
Flacco, Joe, Bal.	9	1	0	-10	1
* Fleener, Coby, Ind.	0	1	0	0	1
Flowers, Brandon, K.C.	0	0	1	64	1
Foote, Larry, Pit.	0	0	2	0	2
Foster, Arian, Hou.	3	1	0	0	1
Gabbert, Blaine, Jac.	5	1	0	0	1
Gates, Antonio, S.D.	0	1	0	0	1
Gilberry, Wallace, Cin.	0	0	3	31	3
Goethel, Travis, Oak.	2	0	0	-20	0
* Gordon, Josh, Cle.	1	0	0	0	0
Gordon, Richard, Oak.	0	0	1	0	1
Gradkowski, Bruce, Cin.	1	2	0	-5	2
* Gradkowski, Gino, Bal.	1	0	0	0	0
Green, A.J., Cin.	2	1	0	0	1
Greene, Shonn, NYJ	4	3	0	0	3
Green-Ellis, BenJarvus, Cin.	3	1	0	0	1
Greenwood, Cory, K.C.	0	0	1	0	1
Gregory, Steve, N.E.	0	0	2	30	2
Gresham, Jermaine, Cin.	2	1	0	0	1
Gronkowski, Rob, N.E.	1	0	0	0	0
Hadnot, Rex, S.D.	0	1	0	0	1
Hanson, Joselio, Oak.	0	0	2	1	2
Hardesty, Montario, Cle.	2	2	0	0	2
Harris, Chris, Den.	0	1	0	0	1
Harris, David, NYJ	0	0	1	0	1
Harris, Ryan, Hou.	0	1	0	0	1
Hartline, Brian, Mia.	1	0	0	0	0
Hasselbeck, Matt, Ten.	3	2	0	-4	2
Hawkins, Andrew, Cin.	1	0	0	0	0
Henne, Chad, Jac.	4	2	0	-2	2
Hernandez, Aaron, N.E.	0	1	0	0	1
Heyward-Bey, Darrius, Oak.	0	1	0	0	1
* Hightower, Dont'a, N.E.	0	0	2	6	2
Hilliard, Lex, NYJ	0	2	0	7	2
Hillis, Peyton, K.C.	2	0	0	0	0
* Hillman, Ronnie, Den.	2	0	0	0	0
* Hilton, T.Y., Ind.	1	0	0	0	0
Hochstein, Russ, K.C.	1	0	0	-4	0
Holliday, Trindon, Hou.-Den.	6	0	0	0	0
Holmes, Santonio, NYJ	1	0	0	0	0
Hood, Ziggy, Pit.	0	0	2	1	2
Houston, Lamarr, Oak.	0	0	1	0	1
Houston, Justin, K.C.	0	0	1	4	1
Incognito, Richie, Mia.	0	2	0	0	2
Jackson, D'Qwell, Cle.	0	0	2	0	2
Jackson, Fred, Buf.	5	0	0	0	0
James, Bradie, Hou.	0	0	2	0	2
Jammer, Quentin, S.D.	0	0	3	0	3
Jennings, Rashad, Jac.	3	0	0	0	0
Johnson, Chris, Ten.	5	0	0	0	0
Johnson, Josh, Cle.	1	0	0	0	0
Johnson, Michael, Cin.	0	0	1	0	1
Johnson, Steve, Buf.	1	0	1	0	1
Johnson, Will, Pit.	0	1	0	0	1
Jones, Donald, Buf.	1	0	0	0	0
Jones, Edgar, K.C.	0	0	2	11	2
Jones, Jacoby, Bal.	2	2	0	0	2
Jones, Reshad, Mia.	1	0	2	24	2
Jones, Taiwan, Oak.	1	2	0	-2	2
Jones-Drew, Maurice, Jac.	2	1	0	0	1
Keisel, Brett, Pit.	0	0	1	0	1
Kelly, Tommy, Oak.	0	0	1	0	1
Kerley, Jeremy, NYJ	4	1	0	1	1
Koppen, Dan, Den.	1	0	0	0	0
Kruger, Paul, Bal.	0	0	1	9	1
Landry, LaRon, NYJ	0	0	0	9	0
* Lane, Jorvorskie, Mia.	3	2	0	0	2
Lechler, Shane, Oak.	0	1	0	0	1
Lefeged, Joe, Ind.	0	0	1	4	1
Leftwich, Byron, Pit.	1	1	0	0	1
Leonhard, Jim, Den.	1	1	0	0	1
Lewis, Marcedes, Jac.	0	1	0	0	1
Lewis, Ray, Bal.	0	0	1	0	1
Liuget, Corey, S.D.	0	0	1	0	1
Lloyd, Brandon, N.E.	0	1	0	0	1
Locker, Jake, Ten.	4	0	0	-2	0
Long, Jake, Mia.	0	1	0	2	1
Lowery, Dwight, Jac.	0	0	1	0	1
* Luck, Andrew, Ind.	10	2	0	-3	2
Lynch, Corey, S.D.	0	0	1	0	1
Maneri, Steve, K.C.	0	1	0	0	1
Manning, Danieal, Hou.	0	0	1	1	1
Manning, Peyton, Den.	2	1	0	0	1
* Martin, Jonathan, Mia.	0	1	0	0	1
* Martin, Keshawn, Hou.	1	1	0	0	1
Massaquoi, Mohamed, Cle.	0	1	0	0	1
Mathews, Ryan, S.D.	2	0	0	0	0
Maualuga, Rey, Cin.	0	0	1	0	1
Mayo, Jerod, N.E.	0	0	1	0	1
Mays, Taylor, Cin.	0	0	1	0	1
McClain, Jameel, Bal.	0	0	1	0	1
McClellan, Albert, Bal.	0	0	2	0	2
McCluster, Dexter, K.C.	2	0	0	0	0
McCourty, Devin, N.E.	1	0	0	0	0
McCourty, Jason, Ten.	0	0	1	0	1
McDaniel, Tony, Mia.	0	0	1	0	1
McElroy, Greg, NYJ	1	0	0	0	0
McFadden, Darren, Oak.	2	0	0	0	0
McGahee, Willis, Den.	5	1	0	0	1
McIntyre, Garrett, NYJ	0	0	1	0	1
McKnight, Joe, NYJ	3	0	0	0	0
McMichael, Randy, S.D.	1	2	0	0	2
Mendenhall, Rashard, Pit.	3	0	0	0	0

	Fum	Own Rec	Opp Rec	Yards	Tot Rec
* Mercilus, Whitney, Hou.	0	0	1	0	1
Mincey, Jeremy, Jac.	0	0	1	0	1
Moeaki, Tony, K.C.	0	1	0	0	1
Moore, Denarius, Oak.	3	2	0	0	2
Moore, Mewelde, Ind.	1	0	0	0	0
Moore, Rahim, Den.	0	0	1	0	1
Moore, Sterling, N.E.	0	0	1	14	1
Moreno, Knowshon, Den.	1	0	0	0	0
Morgan, Derrick, Ten.	0	0	1	0	1
Mosley, C.J., Jac.	0	0	3	0	3
Mundy, Ryan, Pit.	0	0	1	0	1
Myers, Chris, Hou.	0	1	0	0	1
Naanee, Legedu, Mia.	1	0	0	0	0
Newman, Terence, Cin.	0	0	2	8	2
Ninkovich, Rob, N.E.	0	0	4	3	4
Ogbonnaya, Chris, Cle.	1	0	0	0	0
Oher, Michael, Bal.	0	1	0	0	1
Pace, Calvin, NYJ	0	0	1	0	1
Palmer, Carson, Oak.	7	2	0	-3	2
* Palmer, Nathan, Ind.	0	1	0	0	1
Parker, Juqua, Cle.	0	0	1	0	1
* Paulson, David, Pit.	1	0	0	0	0
Peerman, Cedric, Cin.	0	1	0	0	1
Peko, Domata, Cin.	0	0	1	0	1
Phillips, Shaun, S.D.	0	0	3	0	3
* Pierce, Bernard, Bal.	0	1	0	0	1
Pouncey, Maurkice, Pit.	2	0	0	-6	0
Powell, Bilal, NYJ	0	1	0	0	1
Quinn, Brady, K.C.	1	1	0	0	1
* Rainey, Chris, Pit.	4	1	0	0	1
Redding, Cory, Ind.	0	0	1	0	1
Redman, Isaac, Pit.	3	0	0	0	0
Reece, Marcel, Oak.	2	0	0	-23	0
Reed, Ed, Bal.	0	0	3	31	3
Revis, Darrelle, NYJ	0	0	1	0	1
Reynaud, Darius, Ten.	1	0	0	0	0
Rice, Ray, Bal.	1	0	0	0	0
* Richardson, Trent, Cle.	3	3	0	0	3
Ridley, Stevan, N.E.	4	0	0	0	0
Rivers, Philip, S.D.	15	2	0	-8	2
Robertson, Craig, Cle.	0	0	2	2	2
Robinson, Laurent, Jac.	1	0	0	0	0
* Robinson, Trevor, Cin.	1	0	0	-6	0
Roethlisberger, Ben, Pit.	6	3	0	-8	3
Rogers, Justin, Buf.	1	0	0	0	0
Rosario, Dante, S.D.	1	0	1	0	1
Royal, Eddie, S.D.	1	0	0	0	0
Sanchez, Mark, NYJ	14	3	0	-22	3
Sanders, Emmanuel, Pit.	3	0	0	0	0
Schaub, Matt, Hou.	4	2	0	-2	2
Schilens, Chaz, NYJ	1	1	0	0	1
* Schwartz, Mitchell, Cle.	0	1	0	0	1
Scott, Bart, NYJ	0	0	1	38	1
Scott, Bryan, Buf.	0	0	2	8	2
Seymour, Richard, Oak.	0	0	1	0	1
Sharpton, Darryl, Hou.	0	0	1	0	1
Shorts, Cecil, Jac.	1	0	0	0	0
Skrine, Buster, Cle.	0	0	1	0	1
Smith, Andre, Cin.	0	0	1	0	1
Smith, Antonio, Hou.	0	0	1	0	1
Smith, Brad, Buf.	1	1	0	-15	1
Smith, Eric, NYJ	0	0	1	0	1
Smith, Willie, Oak.	0	1	0	0	1
Solder, Nate, N.E.	0	1	0	0	1
Soliai, Paul, Mia.	0	0	1	0	1
Spiller, C.J., Buf.	3	0	0	0	0
Spurlock, Micheal, Jac.	1	0	0	0	0
* Stanford, Julian, Jac.	0	1	0	0	1

	Fum	Own Rec	Opp Rec	Yards	Tot Rec
Starks, Max, Pit.	1	1	0	0	1
Stevens, Craig, Ten.	2	0	0	0	0
* Streater, Rod, Oak.	1	0	0	0	0
Stuckey, Darrell, S.D.	0	1	1	5	2
Talib, Aqib, N.E.	0	0	1	5	1
* Tannehill, Ryan, Mia.	9	1	0	0	1
Tate, Ben, Hou.	1	0	0	0	0
Tate, Brandon, Cin.	4	2	0	0	2
Taylor, Phillip, Cle.	0	0	1	0	1
Thigpen, Marcus, Mia.	1	0	1	0	1
Thomas, Daniel, Mia.	3	1	0	0	1
Thomas, Demaryius, Den.	3	0	0	0	0
Thomas, Joe, Cle.	0	1	0	0	1
Thomas, Mike, Jac.	1	0	0	0	0
* Thompson, Deonte, Bal.	1	0	0	0	0
Timmons, Lawrence, Pit.	0	0	1	1	1
Unrein, Mitch, Den.	0	0	1	0	1
* Upshaw, Courtney, Bal.	0	0	2	5	2
Vereen, Shane, N.E.	1	0	0	0	0
Verner, Alterraun, Ten.	0	0	1	72	1
Wallace, Mike, Pit.	2	1	0	0	1
Washington, Nate, Ten.	1	0	0	0	0
Watson, Benjamin, Cle.	1	0	0	0	0
Watt, J.J., Hou.	0	0	2	7	2
Wayne, Reggie, Ind.	1	1	0	0	1
Webb, Lardarius, Bal.	0	0	1	0	1
Weddle, Eric, S.D.	3	2	0	0	2
* Weeden, Brandon, Cle.	6	2	0	-3	2
Welker, Wes, N.E.	3	0	0	0	0
Wheeler, Philip, Oak.	0	0	1	0	1
Whimper, Guy, Jac.	1	0	0	0	0
Wilfork, Vince, N.E.	0	0	4	2	4
Wilkerson, Muhammad, NYJ	0	0	1	21	1
Williams, Mario, Buf.	0	0	2	0	2
Wilson, Kyle, NYJ	1	1	0	0	1
* Wilson, Tavon, N.E.	0	0	2	0	2
Wimbley, Kamerion, Ten.	0	1	0	2	1
* Winn, Billy, Cle.	0	0	2	35	2
Winston, Eric, K.C.	0	1	0	0	1
Wisniewski, Stefen, Oak.	1	0	0	-5	0
Wood, Eric, Buf.	0	2	0	0	2
Woodhead, Danny, N.E.	1	0	0	0	0
Woodley, LaMarr, Pit.	0	0	1	0	1
Woodyard, Wesley, Den.	0	0	1	12	1
* Wright, Kendall, Ten.	1	0	0	0	0
Yates, T.J., Hou.	2	1	0	0	1
Young, Usama, Cle.	0	0	1	2	1
Zbikowski, Tom, Ind.	1	0	0	0	0

Yards includes aborted plays, own recoveries and opponents' recoveries.

* *Player that was a rookie in 2012*

NFC FUMBLES—INDIVIDUAL

	Fum	Own Rec	Opp Rec	Yards	Tot Rec
Abdul-Quddus, Isa, N.O.	0	0	1	0	1
* Adams, Joe, Car.	4	1	0	0	1
Adams, Michael, Ariz	0	0	2	0	2
* Alexander, Frank, Car.	0	0	2	0	2
Alexander, Lorenzo, Was.	0	0	1	7	1
Allen, Jared, Min.	0	0	1	0	1
Amendola, Danny, St.L	3	0	0	0	0
Austin, Miles, Dal.	1	0	0	0	0
Avant, Jason, Phi.	1	0	0	0	0
Babineaux, Jonathan, Atl.	0	0	1	15	1
Ballard, Christian, Min.	1	2	0	0	2

	Fum	Own Rec	Opp Rec	Yards	Tot Rec		Fum	Own Rec	Opp Rec	Yards	Tot Rec
Banks, Brandon, Was.	4	3	0	5	3	Forté, Matt, Chi.	2	1	0	0	1
* Barclay, Don, G.B.	0	1	0	0	1	Foster, Mason, T.B.	0	0	1	4	1
Barnidge, Gary, Car.	0	0	1	0	1	Frampton, Eric, Dal.	0	1	0	3	1
Bell, Joique, Det.	2	0	0	0	0	Free, Doug, Dal.	0	1	0	0	1
Benn, Arrelious, T.B.	1	0	0	0	0	Freeman, Josh, T.B.	10	1	0	-12	1
Benson, Cedric, G.B.	1	0	0	0	0	Garcon, Pierre, Was.	0	2	0	0	2
Black, Quincy, T.B.	0	1	1	0	2	Gay, William, Ariz	0	0	1	0	1
Blalock, Justin, Atl.	0	1	0	0	1	Gerhart, Toby, Min.	2	0	0	0	0
Boley, Michael, NY-G	0	0	2	70	2	Gibson, Gary, T.B.	0	0	1	0	1
Boothe, Kevin, NY-G	0	1	0	0	1	Ginn, Ted, S.F.	4	1	0	0	1
Bowman, Zack, Chi.	1	0	2	1	2	Godfrey, Charles, Car.	0	0	1	0	1
* Boykin, Brandon, Phi.	1	0	0	0	0	Goldson, Dashon, S.F.	0	0	2	71	2
Bradford, Sam, St.L	7	3	0	-1	3	Gomes, DeJon, Was.	0	0	1	13	1
Bradshaw, Ahmad, NY-G	3	0	0	0	0	Gore, Frank, S.F.	2	4	0	15	4
Branch, Alan, Sea.	0	0	1	0	1	Graham, Brandon, Phi.	0	0	1	0	1
Brees, Drew, N.O.	5	2	0	0	2	Graham, Jimmy, N.O.	1	2	0	0	2
Brown, Andre, NY-G	0	1	0	1	1	Grant, Ryan, G.B.	1	0	0	0	0
* Brown, Bryce, Phi.	4	1	0	0	1	Green, Alex, G.B.	1	0	0	0	0
Brown, Stevie, NY-G	0	0	2	9	2	Greenway, Chad, Min.	0	0	2	0	2
Browner, Brandon, Sea.	0	0	1	0	1	Griffen, Everson, Min.	0	0	2	5	2
Bryant, Dez, Dal.	5	2	0	0	2	* Griffin III, Robert, Was.	12	4	0	-16	4
Burnett, Morgan, G.B.	0	0	1	0	1	Gross, Jordan, Car.	0	1	0	0	1
Bush, Jarrett, G.B.	0	0	1	0	1	Haggan, Mario, St.L	0	1	0	0	1
Bush, Michael, Chi.	1	0	0	0	0	Hall, DeAngelo, Was.	1	1	1	0	2
Bush, Rafael, N.O.	0	0	2	1	2	* Hanna, James, Dal.	0	1	0	0	1
Butler, Victor, Dal.	0	0	1	0	1	Harbor, Clay, Phi.	1	0	0	0	0
* Cadet, Travaris, N.O.	1	0	0	0	0	Hardy, Greg, Car.	0	0	1	0	1
Campbell, Jason, Chi.	2	1	0	0	1	Harrell, Graham, G.B.	1	0	0	-6	0
Carimi, Gabe, Chi.	0	1	0	0	1	Harris, Dwayne, Dal.	1	0	0	0	0
Carr, David, NY-G	1	1	0	0	1	Hartsock, Ben, Car.	0	1	0	0	1
Casillas, Jonathan, N.O.	0	0	2	0	2	Harvin, Percy, Min.	2	2	0	0	2
Celek, Brent, Phi.	1	0	0	0	0	Hatcher, Jason, Dal.	0	0	1	0	1
Chancellor, Kam, Sea.	0	0	2	0	2	Hayden, Kelvin, Chi.	0	0	4	15	4
* Chandler, Nate, Car.	0	0	1	0	1	Hayes, William, St.L	0	0	1	0	1
Church, Barry, Dal.	0	0	1	6	1	* Hekker, Johnny, St.L	2	2	0	0	2
* Claiborne, Morris, Dal.	0	0	2	50	2	Henderson, Devery, N.O.	1	0	0	0	0
Clemens, Kellen, St.L	1	1	0	0	1	Herremans, Todd, Phi.	0	1	0	0	1
Clemons, Chris, Sea.	0	0	1	0	1	Hester, Devin, Chi.	1	0	0	0	0
Cobb, Randall, G.B.	4	3	0	0	3	Hill, Will, NY-G	0	0	1	0	1
Coe, Michael, NY-G	0	0	1	0	1	Holliday, Vonnie, Ariz	0	0	1	0	1
Cole, Trent, Phi.	0	0	1	0	1	Hope, Chris, Atl.	0	0	1	0	1
Collins, Jed, N.O.	1	0	0	0	0	* Hosley, Jayron, NY-G	0	0	1	0	1
Colston, Marques, N.O.	4	0	0	0	0	Hoyer, Brian, Ariz	1	0	0	0	1
Conte, Chris, Chi.	0	0	1	0	1	Hughes, Brandon, Phi.	0	0	1	0	1
Cook, Ryan, Dal.	1	1	0	0	1	Hunter, Kendall, S.F.	1	0	0	0	0
Cordle, Jim, NY-G	0	1	0	0	1	Ingram, Mark, N.O.	0	1	0	1	1
* Cousins, Kirk, Was.	1	1	0	0	1	* Irvin, Bruce, Sea.	0	0	1	35	1
* Crawford, Richard, Was.	0	0	1	10	1	Jackson, DeSean, Phi.	1	1	0	0	1
Culliver, Chris, S.F.	0	0	1	0	1	Jackson, Rob, Was.	0	0	1	0	1
Cutler, Jay, Chi.	8	1	0	-7	1	* James, LaMichael, S.F.	1	0	0	0	1
Dahl, Harvey, St.L	0	1	0	0	1	Jefferson, A.J., Min.	1	0	1	-2	1
* Daniels, Mike, G.B.	0	0	2	43	2	Jenkins, Cullen, Phi.	0	0	1	0	1
Davis, Anthony, S.F.	0	1	0	0	1	* Jenkins, Janoris, St.L	3	0	1	2	1
Davis, Kellen, Chi.	1	0	0	0	0	Jernigan, Jerrel, NY-G	1	0	0	0	0
Davis, Thomas, Car.	0	0	1	-2	1	Jerry, Peria, Atl.	0	0	1	0	1
DeCoud, Thomas, Atl.	0	0	1	0	1	Johnson, Calvin, Det.	3	0	0	0	0
Dixon, Anthony, S.F.	0	1	0	0	1	Johnson, Charles, Car.	0	0	1	0	1
Dotson, Demar, T.B.	0	1	0	0	1	* Johnson, Damaris, Phi.	2	0	0	0	0
Doucet, Early, Ariz	0	1	0	0	1	Johnson, Rashad, Ariz	0	0	1	-1	1
Douglas, Harry, Atl.	1	0	0	0	0	* Johnson, Leonard, T.B.	1	0	1	1	1
* Dunbar, Lance, Dal.	1	0	0	0	0	Jones, Felix, Dal.	2	0	0	0	0
Dunlap, King, Phi.	0	1	0	0	1	Jones, Jason, Sea.	0	0	1	3	1
Edwards, Ray, Atl.	0	0	2	26	2	Jordan, Cameron, N.O.	0	0	2	0	2
Fairley, Nick, Det.	0	0	1	0	1	Joseph, Linval, NY-G	0	0	2	16	2
Feely, Jay, Ariz	1	0	0	0	0	Kaepernick, Colin, S.F.	9	2	0	-22	2
Finley, Jermichael, G.B.	1	0	0	0	0	Kendricks, Lance, St.L	1	1	0	0	1
* Floyd, Michael, Ariz	1	0	0	0	0	Kerrigan, Ryan, Was.	0	0	1	0	1
* Foles, Nick, Phi.	8	2	0	-18	2	Koenen, Michael, T.B.	1	0	0	0	0

	Fum	Own Rec	Opp Rec	Yards	Tot Rec
Kolb, Kevin, Ariz	2	0	0	0	0
* Kuechly, Luke, Car.	0	0	3	9	3
LaFell, Brandon, Car.	1	0	0	0	0
Larsen, Ted, T.B.	0	1	0	0	1
Laurinaitis, James, St.L	0	0	1	4	1
Leach, Mike, Ariz	0	0	1	0	1
Lemon, Orie, Dal.	0	0	1	0	1
Lenon, Paris, Ariz	0	0	1	0	1
Leshoure, Mikel, Det.	3	0	0	0	0
Levy, DeAndre, Det.	0	0	1	0	1
* Lindley, Ryan, Ariz	3	1	0	-10	1
Lofton, Curtis, N.O.	0	0	2	0	2
Logan, Stefan, Det.	6	3	0	0	3
Lumpkin, Kregg, NY-G	1	0	0	0	0
Lynch, Marshawn, Sea.	5	0	0	0	0
Maclin, Jeremy, Phi.	1	0	0	0	0
Manning, Eli, NY-G	5	2	0	0	2
Manningham, Mario, S.F.	2	0	0	0	0
Marshall, Brandon, Chi.	2	1	0	0	1
* Martin, Doug, T.B.	1	1	0	0	1
Maxwell, Byron, Sea.	0	0	1	11	1
McBath, Darcel, S.F.	0	0	1	8	1
McClain, Robert, Atl.	0	0	2	28	2
McCoy, Gerald, T.B.	0	0	1	0	1
McCoy, LeSean, Phi.	4	2	0	0	2
McManis, Sherrick, Chi.	0	1	0	0	1
* McMillian, Jerron, G.B.	0	0	1	3	1
Mebane, Brandon, Sea.	0	0	1	0	1
Meredith, Jamon, T.B.	0	1	0	0	1
Miller, Brit, St.L	1	1	0	0	1
Miller, Bruce, S.F.	0	1	0	0	1
Miller, Zach, Sea.	1	0	0	0	0
Moore, D.J., Chi.	1	0	0	0	0
Moore, William, Atl.	0	0	1	0	1
Morgan, Josh, Was.	1	2	0	13	2
* Morris, Alfred, Was.	4	2	0	0	2
Moss, Randy, S.F.	1	1	0	0	1
Moss, Santana, Was.	2	1	0	-4	1
Munnerlyn, Captain, Car.	1	0	0	0	0
Murphy, Louis, Car.	1	1	0	0	1
Murray, DeMarco, Dal.	3	1	0	0	1
Newton, Cam, Car.	10	3	0	-8	3
Nicholas, Stephen, Atl.	0	0	1	0	1
Ogletree, Kevin, Dal.	0	1	0	0	1
Osgood, Kassim, Det.	0	0	1	0	1
Parrish, Roscoe, T.B.	1	1	0	0	1
Paul, Niles, Was.	1	0	0	0	0
Paysinger, Spencer, NY-G	0	0	1	0	1
* Pead, Isaiah, St.L	2	0	0	0	0
Penn, Donald, T.B.	0	1	0	0	1
Peppers, Julius, Chi.	0	0	4	6	4
Peterson, Adrian, Min.	4	0	0	0	0
Peterson, Patrick, Ariz	7	4	1	60	5
Pettigrew, Brandon, Det.	4	0	0	0	0
Phillips, John, Dal.	0	0	1	0	1
Pierre-Paul, Jason, NY-G	0	0	1	10	1
Ponder, Christian, Min.	7	2	0	0	2
Powell, William, Ariz	2	0	0	0	0
Rachal, Chilo, Chi.	0	1	0	0	1
* Randle, Rueben, NY-G	1	1	0	0	1
Reynolds, Dallas, Phi.	1	0	0	-16	0
* Richardson, Daryl, St.L	3	0	0	0	0
Riley, Perry, Was.	0	0	1	0	1
Rivers, Keith, NY-G	0	0	1	0	1
Roach, Nick, Chi.	0	0	1	0	1
Roberts, Andre, Ariz	1	0	0	0	0
Robison, Brian, Min.	0	0	1	0	1
Rodgers, Aaron, G.B.	5	1	0	0	1
Rogers, Carlos, S.F.	0	0	3	63	3
Rolle, Antrel, NY-G	0	0	1	0	1
Romo, Tony, Dal.	6	2	0	-15	2
Ryan, Jon, Sea.	1	1	0	-14	1
Ryan, Matt, Atl.	3	0	0	-2	0
Saffold, Rodger, St.L	0	1	0	0	1
Sanders, James, Ariz	0	0	1	93	1
Sanford, Jamarca, Min.	0	0	1	0	1
Saturday, Jeff, G.B.	0	2	0	0	2
Scott, Jake, Phi.	0	1	0	0	1
Scott, Jonathan, Chi.	0	2	0	0	2
Sherels, Marcus, Min.	1	1	0	0	1
Sherman, Anthony, Ariz	0	1	0	11	1
Sherman, Richard, Sea.	0	0	1	0	1
Shields, Sam, G.B.	1	1	0	0	1
Shipley, Jordan, T.B.	1	0	0	0	0
* Silatolu, Amini, Car.	0	1	0	0	1
Silva, Ricardo, Det.	0	0	1	0	1
Simpson, Jerome, Min.	2	1	0	0	1
Skelton, John, Ariz	4	2	0	-1	2
Smith, Alex, S.F.	4	2	0	-2	2
* Smith, Harrison, Min.	0	0	1	0	1
Smith, Justin, S.F.	0	0	1	0	1
Smith, Malcolm, Sea.	0	0	1	0	1
Smith, Steve, Car.	1	0	0	0	0
Smith, Will, N.O.	0	0	1	0	1
Snelling, Jason, Atl.	1	0	0	0	0
Spencer, Anthony, Dal.	0	0	1	0	1
Spencer, Chris, Chi.	0	1	0	0	1
Spillman, C.J., S.F.	0	0	1	0	1
Stafford, Matthew, Det.	6	2	0	-7	2
Staley, Joe, S.F.	0	1	0	0	1
Starks, James, G.B.	1	0	0	0	0
Stewart, Jonathan, Car.	2	1	0	0	1
Sullivan, John, Min.	1	0	0	-12	0
Tapp, Darryl, Phi.	0	0	1	4	1
Tate, Golden, Sea.	1	1	0	4	1
Thomas, Pierre, N.O.	0	1	0	0	1
Thomas, Earl, Sea.	0	0	1	0	1
Thomas, Josh, Car.	0	0	1	4	1
Thornton, Cedric, Phi.	1	0	0	0	0
Tillman, Charles, Chi.	0	0	2	0	2
Tolbert, Mike, Car.	0	1	0	0	1
Trufant, Marcus, Sea.	0	0	1	0	1
Tryon, Justin, NY-G	0	0	1	0	1
Tulloch, Stephen, Det.	0	0	2	0	2
* Turbin, Robert, Sea.	0	1	0	0	1
Turner, Michael, Atl.	3	1	0	0	1
Turner, Robert, St.L	0	1	1	0	2
Urlacher, Brian, Chi.	0	0	2	4	2
Vick, Michael, Phi.	11	3	0	-25	3
Walker, Delanie, S.F.	1	0	0	0	0
Walters, Anthony, Chi.	0	0	1	0	1
Ware, DeMarcus, Dal.	0	0	1	0	1
Washington, Daryl, Ariz	0	0	1	3	1
Washington, Leon, Sea.	2	1	0	0	1
Watkins, Danny, Phi.	0	1	0	0	1
Watson, Dekoda, T.B.	0	0	2	0	2
Weatherspoon, Sean, Atl.	0	0	1	0	1
Weems, Eric, Chi.	1	2	1	1	3
Wells, Beanie, Ariz	1	0	0	0	0
Wells, Scott, St.L	1	0	0	0	0
White, Roddy, Atl.	1	1	0	0	1
Whitner, Donte, S.F.	0	0	1	0	1
Williams, Dan, Ariz	0	0	1	0	1
Williams, DeAngelo, Car.	2	0	0	0	0
Williams, Kevin, Min.	0	0	2	0	2
Williams, Kyle, S.F.	1	1	0	0	1

	Fum	Own Rec	Opp Rec	Yards	Tot Rec
Williams, Ryan, Ariz	2	0	0	0	0
Willis, Patrick, S.F.	0	0	1	3	1
* Wilson, David, NY-G	1	0	0	0	0
Wilson, Josh, Was.	0	0	2	30	2
Wilson, Martez, N.O.	0	0	1	0	1
* Wilson, Russell, Sea.	6	3	0	-9	3
Winfield, Antoine, Min.	0	0	1	0	1
Wright, Eric, T.B.	0	0	1	0	1
Wright, Major, Chi.	0	0	2	0	2
Young, Darrel, Was.	0	1	0	0	1
Zuttah, Jeremy, T.B.	0	1	0	0	1

Yards includes aborted plays, own recoveries and opponents' recoveries.

* Player that was a rookie in 2012

AMERICAN FOOTBALL CONFERENCE—FUMBLES

	Fum	Own Rec	Fum OB	TD	Opp Rec	Fum TD Yards	Tot Rec
Houston	12	7	1	0	14	0 38	21
Baltimore	14	8	1	0	12	0 47	20
New England	14	4	3	1	21	3 79	25
Cincinnati	19	8	1	0	16	1 42	24
Jacksonville	20	9	2	0	11	0 -2	20
Indianapolis	21	10	2	0	3	0 1	13
Tennessee	21	6	3	0	5	1 72	11
Cleveland	22	13	1	0	12	0 18	25
Denver	22	6	2	0	8	1 77	14
Oakland	22	11	1	0	8	0 -49	19
Buffalo	23	6	0	0	9	0 -7	15
San Diego	24	11	2	0	14	2 -2	25
Miami	25	9	3	0	6	0 13	15
Kansas City	26	8	1	0	6	1 68	14
N.Y. Jets	32	13	1	0	12	1 68	25
Pittsburgh	33	13	4	0	10	0 11	23
AFC Total	350	142	28	1	167	10 474	309
AFC Average	21.9	8.9	1.8	0.1	10.4	0.6 29.6	19.3

NATIONAL FOOTBALL CONFERENCE—FUMBLES

	Fum	Own Rec	Fum OB	TD	Opp Rec	Fum TD Yards	Tot Rec
Atlanta	9	3	2	0	11	1 67	14
New Orleans	13	6	3	0	11	0 2	17
N.Y. Giants	13	7	0	0	14	1 106	21
Green Bay	16	8	0	0	5	1 40	13
Seattle	16	7	1	0	13	1 30	20
Tampa Bay	16	9	1	0	8	0 -7	17
Chicago	20	12	0	0	20	1 20	32
Dallas	20	10	0	0	9	2 44	19
Minnesota	21	8	2	0	12	0 -9	20
Carolina	22	10	2	1	12	0 3	22
Detroit	24	5	3	0	6	0 -7	11
St. Louis	24	12	4	0	4	1 5	16
Arizona	25	10	2	0	11	1 155	21
San Francisco	26	15	3	1	11	1 136	26
Washington	26	17	3	2	9	1 58	26
Philadelphia	37	13	2	0	5	0 -55	18
NFC Total	328	152	28	4	161	11 588	313
NFC Average	20.5	9.5	1.8	0.3	10.1	0.7 36.8	19.6
NFL Total	678	294	56	5	328	21 1062	622
NFL Average	21.2	9.2	1.8	0.2	10.3	0.7 33.2	19.4

Inside the Numbers

GREATEST COMEBACKS
IN NFL HISTORY
(Most Points Overcome To Win Game)

REGULAR SEASON GAMES
FROM 28 POINTS BEHIND TO WIN:
December 7, 1980, at San Francisco

New Orleans	14	21	0	0	0	— 35
San Francisco	0	7	14	14	3	— 38

NO — Harris 33 pass from Manning (Ricardo kick)
NO — Childs 21 pass from Manning (Ricardo kick)
NO — Holmes 1 run (Ricardo kick)
SF — Solomon 57 punt return (Wersching kick)
NO — Holmes 1 run (Ricardo kick)
NO — Harris 41 pass from Manning (Ricardo kick)
SF — Montana 1 run (Wersching kick)
SF — Clark 71 pass from Montana (Wersching kick)
SF — Solomon 14 pass from Montana (Wersching kick)
SF — Elliott 7 run (Wersching kick)
SF — FG Wersching 36

FROM 26 POINTS BEHIND TO WIN:
September 21, 1997, at Buffalo

Indianapolis	14	12	0	9	— 35
Buffalo	0	10	6	21	— 37

Ind — Bailey 10 pass from Harbaugh (Blanchard kick)
Ind — Faulk 10 run (Blanchard kick)
Ind — FG Blanchard 39
Ind — FG Blanchard 36
Ind — FG Blanchard 49
Ind — FG Blanchard 22
Buff — Johnson 16 pass from Collins (Christie kick)
Buff — FG Christie 27
Buff — A. Smith 15 run (2-pt attempt failed)
Ind — FG Blanchard 25
Buff — Early 4 pass from Collins (Christie kick)
Buff — A. Smith 1 run (Christie kick)
Buff — A. Smith 54 run (Christie kick)
Ind — Harrison 2 pass from Justin (2-pt attempt failed)

FROM 25 POINTS BEHIND TO WIN:
November 8, 1987, at St. Louis

Tampa Bay	7	7	14	0	— 28
St. Louis	0	3	0	28	— 31

TB — Carrier 5 pass from DeBerg (Igwebuike kick)
TB — Carter 3 pass from DeBerg (Igwebuike kick)
StL — FG Gallery 31
TB — Smith 34 pass from DeBerg (Igwebuike kick)
TB — Smith 3 run (Igwebuike kick)
StL — Awalt 4 pass from Lomax (Gallery kick)
StL — Noga 23 fumble recovery (Gallery kick)
StL — J. Smith 11 pass from Lomax (Gallery kick)
StL — J. Smith 17 pass from Lomax (Gallery kick)

FROM 24 POINTS BEHIND TO WIN:
October 27, 1946, at Washington

Philadelphia	0	0	14	14	— 28
Washington	10	14	0	0	— 24

Wash — Rosato 2 run (Poillon kick)
Wash — FG Poillon 28
Wash — Rosato 4 run (Poillon kick)
Wash — Lapka recovered fumble in end zone (Poillon kick)
Phil — Steele 1 run (Lio kick)
Phil — Pritchard 45 pass from Thompson (Lio kick)
Phil — Steinke 7 pass from Thompson (Lio kick)
Phil — Ferrante 30 pass from Thompson (Lio kick)

FROM 24 POINTS BEHIND TO WIN:
October 20, 1957, at Detroit

Baltimore	7	14	6	0	— 27
Detroit	0	3	7	21	— 31

Balt — Mutscheller 15 pass from Unitas (Rechichar kick)
Det — FG Martin 47
Balt — Moore 72 pass from Unitas (Rechichar kick)
Balt — Mutscheller 52 pass from Unitas (Rechichar kick)
Balt — Moore 4 pass from Unitas (kick failed)
Det — Junker 14 pass from Rote (Layne kick)
Det — Cassady 26 pass from Layne (Layne kick)
Det — Johnson 1 run (Layne kick)
Det — Cassady 29 pass from Layne (Layne kick)

FROM 24 POINTS BEHIND TO WIN:
October 25, 1959, at Minneapolis

Philadelphia	0	0	21	7	— 28
Chicago Cardinals	7	10	7	0	— 24

Cardinals — Crow 10 pass from Roach (Conrad kick)
Cardinals — J. Hill 77 blocked field goal return (Conrad kick)
Cardinals — FG Conrad 15
Cardinals — Lane 37 interception return (Conrad kick)
Phil — Barnes 1 run (Walston kick)
Phil — McDonald 29 pass from Van Brocklin (Walston kick)
Phil — Barnes 2 run (Walston kick)
Phil — McDonald 22 pass from Van Brocklin (Walston kick)

FROM 24 POINTS BEHIND TO WIN:
October 23, 1960, at Denver

Boston	10	7	7	0	— 24
Denver	0	0	14	17	— 31

Bos — FG Cappelletti 12
Bos — Colclough 10 pass from Songin (Cappelletti kick)
Bos — Wells 6 pass from Songin (Cappelletti kick)
Bos — Miller 47 pass from Songin (Cappelletti kick)
Den — Carmichael 21 pass from Tripucka (Mingo kick)
Den — Jessup 19 pass from Tripucka (Mingo kick)
Den — Carmichael 35 lateral from Taylor, pass from Tripucka (Mingo kick)
Den — Taylor 8 pass from Tripucka (Mingo kick)
Den — FG Mingo 9

FROM 24 POINTS BEHIND TO WIN:
December 15, 1974, at Miami

New England	21	3	0	3	— 27
Miami	0	17	7	10	— 34

NE — Hannah recovered fumble in end zone (J. Smith kick)
NE — Sanders 23 interception return (J. Smith kick)
NE — Herron 4 pass from Plunkett (J. Smith kick)
NE — FG J. Smith 46
Mia — Nottingham 1 run (Yepremian kick)
Mia — Baker 37 pass from Morrall (Yepremian kick)
Mia — FG Yepremian 28
Mia — Baker 46 pass from Morrall (Yepremian kick)
NE — FG J. Smith 34
Mia — Nottingham 2 run (Yepremian kick)
Mia — FG Yepremian 40

FROM 24 POINTS BEHIND TO WIN:
December 4, 1977, at Minnesota

San Francisco	0	10	14	3	— 27
Minnesota	0	0	7	21	— 28

SF — Delvin Williams 2 run (Wersching kick)
SF — FG Wersching 31
SF — Dave Williams 80 kickoff return (Wersching kick)
SF — Delvin Williams 5 run (Wersching kick)
Minn — McClanahan 15 pass from Lee (Cox kick)
Minn — Rashad 8 pass from Kramer (Cox kick)
Minn — Tucker 9 pass from Kramer (Cox kick)
SF — FG Wersching 31
Minn — S. White 69 pass from Kramer (Cox kick)

FROM 24 POINTS BEHIND TO WIN:
September 23, 1979, at Denver

Seattle	10	10	14	0	— 34
Denver	0	10	21	6	— 37

Sea — FG Herrera 28
Sea — Doornink 5 run (Herrera kick)
Den — FG Turner 27
Sea — Doornink 5 run (Herrera kick)
Den — Armstrong 2 run (Turner kick)
Sea — FG Herrera 22
Sea — McCollum 13 pass from Zorn (Herrera kick)
Sea — Smith 1 run (Herrera kick)
Den — Studdard 2 pass from Morton (Turner kick)
Den — Moses 11 pass from Morton (Turner kick)
Den — Upchurch 35 pass from Morton (Turner kick)
Den — Lytle 1 run (kick failed)

FROM 24 POINTS BEHIND TO WIN:
September 23, 1979, at Cincinnati

Houston	0	10	17	3	— 30
Cincinnati	14	10	0	3	— 27

Cin — Johnson 1 run (Bahr kick)
Cin — Alexander 2 run (Bahr kick)
Cin — Johnson 1 run (Bahr kick)
Cin — FG Bahr 52
Hou — Burrough 35 pass from Pastorini (Fritsch kick)
Hou — FG Fritsch 33
Hou — Campbell 8 run (Fritsch kick)
Hou — Caster 22 pass from Pastorini (Fritsch kick)
Hou — FG Fritsch 47
Cin — FG Bahr 55
Hou — FG Fritsch 29

FROM 24 POINTS BEHIND TO WIN:
November 22, 1982, at Los Angeles

San Diego	10	14	0	0 —	24
L.A. Raiders	0	7	14	7 —	28

SD	—	FG Benirschke 19
SD	—	Scales 29 pass from Fouts (Benirschke kick)
SD	—	Muncie 2 run (Benirschke kick)
SD	—	Muncie 1 run (Benirschke kick)
Raiders	—	Christensen 1 pass from Plunkett (Bahr kick)
Raiders	—	Allen 3 run (Bahr kick)
Raiders	—	Allen 6 run (Bahr kick)
Raiders	—	Hawkins 1 run (Bahr kick)

FROM 24 POINTS BEHIND TO WIN:
September 26, 1988, at Denver

L.A. Raiders	0	0	14	13 3 —	30
Denver	7	17	0	3 0 —	27

Den	—	Dorsett 1 run (Karlis kick)
Den	—	Dorsett 1 run (Karlis kick)
Den	—	Sewell 7 pass from Elway (Karlis kick)
Den	—	FG Karlis 39
Raiders	—	Smith 40 pass from Schroeder (Bahr kick)
Raiders	—	Smith 42 pass from Schroeder (Bahr kick)
Raiders	—	FG Bahr 28
Raiders	—	Allen 4 run (Bahr kick)
Den	—	FG Karlis 25
Raiders	—	FG Bahr 44
Raiders	—	FG Bahr 35

FROM 24 POINTS BEHIND TO WIN:
December 6, 1992, at Tampa

L.A. Rams	0	3	21	7 —	31
Tampa Bay	6	21	0	0 —	27

TB	—	FG Murray 34
TB	—	FG Murray 47
TB	—	Armstrong 81 pass from Testaverde (Murray kick)
TB	—	Jones 26 fumble recovery (Murray kick)
Rams	—	FG Zendejas 18
TB	—	Carrier 10 pass from Testaverde (Murray kick)
Rams	—	Anderson 40 pass from Everett (Zendejas kick)
Rams	—	Chadwick 27 pass from Everett (Zendejas kick)
Rams	—	Lang 1 run (Zendejas kick)
Rams	—	Carter 8 pass from Everett (Zendejas kick)

FROM 24 POINTS BEHIND TO WIN:
October 2, 2011, at Dallas

Detroit	0	3	14	17 —	34
Dallas	3	13	10	0 —	30

Dall	—	Bryant 25 pass from Romo (Bailey kick)
Dall	—	Bryant 6 pass from Romo (Bailey kick)
Dall	—	FG Bailey 41
Det	—	FG Hanson 33
Dall	—	FG Bailey 35
Dall	—	Witten 1 pass from Romo (Bailey kick)
Det	—	Carpenter 34 interception return (Hanson kick)
Det	—	Houston 56 interception return (Hanson kick)
Dall	—	FG Bailey 23
Det	—	Johnson 23 pass from Stafford (Hanson kick)
Det	—	FG Hanson 51
Det	—	Johnson 2 pass from Stafford (Hanson kick)

FROM 24 POINTS BEHIND TO WIN:
October 15, 2012, at San Diego

Denver	0	0	14	21 —	35
San Diego	10	14	0	0 —	24

SD	—	FG Novak
SD	—	Gates 15 pass from Rivers (Novak kick)
SD	—	Jammer 80 interception return (Novak kick)
SD	—	Gates 11 pass from Rivers (Novak kick)
Den	—	D. Thomas 29 pass from Manning (Prater kick)
Den	—	Carter 65 fumble recovery (Prater kick)
Den	—	Decker 7 pass from Manning (Prater kick)
Den	—	Stokley 21 pass from Manning (Prater kick)
Den	—	Harris 46 interception return (Prater kick)

POSTSEASON GAMES
FROM 32 POINTS BEHIND TO WIN:
AFC First-Round Playoff Game
January 3, 1993, at Buffalo

Houston	7	21	7	3	0 —	38
Buffalo	3	0	28	7	3 —	41

Hou	—	Jeffires 3 pass from Moon (Del Greco kick)
Buff	—	FG Christie 36
Hou	—	Slaughter 7 pass from Moon (Del Greco kick)
Hou	—	Duncan 26 pass from Moon (Del Greco kick)
Hou	—	Jeffires 27 pass from Moon (Del Greco kick)
Hou	—	McDowell 58 interception return (Del Greco kick)
Buff	—	Davis 1 run (Christie kick)
Buff	—	Beebe 38 pass from Reich (Christie kick)
Buff	—	Reed 26 pass from Reich (Christie kick)
Buff	—	Reed 18 pass from Reich (Christie kick)
Buff	—	Reed 17 pass from Reich (Christie kick)
Hou	—	FG Del Greco 26
Buff	—	FG Christie 32

FROM 24 POINTS BEHIND TO WIN:
NFC First-Round Playoff Game
January 5, 2003, at San Francisco

N.Y. Giants	7	21	10	0 —	38
San Francisco	7	7	8	17 —	39

SF	—	Owens 76 pass from Garcia (Chandler kick)
NYG	—	Toomer 12 pass from Collins (Bryant kick)
NYG	—	Shockey 2 pass from Collins (Bryant kick)
SF	—	Barlow 1 run (Chandler kick)
NYG	—	Toomer 8 pass from Collins (Bryant kick)
NYG	—	Toomer 24 pass from Collins (Bryant kick)
NYG	—	Barber 6 run (Bryant kick)
NYG	—	FG Bryant 21
SF	—	Owens 26 pass from Garcia (Owens from Garcia)
SF	—	Garcia 14 run (Owens from Garcia)
SF	—	Garcia 14 run (Owens from Garcia)
SF	—	FG Chandler 25
SF	—	Streets 13 pass from Garcia (2-pt attempt failed)

FROM 20 POINTS BEHIND TO WIN:
Western Conference Playoff Game
December 22, 1957, at San Francisco

Detroit	0	7	14	10 —	31
San Francisco	14	10	3	0 —	27

SF	—	Owens 34 pass from Tittle (Soltau kick)
SF	—	McElhenny 47 pass from Tittle (Soltau kick)
Det	—	Junker 4 pass from Rote (Martin kick)
SF	—	Wilson 12 pass from Tittle (Soltau kick)
SF	—	FG Soltau 25
SF	—	FG Soltau 10
Det	—	Tracy 2 run (Martin kick)
Det	—	Tracy 58 run (Martin kick)
Det	—	Gedman 3 run (Martin kick)
Det	—	FG Martin 14

FROM 18 POINTS BEHIND TO WIN:
NFC Divisional Playoff Game
December 23, 1972, at San Francisco

Dallas	3	10	0	17 —	30
San Francisco	7	14	7	0 —	28

SF	—	Washington 97 kickoff return (Gossett kick)
Dall	—	FG Fritsch 37
SF	—	Schreiber 1 run (Gossett kick)
SF	—	Schreiber 1 run (Gossett kick)
Dall	—	FG Fritsch 45
Dall	—	Alworth 28 pass from Morton (Fritsch kick)
SF	—	Schreiber 1 run (Gossett kick)
Dall	—	FG Fritsch 27
Dall	—	Parks 20 pass from Staubach (Fritsch kick)
Dall	—	Sellers 10 pass from Staubach (Fritsch kick)

FROM 18 POINTS BEHIND TO WIN:
AFC Divisional Playoff Game
January 4, 1986, at Miami

Cleveland	7	7	7	0 —	21
Miami	3	0	14	7 —	24

Mia	—	FG Reveiz 51
Cle	—	Newsome 16 pass from Kosar (Bahr kick)
Cle	—	Byner 21 run (Bahr kick)
Cle	—	Byner 66 run (Bahr kick)
Mia	—	Moore 6 pass from Marino (Reveiz kick)
Mia	—	Davenport 31 run (Reveiz kick)
Mia	—	Davenport 1 run (Reveiz kick)

FROM 18 POINTS BEHIND TO WIN:
AFC Championship Playoff Game
January 21, 2007, at Indianapolis

New England	7	14	7	6 —	34
Indianapolis	3	3	15	17 —	38

NE	—	Mankins 0 fumble recovery (Gostkowski kick)
Ind	—	FG Vinatieri 42
NE	—	Dillon 7 run (Gostkowski kick)
NE	—	Samuel 39 interception return (Gostkowski kick)
Ind	—	FG Vinatieri 26
Ind	—	Manning 1 run (Vinatieri kick)
Ind	—	Klecko 1 pass from Manning (Harrison from Manning)
NE	—	Gaffney 6 pass from Brady (Gostkowski kick)
Ind	—	Saturday 0 fumble recovery (Vinatieri kick)
NE	—	FG Gostkowski 28
Ind	—	FG Vinatieri 36
NE	—	FG Gostkowski 43
Ind	—	Addai 3 run (Vinatieri kick)

RECORDS FOR NFL TEAMS FOR MOST POINTS IN A GAME (REGULAR SEASON ONLY)

Note: When the record has been achieved more than once, only the most recent game is shown; summaries are listed in alphabetical order by conference. Bold face indicates team holding record.

BALTIMORE RAVENS
November 11, 2012, at Baltimore

Oakland	0	10	7	3	— 20
Baltimore	10	17	21	7	— 55

TD: Balt—Torrey Smith 2, Joe Flacco, Jacoby Jones, Sam Koch, Dennis Pitta, Ray Rice; Oak—Darrius Heyward-Bey, Denarius Moore. TD Passes: Balt—Joe Flacco 3; Oak—Carson Palmer 2. FG: Balt—Justin Tucker 2; Det—Sebastian Janikowski 2.

BUFFALO BILLS
September 18, 1966, at Buffalo

Miami	3	7	0	14	— 24
Buffalo	21	27	3	7	— 58

TD: Buff—Bobby Burnett 2, Butch Byrd 2, Jack Spikes 2, Bobby Crockett, Jack Kemp; Mia—Dave Kocourek, Bo Roberson, John Roderick. TD Passes: Buff—Jack Kemp, Daryle Lamonica; Mia—George Wilson 3. FG: Buff—Booth Lusteg; Mia—Gene Mingo.

CINCINNATI BENGALS
December 17, 1989, at Cincinnati

Houston	0	0	0	7	— 7
Cincinnati	21	10	21	9	— 61

TD: Cin—Eddie Brown 2, Eric Ball, James Brooks, Ira Hillary, Rodney Holman, Tim McGee, Craig Taylor; Hou—Lorenzo White. TD Passes: Cin—Boomer Esiason 4, Erik Wilhelm. FG: Cin—Jim Breech 2.

CLEVELAND BROWNS
November 7, 1954, at Cleveland

Washington	0	3	0	0	— 3
Cleveland	13	14	21	14	— 62

TD: Cle—Darrell Brewster 2, Mo Bassett, Ken Gorgal, Otto Graham, Dub Jones, Dante Lavelli, Curley Morrison. TD Passes: Cle—George Ratterman 3, Otto Graham. FG: Cle—Lou Groza 2; Wash—Vic Janowicz.

DENVER BRONCOS
October 6, 1963, at Denver

San Diego	13	7	0	14	— 34
Denver	3	14	9	24	— 50

TD: Den—Lionel Taylor 2, Goose Gonsoulin, Gene Prebola, Donnie Stone; SD—Keith Lincoln 2, Lance Alworth, Paul Lowe, Jacque MacKinnon. TD Passes: Den—John McCormick 3; SD—Tobin Rote 3, John Hadl 2. FG: Den—Gene Mingo 5.

HOUSTON TEXANS
November 18, 2012 at Houston

Jacksonville	7	10	10	7	3 — 37
Houston	7	10	3	14	9 — 43

TD: Hou—Garrett Graham 2, James Casey, Andre Johnson, Keshawn Martin; Jax—Marcedes Lewis 2, Justin Blackmon, Cecil Shorts. TD Passes: Hou—Matt Schaub 5; Jax—Chad Henne 4. FG: Hou—Shayne Graham 3; Jax—Josh Scobee 3.

INDIANAPOLIS COLTS
December 12, 1976, at Baltimore

Buffalo	3	3	7	7	— 20
Baltimore Colts	7	13	28	10	— 58

TD: Balt—Roger Carr, Raymond Chester, Glenn Doughty, Roosevelt Leaks, Derrel Luce, Lydell Mitchell, Howard Stevens; Buff—Bob Chandler, O.J. Simpson. TD Passes: Balt—Bert Jones 3; Buff—Gary Marangi. FG: Balt—Toni Linhart 3; Buff—George Jakowenko 2.

JACKSONVILLE JAGUARS
December 23, 2007, at Jacksonville

Oakland	0	3	0	8	— 11
Jacksonville	14	14	7	14	— 49

TD: Oak—Zach Miller; Jax—Richard Angulo, David Garrard, Greg Jones, Matt Jones, Maurice Jones-Drew, Fred Taylor, Reggie Williams. TD Passes: Oak—JaMarcus Russell; Jax—David Garrard 2, Quinn Gray 2. FG: Oak—Sebastian Janikowski.

KANSAS CITY CHIEFS
September 7, 1963, at Denver

Kansas City	14	14	21	10	— 59
Denver	0	7	0	0	— 7

TD: KC—Chris Burford 2, Frank Jackson 2, Dave Grayson, Abner Haynes, Sherrill Headrick, Curtis McClinton; Den—Lionel Taylor. TD Passes: KC—Len Dawson 4, Curtis McClinton; Den—Mickey Slaughter. FG: KC—Tommy Brooker.

MIAMI DOLPHINS
November 24, 1977, at St. Louis

Miami	14	14	20	7	— 55
St. Louis Cardinals	7	0	0	7	— 14

TD: Mia—Nat Moore 3, Gary Davis, Duriel Harris, Leroy Harris, Benny Malone, Andre Tillman; StL—Ike Harris, Terry Metcalf. TD Passes: Mia—Bob Griese 6; StL—Jim Hart.

NEW ENGLAND PATRIOTS
November 18, 2012, at New England

Indianapolis	14	3	0	7	— 24
New England	7	17	14	21	— 59

TD: NE—Julian Edelman 2, Rob Gronkowski 2, Alfonzo Dennard, Stevan Ridley, Aqib Talib, Shane Vereen; Ind—T.Y. Hilton 2, Delone Carter. TD Passes: NE—Tom Brady 3; Ind—Andrew Luck 2. FG: NE—Stephen Gostkowski; Ind—Adam Vinatieri.

NEW YORK JETS
November 17, 1985, at New York

Tampa Bay	14	7	7	0	— 28
New York Jets	17	24	14	7	— 62

TD: NYJ—Mickey Shuler 3, Johnny Hector 2, Tony Paige, Al Toon, Wesley Walker; TB—James Wilder 2, Kevin House, Calvin Magee. TD Passes: NYJ—Ken O'Brien 5; TB—Steve DeBerg 2. FG: NYJ—Pat Leahy 2.

OAKLAND RAIDERS
October 24, 2010, at Denver

Oakland	24	14	21	0	— 59
Denver	0	7	7	0	— 14

TD: Oak—Darren McFadden 4, Michael Bush, Chris Johnson, Zach Miller, Marcel Reese; Den—Knowshon Moreno 2. TD Passes: Oak—Jason Campbell 2; Den—Kyle Orton 2. FG: Oak—Sebastian Janikowski.

PITTSBURGH STEELERS
November 30, 1952, at Pittsburgh

New York Giants	0	0	7	0	— 7
Pittsburgh	14	14	7	28	— 63

TD: Pitt—Lynn Chandnois 2, Dick Hensley 2, Jack Butler, George Hays, Ray Mathews, Ed Modzelewski, Elbie Nickel; NYG—Bill Stribling. TD Passes: Pitt—Jim Finks 4, Gary Kerkorian; NYG—Tom Landry.

SAN DIEGO CHARGERS
December 22, 1963, at San Diego

Denver	7	10	3	0	— 20
San Diego	10	16	10	22	— 58

TD: SD—Paul Lowe 2, Chuck Allen, Bobby Jackson, Dave Kocourek, Keith Lincoln, Jacque MacKinnon; Den—Billy Joe, Donnie Stone. TD Passes: SD—John Hadl, Tobin Rote; Den—Don Breaux. FG: SD—George Blair 3; Den—Gene Mingo 2.

TENNESSEE TITANS
December 9, 1990, at Houston

Cleveland	0	7	7	0	— 14
Houston Oilers	14	31	7	6	— 58

TD: Hou—Lorenzo White 4, Ernest Givins, Leonard Harris, Tony Jones, Terry Kinard; Cle—Eric Metcalf 2. TD Passes: Hou—Warren Moon 2, Cody Carlson; Cle—Bernie Kosar. FG: Hou—Teddy Garcia.

ARIZONA CARDINALS
November 13, 1949, at New York

Chicago Cardinals	7	31	14	13	— 65
New York Bulldogs	7	0	6	7	— 20

TD: Chi—Red Cochran 2, Pat Harder 2, Bill Dewell, Mel Kutner, Bob Ravensburg, Vic Schwall, Charlie Trippi; NY—Joe Golding, Frank Muehlheuser, Johnny Rauch. TD Passes: Chi—Paul Christman 3, Jim Hardy 3; NY—Bobby Layne. FG: Chi—Pat Harder.

ATLANTA FALCONS
September 16, 1973, at New Orleans

Atlanta	0	24	21	17	— 62
New Orleans	0	0	7	0	— 7

TD: Atl—Ken Burrow 2, Eddie Ray 2, Wes Chesson, Tom Hayes, Art Malone, Joe Profit; NO—Bill Butler. TD Passes: Atl—Dick Shiner 3, Bob Lee; NO—Archie Manning. FG: Atl—Nick Mike-Mayer 2.

CAROLINA PANTHERS
December 8, 2002, at Carolina

Cincinnati	7	10	14	0	— 31
Carolina	9	7	21	15	— 52

TD: Car—Steve Smith 3, Dee Brown, Muhsin Muhammad, Al Wallace, Wesley Walls; Cin—Peter Warrick 2, Jon Kitna, Takeo Spikes. TD Passes: Car—Rodney Peete 3; Cin—Jon Kitna 2. FG: Cin—Neil Rackers.

CHICAGO BEARS
December 7, 1980, at Chicago

Green Bay	0	7	0	0	— 7
Chicago	0	28	13	20	— 61

TD: Chi—Walter Payton 3, Brian Baschnagel, Robin Earl, Roland Harper, Willie McClendon, Len Walterscheid, Rickey Watts; GB—James Lofton. TD Passes: Chi—Vince Evans 3; GB—Lynn Dickey.

DALLAS COWBOYS
October 12, 1980, at Dallas

San Francisco	0	7	0	7	— 14
Dallas	14	24	14	7	— 59

TD: Dall—Drew Pearson 3, Ron Springs 2, Tony Dorsett, Billy Joe DuPree, Robert Newhouse; SF—Dwight Clark 2. TD Passes: Dall—Danny White 4; SF—Steve DeBerg 2. FG: Dall—Rafael Septien.

DETROIT LIONS
November 27, 1997, at Detroit

Chicago	14	6	0	0	— 20
Detroit	3	14	17	21	— 55

TD: Det—Herman Moore, Johnnie Morton, Ron Rivers, Barry Sanders 3, Tracy Scroggins; Chi—Raymont Harris, Ricky Proehl. TD Passes: Det—Scott Mitchell 2; Chi—Erik Kramer. FG: Det—Jason Hanson 2; Chi—Jeff Jaeger 2.

GREEN BAY PACKERS
October 7, 1945, at Milwaukee

Detroit	0	7	7	7	— 21
Green Bay	0	41	9	7	— 57

TD: GB—Don Hutson 4, Charley Brock, Irv Comp, Ted Fritsch, Clyde Goodnight; Det—Chuck Fenenbock, John Greene, Bob Westfall. TD Passes: GB—Tex McKay 4, Lou Brock, Irv Comp; Det—Dave Ryan.

MINNESOTA VIKINGS
October 18, 1970, at Minnesota

Dallas	3	3	0	7	— 13
Minnesota	14	20	17	3	— 54

TD: Minn—Clint Jones 2, Ed Sharockman 2, John Beasley, Dave Osborn; Dall—Calvin Hill. TD Pass: Minn—Gary Cuozzo. FG: Minn—Fred Cox 4; Dall—Mike Clark 2.

NEW ORLEANS SAINTS
October 23, 2011, at New Orleans

Indianapolis	0	7	0	0	— 7
New Orleans	21	13	14	14	— 62

TD: NO—Marques Colston 2, Jimmy Graham 2, Darren Sproles 2, Jed Collins, Leigh Torrence; IND—Delone Carter. TD Passes: NO—Drew Brees 5. FG: NO—John Kasay 2.

NEW YORK GIANTS
November 26, 1972, at New York

Philadelphia	3	7	0	0	— 10
New York Giants	14	24	10	14	— 62

TD: NYG—Don Herrmann 2, Ron Johnson 2, Bob Tucker 2, Randy Johnson; Phil—Harold Jackson. TD Passes: NYG—Norm Snead 3, Randy Johnson 2; Phil—John Reaves. FG: NYG—Pete Gogolak 2; Phil—Tom Dempsey.

PHILADELPHIA EAGLES
November 6, 1934, at Philadelphia

Cincinnati Reds	0	0	0	0	— 0
Philadelphia	26	6	12	20	— 64

TD: Phil—Joe Carter 3, Swede Hanson 3, Marvin Ellstrom, Roger Kirkman, Ed Matesic, Ed Storm. TD Passes: Phil—Ed Matesic 2, Albert Weiner 2, Marvin Ellstrom.

ST. LOUIS RAMS
October 22, 1950, at Los Angeles

Baltimore	13	0	7	7	— 27
Los Angeles Rams	21	14	14	21	— 70

TD: LA—Bob Boyd 2, Vitamin T. Smith 2, Tom Fears, Elroy (Crazylegs) Hirsch, Dick Hoerner, Ralph Pasquariello, Dan Towler, Bob Waterfield; Balt—Chet Mutryn 2, Adrian Burk, Billy Stone. TD Passes: LA—Norm Van Brocklin 2, Bob Waterfield 2, Glenn Davis; Balt—Adrian Burk 3.

SAN FRANCISCO 49ERS
October 18, 1992, at San Francisco

Atlanta	7	3	0	7	— 17
San Francisco	21	21	14	0	— 56

TD: SF—Jerry Rice 3, Ricky Watters 3, Brent Jones, Tom Rathman; Atl—Michael Haynes, Jason Phillips. TD Passes: SF—Steve Young 3; Atl—Chris Miller, Wade Wilson. FG: Atl—Norm Johnson.

SEATTLE SEAHAWKS
December 9, 2012, at Seattle

Arizona	0	0	0	0	— 0
Seattle	10	28	13	7	— 58

TD: Sea—Marshawn Lynch 3, Zach Miller, Richard Sherman, Malcolm Smith, Leon Washington. TD Passes: Sea—Russell Wilson. FG: Sea—Steven Hauschka 3.

TAMPA BAY BUCCANEERS
December 23, 2001, at Tampa Bay

New Orleans	0	0	7	14	— 21
Tampa Bay	17	13	3	15	— 48

TD: TB—Mike Alstott, Ronde Barber, Warrick Dunn, Dave Moore, Karl Williams; NO—Joe Horn 2, Eddie Williams. TD Passes: TB—Brad Johnson 3; NO—Aaron Brooks 3. FG: TB—Martin Gramatica 4.

WASHINGTON REDSKINS
November 27, 1966, at Washington

New York Giants	0	14	14	13	— 41
Washington	13	21	14	24	— 72

TD: Wash—A.D. Whitfield 3, Brig Owens 2, Charley Taylor 2, Rickie Harris, Joe Don Looney, Bobby Mitchell; NYG—Allen Jacobs, Homer Jones, Dan Lewis, Joe Morrison, Aaron Thomas, Gary Wood. TD Passes: Wash—Sonny Jurgensen 3; NYG—Gary Wood 2, Tom Kennedy. FG: Wash—Charlie Gogolak.

RECORDS OF NFL TEAMS SINCE 1970 AFL-NFL MERGER

AFC	W	L	T	Pct.	Division Titles	Playoff Berths	Postseason Record	Super Bowl Record
Pittsburgh	404	258	2	.610	20	26	33-20	6-2
Miami	392	270	2	.592	13	22	20-20	2-3
Denver	380	278	6	.577	12	19	18-17	2-4
Baltimore***	150	121	1	.553	4	9	14-7	2-0
New England	363	301	2	.547	14	19	23-16	3-4
Oakland	353	305	6	.536	12	18	22-15	3-1
Indianapolis	331	331	2	.500	13	20	15-18	2-1
Tennessee	322	340	2	.486	5	16	12-16	0-1
Jacksonville**	140	148	0	.486	2	6	5-6	0-0
Kansas City	317	340	7	.483	6	12	3-12	0-0
San Diego	313	346	5	.475	10	12	9-12	0-1
Buffalo	305	357	2	.461	7	13	12-13	0-4
Cincinnati	298	365	1	.450	7	11	5-11	0-2
New York Jets	296	366	2	.447	2	12	10-12	0-0
Houston****	77	99	0	.438	2	2	2-2	0-0
Cleveland+	267	346	3	.436	6	11	4-11	0-0

NFC	W	L	T	Pct.	Division Titles	Playoff Berths	Postseason Record	Super Bowl Record
Dallas	389	275	0	.586	17	26	32-21	5-3
San Francisco	375	285	4	.568	19	23	28-18	5-1
Minnesota	374	288	2	.565	16	25	17-25	0-3
Washington	358	304	2	.541	7	17	20-14	3-2
Green Bay	346	310	8	.527	10	17	18-15	2-1
Philadelphia	337	319	8	.514	8	19	15-19	0-2
Chicago	335	328	1	.505	10	14	10-13	1-1
New York Giants	330	331	3	.499	8	15	20-11	4-1
St. Louis	329	330	5	.499	11	19	16-18	1-2
Seattle*	280	300	0	.483	7	12	9-12	0-1
Carolina**	132	156	0	.458	3	4	6-4	0-1
Atlanta	300	359	5	.455	5	12	7-12	0-1
New Orleans	294	366	4	.446	5	9	6-8	1-0
Arizona	269	389	6	.409	4	6	5-6	0-1
Detroit	268	392	4	.406	3	10	1-10	0-0
Tampa Bay*	229	350	1	.396	6	10	6-9	1-0

Entered NFL in 1976.
**Entered NFL in 1995.*
***Entered NFL in 1996.*
****Entered NFL in 2002.*
+Did not play, 1996-98.*
Oakland totals include L.A. Raiders, 1982-1994.
Tennessee totals include Houston, 1970-1996.
Indianapolis totals include Baltimore, 1970-1983.
St. Louis totals include L.A. Rams, 1970-1994.
Arizona totals include St. Louis, 1970-1987, and Phoenix, 1988-1993.
Tie games before 1972 are not calculated in won-lost percentage.

HOME RECORDS OF NFL TEAMS SINCE 1970 AFL-NFL MERGER

AFC	W	L	T	Pct.
Pittsburgh	239	92	1	.721
Baltimore***	94	41	1	.695
Denver	228	101	4	.692
Miami	223	107	1	.675
New England	207	125	0	.623
Oakland	195	135	2	.591
Jacksonville**	84	60	0	.583
Kansas City	191	137	3	.582
Tennessee	184	147	1	.556
San Diego	179	150	2	.544
Cincinnati	180	151	1	.544
Buffalo	180	152	1	.542
Indianapolis	178	152	2	.539
Houston****	45	43	0	.511
Cleveland+	150	155	2	.492
New York Jets	159	171	1	.482

NFC	W	L	T	Pct.
Minnesota	222	110	1	.668
Dallas	221	111	0	.666
Green Bay	207	120	5	.631
San Francisco	206	123	3	.625
Washington	201	128	2	.611
Chicago	197	134	1	.595
Seattle*	170	121	0	.584
Philadelphia	185	145	3	.560
St. Louis	182	148	2	.552
New York Giants	180	152	1	.542
Atlanta	179	153	1	.539
Detroit	173	158	1	.523
Carolina**	72	72	0	.500
Arizona	163	165	3	.497
Tampa Bay*	139	150	1	.481
New Orleans	157	174	1	.474

Entered NFL in 1976.
**Entered NFL in 1995.*
***Entered NFL in 1996.*
****Entered NFL in 2002.*
+Did not play, 1996-98.*
Oakland totals include L.A. Raiders, 1982-1994.
Tennessee totals include Houston, 1970-1996.
Indianapolis totals include Baltimore, 1970-1983.
St. Louis totals include L.A. Rams, 1970-1994.
Arizona totals include St. Louis, 1970-1987, and Phoenix, 1988-1993.
Tie games before 1972 are not calculated in won-lost percentage.

ROAD RECORDS OF NFL TEAMS SINCE 1970 AFL-NFL MERGER

AFC	W	L	T	Pct.
Miami	169	163	1	.509
Pittsburgh	165	166	1	.498
Oakland	158	170	4	.482
New England	156	176	0	.470
Denver	152	177	2	.462
Indianapolis	153	179	0	.461
Tennessee	138	193	1	.417
New York Jets	137	195	1	.413
Baltimore***	56	80	0	.412
San Diego	134	196	3	.407
Jacksonville**	56	88	0	.389
Kansas City	126	203	4	.384
Cleveland+	117	191	1	.380
Buffalo	125	205	1	.379
Houston****	32	56	0	.364
Cincinnati	118	214	0	.355

NFC	W	L	T	Pct.
San Francisco	169	162	1	.511
Dallas	168	164	0	.506
Washington	157	176	0	.471
Philadelphia	152	174	5	.467
Minnesota	152	178	1	.461
New York Giants	150	179	2	.456
St. Louis	147	182	3	.447
Green Bay	139	190	3	.423
New Orleans	137	192	3	.417
Carolina**	60	84	0	.417
Chicago	138	194	0	.416
Seattle*	110	179	0	.381
Atlanta	121	206	4	.370
Arizona	106	224	3	.322
Tampa Bay*	90	200	0	.310
Detroit	95	234	3	.290

*Entered NFL in 1976.
**Entered NFL in 1995.
***Entered NFL in 1996.
****Entered NFL in 2002.
+Did not play, 1996-98.
Oakland totals include L.A. Raiders, 1982-1994.
Tennessee totals include Houston, 1970-1996.
Indianapolis totals include Baltimore, 1970-1983.
St. Louis totals include L.A. Rams, 1970-1994.
Arizona totals include St. Louis, 1970-1987, and Phoenix, 1988-1993.
Tie games before 1972 are not calculated in won-lost percentage.

RECORDS OF TEAMS ON KICKOFF WEEKEND

AFC	W	L	T	Pct.	Longest W Strk.	Longest L Strk.	Current Streak
Denver	33	19	1	.635	4	4	W-1
Jacksonville	11	7	0	.611	6	3	L-1
San Diego	31	22	0	.585	6	6	W-2
New England	29	24	0	.547	9	3	W-9
Houston	6	5	0	.545	3	3	W-3
Pittsburgh	40	34	4	.541	8	3	L-2
Baltimore	9	8	0	.529	5	4	W-5
Miami	24	22	1	.522	11	5	L-2
Kansas City	27	26	0	.509	7	4	L-2
Tennessee	27	26	0	.509	4	3	L-2
Indianapolis	34	34	1	.500	8	8	L-3
Oakland	25	28	0	.472	5	8	L-1
New York Jets	24	29	0	.453	3	5	W-2
Cleveland	27	33	0	.450	5	8	L-8
Cincinnati	20	25	0	.444	4	4	L-1
Buffalo	21	32	0	.396	6	5	L-1

NFC	W	L	T	Pct.	Longest W Strk.	Longest L Strk.	Current Streak
Dallas	35	17	1	.673	17	5	W-1
Chicago	53	35	5	.602	9	6	W-3
New York Giants	49	34	5	.590	4	3	L-2
Green Bay	52	37	3	.584	5	6	L-1
Minnesota	29	22	1	.569	5	3	W-1
Detroit	44	37	2	.543	10	4	W-2
San Francisco	33	29	1	.532	5	3	W-2
Atlanta	25	22	0	.532	5	3	W-1
Washington	40	37	4	.519	6	5	W-3
St. Louis	38	37	0	.507	5	6	L-6
Philadelphia	33	45	1	.423	5	9	W-2
Arizona	38	52	2	.422	6	7	W-3
Tampa Bay	15	22	0	.405	3	5	W-1
Seattle	13	24	0	.351	3	8	L-2
New Orleans	16	30	0	.348	3	6	L-2
Carolina	6	12	0	.333	3	4	L-4

Kansas City totals include Dallas Texans, 1960-62.
Oakland totals include L.A. Raiders, 1982-1994.
San Diego totals include L.A. Chargers, 1960.
Indianapolis totals include Baltimore, 1953-1983.
Tennessee total include Houston, 1960-1996.
New England totals include Boston, 1960-1970.
St. Louis totals include Cleveland, 1937-1942 and 1944-45, and L.A. Rams, 1946-1994.
Detroit totals include Portsmouth, 1930-33.
Arizona totals include Chi. Cardinals, 1920-1959, St. Louis, 1960-1987, and Phoenix, 1988-1993.
Chicago totals include Decatur, 1920.
Washington totals include Boston Braves, 1932 and Boston Redskins, 1933-36.
NOTE: All tied games occurred prior to 1972, when calculation of ties in percentage as half-win.

RECORDS OF NFL TEAMS, 2003-2012

AFC	W	L	T	Pct.	Division Titles	Playoff Berths	Postseason Record	Super Bowl Record
New England	126	34	0	.788	9	9	14-7	2-2
Indianapolis	112	48	0	.700	7	9	9-8	1-1
Pittsburgh	103	57	0	.644	4	6	10-4	2-1
Baltimore	97	63	0	.606	4	7	9-6	1-0
San Diego	95	65	0	.594	5	5	3-5	0-0
Denver	90	70	0	.563	3	5	2-5	0-0
Tennessee	81	79	0	.506	1	3	1-3	0-0
Cincinnati	79	80	1	.497	2	4	0-4	0-0
New York Jets	77	83	0	.481	0	4	5-4	0-0
Houston	73	87	0	.456	2	2	2-2	0-0
Jacksonville	72	88	0	.450	0	2	1-2	0-0
Kansas City	68	92	0	.425	2	3	0-3	0-0
Miami	68	92	0	.425	1	1	0-1	0-0
Buffalo	63	97	0	.394	0	0	0-0	0-0
Cleveland	52	108	0	.325	0	0	0-0	0-0
Oakland	49	111	0	.306	0	0	0-0	0-0

NFC	W	L	T	Pct.	Division Titles	Playoff Berths	Postseason Record	Super Bowl Record
Green Bay	98	62	0	.613	5	7	7-6	1-0
Philadelphia	91	68	1	.572	4	6	6-6	0-1
Atlanta	91	69	0	.569	3	5	2-5	0-0
Dallas	89	71	0	.556	2	4	1-4	0-0
Chicago	88	72	0	.550	3	3	3-3	0-1
New Orleans	88	72	0	.550	3	4	5-3	1-0
New York Giants	87	73	0	.544	3	5	8-3	2-0
Seattle	85	75	0	.531	5	7	6-7	0-1
Minnesota	81	79	0	.506	2	4	2-4	0-0
Carolina	79	81	0	.494	2	3	5-3	0-1
San Francisco	70	89	1	.441	2	2	3-2	0-1
Tampa Bay	69	91	0	.431	2	2	0-2	0-0
Washington	68	92	0	.425	1	3	1-3	0-0
Arizona	65	95	0	.406	2	2	4-2	0-1
St. Louis	56	103	1	.353	1	2	1-2	0-0
Detroit	48	112	0	.300	0	1	0-1	0-0

HOME RECORDS, 2003-2012

AFC	W - L - T	Pct.
New England	68-12-0	.850
Baltimore	63-17-0	.788
Indianapolis	61-19-0	.763
Pittsburgh	58-22-0	.725
San Diego	53-27-0	.663
Denver	50-30-0	.625
Tennessee	45-35-0	.563
Cincinnati	44-35-1	.556
Jacksonville	44-36-0	.550
New York Jets	44-36-0	.550
Houston	43-37-0	.538
Kansas City	40-40-0	.500
Buffalo	38-42-0	.475
Miami	36-44-0	.450
Cleveland	32-48-0	.400
Oakland	28-52-0	.350

NFC	W - L - T	Pct.
Seattle	56-24-0	.700
Green Bay	54-26-0	.675
Atlanta	52-28-0	.650
Chicago	51-29-0	.638
Minnesota	51-29-0	.638
Dallas	48-32-0	.600
San Francisco	45-34-1	.569
Arizona	45-35-0	.563
New Orleans	45-35-0	.563
Philadelphia	45-35-0	.563
New York Giants	43-37-0	.538
Carolina	41-39-0	.513
Tampa Bay	39-41-0	.488
Washington	36-44-0	.450
St. Louis	33-47-0	.413
Detroit	31-49-0	.388

ROAD RECORDS, 2003-2012

AFC	W-L-T	Pct.
New England	58-22-0	.725
Indianapolis	51-29-0	.638
Pittsburgh	45-35-0	.563
San Diego	42-38-0	.525
Denver	40-40-0	.500
Tennessee	36-44-0	.450
Cincinnati	35-45-0	.438
Baltimore	34-46-0	.425
New York Jets	33-47-0	.413
Miami	32-48-0	.400
Houston	30-50-0	.375
Jacksonville	28-52-0	.350
Kansas City	28-52-0	.350
Buffalo	25-55-0	.313
Oakland	21-59-0	.263
Cleveland	20-60-0	.250

NFC	W-L-T	Pct.
Philadelphia	46-33-1	.581
Green Bay	44-36-0	.550
New York Giants	44-36-0	.550
New Orleans	43-37-0	.538
Dallas	41-39-0	.513
Atlanta	39-41-0	.488
Carolina	38-42-0	.475
Chicago	37-43-0	.463
Washington	32-48-0	.400
Minnesota	30-50-0	.375
Tampa Bay	30-50-0	.375
Seattle	29-51-0	.363
San Francisco	25-55-0	.313
St. Louis	23-56-1	.294
Arizona	20-60-0	.250
Detroit	17-63-0	.213

RECORDS BY MONTHS, 2003-2012

AFC	Sept. W-L-T	Oct. W-L-T	Nov. W-L-T	Dec. W-L-T	Total W-L-T	Pct.
New England	21-10-0	35-7-0	28-11-0	42-6-0	126- 34-0	.788
Indianapolis	23-9-0	25-12-0	31-12-0	33-15-0	112- 48-0	.700
Pittsburgh	20-13-0	25-13-0	25-16-0	33-15-0	103- 57-0	.644
Baltimore	21-11-0	20-17-0	28-16-0	28-19-0	97- 63-0	.606
San Diego	15-18-0	20-20-0	23-16-0	37-11-0	95- 65-0	.594
Denver	22-12-0	20-19-0	24-15-0	24-24-0	90- 70-0	.563
Tennessee	16-17-0	21-20-0	20-17-0	24-25-0	81- 79-0	.506
Cincinnati	17-16-0	15-24-0	23-17-1	24-23-0	79- 80-1	.497
New York Jets	17-16-0	17-22-0	20-19-0	23-26-0	77- 83-0	.481
Houston	14-18-0	20-19-0	17-23-0	22-27-0	73- 87-0	.456
Jacksonville	15-18-0	17-22-0	20-19-0	20-29-0	72- 88-0	.450
Kansas City	13-20-0	22-16-0	14-27-0	19-29-0	68- 92-0	.425
Miami	9-23-0	14-24-0	22-20-0	23-25-0	68- 92-0	.425
Buffalo	15-18-0	15-24-0	15-25-0	18-30-0	63- 97-0	.394
Cleveland	8-26-0	17-21-0	12-28-0	15-33-0	52-108-0	.325
Oakland	12-21-0	14-25-0	11-29-0	12-36-0	49-111-0	.306

December totals include January.

NFC	Sept. W-L-T	Oct. W-L-T	Nov. W-L-T	Dec. W-L-T	Total W-L-T	Pct.
Green Bay	19-15-0	23-15-0	24-17-0	32-15-0	98- 62-0	.613
Philadelphia	19-14-0	21-16-0	21-20-1	30-18-0	91- 68-1	.572
Atlanta	20-14-0	22-14-0	25-18-0	24-23-0	91- 69-0	.569
Dallas	21-10-0	18-22-0	29-13-0	21-26-0	89- 71-0	.556
Chicago	16-16-0	23-15-0	25-17-0	24-24-0	88- 72-0	.550
New Orleans	16-17-0	22-19-0	25-14-0	25-22-0	88- 72-0	.550
New York Giants	20-12-0	31-9-0	15-25-0	21-27-0	87- 73-0	.544
Seattle	21-11-0	15-23-0	22-20-0	27-21-0	85- 75-0	.531
Minnesota	18-16-0	19-19-0	22-18-0	22-26-0	81- 79-0	.506
Carolina	13-19-0	19-21-0	18-22-0	29-19-0	79- 81-0	.494
San Francisco	14-20-0	15-24-0	17-21-1	24-24-0	70- 89-1	.441
Tampa Bay	16-17-0	18-21-0	19-21-0	16-32-0	69- 91-0	.431
Washington	18-14-0	15-26-0	12-27-0	23-25-0	68- 92-0	.425
Arizona	14-20-0	12-25-0	16-25-0	23-25-0	65- 95-0	.406
St. Louis	10-24-0	17-23-0	13-24-1	16-32-0	56-103-1	.353
Detroit	12-20-0	14-24-0	9-33-0	13-35-0	48-112-0	.300

December totals include January.

TAKEAWAYS/GIVEAWAYS, 2003-2012

AFC	Takeaways			Giveaways			Net.Diff.
	Int.	Fum.	Total	Int.	Fum.	Total	
New England	200	124	324	113	90	203	+121
Indianapolis	150	115	265	134	82	216	+ 49
Baltimore	196	112	308	137	126	263	+ 45
Cincinnati	174	123	297	162	99	261	+ 36
San Diego	168	102	270	137	99	236	+ 34
Tennessee	174	102	276	147	118	265	+ 11
Jacksonville	160	88	248	132	111	243	+ 5
Pittsburgh	153	109	262	148	109	257	+ 5
Kansas City	152	108	260	150	107	257	+ 3
New York Jets	155	117	272	170	103	273	- 1
Houston	136	102	238	150	104	254	- 16
Denver	130	109	239	145	118	263	- 24
Buffalo	163	107	270	175	127	302	- 32
Miami	143	103	246	169	115	284	- 38
Cleveland	158	96	254	188	117	305	- 51
Oakland	129	95	224	178	127	305	- 81

NFC	Takeaways			Giveaways			Net.Diff.
	Int.	Fum.	Total	Int.	Fum.	Total	
Atlanta	164	119	283	144	92	236	+ 47
Green Bay	206	84	290	153	99	252	+ 38
Carolina	169	127	296	163	108	271	+ 25
Chicago	196	134	330	192	117	309	+ 21
Seattle	161	116	277	157	104	261	+ 16
N.Y. Giants	160	131	291	168	112	280	+ 11
Minnesota	155	124	279	154	118	272	+ 7
Tampa Bay	172	110	282	169	115	284	- 2
San Francisco	156	113	269	151	123	274	- 5
Philadelphia	163	104	267	148	130	278	- 11
Washington	143	91	234	138	116	254	- 20
New Orleans	135	114	249	164	114	278	- 29
Detroit	136	135	271	199	105	304	- 33
Dallas	139	108	247	180	103	283	- 36
St. Louis	141	117	258	184	116	300	- 42
Arizona	160	122	282	198	137	335	- 53

BEST TAKEAWAY/GIVEAWAY DIFFERENTIAL, SEASON

+43	Washington, 1983
+28	New England, 2010
	San Francisco, 2011
+26	Kansas City, 1990

HIGH AND LOW SINGLE-GAME YARDAGE TOTALS, 2003-2012

Most Total Yards, Game
- 653 Houston vs. Jacksonville, Nov. 18, 2012 (ot)
- 622 New England at Miami, Sept. 12, 2011
- 621 San Francisco vs. Buffalo, Oct. 7, 2012
- 619 New England vs. Tennessee, Oct. 18, 2009
- 617 New Orleans vs. Carolina, Jan. 1, 2012

Fewest Total Yards, Game
- 26 Cleveland at Buffalo, Dec. 12, 2004
- 67 Kansas City at San Diego, Dec. 12, 2010
- 72 Cincinnati at New York Jets, Jan. 3, 2010
- 77 Oakland vs. Atlanta, Nov. 2, 2008
- 86 Tampa Bay vs. New York Giants, Sept. 27, 2009

Most Yards Rushing, Game
- 378 Minnesota vs. San Diego, Nov. 4, 2007
- 375 Jacksonville vs. Indianapolis, Dec. 10, 2006
- 352 Kansas City vs. Indianapolis, Dec. 23, 2012
- 351 Cleveland at Kansas City, Dec. 20, 2009
- 343 Baltimore vs. Cleveland, Sept. 14, 2003

Fewest Yards Rushing, Game
- -18 Detroit at Arizona, Nov. 11, 2007
- -3 Detroit vs. Minnesota, Dec. 10, 2006
- 1 Dallas at Washington, Dec. 30, 2007
- 4 Seattle at Minnesota, Nov. 22, 2009
- 5 New England at Pittsburgh, Oct. 31, 2004

Most Yards Passing, Game
- 516 New England at Miami, Sept. 12, 2011
- 510 New York Giants vs. Tampa Bay, Sept. 16, 2012
- 504 New Orleans vs. Cincinnati, Nov. 19, 2006
- 504 Houston vs. Jacksonville, Nov. 18, 2012 (ot)
- 502 Detroit at Green Bay, Jan. 1, 2012

Fewest Yards Passing, Game
- -7 Tennessee at New England, Oct. 18, 2009
- -5 Houston at Oakland, Dec. 3, 2006
- -3 Cleveland at Buffalo, Dec. 12, 2004
- 0 Oakland at San Diego, Dec. 28, 2003
- Cincinnati at New York Jets, Jan. 3, 2010

NFL INDIVIDUAL LEADERS, 2003-2012

Points
David Akers	1,240
Adam Vinatieri	1,062
Jay Feely	1,057
Sebastian Janikowski	1,038
Shayne Graham	1,018

Passing Yards
Drew Brees	42,414
Peyton Manning	38,869
Tom Brady	38,193
Eli Manning	31,527
Ben Roethlisberger	29,844

Touchdowns
LaDainian Tomlinson	137
Randy Moss	96
Antonio Gates	83
Terrell Owens	82
Adrian Peterson	80

TD Passes
Drew Brees	306
Peyton Manning	298
Tom Brady	288
Eli Manning	211
Brett Favre	194

Field Goals
David Akers	279
Sebastian Janikowski	253
Phil Dawson	239
Jay Feely	238
Jason Hanson	233

Receptions
Reggie Wayne	892
Tony Gonzalez	845
Andre Johnson	818
Jason Witten	806
Anquan Boldin	772

Rushes
LaDainian Tomlinson	2,463
Steven Jackson	2,395
Thomas Jones	2,316
Willis McGahee	1,957
Clinton Portis	1,957

Reception Yards
Reggie Wayne	12,002
Andre Johnson	11,254
Steve Smith	10,426
Larry Fitzgerald	10,413
Anquan Boldin	10,165

Rushing Yards
LaDainian Tomlinson	10,765
Steven Jackson	10,135
Thomas Jones	9,327
Adrian Peterson	8,849
Frank Gore	8,839

Receiving TDs
Randy Moss	96
Antonio Gates	83
Terrell Owens	81
Larry Fitzgerald	77
Reggie Wayne	74

Rushing TDs
LaDainian Tomlinson	121
Adrian Peterson	76
Shaun Alexander	68
Michael Turner	66
Two tied	63

Interceptions
Ed Reed	56
Asante Samuel	50
Charles Woodson	43
DeAngelo Hall	39
Two tied	36

Pass Attempts
Drew Brees	5,596
Peyton Manning	4,976
Tom Brady	4,941
Eli Manning	4,457
Matt Hasselbeck	4,249

Sacks
Jared Allen	117.0
DeMarcus Ware	111.0
Julius Peppers	99.5
John Abraham	94.5
Dwight Freeney	94.5

Completions
Drew Brees	3,700
Peyton Manning	3,333
Tom Brady	3,160
Brett Favre	2,648
Eli Manning	2,612

NFL GAMES IN WHICH A TEAM HAS SCORED 60 OR MORE POINTS

(Home team in CAPITALS)

Regular Season

WASHINGTON 72, New York Giants 41	November 27, 1966
LOS ANGELES RAMS 70, Baltimore 27	October 22, 1950
Chicago Cardinals 65, NEW YORK BULLDOGS 20	November 13, 1949
LOS ANGELES RAMS 65, Detroit 24	October 29, 1950
PHILADELPHIA 64, Cincinnati 0	November 6, 1934
CHICAGO CARDINALS 63, New York Giants 35	October 17, 1948
PITTSBURGH 63, New York Giants 7	November 30, 1952
AKRON 62, Oorang 0	October 29, 1922
CLEVELAND 62, New York Giants 14	December 6, 1953
CLEVELAND 62, Washington 3	November 7, 1954
NEW YORK GIANTS 62, Philadelphia 10	November 26, 1972
Atlanta 62, NEW ORLEANS 7	September 16, 1973
NEW YORK JETS 62, Tampa Bay 28	November 17, 1985
NEW ORLEANS 62, Indianapolis 7	October 23, 2011
CHICAGO 61, San Francisco 20	December 12, 1965
Cincinnati 61, HOUSTON 17	December 17, 1972
CHICAGO 61, Green Bay 7	December 7, 1980
CINCINNATI 61, Houston 7	December 17, 1989
ROCK ISLAND 60, Evansville 0	October 15, 1922
CHICAGO CARDINALS 60, Rochester 0	October 7, 1923

Postseason

Chicago Bears 73, WASHINGTON 0	December 8, 1940
JACKSONVILLE 62, Miami 7	January 15, 2000

YOUNGEST AND OLDEST PLAYERS IN NFL IN 2012

10 Youngest Players

	Birthdate	Games	Starts	Position
Ronnie Hillman, Denver	9/14/1991	14	0	RB
Trent Richardson, Cleveland	7/10/1991	15	15	RB
David Wilson, N.Y. Giants	6/15/1991	16	2	RB
Bryce Brown, Philadelphia	5/14/1991	16	4	RB
Rueben Randle, N.Y. Giants	5/7/1991	16	1	WR
Stephen Hill, N.Y. Jets	4/25/1991	11	8	WR
Lamar Miller, Miami	4/25/1991	13	1	RB
Luke Kuechly, Carolina	4/20/1991	16	16	LB
Josh Gordon, Cleveland	4/13/1991	16	13	WR
Orson Charles, Cincinnati	1/27/1991	16	6	TE

10 Oldest Players

	Birthdate	Games	Starts	Position
Jason Hanson, Detroit	6/17/1970	16	0	K
Adam Vinatieri, Indianapolis	12/28/1972	16	0	K
Olindo Mare, Chicago	6/6/1973	3	0	K
Ben Graham, Detroit	11/2/1973	3	0	P
Sav Rocca, Washington	11/20/1973	16	0	P
Charlie Batch, Pittsburgh	12/5/1974	2	2	QB
David Akers, San Francisco	12/9/1974	16	0	K
Phil Dawson, Cleveland	1/23/1975	16	0	K
Donald Driver, Green Bay	2/2/1975	13	1	WR
Ronde Barber, Tampa Bay	4/7/1975	16	16	S

YOUNGEST AND OLDEST REGULAR STARTERS BY POSITION IN 2012

Minimum: 8 Games Started

	Youngest			Oldest	
QB	2/12/90	Robert Griffin III, Was.	3/24/76	Peyton Manning, Den.
RB	7/10/91	Trent Richardson, Cle.	2/20/81	Fred Jackson, Buff.
WR	4/25/91	Stephen Hill, NYJ	6/23/76	Brandon Stokley, Den.
TE	2/24/90	Dwayne Allen, Ind.	2/27/76	Tony Gonzalez, Atl.
T	12/12/90	Tyron Smith, Dall.	9/21/77	Jeff Backus, Det.
G	3/8/90	Kevin Zeitler, Cin.	8/11/77	Cooper Carlisle, Oak.
C	7/24/89	Maurkice Pouncey, Pitt.	6/18/75	Jeff Saturday, G.B.
		Mike Pouncey, Mia.		
DE	5/18/90	Robert Quinn, Robert, StL	5/6/78	John Abraham, Atl.
DT	12/21/90	Michael Brockers, StL	9/3/77	Casey Hampton, Pitt.
LB	4/20/91	Luke Kuechly, Car.	5/19/75	London Fletcher, Was.
CB	9/19/90	Stephon Gilmore, Buf.	6/24/77	Antoine Winfield, Min.
S	2/11/90	Rahim Moore, Den.	4/7/75	Ronde Barber, T.B.

OLDEST INDIVIDUAL SINGLE-SEASON OR SINGLE-GAME RECORDS IN NFL RECORD & FACT BOOK

Most Points, Game—40, Ernie Nevers, Chi. Cardinals vs. Chi. Bears, Nov. 28, 1929 (6-td, 4-pat)

Most Touchdowns Rushing, Game—6, Ernie Nevers, Chi. Cardinals vs. Chi. Bears, Nov. 28, 1929

Highest Rushing Average Gain, Season (Qualifiers)—8.44, Beattie Feathers, Chi. Bears, 1934 (119-1,004)

Highest Punting Average, Season (Qualifiers)—51.40, Sammy Baugh, Washington, 1940 (35-1,799)

Highest Punting Average, Rookie, Season (Qualifiers)—45.92, Frank Sinkwich, Detroit, 1943 (12-551)

Highest Punting Average, Game (minimum: 4 punts)—61.75, Bob Cifers, Detroit vs. Chi. Bears, Nov. 24, 1946 (4-247)

Highest Average Gain, Pass Receptions, Season (minimum: 24 receptions)—32.58, Don Currivan, Boston, 1947 (24-782)

Highest Average Gain, Passing, Game (minimum: 20 passes)—18.58, Sammy Baugh, Washington vs. Boston, Oct. 31, 1948 (24-446)

Most Touchdowns, Fumble Recoveries, Game—2, Fred (Dippy) Evans, Chi. Bears vs. Washington, Nov. 28, 1948

Most Yards Gained, Intercepted Passes, Rookie, Season—301, Don Doll, Detroit, 1949

Most Passes Had Intercepted, Game—8, Jim Hardy, Chi. Cardinals vs. Philadelphia, Sept. 24, 1950

Highest Kickoff Return Average, Game (minimum: 3 returns)—73.50, Wally Triplett, Detroit vs. Los Angeles, Oct. 29, 1950 (4-294)

Highest Punt Return Average, Season (Qualifiers)—23.00, Herb Rich, Baltimore, 1950 (12-276)

Highest Punt Return Average, Rookie, Season (Qualifiers)—23.00, Herb Rich, Baltimore, 1950 (12-276)

Most Yards Passing, Game—554, Norm Van Brocklin, Los Angeles vs. New York Yanks, Sept. 28, 1951

Most Touchdowns, Punt Returns, Rookie, Season—4, Jack Christiansen, Detroit, 1951

Most Interceptions By, Season—14, Dick (Night Train) Lane, Los Angeles, 1952

Most Interceptions By, Rookie, Season—14, Dick (Night Train) Lane, Los Angeles, 1952

Highest Average Gain, Passing, Season (Qualifiers)—11.17, Tommy O'Connell, Cleveland, 1957 (110-1,229)

Most Yards Gained, Pass Receptions, Rookie, Season—1,473, Bill Groman, Houston, 1960

NFL INDIVIDUAL LEADERS OVER RECENT SEASONS

Last 2 Seasons		Last 3 Seasons		Last 4 Seasons	
Points					
297	David Akers	440	David Akers	579	David Akers
296	Stephen Gostkowski	397	Matt Bryant	494	Mason Crosby
269	Matt Bryant	389	Sebastian Janikowski	484	Sebastian Janikowski
260	Jason Hanson	365	Mason Crosby	477	Stephen Gostkowski
259	Dan Bailey	352	Stephen Gostkowski	471	Lawrence Tynes
Touchdowns					
29	Arian Foster	47	Arian Foster	57	Adrian Peterson
29	Rob Gronkowski	39	Rob Gronkowski	50	Arian Foster
26	Adrian Peterson	39	Adrian Peterson	44	Michael Turner
25	Three tied	34	LeSean McCoy	39	Rob Gronkowski
		34	Michael Turner	39	Ray Rice
Field Goals					
73	David Akers	105	David Akers	137	David Akers
62	Sebastian Janikowski	95	Sebastian Janikowski	121	Sebastian Janikowski
61	Dan Bailey	88	Matt Bryant	106	Dan Carpenter
60	Matt Bryant	81	Dan Carpenter	105	Rob Bironas
57	Stephen Gostkowski	78	Rob Bironas	98	Three tied
Rushes					
629	Arian Foster	956	Arian Foster	1,212	Chris Johnson
600	Marshawn Lynch	857	Michael Turner	1,171	Steven Jackson
556	Adrian Peterson	855	Ray Rice	1,153	Adrian Peterson
548	Ray Rice	854	Chris Johnson	1,109	Ray Rice
540	Frank Gore	847	Steven Jackson	1,040	Maurice Jones-Drew
Rushing Yards					
3,067	Adrian Peterson	4,365	Adrian Peterson	5,748	Adrian Peterson
2,794	Marshawn Lynch	4,264	Arian Foster	5,660	Chris Johnson
2,648	Arian Foster	3,727	Ray Rice	5,066	Ray Rice
2,507	Ray Rice	3,654	Chris Johnson	4,844	Steven Jackson
2,425	Frank Gore	3,531	Marshawn Lynch	4,735	Maurice Jones-Drew
Rushing Touchdowns					
25	Arian Foster	41	Arian Foster	54	Adrian Peterson
24	Adrian Peterson	36	Adrian Peterson	44	Arian Foster
23	Marshawn Lynch	33	Michael Turner	43	Michael Turner
22	Cam Newton	30	BenJarvus Green-Ellis	35	Chris Johnson
21	Two tied	29	Marshawn Lynch	33	Ray Rice
Passes					
1,390	Matthew Stafford	1,905	Drew Brees	2,499	Drew Brees
1,327	Drew Brees	1,752	Matt Ryan	2,305	Tom Brady
1,248	Tom Brady	1,740	Tom Brady	2,203	Matt Ryan
1,181	Matt Ryan	1,664	Eli Manning	2,173	Eli Manning
1,170	Tony Romo	1,650	Philip Rivers	2,136	Philip Rivers
Completions					
890	Drew Brees	1,338	Drew Brees	1,701	Drew Brees
856	Matthew Stafford	1,126	Tom Brady	1,497	Tom Brady
802	Tom Brady	1,126	Matt Ryan	1,389	Matt Ryan
771	Tony Romo	1,061	Philip Rivers	1,378	Philip Rivers
769	Matt Ryan	1,026	Aaron Rodgers	1,376	Aaron Rodgers
Passing Yards					
10,653	Drew Brees	15,273	Drew Brees	19,661	Drew Brees
10,062	Tom Brady	13,962	Tom Brady	18,360	Tom Brady
10,005	Matthew Stafford	12,940	Philip Rivers	17,294	Aaron Rodgers
9,087	Tony Romo	12,883	Eli Manning	17,194	Philip Rivers
8,938	Aaron Rodgers	12,860	Aaron Rodgers	16,904	Eli Manning

Last 2 Seasons		Last 3 Seasons		Last 4 Seasons	

Touchdown Passes

89	Drew Brees	122	Drew Brees	156	Drew Brees
84	Aaron Rodgers	112	Aaron Rodgers	142	Aaron Rodgers
73	Tom Brady	109	Tom Brady	137	Tom Brady
61	Matt Ryan	89	Matt Ryan	113	Eli Manning
61	Matthew Stafford	86	Eli Manning	111	Two tied

Receptions

240	Wes Welker	326	Wes Welker	449	Wes Welker
218	Calvin Johnson	307	Roddy White	392	Reggie Wayne
199	Brandon Marshall	295	Calvin Johnson	392	Roddy White
192	Roddy White	292	Reggie Wayne	386	Brandon Marshall
189	Jason Witten	285	Brandon Marshall	377	Jason Witten

Receiving Yards

3,654	Calvin Johnson	4,765	Calvin Johnson	5,749	Calvin Johnson
2,923	Wes Welker	4,036	Roddy White	5,189	Roddy White
2,722	Brandon Marshall	3,771	Wes Welker	5,119	Wes Welker
2,647	Roddy White	3,736	Brandon Marshall	4,934	Reggie Wayne
2,628	Victor Cruz	3,670	Reggie Wayne	4,875	Andre Johnson

Receiving Touchdowns

28	Rob Gronkowski	38	Rob Gronkowski	38	Rob Gronkowski
22	Jordy Nelson	33	Calvin Johnson	38	Calvin Johnson
21	Four tied	27	Dez Bryant	36	Roddy White
		26	Two tied	34	Marques Colston
				32	Two tied

Interceptions

12	Richard Sherman	15	Ed Reed	24	Asante Samuel
11	Tim Jennings	15	Asante Samuel	19	Charles Woodson
10	Thomas DeCoud	14	Devin McCourty	18	Jairus Byrd
10	Corey Webster	14	Corey Webster	18	Ed Reed
10	Eric Weddle	13	DeAngelo Hall	17	DeAngelo Hall

Sacks

34.0	Jared Allen	46.5	DeMarcus Ware	59.5	Jared Allen
33.5	Aldon Smith	45.0	Jared Allen	57.5	DeMarcus Ware
31.0	DeMarcus Ware	37.5	Jason Babin	44.0	Tamba Hali
30.0	Von Miller	37.5	Cameron Wake	43.0	Cameron Wake
26.0	J.J. Watt	35.5	Tamba Hali	42.5	Clay Matthews

NFL TEAM LEADERS OVER RECENT SEASONS

Highest Won-Lost Percentage

.813	Green Bay	.813	New England	.766	New England
.781	New England	.750	Atlanta	.734	Green Bay
.766	San Francisco	.750	Green Bay	.703	Atlanta
.719	Atlanta	.708	Baltimore	.688	New Orleans
.688	Two tied	.667	Pittsburgh	.672	Baltimore

Most Points

1,070	New England	1,588	New England	2,015	New England
1,008	New Orleans	1,392	New Orleans	1,902	New Orleans
993	Green Bay	1,381	Green Bay	1,842	Green Bay
846	Detroit	1,235	Atlanta	1,651	San Diego
823	New York Giants	1,217	New York Giants	1,619	New York Giants

Most Total Yards

14,048	New Orleans	20,008	New Orleans	26,469	New Orleans
13,694	New England	19,514	New England	25,871	New England
12,877	Detroit	18,300	Detroit	24,222	Houston
12,233	Green Bay	18,281	Philadelphia	24,220	Dallas
12,051	Philadelphia	18,093	Houston	24,028	Green Bay

Last 2 Seasons
Most Rushing Yards
4,952	Minnesota
4,571	Houston
4,535	San Francisco
4,496	Carolina
4,464	Denver

Most Passing Yards
10,344	New Orleans
9,746	New England
9,741	Detroit
8,973	Green Bay
8,930	Dallas

Fewest Turnovers
26	San Francisco
30	Green Bay
33	New England
37	Houston
39	Atlanta

Fewest Points Allowed
502	San Francisco
541	Pittsburgh
560	Seattle
609	Houston
610	Baltimore

Fewest Total Yards Allowed
8,761	Pittsburgh
9,641	San Francisco
9,743	Houston
10,167	New York Jets
10,175	Cincinnati

Fewest Rushing Yards Allowed
2,743	San Francisco
3,047	Pittsburgh
3,096	Houston
3,169	Chicago
3,264	Miami

Fewest Passing Yards Allowed
5,714	Pittsburgh
6,252	New York Jets
6,647	Houston
6,754	Kansas City
6,768	Seattle

Most Opponents' Turnovers
75	Chicago
75	New England
66	New York Giants
63	San Francisco
62	Seattle

Last 3 Seasons
Most Rushing Yards
6,915	Kansas City
6,894	Minnesota
6,613	Houston
6,474	Philadelphia
6,342	Carolina

Most Passing Yards
14,785	New Orleans
13,593	New England
13,551	Detroit
13,097	Green Bay
12,972	Dallas

Fewest Turnovers
43	New England
49	San Francisco
52	Green Bay
55	Houston
56	Atlanta

Fewest Points Allowed
773	Pittsburgh
848	San Francisco
880	Baltimore
904	Chicago
935	Green Bay

Fewest Total Yards Allowed
13,190	Pittsburgh
14,831	New York Jets
14,885	San Francisco
15,114	San Diego
15,339	Baltimore

Fewest Rushing Yards Allowed
4,051	Pittsburgh
4,290	San Francisco
4,610	Chicago
4,847	Houston
4,865	Miami

Fewest Passing Yards Allowed
9,139	Pittsburgh
9,462	New York Jets
10,117	San Diego
10,254	Cincinnati
10,259	Buffalo

Most Opponents' Turnovers
113	New England
110	Chicago
105	New York Giants
93	Green Bay
91	Atlanta

Last 4 Seasons
Most Rushing Yards
8,844	Kansas City
8,840	Carolina
8,812	Minnesota
8,718	New York Jets
8,111	Philadelphia

Most Passing Yards
19,140	New Orleans
18,029	New England
17,277	Green Bay
17,259	Dallas
16,719	Detroit

Fewest Turnovers
65	New England
68	Green Bay
73	San Francisco
81	Atlanta
82	Baltimore

Fewest Points Allowed
1,097	Pittsburgh
1,129	San Francisco
1,141	Baltimore
1,232	Green Bay
1,262	Atlanta

Fewest Total Yards Allowed
18,075	Pittsburgh
18,868	New York Jets
20,107	San Francisco
20,147	Baltimore
20,309	Cincinnati

Fewest Rushing Yards Allowed
5,489	Pittsburgh
5,842	San Francisco
6,433	Minnesota
6,442	Baltimore
6,558	Houston

Fewest Passing Yards Allowed
11,921	New York Jets
12,586	Pittsburgh
13,207	Buffalo
13,465	San Diego
13,503	Cincinnati

Most Opponents' Turnovers
141	New England
138	Chicago
133	Green Bay
129	New York Giants
119	Atlanta

RETIRED UNIFORM NUMBERS IN NFL

AFC

Team	Player	No.
Baltimore	None	
Buffalo	Jim Kelly	12
Cincinnati	Bob Johnson	54
Cleveland	Otto Graham	14
	Jim Brown	32
	Ernie Davis	45
	Don Fleming	46
	Lou Groza	76
Denver	John Elway	7
	Floyd Little	44
Houston	None	
Indianapolis	Peyton Manning	18
	Johnny Unitas	19
	Buddy Young	22
	Lenny Moore	24
	Art Donovan	70
	Jim Parker	77
	Raymond Berry	82
	Gino Marchetti	89
Jacksonville	None	
Kansas City	Jan Stenerud	3
	Len Dawson	16
	Emmitt Thomas	18
	Abner Haynes	28
	Stone Johnson	33
	Mack Lee Hill	36
	Derrick Thomas	58
	Willie Lanier	63
	Bobby Bell	78
	Buck Buchanan	86
Miami	Bob Griese	12
	Dan Marino	13
	Larry Csonka	39
New England	Gino Cappelletti	20
	Mike Haynes	40
	Steve Nelson	57
	John Hannah	73
	Bruce Armstrong	78
	Jim Lee Hunt	79
	Bob Dee	89
New York Jets	Joe Namath	12
	Don Maynard	13
	Curtis Martin	28
	Joe Klecko	73
	Dennis Byrd	90
Oakland	None	
Pittsburgh	Ernie Stautner	70
San Diego	Dan Fouts	14
	Lance Alworth	19
	Junior Seau	55
Tennessee	Warren Moon	1
	Earl Campbell	34
	Jim Norton	43
	Mike Munchak	63
	Elvin Bethea	65
	Bruce Matthews	74

NFC

Team	Player	No.
Arizona	Larry Wilson	8
	Pat Tillman	40
	Stan Mauldin	77
	J.V. Cain	88
	Marshall Goldberg	99
Atlanta	Steve Bartkowski	10
	William Andrews	31
	Jeff Van Note	57
	Tommy Nobis	60
Carolina	Sam Mills	51
Chicago	Bronko Nagurski	3
	George McAfee	5
	George Halas	7
	Willie Galimore	28
	Walter Payton	34
	Gale Sayers	40
	Brian Piccolo	41
	Sid Luckman	42
	Dick Butkus	51
	Bill Hewitt	56
	Bill George	61
	Bulldog Turner	66
	Red Grange	77
Dallas	None	
Detroit	Dutch Clark	7
	Bobby Layne	22
	Doak Walker	37
	Joe Schmidt	56
	Chuck Hughes	85
Green Bay	Tony Canadeo	3
	Don Hutson	14
	Bart Starr	15
	Ray Nitschke	66
	Reggie White	92
Minnesota	Fran Tarkenton	10
	Mick Tingelhoff	53
	Jim Marshall	70
	Korey Stringer	77
	Cris Carter	80
	Alan Page	88
New Orleans	Jim Taylor	31
	Doug Atkins	81
New York Giants	Ray Flaherty	1
	Tuffy Leemans	4
	Mel Hein	7
	Phil Simms	11
	Y.A. Tittle	14
	Frank Gifford	16
	Al Blozis	32
	Joe Morrison	40
	Charlie Conerly	42
	Ken Strong	50
	Lawrence Taylor	56
Philadelphia	Steve Van Buren	15
	Brian Dawkins	20
	Tom Brookshier	40
	Pete Retzlaff	44
	Chuck Bednarik	60
	Al Wistert	70
	Reggie White	92
	Jerome Brown	99
St. Louis	Bob Waterfield	7
	Marshall Faulk	28
	Eric Dickerson	29
	Merlin Olsen	74
	Deacon Jones	75
	Jackie Slater	78
	Isaac Bruce	80
	Jack Youngblood	85
San Francisco	Steve Young	8
	John Brodie	12
	Joe Montana	16
	Joe Perry	34
	Jimmy Johnson	37
	Hugh McElhenny	39
	Ronnie Lott	42
	Charlie Krueger	70
	Leo Nomellini	73
	Bob St. Clair	79
	Jerry Rice	80
	Dwight Clark	87
Seattle	"Fans/the twelfth man"	12
	Walter Jones	71
	Steve Largent	80
	Cortez Kennedy	96
Tampa Bay	Lee Roy Selmon	63
Washington	Sammy Baugh	33

The NFL rates its passers for statistical purposes against a fixed performance standard based on statistical achievements of all qualified pro passers since 1960. The current system replaced one that rated passers in relation to their position in a total group based on various criteria. The current system, which was adopted in 1973, removes inequities that existed in the former method and, at the same time, provides a means of comparing passing performances from one season to the next.

It is important to remember that the system is used to rate passers, not quarterbacks. Statistics do not reflect leadership, play-calling, and other intangible factors that go into making a successful professional quarterback. Four categories are used as a basis for compiling a rating:

—Percentage of completions per attempt
—Average yards gained per attempt
—Percentage of touchdown passes per attempt
—Percentage of interceptions per attempt

The average standard is 1.000. The bottom is .000. To earn a 2.000 rating, a passer must perform at exceptional levels, i.e., 70 percent in completions, 10 percent in touchdowns, 1.5 percent in interceptions, and 11 yards average gain per pass attempt. The maximum a passer can receive in any category is 2.375.

For example, to gain a 2.375 in completion percentage, a passer would have to complete 77.5 percent of his passes. The NFL record is 71.23 by Drew Brees (New Orleans, 2011). To gain a 2.375 in percentage of touchdowns, a passer would have to achieve a percentage of 11.9. The record is 13.9 by Sid Luckman (Chicago, 1943). To gain 2.375 in percentage of interceptions, a passer would have to go the entire season without an interception. The 2.375 figure in average yards is 12.50, compared with the NFL record of 11.17 by Tommy O'Connell (Cleveland, 1957).

In order to make the rating more understandable, the point rating is then converted into a scale of 100, with 158.3 being the highest rating a passer can achieve. In cases where statistical performance has been superior, it is possible for a passer to sur-

pass a 100 rating. For example, take Aaron Rodgers' record-setting season in 2011 when he completed 343 of 502 passes for 4,643 yards, 45 touchdowns, and 6 interceptions. The four calculations would be:

—Percentage of Completions—343 of 502 is 68.33 percent. Subtract 30 from the completion percentage (38.33) and multiply the result by 0.05. The result is a point rating of 1.916.
Note: If the result is less than zero (Comp. Pct. less than 30.0), award zero points. If the results are greater than 2.375 (Comp. Pct. greater than 77.5), award 2.375.

—Average Yards Gained Per Attempt—4,643 yards divided by 502 attempts is 9.25. Subtract three yards from yards-per-attempt (6.25) and multiply the result by 0.25. The result is 1.562.
Note: If the result is less than zero (yards per attempt less than 3.0), award zero points. If the result is greater than 2.375 (yards per attempt greater than 12.5), award 2.375 points.

—Percentage of Touchdown Passes—45 touchdowns in 502 attempts is 8.96 percent. Multiply the touchdown percentage by 0.2. The result is 1.793.
Note: If the result is greater than 2.375 (touchdown percentage greater than 11.875), award 2.375.

—Percentage of Interceptions—Six interceptions in 502 attempts is 1.20 percent. Multiply the interception percentage by 0.25 (0.299) and subtract the number from 2.375. The result is 2.076.
Note: If the result is less than zero (interception percentage greater than 9.5), award zero points.

The sum of the four steps is (1.916 + 1.562 + 1.793 + 2.076) 7.348. The sum is then divided by six (1.225) and multiplied by 100. In this case, the result is 122.5. This same formula can be used to determine a passer rating for any player who attempts at least one pass.

The following is a list of the Top 25 single-season passer ratings among qualifying players:

TOP 25 NFL SINGLE-SEASON PASSER RATINGS (QUALIFYING PLAYERS)

Player, Team	Season	Rating	Att.	Comp.	Pct.	Yds.	Yds. Avg.	TD	TD Pct.	Int.	Int. Pct.
Aaron Rodgers, Green Bay	2011	*122.5	502	343	68.3	4,643	9.25	45	9.0	6	1.2
Peyton Manning, Indianapolis	2004	121.1	497	336	67.6	4,557	9.17	49	9.9	10	2.0
Tom Brady, New England	2007	117.2	578	398	68.9	4,806	8.31	*50	8.7	8	1.4
Steve Young, San Francisco	1994	112.8	461	324	70.2	3,969	8.61	35	7.6	10	2.2
Joe Montana, San Francisco	1989	112.4	386	271	70.2	3,521	9.12	26	6.7	8	2.1
Tom Brady, New England	2010	111.0	492	324	65.9	3,900	7.93	36	7.3	4	0.8
Daunte Culpepper, Minnesota	2004	110.9	548	379	69.2	4,717	8.61	39	7.1	11	2.0
Drew Brees, New Orleans	2011	110.6	657	468	*71.2	*5,476	8.33	46	7.0	14	2.1
Milt Plum, Cleveland	1960	110.4	250	151	60.4	2,297	9.19	21	8.4	5	2.0
Sammy Baugh, Washington	1945	109.9	182	128	70.3	1,669	9.17	11	6.0	4	2.2
Drew Brees, New Orleans	2009	109.6	514	363	70.6	4,388	8.54	34	6.6	11	2.1
Kurt Warner, St. Louis	1999	109.2	499	325	65.1	4,353	8.72	41	8.2	13	2.6
Dan Marino, Miami	1984	108.9	564	362	64.2	5,084	9.01	48	8.5	17	3.0
Aaron Rodgers, Green Bay	2012	108.0	552	371	67.2	4,295	7.78	39	7.1	8	1.4
Sid Luckman, Chicago Bears	1943	107.5	202	110	54.5	2,194	10.86	28	13.9	12	5.9
Brett Favre, Minnesota	2009	107.2	531	363	68.4	4,202	7.91	30	5.6	7	1.3
Steve Young, San Francisco	1992	107.0	402	268	66.7	3,465	8.62	25	6.2	7	1.7
Randall Cunningham, Minnesota	1998	106.0	425	259	60.9	3,704	8.72	34	8.0	10	2.4
Peyton Manning, Denver	2012	105.8	583	400	68.6	4,659	7.99	37	6.3	11	1.9
Tom Brady, New England	2011	105.6	611	401	65.6	5,235	8.57	39	6.4	12	2.0
Philip Rivers, San Diego	2008	105.5	478	312	65.3	4,009	8.39	34	7.1	11	2.3
Bart Starr, Green Bay	1966	105.0	251	156	62.2	2,257	8.99	14	5.6	3	1.2
Drew Brees, San Diego	2004	104.8	400	262	65.5	3,159	7.90	27	6.8	7	1.8
Roger Staubach, Dallas	1971	104.8	211	126	59.7	1,882	8.92	15	7.1	4	1.9
Y.A. Tittle, New York Giants	1963	104.8	367	221	60.2	3,145	8.57	36	9.8	14	3.8

*NFL Record

HIGHEST NFL POSTSEASON PASSER RATINGS (MINIMUM: 150 ATTEMPTS)

Player	Games	Att.	Comp.	Pct.	Yards	Avg. Gain	TD	Int.	Rating
Bart Starr	10	213	130	61.0	1,753	8.23	15	3	104.8
Drew Brees	9	391	262	67.0	2,980	7.62	22	4	104.2
Aaron Rodgers	9	292	193	66.1	2,312	7.92	18	5	103.6
Kurt Warner	13	462	307	66.5	3,952	8.55	31	14	102.8
Joe Montana	23	734	460	62.7	5,772	7.86	45	21	95.6
Mark Sanchez	6	157	95	60.5	1,155	7.36	9	3	94.3
Ken Anderson	6	166	110	66.3	1,321	7.96	9	6	93.5
Joe Theismann	10	211	128	60.7	1,782	8.45	11	7	91.4
Eli Manning	11	356	219	61.5	2,516	7.07	17	8	89.3
Peyton Manning	20	761	481	63.2	5,679	7.46	32	12	88.4

HIGHEST NFL POSTSEASON PASSER RATINGS, ACTIVE PLAYERS (MINIMUM: 150 ATTEMPTS)

Player	Games	Att.	Comp.	Pct.	Yards	Avg. Gain	TD	Int.	Rating
Drew Brees	9	391	262	67.0	2,980	7.62	22	4	104.2
Aaron Rodgers	9	292	193	66.1	2,312	7.92	18	5	103.6
Mark Sanchez	6	157	95	60.5	1,155	7.36	9	3	94.3
Eli Manning	11	356	219	61.5	2,516	7.07	17	8	89.3
Peyton Manning	20	761	481	63.2	5,679	7.46	32	12	88.4
Tom Brady	24	887	553	62.3	5,949	6.71	42	22	87.4
Joe Flacco	13	373	207	55.5	2,672	7.16	19	8	86.2
Matt Ryan	5	187	124	66.3	1,230	6.58	9	7	85.2
Matt Hasselbeck	11	406	237	58.4	2,741	6.75	18	9	84.4
Ben Roethlisberger	14	409	248	60.6	3,150	7.70	20	17	83.7

ALL-TIME RANKINGS OF PLAYERS IN FOUR CATEGORIES THAT DETERMINE NFL PASSER RATING
Minimum: 1,500 Attempts

COMPLETION PERCENTAGE	Pct.	Att.	Comp.
Chad Pennington	66.05	2,471	1,632
Aaron Rodgers	65.74	2,665	1,752
Drew Brees	65.62	6,149	4,035
Kurt Warner	65.50	4,070	2,666
Peyton Manning	65.21	7,793	5,082
Tony Romo	64.72	3,240	2,097
Matt Schaub	64.33	2,823	1,816
Steve Young	64.28	4,149	2,667
Tom Brady	63.75	5,958	3,798
Philip Rivers	63.64	3,564	2,268

TOUCHDOWN PERCENTAGE	Pct.	Att.	TD
Sid Luckman	7.86	1,744	137
Frank Ryan	6.99	2,133	149
Aaron Rodgers	6.42	2,665	171
Len Dawson	6.39	3,741	239
Daryle Lamonica	6.31	2,601	164
Sammy Baugh	6.24	2,995	187
Charlie Conerly	6.11	2,833	173
Bob Waterfield	6.00	1,617	97
Earl Morrall	5.99	2,689	161
Sonny Jurgensen	5.98	4,262	255

AVERAGE YARDS PER PASS	Avg.	Att.	Yards
Otto Graham	8.63	1,565	13,499
Sid Luckman	8.42	1,744	14,686
Norm Van Brocklin	8.16	2,895	23,611
Aaron Rodgers	8.13	2,665	21,661
Steve Young	7.98	4,149	33,124
Kurt Warner	7.95	4,070	32,344
Tony Romo	7.94	3,240	25,737
Ben Roethlisberger	7.93	3,762	29,844
Ed Brown	7.85	1,987	15,600
Bart Starr	7.85	3,149	24,718

INTERCEPTION PERCENTAGE	Pct.	Att.	Int.
Aaron Rodgers	1.73	2,665	46
Tom Brady	2.06	5,958	123
Neil O'Donnell	2.11	3,229	68
Donovan McNabb	2.18	5,374	117
Joe Flacco	2.25	2,489	56
Jeff Garcia	2.26	3,676	83
Matt Ryan	2.28	2,637	60
Mark Brunell	2.33	4,640	108
David Garrard	2.37	2,281	54
Jason Campbell	2.38	2,182	52

STARTING RECORDS OF ACTIVE NFL QUARTERBACKS
Minimum: 10 starts

	W - L - T	Pct.
Tom Brady	136-39-0	.777
Matt Ryan	56-22-0	.718
Ben Roethlisberger	87-39-0	.690
Andrew Luck	11- 5-0	.688
Peyton Manning	154-70-0	.688
Russell Wilson	11- 5-0	.688
Joe Flacco	54-26-0	.675
Aaron Rodgers	52-26-0	.667
Philip Rivers	70-42-0	.625
Robert Griffin III	9- 6-0	.600
Andy Dalton	19-13-0	.594
Tony Romo	55-38-0	.591
Drew Brees	99-70-0	.586
Eli Manning	78-57-0	.578
Tim Tebow	8- 6-0	.571
Michael Vick	56-44-1	.559
Jay Cutler	51-42-0	.548
Matt Schaub	44-38-0	.537
Mark Sanchez	33-29-0	.532
Rex Grossman	25-22-0	.532
Matt Hasselbeck	80-72-0	.526
Matt Moore	13-12-0	.520
Alex Smith	38-36-1	.513
Kyle Orton	35-34-0	.507
Shaun Hill	13-13-0	.500
Tarvaris Jackson	17-17-0	.500
Byron Leftwich	24-26-0	.480
John Skelton	8- 9-0	.471
Matt Cassel	29-33-0	.468
Christian Ponder	12-14-0	.462
Charlie Batch	25-30-0	.455
Carson Palmer	54-67-0	.446
Matt Leinart	8-10-0	.444
Ryan Tannehill	7- 9-0	.438
Jason Campbell	31-40-0	.437
Josh Freeman	24-32-0	.429
Kevin Kolb	9-12-0	.429
Trent Edwards	14-19-0	.424
Derek Anderson	18-25-0	.419
Cam Newton	13-19-0	.406
Josh McCown	13-20-0	.394
Chad Henne	14-23-0	.378
Matthew Stafford	17-28-0	.378
Sam Bradford	15-26-1	.369
Jake Locker	4- 7-0	.364
Ryan Fitzpatrick	24-43-1	.360
Kellen Clemens	4- 8-0	.333
Brandon Weeden	5-10-0	.333
Bruce Gradkowski	6-14-0	.300
David Carr	23-56-0	.291
Colt McCoy	6-15-0	.286
Blaine Gabbert	5-19-0	.208
Brady Quinn	4-16-0	.200
Dan Orlovsky	2-10-0	.167
Jimmy Clausen	1- 9-0	.100
Tyler Thigpen	1-11-0	.083

MOST GAME-WINNING DRIVES IN FOURTH QUARTER OR OVERTIME SINCE 1970

48	Peyton Manning, Indianapolis, 1998-2010; Denver, 2012
47	Dan Marino, Miami, 1983-1999
43	Brett Favre, Atlanta, 1991; Green Bay, 1992-2007; New York Jets, 2008; Minnesota, 2009-2010
40	John Elway, Denver, 1983-1998
35	Warren Moon, Houston, 1984-1993; Minnesota, 1994-96; Seattle, 1997-98; Kansas City, 1999-2000

TEAMS THAT FINISHED IN FIRST PLACE IN THEIR DIVISION THE SEASON AFTER FINISHING IN LAST PLACE

Season	Team	Record	Prior Season
1967	Houston	9-4-1	*3-11-0
1968	Minnesota	8-6-0	3-8-3
1970	Cincinnati	8-6-0	4-9-1
1970	San Francisco	10-3-1	4-8-2
1972	Green Bay	10-4-0	4-8-2
1975	Baltimore	10-4-0	2-12-0
1979	Tampa Bay	10-6-0	5-11-0
1981	Cincinnati	12-4-0	6-10-0
1981	Tampa Bay	9-7-0	*5-10-1
1987	Indianapolis	9-6-0	3-13-0
1988	Cincinnati	12-4-0	4-11-0
1990	Cincinnati	9-7-0	8-8-0
1991	Denver	12-4-0	5-11-0
1992	San Diego	11-5-0	4-12-0
1993	Detroit	10-6-0	*5-11-0
1996	Carolina	12-4-0	*7-9-0
1996	Denver	13-3-0	*8-8-0
1997	New York Giants	10-5-1	6-10-0
1999	Indianapolis	13-3-0	3-13-0
1999	St. Louis	13-3-0	*4-12-0
2000	New Orleans	10-6-0	3-13-0
2001	Chicago	13-3-0	5-11-0
2001	New England	11-5-0	5-11-0
2003	Carolina	11-5-0	7-9-0
2003	Kansas City	13-3-0	*8-8-0
2004	Atlanta	11-5-0	5-11-0
2004	San Diego	12-4-0	*4-12-0
2005	Chicago	11-5-0	5-11-0
2005	New York Giants	11-5-0	*6-10-0
2005	Tampa Bay	11-5-0	5-11-0
2006	Baltimore	13-3-0	*6-10-0
2006	New Orleans	10-6-0	3-13-0
2006	Philadelphia	10-6-0	6-10-0
2007	Tampa Bay	9-7-0	4-12-0
2008	Miami	11-5-0	1-15-0
2009	New Orleans	13-3-0	8-8-0
2010	Kansas City	10-6-0	4-12-0
2011	Denver	8-8-0	4-12-0
2011	Houston	10-6-0	*6-10-0
2012	Washington	10-6-0	5-11-0

tied for last place

LONGEST WINNING STREAKS SINCE 1970

23	Indianapolis, 2008-09	(9 in 2008; 14 in 2009)
21	New England, 2006-08	(3 in 2006, 16 in 2007, 2 in 2008)
18	New England, 2003-04	(12 in 2003, 6 in 2004)
16	Miami, 1971-73	(1 in 1971, 14 in 1972, 1 in 1973)
16	Miami, 1983-84	(5 in 1983, 11 in 1984)
16	Pittsburgh, 2004-05	(14 in 2004, 2 in 2005)
15	San Francisco, 1989-90	(5 in 1989, 10 in 1990)
15	Green Bay, 2010-11	(2 in 2010, 13 in 2011)
14	Oakland, 1976-77	(10 in 1976, 4 in 1977)
14	Denver, 1997-98	(1 in 1997, 13 in 1998)
13	Minnesota, 1974-75	(3 in 1974, 10 in 1975)
13	Chicago, 1984-85	(1 in 1984, 12 in 1985)
13	New York Giants, 1989-90	(3 in 1989, 10 in 1990)
13	Indianapolis, 2005	
13	Tennessee, 2007-08	(3 in 2007, 10 in 2008)
13	New Orleans, 2009	
12	Washington, 1990-91	(1 in 1990, 11 in 1991)
11	Pittsburgh, 1975	
11	Baltimore, 1975-76	(9 in 1975, 2 in 1976)
11	Chicago, 1986-87	(7 in 1986, 4 in 1987)
11	Houston, 1993	
11	San Francisco, 1997	
11	Jacksonville, 1999	
11	Indianapolis, 1999	
11	Seattle, 2005	
11	San Diego, 2006-07	(10 in 2006, 1 in 2007)
11	San Diego, 2009	
11	Denver, 2012	(current)

NFL PLAYOFF APPEARANCES BY SEASONS

Team	Number of Seasons in Playoffs
New York Giants	31
Dallas	30
Green Bay	28
Minnesota	27
Pittsburgh	27
St. Louis	27
Chicago	25
Indianapolis	25
Cleveland	24
San Francisco	24
Philadelphia	23
Washington	23
Miami	22
Oakland	21
Tennessee	21
New England	20
Denver	19
Buffalo	17
San Diego	17
Kansas City	16
Detroit	15
New York Jets	14
Atlanta	12
Seattle	12
Cincinnati	11
Tampa Bay	10
Baltimore	9
New Orleans	9
Arizona	8
Jacksonville	6
Carolina	4
Houston	2

TEAMS IN SUPER BOWL CONTENTION (1978-2012)

	With 3 Weeks to Play	With 2 Weeks to Play	With 1 Week to Play
1978	20	17	12
1979	19	15	13
1980	20	14	12
1981	21	20	16
1982	*27	25	*22
1983	24	19	15
1984	18	14	13
1985	21	18	13
1986	19	17	14
1987	19	19	15
1988	21	18	15
1989	21	18	17
1990	23	20	15
1991	20	18	13
1992	20	16	14
1993	20	18	16
1994	25	22	15
1995	*27	21	18
1996	23	21	13
1997	22	18	14
1998	22	19	14
1999	23	20	16
2000	19	17	16
2001	23	16	13
2002	21	21	19
2003	22	17	14
2004	*27	*26	17
2005	18	17	14
2006	25	24	20
2007	23	16	15
2008	22	19	18
2009	24	19	17
2010	23	20	16
2011	22	22	16
2012	24	19	15

RECORD OF TEAMS ON THE ROAD (1970-2012)

Year	W	L	T	Pct.
1970	72	101	9	.420
1971	74	100	8	.429
1972	87	90	5	.492
1973	66	109	7	.382
1974	82	99	1	.453
1975	81	101	0	.445
1976	83	112	1	.426
1977	83	113	0	.423
1978	93	130	1	.417
1979	92	132	0	.411
1980	101	122	1	.453
1981	84	139	1	.377
1982	57	68	1	.456
1983	104	119	1	.467
1984	94	129	1	.422
1985	80	144	0	.357
1986	104	118	2	.469
1987	95	114	1	.455
1988	92	131	1	.413
1989	95	128	1	.426
1990	93	131	0	.415
1991	92	132	0	.411
1992	88	136	0	.393
1993	101	123	0	.451
1994	96	128	0	.429
1995	96	144	0	.400
1996	91	149	0	.379
1997	93	145	2	.392
1998	89	151	0	.371
1999	100	148	0	.403
2000	110	138	0	.444
2001	112	136	0	.452
2002	107	148	1	.420
2003	99	157	0	.387
2004	111	145	0	.434
2005	105	151	0	.410
2006	120	136	0	.469
2007	109	147	0	.426
2008	109	146	1	.428
2009	110	146	0	.430
2010	113	143	0	.441
2011	111	145	0	.434
2012	109	146	1	.428

GAMES DECIDED BY 7 POINTS OR FEWER AND 3 POINTS OR FEWER (1970-2012)

	Games Decided by 7 Points or Fewer	Games Decided by 3 Points or Fewer
1970	59 of 182 (32.4%)	34 of 182 (18.7%)
1971	76 of 182 (41.8%)	35 of 182 (19.2%)
1972	71 of 182 (39.0%)	38 of 182 (20.9%)
1973	60 of 182 (32.9%)	28 of 182 (15.4%)
1974	91 of 182 (50.0%)	37 of 182 (20.3%)
1975	62 of 182 (34.1%)	35 of 182 (19.2%)
1976	73 of 196 (37.2%)	38 of 196 (19.4%)
1977	85 of 196 (43.4%)	36 of 196 (18.4%)
1978	108 of 224 (48.2%)	49 of 224 (21.9%)
1979	104 of 224 (46.4%)	51 of 224 (22.8%)
1980	108 of 224 (48.2%)	58 of 224 (25.9%)
1981	91 of 224 (40.6%)	60 of 224 (26.8%)
1982	61 of 126 (48.4%)	33 of 126 (26.2%)
1983	106 of 224 (47.3%)	54 of 224 (24.1%)
1984	95 of 224 (42.4%)	58 of 224 (25.9%)
1985	87 of 224 (38.8%)	38 of 224 (17.0%)
1986	106 of 224 (47.3%)	48 of 224 (21.4%)
1987	99 of 210 (47.1%)	40 of 210 (19.0%)
1988	113 of 224 (50.4%)	62 of 224 (27.7%)
1989	107 of 224 (47.8%)	55 of 224 (24.6%)
1990	97 of 224 (43.3%)	54 of 224 (24.1%)
1991	112 of 224 (50.0%)	57 of 224 (25.4%)
1992	88 of 224 (39.3%)	48 of 224 (21.4%)
1993	*105 of 224 (46.9%)	53 of 224 (23.7%)

	Games Decided by 7 Points or Fewer	Games Decided by 3 Points or Fewer
1994	115 of 224 (51.3%)	60 of 224 (26.8%)
1995	115 of 240 (47.9%)	61 of 240 (25.4%)
1996	109 of 240 (45.4%)	47 of 240 (19.6%)
1997	111 of 240 (46.3%)	67 of 240 (27.9%)
1998	113 of 240 (47.1%)	50 of 240 (20.8%)
1999	115 of 248 (46.4%)	**64 of 248 (25.8%)
2000	109 of 248 (44.0%)	61 of 248 (24.6%)
2001	121 of 248 (48.8%)	62 of 248 (25.0%)
2002	126 of 256 (49.2%)	63 of 256 (24.6%)
2003	124 of 256 (48.4%)	60 of 256 (23.4%)
2004	116 of 256 (45.3%)	61 of 256 (23.8%)
2005	114 of 256 (44.5%)	60 of 256 (23.4%)
2006	117 of 256 (45.7%)	61 of 256 (23.8%)
2007	110 of 256 (43.0%)	55 of 256 (21.5%)
2008	115 of 256 (44.9%)	50 of 256 (19.5%)
2009	110 of 256 (43.0%)	54 of 256 (21.1%)
2010	121 of 256 (47.3%)	65 of 256 (25.4%)
2011	125 of 256 (48.8%)	50 of 256 (19.5%)
2012	120 of 256 (46.9%)	57 of 256 (22.3%)

*Week record: Dec. 11-13, 1993 (Week 15), 12 of 14 games (86%) decided by 7 points or fewer.
**Week record: Oct. 10-11, 1999 (Week 5), 10 of 14 games (71%) decided by 3 points or fewer.

GAMES DECIDED BY 8 PTS. OR FEWER (1994-2012)

1994	121 of 224 (54.0%)	2006	126 of 256 (49.2%)
1995	123 of 240 (51.3%)	2007	120 of 256 (46.9%)
1996	115 of 240 (47.9%)	2008	118 of 256 (46.1%)
1997	120 of 240 (50.0%)	2009	120 of 256 (46.9%)
1998	120 of 240 (50.0%)	2010	131 of 256 (51.2%)
1999	124 of 248 (50.0%)	2011	132 of 256 (51.6%)
2000	119 of 248 (48.0%)	2012	131 of 256 (51.2%)
2001	*128 of 248 (51.6%)	*Week record: Oct. 14-15,
2002	137 of 256 (53.5%)	2001 (Week 5), 12 of 14
2003	132 of 256 (51.6%)	games (86%) decided by 8
2004	121 of 256 (47.3%)	points or fewer
2005	123 of 256 (48.0%)	

TWO-POINT CONVERSION RESULTS (1994-2012)

1994	59 of 116 (50.9%)	2004	37 of 76 (48.7%)
1995	40 of 104 (38.5%)	2005	27 of 53 (50.9%)
1996	44 of 92 (47.8%)	2006	21 of 41 (51.2%)
1997	47 of 109 (43.1%)	2007	30 of 61 (49.2%)
1998	41 of 105 (39.1%)	2008	28 of 68 (41.2%)
1999	31 of 84 (36.9%)	2009	24 of 60 (40.0%)
2000	35 of 85 (41.2%)	2010	26 of 53 (49.1%)
2001	40 of 90 (44.4%)	2011	23 of 50 (46.0%)
2002	47 of 98 (48.0%)	2012	29 of 58 (50.0%)
2003	29 of 66 (43.9%)		

RECORDS AFTER BYE WEEKS (1990-2012)

AFC		NFC	
Baltimore	12-5	Arizona	10-14
Buffalo	15-9	Atlanta	14-10
Cincinnati	6-17-1	Carolina	8-10
Cleveland	7-12	Chicago	16-8
Denver	18-6	Dallas	16-8
Houston	4-7	Detroit	11-13
Indianapolis	14-10	Green Bay	15- 9
Jacksonville	9-9	Minnesota	17-7
Kansas City	13-11	New Orleans	12-12
Miami	14-10	New York Giants	9-15
New England	14-10	Philadelphia	19-5
New York Jets	12-12	San Francisco	10-13-1
Oakland	9-15	Seattle	6-18
Pittsburgh	15- 9	St. Louis	11-12-1
San Diego	11-12	Tampa Bay	11-13
Tennessee	13-11	Washington	12-12

2012 RECORDS OF TEAMS IN CLOSE GAMES

AFC	Overall Record	Decided by 8 Pts. or Fewer	Decided By 3 Pts. or Fewer
Baltimore	10-6	6-4	5-3
Buffalo	6-10	2-4	1-2
Cincinnati	10-6	5-4	1-1
Cleveland	5-11	3-5	2-2
Denver	13-3	4-2	0-0
Houston	12-4	5-0	1-0
Indianapolis	11-5	9-1	4-0
Jacksonville	2-14	2-5	0-2
Kansas City	2-14	2-4	1-2
Miami	7-9	3-5	2-3
New England	12-4	4-4	1-3
New York Jets	6-10	3-3	2-1
Oakland	4-12	2-4	2-3
Pittsburgh	8-8	5-6	3-5
San Diego	7-9	2-5	1-2
Tennessee	6-10	4-3	3-0

NFC	Overall Record	Decided by 8 Pts. or Fewer	Decided By 3 Pts. or Fewer
Arizona	5-11	3-4	2-2
Atlanta	13-3	7-2	3-0
Carolina	7-9	4-7	0-2
Chicago	10-6	3-4	0-2
Dallas	8-8	7-5	3-2
Detroit	4-12	3-9	1-4
Green Bay	11-5	4-4	1-3
Minnesota	10-6	5-1	2-1
New Orleans	7-9	4-5	1-2
New York Giants	9-7	3-4	0-2
Philadelphia	4-12	4-5	4-2
San Francisco	11-4-1	4-1-1	0-1-1
Seattle	11-5	5-5	2-1
St. Louis	7-8-1	4-3-1	3-1-1
Tampa Bay	7-9	3-7	0-3
Washington	10-6	6-5	3-1

SUPER BOWL CHAMPIONS THAT DID NOT MAKE PLAYOFFS THE FOLLOWING YEAR

New York Giants—Super Bowl XLVI champions did not make playoffs in 2012 season.

Pittsburgh—Super Bowl XLIII champions did not make playoffs in 2009 season.

Pittsburgh—Super Bowl XL champions did not make playoffs in 2006 season.

Tampa Bay—Super Bowl XXXVII champions did not make playoffs in 2003 season.

New England—Super Bowl XXXVI champions did not make playoffs in the 2002 season.

Denver—Super Bowl XXXIII champions did not make playoffs in the 1999 season.

New York Giants—Super Bowl XXV champions did not make playoffs in the 1991 season.

Washington—Super Bowl XXII champions did not make play-offs in the 1988 season.

New York Giants—Super Bowl XXI champions did not make playoffs in the 1987 season.

San Francisco—Super Bowl XVI champions did not make playoffs in the 1982 season.

Oakland—Super Bowl XV champions did not make playoffs in the 1981 season.

Pittsburgh—Super Bowl XIV champions did not make playoffs in the 1980 season.

Kansas City—Super Bowl IV champions did not make playoffs in the 1970 season.

Green Bay—Super Bowl II champions did not make playoffs in the 1968 season.

NON-DIVISION WINNERS THAT PLAYED IN SUPER BOWL

2010	Green Bay Packers ....Super Bowl XLV (Defeated Pittsburgh, 31-25)	
2007	New York Giants ....Super Bowl XLII (Defeated New England, 17-14)	

2005	Pittsburgh Steelers	Super Bowl XL
	(Defeated Seattle, 21-10)	
2000	Baltimore Ravens	Super Bowl XXXV
	(Defeated New York Giants, 34-7)	
1999	Tennessee Titans	Super Bowl XXXIV
	(Lost to St. Louis, 23-16)	
1997	Denver Broncos	Super Bowl XXXII
	(Defeated Green Bay, 31-24)	
1992	Buffalo Bills	Super Bowl XXVII
	(Lost to Dallas, 52-17)	
1985	New England Patriots	Super Bowl XX
	(Lost to Chicago, 46-10)	
1980	Oakland Raiders	Super Bowl XV
	(Defeated Philadelphia, 27-10)	
1975	Dallas Cowboys	Super Bowl X
	(Lost to Pittsburgh, 21-17)	
1969	Kansas City Chiefs	Super Bowl IV
	(Defeated Minnesota, 23-7)	

TEAMS AT OR UNDER .500 IN POSTSEASON PLAY

2011	Denver Broncos	8-8
2010	Seattle Seahawks	7-9
2008	San Diego Chargers	8-8
2006	New York Giants	8-8
2004	Minnesota Vikings	8-8
2004	St. Louis Rams	8-8
1999	Dallas Cowboys	8-8
1999	Detroit Lions	8-8
1991	New York Jets	8-8
1990	New Orleans Saints	8-8
1985	Cleveland Browns	8-8
1982	Cleveland Browns	4-5
1982	Detroit Lions	4-5
1969	Houston Oilers	6-6-2

TEAMS TO BEAT OPPOSING TEAM THREE TIMES IN A SEASON SINCE 1970

Year	Team	Opponent
2009	Dallas Cowboys	Philadelphia Eagles
2008	Pittsburgh Steelers	Baltimore Ravens
2004	St. Louis Rams	Seattle Seahawks
2002	Pittsburgh Steelers	Cleveland Browns
2000	New York Giants	Philadelphia Eagles
1999	Tennessee Titans	Jacksonville Jaguars
1997	Green Bay Packers	Tampa Bay Buccaneers
1997	New England Patriots	Miami Dolphins
1994	Pittsburgh Steelers	Cleveland Browns
1993	Los Angeles Raiders	Denver Broncos
1991	Kansas City Chiefs	Los Angeles Raiders
1986	New York Giants	Washington Redskins
1982	Miami Dolphins	New York Jets

COLDEST NFL GAMES ON RECORD

-13 degrees (-48 degree wind chill)—December 31, 1967, Lambeau Field, Green Bay, Wisconsin, NFL Championship (Green Bay 21, Dallas 17)

-9 degrees (-59 degree wind chill)—January 10, 1982, Riverfront Stadium, Cincinnati, Ohio, AFC Championship (Cincinnati 27, San Diego 7)

-1 degrees (-23 degree wind chill)—January 20, 2008, Lambeau Field, Green Bay, Wisconsin, NFC Championship (New York Giants 23, Green Bay 20 in OT)

TEAM LEADERS

Offense	Most Scored	Fewest Scored
1st Quarter	113 Cin. & N.E.	31 Philadelphia
2nd Quarter	177 New England	54 Kansas City
3rd Quarter	153 Denver	36 Arizona
4th Quarter	162 Dallas	69 Kansas City

Defense	Fewest Allowed	Most Allowed
1st Quarter	42 Cincinnati	155 Tennessee
2nd Quarter	58 Tennessee	144 Indianapolis
3rd Quarter	42 Seattle	146 Oakland
4th Quarter	61 Arizona	158 Detroit

2012 NFL SCORE BY QUARTERS

AFC Offense	1	2	3	4	OT	PTS
New England	113	177	103	161	3	557
Denver	66	116	153	146	0	481
Houston	94	136	100	74	12	416
Baltimore	88	108	98	101	3	398
Cincinnati	113	104	63	111	0	391
Indianapolis	93	96	81	81	6	357
San Diego	99	100	70	81	0	350
Buffalo	84	109	78	70	3	344
Pittsburgh	57	114	71	91	3	336
Tennessee	72	94	66	95	3	330
Cleveland	50	89	69	94	0	302
Oakland	35	89	54	109	3	290
Miami	50	91	71	76	0	288
New York Jets	58	69	67	84	3	281
Jacksonville	50	71	43	88	3	255
Kansas City	42	54	43	69	3	211

NFC Offense	1	2	3	4	OT	PTS
New Orleans	101	154	110	93	3	461
Washington	79	138	95	121	3	436
Green Bay	83	126	89	135	0	433
New York Giants	101	138	73	117	0	429
Atlanta	91	131	68	129	0	419
Seattle	98	122	87	99	6	412
San Francisco	57	110	100	130	0	397
Tampa Bay	94	77	88	124	6	389
Minnesota	101	112	74	89	3	379
Dallas	36	88	84	162	6	376
Chicago	92	93	79	111	0	375
Detroit	61	105	57	146	3	372
Carolina	97	91	76	93	0	357
St. Louis	53	84	56	103	3	299
Philadelphia	31	92	78	79	0	280
Arizona	51	85	36	75	3	250

AFC Defense	1	2	3	4	OT	PTS
Denver	70	81	62	76	0	289
Pittsburgh	60	103	78	70	3	314
Miami	70	92	48	101	6	317
Cincinnati	42	102	80	96	0	320
Houston	77	83	85	83	3	331
New England	67	81	75	108	0	331
Baltimore	70	103	86	82	3	344
San Diego	72	79	69	127	3	350
Cleveland	84	96	75	110	3	368
New York Jets	72	120	69	111	3	375
Indianapolis	69	144	78	96	0	387
Kansas City	95	121	106	100	3	425
Buffalo	89	115	109	122	0	435
Oakland	106	101	146	90	0	443
Jacksonville	66	134	87	142	15	444
Tennessee	155	58	116	136	6	471

NFC Defense	1	2	3	4	OT	PTS
Seattle	51	84	42	68	0	245
San Francisco	54	63	55	98	3	273
Chicago	48	97	54	72	6	277
Atlanta	59	101	55	84	0	299
Green Bay	53	118	80	85	0	336
New York Giants	86	103	84	71	0	344
Minnesota	60	104	77	107	0	348
St. Louis	74	114	63	97	0	348
Arizona	60	136	97	61	3	357
Carolina	80	81	68	128	6	363
Washington	80	114	46	148	0	388
Tampa Bay	71	127	73	123	0	394
Dallas	71	127	79	120	3	400
Detroit	77	137	59	158	6	437
Philadelphia	106	111	83	141	3	444
New Orleans	96	133	96	126	3	454
NFL TOTALS	**2,390**	**3,363**	**2,480**	**3,337**	**81**	**11,651**

INSIDE THE NUMBERS

**2013 TOP 100 TELEVISION MARKETS
(NFL TEAM MARKETS IN BOLD)**

RANK	MARKET	TV HOUSEHOLDS	% of U.S.
1	**New York**	**7,384,340**	**6.468**
2	Los Angeles	5,613,460	4.917
3	**Chicago**	**3,484,800**	**3.052**
4	**Philadelphia**	**2,949,310**	**2.583**
5	**Dallas-Ft. Worth**	**2,588,020**	**2.267**
6	**San Francisco-Oak-San Jose**	**2,502,030**	**2.191**
7	**Boston (Manchester)**	**2,366,690**	**2.073**
8	**Washington, DC (Hagrstwn)**	**2,359,160**	**2.066**
9	**Atlanta**	**2,326,840**	**2.038**
10	**Houston**	**2,215,650**	**1.941**
11	**Detroit**	**1,845,920**	**1.617**
12	**Seattle-Tacoma**	**1,818,900**	**1.593**
13	**Phoenix (Prescott)**	**1,812,040**	**1.587**
14	**Tampa-St. Pete (Sarasota)**	**1,806,560**	**1.582**
15	**Minneapolis-St. Paul**	**1,728,050**	**1.513**
16	**Miami-Ft. Lauderdale**	**1,621,130**	**1.420**
17	**Denver**	**1,566,460**	**1.372**
18	**Cleveland-Akron (Canton)**	**1,485,140**	**1.301**
19	Orlando-Daytona Bch-Melbrn	1,453,170	1.273
20	Sacramnto-Stkton-Modesto	1,387,710	1.215
21	**St. Louis**	**1,243,490**	**1.089**
22	Portland, OR	1,182,180	1.035
23	**Pittsburgh**	**1,165,740**	**1.021**
24	Raleigh-Durham (Fayetvlle)	1,150,350	1.008
25	**Charlotte**	**1,136,420**	**0.995**
26	**Indianapolis**	**1,089,700**	**0.954**
27	**Baltimore**	**1,085,070**	**0.950**
28	**San Diego**	**1,075,120**	**0.942**
29	**Nashville**	**1,014,910**	**0.889**
30	Hartford & New Haven	996,550	0.873
31	**Kansas City**	**931,320**	**0.816**
32	Columbus, OH	930,460	0.815
33	Salt Lake City	917,370	0.803
34	Milwaukee	902,190	0.790
35	**Cincinnati**	**897,890**	**0.786**
36	San Antonio	881,050	0.772
37	Greenvll-Spart-Ashevll-And	846,030	0.741
38	West Palm Beach-Ft. Pierce	794,310	0.696
39	Grand Rapids-Kalmzoo-B.Crk	720,150	0.631
40	Las Vegas	718,990	0.630
41	Oklahoma City	718,770	0.630
42	Birmingham (Ann and Tusc)	717,530	0.628
43	Harrisburg-Lncstr-Leb-York	716,990	0.628
44	Norfolk-Portsmth-Newpt Nws	709,730	0.622
45	Austin	705,280	0.618
46	Greensboro-H.Point-W.Salem	695,100	0.609
47	Albuquerque-Santa Fe	691,450	0.606
48	Louisville	670,880	0.588
49	Memphis	662,830	0.581
50	**Jacksonville**	**659,170**	**0.577**

2013 TOP 100 TELEVISION MARKETS
(NFL TEAM MARKETS IN BOLD)

RANK	MARKET	TV HOUSEHOLDS	% of U.S.
51	**New Orleans**	**641,550**	**0.562**
52	**Buffalo**	**632,150**	**0.554**
53	Providence-New Bedford	606,400	0.531
54	Wilkes Barre-Scranton-Hztn	581,020	0.509
55	Fresno-Visalia	576,820	0.505
56	Little Rock-Pine Bluff	561,760	0.492
57	Richmond-Petersburg	553,390	0.485
58	Albany-Schenectady-Troy	540,050	0.473
59	Tulsa	526,960	0.462
60	Mobile-Pensacola (Ft Walt)	525,990	0.461
61	Knoxville	520,890	0.456
62	Ft. Myers-Naples	502,050	0.440
63	Dayton	498,270	0.436
64	Lexington	485,630	0.425
65	Charleston-Huntington	455,490	0.399
66	Wichita-Hutchinson Plus	450,300	0.394
67	Flint-Saginaw-Bay City	446,010	0.391
68	Roanoke-Lynchburg	445,470	0.390
69	**Green Bay-Appleton**	**441,800**	**0.387**
70	Tucson (Sierra Vista)	438,440	0.384
71	Honolulu	437,790	0.383
72	Des Moines-Ames	427,860	0.375
73	Spokane	420,640	0.368
74	Springfield, MO	414,570	0.363
75	Omaha	414,060	0.363
76	Toledo	409,550	0.359
77	Columbia, SC	398,510	0.349
78	Rochester, NY	395,680	0.347
79	Huntsville-Decatur (Flor)	390,590	0.342
80	Portland-Auburn	389,530	0.341
81	Paducah-Cape Girard-Harsbg	388,340	0.340
82	Shreveport	384,410	0.337
83	Champaign&Sprngfld-Decatur	378,720	0.332
84	Syracuse	377,550	0.331
85	Madison	376,670	0.330
86	Harlingen-Wslco-Brnsvl-McA	364,160	0.319
87	Chattanooga	353,710	0.310
88	Waco-Temple-Bryan	349,540	0.306
89	Colorado Springs-Pueblo	343,990	0.301
90	Cedar Rapids-Wtrlo-IWC&Dub	342,610	0.300
91	El Paso (Las Cruces)	339,130	0.297
92	Savannah	334,750	0.293
93	Jackson, MS	331,500	0.290
94	Baton Rouge	329,620	0.289
95	South Bend-Elkhart	319,860	0.280
96	Tri-Cities, TN-VA	319,060	0.279
97	Burlington-Plattsburgh	316,910	0.278
98	Charleston, SC	316,080	0.277
99	Davenport-R.Island-Moline	303,800	0.266
100	Greenville-N.Bern-Washngtn	303,280	0.266
	TOTAL NFL MARKETS	**53,875,370**	**47.187**
	TOTAL TOP 100 MARKETS	**98,345,310**	**86.137**
	TOTAL MARKETS	**114,173,690**	**100.00**

ALL-TIME REGULAR-SEASON RECORDS OF CURRENT NFL TEAMS

AFC
BALTIMORE RAVENS

	All Games			Home Games			Road Games		
Season	W	L	T	W	L	T	W	L	T
1996	4	12		4	4		0	8	
1997	6	9	1	3	4	1	3	5	
1998	6	10		4	4		2	6	
1999	8	8		4	4		4	4	
2000	12	4		6	2		6	2	
2001	10	6		6	2		4	4	
2002	7	9		4	4		3	5	
2003	10	6		7	1		3	5	
2004	9	7		6	2		3	5	
2005	6	10		6	2		0	8	
2006	13	3		7	1		6	2	
2007	5	11		4	4		1	7	
2008	11	5		6	2		5	3	
2009	9	7		6	2		3	5	
2010	12	4		7	1		5	3	
2011	12	4		8	0		4	4	
2012	10	6		6	2		4	4	
	150	121	1	94	41	1	56	80	

BUFFALO BILLS

	All Games			Home Games			Road Games		
Season	W	L	T	W	L	T	W	L	T
1960	5	8	1	3	4		2	4	1
1961	6	8		2	5		4	3	
1962	7	6	1	3	3	1	4	3	
1963	7	6	1	4	2	1	3	4	
1964	12	2		6	1		6	1	
1965	10	3	1	5	2		5	1	1
1966	9	4	1	4	2	1	5	2	
1967	4	10		2	5		2	5	
1968	1	12	1	1	6		0	6	1
1969	4	10		4	3		0	7	
1970	3	10	1	1	6		2	4	1
1971	1	13		1	6		0	7	
1972	4	9	1	2	4	1	2	5	
1973	9	5		5	2		4	3	
1974	9	5		5	2		4	3	
1975	8	6		3	4		5	2	
1976	2	12		1	6		1	6	
1977	3	11		1	6		2	5	
1978	5	11		4	4		1	7	
1979	7	9		3	5		4	4	
1980	11	5		6	2		5	3	
1981	10	6		7	1		3	5	
1982	4	5		4	1		0	4	
1983	8	8		3	5		5	3	
1984	2	14		2	6		0	8	
1985	2	14		2	6		0	8	
1986	4	12		3	5		1	7	
1987	7	8		4	4		3	4	
1988	12	4		8	0		4	4	
1989	9	7		6	2		3	5	
1990	13	3		8	0		5	3	
1991	13	3		7	1		6	2	
1992	11	5		6	2		5	3	
1993	12	4		6	2		6	2	
1994	7	9		4	4		3	5	
1995	10	6		6	2		4	4	
1996	10	6		7	1		3	5	
1997	6	10		4	4		2	6	
1998	10	6		6	2		4	4	
1999	11	5		6	2		5	3	
2000	8	8		5	3		3	5	
2001	3	13		1	7		2	6	
2002	8	8		5	3		3	5	
2003	6	10		4	4		2	6	
2004	9	7		5	3		4	4	
2005	5	11		4	4		1	7	
2006	7	9		4	4		3	5	
2007	7	9		4	4		3	5	
2008	7	9		3	5		4	4	
2009	6	10		3	5		3	5	
2010	4	12		2	6		2	6	
2011	6	10		5	3		1	7	
2012	6	10		4	4		2	6	
	370	426	8	214	185	4	156	241	4

CINCINNATI BENGALS

	All Games			Home Games			Road Games		
Season	W	L	T	W	L	T	W	L	T
1968	3	11		2	5		1	6	
1969	4	9	1	4	3		0	6	1
1970	8	6		5	2		3	4	
1971	4	10		3	4		1	6	
1972	8	6		4	3		4	3	
1973	10	4		7	0		3	4	
1974	7	7		4	3		3	4	
1975	11	3		6	1		5	2	
1976	10	4		6	1		4	3	
1977	8	6		5	2		3	4	
1978	4	12		3	5		1	7	
1979	4	12		4	4		0	8	
1980	6	10		3	5		3	5	
1981	12	4		6	2		6	2	
1982	7	2		4	0		3	2	
1983	7	9		4	4		3	5	
1984	8	8		5	3		3	5	
1985	7	9		5	3		2	6	
1986	10	6		6	2		4	4	
1987	4	11		1	7		3	4	
1988	12	4		8	0		4	4	
1989	8	8		5	3		3	5	
1990	9	7		5	3		4	4	
1991	3	13		3	5		0	8	
1992	5	11		3	5		2	6	
1993	3	13		3	5		0	8	
1994	3	13		2	6		1	7	
1995	7	9		3	5		4	4	
1996	8	8		6	2		2	6	
1997	7	9		6	2		1	7	
1998	3	13		1	7		2	6	
1999	4	12		2	6		2	6	
2000	4	12		3	5		1	7	
2001	6	10		4	4		2	6	
2002	2	14		1	7		1	7	
2003	8	8		5	3		3	5	
2004	8	8		5	3		3	5	
2005	11	5		5	3		6	2	
2006	8	8		4	4		4	4	
2007	7	9		5	3		2	6	
2008	4	11	1	3	4	1	1	7	
2009	10	6		6	2		4	4	
2010	4	12		3	5		1	7	
2011	9	7		4	4		5	3	
2012	10	6		4	4		6	2	
	305	385	2	186	159	1	119	226	1

CLEVELAND BROWNS*

	All Games			Home Games			Road Games		
Season	W	L	T	W	L	T	W	L	T
1950	10	2		5	1		5	1	
1951	11	1		6	0		5	1	

Season	All Games W	L	T	Home Games W	L	T	Road Games W	L	T
1952	8	4		4	2		4	2	
1953	11	1		6	0		5	1	
1954	9	3		5	1		4	2	
1955	9	2	1	5	1		4	1	1
1956	5	7		1	5		4	2	
1957	9	2	1	6	0		3	2	1
1958	9	3		4	2		5	1	
1959	7	5		3	3		4	2	
1960	8	3	1	4	2		4	1	1
1961	8	5	1	4	3		4	2	1
1962	7	6	1	4	2	1	3	4	
1963	10	4		5	2		5	2	
1964	10	3	1	5	1	1	5	2	
1965	11	3		5	2		6	1	
1966	9	5		5	2		4	3	
1967	9	5		6	1		3	4	
1968	10	4		5	2		5	2	
1969	10	3	1	5	1	1	5	2	
1970	7	7		4	3		3	4	
1971	9	5		4	3		5	2	
1972	10	4		4	3		6	1	
1973	7	5	2	5	1	1	2	4	1
1974	4	10		3	4		1	6	
1975	3	11		3	4		0	7	
1976	9	5		6	1		3	4	
1977	6	8		2	5		4	3	
1978	8	8		5	3		3	5	
1979	9	7		5	3		4	4	
1980	11	5		6	2		5	3	
1981	5	11		3	5		2	6	
1982	4	5		2	2		2	3	
1983	9	7		6	2		3	5	
1984	5	11		2	6		3	5	
1985	8	8		5	3		3	5	
1986	12	4		6	2		6	2	
1987	10	5		5	2		5	3	
1988	10	6		6	2		4	4	
1989	9	6	1	5	2	1	4	4	
1990	3	13		2	6		1	7	
1991	6	10		3	5		3	5	
1992	7	9		4	4		3	5	
1993	7	9		4	4		3	5	
1994	11	5		6	2		5	3	
1995	5	11		3	5		2	6	
1999	2	14		0	8		2	6	
2000	3	13		2	6		1	7	
2001	7	9		4	4		3	5	
2002	9	7		3	5		6	2	
2003	5	11		2	6		3	5	
2004	4	12		3	5		1	7	
2005	6	10		4	4		2	6	
2006	4	12		2	6		2	6	
2007	10	6		7	1		3	5	
2008	4	12		1	7		3	5	
2009	5	11		3	5		2	6	
2010	5	11		3	5		2	6	
2011	4	12		3	5		1	7	
2012	5	11		4	4		1	7	
	447	417	10	243	188	5	204	229	5

*Did not play from 1996-98.

DENVER BRONCOS

Season	All Games W	L	T	Home Games W	L	T	Road Games W	L	T
1960	4	9	1	2	4	1	2	5	
1961	3	11		2	5		1	6	
1962	7	7		3	4		4	3	
1963	2	11	1	2	5		0	6	1

Season	All Games W	L	T	Home Games W	L	T	Road Games W	L	T
1964	2	11	1	2	4	1	0	7	
1965	4	10		2	5		2	5	
1966	4	10		3	4		1	6	
1967	3	11		1	6		2	5	
1968	5	9		3	4		2	5	
1969	5	8	1	4	2	1	1	6	
1970	5	8	1	3	3	1	2	5	
1971	4	9	1	2	4	1	2	5	
1972	5	9		3	4		2	5	
1973	7	5	2	3	3	1	4	2	1
1974	7	6	1	3	3	1	4	3	
1975	6	8		5	2		1	6	
1976	9	5		6	1		3	4	
1977	12	2		6	1		6	1	
1978	10	6		6	2		4	4	
1979	10	6		6	2		4	4	
1980	8	8		4	4		4	4	
1981	10	6		8	0		2	6	
1982	2	7		1	4		1	3	
1983	9	7		6	2		3	5	
1984	13	3		7	1		6	2	
1985	11	5		6	2		5	3	
1986	11	5		7	1		4	4	
1987	10	4	1	7	1		3	3	1
1988	8	8		6	2		2	6	
1989	11	5		6	2		5	3	
1990	5	11		4	4		1	7	
1991	12	4		7	1		5	3	
1992	8	8		7	1		1	7	
1993	9	7		5	3		4	4	
1994	7	9		4	4		3	5	
1995	8	8		6	2		2	6	
1996	13	3		8	0		5	3	
1997	12	4		8	0		4	4	
1998	14	2		8	0		6	2	
1999	6	10		3	5		3	5	
2000	11	5		6	2		5	3	
2001	8	8		6	2		2	6	
2002	9	7		5	3		4	4	
2003	10	6		6	2		4	4	
2004	10	6		6	2		4	4	
2005	13	3		8	0		5	3	
2006	9	7		4	4		5	3	
2007	7	9		5	3		2	6	
2008	8	8		4	4		4	4	
2009	8	8		4	4		4	4	
2010	4	12		3	5		1	7	
2011	8	8		3	5		5	3	
2012	13	3		7	1		6	2	
	419	375	10	252	144	7	167	231	3

HOUSTON TEXANS

Season	All Games W	L	T	Home Games W	L	T	Road Games W	L	T
2002	4	12		2	6		2	6	
2003	5	11		3	5		2	6	
2004	7	9		3	5		4	4	
2005	2	14		2	6		0	8	
2006	6	10		4	4		2	6	
2007	8	8		6	2		2	6	
2008	8	8		6	2		2	6	
2009	9	7		4	4		5	3	
2010	6	10		4	4		2	6	
2011	10	6		5	3		5	3	
2012	12	4		6	2		6	2	
	77	99		45	43		32	56	

INDIANAPOLIS COLTS*

Season	All Games			Home Games			Road Games		
	W	L	T	W	L	T	W	L	T
1953	3	9		2	4		1	5	
1954	3	9		2	4		1	5	
1955	5	6	1	4	1	1	1	5	
1956	5	7		4	2		1	5	
1957	7	5		4	2		3	3	
1958	9	3		6	0		3	3	
1959	9	3		4	2		5	1	
1960	6	6		4	2		2	4	
1961	8	6		5	2		3	4	
1962	7	7		3	4		4	3	
1963	8	6		4	3		4	3	
1964	12	2		7	1		5	1	
1965	10	3	1	5	2		5	1	1
1966	9	5		5	2		4	3	
1967	11	1	2	6	0	1	5	1	1
1968	13	1		6	1		7	0	
1969	8	5	1	4	2	1	4	3	
1970	11	2	1	5	1	1	6	1	
1971	10	4		5	2		5	2	
1972	5	9		2	5		3	4	
1973	4	10		3	4		1	6	
1974	2	12		0	7		2	5	
1975	10	4		5	2		5	2	
1976	11	3		6	1		5	2	
1977	10	4		6	1		4	3	
1978	5	11		2	6		3	5	
1979	5	11		3	5		2	6	
1980	7	9		2	6		5	3	
1981	2	14		1	7		1	7	
1982	0	8	1	0	3	1	0	5	
1983	7	9		3	5		4	4	
1984	4	12		2	6		2	6	
1985	5	11		4	4		1	7	
1986	3	13		1	7		2	6	
1987	9	6		4	4		5	2	
1988	9	7		6	2		3	5	
1989	8	8		6	2		2	6	
1990	7	9		3	5		4	4	
1991	1	15		0	8		1	7	
1992	9	7		4	4		5	3	
1993	4	12		2	6		2	6	
1994	8	8		5	3		3	5	
1995	9	7		5	3		4	4	
1996	9	7		6	2		3	5	
1997	3	13		2	6		1	7	
1998	3	13		3	5		0	8	
1999	13	3		7	1		6	2	
2000	10	6		6	2		4	4	
2001	6	10		3	5		3	5	
2002	10	6		5	3		5	3	
2003	12	4		5	3		7	1	
2004	12	4		7	1		5	3	
2005	14	2		7	1		7	1	
2006	12	4		8	0		4	4	
2007	13	3		6	2		7	1	
2008	12	4		6	2		6	2	
2009	14	2		7	1		7	1	
2010	10	6		6	2		4	4	
2011	2	14		2	6		0	8	
2012	11	5		7	1		4	4	
	464	415	7	253	186	5	211	229	2

*includes Baltimore Colts (1953-1983).

JACKSONVILLE JAGUARS

Season	All Games			Home Games			Road Games		
	W	L	T	W	L	T	W	L	T
1995	4	12		2	6		2	6	
1996	9	7		7	1		2	6	
1997	11	5		7	1		4	4	
1998	11	5		7	1		4	4	
1999	14	2		7	1		7	1	
2000	7	9		4	4		3	5	
2001	6	10		3	5		3	5	
2002	6	10		3	5		3	5	
2003	5	11		5	3		0	8	
2004	9	7		4	4		5	3	
2005	12	4		6	2		6	2	
2006	8	8		6	2		2	6	
2007	11	5		6	2		5	3	
2008	5	11		2	6		3	5	
2009	7	9		5	3		2	6	
2010	8	8		5	3		3	5	
2011	5	11		4	4		1	7	
2012	2	14		1	7		1	7	
	140	148		84	60		56	88	

KANSAS CITY CHIEFS*

Season	All Games			Home Games			Road Games		
	W	L	T	W	L	T	W	L	T
1960	8	6		5	2		3	4	
1961	6	8		4	3		2	5	
1962	11	3		6	1		5	2	
1963	5	7	2	4	3		1	4	2
1964	7	7		4	3		3	4	
1965	7	5	2	5	2		2	3	2
1966	11	2	1	4	2	1	7	0	
1967	9	5		4	3		5	2	
1968	12	2		6	1		6	1	
1969	11	3		6	1		5	2	
1970	7	5	2	4	1	2	3	4	
1971	10	3	1	7	0		3	3	1
1972	8	6		3	4		5	2	
1973	7	5	2	5	1	1	2	4	1
1974	5	9		1	6		4	3	
1975	5	9		3	4		2	5	
1976	5	9		1	6		4	3	
1977	2	12		1	6		1	6	
1978	4	12		3	5		1	7	
1979	7	9		3	5		4	4	
1980	8	8		3	5		5	3	
1981	9	7		5	3		4	4	
1982	3	6		2	2		1	4	
1983	6	10		5	3		1	7	
1984	8	8		5	3		3	5	
1985	6	10		5	3		1	7	
1986	10	6		6	2		4	4	
1987	4	11		3	4		1	7	
1988	4	11	1	4	4		0	7	1
1989	8	7	1	5	3		3	4	1
1990	11	5		6	2		5	3	
1991	10	6		6	2		4	4	
1992	10	6		7	1		3	5	
1993	11	5		7	1		4	4	
1994	9	7		5	3		4	4	
1995	13	3		8	0		5	3	
1996	9	7		5	3		4	4	
1997	13	3		8	0		5	3	
1998	7	9		5	3		2	6	
1999	9	7		6	2		3	5	
2000	7	9		5	3		2	6	
2001	6	10		3	5		3	5	
2002	8	8		6	2		2	6	
2003	13	3		8	0		5	3	
2004	7	9		4	4		3	5	
2005	10	6		7	1		3	5	
2006	9	7		6	2		3	5	
2007	4	12		2	6		2	6	
2008	2	14		1	7		1	7	

Season	All Games W	L	T	Home Games W	L	T	Road Games W	L	T
2009	4	12		1	7		3	5	
2010	10	6		7	1		3	5	
2011	7	9		3	5		4	4	
2012	2	14		1	7		1	7	
	404	388	12	239	158	4	165	230	8

includes Dallas Texans (1960-62).

MIAMI DOLPHINS

Season	All Games W	L	T	Home Games W	L	T	Road Games W	L	T
1966	3	11		2	5		1	6	
1967	4	10		4	3		0	7	
1968	5	8	1	1	5	1	4	3	
1969	3	10	1	2	4	1	1	6	
1970	10	4		6	1		4	3	
1971	10	3	1	6	1		4	2	1
1972	14	0		7	0		7	0	
1973	12	2		7	0		5	2	
1974	11	3		7	0		4	3	
1975	10	4		5	2		5	2	
1976	6	8		3	4		3	4	
1977	10	4		6	1		4	3	
1978	11	5		7	1		4	4	
1979	10	6		6	2		4	4	
1980	8	8		5	3		3	5	
1981	11	4	1	6	1	1	5	3	
1982	7	2		4	0		3	2	
1983	12	4		7	1		5	3	
1984	14	2		7	1		7	1	
1985	12	4		8	0		4	4	
1986	8	8		4	4		4	4	
1987	8	7		4	3		4	4	
1988	6	10		4	4		2	6	
1989	8	8		4	4		4	4	
1990	12	4		7	1		5	3	
1991	8	8		5	3		3	5	
1992	11	5		6	2		5	3	
1993	9	7		4	4		5	3	
1994	10	6		6	2		4	4	
1995	9	7		5	3		4	4	
1996	8	8		4	4		4	4	
1997	9	7		6	2		3	5	
1998	10	6		7	1		3	5	
1999	9	7		5	3		4	4	
2000	11	5		5	3		6	2	
2001	11	5		7	1		4	4	
2002	9	7		7	1		2	6	
2003	10	6		4	4		6	2	
2004	4	12		3	5		1	7	
2005	9	7		5	3		4	4	
2006	6	10		4	4		2	6	
2007	1	15		1	7		0	8	
2008	11	5		5	3		6	2	
2009	7	9		4	4		3	5	
2010	7	9		1	7		6	2	
2011	6	10		4	4		2	6	
2012	7	9		5	3		2	6	
	407	309	4	232	124	3	175	185	1

NEW ENGLAND PATRIOTS*

Season	All Games W	L	T	Home Games W	L	T	Road Games W	L	T
1960	5	9		3	4		2	5	
1961	9	4	1	4	2	1	5	2	
1962	9	4	1	6	1		3	3	1
1963	7	6	1	5	1	1	2	5	
1964	10	3	1	4	2	1	6	1	
1965	4	8	2	1	4	2	3	4	
1966	8	4	2	4	2	1	4	2	1
1967	3	10	1	2	4		1	6	1
1968	4	10		2	5		2	5	
1969	4	10		2	5		2	5	
1970	2	12		1	6		1	6	
1971	6	8		5	2		1	6	
1972	3	11		2	5		1	6	
1973	5	9		3	4		2	5	
1974	7	7		3	4		4	3	
1975	3	11		2	5		1	6	
1976	11	3		6	1		5	2	
1977	9	5		6	1		3	4	
1978	11	5		5	3		6	2	
1979	9	7		6	2		3	5	
1980	10	6		6	2		4	4	
1981	2	14		2	6		0	8	
1982	5	4		3	1		2	3	
1983	8	8		5	3		3	5	
1984	9	7		5	3		4	4	
1985	11	5		7	1		4	4	
1986	11	5		4	4		7	1	
1987	8	7		5	3		3	4	
1988	9	7		7	1		2	6	
1989	5	11		3	5		2	6	
1990	1	15		0	8		1	7	
1991	6	10		4	4		2	6	
1992	2	14		1	7		1	7	
1993	5	11		3	5		2	6	
1994	10	6		5	3		5	3	
1995	6	10		3	5		3	5	
1996	11	5		6	2		5	3	
1997	10	6		6	2		4	4	
1998	9	7		6	2		3	5	
1999	8	8		5	3		3	5	
2000	5	11		3	5		2	6	
2001	11	5		6	2		5	3	
2002	9	7		5	3		4	4	
2003	14	2		8	0		6	2	
2004	14	2		8	0		6	2	
2005	10	6		5	3		5	3	
2006	12	4		5	3		7	1	
2007	16	0		8	0		8	0	
2008	11	5		5	3		6	2	
2009	10	6		8	0		2	6	
2010	14	2		8	0		6	2	
2011	13	3		7	1		6	2	
2012	12	4		6	2		6	2	
	426	369	9	240	155	6	186	214	3

includes Boston Patriots (1960-1970).

NEW YORK JETS*

Season	All Games W	L	T	Home Games W	L	T	Road Games W	L	T
1960	7	7		3	4		4	3	
1961	7	7		5	2		2	5	
1962	5	9		2	5		3	4	
1963	5	8	1	4	2	1	1	6	
1964	5	8	1	5	1	1	0	7	
1965	5	8	1	3	3	1	2	5	
1966	6	6	2	4	3		2	3	2
1967	8	5	1	4	2	1	4	3	
1968	11	3		6	1		5	2	
1969	10	4		5	2		5	2	
1970	4	10		2	5		2	5	
1971	6	8		4	3		2	5	
1972	7	7		4	3		3	4	
1973	4	10		2	4		2	6	
1974	7	7		3	4		4	3	

Season	All Games W	L	T	Home Games W	L	T	Road Games W	L	T
1975	3	11		1	6		2	5	
1976	3	11		2	5		1	6	
1977	3	11		1	6		2	5	
1978	8	8		4	4		4	4	
1979	8	8		6	2		2	6	
1980	4	12		2	6		2	6	
1981	10	5	1	6	2		4	3	1
1982	6	3		3	1		3	2	
1983	7	9		2	6		5	3	
1984	7	9		3	5		4	4	
1985	11	5		7	1		4	4	
1986	10	6		5	3		5	3	
1987	6	9		4	4		2	5	
1988	8	7	1	5	2	1	3	5	
1989	4	12		1	7		3	5	
1990	6	10		3	5		3	5	
1991	8	8		4	4		4	4	
1992	4	12		3	5		1	7	
1993	8	8		3	5		5	3	
1994	6	10		4	4		2	6	
1995	3	13		2	6		1	7	
1996	1	15		0	8		1	7	
1997	9	7		5	3		4	4	
1998	12	4		7	1		5	3	
1999	8	8		4	4		4	4	
2000	9	7		5	3		4	4	
2001	10	6		3	5		7	1	
2002	9	7		5	3		4	4	
2003	6	10		4	4		2	6	
2004	10	6		6	2		4	4	
2005	4	12		4	4		0	8	
2006	10	6		4	4		6	2	
2007	4	12		3	5		1	7	
2008	9	7		5	3		4	4	
2009	9	7		4	4		5	3	
2010	11	5		5	3		6	2	
2011	8	8		6	2		2	6	
2012	6	10		3	5		3	5	
	365	431	8	200	196	5	165	235	3

*includes New York Titans (1960-62).

OAKLAND RAIDERS*

Season	All Games W	L	T	Home Games W	L	T	Road Games W	L	T
1960	6	8		3	4		3	4	
1961	2	12		1	6		1	6	
1962	1	13		1	6		0	7	
1963	10	4		6	1		4	3	
1964	5	7	2	5	2		0	5	2
1965	8	5	1	5	2		3	3	1
1966	8	5	1	3	3	1	5	2	
1967	13	1		7	0		6	1	
1968	12	2		6	1		6	1	
1969	12	1	1	7	0		5	1	1
1970	8	4	2	6	1		2	3	2
1971	8	4	2	5	1	1	3	3	1
1972	10	3	1	5	1	1	5	2	
1973	9	4	1	5	2		4	2	1
1974	12	2		6	1		6	1	
1975	11	3		6	1		5	2	
1976	13	1		7	0		6	1	
1977	11	3		6	1		5	2	
1978	9	7		4	4		5	3	
1979	9	7		6	2		3	5	
1980	11	5		6	2		5	3	
1981	7	9		4	4		3	5	
1982	8	1		4	0		4	1	
1983	12	4		6	2		6	2	

Season	All Games W	L	T	Home Games W	L	T	Road Games W	L	T
1984	11	5		6	2		5	3	
1985	12	4		7	1		5	3	
1986	8	8		3	5		5	3	
1987	5	10		3	5		2	5	
1988	7	9		3	5		4	4	
1989	8	8		7	1		1	7	
1990	12	4		6	2		6	2	
1991	9	7		5	3		4	4	
1992	7	9		5	3		2	6	
1993	10	6		5	3		5	3	
1994	9	7		4	4		5	3	
1995	8	8		4	4		4	4	
1996	7	9		4	4		3	5	
1997	4	12		2	6		2	6	
1998	8	8		4	4		4	4	
1999	8	8		5	3		3	5	
2000	12	4		7	1		5	3	
2001	10	6		5	3		5	3	
2002	11	5		6	2		5	3	
2003	4	12		4	4		0	8	
2004	5	11		3	5		2	6	
2005	4	12		2	6		2	6	
2006	2	14		2	6		0	8	
2007	4	12		2	6		2	6	
2008	5	11		2	6		3	5	
2009	5	11		2	6		3	5	
2010	8	8		5	3		3	5	
2011	8	8		3	5		5	3	
2012	4	12		3	5		1	7	
	430	363	11	239	160	3	191	203	8

*includes Los Angeles Raiders (1982-1994).

PITTSBURGH STEELERS*

Season	All Games W	L	T	Home Games W	L	T	Road Games W	L	T
1933	3	6	2	2	3		1	3	2
1934	2	10		1	5		1	5	
1935	4	8		2	5		2	3	
1936	6	6		4	1		2	5	
1937	4	7		2	4		2	3	
1938	2	9		0	5		2	4	
1939	1	9	1	1	4		0	5	1
1940	2	7	2	1	2	2	1	5	
1941	1	9	1	1	4		0	5	1
1942	7	4		3	2		4	2	
1945	2	8		1	4		1	4	
1946	5	5	1	4	1		1	4	1
1947	8	4		5	1		3	3	
1948	4	8		4	2		0	6	
1949	6	5	1	3	2	1	3	3	
1950	6	6		2	4		4	2	
1951	4	7	1	1	4	1	3	3	
1952	5	7		2	4		3	3	
1953	6	6		3	3		3	3	
1954	5	7		4	2		1	5	
1955	4	8		3	2		1	6	
1956	5	7		3	3		2	4	
1957	6	6		4	2		2	4	
1958	7	4	1	5	1		2	3	1
1959	6	5	1	3	2	1	3	3	
1960	5	6	1	4	2		1	4	1
1961	6	8		4	3		2	5	
1962	9	5		4	3		5	2	
1963	7	4	3	5	0	2	2	4	1
1964	5	9		2	5		3	4	
1965	2	12		1	6		1	6	
1966	5	8	1	3	3	1	2	5	
1967	4	9	1	1	6		3	3	1

Season	All Games W	L	T	Home Games W	L	T	Road Games W	L	T
1968	2	11	1	1	6		1	5	1
1969	1	13		1	6		0	7	
1970	5	9		4	3		1	6	
1971	6	8		5	2		1	6	
1972	11	3		7	0		4	3	
1973	10	4		7	1		3	3	
1974	10	3	1	5	2		5	1	1
1975	12	2		6	1		6	1	
1976	10	4		6	1		4	3	
1977	9	5		6	1		3	4	
1978	14	2		7	1		7	1	
1979	12	4		8	0		4	4	
1980	9	7		6	2		3	5	
1981	8	8		5	3		3	5	
1982	6	3		4	0		2	3	
1983	10	6		4	4		6	2	
1984	9	7		6	2		3	5	
1985	7	9		5	3		2	6	
1986	6	10		4	4		2	6	
1987	8	7		4	3		4	4	
1988	5	11		4	4		1	7	
1989	9	7		4	4		5	3	
1990	9	7		6	2		3	5	
1991	7	9		5	3		2	6	
1992	11	5		7	1		4	4	
1993	9	7		6	2		3	5	
1994	12	4		7	1		5	3	
1995	11	5		6	2		5	3	
1996	10	6		7	1		3	5	
1997	11	5		7	1		4	4	
1998	7	9		5	3		2	6	
1999	6	10		2	6		4	4	
2000	9	7		4	4		5	3	
2001	13	3		7	1		6	2	
2002	10	5	1	5	2	1	5	3	
2003	6	10		4	4		2	6	
2004	15	1		8	0		7	1	
2005	11	5		5	3		6	2	
2006	8	8		5	3		3	5	
2007	10	6		7	1		3	5	
2008	12	4		6	2		6	2	
2009	9	7		6	2		3	5	
2010	12	4		5	3		7	1	
2011	12	4		7	1		5	3	
2012	8	8		5	3		3	5	
	561	511	20	329	204	9	232	307	11

*includes Pittsburgh Pirates (1933-39).

SAN DIEGO CHARGERS*

Season	All Games W	L	T	Home Games W	L	T	Road Games W	L	T
1960	10	4		5	2		5	2	
1961	12	2		6	1		6	1	
1962	4	10		3	4		1	6	
1963	11	3		6	1		5	2	
1964	8	5	1	4	3		4	2	1
1965	9	2	3	4	1	2	5	1	1
1966	7	6	1	5	2		2	4	1
1967	8	5	1	5	2	1	3	3	
1968	9	5		4	3		5	2	
1969	8	6		5	2		3	4	
1970	5	6	3	2	3	2	3	3	1
1971	6	8		6	1		0	7	
1972	4	9	1	2	5		2	4	1
1973	2	11	1	2	5		0	6	1
1974	5	9		3	4		2	5	
1975	2	12		1	6		1	6	
1976	6	8		3	4		3	4	
1977	7	7		3	4		4	3	
1978	9	7		5	3		4	4	
1979	12	4		7	1		5	3	
1980	11	5		6	2		5	3	
1981	10	6		5	3		5	3	
1982	6	3		3	1		3	2	
1983	6	10		4	4		2	6	
1984	7	9		4	4		3	5	
1985	8	8		6	2		2	6	
1986	4	12		2	6		2	6	
1987	8	7		4	3		4	4	
1988	6	10		3	5		3	5	
1989	6	10		4	4		2	6	
1990	6	10		3	5		3	5	
1991	4	12		3	5		1	7	
1992	11	5		6	2		5	3	
1993	8	8		4	4		4	4	
1994	11	5		5	3		6	2	
1995	9	7		5	3		4	4	
1996	8	8		5	3		3	5	
1997	4	12		2	6		2	6	
1998	5	11		4	4		1	7	
1999	8	8		4	4		4	4	
2000	1	15		1	7		0	8	
2001	5	11		4	4		1	7	
2002	8	8		5	3		3	5	
2003	4	12		2	6		2	6	
2004	12	4		7	1		5	3	
2005	9	7		4	4		5	3	
2006	14	2		8	0		6	2	
2007	11	5		7	1		4	4	
2008	8	8		5	3		3	5	
2009	13	3		6	2		7	1	
2010	9	7		6	2		3	5	
2011	8	8		5	3		3	5	
2012	7	9		3	5		4	4	
	399	394	11	226	171	5	173	223	6

*includes Los Angeles Chargers (1960).

TENNESSEE TITANS*

Season	All Games W	L	T	Home Games W	L	T	Road Games W	L	T
1960	10	4		6	1		4	3	
1961	10	3	1	6	1		4	2	1
1962	11	3		6	1		5	2	
1963	6	8		4	3		2	5	
1964	4	10		3	4		1	6	
1965	4	10		3	4		1	6	
1966	3	11		3	4		0	7	
1967	9	4	1	5	2		4	2	1
1968	7	7		3	4		4	3	
1969	6	6	2	4	2	1	2	4	1
1970	3	10	1	1	6		2	4	1
1971	4	9	1	3	3	1	1	6	
1972	1	13		1	6		0	7	
1973	1	13		0	7		1	6	
1974	7	7		3	4		4	3	
1975	10	4		5	2		5	2	
1976	5	9		3	4		2	5	
1977	8	6		5	2		3	4	
1978	10	6		5	3		5	3	
1979	11	5		6	2		5	3	
1980	11	5		6	2		5	3	
1981	7	9		5	3		2	6	
1982	1	8		1	4		0	4	
1983	2	14		2	6		0	8	
1984	3	13		2	6		1	7	
1985	5	11		4	4		1	7	

Season	All Games W	L	T	Home Games W	L	T	Road Games W	L	T
1986	5	11		4	4		1	7	
1987	9	6		5	2		4	4	
1988	10	6		7	1		3	5	
1989	9	7		6	2		3	5	
1990	9	7		6	2		3	5	
1991	11	5		7	1		4	4	
1992	10	6		5	3		5	3	
1993	12	4		7	1		5	3	
1994	2	14		2	6		0	8	
1995	7	9		3	5		4	4	
1996	8	8		2	6		6	2	
1997	8	8		6	2		2	6	
1998	8	8		3	5		5	3	
1999	13	3		8	0		5	3	
2000	13	3		7	1		6	2	
2001	7	9		3	5		4	4	
2002	11	5		6	2		5	3	
2003	12	4		7	1		5	3	
2004	5	11		2	6		3	5	
2005	4	12		3	5		1	7	
2006	8	8		4	4		4	4	
2007	10	6		5	3		5	3	
2008	13	3		7	1		6	2	
2009	8	8		5	3		3	5	
2010	6	10		3	5		3	5	
2011	9	7		5	3		4	4	
2012	6	10		4	4		2	6	
	392	406	6	227	173	2	165	233	4

*includes Houston (1960-1996) and Tennessee Oilers (1997-98)

NFC
ARIZONA CARDINALS*

Season	All Games W	L	T	Home Games W	L	T	Road Games W	L	T
1920	6	2	2	5	1	1	1	1	1
1921	3	3	2	3	3	1	0	0	1
1922	8	3		8	3		0	0	
1923	8	4		8	3		0	1	
1924	5	4	1	5	3	1	0	1	
1925	11	2	1	11	2		0	0	1
1926	5	6	1	3	3		2	3	1
1927	3	7	1	2	3	1	1	4	
1928	1	5		1	1		0	4	
1929	6	6	1	3	2		3	4	1
1930	5	6	2	3	2		2	4	2
1931	5	4		3	0		2	4	
1932	2	6	2	1	2	1	1	4	1
1933	1	9	1	0	4	1	1	5	
1934	5	6		2	2		3	4	
1935	6	4	2	2	2		4	2	2
1936	3	8	1	3	1	1	0	7	
1937	5	5	1	1	3		4	2	1
1938	2	9		1	4		1	5	
1939	1	10		0	4		1	6	
1940	2	7	2	2	1	1	0	6	1
1941	3	7	1	0	3	1	3	4	
1942	3	8		2	2		1	6	
1943	0	10		0	3		0	7	
1945	1	9		0	3		1	6	
1946	6	5		2	2		4	3	
1947	9	3		5	0		4	3	
1948	11	1		5	1		6	0	
1949	6	5	1	2	3	1	4	2	
1950	5	7		3	3		2	4	
1951	3	9		1	5		2	4	
1952	4	8		2	4		2	4	
1953	1	10	1	0	5	1	1	5	
1954	2	10		2	4		0	6	

Season	All Games W	L	T	Home Games W	L	T	Road Games W	L	T
1955	4	7	1	3	2	1	1	5	
1956	7	5		4	2		3	3	
1957	3	9		0	6		3	3	
1958	2	9	1	1	4	1	1	5	
1959	2	10		2	4		0	6	
1960	6	5	1	3	2	1	3	3	
1961	7	7		3	4		4	3	
1962	4	9	1	2	4	1	2	5	
1963	9	5		3	4		6	1	
1964	9	3	2	4	1	1	5	2	1
1965	5	9		2	5		3	4	
1966	8	5	1	5	1	1	3	4	
1967	6	7	1	3	3	1	3	4	
1968	9	4	1	4	2	1	5	2	
1969	4	9	1	3	4		1	5	1
1970	8	5	1	6	1		2	4	1
1971	4	9	1	1	5	1	3	4	
1972	4	9	1	2	5		2	4	1
1973	4	9	1	2	4	1	2	5	
1974	10	4		5	2		5	2	
1975	11	3		6	1		5	2	
1976	10	4		6	1		4	3	
1977	7	7		4	3		3	4	
1978	6	10		3	5		3	5	
1979	5	11		3	5		2	6	
1980	5	11		2	6		3	5	
1981	7	9		5	3		2	6	
1982	5	4		1	3		4	1	
1983	8	7	1	4	3	1	4	4	
1984	9	7		5	3		4	4	
1985	5	11		4	4		1	7	
1986	4	11	1	3	5		1	6	1
1987	7	8		4	3		3	5	
1988	7	9		4	4		3	5	
1989	5	11		2	6		3	5	
1990	5	11		3	5		2	6	
1991	4	12		2	6		2	6	
1992	4	12		3	5		1	7	
1993	7	9		4	4		3	5	
1994	8	8		5	3		3	5	
1995	4	12		3	5		1	7	
1996	7	9		5	3		2	6	
1997	4	12		3	5		1	7	
1998	9	7		5	3		4	4	
1999	6	10		4	4		2	6	
2000	3	13		3	5		0	8	
2001	7	9		3	5		4	4	
2002	5	11		3	5		2	6	
2003	4	12		4	4		0	8	
2004	6	10		5	3		1	7	
2005	5	11		3	5		2	6	
2006	5	11		3	5		2	6	
2007	8	8		6	2		2	6	
2008	9	7		6	2		3	5	
2009	10	6		4	4		6	2	
2010	5	11		4	4		1	7	
2011	8	8		6	2		2	6	
2012	5	11		4	4		1	7	
	501	700	39	296	300	22	205	400	17

*includes Chicago Cardinals (1920-1959), St. Louis Cardinals (1960-1987), and Phoenix Cardinals (1988-1993).

ATLANTA FALCONS

Season	All Games W	L	T	Home Games W	L	T	Road Games W	L	T
1966	3	11		1	6		2	5	
1967	1	12	1	1	5	1	0	7	
1968	2	12		1	6		1	6	

Season	All Games W	L	T	Home Games W	L	T	Road Games W	L	T
1969	6	8		4	3		2	5	
1970	4	8	2	3	4		1	4	2
1971	7	6	1	4	3		3	3	1
1972	7	7		4	3		3	4	
1973	9	5		4	3		5	2	
1974	3	11		2	5		1	6	
1975	4	10		3	4		1	6	
1976	4	10		3	4		1	6	
1977	7	7		4	3		3	4	
1978	9	7		7	1		2	6	
1979	6	10		3	5		3	5	
1980	12	4		6	2		6	2	
1981	7	9		4	4		3	5	
1982	5	4		2	3		3	1	
1983	7	9		4	4		3	5	
1984	4	12		2	6		2	6	
1985	4	12		3	5		1	7	
1986	7	8	1	2	5	1	5	3	
1987	3	12		2	6		1	6	
1988	5	11		2	6		3	5	
1989	3	13		3	5		0	8	
1990	5	11		5	3		0	8	
1991	10	6		6	2		4	4	
1992	6	10		5	3		1	7	
1993	6	10		4	4		2	6	
1994	7	9		5	3		2	6	
1995	9	7		7	1		2	6	
1996	3	13		2	6		1	7	
1997	7	9		3	5		4	4	
1998	14	2		8	0		6	2	
1999	5	11		4	4		1	7	
2000	4	12		3	5		1	7	
2001	7	9		3	5		4	4	
2002	9	6	1	5	3		4	3	1
2003	5	11		2	6		3	5	
2004	11	5		7	1		4	4	
2005	8	8		4	4		4	4	
2006	7	9		3	5		4	4	
2007	4	12		3	5		1	7	
2008	11	5		7	1		4	4	
2009	9	7		6	2		3	5	
2010	13	3		7	1		6	2	
2011	10	6		6	2		4	4	
2012	13	3		7	1		6	2	
	312	402	6	186	173	2	126	229	4

CAROLINA PANTHERS

Season	All Games W	L	T	Home Games W	L	T	Road Games W	L	T
1995	7	9		5	3		2	6	
1996	12	4		8	0		4	4	
1997	7	9		2	6		5	3	
1998	4	12		2	6		2	6	
1999	8	8		5	3		3	5	
2000	7	9		5	3		2	6	
2001	1	15		0	8		1	7	
2002	7	9		4	4		3	5	
2003	11	5		6	2		5	3	
2004	7	9		3	5		4	4	
2005	11	5		5	3		6	2	
2006	8	8		4	4		4	4	
2007	7	9		2	6		5	3	
2008	12	4		8	0		4	4	
2009	8	8		5	3		3	5	
2010	2	14		2	6		0	8	
2011	6	10		3	5		3	5	
2012	7	9		3	5		4	4	
	132	156		72	72		60	84	

CHICAGO BEARS*

Season	All Games W	L	T	Home Games W	L	T	Road Games W	L	T
1920	10	1	2	6	0	1	4	1	1
1921	9	1	1	9	1	1	0	0	
1922	9	3		7	1		2	2	
1923	9	2	1	7	1	1	2	1	
1924	6	1	4	5	0	3	1	1	1
1925	9	5	3	7	1	1	2	4	2
1926	12	1	3	10	0	2	2	1	1
1927	9	3	2	7	1	1	2	2	1
1928	7	5	1	6	3		1	2	1
1929	4	9	2	1	5	2	3	4	
1930	9	4	1	5	2	1	4	2	
1931	8	5		6	3		2	2	
1932	7	1	6	6	1	1	1	0	5
1933	10	2	1	6	0		4	2	1
1934	13	0		5	0		8	0	
1935	6	4	2	1	2	2	5	2	
1936	9	3		3	1		6	2	
1937	9	1	1	4	1		5	0	1
1938	6	5		2	3		4	2	
1939	8	3		4	1		4	2	
1940	8	3		5	0		3	3	
1941	10	1		5	1		5	0	
1942	11	0		6	0		5	0	
1943	8	1	1	5	0		3	1	1
1944	6	3	1	4	0	1	2	3	
1945	3	7		2	3		1	4	
1946	8	2	1	4	1	1	4	1	
1947	8	4		4	2		4	2	
1948	10	2		5	1		5	1	
1949	9	3		5	1		4	2	
1950	9	3		6	0		3	3	
1951	7	5		3	3		4	2	
1952	5	7		3	3		2	4	
1953	3	8	1	1	4	1	2	4	
1954	8	4		4	2		4	2	
1955	8	4		5	1		3	3	
1956	9	2	1	6	0		3	2	1
1957	5	7		2	4		3	3	
1958	8	4		5	1		3	3	
1959	8	4		4	2		4	2	
1960	5	6	1	4	2		1	4	1
1961	8	6		5	2		3	4	
1962	9	5		4	3		5	2	
1963	11	1	2	6	0	1	5	1	1
1964	5	9		2	5		3	4	
1965	9	5		5	2		4	3	
1966	5	7	2	4	1	2	1	6	
1967	7	6	1	3	3	1	4	3	
1968	7	7		2	5		5	2	
1969	1	13		1	6		0	7	
1970	6	8		3	4		3	4	
1971	6	8		4	3		2	5	
1972	4	9	1	1	5	1	3	4	
1973	3	11		1	6		2	5	
1974	4	10		4	3		0	7	
1975	4	10		3	4		1	6	
1976	7	7		4	3		3	4	
1977	9	5		5	2		4	3	
1978	7	9		4	4		3	5	
1979	10	6		6	2		4	4	
1980	7	9		5	3		2	6	
1981	6	10		4	4		2	6	
1982	3	6		2	2		1	4	
1983	8	8		5	3		3	5	
1984	10	6		6	2		4	4	
1985	15	1		8	0		7	1	
1986	14	2		7	1		7	1	

Season	All Games W	L	T	Home Games W	L	T	Road Games W	L	T
1987	11	4		6	2		5	2	
1988	12	4		7	1		5	3	
1989	6	10		4	4		2	6	
1990	11	5		7	1		4	4	
1991	11	5		6	2		5	3	
1992	5	11		4	4		1	7	
1993	7	9		3	5		4	4	
1994	9	7		5	3		4	4	
1995	9	7		5	3		4	4	
1996	7	9		6	2		1	7	
1997	4	12		2	6		2	6	
1998	4	12		3	5		1	7	
1999	6	10		3	5		3	5	
2000	5	11		3	5		2	6	
2001	13	3		7	1		6	2	
2002	4	12		3	5		1	7	
2003	7	9		6	2		1	7	
2004	5	11		2	6		3	5	
2005	11	5		7	1		4	4	
2006	13	3		6	2		7	1	
2007	7	9		4	4		3	5	
2008	9	7		6	2		3	5	
2009	7	9		5	3		2	6	
2010	11	5		5	3		6	2	
2011	8	8		5	3		3	5	
2012	10	6		5	3		5	3	
	722	526	42	424	219	24	298	307	18

includes Decatur Staleys (1920) and Chicago Staleys (1921).

DALLAS COWBOYS

Season	All Games W	L	T	Home Games W	L	T	Road Games W	L	T
1960	0	11	1	0	6		0	5	1
1961	4	9	1	2	4	1	2	5	
1962	5	8	1	2	4	1	3	4	
1963	4	10		3	4		1	6	
1964	5	8	1	2	4	1	3	4	
1965	7	7		5	2		2	5	
1966	10	3	1	6	1		4	2	1
1967	9	5		5	2		4	3	
1968	12	2		5	2		7	0	
1969	11	2	1	6	0	1	5	2	
1970	10	4		6	1		4	3	
1971	11	3		6	1		5	2	
1972	10	4		5	2		5	2	
1973	10	4		6	1		4	3	
1974	8	6		5	2		3	4	
1975	10	4		5	2		5	2	
1976	11	3		6	1		5	2	
1977	12	2		6	1		6	1	
1978	12	4		7	1		5	3	
1979	11	5		6	2		5	3	
1980	12	4		8	0		4	4	
1981	12	4		8	0		4	4	
1982	6	3		3	2		3	1	
1983	12	4		6	2		6	2	
1984	9	7		5	3		4	4	
1985	10	6		7	1		3	5	
1986	7	9		3	5		4	4	
1987	7	8		3	4		4	4	
1988	3	13		1	7		2	6	
1989	1	15		0	8		1	7	
1990	7	9		5	3		2	6	
1991	11	5		6	2		5	3	
1992	13	3		7	1		6	2	
1993	12	4		6	2		6	2	
1994	12	4		6	2		6	2	
1995	12	4		6	2		6	2	

Season	All Games W	L	T	Home Games W	L	T	Road Games W	L	T
1996	10	6		6	2		4	4	
1997	6	10		5	3		1	7	
1998	10	6		6	2		4	4	
1999	8	8		7	1		1	7	
2000	5	11		3	5		2	6	
2001	5	11		4	4		1	7	
2002	5	11		4	4		1	7	
2003	10	6		6	2		4	4	
2004	6	10		4	4		2	6	
2005	9	7		5	3		4	4	
2006	9	7		4	4		5	3	
2007	13	3		6	2		7	1	
2008	9	7		6	2		3	5	
2009	11	5		6	2		5	3	
2010	6	10		2	6		4	4	
2011	8	8		5	3		3	5	
2012	8	8		4	4		4	4	
	456	340	6	257	140	4	199	200	2

DETROIT LIONS*

Season	All Games W	L	T	Home Games W	L	T	Road Games W	L	T
1930	5	6	3	5	1	2	0	5	1
1931	11	3		8	0		3	3	
1932	6	2	4	3	0	2	3	2	2
1933	6	5		4	1		2	4	
1934	10	3		6	2		4	1	
1935	7	3	2	5	0	1	2	3	1
1936	8	4		5	1		3	3	
1937	7	4		4	2		3	2	
1938	7	4		4	3		3	1	
1939	6	5		4	2		2	3	
1940	5	5	1	3	3		2	2	1
1941	4	6	1	3	2		1	4	1
1942	0	11		0	7		0	4	
1943	3	6	1	2	2	1	1	4	
1944	6	3	1	4	2		2	1	1
1945	7	3		4	1		3	2	
1946	1	10		1	5		0	5	
1947	3	9		2	4		1	5	
1948	2	10		2	4		0	6	
1949	4	8		2	4		2	4	
1950	6	6		4	2		2	4	
1951	7	4	1	3	3	1	4	1	
1952	9	3		6	1		3	2	
1953	10	2		5	1		5	1	
1954	9	2	1	5	0	1	4	2	
1955	3	9		3	4		0	5	
1956	9	3		5	1		4	2	
1957	8	4		5	1		3	3	
1958	4	7	1	2	4		2	3	1
1959	3	8	1	2	4		1	4	1
1960	7	5		5	1		2	4	
1961	8	5	1	2	5		6	0	1
1962	11	3		7	0		4	3	
1963	5	8	1	3	3	1	2	5	
1964	7	5	2	3	3	1	4	2	1
1965	6	7	1	2	4	1	4	3	
1966	4	9	1	3	4		1	5	1
1967	5	7	2	3	4		2	3	2
1968	4	8	2	1	4	2	3	4	
1969	9	4	1	5	2		4	2	1
1970	10	4		6	1		4	3	
1971	7	6	1	3	4		4	2	1
1972	8	5	1	5	2		3	3	1
1973	6	7	1	4	3		2	4	1
1974	7	7		5	2		2	5	
1975	7	7		4	3		3	4	

Season	All Games W	L	T	Home Games W	L	T	Road Games W	L	T
1976	6	8		5	2		1	6	
1977	6	8		5	2		1	6	
1978	7	9		5	3		2	6	
1979	2	14		2	6		0	8	
1980	9	7		6	2		3	5	
1981	8	8		7	1		1	7	
1982	4	5		2	3		2	2	
1983	9	7		6	2		3	5	
1984	4	11	1	2	5	1	2	6	
1985	7	9		6	2		1	7	
1986	5	11		1	7		4	4	
1987	4	11		1	6		3	5	
1988	4	12		2	6		2	6	
1989	7	9		4	4		3	5	
1990	6	10		3	5		3	5	
1991	12	4		8	0		4	4	
1992	5	11		3	5		2	6	
1993	10	6		5	3		5	3	
1994	9	7		6	2		3	5	
1995	10	6		7	1		3	5	
1996	5	11		4	4		1	7	
1997	9	7		6	2		3	5	
1998	5	11		4	4		1	7	
1999	8	8		6	2		2	6	
2000	9	7		4	4		5	3	
2001	2	14		2	6		0	8	
2002	3	13		3	5		0	8	
2003	5	11		5	3		0	8	
2004	6	10		3	5		3	5	
2005	5	11		3	5		2	6	
2006	3	13		2	6		1	7	
2007	7	9		5	3		2	6	
2008	0	16		0	8		0	8	
2009	2	14		2	6		0	8	
2010	6	10		4	4		2	6	
2011	10	6		5	3		5	3	
2012	4	12		2	6		2	6	
	510	611	32	318	255	14	192	356	18

*includes Portsmouth Spartans (1930-33).

GREEN BAY PACKERS

Season	All Games W	L	T	Home Games W	L	T	Road Games W	L	T
1921	3	2	1	2	1		1	1	1
1922	4	3	3	4	1	1	0	2	2
1923	7	2	1	4	2	1	3	0	
1924	7	4		5	0		2	4	
1925	8	5		6	0		2	5	
1926	7	3	3	4	1	2	3	2	1
1927	7	2	1	6	1		1	1	1
1928	6	4	3	2	2	2	4	2	1
1929	12	0	1	5	0		7	0	1
1930	10	3	1	6	0		4	3	1
1931	12	2		8	0		4	2	
1932	10	3	1	5	0	1	5	3	
1933	5	7	1	3	2	1	2	5	
1934	7	6		4	2		3	4	
1935	8	4		5	2		3	2	
1936	10	1	1	5	1		5	0	1
1937	7	4		3	2		4	2	
1938	8	3		4	2		4	1	
1939	9	2		4	1		5	1	
1940	6	4	1	4	2		2	2	1
1941	10	1		4	1		6	0	
1942	8	2	1	4	1		4	1	1
1943	7	2	1	2	1	1	5	1	
1944	8	2		5	0		3	2	
1945	6	4		4	1		2	3	

Season	All Games W	L	T	Home Games W	L	T	Road Games W	L	T
1946	6	5		2	3		4	2	
1947	6	5	1	4	2		2	3	1
1948	3	9		2	4		1	5	
1949	2	10		1	5		1	5	
1950	3	9		3	3		0	6	
1951	3	9		2	4		1	5	
1952	6	6		3	3		3	3	
1953	2	9	1	1	5		1	4	1
1954	4	8		2	4		2	4	
1955	6	6		5	1		1	5	
1956	4	8		2	4		2	4	
1957	3	9		1	5		2	4	
1958	1	10	1	1	4	1	0	6	
1959	7	5		4	2		3	3	
1960	8	4		4	2		4	2	
1961	11	3		6	1		5	2	
1962	13	1		7	0		6	1	
1963	11	2	1	6	1		5	1	1
1964	8	5	1	4	3		4	2	1
1965	10	3	1	6	1		4	2	1
1966	12	2		6	1		6	1	
1967	9	4	1	4	2	1	5	2	
1968	6	7	1	2	5		4	2	1
1969	8	6		5	2		3	4	
1970	6	8		4	3		2	5	
1971	4	8	2	3	3	1	1	5	1
1972	10	4		4	3		6	1	
1973	5	7	2	3	2	2	2	5	
1974	6	8		4	3		2	5	
1975	4	10		3	4		1	6	
1976	5	9		4	3		1	6	
1977	4	10		2	5		2	5	
1978	8	7	1	5	2	1	3	5	
1979	5	11		4	4		1	7	
1980	5	10	1	4	4		1	6	1
1981	8	8		4	4		4	4	
1982	5	3	1	3	1		2	2	1
1983	8	8		5	3		3	5	
1984	8	8		5	3		3	5	
1985	8	8		5	3		3	5	
1986	4	12		1	7		3	5	
1987	5	9	1	2	5	1	3	4	
1988	4	12		2	6		2	6	
1989	10	6		6	2		4	4	
1990	6	10		3	5		3	5	
1991	4	12		2	6		2	6	
1992	9	7		6	2		3	5	
1993	9	7		6	2		3	5	
1994	9	7		7	1		2	6	
1995	11	5		7	1		4	4	
1996	13	3		8	0		5	3	
1997	13	3		8	0		5	3	
1998	11	5		7	1		4	4	
1999	8	8		5	3		3	5	
2000	9	7		6	2		3	5	
2001	12	4		7	1		5	3	
2002	12	4		8	0		4	4	
2003	10	6		5	3		5	3	
2004	10	6		4	4		6	2	
2005	4	12		3	5		1	7	
2006	8	8		3	5		5	3	
2007	13	3		7	1		6	2	
2008	6	10		4	4		2	6	
2009	11	5		6	2		5	3	
2010	10	6		7	1		3	5	
2011	15	1		8	0		7	1	
2012	11	5		7	1		4	4	
	690	530	36	398	213	16	292	317	20

MINNESOTA VIKINGS

Season	All Games W	L	T	Home Games W	L	T	Road Games W	L	T
1961	3	11		3	4		0	7	
1962	2	11	1	1	5	1	1	6	
1963	5	8	1	3	4		2	4	1
1964	8	5	1	4	3		4	2	1
1965	7	7		2	5		5	2	
1966	4	9	1	2	5		2	4	1
1967	3	8	3	1	4	2	2	4	1
1968	8	6		4	3		4	3	
1969	12	2		7	0		5	2	
1970	12	2		7	0		5	2	
1971	11	3		5	2		6	1	
1972	7	7		3	4		4	3	
1973	12	2		7	0		5	2	
1974	10	4		4	3		6	1	
1975	12	2		7	0		5	2	
1976	11	2	1	6	0	1	5	2	
1977	9	5		5	2		4	3	
1978	8	7	1	5	3		3	4	1
1979	7	9		5	3		2	6	
1980	9	7		5	3		4	4	
1981	7	9		5	3		2	6	
1982	5	4		4	1		1	3	
1983	8	8		3	5		5	3	
1984	3	13		2	6		1	7	
1985	7	9		4	4		3	5	
1986	9	7		5	3		4	4	
1987	8	7		5	3		3	4	
1988	11	5		7	1		4	4	
1989	10	6		8	0		2	6	
1990	6	10		4	4		2	6	
1991	8	8		4	4		4	4	
1992	11	5		5	3		6	2	
1993	9	7		4	4		5	3	
1994	10	6		6	2		4	4	
1995	8	8		6	2		2	6	
1996	9	7		5	3		4	4	
1997	9	7		5	3		4	4	
1998	15	1		8	0		7	1	
1999	10	6		6	2		4	4	
2000	11	5		7	1		4	4	
2001	5	11		5	3		0	8	
2002	6	10		4	4		2	6	
2003	9	7		6	2		3	5	
2004	8	8		5	3		3	5	
2005	9	7		6	2		3	5	
2006	6	10		3	5		3	5	
2007	8	8		5	3		3	5	
2008	10	6		6	2		4	4	
2009	12	4		8	0		4	4	
2010	6	10		4	4		2	6	
2011	3	13		1	7		2	6	
2012	10	6		7	1		3	5	
	426	355	9	249	143	4	177	212	5

NEW ORLEANS SAINTS

Season	All Games W	L	T	Home Games W	L	T	Road Games W	L	T
1967	3	11		2	5		1	6	
1968	4	9	1	3	4		1	5	1
1969	5	9		3	4		2	5	
1970	2	11	1	2	5		0	6	1
1971	4	8	2	2	4	1	2	4	1
1972	2	11	1	2	5		0	6	1
1973	5	9		5	2		0	7	
1974	5	9		4	3		1	6	
1975	2	12		2	5		0	7	
1976	4	10		2	5		2	5	

Season	All Games W	L	T	Home Games W	L	T	Road Games W	L	T
1977	3	11		2	5		1	6	
1978	7	9		3	5		4	4	
1979	8	8		3	5		5	3	
1980	1	15		0	8		1	7	
1981	4	12		2	6		2	6	
1982	4	5		2	3		2	2	
1983	8	8		5	3		3	5	
1984	7	9		3	5		4	4	
1985	5	11		3	5		2	6	
1986	7	9		4	4		3	5	
1987	12	3		6	1		6	2	
1988	10	6		5	3		5	3	
1989	9	7		5	3		4	4	
1990	8	8		5	3		3	5	
1991	11	5		6	2		5	3	
1992	12	4		6	2		6	2	
1993	8	8		4	4		4	4	
1994	7	9		3	5		4	4	
1995	7	9		4	4		3	5	
1996	3	13		2	6		1	7	
1997	6	10		3	5		3	5	
1998	6	10		4	4		2	6	
1999	3	13		3	5		0	8	
2000	10	6		3	5		7	1	
2001	7	9		3	5		4	4	
2002	9	7		4	4		5	3	
2003	8	8		5	3		3	5	
2004	8	8		3	5		5	3	
2005	3	13		1	7		2	6	
2006	10	6		4	4		6	2	
2007	7	9		3	5		4	4	
2008	8	8		6	2		2	6	
2009	13	3		6	2		7	1	
2010	11	5		5	3		6	2	
2011	13	3		8	0		5	3	
2012	7	9		4	4		3	5	
	306	395	5	165	187	1	141	208	4

NEW YORK GIANTS

Season	All Games W	L	T	Home Games W	L	T	Road Games W	L	T
1925	8	4		7	2		1	2	
1926	8	4	1	5	2	1	3	2	
1927	11	1	1	7	1		4	0	1
1928	4	7	2	1	2	2	3	5	
1929	13	1	1	7	1		6	0	1
1930	13	4		6	2		7	2	
1931	7	6	1	4	2	1	3	4	
1932	4	6	2	3	2	1	1	4	1
1933	11	3		7	0		4	3	
1934	8	5		5	1		3	4	
1935	9	3		4	2		5	1	
1936	5	6	1	3	3	1	2	3	
1937	6	3	2	4	2	1	2	1	1
1938	8	2	1	6	1		2	1	1
1939	9	1	1	6	0		3	1	1
1940	6	4	1	4	3		2	1	1
1941	8	3		5	2		3	1	
1942	5	5	1	3	2	1	2	3	
1943	6	3	1	4	2		2	1	1
1944	8	1	1	5	1		3	0	1
1945	3	6	1	2	4		1	2	1
1946	7	3	1	5	1	1	2	2	
1947	2	8	2	2	3	1	0	5	1
1948	4	8		2	4		2	4	
1949	6	6		2	4		4	2	
1950	10	2		5	1		5	1	
1951	9	2	1	5	1		4	1	1

Season	All Games W	L	T	Home Games W	L	T	Road Games W	L	T
1952	7	5		2	4		5	1	
1953	3	9		2	4		1	5	
1954	7	5		4	2		3	3	
1955	6	5	1	4	1	1	2	4	
1956	8	3	1	4	1	1	4	2	
1957	7	5		3	3		4	2	
1958	9	3		5	1		4	2	
1959	10	2		5	1		5	1	
1960	6	4	2	1	3	2	5	1	
1961	10	3	1	4	2	1	6	1	
1962	12	2		6	1		6	1	
1963	11	3		5	2		6	1	
1964	2	10	2	2	5		0	5	2
1965	7	7		3	4		4	3	
1966	1	12	1	1	6		0	6	1
1967	7	7		5	2		2	5	
1968	7	7		3	4		4	3	
1969	6	8		5	2		1	6	
1970	9	5		5	2		4	3	
1971	4	10		1	6		3	4	
1972	8	6		4	3		4	3	
1973	2	11	1	2	4	1	0	7	
1974	2	12		0	7		2	5	
1975	5	9		2	5		3	4	
1976	3	11		3	4		0	7	
1977	5	9		3	4		2	5	
1978	6	10		5	3		1	7	
1979	6	10		4	4		2	6	
1980	4	12		2	6		2	6	
1981	9	7		4	4		5	3	
1982	4	5		2	3		2	2	
1983	3	12	1	1	7		2	5	1
1984	9	7		6	2		3	5	
1985	10	6		6	2		4	4	
1986	14	2		8	0		6	2	
1987	6	9		5	3		1	6	
1988	10	6		5	3		5	3	
1989	12	4		7	1		5	3	
1990	13	3		7	1		6	2	
1991	8	8		5	3		3	5	
1992	6	10		4	4		2	6	
1993	11	5		6	2		5	3	
1994	9	7		4	4		5	3	
1995	5	11		3	5		2	6	
1996	6	10		3	5		3	5	
1997	10	5	1	6	2		4	3	1
1998	8	8		5	3		3	5	
1999	7	9		4	4		3	5	
2000	12	4		5	3		7	1	
2001	7	9		5	3		2	6	
2002	10	6		5	3		5	3	
2003	4	12		1	7		3	5	
2004	6	10		3	5		3	5	
2005	11	5		7	1		4	4	
2006	8	8		3	5		5	3	
2007	10	6		3	5		7	1	
2008	12	4		7	1		5	3	
2009	8	8		4	4		4	4	
2010	10	6		5	3		5	3	
2011	9	7		4	4		5	3	
2012	9	7		6	2		3	5	
	654	538	33	363	251	16	291	287	17

PHILADELPHIA EAGLES

Season	All Games W	L	T	Home Games W	L	T	Road Games W	L	T
1933	3	5	1	2	3	1	1	2	
1934	4	7		2	4		2	3	

Season	All Games W	L	T	Home Games W	L	T	Road Games W	L	T
1935	2	9		0	5		2	4	
1936	1	11		1	6		0	5	
1937	2	8	1	0	5	1	2	3	
1938	5	6		2	3		3	3	
1939	1	9	1	1	3	1	0	6	
1940	1	10		1	4		0	6	
1941	2	8	1	1	4	1	1	4	
1942	2	9		0	5		2	4	
1944	7	1	2	3	1	2	4	0	
1945	7	3		6	0		1	3	
1946	6	5		3	2		3	3	
1947	8	4		6	1		2	3	
1948	9	2	1	6	0		3	2	1
1949	11	1		6	0		5	1	
1950	6	6		2	4		4	2	
1951	4	8		1	5		3	3	
1952	7	5		4	2		3	3	
1953	7	4	1	5	0	1	2	4	
1954	7	4	1	5	1		2	3	1
1955	4	7	1	4	2		0	5	1
1956	3	8	1	2	3	1	1	5	
1957	4	8		3	3		1	5	
1958	2	9	1	2	4		0	5	1
1959	7	5		5	1		2	4	
1960	10	2		5	1		5	1	
1961	10	4		5	2		5	2	
1962	3	10	1	2	5		1	5	1
1963	2	10	2	1	5	1	1	5	1
1964	6	8		3	4		3	4	
1965	5	9		2	5		3	4	
1966	9	5		5	2		4	3	
1967	6	7	1	5	2		1	5	1
1968	2	12		1	6		1	6	
1969	4	9	1	2	5		2	4	1
1970	3	10	1	3	3	1	0	7	
1971	6	7	1	3	4		3	3	1
1972	2	11	1	0	6	1	2	5	
1973	5	8	1	4	3		1	5	1
1974	7	7		5	2		2	5	
1975	4	10		2	5		2	5	
1976	4	10		2	5		2	5	
1977	5	9		4	3		1	6	
1978	9	7		5	3		4	4	
1979	11	5		5	3		6	2	
1980	12	4		7	1		5	3	
1981	10	6		6	2		4	4	
1982	3	6		1	4		2	2	
1983	5	11		1	7		4	4	
1984	6	9	1	5	3		1	6	1
1985	7	9		4	4		3	5	
1986	5	10	1	2	5	1	3	5	
1987	7	8		4	4		3	4	
1988	10	6		5	3		5	3	
1989	11	5		6	2		5	3	
1990	10	6		6	2		4	4	
1991	10	6		4	4		6	2	
1992	11	5		8	0		3	5	
1993	8	8		3	5		5	3	
1994	7	9		5	3		2	6	
1995	10	6		6	2		4	4	
1996	10	6		5	3		5	3	
1997	6	9	1	6	2		0	7	1
1998	3	13		3	5		0	8	
1999	5	11		4	4		1	7	
2000	11	5		5	3		6	2	
2001	11	5		4	4		7	1	
2002	12	4		7	1		5	3	
2003	12	4		5	3		7	1	

Season	All Games W	L	T	Home Games W	L	T	Road Games W	L	T
2004	13	3		7	1		6	2	
2005	6	10		4	4		2	6	
2006	10	6		5	3		5	3	
2007	8	8		3	5		5	3	
2008	9	6	1	6	2		3	4	1
2009	11	5		6	2		5	3	
2010	10	6		4	4		6	2	
2011	8	8		3	5		5	3	
2012	4	12		2	6		2	6	
	516	557	25	289	253	12	227	304	13

ST. LOUIS RAMS*

Season	All Games W	L	T	Home Games W	L	T	Road Games W	L	T
1937	1	10		0	5		1	5	
1938	4	7		2	2		2	5	
1939	5	5	1	3	2	1	2	3	
1940	4	6	1	3	1	1	1	5	
1941	2	9		1	4		1	5	
1942	5	6		3	2		2	4	
1944	4	6		1	2		3	4	
1945	9	1		4	0		5	1	
1946	6	4	1	3	2		3	2	1
1947	6	6		3	3		3	3	
1948	6	5	1	3	2	1	3	3	
1949	8	2	2	5	1		3	1	2
1950	9	3		5	1		4	2	
1951	8	4		5	2		3	2	
1952	9	3		5	1		4	2	
1953	8	3	1	5	1		3	2	1
1954	6	5	1	3	2	1	3	3	
1955	8	3	1	5	1		3	2	1
1956	4	8		4	2		0	6	
1957	6	6		5	1		1	5	
1958	8	4		4	2		4	2	
1959	2	10		0	6		2	4	
1960	4	7	1	2	3	1	2	4	
1961	4	10		4	3		0	7	
1962	1	12	1	0	7		1	5	1
1963	5	9		3	4		2	5	
1964	5	7	2	3	2	2	2	5	
1965	4	10		3	4		1	6	
1966	8	6		5	2		3	4	
1967	11	1	2	5	1	1	6	0	1
1968	10	3	1	5	2		5	1	1
1969	11	3		5	2		6	1	
1970	9	4	1	3	3	1	6	1	
1971	8	5	1	4	2	1	4	3	
1972	6	7	1	4	3		2	4	1
1973	12	2		7	0		5	2	
1974	10	4		6	1		4	3	
1975	12	2		6	1		6	1	
1976	10	3	1	5	2		5	1	1
1977	10	4		7	0		3	4	
1978	12	4		6	2		6	2	
1979	9	7		4	4		5	3	
1980	11	5		6	2		5	3	
1981	6	10		4	4		2	6	
1982	2	7		1	4		1	3	
1983	9	7		5	3		4	4	
1984	10	6		5	3		5	3	
1985	11	5		6	2		5	3	
1986	10	6		6	2		4	4	
1987	6	9		3	4		3	5	
1988	10	6		4	4		6	2	
1989	11	5		6	2		5	3	
1990	5	11		2	6		3	5	
1991	3	13		2	6		1	7	
1992	6	10		4	4		2	6	
1993	5	11		3	5		2	6	
1994	4	12		3	5		1	7	
1995	7	9		4	4		3	5	
1996	6	10		4	4		2	6	
1997	5	11		2	6		3	5	
1998	4	12		2	6		2	6	
1999	13	3		8	0		5	3	
2000	10	6		5	3		5	3	
2001	14	2		6	2		8	0	
2002	7	9		6	2		1	7	
2003	12	4		8	0		4	4	
2004	8	8		6	2		2	6	
2005	6	10		3	5		3	5	
2006	8	8		4	4		4	4	
2007	3	13		1	7		2	6	
2008	2	14		1	7		1	7	
2009	1	15		0	8		1	7	
2010	7	9		5	3		2	6	
2011	2	14		1	7		1	7	
2012	7	8	1	4	4		3	4	1
	520	514	21	289	223	10	231	291	11

*includes Cleveland Rams (1937-1942, 1944-45) and Los Angeles Rams (1946-1994).

SAN FRANCISCO 49ERS

Season	All Games W	L	T	Home Games W	L	T	Road Games W	L	T
1950	3	9		3	3		0	6	
1951	7	4	1	5	1		2	3	1
1952	7	5		3	3		4	2	
1953	9	3		5	1		4	2	
1954	7	4	1	4	2		3	2	1
1955	4	8		2	4		2	4	
1956	5	6	1	3	3		2	3	1
1957	8	4		5	1		3	3	
1958	6	6		4	2		2	4	
1959	7	5		4	2		3	3	
1960	7	5		3	3		4	2	
1961	7	6	1	5	1	1	2	5	
1962	6	8		1	6		5	2	
1963	2	12		2	5		0	7	
1964	4	10		3	4		1	6	
1965	7	6	1	4	2	1	3	4	
1966	6	6	2	4	2	1	2	4	1
1967	7	7		3	4		4	3	
1968	7	6	1	3	3	1	4	3	
1969	4	8	2	3	3	1	1	5	1
1970	10	3	1	5	1	1	5	2	
1971	9	5		4	3		5	2	
1972	8	5	1	4	2	1	4	3	
1973	5	9		3	4		2	5	
1974	6	8		3	4		3	4	
1975	5	9		2	5		3	4	
1976	8	6		4	3		4	3	
1977	5	9		3	4		2	5	
1978	2	14		2	6		0	8	
1979	2	14		2	6		0	8	
1980	6	10		4	4		2	6	
1981	13	3		7	1		6	2	
1982	3	6		0	5		3	1	
1983	10	6		4	4		6	2	
1984	15	1		7	1		8	0	
1985	10	6		5	3		5	3	
1986	10	5	1	6	2		4	3	1
1987	13	2		6	1		7	1	
1988	10	6		4	4		6	2	
1989	14	2		6	2		8	0	
1990	14	2		6	2		8	0	
1991	10	6		7	1		3	5	

Season	All Games W	L	T	Home Games W	L	T	Road Games W	L	T
1992	14	2		7	1		7	1	
1993	10	6		6	2		4	4	
1994	13	3		7	1		6	2	
1995	11	5		6	2		5	3	
1996	12	4		6	2		6	2	
1997	13	3		8	0		5	3	
1998	12	4		8	0		4	4	
1999	4	12		3	5		1	7	
2000	6	10		4	4		2	6	
2001	12	4		7	1		5	3	
2002	10	6		5	3		5	3	
2003	7	9		6	2		1	7	
2004	2	14		1	7		1	7	
2005	4	12		3	5		1	7	
2006	7	9		4	4		3	5	
2007	5	11		3	5		2	6	
2008	7	9		4	4		3	5	
2009	8	8		6	2		2	6	
2010	6	10		5	3		1	7	
2011	13	3		7	1		6	2	
2012	11	4	1	6	1	1	5	3	
	495	413	14	275	178	8	220	235	6

SEATTLE SEAHAWKS

Season	All Games W	L	T	Home Games W	L	T	Road Games W	L	T
1976	2	12		1	6		1	6	
1977	5	9		3	4		2	5	
1978	9	7		5	3		4	4	
1979	9	7		5	3		4	4	
1980	4	12		0	8		4	4	
1981	6	10		5	3		1	7	
1982	4	5		3	2		1	3	
1983	9	7		5	3		4	4	
1984	12	4		7	1		5	3	
1985	8	8		5	3		3	5	
1986	10	6		7	1		3	5	
1987	9	6		6	2		3	4	
1988	9	7		5	3		4	4	
1989	7	9		3	5		4	4	
1990	9	7		5	3		4	4	
1991	7	9		5	3		2	6	
1992	2	14		1	7		1	7	
1993	6	10		4	4		2	6	
1994	6	10		3	5		3	5	
1995	8	8		5	3		3	5	
1996	7	9		4	4		3	5	
1997	8	8		4	4		4	4	
1998	8	8		6	2		2	6	
1999	9	7		5	3		4	4	
2000	6	10		3	5		3	5	
2001	9	7		6	2		3	5	
2002	7	9		3	5		4	4	
2003	10	6		8	0		2	6	
2004	9	7		5	3		4	4	
2005	13	3		8	0		5	3	
2006	9	7		5	3		4	4	
2007	10	6		7	1		3	5	
2008	4	12		2	6		2	6	
2009	5	11		4	4		1	7	
2010	7	9		5	3		2	6	
2011	7	9		4	4		3	5	
2012	11	5		8	0		3	5	
	280	300		170	121		110	179	

TAMPA BAY BUCCANEERS

Season	All Games W	L	T	Home Games W	L	T	Road Games W	L	T
1976	0	14		0	7		0	7	
1977	2	12		1	6		1	6	
1978	5	11		3	5		2	6	
1979	10	6		5	3		5	3	
1980	5	10	1	2	5	1	3	5	
1981	9	7		6	2		3	5	
1982	5	4		4	1		1	3	
1983	2	14		1	7		1	7	
1984	6	10		6	2		0	8	
1985	2	14		2	6		0	8	
1986	2	14		1	7		1	7	
1987	4	11		2	5		2	6	
1988	5	11		3	5		2	6	
1989	5	11		2	6		3	5	
1990	6	10		4	4		2	6	
1991	3	13		3	5		0	8	
1992	5	11		3	5		2	6	
1993	5	11		3	5		2	6	
1994	6	10		4	4		2	6	
1995	7	9		5	3		2	6	
1996	6	10		5	3		1	7	
1997	10	6		5	3		5	3	
1998	8	8		6	2		2	6	
1999	11	5		7	1		4	4	
2000	10	6		6	2		4	4	
2001	9	7		5	3		4	4	
2002	12	4		6	2		6	2	
2003	7	9		3	5		4	4	
2004	5	11		4	4		1	7	
2005	11	5		6	2		5	3	
2006	4	12		3	5		1	7	
2007	9	7		6	2		3	5	
2008	9	7		6	2		3	5	
2009	3	13		1	7		2	6	
2010	10	6		4	4		6	2	
2011	4	12		3	5		1	7	
2012	7	9		3	5		4	4	
	229	350	1	139	150	1	90	200	

WASHINGTON REDSKINS*

Season	All Games W	L	T	Home Games W	L	T	Road Games W	L	T
1932	4	4	2	2	3	1	2	1	1
1933	5	5	2	4	2		1	3	2
1934	6	6		4	3		2	3	
1935	2	8	1	2	5		0	3	1
1936	7	5		4	3		3	2	
1937	8	3		4	2		4	1	
1938	6	3	2	3	1	1	3	2	1
1939	8	2	1	5	0	1	3	2	
1940	9	2		6	0		3	2	
1941	6	5		4	2		2	3	
1942	10	1		5	1		5	0	
1943	6	3	1	4	2		2	1	1
1944	6	3	1	4	2		2	1	1
1945	8	2		6	0		2	2	
1946	5	5	1	3	2	1	2	3	
1947	4	8		4	2		0	6	
1948	7	5		4	2		3	3	
1949	4	7	1	3	3		1	4	1
1950	3	9		1	5		2	4	
1951	5	7		2	4		3	3	
1952	4	8		1	5		3	3	
1953	6	5	1	3	3		3	2	1
1954	3	9		3	3		0	6	
1955	8	4		3	3		5	1	
1956	6	6		4	2		2	4	

Season	All Games W	L	T	Home Games W	L	T	Road Games W	L	T
1957	5	6	1	2	3	1	3	3	
1958	4	7	1	3	2	1	1	5	
1959	3	9		2	4		1	5	
1960	1	9	2	1	4	1	0	5	1
1961	1	12	1	1	6		0	6	1
1962	5	7	2	3	4		2	3	2
1963	3	11		1	6		2	5	
1964	6	8		4	3		2	5	
1965	6	8		3	4		3	4	
1966	7	7		4	3		3	4	
1967	5	6	3	2	4	1	3	2	2
1968	5	9		3	4		2	5	
1969	7	5	2	4	2	1	3	3	1
1970	6	8		4	3		2	5	
1971	9	4	1	4	2	1	5	2	
1972	11	3		6	1		5	2	
1973	10	4		7	0		3	4	
1974	10	4		6	1		4	3	
1975	8	6		5	2		3	4	
1976	10	4		5	2		5	2	
1977	9	5		5	2		4	3	
1978	8	8		5	3		3	5	
1979	10	6		6	2		4	4	
1980	6	10		4	4		2	6	
1981	8	8		5	3		3	5	
1982	8	1		3	1		5	0	
1983	14	2		7	1		7	1	
1984	11	5		7	1		4	4	
1985	10	6		5	3		5	3	
1986	12	4		7	1		5	3	
1987	11	4		6	1		5	3	
1988	7	9		4	4		3	5	
1989	10	6		4	4		6	2	
1990	10	6		7	1		3	5	
1991	14	2		7	1		7	1	
1992	9	7		6	2		3	5	
1993	4	12		3	5		1	7	
1994	3	13		0	8		3	5	
1995	6	10		4	4		2	6	
1996	9	7		5	3		4	4	
1997	8	7	1	5	2	1	3	5	
1998	6	10		4	4		2	6	
1999	10	6		6	2		4	4	
2000	8	8		4	4		4	4	
2001	8	8		4	4		4	4	
2002	7	9		5	3		2	6	
2003	5	11		3	5		2	6	
2004	6	10		3	5		3	5	
2005	10	6		6	2		4	4	
2006	5	11		3	5		2	6	
2007	9	7		5	3		4	4	
2008	8	8		4	4		4	4	
2009	4	12		3	5		1	7	
2010	6	10		2	6		4	4	
2011	5	11		2	6		3	5	
2012	10	6		5	3		5	3	
	562	533	27	322	237	11	240	296	16

*includes Boston Braves (1932) and Boston Redskins (1933-36).

ALL-TIME REGULAR-SEASON RECORDS OF NFL TEAMS

AFC	W	L	T	Pct.
Miami	407	309	4	.568
Baltimore	150	121	1	.553
Oakland	430	363	11	.542
New England	426	369	9	.536
Indianapolis	464	415	7	.528
Denver	419	375	10	.528
Pittsburgh	561	511	20	.523
Cleveland	447	417	10	.517
Kansas City	404	388	12	.510
San Diego	399	394	11	.503
Tennessee	392	406	6	.491
Jacksonville	140	148	0	.486
Buffalo	370	426	8	.465
N.Y. Jets	365	431	8	.459
Cincinnati	305	385	2	.442
Houston	77	99	0	.438

NFC	W	L	T	Pct.
Chicago	722	526	42	.578
Dallas	456	340	6	.573
Green Bay	690	530	36	.565
N.Y. Giants	654	538	33	.549
Minnesota	426	355	9	.545
San Francisco	495	413	14	.545
Washington	562	533	27	.513
St. Louis	520	514	21	.503
Seattle	280	300	0	.483
Philadelphia	516	557	25	.481
Carolina	132	156	0	.458
Detroit	510	611	32	.455
Atlanta	312	402	6	.437
New Orleans	306	395	5	.437
Arizona	501	700	39	.417
Tampa Bay	229	350	1	.396

From 1920-1971, tie games were not included in win percentage.

History

The Professional Football Hall of Fame is located in Canton, Ohio, site of the National Football League's organizational meeting on September 17, 1920. The NFL recognized Canton as the Hall of Fame site on April 27, 1961. Canton area individuals, foundations, and companies donated almost $400,000 in cash and services to provide funds for the construction of the original two-building complex, which was dedicated on September 7, 1963.

The Hall of Fame celebrates its 50th Anniversary in 2013. Coinciding with the golden anniversary is the completion of a two-year, $27 million dollar expansion and renovation. As part of the project, the Ralph Wilson, Jr. Pro Football Research and Preservation Center, a state-of-the-art archive for the world's largest collection of documents and artifacts, opened in August 2012.

The Pro Football Hall of Fame has undergone four expansions (1971, 1978, 1995, and 2012) over the years that have resulted in the museum growing from its original 19,000 square feet to today's 118,000-square foot facility.

Each year fans travel from all 50 states in the U.S. and more than 60 foreign countries to visit the Hall of Fame. The museum welcomed its nine millionth visitor during the summer of 2012. In addition, the Hall of Fame entertains tens of millions of fans through television broadcasts, traveling exhibits, an in-depth website, and numerous outreach events.

New members of the Pro Football Hall of Fame are elected annually by a 46-member Selection Committee, made up of media representatives from every league city, 13 at-large representatives, and a representative of the Pro Football Writers of America. Between four and seven new members are elected each year. An affirmative vote of approximately 80 percent is needed for election.

Any fan may nominate any eligible player or contributor simply by writing to the Pro Football Hall of Fame. Players and coaches must have last played or coached at least five years before he is eligible. Contributors (administrators, owners, et al.) may be elected while they are still active.

The charter class of 17 enshrinees was elected in 1963 and the honor roll now stands at 280 (164 living as of May 1, 2013) with the election of a seven-man class in 2013. That class consists of Larry Allen, Cris Carter, Curley Culp, Jonathan Ogden, Bill Parcells, Dave Robinson, and Warren Sapp.

ROSTER OF MEMBERS

HERB ADDERLEY
Cornerback. 6-0, 205. Born in Philadelphia, Pennsylvania, June 8, 1939. Michigan State. Inducted in 1980. 1961-69 Green Bay Packers, 1970-72 Dallas Cowboys. **Highlights:** 48 interceptions, 7 touchdowns. Played in four Super Bowls, five Pro Bowls.

TROY AIKMAN
Quarterback. 6-4, 219. Born in West Covina, California, November 21, 1966. Oklahoma, UCLA. Inducted in 2006. 1989-2000 Dallas Cowboys. **Highlights:** His 90 wins in 1990s make him winningest quarterback in that decade. Led Cowboys to three Super Bowl wins. Passed for 32,942 yards, 165 touchdowns. Named to six Pro Bowls.

GEORGE ALLEN
Coach. Born in Detroit, Michigan, April 29, 1918. Died December 31, 1990. Alma College, Eastern Michigan, Marquette, Michigan. Inducted in 2002. 1966-1970 Los Angeles Rams, 1971-77 Washington Redskins. **Highlights:** 118-54-5 overall record. Never suffered a losing season, and ranked tenth in coaching victories at time of retirement.

LARRY ALLEN
Guard-tackle. 6-3, 325. Born in Los Angeles, California, November 27, 1971. Inducted in 2013. 1994-2005 Dallas Cowboys, 2006-07 San Francisco 49ers. **Highlights:** Named first-team All-Pro seven straight seasons. Elected to 11 Pro Bowls. Member of NFL's All-Decade Teams of 1990s and 2000s.

MARCUS ALLEN
Running back. 6-2, 210. Born in San Diego, California, March 26, 1960. Southern California. Inducted in 2003. 1982-1992 Los Angeles Raiders, 1993-1997 Kansas City Chiefs. **Highlights:** First player in NFL history to tally 10,000 rushing yards and 5,000 receiving yards. MVP, Super Bowl XVIII.

LANCE ALWORTH
Wide receiver. 6-0, 184. Born in Houston, Texas, August 3, 1940. Arkansas. Inducted in 1978. 1962-1970 San Diego Chargers, 1971-72 Dallas Cowboys. **Highlights:** 542 receptions for 10,266 yards, 85 touchdowns. All-AFL seven times, seven All-Star games.

DOUG ATKINS
Defensive end. 6-8, 275. Born in Humboldt, Tennessee, May 8, 1930. Tennessee. Inducted in 1982. 1953-54 Cleveland Browns, 1955-1966 Chicago Bears, 1967-69 New Orleans Saints. **Highlights:** Eight Pro Bowls, All-NFL four times. Played for 17 years, 205 games.

MORRIS (RED) BADGRO
End. 6-0, 190. Born in Orillia, Washington, December 1, 1902. Died July 13, 1998. Southern California. Inducted in 1981. 1927-28 New York Yankees, 1930-35 New York Giants, 1936 Brooklyn Dodgers. **Highlights:** First- or second-team All-NFL four times. Scored first touchdown in NFL Championship Game series.

LEM BARNEY
Cornerback. 6-0, 190. Born in Gulfport, Mississippi, September 8, 1945. Jackson State. Inducted in 1992. 1967-1977 Detroit Lions. **Highlights:** 56 interceptions for 1,077 yards, 11 touchdowns (7 defensive, 4 special teams). Seven Pro Bowls, All-NFL/NFC four times.

CLIFF BATTLES
Halfback. 6-1, 195. Born in Akron, Ohio, May 1, 1910. Died April 28, 1981. West Virginia Wesleyan. Inducted in 1968. 1932 Boston Braves, 1933-36 Boston Redskins, 1937 Washington Redskins. **Highlights:** NFL rushing champion 1932, 1937. First to gain more than 200 yards in a game, 1933.

SAMMY BAUGH
Quarterback. 6-2, 180. Born in Temple, Texas, March 17, 1914. Died December 17, 2008. Texas Christian. Inducted in 1963. 1937-1952 Washington Redskins. **Highlights:** Charter enshrinee. Six-time NFL passing leader. NFL passing, punting, interception champ, 1943.

CHUCK BEDNARIK
Center-linebacker. 6-3, 230. Born in Bethlehem, Pennsylvania, May 1, 1925. Pennsylvania. Inducted in 1967. 1949-1962 Philadelphia Eagles. **Highlights:** Eight Pro Bowls. Missed three games in 14 years. Named NFL all-time center, 1969.

BERT BELL
Team owner. Commissioner. Born in Philadelphia, Pennsylvania, February 25, 1895. Died October 11, 1959. Pennsylvania. Inducted in 1963. 1933-1940 Philadelphia Eagles, 1941-42 Pittsburgh Steelers, 1943 Phil-Pitt, 1944 Card-Pitt, 1945-46 Pittsburgh Steelers. Commissioner, 1946-1959. **Highlights:** Charter enshrinee. Built NFL image as commissioner, 1946-1959. Set up long-term television policies.

BOBBY BELL
Linebacker. 6-4, 225. Born in Shelby, North Carolina, June 17, 1940. Minnesota. Inducted in 1983. 1963-1974 Kansas City Chiefs. **Highlights:** 26 interceptions. All-AFL/AFC eight times. Nine career touchdowns, 1 on onside kick return.

RAYMOND BERRY
End. 6-2, 187. Born in Corpus Christi, Texas, February 27, 1933. Southern Methodist. Inducted in 1973. 1955-1967 Baltimore Colts. **Highlights:** 631 receptions for 9,275 yards, 68 touchdowns. Set NFL title game mark with 12 catches for 178 yards, 1958.

ELVIN BETHEA
Defensive end. 6-2, 260. Born in Trenton, New Jersey, March 1, 1946. North Carolina A&T. Inducted in 2003. 1968-1983 Houston Oilers. **Highlights:** Led team in sacks six times. Elected to eight Pro Bowls. Played for 16 years, 210 games.

CHARLES W. BIDWILL SR.
Team owner. Born in Chicago, Illinois, September 16, 1895. Died April 19, 1947. Loyola of Chicago. Inducted in 1967. 1933-1943 Chicago Cardinals, 1944 Card-Pitt, 1945-47 Chicago Cardinals. **Highlights:** Guiding light for NFL during depression years. Built famous "Dream Backfield."

FRED BILETNIKOFF
Wide receiver. 6-1, 190. Born in Erie, Pennsylvania, February 23, 1943. Florida State. Inducted in 1988. 1965-1978 Oakland Raiders. **Highlights:** 589 receptions for 8,974 yards, 76 touchdowns. 40 catches 10 straight years. MVP, Super Bowl XI.

GEORGE BLANDA
Quarterback-kicker. 6-2, 215. Born in Youngwood, Pennsylvania, September 17, 1927. Died September 27, 2010. Kentucky. Inducted in 1981. 1949-1958 Chicago Bears, 1950 Baltimore Colts, 1960-66 Houston Oilers, 1967-1975 Oakland Raiders. **Highlights:** 2,002 career points. 26-season, 340-game career longest in NFL history at retirement.

MEL BLOUNT
Cornerback. 6-3, 205. Born in Vidalia, Georgia, April 10, 1948. Southern University. Inducted in 1989. 1970-1983 Pittsburgh Steelers. **Highlights:** 57 interceptions for 736 yards. NFL defensive MVP, 1975. Started in four Super Bowl victories.

TERRY BRADSHAW
Quarterback. 6-3, 210. Born in Shreveport, Louisiana, September 2, 1948. Louisiana Tech. Inducted in 1989. 1970-1983 Pittsburgh Steelers. **Highlights:** 27,989 yards passing, 212 touchdowns. MVP in Super Bowls XIII, XIV.

BOB (BOOMER) BROWN
Tackle. 6-4, 280. Born in Cleveland, Ohio, December 8, 1941. Nebraska. Inducted in 2004. 1964-68 Philadelphia Eagles, 1969-1970 Los Angeles Rams, 1971-73 Oakland Raiders. **Highlights:** All-NFL seven of 10 seasons, six Pro Bowls. Named to 1960s All-Decade Team.

JIM BROWN
Fullback. 6-2, 228. Born in St. Simons, Georgia, February 17, 1936. Syracuse. Inducted in 1971. 1957-1965 Cleveland Browns. **Highlights:** 12,312 yards rushing, 756 points. Led NFL rushers eight years. Nine consecutive Pro Bowls.

PAUL BROWN
Coach. Born in Norwalk, Ohio, September 7, 1908. Died August 5, 1991. Miami (Ohio). Inducted in 1967. 1946-49 Cleveland Browns (AAFC), 1950-1962 Cleveland Browns. **Highlights:** Built Cleveland dynasty with 167-53-8 record, four AAFC titles, three NFL crowns. Returned to coaching with Cincinnati Bengals after induction, 1968-1975.

ROOSEVELT BROWN
Tackle. 6-3, 255. Born in Charlottesville, Virginia, October 20, 1932. Died June 9, 2004. Morgan State. Inducted in 1975. 1953-1965 New York Giants. **Highlights:** All-NFL eight consecutive years, nine Pro Bowls. NFL's lineman of year, 1956.

WILLIE BROWN
Cornerback. 6-1, 210. Born in Yazoo City, Mississippi, December 2, 1940. Grambling. Inducted in 1984. 1963-66 Denver Broncos, 1967-1978 Oakland Raiders. **Highlights:** 54 interceptions for 472 yards. Scored on 75-yard interception in Super Bowl XI.

BUCK BUCHANAN
Defensive tackle. 6-7, 274. Born in Gainesville, Alabama, September 10, 1940. Died July 16, 1992. Grambling. Inducted in 1990. 1963-1975 Kansas City Chiefs. **Highlights:** Led Chiefs defensive efforts in Super Bowl I, IV. Did not miss a game in 13 years.

NICK BUONICONTI
Linebacker. 5-11, 220. Born in Springfield, Massachusetts, December 15, 1940. Notre Dame. Inducted in 2001. 1962-68 Boston Patriots, 1969-1974, 1976 Miami Dolphins. **Highlights:** All-AFL/AFC eight times. Named to AFL's All-Time Team.

DICK BUTKUS
Linebacker. 6-3, 245. Born in Chicago, Illinois, December 9, 1942. Illinois. Inducted in 1979. 1965-1973 Chicago Bears. **Highlights:** All-NFL six years, eight consecutive Pro Bowls. 27 fumble recoveries.

JACK BUTLER
Cornerback. 6-1, 200. Born in Pittsburgh, Pennsylvania, November 12, 1927. St. Bonaventure. Inducted in 2012. 1951-59 Pittsburgh Steelers. **Highlights:** Retired as NFL's second all-time leading interceptor with 52 career picks returned for 827 yards, 4 TDs. Named to four Pro Bowls and selected to the NFL's All-Decade Team of 1950s.

EARL CAMPBELL
Running back. 5-11, 233. Born in Tyler, Texas, March 29, 1955. Texas. Inducted in 1991. 1978-1984 Houston Oilers, 1984-85 New Orleans Saints. **Highlights:** 9,407 yards rushing, 74 touchdowns. 1,934 yards rushing in 1980, including four games with at least 200 yards.

TONY CANADEO
Halfback. 5-11, 195. Born in Chicago, Illinois, May 5, 1919. Died November 29, 2003. Gonzaga. Inducted in 1974. 1941-44, 1946-1952 Green Bay Packers. **Highlights:** Two-way player. Third player to rush for 1,000 yards in single season, 1949.

JOE CARR
NFL president. Born in Columbus, Ohio, October 23, 1879. Died May 20, 1939. Did not attend college. Inducted in 1963. President, 1921-1939 National Football League. **Highlights:** Charter enshrinee. NFL co-organizer, 1920. Introduced standard player contract.

HARRY CARSON
Linebacker. 6-2, 237. Born in Florence, South Carolina, November 26, 1953. South Carolina State. Inducted in 2006. 1976-1988 New York Giants. **Highlights:** 11 career interceptions. Named to nine Pro Bowls. Named first- or second-team All-NFL six times.

CRIS CARTER
Wide receiver. 6-3, 202. Born in Troy, Ohio, November 25, 1965. Inducted in 2013. 1987-89 Philadelphia Eagles, 1990-2001 Minnesota Vikings, 2002 Miami Dolphins. **Highlights:** Recorded eight straight 1,000-yards seasons. Career statistics include 1,101 receptions for 13,899 yards and 130 TD catches. Elected to eight Pro Bowls. Named to NFL's All-Decade Team of 1990s.

DAVE CASPER
Tight end. 6-4, 240. Born in Bemidji, Minnesota, February 2, 1952. Notre Dame. Inducted in 2002. 1974-1980 Oakland Raiders, 1980-83 Houston Oilers, 1983 Minnesota Vikings, 1984 Los Angeles Raiders. **Highlights:** 378 receptions for 5,216 yards, 52 touchdowns. Five consecutive Pro Bowls.

GUY CHAMBERLIN
End. Coach. 6-2, 196. Born in Blue Springs, Nebraska, January 16, 1894. Died April 4, 1967. Nebraska. Inducted in 1965. 1919 Canton Bulldogs, 1920-21 Decatur Staleys/Chicago Staleys, player-coach 1922-23 Canton Bulldogs, 1924 Cleveland Bulldogs, 1925-26 Frankford Yellowjackets, 1927-28 Chicago Cardinals. **Highlights:** Player-coach of four NFL championship teams. Six-year coaching record of 58-16-7.

JACK CHRISTIANSEN
Safety. 6-1, 185. Born in Sublette, Kansas, December 20, 1928. Died June 29, 1986. Colorado State. Inducted in 1970. 1951-58 Detroit Lions. **Highlights:** 46 interceptions. NFL interception leader, 1953, 1957. Eight punt returns for touchdowns.

EARL (DUTCH) CLARK
Quarterback. 6-0, 185. Born in Fowler, Colorado, October 11, 1906. Died August 5, 1978. Colorado College. Inducted in 1963. 1931-32 Portsmouth Spartans, 1934-38 Detroit Lions. **Highlights:** Charter enshrinee. NFL scoring champion three years. Led Lions to 1935 NFL title.

GEORGE CONNOR
Tackle-linebacker. 6-3, 240. Born in Chicago, Illinois, January 21, 1925. Died March 31, 2003. Holy Cross, Notre Dame. Inducted in 1975. 1948-1955 Chicago Bears. **Highlights:** All-NFL at three positions—T, DT, LB. All-NFL five years. Played in first four Pro Bowls.

JIMMY CONZELMAN
Quarterback. Coach. Team owner. 6-0, 180. Born in St. Louis, Missouri, March 6, 1898. Died July 31, 1970. Washington of St. Louis. Inducted in 1964. 1920 Decatur Staleys, 1921-22 Rock Island Independents, 1922-24 Milwaukee Badgers; owner-coach 1925-26 Detroit Panthers; player-coach 1927-29, coach 1930 Providence Steam Roller; coach 1940-42, 1946-48 Chicago Cardinals. **Highlights:** Player-coach of four NFL teams in 1920s. Coached Cardinals to 1947 NFL crown.

LOU CREEKMUR
Tackle-guard. 6-4, 255. Born in Hopelawn, New Jersey. January 22, 1927. Died July 5, 2009. William & Mary. Inducted in 1996. 1950-59 Detroit Lions. **Highlights:** All-NFL six times, twice at guard and four times at tackle. Selected to eight Pro Bowls and played on three NFL championship teams.

LARRY CSONKA
Running back. 6-3, 235. Born in Stow, Ohio, December 25, 1946. Syracuse. Inducted in 1987. 1968-1974, 1979 Miami Dolphins, 1976-78 New York Giants. **Highlights:** 8,081 yards rushing, 68 touchdowns. MVP Super Bowl VIII. Only 21 fumbles in 1,891 carries and 106 receptions.

CURLEY CULP
Defensive tackle. 6-2, 265. Born in Yuma, Arizona, March 10, 1946. Inducted in 2013. 1968-1974 Kansas City Chiefs, 1974-1980 Houston Oilers, 1980-81 Detroit Lions. **Highlights:** Started in three AFL/AFC championship games and Super Bowl IV. Named to six Pro Bowls. Earned Defensive Player of the Year honors in 1975.

AL DAVIS
Coach-Commissioner-Owner. Born in Brockton, Massachusetts, July 4, 1929. Died October 8, 2011. Wittenberg, Syracuse. Inducted in 1992. 1963-1981, 1995-2011 Oakland Raiders, 1982-1994 Los Angeles Raiders, 1966 American Football League. **Highlights:** Only person to serve in pros as personnel assistant, scout, assistant coach, head coach, general manager, commissioner, team owner/CEO.

WILLIE DAVIS
Defensive end. 6-3, 245. Born in Lisbon, Louisiana, July 24, 1934. Grambling. Inducted in 1981. 1958-59 Cleveland Browns, 1960-69 Green Bay Packers. **Highlights:** All-NFL five seasons, five Pro Bowls. Did not miss game in 12-year career.

DERMONTTI DAWSON
Center. 6-2, 288. Born in Lexington, Kentucky, June 17, 1965. Kentucky. Inducted in 2012. 1988-2000 Pittsburgh Steelers. **Highlights:** Played in 170 straight games. Named first-team All-Pro six consecutive seasons and voted to seven straight Pro Bowls. Is member of the NFL's All-Decade Team of the 1990s.

LEN DAWSON
Quarterback. 6-0, 190. Born in Alliance, Ohio, June 20, 1935. Purdue. Inducted in 1987. 1957-59 Pittsburgh Steelers, 1960-61 Cleveland Browns, 1962 Dallas Texans, 1963-1975 Kansas City Chiefs. **Highlights:** 28,711 yards passing, 239 touchdowns. Four AFL passing crowns. MVP, Super Bowl IV.

FRED DEAN
Defensive end. 6-3, 230. Born in Arcadia, Louisiana, February 24, 1952. Louisiana Tech. Inducted in 2008. 1975-1981 San Diego Chargers, 1981-85 San Francisco 49ers. **Highlights:** Had career-high 17.5 sacks in 1983. Played on two Super Bowl championship teams with 49ers (Super Bowls XVI, XIX).

JOE DeLAMIELLEURE
Guard. 6-3, 254. Born in Detroit, Michigan, March 16, 1951. Michigan State. Inducted in 2003. 1973-1979, 1985 Buffalo Bills, 1980-1984 Cleveland Browns. **Highlights:** Selected All-Pro and All-AFC six consecutive times, 1975-1980. Named to six Pro Bowls. Played 13 years, 185 games.

RICHARD DENT
Defensive end. 6-5, 265. Born in Atlanta, Georgia, December 13, 1960. Tennessee State. Inducted in 2011. 1983-1993, 1995 Chicago Bears, 1994 San Francisco 49ers, 1996 Indianapolis Colts, 1997 Philadelphia Eagles. **Highlights:** Named MVP of Super Bowl XX. Had double-digit sack totals 10 times. Recorded 137.5 career sacks, third most at time of retirement. Named first- or second-team All-NFL four times, voted to four Pro Bowls.

ERIC DICKERSON
Running back. 6-3, 220. Born in Sealy, Texas, September 2, 1960. Southern Methodist. Inducted in 1999. 1983-87 Los Angeles Rams, 1987-1991 Indianapolis Colts, 1992 Los Angeles Raiders, 1993 Atlanta Falcons. **Highlights:** Rushed for 13,259 career yards, including an NFL record 2,105 yards in 1984. All-Pro five times, six Pro Bowls.

DAN DIERDORF
Tackle. 6-3, 290. Born in Canton, Ohio, June 29, 1949. Michigan. Inducted in 1996. 1971-1983 St. Louis Cardinals. **Highlights:** All-Pro five times, played in six Pro Bowls, named NFL's best blocker three times.

MIKE DITKA
Tight end. 6-3, 225. Born in Carnegie, Pennsylvania, October 18, 1939. Pittsburgh. Inducted in 1988. 1961-66 Chicago Bears, 1967-68 Philadelphia Eagles, 1969-1972 Dallas Cowboys. **Highlights:** 427 receptions for 5,812 yards, 43 touchdowns. First tight end selected to Hall of Fame. Five consecutive Pro Bowls.

CHRIS DOLEMAN

Defensive end-linebacker. 6-5, 270. Born in Indianapolis, Indiana, October 16, 1961. Pittsburgh. Inducted in 2012. 1985-1993, 1999 Minnesota Vikings, 1994-95 Atlanta Falcons, 1996-98 San Francisco 49ers. **Highlights:** Career sack total of 150.5 was fourth best all-time at retirement. Recorded 10 or more sacks in a season eight times. Led NFL with 21 sacks, 1989, one short of season record at time. Voted to eight Pro Bowls.

ART DONOVAN

Defensive tackle. 6-3, 265. Born in Bronx, New York, June 5, 1925. Boston College. Inducted in 1968. 1950 Baltimore Colts, 1951 New York Yanks, 1952 Dallas Texans, 1953-1961 Baltimore Colts. **Highlights:** Five Pro Bowls. Vital part of Baltimore's climb to powerhouse status in 1950s.

TONY DORSETT

Running back. 5-11, 184. Born in Rochester, Pennsylvania, April 7, 1954. Pittsburgh. Inducted in 1994. 1977-1987 Dallas Cowboys, 1988 Denver Broncos. **Highlights:** 12,739 yards rushing, 398 receptions, 91 touchdowns. Ran record 99 yards for touchdown vs. Minnesota, January, 1983.

JOHN (PADDY) DRISCOLL

Quarterback. 5-11, 160. Born in Evanston, Illinois, January 11, 1895. Died June 29, 1968. Northwestern. Inducted in 1965. 1919 Hammond Pros, 1920 Decatur Staleys, 1920-25 Chicago Cardinals, 1926-29 Chicago Bears. **Highlights:** All-NFL seven times. Dropkicked record 4 field goals in one game, 1925.

BILL DUDLEY

Halfback. 5-10, 182. Born in Bluefield, Virginia, December 24, 1921. Died February 4, 2010. Virginia. Inducted in 1966. 1942, 1945-46 Pittsburgh Steelers, 1947-49 Detroit Lions, 1950-51, 1953 Washington Redskins. **Highlights:** Won NFL rushing, interception, punt return titles, 1946. All-NFL 1942, 1946, and 1947.

ALBERT GLEN (TURK) EDWARDS

Tackle. 6-2, 260. Born in Mold, Washington, September 28, 1907. Died January 12, 1973. Washington State. Inducted in 1969. 1932 Boston Braves, 1933-36 Boston Redskins, 1937-1940 Washington Redskins. **Highlights:** All-NFL 1932-34, 1936, 1937. Steamrolling blocker, smothering tackler.

CARL ELLER

Defensive end. 6-6, 247. Born in Winston-Salem, North Carolina, January 25, 1942. Minnesota. Inducted in 2004. 1964-1978 Minnesota Vikings, 1979 Seattle Seahawks. **Highlights:** Fixture on Vikings' "Purple People Eaters" defensive line, All-Pro five time, elected to six Pro Bowls.

JOHN ELWAY

Quarterback. 6-3, 215. Born in Port Angeles, Washington, June 28, 1960. Stanford. Inducted in 2004. 1983-1998 Denver Broncos. **Highlights:** Passed for 51,475 yards, 300 touchdowns. Named to nine Pro Bowls. NFL MVP, 1987; MVP, Super Bowl XXXIII.

WEEB EWBANK

Coach. Born in Richmond, Indiana, May 6, 1907. Died November 17, 1998. Miami (Ohio). Inducted in 1978. 1954-1962 Baltimore Colts, 1963-1973 New York Jets. **Highlights:** Only coach to win championships in both NFL, AFL. Led both Colts (1958 and 1959) and Jets (1968) to championships.

MARSHALL FAULK

Running back. 5-10, 208. Born in New Orleans, Louisiana, February 26, 1973. San Diego State. Inducted in 2011. 1994-98 Indianapolis Colts, 1999-2005 St. Louis Rams. **Highlights:** Became second player to eclipse 1,000 yards in rushing and receiving same season when he set then-record for yards from scrimmage, 1999. NFL's MVP in 2000. Rushed for 1,000 yards in seven of first eight seasons.

TOM FEARS

End. 6-2, 215. Born in Guadalajara, Mexico, December 3, 1922. Died January 4, 2000. Santa Clara, UCLA. Inducted in 1970. 1948-1956 Los Angeles Rams. **Highlights:** 400 receptions for 5,397 yards, 38 touchdowns. Led NFL receivers first three seasons. Had then-record 18 receptions in single game.

JIM FINKS

Administrator. Born in St. Louis, Missouri, August 31, 1927. Died May 8, 1994. Tulsa. Inducted 1995. 1964-1973 Minnesota Vikings, 1974-1982 Chicago Bears, 1986-1993 New Orleans Saints. **Highlights:** Developed Vikings, Bears, Saints—all teams with losing records—into winners.

RAY FLAHERTY

Coach. Born in Spokane, Washington, September 1, 1903. Died July 19, 1994. Gonzaga. Inducted in 1976. 1936-1942 Boston/Washington Redskins, 1946-48 New York Yankees (AAFC), 1949 Chicago Hornets (AAFC). **Highlights:** 82-41-5 coaching record. Introduced screen pass in 1937 title game and platoon system.

LEN FORD

Defensive end. 6-4, 260. Born in Washington, D.C., February 18, 1926. Died March 14, 1972. Morgan State, Michigan. Inducted in 1976. 1948-49 Los Angeles Dons (AAFC), 1950-57 Cleveland Browns, 1958 Green Bay Packers. **Highlights:** All-NFL five times, four Pro Bowls. Recovered 20 opponents' fumbles.

DAN FORTMANN

Guard. 6-0, 210. Born in Pearl River, New York, April 11, 1916. Died May 23, 1995. Colgate. Inducted in 1965. 1936-1943 Chicago Bears. **Highlights:** At 20, became youngest starter in NFL. First-or second-team All-NFL every season of career.

DAN FOUTS

Quarterback. 6-3, 210. Born in San Francisco, California, June 10, 1951. Oregon. Inducted in 1993. 1973-1987 San Diego Chargers. **Highlights:** 43,040 passing yards, 254 touchdowns. Six Pro Bowls, NFL MVP, 1982.

BENNY FRIEDMAN

Quarterback. 5-10, 183. Born in Cleveland, Ohio, March 18, 1905. Died November 23, 1982. Michigan. Inducted in 2005. 1927 Cleveland Bulldogs, 1928 Detroit Wolverines, 1929-1931 New York Giants, 1932-34 Brooklyn Dodgers. **Highlights:** NFL's first great passer. Set league mark for touchdowns with 20 in 1929. Led NFL in touchdown passes each of his first four seasons.

FRANK GATSKI

Center. 6-3, 240. Born in Farmington, West Virginia, March 18, 1919. Marshall, Auburn. Died November 22, 2005. Inducted in 1985. 1946-49 Cleveland Browns (AAFC), 1950-56 Cleveland Browns, 1957 Detroit Lions. **Highlights:** Never missed game in high school, college, or pro football. Played 11 championship games, winning eight.

BILL GEORGE

Linebacker. 6-2, 230. Born in Waynesburg, Pennsylvania, October 27, 1929. Died September 30, 1982. Wake Forest. Inducted in 1974. 1952-1965 Chicago Bears, 1966 Los Angeles Rams. **Highlights:** All-NFL eight years, eight consecutive Pro Bowls. 14 years of service, longest of any Bears player.

JOE GIBBS

Coach. Born in Mocksville, North Carolina, November 25, 1940. Cerritos (Calif.) J.C., San Diego State. Inducted in 1996. 1981-1992 Washington Redskins. **Highlights:** 124-60-0 record in regular season, 16-5 in postseason, including four Super Bowl appearances—winning three. Won 10 or more games eight times.

FRANK GIFFORD
Halfback. 6-1, 195. Born in Santa Monica, California, August 16, 1930. Southern California. Inducted in 1977. 1952-1960, 1962-64 New York Giants. **Highlights:** Starred on both offense and defense. Named to eight Pro Bowls, 1956 NFL player of the year.

SID GILLMAN
Coach. Born in Minneapolis, Minnesota, October 26, 1911. Died January 3, 2003. Ohio State. Inducted in 1983. 1955-59 Los Angeles Rams, 1960-69, 1971 Los Angeles/San Diego Chargers, 1973-74 Houston Oilers. **Highlights:** 123-104-7 coaching record. First to win division titles in both NFL, AFL.

OTTO GRAHAM
Quarterback. 6-1, 195. Born in Waukegan, Illinois, December 6, 1921. Died December 17, 2003. Northwestern. Inducted in 1965. 1946-49 Cleveland Browns (AAFC), 1950-55 Cleveland Browns. **Highlights:** 23,584 passing yards, 174 touchdowns. Guided Browns to 10 division or league crowns in 10 years.

HAROLD (RED) GRANGE
Halfback. 6-0, 185. Born in Forksville, Pennsylvania, June 13, 1903. Died January 28, 1991. Illinois. Inducted in 1963. 1925, 1929-1934 Chicago Bears, 1926 New York Yankees (AFL), 1927 New York Yankees. **Highlights:** Charter enshrinee. Nicknamed "Galloping Ghost." Name produced first huge pro football crowds.

BUD GRANT
Coach. Born in Superior, Wisconsin, May 20, 1927. Minnesota. Inducted in 1994. 1967-1983, 1985 Minnesota Vikings. **Highlights:** 168-108-5 coaching record. Led Vikings to 11 division championships, four Super Bowls.

DARRELL GREEN
Cornerback. . 5-8, 176. Born in Houston, Texas, February 15, 1960. Texas A&I. Inducted in 2008. 1983-2002 Washington Redskins. **Highlights:** 54 interceptions, 621 yards, 6 TDs. Played 20 seasons. Recorded interception in NFL record 19 straight seasons. Selected to seven Pro Bowls.

JOE GREENE
Defensive tackle. 6-4, 260. Born in Temple, Texas, September 24, 1946. North Texas State. Inducted in 1987. 1969-1981 Pittsburgh Steelers. **Highlights:** NFL defensive player of the year, 1972, 1974. Four-time Super Bowl champion, 10 Pro Bowls.

FORREST GREGG
Tackle. 6-4, 250. Born in Birthright, Texas, October 18, 1933. Southern Methodist. Inducted in 1977. 1956, 1958-1970 Green Bay Packers, 1971 Dallas Cowboys. **Highlights:** Played 188 consecutive games. Nine Pro Bowls. Played on six NFL championship teams, three Super Bowl winners.

BOB GRIESE
Quarterback. 6-1, 190. Born in Evansville, Indiana, February 3, 1945. Purdue. Inducted in 1990. 1967-1980 Miami Dolphins. **Highlights:** 25,092 passing yards, 192 touchdowns. Led Miami to three AFC titles, Super Bowl VII, VIII wins.

RUSS GRIMM
Guard. 6-3, 273. Born in Scottdale, Pennsylvania, May 2, 1959. Pittsburgh. Inducted in 2010. 1981-1991 Washington Redskins. **Highlights:** Member of famed "Hogs" offensive line, All-NFL four times, four Pro Bowls. Member of All-Decade Team 1980s.

LOU GROZA
Tackle-kicker. 6-3, 250. Born in Martins Ferry, Ohio, January 25, 1924. Died November 29, 2000. Ohio State. Inducted in 1974. 1946-49 Cleveland Browns (AAFC), 1950-59, 1961-67 Cleveland Browns. **Highlights:** 1,608 points in 21 years. Nine Pro Bowls, All-NFL six years. NFL player of the year, 1954.

JOE GUYON
Halfback. 6-1, 180. Born on White Earth Indian Reservation, Minnesota, November 26, 1892. Died November 27, 1971. Carlisle, Georgia Tech. Inducted in 1966. 1919-1920 Canton Bulldogs, 1921 Cleveland Indians, 1922-23 Oorang Indians, 1924 Rock Island Independents, 1924-25 Kansas City Cowboys, 1927 New York Giants. **Highlights:** Touchdown pass gave Giants victory over Bears to win 1927 championship.

GEORGE HALAS
End. Coach. Team owner. Born in Chicago, Illinois, February 2, 1895. Died October 31, 1983. Illinois. Inducted in 1963. Player-coach 1920 Decatur Staleys, 1921 Chicago Staleys, 1922-29 Chicago Bears; coach 1933-1942, 1946-1955, 1958-1967 Chicago Bears. **Highlights:** Charter enshrinee. 324 coaching wins. Only person associated with NFL throughout first 50 years. Coached Bears 40 seasons, won six NFL titles.

JACK HAM
Linebacker. 6-1, 225. Born in Johnstown, Pennsylvania, December 23, 1948. Penn State. Inducted in 1988. 1971-1982 Pittsburgh Steelers. **Highlights:** Won four Super Bowls, 21 opponents' fumbles recovered, 32 interceptions. Eight consecutive Pro Bowls.

DAN HAMPTON
Defensive tackle-defensive end. 6-5, 264. Born in Oklahoma City, Oklahoma, September 19, 1957. Arkansas. Inducted in 2002. 1979-1990 Chicago Bears. **Highlights:** A versatile player, he earned all-pro honors at both defensive tackle and defensive end. Named to four Pro Bowls.

CHRIS HANBURGER
Linebacker. 6-2, 218. Born in Fort Bragg, North Carolina, August 13, 1941. North Carolina. Inducted in 2011. 1965-1978 Washington Redskins. **Highlights:** Leader of dominant Redskins defenses. Named first-team All-NFL four times in five-season span. Voted to nine Pro Bowls. Three fumble recoveries for TDs tied for NFL record at time of his retirement.

JOHN HANNAH
Guard. 6-3, 265. Born in Canton, Georgia, April 4, 1951. Alabama. Inducted in 1991. 1973-1985 New England Patriots. **Highlights:** Renowned as premier guard of era. All-Pro 10 years, nine Pro Bowls.

FRANCO HARRIS
Running back. 6-2, 225. Born in Fort Dix, New Jersey, March 7, 1950. Penn State. Inducted in 1990. 1972-1983 Pittsburgh Steelers, 1984 Seattle Seahawks. **Highlights:** 12,120 rushing yards, 100 total touchdowns. 1,556 rushing yards in 19 postseason games. MVP in Super Bowl IX.

BOB HAYES
Wide receiver. 5-11, 185. Born in Jacksonville, Florida, December 20, 1942. Died September 18, 2002. Florida A&M. Inducted in 2009. 1965-1974 Dallas Cowboys, 1975 San Francisco 49ers. **Highlights:** Olympic gold medalist with world class speed led Cowboys in receiving three times. 371 receptions for 7,414 yards, 71 TDs. Three Pro Bowls.

MIKE HAYNES
Cornerback. 6-2, 195. Born in Denison, Texas, July 1, 1953. Arizona State. Inducted in 1997. 1976-1982 New England Patriots, 1983-89 Los Angeles Raiders. **Highlights:** Defensive rookie of the year. Selected to nine Pro Bowls and intercepted 46 passes, plus one pick in Super Bowl XVIII.

ED HEALEY
Tackle. 6-3, 220. Born in Indian Orchard, Massachusetts, December 28, 1894. Died December 9, 1978. Dartmouth. Inducted in 1964. 1920-22 Rock Island Independents, 1922-27 Chicago Bears. **Highlights:** Two-way star. Perennial all-pro with Bears.

MEL HEIN
Center. 6-2, 225. Born in Redding, California, August 22, 1909. Died January 31, 1992. Washington State. Inducted in 1963. 1931-1945 New York Giants. **Highlights:** Charter enshrinee. 60-minute regular for 15 years. All-NFL eight consecutive years.

TED HENDRICKS
Linebacker. 6-7, 235. Born in Guatemala City, Guatemala, November 1, 1947. Miami. Inducted in 1990. 1969-1973 Baltimore Colts, 1974 Green Bay Packers, 1975-1981 Oakland Raiders, 1982-83 Los Angeles Raiders. **Highlights:** 25 blocked field goals, extra points, and punts, 26 interceptions. Played in 215 consecutive games.

WILBUR (PETE) HENRY
Tackle. 6-0, 250. Born in Mansfield, Ohio, October 31, 1897. Died February 7, 1952. Washington & Jefferson. Inducted in 1963. 1920-23, 1925-26 Canton Bulldogs, 1927 New York Giants, 1927-28 Pottsville Maroons. **Highlights:** Charter enshrinee. Largest player of his time at 250 pounds. Bulwark of Canton's championship lines.

ARNIE HERBER
Quarterback. 6-0, 200. Born in Green Bay, Wisconsin, April 2, 1910. Died October 14, 1969. Wisconsin, Regis College. Inducted in 1966. 1930-1940 Green Bay Packers, 1944-45 New York Giants. **Highlights:** NFL passing leader 1932, 1934, 1936. Came out of retirement to lead 1944 Giants to NFL Eastern crown.

BILL HEWITT
End. 5-11, 191. Born in Bay City, Michigan, October 8, 1909. Died January 14, 1947. Michigan. Inducted in 1971. 1932-36 Chicago Bears, 1937-39 Philadelphia Eagles, 1943 Phil-Pitt. **Highlights:** First to be named all-NFL with two teams—1933, 1934, 1936 Bears; 1937 Eagles.

GENE HICKERSON
Guard. 6-3, 248. Born in Trenton, Tennessee, February 15, 1935. Died October 20, 2008. Mississippi. Inducted in 2007. 1958-1973 Cleveland Browns. **Highlights:** Blocked for three Hall of Fame running backs. Voted to six straight Pro Bowls. Named to NFL's All-Decade Team of the 1960s.

CLARKE HINKLE
Fullback. 5-11, 201. Born in Toronto, Ohio, April 10, 1909. Died November 9, 1988. Bucknell. Inducted in 1964. 1932-1941 Green Bay Packers. **Highlights:** 3,860 yards rushing, 379 points. Fullback on offense, linebacker on defense.

ELROY (CRAZYLEGS) HIRSCH
Halfback-end. 6-2, 190. Born in Wausau, Wisconsin, June 17, 1923. Died January 28, 2004. Wisconsin, Michigan. Inducted in 1968. 1946-48 Chicago Rockets (AAFC), 1949-1957 Los Angeles Rams. **Highlights:** 387 receptions for 7,029 yards, 60 touchdowns. Key part of Rams' revolutionary "three end" offense, 1949.

PAUL HORNUNG
Halfback. 6-2, 220. Born in Louisville, Kentucky, December 23, 1935. Notre Dame. Inducted in 1986. 1957-1962, 1964-66 Green Bay Packers. **Highlights:** 760 points. Led NFL scorers three years, including record 176 points, 1960. Record 19 points scored in 1961 NFL title game.

KEN HOUSTON
Safety. 6-3, 198. Born in Lufkin, Texas, November 12, 1944. Prairie View A&M. Inducted in 1986. 1967-1972 Houston Oilers, 1973-1980 Washington Redskins. **Highlights:** 49 interceptions, 898 yards, 9 touchdowns. NFL's premier strong safety of 1970s. 12 Pro Bowls.

ROBERT (CAL) HUBBARD
Tackle. 6-5, 250. Born in Keytesville, Missouri, October 31, 1900. Died October 17, 1977. Centenary, Geneva. Inducted in 1963. 1927-28, 1936 New York Giants, 1929-1933, 1935 Green Bay Packers, 1936 Pittsburgh Pirates. **Highlights:** Charter enshrinee. Most feared lineman of his time. All-NFL six years, 1927-29, 1931-33.

SAM HUFF
Linebacker. 6-1, 230. Born in Morgantown, West Virginia, October 4, 1934. West Virginia. Inducted in 1982. 1956-1963 New York Giants, 1964-67, 1969 Washington Redskins. **Highlights:** 30 interceptions. Played in six NFL title games, five Pro Bowls. Redskins player-coach, 1969.

LAMAR HUNT
Team owner. Born in El Dorado, Arkansas, August 2, 1932. Died December 13, 2006. Southern Methodist. Inducted in 1972. 1960-2006 Dallas Texans/Kansas City Chiefs. **Highlights:** Driving force behind organization of AFL. Spearheaded merger negotiations with NFL, 1966.

DON HUTSON
End. 6-1, 180. Born in Pine Bluff, Arkansas, January 31, 1913. Died June 26, 1997. Alabama. Inducted in 1963. 1935-1945 Green Bay Packers. **Highlights:** Charter enshrinee. 488 receptions for 7,991 yards, 99 touchdowns. NFL receiving champion eight years. NFL MVP, 1941, 1942.

MICHAEL IRVIN
Wide receiver. 6-2, 207. Born in Ft. Lauderdale, Florida, March 5, 1966. Miami. Inducted in 2007. 1988-1999 Dallas Cowboys. **Highlights:** 750 career receptions for 11,904 yards, 65 touchdowns. Had NFL record eleven 100-yard receiving games, 1995.

RICKEY JACKSON
Linebacker. 6-2, 243. Born in Pahokee, Florida, March 20, 1958. Pittsburgh. Inducted in 2010. 1981-1993 New Orleans Saints, 1994-95 San Francisco 49ers. **Highlights:** Recorded double-digit sacks in six seasons. Six Pro Bowls, named All-Pro four times. Finished career as defensive end with 49ers.

JIMMY JOHNSON
Cornerback. 6-2, 187. Born in Dallas, Texas, March 31, 1938. UCLA. Inducted in 1994. 1961-1976 San Francisco 49ers. **Highlights:** 47 interceptions for 615 yards. Five Pro Bowls. Opposing passers avoided throwing in his area.

JOHN HENRY JOHNSON
Fullback. 6-2, 225. Born in Waterproof, Louisiana, November 24, 1929. Died June 3, 2011. St. Mary's, Arizona State. Inducted in 1987. 1954-56 San Francisco 49ers, 1957-59 Detroit Lions, 1960-65 Pittsburgh Steelers, 1966 Houston Oilers. **Highlights:** 6,803 yards rushing, 55 total touchdowns. Member of San Francisco's "Million-Dollar" backfield.

CHARLIE JOINER
Wide receiver. 5-11, 180. Born in Many, Louisiana, October 14, 1947. Grambling. Inducted in 1996. 1969-1972 Houston Oilers, 1972-75 Cincinnati Bengals, 1976-1986 San Diego Chargers. **Highlights:** 750 receptions for 12,146 yards and 65 touchdowns. Played 18 seasons, 239 games, most ever for wide receiver at time of retirement.

DAVID (DEACON) JONES
Defensive end. 6-5, 260. Born in Eatonville, Florida, December 9, 1938. South Carolina State, Mississippi Vocational. Inducted in 1980. 1961-1971 Los Angeles Rams, 1972-73 San Diego Chargers, 1974 Washington Redskins. **Highlights:** Specialized in quarterback "sacks," a term he invented. Unanimous all-league five consecutive years.

STAN JONES
Guard-defensive tackle. 6-1, 250. Born in Altoona, Pennsylvania, November 24, 1931. Died May 21, 2010. Maryland. Inducted in 1991. 1954-1965 Chicago Bears, 1966 Washington Redskins. **Highlights:** Seven consecutive Pro Bowls. First to rely on weightlifting for football preparation.

HENRY JORDAN
Defensive tackle, 6-3, 240. Born in Emporia, Virginia, January 26, 1935. Died February 21, 1977. Virginia. Inducted in 1995. 1957-58 Cleveland Browns, 1959-1969 Green Bay Packers. **Highlights:** Fixture at DT during Packers' dynasty. Played in four Pro Bowls, seven NFL title games, Super Bowls I, II.

SONNY JURGENSEN
Quarterback. 6-0, 203. Born in Wilmington, North Carolina, August 23, 1934. Duke. Inducted in 1983. 1957-1963 Philadelphia Eagles, 1964-1974 Washington Redskins. **Highlights:** 32,224 yards passing, 255 touchdowns, 82.63 passer rating. Surpassed 3,000 yards passing in five seasons.

JIM KELLY
Quarterback. 6-3, 225. Born in Pittsburgh, Pennsylvania, February 14, 1960. Miami. Inducted in 2002. 1986-1996 Buffalo Bills. **Highlights:** Passed for more than 3,000 yards eight times. Mastered the no-huddle offense that propelled Bills to four consecutive Super Bowls.

LEROY KELLY
Running back. 6-0, 205. Born in Philadelphia, Pennsylvania, May 20, 1942. Morgan State. Inducted in 1994. 1964-1973 Cleveland Browns. **Highlights:** 7,274 yards rushing, 90 total touchdowns, 1,000-yard rusher first three years as starter. Punt return champion 1965.

CORTEZ KENNEDY
Defensive tackle. 6-3, 298. Born in Osceola, Arkansas, August 23, 1968. Northwest Mississippi Community College, Miami. Inducted in 2012. 1990-2000 Seattle Seahawks. **Highlights:** NFL Defensive Player of the Year, 1992. Voted to eight Pro Bowls and selected first-team All-Pro three times. Named to the NFL's All-Decade Team of the 1990s.

WALT KIESLING
Guard. Coach. 6-2, 245. Born in St. Paul, Minnesota, May 27, 1903. Died March 2, 1962. St. Thomas (Minnesota). Inducted in 1966. 1926-27 Duluth Eskimos, 1928 Pottsville Maroons, 1929-1933 Chicago Cardinals, 1934 Chicago Bears, 1935-36 Green Bay Packers, 1937-38 Pittsburgh Pirates; coach, 1939 Pittsburgh Pirates, 1940-42 Pittsburgh Steelers; co-coach, 1943 Phil-Pitt, 1944 Card-Pitt; coach, 1954-56 Pittsburgh Steelers. **Highlights:** 34-year career as pro player, assistant coach, head coach. Led Steelers to first winning season, 1942.

FRANK (BRUISER) KINARD
Tackle. 6-1, 210. Born in Pelahatchie, Mississippi, October 23, 1914. Died September 7, 1985. Mississippi. Inducted in 1971. 1938-1943 Brooklyn Dodgers, 1944 Brooklyn Tigers, 1946-47 New York Yankees (AAFC). **Highlights:** First man to earn both All-NFL, All-AAFC honors. Out because of injury only once.

PAUL KRAUSE
Safety. 6-3, 200. Born in Flint, Michigan, February 19, 1942. Iowa. Inducted in 1998. 1964-67 Washington Redskins, 1968-1979 Minnesota Vikings. **Highlights:** NFL all-time leader with 81 interceptions. Played in eight Pro Bowls. Starting safety in four Super Bowls.

EARL (CURLY) LAMBEAU
Coach. Born in Green Bay, Wisconsin, April 9, 1898. Died June 1, 1965. Notre Dame. Inducted in 1963. 1919-1949 Green Bay Packers, 1950-51 Chicago Cardinals, 1952-53 Washington Redskins. **Highlights:** Charter enshrinee. 229-134-22 coaching record with six NFL championships. Founded pre-NFL Packers, 1919.

JACK LAMBERT
Linebacker. 6-4, 220. Born in Mantua, Ohio, July 8, 1952. Kent State. Inducted in 1990. 1974-1984 Pittsburgh Steelers. **Highlights:** Leader of 'Steel Curtain.' NFL defensive player of year in 1976, nine Pro Bowls.

TOM LANDRY
Coach. Born in Mission, Texas, September 11, 1924. Died February 12, 2000. Texas. Inducted in 1990. 1960-1988 Dallas Cowboys. **Highlights:** 270-178-6 coaching record. 20 consecutive winning seasons. Innovator on offense and defense.

DICK (NIGHT TRAIN) LANE
Cornerback. 6-2, 210. Born in Austin, Texas, April 16, 1928. Died January 29, 2002. Scottsbluff Junior College. Inducted in 1974. 1952-53 Los Angeles Rams, 1954-59 Chicago Cardinals, 1960-65 Detroit Lions. **Highlights:** 68 interceptions for 1,207 yards, 5 touchdowns. Record 14 interceptions as rookie. Seven Pro Bowls.

JIM LANGER
Center. 6-2, 255. Born in Little Falls, Minnesota, May 16, 1948. South Dakota State. Inducted in 1987. 1970-79 Miami Dolphins, 1980-81 Minnesota Vikings. **Highlights:** Played every offensive down in Dolphins' perfect 1972 season. Six Pro Bowls.

WILLIE LANIER
Linebacker. 6-1, 245. Born in Clover, Virginia, August 21, 1945. Morgan State. Inducted in 1986. 1967-1977 Kansas City Chiefs. **Highlights:** 27 interceptions. Defensive star in Super Bowl IV upset. Nicknamed 'Contact' for ferocious tackling.

STEVE LARGENT
Wide receiver. 5-11, 191. Born in Tulsa, Oklahoma, September 28, 1954, Tulsa. Inducted in 1995. 1976-1989 Seattle Seahawks. **Highlights:** 819 receptions for 13,089 yards, 100 touchdowns. Receptions in 177 consecutive games.

YALE LARY
Safety. 5-11, 189. Born in Fort Worth, Texas, November 24, 1930. Texas A&M. Inducted in 1979. 1952-53, 1956-1964 Detroit Lions. **Highlights:** 50 interceptions. Three NFL punting crowns, three touchdowns on punt returns. Nine Pro Bowls.

DANTE LAVELLI
End. 6-0, 199. Born in Hudson, Ohio, February 23, 1923. Died January 20, 2009. Ohio State. Inducted in 1975. 1946-49 Cleveland Browns (AAFC), 1950-56 Cleveland Browns. **Highlights:** 386 receptions for 6,488 yards, 62 touchdowns. 24 catches in six NFL title games.

BOBBY LAYNE
Quarterback. 6-2, 190. Born in Santa Anna, Texas, December 19, 1926. Died December 1, 1986. Texas. Inducted in 1967. 1948 Chicago Bears, 1949 New York Bulldogs, 1950-58 Detroit Lions, 1958-1962 Pittsburgh Steelers. **Highlights:** 26,768 yards passing, 196 touchdowns, 2,451 yards rushing. Late touchdown pass won 1953 NFL title game.

DICK LeBEAU

Cornerback. 6-1, 185. Born in London, Ohio, September 9, 1937. Ohio State. Inducted in 2010. 1959-1972 Detroit Lions. **Highlights:** Recorded 62 career interceptions for 762 yards, 3 TDs, ranked third all-time in interceptions at retirement. Voted to three Pro Bowls.

ALPHONSE (TUFFY) LEEMANS

Fullback. 6-0, 200. Born in Superior, Wisconsin, November 12, 1912. Died January 19, 1979. Oregon, George Washington. Inducted in 1978. 1936-1943 New York Giants. **Highlights:** 3,132 yards rushing, 2,318 yards passing, 422 yards receiving. Led NFL rushers as rookie, 1936.

MARV LEVY

Coach. Born in Chicago, Illinois, August 3, 1925. Wyoming, Coe College, Harvard. Inducted in 2001. 1978-1982 Kansas City Chiefs, 1986-1997 Buffalo Bills. **Highlights:** Led Bills to unprecedented four consecutive Super Bowls. Had 154-120 record. Coaching victories ranked 10th when retired.

BOB LILLY

Defensive tackle. 6-5, 260. Born in Olney, Texas, July 26, 1939. Texas Christian. Inducted in 1980. 1961-1974 Dallas Cowboys. **Highlights:** Eleven Pro Bowls. Played 196 consecutive games. Foundation of great Dallas defensive units.

FLOYD LITTLE

Running back. 5-10, 196. Born in New Haven, Connecticut, July 4, 1942. Syracuse. Inducted in 2010. 1967-1975 Denver Broncos. **Highlights:** Broncos' first 1,000-yard rusher, won NFL rushing title in 1971. Amassed more than 12,000 career all-purpose yards, 54 TDs, five AFL All-Star Games/Pro Bowls.

LARRY LITTLE

Guard. 6-1, 265. Born in Groveland, Georgia, November 2, 1945. Bethune-Cookman. Inducted in 1993. 1967-68 San Diego Chargers, 1969-1980 Miami Dolphins. **Highlights:** Five Pro Bowls, started in three Super Bowls. Epitome of powerful Dolphins rushing game of 1970s.

JAMES LOFTON

Wide receiver. 6-3, 192. Born in Fort Ord, California, July 5, 1956. Stanford. Inducted in 2003. 1978-1986 Green Bay Packers, 1987-88 Los Angeles Raiders, 1989-1992 Buffalo Bills, 1993 Los Angeles Rams, 1993 Philadelphia Eagles. **Highlights:** Played 16 seasons, 233 games. Caught 764 passes for 75 touchdowns and a then-record 14,004 yards. All-Pro four times, eight Pro Bowls.

VINCE LOMBARDI

Coach. Born in Brooklyn, New York, June 11, 1913. Died September 3, 1970. Fordham. Inducted in 1971. 1959-1967 Green Bay Packers, 1969 Washington Redskins. **Highlights:** 105-35-6 coaching record in 10 years, including five NFL titles and victories in Super Bowls I and II.

HOWIE LONG

Defensive end. 6-5, 268. Born in Somerville, Massachusetts, January 6, 1960. Villanova. Inducted in 2000. 1981-1993 Oakland/Los Angeles Raiders. **Highlights:** All-Pro 1983, 1984, 1985. Named All-AFC four times, 1983-1986. Eight Pro Bowls.

RONNIE LOTT

Cornerback-safety. 6-0, 203. Born in Albuquerque, New Mexico, May 8, 1959. Southern California. Inducted in 2000. 1981-1990 San Francisco 49ers, 1991-92 Los Angeles Raiders, 1993-94 New York Jets. **Highlights:** Ten Pro Bowls, 63 career interceptions, and was named to the NFL's 75th Anniversary Team.

SID LUCKMAN

Quarterback. 6-0, 195. Born in Brooklyn, New York, November 21, 1916. Died July 5, 1998. Columbia. Inducted in 1965. 1939-1950 Chicago Bears. **Highlights:** 137 touchdown passes. All-NFL five times. League MVP in 1943.

WILLIAM ROY (LINK) LYMAN

Tackle. 6-2, 252. Born in Table Rock, Nebraska, November 30, 1898. Died December 28, 1972. Nebraska. Inducted in 1964. 1922-23, 1925 Canton Bulldogs, 1924 Cleveland Bulldogs, 1925 Frankford Yellowjackets, 1926-28, 1930-31, 1933-34 Chicago Bears. **Highlights:** Played for four NFL champions. In 16 seasons of college and pro football, played on one losing team.

TOM MACK

Guard. 6-3, 250. Born in Cleveland, Ohio, November 1, 1943. Michigan. Inducted in 1999. 1966-1978 Los Angeles Rams. **Highlights:** Never missed a game in entire 184-game career. Elected to 11 Pro Bowls.

JOHN MACKEY

Tight end. 6-2, 224. Born in New York, New York, September 24, 1941. Died July 6, 2011. Syracuse. Inducted in 1992. 1963-1971 Baltimore Colts, 1972 San Diego Chargers. **Highlights:** 331 receptions for 5,236 yards, 38 touchdowns. Second tight end to enter Hall of Fame.

JOHN MADDEN

Coach. Born in Austin, Minnesota, April 10, 1936. San Mateo Junior College, California Polytechnic College at San Luis Obispo. Inducted in 2006. 1969-1978 Oakland Raiders. **Highlights:** Became one of youngest coaches in history when hired at age 32. 112-39-7 overall record. Owns best regular season winning percentage among coaches with 100 wins.

TIM MARA

Founder-Team Owner. Born in New York, New York, July 29, 1887. Died February 16, 1959. Did not attend college. Inducted in 1963. 1925-1959 New York Giants. **Highlights:** Charter enshrinee. Founder of New York Giants. Built team into powerhouse winning four NFL titles, 10 division titles.

WELLINGTON MARA

Team owner. Born in New York, New York, August 14, 1916. Died October 25, 2005. Fordham. Inducted in 1997. 1937-2005 New York Giants. **Highlights:** Lifetime contributor to NFL and New York Giants. Worked as Giants' ballboy, secretary, vice-president, president and co-CEO. NFC president 1984-present.

GINO MARCHETTI

Defensive end. 6-4, 245. Born in Smithers, West Virginia, January 2, 1927. San Francisco. Inducted in 1972. 1952 Dallas Texans, 1953-1964, 1966 Baltimore Colts. **Highlights:** Named top defensive end of NFL's first 50 years. 10 consecutive Pro Bowls. All-NFL seven times.

DAN MARINO

Quarterback. 6-4, 218. Born in Pittsburgh, Pennsylvania, September 15, 1961. Pittsburgh. Inducted in 2005. 1983-1999 Miami Dolphins. **Highlights:** Held NFL records for career passing yardage (61,361), completions (4,967), attempts (8,358), and touchdowns (420). Voted to nine Pro Bowls.

GEORGE PRESTON MARSHALL

Team owner. Born in Grafton, West Virginia, October 11, 1896. Died August 9, 1969. Randolph-Macon. Inducted in 1963. 1932 Boston Braves, 1933-36 Boston Redskins, 1937-1969 Washington Redskins. **Highlights:** Charter enshrinee. Sponsored progressive rules changes. Organized first team band, pioneered halftime shows.

CURTIS MARTIN

Running back. 5-11, 207. Born in Pittsburgh, Pennsylvania, May 1, 1973. Pittsburgh. Inducted in 2012. 1995-97 New England Patriots, 1998-2005 New York Jets. **Highlights:** Second player in NFL history to start career with 10 straight 1,000-yard rushing seasons. Retired as fourth-leading rusher of all-time with 14,101 yards. Racked up 17,421 combined net yards and 100 career TDs (90 rushing, 10 receiving). NFL rushing title, 2004.

OLLIE MATSON

Halfback. 6-2, 220. Born in Trinity, Texas, May 1, 1930. Died February 19, 2011. San Francisco. Inducted in 1972. 1952, 1954-58 Chicago Cardinals, 1959-1962 Los Angeles Rams, 1963 Detroit Lions, 1964-66 Philadelphia Eagles. **Highlights:** Nine touchdowns on kickoff, punt returns. Traded for nine players in 1959.

BRUCE MATTHEWS

Guard-tackle-center. 6-5, 289. Born in Raleigh, North Carolina, August 8, 1961. Southern California. Inducted in 2007. 1983-2001 Houston Oilers/Tennessee Oilers/Tennessee Titans. **Highlights:** Played in 296 games, most ever by positional player at time of his retirement. Named to a record-tying 14 straight Pro Bowls. All-Pro nine times, All-AFC 12 times.

DON MAYNARD

Wide receiver. 6-1, 185. Born in Crosbyton, Texas, January 25, 1935. Texas Western. Inducted in 1987. 1958 New York Giants, 1960-62 New York Titans, 1963-1972 New York Jets, 1973 St. Louis Cardinals. **Highlights:** 633 receptions for 11,834 yards, 88 touchdowns. At least 50 catches and 1,000 yards in five different seasons.

GEORGE McAFEE

Halfback. 6-0, 177. Born in Corbin, Kentucky, March 13, 1918. Died March 4, 2009. Duke. Inducted in 1966. 1940-41, 1945-1950 Chicago Bears. **Highlights:** Two-way star. 25 interceptions, 234 points. Career punt-return average of 12.78 yards per return.

MIKE McCORMACK

Tackle. 6-4, 250. Born in Chicago, Illinois, June 21, 1930. Kansas. Inducted in 1984. 1951 New York Yanks, 1954-1962 Cleveland Browns. **Highlights:** Excelled as offensive right tackle for eight years. Six Pro Bowls.

RANDALL McDANIEL

Guard. 6-3, 276. Born in Phoenix, Arizona, December 19, 1964. Arizona State. Inducted in 2009. 1988-1999 Minnesota Vikings, 2000-01 Tampa Bay Buccaneers. **Highlights:** 12 Pro Bowls, All-Pro nine straight times. Blocked for six different 1,000-yard rushers, five 3,000-yard passers.

TOMMY McDONALD

Wide receiver. 5-9, 175. Born in Roy, New Mexico, July 26, 1934. Oklahoma. Inducted in 1998. 1957-1963 Philadelphia Eagles, 1964 Dallas Cowboys, 1965-66 Los Angeles Rams, 1967 Atlanta Falcons, 1968 Cleveland Browns. **Highlights:** Recorded 495 receptions for 8,410 yards, 84 touchdowns.

HUGH McELHENNY

Halfback. 6-1, 198. Born in Los Angeles, California, December 31, 1928. Washington. Inducted in 1970. 1952-1960 San Francisco 49ers, 1961-62 Minnesota Vikings, 1963 New York Giants, 1964 Detroit Lions. **Highlights:** 5,281 rushing yards, 360 points. Totaled 11,369 yards rushing, receiving, and returning kicks.

JOHNNY (BLOOD) McNALLY

Halfback. 6-0, 185. Born in New Richmond, Wisconsin, November 27, 1903. Died November 28, 1985. Notre Dame, St. John's (Minnesota). Inducted in 1963. 1925-26 Milwaukee Badgers, 1926-27 Duluth Eskimos, 1928 Pottsville Maroons, 1929-1933, 1935-36 Green Bay Packers, 1934 Pittsburgh Pirates; player-coach, 1937-38 Pittsburgh Pirates. **Highlights:** Charter enshrinee. 49 touchdowns, 297 points in 14 seasons with five teams.

MIKE MICHALSKE

Guard. 6-0, 209. Born in Cleveland, Ohio, April 24, 1903. Died October 26, 1983. Penn State. Inducted in 1964. 1926 New York Yankees (AFL), 1927-28 New York Yankees, 1929-1935, 1937 Green Bay Packers. **Highlights:** Anchored Packers' championship lines, 1929-1931. First guard enshrined in Canton.

WAYNE MILLNER

End. 6-0, 191. Born in Roxbury, Massachusetts, January 31, 1913. Died November 19, 1976. Notre Dame. Inducted in 1968. 1936 Boston Redskins, 1937-1941, 1945 Washington Redskins. **Highlights:** Redskins' all-time leader with 124 catches when retired. 55- and 78-yard touchdown receptions in 1937 NFL Championship Game.

BOBBY MITCHELL

Running back-wide receiver. 6-0, 195. Born in Hot Springs, Arkansas, June 6, 1935. Illinois. Inducted in 1983. 1958-1961 Cleveland Browns, 1962-68 Washington Redskins. **Highlights:** 91 touchdowns, including 8 on kickoff and punt returns. 14,078 combined yards.

RON MIX

Tackle. 6-4, 255. Born in Los Angeles, California, March 10, 1938. Southern California. Inducted in 1979. 1960 Los Angeles Chargers, 1961-69 San Diego Chargers, 1971 Oakland Raiders. **Highlights:** All-AFL nine times. Only two holding penalties in 10 years with the Chargers.

ART MONK

Wide receiver. 6-3, 210. Born in White Plains, New York, December 5, 1957. Syracuse. Inducted in 2008. 1980-1993 Washington Redskins, 1994 New York Jets, 1995 Philadelphia Eagles. **Highlights:** 940 receptions, 12,721 yards, 68 TDs. Set then-single season record, 106 catches, 1984. Had 50 or more catches in a season nine times.

JOE MONTANA

Quarterback. 6-2, 200. Born in New Eagle, Pennsylvania, June, 11, 1956. Notre Dame. Inducted in 2000. 1979-1990, 1992 San Francisco 49ers, 1993-94 Kansas City Chiefs. **Highlights:** MVP in Super Bowl's XVI, XIX, and XXIV. Eight Pro Bowls and All-NFL three times.

WARREN MOON

Quarterback. 6-3, 212. Born in Los Angeles, California, November 18, 1956. West Los Angeles Junior College, Washington. Inducted in 2006. 1984-1993 Houston Oilers, 1994-1996 Minnesota Vikings, 1997-1998 Seattle Seahawks, 1999-2000 Kansas City Chiefs. **Highlights:** Passed for 49,325 yards and 291 touchdowns in 17 NFL seasons. Elected to nine Pro Bowls including eight straight. Threw for 3,000 yards in nine seasons.

LENNY MOORE

Flanker-running back. 6-1, 198. Born in Reading, Pennsylvania, November 25, 1933. Penn State. Inducted in 1975. 1956-1967 Baltimore Colts. **Highlights:** From 1963-65, scored touchdowns in record 18 consecutive games. 113 career touchdowns, 12,451 combined net yards.

MARION MOTLEY

Fullback. 6-1, 238. Born in Leesburg, Georgia, June 5, 1920. Died June 27, 1999. South Carolina State, Nevada. Inducted in 1968. 1946-49 Cleveland Browns (AAFC), 1950-53 Cleveland Browns, 1955 Pittsburgh Steelers. **Highlights:** AAFC's all-time rushing champion. Led league in rushing in first NFL season.

MIKE MUNCHAK
Guard. 6-3, 281. Born in Scranton, Pennsylvania, March 5, 1960. Penn State. Inducted in 2001. 1982-1993 Houston Oilers. **Highlights:** Devastating blocker, All-AFC seven times, elected to nine Pro Bowls.

ANTHONY MUÑOZ
Tackle. 6-6, 278. Born in Ontario, California, August 19, 1958. Southern California. Inducted in 1998. 1980-1992 Cincinnati Bengals. **Highlights:** All-Pro choice 11 consecutive years, 1981-1991. Selected to 11 straight Pro Bowls.

GEORGE MUSSO
Guard-tackle. 6-2, 270. Born in Collinsville, Illinois. April 8, 1910. Died September 5, 2000. Millikin. Inducted in 1982. 1933-1944 Chicago Bears. **Highlights:** First player to achieve All-NFL status at two positions—tackle in 1935 and guard in 1937.

BRONKO NAGURSKI
Fullback. 6-2, 225. Born in Rainy River, Ontario, Canada, November 3, 1908. Died January 7, 1990. Minnesota. Inducted in 1963. 1930-37, 1943 Chicago Bears. **Highlights:** Charter enshrinee. 2,778 rushing yards in nine seasons. All-NFL five times.

JOE NAMATH
Quarterback. 6-2, 200. Born in Beaver Falls, Pennsylvania, May 31, 1943. Alabama. Inducted in 1985. 1965-1976 New York Jets, 1977 Los Angeles Rams. **Highlights:** First quarterback to pass for more than 4,000 yards in season, 1967. Guaranteed, delivered victory over Colts in Super Bowl III.

EARLE (GREASY) NEALE
Coach. Born in Parkersburg, West Virginia, November 5, 1891. Died November 2, 1973. West Virginia Wesleyan. Inducted in 1969. 1941-42, 1944-1950 Philadelphia Eagles; co-coach, 1943 Phil-Pitt. **Highlights:** Turned Eagles into winners with three consecutive division crowns, NFL championships in 1948 and 1949.

ERNIE NEVERS
Fullback. 6-1, 205. Born in Willow River, Minnesota, June 11, 1903. Died May 3, 1976. Stanford. Inducted in 1963. 1926-27 Duluth Eskimos, 1929-1931 Chicago Cardinals. **Highlights:** Charter enshrinee. Holds NFL's longest-standing record, 40 points in one game in 1929.

OZZIE NEWSOME
Tight end. 6-2, 232. Born in Muscle Shoals, Alabama, March 16, 1956. Alabama. Inducted in 1999. 1978-1990 Cleveland Browns. **Highlights:** Finished career as all-time leader among tight ends with 662 receptions for 7,980 yards.

RAY NITSCHKE
Linebacker. 6-3, 235. Born in Elmwood Park, Illinois, December 29, 1936. Died March 8, 1998. Illinois. Inducted in 1978. 1958-1972 Green Bay Packers. **Highlights:** MVP of 1962 title game. Named NFL's all-time linebacker in 1969.

CHUCK NOLL
Coach. Born in Cleveland, Ohio, January 5, 1932. Dayton. Inducted in 1993. 1969-1991 Pittsburgh Steelers. **Highlights:** Coached for 23 years. Only coach to win four Super Bowl titles (IX, X, XIII, XIV).

LEO NOMELLINI
Defensive tackle. 6-3, 264. Born in Lucca, Italy, June 19, 1924. Died October 17, 2000. Minnesota. Inducted in 1969. 1950-1963 San Francisco 49ers. **Highlights:** Played every 49ers game for 14 seasons. 10 Pro Bowls.

JONATHAN OGDEN
Tackle. 6-9, 345. Born in Washington, D.C., July 31, 1974. Inducted in 2013. 1996-2007 Baltimore Ravens. **Highlights:** First-ever draft pick of the Ravens. Named first-team All-Pro six times. Elected to 11 Pro Bowls. Member of NFL's All-Decade Team of 2000s.

MERLIN OLSEN
Defensive tackle. 6-5, 270. Born in Logan, Utah, September 15, 1940. Died March 11, 2010. Utah State. Inducted in 1982. 1962-1976 Los Angeles Rams. **Highlights:** Member of the Fearsome "Foursome." Named" to 14 consecutive Pro Bowls, Rams' all-time team.

JIM OTTO
Center. 6-2, 255. Born in Wausau, Wisconsin, January 5, 1938. Miami. Inducted in 1980. 1960-1974 Oakland Raiders. **Highlights:** Named AFL's all-time center. Played in 210 games, 12 AFL All-Star Games or Pro Bowls, six AFL/AFC title games.

STEVE OWEN
Tackle. Coach. 6-2, 235. Born in Cleo Springs, Oklahoma, April 21, 1898. Died May 17, 1964. Phillips. Inducted in 1966. 1924-25 Kansas City Cowboys, 1925 Cleveland Bulldogs, 1926-1931, 1933 New York Giants; coach, 1930-1953 New York Giants. **Highlights:** Both player and coach. Coached Giants to record of 155-108-17, eight divisional titles, two NFL championships.

ALAN PAGE
Defensive tackle. 6-4, 225. Born in Canton, Ohio, August 7, 1945. Notre Dame. Inducted in 1988. 1967-1978 Minnesota Vikings, 1978-1981 Chicago Bears. **Highlights:** Dominating defensive tackle played in 238 consecutive games, four Super Bowls. Won league MVP honors in 1971.

BILL PARCELLS
Coach. Born in Englewood, New Jersey, August 22, 1941. Inducted in 2013. 1983-1990 New York Giants, 1993-96 New England Patriots, 1997-99 New York Jets, 2003-06 Dallas Cowboys. **Highlights:** Only coach to lead four different teams to the playoffs. Named NFL Coach of the Year twice (1986 and 1994). Led Giants to two Super Bowl titles. Overall record: 183-138-1.

CLARENCE (ACE) PARKER
Quarterback. 5-11, 168. Born in Portsmouth, Virginia, May 17, 1912. Duke. Inducted in 1972. 1937-1941 Brooklyn Dodgers, 1945 Boston Yanks, 1946 New York Yankees (AAFC). **Highlights:** Two-way threat. Two-time All-NFL performer, league MVP in 1940.

JIM PARKER
Guard-tackle. 6-3, 273. Born in Macon, Georgia, April 3, 1934. Died July 18, 2005. Ohio State. Inducted in 1973. 1957-1967 Baltimore Colts. **Highlights:** First full-time offensive lineman elected to Hall of Fame. All-NFL eight consecutive years, eight Pro Bowls.

WALTER PAYTON
Running back. 5-10, 202. Born in Columbia, Mississippi, July 25, 1954. Died November 1, 1999. Jackson State. Inducted in 1993. 1975-1987 Chicago Bears. **Highlights:** NFL's all-time leading rusher with 16,726 yards and combined net yardage with 21,803 at time of retirement.

JOE PERRY
Fullback. 6-0, 200. Born in Stevens, Arkansas, January 22, 1927. Died April 25, 2011. Compton Junior College. Inducted in 1969. 1948-49 San Francisco 49ers (AAFC), 1950-1960, 1963 San Francisco 49ers, 1961-62 Baltimore Colts. **Highlights:** First player in NFL history to gain 1,000 yards two consecutive seasons. 12,532 combined yards.

PETE PIHOS
End. 6-1, 210. Born in Orlando, Florida, October 22, 1923. Died August 16, 2011. Indiana. Inducted in 1970. 1947-1955 Philadelphia Eagles. **Highlights:** Three-time NFL receiving champion. Caught winning touchdown in 1949 NFL Championship Game.

FRITZ POLLARD
Halfback-Coach. 5-9, 165. Born in Chicago, Illinois, January 27, 1894. Died May 11, 1986. Brown. Inducted in 2005. 1919-1921, 1925-26 Akron Pros/Indians, 1922 Milwaukee Badgers, 1923, 1925 Hammond Pros, 1925 Providence Steam Roller. **Highlights:** True pioneer as one of two African American players in the NFL in 1920 and helped lead Akron to league title that season. In 1921, became the league's first black head coach.

JOHN RANDLE
Defensive tackle. 6-1, 278. Born in Hearne, Texas, December 12, 1967. Trinity Valley Community College; Texas A&I. Inducted in 2010. 1990-2000 Minnesota Vikings, 2001-03 Seattle Seahawks. **Highlights:** Undrafted free agent rookie, record eight straight seasons with 10 or more sacks, had 137.5 career sacks. Voted to seven Pro Bowls, named All-Pro/NFC six consecutive years, All-AFC once.

HUGH (SHORTY) RAY
Supervisor of officials 1938-1952. Born in Highland Park, Illinois, September 21, 1884. Died September 16, 1956. Illinois. Inducted in 1966. **Highlights:** Supervisor of Officials, 1938-1952. Streamlined rules to improve game tempo, player safety.

DAN REEVES
Team owner. Born in New York, New York, June 30, 1912. Died April 15, 1971. Georgetown. Inducted in 1967. 1941-45 Cleveland Rams, 1946-1971 Los Angeles Rams. **Highlights:** Moved Rams to Los Angeles in 1946 and opened up West Coast to pro football. First postwar owner to sign African-American player.

MEL RENFRO
Cornerback-safety. 6-0, 192. Born in Houston, Texas, December 30, 1941. Oregon. Inducted in 1996. 1964-1977 Dallas Cowboys. **Highlights:** 52 interceptions for 626 yards and 3 touchdowns. Also added 842 yards on punt returns, 2,246 yards on kickoff returns. Elected to Pro Bowl first 10 seasons.

JERRY RICE
Wide receiver. 6-2, 200. Born in Starksville, Mississippi, October 13, 1962. Mississippi Valley State. Inducted in 2010. 1985-2000 San Francisco 49ers, 2001-04 Oakland Raiders, 2004 Seattle Seahawks. **Highlights:** NFL's all-time reception leader with 1,549 catches for 22,895 yards, 208 total touchdowns. Had 14 seasons with 1,000 yards receiving; 23,546 combined net yards. All-Pro 11 times, Super Bowl XXIII MVP.

LES RICHTER
Linebacker. 6-3, 238. Born in Fresno, California, October 6, 1930. Died June 12, 2010. California. Inducted in 2011. 1954-1962 Los Angeles Rams. **Highlights:** Second overall pick in 1952 by New York Yanks. Rights traded to Rams in exchange for 11 players. Rugged, fierce competitor. Voted to eight straight Pro Bowls. Recorded 16 career interceptions, also handled Rams' placekicking duties early in career.

JOHN RIGGINS
Running back. 6-2, 240. Born in Seneca, Kansas, August 4, 1949. Kansas. Inducted in 1992. 1971-75 New York Jets, 1976-79, 1981-85 Washington Redskins. **Highlights:** 11,352 rushing yards, 116 total touchdowns. MVP of Super Bowl XVII with 166 rushing yards including game-winning 43-yard touchdown.

JIM RINGO
Center. 6-2, 230. Born in Orange, New Jersey, November 21, 1931. Died November 19, 2007. Syracuse. Inducted in 1981. 1953-1963 Green Bay Packers, 1964-67 Philadelphia Eagles. **Highlights:** Ten-time Pro Bowl selection, seven-time All-NFL selection. Started in then-record 182 consecutive games.

WILLIE ROAF
Tackle. 6-5, 300. Born in Pine Bluff, Arkansas, April 18, 1970. Louisiana Tech. Inducted in 2012. 1993-2001 New Orleans Saints, 2002-05 Kansas City Chiefs. **Highlights:** Voted to 11 Pro Bowls, named first-team All-Pro seven times. Member of both the NFL's All-Decade Team of the 1990s and 2000s.

DAVE ROBINSON
Linebacker. 6-3, 245. Born in Mt. Holly, New Jersey, May 3, 1941. Inducted in 2013. 1963-1972 Green Bay Packers, 1973-74 Washington Redskins. **Highlights:** Starting outside linebacker in three NFL championship game and two Super Bowl wins. Recorded 27 career interceptions. Voted to three Pro Bowl Bowls. Named to NFL's All-Decade Team of 1960s.

ANDY ROBUSTELLI
Defensive end. 6-0, 230. Born in Stamford, Connecticut, December 6, 1925. Died May 31, 2011. Arnold College. Inducted in 1971. 1951-55 Los Angeles Rams, 1956-1964 New York Giants. **Highlights:** Anchored defense in eight championship games. Named NFL's top player in 1962.

ART ROONEY
Founder-Team Owner. Born in Coulterville, Pennsylvania, January 27, 1901. Died August 25, 1988. Georgetown, Duquesne. Inducted in 1964. 1933-39 Pittsburgh Pirates, 1940-42, 1945-1988 Pittsburgh Steelers, 1943 Phil-Pitt, 1944 Card-Pitt. **Highlights:** Founded Pittsburgh Pirates in 1933 and renamed them Steelers in 1940. Team won four Super Bowls in 1970s.

DAN ROONEY
Administrator-Team Owner. Born in Pittsburgh, Pennsylvania, July, 20, 1932. Duquesne. Inducted in 2000. 1955-present Pittsburgh Steelers. **Highlights:** Has been on the board of directors for the NFL Trust Fund, NFL Films, and Scheduling Committee. Played a key role in the labor agreement reached in 1993 between the NFL owners and players.

PETE ROZELLE
Commissioner. Born in South Gate, California, March 1, 1926. Died December 6, 1996. Compton Junior College, San Francisco. Inducted in 1985. Commissioner, 1960-1989. **Highlights:** Negotiated first league-wide television contract in 1962. Generally recognized as premiere commissioner in all of sports. Credited with making NFL the nation's most popular sport.

BOB ST. CLAIR
Tackle. 6-9, 265. Born in San Francisco, California, February 18, 1931. San Francisco, Tulsa. Inducted in 1990. 1953-1963 San Francisco 49ers. **Highlights:** Exceptional offensive lineman. Also played goal-line defense and had 10 blocked field goals, 1956.

ED SABOL
Founder-President-Chairman. Born in Atlantic City, New Jersey, September 11, 1916. Ohio State. Inducted in 2011. 1964-1995 NFL Films. **Highlights:** Bid and received rights to film 1962 NFL Championship Game. Two years later, founded NFL Films. During his tenure, NFL Films won 52 Emmys. Vision and innovations changed the way in which sports were presented.

BARRY SANDERS
Running back. 5-8, 203. Born in Wichita, Kansas, July 16, 1968. Oklahoma State. Inducted in 2004. 1989-1998 Detroit Lions. **Highlights:** 15,269 rushing yards, 99 touchdowns. Rushed for 1,000 yards in each of 10 seasons. NFL co-MVP, 1997. Selected to 10 Pro Bowls.

CHARLIE SANDERS
Tight end. 6-4, 230. Born in Richlands, North Carolina, August 25, 1946. Minnesota. Inducted in 2007. 1968-1977 Detroit Lions. **Highlights:** 336 career receptions for 4,817 yards and 31 touchdowns. Selected to seven Pro Bowls. Named to the NFL's All-Decade Team of 1970s.

DEION SANDERS
Cornerback-Kick returner-Punt returner. 6-1, 195. Born in Fort Myers, Florida, August 9, 1967. Florida State. Inducted in 2011. 1989-1993 Atlanta Falcons, 1994 San Francisco 49ers, 1995-99 Dallas Cowboys, 2000 Washington Redskins, 2004-05 Baltimore Ravens. **Highlights:** First-team All-NFL nine times. Voted to the NFL's All-Decade Team of the 1990s at both cornerback and punt returner. 53 career interceptions. Career touchdowns include six on punt returns, three on kickoff returns, nine on interceptions, one fumble recovery, and three receiving.

WARREN SAPP
Defensive tackle. 6-2, 300. Born in Orlando, Florida, December 19, 1972. Inducted in 2013. 1995-2003 Tampa Bay Buccaneers, 2004-07 Oakland Raiders. **Highlights:** Amassed 96.5 career sacks. Named 1999 NFL Defensive Player of the Year. First-team All-Pro four straight seasons. Member of NFL's All-Decade Teams of 1990s and 2000s.

GALE SAYERS
Running back. 6-0, 200. Born in Wichita, Kansas, May 30, 1943. Kansas. Inducted in 1977. 1965-1971 Chicago Bears. **Highlights:** Broke into league by scoring rookie-record 22 touchdowns. Led league in rushing in 1966, 1969. MVP of three Pro Bowls.

JOE SCHMIDT
Linebacker. 6-0, 222. Born in Pittsburgh, Pennsylvania, January 18, 1932. Pittsburgh. Inducted in 1973. 1953-1965 Detroit Lions. **Highlights:** 24 interceptions. Lions' team captain for nine years. Mastered middle linebacker position that evolved in 1950s.

TEX SCHRAMM
Team president-general manager. Born in San Gabriel, California, June 2, 1920. Died July 15, 2003. Texas. Inducted in 1991. 1947-1956 Los Angeles Rams. 1960-1989 Dallas Cowboys. **Highlights:** Played prominent role in AFL-NFL merger. Chairman of Competition Committee from 1966-1988.

LEE ROY SELMON
Defensive end. 6-3, 250. Born in Eufaula, Oklahoma, October 20, 1954. Died September 4, 2011. Oklahoma. Inducted in 1995. 1976-1984 Tampa Bay Buccaneers. **Highlights:** 78½ sacks, 380 quarterback pressures, forced 28 fumbles. Six consecutive Pro Bowl selections.

SHANNON SHARPE
Tight end. 6-2, 230. Born in Chicago, Illinois, June 26, 1968. Savannah State. Inducted in 2011. 1990-99, 2002-03 Denver Broncos, 2000-01 Baltimore Ravens. **Highlights:** Retired as the NFL's all-time leader among tight ends for catches (815), receiving yards (10,060) and TD receptions (62). Selected as first- or second-team All-Pro five times, named to eight Pro Bowls. Played on three Super Bowl championship teams in four seasons.

BILLY SHAW
Guard. 6-2, 258. Born in Natchez, Mississippi, December 15, 1938. Georgia Tech. Inducted in 1999. 1961-69 Buffalo Bills. **Highlights:** First player who played entire career in AFL to be elected to Hall of Fame. Named to AFL's all-time team.

ART SHELL
Tackle. 6-5, 285. Born in Charleston, South Carolina, November 26, 1946. Maryland State-Eastern Shore. Inducted in 1989. 1968-82 Oakland/Los Angeles Raiders. **Highlights:** Cornerstone of Raiders' offensive line in 1970s. 207 regular-season games, 23 postseason games, eight Pro Bowls.

DON SHULA
Coach. Born in Grand River, Ohio, January 4, 1930. John Carroll. Inducted in 1997. 1963-69 Baltimore Colts, 1970-1995 Miami Dolphins. **Highlights:** Won more games (347) than any coach in NFL history. Won two Super Bowl titles, including Super Bowl VII when Dolphins recorded NFL's only perfect season (17-0).

O.J. SIMPSON
Running back. 6-1, 212. Born in San Francisco, California, July 9, 1947. City College (San Francisco), Southern California. Inducted in 1985. 1969-1977 Buffalo Bills, 1978-79 San Francisco 49ers. **Highlights:** In 1973, became first player to rush for 2,000 yards in season. Finished career with four rushing titles, 11,236 yards.

MIKE SINGLETARY
Linebacker. 6-0, 230. Born in Houston, Texas, October 9, 1958. Baylor. Inducted in 1998. 1981-1992 Chicago Bears. **Highlights:** All-Pro choice eight times and All-NFC nine consecutive seasons. Selected to 10 Pro Bowls.

JACKIE SLATER
Tackle. 6-4, 277. Born in Jackson, Mississippi, May 27, 1954. Jackson State. Inducted in 2001. 1976-1995 Los Angeles/St. Louis Rams. **Highlights:** Played 20 seasons, 259 games. Blocked for seven different 1,000-yard rushers. Seven Pro Bowls.

BRUCE SMITH
Defensive end. 6-4, 280. Born in Norfolk, Virginia, June 18, 1963. Virginia Tech. Inducted in 2009. 1985-1999 Buffalo Bills, 2000-03 Washington Redskins. **Highlights:** NFL's all-time leader in sacks with 200. Named All-Pro nine times, 11 Pro Bowls. Selected to NFL's All-Decade Team of 1980s and 1990s.

EMMITT SMITH
Running back. 5-9, 207. Born in Pensacola, Florida, May 15, 1969. Florida. Inducted in 2010. 1990-2002 Dallas Cowboys, 2003-04 Arizona Cardinals. **Highlights:** Won four rushing titles in five years, recorded record 11 straight 1,000-yard seasons. NFL's all-time leading rusher with 18,355 yards, 164 rushing TDs. Won NFL MVP and Super Bowl XXVIII MVP in 1993.

JACKIE SMITH
Tight end. 6-4, 232. Born in Columbia, Mississippi, February 23, 1940. Northwestern State (Louisiana). Inducted in 1994. 1963-1977 St. Louis Cardinals, 1978 Dallas Cowboys. **Highlights:** 480 receptions for 7,918 yards, 40 touchdowns. Third tight end to be elected to Hall of Fame.

JOHN STALLWORTH
Wide receiver. 6-2, 191. Born in Tuscaloosa, Alabama, July 15, 1952. Alabama A&M. Inducted in 2002. 1974-1987 Pittsburgh Steelers. **Highlights:** 537 receptions for 8,723 yards, 63 touchdowns. Scored go-ahead touchdown in Super Bowl XIV on 73-yard reception.

BART STARR
Quarterback. 6-1, 200. Born in Montgomery, Alabama, January 9, 1934. Alabama. Inducted in 1977. 1956-1971 Green Bay Packers. **Highlights:** Quarterbacked Packers to six division titles, five NFL titles, and first two Super Bowls in which he was MVP.

ROGER STAUBACH
Quarterback. 6-3, 202. Born in Cincinnati, Ohio, February 5, 1942. New Mexico Military Institute, Navy. Inducted in 1985. 1969-1979 Dallas Cowboys. **Highlights:** Led Cowboys to four NFC titles and victories in Super Bowls VI, XII. When retired, 83.4 career passer rating was best of all time.

ERNIE STAUTNER
Defensive tackle. 6-2, 235. Born in Prinzing-by-Cham, Bavaria, April 20, 1925. Died February 16, 2006. Boston College. Inducted in 1969. 1950-1963 Pittsburgh Steelers. **Highlights:** Played in nine Pro Bowls and won the best lineman award in 1957. Recorded 3 safeties.

JAN STENERUD
Kicker. 6-2, 190. Born in Fetsund, Norway, November 26, 1942. Montana State. Inducted in 1991. 1967-1979 Kansas City Chiefs, 1980-83 Green Bay Packers, 1984-85 Minnesota Vikings. **Highlights:** 1,699 points on 580 extra points, 373 field goals. First pure placekicker to enter Hall of Fame.

DWIGHT STEPHENSON
Center. 6-2, 255. Born in Murfreesboro, North Carolina, November 20, 1957. Alabama. Inducted in 1998. 1980-87 Miami Dolphins. **Highlights:** Recognized as premier center of his time. All-Pro, All-AFC five straight years. Selected to five Pro Bowls.

HANK STRAM
Coach. Born in Chicago, Illinois, January 3, 1923. Died July 4, 2005. Purdue. Inducted in 2003. 1960-1974 Dallas Texans/Kansas City Chiefs, 1976-1977 New Orleans Saints. **Highlights:** Overall record of 136-100-10. Recorded most wins in AFL history. Guided teams to titles in 1962, 1966, and 1969. Led Chiefs to AFL win in Super Bowl IV.

KEN STRONG
Halfback. 5-11, 210. Born in West Haven, Connecticut, April 21, 1906. Died October 5, 1979. New York University. Inducted in 1967. 1929-1932 Staten Island Stapletons, 1933-35, 1939, 1944-47 New York Giants, 1936-37 New York Yanks (AFL). **Highlights:** Scored 17 points to lead Giants to victory in 1934 'Sneakers' game, led NFL with 64 points, 1933.

JOE STYDAHAR
Tackle. 6-4, 230. Born in Kaylor, Pennsylvania, March 17, 1912. Died March 23, 1977. West Virginia. Inducted in 1967. 1936-1942, 1945-46 Chicago Bears. **Highlights:** One of stalwarts of Bears' 'Monsters of the Midway.' Played on five divisional, three NFL championship teams.

LYNN SWANN
Wide receiver. 5-11, 180. Born in Alcoa, Tennessee, March 7, 1952. Southern California. Inducted in 2001. 1974-1982 Pittsburgh Steelers. **Highlights:** All-AFC three times. Selected to three Pro Bowls. MVP, Super Bowl X.

FRAN TARKENTON
Quarterback. 6-0, 185. Born in Richmond, Virginia, February 3, 1940. Georgia. Inducted in 1986. 1961-66, 1972-78 Minnesota Vikings, 1967-1971 New York Giants. **Highlights:** At retirement, held NFL records for attempts (6,467), completions (3,686), yards (47,003), and touchdowns (342). Four touchdown passes in first NFL game.

CHARLEY TAYLOR
Running back-wide receiver. 6-3, 210. Born in Grand Prairie, Texas, September 28, 1941. Arizona State. Inducted in 1984. 1964-1975, 1977 Washington Redskins. **Highlights:** Won rookie of year honors as running back. Switched to wide receiver and won receiving titles in 1966, 1967.

JIM TAYLOR
Fullback. 6-0, 216. Born in Baton Rouge, Louisiana, September 20, 1935. Hinds Junior College; Louisiana State. Inducted in 1976. 1958-1966 Green Bay Packers, 1967 New Orleans Saints. **Highlights:** 8,597 rushing yards, 558 points. In 1962, led league in rushing and scoring with 19 touchdowns.

LAWRENCE TAYLOR
Linebacker. 6-3, 237. Born in Williamsburg, Virginia, February 4, 1959. North Carolina. Inducted in 1999. 1981-1993 New York Giants. **Highlights:** Redefined the position of outside linebacker. All-Pro nine times, 10 Pro Bowls. NFL MVP in 1986.

DERRICK THOMAS
Linebacker. 6-3, 243. Born in Miami, Florida, January 1, 1967. Died February 8, 2000. Alabama. Inducted in 2009. 1989-1999 Kansas City Chiefs. **Highlights:** Set NFL record with 7 sacks in one game. Recorded most sacks in NFL during 1990s. Nine Pro Bowls. Named to NFL's All-Decade Team of 1990s.

EMMITT THOMAS
Cornerback. 6-2, 192. Born in Angleton, Texas, June 3, 1943. Bishop. Inducted in 2008. 1966-1978 Kansas City Chiefs. **Highlights:** Undrafted free agent. 58 interceptions, 937 yards, 5 TDs. Ranked fifth all-time in interceptions at retirement. Interception leader —AFL, 1969 and NFL, 1974.

THURMAN THOMAS
Running back. 5-10, 198. Born in Houston, Texas, May 16, 1966. Oklahoma State. Inducted in 2007. 1988-1999 Buffalo Bills, 2000 Miami Dolphins. **Highlights:** Amassed 16,532 total yards including 12,074 yards rushing. Scored 88 touchdowns. Only player in history to lead league in yards from scrimmage four straight seasons.

JIM THORPE
Halfback. 6-1, 190. Born in Prague, Oklahoma, May 28, 1888. Died March 28, 1953. Carlisle. Inducted in 1963. 1915-17, 1919-1920, 1926 Canton Bulldogs, 1921 Cleveland Indians, 1922-23 Oorang Indians, 1924 Rock Island Independents, 1925 New York Giants, 1928 Chicago Cardinals. **Highlights:** Charter enshrinee. First president of American Professional Football Association, 1920. Played for 12 seasons.

ANDRE TIPPETT
Linebacker. 6-3, 240. Born in Birmingham, Alabama, December 27, 1959. Iowa; Ellsworth (IA) Jr. College. Inducted in 2008. 1982-1988, 1990-93 New England Patriots. **Highlights:** Recorded 100 career sacks including personal best 18.5 sacks, 1984. Named to five straight Pro Bowls, 1985-89.

Y.A. TITTLE
Quarterback. 6-0, 200. Born in Marshall, Texas, October 24, 1926. Louisiana State. Inducted in 1971. 1948-49 Baltimore Colts (AAFC), 1950 Baltimore Colts, 1951-1960 San Francisco 49ers, 1961-64 New York Giants. **Highlights:** 33,070 yards, 242 touchdowns. 33 touchdown passes in 1962 and 36 in 1963. Three-time league Player of the Year.

GEORGE TRAFTON
Center. 6-2, 235. Born in Chicago, Illinois, December 6, 1896. Died September 5, 1971. Notre Dame. Inducted in 1964. 1920-1932 Decatur Staleys/Chicago Staleys/Chicago Bears. **Highlights:** First center to snap with one hand. Named top NFL center of 1920s.

CHARLEY TRIPPI
Halfback-quarterback. 6-0, 185. Born in Pittston, Pennsylvania, December 14, 1922. Georgia. Inducted in 1968. 1947-1955 Chicago Cardinals. **Highlights:** One of football's most versatile performers. Played halfback five years, quarterback for two, defense for two.

EMLEN TUNNELL
Safety. 6-1, 200. Born in Bryn Mawr, Pennsylvania, March 29, 1925. Died July 22, 1975. Toledo, Iowa. Inducted in 1967. 1948-1958 New York Giants, 1959-1961 Green Bay Packers. **Highlights:** 79 interceptions. Gained more yards on kickoff, punt, and interception returns (924) in 1952 than that season's NFL rushing leader.

CLYDE (BULLDOG) TURNER
Center. 6-2, 235. Born in Plains, Texas, March 10, 1919. Died October 30, 1998. Hardin-Simmons. Inducted in 1966. 1940-1952 Chicago Bears. **Highlights:** Anchored defense for four NFL championship teams, including 4 interceptions in five title games.

JOHNNY UNITAS
Quarterback. 6-1, 195. Born in Pittsburgh, Pennsylvania, May 7, 1933. Died September 11, 2002. Louisville. Inducted in 1979. 1956-1972 Baltimore Colts, 1973 San Diego Chargers. **Highlights:** 40,239 passing yards, 290 touchdowns. Led Colts to two NFL championships. Passed for at least one touchdown in 47 consecutive games.

GENE UPSHAW
Guard. 6-5, 255. Born in Robstown, Texas, August 15, 1945. Died August 20, 2008. Texas A & I. Inducted in 1987. 1967-1981 Oakland Raiders. **Highlights:** Premier guard of his era played in 10 AFL/AFC Championship Games, three Super Bowls, seven Pro Bowls.

NORM VAN BROCKLIN
Quarterback. 6-1, 190. Born in Eagle Butte, South Dakota, March 15, 1926. Died May 2, 1983. Oregon. Inducted in 1971. 1949-1957 Los Angeles Rams, 1958-1960 Philadelphia Eagles. **Highlights:** NFL-record 554 yards passing in 1951 season opener. Guided Eagles to NFL crown as league's Most Outstanding Player in 1960.

STEVE VAN BUREN
Halfback. 6-1, 200. Born in La Ceiba, Honduras, December 28, 1920. Died August 23, 2012. Louisiana State. Inducted in 1965. 1944-1951 Philadelphia Eagles. **Highlights:** Four-time rushing champion. Won 1944 punt-return title and was 1945 kickoff-return champion.

DOAK WALKER
Halfback. 5-11, 173. Born in Dallas, Texas, January 1, 1927. Died September 27, 1998. Southern Methodist. Inducted in 1986. 1950-55 Detroit Lions. **Highlights:** 534 points. Won two NFL scoring titles. Had winning 67-yard scoring run in 1952 title game.

BILL WALSH
Coach. Born in Los Angeles, California, November 30, 1931. Died July 30, 2007. San Jose State. Inducted in 1993. 1979-1988 San Francisco 49ers. **Highlights:** 102-63-1 coaching record. Guided 49ers to three Super Bowl titles (XVI, XIX, XXIII) in 10 years.

PAUL WARFIELD
Wide receiver. 6-0, 188. Born in Warren, Ohio, November 28, 1942. Ohio State. Inducted in 1983. 1964-69, 1976-77 Cleveland Browns, 1970-74 Miami Dolphins. **Highlights:** 8,565 yards receiving, 85 touchdowns. Eight-time Pro Bowl player. Key to both Cleveland and Miami offenses.

BOB WATERFIELD
Quarterback. 6-2, 200. Born in Elmira, New York, July 26, 1920. Died March 25, 1983. UCLA. Inducted in 1965. 1945 Cleveland Rams, 1946-1952 Los Angeles Rams. **Highlights:** NFL MVP as rookie in 1945 and led Rams to NFL title. Grabbed 20 interceptions in limited defensive duties.

MIKE WEBSTER
Center. 6-2, 260. Born in Tomahawk, Wisconsin, March 18, 1952. Died September 24, 2002. Wisconsin. Inducted in 1997. 1974-1988 Pittsburgh Steelers, 1989-1990 Kansas City Chiefs. **Highlights:** Played in 245 games, nine Pro Bowls, and won four Super Bowls during 17-year career.

ROGER WEHRLI
Cornerback. 6-0, 190. Born in New Point, Missouri, November 26, 1947. Missouri. Inducted in 2007. 1969-1982 St. Louis Cardinals. **Highlights:** 40 career interceptions. Named to the NFL's All-Decade Team of 1970s. All-Pro five times, selected to seven Pro Bowls.

ARNIE WEINMEISTER
Defensive tackle. 6-4, 235. Born in Rhein, Saskatchewan, Canada, March 23, 1923. Died June 29, 2000. Washington. Inducted in 1984. 1948-49 New York Yankees (AAFC), 1950-53 New York Giants. **Highlights:** Dominant defensive tackle of his time. Four-time All-NFL selection, four Pro Bowls.

RANDY WHITE
Defensive tackle. 6-4, 265. Born in Pittsburgh, Pennsylvania, January 15, 1953. Maryland. Inducted in 1994. 1975-1988 Dallas Cowboys. **Highlights:** Missed only one game in 14 seasons. Co-MVP of Super Bowl XII. Nine-time Pro Bowl selection.

REGGIE WHITE
Defensive end. 6-5, 291. Born in Chattanooga, Tennessee, December 19, 1961. Died December 26, 2004. Tennessee. Inducted in 2006. 1985-1992 Philadelphia Eagles, 1993-1998 Green Bay Packers, 2000 Carolina Panthers. **Highlights:** Retired as all-time sack leader with 198. Named All-Pro 13 of 15 seasons including 10 as first-team selection. Named to 13 straight Pro Bowls.

DAVE WILCOX
Linebacker. 6-3, 241. Born in Ontario, Oregon, September 29, 1942. Boise State, Oregon. Inducted in 2000. 1964-1974 San Francisco 49ers. **Highlights:** Seven Pro Bowls, All-NFL five times. Missed only one game because of injury.

BILL WILLIS
Guard. 6-2, 215. Born in Columbus, Ohio, October 5, 1921. Died November 27, 2007. Ohio State. Inducted in 1977. 1946-1953 Cleveland Browns (AAFC/NFL). **Highlights:** Two-way player who excelled on defense. Four-time All-NFL player, played in three Pro Bowls.

LARRY WILSON
Safety. 6-0, 190. Born in Rigby, Idaho, March 24, 1938. Utah. Inducted in 1978. 1960-1972 St. Louis Cardinals. **Highlights:** 52 interceptions. Had interception in seven consecutive games in 1966. Made "safety blitz" famous.

RALPH WILSON, JR.
Owner-founder. Born in Columbus, Ohio, October 17, 1918. Virginia, Michigan. Inducted in 2009. 1960-present Buffalo Bills. **Highlights:** Founded team. Bills teams captured back-to-back AFL titles in mid-1960s. Unprecedented four straight Super Bowl appearances.

KELLEN WINSLOW
Tight end. 6-5, 250. Born in St. Louis, Missouri, November 5, 1957. Missouri. Inducted in 1995. 1979-1987 San Diego Chargers **Highlights:** 541 receptions for 6,741 yards, 45 touchdowns. 13 catches, blocked field goal in 1981 playoff win over Miami.

ALEX WOJCIECHOWICZ
Center. 6-0, 235. Born in South River, New Jersey, August 12, 1915. Died July 13, 1992. Fordham. Inducted in 1968. 1938-1946 Detroit Lions, 1946-1950 Philadelphia Eagles. **Highlights:** One of league's first iron men. Played both ways for eight years with Lions.

WILLIE WOOD
Safety. 5-10, 190. Born in Washington, D.C., December 23, 1936. Southern California. Inducted in 1989. 1960-1971 Green Bay Packers. **Highlights:** 48 interceptions. Competed in six NFL Championship Games and Super Bowls I and II.

ROD WOODSON
Cornerback-safety. 6-0, 200. Born in Fort Wayne, Indiana, March 10, 1965. Purdue. Inducted in 2009. 1987-1996 Pittsburgh Steelers, 1997 San Francisco 49ers, 1998-2001 Baltimore Ravens, 2002-03 Oakland Raiders. **Highlights:** 71 interceptions returned for 1,483 yards and NFL record 12 TDs. Named NFL Defensive Player of Year, 1993. Member of NFL's 75th Anniversary Team. 11 Pro Bowls.

RAYFIELD WRIGHT
Tackle. 6-6, 255. Born in Griffin, Georgia, August 23, 1945. Fort Valley State. Inducted in 2006. 1967-1979 Dallas Cowboys. **Highlights:** Named first- or second-team All-Pro and voted to Pro Bowl six straight seasons, 1971-76. Played in six NFC championship games and five Super Bowls. Named to NFL's All-Decade Team of 1970s.

RON YARY
Tackle. 6-5, 255. Born in Chicago, Illinois, July 16, 1946. Cerritos (Calif.) J.C., Southern California. Inducted in 2001. 1968-1981 Minnesota Vikings, 1982 Los Angeles Rams. **Highlights:** All-Pro six consecutive seasons, All-NFC eight consecutive years. Named to seven Pro Bowls. Started in four Super Bowls and five NFL/NFC Championship Games.

STEVE YOUNG
Quarterback. 6-2, 205. Born in Salt Lake City, Utah, October 11, 1961. Brigham Young. Inducted in 2005. 1985-86 Tampa Bay Buccaneers, 1987-1999 San Francisco 49ers. **Highlights:** Led the NFL in passing a record-tying six times. Passed for more than 33,000 yards and 232 touchdowns in career. MVP of Super Bowl XXIX. Elected to seven Pro Bowls.

JACK YOUNGBLOOD
Defensive end. 6-4, 247. Born in Jacksonville, Florida, January 26, 1950. Florida. Inducted in 2001. 1971-1984 Los Angeles Rams. **Highlights:** Played in club-record 201 consecutive games. Played in five NFC Championship Games, one Super Bowl. Named All-Pro five times, All-NFC seven times. Elected to seven consecutive Pro Bowls. Lions.

GARY ZIMMERMAN
Tackle. 6-6, 294. Born in Fullerton, California, December 13, 1961. Oregon. Inducted in 2008. 1986-1992 Minnesota Vikings, 1993-97 Denver Broncos. **Highlights:** Named to seven Pro Bowls. One of handful of players to be named to two NFL All-Decade Teams, 1980s and 1990s.

ENSHRINEES BY YEAR OF INDUCTION
*Deceased
(Date of enshrinement in parentheses)

1963 CHARTER CLASS
(September 7, 1963)
Sammy Baugh*
Bert Bell*
Joe Carr*
Earl (Dutch) Clark*
Harold (Red) Grange*
George Halas*
Mel Hein*
Wilbur (Pete) Henry*
Robert (Cal) Hubbard*
Don Hutson*
Earl (Curly) Lambeau*
Tim Mara*
George Preston Marshall*
John (Blood) McNally*
Bronko Nagurski*
Ernie Nevers*
Jim Thorpe*

CLASS OF 1964
(September 6, 1964)
Jimmy Conzelman*
Ed Healey*
Clarke Hinkle*
William Roy (Link) Lyman*
Mike Michalske*
Art Rooney*
George Trafton*

CLASS OF 1965
(September 12, 1965)
Guy Chamberlin*
John (Paddy) Driscoll*
Dan Fortmann*
Otto Graham*
Sid Luckman*
Steve Van Buren*
Bob Waterfield*

CLASS OF 1966
(September 17, 1966)
Bill Dudley*
Joe Guyon*
Arnie Herber*
Walt Kiesling*
George McAfee*
Steve Owen*
Hugh (Shorty) Ray*
Clyde (Bulldog) Turner*

CLASS OF 1967
(August 5, 1967)
Chuck Bednarik
Charles W. Bidwill Sr.*
Paul Brown*
Bobby Layne*
Dan Reeves*
Ken Strong*
Joe Stydahar*
Emlen Tunnell*

CLASS OF 1968
(August 3, 1968)
Cliff Battles*
Art Donovan
Elroy (Crazylegs) Hirsch*
Wayne Millner*
Marion Motley*
Charley Trippi
Alex Wojciechowicz*

CLASS OF 1969
(September 13, 1969)
Albert Glen (Turk) Edwards*
Earle (Greasy) Neale*
Leo Nomellini*
Joe Perry*
Ernie Stautner*

CLASS OF 1970
(August 8, 1970)
Jack Christiansen*
Tom Fears*
Hugh McElhenny
Pete Pihos*

CLASS OF 1971
(July 31, 1971)
Jim Brown
Bill Hewitt*
Frank (Bruiser) Kinard*
Vince Lombardi*
Andy Robustelli*
Y. A. Tittle
Norm Van Brocklin*

CLASS OF 1972
(July 29, 1972)
Lamar Hunt*
Gino Marchetti
Ollie Matson*
Clarence (Ace) Parker

CLASS OF 1973
(July 28, 1973)
Raymond Berry
Jim Parker*
Joe Schmidt

CLASS OF 1974
(July 27, 1974)
Tony Canadeo*
Bill George*
Lou Groza*
Dick (Night Train) Lane*

CLASS OF 1975
(August 2, 1975)
Roosevelt Brown*
George Connor*
Dante Lavelli*
Lenny Moore

CLASS OF 1976
(July 24, 1976)
Ray Flaherty*
Len Ford*
Jim Taylor

CLASS OF 1977
(July 30, 1977)
Frank Gifford
Forrest Gregg
Gale Sayers
Bart Starr
Bill Willis*

CLASS OF 1978
(July 29, 1978)
Lance Alworth
Weeb Ewbank*
Alphonse (Tuffy) Leemans*
Ray Nitschke*
Larry Wilson

CLASS OF 1979
(July 28, 1979)
Dick Butkus
Yale Lary
Ron Mix
Johnny Unitas*

CLASS OF 1980
(August 2, 1980)
Herb Adderley
David (Deacon) Jones
Bob Lilly
Jim Otto

CLASS OF 1981
(August 1, 1981)
Morris (Red) Badgro*
George Blanda*
Willie Davis
Jim Ringo*

CLASS OF 1982
(August 7, 1982)
Doug Atkins
Sam Huff
George Musso*
Merlin Olsen*

CLASS OF 1983
(July 30, 1983)
Bobby Bell
Sid Gillman*
Sonny Jurgensen
Bobby Mitchell
Paul Warfield

CLASS OF 1984
(July 28, 1984)
Willie Brown
Mike McCormack
Charley Taylor
Arnie Weinmeister*

CLASS OF 1985
(August 3, 1985)
Frank Gatski*
Joe Namath
Pete Rozelle*
O. J. Simpson
Roger Staubach

CLASS OF 1986
(August 2, 1986)
Paul Hornung
Ken Houston
Willie Lanier
Fran Tarkenton
Doak Walker*

CLASS OF 1987
(August 8, 1987)
Larry Csonka
Len Dawson
Joe Greene
John Henry Johnson*
Jim Langer
Don Maynard
Gene Upshaw*

CLASS OF 1988
(July 30, 1988)
Fred Biletnikoff
Mike Ditka
Jack Ham
Alan Page

CLASS OF 1989
(August 5, 1989)
Mel Blount
Terry Bradshaw
Art Shell
Willie Wood

CLASS OF 1990
(August 4, 1990)
Buck Buchanan*
Bob Griese
Franco Harris
Ted Hendricks
Jack Lambert
Tom Landry*
Bob St. Clair

CLASS OF 1991
(July 27, 1991)
Earl Campbell
John Hannah
Stan Jones*
Tex Schramm*
Jan Stenerud

CLASS OF 1992
(August 1, 1992)
Lem Barney
Al Davis*
John Mackey*
John Riggins

CLASS OF 1993
(July 31, 1993)
Dan Fouts
Larry Little
Chuck Noll
Walter Payton*
Bill Walsh*

CLASS OF 1994
(July 30, 1994)
Tony Dorsett
Bud Grant
Jimmy Johnson
Leroy Kelly
Jackie Smith
Randy White

CLASS OF 1995
(July 29, 1995)
Jim Finks*
Henry Jordan*
Steve Largent
Lee Roy Selmon*
Kellen Winslow

CLASS OF 1996
(July 27, 1996)
Lou Creekmur*
Dan Dierdorf
Joe Gibbs
Charlie Joiner
Mel Renfro

CLASS OF 1997
(July 26, 1997)
Mike Haynes
Wellington Mara*
Don Shula
Mike Webster*

CLASS OF 1998
(August 1, 1998)
Paul Krause
Tommy McDonald
Anthony Muñoz
Mike Singletary
Dwight Stephenson

CLASS OF 1999
(August 7, 1999)
Eric Dickerson
Tom Mack
Ozzie Newsome
Billy Shaw
Lawrence Taylor

CLASS OF 2000
(July 29, 2000)
Howie Long
Ronnie Lott
Joe Montana
Dan Rooney
Dave Wilcox

CLASS OF 2001
(August 4, 2001)
Nick Buoniconti
Marv Levy
Mike Munchak
Jackie Slater
Lynn Swann
Ron Yary
Jack Youngblood

CLASS OF 2002
(August 3, 2002)
George Allen*
Dave Casper
Dan Hampton
Jim Kelly
John Stallworth

CLASS OF 2003
(August 3, 2003)
Marcus Allen
Elvin Bethea
Joe DeLamielleure
James Lofton
Hank Stram*

CLASS OF 2004
(August 8, 2004)
Bob (Boomer) Brown
Carl Eller
John Elway
Barry Sanders

CLASS OF 2005
(August 7, 2005)
Benny Friedman*
Dan Marino
Fritz Pollard*
Steve Young

CLASS OF 2006
(August 6, 2006)
Troy Aikman
Harry Carson
John Madden
Warren Moon
Reggie White*
Rayfield Wright

CLASS OF 2007
(August 4, 2007)
Gene Hickerson*
Michael Irvin
Bruce Matthews
Charlie Sanders
Thurman Thomas
Roger Wehrli

CLASS OF 2008
(August 2, 2008)
Fred Dean
Darrell Green
Art Monk
Emmitt Thomas
Andre Tippett
Gary Zimmerman

CLASS OF 2009
(August 8, 2009)
Bob Hayes*
Randall McDaniel
Bruce Smith
Derrick Thomas*
Ralph Wilson, Jr.
Rod Woodson

CLASS OF 2010
(August 7, 2010)
Russ Grimm
Rickey Jackson
Dick LeBeau
Floyd Little
John Randle
Jerry Rice
Emmitt Smith

CLASS OF 2011
(August 6, 2011)
Richard Dent
Marshall Faulk
Chris Hanburger
Les Richter*
Ed Sabol
Deion Sanders
Shannon Sharpe

CLASS OF 2012
(August 4, 2012)
Jack Butler
Dermontti Dawson
Chris Doleman
Cortez Kennedy
Curtis Martin
Willie Roaf

CLASS OF 2013
(August 3, 2013)
Larry Allen
Cris Carter
Curley Culp
Jonathan Ogden
Bill Parcells
Dave Robinson
Warren Sapp

PRO FOOTBALL HALL OF FAME GAME (49)

Date	Winner	Loser	Attendance
August 11, 1962	New York Giants 21 (tie)	St. Louis Cardinals 21 (tie)	14,000
September 8, 1963	Pittsburgh Steelers 16	Cleveland Browns 7	18,462
September 6, 1964	Baltimore Colts 48	Pittsburgh Steelers 17	11,479
September 12, 1965	Washington Redskins 20	Detroit Lions 3	14,416
1966	No game was played		
August 5, 1967	Philadelphia Eagles 28	Cleveland Browns 13	17,304
August 3, 1968	Chicago Bears 30	Dallas Cowboys 24	14,578
September 13, 1969	Green Bay Packers 38	Atlanta Falcons 24	17,411
August 8, 1970	New Orleans Saints 14	Minnesota Vikings 13	17,932
July 31, 1971	Los Angeles Rams (NFC) 17	Houston Oilers (AFC) 6	19,384
July 29, 1972	Kansas City Chiefs (AFC) 23	New York Giants (NFC) 17	19,304
July 28, 1973	San Francisco 49ers (NFC) 20	New England Patriots (AFC) 7	19,685
July 27, 1974	St. Louis Cardinals (NFC) 21	Buffalo Bills (AFC) 13	17,286
August 2, 1975	Washington Redskins (NFC) 17	Cincinnati Bengals (AFC) 9	19,360
July 24, 1976	Denver Broncos (AFC) 10	Detroit Lions (NFC) 7	17,639
July 30, 1977	Chicago Bears (NFC) 20	New York Jets (AFC) 6	19,057
July 29, 1978	Philadelphia Eagles (NFC) 17	Miami Dolphins (AFC) 3	19,255
July 28, 1979	Oakland Raiders (AFC) 20	Dallas Cowboys (NFC) 13	20,648
August 2, 1980*	San Diego Chargers (AFC) 0	Green Bay Packers (NFC) 0	19,972
August 1, 1981	Cleveland Browns (AFC) 24	Atlanta Falcons (NFC) 10	23,921
August 7, 1982	Minnesota Vikings (NFC) 30	Baltimore Colts (AFC) 14	23,379
July 30, 1983	Pittsburgh Steelers (AFC) 27	New Orleans Saints (NFC) 14	23,909
July 28, 1984	Seattle Seahawks (AFC) 38	Tampa Bay Buccaneers (NFC) 0	22,250
August 3, 1985	New York Giants (NFC) 21	Houston Oilers (AFC) 20	23,940
August 2, 1986	New England Patriots (AFC) 21	St. Louis Cardinals (NFC) 16	22,739
August 8, 1987	San Francisco 49ers (NFC) 20	Kansas City Chiefs (AFC) 7	23,826
July 30, 1988	Cincinnati Bengals (AFC) 14	Los Angeles Rams (NFC) 7	23,801
August 5, 1989	Washington Redskins (NFC) 31	Buffalo Bills (AFC) 6	23,948
August 4, 1990	Chicago Bears (NFC) 13	Cleveland Browns (AFC) 0	23,952
July 27, 1991	Detroit Lions (NFC) 14	Denver Broncos (AFC) 3	23,815
August 1, 1992	New York Jets (AFC) 41	Philadelphia Eagles (NFC) 14	23,853
July 31, 1993	Los Angeles Raiders (AFC) 19	Green Bay Packers (NFC) 3	23,863
July 30, 1994	Atlanta Falcons (NFC) 21	San Diego Chargers (AFC) 17	23,185
July 29, 1995	Carolina Panthers (NFC) 20	Jacksonville Jaguars (AFC) 14	24,625
July 27, 1996	Indianapolis Colts (AFC) 10	New Orleans Saints (NFC) 3	23,376
July 26, 1997	Minnesota Vikings (NFC) 28	Seattle Seahawks (AFC) 26	23,846
August 1, 1998	Tampa Bay Buccaneers (NFC) 30	Pittsburgh Steelers (AFC) 6	23,875
August 9, 1999	Cleveland Browns (AFC) 20	Dallas Cowboys (NFC) 17 (OT)	25,156
July 31, 2000	New England Patriots (AFC) 20	San Francisco 49ers (NFC) 0	22,840
August 6, 2001	St. Louis Rams (NFC) 17	Miami Dolphins (AFC) 10	22,736
August 5, 2002	New York Giants (NFC) 34	Houston Texans (AFC) 17	22,461
August 4, 2003**	Kansas City Chiefs (AFC) 9	Green Bay Packers (NFC) 0	22,385
August 9, 2004	Washington Redskins (NFC) 20	Denver Broncos (AFC) 17	22,177
August 8, 2005	Chicago Bears (NFC) 27	Miami Dolphins (AFC) 24	22,292
August 6, 2006	Oakland Raiders (AFC) 16	Philadelphia Eagles (NFC) 10	22,200
August 5, 2007	Pittsburgh Steelers (AFC) 20	New Orleans Saints (NFC) 7	22,302
August 3, 2008	Washington Redskins (NFC) 30	Indianapolis Colts (AFC) 16	22,216
August 9, 2009	Tennessee Titans (AFC) 21	Buffalo Bills (AFC) 18	22,153
August 8, 2010	Dallas Cowboys (NFC) 16	Cincinnati Bengals (AFC) 7	22,364
2011	No game was played		
August 5, 2012	New Orleans Saints (NFC) 17	Arizona Cardinals (NFC) 10	18,100

*Game called with 5:29 remaining in the fourth quarter because of severe thunder and lightning.
**Game called with 5:49 remaining in the third quarter because of lightning and torrential rain.

1869

Rutgers and Princeton played a college soccer football game, the first ever, November 6. The game used modified London Football Association rules. During the next seven years, rugby gained favor with the major eastern schools over soccer, and modern football began to develop from rugby.

1876

At the Massasoit convention, the first rules for American football were written. Walter Camp, who would become known as the father of American football, first became involved with the game.

1892

In an era in which football was a major attraction of local athletic clubs, an intense competition between two Pittsburgh-area clubs, the Allegheny Athletic Association (AAA) and the Pittsburgh Athletic Club (PAC), led to the making of the first professional football player. Former Yale All-America guard William (Pudge) Heffelfinger was paid $500 by the AAA to play in a game against the PAC, becoming the first person to be paid to play football, November 12. The AAA won the game 4-0 when Heffelfinger picked up a PAC fumble and ran 35 yards for a touchdown.

1893

The Pittsburgh Athletic Club signed one of its players, probably halfback Grant Dibert, to the first known pro football contract, which covered all of the PAC's games for the year.

1895

John Brallier became the first football player to openly turn pro, accepting $10 and expenses to play for the Latrobe YMCA against the Jeannette Athletic Club.

1896

The Allegheny Athletic Association team fielded the first completely professional team for its abbreviated two-game season.

1897

The Latrobe Athletic Association football team went entirely professional, becoming the first team to play a full season with only professionals.

1898

A touchdown was changed from four points to five.

Chris O'Brien formed a neighborhood team, which played under the name the Morgan Athletic Club, on the south side of Chicago. The team later became known as the Normals, then the Racine (for a street in Chicago) Cardinals, the Chicago Cardinals, the St. Louis Cardinals, the Phoenix Cardinals, and, in 1994, the Arizona Cardinals. The team remains the oldest continuing operation in pro football.

1900

William C. Temple took over the team payments for the Duquesne Country and Athletic Club, becoming the first known individual club owner.

1902

Baseball's Philadelphia Athletics, managed by Connie Mack, and the Philadelphia Phillies formed professional football teams, joining the Pittsburgh Stars in the first attempt at a pro football league, named the National Football League. The Athletics won the first night football game ever played, 39-0 over Kanaweola AC at Elmira, New York, November 21.

All three teams claimed the pro championship for the year, but the league president, Dave Berry, named the Stars the champions. Pitcher Rube Waddell was with the Athletics, and pitcher Christy Mathewson a fullback for Pittsburgh.

The first World Series of pro football, actually a five-team tournament, was played among a team made up of players from both the Athletics and the Phillies, but simply named New York; the New York Knickerbockers; the Syracuse AC; the Warlow AC; and the Orange (New Jersey) AC at New York's original Madison Square Garden. New York and Syracuse played the first indoor football game before 3,000, December 28. Syracuse, with Glen (Pop) Warner at guard, won 6-0 and went on to win the tournament.

1903

The Franklin (Pa.) Athletic Club won the second and last World Series of pro football over the Oreos AC of Asbury Park, New Jersey; the Watertown Red and Blacks; and the Orange AC.

Pro football was popularized in Ohio when the Massillon Tigers, a strong amateur team, hired four Pittsburgh pros to play in the season-ending game against Akron. At the same time, pro football declined in the Pittsburgh area, and the emphasis on the pro game moved west from Pennsylvania to Ohio.

1904

A field goal was changed from five points to four.

Ohio had at least seven pro teams, with Massillon winning the Ohio Independent Championship, that is, the pro title. Talk surfaced about forming a state-wide league to end spiraling salaries brought about by constant bidding for players and to write universal rules for the game. The feeble attempt to start the league failed.

Halfback Charles Follis signed a contract with the Shelby (Ohio) AC, making him the first known black pro football player.

1905

The Canton AC, later to become known as the Bulldogs, became a professional team. Massillon again won the Ohio League championship.

1906

The forward pass was legalized. The first authenticated pass completion in a pro game came on October 25, when George (Peggy) Parratt of Massillon threw a completion to Dan (Bullet) Riley in a victory over a combined Benwood-Moundsville team.

Arch-rivals Canton and Massillon, the two best pro teams in America, played twice, with Canton winning the first game but Massillon winning the second and the Ohio League championship. A betting scandal and the financial disaster wrought upon the two clubs by paying huge salaries caused a temporary decline in interest in pro football in the two cities and, somewhat throughout Ohio.

1909

A field goal dropped from four points to three.

1912

A touchdown was increased from five points to six.

Jack Cusack revived a strong pro team in Canton.

1913

Jim Thorpe, a former football and track star at the Carlisle Indian School (Pa.) and a double gold medal winner at the 1912 Olympics in Stockholm, played for the Pine Village Pros in Indiana.

1915

Massillon again fielded a major team, reviving the old rivalry with Canton. Cusack signed Thorpe to play for Canton for $250 a game.

1916

With Thorpe and former Carlisle teammate Pete Calac starring, Canton went 9-0-1, won the Ohio League championship, and was acclaimed the pro football champion.

1917

Despite an upset by Massillon, Canton again won the Ohio League championship.

1919

Canton again won the Ohio League championship, despite the team having been turned over from Cusack to Ralph Hay. Thorpe and Calac were joined in the backfield by Joe Guyon.

Earl (Curly) Lambeau and George Calhoun organized the Green Bay Packers. Lambeau's employer at the Indian Packing Company provided $500 for equipment and allowed the team to use the company field for practices. The Packers went 10-1.

1920

Pro football was in a state of confusion due to three major problems: dramatically rising salaries; players continually jumping from one team to another following the highest offer; and the use of college players still enrolled in school. A league in which all the members would follow the same rules seemed the answer. An organizational meeting, at which the Akron Pros, Canton Bulldogs, Cleveland Indians, and Dayton Triangles were represented, was held at the Jordan and Hupmobile auto showroom in Canton, Ohio, August 20. This meeting resulted in the formation of the American Professional Football Conference.

A second organizational meeting was held in Canton, September 17. The teams were from four states—Akron, Canton, Cleveland, and Dayton from Ohio; the Hammond Pros and Muncie Flyers from Indiana; the Rochester Jeffersons from New York; and the Rock Island Independents, Decatur Staleys, and Racine Cardinals from Illinois. The name of the league was changed to the American Professional Football Association. Hoping to capitalize on his fame, the members elected Thorpe president; Stanley Cofall of Cleveland was elected vice president. A membership fee of $100 per team was charged to give an appearance of respectability, but no team ever paid it. Scheduling was left up to the teams, and there were wide variations, both in the overall number of games played and in the number played against APFA member teams.

Four other teams—the Buffalo All-Americans, Chicago Tigers, Columbus Panhandles, and Detroit Heralds—joined the league sometime during the year. On September 26, the first game featuring an APFA team was played at Rock Island's Douglas Park. A crowd of 800 watched the Independents defeat the St. Paul Ideals 48-0. A week later, October 3, the first game matching two APFA teams was held. At Triangle Park, Dayton defeated Columbus 14-0, with Lou Partlow of Dayton scoring the first touchdown in a game between Association teams. The same day, Rock Island defeated Muncie 45-0.

By the beginning of December, most of the teams in the APFA had abandoned their hopes for a championship, and some of them, including the Chicago Tigers and the Detroit Heralds, had finished their seasons, disbanded, and

had their franchises canceled by the Association. Four teams—Akron, Buffalo, Canton, and Decatur—still had championship aspirations, but a series of late-season games among them left Akron as the only undefeated team in the Association. At one of these games, Akron sold tackle Bob Nash to Buffalo for $300 and five percent of the gate receipts—the first APFA player deal.

1921
At the league meeting in Akron, April 30, the championship of the 1920 season was awarded to the Akron Pros. The APFA was reorganized, with Joe Carr of the Columbus Panhandles named president and Carl Storck of Dayton secretary-treasurer. Carr moved the Association's headquarters to Columbus, drafted a league constitution and by-laws, gave teams territorial rights, restricted player movements, developed membership criteria for the franchises, and issued standings for the first time, so that APFA would have a clear champion.

The Association's membership increased to 22 teams, including the Green Bay Packers, who were awarded to John Clair of the Acme Packing Company.

Thorpe moved from Canton to the Cleveland Indians, but he was hurt early in the season and played very little.

A.E. Staley turned the Decatur Staleys over to player-coach George Halas, who moved the team to Cubs Park in Chicago. Staley paid Halas $5,000 to keep the name Staleys for one more year. Halas made halfback Ed (Dutch) Sternaman his partner.

Player-coach Fritz Pollard of the Akron Pros became the first black head coach.

The Staleys claimed the APFA championship with a 9-1-1 record, as did Buffalo at 9-1-2. Carr ruled in favor of the Staleys, giving Halas his first championship.

1922
After admitting the use of players who had college eligibility remaining during the 1921 season, Clair and the Green Bay management with-

drew from the APFA, January 28. Curly Lambeau promised to obey league rules and then used $50 of his own money to buy back the franchise. Bad weather and low attendance plagued the Packers, and Lambeau went broke, but local merchants arranged a $2,500 loan for the club. A public non-profit corporation was set up to operate the team, with Lambeau as head coach and manager.

The American Professional Football Association changed its name to the National Football League, June 24. The Chicago Staleys became the Chicago Bears.

The NFL fielded 18 teams, including the new Oorang Indians of Marion, Ohio, an all-Indian team featuring Thorpe, Joe Guyon, and Pete Calac, and sponsored by the Oorang dog kennels.

Canton, led by player-coach Guy Chamberlin and tackles Link Lyman and Wilbur (Pete) Henry, emerged as the league's first true powerhouse, going 10-0-2.

1923
For the first time, all of the franchises considered to be part of the NFL fielded teams. Thorpe played his second and final season for the Oorang Indians. Against the Bears, Thorpe fumbled, and Halas picked up the ball and returned it 98 yards for a touchdown, a record that would last until 1972.

Canton had its second consecutive undefeated season, going 11-0-1 for the NFL title.

1924
The league had 18 franchises, including new ones in Kansas City, Kenosha, and Frankford, a section of Philadelphia. League champion Canton, successful on the field but not at the box office, was purchased by the owner of the Cleveland franchise, who kept the Canton franchise inactive, while using the best players for his Cleveland team, which he renamed the Bulldogs. Cleveland won the title with a 7-1-1 record.

1925
Five new franchises were admitted to the NFL—the New York Giants, who were award-

ed to Tim Mara and Billy Gibson for $500; the Detroit Panthers, featuring Jimmy Conzelman as owner, coach, and tailback; the Providence Steam Roller; a new Canton Bulldogs team; and the Pottsville Maroons, who had been perhaps the most successful independent pro team. The NFL established its first player limit, at 16 players.

Late in the season, the NFL made its greatest coup in gaining national recognition. Shortly after the University of Illinois season ended in November, All-America halfback Harold (Red) Grange signed a contract to play with the Chicago Bears. On Thanksgiving Day, a crowd of 36,000—the largest in pro football history—watched Grange and the Bears play the Chicago Cardinals to a scoreless tie at Wrigley Field. At the beginning of December, the Bears left on a barnstorming tour that saw them play eight games in 12 days, in St. Louis, Philadelphia, New York City, Washington, Boston, Pittsburgh, Detroit, and Chicago. A crowd of 73,000 watched the game against the Giants at the Polo Grounds, helping assure the future of the troubled NFL franchise in New York. The Bears then played nine more games in the South and West, including a game in Los Angeles, in which 75,000 fans watched them defeat the Los Angeles Tigers in the Los Angeles Memorial Coliseum.

Pottsville and the Chicago Cardinals were the top contenders for the league title, with Pottsville winning a late-season meeting 21-7. Pottsville scheduled a game against a team of former Notre Dame players for Shibe Park in Philadelphia. Frankford lodged a protest not only because the game was in Frankford's protected territory, but because it was being played the same day as a Yellow Jackets home game. Carr gave three different notices forbidding Pottsville to play the game, but Pottsville played anyway, December 12. That day, Carr fined the club, suspended it from all rights and privileges (including the right to play for the NFL championship), and re-turned its franchise to the league. The Cardinals, who ended the season with the best record in the league, were named the 1925 champions.

1926
Grange's manager, C.C. Pyle, told the Bears that Grange wouldn't play for them unless he was paid a five-figure salary and given one-third ownership of the team. The Bears refused. Pyle leased Yankee Stadium in New York City, then petitioned for an NFL franchise. After he was refused, he started the first American Football League. It lasted one season and included Grange's New York Yankees and eight other teams. The AFL champion Philadelphia Quakers played a December game against the New York Giants, seventh in the NFL, and the Giants won 31-0. At the end of the season, the AFL folded.

Halas pushed through a rule that prohibited any team from signing a player whose college class had not graduated.

The NFL grew to 22 teams, including the Duluth Eskimos, who signed All-America fullback Ernie Nevers of Stanford, giving the league a gate attraction to rival Grange. The 15-member Eskimos, dubbed the Iron Men of the North, played 29 exhibition and league games, 28 on the road, and Nevers played in all but 29 minutes of them.

Frankford edged the Bears for the championship, despite Halas having obtained John (Paddy) Driscoll from the Cardinals. On December 4, the Yellow Jackets scored in the final two minutes to defeat the Bears 7-6 and move ahead of them in the standings.

1927
At a special meeting in Cleveland, April 23, Carr decided to secure the NFL's future by eliminating the financially weaker teams and consolidating the quality players onto a limited number of more successful teams. The new-look NFL dropped to 12 teams, and the center of gravity of the league left the Midwest, where the NFL had started, and began to emerge in the large cities of the East. One of the new teams was Grange's New

York Yankees, but Grange suffered a knee injury and the Yankees finished in the middle of the pack. The NFL championship was won by the crosstown rival New York Giants, who posted 10 shutouts in 13 games.

1928
Grange and Nevers both retired from pro football, and Duluth disbanded, as the NFL was reduced to only 10 teams. The Providence Steam Roller of Jimmy Conzelman and Pearce Johnson won the championship, playing in the Cycledrome, a 10,000-seat oval that had been built for bicycle races.

1929
Chris O'Brien sold the Chicago Cardinals to David Jones, July 27.

The NFL added a fourth official, the field judge, July 28.

Grange and Nevers returned to the NFL. Nevers scored six rushing touchdowns and four extra points as the Cardinals beat Grange's Bears 40-6, November 28. The 40 points set a record that remains the NFL's oldest.

Providence became the first NFL team to host a game at night under floodlights, against the Cardinals, November 6.

The Packers added back Johnny Blood (McNally), tackle Cal Hubbard, and guard Mike Michalske, and won their first NFL championship, edging the Giants, who featured quarterback Benny Friedman.

1930
Dayton, the last of the NFL's original franchises, was purchased by William B. Dwyer and John C. Depler, moved to Brooklyn, and renamed the Dodgers. The Portsmouth, Ohio, Spartans entered the league.

The Packers edged the Giants for the title, but the most improved team was the Bears. Halas retired as a player and replaced himself as coach of the Bears with Ralph Jones, who refined the T-formation by introducing wide ends and a halfback in motion. Jones also introduced rookie All-America fullback-tackle Bronko Nagurski.

The Giants defeated a team of former Notre Dame players coached by Knute Rockne 22-0 before 55,000 at the Polo Grounds, December 14. The proceeds went to the New York Unemployment Fund to help those suffering because of the Great Depression, and the easy victory helped give the NFL credibility with the press and the public.

1931
The NFL decreased to 10 teams, and halfway through the season the Frankford franchise folded. Carr fined the Bears, Packers, and Portsmouth $1,000 each for using players whose college classes had not graduated.

The Packers won an unprecedented third consecutive title, beating out the Spartans, who were led by rookie backs Earl (Dutch) Clark and Glenn Presnell.

1932
George Preston Marshall, Vincent Bendix, Jay O'Brien, and M. Dorland Doyle were awarded a franchise for Boston, July 9. Despite the presence of two rookies—halfback Cliff Battles and tackle Glen (Turk) Edwards—the new team, named the Braves, lost money and Marshall was left as the sole owner at the end of the year.

NFL membership dropped to eight teams, the lowest in history. Official statistics were kept for the first time. The Bears and the Spartans finished the season in the first-ever tie for first place. After the season finale, the league office arranged for an additional regular-season game to determine the league champion. The game was moved indoors to Chicago Stadium because of bitter cold and heavy snow. The arena allowed only an 80-yard field that came right to the walls. The goal posts were moved from the end lines to the goal lines and, for safety, inbounds lines or hashmarks where the ball would be put in play were drawn 10 yards from the walls that butted against the sidelines. The Bears won 9-0, December 18, scoring the winning touchdown on a two-yard pass from Nagurski to Grange. The Spartans claimed Nagurski's pass was thrown

from less than five yards behind the line of scrimmage, violating the existing passing rule, but the play stood.

1933
The NFL, which long had followed the rules of college football, made a number of significant changes from the college game for the first time and began to develop rules serving its needs and the style of play it preferred. The innovations from the 1932 championship game—inbounds line or hashmarks and goal posts on the goal lines—were adopted. Also the forward pass was legalized from anywhere behind the line of scrimmage, February 25.

Marshall and Halas pushed through a proposal that divided the NFL into two divisions, with the winners to meet in an annual championship game, July 8.

Three new franchises joined the league—the Pittsburgh Pirates of Art Rooney, the Philadelphia Eagles of Bert Bell and Lud Wray, and the Cincinnati Reds. The Staten Island Stapletons suspended operations for a year, but never returned to the league.

Halas bought out Sternaman, became sole owner of the Bears, and reinstated himself as head coach. Marshall changed the name of the Boston Braves to the Redskins. David Jones sold the Chicago Cardinals to Charles W. Bidwill.

In the first NFL Championship Game scheduled before the season, the Western Division champion Bears defeated the Eastern Division champion Giants 23-21 at Wrigley Field, December 17.

1934
G.A. (Dick) Richards purchased the Portsmouth Spartans, moved them to Detroit, and renamed them the Lions.

Professional football gained new prestige when the Bears were matched against the best college football players in the first Chicago College All-Star Game, August 31. The game ended in a scoreless tie before 79,432 at Soldier Field.

The Cincinnati Reds lost their first eight games, then were suspended from the league for defaulting on payments. The St. Louis Gunners, an independent team, joined the NFL by buying the Cincinnati franchise and went 1-2 the last three weeks.

Rookie Beattie Feathers of the Bears became the NFL's first 1,000-yard rusher, gaining 1,004 on 101 carries. The Thanksgiving Day game between the Bears and the Lions became the first NFL game broadcast nationally, with Graham McNamee the announcer for NBC radio.

In the championship game, on an extremely cold and icy day at the Polo Grounds, the Giants trailed the Bears 13-3 in the third quarter before changing to basketball shoes for better footing. The Giants won 30-13 in what has come to be known as the Sneakers Game, December 9.

The player waiver rule was adopted, December 10.

1935

The NFL adopted Bert Bell's proposal to hold an annual draft of college players, to begin in 1936, with teams selecting in an inverse order of finish, May 19. The inbounds line or hashmarks were moved nearer the center of the field, 15 yards from the sidelines.

All-America end Don Hutson of Alabama joined Green Bay. The Lions defeated the Giants 26-7 in the NFL Championship Game, December 15.

1936

There were no franchise transactions for the first year since the formation of the NFL. It also was the first year in which all member teams played the same number of games.

The Eagles made University of Chicago halfback and Heisman Trophy winner Jay Berwanger the first player ever selected in the NFL draft, February 8. The Eagles traded his rights to the Bears, but Berwanger never played pro football. The first player selected to actually sign was the number-two pick, Riley Smith of Alabama, who was selected by Boston.

A rival league was formed, and it became the second to call itself the American Football League. The Boston Shamrocks were its champions.

Because of poor atten-

dance, Marshall, the owner of the host team, moved the Championship Game from Boston to the Polo Grounds in New York. Green Bay defeated the Redskins 21-6, December 13.

1937

Homer Marshman was granted a Cleveland franchise, named the Rams, February 12. Marshall moved the Redskins to Washington, D.C., February 13. The Redskins signed TCU All-America tailback Sammy Baugh, who led them to a 28-21 victory over the Bears in the NFL Championship Game, December 12.

The Los Angeles Bulldogs had an 8-0 record to win the AFL title, but then the 2-year-old league folded.

1938

At the suggestion of Halas, Hugh (Shorty) Ray became a technical advisor on rules and officiating to the NFL. A new rule called for a 15-yard penalty for roughing the passer.

Rookie Byron (Whizzer) White of the Pittsburgh Pirates led the NFL in rushing. The Giants defeated the Packers 23-17 for the NFL title, December 11.

Marshall, *Los Angeles Times* sports editor Bill Henry, and promoter Tom Gallery established the Pro Bowl game between the NFL champion and a team of pro all-stars.

1939

The New York Giants defeated the Pro All-Stars 13-10 in the first Pro Bowl, at Wrigley Field, Los Angeles, January 15.

Carr, NFL president since 1921, died in Columbus, May 20. Carl Storck was named acting president, May 25.

An NFL game was televised for the first time when NBC broadcast the Brooklyn Dodgers-Philadelphia Eagles game from Ebbets Field to the approximately 1,000 sets then in New York, October 22.

Green Bay defeated New York 27-0 in the NFL Championship Game, December 10 at Milwaukee. NFL attendance exceeded 1 million in a season for the first time, reaching 1,071,200.

1940

A six-team rival league, the third to call itself the American Football League, was formed, and the Columbus Bullies won its championship.

Halas' Bears, with additional coaching by Clark Shaughnessy of Stanford, defeated the Redskins 73-0 in the NFL Championship Game, December 8. The game, which was the most decisive victory in NFL history, popularized the Bears' T-formation with a man-in-motion. It was the first championship carried on network radio, broadcast by Red Barber to 120 stations of the Mutual Broadcasting System, which paid $2,500 for the rights.

Art Rooney sold the Pittsburgh franchise to Alexis Thompson, December 9, then bought part interest in the Philadelphia Eagles.

Bell and Rooney traded the Eagles to Thompson for the Pirates, then re-named their new team the Steelers.

1941

Elmer Layden was named the first Commissioner of the NFL, March 1; Storck, the acting president, resigned, April 5. NFL headquarters were moved to Chicago.

Homer Marshman sold the Rams to Daniel F. Reeves and Fred Levy, Jr.

The league by-laws were revised to provide for playoffs in case there were ties in division races, and sudden-death overtimes in case a playoff game was tied after four quarters. An official *NFL Record Manual* was published for the first time.

Columbus again won the championship of the AFL, but the two-year-old league then folded.

The Bears and the Packers finished in a tie for the Western Division championship, setting up the first divisional playoff game in league history. The Bears won 33-14, then defeated the Giants 37-9 for the NFL championship, December 21.

1942

Players departing for service in World War II depleted the rosters of NFL teams. Halas left the Bears in midseason to join the Navy, and Luke John-

sos and Heartley (Hunk) Anderson served as co-coaches as the Bears went 11-0 in the regular season. The Redskins defeated the Bears 14-6 in the NFL Championship Game, December 13.

1943

The Cleveland Rams, with co-owners Reeves and Levy in the service, were granted permission to suspend operations for one season, April 6. Levy transferred his stock in the team to Reeves, April 16.

The NFL adopted free substitution, April 7. The league also made the wearing of helmets mandatory and approved a 10-game schedule for all teams.

Philadelphia and Pittsburgh were granted permission to merge for one season, June 19. The team, known as Phil-Pitt (and called the Steagles by fans), divided home games between the two cities, and Earle (Greasy) Neale of Philadelphia and Walt Kiesling of Pittsburgh served as co-coaches. The merger automatically dissolved the last day of the season, December 5.

Ted Collins was granted a franchise for Boston, to become active in 1944.

Sammy Baugh led the league in passing, punting, and interceptions. He led the Redskins to a tie with the Giants for the Eastern Division title, and then to a 28-0 victory in a divisional playoff game. The Bears beat the Redskins 41-21 in the NFL Championship Game, December 26.

1944

Collins, who had wanted a franchise in Yankee Stadium in New York, named his new team in Boston the Yanks. Cleveland resumed operations. The Brooklyn Dodgers changed their name to the Tigers.

Coaching from the bench was legalized, April 20.

The Cardinals and the Steelers were granted permission to merge for one year under the name Card-Pitt, April 21. Phil Handler of the Cardinals and Walt Kiesling of the Steelers served as co-coaches. The merger automatically dissolved the last day of the season, December 3.

In the NFL Championship Game, Green Bay defeated the New York Giants 14-7, December 17.

1945

The inbounds lines or hash-marks were moved from 15 yards away from the sidelines to nearer the center of the field—20 yards from the sidelines.

Brooklyn and Boston merged into a team that played home games in both cities and was known simply as The Yanks. The team was coached by former Boston head coach Herb Kopf. In December, the Brooklyn franchise withdrew from the NFL to join the new All-America Football Conference; all the players on its active and reserve lists were assigned to The Yanks, who once again became the Boston Yanks.

Halas rejoined the Bears late in the season after service with the U.S. Navy. Although Halas took over much of the coaching duties, Anderson and Johnsos remained the coaches of record throughout the season.

Steve Van Buren of Philadelphia led the NFL in rushing, kickoff returns, and scoring.

After the Japanese surrendered ending World War II, a count showed that the NFL service roster, limited to men who had played in league games, totaled 638, 21 of whom had died in action.

Rookie quarterback Bob Waterfield led Cleveland to a 15-14 victory over Washington in the NFL Championship Game, December 16.

1946

The contract of Commissioner Layden was not renewed, and Bert Bell, the co-owner of the Steelers, replaced him, January 11. Bell moved the league headquarters from Chicago to the Philadelphia suburb of Bala-Cynwyd.

Free substitution was withdrawn and substitutions were limited to no more than three men at a time. Forward passes were made automatically incomplete upon striking the goal posts, January 11.

The NFL took on a truly national appearance for the first time when Reeves was granted permission by the league to move his NFL champion Rams to Los Angeles.

Halfback Kenny Washington (March 21) and end Woody Strode (May 7) signed with the Los Angeles Rams to become the first African-Americans to play in the NFL in the modern era. Guard Bill Willis (August 6) and running back Marion Motley (August 9) joined the AAFC with the Cleveland Browns.

The rival All-America Football Conference began play with eight teams. The Cleveland Browns, coached by Paul Brown, won the AAFC's first championship, defeating the New York Yankees 14-9.

Bill Dudley of the Steelers led the NFL in rushing, interceptions, and punt returns, and won the league's most valuable player award.

Backs Frank Filchock and Merle Hapes of the Giants were questioned about an attempt by a New York man to fix the championship game with the Bears. Bell suspended Hapes but allowed Filchock to play; he played well, but Chicago won 24-14, December 15.

1947

The NFL added a fifth official, the back judge.

A bonus choice was made for the first time in the NFL draft. One team each year would select the special choice before the first round began. The Chicago Bears won a lottery and the rights to the first choice and drafted back Bob Fenimore of Oklahoma A&M.

The Cleveland Browns again won the AAFC title, defeating the New York Yankees 14-3.

Charles Bidwill, Sr., owner of the Cardinals, died April 19, but his wife and sons retained ownership of the team. On December 28, the Cardinals won the NFL Championship Game 28-21 over the Philadelphia Eagles, who had beaten Pittsburgh 21-0 in a playoff.

1948

Plastic helmets were prohibited. A flexible artificial tee was permitted at the kickoff. Officials other than the referee were equipped with whistles, not horns, January 14.

Fred Mandel sold the Detroit Lions to a syndicate headed by D. Lyle Fife, January 15.

Halfback Fred Gehrke of the Los Angeles Rams painted horns on the Rams' helmets, the first modern helmet emblems in pro football.

The Cleveland Browns won their third straight championship in the AAFC, going 14-0 and then defeating the Buffalo Bills 49-7.

In a blizzard, the Eagles defeated the Cardinals 7-0 in the NFL Championship Game, December 19.

1949

Alexis Thompson sold the champion Eagles to a syndicate headed by James P. Clark, January 15. The Boston Yanks became the New York Bulldogs, sharing the Polo Grounds with the Giants.

Free substitution was adopted for one year, January 20.

The NFL had two 1,000-yard rushers in the same season for the first time—Steve Van Buren of Philadelphia and Tony Canadeo of Green Bay.

The AAFC played its season with a one-division, seven-team format. On December 9, Bell announced a merger agreement in which three AAFC franchises—Cleveland, San Francisco, and Baltimore—would join the NFL in 1950. The Browns won their fourth consecutive AAFC title, defeating the 49ers 21-7, December 11.

In a heavy rain, the Eagles defeated the Rams 14-0 in the NFL Championship Game, December 18.

1950

Unlimited free substitution was restored, opening the way for the era of two platoons and specialization in pro football, January 20.

Curly Lambeau, founder of the franchise and Green Bay's head coach since 1921, resigned under fire, February 1.

The name National Football League was restored after about three months as the National-American Football League. The American and National conferences were created to replace the Eastern and Western divisions, March 3.

The New York Bulldogs became the Yanks and divided the players of the former AAFC Yankees with the Giants. A special allocation draft was held in which the 13 teams drafted the remaining AAFC players, with special consideration for Baltimore, which received 15 choices compared to 10 for other teams.

The Los Angeles Rams became the first NFL team to have all of its games—both home and away—televised. The Washington Redskins followed the Rams in arranging to televise their games; other teams made deals to put selected games on television.

In the first game of the season, former AAFC champion Cleveland defeated NFL champion Philadelphia 35-10. For the first time, deadlocks occurred in both conferences and playoffs were necessary. The Browns defeated the Giants in the American and the Rams defeated the Bears in the National. Cleveland defeated Los Angeles 30-28 in the NFL Championship Game, December 24.

1951

The Pro Bowl game, dormant since 1942, was revived under a new format matching the all-stars of each conference at the Los Angeles Memorial Coliseum. The American Conference defeated the National Conference 28-27, January 14.

Abraham Watner returned the Baltimore franchise and its player contracts back to the NFL for $50,000. Baltimore's former players were made available for drafting at the same time as college players, January 18.

A rule was passed that no tackle, guard, or center would be eligible to catch a forward pass, January 18.

The Rams reversed their television policy and televised only road games.

The NFL Championship Game was televised coast-to-coast for the first time, December 23. The DuMont Network paid $75,000 for the rights to the game, in which the Rams defeated the Browns 24-17.

1952

Ted Collins sold the New York Yanks' franchise back to the NFL, January 19. A new franchise was awarded to a group in Dallas after it purchased the assets of the Yanks, January 24. The new Texans went 1-11, with the owners turning the franchise back to the league in midseason. For the last five games of the season, the commissioner's office operated the Texans as a road team, using Hershey, Pennsylvania, as a home base. At the end of the season the franchise was canceled, the last time an NFL team failed.

The Pittsburgh Steelers abandoned the Single-Wing for the T-formation, the last pro team to do so.

The Detroit Lions won their first NFL championship in 17 years, defeating the Browns 17-7 in the title game, December 28.

1953
A Baltimore group headed by Carroll Rosenbloom was granted a franchise and was awarded the holdings of the defunct Dallas organization, January 23. The team, named the Colts, put together the largest trade in league history, acquiring 10 players from Cleveland in exchange for five.

The names of the American and National conferences were changed to the Eastern and Western conferences, January 24.

Jim Thorpe died, March 28.

Mickey McBride, founder of the Cleveland Browns, sold the franchise to a syndicate headed by Dave R. Jones, June 10.

The NFL policy of blacking out home games was upheld by Judge Allan K. Grim of the U.S. District Court in Philadelphia, November 12.

The Lions again defeated the Browns in the NFL Championship Game, winning 17-16, December 27.

1954
The Canadian Football League began a series of raids on NFL teams, signing quarterback Eddie LeBaron and defensive end Gene Brito of Washington and defensive tackle Arnie Weinmeister of the Giants, among others.

Fullback Joe Perry of the 49ers became the first player in league history to gain 1,000 yards rushing in consecutive seasons.

Cleveland defeated Detroit 56-10 in the NFL Championship Game, December 26.

1955
The sudden-death overtime rule was used for the first time in a preseason game between the Rams and Giants at Portland, Oregon, August 28. The Rams won 23-17 three minutes into overtime.

A rule change declared the ball dead immediately if the ball carrier touched the ground with any part of his body except his hands or feet while in the grasp of an opponent.

The Baltimore Colts made an 80-cent phone call to Johnny Unitas and signed him as a free agent. Another quarterback, Otto Graham, played his last game as the Browns defeated the Rams 38-14 in the NFL Championship Game, December 26. Graham had quarterbacked the Browns to 10 championship-game appearances in 10 years.

NBC replaced DuMont as the network for the title game, paying a rights fee of $100,000.

1956
The NFL Players Association was founded.

Grabbing an opponent's facemask (other than the ball carrier) was made illegal. Using radio receivers to communicate with players on the field was prohibited. A natural leather ball with white end stripes replaced the white ball with black stripes for night games.

The Giants moved from the Polo Grounds to Yankee Stadium.

Halas retired as coach of the Bears, and was replaced by Paddy Driscoll.

CBS became the first network to broadcast some NFL regular-season games to selected television markets across the nation.

The Giants routed the Bears 47-7 in the NFL Championship Game, December 30.

1957
Pete Rozelle was named general manager of the Rams. Anthony J. Morabito, founder and co-owner of the 49ers, died of a heart attack during a game against the Bears at Kezar Stadium, October 28.

An NFL-record crowd of 102,368 saw the 49ers-Rams game at the Los Angeles Memorial Coliseum, November 10.

The Lions came from 20 points down to post a 31-27 playoff victory over the 49ers, December 22. Detroit defeated Cleveland 59-14 in the NFL Championship Game, December 29.

1958
The bonus selection in the draft was eliminated, January 29. The last selection was quarterback King Hill of Rice by the Chicago Cardinals.

Halas reinstated himself as coach of the Bears.

Jim Brown of Cleveland gained an NFL-record 1,527 yards rushing. In a divisional playoff game, the Giants held Brown to eight yards and defeated Cleveland 10-0.

Baltimore, coached by Weeb Ewbank, defeated the Giants 23-17 in the first sudden-death overtime in an NFL Championship Game, December 28. The game ended when Colts fullback Alan Ameche scored on a one-yard touchdown run after 8:15 of overtime.

1959
Vince Lombardi was named head coach of the Green Bay Packers, January 28. Tim Mara, the co-founder of the Giants, died, February 17.

Lamar Hunt of Dallas announced his intentions to form a second pro football league. The first meeting was held in Chicago, August 14, and consisted of Hunt representing Dallas; Bob Howsam, Denver; K.S. (Bud) Adams, Houston; Barron Hilton, Los Angeles; Max Winter and Bill Boyer, Minneapolis; and Harry Wismer, New York City. They made plans to begin play in 1960.

The new league was named the American Football League, August 22. Buffalo, owned by Ralph Wilson, became the seventh franchise, October 28. Boston, owned by William H. Sullivan, became the eighth team, November 22. The first AFL draft, lasting 33 rounds, was held, November 22. Joe Foss was named AFL Commissioner, November 30. An additional draft of 20 rounds

was held by the AFL, December 2.

NFL Commissioner Bert Bell died of a heart attack suffered at Franklin Field, Philadelphia, during the last two minutes of a game between the Eagles and the Steelers, October 11. Treasurer Austin Gunsel was named president in the office of the commissioner, October 14.

The Colts again defeated the Giants in the NFL Championship Game, 31-16, December 27.

1960
Pete Rozelle was elected NFL Commissioner as a compromise choice on the twenty-third ballot, January 26. Rozelle moved the league offices to New York City.

Hunt was elected AFL president for 1960, January 26. Minneapolis withdrew from the AFL, January 27, and the same ownership was given an NFL franchise for Minnesota (to start in 1961), January 28. Dallas received an NFL franchise for 1960, January 28. Oakland received an AFL franchise, January 30.

The AFL adopted the two-point option on points after touchdown, January 28. A no-tampering verbal pact, relative to players' contracts, was agreed to between the NFL and AFL, February 9.

The NFL owners voted to allow the transfer of the Chicago Cardinals to St. Louis, March 13.

The AFL signed a five-year television contract with ABC, June 9.

The Boston Patriots defeated the Buffalo Bills 28-7 before 16,000 at Buffalo in the first AFL preseason game, July 30. The Denver Broncos defeated the Patriots 13-10 before 21,597 at Boston in the first AFL regular-season game, September 9.

Philadelphia defeated Green Bay 17-13 in the NFL Championship Game, December 26.

1961
The Houston Oilers defeated the Los Angeles Chargers 24-16 before 32,183 in the first AFL Championship Game, January 1.

Detroit defeated Cleveland 17-16 in the first Playoff Bowl, or Bert Bell Benefit Bowl, between second-place teams in each conference in Miami, January 7.

End Willard Dewveall of the Bears played out his option and joined the Oilers, becoming the first player to play out his contract and jump from the NFL to the AFL, January 14.

Ed McGah, Wayne Valley, and Robert Osborne bought out their partners in the ownership of the Raiders, January 17. The Chargers were transferred to San Diego, February 10. Dave R. Jones sold the Browns to a group headed by Arthur B. Modell, March 22. The Howsam brothers sold the Broncos to a group headed by Calvin Kunz and Gerry Phipps, May 26.

NBC was awarded a two-year contract for radio and television rights to the NFL Championship Game for $615,000 annually, $300,000 of which was to go directly into the NFL Player Benefit Plan, April 5.

Canton, Ohio, where the league that became the NFL was formed in 1920, was chosen as the site of the Pro Football Hall of Fame, April 27.

A bill legalizing single-network television contracts by professional sports leagues was introduced in Congress by Representative Emanuel Celler. It passed the House and Senate and was signed into law by President John F. Kennedy, September 30.

Houston defeated San Diego 10-3 for the AFL championship, December 24. Green Bay won its first NFL championship since 1944, defeating the New York Giants 37-0, December 31.

1962
The Western Division defeated the Eastern Division 47-27 in the first AFL All-Star Game, played before 20,973 in San Diego, January 7.

Both leagues prohibited grabbing any player's face-mask. The AFL voted to make the scoreboard clock the official timer of the game.

The NFL entered into a single-network agreement with CBS for telecasting all regular-season games for $4.65 million annually, January 10.

Judge Roszel Thompson of the U.S. District Court in Baltimore ruled against the AFL in

its antitrust suit against the NFL, May 21. The AFL had charged the NFL with monopoly and conspiracy in areas of expansion, television, and player signings. The case lasted two and a half years, the trial two months.

McGah and Valley acquired controlling interest in the Raiders, May 24. The AFL assumed financial responsibility for the New York Titans, November 8. With Commissioner Rozelle as referee, Daniel F. Reeves regained the ownership of the Rams, out-bidding his partners in sealed-envelope bidding for the team, November 27.

The Dallas Texans defeated the Oilers 20-17 for the AFL championship at Houston after 17 minutes, 54 seconds of overtime on a 25-yard field goal by Tommy Brooker. The game lasted a then record 77 minutes, 54 seconds, December 23.

Judge Edward Weinfeld of the U.S. District Court in New York City upheld the legality of the NFL's television blackout within a 75-mile radius of home games and denied an injunction that would have forced the championship game between the Giants and the Packers to be televised in the New York City area, December 28. The Packers beat the Giants 16-7 for the NFL title, December 30.

1963
Don Shula, who went on to become the winningest head coach in NFL history, replaced Weeb Ewbank as head coach of the Colts, January 8.

Paul Brown, head coach of the Browns since their inception, was fired on January 9 and replaced the following day by Blanton Collier.

The Dallas Texans transferred to Kansas City, becoming the Chiefs, February 8. The New York Titans were sold to a five-man syndicate headed by David (Sonny) Werblin, March 28. Weeb Ewbank became the Titans' new head coach and the team's name was changed to the Jets, April 15. They began play in the Polo Grounds.

NFL Properties, Inc., was founded to serve as the licensing arm of the NFL.

Rozelle indefinitely sus-

pended Green Bay halfback Paul Hornung and Detroit defensive tackle Alex Karras for placing bets on their own teams and on other NFL games; he also fined five other Detroit players $2,000 each for betting on one game in which they did not participate, and the Detroit Lions Football Company $2,000 on each of two counts for failure to report information promptly and for lack of sideline supervision, April 17.

The AFL allowed the Jets and Raiders to select players from other franchises in hopes of giving the league more competitive balance, May 11.

NBC was awarded exclusive network broadcasting rights for the 1963 NFL Championship Game for $926,000, May 23.

The Pro Football Hall of Fame was dedicated at Canton, Ohio, September 7.

The U.S. Fourth Circuit Court of Appeals reaffirmed the lower court's finding for the NFL in the $10-million suit brought by the AFL, ending three and a half years of litigation, November 21.

Jim Brown of Cleveland rushed for an NFL single-season record 1,863 yards.

Boston defeated Buffalo 26-8 in the first divisional playoff game in AFL history, December 28.

The Bears defeated the Giants 14-10 in the NFL Championship Game, a record sixth and last title for Halas in his thirty-sixth season as the Bears' coach, December 29.

1964
The Chargers defeated the Patriots 51-10 in the AFL Championship Game, January 5.

William Clay Ford, the Lions' president since 1961, purchased the team, January 10. A group representing the late James P. Clark sold the Eagles to a group headed by Jerry Wolman, January 21. Carroll Rosenbloom, the majority owner of the Colts since 1953, acquired complete ownership of the team, January 23.

The AFL signed a five-year, $36-million television contract with NBC to begin with the 1965 season, January 29.

Hornung and Karras were reinstated by Rozelle, March

16.

CBS submitted the winning bid of $14.1 million per year for the NFL regular-season television rights for 1964 and 1965, January 24. CBS acquired the rights to the championship games for 1964 and 1965 for $1.8 million per game, April 17.

Pete Gogolak of Cornell signed a contract with Buffalo, becoming the first soccer-style kicker in pro football.

Buffalo defeated San Diego 20-7 in the AFL Championship Game, December 26. Cleveland defeated Baltimore 27-0 in the NFL Championship Game, December 27.

1965
The NFL teams pledged not to sign college seniors until completion of all their games, including bowl games, and empowered the Commissioner to discipline the clubs up to as much as the loss of an entire draft list for a violation of the pledge, February 15.

The NFL added a sixth official, the line judge, February 19. The color of the officials' penalty flags was changed from white to bright gold, April 5.

Commissioner Rozelle negotiated an agreement on behalf of the NFL clubs to purchase Ed Sabol's Blair Motion Pictures, which was renamed NFL Films, April.

Atlanta was awarded an NFL franchise for 1966, with Rankin Smith, Sr., as owner, June 30. Miami was awarded an AFL franchise for 1966, with Joe Robbie and Danny Thomas as owners, August 16.

Field Judge Burl Toler became the first black official in NFL history, September 19.

According to a Harris survey, sports fans chose professional football (41 percent) as their favorite sport, overtaking baseball (38 percent) for the first time, October.

Green Bay defeated Baltimore 13-10 in sudden-death overtime in a Western Conference playoff game. Don Chandler kicked a 25-yard field goal for the Packers after 13 minutes, 39 seconds of overtime, December 26. The Packers then defeated the Browns 23-12 in the NFL Championship Game, January 2.

In the AFL Championship Game, the Bills defeated the

Chargers, 23-0, December 26.

CBS acquired the rights to the NFL regular-season games in 1966 and 1967, with an option for 1968, for $18.8 million per year, December 29.

1966

The AFL-NFL war reached its peak, as the leagues spent a combined $7 million to sign their 1966 draft choices. The NFL signed 75 percent of its 232 draftees, the AFL 46 percent of its 181. Of the 111 common draft choices, 79 signed with the NFL, 28 with the AFL, and 4 went unsigned.

Buddy Young became the first African-American to work in the league office when Commissioner Rozelle named him director of player relations, February 1.

The rights to the 1966 and 1967 NFL Championship Games were sold to CBS for $2 million per game, February 14.

Foss resigned as AFL Commissioner, April 7. Al Davis, the head coach and general manager of the Raiders, was named to replace him, April 8.

Goal posts offset from the goal line, painted bright yellow, and with uprights 20 feet above the cross-bar were made standard in the NFL, May 16.

A series of secret meetings regarding a possible AFL-NFL merger were held in the spring between Hunt of Kansas City and Tex Schramm of Dallas. Rozelle announced the merger, June 8. Under the agreement, the two leagues would combine to form an expanded league with 24 teams, to be increased to 26 in 1968 and to 28 by 1970 or soon thereafter. All existing franchises would be retained, and no franchises would be transferred outside their metropolitan areas. While maintaining separate schedules through 1969, the leagues agreed to play an annual AFL-NFL World Championship Game beginning in January, 1967, and to hold a combined draft, also beginning in 1967. Preseason games would be held between teams of each league starting in 1967. Official regular-season play would start in 1970 when the two leagues would officially merge to form one league with two conferences.

Rozelle was named Commissioner of the expanded league setup.

Davis rejoined the Raiders, and Milt Woodard was named president of the AFL, July 25.

The St. Louis Cardinals moved into newly constructed Busch Memorial Stadium.

Barron Hilton sold the Chargers to a group headed by Eugene Klein and Sam Schulman, August 25.

Congress approved the AFL-NFL merger, passing legislation exempting the agreement itself from antitrust action, October 21.

New Orleans was awarded an NFL franchise to begin play in 1967, November 1. John Mecom, Jr., of Houston was designated majority stockholder and president of the franchise, December 15.

The NFL was realigned for the 1967-69 seasons into the Capitol and Century Divisions in the Eastern Conference and the Central and Coastal Divisions in the Western Conference, December 2. New Orleans and the New York Giants agreed to switch divisions in 1968 and return to the 1967 alignment in 1969.

The rights to the Super Bowl for four years were sold to CBS and NBC for $9.5 million, December 13.

1967

Green Bay earned the right to represent the NFL in the first AFL-NFL World Championship Game by defeating Dallas 34-27, January 1. The same day, Kansas City defeated Buffalo 31-7 to represent the AFL. The Packers defeated the Chiefs 35-10 before 61,946 fans at the Los Angeles Memorial Coliseum in the first game between AFL and NFL teams, January 15. The winning players' share for the Packers was $15,000 each, and the losing players' share for the Chiefs was $7,500 each. The game was televised by both CBS and NBC.

The "sling-shot" goal post and a six-foot-wide border around the field were made standard in the NFL, February 22.

Baltimore made Bubba Smith, a Michigan State defensive lineman, the first choice in the first combined AFL-NFL draft, March 14.

The AFL awarded a franchise to begin play in 1968 to Cincinnati, May 23. A group with Paul Brown as part owner, general manager, and head coach, was awarded the Cincinnati franchise, September 27.

Arthur B. Modell, the president of the Cleveland Browns, was elected president of the NFL, May 28.

Defensive back Emlen Tunnell of the New York Giants became the first black player to enter the Pro Football Hall of Fame, August 5.

An AFL team defeated an NFL team for the first time, when Denver beat Detroit 13-7 in a preseason game, August 5.

Green Bay defeated Dallas 21-17 for the NFL championship on a last-minute 1-yard quarterback sneak by Bart Starr in 13-below-zero temperature at Green Bay, December 31. The same day, Oakland defeated Houston 40-7 for the AFL championship.

1968

Green Bay defeated Oakland 33-14 in Super Bowl II at Miami, January 14. The game had the first $3-million gate in pro football history.

Vince Lombardi resigned as head coach of the Packers, but remained as general manager, January 28.

Werblin sold his shares in the Jets to his partners Don Lillis, Leon Hess, Townsend Martin, and Phil Iselin, May 21. Lillis assumed the presidency of the club, but then died July 23. Iselin was appointed president, August 6.

Halas retired for the fourth and last time as head coach of the Bears, May 27.

The Oilers left Rice Stadium for the Astrodome and became the first NFL team to play its home games in a domed stadium.

The movie *Heidi* became a footnote in sports history when NBC didn't show the last 50 seconds of the Jets-Raiders game in order to permit the children's special to begin on time. The Raiders scored two touchdowns in the last 42 seconds to win 43-32, November 17.

Ewbank became the first coach to win titles in both the NFL and AFL when his Jets

defeated the Raiders 27-23 for the AFL championship, December 29. The same day, Baltimore defeated Cleveland 34-0.

1969

The AFL established a playoff format for the 1969 season, with the winner in one division playing the runner-up in the other, January 11.

An AFL team won the Super Bowl for the first time, as the Jets defeated the Colts 16-7 at Miami, January 12 in Super Bowl III. The title Super Bowl was recognized by the NFL for the first time.

Vince Lombardi became part owner, executive vice-president, and head coach of the Washington Redskins, February 7.

Wolman sold the Eagles to Leonard Tose, May 1.

Baltimore, Cleveland, and Pittsburgh agreed to join the AFL teams to form the 13-team American Football Conference of the NFL in 1970, May 10. The NFL also agreed on a playoff format that would include one "wild-card" team per conference—the second-place team with the best record.

The NFL announced a three-year agreement with ABC to televise *Monday Night Football*. The new series makes the NFL the first league with a regular series of national telecasts in prime time, May 26.

George Preston Marshall, president emeritus of the Redskins, died at 72, August 9.

The NFL marked its fiftieth year by the wearing of a special patch by each of the 16 teams.

1970

Kansas City defeated Minnesota 23-7 in Super Bowl IV at New Orleans, January 11. The gross receipts of approximately $3.8 million were the largest ever for a one-day sports event.

A special league meeting was held to determine the divisional realignment of the National Football Conference. With no consensus, Rozelle ordered the five most viable plans be written down on sheets of paper. Rozelle's assistant, Thelma Elkjer, picked the winning one out of a vase at random, January 17.

Four-year television contracts, under which CBS would televise all NFC games and NBC all AFC games (except Monday night games) and the two would divide televising the Super Bowl and AFC-NFC Pro Bowl games, were announced, January 26.

Art Modell resigned as president of the NFL, March 12. Milt Woodard resigned as president of the AFL, March 13. Lamar Hunt was elected president of the AFC and George Halas was elected president of the NFC, March 19.

The merged 26-team league adopted rules changes putting names on the backs of players' jerseys, making a point after touchdown worth only one point, and making the scoreboard clock the official timing device of the game, March 18.

The Players Negotiating Committee and the NFL Players Association announced a four-year agreement guaranteeing approximately $4,535,000 annually to player pension and insurance benefits, August 3. The owners also agreed to contribute $250,000 annually to improve or implement items such as disability payments, widows' benefits, maternity benefits, and dental benefits. The agreement also provided for increased preseason game and per diem payments, averaging approximately $2.6 million annually.

The Pittsburgh Steelers moved into Three Rivers Stadium. The Cincinnati Bengals moved to Riverfront Stadium.

Vince Lombardi died of cancer at 57, September 3.

The Super Bowl trophy was renamed the Vince Lombardi trophy, September 10.

Tom Dempsey of New Orleans kicked a game-winning NFL-record 63-yard field goal against Detroit, November 8.

1971

Baltimore defeated Dallas 16-13 on Jim O'Brien's 32-yard field goal with five seconds to go in Super Bowl V at Miami, January 17.

The NFC defeated the AFC 27-6 in the first AFC-NFC Pro Bowl at Los Angeles, January 24.

The Boston Patriots changed their name to the New England Patriots, March 25. Their new stadium, Schaefer Stadium, was dedicated in a 20-14 preseason victory over the Giants.

The Philadelphia Eagles left Franklin Field and played their games at the new Veterans Stadium.

The San Francisco 49ers left Kezar Stadium and moved their games to Candlestick Park.

Daniel F. Reeves, the president and general manager of the Rams, died at 58, April 15.

The Dallas Cowboys moved from the Cotton Bowl into their new home, Texas Stadium, October 24.

Miami defeated Kansas City 27-24 in sudden-death overtime in an AFC Divisional Playoff Game, December 25. Garo Yepremian kicked a 37-yard field goal for the Dolphins after 22 minutes, 40 seconds of overtime, as the game lasted 82 minutes, 40 seconds overall, making it the longest game in history.

1972

Dallas defeated Miami 24-3 in Super Bowl VI at New Orleans, January 16.

The inbounds lines or hashmarks were moved nearer the center of the field, 23 yards, 1 foot, 9 inches from the sidelines, March 23. The method of determining won-lost percentage in standings changed. Tie games, previously not counted in the standings, were made equal to a half-game won and a half-game lost, May 24.

Robert Irsay purchased the Los Angeles Rams and transferred ownership of the club to Carroll Rosenbloom in exchange for the Baltimore Colts, July 13.

William V. Bidwill purchased the stock of his brother Charles (Stormy) Bidwill to become the sole owner of the St. Louis Cardinals, September 2.

The National District Attorneys Association endorsed the position of professional leagues in opposing proposed legalization of gambling on professional team sports, September 28.

Franco Harris' "Immaculate Reception" gave the Steelers their first postseason win ever, 13-7 over the Raiders, December 23.

1973

Rozelle announced that all Super Bowl VII tickets were sold and that the game would be telecast in Los Angeles, the site of the game, on an experimental basis, January 3.

Miami defeated Washington 14-7 in Super Bowl VII at Los Angeles, completing a 17-0 season, the first perfect-record regular-season and postseason mark in NFL history, January 14.

The AFC defeated the NFC 33-28 in the Pro Bowl in Dallas, the first time since 1942 that the game was played outside Los Angeles, January 21.

A jersey numbering system was adopted, April 5: 1-19 for quarterbacks and specialists, 20-49 for running backs and defensive backs, 50-59 for centers and linebackers, 60-79 for defensive linemen and interior offensive linemen other than centers, and 80-89 for wide receivers and tight ends. Players who had been in the NFL in 1972 could continue to use old numbers.

NFL Charities, a nonprofit organization, was created to derive an income from monies generated from NFL Properties' licensing of NFL trademarks and team names, June 26. NFL Charities was set up to support education and charitable activities and to supply economic support to persons formerly associated with professional football who were no longer able to support themselves.

Congress adopted experimental legislation (for three years) requiring any NFL game that had been declared a sell-out 72 hours prior to kickoff to be made available for local televising, September 14. The legislation provided for an annual review to be made by the Federal Communications Commission.

The Buffalo Bills moved their home games from War Memorial Stadium to Rich Stadium in nearby Orchard Park. The Giants tied the Eagles 23-23 in the final game in Yankee Stadium, September 23. The Giants played the rest of their home games at the Yale Bowl in New Haven, Connecti-

cut.

A rival league, the World Football League, was formed and was reported in operation, October 2. It had plans to start play in 1974.

O.J. Simpson of Buffalo became the first player to rush for more than 2,000 yards in a season, gaining 2,003.

1974

Miami defeated Minnesota 24-7 in Super Bowl VIII at Houston, the second consecutive Super Bowl championship for the Dolphins, January 13.

Rozelle was given a 10-year contract effective January 1, 1973, February 27.

Tampa Bay was awarded the twenty-seventh franchise to begin operation in 1976, April 24.

Sweeping rules changes were adopted to add action and tempo to games: one sudden-death overtime period was added for preseason and regular-season games; the goal posts were moved from the goal line to the end lines; kickoffs were moved from the 40- to the 35-yard line; after missed field goals from beyond the 20, the ball was to be returned to the line of scrimmage; restrictions were placed on members of the punting team to open up return possibilities; roll-blocking and cutting of wide receivers was eliminated; the extent of downfield contact a defender could have with an eligible receiver was restricted; the penalties for offensive holding, illegal use of the hands, and tripping were reduced from 15 to 10 yards; wide receivers blocking back toward the ball within three yards of the line of scrimmage were prevented from blocking below the waist, April 25.

Seattle was awarded the twenty-eighth NFL franchise to begin play in 1976, June 4. Lloyd W. Nordstrom, president of the Seattle Seahawks, and Hugh Culverhouse, president of the Tampa Bay Buccaneers, signed franchise agreements, December 5.

The Birmingham Americans defeated the Florida Blazers 22-21 in the WFL World Bowl, winning the league championship, December 5.

1975

Pittsburgh defeated Minnesota 16-6 in Super Bowl IX at New Orleans, the Steelers' first championship since entering the NFL in 1933, January 12.

The Memphis Southmen of the WFL signed Larry Csonka, Jim Kiick, and Paul Warfield of Miami, March 31.

The divisional winners with the highest won-loss percentage were made the home team for the divisional playoffs, and the surviving winners with the highest percentage made home teams for the championship games. Previously, the home sites were pre-determined by division on a rotating basis, June 26.

Referees were equipped with wireless microphones for all preseason, regular-season, and playoff games.

The Lions moved to the new Pontiac Silverdome. The Giants played their home games in Shea Stadium. The Saints moved into the Louisiana Superdome.

The World Football League folded, October 22.

1976

Pittsburgh defeated Dallas 21-17 in Super Bowl X in Miami. The Steelers joined Green Bay and Miami as the only teams to win two Super Bowls; the Cowboys became the first wild-card team to play in the Super Bowl, January 18.

Lloyd Nordstrom, the president of the Seahawks, died at 66, January 20. His brother Elmer succeeded him as majority representative of the team.

The owners adopted the use of two 30-second clocks for all games, visible to both players and fans to note the official time between the ready-for-play signal and snap of the ball, March 16.

A veteran player allocation was held to stock the Seattle and Tampa Bay franchises with 39 players each, March 30-31. In the college draft, Seattle and Tampa Bay each received eight extra choices, April 8-9.

The Giants moved into new Giants Stadium in East Rutherford, New Jersey.

The Steelers defeated the College All-Stars in a storm-shortened Chicago College All-Star Game, the last of the series, July 23. St. Louis defeated San Diego 20-10 in a preseason game before 38,000 in Korakuen Stadium, Tokyo, in the first NFL game outside of North America, August 16.

1977

Oakland defeated Minnesota 32-14 in Super Bowl XI at Pasadena, January 9. The paid attendance was a pro record 103,438.

The NFL Players Association and the NFL Management Council ratified a collective bargaining agreement extending until 1982, covering five football seasons while continuing the pension plan—including years 1974, 1975, and 1976—with contributions totaling more than $55 million. The total cost of the agreement was estimated at $107 million. The agreement called for a college draft at least through 1986; contained a no-strike, no-suit clause; established a 43-man active player limit; reduced pension vesting to four years; provided for increases in minimum salaries and preseason and postseason pay; improved insurance, medical, and dental benefits; modified previous practices in player movement and control; and reaffirmed the NFL Commissioner's disciplinary authority. Additionally, the agreement called for the NFL member clubs to make payments totaling $16 million in the next 10 years to settle various legal disputes, February 25.

The San Francisco 49ers were sold to Edward J. DeBartolo, Jr., March 28.

A 16-game regular season, 4-game preseason was adopted to begin in 1978. A second wild-card team was adopted for the playoffs beginning in 1978, with the wild-card teams to play each other and the winners advancing to a round of eight postseason series, March 29.

The Seahawks were permanently aligned in the AFC Western Division and the Buccaneers in the NFC Central Division, March 31.

Rules changes were adopted to open up the passing game and to cut down on injuries. Defenders were permitted to make contact with eligible receivers only once; the head slap was outlawed; offensive linemen were prohibited from thrusting their hands to an opponent's neck, face, or head; and wide receivers were prohibited from clipping, even in the legal clipping zone.

Rozelle negotiated contracts with the three television networks to televise all NFL regular-season and postseason games, plus selected preseason games, for four years beginning with the 1978 season. ABC was awarded yearly rights to 16 Monday night games, four primetime games, the AFC-NFC Pro Bowl, and the Hall of Fame games. CBS received the rights to all NFC regular-season and postseason games (except those in the ABC package) and to Super Bowls XIV and XVI. NBC received the rights to all AFC regular-season and postseason games (except those in the ABC package) and to Super Bowls XIII and XV. Industry sources considered it the largest single television package ever negotiated, October 12.

1978

Dallas defeated Denver 27-10 in Super Bowl XII, held indoors for the first time, at the Louisiana Superdome in New Orleans, January 15. Dallas' victory was the first for the NFC in six years.

According to a Louis Harris Sports Survey, 70 percent of the nation's sports fans said they followed football, compared to 54 percent who followed baseball. Football increased its lead as the country's favorite, 26 percent to 16 percent for baseball, January 19.

A seventh official, the side judge, was added to the officiating crew, March 14.

The NFL continued a trend toward opening up the game. Rules changes permitted a defender to maintain contact with a receiver within five yards of the line of scrimmage, but restricted contact beyond that point. The pass-blocking rule was interpreted to permit the extending of arms and open hands, March 17.

A study on the use of instant replay as an officiating aid was made during seven nationally televised preseason games.

The NFL played for the first time in Mexico City, with the Saints defeating the Eagles 14-7 in a preseason game, August 5.

Bolstered by the expansion of the regular-season schedule from 14 to 16 weeks, NFL paid attendance exceeded 12 million (12,771,800) for the first time. The per-game average of 57,017 was the third-highest in league history and the most since 1973.

1979

Pittsburgh defeated Dallas 35-31 in Super Bowl XIII at Miami to become the first team ever to win three Super Bowls, January 21.

NFL rules changes emphasized additional player safety. The changes prohibited players on the receiving team from blocking below the waist during kickoffs, punts, and field-goal attempts; prohibited the wearing of torn or altered equipment and exposed pads that could be hazardous; extended the zone in which there could be no crackback blocks; and instructed officials to quickly whistle a play dead when a quarterback was clearly in the grasp of a tackler, March 16.

Carroll Rosenbloom, the president of the Rams, drowned at 72, April 2. His widow, Georgia, assumed control of the club.

1980

Pittsburgh defeated the Los Angeles Rams 31-19 in Super Bowl XIV at Pasadena to become the first team to win four Super Bowls, January 20.

The AFC-NFC Pro Bowl, won 37-27 by the NFC, was played before 48,060 fans at Aloha Stadium in Honolulu, Hawaii. It was the first time in the 30-year history of the Pro Bowl that the game was played in a non-NFL city.

Rules changes placed greater restrictions on contact in the area of the head, neck, and face. Under the heading of "personal foul," players were prohibited from directly striking, swinging, or clubbing on the head, neck, or face. Starting in 1980, a penalty could be called for such contact whether or not the initial contact was made below the neck area.

CBS, with a record bid of $12 million, won the national radio rights to 26 NFL regular-season games, including Monday Night Football, and all 10 postseason games for the 1980-83 seasons.

The Los Angeles Rams moved their home games to Anaheim Stadium in nearby Orange County, California.

The Oakland Raiders joined the Los Angeles Coliseum Commission's antitrust suit against the NFL. The suit contended the league violated antitrust laws in declining to approve a proposed move by the Raiders from Oakland to Los Angeles.

The NFL Draft is televised for the first time by ESPN, April 29.

Television ratings in 1980 were the second-best in NFL history, trailing only the combined ratings of the 1976 season. All three networks posted gains, and NBC's 15.0 rating was its best ever. CBS and ABC had their best ratings since 1977, with 15.3 and 20.8 ratings, respectively. CBS Radio reported a record audience of 7 million for Monday night and special games.

1981
Oakland defeated Philadelphia 27-10 in Super Bowl XV at the Louisiana Superdome in New Orleans, to become the first wild-card team to win a Super Bowl, January 25.

Edgar F. Kaiser, Jr., purchased the Denver Broncos from Gerald and Allan Phipps, February 26.

The owners adopted a disaster plan for re-stocking a team should the club be involved in a fatal accident, March 20.

A CBS-New York Times poll showed that 48 percent of sports fans preferred football to 31 percent for baseball.

The NFL teams hosted 167 representatives from 44 predominantly black colleges during training camps for a total of 289 days. The program was adopted for renewal during each training camp period.

ABC and CBS set all-time rating highs. ABC finished with a 21.7 rating and CBS with a 17.5 rating. NBC was down slightly to 13.9.

1982
San Francisco defeated Cincinnati 26-21 in Super Bowl XVI at the Pontiac Silverdome, in the first Super Bowl held in the North, January 24. The CBS telecast achieved the highest rating of any televised sports event ever, 49.1 with a 73.0 share.

The NFL signed a five-year contract with the three television networks (ABC, CBS, and NBC) to televise all NFL regular-season and postseason games starting with the 1982 season.

A jury ruled against the NFL in the antitrust trial brought by the Los Angeles Coliseum Commission and the Oakland Raiders, May 7. The verdict cleared the way for the Raiders to move to Los Angeles, where they defeated Green Bay 24-3 in their first preseason game, August 29.

The 1982 season was reduced from a 16-game schedule to nine as the result of a 57-day players' strike. The strike was called by the NFLPA at midnight on Monday, September 20, following the Green Bay at New York Giants game. Play resumed November 21-22 following ratification of the Collective Bargaining Agreement by NFL owners, November 17 in New York.

Under the Collective Bargaining Agreement, which was to run through the 1986 season, the NFL draft was extended through 1992 and the veteran free-agent system was left basically unchanged. A minimum salary schedule for years of experience was established; training camp and postseason pay were increased; players' medical, insurance, and retirement benefits were increased; and a severance-pay system was introduced to aid in career transition, a first in professional sports.

Despite the players' strike, the average paid attendance in 1982 was 58,472, the fifth-highest in league history.

1983
Because of the shortened season, the NFL adopted a format of 16 teams competing in a Super Bowl Tournament for the 1982 playoffs. The NFC's number-one seed, Washing-ton, defeated the AFC's number-two seed, Miami, 27-17 in Super Bowl XVII at the Rose Bowl in Pasadena, January 30.

Super Bowl XVII was the second-highest rated live television program of all time, giving the NFL a sweep of the top 10 live programs in television history.

George Halas, the owner of the Bears and the last surviving member of the NFL's second organizational meeting, died at 88, October 31.

1984
The Los Angeles Raiders defeated Washington 38-9 in Super Bowl XVIII at Tampa Stadium, January 22.

An 11-man group headed by H.R. (Bum) Bright purchased the Dallas Cowboys from Clint Murchison, Jr., March 20. Club president Tex Schramm was designated as managing general partner.

Wellington Mara was named president of the NFC, March 20.

Patrick Bowlen purchased a majority interest in the Denver Broncos from Edgar Kaiser, Jr., March 21.

The Colts relocated to Indianapolis, March 28. Their new home became the Hoosier Dome.

The New York Jets moved their home games to Giants Stadium in East Rutherford, New Jersey.

Alex G. Spanos purchased a majority interest in the San Diego Chargers from Eugene V. Klein, August 28.

Houston defeated Pittsburgh 23-20 to mark the one-hundredth overtime game in regular-season play since overtime was adopted in 1974, December 2.

On the field, many all-time records were set: Dan Marino of Miami passed for 5,084 yards and 48 touchdowns; Eric Dickerson of the Los Angeles Rams rushed for 2,105 yards; Art Monk of Washington caught 106 passes; and Walter Payton of Chicago broke Jim Brown's career rushing mark, finishing the season with 13,309 yards.

According to a CBS Sports/New York Times survey, 53 percent of the nation's sports fans said they most enjoyed watching football, compared to 18 percent for baseball, December 2-4.

1985
San Francisco defeated Miami 38-16 in Super Bowl XIX at Stanford Stadium in Stanford, California, January 20. President Ronald Reagan, who took his second oath of office before tossing the coin for the game, was one of 115,936,000 viewers. Super Bowl XIX had a direct economic impact of $113.5 million on the San Francisco Bay area.

NBC Radio and the NFL entered into a two-year agreement granting NBC the radio rights to a 37-game package in each of the 1985-86 seasons, March 6. The package included 27 regular-season games and 10 postseason games.

Norman Braman, in partnership with Edward Leibowitz, bought the Philadelphia Eagles from Leonard Tose, April 29.

A group headed by Tom Benson, Jr., was approved to purchase the New Orleans Saints from John W. Mecom, Jr., June 3.

The NFL owners adopted a resolution calling for a series of overseas preseason games, beginning in 1986, with one game to be played in England/Europe and/or one game in Japan each year. The game would be a fifth preseason game for the clubs involved and all arrangements and selection of the clubs would be under the control of the Commissioner, May 23.

The league-wide conversion to videotape from movie film for coaching study was approved.

A Louis Harris poll in December revealed that pro football remained the sport most followed by Americans. Fifty-nine percent of those surveyed followed pro football, compared with 54 percent who followed baseball.

The Chicago-Miami Monday game had the highest rating, 29.6, and share, 46.0, of any primetime game in NFL history, December 2. The game was viewed in more than 25 million homes.

The NFL showed a ratings increase on all three networks for the season, gaining 4 percent on NBC, 10 on CBS, and

16 on ABC.

1986

Chicago defeated New England 46-10 in Super Bowl XX at the Louisiana Superdome, January 26. The Patriots had earned the right to play the Bears by becoming the first wild-card team to win three consecutive games on the road. The NBC telecast replaced the final episode of M*A*S*H as the most-viewed television program in history, with an audience of 127 million viewers, according to A.C. Nielsen figures. In addition to drawing a 48.3 rating and a 70 percent share in the United States, Super Bowl XX was televised to 59 foreign countries and beamed via satellite to the QE II.

The owners adopted limited use of instant replay as an officiating aid, prohibited players from wearing or otherwise displaying equipment, apparel, or other items that carry commercial names, names of organizations, or personal messages of any type, March 11.

After an 11-week trial, a jury in U.S. District Court in New York awarded the United States Football League one dollar in its $1.7 billion antitrust suit against the NFL. The jury rejected all of the USFL's television-related claims, which were the self-proclaimed heart of the USFL's case. The jury deliberated five days, July 29.

Chicago defeated Dallas 17-6 at Wembley Stadium in London in the first American Bowl. The game drew a sellout crowd of 82,699 and the NBC national telecast in this country produced a 12.4 rating and 36 percent share, making it the highest daytime preseason television audience ever with 10.65-million viewers, August 3.

ABC's NFL Monday Night Football, in its seventeenth season, became the longest-running primetime series in the history of the network.

1987

The New York Giants defeated Denver 39-20 in Super Bowl XXI and captured their first NFL title since 1956. The game, played in Pasadena's Rose Bowl, drew a sellout crowd of 101,063, January 25.

New three-year TV contracts with ABC, CBS, and NBC were announced for 1987-89 at the NFL annual meeting in Maui, Hawaii, March 15. Commissioner Rozelle and Broadcast Committee Chairman Art Modell also announced a three-year contract with ESPN to televise 13 primetime games each season. The ESPN contract was the first with a cable network. However, NFL games on ESPN also were scheduled for regular television in the city of the visiting team and in the home city if the game was sold out 72 hours in advance.

A special payment program was adopted to benefit nearly 1,000 former NFL players who participated in the League before the current Bert Bell NFL Pension Plan was created and made retroactive to the 1959 season. Players covered by the new program spent at least five years in the League and played all or part of their career prior to 1959. Each vested player would receive $60 per month for each year of service in the League for life.

NFL and CBS Radio jointly announced agreement granting CBS the radio rights to a 40-game package in each of the next three NFL seasons, 1987-89, April 7.

Over 400 former NFL players from the pre-1959 era received first payments from NFL owners, July 1.

The NFL's debut on ESPN produced the two highest-rated and most-watched sports programs in basic cable history. The Chicago at Miami game on August 16 drew an 8.9 rating in 3.81 million homes. Those records fell two weeks later when the Los Angeles Raiders at Dallas game achieved a 10.2 cable rating in 4.36 million homes.

The 1987 season was reduced from a 16-game season to 15 as the result of a 24-day players' strike. The strike was called by the NFLPA on Tuesday, September 22, following the New England at New York Jets game. Games scheduled for the third weekend were canceled but the games of weeks four, five, and six were played with replacement teams. Striking players returned for the seventh week of the season, October 25.

In a three-team deal involving 10 players and/or draft choices, the Los Angeles Rams traded running back Eric Dickerson to the Indianapolis Colts for six draft choices and two players. Buffalo obtained the rights to linebacker Cornelius Bennett from Indianapolis, sending Greg Bell and three draft choices to the Rams. The Colts added Owen Gill and three draft choices of their own to complete the deal with the Rams, October 31.

The Chicago at Minnesota game became the highest-rated and most-watched sports program in basic cable history when it drew a 14.4 cable rating in 6.5 million homes, December 6.

1988

Washington defeated Denver 42-10 in Super Bowl XXII to earn its second victory this decade in the NFL Championship Game. The game, played for the first time in San Diego Jack Murphy Stadium, drew a sellout crowd of 73,302. Doug Williams, the game's MVP, became the first African-American quarterback to play in a Super Bowl, January 31.

In a unanimous 3-0 decision, the 2nd Circuit Court of Appeals in New York upheld the verdict of the jury that in July, 1986, had awarded the United States Football League one dollar in its $1.7 billion antitrust suit against the NFL. In a 91-page opinion, Judge Ralph K. Winter said the USFL sought through court decree the success it failed to gain among football fans, March 10.

By a 23-5 margin, owners voted to continue the instant replay system for the third consecutive season with the Instant Replay Official to be assigned to a regular seven-man, on-the-field crew. At the NFL annual meeting in Phoenix, Arizona, a 45-second clock was also approved to replace the 30-second clock. For a normal sequence of plays, the interval between plays was changed to 45 seconds from the time the ball is signaled dead until it is

snapped on the succeeding play.

NFL owners approved the transfer of the Cardinals' franchise from St. Louis to Phoenix; approved two supplemental drafts each year—one prior to training camp and one prior to the regular season; and voted to initiate an annual series of games in Japan/Asia as early as the 1989 preseason, March 14-18.

The NFL Annual Selection Meeting returned to a separate two-day format and for the first time originated on a Sunday. ESPN drew a 3.6 rating during their seven-hour coverage of the draft, which was viewed in 1.6 million homes, April 24-25.

Art Rooney, founder and owner of the Steelers, died at 87, August 25.

Johnny Grier became the first African-American referee in NFL history, September 4.

Commissioner Rozelle announced that two teams would play a preseason game as part of the American Bowl series on August 6, 1989, in the Korakuen Tokyo Dome in Japan, December 16.

1989

San Francisco defeated Cincinnati 20-16 in Super Bowl XXIII. The game, played for the first time at Joe Robbie Stadium in Miami, was attended by a sellout crowd of 75,129, January 22.

Commissioner Rozelle announced his retirement, pending the naming of a successor, March 22 at the NFL annual meeting in Palm Desert, California.

Following the announcement, AFC president Lamar Hunt and NFC president Wellington Mara announced the formation of a six-man search committee composed of Art Modell, Robert Parins, Dan Rooney, and Ralph Wilson. Hunt and Mara served as co-chairmen.

By a 24-4 margin, owners voted to continue the instant replay system for the fourth straight season. A strengthened policy regarding anabolic steroids and masking agents was announced by Commissioner Rozelle. NFL clubs called for strong disciplinary measures in cases of feigned injuries and adopted a joint proposal by the Long-Range Planning and Finance committees regarding player personnel rules, March 19-23.

Two hundred twenty-nine unconditional free agents signed with new teams under management's Plan B system, April 1.

Jerry Jones purchased a majority interest in the Dallas Cowboys from H.R. (Bum) Bright, April 18.

Tex Schramm was named president of the new World League of American Football to work with a six-man committee of Dan Rooney, chairman; Norman Braman, Lamar Hunt, Victor Kiam, Mike Lynn, and Bill Walsh, April 18.

NFL and CBS Radio jointly announced agreement extending CBS's radio rights to an annual 40-game package through the 1994 season, April 18.

As of opening day, September 10, of the 229 Plan B free agents, 111 were active and 23 others were on teams' reserve lists. Ninety-two others were waived and three retired.

Art Shell was named head coach of the Los Angeles Raiders making him the NFL's first black head coach since Fritz Pollard coached the Akron Pros in 1921, October 3.

The site of the New England Patriots at San Francisco 49ers game scheduled for Candlestick Park on October 22 was switched to Stanford Stadium in the aftermath of the Bay Area Earthquake of October 17. The change was announced on October 19.

Paul Tagliabue became the seventh chief executive of the NFL on October 26 when he was chosen to succeed Commissioner Pete Rozelle on the sixth ballot of a three-day meeting in Cleveland, Ohio.

In all, 12 ballots were required to select Tagliabue. Two were conducted at a meeting in Chicago on July 6, and four at a meeting in Dallas on October 10-11. On the twelfth ballot, with Seattle absent, Tagliabue received more than the 19 affirmative votes required for election from among the 27 clubs present.

The transfer from Commis-sioner Rozelle to Commissioner Tagliabue took place at 12:01 A.M. on Sunday, November 5.

NFL Charities donated $1 million through United Way to benefit Bay Area earthquake victims, November 6.

1990

San Francisco defeated Denver 55-10 in Super Bowl XXIV at the Louisiana Superdome, January 28. San Francisco joined Pittsburgh as the NFL's only teams to win four Super Bowls.

The NFL announced revisions in its 1990 draft eligibility rules. College juniors became eligible but must renounce their collegiate football eligibility before applying for the NFL Draft, February 16.

Commissioner Tagliabue announced NFL teams will play their 16-game schedule over 17 weeks in 1990-92 and 16 games over 18 weeks in 1993, February 27.

The NFL revised its playoff format to include two additional wild-card teams (one per conference), which raised the total to six wild-card teams.

Commissioner Tagliabue and Broadcast Committee Chairman Art Modell announced a four-year contract with Turner Broadcasting to televise nine Sunday-night games.

New four-year TV agreements were ratified for 1990-93 for ABC, CBS, NBC, ESPN, and TNT at the NFL annual meeting in Orlando, Florida, March 12. The contracts totaled $3.6 billion, the largest in TV history.

The NFL announced plans to expand its American Bowl series of preseason games. In addition to games in London and Tokyo, American Bowl games were scheduled for Berlin, Germany, and Montreal, Canada, in 1990.

For the fifth straight year, NFL owners voted to continue a limited system of Instant Replay. Beginning in 1990, the replay official will have a two-minute time limit to make a decision. The vote was 21-7, March 12.

Commissioner Tagliabue announced the formation of a Committee on Expansion and Realignment, March 13. He also named a Player Advisory Council, comprised of 12 former NFL players, March 14.

One-hundred eighty-four Plan B unconditional free agents signed with new teams, April 2.

Commissioner Tagliabue appointed Dr. John Lombardo as the League's Drug Advisor for Anabolic Steroids, April 25 and named Dr. Lawrence Brown as the League's Advisor for Drugs of Abuse, May 17.

NFL International Week was celebrated with four preseason games in seven days in Tokyo, London, Berlin, and Montreal. More than 200,000 fans on three continents attended the four games, August 4-11.

Commissioner Tagliabue announced the NFL Teacher of the Month program in which the League furnishes grants and scholarships in recognition of teachers who provided a positive influence upon NFL players in elementary and secondary schools, September 20.

For the first time since 1957, every NFL club won at least one of its first four games, October 1.

The Super Bowl Most Valuable Player trophy was renamed the Pete Rozelle trophy, October 8.

1991

The New York Giants defeated Buffalo 20-19 in Super Bowl XXV to capture their second title in five years. The game was played before a sellout crowd of 73,813 at Tampa Stadium and became the first Super Bowl decided by one point, January 26.

New York businessman Robert Tisch purchased a 50 percent interest in the New York Giants from Mrs. Helen Mara Nugent and her children, Tim Mara and Maura Mara Concannon, February 2.

NFL clubs voted to continue a limited system of Instant Replay for the sixth consecutive year. The vote was 21-7, March 19.

The NFL launched the World League of American Football, the first sports league to operate on a weekly basis on two separate continents, March 23.

NFL Charities presented a $250,000 donation to the United Service Organization. The donation was the second largest single grant ever by NFL Charities, April 5.

Commissioner Tagliabue named Harold Henderson as Executive Vice President for Labor Relations and Chairman of the NFL Management Council Executive Committee, April 8.

NFL clubs approved a recommendation by the Expansion and Realignment Committee to add two teams for the 1994 season, resulting in six divisions of five teams each, May 22.

"NFL International Week" featured six 1990 playoff teams playing nationally televised games in London, Berlin, and Tokyo on July 28 and August 3-4. The games drew more than 150,000 fans.

Paul Brown, founder of the Cleveland Browns and Cincinnati Bengals, died at age 82, August 5.

NFL clubs approved a resolution establishing an international division. A three-year financial plan for the World League was approved by NFL clubs at a meeting in Dallas, October 23.

1992

The NFL agreed to provide a minimum of $2.5 million in financial support to the NFL Alumni Association and assistance to NFL Alumni-related programs. The agreement included contributions from NFL Charities to the Pre-59ers and Dire Need Programs for former players, January 25.

The Washington Redskins defeated the Buffalo Bills 37-24 in Super Bowl XXVI to capture their third world championship in 10 years, January 26. The game was played before a sellout crowd of 63,130 at the Hubert H. Humphrey Metrodome in Minneapolis.

The use in officiating of a limited system of Instant Replay was not approved. The vote was 17-11 in favor of approval (21 votes were required). Instant Replay had been used for six consecutive years (1986-1991), March 18.

St. Louis businessman James Orthwein purchased controlling interest in the New England Patriots from Victor

Kiam, May 11.

In a Harris Poll taken during the NFL offseason, professional football again was declared the nation's most popular sport. Professional football finished atop similar surveys conducted by Harris in 1985 and 1989, May 23.

NFL clubs accepted the report of the Expansion Committee at a league meeting in Pasadena. The report names five cities as finalists for the two expansion teams—Baltimore, Charlotte, Jacksonville, Memphis, and St. Louis, May 19.

At a league meeting in Dallas, NFL clubs approved a proposal by the World League Board of Directors to restructure the World League and place future emphasis on its international success, September 17.

The Professional and Amateur Sports Protection Act made it unlawful for a government entity to operate a lottery or other betting scheme based on pro or collegiate games. Four states that already had such betting were grandfathered, October 6.

NFL teams played their 16-game regular-season schedule over 18 weeks for the only time in league history.

1993
The NFL and lawyers for the players announced a settlement of various lawsuits and an agreement on the terms of a seven-year deal that included a new player system to be in place through the 1999 season, January 6.

Commissioner Tagliabue announced the establishment of the "NFL World Partnership Program" to develop amateur football internationally through a series of clinics conducted by former NFL players and coaches, January 14.

As part of Super Bowl XXVII, the NFL announced the creation of the first NFL Youth Education Town, a facility located in south central Los Angeles for inner city youth, January 25.

The Dallas Cowboys defeated the Buffalo Bills 52-17 in Super Bowl XXVII to capture their first NFL title since 1978. The game was played before a crowd of 98,374 at the Rose Bowl in

Pasadena, California, January 31.

The NFL and the NFL Players Association officially signed a 7-year Collective Bargaining Agreement in Washington, D.C., which guarantees more than $1 billion in pension, health, and post-career benefits for current and retired players—the most extensive benefits plan in pro sports. It was the NFL's first CBA since the 1982 agreement expired in 1987, June 29.

NFL Enterprises, a newly formed division of the NFL responsible for NFL Films, home video, and special domestic and international television programming was announced, August 19.

NFL announced plans to allow fans, for the first time ever, to join players and coaches in selecting the annual AFC and NFC Pro Bowl teams, October 12.

NFL clubs unanimously awarded the league's twenty-ninth franchise to the Carolina Panthers and owner Jerry Richardson at a meeting in Chicago, October 26.

At the same meeting in Chicago, NFL clubs approved a plan to form a European league with joint venture partners, October 27.

Don Shula became the winningest coach in NFL history when Miami beat Philadelphia to give Shula his 325th victory, one more than George Halas, November 14.

NFL clubs awarded the league's thirtieth franchise to the Jacksonville Jaguars and owner Wayne Weaver at a meeting in Chicago, November 30.

The NFL announced new 4-year television agreements with NBC, ABC, ESPN, TNT, and NFL newcomer FOX, which took over the NFC package from CBS, December 18.

The NFL completed its new TV agreements by announcing that NBC would retain the rights to the AFC package, December 20.

1994
The Dallas Cowboys defeated the Buffalo Bills 30-13 in Super Bowl XXVIII to become the fifth team to win back-to-back Super Bowl titles, January 30.

NFL clubs unanimously approved the transfer of the New England Patriots from James Orthwein to Robert Kraft at a meeting in Orlando, February 22.

In a move to increase offensive production, NFL clubs at the league's annual meeting in Orlando adopted a package of changes, including modifications in line play, chucking rules, and the roughing-the-passer rule, plus the adoption of the two-point conversion and moving the spot of the kickoff back to the 30-yard line, March 22.

NFL clubs approved transfer of the majority interest in the Miami Dolphins from the Robbie family to H. Wayne Huizenga, March 23.

The NFL and FOX announced the formation of a joint venture to create a six-team World League to begin play in Europe in April, 1995, March 23.

The Carolina Panthers earned the right to select first in the 1995 NFL draft by winning a coin toss with the Jacksonville Jaguars. The Jaguars received the second selection in the 1995 draft, April 24.

NFL clubs approved the transfer of the Philadelphia Eagles from Norman Braman to Jeffrey Lurie, May 6.

The NFL launched "NFL Sunday Ticket," a new season subscription service for satellite television dish owners, June 1.

An all-time NFL record crowd of 112,376 attended the American Bowl game between Dallas and Houston in Mexico City. It concluded the biggest American Bowl series in NFL history with four games attracting a record 256,666 fans, August 15.

The NFL reached agreement on a new seven-year contract with its game officials, September 22.

The NFL Management Council and the NFL Players Association announced an agreement on the formulation and implementation of the most comprehensive drug and alcohol policy in sports, October 28.

At an NFL meeting in Chicago, Commissioner Tagliabue slotted the two new expansion teams into the AFC Central (Jacksonville Jaguars) and

NFC West (Carolina Panthers) for the 1995 season only. He also appointed a special committee on realignment to make recommendations on the 1996 season and beyond, November 2.

1995
The San Francisco 49ers became the first team to win five Super Bowls when they defeated the San Diego Chargers 49-26 in Super Bowl XXIX at Joe Robbie Stadium in Miami, January 29.

Carolina and Jacksonville stocked their expansion rosters with a total of 66 players from other NFL teams in a veteran player allocation draft in New York, February 16.

CBS Radio and the NFL agreed to a new four-year contract for an annual 53-game package of games, continuing a relationship that spanned 15 of the past 17 years, February 22.

NFL clubs approved the transfer of the Tampa Bay Buccaneers from the estate of the late Hugh Culverhouse to South Florida businessman Malcolm Glazer, March 13.

After a two-year hiatus, the World League of American Football returned to action with six teams in Europe, April 8.

The NFL became the first major sports league to establish a site on the Internet system of on-line computer communication, April 10.

The transfer of the Rams from Los Angeles to St. Louis was approved by a vote of the NFL clubs at a meeting in Dallas, April 12.

ABC's *NFL Monday Night Football* finished the 1994-95 television season as the fifth highest-rated show out of 146 with a 17.8 average rating, the highest finish in the 25-year history of the series, April 18.

The Frankfurt Galaxy defeated the Amsterdam Admirals 26-22 to win the 1995 World Bowl before a crowd of 23,847 in Amsterdam's Olympic Stadium, June 23.

The transfer of the Raiders from Los Angeles to Oakland was approved by a vote of the NFL clubs at a meeting in Chicago, July 22.

Jacksonville Municipal Stadium opened in Jacksonville, Florida before a sold-out crowd of more than 70,000 as the St. Louis Rams defeated the Jacksonville Jaguars 27-10 in their first preseason game, August 18.

NFL Charities and 50 NFL players donated $1 million to the United Negro College Fund in honor of the fiftieth anniversary of the UNCF and the integration of the modern NFL, September 15.

The Trans World Dome opened in St. Louis with a sold-out crowd of 65,598 as the Rams defeated the Carolina Panthers 28-17, November 12.

On the field, many significant records and milestones were achieved: Miami's Dan Marino surpassed Pro Football Hall of Famer Fran Tarkenton in four major passing categories—attempts, completions, yards, and touchdowns—to become the NFL's all-time career leader. San Francisco's Jerry Rice became the all-time reception and receiving-yardage leader.

1996

The Dallas Cowboys won their third Super Bowl title in four years when they defeated the Pittsburgh Steelers 27-17 in Super Bowl XXX at Sun Devil Stadium in Tempe, Arizona, January 28.

An agreement between the NFL and the city of Cleveland regarding the Cleveland Browns' relocation was approved by a vote of the NFL clubs, February 9. According to the agreement, the city of Cleveland retained the Browns' heritage and records, including the name, logo, colors, history, playing records, trophies, and memorabilia, and committed to building a new 72,000-seat stadium for a reactivated Browns' franchise to begin play there no later than 1999. Art Modell received approval to move his franchise to Baltimore and rename it.

The transfer of the Oilers from Houston to Nashville for the 1998 season was approved by a vote of the NFL clubs at a meeting in Atlanta, April 30.

The Scottish Claymores defeated the Frankfurt Galaxy 32-27 to win the 1996 World Bowl in front of 38,982 at Murrayfield Stadium in Edinburgh, Scotland, June 23.

The NFL returned to Balti-

more when the new Baltimore Ravens defeated the Philadelphia Eagles 17-9 in a preseason game before a crowd of 63,804 at Memorial Stadium, August 3.

Ericsson Stadium opened in Charlotte, North Carolina with a crowd of 65,350 as the Carolina Panthers defeated the Chicago Bears 30-12 in a preseason game, August 3.

Former NFL Commissioner Pete Rozelle died at his home in Rancho Santa Fe, California. Rozelle, regarded as the premier commissioner in sports history, led the NFL for 29 years, from 1960-1989, December 6.

1997

Indianapolis Colts owner Robert Irsay died from complications related to a stroke he suffered in 1995. Irsay acquired the club in 1972 when he traded his Los Angeles Rams to Carrol Rosenbloom for the Colts. He later moved the Colts from Baltimore to Indianapolis in 1984, January 14.

The Green Bay Packers won their first NFL title in 29 years by defeating the New England Patriots 35-21 in Super Bowl XXXI at the Louisiana Superdome in New Orleans, January 26.

The rules governing crossownership were modified, permitting NFL club owners to also own teams in other sports in their home market or markets without NFL teams. The vote was 24-5 (one abstention) in favor of approval, March 11.

Washington Redskins owner Jack Kent Cooke died at his home in Washington, D.C. Cooke became majority owner in 1974 and the Redskins won three Super Bowls under his leadership, April 6.

The Barcelona Dragons defeated the Rhein Fire 38-24 to win the 1997 World Bowl in front of 31,100 fans at Estadi Olimpic de Montjuic in Barcelona, Spain, June 22.

NFL clubs approved the transfer of the Seattle Seahawks from Ken Behring to Paul Allen, August 19.

Jack Kent Cooke Stadium opened in Raljon, Maryland with a crowd of 78,270 as the Washington Redskins defeated the Arizona Cardinals 19-13 in overtime, September 14.

The 10,000th regular-season game in NFL history was played when the Seattle Seahawks defeated the Tennessee Oilers 16-13 at the Kingdome in Seattle, October 5.

Atlanta Falcons owner Rankin Smith died of heart failure three days prior to his seventy-third birthday. Smith was the founder of the Falcons and was instrumental in bringing Super Bowls XXVIII and XXXIV to Atlanta, October 26.

1998

The NFL reached agreement on record eight-year television contracts with four networks. ABC (NFL Monday Night Football) and FOX (NFC) retained their previous rights, CBS took over the AFC package from NBC, and ESPN won the right to broadcast the entire Sunday night cable package, January 13.

The World League was renamed the NFL Europe League, January 22.

The Denver Broncos won their first Super Bowl by defeating the defending champion Green Bay Packers 31-24 in Super Bowl XXXII at Qualcomm Stadium in San Diego, January 25.

The NFL clubs approved an extension of the Collective Bargaining Agreement through 2003. The extended CBA also created a $100 million fund for youth football, March 22.

The NFL clubs unanimously approved an expansion team for Cleveland to fulfill the commitment to return the Browns to the field in 1999, March 23.

The Rhein Fire defeated the Frankfurt Galaxy 34-10 to win the 1998 World Bowl in front of 47,846 fans in Frankfurt's Waldstadion—the biggest crowd to witness a World Bowl since 1991, June 14.

NFL clubs approved the transfer of the Minnesota Vikings from a 10-man ownership group to Red McCombs, July 28.

The NFL Stadium at Camden Yards opened in Baltimore, Maryland before a crowd of 65,938 as the Baltimore Ravens defeated the Chicago Bears 19-14 in a preseason game, August 8.

Raymond James Stadium opened in Tampa, Florida before a crowd of 62,410 as the Tampa Bay Buccaneers

defeated the Chicago Bears 27-15, September 20.

Tennessee Oilers owner Bud Adams announced the team will change its name to the Tennessee Titans following the 1998 season. The NFL announced that the name Oilers will be retired—a first in league history, November 14.

1999

The Denver Broncos won their second consecutive Super Bowl title by defeating the NFC champion Atlanta Falcons 34-19 in Super Bowl XXXIII at Pro Player Stadium in Miami, January 31.

Jim Pyne, a center allocated by the Detroit Lions, was the first selection of the Cleveland Browns in the 1999 NFL Expansion Draft. The Browns eventually selected 37 players, February 9.

CBS Radio/Westwood One agreed to a 3-year extension of their exclusive national radio rights to NFL games, March 11.

By a vote of 28-3, the owners adopted an instant replay system as an officiating aid for the 1999 season, March 17.

New York Jets owner Leon Hess died from complications of a blood disease. Hess had been involved in the ownership of the Jets since 1963 and was sole owner of the club since 1984, May 9.

A group led by Washington area businessman Daniel Snyder is approved by NFL clubs as the new owner of the Washington Redskins at a league meeting in Atlanta, May 25.

The Frankfurt Galaxy became the first team in NFL Europe League history to win a second World Bowl by defeating the Barcelona Dragons 38-24 at Rheinstadion, in Düsseldorf, Germany, June 27.

The Cleveland Browns returned to the field for the first time since 1995 and defeated the Dallas Cowboys 20-17 in overtime in the annual Hall of Fame Game at Canton, Ohio, August 9.

Cleveland Browns Stadium opened in Cleveland, Ohio before a crowd of 71,398 as the Minnesota Vikings defeated the Browns in a preseason game, 24-17, August 21.

Adelphia Coliseum opened

in Nashville, Tennessee before a crowd of 65,729 with the Tennessee Titans defeating the Atlanta Falcons 17-3 in a preseason game, August 26.

Houston, Texas and owner Robert McNair were awarded the NFL's thirty-second franchise in a vote of the NFL clubs at a league meeting in Atlanta. The team will begin play in 2002. The NFL clubs also voted to realign into eight divisions of four teams each for the 2002 season, October 6.

Walter Payton, the NFL's all-time leading rusher, died of liver cancer at the age of 45, November 1. The NFL Man of the Year Award, the only NFL award that recognizes a player for his community service activities as well as his excellence on the field, was renamed in his honor shortly after his passing.

Former NFL Commissioner Pete Rozelle, who guided a still-developing league to its position today as America's most popular sport, was named by *The Sporting News* as the most powerful person in sports in the 20th Century, December 15.

2000

New York businessman Robert Wood Johnson IV was approved by NFL clubs as the new owner of the New York Jets at a league meeting, January 18.

The St. Louis Rams won their first Super Bowl by defeating the AFC champion Tennessee Titans 23-16 in Super Bowl XXXIV at the Georgia Dome in Atlanta, January 30.

For the first time in league history, paid attendance topped 16 million for the regular season and more than 65,000 per game, an increase of 1,300 per game over 1998. Paid attendance for all NFL games increased in 1999 for the third year in a row and was the highest ever in the 80-year history of the league. It marked the first time in league history that the 20-million paid attendance mark was reached for all games in a season, March 27.

The Rhein Fire won their second World Bowl in three years, defeating the Scottish Claymores 13-10 to win World

Bowl 2000 in front of 35,680 at Frankfurt's Waldstadion, June 25.

More than 100 of the 136 living members of the Pro Football Hall of Fame gathered to celebrate Pro Football's Greatest Reunion in Canton, Ohio, July 28-31.

Paul Brown Stadium opened in Cincinnati, Ohio with a crowd of 56,180 as the Cincinnati Bengals defeated the Chicago Bears 24-20 in a preseason game, August 19.

Minnesota's Gary Anderson converted a 21-yard field goal against Buffalo to pass George Blanda as the NFL's all-time scoring leader with 2,004 points, October 22.

2001

NFL clubs approved additional league-wide revenue sharing at a special league meeting in Dallas. The teams agreed to pool the visiting team share of gate receipts for all preseason and regular-season games and divide the pool equally starting in 2002, January 17.

The Baltimore Ravens won their first Super Bowl by defeating the NFC champion New York Giants 34-7 in Super Bowl XXXV at Raymond James Stadium in Tampa Bay, January 28.

The *Sports Business Daily* named NFL Commissioner Paul Tagliabue the 2000 Sports Industrialist of the Year, February 28.

NFL owners unanimously approved a realignment plan for the league starting in 2002. With the addition of the Houston Texans, the league's 32 teams will be divided into eight four-team divisions. Seven clubs change divisions, and the Seattle Seahawks change conferences, moving from the AFC to the NFC. A new scheduling format ensures that every team meets every other team in the league at least once every four years, May 22.

The Berlin Thunder won their first World Bowl, defeating the Barcelona Dragons 24-17 to win World Bowl IX in front of 32,116 at Amsterdam ArenA, June 30.

Heinz Field opened in Pittsburgh, Pennsylvania before a crowd of 57,829 with the Pittsburgh Steelers defeating the Detroit Lions 20-7 in a pre-

season game; and INVESCO Field at Mile High opened in Denver, Colorado before a crowd of 74,063 with the Denver Broncos defeating the New Orleans Saints 31-24 in a preseason game, August 25.

President George W. Bush became the first United States President to be involved in an NFL regular-season coin toss as he helped kick off the 2001 season from the White House. Via satellite, President Bush tossed the coin for the 10 regular-season games that started at 1:00 P.M. ET, September 9.

In the wake of the September 11 terrorist attacks, Commissioner Paul Tagliabue postponed the games scheduled for September 16-17, September 13.

The league's 16-game regular season was retained when the postponed Week 2 games were rescheduled for the weekend of January 6-7, September 18.

The NFL and its game officials agreed to a new six-year Collective Bargaining Agreement, ending a two-week lockout of the regular officials, who returned to work on September 23, September 19.

The NFL announced that the league's prohibition of anabolic steroids and related substances had been strengthened to include supplements containing ephedrine and other high-risk supplements, September 27.

The NFL announced that the Super Bowl would be rescheduled from January 27 to February 3 in order to retain the full playoff format for the 2001 season. It will be the first Super Bowl played in February, October 3.

President Bush designated Super Bowl XXXVI as a "National Special Security Event," allowing all security for the game to be coordinated by the Secret Service, November 26.

2002

The NFL and the NFL Players Association agreed to a fourth extension of the 1993 Collective Bargaining Agreement through 2007, January 7.

In an AFC Wild Card matchup, the Oakland Raiders defeated the New York Jets 38-24 in the NFL's first-ever

primetime playoff game, January 12.

In a special meeting in New Orleans, NFL owners voted unanimously to approve the purchase of the Atlanta Falcons to Home Depot co-founder Arthur Blank, February 2.

The New England Patriots won their first Super Bowl by defeating the NFC champion St. Louis Rams 20-17 in Super Bowl XXXVI at the Louisiana Superdome in New Orleans. The game marked the first time in Super Bowl history that the winning points came on the final play, a 48-yard field goal by Patriots kicker Adam Vinatieri, February 3.

Tony Boselli, a five-time Pro Bowl tackle allocated by the Jacksonville Jaguars, was the first selection of the Houston Texans in the 2002 NFL Expansion Draft. The Texans selected 19 players, February 18.

The NFL and Westwood One/CBS Radio Sports announced the renewal of a multiyear agreement for Westwood One/CBS Radio Sports to continue as the exclusive network radio home of the NFL, April 9.

NFL Europe kicked off its tenth season with a record 254 players allocated by NFL clubs, April 13-14.

The Berlin Thunder became the first team to win consecutive World Bowls, defeating the Rhein Fire 26-20 to win World Bowl X in front of 53,109 fans at Rheinstadion, June 22.

Seahawks Stadium opened in Seattle, Washington with an attendance of 52,902 fans as the Indianapolis Colts defeated the Seattle Seahawks 28-10 in a preseason game, August 10.

Gillette Stadium opened in Foxboro, Massachusetts with a crowd of 68,436 fans as the New England Patriots defeated the Philadelphia Eagles 16-15 in a preseason game, August 17.

Reliant Stadium opened in Houston, Texas with 69,432 fans in attendance, the largest non-Super Bowl crowd to ever watch an NFL game in Houston as the Miami Dolphins defeated the Houston Texans 24-3 in a preseason game, August 24.

For the first time, the NFL

season kicked off on a Thursday night in prime time as the San Francisco 49ers defeated the New York Giants 16-13 at Giants Stadium. The game was preceded by "NFL Kickoff Live From Times Square," presented by New York City and the NFL, a football and music festival honoring the resilient spirit of New York and America, September 5.

Week 1 of the 2002 season produced the highest-scoring and most competitive Kickoff Weekend in NFL history. The 16 games averaged 49.3 points per game. A total of 788 points and 89 touchdowns were scored, the most in league history for an opening weekend. Eleven of the 16 games were decided by one score (eight points or less), a Kickoff Weekend record, September 5-9.

Oakland Raiders wide receiver Jerry Rice became the all-time leader in yards from scrimmage, surpassing Pro Football Hall of Fame running back Walter Payton (21,281 yards), September 29.

Cleveland Browns owner Al Lerner, the NFL Finance Committee Chairman and Chairman and CEO of MBNA Corporation, died at the age of 69, October 23.

Dallas Cowboys running back Emmitt Smith became the NFL's all-time rushing leader, surpassing Pro Football Hall of Fame running back Walter Payton (16,726 yards), October 27.

The NFL and NFLPA announced the creation of USA Football, the first national advocacy organization representing all levels of amateur football, December 5.

NFL clubs implemented an expanded program to promote diversity in their coaching and front office ranks based upon recommendations of the NFL Committee on Workplace Diversity, December 19. The committee, appointed by Commissioner Tagliabue on October 31, comprised 10 owners and team executives with Pittsburgh Steelers owner Dan Rooney serving as chairman.

The 2002 season concluded with 25 overtime games, the most in NFL history, December 30.

2003

The Tampa Bay Buccaneers won their first Super Bowl by defeating the AFC champion Oakland Raiders 48-21 in Super Bowl XXXVII at Qualcomm Stadium in San Diego, January 26.

Chicago Bears chairman emeritus Edward W. McCaskey died at the age of 83, April 8.

The Frankfurt Galaxy became the first team to win three World Bowls, defeating the Rhein Fire 35-16 to win World Bowl XI in front of 28,138 fans at Hampden Park, June 14.

Tex Schramm, the legendary team president and general manager of the Dallas Cowboys and a member of the Pro Football Hall of Fame, died at the age of 83, July 15.

Lincoln Financial Field opened in Philadelphia, Pennsylvania with an attendance of 66,279 fans as the New England Patriots defeated the Philadelphia Eagles 24-12 in a preseason game, August 22.

A renovated Lambeau Field opened in Green Bay, Wisconsin with a crowd of 69,831 fans as the Carolina Panthers defeated the Green Bay Packers 20-7 in a preseason game, August 23.

A renovated Soldier Field opened in Chicago, Illinois with an attendance of 61,500 fans as the Green Bay Packers defeated the Chicago Bears 38-23 in a regular season game on ABC's *NFL Monday Night Football*, September 29.

NFL Network, the first 24-hour, year-round television channel dedicated to the NFL and the sport of football, launched on DirecTV, November 4.

2004

The New England Patriots won their second Super Bowl in three years by defeating the NFC champion Carolina Panthers 32-29 in Super Bowl XXXVIII at Reliant Stadium in Houston, February 1.

By a vote of 29-3, NFL owners extended the instant replay system for another five seasons through 2008, March 30.

Steve Bisciotti took over as the controlling owner of the Baltimore Ravens, succeeding Art Modell, who operated the

franchise for 43 years, April 8.

Former Arizona Cardinals safety Pat Tillman was killed in a firefight while on combat patrol with the U.S. Army Rangers in Afghanistan, April 22.

A federal appeals court formally ruled in favor of the NFL's draft eligibility rule in Maurice Clarett's lawsuit, citing federal labor policy in permitting the NFL and the Players Association to set rules for when players can enter the league, May 24.

The Berlin Thunder defeated the Frankfurt Galaxy 30-24 to win World Bowl XII in front of 35,413 fans at Arena AufSchalke, June 12.

The New England Patriots defeated the New York Jets 13-7 for their NFL-record 18th consecutive regular-season victory, October 24.

The NFL reached an agreement on six-year contract extensions with two of its network television partners—CBS and FOX—to run through the 2011 season, November 8.

The NFL and DirecTV announced a five-year extension on the NFL Sunday Ticket subscription television package to run through the 2010 season, November 8.

NFL Europe named the Hamburg Sea Devils as the league's newest team, November 24.

2005

Indianapolis Colts quarterback Peyton Manning set the NFL single-season record with 49 touchdown passes, January 2.

The New England Patriots became the second team in NFL history to win three Super Bowls in four seasons by defeating the Philadelphia Eagles 24-21 in Super Bowl XXXIX at ALLTEL Stadium in Jacksonville, February 6.

The Pat Tillman USO Center opened in Afghanistan. The NFL donated $250,000 to the USO to honor the memory of the former Arizona Cardinals player who died in Afghanistan while serving in the U.S. Army, April 1.

The NFL reached long-term agreements for its Sunday and Monday primetime TV packages. NBC returned to the NFL by acquiring the Sunday night

package for six years (2006-2011). ESPN agreed on an eight-year deal to televise *Monday Night Football* from 2006-2013, April 18.

The NFL strengthened its steroids program by adopting the Olympic testosterone testing standard, tripling the number of times a player can be randomly tested during the offseason from two to six, adding substances to the list of banned substances, and putting new language in the policy to allow for testing of designer drugs and other substances that may have evaded detection, April 27.

NFL owners voted unanimously to approve the sale of the Minnesota Vikings to real-estate developer Zygi Wilf, May 25.

The Amsterdam Admirals defeated the Berlin Thunder 27-21 to win World Bowl XIII in front of 35,134 fans at LTU Arena in Düsseldorf, Germany, June 11.

The NFL designated September 18-19 as "Hurricane Relief Weekend," which concluded with a telethon in conjunction with a Monday Night Football doubleheader on ABC and ESPN. The New York Giants-New Orleans Saints game, originally scheduled for the Louisiana Superdome, was moved to Giants Stadium following Hurricane Katrina. In total, the NFL, its owners, teams, players, and fans contributed $21 million to aid the Hurricane Katrina rebuilding effort, September 19.

An NFL record 103,467 fans attended the Arizona Cardinals' 31-14 victory over the San Francisco 49ers at Mexico City's Azteca Stadium, the first-ever regular-season NFL game played outside the United States, October 2.

Wellington Mara, the New York Giants' president and co-chief executive officer, died at the age of 89, October 25.

Preston Robert Tisch, the Giants' chairman and co-chief executive officer, died at the age of 79, November 15.

2006

The NFL announced that NFL Network would begin airing a "Road To The Playoffs" package of eight primetime regular season NFL games starting in 2006, January 28.

The Pittsburgh Steelers won their fifth Super Bowl, defeating the Seattle Seahawks 21-10 in Super Bowl XL at Ford Field in Detroit, Michigan, February 5.

The NFL clubs approved an extension of the Collective Bargaining Agreement through 2012, March 8.

Commissioner Tagliabue announced his decision to retire by the end of July. The NFL enjoyed an era of unrivaled prosperity in the Tagliabue Era, including labor peace throughout his 17-year tenure, March 20.

NFL clubs unanimously decided to return the name of the official game ball to "The Duke" in honor of the late New York Giants owner Wellington Mara, March 27.

The Amsterdam Admirals defeated the Berlin Thunder 22-7 to win World Bowl XIV in front of 36,286 fans at LTU Arena in Düsseldorf, Germany, May 27.

Roger Goodell became the eighth chief executive of the NFL on August 8 when he was chosen to succeed Paul Tagliabue as commissioner by a unanimous vote of the clubs at a three-day meeting in Chicago, Illinois. The transfer from Commissioner Tagliabue to Commissioner Goodell took place at 6:00 A.M. on Friday, September 1.

Cardinals Stadium opened in Glendale, Arizona with a crowd of 63,400 fans on August 12 as the Arizona Cardinals defeated the Pittsburgh Steelers 21-13 in a preseason game. The facility was later renamed University of Phoenix Stadium on September 26.

President George W. Bush signed into law HR 4954, which included the Internet Gambling Prohibition and Enforcement Act. The bill prohibits online gamblers from using credit cards, checks and electronic fund transfers to place and settle bets, strengthening enforcement of federal and state gambling laws that had been evaded by overseas gambling operations using the Internet, October 13.

NFL owners approved a resolution to stage a limited number of international regular-season games—up to two per season—beginning in 2007 and continuing through

2011, October 24.

The NFL Network broadcast its first-ever regular-season game as the Kansas City Chiefs defeated the Denver Broncos 19-10 at Arrowhead Stadium on Thanksgiving night, November 23.

San Diego Chargers running back LaDainian Tomlinson set the NFL single-season record for touchdowns with 29 on December 10. He finished the season with 31 touchdowns and also set a single-season record for points with 186.

Lamar Hunt, founder of the Kansas City Chiefs and the American Football League, died at the age of 74, December 13.

2007

The Indianapolis Colts won their second Super Bowl, defeating the Chicago Bears 29-17 in Super Bowl XLI at Dolphin Stadium in South Florida, February 4. Both teams were coached by African-Americans: Tony Dungy of the Colts and Lovie Smith of the Bears.

NFL clubs approved additional league-wide revenue sharing at a league meeting in Phoenix, Arizona. The teams agreed to redistribute up to $430 million over a four-year span, retroactive to 2006, March 26.

The NFL announced changes to its long-standing personal conduct policy and programs for players, coaches, and other team and league employees. The modifications focus on expanded educational and support programs in addition to increased levels of discipline for violations of the policy, April 10.

The NFL, NFL Players Association, NFL Retired Players Association, NFL Alumni Association, NFL Charities and Pro Football Hall of Fame formed the first-ever Alliance to coordinate medical support services for former players, May 22.

The Hamburg Sea Devils defeated the Frankfurt Galaxy 37-28 to win World Bowl XV in front of 48,125 fans at Commerzbank-Arena in Frankfurt, Germany, June 23.

The NFL announced it will focus its international business strategy on reaching the

widest possible global audience, including the staging of international regular-season games, and discontinued NFL Europa after 15 seasons of operation, June 29.

NFL owners unanimously approved $10 million in additional Alliance funding for retired players to help pay for joint replacement surgeries and other medical assistance, supplementing the initial $7 million committed in July by Alliance members, October 24.

The New York Giants defeated the Miami Dolphins 13-10 at London's in front of 81,176 fans at Wembley Stadium in the first regular-season game played outside of North America, October 28.

On the field in the 2007 season, many significant records and milestones were achieved: Green Bay quarterback Brett Favre surpassed Pro Football Hall of Famer Dan Marino in both passing categories—touchdowns and yards—to become the NFL's all-time career leader. Patriots quarterback Tom Brady set the single-season record with 50 touchdown passes, including 23 to wide receiver Randy Moss—also a record. New England, which became the first team ever to finish 16-0 in the regular season, scored a record 589 points.

2008

The NFL, United States Olympic Committee, United States Anti-Doping Agency and MLB announced a partnership to form a clean competition anti-doping research collaborative, January 10.

Georgia Frontiere, majority owner of the St. Louis Rams, died at the age of 80, January 18.

The NFL announced it will stage a regular-season game in the United Kingdom during each of the next three seasons, beginning with the New Orleans Saints hosting the San Diego Chargers on October 26, 2008 at London's Wembley Stadium, February 1.

The New York Giants scored with 35 seconds remaining to win their third Super Bowl, defeating the New England Patriots 17-14 in Super Bowl XLII at University of Phoenix Stadium in Glen-

dale, Arizona, February 3.

The NFL set an all-time paid attendance record in 2007 for the sixth consecutive season. Attendance for all 2007 games was 22,256,502, an increase of 56,790 over the previous mark. The Washington Redskins set an all-time NFL regular-season home paid attendance record of 711,471 for eight games, breaking their own record of 708,852 in 2006.

NFL clubs voted unanimously to exercise their option to shorten by two years the current Collective Bargaining Agreement, which now will run through the 2010 season and 2011 NFL Draft, May 20.

Lucas Oil Stadium opened in Indianapolis, Indiana with a crowd of 65,333 as the Buffalo Bills defeated the Indianapolis Colts by a score of 20-7 in a preseason game, August 24.

The NFL established a new fan code of conduct to help support a positive fan environment at all NFL stadiums, August 5.

NFLPA Executive Director and Pro Football Hall of Famer Gene Upshaw died at the age of 63, August 20.

For the first time, an NFL game was broadcast on NBC and also streamed live in its entirety to fans on the Internet via NFL.com and NBCSports.com as the Giants beat the Redskins 16-7 in the 2009 NFL Kickoff game, September 4.

Owners approved a restructured ownership plan for the Pittsburgh Steelers that will keep the team under the control of chairman Dan Rooney and team president Art Rooney II, December 17.

The NFL announced that the 2010 Pro Bowl will be played a week prior to Super Bowl XLIV on Sunday, January 31, 2010. Both games will be played in South Florida, December 30.

In the 256 regular-season games of 2008, 44.1 points per game were scored—the highest average since 1970.

2009

Stephen M. Ross purchased an additional 45 percent of the Miami Dolphins from Wayne Huizenga and became the team's managing partner. Coupled with his April 1, 2008 purchase of 50 percent of the franchise, the stadium, and the excess developable land, Ross now owns 95 percent of the Dolphins and the stadium while Huizenga retains a five percent share of both and remains a 50 percent partner in that land, January 20.

The NFL re-named its minority coaching internship program the Bill Walsh NFL Minority Coaching Fellowship, honoring the Pro Football Hall of Fame coach who conceived of the program, January 29.

The Pittsburgh Steelers scored a touchdown with 42 seconds remaining to claim their NFL-record sixth Super Bowl title, defeating the Arizona Cardinals 27-23 in Super Bowl XLIII at Raymond James Stadium in Tampa Bay, February 1.

The NFL and Westwood One announced a new two-year agreement for Westwood One to continue as the exclusive network radio partner of the NFL, March 12.

The NFLPA selected Washington-based attorney DeMaurice Smith as its new executive director, March 16.

The NFL and DIRECTV announced an agreement to extend DIRECTV's rights to carry NFL Sunday Ticket through the 2014 season, March 23.

The NFL reached an agreement on two-year contract extensions with two of its network television partners – CBS and FOX – to run through the 2013 season, May 19.

The NFL extended by two years its broadcast partnership with NBC to televise the Sunday night package through the 2013 season, August 19.

Cowboys Stadium opened in Arlington, Texas with a crowd of 75,720 as the Dallas Cowboys defeated the Tennessee Titans by a score of 30-10 in a preseason game, August 21.

The NFL announced games that were blacked out in home team markets during the 2009 season would be shown on NFL.com in their entirety on a delayed basis, September 10.

The NFL launched a new "Red Zone Channel," offering fans crucial live action cut-ins of all Sunday afternoon games, September 13.

Pro Football Hall of Fame head coach and broadcaster John Madden was appointed special advisor to Commissioner Goodell, September 10.

NFL appointed former head coach Tony Dungy to lead a new NFL Player Advisory Forum and serve as a special advisor to Commissioner Goodell, November 19.

Commissioner Goodell notified NFL teams of new and expanded guidelines on return-to-play for any player who sustains a concussion, December 2.

2010

For the first time, the Pro Bowl was played in the Super Bowl city the week before the Super Bowl, as the AFC All-Stars beat the NFC All-Stars 41-34 in the 2010 Pro Bowl at Sun Life Stadium in South Florida. The game drew 70,697 fans – the highest attendance for a Pro Bowl since 1959, January 31.

The New Orleans Saints won their first Super Bowl title, defeating the Indianapolis Colts 31-17 in Super Bowl XLIV at Sun Life Stadium in South Florida, February 7.

Dr. Hunt Batjer of Northwestern University Feinberg School of Medicine and Dr. Richard G. Ellenbogen of the University of Washington School of Medicine were named the new co-chairs of the NFL Head, Neck and Spine Medical Committee, March 16.

NFL owners voted to amend postseason overtime rules to a modified sudden death format, guaranteeing at least one possession for each club if the receiving team fails to score a touchdown on its first overtime possession, March 23.

The NFL and NFL Alumni Association announced a new neurological care program for retired players, one of a series of NFL initiatives addressing the quality of life of retired players, March 24.

NFL rules changes emphasized additional player safety. Protection for defenseless players was standardized and expanded, protecting a player who has just completed a catch from blows to the head or neck by an opponent who launches. Additional protection was also given to longsnappers. Play will now stop if a ball carrier's helmet is removed, March 24.

The NFL Draft debuted a new three-day format, with the first two days broadcast in primetime. A record combined total of 45.4 million viewers tuned in to watch the 75th NFL Draft on NFL Network, ESPN and ESPN2, April 22-24.

New Meadowlands Stadium opened in East Rutherford, New Jersey as the New York Giants defeat the New York Jets by a score of 31-16 in a preseason game, August 16.

Stan Kroenke purchased an additional 60 percent of the St. Louis Rams from the Rosenbloom family and became the team's sole owner and chairman, August 25.

A renovated Arrowhead Stadium opened in Kansas City, Missouri as the Philadelphia Eagles defeated the Kansas City Chiefs 20-17 in a preseason game, August 27.

A poster created by the NFL and the Centers for Disease Control and Prevention (CDC) to help educate young athletes on concussions was released to the public. The poster, similar to one on display in NFL locker rooms, stresses the importance of recognizing a concussion, taking time to recover, and not returning to play too soon, October 11.

The NFL, NFL Alumni and Gay Culverhouse Players' Outreach Program announced a partnership to expand services for retired NFL players. The outreach program identifies retired players in need, ensuring they receive comprehensive medical evaluations and assistance in applying for the expanded benefits and services created in recent years by the NFL, October 12.

Commissioner Roger Goodell notified NFL teams that more significant discipline, including suspensions, would be imposed on players that strike an opponent in the head or neck area in violation of the rules, October 20.

The NFL and Westwood One Radio announced the renewal of a multi-year agreement for Westwood One to continue as the exclusive network radio home of the NFL, December 22.

2011

The NFL appointed Pro Football Hall of Famers Ronnie Lott and John Madden as co-chairs of a new Player Safety Advisory Panel. The panel provides recommendations on a variety of safety-related football matters, while taking a long-term view towards making the game safer at every level of the sport, January 4.

The Green Bay Packers won their fourth Super Bowl title, defeating the Pittsburgh Steelers 31-25 in Super Bowl XLV at Cowboys Stadium in North Texas, February 6.

The NFL Head, Neck and Spine Committee announced a new standardized sideline concussion assessment protocol for team medical personnel. The new protocol includes a symptom checklist, limited neurologic examination and balance assessment, February 25.

On the steps of the Pro Football Hall of Fame in Canton, Ohio, Commissioner Goodell & NFLPA Executive Director DeMaurice Smith formally announced a comprehensive settlement of litigation and signed a new 10-year Collective Bargaining Agreement, August 4. The agreement included additional funding for player alumni of $1 billion, including a $620 million "Legacy Fund" to increase benefits for pre-1993 retirees.

A record 107.4 million fans tuned into Kickoff Weekend games on CBS, ESPN, FOX and NBC, September 8, 11-12.

The NFL announced an eight-year extension of its contract with ESPN for the broadcast rights to Monday Night Football through the 2021 season, September 8.

NFL teams, players and fans remembered the courage and resilience that followed the events of September 11, 2001 with special tributes in each stadium and on television during all games on Sunday, September 11.

Al Davis, the Oakland Raiders' owner and Pro Football Hall of Famer, died at the age of 82, October 8.

NFL owners approved a resolution to continue playing regular-season games in the United Kingdom through the 2016 season, October 11.

The NFL reached an agreement on nine-year contract extensions of its Sunday broadcast television packages with CBS, FOX and NBC to run through the 2022 season,

December 14. The agreements also enabled the NFL to expand its Thursday night package of games on NFL Network, which increased from eight to 13 games for the 2012 season.

NFL clubs unanimously approved the majority ownership transfer of the Jacksonville Jaguars from Wayne Weaver to businessman Shahid Khan at a meeting in Dallas, December 14.

On the field, many all-time records were set: 11,356 points were scored, the most of any season in NFL history; New Orleans' Drew Brees passed for 5,476 yards; and Green Bay's Aaron Rodgers led the league with a 122.5 passer rating.

2012

NFL clubs extended Commissioner Goodell's contract through March 31, 2019, January 25.

The New York Giants won their fourth Super Bowl title, defeating the New England Patriots 21-17 in Super Bowl XLVI at Lucas Oil Stadium in Indianapolis, February 5.

The NFL announced a new comprehensive health program, NFL Total Wellness, for former and current players to provide additional resources for physical and mental health issues, July 26.

Art Modell, former owner of the Cleveland Browns-Baltimore Ravens franchise and longtime chairman of the NFL's Broadcast Committee, died at the age of 87, September 6.

NFL Network's *Thursday Night Football* schedule was expanded from eight to 13 regular-season games, debuting with the Green Bay Packers' 23-10 victory against the Chicago Bears, September 13.

The NFL announced an extension of its exclusive radio broadcast agreement with Dial Global through the 2017 season, September 20.

NFL Films President Steve Sabol died at the age of 69, September 18.

The NFL and its game officials agreed to a new eight-year Collective Bargaining Agreement, ending a four-month dispute. The union officials returned to work for Week 4, September 27.

NFL clubs unanimously approved the majority ownership transfer of the Cleveland Browns from Randy Lerner to Jimmy Haslam at a meeting in Chicago, October 16.

The NFL announced the formation of the National Football League Foundation to focus on youth football, health and safety, and community, December 12. The newly created Foundation resulted from the restructuring of the NFL's previous charitable arms – NFL Charities and the NFL Youth Football Fund.

2013

The Baltimore Ravens won their second Super Bowl, defeating the San Francisco 49ers 34-31 in Super Bowl XLVII at the Mercedes-Benz Superdome in New Orleans. The game was viewed by 164.1 million people, making it the most-watched program in U.S. television history, February 3.

GE and the NFL announced the Head Health Initiative, a four-year, $60 million collaboration to advance diagnostic tools for treating concussions and the development of new materials for head protection, March 11.

NFL COMMISSIONERS AND PRESIDENTS*

1920	Jim Thorpe, President
1921-39	Joe Carr, President
1939-41	Carl Storck, President
1941-46	Elmer Layden, Commissioner
1946-1959	Bert Bell, Commissioner
1960-1989	Pete Rozelle, Commissioner
1989-2006	Paul Tagliabue, Commissioner
2006-present	Roger Goodell, Commissioner

NFL treasurer Austin Gunsel served as president in the office of the commissioner following the death of Bert Bell (Oct. 11, 1959) until the election of Pete Rozelle (Jan. 26, 1960).

2012

AMERICAN CONFERENCE

East Division

	W	L	T	Pct.	Pts.	OP
New England	12	4	0	.750	557	331
Miami	7	9	0	.438	288	317
New York Jets	6	10	0	.375	281	375
Buffalo	6	10	0	.375	344	435

North Division

	W	L	T	Pct.	Pts.	OP
Baltimore	10	6	0	.625	398	344
Cincinnati*	10	6	0	.625	391	320
Pittsburgh	8	8	0	.500	336	314
Cleveland	5	11	0	.313	302	368

South Division

	W	L	T	Pct.	Pts.	OP
Houston	12	4	0	.750	416	331
Indianapolis*	11	5	0	.688	357	387
Tennessee	6	10	0	.375	330	471
Jacksonville	2	14	0	.125	255	444

West Division

	W	L	T	Pct.	Pts.	OP
Denver#	13	3	0	.813	481	289
San Diego	7	9	0	.438	350	350
Oakland	4	12	0	.250	290	443
Kansas City	2	14	0	.125	211	425

NATIONAL CONFERENCE

East Division

	W	L	T	Pct.	Pts.	OP
Washington	10	6	0	.625	436	388
New York Giants	9	7	0	.563	429	344
Dallas	8	8	0	.500	376	400
Philadelphia	4	12	0	.250	280	444

North Division

	W	L	T	Pct.	Pts.	OP
Green Bay	11	5	0	.688	433	336
Minnesota*	10	6	0	.625	379	348
Chicago	10	6	0	.625	375	277
Detroit	4	12	0	.250	372	437

South Division

	W	L	T	Pct.	Pts.	OP
Atlanta#	13	3	0	.813	419	299
Carolina	7	9	0	.438	357	363
New Orleans	7	9	0	.438	461	454
Tampa Bay	7	9	0	.438	389	394

West Division

	W	L	T	Pct.	Pts.	OP
San Francisco	11	4	1	.719	397	273
Seattle*	11	5	0	.688	412	245
St. Louis	7	8	1	.469	299	348
Arizona	5	11	0	.313	250	357

2011

AMERICAN CONFERENCE

East Division

	W	L	T	Pct.	Pts.	OP
New England#	13	3	0	.813	513	342
New York Jets	8	8	0	.500	377	363
Miami	6	10	0	.375	329	313
Buffalo	6	10	0	.375	372	434

North Division

	W	L	T	Pct.	Pts.	OP
Baltimore	12	4	0	.750	378	266
Pittsburgh*	12	4	0	.750	325	227
Cincinnati*	9	7	0	.563	344	323
Cleveland	4	12	0	.250	218	307

South Division

	W	L	T	Pct.	Pts.	OP
Houston	10	6	0	.625	381	278
Tennessee	9	7	0	.563	325	317
Jacksonville	5	11	0	.313	243	329
Indianapolis	2	14	0	.125	243	430

West Division

	W	L	T	Pct.	Pts.	OP
Denver	8	8	0	.500	309	390
San Diego	8	8	0	.500	406	377
Oakland	8	8	0	.500	359	433
Kansas City	7	9	0	.438	212	338

NATIONAL CONFERENCE

East Division

	W	L	T	Pct.	Pts.	OP
New York Giants	9	7	0	.563	394	400
Philadelphia	8	8	0	.500	396	328
Dallas	8	8	0	.500	369	347
Washington	5	11	0	.313	288	367

North Division

	W	L	T	Pct.	Pts.	OP
Green Bay#	15	1	0	.938	560	359
Detroit*	10	6	0	.625	474	387
Chicago	8	8	0	.500	353	341
Minnesota	3	13	0	.188	340	449

South Division

	W	L	T	Pct.	Pts.	OP
New Orleans	13	3	0	.813	547	339
Atlanta*	10	6	0	.625	402	350
Carolina	6	10	0	.375	406	429
Tampa Bay	4	12	0	.250	287	494

West Division

	W	L	T	Pct.	Pts.	OP
San Francisco	13	3	0	.813	380	229
Arizona	8	8	0	.500	312	348
Seattle	7	9	0	.438	321	315
St. Louis	2	14	0	.125	193	407

2012 notes

*Wild Card qualifier for playoffs; #Top playoff seed in conference

New York Jets finished ahead of Buffalo based on better record in common games (5-7 to Bills' 3-9). Baltimore finished ahead of Cincinnati based on better division record (4-2 to Bengals' 3-3). New England finished ahead of Houston based on head-to-head victory. Minnesota finished ahead of Chicago based on better division record (4-2 to Bears' 3-3). Carolina finished ahead of New Orleans and Tampa Bay based on better record against common opponents than Tampa Bay (6-4 to Buccaneers' 5-5) and head-to-head sweep over the Saints. New Orleans finished ahead of Tampa Bay based on head-to-head sweep.

Wild Card Playoff Games: HOUSTON 19, Cincinnati 13; BALTIMORE 24, Indianapolis 9

Divisional Playoff Games: NEW ENGLAND 41, Houston 28; Baltimore 38, DENVER 35 (2 OT)

AFC Championship Game: Baltimore 28, NEW ENGLAND 13

Wild Card Playoff Games: GREEN BAY 24, Minnesota 10; Seattle 24, WASHINGTON 14

Divisional Playoff Games: ATLANTA 30, Seattle 28; SAN FRANCISCO 45, Green Bay 31

NFC Championship Game: San Francisco 28, ATLANTA 24

Super Bowl XLVII: Baltimore (AFC) 34, San Francisco (NFC) 31 at Mercedes-Benz Superdome, New Orleans, Louisiana

In Past Standings section, home teams in playoff games are indicated by capital letters.

Playoff Seeds

AFC	NFC
1. Denver	1. Atlanta
2. New England	2. **San Francisco**
3. Houston	3. Green Bay
4. **Baltimore**	4. Washington
5. Indianapolis	5. Seattle
6. Cincinnati	6. Minnesota

2011 notes

*Wild Card qualifier for playoffs; #Top playoff seed in conference

Miami finished ahead of Buffalo based on head-to-head sweep. Baltimore finished ahead of Pittsburgh based on head-to-head sweep. Denver finished ahead of San Diego and Oakland based on best record in common games (Denver 5-5; Oakland 4-6; San Diego 4-6). San Diego finished ahead of Oakland based on better conference record (7-5 to Raiders' 6-6). Cincinnati finished ahead of Tennessee based on head-to-head victory. Philadelphia finished ahead of Dallas based on head-to-head sweep. Atlanta finished ahead of Detroit based on head-to-head victory. San Francisco finished ahead of New Orleans based on better conference record (10-2 to Saints' 9-3).

Wild Card Playoff Games: HOUSTON 31, Cincinnati 10; DENVER 29, Pittsburgh 23 (OT)

Divisional Playoff Games: NEW ENGLAND 45, Denver 10; BALTIMORE 20, Houston 13

AFC Championship Game: NEW ENGLAND 23, Baltimore 20

Wild Card Playoff Games: NEW ORLEANS 45, Detroit 28; NEW YORK GIANTS 24, Atlanta 2

Divisional Playoff Games: SAN FRANCISCO 36, New Orleans 32; New York Giants 37, GREEN BAY 20

NFC Championship Game: New York Giants 20, SAN FRANCISCO 17 (OT)

Super Bowl XLVI: New York Giants (NFC) 21, New England (AFC) 17 at Lucas Oil Stadium, Indianapolis

Playoff Seeds

AFC	NFC
1. New England	1. Green Bay
2. Baltimore	2. San Francisco
3. Houston	3. New Orleans
4. Denver	4. **New York Giants**
5. Pittsburgh	5. Atlanta
6. Cincinnati	6. Detroit

2010

AMERICAN CONFERENCE

East Division

	W	L	T	Pct.	Pts.	OP
New England#	14	2	0	.875	518	313
New York Jets*	11	5	0	.688	367	304
Miami	7	9	0	.438	273	333
Buffalo	4	12	0	.250	283	425

North Division

	W	L	T	Pct.	Pts.	OP
Pittsburgh	12	4	0	.750	375	232
Baltimore*	12	4	0	.750	357	270
Cleveland	5	11	0	.313	271	332
Cincinnati	4	12	0	.250	322	395

South Division

	W	L	T	Pct.	Pts.	OP
Indianapolis	10	6	0	.625	435	388
Jacksonville	8	8	0	.500	353	419
Houston	6	10	0	.375	390	427
Tennessee	6	10	0	.375	356	339

West Division

	W	L	T	Pct.	Pts.	OP
Kansas City	10	6	0	.625	366	326
San Diego	9	7	0	.563	441	322
Oakland	8	8	0	.500	410	371
Denver	4	12	0	.250	344	471

NATIONAL CONFERENCE

East Division

	W	L	T	Pct.	Pts.	OP
Philadelphia	10	6	0	.625	439	377
New York Giants	10	6	0	.625	394	347
Dallas	6	10	0	.375	394	436
Washington	6	10	0	.375	302	377

North Division

	W	L	T	Pct.	Pts.	OP
Chicago	11	5	0	.688	334	286
Green Bay*	10	6	0	.625	388	240
Detroit	6	10	0	.375	362	369
Minnesota	6	10	0	.375	281	348

South Division

	W	L	T	Pct.	Pts.	OP
Atlanta#	13	3	0	.813	414	288
New Orleans*	11	5	0	.688	384	307
Tampa Bay	10	6	0	.625	341	318
Carolina	2	14	0	.125	196	408

West Division

	W	L	T	Pct.	Pts.	OP
Seattle	7	9	0	.438	310	407
St. Louis	7	9	0	.438	289	328
San Francisco	6	10	0	.375	305	346
Arizona	5	11	0	.313	289	434

*Wild Card qualifier for playoffs; #Top playoff seed in conference
Pittsburgh finished ahead of Baltimore based on better division record (5-1 to 4-2). Indianapolis finished ahead of Kansas City based on head-to-head victory. Houston finished ahead of Tennessee based on better division record (3-3 to 2-4). Philadelphia finished ahead of the Giants based on head-to-head sweep. Dallas finished ahead of Washington based on better division record (3-3 to 2-4). Green Bay finished ahead of the Giants and Tampa Bay based on best strength of victory Green Bay .475; Giants .400; Tampa Bay .344). Detroit finished ahead of Minnesota based on better division record (2-4 to 1-5). Seattle finished ahead of St. Louis based on better division record (4-2 to 3-3).

Wild Card Playoff Games: N.Y. Jets 17, INDIANAPOLIS 16; Baltimore 30, KANSAS CITY 7

Divisional Playoff Games: PITTSBURGH 31, Baltimore 24; N.Y. Jets 28, NEW ENGLAND 21

AFC Championship Game: PITTSBURGH 24, N.Y. Jets 19

Wild Card Playoff Games: SEATTLE 41, New Orleans 36; Green Bay 21, PHILADELPHIA 16

Divisional Playoff Games: Green Bay 48, ATLANTA 21; CHICAGO 35, Seattle 24

NFC Championship Game: Green Bay 21, CHICAGO 14

Super Bowl XLV: Green Bay (NFC) 31, Pittsburgh (AFC) 25 at Cowboys Stadium, North Texas

Playoff Seeds

AFC	NFC
1. New England	1. Atlanta
2. Pittsburgh	2. Chicago
3. Indianapolis	3. Philadelphia
4. Kansas City	4. Seattle
5. Baltimore	5. New Orleans
6. N.Y. Jets	6. Green Bay

2009

AMERICAN CONFERENCE

East Division

	W	L	T	Pct.	Pts.	OP
New England	10	6	0	.625	427	285
New York Jets*	9	7	0	.563	348	236
Miami	7	9	0	.438	360	390
Buffalo	6	10	0	.375	258	326

North Division

	W	L	T	Pct.	Pts.	OP
Cincinnati	10	6	0	.625	305	291
Baltimore*	9	7	0	.563	391	261
Pittsburgh	9	7	0	.563	368	324
Cleveland	5	11	0	.313	245	375

South Division

	W	L	T	Pct.	Pts.	OP
Indianapolis#	14	2	0	.875	416	307
Houston	9	7	0	.563	388	333
Tennessee	8	8	0	.500	354	402
Jacksonville	7	9	0	.438	290	380

West Division

	W	L	T	Pct.	Pts.	OP
San Diego	13	3	0	.813	454	320
Denver	8	8	0	.500	326	324
Oakland	5	11	0	.313	197	379
Kansas City	4	12	0	.250	294	424

NATIONAL CONFERENCE

East Division

	W	L	T	Pct.	Pts.	OP
Dallas	11	5	0	.688	361	250
Philadelphia*	11	5	0	.688	429	337
New York Giants	8	8	0	.500	402	427
Washington	4	12	0	.250	266	336

North Division

	W	L	T	Pct.	Pts.	OP
Minnesota	12	4	0	.750	470	312
Green Bay*	11	5	0	.688	461	297
Chicago	7	9	0	.438	327	375
Detroit	2	14	0	.125	262	494

South Division

	W	L	T	Pct.	Pts.	OP
New Orleans#	13	3	0	.813	510	341
Atlanta	9	7	0	.563	363	325
Carolina	8	8	0	.500	315	308
Tampa Bay	3	13	0	.188	244	400

West Division

	W	L	T	Pct.	Pts.	OP
Arizona	10	6	0	.625	375	325
San Francisco	8	8	0	.500	330	281
Seattle	5	11	0	.313	280	390
St. Louis	1	15	0	.063	175	436

*Wild Card qualifier for playoffs; #Top playoff seed in conference
New England finished ahead of Cincinnati based on better strength of victory (.450 to Bengals' .438). Baltimore finished ahead of Pittsburgh based on better division record (3-3 to Steelers' 2-4). New York Jets finished ahead of Baltimore for first Wild Card based on better record vs. common opponents (4-1 to Ravens' 1-4) and ahead of Houston based on better conference record (7-5 to Texans' 6-6). Baltimore was second Wild Card based on better conference record than Houston (7-5 to Texans' 6-6). Dallas finished ahead of Philadelphia based on head-to-head sweep (2-0). Green Bay was first Wild Card ahead of Philadelphia based on better record vs. common opponents (4-1 to Eagles' 3-2).

Wild Card Playoff: New York Jets 24, CINCINNATI 14; Baltimore 33, NEW ENGLAND 14

Divisional Playoff: INDIANAPOLIS 20, Baltimore 3; New York Jets 17, SAN DIEGO 14

AFC Championship: INDIANAPOLIS 30, New York Jets 17

Wild Card Playoff: DALLAS 34, Philadelphia 14; ARIZONA 51, Green Bay 45 (OT)

Divisional Playoff Games: NEW ORLEANS 45, Arizona 14; MINNESOTA 34, Dallas 3

NFC Championship Game: NEW ORLEANS 31, Minnesota 28 (OT)

Super Bowl XLIV: New Orleans (NFC) 31, Indianapolis (AFC) 17 at Sun Life Stadium, South Florida

Playoff Seeds

AFC	NFC
1. Indianapolis	1. New Orleans
2. San Diego	2. Minnesota
3. New England	3. Dallas
4. Cincinnati	4. Arizona
5. New York Jets	5. Green Bay
6. Baltimore	6. Philadelphia

2008

AMERICAN CONFERENCE

East Division

	W	L	T	Pct.	Pts.	OP
Miami	11	5	0	.688	345	317
New England	11	5	0	.688	410	309
New York Jets	9	7	0	.563	405	356
Buffalo	7	9	0	.438	336	342

North Division

	W	L	T	Pct.	Pts.	OP
Pittsburgh	12	4	0	.750	347	223
Baltimore*	11	5	0	.688	385	244
Cincinnati	4	11	1	.281	204	364
Cleveland	4	12	0	.250	232	350

South Division

	W	L	T	Pct.	Pts.	OP
Tennessee#	13	3	0	.813	375	234
Indianapolis*	12	4	0	.750	377	298
Houston	8	8	0	.500	366	394
Jacksonville	5	11	0	.313	302	367

West Division

	W	L	T	Pct.	Pts.	OP
San Diego	8	8	0	.500	439	347
Denver	8	8	0	.500	370	448
Oakland	5	11	0	.313	263	388
Kansas City	2	14	0	.125	291	440

NATIONAL CONFERENCE

East Division

	W	L	T	Pct.	Pts.	OP
New York Giants#	12	4	0	.750	427	294
Philadelphia*	9	6	1	.594	416	289
Dallas	9	7	0	.563	362	365
Washington	8	8	0	.500	265	296

North Division

	W	L	T	Pct.	Pts.	OP
Minnesota	10	6	0	.625	379	333
Chicago	9	7	0	.563	375	350
Green Bay	6	10	0	.375	419	380
Detroit	0	16	0	.000	268	517

South Division

	W	L	T	Pct.	Pts.	OP
Carolina	12	4	0	.750	414	329
Atlanta*	11	5	0	.688	391	325
Tampa Bay	9	7	0	.563	361	323
New Orleans	8	8	0	.500	463	393

West Division

	W	L	T	Pct.	Pts.	OP
Arizona	9	7	0	.563	427	426
San Francisco	7	9	0	.438	339	381
Seattle	4	12	0	.250	294	392
St. Louis	2	14	0	.125	232	465

*Wild Card qualifier for playoffs; #Top playoff seed in conference
Miami finished ahead of New England based on better conference record (8-4 to Patriots' 7-5). Baltimore was second Wild Card ahead of New England based on better conference record (8-4 to Patriots' 7-5). San Diego finished ahead of Denver based on better division record (5-1 to Broncos' 3-3). N.Y. Giants finished ahead of Carolina based on head-to-head victory.

Wild Card Playoff: SAN DIEGO 23, Indianapolis 17;
Baltimore 27, MIAMI 9

Divisional Playoff: Baltimore 13, TENNESSEE 10;
PITTSBURGH 35, San Diego 24

AFC Championship: PITTSBURGH 23, Baltimore 14

Wild Card Playoff: ARIZONA 30, Atlanta 24;
Philadelphia 26, MINNESOTA 14

Divisional Playoff: Arizona 33, CAROLINA 13;
Philadelphia 23, N.Y. GIANTS 11

NFC Championship: ARIZONA 32, Philadelphia 25

Super Bowl XLIII: Pittsburgh (AFC) 27, Arizona (NFC) 23
at Raymond James Stadium, Tampa, Florida

Playoff Seeds

AFC	NFC
1. Tennessee	1. N.Y. Giants
2. Pittsburgh	2. Carolina
3. Miami	3. Minnesota
4. San Diego	**4. Arizona**
5. Indianapolis	5. Atlanta
6. Baltimore	6. Philadelphia

2007

AMERICAN CONFERENCE

East Division

	W	L	T	Pct.	Pts.	OP
New England#	16	0	0	1.000	589	274
Buffalo	7	9	0	.438	252	354
New York Jets	4	12	0	.250	268	355
Miami	1	15	0	.063	267	437

North Division

	W	L	T	Pct.	Pts.	OP
Pittsburgh	10	6	0	.625	393	269
Cleveland	10	6	0	.625	402	382
Cincinnati	7	9	0	.438	380	385
Baltimore	5	11	0	.313	275	384

South Division

	W	L	T	Pct.	Pts.	OP
Indianapolis	13	3	0	.813	450	262
Jacksonville*	11	5	0	.688	411	304
Tennessee*	10	6	0	.625	301	297
Houston	8	8	0	.500	379	384

West Division

	W	L	T	Pct.	Pts.	OP
San Diego	11	5	0	.688	412	284
Denver	7	9	0	.438	320	409
Kansas City	4	12	0	.250	226	335
Oakland	4	12	0	.250	283	398

NATIONAL CONFERENCE

East Division

	W	L	T	Pct.	Pts.	OP
Dallas#	13	3	0	.813	455	325
New York Giants*	10	6	0	.625	373	351
Washington*	9	7	0	.563	334	310
Philadelphia	8	8	0	.500	336	300

North Division

	W	L	T	Pct.	Pts.	OP
Green Bay	13	3	0	.813	435	291
Minnesota	8	8	0	.500	365	311
Detroit	7	9	0	.438	346	444
Chicago	7	9	0	.438	334	348

South Division

	W	L	T	Pct.	Pts.	OP
Tampa Bay	9	7	0	.563	334	270
Carolina	7	9	0	.438	267	347
New Orleans	7	9	0	.438	379	388
Atlanta	4	12	0	.250	259	414

West Division

	W	L	T	Pct.	Pts.	OP
Seattle	10	6	0	.625	393	291
Arizona	8	8	0	.500	404	399
San Francisco	5	11	0	.313	219	364
St. Louis	3	13	0	.188	263	438

*Wild Card qualifier for playoffs; #Top playoff seed in conference
Pittsburgh finished ahead of Cleveland based on head-to-head sweep (2-0). Tennessee finished ahead of Cleveland based on better record vs. common opponents (4-1 to Browns' 3-2). Kansas City finished ahead of Oakland based on better record vs. common opponents (2-10 to Raiders' 1-11). Dallas finished ahead of Green Bay based on head-to-head victory. Detroit finished ahead of Chicago based on head-to-head sweep (2-0). Carolina finished ahead of New Orleans based on better conference record (7-5 to Saints' 6-6).

Wild Card Playoff: Jacksonville 31, PITTSBURGH 29;
SAN DIEGO 17, Tennessee 6

Divisional Playoff: NEW ENGLAND 31, Jacksonville 20;
San Diego 28, INDIANAPOLIS 24

AFC Championship: NEW ENGLAND 21, San Diego 12

Wild Card Playoff: SEATTLE 35, Washington 14;
N.Y. Giants 24, TAMPA BAY 14

Divisional Playoff: GREEN BAY 42, Seattle 20;
N.Y. Giants 21, DALLAS 17

NFC Championship: N.Y. Giants 23, GREEN BAY 20 (OT)

Super Bowl XLII: N.Y. Giants (NFC) 17, New England (AFC) 14
at University of Phoenix Stadium, Glendale, Arizona

Playoff Seeds

AFC	NFC
1. New England	1. Dallas
2. Indianapolis	2. Green Bay
3. San Diego	3. Seattle
4. Pittsburgh	4. Tampa Bay
5. Jacksonville	**5. N.Y. Giants**
6. Tennessee	6. Washington

2006

AMERICAN CONFERENCE

East Division

	W	L	T	Pct.	Pts.	OP
New England	12	4	0	.750	385	237
New York Jets*	10	6	0	.625	316	295
Buffalo	7	9	0	.438	300	311
Miami	6	10	0	.375	260	283

North Division

	W	L	T	Pct.	Pts.	OP
Baltimore	13	3	0	.813	353	201
Cincinnati	8	8	0	.500	373	331
Pittsburgh	8	8	0	.500	353	315
Cleveland	4	12	0	.250	238	356

South Division

	W	L	T	Pct.	Pts.	OP
Indianapolis	12	4	0	.750	427	360
Tennessee	8	8	0	.500	324	400
Jacksonville	8	8	0	.500	371	274
Houston	6	10	0	.375	267	366

West Division

	W	L	T	Pct.	Pts.	OP
San Diego#	14	2	0	.875	492	303
Kansas City*	9	7	0	.563	331	315
Denver	9	7	0	.563	319	305
Oakland	2	14	0	.125	168	332

NATIONAL CONFERENCE

East Division

	W	L	T	Pct.	Pts.	OP
Philadelphia	10	6	0	.625	398	328
Dallas*	9	7	0	.563	425	350
New York Giants*	8	8	0	.500	355	362
Washington	5	11	0	.313	307	376

North Division

	W	L	T	Pct.	Pts.	OP
Chicago#	13	3	0	.813	427	255
Green Bay	8	8	0	.500	301	366
Minnesota	6	10	0	.375	282	327
Detroit	3	13	0	.188	305	398

South Division

	W	L	T	Pct.	Pts.	OP
New Orleans	10	6	0	.625	413	322
Carolina	8	8	0	.500	270	305
Atlanta	7	9	0	.438	292	328
Tampa Bay	4	12	0	.250	211	353

West Division

	W	L	T	Pct.	Pts.	OP
Seattle	9	7	0	.563	335	341
St. Louis	8	8	0	.500	367	381
San Francisco	7	9	0	.438	298	412
Arizona	5	11	0	.313	314	389

*Wild Card qualifier for playoffs; #Top playoff seed in conference
Indianapolis finished ahead of New England on head-to-head victory. Cincinnati finished ahead of Pittsburgh based on better division record (4-2 to Steelers' 3-3). Tennessee finished ahead of Jacksonville based on better division record (4-2 to Jaguars' 2-4). Kansas City finished ahead of Denver based on better division record (4-2 to Broncos' 3-3). New Orleans finished ahead of Philadelphia based on head-to-head victory. N.Y. Giants finished ahead of Carolina and St. Louis based on better conference record (Giants' 7-5 to Panthers' 6-6 and Rams' 6-6) and ahead of Green Bay based on strength of victory (.422 to Packers' .383).

Wild Card Playoff: INDIANAPOLIS 23, Kansas City 8; NEW ENGLAND 37, N.Y. Jets 16
Divisional Playoff: Indianapolis 15, BALTIMORE 6; New England 24, SAN DIEGO 21
AFC Championship: INDIANAPOLIS 38, New England 34
Wild Card Playoff: SEATTLE 21, Dallas 20; PHILADELPHIA 23, N.Y. Giants 20
Divisional Playoff: NEW ORLEANS 27, Philadelphia 24; CHICAGO 27, Seattle 24 (OT)
NFC Championship: CHICAGO 39, New Orleans 14
Super Bowl XLI: Indianapolis (AFC) 29, Chicago (NFC) 17 at Dolphin Stadium, Miami, Florida

Playoff Seeds

AFC	NFC
1. San Diego	**1. Chicago**
2. Baltimore	2. New Orleans
3. Indianapolis	3. Philadelphia
4. New England	4. Seattle
5. N.Y. Jets	5. Dallas
6. Kansas City	6. N.Y. Giants

2005

AMERICAN CONFERENCE

East Division

	W	L	T	Pct.	Pts.	OP
New England	10	6	0	.625	379	338
Miami	9	7	0	.563	318	317
Buffalo	5	11	0	.313	271	367
N.Y. Jets	4	12	0	.250	240	355

North Division

	W	L	T	Pct.	Pts.	OP
Cincinnati	11	5	0	.688	421	350
Pittsburgh*	11	5	0	.688	389	258
Baltimore	6	10	0	.375	265	299
Cleveland	6	10	0	.375	232	301

South Division

	W	L	T	Pct.	Pts.	OP
Indianapolis#	14	2	0	.875	439	247
Jacksonville*	12	4	0	.750	361	269
Tennessee	4	12	0	.250	299	421
Houston	2	14	0	.125	260	431

West Division

	W	L	T	Pct.	Pts.	OP
Denver	13	3	0	.813	395	258
Kansas City	10	6	0	.625	403	325
San Diego	9	7	0	.563	418	312
Oakland	4	12	0	.250	290	383

NATIONAL CONFERENCE

East Division

	W	L	T	Pct.	Pts.	OP
N.Y. Giants	11	5	0	.688	422	314
Washington*	10	6	0	.625	359	293
Dallas	9	7	0	.563	325	308
Philadelphia	6	10	0	.375	310	388

North Division

	W	L	T	Pct.	Pts.	OP
Chicago	11	5	0	.688	260	202
Minnesota	9	7	0	.563	306	344
Detroit	5	11	0	.313	254	345
Green Bay	4	12	0	.250	298	344

South Division

	W	L	T	Pct.	Pts.	OP
Tampa Bay	11	5	0	.688	300	274
Carolina*	11	5	0	.688	391	259
Atlanta	8	8	0	.500	351	341
New Orleans	3	13	0	.188	235	398

West Division

	W	L	T	Pct.	Pts.	OP
Seattle#	13	3	0	.813	452	271
St. Louis	6	10	0	.375	363	429
Arizona	5	11	0	.313	311	387
San Francisco	4	12	0	.250	239	428

*Wild Card qualifier for playoffs; #Top playoff seed in conference
Cincinnati finished ahead of Pittsburgh based on better division record (5-1 to Steelers' 4-2). Baltimore finished ahead of Cleveland based on better division record (2-4 to Browns' 1-5). Tampa Bay finished ahead of Carolina based on better division record (5-1 to Panthers' 4-2). Chicago finished ahead of Tampa Bay, and Tampa Bay finished ahead of the N.Y. Giants, based on better conference record (Bears' 10-2 to Buccaneers' 9-3 to Giants' 8-4).

Wild Card playoff: NEW ENGLAND 28, Jacksonville 3; Pittsburgh 31, CINCINNATI 17
Divisional playoff: DENVER 27, New England 13; Pittsburgh 21, INDIANAPOLIS 18
AFC Championship: Pittsburgh 34, DENVER 17
Wild Card playoffs: Washington 17, TAMPA BAY 10; Carolina 23, NEW YORK GIANTS 0
Divisional playoff: SEATTLE 20, Washington 10; Carolina 29, CHICAGO 21
NFC Championship: SEATTLE 34, Carolina 14
Super Bowl XL: Pittsburgh (AFC) 21, Seattle (NFC) 10 at Ford Field, Detroit, Michigan

Playoff Seeds

AFC	NFC
1. Indianapolis	**1. Seattle**
2. Denver	2. Chicago
3. Cincinnati	3. Tampa Bay
4. New England	4. New York Giants
5. Jacksonville	5. Carolina
6. Pittsburgh	6. Washington

2004

AMERICAN CONFERENCE

East Division

	W	L	T	Pct.	Pts.	OP
New England	14	2	0	.875	437	260
N.Y. Jets*	10	6	0	.625	333	261
Buffalo	9	7	0	.563	395	284
Miami	4	12	0	.250	275	354

North Division

	W	L	T	Pct.	Pts.	OP
Pittsburgh#	15	1	0	.938	372	251
Baltimore	9	7	0	.563	317	268
Cincinnati	8	8	0	.500	374	372
Cleveland	4	12	0	.250	276	390

South Division

	W	L	T	Pct.	Pts.	OP
Indianapolis	12	4	0	.750	522	351
Jacksonville	9	7	0	.563	261	280
Houston	7	9	0	.438	309	339
Tennessee	5	11	0	.313	344	439

West Division

	W	L	T	Pct.	Pts.	OP
San Diego	12	4	0	.750	446	313
Denver*	10	6	0	.625	381	304
Kansas City	7	9	0	.438	483	435
Oakland	5	11	0	.313	320	442

NATIONAL CONFERENCE

East Division

	W	L	T	Pct.	Pts.	OP
Philadelphia#	13	3	0	.813	386	260
N.Y. Giants	6	10	0	.375	303	347
Dallas	6	10	0	.375	293	405
Washington	6	10	0	.375	240	265

North Division

	W	L	T	Pct.	Pts.	OP
Green Bay	10	6	0	.625	424	380
Minnesota*	8	8	0	.500	405	395
Detroit	6	10	0	.375	296	350
Chicago	5	11	0	.313	231	331

South Division

	W	L	T	Pct.	Pts.	OP
Atlanta	11	5	0	.688	340	337
New Orleans	8	8	0	.500	348	405
Carolina	7	9	0	.438	355	339
Tampa Bay	5	11	0	.313	301	304

West Division

	W	L	T	Pct.	Pts.	OP
Seattle	9	7	0	.563	371	373
St. Louis*	8	8	0	.500	319	392
Arizona	6	10	0	.375	284	322
San Francisco	2	14	0	.125	259	452

*Wild Card qualifier for playoffs; #Top playoff seed in conference
Indianapolis finished ahead of San Diego based on head-to-head
victory. N.Y. Jets finished ahead of Denver based on better record
vs. common opponents (5-0 to Broncos' 3-2). St. Louis finished
ahead of New Orleans and Minnesota based on best conference
record (7-5 to Saints' 6-6 to Vikings' 5-7), and Minnesota
finished ahead of New Orleans based on head-to-head victory.
N.Y. Giants finished ahead of Dallas and Washington based on
better head-to-head record (3-1 to Cowboys' 2-2 to Redskins'
1-3), and Dallas finished ahead of Washington based on
head-to-head sweep (2-0).
Wild Card playoffs: N.Y. Jets 20, SAN DIEGO 17 (OT);
INDIANAPOLIS 49, Denver 24
Divisional playoffs: PITTSBURGH 20, N.Y. Jets 17 (OT);
NEW ENGLAND 20, Indianapolis 3
AFC Championship: New England 41, PITTSBURGH 27
Wild Card playoffs: St. Louis 27, SEATTLE 20;
Minnesota 31, GREEN BAY 17
Divisional playoffs: ATLANTA 47, St. Louis 17;
PHILADELPHIA 27, Minnesota 14
NFC Championship: PHILADELPHIA 27, Atlanta 10
Super Bowl XXXIX: New England (AFC) 24, Philadelphia (NFC) 21
at Alltel Stadium, Jacksonville, Florida

Playoff Seeds

AFC	NFC
1. Pittsburgh	**1. Philadelphia**
2. New England	2. Atlanta
3. Indianapolis	3. Green Bay
4. San Diego	4. Seattle
5. N.Y. Jets	5. St. Louis
6. Denver	6. Minnesota

2003

AMERICAN CONFERENCE

East Division

	W	L	T	Pct.	Pts.	OP
New England#	14	2	0	.875	348	238
Miami	10	6	0	.625	311	261
Buffalo	6	10	0	.375	243	279
N.Y. Jets	6	10	0	.375	283	299

North Division

	W	L	T	Pct.	Pts.	OP
Baltimore	10	6	0	.625	391	281
Cincinnati	8	8	0	.500	346	384
Pittsburgh	6	10	0	.375	300	327
Cleveland	5	11	0	.313	254	322

South Division

	W	L	T	Pct.	Pts.	OP
Indianapolis	12	4	0	.750	447	336
Tennessee*	12	4	0	.750	435	324
Jacksonville	5	11	0	.313	276	331
Houston	5	11	0	.313	255	380

West Division

	W	L	T	Pct.	Pts.	OP
Kansas City	13	3	0	.813	484	332
Denver*	10	6	0	.625	381	301
Oakland	4	12	0	.250	270	379
San Diego	4	12	0	.250	313	441

NATIONAL CONFERENCE

East Division

	W	L	T	Pct.	Pts.	OP
Philadelphia#	12	4	0	.750	374	287
Dallas*	10	6	0	.625	289	260
Washington	5	11	0	.313	287	372
N.Y. Giants	4	12	0	.250	243	387

North Division

	W	L	T	Pct.	Pts.	OP
Green Bay	10	6	0	.625	442	307
Minnesota	9	7	0	.563	416	353
Chicago	7	9	0	.438	283	346
Detroit	5	11	0	.313	270	379

South Division

	W	L	T	Pct.	Pts.	OP
Carolina	11	5	0	.688	325	304
New Orleans	8	8	0	.500	340	326
Tampa Bay	7	9	0	.438	301	264
Atlanta	5	11	0	.313	299	422

West Division

	W	L	T	Pct.	Pts.	OP
St. Louis	12	4	0	.750	447	328
Seattle*	10	6	0	.625	404	327
San Francisco	7	9	0	.438	384	337
Arizona	4	12	0	.250	225	452

*Wild Card qualifier for playoffs; #Top playoff seed in conference
Buffalo finished ahead of N.Y. Jets based on better division record
(2-4 to Jets' 1-5). Indianapolis finished ahead of Tennessee based
on head-to-head sweep (2-0). Jacksonville finished ahead of
Houston based on better division record (2-4 to Texans' 1-5).
Denver finished ahead of Miami based on better conference
record (9-3 to Dolphins' 7-5). Oakland finished ahead of San
Diego based on better conference record (3-9 to Chargers' 2-10).
Philadelphia finished ahead of St. Louis based on better
conference record (9-3 to Rams' 8-4). Seattle finished ahead of
Dallas based on better strength of victory (65-95 to Cowboys'
62-98).
Wild Card playoffs: Tennessee 20, BALTIMORE 17;
INDIANAPOLIS 41, Denver 10
Divisional playoffs: NEW ENGLAND 17, Tennessee 14;
Indianapolis 38, KANSAS CITY 31
AFC Championship: NEW ENGLAND 24, Indianapolis 14
Wild Card playoffs: CAROLINA 29, Dallas 10;
GREEN BAY 33, Seattle 27 (OT)
Divisional playoffs: Carolina 29, ST. LOUIS 23 (2OT);
PHILADELPHIA 20, Green Bay 17 (OT)
NFC Championship: Carolina 14, PHILADELPHIA 3
Super Bowl XXXVIII: New England (AFC) 32, Carolina (NFC) 29
at Reliant Stadium, Houston, Texas

Playoff Seeds

AFC	NFC
1. New England	1. Philadelphia
2. Kansas City	2. St. Louis
3. Indianapolis	**3. Carolina**
4. Baltimore	4. Green Bay
5. Tennessee	5. Seattle
6. Denver	6. Dallas

2002

AMERICAN CONFERENCE

East Division

	W	L	T	Pct.	Pts.	OP
N.Y. Jets	9	7	0	.563	359	336
New England	9	7	0	.563	381	346
Miami	9	7	0	.563	378	301
Buffalo	8	8	0	.500	379	397

North Division

	W	L	T	Pct.	Pts.	OP
Pittsburgh	10	5	1	.656	390	345
Cleveland*	9	7	0	.563	344	320
Baltimore	7	9	0	.438	316	354
Cincinnati	2	14	0	.125	279	456

South Division

	W	L	T	Pct.	Pts.	OP
Tennessee	11	5	0	.688	367	324
Indianapolis*	10	6	0	.625	349	313
Jacksonville	6	10	0	.375	328	315
Houston	4	12	0	.250	213	356

West Division

	W	L	T	Pct.	Pts.	OP
Oakland#	11	5	0	.688	450	304
Denver	9	7	0	.563	392	344
San Diego	8	8	0	.500	333	367
Kansas City	8	8	0	.500	467	399

NATIONAL CONFERENCE

East Division

	W	L	T	Pct.	Pts.	OP
Philadelphia#	12	4	0	.750	415	241
N.Y. Giants*	10	6	0	.625	320	279
Washington	7	9	0	.438	307	365
Dallas	5	11	0	.313	217	329

North Division

	W	L	T	Pct.	Pts.	OP
Green Bay	12	4	0	.750	398	328
Minnesota	6	10	0	.375	390	442
Chicago	4	12	0	.250	281	379
Detroit	3	13	0	.188	306	451

South Division

	W	L	T	Pct.	Pts.	OP
Tampa Bay	12	4	0	.750	346	196
Atlanta*	9	6	1	.594	402	314
New Orleans	9	7	0	.563	432	388
Carolina	7	9	0	.438	258	302

West Division

	W	L	T	Pct.	Pts.	OP
San Francisco	10	6	0	.625	367	351
St. Louis	7	9	0	.438	316	369
Seattle	7	9	0	.438	355	369
Arizona	5	11	0	.313	262	417

*Wild Card qualifier for playoffs; #Top playoff seed in conference
New York Jets finished ahead of New England based on better record in common games (8-4 to Patriots' 7-5) and Miami based on better division record (4-2 to Dolphins' 2-4). New England finished ahead of Miami based on better division record (4-2 to Dolphins' 2-4). Cleveland finished ahead of Denver and New England based on better conference record (7-5 to Broncos' 5-7 and Patriots' 6-6). Oakland finished ahead of Tennessee based on better head-to-head record (1-0). San Diego finished ahead of Kansas City based on better division record (3-3 to Chiefs' 2-4). Philadelphia finished ahead of Green Bay and Tampa Bay based on better conference record (11-1 to Packers' 9-3 and Buccaneers' 9-3). Tampa Bay finished ahead of Green Bay based on better head-to-head record (1-0). St. Louis finished ahead of Seattle based on better division record (4-2 to Seahawks' 2-4).

Wild Card playoffs: N.Y. JETS 41, Indianapolis 0;
  PITTSBURGH 36, Cleveland 33
Divisional playoffs: TENNESSEE 34, Pittsburgh 31 (OT);
  OAKLAND 30, N.Y. Jets 10
AFC Championship: OAKLAND 41, Tennessee 24
Wild Card playoffs: Atlanta 27, GREEN BAY 7;
  SAN FRANCISCO 39, N.Y. Giants 38
Divisional playoffs: PHILADELPHIA 20, Atlanta 6;
  TAMPA BAY 31, San Francisco 6
NFC Championship: Tampa Bay 27, PHILADELPHIA 10
Super Bowl XXXVII: Tampa Bay (NFC) 48, Oakland (AFC) 21
  at Qualcomm Stadium, San Diego, California

Playoff Seeds

AFC	NFC
1. Oakland	1. Philadelphia
2. Tennessee	**2. Tampa Bay**
3. Pittsburgh	3. Green Bay
4. N.Y. Jets	4. San Francisco
5. Indianapolis	5. N.Y. Giants
6. Cleveland	6. Atlanta

2001

AMERICAN CONFERENCE

Eastern Division

	W	L	T	Pct.	Pts.	OP
New England	11	5	0	.688	371	272
Miami*	11	5	0	.688	344	290
N.Y. Jets*	10	6	0	.625	308	295
Indianapolis	6	10	0	.375	413	486
Buffalo	3	13	0	.188	265	420

Central Division

	W	L	T	Pct.	Pts.	OP
Pittsburgh#	13	3	0	.813	352	212
Baltimore*	10	6	0	.625	303	265
Cleveland	7	9	0	.438	285	319
Tennessee	7	9	0	.438	336	388
Jacksonville	6	10	0	.375	294	286
Cincinnati	6	10	0	.375	226	309

Western Division

	W	L	T	Pct.	Pts.	OP
Oakland	10	6	0	.625	399	327
Seattle	9	7	0	.563	301	324
Denver	8	8	0	.500	340	339
Kansas City	6	10	0	.375	320	344
San Diego	5	11	0	.313	332	321

NATIONAL CONFERENCE

Eastern Division

	W	L	T	Pct.	Pts.	OP
Philadelphia	11	5	0	.688	343	208
Washington	8	8	0	.500	256	303
N.Y. Giants	7	9	0	.438	294	321
Arizona	7	9	0	.438	295	343
Dallas	5	11	0	.313	246	338

Central Division

	W	L	T	Pct.	Pts.	OP
Chicago	13	3	0	.813	338	203
Green Bay*	12	4	0	.750	390	266
Tampa Bay*	9	7	0	.563	324	280
Minnesota	5	11	0	.313	290	390
Detroit	2	14	0	.125	270	424

Western Division

	W	L	T	Pct.	Pts.	OP
St. Louis#	14	2	0	.875	503	273
San Francisco*	12	4	0	.750	409	282
New Orleans	7	9	0	.438	333	409
Atlanta	7	9	0	.438	291	377
Carolina	1	15	0	.063	253	410

*Wild Card qualifier for playoffs; #Top playoff seed in conference
New England finished ahead of Miami based on better division record (6-2 to Dolphins' 5-3). Baltimore was second Wild Card ahead of N.Y. Jets based on better record against common opponents (3-2 to Jets' 2-2). Cleveland finished ahead of Tennessee based on better division record (5-5 to Titans' 3-7). Jacksonville finished ahead of Cincinnati based on head-to-head record (2-0). N.Y. Giants finished ahead of Arizona based on head-to-head record (2-0). Green Bay was first Wild Card ahead of San Francisco based on better conference record (9-3 to 49ers' 8-4). New Orleans finished ahead of Atlanta based on better division record (4-4 to Falcons' 3-5).

Wild Card playoffs: OAKLAND 38, N.Y. Jets 24;
  Baltimore 20, MIAMI 3
Divisional playoffs: NEW ENGLAND 16, Oakland 13 (OT);
  PITTSBURGH 27, Baltimore 10
AFC Championship: New England 24, PITTSBURGH 17
Wild Card playoffs: PHILADELPHIA 31, Tampa Bay 9;
  GREEN BAY 25, San Francisco 15
Divisional playoffs: Philadelphia 33, CHICAGO 19;
  ST. LOUIS 45, Green Bay 17
NFC Championship: ST. LOUIS 29, Philadelphia 24
Super Bowl XXXVI: New England (AFC) 20, St. Louis (NFC) 17
  at Louisiana Superdome, New Orleans, Louisiana

Playoff Seeds

AFC	NFC
1. Pittsburgh	**1. St. Louis**
2. New England	2. Chicago
3. Oakland	3. Philadelphia
4. Miami	4. Green Bay
5. Baltimore	5. San Francisco
6. N.Y. Jets	6. Tampa Bay

2000

AMERICAN CONFERENCE

Eastern Division

	W	L	T	Pct.	Pts.	OP
Miami	11	5	0	.688	323	226
Indianapolis*	10	6	0	.625	429	326
N.Y. Jets	9	7	0	.563	321	321
Buffalo	8	8	0	.500	315	350
New England	5	11	0	.313	276	338

Central Division

	W	L	T	Pct.	Pts.	OP
Tennessee#	13	3	0	.813	346	191
Baltimore*	12	4	0	.750	333	165
Pittsburgh	9	7	0	.563	321	255
Jacksonville	7	9	0	.438	367	327
Cincinnati	4	12	0	.250	185	359
Cleveland	3	13	0	.188	161	419

Western Division

	W	L	T	Pct.	Pts.	OP
Oakland	12	4	0	.750	479	299
Denver*	11	5	0	.688	485	369
Kansas City	7	9	0	.438	355	354
Seattle	6	10	0	.375	320	405
San Diego	1	15	0	.063	269	440

NATIONAL CONFERENCE

Eastern Division

	W	L	T	Pct.	Pts.	OP
N.Y. Giants#	12	4	0	.750	328	246
Philadelphia*	11	5	0	.688	351	245
Washington	8	8	0	.500	281	269
Dallas	5	11	0	.313	294	361
Arizona	3	13	0	.188	210	443

Central Division

	W	L	T	Pct.	Pts.	OP
Minnesota	11	5	0	.688	397	371
Tampa Bay*	10	6	0	.625	388	269
Green Bay	9	7	0	.563	353	323
Detroit	9	7	0	.563	307	307
Chicago	5	11	0	.313	216	355

Western Division

	W	L	T	Pct.	Pts.	OP
New Orleans	10	6	0	.625	354	305
St. Louis*	10	6	0	.625	540	471
Carolina	7	9	0	.438	310	310
San Francisco	6	10	0	.375	388	422
Atlanta	4	12	0	.250	252	413

*Wild Card qualifier for playoffs; #Top playoff seed in conference
Green Bay finished ahead of Detroit based on better division record (5-3 to Lions' 3-5). New Orleans finished ahead of St. Louis based on better division record (7-1 to Rams' 5-3). Tampa Bay was second Wild Card based on head-to-head victory over St. Louis (1-0).

Wild Card playoffs: MIAMI 23, Indianapolis 17 (OT); BALTIMORE 21, Denver 3
Divisional playoffs: OAKLAND 27, Miami 0; Baltimore 24, TENNESSEE 10
AFC Championship: Baltimore 16, OAKLAND 3
Wild Card playoffs: NEW ORLEANS 31, St. Louis 28; PHILADELPHIA 21, Tampa Bay 3
Divisional playoffs: MINNESOTA 34, New Orleans 16; N.Y. GIANTS 20, Philadelphia 10
NFC Championship: N.Y. GIANTS 41, Minnesota 0
Super Bowl XXXV: Baltimore (AFC) 34, N.Y. Giants (NFC) 7 at Raymond James Stadium, Tampa, Florida

Playoff Seeds

AFC	NFC
1. Tennessee	1. N.Y. Giants
2. Oakland	2. Minnesota
3. Miami	3. New Orleans
4. Baltimore	4. Philadelphia
5. Denver	5. Tampa Bay
6. Indianapolis	6. St. Louis

1999

AMERICAN CONFERENCE

Eastern Division

	W	L	T	Pct.	Pts.	OP
Indianapolis	13	3	0	.813	423	333
Buffalo*	11	5	0	.688	320	229
Miami*	9	7	0	.563	326	336
N.Y. Jets	8	8	0	.500	308	309
New England	8	8	0	.500	299	284

Central Division

	W	L	T	Pct.	Pts.	OP
Jacksonville#	14	2	0	.875	396	217
Tennessee*	13	3	0	.813	392	324
Baltimore	8	8	0	.500	324	277
Pittsburgh	6	10	0	.375	317	320
Cincinnati	4	12	0	.250	283	460
Cleveland	2	14	0	.125	217	437

Western Division

	W	L	T	Pct.	Pts.	OP
Seattle	9	7	0	.563	338	298
Kansas City	9	7	0	.563	390	322
San Diego	8	8	0	.500	269	316
Oakland	8	8	0	.500	390	329
Denver	6	10	0	.375	314	318

NATIONAL CONFERENCE

Eastern Division

	W	L	T	Pct.	Pts.	OP
Washington	10	6	0	.625	443	377
Dallas*	8	8	0	.500	352	276
N.Y. Giants	7	9	0	.438	299	358
Arizona	6	10	0	.375	245	382
Philadelphia	5	11	0	.313	272	357

Central Division

	W	L	T	Pct.	Pts.	OP
Tampa Bay	11	5	0	.688	270	235
Minnesota*	10	6	0	.625	399	335
Detroit*	8	8	0	.500	322	323
Green Bay	8	8	0	.500	357	341
Chicago	6	10	0	.375	272	341

Western Division

	W	L	T	Pct.	Pts.	OP
St. Louis#	13	3	0	.813	526	242
Carolina	8	8	0	.500	421	381
Atlanta	5	11	0	.313	285	380
San Francisco	4	12	0	.250	295	453
New Orleans	3	13	0	.188	260	434

*Wild Card qualifier for playoffs; #Top playoff seed in conference
Miami was third Wild Card ahead of Kansas City based on better record against common opponents (6-1 to Chiefs' 5-3). N.Y. Jets finished ahead of New England based on better division record (4-4 to Patriots' 2-6). Seattle finished ahead of Kansas City based on head-to-head sweep (2-0). San Diego finished ahead of Oakland based on better division record (5-3 to Raiders' 3-5). Dallas was second Wild Card based on better record against common opponents (4-2 to Lions' 3-3) and better conference record than Carolina (7-5 to Panthers' 6-6). Detroit was third Wild Card based on better conference record than Green Bay (7-5 to Packers' 6-6) and head-to-head victory over Carolina.

Wild Card playoffs: TENNESSEE 22, Buffalo 16; Miami 20, SEATTLE 17
Divisional playoffs: JACKSONVILLE 62, Miami 7; Tennessee 19, INDIANAPOLIS 16
AFC Championship: Tennessee 33, JACKSONVILLE 14
Wild Card playoffs: WASHINGTON 27, Detroit 13; MINNESOTA 27, Dallas 10
Divisional playoffs: TAMPA BAY 14, Washington 13; ST. LOUIS 49, Minnesota 37
NFC Championship: ST. LOUIS 11, Tampa Bay 6
Super Bowl XXXIV: St. Louis (NFC) 23, Tennessee (AFC) 16 at Georgia Dome, Atlanta, Georgia

Playoff Seeds

AFC	NFC
1. Jacksonville	1. St. Louis
2. Indianapolis	2. Tampa Bay
3. Seattle	3. Washington
4. Tennessee	4. Minnesota
5. Buffalo	5. Dallas
6. Miami	6. Detroit

1998

AMERICAN CONFERENCE

Eastern Division

	W	L	T	Pct.	Pts.	OP
N.Y. Jets	12	4	0	.750	416	266
Miami*	10	6	0	.625	321	265
Buffalo*	10	6	0	.625	400	333
New England*	9	7	0	.563	337	329
Indianapolis	3	13	0	.188	310	444

Central Division

	W	L	T	Pct.	Pts.	OP
Jacksonville	11	5	0	.688	392	338
Tennessee	8	8	0	.500	330	320
Pittsburgh	7	9	0	.438	263	303
Baltimore	6	10	0	.375	269	335
Cincinnati	3	13	0	.188	268	452

Western Division

	W	L	T	Pct.	Pts.	OP
Denver#	14	2	0	.875	501	309
Oakland	8	8	0	.500	288	356
Seattle	8	8	0	.500	372	310
Kansas City	7	9	0	.438	327	363
San Diego	5	11	0	.313	241	342

NATIONAL CONFERENCE

Eastern Division

	W	L	T	Pct.	Pts.	OP
Dallas	10	6	0	.625	381	275
Arizona*	9	7	0	.563	325	378
N.Y. Giants	8	8	0	.500	287	309
Washington	6	10	0	.375	319	421
Philadelphia	3	13	0	.188	161	344

Central Division

	W	L	T	Pct.	Pts.	OP
Minnesota#	15	1	0	.938	556	296
Green Bay*	11	5	0	.688	408	319
Tampa Bay	8	8	0	.500	314	295
Detroit	5	11	0	.313	306	378
Chicago	4	12	0	.250	276	368

Western Division

	W	L	T	Pct.	Pts.	OP
Atlanta	14	2	0	.875	442	289
San Francisco*	12	4	0	.750	479	328
New Orleans	6	10	0	.375	305	359
Carolina	4	12	0	.250	336	413
St. Louis	4	12	0	.250	285	378

*Wild Card qualifier for playoffs; #Top playoff seed in conference
Miami finished ahead of Buffalo based on better net division points (6 to Bills' 0). Oakland finished ahead of Seattle based on head-to-head sweep (2-0). Carolina finished ahead of St. Louis based on head-to-head sweep (2-0).

Wild Card playoffs: MIAMI 24, Buffalo 17; JACKSONVILLE 25, New England 10
Divisional playoffs: DENVER 38, Miami 3; N.Y. JETS 34, Jacksonville 24
AFC Championship: DENVER 23, N.Y. Jets 10
Wild Card playoffs: Arizona 20, DALLAS 7; SAN FRANCISCO 30, Green Bay 27
Divisional playoffs: ATLANTA 20, San Francisco 18; MINNESOTA 41, Arizona 21
NFC Championship: Atlanta 30, MINNESOTA 27 (OT)
Super Bowl XXXIII: Denver (AFC) 34, Atlanta (NFC) 19, at Pro Player Stadium, Miami, Florida

Playoff Seeds

AFC	NFC
1. Denver	1. Minnesota
2. N.Y. Jets	**2. Atlanta**
3. Jacksonville	3. Dallas
4. Miami	4. San Francisco
5. Buffalo	5. Green Bay
6. New England	6. Arizona

1997

AMERICAN CONFERENCE

Eastern Division

	W	L	T	Pct.	Pts.	OP
New England	10	6	0	.625	369	289
Miami*	9	7	0	.563	339	327
N.Y. Jets	9	7	0	.563	348	287
Buffalo	6	10	0	.375	255	367
Indianapolis	3	13	0	.188	313	401

Central Division

	W	L	T	Pct.	Pts.	OP
Pittsburgh	11	5	0	.688	372	307
Jacksonville*	11	5	0	.688	394	318
Tennessee	8	8	0	.500	333	310
Cincinnati	7	9	0	.438	355	405
Baltimore	6	9	1	.406	326	345

Western Division

	W	L	T	Pct.	Pts.	OP
Kansas City#	13	3	0	.813	375	232
Denver*	12	4	0	.750	472	287
Seattle	8	8	0	.500	365	362
Oakland	4	12	0	.250	324	419
San Diego	4	12	0	.250	266	425

NATIONAL CONFERENCE

Eastern Division

	W	L	T	Pct.	Pts.	OP
N.Y. Giants	10	5	1	.656	307	265
Washington	8	7	1	.531	327	289
Philadelphia	6	9	1	.406	317	372
Dallas	6	10	0	.375	304	314
Arizona	4	12	0	.250	283	379

Central Division

	W	L	T	Pct.	Pts.	OP
Green Bay	13	3	0	.813	422	282
Tampa Bay*	10	6	0	.625	299	263
Detroit*	9	7	0	.563	379	306
Minnesota*	9	7	0	.563	354	359
Chicago	4	12	0	.250	263	421

Western Division

	W	L	T	Pct.	Pts.	OP
San Francisco#	13	3	0	.813	375	265
Carolina	7	9	0	.438	265	314
Atlanta	7	9	0	.438	320	361
New Orleans	6	10	0	.375	237	327
St. Louis	5	11	0	.313	299	359

*Wild Card qualifier for playoffs; #Top playoff seed in conference
Miami finished ahead of N.Y. Jets based on head-to-head sweep (2-0). Pittsburgh finished ahead of Jacksonville based on better net division points (78 to Jaguars' 23). Oakland finished ahead of San Diego based on better division record (2-6 to Chargers' 1-7). San Francisco was top playoff seed based on better conference record than Green Bay (11-1 to Packers' 10-2). Detroit finished ahead of Minnesota based on head-to-head sweep (2-0). Carolina finished ahead of Atlanta based on head-to-head sweep (2-0).

Wild Card playoffs: DENVER 42, Jacksonville 17; NEW ENGLAND 17, Miami 3
Divisional playoffs: PITTSBURGH 7, New England 6; Denver 14, KANSAS CITY 10
AFC Championship: Denver 24, PITTSBURGH 21
Wild Card playoffs: Minnesota 23, N.Y. GIANTS 22; TAMPA BAY 20, Detroit 10
Divisional playoffs: SAN FRANCISCO 38, Minnesota 22; GREEN BAY 21, Tampa Bay 7
NFC Championship: Green Bay 23, SAN FRANCISCO 10
Super Bowl XXXII: Denver (AFC) 31, Green Bay (NFC) 24, at Qualcomm Stadium, San Diego, California

Playoff Seeds

AFC	NFC
1. Kansas City	1. San Francisco
2. Pittsburgh	**2. Green Bay**
3. New England	3. N.Y. Giants
4. Denver	4. Tampa Bay
5. Jacksonville	5. Detroit
6. Miami	6. Minnesota

1996

AMERICAN CONFERENCE

Eastern Division

	W	L	T	Pct.	Pts.	OP
New England	11	5	0	.688	418	313
Buffalo*	10	6	0	.625	319	266
Indianapolis*	9	7	0	.563	317	334
Miami	8	8	0	.500	339	325
N.Y. Jets	1	15	0	.063	279	454

Central Division

	W	L	T	Pct.	Pts.	OP
Pittsburgh	10	6	0	.625	344	257
Jacksonville*	9	7	0	.563	325	335
Cincinnati	8	8	0	.500	372	369
Houston	8	8	0	.500	345	319
Baltimore	4	12	0	.250	371	441

Western Division

	W	L	T	Pct.	Pts.	OP
Denver#	13	3	0	.813	391	275
Kansas City	9	7	0	.563	297	300
San Diego	8	8	0	.500	310	376
Oakland	7	9	0	.438	340	293
Seattle	7	9	0	.438	317	376

NATIONAL CONFERENCE

Eastern Division

	W	L	T	Pct.	Pts.	OP
Dallas	10	6	0	.625	286	250
Philadelphia*	10	6	0	.625	363	341
Washington	9	7	0	.563	364	312
Arizona	7	9	0	.438	300	397
N.Y. Giants	6	10	0	.375	242	297

Central Division

	W	L	T	Pct.	Pts.	OP
Green Bay#	13	3	0	.813	456	210
Minnesota*	9	7	0	.563	298	315
Chicago	7	9	0	.438	283	305
Tampa Bay	6	10	0	.375	221	293
Detroit	5	11	0	.313	302	368

Western Division

	W	L	T	Pct.	Pts.	OP
Carolina	12	4	0	.750	367	218
San Francisco*	12	4	0	.750	398	257
St. Louis	6	10	0	.375	303	409
Atlanta	3	13	0	.188	309	461
New Orleans	3	13	0	.188	229	339

*Wild Card qualifier for playoffs; #Top playoff seed in conference

Jacksonville was second Wild Card ahead of Indianapolis and Kansas City based on better conference record (7-5 to Colts' 6-6 and Chiefs' 5-7). Indianapolis was third Wild Card based on head-to-head victory over Kansas City (1-0). Cincinnati finished ahead of Houston based on better net division points (19 to Oilers' 11). Oakland finished ahead of Seattle based on better division record (3-5 to Seahawks' 2-6). Dallas finished ahead of Philadelphia based on better record against common opponents (7-4 to Eagles' 6-5). Minnesota was third Wild Card based on better conference record than Washington (8-4 to Redskins' 6-6). Carolina finished ahead of San Francisco based on head-to-head sweep (2-0). Atlanta finished ahead of New Orleans based on head-to-head sweep (2-0).

Wild Card playoffs: Jacksonville 30, BUFFALO 27; PITTSBURGH 42, Indianapolis 14
Divisional playoffs: Jacksonville 30, DENVER 27; NEW ENGLAND 28, Pittsburgh 3
AFC Championship: NEW ENGLAND 20, Jacksonville 6
Wild Card playoffs: DALLAS 40, Minnesota 15; SAN FRANCISCO 14, Philadelphia 0
Divisional playoffs: GREEN BAY 35, San Francisco 14; CAROLINA 26, Dallas 17
NFC Championship: GREEN BAY 30, Carolina 13
Super Bowl XXXI: Green Bay (NFC) 35, New England (AFC) 21, at Louisiana Superdome, New Orleans, Louisiana

Playoff Seeds

AFC	NFC
1. Denver	1. Green Bay
2. New England	2. Carolina
3. Pittsburgh	3. Dallas
4. Buffalo	4. San Francisco
5. Jacksonville	5. Philadelphia
6. Indianapolis	6. Minnesota

1995

AMERICAN CONFERENCE

Eastern Division

	W	L	T	Pct.	Pts.	OP
Buffalo	10	6	0	.625	350	335
Indianapolis*	9	7	0	.563	331	316
Miami*	9	7	0	.563	398	332
New England	6	10	0	.375	294	377
N.Y. Jets	3	13	0	.188	233	384

Central Division

	W	L	T	Pct.	Pts.	OP
Pittsburgh	11	5	0	.688	407	327
Cincinnati	7	9	0	.438	349	374
Houston	7	9	0	.438	348	324
Cleveland	5	11	0	.313	289	356
Jacksonville	4	12	0	.250	275	404

Western Division

	W	L	T	Pct.	Pts.	OP
Kansas City#	13	3	0	.813	358	241
San Diego*	9	7	0	.563	321	323
Seattle	8	8	0	.500	363	366
Denver	8	8	0	.500	388	345
Oakland	8	8	0	.500	348	332

NATIONAL CONFERENCE

Eastern Division

	W	L	T	Pct.	Pts.	OP
Dallas#	12	4	0	.750	435	291
Philadelphia*	10	6	0	.625	318	338
Washington	6	10	0	.375	326	359
N.Y. Giants	5	11	0	.313	290	340
Arizona	4	12	0	.250	275	422

Central Division

	W	L	T	Pct.	Pts.	OP
Green Bay	11	5	0	.688	404	314
Detroit*	10	6	0	.625	436	336
Chicago	9	7	0	.563	392	360
Minnesota	8	8	0	.500	412	385
Tampa Bay	7	9	0	.438	238	335

Western Division

	W	L	T	Pct.	Pts.	OP
San Francisco	11	5	0	.688	457	258
Atlanta*	9	7	0	.563	362	349
St. Louis	7	9	0	.438	309	418
Carolina	7	9	0	.438	289	325
New Orleans	7	9	0	.438	319	348

*Wild Card qualifier for playoffs; #Top playoff seed in conference

Indianapolis finished ahead of Miami based on head-to-head sweep (2-0). San Diego was first Wild Card based on head-to-head victory over Indianapolis (1-0). Cincinnati finished ahead of Houston based on better division record (4-4 to Oilers' 3-5). Seattle finished ahead of Denver and Oakland based on best head-to-head record (3-1 to Broncos' 2-2 and Raiders' 1-3). Denver finished ahead of Oakland based on head-to-head sweep (2-0). Philadelphia was first Wild Card ahead of Detroit based on better conference record (9-3 to Lions' 7-5). San Francisco was second playoff seed ahead of Green Bay based on better conference record (8-4 to Packers' 7-5). Atlanta was third Wild Card ahead of Chicago based on better record against common opponents (4-2 to Bears' 3-3). St. Louis finished ahead of Carolina and New Orleans based on best head-to-head record (3-1 to Panthers' 1-3 and Saints' 2-2). Carolina finished ahead of New Orleans based on better conference record (4-8 to 3-9).

Wild Card playoffs: BUFFALO 37, Miami 22; Indianapolis 35, SAN DIEGO 20
Divisional playoffs: PITTSBURGH 40, Buffalo 21; Indianapolis 10, KANSAS CITY 7
AFC Championship: PITTSBURGH 20, Indianapolis 16
Wild Card playoffs: PHILADELPHIA 58, Detroit 37; GREEN BAY 37, Atlanta 20
Divisional playoffs: Green Bay 27, SAN FRANCISCO 17; DALLAS 30, Philadelphia 11
NFC Championship: DALLAS 38, Green Bay 27
Super Bowl XXX: Dallas (NFC) 27, Pittsburgh (AFC) 17, at Sun Devil Stadium, Tempe, Arizona

Playoff Seeds

AFC	NFC
1. Kansas City	1. Dallas
2. Pittsburgh	2. San Francisco
3. Buffalo	3. Green Bay
4. San Diego	4. Philadelphia
5. Indianapolis	5. Detroit
6. Miami	6. Atlanta

1994

AMERICAN CONFERENCE

Eastern Division

	W	L	T	Pct.	Pts.	OP
Miami	10	6	0	.625	389	327
New England*	10	6	0	.625	351	312
Indianapolis	8	8	0	.500	307	320
Buffalo	7	9	0	.438	340	356
N.Y. Jets	6	10	0	.375	264	320

Central Division

	W	L	T	Pct.	Pts.	OP
Pittsburgh#	12	4	0	.750	316	234
Cleveland*	11	5	0	.688	340	204
Cincinnati	3	13	0	.188	276	406
Houston	2	14	0	.125	226	352

Western Division

	W	L	T	Pct.	Pts.	OP
San Diego	11	5	0	.688	381	306
Kansas City*	9	7	0	.563	319	298
L.A. Raiders	9	7	0	.563	303	327
Denver	7	9	0	.438	347	396
Seattle	6	10	0	.375	287	323

NATIONAL CONFERENCE

Eastern Division

	W	L	T	Pct.	Pts.	OP
Dallas	12	4	0	.750	414	248
N.Y. Giants	9	7	0	.563	279	305
Arizona	8	8	0	.500	235	267
Philadelphia	7	9	0	.438	308	308
Washington	3	13	0	.188	320	412

Central Division

	W	L	T	Pct.	Pts.	OP
Minnesota	10	6	0	.625	356	314
Green Bay*	9	7	0	.563	382	287
Detroit*	9	7	0	.563	357	342
Chicago*	9	7	0	.563	271	307
Tampa Bay	6	10	0	.375	251	351

Western Division

	W	L	T	Pct.	Pts.	OP
San Francisco#	13	3	0	.813	505	296
New Orleans	7	9	0	.438	348	407
Atlanta	7	9	0	.438	317	385
L.A. Rams	4	12	0	.250	286	365

*Wild Card qualifier for playoffs; #Top playoff seed in conference
Miami finished ahead of New England based on head-to-head sweep (2-0). Kansas City finished ahead of L.A. Raiders based on head-to-head sweep (2-0). Green Bay was first Wild Card based on best head-to-head record (3-1) vs. Detroit (2-2) and Chicago (1-3) and better conference record (8-4) than N.Y. Giants (6-6). Detroit was second Wild Card based on better division record (4-4) than Chicago (3-5) and head-to-head victory over N.Y. Giants (1-0). Chicago was third Wild Card based on better record against common opponents (4-4) than N.Y. Giants (3-5). New Orleans finished ahead of Atlanta based on head-to-head sweep (2-0).
Wild Card playoffs: MIAMI 27, Kansas City 17; CLEVELAND 20, New England 13
Divisional playoffs: PITTSBURGH 29, Cleveland 9; SAN DIEGO 22, Miami 21
AFC Championship: San Diego 17, PITTSBURGH 13
Wild Card playoffs: GREEN BAY 16, Detroit 12; Chicago 35, MINNESOTA 18
Divisional playoffs: SAN FRANCISCO 44, Chicago 15; DALLAS 35, Green Bay 9
NFC Championship: SAN FRANCISCO 38, Dallas 28
Super Bowl XXIX: San Francisco (NFC) 49, San Diego (AFC) 26, at Joe Robbie Stadium, Miami, Florida

Playoff Seeds

AFC	NFC
1. Pittsburgh	1. **San Francisco**
2. **San Diego**	2. Dallas
3. Miami	3. Minnesota
4. Cleveland	4. Green Bay
5. New England	5. Detroit
6. Kansas City	6. Chicago

1993

AMERICAN CONFERENCE

Eastern Division

	W	L	T	Pct.	Pts.	OP
Buffalo#	12	4	0	.750	329	242
Miami	9	7	0	.563	349	351
N.Y. Jets	8	8	0	.500	270	247
New England	5	11	0	.313	238	286
Indianapolis	4	12	0	.250	189	378

Central Division

	W	L	T	Pct.	Pts.	OP
Houston	12	4	0	.750	368	238
Pittsburgh*	9	7	0	.563	308	281
Cleveland	7	9	0	.438	304	307
Cincinnati	3	13	0	.188	187	319

Western Division

	W	L	T	Pct.	Pts.	OP
Kansas City	11	5	0	.688	328	291
L.A. Raiders*	10	6	0	.625	306	326
Denver*	9	7	0	.563	373	284
San Diego	8	8	0	.500	322	290
Seattle	6	10	0	.375	280	314

NATIONAL CONFERENCE

Eastern Division

	W	L	T	Pct.	Pts.	OP
Dallas#	12	4	0	.750	376	229
N.Y. Giants*	11	5	0	.688	288	205
Philadelphia	8	8	0	.500	293	315
Phoenix	7	9	0	.438	326	269
Washington	4	12	0	.250	230	345

Central Division

	W	L	T	Pct.	Pts.	OP
Detroit	10	6	0	.625	298	292
Minnesota*	9	7	0	.563	277	290
Green Bay*	9	7	0	.563	340	282
Chicago	7	9	0	.438	234	230
Tampa Bay	5	11	0	.313	237	376

Western Division

	W	L	T	Pct.	Pts.	OP
San Francisco	10	6	0	.625	473	295
New Orleans	8	8	0	.500	317	343
Atlanta	6	10	0	.375	316	385
L.A. Rams	5	11	0	.313	221	367

*Wild Card qualifier for playoffs; #Top playoff seed in conference
Buffalo was top playoff seed based on head-to-head victory over Houston (1-0). Denver was second Wild Card ahead of Pittsburgh and Miami based on better conference record (8-4 to Steelers' 7-5 to Dolphins' 6-6). Pittsburgh was third Wild Card ahead of Miami based on head-to-head victory. San Francisco was second playoff seed based on head-to-head victory over Detroit (1-0). Minnesota finished ahead of Green Bay based on head-to-head sweep (2-0).
Wild Card playoffs: KANSAS CITY 27, Pittsburgh 24 (OT); L.A. RAIDERS 42, Denver 24
Divisional playoffs: BUFFALO 29, L.A. Raiders 23; Kansas City 28, HOUSTON 20
AFC Championship: BUFFALO 30, Kansas City 13
Wild Card playoffs: Green Bay 28, DETROIT 24; N.Y. GIANTS 17, Minnesota 10
Divisional playoffs: SAN FRANCISCO 44, N.Y. Giants 3; DALLAS 27, Green Bay 17
NFC Championship: DALLAS 38, San Francisco 21
Super Bowl XXVIII: Dallas (NFC) 30, Buffalo (AFC) 13, at Georgia Dome, Atlanta, Georgia

Playoff Seeds

AFC	NFC
1. Buffalo	1. Dallas
2. Houston	2. San Francisco
3. Kansas City	3. Detroit
4. L.A. Raiders	4. N.Y. Giants
5. Denver	5. Minnesota
6. Pittsburgh	6. Green Bay

1992

AMERICAN CONFERENCE

Eastern Division

	W	L	T	Pct.	Pts.	OP
Miami	11	5	0	.688	340	281
Buffalo*	11	5	0	.688	381	283
Indianapolis	9	7	0	.563	216	302
N.Y. Jets	4	12	0	.250	220	315
New England	2	14	0	.125	205	363

Central Division

	W	L	T	Pct.	Pts.	OP
Pittsburgh#	11	5	0	.688	299	225
Houston*	10	6	0	.625	352	258
Cleveland	7	9	0	.438	272	275
Cincinnati	5	11	0	.313	274	364

Western Division

	W	L	T	Pct.	Pts.	OP
San Diego	11	5	0	.688	335	241
Kansas City*	10	6	0	.625	348	282
Denver	8	8	0	.500	262	329
L.A. Raiders	7	9	0	.438	249	281
Seattle	2	14	0	.125	140	312

NATIONAL CONFERENCE

Eastern Division

	W	L	T	Pct.	Pts.	OP
Dallas	13	3	0	.813	409	243
Philadelphia*	11	5	0	.688	354	245
Washington*	9	7	0	.563	300	255
N.Y. Giants	6	10	0	.375	306	367
Phoenix	4	12	0	.250	243	332

Central Division

	W	L	T	Pct.	Pts.	OP
Minnesota	11	5	0	.688	374	249
Green Bay	9	7	0	.563	276	296
Tampa Bay	5	11	0	.313	267	365
Chicago	5	11	0	.313	295	361
Detroit	5	11	0	.313	273	332

Western Division

	W	L	T	Pct.	Pts.	OP
San Francisco#	14	2	0	.875	431	236
New Orleans*	12	4	0	.750	330	202
Atlanta	6	10	0	.375	327	414
L.A. Rams	6	10	0	.375	313	383

*Wild Card qualifier for playoffs; #Top playoff seed in conference
Pittsburgh was top playoff seed, and Miami was second playoff seed ahead of San Diego, based on conference record (10-2 to Dolphins' 9-3 to Chargers' 9-5). Miami finished ahead of Buffalo based on better conference record (9-3 to Bills' 7-5). Houston was second Wild Card based on head-to-head victory over Kansas City (1-0). Washington was third Wild Card based on better conference record than Green Bay (7-5 to Packers' 6-6). Tampa Bay finished ahead of Chicago and Chicago finished ahead of Detroit based on better conference record (5-9 to Bears' 4-8 and Lions' 3-9). Atlanta finished ahead of L.A. Rams based on better record against common opponents (5-7 to Rams' 4-8).
Wild Card playoffs: SAN DIEGO 17, Kansas City 0;
  BUFFALO 41, Houston 38 (OT)
Divisional playoffs: Buffalo 24, PITTSBURGH 3;
  MIAMI 31, San Diego 0
AFC Championship: Buffalo 29, MIAMI 10
Wild Card playoffs: Washington 24, MINNESOTA 7;
  Philadelphia 36, NEW ORLEANS 20
Divisional playoffs: SAN FRANCISCO 20, Washington 13;
  DALLAS 34, Philadelphia 10
NFC Championship: Dallas 30, SAN FRANCISCO 20
Super Bowl XXVII: Dallas (NFC) 52, Buffalo (AFC) 17,
  at Rose Bowl, Pasadena, California

Playoff Seeds

AFC	NFC
1. Pittsburgh	1. San Francisco
2. Miami	**2. Dallas**
3. San Diego	3. Minnesota
4. Buffalo	4. New Orleans
5. Houston	5. Philadelphia
6. Kansas City	6. Washington

1991

AMERICAN CONFERENCE

Eastern Division

	W	L	T	Pct.	Pts.	OP
Buffalo#	13	3	0	.813	458	318
N.Y. Jets*	8	8	0	.500	314	293
Miami	8	8	0	.500	343	349
New England	6	10	0	.375	211	305
Indianapolis	1	15	0	.063	143	381

Central Division

	W	L	T	Pct.	Pts.	OP
Houston	11	5	0	.688	386	251
Pittsburgh	7	9	0	.438	292	344
Cleveland	6	10	0	.375	293	298
Cincinnati	3	13	0	.188	263	435

Western Division

	W	L	T	Pct.	Pts.	OP
Denver	12	4	0	.750	304	235
Kansas City*	10	6	0	.625	322	252
L.A. Raiders*	9	7	0	.563	298	297
Seattle	7	9	0	.438	276	261
San Diego	4	12	0	.250	274	342

NATIONAL CONFERENCE

Eastern Division

	W	L	T	Pct.	Pts.	OP
Washington#	14	2	0	.875	485	224
Dallas*	11	5	0	.688	342	310
Philadelphia	10	6	0	.625	285	244
N.Y. Giants	8	8	0	.500	281	297
Phoenix	4	12	0	.250	196	344

Central Division

	W	L	T	Pct.	Pts.	OP
Detroit	12	4	0	.750	339	295
Chicago*	11	5	0	.688	299	269
Minnesota	8	8	0	.500	301	306
Green Bay	4	12	0	.250	273	313
Tampa Bay	3	13	0	.188	199	365

Western Division

	W	L	T	Pct.	Pts.	OP
New Orleans	11	5	0	.688	341	211
Atlanta*	10	6	0	.625	361	338
San Francisco	10	6	0	.625	393	239
L.A. Rams	3	13	0	.188	234	390

*Wild Card qualifier for playoffs; #Top playoff seed in conference
N.Y. Jets finished ahead of Miami based on head-to-head sweep (2-0). Chicago was first Wild Card based on better conference record than Dallas (9-3 to Cowboys' 8-4). Atlanta finished ahead of San Francisco based on head-to-head sweep (2-0), and was third Wild Card ahead of Philadelphia based on better conference record (7-5 to Eagles' 6-6).
Wild Card playoffs: KANSAS CITY 10, L.A. Raiders 6;
  HOUSTON 17, N.Y. Jets 10
Divisional playoffs: DENVER 26, Houston 24;
  BUFFALO 37, Kansas City 14
AFC Championship: BUFFALO 10, Denver 7
Wild Card playoffs: Atlanta 27, NEW ORLEANS 20;
  Dallas 17, CHICAGO 13
Divisional playoffs: WASHINGTON 24, Atlanta 7;
  DETROIT 38, Dallas 6
NFC Championship: WASHINGTON 41, Detroit 10
Super Bowl XXVI: Washington (NFC) 37, Buffalo (AFC) 24,
  at Hubert H. Humphrey Metrodome, Minneapolis, Minnesota

Playoff Seeds

AFC	NFC
1. Buffalo	**1. Washington**
2. Denver	2. Detroit
3. Houston	3. New Orleans
4. Kansas City	4. Chicago
5. L.A. Raiders	5. Dallas
6. N.Y. Jets	6. Atlanta

1990

AMERICAN CONFERENCE

Eastern Division

	W	L	T	Pct.	Pts.	OP
Buffalo#	13	3	0	.813	428	263
Miami*	12	4	0	.750	336	242
Indianapolis	7	9	0	.438	281	353
N.Y. Jets	6	10	0	.375	295	345
New England	1	15	0	.063	181	446

Central Division

	W	L	T	Pct.	Pts.	OP
Cincinnati	9	7	0	.563	360	352
Houston*	9	7	0	.563	405	307
Pittsburgh	9	7	0	.563	292	240
Cleveland	3	13	0	.188	228	462

Western Division

	W	L	T	Pct.	Pts.	OP
L.A. Raiders	12	4	0	.750	337	268
Kansas City*	11	5	0	.688	369	257
Seattle	9	7	0	.563	306	286
San Diego	6	10	0	.375	315	281
Denver	5	11	0	.313	331	374

NATIONAL CONFERENCE

Eastern Division

	W	L	T	Pct.	Pts.	OP
N.Y. Giants	13	3	0	.813	335	211
Philadelphia*	10	6	0	.625	396	299
Washington*	10	6	0	.625	381	301
Dallas	7	9	0	.438	244	308
Phoenix	5	11	0	.313	268	396

Central Division

	W	L	T	Pct.	Pts.	OP
Chicago	11	5	0	.688	348	280
Tampa Bay	6	10	0	.375	264	367
Detroit	6	10	0	.375	373	413
Green Bay	6	10	0	.375	271	347
Minnesota	6	10	0	.375	351	326

Western Division

	W	L	T	Pct.	Pts.	OP
San Francisco#	14	2	0	.875	353	239
New Orleans*	8	8	0	.500	274	275
L.A. Rams	5	11	0	.313	345	412
Atlanta	5	11	0	.313	348	365

*Wild Card qualifier for playoffs; #Top playoff seed in conference
Cincinnati finished ahead of Houston and Pittsburgh based on best head-to-head record (3-1 to Oilers' 2-2 to Steelers' 1-3). Houston was Wild Card based on better conference record (8-4) than Seattle (7-5) and Pittsburgh (6-6). Philadelphia finished ahead of Washington based on better division record (5-3 to Redskins' 4-4). Tampa Bay was second in NFC Central based on best head-to-head record (5-1) against Detroit (2-4), Green Bay (3-3), and Minnesota (2-4). Detroit finished third based on best net division points (minus 8) against Green Bay (minus 40). Green Bay finished ahead of Minnesota based on better conference record (5-7 to Vikings' 4-8). The L.A. Rams finished ahead of Atlanta based on net points in division (plus 1 to Falcons' minus 31).
Wild Card playoffs: MIAMI 17, Kansas City 16;
    CINCINNATI 41, Houston 14
Divisional playoffs: BUFFALO 44, Miami 34;
    L.A. RAIDERS 20, Cincinnati 10
AFC Championship: BUFFALO 51, L.A. Raiders 3
Wild Card playoffs: Washington 20, PHILADELPHIA 6;
    CHICAGO 16, New Orleans 6
Divisional playoffs: SAN FRANCISCO 28, Washington 10;
    N.Y. GIANTS 31, Chicago 3
NFC Championship: N.Y. Giants 15, SAN FRANCISCO 13
Super Bowl XXV: N.Y. Giants (NFC) 20, Buffalo (AFC) 19,
    at Tampa Stadium, Tampa, Florida

Playoff Seeds

AFC	NFC
1. Buffalo	1. San Francisco
2. L.A. Raiders	**2. N.Y. Giants**
3. Cincinnati	3. Chicago
4. Miami	4. Philadelphia
5. Kansas City	5. Washington
6. Houston	6. New Orleans

1989

AMERICAN CONFERENCE

Eastern Division

	W	L	T	Pct.	Pts.	OP
Buffalo	9	7	0	.563	409	317
Indianapolis	8	8	0	.500	298	301
Miami	8	8	0	.500	331	379
New England	5	11	0	.313	297	391
N.Y. Jets	4	12	0	.250	253	411

Central Division

	W	L	T	Pct.	Pts.	OP
Cleveland	9	6	1	.594	334	254
Houston*	9	7	0	.563	365	412
Pittsburgh*	9	7	0	.563	265	326
Cincinnati	8	8	0	.500	404	285

Western Division

	W	L	T	Pct.	Pts.	OP
Denver#	11	5	0	.688	362	226
Kansas City	8	7	1	.531	318	286
L.A. Raiders	8	8	0	.500	315	297
Seattle	7	9	0	.438	241	327
San Diego	6	10	0	.375	266	290

NATIONAL CONFERENCE

Eastern Division

	W	L	T	Pct.	Pts.	OP
N.Y. Giants	12	4	0	.750	348	252
Philadelphia*	11	5	0	.688	342	274
Washington	10	6	0	.625	386	308
Phoenix	5	11	0	.313	258	377
Dallas	1	15	0	.063	204	393

Central Division

	W	L	T	Pct.	Pts.	OP
Minnesota	10	6	0	.625	351	275
Green Bay	10	6	0	.625	362	356
Detroit	7	9	0	.438	312	364
Chicago	6	10	0	.375	358	377
Tampa Bay	5	11	0	.313	320	419

Western Division

	W	L	T	Pct.	Pts.	OP
San Francisco#	14	2	0	.875	442	253
L.A. Rams*	11	5	0	.688	426	344
New Orleans	9	7	0	.563	386	301
Atlanta	3	13	0	.188	279	437

*Wild Card qualifier for playoffs; #Top playoff seed in conference
Indianapolis finished ahead of Miami based on better conference record (7-5 vs. Dolphins' 6-8). Houston finished ahead of Pittsburgh based on head-to-head sweep (2-0). The L.A. Rams did not play San Francisco in the divisional playoffs because, from 1970-1989, two teams from the same division could not meet prior to the conference championship game. Philadelphia was first Wild Card ahead of L.A. Rams based on better record against common opponents (7-3 to Rams' 5-4). Minnesota finished ahead of Green Bay based on better division record (6-2 vs. Packers' 5-3).
Wild Card playoff: Pittsburgh 26, HOUSTON 23 (OT)
Divisional playoffs: CLEVELAND 34, Buffalo 30;
    DENVER 24, Pittsburgh 23
AFC Championship: DENVER 37, Cleveland 21
Wild Card playoff: L.A. Rams 21, PHILADELPHIA 7
Divisional playoffs: L.A. Rams 19, N.Y. GIANTS 13 (OT);
    SAN FRANCISCO 41, Minnesota 13
NFC Championship: SAN FRANCISCO 30, L.A. Rams 3
Super Bowl XXIV: San Francisco (NFC) 55, Denver (AFC) 10,
    at Louisiana Superdome, New Orleans, Louisiana

1988

AMERICAN CONFERENCE

Eastern Division

	W	L	T	Pct.	Pts.	OP
Buffalo	12	4	0	.750	329	237
Indianapolis	9	7	0	.563	354	315
New England	9	7	0	.563	250	284
N.Y. Jets	8	7	1	.531	372	354
Miami	6	10	0	.375	319	380

Central Division

	W	L	T	Pct.	Pts.	OP
Cincinnati#	12	4	0	.750	448	329
Cleveland*	10	6	0	.625	304	288
Houston*	10	6	0	.625	424	365
Pittsburgh	5	11	0	.313	336	421

Western Division

	W	L	T	Pct.	Pts.	OP
Seattle	9	7	0	.563	339	329
Denver	8	8	0	.500	327	352
L.A. Raiders	7	9	0	.438	325	369
San Diego	6	10	0	.375	231	332
Kansas City	4	11	1	.281	254	320

NATIONAL CONFERENCE

Eastern Division

	W	L	T	Pct.	Pts.	OP
Philadelphia	10	6	0	.625	379	319
N.Y. Giants	10	6	0	.625	359	304
Washington	7	9	0	.438	345	387
Phoenix	7	9	0	.438	344	398
Dallas	3	13	0	.188	265	381

Central Division

	W	L	T	Pct.	Pts.	OP
Chicago#	12	4	0	.750	312	215
Minnesota*	11	5	0	.688	406	233
Tampa Bay	5	11	0	.313	261	350
Detroit	4	12	0	.250	220	313
Green Bay	4	12	0	.250	240	315

Western Division

	W	L	T	Pct.	Pts.	OP
San Francisco	10	6	0	.625	369	294
L.A. Rams*	10	6	0	.625	407	293
New Orleans	10	6	0	.625	312	283
Atlanta	5	11	0	.313	244	315

*Wild Card qualifier for playoffs; #Top playoff seed in conference
Cincinnati was top playoff seed ahead of Buffalo based on head-to-head victory (1-0). Indianapolis finished ahead of New England based on better record against common opponents (7-5 to Patriots' 6-6). Cleveland finished ahead of Houston based on better division record (4-2 to Oilers' 3-3). Houston did not play Cincinnati, and Minnesota did not play Chicago in the divisional playoffs because, from 1970-1989, two teams from the same division could not meet prior to the conference championship game. Philadelphia finished first in NFC East based on head-to-head sweep of N.Y. Giants (2-0). Washington finished third in NFC East based on better division record (4-4) than Phoenix (3-5). Detroit finished fourth in NFC Central based on head-to-head sweep of Green Bay (2-0). San Francisco finished first in NFC West based on better head-to-head record (3-1) against L.A. Rams (2-2) and New Orleans (1-3). San Francisco finished with second playoff seed ahead of Philadelphia based on better record against common opponents (5-3 to Eagles' 5-4). L.A. Rams finished second in NFC West based on better division record (4-2) than New Orleans (3-3) and earned Wild-Card position based on better conference record (8-4) than N.Y. Giants (9-5) and New Orleans (6-6).
Wild Card playoff: Houston 24, CLEVELAND 23
Divisional playoffs: CINCINNATI 21, Seattle 13;
  BUFFALO 17, Houston 10
AFC Championship: CINCINNATI 21, Buffalo 10
Wild Card playoff: MINNESOTA 28, L.A. Rams 17
Divisional playoffs: CHICAGO 20, Philadelphia 12;
  SAN FRANCISCO 34, Minnesota 9
NFC Championship: San Francisco 28, CHICAGO 3
Super Bowl XXIII: San Francisco (NFC) 20, Cincinnati (AFC) 16,
  at Joe Robbie Stadium, Miami, Florida

1987

AMERICAN CONFERENCE

Eastern Division

	W	L	T	Pct.	Pts.	OP
Indianapolis	9	6	0	.600	300	238
New England	8	7	0	.533	320	293
Miami	8	7	0	.533	362	335
Buffalo	7	8	0	.467	270	305
N.Y. Jets	6	9	0	.400	334	360

Central Division

	W	L	T	Pct.	Pts.	OP
Cleveland	10	5	0	.667	390	239
Houston*	9	6	0	.600	345	349
Pittsburgh	8	7	0	.533	285	299
Cincinnati	4	11	0	.267	285	370

Western Division

	W	L	T	Pct.	Pts.	OP
Denver#	10	4	1	.700	379	288
Seattle*	9	6	0	.600	371	314
San Diego	8	7	0	.533	253	317
L.A. Raiders	5	10	0	.333	301	289
Kansas City	4	11	0	.267	273	388

NATIONAL CONFERENCE

Eastern Division

	W	L	T	Pct.	Pts.	OP
Washington	11	4	0	.733	379	285
Dallas	7	8	0	.467	340	348
St. Louis	7	8	0	.467	362	368
Philadelphia	7	8	0	.467	337	380
N.Y. Giants	6	9	0	.400	280	312

Central Division

	W	L	T	Pct.	Pts.	OP
Chicago	11	4	0	.733	356	282
Minnesota*	8	7	0	.533	336	335
Green Bay	5	9	1	.367	255	300
Tampa Bay	4	11	0	.267	286	360
Detroit	4	11	0	.267	269	384

Western Division

	W	L	T	Pct.	Pts.	OP
San Francisco#	13	2	0	.867	459	253
New Orleans*	12	3	0	.800	422	283
L.A. Rams	6	9	0	.400	317	361
Atlanta	3	12	0	.200	205	436

*Wild Card qualifier for playoffs; #Top playoff seed in conference
New England finished ahead of Miami based on head-to-head sweep (2-0). Houston was first Wild Card ahead of Seattle based on better conference record (7-4 to Seahawks' 5-6). Chicago was second playoff seed ahead of Washington based on better conference record (9-2 to Redskins' 9-3). Dallas finished ahead of St. Louis and Philadelphia based on better division record (4-4 to Cardinals' 3-5 and Eagles' 3-5). St. Louis finished ahead of Philadelphia based on better conference record (7-7 to Eagles' 4-7). Tampa Bay finished ahead of Detroit based on better division record (3-4 to Lions' 2-5).
Wild Card playoff: HOUSTON 23, Seattle 20 (OT)
Divisional playoffs: CLEVELAND 38, Indianapolis 21;
  DENVER 34, Houston 10
AFC Championship: DENVER 38, Cleveland 33
Wild Card playoff: Minnesota 44, NEW ORLEANS 10
Divisional playoffs: Minnesota 36, SAN FRANCISCO 24;
  Washington 21, CHICAGO 17
NFC Championship: WASHINGTON 17, Minnesota 10
Super Bowl XXII: Washington (NFC) 42, Denver (AFC) 10,
  at San Diego Jack Murphy Stadium, San Diego, California
Note: 1987 regular season was reduced from 16 to 15 games for each team due to players' strike.

1986

AMERICAN CONFERENCE
Eastern Division

	W	L	T	Pct.	Pts.	OP
New England	11	5	0	.688	412	307
N.Y. Jets*	10	6	0	.625	364	386
Miami	8	8	0	.500	430	405
Buffalo	4	12	0	.250	287	348
Indianapolis	3	13	0	.188	229	400

Central Division

	W	L	T	Pct.	Pts.	OP
Cleveland#	12	4	0	.750	391	310
Cincinnati	10	6	0	.625	409	394
Pittsburgh	6	10	0	.375	307	336
Houston	5	11	0	.313	274	329

Western Division

	W	L	T	Pct.	Pts.	OP
Denver	11	5	0	.688	378	327
Kansas City*	10	6	0	.625	358	326
Seattle	10	6	0	.625	366	293
L.A. Raiders	8	8	0	.500	323	346
San Diego	4	12	0	.250	335	396

NATIONAL CONFERENCE
Eastern Division

	W	L	T	Pct.	Pts.	OP
N.Y. Giants#	14	2	0	.875	371	236
Washington*	12	4	0	.750	368	296
Dallas	7	9	0	.438	346	337
Philadelphia	5	10	1	.344	256	312
St. Louis	4	11	1	.281	218	351

Central Division

	W	L	T	Pct.	Pts.	OP
Chicago	14	2	0	.875	352	187
Minnesota	9	7	0	.563	398	273
Detroit	5	11	0	.313	277	326
Green Bay	4	12	0	.250	254	418
Tampa Bay	2	14	0	.125	239	473

Western Division

	W	L	T	Pct.	Pts.	OP
San Francisco	10	5	1	.656	374	247
L.A. Rams*	10	6	0	.625	309	267
Atlanta	7	8	1	.469	280	280
New Orleans	7	9	0	.438	288	287

*Wild Card qualifier for playoffs; #Top playoff seed in conference
Denver was second playoff seed ahead of New England based on head-to-head victory (1-0). N.Y. Jets were first Wild Card based on better conference record (8-4) than Kansas City (9-5), Seattle (7-5), and Cincinnati (7-5). Kansas City was second Wild Card based on better conference record (9-5) than Seattle (7-5) and Cincinnati (7-5). N.Y. Giants were top playoff seed based on better conference record than Chicago (11-1 to Bears' 10-2). Washington did not play the N.Y. Giants in the divisional playoffs because, from 1970-1989, two teams from the same division could not meet prior to the conference championship game.
Wild Card playoff: N.Y. JETS 35, Kansas City 15
Divisional playoffs: CLEVELAND 23, N.Y. Jets 20 (OT);
   DENVER 22, New England 17
AFC Championship: Denver 23, CLEVELAND 20 (OT)
Wild Card playoff: WASHINGTON 19, L.A. Rams 7
Divisional playoffs: Washington 27, CHICAGO 13
   N.Y. GIANTS 49, San Francisco 3
NFC Championship: N.Y. GIANTS 17, Washington 0
Super Bowl XXI: N.Y. Giants (NFC) 39, Denver (AFC) 20,
   at Rose Bowl, Pasadena, California

1985

AMERICAN CONFERENCE
Eastern Division

	W	L	T	Pct.	Pts.	OP
Miami	12	4	0	.750	428	320
N.Y. Jets*	11	5	0	.688	393	264
New England*	11	5	0	.688	362	290
Indianapolis	5	11	0	.313	320	386
Buffalo	2	14	0	.125	200	381

Central Division

	W	L	T	Pct.	Pts.	OP
Cleveland	8	8	0	.500	287	294
Cincinnati	7	9	0	.438	441	437
Pittsburgh	7	9	0	.438	379	355
Houston	5	11	0	.313	284	412

Western Division

	W	L	T	Pct.	Pts.	OP
L.A. Raiders#	12	4	0	.750	354	308
Denver	11	5	0	.688	380	329
Seattle	8	8	0	.500	349	303
San Diego	8	8	0	.500	467	435
Kansas City	6	10	0	.375	317	360

NATIONAL CONFERENCE
Eastern Division

	W	L	T	Pct.	Pts.	OP
Dallas	10	6	0	.625	357	333
N.Y. Giants*	10	6	0	.625	399	283
Washington	10	6	0	.625	297	312
Philadelphia	7	9	0	.438	286	310
St. Louis	5	11	0	.313	278	414

Central Division

	W	L	T	Pct.	Pts.	OP
Chicago#	15	1	0	.938	456	198
Green Bay	8	8	0	.500	337	355
Minnesota	7	9	0	.438	346	359
Detroit	7	9	0	.438	307	366
Tampa Bay	2	14	0	.125	294	448

Western Division

	W	L	T	Pct.	Pts.	OP
L.A. Rams	11	5	0	.688	340	277
San Francisco*	10	6	0	.625	411	263
New Orleans	5	11	0	.313	294	401
Atlanta	4	12	0	.250	282	452

*Wild Card qualifier for playoffs; #Top playoff seed in conference
L.A. Raiders were top playoff seed ahead of Miami based on better record against common opponents (5-1 to 4-2). N.Y. Jets were first Wild Card based on better conference record (9-3) than New England (8-4) and Denver (8-4). New England was second Wild Card ahead of Denver based on better record against common opponents (4-2 to Broncos' 3-3). Cincinnati finished ahead of Pittsburgh based on head-to-head sweep (2-0). Seattle finished ahead of San Diego based on head-to-head sweep (2-0). Dallas finished ahead of N.Y. Giants and Washington based on head-to-head record (4-0 to Giants' 1-3 and Redskins' 1-3). N.Y. Giants were first Wild Card based on better conference record (8-4) than San Francisco (7-5) and Washington (6-6). San Francisco was second Wild Card based on head-to-head victory over Washington (1-0). Minnesota finished ahead of Detroit based on better division record (3-5 to Lions' 2-6).
Wild Card playoff: New England 26, N.Y. JETS 14
Divisional playoffs: MIAMI 24, Cleveland 21;
   New England 27, L.A. RAIDERS 20
AFC Championship: New England 31, MIAMI 14
Wild Card playoff: N.Y. GIANTS 17, San Francisco 3
Divisional playoffs: L.A. RAMS 20, Dallas 0;
   CHICAGO 21, N.Y. Giants 0
NFC Championship: CHICAGO 24, L.A. Rams 0
Super Bowl XX: Chicago (NFC) 46, New England (AFC) 10,
   at Louisiana Superdome, New Orleans, Louisiana

1984

AMERICAN CONFERENCE

Eastern Division

	W	L	T	Pct.	Pts.	OP
Miami#	14	2	0	.875	513	298
New England	9	7	0	.563	362	352
N.Y. Jets	7	9	0	.438	332	364
Indianapolis	4	12	0	.250	239	414
Buffalo	2	14	0	.125	250	454

Central Division

	W	L	T	Pct.	Pts.	OP
Pittsburgh	9	7	0	.563	387	310
Cincinnati	8	8	0	.500	339	339
Cleveland	5	11	0	.313	250	297
Houston	3	13	0	.188	240	437

Western Division

	W	L	T	Pct.	Pts.	OP
Denver	13	3	0	.813	353	241
Seattle*	12	4	0	.750	418	282
L.A. Raiders*	11	5	0	.688	368	278
Kansas City	8	8	0	.500	314	324
San Diego	7	9	0	.438	394	413

NATIONAL CONFERENCE

Eastern Division

	W	L	T	Pct.	Pts.	OP
Washington	11	5	0	.688	426	310
N.Y. Giants*	9	7	0	.563	299	301
St. Louis	9	7	0	.563	423	345
Dallas	9	7	0	.563	308	308
Philadelphia	6	9	1	.406	278	320

Central Division

	W	L	T	Pct.	Pts.	OP
Chicago	10	6	0	.625	325	248
Green Bay	8	8	0	.500	390	309
Tampa Bay	6	10	0	.375	335	380
Detroit	4	11	1	.281	283	408
Minnesota	3	13	0	.188	276	484

Western Division

	W	L	T	Pct.	Pts.	OP
San Francisco#	15	1	0	.938	475	227
L.A. Rams*	10	6	0	.625	346	316
New Orleans	7	9	0	.438	298	361
Atlanta	4	12	0	.250	281	382

*Wild Card qualifier for playoffs; #Top playoff seed in conference
N.Y. Giants finished ahead of St. Louis and Dallas based on best head-to-head record (3-1 to Cardinals' 2-2 and Cowboys' 1-3). St. Louis finished ahead of Dallas based on better division record (5-3 to Cowboys' 3-5).
Wild Card playoff: SEATTLE 13, L.A. Raiders 7
Divisional playoffs: MIAMI 31, Seattle 10;
  Pittsburgh 24, DENVER 17
AFC Championship: MIAMI 45, Pittsburgh 28
Wild Card playoff: N.Y. Giants 16, L.A. RAMS 13
Divisional playoffs: SAN FRANCISCO 21, N.Y. Giants 10;
  Chicago 23, WASHINGTON 19
NFC Championship: SAN FRANCISCO 23, Chicago 0
Super Bowl XIX: San Francisco (NFC) 38, Miami (AFC) 16,
  at Stanford Stadium, Stanford, California

1983

AMERICAN CONFERENCE

Eastern Division

	W	L	T	Pct.	Pts.	OP
Miami	12	4	0	.750	389	250
New England	8	8	0	.500	274	289
Buffalo	8	8	0	.500	283	351
Baltimore	7	9	0	.438	264	354
N.Y. Jets	7	9	0	.438	313	331

Central Division

	W	L	T	Pct.	Pts.	OP
Pittsburgh	10	6	0	.625	355	303
Cleveland	9	7	0	.563	356	342
Cincinnati	7	9	0	.438	346	302
Houston	2	14	0	.125	288	460

Western Division

	W	L	T	Pct.	Pts.	OP
L.A. Raiders#	12	4	0	.750	442	338
Seattle*	9	7	0	.563	403	397
Denver*	9	7	0	.563	302	327
San Diego	6	10	0	.375	358	462
Kansas City	6	10	0	.375	386	367

NATIONAL CONFERENCE

Eastern Division

	W	L	T	Pct.	Pts.	OP
Washington#	14	2	0	.875	541	332
Dallas*	12	4	0	.750	479	360
St. Louis	8	7	1	.531	374	428
Philadelphia	5	11	0	.313	233	322
N.Y. Giants	3	12	1	.219	267	347

Central Division

	W	L	T	Pct.	Pts.	OP
Detroit	9	7	0	.563	347	286
Green Bay	8	8	0	.500	429	439
Chicago	8	8	0	.500	311	301
Minnesota	8	8	0	.500	316	348
Tampa Bay	2	14	0	.125	241	380

Western Division

	W	L	T	Pct.	Pts.	OP
San Francisco	10	6	0	.625	432	293
L.A. Rams*	9	7	0	.563	361	344
New Orleans	8	8	0	.500	319	337
Atlanta	7	9	0	.438	370	389

*Wild Card qualifier for playoffs; #Top playoff seed in conference
L.A. Raiders were top playoff seed ahead of Miami based on head-to-head victory (1-0). Seattle was first Wild Card ahead of Denver based on better division record (5-3 to Broncos' 3-5) after Cleveland was eliminated from three-way tie based on losing head-to-head to both Seattle and Denver. Seattle did not play the L.A. Raiders in the divisional playoffs because, from 1970-1989, two teams from the same division could not meet prior to the conference championship game. New England finished ahead of Buffalo based on head-to-head sweep (2-0). Baltimore finished ahead of N.Y. Jets based on better conference record (5-9 to Jets' 4-8). San Diego finished ahead of Kansas City based on head-to-head sweep (2-0). Green Bay finished ahead of Chicago based on better record against common opponents (4-4 to Bears' 3-5) after Minnesota was eliminated from three-way tie based on conference record (Chicago 7-7 and Green Bay 6-6 to Vikings' 4-8).
Wild Card playoff: SEATTLE 31, Denver 7
Divisional playoffs: Seattle 27, MIAMI 20;
  L.A. RAIDERS 38, Pittsburgh 10
AFC Championship: L.A. RAIDERS 30, Seattle 14
Wild Card playoff: L.A. Rams 24, DALLAS 17
Divisional playoffs: SAN FRANCISCO 24, Detroit 23;
  WASHINGTON 51, L.A. Rams 7
NFC Championship: WASHINGTON 24, San Francisco 21
Super Bowl XVIII: L.A. Raiders (AFC) 38, Washington (NFC) 9,
  at Tampa Stadium, Tampa, Florida

1982

AMERICAN CONFERENCE

	W	L	T	Pct.	Pts.	OP
L.A. Raiders#	8	1	0	.889	260	200
Miami	7	2	0	.778	198	131
Cincinnati	7	2	0	.778	232	177
Pittsburgh	6	3	0	.667	204	146
San Diego	6	3	0	.667	288	221
N.Y. Jets	6	3	0	.667	245	166
New England	5	4	0	.556	143	157
Cleveland	4	5	0	.444	140	182
Buffalo	4	5	0	.444	150	154
Seattle	4	5	0	.444	127	147
Kansas City	3	6	0	.333	176	184
Denver	2	7	0	.222	148	226
Houston	1	8	0	.111	136	245
Baltimore	0	8	1	.056	113	236

NATIONAL CONFERENCE

	W	L	T	Pct.	Pts.	OP
Washington#	8	1	0	.889	190	128
Dallas	6	3	0	.667	226	145
Green Bay	5	3	1	.611	226	169
Minnesota	5	4	0	.556	187	198
Atlanta	5	4	0	.556	183	199
St. Louis	5	4	0	.556	135	170
Tampa Bay	5	4	0	.556	158	178
Detroit	4	5	0	.444	181	176
New Orleans	4	5	0	.444	129	160
N.Y. Giants	4	5	0	.444	164	160
San Francisco	3	6	0	.333	209	206
Chicago	3	6	0	.333	141	174
Philadelphia	3	6	0	.333	191	195
L.A. Rams	2	7	0	.222	200	250

As the result of a 57-day players' strike, the 1982 NFL regular season schedule was reduced from 16 weeks to 9. At the conclusion of the regular season, the NFL conducted a 16-team postseason Super Bowl Tournament. Eight teams from each conference were seeded 1-8 based on their records during the season.

#Top playoff seed in conference

Miami finished ahead of Cincinnati based on better conference record (6-1 to Bengals' 6-2). Pittsburgh finished ahead of San Diego based on better record against common opponents (3-1 to Chargers' 2-1) after N.Y. Jets were eliminated from three-way tie based on conference record (Pittsburgh and San Diego 5-3 to Jets' 2-3). Cleveland finished ahead of Buffalo and Seattle based on better conference record (4-3 to Bills' 3-3 to Seahawks' 3-5). Buffalo finished ahead of Seattle based on better conference record (3-3 to Seahawks' 3-5). Minnesota (4-1), Atlanta (4-3), St. Louis (5-4), Tampa Bay (3-3) seeds were determined by best won-lost record in conference games. Detroit finished ahead of New Orleans and the N.Y. Giants based on best conference record (4-4 to Saints' 3-5 to Giants' 3-5). New Orleans finished ahead of N.Y. Giants based on better record against common opponents (1-3 to Giants' 0-4). San Francisco finished ahead of Chicago, and Chicago finished ahead of Philadelphia, based on conference record (49ers' 2-3 to Bears' 2-5 to Eagles' 1-5).

First round playoff: MIAMI 28, New England 13;
  L.A. RAIDERS 27, Cleveland 10;
  N.Y. Jets 44, CINCINNATI 17;
  San Diego 31, PITTSBURGH 28
Second round playoff: N.Y. Jets 17, L.A. RAIDERS 14;
  MIAMI 34, San Diego 13
AFC Championship: MIAMI 14, N.Y. Jets 0
First round playoff: WASHINGTON 31, Detroit 7;
  GREEN BAY 41, St. Louis 16;
  MINNESOTA 30, Atlanta 24;
  DALLAS 30, Tampa Bay 17
Second round playoff: WASHINGTON 21, Minnesota 7;
  DALLAS 37, Green Bay 26
NFC Championship: WASHINGTON 31, Dallas 17
Super Bowl XVII: Washington (NFC) 27, Miami (AFC) 17,
  at Rose Bowl, Pasadena, California

1981

AMERICAN CONFERENCE

Eastern Division

	W	L	T	Pct.	Pts.	OP
Miami	11	4	1	.719	345	275
N.Y. Jets*	10	5	1	.656	355	287
Buffalo*	10	6	0	.625	311	276
Baltimore	2	14	0	.125	259	533
New England	2	14	0	.125	322	370

Central Division

	W	L	T	Pct.	Pts.	OP
Cincinnati#	12	4	0	.750	421	304
Pittsburgh	8	8	0	.500	356	297
Houston	7	9	0	.438	281	355
Cleveland	5	11	0	.313	276	375

Western Division

	W	L	T	Pct.	Pts.	OP
San Diego	10	6	0	.625	478	390
Denver	10	6	0	.625	321	289
Kansas City	9	7	0	.563	343	290
Oakland	7	9	0	.438	273	343
Seattle	6	10	0	.375	322	388

NATIONAL CONFERENCE

Eastern Division

	W	L	T	Pct.	Pts.	OP
Dallas	12	4	0	.750	367	277
Philadelphia*	10	6	0	.625	368	221
N.Y. Giants*	9	7	0	.563	295	257
Washington	8	8	0	.500	347	349
St. Louis	7	9	0	.438	315	408

Central Division

	W	L	T	Pct.	Pts.	OP
Tampa Bay	9	7	0	.563	315	268
Detroit	8	8	0	.500	397	322
Green Bay	8	8	0	.500	324	361
Minnesota	7	9	0	.438	325	369
Chicago	6	10	0	.375	253	324

Western Division

	W	L	T	Pct.	Pts.	OP
San Francisco#	13	3	0	.813	357	250
Atlanta	7	9	0	.438	426	355
Los Angeles	6	10	0	.375	303	351
New Orleans	4	12	0	.250	207	378

*Wild Card qualifier for playoffs; #Top playoff seed in conference

Baltimore finished ahead of New England based on head-to-head sweep (2-0). San Diego finished ahead of Denver based on better division record (6-2 to Broncos' 5-3). Buffalo was second Wild Card based on head-to-head victory over Denver (1-0). Detroit finished ahead of Green Bay based on better record against common opponents (4-4 to Packers' 3-5).

Wild Card playoff: Buffalo 31, N.Y. JETS 27
Divisional playoffs: San Diego 41, MIAMI 38 (OT);
  CINCINNATI 28, Buffalo 21
AFC Championship: CINCINNATI 27, San Diego 7
Wild Card playoff: N.Y. Giants 27, PHILADELPHIA 21
Divisional playoffs: DALLAS 38, Tampa Bay 0;
  SAN FRANCISCO 38, N.Y. Giants 24
NFC Championship: SAN FRANCISCO 28, Dallas 27
Super Bowl XVI: San Francisco (NFC) 26, Cincinnati (AFC) 21,
  at Silverdome, Pontiac, Michigan

1980

AMERICAN CONFERENCE

Eastern Division

	W	L	T	Pct.	Pts.	OP
Buffalo	11	5	0	.688	320	260
New England	10	6	0	.625	441	325
Miami	8	8	0	.500	266	305
Baltimore	7	9	0	.438	355	387
N.Y. Jets	4	12	0	.250	302	395

Central Division

	W	L	T	Pct.	Pts.	OP
Cleveland	11	5	0	.688	357	310
Houston*	11	5	0	.688	295	251
Pittsburgh	9	7	0	.563	352	313
Cincinnati	6	10	0	.375	244	312

Western Division

	W	L	T	Pct.	Pts.	OP
San Diego#	11	5	0	.688	418	327
Oakland*	11	5	0	.688	364	306
Kansas City	8	8	0	.500	319	336
Denver	8	8	0	.500	310	323
Seattle	4	12	0	.250	291	408

NATIONAL CONFERENCE

Eastern Division

	W	L	T	Pct.	Pts.	OP
Philadelphia	12	4	0	.750	384	222
Dallas*	12	4	0	.750	454	311
Washington	6	10	0	.375	261	293
St. Louis	5	11	0	.313	299	350
N.Y. Giants	4	12	0	.250	249	425

Central Division

	W	L	T	Pct.	Pts.	OP
Minnesota	9	7	0	.563	317	308
Detroit	9	7	0	.563	334	272
Chicago	7	9	0	.438	304	264
Tampa Bay	5	10	1	.344	271	341
Green Bay	5	10	1	.344	231	371

Western Division

	W	L	T	Pct.	Pts.	OP
Atlanta#	12	4	0	.750	405	272
Los Angeles*	11	5	0	.688	424	289
San Francisco	6	10	0	.375	320	415
New Orleans	1	15	0	.063	291	487

*Wild Card qualifier for playoffs; #Top playoff seed in conference
San Diego was top playoff seed based on better conference record than Cleveland and Buffalo (9-3 to Browns' 8-4 and Bills' 8-4). Cleveland was second playoff seed based on better record against common opponents (5-2 to Bills' 5-3). Cleveland finished ahead of Houston based on better conference record (8-4 to Oilers' 7-5). Oakland was first Wild Card based on better conference record than Houston (9-3 to Oilers' 7-5). San Diego finished ahead of Oakland based on better net points in division games (plus 60 net points to Raiders' plus 37). Oakland did not play San Diego in the divisional playoffs because, from 1970-1989, two teams from the same division could not meet prior to the conference championship game. Kansas City finished ahead of Denver based on head-to-head sweep (2-0). Atlanta was top playoff seed based on head-to-head victory over Philadelphia (1-0). Philadelphia finished ahead of Dallas based on better net points in division games (plus 84 net points to Cowboys' plus 50). Minnesota finished ahead of Detroit based on better conference record (8-4 to Lions' 9-5). Tampa Bay finished ahead of Green Bay based on better head-to-head record (1-0-1 to Packers' 0-1-1).
Wild Card playoff: OAKLAND 27, Houston 7
Divisional playoffs: SAN DIEGO 20, Buffalo 14;
   Oakland 14, CLEVELAND 12
AFC Championship: Oakland 34, SAN DIEGO 27
Wild Card playoff: DALLAS 34, Los Angeles 13
Divisional playoffs: PHILADELPHIA 31, Minnesota 16;
   Dallas 30, ATLANTA 27
NFC Championship: PHILADELPHIA 20, Dallas 7
Super Bowl XV: Oakland (AFC) 27, Philadelphia (NFC) 10,
   at Louisiana Superdome, New Orleans, Louisiana

1979

AMERICAN CONFERENCE

Eastern Division

	W	L	T	Pct.	Pts.	OP
Miami	10	6	0	.625	341	257
New England	9	7	0	.563	411	326
N.Y. Jets	8	8	0	.500	337	383
Buffalo	7	9	0	.438	268	279
Baltimore	5	11	0	.313	271	351

Central Division

	W	L	T	Pct.	Pts.	OP
Pittsburgh	12	4	0	.750	416	262
Houston*	11	5	0	.688	362	331
Cleveland	9	7	0	.563	359	352
Cincinnati	4	12	0	.250	337	421

Western Division

	W	L	T	Pct.	Pts.	OP
San Diego#	12	4	0	.750	411	246
Denver*	10	6	0	.625	289	262
Seattle	9	7	0	.563	378	372
Oakland	9	7	0	.563	365	337
Kansas City	7	9	0	.438	238	262

NATIONAL CONFERENCE

Eastern Division

	W	L	T	Pct.	Pts.	OP
Dallas#	11	5	0	.688	371	313
Philadelphia*	11	5	0	.688	339	282
Washington	10	6	0	.625	348	295
N.Y. Giants	6	10	0	.375	237	323
St. Louis	5	11	0	.313	307	358

Central Division

	W	L	T	Pct.	Pts.	OP
Tampa Bay	10	6	0	.625	273	237
Chicago*	10	6	0	.625	306	249
Minnesota	7	9	0	.438	259	337
Green Bay	5	11	0	.313	246	316
Detroit	2	14	0	.125	219	365

Western Division

	W	L	T	Pct.	Pts.	OP
Los Angeles	9	7	0	.563	323	309
New Orleans	8	8	0	.500	370	360
Atlanta	6	10	0	.375	300	388
San Francisco	2	14	0	.125	308	416

*Wild Card qualifier for playoffs; #Top playoff seed in conference
San Diego was top playoff seed based on head-to-head victory over Pittsburgh (1-0). Seattle finished ahead of Oakland based on head-to-head sweep (2-0). Dallas finished ahead of Philadelphia based on better conference record (10-2 to Eagles' 9-3). Philadelphia did not play Dallas in the divisional playoffs because, from 1970-1989, two teams from the same division could not meet prior to the conference championship game. Tampa Bay finished ahead of Chicago based on a better division record (6-2 to Bears' 5-3). Chicago was second Wild Card ahead of Washington based on better net points in all games (57 to Redskins' 53).
Wild Card playoff: HOUSTON 13, Denver 7
Divisional playoffs: Houston 17, SAN DIEGO 14;
   PITTSBURGH 34, Miami 14
AFC Championship: PITTSBURGH 27, Houston 13
Wild Card playoff: PHILADELPHIA 27, Chicago 17
Divisional playoffs: TAMPA BAY 24, Philadelphia 17;
   Los Angeles 21, DALLAS 19
NFC Championship: Los Angeles 9, TAMPA BAY 0
Super Bowl XIV: Pittsburgh (AFC) 31, Los Angeles (NFC) 19,
   at Rose Bowl, Pasadena, California

1978

AMERICAN CONFERENCE

Eastern Division

	W	L	T	Pct.	Pts.	OP
New England	11	5	0	.688	358	286
Miami*	11	5	0	.688	372	254
N.Y. Jets	8	8	0	.500	359	364
Buffalo	5	11	0	.313	302	354
Baltimore	5	11	0	.313	239	421

Central Division

	W	L	T	Pct.	Pts.	OP
Pittsburgh#	14	2	0	.875	356	195
Houston*	10	6	0	.625	283	298
Cleveland	8	8	0	.500	334	356
Cincinnati	4	12	0	.250	252	284

Western Division

	W	L	T	Pct.	Pts.	OP
Denver	10	6	0	.625	282	198
Oakland	9	7	0	.563	311	283
Seattle	9	7	0	.563	345	358
San Diego	9	7	0	.563	355	309
Kansas City	4	12	0	.250	243	327

NATIONAL CONFERENCE

Eastern Division

	W	L	T	Pct.	Pts.	OP
Dallas	12	4	0	.750	384	208
Philadelphia*	9	7	0	.563	270	250
Washington	8	8	0	.500	273	283
St. Louis	6	10	0	.375	248	296
N.Y. Giants	6	10	0	.375	264	298

Central Division

	W	L	T	Pct.	Pts.	OP
Minnesota	8	7	1	.531	294	306
Green Bay	8	7	1	.531	249	269
Detroit	7	9	0	.438	290	300
Chicago	7	9	0	.438	253	274
Tampa Bay	5	11	0	.313	241	259

Western Division

	W	L	T	Pct.	Pts.	OP
Los Angeles#	12	4	0	.750	316	245
Atlanta*	9	7	0	.563	240	290
New Orleans	7	9	0	.438	281	298
San Francisco	2	14	0	.125	219	350

*Wild Card qualifier for playoffs; #Top playoff seed in conference
New England finished ahead of Miami based on better division record (6-2 to Dolphins' 5-3). Buffalo finished ahead of Baltimore based on head-to-head sweep (2-0). Oakland finished ahead of Seattle and San Diego based on better record against common opponents (6-2 to Seahawks' 5-3 and Chargers' 4-4). Atlanta was first Wild Card ahead of Philadelphia based on better record against common opponents (5-2 to Eagles' 5-3). Houston did not play Pittsburgh, and Atlanta did not play Los Angeles in the divisional playoffs because, from 1970-1989, two teams from the same division could not meet prior to the conference championship game. Los Angeles was top playoff seed based on head-to-head victory over Dallas (1-0). St. Louis finished ahead of N.Y. Giants based on better division record (3-5 to Giants' 2-6). Minnesota finished ahead of Green Bay based on better head-to-head record (1-0-1). Detroit finished ahead of Chicago based on better division record (4-4 to Bears' 3-5).
Wild Card playoff: Houston 17, MIAMI 9
Divisional playoffs: Houston 31, NEW ENGLAND 14; PITTSBURGH 33, Denver 10
AFC Championship: PITTSBURGH 34, Houston 5
Wild Card playoff: ATLANTA 14, Philadelphia 13
Divisional playoffs: DALLAS 27, Atlanta 20; LOS ANGELES 34, Minnesota 10
NFC Championship: Dallas 28, LOS ANGELES 0
Super Bowl XIII: Pittsburgh (AFC) 35, Dallas (NFC) 31, at Orange Bowl, Miami, Florida

1977

AMERICAN CONFERENCE

Eastern Division

	W	L	T	Pct.	Pts.	OP
Baltimore	10	4	0	.714	295	221
Miami	10	4	0	.714	313	197
New England	9	5	0	.643	278	217
N.Y. Jets	3	11	0	.214	191	300
Buffalo	3	11	0	.214	160	313

Central Division

	W	L	T	Pct.	Pts.	OP
Pittsburgh	9	5	0	.643	283	243
Houston	8	6	0	.571	299	230
Cincinnati	8	6	0	.571	238	235
Cleveland	6	8	0	.429	269	267

Western Division

	W	L	T	Pct.	Pts.	OP
Denver#	12	2	0	.857	274	148
Oakland*	11	3	0	.786	351	230
San Diego	7	7	0	.500	222	205
Seattle	5	9	0	.357	282	373
Kansas City	2	12	0	.143	225	349

NATIONAL CONFERENCE

Eastern Division

	W	L	T	Pct.	Pts.	OP
Dallas#	12	2	0	.857	345	212
Washington	9	5	0	.643	196	189
St. Louis	7	7	0	.500	272	287
Philadelphia	5	9	0	.357	220	207
N.Y. Giants	5	9	0	.357	181	265

Central Division

	W	L	T	Pct.	Pts.	OP
Minnesota	9	5	0	.643	231	227
Chicago*	9	5	0	.643	255	253
Detroit	6	8	0	.429	183	252
Green Bay	4	10	0	.286	134	219
Tampa Bay	2	12	0	.143	103	223

Western Division

	W	L	T	Pct.	Pts.	OP
Los Angeles	10	4	0	.714	302	146
Atlanta	7	7	0	.500	179	129
San Francisco	5	9	0	.357	220	260
New Orleans	3	11	0	.214	232	336

*Wild Card qualifier for playoffs; #Top playoff seed in conference
Baltimore finished ahead of Miami based on better conference record (9-3 to Dolphins' 8-4). N.Y. Jets finished ahead of Buffalo based on better point-differential in head-to-head competition (1 point). Houston finished ahead of Cincinnati based on better point-differential in head-to-head competition (2 points). Oakland did not play Denver in the divisional playoffs because, from 1970-1989, two teams from the same division could not meet prior to the conference championship game. Minnesota finished ahead of Chicago based on better point-differential in head-to-head competition (3 points). Chicago won Wild Card ahead of Washington based on better net points in conference games (48 to Redskins' 4). Philadelphia finished ahead of N.Y. Giants based on head-to-head sweep (2-0).
Divisional playoffs: DENVER 34, Pittsburgh 21; Oakland 37, BALTIMORE 31 (OT)
AFC Championship: DENVER 20, Oakland 17
Divisional playoffs: DALLAS 37, Chicago 7; Minnesota 14, LOS ANGELES 7
NFC Championship: DALLAS 23, Minnesota 6
Super Bowl XII: Dallas (NFC) 27, Denver (AFC) 10, at Louisiana Superdome, New Orleans, Louisiana

1976

AMERICAN CONFERENCE

Eastern Division

	W	L	T	Pct.	Pts.	OP
Baltimore	11	3	0	.786	417	246
New England*	11	3	0	.786	376	236
Miami	6	8	0	.429	263	264
N.Y. Jets	3	11	0	.214	169	383
Buffalo	2	12	0	.143	245	363

Central Division

	W	L	T	Pct.	Pts.	OP
Pittsburgh	10	4	0	.714	342	138
Cincinnati	10	4	0	.714	335	210
Cleveland	9	5	0	.643	267	287
Houston	5	9	0	.357	222	273

Western Division

	W	L	T	Pct.	Pts.	OP
Oakland#	13	1	0	.929	350	237
Denver	9	5	0	.643	315	206
San Diego	6	8	0	.429	248	285
Kansas City	5	9	0	.357	290	376
Tampa Bay	0	14	0	.000	125	412

NATIONAL CONFERENCE

Eastern Division

	W	L	T	Pct.	Pts.	OP
Dallas	11	3	0	.786	296	194
Washington*	10	4	0	.714	291	217
St. Louis	10	4	0	.714	309	267
Philadelphia	4	10	0	.286	165	286
N.Y. Giants	3	11	0	.214	170	250

Central Division

	W	L	T	Pct.	Pts.	OP
Minnesota#	11	2	1	.821	305	176
Chicago	7	7	0	.500	253	216
Detroit	6	8	0	.429	262	220
Green Bay	5	9	0	.357	218	299

Western Division

	W	L	T	Pct.	Pts.	OP
Los Angeles	10	3	1	.750	351	190
San Francisco	8	6	0	.571	270	190
New Orleans	4	10	0	.286	253	346
Atlanta	4	10	0	.286	172	312
Seattle	2	12	0	.143	229	429

*Wild Card qualifier for playoffs; #Top playoff seed in conference
Baltimore finished ahead of New England based on better division record (7-1 to Patriots' 6-2). Pittsburgh finished ahead of Cincinnati based on head-to-head sweep (2-0). Washington finished ahead of St. Louis based on head-to-head sweep (2-0). New Orleans finished ahead of Atlanta based on better point-differential in head-to-head competition (27 points).
Divisional playoffs: OAKLAND 24, New England 21;
  Pittsburgh 40, BALTIMORE 14
AFC Championship: OAKLAND 24, Pittsburgh 7
Divisional playoffs: MINNESOTA 35, Washington 20;
  Los Angeles 14, DALLAS 12
NFC Championship: MINNESOTA 24, Los Angeles 13
Super Bowl XI: Oakland (AFC) 32, Minnesota (NFC) 14,
  at Rose Bowl, Pasadena, California

1975

AMERICAN CONFERENCE

Eastern Division

	W	L	T	Pct.	Pts.	OP
Baltimore	10	4	0	.714	395	269
Miami	10	4	0	.714	357	222
Buffalo	8	6	0	.571	420	355
N.Y. Jets	3	11	0	.214	258	433
New England	3	11	0	.214	258	358

Central Division

	W	L	T	Pct.	Pts.	OP
Pittsburgh#	12	2	0	.857	373	162
Cincinnati*	11	3	0	.786	340	246
Houston	10	4	0	.714	293	226
Cleveland	3	11	0	.214	218	372

Western Division

	W	L	T	Pct.	Pts.	OP
Oakland	11	3	0	.786	375	255
Denver	6	8	0	.429	254	307
Kansas City	5	9	0	.357	282	341
San Diego	2	12	0	.143	189	345

NATIONAL CONFERENCE

Eastern Division

	W	L	T	Pct.	Pts.	OP
St. Louis	11	3	0	.786	356	276
Dallas*	10	4	0	.714	350	268
Washington	8	6	0	.571	325	276
N.Y. Giants	5	9	0	.357	216	306
Philadelphia	4	10	0	.286	225	302

Central Division

	W	L	T	Pct.	Pts.	OP
Minnesota#	12	2	0	.857	377	180
Detroit	7	7	0	.500	245	262
Chicago	4	10	0	.286	191	379
Green Bay	4	10	0	.286	226	285

Western Division

	W	L	T	Pct.	Pts.	OP
Los Angeles	12	2	0	.857	312	135
San Francisco	5	9	0	.357	255	286
Atlanta	4	10	0	.286	240	289
New Orleans	2	12	0	.143	165	360

*Wild Card qualifier for playoffs; #Top playoff seed in conference
Baltimore finished ahead of Miami based on head-to-head sweep (2-0). Cincinnati did not play Pittsburgh in the divisional playoffs because, from 1970-1989, two teams from the same division could not meet prior to the conference championship game. N.Y. Jets finished ahead of New England based on head-to-head sweep (2-0). Minnesota was top playoff seed based on better Point Rating system than Los Angeles (3 to 6). Chicago finished ahead of Green Bay based on better division record (2-4 to Bears' 1-5).
Divisional playoffs: PITTSBURGH 28, Baltimore 10;
  OAKLAND 31, Cincinnati 28
AFC Championship: PITTSBURGH 16, Oakland 10
Divisional playoffs: LOS ANGELES 35, St. Louis 23;
  Dallas 17, MINNESOTA 14
NFC Championship: Dallas 37, LOS ANGELES 7
Super Bowl X: Pittsburgh (AFC) 21, Dallas (NFC) 17,
  at Orange Bowl, Miami, Florida

1974

AMERICAN CONFERENCE

Eastern Division

	W	L	T	Pct.	Pts.	OP
Miami	11	3	0	.786	327	216
Buffalo*	9	5	0	.643	264	244
N.Y. Jets	7	7	0	.500	279	300
New England	7	7	0	.500	348	289
Baltimore	2	12	0	.143	190	329

Central Division

	W	L	T	Pct.	Pts.	OP
Pittsburgh	10	3	1	.750	305	189
Houston	7	7	0	.500	236	282
Cincinnati	7	7	0	.500	283	259
Cleveland	4	10	0	.286	251	344

Western Division

	W	L	T	Pct.	Pts.	OP
Oakland	12	2	0	.857	355	228
Denver	7	6	1	.536	302	294
Kansas City	5	9	0	.357	233	293
San Diego	5	9	0	.357	212	285

NATIONAL CONFERENCE

Eastern Division

	W	L	T	Pct.	Pts.	OP
St. Louis	10	4	0	.714	285	218
Washington*	10	4	0	.714	320	196
Dallas	8	6	0	.571	297	235
Philadelphia	7	7	0	.500	242	217
N.Y. Giants	2	12	0	.143	195	299

Central Division

	W	L	T	Pct.	Pts.	OP
Minnesota	10	4	0	.714	310	195
Detroit	7	7	0	.500	256	270
Green Bay	6	8	0	.429	210	206
Chicago	4	10	0	.286	152	279

Western Division

	W	L	T	Pct.	Pts.	OP
Los Angeles	10	4	0	.714	263	181
San Francisco	6	8	0	.429	226	236
New Orleans	5	9	0	.357	166	263
Atlanta	3	11	0	.214	111	271

Wild Card qualifier for playoffs

N.Y. Jets finished ahead of New England based on better conference record (5-6 to Patriots' 4-7). Houston finished ahead of Cincinnati based on head-to-head sweep (2-0). Kansas City finished ahead of San Diego based on better point-differential in head-to-head competition (3 points). St. Louis finished ahead of Washington based on head-to-head sweep (2-0).

Divisional playoffs: OAKLAND 28, Miami 26; PITTSBURGH 32, Buffalo 14

AFC Championship: Pittsburgh 24, OAKLAND 13

Divisional playoffs: MINNESOTA 30, St. Louis 14; LOS ANGELES 19, Washington 10

NFC Championship: MINNESOTA 14, Los Angeles 10

Super Bowl IX: Pittsburgh (AFC) 16, Minnesota (NFC) 6, at Tulane Stadium, New Orleans, Louisiana

From 1933-1974, sites for league/conference championship games alternated by division.

1973

AMERICAN CONFERENCE

Eastern Division

	W	L	T	Pct.	Pts.	OP
Miami	12	2	0	.857	343	150
Buffalo	9	5	0	.643	259	230
New England	5	9	0	.357	258	300
N.Y. Jets	4	10	0	.286	240	306
Baltimore	4	10	0	.286	226	341

Central Division

	W	L	T	Pct.	Pts.	OP
Cincinnati	10	4	0	.714	286	231
Pittsburgh*	10	4	0	.714	347	210
Cleveland	7	5	2	.571	234	255
Houston	1	13	0	.071	199	447

Western Division

	W	L	T	Pct.	Pts.	OP
Oakland	9	4	1	.679	292	175
Kansas City	7	5	2	.571	231	192
Denver	7	5	2	.571	354	296
San Diego	2	11	1	.179	188	386

NATIONAL CONFERENCE

Eastern Division

	W	L	T	Pct.	Pts.	OP
Dallas	10	4	0	.714	382	203
Washington*	10	4	0	.714	325	198
Philadelphia	5	8	1	.393	310	393
St. Louis	4	9	1	.321	286	365
N.Y. Giants	2	11	1	.179	226	362

Central Division

	W	L	T	Pct.	Pts.	OP
Minnesota	12	2	0	.857	296	168
Detroit	6	7	1	.464	271	247
Green Bay	5	7	2	.429	202	259
Chicago	3	11	0	.214	195	334

Western Division

	W	L	T	Pct.	Pts.	OP
Los Angeles	12	2	0	.857	388	178
Atlanta	9	5	0	.643	318	224
San Francisco	5	9	0	.357	262	319
New Orleans	5	9	0	.357	163	312

Wild Card qualifier for playoffs

Cincinnati finished ahead of Pittsburgh based on better conference record (8-3 to Steelers' 7-4). N.Y. Jets finished ahead of Baltimore based on head-to-head sweep (2-0). Kansas City finished ahead of Denver based on better division record (4-2 to Broncos' 3-2-1). Dallas finished ahead of Washington based on better point differential in head-to-head games (13 points). San Francisco finished ahead of New Orleans based on better division record (2-4 to Saints' 1-5).

Divisional playoffs: OAKLAND 33, Pittsburgh 14; MIAMI 34, Cincinnati 16

AFC Championship: MIAMI 27, Oakland 10

Divisional playoffs: MINNESOTA 27, Washington 20; DALLAS 27, Los Angeles 16

NFC Championship: Minnesota 27, DALLAS 10

Super Bowl VIII: Miami (AFC) 24, Minnesota (NFC) 7, at Rice Stadium, Houston, Texas

1972

AMERICAN CONFERENCE

Eastern Division

	W	L	T	Pct.	Pts.	OP
Miami	14	0	0	1.000	385	171
N.Y. Jets	7	7	0	.500	367	324
Baltimore	5	9	0	.357	235	252
Buffalo	4	9	1	.321	257	377
New England	3	11	0	.214	192	446

Central Division

	W	L	T	Pct.	Pts.	OP
Pittsburgh	11	3	0	.786	343	175
Cleveland*	10	4	0	.714	268	249
Cincinnati	8	6	0	.571	299	229
Houston	1	13	0	.071	164	380

Western Division

	W	L	T	Pct.	Pts.	OP
Oakland	10	3	1	.750	365	248
Kansas City	8	6	0	.571	287	254
Denver	5	9	0	.357	325	350
San Diego	4	9	1	.321	264	344

NATIONAL CONFERENCE

Eastern Division

	W	L	T	Pct.	Pts.	OP
Washington	11	3	0	.786	336	218
Dallas*	10	4	0	.714	319	240
N.Y. Giants	8	6	0	.571	331	247
St. Louis	4	9	1	.321	193	303
Philadelphia	2	11	1	.179	145	352

Central Division

	W	L	T	Pct.	Pts.	OP
Green Bay	10	4	0	.714	304	226
Detroit	8	5	1	.607	339	290
Minnesota	7	7	0	.500	301	252
Chicago	4	9	1	.321	225	275

Western Division

	W	L	T	Pct.	Pts.	OP
San Francisco	8	5	1	.607	353	249
Atlanta	7	7	0	.500	269	274
Los Angeles	6	7	1	.464	291	286
New Orleans	2	11	1	.179	215	361

Wild Card qualifier for playoffs

Dallas did not play Washington in the divisional playoffs because, from 1970-1989, two teams from the same division could not meet prior to the conference championship game.

Divisional playoffs: PITTSBURGH 13, Oakland 7;
   MIAMI 20, Cleveland 14
AFC Championship: Miami 21, PITTSBURGH 17
Divisional playoffs: Dallas 30, SAN FRANCISCO 28;
   WASHINGTON 16, Green Bay 3
NFC Championship: WASHINGTON 26, Dallas 3
Super Bowl VII: Miami (AFC) 14, Washington (NFC) 7,
   at Memorial Coliseum, Los Angeles, California

1971

AMERICAN CONFERENCE

Eastern Division

	W	L	T	Pct.	Pts.	OP
Miami	10	3	1	.769	315	174
Baltimore*	10	4	0	.714	313	140
New England	6	8	0	.429	238	325
N.Y. Jets	6	8	0	.429	212	299
Buffalo	1	13	0	.071	184	394

Central Division

	W	L	T	Pct.	Pts.	OP
Cleveland	9	5	0	.643	285	273
Pittsburgh	6	8	0	.429	246	292
Houston	4	9	1	.308	251	330
Cincinnati	4	10	0	.286	284	265

Western Division

	W	L	T	Pct.	Pts.	OP
Kansas City	10	3	1	.769	302	208
Oakland	8	4	2	.667	344	278
San Diego	6	8	0	.429	311	341
Denver	4	9	1	.308	203	275

NATIONAL CONFERENCE

Eastern Division

	W	L	T	Pct.	Pts.	OP
Dallas	11	3	0	.786	406	222
Washington*	9	4	1	.692	276	190
Philadelphia	6	7	1	.462	221	302
St. Louis	4	9	1	.308	231	279
N.Y. Giants	4	10	0	.286	228	362

Central Division

	W	L	T	Pct.	Pts.	OP
Minnesota	11	3	0	.786	245	139
Detroit	7	6	1	.538	341	286
Chicago	6	8	0	.429	185	276
Green Bay	4	8	2	.333	274	298

Western Division

	W	L	T	Pct.	Pts.	OP
San Francisco	9	5	0	.643	300	216
Los Angeles	8	5	1	.615	313	260
Atlanta	7	6	1	.538	274	277
New Orleans	4	8	2	.333	266	347

Wild Card qualifier for playoffs

New England finished ahead of N.Y. Jets based on better point-differential in head-to-head competition (13 points).

Divisional playoffs: Miami 27, KANSAS CITY 24 (OT);
   Baltimore 20, CLEVELAND 3
AFC Championship: MIAMI 21, Baltimore 0
Divisional playoffs: Dallas 20, MINNESOTA 12;
   SAN FRANCISCO 24, Washington 20
NFC Championship: DALLAS 14, San Francisco 3
Super Bowl VI: Dallas (NFC) 24, Miami (AFC) 3,
   at Tulane Stadium, New Orleans, Louisiana

From 1920-1971, tie games were not included in winning percentage.

1970

AMERICAN CONFERENCE

Eastern Division

	W	L	T	Pct.	Pts.	OP
Baltimore	11	2	1	.846	321	234
Miami*	10	4	0	.714	297	228
N.Y. Jets	4	10	0	.286	255	286
Buffalo	3	10	1	.231	204	337
Boston Patriots	2	12	0	.143	149	361

Central Division

	W	L	T	Pct.	Pts.	OP
Cincinnati	8	6	0	.571	312	255
Cleveland	7	7	0	.500	286	265
Pittsburgh	5	9	0	.357	210	272
Houston	3	10	1	.231	217	352

Western Division

	W	L	T	Pct.	Pts.	OP
Oakland	8	4	2	.667	300	293
Kansas City	7	5	2	.583	272	244
San Diego	5	6	3	.455	282	278
Denver	5	8	1	.385	253	264

NATIONAL CONFERENCE

Eastern Division

	W	L	T	Pct.	Pts.	OP
Dallas	10	4	0	.714	299	221
N.Y. Giants	9	5	0	.643	301	270
St. Louis	8	5	1	.615	325	228
Washington	6	8	0	.429	297	314
Philadelphia	3	10	1	.231	241	332

Central Division

	W	L	T	Pct.	Pts.	OP
Minnesota	12	2	0	.857	335	143
Detroit*	10	4	0	.714	347	202
Green Bay	6	8	0	.429	196	293
Chicago	6	8	0	.429	256	261

Western Division

	W	L	T	Pct.	Pts.	OP
San Francisco	10	3	1	.769	352	267
Los Angeles	9	4	1	.692	325	202
Atlanta	4	8	2	.333	206	261
New Orleans	2	11	1	.154	172	347

Wild Card qualifier for playoffs

Miami did not play Baltimore, and Detroit did not play Minnesota, in the divisional playoffs because, from 1970-1989, two teams from the same division could not meet prior to the conference championship game. Green Bay finished ahead of Chicago based on better division record (2-4 to Bears' 1-5).

Divisional playoffs: BALTIMORE 17, Cincinnati 0; OAKLAND 21, Miami 14
AFC Championship: BALTIMORE 27, Oakland 17
Divisional playoffs: DALLAS 5, Detroit 0; San Francisco 17, MINNESOTA 14
NFC Championship: Dallas 17, SAN FRANCISCO 10
Super Bowl V: Baltimore (AFC) 16, Dallas (NFC) 13, at Orange Bowl, Miami, Florida

1969 NFL

EASTERN CONFERENCE

Capitol Division

	W	L	T	Pct.	Pts.	OP
Dallas	11	2	1	.846	369	223
Washington	7	5	2	.583	307	319
New Orleans	5	9	0	.357	311	393
Philadelphia	4	9	1	.308	279	377

Century Division

	W	L	T	Pct.	Pts.	OP
Cleveland	10	3	1	.769	351	300
N.Y. Giants	6	8	0	.429	264	298
St. Louis	4	9	1	.308	314	389
Pittsburgh	1	13	0	.071	218	404

WESTERN CONFERENCE

Coastal Division

	W	L	T	Pct.	Pts.	OP
Los Angeles	11	3	0	.786	320	243
Baltimore	8	5	1	.615	279	268
Atlanta	6	8	0	.429	276	268
San Francisco	4	8	2	.333	277	319

Central Division

	W	L	T	Pct.	Pts.	OP
Minnesota	12	2	0	.857	379	133
Detroit	9	4	1	.692	259	188
Green Bay	8	6	0	.571	269	221
Chicago	1	13	0	.071	210	339

Conference championships: Cleveland 38, DALLAS 14; MINNESOTA 23, Los Angeles 20
NFL championship: MINNESOTA 27, Cleveland 7
Super Bowl IV: Kansas City (AFL) 23, Minnesota (NFL) 7, at Tulane Stadium, New Orleans, Louisiana

1969 AFL

EASTERN DIVISION

	W	L	T	Pct.	Pts.	OP
N.Y. Jets	10	4	0	.714	353	269
Houston	6	6	2	.500	278	279
Boston Patriots	4	10	0	.286	266	316
Buffalo	4	10	0	.286	230	359
Miami	3	10	1	.231	233	332

WESTERN DIVISION

	W	L	T	Pct.	Pts.	OP
Oakland	12	1	1	.923	377	242
Kansas City	11	3	0	.786	359	177
San Diego	8	6	0	.571	288	276
Denver	5	8	1	.385	297	344
Cincinnati	4	9	1	.308	280	367

Divisional playoffs: Kansas City 13, N.Y. JETS 6; OAKLAND 56, Houston 7
AFL championship: Kansas City 17, OAKLAND 7

1968 NFL

EASTERN CONFERENCE

Capitol Division

	W	L	T	Pct.	Pts.	OP
Dallas	12	2	0	.857	431	186
N.Y. Giants	7	7	0	.500	294	325
Washington	5	9	0	.357	249	358
Philadelphia	2	12	0	.143	202	351

Century Division

	W	L	T	Pct.	Pts.	OP
Cleveland	10	4	0	.714	394	273
St. Louis	9	4	1	.692	325	289
New Orleans	4	9	1	.308	246	327
Pittsburgh	2	11	1	.154	244	397

WESTERN CONFERENCE

Coastal Division

	W	L	T	Pct.	Pts.	OP
Baltimore	13	1	0	.929	402	144
Los Angeles	10	3	1	.769	312	200
San Francisco	7	6	1	.538	303	310
Atlanta	2	12	0	.143	170	389

Central Division

	W	L	T	Pct.	Pts.	OP
Minnesota	8	6	0	.571	282	242
Chicago	7	7	0	.500	250	333
Green Bay	6	7	1	.462	281	227
Detroit	4	8	2	.333	207	241

Conference championships: CLEVELAND 31, Dallas 20; BALTIMORE 24, Minnesota 14
NFL championship: Baltimore 34, CLEVELAND 0
Super Bowl III: N.Y. Jets (AFL) 16, Baltimore (NFL) 7, at Orange Bowl, Miami, Florida

1968 AFL

EASTERN DIVISION

	W	L	T	Pct.	Pts.	OP
N.Y. Jets	11	3	0	.786	419	280
Houston	7	7	0	.500	303	248
Miami	5	8	1	.385	276	355
Boston Patriots	4	10	0	.286	229	406
Buffalo	1	12	1	.077	199	367

WESTERN DIVISION

	W	L	T	Pct.	Pts.	OP
Oakland	12	2	0	.857	453	233
Kansas City	12	2	0	.857	371	170
San Diego	9	5	0	.643	382	310
Denver	5	9	0	.357	255	404
Cincinnati	3	11	0	.214	215	329

Western Division playoff: OAKLAND 41, Kansas City 6
AFL championship: N.Y. JETS 27, Oakland 23

1967 NFL

EASTERN CONFERENCE

Capitol Division

	W	L	T	Pct.	Pts.	OP
Dallas	9	5	0	.643	342	268
Philadelphia	6	7	1	.462	351	409
Washington	5	6	3	.455	347	353
New Orleans	3	11	0	.214	233	379

Century Division

	W	L	T	Pct.	Pts.	OP
Cleveland	9	5	0	.643	334	297
N.Y. Giants	7	7	0	.500	369	379
St. Louis	6	7	1	.462	333	356
Pittsburgh	4	9	1	.308	281	320

WESTERN CONFERENCE

Coastal Division

	W	L	T	Pct.	Pts.	OP
Los Angeles	11	1	2	.917	398	196
Baltimore	11	1	2	.917	394	198
San Francisco	7	7	0	.500	273	337
Atlanta	1	12	1	.077	175	422

Central Division

	W	L	T	Pct.	Pts.	OP
Green Bay	9	4	1	.692	332	209
Chicago	7	6	1	.538	239	218
Detroit	5	7	2	.417	260	259
Minnesota	3	8	3	.273	233	294

Los Angeles finished ahead of Baltimore based on better point differential in head-to-head games (net 24 points).
Conference championships: DALLAS 52, Cleveland 14;
    GREEN BAY 28, Los Angeles 7
NFL championship: GREEN BAY 21, Dallas 17
Super Bowl II: Green Bay (NFL) 33, Oakland (AFL) 14,
    at Orange Bowl, Miami, Florida

1967 AFL

EASTERN DIVISION

	W	L	T	Pct.	Pts.	OP
Houston	9	4	1	.692	258	199
N.Y. Jets	8	5	1	.615	371	329
Buffalo	4	10	0	.286	237	285
Miami	4	10	0	.286	219	407
Boston Patriots	3	10	1	.231	280	389

WESTERN DIVISION

	W	L	T	Pct.	Pts.	OP
Oakland	13	1	0	.929	468	233
Kansas City	9	5	0	.643	408	254
San Diego	8	5	1	.615	360	352
Denver	3	11	0	.214	256	409

AFL championship: OAKLAND 40, Houston 7

1966 NFL

EASTERN CONFERENCE

	W	L	T	Pct.	Pts.	OP
Dallas	10	3	1	.769	445	239
Cleveland	9	5	0	.643	403	259
Philadelphia	9	5	0	.643	326	340
St. Louis	8	5	1	.615	264	265
Washington	7	7	0	.500	351	355
Pittsburgh	5	8	1	.385	316	347
Atlanta	3	11	0	.214	204	437
N.Y. Giants	1	12	1	.077	263	501

WESTERN CONFERENCE

	W	L	T	Pct.	Pts.	OP
Green Bay	12	2	0	.857	335	163
Baltimore	9	5	0	.643	314	226
Los Angeles	8	6	0	.571	289	212
San Francisco	6	6	2	.500	320	325
Chicago	5	7	2	.417	234	272
Detroit	4	9	1	.308	206	317
Minnesota	4	9	1	.308	292	304

NFL championship: Green Bay 34, DALLAS 27
Super Bowl I: Green Bay (NFL) 35, Kansas City (AFL) 10,
    at Memorial Coliseum, Los Angeles, California

1966 AFL

EASTERN DIVISION

	W	L	T	Pct.	Pts.	OP
Buffalo	9	4	1	.692	358	255
Boston Patriots	8	4	2	.677	315	283
N.Y. Jets	6	6	2	.500	322	312
Houston	3	11	0	.214	335	396
Miami	3	11	0	.214	213	362

WESTERN DIVISION

	W	L	T	Pct.	Pts.	OP
Kansas City	11	2	1	.846	448	276
Oakland	8	5	1	.615	315	288
San Diego	7	6	1	.538	335	284
Denver	4	10	0	.286	196	381

AFL championship: Kansas City 31, BUFFALO 7

1965 NFL

EASTERN CONFERENCE

	W	L	T	Pct.	Pts.	OP
Cleveland	11	3	0	.786	363	325
Dallas	7	7	0	.500	325	280
N.Y. Giants	7	7	0	.500	270	338
Washington	6	8	0	.429	257	301
Philadelphia	5	9	0	.357	363	359
St. Louis	5	9	0	.357	296	309
Pittsburgh	2	12	0	.143	202	397

WESTERN CONFERENCE

	W	L	T	Pct.	Pts.	OP
Green Bay	10	3	1	.769	316	224
Baltimore	10	3	1	.769	389	284
Chicago	9	5	0	.643	409	275
San Francisco	7	6	1	.538	421	402
Minnesota	7	7	0	.500	383	403
Detroit	6	7	1	.462	257	295
Los Angeles	4	10	0	.286	269	328

Western Conference playoff: GREEN BAY 13, Baltimore 10 (OT)
NFL championship: GREEN BAY 23, Cleveland 12

1965 AFL

EASTERN DIVISION

	W	L	T	Pct.	Pts.	OP
Buffalo	10	3	1	.769	313	226
N.Y. Jets	5	8	1	.385	285	303
Boston Patriots	4	8	2	.333	244	302
Houston	4	10	0	.286	298	429

WESTERN DIVISION

	W	L	T	Pct.	Pts.	OP
San Diego	9	2	3	.818	340	227
Oakland	8	5	1	.615	298	239
Kansas City	7	5	2	.583	322	285
Denver	4	10	0	.286	303	392

AFL championship: Buffalo 23, SAN DIEGO 0

1964 NFL

EASTERN CONFERENCE

	W	L	T	Pct.	Pts.	OP
Cleveland	10	3	1	.769	415	293
St. Louis	9	3	2	.750	357	331
Philadelphia	6	8	0	.429	312	313
Washington	6	8	0	.429	307	305
Dallas	5	8	1	.385	250	289
Pittsburgh	5	9	0	.357	253	315
N.Y. Giants	2	10	2	.167	241	399

WESTERN CONFERENCE

	W	L	T	Pct.	Pts.	OP
Baltimore	12	2	0	.857	428	225
Green Bay	8	5	1	.615	342	245
Minnesota	8	5	1	.615	355	296
Detroit	7	5	2	.583	280	260
Los Angeles	5	7	2	.417	283	339
Chicago	5	9	0	.357	260	379
San Francisco	4	10	0	.286	236	330

NFL championship: CLEVELAND 27, Baltimore 0

1964 AFL

EASTERN DIVISION

	W	L	T	Pct.	Pts.	OP
Buffalo	12	2	0	.857	400	242
Boston Patriots	10	3	1	.769	365	297
N.Y. Jets	5	8	1	.385	278	315
Houston	4	10	0	.286	310	355

WESTERN DIVISION

	W	L	T	Pct.	Pts.	OP
San Diego	8	5	1	.615	341	300
Kansas City	7	7	0	.500	366	306
Oakland	5	7	2	.417	303	350
Denver	2	11	1	.154	240	438

AFL championship: BUFFALO 20, San Diego 7

1963 NFL

EASTERN CONFERENCE

	W	L	T	Pct.	Pts.	OP
N.Y. Giants	11	3	0	.786	448	280
Cleveland	10	4	0	.714	343	262
St. Louis	9	5	0	.643	341	283
Pittsburgh	7	4	3	.636	321	295
Dallas	4	10	0	.286	305	378
Washington	3	11	0	.214	279	398
Philadelphia	2	10	2	.167	242	381

WESTERN CONFERENCE

	W	L	T	Pct.	Pts.	OP
Chicago	11	1	2	.917	301	144
Green Bay	11	2	1	.846	369	206
Baltimore	8	6	0	.571	316	285
Detroit	5	8	1	.385	326	265
Minnesota	5	8	1	.385	309	390
Los Angeles	5	9	0	.357	210	350
San Francisco	2	12	0	.143	198	391

NFL championship: CHICAGO 14, N.Y. Giants 10

1963 AFL

EASTERN DIVISION

	W	L	T	Pct.	Pts.	OP
Boston Patriots	7	6	1	.538	327	257
Buffalo	7	6	1	.538	304	291
Houston	6	8	0	.429	302	372
N.Y. Jets	5	8	1	.385	249	399

WESTERN DIVISION

	W	L	T	Pct.	Pts.	OP
San Diego	11	3	0	.786	399	255
Oakland	10	4	0	.714	363	282
Kansas City	5	7	2	.417	347	263
Denver	2	11	1	.154	301	473

Eastern Division playoff: Boston 26, BUFFALO 8
AFL championship: SAN DIEGO 51, Boston 10

1962 NFL

EASTERN CONFERENCE	W	L	T	Pct.	Pts.	OP	WESTERN CONFERENCE	W	L	T	Pct.	Pts.	OP
N.Y. Giants	12	2	0	.857	398	283	Green Bay	13	1	0	.929	415	148
Pittsburgh	9	5	0	.643	312	363	Detroit	11	3	0	.786	315	177
Cleveland	7	6	1	.538	291	257	Chicago	9	5	0	.643	321	287
Washington	5	7	2	.417	305	376	Baltimore	7	7	0	.500	293	288
Dallas Cowboys	5	8	1	.385	398	402	San Francisco	6	8	0	.429	282	331
St. Louis	4	9	1	.308	287	361	Minnesota	2	11	1	.154	254	410
Philadelphia	3	10	1	.231	282	356	Los Angeles	1	12	1	.077	220	334

NFL championship: Green Bay 16, N.Y. GIANTS 7

1962 AFL

EASTERN DIVISION	W	L	T	Pct.	Pts.	OP	WESTERN DIVISION	W	L	T	Pct.	Pts.	OP
Houston	11	3	0	.786	387	270	Dallas Texans	11	3	0	.786	389	233
Boston Patriots	9	4	1	.692	346	295	Denver	7	7	0	.500	353	334
Buffalo	7	6	1	.538	309	272	San Diego	4	10	0	.286	314	392
N.Y. Titans	5	9	0	.357	278	423	Oakland	1	13	0	.071	213	370

AFL championship: Dallas Texans 20, HOUSTON 17 (OT)

1961 NFL

EASTERN CONFERENCE	W	L	T	Pct.	Pts.	OP	WESTERN CONFERENCE	W	L	T	Pct.	Pts.	OP
N.Y. Giants	10	3	1	.769	368	220	Green Bay	11	3	0	.786	391	223
Philadelphia	10	4	0	.714	361	297	Detroit	8	5	1	.615	270	258
Cleveland	8	5	1	.615	319	270	Baltimore	8	6	0	.571	302	307
St. Louis	7	7	0	.500	279	267	Chicago	8	6	0	.571	326	302
Pittsburgh	6	8	0	.429	295	287	San Francisco	7	6	1	.538	346	272
Dallas Cowboys	4	9	1	.308	236	380	Los Angeles	4	10	0	.286	263	333
Washington	1	12	1	.077	174	392	Minnesota	3	11	0	.214	285	407

NFL championship: GREEN BAY 37, N.Y. Giants 0

1961 AFL

EASTERN DIVISION	W	L	T	Pct.	Pts.	OP	WESTERN DIVISION	W	L	T	Pct.	Pts.	OP
Houston	10	3	1	.769	513	242	San Diego	12	2	0	.857	396	219
Boston Patriots	9	4	1	.692	413	313	Dallas Texans	6	8	0	.429	334	343
N.Y. Titans	7	7	0	.500	301	390	Denver	3	11	0	.214	251	432
Buffalo	6	8	0	.429	294	342	Oakland	2	12	0	.143	237	458

AFL championship: Houston 10, SAN DIEGO 3

1960 NFL

EASTERN CONFERENCE	W	L	T	Pct.	Pts.	OP	WESTERN CONFERENCE	W	L	T	Pct.	Pts.	OP
Philadelphia	10	2	0	.833	321	246	Green Bay	8	4	0	.667	332	209
Cleveland	8	3	1	.727	362	217	Detroit	7	5	0	.583	239	212
N.Y. Giants	6	4	2	.600	271	261	San Francisco	7	5	0	.583	208	205
St. Louis	6	5	1	.545	288	230	Baltimore	6	6	0	.500	288	234
Pittsburgh	5	6	1	.455	240	275	Chicago	5	6	1	.455	194	299
Washington	1	9	2	.100	178	309	L.A. Rams	4	7	1	.364	265	297
							Dallas Cowboys	0	11	1	.000	177	369

NFL championship: PHILADELPHIA 17, Green Bay 13

1960 AFL

EASTERN CONFERENCE	W	L	T	Pct.	Pts.	OP	WESTERN CONFERENCE	W	L	T	Pct.	Pts.	OP
Houston	10	4	0	.714	379	285	L.A. Chargers	10	4	0	.714	373	336
N.Y. Titans	7	7	0	.500	382	399	Dallas Texans	8	6	0	.571	362	253
Buffalo	5	8	1	.385	296	303	Oakland	6	8	0	.429	319	388
Boston Patriots	5	9	0	.357	286	349	Denver	4	9	1	.308	309	393

AFL championship: HOUSTON 24, L.A. Chargers 16

1959

EASTERN CONFERENCE	W	L	T	Pct.	Pts.	OP	WESTERN CONFERENCE	W	L	T	Pct.	Pts.	OP
N.Y. Giants	10	2	0	.833	284	170	Baltimore	9	3	0	.750	374	251
Cleveland	7	5	0	.583	270	214	Chi. Bears	8	4	0	.667	252	196
Philadelphia	7	5	0	.583	268	278	Green Bay	7	5	0	.583	248	246
Pittsburgh	6	5	1	.545	257	216	San Francisco	7	5	0	.583	255	237
Washington	3	9	0	.250	185	350	Detroit	3	8	1	.273	203	275
Chi. Cardinals	2	10	0	.167	234	324	Los Angeles	2	10	0	.167	242	315

NFL championship: BALTIMORE 31, N.Y. Giants 16

1958

EASTERN CONFERENCE	W	L	T	Pct.	Pts.	OP	WESTERN CONFERENCE	W	L	T	Pct.	Pts.	OP
N.Y. Giants	9	3	0	.750	246	183	Baltimore	9	3	0	.750	381	203
Cleveland	9	3	0	.750	302	217	Chi. Bears	8	4	0	.667	298	230
Pittsburgh	7	4	1	.636	261	230	Los Angeles	8	4	0	.667	344	278
Washington	4	7	1	.364	214	268	San Francisco	6	6	0	.500	257	324
Chi. Cardinals	2	9	1	.182	261	356	Detroit	4	7	1	.364	261	276
Philadelphia	2	9	1	.182	235	306	Green Bay	1	10	1	.091	193	382

Eastern Conference playoff: N.Y. GIANTS 10, Cleveland 0
NFL championship: Baltimore 23, N.Y. GIANTS 17 (OT)

1957

EASTERN CONFERENCE	W	L	T	Pct.	Pts.	OP	WESTERN CONFERENCE	W	L	T	Pct.	Pts.	OP
Cleveland	9	2	1	.818	269	172	Detroit	8	4	0	.667	251	231
N.Y. Giants	7	5	0	.583	254	211	San Francisco	8	4	0	.667	260	264
Pittsburgh	6	6	0	.500	161	178	Baltimore	7	5	0	.583	303	235
Washington	5	6	1	.455	251	230	Los Angeles	6	6	0	.500	307	278
Philadelphia	4	8	0	.333	173	230	Chi. Bears	5	7	0	.417	203	211
Chi. Cardinals	3	9	0	.250	200	299	Green Bay	3	9	0	.250	218	311

Western Conference playoff: Detroit 31, SAN FRANCISCO 27
NFL championship: DETROIT 59, Cleveland 14

1956

EASTERN CONFERENCE	W	L	T	Pct.	Pts.	OP	WESTERN CONFERENCE	W	L	T	Pct.	Pts.	OP
N.Y. Giants	8	3	1	.727	264	197	Chi. Bears	9	2	1	.818	363	246
Chi. Cardinals	7	5	0	.583	240	182	Detroit	9	3	0	.750	300	188
Washington	6	6	0	.500	183	225	San Francisco	5	6	1	.455	233	284
Cleveland	5	7	0	.417	167	177	Baltimore	5	7	0	.417	270	322
Pittsburgh	5	7	0	.417	217	250	Green Bay	4	8	0	.333	264	342
Philadelphia	3	8	1	.273	143	215	Los Angeles	4	8	0	.333	291	307

NFL championship: N.Y. GIANTS 47, Chi. Bears 7

1955

EASTERN CONFERENCE	W	L	T	Pct.	Pts.	OP	WESTERN CONFERENCE	W	L	T	Pct.	Pts.	OP
Cleveland	9	2	1	.818	349	218	Los Angeles	8	3	1	.727	260	231
Washington	8	4	0	.667	246	222	Chi. Bears	8	4	0	.667	294	251
N.Y. Giants	6	5	1	.545	267	223	Green Bay	6	6	0	.500	258	276
Chi. Cardinals	4	7	1	.364	224	252	Baltimore	5	6	1	.455	214	239
Philadelphia	4	7	1	.364	248	231	San Francisco	4	8	0	.333	216	298
Pittsburgh	4	8	0	.333	195	285	Detroit	3	9	0	.250	230	275

NFL championship: Cleveland 38, LOS ANGELES 14

1954

EASTERN CONFERENCE

	W	L	T	Pct.	Pts.	OP
Cleveland	9	3	0	.750	336	162
Philadelphia	7	4	1	.636	284	230
N.Y. Giants	7	5	0	.583	293	184
Pittsburgh	5	7	0	.417	219	263
Washington	3	9	0	.250	207	432
Chi. Cardinals	2	10	0	.167	183	347

WESTERN CONFERENCE

	W	L	T	Pct.	Pts.	OP
Detroit	9	2	1	.818	337	189
Chi. Bears	8	4	0	.667	301	279
San Francisco	7	4	1	.636	313	251
Los Angeles	6	5	1	.545	314	285
Green Bay	4	8	0	.333	234	251
Baltimore	3	9	0	.250	131	279

NFL championship: CLEVELAND 56, Detroit 10

1953

EASTERN CONFERENCE

	W	L	T	Pct.	Pts.	OP
Cleveland	11	1	0	.917	348	162
Philadelphia	7	4	1	.636	352	215
Washington	6	5	1	.545	208	215
Pittsburgh	6	6	0	.500	211	263
N.Y. Giants	3	9	0	.250	179	277
Chi. Cardinals	1	10	1	.091	190	337

WESTERN CONFERENCE

	W	L	T	Pct.	Pts.	OP
Detroit	10	2	0	.833	271	205
San Francisco	9	3	0	.750	372	237
Los Angeles	8	3	1	.727	366	236
Chi. Bears	3	8	1	.273	218	262
Baltimore	3	9	0	.250	182	350
Green Bay	2	9	1	.182	200	338

NFL championship: DETROIT 17, Cleveland 16

1952

AMERICAN CONFERENCE

	W	L	T	Pct.	Pts.	OP
Cleveland	8	4	0	.667	310	213
N.Y. Giants	7	5	0	.583	234	231
Philadelphia	7	5	0	.583	252	271
Pittsburgh	5	7	0	.417	300	273
Chi. Cardinals	4	8	0	.333	172	221
Washington	4	8	0	.333	240	287

NATIONAL CONFERENCE

	W	L	T	Pct.	Pts.	OP
Detroit	9	3	0	.750	344	192
Los Angeles	9	3	0	.750	349	234
San Francisco	7	5	0	.583	285	221
Green Bay	6	6	0	.500	295	312
Chi. Bears	5	7	0	.417	245	326
Dallas Texans	1	11	0	.083	182	427

National Conference playoff: DETROIT 31, Los Angeles 21
NFL championship: Detroit 17, CLEVELAND 7

1951

AMERICAN CONFERENCE

	W	L	T	Pct.	Pts.	OP
Cleveland	11	1	0	.917	331	152
N.Y. Giants	9	2	1	.818	254	161
Washington	5	7	0	.417	183	296
Pittsburgh	4	7	1	.364	183	235
Philadelphia	4	8	0	.333	234	264
Chi. Cardinals	3	9	0	.250	210	287

NATIONAL CONFERENCE

	W	L	T	Pct.	Pts.	OP
Los Angeles	8	4	0	.667	392	261
Detroit	7	4	1	.636	336	259
San Francisco	7	4	1	.636	255	205
Chi. Bears	7	5	0	.583	286	282
Green Bay	3	9	0	.250	254	375
N.Y. Yanks	1	9	2	.100	241	382

NFL championship: LOS ANGELES 24, Cleveland 17

1950

AMERICAN CONFERENCE

	W	L	T	Pct.	Pts.	OP
Cleveland	10	2	0	.833	310	144
N.Y. Giants	10	2	0	.833	268	150
Philadelphia	6	6	0	.500	254	141
Pittsburgh	6	6	0	.500	180	195
Chi. Cardinals	5	7	0	.417	233	287
Washington	3	9	0	.250	232	326

NATIONAL CONFERENCE

	W	L	T	Pct.	Pts.	OP
Los Angeles	9	3	0	.750	466	309
Chi. Bears	9	3	0	.750	279	207
N.Y. Yanks	7	5	0	.583	366	367
Detroit	6	6	0	.500	321	285
Green Bay	3	9	0	.250	244	406
San Francisco	3	9	0	.250	213	300
Baltimore	1	11	0	.083	213	462

American Conference playoff: CLEVELAND 8, N.Y. Giants 3
National Conference playoff: LOS ANGELES 24, Chi. Bears 14
NFL championship: CLEVELAND 30, Los Angeles 28

1949

EASTERN DIVISION

	W	L	T	Pct.	Pts.	OP
Philadelphia	11	1	0	.917	364	134
Pittsburgh	6	5	1	.545	224	214
N.Y. Giants	6	6	0	.500	287	298
Washington	4	7	1	.364	268	339
N.Y. Bulldogs	1	10	1	.091	153	368

WESTERN DIVISION

	W	L	T	Pct.	Pts.	OP
Los Angeles	8	2	2	.800	360	239
Chi. Bears	9	3	0	.750	332	218
Chi. Cardinals	6	5	1	.545	360	301
Detroit	4	8	0	.333	237	259
Green Bay	2	10	0	.167	114	329

NFL championship: Philadelphia 14, LOS ANGELES 0

1948

EASTERN DIVISION

	W	L	T	Pct.	Pts.	OP
Philadelphia	9	2	1	.818	376	156
Washington	7	5	0	.583	291	287
N.Y. Giants	4	8	0	.333	297	388
Pittsburgh	4	8	0	.333	200	243
Boston	3	9	0	.250	174	372

WESTERN DIVISION

	W	L	T	Pct.	Pts.	OP
Chi. Cardinals	11	1	0	.917	395	226
Chi. Bears	10	2	0	.833	375	151
Los Angeles	6	5	1	.545	327	269
Green Bay	3	9	0	.250	154	290
Detroit	2	10	0	.167	200	407

NFL championship: PHILADELPHIA 7, Chi. Cardinals 0

1947

EASTERN DIVISION

	W	L	T	Pct.	Pts.	OP
Philadelphia	8	4	0	.667	308	242
Pittsburgh	8	4	0	.667	240	259
Boston	4	7	1	.364	168	256
Washington	4	8	0	.333	295	367
N.Y. Giants	2	8	2	.200	190	309

WESTERN DIVISION

	W	L	T	Pct.	Pts.	OP
Chi. Cardinals	9	3	0	.750	306	231
Chi. Bears	8	4	0	.667	363	241
Green Bay	6	5	1	.545	274	210
Los Angeles	6	6	0	.500	259	214
Detroit	3	9	0	.250	231	305

Eastern Division playoff: Philadelphia 21, PITTSBURGH 0
NFL championship: CHI. CARDINALS 28, Philadelphia 21

1946

EASTERN DIVISION

	W	L	T	Pct.	Pts.	OP
N.Y. Giants	7	3	1	.700	236	162
Philadelphia	6	5	0	.545	231	220
Washington	5	5	1	.500	171	191
Pittsburgh	5	5	1	.500	136	117
Boston	2	8	1	.200	189	273

WESTERN DIVISION

	W	L	T	Pct.	Pts.	OP
Chi. Bears	8	2	1	.800	289	193
Los Angeles	6	4	1	.600	277	257
Green Bay	6	5	0	.545	148	158
Chi. Cardinals	6	5	0	.545	260	198
Detroit	1	10	0	.091	142	310

NFL championship: Chi. Bears 24, N.Y. GIANTS 14

1945

EASTERN DIVISION

	W	L	T	Pct.	Pts.	OP
Washington	8	2	0	.800	209	121
Philadelphia	7	3	0	.700	272	133
N.Y. Giants	3	6	1	.333	179	198
Boston	3	6	1	.333	123	211
Pittsburgh	2	8	0	.200	79	220

WESTERN DIVISION

	W	L	T	Pct.	Pts.	OP
Cleveland	9	1	0	.900	244	136
Detroit	7	3	0	.700	195	194
Green Bay	6	4	0	.600	258	173
Chi. Bears	3	7	0	.300	192	235
Chi. Cardinals	1	9	0	.100	98	228

NFL championship: CLEVELAND 15, Washington 14

1944

EASTERN DIVISION

	W	L	T	Pct.	Pts.	OP
N.Y. Giants	8	1	1	.889	206	75
Philadelphia	7	1	2	.875	267	131
Washington	6	3	1	.667	169	180
Boston	2	8	0	.200	82	233
Brooklyn	0	10	0	.000	69	166

WESTERN DIVISION

	W	L	T	Pct.	Pts.	OP
Green Bay	8	2	0	.800	238	141
Chi. Bears	6	3	1	.667	258	172
Detroit	6	3	1	.667	216	151
Cleveland	4	6	0	.400	188	224
Card-Pitt	0	10	0	.000	108	328

NFL championship: Green Bay 14, N.Y. GIANTS 7

1943

EASTERN DIVISION	W	L	T	Pct.	Pts.	OP	WESTERN DIVISION	W	L	T	Pct.	Pts.	OP
Washington	6	3	1	.667	229	137	Chi. Bears	8	1	1	.889	303	157
N.Y. Giants	6	3	1	.667	197	170	Green Bay	7	2	1	.778	264	172
Phil-Pitt	5	4	1	.556	225	230	Detroit	3	6	1	.333	178	218
Brooklyn	2	8	0	.200	65	234	Chi. Cardinals	0	10	0	.000	95	238

Eastern Division playoff: Washington 28, N.Y. GIANTS 0
NFL championship: CHI. BEARS 41, Washington 21

1942

EASTERN DIVISION	W	L	T	Pct.	Pts.	OP	WESTERN DIVISION	W	L	T	Pct.	Pts.	OP
Washington	10	1	0	.909	227	102	Chi. Bears	11	0	0	1.000	376	84
Pittsburgh	7	4	0	.636	167	119	Green Bay	8	2	1	.800	300	215
N.Y. Giants	5	5	1	.500	155	139	Cleveland	5	6	0	.455	150	207
Brooklyn	3	8	0	.273	100	168	Chi. Cardinals	3	8	0	.273	98	209
Philadelphia	2	9	0	.182	134	239	Detroit	0	11	0	.000	38	263

NFL championship: WASHINGTON 14, Chi. Bears 6

1941

EASTERN DIVISION	W	L	T	Pct.	Pts.	OP	WESTERN DIVISION	W	L	T	Pct.	Pts.	OP
N.Y. Giants	8	3	0	.727	238	114	Chi. Bears	10	1	0	.909	396	147
Brooklyn	7	4	0	.636	158	127	Green Bay	10	1	0	.909	258	120
Washington	6	5	0	.545	176	174	Detroit	4	6	1	.400	121	195
Philadelphia	2	8	1	.200	119	218	Chi. Cardinals	3	7	1	.300	127	197
Pittsburgh	1	9	1	.100	103	276	Cleveland	2	9	0	.182	116	244

Western Division playoff: CHI. BEARS 33, Green Bay 14
NFL championship: CHI. BEARS 37, N.Y. Giants 9

1940

EASTERN DIVISION	W	L	T	Pct.	Pts.	OP	WESTERN DIVISION	W	L	T	Pct.	Pts.	OP
Washington	9	2	0	.818	245	142	Chi. Bears	8	3	0	.727	238	152
Brooklyn	8	3	0	.727	186	120	Green Bay	6	4	1	.600	238	155
N.Y. Giants	6	4	1	.600	131	133	Detroit	5	5	1	.500	138	153
Pittsburgh	2	7	2	.222	60	178	Cleveland	4	6	1	.400	171	191
Philadelphia	1	10	0	.091	111	211	Chi. Cardinals	2	7	2	.222	139	222

NFL championship: Chi. Bears 73, WASHINGTON 0

1939

EASTERN DIVISION	W	L	T	Pct.	Pts.	OP	WESTERN DIVISION	W	L	T	Pct.	Pts.	OP
N.Y. Giants	9	1	1	.900	168	85	Green Bay	9	2	0	.818	233	153
Washington	8	2	1	.800	242	94	Chi. Bears	8	3	0	.727	298	157
Brooklyn	4	6	1	.400	108	219	Detroit	6	5	0	.545	145	150
Philadelphia	1	9	1	.100	105	200	Cleveland	5	5	1	.500	195	164
Pittsburgh	1	9	1	.100	114	216	Chi. Cardinals	1	10	0	.091	84	254

NFL championship: GREEN BAY 27, N.Y. Giants 0

1938

EASTERN DIVISION	W	L	T	Pct.	Pts.	OP	WESTERN DIVISION	W	L	T	Pct.	Pts.	OP
N.Y. Giants	8	2	1	.800	194	79	Green Bay	8	3	0	.727	223	118
Washington	6	3	2	.667	148	154	Detroit	7	4	0	.636	119	108
Brooklyn	4	4	3	.500	131	161	Chi. Bears	6	5	0	.545	194	148
Philadelphia	5	6	0	.455	154	164	Cleveland	4	7	0	.364	131	215
Pittsburgh	2	9	0	.182	79	169	Chi. Cardinals	2	9	0	.182	111	168

NFL championship: N.Y. GIANTS 23, Green Bay 17

1937

EASTERN DIVISION	W	L	T	Pct.	Pts.	OP	WESTERN DIVISION	W	L	T	Pct.	Pts.	OP
Washington	8	3	0	.727	195	120	Chi. Bears	9	1	1	.900	201	100
N.Y. Giants	6	3	2	.667	128	109	Green Bay	7	4	0	.636	220	122
Pittsburgh	4	7	0	.364	122	145	Detroit	7	4	0	.636	180	105
Brooklyn	3	7	1	.300	82	174	Chi. Cardinals	5	5	1	.500	135	165
Philadelphia	2	8	1	.200	86	177	Cleveland	1	10	0	.091	75	207

NFL championship: Washington 28, CHI. BEARS 21

1936

EASTERN DIVISION	W	L	T	Pct.	Pts.	OP	WESTERN DIVISION	W	L	T	Pct.	Pts.	OP
Boston	7	5	0	.583	149	110	Green Bay	10	1	1	.909	248	118
Pittsburgh	6	6	0	.500	98	187	Chi. Bears	9	3	0	.750	222	94
N.Y. Giants	5	6	1	.455	115	163	Detroit	8	4	0	.667	235	102
Brooklyn	3	8	1	.273	92	161	Chi. Cardinals	3	8	1	.273	74	143
Philadelphia	1	11	0	.083	51	206							

NFL championship: Green Bay 21, Boston 6, at Polo Grounds, N.Y.

1935

EASTERN DIVISION	W	L	T	Pct.	Pts.	OP	WESTERN DIVISION	W	L	T	Pct.	Pts.	OP
N.Y. Giants	9	3	0	.750	180	96	Detroit	7	3	2	.700	191	111
Brooklyn	5	6	1	.455	90	141	Green Bay	8	4	0	.667	181	96
Pittsburgh	4	8	0	.333	100	209	Chi. Bears	6	4	2	.600	192	106
Boston	2	8	1	.200	65	123	Chi. Cardinals	6	4	2	.600	99	97
Philadelphia	2	9	0	.182	60	179							

NFL championship: DETROIT 26, N.Y. Giants 7
One game between Boston and Philadelphia was canceled.

1934

EASTERN DIVISION	W	L	T	Pct.	Pts.	OP	WESTERN DIVISION	W	L	T	Pct.	Pts.	OP
N.Y. Giants	8	5	0	.615	147	107	Chi. Bears	13	0	0	1.000	286	86
Boston	6	6	0	.500	107	94	Detroit	10	3	0	.769	238	59
Brooklyn	4	7	0	.364	61	153	Green Bay	7	6	0	.538	156	112
Philadelphia	4	7	0	.364	127	85	Chi. Cardinals	5	6	0	.455	80	84
Pittsburgh	2	10	0	.167	51	206	St. Louis	1	2	0	.333	27	61
							Cincinnati	0	8	0	.000	10	243

NFL championship: N.Y. GIANTS 30, Chi. Bears 13

1933

EASTERN DIVISION	W	L	T	Pct.	Pts.	OP	WESTERN DIVISION	W	L	T	Pct.	Pts.	OP
N.Y. Giants	11	3	0	.786	244	101	Chi. Bears	10	2	1	.833	133	82
Brooklyn	5	4	1	.556	93	54	Portsmouth	6	5	0	.545	128	87
Boston	5	5	2	.500	103	97	Green Bay	5	7	1	.417	170	107
Philadelphia	3	5	1	.375	77	158	Cincinnati	3	6	1	.333	38	110
Pittsburgh	3	6	2	.333	67	208	Chi. Cardinals	1	9	1	.100	52	101

NFL championship: CHI. BEARS 23, N.Y. Giants 21

1932

	W	L	T	Pct.
Chicago Bears	7	1	6	.875
Green Bay Packers	10	3	1	.769
Portsmouth Spartans	6	2	4	.750
Boston Braves	4	4	2	.500
New York Giants	4	6	2	.400
Brooklyn Dodgers	3	9	0	.250
Chicago Cardinals	2	6	2	.250
Staten Island Stapletons	2	7	3	.222

Chicago Bears and Portsmouth finished regularly scheduled games tied for first place. Bears won playoff game, which counted in standings, 9-0.

1931

	W	L	T	Pct.
Green Bay Packers	12	2	0	.857
Portsmouth Spartans	11	3	0	.786
Chicago Bears	8	5	0	.615
Chicago Cardinals	5	4	0	.556
New York Giants	7	6	1	.538
Providence Steam Roller	4	4	3	.500
Staten Island Stapletons	4	6	1	.400
Cleveland Indians	2	8	0	.200
Brooklyn Dodgers	2	12	0	.143
Frankford Yellow Jackets	1	6	1	.143

1930

	W	L	T	Pct.
Green Bay Packers	10	3	1	.769
New York Giants	13	4	0	.765
Chicago Bears	9	4	1	.692
Brooklyn Dodgers	7	4	1	.636
Providence Steam Roller	6	4	1	.600
Staten Island Stapletons	5	5	2	.500
Chicago Cardinals	5	6	2	.455
Portsmouth Spartans	5	6	3	.455
Frankford Yellow Jackets	4	13	1	.222
Minneapolis Red Jackets	1	7	1	.125
Newark Tornadoes	1	10	1	.091

1929

	W	L	T	Pct.
Green Bay Packers	12	0	1	1.000
New York Giants	13	1	1	.929
Frankford Yellow Jackets	10	4	5	.714
Chicago Cardinals	6	6	1	.500
Boston Bulldogs	4	4	0	.500
Staten Island Stapletons	3	4	3	.429
Providence Steam Roller	4	6	2	.400
Orange Tornadoes	3	5	4	.375
Chicago Bears	4	9	2	.308
Buffalo Bisons	1	7	1	.125
Minneapolis Red Jackets	1	9	0	.100
Dayton Triangles	0	6	0	.000

1928

	W	L	T	Pct.
Providence Steam Roller	8	1	2	.889
Frankford Yellow Jackets	11	3	2	.786
Detroit Wolverines	7	2	1	.778
Green Bay Packers	6	4	3	.600
Chicago Bears	7	5	1	.583
New York Giants	4	7	2	.364
New York Yankees	4	8	1	.333
Pottsville Maroons	2	8	0	.200
Chicago Cardinals	1	5	0	.167
Dayton Triangles	0	7	0	.000

1927

	W	L	T	Pct.
New York Giants	11	1	1	.917
Green Bay Packers	7	2	1	.778
Chicago Bears	9	3	2	.750
Cleveland Bulldogs	8	4	1	.667
Providence Steam Roller	8	5	1	.615
New York Yankees	7	8	1	.467
Frankford Yellow Jackets	6	9	3	.400
Pottsville Maroons	5	8	0	.385
Chicago Cardinals	3	7	1	.300
Dayton Triangles	1	6	1	.143
Duluth Eskimos	1	8	0	.111
Buffalo Bisons	0	5	0	.000

1926

	W	L	T	Pct.
Frankford Yellow Jackets	14	1	2	.933
Chicago Bears	12	1	3	.923
Pottsville Maroons	10	2	2	.833
Kansas City Cowboys	8	3	0	.727
Green Bay Packers	7	3	3	.700
Los Angeles Buccaneers	6	3	1	.667
New York Giants	8	4	1	.667
Duluth Eskimos	6	5	3	.545
Buffalo Rangers	4	4	2	.500
Chicago Cardinals	5	6	1	.455
Providence Steam Roller	5	7	1	.417
Detroit Panthers	4	6	2	.400
Hartford Blues	3	7	0	.300
Brooklyn Lions	3	8	0	.273
Milwaukee Badgers	2	7	0	.222
Akron Indians	1	4	3	.200
Dayton Triangles	1	4	1	.200
Racine Tornadoes	1	4	0	.200
Columbus Tigers	1	6	0	.143
Canton Bulldogs	1	9	3	.100
Hammond Pros	0	4	0	.000
Louisville Colonels	0	4	0	.000

1925

	W	L	T	Pct.
Chicago Cardinals	11	2	1	.846
Pottsville Maroons	10	2	0	.833
Detroit Panthers	8	2	2	.800
New York Giants	8	4	0	.667
Akron Indians	4	2	2	.667
Frankford Yellow Jackets	13	7	0	.650
Chicago Bears	9	5	3	.643
Rock Island Independents	5	3	3	.625
Green Bay Packers	8	5	0	.615
Providence Steam Roller	6	5	1	.545
Canton Bulldogs	4	4	0	.500
Cleveland Bulldogs	5	8	1	.385
Kansas City Cowboys	2	5	1	.286
Hammond Pros	1	4	0	.200
Buffalo Bisons	1	6	2	.143
Duluth Kelleys	0	3	0	.000
Rochester Jeffersons	0	6	1	.000
Milwaukee Badgers	0	6	0	.000
Dayton Triangles	0	7	1	.000
Columbus Tigers	0	9	0	.000

1924

	W	L	T	Pct.
Cleveland Bulldogs	7	1	1	.875
Chicago Bears	6	1	4	.857
Frankford Yellow Jackets	11	2	1	.846
Duluth Kelleys	5	1	0	.833
Rock Island Independents	5	2	2	.714
Green Bay Packers	7	4	0	.636
Racine Legion	4	3	3	.571
Chicago Cardinals	5	4	1	.556
Buffalo Bisons	6	5	0	.545
Columbus Tigers	4	4	0	.500
Hammond Pros	2	2	1	.500
Milwaukee Badgers	5	8	0	.385
Akron Indians	2	6	0	.250
Dayton Triangles	2	6	0	.250
Kansas City Blues	2	7	0	.222
Kenosha Maroons	0	4	1	.000
Minneapolis Marines	0	6	0	.000
Rochester Jeffersons	0	7	0	.000

1923

	W	L	T	Pct.
Canton Bulldogs	11	0	1	1.000
Chicago Bears	9	2	1	.818
Green Bay Packers	7	2	1	.778
Milwaukee Badgers	7	2	3	.778
Cleveland Indians	3	1	3	.750
Chicago Cardinals	8	4	0	.667
Duluth Kelleys	4	3	0	.571
Buffalo All-Americans	5	4	3	.556
Columbus Tigers	5	4	1	.556
Racine Legion	4	4	2	.500
Toledo Maroons	3	3	2	.500
Rock Island Independents	2	3	3	.400
St. Louis All-Stars	1	4	2	.200
Hammond Pros	1	5	1	.167
Dayton Triangles	1	6	1	.143
Akron Indians	1	6	0	.143
Oorang Indians	1	10	0	.091
Louisville Brecks	0	3	0	.000
Rochester Jeffersons	0	4	0	.000

1922

	W	L	T	Pct.
Canton Bulldogs	10	0	2	1.000
Chicago Bears	9	3	0	.750
Chicago Cardinals	8	3	0	.727
Toledo Maroons	5	2	2	.714
Rock Island Independents	4	2	1	.667
Racine Legion	6	4	1	.600
Dayton Triangles	4	3	1	.571
Green Bay Packers	4	3	3	.571
Buffalo All-Americans	5	4	1	.556
Akron Pros	3	5	2	.375
Milwaukee Badgers	2	4	3	.333
Oorang Indians	3	6	0	.333
Minneapolis Marines	1	3	0	.250
Louisville Brecks	1	3	0	.250
Evansville Crimson Giants	0	3	0	.000
Rochester Jeffersons	0	4	1	.000
Hammond Pros	0	5	1	.000
Columbus Panhandles	0	8	0	.000

1921

	W	L	T	Pct.
Chicago Staleys	9	1	1	.900
Buffalo All-Americans	9	1	2	.900
Akron Pros	8	3	1	.727
Canton Bulldogs	5	2	3	.714
Rock Island Independents	4	2	1	.667
Evansville Crimson Giants	3	2	0	.600
Green Bay Packers	3	2	1	.600
Dayton Triangles	4	4	1	.500
Chicago Cardinals	3	3	2	.500
Rochester Jeffersons	2	3	0	.400
Cleveland Indians	3	5	0	.375
Washington Senators	1	2	0	.333
Cincinnati Celts	1	3	0	.250
Hammond Pros	1	3	1	.250
Minneapolis Marines	1	3	0	.250
Detroit Tigers	1	5	1	.167
Columbus Panhandles	1	8	0	.111
Tonawanda Kardex	0	1	0	.000
Muncie Flyers	0	2	0	.000
Louisville Brecks	0	2	0	.000
New York Giants	0	2	0	.000

1920*

	W	L	T	Pct.
Akron Pros	8	0	3	1.000
Decatur Staleys	10	1	2	.909
Buffalo All-Americans	9	1	1	.900
Chicago Cardinals	6	2	2	.750
Rock Island Independents	6	2	2	.750
Dayton Triangles	5	2	2	.714
Rochester Jeffersons	6	3	2	.667
Canton Bulldogs	7	4	2	.636
Detroit Heralds	2	3	3	.400
Cleveland Tigers	2	4	2	.333
Chicago Tigers	2	5	1	.286
Hammond Pros	2	5	0	.286
Columbus Panhandles	2	6	2	.250
Muncie Flyers	0	1	0	.000

No official standings were maintained for the 1920 season, and the championship was awarded to the Akron Pros in a League meeting on April 30, 1921. Clubs played schedules that included games against nonleague opponents.

WALTER PAYTON NFL MAN OF THE YEAR

The Walter Payton NFL Man of the Year Award is the only NFL award that recognizes a player for his community service activities as well as his excellence on the field. Renamed in 1999 for the legendary Chicago Bears Pro Football Hall of Fame running back, the Walter Payton NFL Man of the Year Award has been given annually since 1970.

YEAR	PLAYER	POS.	TEAM
1970	Johnny Unitas	QB	Baltimore Colts
1971	John Hadl	QB	San Diego Chargers
1972	Willie Lanier	LB	Kansas City Chiefs
1973	Len Dawson	QB	Kansas City Chiefs
1974	George Blanda	QB	Oakland Raiders
1975	Ken Anderson	QB	Cincinnati Bengals
1976	Franco Harris	RB	Pittsburgh Steelers
1977	Walter Payton	RB	Chicago Bears
1978	Roger Staubach	QB	Dallas Cowboys
1979	Joe Greene	DT	Pittsburgh Steelers
1980	Harold Carmichael	WR	Philadelphia Eagles
1981	Lynn Swann	WR	Pittsburgh Steelers
1982	Joe Theismann	QB	Washington Redskins
1983	Rolf Benirschke	K	San Diego Chargers
1984	Marty Lyons	T	New York Jets
1985	Dwight Stephenson	C	Miami Dolphins
1986	Reggie Williams	LB	Cincinnati Bengals
1987	Dave Duerson	S	Chicago Bears
1988	Steve Largent	WR	Seattle Seahawks
1989	Warren Moon	QB	Houston Oilers
1990	Mike Singletary	LB	Chicago Bears
1991	Anthony Muñoz	T	Cincinnati Bengals
1992	John Elway	QB	Denver Broncos
1993	Derrick Thomas	LB	Kansas City Chiefs
1994	Junior Seau	LB	San Diego Chargers
1995	Boomer Esiason	QB	New York Jets
1996	Darrell Green	CB	Washington Redskins
1997	Troy Aikman	QB	Dallas Cowboys
1998	Dan Marino	QB	Miami Dolphins
1999	Cris Carter	WR	Minnesota Vikings
2000*	Derrick Brooks	LB	Tampa Bay Buccaneers
	Jim Flanigan	DT	Chicago Bears
2001	Jerome Bettis	RB	Pittsburgh Steelers
2002	Troy Vincent	CB	Philadelphia Eagles
2003	Will Shields	G	Kansas City Chiefs
2004	Warrick Dunn	RB	Atlanta Falcons
2005	Peyton Manning	QB	Indianapolis Colts
2006*	Drew Brees	QB	New Orleans Saints
	LaDainian Tomlinson	RB	San Diego Chargers
2007	Jason Taylor	DE	Miami Dolphins
2008	Kurt Warner	QB	Arizona Cardinals
2009	Brian Waters	G	Kansas City Chiefs
2010	Madieu Williams	S	Minnesota Vikings
2011	Matt Birk	C	Baltimore Ravens
2012	Jason Witten	TE	Dallas Cowboys

* The award was shared in 2000 and 2006.

RS=REGULAR SEASON
PS=POSTSEASON
*ARIZONA vs. ATLANTA
RS: Cardinals lead series, 14-12
PS: Cardinals lead series, 1-0
1966—Falcons, 16-10 (Atl)
1968—Cardinals, 17-12 (StL)
1971—Cardinals, 26-9 (Atl)
1973—Cardinals, 32-10 (Atl)
1975—Cardinals, 23-20 (StL)
1978—Cardinals, 42-21 (StL)
1980—Falcons, 33-27 (StL) OT
1981—Falcons, 41-20 (Atl)
1982—Cardinals, 23-20 (Atl)
1986—Falcons, 33-13 (Atl)
1987—Cardinals, 34-21 (Atl)
1989—Cardinals, 34-20 (P)
1990—Cardinals, 24-13 (Atl)
1991—Cardinals, 16-10 (P)
1992—Falcons, 20-17 (Atl)
1993—Cardinals, 27-10 (Atl)
1994—Falcons, 10-6 (Atl)
1995—Cardinals, 40-37 (Ariz) OT
1997—Cardinals, 29-26 (Ariz)
1999—Falcons, 37-14 (Atl)
2001—Falcons, 34-14 (Ariz)
2004—Falcons, 6-3 (Atl)
2006—Falcons, 32-10 (Atl)
2007—Cardinals, 30-27 (Ariz) OT
2008—**Cardinals, 30-24 (Ariz)
2010—Falcons, 41-7 (Atl)
2012—Falcons, 23-19 (Atl)
(RS Pts.—Falcons 582, Cardinals 557)
(PS Pts.—Cardinals 30, Falcons 24)
*Franchise known as Phoenix prior to
1994 and in St. Louis prior to 1988*
**NFC First-Round Playoff
*ARIZONA vs. BALTIMORE
RS: Ravens lead series, 4-1
1997—Cardinals, 16-13 (B)
2000—Ravens, 13-7 (A)
2003—Ravens, 26-18 (A)
2007—Ravens, 26-23 (B)
2011—Ravens, 30-27 (B)
(RS Pts.—Ravens 108, Cardinals 91)
*ARIZONA vs. BUFFALO
RS: Bills lead series, 6-4
1971—Cardinals, 28-23 (B)
1975—Bills, 32-14 (StL)
1981—Cardinals, 24-0 (StL)
1984—Cardinals, 37-7 (StL)
1986—Bills, 17-10 (B)
1990—Bills, 45-14 (B)
1999—Bills, 31-21 (A)
2004—Bills, 38-14 (B)
2008—Cardinals, 41-17 (A)
2012—Bills, 19-16 (A) OT
(RS Pts.—Bills 229, Cardinals 219)
*Franchise known as Phoenix prior to
1994 and in St. Louis prior to 1988*
ARIZONA vs. CAROLINA
RS: Panthers lead series, 8-3
PS: Cardinals lead series, 1-0
1995—Panthers, 27-7 (C)
2001—Cardinals, 30-7 (C)
2002—Cardinals, 16-13 (C)
2003—Panthers, 20-17 (A)
2004—Panthers, 35-10 (C)
2005—Panthers, 24-20 (A)
2007—Panthers, 25-10 (A)
2008—Panthers, 27-23 (C)
        *Cardinals, 33-13 (C)
2009—Panthers, 34-21 (A)

2010—Panthers, 19-12 (C)
2011—Cardinals, 28-21 (A)
(RS Pts.—Panthers 252, Cardinals 194)
(PS Pts.—Cardinals 33, Panthers 13)
*NFC Divisional Playoff
*ARIZONA vs. **CHICAGO
RS: Bears lead series, 56-27-6
(NP denotes Normal Park;
Wr denotes Wrigley Field;
Co denotes Comiskey Park;
So denotes Soldier Field;
all Chicago)
1920—Cardinals, 7-6 (NP)
        Staleys, 10-0 (Wr)
1921—Tie, 0-0 (Wr)
1922—Cardinals, 6-0 (Co)
        Cardinals, 9-0 (Co)
1923—Bears, 3-0 (Wr)
1924—Bears, 6-0 (Wr)
        Bears, 21-0 (Co)
1925—Cardinals, 9-0 (Co)
        Tie, 0-0 (Wr)
1926—Bears, 16-0 (Wr)
        Bears, 10-0 (So)
        Tie, 0-0 (Wr)
1927—Bears, 9-0 (NP)
        Cardinals, 3-0 (Wr)
1928—Bears, 15-0 (NP)
        Bears, 34-0 (Wr)
1929—Tie, 0-0 (Wr)
        Cardinals, 40-6 (Co)
1930—Bears, 32-6 (Co)
        Bears, 6-0 (Wr)
1931—Bears, 26-13 (Wr)
        Bears, 18-7 (Wr)
1932—Tie, 0-0 (Wr)
        Bears, 34-0 (Wr)
1933—Bears, 12-9 (Wr)
        Bears, 22-6 (Wr)
1934—Bears, 20-0 (Wr)
        Bears, 17-6 (Wr)
1935—Tie, 7-7 (Wr)
        Bears, 13-0 (Wr)
1936—Bears, 7-3 (Wr)
        Cardinals, 14-7 (Wr)
1937—Bears, 16-7 (Wr)
        Bears, 42-28 (Wr)
1938—Bears, 16-13 (So)
        Bears, 34-28 (Wr)
1939—Bears, 44-7 (Wr)
        Bears, 48-7 (Co)
1940—Cardinals, 21-7 (Co)
        Bears, 31-23 (Wr)
1941—Bears, 53-7 (Wr)
        Bears, 34-24 (Co)
1942—Bears, 41-14 (Wr)
        Bears, 21-7 (Co)
1943—Bears, 20-0 (Wr)
        Bears, 35-24 (Co)
1945—Cardinals, 16-7 (Wr)
        Bears, 28-20 (Co)
1946—Bears, 34-17 (Co)
        Cardinals, 35-28 (Wr)
1947—Cardinals, 31-7 (Co)
        Cardinals, 30-21 (Wr)
1948—Bears, 28-17 (Co)
        Cardinals, 24-21 (Wr)
1949—Bears, 17-7 (Co)
        Bears, 52-21 (Wr)
1950—Bears, 27-6 (Wr)
        Cardinals, 20-10 (Co)
1951—Cardinals, 28-14 (Co)
        Cardinals, 24-14 (Wr)

1952—Cardinals, 21-10 (Co)
        Bears, 10-7 (Wr)
1953—Cardinals, 24-17 (Wr)
1954—Bears, 29-7 (Co)
1955—Cardinals, 53-14 (Co)
1956—Bears, 10-3 (Wr)
1957—Bears, 14-6 (Co)
1958—Bears, 30-14 (Wr)
1959—Bears, 31-7 (So)
1965—Bears, 34-13 (Wr)
1966—Cardinals, 24-17 (StL)
1967—Bears, 30-3 (Wr)
1969—Cardinals, 20-17 (StL)
1972—Bears, 27-10 (StL)
1975—Cardinals, 34-20 (So)
1977—Cardinals, 16-13 (StL)
1978—Bears, 17-10 (So)
1979—Bears, 42-6 (So)
1982—Cardinals, 10-7 (So)
1984—Cardinals, 38-21 (StL)
1990—Bears, 31-21 (P)
1994—Bears, 19-16 (A) OT
1998—Cardinals, 20-7 (A)
2001—Bears, 20-13 (C)
2003—Bears, 28-3 (C)
2006—Cardinals, 24-23 (A)
2009—Cardinals, 41-21 (C)
2012—Bears, 28-13 (A)
(RS Pts.—Bears 1,695, Cardinals 1,127)
*Franchise known as Phoenix prior to
1994, in St. Louis prior to 1988, and in
Chicago prior to 1960*
***Franchise in Decatur prior to 1921 and
known as Staleys prior to 1922*
*ARIZONA vs. CINCINNATI
RS: Bengals lead series, 6-4
1973—Bengals, 42-24 (C)
1979—Bengals, 34-28 (C)
1985—Cardinals, 41-27 (StL)
1988—Bengals, 21-14 (C)
1994—Cardinals, 28-7 (A)
1997—Cardinals, 24-21 (C)
2000—Bengals, 24-13 (C)
2003—Cardinals, 17-14 (A)
2007—Cardinals, 35-27 (C)
2011—Bengals, 23-16 (C)
(RS Pts.—Bengals 243, Cardinals 237)
*Franchise known as Phoenix prior to
1994 and in St. Louis prior to 1988*
*ARIZONA vs. CLEVELAND
RS: Browns lead series, 33-13-3
1950—Browns, 34-24 (Cle)
        Browns, 10-7 (Chi)
1951—Browns, 34-17 (Chi)
        Browns, 49-28 (Chi)
1952—Browns, 28-13 (Cle)
        Browns, 10-0 (Chi)
1953—Browns, 27-7 (Chi)
        Browns, 27-16 (Cle)
1954—Browns, 31-7 (Cle)
        Browns, 35-3 (Chi)
1955—Browns, 26-20 (Chi)
        Browns, 35-24 (Cle)
1956—Cardinals, 9-7 (Chi)
        Cardinals, 24-7 (Cle)
1957—Browns, 17-7 (Chi)
        Browns, 31-0 (Cle)
1958—Browns, 35-28 (Cle)
        Browns, 38-24 (Chi)
1959—Browns, 34-7 (Chi)
        Browns, 17-7 (Cle)
1960—Browns, 28-27 (Cle)
        Tie, 17-17 (StL)

1961—Browns, 20-17 (Cle)
    Browns, 21-10 (StL)
1962—Browns, 34-7 (StL)
    Browns, 38-14 (Cle)
1963—Cardinals, 20-14 (Cle)
    Browns, 24-10 (StL)
1964—Tie, 33-33 (Cle)
    Cardinals, 28-19 (StL)
1965—Cardinals, 49-13 (Cle)
    Browns, 27-24 (StL)
1966—Cardinals, 34-28 (Cle)
    Browns, 38-10 (StL)
1967—Browns, 20-16 (Cle)
    Browns, 20-16 (StL)
1968—Cardinals, 27-21 (Cle)
    Cardinals, 27-16 (StL)
1969—Tie, 21-21 (Cle)
    Browns, 27-21 (StL)
1974—Cardinals, 29-7 (StL)
1979—Browns, 38-20 (StL)
1985—Cardinals, 27-24 (Cle) OT
1988—Browns, 29-21 (P)
1994—Browns, 32-0 (Cle)
2000—Cardinals, 29-21 (A)
2003—Browns, 44-6 (Cle)
2007—Cardinals, 27-21 (A)
2011—Cardinals, 20-17 (A) OT
(RS Pts.—Browns 1,244, Cardinals 879)
*Franchise known as Phoenix prior to
1994, in St. Louis prior to 1988,
and in Chicago prior to 1960*
*ARIZONA vs. DALLAS
RS: Cowboys lead series, 55-30-1
PS: Cardinals lead series, 1-0
1960—Cardinals, 12-10 (StL)
1961—Cardinals, 31-17 (D)
    Cardinals, 31-13 (StL)
1962—Cardinals, 28-24 (D)
    Cardinals, 52-20 (StL)
1963—Cardinals, 34-7 (D)
    Cowboys, 28-24 (StL)
1964—Cardinals, 16-6 (D)
    Cowboys, 31-13 (StL)
1965—Cardinals, 20-13 (StL)
    Cowboys, 27-13 (D)
1966—Tie, 10-10 (StL)
    Cowboys, 31-17 (D)
1967—Cowboys, 46-21 (D)
1968—Cowboys, 27-10 (StL)
1969—Cowboys, 24-3 (D)
1970—Cardinals, 20-7 (StL)
    Cardinals, 38-0 (D)
1971—Cowboys, 16-13 (StL)
    Cowboys, 31-12 (D)
1972—Cowboys, 33-24 (D)
    Cowboys, 27-6 (StL)
1973—Cowboys, 45-10 (D)
    Cowboys, 30-3 (StL)
1974—Cardinals, 31-28 (StL)
    Cowboys, 17-14 (D)
1975—Cowboys, 37-31 (D) OT
    Cardinals, 31-17 (StL)
1976—Cardinals, 21-17 (StL)
    Cowboys, 19-14 (D)
1977—Cowboys, 30-24 (StL)
    Cardinals, 24-17 (D)
1978—Cowboys, 21-12 (D)
    Cowboys, 24-21 (StL) OT
1979—Cowboys, 22-21 (StL)
    Cowboys, 22-13 (D)
1980—Cowboys, 27-24 (StL)
    Cowboys, 31-21 (D)

1981—Cowboys, 30-17 (D)
    Cardinals, 20-17 (StL)
1982—Cowboys, 24-7 (StL)
1983—Cowboys, 34-17 (StL)
    Cowboys, 35-17 (D)
1984—Cardinals, 31-20 (D)
    Cowboys, 24-17 (StL)
1985—Cardinals, 21-10 (StL)
    Cowboys, 35-17 (D)
1986—Cowboys, 31-7 (StL)
    Cowboys, 37-6 (D)
1987—Cardinals, 24-13 (StL)
    Cowboys, 21-16 (D)
1988—Cowboys, 17-14 (P)
    Cardinals, 16-10 (D)
1989—Cardinals, 19-10 (D)
    Cardinals, 24-20 (P)
1990—Cardinals, 20-3 (P)
    Cowboys, 41-10 (D)
1991—Cowboys, 17-9 (P)
    Cowboys, 27-7 (D)
1992—Cowboys, 31-20 (D)
    Cowboys, 16-10 (P)
1993—Cowboys, 17-10 (P)
    Cowboys, 20-15 (D)
1994—Cowboys, 38-3 (D)
    Cowboys, 28-21 (A)
1995—Cowboys, 34-20 (D)
    Cowboys, 37-13 (A)
1996—Cowboys, 17-3 (D)
    Cowboys, 10-6 (A)
1997—Cardinals, 25-22 (A) OT
    Cowboys, 24-6 (D)
1998—Cowboys, 38-10 (D)
    Cowboys, 35-28 (A)
    **Cardinals, 20-7 (D)
1999—Cowboys, 35-7 (D)
    Cardinals, 13-9 (A)
2000—Cardinals, 32-31 (A)
    Cowboys, 48-7 (D)
2001—Cowboys, 17-3 (D)
    Cardinals, 17-10 (A)
2002—Cardinals, 9-6 (A) OT
2003—Cowboys, 24-7 (D)
2005—Cowboys, 34-13 (D)
2006—Cowboys, 27-10 (A)
2008—Cardinals, 30-24 (A) OT
2010—Cardinals, 27-26 (A)
2011—Cardinals, 19-13 (A) OT
(RS Pts.—Cowboys 1,999, Cardinals 1,483)
(PS Pts.—Cardinals 20, Cowboys 7)
*Franchise known as Phoenix prior to
1994 and in St. Louis prior to 1988*
**NFC First-Round Playoff*
*ARIZONA vs. DENVER
RS: Broncos lead series, 7-1-1
1973—Tie, 17-17 (StL)
1977—Broncos, 7-0 (D)
1989—Broncos, 37-0 (P)
1991—Broncos, 24-19 (D)
1995—Broncos, 38-6 (D)
2001—Broncos, 38-17 (A)
2002—Broncos, 37-7 (D)
2006—Broncos, 37-20 (A)
2010—Cardinals, 43-13 (A)
(RS Pts.—Broncos 248, Cardinals 129)
*Franchise known as Phoenix prior to
1994 and in St. Louis prior to 1988*
*ARIZONA vs. **DETROIT
RS: Lions lead series, 31-25-5
1930—Tie, 0-0 (Port)
    Cardinals, 23-0 (C)

1931—Spartans, 13-3 (Port)
    Cardinals, 20-19 (C)
1932—Tie, 7-7 (Port)
1933—Spartans, 7-6 (Port)
1934—Lions, 6-0 (D)
    Lions, 17-13 (C)
1935—Tie, 10-10 (C)
    Lions, 7-6 (C)
1936—Lions, 39-0 (D)
    Lions, 14-7 (C)
1937—Lions, 16-7 (C)
    Lions, 16-7 (C)
1938—Lions, 10-0 (D)
    Lions, 7-3 (C)
1939—Lions, 21-3 (D)
    Lions, 17-3 (C)
1940—Tie, 0-0 (Buffalo)
    Lions, 43-14 (C)
1941—Tie, 14-14 (C)
    Lions, 21-3 (D)
1942—Cardinals, 13-0 (C)
    Cardinals, 7-0 (D)
1943—Lions, 35-17 (D)
    Lions, 7-0 (Buffalo)
1945—Lions, 10-0 (Milwaukee)
    Lions, 26-0 (D)
1946—Cardinals, 34-14 (C)
    Cardinals, 36-14 (D)
1947—Cardinals, 45-21 (C)
    Cardinals, 17-7 (D)
1948—Cardinals, 56-20 (C)
    Cardinals, 28-14 (D)
1949—Cardinals, 24-7 (C)
    Cardinals, 42-19 (D)
1959—Lions, 45-21 (D)
1961—Lions, 45-14 (StL)
1967—Cardinals, 38-28 (StL)
1969—Lions, 20-0 (D)
1970—Lions, 16-3 (D)
1973—Lions, 20-16 (StL)
1975—Cardinals, 24-13 (D)
1978—Cardinals, 21-14 (StL)
1980—Lions, 20-7 (D)
    Cardinals, 24-23 (StL)
1989—Cardinals, 16-13 (D)
1993—Lions, 26-20 (D)
    Lions, 21-14 (Phx)
1995—Cardinals, 20-17 (D)
1998—Cardinals, 17-15 (D)
1999—Cardinals, 23-19 (A)
2001—Cardinals, 45-38 (A)
2002—Cardinals, 23-20 (A) OT
2003—Lions, 42-24 (D)
2004—Lions, 26-12 (D)
2005—Lions, 29-21 (D)
2006—Cardinals, 17-10 (A)
2007—Cardinals, 31-21 (A)
2009—Cardinals, 31-24 (D)
2012—Cardinals, 38-10 (A)
(RS Pts.—Lions 1,103, Cardinals 981)
*Franchise known as Phoenix prior to
1994, in St. Louis prior to 1988,
and in Chicago prior to 1960*
**Franchise in Portsmouth prior to 1934
and known as the Spartans*
*ARIZONA vs. GREEN BAY
RS: Packers lead series, 44-22-4
PS: Series tied, 1-1
1921—Tie, 3-3 (C)
1922—Cardinals, 16-3 (C)
1924—Cardinals, 3-0 (C)
1925—Cardinals, 9-6 (C)

1926—Cardinals, 13-7 (GB)
    Packers, 3-0 (C)
1927—Packers, 13-0 (GB)
    Tie, 6-6 (C)
1928—Packers, 20-0 (GB)
1929—Packers, 9-2 (GB)
    Packers, 7-6 (C)
    Packers, 12-0 (C)
1930—Packers, 14-0 (GB)
    Cardinals, 13-6 (C)
1931—Packers, 26-7 (GB)
    Cardinals, 21-13 (C)
1932—Packers, 15-7 (GB)
    Packers, 19-9 (C)
1933—Packers, 14-6 (C)
1934—Packers, 15-0 (GB)
    Cardinals, 9-0 (Mil)
    Cardinals, 6-0 (C)
1935—Cardinals, 7-6 (GB)
    Cardinals, 3-0 (Mil)
    Cardinals, 9-7 (C)
1936—Packers, 10-7 (GB)
    Packers, 24-0 (Mil)
    Tie, 0-0 (C)
1937—Cardinals, 14-7 (GB)
    Packers, 34-13 (Mil)
1938—Packers, 28-7 (Mil)
    Packers, 24-22 (Buffalo)
1939—Packers, 14-10 (GB)
    Packers, 27-20 (Mil)
1940—Packers, 31-6 (Mil)
    Packers, 28-7 (C)
1941—Packers, 14-13 (Mil)
    Packers, 17-9 (GB)
1942—Packers, 17-13 (C)
    Packers, 55-24 (GB)
1943—Packers, 28-7 (C)
    Packers, 35-14 (Mil)
1945—Packers, 33-14 (GB)
1946—Packers, 19-7 (C)
    Cardinals, 24-6 (GB)
1947—Cardinals, 14-10 (GB)
    Cardinals, 21-20 (C)
1948—Cardinals, 17-7 (Mil)
    Cardinals, 42-7 (C)
1949—Cardinals, 39-17 (Mil)
    Cardinals, 41-21 (C)
1955—Packers, 31-14 (GB)
1956—Packers, 24-21 (C)
1962—Packers, 17-0 (Mil)
1963—Packers, 30-7 (StL)
1967—Packers, 31-23 (StL)
1969—Packers, 45-28 (GB)
1971—Tie, 16-16 (StL)
1973—Packers, 25-21 (GB)
1976—Cardinals, 29-0 (StL)
1982—**Packers, 41-16 (GB)
1984—Packers, 24-23 (GB)
1985—Cardinals, 43-28 (StL)
1988—Packers, 26-17 (P)
1990—Packers, 24-21 (P)
1999—Packers, 49-24 (GB)
2000—Packers, 29-3 (A)
2003—Cardinals, 20-13 (A)
2006—Packers, 31-14 (GB)
2009—Packers, 33-7 (A)
    **Cardinals, 51-45 (A) OT
2012—Packers, 31-17 (GB)
(RS Pts.—Packers 1,264, Cardinals 908)
(PS Pts.—Packers 86, Cardinals 67)
*Franchise known as Phoenix prior to
1994, in St. Louis prior to 1988,
and in Chicago prior to 1960*

**NFC First-Round Playoff*
ARIZONA vs. HOUSTON
RS: Series tied, 1-1
2005—Texans, 30-19 (H)
2009—Cardinals, 28-21 (A)
(RS Pts.—Texans 51, Cardinals 47)
***ARIZONA vs. **INDIANAPOLIS**
RS: Colts lead series, 8-6
1961—Colts, 16-0 (B)
1964—Colts, 47-27 (B)
1968—Colts, 27-0 (B)
1972—Cardinals, 10-3 (B)
1976—Cardinals, 24-17 (StL)
1978—Colts, 30-17 (StL)
1980—Cardinals, 17-10 (B)
1981—Cardinals, 35-24 (B)
1984—Cardinals, 34-33 (I)
1990—Cardinals, 20-17 (P)
1992—Colts, 16-13 (I)
1996—Colts, 20-13 (I)
2005—Colts, 17-13 (I)
2009—Colts, 31-10 (A)
(RS Pts.—Colts 308, Cardinals 233)
*Franchise known as Phoenix prior to
1994 and in St. Louis prior to 1988*
***Franchise in Baltimore prior to 1984*
ARIZONA vs. JACKSONVILLE
RS: Jaguars lead series, 2-1
2000—Jaguars, 44-10 (J)
2005—Jaguars, 24-17 (A)
2009—Cardinals, 31-17 (J)
(RS Pts.—Jaguars 85, Cardinals 58)
***ARIZONA vs. KANSAS CITY**
RS: Chiefs lead series, 8-2-1
1970—Tie, 6-6 (KC)
1974—Chiefs, 17-13 (StL)
1980—Chiefs, 21-13 (StL)
1983—Chiefs, 38-14 (KC)
1986—Cardinals, 23-14 (StL)
1995—Chiefs, 24-3 (A)
1998—Chiefs, 34-24 (KC)
2001—Cardinals, 24-16 (A)
2002—Chiefs, 49-0 (KC)
2006—Chiefs, 23-20 (A)
2010—Chiefs, 31-13 (KC)
(RS Pts.—Chiefs 273, Cardinals 153)
*Franchise known as Phoenix prior to
1994 and in St. Louis prior to 1988*
***ARIZONA vs. MIAMI**
RS: Dolphins lead series, 8-3
1972—Dolphins, 31-10 (M)
1977—Dolphins, 55-14 (StL)
1978—Dolphins, 24-10 (M)
1981—Dolphins, 20-7 (StL)
1984—Dolphins, 36-28 (M)
1990—Dolphins, 23-3 (M)
1996—Dolphins, 38-10 (A)
1999—Dolphins, 19-16 (M)
2004—Cardinals, 24-23 (M)
2008—Cardinals, 31-10 (A)
2012—Cardinals, 24-21 (A) OT
(RS Pts.—Dolphins 300, Cardinals 177)
*Franchise known as Phoenix prior to
1994 and in St. Louis prior to 1988*
***ARIZONA vs. MINNESOTA**
RS: Vikings lead series, 13-10
PS: Vikings lead series, 2-0
1963—Cardinals, 56-14 (M)
1967—Cardinals, 34-24 (M)
1969—Vikings, 27-10 (StL)
1972—Cardinals, 19-17 (M)
1974—Vikings, 28-24 (StL)
    **Vikings, 30-14 (M)

1977—Cardinals, 27-7 (M)
1979—Cardinals, 37-7 (StL)
1981—Cardinals, 30-17 (StL)
1983—Cardinals, 41-31 (StL)
1991—Vikings, 34-7 (M)
    Vikings, 28-0 (P)
1994—Cardinals, 17-7 (A)
1995—Vikings, 30-24 (A) OT
1996—Vikings, 41-17 (M)
1997—Vikings, 20-19 (A)
1998—**Vikings, 41-21 (M)
2000—Vikings, 31-14 (A)
2003—Cardinals, 18-17 (A)
2006—Vikings, 31-26 (M)
2008—Vikings, 35-14 (A)
2009—Cardinals, 30-17 (A)
2010—Vikings, 27-24 (M) OT
2011—Vikings, 34-10 (M)
2012—Vikings, 21-14 (M)
(RS Pts.—Vikings 545, Cardinals 512)
(PS Pts.—Vikings 71, Cardinals 35)
*Franchise known as Phoenix prior to
1994 and in St. Louis prior to 1988*
***NFC Divisional Playoff*
***ARIZONA vs. **NEW ENGLAND**
RS: Cardinals lead series, 7-6
1970—Cardinals, 31-0 (StL)
1975—Cardinals, 24-17 (StL)
1978—Patriots, 16-6 (StL)
1981—Cardinals, 27-20 (NE)
1984—Cardinals, 33-10 (NE)
1990—Cardinals, 34-14 (P)
1991—Cardinals, 24-10 (P)
1993—Patriots, 23-21 (P)
1996—Patriots, 31-0 (NE)
1999—Patriots, 27-3 (A)
2004—Patriots, 23-12 (A)
2008—Patriots, 47-7 (NE)
2012—Cardinals, 20-18 (NE)
(RS Pts.—Patriots 256, Cardinals 242)
*Franchise known as Phoenix prior to
1994 and in St. Louis prior to 1988*
***Franchise in Boston prior to 1971*
***ARIZONA vs. NEW ORLEANS**
RS: Cardinals lead series, 14-12
PS: Saints lead series, 1-0
1967—Cardinals, 31-20 (StL)
1968—Cardinals, 21-20 (NO)
    Cardinals, 31-17 (StL)
1969—Saints, 51-42 (StL)
1970—Cardinals, 24-17 (StL)
1974—Saints, 14-0 (NO)
1977—Cardinals, 49-31 (StL)
1980—Cardinals, 40-7 (NO)
1981—Cardinals, 30-3 (StL)
1982—Cardinals, 21-7 (NO)
1983—Saints, 28-17 (NO)
1984—Saints, 34-24 (NO)
1985—Cardinals, 28-16 (StL)
1986—Saints, 16-7 (StL)
1987—Cardinals, 24-19 (StL)
1990—Saints, 28-7 (NO)
1991—Saints, 27-3 (P)
1992—Saints, 30-21 (P)
1993—Saints, 20-17 (P)
1996—Cardinals, 28-14 (NO)
1997—Saints, 27-10 (NO)
1998—Cardinals, 19-17 (A)
2000—Saints, 21-10 (A)
2004—Cardinals, 34-10 (A)
2007—Saints, 31-24 (NO)
2009—**Saints, 45-14 (NO)
2010—Cardinals, 30-20 (A)

(RS Pts.—Cardinals 592, Saints 545)
(PS Pts.—Saints 45, Cardinals 14)
*Franchise known as Phoenix prior to 1994 and in St. Louis prior to 1988
**NFC Divisional Playoff
ARIZONA vs. N.Y. GIANTS
RS: Giants lead series, 80-42-2
1926—Giants, 20-0 (NY)
1927—Giants, 28-7 (NY)
1929—Giants, 24-21 (NY)
1930—Giants, 25-12 (NY)
⠀⠀⠀⠀Giants, 13-7 (C)
1935—Cardinals, 14-13 (NY)
1936—Giants, 14-6 (NY)
1938—Giants, 6-0 (NY)
1939—Giants, 17-7 (NY)
1941—Cardinals, 10-7 (NY)
1942—Giants, 21-7 (NY)
1943—Giants, 24-13 (NY)
1946—Giants, 28-24 (NY)
1947—Giants, 35-31 (NY)
1948—Cardinals, 63-35 (NY)
1949—Giants, 41-38 (C)
1950—Cardinals, 17-3 (C)
⠀⠀⠀⠀Giants, 51-21 (NY)
1951—Giants, 28-17 (NY)
⠀⠀⠀⠀Giants, 10-0 (C)
1952—Cardinals, 24-23 (NY)
⠀⠀⠀⠀Giants, 28-6 (C)
1953—Giants, 21-7 (NY)
⠀⠀⠀⠀Giants, 23-20 (C)
1954—Giants, 41-10 (C)
⠀⠀⠀⠀Giants, 31-17 (NY)
1955—Cardinals, 28-17 (C)
⠀⠀⠀⠀Giants, 10-0 (NY)
1956—Cardinals, 35-27 (C)
⠀⠀⠀⠀Giants, 23-10 (NY)
1957—Giants, 27-14 (NY)
⠀⠀⠀⠀Giants, 28-21 (C)
1958—Giants, 37-7 (Buffalo)
⠀⠀⠀⠀Cardinals, 23-6 (NY)
1959—Giants, 9-3 (NY)
⠀⠀⠀⠀Giants, 30-20 (Minn)
1960—Giants, 35-14 (StL)
⠀⠀⠀⠀Cardinals, 20-13 (NY)
1961—Cardinals, 21-10 (NY)
⠀⠀⠀⠀Giants, 24-9 (StL)
1962—Giants, 31-14 (StL)
⠀⠀⠀⠀Giants, 31-28 (NY)
1963—Giants, 38-21 (StL)
⠀⠀⠀⠀Cardinals, 24-17 (NY)
1964—Giants, 34-17 (NY)
⠀⠀⠀⠀Tie, 10-10 (StL)
1965—Giants, 14-10 (NY)
⠀⠀⠀⠀Giants, 28-15 (StL)
1966—Cardinals, 24-19 (StL)
⠀⠀⠀⠀Cardinals, 20-17 (NY)
1967—Giants, 37-20 (StL)
⠀⠀⠀⠀Giants, 37-14 (NY)
1968—Cardinals, 28-21 (NY)
1969—Cardinals, 42-17 (StL)
⠀⠀⠀⠀Giants, 49-6 (NY)
1970—Giants, 35-17 (NY)
⠀⠀⠀⠀Giants, 34-17 (StL)
1971—Giants, 21-20 (StL)
⠀⠀⠀⠀Cardinals, 24-7 (NY)
1972—Giants, 27-21 (NY)
⠀⠀⠀⠀Giants, 13-7 (StL)
1973—Cardinals, 35-27 (StL)
⠀⠀⠀⠀Giants, 24-13 (New Haven)
1974—Cardinals, 23-21 (New Haven)
⠀⠀⠀⠀Cardinals, 26-14 (StL)

1975—Cardinals, 26-14 (StL)
⠀⠀⠀⠀Cardinals, 20-13 (NY)
1976—Cardinals, 27-21 (StL)
⠀⠀⠀⠀Cardinals, 17-14 (NY)
1977—Cardinals, 28-0 (StL)
⠀⠀⠀⠀Giants, 27-7 (NY)
1978—Cardinals, 20-10 (StL)
⠀⠀⠀⠀Giants, 17-0 (NY)
1979—Cardinals, 27-14 (NY)
⠀⠀⠀⠀Cardinals, 29-20 (StL)
1980—Giants, 41-35 (StL)
⠀⠀⠀⠀Cardinals, 23-7 (NY)
1981—Giants, 34-14 (NY)
⠀⠀⠀⠀Giants, 20-10 (StL)
1982—Cardinals, 24-21 (StL)
1983—Tie, 20-20 (StL) OT
⠀⠀⠀⠀Cardinals, 10-6 (NY)
1984—Giants, 16-10 (NY)
⠀⠀⠀⠀Cardinals, 31-21 (StL)
1985—Giants, 27-17 (NY)
⠀⠀⠀⠀Giants, 34-3 (StL)
1986—Giants, 13-6 (StL)
⠀⠀⠀⠀Giants, 27-7 (NY)
1987—Giants, 30-7 (NY)
⠀⠀⠀⠀Cardinals, 27-24 (StL)
1988—Cardinals, 24-17 (P)
⠀⠀⠀⠀Giants, 44-7 (NY)
1989—Giants, 35-7 (NY)
⠀⠀⠀⠀Giants, 20-13 (P)
1990—Giants, 20-19 (NY)
⠀⠀⠀⠀Giants, 24-21 (P)
1991—Giants, 20-9 (NY)
⠀⠀⠀⠀Giants, 21-14 (P)
1992—Giants, 31-21 (NY)
⠀⠀⠀⠀Cardinals, 19-0 (P)
1993—Giants, 19-17 (NY)
⠀⠀⠀⠀Cardinals, 17-6 (P)
1994—Giants, 20-17 (A)
⠀⠀⠀⠀Cardinals, 10-9 (NY)
1995—Giants, 27-21 (NY) OT
⠀⠀⠀⠀Giants, 10-6 (A)
1996—Giants, 16-8 (NY)
⠀⠀⠀⠀Cardinals, 31-23 (A)
1997—Giants, 27-13 (A)
⠀⠀⠀⠀Giants, 19-10 (NY)
1998—Giants, 34-7 (NY)
⠀⠀⠀⠀Giants, 23-19 (A)
1999—Cardinals, 14-3 (A)
⠀⠀⠀⠀Cardinals, 34-24 (NY)
2000—Giants, 21-16 (NY)
⠀⠀⠀⠀Giants, 31-7 (A)
2001—Giants, 17-10 (A)
⠀⠀⠀⠀Giants, 17-13 (NY)
2002—Cardinals, 21-7 (A)
2004—Cardinals, 17-14 (A)
2005—Giants, 42-19 (NY)
2008—Giants, 37-29 (A)
2009—Cardinals, 24-17 (NY)
2011—Giants, 31-27 (A)
(RS Pts.—Giants 2,746, Cardinals 2,126)
*Franchise known as Phoenix prior to 1994, in St. Louis prior to 1988, and in Chicago prior to 1960
ARIZONA vs. N.Y. JETS
RS: Jets lead series, 6-2
1971—Cardinals, 17-10 (StL)
1975—Cardinals, 37-6 (NY)
1978—Jets, 23-10 (NY)
1996—Jets, 31-21 (A)
1999—Jets, 12-7 (NY)
2004—Jets, 13-3 (A)
2008—Jets, 56-35 (NY)
2012—Jets, 7-6 (NY)

(RS Pts.—Jets 158, Cardinals 136)
*Franchise known as Phoenix prior to 1994 and in St. Louis prior to 1988
ARIZONA vs. **OAKLAND
RS: Raiders lead series, 5-3
1973—Raiders, 17-10 (StL)
1983—Cardinals, 34-24 (LA)
1989—Raiders, 16-14 (LA)
1998—Raiders, 23-20 (A)
2001—Cardinals, 34-31 (O) OT
2002—Raiders, 41-20 (A)
2006—Raiders, 22-9 (O)
2010—Cardinals, 24-23 (A)
(RS Pts.— Raiders 197, Cardinals 165)
*Franchise known as Phoenix prior to 1994 and in St. Louis prior to 1988
**Franchise in Los Angeles from 1982-1994
ARIZONA vs. PHILADELPHIA
RS: Cardinals lead series, 55-53-5
PS: Cardinals lead series, 2-1
1935—Cardinals, 12-3 (C)
1936—Cardinals, 13-0 (C)
1937—Tie, 6-6 (P)
1938—Eagles, 7-0 (Erie, Pa.)
1941—Eagles, 21-14 (P)
1945—Eagles, 21-6 (P)
1947—Cardinals, 45-21 (P)
⠀⠀⠀⠀**Cardinals, 28-21 (C)
1948—Cardinals, 21-14 (C)
⠀⠀⠀⠀**Eagles, 7-0 (P)
1949—Eagles, 28-3 (P)
1950—Eagles, 45-7 (C)
⠀⠀⠀⠀Cardinals, 14-10 (P)
1951—Eagles, 17-14 (C)
1952—Eagles, 10-7 (P)
⠀⠀⠀⠀Cardinals, 28-22 (C)
1953—Eagles, 56-17 (C)
⠀⠀⠀⠀Eagles, 38-0 (P)
1954—Eagles, 35-16 (C)
⠀⠀⠀⠀Eagles, 30-14 (P)
1955—Tie, 24-24 (C)
⠀⠀⠀⠀Eagles, 27-3 (P)
1956—Cardinals, 20-6 (P)
⠀⠀⠀⠀Cardinals, 28-17 (C)
1957—Eagles, 38-21 (C)
⠀⠀⠀⠀Cardinals, 31-27 (P)
1958—Tie, 21-21 (C)
⠀⠀⠀⠀Eagles, 49-21 (P)
1959—Eagles, 28-24 (Minn)
⠀⠀⠀⠀Eagles, 27-17 (P)
1960—Eagles, 31-27 (P)
⠀⠀⠀⠀Eagles, 20-6 (StL)
1961—Cardinals, 30-27 (P)
⠀⠀⠀⠀Eagles, 20-7 (StL)
1962—Cardinals, 27-21 (P)
⠀⠀⠀⠀Cardinals, 45-35 (StL)
1963—Cardinals, 28-24 (P)
⠀⠀⠀⠀Cardinals, 38-14 (StL)
1964—Cardinals, 38-13 (P)
⠀⠀⠀⠀Cardinals, 36-34 (StL)
1965—Eagles, 34-27 (P)
⠀⠀⠀⠀Eagles, 28-24 (StL)
1966—Cardinals, 16-13 (StL)
⠀⠀⠀⠀Cardinals, 41-10 (P)
1967—Cardinals, 48-14 (StL)
1968—Cardinals, 45-17 (P)
1969—Eagles, 34-30 (StL)
1970—Cardinals, 35-20 (P)
⠀⠀⠀⠀Cardinals, 23-14 (StL)
1971—Eagles, 37-20 (StL)
⠀⠀⠀⠀Eagles, 19-7 (P)

1972—Tie, 6-6 (P)
    Cardinals, 24-23 (StL)
1973—Cardinals, 34-23 (P)
    Eagles, 27-24 (StL)
1974—Cardinals, 7-3 (StL)
    Cardinals, 13-3 (P)
1975—Cardinals, 31-20 (StL)
    Cardinals, 24-23 (P)
1976—Cardinals, 33-14 (StL)
    Cardinals, 17-14 (P)
1977—Cardinals, 21-17 (P)
    Cardinals, 21-16 (StL)
1978—Cardinals, 16-10 (P)
    Eagles, 14-10 (StL)
1979—Eagles, 24-20 (StL)
    Eagles, 16-13 (P)
1980—Cardinals, 24-14 (StL)
    Eagles, 17-3 (P)
1981—Eagles, 52-10 (StL)
    Eagles, 38-0 (P)
1982—Cardinals, 23-20 (P)
1983—Cardinals, 14-11 (P)
    Cardinals, 31-7 (StL)
1984—Cardinals, 34-14 (P)
    Cardinals, 17-16 (StL)
1985—Eagles, 30-7 (P)
    Eagles, 24-14 (StL)
1986—Cardinals, 13-10 (StL)
    Tie, 10-10 (P) OT
1987—Eagles, 28-23 (StL)
    Cardinals, 31-19 (P)
1988—Eagles, 31-21 (P)
    Eagles, 23-17 (Phx)
1989—Eagles, 17-5 (P)
    Eagles, 31-14 (P)
1990—Cardinals, 23-21 (P)
    Eagles, 23-21 (Phx)
1991—Cardinals, 26-10 (P)
    Eagles, 34-14 (Phx)
1992—Eagles, 31-14 (Phx)
    Eagles, 7-3 (P)
1993—Eagles, 23-17 (P)
    Cardinals, 16-3 (Phx)
1994—Eagles, 17-7 (P)
    Cardinals, 12-6 (A)
1995—Eagles, 31-19 (A)
    Eagles, 21-20 (P)
1996—Cardinals, 36-30 (A)
    Eagles, 29-19 (A)
1997—Eagles, 13-10 (P) OT
    Cardinals, 31-21 (A)
1998—Cardinals, 17-3 (A)
    Cardinals, 20-17 (P) OT
1999—Cardinals, 25-24 (P)
    Cardinals, 21-17 (A)
2000—Eagles, 33-14 (A)
    Eagles, 34-9 (P)
2001—Cardinals, 21-20 (P)
    Eagles, 21-7 (A)
2002—Eagles, 38-14 (P)
2005—Cardinals, 27-21 (A)
2008—Eagles, 48-20 (P)
    ***Cardinals, 32-25 (A)
2011—Cardinals, 21-17 (P)
2012—Cardinals, 27-6 (A)
(RS Pts.—Eagles 2,411, Cardinals 2,201)
(PS Pts.—Cardinals 60, Eagles 53)
*Franchise known as Phoenix prior to
1994, in St. Louis prior to 1988,
and in Chicago prior to 1960
**NFL Championship
***NFC Championship

*ARIZONA vs. **PITTSBURGH
RS: Steelers lead series, 32-23-3
PS: Steelers lead series, 1-0
1933—Pirates, 14-13 (P)
1935—Pirates, 17-13 (P)
1936—Cardinals, 14-6 (C)
1937—Cardinals, 13-7 (P)
1939—Cardinals, 10-0 (P)
1940—Tie, 7-7 (P)
1942—Steelers, 19-3 (P)
1945—Steelers, 23-0 (P)
1946—Steelers, 14-7 (P)
1948—Cardinals, 24-7 (P)
1950—Steelers, 28-17 (C)
    Steelers, 28-7 (P)
1951—Steelers, 28-14 (C)
1952—Steelers, 34-28 (C)
    Steelers, 17-14 (P)
1953—Steelers, 31-28 (P)
    Steelers, 21-17 (C)
1954—Cardinals, 17-14 (C)
    Steelers, 20-17 (P)
1955—Steelers, 14-7 (P)
    Cardinals, 27-13 (C)
1956—Steelers, 14-7 (P)
    Cardinals, 38-27 (C)
1957—Steelers, 29-20 (P)
    Steelers, 27-2 (C)
1958—Steelers, 27-20 (C)
    Steelers, 38-21 (P)
1959—Cardinals, 45-24 (C)
    Steelers, 35-20 (P)
1960—Steelers, 27-14 (P)
    Cardinals, 38-7 (StL)
1961—Steelers, 30-27 (P)
    Cardinals, 20-0 (StL)
1962—Steelers, 26-17 (StL)
    Steelers, 19-7 (P)
1963—Steelers, 23-10 (P)
    Cardinals, 24-23 (StL)
1964—Cardinals, 34-30 (StL)
    Cardinals, 21-20 (P)
1965—Cardinals, 20-7 (P)
    Cardinals, 21-17 (StL)
1966—Steelers, 30-9 (P)
    Cardinals, 6-3 (StL)
1967—Cardinals, 28-14 (P)
    Tie, 14-14 (StL)
1968—Tie, 28-28 (StL)
    Cardinals, 20-10 (P)
1969—Cardinals, 27-14 (P)
    Cardinals, 47-10 (StL)
1972—Steelers, 25-19 (StL)
1979—Steelers, 24-21 (StL)
1985—Steelers, 23-10 (P)
1988—Cardinals, 31-14 (Phx)
1994—Cardinals, 20-17 (A) OT
1997—Steelers, 26-20 (A) OT
2003—Steelers, 28-15 (P)
2007—Cardinals, 21-14 (A)
2008—***Steelers, 27-23 (Tampa Bay)
2011—Steelers, 32-20 (A)
(RS Pts.—Steelers 1,138, Cardinals 1,079)
(PS Pts.—Steelers 27, Cardinals 23)
*Franchise known as Phoenix prior to
1994, in St. Louis prior to 1988,
and in Chicago prior to 1960
**Steelers known as Pirates prior to 1940
***Super Bowl XLIII

*ARIZONA vs. **ST. LOUIS
RS: Series tied, 33-33-2
PS: Rams lead series, 1-0

1937—Cardinals, 6-0 (Cle)
    Cardinals, 13-7 (Chi)
1938—Cardinals, 7-6 (Cle)
    Cardinals, 31-17 (Chi)
1939—Rams, 24-0 (Chi)
    Rams, 14-0 (Cle)
1940—Rams, 26-14 (Cle)
    Cardinals, 17-7 (Chi)
1941—Rams, 10-6 (Cle)
    Cardinals, 7-0 (Chi)
1942—Cardinals, 7-0 (Buffalo)
    Rams, 7-3 (Cle)
1945—Rams, 21-0 (Cle)
    Rams, 35-21 (Chi)
1946—Cardinals, 34-10 (Chi)
    Rams, 17-14 (LA)
1947—Rams, 27-7 (LA)
    Cardinals, 17-10 (Chi)
1948—Cardinals, 27-22 (LA)
    Cardinals, 27-24 (Chi)
1949—Tie, 28-28 (Chi)
    Cardinals, 31-27 (LA)
1951—Rams, 45-21 (LA)
1953—Tie, 24-24 (Chi)
1954—Rams, 28-17 (LA)
1958—Rams, 20-14 (Chi)
1960—Cardinals, 43-21 (LA)
1965—Rams, 27-3 (StL)
1968—Rams, 24-13 (StL)
1970—Rams, 34-13 (LA)
1972—Cardinals, 24-14 (StL)
1975—***Rams, 35-23 (LA)
1976—Cardinals, 30-28 (LA)
1979—Rams, 21-0 (LA)
1980—Rams, 21-13 (StL)
1984—Rams, 16-13 (StL)
1985—Rams, 46-14 (StL)
1986—Rams, 16-10 (StL)
1987—Rams, 27-24 (StL)
1988—Cardinals, 41-27 (LA)
1989—Rams, 37-14 (LA)
1991—Cardinals, 24-14 (LA)
1992—Cardinals, 20-14 (LA)
1993—Cardinals, 38-10 (P)
1994—Rams, 14-12 (LA)
1996—Cardinals, 31-28 (A) OT
1998—Cardinals, 20-17 (StL)
2002—Rams, 27-14 (A)
    Rams, 30-28 (StL)
2003—Rams, 37-13 (StL)
    Rams, 30-27 (A) OT
2004—Rams, 17-10 (StL)
    Cardinals, 31-7 (A)
2005—Rams, 17-12 (A)
    Cardinals, 38-28 (StL)
2006—Rams, 16-14 (A)
    Cardinals, 34-20 (StL)
2007—Cardinals, 34-31 (StL)
    Cardinals, 48-19 (A)
2008—Cardinals, 34-13 (StL)
    Cardinals, 34-10 (A)
2009—Cardinals, 21-13 (StL)
    Cardinals, 31-10 (A)
2010—Cardinals, 17-13 (StL)
    Rams, 19-6 (A)
2011—Cardinals, 19-13 (A) OT
    Cardinals, 23-20 (StL)
2012—Rams, 17-3 (StL)
    Rams, 31-17 (A)
(RS Pts.—Rams 1,350, Cardinals 1,301)
(PS Pts.—Rams 35, Cardinals 23)

*Franchise known as Phoenix prior to 1994, in St. Louis prior to 1988, and in Chicago prior to 1960
**Franchise in Los Angeles prior to 1995 and in Cleveland prior to 1946
***NFC Divisional Playoff

*ARIZONA vs. SAN DIEGO
RS: Chargers lead series, 9-3
1971—Chargers, 20-17 (SD)
1976—Chargers, 43-24 (SD)
1983—Cardinals, 44-14 (StL)
1987—Chargers, 28-24 (SD)
1989—Chargers, 24-13 (P)
1992—Chargers, 27-21 (P)
1995—Chargers, 28-25 (SD)
1998—Cardinals, 16-13 (A)
2001—Cardinals, 20-17 (SD)
2002—Chargers, 23-15 (A)
2006—Chargers, 27-20 (SD)
2010—Chargers, 41-10 (SD)
(RS Pts.—Chargers 305, Cardinals 249)
*Franchise known as Phoenix prior to 1994, in St. Louis prior to 1988,

*ARIZONA vs. SAN FRANCISCO
RS: 49ers lead series, 26-17
1951—Cardinals, 27-21 (SF)
1957—Cardinals, 20-10 (SF)
1962—49ers, 24-17 (StL)
1964—49ers, 23-13 (SF)
1968—49ers, 35-17 (SF)
1971—49ers, 26-14 (StL)
1974—Cardinals, 34-9 (SF)
1976—Cardinals, 23-20 (StL) OT
1978—Cardinals, 16-10 (SF)
1979—Cardinals, 13-10 (StL)
1980—49ers, 24-21 (SF) OT
1982—49ers, 31-20 (StL)
1983—49ers, 42-27 (StL)
1986—49ers, 43-17 (SF)
1987—49ers, 34-28 (SF)
1988—Cardinals, 24-23 (P)
1991—49ers, 14-10 (SF)
1992—49ers, 24-14 (P)
1993—49ers, 28-14 (SF)
1999—49ers, 24-10 (A)
2000—49ers, 27-20 (SF)
2002—49ers, 38-28 (SF)
        49ers, 17-14 (A)
2003—Cardinals, 16-13 (A) OT
        49ers, 50-14 (SF)
2004—49ers, 31-28 (SF) OT
        49ers, 31-28 (A) OT
2005—Cardinals, 31-14 (Mex. City)
        Cardinals, 17-10 (SF)
2006—Cardinals, 34-27 (A)
        Cardinals, 26-20 (SF)
2007—49ers, 20-17 (SF)
        49ers, 37-31 (A) OT
2008—Cardinals, 23-13 (SF)
        Cardinals, 29-24 (A)
2009—49ers, 20-16 (A)
        49ers, 24-9 (SF)
2010—49ers, 27-6 (A)
        49ers, 38-7 (SF)
2011—49ers, 23-7 (SF)
        Cardinals, 21-19 (A)
2012—49ers, 24-3 (A)
        49ers, 27-13 (SF)
(RS Pts.—49ers 1,029, Cardinals 837)
*Franchise known as Phoenix prior to 1994, in St. Louis prior to 1988, and in Chicago prior to 1960

*ARIZONA vs. SEATTLE
RS: Cardinals lead series, 15-13
1976—Cardinals, 30-24 (S)
1983—Cardinals, 33-28 (StL)
1989—Cardinals, 34-24 (S)
1993—Cardinals, 30-27 (S) OT
1995—Cardinals, 20-14 (A) OT
1998—Seahawks, 33-14 (S)
2002—Cardinals, 24-13 (S)
        Seahawks, 27-6 (A)
2003—Seahawks, 38-0 (A)
        Seahawks, 28-10 (S)
2004—Cardinals, 25-17 (A)
        Seahawks, 24-21 (S)
2005—Seahawks, 37-12 (S)
        Seahawks, 33-19 (A)
2006—Seahawks, 21-10 (S)
        Cardinals, 27-21 (A)
2007—Cardinals, 23-20 (A)
        Seahawks, 42-21 (S)
2008—Cardinals, 26-20 (S)
        Cardinals, 34-21 (A)
2009—Cardinals, 27-3 (S)
        Cardinals, 31-20 (A)
2010—Seahawks, 22-10 (S)
        Seahawks, 36-18 (A)
2011—Seahawks, 13-10 (S)
        Cardinals, 23-20 (A) OT
2012—Cardinals, 20-16 (A)
        Seahawks, 58-0 (S)
(RS Pts.—Seahawks 700, Cardinals 558)
*Franchise known as Phoenix prior to 1994 and in St. Louis prior to 1988

*ARIZONA vs. TAMPA BAY
RS: Buccaneers lead series, 9-8
1977—Buccaneers, 17-7 (TB)
1981—Buccaneers, 20-10 (TB)
1983—Cardinals, 34-27 (TB)
1985—Buccaneers, 16-0 (TB)
1986—Cardinals, 30-19 (TB)
        Cardinals, 21-17 (StL)
1987—Cardinals, 31-28 (StL)
        Cardinals, 31-14 (TB)
1988—Cardinals, 30-24 (TB)
1989—Buccaneers, 14-13 (P)
1992—Buccaneers, 23-7 (TB)
        Buccaneers, 7-3 (P)
1996—Cardinals, 13-9 (A)
1997—Buccaneers, 19-18 (TB)
2004—Cardinals, 12-7 (A)
2007—Buccaneers, 17-10 (TB)
2010—Buccaneers, 38-35 (A)
(RS Pts.—Buccaneers 316, Cardinals 305)
*Franchise known as Phoenix prior to 1994 and in St. Louis prior to 1988

*ARIZONA vs. **TENNESSEE
RS: Cardinals lead series, 5-4
1970—Cardinals, 44-0 (StL)
1974—Cardinals, 31-27 (H)
1979—Cardinals, 24-17 (H)
1985—Oilers, 20-10 (StL)
1988—Oilers, 38-20 (H)
1994—Cardinals, 30-12 (H)
1997—Oilers, 41-14 (A)
2005—Cardinals, 20-10 (A)
2009—Titans, 20-17 (T)
(RS Pts.—Cardinals 210, Titans 185)
*Franchise known as Phoenix prior to 1994 and in St. Louis prior to 1988
**Franchise in Houston prior to 1997; known as Oilers prior to 1999

*ARIZONA vs. **WASHINGTON
RS: Redskins lead series, 74-44-2

1932—Cardinals, 9-0 (B)
        Braves, 8-6 (C)
1933—Redskins, 10-0 (C)
        Tie, 0-0 (B)
1934—Redskins, 9-0 (B)
1935—Cardinals, 6-0 (B)
1936—Redskins, 13-10 (B)
1937—Cardinals, 21-14 (W)
1939—Redskins, 28-7 (W)
1940—Redskins, 28-21 (W)
1942—Redskins, 28-0 (W)
1943—Redskins, 13-7 (W)
1945—Redskins, 24-21 (W)
1947—Redskins, 45-21 (W)
1949—Cardinals, 38-7 (C)
1950—Cardinals, 38-28 (W)
1951—Cardinals, 7-3 (C)
        Redskins, 20-17 (W)
1952—Redskins, 23-7 (C)
        Cardinals, 17-6 (W)
1953—Cardinals, 24-13 (C)
        Redskins, 28-17 (W)
1954—Cardinals, 38-16 (C)
        Redskins, 37-20 (W)
1955—Cardinals, 24-10 (W)
        Redskins, 31-0 (C)
1956—Cardinals, 31-3 (W)
        Redskins, 17-14 (C)
1957—Redskins, 37-14 (C)
        Cardinals, 44-14 (W)
1958—Cardinals, 37-10 (C)
        Redskins, 45-31 (W)
1959—Cardinals, 49-21 (C)
        Redskins, 23-14 (W)
1960—Cardinals, 44-7 (StL)
        Cardinals, 26-14 (W)
1961—Cardinals, 24-0 (W)
        Cardinals, 38-24 (StL)
1962—Redskins, 24-14 (W)
        Tie, 17-17 (StL)
1963—Redskins, 21-7 (W)
        Cardinals, 24-20 (StL)
1964—Cardinals, 23-17 (W)
        Cardinals, 38-24 (StL)
1965—Cardinals, 37-16 (W)
        Redskins, 24-20 (StL)
1966—Cardinals, 23-7 (StL)
        Redskins, 26-20 (W)
1967—Cardinals, 27-21 (W)
1968—Cardinals, 41-14 (StL)
1969—Redskins, 33-17 (W)
1970—Cardinals, 27-17 (StL)
        Redskins, 28-27 (W)
1971—Cardinals, 24-17 (StL)
        Redskins, 20-0 (W)
1972—Redskins, 24-10 (W)
        Redskins, 33-3 (StL)
1973—Cardinals, 34-27 (StL)
        Redskins, 31-13 (W)
1974—Cardinals, 17-10 (W)
        Cardinals, 23-20 (StL)
1975—Redskins, 27-17 (W)
        Cardinals, 20-17 (StL) OT
1976—Redskins, 20-10 (StL)
        Redskins, 16-10 (W)
1977—Redskins, 24-14 (W)
        Redskins, 26-20 (StL)
1978—Redskins, 28-10 (StL)
        Cardinals, 27-17 (W)
1979—Redskins, 17-7 (StL)
        Redskins, 30-28 (W)
1980—Redskins, 23-0 (W)
        Redskins, 31-7 (StL)

1981—Cardinals, 40-30 (StL)
    Redskins, 42-21 (W)
1982—Redskins, 12-7 (StL)
    Redskins, 28-0 (W)
1983—Redskins, 38-14 (StL)
    Redskins, 45-7 (W)
1984—Cardinals, 26-24 (StL)
    Redskins, 29-27 (W)
1985—Redskins, 27-10 (W)
    Redskins, 27-16 (StL)
1986—Redskins, 28-21 (W)
    Redskins, 20-17 (StL)
1987—Redskins, 28-21 (W)
    Redskins, 34-17 (StL)
1988—Cardinals, 30-21 (P)
    Redskins, 33-17 (W)
1989—Redskins, 30-28 (W)
    Redskins, 29-10 (P)
1990—Redskins, 31-0 (W)
    Redskins, 38-10 (P)
1991—Redskins, 34-0 (W)
    Redskins, 20-14 (P)
1992—Cardinals, 27-24 (P)
    Redskins, 41-3 (W)
1993—Cardinals, 17-10 (W)
    Cardinals, 36-6 (P)
1994—Cardinals, 19-16 (W) OT
    Cardinals, 17-15 (A)
1995—Redskins, 27-7 (W)
    Cardinals, 24-20 (A)
1996—Cardinals, 37-34 (W) OT
    Cardinals, 27-26 (A)
1997—Redskins, 19-13 (W) OT
    Redskins, 38-28 (A)
1998—Cardinals, 29-27 (A)
    Cardinals, 45-42 (W)
1999—Redskins, 24-10 (A)
    Redskins, 28-3 (W)
2000—Cardinals, 16-15 (A)
    Redskins, 20-3 (W)
2001—Redskins, 20-10 (A)
    Redskins, 20-17 (W)
2002—Redskins, 31-23 (W)
2005—Redskins, 17-13 (A)
2007—Redskins, 21-19 (W)
2008—Redskins, 24-17 (W)
2011—Redskins, 22-21 (W)
(RS Pts.—Redskins 2,667, Cardinals 2,224)
*Franchise known as Phoenix prior to
1994, in St. Louis prior to 1988,
and in Chicago prior to 1960
**Franchise in Boston prior to 1937 and
known as Braves prior to 1933

ATLANTA vs. ARIZONA
RS: Cardinals lead series, 14-12
PS: Cardinals lead series, 1-0;
See Arizona vs. Atlanta
ATLANTA vs. BALTIMORE
RS: Series tied, 2-2
1999—Ravens, 19-13 (A) OT
2002—Falcons, 20-17 (A)
2006—Ravens, 24-10 (B)
2010—Falcons, 26-21 (A)
(RS Pts.—Ravens 81, Falcons 69)
ATLANTA vs. BUFFALO
RS: Falcons lead series, 6-4
1973—Bills, 17-6 (A)
1977—Bills, 3-0 (B)
1980—Falcons, 30-14 (B)
1983—Falcons, 31-14 (A)
1989—Falcons, 30-28 (A)
1992—Bills, 41-14 (B)

1995—Bills, 23-17 (B)
2001—Falcons, 33-30 (A)
2005—Falcons, 24-16 (B)
2009—Falcons, 31-3 (A)
(RS Pts.—Falcons 216, Bills 189)
ATLANTA vs. CAROLINA
RS: Falcons lead series, 23-13
1995—Falcons, 23-20 (A) OT
    Panthers, 21-17 (C)
1996—Panthers, 29-6 (C)
    Falcons, 20-17 (A)
1997—Panthers, 9-6 (A)
    Panthers, 21-12 (C)
1998—Falcons, 19-14 (C)
    Falcons, 51-23 (A)
1999—Falcons, 27-20 (A)
    Panthers, 34-28 (C)
2000—Falcons, 15-10 (C)
    Falcons, 13-12 (A)
2001—Falcons, 24-16 (A)
    Falcons, 10-7 (C)
2002—Falcons, 30-0 (A)
    Falcons, 41-0 (C)
2003—Panthers, 23-3 (C)
    Falcons, 20-14 (A) OT
2004—Falcons, 27-10 (C)
    Falcons, 34-31 (A) OT
2005—Panthers, 24-6 (C)
    Panthers, 44-11 (A)
2006—Falcons, 20-6 (C)
    Panthers, 10-3 (A)
2007—Panthers, 27-20 (A)
    Falcons, 20-13 (C)
2008—Panthers, 24-9 (A)
    Falcons, 45-28 (A)
2009—Falcons, 28-20 (A)
    Panthers, 28-19 (C)
2010—Falcons, 31-10 (C)
    Falcons, 31-10 (A)
2011—Falcons, 31-17 (A)
    Falcons, 31-23 (C)
2012—Falcons, 30-28 (A)
    Panthers, 30-20 (C)
(RS Pts.—Falcons 781, Panthers 673)
ATLANTA vs. CHICAGO
RS: Bears lead series, 13-12
1966—Bears, 23-6 (C)
1967—Bears, 23-14 (A)
1968—Falcons, 16-13 (A)
1969—Falcons, 48-31 (A)
1970—Bears, 23-14 (A)
1972—Falcons, 37-21 (C)
1973—Falcons, 46-6 (A)
1974—Falcons, 13-10 (A)
1976—Falcons, 10-0 (C)
1977—Falcons, 16-10 (C)
1978—Bears, 13-7 (C)
1980—Falcons, 28-17 (A)
1983—Falcons, 20-17 (C)
1985—Bears, 36-0 (C)
1986—Bears, 13-10 (A)
1990—Bears, 30-24 (C)
1992—Bears, 41-31 (A)
1993—Bears, 6-0 (C)
1998—Falcons, 20-13 (A)
2001—Bears, 31-3 (A)
2002—Bears, 14-13 (A)
2005—Bears, 16-3 (C)
2008—Falcons, 22-20 (A)
2009—Falcons, 21-14 (A)
2011—Bears, 30-12 (C)
(RS Pts.—Bears 471, Falcons 434)

ATLANTA vs. CINCINNATI
RS: Bengals lead series, 7-5
1971—Falcons, 9-6 (C)
1975—Bengals, 21-14 (A)
1978—Bengals, 37-7 (C)
1981—Bengals, 30-28 (A)
1984—Bengals, 35-14 (C)
1987—Bengals, 16-10 (A)
1990—Falcons, 38-17 (A)
1993—Bengals, 21-17 (C)
1996—Bengals, 41-31 (C)
2002—Falcons, 30-3 (A)
2006—Falcons, 29-27 (C)
2010—Falcons, 39-32 (A)
(RS Pts.—Bengals 286, Falcons 266)
ATLANTA vs. CLEVELAND
RS: Browns lead series, 10-3
1966—Browns, 49-17 (A)
1968—Browns, 30-7 (C)
1971—Falcons, 31-14 (C)
1976—Browns, 20-17 (A)
1978—Browns, 24-16 (A)
1981—Browns, 28-17 (C)
1984—Browns, 23-7 (A)
1987—Browns, 38-3 (C)
1990—Browns, 13-10 (A)
1993—Falcons, 17-14 (A)
2002—Browns, 24-16 (C)
2006—Browns, 17-13 (A)
2010—Falcons, 20-10 (C)
(RS Pts.—Browns 304, Falcons 191)
ATLANTA vs. DALLAS
RS: Cowboys lead series, 14-9
PS: Cowboys lead series, 2-0
1966—Cowboys, 47-14 (A)
1967—Cowboys, 37-7 (D)
1969—Cowboys, 24-17 (A)
1970—Cowboys, 13-0 (D)
1974—Cowboys, 24-0 (A)
1976—Falcons, 17-10 (A)
1978—*Cowboys, 27-20 (D)
1980—*Cowboys, 30-27 (A)
1985—Cowboys, 24-10 (D)
1986—Falcons, 37-35 (D)
1987—Falcons, 21-10 (D)
1988—Cowboys, 26-20 (D)
1989—Falcons, 27-21 (A)
1990—Falcons, 26-7 (A)
1991—Cowboys, 31-27 (D)
1992—Falcons, 41-17 (A)
1993—Falcons, 27-14 (A)
1995—Cowboys, 28-13 (A)
1996—Cowboys, 32-28 (D)
1999—Cowboys, 24-7 (D)
2001—Falcons, 20-13 (A)
2003—Falcons, 27-13 (D)
2006—Cowboys, 38-28 (A)
2009—Cowboys, 37-21 (D)
2012—Falcons, 19-13 (A)
(RS Pts.—Cowboys 562, Falcons 430)
(PS Pts.—Cowboys 57, Falcons 47)
*NFC Divisional Playoff
ATLANTA vs. DENVER
RS: Broncos lead series, 8-5
PS: Broncos lead series, 1-0
1970—Broncos, 24-10 (A)
1972—Falcons, 23-20 (A)
1975—Falcons, 35-21 (A)
1979—Broncos, 20-17 (A) OT
1982—Falcons, 34-27 (D)
1985—Broncos, 44-28 (A)
1988—Broncos, 30-14 (D)
1994—Broncos, 32-28 (D)

1997—Broncos, 29-21 (A)
1998—*Broncos, 34-19 (South Florida)
2000—Broncos, 42-14 (D)
2004—Falcons, 41-28 (D)
2008—Broncos, 24-20 (A)
2012—Falcons, 27-21 (A)
(RS Pts.—Broncos 362, Falcons 312)
(PS Pts.—Broncos 34, Falcons 19)
*Super Bowl XXXIII

ATLANTA vs. DETROIT
RS: Lions lead series, 23-12
1966—Lions, 28-10 (D)
1967—Lions, 24-3 (D)
1968—Lions, 24-7 (A)
1969—Lions, 27-21 (D)
1971—Lions, 41-38 (D)
1972—Lions, 26-23 (A)
1973—Lions, 31-6 (D)
1975—Lions, 17-14 (A)
1976—Lions, 24-10 (D)
1977—Falcons, 17-6 (A)
1978—Falcons, 14-0 (A)
1979—Lions, 24-23 (D)
1980—Falcons, 43-28 (A)
1983—Falcons, 30-14 (D)
1984—Lions, 27-24 (A) OT
1985—Lions, 28-27 (A)
1986—Falcons, 20-6 (D)
1987—Lions, 30-13 (A)
1988—Lions, 31-17 (D)
1989—Lions, 31-24 (A)
1990—Lions, 21-14 (D)
1993—Lions, 30-13 (D)
1994—Lions, 31-28 (D) OT
1995—Falcons, 34-22 (A)
1996—Lions, 28-24 (D)
1997—Lions, 28-17 (D)
1998—Falcons, 24-17 (D)
2000—Lions, 13-10 (D)
2002—Falcons, 36-15 (A)
2004—Lions, 17-10 (A)
2005—Falcons, 27-7 (D)
2006—Lions, 30-14 (A)
2008—Falcons, 34-21 (A)
2011—Falcons, 23-16 (D)
2012—Falcons, 31-18 (D)
(RS Pts.—Lions 781, Falcons 723)

ATLANTA vs. GREEN BAY
RS: Packers lead series, 13-12
PS: Packers lead series, 2-1
1966—Packers, 56-3 (Mil)
1967—Packers, 23-0 (Mil)
1968—Packers, 38-7 (A)
1969—Packers, 28-10 (GB)
1970—Packers, 27-24 (GB)
1971—Falcons, 28-21 (A)
1972—Falcons, 10-9 (Mil)
1974—Falcons, 10-3 (A)
1975—Packers, 22-13 (GB)
1976—Packers, 24-20 (A)
1979—Falcons, 25-7 (A)
1981—Falcons, 31-17 (GB)
1982—Packers, 38-7 (A)
1983—Falcons, 47-41 (A) OT
1988—Falcons, 20-0 (A)
1989—Packers, 23-21 (Mil)
1991—Falcons, 35-31 (A)
1992—Falcons, 24-10 (A)
1994—Falcons, 21-17 (Mil)
1995—*Packers, 37-20 (GB)
2001—Falcons, 23-20 (GB)
2002—Packers, 37-34 (GB) OT
        *Falcons, 27-7 (GB)

2005—Packers, 33-25 (A)
2008—Falcons, 27-24 (GB)
2010—Falcons, 20-17 (A)
        **Packers, 48-21 (A)
2011—Packers, 25-14 (A)
(RS Pts.—Packers 595, Falcons 495)
(PS Pts.—Packers 92, Falcons 68)
*NFC First-Round Playoff
**NFC Divisional Playoff

ATLANTA vs. HOUSTON
RS: Texans lead series, 2-1
2003—Texans, 17-13 (H)
2007—Falcons, 26-16 (A)
2011—Texans, 17-10 (H)
(RS Pts.—Texans 50, Falcons 49)

ATLANTA vs. *INDIANAPOLIS
RS: Colts lead series, 13-2
1966—Colts, 19-7 (A)
1967—Colts, 38-31 (B)
        Colts, 49-7 (A)
1968—Colts, 28-20 (A)
        Colts, 44-0 (B)
1969—Colts, 21-14 (A)
        Colts, 13-6 (B)
1974—Colts, 17-7 (A)
1986—Colts, 28-23 (A)
1989—Colts, 13-9 (I)
1998—Falcons, 28-21 (A)
2001—Colts, 41-27 (I)
2003—Colts, 38-7 (I)
2007—Colts, 31-13 (A)
2011—Falcons, 31-7 (I)
(RS Pts.—Colts 408, Falcons 230)
*Franchise in Baltimore prior to 1984

ATLANTA vs. JACKSONVILLE
RS: Jaguars lead series, 3-2
1996—Jaguars, 19-17 (J)
1999—Jaguars, 30-7 (A)
2003—Falcons, 21-14 (A)
2007—Jaguars, 13-7 (J)
2011—Falcons, 41-14 (A)
(RS Pts.—Falcons 93, Jaguars 90)

ATLANTA vs. KANSAS CITY
RS: Chiefs lead series, 5-3
1972—Chiefs, 17-14 (A)
1985—Chiefs, 38-10 (KC)
1991—Chiefs, 14-3 (KC)
1994—Chiefs, 30-10 (A)
2000—Falcons, 29-13 (A)
2004—Chiefs, 56-10 (KC)
2008—Falcons, 38-14 (A)
2012—Falcons, 40-24 (KC)
(RS Pts.—Chiefs 206, Falcons 154)

ATLANTA vs. MIAMI
RS: Dolphins lead series, 7-4
1970—Dolphins, 20-7 (A)
1974—Dolphins, 42-7 (M)
1980—Dolphins, 20-17 (A)
1983—Dolphins, 31-24 (M)
1986—Falcons, 20-14 (M)
1992—Dolphins, 21-17 (M)
1995—Dolphins, 21-20 (M)
1998—Falcons, 38-16 (A)
2001—Dolphins, 21-14 (M)
2005—Falcons, 17-10 (M)
2009—Falcons, 19-7 (A)
(RS Pts.—Dolphins 223, Falcons 200)

ATLANTA vs. MINNESOTA
RS: Vikings lead series, 15-10
PS: Series tied, 1-1
1966—Falcons, 20-13 (M)
1967—Falcons, 21-20 (A)
1968—Vikings, 47-7 (M)

1969—Falcons, 10-3 (A)
1970—Vikings, 37-7 (A)
1971—Vikings, 24-7 (M)
1973—Falcons, 20-14 (A)
1974—Vikings, 23-10 (M)
1975—Vikings, 38-0 (M)
1977—Vikings, 14-7 (A)
1980—Vikings, 24-23 (M)
1981—Falcons, 31-30 (A)
1982—*Vikings, 30-24 (M)
1984—Vikings, 27-20 (M)
1985—Falcons, 14-13 (A)
1987—Vikings, 24-13 (M)
1989—Falcons, 43-17 (M)
1991—Vikings, 20-19 (A)
1996—Vikings, 23-17 (A)
1998—**Falcons, 30-27 (M) OT
1999—Vikings, 17-14 (A)
2002—Falcons, 30-24 (M) OT
2003—Vikings, 39-26 (A)
2005—Falcons, 30-10 (A)
2007—Vikings, 24-3 (M)
2008—Falcons, 24-17 (M)
2011—Falcons, 24-14 (A)
(RS Pts.—Vikings 582, Falcons 414)
(PS Pts.—Vikings 57, Falcons 54)
*NFC First-Round Playoff
**NFC Championship

ATLANTA vs. NEW ENGLAND
RS: Series tied, 6-6
1972—Patriots, 21-20 (NE)
1977—Patriots, 16-10 (A)
1980—Falcons, 37-21 (NE)
1983—Falcons, 24-13 (A)
1986—Patriots, 25-17 (NE)
1989—Falcons, 16-15 (A)
1992—Falcons, 34-0 (A)
1995—Falcons, 30-17 (A)
1998—Falcons, 41-10 (NE)
2001—Patriots, 24-10 (A)
2005—Patriots, 31-28 (A)
2009—Patriots, 26-10 (NE)
(RS Pts.—Falcons 277, Patriots 219)

ATLANTA vs. NEW ORLEANS
RS: Falcons lead series, 46-41
PS: Falcons lead series, 1-0
1967—Saints, 27-24 (NO)
1969—Falcons, 45-17 (A)
1970—Falcons, 14-3 (NO)
        Falcons, 32-14 (A)
1971—Falcons, 28-6 (A)
        Falcons, 24-20 (NO)
1972—Falcons, 21-14 (NO)
        Falcons, 36-20 (A)
1973—Falcons, 62-7 (NO)
        Falcons, 14-10 (A)
1974—Saints, 14-13 (NO)
        Saints, 13-3 (A)
1975—Falcons, 14-7 (A)
        Saints, 23-7 (NO)
1976—Saints, 30-0 (NO)
        Falcons, 23-20 (A)
1977—Saints, 21-20 (NO)
        Falcons, 35-7 (A)
1978—Falcons, 20-17 (NO)
        Falcons, 20-17 (A)
1979—Falcons, 40-34 (NO) OT
        Saints, 37-6 (A)
1980—Falcons, 41-14 (NO)
        Falcons, 31-13 (A)
1981—Falcons, 27-0 (A)
        Falcons, 41-10 (NO)

1982—Falcons, 35-0 (A)
  Saints, 35-6 (NO)
1983—Saints, 19-17 (A)
  Saints, 27-10 (NO)
1984—Falcons, 36-28 (NO)
  Saints, 17-13 (A)
1985—Falcons, 31-24 (A)
  Falcons, 16-10 (NO)
1986—Falcons, 31-10 (NO)
  Saints, 14-9 (A)
1987—Saints, 38-0 (A)
1988—Saints, 29-21 (A)
  Saints, 10-9 (NO)
1989—Saints, 20-13 (NO)
  Saints, 26-17 (A)
1990—Falcons, 28-27 (A)
  Saints, 10-7 (NO)
1991—Saints, 27-6 (A)
  Falcons, 23-20 (NO) OT
  *Falcons, 27-20 (NO)
1992—Saints, 10-7 (A)
  Saints, 22-14 (NO)
1993—Saints, 34-31 (A)
  Falcons, 26-15 (NO)
1994—Saints, 33-32 (NO)
  Saints, 29-20 (A)
1995—Falcons, 27-24 (NO) OT
  Falcons, 19-14 (A)
1996—Falcons, 17-15 (A)
  Falcons, 31-15 (NO)
1997—Falcons, 23-17 (NO)
  Falcons, 20-3 (A)
1998—Falcons, 31-23 (A)
  Falcons, 27-17 (NO)
1999—Falcons, 20-17 (NO)
  Falcons, 35-12 (A)
2000—Saints, 21-19 (A)
  Saints, 23-7 (NO)
2001—Falcons, 20-13 (NO)
  Saints, 28-10 (A)
2002—Falcons, 37-35 (NO)
  Falcons, 24-17 (A)
2003—Saints, 45-17 (A)
  Saints, 23-20 (NO) OT
2004—Falcons, 24-21 (A)
  Saints, 26-13 (NO)
2005—Falcons, 34-31 (San Antonio)
  Falcons, 36-17 (A)
2006—Saints, 23-3 (NO)
  Saints, 31-13 (A)
2007—Saints, 22-16 (NO)
  Saints, 34-14 (A)
2008—Falcons, 34-20 (A)
  Saints, 29-25 (NO)
2009—Saints, 35-27 (NO)
  Saints, 26-23 (A)
2010—Falcons, 27-24 (NO) OT
  Saints, 17-14 (A)
2011—Saints, 26-23 (A) OT
  Saints, 45-16 (NO)
2012—Saints, 31-27 (NO)
  Falcons, 23-13 (A)
(RS Pts.—Falcons 1,895, Saints 1,782)
(PS Pts.—Falcons 27, Saints 20)
*NFC First-Round Playoff
ATLANTA vs. N.Y. GIANTS
RS: Falcons lead series, 11-10
PS: Giants lead series, 1-0
1966—Falcons, 27-16 (NY)
1968—Falcons, 24-21 (A)
1971—Giants, 21-17 (A)
1974—Falcons, 14-7 (New Haven)
1977—Falcons, 17-3 (A)

1978—Falcons, 23-20 (A)
1979—Giants, 24-3 (NY)
1981—Giants, 27-24 (A) OT
1982—Falcons, 16-14 (NY)
1983—Giants, 16-13 (A) OT
1984—Giants, 19-7 (A)
1988—Giants, 23-16 (A)
1998—Falcons, 34-20 (NY)
2000—Falcons, 13-6 (A)
2002—Falcons, 17-10 (NY)
2003—Falcons, 27-7 (NY)
2004—Falcons, 14-10 (NY)
2006—Giants, 27-14 (A)
2007—Giants, 31-10 (A)
2009—Giants, 34-31 (NY) OT
2011—*Giants, 24-2 (NY)
2012—Falcons, 34-0 (A)
(RS Pts.—Falcons 388, Giants 363)
(PS Pts.—Giants 24, Falcons 2)
*NFC First-Round Playoff
ATLANTA vs. N.Y. JETS
RS: Falcons lead series, 6-4
1973—Falcons, 28-20 (NY)
1980—Jets, 14-7 (A)
1983—Falcons, 27-21 (NY)
1986—Jets, 28-14 (A)
1989—Jets, 27-7 (NY)
1992—Falcons, 20-17 (A)
1995—Falcons, 13-3 (A)
1998—Jets, 28-3 (NY)
2005—Falcons, 27-14 (A)
2009—Falcons, 10-7 (NY)
(RS Pts.—Jets 179, Falcons 156)
ATLANTA vs. *OAKLAND
RS: Raiders lead series, 7-6
1971—Falcons, 24-13 (A)
1975—Raiders, 37-34 (O) OT
1979—Raiders, 50-19 (O)
1982—Raiders, 38-14 (A)
1985—Raiders, 34-24 (A)
1988—Falcons, 12-6 (LA)
1991—Falcons, 21-17 (A)
1994—Raiders, 30-17 (LA)
1997—Raiders, 36-31 (A)
2000—Raiders, 41-14 (O)
2004—Falcons, 35-10 (A)
2008—Falcons, 24-0 (O)
2012—Falcons, 23-20 (A)
(RS Pts.—Raiders 332, Falcons 292)
*Franchise in Los Angeles from 1982-1994
ATLANTA vs. PHILADELPHIA
RS: Eagles lead series, 15-12-1
PS: Eagles lead series, 2-1
1966—Eagles, 23-10 (P)
1967—Eagles, 38-7 (A)
1969—Falcons, 27-3 (P)
1970—Tie, 13-13 (P)
1973—Falcons, 44-27 (P)
1976—Eagles, 14-13 (A)
1978—*Falcons, 14-13 (A)
1979—Falcons, 14-10 (P)
1980—Falcons, 20-17 (P)
1981—Eagles, 16-13 (P)
1983—Eagles, 28-24 (A)
1984—Falcons, 26-10 (A)
1985—Eagles, 23-17 (P) OT
1986—Eagles, 16-0 (A)
1988—Falcons, 27-24 (P)
1990—Eagles, 24-23 (A)
1994—Falcons, 28-21 (A)
1996—Eagles, 33-18 (A)
1997—Falcons, 20-17 (A)
1998—Falcons, 17-12 (A)

2000—Eagles, 38-10 (P)
2002—**Eagles, 20-6 (P)
2003—Eagles, 23-16 (A)
2004—***Eagles, 27-10 (P)
2005—Falcons, 14-10 (A)
2006—Eagles, 24-17 (P)
2008—Eagles, 27-14 (P)
2009—Eagles, 34-7 (A)
2010—Eagles, 31-17 (P)
2011—Falcons, 35-31 (A)
2012—Falcons, 30-17 (P)
(RS Pts.—Eagles 604, Falcons 521)
(PS Pts.—Eagles 60, Falcons 30)
*NFC First-Round Playoff
**NFC Divisional Playoff
***NFC Championship
ATLANTA vs. PITTSBURGH
RS: Steelers lead series, 12-2-1
1966—Steelers, 57-33 (A)
1968—Steelers, 41-21 (A)
1970—Falcons, 27-16 (A)
1974—Steelers, 24-17 (P)
1978—Steelers, 31-7 (A)
1981—Steelers, 34-20 (A)
1984—Steelers, 35-10 (P)
1987—Steelers, 28-12 (A)
1990—Steelers, 21-9 (P)
1993—Steelers, 45-17 (A)
1996—Steelers, 20-17 (A)
1999—Steelers, 13-9 (P)
2002—Tie, 34-34 (P) OT
2006—Falcons, 41-38 (A) OT
2010—Steelers, 15-9 (P) OT
(RS Pts.—Steelers 452, Falcons 283)
ATLANTA vs. *ST. LOUIS
RS: Rams lead series, 47-26-2
PS: Falcons lead series, 1-0
1966—Rams, 19-14 (A)
1967—Rams, 31-3 (A)
  Rams, 20-3 (LA)
1968—Rams, 27-14 (LA)
  Rams, 17-10 (A)
1969—Rams, 17-7 (LA)
  Rams, 38-6 (A)
1970—Tie, 10-10 (LA)
  Rams, 17-7 (A)
1971—Tie, 20-20 (LA)
  Rams, 24-16 (A)
1972—Falcons, 31-3 (A)
  Rams, 20-7 (LA)
1973—Rams, 31-0 (LA)
  Falcons, 15-13 (A)
1974—Rams, 21-0 (LA)
  Rams, 30-7 (A)
1975—Rams, 22-7 (LA)
  Rams, 16-7 (A)
1976—Rams, 30-14 (A)
  Rams, 59-0 (LA)
1977—Falcons, 17-6 (A)
  Rams, 23-7 (LA)
1978—Rams, 10-0 (LA)
  Falcons, 15-7 (A)
1979—Rams, 20-14 (LA)
  Rams, 34-13 (A)
1980—Falcons, 13-10 (A)
  Rams, 20-17 (LA) OT
1981—Rams, 37-35 (A)
  Rams, 21-16 (LA)
1982—Falcons, 34-17 (A)
1983—Rams, 27-21 (LA)
  Rams, 36-13 (A)
1984—Falcons, 30-28 (LA)
  Rams, 24-10 (A)

1985—Rams, 17-6 (LA)
    Falcons, 30-14 (A)
1986—Falcons, 26-14 (A)
    Rams, 14-7 (LA)
1987—Falcons, 24-20 (A)
    Rams, 33-0 (LA)
1988—Rams, 33-0 (A)
    Rams, 22-7 (LA)
1989—Rams, 31-21 (A)
    Rams, 26-14 (LA)
1990—Rams, 44-24 (LA)
    Falcons, 20-13 (A)
1991—Falcons, 31-14 (A)
    Falcons, 31-14 (LA)
1992—Falcons, 30-28 (A)
    Rams, 38-27 (LA)
1993—Falcons, 30-24 (A)
    Falcons, 13-0 (LA)
1994—Falcons, 31-13 (A)
    Falcons, 8-5 (LA)
1995—Rams, 21-19 (StL)
    Falcons, 31-6 (A)
1996—Rams, 59-16 (StL)
    Rams, 34-27 (A)
1997—Falcons, 34-31 (A)
    Falcons, 27-21 (StL)
1998—Falcons, 37-15 (A)
    Falcons, 21-10 (StL)
1999—Rams, 35-7 (StL)
    Rams, 41-13 (A)
2000—Rams, 41-20 (A)
    Rams, 45-29 (StL)
2001—Rams, 35-6 (A)
    Rams, 31-13 (StL)
2003—Rams, 36-0 (StL)
2004—Falcons, 34-17 (A)
    **Falcons, 47-17 (A)
2007—Rams, 28-16 (StL)
2008—Falcons, 31-27 (A)
2010—Falcons, 34-17 (StL)
(RS Pts.—Rams 1,772, Falcons 1,248)
(PS Pts.—Falcons 47, Rams 17)
Franchise in Los Angeles prior to 1995
**NFC Divisional Playoff*

ATLANTA vs. SAN DIEGO
RS: Falcons lead series, 8-1
1973—Falcons, 41-0 (SD)
1979—Falcons, 28-26 (SD)
1988—Chargers, 10-7 (A)
1991—Falcons, 13-10 (SD)
1994—Falcons, 10-9 (A)
1997—Falcons, 14-3 (SD)
2004—Falcons, 21-20 (A)
2008—Falcons, 22-16 (SD)
2012—Falcons, 27-3 (SD)
(RS Pts.—Falcons 183, Chargers 97)

ATLANTA vs. SAN FRANCISCO
RS: 49ers lead series, 44-29-1
PS: Series tied, 1-1
1966—49ers, 44-7 (A)
1967—49ers, 38-7 (SF)
    49ers, 34-28 (A)
1968—Falcons, 28-13 (SF)
    49ers, 14-12 (A)
1969—Falcons, 24-12 (A)
    Falcons, 21-7 (SF)
1970—Falcons, 21-20 (A)
    49ers, 24-20 (SF)
1971—Falcons, 20-17 (A)
    49ers, 24-3 (SF)
1972—49ers, 49-14 (A)
    49ers, 20-0 (SF)
1973—49ers, 13-9 (A)

    Falcons, 17-3 (SF)
1974—49ers, 16-10 (A)
    49ers, 27-0 (SF)
1975—Falcons, 17-3 (SF)
    Falcons, 31-9 (A)
1976—49ers, 15-0 (SF)
    Falcons, 21-16 (A)
1977—Falcons, 7-0 (SF)
    49ers, 10-3 (A)
1978—Falcons, 20-17 (SF)
    Falcons, 21-10 (A)
1979—49ers, 20-15 (SF)
    Falcons, 31-21 (A)
1980—Falcons, 20-17 (SF)
    Falcons, 35-10 (A)
1981—Falcons, 34-17 (A)
    49ers, 17-14 (SF)
1982—Falcons, 17-7 (SF)
1983—49ers, 24-20 (SF)
    Falcons, 28-24 (A)
1984—49ers, 14-5 (SF)
    49ers, 35-17 (A)
1985—49ers, 35-16 (SF)
    49ers, 38-17 (A)
1986—Tie, 10-10 (A) OT
    49ers, 20-0 (SF)
1987—49ers, 25-17 (A)
    49ers, 35-7 (SF)
1988—Falcons, 34-17 (SF)
    49ers, 13-3 (A)
1989—49ers, 45-3 (SF)
    49ers, 23-10 (A)
1990—49ers, 19-13 (SF)
    49ers, 45-35 (A)
1991—Falcons, 39-34 (SF)
    Falcons, 17-14 (A)
1992—49ers, 56-17 (SF)
    49ers, 41-3 (A)
1993—49ers, 37-30 (SF)
    Falcons, 27-24 (A)
1994—49ers, 42-3 (A)
    49ers, 50-14 (SF)
1995—49ers, 41-10 (SF)
    Falcons, 28-27 (A)
1996—49ers, 39-17 (A)
    49ers, 34-10 (A)
1997—49ers, 34-7 (SF)
    49ers, 35-28 (A)
1998—49ers, 31-20 (SF)
    Falcons, 31-19 (A)
    *Falcons, 20-18 (A)
1999—49ers, 26-7 (SF)
    Falcons, 34-29 (A)
2000—Falcons, 36-28 (A)
    49ers, 16-6 (SF)
2001—49ers, 16-13 (SF) OT
    49ers, 37-31 (A) OT
2004—Falcons, 21-19 (SF)
2007—Falcons, 20-16 (A)
2009—Falcons, 45-10 (SF)
2010—Falcons, 16-14 (A)
2012—**49ers, 28-24 (A)
(RS Pts.—49ers 1,770, Falcons 1,277)
(PS Pts.—49ers 46, Falcons 44)
NFC Divisional Playoff
**NFC Championship*

ATLANTA vs. SEATTLE
RS: Seahawks lead series, 8-5
PS: Falcons lead series, 1-0
1976—Seahawks, 30-13 (S)
1979—Seahawks, 31-28 (A)
1985—Seahawks, 30-26 (S)

1988—Seahawks, 31-20 (A)
1991—Falcons, 26-13 (A)
1997—Falcons, 24-17 (S)
2000—Seahawks, 30-10 (A)
2002—Seahawks, 30-24 (A) OT
2004—Seahawks, 28-26 (S)
2005—Seahawks, 21-18 (S)
2007—Falcons, 44-41 (A)
2010—Falcons, 34-18 (S)
2011—Falcons, 30-28 (S)
2012—*Falcons, 30-28 (A)
(RS Pts.—Seahawks 348, Falcons 323)
(PS Pts.—Falcons 30, Seahawks 28)
NFC Divisional Playoff

ATLANTA vs. TAMPA BAY
RS: Buccaneers lead series, 20-19
1977—Falcons, 17-0 (TB)
1978—Buccaneers, 14-9 (TB)
1979—Falcons, 17-14 (A)
1981—Buccaneers, 24-23 (TB)
1984—Buccaneers, 23-6 (TB)
1986—Falcons, 23-20 (TB) OT
1987—Buccaneers, 48-10 (TB)
1988—Falcons, 17-10 (TB)
1990—Buccaneers, 23-17 (TB)
1991—Falcons, 43-7 (A)
1992—Falcons, 35-7 (TB)
1993—Buccaneers, 31-24 (A)
1994—Falcons, 34-13 (A)
1995—Falcons, 24-21 (TB)
1997—Buccaneers, 31-10 (A)
1999—Buccaneers, 19-10 (TB)
2000—Buccaneers, 27-14 (A)
2002—Buccaneers, 20-6 (A)
    Buccaneers, 34-10 (TB)
2003—Buccaneers, 31-10 (A)
    Falcons, 30-28 (TB)
2004—Falcons, 24-14 (A)
    Buccaneers, 27-0 (TB)
2005—Buccaneers, 30-27 (A)
    Buccaneers, 27-24 (TB) OT
2006—Falcons, 14-3 (A)
    Falcons, 17-6 (TB)
2007—Buccaneers, 31-7 (A)
    Buccaneers, 37-3 (TB)
2008—Buccaneers, 24-9 (TB)
    Falcons, 13-10 (A) OT
2009—Falcons, 20-17 (A)
    Falcons, 20-10 (TB)
2010—Falcons, 27-21 (A)
    Falcons, 28-24 (TB)
2011—Buccaneers, 16-13 (TB)
    Falcons, 45-24 (A)
2012—Falcons, 24-23 (TB)
    Buccaneers, 22-17 (A)
(RS Pts.—Buccaneers 811, Falcons 721)

ATLANTA vs. *TENNESSEE
RS: Titans lead series, 7-6
1972—Falcons, 20-10 (A)
1976—Oilers, 20-14 (H)
1978—Falcons, 20-14 (A)
1981—Falcons, 31-27 (H)
1984—Falcons, 42-10 (A)
1987—Oilers, 37-33 (H)
1990—Falcons, 47-27 (A)
1993—Oilers, 33-17 (H)
1996—Oilers, 23-13 (A)
1999—Titans, 30-17 (T)
2003—Titans, 38-31 (A)
2007—Titans, 20-13 (T)
2011—Falcons, 23-17 (A)
(RS Pts.—Falcons 321, Titans 306)
Franchise in Houston prior to 1997;

known as Oilers prior to 1999
ATLANTA vs. WASHINGTON
RS: Redskins lead series, 14-7-1
PS: Redskins lead series, 1-0
1966—Redskins, 33-20 (W)
1967—Tie, 20-20 (A)
1969—Redskins, 27-20 (W)
1972—Redskins, 24-13 (W)
1975—Redskins, 30-27 (A)
1977—Redskins, 10-6 (W)
1978—Falcons, 20-17 (A)
1979—Redskins, 16-7 (A)
1980—Falcons, 10-6 (A)
1983—Redskins, 37-21 (W)
1984—Redskins, 27-14 (W)
1985—Redskins, 44-10 (A)
1987—Falcons, 21-20 (A)
1989—Redskins, 31-30 (A)
1991—Redskins, 56-17 (W)
    *Redskins, 24-7 (W)
1992—Redskins, 24-17 (W)
1993—Redskins, 30-17 (W)
1994—Falcons, 27-20 (W)
2003—Redskins, 33-31 (A)
2006—Falcons, 24-14 (W)
2009—Falcons, 31-17 (A)
2012—Falcons, 24-17 (W)
(RS Pts.—Redskins 553, Falcons 427)
(PS Pts.—Redskins 24, Falcons 7)
NFC Divisional Playoff

BALTIMORE vs. ARIZONA
RS: Ravens lead series, 4-1;
See Arizona vs. Baltimore
BALTIMORE vs. ATLANTA
RS: Series tied, 2-2;
See Atlanta vs. Baltimore
BALTIMORE vs. BUFFALO
RS: Ravens lead series, 3-2
1999—Bills, 13-10 (Balt)
2004—Ravens, 20-6 (Balt)
2006—Ravens, 19-7 (Balt)
2007—Bills, 19-14 (Buf)
2010—Ravens, 37-34 (Balt) OT
(RS Pts.—Ravens 100, Bills 79)
BALTIMORE vs. CAROLINA
RS: Panthers lead series, 3-1
1996—Panthers, 27-16 (C)
2002—Panthers, 10-7 (C)
2006—Panthers, 23-21 (B)
2010—Ravens, 37-13 (C)
(RS Pts.—Ravens 81, Panthers 73)
BALTIMORE vs. CHICAGO
RS: Series tied, 2-2
1998—Bears, 24-3 (C)
2001—Ravens, 17-6 (B)
2005—Bears, 10-6 (C)
2009—Ravens, 31-7 (C)
(RS Pts.—Ravens 57, Bears 47)
BALTIMORE vs. CINCINNATI
RS: Ravens lead series, 19-15
1996—Bengals, 24-21 (B)
    Bengals, 21-14 (C)
1997—Ravens, 23-10 (B)
    Bengals, 16-14 (C)
1998—Ravens, 31-24 (B)
    Ravens, 20-13 (C)
1999—Ravens, 34-31 (C)
    Ravens, 22-0 (B)
2000—Ravens, 37-0 (B)
    Ravens, 27-7 (C)
2001—Bengals, 21-10 (C)
    Ravens, 16-0 (B)

2002—Ravens, 38-27 (B)
    Ravens, 27-23 (C)
2003—Bengals, 34-26 (C)
    Ravens, 31-13 (B)
2004—Ravens, 23-9 (C)
    Bengals, 27-26 (B)
2005—Bengals, 21-9 (B)
    Bengals, 42-29 (C)
2006—Ravens, 26-20 (B)
    Bengals, 13-7 (C)
2007—Ravens, 27-20 (C)
    Bengals, 21-7 (B)
2008—Ravens, 17-10 (B)
    Ravens, 34-3 (C)
2009—Bengals, 17-14 (B)
    Bengals, 17-7 (C)
2010—Bengals, 15-10 (C)
    Ravens, 13-7 (B)
2011—Ravens, 31-24 (B)
    Ravens, 24-16 (C)
2012—Ravens, 44-13 (B)
    Bengals, 23-17 (C)
(RS Pts.—Ravens 749, Bengals 589)
BALTIMORE vs. CLEVELAND
RS: Ravens lead series, 21-7
1999—Ravens, 17-10 (B)
    Ravens, 41-9 (C)
2000—Ravens, 12-0 (C)
    Ravens, 44-7 (B)
2001—Browns, 24-14 (C)
    Browns, 27-17 (B)
2002—Ravens, 26-21 (C)
    Browns, 14-13 (B)
2003—Ravens, 33-13 (B)
    Ravens, 35-0 (C)
2004—Browns, 20-3 (C)
    Ravens, 27-13 (B)
2005—Ravens, 16-3 (B)
    Browns, 20-16 (C)
2006—Ravens, 15-14 (C)
    Ravens, 27-17 (B)
2007—Browns, 27-13 (C)
    Browns, 33-30 (B) OT
2008—Ravens, 28-10 (B)
    Ravens, 37-27 (C)
2009—Ravens, 34-3 (B)
    Ravens, 16-0 (C)
2010—Ravens, 24-17 (B)
    Ravens, 20-10 (C)
2011—Ravens, 24-10 (C)
    Ravens, 20-14 (B)
2012—Ravens, 23-16 (B)
    Ravens, 25-15 (C)
(RS Pts.—Ravens 650, Browns 394)
BALTIMORE vs. DALLAS
RS: Ravens lead series, 4-0
2000—Ravens, 27-0 (B)
2004—Ravens, 30-10 (B)
2008—Ravens, 33-24 (D)
2012—Ravens, 31-29 (B)
(RS Pts.—Ravens 121, Cowboys 63)
BALTIMORE vs. DENVER
RS: Ravens lead series, 5-4
PS: Ravens lead series, 2-0
1996—Broncos, 45-34 (D)
2000—*Ravens, 21-3 (B)
2001—Ravens, 20-13 (D)
2002—Ravens, 34-23 (B)
2003—Ravens, 26-6 (B)
2005—Broncos, 12-10 (B)
2006—Broncos, 13-3 (D)
2009—Ravens, 30-7 (B)
2010—Ravens, 31-17 (B)

2012—Broncos, 34-17 (B)
    **Ravens, 38-35 (D) 2 OT
(RS Pts.—Ravens 205, Broncos 170)
(PS Pts.—Ravens 59, Broncos 38)
AFC First-Round Playoff
**AFC Divisional Playoff*
BALTIMORE vs. DETROIT
RS: Ravens lead series, 2-1
1998—Ravens, 19-10 (B)
2005—Lions, 35-17 (D)
2009—Ravens, 48-3 (B)
(RS Pts.—Ravens 84, Lions 48)
BALTIMORE vs. GREEN BAY
RS: Packers lead series, 3-1
1998—Packers, 28-10 (GB)
2001—Packers, 31-23 (GB)
2005—Ravens, 48-3 (B)
2009—Packers, 27-14 (GB)
(RS Pts.—Ravens 95, Packers 89)
BALTIMORE vs. HOUSTON
RS: Ravens lead series, 5-1
PS: Ravens lead series, 1-0
2002—Ravens, 23-19 (H)
2005—Ravens, 16-15 (B)
2008—Ravens, 41-13 (H)
2010—Ravens, 34-28 (H) OT
2011—Ravens, 29-14 (B)
    *Ravens, 20-13 (B)
2012—Texans, 43-13 (H)
(RS Pts.—Ravens 156, Texans 132)
(PS Pts.—Ravens 20, Texans 13)
AFC Divisional Playoff
BALTIMORE vs. INDIANAPOLIS
RS: Colts lead series, 7-3
PS: Colts lead series, 2-1
1996—Colts, 26-21 (I)
1998—Ravens, 38-31 (B)
2001—Ravens, 39-27 (B)
2002—Colts, 22-20 (I)
2004—Colts, 20-10 (I)
2005—Colts, 24-7 (B)
2006—*Colts, 15-6 (B)
2007—Colts, 44-20 (B)
2008—Colts, 31-3 (I)
2009—Colts, 17-15 (B)
    *Colts, 20-3 (I)
2011—Ravens, 24-10 (B)
2012—**Ravens, 24-9 (B)
(RS Pts.—Colts 252, Ravens 197)
(PS Pts.—Colts 44, Ravens 33)
AFC Divisional Playoff
**AFC First-Round Playoff*
BALTIMORE vs. JACKSONVILLE
RS: Jaguars lead series, 10-7
1996—Jaguars, 30-27 (J)
    Jaguars, 28-25 (B) OT
1997—Jaguars, 28-27 (B)
    Jaguars, 29-27 (J)
1998—Jaguars, 24-10 (J)
    Jaguars, 45-19 (B)
1999—Jaguars, 6-3 (J)
    Jaguars, 30-23 (B)
2000—Ravens, 39-36 (B)
    Ravens, 15-10 (J)
2001—Ravens, 18-17 (B)
    Ravens, 24-21 (J)
2002—Ravens, 17-10 (B)
2003—Ravens, 24-17 (B)
2005—Jaguars, 30-3 (J)
2008—Ravens, 27-7 (B)
2011—Jaguars, 12-7 (J)
(RS Pts.—Jaguars 380, Ravens 335)

BALTIMORE vs. KANSAS CITY
RS: Series tied, 3-3
PS: Ravens lead series, 1-0
1999—Chiefs, 35-8 (B)
2003—Chiefs, 17-10 (B)
2004—Chiefs, 27-24 (B)
2006—Ravens, 20-10 (KC)
2009—Ravens, 38-24 (B)
2010—*Ravens, 30-7 (KC)
2012—Ravens, 9-6 (KC)
(RS Pts.—Chiefs 119, Ravens 109)
(PS Pts.—Ravens 30, Chiefs 7)
*AFC First-Round Playoff

BALTIMORE vs. MIAMI
RS: Dolphins lead series, 5-3
PS: Ravens lead series, 2-0
1997—Dolphins, 24-13 (B)
2000—Dolphins, 19-6 (M)
2001—*Ravens, 20-3 (M)
2002—Dolphins, 26-7 (M)
2003—Dolphins, 9-6 (M) OT
2004—Ravens, 30-23 (B)
2007—Dolphins, 22-16 (M) OT
2008—Ravens, 27-13 (M)
    *Ravens, 27-9 (M)
2010—Ravens, 26-10 (B)
(RS Pts.—Dolphins 146, Ravens 131)
(PS Pts.—Ravens 47, Dolphins 12)
*AFC First-Round Playoff

BALTIMORE vs. MINNESOTA
RS: Series tied, 2-2
1998—Vikings, 38-28 (B)
2001—Ravens, 19-3 (B)
2005—Ravens, 30-23 (B)
2009—Vikings, 33-31 (M)
(RS Pts.—Ravens 108, Vikings 97)

BALTIMORE vs. NEW ENGLAND
RS: Patriots lead series, 6-1
PS: Ravens lead series, 2-1
1996—Patriots, 46-38 (B)
1999—Patriots, 20-3 (NE)
2004—Patriots, 24-3 (NE)
2007—Patriots, 27-24 (B)
2009—Patriots, 27-21 (NE)
    *Ravens, 33-14 (NE)
2010—Patriots, 23-20 (NE) OT
2011—**Patriots, 23-20 (NE)
2012—Patriots, 31-30 (B)
    **Ravens, 28-13 (NE)
(RS Pts.—Patriots 197, Ravens 140)
(PS Pts.—Ravens 81, Patriots 50)
*AFC First-Round Playoff
**AFC Championship

BALTIMORE vs. NEW ORLEANS
RS: Ravens lead series, 4-1
1996—Ravens, 17-10 (B)
1999—Ravens, 31-8 (B)
2002—Saints, 37-25 (B)
2006—Ravens, 35-22 (NO)
2010—Ravens, 30-24 (B)
(RS Pts.—Ravens 138, Saints 101)

BALTIMORE vs. N.Y. GIANTS
RS: Ravens lead series, 3-1
PS: Ravens lead series, 1-0
1997—Ravens, 24-23 (NY)
2000—*Ravens, 34-7 (Tampa)
2004—Ravens, 37-14 (B)
2008—Giants, 30-10 (NY)
2012—Ravens, 33-14 (B)
(RS Pts.—Ravens 104, Giants 81)
(PS Pts.—Ravens 34, Giants 7)
*Super Bowl XXXV

BALTIMORE vs. N.Y. JETS
RS: Ravens lead series, 7-1
1997—Jets, 19-16 (NY) OT
1998—Ravens, 24-10 (NY)
2000—Ravens, 34-20 (B)
2004—Ravens, 20-17 (NY) OT
2005—Ravens, 13-3 (B)
2007—Ravens, 20-13 (B)
2010—Ravens, 10-9 (NY)
2011—Ravens, 34-17 (B)
(RS Pts.—Ravens 171, Jets 108)

BALTIMORE vs. OAKLAND
RS: Ravens lead series, 6-1
PS: Ravens lead series, 1-0
1996—Ravens, 19-14 (B)
1998—Ravens, 13-10 (B)
2000—*Ravens, 16-3 (O)
2003—Raiders, 20-12 (O)
2006—Ravens, 28-6 (B)
2008—Ravens, 29-10 (B)
2009—Ravens, 21-13 (O)
2012—Ravens, 55-20 (B)
(RS Pts.—Ravens 177, Raiders 93)
(PS Pts.—Ravens 16, Raiders 3)
*AFC Championship

BALTIMORE vs. PHILADELPHIA
RS: Eagles lead series, 2-1-1
1997—Tie, 10-10 (B) OT
2004—Eagles, 15-10 (P)
2008—Ravens, 36-7 (B)
2012—Eagles, 24-23 (P)
(RS Pts.—Ravens 79, Eagles 56)

BALTIMORE vs. PITTSBURGH
RS: Steelers lead series, 19-15
PS: Steelers lead series, 3-0
1996—Steelers, 31-17 (P)
    Ravens, 31-17 (B)
1997—Steelers, 42-34 (B)
    Steelers, 37-0 (P)
1998—Steelers, 20-13 (B)
    Steelers, 16-6 (P)
1999—Steelers, 23-20 (B)
    Ravens, 31-24 (P)
2000—Ravens, 16-0 (P)
    Steelers, 9-6 (B)
2001—Ravens, 13-10 (P)
    Steelers, 26-21 (B)
    *Steelers, 27-10 (P)
2002—Steelers, 31-18 (B)
    Steelers, 34-31 (P)
2003—Steelers, 34-15 (P)
    Ravens, 13-10 (B) OT
2004—Ravens, 30-13 (B)
    Steelers, 20-7 (P)
2005—Steelers, 20-19 (P)
    Ravens, 16-13 (B) OT
2006—Ravens, 27-0 (B)
    Ravens, 31-7 (P)
2007—Steelers, 38-7 (P)
    Ravens, 27-21 (B)
2008—Steelers, 23-20 (P) OT
    Steelers, 13-9 (B)
    **Steelers, 23-14 (P)
2009—Ravens, 20-17 (B) OT
    Steelers, 23-20 (P)
2010—Ravens, 17-14 (P)
    Steelers, 13-10 (B)
    *Steelers, 31-24 (P)
2011—Ravens, 35-7 (B)
    Ravens, 23-20 (P)
2012—Ravens, 13-10 (P)
    Steelers, 23-20 (B)
(RS Pts.—Steelers 659, Ravens 636)

(PS Pts.—Steelers 81, Ravens 48)
*AFC Divisional Playoff
**AFC Championship

BALTIMORE vs. ST. LOUIS
RS: Ravens lead series, 3-2
1996—Ravens, 37-31 (B) OT
1999—Ravens, 27-10 (StL)
2003—Rams, 33-22 (StL)
2007—Ravens, 22-3 (B)
2011—Ravens, 37-7 (StL)
(RS Pts.—Ravens 128, Rams 101)

BALTIMORE vs. SAN DIEGO
RS: Ravens lead series, 5-4
1997—Chargers, 21-17 (SD)
1998—Chargers, 14-13 (SD)
2000—Ravens, 24-3 (B)
2003—Ravens, 24-10 (SD)
2006—Ravens, 16-13 (B)
2007—Chargers, 32-14 (SD)
2009—Ravens, 31-26 (SD)
2011—Chargers, 34-14 (SD)
2012—Ravens, 16-13 (SD) OT
(RS Pts.—Ravens 169, Chargers 166)

BALTIMORE vs. SAN FRANCISCO
RS: Ravens lead series, 3-1
PS: Ravens lead series, 1-0
1996—49ers, 38-20 (SF)
2003—Ravens, 44-6 (B)
2007—Ravens, 9-7 (SF)
2011—Ravens, 16-6 (B)
2012—*Ravens, 34-31 (New Orleans)
(RS Pts.—Ravens 89, 49ers 57)
(PS Pts.—Ravens 34, 49ers 31)
*Super Bowl XLVII

BALTIMORE vs. SEATTLE
RS: Series tied, 2-2
1997—Ravens, 31-24 (B)
2003—Ravens, 44-41 (B) OT
2007—Seahawks, 27-6 (S)
2011—Seahawks, 22-17 (S)
(RS Pts.—Seahawks 114, Ravens 98)

BALTIMORE vs. TAMPA BAY
RS: Series tied, 2-2
2001—Buccaneers, 22-10 (TB)
2002—Buccaneers, 25-0 (B)
2006—Ravens, 27-0 (TB)
2010—Ravens, 17-10 (B)
(RS Pts.—Buccaneers 57, Ravens 54)

BALTIMORE vs. *TENNESSEE
RS: Titans lead series, 9-8
PS: Ravens lead series, 2-1
1996—Oilers, 29-13 (H)
    Oilers, 24-21 (B)
1997—Ravens, 36-10 (T)
    Ravens, 21-19 (B)
1998—Oilers, 12-8 (B)
    Oilers, 16-14 (T)
1999—Titans, 14-11 (T)
    Ravens, 41-14 (B)
2000—Titans, 14-6 (B)
    Ravens, 24-23 (T)
    **Ravens, 24-10 (T)
2001—Ravens, 26-7 (B)
    Ravens, 16-10 (T)
2002—Ravens, 13-12 (B)
2003—***Titans, 20-17 (B)
2005—Titans, 25-10 (T)
2006—Ravens, 27-26 (T)
2008—Titans, 13-10 (B)
    **Ravens, 13-10 (T)
2011—Titans, 26-13 (T)
(RS Pts.—Ravens 310, Titans 294)
(PS Pts.—Ravens 54, Titans 40)

*Franchise in Houston prior to 1997;
known as Oilers prior to 1999
**AFC Divisional Playoff
***AFC First-Round Playoff
BALTIMORE vs. WASHINGTON
RS: Ravens lead series, 3-2
1997—Ravens, 20-17 (W)
2000—Redskins, 10-3 (W)
2004—Ravens, 17-10 (W)
2008—Ravens, 24-10 (B)
2012—Redskins, 31-28 (W) OT
(RS Pts.—Ravens 92, Redskins 78)

BUFFALO vs. ARIZONA
RS: Bills lead series, 6-4;
See Arizona vs. Buffalo
BUFFALO vs. ATLANTA
RS: Falcons lead series, 6-4;
See Atlanta vs. Buffalo
BUFFALO vs. BALTIMORE
RS: Ravens lead series, 3-2;
See Baltimore vs. Buffalo
BUFFALO vs. CAROLINA
RS: Bills lead series, 4-1
1995—Bills, 31-9 (B)
1998—Bills, 30-14 (C)
2001—Bills, 25-24 (B)
2005—Panthers, 13-9 (B)
2009—Bills, 20-9 (C)
(RS Pts.—Bills 115, Panthers 69)
BUFFALO vs. CHICAGO
RS: Bears lead series, 7-4
1970—Bears, 31-13 (C)
1974—Bills, 16-6 (B)
1979—Bears, 7-0 (B)
1988—Bears, 24-3 (C)
1991—Bills, 35-20 (B)
1994—Bears, 20-13 (C)
1997—Bears, 20-3 (C)
2000—Bills, 20-3 (B)
2002—Bills, 33-27 (B) OT
2006—Bears, 40-7 (C)
2010—Bears, 22-19 (Toronto)
(RS Pts.—Bears 220, Bills 162)
BUFFALO vs. CINCINNATI
RS: Bills lead series, 15-10
PS: Bengals lead series, 2-0
1968—Bengals, 34-23 (C)
1969—Bills, 16-13 (B)
1970—Bengals, 43-14 (B)
1973—Bengals, 16-13 (B)
1975—Bengals, 33-24 (C)
1978—Bills, 5-0 (B)
1979—Bills, 51-24 (B)
1980—Bills, 14-0 (C)
1981—Bengals, 27-24 (C) OT
        *Bengals, 28-21 (C)
1983—Bills, 10-6 (C)
1984—Bengals, 52-21 (C)
1985—Bengals, 23-17 (B)
1986—Bengals, 36-33 (C) OT
1988—Bengals, 35-21 (C)
        **Bengals, 21-10 (C)
1989—Bills, 24-7 (B)
1991—Bills, 35-16 (B)
1996—Bills, 31-17 (B)
1998—Bills, 33-20 (C)
2002—Bills, 27-9 (B)
2003—Bills, 22-16 (B) OT
2004—Bills, 33-17 (C)
2005—Bills, 37-27 (C)
2007—Bills, 33-21 (B)
2010—Bills, 49-31 (C)

2011—Bengals, 23-20 (C)
(RS Pts.—Bills 630, Bengals 546)
(PS Pts.—Bengals 49, Bills 31)
*AFC Divisional Playoff
**AFC Championship
BUFFALO vs. CLEVELAND
RS: Browns lead series, 10-7
PS: Browns lead series, 1-0
1972—Browns, 27-10 (C)
1974—Bills, 15-10 (C)
1977—Browns, 27-16 (B)
1978—Browns, 41-20 (C)
1981—Bills, 22-13 (B)
1984—Browns, 13-10 (B)
1985—Browns, 17-7 (C)
1986—Browns, 21-17 (B)
1987—Browns, 27-21 (C)
1989—*Browns, 34-30 (C)
1990—Bills, 42-0 (C)
1995—Bills, 22-19 (C)
2004—Bills, 37-7 (B)
2007—Browns, 8-0 (C)
2008—Browns, 29-27 (B)
2009—Browns, 6-3 (B)
2010—Bills, 13-6 (B)
2012—Bills, 24-14 (C)
(RS Pts.—Bills 306, Browns 285)
(PS Pts.—Browns 34, Bills 30)
*AFC Divisional Playoff
BUFFALO vs. DALLAS
RS: Cowboys lead series, 6-3
PS: Cowboys lead series, 2-0
1971—Cowboys, 49-37 (B)
1976—Cowboys, 17-10 (D)
1981—Cowboys, 27-14 (D)
1984—Bills, 14-3 (B)
1992—*Cowboys, 52-17 (Pasadena)
1993—Bills, 13-10 (D)
        **Cowboys, 30-13 (Atlanta)
1996—Bills, 10-7 (B)
2003—Cowboys, 10-6 (D)
2007—Cowboys, 25-24 (B)
2011—Cowboys, 44-7 (D)
(RS Pts.—Cowboys 192, Bills 135)
(PS Pts.—Cowboys 82, Bills 30)
*Super Bowl XXVII
**Super Bowl XXVIII
BUFFALO vs. DENVER
RS: Bills lead series, 19-15-1
PS: Bills lead series, 1-0
1960—Broncos, 27-21 (B)
        Tie, 38-38 (D)
1961—Broncos, 22-10 (B)
        Bills, 23-10 (D)
1962—Broncos, 23-20 (B)
        Bills, 45-38 (D)
1963—Bills, 30-28 (D)
        Bills, 27-17 (B)
1964—Bills, 30-13 (B)
        Bills, 30-19 (D)
1965—Bills, 30-15 (D)
        Bills, 31-13 (B)
1966—Bills, 38-21 (B)
1967—Bills, 17-16 (D)
        Broncos, 21-20 (B)
1968—Broncos, 34-32 (D)
1969—Bills, 41-28 (B)
1970—Broncos, 25-10 (B)
1975—Bills, 38-14 (B)
1977—Broncos, 26-6 (D)
1979—Broncos, 19-16 (B)
1981—Bills, 9-7 (B)
1984—Broncos, 37-7 (B)

1987—Bills, 21-14 (B)
1989—Broncos, 28-14 (B)
1990—Bills, 29-28 (B)
1991—*Bills, 10-7 (B)
1992—Bills, 27-17 (B)
1994—Bills, 27-20 (B)
1995—Broncos, 22-7 (D)
1997—Broncos, 23-20 (B) OT
2002—Broncos, 28-23 (D)
2005—Broncos, 28-17 (D)
2007—Broncos, 15-14 (B)
2008—Bills, 30-23 (D)
2011—Bills, 40-14 (B)
(RS Pts.—Bills 838, Broncos 771)
(PS Pts.—Bills 10, Broncos 7)
*AFC Championship
BUFFALO vs. DETROIT
RS: Series tied, 4-4-1
1972—Tie, 21-21 (B)
1976—Lions, 27-14 (D)
1979—Bills, 20-17 (D)
1991—Lions, 17-14 (B) OT
1994—Lions, 35-21 (D)
1997—Bills, 22-13 (B)
2002—Bills, 24-17 (B)
2006—Lions, 20-17 (D)
2010—Bills, 14-12 (B)
(RS Pts.—Lions 179, Bills 167)
BUFFALO vs. GREEN BAY
RS: Bills lead series, 7-4
1974—Bills, 27-7 (GB)
1979—Bills, 19-12 (B)
1982—Packers, 33-21 (Mil)
1988—Bills, 28-0 (B)
1991—Bills, 34-24 (Mil)
1994—Bills, 29-20 (B)
1997—Packers, 31-21 (GB)
2000—Bills 27-18 (B)
2002—Packers, 10-0 (GB)
2006—Bills, 24-10 (B)
2010—Packers, 34-7 (GB)
(RS Pts.—Bills 237, Packers 199)
BUFFALO vs. HOUSTON
RS: Series tied, 3-3
2002—Bills, 31-24 (H)
2003—Texans, 12-10 (B)
2005—Bills, 22-7 (B)
2006—Bills, 24-21 (H)
2009—Texans, 31-10 (B)
2012—Texans, 21-9 (H)
(RS Pts.—Texans 116, Bills 106)
BUFFALO vs. *INDIANAPOLIS
RS: Bills lead series, 35-31-1
1970—Tie, 17-17 (Balt)
        Colts, 20-14 (Buff)
1971—Colts, 43-0 (Buff)
        Colts, 24-0 (Balt)
1972—Colts, 17-0 (Buff)
        Colts, 35-7 (Balt)
1973—Bills, 31-13 (Buff)
        Bills, 24-17 (Balt)
1974—Bills, 27-14 (Balt)
        Bills, 6-0 (Buff)
1975—Bills, 38-31 (Balt)
        Colts, 42-35 (Buff)
1976—Colts, 31-13 (Buff)
        Colts, 58-20 (Balt)
1977—Colts, 17-14 (Balt)
        Colts, 31-13 (Buff)
1978—Bills, 24-17 (Buff)
        Bills, 21-14 (Balt)
1979—Bills, 31-13 (Balt)
        Colts, 14-13 (Buff)

1980—Colts, 17-12 (Buff)
    Colts, 28-24 (Balt)
1981—Bills, 35-3 (Balt)
    Bills, 23-17 (Buff)
1982—Bills, 20-0 (Buff)
1983—Bills, 28-23 (Buff)
    Bills, 30-7 (Balt)
1984—Colts, 31-17 (I)
    Bills, 21-15 (Buff)
1985—Colts, 49-17 (I)
    Bills, 21-9 (Buff)
1986—Bills, 24-13 (Buff)
    Colts, 24-14 (I)
1987—Colts, 47-6 (Buff)
    Bills, 27-3 (I)
1988—Bills, 34-23 (Buff)
    Colts, 17-14 (I)
1989—Colts, 37-14 (I)
    Bills, 30-7 (Buff)
1990—Bills, 26-10 (Buff)
    Bills, 31-7 (I)
1991—Bills, 42-6 (Buff)
    Bills, 35-7 (I)
1992—Bills, 38-0 (Buff)
    Colts, 16-13 (I) OT
1993—Bills, 23-9 (Buff)
    Bills, 30-10 (I)
1994—Colts, 27-17 (Buff)
    Colts, 10-9 (I)
1995—Bills, 20-14 (Buff)
    Bills, 16-10 (I)
1996—Bills, 16-13 (Buff) OT
    Colts, 13-10 (I) OT
1997—Bills, 37-35 (B)
    Bills, 9-6 (I)
1998—Bills, 31-24 (I)
    Bills, 34-11 (B)
1999—Colts, 31-14 (I)
    Bills, 31-6 (B)
2000—Colts, 18-16 (B)
    Colts, 44-20 (I)
2001—Colts, 42-26 (I)
    Colts, 30-14 (B)
2003—Colts, 17-14 (B)
2006—Colts, 17-16 (I)
2009—Bills, 30-7 (B)
2012—Colts, 20-13 (I)
(RS Pts.—Bills 1,390, Colts 1,298)
*Franchise in Baltimore prior to 1984
BUFFALO vs. JACKSONVILLE
RS: Bills lead series, 6-5
PS: Jaguars lead series, 1-0
1996—*Jaguars, 30-27 (B)
1997—Jaguars, 20-14 (B)
1998—Bills, 17-16 (B)
2001—Bills, 13-10 (J)
2003—Bills, 38-17 (J)
2004—Jaguars, 13-10 (B)
2006—Bills, 27-24 (B)
2007—Jaguars, 36-14 (J)
2008—Bills, 20-16 (J)
2009—Jaguars, 18-15 (J)
2010—Jaguars, 36-26 (B)
2012—Bills, 34-18 (B)
(RS Pts.—Bills 228, Jaguars 224)
(PS Pts.—Jaguars 30, Bills 27)
*AFC First-Round Playoff
BUFFALO vs. *KANSAS CITY
RS: Bills lead series, 23-17-1
PS: Bills lead series, 2-1
1960—Texans, 45-28 (B)
    Texans, 24-7 (D)

1961—Bills, 27-24 (B)
    Bills, 30-20 (D)
1962—Texans, 41-21 (D)
    Bills, 23-14 (B)
1963—Tie, 27-27 (B)
    Bills, 35-26 (KC)
1964—Bills, 34-17 (B)
    Bills, 35-22 (KC)
1965—Bills, 23-7 (KC)
    Bills, 34-25 (B)
1966—Chiefs, 42-20 (B)
    Bills, 29-14 (KC)
    **Chiefs, 31-7 (B)
1967—Chiefs, 23-13 (KC)
1968—Chiefs, 18-7 (B)
1969—Chiefs, 29-7 (B)
    Chiefs, 22-19 (KC)
1971—Chiefs, 22-9 (KC)
1973—Bills, 23-14 (B)
1976—Bills, 50-17 (B)
1978—Bills, 28-13 (B)
    Chiefs, 14-10 (KC)
1982—Bills, 14-9 (B)
1983—Bills, 14-9 (KC)
1986—Chiefs, 20-17 (B)
    Bills, 17-14 (KC)
1991—Chiefs, 33-6 (KC)
    ***Bills, 37-14 (B)
1993—Chiefs, 23-7 (KC)
    ****Bills, 30-13 (B)
1994—Bills, 44-10 (B)
1996—Bills, 20-9 (B)
1997—Chiefs, 22-16 (KC)
2000—Bills, 21-17 (KC)
2002—Chiefs, 17-16 (KC)
2003—Chiefs, 38-5 (KC)
2005—Bills, 14-3 (B)
2008—Bills, 54-31 (KC)
2009—Bills, 16-10 (KC)
2010—Chiefs, 13-10 (KC) OT
2011—Bills, 41-7 (KC)
2012—Bills, 35-17 (B)
(RS Pts.—Bills 906, Chiefs 822)
(PS Pts.—Bills 74, Chiefs 58)
*Franchise in Dallas prior to 1963 and
known as Texans
**AFL Championship
***AFC Divisional Playoff
****AFC Championship
BUFFALO vs. MIAMI
RS: Dolphins lead series, 56-37-1
PS: Bills lead series, 3-1
1966—Bills, 58-24 (B)
    Bills, 29-0 (M)
1967—Bills, 35-13 (B)
    Dolphins, 17-14 (M)
1968—Tie, 14-14 (M)
    Dolphins, 21-17 (B)
1969—Dolphins, 24-6 (M)
    Bills, 28-3 (B)
1970—Dolphins, 33-14 (B)
    Dolphins, 45-7 (M)
1971—Dolphins, 29-14 (B)
    Dolphins, 34-0 (M)
1972—Dolphins, 24-23 (M)
    Dolphins, 30-16 (B)
1973—Dolphins, 27-6 (M)
    Dolphins, 17-0 (B)
1974—Dolphins, 24-16 (B)
    Dolphins, 35-28 (M)
1975—Dolphins, 35-30 (B)
    Dolphins, 31-21 (M)

1976—Dolphins, 30-21 (B)
    Dolphins, 45-27 (M)
1977—Dolphins, 13-0 (B)
    Dolphins, 31-14 (M)
1978—Dolphins, 31-24 (B)
    Dolphins, 25-24 (B)
1979—Dolphins, 9-7 (B)
    Dolphins, 17-7 (M)
1980—Bills, 17-7 (B)
    Dolphins, 17-14 (M)
1981—Bills, 31-21 (B)
    Dolphins, 16-6 (M)
1982—Dolphins, 9-7 (B)
    Dolphins, 27-10 (M)
1983—Dolphins, 12-0 (B)
    Bills, 38-35 (M) OT
1984—Dolphins, 21-17 (B)
    Dolphins, 38-7 (M)
1985—Dolphins, 23-14 (B)
    Dolphins, 28-0 (M)
1986—Dolphins, 27-14 (M)
    Dolphins, 34-24 (B)
1987—Bills, 34-31 (M) OT
    Bills, 27-0 (B)
1988—Bills, 9-6 (B)
    Bills, 31-6 (M)
1989—Bills, 27-24 (M)
    Bills, 31-17 (B)
1990—Dolphins, 30-7 (M)
    Bills, 24-14 (B)
    *Bills, 44-34 (B)
1991—Bills, 35-31 (B)
    Bills, 41-27 (M)
1992—Dolphins, 37-10 (B)
    Bills, 26-20 (M)
    **Bills, 29-10 (M)
1993—Dolphins, 22-13 (B)
    Bills, 47-34 (M)
1994—Bills, 21-11 (B)
    Bills, 42-31 (M)
1995—Dolphins, 23-6 (M)
    Bills, 23-20 (B)
    ***Bills, 37-22 (B)
1996—Dolphins, 21-7 (B)
    Dolphins, 16-14 (M)
1997—Bills, 9-6 (B)
    Dolphins, 30-13 (M)
1998—Dolphins, 13-7 (M)
    Bills, 30-24 (B)
    ***Dolphins, 24-17 (M)
1999—Bills, 23-18 (M)
    Bills, 23-3 (B)
2000—Dolphins, 22-13 (M)
    Dolphins, 33-6 (B)
2001—Dolphins, 34-27 (B)
    Dolphins, 34-7 (M)
2002—Bills, 23-10 (M)
    Bills, 38-21 (B)
2003—Dolphins, 17-7 (M)
    Dolphins, 20-3 (B)
2004—Bills, 20-13 (B)
    Bills, 42-32 (M)
2005—Bills, 20-14 (B)
    Dolphins, 24-23 (M)
2006—Bills, 16-6 (M)
    Bills, 21-0 (B)
2007—Bills, 13-10 (M)
    Bills, 38-17 (B)
2008—Dolphins, 25-16 (M)
    Dolphins, 16-3 (Toronto)
2009—Dolphins, 38-10 (M)
    Bills, 31-14 (B)

2010—Dolphins, 15-10 (B)
　　　Bills, 17-14 (M)
2011—Dolphins, 35-8 (M)
　　　Dolphins, 30-23 (B)
2012—Bills, 19-14 (B)
　　　Dolphins, 24-10 (M)
(RS Pts.—Dolphins 2,043, Bills 1,743)
(PS Pts.—Bills 127, Dolphins 90)
*AFC Divisional Playoff
**AFC Championship
***AFC First-Round Playoff
BUFFALO vs. MINNESOTA
RS: Vikings lead series, 8-4
1971—Vikings, 19-0 (M)
1975—Vikings, 35-13 (B)
1979—Vikings, 10-3 (M)
1982—Bills, 23-22 (B)
1985—Vikings, 27-20 (B)
1988—Bills, 13-10 (B)
1994—Vikings, 21-17 (B)
1997—Vikings, 34-13 (B)
2000—Vikings, 31-27 (M)
2002—Bills, 45-39 (M) OT
2006—Bills, 17-12 (B)
2010—Vikings, 38-14 (M)
(RS Pts.—Vikings 298, Bills 205)
BUFFALO vs. *NEW ENGLAND
RS: Patriots lead series, 63-41-1
PS: Patriots lead series, 1-0
1960—Bills, 13-0 (Bos)
　　　Bills, 38-14 (Buff)
1961—Patriots, 23-21 (Buff)
　　　Patriots, 52-21 (Bos)
1962—Tie, 28-28 (Buff)
　　　Patriots, 21-10 (Bos)
1963—Bills, 28-21 (Buff)
　　　Patriots, 17-7 (Bos)
　　　**Patriots, 26-8 (Buff)
1964—Patriots, 36-28 (Buff)
　　　Bills, 24-14 (Bos)
1965—Bills, 24-7 (Buff)
　　　Bills, 23-7 (Bos)
1966—Bills, 20-10 (Buff)
　　　Patriots, 14-3 (Bos)
1967—Patriots, 23-0 (Buff)
　　　Bills, 44-16 (Bos)
1968—Patriots, 16-7 (Buff)
　　　Patriots, 23-6 (Bos)
1969—Bills, 23-16 (Buff)
　　　Patriots, 35-21 (Bos)
1970—Bills, 45-10 (Bos)
　　　Patriots, 14-10 (Buff)
1971—Patriots, 38-33 (NE)
　　　Bills, 27-20 (Buff)
1972—Bills, 38-14 (Buff)
　　　Bills, 27-24 (NE)
1973—Bills, 31-13 (NE)
　　　Bills, 37-13 (Buff)
1974—Bills, 30-28 (Buff)
　　　Bills, 29-28 (NE)
1975—Bills, 45-31 (Buff)
　　　Bills, 34-14 (NE)
1976—Patriots, 26-22 (Buff)
　　　Patriots, 20-10 (NE)
1977—Bills, 24-14 (NE)
　　　Patriots, 20-7 (Buff)
1978—Patriots, 14-10 (Buff)
　　　Patriots, 26-24 (NE)
1979—Patriots, 26-6 (Buff)
　　　Bills, 16-13 (NE) OT
1980—Bills, 31-13 (Buff)
　　　Patriots, 24-2 (NE)

1981—Bills, 20-17 (Buff)
　　　Bills, 19-10 (NE)
1982—Patriots, 30-19 (NE)
1983—Patriots, 31-0 (Buff)
　　　Patriots, 21-7 (NE)
1984—Patriots, 21-17 (Buff)
　　　Patriots, 38-10 (NE)
1985—Patriots, 17-14 (Buff)
　　　Patriots, 14-3 (NE)
1986—Patriots, 23-3 (Buff)
　　　Patriots, 22-19 (NE)
1987—Patriots, 14-7 (NE)
　　　Patriots, 13-7 (Buff)
1988—Bills, 16-14 (NE)
　　　Bills, 23-20 (Buff)
1989—Bills, 31-10 (Buff)
　　　Patriots, 33-24 (NE)
1990—Patriots, 27-10 (NE)
　　　Bills, 14-0 (Buff)
1991—Bills, 22-17 (Buff)
　　　Patriots, 16-13 (NE)
1992—Bills, 41-7 (NE)
　　　Bills, 16-7 (Buff)
1993—Bills, 38-14 (Buff)
　　　Bills, 13-10 (NE) OT
1994—Bills, 38-35 (NE)
　　　Patriots, 41-17 (Buff)
1995—Patriots, 27-14 (NE)
　　　Patriots, 35-25 (Buff)
1996—Bills, 17-10 (Buff)
　　　Patriots, 28-25 (NE)
1997—Patriots, 33-6 (NE)
　　　Patriots, 31-10 (Buff)
1998—Bills, 13-10 (Buff)
　　　Patriots, 25-21 (NE)
1999—Bills, 17-7 (Buff)
　　　Bills, 13-10 (NE) OT
2000—Bills, 16-13 (NE) OT
　　　Patriots, 13-10 (Buff) OT
2001—Patriots, 21-11 (NE)
　　　Patriots, 12-9 (Buff) OT
2002—Patriots, 38-7 (Buff)
　　　Patriots, 27-17 (NE)
2003—Bills, 31-0 (Buff)
　　　Patriots, 31-0 (NE)
2004—Patriots, 31-17 (Buff)
　　　Patriots, 29-6 (NE)
2005—Patriots, 21-16 (NE)
　　　Patriots, 35-7 (Buff)
2006—Patriots, 19-17 (NE)
　　　Patriots, 28-6 (Buff)
2007—Patriots, 38-7 (NE)
　　　Patriots, 56-10 (Buff)
2008—Patriots, 20-10 (NE)
　　　Patriots, 13-0 (Buff)
2009—Patriots, 25-24 (NE)
　　　Patriots, 17-10 (Buff)
2010—Patriots, 38-30 (NE)
　　　Patriots, 34-3 (Buff)
2011—Bills, 34-31 (Buff)
　　　Patriots, 49-21 (NE)
2012—Patriots, 52-28 (B)
　　　Patriots, 37-31 (NE)
(RS Pts.—Patriots 2,295, Bills 1,934)
(PS Pts.—Patriots 26, Bills 8)
*Franchise in Boston prior to 1971
**Division Playoff
BUFFALO vs. NEW ORLEANS
RS: Saints lead series, 5-4
1973—Saints, 13-0 (NO)
1980—Bills, 35-26 (NO)
1983—Bills, 27-21 (B)
1989—Saints, 22-19 (B)

1992—Bills, 20-16 (NO)
1998—Bills, 45-33 (NO)
2001—Saints, 24-6 (B)
2005—Saints, 19-7 (San Antonio)
2009—Saints, 27-7 (B)
(RS Pts.—Saints 201, Bills 166)
BUFFALO vs. N.Y. GIANTS
RS: Bills lead series, 6-5
PS: Giants lead series, 1-0
1970—Giants, 20-6 (NY)
1975—Giants, 17-14 (B)
1978—Bills, 41-17 (B)
1987—Bills, 6-3 (B) OT
1990—Bills, 17-13 (NY)
　　　*Giants, 20-19 (Tampa)
1993—Bills, 17-14 (B)
1996—Bills, 23-20 (NY) OT
1999—Giants, 19-17 (B)
2003—Bills, 24-7 (NY)
2007—Giants, 38-21 (B)
2011—Giants, 27-24 (NY)
(RS Pts.—Bills 210, Giants 195)
(PS Pts.—Giants 20, Bills 19)
*Super Bowl XXV
BUFFALO vs. *N.Y. JETS
RS: Bills lead series, 54-50
PS: Bills lead series, 1-0
1960—Titans, 27-3 (NY)
　　　Titans, 17-13 (B)
1961—Bills, 41-31 (B)
　　　Titans, 21-14 (NY)
1962—Titans, 17-6 (B)
　　　Bills, 20-3 (NY)
1963—Bills, 45-14 (B)
　　　Bills, 19-10 (NY)
1964—Bills, 34-24 (B)
　　　Bills, 20-7 (NY)
1965—Bills, 33-21 (B)
　　　Jets, 14-12 (NY)
1966—Bills, 33-23 (NY)
　　　Bills, 14-3 (B)
1967—Bills, 20-17 (B)
　　　Jets, 20-10 (NY)
1968—Bills, 37-35 (B)
　　　Jets, 25-21 (NY)
1969—Jets, 33-19 (B)
　　　Jets, 16-6 (NY)
1970—Bills, 34-31 (B)
　　　Bills, 10-6 (NY)
1971—Jets, 28-17 (NY)
　　　Jets, 20-7 (B)
1972—Jets, 41-24 (B)
　　　Jets, 41-3 (NY)
1973—Bills, 9-7 (B)
　　　Bills, 34-14 (NY)
1974—Bills, 16-12 (B)
　　　Jets, 20-10 (NY)
1975—Bills, 42-14 (B)
　　　Bills, 24-23 (NY)
1976—Jets, 17-14 (NY)
　　　Jets, 19-14 (B)
1977—Jets, 24-19 (B)
　　　Bills, 14-10 (NY)
1978—Jets, 21-20 (B)
　　　Jets, 45-14 (NY)
1979—Bills, 46-31 (B)
　　　Bills, 14-12 (NY)
1980—Bills, 20-10 (B)
　　　Bills, 31-24 (NY)
1981—Bills, 31-0 (B)
　　　Jets, 33-14 (NY)
　　　**Bills, 31-27 (NY)

1983—Jets, 34-10 (B)
    Bills, 24-17 (NY)
1984—Jets, 28-26 (B)
    Jets, 21-17 (NY)
1985—Jets, 42-3 (NY)
    Jets, 27-7 (B)
1986—Jets, 28-24 (B)
    Jets, 14-13 (NY)
1987—Jets, 31-28 (B)
    Bills, 17-14 (NY)
1988—Jets, 37-14 (NY)
    Bills, 9-6 (B) OT
1989—Bills, 34-3 (B)
    Bills, 37-0 (NY)
1990—Bills, 30-7 (NY)
    Bills, 30-27 (B)
1991—Bills, 23-20 (NY)
    Bills, 24-13 (B)
1992—Bills, 24-20 (NY)
    Jets, 24-17 (B)
1993—Bills, 19-10 (NY)
    Bills, 16-14 (B)
1994—Jets, 23-3 (B)
    Jets, 22-17 (NY)
1995—Bills, 29-10 (B)
    Bills, 28-26 (NY)
1996—Bills, 25-22 (NY)
    Bills, 35-10 (B)
1997—Bills, 28-22 (NY)
    Bills, 20-10 (B)
1998—Jets, 34-12 (NY)
    Jets, 17-10 (B)
1999—Bills, 17-3 (B)
    Jets, 17-7 (NY)
2000—Jets, 27-14 (NY)
    Bills, 23-20 (B)
2001—Jets, 42-36 (B)
    Bills, 14-9 (NY)
2002—Jets, 37-31 (B) OT
    Jets, 31-13 (NY)
2003—Jets, 30-3 (NY)
    Bills, 17-6 (B)
2004—Jets, 16-14 (NY)
    Bills, 22-17 (B)
2005—Bills, 27-17 (B)
    Jets, 30-26 (NY)
2006—Jets, 28-20 (B)
    Bills, 31-13 (NY)
2007—Bills, 17-14 (B)
    Bills, 13-3 (NY)
2008—Jets, 26-17 (B)
    Jets, 31-27 (NY)
2009—Bills, 16-13 (NY) OT
    Jets, 19-13 (Toronto)
2010—Jets, 38-14 (B)
    Jets, 38-7 (NY)
2011—Jets, 27-11 (B)
    Jets, 28-24 (NY)
2012—Jets, 48-28 (NY)
    Bills, 28-9 (B)
(RS Pts.—Jets 2,128, Bills 2,107)
(PS Pts.—Bills 31, Jets 27)
*Jets known as Titans prior to 1963
**AFC First-Round Playoff
BUFFALO vs. *OAKLAND
RS: Raiders lead series, 19-17
PS: Bills lead series, 2-0
1960—Bills, 38-9 (B)
    Raiders, 20-7 (O)
1961—Raiders, 31-22 (B)
    Bills, 26-21 (O)
1962—Bills, 14-6 (B)
    Bills, 10-6 (O)

1963—Raiders, 35-17 (O)
    Bills, 12-0 (B)
1964—Bills, 23-20 (B)
    Raiders, 16-13 (O)
1965—Bills, 17-12 (B)
    Bills, 17-14 (O)
1966—Bills, 31-10 (O)
1967—Raiders, 24-20 (B)
    Raiders, 28-21 (O)
1968—Raiders, 48-6 (B)
    Raiders, 13-10 (O)
1969—Raiders, 50-21 (O)
1972—Raiders, 28-16 (O)
1974—Bills, 21-20 (B)
1977—Raiders, 34-13 (O)
1980—Bills, 24-7 (B)
1983—Raiders, 27-24 (B)
1987—Raiders, 34-21 (LA)
1988—Bills, 37-21 (B)
1990—Bills, 38-24 (B)
    **Bills, 51-3 (B)
1991—Bills, 30-27 (LA) OT
1992—Raiders, 20-3 (LA)
1993—Raiders, 25-24 (B)
    ***Bills, 29-23 (B)
1998—Bills, 44-21 (B)
1999—Raiders, 20-14 (B)
2002—Raiders, 49-31 (B)
2004—Raiders, 13-10 (O)
2005—Raiders, 38-17 (O)
2008—Bills, 24-23 (B)
2011—Bills, 38-35 (B)
(RS Pts.—Raiders 829, Bills 754)
(PS Pts.—Bills 80, Raiders 26)
*Franchise in Los Angeles from 1982-1994
**AFC Championship
***AFC Divisional Playoff
BUFFALO vs. PHILADELPHIA
RS: Series tied, 6-6
1973—Bills, 27-26 (B)
1981—Eagles, 20-14 (B)
1984—Eagles, 27-17 (B)
1985—Eagles, 21-17 (P)
1987—Eagles, 17-7 (P)
1990—Bills, 30-23 (B)
1993—Bills, 10-7 (P)
1996—Bills, 24-17 (P)
1999—Bills, 26-0 (B)
2003—Eagles, 23-13 (B)
2007—Eagles, 17-9 (P)
2011—Bills, 31-24 (B)
(RS Pts.—Bills 225, Eagles 222)
BUFFALO vs. PITTSBURGH
RS: Steelers lead series, 12-8
PS: Steelers lead series, 2-1
1970—Steelers, 23-10 (P)
1972—Steelers, 38-21 (B)
1974—*Steelers, 32-14 (P)
1975—Bills, 30-21 (P)
1978—Steelers, 28-17 (B)
1979—Steelers, 28-0 (P)
1980—Bills, 28-13 (B)
1982—Bills, 13-0 (B)
1985—Steelers, 30-24 (P)
1986—Bills, 16-12 (B)
1988—Bills, 36-28 (B)
1991—Bills, 52-34 (B)
1992—Bills, 28-20 (B)
    *Bills, 24-3 (P)
1993—Steelers, 23-0 (P)
1994—Steelers, 23-10 (P)
1995—*Steelers, 40-21 (P)
1996—Steelers, 24-6 (P)

1999—Bills, 24-21 (B)
2001—Steelers, 20-3 (B)
2004—Steelers, 29-24 (B)
2007—Steelers, 26-3 (P)
2010—Steelers, 19-16 (B) OT
(RS Pts.—Steelers 460, Bills 361)
(PS Pts.—Steelers 75, Bills 59)
*AFC Divisional Playoff
BUFFALO vs. *ST. LOUIS
RS: Bills lead series, 6-5
1970—Rams, 19-0 (B)
1974—Rams, 19-14 (LA)
1980—Bills, 10-7 (B) OT
1983—Rams, 41-17 (LA)
1989—Bills, 23-20 (B)
1992—Bills, 40-7 (B)
1995—Bills, 45-27 (StL)
1998—Rams, 34-33 (B)
2004—Bills, 37-17 (B)
2008—Bills, 31-14 (StL)
2012—Rams, 15-12 (B)
(RS Pts.—Bills 262, Rams 220)
*Franchise in Los Angeles prior to 1995
BUFFALO vs. *SAN DIEGO
RS: Chargers lead series, 21-10-2
PS: Bills lead series, 2-1
1960—Chargers, 24-10 (B)
    Bills, 32-3 (LA)
1961—Chargers, 19-11 (B)
    Chargers, 28-10 (SD)
1962—Bills, 35-10 (B)
    Bills, 40-20 (SD)
1963—Chargers, 14-10 (SD)
    Chargers, 23-13 (B)
1964—Bills, 30-3 (B)
    Bills, 27-24 (SD)
    **Bills, 20-7 (B)
1965—Chargers, 34-3 (B)
    Tie, 20-20 (SD)
    **Bills, 23-0 (SD)
1966—Chargers, 27-7 (SD)
    Tie, 17-17 (B)
1967—Chargers, 37-17 (B)
1968—Chargers, 21-6 (B)
1969—Chargers, 45-6 (SD)
1971—Chargers, 20-3 (SD)
1973—Chargers, 34-7 (SD)
1976—Chargers, 34-13 (B)
1979—Chargers, 27-19 (SD)
1980—Bills, 26-24 (SD)
    ***Chargers, 20-14 (SD)
1981—Bills, 28-27 (SD)
1985—Chargers, 14-9 (B)
    Chargers, 40-7 (SD)
1998—Chargers, 16-14 (SD)
2000—Bills, 27-24 (B) OT
2001—Chargers, 27-24 (SD)
2002—Bills, 20-13 (B)
2005—Chargers, 48-10 (SD)
2006—Chargers, 24-21 (B)
2008—Bills, 23-14 (B)
2011—Chargers, 37-10 (SD)
(RS Pts.—Chargers 792, Bills 555)
(PS Pts.—Bills 57, Chargers 27)
*Franchise in Los Angeles prior to 1961
**AFL Championship
***AFC Divisional Playoff
BUFFALO vs. SAN FRANCISCO
RS: 49ers lead series, 6-5
1972—Bills, 27-20 (B)
1980—Bills, 18-13 (SF)
1983—49ers, 23-10 (B)
1989—49ers, 21-10 (SF)

1992—Bills, 34-31 (SF)
1995—49ers, 27-17 (SF)
1998—Bills, 26-21 (B)
2001—49ers, 35-0 (SF)
2004—Bills, 41-7 (SF)
2008—49ers, 10-3 (B)
2012—49ers, 45-3 (SF)
(RS Pts.—49ers 253, Bills 189)
BUFFALO vs. SEATTLE
RS: Seahawks lead series, 7-5
1977—Seahawks, 56-17 (S)
1984—Seahawks, 31-28 (S)
1988—Bills, 13-3 (S)
1989—Seahawks, 17-16 (S)
1995—Bills, 27-21 (S)
1996—Seahawks, 26-18 (S)
1999—Seahawks, 26-16 (S)
2000—Bills, 42-23 (S)
2001—Seahawks, 23-20 (B)
2004—Bills, 38-9 (S)
2008—Bills, 34-10 (B)
2012—Seahawks, 50-17 (Toronto)
(RS Pts.—Seahawks 295, Bills 286)
BUFFALO vs. TAMPA BAY
RS: Buccaneers lead series, 6-3
1976—Bills, 14-9 (TB)
1978—Buccaneers, 31-10 (TB)
1982—Buccaneers, 24-23 (TB)
1986—Buccaneers, 34-28 (TB)
1988—Buccaneers, 10-5 (TB)
1991—Bills, 17-10 (TB)
2000—Buccaneers, 31-17 (TB)
2005—Buccaneers, 19-3 (TB)
2009—Bills, 33-19 (B)
(RS Pts.—Buccaneers 188, Bills 150)
BUFFALO vs. *TENNESSEE
RS: Titans lead series, 27-14
PS: Bills lead series, 2-1
1960—Bills, 25-24 (B)
    Oilers, 31-23 (H)
1961—Bills, 22-12 (H)
    Oilers, 28-16 (B)
1962—Oilers, 28-23 (B)
    Oilers, 17-14 (H)
1963—Oilers, 31-20 (B)
    Oilers, 28-14 (H)
1964—Bills, 48-17 (H)
    Bills, 24-10 (B)
1965—Oilers, 19-17 (B)
    Bills, 29-18 (H)
1966—Bills, 27-20 (B)
    Bills, 42-20 (H)
1967—Oilers, 20-3 (B)
    Oilers, 10-3 (H)
1968—Oilers, 30-7 (B)
    Oilers, 35-6 (H)
1969—Oilers, 17-3 (B)
    Oilers, 28-14 (H)
1971—Oilers, 20-14 (B)
1974—Oilers, 21-9 (B)
1976—Oilers, 13-3 (B)
1978—Oilers, 17-10 (H)
1983—Bills, 30-13 (B)
1985—Bills, 20-0 (B)
1986—Oilers, 16-7 (B)
1987—Bills, 34-30 (B)
1988—**Bills, 17-10 (B)
1989—Bills, 47-41 (H) OT
1990—Oilers, 27-24 (H)
1992—Oilers, 27-3 (H)
    ***Bills, 41-38 (B) OT
1993—Bills, 35-7 (B)
1994—Bills, 15-7 (H)

1995—Oilers, 28-17 (B)
1997—Oilers, 31-14 (T)
1999—***Titans, 22-16 (T)
2000—Bills, 16-13 (B)
2003—Titans, 28-26 (T)
2006—Titans, 30-29 (B)
2009—Titans, 41-17 (T)
2011—Titans, 23-17 (B)
2012—Titans, 35-34 (B)
(RS Pts.—Titans 911, Bills 801)
(PS Pts.—Bills 74, Titans 70)
*Franchise in Houston prior to 1997;
known as Oilers prior to 1999
**AFC Divisional Playoff
***AFC First-Round Playoff
BUFFALO vs. WASHINGTON
RS: Bills lead series, 8-4
PS: Redskins lead series, 1-0
1972—Bills, 24-17 (W)
1977—Redskins, 10-0 (B)
1981—Bills, 21-14 (B)
1984—Redskins, 41-14 (W)
1987—Redskins, 27-7 (B)
1990—Redskins, 29-14 (W)
1991—*Redskins, 37-24 (Minneapolis)
1993—Bills, 24-10 (B)
1996—Bills, 38-13 (B)
1999—Bills, 34-17 (W)
2003—Bills, 24-7 (B)
2007—Bills, 17-16 (W)
2011—Bills, 23-0 (Toronto)
(RS Pts.—Bills 240, Redskins 201)
(PS Pts.—Redskins 37, Bills 24)
*Super Bowl XXVI

CAROLINA vs. ARIZONA
RS: Panthers lead series, 8-3
PS: Cardinals lead series, 1-0;
See Arizona vs. Carolina
CAROLINA vs. ATLANTA
RS: Falcons lead series, 23-13;
See Atlanta vs. Carolina
CAROLINA vs. BALTIMORE
RS: Panthers lead series, 3-1;
See Baltimore vs. Carolina
CAROLINA vs. BUFFALO
RS: Bills lead series, 4-1;
See Buffalo vs. Carolina
CAROLINA vs. CHICAGO
RS: Bears lead series, 5-2
PS: Panthers lead series, 1-0
1995—Bears, 31-27 (Chi)
2002—Panthers, 24-14 (Car)
2005—Bears, 13-3 (Chi)
    *Panthers, 29-21 (Chi)
2008—Panthers, 20-17 (Car)
2010—Bears, 23-6 (Car)
2011—Bears, 34-29 (Chi)
2012—Bears, 23-22 (Chi)
(RS Pts.—Bears 155, Panthers 131)
(PS Pts.—Panthers 29, Bears 21)
*NFC Divisional Playoff
CAROLINA vs. CINCINNATI
RS: Series tied, 2-2
1999—Panthers, 27-3 (Car)
2002—Panthers, 52-31 (Car)
2006—Bengals, 17-14 (Cin)
2010—Bengals, 20-7 (Car)
(RS Pts.—Panthers 100, Bengals 71)
CAROLINA vs. CLEVELAND
RS: Panthers lead series, 3-1
1999—Panthers, 31-17 (Cle)
2002—Panthers, 13-6 (Cle)

2006—Panthers, 20-12 (Car)
2010—Browns, 24-23 (Cle)
(RS Pts.—Panthers 87, Browns 59)
CAROLINA vs. DALLAS
RS: Cowboys lead series, 9-1
PS: Panthers lead series, 2-0
1996—*Panthers, 26-17 (C)
1997—Panthers, 23-13 (D)
1998—Cowboys, 27-20 (D)
2000—Cowboys, 16-13 (C) OT
2002—Cowboys, 14-13 (D)
2003—Cowboys, 24-20 (D)
    **Panthers, 29-10 (C)
2005—Cowboys, 24-20 (C)
2006—Cowboys, 35-14 (C)
2007—Cowboys, 20-13 (C)
2009—Cowboys, 21-7 (D)
2012—Cowboys, 19-14 (C)
(RS Pts.—Cowboys 213, Panthers 157)
(PS Pts.—Panthers 55, Cowboys 27)
*NFC Divisional Playoff
*NFC First-Round Playoff
CAROLINA vs. DENVER
RS: Broncos lead series, 3-1
1997—Broncos, 34-0 (D)
2004—Broncos, 20-17 (D)
2008—Panthers, 30-10 (C)
2012—Broncos, 36-14 (C)
(RS Pts.—Broncos 100, Panthers 61)
CAROLINA vs. DETROIT
RS: Panthers lead series, 4-2
1999—Lions, 24-9 (C)
2002—Panthers, 31-7 (C)
2003—Panthers, 20-14 (C)
2005—Panthers, 21-20 (D)
2008—Panthers, 31-22 (C)
2011—Lions, 49-35 (D)
(RS Pts.—Panthers 147, Lions 136)
CAROLINA vs. GREEN BAY
RS: Packers lead series, 7-4
PS: Packers lead series, 1-0
1996—*Packers, 30-13 (GB)
1997—Packers, 31-10 (C)
1998—Packers, 37-30 (C)
1999—Panthers, 33-31 (GB)
2000—Panthers, 31-14 (C)
2001—Packers, 28-7 (C)
2002—Packers, 17-14 (GB)
2004—Packers, 24-14 (C)
2005—Panthers, 32-29 (C)
2007—Packers, 31-17 (GB)
2008—Panthers, 35-31 (GB)
2011—Packers, 30-23 (C)
(RS Pts.—Packers 303, Panthers 246)
(PS Pts.—Packers 30, Panthers 13)
*NFC Championship
CAROLINA vs. HOUSTON
RS: Texans lead series, 2-1
2003—Texans, 14-10 (H)
2007—Texans, 34-21 (H)
2011—Panthers, 28-13 (H)
(RS Pts.—Texans 61, Panthers 59)
CAROLINA vs. INDIANAPOLIS
RS: Panthers lead series, 4-1
1995—Panthers, 13-10 (C)
1998—Panthers, 27-19 (I)
2003—Panthers, 23-20 (I) OT
2007—Colts, 31-7 (C)
2011—Panthers, 27-19 (I)
(RS Pts.—Colts 99, Panthers 97)
CAROLINA vs. JACKSONVILLE
RS: Jaguars lead series, 3-2
1996—Jaguars, 24-14 (J)

1999—Jaguars, 22-20 (C)
2003—Panthers, 24-23 (C)
2007—Jaguars, 37-6 (J)
2011—Panthers, 16-10 (C)
(RS Pts.—Jaguars 116, Panthers 80)
CAROLINA vs. KANSAS CITY
RS: Chiefs lead series, 3-2
1997—Chiefs, 35-14 (C)
2000—Chiefs, 15-14 (KC)
2004—Panthers, 28-17 (KC)
2008—Panthers, 34-0 (C)
2012—Chiefs, 27-21 (KC)
(RS Pts.—Panthers 111, Chiefs 94)
CAROLINA vs. MIAMI
RS: Dolphins lead series, 4-0
1998—Dolphins, 13-9 (C)
2001—Dolphins, 23-6 (M)
2005—Dolphins, 27-24 (M)
2009—Dolphins, 24-17 (C)
(RS Pts.—Dolphins 87, Panthers 56)
CAROLINA vs. MINNESOTA
RS: Vikings lead series, 6-4
1996—Vikings, 14-12 (M)
1997—Vikings, 21-14 (M)
2000—Vikings, 31-17 (M)
2001—Panthers, 24-13 (M)
2002—Panthers, 21-14 (M)
2005—Panthers, 38-13 (C)
2006—Vikings, 16-13 (M) OT
2008—Vikings, 20-10 (M)
2009—Panthers, 26-7 (C)
2011—Vikings, 24-21 (C)
(RS Pts.—Panthers 196, Vikings 173)
CAROLINA vs. NEW ENGLAND
RS: Series tied, 2-2
PS: Patriots lead series, 1-0
1995—Panthers, 20-17 (NE) OT
2001—Patriots, 38-6 (C)
2003—*Patriots, 32-29 (Houston)
2005—Panthers, 27-17 (C)
2009—Panthers, 20-10 (NE)
(RS Pts.—Patriots 92, Panthers 63)
(PS Pts.—Patriots 32, Panthers 29)
*Super Bowl XXXVIII
CAROLINA vs. NEW ORLEANS
RS: Panthers lead series, 19-17
1995—Panthers, 20-3 (C)
Saints, 34-26 (NO)
1996—Panthers, 22-20 (NO)
Panthers, 19-7 (C)
1997—Panthers, 13-0 (NO)
Saints, 16-13 (C)
1998—Saints, 19-14 (NO)
Panthers, 31-17 (C)
1999—Saints, 19-10 (NO)
Panthers, 45-13 (C)
2000—Saints, 24-6 (NO)
Saints, 20-10 (C)
2001—Saints, 27-25 (C)
Saints, 27-23 (NO)
2002—Saints, 34-24 (C)
Panthers, 10-6 (NO)
2003—Panthers, 19-13 (C)
Panthers, 23-20 (NO) OT
2004—Panthers, 32-21 (NO)
Saints, 21-18 (C)
2005—Saints, 23-20 (C)
Panthers, 27-10 (Baton Rouge)
2006—Panthers, 21-18 (C)
Panthers, 31-21 (NO)
2007—Panthers, 16-13 (NO)
Saints, 31-6 (C)

2008—Panthers, 30-7 (C)
Panthers, 33-31 (NO)
2009—Saints, 30-20 (NO)
Panthers, 23-10 (C)
2010—Saints, 16-14 (NO)
Saints, 34-3 (C)
2011—Saints, 30-27 (C)
Saints, 45-17 (NO)
2012—Panthers, 35-27 (C)
Panthers, 44-38 (NO)
(RS Pts.—Panthers 770, Saints 745)
CAROLINA vs. N.Y. GIANTS
RS: Giants lead series, 4-3
PS: Panthers lead series, 1-0
1996—Panthers, 27-17 (C)
2003—Panthers, 37-24 (NY)
2005—*Panthers, 23-0 (NY)
2006—Giants, 27-13 (C)
2008—Giants, 34-28 (NY) OT
2009—Panthers, 41-9 (NY)
2010—Giants, 31-18 (NY)
2012—Giants, 36-7 (C)
(RS Pts.—Giants 178, Panthers 171)
(PS Pts.—Panthers 23, Giants 0)
*NFC First-Round Playoff
CAROLINA vs. N.Y. JETS
RS: Jets lead series, 3-2
1995—Panthers, 26-15 (C)
1998—Jets, 48-21 (NY)
2001—Jets, 13-12 (C)
2005—Panthers, 30-3 (C)
2009—Jets, 17-6 (NY)
(RS Pts.—Jets 96, Panthers 95)
CAROLINA vs. OAKLAND
RS: Panthers lead series, 3-2
1997—Panthers, 38-14 (C)
2000—Raiders, 52-9 (O)
2004—Raiders, 27-24 (C)
2008—Panthers, 17-6 (O)
2012—Panthers, 17-6 (C)
(RS Pts.— Panthers 105, Raiders 105)
CAROLINA vs. PHILADELPHIA
RS: Eagles lead series, 5-2
PS: Panthers lead series, 1-0
1996—Eagles, 20-9 (P)
1999—Panthers, 33-7 (C)
2003—Eagles, 25-16 (C)
*Panthers, 14-3 (P)
2004—Eagles, 30-8 (P)
2006—Eagles, 27-24 (P)
2009—Eagles, 38-10 (C)
2012—Panthers, 30-22 (P)
(RS Pts.—Eagles 169, Panthers 130)
(PS Pts.—Panthers 14, Eagles 3)
*NFC Championship
CAROLINA vs. PITTSBURGH
RS: Steelers lead series, 4-1
1996—Panthers, 18-14 (C)
1999—Steelers, 30-20 (P)
2002—Steelers, 30-14 (P)
2006—Steelers, 37-3 (C)
2010—Steelers, 27-3 (P)
(RS Pts.—Steelers 138, Panthers 58)
CAROLINA vs. ST. LOUIS
RS: Panthers lead series, 10-8
PS: Panthers lead series, 1-0
1995—Rams, 31-10 (C)
Rams, 28-17 (StL)
1996—Panthers, 45-13 (C)
Panthers, 20-10 (StL)
1997—Panthers, 16-10 (StL)
Rams, 30-18 (StL)

1998—Panthers, 24-20 (StL)
Panthers, 20-13 (C)
1999—Rams, 35-10 (StL)
Rams, 34-21 (C)
2000—Panthers, 27-24 (StL)
Panthers, 16-3 (C)
2001—Rams, 48-14 (StL)
Rams, 38-32 (C)
2003—*Panthers, 29-23 (StL) 2OT
2004—Panthers, 20-7 (C)
2006—Panthers, 15-0 (C)
2007—Panthers, 27-13 (StL)
2010—Rams, 20-10 (StL)
(RS Pts.—Rams 377, Panthers 362)
(PS Pts.—Panthers 29, Rams 23)
*NFC Divisional Playoff
CAROLINA vs. SAN DIEGO
RS: Panthers lead series, 4-1
1997—Panthers, 26-7 (SD)
2000—Panthers, 30-22 (C)
2004—Chargers, 17-6 (C)
2008—Panthers, 26-24 (SD)
2012—Panthers, 31-7 (SD)
(RS Pts.—Panthers 119, Chargers 77)
CAROLINA vs. SAN FRANCISCO
RS: Panthers lead series, 10-7
1995—Panthers, 13-7 (SF)
49ers, 31-10 (C)
1996—Panthers, 23-7 (C)
Panthers, 30-24 (SF)
1997—49ers, 34-21 (C)
49ers, 27-19 (SF)
1998—49ers, 25-23 (SF)
49ers, 31-28 (C) OT
1999—Panthers, 31-29 (SF)
Panthers, 41-24 (C)
2000—Panthers, 38-22 (SF)
Panthers, 34-16 (C)
2001—49ers, 24-14 (SF)
49ers, 25-22 (C) OT
2004—Panthers, 37-27 (SF)
2007—Panthers, 31-14 (C)
2010—Panthers, 23-20 (C)
(RS Pts.—Panthers 438, 49ers 387)
CAROLINA vs. SEATTLE
RS: Seahawks lead series, 3-2
PS: Seahawks lead series, 1-0
2000—Panthers, 26-3 (C)
2004—Seahawks, 23-17 (S)
2005—*Seahawks, 34-14 (S)
2007—Panthers, 13-10 (C)
2010—Seahawks, 31-14 (S)
2012—Seahawks, 16-12 (C)
(RS Pts.—Seahawks 83, Panthers 82)
(PS Pts.—Seahawks 34, Panthers 14)
*NFC Championship
CAROLINA vs. TAMPA BAY
RS: Panthers lead series, 14-11
1995—Buccaneers, 20-13 (C)
1996—Panthers, 24-0 (C)
1998—Buccaneers, 16-13 (TB)
2002—Buccaneers, 12-9 (C)
Buccaneers, 23-10 (TB)
2003—Panthers, 12-9 (TB) OT
Panthers, 27-24 (C)
2004—Panthers, 21-14 (C)
Panthers, 37-20 (TB)
2005—Panthers, 34-14 (TB)
Buccaneers, 20-10 (C)
2006—Panthers, 26-24 (TB)
Panthers, 24-10 (C)
2007—Buccaneers, 20-7 (C)
Panthers, 31-23 (TB)

2008—Buccaneers, 27-3 (TB)
   Panthers, 38-23 (C)
2009—Panthers, 28-21 (TB)
   Panthers, 16-6 (C)
2010—Buccaneers, 20-7 (C)
   Buccaneers, 31-16 (TB)
2011—Panthers, 38-19 (TB)
   Panthers, 48-16 (C)
2012—Buccaneers, 16-10 (TB)
   Buccaneers, 27-21 (C) OT
(RS Pts.—Panthers 523, Buccaneers 455)
CAROLINA vs. *TENNESSEE
RS: Titans lead series, 3-1
1996—Panthers, 31-6 (H)
2003—Titans, 37-17 (C)
2007—Titans, 20-7 (T)
2011—Titans, 30-3 (C)
(RS Pts.—Titans 93, Panthers 58)
*Franchise in Houston prior to 1997;
known as Oilers prior to 1999
CAROLINA vs. WASHINGTON
RS: Redskins lead series, 7-4
1995—Redskins, 20-17 (W)
1997—Redskins, 24-10 (C)
1998—Redskins, 28-25 (C)
1999—Redskins, 38-36 (W)
2000—Redskins, 20-17 (W)
2001—Redskins, 17-14 (W) OT
2003—Panthers, 20-17 (C)
2006—Redskins, 17-13 (W)
2009—Panthers, 20-17 (C)
2011—Panthers, 33-20 (C)
2012—Panthers, 21-13 (W)
(RS Pts.—Redskins 231, Panthers 226)

CHICAGO vs. ARIZONA
RS: Bears lead series, 56-27-6;
See Arizona vs. Chicago
CHICAGO vs. ATLANTA
RS: Bears lead series, 13-12;
See Atlanta vs. Chicago
CHICAGO vs. BALTIMORE
RS: Series tied, 2-2;
See Baltimore vs. Chicago
CHICAGO vs. BUFFALO
RS: Bears lead series, 7-4;
See Buffalo vs. Chicago
CHICAGO vs. CAROLINA
RS: Bears lead series, 5-2
PS: Panthers lead series, 1-0;
See Carolina vs. Chicago
CHICAGO vs. CINCINNATI
RS: Bengals lead series, 6-3
1972—Bengals, 13-3 (Chi)
1980—Bengals, 17-14 (Chi) OT
1986—Bears, 44-7 (Cin)
1989—Bears, 17-14 (Chi)
1992—Bengals, 31-28 (Chi) OT
1995—Bengals, 16-10 (Cin)
2001—Bears, 24-0 (Cin)
2005—Bengals, 24-7 (Chi)
2009—Bengals, 45-10 (Cin)
(RS Pts.—Bengals 167, Bears 157)
CHICAGO vs. CLEVELAND
RS: Browns lead series, 9-5
1951—Browns, 42-21 (Cle)
1954—Browns, 39-10 (Cle)
1960—Browns, 42-0 (Cle)
1961—Bears, 17-14 (Chi)
1967—Browns, 24-0 (Cle)
1969—Browns, 28-24 (Chi)
1972—Bears, 17-0 (Cle)
1980—Browns, 27-21 (Cle)

1986—Bears, 41-31 (Chi)
1989—Browns, 27-7 (Cle)
1992—Browns, 27-14 (Cle)
2001—Bears, 27-21 (Chi) OT
2005—Browns, 20-10 (Cle)
2009—Bears, 30-6 (Chi)
(RS Pts.—Browns 348, Bears 239)
CHICAGO vs. DALLAS
RS: Cowboys lead series, 11-10
PS: Cowboys lead series, 2-0
1960—Bears, 17-7 (C)
1962—Bears, 34-33 (D)
1964—Cowboys, 24-10 (C)
1968—Cowboys, 34-3 (C)
1971—Bears, 23-19 (C)
1973—Cowboys, 20-17 (D)
1976—Cowboys, 31-21 (D)
1977—*Cowboys, 37-7 (D)
1979—Cowboys, 24-20 (D)
1981—Cowboys, 10-9 (D)
1984—Cowboys, 23-14 (C)
1985—Bears, 44-0 (D)
1986—Bears, 24-10 (D)
1988—Bears, 17-7 (C)
1991–**Cowboys, 17-13 (C)
1992—Cowboys, 27-14 (D)
1996—Bears, 22-6 (C)
1997—Cowboys, 27-3 (D)
1998—Bears, 13-12 (C)
2004—Cowboys, 21-7 (D)
2007—Cowboys, 34-10 (C)
2010—Bears, 27-20 (D)
2012—Bears, 34-18 (D)
(RS Pts.—Cowboys 407, Bears 383)
(PS Pts.—Cowboys 54, Bears 20)
*NFC Divisional Playoff
**NFC First-Round Playoff
CHICAGO vs. DENVER
RS: Series tied, 7-7
1971—Broncos, 6-3 (D)
1973—Bears, 33-14 (D)
1976—Broncos, 28-14 (C)
1978—Broncos, 16-7 (D)
1981—Bears, 35-24 (C)
1983—Bears, 31-14 (C)
1984—Bears, 27-0 (C)
1987—Broncos, 31-29 (D)
1990—Bears, 16-13 (D) OT
1993—Broncos, 13-3 (C)
1996—Broncos, 17-12 (D)
2003—Bears, 19-10 (D)
2007—Bears, 37-34 (C) OT
2011—Broncos, 13-10 (D) OT
(RS Pts.—Bears 276, Broncos 233)
CHICAGO vs. *DETROIT
RS: Bears lead series, 96-65-5
1930—Spartans, 7-6 (P)
   Bears, 14-6 (C)
1931—Bears, 9-6 (C)
   Spartans, 3-0 (P)
1932—Tie, 13-13 (C)
   Tie, 7-7 (P)
   Bears, 9-0 (C)
1933—Bears, 17-14 (C)
   Bears, 17-7 (P)
1934—Bears, 19-16 (D)
   Bears, 10-7 (C)
1935—Tie, 20-20 (C)
   Lions, 14-2 (D)
1936—Bears, 12-10 (C)
   Lions, 13-7 (D)
1937—Bears, 28-20 (C)
   Bears, 13-0 (D)

1938—Lions, 13-7 (C)
   Lions, 14-7 (D)
1939—Lions, 10-0 (C)
   Bears, 23-13 (D)
1940—Bears, 7-0 (C)
   Lions, 17-14 (D)
1941—Bears, 49-0 (C)
   Bears, 24-7 (D)
1942—Bears, 16-0 (C)
   Bears, 42-0 (D)
1943—Bears, 27-21 (D)
   Bears, 35-14 (C)
1944—Tie, 21-21 (C)
   Lions, 41-21 (D)
1945—Lions, 16-10 (D)
   Lions, 35-28 (C)
1946—Bears, 42-6 (C)
   Bears, 45-24 (D)
1947—Bears, 33-24 (C)
   Bears, 34-14 (D)
1948—Bears, 28-0 (C)
   Bears, 42-14 (D)
1949—Bears, 27-24 (C)
   Bears, 28-7 (D)
1950—Bears, 35-21 (D)
   Bears, 6-3 (C)
1951—Bears, 28-23 (C)
   Lions, 41-28 (C)
1952—Bears, 24-23 (C)
   Lions, 45-21 (D)
1953—Lions, 20-16 (C)
   Lions, 13-7 (D)
1954—Lions, 48-23 (D)
   Bears, 28-24 (C)
1955—Bears, 24-14 (D)
   Bears, 21-20 (C)
1956—Lions, 42-10 (D)
   Bears, 38-21 (C)
1957—Bears, 27-7 (D)
   Lions, 21-13 (C)
1958—Bears, 20-7 (D)
   Bears, 21-16 (C)
1959—Bears, 24-14 (D)
   Bears, 25-14 (C)
1960—Bears, 28-7 (C)
   Lions, 36-0 (D)
1961—Bears, 31-17 (D)
   Lions, 16-15 (C)
1962—Lions, 11-3 (D)
   Bears, 3-0 (C)
1963—Bears, 37-21 (D)
   Bears, 24-14 (C)
1964—Lions, 10-0 (C)
   Bears, 27-24 (D)
1965—Bears, 38-10 (C)
   Bears, 17-10 (D)
1966—Lions, 14-3 (D)
   Tie, 10-10 (C)
1967—Bears, 14-3 (C)
   Bears, 27-13 (D)
1968—Lions, 42-0 (D)
   Lions, 28-10 (C)
1969—Lions, 13-7 (D)
   Lions, 20-3 (C)
1970—Lions, 28-14 (D)
   Lions, 16-10 (C)
1971—Bears, 28-23 (D)
   Lions, 28-3 (C)
1972—Lions, 38-24 (C)
   Lions, 14-0 (D)
1973—Lions, 30-7 (C)
   Lions, 40-7 (D)

1974—Bears, 17-9 (C)
Lions, 34-17 (D)
1975—Lions, 27-7 (D)
Bears, 25-21 (C)
1976—Bears, 10-3 (C)
Lions, 14-10 (D)
1977—Bears, 30-20 (C)
Bears, 31-14 (D)
1978—Bears, 19-0 (D)
Lions, 21-17 (C)
1979—Bears, 35-7 (C)
Lions, 20-0 (D)
1980—Bears, 24-7 (C)
Bears, 23-17 (D) OT
1981—Lions, 48-17 (D)
Lions, 23-7 (C)
1982—Lions, 17-10 (D)
Bears, 20-17 (C)
1983—Lions, 31-17 (D)
Lions, 38-17 (C)
1984—Bears, 16-14 (C)
Bears, 30-13 (D)
1985—Bears, 24-3 (C)
Bears, 37-17 (D)
1986—Bears, 13-7 (C)
Bears, 16-13 (D)
1987—Bears, 30-10 (C)
1988—Bears, 24-7 (D)
Bears, 13-12 (C)
1989—Bears, 47-27 (D)
Lions, 27-17 (C)
1990—Bears, 23-17 (C) OT
Lions, 38-21 (D)
1991—Bears, 20-10 (C)
Lions, 16-6 (D)
1992—Bears, 27-24 (C)
Lions, 16-3 (D)
1993—Bears, 10-6 (D)
Lions, 20-14 (C)
1994—Lions, 21-16 (D)
Bears, 20-10 (C)
1995—Lions, 24-17 (C)
Lions, 27-7 (D)
1996—Lions, 35-16 (D)
Bears, 31-14 (C)
1997—Lions, 32-7 (C)
Lions, 55-20 (D)
1998—Lions, 31-27 (C)
Lions, 26-3 (D)
1999—Lions, 21-17 (D)
Bears, 28-10 (C)
2000—Lions, 21-14 (C)
Bears, 23-20 (D)
2001—Bears, 13-10 (C)
Bears, 24-0 (D)
2002—Lions, 23-20 (D) OT
Bears, 20-17 (C) OT
2003—Bears, 24-16 (C)
Lions, 12-10 (D)
2004—Lions, 20-16 (C)
Lions, 19-13 (D)
2005—Bears, 38-6 (C)
Bears, 19-13 (D) OT
2006—Bears, 34-7 (C)
Bears, 26-21 (D)
2007—Lions, 37-27 (D)
Lions, 16-7 (C)
2008—Bears, 34-7 (D)
Bears, 27-23 (C)
2009—Bears, 48-24 (C)
Bears, 37-23 (D)
2010—Bears, 19-14 (C)
Bears, 24-20 (D)

2011—Lions, 24-13 (D)
Bears, 37-13 (C)
2012—Bears, 13-7 (C)
Bears, 26-24 (D)
(RS Pts.—Bears 3,205, Lions 2,895)
*Franchise in Portsmouth prior to 1934
and known as the Spartans
CHICAGO vs. GREEN BAY
RS: Bears lead series, 91-87-6
PS: Series tied, 1-1
1921—Staleys, 20-0 (C)
1923—Bears, 3-0 (GB)
1924—Bears, 3-0 (C)
1925—Packers, 14-10 (GB)
Bears, 21-0 (C)
1926—Tie, 6-6 (GB)
Bears, 19-13 (C)
Tie, 3-3 (C)
1927—Bears, 7-6 (GB)
Bears, 14-6 (C)
1928—Tie, 12-12 (GB)
Packers, 16-6 (C)
Packers, 6-0 (C)
1929—Packers, 23-0 (GB)
Packers, 14-0 (C)
Packers, 25-0 (C)
1930—Packers, 7-0 (GB)
Packers, 13-12 (C)
Bears, 21-0 (C)
1931—Packers, 7-0 (GB)
Packers, 6-2 (C)
Bears, 7-6 (C)
1932—Tie, 0-0 (GB)
Packers, 2-0 (C)
Bears, 9-0 (C)
1933—Bears, 14-7 (GB)
Bears, 10-7 (C)
Bears, 7-6 (C)
1934—Bears, 24-10 (GB)
Bears, 27-14 (C)
1935—Packers, 7-0 (GB)
Packers, 17-14 (C)
1936—Bears, 30-3 (GB)
Packers, 21-10 (C)
1937—Bears, 14-2 (GB)
Packers, 24-14 (C)
1938—Bears, 2-0 (GB)
Packers, 24-17 (C)
1939—Packers, 21-16 (GB)
Bears, 30-27 (C)
1940—Bears, 41-10 (GB)
Bears, 14-7 (C)
1941—Bears, 25-17 (GB)
Packers, 16-14 (C)
**Bears, 33-14 (C)
1942—Bears, 44-28 (GB)
Bears, 38-7 (C)
1943—Tie, 21-21 (GB)
Bears, 21-7 (C)
1944—Packers, 42-28 (GB)
Bears, 21-0 (C)
1945—Packers, 31-21 (GB)
Bears, 28-24 (C)
1946—Bears, 30-7 (GB)
Bears, 10-7 (C)
1947—Packers, 29-20 (GB)
Bears, 20-17 (C)
1948—Bears, 45-7 (GB)
Bears, 7-6 (C)
1949—Bears, 17-0 (GB)
Bears, 24-3 (C)
1950—Packers, 31-21 (GB)
Bears, 28-14 (C)

1951—Bears, 31-20 (GB)
Bears, 24-13 (C)
1952—Bears, 24-14 (GB)
Packers, 41-28 (C)
1953—Bears, 17-13 (GB)
Tie, 21-21 (C)
1954—Bears, 10-3 (GB)
Bears, 28-23 (C)
1955—Packers, 24-3 (GB)
Bears, 52-31 (C)
1956—Bears, 37-21 (GB)
Bears, 38-14 (C)
1957—Packers, 21-17 (GB)
Bears, 21-14 (C)
1958—Bears, 34-20 (GB)
Bears, 24-10 (C)
1959—Packers, 9-6 (GB)
Bears, 28-17 (C)
1960—Bears, 17-14 (GB)
Packers, 41-13 (C)
1961—Packers, 24-0 (GB)
Packers, 31-28 (C)
1962—Packers, 49-0 (GB)
Packers, 38-7 (C)
1963—Bears, 10-3 (GB)
Bears, 26-7 (C)
1964—Packers, 23-12 (GB)
Packers, 17-3 (C)
1965—Packers, 23-14 (GB)
Bears, 31-10 (C)
1966—Packers, 17-0 (GB)
Packers, 13-6 (C)
1967—Packers, 13-10 (GB)
Packers, 17-13 (C)
1968—Bears, 13-10 (GB)
Packers, 28-27 (C)
1969—Packers, 17-0 (GB)
Packers, 21-3 (C)
1970—Packers, 20-19 (GB)
Bears, 35-17 (C)
1971—Packers, 17-14 (C)
Packers, 31-10 (GB)
1972—Packers, 20-17 (GB)
Packers, 23-17 (C)
1973—Bears, 31-17 (GB)
Packers, 21-0 (C)
1974—Bears, 10-9 (C)
Packers, 20-3 (Mil)
1975—Bears, 27-14 (C)
Packers, 28-7 (GB)
1976—Bears, 24-13 (C)
Bears, 16-10 (GB)
1977—Bears, 26-0 (GB)
Bears, 21-10 (C)
1978—Packers, 24-14 (GB)
Bears, 14-0 (C)
1979—Bears, 6-3 (C)
Bears, 15-14 (GB)
1980—Packers, 12-6 (GB) OT
Bears, 61-7 (C)
1981—Packers, 16-9 (C)
Packers, 21-17 (GB)
1983—Packers, 31-28 (GB)
Bears, 23-21 (C)
1984—Bears, 9-7 (GB)
Packers, 20-14 (C)
1985—Bears, 23-7 (C)
Bears, 16-10 (GB)
1986—Bears, 25-12 (GB)
Bears, 12-10 (C)
1987—Bears, 26-24 (GB)
Bears, 23-10 (C)

1988—Bears, 24-6 (GB)
    Bears, 16-0 (C)
1989—Packers, 14-13 (GB)
    Packers, 40-28 (C)
1990—Bears, 31-13 (GB)
    Bears, 27-13 (C)
1991—Bears, 10-0 (GB)
    Bears, 27-13 (C)
1992—Bears, 30-10 (GB)
    Packers, 17-3 (C)
1993—Packers, 17-3 (GB)
    Bears, 30-17 (C)
1994—Packers, 33-6 (C)
    Packers, 40-3 (GB)
1995—Packers, 27-24 (C)
    Packers, 35-28 (GB)
1996—Packers, 37-6 (C)
    Packers, 28-17 (GB)
1997—Packers, 38-24 (GB)
    Packers, 24-23 (C)
1998—Packers, 26-20 (GB)
    Packers, 16-13 (C)
1999—Bears, 14-13 (GB)
    Packers, 35-19 (C)
2000—Bears, 27-24 (GB)
    Packers, 28-6 (C)
2001—Packers, 20-12 (C)
    Packers, 17-7 (GB)
2002—Packers, 34-21 (C)
    Packers, 30-20 (GB)
2003—Packers, 38-23 (C)
    Packers, 34-21 (GB)
2004—Bears, 21-10 (GB)
    Packers, 31-14 (C)
2005—Bears, 19-7 (C)
    Bears, 24-17 (GB)
2006—Bears, 26-0 (GB)
    Packers, 26-7 (C)
2007—Bears, 27-20 (GB)
    Bears, 35-7 (C)
2008—Packers, 37-3 (GB)
    Bears, 20-17 (C) OT
2009—Packers, 21-15 (GB)
    Packers, 21-14 (C)
2010—Bears, 20-17 (C)
    Packers, 10-3 (GB)
    ***Packers, 21-14 (C)
2011—Packers, 27-17 (C)
    Packers, 35-21 (GB)
2012—Packers, 23-10 (GB)
    Packers, 21-13 (C)
(RS Pts.—Bears 3,121, Packers 3,054)
(PS Pts.—Bears 47, Packers 35)
*Bears known as Staleys prior to 1922
**Division Playoff
***NFC Championship
CHICAGO vs. HOUSTON
RS: Texans lead series, 3-0
2004—Texans, 24-5 (C)
2008—Texans, 31-24 (H)
2012—Texans, 13-6 (C)
(RS Pts.—Texans 68, Bears 35)
CHICAGO vs. *INDIANAPOLIS
RS: Colts lead series, 22-19
PS: Colts lead series, 1-0
1953—Colts, 13-9 (B)
    Colts, 16-14 (C)
1954—Bears, 28-9 (C)
    Bears, 28-13 (B)
1955—Colts, 23-17 (B)
    Bears, 38-10 (C)
1956—Colts, 28-21 (B)
    Bears, 58-27 (C)

1957—Colts, 21-10 (B)
    Colts, 29-14 (C)
1958—Colts, 51-38 (B)
    Colts, 17-0 (C)
1959—Bears, 26-21 (B)
    Colts, 21-7 (C)
1960—Colts, 42-7 (B)
    Colts, 24-20 (C)
1961—Colts, 24-10 (C)
    Bears, 21-20 (B)
1962—Bears, 35-15 (C)
    Bears, 57-0 (B)
1963—Bears, 10-3 (C)
    Bears, 17-7 (B)
1964—Colts, 52-0 (B)
    Colts, 40-24 (C)
1965—Colts, 26-21 (C)
    Bears, 13-0 (B)
1966—Bears, 27-17 (C)
    Colts, 21-16 (B)
1967—Colts, 24-3 (C)
1968—Colts, 28-7 (B)
1969—Colts, 24-21 (C)
1970—Colts, 21-20 (B)
1975—Colts, 35-7 (C)
1983—Colts, 22-19 (B) OT
1985—Bears, 17-10 (C)
1988—Bears, 17-13 (I)
1991—Bears, 31-17 (I)
2000—Bears, 27-24 (C)
2004—Colts, 41-10 (C)
2006—**Colts, 29-17 (South Florida)
2008—Bears, 29-13 (I)
2012—Bears, 41-21 (C)
(RS Pts.—Colts 869, Bears 849)
(PS: Pts.—Colts 29, Bears 17)
*Franchise in Baltimore prior to 1984
**Super Bowl XLI
CHICAGO vs. JACKSONVILLE
RS: Bears lead series, 4-2
1995—Bears, 30-27 (J)
1998—Jaguars, 24-23 (C)
2001—Bears, 33-13 (C)
2004—Jaguars, 22-3 (J)
2008—Bears, 23-10 (C)
2012—Bears, 41-3 (J)
(RS Pts.—Bears 153, Jaguars 99)
CHICAGO vs. KANSAS CITY
RS: Bears lead series, 6-5
1973—Chiefs, 19-7 (KC)
1977—Bears, 28-27 (C)
1981—Bears, 16-13 (KC) OT
1987—Bears, 31-28 (C)
1990—Chiefs, 21-10 (C)
1993—Bears, 19-17 (KC)
1996—Chiefs, 14-10 (KC)
1999—Bears, 20-17 (C)
2003—Chiefs, 31-3 (KC)
2007—Bears, 20-10 (C)
2011—Chiefs, 10-3 (C)
(RS Pts.—Chiefs 207, Bears 167)
CHICAGO vs. MIAMI
RS: Dolphins lead series, 7-4
1971—Dolphins, 34-3 (M)
1975—Dolphins, 46-13 (C)
1979—Dolphins, 31-16 (M)
1985—Dolphins, 38-24 (M)
1988—Bears, 34-7 (C)
1991—Dolphins, 16-13 (C) OT
1994—Bears, 17-14 (M)
1997—Bears, 36-33 (M) OT
2002—Dolphins, 27-9 (M)
2006—Dolphins, 31-13 (C)

2010—Bears, 16-0 (M)
(RS Pts.—Dolphins 277, Bears 194)
CHICAGO vs. MINNESOTA
RS: Vikings lead series, 53-48-2
PS: Bears lead series, 1-0
1961—Vikings, 37-13 (M)
    Bears, 52-35 (C)
1962—Bears, 13-0 (M)
    Bears, 31-30 (C)
1963—Bears, 28-7 (M)
    Tie, 17-17 (C)
1964—Bears, 34-28 (M)
    Vikings, 41-14 (C)
1965—Bears, 45-37 (M)
    Vikings, 24-17 (C)
1966—Bears, 13-10 (M)
    Bears, 41-28 (C)
1967—Bears, 17-7 (M)
    Tie, 10-10 (C)
1968—Bears, 27-17 (M)
    Bears, 26-24 (C)
1969—Vikings, 31-0 (C)
    Vikings, 31-14 (M)
1970—Vikings, 24-0 (M)
    Vikings, 16-13 (C)
1971—Bears, 20-17 (M)
    Vikings, 27-10 (C)
1972—Bears, 13-10 (C)
    Vikings, 23-10 (M)
1973—Vikings, 22-13 (C)
    Vikings, 31-13 (M)
1974—Vikings, 11-7 (M)
    Vikings, 17-0 (C)
1975—Vikings, 28-3 (M)
    Vikings, 13-9 (C)
1976—Vikings, 20-19 (M)
    Bears, 14-13 (C)
1977—Vikings, 22-16 (M) OT
    Bears, 10-7 (C)
1978—Vikings, 24-20 (C)
    Vikings, 17-14 (M)
1979—Bears, 26-7 (C)
    Vikings, 30-27 (M)
1980—Vikings, 34-14 (C)
    Vikings, 13-7 (M)
1981—Vikings, 24-21 (M)
    Bears, 10-9 (C)
1982—Vikings, 35-7 (M)
1983—Vikings, 23-14 (C)
    Bears, 19-13 (M)
1984—Bears, 16-7 (C)
    Bears, 34-3 (M)
1985—Bears, 33-24 (M)
    Bears, 27-9 (C)
1986—Bears, 23-0 (C)
    Vikings, 23-7 (M)
1987—Bears, 27-7 (C)
    Bears, 30-24 (M)
1988—Vikings, 31-7 (C)
    Vikings, 28-27 (M)
1989—Bears, 38-7 (C)
    Vikings, 27-16 (M)
1990—Bears, 19-16 (C)
    Vikings, 41-13 (M)
1991—Bears, 10-6 (C)
    Bears, 34-17 (M)
1992—Vikings, 21-20 (M)
    Vikings, 38-10 (C)
1993—Vikings, 10-7 (M)
    Vikings, 19-12 (C)
1994—Vikings, 42-14 (C)
    Vikings, 33-27 (M) OT
    *Bears, 35-18 (M)

1995—Bears, 31-14 (C)
    Bears, 14-6 (M)
1996—Vikings, 20-14 (C)
    Bears, 15-13 (M)
1997—Vikings, 27-24 (C)
    Vikings, 29-22 (M)
1998—Vikings, 31-28 (C)
    Vikings, 48-22 (M)
1999—Bears, 24-22 (M)
    Vikings, 27-24 (C) OT
2000—Vikings, 30-27 (M)
    Vikings, 28-16 (C)
2001—Bears, 17-10 (C)
    Bears, 13-6 (M)
2002—Bears, 27-23 (C)
    Vikings, 25-7 (M)
2003—Vikings, 24-13 (M)
    Bears, 13-10 (C)
2004—Vikings, 27-22 (M)
    Bears, 24-14 (C)
2005—Bears, 28-3 (C)
    Vikings, 34-10 (M)
2006—Bears, 19-16 (M)
    Bears, 23-13 (C)
2007—Vikings, 34-31 (C)
    Vikings, 20-13 (M)
2008—Bears, 48-41 (C)
    Vikings, 34-14 (M)
2009—Vikings, 36-10 (M)
    Bears, 36-30 (C) OT
2010—Bears, 27-13 (C)
    Bears, 40-14 (M)
2011—Bears, 39-10 (C)
    Bears, 17-13 (M)
2012—Bears, 28-10 (C)
    Vikings, 21-14 (M)
RS Pts.—Vikings 2,153, Bears 2,006)
(PS Pts.—Bears 35, Vikings 18)
*NFC First-Round Playoff
CHICAGO vs. NEW ENGLAND
RS: Patriots lead series, 8-3
PS: Bears lead series, 1-0
1973—Patriots, 13-10 (C)
1979—Patriots, 27-7 (C)
1982—Bears, 26-13 (C)
1985—Bears, 20-7 (C)
    *Bears, 46-10 (New Orleans)
1988—Patriots, 30-7 (NE)
1994—Patriots, 13-3 (C)
1997—Patriots, 31-3 (NE)
2000—Bears, 24-17 (C)
2002—Patriots, 33-30 (C)
2006—Patriots, 17-13 (NE)
2010—Patriots, 36-7 (C)
(RS Pts.—Patriots 237, Bears 150)
(PS Pts.—Bears 46, Patriots 10)
*Super Bowl XX
CHICAGO vs. NEW ORLEANS
RS: Bears lead series, 13-12
PS: Bears lead series, 2-0
1968—Bears, 23-17 (NO)
1970—Bears, 24-3 (NO)
1971—Bears, 35-14 (C)
1973—Saints, 21-16 (NO)
1974—Bears, 24-10 (C)
1975—Bears, 42-17 (NO)
1977—Saints, 42-24 (C)
1980—Saints, 22-3 (C)
1982—Saints, 10-0 (C)
1983—Saints, 34-31 (NO) OT
1984—Bears, 20-7 (C)
1987—Saints, 19-17 (C)
1990—*Bears, 16-6 (C)

1991—Bears, 20-17 (NO)
1992—Saints, 28-6 (NO)
1994—Bears, 17-7 (C)
1996—Saints, 27-24 (NO)
1997—Saints, 20-17 (C)
1999—Bears, 14-10 (C)
2000—Saints, 31-10 (C)
2002—Saints, 29-23 (C)
2003—Saints, 20-13 (NO)
2005—Bears, 20-17 (Baton Rouge)
2006—**Bears, 39-14 (C)
2007—Bears, 33-25 (C)
2008—Bears, 27-24 (C) OT
2011—Saints, 30-13 (NO)
(RS Pts.—Bears 515, Saints 482)
(PS Pts.—Bears 55, Saints 20)
*NFC First-Round Playoff
**NFC Championship
CHICAGO vs. N.Y. GIANTS
RS: Bears lead series, 27-19-2
PS: Bears lead series, 5-3
1925—Bears, 19-7 (NY)
    Giants, 9-0 (C)
1926—Bears, 7-0 (C)
1927—Giants, 13-7 (NY)
1928—Bears, 13-0 (C)
1929—Giants, 26-14 (C)
    Giants, 34-0 (NY)
    Giants, 14-9 (C)
1930—Bears, 12-0 (C)
    Bears, 12-0 (NY)
1931—Bears, 6-0 (C)
    Bears, 12-6 (NY)
    Giants, 25-6 (C)
1932—Bears, 28-8 (NY)
    Bears, 6-0 (C)
1933—Bears, 14-10 (C)
    Giants, 3-0 (NY)
    *Bears, 23-21 (C)
1934—Bears, 27-7 (C)
    Bears, 10-9 (NY)
    *Giants, 30-13 (NY)
1935—Bears, 20-3 (NY)
    Giants, 3-0 (C)
1936—Bears, 25-7 (NY)
1937—Tie, 3-3 (NY)
1939—Giants, 16-13 (NY)
1940—Bears, 37-21 (NY)
1941—*Bears, 37-9 (C)
1942—Bears, 26-7 (NY)
1943—Bears, 56-7 (NY)
1946—Giants, 14-0 (NY)
    *Bears, 24-14 (NY)
1948—Bears, 35-14 (C)
1949—Giants, 35-28 (NY)
1956—Tie, 17-17 (NY)
    *Giants, 47-7 (NY)
1962—Giants, 26-24 (C)
1963—*Bears, 14-10 (C)
1965—Bears, 35-14 (NY)
1967—Bears, 34-7 (C)
1969—Giants, 28-24 (NY)
1970—Bears, 24-16 (NY)
1974—Bears, 16-13 (C)
1977—Bears, 12-9 (NY) OT
1985—**Bears, 21-0 (C)
1987—Bears, 34-19 (C)
1990—**Giants, 31-3 (NY)
1991—Bears, 20-17 (C)
1992—Giants, 27-14 (C)
1993—Giants, 26-20 (C)
1995—Bears, 27-24 (NY)
2000—Giants, 14-7 (C)

2004—Bears, 28-21 (NY)
2006—Bears, 38-20 (NY)
2007—Giants, 21-16 (C)
2010—Giants, 17-3 (NY)
(RS Pts.—Bears 826, Giants 649)
(PS Pts.—Giants 162, Bears 142)
*NFL Championship
**NFC Divisional Playoff
CHICAGO vs. N.Y. JETS
RS: Bears lead series, 7-3
1974—Jets, 23-21 (C)
1979—Bears, 23-13 (C)
1985—Bears, 19-6 (NY)
1991—Bears, 19-13 (C) OT
1994—Bears, 19-7 (NY)
1997—Jets, 23-15 (C)
2000—Jets, 17-10 (NY)
2002—Bears, 20-13 (C)
2006—Bears, 10-0 (NY)
2010—Bears, 38-34 (NY)
(RS Pts.—Bears 194, Jets 149)
CHICAGO vs. *OAKLAND
RS: Raiders lead series, 7-6
1972—Raiders, 28-21 (O)
1976—Raiders, 28-27 (C)
1978—Raiders, 25-19 (C) OT
1981—Bears, 23-6 (O)
1984—Bears, 17-6 (C)
1987—Bears, 6-3 (LA)
1990—Raiders, 24-10 (LA)
1993—Raiders, 16-14 (C)
1996—Bears, 19-17 (C)
1999—Raiders, 24-17 (O)
2003—Bears, 24-21 (C)
2007—Bears, 17-6 (O)
2011—Raiders, 25-20 (O)
(RS Pts.—Bears 234, Raiders 229)
*Franchise in Los Angeles from 1982-1994
CHICAGO vs. PHILADELPHIA
RS: Bears lead series, 28-9-1
PS: Eagles lead series, 2-1
1933—Tie, 3-3 (P)
1935—Bears, 39-0 (P)
1936—Bears, 17-0 (P)
    Bears, 28-7 (P)
1938—Bears, 28-6 (P)
1939—Bears, 27-14 (C)
1941—Bears, 49-14 (P)
1942—Bears, 45-14 (C)
1944—Bears, 28-7 (P)
1946—Bears, 21-14 (C)
1947—Bears, 40-7 (C)
1948—Eagles, 12-7 (P)
1949—Bears, 38-21 (C)
1955—Bears, 17-10 (C)
1961—Eagles, 16-14 (P)
1963—Bears, 16-7 (C)
1968—Bears, 29-16 (P)
1970—Bears, 20-16 (C)
1972—Bears, 21-12 (P)
1975—Bears, 15-13 (P)
1979—*Eagles, 27-17 (P)
1980—Eagles, 17-14 (P)
1983—Bears, 7-6 (P)
    Bears, 17-14 (C)
1986—Bears, 13-10 (C) OT
1987—Bears, 35-3 (P)
1988—**Bears, 20-12 (C)
1989—Bears, 27-13 (C)
1993—Bears, 17-6 (P)
1994—Eagles, 30-22 (P)
1995—Bears, 20-14 (C)
1999—Eagles, 20-16 (C)

2000—Eagles, 13-9 (P)
2001—**Eagles, 33-19 (C)
2002—Eagles, 19-13 (C)
2004—Eagles, 19-9 (C)
2007—Bears, 19-16 (P)
2008—Bears, 24-20 (C)
2009—Eagles, 24-20 (C)
2010—Bears, 31-26 (C)
2011—Bears, 30-24 (P)
(RS Pts.—Bears 845, Eagles 503)
(PS Pts.—Eagles 72, Bears 56)
NFC First-Round Playoff
**NFC Divisional Playoff*
CHICAGO vs. *PITTSBURGH
RS: Bears lead series, 17-7-1
1934—Bears, 28-0 (P)
1935—Bears, 23-7 (P)
1936—Bears, 27-9 (P)
     Bears, 26-7 (C)
1937—Bears, 7-0 (P)
1939—Bears, 32-0 (P)
1941—Bears, 34-7 (C)
1945—Bears, 28-7 (C)
1947—Bears, 49-7 (C)
1949—Bears, 30-21 (C)
1958—Steelers, 24-10 (P)
1959—Bears, 27-21 (C)
1963—Tie, 17-17 (P)
1967—Steelers, 41-13 (P)
1969—Bears, 38-7 (C)
1971—Bears, 17-15 (C)
1975—Steelers, 34-3 (P)
1980—Steelers, 38-3 (P)
1986—Bears, 13-10 (C) OT
1989—Bears, 20-0 (P)
1992—Bears, 30-6 (C)
1995—Steelers, 37-34 (C) OT
1998—Steelers, 17-12 (P)
2005—Steelers, 21-9 (P)
2009—Bears, 17-14 (C)
(RS Pts.—Bears 547, Steelers 367)
Steelers known as Pirates prior to 1940
CHICAGO vs. *ST. LOUIS
RS: Bears lead series, 51-34-3
PS: Series tied, 1-1
1937—Bears, 20-2 (Cle)
     Bears, 15-7 (C)
1938—Rams, 14-7 (C)
     Rams, 23-21 (Cle)
1939—Bears, 30-21 (Cle)
     Bears, 35-21 (C)
1940—Bears, 21-14 (Cle)
     Bears, 47-25 (C)
1941—Bears, 48-21 (Cle)
     Bears, 31-13 (C)
1942—Bears, 21-7 (Cle)
     Bears, 47-0 (C)
1944—Rams, 19-7 (Cle)
     Bears, 28-21 (C)
1945—Bears, 17-0 (Cle)
     Rams, 41-21 (C)
1946—Tie, 28-28 (C)
     Bears, 27-21 (LA)
1947—Bears, 41-21 (LA)
     Rams, 17-14 (C)
1948—Bears, 42-21 (C)
     Bears, 21-6 (LA)
1949—Rams, 31-16 (C)
     Rams, 27-24 (LA)
1950—Bears, 24-20 (LA)
     Bears, 24-14 (C)
     **Rams, 24-14 (LA)
1951—Rams, 42-17 (C)

1952—Rams, 31-7 (LA)
     Rams, 40-24 (C)
1953—Rams, 38-24 (LA)
     Bears, 24-21 (C)
1954—Rams, 42-38 (LA)
     Bears, 24-13 (C)
1955—Bears, 31-20 (LA)
     Bears, 24-3 (C)
1956—Bears, 35-24 (LA)
     Bears, 30-21 (C)
1957—Bears, 34-26 (C)
     Bears, 16-10 (LA)
1958—Bears, 31-10 (C)
     Rams, 41-35 (LA)
1959—Rams, 28-21 (C)
     Bears, 26-21 (LA)
1960—Bears, 34-27 (C)
     Tie, 24-24 (LA)
1961—Bears, 21-17 (LA)
     Bears, 28-24 (C)
1962—Bears, 27-23 (LA)
     Bears, 30-14 (C)
1963—Bears, 52-14 (LA)
     Bears, 6-0 (C)
1964—Bears, 38-17 (C)
     Bears, 34-24 (LA)
1965—Rams, 30-28 (LA)
     Bears, 31-6 (C)
1966—Rams, 31-17 (LA)
     Bears, 17-10 (C)
1967—Rams, 28-17 (C)
1968—Bears, 17-16 (LA)
1969—Rams, 9-7 (C)
1971—Rams, 17-3 (LA)
1972—Tie, 13-13 (C)
1973—Rams, 26-0 (C)
1975—Rams, 38-10 (LA)
1976—Rams, 20-12 (LA)
1977—Bears, 24-23 (C)
1979—Bears, 27-23 (C)
1981—Rams, 24-7 (C)
1982—Bears, 34-26 (LA)
1983—Rams, 21-14 (LA)
1984—Rams, 29-13 (LA)
1985—***Bears, 24-0 (C)
1986—Bears, 20-17 (C)
1988—Rams, 23-3 (LA)
1989—Bears, 20-10 (C)
1990—Bears, 38-9 (C)
1993—Rams, 20-6 (LA)
1994—Bears, 27-13 (C)
1995—Rams, 34-28 (StL)
1996—Bears, 35-9 (C)
1997—Bears, 13-10 (StL)
1998—Rams, 20-12 (C)
1999—Rams, 34-12 (StL)
2002—Rams, 21-16 (StL)
2003—Rams, 23-21 (C)
2006—Bears, 42-27 (StL)
2008—Bears, 27-3 (StL)
2009—Bears, 17-9 (C)
2012—Bears, 23-6 (C)
(RS Pts.—Bears 2,043, Rams 1,768)
(PS Pts.—Bears 38, Rams 24)
Franchise in Los Angeles prior to 1995 and in Cleveland prior to 1946
**Conference Playoff*
***NFC Championship*
CHICAGO vs. SAN DIEGO
RS: Bears lead series, 6-5
1970—Chargers, 20-7 (C)
1974—Chargers, 28-21 (SD)
1978—Chargers, 40-7 (SD)

1981—Bears, 20-17 (C) OT
1984—Chargers, 20-7 (SD)
1993—Bears, 16-13 (SD)
1996—Bears, 27-14 (C)
1999—Bears, 23-20 (SD) OT
2003—Bears, 20-7 (C)
2007—Chargers, 14-3 (SD)
2011—Bears, 31-20 (C)
(RS Pts.—Chargers 213, Bears 182)
CHICAGO vs. SAN FRANCISCO
RS: Series tied, 29-29-1
PS: 49ers lead series, 3-0
1950—Bears, 32-20 (SF)
     Bears, 17-0 (C)
1951—Bears, 13-7 (C)
1952—49ers, 40-16 (C)
     Bears, 20-17 (SF)
1953—49ers, 35-28 (C)
     49ers, 24-14 (SF)
1954—49ers, 31-24 (C)
     Bears, 31-27 (SF)
1955—49ers, 20-19 (C)
     Bears, 34-23 (SF)
1956—Bears, 31-7 (C)
     Bears, 38-21 (SF)
1957—49ers, 21-17 (C)
     49ers, 21-17 (SF)
1958—Bears, 28-6 (C)
     Bears, 27-14 (SF)
1959—49ers, 20-17 (SF)
     Bears, 14-3 (C)
1960—Bears, 27-10 (C)
     49ers, 25-7 (SF)
1961—Bears, 31-0 (C)
     49ers, 41-31 (SF)
1962—Bears, 30-14 (C)
     49ers, 34-27 (C)
1963—49ers, 20-14 (SF)
     Bears, 27-7 (C)
1964—49ers, 31-21 (SF)
     Bears, 23-21 (C)
1965—49ers, 52-24 (SF)
     Bears, 61-20 (C)
1966—Tie, 30-30 (C)
     49ers, 41-14 (SF)
1967—Bears, 28-14 (C)
1968—Bears, 27-19 (C)
1969—49ers, 42-21 (SF)
1970—49ers, 37-16 (C)
1971—49ers, 13-0 (SF)
1972—49ers, 34-21 (C)
1974—49ers, 34-0 (C)
1975—49ers, 31-3 (SF)
1976—Bears, 19-12 (SF)
1978—Bears, 16-13 (SF)
1979—Bears, 28-27 (SF)
1981—49ers, 28-17 (SF)
1983—Bears, 13-3 (C)
1984—*49ers, 23-0 (SF)
1985—Bears, 26-10 (C)
1987—49ers, 41-0 (SF)
1988—Bears, 10-9 (C)
     *49ers, 28-3 (C)
1989—49ers, 26-0 (C)
1991—Bears, 52-14 (SF)
1994—**49ers, 44-15 (SF)
2000—49ers, 17-0 (SF)
2001—Bears, 37-31 (C) OT
2003—49ers, 49-7 (SF)
2004—Bears, 23-13 (C)
2005—Bears, 17-9 (C)
2006—Bears, 41-10 (C)
2009—49ers, 10-6 (SF)

2012—49ers, 32-7 (SF)
(RS Pts.—49ers 1,319, Bears 1,201)
(PS Pts.—49ers 95, Bears 18)
*NFC Championship
**NFC Divisional Playoff
CHICAGO vs. SEATTLE
RS: Seahawks lead series, 10-4
PS: Bears lead series, 2-0
1976—Bears, 34-7 (S)
1978—Seahawks, 31-29 (C)
1982—Seahawks, 20-14 (S)
1984—Seahawks, 38-9 (S)
1987—Seahawks, 34-21 (C)
1990—Bears, 17-0 (C)
1999—Seahawks, 14-13 (C)
2003—Seahawks, 24-17 (S)
2006—Bears, 37-6 (C)
　　　*Bears, 27-24 (C) OT
2007—Seahawks, 30-23 (S)
2009—Bears, 25-19 (S)
2010—Seahawks, 23-20 (C)
　　　*Bears, 35-24 (C)
2011—Seahawks, 38-14 (C)
2012—Seahawks, 23-17 (C) OT
(RS Pts.—Seahawks 307, Bears 290)
(PS Pts.—Bears 62, Seahawks 48)
*NFC Divisional Playoff
CHICAGO vs. TAMPA BAY
RS: Bears lead series, 36-18
1977—Bears, 10-0 (TB)
1978—Buccaneers, 33-19 (TB)
　　　Bears, 14-3 (C)
1979—Buccaneers, 17-13 (C)
　　　Bears, 14-0 (C)
1980—Bears, 23-0 (C)
　　　Bears, 14-13 (TB)
1981—Bears, 28-17 (C)
　　　Buccaneers, 20-10 (TB)
1982—Buccaneers, 26-23 (TB) OT
1983—Bears, 17-10 (C)
　　　Bears, 27-0 (TB)
1984—Bears, 34-14 (C)
　　　Bears, 44-9 (TB)
1985—Bears, 38-28 (C)
　　　Bears, 27-19 (TB)
1986—Bears, 23-3 (TB)
　　　Bears, 48-14 (C)
1987—Bears, 20-3 (C)
　　　Bears, 27-26 (TB)
1988—Bears, 28-10 (C)
　　　Bears, 27-15 (TB)
1989—Buccaneers, 42-35 (TB)
　　　Buccaneers, 32-31 (C)
1990—Bears, 26-6 (TB)
　　　Bears, 27-14 (C)
1991—Bears, 21-20 (TB)
　　　Bears, 27-0 (C)
1992—Bears, 31-14 (C)
　　　Buccaneers, 20-10 (TB)
1993—Bears, 47-17 (C)
　　　Buccaneers, 13-10 (TB)
1994—Bears, 21-9 (C)
　　　Bears, 20-6 (TB)
1995—Bears, 25-6 (TB)
　　　Bears, 31-10 (C)
1996—Bears, 13-10 (C)
　　　Buccaneers, 34-19 (TB)
1997—Bears, 13-7 (C)
　　　Buccaneers, 31-15 (TB)
1998—Buccaneers, 27-15 (TB)
　　　Buccaneers, 31-17 (C)
1999—Buccaneers, 6-3 (TB)
　　　Buccaneers, 20-6 (C)

2000—Buccaneers, 41-0 (TB)
　　　Bears, 13-10 (C)
2001—Bears, 27-24 (TB)
　　　Bears, 27-3 (C)
2002—Buccaneers, 15-0 (C)
2004—Buccaneers, 19-7 (TB)
2005—Bears, 13-10 (TB)
2006—Bears, 34-31 (C) OT
2008—Buccaneers, 27-24 (C) OT
2011—Bears, 24-18 (London)
(RS Pts.—Bears 1,167, Buccaneers 853)
CHICAGO vs. *TENNESSEE
RS: Bears lead series, 6-5
1973—Bears, 35-14 (C)
1977—Oilers, 47-0 (H)
1980—Oilers, 10-6 (C)
1986—Bears, 20-7 (H)
1989—Oilers, 33-28 (C)
1992—Oilers, 24-7 (H)
1995—Bears, 35-32 (C)
1998—Bears, 23-20 (T)
2004—Bears, 19-17 (T) OT
2008—Titans, 21-14 (C)
2012—Bears, 51-20 (T)
(RS Pts.—Titans 245, Bears 238)
*Franchise in Houston prior to 1997;
known as Oilers prior to 1999
CHICAGO vs. *WASHINGTON
RS: Bears lead series, 20-19-1
PS: Redskins lead series, 4-3
1932—Tie, 7-7 (B)
1933—Bears, 7-0 (C)
　　　Redskins, 10-0 (B)
1934—Bears, 21-0 (B)
1935—Bears, 30-14 (B)
1936—Bears, 26-0 (B)
1937—**Redskins, 28-21 (C)
1938—Bears, 31-7 (C)
1940—Redskins, 7-3 (W)
　　　**Bears, 73-0 (W)
1941—Bears, 35-21 (C)
1942—**Redskins, 14-6 (W)
1943—Redskins, 21-7 (W)
　　　**Bears, 41-21 (C)
1945—Redskins, 28-21 (W)
1946—Bears, 24-20 (C)
1947—Bears, 56-20 (W)
1948—Bears, 48-13 (C)
1949—Bears, 31-21 (W)
1951—Bears, 27-0 (W)
1953—Bears, 27-24 (W)
1957—Redskins, 14-3 (C)
1964—Redskins, 27-20 (W)
1968—Redskins, 38-28 (C)
1971—Bears, 16-15 (C)
1974—Redskins, 42-0 (W)
1976—Bears, 33-7 (C)
1978—Bears, 14-10 (W)
1980—Bears, 35-21 (W)
1981—Redskins, 24-7 (C)
1984—***Bears, 23-19 (W)
1985—Bears, 45-10 (C)
1986—***Redskins, 27-13 (C)
1987—***Redskins, 21-17 (C)
1988—Bears, 34-14 (W)
1989—Redskins, 38-14 (W)
1990—Redskins, 10-9 (W)
1991—Bears, 20-7 (C)
1996—Redskins, 10-3 (W)
1997—Redskins, 31-8 (C)
1999—Redskins, 48-22 (W)
2001—Bears, 20-15 (W)
2003—Bears, 27-24 (C)

2004—Redskins, 13-10 (C)
2005—Redskins, 9-7 (W)
2007—Redskins, 24-16 (W)
2010—Redskins, 17-14 (C)
(RS Pts.—Bears 793, Redskins 694)
(PS Pts.—Bears 194, Redskins 130)
*Franchise in Boston prior to 1937 and
known as Braves prior to 1933
**NFL Championship
***NFC Divisional Playoff

CINCINNATI vs. ARIZONA
RS: Bengals lead series, 6-4;
See Arizona vs. Cincinnati
CINCINNATI vs. ATLANTA
RS: Bengals lead series, 7-5;
See Atlanta vs. Cincinnati
CINCINNATI vs. BALTIMORE
RS: Ravens lead series, 19-15;
See Baltimore vs. Cincinnati
CINCINNATI vs. BUFFALO
RS: Bills lead series, 15-10
PS: Bengals lead series, 2-0;
See Buffalo vs. Cincinnati
CINCINNATI vs. CAROLINA
RS: Series tied, 2-2;
See Carolina vs. Cincinnati
CINCINNATI vs. CHICAGO
RS: Bengals lead series, 6-3;
See Chicago vs. Cincinnati
CINCINNATI vs. CLEVELAND
RS: Bengals lead series, 42-37
1970—Browns, 30-27 (Cle)
　　　Bengals, 14-10 (Cin)
1971—Browns, 27-24 (Cin)
　　　Browns, 31-27 (Cle)
1972—Browns, 27-6 (Cle)
　　　Browns, 27-24 (Cin)
1973—Browns, 17-10 (Cle)
　　　Bengals, 34-17 (Cin)
1974—Bengals, 33-7 (Cin)
　　　Bengals, 34-24 (Cle)
1975—Bengals, 24-17 (Cin)
　　　Browns, 35-23 (Cle)
1976—Bengals, 45-24 (Cle)
　　　Bengals, 21-6 (Cin)
1977—Browns, 13-3 (Cin)
　　　Bengals, 10-7 (Cle)
1978—Browns, 13-10 (Cle) OT
　　　Bengals, 48-16 (Cin)
1979—Bengals, 28-27 (Cle)
　　　Bengals, 16-12 (Cin)
1980—Browns, 31-7 (Cle)
　　　Browns, 27-24 (Cin)
1981—Browns, 20-17 (Cin)
　　　Bengals, 41-21 (Cle)
1982—Bengals, 23-10 (Cin)
1983—Browns, 17-7 (Cle)
　　　Bengals, 28-21 (Cin)
1984—Bengals, 12-9 (Cin)
　　　Bengals, 20-17 (Cle) OT
1985—Bengals, 27-10 (Cin)
　　　Browns, 24-6 (Cle)
1986—Bengals, 30-13 (Cle)
　　　Browns, 34-3 (Cin)
1987—Browns, 34-0 (Cle)
　　　Browns, 38-24 (Cin)
1988—Bengals, 24-17 (Cin)
　　　Browns, 23-16 (Cle)
1989—Bengals, 21-14 (Cle)
　　　Bengals, 21-0 (Cin)
1990—Bengals, 34-13 (Cle)
　　　Bengals, 21-14 (Cin)

1991—Browns, 14-13 (Cle)
    Bengals, 23-21 (Cin)
1992—Bengals, 30-10 (Cin)
    Browns, 37-21 (Cle)
1993—Browns, 27-14 (Cle)
    Browns, 28-17 (Cin)
1994—Browns, 28-20 (Cin)
    Browns, 37-13 (Cle)
1995—Browns, 29-26 (Cin) OT
    Browns, 26-10 (Cle)
1999—Bengals, 18-17 (Cle)
    Bengals, 44-28 (Cin)
2000—Browns, 24-7 (Cin)
    Bengals, 12-3 (Cle)
2001—Bengals, 24-14 (Cin)
    Browns, 18-0 (Cle)
2002—Browns, 20-7 (Cle)
    Browns, 27-20 (Cin)
2003—Bengals, 21-14 (Cle)
    Browns, 22-14 (Cin)
2004—Browns, 34-17 (Cle)
    Bengals, 58-48 (Cin)
2005—Bengals, 27-13 (Cle)
    Bengals, 23-20 (Cin)
2006—Bengals, 34-17 (Cin)
    Bengals, 30-0 (Cle)
2007—Browns, 51-45 (Cle)
    Bengals, 19-14 (Cin)
2008—Browns, 20-12 (Cin)
    Bengals, 14-0 (Cle)
2009—Bengals, 23-20 (Cle) OT
    Bengals, 16-7 (Cin)
2010—Browns, 23-20 (Cle)
    Bengals, 19-17 (Cin)
2011—Bengals, 27-17 (Cle)
    Bengals, 23-20 (Cin)
2012—Bengals, 34-27 (Cin)
    Browns, 34-24 (Cle)
(RS Pts.—Bengals 1,685, Browns 1,621)
CINCINNATI vs. DALLAS
RS: Cowboys lead series, 7-4
1973—Cowboys, 38-10 (D)
1979—Cowboys, 38-13 (D)
1985—Bengals, 50-24 (C)
1988—Bengals, 38-24 (D)
1991—Cowboys, 35-23 (D)
1994—Cowboys, 23-20 (C)
1997—Bengals, 31-24 (C)
2000—Cowboys, 23-6 (D)
2004—Bengals, 26-3 (C)
2008—Cowboys, 31-22 (D)
2012—Cowboys, 20-19 (C)
(RS Pts.—Cowboys 283, Bengals 258)
CINCINNATI vs. DENVER
RS: Broncos lead series, 19-8
1968—Bengals, 24-10 (C)
    Broncos, 10-7 (D)
1969—Broncos, 30-23 (C)
    Broncos, 27-16 (D)
1971—Bengals, 24-10 (C)
1972—Bengals, 21-10 (C)
1973—Broncos, 28-10 (D)
1975—Bengals, 17-16 (D)
1976—Bengals, 17-7 (C)
1977—Broncos, 24-13 (C)
1979—Broncos, 10-0 (D)
1981—Bengals, 38-21 (C)
1983—Broncos, 24-17 (D)
1984—Broncos, 20-17 (D)
1986—Broncos, 34-28 (D)
1991—Broncos, 45-14 (D)
1994—Broncos, 15-13 (D)
1996—Broncos, 14-10 (C)

1997—Broncos, 38-20 (D)
1998—Broncos, 33-26 (C)
2000—Bengals, 31-21 (C)
2003—Broncos, 30-10 (C)
2004—Bengals, 23-10 (C)
2006—Broncos, 24-23 (D)
2009—Broncos, 12-7 (C)
2011—Broncos, 24-22 (D)
2012—Broncos, 31-23 (C)
(RS Pts.—Broncos 578, Bengals 494)
CINCINNATI vs. DETROIT
RS: Bengals lead series, 7-3
1970—Lions, 38-3 (D)
1974—Lions, 23-19 (C)
1983—Bengals, 17-9 (C)
1986—Bengals, 24-17 (D)
1989—Bengals, 42-7 (C)
1992—Lions, 19-13 (C)
1998—Bengals, 34-28 (D) OT
2001—Bengals, 31-27 (D)
2005—Bengals, 41-17 (D)
2009—Bengals, 23-13 (C)
(RS Pts.—Bengals 247, Lions 198)
CINCINNATI vs. GREEN BAY
RS: Bengals lead series, 6-5
1971—Packers, 20-17 (GB)
1976—Bengals, 28-7 (C)
1977—Bengals, 17-7 (Mil)
1980—Packers, 14-9 (GB)
1983—Bengals, 34-14 (C)
1986—Bengals, 34-28 (Mil)
1992—Packers, 24-23 (GB)
1995—Packers, 24-10 (GB)
1998—Packers, 13-6 (C)
2005—Bengals, 21-14 (C)
2009—Bengals, 31-24 (GB)
(RS Pts.—Bengals 230, Packers 189)
CINCINNATI vs. HOUSTON
RS: Series tied, 3-3
PS: Texans lead series, 2-0
2002—Bengals, 38-3 (H)
2003—Bengals, 34-27 (C)
2005—Bengals, 16-10 (C)
2008—Texans, 35-6 (H)
2009—Texans, 28-17 (C)
2011—Texans, 20-19 (C)
    *Texans, 31-10 (H)
2012—*Texans, 19-13 (H)
(RS Pts.—Bengals 130, Texans 123)
(PS Pts.—Texans 50, Bengals 23)
*AFC First-Round Playoff
CINCINNATI vs. *INDIANAPOLIS
RS: Colts lead series, 16-9
PS: Colts lead series, 1-0
1970—**Colts, 17-0 (B)
1972—Colts, 20-19 (C)
1974—Bengals, 24-14 (B)
1976—Colts, 28-27 (B)
1979—Colts, 38-28 (B)
1980—Bengals, 34-33 (C)
1981—Bengals, 41-19 (B)
1982—Bengals, 20-17 (B)
1983—Colts, 34-31 (C)
1987—Bengals, 23-21 (I)
1989—Colts, 23-12 (C)
1990—Colts, 34-20 (C)
1992—Colts, 21-17 (C)
1993—Colts, 9-6 (C)
1994—Colts, 17-13 (C)
1995—Bengals, 24-21 (I) OT
1996—Bengals, 31-24 (C)
1997—Bengals, 28-13 (I)
1998—Colts, 39-26 (I)

1999—Colts, 31-10 (I)
2002—Colts, 28-21 (I)
2005—Colts, 45-37 (C)
2006—Colts, 34-16 (I)
2008—Colts, 35-3 (I)
2010—Colts, 23-17 (I)
2011—Bengals, 27-17 (C)
(RS Pts.—Colts 638, Bengals 555)
(PS Pts.—Colts 17, Bengals 0)
*Franchise in Baltimore prior to 1984
**AFC Divisional Playoff
CINCINNATI vs. JACKSONVILLE
RS: Jaguars lead series, 11-8
1995—Bengals, 24-17 (C)
    Bengals, 17-13 (J)
1996—Bengals, 28-21 (C)
    Jaguars, 30-27 (J)
1997—Jaguars, 21-13 (J)
    Bengals, 31-26 (C)
1998—Jaguars, 24-11 (J)
    Jaguars, 34-17 (C)
1999—Jaguars, 41-10 (C)
    Jaguars, 24-7 (J)
2000—Jaguars, 13-0 (J)
    Bengals, 17-14 (C)
2001—Jaguars, 30-13 (J)
    Jaguars, 14-10 (C)
2002—Jaguars, 29-15 (C)
2005—Jaguars, 23-20 (J)
2008—Bengals, 21-19 (C)
2011—Bengals, 30-20 (J)
2012—Bengals, 27-10 (J)
(RS Pts.—Jaguars 423, Bengals 338)
CINCINNATI vs. KANSAS CITY
RS: Bengals lead series, 14-13
1968—Chiefs, 13-3 (KC)
    Chiefs, 16-9 (C)
1969—Bengals, 24-19 (C)
    Chiefs, 42-22 (KC)
1970—Chiefs, 27-19 (C)
1972—Bengals, 23-16 (KC)
1973—Bengals, 14-6 (C)
1974—Bengals, 33-6 (C)
1976—Bengals, 27-24 (KC)
1977—Bengals, 27-7 (KC)
1978—Chiefs, 24-23 (C)
1979—Chiefs, 10-7 (C)
1980—Bengals, 20-6 (KC)
1983—Chiefs, 20-15 (KC)
1984—Chiefs, 27-22 (C)
1986—Chiefs, 24-14 (KC)
1987—Bengals, 30-27 (C) OT
1988—Chiefs, 31-28 (KC)
1989—Bengals, 21-17 (KC)
1993—Chiefs, 17-15 (KC)
2003—Bengals, 24-19 (C)
2005—Chiefs, 37-3 (KC)
2006—Bengals, 23-10 (KC)
2007—Chiefs, 27-20 (KC)
2008—Bengals, 16-6 (C)
2009—Bengals, 17-10 (C)
2012—Bengals, 28-6 (KC)
(RS Pts.—Bengals 527, Chiefs 494)
CINCINNATI vs. MIAMI
RS: Dolphins lead series, 14-5
PS: Dolphins lead series, 1-0
1968—Dolphins, 24-22 (C)
    Bengals, 38-21 (M)
1969—Bengals, 27-21 (C)
1971—Dolphins, 23-13 (C)
1973—*Dolphins, 34-16 (M)
1974—Dolphins, 24-3 (M)
1977—Bengals, 23-17 (C)

1978—Dolphins, 21-0 (M)
1980—Dolphins, 17-16 (M)
1983—Dolphins, 38-14 (M)
1987—Dolphins, 20-14 (C)
1989—Dolphins, 20-13 (C)
1991—Dolphins, 37-13 (M)
1994—Dolphins, 23-7 (C)
1995—Dolphins, 26-23 (C)
2000—Bengals, 31-16 (C)
2004—Bengals, 16-13 (C)
2007—Bengals, 38-25 (M)
2010—Dolphins, 22-14 (C)
2012—Dolphins, 17-13 (C)
(RS Pts.—Dolphins 440, Bengals 323)
(PS Pts.—Dolphins 34, Bengals 16)
*AFC Divisional Playoff
CINCINNATI vs. MINNESOTA
RS: Vikings lead series, 6-5
1973—Bengals, 27-0 (C)
1977—Vikings, 42-10 (M)
1980—Bengals, 14-0 (C)
1983—Vikings, 20-14 (M)
1986—Bengals, 24-20 (C)
1989—Vikings, 29-21 (M)
1992—Vikings, 42-7 (C)
1995—Bengals, 27-24 (C)
1998—Vikings, 24-3 (M)
2005—Bengals, 37-8 (C)
2009—Vikings, 30-10 (M)
(RS Pts.—Vikings 239, Bengals 194)
CINCINNATI vs. *NEW ENGLAND
RS: Patriots lead series, 14-8
1968—Patriots, 33-14 (B)
1969—Patriots, 25-14 (C)
1970—Bengals, 45-7 (C)
1972—Bengals, 31-7 (NE)
1975—Bengals, 27-10 (C)
1978—Patriots, 10-3 (C)
1979—Patriots, 20-14 (C)
1984—Patriots, 20-14 (NE)
1985—Patriots, 34-23 (NE)
1986—Bengals, 31-7 (NE)
1988—Patriots, 27-21 (NE)
1990—Bengals, 41-7 (C)
1991—Bengals, 29-7 (C)
1992—Bengals, 20-10 (C)
1993—Patriots, 7-2 (NE)
1994—Patriots, 31-28 (C)
2000—Patriots, 16-13 (NE)
2001—Bengals, 23-17 (C)
2004—Patriots, 35-28 (NE)
2006—Patriots, 38-13 (C)
2007—Patriots, 34-13 (C)
2010—Patriots, 38-24 (NE)
(RS Pts.—Bengals 471, Patriots 440)
*Franchise in Boston prior to 1971
CINCINNATI vs. NEW ORLEANS
RS: Series tied, 6-6
1970—Bengals, 26-6 (C)
1975—Bengals, 21-0 (NO)
1978—Saints, 20-18 (C)
1981—Saints, 17-7 (NO)
1984—Bengals, 24-21 (NO)
1987—Saints, 41-24 (C)
1990—Saints, 21-7 (C)
1993—Saints, 20-13 (NO)
1996—Bengals, 30-15 (C)
2002—Bengals, 20-13 (C)
2006—Bengals, 31-16 (NO)
2010—Saints, 34-30 (C)
(RS Pts.—Bengals 251, Saints 224)
CINCINNATI vs. N.Y. GIANTS
RS: Bengals lead series, 6-3

1972—Bengals, 13-10 (C)
1977—Bengals, 30-13 (C)
1985—Bengals, 35-30 (C)
1991—Bengals, 27-24 (C)
1994—Giants, 27-20 (NY)
1997—Giants, 29-27 (NY)
2004—Bengals, 23-22 (C)
2008—Giants, 26-23 (NY) OT
2012—Bengals, 31-13 (C)
(RS Pts.—Bengals 229, Giants 194)
CINCINNATI vs. N.Y. JETS
RS: Jets lead series, 15-7
PS: Jets lead series, 2-0
1968—Jets, 27-14 (NY)
1969—Jets, 21-7 (C)
         Jets, 40-7 (NY)
1971—Jets, 35-21 (NY)
1973—Bengals, 20-14 (C)
1976—Bengals, 42-3 (NY)
1981—Bengals, 31-30 (NY)
1982—*Jets, 44-17 (C)
1984—Jets, 43-23 (NY)
1985—Jets, 29-20 (C)
1986—Bengals, 52-21 (C)
1987—Bengals, 27-20 (NY)
1988—Bengals, 36-19 (C)
1990—Bengals, 25-20 (C)
1992—Jets, 17-14 (NY)
1993—Jets, 17-12 (NY)
1997—Jets, 31-14 (C)
2001—Jets, 15-14 (NY)
2004—Jets, 31-24 (NY)
2007—Bengals, 38-31 (NY)
2008—Jets, 26-14 (NY)
2009—Jets, 37-0 (NY)
         *Jets, 24-14 (C)
2010—Jets, 26-10 (NY)
(RS Pts.—Jets 560, Bengals 458)
(PS Pts.—Jets 68, Bengals 31)
*AFC First-Round Playoff
CINCINNATI vs. *OAKLAND
RS: Raiders lead series, 18-9
PS: Raiders lead series, 2-0
1968—Raiders, 31-10 (O)
         Raiders, 34-0 (C)
1969—Bengals, 31-17 (C)
         Raiders, 37-17 (O)
1970—Bengals, 31-21 (C)
1971—Raiders, 31-27 (O)
1972—Raiders, 20-14 (C)
1974—Raiders, 30-27 (O)
1975—Bengals, 14-10 (C)
         **Raiders, 31-28 (O)
1976—Raiders, 35-20 (O)
1978—Raiders, 34-21 (C)
1980—Raiders, 28-17 (O)
1982—Bengals, 31-17 (C)
1983—Raiders, 20-10 (C)
1985—Bengals, 13-6 (LA)
1988—Bengals, 45-21 (LA)
1989—Raiders, 28-7 (LA)
1990—Raiders, 24-7 (LA)
         **Raiders, 20-10 (LA)
1991—Bengals, 38-14 (C)
1992—Bengals, 24-21 (C) OT
1993—Bengals, 16-10 (C)
1995—Raiders, 20-17 (C)
1998—Raiders, 27-10 (C)
2003—Bengals, 23-20 (O)
2006—Bengals, 27-10 (C)
2009—Raiders, 20-17 (O)
2012—Bengals, 34-10 (C)
(RS Pts.—Raiders 630, Bengals 514)

(PS Pts.—Raiders 51, Bengals 38)
*Franchise in Los Angeles from 1982-1994
**AFC Divisional Playoff
CINCINNATI vs. PHILADELPHIA
RS: Bengals lead series, 8-3-1
1971—Bengals, 37-14 (C)
1975—Bengals, 31-0 (P)
1979—Bengals, 37-13 (C)
1982—Bengals, 18-14 (P)
1988—Bengals, 28-24 (P)
1991—Eagles, 17-10 (P)
1994—Bengals, 33-30 (C)
1997—Eagles, 44-42 (P)
2000—Eagles, 16-7 (P)
2004—Bengals, 38-10 (P)
2008—Tie, 13-13 (C) OT
2012—Bengals, 34-13 (P)
(RS Pts.—Bengals 328, Eagles 208)
CINCINNATI vs. PITTSBURGH
RS: Steelers lead series, 52-33
PS: Steelers lead series, 1-0
1970—Steelers, 21-10 (P)
         Bengals, 34-7 (C)
1971—Steelers, 21-10 (P)
         Steelers, 21-13 (C)
1972—Bengals, 15-10 (C)
         Steelers, 40-17 (P)
1973—Bengals, 19-7 (C)
         Steelers, 20-13 (P)
1974—Bengals, 17-10 (C)
         Steelers, 27-3 (P)
1975—Steelers, 30-24 (C)
         Steelers, 35-14 (P)
1976—Steelers, 23-6 (C)
         Steelers, 7-3 (C)
1977—Steelers, 20-14 (P)
         Bengals, 17-10 (C)
1978—Steelers, 28-3 (C)
         Steelers, 7-6 (P)
1979—Bengals, 34-10 (C)
         Steelers, 37-17 (P)
1980—Bengals, 30-28 (C)
         Bengals, 17-16 (P)
1981—Bengals, 34-7 (C)
         Bengals, 17-10 (P)
1982—Steelers, 26-20 (P) OT
1983—Steelers, 24-14 (C)
         Bengals, 23-10 (P)
1984—Steelers, 38-17 (P)
         Bengals, 22-20 (C)
1985—Bengals, 37-24 (P)
         Bengals, 26-21 (C)
1986—Bengals, 24-22 (C)
         Steelers, 30-9 (P)
1987—Steelers, 23-20 (P)
         Steelers, 30-16 (C)
1988—Bengals, 17-12 (P)
         Bengals, 42-7 (C)
1989—Bengals, 41-10 (C)
         Bengals, 26-16 (P)
1990—Bengals, 27-3 (C)
         Bengals, 16-12 (P)
1991—Steelers, 33-27 (C) OT
         Steelers, 17-10 (P)
1992—Steelers, 20-0 (C)
         Steelers, 21-9 (C)
1993—Steelers, 34-7 (C)
         Steelers, 24-16 (C)
1994—Steelers, 14-10 (P)
         Steelers, 38-15 (C)
1995—Bengals, 27-9 (P)
         Steelers, 49-31 (C)

1996—Steelers, 20-10 (P)
    Bengals, 34-24 (C)
1997—Steelers, 26-10 (C)
    Steelers, 20-3 (P)
1998—Bengals, 25-20 (C)
    Bengals, 25-24 (P)
1999—Steelers, 17-3 (C)
    Bengals, 27-20 (P)
2000—Steelers, 15-0 (P)
    Steelers, 48-28 (C)
2001—Steelers, 16-7 (P)
    Bengals, 26-23 (C) OT
2002—Steelers, 34-7 (C)
    Steelers, 29-21 (P)
2003—Steelers, 17-10 (C)
    Bengals, 24-20 (P)
2004—Steelers, 28-17 (P)
    Steelers, 19-14 (C)
2005—Steelers, 27-13 (C)
    Bengals, 38-31 (P)
    *Steelers, 31-17 (C)
2006—Bengals, 28-20 (P)
    Steelers, 23-17 (C) OT
2007—Steelers, 24-13 (C)
    Steelers, 24-10 (P)
2008—Steelers, 38-10 (C)
    Steelers, 27-10 (P)
2009—Bengals, 23-20 (C)
    Bengals, 18-12 (P)
2010—Steelers, 27-21 (C)
    Steelers, 23-7 (P)
2011—Steelers, 24-17 (C)
    Steelers, 35-7 (P)
2012—Steelers, 24-17 (C)
    Bengals, 13-10 (P)
(RS Pts.—Steelers 1,848, Bengals 1,489)
(PS Pts.—Steelers 31, Bengals 17)
*AFC First-Round Playoff
CINCINNATI vs. *ST. LOUIS
RS: Bengals lead series, 7-5
1972—Rams, 15-12 (LA)
1976—Bengals, 20-12 (C)
1978—Bengals, 20-19 (LA)
1981—Bengals, 24-10 (C)
1984—Rams, 24-14 (C)
1990—Bengals, 34-31 (LA) OT
1993—Bengals, 15-3 (C)
1996—Rams, 26-16 (StL)
1999—Bengals, 38-10 (C)
2003—Rams, 27-10 (StL)
2007—Bengals, 19-10 (C)
2011—Bengals, 20-13 (StL)
(RS Pts.—Rams 228, Bengals 214)
*Franchise in Los Angeles prior to 1995
CINCINNATI vs. SAN DIEGO
RS: Chargers lead series, 19-12
PS: Bengals lead series, 1-0
1968—Chargers, 29-13 (SD)
    Chargers, 31-10 (C)
1969—Bengals, 34-20 (C)
    Chargers, 21-14 (SD)
1970—Bengals, 17-14 (SD)
1971—Bengals, 31-0 (C)
1973—Bengals, 20-13 (SD)
1974—Chargers, 20-17 (C)
1975—Bengals, 47-17 (C)
1977—Chargers, 24-3 (SD)
1978—Chargers, 22-13 (SD)
1979—Chargers, 26-24 (C)
1980—Chargers, 31-14 (C)
1981—Chargers, 40-17 (SD)
    *Bengals, 27-7 (C)
1982—Chargers, 50-34 (SD)

1985—Chargers, 44-41 (C)
1987—Chargers, 10-9 (C)
1988—Bengals, 27-10 (C)
1990—Bengals, 21-16 (SD)
1992—Chargers, 27-10 (SD)
1994—Chargers, 27-10 (SD)
1996—Chargers, 27-14 (SD)
1997—Bengals, 38-31 (C)
1999—Chargers, 34-7 (C)
2001—Chargers, 28-14 (SD)
2002—Chargers, 34-6 (C)
2003—Bengals, 34-27 (SD)
2006—Chargers, 49-41 (C)
2009—Chargers, 27-24 (SD)
2010—Bengals, 34-20 (C)
2012—Bengals, 20-13 (SD)
(RS Pts.—Chargers 759, Bengals 681)
(PS Pts.—Bengals 27, Chargers 7)
*AFC Championship
CINCINNATI vs. SAN FRANCISCO
RS: 49ers lead series, 9-3
PS: 49ers lead series, 2-0
1974—Bengals, 21-3 (SF)
1978—49ers, 28-12 (SF)
1981—49ers, 21-3 (C)
    *49ers, 26-21 (Detroit)
1984—49ers, 23-17 (SF)
1987—49ers, 27-26 (C)
1988—**49ers, 20-16 (South Florida)
1990—49ers, 20-17 (C) OT
1993—Bengals, 21-8 (SF)
1996—49ers, 28-21 (SF)
1999—Bengals, 44-30 (C)
2003—Bengals, 41-38 (C)
2007—49ers, 20-13 (SF)
2011—49ers, 13-8 (C)
(RS Pts.—49ers 272, Bengals 231)
(PS Pts.—49ers 46, Bengals 37)
*Super Bowl XVI
**Super Bowl XXIII
CINCINNATI vs. SEATTLE
RS: Series tied, 9-9
PS: Bengals lead series, 1-0
1977—Bengals, 42-20 (C)
1981—Bengals, 27-21 (C)
1982—Bengals, 24-10 (C)
1984—Seahawks, 26-6 (C)
1985—Seahawks, 28-24 (C)
1986—Bengals, 34-7 (C)
1987—Bengals, 17-10 (S)
1988—*Bengals, 21-13 (C)
1989—Seahawks, 24-17 (C)
1990—Seahawks, 31-16 (S)
1991—Bengals, 13-7 (C)
1992—Bengals, 21-3 (S)
1993—Seahawks, 19-10 (C)
1994—Bengals, 20-17 (S) OT
1995—Seahawks, 24-21 (S)
1999—Seahawks, 37-20 (S)
2003—Bengals, 27-24 (C)
2007—Seahawks, 24-21 (S)
2011—Bengals, 34-12 (S)
(RS Pts.—Bengals 388, Seahawks 350)
(PS Pts.—Bengals 21, Seahawks 13)
*AFC Divisional Playoff
CINCINNATI vs. TAMPA BAY
RS: Buccaneers lead series, 7-3
1976—Bengals, 21-0 (C)
1980—Buccaneers, 17-12 (C)
1983—Bengals, 23-17 (TB)
1989—Bengals, 56-23 (C)
1995—Buccaneers, 19-16 (TB)
1998—Buccaneers, 35-0 (C)

2001—Buccaneers, 16-13 (C) OT
2002—Buccaneers, 35-7 (C)
2006—Buccaneers, 14-13 (TB)
2010—Buccaneers, 24-21 (C)
(RS Pts.— Buccaneers 200, Bengals 182)
CINCINNATI vs. *TENNESSEE
RS: Titans lead series, 39-32-1
PS: Bengals lead series, 1-0
1968—Oilers, 27-17 (C)
1969—Tie, 31-31 (H)
1970—Oilers, 20-13 (C)
    Bengals, 30-20 (H)
1971—Oilers, 10-6 (H)
    Bengals, 28-13 (C)
1972—Bengals, 30-7 (C)
    Bengals, 61-17 (H)
1973—Bengals, 24-10 (C)
    Bengals, 27-24 (H)
1974—Oilers, 34-21 (C)
    Oilers, 20-3 (H)
1975—Bengals, 21-19 (H)
    Bengals, 23-19 (C)
1976—Bengals, 27-7 (H)
    Bengals, 31-27 (C)
1977—Bengals, 13-10 (C) OT
    Oilers, 21-16 (H)
1978—Bengals, 28-13 (C)
    Oilers, 17-10 (H)
1979—Oilers, 30-27 (C) OT
    Oilers, 42-21 (H)
1980—Oilers, 13-10 (C)
    Oilers, 23-3 (H)
1981—Oilers, 17-10 (H)
    Bengals, 34-21 (C)
1982—Bengals, 27-6 (C)
    Bengals, 35-27 (H)
1983—Bengals, 55-14 (H)
    Bengals, 38-10 (C)
1984—Bengals, 13-3 (C)
    Bengals, 31-13 (H)
1985—Oilers, 44-27 (H)
    Bengals, 45-27 (C)
1986—Bengals, 31-28 (C)
    Oilers, 32-28 (H)
1987—Bengals, 31-29 (C)
    Oilers, 21-17 (H)
1988—Bengals, 44-21 (C)
    Oilers, 41-6 (H)
1989—Oilers, 26-24 (H)
    Bengals, 61-7 (C)
1990—Oilers, 48-17 (H)
    Bengals, 40-20 (C)
    **Bengals, 41-14 (C)
1991—Oilers, 30-7 (C)
    Oilers, 35-3 (H)
1992—Bengals, 38-24 (C)
    Oilers, 26-10 (H)
1993—Oilers, 28-12 (H)
    Oilers, 38-3 (C)
1994—Oilers, 20-13 (H)
    Bengals, 34-31 (C)
1995—Oilers, 38-28 (C)
    Bengals, 32-25 (H)
1996—Oilers, 30-27 (C) OT
    Bengals, 21-13 (H)
1997—Oilers, 30-7 (T)
    Bengals, 41-14 (C)
1998—Oilers, 23-14 (C)
    Oilers, 44-14 (T)
1999—Titans, 36-35 (T)
    Titans, 24-14 (C)
2000—Titans, 23-14 (C)
    Titans, 35-3 (T)

2001—Titans, 20-7 (C)
    Bengals, 23-21 (T)
2002—Titans, 30-24 (C)
2004—Titans, 27-20 (T)
2005—Bengals, 31-23 (T)
2007—Bengals, 35-6 (C)
2008—Titans, 24-7 (C)
2011—Bengals, 24-17 (T)
(RS Pts.—Titans 1,680, Bengals 1,660)
(PS Pts.—Bengals 41, Titans 14)
*Franchise in Houston prior to 1997;
known as Oilers prior to 1999
**AFC First-Round Playoff
CINCINNATI vs. WASHINGTON
RS: Bengals lead series, 5-4
1970—Redskins, 20-0 (W)
1974—Bengals, 28-17 (C)
1979—Redskins, 28-14 (W)
1985—Redskins, 27-24 (W)
1988—Bengals, 20-17 (C) OT
1991—Redskins, 34-27 (C)
2004—Bengals, 17-10 (W)
2008—Bengals, 20-13 (C)
2012—Bengals, 38-31 (W)
(RS Pts.—Redskins 197, Bengals 188)

CLEVELAND vs. ARIZONA
RS: Browns lead series, 33-13-3;
See Arizona vs. Cleveland
CLEVELAND vs. ATLANTA
RS: Browns lead series, 10-3;
See Atlanta vs. Cleveland
CLEVELAND vs. BALTIMORE
RS: Ravens lead series, 21-7;
See Baltimore vs. Cleveland
CLEVELAND vs. BUFFALO
RS: Browns lead series, 10-7
PS: Browns lead series, 1-0;
See Buffalo vs. Cleveland
CLEVELAND vs. CAROLINA
RS: Panthers lead series, 3-1;
See Carolina vs. Cleveland
CLEVELAND vs. CHICAGO
RS: Browns lead series, 9-5;
See Chicago vs. Cleveland
CLEVELAND vs. CINCINNATI
RS: Bengals lead series, 42-37;
See Cincinnati vs. Cleveland
CLEVELAND vs. DALLAS
RS: Browns lead series, 15-12
PS: Browns lead series, 2-1
1960—Browns, 48-7 (D)
1961—Browns, 25-7 (C)
    Browns, 38-17 (D)
1962—Browns, 19-10 (C)
    Cowboys, 45-21 (D)
1963—Browns, 41-24 (D)
    Browns, 27-17 (C)
1964—Browns, 27-6 (C)
    Browns, 20-16 (D)
1965—Browns, 23-17 (C)
    Browns, 24-17 (D)
1966—Browns, 30-21 (C)
    Cowboys, 26-14 (D)
1967—Cowboys, 21-14 (C)
    *Cowboys, 52-14 (D)
1968—Cowboys, 28-7 (D)
    *Browns, 31-20 (C)
1969—Browns, 42-10 (C)
    *Browns, 38-14 (D)
1970—Cowboys, 6-2 (C)
1974—Cowboys, 41-17 (D)
1979—Browns, 26-7 (C)

1982—Cowboys, 31-14 (D)
1985—Cowboys, 20-7 (D)
1988—Browns, 24-21 (C)
1991—Cowboys, 26-14 (C)
1994—Browns, 19-14 (D)
2004—Cowboys, 19-12 (D)
2008—Cowboys, 28-10 (C)
2012—Cowboys, 23-20 (D) OT
(RS Pts.—Browns 585, Cowboys 525)
(PS Pts.—Cowboys 86, Browns 83)
*Conference Championship
CLEVELAND vs. DENVER
RS: Broncos lead series, 19-5
PS: Broncos lead series, 3-0
1970—Browns, 27-13 (D)
1971—Broncos, 27-0 (C)
1972—Browns, 27-20 (D)
1974—Browns, 23-21 (C)
1975—Broncos, 16-15 (D)
1976—Broncos, 44-13 (D)
1978—Broncos, 19-7 (C)
1980—Broncos, 19-16 (C)
1981—Broncos, 23-20 (D) OT
1983—Broncos, 27-6 (D)
1984—Broncos, 24-14 (C)
1986—*Broncos, 23-20 (C) OT
1987—*Broncos, 38-33 (D)
1988—Broncos, 30-7 (D)
1989—Browns, 16-13 (C)
    *Broncos, 37-21 (D)
1990—Browns, 30-29 (D)
1991—Broncos, 17-7 (D)
1992—Browns, 12-0 (C)
1993—Broncos, 29-14 (C)
1994—Browns, 26-14 (D)
2000—Broncos, 44-10 (D)
2003—Broncos, 23-20 (D) OT
2006—Broncos, 17-7 (C)
2008—Broncos, 34-30 (C)
2009—Broncos, 27-6 (D)
2012—Broncos, 34-12 (D)
(RS Pts.—Broncos 588, Browns 341)
(PS Pts.—Broncos 98, Browns 74)
*AFC Championship
CLEVELAND vs. DETROIT
RS: Lions lead series, 14-4
PS: Lions lead series, 3-1
1952—Lions, 17-6 (D)
    *Lions, 17-7 (C)
1953—*Lions, 17-16 (D)
1954—Lions, 14-10 (C)
    *Browns, 56-10 (C)
1957—Lions, 20-7 (D)
    *Lions, 59-14 (D)
1958—Lions, 30-10 (C)
1963—Lions, 38-10 (D)
1964—Browns, 37-21 (C)
1967—Lions, 31-14 (D)
1969—Lions, 28-21 (C)
1970—Lions, 41-24 (C)
1975—Lions, 21-10 (D)
1983—Browns, 31-26 (D)
1986—Browns, 24-21 (C)
1989—Lions, 13-10 (D)
1992—Lions, 24-14 (D)
1995—Lions, 38-20 (D)
2001—Browns, 24-14 (C)
2005—Lions, 13-10 (C)
2009—Lions, 38-37 (D)
(RS Pts.—Lions 448, Browns 319)
(PS Pts.—Lions 103, Browns 93)
*NFL Championship

CLEVELAND vs. GREEN BAY
RS: Packers lead series, 10-7
PS: Packers lead series, 1-0
1953—Browns, 27-0 (Mil)
1955—Browns, 41-10 (C)
1956—Browns, 24-7 (Mil)
1961—Packers, 49-17 (C)
1964—Packers, 28-21 (Mil)
1965—*Packers, 23-12 (GB)
1966—Packers, 21-20 (C)
1967—Packers, 55-7 (Mil)
1969—Browns, 20-7 (C)
1972—Packers, 26-10 (C)
1980—Browns, 26-21 (C)
1983—Packers, 35-21 (Mil)
1986—Packers, 17-14 (C)
1992—Browns, 17-6 (C)
1995—Packers, 31-20 (C)
2001—Packers, 30-7 (GB)
2005—Browns, 26-24 (GB)
2009—Packers, 31-3 (C)
(RS Pts.—Packers 398, Browns 321)
(PS Pts.—Packers 23, Browns 12)
*NFL Championship
CLEVELAND vs. HOUSTON
RS: Texans lead series, 4-3
2002—Browns, 34-17 (C)
2004—Browns, 22-14 (H)
2005—Texans, 19-16 (H)
2006—Texans, 14-6 (H)
2007—Browns, 27-17 (H)
2008—Texans, 16-6 (C)
2011—Texans, 30-12 (H)
(RS Pts.—Texans 127, Browns 123)
CLEVELAND vs. *INDIANAPOLIS
RS: Browns lead series, 14-13
PS: Series tied, 2-2
1956—Colts, 21-7 (C)
1959—Browns, 38-31 (B)
1962—Colts, 36-14 (C)
1964—**Browns, 27-0 (C)
1968—Browns, 30-20 (B)
    **Colts, 34-0 (C)
1971—Browns, 14-13 (B)
    ***Colts, 20-3 (C)
1973—Browns, 24-14 (C)
1975—Colts, 21-7 (B)
1978—Browns, 45-24 (B)
1979—Browns, 13-10 (C)
1980—Browns, 28-27 (B)
1981—Browns, 42-28 (C)
1983—Browns, 41-23 (C)
1986—Browns, 24-9 (I)
1987—Colts, 9-7 (C)
    ***Browns, 38-21 (C)
1988—Browns, 23-17 (C)
1989—Colts, 23-17 (I) OT
1991—Browns, 31-0 (I)
1992—Colts, 14-3 (I)
1993—Colts, 23-10 (I)
1994—Browns, 21-14 (I)
1999—Colts, 29-28 (C)
2002—Colts, 28-23 (C)
2003—Colts, 9-6 (C)
2005—Colts, 13-6 (I)
2008—Colts, 10-6 (C)
2011—Browns, 27-19 (I)
2012—Colts, 17-13 (I)
(RS Pts.—Browns 548, Colts 502)
(PS Pts.—Colts 75, Browns 68)
*Franchise in Baltimore prior to 1984
**NFL Championship
***AFC Divisional Playoff

CLEVELAND vs. JACKSONVILLE
RS: Jaguars lead series, 9-5
1995—Jaguars, 23-15 (C)
　　　Jaguars, 24-21 (J)
1999—Jaguars, 24-7 (J)
　　　Jaguars, 24-14 (C)
2000—Jaguars, 27-7 (C)
　　　Jaguars, 48-0 (J)
2001—Browns, 23-14 (J)
　　　Jaguars, 15-10 (C)
2002—Browns, 21-20 (J)
2005—Jaguars, 20-14 (C)
2008—Browns, 23-17 (J)
2009—Browns, 23-17 (C)
2010—Jaguars, 24-20 (J)
2011—Browns, 14-10 (C)
(RS Pts.—Jaguars 307, Browns 212)
CLEVELAND vs. KANSAS CITY
RS: Browns lead series, 11-10-2
1971—Chiefs, 13-7 (KC)
1972—Chiefs, 31-7 (C)
1973—Tie, 20-20 (KC)
1975—Browns, 40-14 (C)
1976—Chiefs, 39-14 (KC)
1977—Browns, 44-7 (C)
1978—Chiefs, 17-3 (KC)
1979—Browns, 27-24 (KC)
1980—Browns, 20-13 (C)
1984—Chiefs, 10-6 (KC)
1986—Browns, 20-7 (C)
1988—Browns, 6-3 (KC)
1989—Tie, 10-10 (C) OT
1990—Chiefs, 34-0 (KC)
1991—Browns, 20-15 (C)
1994—Browns, 20-13 (KC)
1995—Browns, 35-17 (C)
2002—Chiefs, 40-39 (C)
2003—Chiefs, 41-20 (KC)
2006—Browns, 31-28 (C) OT
2009—Browns, 41-34 (KC)
2010—Chiefs, 16-14 (C)
2012—Browns, 30-7 (C)
(RS Pts.—Browns 467, Chiefs 460)
CLEVELAND vs. MIAMI
RS: Browns lead series, 8-7
PS: Dolphins lead series, 2-0
1970—Browns, 28-0 (M)
1972—*Dolphins, 20-14 (M)
1973—Dolphins, 17-9 (C)
1976—Browns, 17-13 (C)
1979—Browns, 30-24 (C) OT
1985—*Dolphins, 24-21 (M)
1986—Browns, 26-16 (C)
1988—Dolphins, 38-31 (M)
1989—Dolphins, 13-10 (M) OT
1990—Dolphins, 30-13 (C)
1992—Dolphins, 27-23 (C)
1993—Dolphins, 24-14 (C)
2004—Dolphins, 10-7 (M)
2005—Browns, 22-0 (C)
2007—Browns, 41-31 (C)
2010—Browns, 13-10 (M)
2011—Browns, 17-16 (C)
(RS Pts.—Browns 301, Dolphins 269)
(PS Pts.—Dolphins 44, Browns 35)
*AFC Divisional Playoff
CLEVELAND vs. MINNESOTA
RS: Vikings lead series, 10-3
PS: Vikings lead series, 1-0
1965—Vikings, 27-17 (C)
1967—Browns, 14-10 (C)
1969—Vikings, 51-3 (M)
　　　*Vikings, 27-7 (M)

1973—Vikings, 26-3 (M)
1975—Vikings, 42-10 (C)
1980—Vikings, 28-23 (M)
1983—Vikings, 27-21 (C)
1986—Browns, 23-20 (M)
1989—Browns, 23-17 (C) OT
1992—Vikings, 17-13 (M)
1995—Vikings, 27-11 (M)
2005—Vikings, 24-12 (M)
2009—Vikings, 34-20 (C)
(RS Pts.—Vikings 350, Browns 193)
(PS Pts.—Vikings 27, Browns 7)
*NFL Championship
CLEVELAND vs. NEW ENGLAND
RS: Browns lead series, 12-9
PS: Browns lead series, 1-0
1971—Browns, 27-7 (C)
1974—Browns, 21-14 (NE)
1977—Browns, 30-27 (C) OT
1980—Patriots, 34-17 (NE)
1982—Browns, 10-7 (C)
1983—Browns, 30-0 (NE)
1984—Patriots, 17-16 (C)
1985—Browns, 24-20 (C)
1987—Browns, 20-10 (NE)
1991—Browns, 20-0 (NE)
1992—Browns, 19-17 (NE)
1993—Patriots, 20-17 (C)
1994—Browns, 13-6 (C)
　　　*Browns, 20-13 (C)
1995—Patriots, 17-14 (NE)
1999—Patriots, 19-7 (C)
2000—Browns, 19-11 (C)
2001—Patriots, 27-16 (NE)
2003—Patriots, 9-3 (NE)
2004—Patriots, 42-15 (C)
2007—Patriots, 34-17 (NE)
2010—Browns, 34-14 (C)
(RS Pts.—Browns 389, Patriots 352)
(PS Pts.—Browns 20, Patriots 13)
*AFC First-Round Playoff
CLEVELAND vs. NEW ORLEANS
RS: Browns lead series, 12-4
1967—Browns, 42-7 (NO)
1968—Browns, 24-10 (NO)
　　　Browns, 35-17 (C)
1969—Browns, 27-17 (NO)
1971—Browns, 21-17 (NO)
1975—Browns, 17-16 (C)
1978—Browns, 24-16 (NO)
1981—Browns, 20-17 (C)
1984—Saints, 16-14 (C)
1987—Saints, 28-21 (NO)
1990—Saints, 25-20 (NO)
1993—Browns, 17-13 (C)
1999—Browns, 21-16 (NO)
2002—Browns, 24-15 (NO)
2006—Saints, 19-14 (C)
2010—Browns, 30-17 (NO)
(RS Pts.—Browns 371, Saints 266)
CLEVELAND vs. N.Y. GIANTS
RS: Browns lead series, 26-20-2
PS: Series tied, 1-1
1950—Giants, 6-0 (C)
　　　Giants, 17-13 (NY)
　　　*Browns, 8-3 (C)
1951—Browns, 14-13 (C)
　　　Browns, 10-0 (NY)
1952—Giants, 17-9 (C)
　　　Giants, 37-34 (NY)
1953—Browns, 7-0 (NY)
　　　Browns, 62-14 (C)

1954—Browns, 24-14 (C)
　　　Browns, 16-7 (NY)
1955—Browns, 24-14 (C)
　　　Tie, 35-35 (NY)
1956—Giants, 21-9 (C)
　　　Browns, 24-7 (NY)
1957—Browns, 6-3 (C)
　　　Browns, 34-28 (NY)
1958—Giants, 21-17 (C)
　　　Giants, 13-10 (NY)
　　　*Giants, 10-0 (NY)
1959—Giants, 10-6 (C)
　　　Giants, 48-7 (NY)
1960—Giants, 17-13 (C)
　　　Browns, 48-34 (NY)
1961—Giants, 37-21 (C)
　　　Tie, 7-7 (NY)
1962—Browns, 17-7 (C)
　　　Giants, 17-13 (NY)
1963—Browns, 35-24 (NY)
　　　Giants, 33-6 (C)
1964—Browns, 42-20 (C)
　　　Browns, 52-20 (NY)
1965—Browns, 38-14 (NY)
　　　Browns, 34-21 (C)
1966—Browns, 28-7 (NY)
　　　Browns, 49-40 (C)
1967—Giants, 38-34 (NY)
　　　Browns, 24-14 (C)
1968—Browns, 45-10 (C)
1969—Browns, 28-17 (C)
　　　Giants, 27-14 (NY)
1973—Browns, 12-10 (C)
1977—Browns, 21-7 (NY)
1985—Browns, 35-33 (NY)
1991—Giants, 13-10 (C)
1994—Browns, 16-13 (C)
2000—Giants, 24-3 (C)
2004—Giants, 27-10 (NY)
2008—Browns, 35-14 (C)
2012—Giants, 41-27 (NY)
(RS Pts.—Browns 1,075, Giants 914)
(PS Pts.—Giants 13, Browns 8)
*Conference Playoff
CLEVELAND vs. N.Y. JETS
RS: Browns lead series, 12-8
PS: Browns lead series, 1-0
1970—Browns, 31-21 (C)
1972—Browns, 26-10 (NY)
1976—Browns, 38-17 (C)
1978—Browns, 37-34 (C) OT
1979—Browns, 25-22 (NY) OT
1980—Browns, 17-14 (C)
1981—Jets, 14-13 (C)
1983—Browns, 10-7 (C)
1984—Jets, 24-20 (C)
1985—Jets, 37-10 (NY)
1986—*Browns, 23-20 (C) OT
1988—Jets, 23-3 (C)
1989—Browns, 38-24 (C)
1990—Jets, 24-21 (NY)
1991—Jets, 17-14 (C)
1994—Browns, 27-7 (C)
2002—Browns, 24-21 (NY)
2004—Jets, 10-7 (C)
2006—Browns, 20-13 (C)
2007—Browns, 24-18 (NY)
2010—Jets, 26-20 (NY) OT
(RS Pts.—Browns 425, Jets 383)
(PS Pts.—Browns 23, Jets 20)
*AFC Divisional Playoff

CLEVELAND vs. *OAKLAND
RS: Raiders lead series, 11-9
PS: Raiders lead series, 2-0
1970—Raiders, 23-20 (O)
1971—Raiders, 34-20 (C)
1973—Browns, 7-3 (O)
1974—Raiders, 40-24 (C)
1975—Raiders, 38-17 (O)
1977—Raiders, 26-10 (C)
1979—Raiders, 19-14 (O)
1980—**Raiders, 14-12 (C)
1982—***Raiders, 27-10 (LA)
1985—Raiders, 21-20 (C)
1986—Raiders, 27-14 (LA)
1987—Browns, 24-17 (LA)
1992—Browns, 28-16 (LA)
1993—Browns, 19-16 (LA)
2000—Raiders, 36-10 (O)
2003—Browns, 13-7 (C)
2005—Browns, 9-7 (O)
2006—Browns, 24-21 (O)
2007—Raiders, 26-24 (O)
2009—Browns, 23-9 (C)
2011—Raiders, 24-17 (O)
2012—Browns, 20-17 (O)
(RS Pts.—Raiders 427, Browns 357)
(PS Pts.—Raiders 41, Browns 22)
*Franchise in Los Angeles from 1982-1994
**AFC Divisional Playoff
***AFC First-Round Playoff
CLEVELAND vs. PHILADELPHIA
RS: Browns lead series, 31-16-1
1950—Browns, 35-10 (P)
        Browns, 13-7 (C)
1951—Browns, 20-17 (C)
        Browns, 24-9 (P)
1952—Browns, 49-7 (P)
        Eagles, 28-20 (C)
1953—Browns, 37-13 (C)
        Eagles, 42-27 (P)
1954—Eagles, 28-10 (C)
        Browns, 6-0 (C)
1955—Browns, 21-17 (C)
        Eagles, 33-17 (P)
1956—Browns, 16-0 (P)
        Browns, 17-14 (C)
1957—Browns, 24-7 (C)
        Eagles, 17-7 (P)
1958—Browns, 28-14 (C)
        Browns, 21-14 (P)
1959—Browns, 28-7 (C)
        Browns, 28-21 (P)
1960—Browns, 41-24 (P)
        Eagles, 31-29 (C)
1961—Eagles, 27-20 (P)
        Browns, 45-24 (C)
1962—Eagles, 35-7 (P)
        Tie, 14-14 (C)
1963—Browns, 37-7 (C)
        Browns, 23-17 (P)
1964—Browns, 28-20 (P)
        Browns, 38-24 (C)
1965—Browns, 35-17 (P)
        Browns, 38-34 (C)
1966—Browns, 27-7 (C)
        Eagles, 33-21 (P)
1967—Eagles, 28-24 (P)
1968—Browns, 47-13 (C)
1969—Browns, 27-20 (P)
1972—Browns, 27-17 (P)
1976—Browns, 24-3 (C)
1979—Browns, 24-19 (P)
1982—Eagles, 24-21 (C)

1988—Browns, 19-3 (C)
1991—Eagles, 32-30 (C)
1994—Browns, 26-7 (P)
2000—Eagles, 35-24 (C)
2004—Eagles, 34-31 (C) OT
2008—Eagles, 30-10 (P)
2012—Eagles, 17-16 (C)
(RS Pts.—Browns 1,201, Eagles 901)
CLEVELAND vs. PITTSBURGH
RS: Steelers lead series, 63-57
PS: Steelers lead series, 2-0
1950—Browns, 30-17 (P)
        Browns, 45-7 (C)
1951—Browns, 17-0 (C)
        Browns, 28-0 (P)
1952—Browns, 21-20 (P)
        Browns, 29-28 (C)
1953—Browns, 34-16 (C)
        Browns, 20-16 (P)
1954—Steelers, 55-27 (P)
        Browns, 42-7 (C)
1955—Browns, 41-14 (C)
        Browns, 30-7 (P)
1956—Browns, 14-10 (P)
        Steelers, 24-16 (C)
1957—Browns, 23-12 (P)
        Browns, 24-0 (C)
1958—Browns, 45-12 (C)
        Browns, 27-10 (C)
1959—Steelers, 17-7 (P)
        Steelers, 21-20 (C)
1960—Browns, 28-20 (C)
        Steelers, 14-10 (P)
1961—Browns, 30-28 (P)
        Steelers, 17-13 (C)
1962—Browns, 41-14 (P)
        Browns, 35-14 (C)
1963—Browns, 35-23 (C)
        Steelers, 9-7 (P)
1964—Steelers, 23-7 (C)
        Browns, 30-17 (P)
1965—Browns, 24-19 (C)
        Browns, 42-21 (P)
1966—Browns, 41-10 (C)
        Steelers, 16-6 (P)
1967—Browns, 21-10 (C)
        Browns, 34-14 (P)
1968—Browns, 31-24 (C)
        Browns, 45-24 (P)
1969—Browns, 42-31 (C)
        Browns, 24-3 (P)
1970—Browns, 15-7 (C)
        Steelers, 28-9 (P)
1971—Browns, 27-17 (C)
        Steelers, 26-9 (P)
1972—Browns, 26-24 (C)
        Steelers, 30-0 (P)
1973—Steelers, 33-6 (P)
        Browns, 21-16 (C)
1974—Browns, 20-16 (P)
        Steelers, 26-16 (C)
1975—Steelers, 42-6 (C)
        Steelers, 31-17 (P)
1976—Steelers, 31-14 (P)
        Browns, 18-16 (C)
1977—Steelers, 28-14 (C)
        Steelers, 35-31 (P)
1978—Steelers, 15-9 (P) OT
        Steelers, 34-14 (C)
1979—Steelers, 51-35 (C)
        Steelers, 33-30 (P) OT
1980—Browns, 27-26 (C)
        Steelers, 16-13 (P)

1981—Steelers, 13-7 (P)
        Steelers, 32-10 (C)
1982—Browns, 10-9 (C)
        Steelers, 37-21 (P)
1983—Steelers, 44-17 (P)
        Browns, 30-17 (C)
1984—Browns, 20-10 (C)
        Steelers, 23-20 (P)
1985—Browns, 17-7 (C)
        Steelers, 10-9 (P)
1986—Browns, 27-24 (P)
        Browns, 37-31 (C) OT
1987—Browns, 34-10 (C)
        Browns, 19-13 (P)
1988—Browns, 23-9 (P)
        Browns, 27-7 (C)
1989—Browns, 51-0 (P)
        Steelers, 17-7 (C)
1990—Browns, 13-3 (C)
        Steelers, 35-0 (P)
1991—Browns, 17-14 (C)
        Steelers, 17-10 (P)
1992—Browns, 17-9 (C)
        Steelers, 23-13 (P)
1993—Browns, 28-23 (C)
        Steelers, 16-9 (P)
1994—Steelers, 17-10 (C)
        Steelers, 17-7 (P)
        *Steelers, 29-9 (P)
1995—Steelers, 20-3 (P)
        Steelers, 20-17 (C)
1999—Steelers, 43-0 (C)
        Browns, 16-15 (P)
2000—Browns, 23-20 (C)
        Steelers, 22-0 (P)
2001—Steelers, 15-12 (C) OT
        Steelers, 28-7 (P)
2002—Steelers, 16-13 (P) OT
        Steelers, 23-20 (C)
        **Steelers, 36-33 (P)
2003—Browns, 33-13 (P)
        Steelers, 13-6 (C)
2004—Steelers, 34-23 (P)
        Steelers, 24-10 (C)
2005—Steelers, 34-21 (P)
        Steelers, 41-0 (C)
2006—Steelers, 24-20 (C)
        Steelers, 27-7 (P)
2007—Steelers, 34-7 (C)
        Steelers, 31-28 (P)
2008—Steelers, 10-6 (C)
        Steelers, 31-0 (P)
2009—Steelers, 27-14 (P)
        Browns, 13-6 (C)
2010—Steelers, 28-10 (P)
        Steelers, 41-9 (C)
2011—Steelers, 14-3 (P)
        Steelers, 13-9 (C)
2012—Browns, 20-14 (C)
        Steelers, 24-10 (P)
(RS Pts.—Steelers 2,421, Browns 2,329)
(PS Pts.—Steelers 65, Browns 42)
*AFC Divisional Playoff
**AFC First-Round Playoff
CLEVELAND vs. *ST. LOUIS
RS: Rams lead series, 10-9
PS: Browns lead series, 2-1
1950—**Browns, 30-28 (C)
1951—Browns, 38-23 (LA)
        **Rams, 24-17 (LA)
1952—Browns, 37-7 (C)
1955—**Browns, 38-14 (LA)
1957—Browns, 45-31 (C)

1958—Browns, 30-27 (LA)
1963—Browns, 20-6 (C)
1965—Rams, 42-7 (LA)
1968—Rams, 24-6 (C)
1973—Rams, 30-17 (LA)
1977—Rams, 9-0 (C)
1978—Browns, 30-19 (C)
1981—Rams, 27-16 (LA)
1984—Rams, 20-17 (LA)
1987—Browns, 30-17 (C)
1990—Rams, 38-23 (C)
1993—Browns, 42-14 (LA)
1999—Rams, 34-3 (StL)
2003—Rams, 26-20 (C)
2007—Browns, 27-20 (StL)
2011—Rams, 13-12 (C)
(RS Pts.—Rams 427, Browns 420)
(PS Pts.—Browns 85, Rams 66)
Franchise in Los Angeles prior to 1995
**NFL Championship*
CLEVELAND vs. SAN DIEGO
RS: Chargers lead series, 14-8-1
1970—Chargers, 27-10 (C)
1972—Browns, 21-17 (SD)
1973—Tie, 16-16 (C)
1974—Chargers, 36-35 (SD)
1976—Browns, 21-17 (C)
1977—Chargers, 37-14 (SD)
1981—Chargers, 44-14 (C)
1982—Chargers, 30-13 (C)
1983—Browns, 30-24 (SD) OT
1985—Browns, 21-7 (SD)
1986—Chargers, 47-17 (C)
1987—Chargers, 27-24 (SD) OT
1990—Chargers, 24-14 (C)
1991—Browns, 30-24 (SD) OT
1992—Chargers, 14-13 (C)
1995—Chargers, 31-13 (SD)
1999—Chargers, 23-10 (SD)
2001—Browns, 20-16 (C)
2003—Chargers, 26-20 (C)
2004—Chargers, 21-0 (C)
2006—Chargers, 32-25 (SD)
2009—Chargers, 30-23 (C)
2012—Browns, 7-6 (C)
(RS Pts.—Chargers 546, Browns 441)
CLEVELAND vs. SAN FRANCISCO
RS: Browns lead series, 11-7
1950—Browns, 34-14 (C)
1951—49ers, 24-10 (SF)
1953—Browns, 23-21 (C)
1955—Browns, 38-3 (SF)
1959—49ers, 21-20 (C)
1962—Browns, 13-10 (SF)
1968—Browns, 33-21 (SF)
1970—49ers, 34-31 (SF)
1974—Browns, 7-0 (C)
1978—Browns, 24-7 (C)
1981—Browns, 15-12 (SF)
1984—49ers, 41-7 (C)
1987—49ers, 38-24 (SF)
1990—49ers, 20-17 (SF)
1993—Browns, 23-13 (C)
2003—Browns, 13-12 (SF)
2007—Browns, 20-7 (C)
2011—49ers, 20-10 (SF)
(RS Pts.—Browns 362, 49ers 318)
CLEVELAND vs. SEATTLE
RS: Seahawks lead series, 11-6
1977—Seahawks, 20-19 (S)
1978—Seahawks, 47-24 (S)
1979—Seahawks, 29-24 (C)
1980—Browns, 27-3 (S)

1981—Seahawks, 42-21 (S)
1982—Browns, 21-7 (S)
1983—Seahawks, 24-9 (C)
1984—Seahawks, 33-0 (S)
1985—Seahawks, 31-13 (S)
1988—Seahawks, 16-10 (C)
1989—Browns, 17-7 (S)
1993—Seahawks, 22-5 (S)
1994—Browns, 35-9 (C)
2001—Seahawks, 9-6 (C)
2003—Seahawks, 34-7 (S)
2007—Browns, 33-30 (C) OT
2011—Browns, 6-3 (C)
(RS Pts.—Seahawks 366, Browns 277)
CLEVELAND vs. TAMPA BAY
RS: Browns lead series, 5-3
1976—Browns, 24-7 (TB)
1980—Browns, 34-27 (TB)
1983—Browns, 20-0 (C)
1989—Browns, 42-31 (TB)
1995—Browns, 22-6 (C)
2002—Buccaneers 17-3 (TB)
2006—Buccaneers, 22-7 (C)
2010—Buccaneers, 17-14 (TB)
(RS Pts.—Browns 166, Buccaneers 127)
CLEVELAND vs. *TENNESSEE
RS: Browns lead series, 33-28
PS: Titans lead series, 1-0
1970—Browns, 28-14 (C)
Browns, 21-10 (H)
1971—Browns, 31-0 (C)
Browns, 37-24 (H)
1972—Browns, 23-17 (H)
Browns, 20-0 (C)
1973—Browns, 42-13 (C)
Browns, 23-13 (H)
1974—Browns, 20-7 (C)
Oilers, 28-24 (H)
1975—Oilers, 40-10 (C)
Oilers, 21-10 (H)
1976—Browns, 21-7 (H)
Browns, 13-10 (C)
1977—Browns, 24-23 (H)
Oilers, 19-15 (C)
1978—Browns, 16-13 (C)
Oilers, 14-10 (H)
1979—Oilers, 31-10 (H)
Browns, 14-7 (C)
1980—Oilers, 16-7 (C)
Browns, 17-14 (H)
1981—Oilers, 9-3 (C)
Oilers, 17-13 (H)
1982—Browns, 20-14 (H)
1983—Browns, 25-19 (C) OT
Oilers, 34-27 (H)
1984—Browns, 27-10 (C)
Browns, 27-20 (H)
1985—Browns, 21-6 (H)
Browns, 28-21 (C)
1986—Browns, 23-20 (H)
Browns, 13-10 (C) OT
1987—Oilers, 15-10 (C)
Browns, 40-7 (H)
1988—Oilers, 24-17 (H)
Browns, 28-23 (C)
**Oilers, 24-23 (C)
1989—Browns, 28-17 (C)
Browns, 24-20 (H)
1990—Oilers, 35-23 (C)
Oilers, 58-14 (H)
1991—Browns, 28-24 (H)
Oilers, 17-14 (C)

1992—Browns, 24-14 (H)
Oilers, 17-14 (C)
1993—Oilers, 27-20 (C)
Oilers, 19-17 (H)
1994—Browns, 11-8 (H)
Browns, 34-10 (C)
1995—Browns, 14-7 (H)
Oilers, 37-10 (C)
1999—Titans, 26-9 (T)
Titans, 33-21 (C)
2000—Titans, 24-10 (T)
Titans, 24-0 (C)
2001—Titans, 31-15 (C)
Browns, 41-38 (T)
2002—Browns, 31-28 (T) OT
2005—Browns, 20-14 (C)
2008—Titans, 28-9 (T)
2011—Titans, 31-13 (C)
(RS Pts.—Browns 1,195, Titans 1,184)
(PS Pts.—Titans 24, Browns 23)
Franchise in Houston prior to 1997;
known as Oilers prior to 1999
**AFC First-Round Playoff*
CLEVELAND vs. WASHINGTON
RS: Browns lead series, 33-11-1
1950—Browns, 20-14 (C)
Browns, 45-21 (W)
1951—Browns, 45-0 (C)
1952—Browns, 19-15 (C)
Browns, 48-24 (W)
1953—Browns, 30-14 (W)
Browns, 27-3 (C)
1954—Browns, 62-3 (C)
Browns, 34-14 (W)
1955—Redskins, 27-17 (C)
Browns, 24-14 (W)
1956—Redskins, 20-9 (W)
Redskins, 20-17 (C)
1957—Browns, 21-17 (C)
Tie, 30-30 (W)
1958—Browns, 20-10 (W)
Browns, 21-14 (C)
1959—Browns, 34-7 (C)
Browns, 31-17 (W)
1960—Browns, 31-10 (W)
Browns, 27-16 (C)
1961—Browns, 31-7 (C)
Browns, 17-6 (W)
1962—Redskins, 17-16 (C)
Redskins, 17-9 (W)
1963—Browns, 37-14 (C)
Browns, 27-20 (W)
1964—Browns, 27-13 (W)
Browns, 34-24 (C)
1965—Browns, 17-7 (W)
Browns, 24-16 (C)
1966—Browns, 38-14 (W)
Browns, 14-3 (C)
1967—Browns, 42-37 (C)
1968—Browns, 24-21 (C)
1969—Browns, 27-23 (C)
1971—Browns, 20-13 (C)
1975—Redskins, 23-7 (C)
1979—Redskins, 13-9 (C)
1985—Redskins, 14-7 (C)
1988—Browns, 17-13 (W)
1991—Redskins, 42-17 (W)
2004—Browns, 17-13 (C)
2008—Redskins, 14-11 (W)
2012—Redskins, 38-21 (C)
(RS Pts.—Browns 1,122, Redskins 732)

DALLAS vs. ARIZONA
RS: Cowboys lead series, 55-30-1
PS: Cardinals lead series, 1-0;
See Arizona vs. Dallas
DALLAS vs. ATLANTA
RS: Cowboys lead series, 14-9
PS: Cowboys lead series, 2-0;
See Atlanta vs. Dallas
DALLAS vs. BALTIMORE
RS: Ravens lead series, 4-0;
See Baltimore vs. Dallas
DALLAS vs. BUFFALO
RS: Cowboys lead series, 6-3
PS: Cowboys lead series, 2-0;
See Buffalo vs. Dallas
DALLAS vs. CAROLINA
RS: Cowboys lead series, 9-1
PS: Panthers lead series, 2-0;
See Carolina vs. Dallas
DALLAS vs. CHICAGO
RS: Cowboys lead series, 11-10
PS: Cowboys lead series, 2-0;
See Chicago vs. Dallas
DALLAS vs. CINCINNATI
RS: Cowboys lead series, 7-4;
See Cincinnati vs. Dallas
DALLAS vs. CLEVELAND
RS: Browns lead series, 15-12
PS: Browns lead series, 2-1;
See Cleveland vs. Dallas
DALLAS vs. DENVER
RS: Broncos lead series, 6-4
PS: Cowboys lead series, 1-0
1973—Cowboys, 22-10 (Den)
1977—Cowboys, 14-6 (Dal)
        *Cowboys, 27-10 (New Orleans)
1980—Broncos, 41-20 (Den)
1986—Broncos, 29-14 (Den)
1992—Cowboys, 31-27 (Den)
1995—Cowboys, 31-21 (Dal)
1998—Broncos, 42-23 (Den)
2001—Broncos, 26-24 (Dal)
2005—Broncos, 24-21 (Dal) OT
2009—Broncos, 17-10 (Den)
(RS Pts.—Broncos 243, Cowboys 210)
(PS Pts.—Cowboys 27, Broncos 10)
*Super Bowl XII
DALLAS vs. DETROIT
RS: Cowboys lead series, 12-10
PS: Series tied, 1-1
1960—Lions, 23-14 (Det)
1963—Cowboys, 17-14 (Dal)
1968—Cowboys, 59-13 (Dal)
1970—*Cowboys, 5-0 (Dal)
1972—Cowboys, 28-24 (Dal)
1975—Cowboys, 36-10 (Det)
1977—Cowboys, 37-0 (Dal)
1981—Lions, 27-24 (Det)
1985—Lions, 26-21 (Det)
1986—Cowboys, 31-7 (Det)
1987—Lions, 27-17 (Det)
1991—Lions, 34-10 (Det)
        *Lions, 38-6 (Det)
1992—Cowboys, 37-3 (Det)
1994—Lions, 20-17 (Dal) OT
2001—Lions, 15-10 (Det)
2002—Lions, 9-7 (Det)
2003—Cowboys, 38-7 (Det)
2004—Cowboys, 31-21 (Dal)
2005—Cowboys, 20-7 (Dal)
2006—Lions, 39-31 (Dal)
2007—Cowboys, 28-27 (Det)

2010—Cowboys, 35-19 (Dal)
2011—Lions, 34-30 (Dal)
(RS Pts.—Cowboys 578, Lions 406)
(PS Pts.—Lions 38, Cowboys 11)
*NFC Divisional Playoff
DALLAS vs. GREEN BAY
RS: Series tied, 12-12
PS: Cowboys lead series, 4-2
1960—Packers, 41-7 (GB)
1964—Packers, 45-21 (D)
1965—Packers, 13-3 (Mil)
1966—*Packers, 34-27 (D)
1967—*Packers, 21-17 (GB)
1968—Packers, 28-17 (D)
1970—Cowboys, 16-3 (D)
1972—Packers, 16-13 (Mil)
1975—Packers, 19-17 (D)
1978—Cowboys, 42-14 (Mil)
1980—Cowboys, 28-7 (Mil)
1982—**Cowboys, 37-26 (D)
1984—Cowboys, 20-6 (D)
1989—Packers, 31-13 (GB)
        Packers, 20-10 (D)
1991—Cowboys, 20-17 (Mil)
1993—Cowboys, 36-14 (D)
        ***Cowboys, 27-17 (D)
1994—Cowboys, 42-31 (D)
        ***Cowboys, 35-9 (D)
1995—Cowboys, 34-24 (D)
        ****Cowboys, 38-27 (D)
1996—Cowboys, 21-6 (D)
1997—Packers, 45-17 (GB)
1999—Cowboys, 27-13 (D)
2004—Packers, 41-20 (GB)
2007—Cowboys, 37-27 (D)
2008—Cowboys, 27-16 (GB)
2009—Packers, 17-7 (D)
2010—Packers, 45-7 (GB)
(RS Pts.—Packers, 539, Cowboys 502)
(PS Pts.—Cowboys 181, Packers 134)
*NFL Championship
**NFC Second-Round Playoff
***NFC Divisional Playoff
****NFC Championship
DALLAS vs. HOUSTON
RS: Cowboys lead series, 2-1
2002—Texans, 19-10 (H)
2006—Cowboys, 34-6 (D)
2010—Cowboys, 27-13 (H)
(RS Pts.—Cowboys 71, Texans 38)
DALLAS vs. *INDIANAPOLIS
RS: Cowboys lead series, 9-5
PS: Colts lead series, 1-0
1960—Colts, 45-7 (D)
1967—Colts, 23-17 (B)
1969—Cowboys, 27-10 (D)
1970—**Colts, 16-13 (Miami)
1972—Cowboys, 21-0 (B)
1976—Cowboys, 30-27 (D)
1978—Cowboys, 38-0 (D)
1981—Cowboys, 37-13 (B)
1984—Cowboys, 22-3 (D)
1993—Cowboys, 27-3 (I)
1996—Colts, 25-24 (D)
1999—Colts, 34-24 (I)
2002—Colts, 20-3 (I)
2006—Cowboys, 21-14 (D)
2010—Cowboys, 38-35 (I) OT
(RS Pts.—Cowboys 336, Colts 252)
(PS Pts.—Colts 16, Cowboys 13)
*Franchise in Baltimore prior to 1984
**Super Bowl V

DALLAS vs. JACKSONVILLE
RS: Jaguars lead series, 3-2
1997—Cowboys, 26-22 (D)
2000—Jaguars, 23-17 (D) OT
2002—Cowboys, 21-19 (D)
2006—Jaguars, 24-17 (J)
2010—Jaguars, 35-17 (D)
(RS Pts.—Jaguars 123, Cowboys 98)
DALLAS vs. KANSAS CITY
RS: Cowboys lead series, 6-3
1970—Cowboys, 27-16 (KC)
1975—Chiefs, 34-31 (D)
1983—Cowboys, 41-21 (D)
1989—Chiefs, 36-28 (KC)
1992—Cowboys, 17-10 (D)
1995—Cowboys, 24-12 (D)
1998—Chiefs, 20-17 (KC)
2005—Cowboys, 31-28 (D)
2009—Cowboys, 26-20 (KC) OT
(RS Pts.—Cowboys 242, Chiefs 197)
DALLAS vs. MIAMI
RS: Dolphins lead series, 7-5
PS: Cowboys lead series, 1-0
1971—*Cowboys, 24-3 (New Orleans)
1973—Dolphins, 14-7 (D)
1978—Dolphins, 23-16 (M)
1981—Cowboys, 28-27 (D)
1984—Dolphins, 28-21 (M)
1987—Dolphins, 20-14 (D)
1989—Dolphins, 17-14 (D)
1993—Dolphins, 16-14 (D)
1996—Cowboys, 29-10 (M)
1999—Cowboys, 20-0 (D)
2003—Dolphins, 40-21 (D)
2007—Cowboys, 37-20 (M)
2011—Cowboys, 20-19 (D)
(RS Pts.—Cowboys 241, Dolphins 234)
(PS Pts.—Cowboys 24, Dolphins 3)
*Super Bowl VI
DALLAS vs. MINNESOTA
RS: Vikings lead series, 11-10
PS: Cowboys lead series, 4-3
1961—Cowboys, 21-7 (D)
        Cowboys, 28-0 (M)
1966—Cowboys, 28-17 (D)
1968—Cowboys, 20-7 (M)
1970—Vikings, 54-13 (M)
1971—*Cowboys, 20-12 (M)
1973—**Vikings, 27-10 (D)
1974—Vikings, 23-21 (D)
1975—*Cowboys, 17-14 (M)
1977—Vikings, 16-10 (M) OT
        **Cowboys, 23-6 (D)
1978—Vikings, 21-10 (D)
1979—Cowboys, 36-20 (M)
1982—Vikings, 31-27 (M)
1983—Cowboys, 37-24 (M)
1987—Vikings, 44-38 (D) OT
1988—Vikings, 43-3 (D)
1993—Cowboys, 37-20 (M)
1995—Cowboys, 23-17 (M) OT
1996—***Cowboys, 40-15 (D)
1998—Vikings, 46-36 (D)
1999—Vikings, 27-17 (M)
        ***Vikings, 27-10 (M)
2000—Vikings, 27-15 (D)
2004—Vikings, 35-17 (M)
2007—Cowboys, 24-14 (D)
2009—*Vikings, 34-3 (M)
2010—Vikings, 24-21 (M)
(RS Pts.—Vikings 511, Cowboys 488)
(PS Pts.—Vikings 135, Cowboys 123)
*NFC Divisional Playoff

**NFC Championship*
***NFC First-Round Playoff*
DALLAS vs. NEW ENGLAND
RS: Cowboys lead series, 7-4
1971—Cowboys, 44-21 (D)
1975—Cowboys, 34-31 (NE)
1978—Cowboys, 17-10 (D)
1981—Cowboys, 35-21 (NE)
1984—Cowboys, 20-17 (D)
1987—Cowboys, 23-17 (NE) OT
1996—Cowboys, 12-6 (D)
1999—Patriots, 13-6 (NE)
2003—Patriots, 12-0 (NE)
2007—Patriots, 48-27 (D)
2011—Patriots, 20-16 (NE)
(RS Pts.—Cowboys 234, Patriots 216)
DALLAS vs. NEW ORLEANS
RS: Cowboys lead series, 15-10
1967—Cowboys, 14-10 (D)
　　　Cowboys, 27-10 (NO)
1968—Cowboys, 17-3 (NO)
1969—Cowboys, 21-17 (NO)
　　　Cowboys, 33-17 (D)
1971—Saints, 24-14 (NO)
1973—Cowboys, 40-3 (D)
1976—Cowboys, 24-6 (NO)
1978—Cowboys, 27-7 (D)
1982—Cowboys, 21-7 (D)
1983—Cowboys, 21-20 (D)
1984—Cowboys, 30-27 (D) OT
1988—Saints, 20-17 (NO)
1989—Saints, 28-0 (NO)
1990—Cowboys, 17-13 (D)
1991—Cowboys, 23-14 (D)
1994—Cowboys, 24-16 (NO)
1998—Saints, 22-3 (NO)
1999—Saints, 31-24 (NO)
2003—Saints, 13-7 (NO)
2004—Saints, 27-13 (D)
2006—Saints, 42-17 (D)
2009—Cowboys, 24-17 (NO)
2010—Saints, 30-27 (D)
2012—Saints, 34-31 (D) OT
(RS Pts.—Cowboys 516, Saints 458)
DALLAS vs. N.Y. GIANTS
RS: Cowboys lead series, 57-42-2
PS: Giants lead series, 1-0
1960—Tie, 31-31 (NY)
1961—Giants, 31-10 (D)
　　　Cowboys, 17-16 (NY)
1962—Giants, 41-10 (D)
　　　Giants, 41-31 (NY)
1963—Giants, 37-21 (NY)
　　　Giants, 34-27 (D)
1964—Tie, 13-13 (D)
　　　Cowboys, 31-21 (NY)
1965—Cowboys, 31-2 (D)
　　　Cowboys, 38-20 (NY)
1966—Cowboys, 52-7 (D)
　　　Cowboys, 17-7 (NY)
1967—Cowboys, 38-24 (D)
1968—Giants, 27-21 (D)
　　　Cowboys, 28-10 (NY)
1969—Cowboys, 25-3 (D)
1970—Cowboys, 28-10 (D)
　　　Giants, 23-20 (NY)
1971—Cowboys, 20-13 (D)
　　　Cowboys, 42-14 (NY)
1972—Cowboys, 23-14 (NY)
　　　Giants, 23-3 (D)
1973—Cowboys, 45-28 (D)
　　　Cowboys, 23-10 (New Haven)

1974—Giants, 14-6 (D)
　　　Cowboys, 21-7 (New Haven)
1975—Cowboys, 13-7 (NY)
　　　Cowboys, 14-3 (D)
1976—Cowboys, 24-14 (NY)
　　　Cowboys, 9-3 (D)
1977—Cowboys, 41-21 (D)
　　　Cowboys, 24-10 (NY)
1978—Cowboys, 34-24 (NY)
　　　Cowboys, 24-3 (D)
1979—Cowboys, 16-14 (NY)
　　　Cowboys, 28-7 (D)
1980—Cowboys, 24-3 (D)
　　　Giants, 38-35 (NY)
1981—Cowboys, 18-10 (D)
　　　Giants, 13-10 (NY) OT
1983—Cowboys, 28-13 (D)
　　　Cowboys, 38-20 (NY)
1984—Giants, 28-7 (NY)
　　　Giants, 19-7 (D)
1985—Cowboys, 30-29 (NY)
　　　Cowboys, 28-21 (D)
1986—Cowboys, 31-28 (D)
　　　Giants, 17-14 (NY)
1987—Cowboys, 16-14 (NY)
　　　Cowboys, 33-24 (D)
1988—Giants, 12-10 (D)
　　　Giants, 29-21 (NY)
1989—Giants, 30-13 (D)
　　　Giants, 15-0 (NY)
1990—Giants, 28-7 (D)
　　　Giants, 31-17 (NY)
1991—Cowboys, 21-16 (D)
　　　Giants, 22-9 (NY)
1992—Cowboys, 34-28 (NY)
　　　Cowboys, 30-3 (D)
1993—Cowboys, 31-9 (D)
　　　Cowboys, 16-13 (NY) OT
1994—Cowboys, 38-10 (D)
　　　Giants, 15-10 (NY)
1995—Cowboys, 35-0 (NY)
　　　Cowboys, 21-20 (D)
1996—Cowboys, 27-0 (D)
　　　Giants, 20-6 (NY)
1997—Giants, 20-17 (NY)
　　　Giants, 20-7 (D)
1998—Cowboys, 31-7 (NY)
　　　Cowboys, 16-6 (D)
1999—Giants, 13-10 (NY)
　　　Cowboys, 26-18 (D)
2000—Giants, 19-14 (NY)
　　　Giants, 17-13 (D)
2001—Giants, 27-24 (NY) OT
　　　Cowboys, 20-13 (D)
2002—Cowboys, 21-17 (D)
　　　Giants, 37-7 (NY)
2003—Cowboys, 35-32 (NY) OT
　　　Cowboys, 19-3 (D)
2004—Giants, 26-10 (D)
　　　Giants, 28-24 (NY)
2005—Cowboys, 16-13 (D) OT
　　　Giants, 17-10 (NY)
2006—Giants, 36-22 (D)
　　　Cowboys, 23-20 (NY)
2007—Cowboys, 45-35 (D)
　　　Cowboys, 31-20 (NY)
　　　*Giants, 21-17 (D)
2008—Giants, 35-14 (NY)
　　　Cowboys, 20-8 (D)
2009—Cowboys, 33-31 (D)
　　　Giants, 31-24 (NY)
2010—Giants, 41-35 (D)
　　　Cowboys, 33-20 (NY)

2011—Giants, 37-34 (D)
　　　Giants, 31-14 (NY)
2012—Cowboys, 24-17 (NY)
　　　Giants, 29-24 (D)
(RS Pts.—Cowboys 2,254, Giants 1,935)
(PS Pts.—Giants 21, Cowboys 17)
**NFC Divisional Playoff*
DALLAS vs. N.Y. JETS
RS: Cowboys lead series, 7-3
1971—Cowboys, 52-10 (D)
1975—Cowboys, 31-21 (NY)
1978—Cowboys, 30-7 (NY)
1987—Cowboys, 38-24 (NY)
1990—Jets, 24-9 (D)
1993—Cowboys, 28-7 (NY)
1999—Jets, 22-21 (D)
2003—Cowboys, 17-6 (NY)
2007—Cowboys, 34-3 (D)
2011—Jets, 27-24 (NY)
(RS Pts.—Cowboys 284, Jets 151)
DALLAS vs. *OAKLAND
RS: Raiders lead series, 6-4
1974—Raiders, 27-23 (O)
1980—Cowboys, 19-13 (O)
1983—Raiders, 40-38 (D)
1986—Raiders, 17-13 (D)
1992—Cowboys, 28-13 (LA)
1995—Cowboys, 34-21 (O)
1998—Raiders, 13-12 (D)
2001—Raiders, 28-21 (O)
2005—Raiders, 19-13 (O)
2009—Cowboys, 24-7 (O)
(RS Pts.—Cowboys 225, Raiders 198)
**Franchise in Los Angeles from 1982-1994*
DALLAS vs. PHILADELPHIA
RS: Cowboys lead series, 58-46
PS: Cowboys lead series, 3-1
1960—Eagles, 27-25 (P)
1961—Eagles, 43-7 (D)
　　　Eagles, 35-13 (P)
1962—Cowboys, 41-19 (D)
　　　Eagles, 28-14 (P)
1963—Eagles, 24-21 (P)
　　　Cowboys, 27-20 (D)
1964—Eagles, 17-14 (D)
　　　Eagles, 24-14 (P)
1965—Eagles, 35-24 (D)
　　　Cowboys, 21-19 (P)
1966—Cowboys, 56-7 (D)
　　　Eagles, 24-23 (P)
1967—Eagles, 21-14 (P)
　　　Cowboys, 38-17 (D)
1968—Cowboys, 45-13 (P)
　　　Cowboys, 34-14 (D)
1969—Cowboys, 38-7 (P)
　　　Cowboys, 49-14 (D)
1970—Cowboys, 17-7 (P)
　　　Cowboys, 21-17 (D)
1971—Cowboys, 42-7 (P)
　　　Cowboys, 20-7 (D)
1972—Cowboys, 28-6 (D)
　　　Cowboys, 28-7 (P)
1973—Eagles, 30-16 (P)
　　　Cowboys, 31-10 (D)
1974—Eagles, 13-10 (P)
　　　Cowboys, 31-24 (D)
1975—Cowboys, 20-17 (D)
　　　Cowboys, 27-17 (D)
1976—Cowboys, 27-7 (D)
　　　Cowboys, 26-7 (P)
1977—Cowboys, 16-10 (P)
　　　Cowboys, 24-14 (D)

1978—Cowboys, 14-7 (D)
　　　　Cowboys, 31-13 (P)
1979—Eagles, 31-21 (D)
　　　　Cowboys, 24-17 (P)
1980—Eagles, 17-10 (P)
　　　　Cowboys, 35-27 (D)
　　　　*Eagles, 20-7 (P)
1981—Cowboys, 17-14 (D)
　　　　Cowboys, 21-10 (D)
1982—Eagles, 24-20 (D)
1983—Cowboys, 37-7 (D)
　　　　Cowboys, 27-20 (P)
1984—Cowboys, 23-17 (D)
　　　　Cowboys, 26-10 (P)
1985—Eagles, 16-14 (P)
　　　　Cowboys, 34-17 (D)
1986—Cowboys, 17-14 (P)
　　　　Eagles, 23-21 (D)
1987—Cowboys, 41-22 (D)
　　　　Eagles, 37-20 (P)
1988—Eagles, 24-23 (P)
　　　　Eagles, 23-7 (D)
1989—Eagles, 27-0 (D)
　　　　Eagles, 20-10 (P)
1990—Eagles, 21-20 (D)
　　　　Eagles, 17-3 (P)
1991—Eagles, 24-0 (D)
　　　　Cowboys, 25-13 (P)
1992—Eagles, 31-7 (P)
　　　　Cowboys, 20-10 (D)
　　　　**Cowboys, 34-10 (D)
1993—Cowboys, 23-10 (P)
　　　　Cowboys, 23-17 (D)
1994—Cowboys, 24-13 (D)
　　　　Cowboys, 31-19 (P)
1995—Cowboys, 34-12 (D)
　　　　Eagles, 20-17 (P)
　　　　**Cowboys, 30-11 (D)
1996—Cowboys, 23-19 (P)
　　　　Eagles, 31-21 (D)
1997—Cowboys, 21-20 (D)
　　　　Eagles, 13-12 (P)
1998—Cowboys, 34-0 (P)
　　　　Cowboys, 13-9 (D)
1999—Eagles, 13-10 (P)
　　　　Cowboys, 20-10 (D)
2000—Eagles, 41-14 (D)
　　　　Eagles, 16-13 (P) OT
2001—Eagles, 40-18 (P)
　　　　Eagles, 36-3 (D)
2002—Eagles, 44-13 (P)
　　　　Eagles, 27-3 (D)
2003—Cowboys, 23-21 (D)
　　　　Eagles, 36-10 (P)
2004—Eagles, 49-21 (D)
　　　　Eagles, 12-7 (P)
2005—Cowboys, 33-10 (D)
　　　　Cowboys, 21-20 (P)
2006—Eagles, 38-24 (P)
　　　　Eagles, 23-7 (D)
2007—Eagles, 38-17 (P)
　　　　Eagles, 10-6 (D)
2008—Cowboys, 41-37 (D)
　　　　Eagles, 44-6 (P)
2009—Cowboys, 20-16 (P)
　　　　Cowboys, 24-0 (D)
　　　　***Cowboys, 34-14 (D)
2010—Eagles, 30-27 (D)
　　　　Cowboys, 14-13 (P)
2011—Eagles, 34-7 (P)
　　　　Eagles, 20-7 (D)
2012—Cowboys, 38-23 (P)
　　　　Cowboys, 38-33 (D)

(RS Pts.—Cowboys 2,252, Eagles 2,057)
(PS Pts.—Cowboys 105, Eagles 55)
*NFC Championship
**NFC Divisional Playoff
***NFC First-Round Playoff
DALLAS vs. PITTSBURGH
RS: Cowboys lead series, 15-13
PS: Steelers lead series, 2-1
1960—Steelers, 35-28 (D)
1961—Cowboys, 27-24 (D)
　　　　Steelers, 37-7 (P)
1962—Steelers, 30-28 (D)
　　　　Cowboys, 42-27 (P)
1963—Steelers, 27-21 (P)
　　　　Steelers, 24-19 (D)
1964—Steelers, 23-17 (P)
　　　　Cowboys, 17-14 (D)
1965—Steelers, 22-13 (P)
　　　　Cowboys, 24-17 (D)
1966—Cowboys, 52-21 (D)
　　　　Cowboys, 20-7 (P)
1967—Cowboys, 24-21 (P)
1968—Cowboys, 28-7 (D)
1969—Cowboys, 10-7 (P)
1972—Cowboys, 17-13 (D)
1975—*Steelers, 21-17 (Miami)
1977—Steelers, 28-13 (P)
1978—**Steelers, 35-31 (Miami)
1979—Steelers, 14-3 (P)
1982—Steelers, 36-28 (D)
1985—Cowboys, 27-13 (D)
1988—Steelers, 24-21 (P)
1991—Cowboys, 20-10 (D)
1994—Cowboys, 26-9 (P)
1995—***Cowboys, 27-17 (Tempe)
1997—Cowboys, 37-7 (P)
2004—Steelers, 24-20 (D)
2008—Steelers, 20-13 (P)
2012—Cowboys, 27-24 (D)
(RS Pts.—Cowboys 629, Steelers 565)
(PS Pts.—Cowboys 75, Steelers 73)
*Super Bowl X
**Super Bowl XIII
***Super Bowl XXX
DALLAS vs. *ST. LOUIS
RS: Series tied, 11-11
PS: Series tied, 4-4
1960—Rams, 38-13 (D)
1962—Cowboys, 27-17 (LA)
1967—Rams, 35-13 (D)
1969—Rams, 24-23 (LA)
1971—Cowboys, 28-21 (D)
1973—Rams, 37-31 (LA)
　　　　**Cowboys, 27-16 (D)
1975—Cowboys, 18-7 (D)
　　　　***Cowboys, 37-7 (LA)
1976—**Rams, 14-12 (D)
1978—Rams, 27-14 (LA)
　　　　***Cowboys, 28-0 (LA)
1979—Cowboys, 30-6 (D)
　　　　**Rams, 21-19 (D)
1980—Rams, 38-14 (LA)
　　　　****Cowboys, 34-13 (D)
1981—Cowboys, 29-17 (D)
1983—****Rams, 24-17 (D)
1984—Cowboys, 20-13 (LA)
1985—**Rams, 20-0 (LA)
1986—Rams, 29-10 (LA)
1987—Cowboys, 29-21 (LA)
1989—Rams, 35-31 (D)
1990—Cowboys, 24-21 (LA)
1992—Rams, 27-23 (D)
2002—Cowboys, 13-10 (StL)

2005—Rams, 20-10 (D)
2007—Cowboys, 35-7 (D)
2008—Rams, 34-14 (StL)
2011—Cowboys, 34-7 (D)
(RS Pts.—Rams 491, Cowboys 483)
(PS Pts.—Cowboys 174, Rams 115)
*Franchise in Los Angeles prior to 1995
**NFC Divisional Playoff
***NFC Championship
****NFC First-Round Playoff
DALLAS vs. SAN DIEGO
RS: Cowboys lead series, 6-3
1972—Cowboys, 34-28 (SD)
1980—Cowboys, 42-31 (D)
1983—Chargers, 24-23 (SD)
1986—Cowboys, 24-21 (SD)
1990—Cowboys, 17-14 (D)
1995—Cowboys, 23-9 (SD)
2001—Chargers, 32-21 (D)
2005—Cowboys, 28-24 (SD)
2009—Chargers, 20-17 (D)
(RS Pts.—Cowboys 229, Chargers 203)
DALLAS vs. SAN FRANCISCO
RS: 49ers lead series, 14-11-1
PS: Cowboys lead series, 5-2
1960—49ers, 26-14 (D)
1963—49ers, 31-24 (SF)
1965—Cowboys, 39-31 (D)
1967—49ers, 24-16 (SF)
1969—Tie, 24-24 (D)
1970—*Cowboys, 17-10 (SF)
1971—*Cowboys, 14-3 (D)
1972—49ers, 31-10 (D)
　　　　**Cowboys, 30-28 (SF)
1974—Cowboys, 20-14 (D)
1977—Cowboys, 42-35 (SF)
1979—Cowboys, 21-13 (SF)
1980—Cowboys, 59-14 (D)
1981—49ers, 45-14 (SF)
　　　　*49ers, 28-27 (SF)
1983—49ers, 42-17 (SF)
1985—49ers, 31-16 (D)
1989—49ers, 31-14 (D)
1990—49ers, 24-6 (D)
1992—*Cowboys, 30-20 (SF)
1993—Cowboys, 26-17 (D)
　　　　*Cowboys, 38-21 (D)
1994—49ers, 21-14 (SF)
　　　　*49ers, 38-28 (SF)
1995—49ers, 38-20 (D)
1996—Cowboys, 20-17 (SF) OT
1997—49ers, 17-10 (SF)
2000—49ers, 41-24 (D)
2001—Cowboys, 27-21 (D)
2002—49ers, 31-27 (D)
2005—Cowboys, 34-31 (SF)
2008—Cowboys, 35-22 (D)
2011—Cowboys, 27-24 (SF) OT
(RS Pts.—49ers 696, Cowboys 600)
(PS Pts.—Cowboys 184, 49ers 148)
*NFC Championship
**NFC Divisional Playoff
DALLAS vs. SEATTLE
RS: Cowboys lead series, 9-5
PS: Seahawks lead series, 1-0
1976—Cowboys, 28-13 (S)
1980—Cowboys, 51-7 (D)
1983—Cowboys, 35-10 (S)
1986—Seahawks, 31-14 (D)
1992—Cowboys, 27-0 (D)
1998—Cowboys, 30-22 (D)
2001—Seahawks, 29-3 (S)
2002—Seahawks, 17-14 (D)

2004—Cowboys, 43-39 (S)
2005—Seahawks, 13-10 (S)
2006—*Seahawks, 21-20 (S)
2008—Cowboys, 34-9 (D)
2009—Cowboys, 38-17 (D)
2011—Cowboys, 23-13 (D)
2012—Seahawks, 27-7 (S)
(RS Pts.—Cowboys 357, Seahawks 247)
(PS Pts.—Seahawks 21, Cowboys 20)
*NFC First-Round Playoff
DALLAS vs. TAMPA BAY
RS: Cowboys lead series, 11-3
PS: Cowboys lead series, 2-0
1977—Cowboys, 23-7 (D)
1980—Cowboys, 28-17 (D)
1981—*Cowboys, 38-0 (D)
1982—Cowboys, 14-9 (D)
       **Cowboys, 30-17 (D)
1983—Cowboys, 27-24 (D) OT
1990—Cowboys, 14-10 (D)
       Cowboys, 17-13 (TB)
2000—Buccaneers, 27-7 (TB)
2001—Buccaneers, 10-6 (D)
2003—Buccaneers, 16-0 (TB)
2006—Cowboys, 38-10 (D)
2008—Cowboys, 13-9 (D)
2009—Cowboys, 34-21 (TB)
2011—Cowboys, 31-15 (TB)
2012—Cowboys, 16-10 (D)
(RS Pts.—Cowboys 268, Buccaneers 198)
(PS Pts.—Cowboys 68, Buccaneers 17)
*NFC Divisional Playoff
**NFC First-Round Playoff
DALLAS vs. *TENNESSEE
RS: Cowboys lead series, 7-6
1970—Cowboys, 52-10 (D)
1974—Cowboys, 10-0 (H)
1979—Oilers, 30-24 (D)
1982—Cowboys, 37-7 (H)
1985—Cowboys, 17-10 (H)
1988—Cowboys, 25-17 (D)
1991—Oilers, 26-23 (H) OT
1994—Cowboys, 20-17 (D)
1997—Oilers, 27-14 (D)
2000—Titans, 31-0 (T)
2002—Cowboys, 21-13 (D)
2006—Cowboys, 45-14 (T)
2010—Titans, 34-27 (D)
(RS Pts.—Cowboys 307, Titans 244)
*Franchise in Houston prior to 1997;
known as Oilers prior to 1999
DALLAS vs. WASHINGTON
RS: Cowboys lead series, 62-40-2
PS: Redskins lead series, 2-0
1960—Redskins, 26-14 (W)
1961—Tie, 28-28 (D)
       Redskins, 34-24 (W)
1962—Tie, 35-35 (D)
       Cowboys, 38-10 (W)
1963—Redskins, 21-17 (W)
       Cowboys, 35-20 (D)
1964—Cowboys, 24-18 (D)
       Redskins, 28-16 (W)
1965—Cowboys, 27-7 (D)
       Redskins, 34-31 (W)
1966—Cowboys, 31-30 (W)
       Redskins, 34-31 (D)
1967—Cowboys, 17-14 (W)
       Redskins, 27-20 (D)
1968—Cowboys, 44-24 (W)
       Cowboys, 29-20 (D)
1969—Cowboys, 41-28 (W)
       Cowboys, 20-10 (D)

1970—Cowboys, 45-21 (W)
       Cowboys, 34-0 (D)
1971—Redskins, 20-16 (D)
       Cowboys, 13-0 (D)
1972—Redskins, 24-20 (W)
       Cowboys, 34-24 (D)
       *Redskins, 26-3 (W)
1973—Cowboys, 14-7 (W)
       Cowboys, 27-7 (D)
1974—Redskins, 28-21 (W)
       Cowboys, 24-23 (D)
1975—Redskins, 30-24 (W) OT
       Cowboys, 31-10 (D)
1976—Cowboys, 20-7 (W)
       Redskins, 27-14 (D)
1977—Cowboys, 34-16 (D)
       Cowboys, 14-7 (W)
1978—Redskins, 9-5 (W)
       Cowboys, 37-10 (D)
1979—Redskins, 34-20 (W)
       Cowboys, 35-34 (D)
1980—Cowboys, 17-3 (W)
       Cowboys, 14-10 (D)
1981—Cowboys, 26-10 (W)
       Cowboys, 24-10 (D)
1982—Cowboys, 24-10 (W)
       *Redskins, 31-17 (W)
1983—Cowboys, 31-30 (W)
       Redskins, 31-10 (D)
1984—Redskins, 34-14 (W)
       Redskins, 30-28 (D)
1985—Cowboys, 44-14 (D)
       Cowboys, 13-7 (W)
1986—Cowboys, 30-6 (D)
       Redskins, 41-14 (W)
1987—Redskins, 13-7 (D)
       Redskins, 24-20 (W)
1988—Redskins, 35-17 (D)
       Cowboys, 24-17 (W)
1989—Redskins, 30-7 (D)
       Cowboys, 13-3 (W)
1990—Redskins, 19-15 (W)
       Cowboys, 27-17 (D)
1991—Redskins, 33-31 (D)
       Cowboys, 24-21 (W)
1992—Cowboys, 23-10 (W)
       Redskins, 20-17 (D)
1993—Redskins, 35-16 (W)
       Cowboys, 38-3 (D)
1994—Cowboys, 34-7 (W)
       Cowboys, 31-7 (D)
1995—Redskins, 27-23 (W)
       Redskins, 24-17 (D)
1996—Cowboys, 21-10 (D)
       Redskins, 37-10 (W)
1997—Redskins, 21-16 (W)
       Cowboys, 17-14 (D)
1998—Cowboys, 31-10 (W)
       Cowboys, 23-7 (D)
1999—Cowboys, 41-35 (W) OT
       Cowboys, 38-20 (D)
2000—Cowboys, 27-21 (W)
       Cowboys, 32-13 (D)
2001—Cowboys, 9-7 (D)
       Cowboys, 20-14 (W)
2002—Cowboys, 27-20 (D)
       Redskins, 20-14 (W)
2003—Cowboys, 21-14 (D)
       Cowboys, 27-0 (W)
2004—Cowboys, 21-18 (W)
       Cowboys, 13-10 (D)
2005—Redskins, 14-13 (D)
       Redskins, 35-7 (W)

2006—Cowboys, 27-10 (D)
       Redskins, 22-19 (W)
2007—Cowboys, 28-23 (D)
       Redskins, 27-6 (W)
2008—Redskins, 26-24 (D)
       Cowboys, 14-10 (W)
2009—Cowboys, 7-6 (D)
       Cowboys, 17-0 (W)
2010—Redskins, 13-7 (W)
       Cowboys, 33-30 (D)
2011—Cowboys, 18-16 (D)
       Cowboys, 27-24 (W) OT
2012—Redskins, 38-31 (D)
       Redskins, 28-18 (W)
(RS Pts.—Cowboys 2,374, Redskins 1,987)
(PS Pts.—Redskins 57, Cowboys 20)
*NFC Championship

DENVER vs. ARIZONA
RS: Broncos lead series, 7-1-1;
See Arizona vs. Denver
DENVER vs. ATLANTA
RS: Broncos lead series, 8-5
PS: Broncos lead series, 1-0;
See Atlanta vs. Denver
DENVER vs. BALTIMORE
RS: Ravens lead series, 5-4
PS: Ravens lead series, 2-0;
See Baltimore vs. Denver
DENVER vs. BUFFALO
RS: Bills lead series, 19-15-1
PS: Bills lead series, 1-0;
See Buffalo vs. Denver
DENVER vs. CAROLINA
RS: Broncos lead series, 3-1;
See Carolina vs. Denver
DENVER vs. CHICAGO
RS: Series tied, 7-7;
See Chicago vs. Denver
DENVER vs. CINCINNATI
RS: Broncos lead series, 19-8;
See Cincinnati vs. Denver
DENVER vs. CLEVELAND
RS: Broncos lead series, 19-5
PS: Broncos lead series, 3-0;
See Cleveland vs. Denver
DENVER vs. DALLAS
RS: Broncos lead series, 6-4
PS: Cowboys lead series, 1-0;
See Dallas vs. Denver
DENVER vs. DETROIT
RS: Broncos lead series, 6-5
1971—Lions, 24-20 (Den)
1974—Broncos, 31-27 (Det)
1978—Lions, 17-14 (Det)
1981—Broncos, 27-21 (Den)
1984—Broncos, 28-7 (Det)
1987—Broncos, 34-0 (Den)
1990—Lions, 40-27 (Det)
1999—Broncos, 17-7 (Det)
2003—Broncos, 20-16 (Den)
2007—Lions, 44-7 (Det)
2011—Lions, 45-10 (Den)
(RS Pts.—Lions 248, Broncos 235)
DENVER vs. GREEN BAY
RS: Packers lead series, 6-5-1
PS: Broncos lead series, 1-0
1971—Packers, 34-13 (Mil)
1975—Broncos, 23-13 (D)
1978—Broncos, 16-3 (D)
1984—Broncos, 17-14 (D)
1987—Tie, 17-17 (Mil) OT
1990—Broncos, 22-13 (D)

1993—Packers, 30-27 (GB)
1996—Packers, 41-6 (GB)
1997—*Broncos, 31-24 (San Diego)
1999—Broncos, 31-10 (D)
2003—Packers, 31-3 (GB)
2007—Packers, 19-13 (D) OT
2011—Packers, 49-23 (GB)
(RS Pts.—Packers 274, Broncos 211)
(PS Pts.—Broncos 31, Packers 24)
*Super Bowl XXXII
DENVER vs. HOUSTON
RS: Series tied, 2-2
2004—Broncos, 31-13 (D)
2007—Texans, 31-13 (H)
2010—Broncos, 24-23 (D)
2012—Texans, 31-25 (D)
(RS Pts.—Texans 98, Broncos 93)
DENVER vs. *INDIANAPOLIS
RS: Broncos lead series, 11-8
PS: Colts lead series, 2-0
1974—Broncos, 17-6 (B)
1977—Broncos, 27-13 (D)
1978—Colts, 7-6 (B)
1981—Broncos, 28-10 (D)
1983—Broncos, 17-10 (B)
        Broncos, 21-19 (D)
1985—Broncos, 15-10 (I)
1988—Colts, 55-23 (I)
1989—Broncos, 14-3 (D)
1990—Broncos, 27-17 (I)
1993—Broncos, 35-13 (D)
2001—Colts, 29-10 (I)
2002—Colts, 23-20 (D) OT
2003—Broncos, 31-17 (I)
        **Colts, 41-10 (I)
2004—Broncos, 33-14 (D)
        **Colts, 49-24 (I)
2006—Colts, 34-31 (D)
2007—Colts, 38-20 (I)
2009—Colts, 28-16 (I)
2010—Colts, 27-13 (D)
(RS Pts.—Broncos 404, Colts 373)
(PS Pts.—Colts 90, Broncos 34)
*Franchise in Baltimore prior to 1984
**AFC First-Round Playoff
DENVER vs. JACKSONVILLE
RS: Jaguars lead series, 5-3
PS: Series tied, 1-1
1995—Broncos, 31-23 (D)
1996—*Jaguars, 30-27 (D)
1997—**Broncos, 42-17 (D)
1998—Broncos, 37-24 (D)
1999—Jaguars, 27-24 (J)
2004—Jaguars, 7-6 (J)
2005—Broncos, 20-7 (J)
2007—Jaguars, 23-14 (D)
2008—Jaguars, 24-17 (D)
2010—Jaguars, 24-17 (J)
(RS Pts.—Broncos 166, Jaguars 159)
(PS Pts.—Broncos 69, Jaguars 47)
*AFC Divisional Playoff
**AFC First-Round Playoff
DENVER vs. *KANSAS CITY
RS: Chiefs lead series, 56-49
PS: Broncos lead series, 1-0
1960—Texans, 17-14 (D)
        Texans, 34-7 (Dal)
1961—Texans, 19-12 (D)
        Texans, 49-21 (Dal)
1962—Texans, 24-3 (D)
        Texans, 17-10 (Dal)
1963—Chiefs, 59-7 (D)
        Chiefs, 52-21 (KC)

1964—Broncos, 33-27 (D)
        Chiefs, 49-39 (KC)
1965—Chiefs, 31-23 (D)
        Chiefs, 45-35 (KC)
1966—Chiefs, 37-10 (D)
        Chiefs, 56-10 (D)
1967—Chiefs, 52-9 (KC)
        Chiefs, 38-24 (D)
1968—Chiefs, 34-2 (KC)
        Chiefs, 30-7 (D)
1969—Chiefs, 26-13 (D)
        Chiefs, 31-17 (KC)
1970—Broncos, 26-13 (D)
        Chiefs, 16-0 (KC)
1971—Chiefs, 16-3 (D)
        Chiefs, 28-10 (KC)
1972—Chiefs, 45-24 (D)
        Chiefs, 24-21 (KC)
1973—Chiefs, 16-14 (KC)
        Broncos, 14-10 (D)
1974—Broncos, 17-14 (KC)
        Chiefs, 42-34 (D)
1975—Broncos, 37-33 (D)
        Chiefs, 26-13 (KC)
1976—Broncos, 35-26 (KC)
        Broncos, 17-16 (D)
1977—Broncos, 23-7 (D)
        Broncos, 14-7 (KC)
1978—Broncos, 23-17 (KC) OT
        Broncos, 24-3 (D)
1979—Broncos, 24-10 (KC)
        Broncos, 20-3 (D)
1980—Chiefs, 23-17 (D)
        Chiefs, 31-14 (KC)
1981—Chiefs, 28-14 (KC)
        Broncos, 16-13 (D)
1982—Chiefs, 37-16 (D)
1983—Broncos, 27-24 (D)
        Chiefs, 48-17 (KC)
1984—Broncos, 21-0 (D)
        Chiefs, 16-13 (KC)
1985—Broncos, 30-10 (KC)
        Broncos, 14-13 (D)
1986—Broncos, 38-17 (D)
        Chiefs, 37-10 (KC)
1987—Broncos, 26-17 (KC)
        Broncos, 20-17 (D)
1988—Chiefs, 20-13 (KC)
        Broncos, 17-11 (D)
1989—Broncos, 34-20 (D)
        Broncos, 16-13 (KC)
1990—Broncos, 24-23 (D)
        Chiefs, 31-20 (KC)
1991—Broncos, 19-16 (D)
        Broncos, 24-20 (KC)
1992—Broncos, 20-19 (D)
        Chiefs, 42-20 (KC)
1993—Chiefs, 15-7 (KC)
        Broncos, 27-21 (D)
1994—Chiefs, 31-28 (D)
        Broncos, 20-17 (KC) OT
1995—Chiefs, 21-7 (D)
        Chiefs, 20-17 (KC)
1996—Chiefs, 17-14 (KC)
        Broncos, 34-7 (D)
1997—Broncos, 19-3 (D)
        Chiefs, 24-22 (KC)
        **Broncos, 14-10 (KC)
1998—Broncos, 30-7 (KC)
        Broncos, 35-31 (D)
1999—Chiefs, 26-10 (KC)
        Chiefs, 16-10 (D)

2000—Chiefs, 23-22 (D)
        Chiefs, 20-7 (KC)
2001—Broncos, 20-6 (D)
        Chiefs, 26-23 (KC) OT
2002—Broncos, 37-34 (KC) OT
        Broncos, 31-24 (D)
2003—Chiefs, 24-23 (KC)
        Broncos, 45-27 (D)
2004—Broncos, 34-24 (D)
        Chiefs, 45-17 (KC)
2005—Broncos, 30-10 (D)
        Chiefs, 31-27 (KC)
2006—Broncos, 9-6 (D) OT
        Chiefs, 19-10 (KC)
2007—Broncos, 27-11 (KC)
        Broncos, 41-7 (D)
2008—Chiefs, 33-19 (KC)
        Broncos, 24-17 (D)
2009—Broncos, 44-13 (KC)
        Chiefs, 44-24 (D)
2010—Broncos, 49-29 (D)
        Chiefs, 10-6 (KC)
2011—Broncos, 17-10 (KC)
        Chiefs, 7-3 (D)
2012—Broncos, 17-9 (KC)
        Broncos, 38-3 (D)
(RS Pts.—Chiefs 2,413, Broncos 2,134)
(PS Pts.—Broncos 14, Chiefs 10)
*Franchise in Dallas prior to 1963 and
known as Texans
**AFC Divisional Playoff
DENVER vs. MIAMI
RS: Dolphins lead series, 11-4-1
PS: Broncos lead series, 1-0
1966—Dolphins, 24-7 (M)
        Broncos, 17-7 (D)
1967—Dolphins, 35-21 (M)
1968—Broncos, 21-14 (D)
1969—Dolphins, 27-24 (M)
1971—Tie, 10-10 (D)
1975—Dolphins, 14-13 (M)
1985—Dolphins, 30-26 (D)
1998—Dolphins, 31-21 (M)
        *Broncos, 38-3 (D)
1999—Dolphins, 38-21 (D)
2001—Dolphins, 21-10 (M)
2002—Dolphins, 24-22 (D)
2004—Broncos, 20-17 (D)
2005—Dolphins, 34-10 (M)
2008—Dolphins, 26-17 (D)
2011—Broncos, 18-15 (M) OT
(RS Pts.—Dolphins 367, Broncos 278)
(PS Pts.—Broncos 38, Dolphins 3)
*AFC Divisional Playoff
DENVER vs. MINNESOTA
RS: Vikings lead series, 7-6
1972—Vikings, 23-20 (M)
1978—Vikings, 12-9 (M) OT
1981—Broncos, 19-17 (D)
1984—Broncos, 42-21 (D)
1987—Vikings, 34-27 (M)
1990—Vikings, 27-22 (M)
1991—Broncos, 13-6 (M)
1993—Vikings, 26-23 (D)
1996—Broncos, 21-17 (M)
1999—Vikings, 23-20 (D)
2003—Vikings, 28-20 (M)
2007—Broncos, 22-19 (D) OT
2011—Broncos, 35-32 (M)
(RS Pts.—Broncos 293, Vikings 285)
DENVER vs. *NEW ENGLAND
RS: Broncos lead series, 25-18
PS: Broncos lead series, 2-1

1960—Broncos, 13-10 (B)
　　　Broncos, 31-24 (D)
1961—Patriots, 45-17 (B)
　　　Patriots, 28-24 (D)
1962—Patriots, 41-16 (B)
　　　Patriots, 33-29 (D)
1963—Broncos, 14-10 (D)
　　　Patriots, 40-21 (B)
1964—Patriots, 39-10 (D)
　　　Patriots, 12-7 (B)
1965—Broncos, 27-10 (B)
　　　Patriots, 28-20 (D)
1966—Patriots, 24-10 (D)
　　　Broncos, 17-10 (B)
1967—Broncos, 26-21 (D)
1968—Patriots, 20-17 (D)
　　　Broncos, 35-14 (B)
1969—Broncos, 35-7 (D)
1972—Broncos, 45-21 (D)
1976—Patriots, 38-14 (NE)
1979—Broncos, 45-10 (D)
1980—Patriots, 23-14 (NE)
1984—Broncos, 26-19 (D)
1986—Broncos, 27-20 (D)
　　　**Broncos, 22-17 (D)
1987—Broncos, 31-20 (D)
1988—Broncos, 21-10 (D)
1991—Broncos, 9-6 (NE)
　　　Broncos, 20-3 (D)
1995—Broncos, 37-3 (NE)
1996—Broncos, 34-8 (NE)
1997—Broncos, 34-13 (D)
1998—Broncos, 27-21 (D)
1999—Patriots, 24-23 (NE)
2000—Patriots, 28-19 (D)
2001—Broncos, 31-20 (D)
2002—Broncos, 24-16 (NE)
2003—Patriots, 30-26 (D)
2005—Broncos, 28-20 (D)
　　　**Broncos, 27-13 (D)
2006—Broncos, 17-7 (NE)
2008—Patriots, 41-7 (NE)
2009—Broncos, 20-17 (D) OT
2011—Patriots, 41-23 (D)
　　　**Patriots, 45-10 (NE)
2012—Patriots, 31-21 (NE)
(RS Pts.—Broncos 992, Patriots 906)
(PS Pts.—Patriots 75, Broncos 59)
*Franchise in Boston prior to 1971
**AFC Divisional Playoff
DENVER vs. NEW ORLEANS
RS: Broncos lead series, 8-2
1970—Broncos, 31-6 (NO)
1974—Broncos, 33-17 (D)
1979—Broncos, 10-3 (D)
1985—Broncos, 34-23 (D)
1988—Saints, 42-0 (NO)
1994—Saints, 30-28 (D)
2000—Broncos, 38-23 (NO)
2004—Broncos, 34-13 (NO)
2008—Broncos, 34-32 (D)
2012—Broncos, 34-14 (D)
(RS Pts.—Broncos 276, Saints 203)
DENVER vs. N.Y. GIANTS
RS: Series tied, 5-5
PS: Giants lead series, 1-0
1972—Giants, 29-17 (NY)
1976—Broncos, 14-13 (D)
1980—Broncos, 14-9 (NY)
1986—Giants, 19-16 (NY)
　　　*Giants, 39-20 (Pasadena)
1989—Giants, 14-7 (D)
1992—Broncos, 27-13 (D)

1998—Giants, 20-16 (NY)
2001—Broncos, 31-20 (D)
2005—Giants, 24-23 (NY)
2009—Broncos, 26-6 (D)
(RS Pts.—Broncos 191, Giants 167)
(PS Pts.—Giants 39, Broncos 20)
*Super Bowl XXI
DENVER vs. *N.Y. JETS
RS: Broncos lead series, 17-15-1
PS: Broncos lead series, 1-0
1960—Titans, 28-24 (NY)
　　　Titans, 30-27 (D)
1961—Titans, 35-28 (NY)
　　　Broncos, 27-10 (D)
1962—Broncos, 32-10 (NY)
　　　Titans, 46-45 (D)
1963—Tie, 35-35 (NY)
　　　Jets, 14-9 (D)
1964—Jets, 30-6 (NY)
　　　Broncos, 20-16 (D)
1965—Broncos, 16-13 (D)
　　　Jets, 45-10 (NY)
1966—Jets, 16-7 (D)
1967—Jets, 38-24 (D)
　　　Broncos, 33-24 (NY)
1968—Broncos, 21-13 (NY)
1969—Broncos, 21-19 (D)
1973—Broncos, 40-28 (NY)
1976—Broncos, 46-3 (D)
1978—Jets, 31-28 (D)
1980—Broncos, 31-24 (D)
1986—Jets, 22-10 (NY)
1992—Broncos, 27-16 (D)
1993—Broncos, 26-20 (NY)
1994—Jets, 25-22 (NY) OT
1996—Broncos, 31-6 (D)
1998—**Broncos, 23-10 (D)
1999—Jets, 21-13 (D)
2000—Broncos, 30-23 (NY)
2002—Jets, 19-13 (NY)
2005—Broncos, 27-0 (D)
2008—Broncos, 34-17 (NY)
2010—Jets, 24-20 (D)
2011—Broncos, 17-13 (D)
(RS Pts.—Broncos 800, Jets 714)
(PS Pts.—Broncos 23, Jets 10)
*Jets known as Titans prior to 1963
**AFC Championship
DENVER vs. *OAKLAND
RS: Raiders lead series, 59-44-2
PS: Series tied, 1-1
1960—Broncos, 31-14 (D)
　　　Raiders, 48-10 (O)
1961—Raiders, 33-19 (O)
　　　Broncos, 27-24 (D)
1962—Raiders, 44-7 (D)
　　　Broncos, 23-6 (O)
1963—Raiders, 26-10 (D)
　　　Raiders, 35-31 (O)
1964—Raiders, 40-7 (O)
　　　Tie, 20-20 (D)
1965—Raiders, 28-20 (D)
　　　Raiders, 24-13 (O)
1966—Raiders, 17-3 (D)
　　　Raiders, 28-10 (O)
1967—Raiders, 51-0 (O)
　　　Raiders, 21-17 (D)
1968—Raiders, 43-7 (D)
　　　Raiders, 33-27 (O)
1969—Raiders, 24-14 (D)
　　　Raiders, 41-10 (O)
1970—Raiders, 35-23 (O)
　　　Raiders, 24-19 (D)

1971—Raiders, 27-16 (D)
　　　Raiders, 21-13 (O)
1972—Broncos, 30-23 (O)
　　　Raiders, 37-20 (D)
1973—Tie, 23-23 (D)
　　　Raiders, 21-17 (O)
1974—Raiders, 28-17 (D)
　　　Broncos, 20-17 (O)
1975—Raiders, 42-17 (O)
　　　Raiders, 17-10 (D)
1976—Raiders, 17-10 (D)
　　　Raiders, 19-6 (O)
1977—Broncos, 30-7 (O)
　　　Raiders, 24-14 (D)
　　　**Broncos, 20-17 (D)
1978—Broncos, 14-6 (D)
　　　Broncos, 21-6 (O)
1979—Raiders, 27-3 (O)
　　　Raiders, 14-10 (D)
1980—Raiders, 9-3 (O)
　　　Raiders, 24-21 (D)
1981—Broncos, 9-7 (D)
　　　Broncos, 17-0 (O)
1982—Raiders, 27-10 (LA)
1983—Raiders, 22-7 (D)
　　　Raiders, 22-20 (LA)
1984—Broncos, 16-13 (D)
　　　Broncos, 22-19 (LA) OT
1985—Raiders, 31-28 (LA) OT
　　　Raiders, 17-14 (D) OT
1986—Broncos, 38-36 (D)
　　　Broncos, 21-10 (LA)
1987—Broncos, 30-14 (D)
　　　Broncos, 23-17 (LA)
1988—Raiders, 30-27 (D) OT
　　　Raiders, 21-20 (LA)
1989—Broncos, 31-21 (D)
　　　Raiders, 16-13 (LA) OT
1990—Raiders, 14-9 (LA)
　　　Raiders, 23-20 (D)
1991—Raiders, 16-13 (LA)
　　　Raiders, 17-16 (D)
1992—Broncos, 17-13 (D)
　　　Raiders, 24-0 (LA)
1993—Raiders, 23-20 (D)
　　　Raiders, 33-30 (LA) OT
　　　***Raiders, 42-24 (LA)
1994—Raiders, 48-16 (D)
　　　Raiders, 23-13 (LA)
1995—Broncos, 27-0 (D)
　　　Broncos, 31-28 (O)
1996—Broncos, 22-21 (O)
　　　Broncos, 24-19 (D)
1997—Raiders, 28-25 (O)
　　　Broncos, 31-3 (D)
1998—Broncos, 34-17 (O)
　　　Broncos, 40-14 (D)
1999—Broncos, 16-13 (O)
　　　Broncos, 27-21 (D) OT
2000—Broncos, 33-24 (D)
　　　Broncos, 27-24 (O)
2001—Raiders, 38-28 (O)
　　　Broncos, 23-17 (D)
2002—Raiders, 34-10 (D)
　　　Raiders, 28-16 (O)
2003—Broncos, 31-10 (D)
　　　Broncos, 22-8 (O)
2004—Broncos, 31-3 (D)
　　　Raiders, 25-24 (D)
2005—Broncos, 31-17 (O)
　　　Broncos, 22-3 (D)
2006—Broncos, 13-3 (D)
　　　Broncos, 17-13 (O)

2007—Broncos, 23-20 (D) OT
    Raiders, 34-20 (O)
2008—Broncos, 41-14 (O)
    Raiders, 31-10 (D)
2009—Broncos, 23-3 (O)
    Raiders, 20-19 (D)
2010—Raiders, 59-14 (O)
    Raiders, 39-23 (O)
2011—Raiders, 23-20 (D)
    Broncos, 38-24 (O)
2012—Broncos, 37-6 (D)
    Broncos, 26-13 (O)
(RS Pts.—Raiders 2,285, Broncos 2,099)
(PS Pts.—Raiders 59, Broncos 44)
*Franchise in Los Angeles from 1982-1994
**AFC Championship
***AFC First-Round Playoff

DENVER vs. PHILADELPHIA
RS: Eagles lead series, 7-4
1971—Eagles, 17-16 (P)
1975—Broncos, 25-10 (D)
1980—Eagles, 27-6 (P)
1983—Eagles, 13-10 (D)
1986—Broncos, 33-7 (P)
1989—Eagles, 28-24 (D)
1992—Eagles, 30-0 (P)
1995—Eagles, 31-13 (P)
1998—Broncos, 41-16 (D)
2005—Broncos, 49-21 (D)
2009—Eagles, 30-27 (P)
(RS Pts.—Broncos 244, Eagles 230)

DENVER vs. PITTSBURGH
RS: Broncos lead series, 14-7-1
PS: Broncos lead series, 4-3
1970—Broncos, 16-13 (D)
1971—Broncos, 22-10 (P)
1973—Broncos, 23-13 (P)
1974—Tie, 35-35 (D) OT
1975—Steelers, 20-9 (P)
1977—Broncos, 21-7 (D)
    *Broncos, 34-21 (D)
1978—Steelers, 21-17 (D)
    *Steelers, 33-10 (P)
1979—Steelers, 42-7 (P)
1983—Broncos, 14-10 (P)
1984—*Steelers, 24-17 (D)
1985—Broncos, 31-23 (P)
1986—Broncos, 21-10 (P)
1988—Steelers, 39-21 (P)
1989—Broncos, 34-7 (D)
    *Broncos, 24-23 (D)
1990—Steelers, 34-17 (D)
1991—Broncos, 20-13 (D)
1993—Broncos, 37-13 (D)
1997—Broncos, 35-24 (P)
    **Broncos, 24-21 (P)
2003—Broncos, 17-14 (D)
2005—**Steelers, 34-17 (D)
2006—Broncos, 31-20 (P)
2007—Broncos, 31-28 (D)
2009—Steelers, 28-10 (D)
2011—***Broncos, 29-23 (D) OT
2012—Broncos, 31-19 (D)
(RS Pts.—Broncos 489, Steelers 454)
(PS Pts.—Steelers 179, Broncos 155)
*AFC Divisional Playoff
**AFC Championship
***AFC First-Round Playoff

DENVER vs. *ST. LOUIS
RS: Rams lead series, 7-5
1972—Broncos, 16-10 (LA)
1974—Rams, 17-10 (D)
1979—Rams, 13-9 (D)

1982—Broncos, 27-24 (LA)
1985—Rams, 20-16 (LA)
1988—Broncos, 35-24 (D)
1994—Rams, 27-21 (LA)
1997—Broncos, 35-14 (D)
2000—Rams, 41-36 (StL)
2002—Broncos, 23-16 (D)
2006—Rams, 18-10 (StL)
2010—Rams, 36-33 (D)
(RS Pts.—Broncos 271, Rams 260)
*Franchise in Los Angeles prior to 1995

DENVER vs. *SAN DIEGO
RS: Broncos lead series, 57-48-1
1960—Chargers, 23-19 (D)
    Chargers, 41-33 (LA)
1961—Chargers, 37-0 (SD)
    Chargers, 19-16 (D)
1962—Broncos, 30-21 (D)
    Broncos, 23-20 (SD)
1963—Broncos, 50-34 (D)
    Chargers, 58-20 (SD)
1964—Chargers, 42-14 (SD)
    Chargers, 31-20 (D)
1965—Chargers, 34-31 (SD)
    Chargers, 33-21 (D)
1966—Chargers, 24-17 (SD)
    Broncos, 20-17 (D)
1967—Chargers, 38-21 (D)
    Chargers, 24-20 (SD)
1968—Chargers, 55-24 (D)
    Chargers, 47-23 (D)
1969—Broncos, 13-0 (D)
    Chargers, 45-24 (SD)
1970—Chargers, 24-21 (SD)
    Tie, 17-17 (D)
1971—Broncos, 20-16 (D)
    Chargers, 45-17 (SD)
1972—Chargers, 37-14 (SD)
    Broncos, 38-13 (D)
1973—Broncos, 30-19 (D)
    Broncos, 42-28 (SD)
1974—Broncos, 27-7 (D)
    Chargers, 17-0 (SD)
1975—Broncos, 27-17 (SD)
    Broncos, 13-10 (D) OT
1976—Broncos, 26-0 (D)
    Broncos, 17-0 (SD)
1977—Broncos, 17-14 (SD)
    Broncos, 17-9 (D)
1978—Broncos, 27-14 (D)
    Chargers, 23-0 (SD)
1979—Broncos, 7-0 (D)
    Chargers, 17-7 (SD)
1980—Chargers, 30-13 (D)
    Broncos, 20-13 (SD)
1981—Broncos, 42-24 (D)
    Chargers, 34-17 (SD)
1982—Chargers, 23-3 (D)
    Chargers, 30-20 (SD)
1983—Broncos, 14-6 (D)
    Chargers, 31-7 (SD)
1984—Broncos, 16-13 (SD)
    Broncos, 16-13 (D)
1985—Chargers, 30-10 (SD)
    Broncos, 30-24 (D) OT
1986—Broncos, 31-14 (SD)
    Chargers, 9-3 (D)
1987—Broncos, 31-17 (SD)
    Broncos, 24-0 (D)
1988—Broncos, 34-3 (D)
    Broncos, 12-0 (SD)
1989—Broncos, 16-10 (D)
    Chargers, 19-16 (SD)

1990—Chargers, 19-7 (SD)
    Broncos, 20-10 (D)
1991—Broncos, 27-19 (D)
    Broncos, 17-14 (SD)
1992—Broncos, 21-13 (D)
    Chargers, 24-21 (SD)
1993—Broncos, 34-17 (D)
    Chargers, 13-10 (SD)
1994—Chargers, 37-34 (D)
    Broncos, 20-15 (SD)
1995—Chargers, 17-6 (SD)
    Broncos, 30-27 (D)
1996—Broncos, 28-17 (D)
    Chargers, 16-10 (SD)
1997—Broncos, 38-28 (SD)
    Broncos, 38-3 (D)
1998—Broncos, 27-10 (D)
    Broncos, 31-16 (SD)
1999—Broncos, 33-17 (SD)
    Chargers, 12-6 (D)
2000—Broncos, 21-7 (SD)
    Broncos, 38-37 (D)
2001—Chargers, 27-10 (SD)
    Broncos, 26-16 (D)
2002—Broncos, 26-9 (D)
    Chargers, 30-27 (SD) OT
2003—Broncos, 37-13 (D)
    Broncos, 37-8 (D)
2004—Broncos, 23-13 (D)
    Chargers, 20-17 (SD)
2005—Broncos, 20-17 (D)
    Broncos, 23-7 (SD)
2006—Chargers, 35-27 (D)
    Chargers, 48-20 (SD)
2007—Chargers, 41-3 (D)
    Chargers, 23-3 (SD)
2008—Broncos, 39-38 (D)
    Chargers, 52-21 (SD)
2009—Broncos, 34-23 (SD)
    Chargers, 32-3 (D)
2010—Chargers, 35-14 (SD)
    Chargers, 33-28 (D)
2011—Chargers, 29-24 (D)
    Broncos, 16-13 (SD) OT
2012—Broncos, 35-24 (SD)
    Broncos, 30-23 (D)
(RS Pts.—Chargers 2,312, Broncos 2,258)
*Franchise in Los Angeles prior to 1961

DENVER vs. SAN FRANCISCO
RS: Series tied, 6-6
PS: 49ers lead series, 1-0
1970—49ers, 19-14 (SF)
1973—49ers, 36-34 (D)
1979—Broncos, 38-28 (SF)
1982—Broncos, 24-21 (D)
1985—Broncos, 17-16 (D)
1988—Broncos, 16-13 (SF) OT
1989—*49ers, 55-10 (New Orleans)
1994—49ers, 42-19 (SF)
1997—Broncos, 34-17 (SF)
2000—Broncos, 38-9 (D)
2002—Broncos, 24-14 (SF)
2006—49ers, 26-23 (D) OT
2010—49ers, 24-16 (London)
(RS Pts.—49ers 282, Broncos 280)
(PS Pts.—49ers 55, Broncos 10)
*Super Bowl XXIV

DENVER vs. SEATTLE
RS: Broncos lead series, 34-18
PS: Seahawks lead series, 1-0
1977—Broncos, 24-13 (S)
1978—Broncos, 28-7 (D)
    Broncos, 20-17 (S) OT

1979—Broncos, 37-34 (D)
    Seahawks, 28-23 (S)
1980—Broncos, 36-20 (D)
    Broncos, 25-17 (S)
1981—Seahawks, 13-10 (S)
    Broncos, 23-13 (D)
1982—Seahawks, 17-10 (D)
    Seahawks, 13-11 (S)
1983—Seahawks, 27-19 (S)
    Broncos, 38-27 (D)
    *Seahawks, 31-7 (S)
1984—Seahawks, 27-24 (D)
    Broncos, 31-14 (S)
1985—Broncos, 13-10 (D) OT
    Broncos, 27-24 (S)
1986—Broncos, 20-13 (D)
    Seahawks, 41-16 (S)
1987—Broncos, 40-17 (D)
    Seahawks, 28-21 (S)
1988—Seahawks, 21-14 (D)
    Seahawks, 42-14 (S)
1989—Broncos, 24-21 (S) OT
    Broncos, 41-14 (D)
1990—Broncos, 34-31 (D) OT
    Seahawks, 17-12 (S)
1991—Broncos, 16-10 (D)
    Seahawks, 13-10 (S)
1992—Seahawks, 16-13 (S) OT
    Broncos, 10-6 (D)
1993—Broncos, 28-17 (D)
    Broncos, 17-9 (S)
1994—Broncos, 16-9 (S)
    Broncos, 17-10 (D)
1995—Seahawks, 27-10 (S)
    Seahawks, 31-27 (D)
1996—Broncos, 30-20 (S)
    Broncos, 34-7 (D)
1997—Broncos, 35-14 (S)
    Broncos, 30-27 (D)
1998—Broncos, 21-16 (S)
    Broncos, 28-21 (D)
1999—Seahawks, 20-17 (S)
    Broncos, 36-30 (D) OT
2000—Broncos, 38-31 (S)
    Broncos, 31-24 (D)
2001—Seahawks, 34-21 (S)
    Broncos, 20-7 (D)
2002—Broncos, 31-9 (S)
2006—Seahawks, 23-20 (D)
2010—Broncos, 31-14 (D)
(RS Pts.—Broncos 1,222, Seahawks 1,011)
(PS Pts.—Seahawks 31, Broncos 7)
*AFC First-Round Playoff
DENVER vs. TAMPA BAY
RS: Broncos lead series, 6-2
1976—Broncos, 48-13 (D)
1981—Broncos, 24-7 (TB)
1993—Buccaneers, 17-10 (D)
1996—Broncos, 27-23 (D)
1999—Buccaneers, 13-10 (TB)
2004—Broncos, 16-13 (TB)
2008—Broncos, 16-13 (D)
2012—Broncos, 31-23 (D)
(RS Pts.—Broncos 182, Buccaneers 122)
DENVER vs. *TENNESSEE
RS: Titans lead series, 21-14-1
PS: Broncos lead series, 2-1
1960—Oilers, 45-25 (D)
    Oilers, 20-10 (H)
1961—Oilers, 55-14 (D)
    Oilers, 45-14 (H)
1962—Broncos, 20-10 (D)
    Oilers, 34-17 (H)

1963—Oilers, 20-14 (H)
    Oilers, 33-24 (D)
1964—Oilers, 38-17 (D)
    Oilers, 34-15 (H)
1965—Broncos, 28-17 (D)
    Broncos, 31-21 (H)
1966—Oilers, 45-7 (H)
    Broncos, 40-38 (D)
1967—Oilers, 10-6 (H)
    Oilers, 20-18 (D)
1968—Oilers, 38-17 (H)
1969—Oilers, 24-21 (H)
    Tie, 20-20 (D)
1970—Oilers, 31-21 (H)
1972—Broncos, 30-17 (D)
1973—Broncos, 48-20 (H)
1974—Broncos, 37-14 (D)
1976—Oilers, 17-3 (H)
1977—Broncos, 24-14 (H)
1979—**Oilers, 13-7 (H)
1980—Oilers, 20-16 (D)
1983—Broncos, 26-14 (H)
1985—Broncos, 31-20 (D)
1987—Oilers, 40-10 (D)
    ***Broncos, 34-10 (D)
1991—Oilers, 42-14 (H)
    ***Broncos, 26-24 (D)
1992—Broncos, 27-21 (D)
1995—Oilers, 42-33 (H)
2004—Broncos, 37-16 (T)
2007—Broncos, 34-20 (D)
2010—Broncos, 26-20 (T)
2011—Titans, 17-14 (T)
(RS Pts.—Titans 952, Broncos 789)
(PS Pts.—Broncos 67, Titans 47)
*Franchise in Houston prior to 1997;
known as the Oilers prior to 1999
**AFC First-Round Playoff
***AFC Divisional Playoff
DENVER vs. WASHINGTON
RS: Broncos lead series, 6-5
PS: Redskins lead series, 1-0
1970—Redskins, 19-3 (D)
1974—Redskins, 30-3 (W)
1980—Broncos, 20-17 (D)
1986—Broncos, 31-30 (D)
1987—*Redskins, 42-10 (San Diego)
1989—Broncos, 14-10 (W)
1992—Redskins, 34-3 (W)
1995—Broncos, 38-31 (S)
1998—Broncos, 38-16 (W)
2001—Redskins, 17-10 (D)
2005—Broncos, 21-19 (D)
2009—Redskins, 27-17 (W)
(RS Pts.—Redskins 250, Broncos 198)
(PS Pts.—Redskins 42, Broncos 10)
*Super Bowl XXII

DETROIT vs. ARIZONA
RS: Lions lead series, 31-25-5;
See Arizona vs. Detroit
DETROIT vs. ATLANTA
RS: Lions lead series, 23-12;
See Atlanta vs. Detroit
DETROIT vs. BALTIMORE
RS: Ravens lead series, 2-1;
See Baltimore vs. Detroit
DETROIT vs. BUFFALO
RS: Series tied, 4-4-1;
See Buffalo vs. Detroit
DETROIT vs. CAROLINA
RS: Panthers lead series, 4-2;
See Carolina vs. Detroit

DETROIT vs. CHICAGO
RS: Bears lead series, 96-65-5;
See Chicago vs. Detroit
DETROIT vs. CINCINNATI
RS: Bengals lead series, 7-3;
See Cincinnati vs. Detroit
DETROIT vs. CLEVELAND
RS: Lions lead series, 14-4
PS: Lions lead series, 3-1;
See Cleveland vs. Detroit
DETROIT vs. DALLAS
RS: Cowboys lead series, 12-10
PS: Series tied, 1-1;
See Dallas vs. Detroit
DETROIT vs. DENVER
RS: Broncos lead series, 6-5;
See Denver vs. Detroit
DETROIT vs. GREEN BAY
RS: Packers lead series, 93-65-7
PS: Packers lead series, 2-0
1930—Packers, 47-13 (GB)
    Tie, 6-6 (P)
1932—Packers, 15-10 (GB)
    Spartans, 19-0 (P)
1933—Packers, 17-0 (GB)
    Spartans, 7-0 (P)
1934—Lions, 3-0 (GB)
    Packers, 3-0 (D)
1935—Packers, 13-9 (Mil)
    Packers, 31-7 (GB)
    Lions, 20-10 (D)
1936—Packers, 20-18 (GB)
    Packers, 26-17 (D)
1937—Packers, 26-6 (GB)
    Packers, 14-13 (D)
1938—Lions, 17-7 (GB)
    Packers, 28-7 (D)
1939—Packers, 26-7 (GB)
    Packers, 12-7 (D)
1940—Lions, 23-14 (GB)
    Packers, 50-7 (D)
1941—Packers, 23-0 (GB)
    Packers, 24-7 (D)
1942—Packers, 38-7 (Mil)
    Packers, 28-7 (D)
1943—Packers, 35-14 (GB)
    Packers, 27-6 (D)
1944—Packers, 27-6 (Mil)
    Packers, 14-0 (D)
1945—Packers, 57-21 (Mil)
    Lions, 14-3 (D)
1946—Packers, 10-7 (Mil)
    Packers, 9-0 (D)
1947—Packers, 34-17 (GB)
    Packers, 35-14 (D)
1948—Packers, 33-21 (GB)
    Lions, 24-20 (D)
1949—Packers, 16-14 (Mil)
    Lions, 21-7 (D)
1950—Lions, 45-7 (GB)
    Lions, 24-21 (D)
1951—Lions, 24-17 (GB)
    Lions, 52-35 (D)
1952—Lions, 52-17 (GB)
    Lions, 48-24 (D)
1953—Lions, 14-7 (GB)
    Lions, 34-15 (D)
1954—Lions, 21-17 (GB)
    Lions, 28-24 (D)
1955—Packers, 20-17 (GB)
    Lions, 24-10 (D)
1956—Lions, 20-16 (GB)
    Packers, 24-20 (D)

1957—Lions, 24-14 (GB)
    Lions, 18-6 (D)
1958—Tie, 13-13 (GB)
    Lions, 24-14 (D)
1959—Packers, 28-10 (GB)
    Packers, 24-17 (D)
1960—Packers, 28-9 (GB)
    Lions, 23-10 (D)
1961—Lions, 17-13 (Mil)
    Packers, 17-9 (D)
1962—Packers, 9-7 (GB)
    Lions, 26-14 (D)
1963—Packers, 31-10 (Mil)
    Tie, 13-13 (D)
1964—Packers, 14-10 (D)
    Packers, 30-7 (GB)
1965—Packers, 31-21 (D)
    Lions, 12-7 (GB)
1966—Packers, 23-14 (GB)
    Packers, 31-7 (D)
1967—Tie, 17-17 (GB)
    Packers, 27-17 (D)
1968—Lions, 23-17 (GB)
    Tie, 14-14 (D)
1969—Packers, 28-17 (D)
    Lions, 16-10 (GB)
1970—Lions, 40-0 (GB)
    Lions, 20-0 (D)
1971—Lions, 31-28 (D)
    Tie, 14-14 (Mil)
1972—Packers, 24-23 (D)
    Packers, 33-7 (GB)
1973—Tie, 13-13 (GB)
    Lions, 34-0 (D)
1974—Packers, 21-19 (Mil)
    Lions, 19-17 (D)
1975—Lions, 30-16 (Mil)
    Lions, 13-10 (D)
1976—Packers, 24-14 (GB)
    Lions, 27-6 (D)
1977—Lions, 10-6 (D)
    Packers, 10-9 (GB)
1978—Packers, 13-7 (D)
    Packers, 35-14 (Mil)
1979—Packers, 24-16 (Mil)
    Packers, 18-13 (D)
1980—Lions, 29-7 (Mil)
    Lions, 24-3 (D)
1981—Lions, 31-27 (D)
    Packers, 31-17 (GB)
1982—Lions, 30-10 (GB)
    Lions, 27-24 (D)
1983—Lions, 38-14 (D)
    Lions, 23-20 (Mil) OT
1984—Packers, 41-9 (GB)
    Lions, 31-28 (D)
1985—Packers, 43-10 (GB)
    Packers, 26-23 (D)
1986—Lions, 21-14 (GB)
    Packers, 44-40 (D)
1987—Lions, 19-16 (GB) OT
    Packers, 34-33 (D)
1988—Lions, 19-9 (Mil)
    Lions, 30-14 (D)
1989—Packers, 23-20 (Mil) OT
    Lions, 31-22 (D)
1990—Packers, 24-21 (D)
    Lions, 24-17 (GB)
1991—Lions, 23-14 (D)
    Lions, 21-17 (GB)
1992—Packers, 27-13 (D)
    Packers, 38-10 (Mil)

1993—Packers, 26-17 (Mil)
    Lions, 30-20 (D)
    **Packers, 28-24 (D)
1994—Packers, 38-30 (Mil)
    Lions, 34-31 (D)
    **Packers, 16-12 (GB)
1995—Packers, 30-21 (GB)
    Lions, 24-16 (D)
1996—Packers, 28-18 (GB)
    Packers, 31-3 (D)
1997—Lions, 26-15 (D)
    Packers, 20-10 (GB)
1998—Packers, 38-19 (GB)
    Lions, 27-20 (D)
1999—Lions, 23-15 (D)
    Packers, 26-17 (GB)
2000—Lions, 31-24 (D)
    Packers, 26-13 (GB)
2001—Packers, 28-6 (GB)
    Packers, 29-27 (D)
2002—Packers, 37-31 (D)
    Packers, 40-14 (GB)
2003—Packers, 31-6 (D)
    Lions, 22-14 (D)
2004—Packers, 38-10 (D)
    Packers, 16-13 (GB)
2005—Lions, 17-3 (D)
    Packers, 16-13 (GB) OT
2006—Packers, 31-24 (D)
    Packers, 17-9 (GB)
2007—Packers, 37-26 (D)
    Packers, 34-13 (GB)
2008—Packers, 48-25 (D)
    Packers, 31-21 (GB)
2009—Packers, 26-0 (GB)
    Packers, 34-12 (D)
2010—Packers, 28-26 (GB)
    Lions, 7-3 (D)
2011—Packers, 27-15 (D)
    Packers, 45-41 (GB)
2012—Packers, 24-20 (D)
    Packers, 27-20 (GB)
(RS Pts.—Packers 3,509, Lions 2,985)
(PS Pts.—Packers 44, Lions 36)
*Franchise in Portsmouth prior to 1934
and known as the Spartans
**NFC First-Round Playoff
DETROIT vs. HOUSTON
RS: Texans lead series, 2-1
2004—Lions, 28-16 (D)
2008—Texans, 28-21 (H)
2012—Texans, 34-31 (D) OT
(RS Pts.—Lions 80, Texans 78)
DETROIT vs. *INDIANAPOLIS
RS: Colts lead series, 21-18-2
1953—Lions, 27-17 (B)
    Lions, 17-7 (D)
1954—Lions, 35-0 (D)
    Lions, 27-3 (B)
1955—Colts, 28-13 (B)
    Lions, 24-14 (D)
1956—Lions, 31-14 (B)
    Lions, 27-3 (D)
1957—Colts, 34-14 (B)
    Lions, 31-27 (D)
1958—Colts, 28-15 (B)
    Colts, 40-14 (D)
1959—Colts, 21-9 (B)
    Colts, 31-24 (D)
1960—Lions, 30-17 (D)
    Lions, 20-15 (B)
1961—Lions, 16-15 (B)
    Colts, 17-14 (D)

1962—Lions, 29-20 (B)
    Lions, 21-14 (D)
1963—Colts, 25-21 (D)
    Colts, 24-21 (B)
1964—Colts, 34-0 (D)
    Lions, 31-14 (B)
1965—Colts, 31-7 (B)
    Tie, 24-24 (D)
1966—Colts, 45-14 (B)
    Lions, 20-14 (D)
1967—Colts, 41-7 (B)
1968—Colts, 27-10 (B)
1969—Tie, 17-17 (B)
1973—Colts, 29-27 (D)
1977—Lions, 13-10 (B)
1980—Colts, 10-9 (D)
1985—Colts, 14-6 (I)
1991—Lions, 33-24 (I)
1997—Lions, 32-10 (D)
2000—Colts, 30-18 (I)
2004—Colts, 41-9 (D)
2008—Colts, 31-21 (I)
2012—Colts, 35-33 (D)
(RS Pts.—Colts 895, Lions 811)
*Franchise in Baltimore prior to 1984
DETROIT vs. JACKSONVILLE
RS: Jaguars lead series, 3-2
1995—Lions, 44-0 (D)
1998—Jaguars, 37-22 (J)
2004—Jaguars, 23-17 (J) OT
2008—Jaguars, 38-14 (D)
2012—Lions, 31-14 (J)
(RS Pts.—Lions 128, Jaguars 112)
DETROIT vs. KANSAS CITY
RS: Chiefs lead series, 7-5
1971—Lions, 32-21 (D)
1975—Chiefs, 24-21 (KC) OT
1980—Chiefs, 20-17 (KC)
1981—Lions, 27-10 (D)
1987—Chiefs, 27-20 (D)
1988—Lions, 7-6 (KC)
1990—Chiefs, 43-24 (KC)
1996—Chiefs, 28-24 (D)
1999—Chiefs, 31-21 (KC)
2003—Chiefs, 45-17 (KC)
2007—Lions, 25-20 (D)
2011—Lions, 48-3 (D)
(RS Pts.—Lions 283, Chiefs 278)
DETROIT vs. MIAMI
RS: Dolphins lead series, 7-3
1973—Dolphins, 34-7 (M)
1979—Dolphins, 28-10 (D)
1985—Lions, 31-21 (D)
1991—Lions, 17-13 (D)
1994—Dolphins, 27-20 (M)
1997—Dolphins, 33-30 (M)
2000—Dolphins, 23-8 (D)
2002—Dolphins, 49-21 (M)
2006—Dolphins, 27-10 (D)
2010—Lions, 34-27 (M)
(RS Pts.—Dolphins 282, Lions 188)
DETROIT vs. MINNESOTA
RS: Vikings lead series, 68-33-2
1961—Lions, 37-10 (M)
    Lions, 13-7 (D)
1962—Lions, 17-6 (M)
    Lions, 37-23 (D)
1963—Lions, 28-10 (D)
    Vikings, 34-31 (M)
1964—Lions, 24-20 (M)
    Tie, 23-23 (D)
1965—Lions, 31-29 (M)
    Vikings, 29-7 (D)

1966—Lions, 32-31 (M)
 Vikings, 28-16 (D)
1967—Tie, 10-10 (M)
 Lions, 14-3 (D)
1968—Vikings, 24-10 (M)
 Vikings, 13-6 (D)
1969—Vikings, 24-10 (M)
 Vikings, 27-0 (D)
1970—Vikings, 30-17 (D)
 Vikings, 24-20 (M)
1971—Vikings, 16-13 (D)
 Vikings, 29-10 (M)
1972—Vikings, 34-10 (D)
 Vikings, 16-14 (M)
1973—Vikings, 23-9 (D)
 Vikings, 28-7 (M)
1974—Vikings, 7-6 (D)
 Lions, 20-16 (M)
1975—Vikings, 25-19 (M)
 Lions, 17-10 (D)
1976—Vikings, 10-9 (D)
 Vikings, 31-23 (M)
1977—Vikings, 14-7 (M)
 Vikings, 30-21 (D)
1978—Vikings, 17-7 (M)
 Lions, 45-14 (D)
1979—Vikings, 13-10 (D)
 Vikings, 14-7 (M)
1980—Lions, 27-7 (D)
 Vikings, 34-0 (M)
1981—Vikings, 26-24 (M)
 Lions, 45-7 (D)
1982—Vikings, 34-31 (D)
1983—Vikings, 20-17 (M)
 Lions, 13-2 (D)
1984—Vikings, 29-28 (D)
 Lions, 16-14 (M)
1985—Vikings, 16-13 (M)
 Lions, 41-21 (D)
1986—Lions, 13-10 (M)
 Vikings, 24-10 (D)
1987—Vikings, 34-19 (M)
 Vikings, 17-14 (D)
1988—Vikings, 44-17 (M)
 Vikings, 23-0 (D)
1989—Vikings, 24-17 (M)
 Vikings, 20-7 (D)
1990—Vikings, 34-27 (M)
 Vikings, 17-7 (D)
1991—Lions, 24-20 (D)
 Lions, 34-14 (M)
1992—Lions, 31-17 (D)
 Vikings, 31-14 (M)
1993—Lions, 30-27 (M)
 Vikings, 13-0 (D)
1994—Vikings, 10-3 (M)
 Lions, 41-19 (D)
1995—Vikings, 20-10 (M)
 Lions, 44-38 (D)
1996—Vikings, 17-13 (M)
 Vikings, 24-22 (D)
1997—Lions, 38-15 (D)
 Lions, 14-13 (M)
1998—Vikings, 29-6 (M)
 Vikings, 34-13 (D)
1999—Lions, 25-23 (D)
 Vikings, 24-17 (M)
2000—Vikings, 31-24 (D)
 Vikings, 24-17 (M)
2001—Vikings, 31-26 (M)
 Lions, 27-24 (D)
2002—Vikings, 31-24 (M)
 Vikings, 38-36 (D)

2003—Vikings, 23-13 (D)
 Vikings, 24-14 (M)
2004—Vikings, 22-19 (M)
 Vikings, 28-27 (D)
2005—Vikings, 27-14 (M)
 Vikings, 21-16 (D)
2006—Vikings, 26-17 (M)
 Vikings, 30-20 (D)
2007—Lions, 20-17 (D) OT
 Vikings, 42-10 (M)
2008—Vikings, 12-10 (M)
 Vikings, 20-16 (D)
2009—Vikings, 27-13 (D)
 Vikings, 27-10 (M)
2010—Vikings, 24-10 (M)
 Lions, 20-13 (D)
2011—Lions, 26-23 (M) OT
 Lions, 34-28 (D)
2012—Vikings, 20-13 (D)
 Vikings, 34-24 (M)
(RS Pts.—Vikings 2,257, Lions 1,909)
DETROIT vs. NEW ENGLAND
RS: Patriots lead series, 6-4
1971—Lions, 34-7 (NE)
1976—Lions, 30-10 (D)
1979—Patriots, 24-17 (NE)
1985—Patriots, 23-6 (NE)
1993—Lions, 19-16 (NE) OT
1994—Patriots, 23-17 (D)
2000—Lions, 34-9 (D)
2002—Patriots, 20-12 (D)
2006—Patriots, 28-21 (NE)
2010—Patriots, 45-24 (D)
(RS Pts.—Lions 214, Patriots 205)
DETROIT vs. NEW ORLEANS
RS: Saints lead series, 11-9-1
PS: Saints lead series, 1-0
1968—Tie, 20-20 (D)
1970—Saints, 19-17 (NO)
1972—Lions, 27-14 (D)
1973—Saints, 20-13 (NO)
1974—Lions, 19-14 (D)
1976—Saints, 17-16 (NO)
1977—Lions, 23-19 (D)
1979—Saints, 17-7 (NO)
1980—Lions, 24-13 (D)
1988—Saints, 22-14 (D)
1989—Lions, 21-14 (D)
1990—Lions, 27-10 (NO)
1992—Saints, 13-7 (D)
1993—Saints, 14-3 (NO)
1997—Saints, 35-17 (NO)
2000—Lions, 14-10 (NO)
2002—Lions, 26-21 (D)
2005—Lions, 13-12 (San Antonio)
2008—Saints, 42-7 (D)
2009—Saints, 45-27 (NO)
2011—Saints, 31-17 (NO)
 *Saints, 45-28 (NO)
(RS Pts.—Saints 422, Lions 359)
(PS Pts.—Saints 45, Lions 28)
*NFC First-Round Playoff
*DETROIT vs. N.Y. GIANTS
RS: Lions lead series, 20-19-1
PS: Lions lead series, 1-0
1930—Giants, 19-6 (P)
1931—Spartans, 14-6 (P)
 Giants, 14-0 (NY)
1932—Spartans, 7-0 (P)
 Spartans, 6-0 (NY)
1933—Spartans, 17-7 (P)
 Giants, 13-10 (NY)
1934—Lions, 9-0 (D)

1935—**Lions, 26-7 (D)
1936—Giants, 14-7 (NY)
 Lions, 38-0 (D)
1937—Lions, 17-0 (NY)
1939—Lions, 18-14 (D)
1941—Giants, 20-13 (NY)
1943—Tie, 0-0 (D)
1945—Giants, 35-14 (NY)
1947—Lions, 35-7 (D)
1949—Lions, 45-21 (NY)
1953—Lions, 27-16 (NY)
1955—Giants, 24-19 (D)
1958—Giants, 19-17 (D)
1962—Giants, 17-14 (NY)
1964—Lions, 26-3 (D)
1967—Lions, 30-7 (NY)
1969—Lions, 24-0 (D)
1972—Lions, 30-16 (D)
1974—Lions, 20-19 (D)
1976—Giants, 24-10 (NY)
1982—Giants, 13-6 (D)
1983—Lions, 15-9 (D)
1988—Giants, 30-10 (NY)
 Giants, 13-10 (D) OT
1989—Giants, 24-14 (NY)
1990—Giants, 20-0 (NY)
1994—Lions, 28-25 (NY) OT
1996—Giants, 35-7 (D)
1997—Giants, 26-20 (D) OT
2000—Lions, 31-21 (NY)
2004—Lions, 28-13 (NY)
2007—Giants, 16-10 (D)
2010—Giants, 28-20 (NY)
(RS Pts.—Lions 672, Giants 588)
(PS Pts.—Lions 26, Giants 7)
*Franchise in Portsmouth prior to 1934
and known as the Spartans
**NFL Championship
DETROIT vs. N.Y. JETS
RS: Series tied, 6-6
1972—Lions, 37-20 (D)
1979—Jets, 31-10 (NY)
1982—Jets, 28-13 (D)
1985—Lions, 31-20 (D)
1988—Jets, 17-10 (D)
1991—Lions, 34-20 (D)
1994—Lions, 18-7 (NY)
1997—Lions, 13-10 (D)
2000—Lions, 10-7 (NY)
2002—Jets, 31-14 (D)
2006—Jets, 31-24 (NY)
2010—Jets, 23-20 (D) OT
(RS Pts.—Jets 245, Lions 234)
DETROIT vs. *OAKLAND
RS: Raiders lead series, 6-5
1970—Lions, 28-14 (D)
1974—Raiders, 35-13 (O)
1978—Raiders, 29-17 (O)
1981—Lions, 16-0 (D)
1984—Raiders, 24-3 (D)
1987—Raiders, 27-7 (LA)
1990—Raiders, 38-31 (D)
1996—Raiders, 37-21 (O)
2003—Lions, 23-13 (D)
2007—Lions, 36-21 (O)
2011—Lions, 28-27 (O)
(RS Pts.—Raiders 265, Lions 223)
*Franchise in Los Angeles from 1982-1994
*DETROIT vs. PHILADELPHIA
RS: Eagles lead series, 14-13-2
PS: Eagles lead series, 1-0
1933—Spartans, 25-0 (P)
1934—Lions, 10-0 (P)

1935—Lions, 35-0 (D)
1936—Lions, 23-0 (P)
1938—Eagles, 21-7 (D)
1940—Lions, 21-0 (P)
1941—Lions, 21-17 (D)
1945—Lions, 28-24 (D)
1948—Eagles, 45-21 (P)
1949—Eagles, 22-14 (D)
1951—Lions, 28-10 (P)
1954—Tie, 13-13 (D)
1957—Lions, 27-16 (P)
1960—Eagles, 28-10 (P)
1961—Eagles, 27-24 (D)
1965—Lions, 35-28 (P)
1968—Eagles, 12-0 (D)
1971—Eagles, 23-20 (D)
1974—Eagles, 28-17 (P)
1977—Lions, 17-13 (D)
1979—Eagles, 44-7 (P)
1984—Tie, 23-23 (D) OT
1986—Lions, 13-11 (P)
1995—**Eagles, 58-37 (P)
1996—Eagles, 24-17 (P)
1998—Eagles, 10-9 (P)
2004—Eagles, 30-13 (D)
2007—Eagles, 56-21 (P)
2010—Eagles, 35-32 (D)
2012—Lions, 26-23 (P) OT
(RS Pts.—Eagles 583, Lions 557)
(PS Pts.—Eagles 58, Lions 37)
*Franchise in Portsmouth prior to 1934
and known as the Spartans
**NFC First-Round Playoff
DETROIT vs. *PITTSBURGH
RS: Steelers lead series, 15-14-1
1934—Lions, 40-7 (D)
1936—Lions, 28-3 (D)
1937—Lions, 7-3 (D)
1938—Lions, 16-7 (D)
1940—Steelers, 10-7 (D)
1942—Steelers, 35-7 (D)
1946—Lions, 17-7 (D)
1947—Steelers, 17-10 (P)
1948—Lions, 17-14 (D)
1949—Steelers, 14-7 (P)
1950—Lions, 10-7 (D)
1952—Lions, 31-6 (P)
1953—Lions, 38-21 (P)
1955—Lions, 31-28 (P)
1956—Lions, 45-7 (D)
1959—Tie, 10-10 (P)
1962—Lions, 45-7 (D)
1966—Steelers, 17-3 (P)
1967—Steelers, 24-14 (D)
1969—Steelers, 16-13 (P)
1973—Steelers, 24-10 (P)
1983—Lions, 45-3 (D)
1986—Steelers, 27-17 (P)
1989—Steelers, 23-3 (P)
1992—Steelers, 17-14 (P)
1995—Steelers, 23-20 (P)
1998—Lions, 19-16 (D) OT
2001—Steelers, 47-14 (P)
2005—Steelers, 35-21 (P)
2009—Steelers, 28-20 (P)
(RS Pts.—Lions 579, Steelers 503)
*Steelers known as Pirates prior to 1940
DETROIT vs. *ST. LOUIS
RS: Rams lead series, 42-39-1
PS: Lions lead series, 1-0
1937—Lions, 28-0 (C)
        Lions, 27-7 (D)

1938—Rams, 21-17 (C)
        Lions, 6-0 (D)
1939—Lions, 15-7 (D)
        Rams, 14-3 (C)
1940—Lions, 6-0 (D)
        Rams, 24-0 (C)
1941—Lions, 17-7 (D)
        Lions, 14-0 (C)
1942—Rams, 14-0 (D)
        Rams, 27-7 (C)
1944—Rams, 20-17 (D)
        Lions, 26-14 (C)
1945—Rams, 28-21 (D)
1946—Rams, 35-14 (LA)
        Rams, 41-20 (D)
1947—Rams, 27-13 (D)
        Rams, 28-17 (LA)
1948—Rams, 44-7 (LA)
        Rams, 34-27 (D)
1949—Rams, 27-24 (LA)
        Rams, 21-10 (D)
1950—Rams, 30-28 (D)
        Rams, 65-24 (LA)
1951—Rams, 27-21 (D)
        Lions, 24-22 (LA)
1952—Lions, 17-14 (LA)
        Lions, 24-16 (D)
        **Lions, 31-21 (D)
1953—Lions, 31-19 (D)
        Rams, 37-24 (LA)
1954—Lions, 21-3 (D)
        Lions, 27-24 (LA)
1955—Rams, 17-10 (D)
        Rams, 24-13 (LA)
1956—Lions, 24-21 (D)
        Lions, 16-7 (LA)
1957—Lions, 10-7 (D)
        Rams, 35-17 (LA)
1958—Rams, 42-28 (D)
        Lions, 41-24 (LA)
1959—Lions, 17-7 (LA)
        Lions, 23-17 (D)
1960—Rams, 48-35 (LA)
        Lions, 12-10 (D)
1961—Lions, 14-13 (D)
        Lions, 28-10 (LA)
1962—Lions, 13-10 (D)
        Lions, 12-3 (LA)
1963—Lions, 23-2 (LA)
        Rams, 28-21 (D)
1964—Tie, 17-17 (LA)
        Lions, 37-17 (D)
1965—Lions, 20-0 (D)
        Lions, 31-7 (LA)
1966—Rams, 14-7 (D)
        Rams, 23-3 (LA)
1967—Rams, 31-7 (D)
1968—Rams, 10-7 (LA)
1969—Lions, 28-0 (D)
1970—Lions, 28-23 (LA)
1971—Rams, 21-13 (D)
1972—Rams, 34-17 (LA)
1974—Rams, 16-13 (LA)
1975—Rams, 20-0 (D)
1976—Rams, 20-17 (D)
1980—Lions, 41-20 (LA)
1981—Rams, 20-13 (LA)
1982—Lions, 19-14 (LA)
1983—Rams, 21-10 (LA)
1986—Rams, 14-10 (LA)
1987—Rams, 37-16 (D)
1988—Rams, 17-10 (LA)
1991—Lions, 21-10 (D)

1993—Lions, 16-13 (LA)
1999—Lions, 31-27 (D)
2001—Rams, 35-0 (D)
2003—Lions, 30-20 (D)
2006—Rams, 41-34 (StL)
2009—Rams, 17-10 (D)
2010—Lions, 44-6 (D)
2012—Lions, 27-23 (D)
(RS Pts.—Rams 1,605, Lions 1,516)
(PS Pts.—Lions 31, Rams 21)
*Franchise in Los Angeles prior to 1995
and in Cleveland prior to 1946
**Conference Playoff
DETROIT vs. SAN DIEGO
RS: Chargers lead series, 6-4
1972—Lions, 34-20 (D)
1977—Lions, 20-0 (D)
1978—Lions, 31-14 (D)
1981—Chargers, 28-23 (SD)
1984—Chargers, 27-24 (SD)
1996—Chargers, 27-21 (SD)
1999—Chargers, 20-10 (D)
2003—Chargers, 14-7 (D)
2007—Chargers, 51-14 (SD)
2011—Lions, 38-10 (D)
(RS Pts.—Lions 222, Chargers 211)
DETROIT vs. SAN FRANCISCO
RS: 49ers lead series, 36-26-1
PS: Series tied, 1-1
1950—Lions, 24-7 (D)
        49ers, 28-27 (SF)
1951—49ers, 20-10 (D)
        49ers, 21-17 (SF)
1952—49ers, 17-3 (SF)
        49ers, 28-0 (D)
1953—Lions, 24-21 (D)
        Lions, 14-10 (SF)
1954—49ers, 37-31 (SF)
        Lions, 48-7 (D)
1955—49ers, 27-24 (D)
        49ers, 38-21 (SF)
1956—Lions, 20-17 (D)
        Lions, 17-13 (SF)
1957—49ers, 35-31 (SF)
        Lions, 31-10 (D)
        *Lions, 31-27 (SF)
1958—49ers, 24-21 (SF)
        Lions, 35-21 (D)
1959—49ers, 34-13 (D)
        49ers, 33-7 (SF)
1960—49ers, 24-21 (SF)
        Lions, 24-0 (SF)
1961—49ers, 49-0 (D)
        Tie, 20-20 (SF)
1962—Lions, 45-24 (D)
        Lions, 38-24 (SF)
1963—Lions, 26-3 (D)
        Lions, 45-7 (SF)
1964—Lions, 26-17 (SF)
        Lions, 24-7 (D)
1965—49ers, 27-21 (D)
        49ers, 17-14 (SF)
1966—49ers, 27-24 (SF)
        49ers, 41-14 (D)
1967—Lions, 45-3 (SF)
1968—49ers, 14-7 (D)
1969—Lions, 26-14 (SF)
1970—Lions, 28-7 (D)
1971—49ers, 31-27 (SF)
1973—Lions, 30-20 (D)
1974—Lions, 17-13 (D)
1975—Lions, 28-17 (SF)
1977—49ers, 28-7 (SF)

1978—Lions, 33-14 (D)
1980—Lions, 17-13 (D)
1981—Lions, 24-17 (D)
1983—**49ers, 24-23 (SF)
1984—49ers, 30-27 (D)
1985—Lions, 23-21 (D)
1988—49ers, 20-13 (SF)
1991—49ers, 35-3 (SF)
1992—49ers, 24-6 (SF)
1993—49ers, 55-17 (D)
1994—49ers, 27-21 (D)
1995—Lions, 27-24 (D)
1996—49ers, 24-14 (SF)
1998—49ers, 35-13 (D)
2001—49ers, 21-13 (SF)
2003—49ers, 24-17 (SF)
2006—49ers, 19-13 (SF)
2008—49ers, 31-13 (SF)
2009—49ers, 20-6 (SF)
2011—49ers, 25-19 (D)
2012—49ers, 27-19 (SF)
(RS Pts.—49ers 1,378, Lions 1,302)
(PS Pts.—Lions 54, 49ers 51)
*Conference Playoff
**NFC Divisional Playoff
DETROIT vs. SEATTLE
RS: Seahawks lead series, 7-5
1976—Lions, 41-14 (S)
1978—Seahawks, 28-16 (S)
1984—Seahawks, 38-17 (S)
1987—Seahawks, 37-14 (D)
1990—Seahawks, 30-10 (S)
1993—Lions, 30-10 (D)
1996—Lions, 17-16 (D)
1999—Lions, 28-20 (S)
2003—Seahawks, 35-14 (S)
2006—Seahawks, 9-6 (D)
2009—Seahawks, 32-20 (S)
2012—Lions, 28-24 (D)
(RS Pts.—Seahawks 293, Lions 241)
DETROIT vs. TAMPA BAY
RS: Lions lead series, 29-25
PS: Buccaneers lead series, 1-0
1977—Lions, 16-7 (D)
1978—Lions, 15-7 (TB)
Lions, 34-23 (D)
1979—Buccaneers, 31-16 (TB)
Buccaneers, 16-14 (D)
1980—Lions, 24-10 (TB)
Lions, 27-14 (D)
1981—Buccaneers, 28-10 (TB)
Buccaneers, 20-17 (D)
1982—Buccaneers, 23-21 (TB)
1983—Lions, 11-0 (TB)
Lions, 23-20 (D)
1984—Buccaneers, 21-17 (TB)
Lions, 13-7 (D) OT
1985—Lions, 30-9 (D)
Buccaneers, 19-16 (TB) OT
1986—Buccaneers, 24-20 (D)
Lions, 38-17 (TB)
1987—Buccaneers, 31-27 (D)
Lions, 20-10 (TB)
1988—Buccaneers, 23-20 (TB)
Buccaneers, 21-10 (TB)
1989—Lions, 17-16 (TB)
Lions, 33-7 (D)
1990—Buccaneers, 38-21 (D)
Buccaneers, 23-20 (TB)
1991—Lions, 31-3 (D)
Buccaneers, 30-21 (TB)
1992—Buccaneers, 27-23 (D)
Lions, 38-7 (TB)

1993—Buccaneers, 27-10 (TB)
Lions, 23-0 (D)
1994—Buccaneers, 24-14 (TB)
Lions, 14-9 (D)
1995—Lions, 27-24 (D)
Lions, 37-10 (TB)
1996—Lions, 21-6 (D)
Lions, 27-0 (TB)
1997—Buccaneers, 24-17 (D)
Lions, 27-9 (TB)
*Buccaneers, 20-10 (TB)
1998—Lions, 27-6 (D)
Lions, 28-25 (TB)
1999—Lions, 20-3 (D)
Buccaneers, 23-16 (TB)
2000—Buccaneers, 31-10 (D)
Lions, 28-14 (D)
2001—Buccaneers, 20-17 (D)
Buccaneers, 15-12 (TB)
2002—Buccaneers, 23-20 (D)
2005—Buccaneers, 17-13 (TB)
2007—Lions, 23-16 (D)
2008—Buccaneers, 38-20 (D)
2010—Lions, 23-20 (TB) OT
2011—Lions, 27-20 (TB)
(RS Pts—Lions 1,144, Buccaneers 936)
(PS Pts.—Buccaneers 20, Lions 10)
*NFC First-Round Playoff
DETROIT vs. *TENNESSEE
RS: Titans lead series, 8-3
1971—Lions, 31-7 (H)
1975—Oilers, 24-8 (H)
1983—Oilers, 27-17 (H)
1986—Lions, 24-13 (D)
1989—Oilers, 35-31 (H)
1992—Oilers, 24-21 (D)
1995—Lions, 24-17 (H)
2001—Titans, 27-24 (D)
2004—Titans, 24-19 (T)
2008—Titans, 47-10 (D)
2012—Titans, 44-41 (T) OT
(RS Pts.—Titans 289, Lions 250)
*Franchise in Houston prior to 1997;
known as Oilers prior to 1999
DETROIT vs. **WASHINGTON
RS: Redskins lead series, 27-12
PS: Redskins lead series, 3-0
1932—Spartans, 10-0 (P)
1933—Spartans, 13-0 (B)
1934—Lions, 24-0 (D)
1935—Lions, 17-7 (B)
Lions, 14-0 (D)
1938—Redskins, 7-5 (D)
1939—Redskins, 31-7 (W)
1940—Redskins, 20-14 (D)
1942—Redskins, 15-3 (D)
1943—Redskins, 42-20 (W)
1946—Redskins, 17-16 (W)
1947—Lions, 38-21 (D)
1948—Redskins, 46-21 (W)
1951—Lions, 35-17 (D)
1956—Redskins, 18-17 (W)
1965—Lions, 14-10 (D)
1968—Redskins, 14-3 (W)
1970—Redskins, 31-10 (W)
1973—Redskins, 20-0 (D)
1976—Redskins, 20-7 (W)
1978—Redskins, 21-19 (D)
1979—Redskins, 27-24 (D)
1981—Redskins, 33-31 (W)
1982—***Redskins, 31-7 (W)
1983—Redskins, 38-17 (W)
1984—Redskins, 28-14 (W)

1985—Redskins, 24-3 (W)
1987—Redskins, 20-13 (W)
1990—Redskins, 41-38 (D) OT
1991—Redskins, 45-0 (W)
****Redskins, 41-10 (W)
1992—Redskins, 13-10 (W)
1995—Redskins, 36-30 (W) OT
1997—Redskins, 30-7 (W)
1999—Lions, 33-17 (D)
***Redskins, 27-13 (W)
2000—Lions, 15-10 (D)
2004—Redskins, 17-10 (D)
2007—Redskins, 34-3 (W)
2008—Redskins, 25-17 (D)
2009—Lions, 19-14 (D)
2010—Lions, 37-25 (D)
(RS Pts.—Redskins 834, Lions 628)
(PS Pts.—Redskins 99, Lions 30)
*Franchise in Portsmouth prior to 1934
and known as the Spartans.
**Franchise in Boston prior to 1937.
***NFC First-Round Playoff
****NFC Championship

GREEN BAY vs. ARIZONA
RS: Packers lead series, 44-22-4
PS: Series tied, 1-1;
See Arizona vs. Green Bay
GREEN BAY vs. ATLANTA
RS: Packers lead series, 13-12
PS: Packers lead series, 2-1;
See Atlanta vs. Green Bay
GREEN BAY vs. BALTIMORE
RS: Packers lead series, 3-1;
See Baltimore vs. Green Bay
GREEN BAY vs. BUFFALO
RS: Bills lead series, 7-4;
See Buffalo vs. Green Bay
GREEN BAY vs. CAROLINA
RS: Packers lead series, 7-4
PS: Packers lead series, 1-0;
See Carolina vs. Green Bay
GREEN BAY vs. CHICAGO
RS: Bears lead series, 91-87-6
PS: Series tied, 1-1;
See Chicago vs. Green Bay
GREEN BAY vs. CINCINNATI
RS: Bengals lead series, 6-5;
See Cincinnati vs. Green Bay
GREEN BAY vs. CLEVELAND
RS: Packers lead series, 10-7
PS: Packers lead series, 1-0;
See Cleveland vs. Green Bay
GREEN BAY vs. DALLAS
RS: Series tied, 12-12
PS: Cowboys lead series, 4-2;
See Dallas vs. Green Bay
GREEN BAY vs. DENVER
RS: Packers lead series, 6-5-1
PS: Broncos lead series, 1-0;
See Denver vs. Green Bay
GREEN BAY vs. DETROIT
RS: Packers lead series, 93-65-7
PS: Packers lead series, 2-0;
See Detroit vs. Green Bay
GREEN BAY vs. HOUSTON
RS: Packers lead series, 2-1
2004—Packers, 16-13 (H)
2008—Texans, 24-21 (GB)
2012—Packers, 42-24 (H)
(RS Pts.—Packers 79, Texans 61)

GREEN BAY vs. *INDIANAPOLIS
RS: Colts lead series, 21-20-1
PS: Packers lead series, 1-0
1953—Packers, 37-14 (GB)
　　　Packers, 35-24 (B)
1954—Packers, 7-6 (B)
　　　Packers, 24-13 (Mil)
1955—Colts, 24-20 (Mil)
　　　Colts, 14-10 (B)
1956—Packers, 38-33 (Mil)
　　　Colts, 28-21 (B)
1957—Colts, 45-17 (Mil)
　　　Packers, 24-21 (B)
1958—Colts, 24-17 (Mil)
　　　Colts, 56-0 (B)
1959—Colts, 38-21 (B)
　　　Colts, 28-24 (Mil)
1960—Packers, 35-21 (GB)
　　　Colts, 38-24 (B)
1961—Packers, 45-7 (GB)
　　　Colts, 45-21 (B)
1962—Packers, 17-6 (B)
　　　Packers, 17-13 (GB)
1963—Packers, 31-20 (GB)
　　　Packers, 34-20 (B)
1964—Colts, 21-20 (GB)
　　　Colts, 24-21 (B)
1965—Packers, 20-17 (Mil)
　　　Packers, 42-27 (B)
　　　**Packers, 13-10 (GB) OT
1966—Packers, 24-3 (Mil)
　　　Packers, 14-10 (B)
1967—Colts, 13-10 (B)
1968—Colts, 16-3 (GB)
1969—Colts, 14-6 (B)
1970—Colts, 13-10 (Mil)
1974—Packers, 20-13 (B)
1982—Tie, 20-20 (B) OT
1985—Colts, 37-10 (I)
1988—Colts, 20-13 (GB)
1991—Packers, 14-10 (Mil)
1997—Colts, 41-38 (I)
2000—Packers, 26-24 (GB)
2004—Colts, 45-31 (I)
2008—Packers, 34-14 (GB)
2012—Colts, 30-27 (I)
(RS Pts.—Colts 950, Packers 922)
(PS Pts.—Packers 13, Colts 10)
*Franchise in Baltimore prior to 1984
**Conference Playoff

GREEN BAY vs. JACKSONVILLE
RS: Packers lead series, 3-2
1995—Packers, 24-14 (J)
2001—Packers, 28-21 (J)
2004—Jaguars, 28-25 (GB)
2008—Jaguars, 20-16 (J)
2012—Packers, 24-15 (GB)
(RS Pts.—Packers 117, Jaguars 98)

GREEN BAY vs. KANSAS CITY
RS: Chiefs lead series, 7-2-1
PS: Packers lead series, 1-0
1966—*Packers, 35-10 (Los Angeles)
1973—Tie, 10-10 (Mil)
1977—Chiefs, 20-10 (KC)
1987—Packers, 23-3 (KC)
1989—Packers, 21-3 (GB)
1990—Chiefs, 17-3 (GB)
1993—Chiefs, 23-16 (KC)
1996—Chiefs, 27-20 (KC)
2003—Chiefs, 40-34 (GB) OT
2007—Packers, 33-22 (KC)
2011—Chiefs, 19-14 (KC)
(RS Pts.—Chiefs 202, Packers 166)

(PS Pts.—Packers 35, Chiefs 10)
*Super Bowl I

GREEN BAY vs. MIAMI
RS: Dolphins lead series, 10-3
1971—Dolphins, 27-6 (Mia)
1975—Dolphins, 31-7 (GB)
1979—Dolphins, 27-7 (Mia)
1985—Dolphins, 34-24 (GB)
1988—Dolphins, 24-17 (Mia)
1989—Dolphins, 23-20 (Mia)
1991—Dolphins, 16-13 (Mia)
1994—Dolphins, 24-14 (Mil)
1997—Packers, 23-18 (GB)
2000—Dolphins, 28-20 (Mia)
2002—Packers, 24-10 (GB)
2006—Packers, 34-24 (M)
2010—Dolphins, 23-20 (GB) OT
(RS Pts.—Dolphins 309, Packers 229)

GREEN BAY vs. MINNESOTA
RS: Packers lead series, 54-48-1
PS: Series tied, 1-1
1961—Packers, 33-7 (Minn)
　　　Packers, 28-10 (Mil)
1962—Packers, 34-7 (GB)
　　　Packers, 48-21 (Minn)
1963—Packers, 37-28 (Minn)
　　　Packers, 28-7 (GB)
1964—Vikings, 24-23 (GB)
　　　Packers, 42-13 (Minn)
1965—Packers, 38-13 (Minn)
　　　Packers, 24-19 (GB)
1966—Vikings, 20-17 (GB)
　　　Packers, 28-16 (Minn)
1967—Vikings, 10-7 (Mil)
　　　Packers, 30-27 (Minn)
1968—Vikings, 26-13 (Mil)
　　　Vikings, 14-10 (Minn)
1969—Vikings, 19-7 (Minn)
　　　Vikings, 9-7 (Mil)
1970—Packers, 13-10 (Mil)
　　　Vikings, 10-3 (Minn)
1971—Vikings, 24-13 (GB)
　　　Vikings, 3-0 (Minn)
1972—Vikings, 27-13 (GB)
　　　Packers, 23-7 (Minn)
1973—Vikings, 11-3 (Minn)
　　　Vikings, 31-7 (GB)
1974—Vikings, 32-17 (GB)
　　　Packers, 19-7 (Minn)
1975—Vikings, 28-17 (GB)
　　　Vikings, 24-3 (Minn)
1976—Vikings, 17-10 (Mil)
　　　Vikings, 20-9 (Minn)
1977—Vikings, 19-7 (Minn)
　　　Vikings, 13-6 (GB)
1978—Vikings, 21-7 (Minn)
　　　Tie, 10-10 (GB) OT
1979—Vikings, 27-21 (Minn) OT
　　　Packers, 19-7 (Mil)
1980—Packers, 16-3 (GB)
　　　Packers, 25-13 (Minn)
1981—Vikings, 30-13 (Mil)
　　　Packers, 35-23 (Minn)
1982—Packers, 26-7 (Mil)
1983—Vikings, 20-17 (GB) OT
　　　Packers, 29-21 (Minn)
1984—Packers, 45-17 (Mil)
　　　Packers, 38-14 (Minn)
1985—Packers, 20-17 (Mil)
　　　Packers, 27-17 (Minn)
1986—Vikings, 42-7 (Minn)
　　　Vikings, 32-6 (GB)

1987—Packers, 23-16 (Minn)
　　　Packers, 16-10 (Mil)
1988—Packers, 34-14 (Minn)
　　　Packers, 18-6 (GB)
1989—Vikings, 26-14 (Minn)
　　　Packers, 20-19 (Mil)
1990—Packers, 24-10 (Mil)
　　　Vikings, 23-7 (Minn)
1991—Vikings, 35-21 (GB)
　　　Packers, 27-7 (Minn)
1992—Vikings, 23-20 (GB) OT
　　　Vikings, 27-7 (Minn)
1993—Vikings, 15-13 (GB)
　　　Vikings, 21-17 (Minn)
1994—Packers, 16-10 (GB)
　　　Vikings, 13-10 (Minn) OT
1995—Packers, 38-21 (GB)
　　　Vikings, 27-24 (Minn)
1996—Vikings, 30-21 (Minn)
　　　Packers, 38-10 (GB)
1997—Packers, 38-32 (GB)
　　　Packers, 27-11 (Minn)
1998—Vikings, 37-24 (GB)
　　　Vikings, 28-14 (Minn)
1999—Packers, 23-20 (GB)
　　　Vikings, 24-20 (Minn)
2000—Packers, 26-20 (GB) OT
　　　Packers, 33-28 (Minn)
2001—Vikings, 35-13 (Minn)
　　　Packers, 24-13 (GB)
2002—Vikings, 31-21 (Minn)
　　　Packers, 26-22 (GB)
2003—Vikings, 30-25 (GB)
　　　Packers, 30-27 (Minn)
2004—Packers, 34-31 (GB)
　　　Packers, 34-31 (Minn)
　　　*Vikings, 31-17 (GB)
2005—Vikings, 23-20 (Minn)
　　　Vikings, 20-17 (GB)
2006—Packers, 23-17 (Minn)
　　　Packers, 9-7 (GB)
2007—Packers, 23-16 (Minn)
　　　Packers, 34-0 (GB)
2008—Packers, 24-19 (GB)
　　　Vikings, 28-27 (Minn)
2009—Vikings, 30-23 (Minn)
　　　Vikings, 38-26 (GB)
2010—Packers, 28-24 (GB)
　　　Packers, 31-3 (Minn)
2011—Packers, 33-27 (GB)
　　　Packers, 45-7 (GB)
2012—Packers, 23-14 (GB)
　　　Vikings, 37-34 (M)
　　　*Packers, 24-10 (GB)
(RS Pts.—Packers 2,218, Vikings 1,987)
(PS Pts.—Packers 41, Vikings 41)
*NFC First-Round Playoff

GREEN BAY vs. NEW ENGLAND
RS: Patriots lead series, 5-4
PS: Packers lead series, 1-0
1973—Patriots, 33-24 (NE)
1979—Packers, 27-14 (GB)
1985—Patriots, 26-20 (NE)
1988—Packers, 45-3 (Mil)
1994—Patriots, 17-16 (NE)
1996—*Packers, 35-21 (New Orleans)
1997—Packers, 28-10 (NE)
2002—Packers, 28-10 (NE)
2006—Patriots, 35-0 (GB)
2010—Patriots, 31-27 (NE)
(RS Pts.—Packers 215, Patriots 179)
(PS Pts.—Packers 35, Patriots 21)
*Super Bowl XXXI

GREEN BAY vs. NEW ORLEANS
RS: Packers lead series, 16-7
1968—Packers, 29-7 (Mil)
1971—Saints, 29-21 (Mil)
1972—Packers, 30-20 (NO)
1973—Packers, 30-10 (Mil)
1975—Saints, 20-19 (NO)
1976—Packers, 32-27 (Mil)
1977—Packers, 24-20 (Mil)
1978—Packers, 28-17 (Mil)
1979—Packers, 28-19 (Mil)
1981—Packers, 35-7 (NO)
1984—Packers, 23-13 (NO)
1985—Packers, 38-14 (Mil)
1986—Saints, 24-10 (NO)
1987—Saints, 33-24 (NO)
1989—Packers, 35-34 (GB)
1993—Packers, 19-17 (NO)
1995—Packers, 34-23 (NO)
2002—Saints, 35-20 (NO)
2005—Packers, 52-3 (GB)
2006—Saints, 34-27 (GB)
2008—Saints, 51-29 (NO)
2011—Packers, 42-34 (GB)
2012—Packers, 28-27 (GB)
(RS Pts.—Packers 657, Saints 518)

GREEN BAY vs. N.Y. GIANTS
RS: Packers lead series, 27-22-2
PS: Packers lead series, 4-3
1928—Giants, 6-0 (GB)
    Packers, 7-0 (NY)
1929—Packers, 20-6 (NY)
1930—Packers, 14-7 (GB)
    Giants, 13-6 (NY)
1931—Packers, 27-7 (GB)
    Packers, 14-10 (NY)
1932—Packers, 13-0 (GB)
    Giants, 6-0 (NY)
1933—Packers, 10-7 (Mil)
    Giants, 17-6 (NY)
1934—Packers, 20-6 (Mil)
    Giants, 17-3 (NY)
1935—Packers, 16-7 (GB)
1936—Packers, 26-14 (NY)
1937—Giants, 10-0 (NY)
1938—Giants, 15-3 (NY)
    *Giants, 23-17 (NY)
1939—*Packers, 27-0 (Mil)
1940—Giants, 7-3 (NY)
1942—Tie, 21-21 (NY)
1943—Packers, 35-21 (NY)
1944—Giants, 24-0 (NY)
    *Packers, 14-7 (NY)
1945—Packers, 23-14 (NY)
1947—Tie, 24-24 (NY)
1948—Giants, 49-3 (Mil)
1949—Giants, 30-10 (GB)
1952—Packers, 17-3 (NY)
1957—Giants, 31-17 (GB)
1959—Giants, 20-3 (NY)
1961—Packers, 20-17 (Mil)
    *Packers, 37-0 (GB)
1962—*Packers, 16-7 (NY)
1967—Packers, 48-21 (NY)
1969—Packers, 20-10 (Mil)
1971—Giants, 42-40 (GB)
1973—Packers, 16-14 (New Haven)
1975—Packers, 40-14 (Mil)
1980—Giants, 27-21 (NY)
1981—Packers, 27-14 (NY)
    Packers, 26-24 (Mil)
1982—Packers, 27-19 (NY)
1983—Giants, 27-3 (NY)

1985—Packers, 23-20 (GB)
1986—Giants, 55-24 (NY)
1987—Giants, 20-10 (NY)
1992—Giants, 27-7 (NY)
1995—Packers, 14-6 (GB)
1998—Packers, 37-3 (NY)
2001—Packers, 34-25 (NY)
2004—Giants, 14-7 (GB)
2007—Packers, 35-13 (NY)
    **Giants, 23-20 (GB) OT
2010—Packers, 45-17 (GB)
2011—Packers, 38-35 (NY)
    ***Giants, 37-20 (GB)
2012—Giants, 38-10 (NY)
(RS Pts.—Packers 910, Giants 897)
(PS Pts.—Packers 151, Giants 97)
*NFL Championship
**NFC Championship Game
***NFC Divisional Playoff

GREEN BAY vs. N.Y. JETS
RS: Jets lead series, 8-3
1973—Packers, 23-7 (Mil)
1979—Jets, 27-22 (GB)
1981—Jets, 28-3 (NY)
1982—Jets, 15-13 (NY)
1985—Jets, 24-3 (Mil)
1991—Jets, 19-16 (NY) OT
1994—Packers, 17-10 (GB)
2000—Jets, 20-16 (GB)
2002—Jets, 42-17 (NY)
2006—Jets, 38-10 (GB)
2010—Packers, 9-0 (NY)
(RS Pts.—Jets 230, Packers 149)

GREEN BAY vs. *OAKLAND
RS: Packers lead series, 6-5
PS: Packers lead series, 1-0
1967—**Packers, 33-14 (Miami)
1972—Raiders, 20-14 (GB)
1976—Raiders, 18-14 (O)
1978—Raiders, 28-3 (GB)
1984—Raiders, 28-7 (LA)
1987—Raiders, 20-0 (GB)
1990—Packers, 29-16 (LA)
1993—Packers, 28-0 (GB)
1999—Packers, 28-24 (GB)
2003—Packers, 41-7 (O)
2007—Packers, 38-7 (GB)
2011—Packers, 46-16 (GB)
(RS Pts.—Packers 248, Raiders 184)
(PS Pts.—Packers 33, Raiders 14)
*Franchise in Los Angeles from 1982-1994
**Super Bowl II

GREEN BAY vs. PHILADELPHIA
RS: Packers lead series, 24-13
PS: Eagles lead series, 2-1
1933—Packers, 35-9 (GB)
    Packers, 10-0 (P)
1934—Packers, 19-6 (GB)
1935—Packers, 13-6 (P)
1937—Packers, 37-7 (Mil)
1939—Packers, 23-16 (P)
1940—Packers, 27-20 (GB)
1942—Packers, 7-0 (P)
1946—Packers, 19-7 (P)
1947—Eagles, 28-14 (P)
1951—Packers, 37-24 (GB)
1952—Packers, 12-10 (Mil)
1954—Packers, 37-14 (P)
1958—Packers, 38-35 (GB)
1960—*Eagles, 17-13 (P)
1962—Packers, 49-0 (P)
1968—Packers, 30-13 (GB)
1970—Packers, 30-17 (Mil)

1974—Eagles, 36-14 (P)
1976—Packers, 28-13 (GB)
1978—Eagles, 10-3 (P)
1979—Eagles, 21-10 (GB)
1987—Packers, 16-10 (GB) OT
1990—Eagles, 31-0 (P)
1991—Eagles, 20-3 (GB)
1992—Packers, 27-24 (Mil)
1993—Eagles, 20-17 (GB)
1994—Eagles, 13-7 (P)
1996—Packers, 39-13 (GB)
1997—Eagles, 10-9 (P)
1998—Packers, 24-16 (GB)
2000—Packers, 6-3 (GB)
2003—Eagles, 17-14 (GB)
    **Eagles, 20-17 (P) OT
2004—Eagles, 47-17 (P)
2005—Eagles, 19-14 (P)
2006—Eagles, 31-9 (P)
2007—Packers, 16-13 (GB)
2010—Packers, 27-20 (P)
    ***Packers, 21-16 (P)
(RS Pts.—Packers 737, Eagles 599)
(PS Pts.—Eagles 53, Packers 51)
*NFL Championship
**NFC Divisional Playoff
***NFC First-Round Playoff

GREEN BAY vs. *PITTSBURGH
RS: Packers lead series, 18-14
PS: Packers lead series, 1-0
1933—Packers, 47-0 (GB)
1935—Packers, 27-0 (GB)
    Packers, 34-14 (P)
1936—Packers, 42-10 (Mil)
1938—Packers, 20-0 (GB)
1940—Packers, 24-3 (Mil)
1941—Packers, 54-7 (P)
1942—Packers, 24-21 (Mil)
1946—Packers, 17-7 (GB)
1947—Steelers, 18-17 (Mil)
1948—Steelers, 38-7 (P)
1949—Steelers, 30-7 (Mil)
1951—Packers, 35-33 (GB)
    Steelers, 28-7 (P)
1953—Steelers, 31-14 (P)
1954—Steelers, 21-20 (GB)
1957—Packers, 27-10 (P)
1960—Packers, 19-13 (P)
1963—Packers, 33-14 (Mil)
1965—Packers, 41-9 (P)
1967—Steelers, 24-17 (GB)
1969—Packers, 38-34 (P)
1970—Packers, 20-12 (P)
1975—Steelers, 16-13 (P)
1980—Steelers, 22-20 (P)
1983—Packers, 25-21 (GB)
1986—Steelers, 27-3 (P)
1992—Packers, 17-3 (GB)
1995—Packers, 24-19 (GB)
1998—Steelers, 27-20 (P)
2005—Steelers, 20-10 (GB)
2009—Steelers, 37-36 (P)
2010—**Packers, 31-25 (North Texas)
(RS Pts.—Packers 755, Steelers 573)
(PS Pts.—Packers 31, Steelers 25)
*Steelers known as Pirates prior to 1940
**Super Bowl XLV

GREEN BAY vs. *ST. LOUIS
RS: Rams lead series, 45-44-2
PS: Series tied, 1-1
1937—Packers, 35-10 (C)
    Packers, 35-7 (GB)

1938—Packers, 26-17 (GB)
   Packers, 28-7 (C)
1939—Rams, 27-24 (GB)
   Packers, 7-6 (C)
1940—Packers, 31-14 (GB)
   Tie, 13-13 (C)
1941—Packers, 24-7 (Mil)
   Packers, 17-14 (C)
1942—Packers, 45-28 (GB)
   Packers, 30-12 (C)
1944—Packers, 30-21 (GB)
   Packers, 42-7 (C)
1945—Rams, 27-14 (GB)
   Rams, 20-7 (C)
1946—Rams, 21-17 (Mil)
   Rams, 38-17 (LA)
1947—Packers, 17-14 (Mil)
   Packers, 30-10 (LA)
1948—Packers, 16-0 (GB)
   Rams, 24-10 (LA)
1949—Rams, 48-7 (GB)
   Rams, 35-7 (LA)
1950—Rams, 45-14 (Mil)
   Rams, 51-14 (LA)
1951—Rams, 28-0 (Mil)
   Rams, 42-14 (LA)
1952—Rams, 30-28 (Mil)
   Rams, 45-27 (LA)
1953—Rams, 38-20 (Mil)
   Rams, 33-17 (LA)
1954—Packers, 35-17 (Mil)
   Rams, 35-27 (LA)
1955—Packers, 30-28 (Mil)
   Rams, 31-17 (LA)
1956—Packers, 42-17 (Mil)
   Rams, 49-21 (LA)
1957—Rams, 31-27 (Mil)
   Rams, 42-17 (LA)
1958—Rams, 20-7 (GB)
   Rams, 34-20 (LA)
1959—Rams, 45-6 (Mil)
   Packers, 38-20 (LA)
1960—Rams, 33-31 (Mil)
   Packers, 35-21 (LA)
1961—Packers, 35-17 (GB)
   Packers, 24-17 (LA)
1962—Packers, 41-10 (Mil)
   Packers, 20-17 (LA)
1963—Packers, 42-10 (GB)
   Packers, 31-14 (LA)
1964—Rams, 27-17 (Mil)
   Tie, 24-24 (LA)
1965—Packers, 6-3 (Mil)
   Rams, 21-10 (LA)
1966—Packers, 24-13 (GB)
   Packers, 27-23 (LA)
1967—Rams, 27-24 (LA)
   **Packers, 28-7 (Mil)
1968—Rams, 16-14 (Mil)
1969—Rams, 34-21 (LA)
1970—Rams, 31-21 (GB)
1971—Rams, 30-13 (LA)
1973—Rams, 24-7 (LA)
1974—Packers, 17-6 (Mil)
1975—Rams, 22-5 (LA)
1977—Rams, 24-6 (Mil)
1978—Rams, 31-14 (LA)
1980—Rams, 51-21 (LA)
1981—Rams, 35-23 (LA)
1982—Packers, 35-23 (Mil)
1983—Packers, 27-24 (Mil)
1984—Packers, 31-6 (Mil)
1985—Rams, 34-17 (LA)

1988—Rams, 34-7 (GB)
1989—Rams, 41-38 (LA)
1990—Packers, 36-24 (GB)
1991—Rams, 23-21 (LA)
1992—Packers, 28-13 (GB)
1993—Packers, 36-6 (Mil)
1994—Packers, 24-17 (GB)
1995—Rams, 17-14 (GB)
1996—Packers, 24-9 (StL)
1997—Packers, 17-7 (GB)
2001—***Rams, 45-17 (StL)
2003—Rams, 34-24 (StL)
2004—Packers, 45-17 (GB)
2006—Rams, 23-20 (GB)
2007—Packers, 33-14 (StL)
2009—Packers, 36-17 (StL)
2011—Packers, 24-3 (GB)
2012—Packers, 30-20 (StL)
(RS Pts.—Rams 2,095, Packers 2,070)
(PS Pts.—Rams 52, Packers 45)
*Franchise in Los Angeles prior to 1995
and in Cleveland prior to 1946
**Conference Championship
***NFC Divisional Playoff

GREEN BAY vs. SAN DIEGO
RS: Packers lead series, 9-1
1970—Packers, 22-20 (SD)
1974—Packers, 34-0 (GB)
1978—Packers, 24-3 (SD)
1984—Chargers, 34-28 (GB)
1993—Packers, 20-13 (SD)
1996—Packers, 42-10 (GB)
1999—Packers, 31-3 (SD)
2003—Packers, 38-21 (SD)
2007—Packers, 31-24 (GB)
2011—Packers, 45-38 (SD)
(RS Pts.—Packers 315, Chargers 166)

GREEN BAY vs. SAN FRANCISCO
RS: Packers lead series, 30-26-1
PS: Packers lead series, 4-2
1950—Packers, 25-21 (GB)
   49ers, 30-14 (SF)
1951—Packers, 31-19 (SF)
1952—49ers, 24-14 (SF)
1953—49ers, 37-7 (Mil)
   49ers, 48-14 (SF)
1954—49ers, 23-17 (Mil)
   49ers, 35-0 (SF)
1955—Packers, 27-21 (Mil)
   Packers, 28-7 (SF)
1956—49ers, 17-16 (GB)
   49ers, 38-20 (SF)
1957—49ers, 24-14 (Mil)
   49ers, 27-20 (SF)
1958—49ers, 33-12 (Mil)
   49ers, 48-21 (SF)
1959—Packers, 21-20 (GB)
   Packers, 36-14 (SF)
1960—Packers, 41-14 (Mil)
   Packers, 13-0 (SF)
1961—Packers, 30-10 (GB)
   49ers, 22-21 (SF)
1962—Packers, 31-13 (Mil)
   Packers, 31-21 (SF)
1963—Packers, 28-10 (Mil)
   Packers, 21-17 (SF)
1964—Packers, 24-14 (Mil)
   49ers, 24-14 (SF)
1965—Packers, 27-10 (GB)
   Tie, 24-24 (SF)
1966—49ers, 21-20 (SF)
   Packers, 20-7 (Mil)
1967—Packers, 13-0 (GB)

1968—49ers, 27-20 (SF)
1969—Packers, 14-7 (Mil)
1970—49ers, 26-10 (SF)
1972—Packers, 34-24 (Mil)
1973—49ers, 20-6 (SF)
1974—49ers, 7-6 (SF)
1976—Packers, 26-14 (GB)
1977—Packers, 16-14 (Mil)
1980—Packers, 23-16 (Mil)
1981—49ers, 13-3 (Mil)
1986—49ers, 31-17 (Mil)
1987—49ers, 23-12 (GB)
1989—Packers, 21-17 (SF)
1990—49ers, 24-20 (GB)
1995—*Packers, 27-17 (SF)
1996—Packers, 23-20 (GB) OT
   *Packers, 35-14 (GB)
1997—**Packers, 23-10 (SF)
1998—Packers, 36-22 (GB)
   ***49ers, 30-27 (SF)
1999—Packers, 20-3 (SF)
2000—Packers, 31-28 (GB)
2001—***Packers, 25-15 (GB)
2002—Packers, 20-14 (SF)
2003—Packers, 20-10 (GB)
2006—Packers, 30-19 (GB)
2009—Packers, 30-24 (GB)
2010—Packers, 34-16 (GB)
2012—49ers, 30-22 (GB)
   *49ers, 45-31 (SF)
(RS Pts.—49ers 1,166, Packers 1,165)
(PS Pts.—Packers 168, 49ers 131)
*NFC Divisional Playoff
**NFC Championship
***NFC First-Round Playoff

GREEN BAY vs. SEATTLE
RS: Packers lead series, 8-6
PS: Packers lead series, 2-0
1976—Packers, 27-20 (Mil)
1978—Packers, 45-28 (Mil)
1981—Packers, 34-24 (GB)
1984—Seahawks, 30-24 (Mil)
1987—Seahawks, 24-13 (S)
1990—Seahawks, 20-14 (Mil)
1996—Packers, 31-10 (S)
1999—Seahawks, 27-7 (GB)
2003—Packers, 35-13 (GB)
   *Packers, 33-27 (GB) OT
2005—Packers, 23-17 (GB)
2006—Seahawks, 34-24 (S)
2007—**Packers, 42-20 (GB)
2008—Packers, 27-17 (S)
2009—Packers, 48-10 (GB)
2012—Seahawks, 14-12 (S)
(RS Pts.—Packers 364, Seahawks 288)
(PS Pts.—Packers 75, Seahawks 47)
*NFC First-Round Playoff
**NFC Divisional Playoff

GREEN BAY vs. TAMPA BAY
RS: Packers lead series, 30-21-1
PS: Packers lead series, 1-0
1977—Packers, 13-0 (TB)
1978—Packers, 9-7 (GB)
   Packers, 17-7 (TB)
1979—Buccaneers, 21-10 (GB)
   Buccaneers, 21-3 (TB)
1980—Tie, 14-14 (TB) OT
   Buccaneers, 20-17 (Mil)
1981—Buccaneers, 21-10 (GB)
   Buccaneers, 37-3 (TB)
1983—Packers, 55-14 (GB)
   Packers, 12-9 (TB) OT

1984—Buccaneers, 30-27 (TB) OT
    Packers, 27-14 (GB)
1985—Packers, 21-0 (GB)
    Packers, 20-17 (TB)
1986—Packers, 31-7 (Mil)
    Packers, 21-7 (TB)
1987—Buccaneers, 23-17 (Mil)
1988—Buccaneers, 13-10 (GB)
    Buccaneers, 27-24 (TB)
1989—Buccaneers, 23-21 (GB)
    Packers, 17-16 (TB)
1990—Buccaneers, 26-14 (TB)
    Packers, 20-10 (Mil)
1991—Packers, 15-13 (GB)
    Packers, 27-0 (TB)
1992—Buccaneers, 31-3 (TB)
    Packers, 19-14 (Mil)
1993—Packers, 37-14 (TB)
    Packers, 13-10 (GB)
1994—Packers, 30-3 (GB)
    Packers, 34-19 (TB)
1995—Packers, 35-13 (GB)
    Buccaneers, 13-10 (TB) OT
1996—Packers, 34-3 (TB)
    Packers, 13-7 (GB)
1997—Packers, 21-16 (GB)
    Packers, 17-6 (TB)
    *Packers, 21-7 (GB)
1998—Packers, 23-15 (GB)
    Buccaneers, 24-22 (TB)
1999—Packers, 26-23 (GB)
    Buccaneers, 29-10 (TB)
2000—Buccaneers, 20-15 (TB)
    Packers, 17-14 (GB) OT
2001—Buccaneers, 14-10 (TB)
    Packers, 21-20 (GB)
2002—Buccaneers, 21-7 (TB)
2003—Packers, 20-13 (TB)
2005—Buccaneers, 17-16 (GB)
2008—Buccaneers, 30-21 (TB)
2009—Buccaneers, 38-28 (TB)
2011—Packers, 35-26 (GB)
(RS Pts.—Packers 1,012, Buccaneers 850)
(PS Pts.—Packers 21, Buccaneers 7)
*NFC Divisional Playoff

GREEN BAY vs. *TENNESSEE
RS: Titans lead series, 6-5
1972—Packers, 23-10 (H)
1977—Oilers, 16-10 (GB)
1980—Oilers, 22-3 (GB)
1983—Packers, 41-38 (H) OT
1986—Oilers, 31-3 (GB)
1992—Packers, 16-14 (H)
1998—Packers, 30-22 (GB)
2001—Titans, 26-20 (T)
2004—Titans, 48-27 (GB)
2008—Titans, 19-16 (T) OT
2012—Packers, 55-7 (GB)
(RS Pts.—Titans 253, Packers 244)
*Franchise in Houston prior to 1997;
known as Oilers prior to 1999

GREEN BAY vs. *WASHINGTON
RS: Packers lead series, 17-13-1
PS: Series tied, 1-1
1932—Packers, 21-0 (B)
1933—Tie, 7-7 (GB)
    Redskins, 20-7 (B)
1934—Packers, 10-0 (B)
1936—Packers, 31-2 (GB)
    Packers, 7-3 (B)
    **Packers, 21-6 (New York)
1937—Redskins, 14-6 (W)
1939—Packers, 24-14 (Mil)

1941—Packers, 22-17 (W)
1943—Redskins, 33-7 (Mil)
1946—Packers, 20-7 (W)
1947—Packers, 27-10 (Mil)
1948—Redskins, 23-7 (Mil)
1949—Redskins, 30-0 (W)
1950—Packers, 35-21 (Mil)
1952—Packers, 35-20 (Mil)
1958—Redskins, 37-21 (W)
1959—Packers, 21-0 (GB)
1968—Packers, 27-7 (W)
1972—Redskins, 21-16 (W)
    ***Redskins, 16-3 (W)
1974—Redskins, 17-6 (GB)
1977—Redskins, 10-9 (W)
1979—Redskins, 38-21 (W)
1983—Packers, 48-47 (GB)
1986—Redskins, 16-7 (GB)
1988—Redskins, 20-17 (Mil)
2001—Packers, 37-0 (GB)
2002—Packers, 30-9 (GB)
2004—Packers, 28-14 (W)
2007—Packers, 17-14 (GB)
2010—Redskins, 16-13 (W) OT
(RS Pts.—Packers 584, Redskins 487)
(PS Pts.—Packers 24, Redskins 22)
*Franchise in Boston prior to 1937 and
known as Braves prior to 1933
**NFL Championship
***NFC Divisional Playoff

HOUSTON vs. ARIZONA
RS: Series tied, 1-1;
See Arizona vs. Houston
HOUSTON vs. ATLANTA
RS: Texans lead series, 2-1;
See Atlanta vs. Houston
HOUSTON vs. BALTIMORE
RS: Ravens lead series, 5-1
PS: Ravens lead series, 1-0;
See Baltimore vs. Houston
HOUSTON vs. BUFFALO
RS: Series tied, 3-3;
See Buffalo vs. Houston
HOUSTON vs. CAROLINA
RS: Texans lead series, 2-1;
See Carolina vs. Houston
HOUSTON vs. CHICAGO
RS: Texans lead series, 3-0;
See Chicago vs. Houston
HOUSTON vs. CINCINNATI
RS: Series tied, 3-3
PS: Texans lead series, 2-0;
See Cincinnati vs. Houston
HOUSTON vs. CLEVELAND
RS: Texans lead series, 4-3;
See Cleveland vs. Houston
HOUSTON vs. DALLAS
RS: Cowboys lead series, 2-1;
See Dallas vs. Houston
HOUSTON vs. DENVER
RS: Series tied, 2-2;
See Denver vs. Houston
HOUSTON vs. DETROIT
RS: Texans lead series, 2-1;
See Detroit vs. Houston
HOUSTON vs. GREEN BAY
RS: Packers lead series, 2-1;
See Green Bay vs. Houston
HOUSTON vs. INDIANAPOLIS
RS: Colts lead series, 18-4
2002—Colts, 23-3 (H)
    Colts, 19-3 (I)

2003—Colts, 30-21 (I)
    Colts, 20-17 (H)
2004—Colts, 49-14 (I)
    Colts, 23-14 (H)
2005—Colts, 38-20 (H)
    Colts, 31-17 (I)
2006—Colts, 43-24 (I)
    Texans, 27-24 (H)
2007—Colts, 30-24 (H)
    Colts, 38-15 (I)
2008—Colts, 31-27 (H)
    Colts, 33-27 (I)
2009—Colts, 20-17 (I)
    Colts, 35-27 (H)
2010—Texans, 34-24 (H)
    Colts, 30-17 (I)
2011—Texans, 34-7 (H)
    Colts, 19-16 (I)
2012—Texans, 29-17 (H)
    Colts, 28-16 (I)
(RS Pts.—Colts 612, Texans 443)
HOUSTON vs. JACKSONVILLE
RS: Texans lead series, 13-9
2002—Texans, 21-19 (J)
    Jaguars, 24-21 (H)
2003—Texans, 24-20 (H)
    Jaguars, 27-0 (J)
2004—Texans, 20-6 (H)
    Texans, 21-0 (J)
2005—Jaguars, 21-14 (J)
    Jaguars, 38-20 (H)
2006—Texans, 27-7 (H)
    Texans, 13-10 (J)
2007—Jaguars, 37-17 (J)
    Texans, 42-28 (H)
2008—Jaguars, 30-27 (J) OT
    Texans, 30-17 (H)
2009—Jaguars, 31-24 (H)
    Jaguars, 23-18 (J)
2010—Jaguars, 31-24 (J)
    Texans, 34-17 (H)
2011—Texans, 24-14 (H)
    Texans, 20-13 (J)
2012—Texans, 27-7 (J)
    Texans, 43-37 (H) OT
(RS Pts.—Texans 511, Jaguars 457)
HOUSTON vs. KANSAS CITY
RS: Texans lead series, 3-2
2003—Chiefs, 42-14 (H)
2004—Texans, 24-21 (KC)
2005—Chiefs, 45-17 (H)
2007—Texans, 20-3 (H)
2010—Texans, 35-31 (H)
(RS Pts.—Chiefs 142, Texans 110)
HOUSTON vs. MIAMI
RS: Texans lead series, 7-0
2003—Texans, 21-20 (M)
2006—Texans, 17-15 (H)
2007—Texans, 22-19 (H)
2008—Texans, 29-28 (H)
2009—Texans, 27-20 (M)
2011—Texans, 23-13 (M)
2012—Texans, 30-10 (H)
(RS Pts.—Texans 169, Dolphins 125)
HOUSTON vs. MINNESOTA
RS: Vikings lead series, 3-0
2004—Vikings, 34-28 (H) OT
2008—Vikings, 28-21 (M)
2012—Vikings, 23-6 (H)
(RS Pts.—Vikings 85, Texans 55)
HOUSTON vs. NEW ENGLAND
RS: Patriots lead series, 3-1
PS: Patriots lead series, 1-0

2003—Patriots, 23-20 (H) OT
2006—Patriots, 40-7 (NE)
2009—Texans, 34-27 (H)
2012—Patriots, 42-14 (NE)
    *Patriots, 41-28 (NE)
(RS Pts.—Patriots 132, Texans 75)
(PS Pts.—Patriots 41, Texans 28)
*AFC Divisional Playoff
HOUSTON vs. NEW ORLEANS
RS: Saints lead series, 2-1
2003—Saints, 31-10 (NO)
2007—Texans, 23-10 (H)
2011—Saints, 40-33 (NO)
(RS Pts.—Saints 81, Texans 66)
HOUSTON vs. N.Y. GIANTS
RS: Giants lead series, 2-1
2002—Texans, 16-14 (H)
2006—Giants, 14-10 (NY)
2010—Giants, 34-10 (H)
(RS Pts.—Giants 62, Texans 36)
HOUSTON vs. N.Y. JETS
RS: Jets lead series, 5-1
2003—Jets, 19-14 (H)
2004—Jets, 29-7 (NY)
2006—Jets, 26-11 (NY)
2009—Jets, 24-7 (H)
2010—Jets, 30-27 (NY)
2012—Texans, 23-17 (NY)
(RS Pts.—Jets 145, Texans 89)
HOUSTON vs. OAKLAND
RS: Texans lead series, 5-2
2004—Texans, 30-17 (H)
2006—Texans, 23-14 (O)
2007—Texans, 24-17 (O)
2008—Raiders, 27-16 (O)
2009—Texans, 29-6 (H)
2010—Texans, 31-24 (O)
2011—Raiders, 25-20 (H)
(RS Pts.—Texans 173, Raiders 130)
HOUSTON vs. PHILADELPHIA
RS: Eagles lead series, 3-0
2002—Eagles, 35-17 (P)
2006—Eagles, 24-10 (H)
2010—Eagles, 34-24 (P)
(RS Pts.—Eagles 93, Texans 51)
HOUSTON vs. PITTSBURGH
RS: Series tied, 2-2
2002—Texans, 24-6 (P)
2005—Steelers, 27-7 (H)
2008—Steelers, 38-17 (P)
2011—Texans, 17-10 (H)
(RS Pts.—Steelers 81, Texans 65)
HOUSTON vs. ST. LOUIS
RS: Series tied, 1-1
2005—Rams, 33-27 (H) OT
2009—Texans, 16-13 (StL)
(RS Pts.—Rams 46, Texans 43)
HOUSTON vs. SAN DIEGO
RS: Chargers lead series, 4-0
2002—Chargers, 24-3 (SD)
2004—Chargers, 27-20 (H)
2007—Chargers, 35-10 (SD)
2010—Chargers, 29-23 (H)
(RS Pts.—Chargers 115, Texans 56)
HOUSTON vs. SAN FRANCISCO
RS: Series tied, 1-1
2005—49ers, 20-17 (SF) OT
2009—Texans, 24-21 (H)
(RS Pts.—Texans 41, 49ers 41)
HOUSTON vs. SEATTLE
RS: Series tied, 1-1
2005—Seahawks, 42-10 (S)
2009—Texans, 34-7 (H)

(RS Pts.—Seahawks 49, Texans 44)
HOUSTON vs. TAMPA BAY
RS: Texans lead series, 2-1
2003—Buccaneers, 16-3 (TB)
2007—Texans, 28-14 (H)
2011—Texans, 37-9 (TB)
(RS Pts.—Texans 68, Buccaneers 39)
HOUSTON vs. TENNESSEE
RS: Titans lead series, 14-8
2002—Titans, 17-10 (T)
    Titans, 13-3 (H)
2003—Titans, 38-17 (T)
    Titans, 27-24 (H)
2004—Texans, 20-10 (T)
    Texans, 31-21 (H)
2005—Titans, 34-20 (H)
    Titans, 13-10 (T)
2006—Titans, 28-22 (T)
    Titans, 26-20 (H) OT
2007—Titans, 38-36 (H)
    Titans, 28-20 (T)
2008—Titans, 31-12 (H)
    Texans, 13-12 (H)
2009—Texans, 34-31 (T)
    Titans, 20-17 (H)
2010—Texans, 20-0 (H)
    Titans, 31-17 (T)
2011—Texans, 41-7 (T)
    Titans, 23-22 (H)
2012—Texans, 38-14 (H)
    Texans, 24-10 (T)
(RS Pts.—Titans 472, Texans 471)
HOUSTON vs. WASHINGTON
RS: Redskins lead series, 2-1
2002—Redskins, 26-10 (W)
2006—Redskins, 31-15 (H)
2010—Texans, 30-27 (W) OT
(RS Pts.—Redskins 84, Texans 55)

INDIANAPOLIS vs. ARIZONA
RS: Colts lead series, 8-6;
See Arizona vs. Indianapolis
INDIANAPOLIS vs. ATLANTA
RS: Colts lead series, 13-2;
See Atlanta vs. Indianapolis
INDIANAPOLIS vs. BALTIMORE
RS: Colts lead series, 7-3
PS: Colts lead series, 2-1;
See Baltimore vs. Indianapolis
INDIANAPOLIS vs. BUFFALO
RS: Bills lead series, 35-31-1;
See Buffalo vs. Indianapolis
INDIANAPOLIS vs. CAROLINA
RS: Panthers lead series, 4-1;
See Carolina vs. Indianapolis
INDIANAPOLIS vs. CHICAGO
RS: Colts lead series, 22-19
PS: Colts lead series, 1-0;
See Chicago vs. Indianapolis
INDIANAPOLIS vs. CINCINNATI
RS: Colts lead series, 16-9
PS: Colts lead series, 1-0;
See Cincinnati vs. Indianapolis
INDIANAPOLIS vs. CLEVELAND
RS: Browns lead series, 14-13
PS: Series tied, 2-2;
See Cleveland vs. Indianapolis
INDIANAPOLIS vs. DALLAS
RS: Cowboys lead series, 9-5
PS: Colts lead series, 1-0;
See Dallas vs. Indianapolis
INDIANAPOLIS vs. DENVER
RS: Broncos lead series, 11-8

PS: Colts lead series, 2-0;
See Denver vs. Indianapolis
INDIANAPOLIS vs. DETROIT
RS: Colts lead series, 21-18-2;
See Detroit vs. Indianapolis
INDIANAPOLIS vs. GREEN BAY
RS: Colts lead series, 21-20-1
PS: Packers lead series, 1-0;
See Green Bay vs. Indianapolis
INDIANAPOLIS vs. HOUSTON
RS: Colts lead series, 18-4;
See Houston vs. Indianapolis
INDIANAPOLIS vs. JACKSONVILLE
RS: Colts lead series, 16-8
1995—Colts, 41-31 (J)
2000—Colts, 43-14 (I)
2002—Colts, 28-25 (J)
    Colts, 20-13 (I)
2003—Colts, 23-13 (I)
    Jaguars, 28-23 (J)
2004—Colts, 24-17 (J)
    Jaguars, 27-24 (I)
2005—Colts, 10-3 (I)
    Colts, 26-18 (J)
2006—Colts, 21-14 (I)
    Jaguars, 44-17 (J)
2007—Colts, 29-7 (J)
    Colts, 28-25 (I)
2008—Jaguars, 23-21 (I)
    Colts, 31-24 (J)
2009—Colts, 14-12 (I)
    Colts, 35-31 (J)
2010—Jaguars, 31-28 (J)
    Colts, 34-24 (I)
2011—Jaguars, 17-3 (I)
    Jaguars, 19-13 (J)
2012—Jaguars, 22-17 (I)
    Colts, 27-10 (J)
(RS Pts.—Colts 580, Jaguars 492)
*INDIANAPOLIS vs. KANSAS CITY
RS: Colts lead series, 11-8
PS: Colts lead series, 3-0
1970—Chiefs, 44-24 (B)
1972—Chiefs, 24-10 (KC)
1975—Colts, 28-14 (B)
1977—Colts, 17-6 (KC)
1979—Chiefs, 14-0 (KC)
    Chiefs, 10-7 (B)
1980—Colts, 31-24 (KC)
    Chiefs, 38-28 (B)
1985—Colts, 20-7 (KC)
1990—Colts, 23-19 (I)
1995—**Colts, 10-7 (KC)
1996—Colts, 24-19 (KC)
1999—Colts, 25-17 (I)
2000—Colts, 27-14 (KC)
2001—Colts, 35-28 (KC)
2003—**Colts, 38-31 (KC)
2004—Chiefs, 45-35 (KC)
2006—***Colts, 23-8 (I)
2007—Colts, 13-10 (I)
2010—Colts, 19-9 (I)
2011—Chiefs, 28-24 (I)
2012—Colts, 20-13 (KC)
(RS Pts.—Colts 397, Chiefs 396)
(PS Pts.—Colts 71, Chiefs 46)
Franchise in Baltimore prior to 1984
**AFC Divisional Playoff*
***AFC First-Round Playoff*
*INDIANAPOLIS vs. MIAMI
RS: Dolphins lead series, 44-25
PS: Dolphins lead series, 2-0

1970—Colts, 35-0 (B)
　　　Dolphins, 34-17 (M)
1971—Dolphins, 17-14 (M)
　　　Colts, 14-3 (B)
　　　**Dolphins, 21-0 (M)
1972—Dolphins, 23-0 (B)
　　　Dolphins, 16-0 (M)
1973—Dolphins, 44-0 (M)
　　　Colts, 16-3 (B)
1974—Dolphins, 17-7 (M)
　　　Dolphins, 17-16 (B)
1975—Colts, 33-17 (M)
　　　Colts, 10-7 (B) OT
1976—Colts, 28-14 (B)
　　　Colts, 17-16 (M)
1977—Colts, 45-28 (B)
　　　Dolphins, 17-6 (M)
1978—Dolphins, 42-0 (B)
　　　Dolphins, 26-8 (M)
1979—Dolphins, 19-0 (M)
　　　Dolphins, 28-24 (B)
1980—Colts, 30-17 (M)
　　　Dolphins, 24-14 (B)
1981—Dolphins, 31-28 (B)
　　　Dolphins, 27-10 (M)
1982—Dolphins, 24-20 (M)
　　　Dolphins, 34-7 (B)
1983—Dolphins, 21-7 (B)
　　　Dolphins, 37-0 (M)
1984—Dolphins, 44-7 (M)
　　　Dolphins, 35-17 (I)
1985—Dolphins, 30-13 (M)
　　　Dolphins, 34-20 (I)
1986—Dolphins, 30-10 (M)
　　　Dolphins, 17-13 (I)
1987—Dolphins, 23-10 (I)
　　　Colts, 40-21 (M)
1988—Colts, 15-13 (I)
　　　Colts, 31-28 (M)
1989—Dolphins, 19-13 (M)
　　　Colts, 42-13 (I)
1990—Dolphins, 27-7 (I)
　　　Dolphins, 23-17 (M)
1991—Dolphins, 17-6 (M)
　　　Dolphins, 10-6 (I)
1992—Colts, 31-20 (M)
　　　Dolphins, 28-0 (I)
1993—Dolphins, 24-20 (I)
　　　Dolphins, 41-27 (M)
1994—Dolphins, 22-21 (M)
　　　Colts, 10-6 (I)
1995—Colts, 27-24 (M) OT
　　　Colts, 36-28 (I)
1996—Colts, 10-6 (I)
　　　Dolphins, 37-13 (M)
1997—Dolphins, 16-10 (M)
　　　Colts, 41-0 (I)
1998—Dolphins, 24-15 (I)
　　　Dolphins, 27-14 (M)
1999—Dolphins, 34-31 (I)
　　　Colts, 37-34 (M)
2000—Dolphins, 17-14 (I)
　　　Colts, 20-13 (M)
　　　***Dolphins 23-17 (M) OT
2001—Dolphins, 27-24 (I)
　　　Dolphins, 41-6 (M)
2002—Dolphins, 21-13 (I)
2003—Colts, 23-17 (M)
2006—Colts, 27-22 (I)
2009—Colts, 27-23 (M)
2012—Colts, 23-20 (I)
(RS Pts.—Dolphins 1,559, Colts 1,193)
(PS Pts.—Dolphins 44, Colts 17)

*Franchise in Baltimore prior to 1984
**AFC Championship
***AFC First-Round Playoff
*INDIANAPOLIS vs. MINNESOTA
RS: Colts lead series, 15-7-1
PS: Colts lead series, 1-0
1961—Colts, 34-33 (B)
　　　Vikings, 28-20 (M)
1962—Colts, 34-7 (M)
　　　Colts, 42-17 (B)
1963—Colts, 37-34 (M)
　　　Colts, 41-10 (B)
1964—Vikings, 34-24 (M)
　　　Colts, 17-14 (B)
1965—Colts, 35-16 (B)
　　　Colts, 41-21 (M)
1966—Colts, 38-23 (M)
　　　Colts, 20-17 (B)
1967—Tie, 20-20 (M)
1968—Colts, 21-9 (B)
　　　**Colts, 24-14 (B)
1969—Vikings, 52-14 (M)
1971—Vikings, 10-3 (M)
1982—Vikings, 13-10 (M)
1988—Vikings, 12-3 (M)
1997—Vikings, 39-28 (M)
2000—Colts, 31-10 (I)
2004—Colts, 31-28 (I)
2008—Colts, 18-15 (M)
2012—Colts, 23-20 (I)
(RS Pts.—Colts 585, Vikings 482)
(PS Pts.—Colts 24, Vikings 14)
*Franchise in Baltimore prior to 1984
**Conference Championship
*INDIANAPOLIS vs. **NEW ENGLAND
RS: Patriots lead series, 45-28
PS: Patriots lead series, 2-1
1970—Colts, 14-6 (Bos)
　　　Colts, 27-3 (Balt)
1971—Colts, 23-3 (NE)
　　　Patriots, 21-17 (Balt)
1972—Colts, 24-17 (NE)
　　　Colts, 31-0 (Balt)
1973—Patriots, 24-16 (NE)
　　　Colts, 18-13 (Balt)
1974—Patriots, 42-3 (NE)
　　　Patriots, 27-17 (Balt)
1975—Patriots, 21-10 (NE)
　　　Colts, 34-21 (Balt)
1976—Colts, 27-13 (NE)
　　　Patriots, 21-14 (Balt)
1977—Patriots, 17-3 (NE)
　　　Colts, 30-24 (Balt)
1978—Colts, 34-27 (NE)
　　　Patriots, 35-14 (Balt)
1979—Colts, 31-26 (Balt)
　　　Patriots, 50-21 (NE)
1980—Patriots, 37-21 (Balt)
　　　Patriots, 47-21 (NE)
1981—Colts, 29-28 (NE)
　　　Colts, 23-21 (Balt)
1982—Patriots, 24-13 (Balt)
1983—Colts, 29-23 (NE) OT
　　　Colts, 12-7 (Balt)
1984—Patriots, 50-17 (I)
　　　Patriots, 16-10 (NE)
1985—Patriots, 34-15 (NE)
　　　Patriots, 38-31 (I)
1986—Patriots, 33-3 (NE)
　　　Patriots, 30-21 (I)
1987—Colts, 30-16 (I)
　　　Patriots, 24-0 (NE)

1988—Patriots, 21-17 (NE)
　　　Colts, 24-21 (I)
1989—Patriots, 23-20 (I) OT
　　　Patriots, 22-16 (NE)
1990—Patriots, 16-14 (I)
　　　Colts, 13-10 (NE)
1991—Patriots, 16-7 (I)
　　　Patriots, 23-17 (NE) OT
1992—Patriots, 37-34 (I) OT
　　　Colts, 6-0 (NE)
1993—Colts, 9-6 (I)
　　　Patriots, 38-0 (NE)
1994—Patriots, 12-10 (I)
　　　Patriots, 28-13 (NE)
1995—Colts, 24-10 (NE)
　　　Colts, 10-7 (I)
1996—Patriots, 27-9 (I)
　　　Patriots, 27-13 (NE)
1997—Patriots, 31-6 (I)
　　　Patriots, 20-17 (NE)
1998—Patriots, 29-6 (NE)
　　　Patriots, 21-16 (I)
1999—Patriots, 31-28 (NE)
　　　Colts, 20-15 (I)
2000—Patriots, 24-16 (NE)
　　　Colts, 30-23 (I)
2001—Patriots, 44-13 (NE)
　　　Patriots, 38-17 (I)
2003—Patriots, 38-34 (I)
　　　***Patriots, 24-14 (NE)
2004—Patriots, 27-24 (NE)
　　　****Patriots, 20-3 (NE)
2005—Colts, 40-21 (NE)
2006—Colts, 27-20 (NE)
　　　***Colts, 38-34 (I)
2007—Patriots, 24-20 (I)
2008—Colts, 18-15 (I)
2009—Colts, 35-34 (I)
2010—Patriots, 31-28 (NE)
2011—Patriots, 31-24 (NE)
2012—Patriots, 59-24 (NE)
(RS Pts.—Patriots 1,759, Colts 1,382)
(PS Pts.—Patriots 78, Colts 55)
*Franchise in Baltimore prior to 1984
**Franchise in Boston prior to 1971
***AFC Championship
****AFC Divisional Playoff
*INDIANAPOLIS vs. NEW ORLEANS
RS: Saints lead series, 6-5
PS: Saints lead series, 1-0
1967—Colts, 30-10 (B)
1969—Colts, 30-10 (NO)
1973—Colts, 14-10 (B)
1986—Saints, 17-14 (I)
1989—Saints, 41-6 (NO)
1995—Saints, 17-14 (NO)
1998—Saints, 19-13 (I) OT
2001—Saints, 34-20 (NO)
2003—Colts, 55-21 (NO)
2007—Colts, 41-10 (I)
2009—**Saints 31-17 (South Florida)
2011—Saints, 62-7 (NO)
(RS Pts.—Saints 251, Colts 244)
(PS Pts.—Saints 31, Colts 17)
*Franchise in Baltimore prior to 1984
**Super Bowl XLIV
*INDIANAPOLIS vs. N.Y. GIANTS
RS: Colts lead series, 8-6
PS: Colts lead series, 2-0
1954—Colts, 20-14 (B)
1955—Giants, 17-7 (NY)
1958—Giants, 24-21 (NY)
　　　**Colts, 23-17 (NY) OT

1959—**Colts, 31-16 (B)
1963—Giants, 37-28 (B)
1968—Colts, 26-0 (NY)
1971—Colts, 31-7 (NY)
1975—Colts, 21-0 (NY)
1979—Colts, 31-7 (NY)
1990—Giants, 24-7 (I)
1993—Giants, 20-6 (NY)
1999—Colts, 27-19 (NY)
2002—Giants, 44-27 (I)
2006—Colts, 26-21 (NY)
2010—Colts, 38-14 (I)
(RS Pts.—Colts 316, Giants 248)
(PS Pts.—Colts 54, Giants 33)
*Franchise in Baltimore prior to 1984
**NFL Championship
INDIANAPOLIS vs. N.Y. JETS
RS: Colts lead series, 40-27
PS: Jets lead series, 3-1
1968—**Jets 16-7 (Miami)
1970—Colts, 29-22 (NY)
         Colts, 35-20 (B)
1971—Colts, 22-0 (B)
         Colts, 14-13 (NY)
1972—Jets, 44-34 (B)
         Jets, 24-20 (NY)
1973—Jets, 34-10 (B)
         Jets, 20-17 (NY)
1974—Colts, 35-20 (NY)
         Jets, 45-38 (B)
1975—Colts, 45-28 (NY)
         Colts, 52-19 (B)
1976—Colts, 20-0 (NY)
         Colts, 33-16 (B)
1977—Colts, 20-12 (NY)
         Colts, 33-12 (B)
1978—Jets, 33-10 (B)
         Jets, 24-16 (NY)
1979—Colts, 10-8 (B)
         Jets, 30-17 (NY)
1980—Colts, 17-14 (NY)
         Colts, 35-21 (B)
1981—Jets, 41-14 (B)
         Jets, 25-0 (NY)
1982—Jets, 37-0 (NY)
1983—Colts, 17-14 (NY)
         Jets, 10-6 (B)
1984—Jets, 23-14 (I)
         Colts, 9-5 (NY)
1985—Jets, 25-20 (NY)
         Jets, 35-17 (I)
1986—Jets, 26-7 (I)
         Jets, 31-16 (NY)
1987—Colts, 6-0 (I)
         Colts, 19-14 (NY)
1988—Colts, 38-14 (I)
         Jets, 34-16 (NY)
1989—Colts, 17-10 (NY)
         Colts, 27-10 (I)
1990—Colts, 17-14 (I)
         Colts, 29-21 (NY)
1991—Jets, 17-6 (I)
         Colts, 28-27 (NY)
1992—Colts, 6-3 (I) OT
         Colts, 10-6 (NY)
1993—Jets, 31-17 (I)
         Colts, 9-6 (NY)
1994—Jets, 16-6 (NY)
         Colts, 28-25 (I)
1995—Colts, 27-24 (NY) OT
         Colts, 17-10 (I)
1996—Colts, 21-7 (NY)
         Colts, 34-29 (I)

1997—Jets, 16-12 (I)
         Colts, 22-14 (NY)
1998—Jets, 44-6 (NY)
         Colts, 24-23 (I)
1999—Colts, 16-13 (NY)
         Colts, 13-6 (I)
2000—Colts, 23-15 (I)
         Jets, 27-17 (NY)
2001—Colts, 45-24 (NY)
         Jets, 29-28 (I)
2002—***Jets, 41-0 (NY)
2003—Colts, 38-31 (I)
2006—Colts, 31-28 (NY)
2009—Jets, 29-15 (I)
         ****Colts, 30-17 (I)
2010—***Jets, 17-16 (I)
2012—Jets, 35-9 (NY)
(RS Pts.—Jets 1,383, Colts 1,359)
(PS Pts.—Jets 91, Colts 53)
*Franchise in Baltimore prior to 1984
**Super Bowl III
***AFC First-Round Playoff
****AFC Championship
INDIANAPOLIS vs. **OAKLAND
RS: Raiders lead series, 7-5
PS: Series tied, 1-1
1970—***Colts, 27-17 (B)
1971—Colts, 37-14 (O)
1973—Raiders, 34-21 (B)
1975—Raiders, 31-20 (B)
1977—****Raiders, 37-31 (B) OT
1984—Raiders, 21-7 (LA)
1986—Colts, 30-24 (LA)
1991—Raiders, 16-0 (LA)
1995—Raiders, 30-17 (O)
2000—Raiders, 38-31 (I)
2001—Raiders, 23-18 (I)
2004—Colts, 35-14 (I)
2007—Colts, 21-14 (O)
2010—Colts, 31-26 (O)
(RS Pts.—Raiders 285, Colts 268)
(PS Pts.—Colts 58, Raiders 54)
*Franchise in Baltimore prior to 1984
**Franchise in Los Angeles from
1982-1994
***AFC Championship
****AFC Divisional Playoff
INDIANAPOLIS vs. PHILADELPHIA
RS: Colts lead series, 10-7
1953—Eagles, 45-14 (P)
1965—Colts, 34-24 (B)
1967—Colts, 38-6 (P)
1969—Colts, 24-20 (B)
1970—Colts, 29-10 (B)
1974—Eagles, 30-10 (P)
1978—Eagles, 17-14 (B)
1981—Eagles, 38-13 (P)
1983—Colts, 22-21 (P)
1984—Eagles, 16-7 (P)
1990—Colts, 24-23 (P)
1993—Eagles, 20-10 (I)
1996—Colts, 37-10 (I)
1999—Colts, 44-17 (P)
2002—Colts, 35-13 (P)
2006—Colts, 45-21 (I)
2010—Eagles, 26-24 (P)
(RS Pts.—Colts 424, Eagles 357)
*Franchise in Baltimore prior to 1984
INDIANAPOLIS vs. PITTSBURGH
RS: Steelers lead series, 14-6
PS: Steelers lead series, 5-0
1957—Steelers, 19-13 (B)
1968—Colts, 41-7 (P)

1971—Colts, 34-21 (B)
1974—Steelers, 30-0 (P)
1975—**Steelers, 28-10 (P)
1976—**Steelers, 40-14 (B)
1977—Colts, 31-21 (B)
1978—Steelers, 35-13 (P)
1979—Steelers, 17-13 (P)
1980—Steelers, 20-17 (B)
1983—Steelers, 24-13 (B)
1984—Colts, 17-16 (I)
1985—Steelers, 45-3 (P)
1987—Steelers, 21-7 (P)
1991—Steelers, 21-3 (I)
1992—Steelers, 30-14 (P)
1994—Steelers, 31-21 (P)
1995—***Steelers, 20-16 (P)
1996—****Steelers, 42-14 (P)
1997—Steelers, 24-22 (P)
2002—Steelers, 28-10 (P)
2005—Colts, 26-7 (I)
         **Steelers, 21-18 (I)
2008—Colts, 24-20 (P)
2011—Steelers, 23-20 (I)
(RS Pts.—Steelers 460, Colts 342)
(PS Pts.—Steelers 151, Colts 72)
*Franchise in Baltimore prior to 1984
**AFC Divisional Playoff
***AFC Championship
****AFC First-Round Playoff
INDIANAPOLIS vs. **ST. LOUIS
RS: Colts lead series, 23-17-2
1953—Rams, 21-13 (B)
         Rams, 45-2 (LA)
1954—Rams, 48-0 (B)
         Colts, 22-21 (LA)
1955—Tie, 17-17 (B)
         Rams, 20-14 (LA)
1956—Colts, 56-21 (B)
         Rams, 31-7 (LA)
1957—Colts, 31-14 (B)
         Rams, 37-21 (LA)
1958—Colts, 34-7 (B)
         Rams, 30-28 (LA)
1959—Colts, 35-21 (B)
         Colts, 45-26 (LA)
1960—Colts, 31-17 (B)
         Rams, 10-3 (LA)
1961—Colts, 27-24 (B)
         Rams, 34-17 (LA)
1962—Colts, 30-27 (B)
         Colts, 14-2 (LA)
1963—Rams, 17-16 (LA)
         Colts, 19-16 (B)
1964—Colts, 35-20 (B)
         Colts, 24-7 (LA)
1965—Colts, 35-20 (B)
         Colts, 20-17 (LA)
1966—Colts, 17-3 (LA)
         Rams, 23-7 (B)
1967—Tie, 24-24 (B)
         Rams, 34-10 (LA)
1968—Colts, 27-10 (B)
         Colts, 28-24 (LA)
1969—Rams, 27-20 (B)
         Colts, 13-7 (LA)
1971—Colts, 24-17 (B)
1975—Rams, 24-13 (LA)
1986—Rams, 24-7 (I)
1989—Rams, 31-17 (LA)
1995—Colts, 21-18 (I)
2001—Rams, 42-17 (StL)
2005—Colts, 45-28 (I)
2009—Colts, 42-6 (StL)

(RS Pts.—Colts 928, Rams 912)
*Franchise in Baltimore prior to 1984
**Franchise in Los Angeles prior to 1995
INDIANAPOLIS vs. SAN DIEGO
RS: Chargers lead series, 15-9
PS: Chargers lead series, 2-1
1970—Colts, 16-14 (SD)
1972—Chargers, 23-20 (B)
1976—Colts, 37-21 (SD)
1981—Chargers, 43-14 (B)
1982—Chargers, 44-26 (SD)
1984—Chargers, 38-10 (I)
1986—Chargers, 17-3 (I)
1987—Chargers, 16-13 (I)
 Colts, 20-7 (SD)
1988—Colts, 16-0 (SD)
1989—Colts, 10-6 (I)
1992—Chargers, 34-14 (I)
 Chargers, 26-0 (SD)
1993—Chargers, 31-0 (I)
1995—Chargers, 27-24 (I)
 **Colts, 35-20 (SD)
1996—Chargers, 26-19 (I)
1997—Chargers, 35-19 (SD)
1998—Colts, 17-12 (I)
1999—Colts, 27-19 (SD)
2004—Colts, 34-31 (I) OT
2005—Chargers, 26-17 (I)
2007—Chargers, 23-21 (SD)
 ***Chargers, 28-24 (I)
2008—Colts, 23-20 (SD)
 **Chargers, 23-17 (SD) OT
2010—Chargers, 36-14 (I)
(RS Pts.—Chargers 575, Colts 414)
(PS Pts.—Colts 76, Chargers 71)
*Franchise in Baltimore prior to 1984
**AFC First-Round Playoff
***AFC Divisional Playoff
INDIANAPOLIS vs. SAN FRANCISCO
RS: Colts lead series, 24-18
1953—49ers, 38-21 (B)
 49ers, 45-14 (SF)
1954—Colts, 17-13 (B)
 49ers, 10-7 (SF)
1955—Colts, 26-14 (B)
 49ers, 35-24 (SF)
1956—49ers, 20-17 (B)
 49ers, 30-17 (SF)
1957—Colts, 27-21 (B)
 49ers, 17-13 (SF)
1958—Colts, 35-27 (B)
 49ers, 21-12 (SF)
1959—Colts, 45-14 (B)
 Colts, 34-14 (SF)
1960—49ers, 30-22 (B)
 49ers, 34-10 (SF)
1961—Colts, 20-17 (B)
 Colts, 27-24 (SF)
1962—49ers, 21-13 (B)
 Colts, 22-3 (SF)
1963—Colts, 20-14 (I)
 Colts, 20-3 (B)
1964—Colts, 37-7 (B)
 Colts, 14-3 (SF)
1965—Colts, 27-24 (B)
 Colts, 34-28 (SF)
1966—Colts, 36-14 (B)
 Colts, 30-14 (SF)
1967—Colts, 41-7 (B)
 Colts, 26-9 (SF)
1968—Colts, 27-10 (B)
 Colts, 42-14 (SF)

1969—49ers, 24-21 (B)
 49ers, 20-17 (SF)
1972—49ers, 24-21 (SF)
1986—49ers, 35-14 (SF)
1989—49ers, 30-24 (I)
1995—Colts, 18-17 (I)
1998—49ers, 34-31 (SF)
2001—49ers, 40-21 (I)
2005—Colts, 28-3 (SF)
2009—Colts, 18-14 (I)
(RS Pts.—Colts 990, 49ers 836)
*Franchise in Baltimore prior to 1984
INDIANAPOLIS vs. SEATTLE
RS: Colts lead series, 6-4
1977—Colts, 29-14 (S)
1978—Colts, 17-14 (S)
1991—Seahawks, 31-3 (S)
1994—Colts, 17-15 (I)
 Colts, 31-19 (S)
1997—Seahawks, 31-3 (I)
1998—Seahawks, 27-23 (S)
2000—Colts, 37-24 (S)
2005—Seahawks, 28-13 (S)
2009—Colts, 34-17 (I)
(RS Pts.—Seahawks 220, Colts 207)
*Franchise in Baltimore prior to 1984
INDIANAPOLIS vs. TAMPA BAY
RS: Colts lead series, 7-5
1976—Colts, 42-17 (B)
1979—Buccaneers, 29-26 (B) OT
1985—Colts, 31-23 (TB)
1987—Colts, 24-6 (I)
1988—Colts, 35-31 (I)
1991—Buccaneers, 17-3 (TB)
1992—Colts, 24-14 (TB)
1994—Buccaneers, 24-10 (TB)
1997—Buccaneers, 31-28 (I)
2003—Colts, 38-35 (TB) OT
2007—Colts, 33-14 (I)
2011—Buccaneers, 24-17 (TB)
(RS Pts.—Colts 311, Buccaneers 265)
*Franchise in Baltimore prior to 1984
INDIANAPOLIS vs. **TENNESSEE
RS: Colts lead series, 23-13
PS: Titans lead series, 1-0
1970—Colts, 24-20 (H)
1973—Oilers, 31-27 (B)
1976—Colts, 38-14 (B)
1979—Oilers, 28-16 (B)
1980—Oilers, 21-16 (H)
1983—Colts, 20-10 (B)
1984—Colts, 35-21 (H)
1985—Colts, 34-16 (I)
1986—Oilers, 31-17 (H)
1987—Colts, 51-27 (I)
1988—Oilers, 17-14 (I) OT
1990—Oilers, 24-10 (H)
1992—Oilers, 20-10 (I)
1994—Colts, 45-21 (I)
1999—***Titans, 19-16 (I)
2002—Titans, 23-15 (I)
 Titans, 27-17 (T)
2003—Colts, 33-7 (I)
 Colts, 29-27 (T)
2004—Colts, 31-17 (T)
 Colts, 51-24 (I)
2005—Colts, 31-10 (T)
 Colts, 35-3 (I)
2006—Colts, 14-13 (I)
 Titans, 20-17 (T)
2007—Colts, 22-20 (T)
 Titans, 16-10 (I)

2008—Titans, 31-21 (T)
 Colts, 23-0 (I)
2009—Colts, 31-9 (T)
 Colts, 27-17 (I)
2010—Colts, 30-28 (T)
 Colts, 23-20 (I)
2011—Titans, 27-10 (T)
 Colts, 27-13 (I)
2012—Colts, 19-13 (T) OT
 Colts, 27-23 (I)
(RS Pts.—Colts 900, Titans 689)
(PS Pts.—Titans 19, Colts 16)
*Franchise in Baltimore prior to 1984
**Franchise in Houston prior to 1997;
known as Oilers prior to 1999
***AFC Divisional Playoff
INDIANAPOLIS vs. WASHINGTON
RS: Colts lead series, 19-10
1953—Colts, 27-17 (B)
1954—Redskins, 24-21 (W)
1955—Redskins, 14-13 (B)
1956—Colts, 19-17 (B)
1957—Colts, 21-17 (W)
1958—Colts, 35-10 (B)
1959—Redskins, 27-24 (W)
1960—Colts, 20-0 (B)
1961—Colts, 27-6 (W)
1962—Colts, 34-21 (B)
1963—Colts, 36-20 (W)
1964—Colts, 45-17 (B)
1965—Colts, 38-7 (W)
1966—Colts, 37-10 (B)
1967—Colts, 17-13 (W)
1969—Colts, 41-17 (B)
1973—Redskins, 22-14 (W)
1977—Colts, 10-3 (B)
1978—Colts, 21-17 (B)
1981—Redskins, 38-14 (W)
1984—Redskins, 35-7 (I)
1990—Colts, 35-28 (I)
1993—Redskins, 30-24 (W)
1994—Redskins, 41-27 (I)
1996—Redskins, 31-16 (W)
1999—Colts, 24-21 (I)
2002—Redskins, 26-21 (W)
2006—Colts, 36-22 (I)
2010—Colts, 27-24 (W)
(RS Pts.—Colts 731, Redskins 575)
*Franchise in Baltimore prior to 1984

JACKSONVILLE vs. ARIZONA
RS: Jaguars lead series, 2-1;
See Arizona vs. Jacksonville
JACKSONVILLE vs. ATLANTA
RS: Jaguars lead series, 3-2;
See Atlanta vs. Jacksonville
JACKSONVILLE vs. BALTIMORE
RS: Jaguars lead series, 10-7;
See Baltimore vs. Jacksonville
JACKSONVILLE vs. BUFFALO
RS: Bills lead series, 6-5
PS: Jaguars lead series, 1-0;
See Buffalo vs. Jacksonville
JACKSONVILLE vs. CAROLINA
RS: Jaguars lead series, 3-2;
See Carolina vs. Jacksonville
JACKSONVILLE vs. CHICAGO
RS: Bears lead series, 4-2;
See Chicago vs. Jacksonville
JACKSONVILLE vs. CINCINNATI
RS: Jaguars lead series, 11-8;
See Cincinnati vs. Jacksonville

JACKSONVILLE vs. CLEVELAND
RS: Jaguars lead series, 9-5;
See Cleveland vs. Jacksonville
JACKSONVILLE vs. DALLAS
RS: Jaguars lead series, 3-2;
See Dallas vs. Jacksonville
JACKSONVILLE vs. DENVER
RS: Jaguars lead series, 5-3
PS: Series tied, 1-1;
See Denver vs. Jacksonville
JACKSONVILLE vs. DETROIT
RS: Jaguars lead series, 3-2;
See Detroit vs. Jacksonville
JACKSONVILLE vs. GREEN BAY
RS: Packers lead series, 3-2;
See Green Bay vs. Jacksonville
JACKSONVILLE vs. HOUSTON
RS: Texans lead series, 13-9;
See Houston vs. Jacksonville
JACKSONVILLE vs. INDIANAPOLIS
RS: Colts lead series, 16-8;
See Indianapolis vs. Jacksonville
JACKSONVILLE vs. KANSAS CITY
RS: Jaguars lead series, 6-3
1997—Jaguars, 24-10 (J)
1998—Jaguars, 21-16 (J)
2001—Chiefs, 30-26 (J)
2002—Jaguars, 23-16 (KC)
2004—Jaguars, 22-16 (J)
2006—Chiefs, 35-30 (KC)
2007—Jaguars, 17-7 (KC)
2009—Jaguars, 24-21 (J)
2010—Chiefs, 42-20 (KC)
(RS Pts.—Jaguars 207, Chiefs 193)
JACKSONVILLE vs. MIAMI
RS: Dolphins lead series, 3-2
PS: Jaguars lead series, 1-0
1998—Jaguars, 28-21 (J)
1999—*Jaguars, 62-7 (J)
2003—Dolphins, 24-10 (J)
2006—Jaguars, 24-10 (M)
2009—Dolphins, 14-10 (J)
2012—Dolphins, 24-3 (M)
(RS Pts.—Dolphins, 93, Jaguars 75)
(PS Pts.—Jaguars 62, Dolphins 7)
*AFC Divisional Playoff
JACKSONVILLE vs. MINNESOTA
RS: Vikings lead series, 4-1
1998—Vikings, 50-10 (M)
2001—Jaguars, 33-3 (M)
2004—Vikings, 27-16 (M)
2008—Vikings, 30-12 (J)
2012—Vikings, 26-23 (M) OT
(RS Pts.—Vikings 136, Jaguars 94)
JACKSONVILLE vs. NEW ENGLAND
RS: Patriots lead series, 6-0
PS: Patriots lead series, 3-1
1996—Patriots, 28-25 (NE) OT
        *Patriots, 20-6 (NE)
1997—Patriots, 26-20 (J)
1998—**Jaguars, 25-10 (J)
2003—Patriots, 27-13 (NE)
2005—**Patriots, 28-3 (NE)
2006—Patriots, 24-21 (J)
2007—***Patriots, 31-20 (NE)
2009—Patriots, 35-7 (NE)
2012—Patriots, 23-16 (J)
(RS Pts.—Patriots 163, Jaguars 102)
(PS Pts.—Patriots 89, Jaguars 54)
*AFC Championship
**AFC First-Round Playoff
***AFC Divisional Playoff

JACKSONVILLE vs. NEW ORLEANS
RS: Saints lead series, 3-2
1996—Saints, 17-13 (NO)
1999—Jaguars, 41-23 (J)
2003—Jaguars, 20-19 (J)
2007—Saints, 41-24 (NO)
2011—Saints, 23-10 (J)
(RS Pts.—Saints 123, Jaguars 108)
JACKSONVILLE vs. N.Y. GIANTS
RS: Giants lead series, 3-2
1997—Jaguars, 40-13 (J)
2000—Giants, 28-25 (NY)
2002—Giants, 24-17 (NY)
2006—Jaguars, 26-10 (J)
2010—Giants, 24-20 (NY)
(RS Pts.—Jaguars 128, Giants 99)
JACKSONVILLE vs. N.Y. JETS
RS: Jaguars lead series, 6-4
PS: Jets lead series, 1-0
1995—Jets, 27-10 (NY)
1996—Jaguars, 21-17 (J)
1998—*Jets, 34-24 (NY)
1999—Jaguars, 16-6 (NY)
2002—Jaguars, 28-3 (J)
2003—Jets, 13-10 (NY)
2005—Jaguars, 26-20 (NY) OT
2006—Jaguars, 41-0 (J)
2009—Jaguars, 24-22 (NY)
2011—Jets, 32-3 (NY)
2012—Jets, 17-10 (J)
(RS Pts.—Jaguars 189, Jets 157)
(PS Pts.—Jets 34, Jaguars 24)
*AFC Divisional Playoff
JACKSONVILLE vs. OAKLAND
RS: Jaguars lead series, 4-2
1996—Raiders, 17-3 (O)
1997—Jaguars, 20-9 (O)
2004—Jaguars, 13-6 (O)
2007—Jaguars, 49-11 (J)
2010—Jaguars, 38-31 (J)
2012—Raiders, 26-23 (O) OT
(RS Pts.—Jaguars 146, Raiders 100)
JACKSONVILLE vs. PHILADELPHIA
RS: Jaguars lead series, 3-1
1997—Jaguars, 38-21 (J)
2002—Jaguars, 28-25 (J)
2006—Jaguars, 13-6 (P)
2010—Eagles, 28-3 (J)
(RS Pts.—Jaguars 82, Eagles 80)
JACKSONVILLE vs. PITTSBURGH
RS: Jaguars lead series, 11-10
PS: Jaguars lead series, 1-0
1995—Jaguars, 20-16 (J)
        Steelers, 24-7 (P)
1996—Jaguars, 24-9 (J)
        Steelers, 28-3 (P)
1997—Jaguars, 30-21 (J)
        Steelers, 23-17 (P) OT
1998—Steelers, 30-15 (P)
        Jaguars, 21-3 (J)
1999—Jaguars, 17-3 (P)
        Jaguars, 20-6 (J)
2000—Steelers, 24-13 (J)
        Jaguars, 34-24 (P)
2001—Jaguars, 21-3 (J)
        Steelers, 20-7 (P)
2002—Steelers, 25-23 (J)
2004—Steelers, 17-16 (J)
2005—Jaguars, 23-17 (P) OT
2006—Jaguars, 9-0 (J)
2007—Jaguars, 29-22 (P)
        *Jaguars, 31-29 (P)
2008—Steelers, 26-21 (J)

2011—Steelers, 17-13 (P)
(RS Pts.—Jaguars 383, Steelers 358)
(PS Pts.—Jaguars 31, Steelers 29)
*AFC First-Round Playoff
JACKSONVILLE vs. ST. LOUIS
RS: Rams lead series, 2-1
1996—Rams, 17-14 (StL)
2005—Rams, 24-21 (StL)
2009—Jaguars, 23-20 (J) OT
(RS Pts.—Rams 61, Jaguars 58)
JACKSONVILLE vs. SAN DIEGO
RS: Chargers lead series, 3-2
2003—Jaguars, 27-21 (J)
2004—Chargers, 34-21 (SD)
2007—Jaguars, 24-17 (J)
2010—Chargers, 38-13 (SD)
2011—Chargers, 38-14 (J)
(RS Pts.—Chargers 148, Jaguars 99)
JACKSONVILLE vs. SAN FRANCISCO
RS: Jaguars lead series, 2-1
1999—Jaguars, 41-3 (J)
2005—Jaguars, 10-9 (J)
2009—49ers, 20-3 (SF)
(RS Pts.—Jaguars 54, 49ers 32)
JACKSONVILLE vs. SEATTLE
RS: Seahawks lead series, 4-2
1995—Seahawks, 47-30 (J)
1996—Jaguars, 20-13 (J)
2000—Seahawks, 28-21 (J)
2001—Seahawks, 24-15 (S)
2005—Jaguars, 26-14 (J)
2009—Seahawks, 41-0 (S)
(RS Pts.—Seahawks 167, Jaguars 112)
JACKSONVILLE vs. TAMPA BAY
RS: Jaguars lead series, 4-1
1995—Buccaneers, 17-16 (TB)
1998—Jaguars, 29-24 (J)
2003—Jaguars, 17-10 (J)
2007—Jaguars, 24-23 (TB)
2011—Jaguars, 41-14 (J)
(RS Pts.—Jaguars 127, Buccaneers 88)
JACKSONVILLE vs. *TENNESSEE
RS: Titans lead series, 20-16
PS: Titans lead, 1-0
1995—Oilers, 10-3 (J)
        Jaguars, 17-16 (H)
1996—Oilers, 34-27 (J)
        Jaguars, 23-17 (H)
1997—Jaguars, 30-24 (T)
        Jaguars, 17-9 (J)
1998—Jaguars, 27-22 (T)
        Oilers, 16-13 (J)
1999—Titans, 20-19 (J)
        Titans, 41-14 (T)
        **Titans, 33-14 (J)
2000—Titans, 27-13 (T)
        Jaguars, 16-13 (J)
2001—Jaguars, 13-6 (J)
        Titans, 28-24 (T)
2002—Titans, 23-14 (T)
        Titans, 28-10 (J)
2003—Titans, 30-17 (J)
        Titans, 10-3 (T)
2004—Jaguars, 15-12 (T)
        Titans, 18-15 (J)
2005—Jaguars, 31-28 (T)
        Jaguars, 40-13 (J)
2006—Jaguars, 37-7 (J)
        Titans, 24-17 (T)
2007—Titans, 13-10 (J)
        Jaguars, 28-13 (T)
2008—Titans, 17-10 (T)
        Titans, 24-14 (J)

2009—Jaguars, 37-17 (J)
   Titans, 30-13 (T)
2010—Titans, 30-3 (J)
   Jaguars, 17-6 (T)
2011—Jaguars, 16-14 (J)
   Titans, 23-17 (T)
2012—Jaguars, 24-19 (J)
   Titans, 38-20 (T)
(RS Pts.—Titans 720, Jaguars 664)
(PS Pts.—Titans 33, Jaguars 14)
*Franchise in Houston prior to 1997;
known as Oilers prior to 1999
**AFC Championship

JACKSONVILLE vs. WASHINGTON
RS: Redskins lead series, 4-1
1997—Redskins, 24-12 (W)
2000—Redskins, 35-16 (J)
2002—Jaguars, 26-7 (J)
2006—Redskins, 36-30 (W) OT
2010—Redskins, 20-17 (J) OT
(RS Pts.—Redskins 122, Jaguars 101)

KANSAS CITY vs. ARIZONA
RS: Chiefs lead series, 8-2-1;
See Arizona vs. Kansas City
KANSAS CITY vs. ATLANTA
RS: Chiefs lead series, 5-3;
See Atlanta vs. Kansas City
KANSAS CITY vs. BALTIMORE
RS: Series tied, 3-3
PS: Ravens lead series, 1-0;
See Baltimore vs. Kansas City
KANSAS CITY vs. BUFFALO
RS: Bills lead series, 23-17-1
PS: Bills lead series, 2-1;
See Buffalo vs. Kansas City
KANSAS CITY vs. CAROLINA
RS: Chiefs lead series, 3-2;
See Carolina vs. Kansas City
KANSAS CITY vs. CHICAGO
RS: Bears lead series, 6-5;
See Chicago vs. Kansas City
KANSAS CITY vs. CINCINNATI
RS: Bengals lead series, 14-13;
See Cincinnati vs. Kansas City
KANSAS CITY vs. CLEVELAND
RS: Browns lead series, 11-10-2;
See Cleveland vs. Kansas City
KANSAS CITY vs. DALLAS
RS: Cowboys lead series, 6-3;
See Dallas vs. Kansas City
KANSAS CITY vs. DENVER
RS: Chiefs lead series, 56-49
PS: Broncos lead series, 1-0;
See Denver vs. Kansas City
KANSAS CITY vs. DETROIT
RS: Chiefs lead series, 7-5;
See Detroit vs. Kansas City
KANSAS CITY vs. GREEN BAY
RS: Chiefs lead series, 7-2-1
PS: Packers lead series, 1-0;
See Green Bay vs. Kansas City
KANSAS CITY vs. HOUSTON
RS: Texans lead series, 3-2;
See Houston vs. Kansas City
KANSAS CITY vs. INDIANAPOLIS
RS: Colts lead series, 11-8
PS: Colts lead series, 3-0;
See Indianapolis vs. Kansas City
KANSAS CITY vs. JACKSONVILLE
RS: Jaguars lead series, 6-3;
See Jacksonville vs. Kansas City

KANSAS CITY vs. MIAMI
RS: Dolphins lead series, 13-12
PS: Dolphins lead series, 3-0
1966—Chiefs, 34-16 (KC)
   Chiefs, 19-18 (M)
1967—Chiefs, 24-0 (M)
   Chiefs, 41-0 (KC)
1968—Chiefs, 48-3 (M)
1969—Chiefs, 17-10 (KC)
1971—*Dolphins, 27-24 (KC) OT
1972—Dolphins, 20-10 (KC)
1974—Dolphins, 9-3 (M)
1976—Chiefs, 20-17 (M) OT
1981—Dolphins, 17-7 (KC)
1983—Dolphins, 14-6 (M)
1985—Dolphins, 31-0 (M)
1987—Dolphins, 42-0 (M)
1989—Chiefs, 26-21 (KC)
   Chiefs, 27-24 (M)
1990—**Dolphins, 17-16 (M)
1991—Chiefs, 42-7 (KC)
1993—Dolphins, 30-10 (M)
1994—Dolphins, 45-28 (M)
   **Dolphins, 27-17 (M)
1995—Dolphins, 13-6 (M)
1997—Dolphins, 17-14 (M)
2002—Chiefs, 48-30 (KC)
2005—Chiefs, 30-20 (M)
2006—Dolphins, 13-10 (M)
2008—Dolphins, 38-31 (KC)
2011—Dolphins, 31-3 (KC)
(RS Pts.—Chiefs 504, Dolphins 486)
(PS Pts.—Dolphins 71, Chiefs 57)
*AFC Divisional Playoff
**AFC First-Round Playoff
KANSAS CITY vs. MINNESOTA
RS: Chiefs lead series, 6-4
PS: Chiefs lead series, 1-0
1969—*Chiefs, 23-7 (New Orleans)
1970—Vikings, 27-10 (M)
1974—Vikings, 35-15 (KC)
1981—Chiefs, 10-6 (M)
1990—Chiefs, 24-21 (KC)
1993—Vikings, 30-10 (M)
1996—Chiefs, 21-6 (M)
1999—Chiefs, 31-28 (KC)
2003—Vikings, 45-20 (M)
2007—Chiefs, 13-10 (KC)
2011—Chiefs, 22-17 (KC)
(RS Pts.—Vikings 225, Chiefs 176)
(PS Pts.—Chiefs 23, Vikings 7)
*Super Bowl IV
KANSAS CITY vs. **NEW ENGLAND
RS: Chiefs lead series, 16-13-3
1960—Patriots, 42-14 (B)
   Texans, 34-0 (D)
1961—Patriots, 18-17 (D)
   Patriots, 28-21 (B)
1962—Texans, 42-28 (D)
   Texans, 27-7 (B)
1963—Tie, 24-24 (B)
   Chiefs, 35-3 (KC)
1964—Patriots, 24-7 (B)
   Patriots, 31-24 (KC)
1965—Chiefs, 27-17 (KC)
   Tie, 10-10 (B)
1966—Chiefs, 43-24 (B)
   Tie, 27-27 (KC)
1967—Chiefs, 33-10 (B)
1968—Chiefs, 31-17 (KC)
1969—Chiefs, 31-0 (B)
1970—Chiefs, 23-10 (KC)
1973—Chiefs, 10-7 (NE)

1977—Patriots, 21-17 (NE)
1981—Patriots, 33-17 (NE)
1990—Chiefs, 37-7 (NE)
1992—Chiefs, 27-20 (KC)
1995—Chiefs, 31-26 (KC)
1998—Patriots, 40-10 (NE)
1999—Chiefs, 16-14 (KC)
2000—Patriots, 30-24 (NE)
2002—Patriots, 41-38 (NE) OT
2004—Patriots, 27-19 (KC)
2005—Chiefs, 26-16 (KC)
2008—Patriots, 17-10 (NE)
2011—Patriots, 34-3 (NE)
(RS Pts.—Chiefs 755, Patriots 653)
*Franchise located in Dallas prior to 1963
and known as Texans
**Franchise in Boston prior to 1971
KANSAS CITY vs. NEW ORLEANS
RS: Series tied, 5-5
1972—Chiefs, 20-17 (NO)
1976—Saints, 27-17 (KC)
1982—Saints, 27-17 (NO)
1985—Chiefs, 47-27 (NO)
1991—Saints, 17-10 (KC)
1994—Saints, 30-17 (NO)
1997—Chiefs, 25-13 (NO)
2004—Saints, 27-20 (NO)
2008—Saints, 30-20 (KC)
2012—Chiefs, 27-24 (NO)
(RS Pts.—Chiefs 233, Saints 226)
KANSAS CITY vs. N.Y. GIANTS
RS: Giants lead series, 10-2
1974—Giants, 33-27 (KC)
1978—Giants, 26-10 (NY)
1979—Giants, 21-17 (KC)
1983—Chiefs, 38-17 (KC)
1984—Giants, 28-27 (NY)
1988—Giants, 28-12 (NY)
1992—Giants, 35-21 (NY)
1995—Chiefs, 20-17 (KC) OT
1998—Giants, 28-7 (NY)
2001—Giants, 13-3 (KC)
2005—Giants, 27-17 (NY)
2009—Giants, 27-16 (KC)
(RS Pts.—Giants 300, Chiefs 215)
***KANSAS CITY vs. **N.Y. JETS**
RS: Jets lead series, 17-16-1
PS: Series tied, 1-1
1960—Titans, 37-35 (D)
   Titans, 41-35 (NY)
1961—Titans, 28-7 (NY)
   Texans, 35-24 (D)
1962—Texans, 20-17 (D)
   Texans, 52-31 (NY)
1963—Jets, 17-0 (NY)
   Chiefs, 48-0 (KC)
1964—Jets, 27-14 (NY)
   Chiefs, 24-7 (KC)
1965—Chiefs, 14-10 (NY)
   Jets, 13-10 (KC)
1966—Chiefs, 32-24 (NY)
1967—Chiefs, 42-18 (KC)
   Chiefs, 21-7 (NY)
1968—Jets, 20-19 (KC)
1969—Chiefs, 34-16 (NY)
   ***Chiefs, 13-6 (NY)
1971—Jets, 13-10 (NY)
1974—Chiefs, 24-16 (KC)
1975—Jets, 30-24 (KC)
1982—Chiefs, 37-13 (KC)
1984—Jets, 17-16 (KC)
   Jets, 28-7 (NY)
1986—****Jets, 35-15 (NY)

1987—Jets, 16-9 (KC)
1988—Tie, 17-17 (NY)
    Chiefs, 38-34 (KC)
1992—Chiefs, 23-7 (NY)
1998—Jets, 20-17 (KC)
2001—Jets, 27-7 (NY)
2002—Chiefs, 29-25 (NY)
2005—Chiefs, 27-7 (KC)
2007—Jets, 13-10 (NY) OT
2008—Jets, 28-24 (NY)
2011—Jets, 37-10 (NY)
(RS Pts.—Chiefs 771, Jets 685)
(PS Pts.—Jets 41, Chiefs 28)
*Franchise in Dallas prior to 1963 and known as Texans
**Jets known as Titans prior to 1963
***Inter-Divisional Playoff
****AFC First-Round Playoff
*KANSAS CITY vs. **OAKLAND
RS: Chiefs lead series, 53-50-2
PS: Chiefs lead series, 2-1
1960—Texans, 34-16 (O)
    Raiders, 20-19 (D)
1961—Texans, 42-35 (O)
    Texans, 43-11 (D)
1962—Texans, 26-16 (O)
    Texans, 35-7 (D)
1963—Raiders, 10-7 (O)
    Raiders, 22-7 (KC)
1964—Chiefs, 21-9 (O)
    Chiefs, 42-7 (KC)
1965—Raiders, 37-10 (O)
    Chiefs, 14-7 (KC)
1966—Chiefs, 32-10 (O)
    Raiders, 34-13 (KC)
1967—Raiders, 23-21 (O)
    Raiders, 44-22 (KC)
1968—Chiefs, 24-10 (KC)
    Raiders, 38-21 (O)
    ***Raiders, 41-6 (O)
1969—Raiders, 27-24 (KC)
    Raiders, 10-6 (O)
    ****Chiefs, 17-7 (O)
1970—Tie, 17-17 (KC)
    Raiders, 20-6 (O)
1971—Tie, 20-20 (O)
    Chiefs, 16-14 (KC)
1972—Chiefs, 27-14 (KC)
    Raiders, 26-3 (O)
1973—Chiefs, 16-3 (O)
    Raiders, 37-7 (O)
1974—Raiders, 27-7 (O)
    Raiders, 7-6 (KC)
1975—Chiefs, 42-10 (KC)
    Raiders, 28-20 (O)
1976—Raiders, 24-21 (KC)
    Raiders, 21-10 (O)
1977—Raiders, 37-28 (KC)
    Raiders, 21-20 (O)
1978—Raiders, 28-6 (O)
    Raiders, 20-10 (KC)
1979—Chiefs, 35-7 (KC)
    Chiefs, 24-21 (O)
1980—Raiders, 27-14 (KC)
    Chiefs, 31-17 (O)
1981—Chiefs, 27-0 (KC)
    Chiefs, 28-17 (O)
1982—Raiders, 21-16 (KC)
1983—Raiders, 21-20 (LA)
    Raiders, 28-20 (KC)
1984—Raiders, 22-20 (KC)
    Raiders, 17-7 (LA)

1985—Chiefs, 36-20 (KC)
    Raiders, 19-10 (LA)
1986—Raiders, 24-17 (KC)
    Chiefs, 20-17 (LA)
1987—Raiders, 35-17 (LA)
    Chiefs, 16-10 (KC)
1988—Raiders, 27-17 (KC)
    Raiders, 17-10 (LA)
1989—Chiefs, 24-19 (KC)
    Raiders, 20-14 (LA)
1990—Chiefs, 9-7 (KC)
    Chiefs, 27-24 (LA)
1991—Chiefs, 24-21 (KC)
    Chiefs, 27-21 (LA)
    *****Chiefs, 10-6 (KC)
1992—Chiefs, 27-7 (KC)
    Raiders, 28-7 (LA)
1993—Chiefs, 24-9 (KC)
    Chiefs, 31-20 (LA)
1994—Chiefs, 13-3 (KC)
    Chiefs, 19-9 (LA)
1995—Chiefs, 23-17 (KC) OT
    Chiefs, 29-23 (O)
1996—Chiefs, 19-3 (KC)
    Raiders, 26-7 (O)
1997—Chiefs, 28-27 (O)
    Chiefs, 30-0 (KC)
1998—Chiefs, 28-8 (KC)
    Chiefs, 31-24 (O)
1999—Chiefs, 37-34 (O)
    Raiders, 41-38 (KC) OT
2000—Raiders, 20-17 (KC)
    Raiders, 49-31 (O)
2001—Raiders, 27-24 (KC)
    Raiders, 28-26 (O)
2002—Chiefs, 20-10 (KC)
    Raiders, 24-0 (O)
2003—Chiefs, 17-10 (O)
    Chiefs, 27-24 (KC)
2004—Chiefs, 34-27 (O)
    Chiefs, 31-30 (KC)
2005—Chiefs, 23-17 (O)
    Chiefs, 27-23 (KC)
2006—Chiefs, 17-13 (KC)
    Chiefs, 20-9 (O)
2007—Chiefs, 12-10 (O)
    Raiders, 20-17 (KC)
2008—Raiders, 23-8 (KC)
    Chiefs, 20-13 (O)
2009—Raiders, 13-10 (KC)
    Chiefs, 16-10 (O)
2010—Raiders, 23-20 (O) OT
    Raiders, 31-10 (KC)
2011—Chiefs, 28-0 (O)
    Raiders, 16-13 (KC) OT
2012—Raiders, 26-16 (KC)
    Raiders, 15-0 (O)
(RS Pts.—Chiefs 2,130, Raiders 2,036)
(PS Pts.—Raiders 54, Chiefs 33)
*Franchise in Dallas prior to 1963 and known as Texans
**Franchise in Los Angeles from 1982-1994
***Division Playoff
****AFL Championship
*****AFC First-Round Playoff
KANSAS CITY vs. PHILADELPHIA
RS: Eagles lead series, 4-2
1972—Eagles, 21-20 (KC)
1992—Chiefs, 24-17 (KC)
1998—Chiefs, 24-21 (P)
2001—Eagles, 23-10 (KC)
2005—Eagles, 37-31 (KC)

2009—Eagles, 34-14 (P)
(RS Pts.—Eagles 153, Chiefs 123)
KANSAS CITY vs. PITTSBURGH
RS: Steelers lead series, 19-9
PS: Chiefs lead series, 1-0
1970—Chiefs, 31-14 (P)
1971—Chiefs, 38-16 (KC)
1972—Steelers, 16-7 (P)
1974—Steelers, 34-24 (KC)
1975—Steelers, 28-3 (P)
1976—Steelers, 45-0 (KC)
1978—Steelers, 27-24 (P)
1979—Steelers, 30-3 (KC)
1980—Steelers, 21-16 (P)
1981—Chiefs, 37-33 (P)
1982—Steelers, 35-14 (P)
1984—Chiefs, 37-27 (P)
1985—Steelers, 36-28 (KC)
1986—Chiefs, 24-19 (P)
1987—Steelers, 17-16 (KC)
1988—Steelers, 16-10 (P)
1989—Steelers, 23-17 (P)
1992—Steelers, 27-3 (KC)
1993—*Chiefs, 27-24 (KC) OT
1996—Steelers, 17-7 (KC)
1997—Chiefs, 13-10 (KC)
1998—Steelers, 20-13 (KC)
1999—Chiefs, 35-19 (KC)
2001—Steelers, 20-17 (KC)
2003—Chiefs, 41-20 (KC)
2006—Steelers, 45-7 (P)
2009—Chiefs, 27-24 (KC) OT
2011—Steelers, 13-9 (KC)
2012—Steelers, 16-13 (P) OT
(RS Pts.—Steelers 668, Chiefs 514)
(PS Pts.—Chiefs 27, Steelers 24)
*AFC First-Round Playoff
KANSAS CITY vs. *ST. LOUIS
RS: Chiefs lead series, 6-4
1973—Rams, 23-13 (KC)
1982—Rams, 20-14 (LA)
1985—Rams, 16-0 (KC)
1991—Chiefs, 27-20 (LA)
1994—Rams, 16-0 (KC)
1997—Chiefs, 28-20 (StL)
2000—Chiefs, 54-34 (KC)
2002—Chiefs, 49-10 (KC)
2006—Chiefs, 31-17 (StL)
2010—Chiefs, 27-13 (StL)
(RS Pts.—Chiefs 243, Rams 189)
*Franchise in Los Angeles prior to 1995
*KANSAS CITY vs. **SAN DIEGO
RS: Series tied, 52-52-1
PS: Chargers lead series, 1-0
1960—Chargers, 21-20 (LA)
    Texans, 17-0 (D)
1961—Chargers, 26-10 (D)
    Chargers, 24-14 (SD)
1962—Chargers, 32-28 (SD)
    Texans, 26-17 (D)
1963—Chargers, 24-10 (SD)
    Chargers, 38-17 (KC)
1964—Chargers, 28-14 (KC)
    Chiefs, 49-6 (SD)
1965—Tie, 10-10 (SD)
    Chiefs, 31-7 (KC)
1966—Chiefs, 24-14 (SD)
    Chiefs, 27-17 (SD)
1967—Chargers, 45-31 (SD)
    Chargers, 17-16 (KC)
1968—Chiefs, 27-20 (SD)
    Chiefs, 40-3 (SD)

1969—Chiefs, 27-9 (SD)
  Chiefs, 27-3 (KC)
1970—Chiefs, 26-14 (KC)
  Chargers, 31-13 (SD)
1971—Chargers, 21-14 (SD)
  Chiefs, 31-10 (KC)
1972—Chiefs, 26-14 (SD)
  Chargers, 27-17 (KC)
1973—Chiefs, 19-0 (SD)
  Chiefs, 33-6 (KC)
1974—Chiefs, 24-14 (SD)
  Chargers, 14-7 (KC)
1975—Chiefs, 12-10 (SD)
  Chargers, 28-20 (KC)
1976—Chargers, 30-16 (KC)
  Chiefs, 23-20 (SD)
1977—Chargers, 23-7 (KC)
  Chiefs, 21-16 (SD)
1978—Chargers, 29-23 (SD) OT
  Chiefs, 23-0 (KC)
1979—Chargers, 20-14 (KC)
  Chargers, 28-7 (SD)
1980—Chargers, 24-7 (KC)
  Chargers, 20-7 (SD)
1981—Chargers, 42-31 (KC)
  Chargers, 22-20 (SD)
1982—Chiefs, 19-12 (KC)
1983—Chargers, 17-14 (KC)
  Chargers, 41-38 (SD)
1984—Chiefs, 31-13 (KC)
  Chiefs, 42-21 (SD)
1985—Chargers, 31-20 (SD)
  Chiefs, 38-34 (KC)
1986—Chiefs, 42-41 (KC)
  Chiefs, 24-23 (SD)
1987—Chiefs, 20-13 (KC)
  Chargers, 42-21 (SD)
1988—Chargers, 24-23 (KC)
  Chargers, 24-13 (SD)
1989—Chargers, 21-6 (SD)
  Chargers, 20-13 (KC)
1990—Chiefs, 27-10 (KC)
  Chiefs, 24-21 (SD)
1991—Chiefs, 14-13 (SD)
  Chiefs, 20-17 (KC) OT
1992—Chiefs, 24-10 (SD)
  Chiefs, 16-14 (KC)
  ***Chargers, 17-0 (SD)
1993—Chiefs, 17-14 (SD)
  Chiefs, 28-24 (KC)
1994—Chargers, 20-6 (SD)
  Chargers, 14-13 (KC)
1995—Chiefs, 29-23 (KC) OT
  Chiefs, 22-7 (SD)
1996—Chargers, 22-19 (SD)
  Chargers, 28-14 (KC)
1997—Chiefs, 31-3 (KC)
  Chiefs, 29-7 (SD)
1998—Chiefs, 23-7 (KC)
  Chargers, 38-37 (SD)
1999—Chargers, 21-14 (SD)
  Chiefs, 34-0 (KC)
2000—Chiefs, 42-10 (KC)
  Chargers, 17-16 (SD)
2001—Chiefs, 25-20 (SD)
  Chiefs, 20-17 (KC)
2002—Chargers, 35-34 (SD)
  Chiefs, 24-22 (KC)
2003—Chiefs, 27-14 (KC)
  Chiefs, 28-24 (SD)
2004—Chargers, 34-31 (KC)
  Chargers, 24-17 (SD)

2005—Chargers, 28-20 (SD)
  Chiefs, 20-7 (KC)
2006—Chiefs, 30-27 (KC)
  Chargers, 20-9 (SD)
2007—Chiefs, 30-16 (SD)
  Chargers, 24-10 (KC)
2008—Chargers, 20-19 (SD)
  Chargers, 22-21 (KC)
2009—Chargers, 37-7 (KC)
  Chargers, 43-14 (SD)
2010—Chiefs, 21-14 (KC)
  Chargers, 31-0 (SD)
2011—Chargers, 20-17 (SD)
  Chiefs, 23-20 (KC) OT
2012—Chargers, 37-20 (KC)
  Chargers, 31-13 (SD)
(RS Pts.—Chiefs 2,249, Chargers 2,128)
(PS Pts.—Chargers 17, Chiefs 0)
*Franchise in Dallas prior to 1963 and
known as Texans
**Franchise in Los Angeles prior to 1961
***AFC First-Round Playoff
KANSAS CITY vs. SAN FRANCISCO
RS: 49ers lead series, 6-5
1971—Chiefs, 26-17 (SF)
1975—49ers, 20-3 (KC)
1982—49ers, 26-13 (KC)
1985—49ers, 31-3 (SF)
1991—49ers, 28-14 (SF)
1994—Chiefs, 24-17 (KC)
1997—Chiefs, 44-9 (KC)
2000—49ers, 21-7 (SF)
2002—49ers, 17-13 (SF)
2006—Chiefs, 41-10 (KC)
2010—Chiefs, 31-10 (KC)
(PS Pts.—Chiefs 219, 49ers 196)
KANSAS CITY vs. SEATTLE
RS: Chiefs lead series, 32-18
1977—Seahawks, 34-31 (KC)
1978—Seahawks, 13-10 (KC)
  Seahawks, 23-19 (S)
1979—Chiefs, 24-6 (S)
  Chiefs, 37-21 (KC)
1980—Seahawks, 17-16 (KC)
  Chiefs, 31-30 (S)
1981—Chiefs, 20-14 (S)
  Chiefs, 40-13 (KC)
1983—Chiefs, 17-13 (KC)
  Seahawks, 51-48 (S) OT
1984—Seahawks, 45-0 (S)
  Chiefs, 34-7 (KC)
1985—Chiefs, 28-7 (KC)
  Seahawks, 24-6 (S)
1986—Seahawks, 23-17 (S)
  Chiefs, 27-7 (KC)
1987—Seahawks, 43-14 (S)
  Chiefs, 41-20 (KC)
1988—Seahawks, 31-10 (S)
  Chiefs, 27-24 (KC)
1989—Chiefs, 20-16 (S)
  Chiefs, 20-10 (KC)
1990—Seahawks, 19-7 (S)
  Seahawks, 17-16 (KC)
1991—Chiefs, 20-13 (KC)
  Chiefs, 19-6 (S)
1992—Chiefs, 26-7 (KC)
  Chiefs, 24-14 (S)
1993—Chiefs, 31-16 (S)
  Chiefs, 34-24 (KC)
1994—Chiefs, 38-23 (KC)
  Seahawks, 10-9 (S)
1995—Chiefs, 34-10 (S)
  Chiefs, 26-3 (KC)

1996—Chiefs, 35-17 (S)
  Chiefs, 34-16 (KC)
1997—Chiefs, 20-17 (KC) OT
  Chiefs, 19-14 (S)
1998—Chiefs, 17-6 (KC)
  Seahawks, 24-12 (S)
1999—Seahawks, 31-19 (KC)
  Seahawks, 23-14 (S)
2000—Chiefs, 24-17 (KC)
  Chiefs, 24-19 (S)
2001—Chiefs, 19-7 (KC)
  Seahawks, 21-18 (S)
2002—Seahawks, 39-32 (S)
2006—Chiefs, 35-28 (KC)
2010—Chiefs, 42-24 (S)
(RS Pts.—Chiefs 1,185, Seahawks 957)
KANSAS CITY vs. TAMPA BAY
RS: Buccaneers lead series, 6-5
1976—Chiefs, 28-19 (TB)
1978—Buccaneers, 30-13 (KC)
1979—Buccaneers, 3-0 (TB)
1981—Chiefs, 19-10 (KC)
1984—Chiefs, 24-20 (KC)
1986—Chiefs, 27-20 (KC)
1993—Chiefs, 27-3 (TB)
1999—Buccaneers, 17-10 (TB)
2004—Buccaneers, 34-31 (TB)
2008—Buccaneers, 30-27 (KC) OT
2012—Buccaneers, 38-10 (TB)
(RS Pts.—Buccaneers 224, Chiefs 216)
***KANSAS CITY vs. **TENNESSEE**
RS: Chiefs lead series, 26-20
PS: Chiefs lead series, 2-0
1960—Oilers, 20-10 (H)
  Texans, 24-0 (D)
1961—Texans, 26-21 (D)
  Oilers, 38-7 (H)
1962—Texans, 31-7 (H)
  Oilers, 14-6 (D)
  ***Texans, 20-17 (H) OT
1963—Chiefs, 28-7 (KC)
  Oilers, 28-7 (H)
1964—Chiefs, 28-7 (KC)
  Chiefs, 28-19 (H)
1965—Chiefs, 52-21 (KC)
  Oilers, 38-36 (H)
1966—Chiefs, 48-23 (KC)
1967—Chiefs, 25-20 (H)
  Oilers, 24-19 (KC)
1968—Chiefs, 26-21 (H)
  Chiefs, 24-10 (KC)
1969—Chiefs, 24-0 (KC)
1970—Chiefs, 24-9 (KC)
1971—Chiefs, 20-16 (H)
1973—Chiefs, 38-14 (KC)
1974—Chiefs, 17-7 (H)
1975—Oilers, 17-13 (KC)
1977—Oilers, 34-20 (H)
1978—Oilers, 20-17 (KC)
1979—Oilers, 20-6 (H)
1980—Chiefs, 21-20 (KC)
1981—Chiefs, 23-10 (KC)
1983—Chiefs, 13-10 (H) OT
1984—Oilers, 17-16 (KC)
1985—Oilers, 23-20 (H)
1986—Chiefs, 27-13 (H)
1988—Oilers, 7-6 (H)
1989—Chiefs, 34-0 (KC)
1990—Chiefs, 27-10 (KC)
1991—Oilers, 17-7 (H)
1992—Oilers, 23-20 (H) OT
1993—Oilers, 30-0 (H)
  ****Chiefs, 28-20 (H)

1994—Chiefs, 31-9 (KC)
1995—Chiefs, 20-13 (KC)
1996—Chiefs, 20-19 (H)
2000—Titans, 17-14 (T) OT
2004—Chiefs, 49-38 (T)
2007—Titans, 26-17 (KC)
2008—Titans, 34-10 (KC)
2010—Chiefs, 34-14 (KC)
(RS Pts.—Chiefs 996, Titans 822)
(PS Pts.—Chiefs 48, Titans 37)
*Franchise in Dallas prior to 1963 and known as Texans
**Franchise in Houston prior to 1997; known as Oilers prior to 1999
***AFL Championship
****AFC Divisional Playoff

KANSAS CITY vs. WASHINGTON
RS: Chiefs lead series, 7-1
1971—Chiefs, 27-20 (KC)
1976—Chiefs, 33-30 (W)
1983—Redskins, 27-12 (W)
1992—Chiefs, 35-16 (KC)
1995—Chiefs, 24-3 (KC)
2001—Chiefs, 45-13 (W)
2005—Chiefs, 28-21, (KC)
2009—Chiefs, 14-6 (W)
(RS Pts.—Chiefs 218, Redskins 136)

MIAMI vs. ARIZONA
RS: Dolphins lead series, 8-3;
See Arizona vs. Miami

MIAMI vs. ATLANTA
RS: Dolphins lead series, 7-4;
See Atlanta vs. Miami

MIAMI vs. BALTIMORE
RS: Dolphins lead series, 5-3
PS: Ravens lead series, 2-0;
See Baltimore vs. Miami

MIAMI vs. BUFFALO
RS: Dolphins lead series, 56-37-1
PS: Bills lead series, 3-1;
See Buffalo vs. Miami

MIAMI vs. CAROLINA
RS: Dolphins lead series, 4-0;
See Carolina vs. Miami

MIAMI vs. CHICAGO
RS: Dolphins lead series, 7-4;
See Chicago vs. Miami

MIAMI vs. CINCINNATI
RS: Dolphins lead series, 14-5
PS: Dolphins lead series, 1-0;
See Cincinnati vs. Miami

MIAMI vs. CLEVELAND
RS: Browns lead series, 8-7
PS: Dolphins lead series, 2-0;
See Cleveland vs. Miami

MIAMI vs. DALLAS
RS: Dolphins lead series, 7-5
PS: Cowboys lead series, 1-0;
See Dallas vs. Miami

MIAMI vs. DENVER
RS: Dolphins lead series, 11-4-1
PS: Broncos lead series, 1-0;
See Denver vs. Miami

MIAMI vs. DETROIT
RS: Dolphins lead series, 7-3;
See Detroit vs. Miami

MIAMI vs. GREEN BAY
RS: Dolphins lead series, 10-3;
See Green Bay vs. Miami

MIAMI vs. HOUSTON
RS: Texans lead series, 7-0;
See Houston vs. Miami

MIAMI vs. INDIANAPOLIS
RS: Dolphins lead series, 44-25
PS: Dolphins lead series, 2-0;
See Indianapolis vs. Miami

MIAMI vs. JACKSONVILLE
RS: Dolphins lead series, 3-2
PS: Jaguars lead series, 1-0;
See Jacksonville vs. Miami

MIAMI vs. KANSAS CITY
RS: Dolphins lead series, 13-12
PS: Dolphins lead series, 3-0;
See Kansas City vs. Miami

MIAMI vs. MINNESOTA
RS: Dolphins lead series, 6-4
PS: Dolphins lead series, 1-0
1972—Dolphins, 16-14 (Minn)
1973—*Dolphins, 24-7 (Houston)
1976—Vikings, 29-7 (Mia)
1979—Dolphins, 27-12 (Minn)
1982—Dolphins, 22-14 (Mia)
1988—Dolphins, 24-7 (Mia)
1994—Vikings, 38-35 (Minn)
2000—Vikings, 13-7 (Minn)
2002—Vikings, 20-17 (Minn)
2006—Dolphins, 24-20 (Mia)
2010—Dolphins, 14-10 (Minn)
(RS Pts.—Dolphins 193, Vikings 177)
(PS Pts.—Dolphins 24, Vikings 7)
*Super Bowl VIII

MIAMI vs. *NEW ENGLAND
RS: Dolphins lead series, 49-43
PS: Patriots lead series, 2-1
1966—Patriots, 20-14 (M)
1967—Patriots, 41-10 (B)
        Dolphins, 41-32 (M)
1968—Dolphins, 34-10 (B)
        Dolphins, 38-7 (M)
1969—Dolphins, 17-16 (B)
        Patriots, 38-23 (Tampa)
1970—Patriots, 27-14 (B)
        Dolphins, 37-20 (M)
1971—Dolphins, 41-3 (M)
        Patriots, 34-13 (NE)
1972—Dolphins, 52-0 (M)
        Dolphins, 37-21 (NE)
1973—Dolphins, 44-23 (M)
        Dolphins, 30-14 (NE)
1974—Patriots, 34-24 (NE)
        Patriots, 34-27 (M)
1975—Dolphins, 22-14 (NE)
        Dolphins, 20-7 (M)
1976—Patriots, 30-14 (NE)
        Dolphins, 10-3 (M)
1977—Dolphins, 17-5 (M)
        Patriots, 14-10 (NE)
1978—Patriots, 33-24 (NE)
        Dolphins, 23-3 (M)
1979—Patriots, 28-13 (NE)
        Dolphins, 39-24 (M)
1980—Patriots, 34-0 (NE)
        Dolphins, 16-13 (M) OT
1981—Dolphins, 30-27 (NE) OT
        Dolphins, 24-14 (M)
1982—Patriots, 3-0 (NE)
        **Dolphins, 28-13 (M)
1983—Dolphins, 34-24 (M)
        Patriots, 17-6 (NE)
1984—Dolphins, 28-7 (M)
        Dolphins, 44-24 (NE)
1985—Patriots, 17-13 (NE)
        Dolphins, 30-27 (M)
        ***Patriots, 31-14 (M)

1986—Patriots, 34-7 (NE)
        Patriots, 34-27 (M)
1987—Patriots, 28-21 (NE)
        Patriots, 24-10 (M)
1988—Patriots, 21-10 (NE)
        Patriots, 6-3 (M)
1989—Dolphins, 24-10 (NE)
        Dolphins, 31-10 (M)
1990—Dolphins, 27-24 (NE)
        Dolphins, 17-10 (M)
1991—Dolphins, 20-10 (NE)
        Dolphins, 30-20 (M)
1992—Dolphins, 38-17 (M)
        Dolphins, 16-13 (NE) OT
1993—Dolphins, 17-13 (M)
        Patriots, 33-27 (NE) OT
1994—Dolphins, 39-35 (M)
        Dolphins, 23-3 (NE)
1995—Dolphins, 20-3 (NE)
        Patriots, 34-17 (M)
1996—Dolphins, 24-10 (M)
        Patriots, 42-23 (NE)
1997—Patriots, 27-24 (NE)
        Patriots, 14-12 (M)
        **Patriots, 17-3 (NE)
1998—Dolphins, 12-9 (M) OT
        Patriots, 26-23 (NE)
1999—Dolphins, 31-30 (NE)
        Dolphins, 27-17 (M)
2000—Dolphins, 10-3 (M)
        Dolphins, 27-24 (NE)
2001—Dolphins, 30-10 (M)
        Patriots, 20-13 (NE)
2002—Dolphins, 26-13 (M)
        Patriots, 27-24 (NE) OT
2003—Patriots, 19-13 (M) OT
        Patriots, 12-0 (NE)
2004—Patriots, 24-10 (NE)
        Dolphins, 29-28 (M)
2005—Patriots, 23-16 (M)
        Dolphins, 28-26 (NE)
2006—Patriots, 20-10 (NE)
        Dolphins, 21-0 (M)
2007—Patriots, 49-28 (M)
        Patriots, 28-7 (NE)
2008—Dolphins, 38-13 (NE)
        Patriots, 48-28 (M)
2009—Patriots, 27-17 (NE)
        Dolphins, 22-21 (M)
2010—Patriots, 41-14 (M)
        Patriots, 38-7 (NE)
2011—Patriots, 38-24 (M)
        Patriots, 27-24 (NE)
2012—Patriots, 23-16 (M)
        Patriots, 28-0 (NE)
(RS Pts.—Dolphins 2,002, Patriots 1,922)
(PS Pts.—Patriots 61, Dolphins 45)
*Franchise in Boston prior to 1971
**AFC First-Round Playoff
***AFC Championship

MIAMI vs. NEW ORLEANS
RS: Dolphins lead series, 6-4
1970—Dolphins, 21-10 (M)
1974—Dolphins, 21-0 (NO)
1980—Dolphins, 21-16 (M)
1983—Saints, 17-7 (NO)
1986—Dolphins, 31-27 (NO)
1992—Saints, 24-13 (NO)
1995—Saints, 33-30 (NO)
1998—Dolphins, 30-10 (M)
2005—Dolphins, 21-6 (Baton Rouge)
2009—Saints, 46-34 (M)
(RS Pts.—Dolphins 229, Saints 189)

MIAMI vs. N.Y. GIANTS
RS: Giants lead series, 5-2
1972—Dolphins, 23-13 (NY)
1990—Giants, 20-3 (NY)
1993—Giants, 19-14 (M)
1996—Giants, 17-7 (M)
2003—Dolphins, 23-10 (NY)
2007—Giants, 13-10 (London)
2011—Giants, 20-17 (NY)
(RS Pts.—Giants 112, Dolphins 97)

MIAMI vs. N.Y. JETS
RS: Jets lead series, 49-44-1
PS: Dolphins lead series, 1-0
1966—Jets, 19-14 (M)
    Jets, 30-13 (NY)
1967—Jets, 29-7 (NY)
    Jets, 33-14 (M)
1968—Jets, 35-17 (NY)
    Jets, 31-7 (M)
1969—Jets, 34-31 (NY)
    Jets, 27-9 (M)
1970—Dolphins, 20-6 (NY)
    Dolphins, 16-10 (M)
1971—Jets, 14-10 (M)
    Dolphins, 30-14 (NY)
1972—Dolphins, 27-17 (NY)
    Dolphins, 28-24 (M)
1973—Dolphins, 31-3 (M)
    Dolphins, 24-14 (NY)
1974—Dolphins, 21-17 (M)
    Jets, 17-14 (NY)
1975—Dolphins, 43-0 (NY)
    Dolphins, 27-7 (M)
1976—Dolphins, 16-0 (M)
    Dolphins, 27-7 (NY)
1977—Dolphins, 21-17 (M)
    Dolphins, 14-10 (NY)
1978—Jets, 33-20 (NY)
    Jets, 24-13 (M)
1979—Jets, 33-27 (NY)
    Jets, 27-24 (M)
1980—Jets, 17-14 (NY)
    Jets, 24-17 (M)
1981—Tie, 28-28 (M) OT
    Jets, 16-15 (NY)
1982—Dolphins, 45-28 (NY)
    Dolphins, 20-19 (M)
    *Dolphins, 14-0 (M)
1983—Dolphins, 32-14 (NY)
    Dolphins, 34-14 (M)
1984—Dolphins, 31-17 (NY)
    Dolphins, 28-17 (M)
1985—Jets, 23-7 (NY)
    Dolphins, 21-17 (M)
1986—Jets, 51-45 (NY) OT
    Dolphins, 45-3 (M)
1987—Jets, 37-31 (NY) OT
    Dolphins, 37-28 (M)
1988—Jets, 44-30 (M)
    Jets, 38-34 (NY)
1989—Jets, 40-33 (NY)
    Dolphins, 31-23 (NY)
1990—Dolphins, 20-16 (M)
    Dolphins, 17-3 (NY)
1991—Jets, 41-23 (NY)
    Jets, 23-20 (M) OT
1992—Jets, 26-14 (NY)
    Dolphins, 19-17 (M)
1993—Jets, 24-14 (M)
    Jets, 27-10 (NY)
1994—Dolphins, 28-14 (M)
    Dolphins, 28-24 (NY)

1995—Dolphins, 52-14 (M)
    Jets, 17-16 (NY)
1996—Dolphins, 36-27 (M)
    Dolphins, 31-28 (NY)
1997—Dolphins, 31-20 (NY)
    Dolphins, 24-17 (M)
1998—Jets, 20-9 (NY)
    Jets, 21-16 (M)
1999—Jets, 28-20 (NY)
    Jets, 38-31 (M)
2000—Jets, 40-37 (NY) OT
    Jets, 20-3 (M)
2001—Jets, 21-17 (NY)
    Jets, 24-0 (M)
2002—Dolphins, 30-3 (M)
    Jets, 13-10 (NY)
2003—Dolphins, 21-10 (NY)
    Dolphins, 23-21 (M)
2004—Jets, 17-9 (M)
    Jets, 41-14 (NY)
2005—Jets, 17-7 (NY)
    Dolphins, 24-20 (M)
2006—Jets, 20-17 (M)
    Jets, 13-10 (M)
2007—Jets, 31-28 (NY)
    Jets, 40-13 (M)
2008—Jets, 20-14 (M)
    Dolphins, 24-17 (NY)
2009—Dolphins, 31-27 (M)
    Dolphins, 30-25 (NY)
2010—Jets, 31-23 (M)
    Dolphins, 10-6 (NY)
2011—Jets, 24-6 (NY)
    Dolphins, 19-17 (M)
2012—Jets, 23-20 (M) OT
    Dolphins, 30-9 (M)
(RS Pts.—Dolphins 2,072, Jets 2,025)
(PS Pts.—Dolphins 14, Jets 0)
*AFC Championship

MIAMI vs. *OAKLAND
RS: Raiders lead series, 16-15-1
PS: Raiders lead series, 3-1
1966—Raiders, 23-14 (M)
    Raiders, 21-10 (O)
1967—Raiders, 31-17 (O)
1968—Raiders, 47-21 (M)
1969—Raiders, 20-17 (O)
    Tie, 20-20 (M)
1970—Dolphins, 20-13 (M)
    **Raiders, 21-14 (O)
1973—Raiders, 12-7 (O)
    ***Dolphins, 27-10 (M)
1974—**Raiders, 28-26 (O)
1975—Raiders, 31-21 (M)
1978—Dolphins, 23-6 (M)
1979—Raiders, 13-3 (O)
1980—Raiders, 16-10 (O)
1981—Raiders, 33-17 (M)
1983—Raiders, 27-14 (LA)
1984—Raiders, 45-34 (M)
1986—Raiders, 30-28 (M)
1988—Dolphins, 24-14 (LA)
1990—Raiders, 13-10 (M)
1992—Dolphins, 20-7 (M)
1994—Dolphins, 20-17 (M) OT
1996—Raiders, 17-7 (O)
1997—Dolphins, 34-16 (O)
1998—Dolphins, 27-17 (O)
1999—Dolphins, 16-9 (O)
2000—**Raiders, 27-0 (O)
2001—Dolphins, 18-15 (M)
2002—Dolphins, 23-17 (M)
2005—Dolphins, 33-21 (O)

2007—Raiders, 35-17 (M)
2008—Dolphins, 17-15 (M)
2010—Dolphins, 33-17 (O)
2011—Dolphins, 34-14 (M)
2012—Dolphins, 35-13 (M)
(RS Pts.—Raiders 645, Dolphins 644)
(PS Pts.—Raiders 86, Dolphins 67)
*Franchise in Los Angeles from 1982-1994
**AFC Divisional Playoff
***AFC Championship

MIAMI vs. PHILADELPHIA
RS: Dolphins lead series, 7-6
1970—Eagles, 24-17 (P)
1975—Dolphins, 24-16 (M)
1978—Eagles, 17-3 (P)
1981—Dolphins, 13-10 (M)
1984—Dolphins, 24-23 (M)
1987—Dolphins, 28-10 (P)
1990—Dolphins, 23-20 (M) OT
1993—Dolphins, 19-14 (P)
1996—Eagles, 35-28 (P)
1999—Dolphins, 16-13 (M)
2003—Eagles, 34-27 (M)
2007—Eagles, 17-7 (P)
2011—Eagles, 26-10 (M)
(RS Pts.—Eagles 259, Dolphins 239)

MIAMI vs. PITTSBURGH
RS: Steelers lead series, 12-9
PS: Dolphins lead series, 2-1
1971—Dolphins, 24-21 (M)
1972—*Dolphins, 21-17 (P)
1973—Dolphins, 30-26 (M)
1976—Steelers, 14-3 (P)
1979—**Steelers, 34-14 (P)
1980—Steelers, 23-10 (P)
1981—Dolphins, 30-10 (M)
1984—Dolphins, 31-7 (P)
    *Dolphins, 45-28 (M)
1985—Dolphins, 24-20 (M)
1987—Dolphins, 35-24 (M)
1988—Steelers, 40-24 (P)
1989—Steelers, 34-14 (M)
1990—Dolphins, 28-6 (P)
1993—Steelers, 21-20 (M)
1994—Steelers, 16-13 (P) OT
1995—Dolphins, 23-10 (M)
1996—Steelers, 24-17 (M)
1998—Dolphins, 21-0 (M)
2004—Steelers, 13-3 (M)
2006—Steelers, 28-17 (P)
2007—Steelers, 3-0 (M)
2009—Steelers, 30-24 (M)
2010—Steelers, 23-22 (M)
(RS Pts.—Dolphins 413, Steelers 393)
(PS Pts.—Dolphins 80, Steelers 79)
*AFC Championship
**AFC Divisional Playoff

MIAMI vs. *ST. LOUIS
RS: Dolphins lead series, 10-2
1971—Dolphins, 20-14 (LA)
1976—Rams, 31-28 (M)
1980—Dolphins, 35-14 (LA)
1983—Dolphins, 30-14 (M)
1986—Dolphins, 37-31 (LA) OT
1992—Dolphins, 26-10 (M)
1995—Dolphins, 41-22 (StL)
1998—Dolphins, 14-0 (M)
2001—Rams, 42-10 (StL)
2004—Dolphins, 31-14 (M)
2008—Dolphins, 16-12 (StL)
2012—Dolphins, 17-14 (M)
(RS Pts.—Dolphins 305, Rams 218)
*Franchise in Los Angeles prior to 1995

MIAMI vs. SAN DIEGO
RS: Series tied, 12-12
PS: Series tied, 2-2
1966—Chargers, 44-10 (SD)
1967—Chargers, 24-0 (SD)
      Dolphins, 41-24 (M)
1968—Chargers, 34-28 (SD)
1969—Chargers, 21-14 (M)
1972—Dolphins, 24-10 (M)
1974—Dolphins, 28-21 (SD)
1977—Chargers, 14-13 (M)
1978—Dolphins, 28-21 (SD)
1980—Chargers, 27-24 (M) OT
1981—*Chargers, 41-38 (M) OT
1982—**Dolphins, 34-13 (M)
1984—Chargers, 34-28 (SD) OT
1986—Chargers, 50-28 (SD)
1988—Dolphins, 31-28 (M)
1991—Chargers, 38-30 (SD)
1992—*Dolphins, 31-0 (M)
1993—Chargers, 45-20 (SD)
1994—*Chargers, 22-21 (SD)
1995—Dolphins, 24-14 (SD)
1999—Dolphins, 12-9 (M)
2000—Dolphins, 17-7 (SD)
2002—Dolphins, 30-3 (M)
2003—Dolphins, 26-10 (Ariz)
2005—Dolphins, 23-21 (SD)
2008—Dolphins, 17-10 (M)
2009—Chargers, 23-13 (SD)
2011—Chargers, 26-16 (SD)
(RS Pts.—Chargers 558, Dolphins 525)
(PS Pts.—Dolphins 124, Chargers 76)
*AFC Divisional Playoff
**AFC Second-Round Playoff

MIAMI vs. SAN FRANCISCO
RS: Dolphins lead series, 6-5
PS: 49ers lead series, 1-0
1973—Dolphins, 21-13 (M)
1977—Dolphins, 19-15 (SF)
1980—Dolphins, 17-13 (M)
1983—Dolphins, 20-17 (SF)
1984—*49ers, 38-16 (Stanford)
1986—49ers, 31-16 (M)
1992—49ers, 27-3 (SF)
1995—49ers, 44-20 (M)
2001—49ers, 21-0 (SF)
2004—Dolphins, 24-17 (SF)
2008—Dolphins, 14-9 (M)
2012—49ers, 27-13 (SF)
(RS Pts.—49ers 237, Dolphins 167)
(PS Pts.—49ers 38, Dolphins 16)
*Super Bowl XIX

MIAMI vs. SEATTLE
RS: Dolphins lead series, 8-3
PS: Dolphins lead series, 2-1
1977—Dolphins, 31-13 (M)
1979—Dolphins, 19-10 (M)
1983—*Seahawks, 27-20 (M)
1984—*Dolphins, 31-10 (M)
1987—Seahawks, 24-20 (S)
1990—Dolphins, 24-17 (M)
1992—Dolphins, 19-17 (S)
1996—Seahawks, 22-15 (M)
1999—**Dolphins, 20-17 (S)
2000—Dolphins, 23-0 (M)
2001—Dolphins, 24-20 (S)
2004—Seahawks, 24-17 (S)
2008—Dolphins, 21-19 (M)
2012—Dolphins, 24-21 (M)
(RS Pts.—Dolphins 237, Seahawks 187)
(PS Pts.—Dolphins 71, Seahawks 54)
*AFC Divisional Playoff

*AFC First-Round Playoff

MIAMI vs. TAMPA BAY
RS: Dolphins lead series, 5-4
1976—Dolphins, 23-20 (TB)
1982—Buccaneers, 23-17 (TB)
1985—Dolphins, 41-38 (M)
1988—Dolphins, 17-14 (TB)
1991—Dolphins, 33-14 (M)
1997—Buccaneers, 31-21 (TB)
2000—Buccaneers, 16-13 (M)
2005—Buccaneers, 27-13 (TB)
2009—Dolphins, 25-23 (M)
(RS Pts.—Buccaneers 206, Dolphins 203)

MIAMI vs. *TENNESSEE
RS: Dolphins lead series, 18-15
PS: Titans lead series, 1-0
1966—Dolphins, 20-13 (H)
      Dolphins, 29-28 (M)
1967—Oilers, 17-14 (H)
      Oilers, 41-10 (M)
1968—Oilers, 24-10 (M)
      Dolphins, 24-7 (H)
1969—Oilers, 22-10 (H)
      Oilers, 32-7 (M)
1970—Dolphins, 20-10 (H)
1972—Dolphins, 34-13 (M)
1975—Oilers, 20-19 (H)
1977—Dolphins, 27-7 (M)
1978—Oilers, 35-30 (H)
      **Oilers, 17-9 (H)
1979—Oilers, 9-6 (H)
1981—Dolphins, 16-10 (H)
1983—Dolphins, 24-17 (H)
1984—Dolphins, 28-10 (M)
1985—Oilers, 26-23 (H)
1986—Dolphins, 28-7 (M)
1989—Oilers, 39-7 (H)
1991—Oilers, 17-13 (M)
1992—Dolphins, 19-16 (M)
1996—Dolphins, 23-20 (H)
1997—Dolphins, 16-13 (M) OT
1999—Dolphins, 17-0 (M)
2001—Dolphins, 31-23 (T)
2003—Titans, 31-7 (T)
2004—Titans, 17-7 (M)
2005—Dolphins, 24-10 (M)
2006—Dolphins, 13-10 (M)
2009—Titans, 27-24 (T) OT
2010—Dolphins, 29-17 (M)
2012—Titans, 37-3 (M)
(RS Pts.—Titans 625, Dolphins 612)
(PS Pts.—Titans 17, Dolphins 9)
*Franchise in Houston prior to 1997; known as Oilers prior to 1999
**AFC First-Round Playoff

MIAMI vs. WASHINGTON
RS: Dolphins lead series, 7-4
PS: Series tied, 1-1
1972—*Dolphins, 14-7 (Los Angeles)
1974—Redskins, 20-17 (W)
1978—Dolphins, 16-0 (W)
1981—Dolphins, 13-10 (M)
1982—**Redskins, 27-17 (Pasadena)
1984—Dolphins, 35-17 (M)
1987—Dolphins, 23-21 (M)
1990—Redskins, 42-20 (W)
1993—Dolphins, 17-10 (M)
1999—Redskins, 21-10 (M)
2003—Dolphins, 24-23 (M)
2007—Redskins, 16-13 (W) OT
2011—Dolphins, 20-9 (M)
(RS Pts.—Dolphins 208, Redskins 189)
(PS Pts.—Redskins 34, Dolphins 31)

*Super Bowl VII
**Super Bowl XVII

MINNESOTA vs. ARIZONA
RS: Vikings lead series, 13-10
PS: Vikings lead series, 2-0;
See Arizona vs. Minnesota

MINNESOTA vs. ATLANTA
RS: Vikings lead series, 15-10
PS: Series tied, 1-1;
See Atlanta vs. Minnesota

MINNESOTA vs. BALTIMORE
RS: Series tied, 2-2;
See Baltimore vs. Minnesota

MINNESOTA vs. BUFFALO
RS: Vikings lead series, 8-4;
See Buffalo vs. Minnesota

MINNESOTA vs. CAROLINA
RS: Vikings lead series, 6-4;
See Carolina vs. Minnesota

MINNESOTA vs. CHICAGO
RS: Vikings lead series, 53-48-2
PS: Bears lead series, 1-0;
See Chicago vs. Minnesota

MINNESOTA vs. CINCINNATI
RS: Vikings lead series, 6-5;
See Cincinnati vs. Minnesota

MINNESOTA vs. CLEVELAND
RS: Vikings lead series, 10-3
PS: Vikings lead series, 1-0;
See Cleveland vs. Minnesota

MINNESOTA vs. DALLAS
RS: Vikings lead series, 11-10
PS: Cowboys lead series, 4-3;
See Dallas vs. Minnesota

MINNESOTA vs. DENVER
RS: Vikings lead series, 7-6;
See Denver vs. Minnesota

MINNESOTA vs. DETROIT
RS: Vikings lead series, 68-33-2;
See Detroit vs. Minnesota

MINNESOTA vs. GREEN BAY
RS: Packers lead series, 54-48-1
PS: Series tied, 1-1;
See Green Bay vs. Minnesota

MINNESOTA vs. HOUSTON
RS: Vikings lead series, 3-0;
See Houston vs. Minnesota

MINNESOTA vs. INDIANAPOLIS
RS: Colts lead series, 15-7-1
PS: Colts lead series, 1-0;
See Indianapolis vs. Minnesota

MINNESOTA vs. JACKSONVILLE
RS: Vikings lead series, 4-1;
See Jacksonville vs. Minnesota

MINNESOTA vs. KANSAS CITY
RS: Chiefs lead series, 6-4
PS: Chiefs lead series, 1-0;
See Kansas City vs. Minnesota

MINNESOTA vs. MIAMI
RS: Dolphins lead series, 6-4
PS: Dolphins lead series, 1-0;
See Miami vs. Minnesota

MINNESOTA vs. *NEW ENGLAND
RS: Patriots lead series, 7-4
1970—Vikings, 35-14 (B)
1974—Patriots, 17-14 (M)
1979—Patriots, 27-23 (NE)
1988—Vikings, 36-6 (M)
1991—Patriots, 26-23 (NE) OT
1994—Patriots, 26-20 (NE) OT
1997—Vikings, 23-18 (M)
2000—Vikings, 21-13 (NE)

2002—Patriots, 24-17 (NE)
2006—Patriots, 31-7 (M)
2010—Patriots, 28-18 (NE)
(RS Pts.—Vikings 237, Patriots 230)
*Franchise in Boston prior to 1971
MINNESOTA vs. NEW ORLEANS
RS: Vikings lead series, 18-9
PS: Vikings lead series, 2-1
1968—Saints, 20-17 (NO)
1970—Vikings, 26-0 (M)
1971—Vikings, 23-10 (NO)
1972—Vikings, 37-6 (M)
1974—Vikings, 29-9 (M)
1975—Vikings, 20-7 (NO)
1976—Vikings, 40-9 (NO)
1978—Saints, 31-24 (NO)
1980—Vikings, 23-20 (NO)
1981—Vikings, 20-10 (M)
1983—Saints, 17-16 (NO)
1985—Saints, 30-23 (M)
1986—Vikings, 33-17 (M)
1987—*Vikings, 44-10 (NO)
1988—Vikings, 45-3 (M)
1990—Vikings, 32-3 (M)
1991—Saints, 26-0 (NO)
1993—Saints, 17-14 (M)
1994—Vikings, 21-20 (M)
1995—Vikings, 43-24 (M)
1998—Vikings, 31-24 (M)
2000—**Vikings, 34-16 (M)
2001—Saints, 28-15 (NO)
2002—Vikings, 32-31 (NO)
2004—Vikings, 38-31 (NO)
2005—Vikings, 33-16 (M)
2008—Vikings, 30-27 (NO)
2009—***Saints, 31-28 (NO) OT
2010—Saints, 14-9 (NO)
2011—Saints, 42-20 (M)
(RS Pts.—Vikings 694, Saints 492)
(PS Pts.—Vikings 106, Saints 57)
*NFC First-Round Playoff
**NFC Divisional Playoff
***NFC Championship
MINNESOTA vs. N.Y. GIANTS
RS: Vikings lead series, 13-9
PS: Giants lead series, 2-1
1964—Vikings, 30-21 (NY)
1965—Vikings, 40-14 (M)
1967—Vikings, 27-24 (M)
1969—Giants, 24-23 (NY)
1971—Vikings, 17-10 (NY)
1973—Vikings, 31-7 (New Haven)
1976—Vikings, 24-7 (M)
1986—Giants, 22-20 (M)
1989—Giants, 24-14 (NY)
1990—Giants, 23-15 (NY)
1993—*Giants, 17-10 (NY)
1994—Vikings, 27-10 (NY)
1996—Giants, 15-10 (NY)
1997—*Vikings, 23-22 (NY)
1999—Vikings, 34-17 (NY)
2000—**Giants, 41-0 (NY)
2001—Vikings, 28-16 (M)
2002—Giants, 27-20 (M)
2003—Giants, 29-17 (M)
2004—Giants, 34-13 (M)
2005—Vikings, 24-21 (NY)
2007—Vikings, 41-17 (NY)
2008—Vikings, 20-19 (M)
2009—Vikings, 44-7 (M)
2010—Giants, 21-3 (Detroit)
(RS Pts.—Vikings 522, Giants 409)
(PS Pts.—Giants 80, Vikings 33)

*NFC First-Round Playoff
**NFC Championship
MINNESOTA vs. N.Y. JETS
RS: Jets lead series, 8-1
1970—Jets, 20-10 (NY)
1975—Vikings, 29-21 (M)
1979—Jets, 14-7 (NY)
1982—Jets, 42-14 (M)
1994—Jets, 31-21 (M)
1997—Jets, 23-21 (NY)
2002—Jets, 20-7 (NY)
2006—Jets, 26-13 (M)
2010—Jets, 29-20 (NY)
(RS Pts.—Jets 226, Vikings 142)
MINNESOTA vs. *OAKLAND
RS: Raiders lead series, 9-4
PS: Raiders lead series, 1-0
1973—Vikings, 24-16 (M)
1976—**Raiders, 32-14 (Pasadena)
1977—Raiders, 35-13 (O)
1978—Raiders, 27-20 (O)
1981—Raiders, 36-10 (M)
1984—Raiders, 23-20 (LA)
1987—Vikings, 31-20 (M)
1990—Raiders, 28-24 (M)
1993—Raiders, 24-7 (LA)
1996—Vikings, 16-13 (O) OT
1999—Raiders, 22-17 (M)
2003—Raiders, 28-18 (O)
2007—Vikings, 29-22 (M)
2011—Raiders, 27-21 (M)
(RS Pts.—Raiders 321, Vikings 250)
(PS Pts.—Raiders 32, Vikings 14)
*Franchise in Los Angeles from 1982-1994
**Super Bowl XI
MINNESOTA vs. PHILADELPHIA
RS: Vikings lead series, 12-9
PS: Eagles lead series, 3-0
1962—Vikings, 31-21 (M)
1963—Vikings, 34-13 (P)
1968—Vikings, 24-17 (P)
1971—Vikings, 13-0 (P)
1973—Vikings, 28-21 (M)
1976—Vikings, 31-12 (P)
1978—Vikings, 28-27 (M)
1980—Eagles, 42-7 (M)
       *Eagles, 31-16 (P)
1981—Vikings, 35-23 (M)
1984—Eagles, 19-17 (P)
1985—Vikings, 28-23 (M)
       Eagles, 37-35 (M)
1988—Vikings, 23-21 (M)
1989—Eagles, 10-9 (P)
1990—Eagles, 32-24 (M)
1992—Eagles, 28-17 (P)
1997—Vikings, 28-19 (M)
2001—Eagles, 48-17 (M)
2004—Eagles, 27-16 (P)
       *Eagles, 27-14 (P)
2007—Eagles, 23-16 (M)
2008—**Eagles, 26-14 (M)
2010—Vikings, 24-14 (P)
(RS Pts.—Vikings 485, Eagles 477)
(PS Pts.—Eagles 84, Vikings 44)
*NFC Divisional Playoff
**NFC First-Round Playoff
MINNESOTA vs. PITTSBURGH
RS: Vikings lead series, 8-7
PS: Steelers lead series, 1-0
1962—Steelers, 39-31 (P)
1964—Vikings, 30-10 (M)
1967—Vikings, 41-27 (P)
1969—Vikings, 52-14 (M)

1972—Steelers, 23-10 (P)
1974—*Steelers, 16-6 (New Orleans)
1976—Vikings, 17-6 (M)
1980—Steelers, 23-17 (M)
1983—Vikings, 17-14 (P)
1986—Vikings, 31-7 (M)
1989—Steelers, 27-14 (P)
1992—Vikings, 6-3 (P)
1995—Vikings, 44-24 (P)
2001—Steelers, 21-16 (P)
2005—Steelers, 18-3 (M)
2009—Steelers, 27-17 (P)
(RS Pts.—Vikings 346, Steelers 283)
(PS Pts.—Steelers 16, Vikings 6)
*Super Bowl IX
MINNESOTA vs. *ST. LOUIS
RS: Vikings lead series, 19-14-2
PS: Vikings lead series, 5-2
1961—Rams, 31-17 (LA)
       Vikings, 42-21 (M)
1962—Vikings, 38-14 (LA)
       Tie, 24-24 (M)
1963—Rams, 27-24 (LA)
       Vikings, 21-13 (M)
1964—Rams, 22-13 (LA)
       Vikings, 34-13 (M)
1965—Vikings, 38-35 (LA)
       Vikings, 24-13 (M)
1966—Vikings, 35-7 (M)
       Rams, 21-6 (LA)
1967—Rams, 39-3 (LA)
1968—Rams, 31-3 (M)
1969—Vikings, 20-13 (LA)
       **Vikings, 23-20 (M)
1970—Vikings, 13-3 (M)
1972—Vikings, 45-41 (LA)
1973—Vikings, 10-9 (M)
1974—Rams, 20-17 (LA)
       ***Vikings, 14-10 (M)
1976—Tie, 10-10 (M) OT
       ***Vikings, 24-13 (M)
1977—Rams, 35-3 (LA)
       ****Vikings, 14-7 (LA)
1978—Rams, 34-17 (M)
       ****Rams, 34-10 (LA)
1979—Rams, 27-21 (LA) OT
1985—Rams, 13-10 (LA)
1987—Vikings, 21-16 (LA)
1988—*****Vikings, 28-17 (M)
1989—Rams, 23-21 (M) OT
1991—Vikings, 20-14 (M)
1992—Vikings, 31-17 (LA)
1998—Vikings, 38-31 (StL)
1999—****Rams, 49-37 (StL)
2000—Rams, 40-29 (StL)
2003—Rams, 48-17 (StL)
2005—Vikings, 27-13 (M)
2006—Rams, 41-21 (M)
2009—Vikings, 38-10 (StL)
2012—Vikings, 36-22 (StL)
(RS Pts.—Rams 789, Vikings 789)
(PS Pts.—Rams 150, Vikings 150)
*Franchise in Los Angeles prior to 1995
**Conference Championship
***NFC Championship
****NFC Divisional Playoff
*****NFC First-Round Playoff
MINNESOTA vs. SAN DIEGO
RS: Chargers lead series, 6-5
1971—Chargers, 30-14 (SD)
1975—Vikings, 28-13 (M)
1978—Chargers, 13-7 (M)
1981—Vikings, 33-31 (SD)

1984—Chargers, 42-13 (M)
1985—Vikings, 21-17 (M)
1993—Chargers, 30-17 (M)
1999—Vikings, 35-27 (M)
2003—Chargers, 42-28 (SD)
2007—Vikings, 35-17 (M)
2011—Chargers, 24-17 (SD)
(RS Pts.—Chargers 286, Vikings 248)
MINNESOTA vs. SAN FRANCISCO
RS: Vikings lead series, 21-18-1
PS: 49ers lead series, 4-1
1961—49ers, 38-24 (M)
    49ers, 38-28 (SF)
1962—49ers, 21-7 (SF)
    49ers, 35-12 (M)
1963—Vikings, 24-20 (SF)
    Vikings, 45-14 (M)
1964—Vikings, 27-22 (SF)
    Vikings, 24-7 (M)
1965—Vikings, 42-41 (SF)
    49ers, 45-24 (M)
1966—Tie, 20-20 (SF)
    Vikings, 28-3 (M)
1967—49ers, 27-21 (M)
1968—Vikings, 30-20 (SF)
1969—Vikings, 10-7 (M)
1970—*49ers, 17-14 (M)
1971—49ers, 13-9 (M)
1972—49ers, 20-17 (SF)
1973—Vikings, 17-13 (SF)
1975—Vikings, 27-17 (M)
1976—49ers, 20-16 (SF)
1977—Vikings, 28-27 (M)
1979—Vikings, 28-22 (M)
1983—49ers, 48-17 (M)
1984—49ers, 51-7 (SF)
1985—Vikings, 28-21 (M)
1986—Vikings, 27-24 (SF) OT
1987—*Vikings, 36-24 (SF)
1988—49ers, 24-21 (SF)
    *49ers, 34-9 (SF)
1989—*49ers, 41-13 (SF)
1990—49ers, 20-17 (M)
1991—Vikings, 17-14 (M)
1992—49ers, 20-17 (M)
1993—49ers, 38-19 (SF)
1994—Vikings, 21-14 (M)
1995—Vikings, 37-30 (M)
1997—49ers, 28-17 (SF)
    *49ers, 38-22 (SF)
1999—Vikings, 40-16 (M)
2003—Vikings, 35-7 (M)
2006—49ers, 9-3 (SF)
2007—Vikings, 27-7 (SF)
2009—Vikings, 27-24 (M)
2012—Vikings, 24-13 (M)
(RS Pts.—49ers 905, Vikings 902)
(PS Pts.—49ers 154, Vikings 94)
*NFC Divisional Playoff
MINNESOTA vs. SEATTLE
RS: Seahawks lead series, 7-5
1976—Vikings, 27-21 (M)
1978—Seahawks, 29-28 (S)
1984—Seahawks, 20-12 (M)
1987—Seahawks, 28-17 (S)
1990—Vikings, 24-21 (S)
1996—Seahawks, 42-23 (M)
2002—Seahawks, 48-23 (S)
2003—Vikings, 34-7 (M)
2004—Vikings, 27-23 (M)
2006—Vikings, 31-13 (S)
2009—Vikings, 35-9 (M)
2012—Seahawks, 30-20 (S)

(RS Pts.—Vikings 297, Seahawks 295)
MINNESOTA vs. TAMPA BAY
RS: Vikings lead series, 31-22
1977—Vikings, 9-3 (TB)
1978—Buccaneers, 16-10 (M)
    Vikings, 24-7 (TB)
1979—Buccaneers, 12-10 (M)
    Vikings, 23-22 (TB)
1980—Vikings, 38-30 (M)
    Vikings, 21-10 (TB)
1981—Buccaneers, 21-13 (TB)
    Vikings, 25-10 (M)
1982—Vikings, 17-10 (M)
1983—Vikings, 19-16 (TB) OT
    Buccaneers, 17-12 (M)
1984—Buccaneers, 35-31 (TB)
    Vikings, 27-24 (M)
1985—Vikings, 31-16 (TB)
    Vikings, 26-7 (M)
1986—Vikings, 23-10 (M)
    Vikings, 45-13 (TB)
1987—Buccaneers, 20-10 (TB)
    Vikings, 23-17 (M)
1988—Vikings, 14-13 (M)
    Vikings, 49-20 (TB)
1989—Vikings, 17-3 (M)
    Vikings, 24-10 (TB)
1990—Buccaneers, 23-20 (M) OT
    Buccaneers, 26-13 (TB)
1991—Vikings, 28-13 (M)
    Vikings, 26-24 (TB)
1992—Vikings, 26-20 (M)
    Vikings, 35-7 (TB)
1993—Vikings, 15-0 (M)
    Buccaneers, 23-10 (TB)
1994—Vikings, 36-13 (TB)
    Buccaneers, 20-17 (M) OT
1995—Buccaneers, 20-17 (TB) OT
    Vikings, 31-17 (M)
1996—Buccaneers, 24-13 (TB)
    Vikings, 21-10 (M)
1997—Buccaneers, 28-14 (M)
    Vikings, 10-6 (TB)
1998—Vikings, 31-7 (M)
    Buccaneers, 27-24 (TB)
1999—Vikings, 21-14 (M)
    Buccaneers, 24-17 (TB)
2000—Vikings, 30-23 (M)
    Buccaneers, 41-13 (TB)
2001—Vikings, 20-16 (M)
    Buccaneers, 41-14 (TB)
2002—Buccaneers, 38-24 (TB)
2005—Buccaneers, 24-13 (M)
2008—Buccaneers, 19-13 (TB)
2011—Buccaneers, 24-20 (M)
2012—Buccaneers, 36-17 (M)
(RS Pts.—Vikings 1,130, Buccaneers 970)
MINNESOTA vs. *TENNESSEE
RS: Vikings lead series, 8-4
1974—Vikings, 51-10 (M)
1980—Oilers, 20-16 (H)
1983—Vikings, 34-14 (M)
1986—Oilers, 23-10 (H)
1989—Vikings, 38-7 (M)
1992—Oilers, 17-13 (M)
1995—Vikings, 23-17 (M) OT
1998—Vikings, 26-16 (T)
2001—Vikings, 42-24 (M)
2004—Vikings, 20-3 (M)
2008—Titans, 30-17 (T)
2012—Vikings, 30-7 (M)
(RS Pts.—Vikings 320, Titans 188)
*Franchise in Houston prior to 1997;

known as Oilers prior to 1999
MINNESOTA vs. WASHINGTON
RS: Redskins lead series, 9-8
PS: Redskins lead series, 3-2
1968—Vikings, 27-14 (M)
1970—Vikings, 19-10 (W)
1972—Redskins, 24-21 (M)
1973—*Vikings, 27-20 (M)
1975—Redskins, 31-30 (M)
1976—*Vikings, 35-20 (M)
1980—Vikings, 39-14 (W)
1982—**Redskins, 21-7 (W)
1984—Redskins, 31-17 (M)
1986—Redskins, 44-38 (W) OT
1987—Redskins, 27-24 (M) OT
    ***Redskins, 17-10 (W)
1992—Redskins, 15-13 (M)
    ****Redskins, 24-7 (M)
1993—Vikings, 14-9 (M)
1998—Vikings, 41-7 (M)
2004—Redskins, 21-18 (W)
2006—Vikings, 19-16 (W)
2007—Redskins, 32-21 (M)
2010—Vikings, 17-13 (M)
2011—Vikings, 33-26 (W)
2012—Redskins, 38-26 (W)
(RS Pts.—Vikings 417, Redskins 372)
(PS Pts.—Redskins 102, Vikings 86)
*NFC Divisional Playoff
**NFC Second-Round Playoff
***NFC Championship
****NFC First-Round Playoff

NEW ENGLAND vs. ARIZONA
RS: Cardinals lead series, 7-6;
See Arizona vs. New England
NEW ENGLAND vs. ATLANTA
RS: Series tied, 6-6;
See Atlanta vs. New England
NEW ENGLAND vs. BALTIMORE
RS: Patriots lead series, 6-1
PS: Ravens lead series, 2-1;
See Baltimore vs. New England
NEW ENGLAND vs. BUFFALO
RS: Patriots lead series, 63-41-1
PS: Patriots lead series, 1-0;
See Buffalo vs. New England
NEW ENGLAND vs. CAROLINA
RS: Series tied, 2-2
PS: Patriots lead series, 1-0;
See Carolina vs. New England
NEW ENGLAND vs. CHICAGO
RS: Patriots lead series, 8-3
PS: Bears lead series, 1-0;
See Chicago vs. New England
NEW ENGLAND vs. CINCINNATI
RS: Patriots lead series, 14-8;
See Cincinnati vs. New England
NEW ENGLAND vs. CLEVELAND
RS: Browns lead series, 12-9
PS: Browns lead series, 1-0;
See Cleveland vs. New England
NEW ENGLAND vs. DALLAS
RS: Cowboys lead series, 7-4;
See Dallas vs. New England
NEW ENGLAND vs. DENVER
RS: Broncos lead series, 25-18
PS: Broncos lead series, 2-1;
See Denver vs. New England
NEW ENGLAND vs. DETROIT
RS: Patriots lead series, 6-4;
See Detroit vs. New England

NEW ENGLAND vs. GREEN BAY
RS: Patriots lead series, 5-4
PS: Packers lead series, 1-0;
See Green Bay vs. New England
NEW ENGLAND vs. HOUSTON
RS: Patriots lead series, 3-1
PS: Patriots lead series, 1-0;
See Houston vs. New England
NEW ENGLAND vs. INDIANAPOLIS
RS: Patriots lead series, 45-28
PS: Patriots lead series, 2-1;
See Indianapolis vs. New England
NEW ENGLAND vs. JACKSONVILLE
RS: Patriots lead series, 6-0
PS: Patriots lead series, 3-1;
See Jacksonville vs. New England
NEW ENGLAND vs. KANSAS CITY
RS: Chiefs lead series, 16-13-3;
See Kansas City vs. New England
NEW ENGLAND vs. MIAMI
RS: Dolphins lead series, 49-43
PS: Patriots lead series, 2-1;
See Miami vs. New England
NEW ENGLAND vs. MINNESOTA
RS: Patriots lead series, 7-4;
See Minnesota vs. New England
NEW ENGLAND vs. NEW ORLEANS
RS: Patriots lead series, 8-4
1972—Patriots, 17-10 (NO)
1976—Patriots, 27-6 (NE)
1980—Patriots, 38-27 (NO)
1983—Patriots, 7-0 (NE)
1986—Patriots, 21-20 (NO)
1989—Saints, 28-24 (NE)
1992—Saints, 31-14 (NE)
1995—Saints, 31-17 (NE)
1998—Patriots, 30-27 (NO)
2001—Patriots, 34-17 (NE)
2005—Patriots, 24-17 (NE)
2009—Saints, 38-17 (NO)
(RS Pts.—Patriots 270, Saints 252)
*NEW ENGLAND vs. N.Y. GIANTS
RS: Patriots lead series, 5-4
PS: Giants lead series, 2-0;
1970—Giants, 16-0 (B)
1974—Patriots, 28-20 (New Haven)
1987—Giants, 17-10 (NY)
1990—Giants, 13-10 (NE)
1996—Patriots, 23-22 (NY)
1999—Patriots, 16-14 (NE)
2003—Patriots, 17-6 (NE)
2007—Patriots, 38-35 (NY)
　　　**Giants, 17-14 (Arizona)
2011—Giants, 24-20 (NE)
　　　***Giants, 21-17 (Indianapolis)
(RS Pts.—Giants 167, Patriots 162)
(PS Pts.—Giants 38, Patriots 31)
*Franchise in Boston prior to 1971
**Super Bowl XLII
***Super Bowl XLVI
*NEW ENGLAND vs. **N.Y. JETS
RS: Patriots lead series, 53-51-1
PS: Patriots lead series, 2-1
1960—Patriots, 28-24 (NY)
　　　Patriots, 38-21 (B)
1961—Titans, 21-20 (B)
　　　Titans, 37-30 (NY)
1962—Patriots, 43-14 (NY)
　　　Patriots, 24-17 (B)
1963—Patriots, 38-14 (B)
　　　Jets, 31-24 (NY)
1964—Patriots, 26-10 (B)
　　　Jets, 35-14 (NY)

1965—Jets, 30-20 (B)
　　　Patriots, 27-23 (NY)
1966—Tie, 24-24 (B)
　　　Jets, 38-28 (NY)
1967—Jets, 30-23 (NY)
　　　Jets, 29-24 (B)
1968—Jets, 47-31 (Birmingham)
　　　Jets, 48-14 (NY)
1969—Jets, 23-14 (B)
　　　Jets, 23-17 (NY)
1970—Jets, 31-21 (B)
　　　Jets, 17-3 (NY)
1971—Patriots, 20-0 (NE)
　　　Jets, 13-6 (NY)
1972—Patriots, 41-13 (NE)
　　　Jets, 34-10 (NY)
1973—Jets, 9-7 (NE)
　　　Jets, 33-13 (NY)
1974—Patriots, 24-0 (NY)
　　　Jets, 21-16 (NE)
1975—Jets, 36-7 (NY)
　　　Jets, 30-28 (NE)
1976—Patriots, 41-7 (NE)
　　　Patriots, 38-24 (NY)
1977—Jets, 30-27 (NY)
　　　Patriots, 24-13 (NE)
1978—Patriots, 55-21 (NE)
　　　Patriots, 19-17 (NY)
1979—Patriots, 56-3 (NE)
　　　Jets, 27-26 (NY)
1980—Patriots, 21-11 (NY)
　　　Patriots, 34-21 (NE)
1981—Jets, 28-24 (NY)
　　　Jets, 17-6 (NE)
1982—Jets, 31-7 (NE)
1983—Patriots, 23-13 (NE)
　　　Jets, 26-3 (NY)
1984—Patriots, 28-21 (NY)
　　　Patriots, 30-20 (NE)
1985—Patriots, 20-13 (NE)
　　　Jets, 16-13 (NY) OT
　　　***Patriots, 26-14 (NY)
1986—Patriots, 20-6 (NY)
　　　Jets, 31-24 (NE)
1987—Jets, 43-24 (NY)
　　　Patriots, 42-20 (NE)
1988—Patriots, 28-3 (NE)
　　　Patriots, 14-13 (NY)
1989—Patriots, 27-24 (NY)
　　　Jets, 27-26 (NE)
1990—Jets, 37-13 (NE)
　　　Jets, 42-7 (NY)
1991—Jets, 28-21 (NE)
　　　Patriots, 6-3 (NY)
1992—Jets, 30-21 (NY)
　　　Patriots, 24-3 (NE)
1993—Jets, 45-7 (NE)
　　　Jets, 6-0 (NE)
1994—Jets, 24-17 (NY)
　　　Patriots, 24-13 (NE)
1995—Patriots, 20-7 (NY)
　　　Patriots, 31-28 (NE)
1996—Patriots, 31-27 (NY)
　　　Patriots, 34-10 (NE)
1997—Patriots, 27-24 (NE) OT
　　　Jets, 24-19 (NY)
1998—Jets, 24-14 (NE)
　　　Jets, 31-10 (NY)
1999—Patriots, 30-28 (NY)
　　　Jets, 24-17 (NE)
2000—Jets, 20-19 (NY)
　　　Jets, 34-17 (NE)
2001—Jets, 10-3 (NE)

　　　Patriots, 17-16 (NY)
2002—Patriots, 44-7 (NY)
　　　Jets, 30-17 (NE)
2003—Patriots, 23-16 (NE)
　　　Patriots, 21-16 (NY)
2004—Patriots, 13-7 (NE)
　　　Patriots, 23-7 (NY)
2005—Patriots, 16-3 (NE)
　　　Patriots, 31-21 (NE)
2006—Patriots, 24-17 (NY)
　　　Jets, 17-14 (NE)
　　　***Patriots, 37-16 (NE)
2007—Patriots, 38-14 (NY)
　　　Patriots, 20-10 (NE)
2008—Patriots, 19-10 (NY)
　　　Jets, 34-31 (NE) OT
2009—Jets, 16-9 (NY)
　　　Patriots, 31-14 (NE)
2010—Jets, 28-14 (NY)
　　　Patriots, 45-3 (NE)
　　　****Jets, 28-21 (NE)
2011—Patriots, 30-21 (NE)
　　　Patriots, 37-16 (NY)
2012—Patriots, 29-26 (NE) OT
　　　Patriots, 49-19 (NY)
(RS Pts.—Patriots 2,382, Jets 2,220)
(PS Pts.—Patriots 84, Jets 58)
*Franchise in Boston prior to 1971
**Jets known as Titans prior to 1963
***AFC First-Round Playoff
****AFC Divisional Playoff
*NEW ENGLAND vs. **OAKLAND
RS: Patriots lead series, 15-14-1
PS: Patriots lead series, 2-1
1960—Raiders, 27-14 (O)
　　　Patriots, 34-28 (B)
1961—Patriots, 20-17 (B)
　　　Patriots, 35-21 (O)
1962—Patriots, 26-16 (B)
　　　Raiders, 20-0 (O)
1963—Patriots, 20-14 (O)
　　　Patriots, 20-14 (B)
1964—Patriots, 17-14 (O)
　　　Tie, 43-43 (B)
1965—Patriots, 24-10 (B)
　　　Raiders, 30-21 (O)
1966—Patriots, 24-21 (B)
1967—Raiders, 35-7 (O)
　　　Raiders, 48-14 (B)
1968—Raiders, 41-10 (B)
1969—Raiders, 38-23 (B)
1971—Patriots, 20-6 (NE)
1974—Raiders, 41-26 (O)
1976—Patriots, 48-17 (NE)
　　　***Raiders, 24-21 (O)
1978—Patriots, 21-14 (O)
1981—Raiders, 27-17 (O)
1985—Raiders, 35-20 (NE)
　　　***Patriots, 27-20 (LA)
1987—Patriots, 26-23 (NE)
1989—Raiders, 24-21 (LA)
1994—Patriots, 21-17 (NE)
2001—***Patriots, 16-13 (NE) OT
2002—Raiders, 27-20 (O)
2005—Patriots, 30-20 (NE)
2008—Patriots, 49-26 (O)
2011—Patriots, 31-19 (O)
(RS Pts.—Raiders 751, Patriots 684)
(PS Pts.—Patriots 64, Raiders 57)
*Franchise in Boston prior to 1971
**Franchise in Los Angeles from 1982-1994
***AFC Divisional Playoff

NEW ENGLAND vs. PHILADELPHIA
RS: Eagles lead series, 6-5
PS: Patriots lead series, 1-0
1973—Eagles, 24-23 (P)
1977—Patriots, 14-6 (NE)
1978—Patriots, 24-14 (NE)
1981—Eagles, 13-3 (P)
1984—Eagles, 27-17 (P)
1987—Eagles, 34-31 (NE) OT
1990—Eagles, 48-20 (P)
1999—Eagles, 24-9 (P)
2003—Patriots, 31-10 (P)
2004—*Patriots, 24-21 (Jacksonville)
2007—Patriots, 31-28 (NE)
2011—Patriots, 38-20 (P)
(RS Pts.—Eagles 248, Patriots 241)
(PS Pts.—Patriots 24, Eagles 21)
*Super Bowl XXXIX
NEW ENGLAND vs. PITTSBURGH
RS: Steelers lead series, 14-8
PS: Patriots lead series, 3-1
1972—Steelers, 33-3 (P)
1974—Steelers, 21-17 (NE)
1976—Patriots, 30-27 (P)
1979—Steelers, 16-13 (NE) OT
1981—Steelers, 27-21 (P) OT
1982—Steelers, 37-14 (P)
1983—Patriots, 28-23 (P)
1986—Patriots, 34-0 (P)
1989—Steelers, 28-10 (P)
1990—Steelers, 24-3 (P)
1991—Steelers, 20-6 (P)
1993—Steelers, 17-14 (P)
1995—Steelers, 41-27 (P)
1996—*Patriots, 28-3 (NE)
1997—Steelers, 24-21 (NE) OT
        *Steelers, 7-6 (P)
1998—Patriots, 23-9 (P)
2001—**Patriots, 24-17 (P)
2002—Patriots, 30-14 (NE)
2004—Steelers, 34-20 (P)
        **Patriots, 41-27 (P)
2005—Patriots, 23-20 (P)
2007—Patriots, 34-13 (NE)
2008—Steelers, 33-10 (NE)
2010—Patriots, 39-26 (P)
2011—Steelers, 25-17 (P)
(RS Pts.—Steelers 512, Patriots 437)
(PS Pts.—Patriots 99, Steelers 54)
*AFC Divisional Playoff
**AFC Championship
NEW ENGLAND vs. *ST. LOUIS
RS: Patriots lead series, 6-5
PS: Patriots lead series, 1-0
1974—Patriots, 20-14 (NE)
1980—Rams, 17-14 (NE)
1983—Patriots, 21-7 (LA)
1986—Patriots, 30-28 (LA)
1989—Rams, 24-20 (NE)
1992—Rams, 14-0 (LA)
1998—Rams, 32-18 (StL)
2001—Rams, 24-17 (NE)
        **Patriots, 20-17 (New Orleans)
2004—Patriots, 40-22 (StL)
2008—Patriots, 23-16 (StL)
2012—Patriots, 45-7 (London)
(RS Pts.—Patriots 248, Rams 205)
(PS Pts.—Patriots 20, Rams 17)
*Franchise in Los Angeles prior to 1995
**Super Bowl XXXVI
NEW ENGLAND vs. **SAN DIEGO
RS: Patriots lead series, 20-14-2
PS: Patriots lead series, 2-1

1960—Patriots, 35-0 (LA)
        Chargers, 45-16 (B)
1961—Chargers, 38-27 (B)
        Patriots, 41-0 (SD)
1962—Patriots, 24-20 (B)
        Patriots, 20-14 (SD)
1963—Chargers, 17-13 (SD)
        Chargers, 7-6 (B)
        ***Chargers, 51-10 (SD)
1964—Patriots, 33-28 (SD)
        Chargers, 26-17 (B)
1965—Tie, 10-10 (B)
        Patriots, 22-6 (SD)
1966—Chargers, 24-0 (SD)
        Patriots, 35-17 (B)
1967—Chargers, 28-14 (SD)
        Tie, 31-31 (SD)
1968—Chargers, 27-17 (B)
1969—Chargers, 13-10 (B)
        Chargers, 28-18 (SD)
1970—Chargers, 16-14 (B)
1973—Patriots, 30-14 (NE)
1975—Patriots, 33-19 (SD)
1977—Patriots, 24-20 (SD)
1978—Patriots, 28-23 (NE)
1979—Patriots, 27-21 (NE)
1983—Patriots, 37-21 (NE)
1994—Patriots, 23-17 (NE)
1996—Patriots, 45-7 (SD)
1997—Patriots, 41-7 (NE)
2001—Patriots, 29-26 (NE) OT
2002—Chargers, 21-14 (SD)
2005—Chargers, 41-17 (NE)
2006—****Patriots, 24-21 (SD)
2007—Patriots, 38-14 (NE)
        *****Patriots, 21-12 (NE)
2008—Chargers, 30-10 (SD)
2010—Patriots, 23-20 (SD)
2011—Patriots, 35-21 (NE)
(RS Pts.—Patriots 860, Chargers 720)
(PS Pts.—Chargers 84, Patriots 55)
*Franchise in Boston prior to 1971
**Franchise in Los Angeles prior to 1961
***AFL Championship
****AFC Divisional Playoff
*****AFC Championship
NEW ENGLAND vs. SAN FRANCISCO
RS: 49ers lead series, 8-4
1971—49ers, 27-10 (SF)
1975—Patriots, 24-16 (NE)
1980—49ers, 21-17 (SF)
1983—49ers, 33-13 (NE)
1986—49ers, 29-24 (NE)
1989—49ers, 37-20 (SF)
1992—49ers, 24-12 (NE)
1995—49ers, 28-3 (SF)
1998—Patriots, 24-21 (NE)
2004—Patriots, 21-7 (NE)
2008—Patriots, 30-21 (SF)
2012—49ers, 41-34 (NE)
(RS Pts.—49ers 305, Patriots 232)
NEW ENGLAND vs. SEATTLE
RS: Series tied, 8-8
1977—Patriots, 31-0 (NE)
1980—Patriots, 37-31 (S)
1982—Patriots, 16-0 (S)
1983—Seahawks, 24-6 (S)
1984—Patriots, 38-23 (NE)
1985—Patriots, 20-13 (S)
1986—Seahawks, 38-31 (NE)
1988—Patriots, 13-7 (NE)
1989—Seahawks, 24-3 (NE)
1990—Seahawks, 33-20 (NE)

1992—Seahawks, 10-6 (NE)
1993—Seahawks, 17-14 (NE)
        Seahawks, 10-9 (S)
2004—Patriots, 30-20 (NE)
2008—Patriots, 24-21 (S)
2012—Seahawks, 24-23 (S)
(RS Pts.—Patriots 321, Seahawks 295)
NEW ENGLAND vs. TAMPA BAY
RS: Patriots lead series, 5-2
1976—Patriots, 31-14 (TB)
1985—Patriots, 32-14 (TB)
1988—Patriots, 10-7 (NE) OT
1997—Buccaneers, 27-7 (TB)
2000—Buccaneers, 21-16 (NE)
2005—Patriots, 28-0 (NE)
2009—Patriots, 35-7 (London)
(RS Pts.—Patriots 159, Buccaneers 90)
*NEW ENGLAND vs. **TENNESSEE
RS: Patriots lead series, 22-15-1
PS: Series tied, 1-1
1960—Patriots, 24-10 (B)
        Oilers, 37-21 (H)
1961—Tie, 31-31 (B)
        Oilers, 27-15 (H)
1962—Patriots, 34-21 (B)
        Oilers, 21-17 (H)
1963—Patriots, 45-3 (B)
        Patriots, 46-28 (H)
1964—Patriots, 25-24 (B)
        Patriots, 34-17 (H)
1965—Oilers, 31-10 (H)
        Patriots, 42-14 (B)
1966—Patriots, 27-21 (B)
        Patriots, 38-14 (H)
1967—Patriots, 18-7 (B)
        Oilers, 27-6 (H)
1968—Oilers, 16-0 (B)
        Oilers, 45-17 (H)
1969—Patriots, 24-0 (B)
        Oilers, 27-23 (H)
1971—Patriots, 28-20 (NE)
1973—Patriots, 32-0 (H)
1975—Oilers, 7-0 (NE)
1978—Patriots, 26-23 (NE)
        ***Oilers, 31-14 (NE)
1980—Oilers, 38-34 (H)
1981—Patriots, 38-10 (NE)
1982—Patriots, 29-21 (NE)
1987—Patriots, 21-7 (H)
1988—Oilers, 31-6 (H)
1989—Patriots, 23-13 (NE)
1991—Patriots, 24-20 (NE)
1993—Oilers, 28-14 (NE)
1998—Patriots, 27-16 (NE)
2002—Titans, 24-7 (T)
2003—Patriots, 38-30 (NE)
        ***Patriots, 17-14 (NE)
2006—Patriots, 40-23 (T)
2009—Patriots, 59-0 (NE)
2012—Patriots, 34-13 (T)
(RS Pts.—Patriots 960, Titans 762)
(PS Pts.—Titans 45, Patriots 31)
*Franchise in Boston prior to 1971
**Franchise in Houston prior to 1997;
known as Oilers prior to 1999
***AFC Divisional Playoff
NEW ENGLAND vs. WASHINGTON
RS: Redskins lead series, 6-3
1972—Patriots, 24-23 (NE)
1978—Redskins, 16-14 (NE)
1981—Redskins, 24-22 (W)
1984—Redskins, 26-10 (NE)
1990—Redskins, 25-10 (NE)

1996—Redskins, 27-22 (NE)
2003—Redskins, 20-17 (W)
2007—Patriots, 52-7 (NE)
2011—Patriots, 34-27 (W)
(RS Pts.—Patriots 205, Redskins 195)

NEW ORLEANS vs. ARIZONA
RS: Cardinals lead series, 14-12
PS: Saints lead series, 1-0;
See Arizona vs. New Orleans
NEW ORLEANS vs. ATLANTA
RS: Falcons lead series, 46-41
PS: Falcons lead series, 1-0;
See Atlanta vs. New Orleans
NEW ORLEANS vs. BALTIMORE
RS: Ravens lead series, 4-1;
See Baltimore vs. New Orleans
NEW ORLEANS vs. BUFFALO
RS: Saints lead series, 5-4;
See Buffalo vs. New Orleans
NEW ORLEANS vs. CAROLINA
RS: Panthers lead series, 19-17;
See Carolina vs. New Orleans
NEW ORLEANS vs. CHICAGO
RS: Bears lead series, 13-12
PS: Bears lead series, 2-0;
See Chicago vs. New Orleans
NEW ORLEANS vs. CINCINNATI
RS: Series tied, 6-6;
See Cincinnati vs. New Orleans
NEW ORLEANS vs. CLEVELAND
RS: Browns lead series, 12-4;
See Cleveland vs. New Orleans
NEW ORLEANS vs. DALLAS
RS: Cowboys lead series, 15-10;
See Dallas vs. New Orleans
NEW ORLEANS vs. DENVER
RS: Broncos lead series, 8-2;
See Denver vs. New Orleans
NEW ORLEANS vs. DETROIT
RS: Saints lead series, 11-9-1
PS: Saints lead series, 1-0;
See Detroit vs. New Orleans
NEW ORLEANS vs. GREEN BAY
RS: Packers lead series, 16-7;
See Green Bay vs. New Orleans
NEW ORLEANS vs. HOUSTON
RS: Saints lead series, 2-1;
See Houston vs. New Orleans
NEW ORLEANS vs. INDIANAPOLIS
RS: Saints lead series, 6-5
PS: Saints lead series, 1-0;
See Indianapolis vs. New Orleans
NEW ORLEANS vs. JACKSONVILLE
RS: Saints lead series, 3-2;
See Jacksonville vs. New Orleans
NEW ORLEANS vs. KANSAS CITY
RS: Series tied, 5-5;
See Kansas City vs. New Orleans
NEW ORLEANS vs. MIAMI
RS: Dolphins lead series, 6-4;
See Miami vs. New Orleans
NEW ORLEANS vs. MINNESOTA
RS: Vikings lead series, 18-9
PS: Vikings lead series, 2-1;
See Minnesota vs. New Orleans
NEW ORLEANS vs. NEW ENGLAND
RS: Patriots lead series, 8-4;
See New England vs. New Orleans
NEW ORLEANS vs. N.Y. GIANTS
RS: Giants lead series, 15-12
1967—Giants, 27-21 (NY)
1968—Giants, 38-21 (NY)

1969—Saints, 25-24 (NY)
1970—Saints, 14-10 (NO)
1972—Giants, 45-21 (NY)
1975—Giants, 28-14 (NY)
1978—Saints, 28-17 (NO)
1979—Saints, 24-14 (NO)
1981—Giants, 20-7 (NY)
1984—Saints, 10-3 (NY)
1985—Giants, 21-13 (NO)
1986—Giants, 20-17 (NY)
1987—Saints, 23-14 (NO)
1988—Giants, 13-12 (NO)
1993—Giants, 24-14 (NO)
1994—Saints, 27-22 (NO)
1995—Giants, 45-29 (NY)
1996—Saints 17-3 (NY)
1997—Giants, 14-9 (NY)
1999—Giants, 31-3 (NY)
2001—Giants, 21-13 (NY)
2003—Giants, 45-7 (NO)
2005—Giants, 27-10 (NY*)
2006—Saints, 30-7 (NY)
2009—Saints, 48-27 (NO)
2011—Saints, 49-24 (NO)
2012—Giants, 52-27 (NY)
(RS Pts.—Giants 598, Saints 571)
*Saints home game
NEW ORLEANS vs. N.Y. JETS
RS: Saints lead series, 6-5
1972—Jets, 18-17 (NY)
1977—Jets, 16-13 (NO)
1980—Saints, 21-20 (NY)
1983—Jets, 31-28 (NY)
1986—Jets, 28-23 (NY)
1989—Saints, 29-14 (NO)
1992—Saints, 20-0 (NY)
1995—Saints, 12-0 (NY)
2001—Jets, 16-9 (NO)
2005—Saints, 21-19 (NY)
2009—Saints, 24-10 (NO)
(RS Pts.—Saints 217, Jets 172)
NEW ORLEANS vs. *OAKLAND
RS: Saints lead series, 6-5-1
1971—Tie, 21-21 (NO)
1975—Raiders, 48-10 (O)
1979—Raiders, 42-35 (NO)
1985—Raiders, 23-13 (LA)
1988—Saints, 20-6 (NO)
1991—Saints, 27-0 (NO)
1994—Raiders, 24-19 (LA)
1997—Saints, 13-10 (O)
2000—Raiders, 31-22 (NO)
2004—Saints, 31-26 (O)
2008—Saints, 34-3 (NO)
2012—Saints, 38-17 (O)
(RS Pts.—Saints 283, Raiders 251)
*Franchise in Los Angeles from 1982-1994
NEW ORLEANS vs. PHILADELPHIA
RS: Eagles lead series, 15-11
PS: Series tied, 1-1
1967—Saints, 31-24 (NO)
       Eagles, 48-21 (P)
1968—Eagles, 29-17 (P)
1969—Eagles, 13-10 (P)
       Saints, 26-17 (NO)
1972—Saints, 21-3 (NO)
1974—Saints, 14-10 (NO)
1977—Eagles, 28-7 (P)
1978—Eagles, 24-17 (NO)
1979—Eagles, 26-14 (NO)
1980—Eagles, 34-21 (NO)
1981—Eagles, 31-14 (NO)
1983—Saints, 20-17 (P) OT

1985—Saints, 23-21 (NO)
1987—Eagles, 27-17 (P)
1989—Saints, 30-20 (NO)
1991—Saints, 13-6 (P)
1992—Eagles, 15-13 (P)
       *Eagles, 36-20 (NO)
1993—Eagles, 37-26 (P)
1995—Eagles, 15-10 (NO)
2000—Eagles, 21-7 (NO)
2003—Eagles, 33-20 (P)
2006—Saints, 27-24 (NO)
       **Saints, 27-24 (NO)
2007—Eagles, 38-23 (NO)
2009—Saints, 48-22 (P)
2012—Saints, 28-13 (NO)
(RS Pts.—Eagles 596, Saints 518)
(PS Pts.—Eagles 60, Saints 47)
*NFC First-Round Playoff
**NFC Divisional Playoff
NEW ORLEANS vs. PITTSBURGH
RS: Series tied, 7-7
1967—Steelers, 14-10 (NO)
1968—Saints, 16-12 (P)
       Saints, 24-14 (NO)
1969—Saints, 27-24 (NO)
1974—Steelers, 28-7 (NO)
1978—Steelers, 20-14 (P)
1981—Steelers, 20-6 (NO)
1984—Saints, 27-24 (NO)
1987—Saints, 20-16 (P)
1990—Steelers, 9-6 (NO)
1993—Steelers, 37-14 (P)
2002—Saints, 32-29 (NO)
2006—Steelers, 38-31 (P)
2010—Saints, 20-10 (NO)
(RS Pts.—Steelers 295, Saints 254)
NEW ORLEANS vs. *ST. LOUIS
RS: Rams lead series, 39-31
PS: Saints lead series, 1-0
1967—Rams, 27-13 (NO)
1969—Rams, 36-17 (LA)
1970—Rams, 30-17 (NO)
       Rams, 34-16 (LA)
1971—Saints, 24-20 (NO)
       Rams, 45-28 (LA)
1972—Rams, 34-14 (LA)
       Saints, 19-16 (NO)
1973—Rams, 29-7 (LA)
       Rams, 24-13 (NO)
1974—Rams, 24-0 (LA)
       Saints, 20-7 (NO)
1975—Rams, 38-14 (LA)
       Rams, 14-7 (NO)
1976—Rams, 16-10 (NO)
       Rams, 33-14 (LA)
1977—Rams, 14-7 (LA)
       Saints, 27-26 (NO)
1978—Rams, 26-20 (NO)
       Saints, 10-3 (LA)
1979—Rams, 35-17 (NO)
       Saints, 29-14 (LA)
1980—Rams, 45-31 (NO)
       Rams, 27-7 (NO)
1981—Saints, 23-17 (NO)
       Saints, 21-13 (LA)
1983—Rams, 30-27 (LA)
       Rams, 26-24 (NO)
1984—Rams, 28-10 (NO)
       Rams, 34-21 (LA)
1985—Rams, 28-10 (LA)
       Saints, 29-3 (LA)
1986—Saints, 6-0 (NO)
       Rams, 26-13 (LA)

1987—Saints, 37-10 (NO)
 Saints, 31-14 (LA)
1988—Rams, 12-10 (NO)
 Saints, 14-10 (LA)
1989—Saints, 40-21 (LA)
 Rams, 20-17 (NO) OT
1990—Saints, 24-20 (LA)
 Saints, 20-17 (NO)
1991—Saints, 24-7 (NO)
 Saints, 24-17 (LA)
1992—Saints, 13-10 (NO)
 Saints, 37-14 (LA)
1993—Saints, 37-6 (LA)
 Rams, 23-20 (NO)
1994—Saints, 37-34 (NO)
 Saints, 31-15 (LA)
1995—Rams, 17-13 (StL)
 Saints, 19-10 (NO)
1996—Saints, 26-10 (NO)
 Rams, 14-13 (StL)
1997—Rams, 38-24 (StL)
 Rams, 34-27 (NO)
1998—Saints, 24-17 (StL)
 Saints, 24-3 (NO)
1999—Rams, 43-12 (StL)
 Rams, 30-14 (NO)
2000—Saints, 31-24 (StL)
 Rams, 26-21 (NO)
 **Saints, 31-28 (NO)
2001—Saints, 34-31 (StL)
 Rams, 34-21 (NO)
2004—Saints, 28-25 (StL) OT
2005—Rams, 28-17 (StL)
2007—Rams, 37-29 (NO)
2009—Saints, 28-23 (StL)
2010—Saints, 31-13 (NO)
2011—Rams, 31-21 (StL)
(RS Pts.—Rams 1,576, Saints 1,422)
(PS Pts.—Saints 31, Rams 28)
*Franchise in Los Angeles prior to 1995
**NFC First-Round Playoff
NEW ORLEANS vs. SAN DIEGO
RS: Chargers lead series, 7-4
1973—Chargers, 17-14 (SD)
1977—Chargers, 14-0 (NO)
1979—Chargers, 35-0 (NO)
1988—Saints, 23-17 (SD)
1991—Chargers, 24-21 (SD)
1994—Chargers, 36-22 (NO)
1997—Chargers, 20-6 (NO)
2000—Saints, 28-27 (SD)
2004—Chargers, 43-17 (SD)
2008—Saints, 37-32 (London)
2012—Saints, 31-24 (NO)
(RS Pts.—Chargers 289, Saints 199)
NEW ORLEANS vs. SAN FRANCISCO
RS: 49ers lead series, 46-24-2
PS: 49ers lead series, 1-0
1967—49ers, 27-13 (SF)
1969—Saints, 43-38 (NO)
1970—Tie, 20-20 (SF)
 49ers, 38-27 (NO)
1971—49ers, 38-20 (NO)
 Saints, 26-20 (SF)
1972—49ers, 37-2 (NO)
 Tie, 20-20 (SF)
1973—49ers, 40-0 (SF)
 Saints, 16-10 (NO)
1974—49ers, 17-13 (NO)
 49ers, 35-21 (SF)
1975—49ers, 35-21 (SF)
 49ers, 16-6 (NO)

1976—49ers, 33-3 (SF)
 49ers, 27-7 (NO)
1977—49ers, 10-7 (NO) OT
 49ers, 20-17 (SF)
1978—Saints, 14-7 (SF)
 Saints, 24-13 (NO)
1979—Saints, 30-21 (SF)
 Saints, 31-20 (NO)
1980—49ers, 26-23 (NO)
 49ers, 38-35 (SF) OT
1981—49ers, 21-14 (SF)
 49ers, 21-17 (NO)
1982—Saints, 23-20 (SF)
1983—49ers, 32-13 (NO)
 49ers, 27-0 (SF)
1984—49ers, 30-20 (SF)
 49ers, 35-3 (NO)
1985—Saints, 20-17 (SF)
 49ers, 31-19 (NO)
1986—49ers, 26-17 (SF)
 Saints, 23-10 (NO)
1987—49ers, 24-22 (NO)
 Saints, 26-24 (SF)
1988—49ers, 34-33 (NO)
 49ers, 30-17 (SF)
1989—49ers, 24-20 (NO)
 49ers, 31-13 (SF)
1990—49ers, 13-12 (NO)
 Saints, 13-10 (SF)
1991—Saints, 10-3 (NO)
 49ers, 38-24 (SF)
1992—49ers, 16-10 (NO)
 49ers, 21-20 (SF)
1993—Saints, 16-13 (NO)
 49ers, 42-7 (SF)
1994—49ers, 24-13 (SF)
 49ers, 35-14 (NO)
1995—49ers, 24-22 (NO)
 Saints, 11-7 (SF)
1996—49ers, 27-11 (SF)
 49ers, 24-17 (NO)
1997—49ers, 33-7 (SF)
 49ers, 23-0 (NO)
1998—49ers, 31-0 (NO)
 49ers, 31-20 (SF)
1999—49ers, 28-21 (SF)
 Saints, 24-6 (NO)
2000—Saints, 31-15 (NO)
 Saints, 31-27 (SF)
2001—49ers, 28-27 (SF)
 49ers, 38-0 (NO)
2002—Saints, 35-27 (NO)
2004—Saints, 30-27 (NO)
2006—Saints, 34-10 (NO)
2007—Saints, 31-10 (SF)
2008—Saints, 31-17 (NO)
2010—Saints, 25-22 (NO)
2011—*49ers, 36-32 (SF)
2012—49ers, 31-21 (NO)
(RS Pts.—49ers 1,744, Saints 1,307)
(PS Pts.—49ers 36, Saints 32)
*NFC Divisional Playoff
NEW ORLEANS vs. SEATTLE
RS: Saints lead series, 6-5
PS: Seahawks lead series, 1-0
1976—Saints, 51-27 (S)
1979—Seahawks, 38-24 (S)
1985—Seahawks, 27-3 (NO)
1988—Saints, 20-19 (S)
1991—Saints, 27-24 (NO)
1997—Saints, 20-17 (NO) OT
2000—Seahawks, 20-10 (S)
2003—Seahawks, 27-10 (S)

2004—Seahawks, 21-7 (NO)
2007—Saints, 28-17 (S)
2010—Saints, 34-19 (NO)
 *Seahawks, 41-36 (S)
(RS Pts.—Seahawks 256, Saints 234)
(PS Pts.—Seahawks 41, Saints 36)
*NFC First-Round Playoff
NEW ORLEANS vs. TAMPA BAY
RS: Saints lead series, 25-17
1977—Buccaneers, 33-14 (NO)
1978—Saints, 17-10 (TB)
1979—Saints, 42-14 (TB)
1981—Buccaneers, 31-14 (NO)
1982—Buccaneers, 13-10 (NO)
1983—Saints, 24-21 (TB)
1984—Saints, 17-13 (NO)
1985—Saints, 20-13 (NO)
1986—Saints, 38-7 (NO)
1987—Saints, 44-34 (NO)
1988—Saints, 13-9 (NO)
1989—Buccaneers, 20-10 (TB)
1990—Saints, 35-7 (NO)
1991—Saints, 23-7 (NO)
1992—Saints, 23-21 (NO)
1994—Saints, 9-7 (TB)
1996—Buccaneers, 13-7 (TB)
1998—Saints, 9-3 (NO)
1999—Buccaneers, 31-16 (NO)
2001—Buccaneers, 48-21 (TB)
2002—Saints, 26-20 (TB) OT
 Saints, 23-20 (NO)
2003—Saints, 17-14 (TB)
 Buccaneers, 14-7 (NO)
2004—Buccaneers, 20-17 (NO)
 Saints, 21-17 (NO)
2005—Buccaneers, 10-3 (Baton Rouge)
 Buccaneers, 27-13 (TB)
2006—Saints, 24-21 (NO)
 Saints, 31-14 (TB)
2007—Buccaneers, 31-14 (TB)
 Buccaneers, 27-23 (NO)
2008—Saints, 24-20 (NO)
 Buccaneers, 23-20 (TB)
2009—Saints, 38-7 (TB)
 Buccaneers, 20-17 (NO) OT
2010—Saints, 31-6 (NO)
 Buccaneers, 23-13 (NO)
2011—Buccaneers, 26-20 (TB)
 Saints, 27-16 (NO)
2012—Saints, 35-28 (TB)
 Saints, 41-0 (NO)
(RS Pts.—Saints 891, Buccaneers 759)
NEW ORLEANS vs. *TENNESSEE
RS: Titans lead series, 7-5-1
1971—Tie, 13-13 (H)
1976—Oilers, 31-26 (NO)
1978—Oilers, 17-12 (NO)
1981—Saints, 27-24 (H)
1984—Saints, 27-10 (H)
1987—Saints, 24-10 (NO)
1990—Oilers, 23-10 (H)
1993—Saints, 33-21 (NO)
1996—Oilers, 31-14 (NO)
1999—Titans, 24-21 (NO)
2003—Titans, 27-12 (T)
2007—Titans, 31-14 (NO)
2011—Saints, 22-17 (T)
(RS Pts.—Titans 279, Saints 255)
*Franchise in Houston prior to 1997;
known as Oilers prior to 1999

NEW ORLEANS vs. WASHINGTON
RS: Redskins lead series, 16-8
1967—Redskins, 30-10 (NO)
 Saints, 30-14 (W)
1968—Saints, 37-17 (NO)
1969—Redskins, 26-20 (NO)
 Redskins, 17-14 (W)
1971—Redskins, 24-14 (W)
1973—Saints, 19-3 (NO)
1975—Redskins, 41-3 (W)
1979—Saints, 14-10 (W)
1980—Redskins, 22-14 (W)
1982—Redskins, 27-10 (NO)
1986—Redskins, 14-6 (NO)
1988—Redskins, 27-24 (W)
1989—Redskins, 16-14 (NO)
1990—Redskins, 31-17 (W)
1992—Saints, 20-3 (NO)
1994—Redskins, 38-24 (NO)
2001—Redskins, 40-10 (NO)
2002—Saints, 43-27 (W)
2003—Saints, 24-20 (W)
2006—Redskins, 16-10 (NO)
2008—Redskins, 29-24 (W)
2009—Saints, 33-30 (W) OT
2012—Redskins, 40-32 (NO)
(RS Pts.—Redskins 562, Saints 466)

N.Y. GIANTS vs. ARIZONA
RS: Giants lead series, 80-42-2;
See Arizona vs. N.Y. Giants
N.Y. GIANTS vs. ATLANTA
RS: Falcons lead series, 11-10
PS: Giants lead series, 1-0;
See Atlanta vs. N.Y. Giants
N.Y. GIANTS vs. BALTIMORE
RS: Ravens lead series, 3-1
PS: Ravens lead series, 1-0;
See Baltimore vs. N.Y. Giants
N.Y. GIANTS vs. BUFFALO
RS: Bills lead series, 6-5
PS: Giants lead series, 1-0;
See Buffalo vs. N.Y. Giants
N.Y. GIANTS vs. CAROLINA
RS: Giants lead series, 4-3
PS: Panthers lead series, 1-0;
See Carolina vs. N.Y. Giants
N.Y. GIANTS vs. CHICAGO
RS: Bears lead series, 27-19-2
PS: Bears lead series, 5-3;
See Chicago vs. N.Y. Giants
N.Y. GIANTS vs. CINCINNATI
RS: Bengals lead series, 6-3;
See Cincinnati vs. N.Y. Giants
N.Y. GIANTS vs. CLEVELAND
RS: Browns lead series, 26-20-2
PS: Series tied, 1-1;
See Cleveland vs. N.Y. Giants
N.Y. GIANTS vs. DALLAS
RS: Cowboys lead series, 57-42-2
PS: Giants lead series, 1-0;
See Dallas vs. N.Y. Giants
N.Y. GIANTS vs. DENVER
RS: Series tied, 5-5
PS: Giants lead series, 1-0;
See Denver vs. N.Y. Giants
N.Y. GIANTS vs. DETROIT
RS: Lions lead series, 20-19-1
PS: Lions lead series, 1-0;
See Detroit vs. N.Y. Giants
N.Y. GIANTS vs. GREEN BAY
RS: Packers lead series, 27-22-2
PS: Packers lead series, 4-3;

See Green Bay vs. N.Y. Giants
N.Y. GIANTS vs. HOUSTON
RS: Giants lead series, 2-1;
See Houston vs. N.Y. Giants
N.Y. GIANTS vs. INDIANAPOLIS
RS: Colts lead series, 8-6
PS: Colts lead series, 2-0;
See Indianapolis vs. N.Y. Giants
N.Y. GIANTS vs. JACKSONVILLE
RS: Giants lead series, 3-2;
See Jacksonville vs. N.Y. Giants
N.Y. GIANTS vs. KANSAS CITY
RS: Giants lead series, 10-2;
See Kansas City vs. N.Y. Giants
N.Y. GIANTS vs. MIAMI
RS: Giants lead series, 5-2;
See Miami vs. N.Y. Giants
N.Y. GIANTS vs. MINNESOTA
RS: Vikings lead series, 13-9
PS: Giants lead series, 2-1;
See Minnesota vs. N.Y. Giants
N.Y. GIANTS vs. NEW ENGLAND
RS: Patriots lead series, 5-4
PS: Giants lead series, 2-0;
See New England vs. N.Y. Giants
N.Y. GIANTS vs. NEW ORLEANS
RS: Giants lead series, 15-12;
See New Orleans vs. N.Y. Giants
N.Y. GIANTS vs. N.Y. JETS
RS: Giants lead series, 8-4
1970—Giants, 22-10 (NYJ)
1974—Jets, 26-20 (New Haven) OT
1981—Jets, 26-7 (NYG)
1984—Giants, 20-10 (NYJ)
1987—Giants, 20-7 (NYG)
1988—Jets, 27-21 (NYJ)
1993—Jets, 10-6 (NYG)
1996—Giants, 13-6 (NYJ)
1999—Giants, 41-28 (NYG)
2003—Giants, 31-28 (NYJ) OT
2007—Giants, 35-24 (NYG)
2011—Giants, 29-14 (NYJ)
(RS Pts.—Giants 265, Jets 216)
N.Y. GIANTS vs. *OAKLAND
RS: Raiders lead series, 7-4
1973—Raiders, 42-0 (O)
1980—Raiders, 33-17 (NY)
1983—Raiders, 27-12 (LA)
1986—Giants, 14-9 (LA)
1989—Giants, 34-17 (NY)
1992—Raiders, 13-10 (LA)
1995—Raiders, 17-13 (NY)
1998—Raiders, 20-17 (O)
2001—Raiders, 28-10 (NY)
2005—Giants, 30-21 (O)
2009—Giants, 44-7 (NY)
(RS Pts.—Raiders 234, Giants 201)
*Franchise in Los Angeles from 1982-1994
N.Y. GIANTS vs. PHILADELPHIA
RS: Giants lead series, 81-73-2
PS: Series tied, 2-2
1933—Giants, 56-0 (NY)
 Giants, 20-14 (P)
1934—Giants, 17-0 (NY)
 Eagles, 6-0 (P)
1935—Giants, 10-0 (NY)
 Giants, 21-14 (P)
1936—Eagles, 10-7 (P)
 Giants, 21-17 (NY)
1937—Giants, 16-7 (P)
 Giants, 21-0 (NY)
1938—Eagles, 14-10 (P)
 Giants, 17-7 (NY)

1939—Giants, 13-3 (P)
 Giants, 27-10 (NY)
1940—Giants, 20-14 (P)
 Giants, 17-7 (NY)
1941—Giants, 24-0 (P)
 Giants, 16-0 (NY)
1942—Giants, 35-17 (NY)
 Giants, 14-0 (P)
1944—Eagles, 24-17 (NY)
 Tie, 21-21 (P)
1945—Eagles, 38-17 (P)
 Giants, 28-21 (NY)
1946—Eagles, 24-14 (P)
 Giants, 45-17 (NY)
1947—Eagles, 23-0 (P)
 Eagles, 41-24 (NY)
1948—Eagles, 45-0 (P)
 Eagles, 35-14 (NY)
1949—Eagles, 24-3 (NY)
 Eagles, 17-3 (P)
1950—Giants, 7-3 (NY)
 Giants, 9-7 (P)
1951—Giants, 26-24 (NY)
 Giants, 23-7 (P)
1952—Giants, 31-7 (P)
 Eagles, 14-10 (NY)
1953—Eagles, 30-7 (P)
 Giants, 37-28 (NY)
1954—Giants, 27-14 (NY)
 Eagles, 29-14 (P)
1955—Eagles, 27-17 (P)
 Giants, 31-7 (NY)
1956—Giants, 20-3 (NY)
 Giants, 21-7 (P)
1957—Giants, 24-20 (P)
 Giants, 13-0 (NY)
1958—Eagles, 27-24 (P)
 Giants, 24-10 (NY)
1959—Eagles, 49-21 (P)
 Giants, 24-7 (NY)
1960—Eagles, 17-10 (NY)
 Eagles, 31-23 (P)
1961—Giants, 38-21 (NY)
 Giants, 28-24 (P)
1962—Giants, 29-13 (P)
 Giants, 19-14 (NY)
1963—Giants, 37-14 (P)
 Giants, 42-14 (NY)
1964—Eagles, 38-7 (P)
 Eagles, 23-17 (NY)
1965—Giants, 16-14 (P)
 Giants, 35-27 (NY)
1966—Eagles, 35-17 (P)
 Eagles, 31-3 (NY)
1967—Giants, 44-7 (NY)
1968—Giants, 34-25 (P)
 Giants, 7-6 (NY)
1969—Eagles, 23-20 (NY)
1970—Giants, 30-23 (NY)
 Eagles, 23-20 (P)
1971—Eagles, 23-7 (P)
 Eagles, 41-28 (NY)
1972—Giants, 27-12 (P)
 Giants, 62-10 (NY)
1973—Tie, 23-23 (NY)
 Eagles, 20-16 (P)
1974—Eagles, 35-7 (P)
 Eagles, 20-7 (New Haven)
1975—Giants, 23-14 (P)
 Eagles, 13-10 (NY)
1976—Eagles, 20-7 (P)
 Eagles, 10-0 (NY)

1977—Eagles, 28-10 (NY)
　　　Eagles, 17-14 (P)
1978—Eagles, 19-17 (NY)
　　　Eagles, 20-3 (P)
1979—Eagles, 23-17 (P)
　　　Eagles, 17-13 (NY)
1980—Eagles, 35-3 (P)
　　　Eagles, 31-16 (NY)
1981—Eagles, 24-10 (NY)
　　　Giants, 20-10 (P)
　　　*Giants, 27-21 (P)
1982—Giants, 23-7 (NY)
　　　Giants, 26-24 (P)
1983—Eagles, 17-13 (NY)
　　　Giants, 23-0 (P)
1984—Giants, 28-27 (NY)
　　　Eagles, 24-10 (P)
1985—Giants, 21-0 (NY)
　　　Giants, 16-10 (P) OT
1986—Giants, 35-3 (NY)
　　　Giants, 17-14 (P)
1987—Giants, 20-17 (P)
　　　Giants, 23-20 (NY) OT
1988—Eagles, 24-13 (P)
　　　Eagles, 23-17 (NY) OT
1989—Eagles, 21-19 (P)
　　　Eagles, 24-17 (NY)
1990—Giants, 27-20 (NY)
　　　Eagles, 31-13 (P)
1991—Eagles, 30-7 (P)
　　　Eagles, 19-14 (NY)
1992—Eagles, 47-34 (NY)
　　　Eagles, 20-10 (P)
1993—Giants, 21-10 (NY)
　　　Giants, 7-3 (P)
1994—Giants, 28-23 (NY)
　　　Giants, 16-13 (P)
1995—Giants, 17-14 (NY)
　　　Eagles, 28-19 (P)
1996—Giants, 19-10 (NY)
　　　Eagles, 24-0 (P)
1997—Giants, 31-17 (NY)
　　　Giants, 31-21 (P)
1998—Giants, 20-0 (NY)
　　　Giants, 20-10 (P)
1999—Giants, 16-15 (NY)
　　　Giants, 23-17 (P) OT
2000—Giants, 33-18 (P)
　　　Giants, 24-7 (NY)
　　　**Giants, 20-10 (NY)
2001—Eagles, 10-9 (NY)
　　　Eagles, 24-21 (P)
2002—Eagles, 17-3 (P)
　　　Giants, 10-7 (NY) OT
2003—Giants, 14-10 (NY)
　　　Eagles, 28-10 (P)
2004—Eagles, 31-17 (P)
　　　Eagles, 27-6 (NY)
2005—Giants, 27-17 (NY)
　　　Giants, 26-23 (P) OT
2006—Giants, 30-24 (P) OT
　　　Giants, 36-22 (NY)
　　　*Eagles, 23-20 (P)
2007—Giants, 16-3 (NY)
　　　Giants, 16-13 (P)
2008—Giants, 36-31 (P)
　　　Eagles, 20-14 (NY)
　　　**Eagles, 23-11 (NY)
2009—Eagles, 40-17 (P)
　　　Eagles, 45-38 (NY)
2010—Eagles, 27-17 (P)
　　　Eagles, 38-31 (NY)

2011—Giants, 29-16 (P)
　　　Eagles, 17-10 (NY)
2012—Eagles, 19-17 (P)
　　　Giants, 42-7 (NY)
(RS Pts.—Giants 3,007, Eagles 2,876)
(PS Pts.—Giants 78, Eagles 77)
*NFC First-Round Playoff
**NFC Divisional Playoff
N.Y. GIANTS vs. *PITTSBURGH
RS: Giants lead series, 44-29-3
1933—Giants, 23-2 (P)
　　　Giants, 27-3 (NY)
1934—Giants, 14-12 (P)
　　　Giants, 17-7 (NY)
1935—Giants, 42-7 (P)
　　　Giants, 13-0 (NY)
1936—Pirates, 10-7 (P)
1937—Giants, 10-7 (P)
　　　Giants, 17-0 (NY)
1938—Giants, 27-14 (P)
　　　Pirates, 13-10 (NY)
1939—Giants, 14-7 (P)
　　　Giants, 23-7 (NY)
1940—Tie, 10-10 (P)
　　　Giants, 12-0 (NY)
1941—Giants, 37-10 (P)
　　　Giants, 28-7 (NY)
1942—Steelers, 13-10 (P)
　　　Steelers, 17-9 (NY)
1945—Giants, 34-6 (P)
　　　Steelers, 21-7 (NY)
1946—Giants, 17-14 (P)
　　　Giants, 7-0 (NY)
1947—Steelers, 38-21 (NY)
　　　Steelers, 24-7 (P)
1948—Giants, 34-27 (NY)
　　　Steelers, 38-28 (P)
1949—Steelers, 28-7 (P)
　　　Steelers, 21-17 (NY)
1950—Giants, 18-7 (P)
　　　Steelers, 17-6 (NY)
1951—Tie, 13-13 (P)
　　　Giants, 14-0 (NY)
1952—Steelers, 63-7 (P)
1953—Steelers, 24-14 (P)
　　　Steelers, 14-10 (NY)
1954—Giants, 30-6 (P)
　　　Giants, 24-3 (NY)
1955—Steelers, 30-23 (P)
　　　Steelers, 19-17 (NY)
1956—Giants, 38-10 (NY)
　　　Giants, 17-14 (P)
1957—Giants, 35-0 (NY)
　　　Steelers, 21-10 (P)
1958—Giants, 17-6 (NY)
　　　Steelers, 31-10 (P)
1959—Giants, 21-16 (P)
　　　Steelers, 14-9 (NY)
1960—Giants, 19-17 (P)
　　　Giants, 27-24 (NY)
1961—Giants, 17-14 (P)
　　　Giants, 42-21 (NY)
1962—Giants, 31-27 (P)
　　　Steelers, 20-17 (NY)
1963—Steelers, 31-0 (P)
　　　Giants, 33-17 (NY)
1964—Steelers, 27-24 (P)
　　　Steelers, 44-17 (NY)
1965—Giants, 23-13 (P)
　　　Giants, 35-10 (NY)
1966—Tie, 34-34 (P)
　　　Steelers, 47-28 (NY)

1967—Giants, 27-24 (P)
　　　Giants, 28-20 (NY)
1968—Giants, 34-20 (P)
1969—Giants, 10-7 (NY)
　　　Giants, 21-17 (P)
1971—Steelers, 17-13 (P)
1976—Steelers, 27-0 (NY)
1985—Giants, 28-10 (NY)
1991—Giants, 23-20 (P)
1994—Steelers, 10-6 (NY)
2000—Giants, 30-10 (NY)
2004—Steelers, 33-30 (NY)
2008—Giants, 21-14 (P)
2012—Steelers, 24-20 (NY)
(RS Pts.—Giants 1,500, Steelers 1,270)
*Steelers known as Pirates prior to 1940
N.Y. GIANTS vs. *ST. LOUIS
RS: Rams lead series, 25-14
PS: Series tied, 1-1
1938—Giants, 28-0 (NY)
1940—Rams, 13-0 (NY)
1941—Giants, 49-14 (NY)
1945—Rams, 21-17 (NY)
1946—Rams, 31-21 (NY)
1947—Rams, 34-10 (LA)
1948—Rams, 52-37 (NY)
1953—Rams, 21-7 (LA)
1954—Rams, 17-16 (NY)
1959—Giants, 23-21 (LA)
1961—Giants, 24-14 (NY)
1966—Rams, 55-14 (LA)
1968—Giants, 24-21 (LA)
1970—Rams, 31-3 (NY)
1973—Rams, 40-6 (LA)
1976—Rams, 24-10 (LA)
1978—Rams, 20-17 (NY)
1979—Giants, 20-14 (LA)
1980—Rams, 28-7 (NY)
1981—Giants, 10-7 (NY)
1983—Rams, 16-6 (NY)
1984—Rams, 33-12 (LA)
　　　**Giants, 16-13 (LA)
1985—Giants, 24-19 (NY)
1988—Rams, 45-31 (NY)
1989—Rams, 31-10 (LA)
　　　***Rams, 19-13 (NY) OT
1990—Giants, 31-7 (LA)
1991—Rams, 19-13 (NY)
1992—Rams, 38-17 (LA)
1993—Giants, 20-10 (NY)
1994—Rams, 17-10 (LA)
1997—Rams, 13-3 (StL)
1999—Rams, 31-10 (StL)
2000—Rams, 38-24 (NY)
2001—Rams, 15-14 (StL)
2002—Giants, 26-21 (StL)
2003—Giants, 23-13 (NY)
2005—Giants, 44-24 (NY)
2008—Giants, 41-13 (StL)
2011—Giants, 28-16 (NY)
(RS Pts.—Rams 900, Giants 727)
(PS Pts.—Rams 32, Giants 29)
*Franchise in Los Angeles prior to 1995
and in Cleveland prior to 1946
**NFC First-Round Playoff
***NFC Divisional Playoff
N.Y. GIANTS vs. SAN DIEGO
RS: Series tied, 5-5
1971—Giants, 35-17 (NY)
1975—Giants, 35-24 (NY)
1980—Chargers, 44-7 (SD)
1983—Chargers, 41-34 (NY)
1986—Giants, 20-7 (NY)

1989—Giants, 20-13 (SD)
1995—Chargers, 27-17 (NY)
1998—Giants, 34-16 (SD)
2005—Chargers, 45-23 (SD)
2009—Chargers, 21-20 (NY)
(RS Pts.—Chargers 255, Giants 245)
N.Y. GIANTS vs. SAN FRANCISCO
RS: Giants lead series, 15-14
PS: Series tied, 4-4
1952—Giants, 23-14 (NY)
1956—Giants, 38-21 (SF)
1957—49ers, 27-17 (NY)
1960—Giants, 21-19 (SF)
1963—Giants, 48-14 (NY)
1968—49ers, 26-10 (NY)
1972—Giants, 23-17 (SF)
1975—Giants, 26-23 (SF)
1977—Giants, 20-17 (NY)
1978—Giants, 27-10 (NY)
1979—Giants, 32-16 (NY)
1980—49ers, 12-0 (SF)
1981—49ers, 17-10 (SF)
      *49ers, 38-24 (SF)
1984—49ers, 31-10 (NY)
      *49ers, 21-10 (SF)
1985—**Giants, 17-3 (NY)
1986—Giants, 21-17 (SF)
      *Giants, 49-3 (NY)
1987—49ers, 41-21 (NY)
1988—49ers, 20-17 (NY)
1989—49ers, 34-24 (SF)
1990—49ers, 7-3 (SF)
      ***Giants, 15-13 (SF)
1991—Giants, 16-14 (NY)
1992—49ers, 31-14 (NY)
1993—*49ers, 44-3 (SF)
1995—49ers, 20-6 (SF)
1998—49ers, 31-7 (SF)
2002—49ers, 16-13 (NY)
      **49ers, 39-38 (SF)
2005—Giants, 24-6 (SF)
2007—Giants, 33-15 (NY)
2008—Giants, 29-17 (NY)
2011—49ers, 27-20 (SF)
      ***Giants, 20-17 (SF) OT
2012—Giants, 26-3 (SF)
(RS Pts.—Giants 579, 49ers 563)
(PS Pts.—49ers 178, Giants 176)
*NFC Divisional Playoff
**NFC First-Round Playoff
***NFC Championship
N.Y. GIANTS vs. SEATTLE
RS: Giants lead series, 9-6
1976—Giants, 28-16 (NY)
1980—Giants, 27-21 (S)
1981—Giants, 32-0 (S)
1983—Seahawks, 17-12 (NY)
1986—Seahawks, 17-12 (S)
1989—Giants, 15-3 (NY)
1992—Giants, 23-10 (NY)
1995—Seahawks, 30-28 (S)
2001—Giants, 27-24 (NY)
2002—Giants, 9-6 (NY)
2005—Seahawks, 24-21 (S) OT
2006—Seahawks, 42-30 (S)
2008—Giants, 44-6 (NY)
2010—Giants, 41-7 (S)
2011—Seahawks, 36-25 (NY)
(RS Pts.—Giants 374, Seahawks 259)
N.Y. GIANTS vs. TAMPA BAY
RS: Giants lead series, 12-6
PS: Giants lead series, 1-0
1977—Giants, 10-0 (TB)

1978—Giants, 19-13 (TB)
      Giants, 17-14 (NY)
1979—Giants, 17-14 (NY)
      Buccaneers, 31-3 (TB)
1980—Buccaneers, 30-13 (TB)
1984—Giants, 17-14 (NY)
      Buccaneers, 20-17 (TB)
1985—Giants, 22-20 (NY)
1991—Giants, 21-14 (TB)
1993—Giants, 23-7 (NY)
1997—Buccaneers, 20-8 (NY)
1998—Buccaneers, 20-3 (TB)
1999—Giants, 17-13 (TB)
2003—Buccaneers, 19-13 (TB)
2006—Giants, 17-3 (NY)
2007—*Giants, 24-14 (TB)
2009—Giants, 24-0 (TB)
2012—Giants, 41-34 (NY)
(RS Pts.—Giants 302, Buccaneers 286)
(PS Pts.—Giants 24, Buccaneers 14)
*NFC First-Round Playoff
N.Y. GIANTS vs. *TENNESSEE
RS: Series tied, 5-5
1973—Giants, 34-14 (NY)
1982—Giants, 17-14 (NY)
1985—Giants, 35-14 (H)
1991—Giants, 24-20 (NY)
1994—Giants, 13-10 (H)
1997—Oilers, 10-6 (T)
2000—Titans, 28-14 (T)
2002—Titans, 32-29 (NY) OT
2006—Titans, 24-21 (T)
2010—Titans, 29-10 (NY)
(RS Pts.—Giants 203, Titans 195)
*Franchise in Houston prior to 1997;
known as Oilers prior to 1999
N.Y. GIANTS vs. *WASHINGTON
RS: Giants lead series, 92-64-4
PS: Series tied, 1-1
1932—Braves, 14-6 (B)
      Tie, 0-0 (NY)
1933—Redskins, 21-20 (B)
      Giants, 7-0 (NY)
1934—Giants, 16-13 (B)
      Giants, 3-0 (NY)
1935—Giants, 20-12 (B)
      Giants, 17-6 (NY)
1936—Giants, 7-0 (B)
      Redskins, 14-0 (NY)
1937—Redskins, 13-3 (W)
      Redskins, 49-14 (NY)
1938—Giants, 10-7 (W)
      Giants, 36-0 (NY)
1939—Tie, 0-0 (W)
      Giants, 9-7 (NY)
1940—Redskins, 21-7 (W)
      Giants, 21-7 (NY)
1941—Giants, 17-10 (NY)
      Giants, 20-13 (NY)
1942—Giants, 14-7 (W)
      Redskins, 14-7 (NY)
1943—Giants, 14-10 (NY)
      Giants, 31-7 (W)
      **Redskins, 28-0 (NY)
1944—Giants, 16-13 (NY)
      Giants, 31-0 (W)
1945—Redskins, 24-14 (NY)
      Redskins, 17-0 (W)
1946—Redskins, 24-14 (W)
      Giants, 31-0 (NY)
1947—Redskins, 28-20 (W)
      Giants, 35-10 (NY)

1948—Redskins, 41-10 (W)
      Redskins, 28-21 (NY)
1949—Giants, 45-35 (W)
      Giants, 23-7 (NY)
1950—Giants, 21-17 (W)
      Giants, 24-21 (NY)
1951—Giants, 35-14 (W)
      Giants, 28-14 (NY)
1952—Giants, 14-10 (W)
      Redskins, 27-17 (NY)
1953—Redskins, 13-9 (W)
      Redskins, 24-21 (NY)
1954—Giants, 51-21 (W)
      Giants, 24-7 (NY)
1955—Giants, 35-7 (W)
      Giants, 27-20 (W)
1956—Redskins, 33-7 (W)
      Giants, 28-14 (NY)
1957—Giants, 24-20 (W)
      Redskins, 31-14 (NY)
1958—Giants, 21-14 (W)
      Giants, 30-0 (NY)
1959—Giants, 45-14 (NY)
      Giants, 24-10 (W)
1960—Tie, 24-24 (NY)
      Giants, 17-3 (W)
1961—Giants, 24-21 (W)
      Giants, 53-0 (NY)
1962—Giants, 49-34 (NY)
      Giants, 42-24 (W)
1963—Giants, 24-14 (W)
      Giants, 44-14 (NY)
1964—Giants, 13-10 (NY)
      Redskins, 36-21 (W)
1965—Redskins, 23-7 (NY)
      Giants, 27-10 (W)
1966—Giants, 13-10 (NY)
      Redskins, 72-41 (W)
1967—Redskins, 38-34 (W)
1968—Giants, 48-21 (NY)
      Giants, 13-10 (W)
1969—Redskins, 20-14 (W)
1970—Giants, 35-33 (NY)
      Giants, 27-24 (W)
1971—Redskins, 30-3 (NY)
      Redskins, 23-7 (W)
1972—Redskins, 23-16 (NY)
      Redskins, 27-13 (W)
1973—Redskins, 21-3 (New Haven)
      Redskins, 27-24 (W)
1974—Redskins, 13-10 (New Haven)
      Redskins, 24-3 (W)
1975—Redskins, 49-13 (W)
      Redskins, 21-13 (NY)
1976—Redskins, 19-17 (W)
      Giants, 12-9 (NY)
1977—Giants, 20-17 (NY)
      Giants, 17-6 (W)
1978—Giants, 17-6 (NY)
      Redskins, 16-13 (W) OT
1979—Redskins, 27-0 (W)
      Giants, 14-6 (NY)
1980—Redskins, 23-21 (NY)
      Redskins, 16-13 (W)
1981—Giants, 17-7 (W)
      Redskins, 30-27 (NY) OT
1982—Redskins, 27-17 (NY)
      Redskins, 15-14 (W)
1983—Redskins, 33-17 (NY)
      Redskins, 31-22 (W)
1984—Redskins, 30-14 (W)
      Giants, 37-13 (NY)

1985—Giants, 17-3 (NY)
    Redskins, 23-21 (W)
1986—Giants, 27-20 (NY)
    Giants, 24-14 (W)
    ***Giants, 17-0 (NY)
1987—Redskins, 38-12 (NY)
    Redskins, 23-19 (W)
1988—Giants, 27-20 (NY)
    Giants, 24-23 (W)
1989—Giants, 27-24 (W)
    Giants, 20-17 (NY)
1990—Giants, 24-20 (W)
    Giants, 21-10 (NY)
1991—Redskins, 17-13 (NY)
    Redskins, 34-17 (W)
1992—Giants, 24-7 (W)
    Redskins, 28-10 (NY)
1993—Giants, 41-7 (W)
    Giants, 20-6 (NY)
1994—Giants, 31-23 (NY)
    Giants, 21-19 (W)
1995—Giants, 24-15 (W)
    Giants, 20-13 (NY)
1996—Redskins, 31-10 (NY)
    Redskins, 31-21 (W)
1997—Tie, 7-7 (W) OT
    Giants, 30-10 (NY)
1998—Giants, 31-24 (NY)
    Redskins, 21-14 (W)
1999—Redskins, 50-21 (W)
    Redskins, 23-13 (W)
2000—Redskins, 16-6 (NY)
    Giants, 9-7 (W)
2001—Giants, 23-9 (NY)
    Redskins, 35-21 (W)
2002—Giants, 19-17 (NY)
    Giants, 27-21 (W)
2003—Giants, 24-21 (W) OT
    Redskins, 20-7 (NY)
2004—Giants, 20-14 (NY)
    Redskins, 31-7 (W)
2005—Giants, 36-0 (NY)
    Redskins, 35-20 (W)
2006—Giants, 19-3 (NY)
    Giants, 34-28 (W)
2007—Giants, 24-17 (W)
    Redskins, 22-10 (NY)
2008—Giants, 16-7 (NY)
    Giants, 23-7 (W)
2009—Giants, 23-17 (NY)
    Giants, 45-12 (W)
2010—Giants, 31-7 (NY)
    Giants, 17-14 (W)
2011—Redskins, 28-14 (W)
    Redskins, 23-10 (NY)
2012—Giants, 27-23 (NY)
    Redskins, 17-16 (W)
(RS Pts.—Giants 3,201, Redskins 2,885)
(PS Pts.—Redskins 28, Giants 17)
*Franchise in Boston prior to 1937 and
known as Braves prior to 1933
**Division Playoff
***NFC Championship

N.Y. JETS vs. ARIZONA
RS: Jets lead series, 6-2;
See Arizona vs. N.Y. Jets
N.Y. JETS vs. ATLANTA
RS: Falcons lead series, 6-4;
See Atlanta vs. N.Y. Jets
N.Y. JETS vs. BALTIMORE
RS: Ravens lead series, 7-1;
See Baltimore vs. N.Y. Jets

N.Y. JETS vs. BUFFALO
RS: Bills lead series, 54-50
PS: Bills lead series, 1-0;
See Buffalo vs. N.Y. Jets
N.Y. JETS vs. CAROLINA
RS: Jets lead series, 3-2;
See Carolina vs. N.Y. Jets
N.Y. JETS vs. CHICAGO
RS: Bears lead series, 7-3;
See Chicago vs. N.Y. Jets
N.Y. JETS vs. CINCINNATI
RS: Jets lead series, 15-7
PS: Jets lead series, 2-0;
See Cincinnati vs. N.Y. Jets
N.Y. JETS vs. CLEVELAND
RS: Browns lead series, 12-8
PS: Browns lead series, 1-0;
See Cleveland vs. N.Y. Jets
N.Y. JETS vs. DALLAS
RS: Cowboys lead series, 7-3;
See Dallas vs. N.Y. Jets
N.Y. JETS vs. DENVER
RS: Broncos lead series, 17-15-1
PS: Broncos lead series, 1-0;
See Denver vs. N.Y. Jets
N.Y. JETS vs. DETROIT
RS: Series tied, 6-6;
See Detroit vs. N.Y. Jets
N.Y. JETS vs. GREEN BAY
RS: Jets lead series, 8-3;
See Green Bay vs. N.Y. Jets
N.Y. JETS vs. HOUSTON
RS: Jets lead series, 5-1;
See Houston vs. N.Y. Jets
N.Y. JETS vs. INDIANAPOLIS
RS: Colts lead series, 40-27
PS: Jets lead series, 3-1;
See Indianapolis vs. N.Y. Jets
N.Y. JETS vs. JACKSONVILLE
RS: Jaguars lead series, 6-4
PS: Jets lead series, 1-0;
See Jacksonville vs. N.Y. Jets
N.Y. JETS vs. KANSAS CITY
RS: Jets lead series, 17-16-1
PS: Series tied, 1-1;
See Kansas City vs. N.Y. Jets
N.Y. JETS vs. MIAMI
RS: Jets lead series, 49-44-1
PS: Dolphins lead series, 1-0;
See Miami vs. N.Y. Jets
N.Y. JETS vs. MINNESOTA
RS: Jets lead series, 8-1;
See Minnesota vs. N.Y. Jets
N.Y. JETS vs. NEW ENGLAND
RS: Patriots lead series, 53-51-1
PS: Patriots lead series, 2-1;
See New England vs. N.Y. Jets
N.Y. JETS vs. NEW ORLEANS
RS: Saints lead series, 6-5;
See New Orleans vs. N.Y. Jets
N.Y. JETS vs. N.Y. GIANTS
RS: Giants lead series, 8-4;
See N.Y. Giants vs. N.Y. Jets
***N.Y. JETS vs. **OAKLAND**
RS: Raiders lead series, 21-15-2
PS: Series tied, 2-2
1960—Raiders, 28-27 (NY)
    Titans, 31-28 (O)
1961—Titans, 14-6 (O)
    Titans, 23-12 (NY)
1962—Titans, 28-17 (O)
    Titans, 31-21 (NY)

1963—Jets, 10-7 (NY)
    Raiders, 49-26 (O)
1964—Jets, 35-13 (NY)
    Raiders, 35-26 (O)
1965—Tie, 24-24 (NY)
    Raiders, 24-14 (O)
1966—Raiders, 24-21 (NY)
    Tie, 28-28 (O)
1967—Jets, 27-14 (NY)
    Raiders, 38-29 (O)
1968—Raiders, 43-32 (O)
    ***Jets, 27-23 (NY)
1969—Raiders, 27-14 (NY)
1970—Raiders, 14-13 (NY)
1972—Raiders, 24-16 (O)
1977—Raiders, 28-27 (NY)
1979—Jets, 28-19 (NY)
1982—****Jets, 17-14 (LA)
1985—Raiders, 31-0 (LA)
1989—Raiders, 14-7 (NY)
1993—Raiders, 24-20 (LA)
1995—Raiders, 47-10 (NY)
1996—Raiders, 34-13 (NY)
1997—Jets 23-22 (NY)
1999—Raiders, 24-23 (O)
2000—Raiders, 31-7 (O)
2001—Jets, 24-22 (O)
    *****Raiders, 38-24 (O)
2002—Raiders, 26-20 (O)
    ****Raiders, 30-10 (O)
2003—Jets, 27-24 (O) OT
2005—Jets, 26-10 (NY)
2006—Jets, 23-3 (NY)
2008—Raiders, 16-13 (O) OT
2009—Jets, 38-0 (O)
2011—Raiders, 34-24 (O)
(RS Pts.—Raiders 885, Jets 822)
(PS Pts.—Raiders 105, Jets 78)
*Jets known as Titans prior to 1963
**Franchise in Los Angeles from
1982-1994
***AFL Championship
****AFC Second-Round Playoff
*****AFC First-Round Playoff
N.Y. JETS vs. PHILADELPHIA
RS: Eagles lead series, 9-0
1973—Eagles, 24-23 (P)
1977—Eagles, 27-0 (P)
1978—Eagles, 17-9 (P)
1987—Eagles, 38-27 (NY)
1993—Eagles, 35-30 (NY)
1996—Eagles, 21-20 (NY)
2003—Eagles, 24-17 (P)
2007—Eagles, 16-9 (NY)
2011—Eagles, 45-19 (P)
(RS Pts.—Eagles 247, Jets 154)
N.Y. JETS vs. PITTSBURGH
RS: Steelers lead series, 16-4
PS: Steelers lead series, 2-0
1970—Steelers, 21-17 (P)
1973—Steelers, 26-14 (P)
1975—Steelers, 20-7 (NY)
1977—Steelers, 23-20 (NY)
1978—Steelers, 28-17 (NY)
1981—Steelers, 38-10 (P)
1983—Steelers, 34-7 (NY)
1984—Steelers, 23-17 (NY)
1986—Steelers, 45-24 (NY)
1988—Jets, 24-20 (NY)
1989—Steelers, 13-0 (NY)
1990—Steelers, 24-7 (NY)
1992—Steelers, 27-10 (P)
2000—Steelers, 20-3 (NY)

2001—Steelers, 18-7 (P)
2003—Jets, 6-0 (NY)
2004—Steelers, 17-6 (P)
  *Steelers, 20-17 (P) OT
2007—Jets, 19-16 (NY) OT
2010—Jets, 22-17 (P)
  **Steelers, 24-19 (P)
2012—Steelers, 27-10 (P)
(RS Pts.—Steelers 457, Jets 247)
(PS Pts.—Steelers 44, Jets 36)
*AFC Divisional Playoff
**AFC Championship
N.Y. JETS vs. *ST. LOUIS
RS: Rams lead series, 9-4
1970—Jets, 31-20 (LA)
1974—Rams, 20-13 (NY)
1980—Rams, 38-13 (LA)
1983—Jets, 27-24 (NY) OT
1986—Rams, 17-3 (NY)
1989—Rams, 38-14 (LA)
1992—Rams, 18-10 (LA)
1995—Rams, 23-20 (NY)
1998—Rams, 30-10 (StL)
2001—Rams, 34-14 (NY)
2004—Rams, 32-29 (StL) OT
2008—Jets, 47-3 (NY)
2012—Jets, 27-13 (StL)
(RS Pts.—Rams 310, Jets 258)
*Franchise in Los Angeles prior to 1995
N.Y. JETS vs. **SAN DIEGO
RS: Chargers lead series, 20-12-1
PS: Jets lead series, 2-0
1960—Chargers, 21-7 (NY)
  Chargers, 50-43 (LA)
1961—Chargers, 25-10 (NY)
  Chargers, 48-13 (SD)
1962—Chargers, 40-14 (SD)
  Titans, 23-3 (NY)
1963—Chargers, 24-20 (SD)
  Chargers, 53-7 (NY)
1964—Tie, 17-17 (NY)
  Chargers, 38-3 (SD)
1965—Chargers, 34-9 (NY)
  Chargers, 38-7 (SD)
1966—Jets, 17-16 (NY)
  Chargers, 42-27 (SD)
1967—Jets, 42-31 (SD)
1968—Jets, 23-20 (NY)
  Jets, 37-15 (SD)
1969—Chargers, 34-27 (SD)
1971—Chargers, 49-21 (SD)
1974—Jets, 27-14 (NY)
1975—Chargers, 24-16 (SD)
1983—Jets, 41-29 (SD)
1989—Jets, 20-17 (SD)
1990—Chargers, 39-3 (NY)
  Chargers, 38-17 (SD)
1991—Jets, 24-3 (NY)
1994—Chargers, 21-6 (NY)
2002—Jets, 44-13 (SD)
2004—Jets, 34-28 (SD)
  ***Jets, 20-17 (SD) OT
2005—Chargers, 31-26 (NY)
2008—Chargers, 48-29 (SD)
2009—****Jets, 17-14 (SD)
2011—Jets, 27-21 (NY)
2012—Chargers, 27-17 (NY)
(RS Pts.—Chargers 951, Jets 698)
(PS Pts.—Jets 37, Chargers 31)
*Jets known as Titans prior to 1963
**Franchise in Los Angeles prior to 1961
***AFC First-Round Playoff
****AFC Divisional Playoff

N.Y. JETS vs. SAN FRANCISCO
RS: 49ers lead series, 10-2
1971—49ers, 24-21 (NY)
1976—49ers, 17-6 (SF)
1980—49ers, 37-27 (NY)
1983—Jets, 27-13 (SF)
1986—49ers, 24-10 (SF)
1989—49ers, 23-10 (NY)
1992—49ers, 31-14 (NY)
1998—49ers, 36-30 (SF) OT
2001—49ers, 19-17 (NY)
2004—Jets, 22-14 (NY)
2008—49ers, 24-14 (SF)
2012—49ers, 34-0 (NY)
(RS Pts.—49ers 296, Jets 198)
N.Y. JETS vs. SEATTLE
RS: Seahawks lead series, 10-8
1977—Seahawks, 17-0 (NY)
1978—Seahawks, 24-17 (NY)
1979—Seahawks, 30-7 (S)
1980—Seahawks, 27-17 (NY)
1981—Seahawks, 19-3 (NY)
  Seahawks, 27-23 (S)
1983—Seahawks, 17-10 (NY)
1985—Jets, 17-14 (NY)
1986—Jets, 38-7 (S)
1987—Jets, 30-14 (NY)
1991—Seahawks, 20-13 (S)
1995—Jets, 16-10 (S)
1997—Jets, 41-3 (S)
1998—Jets, 32-31 (NY)
1999—Jets, 19-9 (NY)
2004—Jets, 37-14 (NY)
2008—Seahawks, 13-3 (S)
2012—Seahawks, 28-7 (S)
(RS Pts.—Jets 330, Seahawks 324)
N.Y. JETS vs. TAMPA BAY
RS: Jets lead series, 9-1
1976—Jets, 34-0 (NY)
1982—Jets, 32-17 (NY)
1984—Buccaneers, 41-21 (TB)
1985—Jets, 62-28 (NY)
1990—Jets, 16-14 (TB)
1991—Jets, 16-13 (NY)
1997—Jets, 31-0 (NY)
2000—Jets, 21-17 (TB)
2005—Jets, 14-12 (NY)
2009—Jets, 26-3 (TB)
(RS Pts.—Jets 273, Buccaneers 145)
N.Y. JETS vs. **TENNESSEE
RS: Titans lead series, 22-17-1
PS: Titans lead series, 1-0
1960—Oilers, 27-21 (H)
  Oilers, 42-28 (NY)
1961—Oilers, 49-13 (H)
  Oilers, 48-21 (NY)
1962—Oilers, 56-17 (H)
  Oilers, 44-10 (NY)
1963—Jets, 24-17 (NY)
  Oilers, 31-27 (H)
1964—Jets, 24-21 (NY)
  Oilers, 33-17 (H)
1965—Oilers, 27-21 (H)
  Jets, 41-14 (NY)
1966—Jets, 52-13 (NY)
  Oilers, 24-0 (H)
1967—Tie, 28-28 (NY)
1968—Jets, 20-14 (H)
  Jets, 26-7 (NY)
1969—Jets, 26-17 (NY)
  Jets, 34-26 (H)
1972—Oilers, 26-20 (H)
1974—Oilers, 27-22 (NY)

1977—Oilers, 20-0 (H)
1979—Oilers, 27-24 (H) OT
1980—Jets, 31-28 (NY) OT
1981—Jets, 33-17 (NY)
1984—Oilers, 31-20 (H)
1988—Jets, 45-3 (NY)
1990—Jets, 17-12 (H)
1991—Oilers, 23-20 (NY)
  ***Oilers, 17-10 (H)
1993—Oilers, 24-0 (H)
1994—Oilers, 24-10 (H)
1995—Oilers, 23-6 (H)
1996—Oilers, 35-10 (NY)
1998—Jets, 24-3 (T)
2003—Jets, 24-17 (NY)
2006—Jets, 23-16 (T)
2007—Titans, 10-6 (T)
2008—Jets, 34-13 (T)
2009—Jets, 24-17 (NY)
2012—Titans, 14-10 (T)
(RS Pts.—Titans 948, Jets 853)
(PS Pts.—Titans 17, Jets 10)
*Jets known as Titans prior to 1963
**Franchise in Houston prior to 1997;
known as Oilers prior to 1999
***AFC First-Round Playoff
N.Y. JETS vs. WASHINGTON
RS: Redskins lead series, 8-2
1972—Redskins, 35-17 (NY)
1976—Redskins, 37-16 (NY)
1978—Redskins, 23-3 (W)
1987—Redskins, 17-16 (W)
1993—Jets, 3-0 (W)
1996—Redskins, 31-16 (W)
1999—Redskins, 27-20 (NY)
2003—Jets, 16-13 (W)
2007—Redskins, 23-20 (NY) OT
2011—Jets, 34-19 (W)
(RS Pts.—Redskins 228, Jets 158)

OAKLAND vs. ARIZONA
RS: Raiders lead series, 5-3;
See Arizona vs. Oakland
OAKLAND vs. ATLANTA
RS: Raiders lead series, 7-6;
See Atlanta vs. Oakland
OAKLAND vs. BALTIMORE
RS: Ravens lead series, 6-1
PS: Ravens lead series, 1-0;
See Baltimore vs. Oakland
OAKLAND vs. BUFFALO
RS: Raiders lead series, 19-17
PS: Bills lead series, 2-0;
See Buffalo vs. Oakland
OAKLAND vs. CAROLINA
RS: Panthers lead series, 3-2;
See Carolina vs. Oakland
OAKLAND vs. CHICAGO
RS: Raiders lead series, 7-6;
See Chicago vs. Oakland
OAKLAND vs. CINCINNATI
RS: Raiders lead series, 18-9
PS: Raiders lead series, 2-0;
See Cincinnati vs. Oakland
OAKLAND vs. CLEVELAND
RS: Raiders lead series, 11-9
PS: Raiders lead series, 2-0;
See Cleveland vs. Oakland
OAKLAND vs. DALLAS
RS: Raiders lead series, 6-4;
See Dallas vs. Oakland
OAKLAND vs. DENVER
RS: Raiders lead series, 59-44-2

PS: Series tied, 1-1;
See Denver vs. Oakland

OAKLAND vs. DETROIT
RS: Raiders lead series, 6-5;
See Detroit vs. Oakland

OAKLAND vs. GREEN BAY
RS: Packers lead series, 6-5
PS: Packers lead series, 1-0;
See Green Bay vs. Oakland

OAKLAND vs. HOUSTON
RS: Texans lead series, 5-2;
See Houston vs. Oakland

OAKLAND vs. INDIANAPOLIS
RS: Raiders lead series, 7-5
PS: Series tied, 1-1;
See Indianapolis vs. Oakland

OAKLAND vs. JACKSONVILLE
RS: Jaguars lead series, 4-2;
See Jacksonville vs. Oakland

OAKLAND vs. KANSAS CITY
RS: Chiefs lead series, 53-50-2
PS: Chiefs lead series, 2-1;
See Kansas City vs. Oakland

OAKLAND vs. MIAMI
RS: Raiders lead series, 16-15-1
PS: Raiders lead series, 3-1;
See Miami vs. Oakland

OAKLAND vs. MINNESOTA
RS: Raiders lead series, 9-4
PS: Raiders lead series, 1-0;
See Minnesota vs. Oakland

OAKLAND vs. NEW ENGLAND
RS: Patriots lead series, 15-14-1
PS: Patriots lead series, 2-1;
See New England vs. Oakland

OAKLAND vs. NEW ORLEANS
RS: Saints lead series, 6-5-1;
See New Orleans vs. Oakland

OAKLAND vs. N.Y. GIANTS
RS: Raiders lead series, 7-4;
See N.Y. Giants vs. Oakland

OAKLAND vs. N.Y. JETS
RS: Raiders lead series, 21-15-2
PS: Series tied, 2-2;
See N.Y. Jets vs. Oakland

*OAKLAND vs. PHILADELPHIA
RS: Series tied, 5-5
PS: Raiders lead series, 1-0
1971—Raiders, 34-10 (O)
1976—Raiders, 26-7 (P)
1980—Eagles, 10-7 (P)
    **Raiders, 27-10 (New Orleans)
1986—Eagles, 33-27 (LA) OT
1989—Eagles, 10-7 (P)
1992—Eagles, 31-10 (P)
1995—Raiders, 48-17 (O)
2001—Raiders, 20-10 (P)
2005—Eagles, 23-20 (P)
2009—Raiders, 13-9 (O)
(RS Pts.—Raiders 212, Eagles 160)
(PS Pts.—Raiders 27, Eagles 10)
*Franchise in Los Angeles from 1982-1994
**Super Bowl XV

*OAKLAND vs. PITTSBURGH
RS: Raiders lead series, 11-9
PS: Series tied, 3-3
1970—Raiders, 31-14 (O)
1972—Steelers, 34-28 (P)
    **Steelers, 13-7 (P)
1973—Raiders, 17-9 (O)
    **Raiders, 33-14 (O)
1974—Raiders, 17-0 (P)
    ***Steelers, 24-13 (O)

1975—***Steelers, 16-10 (P)
1976—Raiders, 31-28 (O)
    ***Raiders, 24-7 (O)
1977—Raiders, 16-7 (P)
1980—Raiders, 45-34 (P)
1981—Raiders, 30-27 (O)
1983—**Raiders, 38-10 (LA)
1984—Steelers, 13-7 (LA)
1990—Raiders, 20-3 (LA)
1994—Steelers, 21-3 (LA)
1995—Steelers, 29-10 (O)
2000—Steelers, 21-20 (P)
2002—Raiders, 30-17 (P)
2003—Steelers, 27-7 (P)
2004—Steelers, 24-21 (P)
2006—Raiders, 20-13 (O)
2009—Raiders, 27-24 (P)
2010—Steelers, 35-3 (P)
2012—Raiders, 34-31 (O)
(RS Pts.—Steelers 419, Raiders 409)
(PS Pts.—Raiders 125, Steelers 84)
*Franchise in Los Angeles from 1982-1994
**AFC Divisional Playoff
***AFC Championship

*OAKLAND vs. **ST. LOUIS
RS: Raiders lead series, 8-4
1972—Raiders, 45-17 (O)
1977—Rams, 20-14 (LA)
1979—Raiders, 24-17 (LA)
1982—Raiders, 37-31 (LA Raiders)
1985—Raiders, 16-6 (LA Rams)
1988—Rams, 22-17 (LA Raiders)
1991—Raiders, 20-17 (LA Raiders)
1994—Raiders, 20-17 (LA Rams)
1997—Raiders, 35-17 (O)
2002—Rams, 28-13 (StL)
2006—Rams, 20-0 (O)
2010—Raiders, 16-14 (O)
(RS Pts.—Raiders 257, Rams 226)
*Franchise in Los Angeles from 1982-1994
**Franchise in Los Angeles prior to 1995

*OAKLAND vs. **SAN DIEGO
RS: Raiders lead series, 57-47-2
PS: Raiders lead series, 1-0
1960—Chargers, 52-28 (LA)
    Chargers, 41-17 (O)
1961—Chargers, 44-0 (SD)
    Chargers, 41-10 (O)
1962—Chargers, 42-33 (O)
    Chargers, 31-21 (SD)
1963—Raiders, 34-33 (O)
    Raiders, 41-27 (O)
1964—Chargers, 31-17 (SD)
    Raiders, 21-20 (O)
1965—Chargers, 17-6 (O)
    Chargers, 24-14 (SD)
1966—Chargers, 29-20 (O)
    Raiders, 41-19 (SD)
1967—Raiders, 51-10 (O)
    Raiders, 41-21 (SD)
1968—Chargers, 23-14 (O)
    Raiders, 34-27 (SD)
1969—Raiders, 24-12 (SD)
    Raiders, 21-16 (O)
1970—Tie, 27-27 (SD)
    Raiders, 20-17 (O)
1971—Raiders, 34-0 (SD)
    Raiders, 34-33 (O)
1972—Tie, 17-17 (O)
    Raiders, 21-19 (SD)
1973—Raiders, 27-17 (SD)
    Raiders, 31-3 (O)

1974—Raiders, 14-10 (SD)
    Raiders, 17-10 (O)
1975—Raiders, 6-0 (SD)
    Raiders, 25-0 (O)
1976—Raiders, 27-17 (SD)
    Raiders, 24-0 (O)
1977—Raiders, 24-0 (O)
    Chargers, 12-7 (SD)
1978—Raiders, 21-20 (SD)
    Chargers, 27-23 (O)
1979—Chargers, 30-10 (SD)
    Raiders, 45-22 (O)
1980—Chargers, 30-24 (SD) OT
    Raiders, 38-24 (O)
    ***Raiders, 34-27 (SD)
1981—Chargers, 55-21 (O)
    Chargers, 23-10 (SD)
1982—Raiders, 28-24 (LA)
    Raiders, 41-34 (SD)
1983—Raiders, 42-10 (SD)
    Raiders, 30-14 (LA)
1984—Raiders, 33-30 (LA)
    Raiders, 44-37 (SD)
1985—Raiders, 34-21 (LA)
    Chargers, 40-34 (SD) OT
1986—Raiders, 17-13 (LA)
    Raiders, 37-31 (SD) OT
1987—Chargers, 23-17 (LA)
    Chargers, 16-14 (SD)
1988—Raiders, 24-13 (LA)
    Raiders, 13-3 (SD)
1989—Raiders, 40-14 (LA)
    Chargers, 14-12 (SD)
1990—Raiders, 24-9 (SD)
    Raiders, 17-12 (LA)
1991—Chargers, 21-13 (LA)
    Raiders, 9-7 (SD)
1992—Chargers, 27-3 (SD)
    Chargers, 36-14 (LA)
1993—Chargers, 30-23 (LA)
    Raiders, 12-7 (SD)
1994—Chargers, 26-24 (LA)
    Raiders, 24-17 (SD)
1995—Raiders, 17-7 (O)
    Chargers, 12-6 (SD)
1996—Chargers, 40-34 (O)
    Raiders, 23-14 (SD)
1997—Chargers, 25-10 (O)
    Raiders, 38-13 (SD)
1998—Raiders, 7-6 (O)
    Raiders, 17-10 (SD)
1999—Raiders, 28-9 (O)
    Chargers, 23-20 (SD)
2000—Raiders, 9-6 (O)
    Raiders, 15-13 (SD)
2001—Raiders, 34-24 (O)
    Raiders, 13-6 (SD)
2002—Chargers, 27-21 (O) OT
    Raiders, 27-7 (SD)
2003—Raiders, 34-31 (O) OT
    Chargers, 21-14 (SD)
2004—Chargers, 42-14 (SD)
    Chargers, 23-17 (O)
2005—Chargers, 27-14 (O)
    Chargers, 34-10 (SD)
2006—Chargers, 27-0 (O)
    Chargers, 21-14 (SD)
2007—Chargers, 28-14 ((SD)
    Chargers, 30-17 (O)
2008—Chargers, 28-18 (O)
    Chargers, 34-7 (SD)
2009—Chargers, 24-20 (O)
    Chargers, 24-16 (SD)

2010—Raiders, 35-27 (O)
    Raiders, 28-13 (SD)
2011—Raiders, 24-17 (SD)
    Chargers, 38-26 (O)
2012—Chargers, 22-14 (O)
    Chargers, 24-21 (SD)
(RS Pts.—Raiders 2,334, Chargers 2,279)
(PS Pts.—Raiders 34, Chargers 27)
*Franchise in Los Angeles from 1982-1994
**Franchise in Los Angeles prior to 1961
***AFC Championship
OAKLAND vs. SAN FRANCISCO
RS: Series tied, 6-6
1970—49ers, 38-7 (O)
1974—Raiders, 35-24 (SF)
1979—Raiders, 23-10 (O)
1982—Raiders, 23-17 (SF)
1985—49ers, 34-10 (LA)
1988—Raiders, 9-3 (SF)
1991—Raiders, 12-6 (LA)
1994—49ers, 44-14 (SF)
2000—Raiders, 34-28 (SF) OT
2002—49ers, 23-20 (O) OT
2006—Raiders, 34-20 (SF)
2010—49ers, 17-9 (SF)
(RS Pts.—49ers 278, Raiders 216)
*Franchise in Los Angeles from 1982-1994
OAKLAND vs. SEATTLE
RS: Raiders lead series, 28-23
PS: Series tied, 1-1
1977—Raiders, 44-7 (O)
1978—Seahawks, 27-7 (S)
    Seahawks, 17-16 (O)
1979—Seahawks, 27-10 (S)
    Seahawks, 29-24 (O)
1980—Raiders, 33-14 (O)
    Raiders, 19-17 (S)
1981—Raiders, 20-10 (O)
    Raiders, 32-31 (S)
1982—Raiders, 28-23 (LA)
1983—Seahawks, 38-36 (S)
    Seahawks, 34-21 (LA)
    **Raiders, 30-14 (LA)
1984—Raiders, 28-14 (LA)
    Seahawks, 17-14 (S)
    ***Seahawks, 13-7 (S)
1985—Seahawks, 33-3 (S)
    Raiders, 13-3 (LA)
1986—Raiders, 14-10 (LA)
    Seahawks, 37-0 (S)
1987—Seahawks, 35-13 (LA)
    Raiders, 37-14 (S)
1988—Seahawks, 35-27 (S)
    Seahawks, 43-37 (LA)
1989—Seahawks, 24-20 (LA)
    Seahawks, 23-17 (S)
1990—Raiders, 17-13 (S)
    Raiders, 24-17 (LA)
1991—Raiders, 23-20 (S) OT
    Raiders, 31-7 (LA)
1992—Raiders, 19-0 (S)
    Raiders, 20-3 (LA)
1993—Raiders, 17-13 (S)
    Raiders, 27-23 (LA)
1994—Seahawks, 38-9 (LA)
    Raiders, 17-16 (S)
1995—Raiders, 34-14 (O)
    Seahawks, 44-10 (S)
1996—Raiders, 27-21 (S)
    Seahawks, 28-21 (O)
1997—Seahawks, 45-34 (S)
    Seahawks, 22-21 (O)

1998—Raiders, 31-18 (S)
    Raiders, 20-17 (O)
1999—Seahawks, 22-21 (S)
    Raiders, 30-21 (O)
2000—Raiders, 31-3 (O)
    Seahawks, 27-24 (S)
2001—Raiders, 38-14 (O)
    Seahawks, 34-27 (S)
2002—Raiders, 31-17 (O)
2006—Seahawks, 16-0 (S)
2010—Raiders, 33-3 (O)
(RS Pts.—Raiders 1,150, Seahawks 1,078)
(PS Pts.—Raiders 37, Seahawks 27)
*Franchise in Los Angeles from 1982-1994
**AFC Championship
***AFC First-Round Playoff
OAKLAND vs. TAMPA BAY
RS: Raiders lead series, 6-2
PS: Buccaneers lead series, 1-0
1976—Raiders, 49-16 (O)
1981—Raiders, 18-16 (O)
1993—Raiders, 27-20 (LA)
1996—Buccaneers, 20-17 (TB) OT
1999—Raiders, 45-0 (O)
2002—**Buccaneers, 48-21 (San Diego)
2004—Raiders, 30-20 (O)
2008—Raiders, 31-24 (TB)
2012—Buccaneers, 42-32 (O)
(RS Pts.—Raiders 249, Buccaneers 158)
(PS Pts.—Buccaneers 48, Raiders 21)
*Franchise in Los Angeles from 1982-1994
**Super Bowl XXXVII
OAKLAND vs. **TENNESSEE
RS: Raiders lead series, 23-19
PS: Raiders lead series, 4-0
1960—Oilers, 37-22 (O)
    Raiders, 14-13 (H)
1961—Oilers, 55-0 (H)
    Oilers, 47-16 (O)
1962—Oilers, 28-20 (O)
    Oilers, 32-17 (H)
1963—Raiders, 24-13 (H)
    Raiders, 52-49 (O)
1964—Oilers, 42-28 (H)
    Raiders, 20-10 (O)
1965—Raiders, 21-17 (O)
    Raiders, 33-21 (H)
1966—Raiders, 31-0 (H)
    Raiders, 38-23 (O)
1967—Raiders, 19-7 (H)
    ***Raiders, 40-7 (O)
1968—Raiders, 24-15 (H)
1969—Raiders, 21-17 (O)
    ****Raiders, 56-7 (O)
1971—Raiders, 41-21 (O)
1972—Raiders, 34-0 (H)
1973—Raiders, 17-6 (H)
1975—Oilers, 27-26 (O)
1976—Raiders, 14-13 (O)
1977—Raiders, 34-29 (O)
1978—Raiders, 21-17 (O)
1979—Oilers, 31-17 (H)
1980—*****Raiders, 27-7 (O)
1981—Oilers, 17-16 (H)
1983—Raiders, 20-6 (LA)
1984—Raiders, 24-14 (H)
1986—Raiders, 28-17 (H)
1988—Oilers, 38-35 (H)
1989—Oilers, 23-7 (H)
1991—Oilers, 47-17 (H)
1994—Raiders, 17-14 (LA)
1997—Oilers, 24-21 (T) OT
1999—Titans, 21-14 (T)

2001—Titans, 13-10 (O)
2002—Raiders, 52-25 (O)
    ******Raiders, 41-24 (O)
2003—Titans, 25-20 (T)
2004—Raiders, 40-35 (O)
2005—Raiders, 34-25 (T)
2007—Titans, 13-9 (T)
2010—Titans, 38-13 (T)
(RS Pts.—Titans 996, Raiders 950)
(PS Pts.—Raiders 164, Titans 45)
*Franchise in Los Angeles from 1982-1994
**Franchise in Houston prior to 1997;
known as Oilers prior to 1999
***AFL Championship
****Inter-Divisional Playoff
*****AFC First-Round Playoff
******AFC Championship
OAKLAND vs. WASHINGTON
RS: Raiders lead series, 7-4
PS: Raiders lead series, 1-0
1970—Raiders, 34-20 (O)
1975—Raiders, 26-23 (W) OT
1980—Raiders, 24-21 (O)
1983—Redskins, 37-35 (W)
    **Raiders, 38-9 (Tampa)
1986—Redskins, 10-6 (W)
1989—Raiders, 37-24 (LA)
1992—Raiders, 21-20 (W)
1995—Raiders, 20-8 (W)
1998—Redskins, 29-19 (O)
2005—Raiders, 16-13 (W)
2009—Redskins, 34-13 (O)
(RS Pts.—Raiders 251, Redskins 239)
(PS Pts.—Raiders 38, Redskins 9)
*Franchise in Los Angeles from
1982-1994
**Super Bowl XVIII

PHILADELPHIA vs. ARIZONA
RS: Cardinals lead series, 55-53-5
PS: Cardinals lead series, 2-1;
See Arizona vs. Philadelphia
PHILADELPHIA vs. ATLANTA
RS: Eagles lead series, 15-12-1
PS: Eagles lead series, 2-1;
See Atlanta vs. Philadelphia
PHILADELPHIA vs. BALTIMORE
RS: Eagles lead series, 2-1-1;
See Baltimore vs. Philadelphia
PHILADELPHIA vs. BUFFALO
RS: Series tied, 6-6;
See Buffalo vs. Philadelphia
PHILADELPHIA vs. CAROLINA
RS: Eagles lead series, 5-2
PS: Panthers lead series, 1-0;
See Carolina vs. Philadelphia
PHILADELPHIA vs. CHICAGO
RS: Bears lead series, 28-9-1
PS: Eagles lead series, 2-1;
See Chicago vs. Philadelphia
PHILADELPHIA vs. CINCINNATI
RS: Bengals lead series, 8-3-1;
See Cincinnati vs. Philadelphia
PHILADELPHIA vs. CLEVELAND
RS: Browns lead series, 31-16-1;
See Cleveland vs. Philadelphia
PHILADELPHIA vs. DALLAS
RS: Cowboys lead series, 58-46
PS: Cowboys lead series, 3-1;
See Dallas vs. Philadelphia
PHILADELPHIA vs. DENVER
RS: Eagles lead series, 7-4;
See Denver vs. Philadelphia

PHILADELPHIA vs. DETROIT
RS: Eagles lead series, 14-13-2
PS: Eagles lead series, 1-0;
See Detroit vs. Philadelphia
PHILADELPHIA vs. GREEN BAY
RS: Packers lead series, 24-13
PS: Eagles lead series, 2-1;
See Green Bay vs. Philadelphia
PHILADELPHIA vs. HOUSTON
RS: Eagles lead series, 3-0;
See Houston vs. Philadelphia
PHILADELPHIA vs. INDIANAPOLIS
RS: Colts lead series, 10-7;
See Indianapolis vs. Philadelphia
PHILADELPHIA vs. JACKSONVILLE
RS: Jaguars lead series, 3-1;
See Jacksonville vs. Philadelphia
PHILADELPHIA vs. KANSAS CITY
RS: Eagles lead series, 4-2;
See Kansas City vs. Philadelphia
PHILADELPHIA vs. MIAMI
RS: Dolphins lead series, 6-0;
See Miami vs. Philadelphia
PHILADELPHIA vs. MINNESOTA
RS: Vikings lead series, 12-9
PS: Eagles lead series, 3-0;
See Minnesota vs. Philadelphia
PHILADELPHIA vs. NEW ENGLAND
RS: Eagles lead series, 6-5
PS: Patriots lead series, 1-0;
See New England vs. Philadelphia
PHILADELPHIA vs. NEW ORLEANS
RS: Eagles lead series, 15-11
PS; Series tied, 1-1;
See New Orleans vs. Philadelphia
PHILADELPHIA vs. N.Y. GIANTS
RS: Giants lead series, 81-73-2
PS: Series tied, 2-2;
See N.Y. Giants vs. Philadelphia
PHILADELPHIA vs. N.Y. JETS
RS: Eagles lead series, 9-0;
See N.Y. Jets vs. Philadelphia
PHILADELPHIA vs. OAKLAND
RS: Series tied, 5-5
PS: Raiders lead series, 1-0;
See Oakland vs. Philadelphia
PHILADELPHIA vs. *PITTSBURGH
RS: Eagles lead series, 46-28-3
PS: Eagles lead series, 1-0
1933—Eagles, 25-6 (Phila)
1934—Eagles, 17-0 (Pitt)
    Pirates, 9-7 (Phila)
1935—Pirates, 17-7 (Phila)
    Eagles, 17-6 (Pitt)
1936—Eagles, 17-0 (Pitt)
    Pirates, 6-0 (Johnstown, Pa.)
1937—Pirates, 27-14 (Pitt)
    Pirates, 16-7 (Pitt)
1938—Pirates, 27-7 (Buffalo)
    Eagles, 14-7 (Charleston, W. Va.)
1939—Eagles, 17-14 (Phila)
    Pirates, 24-12 (Pitt)
1940—Steelers, 7-3 (Pitt)
    Eagles, 7-0 (Phila)
1941—Eagles, 10-7 (Pitt)
    Tie, 7-7 (Phila)
1942—Eagles, 24-14 (Pitt)
    Steelers, 14-0 (Phila)
1945—Eagles, 45-3 (Pitt)
    Eagles, 30-6 (Phila)
1946—Steelers, 10-7 (Pitt)
    Eagles, 10-7 (Phila)

1947—Steelers, 35-24 (Pitt)
    Eagles, 21-0 (Phila)
    **Eagles, 21-0 (Pitt)
1948—Eagles, 34-7 (Pitt)
    Eagles, 17-0 (Phila)
1949—Eagles, 38-7 (Pitt)
    Eagles, 34-17 (Phila)
1950—Eagles, 17-10 (Pitt)
    Steelers, 9-7 (Phila)
1951—Eagles, 34-13 (Pitt)
    Steelers, 17-13 (Phila)
1952—Eagles, 31-25 (Pitt)
    Eagles, 26-21 (Phila)
1953—Eagles, 23-17 (Phila)
    Eagles, 35-7 (Pitt)
1954—Eagles, 24-22 (Phila)
    Steelers, 17-7 (Pitt)
1955—Steelers, 13-7 (Pitt)
    Eagles, 24-0 (Phila)
1956—Eagles, 35-21 (Pitt)
    Eagles, 14-7 (Phila)
1957—Steelers, 6-0 (Pitt)
    Eagles, 7-6 (Phila)
1958—Steelers, 24-3 (Pitt)
    Steelers, 31-24 (Phila)
1959—Steelers, 28-24 (Phila)
    Steelers, 31-0 (Pitt)
1960—Eagles, 34-7 (Phila)
    Steelers, 27-21 (Pitt)
1961—Eagles, 21-16 (Phila)
    Eagles, 35-24 (Pitt)
1962—Steelers, 13-7 (Pitt)
    Steelers, 26-17 (Phila)
1963—Tie, 21-21 (Phila)
    Tie, 20-20 (Pitt)
1964—Eagles, 21-7 (Phila)
    Eagles, 34-10 (Pitt)
1965—Steelers, 20-14 (Phila)
    Eagles, 47-13 (Pitt)
1966—Eagles, 31-14 (Pitt)
    Eagles, 27-23 (Phila)
1967—Eagles, 34-24 (Phila)
1968—Steelers, 6-3 (Pitt)
1969—Eagles, 41-27 (Phila)
1970—Eagles, 30-20 (Phila)
1974—Steelers, 27-0 (Pitt)
1979—Eagles, 17-14 (Phila)
1988—Eagles, 27-26 (Phila)
1991—Eagles, 23-14 (Phila)
1994—Steelers, 14-3 (Pitt)
1997—Eagles, 23-20 (Phila)
2000—Eagles, 26-23 (Pitt) OT
2004—Steelers, 27-3 (Pitt)
2008—Eagles, 15-6 (Phila)
2012—Steelers, 16-14 (Pitt)
(RS Pts.—Eagles 1,443, Steelers 1,113)
(PS Pts.—Eagles 21, Steelers 0)
*Steelers known as Pirates prior to 1940
**Division Playoff
PHILADELPHIA vs. *ST. LOUIS
RS: Eagles lead series, 18-17-1
PS: Rams lead series, 2-1
1937—Rams, 21-3 (P)
1939—Rams, 35-13 (Colorado Springs)
1940—Rams, 21-13 (C)
1942—Rams, 24-14 (Akron)
1944—Eagles, 26-13 (P)
1945—Eagles, 28-14 (P)
1946—Eagles, 25-14 (LA)
1947—Eagles, 14-7 (P)
1948—Tie, 28-28 (LA)
1949—Eagles, 38-14 (P)
    **Eagles, 14-0 (LA)

1950—Eagles, 56-20 (P)
1955—Rams, 23-21 (P)
1956—Rams, 27-7 (LA)
1957—Rams, 17-13 (LA)
1959—Eagles, 23-20 (P)
1964—Rams, 20-10 (LA)
1967—Rams, 33-17 (LA)
1969—Rams, 23-17 (P)
1972—Rams, 34-3 (P)
1975—Rams, 42-3 (P)
1977—Rams, 20-0 (LA)
1978—Rams, 16-14 (P)
1983—Eagles, 13-9 (P)
1985—Rams, 17-6 (P)
1986—Eagles, 34-20 (P)
1988—Eagles, 30-24 (P)
1989—***Rams, 21-7 (P)
1990—Eagles, 27-21 (LA)
1995—Eagles, 20-9 (P)
1998—Eagles, 17-14 (P)
1999—Eagles, 38-31 (P)
2001—Eagles, 20-17 (P) OT
    ****Rams, 29-24 (StL)
2002—Eagles, 10-3 (P)
2004—Rams, 20-7 (StL)
2005—Eagles, 17-16 (StL)
2008—Eagles, 38-3 (P)
2011—Eagles, 31-13 (StL)
(RS Pts.—Rams 706, Eagles 691)
(PS Pts.—Rams 50, Eagles 45)
*Franchise in Los Angeles prior to 1995
and in Cleveland prior to 1946
**NFL Championship
***NFC First-Round Playoff
****NFC Championship
PHILADELPHIA vs. SAN DIEGO
RS: Chargers lead series, 6-4
1974—Eagles, 13-7 (SD)
1980—Chargers, 22-21 (SD)
1985—Chargers, 20-14 (SD)
1986—Eagles, 23-7 (P)
1989—Chargers, 20-17 (SD)
1995—Chargers, 27-21 (P)
1998—Chargers, 13-10 (SD)
2001—Eagles, 24-14 (P)
2005—Eagles, 20-17 (P)
2009—Chargers, 31-23 (SD)
(RS Pts.—Eagles 186, Chargers 178)
PHILADELPHIA vs. SAN FRANCISCO
RS: 49ers lead series, 17-12-1
PS: 49ers lead series, 1-0
1951—Eagles, 21-14 (P)
1953—49ers, 31-21 (SF)
1956—Tie, 10-10 (P)
1958—49ers, 30-24 (P)
1959—49ers, 24-14 (P)
1964—49ers, 28-24 (P)
1966—Eagles, 35-34 (SF)
1967—49ers, 28-27 (P)
1969—49ers, 14-13 (P)
1971—49ers, 31-3 (P)
1973—49ers, 38-28 (SF)
1975—Eagles, 27-17 (P)
1983—49ers, 22-17 (SF)
1984—49ers, 21-9 (P)
1985—49ers, 24-13 (SF)
1989—49ers, 38-28 (P)
1991—49ers, 23-7 (P)
1992—49ers, 20-14 (SF)
1993—Eagles, 37-34 (SF) OT
1994—Eagles, 40-8 (SF)
1996—*49ers, 14-0 (SF)
1997—49ers, 24-12 (P)

2001—49ers, 13-3 (SF)
2002—Eagles, 38-17 (SF)
2003—49ers, 31-28 (P) OT
2005—Eagles, 42-3 (P)
2006—Eagles, 38-24 (SF)
2008—Eagles, 40-26 (SF)
2009—Eagles, 27-13 (P)
2010—Eagles, 27-24 (SF)
2011—49ers, 24-23 (P)
(RS Pts.—Eagles 695, 49ers 683)
(PS Pts.—49ers 14, Eagles 0)
*NFC First-Round Playoff
PHILADELPHIA vs. SEATTLE
RS: Eagles lead series, 7-6
1976—Eagles, 27-10 (P)
1980—Eagles, 27-20 (S)
1986—Seahawks, 24-20 (S)
1989—Eagles, 31-7 (P)
1992—Eagles, 20-17 (S) OT
1995—Seahawks, 26-14 (S)
1998—Seahawks, 38-0 (P)
2001—Eagles, 27-3 (S)
2002—Eagles, 27-20 (S)
2005—Seahawks, 42-0 (P)
2007—Seahawks, 28-24 (P)
2008—Eagles, 26-7 (S)
2011—Seahawks, 31-14 (S)
(RS Pts.—Seahawks 273, Eagles 257)
PHILADELPHIA vs. TAMPA BAY
RS: Eagles lead series, 7-5
PS: Series tied, 2-2
1977—Eagles, 13-3 (P)
1979—*Buccaneers, 24-17 (TB)
1981—Eagles, 20-10 (P)
1988—Eagles, 41-14 (TB)
1991—Buccaneers, 14-13 (TB)
1995—Buccaneers, 21-6 (P)
1999—Buccaneers, 19-5 (P)
2000—**Eagles, 21-3 (P)
2001—Eagles, 17-13 (TB)
      **Eagles, 31-9 (P)
2002—Eagles, 20-10 (P)
      ***Buccaneers, 27-10 (P)
2003—Buccaneers, 17-0 (P)
2006—Buccaneers, 23-21 (TB)
2009—Eagles, 33-14 (P)
2012—Eagles, 23-21 (TB)
(RS Pts.—Eagles 212, Buccaneers 179)
(PS Pts.—Eagles 79, Buccaneers 63)
*NFC Divisional Playoff
**NFC First-Round Playoff
***NFC Championship
PHILADELPHIA vs. *TENNESSEE
RS: Eagles lead series, 6-4
1972—Eagles, 18-17 (H)
1979—Eagles, 26-20 (H)
1982—Eagles, 35-14 (P)
1988—Eagles, 32-23 (P)
1991—Eagles, 13-6 (H)
1994—Eagles, 21-6 (P)
2000—Titans, 15-13 (P)
2002—Titans, 27-24 (T)
2006—Titans, 31-13 (P)
2010—Titans, 37-19 (T)
(RS Pts.—Eagles 214, Titans 196)
*Franchise in Houston prior to 1997;
known as Oilers prior to 1999
PHILADELPHIA vs. *WASHINGTON
RS: Redskins lead series, 80-70-5
PS: Redskins lead series, 1-0
1934—Redskins, 6-0 (B)
      Redskins, 14-7 (P)
1935—Eagles, 7-6 (B)

1936—Redskins, 26-3 (P)
      Redskins, 17-7 (B)
1937—Eagles, 14-0 (W)
      Redskins, 10-7 (P)
1938—Redskins, 26-23 (P)
      Redskins, 20-14 (W)
1939—Redskins, 7-0 (P)
      Redskins, 7-6 (W)
1940—Redskins, 34-17 (P)
      Redskins, 13-6 (W)
1941—Redskins, 21-17 (P)
      Redskins, 20-14 (W)
1942—Redskins, 14-10 (P)
      Redskins, 30-27 (W)
1944—Tie, 31-31 (P)
      Eagles, 37-7 (W)
1945—Redskins, 24-14 (W)
      Eagles, 16-0 (P)
1946—Eagles, 28-24 (W)
      Redskins, 27-10 (P)
1947—Eagles, 45-42 (P)
      Eagles, 38-14 (W)
1948—Eagles, 45-0 (W)
      Eagles, 42-21 (P)
1949—Eagles, 49-14 (P)
      Eagles, 44-21 (W)
1950—Eagles, 35-3 (P)
      Eagles, 33-0 (W)
1951—Redskins, 27-23 (P)
      Eagles, 35-21 (W)
1952—Eagles, 38-20 (P)
      Redskins, 27-21 (W)
1953—Tie, 21-21 (P)
      Redskins, 10-0 (W)
1954—Eagles, 49-21 (W)
      Eagles, 41-33 (P)
1955—Redskins, 31-30 (P)
      Redskins, 34-21 (W)
1956—Eagles, 13-9 (P)
      Redskins, 19-17 (W)
1957—Eagles, 21-12 (P)
      Redskins, 42-7 (W)
1958—Redskins, 24-14 (P)
      Redskins, 20-0 (W)
1959—Eagles, 30-23 (P)
      Eagles, 34-14 (W)
1960—Eagles, 19-13 (P)
      Eagles, 38-28 (W)
1961—Eagles, 14-7 (P)
      Eagles, 27-24 (W)
1962—Redskins, 27-21 (P)
      Eagles, 37-14 (W)
1963—Eagles, 37-24 (W)
      Redskins, 13-10 (P)
1964—Redskins, 35-20 (W)
      Redskins, 21-10 (P)
1965—Redskins, 23-21 (W)
      Eagles, 21-14 (P)
1966—Redskins, 27-13 (P)
      Eagles, 37-28 (W)
1967—Eagles, 35-24 (P)
      Tie, 35-35 (W)
1968—Redskins, 17-14 (W)
      Redskins, 16-10 (P)
1969—Tie, 28-28 (W)
      Redskins, 34-29 (P)
1970—Redskins, 33-21 (P)
      Redskins, 24-6 (W)
1971—Tie, 7-7 (W)
      Redskins, 20-13 (P)
1972—Redskins, 14-0 (W)
      Redskins, 23-7 (P)

1973—Redskins, 28-7 (P)
      Redskins, 38-20 (W)
1974—Redskins, 27-20 (P)
      Redskins, 26-7 (W)
1975—Eagles, 26-10 (P)
      Eagles, 26-3 (W)
1976—Redskins, 20-17 (P) OT
      Redskins, 24-0 (W)
1977—Redskins, 23-17 (W)
      Redskins, 17-14 (P)
1978—Redskins, 35-30 (P)
      Eagles, 17-10 (P)
1979—Eagles, 28-17 (P)
      Redskins, 17-7 (W)
1980—Eagles, 24-14 (P)
      Eagles, 24-0 (W)
1981—Eagles, 36-13 (P)
      Redskins, 15-13 (W)
1982—Redskins, 37-34 (P) OT
      Redskins, 13-9 (W)
1983—Redskins, 23-13 (P)
      Redskins, 28-24 (W)
1984—Redskins, 20-0 (W)
      Eagles, 16-10 (P)
1985—Eagles, 19-6 (W)
      Redskins, 17-12 (P)
1986—Redskins, 41-14 (W)
      Redskins, 21-14 (P)
1987—Redskins, 34-24 (W)
      Eagles, 31-27 (P)
1988—Redskins, 17-10 (W)
      Redskins, 20-19 (P)
1989—Eagles, 42-37 (W)
      Redskins, 10-3 (P)
1990—Redskins, 13-7 (W)
      Eagles, 28-14 (P)
      **Redskins, 20-6 (P)
1991—Redskins, 23-0 (W)
      Eagles, 24-22 (P)
1992—Redskins, 16-12 (W)
      Eagles, 17-13 (P)
1993—Eagles, 34-31 (W)
      Eagles, 17-14 (P)
1994—Eagles, 21-17 (P)
      Eagles, 31-29 (W)
1995—Eagles, 37-34 (P) OT
      Eagles, 14-7 (W)
1996—Eagles, 17-14 (W)
      Redskins, 26-21 (P)
1997—Eagles, 24-10 (P)
      Redskins, 35-32 (W)
1998—Eagles, 17-12 (P)
      Redskins, 28-3 (W)
1999—Eagles, 35-28 (P)
      Redskins, 20-17 (W) OT
2000—Redskins, 17-14 (P)
      Eagles, 23-20 (W)
2001—Redskins, 13-3 (P)
      Eagles, 20-6 (W)
2002—Eagles, 37-7 (W)
      Eagles, 34-21 (P)
2003—Eagles, 27-25 (P)
      Eagles, 31-7 (W)
2004—Eagles, 28-6 (P)
      Eagles, 17-14 (W)
2005—Redskins, 17-10 (W)
      Redskins, 31-20 (P)
2006—Eagles, 27-3 (P)
      Eagles, 21-19 (W)
2007—Redskins, 20-12 (P)
      Eagles, 33-25 (W)
2008—Redskins, 23-17 (P)
      Redskins, 10-3 (W)

2009—Eagles, 27-17 (W)
    Eagles, 27-24 (P)
2010—Redskins, 17-12 (P)
    Eagles, 59-28 (W)
2011—Eagles, 20-13 (W)
    Eagles, 34-10 (P)
2012—Redskins, 31-6 (W)
    Redskins, 27-20 (P)
(RS Pts.—Eagles 3,198, Redskins 3,035)
(PS Pts.—Redskins 20, Eagles 6)
*Franchise in Boston prior to 1937
**NFC First-Round Playoff

PITTSBURGH vs. ARIZONA
RS: Steelers lead series, 32-23-3
PS: Steelers lead series, 1-0;
See Arizona vs. Pittsburgh
PITTSBURGH vs. ATLANTA
RS: Steelers lead series, 12-2-1;
See Atlanta vs. Pittsburgh
PITTSBURGH vs. BALTIMORE
RS: Steelers lead series, 19-15
PS: Steelers lead series, 3-0;
See Baltimore vs. Pittsburgh
PITTSBURGH vs. BUFFALO
RS: Steelers lead series, 12-8
PS: Steelers lead series, 2-1;
See Buffalo vs. Pittsburgh
PITTSBURGH vs. CAROLINA
RS: Steelers lead series, 4-1;
See Carolina vs. Pittsburgh
PITTSBURGH vs. CHICAGO
RS: Bears lead series, 17-7-1;
See Chicago vs. Pittsburgh
PITTSBURGH vs. CINCINNATI
RS: Steelers lead series, 52-33
PS: Steelers lead series, 1-0;
See Cincinnati vs. Pittsburgh
PITTSBURGH vs. CLEVELAND
RS: Steelers lead series, 63-57
PS: Steelers lead series, 2-0;
See Cleveland vs. Pittsburgh
PITTSBURGH vs. DALLAS
RS: Cowboys lead series, 15-13
PS: Steelers lead series, 2-1;
See Dallas vs. Pittsburgh
PITTSBURGH vs. DENVER
RS: Broncos lead series, 14-7-1
PS: Broncos lead series, 4-3;
See Denver vs. Pittsburgh
PITTSBURGH vs. DETROIT
RS: Steelers lead series, 15-14-1;
See Detroit vs. Pittsburgh
PITTSBURGH vs. GREEN BAY
RS: Packers lead series, 18-14
PS: Packers lead series, 1-0;
See Green Bay vs. Pittsburgh
PITTSBURGH vs. HOUSTON
RS: Series tied, 2-2;
See Houston vs. Pittsburgh
PITTSBURGH vs. INDIANAPOLIS
RS: Steelers lead series, 14-6
PS: Steelers lead series, 5-0;
See Indianapolis vs. Pittsburgh
PITTSBURGH vs. JACKSONVILLE
RS: Jaguars lead series, 11-10
PS: Jaguars lead series, 1-0;
See Jacksonville vs. Pittsburgh
PITTSBURGH vs. KANSAS CITY
RS: Steelers lead series, 19-9
PS: Chiefs lead series, 1-0;
See Kansas City vs. Pittsburgh

PITTSBURGH vs. MIAMI
RS: Steelers lead series, 12-9
PS: Dolphins lead series, 2-1;
See Miami vs. Pittsburgh
PITTSBURGH vs. MINNESOTA
RS: Vikings lead series, 8-7
PS: Steelers lead series, 1-0;
See Minnesota vs. Pittsburgh
PITTSBURGH vs. NEW ENGLAND
RS: Steelers lead series, 14-8
PS: Steelers lead series, 3-1;
See New England vs. Pittsburgh
PITTSBURGH vs. NEW ORLEANS
RS: Series tied, 7-7;
See New Orleans vs. Pittsburgh
PITTSBURGH vs. N.Y. GIANTS
RS: Giants lead series, 44-29-3;
See N.Y. Giants vs. Pittsburgh
PITTSBURGH vs. N.Y. JETS
RS: Steelers lead series, 16-4
PS: Steelers lead series, 2-0;
See N.Y. Jets vs. Pittsburgh
PITTSBURGH vs. OAKLAND
RS: Raiders lead series, 11-9
PS: Series tied, 3-3;
See Oakland vs. Pittsburgh
PITTSBURGH vs. PHILADELPHIA
RS: Eagles lead series, 46-28-3
PS: Eagles lead series, 1-0;
See Philadelphia vs. Pittsburgh
*PITTSBURGH vs. **ST. LOUIS
RS: Rams lead series, 15-7-2
PS: Steelers lead series, 1-0
1938—Rams, 13-7 (New Orleans)
1939—Tie, 14-14 (C)
1941—Rams, 17-14 (Akron)
1947—Rams, 48-7 (P)
1948—Rams, 31-14 (LA)
1949—Tie, 7-7 (P)
1952—Rams, 28-14 (LA)
1955—Rams, 27-26 (LA)
1956—Steelers, 30-13 (P)
1961—Rams, 24-14 (LA)
1964—Rams, 26-14 (P)
1968—Rams, 45-10 (LA)
1971—Rams, 23-14 (P)
1975—Rams, 10-3 (LA)
1978—Rams, 10-7 (LA)
1979—***Steelers, 31-19 (Pasadena)
1981—Steelers, 24-0 (P)
1984—Steelers, 24-14 (P)
1987—Rams, 31-21 (LA)
1990—Steelers, 41-10 (P)
1993—Rams, 27-0 (LA)
1996—Steelers, 42-6 (P)
2003—Rams, 33-21 (P)
2007—Steelers, 41-24 (StL)
2011—Steelers, 27-0 (P)
(RS Pts.—Rams 481, Steelers 436)
(PS Pts.—Steelers 31, Rams 19)
*Steelers known as Pirates prior to 1940
**Franchise in Los Angeles prior to 1995
and in Cleveland prior to 1946
***Super Bowl XIV
PITTSBURGH vs. SAN DIEGO
RS: Steelers lead series, 21-7
PS: Chargers lead series, 2-1
1971—Steelers, 21-17 (P)
1972—Steelers, 24-2 (SD)
1973—Steelers, 38-21 (P)
1975—Steelers, 37-0 (SD)
1976—Steelers, 23-0 (P)
1977—Steelers, 10-9 (SD)

1979—Chargers, 35-7 (SD)
1980—Chargers, 26-17 (SD)
1982—*Chargers, 31-28 (P)
1983—Steelers, 26-3 (P)
1984—Steelers, 52-24 (P)
1985—Chargers, 54-44 (SD)
1987—Steelers, 20-16 (SD)
1988—Chargers, 20-14 (SD)
1989—Steelers, 20-17 (P)
1990—Steelers, 36-14 (P)
1991—Steelers, 26-20 (P)
1992—Steelers, 23-6 (SD)
1993—Steelers,.16-3 (P)
1994—Chargers, 37-34 (SD)
    **Chargers, 17-13 (P)
1995—Steelers, 31-16 (P)
1996—Steelers, 16-3 (P)
2000—Steelers, 34-21 (SD)
2003—Steelers, 40-24 (P)
2005—Steelers, 24-22 (SD)
2006—Chargers, 23-13 (SD)
2008—Steelers, 11-10 (P)
    ***Steelers, 35-24 (P)
2009—Steelers, 38-28 (P)
2012—Chargers, 34-24 (P)
(RS Pts.—Steelers 719, Chargers 505)
(PS Pts.—Steelers 76, Chargers 72)
*AFC First-Round Playoff
**AFC Championship
***AFC Divisional Playoff
PITTSBURGH vs. SAN FRANCISCO
RS: 49ers lead series, 11-9
1951—49ers, 28-24 (P)
1952—Steelers, 24-7 (SF)
1954—49ers, 31-3 (SF)
1958—49ers, 23-20 (SF)
1961—Steelers, 20-10 (P)
1965—49ers, 27-17 (SF)
1968—49ers, 45-28 (P)
1973—Steelers, 37-14 (SF)
1977—Steelers, 27-0 (P)
1978—Steelers, 24-7 (SF)
1981—49ers, 17-14 (P)
1984—Steelers, 20-17 (SF)
1987—Steelers, 30-17 (P)
1990—49ers, 27-7 (SF)
1993—49ers, 24-13 (P)
1996—49ers, 25-15 (P)
1999—Steelers, 27-6 (SF)
2003—49ers, 30-14 (SF)
2007—Steelers, 37-16 (P)
2011—49ers, 20-3 (SF)
(RS Pts.—Steelers 404, 49ers 391)
PITTSBURGH vs. SEATTLE
RS: Series tied, 8-8
PS: Steelers lead series, 1-0
1977—Steelers, 30-20 (P)
1978—Steelers, 21-10 (P)
1981—Seahawks, 24-21 (S)
1982—Seahawks, 16-0 (S)
1983—Steelers, 27-21 (S)
1986—Seahawks, 30-0 (S)
1987—Steelers, 13-9 (P)
1991—Seahawks, 27-7 (P)
1992—Steelers, 20-14 (P)
1993—Seahawks, 16-6 (S)
1994—Seahawks, 30-13 (S)
1998—Steelers, 13-10 (P)
1999—Seahawks, 29-10 (P)
2003—Seahawks, 23-16 (S)
2005—*Steelers, 21-10 (Detroit)
2007—Steelers, 21-0 (P)
2011—Steelers, 24-0 (P)

(RS Pts.—Seahawks 279, Steelers 242)
(PS Pts.—Steelers 21, Seahawks 10)
*Super Bowl XL
PITTSBURGH vs. TAMPA BAY
RS: Steelers lead series, 8-1
1976—Steelers, 42-0 (P)
1980—Steelers, 24-21 (TB)
1983—Steelers, 17-12 (P)
1989—Steelers, 31-22 (TB)
1998—Buccaneers, 16-3 (TB)
2001—Steelers, 17-10 (TB)
2002—Steelers, 17-7 (TB)
2006—Steelers, 20-3 (P)
2010—Steelers, 38-13 (TB)
(RS Pts.—Steelers 209, Buccaneers 104)
PITTSBURGH vs. *TENNESSEE
RS: Steelers lead series, 41-30
PS: Steelers lead series, 3-1
1970—Oilers, 19-7 (P)
　　　Steelers, 7-3 (H)
1971—Steelers, 23-16 (P)
　　　Oilers, 29-3 (H)
1972—Steelers, 24-7 (P)
　　　Steelers, 9-3 (H)
1973—Steelers, 36-7 (H)
　　　Steelers, 33-7 (P)
1974—Steelers, 13-7 (H)
　　　Oilers, 13-10 (P)
1975—Steelers, 24-17 (P)
　　　Steelers, 32-9 (H)
1976—Steelers, 32-16 (P)
　　　Steelers, 21-0 (H)
1977—Oilers, 27-10 (H)
　　　Steelers, 27-10 (P)
1978—Oilers, 24-17 (P)
　　　Steelers, 13-3 (H)
　　　**Steelers, 34-5 (P)
1979—Steelers, 38-7 (P)
　　　Oilers, 20-17 (H)
　　　**Steelers, 27-13 (P)
1980—Steelers, 31-17 (P)
　　　Oilers, 6-0 (H)
1981—Steelers, 26-13 (P)
　　　Oilers, 21-20 (H)
1982—Steelers, 24-10 (H)
1983—Steelers, 40-28 (H)
　　　Steelers, 17-10 (P)
1984—Steelers, 35-7 (P)
　　　Oilers, 23-20 (H) OT
1985—Steelers, 20-0 (P)
　　　Steelers, 30-7 (H)
1986—Steelers, 22-16 (H) OT
　　　Steelers, 21-10 (P)
1987—Oilers, 23-3 (P)
　　　Oilers, 24-16 (H)
1988—Oilers, 34-14 (P)
　　　Steelers, 37-34 (H)
1989—Oilers, 27-0 (H)
　　　Oilers, 23-16 (P)
　　　***Steelers, 26-23 (H) OT
1990—Steelers, 20-9 (P)
　　　Oilers, 34-14 (H)
1991—Steelers, 26-14 (P)
　　　Oilers, 31-6 (H)
1992—Steelers, 29-24 (H)
　　　Steelers, 21-20 (P)
1993—Oilers, 23-3 (H)
　　　Oilers, 26-17 (H)
1994—Steelers, 30-14 (P)
　　　Steelers, 12-9 (H) OT
1995—Steelers, 34-17 (H)
　　　Steelers, 21-7 (H)

1996—Steelers, 30-16 (P)
　　　Oilers, 23-13 (H)
1997—Steelers, 37-24 (P)
　　　Oilers, 16-6 (T)
1998—Oilers, 41-31 (P)
　　　Oilers, 23-14 (T)
1999—Titans, 16-10 (T)
　　　Titans, 47-36 (P)
2000—Titans, 23-20 (P)
　　　Titans, 9-7 (T)
2001—Steelers, 34-7 (P)
　　　Steelers, 34-24 (T)
2002—Titans, 31-23 (T)
　　　****Titans, 34-31 (T) OT
2003—Titans, 30-13 (P)
2005—Steelers, 34-7 (P)
2008—Titans, 31-14 (T)
2009—Steelers, 13-10 (P) OT
2010—Steelers, 19-11 (T)
2011—Steelers, 38-17 (P)
2012—Titans, 26-23 (T)
(RS Pts.—Steelers 1,470, Titans 1,237)
(PS Pts.—Steelers 118, Titans 75)
*Franchise in Houston prior to 1997;
known as Oilers prior to 1999
**AFC Championship
***AFC First-Round Playoff
****AFC Divisional Playoff
PITTSBURGH vs. **WASHINGTON
RS: Redskins lead series, 42-32-3
1933—Redskins, 21-6 (P)
　　　Pirates, 16-14 (B)
1934—Redskins, 7-0 (P)
　　　Redskins, 39-0 (B)
1935—Pirates, 6-0 (P)
　　　Redskins, 13-3 (B)
1936—Pirates, 10-0 (P)
　　　Redskins, 30-0 (B)
1937—Redskins, 34-20 (W)
　　　Pirates, 21-13 (P)
1938—Redskins, 7-0 (P)
　　　Redskins, 15-0 (W)
1939—Redskins, 44-14 (W)
　　　Redskins, 21-14 (P)
1940—Redskins, 40-10 (P)
　　　Redskins, 37-10 (W)
1941—Redskins, 24-20 (P)
　　　Redskins, 23-3 (W)
1942—Redskins, 28-14 (W)
　　　Redskins, 14-0 (P)
1945—Redskins, 14-0 (P)
　　　Redskins, 24-0 (W)
1946—Tie, 14-14 (W)
　　　Steelers, 14-7 (P)
1947—Redskins, 27-26 (W)
　　　Steelers, 21-14 (P)
1948—Redskins, 17-14 (W)
　　　Steelers, 10-7 (P)
1949—Redskins, 27-14 (P)
　　　Redskins, 27-14 (W)
1950—Steelers, 26-7 (W)
　　　Redskins, 24-7 (P)
1951—Redskins, 22-7 (P)
　　　Steelers, 20-10 (W)
1952—Redskins, 28-24 (P)
　　　Steelers, 24-23 (W)
1953—Redskins, 17-9 (P)
　　　Steelers, 14-13 (W)
1954—Steelers, 37-7 (P)
　　　Redskins, 17-14 (W)
1955—Redskins, 23-14 (P)
　　　Redskins, 28-17 (W)

1956—Steelers, 30-13 (P)
　　　Steelers, 23-0 (W)
1957—Steelers, 28-7 (P)
　　　Redskins, 10-3 (W)
1958—Steelers, 24-16 (P)
　　　Tie, 14-14 (W)
1959—Redskins, 23-17 (P)
　　　Steelers, 27-6 (W)
1960—Tie, 27-27 (W)
　　　Steelers, 22-10 (P)
1961—Steelers, 20-0 (P)
　　　Steelers, 30-14 (W)
1962—Steelers, 23-21 (P)
　　　Steelers, 27-24 (W)
1963—Steelers, 38-27 (P)
　　　Steelers, 34-28 (W)
1964—Redskins, 30-0 (P)
　　　Steelers, 14-7 (W)
1965—Redskins, 31-3 (P)
　　　Redskins, 35-14 (W)
1966—Redskins, 33-27 (P)
　　　Redskins, 24-10 (W)
1967—Redskins, 15-10 (P)
1968—Redskins, 16-13 (W)
1969—Redskins, 14-7 (P)
1973—Steelers, 21-16 (P)
1979—Steelers, 38-7 (P)
1985—Redskins, 30-23 (P)
1988—Redskins, 30-29 (W)
1991—Redskins, 41-14 (P)
1997—Steelers, 14-13 (P)
2000—Steelers, 24-3 (P)
2004—Steelers, 16-7 (P)
2008—Steelers, 23-6 (W)
2012—Steelers, 27-12 (P)
(RS Pts.—Redskins 1,431, Steelers 1,221)
*Steelers known as Pirates prior to 1940
**Franchise in Boston prior to 1937

ST. LOUIS vs. ARIZONA
RS: Series tied, 33-33-2
PS: Rams lead series, 1-0;
See Arizona vs. St. Louis
ST. LOUIS vs. ATLANTA
RS: Rams lead series, 47-26-2
PS: Falcons lead series, 1-0;
See Atlanta vs. St. Louis
ST. LOUIS vs. BALTIMORE
RS: Ravens lead series, 3-2;
See Baltimore vs. St. Louis
ST. LOUIS vs. BUFFALO
RS: Bills lead series, 6-5;
See Buffalo vs. St. Louis
ST. LOUIS vs. CAROLINA
RS: Panthers lead series, 10-8
PS: Panthers lead series, 1-0;
See Carolina vs. St. Louis
ST. LOUIS vs. CHICAGO
RS: Bears lead series, 51-34-3
PS: Series tied, 1-1;
See Chicago vs. St. Louis
ST. LOUIS vs. CINCINNATI
RS: Bengals lead series, 7-5;
See Cincinnati vs. St. Louis
ST. LOUIS vs. CLEVELAND
RS: Rams lead series, 10-9
PS: Browns lead series, 2-1;
See Cleveland vs. St. Louis
ST. LOUIS vs. DALLAS
RS: Series tied, 11-11
PS: Series tied, 4-4;
See Dallas vs. St. Louis

ST. LOUIS vs. DENVER
RS: Rams lead series, 7-5;
See Denver vs. St. Louis
ST. LOUIS vs. DETROIT
RS: Rams lead series, 42-39-1
PS: Lions lead series, 1-0;
See Detroit vs. St. Louis
ST. LOUIS vs. GREEN BAY
RS: Rams lead series, 45-44-2
PS: Series tied, 1-1;
See Green Bay vs. St. Louis
ST. LOUIS vs. HOUSTON
RS: Series tied, 1-1;
See Houston vs. St. Louis
ST. LOUIS vs. INDIANAPOLIS
RS: Colts lead series, 23-17-2;
See Indianapolis vs. St. Louis
ST. LOUIS vs. JACKSONVILLE
RS: Rams lead series, 2-1;
See Jacksonville vs. St. Louis
ST. LOUIS vs. KANSAS CITY
RS: Chiefs lead series; 6-4;
See Kansas City vs. St. Louis
ST. LOUIS vs. MIAMI
RS: Dolphins lead series, 10-2;
See Miami vs. St. Louis
ST. LOUIS vs. MINNESOTA
RS: Vikings lead series, 19-14-2
PS: Vikings lead series, 5-2;
See Minnesota vs. St. Louis
ST. LOUIS vs. NEW ENGLAND
RS: Patriots lead series, 6-5
PS: Patriots lead series, 1-0;
See New England vs. St. Louis
ST. LOUIS vs. NEW ORLEANS
RS: Rams lead series, 39-31
PS: Saints lead series, 1-0;
See New Orleans vs. St. Louis
ST. LOUIS vs. N.Y. GIANTS
RS: Rams lead series, 25-14
PS: Series tied, 1-1;
See N.Y. Giants vs. St. Louis
ST. LOUIS vs. N.Y. JETS
RS: Rams lead series, 9-4;
See N.Y. Jets vs. St. Louis
ST. LOUIS vs. OAKLAND
RS: Raiders lead series, 8-4;
See Oakland vs. St. Louis
ST. LOUIS vs. PHILADELPHIA
RS: Eagles lead series, 18-17-1
PS: Rams lead series, 2-1;
See Philadelphia vs. St. Louis
ST. LOUIS vs. PITTSBURGH
RS: Rams lead series, 15-7-2
PS: Steelers lead series, 1-0;
See Pittsburgh vs. St. Louis
***ST. LOUIS vs. SAN DIEGO**
RS: Rams lead series, 6-4
1970—Rams, 37-10 (LA)
1975—Rams, 13-10 (SD) OT
1979—Chargers, 40-16 (LA)
1988—Chargers, 38-24 (LA)
1991—Rams, 30-24 (LA)
1994—Chargers, 31-17 (SD)
2000—Rams, 57-31 (StL)
2002—Rams, 28-24 (StL)
2006—Chargers, 38-24 (SD)
2010—Rams, 20-17 (StL)
(RS Pts.—Rams 266, Chargers 263)
*Franchise in Los Angeles prior to 1995
***ST. LOUIS vs. SAN FRANCISCO**
RS: Rams lead series, 62-61-3
PS: 49ers lead series, 1-0

1950—Rams, 35-14 (SF)
    Rams, 28-21 (LA)
1951—49ers, 44-17 (SF)
    Rams, 23-16 (LA)
1952—Rams, 35-9 (LA)
    Rams, 34-21 (SF)
1953—49ers, 31-30 (SF)
    49ers, 31-27 (LA)
1954—Tie, 24-24 (LA)
    Rams, 42-34 (SF)
1955—Rams, 23-14 (SF)
    Rams, 27-14 (LA)
1956—49ers, 33-30 (SF)
    Rams, 30-6 (LA)
1957—49ers, 23-20 (SF)
    Rams, 37-24 (LA)
1958—Rams, 33-3 (SF)
    Rams, 56-7 (LA)
1959—49ers, 34-0 (SF)
    49ers, 24-16 (LA)
1960—49ers, 13-9 (SF)
    49ers, 23-7 (LA)
1961—49ers, 35-0 (SF)
    Rams, 17-7 (LA)
1962—Rams, 28-14 (SF)
    49ers, 24-17 (LA)
1963—Rams, 28-21 (LA)
    Rams, 21-17 (SF)
1964—Rams, 42-14 (LA)
    49ers, 28-7 (SF)
1965—49ers, 45-21 (LA)
    49ers, 30-27 (SF)
1966—Rams, 34-3 (LA)
    49ers, 21-13 (SF)
1967—49ers, 27-24 (LA)
    Rams, 17-7 (SF)
1968—Rams, 24-10 (LA)
    Tie, 20-20 (SF)
1969—Rams, 27-21 (SF)
    Rams, 41-30 (LA)
1970—49ers, 20-6 (LA)
    Rams, 30-13 (SF)
1971—Rams, 20-13 (SF)
    Rams, 17-6 (LA)
1972—Rams, 31-7 (LA)
    Rams, 26-16 (SF)
1973—Rams, 40-20 (SF)
    Rams, 31-13 (LA)
1974—Rams, 37-14 (LA)
    Rams, 15-13 (SF)
1975—Rams, 23-14 (LA)
    49ers, 24-23 (LA)
1976—49ers, 16-0 (LA)
    Rams, 23-3 (SF)
1977—Rams, 34-14 (LA)
    Rams, 23-10 (SF)
1978—Rams, 27-10 (LA)
    Rams, 31-28 (SF)
1979—Rams, 27-24 (LA)
    Rams, 26-20 (SF)
1980—Rams, 48-26 (LA)
    Rams, 31-17 (SF)
1981—49ers, 20-17 (SF)
    49ers, 33-31 (LA)
1982—49ers, 30-24 (LA)
    Rams, 21-20 (SF)
1983—Rams, 10-7 (SF)
    49ers, 45-35 (LA)
1984—49ers, 33-0 (LA)
    49ers, 19-16 (SF)
1985—49ers, 28-14 (LA)
    Rams, 27-20 (SF)

1986—Rams, 16-13 (LA)
    49ers, 24-14 (SF)
1987—49ers, 31-10 (LA)
    49ers, 48-0 (SF)
1988—49ers, 24-21 (LA)
    Rams, 38-16 (SF)
1989—Rams, 13-12 (SF)
    49ers, 30-27 (LA)
    **49ers, 30-3 (SF)
1990—Rams, 28-17 (SF)
    49ers, 26-10 (LA)
1991—49ers, 27-10 (SF)
    49ers, 33-10 (LA)
1992—49ers, 27-24 (SF)
    49ers, 27-10 (LA)
1993—49ers, 40-17 (SF)
    49ers, 35-10 (LA)
1994—49ers, 34-19 (LA)
    49ers, 31-27 (SF)
1995—49ers, 44-10 (StL)
    49ers, 41-13 (SF)
1996—49ers, 34-0 (SF)
    49ers, 28-11 (StL)
1997—49ers, 15-12 (StL)
    49ers, 30-10 (SF)
1998—49ers, 28-10 (StL)
    49ers, 38-19 (SF)
1999—Rams, 42-20 (StL)
    Rams, 23-7 (SF)
2000—Rams, 41-24 (StL)
    Rams, 34-24 (SF)
2001—Rams, 30-26 (SF)
    Rams, 27-14 (StL)
2002—Rams, 37-13 (SF)
    Rams, 31-20 (StL)
2003—Rams, 27-24 (StL) OT
    49ers, 30-10 (SF)
2004—Rams, 24-14 (StL)
    Rams, 16-6 (StL)
2005—49ers, 28-25 (SF)
    49ers, 24-20 (StL)
2006—49ers, 20-13 (SF)
    Rams, 20-17 (StL)
2007—49ers, 17-16 (StL)
    Rams, 13-9 (SF)
2008—49ers, 35-16 (StL)
    49ers, 17-16 (SF)
2009—49ers, 35-0 (SF)
    49ers, 28-6 (StL)
2010—49ers, 23-20 (SF) OT
    Rams, 25-17 (StL)
2011—49ers, 26-0 (SF)
    49ers, 34-27 (StL)
2012—Tie, 24-24 (SF) OT
    Rams, 16-13 (StL) OT
(RS Pts.—49ers 2,799, Rams 2,719)
(PS Pts.—49ers 30, Rams 3)
*Franchise in Los Angeles prior to 1995
**NFC Championship
***ST. LOUIS vs. SEATTLE**
RS: Seahawks lead series, 18-11
PS: Rams lead series, 1-0
1976—Rams, 45-6 (LA)
1979—Rams, 24-0 (Sea)
1985—Rams, 35-24 (Sea)
1988—Rams, 31-10 (LA)
1991—Seahawks, 23-9 (Sea)
1997—Seahawks, 17-9 (StL)
2000—Rams, 37-34 (Sea)
2002—Rams, 37-20 (Sea)
    Seahawks, 30-10 (Sea)
2003—Seahawks, 24-23 (Sea)
    Rams, 27-22 (StL)

2004—Rams, 33-27 (Sea) OT
    Rams, 23-12 (StL)
    **Rams, 27-20 (Sea)
2005—Seahawks, 37-31 (StL)
    Seahawks, 31-16 (Sea)
2006—Seahawks, 30-28 (StL)
    Seahawks, 24-22 (Sea)
2007—Seahawks, 33-6 (Sea)
    Seahawks, 24-19 (StL)
2008—Seahawks, 37-13 (Sea)
    Seahawks, 23-20 (StL)
2009—Seahawks, 28-0 (Sea)
    Seahawks, 27-17 (StL)
2010—Rams, 20-3 (StL)
    Seahawks, 16-6 (Sea)
2011—Seahawks, 24-7 (StL)
    Seahawks, 30-13 (Sea)
2012—Rams, 19-13 (StL)
    Seahawks, 20-13 (Sea)
(RS Pts.—Seahawks 649, Rams 593)
(PS Pts.—Rams 27, Seahawks 20)
*Franchise in Los Angeles prior to 1995
**NFC First-Round Playoff
*ST. LOUIS vs. TAMPA BAY
RS: Rams lead series, 10-8
PS: Rams lead series, 2-0
1977—Rams, 31-0 (LA)
1978—Rams, 26-23 (LA)
1979—Buccaneers, 21-6 (TB)
    **Rams, 9-0 (TB)
1980—Buccaneers, 10-9 (TB)
1984—Rams, 34-33 (TB)
1985—Rams, 31-27 (TB)
1986—Rams, 26-20 (LA) OT
1987—Rams, 35-3 (LA)
1990—Rams, 35-14 (TB)
1992—Rams, 31-27 (TB)
1994—Buccaneers, 24-14 (TB)
1999—**Rams, 11-6 (StL)
2000—Buccaneers, 38-35 (TB)
2001—Buccaneers, 24-17 (StL)
2002—Buccaneers, 26-14 (TB)
2004—Rams, 28-21 (StL)
2007—Buccaneers, 24-3 (TB)
2010—Buccaneers, 18-17 (TB)
2012—Rams, 28-13 (TB)
(RS Pts.—Rams 420, Buccaneers 366)
(PS Pts.—Rams 20, Buccaneers 6)
*Franchise in Los Angeles prior to 1995
**NFC Championship
*ST. LOUIS vs. **TENNESSEE
RS: Rams lead series, 6-4
PS: Rams lead series, 1-0
1973—Rams, 31-26 (H)
1978—Rams, 10-6 (H)
1981—Oilers, 27-20 (LA)
1984—Rams, 27-16 (LA)
1987—Oilers, 20-16 (H)
1990—Rams, 17-13 (LA)
1993—Rams, 28-13 (H)
1999—Titans, 24-21 (T)
    ***Rams, 23-16 (Atlanta)
2005—Rams, 31-27 (StL)
2009—Titans, 47-7 (T)
(RS Pts.—Titans, 219, Rams 208)
(PS Pts.—Rams 23, Titans 16)
*Franchise in Los Angeles prior to 1995
**Franchise in Houston prior to 1997;
known as Oilers prior to 1999
***Super Bowl XXXIV
*ST. LOUIS vs. WASHINGTON
RS: Redskins lead series, 22-10-1
PS: Series tied, 2-2

1937—Redskins, 16-7 (C)
1938—Redskins, 37-13 (W)
1941—Redskins, 17-13 (W)
1942—Redskins, 33-14 (W)
1944—Redskins, 14-10 (W)
1945—**Rams, 15-14 (C)
1948—Rams, 41-13 (W)
1949—Rams, 53-27 (LA)
1951—Redskins, 31-21 (W)
1962—Redskins, 20-14 (W)
1963—Redskins, 37-14 (LA)
1967—Tie, 28-28 (LA)
1969—Rams, 24-13 (W)
1971—Redskins, 38-24 (LA)
1974—Redskins, 23-17 (LA)
    ***Rams, 19-10 (LA)
1977—Redskins, 17-14 (W)
1981—Redskins, 30-7 (LA)
1983—Redskins, 42-20 (LA)
    ***Redskins, 51-7 (W)
1986—****Redskins, 19-7 (W)
1987—Rams, 30-26 (W)
1991—Redskins, 27-6 (LA)
1993—Rams, 10-6 (LA)
1994—Redskins, 24-21 (LA)
1995—Redskins, 35-23 (StL)
1996—Redskins, 17-10 (StL)
1997—Rams, 23-20 (W)
2000—Redskins, 33-20 (StL)
2002—Redskins, 20-17 (W)
2005—Redskins, 24-9 (StL)
2006—Rams, 37-31 (StL) OT
2008—Rams, 19-17 (W)
2009—Redskins, 9-7 (W)
2010—Rams, 30-16 (StL)
2011—Redskins, 17-10 (StL)
2012—Rams, 31-28 (StL)
(RS Pts.—Redskins 786, Rams 637)
(PS Pts.—Redskins 94, Rams 48)
*Franchise in Los Angeles prior to 1995
and in Cleveland prior to 1946
**NFL Championship
***NFC Divisional Playoff
****NFC First-Round Playoff

SAN DIEGO vs. ARIZONA
RS: Chargers lead series, 9-3;
See Arizona vs. San Diego
SAN DIEGO vs. ATLANTA
RS: Falcons lead series, 8-1;
See Atlanta vs. San Diego
SAN DIEGO vs. BALTIMORE
RS: Ravens lead series, 5-4;
See Baltimore vs. San Diego
SAN DIEGO vs. BUFFALO
RS: Chargers lead series, 21-10-2
PS: Bills lead series, 2-1;
See Buffalo vs. San Diego
SAN DIEGO vs. CAROLINA
RS: Panthers lead series, 4-1;
See Carolina vs. San Diego
SAN DIEGO vs. CHICAGO
RS: Bears lead series, 6-5;
See Chicago vs. San Diego
SAN DIEGO vs. CINCINNATI
RS: Chargers lead series, 19-12
PS: Bengals lead series, 1-0;
See Cincinnati vs. San Diego
SAN DIEGO vs. CLEVELAND
RS: Chargers lead series, 14-8-1;
See Cleveland vs. San Diego
SAN DIEGO vs. DALLAS
RS: Cowboys lead series, 6-3;

See Dallas vs. San Diego
SAN DIEGO vs. DENVER
RS: Broncos lead series, 57-48-1;
See Denver vs. San Diego
SAN DIEGO vs. DETROIT
RS: Chargers lead series, 6-4;
See Detroit vs. San Diego
SAN DIEGO vs. GREEN BAY
RS: Packers lead series, 9-1;
See Green Bay vs. San Diego
SAN DIEGO vs. HOUSTON
RS: Chargers lead series, 4-0;
See Houston vs. San Diego
SAN DIEGO vs. INDIANAPOLIS
RS: Chargers lead series, 15-9
PS: Chargers lead series, 2-1;
See Indianapolis vs. San Diego
SAN DIEGO vs. JACKSONVILLE
RS: Chargers lead series, 3-2;
See Jacksonville vs. San Diego
SAN DIEGO vs. KANSAS CITY
RS: Series tied, 52-52-1
PS: Chargers lead series, 1-0;
See Kansas City vs. San Diego
SAN DIEGO vs. MIAMI
RS: Series tied, 12-12
PS: Series tied, 2-2;
See Miami vs. San Diego
SAN DIEGO vs. MINNESOTA
RS: Chargers lead series, 6-5;
See Minnesota vs. San Diego
SAN DIEGO vs. NEW ENGLAND
RS: Patriots lead series, 20-14-2
PS: Patriots lead series, 2-1;
See New England vs. San Diego
SAN DIEGO vs. NEW ORLEANS
RS: Chargers lead series, 7-4;
See New Orleans vs. San Diego
SAN DIEGO vs. N.Y. GIANTS
RS: Series tied, 5-5;
See N.Y. Giants vs. San Diego
SAN DIEGO vs. N.Y. JETS
RS: Chargers lead series, 20-12-1
PS: Jets lead series, 2-0;
See N.Y. Jets vs. San Diego
SAN DIEGO vs. OAKLAND
RS: Raiders lead series, 57-47-2
PS: Raiders lead series, 1-0;
See Oakland vs. San Diego
SAN DIEGO vs. PHILADELPHIA
RS: Chargers lead series, 6-4;
See Philadelphia vs. San Diego
SAN DIEGO vs. PITTSBURGH
RS: Steelers lead series, 21-7
PS: Chargers lead series, 2-1;
See Pittsburgh vs. San Diego
SAN DIEGO vs. ST. LOUIS
RS: Rams lead series, 6-4;
See St. Louis vs. San Diego
SAN DIEGO vs. SAN FRANCISCO
RS: Series tied, 6-6
PS: 49ers lead series, 1-0
1972—49ers, 34-3 (SF)
1976—Chargers, 13-7 (SD) OT
1979—Chargers, 31-9 (SD)
1982—Chargers, 41-37 (SF)
1988—49ers, 48-10 (SD)
1991—49ers, 34-14 (SF)
1994—49ers, 38-15 (SD)
    *49ers, 49-26 (South Florida)
1997—49ers, 17-10 (SF)
2000—49ers, 45-17 (SD)
2002—Chargers, 20-17 (SD) OT

2006—Chargers, 48-19 (SF)
2010—Chargers, 34-7 (SD)
(RS Pts.—49ers 312, Chargers 256)
(PS Pts.—49ers 49, Chargers 26)
*Super Bowl XXIX
SAN DIEGO vs. SEATTLE
RS: Seahawks lead series, 26-23
1977—Chargers, 30-28 (Sea)
1978—Chargers, 24-20 (Sea)
      Chargers, 37-10 (SD)
1979—Chargers, 33-16 (Sea)
      Chargers, 20-10 (SD)
1980—Chargers, 34-13 (Sea)
      Chargers, 21-14 (SD)
1981—Chargers, 24-10 (SD)
      Seahawks, 44-23 (Sea)
1983—Seahawks, 34-31 (Sea)
      Chargers, 28-21 (SD)
1984—Seahawks, 31-17 (Sea)
      Seahawks, 24-0 (SD)
1985—Seahawks, 49-35 (SD)
      Seahawks, 26-21 (Sea)
1986—Seahawks, 33-7 (Sea)
      Seahawks, 34-24 (SD)
1987—Seahawks, 34-3 (Sea)
1988—Chargers, 17-6 (SD)
      Seahawks, 17-14 (Sea)
1989—Seahawks, 17-16 (SD)
      Seahawks, 10-7 (Sea)
1990—Chargers, 31-14 (Sea)
      Seahawks, 13-10 (SD) OT
1991—Seahawks, 20-9 (Sea)
      Chargers, 17-14 (SD)
1992—Chargers, 17-6 (SD)
      Chargers, 31-14 (Sea)
1993—Chargers, 18-12 (SD)
      Seahawks, 31-14 (Sea)
1994—Chargers, 24-10 (Sea)
      Chargers, 35-15 (SD)
1995—Chargers, 14-10 (SD)
      Chargers, 35-25 (Sea)
1996—Chargers, 29-7 (SD)
      Seahawks, 32-13 (Sea)
1997—Seahawks, 26-22 (Sea)
      Seahawks, 37-31 (SD)
1998—Seahawks, 27-20 (SD)
      Seahawks, 38-17 (Sea)
1999—Chargers, 13-10 (SD)
      Chargers, 19-16 (Sea)
2000—Seahawks, 20-12 (SD)
      Seahawks, 17-15 (Sea)
2001—Seahawks, 13-10 (Sea) OT
      Seahawks, 25-22 (SD)
2002—Seahawks, 31-28 (SD) OT
2006—Chargers, 20-17 (Sea)
2010—Seahawks, 27-20 (Sea)
(RS Pts.—Seahawks 1,028, Chargers 1,012)
SAN DIEGO vs. TAMPA BAY
RS: Chargers lead series, 8-2
1976—Chargers, 23-0 (TB)
1981—Chargers, 24-23 (TB)
1987—Chargers, 17-13 (SD)
1990—Chargers, 41-10 (SD)
1992—Chargers, 29-14 (SD)
1993—Chargers, 32-17 (TB)
1996—Buccaneers, 25-17 (SD)
2004—Chargers, 31-24 (SD)
2008—Chargers, 41-24 (TB)
2012—Buccaneers, 34-24 (TB)
(RS Pts.—Chargers 279, Buccaneers 184)
***SAN DIEGO vs. **TENNESSEE**
RS: Chargers lead series, 25-13-1
PS: Titans lead series, 3-1

1960—Oilers, 38-28 (H)
      Chargers, 24-21 (LA)
      ***Oilers, 24-16 (H)
1961—Chargers, 34-24 (SD)
      Oilers, 33-13 (H)
      ***Oilers, 10-3 (SD)
1962—Chargers, 42-17 (SD)
      Oilers, 33-27 (H)
1963—Chargers, 27-0 (SD)
      Chargers 20-14 (H)
1964—Chargers, 27-21 (SD)
      Chargers, 20-17 (H)
1965—Chargers, 31-14 (SD)
      Chargers, 37-26 (H)
1966—Chargers, 28-22 (H)
1967—Chargers, 13-3 (SD)
      Oilers, 24-17 (H)
1968—Chargers, 30-14 (SD)
1969—Chargers, 21-17 (H)
1970—Tie, 31-31 (SD)
1971—Oilers, 49-33 (H)
1972—Chargers, 34-20 (SD)
1974—Oilers, 21-14 (H)
1975—Oilers, 33-17 (H)
1976—Chargers, 30-27 (SD)
1978—Chargers, 45-24 (H)
1979—****Oilers, 17-14 (SD)
1984—Chargers, 31-14 (SD)
1985—Oilers, 37-35 (H)
1986—Chargers, 27-0 (SD)
1987—Oilers, 33-18 (H)
1989—Oilers, 34-27 (SD)
1990—Oilers, 17-7 (SD)
1992—Oilers, 27-0 (H)
1993—Chargers, 18-17 (SD)
1998—Chargers, 13-7 (T)
2004—Chargers, 38-17 (SD)
2006—Chargers, 40-7 (SD)
2007—Chargers, 23-17 (T) OT
      *****Chargers, 17-6 (SD)
2009—Chargers, 42-17 (T)
2010—Chargers, 33-25 (SD)
2012—Chargers, 38-10 (SD)
(RS Pts.—Chargers 1,008, Titans 847)
(PS Pts.—Titans 57, Chargers 50)
*Franchise in Los Angeles prior to 1961
**Franchise in Houston prior to 1997;
known as Oilers prior to 1999
***AFL Championship
****AFC Divisional Playoff
*****AFC First-Round Playoff
SAN DIEGO vs. WASHINGTON
RS: Redskins lead series, 6-3
1973—Redskins, 38-0 (W)
1980—Redskins, 40-17 (W)
1983—Chargers, 27-24 (SD)
1986—Redskins, 30-27 (SD)
1989—Redskins, 26-21 (W)
1998—Redskins, 24-20 (W)
2001—Chargers, 30-3 (SD)
2005—Chargers, 23-17 (W) OT
2009—Chargers, 23-20 (SD)
(RS Pts.—Redskins 225, Chargers 185)

SAN FRANCISCO vs. ARIZONA
RS: 49ers lead series, 26-17;
See Arizona vs. San Francisco
SAN FRANCISCO vs. ATLANTA
RS: 49ers lead series, 44-29-1
PS: Series tied, 1-1;
See Atlanta vs. San Francisco
SAN FRANCISCO vs. BALTIMORE
RS: Ravens lead series, 3-1

PS: Ravens lead series, 1-0;
See Baltimore vs. San Francisco
SAN FRANCISCO vs. BUFFALO
RS: 49ers lead series, 6-5;
See Buffalo vs. San Francisco
SAN FRANCISCO vs. CAROLINA
RS: Panthers lead series, 10-7;
See Carolina vs. San Francisco
SAN FRANCISCO vs. CHICAGO
RS: Series tied, 29-29-1
PS: 49ers lead series, 3-0;
See Chicago vs. San Francisco
SAN FRANCISCO vs. CINCINNATI
RS: 49ers lead series, 9-3
PS: 49ers lead series, 2-0;
See Cincinnati vs. San Francisco
SAN FRANCISCO vs. CLEVELAND
RS: Browns lead series, 11-7;
See Cleveland vs. San Francisco
SAN FRANCISCO vs. DALLAS
RS: 49ers lead series, 14-11-1
PS: Cowboys lead series, 5-2;
See Dallas vs. San Francisco
SAN FRANCISCO vs. DENVER
RS: Series tied, 6-6
PS: 49ers lead series, 1-0;
See Denver vs. San Francisco
SAN FRANCISCO vs. DETROIT
RS: 49ers lead series, 36-26-1
PS: Series tied, 1-1;
See Detroit vs. San Francisco
SAN FRANCISCO vs. GREEN BAY
RS: Packers lead series, 30-26-1
PS: Packers lead series, 4-2;
See Green Bay vs. San Francisco
SAN FRANCISCO vs. HOUSTON
RS: Series tied, 1-1;
See Houston vs. San Francisco
SAN FRANCISCO vs. INDIANAPOLIS
RS: Colts lead series, 24-18;
See Indianapolis vs. San Francisco
SAN FRANCISCO vs. JACKSONVILLE
RS: Jaguars lead series, 2-1;
See Jacksonville vs. San Francisco
SAN FRANCISCO vs. KANSAS CITY
RS: 49ers lead series, 6-5;
See Kansas City vs. San Francisco
SAN FRANCISCO vs. MIAMI
RS: Dolphins lead series, 6-5
PS: 49ers lead series, 1-0;
See Miami vs. San Francisco
SAN FRANCISCO vs. MINNESOTA
RS: Vikings lead series, 21-18-1
PS: 49ers lead series, 4-1;
See Minnesota vs. San Francisco
SAN FRANCISCO vs. NEW ENGLAND
RS: 49ers lead series, 8-4;
See New England vs. San Francisco
SAN FRANCISCO vs. NEW ORLEANS
RS: 49ers lead series, 46-24-2
PS: 49ers lead series, 1-0;
See New Orleans vs. San Francisco
SAN FRANCISCO vs. N.Y. GIANTS
RS: Giants lead series, 15-14
PS: Series tied, 4-4;
See N.Y. Giants vs. San Francisco
SAN FRANCISCO vs. N.Y. JETS
RS: 49ers lead series, 10-2;
See N.Y. Jets vs. San Francisco
SAN FRANCISCO vs. OAKLAND
RS: Series tied, 6-6;
See Oakland vs. San Francisco

SAN FRANCISCO vs. PHILADELPHIA
RS: 49ers lead series, 17-12-1
PS: 49ers lead series, 1-0;
See Philadelphia vs. San Francisco

SAN FRANCISCO vs. PITTSBURGH
RS: 49ers lead series, 11-9;
See Pittsburgh vs. San Francisco

SAN FRANCISCO vs. ST. LOUIS
RS: Rams lead series, 62-61-3
PS: 49ers lead series, 1-0;
See St. Louis vs. San Francisco

SAN FRANCISCO vs. SAN DIEGO
RS: Series tied, 6-6
PS: 49ers lead series, 1-0;
See San Diego vs. San Francisco

SAN FRANCISCO vs. SEATTLE
RS: Series tied, 14-14
1976—49ers, 37-21 (Sea)
1979—Seahawks, 35-24 (SF)
1985—49ers, 19-6 (SF)
1988—49ers, 38-7 (Sea)
1991—49ers, 24-22 (Sea)
1997—Seahawks, 38-9 (Sea)
2002—49ers, 28-21 (Sea)
    49ers, 31-24 (SF)
2003—Seahawks, 20-19 (Sea)
    Seahawks, 24-17 (SF)
2004—Seahawks, 34-0 (Sea)
    Seahawks, 42-27 (SF)
2005—Seahawks, 27-25 (SF)
    Seahawks, 41-3 (Sea)
2006—49ers, 20-14 (SF)
    49ers, 24-14 (Sea)
2007—Seahawks, 23-3 (SF)
    Seahawks, 24-0 (Sea)
2008—49ers, 33-30 (Sea) OT
    Seahawks, 34-13 (SF)
2009—49ers, 23-10 (SF)
    Seahawks, 20-17 (Sea)
2010—Seahawks, 31-6 (Sea)
    49ers, 40-21 (SF)
2011—49ers, 33-17 (SF)
    49ers, 19-17 (Sea)
2012—49ers, 13-6 (SF)
    Seahawks, 42-13 (Sea)
(RS Pts.—Seahawks 665, 49ers 558)

SAN FRANCISCO vs. TAMPA BAY
RS: 49ers lead series, 16-4
PS: Buccaneers lead series, 1-0
1977—49ers, 20-10 (SF)
1978—49ers, 6-3 (SF)
1979—49ers, 23-7 (SF)
1980—Buccaneers, 24-23 (SF)
1983—49ers, 35-21 (SF)
1984—49ers, 24-17 (SF)
1986—49ers, 31-7 (TB)
1987—49ers, 24-10 (TB)
1989—49ers, 20-16 (TB)
1990—49ers, 31-7 (SF)
1992—49ers, 21-14 (SF)
1993—49ers, 45-21 (TB)
1994—49ers, 41-16 (SF)
1997—Buccaneers, 13-6 (TB)
2002—*Buccaneers, 31-6 (TB)
2003—49ers, 24-7 (SF)
2004—Buccaneers, 35-3 (TB)
2005—49ers, 15-10 (SF)
2007—49ers, 21-19 (SF)
2010—49ers, 21-0 (SF)
2011—49ers, 48-3 (SF)
(RS Pts.—49ers 461, Buccaneers 281)
(PS Pts.—Buccaneers 31, 49ers 6)
*NFC Divisional Playoff

SAN FRANCISCO vs. *TENNESSEE
RS: 49ers lead series, 7-5
1970—49ers, 30-20 (H)
1975—Oilers, 27-13 (SF)
1978—Oilers, 20-19 (H)
1981—49ers, 28-6 (SF)
1984—49ers, 34-21 (H)
1987—49ers, 27-20 (SF)
1990—49ers, 24-21 (H)
1993—Oilers, 10-7 (SF)
1996—49ers, 10-9 (H)
1999—49ers, 24-22 (SF)
2005—Titans, 33-22 (T)
2009—Titans, 34-27 (SF)
(RS Pts.—49ers 265, Titans 243)
*Franchise in Houston prior to 1997;
known as Oilers prior to 1999

SAN FRANCISCO vs. WASHINGTON
RS: 49ers lead series, 15-9-1
PS: 49ers lead series, 3-1
1952—49ers, 23-17 (W)
1954—49ers, 41-7 (SF)
1955—Redskins, 7-0 (W)
1961—49ers, 35-3 (SF)
1967—Redskins, 31-28 (W)
1969—Tie, 17-17 (SF)
1970—49ers, 26-17 (SF)
1971—*49ers, 24-20 (SF)
1973—Redskins, 33-9 (W)
1976—Redskins, 24-21 (W)
1978—Redskins, 38-20 (W)
1981—49ers, 30-17 (W)
1983—**Redskins, 24-21 (W)
1984—49ers, 37-31 (SF)
1985—49ers, 35-8 (W)
1986—Redskins, 14-6 (W)
1988—49ers, 37-21 (SF)
1990—49ers, 26-13 (SF)
    *49ers, 28-10 (SF)
1992—*49ers, 20-13 (SF)
1994—49ers, 37-22 (W)
1996—49ers, 19-16 (W) OT
1998—49ers, 45-10 (W)
1999—Redskins, 26-20 (SF) OT
2002—49ers, 20-10 (SF)
2004—Redskins, 26-16 (SF)
2005—Redskins, 52-17 (W)
2008—49ers, 27-24 (SF)
2011—49ers, 19-11 (W)
(RS Pts.—49ers 611, Redskins 495)
(PS Pts.—49ers 93, Redskins 67)
*NFC Divisional Playoff
**NFC Championship

SEATTLE vs. ARIZONA
RS: Cardinals lead series, 15-13;
See Arizona vs. Seattle

SEATTLE vs. ATLANTA
RS: Seahawks lead series, 8-5
PS: Falcons lead series 1-0;
See Atlanta vs. Seattle

SEATTLE vs. BALTIMORE
RS: Series tied, 2-2;
See Baltimore vs. Seattle

SEATTLE vs. BUFFALO
RS: Seahawks lead series, 7-5;
See Buffalo vs. Seattle

SEATTLE vs. CAROLINA
RS: Seahawks lead series, 3-2
PS: Seahawks lead series, 1-0;
See Carolina vs. Seattle

SEATTLE vs. CHICAGO
RS: Seahawks lead series, 10-4

PS: Bears lead series, 2-0;
See Chicago vs. Seattle

SEATTLE vs. CINCINNATI
RS: Series tied, 9-9
PS: Bengals lead series, 1-0;
See Cincinnati vs. Seattle

SEATTLE vs. CLEVELAND
RS: Seahawks lead series, 11-6;
See Cleveland vs. Seattle

SEATTLE vs. DALLAS
RS: Cowboys lead series, 9-5
PS: Seahawks lead series, 1-0;
See Dallas vs. Seattle

SEATTLE vs. DENVER
RS: Broncos lead series, 34-18
PS: Seahawks lead series, 1-0;
See Denver vs. Seattle

SEATTLE vs. DETROIT
RS: Seahawks lead series, 7-5;
See Detroit vs. Seattle

SEATTLE vs. GREEN BAY
RS: Packers lead series, 8-6
PS: Packers lead series, 2-0;
See Green Bay vs. Seattle

SEATTLE vs. HOUSTON
RS: Series tied, 1-1;
See Houston vs. Seattle

SEATTLE vs. INDIANAPOLIS
RS: Colts lead series, 6-4;
See Indianapolis vs. Seattle

SEATTLE vs. JACKSONVILLE
RS: Seahawks lead series, 4-2;
See Jacksonville vs. Seattle

SEATTLE vs. KANSAS CITY
RS: Chiefs lead series, 32-18;
See Kansas City vs. Seattle

SEATTLE vs. MIAMI
RS: Dolphins lead series, 8-3
PS: Dolphins lead series, 2-1;
See Miami vs. Seattle

SEATTLE vs. MINNESOTA
RS: Seahawks lead series, 7-5;
See Minnesota vs. Seattle

SEATTLE vs. NEW ENGLAND
RS: Series tied, 8-8;
See New England vs. Seattle

SEATTLE vs. NEW ORLEANS
RS: Saints lead series, 6-5
PS: Seahawks lead series, 1-0;
See New Orleans vs. Seattle

SEATTLE vs. N.Y. GIANTS
RS: Giants lead series, 9-6;
See N.Y. Giants vs. Seattle

SEATTLE vs. N.Y. JETS
RS: Seahawks lead series, 10-8;
See N.Y. Jets vs. Seattle

SEATTLE vs. OAKLAND
RS: Raiders lead series, 28-23
PS: Series tied, 1-1;
See Oakland vs. Seattle

SEATTLE vs. PHILADELPHIA
RS: Eagles lead series, 7-6;
See Philadelphia vs. Seattle

SEATTLE vs. PITTSBURGH
RS: Series tied, 8-8
PS: Steelers lead series, 1-0;
See Pittsburgh vs. Seattle

SEATTLE vs. ST. LOUIS
RS: Seahawks lead series, 18-11
PS: Rams lead series, 1-0;
See St. Louis vs. Seattle

SEATTLE vs. SAN DIEGO
RS: Seahawks lead series, 26-23;

See San Diego vs. Seattle
SEATTLE vs. SAN FRANCISCO
RS: Series tied, 14-14;
See San Francisco vs. Seattle
SEATTLE vs. TAMPA BAY
RS: Seahawks lead series, 7-4
1976—Seahawks, 13-10 (TB)
1977—Seahawks, 30-23 (S)
1994—Seahawks, 22-21 (S)
1996—Seahawks, 17-13 (TB)
1999—Buccaneers, 16-3 (S)
2004—Seahawks, 10-6 (TB)
2006—Seahawks, 23-7 (TB)
2007—Seahawks, 20-6 (S)
2008—Buccaneers, 20-10 (TB)
2009—Buccaneers, 24-7 (S)
2010—Buccaneers, 35-15 (TB)
(RS Pts.—Buccaneers 184, Seahawks 170)
SEATTLE vs. *TENNESSEE
RS: Seahawks lead series, 9-5
PS: Titans lead series, 1-0
1977—Oilers, 22-10 (S)
1979—Seahawks, 34-14 (S)
1980—Seahawks, 26-7 (H)
1981—Oilers, 35-17 (H)
1982—Oilers, 23-21 (H)
1987—**Oilers, 23-20 (H) OT
1988—Seahawks, 27-24 (S)
1990—Seahawks, 13-10 (S) OT
1993—Oilers, 24-14 (H)
1994—Seahawks, 16-14 (H)
1996—Seahawks, 23-16 (S)
1997—Seahawks, 16-13 (S)
1998—Seahawks, 20-18 (S)
2005—Seahawks, 28-24 (T)
2009—Titans, 17-13 (S)
(RS Pts.—Seahawks 278, Titans 261)
(PS Pts.—Titans 23, Seahawks 20)
*Franchise in Houston prior to 1997;
known as Oilers prior to 1999
**AFC First-Round Playoff
SEATTLE vs. WASHINGTON
RS: Redskins lead series, 11-4
PS: Seahawks lead series, 3-0
1976—Redskins, 31-7 (W)
1980—Seahawks, 14-0 (W)
1983—Redskins, 27-17 (S)
1986—Redskins, 19-14 (W)
1989—Redskins, 29-0 (S)
1992—Redskins, 16-3 (S)
1994—Seahawks, 28-7 (W)
1995—Seahawks, 27-20 (W)
1998—Seahawks, 24-14 (S)
2001—Redskins, 27-14 (W)
2002—Redskins, 14-3 (S)
2003—Redskins, 27-20 (W)
2005—Redskins, 20-17 (W) OT
    *Seahawks, 20-10 (S)
2007—**Seahawks, 35-14 (S)
2008—Redskins, 20-17 (S)
2011—Redskins, 23-17 (S)
2012—**Seahawks, 24-14 (W)
(RS Pts.—Redskins 294, Seahawks 222)
(PS Pts.—Seahawks 79, Redskins 38)
*NFC Divisional Playoff
**NFC First-Round Playoff

TAMPA BAY vs. ARIZONA
RS: Buccaneers lead series, 9-8;
See Arizona vs. Tampa Bay
TAMPA BAY vs. ATLANTA
RS: Buccaneers lead series, 20-19;
See Atlanta vs. Tampa Bay

TAMPA BAY vs. BALTIMORE
RS: Series tied, 2-2;
See Baltimore vs. Tampa Bay
TAMPA BAY vs. BUFFALO
RS: Buccaneers lead series, 6-3;
See Buffalo vs. Tampa Bay
TAMPA BAY vs. CAROLINA
RS: Panthers lead series, 14-11;
See Carolina vs. Tampa Bay
TAMPA BAY vs. CHICAGO
RS: Bears lead series, 36-18;
See Chicago vs. Tampa Bay
TAMPA BAY vs. CINCINNATI
RS: Buccaneers lead series, 7-3;
See Cincinnati vs. Tampa Bay
TAMPA BAY vs. CLEVELAND
RS: Browns lead series, 5-3;
See Cleveland vs. Tampa Bay
TAMPA BAY vs. DALLAS
RS: Cowboys lead series, 11-3
PS: Cowboys lead series, 2-0;
See Dallas vs. Tampa Bay
TAMPA BAY vs. DENVER
RS: Broncos lead series, 6-2;
See Denver vs. Tampa Bay
TAMPA BAY vs. DETROIT
RS: Lions lead series, 29-25
PS: Buccaneers lead series, 1-0;
See Detroit vs. Tampa Bay
TAMPA BAY vs. GREEN BAY
RS: Packers lead series, 30-21-1
PS: Packers lead series, 1-0;
See Green Bay vs. Tampa Bay
TAMPA BAY vs. HOUSTON
RS: Texans lead series, 2-1;
See Houston vs. Tampa Bay
TAMPA BAY vs. INDIANAPOLIS
RS: Colts lead series, 7-5;
See Indianapolis vs. Tampa Bay
TAMPA BAY vs. JACKSONVILLE
RS: Jaguars lead series, 4-1;
See Jacksonville vs. Tampa Bay
TAMPA BAY vs. KANSAS CITY
RS: Buccaneers lead series, 6-5;
See Kansas City vs. Tampa Bay
TAMPA BAY vs. MIAMI
RS: Dolphins lead series, 5-4;
See Miami vs. Tampa Bay
TAMPA BAY vs. MINNESOTA
RS: Vikings lead series, 31-22;
See Minnesota vs. Tampa Bay
TAMPA BAY vs. NEW ENGLAND
RS: Patriots lead series, 5-2;
See New England vs. Tampa Bay
TAMPA BAY vs. NEW ORLEANS
RS: Saints lead series, 25-17;
See New Orleans vs. Tampa Bay
TAMPA BAY vs. N.Y. GIANTS
RS: Giants lead series, 12-6
PS: Giants lead series, 1-0;
See N.Y. Giants vs. Tampa Bay
TAMPA BAY vs. N.Y. JETS
RS: Jets lead series, 9-1;
See N.Y. Jets vs. Tampa Bay
TAMPA BAY vs. OAKLAND
RS: Raiders lead series, 6-2
PS: Buccaneers lead series, 1-0;
See Oakland vs. Tampa Bay
TAMPA BAY vs. PHILADELPHIA
RS: Eagles lead series, 7-5
PS: Series tied, 2-2;
See Philadelphia vs. Tampa Bay
TAMPA BAY vs. PITTSBURGH

RS: Steelers lead series, 8-1;
See Pittsburgh vs. Tampa Bay
TAMPA BAY vs. ST. LOUIS
RS: Rams lead series, 10-8
PS: Rams lead series, 2-0;
See St. Louis vs. Tampa Bay
TAMPA BAY vs. SAN DIEGO
RS: Chargers lead series, 8-2;
See San Diego vs. Tampa Bay
TAMPA BAY vs. SAN FRANCISCO
RS: 49ers lead series, 16-4
PS: Buccaneers lead series, 1-0;
See San Francisco vs. Tampa Bay
TAMPA BAY vs. SEATTLE
RS: Seahawks lead series, 7-4;
See Seattle vs. Tampa Bay
TAMPA BAY vs. *TENNESSEE
RS: Titans lead series, 8-2
1976—Oilers, 20-0 (H)
1980—Oilers, 20-14 (H)
1983—Buccaneers, 33-24 (TB)
1989—Oilers, 20-17 (H)
1995—Oilers, 19-7 (H)
1998—Oilers, 31-22 (TB)
2001—Titans, 31-28 (Tenn) OT
2003—Titans, 33-13 (Tenn)
2007—Buccaneers, 13-10 (TB)
2011—Titans, 23-17 (Tenn)
(RS Pts.—Titans 231, Buccaneers 164)
*Franchise in Houston prior to 1997;
known as Oilers prior to 1999
TAMPA BAY vs. WASHINGTON
RS: Series tied, 9-9
PS: Series tied, 1-1
1977—Redskins, 10-0 (TB)
1982—Redskins, 21-13 (TB)
1989—Redskins, 32-28 (W)
1993—Redskins, 23-17 (TB)
1994—Buccaneers, 26-21 (TB)
    Buccaneers, 17-14 (W)
1995—Buccaneers, 14-6 (TB)
1996—Buccaneers, 24-10 (TB)
1998—Redskins, 20-16 (W)
1999—*Buccaneers, 14-13 (TB)
2000—Redskins, 20-17 (W) OT
2003—Buccaneers, 35-13 (W)
2004—Redskins, 16-10 (W)
2005—Buccaneers, 36-35 (TB)
    **Redskins, 17-10 (TB)
2006—Buccaneers, 20-17 (TB)
2007—Buccaneers, 19-13 (TB)
2009—Redskins, 16-13 (W)
2010—Buccaneers, 17-16 (W)
2012—Redskins, 24-22 (TB)
(RS Pts.—Buccaneers 344, Redskins 327)
(PS Pts.—Redskins 30, Buccaneers 24)
*NFC Divisional Playoff
**NFC First-Round Playoff

TENNESSEE VS. ARIZONA
RS: Cardinals lead series, 5-4;
See Arizona vs. Tennessee
TENNESSEE VS. ATLANTA
RS: Titans lead series, 7-6;
See Atlanta vs. Tennessee
TENNESSEE VS. BALTIMORE
RS: Titans lead series, 9-8
PS: Ravens lead series, 2-1;
See Baltimore vs. Tennessee
TENNESSEE VS. BUFFALO
RS: Titans lead series, 27-14
PS: Bills lead series, 2-1;
See Buffalo vs. Tennessee

TENNESSEE vs. CAROLINA
RS: Titans lead series, 3-1;
See Carolina vs. Tennessee
TENNESSEE vs. CHICAGO
RS: Bears lead series, 6-5;
See Chicago vs. Tennessee
TENNESSEE vs. CINCINNATI
RS: Titans lead series, 39-32-1
PS: Bengals lead series, 1-0;
See Cincinnati vs. Tennessee
TENNESSEE vs. CLEVELAND
RS: Browns lead series, 33-28
PS: Titans lead series, 1-0;
See Cleveland vs. Tennessee
TENNESSEE vs. DALLAS
RS: Cowboys lead series, 7-6;
See Dallas vs. Tennessee
TENNESSEE vs. DENVER
RS: Titans lead series, 21-14-1
PS: Broncos lead series, 2-1;
See Denver vs. Tennessee
TENNESSEE vs. DETROIT
RS: Titans lead series, 8-3;
See Detroit vs. Tennessee
TENNESSEE vs. GREEN BAY
RS: Titans lead series, 6-5;
See Green Bay vs. Tennessee
TENNESSEE vs. HOUSTON
RS: Titans lead series, 14-8;
See Houston vs. Tennessee
TENNESSEE vs. INDIANAPOLIS
RS: Colts lead series, 23-13
PS: Titans lead series, 1-0;
See Indianapolis vs. Tennessee
TENNESSEE vs. JACKSONVILLE
RS: Titans lead series, 20-16
PS: Titans lead series, 1-0;
See Jacksonville vs. Tennessee
TENNESSEE vs. KANSAS CITY
RS: Chiefs lead series, 26-20
PS: Chiefs lead series, 2-0;
See Kansas City vs. Tennessee
TENNESSEE vs. MIAMI
RS: Dolphins lead series, 18-15
PS: Titans lead series, 1-0;
See Miami vs. Tennessee
TENNESSEE vs. MINNESOTA
RS: Vikings lead series, 8-4;
See Minnesota vs. Tennessee
TENNESSEE vs. NEW ENGLAND
RS: Patriots lead series, 22-15-1
PS: Series tied, 1-1;
See New England vs. Tennessee
TENNESSEE vs. NEW ORLEANS
RS: Titans lead series, 7-5-1;
See New Orleans vs. Tennessee
TENNESSEE vs. N.Y. GIANTS
RS: Series tied, 5-5;
See N.Y. Giants vs. Tennessee
TENNESSEE vs. N.Y. JETS
RS: Titans lead series, 22-17-1
PS: Titans lead series, 1-0;
See N.Y. Jets vs. Tennessee
TENNESSEE vs. OAKLAND
RS: Raiders lead series, 23-19
PS: Raiders lead series, 4-0;
See Oakland vs. Tennessee
TENNESSEE vs. PHILADELPHIA
RS: Eagles lead series, 6-4;
See Philadelphia vs. Tennessee
TENNESSEE vs. PITTSBURGH
RS: Steelers lead series, 41-30
PS: Steelers lead series, 3-1;

See Pittsburgh vs. Tennessee
TENNESSEE vs. ST. LOUIS
RS: Rams lead series, 6-4
PS: Rams lead series, 1-0;
See St. Louis vs. Tennessee
TENNESSEE vs. SAN DIEGO
RS: Chargers lead series, 25-13-1
PS: Titans lead series, 3-1;
See San Diego vs. Tennessee
TENNESSEE vs. SAN FRANCISCO
RS: 49ers lead series, 7-5;
See San Francisco vs. Tennessee
TENNESSEE vs. SEATTLE
RS: Seahawks lead series, 9-5
PS: Titans lead series, 1-0;
See Seattle vs. Tennessee
TENNESSEE vs. TAMPA BAY
RS: Titans lead series, 8-2;
See Tampa Bay vs. Tennessee
*TENNESSEE vs. WASHINGTON
RS: Titans lead series, 6-5
1971—Redskins, 22-13 (W)
1975—Oilers, 13-10 (H)
1979—Oilers, 29-27 (W)
1985—Redskins, 16-13 (W)
1988—Oilers, 41-17 (H)
1991—Redskins, 16-13 (W) OT
1997—Oilers, 28-14 (T)
2000—Titans, 27-21 (W)
2002—Redskins, 31-14 (T)
2006—Titans, 25-22 (W)
2010—Redskins, 19-16 (T) OT
(RS—Titans 232, Redskins 215)
*Franchise in Houston prior to 1997;
known as Oilers prior to 1999*

WASHINGTON vs. ARIZONA
RS: Redskins lead series, 74-44-2;
See Arizona vs. Washington
WASHINGTON vs. ATLANTA
RS: Redskins lead series, 14-7-1
PS: Redskins lead series, 1-0;
See Atlanta vs. Washington
WASHINGTON vs. BALTIMORE
RS: Ravens lead series, 3-2;
See Baltimore vs. Washington
WASHINGTON vs. BUFFALO
RS: Bills lead series, 8-4
PS: Redskins lead series, 1-0;
See Buffalo vs. Washington
WASHINGTON vs. CAROLINA
RS: Redskins lead series, 7-4;
See Carolina vs. Washington
WASHINGTON vs. CHICAGO
RS: Bears lead series, 20-19-1
PS: Redskins lead series, 4-3;
See Chicago vs. Washington
WASHINGTON vs. CINCINNATI
RS: Bengals lead series, 5-4;
See Cincinnati vs. Washington
WASHINGTON vs. CLEVELAND
RS: Browns lead series, 33-11-1;
See Cleveland vs. Washington
WASHINGTON vs. DALLAS
RS: Cowboys lead series, 62-40-2
PS: Redskins lead series, 2-0;
See Dallas vs. Washington
WASHINGTON vs. DENVER
RS: Broncos lead series, 6-5
PS: Redskins lead series, 1-0;
See Denver vs. Washington
WASHINGTON vs. DETROIT
RS: Redskins lead series, 27-12

PS: Redskins lead series, 3-0;
See Detroit vs. Washington
WASHINGTON vs. GREEN BAY
RS: Packers lead series, 17-13-1
PS: Series tied, 1-1;
See Green Bay vs. Washington
WASHINGTON vs. HOUSTON
RS: Redskins lead series, 2-1;
See Houston vs. Washington
WASHINGTON vs. INDIANAPOLIS
RS: Colts lead series, 19-10;
See Indianapolis vs. Washington
WASHINGTON vs. JACKSONVILLE
RS: Redskins lead series, 4-1;
See Jacksonville vs. Washington
WASHINGTON vs. KANSAS CITY
RS: Chiefs lead series, 7-1;
See Kansas City vs. Washington
WASHINGTON vs. MIAMI
RS: Dolphins lead series, 7-4
PS: Series tied, 1-1;
See Miami vs. Washington
WASHINGTON vs. MINNESOTA
RS: Redskins lead series, 9-8
PS: Redskins lead series, 3-2;
See Minnesota vs. Washington
WASHINGTON vs. NEW ENGLAND
RS: Redskins lead series, 6-3;
See New England vs. Washington
WASHINGTON vs. NEW ORLEANS
RS: Redskins lead series, 16-8;
See New Orleans vs. Washington
WASHINGTON vs. N.Y. GIANTS
RS: Giants lead series, 92-64-4
PS: Series tied, 1-1;
See N.Y. Giants vs. Washington
WASHINGTON vs. N.Y. JETS
RS: Redskins lead series, 8-2;
See N.Y. Jets vs. Washington
WASHINGTON vs. OAKLAND
RS: Raiders lead series, 7-4
PS: Raiders lead series, 1-0;
See Oakland vs. Washington
WASHINGTON vs. PHILADELPHIA
RS: Redskins lead series, 80-70-5
PS: Redskins lead series, 1-0;
See Philadelphia vs. Washington
WASHINGTON vs. PITTSBURGH
RS: Redskins lead series, 42-32-3;
See Pittsburgh vs. Washington
WASHINGTON vs. ST. LOUIS
RS: Redskins lead series, 22-10-1
PS: Series tied, 2-2;
See St. Louis vs. Washington
WASHINGTON vs. SAN DIEGO
RS: Redskins lead series, 6-3;
See San Diego vs. Washington
WASHINGTON vs. SAN FRANCISCO
RS: 49ers lead series, 15-9-1
PS: 49ers lead series, 3-1;
See San Francisco vs. Washington
WASHINGTON vs. SEATTLE
RS: Redskins lead series, 11-4
PS: Seahawks lead series, 3-0;
See Seattle vs. Washington
WASHINGTON vs. TAMPA BAY
RS: Series tied, 9-9
PS: Series tied, 1-1;
See Tampa Bay vs. Washington
WASHINGTON vs. TENNESSEE
RS: Titans lead series, 6-5;
See Tennessee vs. Washington

INTERCONFERENCE GAMES

AFC VS. NFC (REGULAR SEASON), 1970-2012

	Balt	Buff	Cin	Cle	Den	Hou	Ind	Jax	KC	Mia
1970		0-3	1-2	0-3	2-2		3-0		0-2-1	2-1
1971		0-3	1-2	2-1	1-3		2-1		2-1	3-0
1972		2-0-1	2-1	1-2	1-3		0-3		2-1	3-0
1973		2-1	2-1	1-2	0-3-1		2-1		1-1-1	3-0
1974		2-1	2-1	1-2	2-2		1-2		1-2	2-1
1975		1-2	3-0	1-3	2-1		2-1		2-1	3-0
1976		0-2	2-0	2-0	2-0		0-2		1-1	0-2
1977		1-1	2-1	1-1	1-1		1-1		1-1	2-0
1978		1-1	2-2	4-0	2-2		2-2		0-2	3-1
1979		2-2	2-2	3-1	3-1		1-1		0-2	4-0
1980		3-1	2-2	3-1	3-1		1-1		2-0	4-0
1981		1-3	2-2	3-1	3-1		0-4		2-2	3-1
1982		1-2	1-0	0-2	2-1		0-1-1		0-3	1-1
1983		1-3	3-1	2-2	0-2		2-0		2-2	3-1
1984		1-3	2-2	1-3	3-1		0-4		1-1	4-0
1985		0-2	2-2	1-3	3-1		3-1		2-2	3-1
1986		1-1	3-1	2-2	3-1		1-3		1-1	2-2
1987		1-2	1-2	2-2	2-1-1		1-0		1-2	3-0
1988		2-2	4-0	4-0	3-1		2-2		0-2	3-1
1989		1-3	2-2	3-1	2-2		1-3		2-0	2-0
1990		3-1	1-3	1-3	1-3		2-2		4-0	2-2
1991		3-1	1-3	0-4	2-0		0-4		2-2	3-1
1992		4-0	1-3	2-2	1-3		2-0		2-2	2-2
1993		4-0	2-2	3-1	1-3		0-4		2-2	3-1
1994		1-3	1-3	3-1	1-3		0-2		3-1	2-2
1995		3-1	2-2	1-3	2-2		2-2	0-4	3-1	2-2
1996	2-2	4-0	2-2		3-1		3-1	2-2	4-0	1-3
1997	2-1-1	1-3	2-2		3-1		1-3	2-2	4-0	1-3
1998	1-3	3-1	1-3		3-1		0-4	3-1	3-1	3-1
1999	2-1	3-1	1-2	1-2	2-2		4-0	4-0	2-2	2-2
2000	2-1	2-2	1-2	0-3	3-1		2-2	2-2	2-2	2-2
2001	2-2	1-3	1-2	1-2	3-1		1-3	1-2	1-3	2-2
2002	0-4	3-1	1-3	2-2	4-0	2-2	2-2	2-2	2-2	2-2
2003	3-1	2-2	2-2	2-2	1-3	2-2	3-1	2-2	3-1	3-1
2004	3-1	4-0	4-0	1-3	3-1	1-3	4-0	3-1	1-3	2-2
2005	2-2	0-4	4-0	2-2	3-1	1-3	3-1	3-1	1-3	2-2
2006	3-1	2-2	2-2	1-3	1-3	0-4	3-1	3-1	4-0	3-1
2007	3-1	1-3	1-3	3-1	1-3	3-1	4-0	3-1	1-3	0-4
2008	3-1	2-2	1-2-1	1-3	3-1	3-1	2-2	2-2	0-4	3-1
2009	2-2	2-2	3-1	0-4	2-2	3-1	4-0	1-3	1-3	2-2
2010	3-1	1-3	1-3	2-2	1-3	1-3	2-2	1-3	4-0	2-2
2011	3-1	2-2	3-1	1-3	2-2	2-2	0-4	1-3	3-1	1-3
2012	2-2	1-3	3-1	0-4	3-1	2-2	3-1	0-4	2-2	2-2
Total	38-27-1	75-78-1	82-73-1	64-82	89-71-2	20-24	72-74-1	35-36	77-67-2	100-57

AFC VS. NFC (REGULAR SEASON), 1970-2012

	NE	NYJ	Oak	Pitt	SD	Sea	TB	Ten	TOTALS
1970	0-3	2-1	1-2	0-3	1-2			0-3	12-27-1
1971	0-3	0-3	1-1-1	1-2	2-1			0-2-1	15-23-2
1972	3-0	1-2	3-0	2-1	0-3			0-3	20-19-1
1973	2-1	0-3	2-1	3-0	1-2			0-3	19-19-2
1974	3-0	2-1	3-0	3-0	1-2			0-3	23-17
1975	1-2	0-3	3-0	2-1	0-3			3-0	23-17
1976	1-1	0-2	3-0	1-1	2-0		0-1	2-0	16-12
1977	2-0	1-1	1-1	2-0	1-1	1-0		2-0	19-9
1978	2-2	1-3	4-0	3-1	2-2	3-1		2-2	31-21
1979	3-1	3-1	4-0	3-1	3-1	3-1		2-2	36-16
1980	1-3	1-3	2-2	4-0	2-2	1-3		4-0	33-19
1981	0-4	2-0	2-2	3-1	2-2	0-2		1-3	24-28
1982	0-1	4-0	3-0	1-0	1-0	1-0		0-3	15-14-1
1983	2-2	3-1	2-2	2-2	2-2	1-3		1-3	26-26
1984	0-4	0-2	3-1	3-1	4-0	4-0		0-4	26-26
1985	3-1	2-2	3-1	1-3	1-1	2-2		1-3	27-25
1986	3-1	2-2	1-3	2-2	0-4	3-1		2-2	26-26
1987	0-3	0-4	2-2	2-2	2-0	4-0		2-2	23-22-1
1988	2-2	2-0	1-3	1-3	2-2	1-3		3-1	30-22
1989	0-4	1-3	2-2	3-1	2-2	0-4		3-1	24-28
1990	0-4	2-0	3-1	3-1	1-1	2-2		1-3	26-26
1991	1-1	2-2	2-2	0-4	1-3	1-3		1-3	19-33
1992	0-4	0-4	2-2	1-3	2-0	0-4		3-1	22-30
1993	1-1	2-2	3-1	2-2	2-2	0-2		2-2	27-25
1994	4-0	1-3	3-1	2-2	2-2	2-0		0-4	25-27
1995	0-4	0-4	3-1	2-2	3-1	3-1		1-3	27-33
1996	2-2	1-3	1-3	2-2	1-3	2-2		2-2	32-28
1997	1-3	3-1	2-2	2-2	1-3	2-2		4-0	31-28-1
1998	2-2	2-2	3-1	2-2	1-3	3-1		1-3	31-29
1999	3-1	2-2	3-1	3-0	1-3	2-2		3-1	38-22
2000	0-4	3-1	4-0	1-2	0-4	2-2		4-0	30-30
2001	3-1	2-2	3-1	3-0	2-2	1-3		3-1	30-30
2002	3-1	3-1	2-2	2-1-1	2-2			2-2	34-29-1
2003	3-1	0-4	1-3	1-3	2-2			4-0	34-30
2004	4-0	3-1	2-2	4-0	3-1			2-2	44-20
2005	3-1	1-3	2-2	4-0	2-2			1-3	34-30
2006	4-0	3-1	1-3	3-1	4-0			3-1	40-24
2007	4-0	0-4	0-4	3-1	2-2			3-1	32-32
2008	4-0	2-2	1-3	2-2	1-3			4-0	34-29-1
2009	3-1	2-2	1-3	3-1	4-0			4-0	37-27
2010	4-0	2-2	2-2	3-1	2-2			3-1	34-30
2011	3-1	2-2	2-2	3-1	1-3			2-2	31-33
2012	1-3	2-2	0-4	3-1	0-4			1-3	25-39
Total	**81-73**	**67-87**	**92-69-1**	**96-59-1**	**71-80**	**44-44**	**0-1**	**82-78-1**	**1,185-1,080-11**

NFC VS. AFC (REGULAR SEASON), 1970-2012

	Ariz	Atl	Car	Chi	Dall	Det	GB	Minn	NO
1970	2-0-1	1-2		1-2	3-0	3-0	2-1	2-1	0-3
1971	2-1	3-0		1-2	3-0	4-0	2-1	2-1	0-1-2
1972	1-2	2-2		1-2	3-0	2-0-1	2-1	1-2	0-3
1973	0-2-1	2-1		2-2	2-1	0-3	1-1-1	2-1	1-2
1974	2-1	0-3		0-3	2-1	1-2	2-1	2-1	0-3
1975	2-1	1-2		0-3	2-1	1-2	0-3	4-0	0-3
1976	1-1	0-2		0-2	2-0	2-0	0-2	2-0	1-2
1977	0-2	0-2		1-1	1-1	2-0	0-3	1-1	0-2
1978	0-4	1-3		0-4	3-1	2-2	2-2	1-3	1-3
1979	1-3	1-3		2-2	1-3	0-4	1-3	1-3	0-4
1980	1-1	2-2		0-4	3-1	0-2	1-3	1-3	1-3
1981	3-1	1-3		4-0	4-0	2-2	1-1	1-3	2-2
1982		1-1		1-1	2-1	0-1	1-1-1	1-3	1-0
1983	3-1	3-1		1-1	2-2	1-3	2-2	4-0	1-3
1984	3-1	1-3		2-2	2-2	0-4	0-4	0-4	3-1
1985	2-2	0-4		3-1	3-1	2-2	0-4	2-0	0-4
1986	1-1	1-3		4-0	1-3	1-3	1-3	1-3	1-3
1987	0-1	0-4		2-2	2-1	0-4	1-2-1	2-1	4-0
1988	1-3	1-3		3-1	0-4	1-1	1-3	2-2	4-0
1989	1-3	2-2		2-2	0-2	1-3	0-2	2-2	4-0
1990	2-2	2-2		2-2	1-1	1-3	1-3	2-2	2-2
1991	1-1	3-1		2-2	3-1	4-0	1-3	0-2	3-1
1992	0-2	2-2		1-3	4-0	2-2	3-1	3-1	3-1
1993	1-1	1-3		2-2	2-2	2-0	3-1	2-2	2-2
1994	3-1	1-3		3-1	3-1	2-2	1-3	2-2	1-3
1995	1-3	2-2	3-1	2-2	4-0	3-1	4-0	3-1	4-0
1996	0-4	0-4	3-1	2-2	2-2	1-3	3-1	1-3	1-3
1997	1-3	2-2	2-2	2-2	2-2	2-2	3-1	3-1	2-2
1998	1-3	3-1	1-3	2-2	1-3	1-3	3-1	4-0	1-3
1999	0-4	0-4	2-2	2-2	1-3	1-3	2-2	2-2	0-4
2000	1-3	1-3	2-2	2-2	1-3	2-2	1-3	3-1	1-3
2001	3-1	1-3	0-4	3-1	0-4	0-4	3-1	1-3	2-2
2002	0-4	2-1-1	3-1	1-3	2-2	0-4	3-1	1-3	2-2
2003	1-3	1-3	2-2	3-1	2-2	1-3	3-1	2-2	1-3
2004	1-3	3-1	1-3	1-3	1-3	1-3	1-3	3-1	2-2
2005	1-3	3-1	3-1	1-3	2-2	2-2	0-4	1-3	2-2
2006	0-4	2-2	2-2	2-2	3-1	1-3	1-3	0-4	1-3
2007	3-1	1-3	0-4	3-1	3-1	3-1	4-0	2-2	1-3
2008	2-2	3-1	4-0	2-2	2-2	0-4	1-3	2-2	3-1
2009	2-2	3-1	0-4	2-2	2-2	1-3	2-2	3-1	4-0
2010	2-2	3-1	0-4	3-1	2-2	1-3	2-2	1-3	2-2
2011	1-3	3-1	3-1	1-3	2-2	4-0	3-1	0-4	4-0
2012	2-2	4-0	2-2	3-1	3-1	1-3	3-1	3-1	2-2
Total	55-88-2	69-91-1	33-39	77-82	89-67	61-92-1	71-84-3	78-80	70-88-2

NFC VS. AFC (REGULAR SEASON), 1970-2012

	NYG	Phil	StL	SF	Sea	TB	Wash	TOTALS
1970	3-0	2-1	2-1	4-0			2-1	27-12-1
1971	1-2	1-2	1-2	2-1			1-2	23-15-2
1972	1-2	2-1	1-2	2-1			1-2	19-20-1
1973	1-2	2-1	3-0	1-2			2-1	19-19-2
1974	1-2	2-1	3-1	0-3			2-1	17-23
1975	2-1	0-3	3-0	1-2			1-2	17-23
1976	0-2	0-2	1-1	1-1	1-0		1-1	12-16
1977	0-2	1-1	2-0	0-2		0-1	1-1	9-19
1978	1-1	3-1	2-2	1-3		2-0	2-2	21-31
1979	1-1	2-2	2-2	0-4		2-0	2-2	16-36
1980	1-3	3-1	2-2	2-2		1-3	1-3	19-33
1981	1-1	3-1	1-3	3-1		0-4	2-2	28-24
1982	1-0	2-1	1-2	1-3		2-1		14-15-1
1983	0-4	1-1	1-3	2-2		1-3	4-0	26-26
1984	2-0	3-1	3-1	3-1		1-1	3-1	26-26
1985	2-2	1-1	3-1	3-1		0-4	4-0	25-27
1986	3-1	2-2	2-2	4-0		1-1	3-1	26-26
1987	2-1	3-1	1-2	3-1		0-2	2-1	22-23-1
1988	1-1	2-2	2-2	2-2		1-3	1-3	22-30
1989	4-0	3-1	3-1	4-0		0-4	2-2	28-24
1990	3-1	1-3	2-2	4-0		0-2	3-1	26-26
1991	3-1	4-0	1-3	3-1		1-3	4-0	33-19
1992	2-2	3-1	2-2	3-1		0-2	2-2	30-22
1993	2-2	2-2	2-2	2-2		1-3	1-3	25-27
1994	3-1	1-3	2-2	3-1		1-1	1-1	27-25
1995	0-4	1-3	1-3	3-1		2-2	0-4	33-27
1996	2-2	2-2	2-2	4-0		2-2	3-1	28-32
1997	1-3	2-1-1	0-4	2-2		3-1	1-3	28-31-1
1998	3-1	0-4	3-1	2-2		2-2	2-2	29-31
1999	2-2	1-3	3-1	1-3		3-1	2-2	22-38
2000	3-1	3-1	3-1	2-2		3-1	2-2	30-30
2001	2-2	3-1	4-0	4-0		2-2	2-2	30-30
2002	2-2	1-3	2-2	2-2	2-2	3-1	3-1	29-34-1
2003	1-3	3-1	4-0	1-3	2-2	1-3	2-2	30-34
2004	1-3	2-2	1-3	0-4	1-3	1-3	0-4	20-44
2005	3-1	3-1	3-1	1-3	3-1	2-2	0-4	30-34
2006	1-3	1-3	2-2	2-2	2-2	2-2	2-2	24-40
2007	3-1	3-1	0-4	1-3	2-2	1-3	2-2	32-32
2008	3-1	2-1-1	0-4	2-2	1-3	1-3	1-3	29-34-1
2009	2-2	2-2	0-4	1-3	1-3	0-4	2-2	27-37
2010	2-2	3-1	2-2	2-2	1-3	2-2	2-2	30-34
2011	4-0	2-2	1-3	3-1	1-3	1-3	0-4	33-31
2012	1-3	2-2	1-3	4-0	3-1	3-1	2-2	39-25
Total	77-71	85-70-2	80-81	91-72	20-25	48-76	76-79	1,080-1,185-11

INTERCONFERENCE GAMES

INTERCONFERENCE VICTORIES, 1970-2012

	AFC	NFC	Tie
1970	12	27	1
1971	15	23	2
1972	20	19	1
1973	19	19	2
1974	23	17	0
1975	23	17	0
1976	16	12	0
1977	19	9	0
1978	31	21	0
1979	36	16	0
1980	33	19	0
1981	24	28	0
1982	15	14	1
1983	26	26	0
1984	26	26	0
1985	27	25	0
1986	26	26	0
1987	23	22	1
1988	30	22	0
1989	24	28	0
1990	26	26	0
1991	19	33	0
1992	22	30	0
1993	27	25	0
1994	25	27	0
1995	27	33	0
1996	32	28	0
1997	31	28	1
1998	31	29	0
1999	38	22	0
2000	30	30	0
2001	30	30	0
2002	34	29	1
2003	34	30	0
2004	44	20	0
2005	34	30	0
2006	40	24	0
2007	32	32	0
2008	34	29	1
2009	37	27	0
2010	34	30	0
2011	31	33	0
2012	25	39	0
Total	1,185	1,080	11

REGULAR SEASON INTERCONFERENCE RECORDS, 1970-2012

AMERICAN FOOTBALL CONFERENCE

East	W	L	T	Pct.
Miami	100	57	0	.637
New England	81	73	1	.526
Buffalo	75	78	1	.490
New York Jets	67	87	0	.435
North	**W**	**L**	**T**	**Pct.**
Pittsburgh	96	59	1	.619
Baltimore	38	27	1	.585
Cincinnati	82	73	1	.529
Cleveland	64	82	0	.438
South	**W**	**L**	**T**	**Pct.**
Tennessee	82	78	1	.513
Indianapolis	72	74	1	.493
Jacksonville	35	36	0	.493
Houston	20	24	0	.455
West	**W**	**L**	**T**	**Pct.**
Oakland	92	69	1	.571
Denver	89	71	2	.556
Kansas City	77	67	2	.535
San Diego	71	80	0	.470

NATIONAL FOOTBALL CONFERENCE

East	W	L	T	Pct.
Dallas	89	67	0	.571
Philadelphia	85	70	2	.548
New York Giants	77	71	0	.520
Washington	76	79	0	.490
North	**W**	**L**	**T**	**Pct.**
Minnesota	78	80	0	.494
Chicago	77	82	0	.484
Green Bay	71	84	3	.458
Detroit	61	92	1	.399
South	**W**	**L**	**T**	**Pct.**
Carolina	33	39	0	.458
New Orleans	70	88	2	.443
Atlanta	69	91	1	.431
Tampa Bay*	48	77	0	.384
West	**W**	**L**	**T**	**Pct.**
San Francisco	91	72	0	.558
St. Louis	80	81	0	.497
Seattle* #	64	69	0	.481
Arizona	55	88	2	.385

* Records include one game played between Seattle and Tampa Bay, won by the Seahawks 13-10, in their inaugural season (1976) when Seattle competed in the NFC and Tampa Bay in the AFC.

\# Seattle was a member of the AFC from 1977-2001.

From 1970-71, tie games were not included in winning percentage.

SUPER BOWL COMPOSITE STANDINGS

	W	L	Pct.	Pts.	OP
Baltimore Ravens	2	0	1.000	68	38
New Orleans Saints	1	0	1.000	31	17
New York Jets	1	0	1.000	16	7
Tampa Bay Buccaneers	1	0	1.000	48	21
San Francisco 49ers	5	1	.833	219	123
Green Bay Packers	4	1	.800	158	101
New York Giants	4	1	.800	104	104
Pittsburgh Steelers	6	2	.750	193	164
Dallas Cowboys	5	3	.625	221	132
Oakland/L.A. Raiders	3	2	.600	132	114
Washington Redskins	3	2	.600	122	103
Indianapolis/Baltimore Colts	2	2	.500	69	77
Chicago Bears	1	1	.500	63	39
Kansas City Chiefs	1	1	.500	33	42
New England Patriots	3	4	.429	138	186
Miami Dolphins	2	3	.400	74	103
Denver Broncos	2	4	.333	115	206
St. Louis/L.A. Rams	1	2	.333	59	67
Arizona Cardinals	0	1	.000	23	27
Atlanta Falcons	0	1	.000	19	34
Carolina Panthers	0	1	.000	29	32
San Diego Chargers	0	1	.000	26	49
Seattle Seahawks	0	1	.000	10	21
Tennessee Titans	0	1	.000	16	23
Cincinnati Bengals	0	2	.000	37	46
Philadelphia Eagles	0	2	.000	31	51
Buffalo Bills	0	4	.000	73	139
Minnesota Vikings	0	4	.000	34	95

SUPER BOWL HOST CITIES

New Orleans	10	
South Florida	10	
Los Angeles	7	(LA Coliseum 2, Rose Bowl 5)
Tampa Bay	4	
San Diego	3	
Arizona	2	
Atlanta	2	
Detroit	2	
Houston	2	
Indianapolis	1	
Jacksonville	1	
Minneapolis	1	
North Texas	1	
Stanford	1	

FUTURE SUPER BOWL SITES

Super Bowl XLVIII Feb. 2, 2014 MetLife Stadium
(awarded May 25, 2010) New York-New Jersey

Super Bowl XLIX Feb. 1, 2015 University of Phoenix Stadium
(awarded October 11, 2011) Arizona

Super Bowl L Feb. 7, 2016* Levi's Stadium
(awarded May 21, 2013) San Francisco

Super Bowl LI Feb. 5, 2017* Reliant Stadium
(awarded May 21, 2013) Houston

*Tentative date

PETE ROZELLE TROPHY/SUPER BOWL MVPs*

Super Bowl I	— QB Bart Starr, Green Bay
Super Bowl II	— QB Bart Starr, Green Bay
Super Bowl III	— QB Joe Namath, N.Y. Jets
Super Bowl IV	— QB Len Dawson, Kansas City
Super Bowl V	— LB Chuck Howley, Dallas
Super Bowl VI	— QB Roger Staubach, Dallas
Super Bowl VII	— S Jake Scott, Miami
Super Bowl VIII	— RB Larry Csonka, Miami
Super Bowl IX	— RB Franco Harris, Pittsburgh
Super Bowl X	— WR Lynn Swann, Pittsburgh
Super Bowl XI	— WR Fred Biletnikoff, Oakland
Super Bowl XII	— DT Randy White and
	DE Harvey Martin, Dallas
Super Bowl XIII	— QB Terry Bradshaw, Pittsburgh
Super Bowl XIV	— QB Terry Bradshaw, Pittsburgh
Super Bowl XV	— QB Jim Plunkett, Oakland
Super Bowl XVI	— QB Joe Montana, San Francisco
Super Bowl XVII	— RB John Riggins, Washington
Super Bowl XVIII	— RB Marcus Allen, L.A. Raiders
Super Bowl XIX	— QB Joe Montana, San Francisco
Super Bowl XX	— DE Richard Dent, Chicago
Super Bowl XXI	— QB Phil Simms, N.Y. Giants
Super Bowl XXII	— QB Doug Williams, Washington
Super Bowl XXIII	— WR Jerry Rice, San Francisco
Super Bowl XXIV	— QB Joe Montana, San Francisco
Super Bowl XXV	— RB Ottis Anderson, N.Y. Giants
Super Bowl XXVI	— QB Mark Rypien, Washington
Super Bowl XXVII	— QB Troy Aikman, Dallas
Super Bowl XXVIII	— RB Emmitt Smith, Dallas
Super Bowl XXIX	— QB Steve Young, San Francisco
Super Bowl XXX	— CB Larry Brown, Dallas
Super Bowl XXXI	— KR-PR Desmond Howard, Green Bay
Super Bowl XXXII	— RB Terrell Davis, Denver
Super Bowl XXXIII	— QB John Elway, Denver
Super Bowl XXXIV	— QB Kurt Warner, St. Louis
Super Bowl XXXV	— LB Ray Lewis, Baltimore
Super Bowl XXXVI	— QB Tom Brady, New England
Super Bowl XXXVII	— S Dexter Jackson, Tampa Bay
Super Bowl XXXVIII	— QB Tom Brady, New England
Super Bowl XXXIX	— WR Deion Branch, New England
Super Bowl XL	— WR Hines Ward, Pittsburgh
Super Bowl XLI	— QB Peyton Manning, Indianapolis
Super Bowl XLII	— QB Eli Manning, N.Y. Giants
Super Bowl XLIII	— WR Santonio Holmes, Pittsburgh
Super Bowl XLIV	— QB Drew Brees, New Orleans
Super Bowl XLV	— QB Aaron Rodgers, Green Bay
Super Bowl XLVI	— QB Eli Manning, N.Y. Giants
Super Bowl XLVII	— QB Joe Flacco, Baltimore

* Award named Pete Rozelle Trophy since Super Bowl XXV.

SUPER BOWL MVP BY POSITION

Quarterback	26
Running Back	7
Wide Receiver	6
Defensive End	2
Linebacker	2
Safety	2
Cornerback	1
Defensive Tackle	1
Kick Returner-Punt Returner	1

A defensive end and defensive tackle shared the Super Bowl XII MVP award.

RESULTS

NFC leads AFC, 25-22

Super Bowl	Date	Winner (Share)	Loser (Share)	Score	Site	Attendance
XLVII	2-3-13	Baltimore ($88,000)	San Francisco ($44,000)	34-31	New Orleans	71,024
XLVI	2-5-12	N.Y. Giants ($88,000)	New England ($44,000)	21-17	Indianapolis	68,658
XLV	2-6-11	Green Bay ($83,000)	Pittsburgh ($42,000)	31-25	North Texas	91,060
XLIV	2-7-10	New Orleans ($83,000)	Indianapolis ($42,000)	31-17	South Florida	74,059
XLIII	2-1-09	Pittsburgh ($78,000)	Arizona ($40,000)	27-23	Tampa Bay	70,774
XLII	2-3-08	N.Y. Giants ($78,000)	New England ($40,000)	17-14	Arizona	71,101
XLI	2-4-07	Indianapolis ($73,000)	Chicago ($38,000)	29-17	South Florida	74,512
XL	2-5-06	Pittsburgh ($73,000)	Seattle ($38,000)	21-10	Detroit	68,206
XXXIX	2-6-05	New England ($68,000)	Philadelphia ($36,500)	24-21	Jacksonville	78,125
XXXVIII	2-1-04	New England ($68,000)	Carolina ($36,500)	32-29	Houston	71,525
* XXXVII	1-26-03	Tampa Bay ($63,000)	Oakland ($35,000)	48-21	San Diego	67,603
* XXXVI	2-3-02	New England ($63,000)	St. Louis ($34,500)	20-17	New Orleans	72,922
XXXV	1-28-01	Baltimore ($58,000)	N.Y. Giants ($34,500)	34-7	Tampa Bay	71,921
* XXXIV	1-30-00	St. Louis ($58,000)	Tennessee ($33,000)	23-16	Atlanta	72,625
XXXIII	1-31-99	Denver ($53,000)	Atlanta ($32,500)	34-19	South Florida	74,803
XXXII	1-25-98	Denver ($48,000)	Green Bay ($29,000)	31-24	San Diego	68,912
XXXI	1-26-97	Green Bay ($48,000)	New England ($29,000)	35-21	New Orleans	72,301
XXX	1-28-96	Dallas ($42,000)	Pittsburgh ($27,000)	27-17	Arizona	76,347
XXIX	1-29-95	San Francisco ($42,000)	San Diego ($26,000)	49-26	South Florida	74,107
* XXVIII	1-30-94	Dallas ($38,000)	Buffalo ($23,500)	30-13	Atlanta	72,817
XXVII	1-31-93	Dallas ($36,000)	Buffalo ($18,000)	52-17	Pasadena	98,374
XXVI	1-26-92	Washington ($36,000)	Buffalo ($18,000)	37-24	Minneapolis	63,130
* XXV	1-27-91	N.Y. Giants ($36,000)	Buffalo ($18,000)	20-19	Tampa Bay	73,813
XXIV	1-28-90	San Francisco ($36,000)	Denver ($18,000)	55-10	New Orleans	72,919
XXIII	1-22-89	San Francisco ($36,000)	Cincinnati ($18,000)	20-16	South Florida	75,129
XXII	1-31-88	Washington ($36,000)	Denver ($18,000)	42-10	San Diego	73,302
XXI	1-25-87	N.Y. Giants ($36,000)	Denver ($18,000)	39-20	Pasadena	101,063
XX	1-26-86	Chicago ($36,000)	New England ($18,000)	46-10	New Orleans	73,818
XIX	1-20-85	San Francisco ($36,000)	Miami ($18,000)	38-16	Stanford	84,059
XVIII	1-22-84	L.A. Raiders ($36,000)	Washington ($18,000)	38-9	Tampa Bay	72,920
* XVII	1-30-83	Washington ($36,000)	Miami ($18,000)	27-17	Pasadena	103,667
XVI	1-24-82	San Francisco ($18,000)	Cincinnati ($9,000)	26-21	Pontiac	81,270
XV	1-25-81	Oakland ($18,000)	Philadelphia ($9,000)	27-10	New Orleans	76,135
XIV	1-20-80	Pittsburgh ($18,000)	Los Angeles ($9,000)	31-19	Pasadena	103,985
XIII	1-21-79	Pittsburgh ($18,000)	Dallas ($9,000)	35-31	South Florida	79,484
XII	1-15-78	Dallas ($18,000)	Denver ($9,000)	27-10	New Orleans	75,583
XI	1-9-77	Oakland ($15,000)	Minnesota ($7,500)	32-14	Pasadena	103,438
X	1-18-76	Pittsburgh ($15,000)	Dallas ($7,500)	21-17	South Florida	80,187
IX	1-12-75	Pittsburgh ($15,000)	Minnesota ($7,500)	16-6	New Orleans	80,997
VIII	1-13-74	Miami ($15,000)	Minnesota ($7,500)	24-7	Houston	71,882
VII	1-14-73	Miami ($15,000)	Washington ($7,500)	14-7	Los Angeles	90,182
VI	1-16-72	Dallas ($15,000)	Miami ($7,500)	24-3	New Orleans	81,023
V	1-17-71	Baltimore ($15,000)	Dallas ($7,500)	16-13	South Florida	79,204
* IV	1-11-70	Kansas City ($15,000)	Minnesota ($7,500)	23-7	New Orleans	80,562
III	1-12-69	N.Y. Jets ($15,000)	Baltimore ($7,500)	16-7	South Florida	75,389
II	1-14-68	Green Bay ($15,000)	Oakland ($7,500)	33-14	South Florida	75,546
I	1-15-67	Green Bay ($15,000)	Kansas City ($7,500)	35-10	Los Angeles	61,946

* One week between conference championship games and Super Bowl; all others had two weeks between conference championship games and Super Bowl.

For historical Super Bowl game recaps, box scores, and video highlights, please visit www.NFL.com/SuperBowl.

SUPER BOWL XLVII
Mercedes-Benz Superdome,
New Orleans, Louisiana
February 3, 2013, Attendance: 71,024
BALTIMORE 34, SAN FRANCISCO 31—
Joe Flacco passed for 3 touchdowns and the Ravens held off a second-half rally to win the second Super Bowl in franchise history. The loss for the 49ers marked their franchise's first defeat in six Super Bowls. Jacoby Jones played a pivotal role for the Ravens. His 17-yard punt return less than two minutes into the game gave Baltimore the ball near midfield. On third-and-9 from the 49ers' 18, Flacco's pass fell incomplete. However, Ahmad Brooks lined up offside, giving the Ravens another opportunity. On the next play, Flacco completed a 13-yard touchdown pass to Anquan Boldin. The 49ers responded with a field goal, and on their next possession drove to the Ravens' 24 only to have Courtney Upshaw force LaMichael James to fumble. Arthur Jones recovered for Baltimore, sparking a 75-yard touchdown drive capped by Flacco's 1-yard touchdown pass to Dennis Pitta for a 14-3 lead.

On the next play from scrimmage, Ed Reed intercepted Colin Kaepernick's deep pass. The Ravens drove to the 49ers' 14, but on fourth-and-9 kicker Justin Tucker took a direct snap and attempted to gain the first down running left but was stopped by Darcel McBath. The Ravens forced a punt and Flacco connected with Jacoby Jones on a 56-yard touchdown pass deep down the middle for a 21-3 lead. The 49ers added a field goal as the first half expired, but Jones returned the opening kickoff of the second half a Super Bowl-record 108 yards for a 28-6 lead. Faced with third-and-13 from their own 40 with 13:04 left in the third quarter, a power outage at the Mercedes-Benz Superdome delayed the game for 34 minutes. Following the resumption of play, the teams exchanged punts. Kaepernick completed a key 9-yard pass to Randy Moss on third-and-8 and an 18-yard pass to Vernon Davis to set up his 31-yard scoring pass to Michael Crabtree. The 49ers' defense forced a three-and-out, and Ted Ginn Jr. returned the punt 32 yards to set up Frank Gore's 6-yard touchdown run to trim the deficit to 28-20 with 4:59 left in the third quarter. Two plays later Ray Rice fumbled and Tarell Brown recovered. David Akers missed a 39-yard field goal, but a running into the kicker penalty gave him a second chance and Akers converted from 34 yards to cut the lead to 28-23. The Ravens drove to the 49ers' 1, but were stopped on two successive plays and settled for Tucker's 19-yard field goal with 12:54 remaining for a 31-23 lead. On the ensuing possession, a 32-yard catch by Moss and 21-yard run by Gore set up Kaepernick's 15-yard scramble around left end for a touchdown. But his 2-point conversion attempt pass to Moss was overthrown, allowing the Ravens to maintain a 31-29 lead with 9:57 to play. Tucker capped the ensuing 10-play drive with a 38-yard field goal for a 34-29 advantage with 4:19 to play. A 24-yard catch by Crabtree and 33-yard run by Gore put the ball at the Ravens' 7 with 2:39 to play. James was stopped for a 2-yard gain on first down, and Kaepernick threw two incompletions to set up fourth-and-goal from the Ravens' 5. Kaepernick attempted a fade pass to the right corner of the end zone but his pass landed on Crabtree's ahead and out of bounds. On fourth-and-7 from the Ravens' 8 with 12 seconds remaining, punter Sam Koch ran along the back of the end zone before Chris Culliver forced him out with four seconds left for a safety. Ginn returned the free kick 31 yards to midfield as time expired. Flacco, who was named the most valuable player, completed 22 of 33 passes for 287 yards and 3 touchdowns. Boldin caught 6 passes for 104 yards. Kaepernick was 16 of 28 for 302 yards and 1 touchdown, with 1 interception. Gore carried 19 times for 110 yards. Davis had 6 catches for 104 yards and Crabtree added 5 receptions for 109 yards.

Baltimore (34)   San Francisco (31)

Offense

Torrey Smith	WR	Michael Crabtree
Bryant McKinnie	LT	Joe Staley
Kelechi Osemele	LG	Mike Iupati
Matt Birk	C	Jonathan Goodwin
Marshal Yanda	RG	Alex Boone
Michael Oher	RT	Anthony Davis
Anquan Boldin	WR/TE	Vernon Davis
Jacoby Jones	WR	Randy Moss
Joe Flacco	QB	Colin Kaepernick
Ray Rice	RB	Frank Gore
Vonta Leach	FB/TE	Delanie Walker

Defense

Haloti Ngata	DT	Ray McDonald
Ma'ake Kemoeatu	NT	Isaac Sopoaga
Arthur Jones	DE/DT	Justin Smith
Terrell Suggs	RUSH/OLB	Ahmad Brooks
Dannell Ellerbe	WILL/ILB	NaVorro Bowman
Ray Lewis	MIKE/ILB	Patrick Willis
Courtney Upshaw	SAM/OLB	Aldon Smith
Corey Graham	LCB	Carlos Rogers
Cary Williams	RCB	Tarell Brown
Ed Reed	FS	Dashon Goldson
Bernard Pollard	SS	Donte Whitner

SUBSTITUTIONS

BALTIMORE—Specialists: K—Justin Tucker. P—Sam Koch. LS—Morgan Cox. Offense: RB—Anthony Allen, Bernard Pierce. WR—Tandon Doss, David Reed. TE—Billy Bajema, Ed Dickson, Dennis Pitta. G—Bobbie Williams. G/C—Gino Gradkowski. Defense: DE—Pernell McPhee, DeAngelo Tyson. NT—Terrence Cody. LB—Brendon Ayanbadejo, Josh Bynes, Paul Kruger, Albert McClellan. CB—Chykie Brown, Jimmy Smith. S—Sean Considine, James Ihedigbo. DNP: QB—Tyrod Taylor. Not Active: WR/RS—Deonte Thompson. G/T—Ramon Harewood. DT—Bryan Hall. LB—Adrian Hamilton. CB—Asa Jackson, Chris Johnson. S—Omar Brown.

SAN FRANCISCO—Specialists: K—David Akers. P—Andy Lee. TE/LS—Brian Jennings. Offense: RB—Anthony Dixon, LaMichael James. FB—Bruce Miller. WR—Ted Ginn, A.J. Jenkins. TE—Garrett Celek. G—Leonard Davis, Daniel Kilgore. Defense: DT/FB—Will Tukuafu. DT—Ricky Jean Francois. LB—Tavares Gooden, Larry Grant, Clark Haggans, Michael Wilhoite. CB—Tramaine Brock, Perrish Cox, Chris Culliver. S—Darcel McBath, C.J. Spillman. DNP: QB—Alex Smith. WR—Chad Hall. Not Active: QB—Scot Tolzein. RB—Jewel Hampton. G—Joe Looney. NT—Ian Williams. DT—Tony Jerod-Eddie. LB—Cam Johnson. S—Trenton Robinson.

OFFICIALS

Referee—Jerome Boger. Umpire—Darrell Jenkins. Head Linesman—Steve Stelljes. Line Judge—Byron Boston. Side Judge—Joe Larrew. Field Judge—Craig Wrolstad. Back Judge—Dino Paganelli. Replay Official—Bill Spyksma.

SCORING

Baltimore (AFC)		7 14 7 6 — 34
San Francisco (NFC)		3 3 17 8 — 31

Balt	—	Boldin 13 pass from Flacco (Tucker kick) (10:36)
SF	—	FG Akers 36 (3:58)
Balt	—	Pitta 1 pass from Flacco (Tucker kick) (7:10)
Balt	—	J. Jones 56 pass from Flacco (Tucker kick) (1:45)
SF	—	FG Akers 27 (0:00)
Balt	—	J. Jones 108 kickoff return (Tucker kick) (14:49)
SF	—	Crabtree 31 pass from Kaepernick (Akers kick) (7:20)
SF	—	Gore 6 run (Akers kick) (4:59)
SF	—	FG Akers 34 (3:10)
Balt	—	FG Tucker 19 (12:54)
SF	—	Kaepernick 15 run (pass failed) (9:57)
Balt	—	FG Tucker 38 (4:19)
SF	—	Safety, Culliver forced Koch out of end zone (0:04)

TEAM STATISTICS

	BALT	SF
Total First Downs	21	23
Rushing	6	9
Passing	13	13
Penalty	2	1
Total Net Yardage	367	468
Total Offensive Plays	70	60
Avg. Gain Per Offensive Play	5.2	7.8
Rushes	35	29
Yards Gained Rushing (Net)	93	182
Avg. Yards per Rush	2.7	6.3
Passes Attempted	33	28
Passes Completed	22	16
Had Intercepted	0	1
Tackled Attempting to Pass	2	3
Yards Lost Attempting to Pass	13	16
Yards Gained Passing (Net)	274	286
Punts	3	3
Avg. Distance	47.0	53.0
Punt Returns	2	1
Punt Return Yardage	28	32
Kickoff Returns	5	4
Kickoff Return Yardage	206	106
Interception Return Yardage	6	0
Total Return Yardage (excl. Kickoff)	34	32
Fumbles	2	1
Fumbles Lost	1	1
Own Fumbles Recovered	1	0
Opponent Fumbles Recovered	1	1
Penalties	2	5
Yards Penalized	20	33
Field Goals	2	3
Field Goals Attempted	2	3
Third-Down Efficiency	9/16	2/9
Fourth-Down Efficiency	0/2	0/1
Time of Possession	32:23	27:37

INDIVIDUAL STATISTICS

RUSHING: Balt: Rice 20-59-0, Pierce 12-33-0, Tucker 1-8-0, Leach 1-1-0, Koch 1-(-8)-0. SF: Gore 19-110-1, Kaepernick 7-62-1, James 3-10-0.

PASSING: Balt: Flacco 33-22-287-3-0. SF: Kaepernick 28-16-302-1-1.

RECEIVING: Balt: Boldin 6-104-1, Pitta 4-26-1, Rice 4-19-0, Leach 3-10-0, Dickson 2-37-0, T. Smith 2-35-0, J. Jones 1-56-1. SF: Davis 6-104-0, Crabtree 5-109-1, Walker 3-48-0, Moss 2-41-0.

KICKOFF RETURNS: Balt: J. Jones 5-206-1. SF: James 3-75-0, Ginn 1-31-0.

PUNT RETURNS: Balt: J. Jones 2-28-0. SF: Ginn 1-32-0.

PUNTING: Balt: Koch 3-141-47.0. SF: Lee 3-159-53.0.

INTERCEPTIONS: Balt: Reed 1-6-0. SF: None.

SACKS: Balt: Kruger 2, A. Jones 1. SF: Brooks 1, McDonald 1.

PLAYOFF GAME SUMMARIES

AFC CHAMPIONSHIP GAME RESULTS
Includes AFL Championship Games (1960-69)

Season	Date	Winner (Share)	Loser (Share)	Score	Site	Attendance
2012	Jan. 20	Baltimore ($40,000)	New England ($40,000)	28-13	Foxborough	68,756
2011	Jan. 22	New England ($40,000)	Baltimore ($40,000)	23-20	Foxborough	68,756
2010	Jan. 23	Pittsburgh ($38,000)	N.Y. Jets ($38,000)	24-19	Pittsburgh	66,662
2009	Jan. 24	Indianapolis ($38,000)	N.Y. Jets ($38,000)	30-17	Indianapolis	67,650
2008	Jan. 18	Pittsburgh ($37,500)	Baltimore ($37,500)	23-14	Pittsburgh	65,350
2007	Jan. 20	New England ($37,500)	San Diego ($37,500)	21-12	Foxborough	68,756
2006	Jan. 21	Indianapolis ($37,000)	New England ($37,000)	38-34	Indianapolis	57,433
2005	Jan. 22	Pittsburgh ($37,000)	Denver ($37,000)	34-17	Denver	76,775
2004	Jan. 23	New England ($36,500)	Pittsburgh ($36,500)	41-27	Pittsburgh	65,242
2003	Jan. 18	New England ($36,500)	Indianapolis ($36,500)	24-14	Foxborough	68,436
2002	Jan. 19	Oakland ($35,000)	Tennessee ($35,000)	41-24	Oakland	62,544
2001	Jan. 27	New England ($34,500)	Pittsburgh ($34,500)	24-17	Pittsburgh	64,704
2000	Jan. 14	Baltimore ($34,500)	Oakland ($34,500)	16-3	Oakland	62,784
1999	Jan. 23	Tennessee ($33,000)	Jacksonville ($33,000)	33-14	Jacksonville	75,206
1998	Jan. 17	Denver ($32,500)	N.Y. Jets ($32,500)	23-10	Denver	75,482
1997	Jan. 11	Denver ($30,000)	Pittsburgh ($30,000)	24-21	Pittsburgh	61,382
1996	Jan. 12	New England ($29,000)	Jacksonville ($29,000)	20-6	Foxborough	60,190
1995	Jan. 14	Pittsburgh ($27,000)	Indianapolis ($27,000)	20-16	Pittsburgh	61,062
1994	Jan. 15	San Diego ($26,000)	Pittsburgh ($26,000)	17-13	Pittsburgh	61,545
1993	Jan. 23	Buffalo ($23,500)	Kansas City ($23,500)	30-13	Buffalo	76,642
1992	Jan. 17	Buffalo ($18,000)	Miami ($18,000)	29-10	Miami	72,703
1991	Jan. 12	Buffalo ($18,000)	Denver ($18,000)	10-7	Buffalo	80,272
1990	Jan. 20	Buffalo ($18,000)	L.A. Raiders ($18,000)	51-3	Buffalo	80,325
1989	Jan. 14	Denver ($18,000)	Cleveland ($18,000)	37-21	Denver	76,046
1988	Jan. 8	Cincinnati ($18,000)	Buffalo ($18,000)	21-10	Cincinnati	59,747
1987	Jan. 17	Denver ($18,000)	Cleveland ($18,000)	38-33	Denver	76,197
1986	Jan. 11	Denver ($18,000)	Cleveland ($18,000)	23-20*	Cleveland	79,973
1985	Jan. 12	New England ($18,000)	Miami ($18,000)	31-14	Miami	75,662
1984	Jan. 6	Miami ($18,000)	Pittsburgh ($18,000)	45-28	Miami	76,029
1983	Jan. 8	L.A. Raiders ($18,000)	Seattle ($18,000)	30-14	Los Angeles	91,445
1982	Jan. 23	Miami ($18,000)	N.Y. Jets ($18,000)	14-0	Miami	67,396
1981	Jan. 10	Cincinnati ($9,000)	San Diego ($9,000)	27-7	Cincinnati	46,302
1980	Jan. 11	Oakland ($9,000)	San Diego ($9,000)	34-27	San Diego	52,675
1979	Jan. 6	Pittsburgh ($9,000)	Houston ($9,000)	27-13	Pittsburgh	50,475
1978	Jan. 7	Pittsburgh ($9,000)	Houston ($9,000)	34-5	Pittsburgh	50,725
1977	Jan. 1	Denver ($9,000)	Oakland ($9,000)	20-17	Denver	75,044
1976	Dec. 26	Oakland ($8,500)	Pittsburgh ($5,500)	24-7	Oakland	53,821
1975	Jan. 4	Pittsburgh ($8,500)	Oakland ($5,500)	16-10	Pittsburgh	50,609
1974	Dec. 29	Pittsburgh ($8,500)	Oakland ($5,500)	24-13	Oakland	53,800
1973	Dec. 30	Miami ($8,500)	Oakland ($5,500)	27-10	Miami	79,325
1972	Dec. 31	Miami ($8,500)	Pittsburgh ($5,500)	21-17	Pittsburgh	50,845
1971	Jan. 2	Miami ($8,500)	Baltimore ($5,500)	21-0	Miami	76,622
1970	Jan. 3	Baltimore ($8,500)	Oakland ($5,500)	27-17	Baltimore	54,799
1969	Jan. 4	Kansas City ($7,755)	Oakland ($6,252)	17-7	Oakland	53,564
1968	Dec. 29	N.Y. Jets ($7,007)	Oakland ($5,349)	27-23	New York	62,627
1967	Dec. 31	Oakland ($6,321)	Houston ($4,996)	40-7	Oakland	53,330
1966	Jan. 1	Kansas City ($5,309)	Buffalo ($3,799)	31-7	Buffalo	42,080
1965	Dec. 26	Buffalo ($5,189)	San Diego ($3,447)	23-0	San Diego	30,361
1964	Dec. 26	Buffalo ($2,668)	San Diego ($1,738)	20-7	Buffalo	40,242
1963	Jan. 5	San Diego ($2,498)	Boston ($1,596)	51-10	San Diego	30,127
1962	Dec. 23	Dallas ($2,206)	Houston ($1,471)	20-17*	Houston	37,981
1961	Dec. 24	Houston ($1,792)	San Diego ($1,111)	10-3	San Diego	29,556
1960	Jan. 1	Houston ($1,025)	L.A. Chargers ($718)	24-16	Houston	32,183

*Overtime

AFC CHAMPIONSHIP GAME COMPOSITE STANDINGS

	W	L	Pct.	Pts.	OP
Cincinnati Bengals	2	0	1.000	48	17
Buffalo Bills	6	2	.750	180	92
Denver Broncos	6	2	.750	189	166
Kansas City Chiefs*	3	1	.750	81	61
Miami Dolphins	5	2	.714	152	115
New England Patriots**	7	3	.700	241	227
Pittsburgh Steelers	8	7	.533	332	303
Indianapolis Colts#	3	3	.500	125	133
Baltimore Ravens	2	2	.500	78	62
Tennessee Titans##	3	5	.375	133	195
Oakland Raiders###	5	9	.357	272	304
New York Jets	1	4	.200	73	114
San Diego Chargers***	2	7	.222	140	182
Seattle Seahawks	0	1	.000	14	30
Jacksonville Jaguars	0	2	.000	20	53
Cleveland Browns	0	3	.000	74	98

   * One game played when franchise was in Dallas (Texans) (Won 20-17)

  ** One game played when franchise was in Boston (Lost 51-10)

 *** One game played when franchise was in Los Angeles (Lost 24-16)

   # Two games played when franchise was in Baltimore (Won 27-17, lost 21-0)

  ## Six games played when franchise was in Houston and known as Oilers (Won 2, lost 4)

 ### Two games played when franchise was in Los Angeles (Won 30-14, lost 51-3)

2012 AFC CHAMPIONSHIP GAME

Gillette Stadium, Foxborough, Massachusetts
January 20, 2013, Attendance: 68,756

BALTIMORE 28, NEW ENGLAND 13—Joe Flacco threw 2 fourth-quarter touchdown passes to Anquan Boldin to overcome a six-point halftime deficit and win the second AFC title in franchise history. Stephen Gostkowski's 31-yard field goal capped a 67-yard drive in the middle of the first quarter to give New England a 3-0 lead. A 17-yard pass from Flacco to Dennis Pitta sparked a 90-yard drive that culminated with Ray Rice's 2-yard touchdown run. New England answered with an 11-play, 79-yard drive in which Tom Brady completed 5 of 6 passes, including a 1-yard scoring pass to Wes Welker, for a 10-7 lead. The Patriots' defense forced a three-and-out with 2:32 left in the half. The Patriots reached the Ravens' 34, and on fourth-and-1 Danny Woodhead took a direct snap and ran seven yards for a first down. Gostkowswki finished the drive with a 25-yard field goal as the half expired for a 13-7 lead. The Ravens marched 87 yards in 10 plays in the middle of the third quarter, with three catches by Pitta, including a 5-yard scoring reception, to give Baltimore a 14-13 lead. The Ravens' defense forced a punt, and Torrey Smith's 23-yard catch highlighted a 63-yard drive that was capped by Flacco's 3-yard touchdown pass to Boldin on the first play of the fourth quarter for a 21-13 lead. Bernard Pollard forced Stevan Ridley to fumble for the Patriots five plays later. Arthur Jones recovered at the Patriots' 47. On the next four plays, Flacco completed a 16-yard pass to Smith, scrambled for 14 yards, connected for a 6-yard pass with Jacoby Jones and finished the drive with an 11-yard scoring pass to Boldin with 11:13 to play. The Patriots drove to the Ravens' 19, but Brady threw three consecutive incomplete passes to end the threat. The Patriots' defense forced a three-and-out and Brady immediately completed a 36-yard pass to Wes Welker to reach the Ravens' 24. But on the next play Dannell Ellerbe intercepted Brady's pass intended for Aaron Hernandez with 6:49 to play. The Patriots regained possession one last time and drove to the Ravens' 22 but Cary Williams intercepted Brady's pass intendend for Brandon Lloyd in the end zone with 1:06 to play. Flacco was 21 of 36 for 240 yards and 3 touchdowns. Brady was 29 of 54 for 320 yards and 1 touchdown, with 2 interceptions, and surpassed Brett Favre for the most passing yards in NFL postseason history. Welker had 8 receptions for 117 yards.

Baltimore (28)	Offense	New England (13)
Torrey Smith	WR	Wes Welker
Bryant McKinnie	LT	Nate Solder
Kelechi Osemele	LG	Logan Mankins
Matt Birk	C	Ryan Wendell
Marshal Yanda	RG	Dan Connolly
Michael Oher	RT	Sebastian Vollmer
Ed Dickson	TE	Michael Hoomanawanui
Anquan Boldin	WR	Brandon Lloyd
Joe Flacco	QB	Tom Brady
Dennis Pitta	TE	Aaron Hernandez
Ray Rice	RB	Stevan Ridley
	Defense	
Haloti Ngata	DT/DE	Justin Francis
Maake Kemoeatu	NT/DT	Vince Wilfork
Paul Kruger	DE/DT	Kyle Love
Terrell Suggs	RUSH/RE	Rob Ninkovich
Dannell Ellerbe	WILL/LB	Jerod Mayo
Ray Lewis	MIKE/LB	Brandon Spikes
Chykie Brown	DB/LB	Dont'a Hightower
Corey Graham	LCB	Aqib Talib
Cary Williams	RCB	Alfonzo Dennard
Bernard Pollard	SS/S	Steve Gregory
Ed Reed	FS/S	Devin McCourty

SUBSTITUTIONS

BALTIMORE—Specialists: K—Justin Tucker. P—Sam Koch. LS—Morgan Cox. Offense: RB—Anthony Allen, Bernard Pierce. FB—Vonta Leach. WR/RS—Jacoby Jones, David Reed. WR—Tandon Doss. TE—Billy Bajema. G—Bobbie Williams. G/C—Gino Gradkowski. Defense: NT—Terrence Cody. DE—Arthur Jones, Pernell McPhee. LB—Brendon Ayanbadejo, Josh Byrnes, Albert McClellan, Courtney Upshaw. CB—Chris Johnson, Jimmy Smith. S—Sean Considine, James Ihedigbo. Did Not Play: QB—Tyrod Taylor. Not Active: WR/RS—Deonte Thompson. G/T—Ramon Harewood. DT—Bryan Hall. DE—DeAngelo Tyson. LB—Adrian Hamilton. CB—Asa Jackson. S—Omar Brown.

NEW ENGLAND—Specialists: K—Stephen Gostkowski. P—Zoltan Mesko. LS—Danny Aiken. Offense: RB—Brandon Bolden, Shane Vereen, Danny Woodhead. WR—Deion Branch, Matthew Slater. TE—Daniel Fells. OL—Marcus Cannon, Donald Thomas. Defense: DE—Jermaine Cunningham, Chandler Jones, Trevor Scott. DL—Brandon Deaderick. LB—Niko Koutouvides, Mike Rivera, Tracy White. CB—Kyle Arrington, Marquice Cole. DB—Nate Ebner, Tavon Wilson. S—Patrick Chung. DNP: QB—Ryan Mallett. Not Active: WR—Kamar Aiken. OL—Nick McDonald, Markus Zusevics. DE—Jake Bequette. DL—Marcus Fortson. DB—Malcolm Williams. FS—Derrick Martin.

OFFICIALS

Referee—Bill Leavy. Umpire—Chad Brown. Head Linesman—Tony Veteri. Line Judge—Jeff Seeman. Side Judge—Doug Rosenbaum. Field Judge—Scott Steenson. Back Judge—Perry Paganelli. Replay Official—Mark Burns.

SCORING

Baltimore	0	7	7	14	—	28
New England	3	10	0	0	—	13

NE	—	FG Gostkowski 31
Balt	—	Rice 2 run (Tucker kick)
NE	—	Welker 1 pass from Brady (Gostkowski kick)
NE	—	FG Gostkowski 25
Balt	—	Pitta 5 pass from Flacco (Tucker kick)
Balt	—	Boldin 3 pass from Flacco (Tucker kick)
Balt	—	Boldin 11 pass from Flacco (Tucker kick)

TEAM STATISTICS

	BALT	NE
Total First Downs	25	28
Rushing	9	6
Passing	15	19
Penalty	1	3
Total Net Yardage	356	428
Total Offensive Plays	71	82
Average Gain Per Offensive Play	5.0	5.2
Rushes	33	28
Yards Gained Rushing (Net)	121	108
Average Yards per Rush	3.7	3.9
Passes Attempted	36	54
Passes Completed	21	29
Had Intercepted	0	2
Tackled Attempting to Pass	2	0
Yards Lost Attempting to Pass	5	0
Yards Gained Passing (Net)	235	320
Punts	7	5
Average Distance	44.7	35.8
Punt Returns	1	4
Punt Return Yardage	11	56
Kickoff Returns	3	4
Kickoff Return Yardage	32	89
Interception Return Yardage	2	19
Total Return Yardage (not incl. kickoffs)	13	56
Fumbles	1	1
Fumbles Lost	0	1
Own Fumbles Recovered	1	0
Opponent Fumbles Recovered	1	0
Penalties	1	1
Yards Penalized	0	1
Field Goals	0	2
Field Goals Attempted	0	2
Third-Down Efficiency	5/12	7/15
Fourth-Down Efficiency	0/0	1/2
Time of Possession	31:06	28:54

PLAYOFF GAME SUMMARIES

INDIVIDUAL STATISTICS
RUSHING: BALT: Pierce 9-52-0, Rice 19-48-1, Flacco 3-12-0, Leach 2-9-0. NE: Ridley 18-70-0, Vereen 4-16-0, Woodhead 3-11-0, Hernandez 1-6-0, Brady 2-5-0.
PASSING: BALT: Flacco 36-21-240-3-0.
NE: Brady 54-29-320-1-2.
RECEIVING: BALT: Boldin 5-60-2, Pitta 5-55-1, T. Smith 4-69-0, Rice 3-22-0, Leach 2-20-0, Pierce 1-8-0, J. Jones 1-6-0.
NE: Hernandez 9-83-0, Welker 8-117-1, Lloyd 7-70-0, Vereen

2-22-0, Branch 2-16-0, Woodhead 1-12-0
KICKOFF RETURNS: BALT: J. Jones 3-32-0. NE: McCourty 4-89-0.
PUNT RETURNS: BALT: J. Jones 1-11-0. NE: Welker 4-56-0.
PUNTING: BALT: Koch 7-313-44.7. NE: Mesko 5-179-35.8.
INTERCEPTIONS: BALT: Ellerbe 1-2-0, C. Williams 1-0-0.
NE: None.
SACKS: BALT: None. NE: Ninkovich 2.

NFC CHAMPIONSHIP GAME RESULTS
Includes NFL Championship Games (1933-1969)

Season	Date	Winner (Share)	Loser (Share)	Score	Site	Attendance
2012	Jan. 20	San Francisco ($40,000)	Atlanta ($40,000)	28-24	Atlanta	70,863
2011	Jan. 22	N.Y. Giants ($40,000)	San Francisco ($40,000)	20-17*	San Francisco	69,732
2010	Jan. 23	Green Bay ($38,000)	Chicago ($38,000)	21-14	Chicago	62,377
2009	Jan. 24	New Orleans ($38,000)	Minnesota ($38,000)	31-28*	New Orleans	71,276
2008	Jan. 18	Arizona ($37,500)	Philadelphia ($37,500)	32-25	Glendale	70,650
2007	Jan. 20	N.Y. Giants ($37,500)	Green Bay ($37,500)	23-20*	Green Bay	72,740
2006	Jan. 21	Chicago ($37,000)	New Orleans ($37,000)	39-14	Chicago	61,817
2005	Jan. 22	Seattle ($37,000)	Carolina ($37,000)	34-14	Seattle	67,837
2004	Jan. 23	Philadelphia ($36,500)	Atlanta ($36,500)	27-10	Philadelphia	67,717
2003	Jan. 18	Carolina ($36,500)	Philadelphia ($36,500)	14-3	Philadelphia	67,862
2002	Jan. 19	Tampa Bay ($35,000)	Philadelphia ($35,000)	27-10	Philadelphia	66,713
2001	Jan. 27	St. Louis ($34,500)	Philadelphia ($34,500)	29-24	St. Louis	66,502
2000	Jan. 14	N.Y. Giants ($34,500)	Minnesota ($34,500)	41-0	East Rutherford	79,310
1999	Jan. 23	St. Louis ($33,000)	Tampa Bay ($33,000)	11-6	St. Louis	66,396
1998	Jan. 17	Atlanta ($32,500)	Minnesota ($32,500)	30-27*	Minneapolis	64,060
1997	Jan. 11	Green Bay ($30,000)	San Francisco ($30,000)	23-10	San Francisco	68,987
1996	Jan. 12	Green Bay ($29,000)	Carolina ($29,000)	30-13	Green Bay	60,216
1995	Jan. 14	Dallas ($27,000)	Green Bay ($27,000)	38-27	Dallas	65,135
1994	Jan. 15	San Francisco ($26,000)	Dallas ($26,000)	38-28	San Francisco	69,125
1993	Jan. 23	Dallas ($23,500)	San Francisco ($23,500)	38-21	Dallas	64,902
1992	Jan. 17	Dallas ($18,000)	San Francisco ($18,000)	30-20	San Francisco	64,920
1991	Jan. 12	Washington ($18,000)	Detroit ($18,000)	41-10	Washington	55,585
1990	Jan. 20	N.Y. Giants ($18,000)	San Francisco ($18,000)	15-13	San Francisco	65,750
1989	Jan. 14	San Francisco ($18,000)	L.A. Rams ($18,000)	30-3	San Francisco	65,634
1988	Jan. 8	San Francisco ($18,000)	Chicago ($18,000)	28-3	Chicago	66,946
1987	Jan. 17	Washington ($18,000)	Minnesota ($18,000)	17-10	Washington	55,212
1986	Jan. 11	New York Giants ($18,000)	Washington ($18,000)	17-0	East Rutherford	76,891
1985	Jan. 12	Chicago ($18,000)	L.A. Rams ($18,000)	24-0	Chicago	66,030
1984	Jan. 6	San Francisco ($18,000)	Chicago ($18,000)	23-0	San Francisco	61,336
1983	Jan. 8	Washington ($18,000)	San Francisco ($18,000)	24-21	Washington	55,363
1982	Jan. 22	Washington ($18,000)	Dallas ($18,000)	31-17	Washington	55,045
1981	Jan. 10	San Francisco ($9,000)	Dallas ($9,000)	28-27	San Francisco	60,525
1980	Jan. 11	Philadelphia ($9,000)	Dallas ($9,000)	20-7	Philadelphia	71,522
1979	Jan. 6	Los Angeles ($9,000)	Tampa Bay ($9,000)	9-0	Tampa	72,033
1978	Jan. 7	Dallas ($9,000)	Los Angeles ($9,000)	28-0	Los Angeles	71,086
1977	Jan. 1	Dallas ($9,000)	Minnesota ($9,000)	23-6	Dallas	64,293
1976	Dec. 26	Minnesota ($8,500)	Los Angeles ($5,500)	24-13	Minneapolis	48,379
1975	Jan. 4	Dallas ($8,500)	Los Angeles ($5,500)	37-7	Los Angeles	88,919
1974	Dec. 29	Minnesota ($8,500)	Los Angeles ($5,500)	14-10	Minneapolis	48,444
1973	Dec. 30	Minnesota ($8,500)	Dallas ($5,500)	27-10	Dallas	64,422
1972	Dec. 31	Washington ($8,500)	Dallas ($5,500)	26-3	Washington	53,129
1971	Jan. 2	Dallas ($8,500)	San Francisco ($5,500)	14-3	Dallas	63,409
1970	Jan. 3	Dallas ($8,500)	San Francisco ($5,500)	17-10	San Francisco	59,364
1969	Jan. 4	Minnesota ($7,930)	Cleveland ($5,118)	27-7	Minneapolis	46,503
1968	Dec. 29	Baltimore ($9,306)	Cleveland ($5,963)	34-0	Cleveland	78,410
1967	Dec. 31	Green Bay ($7,950)	Dallas ($5,299)	21-17	Green Bay	50,861
1966	Jan. 1	Green Bay ($9,813)	Dallas ($6,527)	34-27	Dallas	74,152
1965	Jan. 2	Green Bay ($7,819)	Cleveland ($5,288)	23-12	Green Bay	50,777
1964	Dec. 27	Cleveland ($8,052)	Baltimore ($5,571)	27-0	Cleveland	79,544
1963	Dec. 29	Chicago ($5,899)	New York ($4,218)	14-10	Chicago	45,801
1962	Dec. 30	Green Bay ($5,888)	New York ($4,166)	16-7	New York	64,892
1961	Dec. 31	Green Bay ($5,195)	New York ($3,339)	37-0	Green Bay	39,029
1960	Dec. 26	Philadelphia ($5,116)	Green Bay ($3,105)	17-13	Philadelphia	67,325
1959	Dec. 27	Baltimore ($4,674)	New York ($3,083)	31-16	Baltimore	57,545
1958	Dec. 28	Baltimore ($4,718)	New York ($3,111)	23-17*	New York	64,185
1957	Dec. 29	Detroit ($4,295)	Cleveland ($2,750)	59-14	Detroit	55,263
1956	Dec. 30	New York ($3,779)	Chi. Bears ($2,485)	47-7	New York	56,836
1955	Dec. 26	Cleveland ($3,508)	Los Angeles ($2,316)	38-14	Los Angeles	85,693
1954	Dec. 26	Cleveland ($2,478)	Detroit ($1,585)	56-10	Cleveland	43,827

Season	Date	Winner (Share)	Loser (Share)	Score	Site	Attendance
1953	Dec. 27	Detroit ($2,424)	Cleveland ($1,654)	17-16	Detroit	54,577
1952	Dec. 28	Detroit ($2,274)	Cleveland ($1,712)	17-7	Cleveland	50,934
1951	Dec. 23	Los Angeles ($2,108)	Cleveland ($1,483)	24-17	Los Angeles	57,522
1950	Dec. 24	Cleveland ($1,113)	Los Angeles ($686)	30-28	Cleveland	29,751
1949	Dec. 18	Philadelphia ($1,094)	Los Angeles ($739)	14-0	Los Angeles	27,980
1948	Dec. 19	Philadelphia ($1,540)	Chi. Cardinals ($874)	7-0	Philadelphia	36,309
1947	Dec. 28	Chi. Cardinals ($1,132)	Philadelphia ($754)	28-21	Chicago	30,759
1946	Dec. 15	Chi. Bears ($1,975)	New York ($1,295)	24-14	New York	58,346
1945	Dec. 16	Cleveland ($1,469)	Washington ($902)	15-14	Cleveland	32,178
1944	Dec. 17	Green Bay ($1,449)	New York ($814)	14-7	New York	46,016
1943	Dec. 26	Chi. Bears ($1,146)	Washington ($765)	41-21	Chicago	34,320
1942	Dec. 13	Washington ($965)	Chi. Bears ($637)	14-6	Washington	36,006
1941	Dec. 21	Chi. Bears ($430)	New York ($288)	37-9	Chicago	13,341
1940	Dec. 8	Chi. Bears ($873)	Washington ($606)	73-0	Washington	36,034
1939	Dec. 10	Green Bay ($703.97)	New York ($455.57)	27-0	Milwaukee	32,279
1938	Dec. 11	New York ($504.45)	Green Bay ($368.81)	23-17	New York	48,120
1937	Dec. 12	Washington ($225.90)	Chi. Bears ($127.78)	28-21	Chicago	15,870
1936	Dec. 13	Green Bay ($250)	Boston ($180)	21-6	New York	29,545
1935	Dec. 15	Detroit ($313.35)	New York ($200.20)	26-7	Detroit	15,000
1934	Dec. 9	New York ($621)	Chi. Bears ($414.02)	30-13	New York	35,059
1933	Dec. 17	Chi. Bears ($210.34)	New York ($140.22)	23-21	Chicago	26,000

*Overtime

NFC CHAMPIONSHIP GAME COMPOSITE STANDINGS

	W	L	Pct.	Pts.	OP
Seattle Seahawks	1	0	1.000	34	14
Baltimore Colts	3	1	.750	88	60
Green Bay Packers	11	4	.733	344	214
Detroit Lions	4	2	.667	139	141
Arizona Cardinals**	2	1	.667	60	53
Washington Redskins*	7	5	.583	222	255
Chicago Bears	8	7	.533	339	280
Dallas Cowboys	8	8	.500	361	319
Philadelphia Eagles	5	5	.500	168	160
Atlanta Falcons	1	2	.333	64	82
New Orleans Saints	1	1	.500	45	67
Minnesota Vikings	4	5	.444	163	182
New York Giants	8	11	.421	324	359
San Francisco 49ers	6	8	.429	290	266
Cleveland Browns	4	7	.364	224	253
St. Louis Rams***	5	9	.357	163	300
Carolina Panthers	1	2	.333	41	67
Tampa Bay Buccaneers	1	2	.333	33	30

*One game played when franchise was in Boston (Lost 21-6)
**Both games played when franchise was in Chicago (Won 28-21, lost 7-0)
***One game played when franchise was in Cleveland (Won 15-14), and 11 games when franchise was in Los Angeles (Won 2, lost 9, scored 108 points, allowed 256 points).

2012 NFC CHAMPIONSHIP GAME
Georgia Dome, Atlanta, Georgia
January 20, 2013, Attendance: 70,863
SAN FRANCISCO 28, ATLANTA 24—Frank Gore rushed for 2 touchdowns and the 49ers rallied from a 17-0 deficit to register the franchise's first NFC championship in 18 years. The Falcons rolled up 297 total yards in the first half, scoring on their first three possessions. On their first drive, Matt Ryan completed a 16-yard pass to Roddy White on third-and-9 to set up his 46-yard touchdown pass deep down the left side to Julio Jones. The Falcons' defense forced a three-and-out and Jones caught a 27-yard pass on third down to keep alive a 65-yard drive capped by Matt Bryant's 35-yard field goal for a 10-0 lead. After another three-and-out by the Falcons' defense, Jones stayed in-bounds with his 20-yard touchdown catch along the left side of the end zone for a 17-0 lead one play into the second quarter. The 49ers responded with touchdown drives of 80 and 82 yards on their next two possessions. Vernon Davis had a 27-yard catch on third-and-7 to

keep the first drive going to set up LaMichael James' 15-yard scoring run. Davis had a pair of 25-yard catches on the second drive before his 4-yard scoring grab trimmed the deficit to 17-14 with 1:55 left in the half. The Falcons answered, as Ryan completed 6 of 7 passes on the ensuing drive, capped by Tony Gonzalez' 10-yard catch with 25 seconds left in the half to stretch the halftime lead to 24-14. Colin Kaepernick completed passes of 21 and 17 yards to Randy Moss to begin the second half, and Gore culminated the 82-yard drive with his 5-yard touchdown run to pull within 24-21. The 49ers' defense then forced turnovers on each of the Falcons' next two possessions, but San Francisco failed to capitalize as David Akers missed a field-goal attempt to conclude the first drive and Dunta Robinson forced Michael Crabtree to fumble near the goal line and Stephen Nicholas recovered at the 1-yard line. Three plays later, Carlos Rogers forced Gonzalez out of bounds 1-yard shy of a first down, forcing the Falcons to punt from their own end zone with 11:46 to play. Ted Ginn Jr. returned the punt 20 yards, and Gore's 9-yard run around right end gave San Francisco its first lead, 28-24, with 8:23 to play. The Falcons drove more than seven minutes, converted two third downs, and reached the 49ers' 10-yard-line, but Ryan's pass on fourth-and-4 was incomplete with 1:09 to play. Kaepernick completed 16 of 21 passes for 233 yards and 1 touchdown. Davis had 5 catches for 106 yards. Ryan was 30 of 42 for 396 yards and 3 touchdowns, with 1 interception. Jones had 11 catches for 182 yards and White added 7 catches for 100 yards.

San Francisco (28)	Offense	Atlanta (24)
Michael Crabtree	WR	Julio Jones
Joe Staley	LT	Sam Baker
Mike Iupati	LG	Justin Blalock
Jonathan Goodwin	C	Todd McClure
Alex Boone	RG	Peter Konz
Anthony Davis	RT	Tyson Clabo
Vernon Davis	TE	Tony Gonzalez
Randy Moss	WR	Roddy White
Colin Kaepernick	QB	Matt Ryan
Brad Miller	FB/WR	Harry Douglas
Frank Gore	RB	Michael Turner
	Defense	
Ray McDonald	LDT/LE	John Abraham
Justin Smith	RDT/DT	Corey Peters
Ahmad Brooks	OLB/DT	Vance Walker
NaVorro Bowman	ILB/RE	Jonathan Babineaux
Patrick Willis	ILB/OLB	Sean Weatherspoon
Aldon Smith	OLB/MLB	Akeem Dent

PLAYOFF GAME SUMMARIES

Chris Culliver	NB/OLB	Stephen Nicholas	
Carlos Rogers	LCB/CB	Dunta Robinson	
Tarell Brown	RCB/CB	Asante Samuel	
Donte Whitner	SS/S	William Moore	
Dashon Goldson	FS/S	Thomas DeCoud	

SUBSTITUTIONS

SAN FRANCISCO—Specialists: K—David Akers. P—Andy Lee. LS/TE—Brian Jennings. Offense: RB—Anthony Dixon, LaMichael James. WR—Ted Ginn, Chad Hall. TE—Garrett Celek, Delanie Walker. G—Leonard Davis, Daniel Kilgore. Defense: NT—Isaac Sopoaga. DT/FB—Will Tukuafu. DT—Ricky Jean Francois. LB—Tavares Gooden, Larry Grant, Clark Haggans, Michael Wilhoite. CB—Tramaine Brock, Perrish Cox. S—Darcel McBath, C.J. Spillman. Did Not Play: QB—Alex Smith. WR—A.J. Jenkins. Not Active: QB—Scott Tolzien. RB—Jewel Hampton. G—Joe Looney. NT—Ian Williams. DT—Tony Jerod-Eddie. LB—Cam Johnson. S—Trenton Robinson.

ATLANTA—Specialists: K—Matt Bryant. P—Matt Bosher. LS—Josh Harris. Offense: RB—Jacquizz Rodgers, Antone Smith, Jason Snelling. FB—Mike Cox. WR—Drew Davis. TE—Chase Coffman, Michael Palmer. OL—Mike Johnson. Defense: DT—Peria Jerry. DE—Kroy Biermann, Jonathan Massaquoi, Cliff Matthews. LB—Robert James, Mike Peterson. CB—Robert McClain, Christopher Owens. S—Chris Hope, Charles Mitchell. Did Not Play: QB—Luke McCown. C—Joe Hawley. CB—Dominique Franks. Not Active: QB—Dominique Davis. WR—Tim Toone. G—Harland Gunn, Phillipkeith Manley. T—Lamar Holmes. DT—Travain Robertson. DE—Lawrence Sidbury.

OFFICIALS

Referee—Terry McAulay. Umpire—Carl Paganelli. Head Linesman—Wayne Mackie. Line Judge—Tom Stephan. Side Judge—Allen Baynes. Field Judge—Gary Cavaletto. Back Judge—Tony Steratore. Reply Official—Earnie Frantz.

SCORING

San Francisco	0	14	7	7	—	28
Atlanta	10	14	0	0	—	24

Atl	—	Jones 46 pass from Ryan (Bryant kick)
Atl	—	FG Bryant 35
Atl	—	Jones 20 pass from Ryan (Bryant kick)
SF	—	James 15 run (Akers kick)
SF	—	Davis 4 pass from Kaepernick (Akers kick)
Atl	—	Gonzalez 10 pass from Ryan (Bryant kick)
SF	—	Gore 5 run (Akers kick)
SF	—	Gore 9 run (Akers kick)

TEAM STATISTICS

	SF	ATL
Total First Downs	21	27
Rushing	8	5
Passing	11	21
Penalty	2	1
Total Net Yardage	373	477
Total Offensive Plays	51	66
Average Gain Per Offensive Play	7.3	7.2
Rushes	29	23
Yards Gained Rushing (Net)	149	81
Average Yards per Rush	5.1	3.5
Passes Attempted	21	42
Passes Completed	16	30
Had Intercepted	0	1
Tackled Attempting to Pass	1	1
Yards Lost Attempting to Pass	9	0
Yards Gained Passing (Net)	224	396
Punts	3	2
Average Distance	50.3	45.0
Punt Returns	1	3
Punt Return Yardage	20	6
Kickoff Returns	3	0
Kickoff Return Yardage	64	0
Interception Return Yardage	6	0
Total Return Yardage (excluding Kickoffs)	26	6
Fumbles	1	1
Fumbles Lost	1	1
Own Fumbles Recovered	0	0
Opponent Fumbles Recovered	1	1
Penalties	4	2
Yards Penalized	24	30
Field Goals	0	1
Field Goals Attempted	1	1
Third-Down Efficiency	2/6	5/9
Fourth-Down Efficiency	0/0	0/1
Time of Possession	27:56	32:04

INDIVIDUAL STATISTICS

RUSHING: SF: Gore 21-90-2, James 5-34-1, Kaepernick 2-21-0, Dixon 1-4-0. ATL: Rodgers 10-32-0, Turner 8-30-0, Snelling 2-12-0, Cox 1-4-0, Ryan 2-3-0.

PASSING: SF: Kaepernick 21-16-233-1-0. ATL: Ryan 42-30-396-3-1.

RECEIVING: SF: Crabtree 6-57-0, Davis 5-106-1, Moss 3-46-0, Walker 1-20-0, James 1-4-0. ATL: Jones 11-182-2, Gonzalez 8-78-1, White 7-100-0, Douglas 3-31-0, Snelling 1-5-0.

KICKOFF RETURNS: SF: James 3-64-0. ATL : None.

PUNT RETURNS: SF: Ginn 1-20-0. ATL : Douglas 3-6-0.

PUNTING: SF: Lee 3-151-50.3. ATL: Bosher 2-90-45.0.

INTERCEPTIONS: SF: Culliver 1-6-0. SF: None.

SACKS: SF: Sopoaga 1. ATL: Peters 1.

AFC DIVISIONAL PLAYOFF GAMES RESULTS

Includes Second-Round Playoff Games (1982), AFC Inter-Divisional Games (1969), and special playoff games to break ties for AFC Division Championships (1963, 1968)

Season	Date	Winner (Share)	Loser (Share)	Score	Site	Attendance
2012	Jan. 13	New England ($22,000)	Houston ($22,000)	41-28	Foxborough	68,756
	Jan. 12	Baltimore ($22,000)	Denver ($22,000)	38-35*	Denver	76,732
2011	Jan. 15	Baltimore ($22,000)	Houston ($22,000)	20-13	Baltimore	71,547
	Jan. 14	New England ($22,000)	Denver ($22,000)	45-10	Foxborough	68,756
2010	Jan. 16	N.Y. Jets ($21,000)	New England ($21,000)	28-21	Foxborough	68,756
	Jan. 15	Pittsburgh ($21,000)	Baltimore ($21,000)	31-24	Pittsburgh	64,879
2009	Jan. 17	N.Y. Jets ($21,000)	San Diego ($21,000)	17-14	San Diego	69,498
	Jan. 16	Indianapolis ($21,000)	Baltimore ($21,000)	20-3	Indianapolis	67,535
2008	Jan. 11	Pittsburgh ($20,000)	San Diego ($20,000)	35-24	Pittsburgh	63,899
	Jan. 10	Baltimore ($20,000)	Tennessee ($20,000)	13-10	Nashville	69,143
2007	Jan. 13	San Diego ($20,000)	Indianapolis ($20,000)	28-24	Indianapolis	56,950
	Jan. 12	New England ($20,000)	Jacksonville ($20,000)	31-20	Foxborough	68,756
2006	Jan. 14	New England ($19,000)	San Diego ($19,000)	24-21	San Diego	68,810
	Jan. 13	Indianapolis ($19,000)	Baltimore ($19,000)	15-6	Baltimore	71,162
2005	Jan. 15	Pittsburgh ($19,000)	Indianapolis ($19,000)	21-18	Indianapolis	57,449
	Jan. 14	Denver ($19,000)	New England ($19,000)	27-13	Denver	76,238
2004	Jan. 16	New England ($18,000)	Indianapolis ($18,000)	20-3	Foxborough	68,756
	Jan. 15	Pittsburgh ($18,000)	N.Y. Jets ($18,000)	20-17*	Pittsburgh	64,915

Season	Date	Winner (Share)	Loser (Share)	Score	Site	Attendance
2003	Jan. 11	Indianapolis ($18,000)	Kansas City ($18,000)	38-31	Kansas City	79,159
	Jan. 10	New England ($18,000)	Tennessee ($18,000)	17-14	Foxborough	68,436
2002	Jan. 12	Oakland ($17,000)	N.Y. Jets ($17,000)	30-10	Oakland	62,207
	Jan. 11	Tennessee ($17,000)	Pittsburgh ($17,000)	34-31*	Nashville	68,809
2001	Jan. 20	Pittsburgh ($17,000)	Baltimore ($17,000)	27-10	Pittsburgh	63,976
	Jan. 19	New England ($17,000)	Oakland ($17,000)	16-13*	Foxborough	60,292
2000	Jan. 7	Baltimore ($16,000)	Tennessee ($16,000)	24-10	Nashville	68,527
	Jan. 6	Oakland ($16,000)	Miami ($16,000)	27-0	Oakland	61,998
1999	Jan. 16	Tennessee ($16,000)	Indianapolis ($16,000)	19-16	Indianapolis	57,097
	Jan. 15	Jacksonville ($16,000)	Miami ($16,000)	62-7	Jacksonville	75,173
1998	Jan. 10	N.Y. Jets ($15,000)	Jacksonville ($15,000)	34-24	East Rutherford	78,817
	Jan. 9	Denver ($15,000)	Miami ($15,000)	38-3	Denver	75,729
1997	Jan. 4	Denver ($15,000)	Kansas City ($15,000)	14-10	Kansas City	76,965
	Jan. 3	Pittsburgh ($15,000)	New England ($15,000)	7-6	Pittsburgh	61,228
1996	Jan. 5	New England ($14,000)	Pittsburgh ($14,000)	28-3	Foxborough	60,188
	Jan. 4	Jacksonville ($14,000)	Denver ($14,000)	30-27	Denver	75,678
1995	Jan. 7	Indianapolis ($13,000)	Kansas City ($13,000)	10-7	Kansas City	77,594
	Jan. 6	Pittsburgh ($13,000)	Buffalo ($13,000)	40-21	Pittsburgh	59,072
1994	Jan. 8	San Diego ($12,000)	Miami ($12,000)	22-21	San Diego	63,381
	Jan. 7	Pittsburgh ($12,000)	Cleveland ($12,000)	29-9	Pittsburgh	58,185
1993	Jan. 16	Kansas City ($12,000)	Houston ($12,000)	28-20	Houston	64,011
	Jan. 15	Buffalo ($12,000)	L.A. Raiders ($12,000)	29-23	Buffalo	61,923
1992	Jan. 10	Miami ($10,000)	San Diego ($10,000)	31-0	Miami	71,224
	Jan. 9	Buffalo ($10,000)	Pittsburgh ($10,000)	24-3	Pittsburgh	60,407
1991	Jan. 5	Buffalo ($10,000)	Kansas City ($10,000)	37-14	Buffalo	80,182
	Jan. 4	Denver ($10,000)	Houston ($10,000)	26-24	Denver	75,301
1990	Jan. 13	L.A. Raiders ($10,000)	Cincinnati ($10,000)	20-10	Los Angeles	92,045
	Jan. 12	Buffalo ($10,000)	Miami ($10,000)	44-34	Buffalo	77,087
1989	Jan. 7	Denver ($10,000)	Pittsburgh ($10,000)	24-23	Denver	75,477
	Jan. 6	Cleveland ($10,000)	Buffalo ($10,000)	34-30	Cleveland	78,921
1988	Jan. 1	Buffalo ($10,000)	Houston ($10,000)	17-10	Buffalo	79,532
	Dec. 31	Cincinnati ($10,000)	Seattle ($10,000)	21-13	Cincinnati	58,560
1987	Jan. 10	Denver ($10,000)	Houston ($10,000)	34-10	Denver	75,440
	Jan. 9	Cleveland ($10,000)	Indianapolis ($10,000)	38-21	Cleveland	79,372
1986	Jan. 4	Denver ($10,000)	New England ($10,000)	22-17	Denver	75,262
	Jan. 3	Cleveland ($10,000)	N.Y. Jets ($10,000)	23-20*	Cleveland	79,720
1985	Jan. 5	New England ($10,000)	L.A. Raiders ($10,000)	27-20	Los Angeles	87,163
	Jan. 4	Miami ($10,000)	Cleveland ($10,000)	24-21	Miami	74,667
1984	Dec. 30	Pittsburgh ($10,000)	Denver ($10,000)	24-17	Denver	74,981
	Dec. 29	Miami ($10,000)	Seattle ($10,000)	31-10	Miami	73,469
1983	Jan. 1	L.A. Raiders ($10,000)	Pittsburgh ($10,000)	38-10	Los Angeles	90,380
	Dec. 31	Seattle ($10,000)	Miami ($10,000)	27-20	Miami	74,136
1982	Jan. 16	Miami ($10,000)	San Diego ($10,000)	34-13	Miami	71,383
	Jan. 15	N.Y. Jets ($10,000)	L.A. Raiders ($10,000)	17-14	Los Angeles	90,038
1981	Jan. 3	Cincinnati ($5,000)	Buffalo ($5,000)	28-21	Cincinnati	55,420
	Jan. 2	San Diego ($5,000)	Miami ($5,000)	41-38*	Miami	73,735
1980	Jan. 4	Oakland ($5,000)	Cleveland ($5,000)	14-12	Cleveland	78,245
	Jan. 3	San Diego ($5,000)	Buffalo ($5,000)	20-14	San Diego	52,253
1979	Dec. 30	Pittsburgh ($5,000)	Miami ($5,000)	34-14	Pittsburgh	50,214
	Dec. 29	Houston ($5,000)	San Diego ($5,000)	17-14	San Diego	51,192
1978	Dec. 31	Houston ($5,000)	New England ($5,000)	31-14	Foxborough	60,735
	Dec. 30	Pittsburgh ($5,000)	Denver ($5,000)	33-10	Pittsburgh	50,230
1977	Dec. 24	Oakland ($5,000)	Baltimore ($5,000)	37-31*	Baltimore	59,925
	Dec. 24	Denver ($5,000)	Pittsburgh ($5,000)	34-21	Denver	75,059
1976	Dec. 19	Pittsburgh [$]	Baltimore [$]	40-14	Baltimore	59,296
	Dec. 18	Oakland [$]	New England [$]	24-21	Oakland	53,050
1975	Dec. 28	Oakland [$]	Cincinnati [$]	31-28	Oakland	53,030
	Dec. 27	Pittsburgh [$]	Baltimore [$]	28-10	Pittsburgh	49,557
1974	Dec. 22	Pittsburgh [$]	Buffalo [$]	32-14	Pittsburgh	49,841
	Dec. 21	Oakland [$]	Miami [$]	28-26	Oakland	53,023
1973	Dec. 23	Miami [$]	Cincinnati [$]	34-16	Miami	78,928
	Dec. 22	Oakland [$]	Pittsburgh [$]	33-14	Oakland	52,646
1972	Dec. 24	Miami [$]	Cleveland [$]	20-14	Miami	78,916
	Dec. 23	Pittsburgh [$]	Oakland [$]	13-7	Pittsburgh	50,327
1971	Dec. 26	Baltimore [$]	Cleveland [$]	20-3	Cleveland	70,734
	Dec. 25	Miami [$]	Kansas City [$]	27-24*	Kansas City	50,374
1970	Dec. 27	Oakland [$]	Miami [$]	21-14	Oakland	52,594
	Dec. 26	Baltimore [$]	Cincinnati [$]	17-0	Baltimore	49,694
1969	Dec. 21	Oakland [$]	Houston [$]	56-7	Oakland	53,539
	Dec. 20	Kansas City [$]	N.Y. Jets [$]	13-6	New York	62,977
1968	Dec. 22	Oakland [$]	Kansas City [$]	41-6	Oakland	53,605
1963	Dec. 28	Boston [$]	Buffalo [$]	26-8	Buffalo	33,044

*Overtime

$ Players received 1/14 of annual salary for playoff appearances.

2012 AFC DIVISIONAL PLAYOFF GAMES

Gillette Stadium, Foxborough, Massachusetts
January 13, 2013, Attendance: 68,756

NEW ENGLAND 41, HOUSTON 28—Tom Brady passed for 3 touchdowns and Shane Vereen scored 3 times as the Patriots led by as many as 25 points en route to victory. The teams combined for 882 yards (457 for New England) and 69 points. Danieal Manning began the game with a 94-yard kickoff return to set up Shayne Graham's 27-yard field goal. Late in the first quarter the Patriots began a stretch of scoring drives consisting of 65, 80, and 65 yards, the last of which was set up by Wes Welker's 47-yard reception and capped by Vereen's second touchdown, for a 17-3 lead. Manning's 35-yard kickoff return, and a horsecollar-tackle penalty on New England, set up Arian Foster's 1-yard touchdown run with 1:15 left in the half. The Texans' defense forced a three-and-out and Matt Schaub completed two passes to Owen Daniels. Graham ended the half with a 55-yard field goal, suddenly pulling Houston to within 17-13. The Patriots responded with a touchdown on the first drive of the second half, highlighted by Aaron Hernandez' 40-yard catch and run. Later in the third quarter Rob Ninkovich intercepted Schaub's pass, and Stevan Ridley had a 23-yard run to set up Brandon Lloyd's 5-yard touchdown catch for a 31-13 lead. Early in the fourth quarter, Schaub's fourth-and-1 pass fell incomplete and on the next play Brady completed a 33-yard touchdown pass to Vereen to give New England a 38-13 lead with 13:07 to play. Manning had a 69-yard kickoff return to set up DeVier Posey's 25-yard touchdown catch. Foster scored, and Andre Johnson caught a 2-point conversion pass, to pull Houston to within 38-28 with 5:11 to play, but Ninkovich recovered the onside kick and Stephen Gostkowski made a 38-yard field goal with 1:14 to play. Brady was 25 of 40 for 344 yards and 3 touchdowns. Welker had 8 catches for 131 yards. Schaub completed 34 of 51 passes for 343 yards and 2 touchdowns, with 2 interceptions.

Houston	3	10	0	15	—	28
New England	7	10	14	10	—	41

Hou — FG Graham 27
NE — Vereen 1 run (Gostkowski kick)
NE — FG Gostkowski 37
NE — Vereen 8 pass from Brady (Gostkowski kick)
Hou — Foster 1 run (Graham kick)
Hou — FG Graham 55
NE — Ridley 8 run (Gostkowski kick)
NE — Lloyd 5 pass from Brady (Gostkowski kick)
NE — Vereen 33 pass from Brady (Gostkowski kick)
Hou — Posey 25 pass from Schaub (Graham kick)
Hou — Foster 1 pass from Schaub
  (Johnson pass from Schaub)
NE — FG Gostkowski 38

Sports Authority Field at Mile High, Denver, Colorado
January 12, 2013, Attendance: 76,732

BALTIMORE 38, DENVER 35 (2 OT)—Corey Graham's interception set up Justin Tucker's 47-yard field goal with 13:24 left in the second overtime to conclude the third-longest game in NFL history. The Ravens forced overtime when Joe Flacco completed a 70-yard touchdown pass to Jacoby Jones with just 31 seconds remaining in regulation. Denver's defense began the game by forcing a punt and Trindon Holliday returned it 90 yards for a touchdown. Baltimore needed just four plays to tie the game on Flacco's 59-yard touchdown pass to Torrey Smith, and took a 14-7 lead three plays later on Graham's 39-yard interception return for a score. The Broncos answered with a 74-yard touchdown drive to tie the game, and an 86-yard drive, capped by Peyton Manning's 14-yard touchdown pass to Knowshon Moreno, to take a 21-14 lead with 7:26 left in the half. With 1:16 remaining in the half Matt Prater's 52-yard field goal attempt was short, and Flacco completed a 32-yard touchdown pass to Smith three plays later to tie the game. Holliday returned the opening kickoff of the second half 104 yards for a touchdown, thus becoming the first player in NFL postseason annals to return both a punt and kickoff for a touchdown in the same game. Late in the third quarter Pernell McPhee sacked Manning and forced him to fumble. Paul Kruger recovered at the Broncos' 37. Ray Rice's 32-yard run moments later set up his 1-yard touchdown to tie the game at 28 entering the fourth quarter. Manning's 17-yard touchdown pass to Demaryius Thomas capped a 10-play, 88-yard drive to give Denver a 35-28 lead with 7:11 remaining. The Ravens drove to the Broncos' 31, but Flacco's fourth-and-5 pass fell incomplete with 3:12 to play. Ronnie Hillman rushed for one first down and forced the Ravens to use up their timeouts before Britton Colquitt punted. With 1:09 to play on their own 23-yard-line and no timeouts, Flacco threw an incomplete pass on first down and scrambled the middle for 7 yards, forcing third-and-3. With the clock running, Flacco fired deep down the right sideline for Jones, who got behind the defense, caught the ball at the Broncos' 20 and raced untouched for the tying touchdown. In overtime, only one play was snapped in the other team's territory during the first 14 minutes. On second-and-6 from their own 38-yard-line, Manning's short pass for Brandon Stokley was intercepted by Graham at the Broncos' 45. An 11-yard run by Rice set up Tucker's game-winning kick. Flacco was 18 of 34 for 331 yards and 3 touchdowns. Rice carried 30 times for 131 yards. Manning was 28 of 43 for 290 yards and 3 touchdowns, with 2 interceptions.

Baltimore	14	7	7	7	0	3	—	38
Denver	14	7	7	7	0	0	—	35

Den — Holliday 90 punt return (Prater kick)
Balt — Smith 59 pass from Flacco (Tucker kick)
Balt — Graham 39 interception return (Tucker kick)
Den — Stokley 15 pass from Manning (Prater kick)
Den — Moreno 14 pass from Manning (Prater kick)
Balt — Smith 32 pass from Flacco (Tucker kick)
Den — Holliday 104 kickoff return (Prater kick)
Balt — Rice 1 run (Tucker kick)
Den — Thomas 17 pass from Manning (Prater kick)
Balt — J. Jones 70 pass from Flacco (Tucker kick)
Balt — FG Tucker 47

NFC DIVISIONAL PLAYOFF GAMES RESULTS

Includes Second-Round Playoff Games (1982), NFL Conference Championship Games (1967-69), and special playoff games to break ties for NFL Division or Conference Championships (1941, 1943, 1947, 1950, 1952, 1957, 1958, 1965)

Season	Date	Winner (Share)	Loser (Share)	Score	Site	Attendance
2012	Jan. 13	Atlanta ($22,000)	Seattle ($22,000)	30-28	Atlanta	70,366
	Jan. 12	San Francisco ($22,000)	Green Bay ($22,000)	45-31	San Francisco	69,732
2011	Jan. 15	N.Y. Giants ($22,000)	Green Bay ($22,000)	37-20	Green Bay	72,080
	Jan. 14	San Francisco ($22,000)	New Orleans ($22,000)	36-32	San Francisco	69,732
2010	Jan. 16	Chicago ($21,000)	Seattle ($21,000)	35-24	Chicago	62,265
	Jan. 15	Green Bay ($21,000)	Atlanta ($21,000)	48-21	Atlanta	69,210
2009	Jan. 17	Minnesota ($21,000)	Dallas ($21,000)	34-3	Minneapolis	63,547
	Jan. 16	New Orleans ($21,000)	Arizona ($21,000)	45-14	New Orleans	70,149
2008	Jan. 11	Philadelphia ($20,000)	N.Y. Giants ($20,000)	23-11	East Rutherford	79,193
	Jan. 10	Arizona ($20,000)	Carolina ($20,000)	33-13	Charlotte	73,695
2007	Jan. 13	N.Y. Giants ($20,000)	Dallas ($20,000)	21-17	Dallas	63,660
	Jan. 12	Green Bay ($20,000)	Seattle ($20,000)	42-20	Green Bay	72,168

Season	Date	Winner (Share)	Loser (Share)	Score	Site	Attendance
2006	Jan. 14	Chicago ($19,000)	Seattle ($19,000)	27-24*	Chicago	62,184
	Jan. 13	New Orleans ($19,000)	Philadelphia ($19,000)	27-24	New Orleans	70,001
2005	Jan. 15	Carolina ($19,000)	Chicago ($19,000)	29-21	Chicago	62,209
	Jan. 14	Seattle ($19,000)	Washington ($19,000)	20-10	Seattle	67,551
2004	Jan. 16	Philadelphia ($18,000)	Minnesota ($18,000)	27-14	Philadelphia	67,722
	Jan. 15	Atlanta ($18,000)	St. Louis ($18,000)	47-17	Atlanta	70,709
2003	Jan. 11	Philadelphia ($18,000)	Green Bay ($18,000)	20-17*	Philadelphia	67,707
	Jan. 10	Carolina ($18,000)	St. Louis ($18,000)	29-23*	St. Louis	66,165
2002	Jan. 12	Tampa Bay ($17,000)	San Francisco ($17,000)	31-6	Tampa	65,599
	Jan. 11	Philadelphia ($17,000)	Atlanta ($17,000)	20-6	Philadelphia	66,452
2001	Jan. 20	St. Louis ($17,000)	Green Bay ($17,000)	45-17	St. Louis	66,338
	Jan. 19	Philadelphia ($17,000)	Chicago ($17,000)	33-19	Chicago	66,944
2000	Jan. 7	N.Y. Giants ($16,000)	Philadelphia ($16,000)	20-10	East Rutherford	78,765
	Jan. 6	Minnesota ($16,000)	New Orleans ($16,000)	34-16	Minneapolis	63,881
1999	Jan. 16	St. Louis ($16,000)	Minnesota ($16,000)	49-37	St. Louis	66,194
	Jan. 15	Tampa Bay ($16,000)	Washington ($16,000)	14-13	Tampa	65,835
1998	Jan. 10	Minnesota ($15,000)	Arizona ($15,000)	41-21	Minneapolis	63,760
	Jan. 9	Atlanta ($15,000)	San Francisco ($15,000)	20-18	Atlanta	70,262
1997	Jan. 4	Green Bay ($15,000)	Tampa Bay ($15,000)	21-7	Green Bay	60,327
	Jan. 3	San Francisco ($15,000)	Minnesota ($15,000)	38-22	San Francisco	65,018
1996	Jan. 5	Carolina ($14,000)	Dallas ($14,000)	26-17	Charlotte	72,808
	Jan. 4	Green Bay ($14,000)	San Francisco ($14,000)	35-14	Green Bay	60,787
1995	Jan. 7	Dallas ($13,000)	Philadelphia ($13,000)	30-11	Dallas	64,371
	Jan. 6	Green Bay ($13,000)	San Francisco ($13,000)	27-17	San Francisco	69,311
1994	Jan. 8	Dallas ($12,000)	Green Bay ($12,000)	35-9	Dallas	64,745
	Jan. 7	San Francisco ($12,000)	Chicago ($12,000)	44-15	San Francisco	64,644
1993	Jan. 16	Dallas ($12,000)	Green Bay ($12,000)	27-17	Dallas	64,790
	Jan. 15	San Francisco ($12,000)	N.Y. Giants ($12,000)	44-3	San Francisco	67,143
1992	Jan. 10	Dallas ($10,000)	Philadelphia ($10,000)	34-10	Dallas	63,721
	Jan. 9	San Francisco ($10,000)	Washington ($10,000)	20-13	San Francisco	64,991
1991	Jan. 5	Detroit ($10,000)	Dallas ($10,000)	38-6	Detroit	78,290
	Jan. 4	Washington ($10,000)	Atlanta ($10,000)	24-7	Washington	55,181
1990	Jan. 13	N.Y. Giants ($10,000)	Chicago ($10,000)	31-3	East Rutherford	77,025
	Jan. 12	San Francisco ($10,000)	Washington ($10,000)	28-10	San Francisco	65,292
1989	Jan. 7	L.A. Rams ($10,000)	N.Y. Giants ($10,000)	19-13*	East Rutherford	76,526
	Jan. 6	San Francisco ($10,000)	Minnesota ($10,000)	41-13	San Francisco	64,918
1988	Jan. 1	San Francisco ($10,000)	Minnesota ($10,000)	34-9	San Francisco	61,848
	Dec. 31	Chicago ($10,000)	Philadelphia ($10,000)	20-12	Chicago	65,534
1987	Jan. 10	Washington ($10,000)	Chicago ($10,000)	21-17	Chicago	65,268
	Jan. 9	Minnesota ($10,000)	San Francisco ($10,000)	36-24	San Francisco	63,008
1986	Jan. 4	N.Y. Giants ($10,000)	San Francisco ($10,000)	49-3	East Rutherford	75,691
	Jan. 3	Washington ($10,000)	Chicago ($10,000)	27-13	Chicago	65,524
1985	Jan. 5	Chicago ($10,000)	N.Y. Giants ($10,000)	21-0	Chicago	65,670
	Jan. 4	L.A. Rams ($10,000)	Dallas ($10,000)	20-0	Anaheim	66,581
1984	Dec. 30	Chicago ($10,000)	Washington ($10,000)	23-19	Washington	55,431
	Dec. 29	San Francisco ($10,000)	N.Y. Giants ($10,000)	21-10	San Francisco	60,303
1983	Jan. 1	Washington ($10,000)	L.A. Rams ($10,000)	51-7	Washington	54,440
	Dec. 31	San Francisco ($10,000)	Detroit ($10,000)	24-23	San Francisco	59,979
1982	Jan. 16	Dallas ($10,000)	Green Bay ($10,000)	37-26	Dallas	63,972
	Jan. 15	Washington ($10,000)	Minnesota ($10,000)	21-7	Washington	54,593
1981	Jan. 3	San Francisco ($5,000)	N.Y. Giants ($5,000)	38-24	San Francisco	58,360
	Jan. 2	Dallas ($5,000)	Tampa Bay ($5,000)	38-0	Dallas	64,848
1980	Jan. 4	Dallas ($5,000)	Atlanta ($5,000)	30-27	Atlanta	59,793
	Jan. 3	Philadelphia ($5,000)	Minnesota ($5,000)	31-16	Philadelphia	70,178
1979	Dec. 30	Los Angeles ($5,000)	Dallas ($5,000)	21-19	Dallas	64,792
	Dec. 29	Tampa Bay ($5,000)	Philadelphia ($5,000)	24-17	Tampa	71,402
1978	Dec. 31	Los Angeles ($5,000)	Minnesota ($5,000)	34-10	Los Angeles	70,436
	Dec. 30	Dallas ($5,000)	Atlanta ($5,000)	27-20	Dallas	63,406
1977	Dec. 26	Dallas ($5,000)	Chicago ($5,000)	37-7	Dallas	63,260
	Dec. 26	Minnesota ($5,000)	Los Angeles ($5,000)	14-7	Los Angeles	70,203
1976	Dec. 19	Los Angeles [$]	Dallas [$]	14-12	Dallas	63,283
	Dec. 18	Minnesota [$]	Washington [$]	35-20	Minneapolis	47,466
1975	Dec. 28	Dallas [$]	Minnesota [$]	17-14	Minneapolis	48,050
	Dec. 27	Los Angeles [$]	St. Louis [$]	35-23	Los Angeles	73,459
1974	Dec. 22	Los Angeles [$]	Washington [$]	19-10	Los Angeles	77,925
	Dec. 21	Minnesota [$]	St. Louis [$]	30-14	Minneapolis	48,150
1973	Dec. 23	Dallas [$]	Los Angeles [$]	27-16	Dallas	63,272
	Dec. 22	Minnesota [$]	Washington [$]	27-20	Minneapolis	48,040
1972	Dec. 24	Washington [$]	Green Bay [$]	16-3	Washington	52,321
	Dec. 23	Dallas [$]	San Francisco [$]	30-28	San Francisco	59,746
1971	Dec. 26	San Francisco [$]	Washington [$]	24-20	San Francisco	45,327
	Dec. 25	Dallas [$]	Minnesota [$]	20-12	Minneapolis	47,307
1970	Dec. 27	San Francisco [$]	Minnesota [$]	17-14	Minneapolis	45,103
	Dec. 26	Dallas [$]	Detroit [$]	5-0	Dallas	69,613
1969	Dec. 28	Cleveland [$]	Dallas [$]	38-14	Dallas	69,321
	Dec. 27	Minnesota [$]	Los Angeles [$]	23-20	Minneapolis	47,900

Season	Date	Winner (Share)	Loser (Share)	Score	Site	Attendance
1968	Dec. 22	Baltimore [$]	Minnesota [$]	24-14	Baltimore	60,238
	Dec. 21	Cleveland [$]	Dallas [$]	31-20	Cleveland	81,497
1967	Dec. 24	Dallas [$]	Cleveland [$]	52-14	Dallas	70,786
	Dec. 23	Green Bay [$]	Los Angeles [$]	28-7	Milwaukee	49,861
1965	Dec. 26	Green Bay [$]	Baltimore [$]	13-10*	Green Bay	50,484
1958	Dec. 21	N.Y. Giants (#)	Cleveland (#)	10-0	New York	61,274
1957	Dec. 22	Detroit (#)	San Francisco (#)	31-27	San Francisco	60,118
1952	Dec. 21	Detroit (#)	Los Angeles (#)	31-21	Detroit	47,645
1950	Dec. 17	Los Angeles (#)	Chicago Bears (#)	24-14	Los Angeles	83,501
	Dec. 17	Cleveland (#)	N.Y. Giants (#)	8-3	Cleveland	33,054
1947	Dec. 21	Philadelphia (#)	Pittsburgh (#)	21-0	Pittsburgh	35,729
1943	Dec. 19	Washington (¢)	N.Y. Giants (¢)	28-0	New York	42,800
1941	Dec. 14	Chicago Bears (¢)	Green Bay (¢)	33-14	Chicago	43,425

*Overtime
$ Players received 1/14 of annual salary for playoff appearances.
# Players received 1/12 of annual salary for playoff appearances.
¢ Players received 1/10 of annual salary for playoff appearances.

2012 NFC DIVISIONAL PLAYOFF GAMES

Georgia Dome, Atlanta, Georgia
January 13, 2013, Attendance: 70,366
ATLANTA 30, SEATTLE 28—Matt Bryant made a 49-yard field goal with eight seconds remaining, after having blown a 20-point lead, to give Atlanta its first postseason playoff victory in eight years. The Falcons took a 3-0 in the first quarter when Sean Weatherspoon forced Marshawn Lynch to fumble. Jonathan Babineaux recovered to spark a 61-yard touchdown drive, keyed by Roddy White's 17-yard catch on third-and-14, and capped by Matt Ryan's 1-yard touchdown pass to Tony Gonzalez. The Falcons scored on their next two possessions as well, with White's 47-yard touchdown catch deep down the middle of the field staking Atlanta to a 20-0 lead with 4:16 left in the half. Seattle drove the Falcons' 11 with 17 seconds left, but Babineaux sacked Russell Wilson and the half expired before the Seahawks could attempt a field goal. Seattle opened the third quarter with an 80-yard touchdown drive, but Atlanta answered with a 7-play, 80-yard drive and took a 27-7 lead on Jason Snelling's 5-yard touchdown catch with 2:11 left in the third quarter. The Seahawks answered with another 80-yard touchdown drive, and four plays later Earl Thomas intercepted Ryan's pass. Wilson quickly connected on passes of 24 yards to Sidney Rice and 30 yards to Robert Turbin, setting up Zach Miller's 3-yard scoring catch to pull Seattle to within 27-21 with 9:13 remaining. With 3:00 left, Seattle began a drive on its own 39-yard-line. Wilson completed a 19-yard pass to Golden Tate and, on third-and-5, a 24-yard short pass-and-run to Lynch. With 31 seconds left Lynch scored on a 2-yard run to give Seattle a 28-27 lead. Jacquizz Rodgers returned the kickoff 34 yards to the Falcons' 28 with 25 seconds left and two time outs. Ryan completed a 22-yard pass to Harry Douglas and, after a timeout, connected with Gonzalez on a 19-yard pass to the Seahawks' 31 with 13 seconds left. Bryant then made the winning 49-yard field goal. Ryan completed 24 of 35 passes for 250 yards and 3 touchdowns, with 2 interceptions. Wilson was 24 of 36 for 385 yards and 2 touchdowns, with 1 interception. Miller had 8 catches for 142 yards and Tate added 6 receptions for 103 yards.

	1	2	3	4		T
Seattle	0	0	7	21	—	28
Atlanta	10	10	7	3	—	30

Atl — FG Bryant 39
Atl — Gonzalez 1 pass from Ryan (Bryant kick)
Atl — FG Bryant 37
Atl — White 47 pass from Ryan (Bryant kick)
Sea — Tate 29 pass from Wilson (Longwell kick)
Atl — Snelling 5 pass from Ryan (Bryant kick)
Sea — Wilson 1 run (Longwell kick)
Sea — Miller 3 pass from Wilson (Longwell kick)
Sea — Lynch 2 run (Longwell kick)
Atl — FG Bryant 49

Candlestick Park, San Francisco, California
January 12, 2013, Attendance: 69,732
SAN FRANCISCO 45, GREEN BAY 31—Colin Kaepernick passed for 263 yards and 2 touchdowns, and added an NFL quarterback-record 181 rushing yards and two more scores, as the 49ers pulled away from the Packers. Making his first postseason start, Kaepernick was the catalyst for the 49ers offense that generated 579 total yards. The game began, however, with Sam Shields intercepting Kaepernick's second pass of the game and returning it 52 yards for a touchdown to give Green Bay a 7-0 lead. On the next possession, Frank Gore's 45-yard catch on third-and-10 set up Kaepernick' 20-yard touchdown run on third-and-8 to tie the game. Aaron Rodgers' 44-yard pass to James Jones on third-and-5 led to Dwayne Harris' 18-yard touchdown catch for the Packers. The Packers' defense then forced a punt, by Jeremy Ross muffed the punt and C.J. Spillman recovered at the Packers' 9. Michael Crabtree caught a short pass at the 9-yard line and reached the end zone to tie the game. On the next possession Tarell Brown intercepted Rodgers' pass. The 49ers drove 48 yards, highlighted by Kaepernick's 15-yard scramble on third-and-9, and culminated with Crabtree's 20-yard touchdown catch, for a 21-14 lead. The Packers quickly responded with an 80-yard touchdown drive, and San Francisco ended the half with a 36-yard field goal from David Akers for a 24-21 halftime lead. Mason Crosby's 31-yard field goal midway through the third quarter tied the game, but Kaepernick's 56-yard touchdown run around right end vaulted the 49ers back into the lead. The 49ers' defense forced a punt, and the offense answered with a 93-yard touchdown drive, keyed by Vernon Davis' 44-yard catch, to take a 38-24 advantage. After another Green Bay punt, the 49ers put the game away with a second 93-yard touchdown drive that ended with Anthony Dixon's 2-yard run with 3:34 remaining. Kaepernick was 17 of 31 for 263 yards and 2 touchdowns, with 1 interception. Crabtree had 9 receptions for 119 yards, while Gore added 23 carries for 119 rushing yards. Rodgers completed 26 of 39 for 257 yards and 2 touchdowns, with 1 interception.

	1	2	3	4		T
Green Bay	14	7	3	7	—	31
San Francisco	7	17	7	14	—	45

GB — Shields 52 interception return (Crosby kick)
SF — Kaepernick 20 run (Akers kick)
GB — Harris 18 run (Crosby kick)
SF — Crabtree 12 pass from Kaepernick (Akers kick)
SF — Crabtree 20 pass from Kaepernick (Akers kick)
GB — J. Jones 20 pass from Rodgers (Crosby kick)
SF — FG Akers 36
GB — FG Crosby 31
SF — Kaepernick 56 run (Akers kick)
SF — Gore 2 run (Akers kick)
SF — Dixon 2 run (Akers kick)
GB — Jennings 3 pass from Rodgers (Crosby kick)

AFC WILD CARD PLAYOFF GAMES RESULTS

Season	Date	Winner (Share)	Loser (Share)	Score	Site	Attendance
2012	Jan. 6	Baltimore ($22,000)	Indianapolis ($20,000)	24-9	Baltimore	71,379
	Jan. 5	Houston ($22,000)	Cincinnati ($20,000)	19-13	Houston	71,738

Season	Date	Winner (Share)	Loser (Share)	Score	Site	Attendance
2011	Jan. 8	Denver ($22,000)	Pittsburgh ($20,000)	29-23*	Denver	75,970
	Jan. 7	Houston ($22,000)	Cincinnati ($20,000)	31-10	Houston	71,725
2010	Jan. 9	Baltimore ($19,000)	Kansas City ($21,000)	30-7	Kansas City	72,190
	Jan. 8	N.Y. Jets ($19,000)	Indianapolis ($21,000)	17-16	Indianapolis	65,332
2009	Jan. 10	Baltimore ($19,000)	New England ($21,000)	33-14	Foxborough	68,756
	Jan. 9	N.Y. Jets ($19,000)	Cincinnati ($21,000)	24-14	Cincinnati	63,686
2008	Jan. 4	Baltimore ($18,000)	Miami ($20,000)	27-9	Miami	74,240
	Jan. 3	San Diego ($20,000)	Indianapolis ($18,000)	23-17*	San Diego	68,082
2007	Jan. 6	San Diego ($20,000)	Tennessee ($18,000)	17-6	San Diego	65,640
	Jan. 5	Jacksonville ($18,000)	Pittsburgh ($20,000)	31-29	Pittsburgh	63,629
2006	Jan. 7	New England ($19,000)	N.Y. Jets ($17,000)	37-16	Foxborough	68,756
	Jan. 6	Indianapolis ($19,000)	Kansas City ($17,000)	23-8	Indianapolis	57,215
2005	Jan. 8	Pittsburgh ($17,000)	Cincinnati ($19,000)	31-17	Cincinnati	65,870
	Jan. 7	New England ($19,000)	Jacksonville ($17,000)	28-3	Foxborough	68,756
2004	Jan. 9	Indianapolis ($18,000)	Denver ($15,000)	49-24	Indianapolis	56,609
	Jan. 8	N.Y. Jets ($15,000)	San Diego ($18,000)	20-17*	San Diego	67,536
2003	Jan. 4	Indianapolis ($18,000)	Denver ($15,000)	41-10	Indianapolis	56,586
	Jan. 3	Tennessee ($15,000)	Baltimore ($18,000)	20-17	Baltimore	69,452
2002	Jan. 5	Pittsburgh ($17,000)	Cleveland ($12,500)	36-33	Pittsburgh	62,595
	Jan. 4	N.Y. Jets ($17,000)	Indianapolis ($12,500)	41-0	East Rutherford	78,524
2001	Jan. 13	Baltimore ($12,500)	Miami ($12,500)	20-3	Miami	72,251
	Jan. 12	Oakland ($17,000)	N.Y. Jets ($12,500)	38-24	Oakland	61,503
2000	Dec. 31	Baltimore (12,500)	Denver ($12,500)	21-3	Baltimore	69,638
	Dec. 30	Miami ($16,000)	Indianapolis ($12,500)	23-17*	Miami	73,193
1999	Jan. 9	Miami ($10,000)	Seattle ($16,000)	20-17	Seattle	66,170
	Jan. 8	Tennessee ($10,000)	Buffalo ($10,000)	22-16	Nashville	66,672
1998	Jan. 3	Jacksonville ($15,000)	New England ($10,000)	25-10	Jacksonville	71,139
	Jan. 2	Miami ($10,000)	Buffalo ($10,000)	24-17	Miami	72,698
1997	Dec. 28	New England ($15,000)	Miami ($10,000)	17-3	Foxborough	60,041
	Dec. 27	Denver ($10,000)	Jacksonville ($10,000)	42-17	Denver	74,481
1996	Dec. 29	Pittsburgh ($14,000)	Indianapolis ($10,000)	42-14	Pittsburgh	58,078
	Dec. 28	Jacksonville ($10,000)	Buffalo ($10,000)	30-27	Buffalo	70,213
1995	Dec. 31	Indianapolis ($7,500)	San Diego ($7,500)	35-20	San Diego	61,182
	Dec. 30	Buffalo ($13,000)	Miami ($7,500)	37-22	Buffalo	73,103
1994	Jan. 1	Cleveland ($7,500)	New England ($7,500)	20-13	Cleveland	77,452
	Dec. 31	Miami ($12,000)	Kansas City ($7,500)	27-17	Miami	67,487
1993	Jan. 9	L.A. Raiders ($7,500)	Denver ($7,500)	42-24	Los Angeles	65,314
	Jan. 8	Kansas City ($12,000)	Pittsburgh ($7,500)	27-24*	Kansas City	74,515
1992	Jan. 3	Buffalo ($6,000)	Houston ($6,000)	41-38*	Buffalo	75,141
	Jan. 2	San Diego ($10,000)	Kansas City ($6,000)	17-0	San Diego	58,278
1991	Dec. 29	Houston ($10,000)	N.Y. Jets ($6,000)	17-10	Houston	61,485
	Dec. 28	Kansas City ($6,000)	L.A. Raiders ($6,000)	10-6	Kansas City	75,827
1990	Jan. 6	Cincinnati ($10,000)	Houston ($6,000)	41-14	Cincinnati	60,012
	Jan. 5	Miami ($6,000)	Kansas City ($6,000)	17-16	Miami	67,276
1989	Dec. 31	Pittsburgh ($6,000)	Houston ($6,000)	26-23*	Houston	59,406
1988	Dec. 26	Houston ($6,000)	Cleveland ($6,000)	24-23	Cleveland	75,896
1987	Jan. 3	Houston ($6,000)	Seattle ($6,000)	23-20*	Houston	50,519
1986	Dec. 28	N.Y. Jets ($6,000)	Kansas City ($6,000)	35-15	East Rutherford	75,210
1985	Dec. 28	New England ($6,000)	N.Y. Jets ($6,000)	26-14	East Rutherford	75,945
1984	Dec. 22	Seattle ($6,000)	L.A. Raiders ($6,000)	13-7	Seattle	62,049
1983	Dec. 24	Seattle ($6,000)	Denver ($6,000)	31-7	Seattle	64,275
1982	Jan. 9	N.Y. Jets ($6,000)	Cincinnati ($6,000)	44-17	Cincinnati	57,560
	Jan. 9	San Diego ($6,000)	Pittsburgh ($6,000)	31-28	Pittsburgh	53,546
	Jan. 8	L.A. Raiders ($6,000)	Cleveland ($6,000)	27-10	Los Angeles	56,555
	Jan. 8	Miami ($6,000)	New England ($6,000)	28-13	Miami	68,842
1981	Dec. 27	Buffalo ($3,000)	N.Y. Jets ($3,000)	31-27	New York	57,050
1980	Dec. 28	Oakland ($3,000)	Houston ($3,000)	27-7	Oakland	53,333
1979	Dec. 23	Houston ($3,000)	Denver ($3,000)	13-7	Houston	48,776
1978	Dec. 24	Houston ($3,000)	Miami ($3,000)	17-9	Miami	72,445

*Overtime

2012 AFC WILD CARD PLAYOFF GAMES

M&T Bank Stadium, Baltimore, Maryland
January 6, 2013, Attendance: 71,379
BALTIMORE 24, INDIANAPOLIS 9—Joe Flacco passed for 282 yards and 2 touchdowns as the Ravens began their Super Bowl march by defeating the Colts. The Ravens had a chance to score early, but Cory Redding forced Ray Rice to fumble at the Colts' 11 and Lawrence Guy recovered. Baltimore then drove 59 yards, but on third-and-5 Paul Kruger sacked Andrew Luck and forced him to fumble. Pernell McPhee recovered for the Ravens. After an exchange of field goals, Jacoby Jones returned the kickoff 37 yards. Flacco completed a short pass to Rice, who gained 47 yards to the Colts' 2-yard-line to set up Vonta Leach's touchdown run for a 10-3 lead. Luck completed a 25-yard pass to T.Y. Hilton just before halftime to set up Adam Vinatieri's 52-yard field goal as the half expired to pull the Colts to within 10-6. In the middle of the third quarter Flacco completed a long 46-yard pass to Anquan Boldin to set up Dennis Pitta's 20-yard scoring catch for a 17-6 lead. The Colts responded with a 15-play scoring drive that ended in the final minute of the third quarter with Vinatieri's

third field goal. Joe Lefeged then forced Rice to fumble and Pat Angerer fell on the loose ball at the Colts' 29. Vick Ballard's 24-yard run on the ensuing possession but the Colts in scoring range, but Vinatieri's 40-yard field-goal attempt sailed wide right with 11:44 to play. Three plays later, on third-and-1, Bernard Pierce broke free for a 43-yard run to set up Flacco's 18-yard scoring pass to Boldin with 9:14 to play. The Colts again drove deep into Ravens' territory but Cary Williams intercepted Luck's fourth-and-1 pass from the Ravens' 18 with 5:24 remaining to quell Baltimore's final scoring threat. Flacco was 12 of 23 for 282 yards and 2 touchdowns. Pierce carried 13 times for 103 yards, and Boldin had 5 receptions for 145 yards. Kruger had 2.5 sacks for the Ravens. Luck was 28 of 54 for 288 yards, with 1 interception. Reggie Wayne had 9 catches for 114 yards.

| Indianapolis | 0 | 6 | 3 | 0 | — | 9 |
| Baltimore | 0 | 10 | 7 | 7 | — | 24 |

Balt — FG Tucker 23
Ind — FG Vinatieri 47
Balt — Leach 2 run (Tucker kick)
Ind — FG Vinatieri 52
Balt — Pitta 20 pass from Flacco (Tucker kick)
Ind — FG Vinatieri 26
Balt — Boldin 18 pass from Flacco (Tucker kick)

Reliant Stadium, Houston, Texas
January 5, 2013, Attendance: 71,738
HOUSTON 19, CINCINNATI 13—Arian Foster rushed for 140 yards and 1 touchdown as the Texans defeated the Bengals in the wild-card round of the playoffs for the second consecutive year. The Texans had more than twice as many yards as the Bengals (420-198) and maintained possession for 38 minutes, 49 seconds. The Texans had scoring drives of 65 and 60 yards to take a 6-0 lead, but Leon Hall intercepted a short pass and returned it 21 yards for a touchdown to give Cincinnati a 7-6 lead in the second quarter despite not having run a play in Texans' territory. On the ensuing drive Foster had three carries of at least 11 yards, with Shayne Graham capping the 76-yard drive with his third field goal of the half for a 9-7 Houston halftime lead. The Texans' defense forced another three-and-out to begin the second half, and Matt Schaub completed a 22-yard pass to Andre Johnson to set up Foster's 1-yard touchdown run for a 16-7 lead. Andy Dalton responded with the Bengals' best drive of the game, highlighted by his 45-yard pass to A.J. Green, to set up Josh Brown's 34-yard field goal. Graham's fourth field goal was set up by Johnathan Joseph's interception and staked the Texans to a 19-10 lead with 14:17 to play. Brandon Tate returned the ensuing kickoff 43 yards, and BenJarvus Green Ellis gained 2 yards on fourth-and-1, en route to Brown's 47-yard field goal with 9:03 to play to pull the Bengals within 19-13. The Bengals' defense forced a punt, and Dalton drove the Bengals to the Texans' 35, but on fourth-and-11 his completed pass to Marvin Jones netted just eight yards with 2:44 to play. Faced with third-and-2 from the Texans' 36, Schaub completed a 7-yard pass to Garrett Graham to help Houston maintain possession with 2:33 to play. Two plays later, Foster gained 10 yards on second-and-8 to clinch the victory. Schaub was 29 of 38 for 262 yards, with 1 interception. Foster rushed 32 times for 140 yards. Dalton was 14 of 30 for 127 yards, with 1 interception.

| Cincinnati | 0 | 7 | 3 | 3 | — | 13 |
| Houston | 3 | 6 | 7 | 3 | — | 19 |

Hou — FG Graham 48
Hou — FG Graham 27
Cin — Hall 21 interception return (Brown kick)
Hou — FG Graham 22
Hou — Foster 1 run (Graham kick)
Cin — FG Brown 34
Hou — FG Graham 24
Cin — FG Brown 47

NFC WILD CARD PLAYOFF GAMES RESULTS

Season	Date	Winner (Share)	Loser (Share)	Score	Site	Attendance
2012	Jan. 6	Seattle ($20,000)	Washington ($22,000)	24-14	Washington	84,325
	Jan. 5	Green Bay ($22,000)	Minnesota ($20,000)	24-10	Green Bay	71,548
2011	Jan. 8	N.Y. Giants ($22,000)	Atlanta ($20,000)	24-2	East Rutherford	79,909
	Jan. 7	New Orleans ($22,000)	Detroit ($20,000)	45-28	New Orleans	73,038
2010	Jan. 9	Green Bay ($19,000)	Philadelphia ($21,000)	21-16	Philadelphia	69,144
	Jan. 8	Seattle ($21,000)	New Orleans ($19,000)	41-36	Seattle	66,336
2009	Jan. 10	Arizona ($21,000)	Green Bay ($19,000)	51-45*	Glendale	61,926
	Jan. 9	Dallas ($21,000)	Philadelphia ($19,000)	34-14	Dallas	92,951
2008	Jan. 4	Philadelphia ($18,000)	Minnesota ($20,000)	26-14	Minneapolis	61,746
	Jan. 3	Arizona ($20,000)	Atlanta ($18,000)	30-24	Glendale	62,848
2007	Jan. 6	N.Y. Giants ($18,000)	Tampa Bay ($20,000)	24-14	Tampa	65,621
	Jan. 5	Seattle ($20,000)	Washington ($18,000)	35-14	Seattle	68,297
2006	Jan. 7	Philadelphia ($19,000)	N.Y. Giants ($17,000)	23-20	Philadelphia	69,094
	Jan. 6	Seattle ($19,000)	Dallas ($17,000)	21-20	Seattle	68,058
2005	Jan. 8	Carolina ($17,000)	N.Y. Giants ($19,000)	23-0	East Rutherford	79,378
	Jan. 7	Washington ($17,000)	Tampa Bay ($19,000)	17-10	Tampa	65,514
2004	Jan. 9	Minnesota ($15,000)	Green Bay ($18,000)	31-17	Green Bay	71,075
	Jan. 8	St. Louis ($15,000)	Seattle ($18,000)	27-20	Seattle	65,397
2003	Jan. 4	Green Bay ($18,000)	Seattle ($15,000)	33-27*	Green Bay	71,457
	Jan. 3	Carolina ($18,000)	Dallas ($15,000)	29-10	Charlotte	73,014
2002	Jan. 5	San Francisco ($17,000)	N.Y. Giants ($12,500)	39-38	San Francisco	66,318
	Jan. 4	Atlanta ($12,500)	Green Bay ($17,000)	27-7	Green Bay	65,358
2001	Jan. 13	Green Bay ($12,500)	San Francisco ($12,500)	25-15	Green Bay	59,825
	Jan. 12	Philadelphia ($17,000)	Tampa Bay ($12,500)	31-9	Philadelphia	65,847
2000	Dec. 31	Philadelphia ($12,500)	Tampa Bay ($12,500)	21-3	Philadelphia	65,813
	Dec. 30	New Orleans ($16,000)	St. Louis ($12,500)	31-28	New Orleans	64,900
1999	Jan. 9	Minnesota ($10,000)	Dallas ($10,000)	27-10	Minneapolis	64,056
	Jan. 8	Washington ($16,000)	Detroit ($10,000)	27-13	Washington	79,411
1998	Jan. 3	San Francisco ($10,000)	Green Bay ($10,000)	30-27	San Francisco	66,506
	Jan. 2	Arizona ($10,000)	Dallas ($15,000)	20-7	Dallas	62,969
1997	Dec. 28	Tampa Bay ($10,000)	Detroit ($10,000)	20-10	Tampa	73,361
	Dec. 27	Minnesota ($10,000)	N.Y. Giants ($15,000)	23-22	East Rutherford	77,497
1996	Dec. 29	San Francisco ($10,000)	Philadelphia ($10,000)	14-0	San Francisco	56,460
	Dec. 28	Dallas ($14,000)	Minnesota ($10,000)	40-15	Dallas	64,682
1995	Dec. 31	Green Bay ($13,000)	Atlanta ($7,500)	37-20	Green Bay	60,453
	Dec. 30	Philadelphia ($7,500)	Detroit ($7,500)	58-37	Philadelphia	66,099

NFC WILD CARD PLAYOFF GAMES RESULTS

Season	Date	Winner (Share)	Loser (Share)	Score	Site	Attendance
1994	Jan. 1	Chicago ($7,500)	Minnesota ($12,000)	35-18	Minnesota	60,347
	Dec. 31	Green Bay ($7,500)	Detroit ($7,500)	16-12	Green Bay	58,125
1993	Jan. 9	N.Y. Giants ($7,500)	Minnesota ($7,500)	17-10	East Rutherford	75,089
	Jan. 8	Green Bay ($7,500)	Detroit ($12,000)	28-24	Detroit	68,479
1992	Jan. 3	Philadelphia ($6,000)	New Orleans ($6,000)	36-20	New Orleans	68,893
	Jan. 2	Washington ($6,000)	Minnesota ($10,000)	24-7	Minnesota	57,353
1991	Dec. 29	Dallas ($6,000)	Chicago ($6,000)	17-13	Chicago	62,594
	Dec. 28	Atlanta ($6,000)	New Orleans ($10,000)	27-20	New Orleans	68,794
1990	Jan. 6	Chicago ($10,000)	New Orleans ($6,000)	16-6	Chicago	60,767
	Jan. 5	Washington ($6,000)	Philadelphia ($6,000)	20-6	Philadelphia	65,287
1989	Dec. 31	L.A. Rams ($6,000)	Philadelphia ($6,000)	21-7	Philadelphia	65,479
1988	Dec. 26	Minnesota ($6,000)	L.A. Rams ($6,000)	28-17	Minnesota	61,204
1987	Jan. 3	Minnesota ($6,000)	New Orleans ($6,000)	44-10	New Orleans	68,546
1986	Dec. 28	Washington ($6,000)	L.A. Rams ($6,000)	19-7	Washington	54,567
1985	Dec. 29	N.Y. Giants ($6,000)	San Francisco ($6,000)	17-3	East Rutherford	75,131
1984	Dec. 23	N.Y. Giants ($6,000)	L.A. Rams ($6,000)	16-13	Anaheim	67,037
1983	Dec. 26	L.A. Rams ($6,000)	Dallas ($6,000)	24-17	Dallas	62,118
1982	Jan. 9	Dallas ($6,000)	Tampa Bay ($6,000)	30-17	Dallas	65,042
	Jan. 9	Minnesota ($6,000)	Atlanta ($6,000)	30-24	Minnesota	60,560
	Jan. 8	Green Bay ($6,000)	St. Louis ($6,000)	41-16	Green Bay	54,282
	Jan. 8	Washington ($6,000)	Detroit ($6,000)	31-7	Washington	55,045
1981	Dec. 27	N.Y. Giants ($3,000)	Philadelphia ($3,000)	27-21	Philadelphia	71,611
1980	Dec. 28	Dallas ($3,000)	Los Angeles ($3,000)	34-13	Dallas	63,052
1979	Dec. 23	Philadelphia ($3,000)	Chicago ($3,000)	27-17	Philadelphia	69,397
1978	Dec. 24	Atlanta ($3,000)	Philadelphia ($3,000)	14-13	Atlanta	59,403

*Overtime

2012 NFC WILD CARD PLAYOFF GAMES

FedExField, Landover, Maryland
January 6, 2013, Attendance: 84,325
SEATTLE 24, WASHINGTON 14—Marshawn Lynch rushed for 132 yards and his 27-yard touchdown run midway through the fourth quarter lifted the Seahawks to the franchise's first road postseason victory since 1983. The Redskins began the game with touchdown drives of 80 and 54 yards, both capped by 4-yard touchdown passes by Robert Griffin III, to stake the Redskins to a 14-0 lead with 2:26 left in the first quarter. Griffin appeared to tweak his knee just before the second touchdown, however, and the Seahawks' defense allowed just 74 total yards in the game's final three quarters. Trailing 14-0, the Redskins' defense immediately forced Seattle into a third-and-12 situation, but Russell Wilson completed a 12-yard pass to Zach Miller for a first down. Wilson's 19-yard scramble and 27-yard pass moments later to Sidney Rice highlighted a drive that culminated with Steven Hauschka's 32-yard field goal. The Seahawks' defense forced a three-and-out, and Lynch had a 20-yard run on the ensuing drive en route to Michael Robinson's 4-yard touchdown catch to pull the Seahawks within 14-10. Two plays later, Earl Thomas intercepted Griffin's deep pass, and Wilson's 33-yard pass to Doug Baldwin set up Hauschka's 29-yard field goal as the half expired. Trailing 14-13 in the fourth quarter, Wilson and Miller hooked up for another key third-down conversion, 22 yards on third-and-10, to set up Lynch's 27-yard touchdown run, which came on third-and-5 with 7:08 to play. Wilson completed the 2-point conversion pass to Miller to take a 21-14 lead. After the kickoff, Bruce Irvin sacked Griffin for a 12-yard loss. On the next play from scrimmage, Griffin fumbled the snap and Clinton McDonald recovered at the Redskins' 5. The Redskins' defense held Seattle to a field goal with 5:32 to play. Kirk Cousins entered the game at quarterback, but Washington was unable to drive past midfield on its final two possessions. Wilson was 15 of 26 for 187 yards and 1 touchdown. Lynch carried 20 times for 132 yards. Griffin was 10 of 19 for 84 yards and 2 touchdowns, with 1 interception. Cousins completed 3 of 10 passes for 31 yards.

Seattle	0	13	0	11	—	24
Washington	14	0	0	0	—	14

Wash — Royster 4 pass from Griffin (Forbath kick)
Wash — Paulsen 4 pass from Griffin (Forbath kick)
Sea — FG Hauschka 32

Sea — Robinson 4 pass from Wilson (Hauschka kick)
Sea — FG Hauschka 29
Sea — Lynch 27 run (Miller pass from Wilson)
Sea — FG Hauschka 22

Lambeau Field, Green Bay, Wisconsin
January 5, 2013, Attendance: 71,548
GREEN BAY 24, MINNESOTA 10—Aaron Rodgers passed for 274 yards and 1 touchdown and John Kuhn scored 3 touchdowns as the Packers defeated the Vikings. Minnesota played the game without Christian Ponder, who suffered an elbow injury in week 17. Joe Webb, who had not attempted a pass all season, completed 11 of 30 passes for 180 yards and 1 touchdown, with 1 interception, and carried seven times for 68 yards. Webb's versatility was on display on the Vikings' first drive, as Minnesota drove 53 yards in 10 plays to take a 3-0 lead on Blair Walsh's 33-yard field goal. The Packers' defense allowed just three first downs the rest of the half, while the offense had scoring drives of 82, 72, and 62 yards. The last drive was highlighted by passes of 22 and 23 yards from Rodgers to Jordy Nelson, and capped by Kuhn's 3-yard touchdown run for a 17-3 lead with 38 seconds left in half. Green Bay opened the second half with the ball and methodically drove 80 yards in 12 plays. The possession was kept alive when Minnesota was flagged for 12 men on the field during a field-goal attempt on fourth-and-4, and culminated with Rodgers' 9-yard touchdown pass to Kuhn. The Vikings pierced the goal line for the first time with 3:39 to play when Webb connected on a deep 50-yard touchdown pass to Michael Jenkins, but Rodgers completed a 6-yard pass to Nelson on third-and-5 with 3:20 left to help Green Bay clinch the victory. Rodgers was 23 of 33 for 274 yards and 1 touchdown. Adrian Peterson, who in 2012 established the second-highest single-season rushing total in NFL history, carried the ball 22 times for 99 yards.

Minnesota	3	0	0	7	—	10
Green Bay	7	10	7	0	—	24

Minn — FG Walsh 33
GB — Harris 9 run (Crosby kick)
GB — FG Crosby 20
GB — Kuhn 3 run (Crosby kick)
GB — Kuhn 9 pass from Rodgers (Crosby kick)
Minn — Jenkins 50 pass from Webb (Walsh kick)

Includes AFL All-Star Game played after the 1961-69 seasons.

Date	Result/Honored players	Site (attendance)
Jan. 15, 1939	New York Giants 13, Pro All-Stars 10	Wrigley Field, Los Angeles (20,000)
Jan. 14, 1940	Green Bay 16, NFL All-Stars 7	Gilmore Stadium, Los Angeles (18,000)
Dec. 29, 1940	Chicago Bears 28, NFL All-Stars 14	Gilmore Stadium, Los Angeles (21,624)
Jan. 4, 1942	Chicago Bears 35, NFL All-Stars 24	Polo Grounds, New York (17,725)
Dec. 27, 1942	NFL All-Stars 17, Washington 14	Shibe Park, Philadelphia (18,671)
Jan. 14, 1951	American Conf. 28, National Conf. 27	Los Angeles Memorial Coliseum (53,676)
	Otto Graham, Cleveland, player of the game	
Jan. 12, 1952	National Conf. 30, American Conf. 13	Los Angeles Memorial Coliseum (19,400)
	Dan Towler, Los Angeles, player of the game	
Jan. 10, 1953	National Conf. 27, American Conf. 7	Los Angeles Memorial Coliseum (34,208)
	Don Doll, Detroit, player of the game	
Jan. 17, 1954	East 20, West 9	Los Angeles Memorial Coliseum (44,214)
	Chuck Bednarik, Philadelphia, player of the game	
Jan. 16, 1955	West 26, East 19	Los Angeles Memorial Coliseum (43,972)
	Billy Wilson, San Francisco, player of the game	
Jan. 15, 1956	East 31, West 30	Los Angeles Memorial Coliseum (37,867)
	Ollie Matson, Chi. Cardinals, player of the game	
Jan. 13, 1957	West 19, East 10	Los Angeles Memorial Coliseum (44,177)
	Bert Rechichar, Baltimore, outstanding back	
	Ernie Stautner, Pittsburgh, outstanding lineman	
Jan. 12, 1958	West 26, East 7	Los Angeles Memorial Coliseum (66,634)
	Hugh McElhenny, San Francisco, outstanding back	
	Gene Brito, Washington, outstanding lineman	
Jan. 11, 1959	East 28, West 21	Los Angeles Memorial Coliseum (72,250)
	Frank Gifford, N.Y. Giants, outstanding back	
	Doug Atkins, Chi. Bears, outstanding lineman	
Jan. 17, 1960	West 38, East 21	Los Angeles Memorial Coliseum (56,876)
	Johnny Unitas, Baltimore, outstanding back	
	Gene (Big Daddy) Lipscomb, Baltimore, outstanding lineman	
Jan. 15, 1961	West 35, East 31	Los Angeles Memorial Coliseum (62,971)
	Johnny Unitas, Baltimore, outstanding back	
	Sam Huff, N.Y. Giants, outstanding lineman	
Jan. 7, 1962	AFL West 47, East 27	Balboa Stadium, San Diego (20,973)
	Cotton Davidson, Dallas Texans, player of the game	
Jan. 14, 1962	NFL West 31, East 30	Los Angeles Memorial Coliseum (57,409)
	Jim Brown, Cleveland, outstanding back	
	Henry Jordan, Green Bay, outstanding lineman	
Jan. 13, 1963	AFL West 21, East 14	Balboa Stadium, San Diego (27,641)
	Curtis McClinton, Dallas Texans, outstanding offensive player	
	Earl Faison, San Diego, outstanding defensive player	
Jan. 13, 1963	NFL East 30, West 20	Los Angeles Memorial Coliseum (61,374)
	Jim Brown, Cleveland, outstanding back	
	Gene (Big Daddy) Lipscomb, Pittsburgh, outstanding lineman	
Jan. 12, 1964	NFL West 31, East 17	Los Angeles Memorial Coliseum (67,242)
	Johnny Unitas, Baltimore, player of the game	
	Gino Marchetti, Baltimore, outstanding lineman	
Jan. 19, 1964	AFL West 27, East 24	Balboa Stadium, San Diego (20,016)
	Keith Lincoln, San Diego, outstanding offensive player	
	Archie Matsos, Oakland, outstanding defensive player	
Jan. 10, 1965	NFL West 34, East 14	Los Angeles Memorial Coliseum (60,598)
	Fran Tarkenton, Minnesota, outstanding back	
	Terry Barr, Detroit, outstanding lineman	
Jan. 16, 1965	AFL West 38, East 14	Jeppesen Stadium, Houston (15,446)
	Keith Lincoln, San Diego, outstanding offensive player	
	Willie Brown, Denver, outstanding defensive player	
Jan. 15, 1966	AFL All-Stars 30, Buffalo 19	Rice Stadium, Houston (35,572)
	Joe Namath, N.Y. Jets, most valuable player, offense	
	Frank Buncom, San Diego, most valuable player, defense	
Jan. 15, 1966	NFL East 36, West 7	Los Angeles Memorial Coliseum (60,124)
	Jim Brown, Cleveland, outstanding back	
	Dale Meinert, St. Louis, outstanding lineman	
Jan. 21, 1967	AFL East 30, West 23	Oakland-Alameda County Coliseum (18,876)
	Babe Parilli, Boston, outstanding offensive player	
	Verlon Biggs, N.Y. Jets, outstanding defensive player	
Jan. 22, 1967	NFL East 20, West 10	Los Angeles Memorial Coliseum (15,062)
	Gale Sayers, Chicago, outstanding back	
	Floyd Peters, Philadelphia, outstanding lineman	
Jan. 21, 1968	AFL East 25, West 24	Gator Bowl, Jacksonville, Fla. (40,103)
	Joe Namath and Don Maynard, N.Y. Jets, out. off. players	
	Leslie (Speedy) Duncan, San Diego, out. def. player	
Jan. 21, 1968	NFL West 38, East 20	Los Angeles Memorial Coliseum (53,289)
	Gale Sayers, Chicago, outstanding back	
	Dave Robinson, Green Bay, outstanding lineman	
Jan. 19, 1969	AFL West 38, East 25	Gator Bowl, Jacksonville, Fla. (41,058)
	Len Dawson, Kansas City, outstanding offensive player	
	George Webster, Houston, outstanding defensive player	
Jan. 19, 1969	NFL West 10, East 7	Los Angeles Memorial Coliseum (32,050)
	Roman Gabriel, Los Angeles, outstanding back	
	Merlin Olsen, Los Angeles, outstanding lineman	
Jan. 17, 1970	AFL West 26, East 3	Astrodome, Houston (30,170)
	John Hadl, San Diego, player of the game	
Jan. 18, 1970	NFL West 16, East 13	Los Angeles Memorial Coliseum (57,786)
	Gale Sayers, Chicago, outstanding back	
	George Andrie, Dallas, outstanding lineman	

Jan. 24, 1971	NFC 27, AFC 6	Los Angeles Memorial Coliseum (48,222)

Mel Renfro, Dallas, outstanding back
Fred Carr, Green Bay, outstanding lineman

Jan. 23, 1972	AFC 26, NFC 13	Los Angeles Memorial Coliseum (53,647)

Jan Stenerud, Kansas City, outstanding offensive player
Willie Lanier, Kansas City, outstanding defensive player

Jan. 21, 1973	AFC 33, NFC 28	Texas Stadium, Irving (37,091)

O.J. Simpson, Buffalo, player of the game

Jan. 20, 1974	AFC 15, NFC 13	Arrowhead Stadium, Kansas City (66,918)

Garo Yepremian, Miami, player of the game

Jan. 20, 1975	NFC 17, AFC 10	Orange Bowl, Miami (26,484)

James Harris, Los Angeles, player of the game

Jan. 26, 1976	NFC 23, AFC 20	Louisiana Superdome, New Orleans (30,546)

Billy Johnson, Houston, player of the game

Jan. 17, 1977	AFC 24, NFC 14	Kingdome, Seattle (64,752)

Mel Blount, Pittsburgh, player of the game

Jan. 23, 1978	NFC 14, AFC 13	Tampa Stadium (51,337)

Walter Payton, Chicago, player of the game

Jan. 29, 1979	NFC 13, AFC 7	Los Angeles Memorial Coliseum (46,281)

Ahmad Rashad, Minnesota, player of the game

Jan. 27, 1980	NFC 37, AFC 27	Aloha Stadium, Honolulu (49,800)

Chuck Muncie, New Orleans, player of the game

Feb. 1, 1981	NFC 21, AFC 7	Aloha Stadium, Honolulu (50,360)

Eddie Murray, Detroit, player of the game

Jan. 31, 1982	AFC 16, NFC 13	Aloha Stadium, Honolulu (50,402)

Kellen Winslow, San Diego, and Lee Roy Selmon, Tampa Bay, players of the game

Feb. 6, 1983	NFC 20, AFC 19	Aloha Stadium, Honolulu (49,883)

Dan Fouts, San Diego, and John Jefferson, Green Bay, players of the game

Jan. 29, 1984	NFC 45, AFC 3	Aloha Stadium, Honolulu (50,445)

Joe Theismann, Washington, player of the game

Jan. 27, 1985	AFC 22, NFC 14	Aloha Stadium, Honolulu (50,385)

Mark Gastineau, N.Y. Jets, player of the game

Feb. 2, 1986	NFC 28, AFC 24	Aloha Stadium, Honolulu (50,101)

Phil Simms, N.Y. Giants, player of the game

Feb. 1, 1987	AFC 10, NFC 6	Aloha Stadium, Honolulu (50,101)

Reggie White, Philadelphia, player of the game

Feb. 7, 1988	AFC 15, NFC 6	Aloha Stadium, Honolulu (50,113)

Bruce Smith, Buffalo, player of the game

Jan. 29, 1989	NFC 34, AFC 3	Aloha Stadium, Honolulu (50,113)

Randall Cunningham, Philadelphia, player of the game

Feb. 4, 1990	NFC 27, AFC 21	Aloha Stadium, Honolulu (50,445)

Jerry Gray, L.A. Rams, player of the game

Feb. 3, 1991	AFC 23, NFC 21	Aloha Stadium, Honolulu (50,345)

Jim Kelly, Buffalo, player of the game

Feb. 2, 1992	NFC 21, AFC 15	Aloha Stadium, Honolulu (50,209)

Michael Irvin, Dallas, player of the game

Feb. 7, 1993	AFC 23, NFC 20 (OT)	Aloha Stadium, Honolulu (50,007)

Steve Tasker, Buffalo, player of the game

Feb. 6, 1994	NFC 17, AFC 3	Aloha Stadium, Honolulu (50,026)

Andre Rison, Atlanta, player of the game

Feb. 5, 1995	AFC 41, NFC 13	Aloha Stadium, Honolulu (50,529)

Marshall Faulk, Indianapolis, player of the game

Feb. 4, 1996	NFC 20, AFC 13	Aloha Stadium, Honolulu (50,034)

Jerry Rice, San Francisco, player of the game

Feb. 2, 1997	AFC 26, NFC 23 (OT)	Aloha Stadium, Honolulu (50,031)

Mark Brunell, Jacksonville, player of the game

Feb. 1, 1998	AFC 29, NFC 24	Aloha Stadium, Honolulu (49,995)

Warren Moon, Seattle, player of the game

Feb. 7, 1999	AFC 23, NFC 10	Aloha Stadium, Honolulu (50,075)

Keyshawn Johnson, N.Y. Jets and Ty Law, New England, co-players of the game

Feb. 6, 2000	NFC 51, AFC 31	Aloha Stadium, Honolulu (50,112)

Randy Moss, Minnesota, player of the game

Feb. 4, 2001	AFC 38, NFC 17	Aloha Stadium, Honolulu (50,128)

Rich Gannon, Oakland, player of the game

Feb. 9, 2002	AFC 38, NFC 30	Aloha Stadium, Honolulu (50,301)

Rich Gannon, Oakland, player of the game

Feb. 2, 2003	AFC 45, NFC 20	Aloha Stadium, Honolulu (50,125)

Ricky Williams, Miami, player of the game

Feb. 8, 2004	NFC 55, AFC 52	Aloha Stadium, Honolulu (50,127)

Marc Bulger, St. Louis, player of the game

Feb. 13, 2005	AFC 38, NFC 27	Aloha Stadium, Honolulu (50,225)

Peyton Manning, Indianapolis, player of the game

Feb. 12, 2006	NFC 23, AFC 17	Aloha Stadium, Honolulu (50,190)

Derrick Brooks, Tampa Bay, player of the game

Feb. 10, 2007	AFC 31, NFC 28	Aloha Stadium, Honolulu (50,410)

Carson Palmer, Cincinnati, player of the game

Feb. 10, 2008	NFC 42, AFC 30	Aloha Stadium, Honolulu (50,044)

Adrian Peterson, Minnesota, most valuable player

Feb. 8, 2009	NFC 30, AFC 21	Aloha Stadium, Honolulu (49,958)

Larry Fitzgerald, Arizona, most valuable player

Jan. 31, 2010	AFC 41, NFC 34	Sun Life Stadium, South Florida (70,697)

Matt Schaub, Houston, most valuable player

Jan. 30, 2011	NFC 55, AFC 41	Aloha Stadium, Honolulu (49,331)

DeAngelo Hall, Washington, most valuable player

Jan. 29, 2012	AFC 59, NFC 41	Aloha Stadium, Honolulu (48,423)

Brandon Marshall, Miami, most valuable player

Jan. 27, 2013	NFC 62, AFC 35	Aloha Stadium, Honolulu (47,134)

Kyle Rudolph, Minnesota, most valuable player

SUNDAY NIGHT WON-LOST RECORDS, 1978-2012

AMERICAN FOOTBALL CONFERENCE

	Balt.	Buff.	Cin.	Clev.	Den.	Hou.	Ind.	Jax.	K.C.	Mia.	N.E.	N.Y.J.	Oak.	Pitt.	S.D.	Tenn.
Total	13-10	10-10	3-11	1-9	20-15	2-4	18-19	5-6	10-5	19-8	18-16	10-13	16-18	19-19	16-16	11-9
2012	2-0	0-1		2-0		1-1					0-2			1-2	0-1	
2011	2-1						0-2		0-1		1-0	1-2		2-1	1-0	
2010	0-1						2-1	0-1			2-0	1-0		1-2	1-0	
2009	1-0	0-1			3-0						0-1	1-0		1-1	0-1	0-1
2008	1-0		0-1	0-1			2-1	0-1			0-2			2-0	2-1	
2007	0-1	0-1	0-1	1-0			1-2				3-0			1-1	1-1	1-0
2006			2-2		3-0				0-1		0-2		0-1	0-1	3-0	
2005	1-1	0-1	0-1	0-1		0-2	1-0	1-0	2-0		1-0	0-1	0-2	1-0	2-0	
2004	2-1	0-1	1-0	0-2	1-1	0-1	0-1	0-1	1-2	1-0			2-0	2-0		
2003	1-1	0-2		1-0	1-0		1-1	1-0	1-0	2-0	1-0		0-1	0-2		1-0
2002	1-0		0-1	0-1	0-2	1-0	1-1	0-1		1-1	0-2	2-0	2-0	0-1		
2001	0-1	0-1		2-0			0-2			1-0	0-1	2-0	1-1	1-0		0-1
2000	1-1	1-0					1-0	1-1		1-0		0-2	2-0	0-1	0-1	0-1
1999		2-0	0-1	0-1			1-0	1-0	1-0	2-0	0-1	0-1	1-0			0-1
1998	1-0	1-0	0-1	1-0		0-1	0-1	2-0	0-1	1-0	1-0		1-1		0-1	1-0
1997	0-1			1-0		0-1				1-1	1-0	0-1	1-0	2-0	0-2	
1996	0-1	1-1	0-1	1-1			1-0	1-0		1-0	2-0		0-1		1-1	1-0
1995		0-2		2-1				0-1	1-0	1-0	0-1	0-1	1-1		0-1	0-1
1994		1-0	0-1	0-1			0-1		2-0	2-1	1-0	0-1	1-1	0-1	1-0	
1993		1-0	0-1	0-1			0-3		0-1	1-0	0-1	1-1	1-0	0-1	0-2	2-1
1992		1-1	1-0	2-0			0-1		1-1	1-0	0-1	1-1	0-2	1-0	1-0	1-1
1991		1-0	0-1	0-1	2-0		0-2			1-0	0-1		2-0	1-1	0-1	2-0
1990		1-0	1-1	0-2						1-0			0-1	1-2	0-1	1-1
1989							1-0			1-0	0-1	0-1	0-2		1-0	
1988				0-1						0-1	1-0		1-0	1-0	0-1	1-1
1987			0-1	0-1							2-0	0-1	0-1		1-0	
1986																
1985														0-1	1-0	
1984			0-1	1-0												
1983													1-0			
1982																
1981																
1980															0-1	
1979																
1978				1-0							1-0		0-2	0-1		

SUNDAY NIGHT FOOTBALL ALL-TIME STANDINGS

AMERICAN FOOTBALL CONFERENCE

East	W	L	T	Pct.	South	W	L	T	Pct.
Miami	19	8	0	.704	Tennessee	11	9	0	.550
New England	18	16	0	.529	Indianapolis	18	19	0	.486
Buffalo	10	10	0	.500	Jacksonville	5	6	0	.455
New York Jets	10	13	0	.435	Houston	2	4	0	.333

North	W	L	T	Pct.	West	W	L	T	Pct.
Baltimore	13	10	0	.565	Kansas City	10	5	0	.667
Pittsburgh	19	19	0	.500	Denver	20	15	0	.571
Cincinnati	3	11	0	.214	San Diego	16	16	0	.500
Cleveland	1	9	0	.100	Oakland	16	18	0	.471

SUNDAY NIGHT WON-LOST RECORDS, 1978-2012
NATIONAL FOOTBALL CONFERENCE

	Ariz.	Atl.	Car.	Chi.	Dall.	Det.	G.B.	Minn.	N.O.	N.Y.G.	Phil.	St. L.	S.F.	Sea.	T.B.	Wash.
Total	7-13	9-8	5-7	14-19	21-25	5-10	21-6	15-16	15-13	18-23-1	18-14	10-12	13-10	17-11	6-11	16-15-1
2012		1-0	0-1	1-2	0-2	2-1			1-1	1-1	1-1		2-1	1-0		1-0
2011		1-1	1-1	0-4	0-1	2-0	0-1		2-0	2-1	2-1					
2010			0-1	0-3			3-1	0-1	1-0	1-3	3-0	0-1	0-1	1-0		1-1
2009	2-1	1-0	1-0	0-3	2-1		1-0	0-2		1-2	2-1					0-1
2008			0-1	2-1	3-0		0-1	1-0		2-1	0-2			0-1	1-0	0-2
2007			1-1	3-0			0-1	0-1	1-0	1-2	0-3			0-1		2-0
2006			0-1	2-1	2-1		1-0		1-0	0-2	0-1			1-1		0-1
2005	1-0	0-1	1-0	0-1	0-1	1-0	0-1	1-0	0-1	0-1	0-1	1-0	0-1	1-0		1-0
2004		1-0	0-1				1-0	1-0	0-1	1-0	1-0	1-0	0-2		0-1	0-2
2003		1-0	0-1	0-1	0-1		1-0	1-1	1-1	0-1		1-0	0-1	1-0	0-1	0-1
2002	0-1	1-0	0-1		1-0		0-2		1-0	1-0		1-0		1-0	1-1	1-0
2001	0-1		0-1	1-0	0-1			0-1	0-2		2-0	1-0	2-0	1-1		1-0
2000	1-1	0-1	1-0	0-2	0-2		1-0	1-0		2-1	1-0	0-1				1-0
1999	0-2	0-1	1-0		0-1	1-0	1-0	0-1	0-1	0-1			0-1	2-0	0-2	2-0
1998	1-0	1-0	0-1	0-2	1-0	1-0		2-0	0-1	0-1	0-1	1-0	0-2	0-1		0-1
1997	1-0	0-1	1-1	1-1	0-1	0-2	1-0	1-0	1-0	0-0-1	0-1	0-1	0-1	1-0	1-0	1-0-1
1996	0-1	0-1	1-0		0-1	1-0	2-0	0-1		0-2	1-0	0-1	1-0	0-1	0-1	1-0
1995	0-1	0-2	0-1	1-0				1-1	0-1	1-0	1-0	2-0	1-0	1-0	1-0	0-1
1994	1-1		1-0		1-1				1-0	1-0	1-0	0-1	1-0	0-1	0-1	0-1
1993	0-1		1-0	1-0	1-0	2-0	1-2		1-0	0-1	1-0	1-0	0-1	1-0		1-0
1992	0-1		0-1				1-0		1-1	1-1	1-0	1-1	1-0	0-1	0-1	0-1
1991	0-1	1-0		1-0	0-1		1-1	1-1		0-1		0-2		1-1	0-1	2-0
1990	0-1	1-0	1-1	0-1	1-1	0-1	2-0		1-0		0-2	0-1	1-0	2-0	1-0	1-0
1989			0-1	1-0				1-0	0-1			1-0		1-0		0-1
1988				0-1				1-0	0-1			1-0	0-1	1-0		0-1
1987			1-0	0-1					1-0			0-1	2-0	1-0		0-1
1986				0-1								1-0				
1985				1-0						0-1						
1984				1-0				0-1								
1983				0-1												
1982		1-0											0-1			
1981				1-0								0-1				
1980				1-0												
1979				1-0									0-1			
1978													1-0			

SUNDAY NIGHT FOOTBALL ALL-TIME STANDINGS
NATIONAL FOOTBALL CONFERENCE

East	W	L	T	Pct.	South	W	L	T	Pct.
Philadelphia	18	14	0	.563	New Orleans	15	13	0	.536
Washington	16	15	1	.516	Atlanta	9	8	0	.529
Dallas	21	25	0	.457	Carolina	5	7	0	.417
New York Giants	18	23	1	.440	Tampa Bay	6	11	0	.353

North	W	L	T	Pct.	West	W	L	T	Pct.
Green Bay	21	6	0	.778	Seattle	17	11	0	.607
Minnesota	15	16	0	.484	San Francisco	13	10	0	.565
Chicago	14	19	0	.424	St. Louis	10	12	0	.455
Detroit	5	10	0	.333	Arizona	7	13	0	.350

MONDAY NIGHT WON-LOST RECORDS, 1970-2012
AMERICAN FOOTBALL CONFERENCE

	Balt.	Buff.	Cin.	Cle.	Den.	Hou.	Ind.	Jax.	K.C.	Mia.	N.E.	N.Y.J.	Oak.	Pitt.	S.D.	Tenn.
Total	8-9	17-23	9-20	15-14	28-36-1	2-4	21-12	8-7	22-17	40-38	22-22	19-27	37-26-1	40-23	21-18	21-16
2012	1-0	0-1		1-1		1-1	0-1			1-0	0-2	0-1		1-0	1-1	1-0
2011	0-1			0-1			0-1	1-1	1-1	0-2	2-0	1-0	1-0	0-1	1-1	
2010	2-0		0-1	0-1		0-2	1-0	0-1	1-0	0-1	2-0	1-2		1-0	1-1	1-0
2009	1-1	0-1		0-1	1-1	1-0				1-1	1-1	0-1	0-1	1-0	1-1	1-0
2008	0-1	0-1		2-1	1-1	1-0	0-1	0-1			1-0	0-1	0-1	2-0	1-0	1-0
2007	0-3	0-1	1-1		1-2		1-0	0-1	0-1	2-0				2-0	1-0	1-1
2006	0-1	0-1			1-0		1-0	2-0	0-1	0-1	1-0	1-0	0-2	0-1	1-0	
2005	1-1				1-0		3-0		0-1		1-1	0-2		2-1	0-1	
2004	0-1	1-0			0-1		1-0		2-1	1-1	1-1	1-0				1-1
2003			0-1		1-1		1-0		1-1	1-0	1-0		0-3	0-1	0-1	0-1
2002	1-0				0-2		0-1			1-1	1-1	0-1	2-0	2-1		1-0
2001	2-0				1-1		0-1	0-1	1-0			0-1	1-0	1-0		0-2
2000		0-1			1-1		2-0	0-2	1-1	0-1	1-1	2-0	0-1			3-0
1999		1-0			1-2			2-0		1-2	0-1	2-1	0-1	1-0		
1998					2-1			2-0	0-2	1-2	1-2	1-0		2-1		
1997		1-1			2-1		0-1	1-0	2-0	1-2	1-2			0-2	0-2	
1996		0-2			1-0	1-0			0-2	1-2			2-1	3-0	1-1	
1995		1-1	0-2		1-0				1-1	2-1	1-0		0-2	1-1	1-1	
1994		1-1			0-2				1-1	1-0			1-1	2-0	0-1	0-3
1993		2-1		1-0	0-2	0-1			2-0	1-2			1-0	3-0	2-0	0-1
1992		2-0	0-1	0-1	0-2				1-0	2-1		0-1		0-2	1-0	1-0
1991		2-1	0-2						2-1	1-1		0-1	0-2	0-1		1-1
1990		1-1	1-1	1-1	1-1	0-1			0-1	0-1		0-1	2-0	1-0		1-0
1989		1-2	1-2	1-1	2-0							0-1	1-0			1-0
1988		2-0		1-2	0-2	1-1				1-1			1-1	1-1		1-0
1987				1-0	2-1				1-1	1-1	2-1	1-1				
1986		1-0	1-0	1-1					1-2	1-0	1-1	0-1		0-2	0-1	
1985		1-0	1-0	1-0					2-1	0-1	1-0		2-0	0-2	0-1	
1984	0-1	0-1			1-0				3-0		0-1	2-1	1-1	1-2		
1983	0-1	0-2				0-1			1-1		2-0		1-0	1-0	1-1	
1982	0-1	0-1							1-1		1-0		1-0	1-1	1-1	0-1
1981		1-1		0-1	1-0				1-1	0-1			2-1	1-1	2-1	0-1
1980			1-1		1-2				1-1	1-2	1-0		3-0	0-2	1-0	2-0
1979			1-0		0-2				0-2	0-2	1-1		2-0	2-1	1-0	2-0
1978		1-2			1-1	2-1			2-1	0-2			1-0	1-1	1-0	2-0
1977	0-1	0-1	1-0			1-1	0-1		1-0	0-1			2-0	2-0		
1976		0-2	1-1			2-0			0-1	1-1	1-0	0-1	2-0	0-1		0-1
1975		0-2	1-0						1-0	1-1	0-1	0-1	2-0	1-0	1-0	0-1
1974	1-0	0-1		0-2					1-0	2-0		0-1	0-1	2-0		
1973	1-0		0-1	0-0-1					1-1	2-0		0-1	0-0-1	1-1		
1972		1-0					1-0		1-0	1-0	0-1	0-1	2-0		0-1	0-1
1971		0-1					1-1		2-0	1-0		0-1	1-0	0-1	1-0	
1970			0-1	2-0			1-1		1-0	1-0		0-1	1-0	1-0	0-1	0-1

MONDAY NIGHT FOOTBALL ALL-TIME STANDINGS
AMERICAN FOOTBALL CONFERENCE

East	W	L	T	Pct.	South	W	L	T	Pct.
Miami	40	38	0	.513	Indianapolis	21	12	0	.636
New England	22	22	0	.500	Tennessee	21	16	0	.568
Buffalo	17	23	0	.425	Jacksonville	8	7	0	.533
New York Jets	19	27	0	.413	Houston	2	4	0	.333

North	W	L	T	Pct.	West	W	L	T	Pct.
Pittsburgh	40	23	0	.635	Oakland	37	26	1	.586
Cleveland	15	14	0	.517	Kansas City	22	17	0	.564
Baltimore	8	9	0	.471	San Diego	21	18	0	.538
Cincinnati	9	20	0	.310	Denver	28	36	1	.438

From 1970-71, tie games were not included in winning percentage.

MONDAY NIGHT WON-LOST RECORDS, 1970-2012
NATIONAL FOOTBALL CONFERENCE

	Ariz.	Atl.	Car.	Chi.	Dall.	Det.	G.B.	Minn.	N.O.	N.Y.G.	Phil.	St.L.	S.F.	Sea.	T.B.	Wash.
Total	6-15-1	10-24	6-4	25-35	43-31	12-14-1	28-30-1	26-28	16-17	21-33-1	27-25	26-29	43-25	18-8	9-9	27-34
2012	0-1	1-0	1-0	2-1	0-1	0-1	0-1		1-0	0-1	0-2		2-0	1-0		1-0
2011		0-1	1-1	1-0	1-0	1-0		0-1	2-0	1-1	0-1	0-2	1-0	1-0	1-0	0-1
2010	0-1	0-1		2-0	0-1		0-1	0-2	2-0	1-0	1-0		1-1			0-1
2009	0-1	0-1	0-1	1-0	1-0		1-1	1-1	2-0	1-0	1-0		1-0			0-2
2008	1-0		1-0	1-0	1-0		1-2	1-1	1-1	0-1	1-1		0-1		0-1	0-1
2007	0-1	0-2		0-1	1-0		1-0	1-0	1-1	1-0	0-1		1-1	1-0		1-0
2006	0-1	0-1	1-1	2-0	0-1		0-2	1-1	1-0	1-1	2-0	0-1	2-0	0-1		0-1
2005		3-0	1-0	1-1			0-3	1-0	0-2	1-0	0-3	0-1	1-0			1-0
2004		0-1		2-1			2-1	0-2			2-1	2-1		0-1	0-1	0-1	
2003		0-1	0-1	1-0			2-1		0-2		2-1	2-0	1-0	2-1		
2002				0-3			2-0		0-1		3-0	2-1	1-2	0-1	1-1	0-1
2001				1-0	0-1		2-0	1-1	0-1	0-3	1-0	2-1	1-0		1-0	0-2
2000		1-0		1-1			1-1	1-1				1-2		0-1	1-1	1-2
1999	0-1	1-2		1-2			1-2	2-1		1-0			1-2	1-0	1-0	
1998				2-0	1-1		0-3	1-0		0-2	0-1		3-0		1-1	0-1
1997			1-1	1-1	1-2		3-0	0-1			0-2		3-0			1-0
1996		0-1	2-0	2-1	0-2		2-1	0-1			0-2		2-1			
1995	0-1			1-2	3-0	2-0	1-0	0-2		0-1	0-1		2-1			
1994				0-2	2-1	1-0	1-0	2-0	0-2	1-2	2-0		2-1			
1993		0-1	0-1	1-1			0-1	1-0	0-2	1-0	1-1		1-2			1-2
1992		0-2	0-3	2-1	0-1			1-0	1-0	1-0	1-0		2-0	1-0		1-2
1991			2-1	0-1				0-1	1-0	2-1	2-1	0-1	2-1			2-0
1990						0-1		0-1	1-1	1-1	2-0	0-3	3-0	1-0		0-1
1989			1-1					1-1	1-1	2-1	0-2	0-2	3-0	1-0		0-2
1988	0-1		1-2	1-1				1-0	1-0	1-1	1-0	1-0	1-1	1-0		0-2
1987		1-2		2-1				1-0		0-3		1-2	2-0	0-2		1-1
1986	0-1		2-1	2-0	0-1	0-1				2-1		1-0	0-2	2-0		1-1
1985	1-1		1-1	1-1		0-1				0-1		2-1	1-2	0-2		2-1
1984		0-2	0-1	1-1	0-1	0-1		1-0	0-1			1-1	2-0	2-0		1-1
1983	0-0-1	0-1		1-1	2-0	2-1	0-1	0-1		1-1-1		1-0	1-0		0-1	1-2
1982				1-2		0-1	1-0	1-0		0-1					1-0	
1981		1-2	0-2	2-0	1-0		0-3					1-1	2-0	1-0		
1980		1-1		1-1					0-1	0-1	1-0	2-0		0-1	0-1	0-2
1979		1-2		0-2		1-0	0-1	0-1		0-1	1-1	1-0		2-0		1-0
1978		1-0	0-3	1-1			2-0					0-2	0-1			1-1
1977	2-0			1-0	1-1		0-1	0-1				1-1	0-2			1-1
1976	0-1			1-0				1-1				0-1	0-2	2-0		2-0
1975	0-1			0-1	1-1	0-1				1-0	0-1	1-0				1-0
1974	0-1	0-1		1-0	0-1	1-0	0-1	1-0	0-1		1-0	1-1	0-2			2-0
1973		1-1		0-1	1-1	1-0	1-1	0-1	0-1	0-1		1-0	1-0			1-1
1972	0-1	0-1		1-0	1-0	0-2	1-0	0-2	0-1	1-0	0-1	1-0	0-1			2-0
1971	1-1	1-0		0-1	1-0	0-1-1	0-1-1	2-0		0-1		0-2	0-1			1-0
1970	1-0	0-1		0-1	0-1	2-0	1-1	1-0		0-1	1-0	0-2				0-1

MONDAY NIGHT FOOTBALL ALL-TIME STANDINGS
NATIONAL FOOTBALL CONFERENCE

East	W	L	T	Pct.	South	W	L	T	Pct.
Dallas	43	31	0	.581	Carolina	6	4	0	.600
Philadelphia	27	25	0	.519	Tampa Bay	9	9	0	.500
Washington	27	34	0	.443	New Orleans	16	17	0	.485
New York Giants	21	33	1	.391	Atlanta	10	24	0	.294

North	W	L	T	Pct.	West	W	L	T	Pct.
Green Bay	28	30	1	.483	Seattle	18	8	0	.692
Minnesota	26	28	0	.481	San Francisco	43	25	0	.632
Detroit	12	14	1	.462	St. Louis	26	29	0	.473
Chicago	25	35	0	.417	Arizona	6	15	1	.295

From 1970-71, tie games were not included in winning percentage.

Compiled by Elias Sports Bureau
*NFL record.

MONDAY NIGHT RECORDS

SCORING
TOUCHDOWNS
Most Touchdowns, Career
36 Jerry Rice, San Francisco, 1985-2000;
    Oakland, 2001-04; Seattle 2004
24 Emmitt Smith, Dallas, 1990-2002; Arizona 2003-04
20 Terrell Owens, San Francisco, 1996-2003;
    Philadelphia, 2004-05; Dallas, 2006-08;
    Buffalo, 2009; Cincinnati, 2010
Most Touchdowns, Game
4   Ron Johnson, N.Y. Giants at Philadelphia,
    Oct. 2, 1972
    Earl Campbell, Houston vs. Miami, Nov. 20, 1978
    Marcus Allen, L.A. Raiders vs. San Diego,
    Sept. 24, 1984
    Eric Dickerson, Indianapolis vs. Denver,
    Oct. 31, 1988
    Emmitt Smith, Dallas at N.Y. Giants, Sept. 4, 1995
    Marshall Faulk, St. Louis at Tampa Bay,
    Dec. 18, 2000

FIELD GOALS
Most Field Goals, Career
51 Gary Anderson, Pittsburgh, 1982-1994; Philadelphia,
    1995-96; San Francisco, 1997;
    Minnesota, 1998-2002; Tennessee, 2003-04
50 Jason Elam, Denver, 1993-2007; Atlanta, 2008-09
42 Ryan Longwell, Green Bay, 1997-2005;
    Minnesota, 2006-2011; Seattle, 2012
Most Field Goals, Game
7   Chris Boniol, Dallas vs. Green Bay, Nov. 18, 1996*
    Billy Cundiff, Dallas at N.Y. Giants, Sept. 15, 2003 (OT)*
6   Dan Bailey, Dallas vs. Washington, Sept. 26, 2011
5   Tim Mazzetti, Atlanta vs. Los Angeles, Oct. 30, 1978
    Roger Ruzek, Dallas at L.A. Rams, Dec. 21, 1987
    Rich Karlis, Minnesota vs. Cincinnati, Dec. 25, 1989
    Nick Lowery, Kansas City vs. Denver, Sept. 20, 1993
    Chris Jacke, Green Bay vs. San Francisco,
    Oct. 14, 1996 (OT)
    Richie Cunningham, Dallas vs. Philadelphia,
    Sept. 15, 1997
    Phil Dawson, Cleveland vs. Buffalo, Nov. 17, 2008
    Nick Folk, N.Y. Jets vs. Minnesota, Oct. 11, 2010
    Nate Kaeding, San Diego at Oakland, Sept. 10, 2012

RUSHING
YARDS GAINED
Most Yards Gained, Career
2,434 Emmitt Smith, Dallas, 1990-2002; Arizona, 2003-04
1,897 Tony Dorsett, Dallas, 1977-1987; Denver, 1988
1,769 Thurman Thomas, Buffalo, 1988-1999; Miami, 2000
Most Yards Gained, Game
221 Bo Jackson, L.A. Raiders at Seattle, Nov. 30, 1987
216 Ricky Williams, Miami vs. Chicago, Dec. 9, 2002
214 Thurman Thomas, Buffalo at N.Y. Jets,
     Sept. 24, 1990
Longest Run From Scrimmage, Game
99 Tony Dorsett, Dallas at Minnesota,
    Jan. 3, 1983 (TD)*
94 Chris Johnson, Tennessee vs. N.Y. Jets,
    Dec. 17, 2012 (TD)
91 Bo Jackson, L.A. Raiders at Seattle,
    Nov. 30, 1987 (TD)
TOUCHDOWNS
Most Rushing Touchdowns, Career
23 Emmitt Smith, Dallas, 1990-2002; Arizona, 2003-04

17 Marcus Allen, L.A. Raiders, 1982-1992;
    Kansas City, 1993-97
14 Eric Dickerson, L.A. Rams, 1983-87; Indianapolis,
    1987-1991; L.A. Raiders, 1992; Atlanta, 1993
Most Rushing Touchdowns, Game
4   Earl Campbell, Houston vs. Miami, Nov. 20, 1978
    Eric Dickerson, Indianapolis vs. Denver,
    Oct. 31, 1988
    Emmitt Smith, Dallas at N.Y. Giants, Sept. 4, 1995

PASSING
YARDS GAINED
Most Yards Gained, Career
9,654 Dan Marino, Miami, 1983-1999
9,068 Brett Favre, Atlanta, 1991; Green Bay, 1992-2007;
       N.Y. Jets, 2008; Minnesota, 2009-2010
5,148 Joe Montana, San Francisco, 1979-1992;
       Kansas City, 1993-94
Most Yards Gained, Game
517 Tom Brady, New England vs. Miami, Sept. 12, 2011
458 Joe Montana, San Francisco at L.A. Rams,
     Dec. 11, 1989
448 Marc Bulger, St. Louis at Green Bay, Nov. 29, 2004
Longest Pass Play
99 Brett Favre to Robert Brooks, Green Bay at Chicago,
    Sept. 11, 1995 (TD)*
    Tom Brady to Wes Welker, New England vs. Miami,
    Sept. 12, 2011*
97 Bernie Kosar to Webster Slaughter, Cleveland vs.
    Chicago, Oct. 23, 1989 (TD)
95 Joe Montana to John Taylor, San Francisco at
    L.A. Rams, Dec. 11, 1989 (TD)
TOUCHDOWNS
Most Touchdown Passes, Career
74 Dan Marino, Miami, 1983-1999
69 Brett Favre, Atlanta, 1991; Green Bay, 1992-2007;
    N.Y. Jets, 2008; Minnesota, 2009-2010
42 Steve Young, Tampa Bay, 1985-86; San Francisco,
    1987-1999
Most Touchdown Passes, Game
5   Dave Krieg, Seattle vs. L.A. Raiders, Nov. 28, 1988
    Jim Kelly, Buffalo vs. Cincinnati, Oct. 21, 1991
    Vinny Testaverde, N.Y. Jets vs. Miami,
    Oct. 23, 2000 (OT)
    Ben Roethlisberger, Pittsburgh vs. Baltimore,
    Nov. 5, 2007
    Drew Brees, New Orleans vs. New England,
    Nov. 30, 2009

RECEIVING
PASS RECEPTIONS
Most Pass Receptions, Career
254 Jerry Rice, San Francisco, 1985-2000;
     Oakland, 2001-04; Seattle, 2004
124 Andre Reed, Buffalo, 1985-1999; Washington, 2000
123 Cris Carter, Philadelphia, 1987-89; Minnesota,
     1990-2001; Miami, 2002
Most Pass Receptions, Game
14   Herman Moore, Detroit vs. Chicago, Dec. 4, 1995
     Jerry Rice, San Francisco vs. Minnesota,
     Dec. 18, 1995
13   Andre Reed, Buffalo vs. Denver, Sept. 18, 1989
     Terrell Owens, San Francisco vs. Philadelphia,
     Nov. 25, 2002
     Darren McFadden, Oakland vs. San Diego,
     Sept. 10, 2012
     Jason Witten, Dallas vs. Chicago, Oct. 1, 2012
YARDS GAINED
Most Yards Gained, Career
4,029 Jerry Rice, San Francisco, 1985-2000;
       Oakland, 2001-04; Seattle, 2004

1,783 Andre Reed, Buffalo, 1985-1999; Washington, 2000
1,697 Terrell Owens, San Francisco, 1996-2003;
Philadelphia, 2004-05; Dallas, 2006-08;
Buffalo, 2009; Cincinnati, 2010

Most Yards Gained, Game
289 Jerry Rice, San Francisco vs. Minnesota,
Dec. 18, 1995
286 John Taylor, San Francisco at L.A. Rams,
Dec. 11, 1989
260 Wes Chandler, San Diego vs. Cincinnati,
Dec. 20, 1982

TOUCHDOWN
Most Receiving Touchdowns, Career
34 Jerry Rice, San Francisco, 1985-2000;
Oakland, 2001-04; Seattle, 2004
20 Terrell Owens, San Francisco, 1996-2003;
Philadelphia, 2004-05; Dallas, 2006-08;
Buffalo, 2009; Cincinnati, 2010
18 Randy Moss, Minnesota, 1998-2004;
Oakland, 2005-06; New England, 2007-2010;
Minnesota, 2010; Tennessee, 2010;
San Francisco, 2012

Most Receiving Touchdowns, Game
3 Ron Johnson, N.Y. Giants at Philadelphia,
Oct. 2, 1972
Wesley Walker, N.Y. Jets at Detroit, Dec. 6, 1982
Steve Largent, Seattle at San Diego, Oct. 29, 1984
Mark Clayton, Miami vs. Dallas, Dec. 17, 1984
Jerry Rice, San Francisco vs. Chicago,
Dec. 14, 1987
Jerry Rice, San Francisco vs. Minnesota,
Dec. 18, 1995
Lamar Thomas, Miami vs. Denver, Dec. 21, 1998
Ed McCaffrey, Denver vs. Miami, Sept. 13, 1999
Randy Moss, Minnesota vs. N.Y. Giants,
Nov. 19, 2001
Isaac Bruce, St. Louis at New Orleans,
Dec. 17, 2001
Terrell Owens, Philadelphia at Dallas, Nov. 15, 2004
Drew Bennett, Tennessee vs. Kansas City,
Dec. 13, 2004
Marvin Harrison, Indianapolis vs. Cincinnati,
Dec. 18, 2006

YARDS FROM SCRIMMAGE
Most Scrimmage Yards, Career
4,116 Jerry Rice, San Francisco, 1985-2000;
Oakland, 2001-04; Seattle, 2004
2,836 Emmitt Smith, Dallas, 1990-2002; Arizona, 2003-04
2,567 Tony Dorsett, Dallas, 1977-1987; Denver, 1988

INTERCEPTIONS BY
Most Interceptions, Career
11 Everson Walls, Dallas, 1981-89; N.Y. Giants,
1990-92; Cleveland, 1992-93
9 Merton Hanks, San Francisco, 1991-98;
Seattle, 1999
8 Emmitt Thomas, Kansas City, 1966-1978
Darren Sharper, Green Bay, 1997-2004; Minnesota,
2005-08; New Orleans, 2009-2010

Most Interceptions, Game
4 Dick Anderson, Miami vs. Pittsburgh, Dec. 3, 1973*
3 Johnny Robinson, Kansas City at Baltimore,
Sept. 28, 1970
Charlie Babb, Miami vs. Oakland, Sept. 22, 1975
Charles Phillips, Oakland vs. Denver, Dec. 8, 1975
Mark Murphy, Washington at San Diego,
Oct. 31, 1983
Ken Easley, Seattle at San Diego, Oct. 29, 1984
Dwayne Harper, San Diego vs. Oakland,
Nov. 27, 1995

Marcus Coleman, N.Y. Jets vs. Miami,
Oct. 23, 2000 (OT)
Keith Bulluck, Tennessee vs. New Orleans,
Sept. 24, 2007

Longest Interception Return
102 Eddie Anderson, L.A. Raiders at Miami,
Dec. 14, 1992 (TD)
101 Lito Sheppard, Philadelphia at Dallas,
Nov. 15, 2004 (TD)
100 Darrelle Revis, N.Y. Jets vs. Miami,
Oct. 17, 2011 (TD)

SACKS
Most Sacks, Career
24.5 Bruce Smith, Buffalo, 1985-1999; Washington,
2000-03
20.0 Richard Dent, Chicago, 1983-1993, 1995;
San Francisco, 1994; Indianapolis, 1996;
Philadelphia, 1997
18.0 Kevin Greene, L.A. Rams, 1985-1992; Pittsburgh,
1993-95; Carolina, 1996, 1998-99;
San Francisco, 1997

PUNTING
Highest Punt Average, Career (Minimum: 25 Punts)
48.53 Shane Lechler, Oakland, 2000-2012
47.78 Mike Scifres, San Diego, 2003-2012
47.31 Andy Lee, San Francisco, 2004-2012

Longest Punt
90 Rodney Williams, N.Y. Giants at Denver,
Sept. 10, 2001
83 Bryan Barker, Jacksonville vs. N.Y. Jets,
Oct. 11, 1999
77 Shane Lechler, Oakland vs. Denver, Sept. 12, 2011

PUNT RETURNS
Longest Punt Return
95 John Taylor, San Francisco vs. Washington,
Nov. 21, 1988 (TD)
94 Dennis McKinnon, Chicago vs. N.Y. Giants,
Sept. 14, 1987 (TD)
Dexter McCluster, Kansas City vs. San Diego,
Sept. 13, 2010 (TD)
93 Dez Bryant, Dallas vs. N.Y. Giants,
Oct. 25, 2010 (TD)

KICKOFF RETURNS
Longest Kickoff Return
105 Terry Fair, Detroit vs. Tampa Bay,
Sept. 28, 1998 (TD)
104 Allen Rossum, San Francisco vs. Arizona,
Nov. 10, 2008 (TD)
103 Terrence McGee, Buffalo vs. Dallas,
Oct. 8, 2007 (TD)
Brandon Tate, New England at Miami,
Oct. 4, 2010 (TD)
David Reed, Baltimore at Houston,
Dec. 13, 2010 (TD)

FUMBLES
Longest Fumble Return
99 Don Griffin, San Francisco vs. Chicago,
Dec. 23, 1991 (TD)
96 Joe Lavender, Philadelphia vs. Dallas,
Sept. 23, 1974 (TD)
93 Adam Archuleta, St. Louis vs. Tampa Bay,
Oct. 18, 2004 (TD)

NFL INTERNATIONAL GAMES (69)

REGULAR SEASON GAMES (12)
(Home Team in capitals)

Date	Site	Teams
October 2, 2005	Mexico City, Mexico	ARIZONA 31, San Francisco 14
October 28, 2007	London, England	N.Y. Giants 13, MIAMI 10
October 26, 2008	London, England	NEW ORLEANS 37, San Diego 32
December 7, 2008	Toronto, Canada	Miami 16, BUFFALO 3
October 25, 2009	London, England	New England 35, TAMPA BAY 7
December 3, 2009	Toronto, Canada	N.Y. Jets 19, BUFFALO 13
October 31, 2010	London, England	SAN FRANCISCO 24, Denver 16
November 7, 2010	Toronto, Canada	Chicago 22, BUFFALO 19
October 23, 2011	London, England	Chicago 24, TAMPA BAY 18
October 30, 2011	Toronto, Canada	BUFFALO 23, Washington 0
October 28, 2012	London, England	New England 45, ST. LOUIS 7
December 16, 2012	Toronto, Canada	Seattle 50, BUFFALO 17

PRESEASON GAMES (57)

Date	Site	Teams
August 12, 1950	Ottawa, Canada	N.Y. Giants 27, Ottawa Rough Riders 6
August 11, 1951	Ottawa, Canada	N.Y. Giants 41, Ottawa Rough Riders 18
August 5, 1959	Toronto, Canada	Chi. Cardinals 55, Tor. Argonauts 26
August 3, 1960	Toronto, Canada	Pittsburgh 43, Toronto Argonauts 16
August 15, 1960	Toronto, Canada	Chicago 16, N.Y. Giants 7
August 2, 1961	Toronto, Canada	St. Louis 36, Toronto Argonauts 7
August 5, 1961	Montreal, Canada	Chicago 34, Montreal Alouettes 16
August 8, 1961	Hamilton, Canada	Hamilton Tiger-Cats 38, Buffalo 21
August 25, 1969	Montreal, Canada	Detroit 22, Boston 9
September 11, 1969	Montreal, Canada	Pittsburgh 17, N.Y. Giants 13
August 16, 1976	Tokyo, Japan	St. Louis 20, San Diego 10
August 5, 1978	Mexico City, Mexico	New Orleans 14, Philadelphia 7
August 6, 1983	London, England	Minnesota 28, St. Louis 10
* August 3, 1986	London, England	Chicago 17, Dallas 6
* August 9, 1987	London, England	L.A. Rams 28, Denver 27
* July 31, 1988	London, England	Miami 27, San Francisco 21
August 14, 1988	Goteborg, Sweden	Minnesota 28, Chicago 21
August 18, 1988	Montreal, Canada	N.Y. Jets 11, Cleveland 7
* August 5, 1989	Tokyo, Japan	L.A. Rams 16, San Francisco 13 (OT)
* August 6, 1989	London, England	Philadelphia 17, Cleveland 13
* August 4, 1990	Tokyo, Japan	Denver 10, Seattle 7
* August 5, 1990	London, England	New Orleans 17, L.A. Raiders 10
* August 9, 1990	Montreal, Canada	Pittsburgh 30, New England 14
* August 11, 1990	Berlin, Germany	L.A. Rams 19, Kansas City 3
* July 28, 1991	London, England	Buffalo 17, Philadelphia 13
* August 3, 1991	Berlin, Germany	San Francisco 21, Chicago 7
* August 3, 1991	Tokyo, Japan	Miami 19, L.A. Raiders 17
* August 1, 1992	Tokyo, Japan	Houston 34, Dallas 23
* August 15, 1992	Berlin, Germany	Miami 31, Denver 27
* August 16, 1992	London, England	San Francisco 17, Washington 15
* July 31, 1993	Tokyo, Japan	New Orleans 28, Philadelphia 16
* August 1, 1993	Barcelona, Spain	San Francisco 21, Pittsburgh 14
* August 7, 1993	Berlin, Germany	Minnesota 20, Buffalo 6
* August 8, 1993	London, England	Dallas 13, Detroit 13 (OT)
August 14, 1993	Toronto, Canada	Cleveland 12, New England 9
* July 31, 1994	Barcelona, Spain	L.A. Raiders 25, Denver 22
* August 6, 1994	Tokyo, Japan	Minnesota 17, Kansas City 9
* August 13, 1994	Berlin, Germany	N.Y. Giants 28, San Diego 20
* August 15, 1994	Mexico City, Mexico	Houston 6, Dallas 0
* August 5, 1995	Tokyo, Japan	Denver 24, San Francisco 10
* August 12, 1995	Toronto, Canada	Buffalo 9, Dallas 7
* July 27, 1996	Tokyo, Japan	San Diego 20, Pittsburgh 10
* August 5, 1996	Monterrey, Mexico	Kansas City 32, Dallas 6
* July 27, 1997	Dublin, Ireland	Pittsburgh 30, Chicago 17
* August 4, 1997	Mexico City, Mexico	Miami 38, Denver 19
* August 16, 1997	Toronto, Canada	Green Bay 35, Buffalo 3
* August 1, 1998	Tokyo, Japan	Green Bay 27, Kansas City 24 (OT)
* August 15, 1998	Vancouver, Canada	San Francisco 24, Seattle 21
* August 17, 1998	Mexico City, Mexico	New England 21, Dallas 3
* August 7, 1999	Sydney, Australia	Denver 20, San Diego 17
* August 5, 2000	Tokyo, Japan	Atlanta 20, Dallas 9

INTERNATIONAL GAMES / NFL OPENING KICKOFF WEEKEND

Date	Site	Teams
* August 19, 2000	Mexico City, Mexico	Indianapolis 24, Pittsburgh 23
* August 27, 2001	Mexico City, Mexico	Dallas 21, Oakland 6
* August 3, 2002	Osaka, Japan	Washington 38, San Francisco 7
* August 2, 2003	Tokyo, Japan	Tampa Bay 30, N.Y. Jets 14
* August 6, 2005	Tokyo, Japan	Atlanta 27, Indianapolis 21
August 14, 2008	Toronto, Canada	Buffalo 24, Pittsburgh 21
August 19, 2010	Toronto, Canada	Buffalo 34, Indianapolis 21
* *American Bowl Game*		

NFL OPENING KICKOFF GAMES (11)
(Home Team in capitals)
The first site listed each year designates location of Thursday Night NFL Kickoff Weekend game; subsequent locations indicate site(s) of NFL Kickoff Weekend concert.

Date	Sites	Teams
Sept. 5, 2002	Giants Stadium (East Rutherford, New Jersey) Times Square (New York, New York)	San Francisco 16, N.Y. GIANTS 13
Sept. 4, 2003	FedExField (Landover, Maryland) National Mall (Washington, D.C.)	WASHINGTON 16, N.Y. Jets 13
Sept. 9, 2004	Gillette Stadium (Foxboro, Massachusetts) Metropolitan Park (Jacksonville, Florida)	NEW ENGLAND 27, Indianapolis 24
Sept. 8, 2005	Gillette Stadium (Foxboro, Massachusetts) Detroit, Michigan Los Angeles Coliseum (Los Angeles, California)	NEW ENGLAND 30, Oakland 20
Sept. 7, 2006	Heinz Field (Pittsburgh, Pennsylvania) Miami, Florida	PITTSBURGH 28, Miami 17
Sept. 6, 2007	RCA Dome (Indianapolis, Indianapolis)	INDIANAPOLIS 41, New Orleans 10
Sept. 4, 2008	Giants Stadium (East Rutherford, New Jersey) Columbus Circle (New York, New York)	N.Y. GIANTS 16, Washington 7
Sept. 10, 2009	Heinz Field (Pittsburgh, Pennsylvania) Point State Park (Pittsburgh, Pennsylvania)	PITTSBURGH 13, Tennessee 10 (OT)
Sept. 9, 2010	Louisiana Superdome (New Orleans, Louisiana) Jackson Square (New Orleans, Louisiana)	NEW ORLEANS 14, Minnesota 9
Sept. 8, 2011	Lambeau Field (Green Bay, Wisconsin)	GREEN BAY 42, New Orleans 34
Sept. 5, 2012*	MetLife Stadium (East Rutherford, New Jersey) Rockefeller Center (New York, New York)	Dallas 24, N.Y. GIANTS 17

Wednesday night

MODIFIED SUDDEN DEATH OVERTIME

For the 2010 postseason, the NFL installed a modified sudden death system to determine the winner when the score is tied at the end of regulation. In 2012, the system was expanded to cover all NFL games, including regular-season and preseason games.

Modified sudden death guarantees each team a possession or the opportunity to possess, unless the team that receives the opening kickoff scores a touchdown on its initial possession.

Key Definitions:

Possession: Actual possession of the ball with complete control. The defense gains possession when it catches, intercepts, or recovers a loose ball.

Opportunity to possess: The opportunity to possess occurs only during kicking plays. A kickoff is an opportunity to possess for the receiving team. If the kicking team legally recovers the kick, the receiving team is considered to have had its opportunity. A punt or a field goal that crosses the line of scrimmage and is muffed by the receiving team is considered to be an opportunity to possess for the receivers. Normal touching rules by the kicking team apply.

REGULAR SEASON

At the end of regulation time, the Referee will immediately toss coin at center of field in accordance with rules pertaining to the usual pregame toss. The captain of the visiting team will call the toss prior to the coin being flipped.

Following a three-minute intermission after the end of the regulation game, there shall be a maximum of one 15-minute period. Each team must possess or have the opportunity to possess the ball unless the team that has the ball first scores a touchdown on its initial possession. Play continues in sudden death until a winner is determined, and the game automatically ends upon any score (by safety, field goal, or touchdown) or when a score is awarded by Referee for a palpably unfair act. Each team shall be entitled to two timeouts, and if there is an excess timeout, the usual rules shall apply. Try is not attempted if touchdown scored. Disqualified players are not allowed to return.

If the score is tied at the end of a 15-minute overtime period, the game shall result in a tie.

Instant Replay: No challenges. Reviews to be initiated by the replay official.

POSTSEASON

At the end of regulation time, the Referee will immediately toss coin at center of field in accordance with rules pertaining to the usual pregame toss. The captain of the visiting team will call the toss prior to the coin being flipped.

Following a three-minute intermission after the end of the regulation game, play will be continued in 15-minute periods until a winner is declared. Each team must possess or have the opportunity to possess the ball unless the team that has the ball first scores a touchdown on its initial possession. Play continues in sudden death until a winner is determined, and the game automatically ends upon any score (by safety, field goal, or touchdown) or when a score is awarded by Referee for a palpably unfair act. Each team has three time outs per half and all general timing provisions apply as during a regular game. Try is not attempted if touchdown scored. Disqualified players are not allowed to return.

Instant Replay: No challenges. Reviews to be initiated by the replay official.

italic indicates Monday-night game
# indicates Thursday/Saturday/Sunday-night game
+ indicates Thanksgiving Day game

REGULAR SEASON

Sept. 9, 2012—Minnesota 26, Jacksonville 23, at Minnesota; Vikings win toss. Harvin returns kickoff 30 yards. Drive begins on Minnesota 25. Walsh kicks 38-yard field goal. Parmele returns kickoff 21 yards. Drive begins on Jacksonville 23. Drive ends on Jacksonville 31 at 4:54.

Sept. 23, 2012—New York Jets 23, Miami 20, at Miami; Jets win toss. Touchback. Drive begins on Jets 20. Drive ends on Miami 45. Malone punts 35 yards and Bess makes fair catch at Miami 10. Carpenter misses 48-yard field goal. Drive begins on Jets 38. Folk kicks 33-yard field goal at 8:56.

Sept. 23, 2012—Kansas City 27, New Orleans 24, at New Orleans; Chiefs win toss. Touchback. Drive begins on Kansas City 20. Drive ends on New Orleans 46. Colquitt punts 43 yards to New Orleans 3. Drive begins on New Orleans 3. Drive ends on New Orleans 3. Morstead punts 60 yards to Kansas City 37 and Arenas returns punt 10 yards. Drive begins on Kansas City 47. Succop kicks 31-yard field goal at 8:33.

Sept. 23, 2012—Tennessee 44, Detroit 41, at Tennessee; Titans win toss. Reynaud returns kickoff 25 yards. Drive begins on Tennessee 20. Bironas kicks 26-yard field goal. Logan returns kickoff 23 yards. Drive begins on Detroit 22. Drive ends on Tennessee 7 at 8:25.

Sept. 30, 2012—Arizona 24, Miami 21, at Arizona; Cardinals win toss. Powell returns kickoff 41 yards. Drive begins on Arizona 34. Drive ends on Arizona 31. Zastudil punts 57 yards and Bess returns for 9 yards. Drive begins on Miami 21. Tannehill pass to Hartline is intercepted by Rhodes, who returns it 5 yards. Drive begins on Miami 47. Feely kicks 46-yard field goal at 6:31.

Oct. 14, 2012—Detroit 26, Philadelphia 23, at Philadelphia; Eagles win toss. Boykin returns kickoff 23 yards. Drive begins on Philadelphia 25. Drive ends on Philadelphia 4. McBriar punts 57 yards and Logan returns punt 10 yards. Drive begins at 50. Hanson kicks 45-yard field goal at 4:00.

Oct. 14, 2012—Buffalo 19, Arizona 16, at Arizona; Bills win toss. Touchback. Drive begins on Buffalo 20. Drive ends on Arizona 40. Powell punts 40 yards. Touchback. Drive begins on Arizona 20. Skelton's pass to Housler is intercepted by Byrd, who returns it 29 yards. Drive begins on Arizona 6. Lindell kicks 25-yard field goal at 3:50.

Oct. 21, 2012—New England 29, New York Jets 26, at New England; Patriots win toss. McCourty returns kickoff 17 yards. Drive begins on New England 18. Gostkowski kicks 48-yard field goal. McKnight returns kickoff 19 yards. Drive begins at Jets 15. Ninkovich sacks Sanchez and recovers fumble at Jets 25 at 7:32.

Oct. 21, 2012—Oakland 26, Jacksonville 23, at Oakland; Jaguars win toss. Thomas returns kickoff 14 yards. Drive begins on Jacksonville 19. Henne completes pass to Shorts for 8 yards, and Houston forces fumble, which is recovered by Hanson. Drive begins at Jacksonville 21. Janikowski kicks 40-yard field goal at 2:06.

Oct. 28, 2012—Indianapolis 19, Tennessee 13, at Tennessee; Colts win toss. Touchback. Drive begins on Indianapolis 20. Luck completes 16-yard touchdown pass to Ballard at 4:49.

Nov. 11, 2012—San Francisco 24, St. Louis 24, at San Francisco; Rams win toss. Pead returns kickoff 21 yards. Drive begins on St. Louis 18. Drive ends on St. Louis 27. J. Hekker punts 45 yards and Ginn returns for 12 yards. Drive begins on San Francisco 40. Akers misses 41-yard field goal. Drive begins on St. Louis 31. Zuerlein misses 58-yard field goal. Drive begins on San Francisco 48. Drive ends on San Francisco 43. Lee punts 46 yards and Amendola returns for 3 yards. Drive begins on St. Louis 14. Bradford completes pass to Gibson for 24 yards to St. Louis 49 as time expires.

* **Nov. 12, 2012—Pittsburgh 16, Kansas City 13,** at Pittsburgh; Chiefs win toss. Wylie returns kickoff 20 yards. Drive begins on Kansas City 15. Cassel's pass to Bowe intercepted by Timmons, who returns for 23 yards. Drive begins on Kansas City

5. Suisham kicks 23-yard field goal at 0:55.

Nov. 18, 2012—Tampa Bay 27, Carolina 21, at Carolina; Buccaneers win toss. Touchback. Drive begins on Tampa Bay 20. Freeman completes 15-yard touchdown pass to Clark at 4:20.

Nov. 18, 2012—Dallas 23, Cleveland 20, at Dallas; Cowboys win toss. Touchback. Drive begins on Dallas 20. Drive ends on Cleveland 41. Moorman punts 31 yards. Drive begins on Cleveland 10. Drive ends on Cleveland 16. Hodges punts 52 yards and Harris returns for 20 yards. Drive begins on Cleveland 48. Bailey kicks 38-yard field goal at 8:53.

Nov. 18, 2012—Houston 43, Jacksonville 37, at Houston; Texans win toss. Touchback. Drive begins on Houston 20. Graham kicks 25-yard field goal. Jennings returns kickoff 29 yards. Drive begins on Jacksonville 32. Scobee kicks 33-yard field goal. Touchback. Henne throws incomplete pass to Blackmon on fourth down. Drive ends on Houston 47. Schaub completes 48-yard touchdown pass to A. Johnson at 12:59.

+**Nov. 22, 2012—Houston 34, Detroit 31,** at Detroit; Lions win toss. Touchback. Drive begins on Detroit 20. Graham misses 51-yard field goal. Drive begins at Detroit 41. Drive ends at Houston 45. Harris punts 36 yards. Drive begins at Houston 9. Houston intercepts Schaub's pass and returns for 2 yards. Drive begins on Houston 41. Hanson misses 47-yard field goal. Drive begins on Houston 37. M. Schaub pass to J. Casey for 15 yards. M. Schaub pass to A. Johnson for 23 yards. M. Schaub pass to J. Casey for 11 yards. S. Graham kicks 32-yard field goal at 12:39.

Nov. 25, 2012—Baltimore 16, San Diego 13, at San Diego; Chargers win toss. Carr returns kickoff 25 yards. Drive begins on San Diego 16. Drive ends on 50. Scifres punts 39 yards. Drive begins on Baltimore 11. Drive ends on Baltimore 48. Koch punts 52 yards. Touchback. Drive begins on San Diego 20. Drive ends on San Diego 27. Scifres punts 63 yards and J. Jones returns for 1 yard. Drive begins on Baltimore 11. Tucker kicks 38-yard field goal at 13:53.

Dec. 2, 2012—Seattle 23, Chicago 17, at Chicago; Seahawks win toss. Touchback. Drive begins on Seattle 20. Wilson completes 13-yard touchdown pass to Rice at 7:27.

Dec. 2, 2012—St. Louis 16, San Francisco 13, at St. Louis; Rams win toss. Touchback. Drive begins on St. Louis 20. Drive ends on St. Louis 33. Hekker punts 47 yards. Drive begins on San Francisco 20. Drive ends on San Francisco 28. Lee punts 60 yards and Pettis returns for 15 yards. Drive begins on St. Louis 27. Drive ends on St. Louis 36. Hekker punts 14 yards. Drive begins on 50. Akers misses 51-yard field goal. Drive begins on St. Louis 41. Zuerlein kicks 54-yard field goal at 14:34.

Dec. 9, 2012—Washington 31, Baltimore 28, at Washington; Ravens win toss. J. Jones returns kickoff 27 yards. Drive begins on Baltimore 25. Drive ends on Baltimore 32. Koch punts 56 yards and Crawford returns for 64 yards. Drive begins on Baltimore 24. Forbath kicks 34-yard field goal at 3:23.

Dec. 16, 2012— Dallas 27, Pittsburgh 24, at Dallas; Steelers win toss. Touchback. Drive begins on Pittsburgh 20. Roethlisberger's pass intercepted by Carr, who returns it for 36 yards. Drive begins on Pittsburgh 1. Bailey kicks 21-yard field goal at 1:24.

Dec. 23, 2012— New Orleans 34, Dallas 31, at Dallas; Cowboys win toss. Touchback. Drive begins on Dallas 20. Drive ends on Dallas 36. Moorman punts 46 yards and Sproles returns for 8 yards. Drive begins on New Orleans 26. Hartley kicks 20-yard field goal at 4:27.

2012 POSTSEASON

Jan. 12, 2013—Baltimore 38, Denver 35, at Denver in AFC Divisional Playoff Game; Ravens win toss. Touchback. Drive begins on Baltimore 20. Drive ends on Baltimore 49. Koch punts 35 yards. Fair catch by Leonhard. Drive begins on Denver 16. Drive ends on Denver 39. Colquitt punts 55 yards and Reed returns for no gain. Drive begins on Baltimore 6. Drive ends on Baltimore 34. Koch punts 52 yards and Holliday returns for -7 yards. Drive begins on Denver 7. Manning's pass intended for Stokley intercepted by Graham, who returns for no gain, at Denver 45. Drive begins at Denver 45. Tucker kicks 47-yard field goal at 16:42.

NFL POSTSEASON OVERTIME GAMES
(BY LENGTH OF GAME)

Date	Game	Time
Dec. 25, 1971	Miami 27, KANSAS CITY 24	82:40
Dec. 23, 1962	Dallas Texans 20, HOUSTON 17	77:54
Jan. 3, 1987	CLEVELAND 23, N.Y. Jets 20	77:02
Jan. 12, 2013	Baltimore 38, DENVER 35	76:42
Dec. 24, 1977	Oakland 37, BALTIMORE 31	75:43
Jan. 10, 2004	Carolina 29, ST. LOUIS 23	75:10
Jan. 8, 2005	N.Y. Jets 20, SAN DIEGO 17	74:55
Jan 2, 1982	San Diego 41, MIAMI 38	73:52
Dec. 26, 1965	GREEN BAY 13, Baltimore 10	73:39
Jan. 17, 1999	Atlanta 30, MINNESOTA 27	71:52
Dec. 30, 2000	MIAMI 23, Indianapolis 17	71:16
Jan. 15, 2005	PITTSBURGH 20, N.Y. Jets 17	71:04
Jan. 8, 1994	KANSAS CITY 27, Pittsburgh 24	71:03
Jan. 19, 2002	NEW ENGLAND 16, Oakland 13	68:29
Dec. 28, 1958	Baltimore 23, N.Y. GIANTS 17	68:15
Jan. 3, 1988	HOUSTON 23, Seattle 20	68:05
Jan. 22, 2012	N.Y. Giants 20, SAN FRANCISCO 17	67:54
Jan. 3, 2009	SAN DIEGO 23, Indianapolis 17	66:12
Jan. 11, 1987	Denver 23, CLEVELAND 20	65:38
Jan. 14, 2007	CHICAGO 27, Seattle 24	64:53
Jan. 11, 2004	PHILADELPHIA 20, Green Bay 17	64:48
Jan. 24, 2010	NEW ORLEANS 31, Minnesota 28	64:45
Jan. 4, 2004	GREEN BAY 33, Seattle 27	64:25
Dec. 31, 1989	Pittsburgh 26, HOUSTON 23	63:26
Jan. 3, 1993	BUFFALO 41, Houston 38	63:06
Jan. 20, 2008	N.Y. Giants 23, GREEN BAY 20	62:26
Jan. 11, 2003	TENNESSEE 34, Pittsburgh 31	62:15
Jan. 10, 2010	ARIZONA 51, Green Bay 45	61:18
Jan. 7, 1990	L.A. Rams 19, N.Y. GIANTS 13	61:06
Jan. 8, 2012	DENVER 29, Pittsburgh 23	60:11

Home team in CAPS

OVERTIME GAMES BY YEAR
(REGULAR SEASON)

2012-22	2002-25*	1992-10	1982- 4
2011-13	2001-17	1991-15	1981-10
2010-19	2000-13	1990-10	1980-13
2009-13	1999-11	1989-11	1979-12
2008-15	1998-7	1988- 9	1978-11
2007-15	1997-17	1987-13	1977-6
2006-11	1996-14	1986-16	1976-5
2005-14	1995-21	1985-10	1975-9
2004-12	1994-16	1984- 9	1974-2
2003-23	1993-7	1983-19	

*Record

OVERTIME WON-LOST RECORDS, 1974-2012
(REGULAR SEASON)

Team	Win	Loss	Tie	Pct.
AFC				
Baltimore	10	8	1	.553
Buffalo	19	12	0	.609
Cincinnati	15	11	1	.574
Cleveland	16	17	1	.485
Denver	25	15	2	.619
Houston	3	7	0	.300
Indianapolis	13	10	1	.563
Jacksonville	7	7	0	.500
Kansas City	14	19	2	.426
Miami	13	22	1	.371
New England	18	20	0	.474
N.Y. Jets	19	17	2	.528
Oakland	17	17	0	.500
Pittsburgh	21	15	2	.581
San Diego	12	20	0	.375
Tennessee	15	19	0	.441
NFC				
Arizona	23	16	2	.588
Atlanta	13	20	2	.397
Carolina	4	10	0	.286
Chicago	22	17	0	.564
Dallas	19	14	0	.576
Detroit	15	18	1	.456
Green Bay	11	15	4	.431
Minnesota	19	18	2	.514
New Orleans	10	12	0	.455
N.Y. Giants	18	14	2	.563
Philadelphia	11	17	4	.400
St. Louis	13	11	2	.542
San Francisco	19	15	2	.559
Seattle	9	18	0	.333
Tampa Bay	15	16	1	.484
Washington	23	14	1	.622

OVERTIME GAME SUMMARY—1974-2012

There have been 499 overtime games in regular season play since the rule was adopted in 1974 (22 in 2012 season). Breakdown follows:

RESULTS

265(13) times the team which won the toss won the game (53.1%)

216 (8) times the team which lost the toss won the game (43.3%)

18 (1) games ended tied (3.6%). Last time: Nov. 11, 2012, St. Louis 24 at San Francisco 24.

POSSESSIONS

356(19) times both teams had at least one possession (71.3%)

143 (3) times the team which won the toss drove for winning score (104 FG, 39 TD) (28.7%)

Of the 499 overtime games, there were 13 miscellaneous situations in which non-standard possessions took place:

9 (0) times the defense or special teams won without registering an official possession (5 INT, 2 blocked punts, 1 FR, 1 blocked FG) (1.8%)

1 (0) times the special teams forced a fumble on the opening kickoff and drove for winning score (0.2%)

1 (0) times the punting team recovered a muffed punt and drove for winning score with team muffing punt having no official possessions (0.2%)

2 (0) times the team that won the toss elected to kick and the team receiving the ball drove for winning score (0.4%)

SCORING

356(17) games were decided by a field goal (71.3%)
123 (4) games were decided by a touchdown (24.6%)
2 (0) games were decided by a safety (0.4%)
18 (1) games ended tied (3.6%). Last time: Nov. 11, 2012, St. Louis 24 at San Francisco 24.

COIN TOSS

490(22) times the team which won the toss elected to receive (98.2%)
9 (0) times the team which won the toss elected to kick off (4 wins) (1.8%)

Note: The number in parentheses is the 2012 Season Total.

MOST OVERTIME GAMES, SEASON

5	Green Bay Packers, 1983
4	Denver Broncos, 1985, 2007
	Cleveland Browns, 1989
	Minnesota Vikings, 1994, 1995
	Arizona Cardinals, 1995, 1997
	San Francisco 49ers, 2001
	Atlanta Falcons, 2002
	San Diego Chargers, 2002
	Carolina Panthers, 2003
	Washington Redskins, 2010
	Arizona Cardinals, 2011

LONGEST CONSECUTIVE GAME STREAKS WITHOUT OVERTIME (Current)

60   Cincinnati Bengals (Last OT Game, 10/4/2009 vs. Cleveland Browns)
(Record: 110, St. Louis/Phoenix Cardinals, 12/7/86-12/19/93)

There have been 30 overtime postseason games dating back to 1958. In 24 cases, both teams had at least one possession. Last time: 1/12/13, Baltimore 38, DENVER 35.

SHORTEST OVERTIME GAMES

0:11	*DENVER 29, Pittsburgh 23; 1/8/12
0:14	New York Jets 37, BUFFALO 31; 9/8/02
0:16	CHICAGO 37, San Francisco 31; 10/28/01
0:16	Green Bay 19, DENVER 13; 10/29/07
0:17	NEW ORLEANS 20, Seattle 17; 11/16/97
0:21	Chicago 23, DETROIT 17; 11/27/80
0:30	Baltimore 29, NEW ENGLAND 23; 9/4/83
0:34	San Diego 23, WASHINGTON 17; 11/27/05
0:55	New York Giants 16, PHILADELPHIA 10; 9/29/85
0:55	PITTSBURGH 16, Kansas City 13; 11/12/12

Postseason game

LONGEST OVERTIME GAMES (ALL POSTSEASON GAMES)

22:40	Miami 27, KANSAS CITY 24; 12/25/71
17:54	Dallas Texans 20, HOUSTON 17; 12/23/62
17:02	CLEVELAND 23, New York Jets 20; 1/3/87
16:42	Baltimore 38, DENVER 35; 1/12/13
15:43	Oakland 37, BALTIMORE 31; 12/24/77
15:10	Carolina 29, ST. LOUIS 23; 1/10/04

OVERTIME SCORING SUMMARY

356	were decided by a field goal
59	were decided by a touchdown pass
32	were decided by a touchdown run
18	were decided by an interception
3	were decided by a fumble recovery (Baltimore 29, New England 23, 9/4/83; Denver 36, Seattle 30, 12/19/99; San Francisco 37, Arizona 31, 11/24/07)
2	were decided on a fake field goal/touchdown pass (Minnesota 22, Chicago 16, 10/16/77; Cleveland 23, Minnesota 17, 12/17/89)
2	were decided by a kickoff return (Chicago 23, Detroit 17, 11/27/80; New York Jets 37, Buffalo 31, 9/8/02)
2	were decided by a safety (Minnesota 23, Los Angeles Rams 21, 11/5/89; Chicago 19, Tennessee 17, 11/14/04)
2	were decided by a punt return (Kansas City 29, San Diego 23, 10/9/95; Arizona 19, St. Louis 13, 11/6/11)
1	was decided on a fake field goal/touchdown run (Los Angeles Rams 27, Minnesota 21, 12/2/79)
1	was decided on a blocked field goal (Denver 30, San Diego 24, 11/17/85)
1	was decided on a blocked field goal/recovery by kicker (Green Bay 12, Chicago 6, 9/7/80)
1	was decided on a blocked field goal/recovery by kicking team (Philadelphia 23, New York Giants 17, 11/20/88)
1	was decided by a blocked punt (Arizona 30, Dallas 24, 10/12/08)
18	ended tied

OVERTIME RECORDS (REGULAR SEASON)

Longest Touchdown Pass

99 Yards — Ron Jaworski to Mike Quick, Philadelphia 23, Atlanta 17 (11/10/85)
82 Yards — Tom Brady to Troy Brown, New England 19, Miami 13 (10/19/03); Brett Favre to Greg Jennings, Green Bay 19, Denver 13 (10/29/07)
76 Yards — Troy Aikman to Raghib Ismail, Dallas 41, Washington 35 (9/12/99)

Longest Touchdown Run

96 Yards — Garrison Hearst, San Francisco 36, New York Jets 30 (9/6/98)
60 Yards — Herschel Walker, Dallas 23, New England 17 (11/15/87)
50 Yards — Rashard Mendenhall, Pittsburgh 15, Atlanta 9 (9/12/10)

Longest Field Goal

57 Yards — Sebastian Janikowski, Oakland 16, New York Jets 13 (10/19/08)
54 Yards — Greg Zuerlein, St. Louis 16, San Francisco 13 (12/2/12)
53 Yards — Chris Jacke, Green Bay 23, San Francisco 20 (10/4/96)

Longest Touchdown Plays

99 Yards — (Pass) Ron Jaworski to Mike Quick, Philadelphia 23, Atlanta 17 (11/10/85)
99 Yards — (Punt return) Patrick Peterson, Arizona 19, St. Louis 13 (11/6/11)
96 Yards — (Run) Garrison Hearst, San Francisco 36, New York Jets 30 (9/6/98)
96 Yards — (Kickoff return) Chad Morton, New York Jets 37, Buffalo 31 (9/8/02)
95 Yards — (Kickoff return) Dave Williams, Chicago 23, Detroit 17 (11/27/80)

THANKSGIVING DAY FOOTBALL, 1920-2012
(Home Team in capitals, games listed in chronological order.)
(AFL)-American Football League, 1960-69.

Nov. 25, 1920
AKRON PROS 7, Canton Bulldogs 0
Decatur Staleys 6, CHICAGO TIGERS 0
ELYRIA (OH) ATHLETICS* 0, Columbus Panhandles 0
DAYTON TRIANGLES 28, Detroit Heralds 0
CHICAGO BOOSTERS* 27, Hammond Pros 0
All-Tonawanda (NY) 14, ROCHESTER JEFFERSONS 3
* Non league team. Games between league teams and non league teams counted in standings in 1920.

Nov. 24, 1921
Canton Bulldogs 14, AKRON PROS 0
Buffalo All-Americans 7, CHICAGO STALEYS 6

Nov. 30, 1922
Buffalo All-Americans 21, ROCHESTER JEFFERSONS 0
CHICAGO CARDINALS 6, Chicago Bears 0
RACINE LEGION 3, Milwaukee Badgers 0
Oorang Indians 18, COLUMBUS PANHANDLES 6
CANTON BULLDOGS 14, Akron Pros 0

Nov. 29, 1923
CANTON BULLDOGS 28, Toledo Maroons 0
CHICAGO BEARS 3, Chicago Cardinals 0
GREEN BAY PACKERS 19, Hammond Pros 0
Milwaukee Badgers 16, RACINE LEGION 0
AKRON PROS 2, Buffalo All-Americans 0

Nov. 27, 1924
AKRON PROS 22, Buffalo Bisons 0
Chicago Bears 21, CHICAGO CARDINALS 0
FRANKFORD YELLOWJACKETS 32, Dayton Triangles 7
CLEVELAND BULLDOGS 53, Milwaukee Badgers 10 (at Canton, Ohio)
Green Bay Packers 17, KANSAS CITY BLUES 6

Nov. 26, 1925
CHICAGO BEARS 0, Chicago Cardinals 0
Kansas City Cowboys 17, CLEVELAND BULLDOGS 0 (at Hartford, Connecticut)
Rock Island Independents 6, DETROIT PANTHERS 3
POTTSVILLE MAROONS 31, Green Bay Packers 0

Nov. 25, 1926
New York Giants 17, BROOKLYN LIONS 0
Los Angeles Buccaneers 9, DETROIT PANTHERS 6
CHICAGO BEARS 0, Chicago Cardinals 0
FRANKFORD YELLOWJACKETS 20, Green Bay Packers 14
POTTSVILLE MAROONS 8, Providence Steam Roller 0
CANTON BULLDOGS 0, Akron Pros 0

Nov. 24, 1927
Chicago Cardinals 3, CHICAGO BEARS 0
POTTSVILLE MAROONS 6, Providence Steam Roller 0
Green Bay Packers 17, FRANKFORD YELLOWJACKETS 9
Cleveland Bulldogs 30, NEW YORK YANKEES 19

Nov. 29, 1928
Providence Steam Roller 7, POTTSVILLE MAROONS 0
DETROIT WOLVERINES 33, Dayton Triangles 0
FRANKFORD YELLOWJACKETS 2, Green Bay Packers 0
CHICAGO BEARS 34, Chicago Cardinals 0

Nov. 28, 1929
New York Giants 21, STATEN ISLAND STAPLETONS 7
FRANKFORD YELLOWJACKETS 0, Green Bay Packers 0
Chicago Cardinals 40, CHICAGO BEARS 6

Nov. 27, 1930
STATEN ISLAND STAPLETONS 7, New York Giants 6
BROOKLYN DODGERS 33, Providence Steam Roller 12
Green Bay Packers 25, FRANKFORD YELLOWJACKETS 7
CHICAGO BEARS 6, Chicago Cardinals 0

Nov. 26, 1931
Green Bay Packers 38, PROVIDENCE STEAM ROLLER 7
STATEN ISLAND STAPLETONS 9, New York Giants 6
CHICAGO BEARS 18, Chicago Cardinals 7

Nov. 24, 1932
CHICAGO BEARS 34, Chicago Cardinals 0
Green Bay Packers 7, BROOKLYN DODGERS 0
STATEN ISLAND STAPLETONS 13, New York Giants 13

Nov. 30, 1933
Chicago Bears 22, CHICAGO CARDINALS 6
New York Giants 10, BROOKLYN DODGERS 0

Nov. 29, 1934
CHICAGO CARDINALS 6, Green Bay Packers 0
Chicago Bears 19, DETROIT LIONS 16
New York Giants 27, BROOKLYN DODGERS 0

Nov. 28, 1935	New York Giants 21, BROOKLYN DODGERS 0
	CHICAGO CARDINALS 9, Green Bay Packers 7
	DETROIT LIONS 14, Chicago Bears 2
Nov. 26, 1936	DETROIT LIONS 13, Chicago Bears 7
	New York Giants 14, BROOKLYN DODGERS 0
Nov. 25, 1937	Chicago Bears 13, DETROIT LIONS 0
	BROOKLYN DODGERS 13, New York Giants 13
Nov. 24, 1938	DETROIT LIONS 14, Chicago Bears 7
	BROOKLYN DODGERS 7, New York Giants 7
Nov. 23, 1939#	PHILADELPHIA EAGLES 17, Pittsburgh Steelers 14
Nov. 28, 1940#	PHILADELPHIA EAGLES 7, Pittsburgh Steelers 0

In 1939 and 1940, President Roosevelt moved Thanksgiving one week earlier. Various states celebrated on the date declared by the President, while other states recognized the traditional fourth Thursday of the month. In 1941, Thanksgiving was sanctioned by Congress to be celebrated on the fourth Thursday of November, which it has been ever since.

Nov. 22, 1945	Cleveland Rams 28, DETROIT LIONS 21
Nov. 28, 1946	Boston Yanks 34, DETROIT LIONS 10
Nov. 27, 1947	Chicago Bears 34, DETROIT LIONS 14
Nov. 25, 1948	Chicago Cardinals 28, DETROIT LIONS 14
Nov. 24, 1949	Chicago Bears 28, DETROIT LIONS 7
Nov. 23, 1950	DETROIT LIONS 49, New York Yanks 14
	Pittsburgh Steelers 28, CHICAGO CARDINALS 17
Nov. 22, 1951	DETROIT LIONS 52, Green Bay Packers 35
Nov. 27, 1952	DETROIT LIONS 48, Green Bay Packers 24
	DALLAS TEXANS 27, Chicago Bears 23 (at Akron, Ohio)
Nov. 26, 1953	DETROIT LIONS 34, Green Bay Packers 15
Nov. 25, 1954	DETROIT LIONS 28, Green Bay Packers 24
Nov. 24, 1955	DETROIT LIONS 24, Green Bay Packers 10
Nov. 22, 1956	Green Bay Packers 24, DETROIT LIONS 20
Nov. 28, 1957	DETROIT LIONS 18, Green Bay Packers 6
Nov. 27, 1958	DETROIT LIONS 24, Green Bay Packers 14
Nov. 26, 1959	Green Bay Packers 24, DETROIT LIONS 17
Nov. 24, 1960	DETROIT LIONS 23, Green Bay Packers 10
	(AFL) - NEW YORK TITANS 41, Dallas Texans 35
Nov. 23, 1961	Green Bay Packers 17, DETROIT LIONS 9
	(AFL) - NEW YORK TITANS 21, Buffalo Bills 14
Nov. 22, 1962	DETROIT LIONS 26, Green Bay Packers 14
	(AFL) - New York Titans 46, DENVER BRONCOS 45
Nov. 28, 1963	DETROIT LIONS 13, Green Bay Packers 13
	(AFL) - Oakland Raiders 26, DENVER BRONCOS 10
Nov. 26, 1964	Chicago Bears 27, DETROIT LIONS 24
	(AFL) - Buffalo Bills 27, SAN DIEGO CHARGERS 24
Nov. 25, 1965	DETROIT LIONS 24, Baltimore Colts 24
	(AFL) - SAN DIEGO CHARGERS 20, Buffalo Bills 20
Nov. 24, 1966	San Francisco 49ers 41, DETROIT LIONS 14
	DALLAS COWBOYS 26, Cleveland Browns 14
	(AFL) - Buffalo Bills 31, OAKLAND RAIDERS 10
Nov. 23, 1967	Los Angeles Rams 31, DETROIT LIONS 7
	DALLAS COWBOYS 46, St. Louis Cardinals 21
	(AFL) - Oakland Raiders 44, KANSAS CITY CHIEFS 22
	(AFL) - SAN DIEGO CHARGERS 24, Denver Broncos 20

Nov. 28, 1968	Philadelphia Eagles 12, DETROIT LIONS 0 DALLAS COWBOYS 29, Washington Redskins 20 (AFL) - OAKLAND RAIDERS 13, Buffalo Bills 10 (AFL) - KANSAS CITY CHIEFS 24, Houston Oilers 10
Nov. 27, 1969	Minnesota Vikings 27, DETROIT LIONS 0 DALLAS COWBOYS 24, San Francisco 49ers 24 (AFL) - KANSAS CITY CHIEFS 31, Denver Broncos 17 (AFL) - San Diego Chargers 21, HOUSTON OILERS 17
Nov. 26, 1970	DETROIT LIONS 28, Oakland Raiders 14 DALLAS COWBOYS 16, Green Bay Packers 3
Nov. 25, 1971	DETROIT LIONS 32, Kansas City Chiefs 21 DALLAS COWBOYS 28, Los Angeles Rams 21
Nov. 23, 1972	DETROIT LIONS 37, New York Jets 20 San Francisco 49ers 31, DALLAS COWBOYS 10
Nov. 22, 1973	Washington Redskins 20, DETROIT LIONS 0 Miami Dolphins 14, DALLAS COWBOYS 7
Nov. 28, 1974	Denver Broncos 31, DETROIT LIONS 27 DALLAS COWBOYS 24, Washington Redskins 23
Nov. 27, 1975	Los Angeles Rams 20, DETROIT LIONS 0 Buffalo Bills 32, ST. LOUIS CARDINALS 14
Nov. 25, 1976	DETROIT LIONS 27, Buffalo Bills 14 DALLAS COWBOYS 19, St. Louis Cardinals 14
Nov. 24, 1977	Chicago Bears 31, DETROIT LIONS 14 Miami Dolphins 55, ST. LOUIS CARDINALS 14
Nov. 23, 1978	DETROIT LIONS 17, Denver Broncos 14 DALLAS COWBOYS 37, Washington Redskins 10
Nov. 22, 1979	DETROIT LIONS 20, Chicago Bears 0 Houston Oilers 30, DALLAS COWBOYS 24
Nov. 27, 1980	Chicago Bears 23, DETROIT LIONS 17 (OT) DALLAS COWBOYS 51, Seattle Seahawks 7
Nov. 26, 1981	DETROIT LIONS 27, Kansas City Chiefs 10 DALLAS COWBOYS 10, Chicago Bears 9
Nov. 25, 1982	New York Giants 13, DETROIT LIONS 6 DALLAS COWBOYS 31, Cleveland Browns 14
Nov. 24, 1983	DETROIT LIONS 45, Pittsburgh Steelers 3 DALLAS COWBOYS 35, St. Louis Cardinals 17
Nov. 22, 1984	DETROIT LIONS 31, Green Bay Packers 28 DALLAS COWBOYS 20, New England Patriots 17
Nov. 28, 1985	DETROIT LIONS 31, New York Jets 20 DALLAS COWBOYS 35, St. Louis Cardinals 17
Nov. 27, 1986	Green Bay Packers 44, DETROIT LIONS 40 Seattle Seahawks 31, DALLAS COWBOYS 14
Nov. 26, 1987	Kansas City Chiefs 27, DETROIT LIONS 20 Minnesota Vikings 44, DALLAS COWBOYS 38 (OT)
Nov. 24, 1988	Minnesota Vikings 23, DETROIT LIONS 0 Houston Oilers 25, DALLAS COWBOYS 17
Nov. 23, 1989	DETROIT LIONS 13, Cleveland Browns 10 Philadelphia Eagles 27, DALLAS COWBOYS 0
Nov. 22, 1990	DETROIT LIONS 40, Denver Broncos 27 DALLAS COWBOYS 27, Washington Redskins 17
Nov. 28, 1991	DETROIT LIONS 16, Chicago Bears 6 DALLAS COWBOYS 20, Pittsburgh Steelers 10
Nov. 26, 1992	Houston Oilers 24, DETROIT LIONS 21 DALLAS COWBOYS 30, New York Giants 3
Nov. 25, 1993	Chicago Bears 10, DETROIT LIONS 6 Miami Dolphins 16, DALLAS COWBOYS 14

Nov. 24, 1994	DETROIT LIONS 35, Buffalo Bills 21
	DALLAS COWBOYS 42, Green Bay Packers 31
Nov. 23, 1995	DETROIT LIONS 44, Minnesota Vikings 38
	DALLAS COWBOYS 24, Kansas City Chiefs 12
Nov. 28, 1996	Kansas City Chiefs 28, DETROIT LIONS 24
	DALLAS COWBOYS 21, Washington Redskins 10
Nov. 27, 1997	DETROIT LIONS 55, Chicago Bears 20
	Tennessee Titans 27, DALLAS COWBOYS 14
Nov. 26, 1998	DETROIT LIONS 19, Pittsburgh Steelers 16 (OT)
	Minnesota Vikings 46, DALLAS COWBOYS 36
Nov. 25, 1999	DETROIT LIONS 21, Chicago Bears 17
	DALLAS COWBOYS 20, Miami Dolphins 0
Nov. 23, 2000	DETROIT LIONS 34, New England Patriots 9
	Minnesota Vikings 27, DALLAS COWBOYS 15
Nov. 22, 2001	Green Bay Packers 29, DETROIT LIONS 27
	Denver Broncos 26, DALLAS COWBOYS 24
Nov. 28, 2002	New England Patriots 20, DETROIT LIONS 12
	DALLAS COWBOYS 27, Washington Redskins 20
Nov. 27, 2003	DETROIT LIONS 22, Green Bay Packers 14
	Miami Dolphins 40, DALLAS COWBOYS 21
Nov. 25, 2004	Indianapolis Colts 41, DETROIT LIONS 9
	DALLAS COWBOYS 21, Chicago Bears 7
Nov. 24, 2005	Atlanta Falcons 27, DETROIT LIONS 7
	Denver Broncos 24, DALLAS COWBOYS 21 (OT)
Nov. 23, 2006	Miami Dolphins 27, DETROIT LIONS 10
	DALLAS COWBOYS 38, Tampa Bay Buccaneers 10
	KANSAS CITY CHIEFS 19, Denver Broncos 10
Nov. 22, 2007	Green Bay Packers 37, DETROIT LIONS 26
	DALLAS COWBOYS 34, New York Jets 3
	Indianapolis Colts 31, ATLANTA FALCONS 13
Nov. 27, 2008	Tennessee Titans 47, DETROIT LIONS 10
	DALLAS COWBOYS 34, Seattle Seahawks 9
	PHILADELPHIA EAGLES 48, Arizona Cardinals 20
Nov. 26, 2009	Green Bay Packers 34, DETROIT LIONS 12
	DALLAS COWBOYS 24, Oakland Raiders 7
	DENVER BRONCOS 26, New York Giants 6
Nov. 25, 2010	New England Patriots 45, DETROIT LIONS 24
	New Orleans Saints 30, DALLAS COWBOYS 27
	NEW YORK JETS 26, Cincinnati Bengals 10
Nov. 24, 2011	Green Bay Packers 27, DETROIT LIONS 15
	DALLAS COWBOYS 20, Miami Dolphins 19
	BALTIMORE RAVENS 16, San Francisco 49ers 6
Nov. 22, 2012	Houston Texans 34, DETROIT LIONS 31 (OT)
	Washington Redskins 38, DALLAS COWBOYS 31
	New England Patriots 49, NEW YORK JETS 19

THANKSGIVING DAY RECORDS
*NFL record; stats compiled by Elias Sports Bureau.

SCORING / Most Touchdowns, Game
- 6   Ernie Nevers, Chi. Cardinals vs. Chi. Bears, Nov. 28, 1929*
- 4   Doc Elliott, Cleveland vs. Milwaukee, Nov. 27, 1924
  - Sterling Sharpe, Green Bay at Dallas, Nov. 24, 1994
  - Brian Westbrook, Philadelphia vs. Arizona, Nov. 27, 2008
- 3   By many players

RUSHING / Most Yards Rushing, Game
- 273   O.J. Simpson, Buffalo at Detroit, Nov. 25, 1976
- 198   Bob Hoernschemeyer, Detroit vs. N.Y. Yankees, Nov. 23, 1950
- 195   Earl Campbell, Houston at Dallas, Nov. 22, 1979

PASSING / Most Yards Passing, Game
- 455   Troy Aikman, Dallas vs. Minnesota, Nov. 26, 1998
- 441   Matthew Stafford, Detroit vs. Houston, Nov. 22, 2012 (OT)
  - Tony Romo, Dallas vs. Washington, Nov. 22, 2012
- 410   Scott Mitchell, Detroit vs. Minnesota, Nov. 23, 1995

PASS RECEIVING
RECEPTIONS / Most Pass Receptions, Game
- 12   Brett Perriman, Detroit vs. Minnesota, Nov. 23, 1995
  - Marvin Harrison, Indianapolis at Detroit, Nov. 25, 2004
- 11   Daryl Johnston, Dallas vs. Miami, Nov. 25, 1993
  - Michael Irvin, Dallas vs. Kansas City, Nov. 23, 1995

YARDS GAINED / Most Yards on Pass Receptions, Game
- 303   Jim Benton, Cleveland at Detroit, Nov. 22, 1945
- 188   Andre Johnson, Houston at Detroit, Nov. 22, 2012 (OT)
- 185   Lance Alworth, San Diego vs. Buffalo, Nov. 26, 1964

ASSOCIATED PRESS NFL MOST OUTSTANDING/VALUABLE PLAYERS

THE FOLLOWING AWARDS WERE NAMED BY ASSOCIATED PRESS IN BALLOTING BY A NATIONWIDE PANEL OF MEDIA.

NFL MOST OUTSTANDING PLAYER AWARD

YEAR	PLAYER	POS.	TEAM	ACCOMPLISHMENTS
1957	Jim Brown	RB	Cleveland Browns	Rushed for league-leading 942 yards and added 9 touchdowns as a rookie.
1958	Jim Brown	RB	Cleveland Browns	Rushed for NFL-record 1,527 yards and added 17 touchdowns. Led Browns to 9-3 record.
1959	Charley Conerly	QB	New York Giants	Passed for 14 touchdowns and only 4 interceptions. Led offense to division-leading 284 points.
1960	Norm Van Brocklin	QB	Philadelphia Eagles	Guided Eagles to first division title since 1949. Passed for 2,471 yards and 24 touchdowns.

NFL MOST VALUABLE PLAYER AWARD

YEAR	PLAYER	POS.	TEAM	ACCOMPLISHMENTS
1961	Paul Hornung	RB	Green Bay Packers	Led league in scoring for second straight season with 146 points (10 TD, 15 FG, 41 PAT).
1962	Jim Taylor	RB	Green Bay Packers	League rushing champion with 1,474 yards. Scored all-time record 19 touchdowns.
1963	Y.A. Tittle	QB	New York Giants	Set all-time season record with 36 touchdown passes. Guided league's top offense (5,024 yards).
1964	Johnny Unitas	QB	Baltimore Colts	Guided Colts to NFL's best record (12-2) and league's top offensive attack (4,779 yards).
1965	Jim Brown	RB	Cleveland Browns	Leader of NFL's top rushing attack. Led league with 1,544 yards, added 21 total touchdowns.
1966	Bart Starr	QB	Green Bay Packers	Passed for 14 touchdowns and only 3 interceptions. Led Packers to league-best 12-2 record.
1967	Johnny Unitas	QB	Baltimore Colts	Passed for 3,428 yards and 20 touchdowns. Led Colts to 11-1-2 record.
1968	Earl Morrall	QB	Baltimore Colts	Guided Colts to NFL-best 13-1 record. Led league with 26 touchdown passes.
1969	Roman Gabriel	QB	Los Angeles Rams	Led NFL with 24 touchdown passes. Guided Rams to 11-3 record.
1970	John Brodie	QB	San Francisco 49ers	Took 49ers to first division title. Threw NFL-best 24 touchdown passes.
1971	Alan Page	DT	Minnesota Vikings	Led defense that allowed NFL-low 139 points. Vikings won fourth straight NFC Central title.
1972	Larry Brown	RB	Washington Redskins	Led conference with 1,216 rushing yards. Redskins had NFC-best 11-3 record.
1973	O.J. Simpson	RB	Buffalo Bills	Rushed for all-time record 2,003 yards, including three 200-yard performances.
1974	Ken Stabler	QB	Oakland Raiders	Led league with 26 touchdown passes and only 12 interceptions. Raiders had NFL-best 12-2 record.
1975	Fran Tarkenton	QB	Minnesota Vikings	Tied for league-best 12-2 record. Led NFC with 91.7 passer rating.
1976	Bert Jones	QB	Baltimore Colts	Threw 24 touchdowns and only 9 interceptions for 102.5 passer rating.
1977	Walter Payton	RB	Chicago Bears	Rushed for league-leading 1,852 yards and 16 total touchdowns.
1978	Terry Bradshaw	QB	Pittsburgh Steelers	Led Steelers to league-leading 14-2 mark. Set club record with 28 touchdown passes.
1979	Earl Campbell	RB	Houston Oilers	Led league with 1,697 rushing yards and 19 touchdowns.
1980	Brian Sipe	QB	Cleveland Browns	NFL-best 91.4 passer rating. Set Browns' records with 30 touchdown passes and 4,132 yards.
1981	Ken Anderson	QB	Cincinnati Bengals	Led Bengals to first division title since 1973. NFL-high 98.5 passer rating.
1982	Mark Moseley	K	Washington Redskins	Converted 20 of 21 FGs. Set consecutive field-goal record at 23 (including last three in '81).
1983	Joe Theismann	QB	Washington Redskins	Leader of offense that scored NFL record 541 points. Redskins had NFL-best 14-2 record.
1984	Dan Marino	QB	Miami Dolphins	Set NFL records with 5,084 yards and 48 touchdown passes. Led Dolphins to AFC-best 14-2 mark.
1985	Marcus Allen	RB	Los Angeles Raiders	Rushed for league-leading 1,759 yards. Tied for AFC lead with 11 rushing touchdowns.
1986	Lawrence Taylor	LB	New York Giants	Recorded league-high 20.5 sacks, and led Giants' second-ranked defense (297.3).
1987	John Elway	QB	Denver Broncos	In 12 games, passed for 19 touchdowns and 3,198 yards, including four 300-yard games.
1988	Boomer Esiason	QB	Cincinnati Bengals	Led NFL with 97.4 passer rating. Tied for AFC lead with 28 TD passes.
1989	Joe Montana	QB	San Francisco 49ers	Set NFL record with 112.4 passer rating, including 70.2 completion percentage.
1990	Joe Montana	QB	San Francisco 49ers	Led 49ers to league-best 14-2 record. Completed NFC-high 61.7 percent of passes.
1991	Thurman Thomas	RB	Buffalo Bills	Recorded league-high 2,038 yards from scrimmage (1,407 rushing, 631 receiving).
1992	Steve Young	QB	San Francisco 49ers	NFL's top passer with 107.0 rating. Led 49ers to NFL-best 14-2 record.

1993	Emmitt Smith	RB	Dallas Cowboys	Led league in rushing (1,486 yards) for third straight year despite missing first two games.
1994	Steve Young	QB	San Francisco 49ers	Compiled NFL all-time best 112.8 passer rating. Completed more than 70 percent of his passes.
1995	Brett Favre	QB	Green Bay Packers	Led league with 38 touchdown passes and NFC with 99.5 passer rating.
1996	Brett Favre	QB	Green Bay Packers	Led Packers to top conference record (13-3). Threw NFL-best 39 touchdown passes.
1997*	Brett Favre	QB	Green Bay Packers	Led league with 35 touchdown passes. Led NFC with 3,867 passing yards.
	Barry Sanders	RB	Detroit Lions	Rushed for all-time second-best 2,053 yards, including record 14 straight 100-yard games.
1998	Terrell Davis	RB	Denver Broncos	Rushed for 2,008 yards and scored league-best 23 total touchdowns.
1999	Kurt Warner	QB	St. Louis Rams	Became the second QB in history to have 40 touchdown passes in a season (41).
2000	Marshall Faulk	RB	St. Louis Rams	Set NFL record with 26 touchdowns and led NFC with 2,189 yards from scrimmage.
2001	Kurt Warner	QB	St. Louis Rams	Led NFL with 4,830 passing yards, 36 touchdowns, 68.7 completion percentage, and 101.4 passer rating.
2002	Rich Gannon	QB	Oakland Raiders	Set single-season records with 10 300-yard passing games and 418 completions, and led NFL with 4,689 passing yards.
2003*	Peyton Manning	QB	Indianapolis Colts	Led NFL with 4,267 passing yards, had AFC-best 29 touchdown passes, and posted 99.0 passer rating.
	Steve McNair	QB	Tennessee Titans	Posted NFL-best 100.4 passer rating, passing for 3,215 yards with 24 touchdowns against 7 interceptions.
2004	Peyton Manning	QB	Indianapolis Colts	Set NFL records with 49 touchdown passes and 121.1 passer rating while passing for 4,557 yards.
2005	Shaun Alexander	RB	Seattle Seahawks	Set NFL record with 28 touchdowns and led league with 1,880 rushing yards.
2006	LaDainian Tomlinson	RB	San Diego Chargers	Set NFL record for touchdowns (31) and points scored (186). Rushed for team-record 1,815 yards.
2007	Tom Brady	QB	New England Patriots	Set NFL record with 50 passing touchdowns. Led New England to first 16-0 regular-season record in league history.
2008	Peyton Manning	QB	Indianapolis Colts	Threw for 4,002 yards and 27 touchdowns and 95.0 passer rating. Led Indianapolis to 12-4 record.
2009	Peyton Manning	QB	Indianapolis Colts	Threw for 4,500 yards with 33 touchdowns for 99.9 passer rating while leading Colts to NFL-best 14-2 record.
2010	Tom Brady	QB	New England Patriots	Led league with 111.0 passer rating, throwing for 3,900 yards and 36 touchdowns while guiding Patriots to NFL-best 14-2 record.
2011	Aaron Rodgers	QB	Green Bay Packers	Set NFL record with 122.5 passer rating. Guided Green Bay to NFL-best 15-1 record.
2012	Adrian Peterson	RB	Minnesota Vikings	Rushed for league-leading 2,096 yards and scored 13 total touchdowns.

Total Associated Press NFL MVPs: 54
Four-time Winner: Peyton Manning
Three-time Winner: Brett Favre
Two-time Winners: Tom Brady, Joe Montana, Johnny Unitas, Kurt Warner, Steve Young
* The award was shared in 1997 and 2003.

ASSOCIATED PRESS MVPs WHO WON SUPER BOWL/NFL CHAMPIONSHIP IN SAME SEASON: 13

1961	Paul Hornung	Green Bay Packers
1962	Jim Taylor	Green Bay Packers
1966	Bart Starr	Green Bay Packers
1968	Earl Morrall	Baltimore Colts
1978	Terry Bradshaw	Pittsburgh Steelers
1982	Mark Moseley	Washington Redskins
1986	Lawrence Taylor	New York Giants
1989	Joe Montana	San Francisco 49ers
1993	Emmitt Smith	Dallas Cowboys
1994	Steve Young	San Francisco 49ers
1996	Brett Favre	Green Bay Packers
1998	Terrell Davis	Denver Broncos
1999	Kurt Warner	St. Louis Rams

ASSOCIATED PRESS NFL MVP BY POSITION

Quarterback:	35	Kicker:	1
Running Back:	16	Linebacker:	1
Defensive Tackle:	1		

ASSOCIATED PRESS MVPs BY TEAM

8	Indianapolis/Baltimore Colts	2	Buffalo Bills
			Cincinnati Bengals
7	Green Bay Packers		Cleveland Browns
			Denver Broncos
5	San Francisco 49ers		Houston Oilers/Tennessee Titans
			New England Patriots
4	St. Louis/Los Angeles Rams		New York Giants
3	Minnesota Vikings		
	Oakland/Los Angeles Raiders	1	Chicago Bears
	Washington Redskins		Dallas Cowboys
			Detroit Lions
			Miami Dolphins
			Pittsburgh Steelers
			San Diego Chargers
			Seattle Seahawks

AP OFFENSIVE PLAYER OF THE YEAR

1973	O.J. Simpson	RB	Buffalo Bills
1974	Ken Stabler	QB	Oakland Raiders
1975	Fran Tarkenton	QB	Minnesota Vikings
1976	Bert Jones	QB	Baltimore Colts
1977	Walter Payton	RB	Chicago Bears
1978	Earl Campbell	RB	Houston Oilers
1979	Earl Campbell	RB	Houston Oilers
1980	Earl Campbell	RB	Houston Oilers
1981	Ken Anderson	QB	Cincinnati Bengals
1982	Dan Fouts	QB	San Diego Chargers
1983	Joe Theismann	QB	Washington Redskins
1984	Dan Marino	QB	Miami Dolphins
1985	Marcus Allen	RB	Los Angeles Raiders
1986	Eric Dickerson	RB	Los Angeles Rams
1987	Jerry Rice	WR	San Francisco 49ers
1988	Roger Craig	RB	San Francisco 49ers
1989	Joe Montana	QB	San Francisco 49ers
1990	Warren Moon	QB	Houston Oilers
1991	Thurman Thomas	RB	Buffalo Bills
1992	Steve Young	QB	San Francisco 49ers
1993	Jerry Rice	WR	San Francisco 49ers
1994	Barry Sanders	RB	Detroit Lions
1995	Brett Favre	QB	Green Bay Packers
1996	Terrell Davis	RB	Denver Broncos
1997	Barry Sanders	RB	Detroit Lions
1998	Terrell Davis	RB	Denver Broncos
1999	Marshall Faulk	RB	St. Louis Rams
2000	Marshall Faulk	RB	St. Louis Rams
2001	Marshall Faulk	RB	St. Louis Rams
2002	Priest Holmes	RB	Kansas City Chiefs
2003	Jamal Lewis	RB	Baltimore Ravens
2004	Peyton Manning	QB	Indianapolis Colts
2005	Shaun Alexander	RB	Seattle Seahawks
2006	LaDainian Tomlinson	RB	San Diego Chargers
2007	Tom Brady	QB	New England Patriots
2008	Drew Brees	QB	New Orleans Saints
2009	Chris Johnson	RB	Tennessee Titans
2010	Tom Brady	QB	New England Patriots
2011	Drew Brees	QB	New Orleans Saints
2012	Adrian Peterson	RB	Minnesota Vikings

AP OFFENSIVE ROOKIE OF THE YEAR

1957	Jim Brown	RB	Cleveland Browns
1958	Jimmy Orr	WR	Pittsburgh Steelers
1959	Nick Pietrosante	RB	Detroit Lions
1960	Gail Cogdill	WR	Detroit Lions
1961	Mike Ditka	TE	Chicago Bears
1962	Ron Bull	RB	Chicago Bears
1963	Paul Flatley	WR	Minnesota Vikings
1964	Charley Taylor	WR	Washington Redskins
1965	Gale Sayers	RB	Chicago Bears
1966	Johnny Roland	RB	St. Louis Cardinals
1967	Mel Farr	RB	Detroit Lions
1968	Earl McCullouch	WR	Detroit Lions
1969	Calvin Hill	RB	Dallas Cowboys
1970	Duane Thomas	RB	Dallas Cowboys
1971	John Brockington	RB	Green Bay Packers
1972	Franco Harris	RB	Pittsburgh Steelers
1973	Chuck Foreman	RB	Minnesota Vikings
1974	Don Woods	RB	San Diego Chargers
1975	Mike Thomas	RB	Washington Redskins
1976	Sammy White	WR	Minnesota Vikings
1977	Tony Dorsett	RB	Dallas Cowboys
1978	Earl Campbell	RB	Houston Oilers
1979	Ottis Anderson	RB	St. Louis Cardinals
1980	Billy Sims	RB	Detroit Lions
1981	George Rogers	RB	New Orleans Saints

1982	Marcus Allen	RB	Los Angeles Raiders
1983	Eric Dickerson	RB	Los Angeles Rams
1984	Louis Lipps	WR	Pittsburgh Steelers
1985	Eddie Brown	WR	Cincinnati Bengals
1986	Rueben Mayes	RB	New Orleans Saints
1987	Troy Stradford	RB	Miami Dolphins
1988	John Stephens	RB	New England Patriots
1989	Barry Sanders	RB	Detroit Lions
1990	Emmitt Smith	RB	Dallas Cowboys
1991	Leonard Russell	RB	New England Patriots
1992	Carl Pickens	WR	Cincinnati Bengals
1993	Jerome Bettis	RB	Los Angeles Rams
1994	Marshall Faulk	RB	Indianapolis Colts
1995	Curtis Martin	RB	New England Patriots
1996	Eddie George	RB	Houston Oilers
1997	Warrick Dunn	RB	Tampa Bay Buccaneers
1998	Randy Moss	WR	Minnesota Vikings
1999	Edgerrin James	RB	Indianapolis Colts
2000	Mike Anderson	RB	Denver Broncos
2001	Anthony Thomas	RB	Chicago Bears
2002	Clinton Portis	RB	Denver Broncos
2003	Anquan Boldin	WR	Arizona Cardinals
2004	Ben Roethlisberger	QB	Pittsburgh Steelers
2005	Carnell Williams	RB	Tampa Bay Buccaneers
2006	Vince Young	QB	Tennessee Titans
2007	Adrian Peterson	RB	Minnesota Vikings
2008	Matt Ryan	QB	Atlanta Falcons
2009	Percy Harvin	WR	Minnesota Vikings
2010	Sam Bradford	QB	St. Louis Rams
2011	Cam Newton	QB	Carolina Panthers
2012	Robert Griffin III	QB	Washington Redskins

AP DEFENSIVE PLAYER OF THE YEAR

1971	Alan Page	DT	Minnesota Vikings
1972	Joe Greene	DT	Pittsburgh Steelers
1973	Dick Anderson	S	Miami Dolphins
1974	Joe Greene	DT	Pittsburgh Steelers
1975	Mel Blount	CB	Pittsburgh Steelers
1976	Jack Lambert	LB	Pittsburgh Steelers
1977	Harvey Martin	DE	Dallas Cowboys
1978	Randy Gradishar	LB	Denver Broncos
1979	Lee Roy Selmon	DE	Tampa Bay Buccaneers
1980	Lester Hayes	CB	Oakland Raiders
1981	Lawrence Taylor	LB	New York Giants
1982	Lawrence Taylor	LB	New York Giants
1983	Doug Betters	DE	Miami Dolphins
1984	Kenny Easley	S	Seattle Seahawks
1985	Mike Singletary	LB	Chicago Bears
1986	Lawrence Taylor	LB	New York Giants
1987	Reggie White	DT	Philadelphia Eagles
1988	Mike Singletary	LB	Chicago Bears
1989	Keith Millard	DT	Minnesota Vikings
1990	Bruce Smith	DE	Buffalo Bills
1991	Pat Swilling	LB	New Orleans Saints
1992	Cortez Kennedy	DT	Seattle Seahawks
1993	Rod Woodson	CB	Pittsburgh Steelers
1994	Deion Sanders	CB	San Francisco 49ers
1995	Bryce Paup	LB	Buffalo Bills
1996	Bruce Smith	DE	Buffalo Bills
1997	Dana Stubblefield	DT	San Francisco 49ers
1998	Reggie White	DE	Green Bay Packers
1999	Warren Sapp	DT	Tampa Bay Buccaneers
2000	Ray Lewis	LB	Baltimore Ravens
2001	Michael Strahan	DE	New York Giants
2002	Derrick Brooks	LB	Tampa Bay Buccaneers
2003	Ray Lewis	LB	Baltimore Ravens
2004	Ed Reed	S	Baltimore Ravens
2005	Brian Urlacher	LB	Chicago Bears
2006	Jason Taylor	DE	Miami Dolphins

2007	Bob Sanders	S	Indianapolis Colts
2008	James Harrison	LB	Pittsburgh Steelers
2009	Charles Woodson	CB	Green Bay Packers
2010	Troy Polamalu	S	Pittsburgh Steelers
2011	Terrell Suggs	LB	Baltimore Ravens
2012	J.J. Watt	DE	Houston Texans

AP DEFENSIVE ROOKIE OF THE YEAR

1967	Lem Barney	CB	Detroit Lions
1968	Claude Humphrey	DE	Atlanta Falcons
1969	Joe Greene	DT	Pittsburgh Steelers
1970	Bruce Taylor	CB	San Francisco 49ers
1971	Isiah Robertson	LB	Los Angeles Rams
1972	Willie Buchanon	CB	Green Bay Packers
1973	Wally Chambers	DT	Chicago Bears
1974	Jack Lambert	LB	Pittsburgh Steelers
1975	Robert Brazile	LB	Houston Oilers
1976	Mike Haynes	S	New England Patriots
1977	A.J. Duhe	DT	Miami Dolphins
1978	Al Baker	DE	Detroit Lions
1979	Jim Haslett	LB	Buffalo Bills
1980*	Buddy Curry	LB	Atlanta Falcons
	Al Richardson	LB	Atlanta Falcons
1981	Lawrence Taylor	LB	New York Giants
1982	Chip Banks	LB	Cleveland Browns
1983	Vernon Maxwell	LB	Baltimore Colts
1984	Bill Maas	NT	Kansas City Chiefs
1985	Duane Bickett	LB	Indianapolis Colts
1986	John Offerdahl	LB	Miami Dolphins
1987	Shane Conlan	LB	Buffalo Bills
1988	Erik McMillan	S	New York Jets
1989	Derrick Thomas	LB	Kansas City Chiefs
1990	Mark Carrier	S	Chicago Bears
1991	Mike Croel	LB	Denver Broncos
1992	Dale Carter	CB	Kansas City Chiefs
1993	Dana Stubblefield	DT	San Francisco 49ers
1994	Tim Bowens	DT	Miami Dolphins
1995	Hugh Douglas	DE	New York Jets
1996	Simeon Rice	DE	Arizona Cardinals
1997	Peter Boulware	LB	Baltimore Ravens
1998	Charles Woodson	CB	Oakland Raiders
1999	Jevon Kearse	DE	Tennessee Titans
2000	Brian Urlacher	LB	Chicago Bears
2001	Kendrell Bell	LB	Pittsburgh Steelers
2002	Julius Peppers	DE	Carolina Panthers
2003	Terrell Suggs	LB	Baltimore Ravens
2004	Jonathan Vilma	LB	New York Jets
2005	Shawne Merriman	LB	San Diego Chargers
2006	DeMeco Ryans	LB	Houston Texans
2007	Patrick Willis	LB	San Francisco 49ers
2008	Jerod Mayo	LB	New England Patriots
2009	Brian Cushing	LB	Houston Texans
2010	Ndamukong Suh	DT	Detroit Lions
2011	Von Miller	LB	Denver Broncos
2012	Luke Kuechly	LB	Carolina Panthers

*The award was shared in 1980.

AP COMEBACK PLAYER OF THE YEAR

1998	Doug Flutie	QB	Buffalo Bills
1999	Bryant Young	DT	San Francisco 49ers
2000	Joe Johnson	DE	New Orleans Saints
2001	Garrison Hearst	RB	San Francisco 49ers
2002	Tommy Maddox	QB	Pittsburgh Steelers
2003	Jon Kitna	QB	Cincinnati Bengals
2004	Drew Brees	QB	San Diego Chargers
2005*	Steve Smith	WR	Carolina Panthers
	Tedy Bruschi	LB	New England Patriots
2006	Chad Pennington	QB	New York Jets

2007	Greg Ellis	DE	Dallas Cowboys
2008	Chad Pennington	QB	Miami Dolphins
2009	Tom Brady	QB	New England Patriots
2010	Michael Vick	QB	Philadelphia Eagles
2011	Matthew Stafford	QB	Detroit Lions
2012	Peyton Manning	QB	Denver Broncos

*The award was shared in 2005.

AP COACH OF THE YEAR

1957	George Wilson	Detroit Lions
1958	Weeb Ewbank	Baltimore Colts
1959	Vince Lombardi	Green Bay Packers
1960	Buck Shaw	Philadelphia Eagles
1961	Allie Sherman	New York Giants
1962	Allie Sherman	New York Giants
1963	George Halas	Chicago Bears
1964	Don Shula	Baltimore Colts
1965	George Halas	Chicago Bears
1966	Tom Landry	Dallas Cowboys
1967*	George Allen	Los Angeles Rams
	Don Shula	Baltimore Colts
1968	Don Shula	Baltimore Colts
1969	Bud Grant	Minnesota Vikings
1970	Paul Brown	Cincinnati Bengals
1971	George Allen	Washington Redskins
1972	Don Shula	Miami Dolphins
1973	Chuck Knox	Los Angeles Rams
1974	Don Coryell	St. Louis Cardinals
1975	Ted Marchibroda	Baltimore Colts
1976	Forrest Gregg	Cleveland Browns
1977	Red Miller	Denver Broncos
1978	Jack Patera	Seattle Seahawks
1979	Jack Pardee	Washington Redskins
1980	Chuck Knox	Buffalo Bills
1981	Bill Walsh	San Francisco 49ers
1982	Joe Gibbs	Washington Redskins
1983	Joe Gibbs	Washington Redskins
1984	Chuck Knox	Seattle Seahawks
1985	Mike Ditka	Chicago Bears
1986	Bill Parcells	New York Giants
1987	Jim Mora	New Orleans Saints
1988	Mike Ditka	Chicago Bears
1989	Lindy Infante	Green Bay Packers
1990	Jimmy Johnson	Dallas Cowboys
1991	Wayne Fontes	Detroit Lions
1992	Bill Cowher	Pittsburgh Steelers
1993	Dan Reeves	New York Giants
1994	Bill Parcells	New England Patriots
1995	Ray Rhodes	Philadelphia Eagles
1996	Dom Capers	Carolina Panthers
1997	Jim Fassel	New York Giants
1998	Dan Reeves	Atlanta Falcons
1999	Dick Vermeil	St. Louis Rams
2000	Jim Haslett	New Orleans Saints
2001	Dick Jauron	Chicago Bears
2002	Andy Reid	Philadelphia Eagles
2003	Bill Belichick	New England Patriots
2004	Marty Schottenheimer	San Diego Chargers
2005	Lovie Smith	Chicago Bears
2006	Sean Payton	New Orleans Saints
2007	Bill Belichick	New England Patriots
2008	Mike Smith	Atlanta Falcons
2009	Marvin Lewis	Cincinnati Bengals
2010	Bill Belichick	New England Patriots
2011	Jim Harbaugh	San Francisco 49ers
2012	Bruce Arians	Indianapolis Colts

*The award was shared in 1967.

NUMBER-ONE DRAFT CHOICES

Season	Date	Team	Player	Position	College
2013	April 25-27	Kansas City	Eric Fisher	T	Central Michigan
2012	April 26-28	Indianapolis	Andrew Luck	QB	Stanford
2011	April 28-30	Carolina	Cam Newton	QB	Auburn
2010	April 22-24	St. Louis	Sam Bradford	QB	Oklahoma
2009	April 25-26	Detroit	Matthew Stafford	QB	Georgia
2008	April 26-27	Miami	Jake Long	T	Michigan
2007	April 28-29	Oakland	JaMarcus Russell	QB	Louisiana State
2006	April 29-30	Houston	Mario Williams	DE	North Carolina State
2005	April 23-24	San Francisco	Alex Smith	QB	Utah
2004	April 24-25	San Diego	Eli Manning	QB	Mississippi
2003	April 26-27	Cincinnati	Carson Palmer	QB	Southern California
2002	April 20-21	Houston	David Carr	QB	Fresno State
2001	April 21-22	Atlanta	Michael Vick	QB	Virginia Tech
2000	April 15-16	Cleveland	Courtney Brown	DE	Penn State
1999	April 17-18	Cleveland	Tim Couch	QB	Kentucky
1998	April 18-19	Indianapolis	Peyton Manning	QB	Tennessee
1997	April 19-20	St. Louis	Orlando Pace	T	Ohio State
1996	April 20-21	New York Jets	Keyshawn Johnson	WR	Southern California
1995	April 22-23	Cincinnati	Ki-Jana Carter	RB	Penn State
1994	April 24-25	Cincinnati	Dan Wilkinson	DT	Ohio State
1993	April 25-26	New England	Drew Bledsoe	QB	Washington State
1992	April 26-27	Indianapolis	Steve Emtman	DT	Washington
1991	April 21-22	Dallas	Russell Maryland	DT	Miami
1990	April 22-23	Indianapolis	Jeff George	QB	Illinois
1989	April 23-24	Dallas	Troy Aikman	QB	UCLA
1988	April 24-25	Atlanta	Aundray Bruce	LB	Auburn
1987	April 28-29	Tampa Bay	Vinny Testaverde	QB	Miami
1986	April 29-30	Tampa Bay	Bo Jackson	RB	Auburn
1985	April 30-May 1	Buffalo	Bruce Smith	DE	Virginia Tech
1984	May 1-2	New England	Irving Fryar	WR	Nebraska
1983	April 26-27	Baltimore	John Elway	QB	Stanford
1982	April 27-28	New England	Kenneth Sims	DT	Texas
1981	April 28-29	New Orleans	George Rogers	RB	South Carolina
1980	April 29-30	Detroit	Billy Sims	RB	Oklahoma
1979	May 3-4	Buffalo	Tom Cousineau	LB	Ohio State
1978	May 2-3	Houston	Earl Campbell	RB	Texas
1977	May 3-4	Tampa Bay	Ricky Bell	RB	Southern California
1976	April 8-9	Tampa Bay	Lee Roy Selmon	DE	Oklahoma
1975	January 28-29	Atlanta	Steve Bartkowski	QB	California
1974	January 29-30	Dallas	Ed Jones	DE	Tennessee State
1973	January 30-31	Houston	John Matuszak	DE	Tampa
1972	February 1-2	Buffalo	Walt Patulski	DE	Notre Dame
1971	January 28-29	New England	Jim Plunkett	QB	Stanford
1970	January 27-28	Pittsburgh	Terry Bradshaw	QB	Louisiana Tech
1969	January 28-29	Buffalo (AFL)	O.J. Simpson	RB	Southern California
1968	January 30-31	Minnesota	Ron Yary	T	Southern California
1967	March 14	Baltimore	Bubba Smith	DT	Michigan State
1966	November 27, 1965	Atlanta	Tommy Nobis	LB	Texas
	November 28, 1965	Miami (AFL)	Jim Grabowski	RB	Illinois
1965	November 28, 1964	New York Giants	Tucker Frederickson	RB	Auburn
	November 28, 1964	Houston (AFL)	Lawrence Elkins	E	Baylor
1964	December 2, 1963	San Francisco	Dave Parks	E	Texas Tech
	November 30, 1963	Boston (AFL)	Jack Concannon	QB	Boston College
1963	December 3, 1962	Los Angeles	Terry Baker	QB	Oregon State
	December 1, 1962	Kansas City (AFL)	Buck Buchanan	DT	Grambling
1962	December 4, 1961	Washington	Ernie Davis	RB	Syracuse
	December 2, 1961	Oakland (AFL)	Roman Gabriel	QB	North Carolina State
1961	December 27-28, 1960	Minnesota	Tommy Mason	RB	Tulane
	November 23, 1960	Buffalo (AFL)	Ken Rice	G	Auburn
1960	Secret Draft	Los Angeles	Billy Cannon	RB	Louisiana State
	November 22, December 2, 1959	(AFL had no formal first pick)			

NUMBER-ONE DRAFT CHOICES

Season	Date	Team	Player	Position	College
1959	December 2, 1958	Green Bay	Randy Duncan	QB	Iowa
1958	December 2, 1957	Chicago Cardinals	King Hill	QB	Rice
1957	November 27, 1956	Green Bay	Paul Hornung	HB	Notre Dame
1956	November 29, 1955	Pittsburgh	Gary Glick	DB	Colorado A&M
1955	January 27-28	Baltimore	George Shaw	QB	Oregon
1954	January 28	Cleveland	Bobby Garrett	QB	Stanford
1953	January 22	San Francisco	Harry Babcock	E	Georgia
1952	January 17	Los Angeles	Bill Wade	QB	Vanderbilt
1951	January 18-19	New York Giants	Kyle Rote	HB	Southern Methodist
1950	January 21-22	Detroit	Leon Hart	E	Notre Dame
1949	December 21, 1948	Philadelphia	Chuck Bednarik	C	Pennsylvania
1948	December 19, 1947	Washington	Harry Gilmer	QB	Alabama
1947	December 16, 1946	Chicago Bears	Bob Fenimore	HB	Oklahoma A&M
1946	January 14	Boston	Frank Dancewicz	QB	Notre Dame
1945	April 6	Chicago Cardinals	Charley Trippi	HB	Georgia
1944	April 19	Boston	Angelo Bertelli	QB	Notre Dame
1943	April 8	Detroit	Frank Sinkwich	HB	Georgia
1942	December 22, 1941	Pittsburgh	Bill Dudley	HB	Virginia
1941	December 10, 1940	Chicago Bears	Tom Harmon	HB	Michigan
1940	December 9, 1939	Chicago Cardinals	George Cafego	HB	Tennessee
1939	December 8, 1938	Chicago Cardinals	Ki Aldrich	C	Texas Christian
1938	December 12, 1937	Cleveland	Corbett Davis	FB	Indiana
1937	December 12, 1936	Philadelphia	Sam Francis	FB	Nebraska
1936	February 8	Philadelphia	Jay Berwanger	HB	Chicago

Note: From 1947 through 1958, the first selection in the draft was a Bonus pick, awarded to the winner of a random draw. That club, in turn, forfeited its last-round draft choice. The winner of the Bonus choice was eliminated from future draws. The system was abolished after 1958, by which time all clubs had received a Bonus choice.

NUMBER-ONE DRAFT CHOICES BY POSITION
Quarterbacks: 31
Running Backs: 23
Defensive Linemen: 13
Offensive Linemen: 7
Wide Receivers: 6
Linebackers: 3
Defensive Backs: 1

NFL DRAFT, NUMBER OF ROUNDS
1936: 9
1937: 10
1938-1942: 22
1943-1948: 32
1949: 25
1950-59: 30
1960-66: 20
1967-1976: 17
1977-1992: 12
1993: 8
1994-2013: 7

FIRST-ROUND SELECTIONS

If club had no first-round selection, first player drafted is listed with round in parentheses.

ARIZONA CARDINALS
Year Player, College, Position
1936 Jim Lawrence, Texas Christian, B
1937 Ray Buivid, Marquette, B
1938 Jack Robbins, Arkansas, B
1939 Charles (Ki) Aldrich, TCU, C
1940 George Cafego, Tennessee, B
1941 John Kimbrough, Texas A&M, B
1942 Steve Lach, Duke, B
1943 Glenn Dobbs, Tulsa, B
1944 Pat Harder, Wisconsin, B
1945 Charley Trippi, Georgia, B
1946 Dub Jones, Louisiana State, B
1947 DeWitt (Tex) Coulter, Army, T
1948 Jim Spavital, Oklahoma A&M, B
1949 Bill Fischer, Notre Dame, G
1950 Jack Jennings, Ohio State, T (2)
1951 Jerry Groom, Notre Dame, C
1952 Ollie Matson, San Francisco, B
1953 Johnny Olszewski, California, B
1954 Lamar McHan, Arkansas, B
1955 Max Boydston, Oklahoma, E
1956 Joe Childress, Auburn, B
1957 Jerry Tubbs, Oklahoma, C
1958 King Hill, Rice, B
      John David Crow, Texas A&M, B
1959 Bill Stacy, Mississippi State, B
1960 George Izo, Notre Dame, QB
1961 Ken Rice, Auburn, T
1962 Fate Echols, Northwestern, DT
      Irv Goode, Kentucky, C
1963 Jerry Stovall, Louisiana State, S
      Don Brumm, Purdue, DE
1964 Ken Kortas, Louisville, DT
1965 Joe Namath, Alabama, QB
1966 Carl McAdams, Oklahoma, LB
1967 Dave Williams, Washington, WR
1968 MacArthur Lane, Utah State, RB
1969 Roger Wehrli, Missouri, DB
1970 Larry Stegent, Texas A&M, RB
1971 Norm Thompson, Utah, CB
1972 Ahmad Rashad, Oregon, RB-WR
1973 Dave Butz, Purdue, DT
1974 J.V. Cain, Colorado, TE
1975 Tim Gray, Texas A&M, DB
1976 Mike Dawson, Arizona, DT
1977 Steve Pisarkiewicz, Missouri, QB
1978 Steve Little, Arkansas, K
      Ken Greene, Washington State, DB
1979 Ottis Anderson, Miami, RB
1980 Curtis Greer, Michigan, DE
1981 E.J. Junior, Alabama, LB
1982 Luis Sharpe, UCLA, T
1983 Leonard Smith, McNeese St., DB
1984 Clyde Duncan, Tennessee, WR
1985 Freddie Joe Nunn, Mississippi, LB
1986 Anthony Bell, Michigan State, LB
1987 Kelly Stouffer, Colorado State, QB
1988 Ken Harvey, California, LB
1989 Eric Hill, Louisiana State, LB
      Joe Wolf, Boston College, G
1990 Anthony Thompson, Indiana, RB (2)
1991 Eric Swann, No College, DE
1992 Tony Sacca, Penn State, QB (2)
1993 Garrison Hearst, Georgia, RB

Ernest Dye, South Carolina, T
1994 Jamir Miller, UCLA, LB
1995 Frank Sanders, Auburn, WR (2)
1996 Simeon Rice, Illinois, DE
1997 Tom Knight, Iowa, DB
1998 Andre Wadsworth, Florida St., DE
1999 David Boston, Ohio State, WR
      L.J. Shelton, Eastern Michigan, T
2000 Thomas Jones, Virginia, RB
2001 Leonard Davis, Texas, T
2002 Wendell Bryant, Wisconsin, DT
2003 Bryant Johnson, Penn State, WR
      Calvin Pace, Wake Forest, DE
2004 Larry Fitzgerald, Pittsburgh, WR
2005 Antrel Rolle, Miami, DB
2006 Matt Leinart, So. California, QB
2007 Levi Brown, Penn State, T
2008 Dominique Rodgers-Cromartie, Tenn. St., DB
2009 Beanie Wells, Ohio State, RB
2010 Dan Williams, Tennessee, DT
2011 Patrick Peterson, Louisiana St., DB
2012 Michael Floyd, Notre Dame, WR
2013 Jonathan Cooper, North Carolina, G

ATLANTA FALCONS
Year Player, College, Position
1966 Tommy Nobis, Texas, LB
      Randy Johnson, Texas A&I, QB
1967 Leo Carroll, San Diego St., DE (2)
1968 Claude Humphrey, Tennessee St., DE
1969 George Kunz, Notre Dame, T
1970 John Small, Citadel, LB
1971 Joe Profit, Northeast Louisiana, RB
1972 Clarence Ellis, Notre Dame, DB
1973 Greg Marx, Notre Dame, DT (2)
1974 Gerald Tinker, Kent State, WR (2)
1975 Steve Bartkowski, California, QB
1976 Bubba Bean, Texas A&M, RB
1977 Warren Bryant, Kentucky, T
      Wilson Faumuina, San Jose St., DT
1978 Mike Kenn, Michigan, T
1979 Don Smith, Miami, DE
1980 Junior Miller, Nebraska, TE
1981 Bobby Butler, Florida State, DB
1982 Gerald Riggs, Arizona State, RB
1983 Mike Pitts, Alabama, DE
1984 Rick Bryan, Oklahoma, DT
1985 Bill Fralic, Pittsburgh, T
1986 Tony Casillas, Oklahoma, NT
      Tim Green, Syracuse, LB
1987 Chris Miller, Oregon, QB
1988 Aundray Bruce, Auburn, LB
1989 Deion Sanders, Florida State, DB
      Shawn Collins, No. Arizona, WR
1990 Steve Broussard, Washington St., RB
1991 Bruce Pickens, Nebraska, DB
      Mike Pritchard, Colorado, WR
1992 Bob Whitfield, Stanford, T
      Tony Smith, So. Mississippi, RB
1993 Lincoln Kennedy, Washington, T
1994 Bert Emanuel, Rice, WR (2)
1995 Devin Bush, Florida State, DB
1996 Shannon Brown, Alabama, DT (3)
1997 Michael Booker, Nebraska, DB
1998 Keith Brooking, Georgia Tech, LB
1999 Patrick Kerney, Virginia, DE
2000 Travis Claridge, So. California, T (2)
2001 Michael Vick, Virginia Tech, QB
2002 T.J. Duckett, Michigan State, RB
2003 Bryan Scott, Penn State, DB (2)

2004 DeAngelo Hall, Virginia Tech, DB
      Michael Jenkins, Ohio State, WR
2005 Roddy White, Ala.-Birmingham, WR
2006 Jimmy Williams, Virginia Tech, DB (2)
2007 Jamaal Anderson, Arkansas, DE
2008 Matt Ryan, Boston College, QB
      Sam Baker, So. California, T
2009 Peria Jerry, Mississippi, DT
2010 Sean Weatherspoon, Missouri, LB
2011 Julio Jones, Alabama, WR
2012 Peter Konz, Wisconsin, G (2)
2013 Desmond Trufant, Washington, DB

BALTIMORE RAVENS
Year Player, College, Position
1996 Jonathan Ogden, UCLA, T
      Ray Lewis, Miami, LB
1997 Peter Boulware, Florida State, DE
1998 Duane Starks, Miami, DB
1999 Chris McAlister, Arizona, DB
2000 Jamal Lewis, Tennessee, RB
      Travis Taylor, Florida, WR
2001 Todd Heap, Arizona State, TE
2002 Ed Reed, Miami, DB
2003 Terrell Suggs, Arizona State, DE
      Kyle Boller, California, QB
2004 Dwan Edwards, Oregon St., DT (2)
2005 Mark Clayton, Oklahoma, WR
2006 Haloti Ngata, Oregon, DT
2007 Ben Grubbs, Auburn, G
2008 Joe Flacco, Delaware, QB
2009 Michael Oher, Mississippi, T
2010 Sergio Kindle, Texas, LB (2)
2011 Jimmy Smith, Colorado, DB
2012 Courtney Upshaw, Alabama, LB (2)
2013 Matt Elam, Florida, DB

BUFFALO BILLS
Year Player, College, Position
1960 Richie Lucas, Penn State, QB
1961 Ken Rice, Auburn, T
1962 Ernie Davis, Syracuse, RB
1963 Dave Behrman, Michigan State, C
1964 Carl Eller, Minnesota, DE
1965 Jim Davidson, Ohio State, T
1966 Mike Dennis, Mississippi, RB
1967 John Pitts, Arizona State, S
1968 Haven Moses, San Diego St., WR
1969 O.J. Simpson, So. California, RB
1970 Al Cowlings, So. California, DE
1971 J.D. Hill, Arizona State, WR
1972 Walt Patulski, Notre Dame, DE
1973 Paul Seymour, Michigan, TE
      Joe DeLamielleure, Michigan St., G
1974 Reuben Gant, Oklahoma State, TE
1975 Tom Ruud, Nebraska, LB
1976 Mario Clark, Oregon, DB
1977 Phil Dokes, Oklahoma State, DT
1978 Terry Miller, Oklahoma State, RB
1979 Tom Cousineau, Ohio State, LB
      Jerry Butler, Clemson, WR
1980 Jim Ritcher, North Carolina St., C
1981 Booker Moore, Penn State, RB
1982 Perry Tuttle, Clemson, WR
1983 Tony Hunter, Notre Dame, TE
      Jim Kelly, Miami, QB
1984 Greg Bell, Notre Dame, RB
1985 Bruce Smith, Virginia Tech, DE
      Derrick Burroughs, Memphis St., DB
1986 Ronnie Harmon, Iowa, RB

	Will Wolford, Vanderbilt, T
1987	Shane Conlan, Penn State, LB
1988	Thurman Thomas, Oklahoma St., RB (2)
1989	Don Beebe, Chadron, Neb., WR (3)
1990	James Williams, Fresno State, DB
1991	Henry Jones, Illinois, DB
1992	John Fina, Arizona, T
1993	Thomas Smith, North Carolina, DB
1994	Jeff Burris, Notre Dame, DB
1995	Ruben Brown, Pittsburgh, G
1996	Eric Moulds, Mississippi St., WR
1997	Antowain Smith, Houston, RB
1998	Sam Cowart, Florida State, LB (2)
1999	Antoine Winfield, Ohio State, DB
2000	Erik Flowers, Arizona State, DE
2001	Nate Clements, Ohio State, DB
2002	Mike Williams, Texas, T
2003	Willis McGahee, Miami, RB
2004	Lee Evans, Wisconsin, WR
	J.P. Losman, Tulane, QB
2005	Roscoe Parrish, Miami, WR (2)
2006	Donte' Whitner, Ohio State, DB
	John McCargo, North Carolina St., DT
2007	Marshawn Lynch, California, RB
2008	Leodis McKelvin, Troy, DB
2009	Aaron Maybin, Penn State, DE
	Eric Wood, Louisville, C
2010	C.J. Spiller, Clemson, RB
2011	Marcell Dareus, Alabama, DT
2012	Stephon Gilmore, South Carolina, DB
2013	E.J. Manuel, Florida State, QB

CAROLINA PANTHERS
Year   Player, College, Position

1995	Kerry Collins, Penn State, QB
	Tyrone Poole, Ft. Valley State, DB
	Blake Brockermeyer, Texas, T
1996	Tim Biakabutuka, Michigan, RB
1997	Rae Carruth, Colorado, WR
1998	Jason Peter, Nebraska, DT
1999	Chris Terry, Georgia, T (2)
2000	Rashard Anderson, Jackson St., DB
2001	Dan Morgan, Miami, LB
2002	Julius Peppers, North Carolina, DE
2003	Jordan Gross, Utah, T
2004	Chris Gamble, Ohio State, DB
2005	Thomas Davis, Georgia, DB
2006	DeAngelo Williams, Memphis, RB
2007	Jon Beason, Miami, LB
2008	Jonathan Stewart, Oregon, RB
	Jeff Otah, Pittsburgh, T
2009	Everette Brown, Florida St., DE (2)
2010	Jimmy Clausen, Notre Dame, QB (2)
2011	Cam Newton, Auburn, QB
2012	Luke Kuechly, Boston College, LB
2013	Star Lotulelei, Utah, DT

CHICAGO BEARS
Year   Player, College, Position

1936	Joe Stydahar, West Virginia, T
1937	Les McDonald, Nebraska, E
1938	Joe Gray, Oregon State, B
1939	Sid Luckman, Columbia, QB
	Bill Osmanski, Holy Cross, B
1940	Clyde (Bulldog) Turner, Hardin-Simmons, C
1941	Tom Harmon, Michigan, B
	Norm Standlee, Stanford, B
	Don Scott, Ohio State, B
1942	Frankie Albert, Stanford, B
1943	Bob Steber, Missouri, B

1944	Ray Evans, Kansas, B
1945	Don Lund, Michigan, B
1946	Johnny Lujack, Notre Dame, QB
1947	Bob Fenimore, Oklahoma State, B
	Don Kindt, Wisconsin, B
1948	Bobby Layne, Texas, QB
	Max Bumgardner, Texas, E
1949	Dick Harris, Texas, C
1950	Chuck Hunsinger, Florida, B
	Fred Morrison, Ohio State, B
1951	Bob Williams, Notre Dame, B
	Billy Stone, Bradley, B
	Gene Schroeder, Virginia, E
1952	Jim Dooley, Miami, B
1953	Billy Anderson, Compton (Calif.) J.C., B
1954	Stan Wallace, Illinois, B
1955	Ron Drzewiecki, Marquette, B
1956	Menan (Tex) Schriewer, Texas, E
1957	Earl Leggett, Louisiana State, T
1958	Chuck Howley, West Virginia, G
1959	Don Clark, Ohio State, B
1960	Roger Davis, Syracuse, G
1961	Mike Ditka, Pittsburgh, E
1962	Ronnie Bull, Baylor, RB
1963	Dave Behrman, Michigan State, C
1964	Dick Evey, Tennessee, DT
1965	Dick Butkus, Illinois, LB
	Gale Sayers, Kansas, RB
	Steve DeLong, Tennessee, T
1966	George Rice, Louisiana State, DT
1967	Loyd Phillips, Arkansas, DE
1968	Mike Hull, Southern California, RB
1969	Rufus Mayes, Ohio State, T
1970	George Farmer, UCLA, WR (3)
1971	Joe Moore, Missouri, RB
1972	Lionel Antoine, Southern Illinois, T
	Craig Clemons, Iowa, DB
1973	Wally Chambers, Eastern Kentucky, DE
1974	Waymond Bryant, Tennessee St., LB
	Dave Gallagher, Michigan, DT
1975	Walter Payton, Jackson State, RB
1976	Dennis Lick, Wisconsin, T
1977	Ted Albrecht, California, T
1978	Brad Shearer, Texas, DT (3)
1979	Dan Hampton, Arkansas, DT
	Al Harris, Arizona State, DE
1980	Otis Wilson, Louisville, LB
1981	Keith Van Horne, So. California, T
1982	Jim McMahon, Brigham Young, QB
1983	Jim Covert, Pittsburgh, T
	Willie Gault, Tennessee, WR
1984	Wilber Marshall, Florida, LB
1985	William Perry, Clemson, DT
1986	Neal Anderson, Florida, RB
1987	Jim Harbaugh, Michigan, QB
1988	Brad Muster, Stanford, RB
	Wendell Davis, Louisiana St., WR
1989	Donnell Woolford, Clemson, DB
	Trace Armstrong, Florida, DE
1990	Mark Carrier, So. California, DB
1991	Stan Thomas, Texas, T
1992	Alonzo Spellman, Ohio State, DE
1993	Curtis Conway, So. California, WR
1994	John Thierry, Alcorn State, DE
1995	Rashaan Salaam, Colorado, RB
1996	Walt Harris, Mississippi State, DB
1997	John Allred, So. California, TE (2)
1998	Curtis Enis, Penn State, RB
1999	Cade McNown, UCLA, QB
2000	Brian Urlacher, New Mexico, LB

2001	David Terrell, Michigan, WR
2002	Marc Colombo, Boston College, T
2003	Michael Haynes, Penn State, DE
	Rex Grossman, Florida, QB
2004	Tommie Harris, Oklahoma, DT
2005	Cedric Benson, Texas, RB
2006	Danieal Manning, Abilene Christian, DB (2)
2007	Greg Olsen, Miami, TE
2008	Chris Williams, Vanderbilt, T
2009	Jarron Gilbert, San Jose State, DT (3)
2010	Major Wright, Florida, DB (3)
2011	Gabe Carimi, Wisconsin, T
2012	Shea McClellin, Boise State, DE
2013	Kyle Long, Oregon, G

CINCINNATI BENGALS
Year   Player, College, Position

1968	Bob Johnson, Tennessee, C
1969	Greg Cook, Cincinnati, QB
1970	Mike Reid, Penn State, DT
1971	Vernon Holland, Tennessee St., T
1972	Sherman White, California, DE
1973	Isaac Curtis, San Diego State, WR
1974	Bill Kollar, Montana State, DT
1975	Glenn Cameron, Florida, LB
1976	Billy Brooks, Oklahoma, WR
	Archie Griffin, Ohio State, RB
1977	Eddie Edwards, Miami, DT
	Wilson Whitley, Houston, DT
	Mike Cobb, Michigan State, TE
1978	Ross Browner, Notre Dame, DT
	Blair Bush, Washington, C
1979	Jack Thompson, Washington St., QB
	Charles Alexander, Louisiana St., RB
1980	Anthony Muñoz, So. California, T
1981	David Verser, Kansas, WR
1982	Glen Collins, Mississippi State, DE
1983	Dave Rimington, Nebraska, C
1984	Ricky Hunley, Arizona, LB
	Pete Koch, Maryland, DE
	Brian Blados, North Carolina, T
1985	Eddie Brown, Miami, WR
	Emanuel King, Alabama, LB
1986	Joe Kelly, Washington, LB
	Tim McGee, Tennessee, WR
1987	Jason Buck, Brigham Young, DE
1988	Rickey Dixon, Oklahoma, DB
1989	Eric Ball, UCLA, RB (2)
1990	James Francis, Baylor, LB
1991	Alfred Williams, Colorado, LB
1992	David Klingler, Houston, QB
	Darryl Williams, Miami, DB
1993	John Copeland, Alabama, DE
1994	Dan Wilkinson, Ohio State, DT
1995	Ki-Jana Carter, Penn State, RB
1996	Willie Anderson, Auburn, T
1997	Reinard Wilson, Florida State, LB
1998	Takeo Spikes, Auburn, LB
	Brian Simmons, North Carolina, LB
1999	Akili Smith, Oregon, QB
2000	Peter Warrick, Florida State, WR
2001	Justin Smith, Missouri, DE
2002	Levi Jones, Arizona State, T
2003	Carson Palmer, Southern California, QB
2004	Chris Perry, Michigan, RB
2005	David Pollack, Georgia, LB
2006	Johnathan Joseph, South Carolina, DB
2007	Leon Hall, Michigan, DB
2008	Keith Rivers, So. California, LB
2009	Andre Smith, Alabama, T

2010 Jermaine Gresham, Oklahoma, TE
2011 A.J. Green, Georgia, WR
2012 Dre Kirkpatrick, Alabama, DB
     Kevin Zeitler, Wisconsin, G
2013 Tyler Eifert, Notre Dame, TE

CLEVELAND BROWNS
Year Player, College, Position
1950 Ken Carpenter, Oregon State, B
1951 Ken Konz, Louisiana State, B
1952 Bert Rechichar, Tennessee, DB
     Harry Agganis, Boston U., QB
1953 Doug Atkins, Tennessee, DE
1954 Bobby Garrett, Stanford, QB
     John Bauer, Illinois, G
1955 Kurt Burris, Oklahoma, C
1956 Preston Carpenter, Arkansas, B
1957 Jim Brown, Syracuse, RB
1958 Jim Shofner, Texas Christian, DB
1959 Rich Kreitling, Illinois, DE
1960 Jim Houston, Ohio State, DE
1961 Bobby Crespino, Mississippi, TE
1962 Gary Collins, Maryland, WR
     Leroy Jackson, Western Illinois, RB
1963 Tom Hutchinson, Kentucky, WR
1964 Paul Warfield, Ohio State, WR
1965 James Garcia, Purdue, T (2)
1966 Milt Morin, Massachusetts, TE
1967 Bob Matheson, Duke, LB
1968 Marvin Upshaw, Trinity, Tex., DT-DE
1969 Ron Johnson, Michigan, RB
1970 Mike Phipps, Purdue, QB
     Bob McKay, Texas, T
1971 Clarence Scott, Kansas State, CB
1972 Thom Darden, Michigan, DB
1973 Steve Holden, Arizona State, WR
     Pete Adams, Southern California, T
1974 Billy Corbett, Johnson C. Smith, T (2)
1975 Mack Mitchell, Houston, DE
1976 Mike Pruitt, Purdue, RB
1977 Robert Jackson, Texas A&M, LB
1978 Clay Matthews, So. California, LB
     Ozzie Newsome, Alabama, TE
1979 Willis Adams, Houston, WR
1980 Charles White, So. California, RB
1981 Hanford Dixon, So. Mississippi, DB
1982 Chip Banks, So. California, LB
1983 Ron Brown, Arizona State, WR (2)
1984 Don Rogers, UCLA, DB
1985 Greg Allen, Florida State, RB (2)
1986 Webster Slaughter, San Diego St., WR (2)
1987 Mike Junkin, Duke, LB
1988 Clifford Charlton, Florida, LB
1989 Eric Metcalf, Texas, RB
1990 Leroy Hoard, Michigan, RB (2)
1991 Eric Turner, UCLA, DB
1992 Tommy Vardell, Stanford, RB
1993 Steve Everitt, Michigan, C
1994 Antonio Langham, Alabama, DB
     Derrick Alexander, Michigan, WR
1995 Craig Powell, Ohio State, LB
1999 Tim Couch, Kentucky, QB
2000 Courtney Brown, Penn State, DE
2001 Gerard Warren, Florida, DT
2002 William Green, Boston College, RB
2003 Jeff Faine, Norte Dame, C
2004 Kellen Winslow, Miami, TE
2005 Braylon Edwards, Michigan, WR
2006 Kamerion Wimbley, Florida St., DE
2007 Joe Thomas, Wisconsin, T

     Brady Quinn, Notre Dame, QB
2008 Beau Bell, Nevada-Las Vegas, LB (4)
2009 Alex Mack, California, C
2010 Joe Haden, Florida, DB
2011 Phil Taylor, Baylor, DT
2012 Trent Richardson, Alabama, RB
     Brandon Weeden, Oklahoma St., QB
2013 Barkevious Mingo, Louisiana St., DE

DALLAS COWBOYS
Year Player, College, Position
1960 None
1961 Bob Lilly, Texas Christian, DT
1962 Sonny Gibbs, TCU, QB (2)
1963 Lee Roy Jordan, Alabama, LB
1964 Scott Appleton, Texas, DT
1965 Craig Morton, California, QB
1966 John Niland, Iowa, G
1967 Phil Clark, Northwestern, DB (3)
1968 Dennis Homan, Alabama, WR
1969 Calvin Hill, Yale, RB
1970 Duane Thomas, West Texas St., RB
1971 Tody Smith, So. California, DE
1972 Bill Thomas, Boston College, RB
1973 Billy Joe DuPree, Michigan St., TE
1974 Ed (Too Tall) Jones, Tennessee St., DE
     Charley Young, North Carolina St., RB
1975 Randy White, Maryland, LB
     Thomas Henderson, Langston, LB
1976 Aaron Kyle, Wyoming, DB
1977 Tony Dorsett, Pittsburgh, RB
1978 Larry Bethea, Michigan State, DE
1979 Robert Shaw, Tennessee, C
1980 Bill Roe, Colorado, LB (3)
1981 Howard Richards, Missouri, T
1982 Rod Hill, Kentucky State, DB
1983 Jim Jeffcoat, Arizona State, DE
1984 Billy Cannon, Jr., Texas A&M, LB
1985 Kevin Brooks, Michigan, DE
1986 Mike Sherrard, UCLA, WR
1987 Danny Noonan, Nebraska, DT
1988 Michael Irvin, Miami, WR
1989 Troy Aikman, UCLA, QB
1990 Emmitt Smith, Florida, RB
1991 Russell Maryland, Miami, DT
     Alvin Harper, Tennessee, WR
     Kelvin Pritchett, Mississippi, DT
1992 Kevin Smith, Texas A&M, DB
     Robert Jones, East Carolina, LB
1993 Kevin Williams, Miami, WR (2)
1994 Shante Carver, Arizona State, DE
1995 Sherman Williams, Alabama, RB (2)
1996 Kavika Pittman, McNeese St., DE (2)
1997 David LaFleur, Louisiana State, TE
1998 Greg Ellis, North Carolina, DE
1999 Ebenezer Ekuban, North Carolina, DE
2000 Dwayne Goodrich, Tennessee, DB (2)
2001 Quincy Carter, Georgia, QB (2)
2002 Roy Williams, Oklahoma, DB
2003 Terence Newman, Kansas State, DB
2004 Julius Jones, Notre Dame, RB (2)
2005 DeMarcus Ware, Troy, DE
     Marcus Spears, Louisiana St., DE
2006 Bobby Carpenter, Ohio State, LB
2007 Anthony Spencer, Purdue, LB
2008 Felix Jones, Arkansas, RB
     Mike Jenkins, South Florida, DB
2009 Jason Williams, Western Illinois, LB (3)
2010 Dez Bryant, Oklahoma State, WR
2011 Tyron Smith, Southern California, T

2012 Morris Claiborne, Louisiana St., DB
2013 Travis Frederick, Wisconsin, C

DENVER BRONCOS
Year Player, College, Position
1960 Roger LeClerc, Trinity, Conn., C
1961 Bob Gaiters, New Mexico St., RB
1962 Merlin Olsen, Utah State, DT
1963 Kermit Alexander, UCLA, CB
1964 Bob Brown, Nebraska, T
1965 Dick Butkus, Illinois, LB (2)
1966 Jerry Shay, Purdue, DT
1967 Floyd Little, Syracuse, RB
1968 Curley Culp, Arizona State, DE (2)
1969 Grady Cavness, Texas-El Paso, DB (2)
1970 Bob Anderson, Colorado, RB
1971 Marv Montgomery, So. California, T
1972 Riley Odoms, Houston, TE
1973 Otis Armstrong, Purdue, RB
1974 Randy Gradishar, Ohio State, LB
1975 Louis Wright, San Jose State, DB
1976 Tom Glassic, Virginia, G
1977 Steve Schindler, Boston College, G
1978 Don Latimer, Miami, DT
1979 Kelvin Clark, Nebraska, T
1980 Rulon Jones, Utah State, DE (2)
1981 Dennis Smith, So. California, DB
1982 Gerald Willhite, San Jose St., RB
1983 Chris Hinton, Northwestern, G
1984 Andre Townsend, Mississippi, DE (2)
1985 Steve Sewell, Oklahoma, RB
1986 Jim Juriga, Illinois, T (4)
1987 Ricky Nattiel, Florida, WR
1988 Ted Gregory, Syracuse, NT
1989 Steve Atwater, Arkansas, DB
1990 Alton Montgomery, Houston, DB (2)
1991 Mike Croel, Nebraska, LB
1992 Tommy Maddox, UCLA, QB
1993 Dan Williams, Toledo, DE
1994 Allen Aldridge, Houston, LB (2)
1995 Jamie Brown, Florida A&M, T (4)
1996 John Mobley, Kutztown, LB
1997 Trevor Pryce, Clemson, DT
1998 Marcus Nash, Tennessee, WR
1999 Al Wilson, Tennessee, LB
2000 Deltha O'Neal, California, DB
2001 Willie Middlebrooks, Minnesota, DB
2002 Ashley Lelie, Hawaii, WR
2003 George Foster, Georgia, T
2004 D.J. Williams, Miami, LB
2005 Darrent Williams, Oklahoma St., DB (2)
2006 Jay Cutler, Vanderbilt, QB
2007 Jarvis Moss, Florida, DE
2008 Ryan Clady, Boise State, T
2009 Knowshon Moreno, Georgia, RB
     Robert Ayers, Tennessee, DE
2010 Demaryius Thomas, Georgia Tech, WR
     Tim Tebow, Florida, QB
2011 Von Miller, Texas A&M, LB
2012 Derek Wolfe, Cincinnati, DT (2)
2013 Sylvester Williams, North Carolina, DT

DETROIT LIONS
Year Player, College, Position
1936 Sid Wagner, Michigan State, G
1937 Lloyd Cardwell, Nebraska, B
1938 Alex Wojciechowicz, Fordham, C
1939 John Pingel, Michigan State, B
1940 Doyle Nave, Southern California, B
1941 Jim Thomason, Texas A&M, B

1942 Bob Westfall, Michigan, B
1943 Frank Sinkwich, Georgia, B
1944 Otto Graham, Northwestern, B
1945 Frank Szymanski, Notre Dame, C
1946 Bill Dellastatious, Missouri, B
1947 Glenn Davis, Army, B
1948 Y.A. Tittle, Louisiana State, B
1949 John Rauch, Georgia, B
1950 Leon Hart, Notre Dame, E
      Joe Watson, Rice, C
1951 Dick Stanfel, San Francisco, G (2)
1952 Yale Lary, Texas A&M, B (3)
1953 Harley Sewell, Texas, G
1954 Dick Chapman, Rice, T
1955 Dave Middleton, Auburn, B
1956 Hopalong Cassady, Ohio State, B
1957 Bill Glass, Baylor, G
1958 Alex Karras, Iowa, T
1959 Nick Pietrosante, Notre Dame, B
1960 John Robinson, Louisiana State, S
1961 Danny LaRose, Missouri, T (2)
1962 John Hadl, Kansas, QB
1963 Daryl Sanders, Ohio State, T
1964 Pete Beathard, So. California, QB
1965 Tom Nowatzke, Indiana, RB
1966 Nick Eddy, Notre Dame, RB (2)
1967 Mel Farr, UCLA, RB
1968 Greg Landry, Massachusetts, QB
      Earl McCullouch, So. California, WR
1969 Altie Taylor, Utah State, RB (2)
1970 Steve Owens, Oklahoma, RB
1971 Bob Bell, Cincinnati, DT
1972 Herb Orvis, Colorado, DE
1973 Ernie Price, Texas A&I, DE
1974 Ed O'Neil, Penn State, LB
1975 Lynn Boden, South Dakota St., G
1976 James Hunter, Grambling, DB
      Lawrence Gaines, Wyoming, RB
1977 Walt Williams, New Mexico St., DB (2)
1978 Luther Bradley, Notre Dame, DB
1979 Keith Dorney, Penn State, T
1980 Billy Sims, Oklahoma, RB
1981 Mark Nichols, San Jose State, WR
1982 Jimmy Williams, Nebraska, LB
1983 James Jones, Florida, RB
1984 David Lewis, California, TE
1985 Lomas Brown, Florida, T
1986 Chuck Long, Iowa, QB
1987 Reggie Rogers, Washington, DE
1988 Bennie Blades, Miami, DB
1989 Barry Sanders, Oklahoma St., RB
1990 Andre Ware, Houston, QB
1991 Herman Moore, Virginia, WR
1992 Robert Porcher, South Carolina St., DE
1993 Ryan McNeil, Miami, DB (2)
1994 Johnnie Morton, So. California, WR
1995 Luther Elliss, Utah, DT
1996 Reggie Brown, Texas A&M, LB
      Jeff Hartings, Penn State, G
1997 Bryant Westbrook, Texas, DB
1998 Terry Fair, Tennessee, DB
1999 Chris Claiborne, So. California, LB
      Aaron Gibson, Wisconsin, T
2000 Stockar McDougle, Oklahoma, T
2001 Jeff Backus, Michigan, T
2002 Joey Harrington, Oregon, QB
2003 Charles Rogers, Michigan State, WR
2004 Roy Williams, Texas, WR
      Kevin Jones, Virginia Tech, RB
2005 Mike Williams, So. California, WR

2006 Ernie Sims, Florida State, LB
2007 Calvin Johnson, Georgia Tech, WR
2008 Gosder Cherilus, Boson College, T
2009 Matthew Stafford, Georgia, QB
      Brandon Pettigrew, Oklahoma St., TE
2010 Ndamukong Suh, Nebraska, DT
      Jahvid Best, California, RB
2011 Nick Fairley, Auburn, DT
2012 Riley Reiff, Iowa, T
2013 Ezekiel Ansah, Brigham Young, DE

GREEN BAY PACKERS
Year Player, College, Position
1936 Russ Letlow, San Francisco, G
1937 Eddie Jankowski, Wisconsin, B
1938 Cecil Isbell, Purdue, B
1939 Larry Buhler, Minnesota, B
1940 Harold Van Every, Minnesota, B
1941 George Paskvan, Wisconsin, B
1942 Urban Odson, Minnesota, T
1943 Dick Wildung, Minnesota, T
1944 Merv Pregulman, Michigan, G
1945 Walt Schlinkman, Texas Tech, B
1946 Johnny Strzykalski, Marquette, B
1947 Ernie Case, UCLA, B
1948 Earl (Jug) Girard, Wisconsin, B
1949 Stan Heath, Nevada, B
1950 Clayton Tonnemaker, Minnesota, C
1951 Bob Gain, Kentucky, T
1952 Babe Parilli, Kentucky, QB
1953 Al Carmichael, So. California, B
1954 Art Hunter, Notre Dame, T
      Veryl Switzer, Kansas State, B
1955 Tom Bettis, Purdue, G
1956 Jack Losch, Miami, B
1957 Paul Hornung, Notre Dame, B
      Ron Kramer, Michigan, E
1958 Dan Currie, Michigan State, C
1959 Randy Duncan, Iowa, B
1960 Tom Moore, Vanderbilt, RB
1961 Herb Adderley, Michigan State, CB
1962 Earl Gros, Louisiana State, RB
1963 Dave Robinson, Penn State, LB
1964 Lloyd Voss, Nebraska, DT
1965 Donny Anderson, Texas Tech, RB
      Lawrence Elkins, Baylor, E
1966 Jim Grabowski, Illinois, RB
      Gale Gillingham, Minnesota, T
1967 Bob Hyland, Boston College, C
      Don Horn, San Diego State, QB
1968 Fred Carr, Texas-El Paso, LB
      Bill Lueck, Arizona, G
1969 Rich Moore, Villanova, DT
1970 Mike McCoy, Notre Dame, DT
      Rich McGeorge, Elon, TE
1971 John Brockington, Ohio State, RB
1972 Willie Buchanon, San Diego St., DB
      Jerry Tagge, Nebraska, QB
1973 Barry Smith, Florida State, WR
1974 Barty Smith, Richmond, RB
1975 Bill Bain, So. California, G (2)
1976 Mark Koncar, Colorado, T
1977 Mike Butler, Kansas, DE
      Ezra Johnson, Morris Brown, DE
1978 James Lofton, Stanford, WR
      John Anderson, Michigan, LB
1979 Eddie Lee Ivery, Georgia Tech, RB
1980 Bruce Clark, Penn State, DE
      George Cumby, Oklahoma, LB
1981 Rich Campbell, California, QB

1982 Ron Hallstrom, Iowa, G
1983 Tim Lewis, Pittsburgh, DB
1984 Alphonso Carreker, Florida St., DE
1985 Ken Ruettgers, So. California, T
1986 Kenneth Davis, TCU, RB (2)
1987 Brent Fullwood, Auburn, RB
1988 Sterling Sharpe, South Carolina, WR
1989 Tony Mandarich, Michigan State, T
1990 Tony Bennett, Mississippi, LB
      Darrell Thompson, Minnesota, RB
1991 Vinnie Clark, Ohio State, DB
1992 Terrell Buckley, Florida State, DB
1993 Wayne Simmons, Clemson, LB
      George Teague, Alabama, DB
1994 Aaron Taylor, Notre Dame, T
1995 Craig Newsome, Arizona State, DB
1996 John Michels, Southern California, T
1997 Ross Verba, Iowa, T
1998 Vonnie Holliday, North Carolina, DT
1999 Antuan Edwards, Clemson, DB
2000 Bubba Franks, Miami, TE
2001 Jamal Reynolds, Florida State, DE
2002 Javon Walker, Florida State, WR
2003 Nick Barnett, Oregon State, LB
2004 Ahmad Carroll, Arkansas, DB
2005 Aaron Rodgers, California, QB
2006 A.J. Hawk, Ohio State, LB
2007 Justin Harrell, Tennessee, DT
2008 Jordy Nelson, Kansas State, WR (2)
2009 B.J. Raji, Boston College, DT
      Clay Matthews, So. California, LB
2010 Bryan Bulaga, Iowa, T
2011 Derek Sherrod, Mississippi State, T
2012 Nick Perry, Southern California, LB
2013 Datone Jones, UCLA, DE

HOUSTON TEXANS
Year Player, College, Position
2002 David Carr, Fresno State, QB
2003 Andre Johnson, Miami, WR
2004 Dunta Robinson, South Carolina, DB
      Jason Babin, Western Michigan, LB
2005 Travis Johnson, Florida State, DE
2006 Mario Williams, North Carolina St., DE
2007 Amobi Okoye, Louisville, DT
2008 Duane Brown, Virginia Tech, T
2009 Brian Cushing, So. California, LB
2010 Kareem Jackson, Alabama, DB
2011 J.J. Watt, Wisconsin, DE
2012 Whitney Mercilus, Illinois, LB
2013 DeAndre Hopkins, Clemson, WR

INDIANAPOLIS COLTS
Year Player, College, Position
1953 Billy Vessels, Oklahoma, B
1954 Cotton Davidson, Baylor, B
1955 George Shaw, Oregon, B
      Alan Ameche, Wisconsin, FB
1956 Lenny Moore, Penn State, B
1957 Jim Parker, Ohio State, G
1958 Lenny Lyles, Louisville, B
1959 Jackie Burkett, Auburn, C
1960 Ron Mix, Southern California, T
1961 Tom Matte, Ohio State, RB
1962 Wendell Harris, Louisiana State, S
1963 Bob Vogel, Ohio State, T
1964 Marv Woodson, Indiana, CB
1965 Mike Curtis, Duke, LB
1966 Sam Ball, Kentucky, T
1967 Bubba Smith, Michigan State, DT

	Jim Detwiler, Michigan, RB
1968	John Williams, Minnesota, G
1969	Eddie Hinton, Oklahoma, WR
1970	Norman Bulaich, Texas Christian, RB
1971	Don McCauley, North Carolina, RB
	Leonard Dunlap, North Texas St., DB
1972	Tom Drougas, Oregon, T
1973	Bert Jones, Louisiana State, QB
	Joe Ehrmann, Syracuse, DT
1974	John Dutton, Nebraska, DE
	Roger Carr, Louisiana Tech, WR
1975	Ken Huff, North Carolina, G
1976	Ken Novak, Purdue, DT
1977	Randy Burke, Kentucky, WR
1978	Reese McCall, Auburn, TE
1979	Barry Krauss, Alabama, LB
1980	Curtis Dickey, Texas A&M, RB
	Derrick Hatchett, Texas, DB
1981	Randy McMillan, Pittsburgh, RB
	Donnell Thompson, North Carolina, DT
1982	Johnie Cooks, Mississippi St., LB
	Art Schlichter, Ohio State, QB
1983	John Elway, Stanford, QB
1984	Leonard Coleman, Vanderbilt, DB
	Ron Solt, Maryland, G
1985	Duane Bickett, So. California, LB
1986	Jon Hand, Alabama, DE
1987	Cornelius Bennett, Alabama, LB
1988	Chris Chandler, Washington, QB (3)
1989	Andre Rison, Michigan State, WR
1990	Jeff George, Illinois, QB
1991	Shane Curry, Miami, DE (2)
1992	Steve Emtman, Washington, DT
	Quentin Coryatt, Texas A&M, LB
1993	Sean Dawkins, California, WR
1994	Marshall Faulk, San Diego St., RB
	Trev Alberts, Nebraska, LB
1995	Ellis Johnson, Florida, DT
1996	Marvin Harrison, Syracuse, WR
1997	Tarik Glenn, California, T
1998	Peyton Manning, Tennessee, QB
1999	Edgerrin James, Miami, RB
2000	Rob Morris, Brigham Young, LB
2001	Reggie Wayne, Miami, WR
2002	Dwight Freeney, Syracuse, DE
2003	Dallas Clark, Iowa, TE
2004	Bob Sanders, Iowa, DB (2)
2005	Marlin Jackson, Michigan, DB
2006	Joseph Addai, Louisiana State, RB
2007	Anthony Gonzalez, Ohio State, WR
2008	Mike Pollak, Arizona State, G (2)
2009	Donald Brown, Connecticut, RB
2010	Jerry Hughes, Texas Christian, DE
2011	Anthony Castonzo, Boston College, T
2012	Andrew Luck, Stanford, QB
2013	Bjoern Werner, Florida State, DE

JACKSONVILLE JAGUARS
Year Player, College, Position

1995	Tony Boselli, Southern California, T
	James Stewart, Tennessee, RB
1996	Kevin Hardy, Illinois, LB
1997	Renaldo Wynn, Notre Dame, DT
1998	Fred Taylor, Florida, RB
	Donovin Darius, Syracuse, DB
1999	Fernando Bryant, Alabama, DB
2000	R. Jay Soward, So. California, WR
2001	Marcus Stroud, Georgia, DT
2002	John Henderson, Tennessee, DT
2003	Byron Leftwich, Marshall, QB

2004	Reggie Williams, Washington, WR
2005	Matt Jones, Arkansas, WR
2006	Marcedes Lewis, UCLA, TE
2007	Reggie Nelson, Florida, DB
2008	Derrick Harvey, Florida, DE
2009	Eugene Monroe, Virginia, T
2010	Tyson Alualu, California, DT
2011	Blaine Gabbert, Missouri, QB
2012	Justin Blackmon, Oklahoma St., WR
2013	Luke Joeckel, Texas A&M, T

KANSAS CITY CHIEFS
Year Player, College, Position

1960	Don Meredith, So. Methodist, QB
1961	E.J. Holub, Texas Tech, C
1962	Ronnie Bull, Baylor, RB
1963	Buck Buchanan, Grambling, DT
	Ed Budde, Michigan State, G
1964	Pete Beathard, So. California, QB
1965	Gale Sayers, Kansas, RB
1966	Aaron Brown, Minnesota, DE
1967	Gene Trosch, Miami, DE-DT
1968	Mo Moorman, Texas A&M, G
	George Daney, Texas-El Paso, G
1969	Jim Marsalis, Tennessee State, CB
1970	Sid Smith, Southern California, T
1971	Elmo Wright, Houston, WR
1972	Jeff Kinney, Nebraska, RB
1973	Gary Butler, Rice, TE (2)
1974	Woody Green, Arizona State, RB
1975	Elmore Stephens, Kentucky, TE (2)
1976	Rod Walters, Iowa, G
1977	Gary Green, Baylor, DB
1978	Art Still, Kentucky, DE
1979	Mike Bell, Colorado State, DE
	Steve Fuller, Clemson, QB
1980	Brad Budde, Southern California, G
1981	Willie Scott, South Carolina, TE
1982	Anthony Hancock, Tennessee, WR
1983	Todd Blackledge, Penn State, QB
1984	Bill Maas, Pittsburgh, DT
	John Alt, Iowa, T
1985	Ethan Horton, North Carolina, RB
1986	Brian Jozwiak, West Virginia, T
1987	Paul Palmer, Temple, RB
1988	Neil Smith, Nebraska, DE
1989	Derrick Thomas, Alabama, LB
1990	Percy Snow, Michigan State, LB
1991	Harvey Williams, Louisiana St., RB
1992	Dale Carter, Tennessee, DB
1993	Will Shields, Nebraska, G (3)
1994	Greg Hill, Texas A&M, RB
1995	Trezelle Jenkins, Michigan, T
1996	Jerome Woods, Memphis, DB
1997	Tony Gonzalez, California, TE
1998	Victor Riley, Auburn, T
1999	John Tait, Brigham Young, T
2000	Sylvester Morris, Jackson St., WR
2001	Eric Downing, Syracuse, DT (3)
2002	Ryan Sims, North Carolina, DT
2003	Larry Johnson, Penn State, RB
2004	Junior Siavii, Oregon, DT (2)
2005	Derrick Johnson, Texas, LB
2006	Tamba Hali, Penn State, DE
2007	Dwayne Bowe, Louisiana State, WR
2008	Glenn Dorsey, Louisiana State, DT
	Branden Albert, Virginia, T
2009	Tyson Jackson, Louisiana State, DE
2010	Eric Berry, Tennessee, DB
2011	Jonathan Baldwin, Pittsburgh, WR

2012	Dontari Poe, Memphis, NT
2013	Eric Fisher, Central Michigan, T

MIAMI DOLPHINS
Year Player, College, Position

1966	Jim Grabowski, Illinois, RB
	Rick Norton, Kentucky, QB
1967	Bob Griese, Purdue, QB
1968	Larry Csonka, Syracuse, RB
	Doug Crusan, Indiana, T
1969	Bill Stanfill, Georgia, DE
1970	Jim Mandich, Michigan, TE (2)
1971	Otto Stowe, Iowa State, WR (2)
1972	Mike Kadish, Notre Dame, DT
1973	Chuck Bradley, Oregon, C (2)
1974	Donald Reese, Jackson State, DE
1975	Darryl Carlton, Tampa, T
1976	Larry Gordon, Arizona State, LB
	Kim Bokamper, San Jose State, LB
1977	A.J. Duhe, Louisiana State, DT
1978	Guy Benjamin, Stanford, QB (2)
1979	Jon Giesler, Michigan, T
1980	Don McNeal, Alabama, DB
1981	David Overstreet, Oklahoma, RB
1982	Roy Foster, Southern California, G
1983	Dan Marino, Pittsburgh, QB
1984	Jackie Shipp, Oklahoma, LB
1985	Lorenzo Hampton, Florida, RB
1986	John Offerdahl, Western Michigan, LB (2)
1987	John Bosa, Boston College, DE
1988	Eric Kumerow, Ohio State, DE
1989	Sammie Smith, Florida State, RB
	Louis Oliver, Florida, DB
1990	Richmond Webb, Texas A&M, T
1991	Randal Hill, Miami, WR
1992	Troy Vincent, Wisconsin, DB
	Marco Coleman, Georgia Tech, LB
1993	O.J. McDuffie, Penn State, WR
1994	Tim Bowens, Mississippi, DT
1995	Billy Milner, Houston, T
1996	Daryl Gardener, Baylor, DT
1997	Yatil Green, Miami, WR
1998	John Avery, Mississippi, RB
1999	J.J. Johnson, Mississippi St., RB (2)
2000	Todd Wade, Mississippi, T (2)
2001	Jamar Fletcher, Wisconsin, DB
2002	Seth McKinney, Texas A&M, C (3)
2003	Eddie Moore, Tennessee, LB (2)
2004	Vernon Carey, Miami, T
2005	Ronnie Brown, Auburn, RB
2006	Jason Allen, Tennessee, DB
2007	Ted Ginn, Ohio State, WR
2008	Jake Long, Michigan, T
2009	Vontae Davis, Illinois, DB
2010	Jared Odrick, Penn State, DT
2011	Mike Pouncey, Florida, C
2012	Ryan Tannehill, Texas A&M, QB
2013	Dion Jordan, Oregon, DE

MINNESOTA VIKINGS
Year Player, College, Position

1961	Tommy Mason, Tulane, RB
1962	Bill Miller, Miami, WR (3)
1963	Jim Dunaway, Mississippi, T
1964	Carl Eller, Minnesota, DE
1965	Jack Snow, Notre Dame, WR
1966	Jerry Shay, Purdue, DT
1967	Clint Jones, Michigan State, RB
	Gene Washington, Michigan St., WR
	Alan Page, Notre Dame, DT

1968	Ron Yary, Southern California, T
1969	Ed White, California, G (2)
1970	John Ward, Oklahoma State, DT
1971	Leo Hayden, Ohio State, RB
1972	Jeff Siemon, Stanford, LB
1973	Chuck Foreman, Miami, RB
1974	Fred McNeill, UCLA, LB
	Steve Riley, Southern California, T
1975	Mark Mullaney, Colorado State, DE
1976	James White, Oklahoma State, DT
1977	Tommy Kramer, Rice, QB
1978	Randy Holloway, Pittsburgh, DE
1979	Ted Brown, North Carolina St., RB
1980	Doug Martin, Washington, DT
1981	Mardye McDole, Mississippi St., WR (2)
1982	Darrin Nelson, Stanford, RB
1983	Joey Browner, So. California, DB
1984	Keith Millard, Washington St., DE
1985	Chris Doleman, Pittsburgh, LB
1986	Gerald Robinson, Auburn, DE
1987	D.J. Dozier, Penn State, RB
1988	Randall McDaniel, Arizona State, G
1989	David Braxton, Wake Forest, LB (2)
1990	Mike Jones, Texas A&M, TE (3)
1991	Carlos Jenkins, Michigan St., LB (3)
1992	Robert Harris, Southern Univ., DE (2)
1993	Robert Smith, Ohio State, RB
1994	DeWayne Washington, N. Carolina St., DB
	Todd Steussie, California, T
1995	Derrick Alexander, Florida St., DE
	Korey Stringer, Ohio State, T
1996	Duane Clemons, California, DE
1997	Dwayne Rudd, Alabama, LB
1998	Randy Moss, Marshall, WR
1999	Daunte Culpepper, Central Florida, QB
	Dimitrius Underwood, Michigan St., DE
2000	Chris Hovan, Boston College, DT
2001	Michael Bennett, Wisconsin, RB
2002	Bryant McKinnie, Miami, T
2003	Kevin Williams, Oklahoma State, DT
2004	Kenechi Udeze, Southern California, DE
2005	Troy Williamson, South Carolina, WR
	Erasmus James, Wisconsin, DE
2006	Chad Greenway, Iowa, LB
2007	Adrian Peterson, Oklahoma, RB
2008	Tyrell Johnson, Arkansas State, DB (2)
2009	Percy Harvin, Florida, WR
2010	Chris Cook, Virginia, DB (2)
2011	Christian Ponder, Florida State, QB
2012	Matt Kalil, Southern California, T
	Harrison Smith, Notre Dame, DB
2013	Shariff Floyd, Florida, DT
	Xavier Rhodes, Florida State, DB
	Cordarrelle Patterson, Tennessee, WR

NEW ENGLAND PATRIOTS

Year	Player, College, Position
1960	Ron Burton, Northwestern, RB
1961	Tommy Mason, Tulane, RB
1962	Gary Collins, Maryland, WR
1963	Art Graham, Boston College, WR
1964	Jack Concannon, Boston College, QB
1965	Jerry Rush, Michigan State, DE
1966	Karl Singer, Purdue, T
1967	John Charles, Purdue, S
1968	Dennis Byrd, North Carolina St., DE
1969	Ron Sellers, Florida State, WR
1970	Phil Olsen, Utah State, DE
1971	Jim Plunkett, Stanford, QB
1972	Tom Reynolds, San Diego St., WR (2)

1973	John Hannah, Alabama, G
	Sam Cunningham, So. California, RB
	Darryl Stingley, Purdue, WR
1974	Steve Corbett, Boston College, G (2)
1975	Russ Francis, Oregon, TE
1976	Mike Haynes, Arizona State, DB
	Pete Brock, Colorado, C
	Tim Fox, Ohio State, DB
1977	Raymond Clayborn, Texas, DB
	Stanley Morgan, Tennessee, WR
1978	Bob Cryder, Alabama, G
1979	Rick Sanford, South Carolina, DB
1980	Roland James, Tennessee, DB
	Vagas Ferguson, Notre Dame, RB
1981	Brian Holloway, Stanford, T
1982	Kenneth Sims, Texas, DT
	Lester Williams, Miami, DT
1983	Tony Eason, Illinois, QB
1984	Irving Fryar, Nebraska, WR
1985	Trevor Matich, Brigham Young, C
1986	Reggie Dupard, So. Methodist, RB
1987	Bruce Armstrong, Louisville, T
1988	John Stephens, Northwestern St., La., RB
1989	Hart Lee Dykes, Oklahoma St., WR
1990	Chris Singleton, Arizona, LB
	Ray Agnew, North Carolina St., DE
1991	Pat Harlow, Southern California, T
	Leonard Russell, Arizona St., RB
1992	Eugene Chung, Virginia Tech, T
1993	Drew Bledsoe, Washington St., QB
1994	Willie McGinest, So. California, DE
1995	Ty Law, Michigan, DB
1996	Terry Glenn, Ohio State, WR
1997	Chris Canty, Kansas State, DB
1998	Robert Edwards, Georgia, RB
	Tebucky Jones, Syracuse, DB
1999	Damien Woody, Boston College, C
	Andy Katzenmoyer, Ohio State, LB
2000	Adrian Klemm, Hawaii, T (2)
2001	Richard Seymour, Georgia, DT
2002	Daniel Graham, Colorado, TE
2003	Ty Warren, Texas A&M, DT
2004	Vince Wilfork, Miami, DT
	Ben Watson, Georgia, TE
2005	Logan Mankins, Fresno State, G
2006	Laurence Maroney, Minnesota, RB
2007	Brandon Meriweather, Miami, DB
2008	Jerod Mayo, Tennessee, LB
2009	Patrick Chung, Oregon, DB (2)
2010	Devin McCourty, Rutgers, DB
2011	Nate Solder, Colorado, T
2012	Chandler Jones, Syracuse, DE
	Dont'a Hightower, Alabama, LB
2013	Jamie Collins, So. Mississippi, LB (2)

NEW ORLEANS SAINTS

Year	Player, College, Position
1967	Les Kelley, Alabama, RB
1968	Kevin Hardy, Notre Dame, DE
1969	John Shinners, Xavier, G
1970	Ken Burrough, Texas Southern, WR
1971	Archie Manning, Mississippi, QB
1972	Royce Smith, Georgia, G
1973	Derland Moore, Oklahoma, DE (2)
1974	Rick Middleton, Ohio State, LB
1975	Larry Burton, Purdue, WR
	Kurt Schumacher, Ohio State, T
1976	Chuck Muncie, California, RB
1977	Joe Campbell, Maryland, DE
1978	Wes Chandler, Florida, WR

1979	Russell Erxleben, Texas, P-K
1980	Stan Brock, Colorado, T
1981	George Rogers, South Carolina, RB
1982	Lindsay Scott, Georgia, WR
1983	Steve Korte, Arkansas, G (2)
1984	James Geathers, Wichita State, DE
1985	Alvin Toles, Tennessee, LB
1986	Jim Dombrowski, Virginia, T
1987	Shawn Knight, Brigham Young, DT
1988	Craig Heyward, Pittsburgh, RB
1989	Wayne Martin, Arkansas, DE
1990	Renaldo Turnbull, West Virginia, DE
1991	Wesley Carroll, Miami, WR (2)
1992	Vaughn Dunbar, Indiana, RB
1993	Willie Roaf, Louisiana Tech, T
	Irv Smith, Notre Dame, TE
1994	Joe Johnson, Louisville, DE
1995	Mark Fields, Washington State, LB
1996	Alex Molden, Oregon, DB
1997	Chris Naeole, Colorado, G
1998	Kyle Turley, San Diego State, T
1999	Ricky Williams, Texas, RB
2000	Darren Howard, Kansas St., DE (2)
2001	Deuce McAllister, Mississippi, RB
2002	Donte' Stallworth, Tennessee, WR
	Charles Grant, Georgia, DE
2003	Johnathan Sullivan, Georgia, DT
2004	Will Smith, Ohio State, DE
2005	Jammal Brown, Oklahoma, T
2006	Reggie Bush, So. California, RB
2007	Robert Meachem, Tennessee, WR
2008	Sedrick Ellis, So. California, DT
2009	Malcolm Jenkins, Ohio State, DB
2010	Patrick Robinson, Florida State, DB
2011	Cameron Jordan, California, DE
	Mark Ingram, Alabama, RB
2012	Akiem Hicks, Regina, DT (3)
2013	Kenny Vaccaro, Texas, DB

NEW YORK GIANTS

Year	Player, College, Position
1936	Art Lewis, Ohio U., T
1937	Ed Widseth, Minnesota, T
1938	George Karamatic, Gonzaga, B
1939	Walt Neilson, Arizona, B
1940	Grenville Lansdell, So. California, B
1941	George Franck, Minnesota, B
1942	Merle Hapes, Mississippi, B
1943	Steve Filipowicz, Fordham, B
1944	Billy Hillenbrand, Indiana, B
1945	Elmer Barbour, Wake Forest, B
1946	George Connor, Notre Dame, T
1947	Vic Schwall, Northwestern, B
1948	Tony Minisi, Pennsylvania, B
1949	Paul Page, Southern Methodist, B
1950	Travis Tidwell, Auburn, B
1951	Kyle Rote, Southern Methodist, B
	Jim Spavital, Oklahoma A&M, B
1952	Frank Gifford, Southern California, B
1953	Bobby Marlow, Alabama, B
1954	Ken Buck, Pacific, C (2)
1955	Joe Heap, Notre Dame, B
1956	Henry Moore, Arkansas, B (2)
1957	Sam DeLuca, South Carolina, T (2)
1958	Phil King, Vanderbilt, B
1959	Lee Grosscup, Utah, B
1960	Lou Cordileone, Clemson, G
1961	Bruce Tarbox, Syracuse, G (2)
1962	Jerry Hillebrand, Colorado, LB
1963	Frank Lasky, Florida, T (2)

1964	Joe Don Looney, Oklahoma, RB
1965	Tucker Frederickson, Auburn, RB
1966	Francis Peay, Missouri, T
1967	Louis Thompson, Alabama, DT (4)
1968	Dick Buzin, Penn State, T (2)
1969	Fred Dryer, San Diego State, DE
1970	Jim Files, Oklahoma, LB
1971	Rocky Thompson, West Texas St., WR
1972	Eldridge Small, Texas A&I, DB
	Larry Jacobson, Nebraska, DE
1973	Brad Van Pelt, Michigan St., LB (2)
1974	John Hicks, Ohio State, G
1975	Al Simpson, Colorado State, T (2)
1976	Troy Archer, Colorado, DE
1977	Gary Jeter, Southern California, DT
1978	Gordon King, Stanford, T
1979	Phil Simms, Morehead State, QB
1980	Mark Haynes, Colorado, DB
1981	Lawrence Taylor, North Carolina, LB
1982	Butch Woolfolk, Michigan, RB
1983	Terry Kinard, Clemson, DB
1984	Carl Banks, Michigan State, LB
	William Roberts, Ohio State, T
1985	George Adams, Kentucky, RB
1986	Eric Dorsey, Notre Dame, DE
1987	Mark Ingram, Michigan State, WR
1988	Eric Moore, Indiana, T
1989	Brian Williams, Minnesota, C-G
1990	Rodney Hampton, Georgia, RB
1991	Jarrod Bunch, Michigan, RB
1992	Derek Brown, Notre Dame, TE
1993	Michael Strahan, Texas Southern, DE (2)
1994	Thomas Lewis, Indiana, WR
1995	Tyrone Wheatley, Michigan, RB
1996	Cedric Jones, Oklahoma, DE
1997	Ike Hilliard, Florida, WR
1998	Shaun Williams, UCLA, DB
1999	Luke Petitgout, Notre Dame, T
2000	Ron Dayne, Wisconsin, RB
2001	Will Allen, Syracuse, DB
2002	Jeremy Shockey, Miami, TE
2003	William Joseph, Miami, DT
2004	Philip Rivers, North Carolina St., QB
2005	Corey Webster, Louisiana St., DB (2)
2006	Mathias Kiwanuka, Boston College, DE
2007	Aaron Ross, Texas, DB
2008	Kenny Phillips, Miami, DB
2009	Hakeem Nicks, North Carolina, WR
2010	Jason Pierre-Paul, South Florida, DE
2011	Prince Amukamara, Nebraska, DB
2012	David Wilson, Virginia Tech, RB
2013	Justin Pugh, Syracuse, T

NEW YORK JETS

Year Player, College, Position

1960	George Izo, Notre Dame, QB
1961	Tom Brown, Minnesota, G
1962	Sandy Stephens, Minnesota, QB
1963	Jerry Stovall, Louisiana State, S
1964	Matt Snell, Ohio State, RB
1965	Joe Namath, Alabama, QB
	Tom Nowatzke, Indiana, RB
1966	Bill Yearby, Michigan, DT
1967	Paul Seiler, Notre Dame, T
1968	Lee White, Weber State, RB
1969	Dave Foley, Ohio State, T
1970	Steve Tannen, Florida, CB
1971	John Riggins, Kansas, RB
1972	Jerome Barkum, Jackson St., WR
	Mike Taylor, Michigan, LB

1973	Burgess Owens, Miami, DB
1974	Carl Barzilauskas, Indiana, DT
1975	Anthony Davis, So. California, RB (2)
1976	Richard Todd, Alabama, QB
1977	Marvin Powell, So. California, T
1978	Chris Ward, Ohio State, T
1979	Marty Lyons, Alabama, DE
1980	Johnny (Lam) Jones, Texas, WR
1981	Freeman McNeil, UCLA, RB
1982	Bob Crable, Notre Dame, LB
1983	Ken O'Brien, Cal-Davis, QB
1984	Russell Carter, So. Methodist, DB
	Ron Faurot, Arkansas, DE
1985	Al Toon, Wisconsin, WR
1986	Mike Haight, Iowa, T
1987	Roger Vick, Texas A&M, RB
1988	Dave Cadigan, So. California, T
1989	Jeff Lageman, Virginia, LB
1990	Blair Thomas, Penn State, RB
1991	Browning Nagle, Louisville, QB (2)
1992	Johnny Mitchell, Nebraska, TE
1993	Marvin Jones, Florida State, LB
1994	Aaron Glenn, Texas A&M, DB
1995	Kyle Brady, Penn State, TE
	Hugh Douglas, Central St., Ohio, DE
1996	Keyshawn Johnson, So. California, WR
1997	James Farrior, Virginia, LB
1998	Dorian Boose, Washington St., DE (2)
1999	Randy Thomas, Mississippi St., G (2)
2000	Shaun Ellis, Tennessee, DE
	John Abraham, South Carolina, LB
	Chad Pennington, Marshall, QB
	Anthony Becht, West Virginia, TE
2001	Santana Moss, Miami, WR
2002	Bryan Thomas, Ala.-Birmingham, DE
2003	Dewayne Robertson, Kentucky, DT
2004	Jonathan Vilma, Miami, LB
2005	Mike Nugent, Ohio State, K (2)
2006	D'Brickashaw Ferguson, Virginia, T
	Nick Mangold, Ohio State, C
2007	Darrelle Revis, Pittsburgh, DB
2008	Vernon Gholston, Ohio State, LB
	Dustin Keller, Purdue, TE
2009	Mark Sanchez, So. California, QB
2010	Kyle Wilson, Boise State, DB
2011	Muhammad Wilkerson, Temple, DT
2012	Quinton Coples, North Carolina, DE
2013	Dee Milliner, Alabama, DB
	Sheldon Richardson, Missouri, DT

OAKLAND RAIDERS

Year Player, College, Position

1960	Dale Hackbart, Wisconsin, CB
1961	Joe Rutgens, Illinois, DT
1962	Roman Gabriel, North Carolina St., QB
1963	George Wilson, Alabama, RB (6)
1964	Tony Lorick, Arizona State, RB
1965	Harry Schuh, Memphis State, T
1966	Rodger Bird, Kentucky, S
1967	Gene Upshaw, Texas A&I, G
1968	Eldridge Dickey, Tennessee St., QB
1969	Art Thoms, Syracuse, DT
1970	Raymond Chester, Morgan St., TE
1971	Jack Tatum, Ohio State, S
1972	Mike Siani, Villanova, WR
1973	Ray Guy, Southern Mississippi, P
1974	Henry Lawrence, Florida A&M, T
1975	Neal Colzie, Ohio State, DB
1976	Charles Philyaw, Texas Southern, DT (2)
1977	Mike Davis, Colorado, DB (2)

1978	Dave Browning, Washington, DE (2)
1979	Willie Jones, Florida State, DE (2)
1980	Marc Wilson, Brigham Young, QB
1981	Ted Watts, Texas Tech, DB
	Curt Marsh, Washington, T
1982	Marcus Allen, So. California, RB
1983	Don Mosebar, So. California, T
1984	Sean Jones, Northeastern, DE (2)
1985	Jessie Hester, Florida State, WR
1986	Bob Buczkowski, Pittsburgh, DE
1987	John Clay, Missouri, T
1988	Tim Brown, Notre Dame, WR
	Terry McDaniel, Tennessee, DB
	Scott Davis, Illinois, DE
1989	Jeff Francis, Tennessee, QB (6)
1990	Anthony Smith, Arizona, DE
1991	Todd Marinovich, So. California, QB
1992	Chester McGlockton, Clemson, DE
1993	Patrick Bates, Texas A&M, DB
1994	Rob Fredrickson, Michigan St., LB
1995	Napoleon Kaufman, Washington, RB
1996	Rickey Dudley, Ohio State, TE
1997	Darrell Russell, Southern California, DT
1998	Charles Woodson, Michigan, DB
	Mo Collins, Florida, T
1999	Matt Stinchcomb, Georgia, T
2000	Sebastian Janikowski, Florida St., K
2001	Derrick Gibson, Florida State, DB
2002	Phillip Buchanon, Miami, DB
	Napoleon Harris, Northwestern, LB
2003	Nnamdi Asomugha, California, DB
	Tyler Brayton, Colorado, DE
2004	Robert Gallery, Iowa, T
2005	Fabian Washington, Nebraska, DB
2006	Michael Huff, Texas, DB
2007	JaMarcus Russell, Louisiana State, QB
2008	Darren McFadden, Arkansas, RB
2009	Darrius Heyward-Bey, Maryland, WR
2010	Rolando McClain, Alabama, LB
2011	Stefan Wisniewski, Penn State, C (2)
2012	Tony Bergstrom, Utah, G (3)
2013	D.J. Hayden, Houston, DB

PHILADELPHIA EAGLES

Year Player, College, Position

1936	Jay Berwanger, Chicago, B
1937	Sam Francis, Nebraska, B
1938	Jim McDonald, Ohio State, B
1939	Davey O'Brien, Texas Christian, B
1940	George McAfee, Duke, B
1941	Art Jones, Richmond, B (2)
1942	Pete Kmetovic, Stanford, B
1943	Joe Muha, Virginia Military, B
1944	Steve Van Buren, Louisiana St., B
1945	John Yonaker, Notre Dame, E
1946	Leo Riggs, Southern California, B
1947	Neill Armstrong, Oklahoma A&M, E
1948	Clyde (Smackover) Scott, Arkansas, B
1949	Chuck Bednarik, Pennsylvania, C
	Frank Tripucka, Notre Dame, B
1950	Harry (Bud) Grant, Minnesota, E
1951	Ebert Van Buren, Louisiana St., B
	Chet Mutryn, Xavier, B
1952	Johnny Bright, Drake, B
1953	Al Conway, Army, B (2)
1954	Neil Worden, Notre Dame, B
1955	Dick Bielski, Maryland, B
1956	Bob Pellegrini, Maryland, C
1957	Clarence Peaks, Michigan State, B
1958	Walt Kowalczyk, Michigan State, B

1959 J.D. Smith, Rice, T (2)
1960 Ron Burton, Northwestern, RB
1961 Art Baker, Syracuse, RB
1962 Pete Case, Georgia, G (2)
1963 Ed Budde, Michigan State, G
1964 Bob Brown, Nebraska, T
1965 Ray Rissmiller, Georgia, T (2)
1966 Randy Beisler, Indiana, DE
1967 Harry Jones, Arkansas, RB
1968 Tim Rossovich, So. California, DE
1969 Leroy Keyes, Purdue, RB
1970 Steve Zabel, Oklahoma, TE
1971 Richard Harris, Grambling, DE
1972 John Reaves, Florida, QB
1973 Jerry Sisemore, Texas, T
    Charle Young, So. California, TE
1974 Mitch Sutton, Kansas, DT (3)
1975 Bill Capraun, Miami, T (7)
1976 Mike Smith, Florida, DE (4)
1977 Skip Sharp, Kansas, DB (5)
1978 Reggie Wilkes, Georgia Tech, LB (3)
1979 Jerry Robinson, UCLA, LB
1980 Roynell Young, Alcorn State, DB
1981 Leonard Mitchell, Houston, DE
1982 Mike Quick, North Carolina St., WR
1983 Michael Haddix, Mississippi St., RB
1984 Kenny Jackson, Penn State, WR
1985 Kevin Allen, Indiana, T
1986 Keith Byars, Ohio State, RB
1987 Jerome Brown, Miami, DT
1988 Keith Jackson, Oklahoma, TE
1989 Jessie Small, Eastern Kentucky, LB (2)
1990 Ben Smith, Georgia, DB
1991 Antone Davis, Tennessee, T
1992 Siran Stacy, Alabama, RB (2)
1993 Lester Holmes, Jackson State, T
    Leonard Renfro, Colorado, DT
1994 Bernard Williams, Georgia, T
1995 Mike Mamula, Boston College, DE
1996 Jermane Mayberry, Texas A&M-Kingsville, T
1997 Jon Harris, Virginia, DE
1998 Tra Thomas, Florida State, T
1999 Donovan McNabb, Syracuse, QB
2000 Corey Simon, Florida State, DT
2001 Freddie Mitchell, UCLA, WR
2002 Lito Sheppard, Florida, DB
2003 Jerome McDougle, Miami, DE
2004 Shawn Andrews, Arkansas, T
2005 Mike Patterson, So. California, DT
2006 Brodrick Bunkley, Florida State, DT
2007 Kevin Kolb, Houston, QB (2)
2008 Trevor Laws, Notre Dame, DT (2)
2009 Jeremy Maclin, Missouri, WR
2010 Brandon Graham, Michigan, DE
2011 Danny Watkins, Baylor, G
2012 Fletcher Cox, Mississippi St., DT
2013 Lane Johnson, Oklahoma, T

PITTSBURGH STEELERS
Year Player, College, Position
1936 Bill Shakespeare, Notre Dame, B
1937 Mike Basrak, Duquesne, C
1938 Byron (Whizzer) White, Colorado, B (3)
1939 Bill Patterson, Baylor, B (3)
1940 Kay Eakin, Arkansas, B
1941 Chet Gladchuk, Boston College, C (2)
1942 Bill Dudley, Virginia, B
1943 Bill Daley, Minnesota, B
1944 Johnny Podesto, St. Mary's, Calif., B
1945 Paul Duhart, Florida, B

1946 Felix (Doc) Blanchard, Army, B
1947 Hub Bechtol, Texas, E
1948 Dan Edwards, Georgia, E
1949 Bobby Gage, Clemson, B
1950 Lynn Chandnois, Michigan St., B
1951 Butch Avinger, Alabama, B
1952 Ed Modzelewski, Maryland, B
1953 Ted Marchibroda, St. Bonaventure, B
1954 Johnny Lattner, Notre Dame, B
1955 Frank Varrichione, Notre Dame, T
1956 Gary Glick, Colorado A&M, B
    Art Davis, Mississippi State, B
1957 Len Dawson, Purdue, B
1958 Larry Krutko, West Virginia, B (2)
1959 Tom Barnett, Purdue, B (8)
1960 Jack Spikes, Texas Christian, RB
1961 Myron Pottios, Notre Dame, LB (2)
1962 Bob Ferguson, Ohio State, RB
1963 Frank Atkinson, Stanford, T (8)
1964 Paul Martha, Pittsburgh, S
1965 Roy Jefferson, Utah, WR (2)
1966 Dick Leftridge, West Virginia, RB
1967 Don Shy, San Diego State, RB (2)
1968 Mike Taylor, Southern California, T
1969 Joe Greene, North Texas State, DT
1970 Terry Bradshaw, Louisiana Tech, QB
1971 Frank Lewis, Grambling, WR
1972 Franco Harris, Penn State, RB
1973 J.T. Thomas, Florida State, DB
1974 Lynn Swann, So. California, WR
1975 Dave Brown, Michigan, DB
1976 Bennie Cunningham, Clemson, TE
1977 Robin Cole, New Mexico, LB
1978 Ron Johnson, Eastern Michigan, DB
1979 Greg Hawthorne, Baylor, RB
1980 Mark Malone, Arizona State, QB
1981 Keith Gary, Oklahoma, DE
1982 Walter Abercrombie, Baylor, RB
1983 Gabriel Rivera, Texas Tech, DT
1984 Louis Lipps, So. Mississippi, WR
1985 Darryl Sims, Wisconsin, DE
1986 John Rienstra, Temple, G
1987 Rod Woodson, Purdue, DB
1988 Aaron Jones, Eastern Kentucky, DE
1989 Tim Worley, Georgia, RB
    Tom Ricketts, Pittsburgh, T
1990 Eric Green, Liberty, TE
1991 Huey Richardson, Florida, DE
1992 Leon Searcy, Miami, T
1993 Deon Figures, Colorado, DB
1994 Charles Johnson, Colorado, WR
1995 Mark Bruener, Washington, TE
1996 Jamain Stephens, North Carolina A&T, T
1997 Chad Scott, Maryland, DB
1998 Alan Faneca, Louisiana State, G
1999 Troy Edwards, Louisiana Tech, WR
2000 Plaxico Burress, Michigan St., WR
2001 Casey Hampton, Texas, DT
2002 Kendall Simmons, Auburn, G
2003 Troy Polamalu, Southern California, DB
2004 Ben Roethlisberger, Miami (OH), QB
2005 Heath Miller, Virginia, TE
2006 Santonio Holmes, Ohio State, WR
2007 Lawrence Timmons, Florida State, LB
2008 Rashard Mendenhall, Illinois, RB
2009 Evander Hood, Missouri, DE
2010 Maurkice Pouncey, Florida, C
2011 Cameron Heyward, Ohio State, DE
2012 David DeCastro, Stanford, G
2013 Jarvis Jones, Georgia, LB

ST. LOUIS RAMS
Year Player, College, Position
1937 Johnny Drake, Purdue, B
1938 Corbett Davis, Indiana, B
1939 Parker Hall, Mississippi, B
1940 Ollie Cordill, Rice, B
1941 Rudy Mucha, Washington, C
1942 Jack Wilson, Baylor, B
1943 Mike Holovak, Boston College, B
1944 Tony Butkovich, Illinois, B
1945 Elroy (Crazylegs) Hirsch, Wisconsin, B
1946 Emil Sitko, Notre Dame, B
1947 Herman Wedemeyer, St. Mary's, Calif., B
1948 Tom Keane, West Virginia, B (2)
1949 Bobby Thomason, Virginia Military, B
1950 Ralph Pasqualriello, Villanova, B
    Stan West, Oklahoma, G
1951 Bud McFadin, Texas, G
1952 Bill Wade, Vanderbilt, QB
    Bob Carey, Michigan State, E
1953 Donn Moomaw, UCLA, C
    Ed Barker, Washington State, E
1954 Ed Beatty, Cincinnati, C
1955 Larry Morris, Georgia Tech, C
1956 Joe Marconi, West Virginia, B
    Charles Horton, Vanderbilt, B
1957 Jon Arnett, Southern California, B
    Del Shofner, Baylor, E
1958 Lou Michaels, Kentucky, T
    Jim Phillips, Auburn, E
1959 Dick Bass, Pacific, B
    Paul Dickson, Baylor, T
1960 Billy Cannon, Louisiana State, RB
1961 Marlin McKeever, So. California, E-LB
1962 Roman Gabriel, North Carolina St., QB
    Merlin Olsen, Utah State, DT
1963 Terry Baker, Oregon State, QB
    Rufus Guthrie, Georgia Tech, G
1964 Bill Munson, Utah State, QB
1965 Clancy Williams, Washington St., CB
1966 Tom Mack, Michigan, G
1967 Willie Ellison, Texas Southern, RB (2)
1968 Gary Beban, UCLA, QB (2)
1969 Larry Smith, Florida, RB
    Jim Seymour, Notre Dame, WR
    Bob Klein, Southern California, TE
1970 Jack Reynolds, Tennessee, LB
1971 Isiah Robertson, Southern, LB
    Jack Youngblood, Florida, DE
1972 Jim Bertelsen, Texas, RB (2)
1973 Cullen Bryant, Colorado, DB (2)
1974 John Cappelletti, Penn State, RB
1975 Mike Fanning, Notre Dame, DT
    Dennis Harrah, Miami, T
    Doug France, Ohio State, T
1976 Kevin McLain, Colorado State, LB
1977 Bob Brudzinski, Ohio State, LB
1978 Elvis Peacock, Oklahoma, RB
1979 George Andrews, Nebraska, LB
    Kent Hill, Georgia Tech, T
1980 Johnnie Johnson, Texas, DB
1981 Mel Owens, Michigan, LB
1982 Barry Redden, Richmond, RB
1983 Eric Dickerson, So. Methodist, RB
1984 Hal Stephens, East Carolina, DE (5)
1985 Jerry Gray, Texas, DB
1986 Mike Schad, Queen's Univ., Canada, T
1987 Donald Evans, Winston-Salem, DE (2)
1988 Gaston Green, UCLA, RB

Aaron Cox, Arizona State, WR
1989 Bill Hawkins, Miami, DE
Cleveland Gary, Miami, RB
1990 Bern Brostek, Washington, C
1991 Todd Lyght, Notre Dame, DB
1992 Sean Gilbert, Pittsburgh, DE
1993 Jerome Bettis, Notre Dame, RB
1994 Wayne Gandy, Auburn, T
1995 Kevin Carter, Florida, DE
1996 Lawrence Phillips, Nebraska, RB
Eddie Kennison, Louisiana St., WR
1997 Orlando Pace, Ohio State, T
1998 Grant Wistrom, Nebraska, DE
1999 Torry Holt, North Carolina St., WR
2000 Trung Canidate, Arizona, RB
2001 Damione Lewis, Miami, DT
Adam Archuleta, Arizona State, DB
Ryan Pickett, Ohio State, DT
2002 Robert Thomas, UCLA, LB
2003 Jimmy Kennedy, Penn State, DT
2004 Steven Jackson, Oregon State, RB
2005 Alex Barron, Florida State, T
2006 Tye Hill, Clemson, DB
2007 Adam Carriker, Nebraska, DE
2008 Chris Long, Virginia, DE
2009 Jason Smith, Baylor, T
2010 Sam Bradford, Oklahoma, QB
2011 Robert Quinn, North Carolina, DE
2012 Michael Brockers, Louisiana St., DT
2013 Tavon Austin, West Virginia, WR
Alec Ogletree, Georgia, LB

SAN DIEGO CHARGERS
Year Player, College, Position
1960 Monty Stickles, Notre Dame, E
1961 Earl Faison, Indiana, DE
1962 Bob Ferguson, Ohio State, RB
1963 Walt Sweeney, Syracuse, G
1964 Ted Davis, Georgia Tech, LB
1965 Steve DeLong, Tennessee, DE
1966 Don Davis, Cal St.-Los Angeles, DT
1967 Ron Billingsley, Wyoming, DE
1968 Russ Washington, Missouri, DT
Jimmy Hill, Texas A&I, DB
1969 Marty Domres, Columbia, QB
Bob Babich, Miami, Ohio, LB
1970 Walker Gillette, Richmond, WR
1971 Leon Burns, Long Beach State, RB
1972 Pete Lazetich, Stanford, DE (2)
1973 Johnny Rodgers, Nebraska, WR
1974 Bo Matthews, Colorado, RB
Don Goode, Kansas, LB
1975 Gary Johnson, Grambling, DT
Mike Williams, Louisiana State, DB
1976 Joe Washington, Oklahoma, RB
1977 Bob Rush, Memphis State, C
1978 John Jefferson, Arizona State, WR
1979 Kellen Winslow, Missouri, TE
1980 Ed Luther, San Jose State, QB (4)
1981 James Brooks, Auburn, RB
1982 Hollis Hall, Clemson, DB (7)
1983 Billy Ray Smith, Arkansas, LB
Gary Anderson, Arkansas, WR
Gill Byrd, San Jose State, DB
1984 Mossy Cade, Texas, DB
1985 Jim Lachey, Ohio State, G
1986 Leslie O'Neal, Oklahoma State, DE
James FitzPatrick, So. California, T
1987 Rod Bernstine, Texas A&M, TE
1988 Anthony Miller, Tennessee, WR

1989 Burt Grossman, Pittsburgh, DE
1990 Junior Seau, So. California, LB
1991 Stanley Richard, Texas, DB
1992 Chris Mims, Tennessee, DE
1993 Darrien Gordon, Stanford, DB
1994 Isaac Davis, Arkansas, G (2)
1995 Terrance Shaw, Stephen F. Austin, DB (2)
1996 Bryan Still, Virginia Tech, WR (2)
1997 Freddie Jones, North Carolina, TE (2)
1998 Ryan Leaf, Washington State, QB
1999 Jermaine Fazande, Oklahoma, RB (2)
2000 Rogers Beckett, Marshall, DB (2)
2001 LaDainian Tomlinson, TCU, RB
2002 Quentin Jammer, Texas, DB
2003 Sammy Davis, Texas A&M, DB
2004 Eli Manning, Mississippi, QB
2005 Shawne Merriman, Maryland, LB
Luis Castillo, Northwestern, DT
2006 Antonio Cromartie, Florida State, DB
2007 Craig Davis, Louisiana State, WR
2008 Antoine Cason, Arizona, DB
2009 Larry English, Northern Illinois, LB
2010 Ryan Mathews, Fresno State, RB
2011 Corey Liuget, Illinois, DE
2012 Melvin Ingram, South Carolina, LB
2013 D.J. Fluker, Alabama, T

SAN FRANCISCO 49ERS
Year Player, College, Position
1950 Leo Nomellini, Minnesota, T
1951 Y.A. Tittle, Louisiana State, B
1952 Hugh McElhenny, Washington, B
1953 Harry Babcock, Georgia, E
Tom Stolhandske, Texas, E
1954 Bernie Faloney, Maryland, B
1955 Dickie Moegle, Rice, B
1956 Earl Morrall, Michigan State, B
1957 John Brodie, Stanford, B
1958 Jim Pace, Michigan, B
Charlie Krueger, Texas A&M, T
1959 Dave Baker, Oklahoma, B
Dan James, Ohio State, C
1960 Monty Stickles, Notre Dame, E
1961 Jimmy Johnson, UCLA, CB
Bernie Casey, Bowling Green, WR
Bill Kilmer, UCLA, QB
1962 Lance Alworth, Arkansas, WR
1963 Kermit Alexander, UCLA, CB
1964 Dave Parks, Texas Tech, WR
1965 Ken Willard, North Carolina, RB
George Donnelly, Illinois, DB
1966 Stan Hindman, Mississippi, DE
1967 Steve Spurrier, Florida, QB
Cas Banaszek, Northwestern, T
1968 Forrest Blue, Auburn, C
1969 Ted Kwalick, Penn State, TE
Gene Washington, Stanford, WR
1970 Cedrick Hardman, North Texas St., DE
Bruce Taylor, Boston U., DB
1971 Tim Anderson, Ohio State, DB
1972 Terry Beasley, Auburn, WR
1973 Mike Holmes, Texas Southern, DB
1974 Wilbur Jackson, Alabama, RB
Bill Sandifer, UCLA, DT
1975 Jimmy Webb, Mississippi St., DT
1976 Randy Cross, UCLA, C (2)
1977 Elmo Boyd, Eastern Kentucky, WR (3)
1978 Ken MacAfee, Notre Dame, TE
Dan Bunz, Cal St.-Long Beach, LB
1979 James Owens, UCLA, WR (2)

1980 Earl Cooper, Rice, RB
Jim Stuckey, Clemson, DT
1981 Ronnie Lott, So. California, DB
1982 Bubba Paris, Michigan, T (2)
1983 Roger Craig, Nebraska, RB (2)
1984 Todd Shell, Brigham Young, LB
1985 Jerry Rice, Mississippi Valley St., WR
1986 Larry Roberts, Alabama, DE (2)
1987 Harris Barton, North Carolina, T
Terrence Flagler, Clemson, RB
1988 Danny Stubbs, Miami, DE (2)
1989 Keith DeLong, Tennessee, LB
1990 Dexter Carter, Florida State, RB
1991 Ted Washington, Louisville, DT
1992 Dana Hall, Washington, DB
1993 Dana Stubblefield, Kansas, DT
Todd Kelly, Tennessee, DE
1994 Bryant Young, Notre Dame, DT
William Floyd, Florida State, RB
1995 J.J. Stokes, UCLA, WR
1996 Israel Ifeanyi, So.California, DE (2)
1997 Jim Druckenmiller, Virginia Tech, QB
1998 R.W. McQuarters, Oklahoma St., DB
1999 Reggie McGrew, Florida, DT
2000 Julian Peterson, Michigan St., LB
Ahmed Plummer, Ohio State, DB
2001 Andre Carter, California, DE
2002 Mike Rumph, Miami, DB
2003 Kwame Harris, Stanford, T
2004 Rashaun Woods, Oklahoma St., WR
2005 Alex Smith, Utah, QB
2006 Vernon Davis, Maryland, TE
Manny Lawson, North Carolina St., DE
2007 Patrick Willis, Mississippi, LB
Joe Staley, Central Michigan, T
2008 Kentwan Balmer, North Carolina, DT
2009 Michael Crabtree, Texas Tech, WR
2010 Anthony Davis, Rutgers, T
Mike Iupati, Idaho, G
2011 Aldon Smith, Missouri, LB
2012 A.J. Jenkins, Illinois, WR
2013 Eric Reid, Louisiana State, DB

SEATTLE SEAHAWKS
Year Player, College, Position
1976 Steve Niehaus, Notre Dame, DT
1977 Steve August, Tulsa, G
1978 Keith Simpson, Memphis St., DB
1979 Manu Tuiasosopo, UCLA, DT
1980 Jacob Green, Texas A&M, DE
1981 Ken Easley, UCLA, DB
1982 Jeff Bryant, Clemson, DE
1983 Curt Warner, Penn State, RB
1984 Terry Taylor, Southern Illinois, DB
1985 Owen Gill, Iowa, RB (2)
1986 John L. Williams, Florida, RB
1987 Tony Woods, Pittsburgh, LB
1988 Brian Blades, Miami, WR (2)
1989 Andy Heck, Notre Dame, T
1990 Cortez Kennedy, Miami, DT
1991 Dan McGwire, San Diego St., QB
1992 Ray Roberts, Virginia, T
1993 Rick Mirer, Notre Dame, QB
1994 Sam Adams, Texas A&M, DT
1995 Joey Galloway, Ohio State, WR
1996 Pete Kendall, Boston College, T
1997 Shawn Springs, Ohio State, DB
Walter Jones, Florida State, T
1998 Anthony Simmons, Clemson, LB
1999 Lamar King, Saginaw Valley St., DE

2000	Shaun Alexander, Alabama, RB
	Chris McIntosh, Wisconsin, T
2001	Koren Robinson, North Carolina St., WR
	Steve Hutchinson, Michigan, G
2002	Jerramy Stevens, Washington, TE
2003	Marcus Trufant, Washington State, DB
2004	Marcus Tubbs, Texas, DT
2005	Chris Spencer, Mississippi, C
2006	Kelly Jennings, Miami, DB
2007	Josh Wilson, Maryland, DB (2)
2008	Lawrence Jackson, So. California, DE
2009	Aaron Curry, Wake Forest, LB
2010	Russell Okung, Oklahoma State, T
	Earl Thomas, Texas, DB
2011	James Carpenter, Alabama, T
2012	Bruce Irvin, West Virginia, DE
2013	Christine Michael, Texas A&M, RB (2)

TAMPA BAY BUCCANEERS
Year Player, College, Position

1976	Lee Roy Selmon, Oklahoma, DT
1977	Ricky Bell, Southern California, RB
1978	Doug Williams, Grambling, QB
1979	Greg Roberts, Oklahoma, G (2)
1980	Ray Snell, Wisconsin, G
1981	Hugh Green, Pittsburgh, LB
1982	Sean Farrell, Penn State, G
1983	Randy Grimes, Baylor, C (2)
1984	Keith Browner, So. California, LB (2)
1985	Ron Holmes, Washington, DE
1986	Bo Jackson, Auburn, RB
	Roderick Jones, So. Methodist, DB
1987	Vinny Testaverde, Miami, QB
1988	Paul Gruber, Wisconsin, T
1989	Broderick Thomas, Nebraska, LB
1990	Keith McCants, Alabama, LB
1991	Charles McRae, Tennessee, T
1992	Courtney Hawkins, Michigan St., WR (2)
1993	Eric Curry, Alabama, DE
1994	Trent Dilfer, Fresno State, QB
1995	Warren Sapp, Miami, DT
	Derrick Brooks, Florida State, LB
1996	Regan Upshaw, California, DE
	Marcus Jones, North Carolina, DT
1997	Warrick Dunn, Florida State, RB
	Reidel Anthony, Florida, WR
1998	Jacquez Green, Florida, WR (2)
1999	Anthony McFarland, Louisiana St., DT
2000	Cosey Coleman, Tennessee, G (2)
2001	Kenyatta Walker, Florida, T
2002	Marquise Walker, Michigan, WR (3)
2003	Dewayne White, Louisville, DE (2)
2004	Michael Clayton, Louisiana St., WR
2005	Carnell Williams, Auburn, RB
2006	Davin Joseph, Oklahoma, G
2007	Gaines Adams, Clemson, DE
2008	Aqib Talib, Kansas, DB
2009	Josh Freeman, Kansas State, QB
2010	Gerald McCoy, Oklahoma, DT
2011	Adrian Clayborn, Iowa, DE
2012	Mark Barron, Alabama, DB
	Doug Martin, Boise State, RB
2013	Johnthan Banks, Mississippi St., DB (2)

TENNESSEE TITANS
Year Player, College, Position

1960	Billy Cannon, Louisiana State, RB
1961	Mike Ditka, Pittsburgh, E
1962	Ray Jacobs, Howard Payne, DT
1963	Danny Brabham, Arkansas, LB

1964	Scott Appleton, Texas, DT
1965	Lawrence Elkins, Baylor, WR
1966	Tommy Nobis, Texas, LB
1967	George Webster, Michigan St., LB
	Tom Regner, Notre Dame, G
1968	Mac Haik, Mississippi, WR (2)
1969	Ron Pritchard, Arizona State, LB
1970	Doug Wilkerson, N. Carolina Central, G
1971	Dan Pastorini, Santa Clara, QB
1972	Greg Sampson, Stanford, DE
1973	John Matuszak, Tampa, DE
	George Amundson, Iowa State, RB
1974	Steve Manstedt, Nebraska, LB (4)
1975	Robert Brazile, Jackson State, LB
	Don Hardeman, Texas A&I, RB
1976	Mike Barber, Louisiana Tech, TE (2)
1977	Morris Towns, Missouri, T
1978	Earl Campbell, Texas, RB
1979	Mike Stensrud, Iowa State, DE (2)
1980	Angelo Fields, Michigan St., T (2)
1981	Michael Holston, Morgan St., WR (3)
1982	Mike Munchak, Penn State, G
1983	Bruce Matthews, So. California, T
1984	Dean Steinkuhler, Nebraska, T
1985	Ray Childress, Texas A&M, DE
	Richard Johnson, Wisconsin, DB
1986	Jim Everett, Purdue, QB
1987	Alonzo Highsmith, Miami, RB
	Haywood Jeffires, North Carolina St., WR
1988	Lorenzo White, Michigan State, RB
1989	David Williams, Florida, T
1990	Lamar Lathon, Houston, LB
1991	Mike Dumas, Indiana, DB (2)
1992	Eddie Robinson, Alabama St., LB (2)
1993	Brad Hopkins, Illinois, T
1994	Henry Ford, Arkansas, DE
1995	Steve McNair, Alcorn State, QB
1996	Eddie George, Ohio State, RB
1997	Kenny Holmes, Miami, DE
1998	Kevin Dyson, Utah, WR
1999	Jevon Kearse, Florida, DE
2000	Keith Bulluck, Syracuse, LB
2001	Andre Dyson, Utah, DB (2)
2002	Albert Haynesworth, Tennessee, DT
2003	Andre Woolfolk, Oklahoma, DB
2004	Ben Troupe, Florida, TE (2)
2005	Adam Jones, West Virginia, DB
2006	Vince Young, Texas, QB
2007	Michael Griffin, Texas, DB
2008	Chris Johnson, East Carolina, RB
2009	Kenny Britt, Rutgers, WR
2010	Derrick Morgan, Georgia Tech, DE
2011	Jake Locker, Washington, QB
2012	Kendall Wright, Baylor, WR
2013	Chance Warmack, Alabama, G

WASHINGTON REDSKINS
Year Player, College, Position

1936	Riley Smith, Alabama, B
1937	Sammy Baugh, Texas Christian, B
1938	Andy Farkas, Detroit, B
1939	I.B. Hale, Texas Christian, T
1940	Ed Boell, New York U., B
1941	Forest Evashevski, Michigan, B
1942	Orban (Spec) Sanders, Texas, B
1943	Jack Jenkins, Missouri, B
1944	Mike Micka, Colgate, B
1945	Jim Hardy, Southern California, B
1946	Cal Rossi, UCLA, B*
1947	Cal Rossi, UCLA, B
1948	Harry Gilmer, Alabama, B

	Lowell Tew, Alabama, B
1949	Rob Goode, Texas A&M, B
1950	George Thomas, Oklahoma, B
1951	Leon Heath, Oklahoma, B
1952	Larry Isbell, Baylor, B
1953	Jack Scarbath, Maryland, B
1954	Steve Meilinger, Kentucky, E
1955	Ralph Guglielmi, Notre Dame, B
1956	Ed Vereb, Maryland, B
1957	Don Bosseler, Miami, B
1958	Mike Sommer, George Washington, B (2)
1959	Don Allard, Boston College, B
1960	Richie Lucas, Penn State, QB
1961	Norman Snead, Wake Forest, QB
	Joe Rutgens, Illinois, DT
1962	Ernie Davis, Syracuse, RB
1963	Pat Richter, Wisconsin, TE
1964	Charley Taylor, Arizona St., RB-WR
1965	Bob Breitenstein, Tulsa, T (2)
1966	Charlie Gogolak, Princeton, K
1967	Ray McDonald, Idaho, RB
1968	Jim Smith, Oregon, DB
1969	Eugene Epps, Texas-El Paso, DB (2)
1970	Bill Bundige, Colorado, DT (2)
1971	Cotton Speyrer, Texas, WR (2)
1972	Moses Denson, Maryland St., RB (8)
1973	Charles Cantrell, Lamar, G (5)
1974	Jon Keyworth, Colorado, TE (6)
1975	Mike Thomas, Nevada-Las Vegas, RB (6)
1976	Mike Hughes, Baylor, G (5)
1977	Duncan McColl, Stanford, DE (4)
1978	Tony Green, Florida, RB (6)
1979	Don Warren, San Diego St., TE (4)
1980	Art Monk, Syracuse, WR
1981	Mark May, Pittsburgh, T
1982	Vernon Dean, San Diego St., DB (2)
1983	Darrell Green, Texas A&I, DB
1984	Bob Slater, Oklahoma, DT (2)
1985	Tory Nixon, San Diego St., DB (2)
1986	Markus Koch, Boise State, DE (2)
1987	Brian Davis, Nebraska, DB (2)
1988	Chip Lohmiller, Minnesota, K (2)
1989	Tracy Rocker, Auburn, DT (3)
1990	Andre Collins, Penn State, LB (2)
1991	Bobby Wilson, Michigan State, DT
1992	Desmond Howard, Michigan, WR
1993	Tom Carter, Notre Dame, DB
1994	Heath Shuler, Tennessee, QB
1995	Michael Westbrook, Colorado, WR
1996	Andre Johnson, Penn State, T
1997	Kenard Lang, Miami, DE
1998	Stephen Alexander, Oklahoma, TE (2)
1999	Champ Bailey, Georgia, DB
2000	LaVar Arrington, Penn State, LB
	Chris Samuels, Alabama, T
2001	Rod Gardner, Clemson, WR
2002	Patrick Ramsey, Tulane, QB
2003	Taylor Jacobs, Florida, WR (2)
2004	Sean Taylor, Miami, DB
2005	Carlos Rogers, Auburn, DB
	Jason Campbell, Auburn, QB
2006	Rocky McIntosh, Miami, LB (2)
2007	LaRon Landry, Louisiana State, DB
2008	Devin Thomas, Michigan State, WR (2)
2009	Brian Orakpo, Texas, DE
2010	Trent Williams, Oklahoma, T
2011	Ryan Kerrigan, Purdue, LB
2012	Robert Griffin III, Baylor, QB
2013	David Amerson, North Carolina St., DB (2)

Choice lost because of ineligibility

NFL'S 10 HIGHEST SCORING WEEKENDS

Point Total	Date	Weekend
837	November 20-24, 2008	12th
791	September 5, 9-10, 2012	1st
788	December 29-30, 2007	17th
788	December 5-6, 2004	13th
788	September 5, 8-9, 2002	1st
779	December 16, 19-20, 2010	15th
765	September 13, 16-17, 2012	2nd
762	November 10-11, 1996	11th
761	October 16-17, 1983	7th
759	October 2-3, 2011	4th
759	January 1, 2012	17th

TOP 10 TELEVISED SPORTS EVENTS OF ALL-TIME
(Based on Nielsen Company Figures)

Program	Date	Network	Share	Rating
Super Bowl XVI	1/24/82	CBS	73%	49.1
Super Bowl XVII	1/30/83	NBC	69%	48.6
Winter Olympics	2/23/94	CBS	64%	48.5
Super Bowl XX	1/26/86	NBC	70%	48.3
Super Bowl XII	1/15/78	CBS	67%	47.2
Super Bowl XIII	1/21/79	NBC	74%	47.1
Super Bowl XLVI	2/5/12	NBC	71%	47.0
Super Bowl XVIII	1/22/84	CBS	71%	46.4
Super Bowl XIX	1/20/85	ABC	63%	46.4
Super Bowl XLVII	2/3/13	CBS	69%	46.4

TEN MOST WATCHED TV PROGRAMS & ESTIMATED TOTAL NUMBER OF VIEWERS
(Based on Nielsen Company Figures)

Program	Date	Network	*Total Viewers
Super Bowl XLVII	Feb. 3, 2013	CBS	164,100,000
Super Bowl XLV	Feb. 6, 2011	FOX	162,900,000
Super Bowl XLVI	Feb. 5, 2012	NBC	159,200,000
Super Bowl XLIV	Feb. 7, 2010	CBS	153,400,000
Super Bowl XLIII	Feb. 1, 2009	NBC	151,600,000
Super Bowl XLII	Feb. 3, 2008	FOX	148,300,000
Super Bowl XXXVIII	Feb. 1, 2004	CBS	144,400,000
Super Bowl XL	Feb. 5, 2006	ABC	141,400,000
Super Bowl XLI	Feb. 4, 2007	CBS	139,800,000
Super Bowl XXXVII	Jan. 26, 2003	ABC	138,900,000

NFL'S TOP FIVE PAID ATTENDANCE TOTALS FOR ALL GAMES

Year	Preseason	Regular Season	Postseason	All Games
2007	4,119,278	17,345,205	792,019	22,256,502
2006	4,083,282	17,340,879	775,551	22,199,712
2008	3,995,942	17,055,982	806,840	21,858,764
2005	3,977,388	17,012,453	802,255	21,792,096
2004	3,918,848	17,000,811	788,965	21,708,624

TEN HIGHEST-RATED *NFL MONDAY NIGHT FOOTBALL* GAMES OF ALL-TIME
(Based on Nielsen Company Figures)

Game	Date	Share	Rating
Chicago at Miami	12/2/85	46%	29.6
N.Y. Giants at San Francisco	12/3/90	42%	26.9
Dallas at Washington	10/2/78	43%	26.8
Pittsburgh at San Diego	12/22/80	40%	25.3
Philadelphia at Miami	11/30/81	40%	25.3
Pittsburgh at Houston	12/10/79	40%	25.1
Dallas at Miami	12/17/84	40%	25.1
Pittsburgh at Dallas	9/13/82	42%	24.9
Cincinnati at Oakland	12/6/76	40%	24.7
Dallas at Washington	10/8/73	40%	24.6
Minnesota at Atlanta	11/19/73	40%	24.6

NFL'S 10 BIGGEST SINGLE-GAME ATTENDANCE TOTALS

Date	Site	Game	Teams	Attendance
August 15, 1994	Azteca Stadium	American Bowl (Mexico City)	Cowboys vs. Oilers	112,376
August 17, 1998	Azteca Stadium	American Bowl (Mexico City)	Cowboys vs. Patriots	106,424
August 22, 1947	Soldier Field	College All-Star	Bears vs. All-Stars	105,840
September 20, 2009	Cowboys Stadium	Regular Season	Cowboys vs. Giants	105,121
August 4, 1997	Estadio Guillermo Canedo	American Bowl (Mexico City)	Broncos vs. Dolphins	104,629
January 20, 1980	Rose Bowl	Super Bowl XIV	Steelers vs. Rams	103,985
January 30, 1983	Rose Bowl	Super Bowl XVII	Redskins vs. Dolphins	103,667
October 2, 2005	Azteca Stadium	Regular Season	49ers at Cardinals	103,467
January 9, 1977	Rose Bowl	Super Bowl XI	Raiders vs. Vikings	103,438
November 10, 1957	L.A. Coliseum	Regular Season	49ers at Rams	102,368

NFL'S TOP 10 PAID ATTENDANCE WEEKENDS

Weekend	Games	Attendance
September 8, 11-12, 2005	16	1,115,018
December 6, 9-10, 2007	16	1,113,376
November 20-21, 2005	16	1,112,555
December 27-28, 2003	16	1,106,818
November 19-20, 2006	16	1,106,739
September 23-24, 2007	16	1,103,570
December 24-26, 2005	16	1,102,701
September 7, 10-11, 2006	16	1,102,102
September 9, 12-13, 2004	16	1,101,332
December 7, 10-11, 2006	16	1,099,794

NFL'S TOP 10 TEAM SINGLE-SEASON HOME PAID ATTENDANCE TOTALS

Year	Club	Games	Attendance
2007	Washington Redskins	8	711,471
2008	Washington Redskins	8	710,049
2006	Washington Redskins	8	708,952
2004	Washington Redskins	8	707,920
2005	Washington Redskins	8	707,614
2009	Washington Redskins	8	681,703
2010	Washington Redskins	8	680,966
2003	Washington Redskins	8	667,033
2002	Washington Redskins	8	663,536
2001	Washington Redskins	8	661,970

NFL PAID ATTENDANCE

For detailed 2012 attendance, see page 246.

Year	Regular Season		Average	Postseason	Total
2012	16,658,950	(256 games)	65,074	821,433 (12)	17,480,383
2011	16,562,706	(256 games)	64,698	828,457 (12)	17,391,163
2010	16,569,514	(255 games****)	64,978	800,426 (12)	17,369,940
2009	16,651,126	(256 games)	65,043	823,882 (12)	17,475,008
2008	17,055,982	(256 games)	66,625	806,840 (12)	17,862,822
2007	17,345,205	(256 games)	#67,755	792,019 (12)	#18,137,224
2006	17,340,879	(256 games)	67,738	775,551 (12)	18,116,430
2005	17,012,453	(256 games)	66,455	802,255 (12)	17,814,708
2004	17,000,811	(256 games)	66,409	788,965 (12)	17,789,776
2003	16,913,584	(255 games***)	66,328	805,546 (12)	17,719,130
2002	16,833,310	(256 games)	65,755	781,944 (12)	17,615,254
2001	16,166,258	(248 games)	65,187	766,905 (12)	16,933,163
2000	16,387,289	(248 games)	66,078	809,132 (12)	17,196,421
1999	16,206,640	(248 games)	65,349	793,759 (12)	17,000,399
1998	15,364,873	(240 games)	64,020	822,885 (12)	16,187,758
1997	14,967,314	(240 games)	62,364	801,879 (12)	15,769,193
1996	14,612,417	(240 games)	60,885	769,310 (12)	15,381,727
1995	15,043,562	(240 games)	62,682	790,906 (12)	15,834,468
1994	14,030,435	(224 games)	62,636	779,738 (12)	14,810,173
1993	13,966,843	(224 games)	62,352	814,607 (12)	14,781,450
1992	13,828,887	(224 games)	61,736	815,910 (12)	14,644,797
1991	13,841,459	(224 games)	61,792	813,247 (12)	14,654,706
1990	13,959,896	(224 games)	62,321	847,543 (12)	14,807,439
1989	13,625,662	(224 games)	60,829	685,771 (10)	14,311,433
1988	13,539,848	(224 games)	60,446	658,317 (10)	14,198,165
1987	11,406,166	(210 games**)	54,315	656,977 (10)	12,063,143
1986	13,588,551	(224 games)	60,663	734,002 (10)	14,322,553
1985	13,345,047	(224 games)	59,567	710,768 (10)	14,055,815
1984	13,398,112	(224 games)	59,813	665,194 (10)	14,063,306
1983	13,277,222	(224 games)	59,273	675,513 (10)	13,952,735
1982	7,367,438	(126 games*)	58,472	#1,033,153 (16)	8,400,591
1981	13,606,990	(224 games)	60,745	637,763 (10)	14,244,753
1980	13,392,230	(224 games)	59,787	624,430 (10)	14,016,660
1979	13,182,039	(224 games)	58,848	630,326 (10)	13,812,365
1978	12,771,800	(224 games)	57,017	624,388 (10)	13,396,188
1977	11,018,632	(196 games)	56,218	534,925 (8)	11,553,557
1976	11,070,543	(196 games)	56,482	492,884 (8)	11,563,427
1975	10,213,193	(182 games)	56,116	475,919 (8)	10,689,112
1974	10,236,322	(182 games)	56,244	438,664 (8)	10,674,986
1973	10,730,933	(182 games)	58,961	525,433 (8)	11,256,366
1972	10,445,827	(182 games)	57,395	483,345 (8)	10,929,172
1971	10,076,035	(182 games)	55,363	483,891 (8)	10,559,926
1970	9,533,333	(182 games)	52,381	458,493 (8)	9,991,826
1969	6,096,127	(112 games) NFL	54,430	162,279 (3)	6,258,406
	2,843,373	(70 games) AFL	40,620	167,088 (3)	3,010,461
1968	5,882,313	(112 games) NFL	52,521	215,902 (3)	6,098,215
	2,635,004	(70 games) AFL	37,643	114,438 (2)	2,749,442
1967	5,938,924	(112 games) NFL	53,026	166,208 (3)	6,105,132
	2,295,697	(63 games) AFL	36,439	53,330 (1)	2,349,027
1966	5,337,044	(105 games) NFL	50,829	74,152 (1)	5,411,196
	2,160,369	(63 games) AFL	34,291	42,080 (1)	2,202,449
1965	4,634,021	(98 games) NFL	47,286	100,304 (2)	4,734,325
	1,782,384	(56 games) AFL	31,828	30,361 (1)	1,812,745

PAID ATTENDANCE

Year	Regular Season			Average	Postseason	Total
1964	4,563,049	(98 games)	NFL	46,562	79,544 (1)	4,642,593
	1,447,875	(56 games)	AFL	25,855	40,242 (1)	1,488,117
1963	4,163,643	(98 games)	NFL	42,486	45,801 (1)	4,209,444
	1,208,697	(56 games)	AFL	21,584	63,171 (2)	1,271,868
1962	4,003,421	(98 games)	NFL	40,851	64,892 (1)	4,068,313
	1,147,302	(56 games)	AFL	20,487	37,981 (1)	1,185,283
1961	3,986,159	(98 games)	NFL	40,675	39,029 (1)	4,025,188
	1,002,657	(56 games)	AFL	17,904	29,556 (1)	1,032,213
1960	3,128,296	(78 games)	NFL	40,106	67,325 (1)	3,195,621
	926,156	(56 games)	AFL	16,538	32,183 (1)	958,339
1959	3,140,000	(72 games)		43,617	57,545 (1)	3,197,545
1958	3,006,124	(72 games)		41,752	123,659 (2)	3,129,783
1957	2,836,318	(72 games)		39,393	119,579 (2)	2,955,897
1956	2,551,263	(72 games)		35,434	56,836 (1)	2,608,099
1955	2,521,836	(72 games)		35,026	85,693 (1)	2,607,529
1954	2,190,571	(72 games)		30,425	43,827 (1)	2,234,398
1953	2,164,585	(72 games)		30,064	54,577 (1)	2,219,162
1952	2,052,126	(72 games)		28,502	97,507 (2)	2,149,633
1951	1,913,019	(72 games)		26,570	57,522 (1)	1,970,541
1950	1,977,753	(78 games)		25,356	136,647 (3)	2,114,400
1949	1,391,735	(60 games)		23,196	27,980 (1)	1,419,715
1948	1,525,243	(60 games)		25,421	36,309 (1)	1,561,552
1947	1,837,437	(60 games)		30,624	66,268 (2)	1,903,705
1946	1,732,135	(55 games)		31,493	58,346 (1)	1,790,481
1945	1,270,401	(50 games)		25,408	32,178 (1)	1,302,579
1944	1,019,649	(50 games)		20,393	46,016 (1)	1,065,665
1943	969,128	(40 games)		24,228	71,315 (2)	1,040,443
1942	887,920	(55 games)		16,144	36,006 (1)	923,926
1941	1,108,615	(55 games)		20,157	55,870 (2)	1,164,485
1940	1,063,025	(55 games)		19,328	36,034 (1)	1,099,059
1939	1,071,200	(55 games)		19,476	32,279 (1)	1,103,479
1938	937,197	(55 games)		17,040	48,120 (1)	985,317
1937	963,039	(55 games)		17,510	15,878 (1)	978,917
1936	816,007	(54 games)		15,111	29,545 (1)	845,552
1935	638,178	(53 games)		12,041	15,000 (1)	653,178
1934	492,684	(60 games)		8,211	35,059 (1)	527,743

Record

*Players' 57-day strike reduced 224-game schedule to 126 games.
**Players' 24-day strike reduced 224-game schedule to 210 games.
***The Week 8 Miami at San Diego game is not included. The game was moved to Arizona due to the San Diego wildfires and tickets were distributed at no charge.
****The Week 14 N.Y. Giants at Minnesota game is not included. The game was moved to Detroit due to the Minneapolis blizzard. Original game tickets were cross-honored at Ford Field. Remaining tickets were distributed at no charge.

Records

Compiled by Elias Sports Bureau.

The following records reflect all available official information on the National Football League from its formation in 1920 to date. Also included are all applicable records from the American Football League, 1960-69.

Individuals eligible for Rookie records are players who were in their first season of professional football and had not been on the roster of another professional football team, including teams in other leagues, for any regular-season or postseason games in a previous season. Eligible players, therefore, include those who were under contract to a National Football League club for a previous season but were terminated prior to their club's first regular-season game and not re-signed, or who were placed on Reserve/Injured (or another category of the Reserve List) prior to their club's first regular-season game and were not activated during the rest of the regular season or postseason.

INDIVIDUAL RECORDS

SERVICE
Most Seasons
- 26   George Blanda, Chi. Bears, 1949, 1950-58; Baltimore, 1950; Houston, 1960-66; Oakland, 1967-1975
- 25   Morten Andersen, New Orleans, 1982-1994; Atlanta, 1995-2000; N.Y. Giants, 2001; Kansas City, 2002-03; Minnesota, 2004; Atlanta, 2006-07
- 23   Gary Anderson, Pittsburgh, 1982-1994; Philadelphia, 1995-96; San Francisco, 1997; Minnesota, 1998-2002; Tennessee, 2003-04
-      John Carney, Tampa Bay, 1988-89; L.A. Rams, 1990: San Diego, 1990-2000; New Orleans, 2001-06; Jacksonville, 2007; Kansas City, 2007; N.Y. Giants, 2008; New Orleans, 2009-2010

Most Seasons, One Club
- 21   Jason Hanson, Detroit, 1992-2012
- 20   Jackie Slater, L.A. Rams, 1976-1994; St. Louis, 1995
-      Darrell Green, Washington, 1983-2002
- 19   Jim Marshall, Minnesota, 1961-1979
-      Bruce Matthews, Houston, 1983-1996; Tennessee, 1997-2001

Most Games Played, Career
- 382   Morten Andersen, New Orleans, 1982-1994; Atlanta, 1995-2000; N.Y. Giants, 2001; Kansas City, 2002-03; Minnesota, 2004; Atlanta, 2006-07
- 353   Gary Anderson, Pittsburgh, 1982-1994; Philadelphia, 1995-96; San Francisco, 1997; Minnesota, 1998-2002; Tennessee, 2003-04
- 352   Jeff Feagles, New England, 1988-89; Philadelphia, 1990-93; Arizona, 1994-97; Seattle, 1998-2002; N.Y. Giants, 2003-09

Most Consecutive Games Played, Career
- 352   Jeff Feagles, New England, 1988-89; Philadelphia, 1990-93; Arizona, 1994-97; Seattle, 1998-2002; N.Y. Giants, 2003-09
- 299   Brett Favre, Green Bay, 1992-2007; N.Y. Jets, 2008; Minnesota, 2009-2010
- 282   Jim Marshall, Cleveland, 1960; Minnesota, 1961-1979

SCORING
Most Seasons Leading League
- 5   Don Hutson, Green Bay, 1940-44
-    Gino Cappelletti, Boston, 1961, 1963-66
- 3   Earl (Dutch) Clark, Portsmouth, 1932; Detroit, 1935-36
-    Pat Harder, Chi. Cardinals, 1947-49
-    Paul Hornung, Green Bay, 1959-1961
- 2   By 11 players

Most Consecutive Seasons Leading League
- 5   Don Hutson, Green Bay, 1940-44
- 4   Gino Cappelletti, Boston, 1963-66
- 3   Pat Harder, Chi. Cardinals, 1947-49
-    Paul Hornung, Green Bay, 1959-1961

POINTS
Most Points, Career
- 2,544   Morten Andersen, New Orleans, 1982-1994; Atlanta, 1995-2000; N.Y. Giants, 2001; Kansas City, 2002-03; Minnesota, 2004; Atlanta, 2006-07 (849-pat, 565-fg)
- 2,434   Gary Anderson, Pittsburgh, 1982-1994; Philadelphia 1995-96; San Francisco, 1997; Minnesota, 1998-2002; Tennessee, 2003-04 (820-pat, 538-fg)
- 2,150   Jason Hanson, Detroit, 1992-2012 (665-pat, 495-fg)

Most Points, Season
- 186   LaDainian Tomlinson, San Diego, 2006 (31-td)
- 176   Paul Hornung, Green Bay, 1960 (15-td, 41-pat, 15-fg)
- 168   Shaun Alexander, Seattle, 2005 (28-td)

Most Points, No Touchdowns, Season
- 166   David Akers, San Francisco, 2011 (34-pat, 44-fg)
- 164   Gary Anderson, Minnesota, 1998 (59-pat, 35-fg)
- 163   Jeff Wilkins, St. Louis, 2003 (46-pat, 39-fg)

Most Seasons, 100 or More Points
- 16   Jason Elam, Denver, 1993-2007; Atlanta, 2008
- 15   Adam Vinatieri, New England, 1996-2005; Indianapolis, 2006-08, 2010, 2012
- 14   Gary Anderson, Pittsburgh, 1983-85, 1988, 1991-94; Philadelphia 1996; San Francisco, 1997; Minnesota, 1998-2000; Tennessee, 2003
-    Morten Andersen, New Orleans, 1985-89, 1991-94; Atlanta, 1995, 1997-98; Kansas City, 2002-03

Most Points, Rookie Season
- 144   Kevin Butler, Chicago, 1985 (51-pat, 31-fg)
- 141   Mason Crosby, Green Bay, 2007 (48-pat, 31-fg)
-    Blair Walsh, Minnesota, 2012 (36-pat, 35-fg)
- 135   Dan Bailey, Dallas, 2011 (39-pat, 32-fg)

Most Points, Game
- 40   Ernie Nevers, Chi. Cardinals vs. Chi. Bears, Nov. 28, 1929 (6-td, 4-pat)
- 36   Dub Jones, Cleveland vs. Chi. Bears, Nov. 25, 1951 (6-td)
-    Gale Sayers, Chicago vs. San Francisco, Dec. 12, 1965 (6-td)
- 33   Paul Hornung, Green Bay vs. Baltimore, Oct. 8, 1961 (4-td, 6-pat, 1-fg)

Most Consecutive Games Scoring
- 360   Morten Andersen, New Orleans, 1983-1994; Atlanta, 1995-2000; N.Y. Giants, 2001; Kansas City, 2002-03; Minnesota, 2004; Atlanta, 2006-07
- 263   Jason Elam, Denver, 1993-2007; Atlanta, 2008-09
- 186   Jim Breech, Oakland, 1979; Cincinnati, 1980-1992

TOUCHDOWNS
Most Seasons Leading League
- 8   Don Hutson, Green Bay, 1935-38, 1941-44
- 3   Jim Brown, Cleveland, 1958-59, 1963
-    Lance Alworth, San Diego, 1964-66
-    Emmitt Smith, Dallas, 1992, 1994-95
- 2   By many players

Most Consecutive Seasons Leading League
- 4   Don Hutson, Green Bay, 1935-38, 1941-44
- 3   Lance Alworth, San Diego, 1964-66
- 2   By many players

Most Touchdowns, Career
- 208   Jerry Rice, San Francisco, 1985-2000; Oakland, 2001-04; Seattle, 2004 (10-r, 197-p, 1-ret)
- 175   Emmitt Smith, Dallas, 1990-2002; Arizona, 2003-04 (164-r, 11-p)
- 162   LaDainian Tomlinson, San Diego, 2001-09; N.Y. Jets, 2010-11 (145-r, 17-p)

Most Touchdowns, Season
- 31   LaDainian Tomlinson, San Diego, 2006 (28-r, 3-p)
- 28   Shaun Alexander, Seattle, 2005 (27-r, 1-p)
- 27   Priest Holmes, Kansas City, 2003 (27-r)

Most Touchdowns, Rookie, Season
- 22   Gale Sayers. Chicago, 1965 (14-r, 6-p)
- 20   Eric Dickerson, Rams, 1983 (18-r, 2-p)
- 17   Fred Taylor, Jacksonville, 1998 (14-r, 3-p)
  - Randy Moss, Minnesota, 1998 (17-p)
  - Edgerrin James, Indianapolis, 1999 (13-r, 4-p)
  - Clinton Portis, Denver, 2002 (15-r, 2-p)

Most Touchdowns, Game
- 6   Ernie Nevers, Chi. Cardinals vs. Chi. Bears, Nov. 28, 1929 (6-r)
  - Dub Jones, Cleveland vs. Chi. Bears, Nov. 25, 1951 (4-r, 2-p)
  - Gale Sayers, Chicago vs. San Francisco, Dec. 12, 1965 (4-r, 1-p, 1-ret)
- 5   Jimmy Conzelman, Rhode Island vs. Evansville, Oct. 15, 1922 (5-r)
  - Bob Shaw, Chi. Cardinals vs. Baltimore, Oct. 2, 1950 (5-p)
  - Jim Brown, Cleveland vs. Baltimore, Nov. 1, 1959 (5-r)
  - Abner Haynes, Dall. Texans vs. Oakland, Nov. 26, 1961 (4-r, 1-p)
  - Billy Cannon, Houston vs. N.Y. Titans, Dec. 10, 1961 (3-r, 2-p)
  - Cookie Gilchrist, Buffalo vs. N.Y. Jets, Dec. 8, 1963 (5-r)
  - Paul Hornung, Green Bay vs. Baltimore, Dec. 12, 1965 (3-r, 2-p)
  - Kellen Winslow, San Diego vs. Oakland, Nov. 22, 1981 (5-p)
  - Jerry Rice, San Francisco vs. Atlanta, Oct. 14, 1990 (5-p)
  - James Stewart, Jacksonville vs. Philadelphia, Oct. 12, 1997 (5-r)
  - Shaun Alexander, Seattle vs. Minnesota, Sept. 29, 2002 (4-r, 1-p)
  - Clinton Portis, Denver vs. Kansas City, Dec. 7, 2003 (5-r)
- 4   By many players. Last time:
  - Doug Martin, Tampa Bay vs. Oakland, Nov. 4, 2012 (4-r)

Most Consecutive Games Scoring Touchdowns
- 18   Lenny Moore, Baltimore, 1963-65
  - LaDainian Tomlinson, San Diego, 2004-05
- 14   O.J. Simpson, Buffalo, 1975
- 13   John Riggins, Washington, 1982-83
  - George Rogers, Washington, 1985-86
  - Jerry Rice, San Francisco, 1986-87

POINTS AFTER TOUCHDOWN

Most Seasons Leading League
- 8   George Blanda, Chi. Bears, 1956; Houston, 1961-62; Oakland, 1967-69, 1972, 1974
- 4   Bob Waterfield, Cleveland, 1945; Los Angeles, 1946, 1950, 1952
- 3   Earl (Dutch) Clark, Portsmouth, 1932; Detroit, 1935-36 Jack Manders, Chi. Bears, 1933-35
  - Don Hutson, Green Bay, 1941-42, 1945

Most (Kicking) Points After Touchdown Attempted, Career
- 959   George Blanda, Chi. Bears, 1949, 1950-58; Baltimore, 1950; Houston, 1960-66; Oakland, 1967-1975
- 859   Morten Andersen, New Orleans, 1982-1994; Atlanta, 1995-2000; N.Y. Giants, 2001; Kansas City, 2002-03; Minnesota, 2004; Atlanta, 2006-07
- 827   Gary Anderson, Pittsburgh, 1982-1994; Philadelphia 1995-96; San Francisco, 1997; Minnesota, 1998-2002; Tennessee, 2003-04

Most (Kicking) Points After Touchdown Attempted, Season
- 74   Stephen Gostkowski, New England, 2007
- 70   Uwe von Schamann, Miami, 1984
- 69   Mason Crosby, Green Bay, 2011

Most (Kicking) Points After Touchdown Attempted, Game
- 10   Charlie Gogolak, Washington vs. N.Y. Giants, Nov. 27, 1966
- 9   Pat Harder, Chi. Cardinals vs. N.Y. Giants, Oct. 17, 1948; vs. N.Y. Bulldogs, Nov. 13, 1949
  - Bob Waterfield, Los Angeles vs. Baltimore, Oct. 22, 1950
  - Bob Thomas, Chicago vs. Green Bay, Dec. 7, 1980
- 8   By many players

Most (One-Point) Points After Touchdown, Career
- 943   George Blanda, Chi. Bears, 1949, 1950-58; Baltimore, 1950; Houston, 1960-66; Oakland, 1967-1975
- 849   Morten Andersen, New Orleans, 1982-1994; Atlanta, 1995-2000; N.Y. Giants, 2001; Kansas City, 2002-03; Minnesota, 2004, Atlanta, 2006-07
- 820   Gary Anderson, Pittsburgh, 1982-1994; Philadelphia 1995-96; San Francisco, 1997; Minnesota, 1998-2002; Tennessee, 2003-04

Most (One-Point) Points After Touchdown, Season
- 74   Stephen Gostkowski, New England, 2007
- 68   Mason Crosby, Green Bay, 2011
- 66   Uwe von Schamann, Miami, 1984
  - Stephen Gostkowski, New England, 2012

Most (One-Point) Points After Touchdown, Game
- 9   Pat Harder, Chi. Cardinals vs. N.Y. Giants, Oct. 17, 1948
  - Bob Waterfield, Los Angeles vs. Baltimore, Oct. 22, 1950
  - Charlie Gogolak, Washington vs. N.Y. Giants, Nov. 27, 1966
- 8   By many players

Most Consecutive (Kicking) Points After Touchdown
- 422   Matt Stover, Baltimore, 1996-2008; Indianapolis, 2009
- 371   Jason Elam, Denver, 1993-2002
  - Jeff Wilkins, St. Louis, 1999-2007
- 322   Jay Feely, Atlanta, 2002-04; N.Y. Giants, 2005-06; Miami, 2007; N.Y. Jets, 2008-09; Arizona, 2010-12 (current)

Highest (Kicking) Points After Touchdown Percentage, Career (200 points after touchdown)
- 100.00   Nick Folk, Dallas, 2007-09; N.Y. Jets, 2010-12 (242-242)
- 99.75   Rian Lindell, Seattle, 2000-02; Buffalo, 2003-2012 (401-402)
- 99.72   Stephen Gostkowski, New England, 2006-2011 (355-356)

Most (Kicking) Points After Touchdown, No Misses, Season
- 74   Stephen Gostkowski, New England, 2007
- 66   Stephen Gostkowski, New England, 2012
- 64   Jeff Wilkins, St. Louis, 1999

Most (Kicking) Points After Touchdown, No Misses, Game
- 9   Pat Harder, Chi. Cardinals vs. N.Y. Giants, Oct. 17, 1948

Bob Waterfield, Los Angeles vs. Baltimore,
    Oct. 22, 1950
  8   By many players

Most Two-Point Conversions, Career
Two-point conversions include AFL (1960-69) and NFL (since 1994).
  7   Marshall Faulk, Indianapolis, 1994-98; St. Louis, 1999-2005
  6   Terance Mathis, Atlanta, 1994-2001; Pittsburgh, 2002
  5   Cris Carter, Minnesota, 1994-2001; Miami, 2002
     Rob Moore, N.Y. Jets, 1994; Arizona, 1995-99
     Willie Jackson, Jacksonville, 1995-97; Cincinnati, 1998-99; New Orleans, 2000-01; Washington, 2002
     Keenan McCardell, Cleveland, 1994-95; Jacksonville, 1996-2001; Tampa Bay, 2002-03; San Diego, 2004-06, Washington, 2007
     Marvin Harrison, Indianapolis, 1996-2008
     Marcus Pollard, Indianapolis, 1995-2004; Detroit, 2005-06; Seattle, 2007; Atlanta, 2008
     Todd Heap, Baltimore, 2001-2010; Arizona, 2011-12
     Hines Ward, Pittsburgh, 1998-2011
     Edgerrin James, Indianapolis, 1999-2005; Arizona, 2006-08; Seattle, 2009

Most Two-Point Conversions, Season
  4   Todd Heap, Baltimore, 2003
  3   Gino Cappelletti, Boston, 1960
     Richie Lucas, Buffalo, 1961
     Ronnie Harmon, San Diego, 1994
     Haywood Jeffires, Houston, 1994
     Tom Tupa, Cleveland, 1994
     Terance Mathis, Atlanta, 1995
     Lamar Smith, Seattle, 1996
     Cris Carter, Minnesota, 1997
     Terrell Davis, Denver, 1997
     James Stewart, Detroit, 2000
     Hines Ward, Pittsburgh, 2002
     Brian Finneran, Atlanta, 2005
     Reggie Bush, New Orleans, 2007
  2   By many players

Most Two-Point Conversions, Game
  2   Brett Perriman, Detroit vs. Green Bay, Nov. 6, 1994

     Michael Jackson, Baltimore vs. New England, Oct. 6, 1996
     Terrell Davis, Denver vs. Atlanta, Sept. 28, 1997
     Charles Johnson, Pittsburgh vs. Tennessee, Nov. 1, 1998
     Marshall Faulk, St. Louis vs. Atlanta, Oct. 15, 2000
     Todd Heap, Baltimore vs. Cincinnati, Oct. 19, 2003
     Reggie Bush, New Orleans vs. St. Louis, Nov. 11, 2007
     Tarvaris Jackson, Minnesota vs. Denver, Dec. 30, 2007 (ot)
     Mewelde Moore, Pittsburgh vs. New England, Nov. 14, 2010
     Lance Moore, New Orleans vs. Houston, Sept. 25, 2011

FIELD GOALS
Most Seasons Leading League
  5   Lou Groza, Cleveland, 1950, 1952-54, 1957
  4   Jack Manders, Chi. Bears, 1933-34, 1936-37
     Ward Cuff, N.Y. Giants, 1938-39, 1943; Green Bay, 1947
     Mark Moseley, Washington, 1976-77, 1979, 1982
  3   Bob Waterfield, Los Angeles, 1947, 1949, 1951
     Gino Cappelletti, Boston, 1961, 1963-64
     Fred Cox, Minnesota, 1965, 1969-1970
     Jan Stenerud, Kansas City, 1967, 1970, 1975

Most Consecutive Seasons Leading League
  3   Lou Groza, Cleveland, 1952-54
  2   Jack Manders, Chi. Bears, 1933-34
     Armand Niccolai, Pittsburgh, 1935-36
     Jack Manders, Chi. Bears, 1936-37
     Ward Cuff, N.Y. Giants, 1938-39
     Clark Hinkle, Green Bay, 1940-41
     Cliff Patton, Philadelphia, 1948-49
     Gino Cappelletti, Boston, 1963-64
     Jim Turner, N.Y. Jets, 1968-69
     Fred Cox, Minnesota, 1969-1970
     Mark Moseley, Washington, 1976-77
     Chip Lohmiller, Washington, 1991-92
     Pete Stoyanovich, Miami, 1991-92

Most Field Goals Attempted, Career
  709   Morten Andersen, New Orleans, 1982-1994; Atlanta, 1995-2000; N.Y. Giants, 2001; Kansas City, 2002-03; Minnesota, 2004; Atlanta, 2006-07
  672   Gary Anderson, Pittsburgh, 1982-1994; Philadelphia, 1995-96; San Francisco, 1997; Minnesota, 1998-2002; Tennessee, 2003-04
  641   George Blanda, Chi. Bears, 1949, 1950-58; Baltimore, 1950; Houston, 1960-66; Oakland, 1967-1975

Most Field Goals Attempted, Season
  52   David Akers, San Francisco, 2011
  49   Bruce Gossett, Los Angeles, 1966
     Curt Knight, Washington, 1971
  48   Chester Marcol, Green Bay, 1972

Most Field Goals Attempted, Game
  9   Jim Bakken, St. Louis vs. Pittsburgh, Sept. 24, 1967
  8   Lou Michaels, Pittsburgh vs. St. Louis, Dec. 2, 1962
     Garo Yepremian, Detroit vs. Minnesota, Nov. 13, 1966
     Jim Turner, N.Y. Jets vs. Buffalo, Nov. 3, 1968
     Billy Cundiff, Dallas vs. N.Y. Giants, Sept. 15, 2003 (ot)
     Rob Bironas, Tennessee vs. Houston, Oct. 21, 2007
  7   By many players

Most Field Goals, Career
  565   Morten Andersen, New Orleans, 1982-1994; Atlanta, 1995-2000; N.Y. Giants, 2001; Kansas City, 2002-03; Minnesota, 2004; Atlanta, 2006-07
  538   Gary Anderson, Pittsburgh, 1982-1994; Philadelphia, 1995-96; San Francisco, 1997; Minnesota, 1998-2002; Tennessee, 2003-04
  495   Jason Hanson, Detroit, 1992-2012

Most Field Goals, Season
  44   David Akers, San Francisco, 2011
  40   Neil Rackers, Arizona, 2005
  39   Olindo Mare, Miami, 1999
     Jeff Wilkins, St. Louis, 2003

Most Field Goals, Rookie, Season
  35   Ali Haji-Sheikh, N.Y. Giants, 1983
     Blair Walsh, Minnesota, 2012
  34   Richie Cunningham, Dallas, 1997
  33   Chester Marcol, Green Bay, 1972

Most Field Goals, Game
  8   Rob Bironas, Tennessee vs. Houston, Oct. 21, 2007
  7   Jim Bakken, St. Louis vs. Pittsburgh, Sept. 24, 1967
     Rich Karlis, Minnesota vs. L.A. Rams, Nov. 5, 1989 (ot)
     Chris Boniol, Dallas vs. Green Bay, Nov. 18, 1996
     Billy Cundiff, Dallas vs. N.Y. Giants, Sept. 15, 2003 (ot)
     Shayne Graham, Cincinnati vs. Baltimore, Nov. 11, 2007
  6   By many players

Most Field Goals, One Quarter
  4   Garo Yepremian, Detroit vs. Minnesota, Nov. 13, 1966 (second quarter)
     Curt Knight, Washington vs. N.Y. Giants, Nov. 15, 1970 (second quarter)

Roger Ruzek, Dallas vs. N.Y. Giants, Nov. 2, 1987
(fourth quarter)
Cary Blanchard, Indianapolis vs. Buffalo,
Sept. 21 1997 (second quarter)
Sebastian Janikowski, Oakland vs. Chicago,
Oct. 5, 2003 (second quarter)
Jeff Wilkins, St. Louis vs. Baltimore, Nov. 9, 2003
(fourth quarter)
Lawrence Tynes, Kansas City vs. New England,
Nov. 27, 2005 (second quarter)
Shayne Graham, Cincinnati vs. Baltimore,
Nov. 11, 2007 (fourth quarter)
3   By many players
Most Consecutive Games Scoring Field Goals
38   Matt Stover, Baltimore, 1999-2001
33   David Akers, Philadelphia, 2010;
San Francisco, 2011-12 (current)
31   Fred Cox, Minnesota, 1968-1970
Most Consecutive Field Goals
42   Mike Vanderjagt, Indianapolis, 2002-04
40   Gary Anderson, San Francisco, 1997;
Minnesota, 1998
36   Matt Stover, Baltimore, 2005-06
Longest Field Goal
63   Tom Dempsey, New Orleans vs. Detroit, Nov. 8, 1970
Jason Elam, Denver vs. Jacksonville, Oct. 25, 1998
Sebastian Janikowski, Oakland vs. Denver,
Sept. 12, 2011
David Akers, San Francisco vs. Green Bay,
Sept. 9, 2012

62   Matt Bryant, Tampa Bay vs. Philadelphia,
Oct. 22, 2006
61   Sebastian Janikowski, Oakland vs. Cleveland,
Dec. 27, 2009
Jay Feely, Arizona vs. Buffalo, Oct. 14, 2012
Highest Field Goal Pct., Career (100 field goals)
86.19   Nate Kaeding, San Diego, 2004-2011; Miami, 2012
(181-210)
86.47   Mike Vanderjagt, Indianapolis, 1998-2005; Dallas,
2006 (230-266)
85.60   Rob Bironas, Tennessee, 2005-2012 (214-250)
Highest Field Goal Pct., Season (Qualifiers)
100.00   Tony Zendejas, L.A. Rams, 1991 (17-17)
Gary Anderson, Minnesota, 1998 (35-35)
Jeff Wilkins, St. Louis, 2000 (17-17)
Mike Vanderjagt, Indianapolis, 2003 (37-37)
96.43   Chris Boniol, Dallas, 1995 (28-27)
96.30   Norm Johnson, Atlanta, 1993 (27-26)
Pete Stoyanovich, Kansas City, 1997 (27-26)
Most Field Goals, No Misses, Game
8   Rob Bironas, Tennessee vs. Houston, Oct. 21, 2007
7   Rich Karlis, Minnesota vs. L.A. Rams, Nov. 5, 1989
(ot)
Chris Boniol, Dallas vs. Green Bay, Nov. 18, 1996
Shayne Graham, Cincinnati vs. Baltimore,
Nov. 11, 2007
6   By many players
Most Field Goals, 50 or More Yards, Career
52   Jason Hanson, Detroit, 1992-2012
42   John Kasay, Seattle, 1991-94; Carolina, 1995-99,
2001-2010; New Orleans, 2011
Sebastian Janikowski, Oakland, 2000-2012
40   Morten Andersen, New Orleans, 1982-1994;
Atlanta, 1995-2000; N.Y. Giants, 2001;
Kansas City, 2002-03; Minnesota, 2004;
Atlanta, 2006-07
Most Field Goals, 50 or More Yards, Season
10   Blair Walsh, Minnesota, 2012
8   Morten Andersen, Atlanta, 1995

Jason Hanson, Detroit, 2008
7   David Akers, San Francisco, 2011
Phil Dawson, Cleveland, 2011
Sebastian Janikowski, Oakland, 2011
Phil Dawson, Cleveland, 2012
Greg Zuerlein, St. Louis, 2012
Most Field Goals, 50 or More Yards, Game
3   Morten Andersen, Atlanta vs. New Orleans,
Dec. 10, 1995
Neil Rackers, Arizona vs. Seattle, Oct. 24, 2004
Kris Brown, Houston vs. Miami, Oct. 7, 2007
Conner Barth, Tampa Bay vs. Miami, Nov. 15, 2009
Sebastian Janikowski, Oakland vs. Houston,
Oct. 9, 2011
Josh Scobee, Jacksonville vs. Baltimore,
Oct. 24, 2011
Phil Dawson, Cleveland vs. Baltimore,
Sept. 27, 2012
Blair Walsh, Minnesota vs. St. Louis, Dec. 16, 2012
2   By many players. Last time: Sebastian Janikowski,
Oakland vs. Kansas City, Dec. 16, 2012

SAFETIES
Most Safeties, Career
4   Ted Hendricks, Baltimore, 1969-1973; Green Bay,
1974; Oakland, 1975-1981; L.A. Raiders, 1982-83
Doug English, Detroit, 1975-79, 1981-85
Jared Allen, Kansas City, 2004-07;
Minnesota, 2008-2012
3   Bill McPeak, Pittsburgh, 1949-1957
Charlie Krueger, San Francisco, 1959-1973
Ernie Stautner, Pittsburgh, 1950-1963
Jim Katcavage, N.Y. Giants, 1956-1968
Roger Brown, Detroit, 1960-66; Los Angeles,
1967-69
Bruce Maher, Detroit, 1960-67; N.Y. Giants, 1968-69
Ron McDole, St. Louis, 1961; Houston, 1962;
Buffalo, 1963-1970; Washington, 1971-78
Alan Page, Minnesota, 1967-1978; Chicago,
1979-1981
Lyle Alzado, Denver, 1971-78; Cleveland,
1979-1981; L.A. Raiders, 1982-85
Rulon Jones, Denver, 1980-88
Steve McMichael, New England, 1980; Chicago,
1981-1993; Green Bay, 1994
Kevin Greene, L.A. Rams, 1985-1992; Pittsburgh,
1993-95; Carolina, 1996, 1998-99;
San Francisco, 1997
Burt Grossman, San Diego, 1989-1993;
Philadelphia, 1994
Eric Swann, Phoenix, 1991-93; Arizona, 1994-99;
Carolina, 2000
Dan Saleaumua, Detroit, 1987-88; Kansas City,
1989-1996; Seattle, 1997-98
Derrick Thomas, Kansas City, 1989-1999
Bryant Young, San Francisco, 1994-2007
Jason Taylor, Miami, 1997-2007; Washington, 2008;
Miami, 2009; N.Y. Jets, 2010; Miami, 2011
2   By many players
Most Safeties, Season
2   Tom Nash, Green Bay, 1932
Willie Wilkin, Washington, 1942
Roger Brown, Detroit, 1962
Ron McDole, Buffalo, 1964
Alan Page, Minnesota, 1971
Fred Dryer, Los Angeles, 1973
Benny Barnes, Dallas, 1973
James Young, Houston, 1977
Doug English, Detroit, 1983
Don Blackmon, New England, 1985

Tim Harris, Green Bay, 1988
Brian Jordan, Atlanta, 1991
Burt Grossman, San Diego, 1992
Rod Stephens, Seattle, 1993
Bryant Young, San Francisco, 1996
Jared Allen, Minnesota, 2008
Jameel McClain, Baltimore, 2008

Most Safeties, Game
2   Fred Dryer, Los Angeles vs. Green Bay,
     Oct. 21, 1973

RUSHING

Most Seasons Leading League
8   Jim Brown, Cleveland, 1957-1961, 1963-65
4   Steve Van Buren, Philadelphia, 1945, 1947-49
     O.J. Simpson, Buffalo, 1972-73, 1975-76
     Eric Dickerson, L.A. Rams, 1983-84, 1986;
       Indianapolis, 1988
     Emmitt Smith, Dallas, 1991-93, 1995
     Barry Sanders, Detroit, 1990, 1994, 1996-97
3   Earl Campbell, Houston, 1978-1980

Most Consecutive Seasons Leading League
5   Jim Brown, Cleveland, 1957-1961
3   Steve Van Buren, Philadelphia, 1947-49
     Jim Brown, Cleveland, 1963-65
     Earl Campbell, Houston, 1978-1980
     Emmitt Smith, Dallas, 1991-93
2   By many players

ATTEMPTS

Most Seasons Leading League
6   Jim Brown, Cleveland, 1958-59, 1961, 1963-65
4   Steve Van Buren, Philadelphia, 1947-1950
     Walter Payton, Chicago, 1976-79
3   Cookie Gilchrist, Buffalo, 1963-64; Denver, 1965
     Jim Nance, Boston, 1966-67, 1969
     O.J. Simpson, Buffalo, 1973-75
     Eric Dickerson, L.A. Rams, 1983, 1986;
       Indianapolis, 1988
     Emmitt Smith, Dallas, 1991, 1994-95

Most Consecutive Seasons Leading League
4   Steve Van Buren, Philadelphia, 1947-1950
     Walter Payton, Chicago, 1976-79
3   Jim Brown, Cleveland, 1963-65
     Cookie Gilchrist, Buffalo, 1963-64; Denver, 1965
     O.J. Simpson, Buffalo, 1973-75
2   By many players

Most Attempts, Career
4,409   Emmitt Smith, Dallas, 1990-2002; Arizona, 2003-04
3,838   Walter Payton, Chicago, 1975-1987
3,518   Curtis Martin, New England, 1995-97;
         N.Y. Jets, 1998-2005

Most Attempts, Season
416   Larry Johnson, Kansas City, 2006
410   Jamal Anderson, Atlanta, 1998
407   James Wilder, Tampa Bay, 1984

Most Attempts, Rookie, Season
390   Eric Dickerson, L.A. Rams, 1983
378   George Rogers, New Orleans, 1981
369   Edgerrin James, Indianapolis, 1999

Most Attempts, Game
45   Jamie Morris, Washington vs. Cincinnati,
     Dec. 17, 1988 (ot)
43   Butch Woolfolk, N.Y. Giants vs. Philadelphia,
     Nov. 20, 1983
     James Wilder, Tampa Bay vs. Green Bay,
     Sept. 30, 1984 (ot)
     Rudi Johnson, Cincinnati vs. Houston, Nov. 9, 2003
42   James Wilder, Tampa Bay vs. Pittsburgh,
     Oct. 30, 1983

Terrell Davis, Denver vs. Buffalo, Oct. 26, 1997 (ot)
Ricky Williams, Miami vs. Buffalo, Sept. 21, 2003

YARDS GAINED

Most Yards Gained, Career
18,355   Emmitt Smith, Dallas, 1990-2002; Arizona, 2003-04
16,726   Walter Payton, Chicago, 1975-1987
15,269   Barry Sanders, Detroit, 1989-1998

Most Seasons, 1,000 or More Yards Rushing
11   Emmitt Smith, Dallas, 1991-2001
10   Walter Payton, Chicago, 1976-1981, 1983-86
     Barry Sanders, Detroit, 1989-1998
     Curtis Martin, New England, 1995-97; N.Y. Jets,
       1998-2004
8   Franco Harris, Pittsburgh, 1972, 1974-79, 1983
     Tony Dorsett, Dallas, 1977-1981, 1983-85
     Thurman Thomas, Buffalo, 1989-1996
     Jerome Bettis, L.A. Rams, 1993-94; Pittsburgh,
       1996-2001
     LaDainian Tomlinson, San Diego, 2001-08
     Steven Jackson, St. Louis, 2005-2012

Most Consecutive Seasons, 1,000 or More Yards Rushing
11   Emmitt Smith, Dallas, 1991-2001
10   Barry Sanders, Detroit, 1989-1998
     Curtis Martin, New England, 1995-97; N.Y. Jets,
       1998-2004
8   Thurman Thomas, Buffalo, 1989-1996
     LaDainian Tomlinson, San Diego, 2001-08
     Steven Jackson, St. Louis, 2005-2012

Most Yards Gained, Season
2,105   Eric Dickerson, L.A. Rams, 1984
2,097   Adrian Peterson, Minnesota, 2012
2,066   Jamal Lewis, Baltimore, 2003

Most Yards Gained, Rookie, Season
1,808   Eric Dickerson, L.A. Rams, 1983
1,674   George Rogers, New Orleans, 1981
1,613   Alfred Morris, Washington, 2012

Most Yards Gained, Game
296   Adrian Peterson, Minnesota vs. San Diego,
     Nov. 4, 2007
295   Jamal Lewis, Baltimore vs. Cleveland,
     Sept. 14, 2003
286   Jerome Harrison, Cleveland vs. Kansas City,
     Dec. 20, 2009

Most Games, 200 or More Yards Rushing, Career
6   O.J. Simpson, Buffalo, 1969-1977; San Francisco,
     1978-79
5   Tiki Barber, N.Y. Giants, 1997-2006
4   Jim Brown, Cleveland, 1957-1965
     Earl Campbell, Houston, 1978-1984; New Orleans,
     1984-85
     Barry Sanders, Detroit, 1989-1998
     LaDainian Tomlinson, San Diego, 2001-09;
     N.Y. Jets, 2010-11
     Adrian Peterson, Minnesota, 2007-2012

Most Games, 200 or More Yards Rushing, Season
4   Earl Campbell, Houston, 1980
3   O.J. Simpson, Buffalo, 1973
     Tiki Barber, N.Y. Giants, 2005
2   Jim Brown, Cleveland, 1963
     O.J. Simpson, Buffalo, 1976
     Walter Payton, Chicago, 1977
     Eric Dickerson, L.A. Rams, 1984
     Greg Bell, L.A. Rams, 1989
     Terrell Davis, Denver, 1997
     Barry Sanders, Detroit, 1997
     Corey Dillon, Cincinnati, 2000
     Marshall Faulk, St. Louis, 2000
     LaDainian Tomlinson, San Diego, 2002
     Ricky Williams, Miami, 2002

Jamal Lewis, Baltimore, 2003
LaDainian Tomlinson, San Diego, 2003
Larry Johnson, Kansas City, 2005
Willie Parker, Pittsburgh, 2006
Adrian Peterson, Minnesota, 2007
Michael Turner, Atlanta, 2008
Jamaal Charles, Kansas City, 2012
Adrian Peterson, Minnesota, 2012

Most Consecutive Games, 200 or More Yards Rushing
2   O.J. Simpson, Buffalo, 1973, 1976
    Earl Campbell, Houston, 1980
    Ricky Williams, Miami, 2002

Most Games, 100 or more Yards Rushing, Career
78 Emmitt Smith, Dallas, 1990-2002; Arizona, 2003-04
77 Walter Payton, Chicago, 1975-1987
76 Barry Sanders, Detroit, 1989-1998

Most Games, 100 or More Yards Rushing, Season
14 Barry Sanders, Detroit, 1997
12 Eric Dickerson, L.A. Rams, 1984
    Barry Foster, Pittsburgh, 1992
    Jamal Anderson, Atlanta, 1998
    Jamal Lewis, Baltimore, 2003
    Chris Johnson, Tennessee, 2009
11 O.J. Simpson, Buffalo, 1973
    Earl Campbell, Houston, 1979
    Marcus Allen, L.A. Raiders, 1985
    Eric Dickerson, L.A. Rams, 1986
    Emmitt Smith, Dallas, 1995
    Terrell Davis, Denver, 1998
    Shaun Alexander, Seattle, 2005
    Larry Johnson, Kansas City, 2006

Most Consecutive Games, 100 or More Yards Rushing
14 Barry Sanders, Detroit, 1997
12 Chris Johnson, Tennessee, 2009-2010
11 Marcus Allen, L.A. Raiders, 1985-86

Longest Run from Scrimmage
99 Tony Dorsett, Dallas vs. Minnesota, Jan. 3, 1983
    (TD)
98 Ahman Green, Green Bay vs. Denver, Dec. 28, 2003
    (TD)
97 Andy Uram, Green Bay vs. Chi. Cardinals,
    Oct. 8, 1939 (TD)
    Bob Gage, Pittsburgh vs. Chi. Bears, Dec. 4, 1949
    (TD)

AVERAGE GAIN
Highest Average Gain, Career (750 attempts)
7.02 Michael Vick, Atlanta, 2001-06; Philadelphia,
     2009-2012 (791-5,551)
6.36 Randall Cunningham, Philadelphia, 1985-1995;
     Minnesota, 1997-99; Dallas, 2000; Baltimore,
     2001 (775-4,928)
5.79 Jamaal Charles, Kansas City, 2008-2012
     (784-4,536)

Highest Average Gain, Season (Qualifiers)
8.45 Michael Vick, Atlanta, 2006 (123-1,039)
8.44 Beattie Feathers, Chi. Bears, 1934 (119-1,004)
7.98 Randall Cunningham, Philadelphia, 1990 (118-942)

Highest Average Gain, Game (10 attempts)
17.30 Michael Vick, Atlanta vs. Minnesota, Dec. 1, 2002
      (10-173)
17.09 Marion Motley, Cleveland vs. Pittsburgh,
      Oct. 29, 1950 (11-188)
16.70 Billy Grimes, Green Bay vs. N.Y. Yanks, Oct. 8, 1950
      (10-167)

TOUCHDOWNS
Most Seasons Leading League
5 Jim Brown, Cleveland, 1957-59, 1963, 1965
4 Steve Van Buren, Philadelphia, 1945, 1947-49

3 Abner Haynes, Dall. Texans, 1960-62
   Cookie Gilchrist, Buffalo, 1962-64
   Paul Lowe, L.A. Chargers, 1960; San Diego, 1961,
    1965
   Leroy Kelly, Cleveland, 1966-68
   Emmitt Smith, Dallas, 1992, 1994-95
   LaDainian Tomlinson, San Diego, 2004, 2006-07

Most Consecutive Seasons Leading League
3 Steve Van Buren, Philadelphia, 1947-49
   Jim Brown, Cleveland, 1957-59
   Abner Haynes, Dall. Texans, 1960-62
   Cookie Gilchrist, Buffalo, 1962-64
   Leroy Kelly, Cleveland, 1966-68

Most Touchdowns, Career
164 Emmitt Smith, Dallas, 1990-2002; Arizona, 2003-04
145 LaDainian Tomlinson, San Diego, 2001-09;
     N.Y. Jets, 2010-11
123 Marcus Allen, L.A. Raiders, 1982-1992; Kansas City,
     1993-97

Most Rushing Touchdowns, Season
28 LaDainian Tomlinson, San Diego, 2006
27 Priest Holmes, Kansas City, 2003
    Shaun Alexander, Seattle, 2005
25 Emmitt Smith, Dallas, 1995

Most Touchdowns, Rookie, Season
18 Eric Dickerson, L.A. Rams, 1983
15 Ickey Woods, Cincinnati, 1988
    Mike Anderson, Denver, 2000
    Clinton Portis, Denver, 2002
14 Gale Sayers, Chicago, 1965
    Barry Sanders, Detroit, 1989
    Curtis Martin, New England, 1995
    Fred Taylor, Jacksonville, 1998
    Cam Newton, Carolina, 2011

Most Touchdowns, Game
6 Ernie Nevers, Chi. Cardinals vs. Chi. Bears,
    Nov. 28, 1929
5 Jimmy Conzelman, Rhode Island vs. Evansville,
    Oct. 15, 1922
   Jim Brown, Cleveland vs. Baltimore, Nov. 1, 1959
   Cookie Gilchrist, Buffalo vs. N.Y. Jets, Dec. 8, 1963
   James Stewart, Jacksonville vs. Philadelphia,
    Oct. 12, 1997
   Clinton Portis, Denver vs. Kansas City, Dec. 7, 2003
4 By many players

Most Consecutive Games Rushing for Touchdowns
18 LaDainian Tomlinson, San Diego, 2004-05
13 John Riggins, Washington, 1982-83
    George Rogers, Washington, 1985-86
11 Lenny Moore, Baltimore, 1963-64
    Emmitt Smith, Dallas, 1994-95
    Emmitt Smith, Dallas, 1995
    Priest Holmes, Kansas City, 2002

PASSING
Most Seasons Leading League (Passer Rating)
6 Sammy Baugh, Washington, 1937, 1940, 1943,
    1945, 1947, 1949
   Steve Young San Francisco, 1991-94, 1996-97
4 Len Dawson, Dall. Texans; 1962; Kansas City, 1964,
    1966, 1968
   Roger Staubach, Dallas, 1971, 1973, 1978-79
   Ken Anderson, Cincinnati, 1974-75, 1981-82
3 Arnie Herber, Green Bay, 1932, 1934, 1936
   Norm Van Brocklin, Los Angeles, 1950, 1952, 1954
   Bart Starr, Green Bay, 1962, 1964, 1966
   Peyton Manning, Indianapolis, 2004-06

Most Consecutive Seasons Leading League (Passer Rating)
4 Steve Young, San Francisco, 1991-94
3 Peyton Manning, Indianapolis, 2004-06

2 Cecil Isbell, Green Bay, 1941-42
   Milt Plum, Cleveland, 1960-61
   Ken Anderson, Cincinnati, 1974-75, 1981-82
   Roger Staubach, Dallas, 1978-79
   Steve Young, San Francisco, 1996-97
   Aaron Rodgers, Green Bay, 2011-12

PASSER RATING
Highest Passer Rating, Career (1,500 attempts)
104.9 Aaron Rodgers, Green Bay, 2005-2012
 96.8 Steve Young, Tampa Bay, 1985-86; San Francisco, 1987-1999
 96.6 Tom Brady, New England, 2000-2012
Highest Passer Rating, Season (Qualifiers)
122.5 Aaron Rodgers, Green Bay, 2011
121.1 Peyton Manning, Indianapolis, 2004
117.2 Tom Brady, New England, 2007
Highest Passer Rating, Rookie, Season (Qualifiers)
102.4 Robert Griffin III, Washington, 2012
100.0 Russell Wilson, Seattle, 2012
 98.1 Ben Roethlisberger, Pittsburgh, 2004

ATTEMPTS
Most Seasons Leading League
5 Dan Marino, Miami, 1984, 1986, 1988, 1992, 1997
4 Sammy Baugh, Washington, 1937, 1943, 1947-48
   Johnny Unitas, Baltimore, 1957, 1959-1961
   George Blanda, Chi. Bears, 1953; Houston, 1963-65
3 Arnie Herber, Green Bay, 1932, 1934, 1936
   Sonny Jurgensen, Washington, 1966-67, 1969
   Drew Bledsoe, New England, 1994-96
   Brett Favre, Green Bay, 1999, 2005-06
Most Consecutive Seasons Leading League
3 Johnny Unitas, Baltimore, 1959-1961
   George Blanda, Houston, 1963-65
   Drew Bledsoe, New England, 1994-96
2 By many players
Most Passes Attempted, Career
10,169 Brett Favre, Atlanta, 1991; Green Bay, 1992-2007; N.Y. Jets, 2008; Minnesota, 2009-2010
 8,358 Dan Marino, Miami, 1983-1999
 7,793 Peyton Manning, Indianapolis, 1998-2010; Denver, 2012
Most Passes Attempted, Season
727 Matthew Stafford, Detroit, 2012
691 Drew Bledsoe, New England, 1994
679 Peyton Manning, Indianapolis, 2010
Most Passes Attempted, Rookie, Season
627 Andrew Luck, Indianapolis, 2012
590 Sam Bradford, St. Louis, 2010
575 Peyton Manning, Indianapolis, 1998
Most Passes Attempted, Game
70 Drew Bledsoe, New England vs. Minnesota, Nov. 13, 1994
69 Vinny Testaverde, N.Y. Jets vs. Baltimore, Dec. 24, 2000
68 George Blanda, Houston vs. Buffalo, Nov. 1, 1964
    Jon Kitna, Cincinnati vs. Pittsburgh, Dec. 30, 2001

COMPLETIONS
Most Seasons Leading League
6 Dan Marino, Miami, 1984-86, 1988, 1992, 1997
5 Sammy Baugh, Washington, 1937, 1943, 1945, 1947-48
4 George Blanda, Chi. Bears, 1953; Houston, 1963-65
   Sonny Jurgensen, Philadelphia, 1961; Washington, 1966-67, 1969
Most Consecutive Seasons Leading League
3 George Blanda, Houston, 1963-65
   Dan Marino, Miami, 1984-86

2 By many players
Most Passes Completed, Career
6,300 Brett Favre, Atlanta, 1991; Green Bay, 1992-2007; N.Y. Jets, 2008, Minnesota, 2009-2010
5,082 Peyton Manning, Indianapolis, 1998-2010; Denver, 2012
4,967 Dan Marino, Miami, 1983-1999
Most Passes Completed, Season
468 Drew Brees, New Orleans, 2011
450 Peyton Manning, Indianapolis, 2010
448 Drew Brees, New Orleans, 2010
Most Passes Completed, Rookie, Season
354 Sam Bradford, St. Louis, 2010
339 Andrew Luck, Indianapolis, 2012
326 Peyton Manning, Indianapolis, 1998
Most Passes Completed, Game
45 Drew Bledsoe, New England vs. Minnesota, Nov. 13, 1994 (ot)
43 Rich Gannon, Oakland vs. Pittsburgh, Sept. 15, 2002
    Matt Schaub, Houston vs. Jacksonville, Nov. 18, 2012 (ot)
42 Richard Todd, N.Y. Jets vs. San Francisco, Sept. 21, 1980
    Vinny Testaverde, N.Y. Jets vs. Seattle, Dec. 6, 1998
Most Consecutive Passes Completed
24 Donovan McNabb, Philadelphia vs. N.Y. Giants (10), Nov. 28, 2004; vs. Green Bay (14), Dec. 5, 2004
    Matt Schaub, Houston vs. Jacksonville, Nov. 18, 2012 (ot)
23 Peyton Manning, Indianapolis vs. Detroit (6), Dec. 14, 2008; vs. Jacksonville (17), Dec. 18, 2008
22 Joe Montana, San Francisco vs. Cleveland (5), Nov. 29, 1987; vs. Green Bay (17), Dec. 6, 1987
    Mark Brunell, Washington vs. Houston, Sept. 24, 2006
    David Carr, Houston vs. Buffalo, Nov. 19, 2006
    Matt Ryan, Atlanta vs. N.Y. Giants (10), Dec. 16, 2012; vs. Detroit (12), Dec. 22, 2012

COMPLETION PERCENTAGE
Most Seasons Leading League
8 Len Dawson, Dall. Texans, 1962; Kansas City, 1964-69, 1975
7 Sammy Baugh, Washington, 1940, 1942-43, 1945, 1947-49
5 Joe Montana, San Francisco, 1980-81, 1985, 1987, 1989
   Steve Young, San Francisco, 1992, 1994-97
Most Consecutive Seasons Leading League
6 Len Dawson, Kansas City, 1964-69
4 Steve Young, San Francisco, 1994-97
3 Sammy Baugh, Washington, 1947-49
   Otto Graham, Cleveland, 1953-55
   Milt Plum, Cleveland, 1959-1961
   Kurt Warner, St. Louis, 1999-2001
   Drew Brees, New Orleans, 2009-2011
Highest Completion Percentage, Career (1,500 attempts)
66.05 Chad Pennington, N.Y. Jets, 2000-07; Miami, 2008-2010 (2,471-1,632)
65.74 Aaron Rodgers, Green Bay, 2005-2012 (2,665-1,752)
65.62 Drew Brees, San Diego, 2001-05; New Orleans, 2006-2012 (6,149-4,035)
Highest Completion Percentage, Season (Qualifiers)
71.23 Drew Brees, New Orleans, 2011 (657-468)
70.62 Drew Brees, New Orleans, 2009 (514-363)
70.55 Ken Anderson, Cincinnati, 1982 (309-218)

Highest Completion Percentage, Rookie, Season (Qualifiers)
66.44 Ben Roethlisberger, Pittsburgh, 2004 (295-196)
65.65 Robert Griffin III, Washington, 2012 (393-258)
64.12 Russell Wilson, Seattle, 2012 (393-252)

Highest Completion Percentage, Game (20 attempts)
92.31 Kurt Warner, Arizona vs. Jacksonville, Sept. 20, 2009 (26-24)
91.30 Vinny Testaverde, Cleveland vs. L.A. Rams, Dec. 26, 1993 (23-21)
90.91 Ken Anderson, Cincinnati vs. Pittsburgh, Nov. 10, 1974 (22-20)

YARDS GAINED

Most Seasons Leading League
5 Sonny Jurgensen, Philadelphia, 1961-62; Washington, 1966-67, 1969
   Dan Marino, Miami, 1984-86, 1988, 1992
4 Sammy Baugh, Washington, 1937, 1940, 1947-48
   Johnny Unitas, Baltimore, 1957, 1959-1960, 1963
   Dan Fouts, San Diego, 1979-1982
   Drew Brees, New Orleans, 2006, 2008, 2011-12
3 Arnie Herber, Green Bay, 1932, 1934, 1936
   Sid Luckman, Chi. Bears, 1943, 1945-46
   John Brodie, San Francisco, 1965, 1968, 1970
   John Hadl, San Diego, 1965, 1968, 1971
   Joe Namath, N.Y. Jets, 1966-67, 1972

Most Consecutive Seasons Leading League
4 Dan Fouts, San Diego, 1979-1982
3 Dan Marino, Miami, 1984-86
2 By many players

Most Yards Gained, Career
71,838 Brett Favre, Atlanta, 1991; Green Bay, 1992-2007; N.Y. Jets, 2008, Minnesota, 2009-2010
61,361 Dan Marino, Miami, 1983-1999
59,487 Peyton Manning, Indianapolis, 1998-2010; Denver, 2012

Most Seasons, 3,000 or More Yards Passing
18 Brett Favre, Green Bay, 1992-2007; N.Y. Jets, 2008; Minnesota, 2009
14 Peyton Manning, Indianapolis, 1998-2010; Denver, 2012
13 Dan Marino, Miami, 1984-1992, 1994-95, 1997-98

Most Yards Gained, Season
5,476 Drew Brees, New Orleans, 2011
5,235 Tom Brady, New England, 2011
5,177 Drew Brees, New Orleans, 2012

Most Yards Gained, Rookie, Season
4,374 Andrew Luck, Indianapolis, 2012
4,051 Cam Newton, Carolina, 2011
3,739 Peyton Manning, Indianapolis, 1998

Most Yards Gained, Game
554 Norm Van Brocklin, Los Angeles vs. N.Y. Yanks, Sept. 28, 1951
527 Warren Moon, Houston vs. Kansas City, Dec. 16, 1990
     Matt Schaub, Houston vs. Jacksonville, Nov. 18, 2012 (ot)
522 Boomer Esiason, Arizona vs. Washington, Nov. 10, 1996 (ot)

Most Games, 400 or More Yards Passing, Career
13 Dan Marino, Miami, 1983-1999
9 Drew Brees, San Diego, 2001-05; New Orleans, 2006-2012
8 Peyton Manning, Indianapolis, 1998-2010; Denver, 2012

Most Games, 400 or More Yards Passing, Season
4 Dan Marino, Miami, 1984
3 Dan Marino, Miami, 1986
   Eli Manning, N.Y. Giants, 2011
   Tony Romo, Dallas, 2012

2 By many players

Most Consecutive Games, 400 or More Yards Passing
2 Dan Fouts, San Diego, 1982
   Dan Marino, Miami, 1984
   Phil Simms, N.Y. Giants, 1985
   Billy Volek, Tennessee, 2004
   Matt Cassel, New England, 2008
   Tom Brady, New England, 2011
   Cam Newton, Carolina, 2011

Most Games, 300 or More Yards Passing, Career
72 Peyton Manning, Indianapolis, 1998-2010; Denver, 2012
67 Drew Brees, San Diego, 2001-05; New Orleans, 2006-2012
63 Dan Marino, Miami, 1983-1999
    Peyton Manning, Indianapolis, 1998-2010

Most Games, 300 or More Yards Passing, Season
13 Drew Brees, New Orleans, 2011
11 Tom Brady, New England, 2011
10 Rich Gannon, Oakland, 2002
    Drew Brees, New Orleans, 2008
    Drew Brees, New Orleans, 2012

Most Consecutive Games, 300 or More Yards Passing
9 Drew Brees, New Orleans, 2011-12
6 Steve Young, San Francisco, 1998
   Kurt Warner, St. Louis, 2000
   Rich Gannon, Oakland, 2002
5 Joe Montana, San Francisco, 1982
   Kerry Collins, N.Y. Giants, 2001-02
   Drew Brees, New Orleans, 2006
   Kurt Warner, Arizona, 2008
   Tom Brady, New England, 2009
   Peyton Manning, Indianapolis, 2009
   Drew Brees, New Orleans, 2011
   Peyton Manning, Denver, 2012
   Drew Brees, New Orleans, 2012

Longest Pass Completion (All TDs except as noted)
99 Frank Filchock (to Farkas), Washington vs. Pittsburgh, Oct. 15, 1939
    George Izo (to Mitchell), Washington vs. Cleveland, Sept. 15, 1963
    Karl Sweetan (to Studstill), Detroit vs. Baltimore, Oct. 16, 1966
    Sonny Jurgensen (to Allen), Washington vs. Chicago, Sept. 15, 1968
    Jim Plunkett (to Branch), L.A. Raiders vs. Washington, Oct. 2, 1983
    Ron Jaworski (to Quick), Philadelphia vs. Atlanta, Nov. 10, 1985
    Stan Humphries (to Martin), San Diego vs. Seattle, Sept. 18, 1994
    Brett Favre (to Brooks), Green Bay vs. Chicago, Sept. 11, 1995
    Trent Green (to Boerigter), Kansas City vs. San Diego, Dec. 22, 2002
    Jeff Garcia (to Davis), Cleveland vs. Cincinnati, Oct. 17, 2004
    Gus Frerotte (to Berrian), Minnesota vs. Chicago, Nov. 30, 2008
    Tom Brady (to Welker), New England vs. Miami, Sept. 12, 2011
    Eli Manning (to Cruz), N.Y. Giants vs. N.Y. Jets, Dec. 24, 2011
98 Doug Russell (to Tinsley), Chi. Cardinals vs. Cleveland, Nov. 27, 1938
    Ogden Compton (to Lane), Chi. Cardinals vs. Green Bay, Nov. 13, 1955
    Bill Wade (to Farrington), Chicago Bears vs. Detroit, Oct. 8, 1961

Jacky Lee (to Dewveall), Houston vs. San Diego,
   Nov. 25, 1962
Earl Morrall (to Jones), N.Y. Giants vs. Pittsburgh,
   Sept. 11, 1966
Jim Hart (to Rashad), St. Louis vs. Los Angeles,
   Dec. 10, 1972 (no TD)
Bobby Hebert (to Haynes), Atlanta vs. New Orleans,
   Sept. 12, 1993
Charlie Batch (to Morton), Detroit vs. Chicago,
   Oct. 4, 1998
Ryan Fitzpatrick (to Owens), Buffalo vs. Jacksonville,
   Nov. 22, 2009
97 Pat Coffee (to Tinsley), Chi. Cardinals vs. Chi. Bears,
   Dec. 5, 1937
Bobby Layne (to Box), Detroit vs. Green Bay,
   Nov. 26, 1953
George Shaw (to Tarr), Denver vs. Boston,
   Sept. 21, 1962
Bernie Kosar (to Slaughter), Cleveland vs. Chicago,
   Oct. 23, 1989
Steve Young (to Taylor), San Francisco vs. Atlanta,
   Nov. 3, 1991

AVERAGE GAIN
Most Seasons Leading League
7 Sid Luckman, Chi. Bears, 1939-1943, 1946-47
5 Steve Young, San Francisco, 1991-94, 1997
3 Arnie Herber, Green Bay, 1932, 1934, 1936
   Norm Van Brocklin, Los Angeles, 1950, 1952, 1954
   Len Dawson, Dall. Texans, 1962; Kansas City, 1966,
   1968
   Bart Starr, Green Bay, 1966-68
   Kurt Warner, St. Louis, 1999-2001
   Philip Rivers, San Diego, 2008-2010
Most Consecutive Seasons Leading League
5 Sid Luckman, Chi. Bears, 1939-1943
4 Steve Young, San Francisco, 1991-94
3 Bart Starr, Green Bay, 1966-68
   Kurt Warner, St. Louis, 1999-2001
   Philip Rivers, San Diego, 2008-2010
Highest Average Gain, Career (1,500 Attempts)
8.63 Otto Graham, Cleveland, 1950-55 (1,565-13,499)
8.42 Sid Luckman, Chi. Bears, 1939-1950 (1,744-14,686)
8.16 Norm Van Brocklin, Los Angeles, 1949-1957;
   Philadelphia, 1958-1960 (2,895-23,611)
Highest Average Gain, Season (Qualifiers)
11.17 Tommy O'Connell, Cleveland, 1957 (110-1,229)
10.86 Sid Luckman, Chi. Bears, 1943 (202-2,194)
10.55 Otto Graham, Cleveland, 1953 (258-2,722)
Highest Average Gain, Rookie, Season (Qualifiers)
9.411 Greg Cook, Cincinnati, 1969 (197-1,854)
9.409 Bob Waterfield, Cleveland, 1945 (171-1,609)
8.88 Ben Roethlisberger, Pittsburgh, 2004 (295-2,621)
Highest Average Gain, Game (20 attempts)
18.58 Sammy Baugh, Washington vs. Boston,
   Oct. 31, 1948 (24-446)
18.50 Johnny Unitas, Baltimore vs. Atlanta, Nov. 12, 1967
   (20-370)
17.71 Joe Namath, N.Y. Jets vs. Baltimore, Sept. 24, 1972
   (28-496)

TOUCHDOWNS
Most Seasons Leading League
4 Johnny Unitas, Baltimore, 1957-1960
   Len Dawson, Dall. Texans, 1962; Kansas City, 1963,
   1965-66
   Steve Young, San Francisco, 1992-94, 1998
   Brett Favre, Green Bay, 1995-97, 2003
   Drew Brees, New Orleans, 2008-09, 2011-12
3 Arnie Herber, Green Bay, 1932, 1934, 1936

Sid Luckman, Chi. Bears, 1943, 1945-46
Y.A. Tittle, San Francisco, 1955; N.Y. Giants, 1962-63
Dan Marino, Miami, 1984-86
Peyton Manning, Indianapolis, 2000, 2004, 2006
Tom Brady, New England, 2002, 2007, 2010
2 By many players
Most Consecutive Seasons Leading League
4 Johnny Unitas, Baltimore, 1957-1960
3 Dan Marino, Miami, 1984-86
   Steve Young, San Francisco, 1992-94
   Brett Favre, Green Bay, 1995-97
2 By many players
Most Touchdown Passes, Career
508 Brett Favre, Atlanta, 1991; Green Bay, 1992-2007;
   N.Y. Jets, 2008, Minnesota, 2009-2010
436 Peyton Manning, Indianapolis, 1998-2010;
   Denver, 2012
420 Dan Marino, Miami, 1983-1999
Most Touchdown Passes, Season
50 Tom Brady, New England, 2007
49 Peyton Manning, Indianapolis, 2004
48 Dan Marino, Miami, 1984
Most Touchdown Passes, Rookie, Season
26 Peyton Manning, Indianapolis, 1998
   Russell Wilson, Seattle, 2012
23 Andrew Luck, Indianapolis, 2012
22 Charlie Conerly, N.Y. Giants, 1948
Most Touchdown Passes, Game
7 Sid Luckman, Chi. Bears vs. N.Y. Giants,
   Nov. 14, 1943
   Adrian Burk, Philadelphia vs. Washington,
   Oct. 17, 1954
   George Blanda, Houston vs. N.Y. Titans,
   Nov. 19, 1961
   Y.A. Tittle, N.Y. Giants vs. Washington, Oct. 28, 1962
   Joe Kapp, Minnesota vs. Baltimore, Sept. 28, 1969
6 By many players. Last time:
   Aaron Rodgers, Green Bay vs. Houston,
   Oct. 14, 2012
Most Games, Four or More Touchdown Passes, Career
23 Brett Favre, Atlanta, 1991; Green Bay, 1992-2007;
   N.Y. Jets, 2008; Minnesota, 2009-2010
22 Peyton Manning, Indianapolis, 1998-2010;
   Denver, 2012
21 Dan Marino, Miami, 1983-1999
Most Games, Four or More Touchdown Passes, Season
6 Dan Marino, Miami, 1984
   Peyton Manning, Indianapolis, 2004
5 Dan Marino, Miami, 1986
   Brett Favre, Green Bay, 1996
   Donovan McNabb, Philadelphia, 2004
   Tom Brady, New England, 2007
   Drew Brees, New Orleans, 2011
   Aaron Rodgers, Green Bay, 2011
4 George Blanda, Houston, 1961
   Vince Ferragamo, Los Angeles, 1980
   Steve Young, San Francisco, 1994
   Randall Cunningham, Minnesota, 1998
   Daunte Culpepper, Minnesota, 2004
   Tony Romo, Dallas, 2007
   Peyton Manning, Indianapolis, 2009
   Matthew Stafford, Detroit, 2011
   Drew Brees, New Orleans, 2012
   Aaron Rodgers, Green Bay, 2012
Most Consecutive Games, Four or More Touchdown Passes
5 Peyton Manning, Indianapolis, 2004
4 Dan Marino, Miami, 1984
3 Drew Brees, 2011
Most Consecutive Games, Touchdown Passes
54 Drew Brees, New Orleans, 2009-2012

   48   Tom Brady, New England, 2010-12 (current)
   47   Johnny Unitas, Baltimore, 1956-1960

HAD INTERCEPTED
Most Consecutive Passes Attempted, None Intercepted
  358   Tom Brady, New England, 2010-11
  308   Bernie Kosar, Cleveland, 1990-91
  294   Bart Starr, Green Bay, 1964-65
Most Passes Had Intercepted, Career
  336   Brett Favre, Atlanta, 1991; Green Bay, 1992-2007;
         N.Y. Jets, 2008; Minnesota, 2009-2010
  277   George Blanda, Chi. Bears, 1949, 1950-58; Baltimore,
         1950; Houston, 1960-66; Oakland, 1967-1975
  268   John Hadl, San Diego, 1962-1972; Los Angeles,
         1973-74; Green Bay, 1974-75; Houston, 1976-77
Most Passes Had Intercepted, Season
   42   George Blanda, Houston, 1962
   35   Vinny Testaverde, Tampa Bay, 1988
   34   Frank Tripucka, Denver, 1960
Most Passes Had Intercepted, Game
    8   Jim Hardy, Chi. Cardinals vs. Philadelphia,
         Sept. 24, 1950
    7   Parker Hall, Cleveland vs. Green Bay, Nov. 8, 1942
         Frank Sinkwich, Detroit vs. Green Bay, Oct. 24, 1943
         Bob Waterfield, Los Angeles vs. Green Bay,
         Oct. 17, 1948
         Zeke Bratkowski, Chicago vs. Baltimore,
         Oct. 2, 1960
         Tommy Wade, Pittsburgh vs. Philadelphia,
         Dec. 12, 1965
         Ken Stabler, Oakland vs. Denver, Oct. 16, 1977
         Steve DeBerg, Tampa Bay vs. San Francisco,
         Sept. 7, 1986
         Ty Detmer, Detroit vs. Cleveland, Sept. 23, 2001
    6   By many players
Most Attempts, No Interceptions, Game
   70   Drew Bledsoe, New England vs. Minnesota,
         Nov. 13, 1994 (ot)
   63   Rich Gannon, Minnesota vs. New England,
         Oct. 20, 1991 (ot)
   61   Matthew Stafford, Detroit vs. Houston,
         Nov. 22, 2012 (ot)

LOWEST PERCENTAGE, PASSES HAD INTERCEPTED
Most Seasons Leading League, Lowest Percentage, Passes Had Intercepted
    5   Sammy Baugh, Washington, 1940, 1942, 1944-45,
         1947
    3   Charlie Conerly, N.Y. Giants, 1950, 1956, 1959
         Bart Starr, Green Bay, 1962, 1964, 1966
         Roger Staubach, Dallas, 1971, 1977, 1979
         Ken Anderson, Cincinnati, 1972, 1981-82
         Ken O'Brien, N.Y. Jets, 1985, 1987-88
    2   By many players
Lowest Pct., Passes Had Intercepted, Career (1,500 attempts)
  1.73   Aaron Rodgers, Green Bay, 2005-2012 (2,665-46)
  2.06   Tom Brady, New England, 2000-2012 (5,958-123)
  2.11   Neil O'Donnell, Pittsburgh, 1991-95; N.Y. Jets, 1996-
         97; Cincinnati, 1998; Tennessee, 1999-2003
         (3,229-68)
Lowest Pct., Passes Had Intercepted, Season (Qualifiers)
  0.41   Damon Huard, Kansas City, 2006 (244-1)
  0.66   Joe Ferguson, Buffalo, 1976 (151-1)
  0.81   Tom Brady, New England, 2010 (492-4)
Lowest Pct., Passes Had Intercepted, Rookie, Season (Qualifiers)
  1.27   Robert Griffin III, Washington, 2012 (393-5)
  1.89   Nick Foles, Philadelphia, 2012 (265-5)
  1.98   Charlie Batch, Detroit, 1998 (303-6)

TIMES SACKED
Times Sacked has been compiled since 1963.
Most Times Sacked, Career
  525   Brett Favre, Atlanta, 1991; Green Bay, 1992-2007;
         N.Y. Jets, 2008; Minnesota, 2009-2010
  516   John Elway, Denver, 1983-1998
  494   Dave Krieg, Seattle, 1980-1991; Kansas City,
         1992-93; Detroit, 1994; Arizona, 1995;
         Chicago, 1996; Tennessee, 1997-98
Most Times Sacked, Season
   76   David Carr, Houston, 2002
   72   Randall Cunningham, Philadelphia, 1986
   68   David Carr, Houston, 2005
Most Times Sacked, Game
   12   Bert Jones, Baltimore vs. St. Louis, Oct. 26, 1980
         Warren Moon, Houston vs. Dallas, Sept. 29, 1985
         Donovan McNabb, Philadelphia vs. N.Y. Giants,
         Sept. 30, 2007
   11   Charley Johnson, St. Louis vs. N.Y. Giants,
         Nov. 1, 1964
         Bart Starr, Green Bay vs. Detroit, Nov. 7, 1965
         Jack Kemp, Buffalo vs. Oakland, Oct. 15, 1967
         Bob Berry, Atlanta vs. St. Louis, Nov. 24, 1968
         Greg Landry, Detroit vs. Dallas, Oct. 6, 1975
         Ron Jaworski, Philadelphia vs. St. Louis,
         Dec. 18, 1983
         Paul McDonald, Cleveland vs. Kansas City,
         Sept. 30, 1984
         Archie Manning, Minnesota vs. Chicago,
         Oct. 28, 1984
         Steve Pelluer, Dallas vs. San Diego, Nov. 16, 1986
         Randall Cunningham, Philadelphia vs. L.A. Raiders,
         Nov. 30, 1986 (ot)
         David Norrie, N.Y. Jets vs. Dallas, Oct. 4, 1987
         Troy Aikman, Dallas vs. Philadelphia, Sept. 15, 1991
         Bernie Kosar, Cleveland vs. Indianapolis,
         Sept. 6, 1992
         Greg McElroy, N.Y. Jets vs. San Diego,
         Dec. 23, 2012
   10   By many players

RECEIVING
Most Seasons Leading League
    8   Don Hutson, Green Bay, 1936-37, 1939, 1941-45
    5   Lionel Taylor, Denver, 1960-63, 1965
    3   Tom Fears, Los Angeles, 1948-1950
         Pete Pihos, Philadelphia, 1953-55
         Billy Wilson, San Francisco, 1954, 1956-57
         Raymond Berry, Baltimore, 1958-1960
         Lance Alworth, San Diego, 1966, 1968-69
         Sterling Sharpe, Green Bay, 1989, 1992-93
         Wes Welker, New England, 2007, 2009, 2011
Most Consecutive Seasons Leading League
    5   Don Hutson, Green Bay, 1941-45
    4   Lionel Taylor, Denver, 1960-63
    3   Tom Fears, Los Angeles, 1948-1950
         Pete Pihos, Philadelphia, 1953-55
         Raymond Berry, Baltimore, 1958-1960
Most Pass Receptions, Career
 1,549   Jerry Rice, San Francisco, 1985-2000; Oakland,
         2001-04; Seattle, 2004
 1,242   Tony Gonzalez, Kansas City, 1997-2008; Atlanta,
         2009-2012
 1,102   Marvin Harrison, Indianapolis, 1996-2008
Most Seasons, 50 or More Pass Receptions
   17   Jerry Rice, San Francisco, 1986-1996, 1998-2000;
         Oakland, 2001-03
   15   Tony Gonzalez, Kansas City, 1998-2008; Atlanta,
         2009-2012

13 Andre Reed, Buffalo, 1986-1994, 1996-99
   Terrell Owens, San Francisco, 1997-2003;
      Philadelphia, 2004; Dallas, 2006-08;
      Buffalo, 2009; Cincinnati, 2010

Most Pass Receptions, Season
143 Marvin Harrison, Indianapolis, 2002
123 Herman Moore, Detroit, 1995
   Wes Welker, New England, 2009
122 Cris Carter, Minnesota, 1994
   Jerry Rice, San Francisco, 1995
   Cris Carter, Minnesota, 1995
   Wes Welker, New England, 2011
   Calvin Johnson, Detroit, 2012

Most Pass Receptions, Rookie, Season
101 Anquan Boldin, Arizona, 2003
91 Eddie Royal, Denver, 2008
90 Terry Glenn, New England, 1996

Most Pass Receptions, Game
21 Brandon Marshall, Denver vs. Indianapolis,
      Dec. 13, 2009
20 Terrell Owens, San Francisco vs. Chicago,
      Dec. 17, 2000
18 Tom Fears, Los Angeles vs. Green Bay, Dec. 3, 1950
   Brandon Marshall, Denver vs. San Diego,
      Sept. 14, 2008
   Jason Witten, Dallas vs. N.Y. Giants, Oct. 28, 2012

Most Consecutive Games, Pass Receptions
274 Jerry Rice, San Francisco, 1985-2000; Oakland,
      2001-04
195 Tony Gonzalez, Kansas City, 2000-08; Atlanta,
      2009-2012 (current)
190 Marvin Harrison, Indianapolis, 1996-2008

YARDS GAINED
Most Seasons Leading League
7 Don Hutson, Green Bay, 1936, 1938-39, 1941-44
6 Jerry Rice, San Francisco, 1986, 1989-1990,
      1993-95
3 Raymond Berry, Baltimore, 1957, 1959-1960
   Lance Alworth, San Diego, 1965-66, 1968

Most Consecutive Seasons Leading League
4 Don Hutson, Green Bay, 1941-44
3 Jerry Rice, San Francisco, 1993-95
2 By many players

Most Yards Gained, Career
22,895 Jerry Rice, San Francisco, 1985-2000; Oakland,
      2001-04; Seattle, 2004
15,934 Terrell Owens, San Francisco, 1996-2003;
      Philadelphia, 2004-05; Dallas, 2006-08;
      Buffalo, 2009; Cincinnati, 2010
15,292 Randy Moss, Minnesota, 1998-2004, 2010;
      Oakland, 2005-06; New England, 2007-2010;
      Tennessee, 2010; San Francisco, 2012

Most Seasons, 1,000 or More Yards, Pass Receiving
14 Jerry Rice, San Francisco, 1986-1996, 1998;
      Oakland, 2001-02
10 Randy Moss, Minnesota, 1998-2003; Oakland,
      2005; New England, 2007-09
9 Tim Brown, L.A. Raiders, 1993-94; Oakland,
      1995-2001
   Jimmy Smith, Jacksonville, 1996-2002, 2004-05
   Terrell Owens, San Francisco, 1998, 2000-03;
      Philadelphia, 2004; Dallas, 2006-08

Most Yards Gained, Season
1,964 Calvin Johnson, Detroit, 2012
1,848 Jerry Rice, San Francisco, 1995
1,781 Isaac Bruce, St. Louis, 1995

Most Yards Gained, Rookie, Season
1,473 Bill Groman, Houston, 1960
1,377 Anquan Boldin, Arizona, 2003

1,313 Randy Moss, Minnesota, 1998

Most Yards Gained, Game
336 Flipper Anderson, L.A. Rams vs. New Orleans,
      Nov. 26, 1989
309 Stephone Paige, Kansas City vs. San Diego,
      Dec. 22, 1985
303 Jim Benton, Cleveland vs. Detroit, Nov. 22, 1945

Most Games, 200 or More Yards Pass Receiving, Career
5 Lance Alworth, San Diego, 1962-1970; Dallas,
      1971-72
4 Don Hutson, Green Bay, 1935-45
   Charley Hennigan, Houston, 1960-66
   Jerry Rice, San Francisco, 1985-2000; Oakland,
      2001-04; Seattle, 2004
   Calvin Johnson, Detroit, 2012
3 Don Maynard, N.Y. Giants, 1958; N.Y. Jets,
      1960-1972; St. Louis, 1973
   Wes Chandler, New Orleans, 1978-1981; San Diego,
      1981-87; San Francisco, 1988
   Isaac Bruce, L.A. Rams, 1994; St. Louis, 1995-2007;
      San Francisco, 2008
   Terrell Owens, San Francisco, 1996-2003;
      Philadelphia, 2004-05; Dallas, 2006-08; Buffalo,
      2009; Cincinnati, 2010

Most Games, 200 or More Yards Pass Receiving, Season
3 Charley Hennigan, Houston, 1961
2 Don Hutson, Green Bay, 1942
   Gene Roberts, N.Y. Giants, 1949
   Lance Alworth, San Diego, 1963
   Don Maynard, N.Y. Jets, 1968
   Calvin Johnson, Detroit, 2011
   Calvin Johnson, Detroit, 2012

Most Games, 100 or More Yards Pass Receiving, Career
76 Jerry Rice, San Francisco, 1985-2000; Oakland,
      2001-04; Seattle, 2004
64 Randy Moss, Minnesota, 1998-2004, 2010;
      Oakland, 2005-06; New England, 2007-2010;
      Tennessee, 2010; San Francisco, 2012
59 Marvin Harrison, Indianapolis, 1996-2008

Most Games, 100 or More Yards Pass Receiving, Season
11 Michael Irvin, Dallas, 1995
   Calvin Johnson, Detroit, 2012
10 Charley Hennigan, Houston, 1961
   Herman Moore, Detroit, 1995
   Marvin Harrison, Indianapolis, 2002
   Torry Holt, St. Louis, 2003
9 Elroy (Crazylegs) Hirsch, Los Angeles, 1951
   Bill Groman, Houston, 1960
   Lance Alworth, San Diego, 1965
   Don Maynard, N.Y. Jets, 1967
   Stanley Morgan, New England, 1986
   Mark Carrier, Tampa Bay, 1989
   Robert Brooks, Green Bay, 1995
   Isaac Bruce, St. Louis, 1995
   Jerry Rice, San Francisco, 1995
   Marvin Harrison, Indianapolis, 1999
   Jimmy Smith, Jacksonville, 1999
   David Boston, Arizona, 2001
   Steve Smith, Carolina, 2005
   Randy Moss, New England, 2007

Most Consecutive Games, 100 or More Yards Pass Receiving
8 Calvin Johnson, Detroit, 2012
7 Charley Hennigan, Houston, 1961
   Michael Irvin, Dallas, 1995
6 Raymond Berry, Baltimore, 1960
   Bill Groman, Houston, 1961
   Pat Studstill, Detroit, 1966
   Isaac Bruce, St. Louis, 1995
   Mike Wallace, Pittsburgh, 2010-11

Longest Pass Reception (All TDs except as noted)

99   Andy Farkas (from Filchock), Washington vs. Pittsburgh, Oct. 15, 1939

     Bobby Mitchell (from Izo), Washington vs. Cleveland, Sept. 15, 1963

     Pat Studstill (from Sweetan), Detroit vs. Baltimore, Oct. 16, 1966

     Gerry Allen (from Jurgensen), Washington vs. Chicago, Sept. 15, 1968

     Cliff Branch (from Plunkett), L.A. Raiders vs. Washington, Oct. 2, 1983

     Mike Quick (from Jaworski), Philadelphia vs. Atlanta, Nov. 10, 1985

     Tony Martin (from Humphries), San Diego vs. Seattle, Sept. 18, 1994

     Robert Brooks (from Favre), Green Bay vs. Chicago, Sept. 11, 1995

     Marc Boerigter (from Green), Kansas City vs. San Diego, Dec. 22, 2002

     Andre Davis (from Garcia), Cleveland vs. Cincinnati, Oct. 17, 2004

     Bernard Berrian (from Frerotte), Minnesota vs. Chicago, Nov. 30, 2008

     Wes Welker (from Brady), New England vs. Miami, Sept. 12, 2011

     Victor Cruz (from Manning), N.Y. Giants vs. N.Y. Jets, Dec. 24, 2011

98   Gaynell Tinsley (from Russell), Chi. Cardinals vs. Cleveland, Nov. 17, 1938

     Dick (Night Train) Lane (from Compton), Chi. Cardinals vs. Green Bay, Nov. 13, 1955

     John Farrington (from Wade), Chicago vs. Detroit, Oct. 8, 1961

     Willard Dewveall (from Lee), Houston vs. San Diego, Nov. 25, 1962

     Homer Jones (from Morrall), N.Y. Giants vs. Pittsburgh, Sept. 11, 1966

     Ahmad Rashad (from Hart), St. Louis vs. Los Angeles, Dec. 10, 1972 (no TD)

     Michael Haynes (from Hebert), Atlanta vs. New Orleans, Sept. 12, 1993

     Johnnie Morton (from Batch), Detroit vs. Chicago, Oct. 4, 1998

     Terrell Owens (from Fitzpatrick), Buffalo vs. Jacksonville, Nov. 22, 2009

97   Gaynell Tinsley (from Coffee), Chi. Cardinals vs. Chi. Bears, Dec. 5, 1937

     Cloyce Box (from Layne), Detroit vs. Green Bay, Nov. 26, 1953

     Jerry Tarr (from Shaw), Denver vs. Boston, Sept. 21, 1962

     Webster Slaughter (from Kosar), Cleveland vs. Chicago, Oct. 23, 1989

     John Taylor (from Young), San Francisco vs. Atlanta, Nov. 3, 1991

AVERAGE GAIN

Highest Avg. Gain, Career (200 receptions)

22.26   Homer Jones, N.Y. Giants, 1964-69; Cleveland, 1970 (224-4,986)

20.83   Buddy Dial, Pittsburgh, 1959-1963; Dallas, 1964-66 (261-5,436)

20.24   Harlon Hill, Chi. Bears, 1954-1961; Pittsburgh, 1962; Detroit, 1962 (233-4,717)

Highest Avg. Gain, Season (24 receptions)

32.58   Don Currivan, Boston, 1947 (24-782)

31.44   Bucky Pope, Los Angeles, 1964 (25-786)

28.60   Bobby Duckworth, San Diego, 1984 (25-715)

Highest Average Gain, Game (3 receptions)

63.00   Torry Holt, St. Louis vs. Atlanta, Sept. 24, 2000 (3-189)

60.67   Bill Groman, Houston vs. Denver, Nov. 20, 1960 (3-182)

     Homer Jones, N.Y. Giants vs. Washington, Dec. 12, 1965 (3-182)

60.33   Don Currivan, Boston vs. Washington, Nov. 30, 1947 (3-181)

TOUCHDOWNS

Most Seasons Leading League

9   Don Hutson, Green Bay, 1935-38, 1940-44

6   Jerry Rice, San Francisco, 1986-87, 1989-1991, 1993

5   Randy Moss, Minnesota, 1998, 2000, 2003; New England, 2007, 2009

Most Consecutive Seasons Leading League

5   Don Hutson, Green Bay, 1940-44

4   Don Hutson, Green Bay, 1935-38

3   Lance Alworth, San Diego, 1964-66

    Jerry Rice, San Francisco, 1989-1991

Most Touchdowns, Career

197   Jerry Rice, San Francisco, 1985-2000; Oakland, 2001-04; Seattle, 2004

156   Randy Moss, Minnesota, 1998-2004, 2010; Oakland, 2005-06; New England, 2007-2010; Tennessee, 2010; San Francisco, 2012

153   Terrell Owens, San Francisco, 1996-2003; Philadelphia, 2004-05; Dallas, 2006-08; Buffalo, 2009; Cincinnati, 2010

Most Touchdowns, Season

23   Randy Moss, New England, 2007

22   Jerry Rice, San Francisco, 1987

18   Mark Clayton, Miami, 1984

    Sterling Sharpe, Green Bay, 1994

Most Touchdowns, Rookie, Season

17   Randy Moss, Minnesota, 1998

13   Bill Howton, Green Bay, 1952

    John Jefferson, San Diego, 1978

12   Harlon Hill, Chi. Bears, 1954

    Bill Groman, Houston, 1960

    Mike Ditka, Chicago, 1961

    Bob Hayes, Dallas, 1965

Most Touchdowns, Game

5   Bob Shaw, Chi. Cardinals vs. Baltimore, Oct. 2, 1950

    Kellen Winslow, San Diego vs. Oakland, Nov. 22, 1981

    Jerry Rice, San Francisco vs. Atlanta, Oct. 14, 1990

4   By many players. Last time:

    Randy Moss, New England vs. Buffalo, Nov. 18, 2007

    Terrell Owens, Dallas vs. Washington, Nov. 18, 2007

Most Consecutive Games, Touchdowns

13   Jerry Rice, San Francisco, 1986-87

11   Elroy (Crazylegs) Hirsch, Los Angeles, 1950-51

    Buddy Dial, Pittsburgh, 1959-1960

10   Carl Pickens, Cincinnati, 1994-95

    Randy Moss, Minnesota, 2003-04

YARDS FROM SCRIMMAGE

Most Scrimmage Yards, Career

23,540   Jerry Rice, San Francisco 1985-2000; Oakland, 2001-04; Seattle, 2004

21,579   Emmitt Smith, Dallas, 1990-2002; Arizona, 2003-04

21,264   Walter Payton, Chicago, 1975-1987

Most Scrimmage Yards, Season

2,509   Chris Johnson, Tennessee, 2009

2,429   Marshall Faulk, St. Louis, 1999

2,390   Tiki Barber, N.Y. Giants, 2005

Most Scrimmage Yards, Rookie, Season
- 2,212   Eric Dickerson, L.A. Rams, 1983
- 2,139   Edgerrin James, Indianapolis, 1999
- 1,926   Doug Martin, Tampa Bay, 2012

Most Scrimmage Yards, Game
- 336   Flipper Anderson, L.A. Rams vs. New Orleans, Nov. 26, 1989 (ot)
- 330   Billy Cannon, Houston vs. N.Y. Titans, Dec. 10, 1961
- 315   Adrian Peterson, Minnesota vs. San Diego, Nov. 4, 2007

INTERCEPTIONS BY

Most Seasons Leading League
- 3   Everson Walls, Dallas, 1981-82, 1985
  Ed Reed, Baltimore, 2004, 2008, 2010
- 2   Dick (Night Train) Lane, Los Angeles, 1952; Chi. Cardinals, 1954
  Jack Christiansen, Detroit, 1953, 1957
  Milt Davis, Baltimore, 1957, 1959
  Dick Lynch, N.Y. Giants, 1961, 1963
  Johnny Robinson, Kansas City, 1966, 1970
  Bill Bradley, Philadelphia, 1971-72
  Emmitt Thomas, Kansas City, 1969, 1974
  Ronnie Lott, San Francisco, 1986; L.A. Raiders, 1991
  Rod Woodson, Baltimore, 1999; Oakland, 2002
  Ty Law, New England, 1998; N.Y. Jets, 2005
  Darren Sharper, Green Bay, 2000; New Orleans, 2009
  Asante Samuel, New England, 2006; Philadelphia, 2009
  Charles Woodson, Green Bay, 2009, 2011

Most Interceptions By, Career
- 81   Paul Krause, Washington, 1964-67; Minnesota, 1968-1979
- 79   Emlen Tunnell, N.Y. Giants, 1948-1958; Green Bay, 1959-1961
- 71   Rod Woodson, Pittsburgh, 1987-1996; San Francisco, 1997; Baltimore, 1998-2001; Oakland, 2002-03

Most Interceptions By, Season
- 14   Dick (Night Train) Lane, Los Angeles, 1952
- 13   Dan Sandifer, Washington, 1948
  Orban (Spec) Sanders, N.Y. Yanks, 1950
  Lester Hayes, Oakland, 1980
- 12   By nine players

Most Interceptions By, Rookie, Season
- 14   Dick (Night Train) Lane, Los Angeles, 1952
- 13   Dan Sandifer, Washington, 1948
- 12   Woodley Lewis, Los Angeles, 1950
  Paul Krause, Washington, 1964

Most Interceptions By, Game
- 4   Sammy Baugh, Washington vs. Detroit, Nov. 14, 1943
  Dan Sandifer, Washington vs. Boston, Oct. 31, 1948
  Don Doll, Detroit vs. Chi. Cardinals, Oct. 23, 1949
  Bob Nussbaumer, Chi. Cardinals vs. N.Y. Bulldogs, Nov. 13, 1949
  Russ Craft, Philadelphia vs. Chi. Cardinals, Sept. 24, 1950
  Bobby Dillon, Green Bay vs. Detroit, Nov. 26, 1953
  Jack Butler, Pittsburgh vs. Washington, Dec. 13, 1953
  Austin (Goose) Gonsoulin, Denver vs. Buffalo, Sept. 18, 1960
  Jerry Norton, St. Louis vs. Washington, Nov. 20, 1960; vs. Pittsburgh, Nov. 26, 1961
  Dave Baker, San Francisco vs. L.A. Rams, Dec. 4, 1960
  Bobby Ply, Dall. Texans vs. San Diego, Dec. 16, 1962
  Bobby Hunt, Kansas City vs. Houston, Oct. 4, 1964
  Willie Brown, Denver vs. N.Y. Jets, Nov. 15, 1964
  Dick Anderson, Miami vs. Pittsburgh, Dec. 3, 1973
  Willie Buchanon, Green Bay vs. San Diego, Sept. 24, 1978

Deron Cherry, Kansas City vs. Seattle, Sept. 29, 1985
Kwamie Lassiter, Arizona vs. San Diego, Dec. 27, 1998
Deltha O'Neal, Denver vs. Kansas City, Oct. 7, 2001
DeAngelo Hall, Washington vs. Chicago, Oct. 24, 2010

Most Consecutive Games, Passes Intercepted By
- 8   Tom Morrow, Oakland, 1962-63
- 7   Tom Landry, N.Y. Giants, 1950-51
  Paul Krause, Washington, 1964
  Larry Wilson, St. Louis, 1966
  Ben Davis, Cleveland, 1968
- 6   By many players.
  Last time: Brian Russell, Minnesota, 2003

YARDS GAINED

Most Seasons Leading League
- 3   Darren Sharper, Green Bay, 2002; Minnesota, 2005; New Orleans, 2009
- 2   Dick (Night Train) Lane, Los Angeles, 1952; Chi. Cardinals, 1954
  Herb Adderley, Green Bay, 1965, 1969
  Dick Anderson, Miami, 1968, 1970
  Ed Reed, Baltimore, 2004, 2010

Most Yards Gained, Career
- 1,541   Ed Reed, Baltimore, 2002-2012
- 1,483   Rod Woodson, Pittsburgh, 1987-1996; San Francisco, 1997; Baltimore, 1998-2001; Oakland, 2002-03
- 1,412   Darren Sharper, Green Bay, 1997-2004; Minnesota, 2005-08; New Orleans, 2009-2010

Most Yards Gained, Season
- 376   Darren Sharper, New Orleans, 2009
- 358   Ed Reed, Baltimore, 2004
- 349   Charlie McNeil, San Diego, 1961

Most Yards Gained, Rookie, Season
- 301   Don Doll, Detroit, 1949
- 298   Dick (Night Train) Lane, Los Angeles, 1952
- 275   Woodley Lewis, Los Angeles, 1950

Most Yards Gained, Game
- 177   Charlie McNeil, San Diego vs. Houston, Sept. 24, 1961
- 170   Louis Oliver, Miami vs. Buffalo, Oct. 4, 1992
- 167   Dick Jauron, Detroit vs. Chicago, Nov. 18, 1973

Longest Return (All TDs)
- 107   Ed Reed, Baltimore vs. Philadelphia, Nov. 23, 2008
- 106   Ed Reed, Baltimore vs. Cleveland, Nov. 7, 2004
- 103   Vencie Glenn, San Diego vs. Denver, Nov. 29, 1987
  Louis Oliver, Miami vs. Buffalo, Oct. 4, 1992

TOUCHDOWNS

Most Touchdowns, Career
- 12   Rod Woodson, Pittsburgh, 1987-1996; San Francisco, 1997; Baltimore, 1998-2001; Oakland, 2002-03
- 11   Darren Sharper, Green Bay, 1997-2004; Minnesota, 2005-08; New Orleans, 2009-2010
  Charles Woodson, Oakland, 1998-2005; Green Bay, 2006-2012
- 9   Ken Houston, Houston, 1967-1972; Washington, 1973-1980
  Aeneas Williams, Phoenix, 1991-93; Arizona, 1994-2000; St. Louis, 2001-04
  Deion Sanders, Atlanta, 1989-1993; San Francisco, 1994; Dallas, 1995-99; Washington, 2000; Baltimore, 2004-05

Most Touchdowns, Season
- 4   Ken Houston, Houston, 1971
  Jim Kearney, Kansas City, 1972
  Eric Allen, Philadelphia, 1993
- 3   Dick Harris, San Diego, 1961
  Dick Lynch, N.Y. Giants, 1963

Herb Adderley, Green Bay, 1965
Lem Barney, Detroit, 1967
Miller Farr, Houston, 1967
Monte Jackson, Los Angeles, 1976
Rod Perry, Los Angeles, 1978
Ronnie Lott, San Francisco, 1981
Lloyd Burruss, Kansas City, 1986
Wayne Haddix, Tampa Bay, 1990
Robert Massey, Phoenix, 1992
Ray Buchanan, Indianapolis, 1994
Deion Sanders, San Francisco, 1994
Mark McMillian, Kansas City, 1997
Otis Smith, N.Y. Jets, 1997
Jimmy Hitchcock, Minnesota, 1998
Eric Allen, Oakland, 2000
Derrick Brooks, Tampa Bay, 2002
Antrel Rolle, Arizona, 2007
Nick Collins, Green Bay, 2008
Darren Sharper, New Orleans, 2009
Charles Woodson, Green Bay, 2009
Janoris Jenkins, St. Louis, 2012
Charles Tillman, Chicago, 2012
2   By many players

Most Touchdowns, Rookie, Season
3   Lem Barney, Detroit, 1967
    Ronnie Lott, San Francisco, 1981
    Janoris Jenkins, St. Louis, 2012
2   By many players

Most Touchdowns, Game
2   Guy Chamberlain, Canton vs. Chi. Cardinals,
     Nov. 26, 1922
    Hoot Flanagan, Pottsville vs. Frankford,
     Nov. 29, 1925
    Tom Leary, Newark vs. Frankford, Oct. 4, 1930
    Bill Blackburn, Chi. Cardinals vs. Boston,
     Oct. 24, 1948
    Dan Sandifer, Washington vs. Boston, Oct. 31, 1948
    Bob Franklin, Cleveland vs. Chicago, Dec. 11, 1960
    Bill Stacy, St. Louis vs. Dall. Cowboys, Nov. 5, 1961
    Jerry Norton, St. Louis vs. Pittsburgh, Nov. 26, 1961
    Miller Farr, Houston vs. Buffalo, Dec. 7, 1968
    Ken Houston, Houston vs. San Diego, Dec. 19, 1971
    Jim Kearney, Kansas City vs. Denver, Oct. 1, 1972
    Lemar Parrish, Cincinnati vs. Houston, Dec. 17, 1972
    Dick Anderson, Miami vs. Pittsburgh, Dec. 3, 1973
    Prentice McCray, New England vs. N.Y. Jets,
     Nov. 21, 1976
    Kenny Johnson, Atlanta vs. Green Bay,
     Nov. 27, 1983 (ot)
    Mike Kozlowski, Miami vs. N.Y. Jets, Dec. 16, 1983
    Dave Brown, Seattle vs. Kansas City, Nov. 4, 1984
    Lloyd Burruss, Kansas City vs. San Diego,
     Oct. 19, 1986
    Henry Jones, Buffalo vs. Indianapolis, Sept. 20, 1992
    Robert Massey, Phoenix vs. Washington, Oct. 4, 1992
    Eric Allen, Philadelphia vs. New Orleans,
     Dec. 26, 1993
    Ken Norton, San Francisco vs. St. Louis,
     Oct. 22, 1995
    Otis Smith, N.Y. Jets vs. Tampa Bay, Dec. 14, 1997
    Dewayne Washington, Pittsburgh vs. Jacksonville,
     Nov. 22, 1998
    Aaron Glenn, Houston vs. Pittsburgh, Dec. 8, 2002
    Ronde Barber, Tampa Bay vs. Philadelphia,
     Oct. 22, 2006
    Antrel Rolle, Arizona vs. Cincinnati, Nov. 18, 2007
    Derrick Johnson, Kansas City vs. Denver,
     Jan. 3, 2010
    David Bowens, Cleveland vs. New Orleans,
     Oct. 24, 2010

Janoris Jenkins, St. Louis vs. Arizona, Nov. 25, 2012
Zach Brown, Tennessee vs. Jacksonville,
    Dec. 30, 2012

PUNTING
Most Punts, Career
1,713   Jeff Feagles, New England, 1988-89; Philadelphia,
       1990-93; Arizona, 1994-97; Seattle, 1998-
       2002; N.Y. Giants, 2003-09
1,401   Sean Landeta, N.Y. Giants, 1985-1993; L.A. Rams,
       1993-94; St. Louis, 1995-96; Tampa Bay, 1997;
       Green Bay, 1998; Philadelphia, 1999-2002;
       St. Louis, 2003-04; Philadelphia, 2005
1,339   Brad Maynard, N.Y. Giants, 1997-2000; Chicago,
       2001-2010; Cleveland, 2011

Most Punts, Season
114   Bob Parsons, Chicago, 1981
     Chad Stanley, Houston, 2002
112   Dave Zastudil, Arizona, 2012
111   Brad Maynard, N.Y. Giants, 1997

Most Punts, Rookie, Season
111   Brad Maynard, N.Y. Giants, 1997
108   John Teltschik, Philadelphia, 1986
101   Daniel Pope, Kansas City, 1999

Most Punts, Game
16   Leo Araguz, Oakland vs. San Diego, Oct. 11, 1998
15   John Teltschik, Philadelphia vs. N.Y. Giants,
     Dec. 6, 1987 (ot)
14   Dick Nesbitt, Chi. Cardinals vs. Chi. Bears,
     Nov. 30, 1933
    Keith Molesworth, Chi. Bears vs. Green Bay,
     Dec. 10, 1933
    Sammy Baugh, Washington vs. Philadelphia,
     Nov. 5, 1939
    Carl Kinscherf, N.Y. Giants vs. Detroit, Nov. 7, 1943
    George Taliaferro, N.Y. Yanks vs. Los Angeles,
     Sept. 28, 1951

Longest Punt
98   Steve O'Neal, N.Y. Jets vs. Denver, Sept. 21, 1969
94   Joe Lintzenich, Chi. Bears vs. N.Y. Giants, Nov. 16, 1931
93   Shawn McCarthy, New England vs. Buffalo,
     Nov. 3, 1991

AVERAGE YARDAGE
Highest Average, Punting, Career (250 punts)
47.55   Shane Lechler, Oakland, 2000-2012 (1,014-48,215)
46.43   Brandon Fields, Miami, 2007-2012 (451-20,942)
46.15   Britton Colquitt, Denver, 2010-12 (254-11,723)

Highest Avg. Punting, Season (Qualifiers)
51.40   Sammy Baugh, Washington, 1940 (35-1,799)
51.14   Shane Lechler, Oakland, 2009 (96-4,909)
50.90   Andy Lee, San Francisco, 2011 (78-3,970)

Highest Avg. Punting, Rookie, Season
47.84   Bryan Anger, Jacksonville, 2012 (91-4,353)
46.74   Brett Kern, Denver, 2008 (46-2,150)
45.92   Frank Sinkwich, Detroit, 1943 (12-551)

Highest Avg. Punting, Game (4 punts)
61.75   Bob Cifers, Detroit vs. Chi. Bears, Nov. 24, 1946
       (4-247)
61.60   Roy McKay, Green Bay vs. Chi. Cardinals,
       Oct. 28, 1945 (5-308)
60.00   Jon Ryan, Seattle vs. New England, Oct. 14, 2012
       (4-240)

NET AVERAGE
Net average has been compiled since 1976.
Highest Net Average, Punting, Career (250 punts)
39.47   Britton Colquitt, Kansas City, 2010-2012
       (254-10,025)
39.23   Andy Lee, San Francisco, 2004-2012 (793-31,109)

39.17   Brett Kern, Denver, 2008-09; Tennessee, 2009-2012
        (356-13,945))

Highest Net Average, Punting, Season (Qualifiers)
43.99   Andy Lee, San Francisco, 2011 (79-3,475)
43.85   Shane Lechler, Oakland, 2009 (96-4,210)
43.24   Andy Lee, San Francisco, 2012 (67-2,897)

Highest Net Average, Punting, Rookie, Season (Qualifiers)
40.85   Bryan Anger, Jacksonville, 2012 (92-3,758)
39.93   Johnny Hekker, St. Louis, 2012 (82-3,274)
38.87   Matt Bosher, Atlanta, 2011 (71-2,760)

Highest Net Average, Punting, Game (4 punts)
59.50   Rohn Stark, Indianapolis vs. Houston,
            Sept. 13, 1992 (4-238)
54.20   Andy Lee, San Francisco vs. Seattle, Sept. 11, 2011
            (5-271)
54.00   Andy Lee, San Francisco vs. New England,
            Dec. 16, 2012 (5-270)

PUNTS HAD BLOCKED
Most Consecutive Punts, None Blocked
1,177   Chris Gardocki, Chicago, 1992-94; Indianapolis,
            1995-98; Cleveland, 1999-2003; Pittsburgh,
            2004-06
878   Bryan Barker, Kansas City, 1993; Philadelphia, 1994;
            Jacksonville, 1995-2000; Washington,
            2001-03; Green Bay, 2004; St. Louis, 2005
735   Brian Moorman, Buffalo, 2002-2011

Most Punts Had Blocked, Career
14   Herman Weaver, Detroit, 1970-76; Seattle, 1977-1980
        Harry Newsome, Pittsburgh, 1985-89; Minnesota,
            1990-93
12   Jerrel Wilson, Kansas City, 1963-1977;
            New England, 1978
        Tom Blanchard, N.Y. Giants, 1971-73; New Orleans,
            1974-78; Tampa Bay, 1979-1981
        Jeff Feagles, New England, 1988-89; Philadelphia,
            1990-93; Arizona, 1994-97; Seattle, 1998-2002;
            N.Y. Giants, 2003-09
11   David Lee, Baltimore, 1966-1978

Most Punts Had Blocked, Season
6   Harry Newsome, Pittsburgh, 1988
4   Bryan Wagner, Cleveland, 1990
        Mike Scifres, San Diego, 2010
3   By many players

PUNTS INSIDE THE 20
Punts Inside the 20 have been compiled since 1976.
Most Punts Inside the 20, Career
554   Jeff Feagles, New England, 1988-89; Philadelphia,
            1990-93; Arizona, 1994-97; Seattle, 1998-2002;
            N.Y. Giants, 2003-09
439   Brad Maynard, N.Y. Giants, 1997-2000; Chicago,
            2001-2010; Cleveland, 2011
399   Craig Hentrich, Green Bay, 1994-97; Tennessee,
            1998-2009

Most Punts Inside the 20, Season
46   Dave Zastudil, Arizona, 2012
45   Dustin Colquitt, Kansas City, 2012
42   Andy Lee, San Francisco, 2007
        Ben Graham, Arizona, 2009
        Steve Weatherford, N.Y. Jets, 2010

Most Punts Inside the 20, Game
8   Mark Royals, Pittsburgh vs. Houston, Nov. 6, 1994 (ot)
        Bryan Barker, Jacksonville vs. Baltimore,
            Nov. 14, 1999
7   Josh Miller, Pittsburgh vs. Cincinnati, Dec. 20, 1998
        David Zastudil. Cleveland vs. Buffalo, Oct. 11, 2009
        Thomas Morstead, New Orleans vs. Carolina,
            Jan. 3, 2010
6   By many players

PUNT RETURNS
Most Seasons Leading League
3   Les (Speedy) Duncan, San Diego, 1965-66;
        Washington, 1971
    Rick Upchurch, Denver, 1976, 1978, 1982
2   Dick Christy, N.Y. Titans, 1961-62
    Claude Gibson, Oakland, 1963-64
    Billy (White Shoes) Johnson, Houston, 1975, 1977
    Mel Gray, New Orleans, 1987; Detroit, 1991
    Jermaine Lewis, Baltimore, 1997, 2000
    Roscoe Parrish, Buffalo, 2007-08
    Devin Hester, Chicago, 2010-11

PUNT RETURNS
Most Punt Returns, Career
463   Brian Mitchell, Washington, 1990-99; Philadelphia,
            2000-02; N.Y. Giants, 2003
351   Eric Metcalf, Cleveland, 1989-1994; Atlanta, 1995-
            96; San Diego, 1997; Arizona, 1998; Carolina,
            1999; Washington, 2001; Green Bay, 2002
349   David Meggett, N.Y. Giants, 1989-1994;
            New England, 1995-97; N.Y. Jets, 1998

Most Punt Returns, Season
70   Danny Reece, Tampa Bay, 1979
62   Fulton Walker, Miami-L.A. Raiders, 1985
58   J.T. Smith, Kansas City, 1979
        Greg Pruitt, L.A. Raiders, 1983
        Leo Lewis, Minnesota, 1988
        Desmond Howard, Green Bay, 1996
        Nate Burleson, Seattle, 2007

Most Punt Returns, Rookie, Season
57   Lew Barnes, Chicago, 1986
55   B.J. Sams, Baltimore, 2004
54   James Jones, Dallas, 1980

Most Punt Returns, Game
11   Eddie Brown, Washington vs. Tampa Bay,
            Oct. 9, 1977
10   Theo Bell, Pittsburgh vs. Buffalo, Dec. 16, 1979
        Mike Nelms, Washington vs. New Orleans,
            Dec. 26, 1982
        Ronnie Harris, New England vs. Pittsburgh,
            Dec. 5, 1993
9   Rodger Bird, Oakland vs. Denver, Sept. 10, 1967
        Ralph McGill, San Francisco vs. Atlanta,
            Oct. 29, 1972
        Ed Podolak, Kansas City vs. San Diego,
            Nov. 10, 1974
        Anthony Leonard, San Francisco vs. New Orleans,
            Oct. 17, 1976
        Butch Johnson, Dallas vs. Buffalo, Nov. 15, 1976
        Larry Marshall, Philadelphia vs. Tampa Bay,
            Sept. 18, 1977
        Nesby Glasgow, Baltimore vs. Kansas City,
            Sept. 2, 1979
        Mike Nelms, Washington vs. St. Louis, Dec. 21, 1980
        Leon Bright, N.Y. Giants vs. Philadelphia,
            Dec. 11, 1982
        Pete Shaw, N.Y. Giants vs. Philadelphia,
            Nov. 20, 1983
        Cleotha Montgomery, L.A. Raiders vs. Detroit,
            Dec. 10, 1984
        Phil McConkey, N.Y. Giants vs. Philadelphia,
            Dec. 6, 1987 (ot)
        Andre Hastings, Pittsburgh vs. Cleveland,
            Nov. 13, 1995
        Steve Smith, Carolina vs. Detroit, Sept. 15, 2002
        Reggie Swinton, Arizona vs. Philadelphia,
            Dec. 24, 2005

FAIR CATCHES
Most Fair Catches, Career
- 231   Brian Mitchell, Washington, 1990-99; Philadelphia, 2000-02; N.Y. Giants, 2003
- 162   Tim Brown, L.A. Raiders, 1988-1994; Oakland, 1995-2003; Tampa Bay, 2004
- 144   Glyn Milburn, Denver, 1993-95; Detroit, 1996-97; Chicago, 1998-2001; San Diego, 2001

Most Fair Catches, Season
- 36   Jeremy Kerley, N.Y. Jets, 2012
- 33   Brian Mitchell, Philadelphia, 2000
- 29   Wes Welker, Miami, 2006

Most Fair Catches, Game
- 7   Bake Turner, N.Y. Jets vs. Miami, Nov. 20, 1966
  - Lem Barney, Detroit vs. Chicago, Nov. 21, 1976
  - Bobby Morse, Philadelphia vs. Buffalo, Dec. 27, 1987
  - Chris Carr, Tennessee vs. Jacksonville, Nov. 16, 2008
- 6   Jake Scott, Miami vs. Buffalo, Dec. 20, 1970
  - Greg Pruitt, L.A. Raiders vs. Seattle, Oct. 7, 1984
  - Phil McConkey, San Diego vs. Kansas City, Dec. 17, 1989
  - Gerald McNeil, Houston vs. Pittsburgh, Sept. 16, 1990
  - Bobby Engram, Chicago vs. Minnesota, Sept. 15, 1996
  - Eddie Kennison, New Orleans vs. Baltimore, Dec. 19, 1999
  - R.W. McQuarters, N.Y. Giants vs. Atlanta, Oct. 15, 2007
  - Emanuel Sanders, Pittsburgh vs. Cleveland, Nov. 25, 2012
  - Jeremy Kerley, N.Y. Jets vs. Arizona, Dec. 2, 2012
  - Jeremy Kerley, N.Y. Jets vs. Tennessee, Dec. 17, 2012
- 5   By many players

YARDS GAINED
Most Seasons Leading League
- 3   Alvin Haymond, Baltimore, 1965-66; Los Angeles, 1969
- 2   Bill Dudley, Pittsburgh, 1942, 1946
  - Emlen Tunnell, N.Y. Giants, 1951-52
  - Dick Christy, N.Y. Titans, 1961-62
  - Claude Gibson, Oakland, 1963-64
  - Rodger Bird, Oakland, 1966-67
  - J.T. Smith, Kansas City, 1979-1980
  - Vai Sikahema, St. Louis, 1986-87
  - David Meggett, N.Y. Giants, 1989-1990
  - Tamarick Vanover, Kansas City, 1995, 1999
  - Devin Hester, Chicago, 2006, 2010

Most Yards Gained, Career
- 4,999   Brian Mitchell, Washington, 1990-99; Philadelphia, 2000-02; N.Y. Giants, 2003
- 3,708   Dave Meggett, N.Y. Giants, 1989-1994; New England, 1995-97; N.Y. Jets, 1998
- 3,601   Darrien Gordon, San Diego, 1993-94, 1996; Denver, 1997-98; Oakland, 1999-2000; Atlanta, 2001; Green Bay, 2002

Most Yards Gained, Season
- 875   Desmond Howard, Green Bay, 1996
- 699   Patrick Peterson, Arizona, 2011
- 692   Fulton Walker, Miami-L.A. Raiders, 1985

Most Yards Gained, Rookie, Season
- 699   Patrick Peterson, Arizona, 2011
- 656   Louis Lipps, Pittsburgh, 1984
- 655   Neal Colzie, Oakland, 1975

Most Yards Gained, Game
- 207   LeRoy Irvin, Los Angeles vs. Atlanta, Oct. 11, 1981
- 205   George Atkinson, Oakland vs. Buffalo, Sept. 15, 1968

- 199   Eddie Drummond, Detroit vs. Jacksonville, Nov. 14, 2004 (ot)

Longest Punt Return (All TDs)
- 103   Robert Bailey, L.A. Rams vs. New Orleans, Oct. 23, 1994
- 99   Patrick Peterson, Arizona vs. St. Louis, Nov. 6, 2011
- 98   Gil LeFebvre, Cincinnati vs. Brooklyn, Dec. 3, 1933
  - Charlie West, Minnesota vs. Washington, Nov. 3, 1968
  - Dennis Morgan, Dallas vs. St. Louis, Oct. 13, 1974
  - Terance Mathis, N.Y. Jets vs. Dallas, Nov. 4, 1990
  - Damaris Johnson, Philadelphia vs. Dallas, Dec. 2, 2012

AVERAGE YARDAGE
Highest Average, Career (75 returns)
- 12.78   George McAfee, Chi. Bears, 1940-41, 1945-1950 (112-1,431)
- 12.75   Jack Christiansen, Detroit, 1951-58 (85-1,084)
- 12.55   Claude Gibson, San Diego, 1961-62; Oakland, 1963-65 (110-1,381)

Highest Average, Season (Qualifiers)
- 23.00   Herb Rich, Baltimore, 1950 (12-276)
- 21.47   Jack Christiansen, Detroit, 1952 (15-322)
- 21.28   Dick Christy, N.Y. Titans, 1961 (18-383)

Highest Average, Rookie, Season (Qualifiers)
- 23.00   Herb Rich, Baltimore, 1950 (12-276)
- 20.88   Jerry Davis, Chi. Cardinals, 1948 (16-334)
- 20.73   Frankie Sinkwich, Detroit, 1943 (11-228)

Highest Average, Game
- 53.33   Darius Reynaud, Tennessee vs. Jacksonville, Dec. 30, 2012 (3-160)
- 51.00   Steve Smith, Carolina vs. Cincinnati, Dec. 8, 2002 (3-153)
- 47.67   Chuck Latourette, St. Louis vs. New Orleans, Sept. 29, 1968 (3-143)

TOUCHDOWNS
Most Touchdowns, Career
- 12   Devin Hester, Chicago, 2006-2012
- 10   Eric Metcalf, Cleveland, 1989-1994; Atlanta, 1995-96; San Diego, 1997; Arizona, 1998; Carolina, 1999; Washington, 2001; Green Bay, 2002
- 9   Brian Mitchell, Washington, 1990-99; Philadelphia 2000-02; N.Y. Giants, 2003

Most Touchdowns, Season
- 4   Jack Christiansen, Detroit, 1951
  - Rick Upchurch, Denver, 1976
  - Devin Hester, Chicago, 2007
  - Patrick Peterson, Arizona, 2011
- 3   Emlen Tunnell, N.Y. Giants, 1951
  - Billy (White Shoes) Johnson, Houston, 1975
  - LeRoy Irvin, Los Angeles, 1981
  - Desmond Howard, Green Bay, 1996
  - Darrien Gordon, Denver, 1997
  - Eric Metcalf, San Diego, 1997
  - Devin Hester, Chicago, 2006
  - Adam Jones, Tennessee, 2006
  - Reggie Bush, New Orleans, 2008
  - Johnnie Lee Higgins, Oakland, 2008
  - Devin Hester, Chicago, 2010
- 2   By many players

Most Touchdowns, Rookie, Season
- 4   Jack Christiansen, Detroit, 1951
  - Patrick Peterson, Arizona, 2011
- 3   Devin Hester, Chicago, 2006
- 2   By many players

Most Touchdowns, Game
- 2   Jack Christiansen, Detroit vs. Los Angeles, Oct. 14, 1951; vs. Green Bay, Nov. 22, 1951

Dick Christy, N.Y. Titans vs. Denver, Sept. 24, 1961
Rick Upchurch, Denver vs. Cleveland, Sept. 26, 1976
LeRoy Irvin, Los Angeles vs. Atlanta, Oct. 11, 1981
Vai Sikahema, St. Louis vs. Tampa Bay,
    Dec. 21, 1986
Todd Kinchen, L.A. Rams vs. Atlanta, Dec. 27, 1992
Eric Metcalf, Cleveland vs. Pittsburgh, Oct. 24, 1993;
    San Diego vs. Cincinnati, Nov. 2, 1997
Darrien Gordon, Denver vs. Carolina, Nov. 9, 1997
Jermaine Lewis, Baltimore vs. Seattle, Dec. 7, 1997
    Baltimore vs. N.Y. Jets, Dec. 24, 2000
Steve Smith, Carolina vs. Cincinnati, Dec. 8, 2002
Eddie Drummond, Detroit vs. Jacksonville,
    Nov. 14, 2004 (ot)
Reggie Bush, New Orleans vs. Minnesota,
    Oct. 6, 2008
Darius Reynaud, Tennessee vs. Jacksonville,
    Dec. 30, 2012

KICKOFF RETURNS
Most Seasons Leading League
3 Abe Woodson, San Francisco, 1959, 1962-63
2 Lynn Chandnois, Pittsburgh, 1951-52
    Bobby Jancik, Houston, 1962-63
    Travis Williams, Green Bay, 1967; Los Angeles, 1971
    Mel Gray, Detroit, 1991, 1994
    Michael Bates, Carolina, 1996-97

KICKOFF RETURNS
Most Kickoff Returns, Career
607 Brian Mitchell, Washington, 1990-99; Philadelphia,
     2000-02; N.Y. Giants, 2003
514 Allen Rossum, Philadelphia, 1998-99; Green Bay,
     2000-01; Atlanta, 2002-06; Pittsburgh, 2007;
     San Francisco, 2008-09; Dallas, 2009
426 Dante Hall, Kansas City, 2000-06; St. Louis,
     2007-08
Most Kickoff Returns, Season
82 MarTay Jenkins, Arizona, 2000
73 Josh Scobey, Arizona, 2003
    Chris Carr, Oakland, 2005
70 Tyrone Hughes, New Orleans, 1996
    Michael Lewis, New Orleans, 2002
Most Kickoff Returns, Rookie, Season
73 Josh Scobey, Arizona, 2003
    Chris Carr, Oakland, 2005
67 Ronney Jenkins, San Diego, 2000
64 Tab Perry, Cincinnati, 2005
Most Kickoff Returns, Game
10 Desmond Howard, Oakland vs. Seattle, Oct. 26, 1997
    Richard Alston, Cleveland vs. Cincinnati,
     Nov. 28, 2004
9 Noland Smith, Kansas City vs. Oakland, Nov. 23, 1967
    Dino Hall, Cleveland vs. Pittsburgh, Oct. 7, 1979
    Paul Palmer, Kansas City vs. Seattle, Sept. 20, 1987
    Eric Metcalf, Atlanta vs. San Francisco,
     Sept. 29, 1996; vs. St. Louis, Nov. 10, 1996
    Michael Bates, Carolina vs. Atlanta, Oct. 4, 1998
    Nate Jacquet, Minnesota vs. Philadelphia,
     Nov. 11, 2001
    Ahmad Merritt, Chicago vs. San Francisco,
     Sept. 7, 2003
    Josh Scobey, Arizona vs. Cleveland, Nov. 16, 2003
    Maurice Hicks, San Francisco vs. San Diego,
     Oct. 15, 2006
    Aveion Cason, Detroit vs. San Diego, Dec. 16, 2007
    Allen Rossum, San Francisco vs. Philadelphia,
     Oct. 12, 2008
    Steve Breaston, Arizona vs. New England,
     Dec. 21, 2008

Danny Amendola, St. Louis vs. Tennessee,
    Dec. 13, 2009
Brandon James, Indianapolis vs. San Diego,
    Nov. 28, 2010
8 By many players

YARDS GAINED
Most Seasons Leading League
3 Bruce Harper, N.Y. Jets, 1977-79
    Tyrone Hughes, New Orleans, 1994-96
2 Marshall Goldberg, Chi. Cardinals, 1941-42
    Woodley Lewis, Los Angeles, 1953-54
    Al Carmichael, Green Bay, 1956-57
    Timmy Brown, Philadelphia, 1961, 1963
    Bobby Jancik, Houston, 1963, 1966
    Ron Smith, Atlanta, 1966-67
    Chris Carr, Oakland, 2005-06
Most Yards Gained, Career
14,014 Brian Mitchell, Washington, 1990-99; Philadelphia,
     2000-02; N.Y. Giants, 2003
11,947 Allen Rossum, Philadelphia, 1998-99; Green Bay,
     2000-01; Atlanta, 2002-06; Pittsburgh, 2007;
     San Francisco, 2008-09; Dallas, 2009
10,250 Mel Gray, New Orleans, 1986-88; Detroit, 1989-
     1994; Houston, 1995-96; Tennessee, 1997;
     Philadelphia, 1997
Most Yards Gained, Season
2,186 MarTay Jenkins, Arizona, 2000
1,809 Josh Cribbs, Cleveland, 2007
1,807 Michael Lewis, New Orleans, 2002
Most Yards Gained, Rookie, Season
1,752 Chris Carr, Oakland, 2005
1,684 Josh Scobey, Arizona, 2003
1,577 Justin Miller, N.Y. Jets, 2005
Most Yards Gained, Game
304 Tyrone Hughes, New Orleans vs. L.A. Rams,
    Oct. 23, 1994
299 Ted Ginn, Jr., Miami vs. N.Y. Jets, Nov. 1, 2009
294 Wally Triplett, Detroit vs. Los Angeles, Oct. 29, 1950
Longest Kickoff Return (All TDs)
108 Ellis Hobbs, New England, vs. N.Y. Jets, Sept. 9, 2007
    Randall Cobb, Green Bay vs. New Orleans,
     Sept. 8, 2011
    Jacoby Jones, Baltimore vs. Dallas, Oct. 14, 2012
107 Joe McKnight, N.Y. Jets vs. Baltimore, Oct. 2, 2011
106 Al Carmichael, Green Bay vs. Chi. Bears, Oct. 7, 1956
    Noland Smith, Kansas City vs. Denver, Dec. 17, 1967
    Roy Green, St. Louis vs. Dallas, Oct. 21, 1979
    Brad Smith, N.Y. Jets vs. Indianapolis, Dec. 27, 2009

AVERAGE YARDAGE
Highest Average, Career (75 returns)
30.56 Gale Sayers, Chicago, 1965-1971 (91-2,781)
29.57 Lynn Chandnois, Pittsburgh, 1950-56 (92-2,720)
29.01 Joe McKnight, N.Y. Jets, 2010-12 (76-2,205)
Highest Average, Season (Qualifiers)
41.06 Travis Williams, Green Bay, 1967 (18-739)
37.69 Gale Sayers, Chicago, 1967 (16-603)
35.50 Ollie Matson, Chi. Cardinals, 1958 (14-497)
Highest Average, Rookie, Season (Qualifiers)
41.06 Travis Williams, Green Bay, 1967 (18-739)
33.08 Tom Moore, Green Bay, 1960 (12-397)
32.88 Duriel Harris, Miami, 1976 (17-559)
Highest Average, Game (3 returns)
73.50 Wally Triplett, Detroit vs. Los Angeles, Oct. 29, 1950
     (4-294)
67.33 Lenny Lyles, San Francisco vs. Baltimore,
     Dec. 18, 1960 (3-202)
65.33 Ken Hall, Houston vs. N.Y. titans, Oct. 23, 1960
     (3-196)

TOUCHDOWNS
Most Touchdowns, Career
- 8 Josh Cribbs, Cleveland, 2005-2012
   Leon Washington, N.Y. Jets, 2006-09;
   Seattle, 2010-12
- 6 Ollie Matson, Chi. Cardinals, 1952, 1954-58;
   L.A. Rams, 1959-1962; Detroit, 1963;
   Philadelphia, 1964
   Gale Sayers, Chicago, 1965-1971
   Travis Williams, Green Bay, 1967-1970;
   Los Angeles, 1971
   Mel Gray, New Orleans, 1986-88; Detroit,
   1989-1994; Houston, 1995-96; Tennessee,
   1997; Philadelphia, 1997
   Dante Hall, Kansas City, 2000-06; St. Louis, 2007-08
- 5 By many players

Most Touchdowns, Season
- 4 Travis Williams, Green Bay, 1967
   Cecil Turner, Chicago, 1970
- 3 Verda (Vitamin T) Smith, Los Angeles, 1950
   Abe Woodson, San Francisco, 1963
   Gale Sayers, Chicago, 1967
   Raymond Clayborn, New England, 1977
   Ron Brown, L.A. Rams, 1985
   Mel Gray, Detroit, 1994
   Darrick Vaughn, Atlanta, 2000
   Terrence McGee, Buffalo, 2004
   André Davis, Houston, 2007
   Leon Washington, N.Y. Jets, 2007
   Josh Cribbs, Cleveland, 2009
   Jacoby Ford, Oakland, 2010
   Leon Washington, Seattle, 2010
- 2 By many players

Most Touchdowns, Rookie, Season
- 4 Travis Williams, Green Bay, 1967
- 3 Raymond Clayborn, New England, 1977
   Darrick Vaughn, Atlanta, 2000
   Jacoby Ford, Oakland, 2010
- 2 By many players

Most Touchdowns, Game
- 2 Timmy Brown, Philadelphia vs. Dallas, Nov. 6, 1966
   Travis Williams, Green Bay vs. Cleveland,
   Nov. 12, 1967
   Ron Brown, L.A. Rams vs. Green Bay, Nov. 24, 1985
   Tyrone Hughes, New Orleans vs. L.A. Rams,
   Oct. 23, 1994
   Chad Morton, N.Y. Jets vs. Buffalo, Sept. 8, 2002 (ot)
   Devin Hester, Chicago vs. St. Louis, Dec. 11, 2006
   André Davis, Houston vs. Jacksonville, Dec. 30, 2007
   Ted Ginn, Jr., Miami vs. N.Y. Jets, Nov. 1, 2009
   Josh Cribbs, Cleveland vs. Kansas City, Dec. 20, 2009
   Leon Washington, Seattle vs. San Diego,
   Sept. 26, 2010

COMBINED KICK RETURNS
Most Combined Kick Returns, Career
- 1,070 Brian Mitchell, Washington, 1990-99; Philadelphia,
   2000-02; N.Y. Giants, 2003 (p-463, k-607)
- 821 Allen Rossum, Philadelphia, 1998-99; Green Bay,
   2000-01; Atlanta, 2002-06; Pittsburgh, 2007;
   San Francisco, 2008-09; Dallas, 2009
   (p-307, k-514)
- 711 Glyn Milburn, Denver, 1993-95; Detroit, 1996-97;
   Chicago, 1998-2001; San Diego, 2001 (p-304,
   k-407)

Most Combined Kick Returns, Season
- 114 Michael Lewis, New Orleans, 2002 (p-44, k-70)
   B.J. Sams, Baltimore, 2004 (p-55, k-59)
- 107 Chris Carr, Oakland, 2005 (p-34, k-73)
   Dante Hall, Kansas City, 2005 (p-42, k-65)
- 105 Reggie Swinton, Arizona, 2005 (p-42, k-63)

Most Combined Kick Returns, Game
- 13 Stump Mitchell, St. Louis vs. Atlanta, Oct. 18, 1981
   (p-6, k-7)
   Ronnie Harris, New England vs. Pittsburgh,
   Dec. 5, 1993 (p-10, k-3)
- 12 Mel Renfro, Dallas vs. Green Bay, Nov. 29, 1964
   (p-4, k-8)
   Larry Jones, Washington vs. Dallas, Dec. 13, 1975
   (p-6, k-6)
   Eddie Brown, Washington vs. Tampa Bay,
   Oct. 9, 1977 (p-11, k-1)
   Nesby Glasgow, Baltimore vs. Denver, Sept. 2, 1979
   (p-9, k-3)
   Tim Dwight, Atlanta vs. Detroit, Nov. 12, 2000
   (p-8, k-4)
   Wes Welker, Miami vs. Buffalo, Dec. 5, 2004
   (p-6, k-6)
   Reggie Swinton, Arizona vs. Philadelphia,
   Dec. 24, 2005 (p-9, k-3)
   Devin Hester, Chicago vs. Detroit, Sept. 30, 2007
   (p-5, k-7)
   Brandon James, Indianapolis vs. San Diego,
   Nov. 28, 2010 (p-3, k-9)
- 11 By many players

YARDS GAINED
Most Yards Returned, Career
- 19,013 Brian Mitchell, Washington, 1990-99; Philadelphia,
   2000-02; N.Y. Giants, 2003 (p-4,999; k-14,014)
- 15,003 Allen Rossum, Philadelphia, 1998-99; Green Bay,
   2000-01; Atlanta, 2002-06; Pittsburgh, 2007;
   San Francisco, 2008-09; Dallas, 2009
   (p-3,056; k-11,947)
- 13,003 Mel Gray, New Orleans, 1986-88; Detroit, 1989-
   1994; Houston, 1995-96; Tennessee, 1997;
   Philadelphia, 1997 (p-2,753; k-10,250)

Most Yards Returned, Season
- 2,432 Michael Lewis, New Orleans, 2002 (p-625; k-1,807)
- 2,214 Josh Cribbs, Cleveland, 2007 (p-405; k-1,809)
- 2,187 MarTay Jenkins, Arizona, 2000 (pr-1; k-2,186)

Most Yards Returned, Game
- 347 Tyrone Hughes, New Orleans vs. L.A. Rams,
   Oct. 23, 1994 (p-43; k-304)
- 314 Devin Hester, Chicago vs. Detroit, Sept. 30, 2007
   (p-95; k-219)
- 306 Josh Cribbs, Cleveland vs. Baltimore, Nov. 18, 2007
   (p-61; k-245) (ot)

TOUCHDOWNS
Most Touchdowns, Career
- 17 Devin Hester, Chicago, 2006-2012 (p-12, k-5)
- 13 Brian Mitchell, Washington, 1990-99; Philadelphia,
   2000-02; N.Y. Giants, 2003 (p-9, k-4)
- 12 Eric Metcalf, Cleveland, 1989-1994; Atlanta,
   1995-96; San Diego, 1997; Arizona, 1998;
   Carolina, 1999; Washington, 2001; Green Bay,
   2002 (p-10, k-2)
   Dante Hall, Kansas City, 2000-06;
   St. Louis, 2007-08 (p-6, k-6)

Most Touchdowns, Season
- 6 Devin Hester, Chicago, 2007 (p-4, k-2)
- 5 Devin Hester, Chicago, 2006 (p-3, k-2)
- 4 Jack Christiansen, Detroit, 1951 (p-4)
   Emlen Tunnell, N.Y. Giants, 1951 (p-3, k-1)
   Gale Sayers, Chicago, 1967 (p-1, k-3)
   Travis Williams, Green Bay, 1967 (k-4)
   Cecil Turner, Chicago, 1970 (k-4)
   Billy Johnson, Houston, 1975 (p-3, k-1)
   Rick Upchurch, Denver, 1976 (p-4)

Dante Hall, Kansas City, 2003 (p-2, r-2)
Eddie Drummond, Detroit, 2004 (p-2, k-2)
Josh Cribbs, Cleveland, 2009 (p-1, k-3)
Patrick Peterson, Arizona, 2011 (p-4)

Most Touchdowns, Game
2   Jack Christiansen, Detroit vs. Los Angeles,
    Oct. 14, 1951 (p-2); vs. Green Bay,
    Nov. 22, 1951 (p-2)
   Jim Patton, N.Y. Giants vs. Washington,
    Oct. 30, 1955 (p-1, k-1)
   Bobby Mitchell, Cleveland vs. Philadelphia,
    Nov. 23, 1958 (p-1, k-1)
   Dick Christy, N.Y. Titans vs. Denver, Sept. 24, 1961
    (p-2)
   Al Frazier, Denver vs. Boston, Dec. 3, 1961 (p-1, k-1)
   Timmy Brown, Philadelphia vs. Dallas, Nov. 6, 1966
    (k-2)
   Travis Williams, Green Bay vs. Cleveland,
    Nov. 12, 1967 (k-2); vs. Pittsburgh,
    Nov. 2, 1969 (p-1, k-1)
   Gale Sayers, Chicago vs. San Francisco,
    Dec. 3, 1967 (p-1, k-1)
   Rick Upchurch, Denver vs. Cleveland,
    Sept. 26, 1976 (p-2)
   Eddie Payton, Detroit vs. Minnesota, Dec. 17, 1977
    (p-1, k-1)
   LeRoy Irvin, Los Angeles vs. Atlanta, Oct. 11, 1981
    (p-2)
   Ron Brown, L.A. Rams vs. Green Bay,
    Nov. 24, 1985 (k-2)
   Vai Sikahema, St. Louis vs. Tampa Bay,
    Dec. 21, 1986 (p-2)
   Todd Kinchen, L.A. Rams vs. Atlanta, Dec. 27, 1992
    (p-2)
   Eric Metcalf, Cleveland vs. Pittsburgh, Oct. 24, 1993
    (p-2); San Diego vs. Cincinnati, Nov. 2, 1997
    (p-2)
   Tyrone Hughes, New Orleans vs. L.A. Rams,
    Oct. 23, 1994 (k-2)
   Darrien Gordon, Denver vs. Carolina, Nov. 9, 1997
    (p-2)
   Jermaine Lewis, Baltimore vs. Seattle, Dec. 7, 1997
    (p-2); Baltimore vs. N.Y. Jets, Dec. 24, 2000
    (p-2)
   Chad Morton, N.Y. Jets vs. Buffalo, Sept. 8, 2002
    (ot) (k-2)
   Michael Lewis, New Orleans vs. Washington,
    Oct. 13, 2002 (p-1, k-1)
   Dante Hall, Kansas City vs. St. Louis, Dec. 8, 2002
    (p-1, k-1)
   Steve Smith, Carolina vs. Cincinnati, Dec. 8, 2002
    (p-2)
   Eddie Drummond, Detroit vs. Jacksonville,
    Nov. 14, 2004 (ot) (p-2)
   Devin Hester, Chicago vs. St. Louis, Dec. 11, 2006
    (k-2)
   Darren Sproles, San Diego vs. Indianapolis,
    Nov. 11, 2007 (p-1, k-1)
   Devin Hester, Chicago vs. Denver, Nov. 25, 2007
    (p-1, k-1)
   André Davis, Houston vs. Jacksonville,
    Dec. 30, 2007 (k-2)
   Reggie Bush, New Orleans vs. Minnesota,
    Oct. 6, 2008
   Eddie Royal, Denver vs. San Diego, Oct. 19, 2009
    (p-1, k-1)
   Ted Ginn, Jr., Miami vs. N.Y. Jets, Nov. 1, 2009
    (k-2); San Francisco vs. Seattle, Sept. 11, 2011
    (p-1, k-1)

Josh Cribbs, Cleveland vs. Kansas City,
    Dec. 20, 2009 (k-2)
Leon Washington, Seattle vs. San Diego,
    Sept. 26, 2010 (k-2)
Darius Reynaud, Tennessee vs. Jacksonville,
    Dec. 30, 2012 (p-2)

FUMBLES
Most Fumbles, Career
166 Brett Favre, Atlanta, 1991; Green Bay, 1992-2007;
     N.Y. Jets, 2008; Minnesota, 2009-2010
161 Warren Moon, Houston, 1984-1993; Minnesota,
     1994-96; Seattle, 1997-98; Kansas City,
     1999-2000
153 Dave Krieg, Seattle, 1980-1991; Kansas City,
     1992-93; Detroit, 1994; Arizona, 1995;
     Chicago, 1996; Tennessee, 1997-98

Most Fumbles, Season
23 Kerry Collins, N.Y. Giants, 2001
    Daunte Culpepper, Minnesota, 2002
21 Tony Banks, St. Louis, 1996
    David Carr, Houston, 2002
18 Dave Krieg, Seattle, 1989
    Warren Moon, Houston, 1990

Most Fumbles, Game
7 Len Dawson, Kansas City vs. San Diego,
    Nov. 15, 1964
6 Sam Etcheverry, St. Louis vs. N.Y. Giants,
    Sept. 17, 1961
   Dave Krieg, Seattle vs. Kansas City, Nov. 5, 1989
   Brett Favre, Green Bay vs. Tampa Bay, Dec. 7, 1998
   Kurt Warner, St. Louis vs. N.Y. Giants, Sept. 7, 2003
   Chad Pennington, N.Y. Jets vs. Kansas City,
    Sept. 11, 2005
5 Paul Christman, Chi. Cardinals vs. Green Bay,
    Nov. 10, 1946
   Joe Perry, San Francisco vs. Cleveland,
    Nov. 12, 1950
   Charlie Conerly, N.Y. Giants vs. San Francisco,
    Dec. 1, 1957
   Tom Yewcic, Boston vs. Oakland, Dec. 16, 1962
   Jack Kemp, Buffalo vs. Houston, Oct. 29, 1967
   Roman Gabriel, Philadelphia vs. Oakland,
    Nov. 21, 1976
   Randall Cunningham, Philadelphia vs. L.A. Raiders,
    Nov. 30, 1986 (ot)
   Willie Totten, Buffalo vs. Indianapolis, Oct. 4, 1987
   Dave Walter, Cincinnati vs. Seattle, Oct. 11, 1987
   Dave Krieg, Seattle vs. San Diego, Nov. 25, 1990 (ot)
   Andre Ware, Detroit vs. Green Bay, Dec. 6, 1992
   Steve Beuerlein, Carolina vs. San Francisco,
    Nov. 8, 1998
   Patrick Ramsey, Washington vs. Green Bay,
    Oct. 20, 2002
   Eli Manning, N.Y. Giants vs. Buffalo, Dec. 23, 2007
   Josh Johnson, Tampa Bay vs. Carolina,
    Oct. 18, 2009

FUMBLES RECOVERED
Most Fumbles Recovered, Career, Own and Opponents'
56 Warren Moon, Houston, 1984-1993; Minnesota,
    1994-96; Seattle, 1997-98; Kansas City,
    1999-2000 (56 own)
47 Dave Krieg, Seattle, 1980-1991; Kansas City,
    1992-93; Detroit, 1994; Arizona, 1995; Chica-
    go, 1996; Tennessee, 1997-98 (47 own)
45 Boomer Esiason, Cincinnati, 1984-1992, 1997;
    N.Y. Jets, 1993-95; Arizona, 1996 (45 own)

Most Fumbles Recovered, Season, Own and Opponents'
12 David Carr, Houston, 2002 (12 own)

9 Don Hultz, Minnesota, 1963 (9 opp)
Dave Krieg, Seattle, 1989 (9 own)
Brian Griese, Denver, 1999 (9 own)
Jon Kitna, Seattle, 2000 (9 own)
8 Paul Christman, Chi. Cardinals, 1945 (8 own)
Joe Schmidt, Detroit, 1955 (8 opp)
Bill Butler, Minnesota, 1963 (8 own)
Kermit Alexander, San Francisco, 1965
(4 own, 4 opp)
Jack Lambert, Pittsburgh, 1976 (1 own, 7 opp)
Danny White, Dallas, 1981 (8 own)
Dan Marino, Miami, 1988 (7 own, 1 opp)
Tony Banks, St. Louis, 1998 (8 own)
Ryan Fitzpatrick, Cincinnati, 2008 (8 own)
Donovan McNabb, Washington, 2010 (8 own)

Most Fumbles Recovered, Game, Own and Opponents'
4 Otto Graham, Cleveland vs. N.Y. Giants,
Oct. 25, 1953 (4 own)
Sam Etcheverry, St. Louis vs. N.Y. Giants,
Sept. 17, 1961 (4 own)
Roman Gabriel, Los Angeles vs. San Francisco,
Oct. 12, 1969 (4 own)
Randall Cunningham, Philadelphia vs. L.A. Raiders,
Nov. 30, 1986 (ot) (4 own)
Joe Ferguson, Buffalo vs. Miami, Sept. 18, 1977
(4 own)
Tony Romo, Dallas vs. Washington, Sept. 26, 2011
(4-own)
Patrick Peterson, Arizona vs. Miami,
Sept. 30, 2012 (ot) (3 own, 1 opp)
3 By many players

OWN FUMBLES RECOVERED
Most Own Fumbles Recovered, Career
56 Warren Moon, Houston, 1984-1993; Minnesota,
1994-96; Seattle, 1997-98; Kansas City,
1999-2000
47 Dave Krieg, Seattle, 1980-1991; Kansas City,
1992-93; Detroit, 1994; Arizona, 1995;
Chicago, 1996; Tennessee, 1997-98
45 Boomer Esiason, Cincinnati, 1984-1992, 1997;
N.Y. Jets, 1993-95; Arizona, 1996

Most Own Fumbles Recovered, Season
12 David Carr, Houston, 2002
9 Dave Krieg, Seattle, 1989
Brian Griese, Denver, 1999
Jon Kitna, Seattle, 2000
8 Paul Christman, Chi. Cardinals, 1945
Bill Butler, Minnesota, 1963
Danny White, Dallas, 1981
Tony Banks, St. Louis, 1998
Ryan Fitzpatrick, Cincinnati, 2008
Donovan McNabb, Washington, 2010

Most Own Fumbles Recovered, Game
4 Otto Graham, Cleveland vs. N.Y. Giants, Oct. 25, 1953
Sam Etcheverry, St. Louis vs. N.Y. Giants,
Sept. 17, 1961
Roman Gabriel, Los Angeles vs. San Francisco,
Oct. 12, 1969
Joe Ferguson, Buffalo vs. Miami, Sept. 18, 1977

Randall Cunningham, Philadelphia vs. L.A. Raiders,
Nov. 30, 1986 (ot)
Tony Romo, Dallas vs. Washington, Sept. 26, 2011
3 By many players

OPPONENTS' FUMBLES RECOVERED
Most Opponents' Fumbles Recovered, Career
29 Jim Marshall, Cleveland, 1960; Minnesota, 1961-1979
Jason Taylor, Miami, 1997-2007; Washington, 2008;

Miami, 2009; N.Y. Jets, 2010; Miami, 2011
28 Rickey Jackson, New Orleans, 1981-1993;
San Francisco, 1994-95
26 Kevin Greene, L.A. Rams, 1985-1992; Pittsburgh,
1993-95; Carolina, 1996; San Francisco, 1997;
Carolina, 1998-99
Cornelius Bennett, Buffalo, 1987-1995; Atlanta,
1996-98; Indianapolis, 1999-2000

Most Opponents' Fumbles Recovered, Season
9 Don Hultz, Minnesota, 1963
8 Joe Schmidt, Detroit, 1955
7 Alan Page, Minnesota, 1970
Jack Lambert, Pittsburgh, 1976
Ray Childress, Houston, 1988
Rickey Jackson, New Orleans, 1990

Most Opponents' Fumbles Recovered, Game
3 Corwin Clatt, Chi. Cardinals vs. Detroit, Nov. 6, 1949
Vic Sears, Philadelphia vs. Green Bay, Nov. 2, 1952
Ed Beatty, San Francisco vs. Los Angeles,
Oct. 7, 1956
Ron Carroll, Houston vs. Cincinnati, Oct. 27, 1974
Maurice Spencer, New Orleans vs. Atlanta,
Oct. 10, 1976
Steve Nelson, New England vs. Philadelphia,
Oct. 8, 1978
Charles Jackson, Kansas City vs. Pittsburgh,
Sept. 6, 1981
Willie Buchanon, San Diego vs. Denver,
Sept. 27, 1981
Joey Browner, Minnesota vs. San Francisco,
Sept. 8, 1985
Ray Childress, Houston vs. Washington, Oct. 30, 1988
John Thierry, Chicago vs. Houston, Oct. 22, 1995
Stephen Boyd, Detroit vs. Chicago, Oct. 4, 1998
Darryl Williams, Seattle vs. Kansas City, Oct. 4, 1998
Rod Woodson, Oakland vs. Pittsburgh, Sept. 15, 2002
Brian Young, St. Louis vs. Baltimore, Nov. 9, 2003
2 By many players

YARDS RETURNING FUMBLES
Longest Fumble Run (All TDs)
104 Jack Tatum, Oakland vs. Green Bay, Sept. 24, 1972
Aeneas Williams, Arizona vs. Washington,
Nov. 5, 2000
102 Travis Davis, Pittsburgh vs. Carolina, Dec. 26, 1999
100 Chris Martin, Kansas City vs. Miami, Oct. 13, 1991

TOUCHDOWNS
Most Touchdowns, Career (Total)
6 Jason Taylor, Miami, 1997-2007; Washington, 2008;
Miami, 2009; N.Y. Jets, 2010; Miami, 2011
5 Jessie Tuggle, Atlanta, 1987-2006
4 Bill Thompson, Denver, 1969-1981
Derrick Thomas, Kansas City, 1989-1999
Keith Bulluck, Tennessee, 2000-09;
N.Y. Giants, 2010
Ronde Barber, Tampa Bay, 1997-2012

Most Touchdowns, Season (Total)
2 Harold McPhail, Boston, 1934
Harry Ebding, Detroit, 1937
John Morelli, Boston, 1944
Frank Maznicki, Boston, 1947
Fred (Dippy) Evans, Chi. Bears, 1948
Ralph Heywood, Boston, 1948
Art Tait, N.Y. Yanks, 1951
John Dwyer, Los Angeles, 1952
Leo Sugar, Chi. Cardinals, 1957
Doug Cline, Houston, 1961
Jim Bradshaw, Pittsburgh, 1964
Royce Berry, Cincinnati, 1970

Ahmad Rashad, Buffalo, 1974
Tim Gray, Kansas City, 1977
Charles Phillips, Oakland, 1978
Kenny Johnson, Atlanta, 1981
George Martin, N.Y. Giants, 1981
Del Rodgers, Green Bay, 1982
Mike Douglass, Green Bay, 1983
Shelton Robinson, Seattle, 1983
Erik McMillan, N.Y. Jets, 1989
Les Miller, San Diego, 1990
Seth Joyner, Philadelphia, 1991
Robert Goff, New Orleans, 1992
Willie Clay, Detroit, 1993
Tyrone Hughes, New Orleans, 1994
Chad Brown, Seattle, 1997
Marcus Robertson, Tennessee, 1997
Dwayne Rudd, Minnesota, 1998
Keith McKenzie, Green Bay, 1999
Ronde Barber, Tampa Bay, 2004
Leonard Little, St. Louis, 2004
Antwan Odom, Tennessee, 2005
Adalius Thomas, Baltimore, 2005
Kevin Curtis, Philadelphia, 2007
Kerry Rhodes, Arizona, 2010
Juqua Parker, Philadelphia, 2011

Most Touchdowns, Career (Own recovered)
2   Ken Kavanaugh, Chi. Bears, 1940-41, 1945-1950
    Mike Ditka, Chicago, 1961-66; Philadelphia,
        1967-68; Dallas, 1969-1972
    Gail Cogdill, Detroit, 1960-68; Baltimore, 1968;
        Atlanta, 1969-1970
    Ahmad Rashad, St. Louis, 1972-73; Buffalo, 1974;
        Minnesota, 1976-1982
    Jim Mitchell, Atlanta, 1969-1979
    Drew Pearson, Dallas, 1973-1983
    Del Rodgers, Green Bay, 1982, 1984; San Francisco,
        1987-88
    Alan Ricard, Baltimore, 2001-05
    Kevin Curtis, St. Louis, 2003-06; Philadelphia,
        2007-09; Miami, 2010

Most Touchdowns, Season (Own recovered)
2   Ahmad Rashad, Buffalo, 1974
    Del Rodgers, Green Bay, 1982
    Kevin Curtis, Philadelphia, 2007
1   By many players

Most Touchdowns, Career (Opponents' recovered)
6   Jason Taylor, Miami, 1997-2007; Washington, 2008;
        Miami, 2009; N.Y. Jets, 2010; Miami, 2011
5   Jessie Tuggle, Atlanta, 1987-2000
4   Derrick Thomas, Kansas City, 1989-1999
    Keith Bulluck, Tennessee, 2000-09;
        N.Y. Giants, 2010
    Ronde Barber, Tampa Bay, 1997-2012

Most Touchdowns, Season (Opponents' recovered)
2   Harold McPhail, Boston, 1934
    Harry Ebding, Detroit, 1937
    John Morelli, Boston, 1944
    Frank Maznicki, Boston, 1947
    Fred (Dippy) Evans, Chi. Bears, 1948
    Ralph Heywood, Boston, 1948
    Art Tait, N.Y. Yanks, 1951
    John Dwyer, Los Angeles, 1952
    Leo Sugar, Chi. Cardinals, 1957
    Doug Cline, Houston, 1961
    Jim Bradshaw, Pittsburgh, 1964
    Royce Berry, Cincinnati, 1970
    Tim Gray, Kansas City, 1977
    Charles Phillips, Oakland, 1978
    Kenny Johnson, Atlanta, 1981
    George Martin, N.Y. Giants, 1981

Mike Douglass, Green Bay, 1983
Shelton Robinson, Seattle, 1983
Erik McMillan, N.Y. Jets, 1989
Les Miller, San Diego, 1990
Seth Joyner, Philadelphia, 1991
Robert Goff, New Orleans, 1992
Willie Clay, Detroit, 1993
Tyrone Hughes, New Orleans, 1994
Chad Brown, Seattle, 1997
Marcus Robertson, Tennessee, 1997
Dwayne Rudd, Minnesota, 1998
Keith McKenzie, Green Bay, 1999
Ronde Barber, Tampa Bay, 2004
Leonard Little, St. Louis, 2004
Antwan Odom, Tennessee, 2005
Adalius Thomas, Baltimore, 2005
Kerry Rhodes, Arizona, 2010
Juqua Parker, Philadelphia, 2011

Most Touchdowns, Game (Opponents' recovered)
2   Fred (Dippy) Evans, Chi. Bears vs. Washington,
        Nov. 28, 1948

COMBINED NET YARDS GAINED
Rushing, receiving, interception returns, punt returns, kickoff
returns, and fumble returns

Most Seasons Leading League
5   Jim Brown, Cleveland, 1958-1961, 1964
4   Brian Mitchell, Washington, 1994-96, 1998
3   Cliff Battles, Boston, 1932-33; Washington, 1937
    Gale Sayers, Chicago, 1965-67
    Eric Dickerson, L.A. Rams, 1983-84, 1986
    Thurman Thomas, Buffalo, 1989, 1991-92

Most Consecutive Seasons Leading League
4   Jim Brown, Cleveland, 1958-1961
3   Gale Sayers, Chicago, 1965-67
    Brian Mitchell, Washington, 1994-96
2   Cliff Battles, Boston, 1932-33
    Charley Trippi, Chi. Cardinals, 1948-49
    Timmy Brown, Philadelphia, 1962-63
    Floyd Little, Denver, 1967-68
    James Brooks, San Diego, 1981-82
    Eric Dickerson, L.A. Rams, 1983-84
    Thurman Thomas, Buffalo, 1991-92
    Dante Hall, Kansas City, 2003-04

ATTEMPTS
Most Attempts, Career
4,939   Emmitt Smith, Dallas, 1990-2002; Arizona, 2003-04
4,368   Walter Payton, Chicago, 1975-1987
4,016   Curtis Martin, New England, 1995-97; N.Y. Jets,
            1998-2005

Most Attempts, Season
496   James Wilder, Tampa Bay, 1984
458   Larry Johnson, Kansas City, 2006
455   Eddie George, Tennessee, 2000

Most Attempts, Rookie, Season
442   Eric Dickerson, L.A. Rams, 1983
433   Edgerrin James, Indianapolis, 1999
401   Curtis Martin, New England, 1995

Most Attempts, Game
48   James Wilder, Tampa Bay vs. Pittsburgh, Oct. 30, 1983
     LaDainian Tomlinson, San Diego vs. Denver,
         Dec. 1, 2002 (ot)
47   James Wilder, Tampa Bay vs. Green Bay,
         Sept. 30, 1984 (ot)
     Terrell Davis, Denver vs. Buffalo, Oct. 26, 1997 (ot)
46   Gerald Riggs, Atlanta vs. L.A. Rams, Nov. 17, 1985

YARDS GAINED

Most Yards Gained, Career

23,546	Jerry Rice, San Francisco, 1985-2000; Oakland, 2001-04; Seattle, 2004
23,330	Brian Mitchell, Washington, 1990-99; Philadelphia, 2000-02; N.Y. Giants, 2003
21,803	Walter Payton, Chicago, 1975-1987

Most Yards Gained, Season

2,696	Darren Sproles, New Orleans, 2011
2,690	Derrick Mason, Tennessee, 2000
2,647	Michael Lewis, New Orleans, 2002

Most Yards Gained, Rookie, Season

2,317	Tim Brown, L.A. Raiders, 1988
2,272	Gale Sayers, Chicago, 1965
2,250	Maurice Jones-Drew, Jacksonville, 2006

Most Yards Gained, Game

404	Glyn Milburn, Denver vs. Seattle, Dec. 10, 1995
373	Billy Cannon, Houston vs. N.Y. Titans, Dec. 10. 1961
361	Adrian Peterson, Minnesota vs. Chicago, Oct. 14, 2007

SACKS

Sacks have been compiled since 1982.

Most Seasons Leading League

2	Mark Gastineau, N.Y. Jets, 1983-84
	Reggie White, Philadelphia, 1987-88
	Kevin Greene, Pittsburgh, 1994; Carolina, 1996
	Michael Strahan, N.Y. Giants, 2001, 2003
	DeMarcus Ware, Dallas, 2008, 2010
	Jared Allen, Kansas City, 2007; Minnesota, 2011

Most Sacks, Career

200.0	Bruce Smith, Buffalo, 1985-1999; Washington, 2000-03
198.0	Reggie White, Philadelphia, 1985-1992; Green Bay, 1993-98; Carolina, 2000
160.0	Kevin Greene, L.A. Rams, 1985-1992; Pittsburgh, 1993-95; Carolina, 1996, 1998-99; San Francisco, 1997

Most Sacks, Season

22.5	Michael Strahan, N.Y. Giants, 2001
22.0	Mark Gastineau, N.Y. Jets, 1984
	Jared Allen, Minnesota, 2011
21.0	Reggie White, Philadelphia, 1987
	Chris Doleman, Minnesota, 1989

Most Sacks, Rookie, Season

14.5	Jevon Kearse, Tennessee, 1999
14.0	Aldon Smith, San Francisco, 2011
13.0	Dwight Freeney, Indianapolis, 2002

Most Sacks, Game

7.0	Derrick Thomas, Kansas City vs. Seattle, Nov. 11, 1990
6.0	Fred Dean, San Francisco vs. New Orleans, Nov. 13, 1983
	Derrick Thomas, Kansas City vs. Oakland, Sept. 6, 1998
	Osi Umenyiora, N.Y. Giants vs. Philadelphia, Sept. 30, 2007
5.5	William Gay, Detroit vs. Tampa Bay, Sept. 4, 1983
	Aldon Smith, San Francisco vs. Chicago, Nov. 19, 2012

Most Seasons, 10 or More Sacks

13	Bruce Smith, Buffalo, 1986-1990, 1992-98; Washington, 2000
12	Reggie White, Philadelphia, 1985-1992; Green Bay, 1993, 1995, 1997-98
10	Kevin Greene, L.A. Rams, 1988-1990, 1992; Pittsburgh, 1993-94; Carolina, 1996, 1998-99; San Francisco, 1997

Most Consecutive Seasons, 10 or More Sacks

9	Reggie White, Philadelphia, 1985-1992; Green Bay, 1993
8	John Randle, Minnesota, 1992-99
7	Lawrence Taylor, N.Y. Giants, 1984-1990
	Bruce Smith, Buffalo, 1992-98
	DeMarcus Ware, Dallas, 2006-2012 (current)

Most Consecutive Games, Sack

10	Simon Fletcher, Denver, Nov. 15, 1992-Sept. 20, 1993
	DeMarcus Ware, Dallas, Dec. 16, 2007-Oct. 19, 2008
9	Bruce Smith, Buffalo, Nov. 16, 1986-Oct. 25, 1987
	Kevin Greene, San Francisco-Carolina, Dec. 7, 1997-Oct. 18, 1998
	Dwight Freeney, Indianapolis, Dec. 18, 2008-Nov. 8, 2009
8	By many players

MISCELLANEOUS

Longest Return of Missed Field Goal (All TDs)

109	Antonio Cromartie, San Diego vs. Minnesota, Nov. 4, 2007
108	Nathan Vasher, Chicago vs. San Francisco, Nov. 13, 2005
	Devin Hester, Chicago vs. N.Y. Giants, Nov. 12, 2006
107	Chris McAlister, Baltimore vs. Denver, Sept. 30, 2002

TEAM RECORDS

CHAMPIONSHIPS

Most Seasons League Champion

13	Green Bay, 1929-1931, 1936, 1939, 1944, 1961-62, 1965-67, 1996, 2010
9	Chi. Bears, 1921, 1932-33, 1940-41, 1943, 1946, 1963, 1985
8	N.Y. Giants, 1927, 1934, 1938, 1956, 1986, 1990, 2007, 2011

Most Consecutive Seasons League Champion

3	Green Bay, 1929-1931
	Green Bay, 1965-67
2	Canton, 1922-23
	Chi. Bears, 1932-33
	Chi. Bears, 1940-41
	Philadelphia, 1948-49
	Detroit, 1952-53
	Cleveland, 1954-55
	Baltimore, 1958-59
	Houston, 1960-61
	Green Bay, 1961-62
	Buffalo, 1964-65
	Miami, 1972-73
	Pittsburgh, 1974-75
	Pittsburgh, 1978-79
	San Francisco, 1988-89
	Dallas, 1992-93
	Denver, 1997-98
	New England, 2003-04

Most Times Finishing First, Regular Season

23	N.Y. Giants, 1927, 1933-35, 1938-39, 1941, 1944, 1946, 1956, 1958-59, 1961-63, 1986, 1989-1990, 1997, 2000, 2005, 2008, 2011
	Green Bay, 1929-1931, 1936, 1938-39, 1944, 1960-62, 1965-67, 1972, 1995-97, 2002-04, 2007, 2011-12
22	Chi. Bears, 1921, 1932-34, 1937, 1940-43, 1946, 1956, 1963, 1984-88, 1990, 2001, 2005-06, 2010
21	Dallas, 1966-1971, 1973, 1976-79, 1981, 1985, 1992-96, 1998, 2007, 2009

Most Consecutive Times Finishing First, Regular Season

7	Los Angeles, 1973-79

6 Cleveland, 1950-55
   Dallas, 1966-1971
   Minnesota, 1973-78
   Pittsburgh, 1974-79
5 Oakland, 1972-76
   Chicago, 1984-88
   San Francisco, 1986-1990
   Dallas, 1992-96
   Indianapolis, 2003-07
   New England, 2003-07

GAMES WON
Most Consecutive Games Won
23 Indianapolis, 2008-09
21 New England, 2006-08
18 New England, 2003-04
Most Consecutive Games Without Defeat
25 Canton, 1921-23 (won 22, tied 3)
24 Chi. Bears, 1941-43 (won 23, tied 1)
23 Green Bay, 1928-1930 (won 21, tied 2)
    Indianapolis, 2008-09 (won 23)
Most Games Won, Season
16 New England, 2007
15 San Francisco, 1984
    Chicago, 1985
    Minnesota, 1998
    Pittsburgh, 2004
    Green Bay, 2011
14 By many teams
Most Consecutive Games Won, Season
16 New England, 2007, entire season
14 Miami, 1972, entire season
    Pittsburgh, 2004
    Indianapolis, 2009
13 Chi. Bears, 1934, entire season
    Denver, 1998
    Indianapolis, 2005
    New Orleans, 2009
    Green Bay, 2011
Most Consecutive Games Won, Start of Season
16 New England, 2007, entire season
14 Miami, 1972, entire season
    Indianapolis, 2009
13 Chi. Bears, 1934, entire season
    Denver, 1998
    Indianapolis, 2005
    New Orleans, 2009
    Green Bay, 2011
Most Consecutive Games Won, End of Season
16 New England, 2007, entire season
14 Miami, 1972, entire season
    Pittsburgh, 2004
13 Chi. Bears, 1934, entire season
Most Consecutive Games Without Defeat, Season
16 New England, 2007 (won 16), entire season
14 Miami, 1972 (won 14), entire season
    Pittsburgh, 2004 (won 14)
    Indianapolis, 2009 (won 14)
13 Chi. Bears, 1926 (won 11, tied 2)
    Green Bay, 1929 (won 12, tied 1)
    Chi. Bears, 1934 (won 13), entire season
    Baltimore, 1967 (won 11, tied 2)
    Denver, 1998 (won 13)
    Indianapolis, 2005 (won 13)
    New Orleans, 2009 (won 13)
    Green Bay, 2011 (won 13)
Most Consecutive Games Without Defeat, Start of Season
16 New England, 2007 (won 16), entire season
14 Miami, 1972 (won 14), entire season
    Indianapolis, 2009 (won 14)

13 Chi. Bears, 1926 (won 11, tied 2)
    Green Bay, 1929 (won 12, tied 1), entire season
    Chi. Bears, 1934 (won 13), entire season
    Baltimore, 1967 (won 11, tied 2)
    Denver, 1998 (won 13)
    Indianapolis, 2005 (won 13)
    New Orleans, 2009 (won 13)
    Green Bay, 2011 (won 13)
Most Consecutive Games Without Defeat, End of Season
16 New England, 2007 (won 16), entire season
14 Miami, 1972 (won 14), entire season
    Pittsburgh, 2004 (won 14)
13 Green Bay, 1929 (won 12, tied 1), entire season
    Chi. Bears, 1934 (won 13), entire season
Most Consecutive Home Games Won
27 Miami, 1971-74
25 Green Bay, 1995-98
24 Denver, 1996-98
Most Consecutive Home Games Without Defeat
29 Green Bay, 1928-1933 (won 26, tied 3)
27 Miami, 1971-74 (won 27)
25 Green Bay, 1995-98 (won 25)
Most Consecutive Road Games Won
18 San Francisco, 1988-1990
12 New England, 2006-08
11 L.A. Chargers/San Diego, 1960-61
    San Francisco, 1987-88
    Pittsburgh, 2004-05
    Indianapolis, 2008-09
Most Consecutive Road Games Without Defeat
18 San Francisco, 1988-1990 (won 18)
13 Chi. Bears, 1941-43 (won 12, tied 1)
12 Green Bay, 1928-1930 (won 10, tied 2)
    New England, 2006-08 (won 12)
Most Shutout Games Won or Tied, Season
10 Pottsville, 1926 (won 9, tied 1)
    N.Y. Giants, 1927 (won 9, tied 1)
9   Akron, 1921 (won 8, tied 1)
    Canton, 1922 (won 7, tied 2)
    Frankford, 1926 (won 9)
    Frankford, 1929 (won 6, tied 3)
8   By many teams
Most Consecutive Shutout Games Won or Tied
13 Akron, 1920-21 (won 10, tied 3)
7   Pottsville, 1926 (won 6, tied 1)
    Detroit, 1934 (won 7)
6   Buffalo, 1920-21 (won 5, tied 1)
    Frankford, 1926 (won 6)
    Detroit, 1926 (won 4, tied 2)
    N.Y. Giants, 1926-27 (won 5, tied 1)

GAMES LOST
Most Consecutive Games Lost
26 Tampa Bay, 1976-1977
19 Chi. Cardinals, 1942-43, 1945
    Oakland, 1961-62
    Detroit, 2007-09
18 Houston, 1972-73
Most Consecutive Games Without Victory
26 Tampa Bay, 1976-77 (lost 26)
23 Rochester, 1922-25 (lost 21, tied 2)
    Washington, 1960-61 (lost 20, tied 3)
19 Dayton, 1927-29 (lost 18, tied 1)
    Chi. Cardinals, 1942-43, 1945 (lost 19)
    Oakland, 1961-62 (lost 19)
    Detroit, 2007-09 (lost 19)
Most Games Lost, Season
16 Detroit, 2008
15 New Orleans, 1980
    Dallas, 1989

New England, 1990
Indianapolis, 1991
N.Y. Jets, 1996
San Diego, 2000
Carolina, 2001
Miami, 2007
St. Louis, 2009
14 By many teams

Most Consecutive Games Lost, Season
16 Detroit, 2008, entire season
15 Carolina, 2001
14 Tampa Bay, 1976
     New Orleans, 1980
     Baltimore, 1981
     New England, 1990

Most Consecutive Games Lost, Start of Season
16 Detroit, 2008, entire season
14 Tampa Bay, 1976, entire season
     New Orleans, 1980
13 Oakland, 1962
     Indianapolis, 1986
     Miami, 2007
     Indianapolis, 2011

Most Consecutive Games Lost, End of Season
16 Detroit, 2008, entire season
15 Carolina, 2001
14 Tampa Bay, 1976, entire season
     New England, 1990

Most Consecutive Games Without Victory, Season
16 Detroit, 2008 (lost 16), entire season
15 Carolina, 2001 (lost 15)
14 Tampa Bay, 1976 (lost 14), entire season
     New Orleans, 1980 (lost 14)
     Baltimore, 1981 (lost 14)
     New England, 1990 (lost 14)

Most Consecutive Games Without Victory, Start of Season
16 Detroit, 2008 (lost 16), entire season
14 Tampa Bay, 1976 (lost 14), entire season
     New Orleans, 1980 (lost 14)
13 Washington, 1961 (lost 12, tied 1)
     Oakland, 1962 (lost 13)
     Indianapolis, 1986 (lost 13)
     Miami, 2007 (lost 13)
     Indianapolis, 2011 (lost 13)

Most Consecutive Games Without Victory, End of Season
16 Detroit, 2008 (lost 16), entire season
15 Carolina, 2001
14 Tampa Bay, 1976, (lost 14), entire season
     New England, 1990 (lost 14)

Most Consecutive Home Games Lost
14 Dallas, 1988-89
     St. Louis, 2008-2010
13 Houston, 1972-73
     Tampa Bay, 1976-77
     N.Y. Jets, 1995-97
11 Oakland, 1961-62
     Los Angeles, 1961-63
     Cincinnati, 1998-99

Most Consecutive Home Games Without Victory
14 Dallas, 1988-89 (lost 14)
     St. Louis, 2008-2010 (lost 14)
13 Houston, 1972-73 (lost 13)
     Tampa Bay, 1976-77 (lost 13)
     N.Y. Jets, 1995-97 (lost 13)
     Philadelphia, 1936-38 (lost 12, tied 1)

Most Consecutive Road Games Lost
26 Detroit, 2007-2010
24 Detroit, 2001-03
23 Houston, 1981-84

Most Consecutive Road Games Without Victory
26 Detroit, 2007-2010 (lost 26)
24 Detroit, 2001-03 (lost 24)
23 Houston, 1981-84 (lost 23)

Most Shutout Games Lost or Tied, Season
8 Frankford, 1927 (lost 6, tied 2)
   Brooklyn, 1931 (lost 8)
7 Dayton, 1925 (lost 6, tied 1)
   Orange, 1929 (lost 4, tied 3)
   Frankford, 1931 (lost 6, tied 1)
6 By many teams

Most Consecutive Shutout Games Lost or Tied
8 Rochester, 1922-24 (lost 8)
7 Hammond, 1922-23 (lost 6, tied 1)
6 Providence, 1926-27 (lost 5, tied 1)
   Brooklyn, 1942-43 (lost 6)

TIE GAMES

Most Tie Games, Season
6 Chi. Bears, 1932
5 Frankford, 1929
4 Chi. Bears, 1924
   Orange, 1929
   Portsmouth, 1932

Most Consecutive Tie Games
3 Chi. Bears, 1932
2 By many teams

SCORING

Most Seasons Leading League
10 Chi. Bears, 1932, 1934-35, 1939, 1941-43,
      1946-47, 1956
9 San Francisco, 1953, 1965, 1970, 1987, 1989,
     1992-95
   L.A./St. Louis Rams, 1950-52, 1957, 1967, 1973,
     1999-2001
8 Green Bay, 1931, 1936-38, 1961-62, 1996, 2011

Most Consecutive Seasons Leading League
4 San Francisco, 1992-1995
3 Green Bay, 1936-38
   Chi. Bears, 1941-43
   Los Angeles, 1950-52
   Oakland, 1967-69
   St. Louis, 1999-2001
2 By many teams

POINTS

Most Points, Season
589 New England, 2007
560 Green Bay, 2011
557 New England, 2012

Fewest Points, Season (Since 1932)
37 Cincinnati/St. Louis, 1934
38 Cincinnati, 1933
   Detroit, 1942
51 Pittsburgh, 1934
   Philadelphia, 1936

Most Points, Game
72 Washington vs. N.Y. Giants, Nov. 27, 1966
70 Los Angeles vs. Baltimore, Oct. 22, 1950
66 Rochester vs. *Fort Porter, Oct. 10, 1920
   *Not a member of the American Professional
   Football Association

Most Points, Both Teams, Game
113 Washington (72) vs. N.Y. Giants (41), Nov. 27, 1966
106 Cincinnati (58) vs. Cleveland (48), Nov. 28, 2004
101 Oakland (52) vs. Houston (49), Dec. 22, 1963
    San Diego (54) vs. Pittsburgh (44), Dec. 8, 1985

Fewest Points, Both Teams, Game
- 0   In many games. Last time: N.Y. Giants vs. Detroit, Nov. 7, 1943

Most Points, Shutout Victory Game
- 66   Rochester vs. *Fort Porter, Oct. 10, 1920
  Not a member of the American Professional Football Association
- 64   Philadelphia vs. Cincinnati, Nov. 6, 1934
- 62   Akron vs. Oorang, Oct. 29, 1922

Most Consecutive Games Scoring
- 420   San Francisco, 1977-2004
- 325   Denver, 1992-2012 (current)
- 305   Indianapolis, 1994-2012 (current)

Fewest Points, Shutout Victory, Game
- 2   Akron vs. Buffalo, Nov. 29, 1923
  Kansas City vs. Buffalo, Nov. 21, 1926
  Frankford vs. Green Bay, Nov. 29, 1928
  Green Bay vs. Chi. Bears, Oct. 16, 1932
  Chi. Bears vs. Green Bay, Sept. 18, 1938

Most Points Overcome to Win Game
- 28   San Francisco vs. New Orleans, Dec. 7, 1980 (ot) (trailed 7-35, won 38-35)
- 26   Buffalo vs. Indianapolis, Sept., 21, 1997 (trailed 0-26, won 37-35)
- 25   St. Louis vs. Tampa Bay, Nov. 8, 1987 (trailed 3-28, won 31-28)

Most Points Overcome to Tie Game
- 31   Denver vs. Buffalo, Nov. 27, 1960 (trailed 7-38, tied 38-38)
- 28   Los Angeles vs. Philadelphia, Oct. 3, 1948 (trailed 0-28, tied 28-28)

Most Points, Each Half
- 1st: 49   Green Bay vs. Tampa Bay, Oct. 2, 1983
- 48   Buffalo vs. Miami, Sept. 18, 1966
- 45   Green Bay vs. Cleveland, Nov. 12, 1967
  Indianapolis vs. Denver, Oct. 31, 1988
  Houston vs. Cleveland, Dec. 9, 1990
  Seattle vs. Minnesota, Sept. 29, 2002
  New England vs. Tennessee, Oct. 18, 2009
  Philadelphia vs. Washington, Nov. 15, 2010
- 2nd: 49   Chi. Bears vs. Philadelphia, Nov. 30, 1941
- 48   Chi. Cardinals vs. Baltimore, Oct. 2, 1950
  N.Y. Giants vs. Baltimore, Nov. 19, 1950
- 45   Cincinnati vs. Houston, Dec. 17, 1972
  New England vs. Buffalo, Sept. 30, 2012

Most Points, Both Teams, Each Half
- 1st: 70   Houston (35) vs. Oakland (35), Dec. 22, 1963
- 63   Philadelphia (42) vs. Detroit (21), Sept. 23, 2007
- 62   N.Y. Jets (41) vs. Tampa Bay (21), Nov. 17, 1985
  Indianapolis (35) vs. Cincinnati, Nov. 20, 2005
- 2nd: 66   Cleveland (35) vs. Cincinnati (31), Nov. 28, 2004
- 65   Washington (38) vs. N.Y. Giants (27), Nov. 27, 1966
- 62   L.A. Raiders (31) vs. San Diego (31), Jan. 2, 1983
  Baltimore (38) vs. Seattle (24), Nov. 23, 2003

Most Points, One Quarter
- 41   Green Bay vs. Detroit, Oct. 7, 1945 (second quarter)
  Los Angeles vs. Detroit, Oct. 29, 1950 (third quarter)
- 37   Los Angeles vs. Green Bay, Sept. 21, 1980 (second quarter)
- 35   Chi. Cardinals vs. Boston, Oct. 24, 1948 (third quarter)
  Green Bay vs. Cleveland, Nov. 12, 1967 (first quarter)
  Green Bay vs. Tampa Bay, Oct. 2, 1983 (second quarter)
  New England vs. Tennessee, Oct. 18, 2009 (second quarter)
  New England vs. N.Y. Jets, Nov. 22, 2012 (second quarter)

Most Points, Both Teams, One Quarter
- 49   Oakland (28) vs. Houston (21), Dec. 22, 1963 (second quarter)
- 48   Green Bay (41) vs. Detroit (7), Oct. 7, 1945 (second quarter)
  Los Angeles (41) vs. Detroit (7), Oct. 29, 1950 (third quarter)
  Detroit (34) vs. Chicago (14), Sept. 30, 2007 (fourth quarter)
- 47   St. Louis (27) vs. Philadelphia (20), Dec. 13, 1964 (second quarter)

Most Points, Each Quarter
- 1st: 35   Green Bay vs. Cleveland, Nov. 12, 1967
- 31   Buffalo vs. Kansas City, Sept. 13, 1964
- 28   By 11 teams
- 2nd: 41   Green Bay vs. Detroit, Oct. 7, 1945
- 37   Los Angeles vs. Green Bay, Sept. 21, 1980
- 35   Green Bay vs. Tampa Bay, Oct. 2, 1983
  New England vs. Tennessee, Oct. 18, 2009
  New England vs. N.Y. Jets, Nov. 22, 2012
- 3rd: 41   Los Angeles vs. Detroit, Oct. 29, 1950
- 35   Chi. Cardinals vs. Boston, Oct. 24, 1948
- 28   By 10 teams
- 4th: 34   Detroit vs. Chicago, Sept. 30, 2007
- 31   Oakland vs. Denver, Dec. 17, 1960
  Oakland vs. San Diego, Dec. 8, 1963
  Atlanta vs. Green Bay, Sept. 13, 1981
  New England vs. Buffalo, Sept. 30, 2012
- 30   N.Y. Jets vs. Miami, Oct. 23, 2000

Most Points, Both Teams, Each Quarter
- 1st: 42   Green Bay (35) vs. Cleveland (7), Nov. 12, 1967
- 41   Tennessee (24) vs. Indianapolis (17), Dec. 5, 2004
- 35   Dall. Texans (21) vs. N.Y. Titans (14), Nov. 11, 1962
  Dallas (28) vs. Philadelphia (7), Oct. 19, 1969
  Kansas City (21) vs. Seattle (14), Dec. 11, 1977
  Detroit (21) vs. L.A. Raiders (14), Dec. 10, 1990
  Dallas (21) vs. Atlanta (14), Dec. 22, 1991
  Indianapolis (21) vs. Green Bay (14), Sept 26, 2004
  Miami (21) vs. Buffalo (14), Dec. 5, 2004
  Philadelphia (21) vs. New Orleans (14), Dec. 23, 2007
- 2nd: 49   Oakland (28) vs. Houston (21), Dec. 22, 1963
- 48   Green Bay (41) vs. Detroit (7), Oct. 7, 1945
- 47   St. Louis (27) vs. Philadelphia (20), Dec. 13, 1964
- 3rd: 48   Los Angeles (41) vs. Detroit (7), Oct. 29, 1950
- 42   Washington (28) vs. Philadelphia (14), Oct. 1, 1955
- 41   Green Bay (21) vs. N.Y. Yanks (20), Oct. 8, 1950
- 4th: 48   Detroit (34) vs. Chicago (14), Sept. 30, 2007
- 46   Detroit (25) vs. Tennessee (21), Sept. 23, 2012
- 43   Atlanta (28) vs. Carolina (15), Nov. 23, 2008

TOUCHDOWNS

Most Seasons Leading League, Touchdowns
- 13   Chi. Bears, 1932, 1934-35, 1939, 1941-44, 1946-48, 1956, 1965
- 7   Dallas, 1966, 1968, 1971, 1973, 1977-78, 1980
  San Francisco, 1953, 1970, 1987, 1992-95
  L.A./St. Louis Rams, 1949-1952, 1999-2001
  San Diego, 1963, 1965, 1979, 1981-82, 1985, 2006
  Green Bay, 1932, 1937-38, 1961-62, 1996, 2011
- 6   Oakland, 1967-69, 1972, 1974, 1977
  Baltimore/Indianapolis Colts, 1957-59, 1964, 1976, 2004

Most Consecutive Seasons Leading League, Touchdowns
- 4   Chi. Bears, 1941-44
  Los Angeles, 1949-1952
  San Francisco, 1992-95
- 3   Chi. Bears, 1946-48
  Baltimore, 1957-59
  Oakland, 1967-69

St. Louis, 1999-2001
2 By many teams

Most Touchdowns, Season
75 New England, 2007
70 Miami, 1984
Green Bay, 2011
67 St. Louis, 2000
New England, 2012

Fewest Touchdowns, Season (Since 1932)
3 Cincinnati, 1933
4 Cincinnati/St. Louis, 1934
5 Detroit, 1942

Most Touchdowns, Game
10 Rochester vs. *Fort Porter, Oct. 10, 1920
*Not a member of the American Professional
Football Association
Philadelphia vs. Cincinnati, Nov. 6, 1934
Los Angeles vs. Baltimore, Oct. 22, 1950
Washington vs. N.Y. Giants, Nov. 27, 1966
9 Rock Island vs. Evansville, Oct. 15, 1922
Akron vs. Oorang, Oct. 29, 1922
Racine vs. Louisville, Nov. 5, 1922
Chi. Cardinals vs. Rochester, Oct. 7, 1923
Chi. Cardinals vs. Milwaukee, Dec. 10, 1925
Chi. Cardinals vs. N.Y. Giants, Oct. 17, 1948
Chi. Cardinals vs. N.Y. Bulldogs, Nov. 13, 1949
Los Angeles vs. Detroit, Oct. 29, 1950
Pittsburgh vs. N.Y. Giants, Nov. 30, 1952
Chicago vs. San Francisco, Dec. 12, 1965
Chicago vs. Green Bay, Dec. 7, 1980
8 By many teams

Most Touchdowns, Both Teams, Game
16 Washington (10) vs. N.Y. Giants (6), Nov. 27, 1966
14 Chi. Cardinals (9) vs. N.Y. Giants (5), Oct. 17, 1948
Los Angeles (10) vs. Baltimore (4), Oct. 22, 1950
Houston (7) vs. Oakland (7), Dec. 22, 1963
13 New Orleans (7) vs. St. Louis (6), Nov. 2, 1969
Kansas City (7) vs. Seattle (6), Nov. 27, 1983 (ot)
San Diego (8) vs. Pittsburgh (5), Dec. 8, 1985
N.Y. Jets (7) vs. Miami (6), Sept. 21, 1986 (ot)
Cincinnati (7) vs. Cleveland (6), Nov. 28, 2004

Most Consecutive Games Scoring Touchdowns
166 Cleveland, 1957-1969
151 San Diego, 2002-2012
136 Indianapolis, 2003-2011

POINTS AFTER TOUCHDOWN

Most (One-Point) Points After Touchdown, Season
74 New England, 2007
68 Green Bay, 2011
66 Miami, 1984
New England, 2012

Fewest (One-Point) Points After Touchdown, Season
2 Chi. Cardinals, 1933
3 Cincinnati, 1933
Pittsburgh, 1934
4 Cincinnati/St. Louis, 1934

Most (One-Point) Points After Touchdown, Game
10 Los Angeles vs. Baltimore, Oct. 22, 1950
9 Chi. Cardinals vs. N.Y. Giants, Oct. 17, 1948
Pittsburgh vs. N.Y. Giants, Nov. 30, 1952
Washington vs. N.Y. Giants, Nov. 27, 1966
8 By many teams

Most (One-Point) Points After Touchdown, Both Teams, Game
14 Chi. Cardinals (9) vs. N.Y. Giants (5), Oct. 17, 1948
Houston (7) vs. Oakland (7), Dec. 22, 1963
Washington (9) vs. N.Y. Giants (5), Nov. 27, 1966
13 Los Angeles (10) vs. Baltimore (3), Oct. 22, 1950
Cincinnati (7) vs. Cleveland (6), Nov. 28, 2004
12 In many games

Most Two-Point Conversions, Season
6 Miami, 1994
Minnesota, 1997
5 Arizona, 1995
Baltimore, 1996
Jacksonville, 1996
Chicago, 1997
San Francisco, 1998
Pittsburgh, 2002
St. Louis, 2012
4 By many teams

Most Two-Point Conversions, Game
4 St. Louis vs. Atlanta, Oct. 15, 2000
3 Baltimore vs. New England, Oct. 6, 1996
Pittsburgh vs. Tennessee, Nov. 1, 1998
2 By many teams

Most Two-Point Conversions, Both Teams, Game
5 Baltimore (3) vs. New England (2), Oct. 6, 1996
St. Louis (4) vs. Atlanta (1), Oct. 15, 2000
3 Seattle (2) vs. Kansas City (1), Oct. 23, 1994
Minnesota (2) vs. Seattle (1), Nov. 10, 1996
Pittsburgh (3) vs. Tennessee (0), Nov. 1, 1998
2 In many games

FIELD GOALS

Most Seasons Leading League, Field Goals
11 Green Bay, 1935-36, 1940-43, 1946-47, 1955, 1972, 1974
9 L.A./St. Louis Rams, 1949, 1951, 1958, 1966, 1973, 1978, 2003, 2006, 2010
8 Washington, 1945, 1956, 1971, 1976-77, 1979, 1982, 1992
N.Y. Giants, 1933, 1937, 1939, 1941, 1944, 1959, 1983, 2008

Most Consecutive Seasons Leading League, Field Goals
4 Green Bay, 1940-43
3 Cleveland, 1952-54
2 By many teams

Most Field Goals Attempted, Season
52 San Francisco, 2011
49 Los Angeles, 1966
Washington, 1971
48 Green Bay, 1972

Fewest Field Goals Attempted, Season (Since 1938)
0 Chi. Bears, 1944
2 Cleveland, 1939
Card-Pitt, 1944
Boston, 1946
Chi. Bears, 1947
3 Chi. Bears, 1945
Cleveland, 1945

Most Field Goals Attempted, Game
9 St. Louis vs. Pittsburgh, Sept. 24, 1967
8 Pittsburgh vs. St. Louis, Dec. 2, 1962
Detroit vs. Minnesota, Nov. 13, 1966
N.Y. Jets vs. Buffalo, Nov. 3, 1968
Dallas vs. N.Y. Giants, Sept. 15, 2003 (ot)
Tennessee vs. Houston, Oct. 21, 2007
7 By many teams

Most Field Goals Attempted, Both Teams, Game
11 St. Louis (6) vs. Pittsburgh (5), Nov. 13, 1966
Washington (6) vs. Chicago (5), Nov. 14, 1971
Green Bay (6) vs. Detroit (5), Sept. 29, 1974
Washington (6) vs. N.Y. Giants (5), Nov. 14, 1976
10 In many games

Most Field Goals, Season
44 San Francisco, 2011
43 Arizona, 2005
39 Miami, 1999
St. Louis, 2003

Fewest Field Goals, Season (Since 1932)
- 0 Boston, 1932, 1935
  - Chi. Cardinals, 1932, 1945
  - Green Bay, 1932, 1944
  - N.Y. Giants, 1932
  - Brooklyn, 1944
  - Card-Pitt, 1944
  - Chi. Bears, 1944, 1947
  - Boston, 1946
  - Baltimore, 1950
  - Dallas, 1952

Most Field Goals, Game
- 8 Tennessee vs. Houston, Oct. 21, 2007
- 7 St. Louis vs. Pittsburgh, Sept. 24, 1967
  - Minnesota vs. L.A. Rams, Nov. 5, 1989 (ot)
  - Dallas vs. Green Bay, Nov. 18, 1996
  - Dallas vs. N.Y. Giants, Sept. 15, 2003 (ot)
  - Cincinnati vs. Baltimore, Nov. 11, 2007
- 6 By many teams

Most Field Goals, Both Teams, Game
- 9 San Diego (5) vs. Kansas City (4), Sept. 29, 1996
  - Miami (6) vs. New England (3), Oct. 17, 1999
  - Houston (5) vs. Miami (4), Oct. 7, 2007
  - Dallas (6) vs. Washington (3), Sept. 26, 2011
- 8 Cleveland (4) vs. St. Louis (4), Sept. 20, 1964
  - Chicago (5) vs. Philadelphia (3), Oct. 20, 1968
  - Washington (5) vs. Chicago (3), Nov. 14, 1971
  - Kansas City (5) vs. Buffalo (3), Dec. 19, 1971
  - Detroit (4) vs. Green Bay (4), Sept. 29, 1974
  - Cleveland (5) vs. Denver (3), Oct. 19, 1975
  - New England (4) vs. San Diego (4), Nov. 9, 1975
  - San Francisco (6) vs. New Orleans (2), Oct. 16, 1983
  - Seattle (5) vs. L.A. Raiders (3), Dec. 18, 1988
  - Atlanta (6) vs. New Orleans (2), Nov. 13, 1994
  - Indianapolis (4) vs. San Diego (4), Nov. 3, 1996
  - Dallas (7) vs. N.Y. Giants (1), Sept. 15, 2003 (ot)
  - Oakland (5) vs. Chicago (3), Oct. 5, 2003
  - Buffalo (5) vs. Tennessee (3), Dec. 24, 2006
  - Tennessee (8) vs. Houston (0), Oct. 21, 2007
  - Buffalo (5) vs. Washington (3), Dec. 2, 2007
  - Kansas City (4) vs. Denver (4), Sept. 28, 2008
  - San Francisco (4) vs. Philadelphia (4), Oct. 12, 2008
  - Pittsburgh (4) vs. Cincinnati (4), Nov. 15, 2009
  - Miami (5) vs. Pittsburgh (3), Oct. 24, 2010
  - Oakland (6) vs. Chicago (2), Nov. 27, 2011
- 7 In many games

Most Consecutive Games Scoring Field Goals
- 38 Baltimore, 1999-2001
- 34 New England, 2010-12
  - San Francisco, 2010-12 (current)
- 31 Minnesota, 1968-1970

SAFETIES
Most Safeties, Season
- 4 Cleveland, 1927
  - Detroit, 1962
  - Seattle, 1993
  - San Francisco, 1996
  - Tennessee, 1999
- 3 By many teams

Most Safeties, Game
- 3 L.A. Rams vs. N.Y. Giants, Sept. 30, 1984
- 2 N.Y. Giants vs. Pottsville, Oct. 30, 1927
  - Chi. Bears vs. Pottsville, Nov. 13, 1927
  - Detroit vs. Brooklyn, Dec. 1, 1935
  - N.Y. Giants vs. Pittsburgh, Sept. 17, 1950
  - N.Y. Giants vs. Washington, Nov. 5, 1961
  - Chicago vs. Pittsburgh, Nov. 9, 1969
  - Dallas vs. Philadelphia, Nov. 19, 1972
  - Los Angeles vs. Green Bay, Oct. 21, 1973

- Oakland vs. San Diego, Oct. 26, 1975
- Denver vs. Seattle, Jan. 2, 1983
- New Orleans vs. Cleveland, Sept. 13, 1987
- Buffalo vs. Denver, Nov. 8, 1987
- San Francisco vs. St. Louis, Sept. 8, 1996
- Jacksonville vs. Pittsburgh, Oct. 3, 1999
- Minnesota vs. Atlanta, Oct. 5, 2003
- Dallas vs. Arizona, Oct. 5, 2003
- Buffalo vs. Houston, Nov. 16, 2003
- Minnesota vs. Green Bay, Nov. 9, 2008
- St. Louis vs. Arizona, Nov. 6, 2011 (ot)

Most Safeties, Both Teams, Game
- 3 L.A. Rams (3) vs. N.Y. Giants (0), Sept. 30, 1984
- 2 Chi. Cardinals (1) vs. Frankford (1), Nov. 19, 1927
  - Chi. Cardinals (1) vs. Cincinnati (1), Nov. 12, 1933
  - Chi. Bears (1) vs. San Francisco (1), Oct. 19, 1952
  - Cincinnati (1) vs. Los Angeles (1), Oct. 22, 1972
  - Chi. Bears (1) vs. San Francisco (1), Sept. 19, 1976
  - Baltimore (1) vs. Miami (1), Oct. 29, 1978
  - Atlanta (1) vs. Detroit (1), Oct. 5, 1980
  - Houston (1) vs. Philadelphia (1), Oct. 2, 1988
  - Cleveland (1) vs. Seattle (1), Nov. 14, 1993
  - Arizona (1) vs. Houston (1), Dec. 4, 1994
  - (Also see previous record)

FIRST DOWNS
Most Seasons Leading League
- 9 Chi. Bears, 1935, 1939, 1941, 1943, 1945, 1947-49, 1955
- 7 San Diego, 1965, 1969, 1980-83, 1985
  - L.A./St. Louis Rams, 1946, 1950-51, 1954, 1957, 1973, 2001
  - Baltimore/Indianapolis Colts, 1958-59, 1967, 2003, 2005-06, 2010
- 6 San Francisco, 1965, 1987, 1989, 1993-94, 1998

Most Consecutive Seasons Leading League
- 4 San Diego, 1980-83
- 3 Chi. Bears, 1947-49
  - New England, 2007-09
- 2 By many teams

Most First Downs, Season
- 444 New England, 2012
- 416 New Orleans, 2011
- 399 New England, 2011

Fewest First Downs, Season
- 51 Cincinnati, 1933
- 64 Pittsburgh, 1935
- 67 Philadelphia, 1937

Most First Downs, Game
- 39 N.Y. Jets vs. Miami, Nov. 27, 1988
  - Washington vs. Detroit, Nov. 4, 1990 (ot)
  - Houston vs. Jacksonville, Nov. 18, 2012 (ot)
- 38 Los Angeles vs. N.Y. Giants, Nov. 13, 1966
- 37 Green Bay vs. Philadelphia, Nov. 11, 1962

Fewest First Downs, Game
- 0 N.Y. Giants vs. Green Bay, Oct. 1, 1933
  - Pittsburgh vs. Boston, Oct. 29, 1933
  - Philadelphia vs. Detroit, Sept. 20, 1935
  - N.Y. Giants vs. Washington, Sept. 27, 1942
  - Denver vs. Houston, Sept. 3, 1966

Most First Downs, Both Teams, Game
- 64 Seattle (32) vs. Kansas City (32), Nov. 24, 2002
- 62 San Diego (32) vs. Seattle (30), Sept. 15, 1985
  - Oakland (31) vs. Kansas City (31), Nov. 5, 2000
  - Buffalo (35) vs. New England (27), Nov. 11, 2012
- 61 New England (33) vs. Baltimore (28), Sept. 23, 2012

Fewest First Downs, Both Teams, Game
- 7 Chi. Cardinals (2) vs. Detroit (5), Sept. 15, 1940
- 9 Pittsburgh (1) vs. Boston (8), Oct. 27, 1935
  - Boston (4) vs. Brooklyn (5), Nov. 24, 1935

N.Y. Giants (3) vs. Detroit (6), Nov. 7, 1943
Pittsburgh (4) vs. Chi. Cardinals (5), Nov. 11, 1945
N.Y. Bulldogs (1) vs. Philadelphia (8), Sept. 22, 1949
　10　Philadelphia (4) vs. Brooklyn (6), Nov. 5, 1944
N.Y. Giants (4) vs. Washington (6), Dec. 11, 1960

Most First Downs, Rushing, Season
　181　New England, 1978
　177　Los Angeles, 1973
　176　Chicago, 1985

Fewest First Downs, Rushing, Season
　36　Cleveland, 1942
　　　Boston, 1944
　39　Brooklyn, 1943
　40　Philadelphia, 1940
　　　Detroit, 1945

Most First Downs, Rushing, Game
　25　Philadelphia vs. Washington, Dec. 2, 1951
　23　St. Louis vs. New Orleans, Oct. 5, 1980
　21　Cleveland vs. Philadelphia, Dec. 13, 1959
　　　Green Bay vs. Philadelphia, Nov. 11, 1962
　　　Los Angeles vs. New Orleans, Nov. 25, 1973
　　　Pittsburgh vs. Kansas City, Nov. 7, 1976
　　　New England vs. Denver, Nov. 28, 1976
　　　Oakland vs. Green Bay, Sept. 17, 1978
　　　Buffalo vs. Washington, Nov. 3, 1996
　　　San Francisco vs. Detroit, Dec. 14, 1998
　　　Kansas City vs. Atlanta, Oct. 24, 2004

Fewest First Downs, Rushing, Game
　0　By many teams. Last time:
　　　　Cincinnati vs. Pittsburgh, Dec. 23, 2012
　　　　Arizona vs. Chicago, Dec. 23, 2012

Most First Downs, Rushing, Both Teams, Game
　36　Philadelphia (25) vs. Washington (11), Dec. 2, 1951
　31　Detroit (18) vs. Washington (13), Sept. 30, 1951
　30　Los Angeles (17) vs. Minnesota (13), Nov. 5, 1961
　　　New Orleans (17) vs. Green Bay (13), Sept. 9, 1979
　　　New Orleans (16) vs. San Francisco (14), Nov. 11, 1979
　　　New England (16) vs. Kansas City (14), Oct. 4, 1981
　　　Indianapolis (18) vs. Denver (12), Sept. 30, 2007

Fewest First Downs, Rushing, Both Teams, Game
　1　Oakland (0) vs. Tennessee (1), Sept. 7, 2003
　　　Carolina (0) vs. Detroit (1), Oct. 16, 2005
　2　Houston (0) vs. Denver (2), Dec. 2, 1962
　　　N.Y. Jets, (1) vs. St. Louis (1), Dec. 3, 1995
　　　Miami (1) vs. San Diego (1), Dec. 19, 1999
　　　New Orleans (0) vs. Baltimore (2), Dec. 19, 1999
　　　Baltimore (0) vs. Tennessee (2), Sept. 18, 2005
　　　Pittsburgh (1) vs. Baltimore (1), Nov. 5, 2007
　　　Arizona (1) vs. San Francisco (1), Sept. 13, 2009
　3　In many games

Most First Downs, Passing, Season
　280　New Orleans, 2011
　272　Detroit, 2012
　267　New Orleans, 2012

Fewest First Downs, Passing, Season
　18　Pittsburgh, 1941
　23　Brooklyn, 1942
　　　N.Y. Giants, 1944
　24　N.Y. Giants, 1943

Most First Downs, Passing, Game
　29　N.Y. Giants vs. Cincinnati, Oct. 13, 1985
　28　Tennessee vs. Oakland, Dec. 19, 2004
　27　San Diego vs. Seattle, Sept. 15, 1985
　　　Detroit vs. Green Bay, Jan. 1, 2012

Fewest First Downs, Passing, Game
　0　By many teams. Last time:
　　　　Pittsburgh vs. Tennessee, Sept. 19, 2010

Most First Downs, Passing, Both Teams, Game
　47　Detroit (27) vs. Green Bay (20), Jan. 1, 2012
　44　New Orleans (23) vs. Green Bay (21),

　　　Sept. 30, 2012
　43　San Diego (23) vs. Cincinnati (20), Dec. 20, 1982
　　　Miami (24) vs. N.Y. Jets (19), Sept. 21, 1986 (ot)
　　　Tennessee (28) vs. Oakland (15), Dec. 19, 2004
　　　New England (23) vs. San Diego (20),
　　　　Sept. 18, 2011

Fewest First Downs, Passing, Both Teams, Game
　0　Brooklyn vs. Pittsburgh, Nov. 29, 1942
　1　Green Bay (0) vs. Cleveland (1), Sept. 21, 1941
　　　Pittsburgh (0) vs. Brooklyn (1), Oct. 11, 1942
　　　N.Y. Giants (0) vs. Detroit (1), Nov. 7, 1943
　　　Pittsburgh (0) vs. Chi. Cardinals (1), Nov. 11, 1945
　　　N.Y. Bulldogs (0) vs. Philadelphia (1), Sept. 22, 1949
　　　Chicago (0) vs. Buffalo (1), Oct. 7, 1979
　2　In many games

Most First Downs, Penalty, Season
　47　Buffalo, 2002
　　　Indianapolis, 2004
　44　Dallas, 2005
　43　Denver, 1994
　　　Green Bay, 2012

Fewest First Downs, Penalty, Season
　2　Brooklyn, 1940
　4　Chi. Cardinals, 1940
　　　N.Y. Giants, 1942, 1944
　　　Washington, 1944
　　　Cleveland, 1952
　　　Kansas City, 1969
　5　Brooklyn, 1939
　　　Chi. Bears, 1939
　　　Detroit, 1953
　　　Los Angeles, 1953
　　　Houston, 1982

Most First Downs, Penalty, Game
　11　Denver vs. Houston, Oct. 6, 1985
　10　Dallas vs. Cleveland, Nov. 18, 2012 (ot)
　9　Chi. Bears vs. Cleveland, Nov. 25, 1951
　　　Baltimore vs. Pittsburgh, Oct. 30, 1977
　　　N.Y. Jets vs. Houston, Sept. 18, 1988
　　　Dallas vs. Detroit, Nov. 20, 2005

Most First Downs, Penalty, Both Teams, Game
　13　New England (8) vs. Baltimore (5), Sept. 23, 2012
　12　Buffalo (7) vs. San Francisco (5), Oct. 4, 1998
　　　Detroit (8) vs. Baltimore (4), Oct. 9, 2005
　　　Dallas (10) vs. Cleveland (2), Nov. 18, 2012 (ot)
　11　Chi. Bears (9) vs. Cleveland (2), Nov. 25, 1951
　　　Cincinnati (8) vs. N.Y. Jets (3), Oct. 6, 1985
　　　Denver (11) vs. Houston (0), Oct. 6, 1985
　　　Detroit (6) vs. Dallas (5), Nov. 8, 1987
　　　N.Y. Jets (9) vs. Houston (2), Sept. 18, 1988
　　　Kansas City (8) vs. L.A. Raiders (3), Oct. 3, 1993
　　　Detroit (6) vs. San Diego (5), Nov. 11, 1996
　　　Philadelphia (8) vs. Chicago (3), Nov. 3, 2002
　　　Arizona (6) vs. St. Louis (5), Dec. 3, 2006
　　　Indianapolis (6) vs. Green Bay (5), Oct. 19, 2008

NET YARDS GAINED RUSHING AND PASSING
Most Seasons Leading League
　12　Chi. Bears, 1932, 1934-35, 1939, 1941-44, 1947,
　　　　1949, 1955-56
　9　L.A./St. Louis Rams, 1946, 1950-51, 1954, 1957,
　　　　1973, 1999-2001
　8　San Diego, 1963, 1965, 1980-83, 1985, 2010

Most Consecutive Seasons Leading League
　4　Chi. Bears, 1941-44
　　　San Diego, 1980-83
　3　Baltimore, 1958-1960
　　　Houston, 1960-62
　　　Oakland, 1968-1970
　　　St. Louis, 1999-2001

  2 By many teams

Most Yards Gained, Season
- 7,474 New Orleans, 2011
- 7,075 St. Louis, 2000
- 6,936 Miami, 1984

Fewest Yards Gained, Season
- 1,150 Cincinnati, 1933
- 1,443 Chi. Cardinals, 1934
- 1,486 Chi. Cardinals, 1933

Most Yards Gained, Game
- 735 Los Angeles vs. N.Y. Yanks, Sept. 28, 1951
- 683 Pittsburgh vs. Chi. Cardinals, Dec. 13, 1958
- 682 Chi. Bears vs. N.Y. Giants, Nov. 14, 1943

Fewest Yards Gained, Game
- −7 Seattle vs. Los Angeles, Nov. 4, 1979
- −5 Denver vs. Oakland, Sept. 10, 1967
- 14 Chi. Cardinals vs. Detroit, Sept. 15, 1940

Most Yards Gained, Both Teams, Game
- 1,133 Los Angeles (636) vs. N.Y. Yanks (497), Nov. 19, 1950
- 1,125 Detroit (575) vs. Green Bay (550), Jan. 1, 2012
- 1,111 Houston (653) vs. Jacksonville (458), Nov. 18, 2012 (ot)

Fewest Yards Gained, Both Teams, Game
- 30 Chi. Cardinals (14) vs. Detroit (16), Sept. 15, 1940
- 136 Chi. Cardinals (50) vs. Green Bay (86), Nov. 18, 1934
- 154 N.Y. Giants (51) vs. Washington (103), Dec. 11, 1960

Most Consecutive Games, 400 or More Yards Gained
- 11 San Diego, 1982-83
- 9 New England, 2006-07
- 8 St. Louis, 1999-2000

Most Consecutive Games, 300 or More Yards Gained
- 36 Minnesota, 2002-04
- 30 Minnesota, 1999-2000
-     St. Louis, 2000-02
- 29 Los Angeles, 1949-1951
-     New Orleans, 2008-09

RUSHING
Most Seasons Leading League
- 16 Chi. Bears, 1932, 1934-35, 1939-1942, 1951, 1955-56, 1968, 1977, 1983-86
- 7 Buffalo, 1962, 1964, 1973, 1975, 1982, 1991-92
- 6 Cleveland, 1958-59, 1963, 1965-67
-     San Francisco, 1952-54, 1987, 1998-99
-     Dall. Texans/K.C. Chiefs, 1961, 1966, 1968-69, 1995, 2010

Most Consecutive Seasons Leading League
- 4 Chi. Bears, 1939-1942
-     Chi. Bears, 1983-86
- 3 Detroit, 1936-38
-     San Francisco, 1952-54
-     Cleveland, 1965-67
-     Atlanta, 2004-06
- 2 By many teams

ATTEMPTS
Most Rushing Attempts, Season
- 681 Oakland, 1977
- 674 Chicago, 1984
- 671 New England, 1978

Fewest Rushing Attempts, Season
- 211 Philadelphia, 1982
- 219 San Francisco, 1982
- 225 Houston, 1982

Most Rushing Attempts, Game
- 72 Chi. Bears vs. Brooklyn, Oct. 20, 1935
- 70 Chi. Cardinals vs. Green Bay, Dec. 5, 1948
- 69 Chi. Cardinals vs. Green Bay, Dec. 6, 1936
-     Kansas City vs. Cincinnati, Sept. 3, 1978

Fewest Rushing Attempts, Game
- 6 Chi. Cardinals vs. Boston, Oct. 22, 1933
-     New England vs. Pittsburgh, Oct. 31, 2004
-     Arizona vs. Minnesota, Nov. 26, 2006
- 7 Oakland vs. Buffalo, Oct. 5, 1963
-     Houston vs. N.Y. Giants, Dec. 8, 1985
-     Seattle vs. L.A. Raiders, Nov. 17, 1991
-     Green Bay vs. Miami, Sept. 11, 1994
-     Detroit vs. Minnesota, Dec. 2, 2007
-     Arizona vs. Minnesota, Dec. 14, 2008
- 8 Denver vs. Oakland, Dec. 17, 1960
-     Buffalo vs. St. Louis, Sept. 9, 1984
-     Detroit vs. San Francisco, Oct. 20, 1991
-     Atlanta vs. Detroit, Sept. 5, 1993
-     St. Louis vs. San Francisco, Nov. 2, 2003
-     N.Y. Jets vs. Denver, Nov. 20, 2005
-     St. Louis vs. Carolina, Nov. 19, 2006
-     Detroit vs. Arizona, Nov. 11, 2007
-     San Diego vs. Pittsburgh, Oct. 4, 2009
-     San Diego vs. Oakland, Dec. 5, 2010

Most Rushing Attempts, Both Teams, Game
- 108 Chi. Bears (70) vs. Green Bay (38), Dec. 5, 1948
- 105 Oakland (62) vs. Atlanta (43), Nov. 30, 1975 (ot)
- 104 Chi. Bears (64) vs. Pittsburgh (40), Oct. 18, 1936

Fewest Rushing Attempts, Both Teams, Game
- 16 Chi. Cardinals (6) vs. Boston (10), Oct. 22, 1933
- 30 Minnesota (15) vs. New England (15), Oct. 30, 2006
- 31 Green Bay (12) vs. Pittsburgh (19), Dec. 20, 2009

YARDS GAINED
Most Yards Gained Rushing, Season
- 3,165 New England, 1978
- 3,088 Buffalo, 1973
- 2,986 Kansas City, 1978

Fewest Yards Gained Rushing, Season
- 298 Philadelphia, 1940
- 467 Detroit, 1946
- 471 Boston, 1944

Most Yards Gained Rushing, Game
- 426 Detroit vs. Pittsburgh, Nov. 4, 1934
- 423 N.Y. Giants vs. Baltimore, Nov. 19, 1950
- 420 Boston vs. N.Y. Giants, Oct. 8, 1933

Fewest Yards Gained Rushing, Game
- −53 Detroit vs. Chi. Cardinals, Oct. 17, 1943
- −36 Philadelphia vs. Chi. Bears, Nov. 19, 1939
- −33 Brooklyn vs. Phil-Pitt, Oct. 2, 1943

Most Yards Gained Rushing, Both Teams, Game
- 595 Los Angeles (371) vs. N.Y. Yankees (224), Nov. 18, 1951
- 574 Chi. Bears (396) vs. Pittsburgh (178), Oct. 10, 1934
- 558 Boston (420) vs. N.Y. Giants (138), Oct. 8, 1933

Fewest Yards Gained Rushing, Both Teams, Game
- −15 Detroit (−53) vs. Chi. Cardinals (38), Oct. 17, 1943
- 4 Detroit (−10) vs. Chi. Cardinals (14), Sept. 15, 1940
- 45 San Diego (21) vs. Philadelphia (24), Oct. 23, 2005

AVERAGE GAIN
Highest Average Gain, Rushing, Season
- 5.74 Cleveland, 1963
- 5.65 San Francisco, 1954
- 5.56 San Diego, 1963

Lowest Average Gain, Rushing, Season
- 0.94 Philadelphia, 1940
- 1.45 Boston, 1944
- 1.55 Pittsburgh, 1935

TOUCHDOWNS
Most Touchdowns, Rushing, Season
- 36 Green Bay, 1962
- 33 Pittsburgh, 1976

32 Kansas City, 2003
San Diego, 2006

Fewest Touchdowns, Rushing, Season

1 Brooklyn, 1934
2 Chi. Cardinals, 1933
Cincinnati, 1933
Pittsburgh, 1934
Philadelphia, 1935
Philadelphia, 1936
Philadelphia, 1937
Philadelphia, 1938
Pittsburgh, 1940
Philadelphia, 1972
N.Y. Jets, 1995
Arizona, 2005
3 By many teams

Most Touchdowns, Rushing, Game

9 Rock Island vs. Evansville, Oct. 15, 1922
Racine vs. Louisville, Nov. 5, 1922
8 Chi. Cardinals vs. Rochester, Oct. 7, 1923
Kansas City vs. Atlanta, Oct. 24, 2004
7 By many teams

Most Touchdowns, Rushing, Both Teams, Game

9 Rock Island (9) vs. Evansville (0), Oct. 15, 1922
Racine (9) vs. Louisville (0), Nov. 5, 1922
8 Chi. Cardinals (8) vs. Rochester (0), Oct. 7, 1923
Canton (7) vs. Cleveland (1), Nov. 25, 1923
Los Angeles (6) vs. N.Y. Yanks (2), Nov. 18, 1951
Chi. Bears (5) vs. Green Bay (3), Nov. 6, 1955
Denver (5) vs. Kansas City (3), Dec. 7, 2003
Kansas City (8) vs. Atlanta (0), Oct. 24, 2004
7 In many games

PASSING

ATTEMPTS

Most Passes Attempted, Season

740 Detroit, 2012
709 Minnesota, 1981
699 New England, 1994

Fewest Passes Attempted, Season

102 Cincinnati, 1933
106 Boston, 1933
120 Detroit, 1937

Most Passes Attempted, Game

70 New England vs. Minnesota, Nov. 13, 1994 (ot)
69 N.Y. Jets vs. Baltimore, Dec. 24, 2000
68 Houston vs. Buffalo, Nov 1, 1964
Cincinnati vs. Pittsburgh, Dec. 30, 2001 (ot)

Fewest Passes Attempted, Game

0 Green Bay vs. Portsmouth, Oct. 8, 1933
Detroit vs. Cleveland, Sept. 10, 1937
Pittsburgh vs. Brooklyn, Nov. 16, 1941
Pittsburgh vs. Los Angeles, Nov. 13, 1949
Cleveland vs. Philadelphia, Dec. 3, 1950

Most Passes Attempted, Both Teams, Game

112 New England (70) vs. Minnesota (42),
Nov. 13, 1994 (ot)
109 Detroit (61) vs. Houston (48), Nov. 22, 2012 (ot)
104 Miami (55) vs. N.Y. Jets (49), Oct. 18. 1987 (ot)
N.Y. Jets (58) vs. San Francisco (46),
Sept. 6, 1998 (ot)

Fewest Passes Attempted, Both Teams, Game

4 Chi. Cardinals (1) vs. Detroit (3), Nov. 3, 1935
Detroit (0) vs. Cleveland (4), Sept. 10, 1937
6 Chi. Cardinals (2) vs. Detroit (4), Sept. 15, 1940
8 Brooklyn (2) vs. Philadelphia (6), Oct. 1, 1939

COMPLETIONS

Most Passes Completed, Season

472 New Orleans, 2011
450 Indianapolis, 2010
New Orleans, 2010
445 Detroit, 2012

Fewest Passes Completed, Season

25 Cincinnati, 1933
33 Boston, 1933
34 Chi. Cardinals, 1934

Most Passes Completed, Game

45 New England vs. Minnesota, Nov. 13, 1994 (ot)
43 Washington vs. Detroit, Nov. 4, 1990 (ot)
Oakland vs. Pittsburgh, Sept. 15, 2002
Detroit vs. Tennessee, Sept. 23, 2012 (ot)
Houston vs. Jacksonville, Nov. 18, 2012 (ot)
42 N.Y. Jets vs. San Francisco, Sept. 21, 1980
N.Y. Jets vs. Seattle, Dec. 6, 1998

Fewest Passes Completed, Game

0 By many teams. Last time: Buffalo vs. N.Y. Jets,
Sept. 29, 1974

Most Passes Completed, Both Teams, Game

72 Detroit (43) vs. Tennessee (29), Sept. 23, 2012 (ot)
71 New England (45) vs. Minnesota (26),
Nov. 13, 1994 (ot)
68 San Francisco (37) vs. Atlanta (31), Oct. 6, 1985
Denver (34) vs. Oakland (34), Nov. 11, 2002

Fewest Passes Completed, Both Teams, Game

1 Chi. Cardinals (0) vs. Philadelphia (1), Nov. 8, 1936
Detroit (0) vs. Cleveland (1), Sept. 10, 1937
Chi. Cardinals (0) vs. Detroit (1), Sept. 15, 1940
Brooklyn (0) vs. Pittsburgh (1), Nov. 29, 1942
2 Chi. Cardinals (0) vs. Detroit (2), Nov. 3, 1935
Buffalo (0) vs. N.Y. Jets (2), Sept. 29, 1974
Chi. Cardinals (0) vs. Green Bay (2), Nov. 18, 1934
3 In seven games

YARDS GAINED

Most Seasons Leading League, Passing Yardage

10 San Diego, 1965, 1968, 1971, 1978-1983, 1985
8 Chi. Bears, 1932, 1939, 1941, 1943, 1945, 1949,
1954, 1964
Washington, 1938, 1940, 1944, 1947-48, 1967,
1974, 1989
Balt./Indianapolis, 1957, 1959, 1960, 1963, 1976,
2003-04, 2010
7 Houston, 1960-61, 1963-64, 1990-92
L.A./St. Louis Rams, 1946, 1950-51, 1956,
1999-2001

Most Consecutive Seasons Leading League, Passing Yardage

6 San Diego, 1978-1983
4 Green Bay, 1934-37
3 Miami, 1986-88
Houston, 1990-92
St. Louis, 1999-2001

Most Yards Gained, Passing, Season

5,347 New Orleans, 2011
5,232 St. Louis, 2000
5,084 New England, 2011

Fewest Yards Gained, Passing, Season

302 Chi. Cardinals, 1934
357 Cincinnati, 1933
459 Boston, 1934

Most Yards Gained Passing, Game

554 Los Angeles vs. N.Y. Yankees, Sept. 28, 1951
530 Minnesota vs. Baltimore, Sept. 28, 1969
521 Miami vs. N.Y. Jets, Oct. 23, 1988

Fewest Yards Gained, Passing, Game

–53 Denver vs. Oakland, Sept. 10, 1967

−52   Cincinnati vs. Houston, Oct. 31, 1971
−39   Atlanta vs. San Francisco, Oct. 23, 1976

Most Yards Gained, Passing, Both Teams, Game
971   Detroit (502) vs. Green Bay (469), Jan. 1, 2012
906   New England (516) vs. Miami (390), Sept. 12, 2011
884   N.Y. Jets (449) vs. Miami (435), Sept. 21, 1986 (ot)

Fewest Yards Gained, Passing, Both Teams, Game
−11   Green Bay (−10) vs. Dallas (−1), Oct. 24, 1965
  1   Chi. Cardinals (0) vs. Philadelphia (1), Nov. 8, 1936
  7   Brooklyn (0) vs. Pittsburgh (7), Nov. 29, 1942

TIMES SACKED

Most Seasons Leading League, Fewest Times Sacked
10   Miami, 1973, 1982-1990
 7   Indianapolis, 1999-2000, 2004-06, 2009, 2012
 5   N.Y. Jets, 1965-66, 1968, 1993, 2000

Most Consecutive Seasons Leading League, Fewest Times Sacked
9   Miami, 1982-1990
3   St. Louis, 1974-76
    Indianapolis, 2004-06
2   By many teams

Most Times Sacked, Season
104 Philadelphia, 1986
 78 Arizona, 1997
 76 Houston, 2002

Fewest Times Sacked, Season
7   Miami, 1988
8   San Francisco, 1970
   St. Louis, 1975
9   N.Y. Jets, 1966
   Washington, 1991

Most Times Sacked, Game
12 Pittsburgh vs. Dallas, Nov. 20, 1966
    Baltimore vs. St. Louis, Oct. 26, 1980
    Detroit vs. Chicago, Dec. 16, 1984
    Houston vs. Dallas, Sept. 29, 1985
    Philadelphia vs. N.Y. Giants, Sept. 30, 2007
11 St. Louis vs. N.Y. Giants, Nov. 1, 1964
    Los Angeles vs. Baltimore, Nov. 22, 1964
    Denver vs. Buffalo, Dec. 13, 1964
    Green Bay vs. Detroit, Nov. 7, 1965
    Buffalo vs. Oakland, Oct. 15, 1967
    Denver vs. Oakland, Nov. 5, 1967
    Atlanta vs. St. Louis, Nov. 24, 1968
    Detroit vs. Dallas, Oct. 6, 1975
    Philadelphia vs. St. Louis, Dec. 18, 1983
    Cleveland vs. Kansas City, Sept. 30, 1984
    Minnesota vs. Chicago, Oct. 28, 1984
    Atlanta vs. Cleveland, Nov. 18, 1984
    Dallas vs. San Diego, Nov. 16, 1986
    Philadelphia vs. Detroit, Nov. 16, 1986
    Philadelphia vs. L.A. Raiders, Nov. 30, 1986 (ot)
    L.A. Raiders vs. Seattle, Dec. 8, 1986
    N.Y. Jets vs. Dallas, Oct. 4, 1987
    Philadelphia vs. Chicago, Oct. 4, 1987
    Dallas vs. Philadelphia, Sept. 15, 1991
    Cleveland vs. Indianapolis, Sept. 6, 1992
    N.Y. Jets vs. San Diego, Dec. 23, 2012
10 By many teams

Most Times Sacked, Both Teams, Game
18 Green Bay (10) vs. San Diego (8), Sept. 24, 1978
17 Buffalo (10) vs. N.Y. Titans (7), Nov. 23, 1961
    Pittsburgh (12) vs. Dallas (5), Nov. 20, 1966
    Atlanta (9) vs. Philadelphia (8), Dec. 16, 1984
    Philadelphia (11) vs. L.A. Raiders (6), Nov. 30, 1986 (ot)
16 Los Angeles (11) vs. Baltimore (5), Nov. 22, 1964
    Buffalo (11) vs. Oakland (5), Oct. 15, 1967

COMPLETION PERCENTAGE

Most Seasons Leading League, Completion Percentage
14 San Francisco, 1952, 1957-58, 1965, 1981, 1983, 1987, 1989, 1992-97
11 Washington, 1937, 1939-1940, 1942-45, 1947-48, 1969-1970
 8   Green Bay, 1936, 1941, 1961-62, 1964, 1966, 1968, 1998

Most Consecutive Seasons Leading League, Completion Percentage
6   San Francisco, 1992-97
4   Washington, 1942-45
    Kansas City, 1966-69
3   Cleveland, 1953-55
    St. Louis, 1999-2001
    New Orleans, 2009-2011

Highest Completion Percentage, Season
71.30 New Orleans, 2011 (662-472)
70.65 Cincinnati, 1982 (310-219)
70.25 San Francisco, 1994 (511-359)

Lowest Completion Percentage, Season
22.9 Philadelphia, 1936 (170-39)
24.5 Cincinnati, 1933 (102-25)
25.0 Pittsburgh, 1941 (168-42)

TOUCHDOWNS

Most Touchdowns, Passing, Season
51 Indianapolis, 2004
   Green Bay, 2011
50 New England, 2007
49 Miami, 1984

Fewest Touchdowns, Passing, Season
0   Cincinnati, 1933
    Pittsburgh, 1945
1   Boston, 1932
    Boston, 1933
    Chi. Cardinals, 1934
    Cincinnati/St. Louis, 1934
    Detroit, 1942
2   Chi. Cardinals, 1932
    Stapleton, 1932
    Chi. Cardinals, 1935
    Brooklyn, 1936
    Pittsburgh, 1942

Most Touchdowns, Passing, Game
7   Chi. Bears vs. N.Y. Giants, Nov. 14, 1943
    Philadelphia vs. Washington, Oct. 17, 1954
    Houston vs. N.Y. Titans, Nov. 19, 1961
    Houston vs. N.Y. Titans, Oct. 14, 1962
    N.Y. Giants vs. Washington, Oct. 28, 1962
    Minnesota vs. Baltimore, Sept. 28, 1969
    San Diego vs. Oakland, Nov. 22, 1981
6   By many teams

Most Touchdowns, Passing, Both Teams, Game
12 New Orleans (6) vs. St. Louis (6), Nov. 2, 1969
11 N.Y. Giants (7) vs. Washington (4), Oct. 28, 1962
    Oakland (6) vs. Houston (5), Dec. 22, 1963
    Cincinnati (6) vs. Cleveland, (5), Sept. 16, 2007
    Green Bay (6) vs. Detroit (5), Jan. 1, 2012
10 San Diego (5) vs. Seattle (5), Sept. 15, 1985
    Miami (6) vs. N.Y. Jets (4), Sept. 21, 1986 (ot)
    San Francisco (6) vs. Atlanta (4), Oct. 14, 1990

PASSES HAD INTERCEPTED

Most Passes Had Intercepted, Season
48 Houston, 1962
45 Denver, 1961
41 Card-Pitt, 1944

Fewest Passes Had Intercepted, Season
- 5   Cleveland, 1960
  - Green Bay, 1966
  - Kansas City, 1990
  - N.Y. Giants, 1990
  - New England, 2010
  - San Francisco, 2011
- 6   Green Bay, 1964
  - St. Louis, 1982
  - Dallas, 1993
  - Jacksonville, 2005
  - Washington, 2008
  - Tampa Bay, 2010
- 7   Los Angeles, 1969
  - Denver, 2005
  - Miami, 2008
  - Minnesota, 2009

Most Passes Had Intercepted, Game
- 9   Detroit vs. Green Bay, Oct. 24, 1943
  - Pittsburgh vs. Philadelphia, Dec. 12, 1965
- 8   Green Bay vs. N.Y. Giants, Nov. 21, 1948
  - Chi. Cardinals vs. Philadelphia, Sept. 24, 1950
  - N.Y. Yanks vs. N.Y. Giants, Dec. 16, 1951
  - Denver vs. Houston, Dec. 2, 1962
  - Chi. Bears vs. Detroit, Sept. 22, 1968
  - Baltimore vs. N.Y. Jets, Sept. 23, 1973
- 7   By many teams. Last time: Detroit vs. Cleveland, Sept. 23, 2001

Most Passes Had Intercepted, Both Teams, Game
- 13   Denver (8) vs. Houston (5), Dec. 2, 1962
- 11   Philadelphia (7) vs. Boston (4), Nov. 3, 1935
  - Boston (6) vs. Pittsburgh (5), Dec. 1, 1935
  - Cleveland (7) vs. Green Bay (4), Oct. 30, 1938
  - Green Bay (7) vs. Detroit (4), Oct. 20, 1940
  - Detroit (7) vs. Chi. Bears (4), Nov. 22, 1942
  - Detroit (7) vs. Cleveland (4), Nov. 26, 1944
  - Chi. Cardinals (8) vs. Philadelphia (3), Sept. 24, 1950
  - Washington (7) vs. N.Y. Giants (4), Dec. 8, 1963
  - Pittsburgh (9) vs. Philadelphia (2), Dec 12, 1965
- 10   In many games

PUNTING
Most Seasons Leading League (Average Distance)
- 8   Oakland, 1974-75, 1977-78, 2003-04, 2007, 2009
- 7   Denver 1962-64, 1966-67, 1982, 1999
- 6   Washington, 1940-43, 1945, 1958
  - Kansas City, 1968, 1971-73, 1979, 1984
  - L.A. Rams, 1946, 1949, 1955-56, 1994, 2008

Most Consecutive Seasons Leading League (Average Distance)
- 4   Washington, 1940-43
- 3   Cleveland, 1950-52
  - Denver, 1962-64
  - Kansas City, 1971-73

Most Punts, Season
- 116   Houston, 2002
- 114   Chicago, 1981
- 113   Boston, 1934
  - Brooklyn, 1934
  - Dallas, 2002

Fewest Punts, Season
- 23   San Diego, 1982
- 31   Cincinnati, 1982
- 32   Chi. Bears, 1941
- 33   Washington, 1945
- 34   Houston, 1990

Most Punts, Game
- 17   Chi. Bears vs. Green Bay, Oct. 22, 1933
  - Cincinnati vs. Pittsburgh, Oct. 22, 1933
- 16   Cincinnati vs. Portsmouth, Sept. 17, 1933

- Chi. Cardinals vs. Chi. Bears, Nov. 30, 1933
- Chi. Cardinals vs. Detroit, Sept. 15, 1940
- Oakland vs. San Diego, Oct. 11, 1998
- 15   Chi. Cardinals vs. Cincinnati, Nov. 12, 1933
  - N.Y. Giants vs. Chi. Bears, Nov. 17, 1935
  - Philadelphia vs. N.Y. Giants, Dec. 6, 1987 (ot)

Fewest Punts, Game
- 0   By many teams. Last time:
  - Denver vs. Oakland, Sept. 30, 2012

Most Punts, Both Teams, Game
- 31   Chi. Bears (17) vs. Green Bay (14), Oct. 22, 1933
  - Cincinnati (17), vs. Pittsburgh (14), Oct. 22, 1933
- 29   Chi. Cardinals (15) vs. Cincinnati (14), Nov. 12, 1933
  - Chi. Cardinals (16) vs. Chi. Bears (13), Nov. 30, 1933
  - Chi. Cardinals (16) vs. Detroit (13), Sept. 15, 1940
- 28   Philadelphia (14) vs. Washington (14), Nov. 5, 1939

Fewest Punts, Both Teams, Game
- 0   Buffalo vs. San Francisco, Sept. 13, 1992
- 1   Baltimore (0) vs. Cleveland (1), Nov. 1, 1959
  - Dall. Cowboys (0) vs. Cleveland (1), Dec. 3, 1961
  - Chicago (0) vs. Detroit (1), Oct. 1, 1972
  - San Francisco (0) vs. N.Y. Giants (1), Oct. 15, 1972
  - Green Bay (0) vs. Buffalo (1), Dec. 5, 1982
  - Miami (0) vs. Buffalo (1), Oct. 12, 1986
  - Green Bay (0) vs. Chicago (1), Dec. 17, 1989
  - Oakland (0) vs. Seattle (1), Dec. 5, 1999
  - Tampa Bay (0) vs. Minnesota (1), Oct. 29, 2000
  - New Orleans (0) vs. San Francisco (1), Oct. 20, 2002
  - San Diego (0) vs. Oakland (1), Jan. 1, 2012
- 2   In many games

AVERAGE YARDAGE
Highest Avg. Distance, Punting, Season
- 51.1   Oakland, 2009
- 50.9   San Francisco, 2011
- 50.8   Oakland, 2011

Lowest Average Distance, Punting, Season
- 32.7   Card-Pitt, 1944 (60-1,964)
- 33.8   Cincinnati, 1986 (59-1,996)
- 33.9   Detroit, 1969 (74-2,510)

PUNT RETURNS
Most Seasons Leading League (Average Return)
- 9   Detroit, 1943-45, 1951-52, 1962, 1966, 1969, 1991
- 7   Chi. Cardinals/St. Louis, 1948-49, 1955-56, 1959, 1986-87
- 6   Green Bay, 1950, 1953-54, 1961, 1972, 1996
  - Dallas/Kansas City, 1960, 1968, 1970, 1979-1980, 2003

Most Consecutive Seasons Leading League (Average Return)
- 3   Detroit, 1943-45
- 2   By many teams

Most Punt Returns, Season
- 71   Pittsburgh, 1976
  - Tampa Bay, 1979
  - L.A. Raiders, 1985
- 67   Pittsburgh, 1974
  - Los Angeles, 1978
  - L.A. Raiders, 1984
- 65   San Francisco, 1976

Fewest Punt Returns, Season
- 12   Baltimore, 1981
  - San Diego, 1982
- 14   Los Angeles, 1961
  - Philadelphia, 1962
  - Baltimore, 1982
- 15   Houston, 1960
  - Washington, 1960
  - Oakland, 1961
  - N.Y. Giants, 1969

Philadelphia, 1973
Kansas City, 1982

Most Punt Returns, Game
- 12   Philadelphia vs. Cleveland, Dec. 3, 1950
- 11   Chi. Bears vs. Chi. Cardinals, Oct. 8, 1950
      Washington vs. Tampa Bay, Oct. 9, 1977
- 10   Philadelphia vs. N.Y. Giants, Nov. 26, 1950
      Philadelphia vs. Tampa Bay, Sept. 18, 1977
      Pittsburgh vs. Buffalo, Dec. 16, 1979
      Washington vs. New Orleans, Dec. 26, 1982
      Philadelphia vs. Seattle, Dec. 13, 1992 (ot)
      New England vs. Pittsburgh, Dec. 5, 1993

Most Punt Returns, Both Teams, Game
- 17   Philadelphia (12) vs. Cleveland (5), Dec. 3, 1950
- 16   N.Y. Giants (9) vs. Philadelphia (7), Dec. 12, 1954
      Washington (11) vs. Tampa Bay (5), Oct. 9, 1977
      Oakland (8) vs. San Diego (8), Oct. 11, 1998
- 15   Detroit (8) vs. Cleveland (7), Sept. 27, 1942
      Los Angeles (8) vs. Baltimore (7), Nov. 27, 1966
      Pittsburgh (8) vs. Houston (7), Dec. 1, 1974
      Philadelphia (10) vs. Tampa Bay (5), Sept. 18, 1977
      Baltimore (9) vs. Kansas City (6), Sept. 2, 1979
      Washington (10) vs. New Orleans (5), Dec. 26, 1982
      L.A. Raiders (8) vs. Cleveland (7), Nov. 16, 1986

FAIR CATCHES
Most Fair Catches, Season
- 38   N.Y. Jets, 2012
- 34   Baltimore, 1971
- 33   Philadelphia, 2000

Fewest Fair Catches, Season
- 0   San Diego, 1975
    New England, 1976
    Tampa Bay, 1976
    Pittsburgh, 1977
    Dallas, 1982
- 1   Cleveland, 1974
    San Francisco, 1975
    Kansas City, 1976
    St. Louis, 1976
    San Diego, 1976
    L.A. Rams, 1982
    St. Louis, 1982
    Tampa Bay, 1982
    Arizona, 2001
- 2   By many teams

Most Fair Catches, Game
- 7   Minnesota vs. Dallas, Sept. 25, 1966
    N.Y. Jets vs. Miami, Nov. 20, 1966
    Detroit vs. Chicago, Nov. 21, 1976
    Philadelphia vs. Buffalo, Dec. 27, 1987
    Tennessee vs. Jacksonville, Nov. 16, 2008
- 6   By many teams

YARDS GAINED
Most Yards, Punt Returns, Season
- 875   Green Bay, 1996
- 785   L.A. Raiders, 1985
- 781   Chi. Bears, 1948

Fewest Yards, Punt Returns, Season
- 27   St. Louis, 1965
- 35   N.Y. Giants, 1965
- 37   New England, 1972

Most Yards, Punt Returns, Game
- 231   Detroit vs. San Francisco, Oct. 6, 1963
- 225   Oakland vs. Buffalo, Sept. 15, 1968
- 219   L.A. Rams vs. Atlanta, Oct. 11, 1981

Fewest Yards, Punt Returns, Game
- -28   Washington vs. Dallas, Dec. 11, 1966
- -23   N.Y. Giants vs. Buffalo, Oct. 20, 1975

Pittsburgh vs. Houston, Sept. 20, 1970
- -20   New Orleans vs. Pittsburgh, Oct. 20, 1968

Most Yards, Punt Returns, Both Teams, Game
- 282   L.A. Rams (219) vs. Atlanta (63), Oct. 11, 1981
- 245   Detroit (231) vs. San Francisco (14), Oct. 6, 1963
- 244   Oakland (225) vs. Buffalo (19), Sept. 15, 1968

Fewest Yards, Punt Returns, Both Teams, Game
- -18   Buffalo (-18) vs. Pittsburgh (0), Oct. 29, 1972
- -14   Miami (-14) vs. Boston (0), Nov. 30, 1969
    Tennessee (-14) vs. New Orleans (0),
       Sept. 21, 2003
- -13   N.Y. Giants (-13) vs. Cleveland (0), Nov. 14, 1965

AVERAGE YARDS RETURNING PUNTS
Highest Average, Punt Returns, Season
- 20.2   Chi. Bears, 1941
- 19.1   Chi. Cardinals, 1948
- 18.2   Chi. Cardinals, 1949

Lowest Average, Punt Returns, Season
- 1.2   St. Louis, 1965 (23-27)
- 1.5   N.Y. Giants, 1965 (24-35)
- 1.7   Washington, 1970 (27-45)

TOUCHDOWNS RETURNING PUNTS
Most Touchdowns, Punt Returns, Season
- 5   Chi. Cardinals, 1959
- 4   Chi. Cardinals, 1948
    Detroit, 1951
    N.Y. Giants, 1951
    Denver, 1976
    Chicago, 2007
    Arizona, 2011
- 3   Washington, 1941
    Detroit, 1952
    Pittsburgh, 1952
    Houston, 1975
    Los Angeles, 1981
    Cleveland, 1993
    Green Bay, 1996
    Denver, 1997
    San Diego, 1997
    Chicago, 2006
    Tennessee, 2006
    New Orleans, 2008
    Oakland, 2008
    Chicago, 2010
    Dallas, 2010
    Tennessee, 2012

Most Touchdowns, Punt Returns, Game
- 2   Detroit vs. Los Angeles, Oct. 14, 1951
    Detroit vs. Green Bay, Nov. 22, 1951
    Chi. Cardinals vs. Pittsburgh, Nov. 1, 1959
    Chi. Cardinals vs. N.Y. Giants, Nov. 22, 1959
    N.Y. Titans vs. Denver, Sept. 24, 1961
    Denver vs. Cleveland, Sept. 26, 1976
    Los Angeles vs. Atlanta, Oct. 11, 1981
    St. Louis vs. Tampa Bay, Dec. 21, 1986
    L.A. Rams vs. Atlanta, Dec. 27, 1992
    Cleveland vs. Pittsburgh, Oct. 24, 1993
    San Diego vs. Cincinnati, Nov. 2, 1997
    Denver vs. Carolina, Nov. 9, 1997
    Baltimore vs. Seattle, Dec. 7, 1997
    Baltimore vs. N.Y. Jets, Dec. 24, 2000
    Oakland vs. Tennessee, Sept. 29, 2002
    Carolina vs. Cincinnati, Dec. 8, 2002
    Detroit at Jacksonville, Nov. 14, 2004 (ot)
    New Orleans vs. Minnesota, Oct. 6, 2008
    Tennessee vs. Jacksonville, Dec. 30, 2012

Most Touchdowns, Punt Returns, Both Teams, Game
- 2   Philadelphia (1) vs. Washington (1), Nov. 9, 1952

Kansas City (1) vs. Buffalo (1), Sept. 11, 1966
Baltimore (1) vs. New England (1), Nov. 18, 1979
L.A. Raiders (1) vs. Philadelphia (1),
  Nov. 30, 1986 (ot)
Cincinnati (1) vs. Green Bay (1), Sept. 20, 1992
Oakland (1) vs. Seattle (1), Nov. 15, 1998
Atlanta (1) vs. Tennessee (1), Nov. 23, 2003
San Diego (1) vs. Denver (1), Oct. 19, 2009
St. Louis (1) vs. Arizona (1), Nov. 27, 2011
(Also see previous record)

KICKOFF RETURNS
Most Seasons Leading League (Average Return)
- 8 Washington, 1942, 1947, 1962-63, 1973-74, 1981, 1995
- 6 Chicago Bears, 1943, 1948, 1958, 1966, 1972, 1985
  N.Y. Giants, 1944, 1946, 1949, 1951, 1953, 2004
- 5 Green Bay, 1954, 1964, 1967, 1993, 1998
  New England, 1977, 1980, 1982, 1997, 2006
  Hou. Oilers/ Tenn. Titans, 1960, 1962-63, 1968, 2008

Most Consecutive Seasons Leading League (Average Return)
- 3 Denver, 1965-67
- 2 By many teams

Most Kickoff Returns, Season
- 96 Detroit, 2009
- 89 Cleveland, 1999
- 88 New Orleans, 1980

Fewest Kickoff Returns, Season
- 17 N.Y. Giants, 1944
- 20 N.Y. Giants, 1941, 1943
  Chi. Bears, 1942
- 23 Washington, 1942

Most Kickoff Returns, Game
- 12 N.Y. Giants vs. Washington, Nov. 27, 1966
- 11 Kansas City vs. Buffalo, Nov. 23, 2008
- 10 By many teams

Most Kickoff Returns, Both Teams, Game
- 19 N.Y. Giants (12) vs. Washington (7), Nov. 27, 1966
  Cleveland (10) vs. Cincinnati (9), Nov. 28, 2004
- 18 Houston (10) vs. Oakland (8), Dec. 22, 1963
- 17 Washington (9) vs. Green Bay (8), Oct. 17, 1983
  San Diego (9) vs. Pittsburgh (8), Dec. 8, 1985
  Detroit (9) vs. Green Bay (8), Nov. 27, 1986
  L.A. Raiders (9) vs. Seattle (8), Dec. 18, 1988
  Oakland (10) vs. Seattle (7), Oct. 26, 1997
  Buffalo (9) vs. Minnesota (8), Sept. 15, 2002 (ot)
  Cincinnati (10) vs. Cleveland (7), Sept. 16, 2007
  Kansas City (11) vs. Buffalo (6), Nov. 23, 2008

YARDS GAINED
Most Yards, Kickoff Returns, Season
- 2,296 Arizona, 2000
- 2,173 Houston, 2005
- 2,084 Arizona, 2010

Fewest Yards, Kickoff Returns, Season
- 282 N.Y. Giants, 1940
- 381 Green Bay, 1940
- 424 Chicago, 1963

Most Yards, Kickoff Returns, Game
- 367 Baltimore vs. Minnesota, Dec. 13, 1998
- 362 Detroit vs. Los Angeles, Oct. 29, 1950
- 304 Chi. Bears vs. Green Bay, Nov. 9, 1952
  New Orleans vs. L.A. Rams, Oct. 23, 1994

Most Yards, Kickoff Returns, Both Teams, Game
- 560 Detroit (362) vs. L.A. Rams (198), Oct. 29, 1950
- 511 Baltimore (367) vs. Minnesota (144), Dec. 13, 1998
- 501 New Orleans (304) vs. L.A. Rams (197), Oct. 23, 1994

AVERAGE YARDAGE
Highest Average, Kickoff Returns, Season
- 29.4 Chicago, 1972
- 28.9 Pittsburgh, 1952
- 28.2 Washington, 1962

Lowest Average, Kickoff Returns, Season
- 14.7 N.Y. Jets, 1993 (46-675)
- 15.8 N.Y. Giants, 1993 (32-507)
- 15.9 Tampa Bay, 1993 (58-922)

TOUCHDOWNS
Most Touchdowns, Kickoff Returns, Season
- 4 Green Bay, 1967
  Chicago, 1970
  Detroit, 1994
  Houston, 2007
- 3 Los Angeles, 1950
  Chi. Cardinals, 1954
  San Francisco, 1963
  Denver, 1966
  Chicago, 1967
  New England, 1977
  L.A. Rams, 1985
  Atlanta, 2000
  Buffalo, 2004
  N.Y. Jets, 2007
  Cleveland, 2009
  Oakland, 2010
  Seattle, 2010
- 2 By many teams

Most Touchdowns, Kickoff Returns, Game
- 2 Chi. Bears vs. Green Bay, Sept. 22, 1940
  Chi. Bears vs. Green Bay, Nov. 9, 1952
  Philadelphia vs. Dallas, Nov. 6, 1966
  Green Bay vs. Cleveland, Nov. 12, 1967
  L.A. Rams vs. Green Bay, Nov. 24, 1985
  New Orleans vs. L.A. Rams, Oct. 23, 1994
  Baltimore vs. Minnesota, Dec. 13, 1998
  N.Y. Jets vs. Buffalo, Sept. 8, 2002 (ot)
  Chicago vs. St. Louis, Dec. 11, 2006
  Houston vs. Jacksonville, Dec. 30, 2007
  Miami vs. N.Y. Jets, Nov. 1, 2009
  Cleveland vs. Kansas City, Dec. 20, 2009
  Seattle vs. San Diego, Sept. 26, 2010

Most Touchdowns, Kickoff Returns, Both Teams, Game
- 3 Baltimore (2) vs. Minnesota (1), Dec. 13, 1998
- 2 In many games

FUMBLES
Most Fumbles, Season
- 56 Chi. Bears, 1938
  San Francisco, 1978
- 54 Philadelphia, 1946
- 51 New England, 1973

Fewest Fumbles, Season
- 6 New Orleans, 2011
- 7 Kansas City, 2002
- 8 Cleveland, 1959

Most Fumbles, Game
- 10 Phil-Pitt vs. N.Y. Giants, Oct. 9, 1943
  Detroit vs. Minnesota, Nov. 12, 1967
  Kansas City vs. Houston, Oct. 12, 1969
  San Francisco vs. Detroit, Dec. 17, 1978
- 9 Philadelphia vs. Green Bay, Oct. 13, 1946
  Boston at Oakland, Dec. 16, 1962
  Kansas City vs. San Diego, Nov. 15, 1964
  N.Y. Giants vs. Buffalo, Oct. 20, 1975
  St. Louis vs. Washington, Oct. 25, 1976
  San Diego vs. Green Bay, Sept. 24, 1978

Pittsburgh vs. Cincinnati, Oct. 14, 1979
Cleveland vs. Seattle, Dec. 20, 1981
Cleveland vs. Pittsburgh, Dec. 23, 1990
Oakland vs. Seattle, Dec. 22, 1996
8   By many teams
Most Fumbles, Both Teams, Game
14 Chi. Bears (7) vs. Cleveland (7), Nov. 24, 1940
St. Louis (8) vs. N.Y. Giants (6), Sept. 17, 1961
Kansas City (10) vs. Houston (4), Oct. 12, 1969
13 Washington (8) vs. Pittsburgh (5), Nov. 14, 1937
Philadelphia (7) vs. Boston (6), Dec. 8, 1946
N.Y. Giants (7) vs. Washington (6), Nov. 5, 1950
Kansas City (9) vs. San Diego (4), Nov. 15, 1964
Buffalo (7) vs. Denver (6), Dec. 13, 1964
N.Y. Jets (7) vs. Houston (6), Sept. 12, 1965
Cleveland (7) vs. New Orleans (6), Dec. 12, 1971
Houston (8) vs. Pittsburgh (5), Dec. 9, 1973
St. Louis (9) vs. Washington (4), Oct. 25, 1976
Cleveland (9) vs. Seattle (4), Dec. 20, 1981
Green Bay (7) vs. Detroit (6), Oct. 6, 1985
12 In many games

FUMBLES LOST
Most Fumbles Lost, Season
36 Chi. Cardinals, 1959
31 Green Bay, 1952
29 Chi. Cardinals, 1946
Pittsburgh, 1950
Cleveland, 1978
Fewest Fumbles Lost, Season
2   Kansas City, 2002
3   Philadelphia, 1938
Minnesota, 1980
N.Y. Giants, 2008
4   San Francisco, 1960
Kansas City, 1982
Minnesota, 1998
Detroit, 2003
Atlanta, 2012
Houston, 2012
Most Fumbles Lost, Game
8   St. Louis vs. Washington, Oct. 25, 1976
Cleveland vs. Pittsburgh, Dec. 23, 1990
7   Cincinnati vs. Buffalo, Nov. 30, 1969
Pittsburgh vs. Cincinnati, Oct. 14, 1979
Cleveland vs. Seattle, Dec. 20, 1981
6   By many teams

FUMBLES RECOVERED
Most Fumbles Recovered, Season, Own and Opponents'
58 Minnesota, 1963 (27 own, 31 opp)
51 Chi. Bears, 1938 (37 own, 14 opp)
San Francisco, 1978 (24 own, 27 opp)
50 Philadelphia, 1987 (23 own, 27 opp)
Fewest Fumbles Recovered, Season, Own and Opponents'
7   New Orleans, 2011 (0 own, 7 opp)
Pittsburgh, 2011 (3 own, 4 opp)
9   San Francisco, 1982 (5 own, 4 opp)
10 Jacksonville, 2006 (6 own, 4 opp)
Most Fumbles Recovered, Game, Own and Opponents'
10 Denver vs. Buffalo, Dec. 13, 1964 (5 own, 5 opp)
Pittsburgh vs. Houston, Dec. 9, 1973 (5 own, 5 opp)
Washington vs. St. Louis, Oct. 25, 1976
(2 own, 8 opp)
9   St. Louis vs. N.Y. Giants, Sept. 17, 1961
(6 own, 3 opp)
Houston vs. Cincinnati, Oct. 27, 1974 (4 own, 5 opp)
Kansas City vs. Dallas, Nov. 10, 1975 (4 own, 5 opp)
Green Bay vs. Detroit, Oct. 6, 1985 (5 own, 4 opp)
Pittsburgh vs. Cleveland, Dec. 23, 1990

(1 own, 8 opp)
8   By many teams
Most Own Fumbles Recovered, Season
37 Chi. Bears, 1938
28 Pittsburgh, 1987
27 Philadelphia, 1946
Minnesota, 1963
Fewest Own Fumbles Recovered, Season
0   New Orleans, 2011
1   Indianapolis, 2006
Philadelphia, 2008
2   Washington, 1958
Miami, 2000
Atlanta, 2011
Most Opponents' Fumbles Recovered, Season
31 Minnesota, 1963
29 Cleveland, 1951
28 Green Bay, 1946
Houston, 1977
Seattle, 1983
Fewest Opponents' Fumbles Recovered, Season
3   Los Angeles, 1974
Green Bay, 1995
Miami, 2011
Indianapolis, 2012
4   Philadelphia, 1944
San Francisco, 1982
Jacksonville, 2006
Jacksonville, 2008
Pittsburgh, 2011
San Diego, 2011
St. Louis, 2012
5   Baltimore, 1982
Arizona, 1997
Baltimore, 1998
Chicago, 2003
Oakland, 2006
N.Y. Giants, 2008
Washington, 2008
Buffalo, 2009
Houston, 2010
Jacksonville, 2010
Green Bay, 2012
Philadelphia, 2012
Tennessee, 2012
Most Opponents' Fumbles Recovered, Game
8   Washington vs. St. Louis, Oct. 25, 1976
Pittsburgh vs. Cleveland, Dec. 23, 1990
7   Buffalo vs. Cincinnati, Nov. 30, 1969
Cincinnati vs. Pittsburgh, Oct. 14, 1979
Seattle vs. Cleveland, Dec. 20, 1981
6   By many teams

TOUCHDOWNS
**Most Touchdowns, Fumbles Recovered, Season,
Own and Opponents'**
7   Arizona, 2010 (3 own, 4 opp)
5   Chi. Bears, 1942 (1 own, 4 opp)
Los Angeles, 1952 (1 own, 4 opp)
San Francisco, 1965 (1 own, 4 opp)
Oakland, 1978 (2 own, 3 opp)
4   Chi. Bears, 1948 (1 own, 3 opp)
Boston, 1948 (4 opp)
Denver, 1979 (1 own, 3 opp)
Atlanta, 1981 (1 own, 3 opp)
Denver, 1984 (4 opp)
St. Louis, 1987 (4 opp)
Minnesota, 1989 (4 opp)
Atlanta, 1991 (4 opp)
Philadelphia, 1995 (4 opp)

Atlanta, 1998 (4 opp)
New Orleans, 1998 (4 opp)
Kansas City, 1999 (4 opp)
New England, 2012 (1 own, 3 opp)

Most Touchdowns, Own Fumbles Recovered, Season
3 Arizona, 2010
2 Chi. Bears, 1953
   New England, 1973
   Buffalo, 1974
   Denver, 1975
   Oakland, 1978
   Green Bay, 1982
   New Orleans, 1983
   Cleveland, 1986
   Green Bay, 1989
   Miami, 1996
   Buffalo, 2000
   Philadelphia, 2007
   Washington, 2012

Most Touchdowns, Opponents' Fumbles Recovered, Season
4 Detroit, 1937
   Chi. Bears, 1942
   Boston, 1948
   Los Angeles, 1952
   San Francisco, 1965
   Denver, 1984
   St. Louis, 1987
   Minnesota, 1989
   Atlanta, 1991
   Philadelphia, 1995
   Atlanta, 1998
   New Orleans, 1998
   Kansas City, 1999
   Arizona, 2010
3 By many teams

Most Touchdowns, Fumbles Recovered, Game, Own and Opponents'
2 By many teams

Most Touchdowns, Fumbles Recovered, Game, Both Teams, Own and Opponents'
3 Detroit (2) vs. Minnesota (1), Dec. 9, 1962
    (2 own, 1 opp)
   Green Bay (2) vs. Dallas (1), Nov. 29, 1964 (3 opp)
   Oakland (2) vs. Buffalo (1), Dec. 24, 1967 (3 opp)
   Oakland (2) vs. Philadelphia (1), Sept. 24, 1995
    (3 opp)
   Tennessee (2) vs. Pittsburgh (1), Jan. 2, 2000
    (3 opp)

Most Touchdowns, Own Fumbles Recovered, Game
2 Miami vs. New England, Sept.1, 1996

Most Touchdowns, Opponents' Fumbles Recovered, Game
2 Many times. Last time:
    New England vs. N.Y. Jets, Nov. 22, 2012

Most Touchdowns, Opponents' Fumbles Recovered, Game, Both Teams
3 Green Bay (2) vs. Dallas (1), Nov. 29, 1964
   Oakland (2) vs. Buffalo (1), Dec. 24, 1967
   Oakland (2) vs. Philadelphia (1), Sept. 24, 1995
   Tennessee (2) vs. Pittsburgh (1), Jan. 2, 2000

TURNOVERS
(Number of times losing the ball on interceptions and fumbles.)
Most Turnovers, Season
65 Denver, 1961
63 San Francisco, 1978
58 Chi. Bears, 1947
    Pittsburgh, 1950
    N.Y. Giants, 1983
Fewest Turnovers, Season
10 New England, 2010

San Francisco, 2011
12 Kansas City, 1982
13 Miami, 2008
    N.Y. Giants, 2008

Most Turnovers, Game
12 Detroit vs. Chi. Bears, Nov. 22, 1942
    Chi. Cardinals vs. Philadelphia, Sept. 24, 1950
    Pittsburgh vs. Philadelphia, Dec. 12, 1965
11 San Diego vs. Green Bay, Sept. 24, 1978
10 Washington vs. N.Y. Giants, Dec. 4, 1938
    Pittsburgh vs. Green Bay, Nov. 23, 1941
    Detroit vs. Green Bay, Oct. 24, 1943
    Chi. Cardinals vs. Green Bay, Nov. 10, 1946
    Chi. Cardinals vs. N.Y. Giants, Nov. 2, 1952
    Minnesota vs. Detroit, Dec. 9, 1962
    Houston vs. Oakland, Sept. 7, 1963
    Washington vs. N.Y. Giants, Dec. 8, 1963
    Chicago vs. Detroit, Sept. 22, 1968
    St. Louis vs. Washington, Oct. 25, 1976
    N.Y. Jets vs. New England, Nov. 21, 1976
    San Francisco vs. Dallas, Oct. 12, 1980
    Cleveland vs. Seattle, Dec. 20, 1981
    Detroit vs. Denver, Oct. 7, 1984

Most Turnovers, Both Teams, Game
17 Detroit (12) vs. Chi. Bears (5), Nov. 22, 1942
    Boston (9) vs. Philadelphia (8), Dec. 8, 1946
16 Chi. Cardinals (12) vs. Philadelphia (4),
     Sept. 24, 1950
    Chi. Cardinals (8) vs. Chi. Bears (8), Dec. 7, 1958
    Minnesota (10) vs. Detroit (6), Dec. 9, 1962
    Houston (9) vs. Kansas City (7), Oct. 12, 1969
15 Philadelphia (8) vs. Chi. Cardinals (7), Oct. 3, 1954
    Denver (9) vs. Houston (6), Dec. 2, 1962
    Washington (10) vs. N.Y. Giants (5), Dec. 8, 1963
    St. Louis (9) vs. Kansas City (6), Oct. 2, 1983

PENALTIES
Most Seasons Leading League, Fewest Penalties
13 Miami, 1968, 1976-1984, 1986, 1990-91
9 Pittsburgh, 1946-47, 1950-52, 1954, 1963, 1965,
    1968
8 Boston/New England, 1962, 1964-65, 1973, 1987,
    1989, 1993, 2008

Most Consecutive Seasons Leading League, Fewest Penalties
9 Miami, 1976-1984
3 Pittsburgh, 1950-52
2 By many teams

Most Seasons Leading League, Most Penalties
17 Oakland/L.A. Raiders, 1963, 1966, 1968-69, 1975,
    1982, 1984, 1991, 1993-96, 2003-05, 2010-11
16 Chi. Bears, 1941-44, 1946-49, 1951, 1959-1961,
    1963, 1965, 1968, 1976
8 L.A./St. Louis Rams, 1950, 1952, 1962, 1969,
    1978, 1980, 1997, 2012

Most Consecutive Seasons Leading League, Most Penalties
4 Chi. Bears, 1941-44, 1946-49
   Oakland/L.A. Raiders, 1993-96
3 Chi. Cardinals, 1954-56
   Chi. Bears, 1959-1961
   Oakland, 2003-05

Fewest Penalties, Season
19 Detroit, 1937
21 Boston, 1935
24 Philadelphia, 1936

Most Penalties, Season
163 Oakland, 2011
158 Kansas City, 1998
156 L.A. Raiders, 1994
     Oakland, 1996

Fewest Penalties, Game
- 0 By many teams. Last time:
  - Pittsburgh vs. Dallas, Dec. 16, 2012 (ot)

Most Penalties, Game
- 22 Brooklyn vs. Green Bay, Sept. 17, 1944
  - Chi. Bears vs. Philadelphia, Nov. 26, 1944
  - San Francisco vs. Buffalo, Oct. 4, 1998
- 21 Cleveland vs. Chi. Bears, Nov. 25, 1951
  - Baltimore vs. Detroit, Oct. 9, 2005
- 20 Tampa Bay vs. Seattle, Oct. 17, 1976
  - Oakland vs. Denver, Dec. 15, 1996

Fewest Penalties, Both Teams, Game
- 0 Brooklyn vs. Pittsburgh, Oct. 28, 1934
  - Brooklyn vs. Boston, Sept. 28, 1936
  - Cleveland vs. Chi. Bears, Oct. 9, 1938
  - Pittsburgh vs. Philadelphia, Nov. 10, 1940

Most Penalties, Both Teams, Game
- 37 Cleveland (21) vs. Chi. Bears (16), Nov. 25, 1951
- 35 Tampa Bay (20) vs. Seattle (15), Oct. 17, 1976
- 34 San Francisco (22) vs. Buffalo (12), Oct. 4, 1998

YARDS PENALIZED

Most Seasons Leading League, Fewest Yards Penalized
- 14 Miami, 1967-68, 1973, 1977-1984, 1990-91, 2010
- 10 Boston/Washington, 1935, 1953-54, 1956-58, 1970, 1985, 1995, 1997
- 8 Boston/New England, 1962, 1964-66, 1987, 1989, 1993, 2008

Most Consecutive Seasons Leading League, Fewest Yards Penalized
- 8 Miami, 1977-1984
- 3 Washington, 1956-58
  - Boston, 1964-66
- 2 By many teams

Most Seasons Leading League, Most Yards Penalized
- 15 Chi. Bears, 1935, 1937, 1939-1944, 1946-47, 1949, 1951, 1961-62, 1968
- 14 Oakland/L.A. Raiders, 1963-64, 1968-69, 1975, 1982, 1984, 1991, 1993-94, 1996, 2003, 2010-11
- 6 Buffalo, 1962, 1967, 1970, 1972, 1981, 1983
  - Houston, 1961, 1985-86, 1988-1990

Most Consecutive Seasons Leading League, Most Yards Penalized
- 6 Chi. Bears, 1939-1944
- 3 Houston, 1988-1990
- 2 By many teams

Fewest Yards Penalized, Season
- 139 Detroit, 1937
- 146 Philadelphia, 1937
- 159 Philadelphia, 1936

Most Yards Penalized, Season
- 1,358 Oakland, 2011
- 1,304 Kansas City, 1998
- 1,276 Oakland, 2010

Fewest Yards Penalized, Game
- 0 By many teams. Last time:
  - Pittsburgh vs. Dallas, Dec. 16, 2012 (ot)

Most Yards Penalized, Game
- 212 Tennessee vs. Baltimore, Oct. 10, 1999
- 209 Cleveland vs. Chi. Bears, Nov. 25, 1951
- 191 Philadelphia vs. Seattle, Dec. 13, 1992 (ot)

Fewest Yards Penalized, Both Teams, Game
- 0 Brooklyn vs. Pittsburgh, Oct. 28, 1934
  - Brooklyn vs. Boston, Sept. 28, 1936
  - Cleveland vs. Chi. Bears, Oct. 9, 1938
  - Pittsburgh vs. Philadelphia, Nov. 10, 1940

Most Yards Penalized, Both Teams, Game
- 374 Cleveland (209) vs. Chi. Bears (165), Nov. 25, 1951
- 310 Tampa Bay (190) vs. Seattle (120), Oct. 17, 1976

- Green Bay (175) vs. Baltimore (135), Dec. 7, 2009
- 309 Green Bay (184) vs. Boston (125), Oct. 21, 1945

DEFENSE

SCORING

Most Seasons Leading League, Fewest Points Allowed
- 11 N.Y. Giants, 1927, 1935, 1938-39, 1941, 1944, 1958-59, 1961, 1990, 1993
  - Chi. Bears, 1932, 1936-37, 1942, 1948, 1963, 1985-86, 1988, 2001, 2005
- 7 Cleveland, 1951, 1953-57, 1994
  - Green Bay, 1929, 1935, 1947, 1962, 1965-66, 1996
  - Pittsburgh, 1946, 1976, 1978, 2004, 2008, 2010-11
- 6 Dallas/Kansas City, 1960, 1962, 1968-69, 1995, 1997

Most Consecutive Seasons Leading League, Fewest Points Allowed
- 5 Cleveland, 1953-57
- 3 Buffalo, 1964-66
  - Minnesota, 1969-1971
- 2 By many teams

Fewest Points Allowed, Season (Since 1932)
- 44 Chi. Bears, 1932
- 54 Brooklyn, 1933
- 59 Detroit, 1934

Most Points Allowed, Season
- 533 Baltimore, 1981
- 517 Detroit, 2008
- 501 N.Y. Giants, 1966

Fewest TDs Allowed, Season (Since 1932)
- 6 Chi. Bears, 1932
  - Brooklyn, 1933
- 7 Detroit, 1934
- 8 Green Bay, 1932

Most Touchdowns Allowed, Season
- 68 Baltimore, 1981
- 66 N.Y. Giants, 1966
- 63 Baltimore, 1950
  - Detroit, 2008

FIRST DOWNS

Fewest First Downs Allowed, Season
- 77 Detroit, 1935
- 79 Boston, 1935
- 82 Washington, 1937

Most First Downs Allowed, Season
- 406 Baltimore, 1981
- 380 New Orleans, 2012
- 371 Seattle, 1981

Fewest First Downs Allowed, Rushing, Season
- 35 Chi. Bears, 1942
- 40 Green Bay, 1939
- 41 Brooklyn, 1944

Most First Downs Allowed, Rushing, Season
- 179 Detroit, 1985
- 178 New Orleans, 1980
- 175 Seattle, 1981

Fewest First Downs Allowed, Passing, Season
- 33 Chi. Bears, 1943
- 34 Pittsburgh, 1941
  - Washington, 1943
- 35 Detroit, 1940
  - Philadelphia, 1940
  - Philadelphia, 1944

Most First Downs Allowed, Passing, Season
- 246 Green Bay, 2011
- 245 New England, 2011
- 236 New Orleans, 2012

Fewest First Downs Allowed, Penalty, Season
- 1 Boston, 1944
- 3 Philadelphia, 1940
  Pittsburgh, 1945
  Washington, 1957
- 4 Cleveland, 1940
  Green Bay, 1943
  N.Y. Giants, 1943

Most First Downs Allowed, Penalty, Season
- 58 Oakland, 2011
- 56 Kansas City, 1998
- 48 Houston, 1985

NET YARDS ALLOWED RUSHING AND PASSING

Most Seasons Leading League, Fewest Yards Allowed
- 10 Pittsburgh, 1957, 1974, 1976, 1990, 2001, 2004, 2007-08, 2011-12
- 8 Chi. Bears, 1942-43, 1948, 1958, 1963, 1984-86
- 6 N.Y. Giants, 1938, 1940-41, 1951, 1956, 1959
  Philadelphia, 1944-45, 1949, 1953, 1981, 1991
  Minnesota, 1969-1970, 1975, 1988-89, 1993

Most Consecutive Seasons Leading League, Fewest Yards Allowed
- 3 Boston/Washington, 1935-37
  Chicago, 1984-86
- 2 By many teams

Fewest Yards Allowed, Season
- 1,539 Chi. Cardinals, 1934
- 1,703 Chi. Bears, 1942
- 1,789 Brooklyn, 1933

Most Yards Allowed, Season
- 7,042 New Orleans, 2012
- 6,793 Baltimore, 1981
- 6,585 Green Bay, 2011

RUSHING

Most Seasons Leading League, Fewest Yards Allowed
- 10 Chi. Bears, 1937, 1939, 1942, 1946, 1949, 1963, 1984-85, 1987-88
- 8 Pittsburgh, 1961, 1976, 1982, 1997, 2001-02, 2004, 2010
- 7 Detroit, 1938, 1950, 1952, 1962, 1970, 1980-81
  Philadelphia, 1944-45, 1947-48, 1953, 1990-91
  Dallas, 1966-69, 1972, 1978, 1992

Most Consecutive Seasons Leading League, Fewest Yards Allowed
- 4 Dallas, 1966-69
- 3 Minnesota, 2006-08
- 2 By many teams

Fewest Yards Allowed, Rushing, Season
- 519 Chi. Bears, 1942
- 558 Philadelphia, 1944
- 762 Pittsburgh, 1982

Most Yards Allowed, Rushing, Season
- 3,228 Buffalo, 1978
- 3,106 New Orleans, 1980
- 3,010 Baltimore, 1978

Fewest Touchdowns Allowed, Rushing, Season
- 2 Detroit, 1934
  N.Y. Giants, 1944
  Dallas, 1968
  Minnesota, 1971
- 3 By many teams

Most Touchdowns Allowed, Rushing, Season
- 36 Oakland, 1961
- 31 N.Y. Giants, 1980
  Tampa Bay, 1986
  Detroit, 2008
- 30 Baltimore, 1981

PASSING

Most Seasons Leading League, Fewest Yards Allowed
- 10 Green Bay, 1947-48, 1962, 1964-68, 1996, 2005
- 9 Pittsburgh, 1941, 1946, 1951, 1955, 1974, 1990, 2008, 2011-12
- 7 Washington, 1939, 1942, 1945, 1952-53, 1980, 1985
  Philadelphia 1934, 1936, 1940, 1949, 1981, 1991, 1998

Most Consecutive Seasons Leading League, Fewest Yards Allowed
- 5 Green Bay, 1964-68
- 2 By many teams

Fewest Yards Allowed Passing, Season
- 545 Philadelphia, 1934
- 558 Portsmouth, 1933
- 585 Chi. Cardinals, 1934

Most Yards Allowed, Passing, Season
- 4,796 Green Bay, 2011
- 4,758 Tampa Bay, 2012
- 4,703 New England, 2011

Fewest Touchdowns Allowed, Passing, Season
- 1 Portsmouth, 1932
  Philadelphia, 1934
- 2 Brooklyn, 1933
  Chi. Bears, 1934
- 3 Chi. Bears, 1932
  Green Bay, 1932
  Green Bay, 1934
  Chi. Bears, 1936
  New York, 1939
  New York, 1944

Most Touchdowns Allowed, Passing, Season
- 40 Denver, 1963
- 38 St. Louis, 1969
- 37 Washington, 1961
  Baltimore, 1981

SACKS

Most Seasons Leading League
- 5 Oakland/L.A. Raiders, 1966-68, 1982, 1986
  Dallas, 1966, 1968-69, 1978, 2008
  L.A./St. Louis Rams, 1968, 1970, 1988, 1999, 2012
- 4 New England/Boston, 1961, 1963, 1977, 1979
  Dallas/Kansas City, 1960, 1965, 1969, 1990
  N.Y. Giants, 1963, 1985, 1998, 2007
  Pittsburgh, 1974, 1994, 2001, 2010
- 3 San Francisco, 1967, 1972, 1976
  N.Y. Giants, 1963, 1985, 1998
  New Orleans, 1992, 1997, 2000
  San Diego, 1962, 1980, 2006
  Philadelphia, 1991, 2002, 2011

Most Consecutive Seasons Leading League
- 3 Oakland, 1966-68
- 2 Dallas, 1968-69

Most Sacks, Season
- 72 Chicago, 1984
- 71 Minnesota, 1989
- 70 Chicago, 1987

Fewest Sacks, Season
- 10 Kansas City, 2008
- 11 Baltimore, 1982
- 12 Buffalo, 1982

Most Sacks, Game
- 12 Dallas vs. Pittsburgh, Nov. 20, 1966
  St. Louis vs. Baltimore, Oct. 26, 1980
  Chicago vs. Detroit, Dec. 16, 1984
  Dallas vs. Houston, Sept. 29, 1985
  N.Y. Giants vs. Philadelphia, Sept. 30, 2007

11   N.Y. Giants vs. St. Louis, Nov. 1, 1964
     Baltimore vs. Los Angeles, Nov. 22, 1964
     Buffalo vs. Denver, Dec. 13, 1964
     Detroit vs. Green Bay, Nov. 7, 1965
     Oakland vs. Buffalo, Oct. 15, 1967
     Oakland vs. Denver, Nov. 5, 1967
     St. Louis vs. Atlanta, Nov. 24, 1968
     Dallas vs. Detroit, Oct. 6, 1975
     St. Louis vs. Philadelphia, Dec. 18, 1983
     Kansas City vs. Cleveland, Sept. 30, 1984
     Chicago vs. Minnesota, Oct. 28, 1984
     Cleveland vs. Atlanta, Nov. 18, 1984
     Detroit vs. Philadelphia, Nov. 16, 1986
     San Diego vs. Dallas, Nov. 16, 1986
     L.A. Raiders vs. Philadelphia, Nov. 30, 1986 (ot)
     Seattle vs. L.A. Raiders, Dec. 8, 1986
     Chicago vs. Philadelphia, Oct. 4, 1987
     Dallas vs. N.Y. Jets, Oct. 4, 1987
     Philadelphia vs. Dallas, Sept. 15, 1991
     Indianapolis vs. Cleveland, Sept. 6, 1992
     San Diego vs. N.Y. Jets, Dec. 23, 2012
10   By many teams

Most Opponents Yards Lost Attempting to Pass, Season
666   Oakland, 1967
583   Chicago, 1984
573   San Francisco, 1976

Fewest Opponents Yards Lost Attempting to Pass, Season
62   Kansas City, 2008
72   Jacksonville, 1995
75   Green Bay, 1956

INTERCEPTIONS BY

Most Seasons Leading League
10   N.Y. Giants, 1933, 1937-39, 1944, 1948, 1951,
       1954, 1961, 1997
     Green Bay, 1940, 1942-43, 1947, 1955, 1957,
       1962, 1965, 2009, 2011
 9   Chi. Bears, 1935-36, 1941-42, 1946, 1963, 1985,
       1990, 2012
 6   Kansas City, 1966-1970, 1974

Most Consecutive Seasons Leading League
5   Kansas City, 1966-1970
3   N.Y. Giants, 1937-39
2   By many teams

Most Passes Intercepted, Season
49   San Diego, 1961
42   Green Bay, 1943
41   N.Y. Giants, 1951

Fewest Passes Intercepted By, Season
3   Houston, 1982
4   Detroit, 2008
5   Baltimore, 1982
    Oakland, 2005

Most Passes Intercepted By, Game
9   Green Bay vs. Detroit, Oct. 24, 1943
    Philadelphia vs. Pittsburgh, Dec. 12, 1965
8   N.Y. Giants vs. Green Bay, Nov. 21, 1948
    Philadelphia vs. Chi. Cardinals, Sept. 24, 1950
    N.Y. Giants vs. N.Y. Yanks, Dec. 16, 1951
    Houston vs. Denver, Dec. 2, 1962
    Detroit vs. Chicago, Sept. 22, 1968
    N.Y. Jets vs. Baltimore, Sept. 23, 1973
7   By many teams. Last time:
      Cleveland vs. Detroit, Sept. 23, 2001

Most Consecutive Games, One or More Interceptions By
46   L.A. Chargers/San Diego, 1960-63
37   Detroit, 1960-63
36   Boston, 1944-47

Most Yards Returning Interceptions, Season
929   San Diego, 1961

712   Los Angeles, 1952
700   Baltimore, 2004

Fewest Yards Returning Interceptions, Season
5   Los Angeles, 1959
16   Detroit, 2008
25   Washington, 2006

Most Yards Returning Interceptions, Game
325   Seattle vs. Kansas City, Nov. 4, 1984
314   Los Angeles vs. San Francisco, Oct. 18, 1964
245   Houston vs. N.Y. Jets, Oct. 15, 1967

Most Yards Returning Interceptions, Both Teams, Game
356   Seattle (325) vs. Kansas City (31), Nov. 4, 1984
338   Los Angeles (314) vs. San Francisco (24),
        Oct. 18, 1964
308   Dallas (182) vs. Los Angeles (126), Nov. 2, 1952

Most Touchdowns, Returning Interceptions, Season
9   San Diego, 1961
8   Seattle, 1998
    Chicago, 2012
7   Seattle, 1984
    St. Louis, 1999

Most Touchdowns Returning Interceptions, Game
4   Seattle vs. Kansas City, Nov. 4, 1984
3   Baltimore vs. Green Bay, Nov. 5, 1950
    Cleveland vs. Chicago, Dec. 11, 1960
    Philadelphia vs. Pittsburgh, Dec. 12, 1965
    Baltimore vs. Pittsburgh, Sept. 29, 1968
    Buffalo vs. N.Y. Jets, Sept. 29, 1968
    Houston vs. San Diego, Dec. 19, 1971
    Cincinnati vs. Houston, Dec. 17, 1972
    Tampa Bay vs. New Orleans, Dec. 11, 1977
    Minnesota vs. N.Y. Giants, Nov. 25, 2007
2   By many teams

Most Touchdown Returning Interceptions, Both Teams, Game
4   Philadelphia (3) vs. Pittsburgh (1), Dec. 12, 1965
    Seattle (4) vs. Kansas City (0), Nov. 4, 1984
3   Los Angeles (2) vs. Detroit (1), Nov. 1, 1953
    Cleveland (2) vs. N.Y. Giants (1), Dec. 18, 1960
    Pittsburgh (2) vs. Cincinnati (1), Oct. 10, 1983
    Kansas City (2) vs. San Diego (1), Oct. 19, 1986
    Arizona (2) vs. St. Louis (1), Dec. 30, 2007
    (Also see previous record)

PUNT RETURNS

Fewest Opponents Punt Returns, Season
7   Washington, 1962
    San Diego, 1982
10   Buffalo, 1982
11   Boston, 1962
    New England, 2008

Most Opponents Punt Returns, Season
71   Tampa Bay, 1976, 1977
69   N.Y. Giants, 1953
    Cleveland, 2000
68   Cleveland, 1974
    Cleveland, 1999

Fewest Yards Allowed, Punt Returns, Season
22   Green Bay, 1967
30   Buffalo, 1982
34   Washington, 1962

Most Yards Allowed, Punt Returns, Season
932   Green Bay, 1949
913   Boston, 1947
906   New Orleans, 1974

Lowest Avg. Allowed, Punt Returns, Season
1.20   Chi. Cardinals, 1954
1.22   Cleveland, 1959
1.55   Chi. Cardinals, 1953

Highest Average Allowed, Punt Returns, Season
18.9   San Diego, 2010 (28-528)

18.6   Green Bay, 1949 (50-932)
18.0   Cleveland, 1977 (31-558)
Most Touchdowns Allowed, Punt Returns, Season
4   Los Angeles, 1951
    N.Y. Giants, 1959
    Atlanta, 1992
    Minnesota, 2008
3   Green Bay, 1949
    Chi. Cardinals, 1951
    L.A. Rams, 1951, 1994
    Washington, 1952
    Dallas, 1952
    Pittsburgh, 1959, 1993
    N.Y. Jets, 1968
    Cleveland, 1977
    Atlanta, 1986
    Tampa Bay, 1986
    Arizona, 2002
    Cincinnati, 2002
    Tennessee, 2002
    Carolina, 2011
2   By many teams

KICKOFF RETURNS
Fewest Opponents Kickoff Returns, Season
10   Brooklyn, 1943
13   Denver, 1992
15   Detroit, 1942
    Brooklyn, 1944
Most Opponents Kickoff Returns, Season
93   Indianapolis, 2003
92   Indianapolis, 2004
    New England, 2007
91   Washington, 1983
    Minnesota, 2009
Fewest Yards Allowed, Kickoff Returns, Season
225   Brooklyn, 1943
254   Denver, 1992
293   Brooklyn, 1944
Most Yards Allowed, Kickoff Returns, Season
2,194   St. Louis, 2001
2,115   St. Louis, 1999
2,060   Minnesota, 2009
Lowest Average Allowed, Kickoff Returns, Season
14.3   Cleveland, 1980
14.9   Indianapolis, 1993
15.0   Seattle, 1982
Highest Average Allowed, Kickoff Returns, Season
30.7   Indianapolis, 2011 (19-584)
29.5   N.Y. Jets, 1972 (47-1,386)
29.4   Los Angeles, 1950 (48-1,411)
Most Touchdowns Allowed, Kickoff Returns, Season
4   Minnesota, 1998
    Pittsburgh, 2009
3   Minnesota, 1963, 1970
    Dallas, 1966
    Detroit, 1980
    Pittsburgh, 1986
    Buffalo, 1997
    Atlanta, 2000
    Arizona, 2005
    Indianapolis, 2007
    San Diego, 2010
2   By many teams

FUMBLES
Fewest Opponents Fumbles, Season
11   Cleveland, 1956
    Baltimore, 1982
    Tennessee, 1998

San Diego, 2011
Indianapolis, 2012
12   Green Bay, 1995
    Cincinnati, 1998
    Jacksonville, 2006
    Baltimore, 2007
    Jacksonville, 2010
13   Los Angeles, 1956
    Chicago, 1960
    Cleveland, 1963
    Cleveland, 1965
    Detroit, 1967
    San Diego, 1969
    New England, 2005
    Cleveland, 2006
    San Diego, 2010
    Oakland, 2011
    Pittsburgh, 2011
Most Opponents Fumbles, Season
50   Minnesota, 1963
    San Francisco, 1978
48   N.Y. Giants, 1980
    N.Y. Jets, 1986
47   N.Y. Giants, 1977
    Seattle, 1984
46   Boston, 1948
    Atlanta, 1978
    Denver, 1983
    Washington, 1983

TURNOVERS
(Number of times losing the ball on interceptions and fumbles.)
Fewest Opponents Turnovers, Season
11   Baltimore, 1982
12   Washington, 2006
13   San Francisco, 1982
    Denver, 2008
    Kansas City, 2012
    Philadelphia 2012
Most Opponent Turnovers, Season
66   San Diego, 1961
63   Seattle, 1984
61   Washington, 1983
Most Opponent Turnovers, Game
12   Chi. Bears vs. Detroit, Nov. 22, 1942
    Philadelphia vs. Chi. Cardinals, Sept. 24, 1950
    Philadelphia vs. Pittsburgh, Dec. 12, 1965
11   Green Bay vs. San Diego, Sept. 24, 1978
10   By 14 teams

1,000 YARDS RUSHING IN A SEASON

Year	Player, Team	Att.	Yards	Avg.	Long	T8
2012	Adrian Peterson, Minnesota[5]	348	2,097	6.0	82	12
	*Alfred Morris, Washington	335	1,613	4.8	39	13
	Marshawn Lynch, Seattle[4]	315	1,590	5.0	77	11
	Jamaal Charles, Kansas City[3]	285	1,509	5.3	91	5
	*Doug Martin, Tampa Bay	319	1,454	4.6	70	11
	Arian Foster, Houston[3]	351	1,424	4.1	46	15
	Stevan Ridley, New England	290	1,263	4.4	41	12
	C.J. Spiller, Buffalo	207	1,244	6.0	62	6
	Chris Johnson, Tennessee[5]	276	1,243	4.5	94	6
	Frank Gore, San Francisco[6]	258	1,214	4.7	37	8
	Ray Rice, Baltimore[4]	257	1,143	4.4	46	9
	Matt Forté, Chicago[3]	248	1,094	4.4	46	5
	BenJarvus Green-Ellis, Cincinnati[2]	278	1,094	3.9	48	6
	Shonn Greene, N.Y. Jets[2]	276	1,063	3.9	36	8
	Steven Jackson, St. Louis[8]	257	1,042	4.1	46	4
	Ahmad Bradshaw, N.Y. Giants[2]	221	1,015	4.6	37	6
2011	Maurice Jones-Drew, Jacksonville[3]	343	1,606	4.7	56	8
	Ray Rice, Baltimore[3]	291	1,364	4.7	70	12
	Michael Turner, Atlanta[3]	301	1,340	4.5	81	11
	LeSean McCoy, Philadelphia[2]	273	1,309	4.8	60	17
	Arian Foster, Houston[2]	278	1,224	4.4	43	10
	Frank Gore, San Francisco[5]	282	1,211	4.3	55	8
	Marshawn Lynch, Seattle[3]	285	1,204	4.2	47	12
	Willis McGahee, Denver[4]	249	1,199	4.8	60	4
	Steven Jackson, St. Louis[7]	260	1,145	4.4	47	5
	Ryan Mathews, San Diego	222	1,091	4.9	39	6
	Reggie Bush, Miami	216	1,086	5.0	76	6
	Cedric Benson, Cincinnati[3]	273	1,067	3.9	42	6
	Shonn Greene, N.Y. Jets	253	1,054	4.2	31	6
	Chris Johnson, Tennessee[4]	262	1,047	4.0	48	4
	Beanie Wells, Arizona	245	1,047	4.3	71	10
2010	Arian Foster, Houston	327	1,616	4.9	74	16
	Jamaal Charles, Kansas City[2]	230	1,467	6.4	80	5
	Michael Turner, Atlanta[2]	334	1,371	4.1	55	12
	Chris Johnson, Tennessee[3]	316	1,364	4.3	76	11
	Maurice Jones-Drew, Jacksonville[2]	299	1,324	4.4	37	5
	Adrian Peterson, Minnesota[4]	283	1,298	4.6	80	12
	Rashard Mendenhall, Pittsburgh[2]	324	1,273	3.9	50	13
	Steven Jackson, St. Louis[6]	330	1,241	3.8	42	6
	Ahmad Bradshaw, N.Y. Giants	276	1,235	4.5	48	8
	Ray Rice, Baltimore[2]	307	1,220	4.0	50	5
	Peyton Hillis, Cleveland	270	1,177	4.4	48	11
	Darren McFadden, Oakland	223	1,157	5.2	57	7
	Cedric Benson, Cincinnati[2]	321	1,111	3.5	26	7
	LeSean McCoy, Philadelphia	207	1,080	5.2	62	7
	Matt Forté, Chicago[2]	237	1,069	4.5	68	6
	BenJarvus Green-Ellis, New England	229	1,008	4.4	33	13
	*LeGarrette Blount, Tampa Bay	201	1,007	5.0	53	6
2009	Chris Johnson, Tennessee[2]	358	2,006	5.6	91	14
	Steven Jackson, St. Louis[5]	324	1,416	4.8	58	4
	Thomas Jones, N.Y. Jets[5]	331	1,402	4.2	71	14
	Maurice Jones-Drew, Jacksonville	312	1,391	4.5	80	15
	Adrian Peterson, Minnesota[3]	314	1,383	4.4	64	18
	Ray Rice, Baltimore	254	1,339	5.3	59	7
	Ryan Grant, Green Bay[2]	282	1,253	4.4	62	11
	Cedric Benson, Cincinnati	301	1,251	4.2	42	6
	Jonathan Stewart, Carolina	221	1,133	5.1	67	10
	Ricky Williams, Miami[5]	241	1,121	4.6	68	11
	Jamaal Charles, Kansas City	190	1,120	5.9	76	7
	Frank Gore, San Francisco[4]	229	1,120	4.9	80	10
	DeAngelo Williams, Carolina[2]	216	1,117	5.2	77	7
	Rashard Mendenhall, Pittsburgh	242	1,108	4.6	60	7
	Fred Jackson, Buffalo	237	1,062	4.5	43	2
2008	Adrian Peterson, Minnesota[2]	363	1,760	4.9	67	10
	Michael Turner, Atlanta	376	1,699	4.5	70	17
	DeAngelo Williams, Carolina	273	1,515	5.6	69	18
	Clinton Portis, Washington[6]	342	1,487	4.4	31	9
	Thomas Jones, N.Y. Jets[4]	290	1,312	4.5	59	13

Year	Player, Team	Att.	Yards	Avg.	Long	TD
	*Steve Slaton, Houston	268	1,282	4.8	71	9
	*Matt Forté, Chicago	316	1,238	3.9	50	8
	*Chris Johnson, Tennessee	251	1,228	4.9	66	9
	Ryan Grant, Green Bay	312	1,203	3.9	57	4
	LaDainian Tomlinson, San Diego[8]	292	1,110	3.8	45	11
	Brandon Jacobs, N.Y. Giants[2]	219	1,089	5.0	44	15
	Steven Jackson, St. Louis[4]	253	1,042	4.1	56	7
	Frank Gore, San Francisco[3]	240	1,036	4.3	41	6
	Marshawn Lynch, Buffalo[2]	250	1,036	4.1	50	8
	Derrick Ward, N.Y. Giants	182	1,025	5.6	51	2
	Jamal Lewis, Cleveland[7]	279	1,002	3.6	29	4
2007	LaDainian Tomlinson, San Diego[7]	315	1,474	4.7	49	15
	*Adrian Peterson, Minnesota	238	1,341	5.6	73	12
	Brian Westbrook, Philadelphia[2]	278	1,333	4.8	36	7
	Willie Parker, Pittsburgh[3]	321	1,316	4.1	32	2
	Jamal Lewis, Cleveland[6]	298	1,304	4.4	66	9
	Clinton Portis, Washington[5]	325	1,262	3.9	32	11
	Edgerrin James, Arizona[7]	324	1,222	3.8	27	7
	Willis McGahee, Baltimore[3]	294	1,207	4.1	46	7
	Fred Taylor, Jacksonville[7]	223	1,202	5.4	80	5
	Thomas Jones, N.Y. Jets[3]	310	1,119	3.6	36	1
	*Marshawn Lynch, Buffalo	280	1,115	4.0	56	7
	LenDale White, Tennessee	303	1,110	3.7	28	7
	Frank Gore, San Francisco[2]	260	1,102	4.2	43	5
	Joseph Addai, Indianapolis[2]	261	1,072	4.1	23	12
	Justin Fargas, Oakland	222	1,009	4.6	48	4
	Brandon Jacobs, N.Y. Giants	202	1,009	5.0	43	4
	Steven Jackson, St. Louis[3]	237	1,002	4.2	54	5
2006	LaDainian Tomlinson, San Diego[6]	348	1,815	5.2	85	28
	Larry Johnson, Kansas City[2]	416	1,789	4.3	47	17
	Frank Gore, San Francisco	312	1,695	5.4	72	8
	Tiki Barber, N.Y. Giants[6]	327	1,662	5.1	55	5
	Steven Jackson, St. Louis[2]	346	1,528	4.4	59	13
	Willie Parker, Pittsburgh[2]	337	1,494	4.4	76	13
	Rudi Johnson, Cincinnati[3]	341	1,309	3.8	22	12
	Brian Westbrook, Philadelphia	240	1,217	5.1	71	7
	Chester Taylor, Minnesota	303	1,216	4.0	95	6
	Travis Henry, Tennessee[3]	270	1,211	4.5	70	7
	Thomas Jones, Chicago[2]	296	1,210	4.1	30	6
	Edgerrin James, Arizona[6]	337	1,159	3.4	18	6
	Ladell Betts, Washington	245	1,154	4.7	26	4
	Fred Taylor, Jacksonville[6]	231	1,146	5.0	76	5
	Warrick Dunn, Atlanta[5]	286	1,140	4.0	90	4
	Jamal Lewis, Baltimore[5]	314	1,132	3.6	52	9
	Julius Jones, Dallas	267	1,084	4.1	77	4
	*Joseph Addai, Indianapolis	226	1,081	4.8	41	7
	Ahman Green, Green Bay[6]	266	1,059	4.0	70	5
	Deuce McAllister, New Orleans[4]	244	1,057	4.3	57	10
	Michael Vick, Atlanta	123	1,039	8.5	51	2
	Tatum Bell, Denver	233	1,025	4.4	51	2
	Ronnie Brown, Miami	241	1,008	4.2	47	5
2005	Shaun Alexander, Seattle[5]	370	1,880	5.1	88	27
	Tiki Barber, N.Y. Giants[5]	357	1,860	5.2	95	9
	Larry Johnson, Kansas City	336	1,750	5.2	49	20
	Clinton Portis, Washington[4]	352	1,516	4.3	47	11
	Edgerrin James, Indianapolis[5]	360	1,506	4.2	33	13
	LaDainian Tomlinson, San Diego[5]	339	1,462	4.3	62	18
	Rudi Johnson, Cincinnati[2]	337	1,458	4.3	33	12
	Warrick Dunn, Atlanta[4]	280	1,416	5.1	65	3
	Thomas Jones, Chicago	314	1,335	4.3	42	9
	Willis McGahee, Buffalo[2]	325	1,247	3.8	27	5
	Reuben Droughns, Cleveland[2]	309	1,232	4.0	75	2
	Willie Parker, Pittsburgh	255	1,202	4.7	80	4
	*Carnell Williams, Tampa Bay	290	1,178	4.1	71	6
	Steven Jackson, St. Louis	254	1,046	4.1	51	8
	LaMont Jordan, Oakland	272	1,025	3.8	26	9
	Mike Anderson, Denver[2]	239	1,014	4.2	44	12
2004	Curtis Martin, N.Y. Jets[10]	371	1,697	4.6	25	12
	Shaun Alexander, Seattle[4]	353	1,696	4.8	44	16

Year	Player, Team	Att.	Yards	Avg.	Long	TD
	Corey Dillon, New England[7]	345	1,635	4.7	44	12
	Edgerrin James, Indianapolis[4]	334	1,548	4.6	40	9
	Tiki Barber, N.Y. Giants[4]	322	1,518	4.7	72	13
	Rudi Johnson, Cincinnati	361	1,454	4.0	52	12
	LaDainian Tomlinson, San Diego[4]	339	1,335	3.9	42	17
	Clinton Portis, Washington[3]	343	1,315	3.8	64	5
	Reuben Droughns, Denver	275	1,240	4.5	51	6
	Fred Taylor, Jacksonville[5]	260	1,224	4.7	46	2
	Domanick Davis, Houston[2]	302	1,188	3.9	44	13
	Ahman Green, Green Bay[6]	259	1,163	4.5	90	7
	*Kevin Jones, Detroit	241	1,133	4.7	74	5
	Willis McGahee, Buffalo	284	1,128	4.0	41	13
	Warrick Dunn, Atlanta[3]	265	1,106	4.2	60	9
	Deuce McAllister, New Orleans[3]	269	1,074	4.0	71	9
	Chris Brown, Tennessee	220	1,067	4.9	52	6
	Jamal Lewis, Baltimore[4]	235	1,006	4.3	75	7
2003	Jamal Lewis, Baltimore[3]	387	2,066	5.3	82	14
	Ahman Green, Green Bay[4]	355	1,883	5.3	98	15
	LaDainian Tomlinson, San Diego[3]	313	1,645	5.3	73	13
	Deuce McAllister, New Orleans[2]	351	1,641	4.7	76	8
	Clinton Portis, Denver[2]	290	1,591	5.5	65	14
	Fred Taylor, Jacksonville[4]	345	1,572	4.6	62	6
	Stephen Davis, Carolina[4]	318	1,444	4.5	40	8
	Shaun Alexander, Seattle[3]	326	1,435	4.4	55	14
	Priest Holmes, Kansas City[4]	320	1,420	4.4	31	27
	Ricky Williams, Miami[4]	392	1,372	3.5	45	9
	Travis Henry, Buffalo[2]	331	1,356	4.1	64	10
	Curtis Martin, N.Y. Jets[9]	323	1,308	4.1	56	2
	Edgerrin James, Indianapolis[3]	310	1,259	4.1	43	11
	Tiki Barber, N.Y. Giants[3]	278	1,216	4.4	27	2
	*Domanick Davis, Houston	238	1,031	4.3	51	8
	Eddie George, Tennessee[7]	312	1,031	3.3	27	5
	Kevan Barlow, San Francisco	201	1,024	5.1	78	6
	Anthony Thomas, Chicago[2]	244	1,024	4.2	67	6
2002	Ricky Williams, Miami[3]	383	1,853	4.8	63	16
	LaDainian Tomlinson, San Diego[2]	372	1,683	4.5	76	14
	Priest Holmes, Kansas City[3]	313	1,615	5.2	56	21
	*Clinton Portis, Denver	273	1,508	5.5	59	15
	Travis Henry, Buffalo	325	1,438	4.4	34	13
	Deuce McAllister, New Orleans	325	1,388	4.3	62	13
	Tiki Barber, N.Y. Giants[2]	304	1,387	4.6	70	11
	Jamal Lewis, Baltimore[2]	308	1,327	4.3	75	6
	Fred Taylor, Jacksonville[3]	287	1,314	4.6	63	8
	Corey Dillon, Cincinnati[6]	314	1,311	4.2	67	7
	Michael Bennett, Minnesota	255	1,296	5.1	85	5
	Ahman Green, Green Bay[3]	286	1,240	4.3	43	7
	Shaun Alexander, Seattle[2]	295	1,175	4.0	58	16
	Eddie George, Tennessee[6]	343	1,165	3.4	35	12
	Curtis Martin, N.Y. Jets[8]	261	1,094	4.2	35	7
	Duce Staley, Philadelphia[3]	269	1,029	3.8	57	5
	James Stewart, Detroit[2]	231	1,021	4.4	56	4
2001	Priest Holmes, Kansas City[2]	327	1,555	4.8	41	8
	Curtis Martin, N.Y. Jets[7]	333	1,513	4.5	47	10
	Stephen Davis, Washington[3]	356	1,432	4.0	32	5
	Ahman Green, Green Bay[2]	304	1,387	4.6	83	9
	Marshall Faulk, St. Louis[7]	260	1,382	5.3	71	12
	Shaun Alexander, Seattle	309	1,318	4.3	88	14
	Corey Dillon, Cincinnati[5]	340	1,315	3.9	96	10
	Ricky Williams, New Orleans[2]	313	1,245	4.0	46	6
	*LaDainian Tomlinson, San Diego	339	1,236	3.6	54	10
	Garrison Hearst, San Francisco[4]	252	1,206	4.8	43	4
	*Anthony Thomas, Chicago	278	1,183	4.3	46	7
	Antowain Smith, New England[2]	287	1,157	4.0	44	12
	*Dominic Rhodes, Indianapolis	233	1,104	4.7	77	9
	Jerome Bettis, Pittsburgh[8]	225	1,072	4.8	48	4
	Emmitt Smith, Dallas[11]	261	1,021	3.9	44	3
2000	Edgerrin James, Indianapolis[2]	387	1,709	4.4	30	13
	Robert Smith, Minnesota[4]	295	1,521	5.2	72	7
	Eddie George, Tennessee[5]	403	1,509	3.7	35	14

Year	Player, Team	Att.	Yards	Avg.	Long	TD
	*Mike Anderson, Denver	297	1,487	5.0	80	15
	Corey Dillon, Cincinnati[4]	315	1,435	4.6	80	7
	Fred Taylor, Jacksonville[2]	292	1,399	4.8	71	12
	*Jamal Lewis, Baltimore	309	1,364	4.4	45	6
	Marshall Faulk, St. Louis[6]	253	1,359	5.4	36	18
	Jerome Bettis, Pittsburgh[7]	355	1,341	3.8	30	8
	Stephen Davis, Washington[2]	332	1,318	4.0	50	11
	Ricky Watters, Seattle[7]	278	1,242	4.5	55	7
	Curtis Martin, N.Y. Jets[6]	316	1,204	3.8	55	9
	Emmitt Smith, Dallas[10]	294	1,203	4.1	52	9
	James Stewart, Detroit	339	1,184	3.5	34	10
	Ahman Green, Green Bay	263	1,175	4.5	39	10
	Charlie Garner, San Francisco[2]	258	1,142	4.4	42	7
	Lamar Smith, Miami	309	1,139	3.7	68	14
	Warrick Dunn, Tampa Bay[2]	248	1,133	4.6	70	8
	James Allen, Chicago	290	1,120	3.9	29	2
	Tyrone Wheatley, Oakland	232	1,046	4.5	80	9
	Jamal Anderson, Atlanta[4]	282	1,024	3.6	42	6
	Tiki Barber, N.Y. Giants	213	1,006	4.7	78	8
	Ricky Williams, New Orleans	248	1,000	4.0	26	8
1999	*Edgerrin James, Indianapolis	369	1,553	4.2	72	13
	Curtis Martin, N.Y. Jets[5]	367	1,464	4.0	50	5
	Stephen Davis, Washington	290	1,405	4.8	76	17
	Emmitt Smith, Dallas[9]	329	1,397	4.3	63	11
	Marshall Faulk, St. Louis[5]	253	1,381	5.5	58	7
	Eddie George, Tennessee[4]	320	1,304	4.1	40	9
	Duce Staley, Philadelphia[2]	325	1,273	3.9	29	4
	Charlie Garner, San Francisco	241	1,229	5.1	53	4
	Ricky Watters, Seattle[6]	325	1,210	3.7	45	5
	Corey Dillon, Cincinnati[3]	263	1,200	4.6	50	5
	*Olandis Gary, Denver	276	1,159	4.2	71	7
	Jerome Bettis, Pittsburgh[6]	299	1,091	3.7	35	7
	Dorsey Levens, Green Bay[2]	279	1,034	3.7	36	9
	Robert Smith, Minnesota[3]	221	1,015	4.6	70	2
1998	Terrell Davis, Denver[4]	392	2,008	5.1	70	21
	Jamal Anderson, Atlanta[3]	410	1,846	4.5	48	14
	Garrison Hearst, San Francisco[3]	310	1,570	5.1	96	7
	Barry Sanders, Detroit[10]	343	1,491	4.3	73	4
	Emmitt Smith, Dallas[8]	319	1,332	4.2	32	13
	Marshall Faulk, Indianapolis[4]	324	1,319	4.1	68	6
	Eddie George, Tennessee[3]	348	1,294	3.7	37	5
	Curtis Martin, N.Y. Jets[4]	369	1,287	3.5	60	8
	Ricky Watters, Seattle[5]	319	1,239	3.9	39	9
	*Fred Taylor, Jacksonville	264	1,223	4.6	77	14
	Robert Smith, Minnesota[2]	249	1,187	4.8	74	6
	Jerome Bettis, Pittsburgh[5]	316	1,185	3.8	42	3
	Corey Dillon, Cincinnati[2]	262	1,130	4.3	66	4
	Antowain Smith, Buffalo	300	1,124	3.7	30	8
	*Robert Edwards, New England	291	1,115	3.8	53	9
	Duce Staley, Philadelphia	258	1,065	4.1	64	5
	Gary Brown, N.Y. Giants[2]	247	1,063	4.3	45	5
	Adrian Murrell, Arizona[3]	274	1,042	3.8	32	8
	Warrick Dunn, Tampa Bay	245	1,026	4.2	50	2
	Priest Holmes, Baltimore	233	1,008	4.3	56	7
1997	Barry Sanders, Detroit[9]	335	2,053	6.1	82	11
	Terrell Davis, Denver[3]	369	1,750	4.7	50	15
	Jerome Bettis, Pittsburgh[4]	375	1,665	4.4	34	7
	Dorsey Levens, Green Bay	329	1,435	4.4	52	7
	Eddie George, Tennessee[2]	357	1,399	3.9	30	6
	Napoleon Kaufman, Oakland	272	1,294	4.8	83	6
	Robert Smith, Minnesota	232	1,266	5.5	78	6
	Curtis Martin, New England[3]	274	1,160	4.2	70	4
	*Corey Dillon, Cincinnati	233	1,129	4.8	71	10
	Ricky Watters, Philadelphia[4]	285	1,110	3.9	28	7
	Adrian Murrell, N.Y. Jets[2]	300	1,086	3.6	43	7
	Emmitt Smith, Dallas[7]	261	1,074	4.1	44	4
	Marshall Faulk, Indianapolis[3]	264	1,054	4.0	45	7
	Raymont Harris, Chicago	275	1,033	3.8	68	10
	Garrison Hearst, San Francisco[2]	234	1,019	4.4	51	4

Year	Player, Team	Att.	Yards	Avg.	Long	TD
	Jamal Anderson, Atlanta[2]	290	1,002	3.5	39	7
1996	Barry Sanders, Detroit[8]	307	1,553	5.1	54	11
	Terrell Davis, Denver[2]	345	1,538	4.5	71	13
	Jerome Bettis, Pittsburgh[3]	320	1,431	4.5	50	11
	Ricky Watters, Philadelphia[3]	353	1,411	4.0	56	13
	*Eddie George, Houston	335	1,368	4.1	76	8
	Terry Allen, Washington[4]	347	1,353	3.9	49	21
	Adrian Murrell, N.Y. Jets	301	1,249	4.1	78	6
	Emmitt Smith, Dallas[6]	327	1,204	3.7	42	12
	Curtis Martin, New England[2]	316	1,152	3.6	57	14
	Anthony Johnson, Carolina	300	1,120	3.7	29	6
	*Karim Abdul-Jabbar, Miami	307	1,116	3.6	29	11
	Jamal Anderson, Atlanta	232	1,055	4.5	32	5
	Thurman Thomas, Buffalo[8]	281	1,033	3.7	36	8
1995	Emmitt Smith, Dallas[5]	377	1,773	4.7	60	25
	Barry Sanders, Detroit[7]	314	1,500	4.8	75	11
	*Curtis Martin, New England	368	1,487	4.0	49	14
	Chris Warren, Seattle[4]	310	1,346	4.3	52	15
	Terry Allen, Washington[3]	338	1,309	3.9	28	10
	Ricky Watters, Philadelphia[2]	337	1,273	3.8	57	11
	Errict Rhett, Tampa Bay[2]	332	1,207	3.6	21	11
	Rodney Hampton, N.Y. Giants[5]	306	1,182	3.9	32	10
	*Terrell Davis, Denver	237	1,117	4.7	60	7
	Harvey Williams, Oakland	255	1,114	4.4	60	9
	Craig Heyward, Atlanta	236	1,083	4.6	31	6
	Marshall Faulk, Indianapolis[2]	289	1,078	3.7	40	11
	*Rashaan Salaam, Chicago	296	1,074	3.6	42	10
	Garrison Hearst, Arizona	284	1,070	3.8	38	1
	Edgar Bennett, Green Bay	316	1,067	3.4	23	3
	Thurman Thomas, Buffalo[7]	267	1,005	3.8	49	6
1994	Barry Sanders, Detroit[6]	331	1,883	5.7	85	7
	Chris Warren, Seattle[3]	333	1,545	4.6	41	9
	Emmitt Smith, Dallas[4]	368	1,484	4.0	46	21
	Natrone Means, San Diego	343	1,350	3.9	25	12
	*Marshall Faulk, Indianapolis	314	1,282	4.1	52	11
	Thurman Thomas, Buffalo[6]	287	1,093	3.8	29	7
	Rodney Hampton, N.Y. Giants[4]	327	1,075	3.3	27	6
	Terry Allen, Minnesota[2]	255	1,031	4.0	45	8
	Jerome Bettis, L.A. Rams[2]	319	1,025	3.2	19	3
	*Errict Rhett, Tampa Bay	284	1,011	3.6	27	7
1993	Emmitt Smith, Dallas[3]	283	1,486	5.3	62	9
	*Jerome Bettis, L.A. Rams	294	1,429	4.9	71	7
	Thurman Thomas, Buffalo[5]	355	1,315	3.7	27	6
	Eric Pegram, Atlanta	292	1,185	4.1	29	3
	Barry Sanders, Detroit[5]	243	1,115	4.6	42	3
	Leonard Russell, New England	300	1,088	3.6	21	7
	Rodney Hampton, N.Y. Giants[3]	292	1,077	3.7	20	5
	Chris Warren, Seattle[2]	273	1,072	3.9	45	7
	*Reggie Brooks, Washington	223	1,063	4.8	85	3
	*Ron Moore, Phoenix	263	1,018	3.9	20	9
	Gary Brown, Houston	195	1,002	5.1	26	6
1992	Emmitt Smith, Dallas[2]	373	1,713	4.6	68	18
	Barry Foster, Pittsburgh	390	1,690	4.3	69	11
	Thurman Thomas, Buffalo[4]	312	1,487	4.8	44	9
	Barry Sanders, Detroit[4]	312	1,352	4.3	55	9
	Lorenzo White, Houston	265	1,226	4.6	44	7
	Terry Allen, Minnesota	266	1,201	4.5	51	13
	Reggie Cobb, Tampa Bay	310	1,171	3.8	25	9
	Harold Green, Cincinnati	265	1,170	4.4	53	2
	Rodney Hampton, N.Y. Giants[2]	257	1,141	4.4	63	14
	Cleveland Gary, L.A. Rams	279	1,125	4.0	63	7
	Herschel Walker, Philadelphia[2]	267	1,070	4.0	38	8
	Chris Warren, Seattle	223	1,017	4.6	52	3
	Ricky Watters, San Francisco	206	1,013	4.9	43	9
1991	Emmitt Smith, Dallas	365	1,563	4.3	75	12
	Barry Sanders, Detroit[3]	342	1,548	4.5	69	16
	Thurman Thomas, Buffalo[3]	288	1,407	4.9	33	7
	Rodney Hampton, N.Y. Giants	256	1,059	4.1	44	10
	Earnest Byner, Washington[3]	274	1,048	3.8	32	5

Year	Player, Team	Att.	Yards	Avg.	Long	TD
	Gaston Green, Denver	261	1,037	4.0	63	4
	Christian Okoye, Kansas City[2]	225	1,031	4.6	48	9
1990	Barry Sanders, Detroit[2]	255	1,304	5.1	45	13
	Thurman Thomas, Buffalo[2]	271	1,297	4.8	80	11
	Marion Butts, San Diego	265	1,225	4.6	52	8
	Earnest Byner, Washington[2]	297	1,219	4.1	22	6
	Bobby Humphrey, Denver[2]	288	1,202	4.2	37	7
	Neal Anderson, Chicago[3]	260	1,078	4.1	52	10
	Barry Word, Kansas City	204	1,015	5.0	53	4
	James Brooks, Cincinnati[3]	195	1,004	5.1	56	5
1989	Christian Okoye, Kansas City	370	1,480	4.0	59	12
	*Barry Sanders, Detroit	280	1,470	5.3	34	14
	Eric Dickerson, Indianapolis[7]	314	1,311	4.2	21	7
	Neal Anderson, Chicago[2]	274	1,275	4.7	73	11
	Dalton Hilliard, New Orleans	344	1,262	3.7	40	13
	Thurman Thomas, Buffalo	298	1,244	4.2	38	6
	James Brooks, Cincinnati[2]	221	1,239	5.6	65	7
	*Bobby Humphrey, Denver	294	1,151	3.9	40	7
	Greg Bell, L.A. Rams[3]	272	1,137	4.2	47	15
	Roger Craig, San Francisco[3]	271	1,054	3.9	27	6
	Ottis Anderson, N.Y. Giants[6]	325	1,023	3.1	36	14
1988	Eric Dickerson, Indianapolis[6]	388	1,659	4.3	41	14
	Herschel Walker, Dallas	361	1,514	4.2	38	5
	Roger Craig, San Francisco[2]	310	1,502	4.8	46	9
	Greg Bell, L.A. Rams[2]	288	1,212	4.2	44	16
	*John Stephens, New England	297	1,168	3.9	52	4
	Gary Anderson, San Diego	225	1,119	5.0	36	3
	Neal Anderson, Chicago	249	1,106	4.4	80	12
	Joe Morris, N.Y. Giants[3]	307	1,083	3.5	27	5
	*Ickey Woods, Cincinnati	203	1,066	5.3	56	15
	Curt Warner, Seattle[4]	266	1,025	3.9	29	10
	John Settle, Atlanta	232	1,024	4.4	62	7
	Mike Rozier, Houston	251	1,002	4.0	28	10
1987	Charles White, L.A. Rams	324	1,374	4.2	58	11
	Eric Dickerson, L.A. Rams-Indianapolis[5]	283	1,288	4.6	57	6
1986	Eric Dickerson, L.A. Rams[4]	404	1,821	4.5	42	11
	Joe Morris, N.Y. Giants[2]	341	1,516	4.4	54	14
	Curt Warner, Seattle[3]	319	1,481	4.6	60	13
	*Rueben Mayes, New Orleans	286	1,353	4.7	50	8
	Walter Payton, Chicago[10]	321	1,333	4.2	41	8
	Gerald Riggs, Atlanta[3]	343	1,327	3.9	31	9
	George Rogers, Washington[4]	303	1,203	4.0	42	18
	James Brooks, Cincinnati	205	1,087	5.3	56	5
1985	Marcus Allen, L.A. Raiders[3]	390	1,759	4.6	61	11
	Gerald Riggs, Atlanta[2]	397	1,719	4.3	50	10
	Walter Payton, Chicago[9]	324	1,551	4.8	40	9
	Joe Morris, N.Y. Giants	294	1,336	4.5	65	21
	Freeman McNeil, N.Y. Jets[2]	294	1,331	4.5	69	3
	Tony Dorsett, Dallas[8]	305	1,307	4.3	60	7
	James Wilder, Tampa Bay[2]	365	1,300	3.6	28	10
	Eric Dickerson, L.A. Rams[3]	292	1,234	4.2	43	12
	Craig James, New England	263	1,227	4.7	65	5
	Kevin Mack, Cleveland	222	1,104	5.0	61	7
	Curt Warner, Seattle[2]	291	1,094	3.8	38	8
	George Rogers, Washington[3]	231	1,093	4.7	35	7
	Roger Craig, San Francisco	214	1,050	4.9	62	9
	Earnest Jackson, Philadelphia[2]	282	1,028	3.6	59	5
	Stump Mitchell, St. Louis	183	1,006	5.5	64	7
	Earnest Byner, Cleveland	244	1,002	4.1	36	8
1984	Eric Dickerson, L.A. Rams[2]	379	2,105	5.6	66	14
	Walter Payton, Chicago[8]	381	1,684	4.4	72	11
	James Wilder, Tampa Bay	407	1,544	3.8	37	13
	Gerald Riggs, Atlanta	353	1,486	4.2	57	13
	Wendell Tyler, San Francisco[3]	246	1,262	5.1	40	7
	John Riggins, Washington[5]	327	1,239	3.8	24	14
	Tony Dorsett, Dallas[7]	302	1,189	3.9	31	6
	Earnest Jackson, San Diego	296	1,179	4.0	32	8
	Ottis Anderson, St. Louis[5]	289	1,174	4.1	24	6
	Marcus Allen, L.A. Raiders[2]	275	1,168	4.2	52	13

Year	Player, Team	Att.	Yards	Avg.	Long	TD
	Sammy Winder, Denver	296	1,153	3.9	24	4
	*Greg Bell, Buffalo	262	1,100	4.2	85	7
	Freeman McNeil, N.Y. Jets	229	1,070	4.7	53	5
1983	*Eric Dickerson, L.A. Rams	390	1,808	4.6	85	18
	William Andrews, Atlanta[4]	331	1,567	4.7	27	7
	*Curt Warner, Seattle	335	1,449	4.3	60	13
	Walter Payton, Chicago[7]	314	1,421	4.5	49	6
	John Riggins, Washington[4]	375	1,347	3.6	44	24
	Tony Dorsett, Dallas[6]	289	1,321	4.6	77	8
	Earl Campbell, Houston[5]	322	1,301	4.0	42	12
	Ottis Anderson, St. Louis[4]	296	1,270	4.3	43	5
	Mike Pruitt, Cleveland[4]	293	1,184	4.0	27	10
	George Rogers, New Orleans[2]	256	1,144	4.5	76	5
	Joe Cribbs, Buffalo[3]	263	1,131	4.3	45	3
	Curtis Dickey, Baltimore	254	1,122	4.4	56	4
	Tony Collins, New England	219	1,049	4.8	50	10
	Billy Sims, Detroit[3]	220	1,040	4.7	41	7
	Marcus Allen, L.A. Raiders	266	1,014	3.8	19	9
	Franco Harris, Pittsburgh[8]	279	1,007	3.6	19	5
1981	*George Rogers, New Orleans	378	1,674	4.4	79	13
	Tony Dorsett, Dallas[6]	342	1,646	4.8	75	4
	Billy Sims, Detroit[2]	296	1,437	4.9	51	13
	Wilbert Montgomery, Philadelphia[3]	286	1,402	4.9	41	8
	Ottis Anderson, St. Louis[3]	328	1,376	4.2	28	9
	Earl Campbell, Houston[4]	361	1,376	3.8	43	10
	William Andrews, Atlanta[3]	289	1,301	4.5	29	10
	Walter Payton, Chicago[6]	339	1,222	3.6	39	6
	Chuck Muncie, San Diego[2]	251	1,144	4.6	73	19
	*Joe Delaney, Kansas City	234	1,121	4.8	82	3
	Mike Pruitt, Cleveland[3]	247	1,103	4.5	21	7
	Joe Cribbs, Buffalo[2]	257	1,097	4.3	35	3
	Pete Johnson, Cincinnati	274	1,077	3.9	39	12
	Wendell Tyler, Los Angeles[2]	260	1,074	4.1	69	12
	Ted Brown, Minnesota	274	1,063	3.9	34	6
1980	Earl Campbell, Houston[3]	373	1,934	5.2	55	13
	Walter Payton, Chicago[5]	317	1,460	4.6	69	6
	Ottis Anderson, St. Louis[2]	301	1,352	4.5	52	9
	William Andrews, Atlanta[2]	265	1,308	4.9	33	4
	*Billy Sims, Detroit	313	1,303	4.2	52	13
	Tony Dorsett, Dallas[4]	278	1,185	4.3	56	11
	*Joe Cribbs, Buffalo	306	1,185	3.9	48	11
	Mike Pruitt, Cleveland[2]	249	1,034	4.2	56	6
1979	Earl Campbell, Houston[2]	368	1,697	4.6	61	19
	Walter Payton, Chicago[4]	369	1,610	4.4	43	14
	*Ottis Anderson, St. Louis	331	1,605	4.8	76	8
	Wilbert Montgomery, Philadelphia[2]	338	1,512	4.5	62	9
	Mike Pruitt, Cleveland	264	1,294	4.9	77	9
	Ricky Bell, Tampa Bay	283	1,263	4.5	49	7
	Chuck Muncie, New Orleans	238	1,198	5.0	69	11
	Franco Harris, Pittsburgh[7]	267	1,186	4.4	71	11
	John Riggins, Washington[3]	260	1,153	4.4	66	9
	Wendell Tyler, Los Angeles	218	1,109	5.1	63	9
	Tony Dorsett, Dallas[3]	250	1,107	4.4	41	6
	*William Andrews, Atlanta	239	1,023	4.3	23	3
1978	*Earl Campbell, Houston	302	1,450	4.8	81	13
	Walter Payton, Chicago[3]	333	1,395	4.2	76	11
	Tony Dorsett, Dallas[2]	290	1,325	4.6	63	7
	Delvin Williams, Miami[2]	272	1,258	4.6	58	8
	Wilbert Montgomery, Philadelphia	259	1,220	4.7	47	9
	Terdell Middleton, Green Bay	284	1,116	3.9	76	11
	Franco Harris, Pittsburgh[6]	310	1,082	3.5	37	8
	Mark van Eeghen, Oakland[3]	270	1,080	4.0	34	9
	*Terry Miller, Buffalo	238	1,060	4.5	60	7
	Tony Reed, Kansas City	206	1,053	5.1	62	5
	John Riggins, Washington[2]	248	1,014	4.1	31	5
1977	Walter Payton, Chicago[2]	339	1,852	5.5	73	14
	Mark van Eeghen, Oakland[2]	324	1,273	3.9	27	7
	Lawrence McCutcheon, Los Angeles[4]	294	1,238	4.2	48	7
	Franco Harris, Pittsburgh[5]	300	1,162	3.9	61	11

Year	Player, Team	Att.	Yards	Avg.	Long	TD
	Lydell Mitchell, Baltimore[3]	301	1,159	3.9	64	3
	Chuck Foreman, Minnesota[3]	270	1,112	4.1	51	6
	Greg Pruitt, Cleveland[3]	236	1,086	4.6	78	3
	Sam Cunningham, New England	270	1,015	3.8	31	4
	*Tony Dorsett, Dallas	208	1,007	4.8	84	12
1976	O.J. Simpson, Buffalo[5]	290	1,503	5.2	75	8
	Walter Payton, Chicago	311	1,390	4.5	60	13
	Delvin Williams, San Francisco	248	1,203	4.9	80	7
	Lydell Mitchell, Baltimore[2]	289	1,200	4.2	43	5
	Lawrence McCutcheon, Los Angeles[3]	291	1,168	4.0	40	9
	Chuck Foreman, Minnesota[2]	278	1,155	4.2	46	13
	Franco Harris, Pittsburgh[4]	289	1,128	3.9	30	14
	Mike Thomas, Washington	254	1,101	4.3	28	5
	Rocky Bleier, Pittsburgh	220	1,036	4.7	28	5
	Mark van Eeghen, Oakland	233	1,012	4.3	21	3
	Otis Armstrong, Denver[2]	247	1,008	4.1	31	5
	Greg Pruitt, Cleveland[2]	209	1,000	4.8	64	4
1975	O.J. Simpson, Buffalo[4]	329	1,817	5.5	88	16
	Franco Harris, Pittsburgh[3]	262	1,246	4.8	36	10
	Lydell Mitchell, Baltimore	289	1,193	4.1	70	11
	Jim Otis, St. Louis	269	1,076	4.0	30	5
	Chuck Foreman, Minnesota	280	1,070	3.8	31	13
	Greg Pruitt, Cleveland	217	1,067	4.9	50	8
	John Riggins, N.Y. Jets	238	1,005	4.2	42	8
	Dave Hampton, Atlanta	250	1,002	4.0	22	5
1974	Otis Armstrong, Denver	263	1,407	5.3	43	9
	*Don Woods, San Diego	227	1,162	5.1	56	7
	O.J. Simpson, Buffalo[3]	270	1,125	4.2	41	3
	Lawrence McCutcheon, Los Angeles[2]	236	1,109	4.7	23	3
	Franco Harris, Pittsburgh[2]	208	1,006	4.8	54	5
1973	O.J. Simpson, Buffalo[2]	332	2,003	6.0	80	12
	John Brockington, Green Bay[3]	265	1,144	4.3	53	3
	Calvin Hill, Dallas[2]	273	1,142	4.2	21	6
	Lawrence McCutcheon, Los Angeles	210	1,097	5.2	37	2
	Larry Csonka, Miami[3]	219	1,003	4.6	25	5
1972	O.J. Simpson, Buffalo	292	1,251	4.3	94	6
	Larry Brown, Washington[2]	285	1,216	4.3	38	8
	Ron Johnson, N.Y. Giants[2]	298	1,182	4.0	35	9
	Larry Csonka, Miami[2]	213	1,117	5.2	45	6
	Marv Hubbard, Oakland	219	1,100	5.0	39	4
	*Franco Harris, Pittsburgh	188	1,055	5.6	75	10
	Calvin Hill, Dallas	245	1,036	4.2	26	6
	Mike Garrett, San Diego[2]	272	1,031	3.8	41	6
	John Brockington, Green Bay[2]	274	1,027	3.7	30	8
	Eugene (Mercury) Morris, Miami	190	1,000	5.3	33	12
1971	Floyd Little, Denver	284	1,133	4.0	40	6
	*John Brockington, Green Bay	216	1,105	5.1	52	4
	Larry Csonka, Miami	195	1,051	5.4	28	7
	Steve Owens, Detroit	246	1,035	4.2	23	8
	Willie Ellison, Los Angeles	211	1,000	4.7	80	4
1970	Larry Brown, Washington	237	1,125	4.7	75	5
	Ron Johnson, N.Y. Giants	263	1,027	3.9	68	8
1969	Gale Sayers, Chicago[2]	236	1,032	4.4	28	8
1968	Leroy Kelly, Cleveland[3]	248	1,239	5.0	65	16
	*Paul Robinson, Cincinnati	238	1,023	4.3	87	8
1967	Jim Nance, Boston[2]	269	1,216	4.5	53	7
	Leroy Kelly, Cleveland[2]	235	1,205	5.1	42	11
	Hoyle Granger, Houston	236	1,194	5.1	67	6
	Mike Garrett, Kansas City	236	1,087	4.6	58	9
1966	Jim Nance, Boston	299	1,458	4.9	65	11
	Gale Sayers, Chicago	229	1,231	5.4	58	8
	Leroy Kelly, Cleveland	209	1,141	5.5	70	15
	Dick Bass, Los Angeles[2]	248	1,090	4.4	50	8
1965	Jim Brown, Cleveland[7]	289	1,544	5.3	67	17
	Paul Lowe, San Diego[2]	222	1,121	5.0	59	7
1964	Jim Brown, Cleveland[6]	280	1,446	5.2	71	7
	Jim Taylor, Green Bay[5]	235	1,169	5.0	84	12
	John Henry Johnson, Pittsburgh[2]	235	1,048	4.5	45	7
1963	Jim Brown, Cleveland[5]	291	1,863	6.4	80	12

Year	Player, Team	Att.	Yards	Avg.	Long	TD
	Clem Daniels, Oakland	215	1,099	5.1	74	3
	Jim Taylor, Green Bay[4]	248	1,018	4.1	40	9
	Paul Lowe, San Diego	177	1,010	5.7	66	8
1962	Jim Taylor, Green Bay[3]	272	1,474	5.4	51	19
	John Henry Johnson, Pittsburgh	251	1,141	4.5	40	7
	Cookie Gilchrist, Buffalo	214	1,096	5.1	44	13
	Abner Haynes, Dall. Texans	221	1,049	4.7	71	13
	Dick Bass, Los Angeles	196	1,033	5.3	57	6
	Charlie Tolar, Houston	244	1,012	4.1	25	7
1961	Jim Brown, Cleveland[4]	305	1,408	4.6	38	8
	Jim Taylor, Green Bay[2]	243	1,307	5.4	53	15
1960	Jim Brown, Cleveland[3]	215	1,257	5.8	71	9
	Jim Taylor, Green Bay	230	1,101	4.8	32	11
	John David Crow, St. Louis	183	1,071	5.9	57	6
1959	Jim Brown, Cleveland[2]	290	1,329	4.6	70	14
	J.D. Smith, San Francisco	207	1,036	5.0	73	10
1958	Jim Brown, Cleveland	257	1,527	5.9	65	17
1956	Rick Casares, Chi. Bears	234	1,126	4.8	68	12
1954	Joe Perry, San Francisco[2]	173	1,049	6.1	58	8
1953	Joe Perry, San Francisco	192	1,018	5.3	51	10
1949	Steve Van Buren, Philadelphia[2]	263	1,146	4.4	41	11
	Tony Canadeo, Green Bay	208	1,052	5.1	54	4
1947	Steve Van Buren, Philadelphia	217	1,008	4.6	45	13
1934	*Beattie Feathers, Chi. Bears	119	1,004	8.4	82	8

*First season of professional football.

200 YARDS RUSHING IN A GAME

Date	Player, Team, Opponent	Att.	Yards	TD
Dec. 30, 2012	DeAngelo Williams, Carolina vs. New Orleans	21	210	2
Dec. 30, 2012	*Alfred Morris, Washington vs. Dallas	33	200	3
Dec. 23, 2012	Jamaal Charles, Kansas City vs. Indianapolis	22	226	1
Dec. 16, 2012	Adrian Peterson, Minnesota vs. St. Louis	24	212	1
Dec. 2, 2012	Adrian Peterson, Minnesota vs. Green Bay	21	210	1
Nov. 4, 2012	*Doug Martin, Tampa Bay vs. Oakland	25	251	4
Oct. 7, 2012	Ahmad Bradshaw, N.Y. Giants vs. Cleveland	30	200	1
Sept. 23, 2012	Jamaal Charles, Kansas City vs. New Orleans (OT)	33	233	1
Dec. 18, 2011	Reggie Bush, Miami vs. Buffalo	25	203	1
Dec. 4, 2011	Ray Rice, Baltimore vs. Cleveland	29	204	1
Nov. 27, 2011	Beanie Wells, Arizona vs. St. Louis	27	228	1
Oct. 23, 2011	*DeMarco Murray, Dallas vs. St. Louis	25	253	1
Oct. 2, 2011	Matt Forté, Chicago vs. Carolina	25	205	1
Sept. 12, 2010	Arian Foster, Houston vs. Indianapolis	33	231	3
Jan. 3, 2010	Jamaal Charles, Kansas City vs. Denver	25	259	2
Jan. 3, 2010	Fred Jackson, Buffalo vs. Indianapolis	33	212	0
Dec. 27, 2009	Jonathan Stewart, Carolina vs. N.Y. Giants	28	206	1
Dec. 20, 2009	Jerome Harrison, Cleveland vs. Kansas City	34	286	3
Nov. 1, 2009	Chris Johnson, Tennessee vs. Jacksonville	24	228	2
Oct. 18, 2009	Thomas Jones, N.Y. Jets vs. Buffalo (OT)	22	210	1
Sept. 20, 2009	Frank Gore, San Francisco vs. Seattle	16	207	2
Dec. 28, 2008	Michael Turner, Atlanta vs. St. Louis	25	208	1
Dec. 21, 2008	Derrick Ward, N.Y. Giants vs. Carolina (OT)	15	215	0
Sept. 7, 2008	Michael Turner, Atlanta vs. Detroit	22	220	2
Nov. 4, 2007	*Adrian Peterson, Minnesota vs. San Diego	30	296	3
Oct. 14, 2007	*Adrian Peterson, Minnesota vs. Chicago	20	224	3
Sept. 16, 2007	Jamal Lewis, Cleveland vs. Cincinnati	27	216	1
Dec. 30, 2006	Tiki Barber, N.Y. Giants vs. Washington	23	234	3
Dec. 7, 2006	Willie Parker, Pittsburgh vs. Cleveland	32	223	1
Nov. 27, 2006	Shaun Alexander, Seattle vs. Green Bay	40	201	0
Nov. 19, 2006	Frank Gore, San Francisco vs. Seattle	24	212	0
Nov. 12, 2006	Willie Parker, Pittsburgh vs. New Orleans	22	213	2
Jan. 1, 2006	Larry Johnson, Kansas City vs. Cincinnati	26	201	3
Dec. 31, 2005	Tiki Barber, N.Y. Giants vs. Oakland	28	203	1
Dec. 17, 2005	Tiki Barber, N.Y. Giants vs. Kansas City	29	220	2
Nov. 20, 2005	Larry Johnson, Kansas City vs. Houston	36	211	2
Oct. 30, 2005	Tiki Barber, N.Y. Giants vs. Washington	24	206	1
Nov. 28, 2004	Rudi Johnson, Cincinnati vs. Cleveland	26	202	2
Nov. 21, 2004	Edgerrin James, Indianapolis vs. Chicago	23	204	1
Dec. 28, 2003	Ahman Green, Green Bay vs. Denver	20	218	2
Dec. 28, 2003	LaDainian Tomlinson, San Diego vs. Oakland	31	243	2
Dec. 21, 2003	Jamal Lewis, Baltimore vs. Cleveland	22	205	2

Date	Player, Team, Opponent	Att.	Yards	TD
Dec. 7, 2003	Clinton Portis, Denver vs. Kansas City	22	218	5
Oct. 19, 2003	LaDainian Tomlinson, San Diego vs. Cleveland	26	200	1
Sept. 14, 2003	Jamal Lewis, Baltimore vs. Cleveland	30	295	2
Dec. 29, 2002	*Clinton Portis, Denver vs. Arizona	24	228	2
Dec. 28, 2002	Tiki Barber, N.Y. Giants vs. Philadelphia	32	203	0
Dec. 9, 2002	Ricky Williams, Miami vs. Chicago	31	216	2
Dec. 1, 2002	LaDainian Tomlinson, San Diego vs. Denver	37	220	3
Dec. 1, 2002	Ricky Williams, Miami vs. Buffalo	27	228	2
Sept. 29, 2002	LaDainian Tomlinson, San Diego vs. New England	27	217	2
Dec. 23, 2001	Marshall Faulk, St. Louis vs. Carolina	30	202	2
Nov. 11, 2001	Shaun Alexander, Seattle vs. Oakland	35	266	3
Dec. 24, 2000	Marshall Faulk, St. Louis vs. New Orleans	32	220	2
Dec. 3, 2000	Corey Dillon, Cincinnati vs. Arizona	35	216	1
Dec. 3, 2000	Warrick Dunn, Tampa Bay vs. Dallas	22	210	2
Dec. 3, 2000	*Mike Anderson, Denver vs. New Orleans	37	251	4
Dec. 3, 2000	Curtis Martin, N.Y. Jets vs. Indianapolis	30	203	1
Nov. 19, 2000	Fred Taylor, Jacksonville vs. Pittsburgh	30	234	3
Oct. 22, 2000	Corey Dillon, Cincinnati vs. Denver	22	278	2
Oct. 15, 2000	Marshall Faulk, St. Louis vs. Atlanta	25	208	1
Oct. 15, 2000	Edgerrin James, Indianapolis vs. Seattle	38	219	3
Sept. 24, 2000	Charlie Garner, San Francisco vs. Dallas	36	201	1
Sept. 3, 2000	Duce Staley, Philadelphia vs. Dallas	26	201	1
Nov. 22, 1998	Priest Holmes, Baltimore vs. Cincinnati	36	227	1
Oct. 11, 1998	Terrell Davis, Denver vs. Seattle	30	208	1
Dec. 4, 1997	*Corey Dillon, Cincinnati vs. Tennessee	39	246	4
Nov. 23, 1997	Barry Sanders, Detroit vs. Indianapolis	24	216	2
Oct. 26, 1997	Terrell Davis, Denver vs. Buffalo (OT)	42	207	1
Oct. 19, 1997	Napoleon Kaufman, Oakland vs. Denver	28	227	1
Oct. 12, 1997	Barry Sanders, Detroit vs. Tampa Bay	24	215	2
Sept. 21, 1997	Terrell Davis, Denver vs. Cincinnati	27	215	1
Aug. 31, 1997	Eddie George, Tennessee vs. Oakland (OT)	35	216	1
Sept. 22, 1996	LeShon Johnson, Arizona vs. New Orleans	21	214	2
Nov. 13, 1994	Barry Sanders, Detroit vs. Tampa Bay	26	237	0
Dec. 12, 1993	*Jerome Bettis, L.A. Rams vs. New Orleans	28	212	1
Oct. 31, 1993	Emmitt Smith, Dallas vs. Philadelphia	30	237	1
Nov. 24, 1991	Barry Sanders, Detroit vs. Minnesota	23	220	4
Dec. 23, 1990	James Brooks, Cincinnati vs. Houston	20	201	1
Oct. 14, 1990	Barry Word, Kansas City vs. Detroit	18	200	2
Sept. 24, 1990	Thurman Thomas, Buffalo vs. N.Y. Jets	18	214	0
Dec. 24, 1989	Greg Bell, L.A. Rams vs. New England	26	210	1
Sept. 24, 1989	Greg Bell, L.A. Rams vs. Green Bay	28	221	2
Sept. 17, 1989	Gerald Riggs, Washington vs. Philadelphia	29	221	1
Dec. 18, 1988	Gary Anderson, San Diego vs. Kansas City	34	217	1
Nov. 30, 1987	*Bo Jackson, L.A. Raiders vs. Seattle	18	221	2
Nov. 15, 1987	Charles White, L.A. Rams vs. St. Louis	34	213	1
Dec. 7, 1986	Rueben Mayes, New Orleans vs. Miami	28	203	2
Oct. 5, 1986	Eric Dickerson, L.A. Rams vs. Tampa Bay (OT)	30	207	2
Dec. 21, 1985	George Rogers, Washington vs. St. Louis	34	206	1
Dec. 21, 1985	Joe Morris, N.Y. Giants vs. Pittsburgh	36	202	3
Dec. 9, 1984	Eric Dickerson, L.A. Rams vs. Houston	27	215	2
Nov. 18, 1984	*Greg Bell, Buffalo vs. Dallas	27	206	1
Nov. 4, 1984	Eric Dickerson, L.A. Rams vs. St. Louis	21	208	0
Sept. 2, 1984	Gerald Riggs, Atlanta vs. New Orleans	35	202	2
Nov. 27, 1983	*Curt Warner, Seattle vs. Kansas City (OT)	32	207	3
Nov. 6, 1983	James Wilder, Tampa Bay vs. Minnesota	31	219	1
Sept. 18, 1983	Tony Collins, New England vs. N.Y. Jets	23	212	3
Sept. 4, 1983	George Rogers, New Orleans vs. St. Louis	24	206	2
Dec. 21, 1980	Earl Campbell, Houston vs. Minnesota	29	203	1
Nov. 16, 1980	Earl Campbell, Houston vs. Chicago	31	206	0
Oct. 26, 1980	Earl Campbell, Houston vs. Cincinnati	27	202	2
Oct. 19, 1980	Earl Campbell, Houston vs. Tampa Bay	33	203	0
Nov. 26, 1978	*Terry Miller, Buffalo vs. N.Y. Giants	21	208	2
Dec. 4, 1977	*Tony Dorsett, Dallas vs. Philadelphia	23	206	2
Nov. 20, 1977	Walter Payton, Chicago vs. Minnesota	40	275	1
Oct. 30, 1977	Walter Payton, Chicago vs. Green Bay	23	205	2
Dec. 5, 1976	O.J. Simpson, Buffalo vs. Miami	24	203	1
Nov. 25, 1976	O.J. Simpson, Buffalo vs. Detroit	29	273	2
Oct. 24, 1976	Chuck Foreman, Minnesota vs. Philadelphia	28	200	2
Dec. 14, 1975	Greg Pruitt, Cleveland vs. Kansas City	26	214	3
Sept. 28, 1975	O.J. Simpson, Buffalo vs. Pittsburgh	28	227	1
Dec. 16, 1973	O.J. Simpson, Buffalo vs. N.Y. Jets	34	200	1

Dec. 9, 1973	O.J. Simpson, Buffalo vs. New England	22	219	1
Sept. 16, 1973	O.J. Simpson, Buffalo vs. New England	29	250	2
Dec. 5, 1971	Willie Ellison, Los Angeles vs. New Orleans	26	247	1
Dec. 20, 1970	John (Frenchy) Fuqua, Pittsburgh vs. Philadelphia	20	218	2
Nov. 3, 1968	Gale Sayers, Chicago vs. Green Bay	24	205	0
Oct. 30, 1966	Jim Nance, Boston vs. Oakland	38	208	2
Oct. 10, 1964	John Henry Johnson, Pittsburgh vs. Cleveland	30	200	3
Dec. 8, 1963	Cookie Gilchrist, Buffalo vs. N.Y. Jets	36	243	5
Nov. 3, 1963	Jim Brown, Cleveland vs. Philadelphia	28	223	1
Oct. 20, 1963	Clem Daniels, Oakland vs. N.Y. Jets	27	200	2
Sept. 22, 1963	Jim Brown, Cleveland vs. Dallas	20	232	2
Dec. 10, 1961	Billy Cannon, Houston vs. N.Y. Titans	25	216	3
Nov. 19, 1961	Jim Brown, Cleveland vs. Philadelphia	34	237	4
Dec. 18, 1960	John David Crow, St. Louis vs. Pittsburgh	24	203	0
Nov. 15, 1959	Bobby Mitchell, Cleveland vs. Washington	14	232	3
Nov. 24, 1957	*Jim Brown, Cleveland vs. Los Angeles	31	237	4
Dec. 16, 1956	*Tom Wilson, Los Angeles vs. Green Bay	23	223	0
Nov. 22, 1953	Dan Towler, Los Angeles vs. Baltimore	14	205	1
Nov. 12, 1950	Gene Roberts, N.Y. Giants vs. Chi. Cardinals	26	218	2
Nov. 27, 1949	Steve Van Buren, Philadelphia vs. Pittsburgh	27	205	0
Oct. 8, 1933	Cliff Battles, Boston vs. N.Y. Giants	16	215	1

First season of professional football.

TIMES 200 OR MORE

134 times by 85 players…Simpson 6; Barber 5; Brown, Campbell, Peterson, Sanders, Tomlinson 4; Bell, Charles, Davis, Dickerson, Dillon, Faulk, Lewis 3; Alexander, Gore, James, L. Johnson, Parker, Payton, Portis, Riggs, Rogers, Turner, Williams 2.

4,000 YARDS PASSING IN A SEASON

Year	Player, Team	Att.	Comp.	Pct.	Yards	TD	Int.
2012	Drew Brees, New Orleans[7]	670	422	63.0	5,177	43	19
	Matthew Stafford, Detroit[2]	727	435	59.8	4,967	20	17
	Tony Romo, Dallas[4]	648	425	65.6	4,903	28	19
	Tom Brady, New England[5]	637	401	63.0	4,827	34	8
	Matt Ryan, Atlanta[2]	615	422	68.6	4,719	32	14
	Peyton Manning, Denver[12]	583	400	68.6	4,659	37	11
	*Andrew Luck, Indianapolis	627	339	54.1	4,374	23	18
	Aaron Rodgers, Green Bay[4]	552	371	67.2	4,295	39	8
	Josh Freeman, Tampa Bay	558	306	54.8	4,065	27	17
	Carson Palmer, Oakland[3]	565	345	61.1	4,018	22	14
	Matt Schaub, Houston[3]	544	350	64.3	4,008	22	12
2011	Drew Brees, New Orleans[6]	657	468	71.2	5,476	46	14
	Tom Brady, New England[4]	611	401	65.6	5,235	39	12
	Matthew Stafford, Detroit	663	421	63.5	5,038	41	16
	Eli Manning, N.Y. Giants[3]	589	359	61.0	4,933	29	16
	Aaron Rodgers, Green Bay[3]	502	343	68.3	4,643	45	6
	Philip Rivers, San Diego[4]	582	366	62.9	4,624	27	20
	Tony Romo, Dallas[3]	522	346	66.3	4,184	31	10
	Matt Ryan, Atlanta	566	347	61.3	4,177	29	12
	Ben Roethlisberger, Pittsburgh[2]	513	324	63.2	4,077	21	14
	*Cam Newton, Carolina	517	310	60.0	4,051	21	17
2010	Philip Rivers, San Diego[3]	541	357	66.0	4,710	30	13
	Peyton Manning, Indianapolis[11]	679	450	66.3	4,700	33	17
	Drew Brees, New Orleans[5]	658	448	68.1	4,620	33	22
	Matt Schaub, Houston[2]	574	365	63.6	4,370	24	12
	Eli Manning, N.Y. Giants[2]	539	339	62.9	4,002	31	25
2009	Matt Schaub, Houston	583	396	67.9	4,770	29	15
	Peyton Manning, Indianapolis[10]	571	393	68.8	4,500	33	16
	Tony Romo, Dallas[2]	550	347	63.1	4,483	26	9
	Aaron Rodgers, Green Bay[2]	541	350	64.7	4,434	30	7
	Tom Brady, New England[3]	565	371	65.7	4,398	28	13
	Drew Brees, New Orleans[4]	514	363	70.6	4,388	34	11
	Ben Roethlisberger, Pittsburgh	506	337	66.6	4,328	26	12
	Philip Rivers, San Diego[2]	486	317	65.2	4,254	28	9
	Brett Favre, Minnesota[6]	531	363	68.4	4,202	33	7
	Eli Manning, N.Y. Giants	509	317	62.3	4,021	27	14
2008	Drew Brees, New Orleans[3]	635	413	65.0	5,069	34	17
	Kurt Warner, Arizona[3]	598	401	67.1	4,583	30	14
	Jay Cutler, Denver	616	384	62.3	4,526	25	18

Year	Player, Team	Att.	Comp.	Pct.	Yards	TD	Int.
	Aaron Rodgers, Green Bay	536	341	63.6	4,038	28	13
	Philip Rivers, San Diego	478	312	65.3	4,009	34	11
	Peyton Manning, Indianapolis[9]	555	371	66.8	4,002	27	12
2007	Tom Brady, New England[2]	578	398	68.9	4,806	50	8
	Drew Brees, New Orleans[2]	652	440	67.5	4,423	28	18
	Tony Romo, Dallas	520	335	64.4	4,211	36	19
	Brett Favre, Green Bay[5]	535	356	66.5	4,155	28	15
	Carson Palmer, Cincinnati[2]	575	373	64.9	4,131	26	20
	Jon Kitna, Detroit[2]	561	355	63.3	4,068	18	20
	Peyton Manning, Indianapolis[8]	515	337	65.4	4,040	31	14
2006	Drew Brees, New Orleans	554	356	64.3	4,418	26	11
	Peyton Manning, Indianapolis[7]	557	362	65.0	4,397	31	9
	Marc Bulger, St. Louis	588	370	62.9	4,301	24	8
	Jon Kitna, Detroit	596	372	62.4	4,208	21	22
	Carson Palmer, Cincinnati	520	324	62.3	4,035	28	13
2005	Tom Brady, New England	530	334	63.0	4,110	26	14
	Trent Green, Kansas City[3]	507	317	62.5	4,014	17	10
2004	Daunte Culpepper, Minnesota	548	379	69.2	4,717	39	11
	Trent Green, Kansas City[2]	556	369	66.4	4,591	27	17
	Peyton Manning, Indianapolis[6]	497	336	67.6	4,557	49	10
	Jake Plummer, Denver	521	303	58.2	4,089	27	20
	Brett Favre, Green Bay[4]	540	346	64.1	4,088	30	17
2003	Peyton Manning, Indianapolis[5]	566	379	67.0	4,267	29	10
	Trent Green, Kansas City	523	330	63.1	4,039	24	12
2002	Rich Gannon, Oakland	618	418	67.6	4,689	26	10
	Drew Bledsoe, Buffalo[3]	610	375	61.5	4,359	24	15
	Peyton Manning, Indianapolis[4]	591	392	66.3	4,200	27	19
	Kerry Collins, N.Y. Giants	545	335	61.5	4,073	19	14
2001	Kurt Warner, St. Louis[2]	546	375	68.7	4,830	36	22
	Peyton Manning, Indianapolis[3]	547	343	62.7	4,131	26	23
2000	Peyton Manning, Indianapolis[2]	571	357	62.5	4,413	33	15
	Jeff Garcia, San Francisco	561	355	63.3	4,278	31	10
	Elvis Grbac, Kansas City	547	326	59.6	4,169	28	14
1999	Steve Beuerlein, Carolina	571	343	60.1	4,436	36	15
	Kurt Warner, St. Louis	499	325	65.1	4,353	41	13
	Peyton Manning, Indianapolis	533	331	62.1	4,135	26	15
	Brett Favre, Green Bay[3]	595	341	57.3	4,091	22	23
	Brad Johnson, Washington	519	316	60.9	4,005	24	13
1998	Brett Favre, Green Bay[2]	551	347	63.0	4,212	31	23
	Steve Young, San Francisco[2]	517	322	62.3	4,170	36	12
1996	Mark Brunell, Jacksonville	557	353	63.4	4,367	19	20
	Vinny Testaverde, Baltimore	549	325	59.2	4,177	33	19
	Drew Bledsoe, New England[2]	623	373	59.9	4,086	27	15
1995	Brett Favre, Green Bay	570	359	63.0	4,413	38	13
	Scott Mitchell, Detroit	583	346	59.3	4,338	32	12
	Warren Moon, Minnesota[4]	606	377	62.2	4,228	33	14
	Jeff George, Atlanta	557	336	60.3	4,143	24	11
1994	Drew Bledsoe, New England	691	400	57.9	4,555	25	27
	Dan Marino, Miami[6]	615	385	62.6	4,453	30	17
	Warren Moon, Minnesota[3]	601	371	61.7	4,264	18	19
1993	John Elway, Denver	551	348	63.2	4,030	25	10
	Steve Young, San Francisco	462	314	68.0	4,023	29	16
1992	Dan Marino, Miami[5]	554	330	59.6	4,116	24	16
1991	Warren Moon, Houston[2]	655	404	61.7	4,690	23	21
1990	Warren Moon, Houston	584	362	62.0	4,689	33	13
1989	Don Majkowski, Green Bay	599	353	58.9	4,318	27	20
	Jim Everett, L.A. Rams	518	304	58.7	4,310	29	17
1988	Dan Marino, Miami[4]	606	354	58.4	4,434	28	23
1986	Dan Marino, Miami[3]	623	378	60.7	4,746	44	23
	Jay Schroeder, Washington	541	276	51.0	4,109	22	22
1985	Dan Marino, Miami[2]	567	336	59.3	4,137	30	21
1984	Dan Marino, Miami	564	362	64.2	5,084	48	17
	Neil Lomax, St. Louis	560	345	61.6	4,614	28	16
	Phil Simms, N.Y. Giants	533	286	53.7	4,044	22	18
1983	Lynn Dickey, Green Bay	484	289	59.7	4,458	32	29
	Bill Kenney, Kansas City	603	346	57.4	4,348	24	18
1981	Dan Fouts, San Diego[3]	609	360	59.1	4,802	33	17
1980	Dan Fouts, San Diego[2]	589	348	59.1	4,715	30	24

Year	Player, Team	Att.	Comp.	Pct.	Yards	TD	Int.
	Brian Sipe, Cleveland	554	337	60.8	4,132	30	14
1979	Dan Fouts, San Diego	530	332	62.6	4,082	24	24
1967	Joe Namath, N.Y. Jets	491	258	52.5	4,007	26	28

First season of professional football.

400 YARDS PASSING IN A GAME

Date	Player, Team, Opponent	Att.	Comp.	Yards	TD
Dec. 23, 2012	Drew Brees, New Orleans vs. Dallas (OT)	53	37	446	3
Dec. 23, 2012	Tony Romo, Dallas vs. New Orleans (OT)	43	26	416	4
Dec. 22, 2012	Matthew Stafford, Detroit vs. Atlanta	56	37	443	0
Dec. 16, 2012	Tom Brady, New England vs. San Francisco	65	36	443	1
Nov. 22, 2012	Tony Romo, Dallas vs. Washington	62	37	441	3
Nov. 22, 2012	Matthew Stafford, Detroit vs. Houston (OT)	61	31	441	2
Nov. 18, 2012	Matt Schaub, Houston vs. Jacksonville (OT)	55	43	527	5
Nov. 11, 2012	Matt Ryan, Atlanta vs. New Orleans	52	34	411	3
Nov. 4, 2012	*Andrew Luck, Indianapolis vs. Miami	48	30	433	2
Nov. 4, 2012	Carson Palmer, Oakland vs. Tampa Bay	61	39	414	4
Oct. 28, 2012	Tony Romo, Dallas vs. N.Y. Giants	62	36	437	1
Oct. 21, 2012	Josh Freeman, Tampa Bay vs. New Orleans	42	24	420	3
Sept. 30, 2012	Drew Brees, New Orleans vs. Green Bay	54	35	446	3
Sept. 30, 2012	*Ryan Tannehill, Miami vs. Arizona (OT)	41	26	431	1
Sept. 16, 2012	Eli Manning, N.Y. Giants vs. Tampa Bay	51	31	510	3
Jan. 1, 2012	Carson Palmer, Oakland vs. San Diego	43	28	417	2
Jan. 1, 2012	Matthew Stafford, Detroit vs. Green Bay	59	36	520	5
Jan. 1, 2012	Matt Flynn, Green Bay vs. Detroit	44	31	480	6
Dec. 18, 2011	Drew Brees, New Orleans vs. Minnesota	40	32	412	5
Dec. 11, 2011	Eli Manning, N.Y. Giants vs. Dallas	47	27	400	2
Dec. 4, 2011	Matthew Stafford, Detroit vs. New Orleans	44	31	408	1
Nov. 28, 2011	Eli Manning, N.Y. Giants vs. New Orleans	47	33	406	2
Nov. 27, 2011	Vince Young, Philadelphia vs. New England	48	26	400	1
Oct. 9, 2011	Eli Manning, N.Y. Giants vs. Seattle	39	24	420	3
Oct. 9, 2011	Matt Schaub, Houston vs. Oakland	51	24	416	2
Oct. 2, 2011	Aaron Rodgers, Green Bay vs. Denver	38	29	408	4
Oct. 2, 2011	Michael Vick, Philadelphia vs. San Francisco	46	30	416	2
Sept. 18, 2011	Tom Brady, New England vs. San Diego	40	31	423	3
Sept. 18, 2011	*Cam Newton, Carolina vs. Green Bay	46	28	432	1
Sept. 12, 2011	Chad Henne, Miami vs. New England	49	30	416	2
Sept. 12, 2011	Tom Brady, New England vs. Miami	48	32	517	4
Sept. 11, 2011	*Cam Newton, Carolina vs. Arizona	37	24	422	2
Sept. 8, 2011	Drew Brees, New Orleans vs. Green Bay	49	32	419	3
Dec. 26, 2010	Aaron Rodgers, Green Bay vs. N.Y. Giants	37	25	404	4
Nov. 14, 2010	Matt Cassel, Kansas City vs. Denver	53	33	469	4
Nov. 7, 2010	Brett Favre, Minnesota vs. Arizona (OT)	47	36	446	2
Oct. 24, 2010	Carson Palmer, Cincinnati vs. Atlanta	50	36	412	3
Oct. 10, 2010	Tony Romo, Dallas vs. Tennessee	46	31	406	3
Oct. 10, 2010	Philip Rivers, San Diego vs. Oakland	42	27	431	2
Sept. 26, 2010	Kyle Orton, Denver vs. Indianapolis	57	37	476	1
Sept. 26, 2010	Philip Rivers, San Diego vs. Seattle	53	29	455	2
Sept. 19, 2010	Matt Schaub, Houston vs. Washington	52	38	497	3
Sept. 19, 2010	Donovan McNabb, Washington vs. Houston	38	28	426	1
Sept. 12, 2010	Peyton Manning, Indianapolis vs. Houston	57	40	433	3
Jan. 3, 2010	Kyle Orton, Denver vs. Kansas City	56	32	431	1
Dec. 20, 2009	Ben Roethlisberger, Pittsburgh vs. Green Bay	46	29	503	3
Dec. 6, 2009	Drew Brees, New Orleans vs. Washington (OT)	49	35	419	2
Nov. 22, 2009	Matthew Stafford, Detroit vs. Cleveland	43	26	422	5
Nov. 15, 2009	Donovan McNabb, Philadelphia vs. San Diego	55	35	450	2
Oct. 18, 2009	Ben Roethlisberger, Pittsburgh vs. Cleveland	35	23	417	2
Sept. 20, 2009	Philip Rivers, San Diego vs. Baltimore	45	25	436	2
Dec. 7, 2008	Matt Schaub, Houston vs. Green Bay	42	28	414	2
Nov. 23, 2008	Matt Cassel, New England vs. Miami	43	30	415	3
Nov. 13, 2008	Matt Cassel, New England vs. N.Y. Jets (OT)	51	30	400	3
Nov. 9, 2008	Drew Brees, New Orleans vs. Atlanta	58	31	422	2
Nov. 6, 2008	Jay Cutler, Denver vs. Cleveland	42	24	447	3
Sept. 28, 2008	Kurt Warner, Arizona vs. N.Y. Jets	57	40	472	2
Sept. 21, 2008	Drew Brees, New Orleans vs. Denver	48	39	421	1
Sept. 21, 2008	Brian Griese, Tampa Bay vs. Chicago (OT)	67	38	407	2
Nov. 25, 2007	Kurt Warner, Arizona vs. San Francisco (OT)	48	34	484	2
Nov. 4, 2007	Drew Brees, New Orleans vs. Jacksonville	49	35	445	3

Date	Player, Team, Opponent	Att.	Comp.	Yards	TD
Sept. 23, 2007	Jon Kitna, Detroit vs. Philadelphia	46	29	446	2
Sept. 16, 2007	Carson Palmer, Cincinnati vs. Cleveland	50	33	401	6
Dec. 10, 2006	Chris Weinke, Carolina vs. N.Y. Giants	61	34	423	1
Nov. 26, 2006	Matt Leinart, Arizona vs. Minnesota	51	31	405	1
Nov. 19, 2006	Drew Brees, New Orleans vs. Cincinnati	52	37	510	2
Nov. 12, 2006	Carson Palmer, Cincinnati vs. San Diego	42	31	440	3
Nov. 5, 2006	Ben Roethlisberger, Pittsburgh vs. Denver	54	38	433	1
Oct. 22, 2006	Joey Harrington, Miami vs. Green Bay	62	33	414	2
Sept. 17, 2006	Peyton Manning, Indianapolis vs. Houston	38	26	400	3
Oct. 2, 2005	Marc Bulger, St. Louis vs. N.Y. Giants	62	40	442	2
Jan. 2, 2005	Marc Bulger, St. Louis vs. N.Y. Jets (OT)	39	29	450	3
Dec. 19, 2004	Daunte Culpepper, Minnesota vs. Detroit	35	25	404	3
Dec. 19, 2004	Billy Volek, Tennessee vs. Oakland	60	40	492	4
Dec. 13, 2004	Billy Volek, Tennessee vs. Kansas City	43	29	426	4
Dec. 6, 2004	Matt Hasselbeck, Seattle vs. Dallas	40	28	414	3
Dec. 5, 2004	Peyton Manning, Indianapolis vs. Tennessee	33	25	425	3
Dec. 5, 2004	Donovan McNabb, Philadelphia vs. Green Bay	43	32	464	5
Nov. 29, 2004	Marc Bulger, St. Louis vs. Green Bay	53	35	448	2
Nov. 28, 2004	Kelly Holcomb, Cleveland vs. Cincinnati	39	30	413	5
Oct. 31, 2004	Peyton Manning, Indianapolis vs. Kansas City	44	25	472	5
Oct. 31, 2004	Jake Plummer, Denver vs. Atlanta	55	31	499	4
Oct. 17, 2004	Daunte Culpepper, Minnesota vs. New Orleans	37	26	425	5
Oct. 10. 2004	Tim Rattay, San Francisco vs. Arizona (OT)	57	38	417	2
Nov. 16, 2003	Peyton Manning, Indianapolis vs. N.Y. Jets	36	27	401	1
Oct. 12, 2003	Trent Green, Kansas City vs. Green Bay (OT)	45	27	400	3
Oct. 12, 2003	Steve McNair, Tennessee vs. Houston	27	18	421	3
Dec. 29, 2002	Matt Hasselbeck, Seattle vs. San Diego (OT)	53	36	449	2
Dec. 1, 2002	Matt Hasselbeck, Seattle vs. San Francisco	55	30	427	3
Nov. 10, 2002	Marc Bulger, St. Louis vs. San Diego	48	36	453	4
Nov. 10, 2002	Tommy Maddox, Pittsburgh vs. Atlanta (OT)	41	28	473	4
Oct. 6, 2002	Drew Bledsoe, Buffalo vs. Oakland	53	32	417	2
Sept. 22, 2002	Tom Brady, New England vs. Kansas City (OT)	54	39	410	4
Sept. 15, 2002	Drew Bledsoe, Buffalo vs. Minnesota (OT)	49	35	463	3
Sept. 15, 2002	Rich Gannon, Oakland vs. Pittsburgh	64	43	403	1
Dec. 30, 2001	Jon Kitna, Cincinnati vs. Pittsburgh	68	35	411	2
Dec. 23, 2001	Chris Chandler, Atlanta vs. Buffalo	40	28	431	2
Nov. 18, 2001	Charlie Batch, Detroit vs. Arizona	62	36	436	3
Nov. 18, 2001	Kurt Warner, St. Louis vs. New England	42	30	401	3
Sept. 23, 2001	Peyton Manning, Indianapolis vs. Buffalo	29	23	421	4
Dec. 24, 2000	Vinny Testaverde, N.Y. Jets vs. Baltimore	69	36	481	2
Dec. 17, 2000	Jeff Garcia, San Francisco vs. Chicago	44	36	402	2
Dec. 3, 2000	Aaron Brooks, New Orleans vs. Denver	48	30	441	2
Nov. 19, 2000	Gus Frerotte, Denver vs. San Diego	58	36	462	5
Nov. 5, 2000	Elvis Grbac, Kansas City vs. Oakland	53	39	504	2
Nov. 5, 2000	Trent Green, St. Louis vs. Carolina	42	29	431	2
Sept. 25, 2000	Peyton Manning, Indianapolis vs. Jacksonville	36	23	440	4
Sept. 4, 2000	Kurt Warner, St. Louis vs. Denver	35	25	441	3
Dec. 26, 1999	Brad Johnson, Washington vs. San Francisco (OT)	47	32	471	2
Dec. 5, 1999	Jeff Garcia, San Francisco vs. Cincinnati	49	33	437	3
Nov. 28, 1999	Jim Harbaugh, San Diego vs. Minnesota	39	25	404	1
Nov. 14, 1999	Jim Miller, Chicago vs. Minnesota (OT)	48	34	422	3
Sept. 26, 1999	Peyton Manning, Indianapolis vs. San Diego	54	29	404	2
Dec. 6, 1998	Vinny Testaverde, N.Y. Jets vs. Seattle	63	42	418	2
Dec. 6, 1998	John Elway, Denver vs. Kansas City	32	22	400	2
Nov. 26, 1998	Troy Aikman, Dallas vs. Minnesota	57	34	455	1
Nov. 23, 1998	Drew Bledsoe, New England vs. Miami	54	28	423	2
Nov. 15, 1998	Jake Plummer, Arizona vs. Dallas	56	31	465	3
Oct. 5, 1998	Randall Cunningham, Minnesota vs. Green Bay	32	20	442	4
Sept. 6, 1998	Glenn Foley, N.Y. Jets vs. San Francisco (OT)	58	30	415	3
Nov. 2, 1997	Tony Banks, St. Louis vs. Atlanta	34	23	401	2
Oct. 26, 1997	Warren Moon, Seattle vs. Oakland	44	28	409	5
Nov. 10, 1996	Boomer Esiason, Arizona vs. Washington (OT)	59	35	522	3
Nov. 3, 1996	Drew Bledsoe, New England vs. Miami	41	30	419	3
Oct. 27, 1996	Vinny Testaverde, Baltimore vs. St. Louis (OT)	51	31	429	3
Oct. 20, 1996	Mark Brunell, Jacksonville vs. St. Louis	52	37	421	0
Sept. 22, 1996	Mark Brunell, Jacksonville vs. New England (OT)	39	23	432	3
Dec. 18, 1995	Steve Young, San Francisco vs. Minnesota	49	30	425	3
Nov. 26, 1995	Dave Krieg, Arizona vs. Atlanta (OT)	43	27	413	4

Date	Player, Team, Opponent	Att.	Comp.	Yards	TD
Nov. 23, 1995	Scott Mitchell, Detroit vs. Minnesota	45	30	410	4
Oct. 1, 1995	Dan Marino, Miami vs. Cincinnati	48	33	450	2
Nov. 20, 1994	Warren Moon, Minnesota vs. N.Y. Jets	50	33	400	2
Nov. 13, 1994	Drew Bledsoe, New England vs. Minnesota (OT)	70	45	426	3
Nov. 6, 1994	Warren Moon, Minnesota vs. New Orleans	57	33	420	3
Sept. 25, 1994	Dan Marino, Miami vs. Minnesota	54	29	431	3
Sept. 4, 1994	Dan Marino, Miami vs. New England (OT)	42	23	473	5
Sept. 4, 1994	Drew Bledsoe, New England vs. Miami (OT)	51	32	421	4
Dec. 19, 1993	Steve Beuerlein, Phoenix vs. Seattle	53	34	431	3
Dec. 5, 1993	Brett Favre, Green Bay vs. Chicago	54	36	402	2
Nov. 28, 1993	Steve Young, San Francisco vs. L.A. Rams	32	26	462	4
Oct. 31, 1993	Jeff Hostetler, L.A. Raiders vs. San Diego	32	20	424	2
Sept. 13, 1992	Steve Young, San Francisco vs. Buffalo	37	26	449	3
Sept. 13, 1992	Jim Kelly, Buffalo vs. San Francisco	33	22	403	3
Nov. 10, 1991	Warren Moon, Houston vs. Dallas (OT)	56	41	432	0
Nov. 10, 1991	Mark Rypien, Washington vs. Atlanta	31	16	442	6
Oct. 13, 1991	Warren Moon, Houston vs. N.Y. Jets	50	35	423	2
Dec. 16, 1990	Warren Moon, Houston vs. Kansas City	45	27	527	3
Nov. 4, 1990	Joe Montana, San Francisco vs. Green Bay	40	25	411	3
Oct. 14, 1990	Joe Montana, San Francisco vs. Atlanta	49	32	476	6
Oct. 7, 1990	Boomer Esiason, Cincinnati vs. L.A. Rams (OT)	45	31	490	3
Dec. 23, 1989	Warren Moon, Houston vs. Cleveland	51	32	414	2
Dec. 11, 1989	Joe Montana, San Francisco vs. L.A. Rams	42	30	458	3
Nov. 26, 1989	Jim Everett, L.A. Rams vs. New Orleans (OT)	51	29	454	1
Nov. 26, 1989	Mark Rypien, Washington vs. Chicago	47	30	401	4
Oct. 2, 1989	Randall Cunningham, Philadelphia vs. Chicago	62	32	401	1
Sept. 24, 1989	Joe Montana, San Francisco vs. Philadelphia	34	25	428	5
Sept. 24, 1989	Dan Marino, Miami vs. N.Y. Jets	55	33	427	3
Sept. 17, 1989	Randall Cunningham, Philadelphia vs. Washington	46	34	447	5
Dec. 18, 1988	Dave Krieg, Seattle vs. L.A. Raiders	32	19	410	4
Dec. 12, 1988	Dan Marino, Miami vs. Cleveland	50	30	404	4
Oct. 23, 1988	Dan Marino, Miami vs. N.Y. Jets	60	35	521	3
Oct. 16, 1988	Vinny Testaverde, Tampa Bay vs. Indianapolis	42	25	469	2
Sept. 11, 1988	Doug Williams, Washington vs. Pittsburgh	52	30	430	2
Nov. 29, 1987	Tom Ramsey, New England vs. Philadelphia	53	34	402	3
Nov. 22, 1987	Boomer Esiason, Cincinnati vs. Pittsburgh	53	30	409	0
Sept. 20, 1987	Neil Lomax, St. Louis vs. San Diego	61	32	457	3
Dec. 21, 1986	Boomer Esiason, Cincinnati vs. N.Y. Jets	30	23	425	5
Dec. 14, 1986	Dan Marino, Miami vs. L.A. Rams (OT)	46	29	403	5
Nov. 23, 1986	Bernie Kosar, Cleveland vs. Pittsburgh (OT)	46	28	414	2
Nov. 17, 1986	Joe Montana, San Francisco vs. Washington	60	33	441	0
Nov. 16, 1986	Dan Marino, Miami vs. Buffalo	54	39	404	4
Nov. 10, 1986	Bernie Kosar, Cleveland vs. Miami	50	32	401	0
Nov. 2, 1986	Tommy Kramer, Minnesota vs. Washington (OT)	35	20	490	4
Nov. 2, 1986	Ken O'Brien, N.Y. Jets vs. Seattle	32	26	431	4
Oct. 27, 1986	Jay Schroeder, Washington vs. N.Y. Giants	40	22	420	1
Oct. 12, 1986	Steve Grogan, New England vs. N.Y. Jets	42	23	401	4
Sept. 21, 1986	Ken O'Brien, N.Y. Jets vs. Miami (OT)	43	29	479	4
Sept. 21, 1986	Dan Marino, Miami vs. N.Y. Jets (OT)	50	30	448	6
Sept. 21, 1986	Tony Eason, New England vs. Seattle	45	26	414	3
Dec. 20, 1985	John Elway, Denver vs. Seattle	42	24	432	1
Nov. 10, 1985	Dan Fouts, San Diego vs. L.A. Raiders (OT)	41	26	436	4
Oct. 13, 1985	Phil Simms, N.Y. Giants vs. Cincinnati	62	40	513	1
Oct. 13, 1985	Dave Krieg, Seattle vs. Atlanta	51	33	405	4
Oct. 6, 1985	Phil Simms, N.Y. Giants vs. Dallas	36	18	432	3
Oct. 6, 1985	Joe Montana, San Francisco vs. Atlanta	57	37	429	5
Sept. 19, 1985	Tommy Kramer, Minnesota vs. Chicago	55	28	436	3
Sept. 15, 1985	Dan Fouts, San Diego vs. Seattle	43	29	440	4
Dec. 16, 1984	Neil Lomax, St. Louis vs. Washington	46	37	468	2
Dec. 9, 1984	Dan Marino, Miami vs. Indianapolis	41	29	404	4
Dec. 2, 1984	Dan Marino, Miami vs. L.A. Raiders	57	35	470	4
Nov. 25, 1984	Dave Krieg, Seattle vs. Denver	44	30	406	3
Nov. 4, 1984	Dan Marino, Miami vs. N.Y. Jets	42	23	422	2
Oct. 21, 1984	Dan Fouts, San Diego vs. L.A. Raiders	45	24	410	3
Sept. 30, 1984	Dan Marino, Miami vs. St. Louis	36	24	429	3
Sept. 2, 1984	Phil Simms, N.Y. Giants vs. Philadelphia	30	23	409	4
Dec. 11, 1983	Bill Kenney, Kansas City vs. San Diego	41	31	411	4
Nov. 20, 1983	Dave Krieg, Seattle vs. Denver	42	31	418	3

Date	Player, Team, Opponent	Att.	Comp.	Yards	TD
Oct. 9, 1983	Joe Ferguson, Buffalo vs. Miami (OT)	55	38	419	5
Oct. 2, 1983	Joe Theismann, Washington vs. L.A. Raiders	39	23	417	3
Sept. 25, 1983	Richard Todd, N.Y. Jets vs. L.A. Rams (OT)	50	37	446	2
Dec. 26, 1982	Vince Ferragamo, L.A. Rams vs. Chicago	46	30	509	3
Dec. 20, 1982	Dan Fouts, San Diego vs. Cincinnati	40	25	435	1
Dec. 20, 1982	Ken Anderson, Cincinnati vs. San Diego	56	40	416	2
Dec. 11, 1982	Dan Fouts, San Diego vs. San Francisco	48	33	444	5
Nov. 21, 1982	Joe Montana, San Francisco vs. St. Louis	39	26	408	3
Nov. 15, 1981	Steve Bartkowski, Atlanta vs. Pittsburgh	50	33	416	2
Oct. 25, 1981	Brian Sipe, Cleveland vs. Baltimore	41	30	444	4
Oct. 25, 1981	David Woodley, Miami vs. Dallas	37	21	408	3
Oct. 11, 1981	Tommy Kramer, Minnesota vs. San Diego	43	27	444	4
Dec. 14, 1980	Tommy Kramer, Minnesota vs. Cleveland	49	38	456	4
Nov. 16, 1980	Doug Williams, Tampa Bay vs. Minnesota	55	30	486	4
Oct. 19, 1980	Dan Fouts, San Diego vs. N.Y. Giants	41	26	444	3
Oct. 12, 1980	Lynn Dickey, Green Bay vs. Tampa Bay (OT)	51	35	418	1
Sept. 21, 1980	Richard Todd, N.Y. Jets vs. San Francisco	60	42	447	3
Oct. 3, 1976	James Harris, Los Angeles vs. Miami	29	17	436	2
Nov. 17, 1975	Ken Anderson, Cincinnati vs. Buffalo	46	30	447	2
Nov. 18, 1974	Charley Johnson, Denver vs. Kansas City	42	28	445	2
Dec. 11, 1972	Joe Namath, N.Y. Jets vs. Oakland	46	25	403	1
Sept. 24, 1972	Joe Namath, N.Y. Jets vs. Baltimore	28	15	496	6
Dec. 21, 1969	Don Horn, Green Bay vs. St. Louis	31	22	410	5
Sept. 28, 1969	Joe Kapp, Minnesota vs. Baltimore	43	28	449	7
Sept. 9, 1968	Pete Beathard, Houston vs. Kansas City	48	23	413	2
Nov. 26, 1967	Sonny Jurgensen, Washington vs. Cleveland	50	32	418	3
Oct. 1, 1967	Joe Namath, N.Y. Jets vs. Miami	39	23	415	3
Sept. 17, 1967	Johnny Unitas, Baltimore vs. Atlanta	32	22	401	2
Nov. 13, 1966	Don Meredith, Dallas vs. Washington	29	21	406	2
Nov. 28, 1965	Sonny Jurgensen, Washington vs. Dallas	43	26	411	3
Oct. 24, 1965	Fran Tarkenton, Minnesota vs. San Francisco	35	21	407	3
Nov. 1, 1964	Len Dawson, Kansas City vs. Denver	38	23	435	6
Oct. 25, 1964	Cotton Davidson, Oakland vs. Denver	36	23	427	5
Oct. 16, 1964	Babe Parilli, Boston vs. Oakland	47	25	422	4
Dec. 22, 1963	Tom Flores, Oakland vs. Houston	29	17	407	6
Nov. 17, 1963	Norm Snead, Washington vs. Pittsburgh	40	23	424	2
Nov. 10, 1963	Don Meredith, Dallas vs. San Francisco	48	30	460	3
Oct. 13, 1963	Charley Johnson, St. Louis vs. Pittsburgh	41	20	428	2
Dec. 16, 1962	Sonny Jurgensen, Philadelphia vs. St. Louis	34	15	419	5
Nov. 18, 1962	Bill Wade, Chicago vs. Dall. Cowboys	46	28	466	2
Oct. 28, 1962	Y.A. Tittle, N.Y. Giants vs. Washington	39	27	505	7
Sept. 15, 1962	Frank Tripucka, Denver vs. Buffalo	56	29	447	2
Dec. 17, 1961	Sonny Jurgensen, Philadelphia vs. Detroit	42	27	403	3
Nov. 19, 1961	George Blanda, Houston vs. N.Y. Titans	32	20	418	7
Oct. 29, 1961	George Blanda, Houston vs. Buffalo	32	18	464	4
Oct. 29, 1961	Sonny Jurgensen, Philadelphia vs. Washington	41	27	436	3
Oct. 13, 1961	Jacky Lee, Houston vs. Boston	41	27	457	2
Dec. 13, 1958	Bobby Layne, Pittsburgh vs. Chi. Cardinals	49	23	409	2
Nov. 8, 1953	Bobby Thomason, Philadelphia vs. N.Y. Giants	44	22	437	4
Oct. 4, 1952	Otto Graham, Cleveland vs. Pittsburgh	49	21	401	3
Sept. 28, 1951	Norm Van Brocklin, Los Angeles vs. N.Y. Yanks	41	27	554	5
Dec. 11, 1949	Johnny Lujack, Chi. Bears vs. Chi. Cardinals	39	24	468	6
Oct. 31, 1948	Sammy Baugh, Washington vs. Boston	24	17	446	4
Oct. 31, 1948	Jim Hardy, Los Angeles vs. Chi. Cardinals	53	28	406	3
Nov. 14, 1943	Sid Luckman, Chi. Bears vs. N.Y. Giants	32	21	433	7

*First season of professional football.

TIMES 400 OR MORE

252 times by 120 players...Marino 13; Brees 9; P. Manning 8; Montana, Moon 7; Bledsoe, Fouts 6; Jurgensen, Krieg, Palmer, Stafford 5; Brady, Bulger, Esiason, Kramer, E. Manning, Romo, Schaub, Testaverde, Warner 4; Cassel, Cunningham, Hasselbeck, McNabb, Namath, Rivers, Roethlisberger, Simms, Young 3; Anderson, Blanda, Brunell, Culpepper, Elway, Favre, Garcia, Green, C. Johnson, Kitna, Kosar, Lomax, Meredith, Newton, O'Brien, Orton, Plummer, Rodgers, Rypien, Todd, Volek, D. Williams 2.

---

100 PASS RECEPTIONS IN A SEASON

Year	Player, Team	No.	Yards	Avg.	Long	TD
2012	Calvin Johnson, Detroit	122	1,964	16.1	53	5

Year	Player, Team	No.	Yards	Avg.	Long	TD
	Brandon Marshall, Chicago[4]	118	1,508	12.8	56	11
	Wes Welker, New England[5]	118	1,354	11.5	59	6
	Andre Johnson, Houston[4]	112	1,598	14.3	60	4
	Jason Witten, Dallas	110	1,039	9.4	36	3
	Reggie Wayne, Indianapolis[4]	106	1,355	12.8	33	5
2011	Wes Welker, New England[4]	122	1,569	12.9	99	9
	Roddy White, Atlanta[2]	100	1,296	13.0	43	8
2010	Roddy White, Atlanta	115	1,389	12.1	46	10
	Reggie Wayne, Indianapolis[3]	111	1,355	12.2	50	6
2009	Wes Welker, New England[3]	123	1,348	11.0	58	4
	Steve Smith, N.Y. Giants	107	1,220	11.4	51	7
	Andre Johnson, Houston[3]	101	1,569	15.5	72	9
	Brandon Marshall, Denver[3]	101	1,120	11.1	75	10
	Dallas Clark, Indianapolis	100	1,106	11.1	80	10
	Reggie Wayne, Indianapolis[2]	100	1,264	12.6	65	10
2008	Andre Johnson, Houston[2]	115	1,575	13.7	65	8
	Wes Welker, New England[2]	111	1,165	10.5	64	3
	Brandon Marshall, Denver[2]	104	1,265	12.2	47	6
2007	T.J. Houshmandzadeh, Cincinnati	112	1,143	10.2	42	12
	Wes Welker, New England	112	1,175	10.5	42	8
	Reggie Wayne, Indianapolis	104	1,510	14.5	64	10
	Derrick Mason, Baltimore	103	1,087	10.6	79	5
	Brandon Marshall, Denver	102	1,325	13.0	68	7
	Larry Fitzgerald, Arizona[2]	100	1,409	14.1	48	10
2006	Andre Johnson, Houston	103	1,147	11.1	53	5
2005	Larry Fitzgerald, Arizona	103	1,409	13.7	47	10
	Steve Smith, Carolina	103	1,563	15.2	80	12
	Anquan Boldin, Arizona[2]	102	1,402	13.7	54	7
	Torry Holt, St. Louis[2]	102	1,331	13.0	44	9
2004	Tony Gonzalez, Kansas City	102	1,258	12.3	32	7
2003	Torry Holt, St. Louis	117	1,696	14.5	48	12
	Randy Moss, Minnesota[2]	111	1,632	14.7	72	17
	*Anquan Boldin, Arizona	101	1,377	13.6	71	8
	LaDainian Tomlinson, San Diego	100	725	7.3	73	4
2002	Marvin Harrison, Indianapolis[4]	143	1,722	12.0	69	11
	Hines Ward, Pittsburgh	112	1,329	11.9	72	12
	Randy Moss, Minnesota	106	1,347	12.7	60	7
	Eric Moulds, Buffalo	100	1,292	12.9	70	10
	Terrell Owens, San Francisco	100	1,300	13.0	76	13
2001	Rod Smith, Denver[2]	113	1,343	11.9	65	11
	Jimmy Smith, Jacksonville[2]	112	1,373	12.3	35	8
	Marvin Harrison, Indianapolis[3]	109	1,524	14.0	68	15
	Keyshawn Johnson, Tampa Bay	106	1,266	11.9	47	1
	Troy Brown, New England	101	1,199	11.9	60	5
	Marty Booker, Chicago	100	1,071	10.7	66	8
2000	Marvin Harrison, Indianapolis[2]	102	1,413	13.9	78	14
	Muhsin Muhammad, Carolina	102	1,183	11.6	36	6
	Ed McCaffrey, Denver	101	1,317	13.0	61	9
	Rod Smith, Denver	100	1,602	16.0	49	8
1999	Jimmy Smith, Jacksonville	116	1,636	14.1	62	6
	Marvin Harrison, Indianapolis	115	1,663	14.5	57	12
1997	Tim Brown, Oakland	104	1,408	13.5	59	5
	Herman Moore, Detroit[3]	104	1,293	12.4	79	8
1996	Jerry Rice, San Francisco[4]	108	1,254	11.6	39	8
	Herman Moore, Detroit[2]	106	1,296	12.2	50	9
	Carl Pickens, Cincinnati	100	1,180	11.8	61	12
1995	Herman Moore, Detroit	123	1,686	13.7	69	14
	Jerry Rice, San Francisco[3]	122	1,848	15.1	81	15
	Cris Carter, Minnesota[2]	122	1,371	11.2	60	17
	Isaac Bruce, St. Louis	119	1,781	15.0	72	13
	Michael Irvin, Dallas	111	1,603	14.4	50	10
	Brett Perriman, Detroit	108	1,488	13.8	91	9
	Eric Metcalf, Atlanta	104	1,189	11.4	62	8
	Robert Brooks, Green Bay	102	1,497	14.7	99	13
	Larry Centers, Arizona	101	962	9.5	32	2
1994	Cris Carter, Minnesota	122	1,256	10.3	65	7
	Jerry Rice, San Francisco[2]	112	1,499	13.4	69	13
	Terance Mathis, Atlanta	111	1,342	12.1	81	11
1993	Sterling Sharpe, Green Bay[2]	112	1,274	11.4	54	11

Year	Player, Team	No.	Yards	Avg.	Long	TD
1992	Sterling Sharpe, Green Bay	108	1,461	13.5	76	13
1991	Haywood Jeffires, Houston	100	1,181	11.8	44	7
1990	Jerry Rice, San Francisco	100	1,502	15.0	64	13
1984	Art Monk, Washington	106	1,372	12.9	72	7
1964	Charley Hennigan, Houston	101	1,546	15.3	53	8
1961	Lionel Taylor, Denver	100	1,176	11.8	52	4

*First season of professional football.

1,000 YARDS PASS RECEIVING IN A SEASON

Year	Player, Team	No.	Yards	Avg.	Long	TD
2012	Calvin Johnson, Detroit[4]	122	1,964	16.1	53	5
	Andre Johnson, Houston[6]	112	1,598	14.3	60	4
	Brandon Marshall, Chicago[6]	118	1,508	12.8	56	11
	Demaryius Thomas, Denver	94	1,434	15.3	71	10
	Vincent Jackson, Tampa Bay[4]	72	1,384	19.2	95	8
	Dez Bryant, Dallas	92	1,382	15.0	85	12
	Reggie Wayne, Indianapolis[8]	106	1,355	12.8	33	5
	Wes Welker, New England[5]	118	1,354	11.5	59	6
	Roddy White, Atlanta[6]	92	1,351	14.7	59	7
	A.J. Green, Cincinnati[2]	97	1,350	13.9	73	11
	Julio Jones, Atlanta	79	1,198	15.2	80	10
	Steve Smith, Carolina[7]	73	1,174	16.1	66	4
	Marques Colston, New Orleans[6]	83	1,154	13.9	60	10
	Michael Crabtree, San Francisco	85	1,105	13.0	49	9
	Victor Cruz, N.Y. Giants[2]	86	1,092	12.7	80	10
	Brian Hartline, Miami	74	1,083	14.6	80	1
	Eric Decker, Denver	85	1,064	12.5	55	13
	Steve Johnson, Buffalo[3]	79	1,046	13.2	63	6
	Lance Moore, New Orleans	65	1,041	16.0	51	6
	Jason Witten, Dallas[4]	110	1,039	9.4	36	3
2011	Calvin Johnson, Detroit[3]	96	1,681	17.5	73	16
	Wes Welker, New England[4]	122	1,569	12.9	99	9
	Victor Cruz, N.Y. Giants	82	1,536	18.7	99	9
	Larry Fitzgerald, Arizona[6]	80	1,411	17.6	73	8
	Steve Smith, Carolina[6]	79	1,394	17.6	77	7
	Rob Gronkowski, New England	90	1,327	14.7	52	17
	Jimmy Graham, New Orleans	99	1,310	13.2	59	11
	Roddy White, Atlanta[5]	100	1,296	13.0	43	8
	Jordy Nelson, Green Bay	68	1,263	18.6	93	15
	Brandon Marshall, Miami[5]	81	1,214	15.0	65	6
	Mike Wallace, Pittsburgh[2]	72	1,193	16.6	95	8
	Hakeem Nicks, N.Y. Giants[2]	76	1,192	15.7	68	7
	Dwayne Bowe, Kansas City[3]	81	1,159	14.3	52	5
	Marques Colston, New Orleans[5]	80	1,143	14.3	50	8
	Antonio Brown, Pittsburgh	69	1,108	16.1	79	2
	Vincent Jackson, San Diego[3]	60	1,106	18.4	58	9
	*A.J. Green, Cincinnati	65	1,057	16.3	58	7
	Nate Washington, Tennessee	74	1,023	13.8	57	7
	Steve Johnson, Buffalo[2]	76	1,004	13.2	55	7
2010	Brandon Lloyd, Denver	77	1,448	18.8	71	11
	Roddy White, Atlanta[4]	115	1,389	12.1	46	10
	Reggie Wayne, Indianapolis[7]	111	1,355	12.2	50	6
	Greg Jennings, Green Bay[3]	76	1,265	16.6	86	12
	Mike Wallace, Pittsburgh	60	1,257	20.9	56	10
	Andre Johnson, Houston[5]	86	1,216	14.1	60	8
	Dwayne Bowe, Kansas City[2]	72	1,162	16.1	75	15
	Larry Fitzgerald, Arizona[5]	90	1,137	12.6	41	6
	Calvin Johnson, Detroit[2]	77	1,120	14.6	87	12
	Santana Moss, Washington[4]	93	1,115	12.0	56	6
	Steve Johnson, Buffalo	82	1,073	13.1	45	10
	DeSean Jackson, Philadelphia[2]	47	1,056	22.5	91	6
	Hakeem Nicks, N.Y. Giants	79	1,052	13.3	46	11
	Miles Austin, Dallas[2]	69	1,041	15.1	69	7
	Marques Colston, New Orleans[4]	84	1,023	12.2	43	7
	Brandon Marshall, Miami[4]	86	1,014	11.8	46	3
	Jason Witten, Dallas[3]	94	1,002	10.7	33	9
2009	Andre Johnson, Houston[4]	101	1,569	15.5	72	9
	Wes Welker, New England[3]	123	1,348	11.0	58	4
	Miles Austin, Dallas	81	1,320	16.3	60	11

Year	Player, Team	No.	Yards	Avg.	Long	TD
	Sidney Rice, Minnesota	83	1,321	15.8	63	8
	Randy Moss, New England[10]	83	1,264	15.2	71	13
	Reggie Wayne, Indianapolis[6]	100	1,264	12.6	65	10
	Santonio Holmes, Pittsburgh	79	1,248	15.8	57	5
	Steve Smith, N.Y. Giants	107	1,220	11.4	51	7
	Vincent Jackson, San Diego[2]	68	1,167	17.2	55	9
	Hines Ward, Pittsburgh[6]	95	1,167	12.3	54	6
	Antonio Gates, San Diego[2]	79	1,157	14.6	56	8
	DeSean Jackson, Philadelphia	62	1,156	18.6	71	9
	Roddy White, Atlanta[3]	85	1,153	13.6	90	11
	Brandon Marshall, Denver[3]	101	1,120	11.1	75	10
	Greg Jennings, Green Bay[2]	68	1,113	16.4	83	4
	Dallas Clark, Indianapolis	100	1,106	11.1	80	10
	Larry Fitzgerald, Arizona[4]	97	1,092	11.3	34	13
	Marques Colston, New Orleans[3]	70	1,074	15.3	68	9
	Donald Driver, Green Bay[7]	70	1,061	15.2	71	6
	Chad Johnson, Cincinnati[7]	72	1,047	14.5	50	9
	Jason Witten, Dallas[2]	94	1,030	11.0	69	2
	Derrick Mason, Baltimore[8]	73	1,028	14.1	72	7
	Anquan Boldin, Arizona[5]	84	1,024	12.2	44	4
2008	Andre Johnson, Houston[3]	115	1,575	13.7	65	8
	Larry Fitzgerald, Arizona[3]	96	1,431	14.9	78	12
	Steve Smith, Carolina[5]	78	1,421	18.2	65	6
	Roddy White, Atlanta[2]	88	1,382	15.7	70	7
	Calvin Johnson, Detroit	78	1,331	17.1	96	12
	Greg Jennings, Green Bay	80	1,292	16.1	63	9
	Brandon Marshall, Denver[2]	104	1,265	12.2	47	6
	Antonio Bryant, Tampa Bay[2]	83	1,248	15.0	71	7
	Wes Welker, New England[2]	111	1,165	10.5	64	3
	Reggie Wayne, Indianapolis[5]	82	1,145	14.0	65	6
	Vincent Jackson, San Diego	59	1,098	18.6	60	7
	Tony Gonzalez, Kansas City[4]	96	1,058	11.0	35	10
	Terrell Owens, Dallas[9]	69	1,052	15.2	75	10
	Santana Moss, Washington[3]	79	1,044	13.2	67	6
	Hines Ward, Pittsburgh[5]	81	1,043	12.9	49	7
	Anquan Boldin, Arizona[4]	89	1,038	11.7	79	11
	Derrick Mason, Baltimore[7]	80	1,037	13.0	54	5
	Dwayne Bowe, Kansas City	86	1,022	11.9	36	7
	Lee Evans, Buffalo[2]	63	1,017	16.1	87	3
	Donald Driver, Green Bay[6]	74	1,012	13.7	71	5
	Randy Moss, New England[9]	69	1,008	14.6	76	11
	Steve Breaston, Arizona	77	1,006	13.1	58	3
2007	Reggie Wayne, Indianapolis[4]	104	1,510	14.5	64	10
	Randy Moss, New England[8]	98	1,493	15.2	65	23
	Chad Johnson, Cincinnati[6]	93	1,440	15.5	70	8
	Larry Fitzgerald, Arizona[2]	100	1,409	14.1	48	10
	Terrell Owens, Dallas[8]	81	1,355	16.7	52	15
	Brandon Marshall, Denver	102	1,325	13.0	68	7
	Braylon Edwards, Cleveland	80	1,289	16.1	78	16
	Marques Colston, New Orleans[2]	98	1,202	12.3	45	11
	Roddy White, Atlanta	83	1,202	14.5	69	6
	Torry Holt, St. Louis[8]	93	1,189	12.8	40	7
	Wes Welker, New England	112	1,175	10.5	42	8
	Tony Gonzalez, Kansas City[3]	99	1,172	11.8	31	5
	Bobby Engram, Seattle	94	1,147	12.2	49	6
	Jason Witten, Dallas	96	1,145	11.9	53	7
	T.J. Houshmandzadeh, Cincinnati[2]	112	1,143	10.2	42	12
	Jerricho Cotchery, N.Y. Jets	82	1,130	13.8	50	2
	Kevin Curtis, Philadelphia	77	1,110	14.4	75	6
	Kellen Winslow, Cleveland	82	1,106	13.5	49	5
	Derrick Mason, Baltimore[6]	103	1,087	10.6	79	5
	Donald Driver, Green Bay[5]	82	1,048	12.8	47	2
	Plaxico Burress, N.Y. Giants[4]	70	1,025	14.6	60	12
	Joey Galloway, Tampa Bay[6]	57	1,014	17.8	69	6
	Steve Smith, Carolina[4]	87	1,002	11.5	74	7
2006	Chad Johnson, Cincinnati[5]	87	1,369	15.7	74	7
	Marvin Harrison, Indianapolis[8]	95	1,366	14.4	68	12
	Reggie Wayne, Indianapolis[3]	86	1,310	15.2	51	9
	Roy Williams, Detroit	82	1,310	16.0	60	7

Year	Player, Team	No.	Yards	Avg.	Long	TD
	Donald Driver, Green Bay[4]	92	1,295	14.1	82	8
	Lee Evans, Buffalo	82	1,292	15.8	83	8
	Anquan Boldin, Arizona[3]	83	1,203	14.5	64	4
	Torry Holt, St. Louis[7]	93	1,188	12.8	67	10
	Terrell Owens, Dallas[7]	85	1,180	13.9	56	13
	Steve Smith, Carolina[3]	83	1,166	14.1	72	8
	Andre Johnson, Houston[2]	103	1,147	11.1	53	5
	Isaac Bruce, St. Louis[8]	74	1,098	14.8	45	3
	Laveranues Coles, N.Y. Jets[2]	91	1,098	12.1	58	6
	Mike Furrey, Detroit	98	1,086	11.1	31	6
	Javon Walker, Denver[2]	69	1,084	15.7	83	8
	T.J. Houshmandzadeh, Cincinnati	90	1,081	12.0	40	9
	Joey Galloway, Tampa Bay[5]	62	1,057	17.1	64	7
	Terry Glenn, Dallas[4]	70	1,047	15.0	54	6
	*Marques Colston, New Orleans	70	1,038	14.8	86	8
2005	Steve Smith, Carolina[2]	103	1,563	15.2	80	12
	Santana Moss, Washington[2]	84	1,483	17.7	78	9
	Chad Johnson, Cincinnati[4]	97	1,432	14.8	70	9
	Larry Fitzgerald, Arizona	103	1,409	13.7	47	10
	Anquan Boldin, Arizona[2]	102	1,402	13.7	54	7
	Torry Holt, St. Louis[6]	102	1,331	13.0	44	9
	Joey Galloway, Tampa Bay[4]	83	1,287	15.5	80	10
	Donald Driver, Green Bay[3]	86	1,221	14.2	59	5
	Plaxico Burress, N.Y. Giants[3]	76	1,214	16.0	78	7
	Marvin Harrison, Indianapolis[7]	82	1,146	14.0	80	12
	Terry Glenn, Dallas[3]	62	1,136	18.3	71	7
	Chris Chambers, Miami	82	1,118	13.6	77	11
	Rod Smith, Denver[8]	85	1,105	13.0	72	6
	Eddie Kennison, Kansas City[2]	68	1,102	16.2	55	5
	Antonio Gates, San Diego	89	1,101	12.4	38	10
	Derrick Mason, Baltimore[5]	86	1,073	12.5	39	3
	Reggie Wayne, Indianapolis[2]	83	1,055	12.7	66	5
	Jimmy Smith, Jacksonville[9]	70	1,023	14.6	45	6
	Antonio Bryant, Cleveland	69	1,009	14.6	54	4
	Randy Moss, Oakland[7]	60	1,005	16.8	79	8
2004	Muhsin Muhammad, Carolina[3]	93	1,405	15.1	51	16
	Joe Horn, New Orleans[4]	94	1,399	14.9	57	11
	Javon Walker, Green Bay	89	1,382	15.5	79	12
	Torry Holt, St. Louis[5]	94	1,372	14.6	75	10
	Isaac Bruce, St. Louis[7]	89	1,292	14.5	56	6
	Chad Johnson, Cincinnati[3]	95	1,274	13.4	53	9
	Tony Gonzalez, Kansas City[2]	102	1,258	12.3	32	7
	Drew Bennett, Tennessee	80	1,247	15.6	48	11
	Reggie Wayne, Indianapolis	77	1,210	15.7	71	12
	Donald Driver, Green Bay[2]	84	1,208	14.4	50	9
	Terrell Owens, Philadelphia[6]	77	1,200	15.6	59	14
	Darrell Jackson, Seattle[3]	87	1,199	13.8	56	7
	*Michael Clayton, Tampa Bay	80	1,193	14.9	75	7
	Jimmy Smith, Jacksonville[8]	74	1,172	15.8	65	6
	Derrick Mason, Tennessee[4]	96	1,168	12.2	37	7
	Rod Smith, Denver[7]	79	1,144	14.5	85	7
	Andre Johnson, Houston	79	1,142	14.5	54	6
	Marvin Harrison, Indianapolis[6]	86	1,113	12.9	59	15
	Eddie Kennison, Kansas City	62	1,086	17.5	70	8
	Ashley Lelie, Denver	54	1,084	20.1	58	7
	Brandon Stokley, Indianapolis	68	1,077	15.8	69	10
	Eric Moulds, Buffalo[4]	88	1,043	11.9	49	5
	Nate Burleson, Minnesota	68	1,006	14.8	68	9
	Hines Ward, Pittsburgh[4]	80	1,004	12.6	58	4
2003	Torry Holt, St. Louis[4]	117	1,696	14.5	48	12
	Randy Moss, Minnesota[6]	111	1,632	14.7	72	17
	*Anquan Boldin, Arizona	101	1,377	13.6	71	8
	Chad Johnson, Cincinnati[2]	90	1,355	15.1	82	10
	Derrick Mason, Tennessee[3]	95	1,303	13.7	50	8
	Marvin Harrison, Indianapolis[5]	94	1,272	13.5	79	10
	Laveranues Coles, Washington[2]	82	1,204	14.7	64	6
	Keenan McCardell, Tampa Bay[5]	84	1,174	14.0	76	8
	Hines Ward, Pittsburgh[3]	95	1,163	12.2	50	10
	Darrell Jackson, Seattle[2]	68	1,137	16.7	80	9

Year	Player, Team	No.	Yards	Avg.	Long	TD
	Steve Smith, Carolina	88	1,110	12.6	67	7
	Santana Moss, N.Y. Jets	74	1,105	14.9	65	10
	Terrell Owens, San Francisco[5]	80	1,102	13.8	75	9
	Amani Toomer, N.Y. Giants[5]	63	1,057	16.8	77	5
2002	Marvin Harrison, Indianapolis[4]	143	1,722	12.0	69	11
	Randy Moss, Minnesota[5]	106	1,347	12.7	60	7
	Amani Toomer, N.Y. Giants[4]	82	1,343	16.4	82	8
	Hines Ward, Pittsburgh[2]	112	1,329	11.9	72	12
	Plaxico Burress, Pittsburgh[2]	78	1,325	17.0	62	7
	Joe Horn, New Orleans[3]	88	1,312	14.9	63	7
	Torry Holt, St. Louis[3]	91	1,302	14.3	58	4
	Terrell Owens, San Francisco[4]	100	1,300	13.0	76	13
	Eric Moulds, Buffalo[3]	100	1,292	12.9	70	10
	Laveranues Coles, N.Y. Jets	89	1,264	14.2	43	5
	Peerless Price, Buffalo	94	1,252	13.3	73	9
	Koren Robinson, Seattle	78	1,240	15.9	83	5
	Jerry Rice, Oakland[14]	92	1,211	13.2	75	7
	Marty Booker, Chicago[2]	97	1,189	12.3	54	6
	Chad Johnson, Cincinnati	69	1,166	16.9	72	5
	Keyshawn Johnson, Tampa Bay[4]	76	1,088	14.3	76	5
	Isaac Bruce, St. Louis[6]	79	1,075	13.6	34	7
	Donald Driver, Green Bay	70	1,064	15.2	85	9
	Jimmy Smith, Jacksonville[7]	80	1,027	12.8	47	7
	Rod Smith, Denver[6]	89	1,027	11.5	46	5
	Derrick Mason, Tennessee[2]	79	1,012	12.8	40	5
	Rod Gardner, Washington	71	1,006	14.2	43	8
2001	David Boston, Arizona[2]	98	1,598	16.3	61	8
	Marvin Harrison, Indianapolis[3]	109	1,524	14.0	68	15
	Terrell Owens, San Francisco[3]	93	1,412	15.2	60	16
	Jimmy Smith, Jacksonville[6]	112	1,373	12.3	35	8
	Torry Holt, St. Louis[2]	81	1,363	16.8	51	7
	Rod Smith, Denver[5]	113	1,343	11.9	65	11
	Keyshawn Johnson, Tampa Bay[3]	106	1,266	11.9	47	1
	Joe Horn, New Orleans[2]	83	1,265	15.2	56	9
	Randy Moss, Minnesota[4]	82	1,233	15.0	73	10
	Troy Brown, New England	101	1,199	11.9	60	5
	Tim Brown, Oakland[9]	91	1,165	12.8	46	9
	Johnnie Morton, Detroit[4]	77	1,154	15.0	76	4
	Jerry Rice, Oakland[13]	83	1,139	13.7	40	9
	Derrick Mason, Tennessee	73	1,128	15.5	71	9
	Curtis Conway, San Diego[3]	71	1,125	15.8	72	6
	Keenan McCardell, Jacksonville[4]	93	1,110	11.9	45	6
	Isaac Bruce, St. Louis[5]	64	1,106	17.3	51	6
	Kevin Johnson, Cleveland	84	1,097	13.1	55	9
	Darrell Jackson, Seattle	70	1,081	15.4	64	8
	Marty Booker, Chicago	100	1,071	10.7	66	8
	Qadry Ismail, Baltimore[2]	74	1,059	14.3	77	7
	Amani Toomer, N.Y. Giants[3]	72	1,054	14.6	60	5
	Willie Jackson, New Orleans	81	1,046	12.9	63	5
	Plaxico Burress, Pittsburgh	66	1,008	15.3	43	6
	Hines Ward, Pittsburgh	94	1,003	10.7	34	4
2000	Torry Holt, St. Louis	82	1,635	19.9	85	6
	Rod Smith, Denver[4]	100	1,602	16.0	49	8
	Isaac Bruce, St. Louis[4]	87	1,471	16.9	78	9
	Terrell Owens, San Francisco[2]	97	1,451	15.0	69	13
	Randy Moss, Minnesota[3]	77	1,437	18.7	78	15
	Marvin Harrison, Indianapolis[2]	102	1,413	13.9	78	14
	Derrick Alexander, Kansas City[3]	78	1,391	17.8	81	10
	Joe Horn, New Orleans	94	1,340	14.3	52	8
	Eric Moulds, Buffalo[2]	94	1,326	14.1	52	5
	Ed McCaffrey, Denver[3]	101	1,317	13.0	61	9
	Cris Carter, Minnesota[8]	96	1,274	13.3	53	9
	Jimmy Smith, Jacksonville[5]	91	1,213	13.3	65	8
	Keenan McCardell, Jacksonville[3]	94	1,207	12.8	67	5
	Tony Gonzalez, Kansas City	93	1,203	12.9	39	9
	Muhsin Muhammad, Carolina[2]	102	1,183	11.6	36	6
	David Boston, Arizona	71	1,156	16.3	70	7
	Tim Brown, Oakland[8]	76	1,128	14.8	45	11
	Amani Toomer, N.Y. Giants[2]	78	1,094	14.0	54	7

Year	Player, Team	No.	Yards	Avg.	Long	TD
1999	Marvin Harrison, Indianapolis	115	1,663	14.5	57	12
	Jimmy Smith, Jacksonville[4]	116	1,636	14.1	62	6
	Randy Moss, Minnesota[2]	80	1,413	17.7	67	11
	Marcus Robinson, Chicago	84	1,400	16.7	80	9
	Tim Brown, Oakland[7]	90	1,344	14.9	47	6
	Germane Crowell, Detroit	81	1,338	16.5	77	7
	Muhsin Muhammad, Carolina	96	1,253	13.1	60	8
	Cris Carter, Minnesota[7]	90	1,241	13.8	68	13
	Michael Westbrook, Washington	65	1,191	18.3	65	9
	Amani Toomer, N.Y. Giants	79	1,183	15.0	80	6
	Keyshawn Johnson, N.Y. Jets[2]	89	1,170	13.2	65	8
	Isaac Bruce, St. Louis[3]	77	1,165	15.1	60	12
	Terry Glenn, New England[2]	69	1,147	16.6	67	4
	Albert Connell, Washington	62	1,132	18.3	62	7
	Johnnie Morton, Detroit[3]	80	1,129	14.1	48	5
	Qadry Ismail, Baltimore	68	1,105	16.3	76	6
	Raghib Ismail, Dallas[2]	80	1,097	13.7	76	6
	Patrick Jeffers, Carolina	63	1,082	17.2	88	12
	Antonio Freeman, Green Bay[3]	74	1,074	14.5	51	6
	Bill Schroeder, Green Bay	74	1,051	14.2	51	5
	Marshall Faulk, St. Louis	87	1,048	12.1	57	5
	Tony Martin, Miami[4]	67	1,037	15.5	69	5
	Darnay Scott, Cincinnati	68	1,022	15.0	76	7
	Rod Smith, Denver[3]	79	1,020	12.9	71	4
	Ed McCaffrey, Denver[2]	71	1,018	14.3	78	7
	Terance Mathis, Atlanta[4]	81	1,016	12.5	52	6
1998	Antonio Freeman, Green Bay[2]	84	1,424	17.0	84	14
	Eric Moulds, Buffalo	67	1,368	20.4	84	9
	*Randy Moss, Minnesota	69	1,313	19.0	61	17
	Rod Smith, Denver[2]	86	1,222	14.2	58	6
	Jimmy Smith, Jacksonville[3]	78	1,182	15.2	72	8
	Tony Martin, Atlanta[3]	66	1,181	17.9	62	6
	Jerry Rice, San Francisco[12]	82	1,157	14.1	75	9
	Frank Sanders, Arizona[2]	89	1,145	12.9	42	3
	Terance Mathis, Atlanta[3]	64	1,136	17.8	78	11
	Keyshawn Johnson, N.Y. Jets	83	1,131	13.6	41	10
	Terrell Owens, San Francisco	67	1,097	16.4	79	14
	Wayne Chrebet, N.Y. Jets	75	1,083	14.4	63	8
	Michael Irvin, Dallas[7]	74	1,057	14.3	51	1
	Ed McCaffrey, Denver	64	1,053	16.5	48	10
	O.J. McDuffie, Miami	90	1,050	11.7	61	7
	Joey Galloway, Seattle[3]	65	1,047	16.1	81	10
	Johnnie Morton, Detroit[2]	69	1,028	14.9	98	2
	Raghib Ismail, Carolina	69	1,024	14.8	62	8
	Carl Pickens, Cincinnati[4]	82	1,023	12.5	67	5
	Tim Brown, Oakland[6]	81	1,012	12.5	49	9
	Cris Carter, Minnesota[6]	78	1,011	13.0	54	12
1997	Rob Moore, Arizona[3]	97	1,584	16.3	47	8
	Tim Brown, Oakland[5]	104	1,408	13.5	59	5
	Yancey Thigpen, Pittsburgh[2]	79	1,398	17.7	69	7
	Jimmy Smith, Jacksonville[2]	82	1,324	16.1	75	4
	Irving Fryar, Philadelphia[5]	86	1,316	15.3	72	6
	Herman Moore, Detroit[4]	104	1,293	12.4	79	8
	Antonio Freeman, Green Bay	81	1,243	15.3	58	12
	Michael Irvin, Dallas[6]	75	1,180	15.7	55	9
	Rod Smith, Denver	70	1,180	16.9	78	12
	Keenan McCardell, Jacksonville[2]	85	1,164	13.7	60	5
	Jake Reed, Minnesota[4]	68	1,138	16.7	56	6
	Shannon Sharpe, Denver[3]	72	1,107	15.4	68	3
	Andre Rison, Kansas City[5]	72	1,092	15.2	45	7
	Cris Carter, Minnesota[5]	89	1,069	12.0	43	13
	Johnnie Morton, Detroit	80	1,057	13.2	73	6
	Joey Galloway, Seattle[2]	72	1,049	14.6	53	12
	Frank Sanders, Arizona	75	1,017	13.6	70	4
	Robert Brooks, Green Bay[2]	60	1,010	16.8	48	7
	Derrick Alexander, Baltimore[2]	65	1,009	15.5	92	9
1996	Isaac Bruce, St. Louis[2]	84	1,338	15.9	70	7
	Jake Reed, Minnesota[3]	72	1,320	18.3	82	7
	Herman Moore, Detroit[3]	106	1,296	12.2	50	9

Year	Player, Team	No.	Yards	Avg.	Long	TD
	Jerry Rice, San Francisco[11]	108	1,254	11.6	39	8
	Jimmy Smith, Jacksonville	83	1,244	15.0	62	7
	Michael Jackson, Baltimore	76	1,201	15.8	86	14
	Irving Fryar, Philadelphia[4]	88	1,195	13.6	42	11
	Carl Pickens, Cincinnati[3]	100	1,180	11.8	61	12
	Tony Martin, San Diego[2]	85	1,171	13.8	55	14
	Cris Carter, Minnesota[4]	96	1,163	12.1	43	10
	*Terry Glenn, New England	90	1,132	12.6	37	6
	Keenan McCardell, Jacksonville	85	1,129	13.3	52	3
	Tim Brown, Oakland[4]	90	1,104	12.3	42	9
	Derrick Alexander, Baltimore	62	1,099	17.7	64	9
	Shannon Sharpe, Denver[2]	80	1,062	13.3	51	10
	Curtis Conway, Chicago[2]	81	1,049	13.0	58	7
	Andre Reed, Buffalo[4]	66	1,036	15.7	67	6
	Brett Perriman, Detroit[2]	94	1,021	10.9	44	5
	Rob Moore, Arizona[2]	58	1,016	17.5	69	4
	Henry Ellard, Washington[7]	52	1,014	19.5	51	2
	Charles Johnson, Pittsburgh	60	1,008	16.8	70	3
1995	Jerry Rice, San Francisco[10]	122	1,848	15.1	81	15
	Isaac Bruce, St. Louis	119	1,781	15.0	72	13
	Herman Moore, Detroit[2]	123	1,686	13.7	69	14
	Michael Irvin, Dallas[5]	111	1,603	14.4	50	10
	Robert Brooks, Green Bay	102	1,497	14.7	99	13
	Brett Perriman, Detroit	108	1,488	13.8	91	9
	Cris Carter, Minnesota[3]	122	1,371	11.2	60	17
	Tim Brown, Oakland[3]	89	1,342	15.1	80	10
	Yancey Thigpen, Pittsburgh	85	1,307	15.4	43	5
	Jeff Graham, Chicago	82	1,301	15.9	51	4
	Carl Pickens, Cincinnati[2]	99	1,234	12.5	68	17
	Tony Martin, San Diego	90	1,224	13.6	51	6
	Eric Metcalf, Atlanta	104	1,189	11.4	62	8
	Jake Reed, Minnesota[2]	72	1,167	16.2	55	9
	Quinn Early, New Orleans	81	1,087	13.4	70	8
	Anthony Miller, Denver[5]	59	1,079	18.3	62	14
	Bert Emanuel, Atlanta	74	1,039	14.0	52	5
	*Joey Galloway, Seattle	67	1,039	15.5	59	7
	Terance Mathis, Atlanta[2]	78	1,039	13.3	54	9
	Curtis Conway, Chicago	62	1,037	16.7	76	12
	Henry Ellard, Washington[6]	56	1,005	17.9	59	5
	Mark Carrier, Carolina[2]	66	1,002	15.2	66	3
	Brian Blades, Seattle[4]	77	1,001	13.0	49	4
1994	Jerry Rice, San Francisco[9]	112	1,499	13.4	69	13
	Henry Ellard, Washington[5]	74	1,397	18.9	73	6
	Terance Mathis, Atlanta	111	1,342	12.1	81	11
	Tim Brown, L.A. Raiders[2]	89	1,309	14.7	77	9
	Andre Reed, Buffalo[2]	90	1,303	14.5	83	8
	Irving Fryar, Miami[3]	73	1,270	17.4	54	7
	Cris Carter, Minnesota[2]	122	1,256	10.3	65	7
	Michael Irvin, Dallas[4]	79	1,241	15.7	65	6
	Jake Reed, Minnesota	85	1,175	13.8	59	4
	Ben Coates, New England	96	1,174	12.2	62	7
	Herman Moore, Detroit	72	1,173	16.3	51	11
	Fred Barnett, Philadelphia[2]	78	1,127	14.4	54	5
	Carl Pickens, Cincinnati	71	1,127	15.9	70	11
	Sterling Sharpe, Green Bay[4]	94	1,119	11.9	49	18
	Anthony Miller, Denver[4]	60	1,107	18.5	76	5
	Andre Rison, Atlanta[3]	81	1,088	13.4	69	8
	Brian Blades, Seattle[3]	81	1,088	13.4	45	4
	Rob Moore, N.Y. Jets	78	1,010	12.9	41	6
	Shannon Sharpe, Denver	87	1,010	11.6	44	4
1993	Jerry Rice, San Francisco[8]	98	1,503	15.3	80	15
	Michael Irvin, Dallas[3]	88	1,330	15.1	61	7
	Sterling Sharpe, Green Bay[4]	112	1,274	11.4	54	11
	Andre Rison, Atlanta[3]	86	1,242	14.4	53	15
	Tim Brown, L.A. Raiders	80	1,180	14.8	71	7
	Anthony Miller, San Diego[3]	84	1,162	13.8	66	7
	Cris Carter, Minnesota	86	1,071	12.5	58	9
	Reggie Langhorne, Indianapolis	85	1,038	12.2	72	3
	Irving Fryar, Miami[2]	64	1,010	15.8	65	5

Year	Player, Team	No.	Yards	Avg.	Long	TD
1992	Sterling Sharpe, Green Bay[3]	108	1,461	13.5	76	13
	Michael Irvin, Dallas[2]	78	1,396	17.9	87	7
	Jerry Rice, San Francisco[7]	84	1,201	14.3	80	10
	Andre Rison, Atlanta[2]	93	1,119	12.0	71	11
	Fred Barnett, Philadelphia	67	1,083	16.2	71	6
	Anthony Miller, San Diego[2]	72	1,060	14.7	67	7
	Eric Martin, New Orleans[3]	68	1,041	15.3	52	5
1991	Michael Irvin, Dallas	93	1,523	16.4	66	8
	Gary Clark, Washington[5]	70	1,340	19.1	82	10
	Jerry Rice, San Francisco[6]	80	1,206	15.1	73	14
	Haywood Jeffires, Houston[2]	100	1,181	11.8	44	7
	Michael Haynes, Atlanta	50	1,122	22.4	80	11
	Andre Reed, Buffalo[2]	81	1,113	13.7	55	10
	Drew Hill, Houston[5]	90	1,109	12.3	61	4
	Mark Duper, Miami[4]	70	1,085	15.5	43	5
	James Lofton, Buffalo[6]	57	1,072	18.8	77	8
	Mark Clayton, Miami[5]	70	1,053	15.0	43	12
	Henry Ellard, L.A. Rams[4]	64	1,052	16.4	38	3
	Art Monk, Washington[5]	71	1,049	14.8	64	8
	Irving Fryar, New England	68	1,014	14.9	56	3
	John Taylor, San Francisco[2]	64	1,011	15.8	97	9
	Brian Blades, Seattle[2]	70	1,003	14.3	52	2
1990	Jerry Rice, San Francisco[5]	100	1,502	15.0	64	13
	Henry Ellard, L.A. Rams[3]	76	1,294	17.0	50	4
	Andre Rison, Atlanta	82	1,208	14.7	75	10
	Gary Clark, Washington[4]	75	1,112	14.8	53	8
	Sterling Sharpe, Green Bay[2]	67	1,105	16.5	76	6
	Flipper Anderson, L.A. Rams[2]	51	1,097	21.5	55	4
	Haywood Jeffires, Houston	74	1,048	14.2	87	8
	Stephone Paige, Kansas City	65	1,021	15.7	86	5
	Drew Hill, Houston[4]	74	1,019	13.8	57	5
	Anthony Carter, Minnesota[3]	70	1,008	14.4	56	8
1989	Jerry Rice, San Francisco[4]	82	1,483	18.1	68	17
	Sterling Sharpe, Green Bay	90	1,423	15.8	79	12
	Mark Carrier, Tampa Bay	86	1,422	16.5	78	9
	Henry Ellard, L.A. Rams[2]	70	1,382	19.7	53	8
	Andre Reed, Buffalo	88	1,312	14.9	78	9
	Anthony Miller, San Diego	75	1,252	16.7	69	10
	Webster Slaughter, Cleveland	65	1,236	19.0	97	6
	Gary Clark, Washington[3]	79	1,229	15.6	80	9
	Tim McGee, Cincinnati	65	1,211	18.6	74	8
	Art Monk, Washington[4]	86	1,186	13.8	60	8
	Flipper Anderson, L.A. Rams	44	1,146	26.0	78	5
	Ricky Sanders, Washington[2]	80	1,138	14.2	68	4
	Vance Johnson, Denver	76	1,095	14.4	69	7
	Richard Johnson, Detroit	70	1,091	15.6	75	8
	Eric Martin, New Orleans[2]	68	1,090	16.0	53	8
	John Taylor, San Francisco	60	1,077	18.0	95	10
	Mervyn Fernandez, L.A. Raiders	57	1,069	18.8	75	9
	Anthony Carter, Minnesota[2]	65	1,066	16.4	50	4
	Brian Blades, Seattle	77	1,063	13.8	60	5
	Mark Clayton, Miami[4]	64	1,011	15.8	78	9
1988	Henry Ellard, L.A. Rams	86	1,414	16.4	68	10
	Jerry Rice, San Francisco[3]	64	1,306	20.4	96	9
	Eddie Brown, Cincinnati	53	1,273	24.0	86	9
	Anthony Carter, Minnesota	72	1,225	17.0	67	6
	Ricky Sanders, Washington	73	1,148	15.7	55	12
	Drew Hill, Houston[3]	72	1,141	15.8	57	10
	Mark Clayton, Miami[3]	86	1,129	13.1	45	14
	Roy Green, Phoenix[3]	68	1,097	16.1	52	7
	Eric Martin, New Orleans	85	1,083	12.7	40	7
	Al Toon, N.Y. Jets[2]	93	1,067	11.5	42	5
	Bruce Hill, Tampa Bay	58	1,040	17.9	42	9
	Lionel Manuel, N.Y. Giants	65	1,029	15.8	46	4
1987	J.T. Smith, St. Louis[2]	91	1,117	12.3	38	8
	Jerry Rice, San Francisco[2]	65	1,078	16.6	57	22
	Gary Clark, Washington[2]	56	1,066	19.0	84	7
	Carlos Carson, Kansas City[3]	55	1,044	19.0	81	7

Year	Player, Team	No.	Yards	Avg.	Long	TD
1986	Jerry Rice, San Francisco	86	1,570	18.3	66	15
	Stanley Morgan, New England[3]	84	1,491	17.8	44	10
	Mark Duper, Miami[3]	67	1,313	19.6	85	11
	Gary Clark, Washington	74	1,265	17.1	55	7
	Al Toon, N.Y. Jets	85	1,176	13.8	62	8
	Todd Christensen, L.A. Raiders[3]	95	1,153	12.1	35	8
	Mark Clayton, Miami[2]	60	1,150	19.2	68	10
	*Bill Brooks, Indianapolis	65	1,131	17.4	84	8
	Drew Hill, Houston[2]	65	1,112	17.1	81	5
	Steve Largent, Seattle[8]	70	1,070	15.3	38	9
	Art Monk, Washington[3]	73	1,068	14.6	69	4
	*Ernest Givins, Houston	61	1,062	17.4	60	3
	Cris Collinsworth, Cincinnati[4]	62	1,024	16.5	46	10
	Wesley Walker, N.Y. Jets[2]	49	1,016	20.7	83	12
	J.T. Smith, St. Louis	80	1,014	12.7	45	6
	Mark Bavaro, N.Y. Giants	66	1,001	15.2	41	4
1985	Steve Largent, Seattle[7]	79	1,287	16.3	43	6
	Mike Quick, Philadelphia[3]	73	1,247	17.1	99	11
	Art Monk, Washington[2]	91	1,226	13.5	53	2
	Wes Chandler, San Diego[4]	67	1,199	17.9	75	10
	Drew Hill, Houston	64	1,169	18.3	57	9
	James Lofton, Green Bay[5]	69	1,153	16.7	56	4
	Louis Lipps, Pittsburgh	59	1,134	19.2	51	12
	Cris Collinsworth, Cincinnati[3]	65	1,125	17.3	71	5
	Tony Hill, Dallas[3]	74	1,113	15.0	53	7
	Lionel James, San Diego	86	1,027	11.9	67	6
	Roger Craig, San Francisco	92	1,016	11.0	73	6
1984	Roy Green, St. Louis[2]	78	1,555	19.9	83	12
	John Stallworth, Pittsburgh[3]	80	1,395	17.4	51	11
	Mark Clayton, Miami	73	1,389	19.0	65	18
	Art Monk, Washington	106	1,372	12.9	72	7
	James Lofton, Green Bay[4]	62	1,361	22.0	79	7
	Mark Duper, Miami[2]	71	1,306	18.4	80	8
	Steve Watson, Denver[3]	69	1,170	17.0	73	7
	Steve Largent, Seattle[6]	74	1,164	15.7	65	12
	Tim Smith, Houston[2]	69	1,141	16.5	75	4
	Stacey Bailey, Atlanta	67	1,138	17.0	61	6
	Carlos Carson, Kansas City[2]	57	1,078	18.9	57	4
	Mike Quick, Philadelphia[2]	61	1,052	17.2	90	9
	Todd Christensen, L.A. Raiders[2]	80	1,007	12.6	38	7
	Kevin House, Tampa Bay[2]	76	1,005	13.2	55	5
	Ozzie Newsome, Cleveland[2]	89	1,001	11.2	52	5
1983	Mike Quick, Philadelphia	69	1,409	20.4	83	13
	Carlos Carson, Kansas City	80	1,351	16.9	50	7
	James Lofton, Green Bay[3]	58	1,300	22.4	74	8
	Todd Christensen, L.A. Raiders	92	1,247	13.6	45	12
	Roy Green, St. Louis	78	1,227	15.7	71	14
	Charlie Brown, Washington	78	1,225	15.7	75	8
	Tim Smith, Houston	83	1,176	14.2	47	6
	Kellen Winslow, San Diego[3]	88	1,172	13.3	46	8
	Earnest Gray, N.Y. Giants	78	1,139	14.6	62	5
	Steve Watson, Denver[2]	59	1,133	19.2	78	5
	Cris Collinsworth, Cincinnati[2]	66	1,130	17.1	63	5
	Steve Largent, Seattle[5]	72	1,074	14.9	46	11
	Mark Duper, Miami	51	1,003	19.7	85	10
1982	Wes Chandler, San Diego[3]	49	1,032	21.1	66	9
1981	Alfred Jenkins, Atlanta[2]	70	1,358	19.4	67	13
	James Lofton, Green Bay[2]	71	1,294	18.2	75	8
	Steve Watson, Denver	60	1,244	20.7	95	13
	Frank Lewis, Buffalo[2]	70	1,244	17.8	33	4
	Steve Largent, Seattle[4]	75	1,224	16.3	57	9
	Charlie Joiner, San Diego[4]	70	1,188	17.0	57	7
	Kevin House, Tampa Bay	56	1,176	21.0	84	9
	Wes Chandler, New Orleans/San Diego[2]	69	1,142	16.6	51	6
	Dwight Clark, San Francisco	85	1,105	13.0	78	4
	John Stallworth, Pittsburgh[2]	63	1,098	17.4	55	5
	Kellen Winslow, San Diego[2]	88	1,075	12.2	67	10
	Pat Tilley, St. Louis	66	1,040	15.8	75	3

Year	Player, Team	No.	Yards	Avg.	Long	TD
	Stanley Morgan, New England[2]	44	1,029	23.4	76	6
	Harold Carmichael, Philadelphia[3]	61	1,028	16.9	85	6
	Freddie Scott, Detroit	53	1,022	19.3	48	5
	*Cris Collinsworth, Cincinnati	67	1,009	15.1	74	8
	Joe Senser, Minnesota	79	1,004	12.7	53	8
	Ozzie Newsome, Cleveland	69	1,002	14.5	62	6
	Sammy White, Minnesota	66	1,001	15.2	53	3
1980	John Jefferson, San Diego[3]	82	1,340	16.3	58	13
	Kellen Winslow, San Diego	89	1,290	14.5	65	9
	James Lofton, Green Bay	71	1,226	17.3	47	4
	Charlie Joiner, San Diego[3]	71	1,132	15.9	51	4
	Ahmad Rashad, Minnesota[2]	69	1,095	15.9	76	5
	Steve Largent, Seattle[3]	66	1,064	16.1	67	6
	Tony Hill, Dallas[2]	60	1,055	17.6	58	8
	Alfred Jenkins, Atlanta	57	1,026	18.0	57	6
1979	Steve Largent, Seattle[2]	66	1,237	18.7	55	9
	John Stallworth, Pittsburgh	70	1,183	16.9	65	8
	Ahmad Rashad, Minnesota	80	1,156	14.5	52	9
	John Jefferson, San Diego[2]	61	1,090	17.9	65	10
	Frank Lewis, Buffalo	54	1,082	20.0	55	2
	Wes Chandler, New Orleans	65	1,069	16.4	85	6
	Tony Hill, Dallas	60	1,062	17.7	75	10
	Drew Pearson, Dallas[2]	55	1,026	18.7	56	8
	Wallace Francis, Atlanta	74	1,013	13.7	42	8
	Harold Jackson, New England[3]	45	1,013	22.5	59	7
	Charlie Joiner, San Diego[2]	72	1,008	14.0	39	4
	Stanley Morgan, New England	44	1,002	22.8	63	12
1978	Wesley Walker, N.Y. Jets	48	1,169	24.4	77	8
	Steve Largent, Seattle	71	1,168	16.5	57	8
	Harold Carmichael, Philadelphia[2]	55	1,072	19.5	56	8
	*John Jefferson, San Diego	56	1,001	17.9	46	13
1976	Roger Carr, Baltimore	43	1,112	25.9	79	11
	Cliff Branch, Oakland[2]	46	1,111	24.2	88	12
	Charlie Joiner, San Diego	50	1,056	21.1	81	7
1975	Ken Burrough, Houston	53	1,063	20.1	77	8
1974	Cliff Branch, Oakland	60	1,092	18.2	67	13
	Drew Pearson, Dallas	62	1,087	17.5	50	2
1973	Harold Carmichael, Philadelphia	67	1,116	16.7	73	9
1972	Harold Jackson, Philadelphia[2]	62	1,048	16.9	77	4
	John Gilliam, Minnesota	47	1,035	22.0	66	7
1971	Otis Taylor, Kansas City[2]	57	1,110	19.5	82	7
1970	Gene Washington, San Francisco	53	1,100	20.8	79	12
	Marlin Briscoe, Buffalo	57	1,036	18.2	48	8
	Dick Gordon, Chicago	71	1,026	14.5	69	13
	Gary Garrison, San Diego[2]	44	1,006	22.9	67	12
1969	Warren Wells, Oakland[2]	47	1,260	26.8	80	14
	Harold Jackson, Philadelphia	65	1,116	17.2	65	9
	Roy Jefferson, Pittsburgh[2]	67	1,079	16.1	63	9
	Dan Abramowicz, New Orleans	73	1,015	13.9	49	7
	Lance Alworth, San Diego[7]	64	1,003	15.7	76	4
1968	Lance Alworth, San Diego[6]	68	1,312	19.3	80	10
	Don Maynard, N.Y. Jets[5]	57	1,297	22.8	87	10
	George Sauer, N.Y. Jets[3]	66	1,141	17.3	43	3
	Warren Wells, Oakland	53	1,137	21.5	94	11
	Gary Garrison, San Diego	52	1,103	21.2	84	10
	Roy Jefferson, Pittsburgh	58	1,074	18.5	62	11
	Paul Warfield, Cleveland	50	1,067	21.3	65	12
	Homer Jones, N.Y. Giants[3]	45	1,057	23.5	84	7
	Fred Biletnikoff, Oakland	61	1,037	17.0	82	6
	Lance Rentzel, Dallas	54	1,009	18.7	65	6
1967	Don Maynard, N.Y. Jets[4]	71	1,434	20.2	75	10
	Ben Hawkins, Philadelphia	59	1,265	21.4	87	10
	Homer Jones, N.Y. Giants[2]	49	1,209	24.7	70	13
	Jackie Smith, St. Louis	56	1,205	21.5	76	9
	George Sauer, N.Y. Jets[2]	75	1,189	15.9	61	6
	Lance Alworth, San Diego[5]	52	1,010	19.4	71	9
1966	Lance Alworth, San Diego[4]	73	1,383	18.9	78	13
	Otis Taylor, Kansas City	58	1,297	22.4	89	8

Year	Player, Team	No.	Yards	Avg.	Long	TD
	Pat Studstill, Detroit	67	1,266	18.9	99	5
	Bob Hayes, Dallas[2]	64	1,232	19.3	95	13
	Charlie Frazier, Houston	57	1,129	19.8	79	12
	Charley Taylor, Washington	72	1,119	15.5	86	12
	George Sauer, N.Y. Jets	63	1,081	17.2	77	5
	Homer Jones, N.Y. Giants	48	1,044	21.8	98	8
	Art Powell, Oakland[5]	53	1,026	19.4	46	11
1965	Lance Alworth, San Diego[3]	69	1,602	23.2	85	14
	Dave Parks, San Francisco	80	1,344	16.8	53	12
	Don Maynard, N.Y. Jets[3]	68	1,218	17.9	56	14
	Pete Retzlaff, Philadelphia	66	1,190	18.0	78	10
	Lionel Taylor, Denver[4]	85	1,131	13.3	63	6
	Tommy McDonald, Los Angeles[3]	67	1,036	15.5	51	9
	*Bob Hayes, Dallas	46	1,003	21.8	82	12
1964	Charley Hennigan, Houston[3]	101	1,546	15.3	53	8
	Art Powell, Oakland[4]	76	1,361	17.9	77	11
	Lance Alworth, San Diego[2]	61	1,235	20.2	82	13
	Johnny Morris, Chicago	93	1,200	12.9	63	10
	Elbert Dubenion, Buffalo	42	1,139	27.1	72	10
	Terry Barr, Detroit[2]	57	1,030	18.1	58	9
1963	Bobby Mitchell, Washington[2]	69	1,436	20.8	99	7
	Art Powell, Oakland[3]	73	1,304	17.9	85	16
	Buddy Dial, Pittsburgh[2]	60	1,295	21.6	83	9
	Lance Alworth, San Diego	61	1,205	19.8	85	11
	Del Shofner, N.Y. Giants[4]	64	1,181	18.5	70	9
	Lionel Taylor, Denver[3]	78	1,101	14.1	72	10
	Terry Barr, Detroit	66	1,086	16.5	75	13
	Charley Hennigan, Houston[2]	61	1,051	17.2	83	10
	Sonny Randle, St. Louis[2]	51	1,014	19.9	68	12
	Bake Turner, N.Y. Jets	71	1,009	14.2	53	6
1962	Bobby Mitchell, Washington	72	1,384	19.2	81	11
	Sonny Randle, St. Louis	63	1,158	18.4	86	7
	Tommy McDonald, Philadelphia[2]	58	1,146	19.8	60	10
	Del Shofner, N.Y. Giants[3]	53	1,133	21.4	69	12
	Art Powell, N.Y. Titans[2]	64	1,130	17.7	80	8
	Frank Clarke, Dall. Cowboys	47	1,043	22.2	66	14
	Don Maynard, N.Y. Titans[2]	56	1,041	18.6	86	8
1961	Charley Hennigan, Houston	82	1,746	21.3	80	12
	Lionel Taylor, Denver[2]	100	1,176	11.8	52	4
	Bill Groman, Houston[2]	50	1,175	23.5	80	17
	Tommy McDonald, Philadelphia	64	1,144	17.9	66	13
	Del Shofner, N.Y. Giants[2]	68	1,125	16.5	46	11
	Jim Phillips, Los Angeles	78	1,092	14.0	69	5
	*Mike Ditka, Chicago	56	1,076	19.2	76	12
	Dave Kocourek, San Diego	55	1,055	19.2	76	4
	Buddy Dial, Pittsburgh	53	1,047	19.8	88	12
	R.C. Owens, San Francisco	55	1,032	18.8	54	5
1960	*Bill Groman, Houston	72	1,473	20.5	92	12
	Raymond Berry, Baltimore	74	1,298	17.5	70	10
	Don Maynard, N.Y. Titans	72	1,265	17.6	65	6
	Lionel Taylor, Denver	92	1,235	13.4	80	12
	Art Powell, N.Y. Titans	69	1,167	16.9	76	14
1958	Del Shofner, Los Angeles	51	1,097	21.5	92	8
1956	Bill Howton, Green Bay[2]	55	1,188	21.6	66	12
	Harlon Hill, Chi. Bears[3]	47	1,128	24.0	79	11
1954	Bob Boyd, Los Angeles	53	1,212	22.9	80	6
	*Harlon Hill, Chi. Bears	45	1,124	25.0	76	12
1953	Pete Pihos, Philadelphia	63	1,049	16.7	59	10
1952	*Bill Howton, Green Bay	53	1,231	23.2	90	13
1951	Elroy (Crazylegs) Hirsch, Los Angeles	66	1,495	22.7	91	17
1950	Tom Fears, Los Angeles[2]	84	1,116	13.3	53	7
	Cloyce Box, Detroit	50	1,009	20.2	82	11
1949	Bob Mann, Detroit	66	1,014	15.4	64	4
	Tom Fears, Los Angeles	77	1,013	13.2	51	9
1945	Jim Benton, Cleveland	45	1,067	23.7	84	8
1942	Don Hutson, Green Bay	74	1,211	16.4	73	17

*First season of professional football.

250 YARDS PASS RECEIVING IN A GAME

Date	Player, Team, Opponent	No.	Yards	TD
Nov. 18, 2012	Andre Johnson, Houston vs. Jacksonville (OT)	14	273	1
Sept. 30, 2012	Brian Hartline, Miami vs. Arizona (OT)	12	253	1
Oct. 11, 2009	Miles Austin, Dallas vs. Kansas City (OT)	10	250	2
Nov. 19, 2006	Lee Evans, Buffalo vs. Houston	11	265	2
Nov. 12, 2006	Chad Johnson, Cincinnati vs. San Diego	11	260	2
Nov. 10, 2002	Plaxico Burress, Pittsburgh vs. Atlanta (OT)	9	253	2
Dec. 17, 2000	Terrell Owens, San Francisco vs. Chicago	20	283	1
Sept. 10, 2000	Jimmy Smith, Jacksonville vs. Baltimore	15	291	3
Dec. 12, 1999	Qadry Ismail, Baltimore vs. Pittsburgh	6	258	3
Dec. 18, 1995	Jerry Rice, San Francisco vs. Minnesota	14	289	3
Dec. 11, 1989	John Taylor, San Francisco vs. L.A. Rams	11	286	2
Nov. 26, 1989	Flipper Anderson, L.A. Rams vs. New Orleans (OT)	15	336	1
Oct. 18, 1987	Steve Largent, Seattle vs. Detroit	15	261	3
Oct. 4, 1987	Anthony Allen, Washington vs. St. Louis	7	255	3
Dec. 22, 1985	Stephone Paige, Kansas City vs. San Diego	8	309	2
Dec. 20, 1982	Wes Chandler, San Diego vs. Cincinnati	10	260	2
Sept. 23, 1979	*Jerry Butler, Buffalo vs. N.Y. Jets	10	255	4
Nov. 4, 1962	Sonny Randle, St. Louis vs. N.Y. Giants	16	256	1
Oct. 28, 1962	Del Shofner, N.Y. Giants vs. Washington	11	269	1
Oct. 13, 1961	Charley Hennigan, Houston vs. Boston	13	272	1
Oct. 21, 1956	Billy Howton, Green Bay vs. Los Angeles	7	257	2
Dec. 3, 1950	Cloyce Box, Detroit vs. Baltimore	12	302	4
Nov. 22, 1945	Jim Benton, Cleveland vs. Detroit	10	303	1

*First season of professional football.

2,000 COMBINED NET YARDS GAINED IN A SEASON

Year	Player, Team	Rushing Att.-Yds.	Pass Rec.	Punt Ret.	Kickoff Ret.	Fum. Ret.	Total Yds.
2012	Randall Cobb, Green Bay	10-132	80-954	31-292	38-964	3-0	162-2,342
	Adrian Peterson, Minnesota[2]	348-2,097	40-217	0-0	0-0	0-0	388-2,314
2011	Darren Sproles, New Orleans[4]	87-603	86-710	29-294	40-1,089	0-0	242-2,696
	Antonio Brown, Pittsburgh	7-41	69-1,108	30-325	27-737	0-0	133-2,211
	Ray Rice, Baltimore[2]	291-1,364	76-704	0-0	0-0	0-0	367-2,068
2010	Danny Amendola, St. Louis[2]	7-81	85-689	40-452	50-1,142	0-0	182-2,364
	Arian Foster, Houston	327-1,616	66-604	0-0	0-0	1-0	394-2,221
	Darren Sproles, San Diego[3]	50-267	59-520	24-166	51-1,257	0-0	184-2,210
2009	Fred Jackson, Buffalo	237-1,062	46-371	6-69	41-1,014	0-0	330-2,516
	Josh Cribbs, Cleveland[2]	55-381	20-135	38-452	56-1,542	2-0	171-2,510
	Chris Johnson, Tennessee	358-2,006	50-503	0-0	0-0	1-0	409-2,509
	Jamaal Charles, Kansas City	190-1,120	40-297	0-0	36-925	3-0	269-2,342
	Darren Sproles, San Diego[2]	93-343	45-497	26-183	54-1,300	1-0	219-2,323
	Danny Amendola, St. Louis	3-2	43-326	31-360	66-1,618	1-0	144-2,302
	*Percy Harvin, Minnesota	15-135	60-790	0-0	42-1,156	0-0	117-2,081
	Ray Rice, Baltimore	254-1,339	78-702	0-0	0-0	1-2	333-2,043
2008	Leon Washington, N.Y. Jets[2]	76-448	47-355	29-303	48-1,231	4-(-5)	204-2,332
	Darren Sproles, San Diego	61-330	29-342	22-249	53-1,376	1-(-2)	166-2,295
	Jerious Norwood, Atlanta[2]	95-489	36-338	0-0	51-1,311	0-0	182-2,138
2007	Josh Cribbs, Cleveland	9-61	3-37	30-405	59-1,809	2-0	103-2,312
	Jerious Norwood, Atlanta	103-613	28-277	0-0	52-1,317	0-0	183-2,207
	Brian Westbrook, Philadelphia	278-1,333	90-771	4-79	0-0	0-0	372-2,183
	*Ted Ginn Jr., Miami	4-3	34-420	24-230	63-1,433	2-(-9)	127-2,077
	Leon Washington, N.Y. Jets	71-353	36-213	20-183	47-1,291	1-0	175-2,040
	*Adrian Peterson, Minnesota	238-1,341	19-268	0-0	16-412	3-0	276-2,014
	Maurice Jones-Drew, Jacksonville[2]	167-768	40-407	3-28	31-811	0-0	241-2,014
2006	Steven Jackson, St. Louis	346-1,528	90-806	0-0	0-0	2-0	438-2,334
	LaDainian Tomlinson, San Diego[3]	348-1,815	56-508	0-0	0-0	1-0	405-2,323
	*Maurice Jones-Drew, Jacksonville	166-941	46-436	1-13	31-860	0-0	244-2,250
	Larry Johnson, Kansas City[2]	416-1,789	41-410	0-0	0-0	1-0	458-2,199
	Frank Gore, San Francisco	312-1,695	61-485	0-0	0-0	0-0	373-2,180
	Wes Welker, Miami[2]	0-0	67-687	41-378	48-1,064	1-0	157-2,129
	Tiki Barber, N.Y. Giants[4]	327-1,662	58-465	0-0	0-0	1-0	386-2,127
	Chris Carr, Oakland	0-0	0-0	35-216	69-1,762	1-0	106-2,078
2005	Tiki Barber, N.Y. Giants[3]	357-1,860	54-530	0-0	0-0	1-0	412-2,390
	Dante Hall, Kansas City[4]	7-11	34-436	42-276	65-1,560	2-0	150-2,283
	Wes Welker, Miami	1-5	29-434	43-390	61-1,379	4-0	138-2,208
	Larry Johnson, Kansas City	336-1,750	33-343	0-0	0-0	3-0	372-2,093
2004	Dante Hall, Kansas City[3]	8-56	25-230	23-232	68-1,718	0-0	124-2,236
	Tiki Barber, N.Y. Giants[2]	322-1,518	52-578	0-0	0-0	2-0	376-2,096

Year	Player, Team	Rushing Att.-Yds.	Pass Rec.	Punt Ret.	Kickoff Ret.	Fum. Ret.	Total Yds.
	Edgerrin James, Indianapolis[3]	334-1,548	51-483	0-0	0-0	1-0	386-2,031
2003	Dante Hall, Kansas City[2]	16-73	40-423	29-472	57-1,478	0-0	142-2,446
	LaDainian Tomlinson, San Diego[2]	313-1,645	100-725	0-0	0-0	2-0	415-2,370
	Jamal Lewis, Baltimore	387-2,066	26-205	0-0	0-0	1-0	414-2,271
	Ahman Green, Green Bay	355-1,883	50-367	0-0	0-0	2-0	407-2,250
	Deuce McAllister, New Orleans	351-1,641	69-516	0-0	0-0	3-(-3)	423-2,154
	Priest Holmes, Kansas City[3]	320-1,420	74-690	0-0	0-0	0-0	394-2,110
2002	Michael Lewis, New Orleans	1-15	8-200	44-625	70-1,807	2-0	125-2,647
	Priest Holmes, Kansas City[2]	313-1,615	70-672	0-0	0-0	0-0	383-2,287
	Ricky Williams, Miami	383-1,853	47-363	0-0	0-0	1-0	431-2,216
	LaDainian Tomlinson, San Diego	372-1,683	79-489	0-0	0-0	0-0	451-2,172
	Dante Hall, Kansas City	11-54	20-322	29-390	57-1,354	1-0	118-2,120
2001	Priest Holmes, Kansas City	327-1,555	62-614	0-0	0-0	0-0	389-2,169
	Marshall Faulk, St. Louis[4]	260-1,382	83-765	0-0	0-0	2-0	345-2,147
	Derrick Mason, Tennessee[2]	0-0	73-1,128	20-128	34-748	1-0	128-2,004
2000	Derrick Mason, Tennessee	1-1	63-895	51-662	42-1,132	1-0	158-2,690
	MarTay Jenkins, Arizona	1-(-4)	17-219	1-1	82-2,186	0-0	101-2,402
	Edgerrin James, Indianapolis[2]	387-1,709	63-594	0-0	0-0	0-0	450-2,303
	Marshall Faulk, St. Louis[3]	253-1,359	81-830	0-0	1-18	2-0	337-2,207
	Tiki Barber, N.Y. Giants	213-1,006	70-719	39-332	1-28	5-0	328-2,085
1999	Marshall Faulk, St. Louis[2]	253-1,381	87-1,048	0-0	0-0	0-0	340-2,429
	*Edgerrin James, Indianapolis	369-1,553	62-586	0-0	0-0	2-0	433-2,139
	*Terrence Wilkins, Indianapolis	1-2	42-565	41-388	51-1,134	1-0	136-2,089
	Glyn Milburn, Chicago[2]	16-102	20-151	30-346	61-1,426	2-0	129-2,025
1998	Brian Mitchell, Washington[4]	39-208	44-306	44-506	59-1,337	0-0	186-2,357
	Marshall Faulk, Indianapolis	324-1,319	86-908	0-0	0-0	2-13	412-2,240
	Terrell Davis, Denver[2]	392-2,008	25-217	0-0	0-0	1-0	418-2,225
	Jamal Anderson, Atlanta	410-1,846	27-319	0-0	0-0	1-0	438-2,165
	Garrison Hearst, San Francisco	310-1,570	39-535	0-0	0-0	1-0	350-2,105
1997	Barry Sanders, Detroit[2]	335-2,053	33-305	0-0	0-0	1-0	369-2,358
	Kevin Williams, Arizona	1-(-2)	20-273	40-462	59-1,458	1-0	121-2,191
	Brian Mitchell, Washington[3]	23-107	36-438	38-442	47-1,094	0-0	144-2,081
	Terrell Davis, Denver	369-1,750	42-287	0-0	0-0	2-(-7)	413-2,030
	Jermaine Lewis, Baltimore	3-35	42-648	28-437	41-905	2-0	116-2,025
1995	Brian Mitchell, Washington[2]	46-301	38-324	25-315	55-1,408	1-0	164-2,348
	Emmitt Smith, Dallas[2]	377-1,773	62-375	0-0	0-0	0-0	439-2,148
	Glyn Milburn, Denver	49-266	22-191	31-354	47-1,269	0-0	149-2,080
	Ernie Mills, Pittsburgh	5-39	39-679	0-0	54-1,306	0-0	98-2,024
1994	Brian Mitchell, Washington	78-311	26-236	32-452	58-1,478	0-0	194-2,477
	Barry Sanders, Detroit	331-1,883	44-283	0-0	0-0	0-0	375-2,166
1992	Thurman Thomas, Buffalo[2]	312-1,487	58-626	0-0	0-0	1-0	371-2,113
	Emmitt Smith, Dallas	373-1,713	59-335	0-0	0-0	1-0	433-2,048
	Barry Foster, Pittsburgh	390-1,690	36-344	0-0	0-0	2-(-20)	428-2,014
1991	Thurman Thomas, Buffalo	288-1,407	62-631	0-0	0-0	0-0	350-2,038
1990	Herschel Walker, Minnesota[2]	184-770	35-315	0-0	44-966	4-0	267-2,051
1988	*Tim Brown, L.A. Raiders	14-50	43-725	49-444	41-1,098	7-0	154-2,317
	Roger Craig, San Francisco[2]	310-1,502	76-534	0-0	2-32	2-0	390-2,068
	Eric Dickerson, Indianapolis[4]	388-1,659	36-377	0-0	0-0	1-0	425-2,036
	Herschel Walker, Dallas	361-1,514	53-505	0-0	0-0	3-0	417-2,019
1986	Eric Dickerson, L.A. Rams[3]	404-1,821	26-205	0-0	0-0	2-0	432-2,026
	Gary Anderson, San Diego	127-442	80-871	25-227	24-482	2-0	258-2,022
1985	Lionel James, San Diego	105-516	86-1,027	25-213	36-779	1-0	253-2,535
	Marcus Allen, L.A. Raiders	380-1,759	67-555	0-0	0-0	2-(-6)	449-2,308
	Roger Craig, San Francisco	214-1,050	92-1,016	0-0	0-0	1-0	306-2,066
	Walter Payton, Chicago[4]	324-1,551	49-483	0-0	0-0	1-0	374-2,034
1984	Eric Dickerson, L.A. Rams[2]	379-2,105	21-139	0-0	0-0	4-15	404-2,259
	James Wilder, Tampa Bay	407-1,544	85-685	0-0	0-0	4-0	496-2,229
	Walter Payton, Chicago[3]	381-1,684	45-368	0-0	0-0	1-0	427-2,052
1983	*Eric Dickerson, L.A. Rams	390-1,808	51-404	0-0	0-0	1-0	442-2,212
	William Andrews, Atlanta[2]	331-1,567	59-609	0-0	0-0	2-0	392-2,176
	Walter Payton, Chicago[2]	314-1,421	53-607	0-0	0-0	2-0	369-2,028
1981	*James Brooks, San Diego	109-525	46-329	22-290	40-949	2-0	219-2,093
	William Andrews, Atlanta	289-1,301	81-735	0-0	0-0	0-0	370-2,036
1980	Bruce Harper, N.Y. Jets[2]	45-126	50-634	28-242	49-1,070	3-0	175-2,072
1979	Wilbert Montgomery, Philadelphia	338-1,512	41-494	0-0	1-6	2-0	382-2,012
1978	Bruce Harper, N.Y. Jets	58-303	13-196	30-378	55-1,280	1-0	157-2,157
1977	Walter Payton, Chicago	339-1,852	27-269	0-0	2-95	5-0	373-2,216
	Terry Metcalf, St. Louis[3]	149-739	34-403	14-108	32-772	1-0	230-2,022

Year	Player, Team	Rushing Att.-Yds.	Pass Rec.	Punt Ret.	Kickoff Ret.	Fum. Ret.	Total Yds.
1975	Terry Metcalf, St. Louis[2]	165-816	43-378	23-285	35-960	2-23	268-2,462
	O.J. Simpson, Buffalo[2]	329-1,817	28-426	0-0	0-0	1-0	358-2,243
1974	Mack Herron, New England	231-824	38-474	35-517	28-629	3-0	335-2,444
	Otis Armstrong, Denver	263-1,407	38-405	0-0	16-386	1-0	318-2,198
	Terry Metcalf, St. Louis	152-718	50-377	26-340	20-623	7-0	255-2,058
1973	O.J. Simpson, Buffalo	332-2,003	6-70	0-0	0-0	0-0	338-2,073
1966	Gale Sayers, Chicago[2]	229-1,231	34-447	6-44	23-718	3-0	295-2,440
	Leroy Kelly, Cleveland	209-1,141	32-366	13-104	19-403	0-0	273-2,014
1965	*Gale Sayers, Chicago	166-867	29-507	16-238	21-660	4-0	236-2,272
1963	Timmy Brown, Philadelphia[2]	192-841	36-487	16-152	33-945	2-3	279-2,428
	Jim Brown, Cleveland	291-1,863	24-268	0-0	0-0	0-0	315-2,131
1962	Timmy Brown, Philadelphia	137-545	52-849	6-81	30-831	4-0	229-2,306
	Dick Christy, N.Y. Titans	114-535	62-538	15-250	38-824	2-0	231-2,147
1961	Billy Cannon, Houston	200-948	43-586	9-70	18-439	2-0	272-2,043
1960	*Abner Haynes, Dallas Texans	156-875	55-576	14-215	19-434	4-0	248-2,100

*First season of professional football.

300 COMBINED NET YARDS GAINED IN A GAME

Date	Player, Team, Opponent	No.	Yards	TD
Dec. 9, 2012	*David Wilson, N.Y. Giants vs. New Orleans	17	327	3
Nov. 28, 2010	*Jacoby Ford, Oakland vs. Miami	12	329	2
Nov. 7, 2010	*Jacoby Ford, Oakland vs. Kansas City (OT)	10	306	1
Dec. 20, 2009	Josh Cribbs, Cleveland vs. Kansas City	14	316	2
Oct. 18, 2009	Domenik Hixon, N.Y. Giants vs. New Orleans	12	303	0
Sept. 28, 2008	Steve Breaston, Arizona vs. N.Y. Jets	19	324	0
Sept. 14, 2008	Darren Sproles, San Diego vs. Denver	14	317	2
Nov. 18, 2007	Josh Cribbs, Cleveland vs. Baltimore (OT)	12	309	0
Nov. 4, 2007	*Adrian Peterson, Minnesota vs. San Diego	31	315	3
Oct. 14, 2007	*Adrian Peterson, Minnesota vs. Chicago	25	361	3
Sept. 30, 2007	Devin Hester, Chicago vs. Detroit	13	317	1
Dec. 10, 2006	*Maurice Jones-Drew, Jacksonville vs. Indianapolis	19	303	3
Dec. 14, 2003	Derrick Mason, Tennessee vs. Buffalo	21	302	0
Nov. 16, 2003	Jonathan Carter, N.Y. Jets vs. Indianapolis	7	304	2
Dec. 8, 2002	Steve Smith, Carolina vs. Cincinnati	9	313	3
Nov. 24, 2002	Priest Holmes, Kansas City vs. Seattle	30	307	3
Oct. 13, 2002	Michael Lewis, New Orleans vs. Washington	8	356	2
Dec. 24, 1999	Jason Tucker, Dallas vs. New Orleans	13	331	1
Dec. 7, 1997	Jermaine Lewis, Baltimore vs. Seattle	10	308	3
Dec. 25, 1995	Kevin Williams, Dallas vs. Arizona	16	307	2
Dec. 10, 1995	Glyn Milburn, Denver vs. Seattle	33	404	0
Oct. 23, 1994	Tyrone Hughes, New Orleans vs. L.A. Rams	11	347	2
Dec. 11, 1989	John Taylor, San Francisco vs. L.A. Rams	14	321	2
Nov. 26, 1989	Flipper Anderson, L.A. Rams vs. New Orleans (OT)	15	336	1
Nov. 28, 1988	*Tim Brown, L.A. Raiders vs. Seattle	12	306	1
Dec. 22, 1985	Stephone Paige, Kansas City vs. San Diego	8	309	2
Nov. 10, 1985	Lionel James, San Diego vs. L.A. Raiders (OT)	23	345	0
Sept. 22, 1985	Lionel James, San Diego vs. Cincinnati	20	316	2
Dec. 21, 1975	*Walter Payton, Chicago vs. New Orleans	32	300	1
Nov. 23, 1975	Greg Pruitt, Cleveland vs. Cincinnati	28	304	2
Nov. 1, 1970	Eugene (Mercury) Morris, Miami vs. Baltimore	17	302	0
Oct. 4, 1970	O.J. Simpson, Buffalo vs. N.Y. Jets	26	303	2
Dec. 6, 1969	Jerry LeVias, Houston vs. N.Y. Jets	18	329	1
Nov. 2, 1969	Travis Williams, Green Bay vs. Pittsburgh	11	314	3
Dec. 18, 1966	Gale Sayers, Chicago vs. Minnesota	20	339	2
Dec. 12, 1965	*Gale Sayers, Chicago vs. San Francisco	17	336	6
Nov. 17, 1963	Gary Ballman, Pittsburgh vs. Washington	12	320	2
Dec. 16, 1962	Timmy Brown, Philadelphia vs. St. Louis	19	341	2
Dec. 10, 1961	Billy Cannon, Houston vs. N.Y. Titans	32	373	5
Nov. 19, 1961	Jim Brown, Cleveland vs. Philadelphia	38	313	4
Dec. 3, 1950	Cloyce Box, Detroit vs. Baltimore	13	302	4
Oct. 29, 1950	Wally Triplett, Detroit vs. Los Angeles	11	331	1
Nov. 22, 1945	Jim Benton, Cleveland vs. Detroit	10	303	1

*First season of professional football.

2,000 SCRIMMAGE YARDS GAINED IN A SEASON

Year	Player, Team	Att.	Rushing Yards	Receptions	Receiving Yards	Scrimm. Yards
2012	Adrian Peterson, Minnesota	348	2,097	40	217	2,314
2011	Ray Rice, Baltimore[2]	291	1,364	76	704	2,068
2010	Arian Foster, Houston	327	1,616	66	604	2,220

Year	Player, Team	Att.				
2009	Chris Johnson, Tennessee	358	2,006	50	503	2,509
	Ray Rice, Baltimore	254	1,339	78	702	2,041
2007	Brian Westbrook, Philadelphia	278	1,333	90	771	2,104
2006	Steven Jackson, St. Louis	346	1,528	90	806	2,334
	LaDainian Tomlinson, San Diego[3]	348	1,815	56	508	2,323
	Larry Johnson, Kansas City[2]	416	1,789	41	410	2,199
	Frank Gore, San Francisco	312	1,695	61	485	2,180
	Tiki Barber, N.Y. Giants[3]	327	1,662	58	465	2,127[3]
2005	Tiki Barber, N.Y. Giants[2]	357	1,860	54	530	2,390
	Larry Johnson, Kansas City	336	1,750	33	343	2,093
2004	Tiki Barber, N.Y. Giants	322	1,518	52	578	2,096
	Edgerrin James, Indianapolis[3]	334	1,548	51	483	2,031
2003	LaDainian Tomlinson, San Diego[2]	313	1,645	100	725	2,370
	Jamal Lewis, Baltimore	387	2,066	26	205	2,271
	Ahman Green, Green Bay	355	1,883	50	367	2,250
	Deuce McAllister, New Orleans	351	1,641	69	516	2,157
	Priest Holmes, Kansas City[3]	320	1,420	74	690	2,110
2002	Priest Holmes, Kansas City[2]	313	1,615	70	672	2,287
	Ricky Williams, Miami	383	1,853	47	363	2,216
	LaDainian Tomlinson, San Diego	372	1,683	79	489	2,172
2001	Priest Holmes, Kansas City	327	1,555	62	614	2,169
	Marshall Faulk, St. Louis[4]	260	1,382	83	765	2,147
2000	Edgerrin James, Indianapolis[2]	387	1,709	63	594	2,303
	Marshall Faulk, St. Louis[3]	253	1,359	81	830	2,189
1999	Marshall Faulk, St. Louis[2]	253	1,381	87	1,048	2,429
	*Edgerrin James, Indianapolis	369	1,553	62	586	2,139
1998	Marshall Faulk, Indianapolis	324	1,319	86	908	2,227
	Terrell Davis, Denver[2]	392	2,008	25	217	2,225
	Jamal Anderson, Atlanta	410	1,846	27	319	2,165
	Garrison Hearst, San Francisco	310	1,570	39	535	2,105
1997	Barry Sanders, Detroit[2]	335	2,053	33	305	2,358
	Terrell Davis, Denver	369	1,750	42	287	2,037
1995	Emmitt Smith, Dallas[2]	377	1,773	62	375	2,148
1994	Barry Sanders, Detroit	331	1,883	44	283	2,166
1992	Thurman Thomas, Buffalo[2]	312	1,487	58	626	2,113
	Emmitt Smith, Dallas	373	1,713	59	335	2,048
	Barry Foster, Pittsburgh	390	1,690	36	344	2,034
1991	Thurman Thomas, Buffalo	288	1,407	62	631	2,038
1988	Roger Craig, San Francisco[2]	310	1,502	76	534	2,036
	Eric Dickerson, Indianapolis[4]	388	1,659	36	377	2,036
	Herschel Walker, Dallas	361	1,514	53	505	2,019
1986	Eric Dickerson, L.A. Rams[3]	404	1,821	26	205	2,026
1985	Marcus Allen, L.A. Raiders	380	1,759	67	555	2,314
	Roger Craig, San Francisco	214	1,050	92	1,016	2,066
	Walter Payton, Chicago[4]	324	1,551	49	483	2,034
1984	Eric Dickerson, L. A. Rams[2]	379	2,105	21	139	2,244
	James Wilder, Tampa Bay	407	1,544	85	685	2,229
	Walter Payton, Chicago[3]	381	1,684	45	368	2,052[3]
1983	*Eric Dickerson, L.A. Rams	390	1,808	51	404	2,212
	William Andrews, Atlanta[2]	331	1,567	59	609	2,176
	Walter Payton, Chicago[2]	314	1,421	53	607	2,028
1981	William Andrews, Atlanta	289	1,301	81	735	2,036
1979	Wilbert Montgomery, Philadelphia	338	1,512	41	494	2,006
1977	Walter Payton, Chicago	339	1,852	27	269	2,121
1975	O.J. Simpson, Buffalo[2]	329	1,817	28	426	2,243
1973	O.J. Simpson, Buffalo	332	2,003	6	70	2,073
1963	Jim Brown, Cleveland	291	1,863	24	268	2,131

*First season of professional football.

300 SCRIMMAGE YARDS GAINED IN A GAME

Date	Player, Team, Opponent	Att.	Yards	TD
Nov. 4, 2007	*Adrian Peterson, Minnesota vs. San Diego	31	315	3
Nov. 24, 2002	Priest Holmes, Kansas City vs. Seattle	30	307	3
Nov. 26, 1989	Flipper Anderson, L.A. Rams vs. New Orleans (OT)	15	336	1
Dec. 22, 1985	Stephone Paige, Kansas City vs. San Diego	8	309	2
Dec. 10, 1961	Billy Cannon, Houston vs. N.Y. Titans	30	330	5
Dec. 3, 1950	Cloyce Box, Detroit vs. Baltimore	12	302	4
Nov. 22, 1945	Jim Benton, Cleveland vs. Detroit	10	303	1

*First season of professional football.

TOP 20 SCORERS

Player	Years	TD	FG	PAT	TP
1. Morten Andersen	25	0	565	849	2,544
2. Gary Anderson	23	0	538	820	2,434
3. Jason Hanson	21	0	495	665	2,150
4. John Carney	23	0	478	628	2,062
5. Matt Stover	19	0	471	591	2,004
6. George Blanda	26	9	335	943	2,002
7. Jason Elam	17	0	436	675	1,983
8. John Kasay	20	0	461	587	1,970
9. Adam Vinatieri	17	0	413	626	1,867
10. Norm Johnson	18	0	366	638	1,736
11. Nick Lowery	18	0	383	562	1,711
12. Jan Stenerud	19	0	373	580	1,699
13. Ryan Longwell	15	0	361	604	1,687
14. David Akers	15	0	367	521	1,622
15. Olindo Mare	16	0	356	487	1,555
16. Eddie Murray	19	0	352	538	1,594
17. Al Del Greco	17	0	347	543	1,584
18. Steve Christie	15	0	336	468	1,476
19. Pat Leahy	18	0	304	558	1,470
20. Jim Turner	16	1	304	521	1,439

TOP 20 TOUCHDOWN SCORERS

Player	Years	Rush	Rec.	Total Returns	TD
1. Jerry Rice	20	10	197	1	208
2. Emmitt Smith	15	164	11	0	175
3. LaDainian Tomlinson	11	145	17	0	162
4. Randy Moss	14	0	156	1	157
5. Terrell Owens	15	3	153	0	156
6. Marcus Allen	16	123	21	1	145
7. Marshall Faulk	12	100	36	0	136
8. Cris Carter	16	0	130	1	131
9. Marvin Harrison	13	0	128	0	128
10. Jim Brown	9	106	20	0	126
11. Walter Payton	13	110	15	0	125
12. John Riggins	14	104	12	0	116
13. Lenny Moore	12	63	48	2	113
14. Shaun Alexander	9	100	12	0	112
15. Barry Sanders	10	99	10	0	109
16. Tim Brown	17	1	100	4	105
Don Hutson	11	3	99	3	105
18. Tony Gonzalez	16	0	103	0	103
19. Steve Largent	14	1	100	0	101
20. Franco Harris	13	91	9	0	100
Curtis Martin	11	90	10	0	100

TOP 20 RUSHERS

Player	Years	Att.	Yards	Avg.	Long	TD
1. Emmitt Smith	15	4,409	18,355	4.2	75	164
2. Walter Payton	13	3,838	16,726	4.4	76	110
3. Barry Sanders	10	3,062	15,269	5.0	85	99
4. Curtis Martin	11	3,518	14,101	4.0	70	90
5. LaDainian Tomlinson	11	3,174	13,684	4.3	85	145
6. Jerome Bettis	13	3,479	13,662	3.9	71	91
7. Eric Dickerson	11	2,996	13,259	4.4	85	90
8. Tony Dorsett	12	2,936	12,739	4.3	99	77
9. Jim Brown	9	2,359	12,312	5.2	80	106
10. Marshall Faulk	12	2,836	12,279	4.3	71	100
11. Edgerrin James	11	3,028	12,246	4.0	72	80
12. Marcus Allen	16	3,022	12,243	4.1	61	123
13. Franco Harris	13	2,949	12,120	4.1	75	91
14. Thurman Thomas	13	2,877	12,074	4.2	80	65
15. Fred Taylor	13	2,534	11,695	4.6	80	66
16. John Riggins	14	2,916	11,352	3.9	66	104
17. Corey Dillon	10	2,618	11,241	4.3	96	82
18. O.J. Simpson	11	2,404	11,236	4.7	94	61
19. Warrick Dunn	12	2,669	10,967	4.1	90	49
20. Ricky Watters	10	2,622	10,643	4.1	57	78

TOP 20 PASS RECEIVERS

Player	Years	No.	Yards	Avg.	Long	TD
1. Jerry Rice	20	1,549	22,895	14.8	96	197
2. Tony Gonzalez	15	1,149	13,338	11.6	73	95
3. Marvin Harrison	13	1,102	14,580	13.2	80	128
4. Cris Carter	16	1,101	13,899	12.6	80	130
5. Tim Brown	17	1,094	14,934	13.7	80	100
6. Terrell Owens	15	1,078	15,934	14.8	98	153
7. Isaac Bruce	16	1,024	15,208	14.9	80	91
8. Hines Ward	14	1,000	12,083	12.1	85	85
9. Randy Moss	13	954	14,858	15.6	82	153
10. Andre Reed	16	951	13,198	13.9	83	87
11. Derrick Mason	15	943	12,061	12.8	79	66
12. Art Monk	16	940	12,721	13.5	79	68
13. Torry Holt	11	920	13,382	14.5	85	74
14. Keenan McCardell	16	883	11,373	12.9	76	63
15. Jimmy Smith	12	862	12,287	14.3	75	67
Reggie Wayne	11	862	11,708	13.6	71	73
16. Muhsin Muhammad	14	860	11,438	13.3	72	62
17. Irving Fryar	17	851	12,785	15.0	80	84
18. Rod Smith	12	849	11,389	13.4	85	68
19. Larry Centers	14	827	6,797	8.2	54	28

TOP 20 INTERCEPTORS

Player	Years	No.	Yards	Avg.	Long	TD
1. Paul Krause	16	81	1,185	14.6	81	3
2. Emlen Tunnell	14	79	1,282	16.2	55	4
3. Rod Woodson	17	71	1,483	20.9	98	12
4. Dick (Night Train) Lane	14	68	1,207	17.8	80	5
5. Ken Riley	15	65	596	9.2	66	5
6. Ronnie Lott	14	63	730	11.6	83	5
Darren Sharper	14	63	1,412	22.4	99	11
7. Dave Brown	15	62	698	11.3	90	5
Dick LeBeau	14	62	762	12.3	70	3
9. Emmitt Thomas	13	58	937	16.2	73	5
10. Mel Blount	14	57	736	12.9	52	2
Bobby Boyd	9	57	994	17.4	74	4
Ed Reed	10	57	1,463	25.7	107	6
Eugene Robinson	16	57	762	13.4	49	1
Johnny Robinson	12	57	741	13.0	57	1
Everson Walls	13	57	504	8.8	40	1
16. Lem Barney	11	56	1,077	19.2	71	7
Pat Fischer	17	56	941	16.8	69	4
18. Aeneas Williams	14	55	807	14.7	65	9
19. Eric Allen	14	54	826	15.3	94	8
Willie Brown	16	54	472	8.7	45	2
Darrell Green	20	54	621	11.5	83	6
Charles Woodson	14	54	896	16.6	62	11

TOP 20 PUNTERS (MINIMUM 250 PUNTS)

Player	Years	No.	Yards	Avg.	Long	Blk.
1. Shane Lechler	12	933	44,389	47.6	80	3
2. Andy Lee	8	723	33,069	45.7	82	3
3. Brandon Fields	5	377	17,227	45.7	71	2
4. Donnie Jones	8	648	29,379	45.3	80	3
5. Mat McBriar	8	494	22,369	45.3	75	3
6. Sammy Baugh	16	338	15,245	45.1	85	9
7. Jon Ryan	6	483	21,713	45.0	77	3
8. Mike Scifres	9	492	22,044	44.8	71	5
9. Tommy Davis	11	511	22,833	44.7	82	2
10. Dustin Colquitt	7	574	25,494	44.4	81	3
11. Chris Kluwe	7	551	24,446	44.4	70	1
12. Brett Kern	4	273	12,109	44.4	68	0
13. Yale Lary	11	503	22,279	44.3	74	4
14. Ben Graham	7	462	20,413	44.2	69	2
15. Sam Koch	6	475	20,980	44.2	74	2
16. Todd Sauerbrun	13	889	39,208	44.1	73	9
17. Brian Moorman	11	847	37,177	43.9	84	2
18. Bob Scarpitto	8	283	12,408	43.8	87	4
19. Horace Gillom	7	385	16,872	43.8	80	5
20. Jerry Norton	11	358	15,671	43.8	78	2

TOP 20 COMBINED YARDS GAINED

Player	Years	Tot.	Rush.	Rec.	Int. Ret.	Punt Ret.	Kickoff Ret.	Fumble Ret.
1. Jerry Rice	20	23,546	645	22,895	0	0	6	0
2. Brian Mitchell	14	23,330	1,967	2,336	0	4,999	14,014	14
3. Walter Payton	13	21,803	16,726	4,538	0	0	539	0
4. Emmitt Smith	15	21,583	18,355	3,224	0	0	0	4
5. Tim Brown	17	19,682	190	14,934	0	3,320	1,235	3
6. Marshall Faulk	12	19,190	12,279	6,875	0	0	18	18
7. LaDainian Tomlinson	11	18,456	13,684	4,772	0	0	0	0
8. Barry Sanders	10	18,308	15,269	2,921	0	0	118	0
9. Herschel Walker	12	18,168	8,225	4,859	0	0	5,084	0
10. Marcus Allen	16	17,648	12,243	5,411	0	0	0	-6
11. Curtis Martin	11	17,430	14,101	3,329	0	0	0	0
12. Tiki Barber	10	17,359	10,449	5,183	0	1,181	544	2
13. Eric Metcalf	13	17,230	2,392	5,572	0	3,453	5,813	0
14. Derrick Mason	15	17,150	3	12,061	0	1,590	3,496	0
15. Thurman Thomas	13	16,532	12,074	4,458	0	0	0	0
16. Tony Dorsett	12	16,347	12,739	3,554	0	0	0	54
17. Terrell Owens	15	16,276	251	15,934	0	0	78	13
18. Steve Smith	12	15,869	387	11,452	0	1,652	2,371	7
19. Henry Ellard	16	15,718	50	13,777	0	1,527	364	0
20. Warrick Dunn	12	15,665	10,967	4,339	0	48	310	1

TOP 20 YARDS FROM SCRIMMAGE

Player	Years	Scrimmage Yards	Rushing Yards	Receiving Yards
1. Jerry Rice	20	23,540	645	22,895
2. Emmitt Smith	15	21,579	18,355	3,224
3. Walter Payton	13	21,264	16,726	4,538
4. Marshall Faulk	12	19,154	12,279	6,875
5. LaDainian Tomlinson	11	18,456	13,684	4,772
6. Barry Sanders	10	18,190	15,269	2,921
7. Marcus Allen	16	17,654	12,243	5,411
8. Curtis Martin	11	17,430	14,101	3,329
9. Thurman Thomas	13	16,532	12,074	4,458
10. Tony Dorsett	12	16,293	12,739	3,554
11. Terrell Owens	15	16,185	251	15,934
12. Tiki Barber	10	15,632	10,449	5,183
13. Edgerrin James	11	15,610	12,246	3,364
14. Randy Moss	16	15,451	159	15,292
15. Eric Dickerson	11	15,396	13,259	2,137
16. Isaac Bruce	16	15,347	139	15,208
17. Warrick Dunn	12	15,306	10,967	4,339
18. Tim Brown	17	15,124	190	14,934
19. Jerome Bettis	13	15,111	13,662	1,449
20. Ricky Watters	10	14,891	10,643	4,248

TOP 20 PASSERS

Player	Years	Att.	Comp.	Pct. Comp.	Yards	Avg. Gain	TD	Pct. TD	Int.	Pct. Int.	Rating
1. Aaron Rodgers	8	2,665	1,752	65.7	21,661	8.13	171	6.4	46	1.7	104.9
2. Steve Young	15	4,149	2,667	64.3	33,124	7.98	232	5.6	107	2.6	96.8
3. Tom Brady	13	5,958	3,798	63.8	44,806	7.52	334	5.6	123	2.1	96.6
4. Peyton Manning	14	7,793	5,082	65.2	59,487	7.63	436	5.6	209	2.7	95.7
5. Tony Romo	9	3,240	2,097	64.7	25,737	7.94	177	5.5	91	2.8	95.6
6. Philip Rivers	9	3,564	2,268	63.6	27,891	7.83	189	5.3	93	2.6	94.5
7. Drew Brees	12	6,149	4,035	65.6	45,919	7.47	324	5.3	165	2.7	94.3
8. Kurt Warner	12	4,070	2,666	65.5	32,344	7.95	208	5.1	128	3.1	93.7
9. Ben Roethlisberger	9	3,762	2,374	63.1	29,844	7.93	191	5.1	108	2.9	92.7
10. Joe Montana	15	5,391	3,409	63.2	40,551	7.52	273	5.1	139	2.6	92.3
11. Matt Schaub	9	2,823	1,816	64.3	21,944	7.77	120	4.3	70	2.5	91.9
12. Matt Ryan	5	2,637	1,654	62.7	18,957	7.19	127	4.8	60	2.3	90.9
13. Chad Pennington	11	2,471	1,632	66.0	17,823	7.21	102	4.1	64	2.6	90.1
14. Daunte Culpepper	11	3,199	2,016	63.0	24,153	7.55	149	4.7	106	3.3	87.8
15. Jeff Garcia	11	3,676	2,264	61.6	25,537	6.95	161	4.4	83	2.3	87.5
16. Dan Marino	17	8,358	4,967	59.4	61,361	7.34	420	5.0	252	3.0	86.4
17. Joe Flacco	5	2,489	1,507	60.6	17,633	7.08	102	4.1	56	2.2	86.3
18. Carson Palmer	9	4,110	2,568	62.5	29,465	7.17	189	4.6	130	3.2	86.2
19. Trent Green	11	3,740	2,266	60.6	28,475	7.61	162	4.3	114	3.0	86.0
20. Brett Favre	20	10,169	6,300	62.0	71,838	7.06	508	5.0	336	3.3	86.0

1,500 or more attempts. The passing ratings are based on performance standards established for completion percentage, interception percentage, touchdown percentage, and average gain. Please consult page 312 for more information.

TOP 20 LEADERS IN PASSES COMPLETED

1.	Brett Favre	6,300
2.	Peyton Manning	5,082
3.	Dan Marino	4,967
4.	John Elway	4,123
5.	Drew Brees	4,035
6.	Warren Moon	3,988
7.	Drew Bledsoe	3,839
8.	Tom Brady	3,798
9.	Vinny Testaverde	3,787
10.	Fran Tarkenton	3,686
11.	Kerry Collins	3,487
12.	Joe Montana	3,409
13.	Dan Fouts	3,297
14.	Donovan McNabb	3,170
15.	Dave Krieg	3,105
16.	Matt Hasselbeck	3,029
17.	Boomer Esiason	2,969
18.	Troy Aikman	2,898
19.	Steve DeBerg	2,874
	Jim Kelly	2,874

TOP 20 LEADERS IN PASSING YARDS

1.	Brett Favre	71,838
2.	Dan Marino	61,361
3.	Peyton Manning	59,487
4.	John Elway	51,475
5.	Warren Moon	49,325
6.	Fran Tarkenton	47,003
7.	Vinny Testaverde	46,233
8.	Drew Brees	45,919
9.	Tom Brady	44,806
10.	Drew Bledsoe	44,611
11.	Dan Fouts	43,040
12.	Kerry Collins	40,922
13.	Joe Montana	40,551
14.	Johnny Unitas	40,239
15.	Dave Krieg	38,147
16.	Boomer Esiason	37,920
17.	Donovan McNabb	37,276
18.	Jim Kelly	35,467
19.	Jim Everett	34,837
20.	Jim Hart	34,665

TOP 20 LEADERS IN TOUCHDOWN PASSES

1.	Brett Favre	508
2.	Peyton Manning	436
3.	Dan Marino	420
4.	Fran Tarkenton	342
5.	Tom Brady	334
6.	Drew Brees	324
7.	John Elway	300
8.	Warren Moon	291
9.	Johnny Unitas	290
10.	Vinny Testaverde	275
11.	Joe Montana	273
12.	Dave Krieg	261
13.	Sonny Jurgensen	255
14.	Dan Fouts	254
15.	Drew Bledsoe	251
16.	Boomer Esiason	247
17.	John Hadl	244
18.	Len Dawson	239
19.	Jim Kelly	237
20.	George Blanda	236

TOP 20 LEADERS IN RECEPTION YARDS

1.	Jerry Rice	22,895
2.	Terrell Owens	15,934
3.	Randy Moss	15,292
4.	Isaac Bruce	15,208
5.	Tim Brown	14,934
6.	Marvin Harrison	14,580
7.	Tony Gonzalez	14,268
8.	James Lofton	14,004
9.	Cris Carter	13,899
10.	Henry Ellard	13,777
11.	Torry Holt	13,382
12.	Andre Reed	13,198
13.	Steve Largent	13,089
14.	Reggie Wayne	13,063
15.	Irving Fryar	12,785
16.	Art Monk	12,721
17.	Jimmy Smith	12,287
18.	Charlie Joiner	12,146
19.	Hines Ward	12,083
20.	Derrick Mason	12,061

TOP 20 KICKOFF RETURNERS (MINIMUM 75 RETURNS)

Player	Years	No.	Yards	Avg.	Long	TD
1. Gale Sayers	7	91	2,781	30.6	103	6
2. Lynn Chandnois	7	92	2,720	29.6	93	3
3. Joe McKnight	3	76	2,205	29.0	107	2
4. Abe Woodson	9	193	5,538	28.7	105	5
5. Buddy Young	6	90	2,514	27.9	104	2
6. Percy Harvin	4	114	3,183	27.9	105	5
7. Travis Williams	5	102	2,801	27.5	105	6
8. Joe Arenas	7	139	3,798	27.3	96	1
9. Clifton Smith	3	75	2,038	27.2	97	1
10. Clarence Davis	8	79	2,140	27.1	76	0
11. Danieal Manning	7	115	3,085	26.8	83	1
12. Steve Van Buren	8	76	2,030	26.7	98	3
13. Lenny Lyles	12	81	2,161	26.7	103	3
14. Mercury Morris	8	111	2,947	26.5	105	3
15. Ellis Hobbs	6	141	3,739	26.5	108	3
16. Bobby Jancik	6	158	4,185	26.5	61	0
17. Leodis McKelvin	5	91	2,407	26.5	98	1
18. Mel Renfro	14	85	2,246	26.4	100	2
19. Bobby Mitchell	14	102	2,690	26.4	98	5
20. Terrence McGee	10	207	5,450	26.3	104	5

TOP 20 PUNT RETURNERS (MINIMUM 75 RETURNS)

Player	Years	No.	Yards	Avg.	Long	TD
1. George McAfee	8	112	1,431	12.8	74	2
2. Jack Christiansen	8	85	1,084	12.8	89	8
3. Claude Gibson	5	110	1,381	12.6	85	3
4. Bill Dudley	9	124	1,515	12.2	96	3
5. Devin Hester	7	246	2,985	12.1	89	12
6. Rick Upchurch	9	248	3,008	12.1	92	8
7. Desmond Howard	11	244	2,895	11.9	95	8
8. Patrick Peterson	2	95	1,125	11.8	99	4
19. Billy Johnson	14	282	3,317	11.8	87	6
10. Mack Herron	3	84	982	11.7	66	0
11. Roscoe Parrish	8	165	1,920	11.6	82	3
12. Billy Thompson	13	157	1,814	11.6	60	0
13. Darrien Gordon	9	314	3,601	11.5	94	6
14. Santana Moss	12	112	1,268	11.3	80	3
15. Henry Ellard	16	135	1,527	11.3	83	4
16. Rodger Bird	3	94	1,063	11.3	78	0
17. Bosh Pritchard	6	95	1,072	11.3	81	2
18. Terry Metcalf	6	84	936	11.1	69	1
19. Bob Hayes	11	104	1,158	11.1	90	3
20. Jermaine Lewis	9	295	3,282	11.1	89	6

TOP 20 LEADERS IN SACKS

Player	*Years	No.
1. Bruce Smith	19	200.0
2. Reggie White	15	198.0
3. Kevin Greene	15	160.0
4. Chris Doleman	15	150.5
5. Michael Strahan	15	141.5
6. Jason Taylor	15	139.5
7. Richard Dent	15	137.5
John Randle	14	137.5
9. Leslie O'Neal	13	132.5
Lawrence Taylor	12	132.5
11. Rickey Jackson	14	128.0
12. Derrick Thomas	11	126.5
13. John Abraham	13	122.0
Simeon Rice	12	122.0
15. Clyde Simmons	15	121.5
16. Jared Allen	9	117.0
17. Sean Jones	13	113.0
18. Julius Peppers	11	111.5
19. DeMarcus Ware	8	111.0
20. Greg Townsend	13	109.5

*Years played since 1982 when sacks became an official statistic.

POSTSEASON LEADERS
TOP 10 POSTSEASON RUSHERS

Player		Att.	Yards	Avg.	Long	TD
1.	Emmitt Smith	349	1,586	4.5	65	19
2.	Franco Harris	400	1,556	3.9	50	16
3.	Thurman Thomas	339	1,442	4.3	40	16
4.	Tony Dorsett	302	1,383	4.6	53	9
5.	Marcus Allen	267	1,347	5.0	74	11
6.	Terrell Davis	204	1,140	5.6	62	12
7.	John Riggins	251	996	4.0	43	12
8.	Larry Csonka	225	891	4.0	49	9
9.	Chuck Foreman	229	860	3.8	62	7
10.	Edgerrin James	218	852	3.9	34	6

TOP 10 POSTSEASON PASSERS

Player		Att.	Comp.	Pct. Comp.	Yards	Avg. Gain	TD	Pct. TD	Int.	Pct. Int.	Rating
1.	Bart Starr	213	130	61.0	1,753	8.23	15	7.0	3	1.4	104.8
2.	Drew Brees	391	262	67.0	2,980	7.62	22	5.6	4	1.0	104.2
3.	Aaron Rodgers	292	193	66.1	2,312	7.92	18	6.2	5	1.7	103.6
4.	Kurt Warner	462	307	66.5	3,952	8.55	31	6.7	14	3.0	102.8
5.	Joe Montana	734	460	62.7	5,772	7.86	45	6.1	21	2.9	95.6
6.	Mark Sanchez	157	95	60.5	1,155	7.36	9	5.7	3	1.9	94.3
7.	Ken Anderson	166	110	66.3	1,321	7.96	9	5.4	6	3.6	93.5
8.	Joe Theismann	211	128	60.7	1,782	8.45	11	5.2	7	3.3	91.4
9.	Eli Manning	356	219	61.5	2,516	7.07	17	4.8	8	2.2	89.3
10.	Peyton Manning	761	481	63.2	5,679	7.46	32	4.2	21	2.8	88.4

TOP 10 POSTSEASON PASS RECEIVERS

Player		No.	Yards	Avg.	Long	TD
1.	Jerry Rice	151	2,245	14.9	72	22
2.	Reggie Wayne	92	1,242	13.5	72	9
3.	Hines Ward	88	1,181	13.4	45	10
4.	Michael Irvin	87	1,315	15.1	53	8
5.	Andre Reed	85	1,229	14.5	72	9
6.	Thurman Thomas	76	672	8.8	27	5
7.	Cliff Branch	73	1,289	17.7	72	5
8.	Fred Biletnikoff	70	1,167	16.7	57	10
9.	Art Monk	69	1,062	15.4	48	7
	Wes Welker	69	686	9.9	47	4

TOP 10 POSTSEASON INTERCEPTION LEADERS

Player		Interceptions
1.	Ronnie Lott	9
	Ed Reed	9
	Bill Simpson	9
	Charlie Waters	9
5.	Lester Hayes	8
6.	Willie Brown	7
	Rodney Harrison	7
	Asante Samuel	7
	Dennis Thurman	7
10.	Bobby Bryant	6
	Eric Davis	6
	Glen Edwards	6
	Darrell Green	6
	Cliff Harris	6
	Ty Law	6
	Vernon Perry	6
	Aeneas Williams	6

TOP 10 POSTSEASON SACK LEADERS

Player		Sacks
1.	Willie McGinest	16.0
2.	Bruce Smith	14.5
3.	Reggie White	12.0
	Terrell Suggs	12.0
5.	Charles Haley	11.0
	LaMarr Woodley	11.0
7.	Richard Dent	10.5
8.	Trace Armstrong	10.0
	Charles Mann	10.0
	Tony Tolbert	10.0

Sacks became an official statistic in 1982.

ANNUAL SCORING LEADERS

Year	Player, Team	TD	FG	PAT	TP
2012	Stephen Gostkowski, New England, AFC	0	29	66	153
	Lawrence Tynes, N.Y. Giants, NFC	0	33	46	145
2011	David Akers, San Francisco, NFC	0	44	34	166
	Stephen Gostkowski, New England, AFC	0	28	59	143
2010	David Akers, Philadelphia, NFC	0	32	47	143
	Sebastian Janikowski, Oakland, AFC	0	33	43	142
2009	Nate Kaeding, San Diego, AFC	0	32	50	146
	David Akers, Philadelphia, NFC	0	32	43	139
2008	Stephen Gostkowski, New England, AFC	0	36	40	148
	David Akers, Philadelphia, NFC	0	33	45	144
2007	*Mason Crosby, Green Bay, NFC	0	31	48	141
	Randy Moss, New England, AFC	23	0	0	138
2006	LaDainian Tomlinson, AFC	31	0	0	186
	Robbie Gould, Chicago, NFC	0	32	47	143
2005	Shaun Alexander, Seattle, NFC	28	0	0	168
	Shayne Graham, Cincinnati, AFC	0	28	47	131
2004	Adam Vinatieri, New England, AFC	0	31	48	141
	David Akers, Philadelphia, NFC	0	27	41	122
2003	Jeff Wilkins, St. Louis, NFC	0	39	46	163
	Priest Holmes, Kansas City, AFC	27	0	0	162
2002	Priest Holmes, Kansas City, AFC	24	0	0	144
	Jay Feely, Atlanta, NFC	0	32	42	138
2001	Marshall Faulk, St. Louis, NFC	21	0	0	#128
	Mike Vanderjagt, Indianapolis, AFC	0	28	41	125
2000	Marshall Faulk, St. Louis, NFC	26	0	0	##160
	Matt Stover, Baltimore, AFC	0	35	30	135
1999	Mike Vanderjagt, Indianapolis, AFC	0	34	43	145
	Jeff Wilkins, St. Louis, NFC	0	20	64	124
1998	Gary Anderson, Minnesota, NFC	0	35	59	164
	Steve Christie, Buffalo, AFC	0	33	41	140
1997	Mike Hollis, Jacksonville, AFC	0	31	41	134
	Richie Cunningham, Dallas, NFC	0	34	24	126
1996	John Kasay, Carolina, NFC	0	37	34	145
	Cary Blanchard, Indianapolis, AFC	0	36	27	135
1995	Emmitt Smith, Dallas, NFC	25	0	0	150
	Norm Johnson, Pittsburgh, AFC	0	34	39	141
1994	John Carney, San Diego, AFC	0	34	33	135
	Fuad Reveiz, Minnesota, NFC	0	34	30	132
1993	Jeff Jaeger, L.A. Raiders, AFC	0	35	27	132
	Jason Hanson, Detroit, NFC	0	34	28	130
1992	Pete Stoyanovich, Miami, AFC	0	30	34	124
	Morten Andersen, New Orleans, NFC	0	29	33	120
	Chip Lohmiller, Washington, NFC	0	30	30	120
1991	Chip Lohmiller, Washington, NFC	0	31	56	149
	Pete Stoyanovich, Miami, AFC	0	31	28	121
1990	Nick Lowery, Kansas City, AFC	0	34	37	139
	Chip Lohmiller, Washington, NFC	0	30	41	131
1989	Mike Cofer, San Francisco, NFC	0	29	49	136
	*David Treadwell, Denver, AFC	0	27	39	120
1988	Scott Norwood, Buffalo, AFC	0	32	33	129
	Mike Cofer, San Francisco, NFC	0	27	40	121
1987	Jerry Rice, San Francisco, NFC	23	0	0	138
	Jim Breech, Cincinnati, AFC	0	24	25	97
1986	Tony Franklin, New England, AFC	0	32	44	140
	Kevin Butler, Chicago, NFC	0	28	36	120
1985	*Kevin Butler, Chicago, NFC	0	31	51	144
	Gary Anderson, Pittsburgh, AFC	0	33	40	139
1984	Ray Wersching, San Francisco, NFC	0	25	56	131
	Gary Anderson, Pittsburgh, AFC	0	24	45	117
1983	Mark Moseley, Washington, NFC	0	33	62	161
	Gary Anderson, Pittsburgh, AFC	0	27	38	119
1982	*Marcus Allen, L.A. Raiders, AFC	14	0	0	84
	Wendell Tyler, L.A. Rams, NFC	13	0	0	78
1981	Ed Murray, Detroit, NFC	0	25	46	121
	Rafael Septien, Dallas, NFC	0	27	40	121
	Jim Breech, Cincinnati, AFC	0	22	49	115
	Nick Lowery, Kansas City, AFC	0	26	37	115
1980	John Smith, New England, AFC	0	26	51	129
	*Ed Murray, Detroit, NFC	0	27	35	116
1979	John Smith, New England, AFC	0	23	46	115
	Mark Moseley, Washington, NFC	0	25	39	114

Year	Player, Team	TD	FG	PAT	TP
1978	*Frank Corral, Los Angeles, NFC	0	29	31	118
	Pat Leahy, N.Y. Jets, AFC	0	22	41	107
1977	Errol Mann, Oakland, AFC	0	20	39	99
	Walter Payton, Chicago, NFC	16	0	0	96
1976	Toni Linhart, Baltimore, AFC	0	20	49	109
	Mark Moseley, Washington, NFC	0	22	31	97
1975	O.J. Simpson, Buffalo, AFC	23	0	0	138
	Chuck Foreman, Minnesota, NFC	22	0	0	132
1974	Chester Marcol, Green Bay, NFC	0	25	19	94
	Roy Gerela, Pittsburgh, AFC	0	20	33	93
1973	David Ray, Los Angeles, NFC	0	30	40	130
	Roy Gerela, Pittsburgh, AFC	0	29	36	123
1972	*Chester Marcol, Green Bay, NFC	0	33	29	128
	Bobby Howfield, N.Y. Jets, AFC	0	27	40	121
1971	Garo Yepremian, Miami, AFC	0	28	33	117
	Curt Knight, Washington, NFC	0	29	27	114
1970	Fred Cox, Minnesota, NFC	0	30	35	125
	Jan Stenerud, Kansas City, AFC	0	30	26	116
1969	Jim Turner, N.Y. Jets, AFL	0	32	33	129
	Fred Cox, Minnesota, NFL	0	26	43	121
1968	Jim Turner, N.Y. Jets, AFL	0	34	43	145
	Leroy Kelly, Cleveland, NFL	20	0	0	120
1967	Jim Bakken, St. Louis, NFL	0	27	36	117
	George Blanda, Oakland, AFL	0	20	56	116
1966	Gino Cappelletti, Boston, AFL	6	16	35	119
	Bruce Gossett, Los Angeles, NFL	0	28	29	113
1965	*Gale Sayers, Chicago, NFL	22	0	0	132
	Gino Cappelletti, Boston, AFL	9	17	27	132
1964	Gino Cappelletti, Boston, AFL	7	25	36	#155
	Lenny Moore, Baltimore, NFL	20	0	0	120
1963	Gino Cappelletti, Boston, AFL	2	22	35	113
	Don Chandler, N.Y. Giants, NFL	0	18	52	106
1962	Gene Mingo, Denver, AFL	4	27	32	137
	Jim Taylor, Green Bay, NFL	19	0	0	114
1961	Gino Cappelletti, Boston, AFL	8	17	48	147
	Paul Hornung, Green Bay, NFL	10	15	41	146
1960	Paul Hornung, Green Bay, NFL	15	15	41	176
	*Gene Mingo, Denver, AFL	6	18	33	123
1959	Paul Hornung, Green Bay	7	7	31	94
1958	Jim Brown, Cleveland	18	0	0	108
1957	Sam Baker, Washington	1	14	29	77
	Lou Groza, Cleveland	0	15	32	77
1956	Bobby Layne, Detroit	5	12	33	99
1955	Doak Walker, Detroit	7	9	27	96
1954	Bobby Walston, Philadelphia	11	4	36	114
1953	Gordy Soltau, San Francisco	6	10	48	114
1952	Gordy Soltau, San Francisco	7	6	34	94
1951	Elroy (Crazylegs) Hirsch, Los Angeles	17	0	0	102
1950	*Doak Walker, Detroit	11	8	38	128
1949	Pat Harder, Chi. Cardinals	8	3	45	102
	Gene Roberts, N.Y. Giants	17	0	0	102
1948	Pat Harder, Chi. Cardinals	6	7	53	110
1947	Pat Harder, Chi. Cardinals	7	7	39	102
1946	Ted Fritsch, Green Bay	10	9	13	100
1945	Steve Van Buren, Philadelphia	18	0	2	110
1944	Don Hutson, Green Bay	9	0	31	85
1943	Don Hutson, Green Bay	12	3	36	117
1942	Don Hutson, Green Bay	17	1	33	138
1941	Don Hutson, Green Bay	12	1	20	95
1940	Don Hutson, Green Bay	7	0	15	57
1939	Andy Farkas, Washington	11	0	2	68
1938	Clarke Hinkle, Green Bay	7	3	7	58
1937	Jack Manders, Chi. Bears	5	8	15	69
1936	Earl (Dutch) Clark, Detroit	7	4	19	73
1935	Earl (Dutch) Clark, Detroit	6	1	16	55
1934	Jack Manders, Chi. Bears	3	10	31	79
1933	Ken Strong, N.Y. Giants	6	5	13	64
	Glenn Presnell, Portsmouth	6	6	10	64
1932	Earl (Dutch) Clark, Portsmouth	6	3	10	55

*First season of professional football.
#Cappelletti's total and Faulk's total in 2001 include a two-point conversion.
##Faulk's total in 2000 includes 2 two-point conversions.

ANNUAL TOUCHDOWN LEADERS

Year	Player, Team	TD	Rush	Pass	Ret.
2012	Arian Foster, Houston, AFC	17	15	2	0
	James Jones, Green Bay, NFC	14	0	14	0
2011	LeSean McCoy, Philadelphia, NFC	20	17	3	0
	Rob Gronkowski, New England, AFC	18	1	17	0
2010	Arian Foster, Houston, AFC	18	16	2	0
	Adrian Peterson, Minnesota, NFC	13	12	1	0
2009	Adrian Peterson, Minnesota, NFC	18	18	0	0
	Chris Johnson, Tennessee, AFC	16	14	2	0
	Maurice Jones-Drew, Jacksonville, AFC	16	15	1	0
2008	DeAngelo Williams, Carolina, NFC	20	18	2	0
	Thomas Jones, N.Y. Jets, AFC	15	13	2	0
	LenDale White, Tennessee, AFC	15	15	0	0
2007	Randy Moss, New England, AFC	23	0	23	0
	Terrell Owens, Dallas, NFC	15	0	15	0
2006	LaDainian Tomlinson, San Diego, AFC	31	28	3	0
	Marion Barber, Dallas, NFC	16	14	2	0
	Steven Jackson, St. Louis, NFC	16	13	3	0
2005	Shaun Alexander, Seattle, NFC	28	27	1	0
	Larry Johnson, Kansas City, AFC	21	20	1	0
2004	Shaun Alexander, Seattle, NFC	20	16	4	0
	LaDainian Tomlinson, San Diego, AFC	18	17	1	0
2003	Priest Holmes, Kansas City, AFC	27	27	0	0
	Ahman Green, Green Bay, NFC	20	15	5	0
2002	Priest Holmes, Kansas City, AFC	24	21	3	0
	Shaun Alexander, Seattle, NFC	18	16	2	0
2001	Marshall Faulk, St. Louis, NFC	21	12	9	0
	Shaun Alexander, Seattle, AFC	16	14	2	0
2000	Marshall Faulk, St. Louis, NFC	26	18	8	0
	Edgerrin James, Indianapolis, AFC	18	13	5	0
1999	Stephen Davis, Washington, NFC	17	17	0	0
	*Edgerrin James, Indianapolis, AFC	17	13	4	0
1998	Terrell Davis, Denver, AFC	23	21	2	0
	*Randy Moss, Minnesota, NFC	17	0	17	0
1997	Karim Abdul-Jabbar, Miami, AFC	16	15	1	0
	Barry Sanders, Detroit, NFC	14	11	3	0
1996	Terry Allen, Washington, NFC	21	21	0	0
	Curtis Martin, New England, AFC	17	14	3	0
1995	Emmitt Smith, Dallas, NFC	25	25	0	0
	Carl Pickens, Cincinnati, AFC	17	0	17	0
1994	Emmitt Smith, Dallas, NFC	22	21	1	0
	*Marshall Faulk, Indianapolis, AFC	12	11	1	0
	Natrone Means, San Diego, AFC	12	12	0	0
1993	Jerry Rice, San Francisco, NFC	16	1	15	0
	Marcus Allen, Kansas City, AFC	15	12	3	0
1992	Emmitt Smith, Dallas, NFC	19	18	1	0
	Thurman Thomas, Buffalo, AFC	12	9	3	0
1991	Barry Sanders, Detroit, NFC	17	16	1	0
	Mark Clayton, Miami, AFC	12	0	12	0
	Thurman Thomas, Buffalo, AFC	12	7	5	0
1990	Barry Sanders, Detroit, NFC	16	13	3	0
	Derrick Fenner, Seattle, AFC	15	14	1	0
1989	Dalton Hilliard, New Orleans, NFC	18	13	5	0
	Christian Okoye, Kansas City, AFC	12	12	0	0
	Thurman Thomas, Buffalo, AFC	12	6	6	0
1988	Greg Bell, L.A. Rams, NFC	18	16	2	0
	Eric Dickerson, Indianapolis, AFC	15	14	1	0
	*Ickey Woods, Cincinnati, AFC	15	15	0	0
1987	Jerry Rice, San Francisco, NFC	23	1	22	0
	Johnny Hector, N.Y. Jets, AFC	11	11	0	0
1986	George Rogers, Washington, NFC	18	18	0	0
	Sammy Winder, Denver, AFC	14	9	5	0
1985	Joe Morris, N.Y. Giants, NFC	21	21	0	0
	Louis Lipps, Pittsburgh, AFC	15	1	12	2
1984	Marcus Allen, L.A. Raiders, AFC	18	13	5	0
	Mark Clayton, Miami, AFC	18	0	18	0
	Eric Dickerson, L.A. Rams, NFC	14	14	0	0
	John Riggins, Washington, NFC	14	14	0	0

Year	Player, Team	TD	Rush	Pass	Ret.
1983	John Riggins, Washington, NFC	24	24	0	0
	Pete Johnson, Cincinnati, AFC	14	14	0	0
	*Curt Warner, Seattle, AFC	14	13	1	0
1982	*Marcus Allen, L.A. Raiders, AFC	14	11	3	0
	Wendell Tyler, L.A. Rams, NFC	13	9	4	0
1981	Chuck Muncie, San Diego, AFC	19	19	0	0
	Wendell Tyler, Los Angeles, NFC	17	12	5	0
1980	*Billy Sims, Detroit, NFC	16	13	3	0
	Earl Campbell, Houston, AFC	13	13	0	0
	*Curtis Dickey, Baltimore, AFC	13	11	2	0
	John Jefferson, San Diego, AFC	13	0	13	0
1979	Earl Campbell, Houston, AFC	19	19	0	0
	Walter Payton, Chicago, NFC	16	14	2	0
1978	David Sims, Seattle, AFC	15	14	1	0
	Terdell Middleton, Green Bay, NFC	12	11	1	0
1977	Walter Payton, Chicago, NFC	16	14	2	0
	Nat Moore, Miami, AFC	13	1	12	0
1976	Chuck Foreman, Minnesota, NFC	14	13	1	0
	Franco Harris, Pittsburgh, AFC	14	14	0	0
1975	O.J. Simpson, Buffalo, AFC	23	16	7	0
	Chuck Foreman, Minnesota, NFC	22	13	9	0
1974	Chuck Foreman, Minnesota, NFC	15	9	6	0
	Cliff Branch, Oakland, AFC	13	0	13	0
1973	Larry Brown, Washington, NFC	14	8	6	0
	Floyd Little, Denver, AFC	13	12	1	0
1972	Emerson Boozer, N.Y. Jets, AFC	14	11	3	0
	Ron Johnson, N.Y. Giants, NFC	14	9	5	0
1971	Duane Thomas, Dallas, NFC	13	11	2	0
	Leroy Kelly, Cleveland, AFC	12	10	2	0
1970	Dick Gordon, Chicago, NFC	13	0	13	0
	MacArthur Lane, St. Louis, NFC	13	11	2	0
	Gary Garrison, San Diego, AFC	12	0	12	0
1969	Warren Wells, Oakland, AFL	14	0	14	0
	Tom Matte, Baltimore, NFL	13	11	2	0
	Lance Rentzel, Dallas, NFL	13	0	12	1
1968	Leroy Kelly, Cleveland, NFL	20	16	4	0
	Warren Wells, Oakland, AFL	12	1	11	0
1967	Homer Jones, N.Y. Giants, NFL	14	1	13	0
	Emerson Boozer, N.Y. Jets, AFL	13	10	3	0
1966	Leroy Kelly, Cleveland, NFL	16	15	1	0
	Dan Reeves, Dallas, NFL	16	8	8	0
	Lance Alworth, San Diego, AFL	13	0	13	0
1965	*Gale Sayers, Chicago, NFL	22	14	6	2
	Lance Alworth, San Diego, AFL	14	0	14	0
	Don Maynard, N.Y. Jets, AFL	14	0	14	0
1964	Lenny Moore, Baltimore, NFL	20	16	3	1
	Lance Alworth, San Diego, AFL	15	2	13	0
1963	Art Powell, Oakland, AFL	16	0	16	0
	Jim Brown, Cleveland, NFL	15	12	3	0
1962	Abner Haynes, Dallas, AFL	19	13	6	0
	Jim Taylor, Green Bay, NFL	19	19	0	0
1961	Bill Groman, Houston, AFL	18	1	17	0
	Jim Taylor, Green Bay, NFL	16	15	1	0
1960	Paul Hornung, Green Bay, NFL	15	13	2	0
	Sonny Randle, St. Louis, NFL	15	0	15	0
	Art Powell, N.Y. Titans, AFL	14	0	14	0
1959	Raymond Berry, Baltimore	14	0	14	0
	Jim Brown, Cleveland	14	14	0	0
1958	Jim Brown, Cleveland	18	17	1	0
1957	Lenny Moore, Baltimore	11	3	7	1
1956	Rick Casares, Chi. Bears	14	12	2	0
1955	*Alan Ameche, Baltimore	9	9	0	0
	Harlon Hill, Chi. Bears	9	0	9	0
1954	*Harlon Hill, Chi. Bears	12	0	12	0
1953	Joseph Perry, San Francisco	13	10	3	0
1952	Cloyce Box, Detroit	15	0	15	0
1951	Elroy (Crazylegs) Hirsch, Los Angeles	17	0	17	0
1950	Bob Shaw, Chi. Cardinals	12	0	12	0
1949	Gene Roberts, N.Y. Giants	17	9	8	0
1948	Mal Kutner, Chi. Cardinals	15	1	14	0

2013 NFL Record & Fact Book

Year	Player, Team	TD	Rush	Pass	Ret.
1947	Steve Van Buren, Philadelphia	14	13	0	1
1946	Ted Fritsch, Green Bay	10	9	1	0
1945	Steve Van Buren, Philadelphia	18	15	2	1
1944	Don Hutson, Green Bay	9	0	9	0
	Bill Paschal, N.Y. Giants	9	9	0	0
1943	Don Hutson, Green Bay	12	0	11	1
	*Bill Paschal, N.Y. Giants	12	10	2	0
1942	Don Hutson, Green Bay	17	0	17	0
1941	Don Hutson, Green Bay	12	2	10	0
	George McAfee, Chi. Bears	12	6	3	3
1940	John Drake, Cleveland	9	9	0	0
	Richard Todd, Washington	9	4	4	1
1939	Andrew Farkas, Washington	11	5	5	1
1938	Don Hutson, Green Bay	9	0	9	0
1937	Cliff Battles, Washington	7	5	1	1
	Clarke Hinkle, Green Bay	7	5	2	0
	Don Hutson, Green Bay	7	0	7	0
1936	Don Hutson, Green Bay	9	0	8	1
1935	*Don Hutson, Green Bay	7	0	6	1
1934	*Beattie Feathers, Chi. Bears	9	8	1	0
1933	*Charlie (Buckets) Goldenberg, Green Bay	7	4	1	2
	John (Shipwreck) Kelly, Brooklyn	7	2	3	2
	*Elvin (Kink) Richards, N.Y. Giants	7	4	3	0
1932	Earl (Dutch) Clark, Portsmouth	6	3	3	0
	Red Grange, Chi. Bears	6	3	3	0

First season of professional football.

ANNUAL LEADERS—MOST FIELD GOALS MADE

Year	Player, Team	Att.	Made	Pct.
2012	*Blair Walsh, Minnesota, NFC	38	35	92.1
	Sebastian Janikowski, Oakland, AFC	34	31	91.2
	Shayne Graham, Houston, AFC	38	31	81.6
2011	David Akers, San Francisco, NFC	52	44	84.6
	Mike Nugent, Cincinnati, AFC	38	33	86.8
2010	Josh Brown, St. Louis, NFC	39	33	84.6
	Sebastian Janikowski, Oakland, AFC	41	33	80.5
2009	Nate Kaeding, San Diego, AFC	35	32	91.4
	David Akers, Philadelphia, NFC	37	32	86.5
2008	Stephen Gostkowski, New England, AFC	40	36	90.0
	John Carney, N.Y. Giants, NFC	38	35	92.1
2007	Rob Bironas, Tennessee, AFC	39	35	89.7
	*Mason Crosby, Green Bay, NFC	39	31	79.5
	Robbie Gould, Chicago, NFC	36	31	86.1
2006	Robbie Gould, Chicago, NFC	36	32	88.9
	Jeff Wilkins, St. Louis, NFC	37	32	86.5
	Matt Stover, Baltimore, AFC	30	28	93.3
2005	Neil Rackers, Arizona, NFC	42	40	95.2
	Matt Stover, Baltimore, AFC	34	30	88.2
2004	Adam Vinatieri, New England, AFC	33	31	93.9
	David Akers, Philadelphia, NFC	32	27	84.4
2003	Jeff Wilkins, St. Louis, NFC	42	39	92.9
	Mike Vanderjagt, Indianapolis, AFC	37	37	100.0
2002	Jay Feely, Atlanta, NFC	40	32	80.0
	Martín Gramatica, Tampa Bay, NFC	39	32	82.1
	Adam Vinatieri, New England, AFC	30	27	90.0
2001	Jason Elam, Denver, AFC	36	31	86.1
	*Jay Feely, Atlanta, NFC	37	29	78.4
2000	Matt Stover, Baltimore, AFC	39	35	89.7
	Ryan Longwell, Green Bay, NFC	38	33	86.8
1999	Olindo Mare, Miami, AFC	46	39	84.8
	*Martin Gramatica, Tampa Bay, NFC	32	27	84.4
1998	Al Del Greco, Tennessee, AFC	39	36	92.3
	Gary Anderson, Minnesota, NFC	35	35	100.0
1997	Richie Cunningham, Dallas, NFC	37	34	91.9
	Cary Blanchard, Indianapolis, AFC	41	32	78.1
1996	John Kasay, Carolina, NFC	45	37	82.2
	Cary Blanchard, Indianapolis, AFC	40	36	90.0
1995	Norm Johnson, Pittsburgh, AFC	41	34	82.9
	Morten Andersen, Atlanta, NFC	37	31	83.8

Year	Player, Team	Att.	Made	Pct.
1994	John Carney, San Diego, AFC	38	34	89.5
	Fuad Reveiz, Minnesota, NFC	39	34	87.2
1993	Jeff Jaeger, L.A. Raiders, AFC	44	35	79.5
	Jason Hanson, Detroit, NFC	43	34	79.1
1992	Pete Stoyanovich, Miami, AFC	37	30	81.1
	Chip Lohmiller, Washington, NFC	40	30	75.0
1991	Pete Stoyanovich, Miami, AFC	37	31	83.8
	Chip Lohmiller, Washington, NFC	43	31	72.1
1990	Nick Lowery, Kansas City, AFC	37	34	91.9
	Chip Lohmiller, Washington, NFC	40	30	75.0
1989	Rich Karlis, Minnesota, NFC	39	31	79.5
	*David Treadwell, Denver, AFC	33	27	81.8
1988	Scott Norwood, Buffalo, AFC	37	32	86.5
	Mike Cofer, San Francisco, NFC	38	27	71.1
1987	Morten Andersen, New Orleans, NFC	36	28	77.8
	Dean Biasucci, Indianapolis, AFC	27	24	88.9
	Jim Breech, Cincinnati, AFC	30	24	80.0
1986	Tony Franklin, New England, AFC	41	32	78.0
	Kevin Butler, Chicago, NFC	41	28	68.3
1985	Gary Anderson, Pittsburgh, AFC	42	33	78.6
	Morten Andersen, New Orleans, NFC	35	31	88.6
	*Kevin Butler, Chicago, NFC	37	31	83.8
1984	*Paul McFadden, Philadelphia, NFC	37	30	81.1
	Gary Anderson, Pittsburgh, AFC	32	24	75.0
	Matt Bahr, Cleveland, AFC	32	24	75.0
1983	*Ali-Haji-Sheikh, N.Y. Giants, NFC	42	35	83.3
	*Raul Allegre, Baltimore, AFC	35	30	85.7
1982	Mark Moseley, Washington, NFC	21	20	95.2
	Nick Lowery, Kansas City, AFC	24	19	79.2
1981	Rafael Septien, Dallas, NFC	35	27	77.1
	Nick Lowery, Kansas City, AFC	36	26	72.2
1980	*Ed Murray, Detroit, NFC	42	27	64.3
	John Smith, New England, AFC	34	26	76.5
	Fred Steinfort, Denver, AFC	34	26	76.5
1979	Mark Moseley, Washington, NFC	33	25	75.8
	John Smith, New England, AFC	33	23	69.7
1978	*Frank Corral, Los Angeles, NFC	43	29	67.4
	Pat Leahy, N.Y. Jets, AFC	30	22	73.3
1977	Mark Moseley, Washington, NFC	37	21	56.8
	Errol Mann, Oakland, AFC	28	20	71.4
1976	Mark Moseley, Washington, NFC	34	22	64.7
	Jan Stenerud, Kansas City, AFC	38	21	55.3
1975	Jan Stenerud, Kansas City, AFC	32	22	68.8
	Toni Fritsch, Dallas, NFC	35	22	62.9
1974	Chester Marcol, Green Bay, NFC	39	25	64.1
	Roy Gerela, Pittsburgh, AFC	29	20	69.0
1973	David Ray, Los Angeles, NFC	47	30	63.8
	Roy Gerela, Pittsburgh, AFC	43	29	67.4
1972	*Chester Marcol, Green Bay, NFC	48	33	68.8
	Roy Gerela, Pittsburgh, AFC	41	28	68.3
1971	Curt Knight, Washington, NFC	49	29	59.2
	Garo Yepremian, Miami, AFC	40	28	70.0
1970	Jan Stenerud, Kansas City, AFC	42	30	71.4
	Fred Cox, Minnesota, NFC	46	30	65.2
1969	Jim Turner, N.Y. Jets, AFL	47	32	68.1
	Fred Cox, Minnesota, NFL	37	26	70.3
1968	Jim Turner, N.Y. Jets, AFL	46	34	73.9
	Mac Percival, Chicago, NFL	36	25	69.4
1967	Jim Bakken, St. Louis, NFL	39	27	69.2
	Jan Stenerud, Kansas City, AFL	36	21	58.3
1966	Bruce Gossett, Los Angeles, NFL	49	28	57.1
	Mike Mercer, Oakland-Kansas City, AFL	30	21	70.0
1965	Pete Gogolak, Buffalo, AFL	46	28	60.9
	Fred Cox, Minnesota, NFL	35	23	65.7
1964	Jim Bakken, St. Louis, NFL	38	25	65.8
	Gino Cappelletti, Boston, AFL	39	25	64.1
1963	Jim Martin, Baltimore, NFL	39	24	61.5
	Gino Cappelletti, Boston, AFL	38	22	57.9
1962	Gene Mingo, Denver, AFL	39	27	69.2
	Lou Michaels, Pittsburgh, NFL	42	26	61.9

Year	Player, Team	Att.	Made	Pct.
1961	Steve Myhra, Baltimore, NFL	39	21	53.8
	Gino Cappelletti, Boston, AFL	32	17	53.1
1960	Tommy Davis, San Francisco, NFL	32	19	59.4
	*Gene Mingo, Denver, AFL	28	18	64.3
1959	Pat Summerall, N.Y. Giants	29	20	69.0
1958	Paige Cothren, Los Angeles	25	14	56.0
	*Tom Miner, Pittsburgh	28	14	50.0
1957	Lou Groza, Cleveland	22	15	68.2
1956	Sam Baker, Washington	25	17	68.0
1955	Fred Cone, Green Bay	24	16	66.7
1954	Lou Groza, Cleveland	24	16	66.7
1953	Lou Groza, Cleveland	26	23	88.5
1952	Lou Groza, Cleveland	33	19	57.6
1951	Bob Waterfield, Los Angeles	23	13	56.5
1950	Lou Groza, Cleveland	19	13	68.4
1949	Cliff Patton, Philadelphia	18	9	50.0
	Bob Waterfield, Los Angeles	16	9	56.3
1948	Cliff Patton, Philadelphia	12	8	66.7
1947	Ward Cuff, Green Bay	16	7	43.8
	Pat Harder, Chi. Cardinals	10	7	70.0
	Bob Waterfield, Los Angeles	16	7	43.8
1946	Ted Fritsch, Green Bay	17	9	52.9
1945	Joe Aguirre, Washington	13	7	53.8
1944	Ken Strong, N.Y. Giants	12	6	50.0
1943	Ward Cuff, N.Y. Giants	9	3	33.3
	Don Hutson, Green Bay	5	3	60.0
1942	Bill Daddio, Chi. Cardinals	10	5	50.0
1941	Clarke Hinkle, Green Bay	14	6	42.9
1940	Clarke Hinkle, Green Bay	14	9	64.3
1939	Ward Cuff, N.Y. Giants	16	7	43.8
1938	Ward Cuff, N.Y. Giants	9	5	55.6
	Ralph Kercheval, Brooklyn	13	5	38.5
1937	Jack Manders, Chi. Bears		8	
1936	Jack Manders, Chi. Bears		7	
	Armand Niccolai, Pittsburgh		7	
1935	Armand Niccolai, Pittsburgh		6	
	Bill Smith, Chi. Cardinals		6	
1934	Jack Manders, Chi. Bears		10	
1933	*Jack Manders, Chi. Bears		6	
	Glenn Presnell, Portsmouth		6	
1932	Earl (Dutch) Clark, Portsmouth		3	

*First season of professional football.

ANNUAL RUSHING LEADERS

Year	Player, Team	Att.	Yards	Avg.	TD
2012	Adrian Peterson, Minnesota, NFC	348	2,097	6.0	12
	Jamaal Charles, Kansas City, AFC	285	1,509	5.3	5
2011	Maurice Jones-Drew, Jacksonville, AFC	343	1,606	4.7	8
	Michael Turner, Atlanta, NFC	301	1,340	4.5	11
2010	Arian Foster, Houston, AFC	327	1,616	4.9	16
	Michael Turner, Atlanta, NFC	334	1,371	4.1	12
2009	Chris Johnson, Tennessee, AFC	358	2,006	5.6	14
	Steven Jackson, St. Louis, NFC	324	1,416	4.4	4
2008	Adrian Peterson, Minnesota, NFC	363	1,760	4.9	10
	Thomas Jones, N.Y. Jets, AFC	290	1,312	4.5	13
2007	LaDainian Tomlinson, San Diego, AFC	315	1,474	4.7	15
	*Adrian Peterson, Minnesota, NFC	238	1,341	5.6	12
2006	LaDainian Tomlinson, San Diego, AFC	348	1,815	5.2	28
	Frank Gore, San Francisco, NFC	312	1,695	5.4	8
2005	Shaun Alexander, Seattle, NFC	370	1,880	5.1	27
	Larry Johnson, Kansas City, AFC	336	1,750	5.2	20
2004	Curtis Martin, N.Y. Jets, AFC	371	1,697	4.6	12
	Shaun Alexander, Seattle, NFC	353	1,696	4.8	16
2003	Jamal Lewis, Baltimore, AFC	387	2,066	5.3	14
	Ahman Green, Green Bay, NFC	355	1,883	5.3	15
2002	Ricky Williams, Miami, AFC	383	1,853	4.8	16
	Deuce McAllister, New Orleans, NFC	325	1,388	4.3	13
2001	Priest Holmes, Kansas City, AFC	327	1,555	4.8	8
	Stephen Davis, Washington, NFC	356	1,432	4.0	5

Year	Player, Team	Att.	Yards	Avg.	TD
2000	Edgerrin James, Indianapolis, AFC	387	1,709	4.4	13
	Robert Smith, Minnesota, NFC	295	1,521	5.2	7
1999	*Edgerrin James, Indianapolis, AFC	369	1,553	4.2	13
	Stephen Davis, Washington, NFC	290	1,405	4.8	17
1998	Terrell Davis, Denver, AFC	392	2,008	5.1	21
	Jamal Anderson, Atlanta, NFC	410	1,846	4.5	14
1997	Barry Sanders, Detroit, NFC	335	2,053	6.1	11
	Terrell Davis, Denver, AFC	369	1,750	4.7	15
1996	Barry Sanders, Detroit, NFC	307	1,553	5.1	11
	Terrell Davis, Denver, AFC	345	1,538	4.5	13
1995	Emmitt Smith, Dallas, NFC	377	1,773	4.7	25
	*Curtis Martin, New England, AFC	368	1,487	4.0	14
1994	Barry Sanders, Detroit, NFC	331	1,883	5.7	7
	Chris Warren, Seattle, AFC	333	1,545	4.6	9
1993	Emmitt Smith, Dallas, NFC	283	1,486	5.3	9
	Thurman Thomas, Buffalo, AFC	355	1,315	3.7	6
1992	Emmitt Smith, Dallas, NFC	373	1,713	4.6	18
	Barry Foster, Pittsburgh, AFC	390	1,690	4.3	11
1991	Emmitt Smith, Dallas, NFC	365	1,563	4.3	12
	Thurman Thomas, Buffalo, AFC	288	1,407	4.9	7
1990	Barry Sanders, Detroit, NFC	255	1,304	5.1	13
	Thurman Thomas, Buffalo, AFC	271	1,297	4.8	11
1989	Christian Okoye, Kansas City, AFC	370	1,480	4.0	12
	*Barry Sanders, Detroit, NFC	280	1,470	5.3	14
1988	Eric Dickerson, Indianapolis, AFC	388	1,659	4.3	14
	Herschel Walker, Dallas, NFC	361	1,514	4.2	5
1987	Charles White, L.A. Rams, NFC	324	1,374	4.2	11
	Eric Dickerson, Indianapolis, AFC	223	1,011	4.5	5
1986	Eric Dickerson, L.A. Rams, NFC	404	1,821	4.5	11
	Curt Warner, Seattle, AFC	319	1,481	4.6	13
1985	Marcus Allen, L.A. Raiders, AFC	380	1,759	4.6	11
	Gerald Riggs, Atlanta, NFC	397	1,719	4.3	10
1984	Eric Dickerson, L.A. Rams, NFC	379	2,105	5.6	14
	Earnest Jackson, San Diego, AFC	296	1,179	4.0	8
1983	*Eric Dickerson, L.A. Rams, NFC	390	1,808	4.6	18
	*Curt Warner, Seattle, AFC	335	1,449	4.3	13
1982	Freeman McNeil, N.Y. Jets, AFC	151	786	5.2	6
	Tony Dorsett, Dallas, NFC	177	745	4.2	5
1981	*George Rogers, New Orleans, NFC	378	1,674	4.4	13
	Earl Campbell, Houston, AFC	361	1,376	3.8	10
1980	Earl Campbell, Houston, AFC	373	1,934	5.2	13
	Walter Payton, Chicago, NFC	317	1,460	4.6	6
1979	Earl Campbell, Houston, AFC	368	1,697	4.6	19
	Walter Payton, Chicago, NFC	369	1,610	4.4	14
1978	*Earl Campbell, Houston, AFC	302	1,450	4.8	13
	Walter Payton, Chicago, NFC	333	1,395	4.2	11
1977	Walter Payton, Chicago, NFC	339	1,852	5.5	14
	Mark van Eeghen, Oakland, AFC	324	1,273	3.9	7
1976	O.J. Simpson, Buffalo, AFC	290	1,503	5.2	8
	Walter Payton, Chicago, NFC	311	1,390	4.5	13
1975	O.J. Simpson, Buffalo, AFC	329	1,817	5.5	16
	Jim Otis, St. Louis, NFC	269	1,076	4.0	5
1974	Otis Armstrong, Denver, AFC	263	1,407	5.3	9
	Lawrence McCutcheon, Los Angeles, NFC	236	1,109	4.7	3
1973	O.J. Simpson, Buffalo, AFC	332	2,003	6.0	12
	John Brockington, Green Bay, NFC	265	1,144	4.3	3
1972	O.J. Simpson, Buffalo, AFC	292	1,251	4.3	6
	Larry Brown, Washington, NFC	285	1,216	4.3	8
1971	Floyd Little, Denver, AFC	284	1,133	4.0	6
	*John Brockington, Green Bay, NFC	216	1,105	5.1	4
1970	Larry Brown, Washington, NFC	237	1,125	4.7	5
	Floyd Little, Denver, AFC	209	901	4.3	3
1969	Gale Sayers, Chicago, NFL	236	1,032	4.4	8
	Dickie Post, San Diego, AFL	182	873	4.8	6
1968	Leroy Kelly, Cleveland, NFL	248	1,239	5.0	16
	*Paul Robinson, Cincinnati, AFL	238	1,023	4.3	8
1967	Jim Nance, Boston, AFL	269	1,216	4.5	7
	Leroy Kelly, Cleveland, NFL	235	1,205	5.1	11
1966	Jim Nance, Boston, AFL	299	1,458	4.9	11
	Gale Sayers, Chicago, NFL	229	1,231	5.4	8

Year	Player, Team	Att.	Yards	Avg.	TD
1965	Jim Brown, Cleveland, NFL	289	1,544	5.3	17
	Paul Lowe, San Diego, AFL	222	1,121	5.0	7
1964	Jim Brown, Cleveland, NFL	280	1,446	5.2	7
	Cookie Gilchrist, Buffalo, AFL	230	981	4.3	6
1963	Jim Brown, Cleveland, NFL	291	1,863	6.4	12
	Clem Daniels, Oakland, AFL	215	1,099	5.1	3
1962	Jim Taylor, Green Bay, NFL	272	1,474	5.4	19
	Cookie Gilchrist, Buffalo, AFL	214	1,096	5.1	13
1961	Jim Brown, Cleveland, NFL	305	1,408	4.6	8
	Billy Cannon, Houston, AFL	200	948	4.7	6
1960	Jim Brown, Cleveland, NFL	215	1,257	5.8	9
	*Abner Haynes, Dall. Texans, AFL	156	875	5.6	9
1959	Jim Brown, Cleveland	290	1,329	4.6	14
1958	Jim Brown, Cleveland	257	1,527	5.9	17
1957	*Jim Brown, Cleveland	202	942	4.7	9
1956	Rick Casares, Chi. Bears	234	1,126	4.8	12
1955	*Alan Ameche, Baltimore	213	961	4.5	9
1954	Joe Perry, San Francisco	173	1,049	6.1	8
1953	Joe Perry, San Francisco	192	1,018	5.3	10
1952	Dan Towler, Los Angeles	156	894	5.7	10
1951	Eddie Price, N.Y. Giants	271	971	3.6	7
1950	Marion Motley, Cleveland	140	810	5.8	3
1949	Steve Van Buren, Philadelphia	263	1,146	4.4	11
1948	Steve Van Buren, Philadelphia	201	945	4.7	10
1947	Steve Van Buren, Philadelphia	217	1,008	4.6	13
1946	Bill Dudley, Pittsburgh	146	604	4.1	3
1945	Steve Van Buren, Philadelphia	143	832	5.8	15
1944	Bill Paschal, N.Y. Giants	196	737	3.8	9
1943	*Bill Paschal, N.Y. Giants	147	572	3.9	10
1942	*Bill Dudley, Pittsburgh	162	696	4.3	5
1941	Clarence (Pug) Manders, Brooklyn	111	486	4.4	5
1940	Byron (Whizzer) White, Detroit	146	514	3.5	5
1939	*Bill Osmanski, Chicago	121	699	5.8	7
1938	*Byron (Whizzer) White, Pittsburgh	152	567	3.7	4
1937	Cliff Battles, Washington	216	874	4.0	5
1936	*Alphonse (Tuffy) Leemans, N.Y. Giants	206	830	4.0	2
1935	Doug Russell, Chi. Cardinals	140	499	3.6	0
1934	*Beattie Feathers, Chi. Bears	119	1,004	8.4	8
1933	Jim Musick, Boston	173	809	4.7	5
1932	*Cliff Battles, Boston	148	576	3.9	3

*First season of professional football.

ANNUAL PASSING LEADERS
(Current rating system implemented in 1973)

Year	Player, Team	Att.	Comp.	Yards	TD	Int.	Rating
2012	Aaron Rodgers, Green Bay, NFC	552	371	4,295	39	8	108.0
	Peyton Manning, Denver, AFC	583	400	4,659	37	11	105.8
2011	Aaron Rodgers, Green Bay, NFC	502	343	4,643	45	6	122.5
	Tom Brady, New England, AFC	611	401	5,235	39	12	105.6
2010	Tom Brady, New England, AFC	492	324	3,900	36	4	111.0
	Aaron Rodgers, Green Bay, NFC	475	312	3,922	28	11	101.2
2009	Drew Brees, New Orleans, NFC	514	363	4,388	34	11	109.6
	Philip Rivers, San Diego, AFC	486	317	4,254	28	9	104.4
2008	Philip Rivers, San Diego, AFC	478	312	4,009	34	11	105.5
	Kurt Warner, Arizona, NFC	598	401	4,583	30	14	96.9
2007	Tom Brady, New England, AFC	578	398	4,806	50	8	117.2
	Tony Romo, Dallas, NFC	520	335	4,211	36	19	97.4
2006	Peyton Manning, Indianapolis, AFC	557	362	4,397	31	9	101.0
	Drew Brees, New Orleans, NFC	554	356	4,418	26	11	96.2
2005	Peyton Manning, Indianapolis, AFC	453	305	3,747	28	10	104.1
	Matt Hasselbeck, Seattle, NFC	449	294	3,459	24	9	98.2
2004	Peyton Manning, Indianapolis, AFC	497	336	4,557	49	10	121.1
	Daunte Culpepper, Minnesota, NFC	548	379	4,717	39	11	110.9
2003	Steve McNair, Tennessee, AFC	400	250	3,215	24	7	100.4
	Daunte Culpepper, Minnesota, NFC	454	295	3,479	25	11	96.4
2002	Chad Pennington, N.Y. Jets, AFC	399	275	3,120	22	6	104.2
	Brad Johnson, Tampa Bay, NFC	451	281	3,049	22	6	92.9
2001	Kurt Warner, St. Louis, NFC	546	375	4,830	36	22	101.4
	Rich Gannon, Oakland, AFC	549	361	3,828	27	9	95.5

Year	Player, Team	Att.	Comp.	Yards	TD	Int.	Rating
2000	Brian Griese, Denver, AFC	336	216	2,688	19	4	102.9
	Trent Green, St. Louis, NFC	240	145	2,063	16	5	101.8
1999	Kurt Warner, St. Louis, NFC	499	325	4,353	41	13	109.2
	Peyton Manning, Indianapolis, AFC	533	331	4,135	26	15	90.7
1998	Randall Cunningham, Minnesota, NFC	425	259	3,704	34	10	106.0
	Vinny Testaverde, N.Y. Jets, AFC	421	259	3,256	29	7	101.6
1997	Steve Young, San Francisco, NFC	356	241	3,029	19	6	104.7
	Mark Brunell, Jacksonville, AFC	435	264	3,281	18	7	91.2
1996	Steve Young, San Francisco NFC	316	214	2,410	14	6	97.2
	John Elway, Denver, AFC	466	287	3,328	26	14	89.2
1995	Jim Harbaugh, Indianapolis, AFC	314	200	2,575	17	5	100.7
	Brett Favre, Green Bay, NFC	570	359	4,413	38	13	99.5
1994	Steve Young, San Francisco, NFC	461	324	3,969	35	10	112.8
	Dan Marino, Miami, AFC	615	385	4,453	30	17	89.2
1993	Steve Young, San Francisco, NFC	462	314	4,023	29	16	101.5
	John Elway, Denver, AFC	551	348	4,030	25	10	92.8
1992	Steve Young, San Francisco, NFC	402	268	3,465	25	7	107.0
	Warren Moon, Houston, AFC	346	224	2,521	18	12	89.3
1991	Steve Young, San Francisco, NFC	279	180	2,517	17	8	101.8
	Jim Kelly, Buffalo, AFC	474	304	3,844	33	17	97.6
1990	Jim Kelly, Buffalo, AFC	346	219	2,829	24	9	101.2
	Phil Simms, N.Y. Giants, NFC	311	184	2,284	15	4	92.7
1989	Joe Montana, San Francisco, NFC	386	271	3,521	26	8	112.4
	Boomer Esiason, Cincinnati, AFC	455	258	3,525	28	11	92.1
1988	Boomer Esiason, Cincinnati, AFC	388	223	3,572	28	14	97.4
	Wade Wilson, Minnesota, NFC	332	204	2,746	15	9	91.5
1987	Joe Montana, San Francisco, NFC	398	266	3,054	31	13	102.1
	Bernie Kosar, Cleveland, AFC	389	241	3,033	22	9	95.4
1986	Tommy Kramer, Minnesota, NFC	372	208	3,000	24	10	92.6
	Dan Marino, Miami, AFC	623	378	4,746	44	23	92.5
1985	Ken O'Brien, N.Y. Jets, AFC	488	297	3,888	25	8	96.2
	Joe Montana, San Francisco, NFC	494	303	3,653	27	13	91.3
1984	Dan Marino, Miami, AFC	564	362	5,084	48	17	108.9
	Joe Montana, San Francisco, NFC	432	279	3,630	28	10	102.9
1983	Steve Bartkowski, Atlanta, NFC	432	274	3,167	22	5	97.6
	*Dan Marino, Miami, AFC	296	173	2,210	20	6	96.0
1982	Ken Anderson, Cincinnati, AFC	309	218	2,495	12	9	95.3
	Joe Theismann, Washington, NFC	252	161	2,033	13	9	91.3
1981	Ken Anderson, Cincinnati, AFC	479	300	3,754	29	10	98.4
	Joe Montana, San Francisco, NFC	488	311	3,565	19	12	88.4
1980	Brian Sipe, Cleveland, AFC	554	337	4,132	30	14	91.4
	Ron Jaworski, Philadelphia, NFC	451	257	3,529	27	12	91.0
1979	Roger Staubach, Dallas, NFC	461	267	3,586	27	11	92.3
	Dan Fouts, San Diego, AFC	530	332	4,082	24	24	82.6
1978	Roger Staubach, Dallas, NFC	413	231	3,190	25	16	84.9
	Terry Bradshaw, Pittsburgh, AFC	368	207	2,915	28	20	84.7
1977	Bob Griese, Miami, AFC	307	180	2,252	22	13	87.8
	Roger Staubach, Dallas, NFC	361	210	2,620	18	9	87.0
1976	Ken Stabler, Oakland, AFC	291	194	2,737	27	17	103.4
	James Harris, Los Angeles, NFC	158	91	1,460	8	6	89.6
1975	Ken Anderson, Cincinnati, AFC	377	228	3,169	21	11	93.9
	Fran Tarkenton, Minnesota, NFC	425	273	2,994	25	13	91.8
1974	Ken Anderson, Cincinnati, AFC	328	213	2,667	18	10	95.7
	Sonny Jurgensen, Washington, NFC	167	107	1,185	11	5	94.5
1973	Roger Staubach, Dallas, NFC	286	179	2,428	23	15	94.6
	Ken Stabler, Oakland, AFC	260	163	1,997	14	10	88.3
1972	Norm Snead, N.Y. Giants, NFC	325	196	2,307	17	12	
	Earl Morrall, Miami, AFC	150	83	1,360	11	7	
1971	Roger Staubach, Dallas, NFC	211	126	1,882	15	4	
	Bob Griese, Miami, AFC	263	145	2,089	19	9	
1970	John Brodie, San Francisco, NFC	378	223	2,941	24	10	
	Daryle Lamonica, Oakland, AFC	356	179	2,516	22	15	
1969	Sonny Jurgensen, Washington, NFL	442	274	3,102	22	15	
	*Greg Cook, Cincinnati, AFL	197	106	1,854	15	11	
1968	Len Dawson, Kansas City, AFL	224	131	2,109	17	9	
	Earl Morrall, Baltimore, NFL	317	182	2,909	26	17	
1967	Sonny Jurgensen, Washington, NFL	508	288	3,747	31	16	
	Daryle Lamonica, Oakland, AFL	425	220	3,228	30	20	
1966	Bart Starr, Green Bay, NFL	251	156	2,257	14	3	
	Len Dawson, Kansas City, AFL	284	159	2,527	26	10	

Year	Player, Team	Att.	Comp.	Yards	TD	Int.	Rating
1965	Rudy Bukich, Chicago, NFL	312	176	2,641	20	9	
	John Hadl, San Diego, AFL	348	174	2,798	20	21	
1964	Len Dawson, Kansas City, AFL	354	199	2,879	30	18	
	Bart Starr, Green Bay, NFL	272	163	2,144	15	4	
1963	Y.A. Tittle, N.Y. Giants, NFL	367	221	3,145	36	14	
	Tobin Rote, San Diego, AFL	286	170	2,510	20	17	
1962	Len Dawson, Dallas Texans, AFL	310	189	2,759	29	17	
	Bart Starr, Green Bay, NFL	285	178	2,438	12	9	
1961	George Blanda, Houston, AFL	362	187	3,330	36	22	
	Milt Plum, Cleveland, NFL	302	177	2,416	18	10	
1960	Milt Plum, Cleveland, NFL	250	151	2,297	21	5	
	Jack Kemp, L.A. Chargers, AFL	406	211	3,018	20	25	
1959	Charlie Conerly, N.Y. Giants	194	113	1,706	14	4	
1958	Eddie LeBaron, Washington	145	79	1,365	11	10	
1957	Tommy O'Connell, Cleveland	110	63	1,229	9	8	
1956	Ed Brown, Chicago Bears	168	96	1,667	11	12	
1955	Otto Graham, Cleveland	185	98	1,721	15	8	
1954	Norm Van Brocklin, Los Angeles	260	139	2,637	13	21	
1953	Otto Graham, Cleveland	258	167	2,722	11	9	
1952	Norm Van Brocklin, Los Angeles	205	113	1,736	14	17	
1951	Bob Waterfield, Los Angeles	176	88	1,566	13	10	
1950	Norm Van Brocklin, Los Angeles	233	127	2,061	18	14	
1949	Sammy Baugh, Washington	255	145	1,903	18	14	
1948	Tommy Thompson, Philadelphia	246	141	1,965	25	11	
1947	Sammy Baugh, Washington	354	210	2,938	25	15	
1946	Bob Waterfield, Los Angeles	251	127	1,747	18	17	
1945	Sammy Baugh, Washington	182	128	1,669	11	4	
	Sid Luckman, Chicago Bears	217	117	1,725	14	10	
1944	Frank Filchock, Washington	147	84	1,139	13	9	
1943	Sammy Baugh, Washington	239	133	1,754	23	19	
1942	Cecil Isbell, Green Bay	268	146	2,021	24	14	
1941	Cecil Isbell, Green Bay	206	117	1,479	15	11	
1940	Sammy Baugh, Washington	177	111	1,367	12	10	
1939	*Parker Hall, Cleveland	208	106	1,227	9	13	
1938	Ed Danowski, N.Y. Giants	129	70	848	7	8	
1937	*Sammy Baugh, Washington	171	81	1,127	8	14	
1936	Arnie Herber, Green Bay	173	77	1,239	11	13	
1935	Ed Danowski, N.Y. Giants	113	57	794	10	9	
1934	Arnie Herber, Green Bay	115	42	799	8	12	
1933	*Harry Newman, N.Y. Giants	136	53	973	11	17	
1932	Arnie Herber, Green Bay	101	37	639	9	9	

First season of professional football.

ANNUAL PASSING TOUCHDOWN LEADERS

Year	Player, Team	TD
2012	Drew Brees, New Orleans, NFC	43
	Peyton Manning, Denver, AFC	37
2011	Drew Brees, New Orleans, NFC	46
	Tom Brady, New England, AFC	39
2010	Tom Brady, New England, AFC	36
	Drew Brees, New Orleans, NFC	33
2009	Drew Brees, New Orleans, NFC	34
	Peyton Manning, Indianapolis, AFC	33
2008	Drew Brees, New Orleans, NFC	34
	Philip Rivers, San Diego, AFC	34
2007	Tom Brady, New England, AFC	50
	Tony Romo, Dallas, NFC	36
2006	Peyton Manning, Indianapolis, AFC	31
	Drew Brees, New Orleans, NFC	26
2005	Carson Palmer, Cincinnati, AFC	32
	Jake Delhomme, Carolina, NFC	24
	Matt Hasselbeck, Seattle, NFC	24
	Eli Manning, N.Y. Giants, NFC	24
2004	Peyton Manning, Indianapolis, AFC	49
	Daunte Culpepper, Minnesota, NFC	39
2003	Brett Favre, Green Bay, NFC	32
	Peyton Manning, Indianapolis, AFC	29
2002	Tom Brady, New England, AFC	28
	Aaron Brooks, New Orleans, NFC	27
	Brett Favre, Green Bay, NFC	27

Year	Player, Team	TD
2001	Kurt Warner, St. Louis, NFC	36
	Rich Gannon, Oakland, AFC	27
2000	Daunte Culpepper, Minnesota, NFC	33
	Peyton Manning, Indianapolis, AFC	33
1999	Kurt Warner, St. Louis, NFC	41
	Peyton Manning, Indianapolis, AFC	26
1998	Steve Young, San Francisco, NFC	36
	Vinny Testaverde, N.Y. Jets, AFC	29
1997	Brett Favre, Green Bay, NFC	35
	Jeff George, Oakland, AFC	29
1996	Brett Favre, Green Bay, NFC	39
	Vinny Testaverde, Baltimore, AFC	33
1995	Brett Favre, Green Bay, NFC	38
	Jeff Blake, Cincinnati, AFC	28
1994	Steve Young, San Francisco, NFC	35
	Dan Marino, Miami, AFC	30
1993	Steve Young, San Francisco, NFC	29
	John Elway, Denver, AFC	25
1992	Steve Young, San Francisco, NFC	25
	Dan Marino, Miami, AFC	24
1991	Jim Kelly, Buffalo, AFC	33
	Mark Rypien, Washington, NFC	28
1990	Warren Moon, Houston, AFC	33
	Randall Cunningham, Philadelphia, NFC	30
1989	Jim Everett, L.A. Rams, NFC	29
	Boomer Esiason, Cincinnati, AFC	28

Year	Player, Team	TD	Year	Player, Team	TD
1988	Jim Everett, L.A. Rams, NFC	31	1967	Sonny Jurgensen, Washington, NFL	31
	Boomer Esiason, Cincinnati, AFC	28		Daryle Lamonica, Oakland, AFL	30
	Dan Marino, Miami, AFC	28	1966	Frank Ryan, Cleveland, NFL	29
1987	Joe Montana, San Francisco, NFC	31		Len Dawson, Kansas City, AFL	26
	Dan Marino, Miami, AFC	26	1965	John Brodie, San Francisco, NFL	30
1986	Dan Marino, Miami, AFC	44		Len Dawson, Kansas City, AFL	21
	Tommy Kramer, Minnesota, NFC	24	1964	Babe Parilli, Boston, AFL	31
1985	Dan Marino, Miami, AFC	30		Frank Ryan, Cleveland, NFL	25
	Joe Montana, San Francisco, NFC	27	1963	Y.A. Tittle, N.Y. Giants, NFL	36
1984	Dan Marino, Miami, AFC	48		Len Dawson, Kansas City, AFL	26
	Neil Lomax, St. Louis, NFC	28	1962	Y.A. Tittle, N.Y. Giants, NFL	33
	Joe Montana, San Francisco, NFC	28		Len Dawson, Dallas, AFL	29
1983	Lynn Dickey, Green Bay, NFC	32	1961	George Blanda, Houston, AFL	36
	Joe Ferguson, Buffalo, AFC	26		Sonny Jurgensen, Philadelphia, NFL	32
	Brian Sipe, Cleveland, AFC	26	1960	Al Dorow, N.Y. Titans, AFL	26
1982	Terry Bradshaw, Pittsburgh, AFC	17		Johnny Unitas, Baltimore, NFL	25
	Dan Fouts, San Diego, AFC	17	1959	Johnny Unitas, Baltimore	32
	Joe Montana, San Francisco, NFC	17	1958	Johnny Unitas, Baltimore	19
1981	Dan Fouts, San Diego, AFC	33	1957	Johnny Unitas, Baltimore	24
	Steve Bartkowski, Atlanta, NFC	30	1956	Tobin Rote, Green Bay	18
1980	Steve Bartkowski, Atlanta, NFC	31	1955	Tobin Rote, Green Bay	17
	Dan Fouts, San Diego, AFC	30		Y.A. Tittle, San Francisco	17
	Brian Sipe, Cleveland, AFC	30	1954	Adrian Burk, Philadelphia	23
1979	Steve Grogan, New England, AFC	28	1953	Robert Thomason, Philadelphia	21
	Brian Sipe, Cleveland, AFC	28	1952	Jim Finks, Pittsburgh	20
	Roger Staubach, Dallas, NFC	27		Otto Graham, Cleveland	20
1978	Terry Bradshaw, Pittsburgh, AFC	28	1951	Bobby Layne, Detroit	26
	Roger Staubach, Dallas, NFC	25	1950	George Ratterman, N.Y. Yanks	22
	Fran Tarkenton, Minnesota, NFC	25	1949	Johnny Lujack, Chi. Bears	23
1977	Bob Griese, Miami, AFC	22	1948	Tommy Thompson, Philadelphia	25
	Ron Jaworski, Philadelphia, NFC	18	1947	Sammy Baugh, Washington	25
	Roger Staubach, Dallas, NFC	18	1946	Sid Luckman, Chi. Bears	17
1976	Ken Stabler, Oakland, AFC	27		Bob Waterfield, Los Angeles	17
	Jim Hart, St. Louis, NFC	18	1945	Sid Luckman, Chi. Bears	14
1975	Joe Ferguson, Buffalo, AFC	25		*Bob Waterfield, Cleveland	14
	Fran Tarkenton, Minnesota, NFC	25	1944	Frank Filchock, Washington	13
1974	Ken Stabler, Oakland, AFC	26	1943	Sid Luckman, Chi. Bears	28
	Jim Hart, St. Louis, NFC	20	1942	Cecil Isbell, Green Bay	24
1973	Roman Gabriel, Philadelphia, NFC	23	1941	Cecil Isbell, Green Bay	15
	Roger Staubach, Dallas, NFC	23	1940	Sammy Baugh, Washington	12
	Charley Johnson, Denver, AFC	20	1939	Frank Filchock, Washington	11
1972	Billy Kilmer, Washington, NFC	19	1938	Bob Monnett, Green Bay	9
	Joe Namath, N.Y. Jets, AFC	19	1937	Bernie Masterson, Chi. Bears	9
1971	John Hadl, San Diego, AFC	21	1936	Arnie Herber, Green Bay	11
	John Brodie, San Francisco, NFC	18	1935	Ed Danowski, N.Y. Giants	10
1970	John Brodie, San Francisco, NFC	24	1934	Arnie Herber, Green Bay	8
	John Hadl, San Diego, AFC	22	1933	*Harry Newman, N.Y. Giants	11
	Daryle Lamonica, Oakland, AFC	22	1932	Arnie Herber, Green Bay	9
1969	Daryle Lamonica, Oakland, AFL	34	*First season of professional football.		
	Roman Gabriel, Los Angeles, NFL	24			
1968	John Hadl, San Diego, AFL	27			
	Earl Morrall, Baltimore, NFL	26			

ANNUAL PASS RECEIVING LEADERS

Year	Player, Team	No.	Yards	Avg.	TD
2012	Calvin Johnson, Detroit, NFC	122	1,964	16.1	5
	Wes Welker, New England, AFC	118	1,354	11.5	6
2011	Wes Welker, New England, AFC	122	1,569	12.9	9
	Roddy White, Atlanta, NFC	100	1,296	13.0	8
2010	Roddy White, Atlanta, NFC	115	1,389	12.1	10
	Reggie Wayne, Indianapolis, AFC	111	1,355	12.2	6
2009	Wes Welker, New England, AFC	123	1,348	11.0	4
	Steve Smith, N.Y. Giants, NFC	107	1,220	11.4	7
2008	Andre Johnson, Houston, AFC	115	1,575	13.7	8
	Larry Fitzgerald, Arizona, NFC	96	1,431	14.9	12
2007	T.J. Houshmandzadeh, Cincinnati, AFC	112	1,143	10.2	12
	Wes Welker, New England, AFC	112	1,175	10.5	8
	Larry Fitzgerald, Arizona, NFC	100	1,409	14.1	10
2006	Andre Johnson, Houston, AFC	103	1,147	11.1	5
	Mike Furrey, Detroit, NFC	98	1,086	11.1	6

Year	Player, Team	No.	Yards	Avg.	TD
2005	Steve Smith, Carolina, NFC	103	1,563	15.2	12
	Larry Fitzgerald, Arizona, NFC	103	1,409	13.7	10
	Chad Johnson, Cincinnati, AFC	97	1,432	14.8	9
2004	Tony Gonzalez, Kansas City, AFC	102	1,258	12.3	7
	Joe Horn, New Orleans, NFC	94	1,399	14.9	11
	Torry Holt, St. Louis, NFC	94	1,372	14.6	10
2003	Torry Holt, St. Louis, NFC	117	1,696	14.5	12
	LaDainian Tomlinson, San Diego, AFC	100	725	7.3	4
2002	Marvin Harrison, Indianapolis, AFC	143	1,722	12.0	11
	Randy Moss, Minnesota, NFC	106	1,347	12.7	7
2001	Rod Smith, Denver, AFC	113	1,343	11.9	11
	Keyshawn Johnson, Tampa Bay, NFC	106	1,266	11.9	1
2000	Marvin Harrison, Indianapolis, AFC	102	1,413	13.9	14
	Muhsin Muhammad, Carolina, NFC	102	1,183	11.6	6
1999	Jimmy Smith, Jacksonville, AFC	116	1,636	14.1	6
	Muhsin Muhammad, Carolina, NFC	96	1,253	13.1	8
1998	O.J. McDuffie, Miami, AFC	90	1,050	11.7	7
	Frank Sanders, Arizona, NFC	89	1,145	12.9	3
1997	Tim Brown, Oakland, AFC	104	1,408	13.5	5
	Herman Moore, Detroit, NFC	104	1,293	12.4	8
1996	Jerry Rice, San Francisco, NFC	108	1,254	11.6	8
	Carl Pickens, Cincinnati, AFC	100	1,180	11.8	12
1995	Herman Moore, Detroit, NFC	123	1,686	13.7	14
	Carl Pickens, Cincinnati, AFC	99	1,234	12.5	17
1994	Cris Carter, Minnesota, NFC	122	1,256	10.3	7
	Ben Coates, New England, AFC	96	1,174	12.2	7
1993	Sterling Sharpe, Green Bay, NFC	112	1,274	11.4	11
	Reggie Langhorne, Indianapolis, AFC	85	1,038	12.2	3
1992	Sterling Sharpe, Green Bay, NFC	108	1,461	13.5	13
	Haywood Jeffires, Houston, AFC	90	913	10.1	9
1991	Haywood Jeffires, Houston, AFC	100	1,181	11.8	7
	Michael Irvin, Dallas, NFC	93	1,523	16.4	8
1990	Jerry Rice, San Francisco, NFC	100	1,502	15.0	13
	Haywood Jeffires, Houston, AFC	74	1,048	14.2	8
	Drew Hill, Houston, AFC	74	1,019	13.8	5
1989	Sterling Sharpe, Green Bay, NFC	90	1,423	15.8	12
	Andre Reed, Buffalo, AFC	88	1,312	14.9	9
1988	Al Toon, N.Y. Jets, AFC	93	1,067	11.5	5
	Henry Ellard, L.A. Rams, NFC	86	1,414	16.4	10
1987	J.T. Smith, St. Louis, NFC	91	1,117	12.3	8
	Al Toon, N.Y. Jets, AFC	68	976	14.4	5
1986	Todd Christensen, L.A. Raiders, AFC	95	1,153	12.1	8
	Jerry Rice, San Francisco, NFC	86	1,570	18.3	15
1985	Roger Craig, San Francisco, NFC	92	1,016	11.0	6
	Lionel James, San Diego, AFC	86	1,027	11.9	6
1984	Art Monk, Washington, NFC	106	1,372	12.9	7
	Ozzie Newsome, Cleveland, AFC	89	1,001	11.2	5
1983	Todd Christensen, L.A. Raiders, AFC	92	1,247	13.6	12
	Roy Green, St. Louis, NFC	78	1,227	15.7	14
	Charlie Brown, Washington, NFC	78	1,225	15.7	8
	Earnest Gray, N.Y. Giants, NFC	78	1,139	14.6	5
1982	Dwight Clark, San Francisco, NFC	60	913	15.2	5
	Kellen Winslow, San Diego, AFC	54	721	13.4	6
1981	Kellen Winslow, San Diego, AFC	88	1,075	12.2	10
	Dwight Clark, San Francisco, NFC	85	1,105	13.0	4
1980	Kellen Winslow, San Diego, AFC	89	1,290	14.5	9
	*Earl Cooper, San Francisco, NFC	83	567	6.8	4
1979	Joe Washington, Baltimore, AFC	82	750	9.1	3
	Ahmad Rashad, Minnesota, NFC	80	1,156	14.5	9
1978	Rickey Young, Minnesota, NFC	88	704	8.0	5
	Steve Largent, Seattle, AFC	71	1,168	16.5	8
1977	Lydell Mitchell, Baltimore, AFC	71	620	8.7	4
	Ahmad Rashad, Minnesota, NFC	51	681	13.4	2
1976	MacArthur Lane, Kansas City, AFC	66	686	10.4	1
	Drew Pearson, Dallas, NFC	58	806	13.9	6
1975	Chuck Foreman, Minnesota, NFC	73	691	9.5	9
	Reggie Rucker, Cleveland, AFC	60	770	12.8	3
	Lydell Mitchell, Baltimore, AFC	60	544	9.1	4
1974	Lydell Mitchell, Baltimore, AFC	72	544	7.6	2
	Charles Young, Philadelphia, NFC	63	696	11.0	3

Year	Player, Team	No.	Yards	Avg.	TD
1973	Harold Carmichael, Philadelphia, NFC	67	1,116	16.7	9
	Fred Willis, Houston, AFC	57	371	6.5	1
1972	Harold Jackson, Philadelphia, NFC	62	1,048	16.9	4
	Fred Biletnikoff, Oakland, AFC	58	802	13.8	7
1971	Fred Biletnikoff, Oakland, AFC	61	929	15.2	9
	Bob Tucker, N.Y. Giants, NFC	59	791	13.4	4
1970	Dick Gordon, Chicago, NFC	71	1,026	14.5	13
	Marlin Briscoe, Buffalo, AFC	57	1,036	18.2	8
1969	Dan Abramowicz, New Orleans, NFL	73	1,015	13.9	7
	Lance Alworth, San Diego, AFL	64	1,003	15.7	4
1968	Clifton McNeil, San Francisco, NFL	71	994	14.0	7
	Lance Alworth, San Diego, AFL	68	1,312	19.3	10
1967	George Sauer, N.Y. Jets, AFL	75	1,189	15.9	6
	Charley Taylor, Washington, NFL	70	990	14.1	9
1966	Lance Alworth, San Diego, AFL	73	1,383	18.9	13
	Charley Taylor, Washington, NFL	72	1,119	15.5	12
1965	Lionel Taylor, Denver, AFL	85	1,131	13.3	6
	Dave Parks, San Francisco, NFL	80	1,344	16.8	12
1964	Charley Hennigan, Houston, AFL	101	1,546	15.3	8
	Johnny Morris, Chicago, NFL	93	1,200	12.9	10
1963	Lionel Taylor, Denver, AFL	78	1,101	14.1	10
	Bobby Joe Conrad, St. Louis, NFL	73	967	13.2	10
1962	Lionel Taylor, Denver, AFL	77	908	11.8	4
	Bobby Mitchell, Washington, NFL	72	1,384	19.2	11
1961	Lionel Taylor, Denver, AFL	100	1,176	11.8	4
	Jim (Red) Phillips, Los Angeles, NFL	78	1,092	14.0	5
1960	Lionel Taylor, Denver, AFL	92	1,235	13.4	12
	Raymond Berry, Baltimore, NFL	74	1,298	17.5	10
1959	Raymond Berry, Baltimore	66	959	14.5	14
1958	Raymond Berry, Baltimore	56	794	14.2	9
	Pete Retzlaff, Philadelphia	56	766	13.7	2
1957	Billy Wilson, San Francisco	52	757	14.6	6
1956	Billy Wilson, San Francisco	60	889	14.8	5
1955	Pete Pihos, Philadelphia	62	864	13.9	7
1954	Pete Pihos, Philadelphia	60	872	14.5	10
	Billy Wilson, San Francisco	60	830	13.8	5
1953	Pete Pihos, Philadelphia	63	1,049	16.7	10
1952	Mac Speedie, Cleveland	62	911	14.7	5
1951	Elroy (Crazylegs) Hirsch, Los Angeles	66	1,495	22.7	17
1950	Tom Fears, Los Angeles	84	1,116	13.3	7
1949	Tom Fears, Los Angeles	77	1,013	13.2	9
1948	*Tom Fears, Los Angeles	51	698	13.7	4
1947	Jim Keane, Chi. Bears	64	910	14.2	10
1946	Jim Benton, Los Angeles	63	981	15.6	6
1945	Don Hutson, Green Bay	47	834	17.7	9
1944	Don Hutson, Green Bay	58	866	14.9	9
1943	Don Hutson, Green Bay	47	776	16.5	11
1942	Don Hutson, Green Bay	74	1,211	16.4	17
1941	Don Hutson, Green Bay	58	738	12.7	10
1940	*Don Looney, Philadelphia	58	707	12.2	4
1939	Don Hutson, Green Bay	34	846	24.9	6
1938	Gaynell Tinsley, Chi. Cardinals	41	516	12.6	1
1937	Don Hutson, Green Bay	41	552	13.5	7
1936	Don Hutson, Green Bay	34	536	15.8	8
1935	*Tod Goodwin, N.Y. Giants	26	432	16.6	4
1934	Joe Carter, Philadelphia	16	238	14.9	4
	Morris (Red) Badgro, N.Y. Giants	16	206	12.9	1
1933	John (Shipwreck) Kelly, Brooklyn	22	246	11.2	3
1932	Ray Flaherty, N.Y. Giants	21	350	16.7	3

*First season of professional football.

ANNUAL PASS RECEIVING LEADERS (YARDS)

Year	Player, Team	No.	Yards	Avg.	TD
2012	Calvin Johnson, Detroit, NFC	122	1,964	16.1	5
	Andre Johnson, Houston, AFC	112	1,598	14.3	4
2011	Calvin Johnson, Detroit, NFC	96	1,681	17.5	16
	Wes Welker, New England, AFC	122	1,569	12.9	9
2010	Brandon Lloyd, Denver, AFC	77	1,448	18.8	11
	Roddy White, Atlanta, NFC	115	1,389	12.1	10

Year	Player, Team	No.	Yards	Avg.	TD
2009	Andre Johnson, Houston, AFC	101	1,569	15.5	9
	Miles Austin, Dallas, NFC	81	1,320	16.3	11
2008	Andre Johnson, Houston, AFC	115	1,575	13.7	8
	Larry Fitzgerald, Arizona, NFC	96	1,431	14.9	12
2007	Reggie Wayne, Indianapolis, AFC	104	1,510	14.5	10
	Larry Fitzgerald, Arizona, NFC	100	1,409	14.1	10
2006	Chad Johnson, Cincinnati, AFC	87	1,369	15.7	7
	Roy Williams, Detroit, NFC	82	1,310	16.0	7
2005	Steve Smith, Carolina, NFC	103	1,563	15.2	12
	Chad Johnson, Cincinnati, AFC	97	1,432	14.8	9
2004	Muhsin Muhammad, Carolina, NFC	93	1,405	15.1	16
	Chad Johnson, Cincinnati, AFC	95	1,274	13.4	9
2003	Torry Holt, St. Louis, NFC	117	1,696	14.5	12
	Chad Johnson, Cincinnati, AFC	90	1,355	15.1	10
2002	Marvin Harrison, Indianapolis, AFC	143	1,722	12.0	11
	Randy Moss, Minnesota, NFC	106	1,347	12.7	7
2001	David Boston, Arizona, NFC	98	1,598	16.3	8
	Marvin Harrison, Indianapolis, AFC	109	1,524	14.0	15
2000	Torry Holt, St. Louis, NFC	82	1,635	19.9	6
	Rod Smith, Denver, AFC	100	1,602	16.0	8
1999	Marvin Harrison, Indianapolis, AFC	115	1,663	14.5	12
	Randy Moss, Minnesota, NFC	80	1,413	17.7	11
1998	Antonio Freeman, Green Bay, NFC	84	1,424	17.0	14
	Eric Moulds, Buffalo, AFC	67	1,368	20.4	9
1997	Rob Moore, Arizona, NFC	97	1,584	16.3	8
	Tim Brown, Oakland, AFC	104	1,408	13.5	5
1996	Isaac Bruce, St. Louis, NFC	84	1,338	15.9	7
	Jimmy Smith, Jacksonville, AFC	83	1,244	15.0	7
1995	Jerry Rice, San Francisco, NFC	122	1,848	15.1	15
	Tim Brown, Oakland, AFC	89	1,342	15.1	10
1994	Jerry Rice, San Francisco, NFC	112	1,499	13.4	13
	Tim Brown, L.A. Raiders, AFC	89	1,309	14.7	9
1993	Jerry Rice, San Francisco, NFC	98	1,503	15.3	15
	Tim Brown, L.A. Raiders, AFC	80	1,180	14.8	7
1992	Sterling Sharpe, Green Bay, NFC	108	1,461	13.5	13
	Anthony Miller, San Diego, AFC	72	1,060	14.7	7
1991	Michael Irvin, Dallas, NFC	93	1,523	16.4	8
	Haywood Jeffires, Houston, AFC	100	1,181	11.8	7
1990	Jerry Rice, San Francisco, NFC	100	1,502	15.0	13
	Haywood Jeffires, Houston, AFC	74	1,048	14.2	8
1989	Jerry Rice, San Francisco, NFC	82	1,483	18.1	17
	Andre Reed, Buffalo, AFC	88	1,312	14.9	9
1988	Henry Ellard, L.A. Rams, NFC	86	1,414	16.4	10
	Eddie Brown, Cincinnati, AFC	53	1,273	24.0	9
1987	J.T. Smith, St. Louis, NFC	91	1,117	12.3	8
	Carlos Carson, Kansas City, AFC	55	1,044	19.0	7
1986	Jerry Rice, San Francisco, NFC	86	1,570	18.3	15
	Stanley Morgan, New England, AFC	84	1,491	17.8	10
1985	Steve Largent, Seattle, AFC	79	1,287	16.3	6
	Mike Quick, Philadelphia, NFC	73	1,247	17.1	11
1984	Roy Green, St. Louis, NFC	78	1,555	19.9	12
	John Stallworth, Pittsburgh, AFC	80	1,395	17.4	11
1983	Mike Quick, Philadelphia, NFC	69	1,409	20.4	13
	Carlos Carson, Kansas City, AFC	80	1,351	16.9	7
1982	Wes Chandler, San Diego, AFC	49	1,032	21.1	9
	Dwight Clark, San Francisco, NFC	60	913	15.2	5
1981	Alfred Jenkins, Atlanta, NFC	70	1,358	19.4	13
	Frank Lewis, Buffalo, AFC	70	1,244	17.8	4
	Steve Watson, Denver, AFC	60	1,244	20.7	13
1980	John Jefferson, San Diego, AFC	82	1,340	16.3	13
	James Lofton, Green Bay, NFC	71	1,226	17.3	4
1979	Steve Largent, Seattle, AFC	66	1,237	18.7	9
	Ahmad Rashad, Minnesota, NFC	80	1,156	14.5	9
1978	Wesley Walker, N.Y. Jets, AFC	48	1,169	24.4	8
	Harold Carmichael, Philadelphia, NFC	55	1,072	19.5	8
1977	Drew Pearson, Dallas, NFC	48	870	18.1	2
	Ken Burrough, Houston, AFC	43	816	19.0	8
1976	Roger Carr, Baltimore, AFC	43	1,112	25.9	11
	*Sammy White, Minnesota, NFC	51	906	17.8	10

Year	Player, Team	No.	Yards	Avg.	TD
1975	Ken Burrough, Houston, AFC	53	1,063	20.1	8
	Mel Gray, St. Louis, NFC	48	926	19.3	11
1974	Cliff Branch, Oakland, AFC	60	1,092	18.2	13
	Drew Pearson, Dallas, NFC	62	1,087	17.5	2
1973	Harold Carmichael, Philadelphia, NFC	67	1,116	16.7	9
	*Isaac Curtis, Cincinnati, AFC	45	843	18.7	9
1972	Harold Jackson, Philadelphia, NFC	62	1,048	16.9	4
	Rich Caster, N.Y. Jets, AFC	39	833	21.4	10
1971	Otis Taylor, Kansas City, AFC	57	1,110	19.5	7
	Gene Washington, San Francisco, NFC	46	884	19.2	4
1970	Gene Washington, San Francisco, NFC	53	1,100	20.8	12
	Marlin Briscoe, Buffalo, AFC	57	1,036	18.2	8
1969	Warren Wells, Oakland, AFL	47	1,260	26.8	14
	Harold Jackson, Philadelphia, NFL	65	1,116	17.2	9
1968	Lance Alworth, San Diego, AFL	68	1,312	19.3	10
	Roy Jefferson, Pittsburgh, NFL	58	1,074	18.5	11
1967	Don Maynard, N.Y. Jets, AFL	71	1,434	20.3	10
	Ben Hawkins, Philadelphia, NFL	59	1,265	21.4	10
1966	Lance Alworth, San Diego, AFL	73	1,383	18.9	13
	Pat Studstill, Detroit, NFL	67	1,266	18.9	5
1965	Lance Alworth, San Diego, AFL	69	1,602	23.2	14
	Dave Parks, San Francisco	80	1,344	16.8	12
1964	Charley Hennigan, Houston, AFL	101	1,546	15.3	8
	Johnny Morris, Chicago, NFL	93	1,200	12.9	10
1963	Bobby Mitchell, Washington, NFL	69	1,436	20.8	7
	Art Powell, Oakland, AFL	73	1,304	17.8	16
1962	Bobby Mitchell, Washington, NFL	72	1,384	19.2	11
	Art Powell, N.Y. Titans, AFL	64	1,130	17.6	8
1961	Charley Hennigan, Houston, AFL	82	1,746	21.3	12
	Tommy McDonald, Philadelphia, NFL	64	1,144	17.9	13
1960	*Bill Groman, Houston, AFL	72	1,473	20.5	12
	Raymond Berry, Baltimore, NFL	74	1,298	17.5	10
1959	Raymond Berry, Baltimore	66	959	14.5	14
1958	Del Shofner, Los Angeles	51	1,097	21.5	8
1957	Raymond Berry, Baltimore	47	800	17.0	6
1956	Billy Howton, Green Bay	55	1,188	21.6	12
1955	Pete Pihos, Philadelphia	62	864	13.9	7
1954	Bob Boyd, Los Angeles	53	1,212	22.9	6
1953	Pete Pihos, Philadelphia	63	1,049	16.7	10
1952	*Billy Howton, Green Bay	53	1,231	23.2	13
1951	Elroy (Crazylegs) Hirsch, Los Angeles	66	1,495	22.7	17
1950	Tom Fears, Los Angeles	84	1,116	13.3	7
1949	Bob Mann, Detroit	66	1,014	15.4	4
1948	Mal Kutner, Chi. Cardinals	41	943	23.0	14
1947	Mal Kutner, Chi. Cardinals	43	944	21.9	7
1946	Jim Benton, Los Angeles	63	981	15.5	6
1945	Jim Benton, Cleveland	45	1,067	23.7	8
1944	Don Hutson, Green Bay	58	866	14.6	9
1943	Don Hutson, Green Bay	47	776	16.5	11
1942	Don Hutson, Green Bay	74	1,211	16.4	17
1941	Don Hutson, Green Bay	58	738	12.7	10
1940	*Don Looney, Philadelphia	58	707	12.2	4
1939	Don Hutson, Green Bay	34	846	24.9	6
1938	Don Hutson, Green Bay	32	548	17.1	9
1937	*Gaynell Tinsley, Chi. Cardinals	36	675	18.8	5
1936	Don Hutson, Green Bay	34	526	15.5	8
1935	Charley Malone, Boston	22	433	19.7	2
1934	Harry Ebding, Detroit	9	257	28.6	2
1933	*Paul Moss, Pittsburgh	13	283	21.8	2
1932	Johnny (Blood) McNally, Green Bay	19	326	17.2	3

*First season of professional football.

ANNUAL PUNT RETURN LEADERS

Year	Player, Team	No.	Yards	Avg.	Long	TD
2012	Leodis McKelvin, Buffalo, AFC	23	431	18.7	88	2
	Dwayne Harris, Dallas, NFC	22	354	16.1	78	1
2011	Devin Hester, Chicago, NFC	28	454	16.2	82	1
	Javier Arenas, Kansas City, AFC	32	410	12.8	37	0
2010	Devin Hester, Chicago, NFC	33	564	17.1	89	3
	Julian Edelman, New England, AFC	21	321	15.3	94	1

Year	Player, Team	No.	Yards	Avg.	Long	TD
2009	DeSean Jackson, Philadelphia, NFC	29	441	15.2	85	2
	Wes Welker, New England, AFC	27	338	12.5	69	0
2008	Roscoe Parrish, Buffalo, AFC	21	322	15.3	63	1
	*Clifton Smith, Tampa Bay, NFC	23	324	14.1	70	1
2007	Roscoe Parrish, Buffalo, AFC	27	440	16.3	74	1
	Devin Hester, Chicago, NFC	42	651	15.5	89	4
2006	Adam Jones, Tennessee, AFC	34	440	12.9	90	3
	*Devin Hester, Chicago, NFC	47	600	12.8	84	3
2005	Reno Mahe, Philadelphia, NFC	21	269	12.8	44	0
	B.J. Sams, Baltimore, AFC	33	401	12.2	51	0
2004	Eddie Drummond, Detroit, NFC	24	316	13.2	83	2
	Dennis Northcutt, Cleveland, AFC	36	432	12.0	44	0
2003	Dante Hall, Kansas City, AFC	29	472	16.3	93	2
	Brian Westbrook, Philadelphia, NFC	20	306	15.3	84	2
2002	Jimmy Williams, San Francisco, NFC	20	336	16.8	89	1
	Santana Moss, N.Y. Jets, AFC	25	413	16.5	63	2
2001	Troy Brown, New England, AFC	29	413	14.2	85	2
	Darrien Gordon, Atlanta, NFC	31	437	14.1	74	0
2000	Jermaine Lewis, Baltimore, AFC	36	578	16.1	89	2
	Az-Zahir Hakim, St. Louis, NFC	32	489	15.3	86	1
1999	*Charlie Rogers, Seattle, AFC	22	318	14.5	94	1
	*Mac Cody, Arizona, NFC	32	373	11.7	31	0
1998	Deion Sanders, Dallas, NFC	24	375	15.6	69	1
	Reggie Barlow, Jacksonville, AFC	43	555	12.9	85	1
1997	Jermaine Lewis, Baltimore, AFC	28	437	15.6	89	2
	David Palmer, Minnesota, NFC	34	444	13.1	57	0
1996	Desmond Howard, Green Bay, NFC	58	875	15.1	92	3
	Darrien Gordon, San Diego, AFC	36	537	14.9	81	1
1995	David Palmer, Minnesota, NFC	26	342	13.2	74	1
	Andre Coleman, San Diego, AFC	28	326	11.6	88	1
1994	Brian Mitchell, Washington, NFC	32	452	14.1	78	2
	Darrien Gordon, San Diego, AFC	36	475	13.2	90	2
1993	*Tyrone Hughes, New Orleans, NFC	37	503	13.6	83	2
	Eric Metcalf, Cleveland, AFC	36	464	12.9	91	2
1992	Johnny Bailey, Phoenix, NFC	20	263	13.2	65	0
	Rod Woodson, Pittsburgh, AFC	32	364	11.4	80	1
1991	Mel Gray, Detroit, NFC	25	385	15.4	78	1
	Rod Woodson, Pittsburgh, AFC	28	320	11.4	40	0
1990	Clarence Verdin, Indianapolis, AFC	31	396	12.8	36	0
	*Johnny Bailey, Chicago, NFC	36	399	11.1	95	1
1989	Walter Stanley, Detroit, NFC	36	496	13.8	74	0
	Clarence Verdin, Indianapolis, AFC	23	296	12.9	49	1
1988	John Taylor, San Francisco, NFC	44	556	12.6	95	2
	JoJo Townsell, N.Y. Jets, AFC	35	409	11.7	59	1
1987	Mel Gray, New Orleans, NFC	24	352	14.7	80	0
	Bobby Joe Edmonds, Seattle, AFC	20	251	12.6	40	0
1986	*Bobby Joe Edmonds, Seattle, AFC	34	419	12.3	75	1
	*Vai Sikahema, St. Louis, NFC	43	522	12.1	71	2
1985	Irving Fryar, New England, AFC	37	520	14.1	85	2
	Henry Ellard, L.A. Rams, NFC	37	501	13.5	80	1
1984	Mike Martin, Cincinnati, AFC	24	376	15.7	55	0
	Henry Ellard, L.A. Rams, NFC	30	403	13.4	83	2
1983	*Henry Ellard, L.A. Rams, NFC	16	217	13.6	72	1
	Kirk Springs, N.Y. Jets, AFC	23	287	12.5	76	1
1982	Rick Upchurch, Denver, AFC	15	242	16.1	78	2
	Billy Johnson, Atlanta, NFC	24	273	11.4	71	0
1981	LeRoy Irvin, Los Angeles, NFC	46	615	13.4	84	3
	*James Brooks, San Diego, AFC	22	290	13.2	42	0
1980	J.T. Smith, Kansas City, AFC	40	581	14.5	75	2
	*Kenny Johnson, Atlanta, NFC	23	281	12.2	56	0
1979	John Sciarra, Philadelphia, NFC	16	182	11.4	38	0
	*Tony Nathan, Miami, AFC	28	306	10.9	86	1
1978	Rick Upchurch, Denver, AFC	36	493	13.7	75	1
	Jackie Wallace, Los Angeles, NFC	52	618	11.9	58	0
1977	Billy Johnson, Houston, AFC	35	539	15.4	87	2
	Larry Marshall, Philadelphia, NFC	46	489	10.6	48	0
1976	Rick Upchurch, Denver, AFC	39	536	13.7	92	4
	Eddie Brown, Washington, NFC	48	646	13.5	71	1
1975	Billy Johnson, Houston, AFC	40	612	15.3	83	3
	Terry Metcalf, St. Louis, NFC	23	285	12.4	69	1

Year	Player, Team	No.	Yards	Avg.	Long	TD
1974	Lemar Parrish, Cincinnati, AFC	18	338	18.8	90	2
	Dick Jauron, Detroit, NFC	17	286	16.8	58	0
1973	Bruce Taylor, San Francisco, NFC	15	207	13.8	61	0
	Ron Smith, San Diego, AFC	27	352	13.0	84	2
1972	Ken Ellis, Green Bay, NFC	14	215	15.4	80	1
	Chris Farasopoulos, N.Y. Jets, AFC	17	179	10.5	65	1
1971	Les (Speedy) Duncan, Washington, NFC	22	233	10.6	33	0
	Leroy Kelly, Cleveland, AFC	30	292	9.7	74	0
1970	Ed Podolak, Kansas City, AFC	23	311	13.5	60	0
	*Bruce Taylor, San Francisco, NFC	43	516	12.0	76	0
1969	Alvin Haymond, Los Angeles, NFL	33	435	13.2	52	0
	*Bill Thompson, Denver, AFL	25	288	11.5	40	0
1968	Bob Hayes, Dallas, NFL	15	312	20.8	90	2
	Noland Smith, Kansas City, AFL	18	270	15.0	80	1
1967	Floyd Little, Denver, AFL	16	270	16.9	72	1
	Ben Davis, Cleveland, NFL	18	229	12.7	52	1
1966	Les (Speedy) Duncan, San Diego, AFL	18	238	13.2	81	1
	Johnny Roland, St. Louis, NFL	20	221	11.1	86	1
1965	Leroy Kelly, Cleveland, NFL	17	265	15.6	67	2
	Les (Speedy) Duncan, San Diego, AFL	30	464	15.5	66	2
1964	Bobby Jancik, Houston, AFL	12	220	18.3	82	1
	Tommy Watkins, Detroit, NFL	16	238	14.9	68	2
1963	Dick James, Washington, NFL	16	214	13.4	39	0
	Claude (Hoot) Gibson, Oakland, AFL	26	307	11.8	85	2
1962	Dick Christy, N.Y. Titans, AFL	15	250	16.7	73	2
	Pat Studstill, Detroit, NFL	29	457	15.8	44	0
1961	Dick Christy, N.Y. Titans, AFL	18	383	21.3	70	2
	Willie Wood, Green Bay, NFL	14	225	16.1	72	2
1960	*Abner Haynes, Dall. Texans, AFL	14	215	15.4	46	0
	Abe Woodson, San Francisco, NFL	13	174	13.4	48	0
1959	Johnny Morris, Chi. Bears	14	171	12.2	78	1
1958	Jon Arnett, Los Angeles	18	223	12.4	58	0
1957	Bert Zagers, Washington	14	217	15.5	76	2
1956	Ken Konz, Cleveland	13	187	14.4	65	1
1955	Ollie Matson, Chi. Cardinals	13	245	18.8	78	2
1954	*Veryl Switzer, Green Bay	24	306	12.8	93	1
1953	Charley Trippi, Chi. Cardinals	21	239	11.4	38	0
1952	Jack Christiansen, Detroit	15	322	21.5	79	2
1951	Claude (Buddy) Young, N.Y. Yanks	12	231	19.3	79	1
1950	*Herb Rich, Baltimore	12	276	23.0	86	1
1949	Verda (Vitamin T) Smith, Los Angeles	27	427	15.8	85	1
1948	George McAfee, Chi. Bears	30	417	13.9	60	1
1947	*Walt Slater, Pittsburgh	28	435	15.5	33	0
1946	Bill Dudley, Pittsburgh	27	385	14.3	52	0
1945	*Dave Ryan, Detroit	15	220	14.7	56	0
1944	*Steve Van Buren, Philadelphia	15	230	15.3	55	1
1943	Andy Farkas, Washington	15	168	11.2	33	0
1942	Merlyn Condit, Brooklyn	21	210	10.0	23	0
1941	Byron (Whizzer) White, Detroit	19	262	13.8	64	0

*First season of professional football.

ANNUAL KICKOFF RETURN LEADERS

Year	Player, Team	No.	Yards	Avg.	Long	TD
2012	Jacoby Jones, Baltimore, AFC	38	1,167	30.7	108	2
	Leon Washington, Seattle, NFC	27	784	29.0	98	1
2011	Joe McKnight, N.Y. Jets, AFC	34	1,073	31.6	107	1
	*Randall Cobb, Green Bay, NFC	34	941	27.7	108	1
2010	*David Reed, Baltimore, AFC	21	616	29.3	103	1
	Eric Weems, Atlanta, NFC	40	1,100	27.5	102	1
2009	Clifton Smith, Tampa Bay, NFC	31	902	29.1	83	0
	Josh Cribbs, Cleveland, AFC	56	1,542	27.5	103	3
2008	Danieal Manning, Chicago, NFC	36	1,070	29.7	83	1
	Ellis Hobbs, New England, AFC	45	1,281	28.5	95	1
2007	Josh Cribbs, Cleveland, AFC	59	1,809	30.7	100	2
	*Aundrae Allison, Minnesota, NFC	20	574	28.7	104	1
2006	Justin Miller, N.Y. Jets, AFC	46	1,304	28.3	103	2
	*Devin Hester, Chicago, NFC	20	528	26.4	96	2
2005	Terrence McGee, Buffalo, AFC	46	1,391	30.2	99	1
	Koren Robinson, Minnesota, NFC	47	1,221	26.0	86	1

Year	Player, Team	No.	Yards	Avg.	Long	TD
2004	Willie Ponder, N.Y. Giants, NFC	36	967	26.9	91	1
	Terrence McGee, Buffalo, AFC	52	1,370	26.3	104	3
2003	Jerry Azumah, Chicago, NFC	41	1,191	29.0	89	2
	*Bethel Johnson, New England, AFC	30	847	28.2	92	1
2002	MarTay Jenkins, Arizona, NFC	20	559	28.0	95	1
	Kevin Faulk, New England, AFC	26	725	27.9	87	2
2001	Ronney Jenkins, San Diego, AFC	58	1,541	26.6	93	2
	*Steve Smith, Carolina, NFC	56	1,431	25.6	99	2
2000	*Darrick Vaughn, Atlanta, NFC	39	1,082	27.7	100	3
	Derrick Mason, Tennessee, AFC	42	1,132	27.0	66	0
1999	Tony Horne, St. Louis, NFC	30	892	29.7	101	2
	Tremain Mack, Cincinnati, AFC	51	1,382	27.1	99	1
1998	*Terry Fair, Detroit, NFC	51	1,428	28.0	105	2
	Corey Harris, Baltimore, AFC	35	965	27.6	95	1
1997	Michael Bates, Carolina, NFC	47	1,281	27.3	56	0
	Aaron Glenn, N.Y. Jets, AFC	28	741	26.5	96	1
1996	Michael Bates, Carolina, NFC	33	998	30.2	93	1
	Tamarick Vanover, Kansas City, AFC	33	854	25.9	97	1
1995	Ron Carpenter, N.Y. Jets, AFC	20	553	27.7	58	0
	Brian Mitchell, Washington, NFC	55	1,408	25.6	59	0
1994	Mel Gray, Detroit, NFC	45	1,276	28.4	102	3
	Randy Baldwin, Cleveland, AFC	28	753	26.9	85	1
1993	Robert Brooks, Green Bay, NFC	23	611	26.6	95	1
	*Raghib Ismail, L.A. Raiders, AFC	25	605	24.2	66	0
1992	Jon Vaughn, New England, AFC	20	564	28.2	100	1
	Deion Sanders, Atlanta, NFC	40	1,067	26.7	99	2
1991	Mel Gray, Detroit, NFC	36	929	25.8	71	0
	Nate Lewis, San Diego, AFC	23	578	25.1	95	1
1990	Kevin Clark, Denver, AFC	20	505	25.3	75	0
	David Meggett, N.Y. Giants, NFC	21	492	23.4	58	0
1989	Rod Woodson, Pittsburgh, AFC	36	982	27.3	84	1
	Mel Gray, Detroit, NFC	24	640	26.7	57	0
1988	*Tim Brown, L.A. Raiders, AFC	41	1,098	26.8	97	1
	Donnie Elder, Tampa Bay, NFC	34	772	22.7	51	0
1987	Sylvester Stamps, Atlanta, NFC	24	660	27.5	97	1
	Paul Palmer, Kansas City, AFC	38	923	24.3	95	2
1986	Dennis Gentry, Chicago, NFC	20	576	28.8	91	1
	Lupe Sanchez, Pittsburgh, AFC	25	591	23.6	64	0
1985	Ron Brown, L.A. Rams, NFC	28	918	32.8	98	3
	Glen Young, Cleveland, AFC	35	898	25.7	63	0
1984	*Bobby Humphery, N.Y. Jets, AFC	22	675	30.7	97	1
	Barry Redden, L.A. Rams, NFC	23	530	23.0	40	0
1983	Fulton Walker, Miami, AFC	36	962	26.7	78	0
	Darrin Nelson, Minnesota, NFC	18	445	24.7	50	0
1982	*Mike Mosley, Buffalo, AFC	18	487	27.1	66	0
	Alvin Hall, Detroit, NFC	16	426	26.6	96	1
1981	Mike Nelms, Washington, NFC	37	1,099	29.7	84	0
	Carl Roaches, Houston, AFC	28	769	27.5	96	1
1980	Horace Ivory, New England, AFC	36	992	27.6	98	1
	Rich Mauti, New Orleans, NFC	31	798	25.7	52	0
1979	Larry Brunson, Oakland, AFC	17	441	25.9	89	0
	Jimmy Edwards, Minnesota, NFC	44	1,103	25.1	83	0
1978	Steve Odom, Green Bay, NFC	25	677	27.1	95	1
	*Keith Wright, Cleveland, AFC	30	789	26.3	86	0
1977	*Raymond Clayborn, New England, AFC	28	869	31.0	101	3
	*Wilbert Montgomery, Philadelphia, NFC	23	619	26.9	99	1
1976	*Duriel Harris, Miami, AFC	17	559	32.9	69	0
	Cullen Bryant, Los Angeles, NFC	16	459	28.7	90	1
1975	*Walter Payton, Chicago, NFC	14	444	31.7	70	0
	Harold Hart, Oakland, AFC	17	518	30.5	102	1
1974	Terry Metcalf, St. Louis, NFC	20	623	31.2	94	1
	Greg Pruitt, Cleveland, AFC	22	606	27.5	88	1
1973	Carl Garrett, Chicago, NFC	16	486	30.4	67	0
	*Wallace Francis, Buffalo, AFC	23	687	29.9	101	2
1972	Ron Smith, Chicago, NFC	30	924	30.8	94	1
	*Bruce Laird, Baltimore, AFC	29	843	29.1	73	0
1971	Travis Williams, Los Angeles, NFC	25	743	29.7	105	1
	Eugene (Mercury) Morris, Miami, AFC	15	423	28.2	94	1
1970	Jim Duncan, Baltimore, AFC	20	707	35.4	99	1
	Cecil Turner, Chicago, NFC	23	752	32.7	96	4

Year	Player, Team	No.	Yards	Avg.	Long	TD
1969	Bobby Williams, Detroit, NFL	17	563	33.1	96	1
	*Bill Thompson, Denver, AFL	18	513	28.5	63	0
1968	Preston Pearson, Baltimore, NFL	15	527	35.1	102	2
	*George Atkinson, Oakland, AFL	32	802	25.1	60	0
1967	*Travis Williams, Green Bay, NFL	18	739	41.1	104	4
	*Zeke Moore, Houston, AFL	14	405	28.9	92	1
1966	Gale Sayers, Chicago, NFL	23	718	31.2	93	2
	*Goldie Sellers, Denver, AFL	19	541	28.5	100	2
1965	Tommy Watkins, Detroit, NFL	17	584	34.4	94	0
	Abner Haynes, Denver, AFL	34	901	26.5	60	0
1964	*Clarence Childs, N.Y. Giants, NFL	34	987	29.0	100	1
	Bo Roberson, Oakland, AFL	36	975	27.1	59	0
1963	Abe Woodson, San Francisco, NFL	29	935	32.2	103	3
	Bobby Jancik, Houston, AFL	45	1,317	29.3	53	0
1962	Abe Woodson, San Francisco, NFL	37	1,157	31.3	79	0
	*Bobby Jancik, Houston, AFL	24	826	30.3	61	0
1961	Dick Bass, Los Angeles, NFL	23	698	30.3	64	0
	*Dave Grayson, Dall. Texans, AFL	16	453	28.3	73	0
1960	*Tom Moore, Green Bay, NFL	12	397	33.1	84	0
	Ken Hall, Houston, AFL	19	594	31.3	104	1
1959	Abe Woodson, San Francisco	13	382	29.4	105	1
1958	Ollie Matson, Chi. Cardinals	14	497	35.5	101	2
1957	*Jon Arnett, Los Angeles	18	504	28.0	98	1
1956	*Tom Wilson, Los Angeles	15	477	31.8	103	1
1955	Al Carmichael, Green Bay	14	418	29.9	100	1
1954	Billy Reynolds, Cleveland	14	413	29.5	51	0
1953	Joe Arenas, San Francisco	16	551	34.4	82	0
1952	Lynn Chandnois, Pittsburgh	17	599	35.2	93	2
1951	Lynn Chandnois, Pittsburgh	12	390	32.5	55	0
1950	Verda (Vitamin T) Smith, Los Angeles	22	742	33.7	97	3
1949	*Don Doll, Detroit	21	536	25.5	56	0
1948	*Joe Scott, N.Y. Giants	20	569	28.5	99	1
1947	Eddie Saenz, Washington	29	797	27.5	94	2
1946	Abe Karnofsky, Boston	21	599	28.5	97	1
1945	Steve Van Buren, Philadelphia	13	373	28.7	98	1
1944	Bob Thurbon, Card.-Pitt.	12	291	24.3	55	0
1943	Ken Heineman, Brooklyn	16	444	27.8	69	0
1942	Marshall Goldberg, Chi. Cardinals	15	393	26.2	95	1
1941	Marshall Goldberg, Chi. Cardinals	12	290	24.2	41	0

*First season of professional football.

ANNUAL INTERCEPTION LEADERS

Year	Player, Team	No.	Yards	TD
2012	Tim Jennings, Chicago, NFC	9	105	1
	Jairus Byrd, Buffalo, AFC	5	81	0
	Devin McCourty, New England, AFC	5	53	0
2011	Kyle Arrington, New England, AFC	7	92	0
	Eric Weddle, San Diego, AFC	7	89	0
	Charles Woodson, Green Bay, NFC	7	63	1
2010	Ed Reed, Baltimore, AFC	8	183	0
	Asante Samuel, Philadelphia, NFC	7	70	0
2009	*Jairus Byrd, Buffalo, AFC	9	118	0
	Asante Samuel, Philadelphia, NFC	9	117	0
	Darren Sharper, New Orleans, NFC	9	376	3
	Charles Woodson, Green Bay, NFC	9	179	3
2008	Ed Reed, Baltimore, AFC	9	264	2
	Nick Collins, Green Bay, NFC	7	295	3
	Charles Woodson, Green Bay, NFC	7	169	2
2007	Antonio Cromartie, San Diego, AFC	10	144	1
	O.J. Atogwe, St. Louis, NFC	8	125	1
2006	Champ Bailey, Denver, AFC	10	162	1
	Asante Samuel, New England, AFC	10	120	0
	Walt Harris, San Francisco, NFC	8	84	1
	Charles Woodson, Green Bay, NFC	8	61	1
2005	Ty Law, N.Y. Jets, AFC	10	195	1
	Deltha O'Neal, Cincinnati, AFC	10	103	0
	Darren Sharper, Minnesota, NFC	9	276	2
2004	Ed Reed, Baltimore, AFC	9	358	1
	Ken Lucas, Seattle, NFC	6	46	1
	*Chris Gamble, Carolina, NFC	6	15	0

Year	Player, Team	No.	Yards	TD
2003	Tony Parrish, San Francisco, NFC	9	202	0
	Brian Russell, Minnesota, NFC	9	185	0
	Ed Reed, Baltimore, AFC	7	132	1
	Marcus Coleman, Houston, AFC	7	95	0
	Patrick Surtain, Miami, AFC	7	59	0
2002	Rod Woodson, Oakland, AFC	8	225	2
	Brian Kelly, Tampa Bay, NFC	8	68	0
2001	*Anthony Henry, Cleveland, AFC	10	177	1
	Ronde Barber, Tampa Bay, NFC	10	86	1
2000	Darren Sharper, Green Bay, NFC	9	109	0
	Samari Rolle, Tennessee, AFC	7	140	1
	Brian Walker, Miami, AFC	7	80	0
1999	Rod Woodson, Baltimore, AFC	7	195	2
	Sam Madison, Miami, AFC	7	164	1
	James Hasty, Kansas City, AFC	7	98	2
	Donnie Abraham, Tampa Bay, NFC	7	115	2
	Troy Vincent, Philadelphia, NFC	7	91	0
1998	Ty Law, New England, AFC	9	133	1
	Kwamie Lassiter, Arizona, NFC	8	80	0
1997	Ryan McNeil, St. Louis, NFC	9	127	1
	Mark McMillian, Kansas City, AFC	8	274	3
	Darryl Williams, Seattle, AFC	8	172	1
1996	Tyrone Braxton, Denver, AFC	9	128	1
	Keith Lyle, St. Louis, NFC	9	152	0
1995	*Orlando Thomas, Minnesota, NFC	9	108	1
	Willie Williams, Pittsburgh, AFC	7	122	1

Year	Player, Team	No.	Yards	TD
1994	Eric Turner, Cleveland, AFC	9	199	1
	Aeneas Williams, Arizona, NFC	9	89	0
1993	Eugene Robinson, Seattle, AFC	9	80	0
	Nate Odomes, Buffalo, AFC	9	65	0
	Deion Sanders, Atlanta, NFC	7	91	0
1992	Henry Jones, Buffalo, AFC	8	263	2
	Audray McMillian, Minnesota, NFC	8	157	2
1991	Ronnie Lott, L.A. Raiders, AFC	8	52	0
	Ray Crockett, Detroit, NFC	6	141	1
	Deion Sanders, Atlanta, NFC	6	119	1
	*Aeneas Williams, Phoenix, NFC	6	60	0
	Tim McKyer, Atlanta, NFC	6	24	0
1990	*Mark Carrier, Chicago, NFC	10	39	0
	Richard Johnson, Houston, AFC	8	100	1
1989	Felix Wright, Cleveland, AFC	9	91	1
	Eric Allen, Philadelphia, NFC	8	38	0
1988	Scott Case, Atlanta, NFC	10	47	0
	Erik McMillan, N.Y. Jets, AFC	8	168	2
1987	Barry Wilburn, Washington, NFC	9	135	1
	Mike Prior, Indianapolis, AFC	6	57	0
	Mark Kelso, Buffalo, AFC	6	25	0
	Keith Bostic, Houston, AFC	6	-14	0
1986	Ronnie Lott, San Francisco, NFC	10	134	1
	Deron Cherry, Kansas City, AFC	9	150	0
1985	Everson Walls, Dallas, NFC	9	31	0
	Albert Lewis, Kansas City, AFC	8	59	0
	Eugene Daniel, Indianapolis, AFC	8	53	0
1984	Ken Easley, Seattle, AFC	10	126	2
	*Tom Flynn, Green Bay, NFC	9	106	0
1983	Mark Murphy, Washington, NFC	9	127	0
	Ken Riley, Cincinnati, AFC	8	89	2
	Vann McElroy, L.A. Raiders, AFC	8	68	0
1982	Everson Walls, Dallas, NFC	7	61	0
	Ken Riley, Cincinnati, AFC	5	88	1
	Bobby Jackson, N.Y. Jets, AFC	5	84	1
	Dwayne Woodruff, Pittsburgh, AFC	5	53	0
	Donnie Shell, Pittsburgh, AFC	5	27	0
1981	*Everson Walls, Dallas, NFC	11	133	0
	John Harris, Seattle, AFC	10	155	2
1980	Lester Hayes, Oakland, AFC	13	273	1
	Nolan Cromwell, Los Angeles, NFC	8	140	1
1979	Mike Reinfeldt, Houston, AFC	12	205	0
	Lemar Parrish, Washington, NFC	9	65	0
1978	Thom Darden, Cleveland, AFC	10	200	0
	Ken Stone, St. Louis, NFC	9	139	0
	Willie Buchanon, Green Bay, NFC	9	93	1
1977	Lyle Blackwood, Baltimore, AFC	10	163	0
	Rolland Lawrence, Atlanta, NFC	7	138	0
1976	Monte Jackson, Los Angeles, NFC	10	173	3
	Ken Riley, Cincinnati, AFC	9	141	1
1975	Mel Blount, Pittsburgh, AFC	11	121	0
	Paul Krause, Minnesota, NFC	10	201	0
1974	Emmitt Thomas, Kansas City, AFC	12	214	2
	Ray Brown, Atlanta, NFC	8	164	1
1973	Dick Anderson, Miami, AFC	8	163	2
	Mike Wagner, Pittsburgh, AFC	8	134	0
	Bobby Bryant, Minnesota, NFC	7	105	1
1972	Bill Bradley, Philadelphia, NFC	9	73	0
	Mike Sensibaugh, Kansas City, AFC	8	65	0
1971	Bill Bradley, Philadelphia, NFC	11	248	0
	Ken Houston, Houston, AFC	9	220	4
1970	Johnny Robinson, Kansas City, AFC	10	155	0
	Dick LeBeau, Detroit, NFC	9	96	0
1969	Mel Renfro, Dallas, NFL	10	118	0
	Emmitt Thomas, Kansas City, AFL	9	146	1
1968	Dave Grayson, Oakland, AFL	10	195	1
	Willie Williams, N.Y. Giants, NFL	10	103	0
1967	Miller Farr, Houston, AFL	10	264	3
	*Lem Barney, Detroit, NFL	10	232	3
	Tom Janik, Buffalo, AFL	10	222	2
	Dave Whitsell, New Orleans, NFL	10	178	2
	Dick Westmoreland, Miami, AFL	10	127	1
1966	Larry Wilson, St. Louis, NFL	10	180	2
	Johnny Robinson, Kansas City, AFL	10	136	1
	Bobby Hunt, Kansas City, AFL	10	113	0
1965	W.K. Hicks, Houston, AFL	9	156	0
	Bobby Boyd, Baltimore, NFL	9	78	1
1964	Dainard Paulson, N.Y. Jets, AFL	12	157	1
	*Paul Krause, Washington, NFL	12	140	1
1963	Fred Glick, Houston, AFL	12	180	1
	Dick Lynch, N.Y. Giants, NFL	9	251	3
	Roosevelt Taylor, Chicago, NFL	9	172	1
1962	Lee Riley, N.Y. Titans, AFL	11	122	0
	Willie Wood, Green Bay, NFL	9	132	0
1961	Billy Atkins, Buffalo, AFL	10	158	0
	Dick Lynch, N.Y. Giants, NFL	9	60	0
1960	*Austin (Goose) Gonsoulin, Denver, AFL	11	98	0
	Dave Baker, San Francisco, NFL	10	96	0
	Jerry Norton, St. Louis, NFL	10	96	0
1959	Dean Derby, Pittsburgh	7	127	0
	Milt Davis, Baltimore	7	119	1
	Don Shinnick, Baltimore	7	70	0
1958	Jim Patton, N.Y. Giants	11	183	0
1957	Milt Davis, Baltimore	10	219	2
	Jack Christiansen, Detroit	10	137	1
	Jack Butler, Pittsburgh	10	85	0
1956	Linden Crow, Chi. Cardinals	11	170	0
1955	Will Sherman, Los Angeles	11	101	0
1954	Dick (Night Train) Lane, Chi. Cardinals	10	181	0
1953	Jack Christiansen, Detroit	12	238	1
1952	*Dick (Night Train) Lane, Los Angeles	14	298	2
1951	Otto Schnellbacher, N.Y. Giants	11	194	2
1950	Orban (Spec) Sanders, N.Y. Yanks	13	199	0
1949	Bob Nussbaumer, Chi. Cardinals	12	157	0
1948	*Dan Sandifer, Washington	13	258	2
1947	Frank Reagan, N.Y. Giants	10	203	0
	Frank Seno, Boston	10	100	0
1946	Bill Dudley, Pittsburgh	10	242	1
1945	Roy Zimmerman, Philadelphia	7	90	0
1944	*Howard Livingston, N.Y. Giants	9	172	1
1943	Sammy Baugh, Washington	11	112	0
1942	Clyde (Bulldog) Turner, Chi. Bears	8	96	1
1941	Marshall Goldberg, Chi. Cardinals	7	54	0
	*Art Jones, Pittsburgh	7	35	0
1940	Clarence (Ace) Parker, Brooklyn	6	146	1
	Kent Ryan, Detroit	6	65	0
	Don Hutson, Green Bay	6	24	0

*First season of professional football.

ANNUAL PUNTING LEADERS

Year	Player, Team	No.	Avg.	Long
2012	Brandon Fields, Miami, AFC	74	50.2	67
	Thomas Morstead, New Orleans, NFC	74	50.1	70
2011	Andy Lee, San Francisco, NFC	78	50.9	68
	Shane Lechler, Oakland, AFC	78	50.8	80
2010	Shane Lechler, Oakland, AFC	77	47.0	68
	Mat McBriar, Dallas, NFC	65	47.9	65
2009	Shane Lechler, Oakland, AFC	96	51.1	70
	Andy Lee, San Francisco, NFC	99	47.6	64
2008	Donnie Jones, St. Louis, NFC	82	50.0	68
	Shane Lechler, Oakland, AFC	90	48.8	70
2007	Shane Lechler, Oakland, AFC	73	49.1	70
	Andy Lee, San Francisco, NFC	105	47.3	74
2006	Mat McBriar, Dallas, NFC	56	48.2	75
	Shane Lechler, Oakland, AFC	77	47.5	67
2005	Brian Moorman, Buffalo, AFC	71	45.7	68
	Josh Bidwell, Tampa Bay, NFC	90	45.6	61

Year	Player, Team	No.	Yards	TD
2004	Shane Lechler, Oakland, AFC	73	46.7	67
	Tom Tupa, Washington, NFC	103	44.1	61
2003	Shane Lechler, Oakland, AFC	96	46.9	73
	Todd Sauerbrun, Carolina, NFC	77	44.6	64
2002	Todd Sauerbrun, Carolina, NFC	104	45.5	67
	Chris Hanson, Jacksonville, AFC	81	44.2	64
2001	Todd Sauerbrun, Carolina, NFC	93	47.5	73
	Shane Lechler, Oakland, AFC	73	46.2	65
2000	Darren Bennett, San Diego, AFC	92	46.2	66
	Mitch Berger, Minnesota, NFC	62	44.7	60
1999	Tom Rouen, Denver, AFC	84	46.5	65
	Mitch Berger, Minnesota, NFC	61	45.4	75
1998	Craig Hentrich, Tennessee, AFC	69	47.2	71
	Mark Royals, New Orleans, NFC	88	45.6	64
1997	Mark Royals, New Orleans, NFC	88	45.9	66
	Tom Tupa, New England, AFC	78	45.8	73
1996	John Kidd, Miami, AFC	78	46.3	63
	Matt Turk, Washington, NFC	75	45.1	63
1995	Rick Tuten, Seattle, AFC	83	45.0	73
	Sean Landeta, St. Louis, NFC	83	44.3	63
1994	Sean Landeta, L.A. Rams, NFC	78	44.8	62
	Jeff Gossett, L.A. Raiders, AFC	77	43.9	65
1993	Greg Montgomery, Houston, AFC	54	45.6	77
	Jim Arnold, Detroit, NFC	72	44.5	68
1992	Greg Montgomery, Houston, AFC	53	46.9	66
	Harry Newsome, Minnesota, NFC	72	45.0	84
1991	Reggie Roby, Miami, AFC	54	45.7	64
	Harry Newsome, Minnesota, AFC	68	45.5	65
1990	Mike Horan, Denver, AFC	58	44.4	67
	Sean Landeta, N.Y. Giants, NFC	75	44.1	67
1989	Rich Camarillo, Phoenix, NFC	76	43.4	58
	Greg Montgomery, Houston, AFC	56	43.3	63
1988	Harry Newsome, Pittsburgh, AFC	65	45.4	62
	Jim Arnold, Detroit, NFC	97	42.4	69
1987	Rick Donnelly, Atlanta, NFC	61	44.0	62
	Ralf Mojsiejenko, San Diego, AFC	67	42.9	57
1986	Rohn Stark, Indianapolis, AFC	76	45.2	63
	Sean Landeta, N.Y. Giants, NFC	79	44.8	61
1985	Rohn Stark, Indianapolis, AFC	78	45.9	68
	*Rick Donnelly, Atlanta, NFC	59	43.6	68
1984	Jim Arnold, Kansas City, AFC	98	44.9	63
	*Brian Hansen, New Orleans, NFC	69	43.8	66
1983	Rohn Stark, Baltimore, AFC	91	45.3	68
	Frank Garcia, Tampa Bay, NFC	95	42.2	64
1982	Luke Prestridge, Denver, AFC	45	45.0	65
	Carl Birdsong, St. Louis, NFC	54	43.8	65
1981	Pat McInally, Cincinnati, AFC	72	45.4	62
	Tom Skladany, Detroit, NFC	64	43.5	74
1980	Dave Jennings, N.Y. Giants, NFC	94	44.8	63
	Luke Prestridge, Denver, AFC	70	43.9	57
1979	*Bob Grupp, Kansas City, AFC	89	43.6	74
	Dave Jennings, N.Y. Giants, NFC	104	42.7	72
1978	Pat McInally, Cincinnati, AFC	91	43.1	65
	*Tom Skladany, Detroit, NFC	86	42.5	63
1977	Ray Guy, Oakland, AFC	59	43.3	74
	Tom Blanchard, New Orleans, NFC	82	42.4	66
1976	Marv Bateman, Buffalo, AFC	86	42.8	78
	John James, Atlanta, NFC	101	42.1	67
1975	Ray Guy, Oakland, AFC	68	43.8	64
	Herman Weaver, Detroit, NFC	80	42.0	61
1974	Ray Guy, Oakland, AFC	74	42.2	66
	Tom Blanchard, New Orleans, NFC	88	42.1	71
1973	Jerrel Wilson, Kansas City, AFC	80	45.5	68
	*Tom Wittum, San Francisco, NFC	79	43.7	62
1972	Jerrel Wilson, Kansas City, AFC	66	44.8	69
	Dave Chapple, Los Angeles, NFC	53	44.2	70
1971	Dave Lewis, Cincinnati, AFC	72	44.8	56
	Tom McNeill, Philadelphia, NFC	73	42.0	64
1970	Dave Lewis, Cincinnati, AFC	79	46.2	63
	*Julian Fagan, New Orleans, NFC	77	42.5	64

Year	Player, Team	No.	Yards	TD
1969	David Lee, Baltimore, NFL	57	45.3	66
	Dennis Partee, San Diego, AFL	71	44.6	62
1968	Jerrel Wilson, Kansas City, AFL	63	45.1	70
	Billy Lothridge, Atlanta, NFL	75	44.3	70
1967	Bob Scarpitto, Denver, AFL	105	44.9	73
	Billy Lothridge, Atlanta, NFL	87	43.7	62
1966	Bob Scarpitto, Denver, AFL	76	45.8	70
	*David Lee, Baltimore, NFL	49	45.6	64
1965	Gary Collins, Cleveland, NFL	65	46.7	71
	Jerrel Wilson, Kansas City, AFL	69	45.4	64
1964	Bobby Walden, Minnesota, NFL	72	46.4	73
	Jim Fraser, Denver, AFL	73	44.2	67
1963	Yale Lary, Detroit, NFL	35	48.9	73
	Jim Fraser, Denver, AFL	81	44.4	66
1962	Tommy Davis, San Francisco, NFL	48	45.6	82
	Jim Fraser, Denver, AFL	55	43.6	75
1961	Yale Lary, Detroit, NFL	52	48.4	71
	Billy Atkins, Buffalo, AFL	85	44.5	70
1960	Jerry Norton, St. Louis, NFL	39	45.6	62
	*Paul Maguire, L.A. Chargers, AFL	43	40.5	61
1959	Yale Lary, Detroit	45	47.1	67
1958	Sam Baker, Washington	48	45.4	64
1957	Don Chandler, N.Y. Giants	60	44.6	64
1956	Norm Van Brocklin, Los Angeles	48	43.1	72
1955	Norm Van Brocklin, Los Angeles	60	44.6	61
1954	Pat Brady, Pittsburgh	66	43.2	72
1953	Pat Brady, Pittsburgh	80	46.9	64
1952	Horace Gillom, Cleveland	61	45.7	73
1951	Horace Gillom, Cleveland	73	45.5	66
1950	*Fred (Curly) Morrison, Chi. Bears	57	43.3	65
1949	*Mike Boyda, N.Y. Bulldogs	56	44.2	61
1948	Joe Muha, Philadelphia	57	47.3	82
1947	Jack Jacobs, Green Bay	57	43.5	74
1946	Roy McKay, Green Bay	64	42.7	64
1945	Roy McKay, Green Bay	44	41.2	73
1944	Frank Sinkwich, Detroit	45	41.0	73
1943	Sammy Baugh, Washington	50	45.9	81
1942	Sammy Baugh, Washington	37	48.2	74
1941	Sammy Baugh, Washington	30	48.7	75
1940	Sammy Baugh, Washington	35	51.4	85
1939	*Parker Hall, Cleveland	58	40.8	80

*First season of professional football.

ANNUAL LEADERS IN SACKS (SINCE 1982)

Year	Player, Team	Sacks
2012	J.J. Watt, Houston, AFC	20.5
	Aldon Smith, San Francisco, NFC	19.5
2011	Jared Allen, Minnesota, NFC	22.0
	Terrell Suggs, Baltimore, AFC	14.0
2010	DeMarcus Ware, Dallas, NFC	15.5
	Tamba Hali, Kansas City, AFC	14.5
2009	Elvis Dumervil, Denver, AFC	17.0
	Jared Allen, Minnesota, NFC	14.5
2008	DeMarcus Ware, Dallas, NFC	20.0
	Joey Porter, Miami, AFC	17.5
2007	Jared Allen, Kansas City, AFC	15.5
	Patrick Kerney, Seattle, NFC	14.5
2006	Shawne Merriman, San Diego, AFC	17.0
	Aaron Kampman, Green Bay, NFC	15.5
2005	Derrick Burgess, Oakland, AFC	16.0
	Osi Umenyiora, N.Y. Giants, NFC	14.5
2004	Dwight Freeney, Indianapolis, AFC	16.0
	Bertrand Berry, Arizona, NFC	14.5
2003	Michael Strahan, N.Y. Giants, NFC	18.5
	Adewale Ogunleye, Miami, AFC	15.0
2002	Jason Taylor, Miami, AFC	18.5
	Simeon Rice, Tampa Bay, NFC	15.5
2001	Michael Strahan, N.Y. Giants, NFC	22.5
	Peter Boulware, Baltimore, AFC	15.0

Year	Player, Team	Sacks
2000	La'Roi Glover, New Orleans, NFC	17.0
	Trace Armstrong, Miami, AFC	16.5
1999	Kevin Carter, St. Louis, NFC	17.0
	*Jevon Kearse, Tennessee, AFC	14.5
1998	Michael Sinclair, Seattle, AFC	16.5
	Reggie White, Green Bay, NFC	16.0
1997	John Randle, Minnesota, NFC	15.5
	Bruce Smith, Buffalo, AFC	14.0
1996	Kevin Greene, Carolina, NFC	14.5
	Michael McCrary, Seattle, AFC	13.5
	Bruce Smith, Buffalo, AFC	13.5
1995	Bryce Paup, Buffalo, AFC	17.5
	William Fuller, Philadelphia, NFC	13.0
	Wayne Martin, New Orleans, NFC	13.0
1994	Kevin Greene, Pittsburgh, AFC	14.0
	Ken Harvey, Washington, NFC	13.5
	John Randle, Minnesota, NFC	13.5
1993	Neil Smith, Kansas City, AFC	15.0
	Renaldo Turnbull, New Orleans, NFC	13.0
	Reggie White, Green Bay, NFC	13.0
1992	Clyde Simmons, Philadelphia, NFC	19.0
	Leslie O'Neal, San Diego, AFC	17.0
1991	Pat Swilling, New Orleans, NFC	17.0
	William Fuller, Houston, AFC	15.0
1990	Derrick Thomas, Kansas City, AFC	20.0
	Charles Haley, San Francisco, NFC	16.0
1989	Chris Doleman, Minnesota, NFC	21.0
	Lee Williams, San Diego, AFC	14.0
1988	Reggie White, Philadelphia, NFC	18.0
	Greg Townsend, L.A. Raiders, AFC	11.5
1987	Reggie White, Philadelphia, NFC	21.0
	Andre Tippett, New England, AFC	12.5
1986	Lawrence Taylor, N.Y. Giants, NFC	20.5
	Sean Jones, L.A. Raiders, AFC	15.5
1985	Richard Dent, Chicago, NFC	17.0
	Andre Tippett, New England, AFC	16.5
1984	Mark Gastineau, N.Y. Jets, AFC	22.0
	Richard Dent, Chicago, NFC	17.5
1983	Mark Gastineau, N.Y. Jets, AFC	19.0
	Fred Dean, San Francisco, NFC	17.5
1982	Doug Martin, Minnesota, NFC	11.5
	Jesse Baker, Houston, AFC	7.5

*First season of professional football.

POINTS SCORED

Year	Team	Points
2012	New England, AFC	557
	New Orleans, NFC	461
2011	Green Bay, NFC	560
	New England, AFC	513
2010	New England, AFC	518
	Philadelphia, NFC	439
2009	New Orleans, NFC	510
	San Diego, AFC	454
2008	New Orleans, NFC	463
	San Diego, AFC	439
2007	New England, AFC	589
	Dallas, NFC	455
2006	San Diego, AFC	492
	Chicago, NFC	427
2005	Seattle, NFC	452
	Indianapolis, AFC	439
2004	Indianapolis, AFC	522
	Green Bay, NFC	424
2003	Kansas City, AFC	484
	St. Louis, NFC	447
2002	Kansas City, AFC	467
	New Orleans, NFC	432
2001	St. Louis, NFC	503
	Indianapolis, AFC	413
2000	St. Louis, NFC	540
	Denver, AFC	485
1999	St. Louis, NFC	526
	Indianapolis, AFC	423
1998	Minnesota, NFC	556
	Denver, AFC	501
1997	Denver, AFC	472
	Green Bay, NFC	422
1996	Green Bay, NFC	456
	New England, AFC	418
1995	San Francisco, NFC	457
	Pittsburgh, AFC	407
1994	San Francisco, NFC	505
	Miami, AFC	389
1993	San Francisco, NFC	473
	Denver, AFC	373
1992	San Francisco, NFC	431
	Buffalo, AFC	381
1991	Washington, NFC	485
	Buffalo, AFC	458
1990	Buffalo, AFC	428
	Philadelphia, NFC	396
1989	San Francisco, NFC	442
	Buffalo, AFC	409
1988	Cincinnati, AFC	448
	L.A. Rams, NFC	407
1987	San Francisco, NFC	459
	Cleveland, AFC	390
1986	Miami, AFC	430
	Minnesota, NFC	398
1985	San Diego, AFC	467
	Chicago, NFC	456
1984	Miami, AFC	513
	San Francisco, NFC	475
1983	Washington, NFC	541
	L.A. Raiders, AFC	442
1982	San Diego, AFC	288
	Dallas, NFC	226
	Green Bay, NFC	226
1981	San Diego, AFC	478
	Atlanta, NFC	426
1980	Dallas, NFC	454
	New England, AFC	441
1979	Pittsburgh, AFC	416
	Dallas, NFC	371
1978	Dallas, NFC	384
	Miami, AFC	372
1977	Oakland, AFC	351
	Dallas, NFC	345
1976	Baltimore, AFC	417
	Los Angeles, NFC	351
1975	Buffalo, AFC	420
	Minnesota, NFC	377
1974	Oakland, AFC	355
	Washington, NFC	320
1973	Los Angeles, NFC	388
	Denver, AFC	354
1972	Miami, AFC	385
	San Francisco, NFC	353
1971	Dallas, NFC	406
	Oakland, AFC	344
1970	San Francisco, NFC	352
	Baltimore, AFC	321
1969	Minnesota, NFL	379
	Oakland, AFL	377
1968	Oakland, AFL	453
	Dallas, NFL	431
1967	Oakland, AFL	468
	Los Angeles, NFL	398

Year	Team	Points
1966	Kansas City, AFL	448
	Dallas, NFL	445
1965	San Francisco, NFL	421
	San Diego, AFL	340
1964	Baltimore, NFL	428
	Buffalo, AFL	400
1963	N.Y. Giants, NFL	448
	San Diego, AFL	399
1962	Green Bay, NFL	415
	Dall. Texans, AFL	389
1961	Houston, AFL	513
	Green Bay, NFL	391
1960	N.Y. Titans, AFL	382
	Cleveland, NFL	362
1959	Baltimore	374
1958	Baltimore	381
1957	Los Angeles	307
1956	Chi. Bears	363
1955	Cleveland	349
1954	Detroit	337
1953	San Francisco	372
1952	Los Angeles	349
1951	Los Angeles	392
1950	Los Angeles	466
1949	Philadelphia	364
1948	Chi. Cardinals	395
1947	Chi. Bears	363
1946	Chi. Bears	289
1945	Philadelphia	272
1944	Philadelphia	267
1943	Chi. Bears	303
1942	Chi. Bears	376
1941	Chi. Bears	396
1940	Washington	245
1939	Chi. Bears	298
1938	Green Bay	223
1937	Green Bay	220
1936	Green Bay	248
1935	Chi. Bears	192
1934	Chi. Bears	286
1933	N.Y. Giants	244
1932	Chi. Bears	160

TOTAL YARDS GAINED

Year	Team	Yards
2012	New England, AFC	6,846
	New Orleans, NFC	6,574
2011	New Orleans, NFC	7,474
	New England, AFC	6,848
2010	San Diego, AFC	6,329
	Philadelphia, NFC	6,230
2009	New Orleans, NFC	6,461
	New England, AFC	6,357
2008	New Orleans, NFC	6,571
	Denver, AFC	6,333
2007	New England, AFC	6,580
	Green Bay, NFC	5,931
2006	New Orleans, NFC	6,264
	Indianapolis, AFC	6,070
2005	Kansas City, AFC	6,192
	Seattle, NFC	5,915
2004	Kansas City, AFC	6,695
	Green Bay, NFC	6,357
2003	Minnesota, NFC	6,294
	Kansas City, AFC	5,910
2002	Oakland, AFC	6,237
	Minnesota, NFC	6,192
2001	St. Louis, NFC	6,690
	Indianapolis, AFC	5,955

Year	Team	Yards
2000	St. Louis, NFC	7,075
	Denver, AFC	6,554
1999	St. Louis, NFC	6,412
	Indianapolis, AFC	5,726
1998	San Francisco, NFC	6,800
	Denver, AFC	6,092
1997	Denver, AFC	5,872
	Detroit, NFC	5,798
1996	Denver, AFC	5,791
	Philadelphia, NFC	5,627
1995	Detroit, NFC	6,113
	Denver, AFC	6,040
1994	Miami, AFC	6,078
	San Francisco, NFC	6,060
1993	San Francisco, NFC	6,435
	Miami, AFC	5,812
1992	San Francisco, NFC	6,195
	Buffalo, AFC	5,893
1991	Buffalo, AFC	6,252
	San Francisco, NFC	5,858
1990	Houston, AFC	6,222
	San Francisco, NFC	5,895
1989	San Francisco, NFC	6,268
	Cincinnati, AFC	6,101
1988	Cincinnati, AFC	6,057
	San Francisco, NFC	5,900
1987	San Francisco, NFC	5,987
	Denver, AFC	5,624
1986	Cincinnati, AFC	6,490
	San Francisco, NFC	6,082
1985	San Diego, AFC	6,535
	San Francisco, NFC	5,920
1984	Miami, AFC	6,936
	San Francisco, NFC	6,366
1983	San Diego, AFC	6,197
	Green Bay, NFC	6,172
1982	San Diego, AFC	4,048
	San Francisco, NFC	3,242
1981	San Diego, AFC	6,744
	Detroit, NFC	5,933
1980	San Diego, AFC	6,410
	Los Angeles, NFC	6,006
1979	Pittsburgh, AFC	6,258
	Dallas, NFC	5,968
1978	New England, AFC	5,965
	Dallas, NFC	5,959
1977	Dallas, NFC	4,812
	Oakland, AFC	4,736
1976	Baltimore, AFC	5,236
	St. Louis, NFC	5,136
1975	Buffalo, AFC	5,467
	Dallas, NFC	5,025
1974	Dallas, NFC	4,983
	Oakland, AFC	4,718
1973	Los Angeles, NFC	4,906
	Oakland, AFC	4,773
1972	Miami, AFC	5,036
	N.Y. Giants, NFC	4,483
1971	Dallas, NFC	5,035
	San Diego, AFC	4,738
1970	Oakland, AFC	4,829
	San Francisco, NFC	4,503
1969	Dallas, NFL	5,122
	Oakland, AFL	5,036
1968	Oakland, AFL	5,696
	Dallas, NFL	5,117
1967	N.Y. Jets, AFL	5,152
	Baltimore, NFL	5,008
1966	Dallas, NFL	5,145
	Kansas City, AFL	5,114

Year	Team	Yards
1965	San Francisco, NFL	5,270
	San Diego, AFL	5,188
1964	Buffalo, AFL	5,206
	Baltimore, NFL	4,779
1963	San Diego, AFL	5,153
	N.Y. Giants, NFL	5,024
1962	N.Y. Giants, NFL	5,005
	Houston, AFL	4,971
1961	Houston, AFL	6,288
	Philadelphia, NFL	5,112
1960	Houston, AFL	4,936
	Baltimore, NFL	4,245
1959	Baltimore	4,458
1958	Baltimore	4,539
1957	Los Angeles	4,143
1956	Chi. Bears	4,537
1955	Chi. Bears	4,316
1954	Los Angeles	5,187
1953	Philadelphia	4,811
1952	Cleveland	4,352
1951	Los Angeles	5,506
1950	Los Angeles	5,420
1949	Chi. Bears	4,873
1948	Chi. Cardinals	4,705
1947	Chi. Bears	5,053
1946	Los Angeles	3,793
1945	Washington	3,549
1944	Chi. Bears	3,239
1943	Chi. Bears	4,045
1942	Chi. Bears	3,900
1941	Chi. Bears	4,265
1940	Green Bay	3,400
1939	Chi. Bears	3,988
1938	Green Bay	3,037
1937	Green Bay	3,201
1936	Detroit	3,703
1935	Chi. Bears	3,454
1934	Chi. Bears	3,900
1933	N.Y. Giants	2,973
1932	Chi. Bears	2,755

YARDS RUSHING

Year	Team	Yards
2012	Washington, NFC	2,709
	Kansas City, AFC	2,395
2011	Denver, AFC	2,632
	Carolina, NFC	2,408
2010	Kansas City, AFC	2,627
	Philadelphia, NFC	2,324
2009	N.Y. Jets, AFC	2,756
	Carolina, NFC	2,498
2008	N.Y. Giants, NFC	2,518
	Baltimore, AFC	2,376
2007	Minnesota, NFC	2,634
	Jacksonville, AFC	2,391
2006	Atlanta, NFC	2,939
	San Diego, AFC	2,578
2005	Atlanta, NFC	2,546
	Denver, AFC	2,539
2004	Atlanta, NFC	2,672
	Pittsburgh, AFC	2,464
2003	Baltimore, AFC	2,674
	Green Bay, NFC	2,558
2002	Minnesota, NFC	2,507
	Miami, AFC	2,502
2001	Pittsburgh, AFC	2,774
	San Francisco, NFC	2,244
2000	Oakland, AFC	2,470
	Minnesota, NFC	2,129

Year	Team	Yards
1999	San Francisco, NFC	2,095
	Jacksonville, AFC	2,091
1998	San Francisco, NFC	2,544
	Denver, AFC	2,468
1997	Pittsburgh, AFC	2,479
	Detroit, NFC	2,464
1996	Denver, AFC	2,362
	Washington, NFC	1,910
1995	Kansas City, AFC	2,222
	Dallas, NFC	2,201
1994	Pittsburgh, AFC	2,180
	Detroit, NFC	2,080
1993	N.Y. Giants, NFC	2,210
	Seattle, AFC	2,015
1992	Buffalo, AFC	2,436
	Philadelphia, NFC	2,388
1991	Buffalo, AFC	2,381
	Minnesota, NFC	2,201
1990	Philadelphia, NFC	2,556
	San Diego, AFC	2,257
1989	Cincinnati, AFC	2,483
	Chicago, NFC	2,287
1988	Cincinnati, AFC	2,710
	San Francisco, NFC	2,523
1987	San Francisco, NFC	2,237
	L.A. Raiders, AFC	2,197
1986	Chicago, NFC	2,700
	Cincinnati, AFC	2,533
1985	Chicago, NFC	2,761
	Indianapolis, AFC	2,439
1984	Chicago, NFC	2,974
	N.Y. Jets, AFC	2,189
1983	Chicago, NFC	2,727
	Baltimore, AFC	2,695
1982	Buffalo, AFC	1,371
	Dallas, NFC	1,313
1981	Detroit, NFC	2,795
	Kansas City, AFC	2,633
1980	Los Angeles, NFC	2,799
	Houston, AFC	2,635
1979	N.Y. Jets, AFC	2,646
	St. Louis, NFC	2,582
1978	New England, AFC	3,165
	Dallas, NFC	2,783
1977	Chicago, NFC	2,811
	Oakland, AFC	2,627
1976	Pittsburgh, AFC	2,971
	Los Angeles, NFC	2,528
1975	Buffalo, AFC	2,974
	Dallas, NFC	2,432
1974	Dallas, NFC	2,454
	Pittsburgh, AFC	2,417
1973	Buffalo, AFC	3,088
	Los Angeles, NFC	2,925
1972	Miami, AFC	2,960
	Chicago, NFC	2,360
1971	Miami, AFC	2,429
	Detroit, NFC	2,376
1970	Dallas, NFC	2,300
	Miami, AFC	2,082
1969	Dallas, NFL	2,276
	Kansas City, AFL	2,220
1968	Chicago, NFL	2,377
	Kansas City, AFL	2,227
1967	Cleveland, NFL	2,139
	Houston, AFL	2,122
1966	Kansas City, AFL	2,274
	Cleveland, NFL	2,166
1965	Cleveland, NFL	2,331
	San Diego, AFL	2,085

Year	Team	Yards
1964	Green Bay, NFL	2,276
	Buffalo, AFL	2,040
1963	Cleveland, NFL	2,639
	San Diego, AFL	2,203
1962	Buffalo, AFL	2,480
	Green Bay, NFL	2,460
1961	Green Bay, NFL	2,350
	Dall. Texans, AFL	2,189
1960	St. Louis, NFL	2,356
	Oakland, AFL	2,056
1959	Cleveland	2,149
1958	Cleveland	2,526
1957	Los Angeles	2,142
1956	Chi. Bears	2,468
1955	Chi. Bears	2,388
1954	San Francisco	2,498
1953	San Francisco	2,230
1952	San Francisco	1,905
1951	Chi. Bears	2,408
1950	N.Y. Giants	2,336
1949	Philadelphia	2,607
1948	Chi. Cardinals	2,560
1947	Los Angeles	2,171
1946	Green Bay	1,765
1945	Cleveland	1,714
1944	Philadelphia	1,661
1943	Phil-Pitt	1,730
1942	Chi. Bears	1,881
1941	Chi. Bears	2,263
1940	Chi. Bears	1,818
1939	Chi. Bears	2,043
1938	Detroit	1,893
1937	Detroit	2,074
1936	Detroit	2,885
1935	Chi. Bears	2,096
1934	Chi. Bears	2,847
1933	Boston	2,260
1932	Chi. Bears	1,770

YARDS PASSING

Leadership in this category has been based on net yards since 1952.

Year	Team	Yards
2012	New Orleans, NFC	4,997
	New England, AFC	4,662
2011	New Orleans, NFC	5,347
	New England, AFC	5,084
2010	Indianapolis, AFC	4,609
	New Orleans, NFC	4,441
2009	Houston, AFC	4,654
	New Orleans, NFC	4,355
2008	New Orleans, NFC	4,977
	Denver, AFC	4,471
2007	New England, AFC	4,731
	Green Bay, NFC	4,334
2006	New Orleans, NFC	4,503
	Indianapolis, AFC	4,308
2005	Arizona, NFC	4,437
	New England, AFC	4,120
2004	Indianapolis, AFC	4,623
	Minnesota, NFC	4,516
2003	Indianapolis, AFC	4,179
	St. Louis, NFC	3,961
2002	Oakland, AFC	4,475
	St. Louis, NFC	4,154
2001	St. Louis, NFC	4,663
	Indianapolis, AFC	3,989
2000	St. Louis, NFC	5,232
	Indianapolis, AFC	4,282

Year	Team	Yards
1999	St. Louis, NFC	4,353
	Indianapolis, AFC	4,066
1998	Minnesota, NFC	4,328
	N.Y. Jets, AFC	3,836
1997	Seattle, AFC	3,959
	Green Bay, NFC	3,705
1996	Jacksonville, AFC	4,110
	Philadelphia, NFC	3,745
1995	San Francisco, NFC	4,608
	Miami, AFC	4,210
1994	New England, AFC	4,444
	Minnesota, NFC	4,324
1993	Miami, AFC	4,353
	San Francisco, NFC	4,302
1992	Houston, AFC	4,029
	San Francisco, NFC	3,880
1991	Houston, AFC	4,621
	San Francisco, NFC	3,997
1990	Houston, AFC	4,805
	San Francisco, NFC	4,177
1989	Washington, NFC	4,349
	Miami, AFC	4,216
1988	Miami, AFC	4,516
	Washington, NFC	4,136
1987	Miami, AFC	3,876
	San Francisco, NFC	3,750
1986	Miami, AFC	4,779
	San Francisco, NFC	4,096
1985	San Diego, AFC	4,870
	Dallas, NFC	3,861
1984	Miami, AFC	5,018
	St. Louis, NFC	4,257
1983	San Diego, AFC	4,661
	Green Bay, NFC	4,365
1982	San Diego, AFC	2,927
	San Francisco, NFC	2,502
1981	San Diego, AFC	4,739
	Minnesota, NFC	4,333
1980	San Diego, AFC	4,531
	Minnesota, NFC	3,688
1979	San Diego, AFC	3,915
	San Francisco, NFC	3,641
1978	San Diego, AFC	3,375
	Minnesota, NFC	3,243
1977	Buffalo, AFC	2,530
	St. Louis, NFC	2,499
1976	Baltimore, AFC	2,933
	Minnesota, NFC	2,855
1975	Cincinnati, AFC	3,241
	Washington, NFC	2,917
1974	Washington, NFC	2,978
	Cincinnati, AFC	2,804
1973	Philadelphia, NFC	2,998
	Denver, AFC	2,519
1972	N.Y. Jets, AFC	2,777
	San Francisco, NFC	2,735
1971	San Diego, AFC	3,134
	Dallas, NFC	2,786
1970	San Francisco, NFC	2,923
	Oakland, AFC	2,865
1969	Oakland, AFL	3,271
	San Francisco, NFL	3,158
1968	San Diego, AFL	3,623
	Dallas, NFL	3,026
1967	N.Y. Jets, AFL	3,845
	Washington, NFL	3,730
1966	N.Y. Jets, AFL	3,464
	Dallas, NFL	3,023
1965	San Francisco, NFL	3,487
	San Diego, AFL	3,103

Year	Team	Yards
1964	Houston, AFL	3,527
	Chicago, NFL	2,841
1963	Baltimore, NFL	3,296
	Houston, AFL	3,222
1962	Denver, AFL	3,404
	Philadelphia, NFL	3,385
1961	Houston, AFL	4,392
	Philadelphia, NFL	3,605
1960	Houston, AFL	3,203
	Baltimore, NFL	2,956
1959	Baltimore	2,753
1958	Pittsburgh	2,752
1957	Baltimore	2,388
1956	Los Angeles	2,419
1955	Philadelphia	2,472
1954	Chi. Bears	3,104
1953	Philadelphia	3,089
1952	Cleveland	2,566
1951	Los Angeles	3,296
1950	Los Angeles	3,709
1949	Chi. Bears	3,055
1948	Washington	2,861
1947	Washington	3,336
1946	Los Angeles	2,080
1945	Chi. Bears	1,857
1944	Washington	2,021
1943	Chi. Bears	2,310
1942	Green Bay	2,407
1941	Chi. Bears	2,002
1940	Washington	1,887
1939	Chi. Bears	1,965
1938	Washington	1,536
1937	Green Bay	1,398
1936	Green Bay	1,629
1935	Green Bay	1,449
1934	Green Bay	1,165
1933	N.Y. Giants	1,348
1932	Chi. Bears	1,013

FEWEST POINTS ALLOWED

Year	Team	Points
2012	Seattle, NFC	245
	Denver, AFC	289
2011	Pittsburgh, AFC	227
	San Francisco, NFC	229
2010	Pittsburgh, AFC	232
	Green Bay, NFC	240
2009	N.Y. Jets, AFC	236
	Dallas, NFC	250
2008	Pittsburgh, AFC	223
	Philadelphia, NFC	289
2007	Indianapolis, AFC	262
	Tampa Bay, NFC	270
2006	Baltimore, AFC	201
	Chicago, NFC	255
2005	Chicago, NFC	202
	Indianapolis, AFC	247
2004	Pittsburgh, AFC	251
	Philadelphia, NFC	260
2003	New England, AFC	238
	Dallas, NFC	260
2002	Tampa Bay, NFC	196
	Miami, AFC	301
2001	Chicago, NFC	203
	Pittsburgh, AFC	212
2000	Baltimore, AFC	165
	Philadelphia, NFC	245
1999	Jacksonville, AFC	217
	Tampa Bay, NFC	235

Year	Team	Points
1998	Miami, AFC	265
	Dallas, NFC	275
1997	Kansas City, AFC	232
	Tampa Bay, NFC	263
1996	Green Bay, NFC	210
	Pittsburgh, AFC	257
1995	Kansas City, AFC	241
	San Francisco, NFC	258
1994	Cleveland, AFC	204
	Dallas, NFC	248
1993	N.Y. Giants, NFC	205
	Houston, AFC	238
1992	New Orleans, NFC	202
	Pittsburgh, AFC	225
1991	New Orleans, NFC	211
	Denver, AFC	235
1990	N.Y. Giants, NFC	211
	Pittsburgh, AFC	240
1989	Denver, AFC	226
	N.Y. Giants, NFC	252
1988	Chicago, NFC	215
	Buffalo, AFC	237
1987	Indianapolis, AFC	238
	San Francisco, NFC	253
1986	Chicago, NFC	187
	Seattle, AFC	293
1985	Chicago, NFC	198
	N.Y. Jets, AFC	264
1984	San Francisco, NFC	227
	Denver, AFC	241
1983	Miami, AFC	250
	Detroit, NFC	286
1982	Washington, NFC	128
	Miami, AFC	131
1981	Philadelphia, NFC	221
	Miami, AFC	275
1980	Philadelphia, NFC	222
	Houston, AFC	251
1979	Tampa Bay, NFC	237
	San Diego, AFC	246
1978	Pittsburgh, AFC	195
	Dallas, NFC	208
1977	Atlanta, NFC	129
	Denver, AFC	148
1976	Pittsburgh, AFC	138
	Minnesota, NFC	176
1975	Los Angeles, NFC	135
	Pittsburgh, AFC	162
1974	Los Angeles, NFC	181
	Pittsburgh, AFC	189
1973	Miami, AFC	150
	Minnesota, NFC	168
1972	Miami, AFC	171
	Washington, NFC	218
1971	Minnesota, NFC	139
	Baltimore, AFC	140
1970	Minnesota, NFC	143
	Miami, AFC	228
1969	Minnesota, NFL	133
	Kansas City, AFL	177
1968	Baltimore, NFL	144
	Kansas City, AFL	170
1967	Los Angeles, NFL	196
	Houston, AFL	199
1966	Green Bay, NFL	163
	Buffalo, AFL	255
1965	Green Bay, NFL	224
	Buffalo, AFL	226
1964	Baltimore, NFL	225
	Buffalo, AFL	242

Year	Team	Points
1963	Chicago, NFL	144
	San Diego, AFL	255
1962	Green Bay, NFL	148
	Dall. Texans, AFL	233
1961	San Diego, AFL	219
	N.Y. Giants, NFL	220
1960	San Francisco, NFL	205
	Dall. Texans, AFL	253
1959	N.Y. Giants	170
1958	N.Y. Giants	183
1957	Cleveland	172
1956	Cleveland	177
1955	Cleveland	218
1954	Cleveland	162
1953	Cleveland	162
1952	Detroit	192
1951	Cleveland	152
1950	Philadelphia	141
1949	Philadelphia	134
1948	Chi. Bears	151
1947	Green Bay	210
1946	Pittsburgh	117
1945	Washington	121
1944	N.Y. Giants	75
1943	Washington	137
1942	Chi. Bears	84
1941	N.Y. Giants	114
1940	Brooklyn	120
1939	N.Y. Giants	85
1938	N.Y. Giants	79
1937	Chi. Bears	100
1936	Chi. Bears	94
1935	Green Bay	96
	N.Y. Giants	96
1934	Detroit	59
1933	Brooklyn	54
1932	Chi. Bears	44

FEWEST TOTAL YARDS ALLOWED

Year	Team	Yards
2012	Pittsburgh, AFC	4,413
	San Francisco, NFC	4,710
2011	Pittsburgh, AFC	4,348
	San Francisco, NFC	4,931
2010	San Diego, AFC	4,345
	New Orleans, NFC	4,900
2009	N.Y. Jets, AFC	4,037
	Green Bay, NFC	4,551
2008	Pittsburgh, AFC	3,795
	Philadelphia, NFC	4,389
2007	Pittsburgh, AFC	4,262
	Tampa Bay, NFC	4,454
2006	Baltimore, AFC	4,225
	Chicago, NFC	4,706
2005	Tampa Bay, NFC	4,444
	Pittsburgh, AFC	4,544
2004	Pittsburgh, AFC	4,134
	Washington, NFC	4,281
2003	Dallas, NFC	4,056
	Buffalo, AFC	4,313
2002	Tampa Bay, NFC	4,044
	Miami, AFC	4,656
2001	Pittsburgh, AFC	4,137
	St. Louis, NFC	4,471
2000	Tennessee, AFC	3,813
	Washington, NFC	4,474
1999	Buffalo, AFC	4,045
	Tampa Bay, NFC	4,280
1998	San Diego, AFC	4,208
	Tampa Bay, NFC	4,345

Year	Team	Yards
1997	San Francisco, NFC	4,013
	Denver, AFC	4,671
1996	Green Bay, NFC	4,156
	Pittsburgh, AFC	4,362
1995	San Francisco, NFC	4,398
	Kansas City, AFC	4,549
1994	Dallas, NFC	4,313
	Pittsburgh, AFC	4,326
1993	Minnesota, NFC	4,406
	Pittsburgh, AFC	4,531
1992	Dallas, NFC	3,931
	Houston, AFC	4,211
1991	Philadelphia, NFC	3,549
	Denver, AFC	4,549
1990	Pittsburgh, AFC	4,115
	N.Y. Giants, NFC	4,206
1989	Minnesota, NFC	4,184
	Kansas City, AFC	4,293
1988	Minnesota, NFC	4,091
	Buffalo, AFC	4,578
1987	San Francisco, NFC	4,095
	Cleveland, AFC	4,264
1986	Chicago, NFC	4,130
	L.A. Raiders, AFC	4,804
1985	Chicago, NFC	4,135
	L.A. Raiders, AFC	4,603
1984	Chicago, NFC	3,863
	Cleveland, AFC	4,641
1983	Cincinnati, AFC	4,327
	New Orleans, NFC	4,691
1982	Miami, AFC	2,312
	Tampa Bay, NFC	2,442
1981	Philadelphia, NFC	4,447
	N.Y. Jets, AFC	4,871
1980	Buffalo, AFC	4,101
	Philadelphia, NFC	4,443
1979	Tampa Bay, NFC	3,949
	Pittsburgh, AFC	4,270
1978	Los Angeles, NFC	3,893
	Pittsburgh, AFC	4,168
1977	Dallas, NFC	3,213
	New England, AFC	3,638
1976	Pittsburgh, AFC	3,323
	San Francisco, NFC	3,562
1975	Minnesota, NFC	3,153
	Oakland, AFC	3,629
1974	Pittsburgh, AFC	3,074
	Washington, NFC	3,285
1973	Los Angeles, NFC	2,951
	Oakland, AFC	3,160
1972	Miami, AFC	3,297
	Green Bay, NFC	3,474
1971	Baltimore, AFC	2,852
	Minnesota, NFC	3,406
1970	Minnesota, NFC	2,803
	N.Y. Jets, AFC	3,655
1969	Minnesota, NFL	2,720
	Kansas City, AFL	3,163
1968	Los Angeles, NFL	3,118
	N.Y. Jets, AFL	3,363
1967	Oakland, AFL	3,294
	Green Bay, NFL	3,300
1966	St. Louis, NFL	3,492
	Oakland, AFL	3,910
1965	San Diego, AFL	3,262
	Detroit, NFL	3,557
1964	Green Bay, NFL	3,179
	Buffalo, AFL	3,878
1963	Chicago, NFL	3,176
	Boston, AFL	3,834

Year	Team	Yards
1962	Detroit, NFL	3,217
	Dall. Texans, AFL	3,951
1961	San Diego, AFL	3,726
	Baltimore, NFL	3,782
1960	St. Louis, NFL	3,029
	Buffalo, AFL	3,866
1959	N.Y. Giants	2,843
1958	Chi. Bears	3,066
1957	Pittsburgh	2,791
1956	N.Y. Giants	3,081
1955	Cleveland	2,841
1954	Cleveland	2,658
1953	Philadelphia	2,998
1952	Cleveland	3,075
1951	N.Y. Giants	3,250
1950	Cleveland	3,154
1949	Philadelphia	2,831
1948	Chi. Bears	2,931
1947	Green Bay	3,396
1946	Washington	2,451
1945	Philadelphia	2,073
1944	Philadelphia	1,943
1943	Chi. Bears	2,262
1942	Chi. Bears	1,703
1941	N.Y. Giants	2,368
1940	N.Y. Giants	2,219
1939	Washington	2,116
1938	N.Y. Giants	2,029
1937	Washington	2,123
1936	Boston	2,181
1935	Boston	1,996
1934	Chi. Cardinals	1,539
1933	Brooklyn	1,789

FEWEST RUSHING YARDS ALLOWED

Year	Team	Yards
2012	Tampa Bay, NFC	1,320
	Pittsburgh, AFC	1,450
2011	San Francisco, NFC	1,236
	Baltimore, AFC	1,482
2010	Pittsburgh, AFC	1,004
	Chicago, NFC	1,441
2009	Green Bay, NFC	1,333
	Pittsburgh, AFC	1,438
2008	Minnesota, NFC	1,230
	Pittsburgh, AFC	1,284
2007	Minnesota, NFC	1,185
	Baltimore, AFC	1,268
2006	Minnesota, NFC	985
	Baltimore, AFC	1,214
2005	San Diego, AFC	1,349
	Carolina, NFC	1,465
2004	Pittsburgh, AFC	1,299
	Washington, NFC	1,304
2003	Tennessee, AFC	1,295
	Dallas, NFC	1,425
2002	Pittsburgh, AFC	1,375
	Tampa Bay, NFC	1,554
2001	Pittsburgh, AFC	1,195
	Chicago, NFC	1,313
2000	Baltimore, AFC	970
	N.Y. Giants, NFC	1,156
1999	St. Louis, NFC	1,189
	Baltimore, AFC	1,231
1998	San Diego, AFC	1,140
	Atlanta, NFC	1,203
1997	Pittsburgh, AFC	1,318
	San Francisco, NFC	1,366
1996	Denver, AFC	1,331
	Green Bay, NFC	1,416

Year	Team	Yards
1995	San Francisco, NFC	1,061
	Pittsburgh, AFC	1,321
1994	Minnesota, NFC	1,090
	San Diego, AFC	1,404
1993	Houston, AFC	1,273
	Minnesota, NFC	1,536
1992	Dallas, NFC	1,244
	Buffalo, AFC	1,395
	San Diego, AFC	1,395
1991	Philadelphia, NFC	1,136
	N.Y. Jets, AFC	1,442
1990	Philadelphia, NFC	1,169
	San Diego, AFC	1,515
1989	New Orleans, NFC	1,326
	Denver, AFC	1,580
1988	Chicago, NFC	1,326
	Houston, AFC	1,592
1987	Chicago, NFC	1,413
	Cleveland, AFC	1,433
1986	N.Y. Giants, NFC	1,284
	Denver, AFC	1,651
1985	Chicago, NFC	1,319
	N.Y. Jets, AFC	1,516
1984	Chicago, NFC	1,377
	Pittsburgh, AFC	1,617
1983	Washington, NFC	1,289
	Cincinnati, AFC	1,499
1982	Pittsburgh, AFC	762
	Detroit, NFC	854
1981	Detroit, NFC	1,623
	Kansas City, AFC	1,747
1980	Detroit, NFC	1,599
	Cincinnati, AFC	1,680
1979	Denver, AFC	1,693
	Tampa Bay, NFC	1,873
1978	Dallas, NFC	1,721
	Pittsburgh, AFC	1,774
1977	Denver, AFC	1,531
	Dallas, NFC	1,651
1976	Pittsburgh, AFC	1,457
	Los Angeles, NFC	1,564
1975	Minnesota, NFC	1,532
	Houston, AFC	1,680
1974	Los Angeles, NFC	1,302
	New England, AFC	1,587
1973	Los Angeles, NFC	1,270
	Oakland, AFC	1,470
1972	Dallas, NFC	1,515
	Miami, AFC	1,548
1971	Baltimore, AFC	1,113
	Dallas, NFC	1,144
1970	Detroit, NFC	1,152
	N.Y. Jets, AFC	1,283
1969	Dallas, NFL	1,050
	Kansas City, AFL	1,091
1968	Dallas, NFL	1,195
	N.Y. Jets, AFL	1,195
1967	Dallas, NFL	1,081
	Oakland, AFL	1,129
1966	Buffalo, AFL	1,051
	Dallas, NFL	1,176
1965	San Diego, AFL	1,094
	Los Angeles, NFL	1,409
1964	Buffalo, AFL	913
	Los Angeles, NFL	1,501
1963	Boston, AFL	1,107
	Chicago, NFL	1,442
1962	Detroit, NFL	1,231
	Dall. Texans, AFL	1,250

Year	Team	Yards
1961	Boston, AFL	1,041
	Pittsburgh, NFL	1,463
1960	St. Louis, NFL	1,212
	Dall. Texans, AFL	1,338
1959	N.Y. Giants	1,261
1958	Baltimore	1,291
1957	Baltimore	1,174
1956	N.Y. Giants	1,443
1955	Cleveland	1,189
1954	Cleveland	1,050
1953	Philadelphia	1,117
1952	Detroit	1,145
1951	N.Y. Giants	913
1950	Detroit	1,367
1949	Chi. Bears	1,196
1948	Philadelphia	1,209
1947	Philadelphia	1,329
1946	Chi. Bears	1,060
1945	Philadelphia	817
1944	Philadelphia	558
1943	Phil-Pitt	793
1942	Chi. Bears	519
1941	Washington	1,042
1940	N.Y. Giants	977
1939	Chi. Bears	812
1938	Detroit	1,081
1937	Chi. Bears	933
1936	Boston	1,148
1935	Boston	998
1934	Chi. Cardinals	954
1933	Brooklyn	964

FEWEST PASSING YARDS ALLOWED

Leadership in this category has been based on net yards since 1952.

Year	Team	Yards
2012	Pittsburgh, AFC	2,963
	San Francisco, NFC	3,203
2011	Pittsburgh, AFC	2,751
	St. Louis, NFC	3,301
2010	San Diego, AFC	2,845
	New Orleans, NFC	3,103
2009	N.Y. Jets, AFC	2,459
	Carolina, NFC	3,056
2008	Pittsburgh, AFC	2,511
	Philadelphia, NFC	2,913
2007	Tampa Bay, NFC	2,728
	Indianapolis, AFC	2,764
2006	Oakland, AFC	2,413
	New Orleans, NFC	2,854
2005	Green Bay, NFC	2,680
	N.Y. Jets, AFC	2,755
2004	Tampa Bay, NFC	2,579
	Miami, AFC	2,592
2003	Dallas, NFC	2,631
	Buffalo, AFC	2,707
2002	Tampa Bay, NFC	2,490
	Indianapolis, AFC	2,917
2001	Miami, AFC	2,829
	Philadelphia, NFC	2,864
2000	Tennessee, AFC	2,423
	Washington, NFC	2,621
1999	Buffalo, AFC	2,675
	Tampa Bay, NFC	2,873
1998	Philadelphia, NFC	2,720
	Oakland, AFC	2,876
1997	Dallas, NFC	2,522
	Indianapolis, AFC	2,820
1996	Green Bay, NFC	2,740
	Pittsburgh, AFC	2,947

Year	Team	Yards
1995	N.Y. Jets, AFC	2,740
	Philadelphia, NFC	2,816
1994	Dallas, NFC	2,752
	Houston, AFC	2,795
1993	New Orleans, NFC	2,606
	Cincinnati, AFC	2,798
1992	New Orleans, NFC	2,470
	Kansas City, AFC	2,537
1991	Philadelphia, NFC	2,413
	Denver, AFC	2,755
1990	Pittsburgh, AFC	2,500
	Dallas, NFC	2,639
1989	Minnesota, NFC	2,501
	Kansas City, AFC	2,527
1988	Kansas City, AFC	2,434
	Minnesota, NFC	2,489
1987	San Francisco, NFC	2,484
	L.A. Raiders, AFC	2,727
1986	St. Louis, NFC	2,637
	New England, AFC	2,978
1985	Washington, NFC	2,746
	Pittsburgh, AFC	2,783
1984	New Orleans, NFC	2,453
	Cleveland, AFC	2,696
1983	New Orleans, NFC	2,691
	Cincinnati, AFC	2,828
1982	Miami, AFC	1,027
	Tampa Bay, NFC	1,384
1981	Philadelphia, NFC	2,696
	Buffalo, AFC	2,870
1980	Washington, NFC	2,171
	Buffalo, AFC	2,282
1979	Tampa Bay, NFC	2,076
	Buffalo, AFC	2,530
1978	Buffalo, AFC	1,960
	Los Angeles, NFC	2,048
1977	Atlanta, NFC	1,384
	San Diego, AFC	1,725
1976	Minnesota, NFC	1,575
	Cincinnati, AFC	1,758
1975	Minnesota, NFC	1,621
	Cincinnati, AFC	1,729
1974	Pittsburgh, AFC	1,466
	Atlanta, NFC	1,572
1973	Miami, AFC	1,290
	Atlanta, NFC	1,430
1972	Minnesota, NFC	1,699
	Cleveland, AFC	1,736
1971	Atlanta, NFC	1,638
	Baltimore, AFC	1,739
1970	Minnesota, NFC	1,438
	Kansas City, AFC	2,010
1969	Minnesota, NFL	1,631
	Kansas City, AFL	2,072
1968	Houston, AFL	1,671
	Green Bay, NFL	1,796
1967	Green Bay, NFL	1,377
	Buffalo, AFL	1,825
1966	Green Bay, NFL	1,959
	Oakland, AFL	2,118
1965	Green Bay, NFL	1,981
	San Diego, AFL	2,168
1964	Green Bay, NFL	1,647
	San Diego, AFL	2,518
1963	Chicago, NFL	1,734
	Oakland, AFL	2,589
1962	Green Bay, NFL	1,746
	Oakland, AFL	2,306
1961	Baltimore, NFL	1,913
	San Diego, AFL	2,363

Year	Team	Yards
1960	Chicago, NFL	1,388
	Buffalo, AFL	2,124
1959	N.Y. Giants	1,582
1958	Chi. Bears	1,769
1957	Cleveland	1,300
1956	Cleveland	1,103
1955	Pittsburgh	1,295
1954	Cleveland	1,608
1953	Washington	1,751
1952	Washington	1,580
1951	Pittsburgh	1,687
1950	Cleveland	1,581
1949	Philadelphia	1,607
1948	Green Bay	1,626
1947	Green Bay	1,790
1946	Pittsburgh	939
1945	Washington	1,121
1944	Chi. Bears	1,052
1943	Chi. Bears	980
1942	Washington	1,093
1941	Pittsburgh	1,168
1940	Philadelphia	1,012
1939	Washington	1,116
1938	Chi. Bears	897
1937	Detroit	804
1936	Philadelphia	853
1935	Chi. Cardinals	793
1934	Philadelphia	545
1933	Portsmouth	558

Compiled by Elias Sports Bureau

Super Bowl I, 1/15/67	Super Bowl XXV, 1/27/91
Super Bowl II, 1/14/68	Super Bowl XXVI, 1/26/92
Super Bowl III, 1/12/69	Super Bowl XXVII, 1/31/93
Super Bowl IV, 1/11/70	Super Bowl XXVIII, 1/30/94
Super Bowl V, 1/17/71	Super Bowl XXIX, 1/29/95
Super Bowl VI, 1/16/72	Super Bowl XXX, 1/28/96
Super Bowl VII, 1/14/73	Super Bowl XXXI, 1/26/97
Super Bowl VIII, 1/13/74	Super Bowl XXXII, 1/25/98
Super Bowl IX, 1/12/75	Super Bowl XXXIII, 1/31/99
Super Bowl X, 1/18/76	Super Bowl XXXIV, 1/30/00
Super Bowl XI, 1/9/77	Super Bowl XXXV, 1/28/01
Super Bowl XII, 1/15/78	Super Bowl XXXVI, 2/3/02
Super Bowl XIII, 1/21/79	Super Bowl XXXVII, 1/26/03
Super Bowl XIV, 1/20/80	Super Bowl XXXVIII, 2/1/04
Super Bowl XV, 1/25/81	Super Bowl XXXIX, 2/6/05
Super Bowl XVI, 1/24/82	Super Bowl XL, 2/5/06
Super Bowl XVII, 1/30/83	Super Bowl XLI, 2/4/07
Super Bowl XVIII, 1/22/84	Super Bowl XLII, 2/3/08
Super Bowl XIX, 1/20/85	Super Bowl XLIII, 2/1/09
Super Bowl XX, 1/26/86	Super Bowl XLIV, 2/7/10
Super Bowl XXI, 1/25/87	Super Bowl XLV, 2/6/11
Super Bowl XXII, 1/31/88	Super Bowl XLVI, 2/5/12
Super Bowl XXIII, 1/22/89	Super Bowl XLVII, 2/3/13
Super Bowl XXIV, 1/28/90	

INDIVIDUAL RECORDS

SERVICE
Most Games
- 6   Mike Lodish, Buffalo, XXV-XXVIII; Denver, XXXII-XXXIII
- 5   Marv Fleming, Green Bay, I-II; Miami, VI-VIII
  - Larry Cole, Dallas, V-VI, X, XII-XIII
  - Cliff Harris, Dallas, V-VI, X, XII-XIII
  - Charles Haley, San Francisco, XXIII-XXIV; Dallas, XXVII-XXVIII, XXX
  - D.D. Lewis, Dallas, V-VI, X, XII-XIII
  - Preston Pearson, Baltimore, III; Pittsburgh, IX; Dallas, X, XII-XIII
  - Charlie Waters, Dallas, V-VI, X, XII-XIII
  - Rayfield Wright, Dallas, V-VI, X, XII-XIII
  - Cornelius Bennett, Buffalo, XXV-XXVIII; Atlanta, XXXIII
  - John Elway, Denver, XXI-XXII, XXIV, XXXII-XXXIII
  - Glenn Parker, Buffalo, XXV-XXVIII; N.Y. Giants, XXXV
  - Bill Romanowski, San Francisco, XXIII-XXIV; Denver, XXXII-XXXIII; Oakland, XXXVII
  - Adam Vinatieri, New England, XXXI, XXXVI, XXXVIII, XXXIX; Indianapolis, XLI
  - Tedy Bruschi, New England, XXXI, XXXVI, XXXVIII-XXXIX, XLII
  - Tom Brady, New England, XXXVI, XXXVIII-XXXIX, XLII, XLVI
  - Matt Light, New England, XXXVI, XXXVIII-XXXIX, XLII, XLVI
- 4   By many players

Most Games, Winning Team
- 5   Charles Haley, San Francisco, XXIII-XXIV; Dallas, XXVII-XXVIII, XXX
- 4   By many players

Most Games, Coach
- 6   Don Shula, Baltimore, III; Miami, VI-VIII, XVII, XIX
- 5   Tom Landry, Dallas, V-VI, X, XII-XIII
  - Bill Belichick, New England, XXXVI, XXXVIII-XXXIX, XLII, XLVI
- 4   Bud Grant, Minnesota, IV, VIII-IX, XI
  - Chuck Noll, Pittsburgh, IX-X, XIII-XIV
  - Joe Gibbs, Washington, XVII-XVIII, XXII, XXVI
  - Marv Levy, Buffalo, XXV-XXVIII
  - Dan Reeves, Denver, XXI-XXII, XXIV; Atlanta, XXXIII

Most Games, Winning Team, Coach
- 4   Chuck Noll, Pittsburgh, IX-X, XIII-XIV
- 3   Bill Walsh, San Francisco, XVI, XIX, XXIII

Joe Gibbs, Washington, XVII, XXII, XXVI
Bill Belichick, New England, XXXVI, XXXVIII-XXXIX
- 2   Vince Lombardi, Green Bay, I-II
  - Tom Landry, Dallas, VI, XII
  - Don Shula, Miami, VII-VIII
  - Tom Flores, Oakland, XV; L.A. Raiders, XVIII
  - Bill Parcells, N.Y. Giants, XXI, XXV
  - Jimmy Johnson, Dallas, XXVII-XXVIII
  - George Seifert, San Francisco, XXIV, XXIX
  - Mike Shanahan, Denver, XXXII-XXXIII
  - Tom Coughlin, N.Y. Giants, XLII, XLVI

Most Games, Losing Team, Coach
- 4   Bud Grant, Minnesota, IV, VIII-IX, XI
  - Don Shula, Baltimore, III; Miami, VI, XVII, XIX
  - Marv Levy, Buffalo, XXV-XXVIII
  - Dan Reeves, Denver, XXI-XXII, XXIV; Atlanta, XXXIII
- 3   Tom Landry, Dallas, V, X, XIII

SCORING
POINTS
Most Points, Career
- 48   Jerry Rice, San Francisco-Oakland, 4 games (8-td)
- 34   Adam Vinatieri, New England-Indianapolis, 5 games (7-fg, 13-xp)
- 30   Emmitt Smith, Dallas, 3 games (5-td)

Most Points, Game
- 18   Roger Craig, San Francisco vs. Miami, XIX (3-td)
  - Jerry Rice, San Francisco vs. Denver, XXIV (3-td); vs. San Diego, XXIX (3-td)
  - Ricky Watters, San Francisco vs. San Diego, XXIX (3-td)
  - Terrell Davis, Denver vs. Green Bay, XXXII (3-td)
- 15   Don Chandler, Green Bay vs. Oakland, II (3-pat, 4-fg)
- 14   Ray Wersching, San Francisco vs. Cincinnati, XVI (2-pat, 4-fg)
  - Kevin Butler, Chicago vs. New England, XX (5-pat, 3-fg)

TOUCHDOWNS
Most Touchdowns, Career
- 8   Jerry Rice, San Francisco-Oakland, 4 games (8-p)
- 5   Emmitt Smith, Dallas, 3 games (5-r)
- 4   Franco Harris, Pittsburgh, 4 games (4-r)
  - Roger Craig, San Francisco, 3 games (2-r, 2-p)
  - Thurman Thomas, Buffalo, 4 games (4-r)
  - John Elway, Denver, 5 games (4-r)

Most Touchdowns, Game
- 3   Roger Craig, San Francisco vs. Miami, XIX (1-r, 2-p)
  - Jerry Rice, San Francisco vs. Denver, XXIV (3-p); vs. San Diego, XXIX (3-p)
  - Ricky Watters, San Francisco vs. San Diego, XXIX (1-r, 2-p)
  - Terrell Davis, Denver vs. Green Bay, XXXII (3-r)
- 2   Max McGee, Green Bay vs. Kansas City, I (2-p)
  - Elijah Pitts, Green Bay vs. Kansas City, I (2-r)
  - Bill Miller, Oakland vs. Green Bay, II (2-p)
  - Larry Csonka, Miami vs. Minnesota, VIII (2-r)
  - Pete Banaszak, Oakland vs. Minnesota, XI (2-r)
  - John Stallworth, Pittsburgh vs. Dallas, XIII (2-p)
  - Franco Harris, Pittsburgh vs. Los Angeles, XIV (2-r)
  - Cliff Branch, Oakland vs. Philadelphia, XV (2-p)
  - Dan Ross, Cincinnati vs. San Francisco, XVI (2-p)
  - Marcus Allen, L.A. Raiders vs. Washington, XVIII (2-r)
  - Jim McMahon, Chicago vs. New England, XX (2-r)
  - Ricky Sanders, Washington vs. Denver, XXII (2-p)
  - Timmy Smith, Washington vs. Denver, XXII (2-r)
  - Tom Rathman, San Francisco vs. Denver, XXIV (2-r)
  - Gerald Riggs, Washington vs. Buffalo, XXVI (2-r)
  - Michael Irvin, Dallas vs. Buffalo, XXVII (2-p)
  - Emmitt Smith, Dallas vs. Buffalo, XXVIII (2-r)
  - Emmitt Smith, Dallas vs. Pittsburgh, XXX (2-r)
  - Antonio Freeman, Green Bay vs. Denver, XXXII (2-p)
  - Howard Griffith, Denver vs. Atlanta, XXXIII (2-r)

Eddie George, Tennessee vs. St. Louis, XXXIV (2-r)
Keenan McCardell, Tampa Bay vs. Oakland, XXXVII (2-r)
Dwight Smith, Tampa Bay vs. Oakland, XXXVII (2-ret)
Larry Fitzgerald, Arizona vs. Pittsburgh, XLIII (2-p)
Greg Jennings, Green Bay vs. Pittsburgh, XLV (2-p)
Jacoby Jones, Baltimore vs. San Francisco, XLVII (1-r, 1-ret)

POINTS AFTER TOUCHDOWN
Most (One-Point) Points After Touchdown, Career
13 Adam Vinatieri, New England-Indianapolis, 5 games (13 att)
9 Mike Cofer, San Francisco, 2 games (10 att)
8 Don Chandler, Green Bay, 2 games (8 att)
Roy Gerela, Pittsburgh, 3 games (9 att)
Chris Bahr, Oakland-L.A. Raiders, 2 games (8 att)
Jason Elam, Denver, 2 games (8 att)
Most (One-Point) Points After Touchdown, Game
7 Mike Cofer, San Francisco vs. Denver, XXIV (8 att)
Lin Elliott, Dallas vs. Buffalo, XXVII (7 att)
Doug Brien, San Francisco vs. San Diego, XXIX (7 att)
6 Ali Haji-Sheikh, Washington vs. Denver, XXII (6 att)
Martín Gramatica, Tampa Bay vs. Oakland, XXXVII (6 att)
5 Don Chandler, Green Bay vs. Kansas City, I (5 att)
Roy Gerela, Pittsburgh vs. Dallas, XIII (5 att)
Chris Bahr, L.A. Raiders vs. Washington, XVIII (5 att)
Ray Wersching, San Francisco vs. Miami, XIX (5 att)
Kevin Butler, Chicago vs. New England, XX (5 att)
Most Two-Point Conversions, Game
1 Mark Seay, San Diego vs. San Francisco, XXIX
Alfred Pupunu, San Diego vs. San Francisco, XXIX
Mark Chmura, Green Bay vs. New England, XXXI
Kevin Faulk, New England vs. Carolina, XXXVIII
Lance Moore, New Orleans vs. Indianapolis, XLIV
Antwaan Randle El, Pittsburgh vs. Green Bay, XLV

FIELD GOALS
Field Goals Attempted, Career
10 Adam Vinatieri, New England-Indianapolis, 5 games
6 Jim Turner, N.Y. Jets-Denver, 2 games
Roy Gerela, Pittsburgh, 3 games
Rich Karlis, Denver, 2 games
Jeff Wilkins, St. Louis, 2 games
5 Efren Herrera, Dallas, 1 game
Ray Wersching, San Francisco, 2 games
Jason Elam, Denver, 2 games
Matt Stover, Baltimore-Indianapolis, 2 games
Most Field Goals Attempted, Game
5 Jim Turner, N.Y. Jets vs. Baltimore, III
Efren Herrera, Dallas vs. Denver, XII
4 Don Chandler, Green Bay vs. Oakland, II
Roy Gerela, Pittsburgh vs. Dallas, X
Ray Wersching, San Francisco vs. Cincinnati, XVI
Rich Karlis, Denver vs. N.Y. Giants, XXI
Mike Cofer, San Francisco vs. Cincinnati, XXIII
Jason Elam, Denver vs. Atlanta, XXXIII
Jeff Wilkins, St. Louis vs. Tennessee, XXXIV
Adam Vinatieri, Indianapolis vs. Chicago, XLI
Most Field Goals, Career
7 Adam Vinatieri, New England-Indianapolis, 5 games (10 att)
5 Ray Wersching, San Francisco, 2 games (5 att)
4 Don Chandler, Green Bay, 2 games (4 att)
Jim Turner, N.Y. Jets-Denver, 2 games (6 att)
Uwe von Schamann, Miami, 2 games (4 att)
Jeff Wilkins, St. Louis, 2 games (6 att)
Most Field Goals, Game
4 Don Chandler, Green Bay vs. Oakland, II
Ray Wersching, San Francisco vs. Cincinnati, XVI
3 Jim Turner, N.Y. Jets vs. Baltimore, III
Jan Stenerud, Kansas City vs. Minnesota, IV

Uwe von Schamann, Miami vs. San Francisco, XIX
Kevin Butler, Chicago vs. New England, XX
Jim Breech, Cincinnati vs. San Francisco, XXIII
Chip Lohmiller, Washington vs. Buffalo, XXVI
Eddie Murray, Dallas vs. Buffalo, XXVIII
Jeff Wilkins, St. Louis vs. Tennessee, XXXIV
Adam Vinatieri, Indianapolis vs. Chicago, XLI
Garrett Hartley, New Orleans vs. Indianapolis, XLIV
David Akers, San Francisco vs. Baltimore, XLVII
Longest Field Goal
54 Steve Christie, Buffalo vs. Dallas, XXVIII
51 Jason Elam, Denver vs. Green Bay, XXXII
50 Jeff Wilkins, St. Louis vs. New England, XXXVI
John Kasay, Carolina vs. New England, XXXVIII

SAFETIES
Most Safeties, Game
1 Dwight White, Pittsburgh vs. Minnesota, IX
Reggie Harrison, Pittsburgh vs. Dallas, X
Henry Waechter, Chicago vs. New England, XX
George Martin, N.Y. Giants vs. Denver, XXI
Bruce Smith, Buffalo vs. N.Y. Giants, XXV
Chris Culliver, San Francisco vs. Baltimore, XLVII

RUSHING
ATTEMPTS
Most Attempts, Career
101 Franco Harris, Pittsburgh, 4 games
70 Emmitt Smith, Dallas, 3 games
64 John Riggins, Washington, 2 games
Most Attempts, Game
38 John Riggins, Washington vs. Miami, XVII
34 Franco Harris, Pittsburgh vs. Minnesota, IX
33 Larry Csonka, Miami vs. Minnesota, VIII

YARDS GAINED
Most Yards Gained, Career
354 Franco Harris, Pittsburgh, 4 games
297 Larry Csonka, Miami, 3 games
289 Emmitt Smith, Dallas, 3 games
Most Yards Gained, Game
204 Timmy Smith, Washington vs. Denver, XXII
191 Marcus Allen, L.A. Raiders vs. Washington, XVIII
166 John Riggins, Washington vs. Miami, XVII
Longest Run From Scrimmage
75 Willie Parker, Pittsburgh vs. Seattle, XL (TD)
74 Marcus Allen, L.A. Raiders vs. Washington, XVIII (TD)
58 Tom Matte, Baltimore vs. N.Y. Jets, III
Timmy Smith, Washington vs. Denver, XXII (TD)

AVERAGE GAIN
Highest Average Gain, Career (20 attempts)
9.6 Marcus Allen, L.A. Raiders, 1 game (20-191)
9.3 Timmy Smith, Washington, 1 game (22-204)
5.4 Dominic Rhodes, Indianapolis, 1 game (21-113)
Highest Average Gain, Game (10 attempts)
10.5 Tom Matte, Baltimore vs. N.Y. Jets, III (11-116)
9.6 Marcus Allen, L.A. Raiders vs. Washington, XVIII (20-191)
9.3 Willie Parker, Pittsburgh vs. Seattle, XL (10-93)

TOUCHDOWNS
Most Touchdowns, Career
5 Emmitt Smith, Dallas, 3 games
4 Franco Harris, Pittsburgh, 4 games
Thurman Thomas, Buffalo, 4 games
John Elway, Denver, 4 games
3 Terrell Davis, Denver, 2 games
Most Touchdowns, Game
3 Terrell Davis, Denver vs. Green Bay, XXXII
2 Elijah Pitts, Green Bay vs. Kansas City, I
Larry Csonka, Miami vs. Minnesota, VIII

Pete Banaszak, Oakland vs. Minnesota, XI
Franco Harris, Pittsburgh vs. Los Angeles, XIV
Marcus Allen, L.A. Raiders vs. Washington, XVIII
Jim McMahon, Chicago vs. New England, XX
Timmy Smith, Washington vs. Denver, XXII
Tom Rathman, San Francisco vs. Denver, XXIV
Gerald Riggs, Washington vs. Buffalo, XXVI
Emmitt Smith, Dallas vs. Buffalo, XXVIII
Emmitt Smith, Dallas vs. Pittsburgh, XXX
Howard Griffith, Denver vs. Atlanta, XXXIII
Eddie George, Tennessee vs. St. Louis, XXXIV

PASSING
PASSER RATING
Highest Passer Rating, Career (40 attempts)
127.8   Joe Montana, San Francisco, 4 games
122.8   Jim Plunkett, Oakland-L.A. Raiders, 2 games
112.8   Terry Bradshaw, Pittsburgh, 4 games

ATTEMPTS
Most Passes Attempted, Career
197   Tom Brady, New England, 5 games
152   John Elway, Denver, 5 games
145   Jim Kelly, Buffalo, 4 games
Most Passes Attempted, Game
58   Jim Kelly, Buffalo vs. Washington, XXVI
51   Donovan McNabb, Philadelphia vs. New England, XXXIX
50   Dan Marino, Miami vs. San Francisco, XIX
      Jim Kelly, Buffalo vs. Dallas, XXVIII

COMPLETIONS
Most Passes Completed, Career
127   Tom Brady, New England, 5 games
83   Joe Montana, San Francisco, 4 games
      Kurt Warner, St. Louis-Arizona, 3 games
81   Jim Kelly, Buffalo, 4 games
Most Passes Completed, Game
32   Tom Brady, New England vs. Carolina, XXXVIII
      Drew Brees, New Orleans vs. Indianapolis, XLIV
31   Jim Kelly, Buffalo vs. Dallas, XXVIII
      Kurt Warner, Arizona vs. Pittsburgh, XLIII
      Peyton Manning, Indianapolis vs. New Orleans, XLIV
30   Donovan McNabb, Philadelphia vs. New England, XXXIX
      Eli Manning, N.Y. Giants vs. New England, XLVI
Most Consecutive Completions, Game
16   Tom Brady, New England vs. N.Y. Giants, XLVI
13   Joe Montana, San Francisco vs. Denver, XXIV
10   Phil Simms, N.Y. Giants vs. Denver, XXI
      Troy Aikman, Dallas vs. Pittsburgh, XXX
      Kurt Warner, Arizona vs. Pittsburgh, XLIII
      Drew Brees, New Orleans vs. Indianapolis, XLIV

COMPLETION PERCENTAGE
Highest Completion Percentage, Career (40 attempts)
70.0   Troy Aikman, Dallas, 3 games, (80-56)
68.0   Joe Montana, San Francisco, 4 games (122-83)
67.5   Peyton Manning, Indianapolis, 2 games (83-56)
Highest Completion Percentage, Game (20 attempts)
88.0   Phil Simms, N.Y. Giants vs. Denver, XXI (25-22)
82.1   Drew Brees, New Orleans vs. Indianapolis, XLIV (39-32)
75.9   Joe Montana, San Francisco vs. Denver, XXIV (29-22)

YARDS GAINED
Most Yards Gained, Career
1,277   Tom Brady, New England, 5 games
1,156   Kurt Warner, St. Louis-Arizona, 3 games
1,142   Joe Montana, San Francisco, 4 games
Most Yards Gained, Game
414   Kurt Warner, St. Louis vs. Tennessee, XXXIV

377   Kurt Warner, Arizona vs. Pittsburgh, XLIII
365   Kurt Warner, St. Louis vs. New England, XXXVI
Longest Pass Completion
85   Jake Delhomme (to Muhammad), Carolina vs. New England, XXXVIII (TD)
81   Brett Favre (to Freeman), Green Bay vs. New England, XXXI (TD)
80   Jim Plunkett (to King), Oakland vs. Philadelphia, XV (TD)
      Doug Williams (to Sanders), Washington vs. Denver, XXII (TD)
      John Elway (to R. Smith), Denver vs. Atlanta, XXXIII (TD)

AVERAGE GAIN
Highest Average Gain, Career (40 attempts)
11.10   Terry Bradshaw, Pittsburgh, 4 games (84-932)
9.62   Bart Starr, Green Bay, 2 games (47-452)
9.41   Jim Plunkett, Oakland-L.A. Raiders, 2 games (46-433)
Highest Average Gain, Game (20 attempts)
14.71   Terry Bradshaw, Pittsburgh vs. Los Angeles, XIV (21-309)
12.80   Jim McMahon, Chicago vs. New England, XX (20-256)
12.43   Jim Plunkett, Oakland vs. Philadelphia, XV (21-261)

TOUCHDOWNS
Most Touchdown Passes, Career
11   Joe Montana, San Francisco, 4 games
9   Terry Bradshaw, Pittsburgh, 4 games
      Tom Brady, New England, 5 games
8   Roger Staubach, Dallas, 4 games
Most Touchdown Passes, Game
6   Steve Young, San Francisco vs. San Diego, XXIX
5   Joe Montana, San Francisco vs. Denver, XXIV
4   Terry Bradshaw, Pittsburgh vs. Dallas, XIII
      Doug Williams, Washington vs. Denver, XXII
      Troy Aikman, Dallas vs. Buffalo, XXVII

HAD INTERCEPTED
Lowest Percentage, Passes Had Intercepted, Career (40 attempts)
0.00   Jim Plunkett, Oakland-L.A. Raiders, 2 games (46-0)
      Joe Montana, San Francisco, 4 games (122-0)
1.02   Tom Brady, New England, 5 games (197-2)
1.25   Troy Aikman, Dallas, 3 games (80-1)
Most Attempts, Without Interception
48   Tom Brady, New England vs. N.Y. Giants, XLII
45   Kurt Warner, St. Louis vs. Tennessee, XXXIV
40   Eli Manning, N.Y. Giants vs. New England, XLVI
Most Passes Had Intercepted, Career
8   John Elway, Denver, 5 games
7   Craig Morton, Dallas-Denver, 2 games
      Jim Kelly, Buffalo, 4 games
6   Fran Tarkenton, Minnesota, 3 games
Most Passes Had Intercepted, Game
5   Rich Gannon, Oakland vs. Tampa Bay, XXXVII
4   Craig Morton, Denver vs. Dallas, XII
      Jim Kelly, Buffalo vs. Washington, XXVI
      Drew Bledsoe, New England vs. Green Bay, XXXI
      Kerry Collins, N.Y. Giants vs. Baltimore, XXXV
3   By 11 players

PASS RECEIVING
RECEPTIONS
Most Receptions, Career
33   Jerry Rice, San Francisco-Oakland, 4 games
27   Andre Reed, Buffalo, 4 games
24   Deion Branch, New England, 3 games
Most Receptions, Game
11   Dan Ross, Cincinnati vs. San Francisco, XVI
      Jerry Rice, San Francisco vs. Cincinnati, XXIII
      Deion Branch, New England vs. Philadelphia, XXXIX
      Wes Welker, New England vs. N.Y. Giants, XLII

10 Tony Nathan, Miami vs. San Francisco, XIX
Jerry Rice, San Francisco vs. San Diego, XXIX
Andre Hastings, Pittsburgh vs. Dallas, XXX
Deion Branch, New England vs. Carolina, XXXVIII
Joseph Addai, Indianapolis vs. Chicago, XLI
Hakeem Nicks, N.Y. Giants vs. New England, XLVI
9 Ricky Sanders, Washington vs. Denver, XXII
Antonio Freeman, Green Bay vs. Denver, XXXII
Terrell Owens, Philadelphia vs. New England, XXXIX
Santonio Holmes, Pittsburgh vs. Arizona, XLIII
Jordy Nelson, Green Bay vs. Pittsburgh, XLV
Mike Wallace, Pittsburgh vs. Green Bay, XLV

YARDS GAINED
Most Yards Gained, Career
589 Jerry Rice, San Francisco-Oakland, 4 games
364 Lynn Swann, Pittsburgh, 4 games
323 Andre Reed, Buffalo, 4 games
Most Yards Gained, Game
215 Jerry Rice, San Francisco vs. Cincinnati, XXIII
193 Ricky Sanders, Washington vs. Denver, XXII
162 Isaac Bruce, St. Louis vs. Tennessee, XXXIV
Longest Reception
85 Muhsin Muhammad (from Delhomme), Carolina vs.
New England, XXXVIII
81 Antonio Freeman (from Favre), Green Bay vs.
New England, XXXI (TD)
80 Kenny King (from Plunkett), Oakland vs.
Philadelphia, XV (TD)
Ricky Sanders (from Williams), Washington vs.
Denver, XXII (TD)
Rod Smith (from Elway), Denver vs. Atlanta, XXXIII

AVERAGE GAIN
Highest Average Gain, Career (8 receptions)
24.4 John Stallworth, Pittsburgh, 4 games (11-268)
23.4 Ricky Sanders, Washington, 2 games (10-234)
22.8 Lynn Swann, Pittsburgh, 4 games (16-364)
Highest Average Gain, Game (3 receptions)
40.33 John Stallworth, Pittsburgh vs. Los Angeles, XIV
(3-121)
40.25 Lynn Swann, Pittsburgh vs. Dallas, X (4-161)
38.33 John Stallworth, Pittsburgh vs. Dallas, XIII (3-115)

TOUCHDOWNS
Most Touchdowns, Career
8 Jerry Rice, San Francisco-Oakland, 4 games
3 John Stallworth, Pittsburgh, 4 games
Lynn Swann, Pittsburgh, 4 games
Cliff Branch, Oakland-L.A. Raiders, 3 games
Antonio Freeman, Green Bay, 2 games
2 Max McGee, Green Bay, 2 games
Bill Miller, Oakland, 1 game
Butch Johnson, Dallas, 2 games
Dan Ross, Cincinnati, 1 game
Roger Craig, San Francisco, 3 games
Ricky Sanders, Washington, 2 games
John Taylor, San Francisco, 3 games
Gary Clark, Washington, 2 games
Don Beebe, Buffalo-Green Bay, 4 games
Michael Irvin, Dallas, 3 games
Ricky Watters, San Francisco, 1 game
Jay Novacek, Dallas, 3 games
Keenan McCardell, Tampa Bay, 1 game
Ricky Proehl, St. Louis-Carolina, 3 games
David Givens, New England, 2 games
Mike Vrabel, New England, 4 games
Muhsin Muhammad, Carolina-Chicago, 2 games
Larry Fitzgerald, Arizona, 1 game
Greg Jennings, Green Bay, 1 game
Hines Ward, Pittsburgh, 3 games

Most Touchdowns, Game
3 Jerry Rice, San Francisco vs. Denver, XXIV; vs.
San Diego, XXIX
2 Max McGee, Green Bay vs. Kansas City, I
Bill Miller, Oakland vs. Green Bay, II
John Stallworth, Pittsburgh vs. Dallas, XIII
Cliff Branch, Oakland vs. Philadelphia, XV
Dan Ross, Cincinnati vs. San Francisco, XVI
Roger Craig, San Francisco vs. Miami, XIX
Ricky Sanders, Washington vs. Denver, XXII
Michael Irvin, Dallas vs. Buffalo, XXVII
Ricky Watters, San Francisco vs. San Diego, XXIX
Antonio Freeman, Green Bay vs. Denver, XXXII
Keenan McCardell, Tampa Bay vs. Oakland, XXXVII
Larry Fitzgerald, Arizona vs. Pittsburgh, XLIII
Greg Jennings, Green Bay vs. Pittsburgh, XLV

INTERCEPTIONS BY
Most Interceptions By, Career
3 Chuck Howley, Dallas, 2 games
Rod Martin, Oakland-L.A. Raiders, 2 games
Larry Brown, Dallas, 3 games
2 Randy Beverly, N.Y. Jets, 1 game
Jake Scott, Miami, 3 games
Mike Wagner, Pittsburgh, 3 games
Mel Blount, Pittsburgh, 4 games
Eric Wright, San Francisco, 4 games
Barry Wilburn, Washington, 1 game
Brad Edwards, Washington, 1 game
Thomas Everett, Dallas, 2 games
James Washington, Dallas, 2 games
Darrien Gordon, San Diego-Denver-Oakland,
4 games
Dexter Jackson, Tampa Bay, 1 game
Dwight Smith, Tampa Bay, 1 game
Rodney Harrison, San Diego-New England, 4 games
Most Interceptions By, Game
3 Rod Martin, Oakland vs. Philadelphia, XV
2 Randy Beverly, N.Y. Jets vs. Baltimore, III
Chuck Howley, Dallas vs. Baltimore, V
Jake Scott, Miami vs. Washington, VII
Barry Wilburn, Washington vs. Denver, XXII
Brad Edwards, Washington vs. Buffalo, XXVI
Thomas Everett, Dallas vs. Buffalo, XXVII
Larry Brown, Dallas vs. Pittsburgh, XXX
Darrien Gordon, Denver vs. Atlanta, XXXIII
Dexter Jackson, Tampa Bay vs. Oakland, XXXVII
Dwight Smith, Tampa Bay vs. Oakland, XXXVII
Rodney Harrison, New England vs. Philadelphia,
XXXIX

YARDS GAINED
Most Yards Gained, Career
108 Darrien Gordon, San Diego-Denver-Oakland,
4 games
100 James Harrison, Pittsburgh, 2 games
94 Dwight Smith, Tampa Bay, 1 game
Most Yards Gained, Game
108 Darrien Gordon, Denver vs. Atlanta, XXXIII
100 James Harrison, Pittsburgh vs. Arizona, XLIII
94 Dwight Smith, Tampa Bay vs. Oakland, XXXVII
Longest Return
100 James Harrison, Pittsburgh vs. Arizona, XLIII (TD)
76 Kelly Herndon, Seattle vs. Pittsburgh, XL
75 Willie Brown, Oakland vs. Minnesota, XI (TD)

TOUCHDOWNS
Most Touchdowns, Game
2 Dwight Smith, Tampa Bay vs. Oakland, XXXVII
1 Herb Adderley, Green Bay vs. Oakland, II
Willie Brown, Oakland vs. Minnesota, XI
Jack Squirek, L.A. Raiders vs. Washington, XVIII
Reggie Phillips, Chicago vs. New England, XX

Duane Starks, Baltimore vs. N.Y. Giants, XXXV
Ty Law, New England vs. St. Louis, XXXVI
Derrick Brooks, Tampa Bay vs. Oakland, XXXVII
Kelvin Hayden, Indianapolis vs. Chicago, XLI
James Harrison, Pittsburgh vs. Arizona, XLIII
Tracy Porter, New Orleans vs. Indianapolis, XLIV
Nick Collins, Green Bay vs. Pittsburgh, XLV

PUNTING
Most Punts, Career
17   Mike Eischeid, Oakland-Minnesota, 3 games
     Mike Horan, Denver-St. Louis, 4 games
16   Brad Maynard, N.Y. Giants-Chicago, 2 games
15   Larry Seiple, Miami, 3 games
Most Punts, Game
11   Brad Maynard, N.Y. Giants vs. Baltimore, XXXV
10   Kyle Richardson, Baltimore vs. N.Y. Giants, XXXV
9   Ron Widby, Dallas vs. Baltimore, V
Longest Punt
63   Lee Johnson, Cincinnati vs. San Francisco, XXIII
62   Rich Camarillo, New England vs. Chicago, XX
61   Jerrel Wilson, Kansas City vs. Green Bay, I

AVERAGE YARDAGE
Highest Average, Punting, Career (10 punts)
46.5   Jerrel Wilson, Kansas City, 2 games (11-511)
43.8   Tom Rouen, Denver-Seattle, 3 games (11-482)
43.0   Kyle Richardson, Baltimore, 1 game (10-430)
       Tom Tupa, New England-Tampa Bay, 2 games
       (12-516)
Highest Average, Punting, Game (4 punts)
50.2   Tom Rouen, Seattle vs. Pittsburgh, XL (6-301)
48.8   Bryan Wagner, San Diego vs. San Francisco, XXIX
       (4-195)
48.7   Chris Gardocki, Pittsburgh vs. Seattle, XL (6-292)

PUNT RETURNS
Most Punt Returns, Career
8   Troy Brown, New England, 3 games
6   Willie Wood, Green Bay, 2 games
     Jake Scott, Miami, 3 games
     Theo Bell, Pittsburgh, 2 games
     Mike Nelms, Washington, 1 game
     John Taylor, San Francisco, 3 games
     Desmond Howard, Green Bay, 1 game
     David Meggett, N.Y. Giants-New England, 2 games
     Darrien Gordon, San Diego-Denver-Oakland,
       4 games
5   Dana McLemore, San Francisco, 1 game
Most Punt Returns, Game
6   Mike Nelms, Washington vs. Miami, XVII
     Desmond Howard, Green Bay vs. New England, XXXI
5   Willie Wood, Green Bay vs. Oakland, II
     Dana McLemore, San Francisco vs. Miami, XIX
4   By 10 players
Most Fair Catches, Game
4   Jermaine Lewis, Baltimore vs. N.Y. Giants, XXXV
     Karl Williams, Tampa Bay vs. Oakland, XXXVII
3   Ron Gardin, Baltimore vs. Dallas, V
     Golden Richards, Dallas vs. Pittsburgh, X
     Greg Pruitt, L.A. Raiders vs. Washington, XVIII
     Al Edwards, Buffalo vs. N.Y. Giants, XXV
     David Meggett, N.Y. Giants vs. Buffalo, XXV

YARDS GAINED
Most Yards Gained, Career
94   John Taylor, San Francisco, 3 games
90   Desmond Howard, Green Bay, 1 game
67   David Meggett, N.Y. Giants-New England, 2 games
Most Yards Gained, Game
90   Desmond Howard, Green Bay vs. New England, XXXI
56   John Taylor, San Francisco vs. Cincinnati, XXIII
52   Mike Nelms, Washington vs. Miami, XXII

Longest Return
45   John Taylor, San Francisco vs. Cincinnati, XXIII
34   Darrell Green, Washington vs. L.A. Raiders, XVIII
     Desmond Howard, Green Bay vs. New England, XXXI
     Jermaine Lewis, Baltimore vs. N.Y. Giants, XXXV
     Steve Breaston, Arizona vs. Pittsburgh, XLIII
32   Desmond Howard, Green Bay vs. New England, XXXI
     Ted Ginn, San Francisco vs. Baltimore, XLVII

AVERAGE YARDAGE
Highest Average, Career (4 returns)
15.7   John Taylor, San Francisco, 3 games (6-94)
15.0   Desmond Howard, Green Bay, 1 game (6-90)
11.2   David Meggett, N.Y. Giants-New England, 2 games
       (6-67)
Highest Average, Game (3 returns)
18.7   John Taylor, San Francisco vs. Cincinnati, XXIII (3-56)
15.0   Desmond Howard, Green Bay vs. New England, XXXI
       (6-90)
14.0   Terrence Wilkins, Indianapolis vs. Chicago, XLI
       (3-42)

TOUCHDOWNS
Most Touchdowns, Game
None

KICKOFF RETURNS
Most Kickoff Returns, Career
10   Ken Bell, Denver, 3 games
8   Larry Anderson, Pittsburgh, 2 games
     Fulton Walker, Miami, 2 games
     Andre Coleman, San Diego, 1 game
     Marcus Knight, Oakland, 1 game
7   Preston Pearson, Baltimore-Pittsburgh-Dallas, 5 games
     Stephen Starring, New England, 1 game
     David Meggett, N.Y. Giants-New England, 2 games
Most Kickoff Returns, Game
8   Andre Coleman, San Diego vs. San Francisco, XXIX
     Marcus Knight, Oakland vs. Tampa Bay, XXXVII
7   Stephen Starring, New England vs. Chicago, XX
6   Darren Carrington, Denver vs. San Francisco, XXIV
     Antonio Freeman, Green Bay vs. Denver, XXXII
     Ron Dixon, N.Y. Giants vs. Baltimore, XXXV

YARDS GAINED
Most Yards Gained, Career
283   Fulton Walker, Miami, 2 games
244   Andre Coleman, San Diego, 1 game
210   Tim Dwight, Atlanta, 1 game
Most Yards Gained, Game
244   Andre Coleman, San Diego vs. San Francisco, XXIX
210   Tim Dwight, Atlanta vs. Denver, XXXIII
206   Jacoby Jones, Baltimore vs. San Francisco, XLVII
Longest Return
108   Jacoby Jones, Baltimore vs. San Francisco, XLVII
      (TD)
99   Desmond Howard, Green Bay vs. New England, XXXI
      (TD)
98   Fulton Walker, Miami vs. Washington, XVII (TD)
      Andre Coleman, San Diego vs. San Francisco, XXIX
      (TD)

AVERAGE YARDAGE
Highest Average, Career (4 returns)
42.0   Tim Dwight, Atlanta, 1 game (5-210)
41.2   Jacoby Jones, Baltimore, 1 game (5-206)
38.5   Desmond Howard, Green Bay, 1 game (4-154)
Highest Average, Game (3 returns)
47.5   Fulton Walker, Miami vs. Washington, XVII (4-190)
42.0   Tim Dwight, Atlanta vs. Denver, XXXIII (5-210)
41.2   Jacoby Jones, Baltimore vs. San Francisco, XLVII
       (5-206)

TOUCHDOWNS
Most Touchdowns, Game
1   Fulton Walker, Miami vs. Washington, XVII
    Stanford Jennings, Cincinnati vs. San Francisco, XXIII
    Andre Coleman, San Diego vs. San Francisco, XXIX
    Desmond Howard, Green Bay vs. New England, XXXI
    Tim Dwight, Atlanta vs. Denver, XXXIII
    Ron Dixon, N.Y. Giants vs. Baltimore, XXXV
    Jermaine Lewis, Baltimore vs. N.Y. Giants, XXXV
    Devin Hester, Chicago vs. Indianapolis, XLI
    Jacoby Jones, Baltimore vs. San Francisco, XLVII

FUMBLES
Most Fumbles, Career
5   Roger Staubach, Dallas, 4 games
4   Jim Kelly, Buffalo, 4 games
    Kurt Warner, St. Louis-Arizona, 3 games
3   Franco Harris, Pittsburgh, 4 games
    Terry Bradshaw, Pittsburgh, 4 games
    John Elway, Denver, 5 games
    Frank Reich, Buffalo, 4 games
    Thurman Thomas, Buffalo, 4 games

Most Fumbles, Game
3   Roger Staubach, Dallas vs. Pittsburgh, X
    Jim Kelly, Buffalo vs. Washington, XXVI
    Frank Reich, Buffalo vs. Dallas, XXVII
2   Franco Harris, Pittsburgh vs. Minnesota, IX
    Butch Johnson, Dallas vs. Denver, XII
    Terry Bradshaw, Pittsburgh vs. Dallas, XIII
    Joe Montana, San Francisco vs. Cincinnati, XXIII
    John Elway, Denver vs. San Francisco, XXIV
    Thurman Thomas, Buffalo vs. Dallas, XXVIII
    Rex Grossman, Chicago vs. Indianapolis, XLI
    Eli Manning, N.Y. Giants vs. New England, XLII
    Kurt Warner, Arizona vs. Pittsburgh, XLIII

RECOVERIES
Most Fumbles Recovered, Career
2   Jake Scott, Miami, 3 games (1 own, 1 opp)
    Fran Tarkenton, Minnesota, 3 games (2 own)
    Franco Harris, Pittsburgh, 4 games (2 own)
    Roger Staubach, Dallas, 4 games (2 own)
    Bobby Walden, Pittsburgh, 2 games (2 own)
    John Fitzgerald, Dallas, 4 games (2 own)
    Randy Hughes, Dallas, 3 games (2 opp)
    Butch Johnson, Dallas, 2 games (2 own)
    Mike Singletary, Chicago, 1 game (2 opp)
    John Elway, Denver, 5 games (2 own)
    Jimmie Jones, Dallas, 2 games (2 opp)
    Kenneth Davis, Buffalo, 4 games (2 own)
    Kurt Warner, St. Louis-Arizona, 3 games (2 own)

Most Fumbles Recovered, Game
2   Jake Scott, Miami vs. Minnesota, VIII (1 own, 1 opp)
    Roger Staubach, Dallas vs. Pittsburgh, X (2 own)
    Randy Hughes, Dallas vs. Denver, XII (2 opp)
    Butch Johnson, Dallas vs. Denver, XII (2 own)
    Mike Singletary, Chicago vs. New England, XX (2 opp)
    Jimmie Jones, Dallas vs. Buffalo, XXVII (2 opp)

YARDS GAINED
Most Yards Gained, Game
64   Leon Lett, Dallas vs. Buffalo, XXVII (opp)
49   Mike Bass, Washington vs. Miami, VII (opp)
46   James Washington, Dallas vs. Buffalo, XXVIII (opp)

Longest Return
64   Leon Lett, Dallas vs. Buffalo, XXVII
49   Mike Bass, Washington vs. Miami, VII (TD)
46   James Washington, Dallas vs. Buffalo, XXVIII (TD)

TOUCHDOWNS
Most Touchdowns, Game
1   Mike Bass, Washington vs. Miami, VII (opp 49 yds)

    Mike Hegman, Dallas vs. Pittsburgh, XIII (opp 37 yds)
    Jimmie Jones, Dallas vs. Buffalo, XXVII (opp 2 yds)
    Ken Norton, Dallas vs. Buffalo, XXVII (opp 9 yds)
    James Washington, Dallas vs. Buffalo, XXVIII
    (opp 46 yds)

COMBINED NET YARDS GAINED
(Rushing, receiving, interception returns, punt returns, kickoff returns, and fumble returns)
ATTEMPTS
Most Attempts, Career
108   Franco Harris, Pittsburgh, 4 games
 81   Emmitt Smith, Dallas, 3 games
 72   Roger Craig, San Francisco, 3 games
     Thurman Thomas, Buffalo, 4 games

Most Attempts, Game
39   John Riggins, Washington vs. Miami, XVII
35   Franco Harris, Pittsburgh vs. Minnesota, IX
34   Matt Snell, N.Y. Jets vs. Baltimore, III
    Emmitt Smith, Dallas vs. Buffalo, XXVIII

YARDS GAINED
Most Yards Gained, Career
604   Jerry Rice, San Francisco-Oakland, 4 games
468   Franco Harris, Pittsburgh, 4 games
410   Roger Craig, San Francisco, 3 games

Most Yards Gained, Game
290   Jacoby Jones, Baltimore vs. San Francisco, XLVII
244   Andre Coleman, San Diego vs. San Francisco, XXIX
     Desmond Howard, Green Bay vs. New England, XXXI
235   Ricky Sanders, Washington vs. Denver, XXII

SACKS
Sacks have been compiled since XVII.
Most Sacks, Career
4.5   Charles Haley, San Francisco-Dallas, 5 games
4.0   Justin Tuck, N.Y. Giants, 2 games
3.0   Danny Stubbs, San Francisco, 2 games
     Leonard Marshall, N.Y. Giants, 2 games
     Jeff Wright, Buffalo, 4 games
     Reggie White, Green Bay, 2 games
     Willie McGinest, New England, 4 games
     Tedy Bruschi, New England, 5 games
     Mike Vrabel, New England, 4 games
     Darnell Dockett, Arizona, 1 game
     LaMarr Woodley, Pittsburgh, 2 games

Most Sacks, Game
3.0   Reggie White, Green Bay vs. New England, XXXI
     Darnell Dockett, Arizona vs. Pittsburgh, XLIII
2.0   Dwaine Board, San Francisco vs. Miami, XIX
     Dennis Owens, New England vs. Chicago, XX
     Otis Wilson, Chicago vs. New England, XX
     Leonard Marshall, N.Y. Giants vs. Denver, XXI
     Alvin Walton, Washington vs. Denver, XXII
     Charles Haley, San Francisco vs. Cincinnati, XXIII
     Danny Stubbs, San Francisco vs. Denver, XXIV
     Jeff Wright, Buffalo vs. Dallas, XXVIII
     Raylee Johnson, San Diego vs. San Francisco, XXIX
     Chad Hennings, Dallas vs. Pittsburgh, XXX
     Tedy Bruschi, New England vs. Green Bay, XXXI
     Michael McCrary, Baltimore vs. N.Y. Giants, XXXV
     Simeon Rice, Tampa Bay vs. Oakland, XXXVII
     Mike Vrabel, New England vs. Carolina, XXXVIII
     Adalius Thomas, New England vs. N.Y. Giants, XLII
     Justin Tuck, N.Y. Giants vs. New England, XLII;
     vs. New England, XLVI
     LaMarr Woodley, Pittsburgh vs. Arizona, XLIII
     Paul Kruger, Baltimore vs. San Francisco, XLVII

TEAM RECORDS

GAMES, VICTORIES, DEFEATS
Most Games
- 8 Dallas, V-VI, X, XII-XIII, XXVII-XXVIII, XXX
  Pittsburgh, IX-X, XIII-XIV, XXX, XL, XLIII, XLV
- 7 New England, XX, XXXI, XXXVI, XXXVIII-XXXIX, XLII, XLVI
- 6 Denver, XII, XXI-XXII, XXIV, XXXII-XXXIII
  San Francisco, XVI, XIX, XXIII-XXIV, XXIX, XLVII

Most Consecutive Games
- 4 Buffalo, XXV-XXVIII
- 3 Miami, VI-VIII
- 2 Green Bay, I-II; XXXI-XXXII
  Dallas, V-VI; XII-XIII; XXVII-XXVIII
  Minnesota, VIII-IX
  Pittsburgh, IX-X; XIII-XIV
  Washington, XVII-XVIII
  Denver, XXI-XXII; XXXII-XXXIII
  San Francisco, XXIII-XXIV
  New England, XXXVIII-XXXIX

Most Games Won
- 6 Pittsburgh, IX-X, XIII-XIV, XL, XLIII
- 5 San Francisco, XVI, XIX, XXIII-XXIV, XXIX
  Dallas, VI, XII, XXVII-XXVIII, XXX
- 4 Green Bay, I-II, XXXI, XLV
  N.Y. Giants, XXI, XXV, XLII, XLVI

Most Consecutive Games Won
- 2 Green Bay, I-II
  Miami, VII-VIII
  Pittsburgh, IX-X, XIII-XIV
  San Francisco, XXIII-XXIV
  Dallas, XXVII-XXVIII
  Denver, XXXII-XXXIII
  New England, XXXVIII-XXXIX

Most Games Lost
- 4 Minnesota, IV, VIII-IX, XI
  Denver, XII, XXI-XXII, XXIV
  Buffalo, XXV-XXVIII
  New England, XX, XXXI, XLII, XLVI
- 3 Dallas, V, X, XIII
  Miami, VI, XVII, XIX
- 2 Washington, VII, XVIII
  Cincinnati, XVI, XXII
  L.A./St. Louis Rams, XIV, XXXVI
  Oakland/L.A. Raiders, II, XXXVII
  Philadelphia, XV, XXXIX
  Baltimore/Indianapolis, III, XLIV
  Pittsburgh, XXX, XLV

Most Consecutive Games Lost
- 4 Buffalo, XXV-XXVIII
- 2 Minnesota, VIII-IX
  Denver, XXI-XXII

SCORING
Most Points, Game
- 55 San Francisco vs. Denver, XXIV
- 52 Dallas vs. Buffalo, XXVII
- 49 San Francisco vs. San Diego, XXIX

Fewest Points, Game
- 3 Miami vs. Dallas, VI
- 6 Minnesota vs. Pittsburgh, IX
- 7 By five teams

Most Points, Both Teams, Game
- 75 San Francisco (49) vs. San Diego (26), XXIX
- 69 Dallas (52) vs. Buffalo (17), XXVII
  Tampa Bay (48) vs. Oakland (21), XXXVII
- 66 Pittsburgh (35) vs. Dallas (31), XIII

Fewest Points, Both Teams, Game
- 21 Washington (7) vs. Miami (14), VII
- 22 Minnesota (6) vs. Pittsburgh (16), IX
- 23 Baltimore (7) vs. N.Y. Jets (16), III

Largest Margin of Victory, Game
- 45 San Francisco vs. Denver, XXIV (55-10)
- 36 Chicago vs. New England, XX (46-10)
- 35 Dallas vs. Buffalo, XXVII (52-17)

Most Points, Each Half
- 1st: 35 Washington vs. Denver, XXII
- 2nd: 30 N.Y. Giants vs. Denver, XXI

Most Points, Each Quarter
- 1st: 14 Miami vs. Minnesota, VIII
  Oakland vs. Philadelphia, XV
  Dallas vs. Buffalo, XXVII
  San Francisco vs. San Diego, XXIX
  New England vs. Green Bay, XXXI
  Chicago vs. Indianapolis, XLI
  Green Bay vs. Pittsburgh, XLV
- 2nd: 35 Washington vs. Denver, XXII
- 3rd: 21 Chicago vs. New England, XX
- 4th: 21 Dallas vs. Buffalo, XXVII

Most Points, Both Teams, Each Half
- 1st: 45 Washington (35) vs. Denver (10), XXII
- 2nd: 46 Tampa Bay (28) vs. Oakland (18), XXXVII

Fewest Points, Both Teams, Each Half
- 1st: 2 Minnesota (0) vs. Pittsburgh (2), IX
- 2nd: 7 Miami (0) vs. Washington (7), VII
  Denver (0) vs. Washington (7), XXII

Most Points, Both Teams, Each Quarter
- 1st: 24 New England (14) vs. Green Bay (10), XXXI
- 2nd: 35 Washington (35) vs. Denver (0), XXII
- 3rd: 24 Washington (14) vs. Buffalo (10), XXVI
  San Francisco (17) vs. Baltimore (7), XLVII
- 4th: 37 Carolina (19) vs. New England (18), XXXVIII

TOUCHDOWNS
Most Touchdowns, Game
- 8 San Francisco vs. Denver, XXIV
- 7 Dallas vs. Buffalo, XXVII
  San Francisco vs. San Diego, XXIX
- 6 Washington vs. Denver, XXII
  Tampa Bay vs. Oakland, XXXVII

Fewest Touchdowns, Game
- 0 Miami vs. Dallas, VI
- 1 By 19 teams

Most Touchdowns, Both Teams, Game
- 10 San Francisco (7) vs. San Diego (3), XXIX
- 9 Pittsburgh (5) vs. Dallas (4), XIII
  San Francisco (8) vs. Denver (1), XXIV
  Dallas (7) vs. Buffalo (2), XXVII
  Tampa Bay (6) vs. Oakland (3), XXXVII
- 8 Carolina (4) vs. New England (4), XXXVIII

Fewest Touchdowns, Both Teams, Game
- 2 Baltimore (1) vs. N.Y. Jets (1), III
- 3 In six games

POINTS AFTER TOUCHDOWN
Most (One-Point) Points After Touchdown, Game
- 7 San Francisco vs. Denver, XXIV
  Dallas vs. Buffalo, XXVII
  San Francisco vs. San Diego, XXIX
- 6 Washington vs. Denver, XXII
  Tampa Bay vs. Oakland, XXXVII
- 5 Green Bay vs. Kansas City, I
  Pittsburgh vs. Dallas, XIII
  L.A. Raiders vs. Washington, XVIII
  San Francisco vs. Miami, XIX
  Chicago vs. New England, XX

Most (One-Point) Points After Touchdown, Both Teams, Game
- 9 Pittsburgh (5) vs. Dallas (4), XIII
  Dallas (7) vs. Buffalo (2), XXVII
- 8 San Francisco (7) vs. Denver (1), XXIV
  San Francisco (7) vs. San Diego (1), XXIX
- 7 Washington (6) vs. Denver (1), XXII
  Washington (4) vs. Buffalo (3), XXVI
  Denver (4) vs. Green Bay (3), XXXII

Fewest (One-Point) Points After Touchdown, Both Teams, Game
- 2 Baltimore (1) vs. N.Y. Jets (1), III
  Baltimore (1) vs. Dallas (1), V
  Minnesota (0) vs. Pittsburgh (2), IX

Most Two-Point Conversions, Game
- 2 San Diego vs. San Francisco, XXIX

Most Two-Point Conversions, Both Teams, Game
- 2 San Diego (2) vs. San Francisco (0), XXIX

FIELD GOALS

Most Field Goals Attempted, Game
- 5 N.Y. Jets vs. Baltimore, III
  Dallas vs. Denver, XII
- 4 Green Bay vs. Oakland, II
  Pittsburgh vs. Dallas, XX
  San Francisco vs. Cincinnati, XVI; XXIII
  Denver vs. N.Y. Giants, XXI
  Denver vs. Atlanta, XXXIII
  St. Louis vs. Tennessee, XXXIV
  Indianapolis vs. Chicago, XLI

Most Field Goals Attempted, Both Teams, Game
- 7 N.Y. Jets (5) vs. Baltimore (2), III
  San Francisco (4) vs. Cincinnati (3), XXIII
  St. Louis (4) vs. Tennessee (3), XXXIV
  Denver (4) vs. Atlanta (3), XXXIII
- 6 Dallas (5) vs. Denver (1), XII
- 5 Green Bay (4) vs. Oakland (1), II
  Pittsburgh (4) vs. Dallas (1), X
  Oakland (3) vs. Philadelphia (2), XV
  Denver (4) vs. N.Y. Giants (1), XXI
  Dallas (3) vs. Buffalo (2), XXVIII
  Indianapolis (4) vs. Chicago (1), XLI
  New Orleans (3) vs. Indianapolis (2), XLIV
  San Francisco (3) vs. Baltimore (2), XLVII

Fewest Field Goals Attempted, Both Teams, Game
- 1 Minnesota (0) vs. Miami (1), VIII
  San Francisco (0) vs. Denver (1), XXIV
  Philadelphia (0) vs. New England (1), XXXIX
  New England (0) vs. N.Y. Giants (1), XLII
- 2 Green Bay (0) vs. Kansas City (2), I
  Miami (1) vs. Washington (1), VII
  Minnesota (1) vs. Pittsburgh (1), IX
  Dallas (1) vs. Pittsburgh (1), XIII
  Dallas (1) vs. Buffalo (1), XXVII
  San Diego (1) vs. San Francisco (1), XXIX
  Denver (1) vs. Green Bay (1), XXXII
  Arizona (0) vs. Pittsburgh (2), XLIII

Most Field Goals, Game
- 4 Green Bay vs. Oakland, II
  San Francisco vs. Cincinnati, XVI
- 3 N.Y. Jets vs. Baltimore, III
  Kansas City vs. Minnesota, IV
  Miami vs. San Francisco, XIX
  Chicago vs. New England, XX
  Cincinnati vs. San Francisco, XXIII
  Washington vs. Buffalo, XXVI
  Dallas vs. Buffalo, XXVIII
  St. Louis vs. Tennessee, XXXIV
  Indianapolis vs. Chicago, XLI
  New Orleans vs. Indianapolis, XLIV
  San Francisco vs. Baltimore, XLVII

Most Field Goals, Both Teams, Game
- 5 Cincinnati (3) vs. San Francisco (2), XXIII
  Dallas (3) vs. Buffalo (2), XXVIII
  San Francisco (3) vs. Baltimore (2), XLVII
- 4 Green Bay (4) vs. Oakland (0), II
  San Francisco (4) vs. Cincinnati (0), XVI
  Miami (3) vs. San Francisco (1), XIX
  Chicago (3) vs. New England (1), XX
  Washington (3) vs. Buffalo (1), XXVI
  Atlanta (2) vs. Denver (2), XXXIII
  St. Louis (3) vs. Tennessee (1), XXXIV
  Indianapolis (3) vs. Chicago (1), XLI

New Orleans (3) vs. Indianapolis (1), XLIV
- 3 In 14 games

Fewest Field Goals, Both Teams, Game
- 0 Miami vs. Washington, VII
  Pittsburgh vs. Minnesota, IX
- 1 Green Bay (0) vs. Kansas City (1), I
  Minnesota (0) vs. Miami (1), VIII
  Pittsburgh (0) vs. Dallas (1), XIII
  Washington (0) vs. Denver (1), XXII
  San Francisco (0) vs. Denver (1), XXIV
  San Francisco (0) vs. San Diego (1), XXIX
  Philadelphia (0) vs. New England (1), XXXIX
  Pittsburgh (0) vs. Seattle (1), XLI
  New England (0) vs. N.Y. Giants (1), XLII

SAFETIES

Most Safeties, Game
- 1 Pittsburgh vs. Minnesota, IX; vs. Dallas, X
  Chicago vs. New England, XX
  N.Y. Giants vs. Denver, XXI; vs. New England, XLVI
  Buffalo vs. N.Y. Giants, XXV
  Arizona vs. Pittsburgh, XLIII
  San Francisco vs. Baltimore, XLVII

FIRST DOWNS

Most First Downs, Game
- 31 San Francisco vs. Miami, XIX
- 29 New England vs. Carolina, XXXVIII
- 28 San Francisco vs. Denver, XXIV
  San Francisco vs. San Diego, XXIX

Fewest First Downs, Game
- 9 Minnesota vs. Pittsburgh, IX
  Miami vs. Washington, XVII
- 10 Dallas vs. Baltimore, V
  Miami vs. Dallas, VI
- 11 Denver vs. Dallas, XII
  N.Y. Giants vs. Baltimore, XXXV
  Oakland vs. Tampa Bay, XXXVII
  Chicago vs. Indianapolis, XLI

Most First Downs, Both Teams, Game
- 50 San Francisco (31) vs. Miami (19), XIX
  Tennessee (27) vs. St. Louis (23), XXXIV
- 49 Buffalo (25) vs. Washington (24), XXVI
- 48 San Francisco (28) vs. San Diego (20), XXIX

Fewest First Downs, Both Teams, Game
- 24 Dallas (10) vs. Baltimore (14), V
  N.Y. Giants (11) vs. Baltimore (13), XXXV
- 26 Minnesota (9) vs. Pittsburgh (17), IX
- 27 Pittsburgh (13) vs. Dallas (14), X

RUSHING

Most First Downs, Rushing, Game
- 16 San Francisco vs. Miami, XIX
- 15 Dallas vs. Miami, VI
- 14 Washington vs. Miami, XVII
  San Francisco vs. Denver, XXIV
  Denver vs. Green Bay, XXXII

Fewest First Downs, Rushing, Game
- 1 New England vs. Chicago, XX
  St. Louis vs. Tennessee, XXXIV
  Oakland vs. Tampa Bay, XXXVII
- 2 Minnesota vs. Kansas City, IV; vs. Pittsburgh, IX;
    vs. Oakland, XI
  Pittsburgh vs. Dallas, XIII
  Miami vs. San Francisco, XIX
  N.Y. Giants vs. Baltimore, XXXV
  Arizona vs. Pittsburgh, XLIII
- 3 Miami vs. Dallas, VI
  Philadelphia vs. Oakland, XV
  New England vs. Green Bay, XXXI
  Carolina vs. New England, XXXVIII
  Chicago vs. Indianapolis, XLII
  New England vs. N.Y. Giants, XLII

New Orleans vs. Indianapolis, XLIV

Most First Downs, Rushing, Both Teams, Game
- 21 Washington (14) vs. Miami (7), XVII
- 19 Washington (13) vs. Denver (6), XXII
  San Francisco (14) vs. Denver (5), XXIV
- 18 Dallas (15) vs. Miami (3), VI
  Miami (13) vs. Minnesota (5), VIII
  San Francisco (16) vs. Miami (2), XIX
  N.Y. Giants (10) vs. Buffalo (8), XXV
  Denver (14) vs. Green Bay (4), XXXII

Fewest First Downs, Rushing, Both Teams, Game
- 6 Arizona (2) vs. Pittsburgh (4), XLIII
- 7 Oakland (1) vs. Tampa Bay (6), XXXVIII
  New England (3) vs. N.Y. Giants (4), XLII
- 8 Baltimore (4) vs. Dallas (4), V
  Pittsburgh (2) vs. Dallas (6), XIII
  N.Y. Giants (2) vs. Baltimore (6), XXXV

PASSING
Most First Downs, Passing, Game
- 20 Arizona vs. Pittsburgh, XLIII
- 19 New England vs. Carolina, XXXVIII
- 18 Buffalo vs. Washington, XXVI
  St. Louis vs. Tennessee, XXXIV
  Philadelphia vs. New England, XXXIX
  N.Y. Giants vs. New England, XLVI

Fewest First Downs, Passing, Game
- 1 Denver vs. Dallas, XII
- 2 Miami vs. Washington, XVII
- 4 Miami vs. Minnesota, VIII

Most First Downs, Passing, Both Teams, Game
- 33 N.Y. Giants (18) vs. New England (15), XLVI
- 32 Miami (17) vs. San Francisco (15), XIX
  Philadelphia (18) vs. New England (14), XXXIX
  Arizona (20) vs. Pittsburgh (12), XLIII
  Indianapolis (16) vs. New Orleans (16), XLIV
- 31 San Francisco (17) vs. San Diego (14), XXIX
  St. Louis (18) vs. Tennessee (13), XXXIV
  New England (19) vs. Carolina (12), XXXVIII

Fewest First Downs, Passing, Both Teams, Game
- 9 Denver (1) vs. Dallas (8), XII
- 10 Minnesota (5) vs. Pittsburgh (5), IX
- 11 Dallas (5) vs. Baltimore (6), V
  Miami (2) vs. Washington (9), XVII

PENALTY
Most First Downs, Penalty, Game
- 4 Baltimore vs. Dallas, V
  Miami vs. Minnesota, VIII
  Cincinnati vs. San Francisco, XVI
  Buffalo vs. Dallas, XXVII
  St. Louis vs. Tennessee, XXXIV
  Pittsburgh vs. Arizona, XLIII
- 3 Kansas City vs. Minnesota, IV
  Minnesota vs. Oakland, XI
  Buffalo vs. Washington, XXVI
  Green Bay vs. Denver, XXXII
  N.Y. Giants vs. Baltimore, XXXV
  St. Louis vs. New England, XXXVI
  Tampa Bay vs. Oakland, XXXVII
  New England vs. Carolina, XXXVIII

Most First Downs, Penalty, Both Teams, Game
- 6 Cincinnati (4) vs. San Francisco (2), XVI
  St. Louis (4) vs. Tennessee (2), XXXIV
- 5 Baltimore (4) vs. Dallas (1), V
  Miami (4) vs. Minnesota (1), VIII
  Buffalo (3) vs. Washington (2), XXVI
  Green Bay (3) vs. Denver (2), XXXII
  New England (3) vs. Carolina (2), XXXVIII
  Pittsburgh (4) vs. Arizona (1), XLIII
- 4 Kansas City (3) vs. Minnesota (1), IV
  Buffalo (4) vs. Dallas (0), XXVII
  N.Y. Giants (3) vs. Baltimore (1), XXXV

St. Louis (3) vs. New England (1), XXXVI
Tampa Bay (3) vs. Oakland (1), XXXVII

Fewest First Downs, Penalty, Both Teams, Game
- 0 Dallas vs. Miami, VI
  Miami vs. Washington, VII
  Dallas vs. Pittsburgh, X
  Miami vs. San Francisco, XIX
  Pittsburgh vs. Seattle, XL
  Green Bay vs. Pittsburgh, XLV
- 1 Green Bay (0) vs. Kansas City (1), I
  Miami (0) vs. Washington (1), XVII
  Cincinnati (0) vs. San Francisco (1), XXIII
  San Francisco (0) vs. Denver (1), XXIV
  Dallas (0) vs. Buffalo (1), XXVIII
  Dallas (0) vs. Pittsburgh (1), XXX
  Denver (0) vs. Atlanta (1), XXXIII
  Chicago (0) vs. Indianapolis (1), XLI
  New England (0) vs. N.Y. Giants (1), XLVI

NET YARDS GAINED RUSHING AND PASSING
Most Yards Gained, Game
- 602 Washington vs. Denver, XXII
- 537 San Francisco vs. Miami, XIX
- 481 New England vs. Carolina, XXXVIII

Fewest Yards Gained, Game
- 119 Minnesota vs. Pittsburgh, IX
- 123 New England vs. Chicago, XX
- 152 N.Y. Giants vs. Baltimore, XXXV

Most Yards Gained, Both Teams, Game
- 929 Washington (602) vs. Denver (327), XXII
- 868 New England (481) vs. Carolina (387), XXXVIII
- 851 San Francisco (537) vs. Miami (314), XIX

Fewest Yards Gained, Both Teams, Game
- 396 N.Y. Giants (152) vs. Baltimore (244), XXXV
- 452 Minnesota (119) vs. Pittsburgh (333), IX
- 481 Washington (228) vs. Miami (253), VII
  Denver (156) vs. Dallas (325), XII

RUSHING
ATTEMPTS
Most Attempts, Game
- 57 Pittsburgh vs. Minnesota, IX
- 53 Miami vs. Minnesota, VIII
- 52 Oakland vs. Minnesota, XI
  Washington vs. Miami, XVII

Fewest Attempts, Game
- 9 Miami vs. San Francisco, XIX
- 11 New England vs. Chicago, XX
  Oakland vs. Tampa Bay, XXXVII
- 12 Arizona vs. Pittsburgh, XLIII

Most Attempts, Both Teams, Game
- 81 Washington (52) vs. Miami (29), XVII
- 78 Pittsburgh (57) vs. Minnesota (21), IX
  Oakland (52) vs. Minnesota (26), XI
- 77 Miami (53) vs. Minnesota (24), VIII
  Pittsburgh (46) vs. Dallas (31), X

Fewest Attempts, Both Teams, Game
- 36 Green Bay (13) vs. Pittsburgh (23), XLV
- 37 Arizona (12) vs. Pittsburgh (25), XLIII
  New Orleans (18) vs. Indianapolis (19), XLIV
- 42 New England (16) vs. N.Y. Giants (26), XLII

YARDS GAINED
Most Yards Gained, Game
- 280 Washington vs. Denver, XXII
- 276 Washington vs. Miami, XVII
- 266 Oakland vs. Minnesota, XI

Fewest Yards Gained, Game
- 7 New England vs. Chicago, XX
- 17 Minnesota vs. Pittsburgh, IX
- 19 Oakland vs. Tampa Bay, XXXVII

Most Yards Gained, Both Teams, Game
- 377 Washington (280) vs. Denver (97), XXII

372 Washington (276) vs. Miami (96), XVII
338 N.Y. Giants (172) vs. Buffalo (166), XXV
Fewest Yards Gained, Both Teams, Game
91 Arizona (33) vs. Pittsburgh (58), XLIII
136 New England (45) vs. N.Y. Giants (91), XLII
150 New Orleans (51) vs. Indianapolis (99), XLIV

AVERAGE GAIN
Highest Average Gain, Game
7.00 L.A. Raiders vs. Washington, XVIII (33-231)
Washington vs. Denver, XXII (40-280)
6.64 Buffalo vs. N.Y. Giants, XXV (25-166)
6.28 San Francisco vs. Baltimore, XLVII (29-182)
Lowest Average Gain, Game
0.64 New England vs. Chicago, XX (11-7)
0.81 Minnesota vs. Pittsburgh, IX (21-17)
1.73 Oakland vs. Tampa Bay, XXXVII (11-19)

TOUCHDOWNS
Most Touchdowns, Game
4 Chicago vs. New England, XX
Denver vs. Green Bay, XXXII
3 Green Bay vs. Kansas City, I
Miami vs. Minnesota, VIII
San Francisco vs. Denver, XXIV
Denver vs. Atlanta, XXXIII
2 Oakland vs. Minnesota, XI
Pittsburgh vs. Los Angeles, XIV
L.A. Raiders vs. Washington, XVIII
San Francisco vs. Miami, XIX
N.Y. Giants vs. Denver, XXI
Washington vs. Denver, XXII; vs. Buffalo, XXVI
Buffalo vs. N.Y. Giants, XXV
Dallas vs. Buffalo, XXVIII; vs. Pittsburgh, XXX
Tennessee vs. St. Louis, XXXIV
Pittsburgh vs. Seattle, XL
San Francisco vs. Baltimore, XLVII
Fewest Touchdowns, Game
0 By 33 teams
Most Touchdowns, Both Teams, Game
4 Miami (3) vs. Minnesota (1), VIII
Chicago (4) vs. New England (0), XX
San Francisco (3) vs. Denver (1), XXIV
Denver (4) vs. Green Bay (0), XXXII
3 In nine games
Fewest Touchdowns, Both Teams, Game
0 Pittsburgh vs. Dallas, X
Oakland vs. Philadelphia, XV
Cincinnati vs. San Francisco, XXIII
1 In 17 games

PASSING
ATTEMPTS
Most Passes Attempted, Game
59 Buffalo vs. Washington, XXVI
55 San Diego vs. San Francisco, XXIX
51 Philadelphia vs. New England, XXXIX
Fewest Passes Attempted, Game
7 Miami vs. Minnesota, VIII
11 Miami vs. Washington, VII
14 Pittsburgh vs. Minnesota, IX
Most Passes Attempted, Both Teams, Game
93 San Diego (55) vs. San Francisco (38), XXIX
92 Buffalo (59) vs. Washington (33), XXVI
85 Miami (50) vs. San Francisco (35), XIX
Fewest Passes Attempted, Both Teams, Game
35 Miami (7) vs. Minnesota (28), VIII
39 Miami (11) vs. Washington (28), VII
40 Pittsburgh (14) vs. Minnesota (26), IX
Miami (17) vs. Washington (23), XVII

COMPLETIONS
Most Passes Completed, Game
32 New England vs. Carolina, XXXVIII
New Orleans vs. Indianapolis, XLIV
31 Buffalo vs. Dallas, XXVIII
Arizona vs. Pittsburgh, XLIII
Indianapolis vs. New Orleans, XLIV
30 Philadelphia vs. New England, XXXIX
N.Y. Giants vs. New England, XLVI
Fewest Passes Completed, Game
4 Miami vs. Washington, XVII
6 Miami vs. Minnesota, VIII
8 Miami vs. Washington, VII
Denver vs. Dallas, XII
Most Passes Completed, Both Teams, Game
63 New Orleans (32) vs. Indianapolis (31), XLIV
57 N.Y. Giants (30) vs. New England (27), XLVI
53 Miami (29) vs. San Francisco (24), XIX
Philadelphia (30) vs. New England (23), XXXIX
Fewest Passes Completed, Both Teams, Game
19 Miami (4) vs. Washington (15), XVII
20 Pittsburgh (9) vs. Minnesota (11), IX
22 Miami (8) vs. Washington (14), VII

COMPLETION PERCENTAGE
Highest Completion Percentage, Game (20 attempts)
88.0 N.Y. Giants vs. Denver, XXI (25-22)
82.1 New Orleans vs. Indianapolis, XLIV (39-32)
75.0 San Francisco vs. Denver, XXIV (32-24)
N.Y. Giants vs. New England, XLVI (40-30)
Lowest Completion Percentage, Game (20 attempts)
32.0 Denver vs. Dallas, XII (25-8)
37.9 Denver vs. San Francisco, XXIV (29-11)
38.5 Denver vs. Washington, XXII (39-15)
N.Y. Giants vs. Baltimore, XXXV (39-15)

YARDS GAINED
Most Yards Gained, Game
407 St. Louis vs. Tennessee, XXXIV
374 Arizona vs. Pittsburgh, XLIII
354 New England vs. Carolina, XXXVIII
Fewest Yards Gained, Game
35 Denver vs. Dallas, XII
63 Miami vs. Minnesota, VIII
69 Miami vs. Washington, VII
Most Yards Gained, Both Teams, Game
649 New England (354) vs. Carolina (295), XXXVIII
615 San Francisco (326) vs. Miami (289), XIX
St. Louis (407) vs. Tennessee (208), XXXIV
614 Indianapolis (333) vs. New Orleans (281), XLIV
Fewest Yards Gained, Both Teams, Game
156 Miami (69) vs. Washington (87), VII
186 Pittsburgh (84) vs. Minnesota (102), IX
204 Miami (80) vs. Washington (124), XVII

TIMES SACKED
Most Times Sacked, Game
7 Dallas vs. Pittsburgh, X
New England vs. Chicago, XX
6 Kansas City vs. Green Bay, I
Washington vs. L.A. Raiders, XVIII
Denver vs. San Francisco, XXIV
5 Dallas vs. Denver, XII; vs. Pittsburgh, XIII
Cincinnati vs. San Francisco, XVI; XXIII
Denver vs. Washington, XXII
Buffalo vs. Washington, XXVI
Green Bay vs. New England, XXXI
New England vs. Green Bay, XXXI
Oakland vs. Tampa Bay, XXXVIII
New England vs. N.Y. Giants, XLII
Fewest Times Sacked, Game
0 Baltimore vs. N.Y. Jets, III; vs. Dallas, V

Minnesota vs. Pittsburgh, IX
Pittsburgh vs. Los Angeles, XIV
Philadelphia vs. Oakland, XV
Washington vs. Buffalo, XXVI
Denver vs. Green Bay, XXXII; vs. Atlanta, XXXIII
Tampa Bay vs. Oakland, XXXVII
New England vs. Carolina, XXXVIII
Indianapolis vs. New Orleans, XLIV
1 By 18 teams

Most Times Sacked, Both Teams, Game
10 New England (7) vs. Chicago (3), XX
   Green Bay (5) vs. New England (5), XXXI
9 Kansas City (6) vs. Green Bay (3), I
   Dallas (7) vs. Pittsburgh (2), X
   Dallas (5) vs. Denver (4), XII
   Dallas (5) vs. Pittsburgh (4), XIII
   Cincinnati (5) vs. San Francisco (4), XXIII
8 Washington (6) vs. L.A. Raiders (2), XVIII
   New England (5) vs. N.Y. Giants (3), XLII

Fewest Times Sacked, Both Teams, Game
1 Philadelphia (0) vs. Oakland (1), XV
   Denver (0) vs. Green Bay (1), XXXII
   Indianapolis (0) vs. New Orleans (1), XLIV
2 Baltimore (0) vs. N.Y. Jets (2), III
   Baltimore (0) vs. Dallas (2), V
   Minnesota (0) vs. Pittsburgh (2), IX
   Denver (0) vs. Atlanta (2), XXXIII
   Chicago (1) vs. Indianapolis (1), XLI
3 In five games

TOUCHDOWNS
Most Touchdowns, Game
6 San Francisco vs. San Diego, XXIX
5 San Francisco vs. Denver, XXIV
4 Pittsburgh vs. Dallas, XIII
   Washington vs. Denver, XXII
   Dallas vs. Buffalo, XXVII

Fewest Touchdowns, Game
0 By 19 teams

Most Touchdowns, Both Teams, Game
7 Pittsburgh (4) vs. Dallas (3), XIII
   San Francisco (6) vs. San Diego (1), XXIX
6 Carolina (3) vs. New England (3), XXXVIII
5 Washington (4) vs. Denver (1), XXII
   San Francisco (5) vs. Denver (0), XXIV
   Dallas (4) vs. Buffalo (1), XXVII
   Philadelphia (3) vs. New England (2), XXXIX
   Green Bay (3) vs. Pittsburgh (2), XLV

Fewest Touchdowns, Both Teams, Game
0 N.Y. Jets vs. Baltimore, III
   Miami vs. Minnesota, VIII
   Buffalo vs. Dallas, XXVIII
1 In seven games

INTERCEPTIONS BY
Most Interceptions By, Game
5 Tampa Bay vs. Oakland, XXXVII
4 N.Y. Jets vs. Baltimore, III
   Dallas vs. Denver, XII
   Washington vs. Buffalo, XXVI
   Dallas vs. Buffalo, XXVII
   Green Bay vs. New England, XXXI
   Baltimore vs. N.Y. Giants, XXXV
3 By 13 teams

Most Interceptions By, Both Teams, Game
6 Baltimore (3) vs. Dallas (3), V
   Tampa Bay (5) vs. Oakland (1), XXXVII
5 Washington (4) vs. Buffalo (1), XXVI
4 In 10 games

Fewest Interceptions By, Both Teams, Game
0 Buffalo vs. N.Y. Giants, XXV
   St. Louis vs. Tennessee, XXXIV
1 Oakland (0) vs. Green Bay (1), II

Miami (0) vs. Dallas (1), VI
Minnesota (0) vs. Miami (1), VIII
N.Y. Giants (0) vs. Denver (1), XXI
Cincinnati (0) vs. San Francisco (1), XXIII
New England (0) vs. Carolina (1), XXXVIII
N.Y. Giants (0) vs. New England (1), XLII
Indianapolis (0) vs. New Orleans (1), XLIV
New England (0) vs. N.Y. Giants (1), XLVI
San Francisco (0) vs. Baltimore (1), XLVII

YARDS GAINED
Most Yards Gained, Game
172 Tampa Bay vs. Oakland, XXXVII
136 Denver vs. Atlanta, XXXIII
100 Pittsburgh vs. Arizona, XLIII

Most Yards Gained, Both Teams, Game
184 Tampa Bay (172) vs. Oakland (12), XXXVII
137 Denver (136) vs. Atlanta (1), XXXIII
100 Seattle (76) vs. Pittsburgh (24), XL
    Indianapolis (94) vs. Chicago (6), XLI

TOUCHDOWNS
Most Touchdowns, Game
3 Tampa Bay vs. Oakland, XXXVII
1 Green Bay vs. Oakland, II
   Oakland vs. Minnesota, XI
   L.A. Raiders vs. Washington, XVIII
   Chicago vs. New England, XX
   Baltimore vs. N.Y. Giants, XXXV
   New England vs. St. Louis, XXXVI
   Indianapolis vs. Chicago, XLI
   Pittsburgh vs. Arizona, XLIII
   New Orleans vs. Indianapolis, XLIV
   Green Bay vs. Pittsburgh, XLV

PUNTING
Most Punts, Game
11 N.Y. Giants vs. Baltimore, XXXV
10 Baltimore vs. N.Y. Giants, XXXV
9 Dallas vs. Baltimore, V

Fewest Punts, Game
1 Atlanta vs. Denver, XXXIII
   Denver vs. Atlanta, XXXIII
2 Pittsburgh vs. Los Angeles, XIV
   Denver vs. N.Y. Giants, XXI
   St. Louis vs. Tennessee, XXXIV
   Indianapolis vs. New Orleans, XLIV
   New Orleans vs. Indianapolis, XLIV
3 By 16 teams

Most Punts, Both Teams, Game
21 N.Y. Giants (11) vs. Baltimore (10), XXXV
15 Washington (8) vs. L.A. Raiders (7), XVIII
   New England (8) vs. Green Bay (7), XXXI
13 Dallas (9) vs. Baltimore (4), V
   Pittsburgh (7) vs. Minnesota (6), IX

Fewest Punts, Both Teams, Game
2 Atlanta (1) vs. Denver (1), XXXIII
4 Indianapolis (2) vs. New Orleans (2), XLIV
5 Denver (2) vs. N.Y. Giants (3), XXI
   St. Louis (2) vs. Tennessee (3), XXXIV

AVERAGE YARDAGE
Highest Average, Game (4 punts)
50.17 Seattle vs. Pittsburgh, XL (6-301)
48.75 San Diego vs. San Francisco, XXIX (4-195)
48.67 Pittsburgh vs. Seattle, XL (6-292)

Lowest Average, Game (4 punts)
31.00 Tampa Bay vs. Oakland, XXXVII (5-155)
31.20 Washington vs. Miami, VII (5-156)
32.38 Washington vs. L.A. Raiders, XVIII (8-259)

PUNT RETURNS

Most Punt Returns, Game
- 6   Washington vs. Miami, XVII
  - Green Bay vs. New England, XXXI
- 5   By seven teams

Fewest Punt Returns, Game
- 0   Minnesota vs. Miami, VIII
  - Buffalo vs. N.Y. Giants, XXV
  - Washington vs. Buffalo, XXVI
  - Denver vs. Green Bay, XXXII
  - Green Bay vs. Denver, XXXII
  - Atlanta vs. Denver, XXXIII
  - Denver vs. Atlanta, XXXIII
  - New England vs. N.Y. Giants, XLVI
- 1   By 26 teams

Most Punt Returns, Both Teams, Game
- 10   Green Bay (6) vs. New England (4), XXXI
- 9   Pittsburgh (5) vs. Minnesota (4), IX
- 8   Green Bay (5) vs. Oakland (3), II
  - Baltimore (5) vs. Dallas (3), V
  - Washington (6) vs. Miami (2), XVII
  - N.Y. Giants (5) vs. Baltimore (3), XXXV

Fewest Punt Returns, Both Teams, Game
- 0   Denver vs. Green Bay, XXXII
  - Atlanta vs. Denver, XXXIII
- 1   New England (0) vs. N.Y. Giants (1), XLVI
- 2   Dallas (1) vs. Miami (1), VI
  - Denver (1) vs. N.Y. Giants (1), XXI
  - Buffalo (0) vs. N.Y. Giants (2), XXV
  - Buffalo (1) vs. Dallas (1), XXVIII
  - Indianapolis (1) vs. New Orleans (1), XLIV

YARDS GAINED

Most Yards Gained, Game
- 90   Green Bay vs. New England, XXXI
- 56   San Francisco vs. Cincinnati, XXIII
- 52   Washington vs. Miami, XVII

Fewest Yards Gained, Game
- −1   Dallas vs. Miami, VI
  - Tennessee vs. St. Louis, XXXIV
- 0   By 15 teams

Most Yards Gained, Both Teams, Game
- 120   Green Bay (90) vs. New England (30), XXXI
- 80   N.Y. Giants (46) vs. Baltimore (34), XXXV
- 74   Washington (52) vs. Miami (22), XVII

Fewest Yards Gained, Both Teams, Game
- 0   Denver vs. Green Bay, XXXII
  - Atlanta vs. Denver, XXXIII
- 4   Indianapolis (0) vs. New Orleans (4), XLIV
- 5   Green Bay (0) vs. Pittsburgh (5), XLV

AVERAGE RETURN

Highest Average, Game (3 returns)
- 18.7   San Francisco vs. Cincinnati, XXIII (3-56)
- 15.0   Green Bay vs. New England, XXXI (6-90)
- 14.0   Indianapolis vs. Chicago, XLI (3-42)

TOUCHDOWNS

Most Touchdowns, Game
- None

KICKOFF RETURNS

Most Kickoff Returns, Game
- 9   Denver vs. San Francisco, XXIV
  - Oakland vs. Tampa Bay, XXXVII
- 8   San Diego vs. San Francisco, XXIX
- 7   By eight teams

Fewest Kickoff Returns, Game
- 1   N.Y. Jets vs. Baltimore, III
  - L.A. Raiders vs. Washington, XVIII
  - Washington vs. Buffalo, XXVI
- 2   By 10 teams

Most Kickoff Returns, Both Teams, Game
- 13   Oakland (9) vs. Tampa Bay (4), XXXVII
- 12   Denver (9) vs. San Francisco (3), XXIV
  - San Diego (8) vs. San Francisco (4), XXIX
- 11   Los Angeles (6) vs. Pittsburgh (5), XIV
  - Miami (7) vs. San Francisco (4), XIX
  - New England (7) vs. Chicago (4), XX
  - Green Bay (6) vs. Denver (5), XXXII

Fewest Kickoff Returns, Both Teams, Game
- 5   N.Y. Jets (1) vs. Baltimore (4), III
  - Miami (2) vs. Washington (3), VII
  - Washington (1) vs. Buffalo (4), XXVI
- 6   In five games

YARDS GAINED

Most Yards Gained, Game
- 244   San Diego vs. San Francisco, XXIX
- 227   Atlanta vs. Denver, XXXIII
- 222   Miami vs. Washington, XVII

Fewest Yards Gained, Game
- 16   Washington vs. Buffalo, XXVI
- 17   L.A. Raiders vs. Washington, XVIII
- 25   N.Y. Jets vs. Baltimore, III

Most Yards Gained, Both Teams, Game
- 312   Baltimore (206) vs. San Francisco (106), XLVII
- 292   San Diego (244) vs. San Francisco (48), XXIX
- 289   Green Bay (154) vs. New England (135), XXXI

Fewest Yards Gained, Both Teams, Game
- 78   Miami (33) vs. Washington (45), VII
- 82   Pittsburgh (32) vs. Minnesota (50), IX
- 92   San Francisco (40) vs. Cincinnati (52), XVI

AVERAGE GAIN

Highest Average, Game (3 returns)
- 44.0   Cincinnati vs. San Francisco, XXIII (3-132)
- 41.2   Baltimore vs. San Francisco, XLVII (5-206)
- 38.5   Green Bay vs. New England, XXXI (4-154)

TOUCHDOWNS

Most Touchdowns, Game
- 1   Miami vs. Washington, XVII
  - Cincinnati vs. San Francisco, XXIII
  - San Diego vs. San Francisco, XXIX
  - Green Bay vs. New England, XXXI
  - Atlanta vs. Denver, XXXIII
  - Baltimore vs. N.Y. Giants, XXXV
  - N.Y. Giants vs. Baltimore, XXXV
  - Chicago vs. Indianapolis, XLI
  - Baltimore vs. San Francisco, XLVII

Most Touchdowns, Both Teams, Game
- 2   Baltimore (1) vs. N.Y. Giants (1), XXXV

PENALTIES

Most Penalties, Game
- 12   Dallas vs. Denver, XII
  - Carolina vs. New England, XXXVIII
- 11   Arizona vs. Pittsburgh, XLIII
- 10   Dallas vs. Baltimore, V

Fewest Penalties, Game
- 0   Miami vs. Dallas, VI
  - Pittsburgh vs. Dallas, X
  - Denver vs. San Francisco, XXIV
  - Atlanta vs. Denver, XXXIII
- 1   Green Bay vs. Oakland, II
  - Miami vs. Minnesota, VIII; vs. San Francisco, XIX
  - Buffalo vs. Dallas, XXVIII
- 2   By seven teams

Most Penalties, Both Teams, Game
- 20   Dallas (12) vs. Denver (8), XII
  - Carolina (12) vs. New England (8), XXXVIII
- 18   Arizona (11) vs. Pittsburgh (7), XLIII
- 16   Cincinnati (8) vs. San Francisco (8), XVI

Green Bay (9) vs. Denver (7), XXXII

Fewest Penalties, Both Teams, Game
2   Pittsburgh (0) vs. Dallas (2), X
3   Miami (0) vs. Dallas (3), VI
     Miami (1) vs. San Francisco (2), XIX
4   Denver (0) vs. San Francisco (4), XXIV
     Atlanta (0) vs. Denver (4), XXXIII

YARDS PENALIZED
Most Yards Penalized, Game
133   Dallas vs. Baltimore, X
122   Pittsburgh vs. Minnesota, IX
106   Arizona vs. Pittsburgh, XLIII
Fewest Yards Penalized, Game
0   Miami vs. Dallas, VI
     Pittsburgh vs. Dallas, X
     Denver vs. San Francisco, XXIV
     Atlanta vs. Denver, XXXIII
4   Miami vs. Minnesota, VIII
10   Miami vs. San Francisco, XIX
     San Francisco vs. Miami, XIX
     Buffalo vs. Dallas, XXVIII
Most Yards Penalized, Both Teams, Game
164   Dallas (133) vs. Baltimore (31), V
162   Arizona (106) vs. Pittsburgh (56), XLIII
154   Dallas (94) vs. Denver (60), XII
Fewest Yards Penalized, Both Teams, Game
15   Miami (0) vs. Dallas (15), VI
20   Pittsburgh (0) vs. Dallas (20), X
     Miami (10) vs. San Francisco (10), XIX
38   Denver (0) vs. San Francisco (38), XXIV

FUMBLES
Most Fumbles, Game
8   Buffalo vs. Dallas, XXVII
6   Dallas vs. Denver, XII
     Buffalo vs. Washington, XXVI
5   Baltimore vs. Dallas, V
Fewest Fumbles, Game
0   By 23 teams
Most Fumbles, Both Teams, Game
12   Buffalo (8) vs. Dallas (4), XXVII
10   Dallas (6) vs. Denver (4), XII
8   Dallas (4) vs. Pittsburgh (4), X
Fewest Fumbles, Both Teams, Game
0   Los Angeles vs. Pittsburgh, XIV
     Green Bay vs. New England, XXXI
     Pittsburgh vs. Seattle, XL
     Indianapolis vs. New Orleans, XLIV
1   Oakland (0) vs. Minnesota (1), XI
     Oakland (0) vs. Philadelphia (1), XV
     Denver (0) vs. Washington (1), XXII
     N.Y. Giants (0) vs. Buffalo (1), XXV
     Denver (0) vs. Atlanta (1), XXXIII
2   In 11 games
Most Fumbles Lost, Game
5   Buffalo vs. Dallas, XXVII
4   Baltimore vs. Dallas, V
     Denver vs. Dallas, XII
     New England vs. Chicago, XX
3   Chicago vs. Indianapolis, XLI
Most Fumbles Lost, Both Teams, Game
7   Buffalo (5) vs. Dallas (2), XXVII
6   Denver (4) vs. Dallas (2), XII
     New England (4) vs. Chicago (2), XX
5   Baltimore (4) vs. Dallas (1), V
     Chicago (3) vs. Indianapolis (2), XLI
Fewest Fumbles Lost, Both Teams, Game
0   Green Bay vs. Kansas City, I
     Dallas vs. Pittsburgh, X
     Los Angeles vs. Pittsburgh, XIV
     Denver vs. N.Y. Giants, XXI; vs. Washington, XXII
     Buffalo vs. N.Y. Giants, XXV

San Diego vs. San Francisco, XXIX
Dallas vs. Pittsburgh, XXX
Green Bay vs. New England, XXXI
St. Louis vs. Tennessee, XXXIV
Oakland vs. Tampa Bay, XXXVII
Pittsburgh vs. Seattle, XL
Indianapolis vs. New Orleans, XLIV
New England vs. N.Y. Giants, XLVI
Most Fumbles Recovered, Game
8   Dallas vs. Denver, XII (4 own, 4 opp.)
6   Dallas vs. Buffalo, XXVII (1 own, 5 opp.)
5   Chicago vs. New England, XX (1 own, 4 opp.)

TURNOVERS
(Number of times losing the ball on interceptions and fumbles.)
Most Turnovers, Game
9   Buffalo vs. Dallas, XXVII
8   Denver vs. Dallas, XII
7   Baltimore vs. Dallas, V
Fewest Turnovers, Game
0   Green Bay vs. Oakland, II
     Miami vs. Minnesota, VIII
     Pittsburgh vs. Dallas, X
     Oakland vs. Minnesota, XI; vs. Philadelphia, XV
     N.Y. Giants vs. Denver, XXI; vs. Buffalo, XXV
     San Francisco vs. Denver, XXIV; vs. San Diego, XXIX
     Buffalo vs. N.Y. Giants, XXV
     Dallas vs. Pittsburgh, XXX
     Green Bay vs. New England, XXXI
     St. Louis vs. Tennessee, XXXIV
     Tennessee vs. St. Louis, XXXIV
     Baltimore vs. N.Y. Giants, XXXV
     New England vs. St. Louis, XXXVI
     New Orleans vs. Indianapolis, XLIV
     Green Bay vs. Pittsburgh, XLV
     N.Y. Giants vs. New England, XLVI
1   By many teams
Most Turnovers, Both Teams, Game
11   Baltimore (7) vs. Dallas (4), V
     Buffalo (9) vs. Dallas (2), XXVII
10   Denver (8) vs. Dallas (2), XII
8   New England (6) vs. Chicago (2), XX
     Chicago (5) vs. Indianapolis (3), XLI
Fewest Turnovers, Both Teams, Game
0   Buffalo vs. N.Y. Giants, XXV
     St. Louis vs. Tennessee, XXXIV
1   N.Y. Giants (0) vs. Denver (1), XXI
     New Orleans (0) vs. Indianapolis (1), XLIV
     N.Y. Giants (0) vs. New England (1), XLVI
2   Green Bay (1) vs. Kansas City (1), I
     Miami (0) vs. Minnesota (2), VIII
     Cincinnati (1) vs. San Francisco (1), XXIII
     Carolina (1) vs. New England (1), XXXVIII
     New England (1) vs. N.Y. Giants (1), XLII

Compiled by Elias Sports Bureau

Throughout this all-time postseason record section, the following abbreviations are used to indicate various levels of postseason games:

SB   Super Bowl (1966 to date)

AFC   AFC Championship Game (1970 to date) or AFL Championship Game (1960-69)

NFC   NFC Championship Game (1970 to date) or NFL Championship Game (1933-69)

AFC-D   AFC Divisional Playoff Game (1970 to date), AFC Second-Round Playoff Game (1982), AFL Inter-Divisional Playoff Game (1969), or special playoff game to break tie for AFL Division Championship (1963, 1968)

NFC-D   NFC Divisional Playoff Game (1970 to date), NFC Second-Round Playoff Game (1982), NFL Conference Championship Game (1967-69), or special playoff game to break tie for NFL Division or Conference Championship (1941, 1943, 1947, 1950, 1952, 1957, 1958, 1965)

AFC-FR AFC First-Round Playoff Game (1978 to date)

NFC-FR NFC First-Round Playoff Game (1978 to date)

Year indicates season in which game took place and does not necessarily reflect calendar year.

POSTSEASON GAME COMPOSITE STANDINGS

	W	L	PCT.	PTS.	OP
Baltimore Ravens	14	7	.667	456	326
Green Bay Packers	30	18	.625	1,191	985
Pittsburgh Steelers	33	21	.611	1,283	1,123
Carolina Panthers	6	4	.600	219	203
San Francisco 49ers	28	19	.596	1,201	994
New England Patriots*	24	17	.585	904	834
Oakland Raiders**	25	18	.581	1,028	797
Dallas Cowboys	33	25	.569	1,355	1,098
Washington Redskins***	23	18	.561	833	731
Denver Broncos	18	17	.514	768	900
New York Giants	24	24	.500	865	889
Miami Dolphins	20	20	.500	789	875
Houston Texans	2	2	.500	91	84
Philadelphia Eagles	19	20	.487	757	720
Chicago Bears	17	18	.486	751	726
Buffalo Bills	14	15	.483	681	658
New York Jets	12	13	.480	510	508
Indianapolis Colts****	19	21	.475	794	810
Arizona Cardinals†	6	7	.462	305	361
Jacksonville Jaguars	5	6	.455	262	288
St. Louis Rams††	19	24	.442	770	944
Seattle Seahawks	9	12	.429	473	482
New Orleans Saints	6	8	.429	364	412
Tennessee Titans†††	14	19	.424	579	762
Minnesota Vikings	19	27	.413	910	1,041
Tampa Bay Buccaneers	6	9	.400	230	279
Detroit Lions	7	11	.389	393	449
San Diego Chargers††††	10	16	.385	488	592
Atlanta Falcons	7	12	.368	399	489
Kansas City Chiefs#	8	14	.364	347	475
Cleveland Browns	11	20	.355	629	728
Cincinnati Bengals	5	11	.313	300	362

 *   *Two games played when franchise was in Boston (won 26-8, lost 51-10).*

 **   *12 games played when franchise was in Los Angeles (won 6, lost 6, 268 points scored, 224 points allowed).*

*** *One game played when franchise was in Boston (lost 21-6).*

**** *15 games played when franchise was in Baltimore (won 8, lost 7, 264 points scored, 262 points allowed).*

 †   *Two games played when franchise was in Chicago (won 28-21, lost 7-0), three games played when franchise was in St. Louis (won 30-14, lost 35-23, lost 41-16).*

 ††   *One game played when franchise was in Cleveland (won 15-14), 32 games played when franchise was in Los Angeles (won 12, lost 20, 486 points scored, 683 points allowed).*

 ††† *22 games played when franchise was in Houston and known as the Oilers (won 9, lost 13, 371 points scored, 533 points allowed).*

†††† *One game played when franchise was in Los Angeles (lost 24-16).*

 #   *One game played when franchise was in Dallas Texans (won 20-17).*

INDIVIDUAL RECORDS

SERVICE
Most Games, Career

29   Jerry Rice, San Francisco-Oakland-Seattle (SB 4, NFC 6, AFC 1, NFC-D 11, AFC-D 2, NFC-FR 4, AFC-FR 1)

27   D.D. Lewis, Dallas (SB 5, NFC 9, NFC-D 12, NFC-FR 1)

26   Larry Cole, Dallas (SB 5, NFC 8, NFC-D 12, NFC-FR 1)
      Bill Romanowski, San Francisco-Philadelphia-Denver-Oakland (SB 5, NFC 5, AFC 3, NFC-D 6, AFC-D 4, NFC-FR 1, AFC-FR 2)

Most Games, Head Coach

36   Tom Landry, Dallas
      Don Shula, Baltimore-Miami

26   Bill Belichick, Cleveland-New England

24   Chuck Noll, Pittsburgh
      Mike Holmgren, Green Bay-Seattle
      Joe Gibbs, Washington

Most Championships Won, Head Coach

6   George Halas, Chicago
      Curly Lambeau, Green Bay

5   Vince Lombardi, Green Bay

4   Guy Chamberlin, Canton Bulldogs-Cleveland Bulldogs-Frankford Yellow Jackets
      Chuck Noll, Pittsburgh

Most Games Won, Head Coach

20   Tom Landry, Dallas

19   Don Shula, Baltimore-Miami

18   Bill Belichick, Cleveland-New England

Most Games Lost, Head Coach

17   Don Shula, Baltimore-Miami

16   Tom Landry, Dallas

13   Marty Schottenheimer, Cleveland-Kansas City-San Diego

SCORING
POINTS
Most Points, Career

196   Adam Vinatieri, New England-Indianapolis, 25 games (52-pat, 48-fg)

175   David Akers, Philadelphia-San Francisco, 24 games (58-pat, 39-fg)

153   Gary Anderson, Pittsburgh-Philadelphia-San Francisco-Minnesota-Tennessee, 22 games (57-pat, 32-fg)

Most Points, Game

30   Ricky Watters, NFC-D: San Francisco vs. N.Y. Giants, 1993 (5-td)

19   Pat Harder, NFC-D: Detroit vs. Los Angeles, 1952 (2-td, 4-pat, 1-fg)
      Paul Hornung, NFC: Green Bay vs. N.Y. Giants, 1961 (1-td, 4-pat, 3-fg)

18   By many players

Most Consecutive Games Scoring

25   Adam Vinatieri, New England-Indianapolis, 1996-98, 2001, 2003-08, 2010, 2012 (current)

24   David Akers, Philadelphia-San Francisco, 2000-06, 2008-2012 (current)

19   George Blanda, Chi. Bears-Houston-Oakland, 1956-1975

TOUCHDOWNS
Most Touchdowns, Career

22   Jerry Rice, San Francisco-Oakland-Seattle, 29 games (22-p)

21   Thurman Thomas, Buffalo, 21 games (16-r, 5-p)
      Emmitt Smith, Dallas, 17 games (19-r, 2-p)

17 Franco Harris, Pittsburgh, 19 games (16-r, 1-p)

Most Touchdowns, Game
5   Ricky Watters, NFC-D: San Francisco vs. N.Y. Giants, 1993 (5-r)
3   Andy Farkas, NFC-D: Washington vs. N.Y. Giants, 1943 (3-r)
    Tom Fears, NFC-D: Los Angeles vs. Chi. Bears, 1950 (3-p)
    Otto Graham, NFC: Cleveland vs. Detroit, 1954 (3-r)
    Gary Collins, NFC: Cleveland vs. Baltimore, 1964 (3-p)
    Craig Baynham, NFC-D: Dallas vs. Cleveland, 1967 (2-r, 1-p)
    Fred Biletnikoff, AFC-D: Oakland vs. Kansas City, 1968 (3-p)
    Tom Matte, NFC: Baltimore vs. Cleveland, 1968 (3-r)
    Larry Schreiber, NFC-D: San Francisco vs. Dallas, 1972 (3-r)
    Larry Csonka, AFC: Miami vs. Oakland, 1973 (3-r)
    Franco Harris, AFC-D: Pittsburgh vs. Buffalo, 1974 (3-r)
    Preston Pearson, NFC: Dallas vs. Los Angeles, 1975 (3-p)
    Dave Casper, AFC-D: Oakland vs. Baltimore, 1977 (ot) (3-p)
    Alvin Garrett, NFC-FR: Washington vs. Detroit, 1982 (3-p)
    John Riggins, NFC-D: Washington vs. L.A. Rams, 1983 (3-r)
    Roger Craig, SB: San Francisco vs. Miami, 1984 (1-r, 2-p)
    Jerry Rice, NFC-D: San Francisco vs. Minnesota, 1988 (3-p)
    Jerry Rice, SB: San Francisco vs. Denver, 1989 (3-p)
    Kenneth Davis, AFC: Buffalo vs. L.A. Raiders, 1990 (3-r)
    Andre Reed, AFC-FR: Buffalo vs. Houston, 1992 (ot) (3-p)
    Sterling Sharpe, NFC-FR: Green Bay vs. Detroit, 1993 (3-p)
    Napoleon McCallum, AFC-FR: L.A. Raiders vs. Denver, 1993 (3-r)
    Thurman Thomas, AFC: Buffalo vs. Kansas City, 1993 (3-r)
    William Floyd, NFC-D: San Francisco vs. Chicago, 1994 (3-r)
    Ricky Watters, SB: San Francisco vs. San Diego, 1994 (1-r, 2-p)
    Jerry Rice, SB: San Francisco vs. San Diego, 1994 (3-p)
    Emmitt Smith, NFC: Dallas vs. Green Bay, 1995 (3-r)
    Curtis Martin, AFC-D: New England vs. Pittsburgh, 1996 (3-r)
    Terrell Davis, SB: Denver vs. Green Bay, 1997 (3-r)
    Mario Bates, NFC-D: Arizona vs. Minnesota, 1998 (3-r)
    Leroy Hoard, NFC-D: Minnesota vs. Arizona, 1998 (2-r, 1-p)
    Willie Jackson, NFC-FR: New Orleans vs. St. Louis, 2000 (3-p)
    Amani Toomer, NFC-FR: N.Y. Giants vs. San Francisco, 2002 (3-p)
    Shaun Alexander, NFC-FR: Seattle vs. Green Bay, 2003 (ot) (3-r)
    Ryan Grant, NFC-D: Green Bay vs. Seattle, 2007 (3-r)
    Larry Fitzgerald, NFC: Arizona vs. Philadelphia, 2008 (3-p)
    Sidney Rice, NFC-D: Minnesota vs. Dallas, 2009 (3-p)
    Adrian Peterson, NFC: Minnesota vs. New Orleans, 2009 (3-r)
    Rob Gronkowski, AFC-D: New England vs. Denver, 2011 (3-p)
    Shane Vereen, AFC-D: New England vs. Houston, 2012 (1-r, 2-p)

Most Consecutive Games Scoring Touchdowns
9   Thurman Thomas, Buffalo, 1992-98
8   John Stallworth, Pittsburgh, 1978-1983
    Emmitt Smith, Dallas, 1993-96
7   John Riggins, Washington, 1982-84
    Marcus Allen, L.A. Raiders, 1982-85
    Terrell Davis, Denver, 1996-98
    David Givens, New England, 2003-05

POINTS AFTER TOUCHDOWN
Most (One-Point) Points After Touchdown, Career
58 David Akers, Philadelphia-San Francisco, 24 games (59 att)
57 Gary Anderson, Pittsburgh-Philadelphia-San Francisco-Minnesota-Tennessee, 22 games (57 att)
52 Adam Vinatieri, New England-Indianapolis, 25 games (52 att)

Most (One-Point) Points After Touchdown, Game
8   Lou Groza, NFC: Cleveland vs. Detroit, 1954 (8 att)
    Jim Martin, NFC: Detroit vs. Cleveland, 1957 (8 att)
    George Blanda, AFC-D: Oakland vs. Houston, 1969 (8 att)
    Mike Hollis, AFC-D: Jacksonville vs. Miami, 1999 (8 att)
7   Danny Villanueva, NFC-D: Dallas vs. Cleveland, 1967 (7 att)
    Raul Allegre, NFC-D: N.Y. Giants vs. San Francisco, 1986 (7 att)
    Mike Cofer, SB: San Francisco vs. Denver, 1989 (8 att)
    Lin Elliott, SB: Dallas vs. Buffalo, 1992 (7 att)
    Doug Brien, SB: San Francisco vs. San Diego, 1994 (7 att)
    Gary Anderson, NFC-FR: Philadelphia vs. Detroit, 1995 (7 att)
    Jeff Wilkins, NFC-D: St. Louis vs. Minnesota, 1999 (7 att)
    Mike Vanderjagt, AFC-FR: Indianapolis vs. Denver, 2004 (7 att)
6   George Blair, AFC: San Diego vs. Boston, 1963 (6 att)
    Mark Moseley, NFC-D: Washington vs. L.A. Rams, 1983 (6 att)
    Uwe von Schamann, AFC: Miami vs. Pittsburgh, 1984 (6 att)
    Ali Haji-Sheikh, SB: Washington vs. Denver, 1987 (6 att)
    Scott Norwood, AFC: Buffalo vs. L.A. Raiders, 1990 (7 att)
    Jeff Jaeger, AFC-FR: L.A. Raiders vs. Denver, 1993 (6 att)
    Jason Elam, AFC-FR: Denver vs. Jacksonville, 1997 (6 att)
    Jeff Wilkins, NFC-D: St. Louis vs. Green Bay, 2001 (6 att)
    Martin Gramatica, SB: Tampa Bay vs. Oakland, 2002 (6 att)
    Jay Feely, NFC-D: Atlanta vs. St. Louis, 2004 (6 att)
    Mason Crosby, NFC-D: Green Bay vs. Seattle, 2007 (6 att)
    Neil Rackers, NFC-FR: Arizona vs. Green Bay, 2009 (ot) (6 att)
    Mason Crosby, NFC-FR: Green Bay vs. Arizona, 2009 (ot) (6 att)
    Garrett Hartley, NFC-D: New Orleans vs. Arizona, 2009 (6 att)
    Mason Crosby, NFC-D: Green Bay vs. Atlanta, 2010 (6 att)
    John Kasay, NFC-FR: New Orleans vs. Detroit, 2011 (6 att)
    Stephen Gostkowski, AFC-D: New England vs. Denver, 2011 (6 att)
    David Akers, NFC-D: San Francisco vs. Green Bay, 2012 (6 att)

Most (Kicking) Points After Touchdown, No Misses, Career
57 Gary Anderson, Pittsburgh-Philadelphia-San Francisco-Minnesota-Tennessee, 22 games
52 Adam Vinatieri, New England-Indianapolis, 25 games
49 George Blanda, Chi. Bears-Houston-Oakland, 19 games

Most Two-Point Conversions, Career
2   Terrell Owens, San Francisco-Philadelphia-Dallas, 12 games
    Kevin Faulk, New England, 19 games

Most Two-Point Conversions, Game
2   Terrell Owens, NFC-FR: San Francisco vs. N.Y. Giants, 2002

FIELD GOALS
Most Field Goals Attempted, Career
58 Adam Vinatieri, New England-Indianapolis, 25 games
47 David Akers, Philadelphia-San Francisco, 24 games
40 Gary Anderson, Pittsburgh-Philadelphia-San Francisco-Minnesota-Tennessee, 22 games

Most Field Goals Attempted, Game
6   George Blanda, AFC: Oakland vs. Houston, 1967
    David Ray, NFC-D: Los Angeles vs. Dallas, 1973
    Mark Moseley, AFC-D: Cleveland vs. N.Y. Jets, 1986 (ot)
    Matt Bahr, NFC: N.Y. Giants vs. San Francisco, 1990
    Steve Christie, AFC: Buffalo vs. Miami, 1992
    Jeff Wilkins, NFC-D: St. Louis vs. Carolina, 2003 (2 ot)
5   By many players

Most Field Goals, Career
48 Adam Vinatieri, New England-Indianapolis, 25 games
39 David Akers, Philadelphia-San Francisco, 24 games
32 Gary Anderson, Pittsburgh-Philadelphia-San Francisco-Minnesota-Tennessee, 22 games

Most Field Goals, Game
5   Chuck Nelson, NFC-D: Minnesota vs. San Francisco, 1987

Matt Bahr, NFC: N.Y. Giants vs. San Francisco, 1990
Steve Christie, AFC: Buffalo vs. Miami, 1992
Brad Daluiso, NFC-FR: N.Y. Giants vs. Minnesota, 1997
John Kasay, NFC-FR: Carolina vs. Dallas, 2003
Jeff Wilkins, NFC-D: St. Louis vs. Carolina, 2003 (2 ot)
Adam Vinatieri, AFC: New England vs. Indianapolis, 2003
Adam Vinatieri, AFC-D: Indianapolis vs. Baltimore, 2006

4 Gino Cappelletti, AFC-D: Boston vs. Buffalo, 1963
George Blanda, AFC: Oakland vs. Houston, 1967
Don Chandler, SB: Green Bay vs. Oakland, 1967
Curt Knight, NFC: Washington vs. Dallas, 1972
George Blanda, AFC-D: Oakland vs. Pittsburgh, 1973
Ray Wersching, SB: San Francisco vs. Cincinnati, 1981
Tony Franklin, AFC-FR: New England vs. N.Y. Jets, 1985
Jess Atkinson, NFC-FR: Washington vs. L.A. Rams, 1986
Luis Zendejas, NFC-D: Philadelphia vs. Chicago, 1988
Gary Anderson, AFC-FR: Pittsburgh vs. Houston, 1989 (ot)
Norm Johnson, AFC-D: Pittsburgh vs. Buffalo, 1995
Chris Boniol, NFC-FR: Dallas vs. Minnesota, 1996
John Kasay, NFC-D: Carolina vs. Dallas, 1996
Mike Hollis, AFC-D: Jacksonville vs. New England, 1998
Al Del Greco, AFC-D: Tennessee vs. Indianapolis, 1999
David Akers, NFC-D: Philadelphia vs. Chicago, 2001
Nate Kaeding, AFC-D: San Diego vs. New England, 2007
David Akers, NFC-FR: Philadelphia vs. Minnesota, 2008
Neil Rackers, NFC-D: Arizona vs. Carolina, 2008
Shayne Graham, AFC-FR: Houston vs. Cincinnati, 2012

3 By many players

Most Consecutive Games Scoring Field Goals
13 Toni Fritsch, Dallas-Houston, 1972-79
12 Adam Vinatieri, New England, 1997-2004
11 Jason Elam, Denver-Atlanta, 1997-2000, 2003-05, 2008

Most Consecutive Field Goals
19 David Akers, Philadelphia, 2000-04, 2006, 2008
16 Gary Anderson, Pittsburgh-Philadelphia, 1989-1995
Matt Stover, Baltimore, 2001, 2003, 2006, 2008;
Indianapolis, 2009
15 Rafael Septien, Dallas, 1978-1982

Longest Field Goal
58 Pete Stoyanovich, AFC-FR: Miami vs. Kansas City, 1990
55 Jeff Wilkins, NFC-D: St. Louis vs. Atlanta, 2004
Shayne Graham, AFC-FR: Houston vs. New England, 2012
54 Ed Murray, NFC-D: Detroit vs. San Francisco, 1983
Steve Christie, SB: Buffalo vs. Dallas, 1993
John Carney, AFC-FR: San Diego vs. Indianapolis, 1995

Highest Field Goal Percentage, Career (10 field goals)
92.9 Martin Gramatica, Tampa Bay-Indianapolis-Dallas,
9 games (14-13)
92.0 John Kasay, Carolina-New Orleans, 12 games (25-23)
90.9 Chuck Nelson, L.A. Rams-Minnesota, 6 games (11-10)

SAFETIES
Most Safeties, Game
1 Bill Willis, NFC-D: Cleveland vs. N.Y. Giants, 1950
Carl Eller, NFC-D: Minnesota vs. Los Angeles, 1969
George Andrie, NFC-D: Dallas vs. Detroit, 1970
Alan Page, NFC-D: Minnesota vs. Dallas, 1971
Dwight White, SB: Pittsburgh vs. Minnesota, 1974
Reggie Harrison, SB: Pittsburgh vs. Dallas, 1975
Jim Jensen, NFC-D: Dallas vs. Los Angeles, 1976
Ted Washington, AFC: Houston vs. Pittsburgh, 1978
Randy White, NFC-D: Dallas vs. Los Angeles, 1979
Henry Waechter, SB: Chicago vs. New England, 1985
Rulon Jones, AFC-D: Denver vs. New England, 1986
George Martin, SB: N.Y. Giants vs. Denver, 1986
D.D. Hoggard, AFC: Cleveland vs. Denver, 1987
Bruce Smith, SB: Buffalo vs. N.Y. Giants, 1990
Reggie White, NFC-FR: Philadelphia vs. New Orleans, 1992
Willie Clay, NFC-FR: Detroit vs. Green Bay, 1994
Carnell Lake, AFC-D: Pittsburgh vs. Cleveland, 1994
Reuben Davis, AFC-D: San Diego vs. Miami, 1994
Jevon Kearse, AFC-FR: Tennessee vs. Buffalo, 1999

Brady Smith, NFC-D: Atlanta vs. St. Louis, 2004
Antonio Smith, NFC-FR: Arizona vs. Atlanta, 2008
Mike DeVito, AFC: N.Y. Jets vs. Pittsburgh, 2010
Chris Culliver, SB: San Francisco vs. Baltimore, 2012

RUSHING
ATTEMPTS
Most Attempts, Career
400 Franco Harris, Pittsburgh, 19 games
349 Emmitt Smith, Dallas, 17 games
339 Thurman Thomas, Buffalo, 21 games

Most Attempts, Game
40 Lamar Smith, AFC-FR: Miami vs. Indianapolis, 2000 (ot)
38 Ricky Bell, NFC-D: Tampa Bay vs. Philadelphia, 1979
John Riggins, SB: Washington vs. Miami, 1982
37 Lawrence McCutcheon, NFC-D: Los Angeles vs. St. Louis,
1975
John Riggins, NFC-D: Washington vs. Minnesota, 1982

YARDS GAINED
Most Yards Gained, Career
1,586 Emmitt Smith, Dallas, 17 games
1,556 Franco Harris, Pittsburgh, 19 games
1,442 Thurman Thomas, Buffalo, 21 games

Most Yards Gained, Game
248 Eric Dickerson, NFC-D: L.A. Rams vs. Dallas, 1985
209 Lamar Smith, AFC-FR: Miami vs. Indianapolis, 2000 (ot)
206 Keith Lincoln, AFC: San Diego vs. Boston, 1963

Most Games, 100 or More Yards Rushing, Career
7 Emmitt Smith, Dallas, 17 games
Terrell Davis, Denver, 8 games
6 John Riggins, Washington, 9 games
Thurman Thomas, Buffalo, 21 games
5 Franco Harris, Pittsburgh, 19 games
Marcus Allen, L.A. Raiders-Kansas City, 16 games

Most Consecutive Games, 100 or More Yards Rushing
7 Terrell Davis, Denver, 1997-98
6 John Riggins, Washington, 1982-83
4 Thurman Thomas, Buffalo, 1990-91

Longest Run From Scrimmage
90 Fred Taylor, AFC-D: Jacksonville vs. Miami, 1999 (TD)
83 Ray Rice, AFC-FR: Baltimore vs. New England, 2009 (TD)
80 Roger Craig, NFC-D: San Francisco vs. Minnesota, 1988 (TD)
Charlie Garner, AFC-FR: Oakland vs. N.Y. Jets, 2001 (TD)

AVERAGE GAIN
Highest Average Gain, Career (100 attempts)
5.59 Terrell Davis, Denver, 8 games (204-1,140)
5.04 Marcus Allen, SB: L.A. Raiders-Kansas City, 16 games
(267-1,347)
4.90 Arian Foster, Houston, 4 games (105-515)

Highest Average Gain, Game (10 attempts)
15.90 Elmer Angsman, NFC: Chi. Cardinals vs. Philadelphia,
1947 (10-159)
15.85 Keith Lincoln, AFC: San Diego vs. Boston, 1963 (13-206)
11.31 Colin Kaepernick, NFC-D: San Francisco vs. Green Bay,
2012 (16-181)

TOUCHDOWNS
Most Touchdowns, Career
19 Emmitt Smith, Dallas, 17 games
16 Franco Harris, Pittsburgh, 19 games
Thurman Thomas, Buffalo, 21 games
12 John Riggins, Washington, 9 games
Terrell Davis, Denver, 8 games

Most Touchdowns, Game
5 Ricky Watters, NFC-D: San Francisco vs. N.Y. Giants, 1993
3 Andy Farkas, NFC-D: Washington vs. N.Y. Giants, 1943
Otto Graham, NFC: Cleveland vs. Detroit, 1954
Tom Matte, NFC: Baltimore vs. Cleveland, 1968
Larry Schreiber, NFC-D: San Francisco vs. Dallas, 1972
Larry Csonka, AFC: Miami vs. Oakland, 1973

Franco Harris, AFC-D: Pittsburgh vs. Buffalo, 1974
John Riggins, NFC-D: Washington vs. L.A. Rams, 1983
Kenneth Davis, AFC: Buffalo vs. L.A. Raiders, 1990
Napoleon McCallum, AFC-FR: L.A. Raiders vs. Denver, 1993
Thurman Thomas, AFC: Buffalo vs. Kansas City, 1993
William Floyd, NFC-D: San Francisco vs. Chicago, 1994
Emmitt Smith, NFC: Dallas vs. Green Bay, 1995
Curtis Martin, AFC-D: New England vs. Pittsburgh, 1996
Terrell Davis, SB: Denver vs. Green Bay, 1997
Mario Bates, NFC-D: Arizona vs. Minnesota, 1998
Shaun Alexander, NFC-FR: Seattle vs. Green Bay, 2003 (ot)
Ryan Grant, NFC-D: Green Bay vs. Seattle, 2007
Adrian Peterson, NFC: Minnesota vs. New Orleans, 2009 (ot)

Most Consecutive Games Rushing for Touchdowns
  8   Emmitt Smith, Dallas, 1993-96
      Thurman Thomas, Buffalo, 1992-98
  7   John Riggins, Washington, 1982-84
      Terrell Davis, Denver, 1996-98
  5   Franco Harris, Pittsburgh, 1974-75
      Franco Harris, Pittsburgh, 1977-79
      Curtis Martin, New England-N.Y. Jets, 1996-98
      Jerome Bettis, Pittsburgh, 2004-05

PASSING
PASSER RATING
Highest Passer Rating, Career (150 attempts)
  104.8   Bart Starr, Green Bay, 10 games
  104.2   Drew Brees, San Diego-New Orleans, 9 games
  103.6   Aaron Rodgers, Green Bay, 9 games

ATTEMPTS
Most Passes Attempted, Career
  887   Tom Brady, New England, 24 games
  791   Brett Favre, Green Bay-Minnesota, 24 games
  761   Peyton Manning, Indianapolis-Denver, 20 games
Most Passes Attempted, Game
  65   Steve Young, NFC-D: San Francisco vs. Green Bay, 1995
  64   Bernie Kosar, AFC-D: Cleveland vs. N.Y. Jets, 1986 (ot)
       Dan Marino, AFC-FR: Miami vs. Buffalo, 1995
  63   Drew Brees, NFC-D: New Orleans vs. San Francisco, 2011

COMPLETIONS
Most Passes Completed, Career
  553   Tom Brady, New England, 24 games
  481   Brett Favre, Green Bay-Minnesota, 24 games
        Peyton Manning, Indianapolis-Denver, 20 games
  460   Joe Montana, San Francisco-Kansas City, 23 games
Most Passes Completed, Game
  40   Drew Brees, NFC-D: New Orleans vs. San Francisco, 2011
  39   Drew Brees, NFC-FR: New Orleans vs. Seattle, 2010
  36   Warren Moon, AFC-FR: Houston vs. Buffalo, 1992 (ot)

COMPLETION PERCENTAGE
Highest Completion Percentage, Career (150 attempts)
  67.0   Drew Brees, San Diego-New Orleans, 9 games (391-262)
  66.5   Kurt Warner, St. Louis-Arizona, 13 games (462-307)
  66.3   Matt Ryan, Atlanta, 5 games, (187-124)
Highest Completion Percentage, Game (15 completions)
  92.9   Tom Brady, AFC-D: New England vs. Jacksonville, 2007
         (28-26)
  88.0   Phil Simms, SB: N.Y. Giants vs. Denver, 1986 (25-22)
  87.9   Kurt Warner, NFC-FR: Arizona vs. Green Bay, 2009 (ot)
         (33-29)

YARDS GAINED
Most Yards Gained, Career
  5,949   Tom Brady, New England, 24 games
  5,855   Brett Favre, Green Bay-Minnesota, 24 games
  5,772   Joe Montana, San Francisco-Kansas City, 23 games
Most Yards Gained, Game
  489   Bernie Kosar, AFC-D: Cleveland vs. N.Y. Jets, 1986 (ot)
  466   Drew Brees, NFC-FR: New Orleans vs. Detroit, 2011

  462   Drew Brees, NFC-D: New Orleans vs. San Francisco, 2011
Most Games, 300 or More Yards Passing, Career
  8   Peyton Manning, Indianapolis-Denver, 20 games
  6   Joe Montana, San Francisco-Kansas City, 23 games
      Kurt Warner, St. Louis-Arizona, 13 games
      Tom Brady, New England, 24 games
  5   Dan Fouts, San Diego, 7 games
      Drew Brees, San Diego-New Orleans, 9 games
Most Consecutive Games, 300 or More Yards Passing
  4   Dan Fouts, San Diego, 1979-1981
  3   Jim Kelly, Buffalo, 1989-1990
      Warren Moon, Houston, 1991-93
      Drew Brees, New Orleans, 2010-11 (current)
  2   Daryle Lamonica, Oakland, 1968
      Ken Anderson, Cincinnati, 1981-82
      Terry Bradshaw, Pittsburgh, 1979-1982
      Joe Montana, San Francisco, 1983-84
      Dan Marino, Miami, 1984
      Troy Aikman, Dallas, 1994
      Steve Young, San Francisco, 1994-95
      Kurt Warner, St. Louis, 1999-2000
      Peyton Manning, Indianapolis, 2003
      Marc Bulger, St. Louis, 2003-04
      Matt Hasselbeck, Seattle, 2003-04
      Peyton Manning, Indianapolis, 2007-08
      Donovan McNabb, Philadelphia, 2004, 2008
      Kurt Warner, Arizona, 2008-09
      Peyton Manning, Indianapolis, 2009
      Eli Manning, N.Y. Giants, 2011
      Tom Brady, New England, 2012 (current)
Longest Pass Completion
  96   Trent Dilfer (to Sharpe), AFC: Baltimore vs. Oakland, 2000 (TD)
  94   Troy Aikman (to Harper), NFC-D: Dallas vs. Green Bay,
       1994 (TD)
  93   Daryle Lamonica (to Dubenion), AFC-D: Buffalo vs. Boston,
       1963 (TD)

AVERAGE GAIN
Highest Average Gain, Career (150 attempts)
  8.55   Kurt Warner, St. Louis-Arizona, 13 games (462-3,952)
  8.45   Joe Theismann, Washington, 10 games (211-1,782)
  8.43   Jim Plunkett, Oakland-L.A. Raiders, 10 games (272-2,293)
Highest Average Gain, Game (20 attempts)
  15.05   Tim Tebow, AFC-FR: Denver vs. Pittsburgh, 2011 (21-316)
  14.71   Terry Bradshaw, SB: Pittsburgh vs. Los Angeles, 1979 (21-309)
  14.50   Peyton Manning, AFC-FR: Indianapolis vs. Denver, 2003
          (26-377)

TOUCHDOWNS
Most Touchdown Passes, Career
  45   Joe Montana, San Francisco-Kansas City, 23 games
  44   Brett Favre, Green Bay-Minnesota, 24 games
  42   Tom Brady, New England, 24 games
Most Touchdown Passes, Game
  6   Daryle Lamonica, AFC-D: Oakland vs. Houston, 1969
      Steve Young, SB: San Francisco vs. San Diego, 1994
      Tom Brady, AFC-D: New England vs. Denver, 2011
  5   Sid Luckman, NFC: Chi. Bears vs. Washington, 1943
      Daryle Lamonica, AFC-D: Oakland vs. Kansas City, 1968
      Joe Montana, SB: San Francisco vs. Denver, 1989
      Kurt Warner, NFC-D: St. Louis vs. Minnesota, 1999
      Kerry Collins, NFC: N.Y. Giants vs. Minnesota, 2000
      Peyton Manning, AFC-FR: Indianapolis vs. Denver, 2003
      Kurt Warner, NFC-FR: Arizona vs. Green Bay, 2009 (ot)
  4   Otto Graham, NFC: Cleveland vs. Los Angeles, 1950
      Tobin Rote, NFC: Detroit vs. Cleveland, 1957
      Bart Starr, NFC: Green Bay vs. Dallas, 1966
      Ken Stabler, AFC-D: Oakland vs. Miami, 1974
      Roger Staubach, NFC: Dallas vs. Los Angeles, 1975
      Terry Bradshaw, SB: Pittsburgh vs. Dallas, 1978
      Don Strock, AFC-D: Miami vs. San Diego, 1981 (ot)
      Lynn Dickey, NFC-FR: Green Bay vs. St. Louis, 1982

Dan Marino, AFC: Miami vs. Pittsburgh, 1984
Phil Simms, NFC-D: N.Y. Giants vs. San Francisco, 1986
Doug Williams, SB: Washington vs. Denver, 1987
Jim Kelly, AFC-D: Buffalo vs. Cleveland, 1989
Joe Montana, NFC-D: San Francisco vs. Minnesota, 1989
Warren Moon, AFC-FR: Houston vs. Buffalo, 1992 (ot)
Frank Reich, AFC-FR: Buffalo vs. Houston, 1992 (ot)
Troy Aikman, SB: Dallas vs. Buffalo, 1992
Jeff George, NFC-D: Minnesota vs. St. Louis, 1999
Aaron Brooks, NFC-FR: New Orleans vs. St. Louis, 2000
Kerry Collins, NFC-FR: N.Y. Giants vs. San Francisco, 2002
Peyton Manning, AFC-FR: Indianapolis vs. Denver, 2004
Daunte Culpepper, NFC-FR: Minnesota vs. Green Bay, 2004
Kurt Warner, NFC: Arizona vs. Philadelphia, 2008
Aaron Rodgers, NFC-FR: Green Bay vs. Arizona, 2009 (ot)
Brett Favre, NFC-D: Minnesota vs. Dallas, 2009
Matt Hasselbeck, NFC-FR: Seattle vs. New Orleans, 2010
Drew Brees, NFC-FR: New Orleans vs. San Francisco, 2011

Most Consecutive Games, Touchdown Passes
20   Brett Favre, Green Bay-Minnesota, 1995-2009
18   Tom Brady, New England, 2001-2011
13   Dan Marino, Miami, 1983-1995

HAD INTERCEPTED
Lowest Percentage, Passes Had Intercepted, Career (150 attempts)
1.02   Drew Brees, San Diego-New Orleans, 9 games (391-4)
1.41   Bart Starr, Green Bay, 10 games (213-3)
1.71   Aaron Rodgers, Green Bay, 9 games (292-5)
Most Attempts Without Interception, Game
60   Drew Brees, NFC-FR: New Orleans vs. Seattle, 2010
58   Eli Manning, NFC: N.Y. Giants vs. San Francisco, 2011 (ot)
54   Neil O'Donnell, AFC: Pittsburgh vs. San Diego, 1994
Most Passes Had Intercepted, Career
30   Brett Favre, Green Bay-Minnesota, 24 games
28   Jim Kelly, Buffalo, 17 games
26   Terry Bradshaw, Pittsburgh, 19 games
Most Passes Had Intercepted, Game
6   Frank Filchock, NFC: N.Y. Giants vs. Chi. Bears, 1946
     Bobby Layne, NFC: Detroit vs. Cleveland, 1954
     Norm Van Brocklin, NFC: Los Angeles vs. Cleveland, 1955
     Brett Favre, NFC-D: Green Bay vs. St. Louis, 2001
5   Frank Filchock, NFC: Washington vs. Chi. Bears, 1940
     George Blanda, AFC: Houston vs. San Diego, 1961
     George Blanda, AFC: Houston vs. Dall. Texans, 1962 (ot)
     Y.A. Tittle, NFC: N.Y. Giants vs. Chicago, 1963
     Mike Phipps, AFC-D: Cleveland vs. Miami, 1972
     Dan Pastorini, AFC: Houston vs. Pittsburgh, 1978
     Dan Fouts, AFC-D: San Diego vs. Houston, 1979
     Tommy Kramer, NFC-D: Minnesota vs. Philadelphia, 1980
     Dan Fouts, AFC-D: San Diego vs. Miami, 1982
     Richard Todd, AFC: N.Y. Jets vs. Miami, 1982
     Gary Danielson, NFC-D: Detroit vs. San Francisco, 1983
     Jay Schroeder, AFC: L.A. Raiders vs. Buffalo, 1990
     Rich Gannon, SB: Oakland vs. Tampa Bay, 2002
     Jake Delhomme, NFC-D: Carolina vs. Arizona, 2008
4   By many players

PASS RECEIVING
RECEPTIONS
Most Receptions, Career
151   Jerry Rice, San Francisco-Oakland-Seattle, 29 games
92   Reggie Wayne, Indianapolis, 18 games
88   Hines Ward, Pittsburgh, 18 games
Most Receptions, Game
15   Darren Sproles, NFC-D: New Orleans vs. San Francisco, 2011
13   Kellen Winslow, AFC-D: San Diego vs. Miami, 1981 (ot)
     Thurman Thomas, AFC-D: Buffalo vs. Cleveland, 1989
     Shannon Sharpe, AFC-FR: Denver vs. L.A. Raiders, 1993
     Chad Morton, NFC-D: New Orleans vs. Minnesota, 2000
12   Raymond Berry, NFC: Baltimore vs. N.Y. Giants, 1958
     Michael Irvin, NFC: Dallas vs. San Francisco, 1994

Darrell Jackson, NFC-FR: Seattle vs. St. Louis, 2004
Steve Smith, NFC-D: Carolina vs. Chicago, 2005
Calvin Johnson, NFC-FR: Detroit vs. New Orleans, 2011
Most Consecutive Games, Pass Receptions
28   Jerry Rice, San Francisco-Oakland, 1985-2002
22   Drew Pearson, Dallas, 1973-1983
18   Paul Warfield, Cleveland-Miami, 1964-1974
     Cliff Branch, Oakland/L.A. Raiders, 1974-1983
     Thurman Thomas, Buffalo, 1989-1998
     Shannon Sharpe, Denver-Baltimore-Denver, 1991-2003
     Reggie Wayne, Indianapolis, 2002-2012 (current)

YARDS GAINED
Most Yards Gained, Career
2,245   Jerry Rice, San Francisco-Oakland-Seattle, 29 games
1,315   Michael Irvin, Dallas, 16 games
1,289   Cliff Branch, Oakland/L.A. Raiders, 22 games
Most Yards Gained, Game
240   Eric Moulds, AFC-FR: Buffalo vs. Miami, 1998
227   Anthony Carter, NFC-D: Minnesota vs. San Francisco, 1987
221   Reggie Wayne, AFC-FR: Indianapolis vs. Denver, 2004
Most Games, 100 or More Yards Receiving, Career
8   Jerry Rice, San Francisco-Oakland-Seattle, 29 games
6   Michael Irvin, Dallas, 16 games
5   John Stallworth, Pittsburgh, 18 games
     Andre Reed, Buffalo, 21 games
     Hines Ward, Pittsburgh, 18 games
Most Consecutive Games, 100 or More Yards Receiving, Career
4   Larry Fitzgerald, Arizona, 2008
3   Tom Fears, Los Angeles, 1950-51
     Jerry Rice, San Francisco, 1988-89
     Randy Moss, Minnesota, 1999-2000
2   By many players
Longest Reception
96   Shannon Sharpe (from Dilfer), AFC: Baltimore vs. Oakland, 2000 (TD)
94   Alvin Harper (from Aikman), NFC-D: Dallas vs. Green Bay, 1994 (TD)
93   Elbert Dubenion (from Lamonica), AFC-D: Buffalo vs. Boston, 1963 (TD)

AVERAGE GAIN
Highest Average Gain, Career (20 receptions)
27.3   Alvin Harper, Dallas, 10 games (24-655)
24.8   Vernon Davis, San Francisco, 5 games (22-546)
23.7   Willie Gault, Chicago-L.A. Raiders, 12 games (21-497)
Highest Average Gain, Game (3 receptions)
51.0   Demaryius Thomas, AFC-FR: Denver vs. Pittsburgh, 2011 (4-204)
46.3   Harold Jackson, NFC: Los Angeles vs. Minnesota, 1974 (3-139)
42.7   Billy Cannon, AFC: Houston vs. L.A. Chargers, 1960 (3-128)

TOUCHDOWNS
Most Touchdowns, Career
22   Jerry Rice, San Francisco-Oakland-Seattle, 29 games
12   John Stallworth, Pittsburgh, 18 games
10   Fred Biletnikoff, Oakland, 19 games
     Antonio Freeman, Green Bay-Philadelphia-Green Bay, 16 games
     Randy Moss, Minnesota-New England-San Francisco, 15 games
     Hines Ward, Pittsburgh, 18 games
Most Touchdowns, Game
3   Tom Fears, NFC-D: Los Angeles vs. Chi. Bears, 1950
     Gary Collins, NFC: Cleveland vs. Baltimore, 1964
     Fred Biletnikoff, AFC-D: Oakland vs. Kansas City, 1968
     Preston Pearson, NFC: Dallas vs. Los Angeles, 1975
     Dave Casper, AFC-D: Oakland vs. Baltimore, 1977 (ot)
     Alvin Garrett, NFC-FR: Washington vs. Detroit, 1982
     Jerry Rice, NFC-D: San Francisco vs. Minnesota, 1988
     Jerry Rice, SB: San Francisco vs. Denver, 1989
     Andre Reed, AFC-FR: Buffalo vs. Houston, 1992 (ot)

Sterling Sharpe, NFC-FR: Green Bay vs. Detroit, 1993
Jerry Rice, SB: San Francisco vs. San Diego, 1994
Willie Jackson, NFC-FR: New Orleans vs. St. Louis, 2000
Amani Toomer, NFC-FR: N.Y. Giants vs. San Francisco, 2002
Larry Fitzgerald, NFC: Arizona vs. Philadelphia, 2008
Sidney Rice, NFC-D: Minnesota vs. Dallas, 2009
Rob Gronkowski, AFC-D: New England vs. Denver, 2011

Most Consecutive Games, Touchdown Passes Caught
8   John Stallworth, Pittsburgh, 1978-1983
7   David Givens, New England, 2003-05)
5   James Lofton, Green Bay-Buffalo, 1982-1990
    Randy Moss, Minnesota, 1998-2000
    Antonio Freeman, Green Bay, 1997-2001
    Hines Ward, Pittsburgh, 2002-05
    Larry Fitzgerald, Arizona, 2008-09

INTERCEPTIONS BY

Most Interceptions, Career
9   Charlie Waters, Dallas, 25 games
    Bill Simpson, Los Angeles-Buffalo, 11 games
    Ronnie Lott, San Francisco-L.A. Raiders, 20 games
    Ed Reed, Baltimore, 15 games
8   Lester Hayes, Oakland/L.A. Raiders, 13 games
7   Willie Brown, Oakland, 17 games
    Dennis Thurman, Dallas, 14 games
    Rodney Harrison, San Diego-New England, 13 games
    Asante Samuel, New England-Philadelphia-Atlanta, 21 games

Most Interceptions, Game
4   Vernon Perry, AFC-D: Houston vs. San Diego, 1979
3   Joe Laws, NFC: Green Bay vs. N.Y. Giants, 1944
    Charlie Waters, NFC-D: Dallas vs. Chicago, 1977
    Rod Martin, SB: Oakland vs. Philadelphia, 1980
    Dennis Thurman, NFC-D: Dallas vs. Green Bay, 1982
    A.J. Duhe, AFC: Miami vs. N.Y. Jets, 1982
    Ty Law, AFC: New England vs. Indianapolis, 2003
    Ricky Manning Jr., NFC: Carolina vs. Philadelphia, 2003
2   By many players

Most Consecutive Games, Interceptions
4   Aeneas Williams, Arizona-St. Louis, 1998-2001
    Rodney Harrison, New England, 2004, 2007
3   By many players. Last time:
    Ed Reed, Baltimore, 2006, 2008

YARDS GAINED

Most Yards Gained, Career
227   Asante Samuel, New England-Philadelphia-Atlanta, 21 games
196   Willie Brown, Oakland, 17 games
187   Ronnie Lott, San Francisco-L.A.-Raiders, 20 games

Most Yards Gained, Game
108   Darrien Gordon, SB: Denver vs. Atlanta, 1998
101   George Teague, NFC-FR: Green Bay vs. Detroit, 1993
100   Champ Bailey, AFC-D: Denver vs. New England, 2005
     James Harrison, SB: Pittsburgh vs. Arizona, 2008

Longest Return
101   George Teague, NFC-FR: Green Bay vs. Detroit, 1993 (TD)
100   Champ Bailey, AFC-D: Denver vs. New England, 2005
     James Harrison, SB: Pittsburgh vs. Arizona, 2008 (TD)
98   Darrol Ray, AFC-FR: N.Y. Jets vs. Cincinnati, 1982 (TD)

TOUCHDOWNS

Most Touchdowns, Career
4   Asante Samuel, New England-Philadelphia-Atlanta, 21 games
3   Willie Brown, Oakland, 17 games
2   Lester Hayes, Oakland/L.A. Raiders, 13 games
    Ronnie Lott, San Francisco-L.A. Raiders, 20 games
    Darrell Green, Washington, 18 games
    Melvin Jenkins, Seattle-Detroit, 5 games
    George Teague, Green Bay-Dallas-Miami-Dallas, 12 games
    Aeneas Williams, Arizona-St. Louis, 6 games

Dwight Smith, Tampa Bay, 4 games

Most Touchdowns, Game
2   Aeneas Williams, NFC-D: St. Louis vs. Green Bay, 2001
    Dwight Smith, SB: Tampa Bay vs. Oakland, 2002
1   By many players

PUNTING

Most Punts, Career
111   Ray Guy, Oakland/L.A. Raiders, 22 games
101   Craig Hentrich, Green Bay-Tennessee, 22 games
84   Danny White, Dallas, 18 games
    Sean Landeta, N.Y. Giants-Tampa Bay-Green Bay-Philadelphia-St. Louis, 18 games

Most Punts, Game
14   Dave Jennings, AFC-D: N.Y. Jets vs. Cleveland, 1986 (ot)
12   David Lee, AFC-D: Baltimore vs. Oakland, 1977 (ot)
    Steve Weatherford, NFC: N.Y. Giants vs. San Francisco, 2011 (ot)
11   Ken Strong, NFC: N.Y. Giants vs. Chi. Bears, 1933
    Jim Norton, AFC: Houston vs. Oakland, 1967
    Ode Burrell, AFC-D: Houston vs. Oakland, 1969
    Dale Hatcher, NFC: L.A. Rams vs. Chicago, 1985
    Brad Maynard, SB: N.Y. Giants vs. Baltimore, 2000

Longest Punt
76   Ed Danowski, NFC: N.Y. Giants vs. Detroit, 1935
    Mike Horan, AFC: Denver vs. Buffalo, 1991
72   Charlie Conerly, NFC-D: N.Y. Giants vs. Cleveland, 1950
    Yale Lary, NFC: Detroit vs. Cleveland, 1953
71   Ray Guy, AFC: Oakland vs. San Diego, 1980

AVERAGE YARDAGE

Highest Average, Career (25 punts)
47.9   Andy Lee, San Francisco, 5 games (27-1,294)
44.5   Rich Camarillo, New England, 6 games (35-1,559)
44.4   Todd Sauerbrun, Carolina-Denver-New England, 9 games (43-1,911)

Highest Average, Game (4 punts)
56.0   Ray Guy, AFC: Oakland vs. San Diego, 1980 (4-224)
53.8   Sam Koch, AFC-D: Baltimore vs. Pittsburgh, 2010 (4-215)
53.3   Craig Hentrich, AFC-D: Tennessee vs. Baltimore, 2008 (4-213)

PUNT RETURNS

Most Punt Returns, Career
34   David Meggett, N.Y. Giants-New England-N.Y. Jets, 13 games
    Brian Mitchell, Washington-Philadelphia, 16 games
33   Troy Brown, New England, 20 games
26   Antwaan Randle El, Pittsburgh-Washington, 12 games

Most Punt Returns, Game
8   Kyle Williams, NFC: San Francisco vs. N.Y. Giants, 2011 (ot)
7   Ron Gardin, AFC-D: Baltimore vs. Cincinnati, 1970
    Carl Roaches, AFC-FR: Houston vs. Oakland, 1980
    Gerald McNeil, AFC-D: Cleveland vs. N.Y. Jets, 1986 (ot)
    Phil McConkey, NFC-D: N.Y. Giants vs. San Francisco, 1986
    David Meggett, AFC-D: New England vs. Pittsburgh, 1996
    Reggie Barlow, AFC-FR: Jacksonville vs. New England, 1998
6   By many players

YARDS GAINED

Most Yards Gained, Career
339   Brian Mitchell, Washington-Philadelphia, 16 games
315   Troy Brown, New England, 20 games
312   David Meggett, N.Y. Giants-New England-N.Y. Jets, 13 games

Most Yards Gained, Game
152   Allen Rossum, NFC-D: Atlanta vs. St. Louis, 2004
143   Anthony Carter, NFC-FR: Minnesota vs. New Orleans, 1987

141 Bob Hayes, NFC-D: Dallas vs. Cleveland, 1967

Longest Return

90 Trindon Holliday, AFC-D: Denver vs. Baltimore, 2012 (2 ot) (TD)

88 Jermaine Lewis, AFC-D: Baltimore vs. Pittsburgh, 2001 (TD)

84 Anthony Carter, NFC-FR: Minnesota vs. New Orleans, 1987 (TD)

AVERAGE YARDAGE

Highest Average, Career (10 returns)

23.9 Allen Rossum, Green Bay-Atlanta, 6 games (10-239)

15.3 Robert Brooks, Green Bay, 11 games (14-214)

15.2 Anthony Carter, Minnesota-Detroit, 9 games (17-259)

Highest Average Gain, Game (3 returns)

50.7 Allen Rossum, NFC-D: Atlanta vs. St. Louis, 2004 (3-152)

47.0 Bob Hayes, NFC-D: Dallas vs. Cleveland, 1967 (3-141)

36.3 Reggie Bush, NFC-D: New Orleans vs. Arizona, 2009 (3-109)

TOUCHDOWNS

Most Touchdowns

1 Hugh Gallarneau, NFC-D: Chicago Bears vs. Green Bay, 1941

Bosh Pritchard, NFC-D: Philadelphia vs. Pittsburgh, 1947

Charley Trippi, NFC: Chicago Cardinals vs. Philadelphia, 1947

Verda (Vitamin T) Smith, NFC-D: Los Angeles vs. Detroit, 1952

George (Butch) Byrd, AFC: Buffalo vs. San Diego, 1965

Golden Richards, NFC: Dallas vs. Minnesota, 1973

Wes Chandler, AFC-D: San Diego vs. Miami, 1981 (ot)

Shaun Gayle, NFC-D: Chicago vs. N.Y. Giants, 1985

Anthony Carter, NFC-FR: Minnesota vs. New Orleans, 1987

Darrell Green, NFC-D: Washington vs. Chicago, 1987

Antonio Freeman, NFC-FR: Green Bay vs. Atlanta, 1995

Desmond Howard, NFC-D: Green Bay vs. San Francisco, 1996

Jermaine Lewis, AFC-D: Baltimore vs. Pittsburgh, 2001

Troy Brown, AFC: New England vs. Pittsburgh, 2001

Antwaan Randle El, AFC-FR: Pittsburgh vs. Cleveland, 2002

Santana Moss, AFC-D: N.Y. Jets vs. Pittsburgh, 2004 (ot)

Allen Rossum, NFC-D: Atlanta vs. St. Louis, 2004

Steve Smith, NFC: Carolina vs. Seattle, 2005

Santonio Holmes, AFC: Pittsburgh vs. San Diego, 2008

Reggie Bush, NFC-D: New Orleans vs. Arizona, 2009

Trindon Holliday, AFC-D: Denver vs. Baltimore, 2012 (2 ot)

KICKOFF RETURNS

Most Kickoff Returns, Career

36 Brian Mitchell, Washington-Philadelphia, 16 games

31 Kevin Williams, Dallas-Buffalo, 12 games

29 Fulton Walker, Miami-L.A. Raiders, 10 games

Most Kickoff Returns, Game

8 Marc Logan, AFC-D: Miami vs. Buffalo, 1990

Andre Coleman, SB: San Diego vs. San Francisco, 1994

Marcus Knight, SB: Oakland vs. Tampa Bay, 2002

7 Don Bingham, NFC: Chi. Bears vs. N.Y. Giants, 1956

Reggie Brown, NFC-FR: Atlanta vs. Minnesota, 1982

David Verser, AFC-FR: Cincinnati vs. N.Y. Jets, 1982

Del Rodgers, NFC-D: Green Bay vs. Dallas, 1982

Henry Ellard, NFC-D: L.A. Rams vs. Washington, 1983

Stephen Starring, SB: New England vs. Chicago, 1985

Darick Holmes, AFC-D: Buffalo vs. Pittsburgh, 1995

Antonio Freeman, NFC: Green Bay vs. Dallas, 1995

Roell Preston, NFC-FR: Green Bay vs. San Francisco, 1998

Robert Tate, NFC-D: Minnesota vs. St. Louis, 1999

Fred McAfee, NFC-D: New Orleans vs. Minnesota, 2000

Michael Bates, NFC-D: Dallas vs. Carolina, 2003

Dante Hall, AFC-D: Kansas City vs. Indianapolis, 2003

Michael Lewis, NFC: New Orleans vs. Chicago, 2006

6 By many players

YARDS GAINED

Most Yards Gained, Career

875 Brian Mitchell, Washington-Philadelphia, 16 games

677 Fulton Walker, Miami-L.A. Raiders, 10 games

632 Kevin Williams, Dallas-Buffalo, 12 games

Most Yards Gained, Game

244 Andre Coleman, SB: San Diego vs. San Francisco, 1994

220 Ellis Hobbs, AFC: New England vs. Indianapolis, 2006

216 Danieal Manning, AFC-D: Houston vs. New England, 2012

Longest Return

108 Jacoby Jones, SB: Baltimore vs. San Francisco, 2012 (TD)

104 Trindon Holliday, AFC-D: Denver vs. Baltimore, 2012 (2 ot) (TD)

102 Eric Weems, NFC-D: Atlanta vs. Green Bay, 2010 (TD)

AVERAGE YARDAGE

Highest Average, Career (10 returns)

35.8 Danieal Manning, Chicago-Houston, 9 games (12-429)

30.1 Carl Garrett, Oakland, 5 games (16-481)

30.0 Reggie Barlow, Jacksonville, 8 games (12-360)

Highest Average, Game (3 returns)

56.7 Les (Speedy) Duncan, NFC-D: Washington vs. San Francisco, 1971 (3-170)

54.0 Danieal Manning, AFC-D: Houston vs. New England, 2012 (4-216)

52.7 Trindon Holliday, AFC-D: Denver vs. Baltimore, 2012 (2 ot) (3-158)

TOUCHDOWNS

Most Touchdowns, Career

2 Ron Dixon, N.Y. Giants, 4 games

1 By many players

Most Touchdowns, Game

1 Vic Washington, NFC-D: San Francisco vs. Dallas, 1972

Nat Moore, AFC-D: Miami vs. Oakland, 1974

Marshall Johnson, AFC-D: Baltimore vs. Oakland, 1977 (ot)

Fulton Walker, SB: Miami vs. Washington, 1982

Stanford Jennings, SB: Cincinnati vs. San Francisco, 1988

Eric Metcalf, AFC-D: Cleveland vs. Buffalo, 1989

Andre Coleman, SB: San Diego vs. San Francisco, 1994

Desmond Howard, SB: Green Bay vs. New England, 1996

Chuck Levy, NFC: San Francisco vs. Green Bay, 1997

Tim Dwight, SB: Atlanta vs. Denver, 1998

Kevin Dyson, AFC-FR: Tennessee vs. Buffalo, 1999

Charlie Rogers, AFC-FR: Seattle vs. Miami, 1999

Brian Mitchell, NFC-D: Washington vs. Tampa Bay, 1999

Tony Horne, NFC-D: St. Louis vs. Minnesota, 1999

Derrick Mason, AFC: Tennessee vs. Jacksonville, 1999

Ron Dixon, NFC-D: N.Y. Giants vs. Philadelphia, 2000; SB: N.Y. Giants vs. Baltimore, 2000

Jermaine Lewis, SB: Baltimore vs. N.Y. Giants, 2000

Dante Hall, AFC-D: Kansas City vs. Indianapolis, 2003

Miles Austin, NFC-FR: Dallas vs. Seattle, 2006

Devin Hester, SB: Chicago vs. Indianapolis, 2006

Eric Weems, NFC-D: Atlanta vs. Green Bay, 2010

Trindon Holliday, AFC-D: Denver vs. Baltimore, 2012 (2 ot)

Jacoby Jones, SB: Baltimore vs. San Francisco, 2012

FUMBLES

Most Fumbles, Career

16 Warren Moon, Houston-Minnesota, 10 games

14 John Elway, Denver, 22 games

Donovan McNabb, Philadelphia, 16 games

13 Tony Dorsett, Dallas, 17 games

Most Fumbles, Game

5 Warren Moon, AFC-D: Houston vs. Kansas City, 1993

4 Brian Sipe, AFC-D: Cleveland vs. Oakland, 1980

Randall Cunningham, NFC-FR: Minnesota vs. N.Y. Giants, 1997
3 By many players

RECOVERIES
Most Own Fumbles Recovered, Career
8 Warren Moon, Houston-Minnesota, 10 games
7 John Elway, Denver, 22 games
6 Jim Kelly, Buffalo, 17 games

Most Opponents' Fumbles Recovered, Career
4 Cliff Harris, Dallas, 21 games
Harvey Martin, Dallas, 22 games
Ted Hendricks, Baltimore-Oakland/L.A. Raiders, 21 games
Alvin Walton, Washington, 9 games
Monte Coleman, Washington, 21 games
Dave Thomas, Dallas-Jacksonville-N.Y. Giants, 13 games
3 Paul Krause, Minnesota, 19 games
Jack Lambert, Pittsburgh, 18 games
Fred Dryer, Los Angeles, 14 games
Charlie Waters, Dallas, 25 games
Jack Ham, Pittsburgh, 16 games
Mike Hegman, Dallas, 16 games
Tom Jackson, Denver, 10 games
Rich Milot, Washington, 13 games
Mike Singletary, Chicago, 12 games
Darryl Grant, Washington, 16 games
Wes Hopkins, Philadelphia, 3 games
Wilber Marshall, Chicago-Washington, 15 games
Tyrone Braxton, Denver-Miami-Denver, 19 games
Neil Smith, Kansas City-Denver, 16 games
Tony Brackens, Jacksonville, 7 games
Phil Hansen, Buffalo, 14 games
Carnell Lake, Pittsburgh-Jacksonville-Baltimore, 17 games
Jason Gildon, Pittsburgh, 13 games
Tedy Bruschi, New England, 22 games
Jim Leonhard, Baltimore-N.Y. Jets-Denver, 7 games
Clay Matthews, Green Bay, 8 games
2 By many players

Most Fumbles Recovered, Game, Own and Opponents'
3 Jack Lambert, AFC: Pittsburgh vs. Oakland, 1975 (3 opp)
Ron Jaworski, NFC-FR: Philadelphia vs. N.Y. Giants, 1981 (3 own)
Devin Hester, NFC-D: Chicago vs. Seattle, 2006 (3-own)
2 By many players

YARDS GAINED
Longest Return
93 Andy Russell, AFC-D: Pittsburgh vs. Baltimore, 1975 (opp, TD)
79 Neil Smith, AFC-D: Denver vs. Miami, 1998 (opp, TD)
64 Leon Lett, SB: Dallas vs. Buffalo, 1992 (opp)

TOUCHDOWNS
Most Touchdowns
1 By many players

COMBINED NET YARDS GAINED
Rushing, receiving, interception returns, punt returns, kickoff returns, and fumble returns.
ATTEMPTS
Most Attempts, Career
454 Franco Harris, Pittsburgh, 19 games
417 Thurman Thomas, Buffalo, 21 games
397 Emmitt Smith, Dallas, 17 games

Most Attempts, Game
43 Lamar Smith, AFC-FR: Miami vs. Indianapolis, 2000 (ot)
42 Curtis Martin, AFC-D: N.Y. Jets vs. Jacksonville, 1998
40 Lawrence McCutcheon, NFC-D: Los Angeles vs. St. Louis, 1975
Arian Foster, AFC-FR: Houston vs. Cincinnati, 2012

YARDS GAINED
Most Yards Gained, Career
2,289 Jerry Rice, San Francisco-Oakland-Seattle, 29 games
2,124 Thurman Thomas, Buffalo, 21 games
2,060 Franco Harris, Pittsburgh, 19 games
Most Yards Gained, Game
350 Ed Podolak, AFC-D: Kansas City vs. Miami, 1971 (ot)
329 Keith Lincoln, AFC: San Diego vs. Boston, 1963
328 Darren Sproles, AFC-FR: San Diego vs. Indianapolis, 2008 (ot)

SACKS
Sacks have been compiled since 1982.
Most Sacks, Career
16.0 Willie McGinest, New England, 18 games
14.5 Bruce Smith, Buffalo, 20 games
12.0 Reggie White, Philadelphia-Green Bay, 19 games
Terrell Suggs, Baltimore, 15 games
Most Sacks, Game
4.5 Willie McGinest, AFC-FR: New England vs. Jacksonville, 2005
3.5 Rich Milot, NFC-D: Washington vs. Chicago, 1984
Richard Dent, NFC-D: Chicago vs. N.Y. Giants, 1985
3.0 Richard Dent, NFC-D: Chicago vs. Washington, 1984
Garin Veris, AFC-FR: New England vs. N.Y. Jets, 1985
Gary Jeter, NFC-D: L.A. Rams vs. Dallas, 1985
Carl Hairston, AFC-D: Cleveland vs. N.Y. Jets, 1986 (ot)
Charles Mann, NFC-D: Washington vs. Chicago, 1987
Kevin Greene, NFC-FR: L.A. Rams vs. Minnesota, 1988
Greg Townsend, AFC-D: L.A. Raiders vs. Cincinnati, 1990
Wilber Marshall, NFC: Washington vs. Detroit, 1991
Fred Stokes, NFC-FR: Washington vs. Minnesota, 1992
Pierce Holt, NFC-D: San Francisco vs. Washington, 1992
Tony Casillas, NFC: Dallas vs. San Francisco, 1992
Gerald Williams, AFC-FR: Pittsburgh vs. Kansas City, 1993
Chad Brown, AFC-FR: Pittsburgh vs. Indianapolis, 1996
Reggie White, SB: Green Bay vs. New England, 1996
Warren Sapp, NFC-D: Tampa Bay vs. Green Bay, 1997
Trace Armstrong, AFC-FR: Miami vs. Seattle, 1999
Michael McCrary, AFC-FR: Baltimore vs. Denver, 2000
Willie McGinest, AFC-D: New England vs. Tennessee, 2003
Darnell Dockett, SB: Arizona vs. Pittsburgh, 2008
Ray Edwards, NFC-D: Minnesota vs. Dallas, 2009
James Harrison, AFC-D: Pittsburgh vs. Baltimore, 2010
Terrell Suggs, AFC-D: Baltimore vs. Pittsburgh, 2010

TEAM RECORDS

CHAMPIONSHIPS
Most Seasons League Champion
13 Green Bay, 1929-1931, 1936, 1939, 1944, 1961-62, 1965-67, 1996, 2010
9 Chi. Bears, 1921, 1932-33, 1940-41, 1943, 1946, 1963, 1985
8 N.Y. Giants, 1927, 1934, 1938, 1956, 1986, 1990, 2007, 2011
Most Consecutive Seasons League Champion
3 Green Bay, 1929-1931
Green Bay, 1965-67
2 Canton, 1922-23
Chi. Bears, 1932-33
Chi. Bears, 1940-41
Philadelphia, 1948-49
Detroit, 1952-53
Cleveland, 1954-55
Baltimore, 1958-59
Houston, 1960-61
Green Bay, 1961-62
Buffalo, 1964-65
Miami, 1972-73
Pittsburgh, 1974-75

Pittsburgh, 1978-79
San Francisco, 1988-89
Dallas, 1992-93
Denver, 1997-98
New England, 2003-04

GAMES, VICTORIES, DEFEATS

Most Seasons Participating in Postseason Games
- 31 N.Y. Giants, 1933-35, 1938-39, 1941, 1943-44, 1946, 1950, 1956, 1958-59, 1961-63, 1981, 1984-86, 1989-1990, 1993, 1997, 2000, 2002, 2005-08, 2011
- 30 Dallas, 1966-1973, 1975-1983, 1985, 1991-96, 1998-99, 2003, 2006-07, 2009
- 28 Green Bay, 1936, 1938-39, 1941, 1944, 1960-62, 1965-67, 1972, 1982, 1993-98, 2001-04, 2007, 2009-2012

Most Consecutive Seasons Participating in Postseason Games
- 9 Dallas, 1975-1983
  Indianapolis, 2002-2010
- 8 Dallas, 1966-1973
  Pittsburgh, 1972-79
  Los Angeles, 1973-1980
  San Francisco, 1983-1990
- 7 Houston, 1987-1993
  San Francisco, 1992-98

Most Games
- 58 Dallas, 1966-1973, 1975-1983, 1985, 1991-96, 1998-99, 2003, 2006-07, 2009
- 54 Pittsburgh, 1947, 1972-79, 1982-84, 1989, 1992-97, 2001-02, 2004-05, 2007-08, 2010-11
- 48 N.Y. Giants, 1933-35, 1938-39, 1941, 1943-44, 1946, 1950, 1956, 1958-59, 1961-63, 1981, 1984-86, 1989-1990, 1993, 1997, 2000, 2002, 2005-08, 2011
  Green Bay, 1936, 1938-39, 1941, 1944, 1960-62, 1965-67, 1972, 1982, 1993-98, 2001-04, 2007, 2009-2012

Most Games Won
- 33 Dallas, 1967, 1970-73, 1975, 1977-78, 1980-82, 1991-96, 2009
  Pittsburgh, 1972, 1974-76, 1978-79, 1984, 1989, 1994-97, 2001-02, 2004-05, 2008, 2010
- 30 Green Bay, 1936, 1939, 1944, 1961-62, 1965-67, 1982, 1993-97, 2001, 2003, 2007, 2010, 2012
- 28 San Francisco, 1970-71, 1981, 1983-84, 1988-1990, 1992-94, 1996-98, 2002, 2011-12

Most Consecutive Games Won
- 10 New England, 2001, 2003-05
- 9 Green Bay, 1961-62, 1965-67
- 7 Pittsburgh, 1974-76
  San Francisco, 1988-1990
  Dallas, 1992-94
  Denver, 1997-98

Most Games Lost
- 27 Minnesota, 1968-1971, 1973-78, 1980, 1982, 1987-89, 1992-94, 1996-2000, 2004, 2008-09, 2012
- 25 Dallas, 1966-1970, 1972-73, 1975-76, 1978-1983, 1985, 1991, 1994, 1996, 1998-99, 2003, 2006-07, 2009
- 24 L.A./St. Louis Rams, 1949-1950, 1952, 1955, 1967, 1969, 1973-1980, 1983-86, 1989, 2000-01, 2003-04
  N.Y. Giants, 1933, 1935, 1939, 1941, 1943-44, 1946, 1950, 1958-59, 1961-63, 1981, 1984-85, 1989, 1993, 1997, 2000, 2002, 2005-06, 2008

Most Consecutive Games Lost
- 7 Kansas City, 1993-95, 1997, 2003, 2006, 2010 (current)
  Detroit, 1991, 1993-95, 1997, 1999, 2011 (current)
- 6 N.Y. Giants, 1939, 1941, 1943-44, 1946, 1950
  Cleveland, 1969, 1971-72, 1980, 1982, 1985
  Minnesota, 1988-89, 1992-94, 1996
  Seattle, 1984, 1987-88, 1999, 2003-04
  Dallas, 1996, 1998-99, 2003, 2006-07
- 5 N.Y. Giants, 1958-59, 1961-63

Los Angeles, 1952, 1955, 1967, 1969, 1973
Denver, 1977-79, 1983-84
Baltimore/Indianapolis, 1971, 1975-77, 1987
Philadelphia, 1980-81, 1988-1990
Indianapolis, 1995-96, 1999-2000, 2002
Cincinnati, 1990, 2005, 2009, 2011-12 (current)

SCORING

Most Points, Game
- 73 NFC: Chi. Bears vs. Washington, 1940
- 62 AFC-D: Jacksonville vs. Miami, 1999
- 59 NFC: Detroit vs. Cleveland, 1957

Most Points, Both Teams, Game
- 96 NFC-FR: Arizona (51) vs. Green Bay (45), 2009
- 95 NFC-FR: Philadelphia (58) vs. Detroit (37), 1995
- 86 NFC-D: St. Louis (49) vs. Minnesota (37), 1999

Fewest Points, Both Teams, Game
- 5 NFC-D: Detroit (0) vs. Dallas (5), 1970
- 7 NFC: Chi. Cardinals (0) vs. Philadelphia (7), 1948
- 9 NFC: Tampa Bay (0) vs. Los Angeles (9), 1979

Largest Margin of Victory, Game
- 73 NFC: Chi. Bears vs. Washington, 1940 (73-0)
- 55 AFC-D: Jacksonville vs. Miami, 1999 (62-7)
- 49 AFC-D: Oakland vs. Houston, 1969 (56-7)

Most Points, Shutout Victory, Game
- 73 NFC: Chi. Bears vs. Washington, 1940
- 41 NFC: N.Y. Giants vs. Minnesota, 2000
  AFC-FR: N.Y. Jets vs. Indianapolis, 2002
- 38 NFC-D: Dallas vs. Tampa Bay, 1981

Most Points Overcome to Win Game
- 32 AFC-FR: Buffalo vs. Houston, 1992 (trailed 3-35, won 41-38) (ot)
- 24 NFC-FR: San Francisco vs. N.Y. Giants, 2002 (trailed 14-38, won 39-38)
- 20 NFC-D: Detroit vs. San Francisco, 1957 (trailed 7-27, won 31-27)

Most Points, Each Half

1st:
- 41 AFC: Buffalo vs. L.A. Raiders, 1990
  AFC-D: Jacksonville vs. Miami, 1999
- 38 NFC-D: Washington vs. L.A. Rams, 1983
  NFC-FR: Philadelphia vs. Detroit, 1995
- 35 NFC: Cleveland vs. Detroit, 1954
  AFC-D: Oakland vs. Houston, 1969
  SB: Washington vs. Denver, 1987
  AFC-FR: Indianapolis vs. Denver, 2004
  NFC-D: New Orleans vs. Arizona, 2009
  AFC-D: New England vs. Denver, 2011

2nd:
- 45 NFC: Chi. Bears vs. Washington, 1940
- 35 AFC-FR: Buffalo vs. Houston, 1992
  NFC-D: St. Louis vs. Minnesota, 1999
  NFC-FR: Green Bay vs. Arizona, 2009
  NFC-FR: New Orleans vs. Detroit, 2011
- 32 AFC: Indianapolis vs. New England, 2006

Most Points, Each Quarter

1st:
- 28 AFC-D: Oakland vs. Houston, 1969
- 24 AFC-D: San Diego vs. Miami, 1981
  AFC-D: Jacksonville vs. Miami, 1999
  AFC-D: Baltimore vs. New England, 2009
- 21 NFC: Chi. Bears vs. Washington, 1940
  AFC: San Diego vs. Boston, 1963
  AFC-D: Oakland vs. Kansas City, 1968
  AFC: Oakland vs. San Diego, 1980
  AFC: Buffalo vs. L.A. Raiders, 1990
  NFC: San Francisco vs. Dallas, 1994
  NFC-D: New Orleans vs. Arizona, 2009

2nd:
- 35 SB: Washington vs. Denver, 1987
- 31 NFC-FR: Philadelphia vs. Detroit, 1995
- 28 NFC-D: Green Bay vs. Atlanta, 2010

3rd:
- 28 AFC-FR: Buffalo vs. Houston, 1992
- 26 NFC: Chi. Bears vs. Washington, 1940
- 21 NFC-D: Dallas vs. Cleveland, 1967
  NFC-D: Dallas vs. Tampa Bay, 1981

AFC-D: L.A. Raiders vs. Pittsburgh, 1983
SB: Chicago vs. New England, 1985
NFC-D: N.Y. Giants vs. San Francisco, 1986
AFC: Cleveland vs. Denver, 1987
AFC: Cleveland vs. Denver, 1989
NFC-D: St. Louis vs. Minnesota, 1999

4th: 27   NFC: N.Y. Giants vs. Chi. Bears, 1934
       26   NFC-FR: Philadelphia vs. New Orleans, 1992
       24   NFC: Baltimore vs. N.Y. Giants, 1959
OT: 6   NFC: Baltimore vs. N.Y. Giants, 1958
          AFC-D: Oakland vs. Baltimore, 1977
          NFC-D: L.A. Rams vs. N.Y. Giants, 1989
          AFC-FR: Miami vs. Indianapolis, 2000
          NFC-FR: Green Bay vs. Seattle, 2003
          NFC-D: Carolina vs. St. Louis, 2003
          AFC-FR: San Diego vs. Indianapolis, 2008
          NFC-FR: Arizona vs. Green Bay, 2009
          AFC-FR: Denver vs. Pittsburgh, 2011

TOUCHDOWNS
Most Touchdowns, Game
11   NFC: Chi. Bears vs. Washington, 1940
8   NFC: Cleveland vs. Detroit, 1954
    NFC: Detroit vs. Cleveland, 1957
    AFC-D: Oakland vs. Houston, 1969
    SB: San Francisco vs. Denver, 1989
    AFC-D: Jacksonville vs. Miami, 1999
7   AFC: San Diego vs. Boston, 1963
    NFC-D: Dallas vs. Cleveland, 1967
    NFC-D: N.Y. Giants vs. San Francisco, 1986
    AFC: Buffalo vs. L.A. Raiders, 1990
    SB: Dallas vs. Buffalo, 1992
    SB: San Francisco vs. San Diego, 1994
    NFC-FR: Philadelphia vs. Detroit, 1995
    NFC-D: St. Louis vs. Minnesota, 1999
    AFC-FR: Indianapolis vs. Denver, 2004
    NFC-FR: Arizona vs. Green Bay, 2009 (ot)

Most Touchdowns, Both Teams, Game
13   NFC-FR: Arizona (7) vs. Green Bay (6), 2009 (ot)
12   NFC-FR: Philadelphia (7) vs. Detroit (5), 1995
    NFC-D: St. Louis (7) vs. Minnesota (5), 1999
11   NFC: Chi. Bears (11) vs. Washington (0), 1940

Fewest Touchdowns, Both Teams, Game
0   NFC-D: N.Y. Giants vs. Cleveland, 1950
    NFC-D: Dallas vs. Detroit, 1970
    NFC: Los Angeles vs. Tampa Bay, 1979
    AFC-D: Baltimore vs. Indianapolis, 2006
1   NFC: Chi. Cardinals (0) vs. Philadelphia (1), 1948
    NFC-D: Cleveland (0) vs. N.Y. Giants (1), 1958
    AFC: San Diego (0) vs. Houston (1), 1961
    AFC-D: N.Y. Jets (0) vs. Kansas City (1), 1969
    NFC-D: Green Bay (0) vs. Washington (1), 1972
    NFC-FR: New Orleans (0) vs. Chicago (1), 1990
    NFC: N.Y. Giants (0) vs. San Francisco (1), 1990
    AFC-FR: L.A. Raiders (0) vs. Kansas City (1), 1991
    AFC-D: New England (0) vs. Pittsburgh (1), 1997
    NFC: Tampa Bay (0) vs. St. Louis (1), 1999
    AFC: Oakland (0) vs. Baltimore (1), 2000
2   In many games

POINTS AFTER TOUCHDOWN
Most (One-Point) Points After Touchdown, Game
8   NFC: Cleveland vs. Detroit, 1954
    NFC: Detroit vs. Cleveland, 1957
    AFC-D: Oakland vs. Houston, 1969
    AFC-D: Jacksonville vs. Miami, 1999
7   NFC: Chi. Bears vs. Washington, 1940
    NFC-D: Dallas vs. Cleveland, 1967
    NFC-D: N.Y. Giants vs. San Francisco, 1986
    SB: San Francisco vs. Denver, 1989
    SB: Dallas vs. Buffalo, 1992
    SB: San Francisco vs. San Diego, 1994

NFC-FR: Philadelphia vs. Detroit, 1995
NFC-D: St. Louis vs. Minnesota, 1999
AFC-FR: Indianapolis vs. Denver, 2004
6   AFC: San Diego vs. Boston, 1963
    NFC-D: Washington vs. L.A. Rams, 1983
    AFC: Miami vs. Pittsburgh, 1984
    SB: Washington vs. Denver, 1987
    AFC: Buffalo vs. L.A. Raiders, 1990
    AFC-FR: L.A. Raiders vs. Denver, 1993
    AFC-FR: Denver vs. Jacksonville, 1997
    NFC-D: St. Louis vs. Green Bay, 2001
    SB: Tampa Bay vs. Oakland, 2002
    NFC-D: Atlanta vs. St. Louis, 2004
    NFC-FR: Green Bay vs. Seattle, 2007
    NFC-FR: Arizona vs. Green Bay, 2009 (ot)
    NFC-FR: Green Bay vs. Arizona, 2009 (ot)
    NFC-D: New Orleans vs. Arizona, 2009
    NFC-D: Green Bay vs. Atlanta, 2010
    NFC-FR: New Orleans vs. Detroit, 2011
    AFC-D: New England vs. Denver, 2011
    NFC-D: San Francisco vs. Green Bay, 2012

Most (One-Point) Points After Touchdown, Both Teams, Game
12   NFC-FR: Arizona (6) vs. Green Bay (6), 2009
10   NFC: Detroit (8) vs. Cleveland (2), 1957
    AFC-D: Miami (5) vs. San Diego (5), 1981 (ot)
    AFC: Miami (6) vs. Pittsburgh (4), 1984
    AFC-FR: Buffalo (5) vs. Houston (5), 1992 (ot)
    NFC-FR: Philadelphia (7) vs. Detroit (3), 1995
    AFC-FR: Indianapolis (7) vs. Denver (3), 2004
    NFC-FR: New Orleans (6) vs. Detroit (4), 2011
    AFC-D: Baltimore (5) vs. Denver (5), 2012
    NFC-D: San Francisco (6) vs. Green Bay (4), 2012
9   In many games

Fewest (One-Point) Points After Touchdown, Both Teams, Game
0   NFC-D: N.Y. Giants vs. Cleveland, 1950
    NFC-D: Dallas vs. Detroit, 1970
    NFC: Los Angeles vs. Tampa Bay, 1979
    NFC: St. Louis vs. Tampa Bay, 1999
    AFC-D: Baltimore vs. Indianapolis, 2006

Most Two-Point Conversions, Game
2   SB: San Diego vs. San Francisco, 1994
    NFC-FR: Detroit vs. Philadelphia, 1995
    NFC-FR: San Francisco vs.. N.Y. Giants, 2002
1   By many teams

FIELD GOALS
Most Field Goals, Game
5   NFC-D: Minnesota vs. San Francisco, 1987
    NFC: N.Y. Giants vs. San Francisco, 1990
    AFC: Buffalo vs. Miami, 1992
    NFC-FR: N.Y. Giants vs. Minnesota, 1997
    NFC-FR: Carolina vs. Dallas, 2003
    NFC-D: St. Louis vs. Carolina, 2003 (2 ot)
    AFC: New England vs. Indianapolis, 2003
    AFC-D: Indianapolis vs. Baltimore, 2006
4   AFC-D: Boston vs. Buffalo, 1963
    AFC: Oakland vs. Houston, 1967
    SB: Green Bay vs. Oakland, 1967
    NFC: Washington vs. Dallas, 1972
    AFC-D: Oakland vs. Pittsburgh, 1973
    SB: San Francisco vs. Cincinnati, 1981
    AFC-FR: New England vs. N.Y. Jets, 1985
    NFC-FR: Washington vs. L.A. Rams, 1986
    NFC-D: Philadelphia vs. Chicago, 1988
    AFC-FR: Pittsburgh vs. Houston, 1989 (ot)
    AFC-D: Pittsburgh vs. Buffalo, 1995
    NFC-FR: Dallas vs. Minnesota, 1996
    NFC-D: Carolina vs. Dallas, 1996
    AFC-FR: Jacksonville vs. New England, 1998
    AFC-D: Tennessee vs. Indianapolis, 1999
    NFC-D: Philadelphia vs. Chicago, 2001
    AFC: San Diego vs. New England, 2007

NFC-FR: Philadelphia vs. Minnesota, 2008
NFC-D: Arizona vs. Carolina, 2008
AFC-FR: Houston vs. Cincinnati, 2012
  3 By many teams

Most Field Goals, Both Teams, Game
  8 NFC-FR: N.Y. Giants (5) vs. Minnesota (3), 1997
NFC-D: St. Louis (5) vs. Carolina (3), 2003 (2 ot)
  7 AFC-FR: Pittsburgh (4) vs. Houston (3), 1989 (ot)
NFC: N.Y. Giants (5) vs. San Francisco (2), 1990
NFC-D: Carolina (4) vs. Dallas (3), 1996
AFC-D: Tennessee (4) vs. Indianapolis (3), 1999
AFC-D: Indianapolis (5) vs. Baltimore (2), 2006
  6 NFC-D: Minnesota (5) vs. San Francisco (1), 1987
NFC-D: Philadelphia (4) vs. Chicago (2), 1988
AFC: Buffalo (5) vs. Miami (1), 1992
NFC-FR: Carolina (5) vs. Dallas (1), 2003
AFC-FR: New England (3) vs. N.Y. Jets (3), 2006
NFC-D: N.Y. Giants (3) vs. Philadelphia (3), 2008
AFC-FR: Denver (3) vs. Pittsburgh (3), 2011 (ot)
AFC-FR: Houston (4) vs. Cincinnati (2), 2012

Most Field Goals Attempted, Game
  6 AFC: Oakland vs. Houston, 1967
NFC-D: Los Angeles vs. Dallas, 1973
AFC-D: Cleveland vs. N.Y. Jets, 1986 (ot)
NFC: N.Y. Giants vs. San Francisco, 1990
AFC: Buffalo vs. Miami, 1992
NFC-D: St. Louis vs. Carolina, 2003 (2 ot)
  5 By many teams

Most Field Goals Attempted, Both Teams, Game
 11 NFC-D: St. Louis (6) vs. Carolina (5), 2003 (2 ot)
  9 NFC-D: Philadelphia (5) vs. Chicago (4), 1988
NFC-FR: N.Y. Giants (5) vs. Minnesota (4), 1997
  8 NFC-D: Los Angeles (6) vs. Dallas (2), 1973
NFC-D: Detroit (5) vs. San Francisco (3), 1983
AFC-D: Cleveland (6) vs. N.Y. Jets (2), 1986 (ot)
NFC-D: Minnesota (5) vs. San Francisco (3), 1987
AFC-FR: Houston (4) vs. Pittsburgh (4), 1989 (ot)
NFC-FR: Chicago (4) vs. New Orleans (4), 1990
NFC: N.Y. Giants (6) vs. San Francisco (2), 1990
NFC-D: N.Y. Giants (5) vs. Philadelphia (3), 2008

SAFETIES

Most Safeties, Game
  1 By many teams

Most Safeties, Both Teams, Game
  1 In many games

FIRST DOWNS

Most First Downs, Game
 34 AFC-D: San Diego vs. Miami, 1981 (ot)
NFC-FR: New Orleans vs. Detroit, 2011
 33 AFC-D: Cleveland vs. N.Y. Jets, 1986 (ot)
 32 AFC: Indianapolis vs. New England, 2006
NFC-FR: Green Bay vs. Arizona, 2009 (ot)
NFC-FR: New Orleans vs. Seattle, 2010

Fewest First Downs, Game
  6 NFC: N.Y. Giants vs. Green Bay, 1961
AFC-D: Baltimore vs. Tennessee, 2000
  7 NFC: Green Bay vs. Boston, 1936
NFC-D: Pittsburgh vs. Philadelphia, 1947
NFC: Chi. Cardinals vs. Philadelphia, 1948
NFC: Los Angeles vs. Philadelphia, 1949
NFC-D: Cleveland vs. N.Y. Giants, 1958
AFC-D: Cincinnati vs. Baltimore, 1970
NFC-D: Detroit vs. Dallas, 1970
NFC: Tampa Bay vs. Los Angeles, 1979
AFC-D: Baltimore vs. Pittsburgh, 2001
AFC-FR: Kansas City vs. Indianapolis, 2006
  8 By many teams

Most First Downs, Both Teams, Game
 62 NFC-FR: Green Bay (32) vs. Arizona (30), 2009 (ot)
 59 AFC-D: San Diego (34) vs. Miami (25), 1981 (ot)

 56 NFC-FR: New Orleans (34) vs. Detroit (22), 2011

Fewest First Downs, Both Teams, Game
 15 NFC: Green Bay (7) vs. Boston (8), 1936
 19 N.Y. Giants (9) vs. Green Bay (10), 1939
NFC: Washington (9) vs. Chi. Bears (10), 1942
 20 NFC-D: Cleveland (9) vs. N.Y. Giants (11), 1950

RUSHING

Most First Downs, Rushing, Game
 19 NFC-FR: Dallas vs. Los Angeles, 1980
 18 AFC-D: Miami vs. Cincinnati, 1973
AFC: Miami vs. Oakland, 1973
AFC-D: Pittsburgh vs. Buffalo, 1974
AFC-FR: Buffalo vs. Miami, 1995
AFC-FR: Denver vs. Jacksonville, 1997
 17 AFC-D: Cincinnati vs. Seattle, 1988
AFC: Buffalo vs. Kansas City, 1993

Fewest First Downs, Rushing, Game
  0 NFC: Los Angeles vs. Philadelphia, 1949
AFC-D: Buffalo vs. Boston, 1963
AFC: Oakland vs. Pittsburgh, 1974
NFC-FR: New Orleans vs. Minnesota, 1987
NFC: L.A. Rams vs. San Francisco, 1989
NFC-D: Chicago vs. N.Y. Giants, 1990
AFC-FR: Indianapolis vs. Pittsburgh, 1996
AFC-FR: Seattle vs. Miami, 1999
AFC-D: Miami vs. Jacksonville, 1999
AFC-D: Miami vs. Oakland, 2000
AFC-D: Baltimore vs. Pittsburgh, 2001
AFC-D: Indianapolis vs. New England, 2004
NFC-FR: Philadelphia vs. Dallas, 2009
  1 By many teams

Most First Downs, Rushing, Both Teams, Game
 26 AFC: Buffalo (14) vs. L.A. Raiders (12), 1990
 25 NFC-FR: Dallas (19) vs. Los Angeles (6), 1980
 23 NFC: Cleveland (15) vs. Detroit (8), 1952
AFC-D: Miami (18) vs. Cincinnati (5), 1973
AFC-D: Pittsburgh (18) vs. Buffalo (5), 1974
AFC-FR: Buffalo (18) vs. Miami (5), 1995

Fewest First Downs, Rushing, Both Teams, Game
  2 NFC-FR: New Orleans (1) vs. St. Louis (1), 2000
  5 AFC-D: Buffalo (0) vs. Boston (5), 1963
NFC-D: Washington (1) vs. Tampa Bay (4), 1999
AFC-FR: Cleveland (2) vs. Pittsburgh (3), 2002
AFC-D: Baltimore (2) vs. Indianapolis (3), 2009
  6 NFC: Green Bay (2) vs. Boston (4), 1936
NFC-D: Baltimore (2) vs. Minnesota (4), 1968
AFC-D: Houston (1) vs. Oakland (5), 1969
AFC-FR: N.Y. Jets (1) vs. Houston (5), 1991
AFC-FR: Denver (1) vs. Baltimore (5), 2000
AFC: Pittsburgh (1) vs. Baltimore (5), 2008
SB: Arizona (2) vs. Pittsburgh (4), 2008

PASSING

Most First Downs, Passing, Game
 24 AFC-FR: Pittsburgh vs. Cleveland, 2002
 23 NFC-D: New Orleans vs. San Francisco, 2011
 22 NFC-FR: New Orleans vs. Seattle, 2010

Fewest First Downs, Passing, Game
  0 NFC: Philadelphia vs. Chi. Cardinals, 1948
  1 NFC-D: N.Y. Giants vs. Washington, 1943
NFC: Cleveland vs. Detroit, 1953
SB: Denver vs. Dallas, 1977
  2 By many teams

Most First Downs, Passing, Both Teams, Game
 42 AFC-D: Miami (21) vs. San Diego (21), 1981 (ot)
AFC-FR: Pittsburgh (24) vs. Cleveland (18), 2002
 40 NFC-FR: New Orleans (20) vs. Detroit (20), 2011
 38 AFC-FR: Pittsburgh (19) vs. San Diego (19), 1982
NFC-D: Minnesota (20) vs. St. Louis (18), 1999
NFC-FR: Arizona (21) vs. Green Bay (17), 2009 (ot)

Fewest First Downs, Passing, Both Teams, Game
- 2 NFC: Philadelphia (0) vs. Chi. Cardinals (2), 1948
- 4 NFC-D: Cleveland (2) vs. N.Y. Giants (2), 1950
- 5 NFC: Detroit (2) vs. N.Y. Giants (3), 1935
  NFC: Green Bay (2) vs. N.Y. Giants (3), 1939

PENALTY
Most First Downs, Penalty, Game
- 7 AFC-D: New England vs. Oakland, 1976
  AFC: Tennessee vs. Oakland, 2002
- 6 AFC-D: Cleveland vs. N.Y. Jets, 1986 (ot)
  NFC-D: Chicago vs. Carolina, 2005
  NFC-FR: Green Bay vs. Arizona, 2009 (ot)
  AFC-D: Denver vs. Baltimore, 2012 (2 ot)
- 5 AFC-FR: Cleveland vs. L. A. Raiders, 1982
  NFC-D: San Francisco vs. Minnesota, 1997
  AFC-FR: Miami vs. Buffalo, 1998
  NFC-D: Arizona vs. Minnesota, 1998
  AFC: Pittsburgh vs. New England, 2001
  AFC-D: Pittsburgh vs. Tennessee, 2002 (ot)
  AFC-FR: Cincinnati vs. N.Y. Jets, 2009
Most First Downs, Penalty, Both Teams, Game
- 10 AFC: Tennessee (7) vs. Oakland (3), 2002
- 9 AFC-D: New England (7) vs. Oakland (2), 1976
  AFC-D: Denver (6) vs. Baltimore (3), 2012 (2 ot)
- 8 NFC-FR: Atlanta (4) vs. Minnesota (4), 1982
  AFC-FR: Miami (5) vs. Buffalo (3), 1998
  NFC-FR: Dallas (4) vs. Philadelphia (4), 2009
  NFC-FR: Green Bay (6) vs. Arizona (2), 2009 (ot)

NET YARDS GAINED RUSHING AND PASSING
Most Yards Gained, Game
- 626 NFC-FR: New Orleans vs. Detroit, 2011
- 610 AFC: San Diego vs. Boston, 1963
- 602 SB: Washington vs. Denver, 1987
Fewest Yards Gained, Game
- 86 NFC-D: Cleveland vs. N.Y. Giants, 1958
- 99 NFC: Chi. Cardinals vs. Philadelphia, 1948
- 112 NFC-D: N.Y. Giants vs. Washington, 1943
Most Yards Gained, Both Teams, Game
- 1,038 AFC-FR: Buffalo (536) vs. Miami (502), 1995
  NFC-FR: New Orleans (626) vs. Detroit (412), 2011
- 1,036 AFC-D: San Diego (564) vs. Miami (472), 1981 (ot)
- 1,024 AFC: Miami (569) vs. Pittsburgh (455), 1984
  NFC-FR: Arizona (531) vs. Green Bay (493), 2009 (ot)
Fewest Yards Gained, Both Teams, Game
- 331 NFC: Chi. Cardinals (99) vs. Philadelphia (232), 1948
- 332 NFC-D: N.Y. Giants (150) vs. Cleveland (182), 1950
- 336 NFC: Boston (116) vs. Green Bay (220), 1936

RUSHING
ATTEMPTS
Most Attempts, Game
- 65 NFC: Detroit vs. N.Y. Giants, 1935
- 61 NFC: Philadelphia vs. Los Angeles, 1949
- 59 AFC: New England vs. Miami, 1985
Fewest Attempts, Game
- 8 AFC-D: Miami vs. San Diego, 1994
- 9 SB: Miami vs. San Francisco, 1984
  NFC: Minnesota vs. N.Y. Giants, 2000
- 10 NFC: L.A. Rams vs. San Francisco, 1989
  NFC-FR: Atlanta vs. Green Bay, 1995
  NFC-FR: Detroit vs. Washington, 1999
  NFC-FR: Detroit vs. New Orleans, 2011
Most Attempts, Both Teams, Game
- 109 NFC: Detroit (65) vs. N.Y. Giants (44), 1935
- 97 AFC-D: Baltimore (50) vs. Oakland (47), 1977 (ot)
- 91 NFC: Philadelphia (57) vs. Chi. Cardinals (34), 1948
Fewest Attempts, Both Teams, Game
- 32 AFC-D: Houston (14) vs. Kansas City (18), 1993
- 36 SB: Green Bay (13) vs. Pittsburgh (23), 2010
  NFC-D: New Orleans (14) vs. San Francisco (22), 2011

- 37 SB: Arizona (12) vs. Pittsburgh (25), 2008
  SB: New Orleans (18) vs. Indianapolis (19), 2009

YARDS GAINED
Most Yards Gained, Game
- 382 NFC: Chi. Bears vs. Washington, 1940
- 341 AFC-FR: Buffalo vs. Miami, 1995
- 338 NFC-FR: Dallas vs. Los Angeles, 1980
Fewest Yards Gained, Game
- – 4 NFC-FR: Detroit vs. Green Bay, 1994
- 7 AFC-D: Buffalo vs. Boston, 1963
  SB: New England vs. Chicago, 1985
- 14 AFC-D: Miami vs. Denver, 1998
  AFC: N.Y. Jets vs. Denver, 1998
Most Yards Gained, Both Teams, Game
- 430 NFC-FR: Dallas (338) vs. Los Angeles (92), 1980
- 427 NFC-D: San Francisco (323) vs. Green Bay (104), 2012
- 426 NFC: Cleveland (227) vs. Detroit (199), 1952
Fewest Yards Gained, Both Teams, Game
- 77 NFC-FR: Detroit (–4) vs. Green Bay (81), 1994
- 84 NFC-FR: St. Louis (34) vs. New Orleans (50), 2000
- 90 AFC-D: Buffalo (7) vs. Boston (83), 1963
  NFC-D: Tampa Bay (44) vs. Washington (46), 1999

AVERAGE GAIN
Highest Average Gain, Game
- 9.94 AFC: San Diego vs. Boston, 1963 (32-318)
- 9.29 NFC-D: Green Bay vs. Dallas, 1982 (17-158)
- 8.18 NFC-D: Atlanta vs. St. Louis, 2004 (40-327)
Lowest Average Gain, Game
- – 0.27 NFC-FR: Detroit vs. Green Bay, 1994 (15-(– 4))
- 0.58 AFC-D: Buffalo vs. Boston, 1963 (12-7)
- 0.64 SB: New England vs. Chicago, 1985 (11-7)

TOUCHDOWNS
Most Touchdowns, Game
- 7 NFC: Chi. Bears vs. Washington, 1940
- 6 NFC-D: San Francisco vs. N.Y. Giants, 1993
- 5 NFC: Cleveland vs. Detroit, 1954
  NFC-D: San Francisco vs. Chicago, 1994
  AFC-FR: Pittsburgh vs. Indianapolis, 1996
  AFC-FR: Denver vs. Jacksonville, 1997
Most Touchdowns, Both Teams, Game
- 7 NFC: Chi. Bears (7) vs. Washington (0), 1940
- 6 NFC: Cleveland (5) vs. Detroit (1), 1954
  NFC-D: San Francisco (6) vs. N.Y. Giants (0), 1993
  NFC-D: San Francisco (5) vs. Chicago (1), 1994
  AFC-FR: Denver (5) vs. Jacksonville (1), 1997
- 5 NFC: Chi. Cardinals (3) vs. Philadelphia (2), 1947
  AFC: San Diego (4) vs. Boston (1), 1963
  AFC-D: Cincinnati (3) vs. Buffalo (2), 1981
  AFC-FR: Pittsburgh (5) vs. Indianapolis (0), 1996
  NFC-D: Arizona (3) vs. Minnesota (2), 1998
  NFC-FR: Seattle (3) vs. Green Bay (2), 2003 (ot)
  NFC-D: San Francisco (4) vs. Green Bay (1), 2012

PASSING
ATTEMPTS
Most Attempts, Game
- 66 AFC-FR: Miami vs. Buffalo, 1995
- 65 AFC-D: Cleveland vs. N.Y. Jets, 1986 (ot)
  NFC-D: San Francisco vs. Green Bay, 1995
- 63 NFC-D: New Orleans vs. San Francisco, 2011
Fewest Attempts, Game
- 5 NFC: Detroit vs. N.Y. Giants, 1935
- 6 AFC: Miami vs. Oakland, 1973
- 7 SB: Miami vs. Minnesota, 1973
Most Attempts, Both Teams, Game
- 105 NFC-D: New Orleans (63) vs. San Francisco (42), 2011
- 102 AFC-D: San Diego (54) vs. Miami (48), 1981 (ot)
- 96 AFC: N.Y. Jets (49) vs. Oakland (47), 1968

Fewest Attempts, Both Teams, Game
- 18 NFC: Detroit (5) vs. N.Y. Giants (13), 1935
- 23 NFC: Chi. Cardinals (11) vs. Philadelphia (12), 1948
- 24 NFC-D: Cleveland (9) vs. N.Y. Giants (15), 1950

COMPLETIONS
Most Completions, Game
- 40 NFC-D: New Orleans vs. San Francisco, 2011
- 39 NFC-FR: New Orleans vs. Seattle, 2010
- 36 AFC-FR: Houston vs. Buffalo, 1992 (ot)

Fewest Completions, Game
- 2 NFC: Detroit vs. N.Y. Giants, 1935
- NFC: Philadelphia vs. Chi. Cardinals, 1948
- 3 NFC: N.Y. Giants vs. Chi. Bears, 1941
- NFC: Green Bay vs. N.Y. Giants, 1944
- NFC: Chi. Cardinals vs. Philadelphia, 1947
- NFC: Chi. Cardinals vs. Philadelphia, 1948
- NFC-D: Cleveland vs. N.Y. Giants, 1950
- NFC-D: N.Y. Giants vs. Cleveland, 1950
- NFC: Cleveland vs. Detroit, 1953
- AFC: Miami vs. Oakland, 1973
- 4 NFC: N.Y. Giants vs. Detroit, 1935
- NFC-D: N.Y. Giants vs. Washington, 1943
- NFC-D: Pittsburgh vs. Philadelphia, 1947
- NFC-D: Dallas vs. Detroit, 1970
- AFC: Miami vs. Baltimore, 1971
- SB: Miami vs. Washington, 1982
- AFC-FR: Seattle vs. L.A. Raiders, 1984
- AFC-FR: Baltimore vs. New England, 2009

Most Completions, Both Teams, Game
- 64 AFC-D: San Diego (33) vs. Miami (31), 1981 (ot)
- NFC-D: New Orleans (40) vs. San Francisco (24), 2011
- 63 SB: New Orleans (32) vs. Indianapolis (31), 2009
- 61 NFC-FR: New Orleans (39) vs. Seattle (22), 2010
- NFC-FR: New Orleans (33) vs. Detroit (28), 2011

Fewest Completions, Both Teams, Game
- 5 NFC: Philadelphia (2) vs. Chi. Cardinals (3), 1948
- 6 NFC: Detroit (2) vs. N.Y. Giants (4), 1935
- NFC-D: Cleveland (3) vs. N.Y. Giants (3), 1950
- 11 NFC: Green Bay (3) vs. N.Y. Giants (8), 1944
- NFC-D: Dallas (4) vs. Detroit (7), 1970

COMPLETION PERCENTAGE
Highest Completion Percentage, Game (20 attempts)
- 92.9 AFC-D: New England vs. Jacksonville, 2007 (28-26)
- 88.0 SB: N.Y. Giants vs. Denver, 1986 (25-22)
- 87.9 NFC-FR: Arizona vs. Green Bay, 2009 (33-29) (ot)

Lowest Completion Percentage, Game (20 attempts)
- 18.5 NFC: Tampa Bay vs. Los Angeles, 1979 (27-5)
- 20.0 NFC-D: N.Y. Giants vs. Washington, 1943 (20-4)
- 25.8 NFC: Chi. Bears vs. Washington, 1937 (31-8)

YARDS GAINED
Most Yards Gained, Game
- 483 AFC-D: Cleveland vs. N.Y. Jets, 1986 (ot)
- 459 NFC-FR: New Orleans vs. Detroit, 2011
- 454 AFC-FR: Indianapolis vs. Denver, 2004

Fewest Yards Gained, Game
- 3 NFC: Chi. Cardinals vs. Philadelphia, 1948
- 7 NFC: Philadelphia vs. Chi. Cardinals, 1948
- 9 NFC-D: N.Y. Giants vs. Cleveland, 1950
- NFC: Cleveland vs. Detroit, 1953

Most Yards Gained, Both Teams, Game
- 839 New Orleans (459) vs. Detroit (380), 2011
- 809 AFC-D: San Diego (415) vs. Miami (394), 1981 (ot)
- 779 NFC-FR: Green Bay (404) vs. Arizona (375), 2009 (ot)

Fewest Yards Gained, Both Teams, Game
- 10 NFC: Chi. Cardinals (3) vs. Philadelphia (7), 1948
- 38 NFC-D: N.Y. Giants (9) vs. Cleveland (29), 1950
- 102 NFC-D: Dallas (22) vs. Detroit (80), 1970

TIMES SACKED
Most Times Sacked, Game
- 9 AFC: Kansas City vs. Buffalo, 1966
- NFC: Chicago vs. San Francisco, 1984
- AFC-D: N.Y. Jets vs. Cleveland, 1986 (ot)
- AFC-D: Houston vs. Kansas City, 1993
- 8 NFC: Green Bay vs. Dallas, 1967
- NFC: Minnesota vs. Washington, 1987
- NFC-D: Philadelphia vs. Green Bay, 2003 (ot)
- 7 NFC-D: Dallas vs. Los Angeles, 1973
- SB: Dallas vs. Pittsburgh, 1975
- AFC-FR: Houston vs. Oakland, 1980
- NFC-D: Washington vs. Chicago, 1984
- SB: New England vs. Chicago, 1985
- AFC-FR: Kansas City vs. San Diego, 1992
- AFC-D: Pittsburgh vs. Buffalo, 1992

Most Times Sacked, Both Teams, Game
- 13 AFC: Kansas City (9) vs. Buffalo (4), 1966
- AFC-D: N.Y. Jets (9) vs. Cleveland (4), 1986 (ot)
- 12 NFC-D: Dallas (7) vs. Los Angeles (5), 1973
- NFC-D: Washington (7) vs. Chicago (5), 1984
- NFC: Chicago (9) vs. San Francisco (3), 1984
- AFC-FR: Kansas City (7) vs. San Diego (5), 1992
- 11 AFC-D: Houston (9) vs. Kansas City (2), 1993
- AFC-D: Pittsburgh (6) vs. Baltimore (5), 2010

Fewest Times Sacked, Both Teams, Game
- 0 AFC-D: Buffalo vs. Pittsburgh, 1974
- AFC-FR: Pittsburgh vs. San Diego, 1982
- AFC: Miami vs. Pittsburgh, 1984
- AFC-D: Buffalo vs. Miami, 1990
- AFC-D: Denver vs. Houston, 1991
- AFC-FR: Buffalo vs. Miami, 1995
- AFC-D: Indianapolis vs. Tennessee, 1999
- AFC-D: Indianapolis vs. San Diego, 2007
- NFC-D: N.Y. Giants vs. Philadelphia, 2008
- 1 In many games

TOUCHDOWNS
Most Touchdowns, Game
- 6 AFC-D: Oakland vs. Houston, 1969
- SB: San Francisco vs. San Diego, 1994
- AFC-D: New England vs. Denver, 2011
- 5 NFC: Chi. Bears vs. Washington, 1943
- NFC: Detroit vs. Cleveland, 1957
- AFC-D: Oakland vs. Kansas City, 1968
- SB: San Francisco vs. Denver, 1989
- NFC: St. Louis vs. Minnesota, 1999
- NFC: N.Y. Giants vs. Minnesota, 2000
- AFC-FR: Indianapolis vs. Denver, 2003
- NFC-FR: Arizona vs. Green Bay, 2009 (ot)
- 4 By many teams

Most Touchdowns, Both Teams, Game
- 9 NFC-D: St. Louis (5) vs. Minnesota (4), 1999
- NFC-FR: Arizona (5) vs. Green Bay (4), 2009 (ot)
- 8 AFC-FR: Buffalo (4) vs. Houston (4), 1992 (ot)
- 7 NFC: Chi. Bears (5) vs. Washington (2), 1943
- AFC-D: Oakland (6) vs. Houston (1), 1969
- SB: Pittsburgh (4) vs. Dallas (3), 1978
- AFC-D: Miami (4) vs. San Diego (3), 1981 (ot)
- AFC: Miami (4) vs. Pittsburgh (3), 1984
- AFC-D: Buffalo (4) vs. Cleveland (3), 1989
- SB: San Francisco (6) vs. San Diego (1), 1994
- NFC-FR: Detroit (4) vs. Philadelphia (3), 1995
- NFC-FR: New Orleans (4) vs. St. Louis (3), 2000
- NFC-FR: N.Y. Giants (4) vs. San Francisco (3), 2002
- NFC: Arizona (4) vs. Philadelphia (3), 2008
- NFC-D: New Orleans (4) vs. San Francisco (3), 2011

INTERCEPTIONS BY
Most Interceptions By, Game
- 8 NFC: Chi. Bears vs. Washington, 1940
- 7 NFC: Cleveland vs. Los Angeles, 1955

6   NFC: Green Bay vs. N.Y. Giants, 1939
      NFC: Chi. Bears vs. N.Y. Giants, 1946
      NFC: Cleveland vs. Detroit, 1954
      AFC: San Diego vs. Houston, 1961
      AFC: Buffalo vs. L.A. Raiders, 1990
      NFC-FR: Philadelphia vs. Detroit, 1995
      NFC-D: St. Louis vs. Green Bay, 2001

Most Interceptions By, Both Teams, Game
10   NFC: Cleveland (7) vs. Los Angeles (3), 1955
      AFC: San Diego (6) vs. Houston (4), 1961
9   NFC: Green Bay (6) vs. N.Y. Giants (3), 1939
8   NFC: Chi. Bears (8) vs. Washington (0), 1940
      NFC: Chi. Bears (6) vs. N.Y. Giants (2), 1946
      NFC: Cleveland (6) vs. Detroit (2), 1954
      AFC-FR: Buffalo (4) vs. N.Y. Jets (4), 1981
      AFC: Miami (5) vs. N.Y. Jets (3), 1982

YARDS GAINED
Most Yards Gained, Game
172   SB: Tampa Bay vs. Oakland, 2002
161   NFC-D: St. Louis vs. Green Bay, 2001
138   AFC-FR: N.Y. Jets vs. Cincinnati, 1982
Most Yards Gained, Both Teams, Game
184   SB: Tampa Bay (172) vs. Oakland (12), 2002
161   NFC-D: St. Louis (161) vs. Green Bay (0), 2001
149   NFC: Cleveland (103) vs. Los Angeles (46), 1955

TOUCHDOWNS
Most Touchdowns, Game
3   NFC: Chi. Bears vs. Washington, 1940
      NFC-D: St. Louis vs. Green Bay, 2001
      SB: Tampa Bay vs. Oakland, 2002
2   NFC-D: Los Angeles vs. St. Louis, 1975
      NFC-FR: Philadelphia vs. Detroit, 1995)
      NFC-FR: Seattle vs. Washington, 2007
1   In many games
Most Touchdowns, Both Teams, Game
3   NFC: Chi. Bears (3) vs. Washington (0), 1940
      NFC-D: St. Louis (3) vs. Green Bay (0), 2001
      SB: Tampa Bay (3) vs. Oakland (0), 2002
2   NFC-D: Los Angeles (2) vs. St. Louis (0), 1975
      NFC-D: Dallas (1) vs. Green Bay (1), 1982
      NFC-D: Minnesota (1) vs. San Francisco (1), 1987
      NFC-FR: Detroit (1) vs. Green Bay (1), 1993
      NFC-FR: Philadelphia (2) vs. Detroit (0), 1995
      AFC-FR: Buffalo (1) vs. Jacksonville (1), 1996)
      NFC-FR: Seattle (2) vs. Washington (0), 2007
1   In many games

PUNTING
Most Punts, Game
14   AFC-D: N.Y. Jets vs. Cleveland, 1986 (ot)
13   NFC: N.Y. Giants vs. Chi. Bears, 1933
      AFC-D: Baltimore vs. Oakland, 1977 (ot)
12   NFC: N.Y. Giants vs. San Francisco, 2011 (ot)
Fewest Punts, Game
0   NFC-FR: St. Louis vs. Green Bay, 1982
      AFC-FR: N.Y. Jets vs. Cincinnati, 1982
      AFC-FR: Indianapolis vs. Denver, 2003
      AFC-D: Kansas City vs. Indianapolis, 2003
      AFC-D: Indianapolis vs. Kansas City, 2003
      NFC-D: Green Bay vs. Atlanta, 2010
      NFC-FR: New Orleans vs. Detroit, 2011
1   By many teams
Most Punts, Both Teams, Game
23   NFC: N.Y. Giants (13) vs. Chi. Bears (10), 1933
22   AFC-D: N.Y. Jets (14) vs. Cleveland (8), 1986 (ot)
      NFC: N.Y. Giants (12) vs. San Francisco (10), 2011 (ot)
21   AFC-D: Baltimore (13) vs. Oakland (8), 1977 (ot)
      NFC: L.A. Rams (11) vs. Chicago (10), 1985
      SB: N.Y. Giants (11) vs. Baltimore (10), 2000

Fewest Punts, Both Teams, Game
0   AFC-D: Kansas City vs. Indianapolis, 2003
1   NFC-FR: St. Louis (0) vs. Green Bay (1), 1982
2   AFC-FR: N.Y. Jets (0) vs. Cincinnati (2), 1982
      SB: Atlanta (1) vs. Denver (1), 1998
      AFC-D: Indianapolis (0) vs. Denver (2), 2003
      AFC-D: New England (1) vs. Jacksonville (1), 2007
      NFC-FR: Arizona (1) vs. Green Bay (1), 2009 (ot)

AVERAGE YARDAGE
Highest Average, Punting, Game (4 punts)
56.0   AFC: Oakland vs. San Diego, 1980
53.8   AFC-D: Baltimore vs. Pittsburgh, 2010
53.3   AFC-D: Tennessee vs. Baltimore, 2008
Lowest Average, Punting, Game (4 punts)
24.9   NFC: Washington vs. Chi. Bears, 1937
25.3   AFC-FR: Pittsburgh vs. Houston, 1989
25.5   NFC: Green Bay vs. N.Y. Giants, 1962

PUNT RETURNS
Most Punt Returns, Game
8   NFC: Green Bay vs. N.Y. Giants, 1944
      NFC: San Francisco vs. N.Y. Giants, 2011 (ot)
7   By many teams
Most Punt Returns, Both Teams, Game
14   NFC: San Francisco (8) vs. N.Y. Giants (6), 2011 (ot)
13   AFC-FR: Houston (7) vs. Oakland (6), 1980
12   AFC-D: New England (7) vs. Pittsburgh (5), 1996
Fewest Punt Returns, Both Teams, Game
0   NFC: Chi. Bears vs. N.Y. Giants, 1941
      AFC: Boston vs. San Diego, 1963
      NFC-FR: Green Bay vs. St. Louis, 1982
      AFC-FR: Houston vs. N.Y. Jets, 1991
      AFC-D: Denver vs. Houston, 1991
      NFC-D: San Francisco vs. Washington, 1992
      SB: Denver vs. Green Bay, 1997
      SB: Atlanta vs. Denver, 1998
      AFC-FR: Oakland vs. N.Y. Jets, 2001
      AFC-D: N.Y. Jets vs. Oakland, 2002
      AFC-FR: Denver vs. Indianapolis, 2003
      NFC-D: Carolina vs. St. Louis, 2003
      AFC-D: Indianapolis vs. Kansas City, 2003
      AFC-FR: Kansas City vs. Baltimore, 2010
      NFC-D: Atlanta vs. Green Bay, 2010
1   In many games

YARDS GAINED
Most Yards Gained, Game
155   NFC-D: Dallas vs. Cleveland, 1967
152   NFC-D: Atlanta vs. St. Louis, 2004
150   NFC: Chi. Cardinals vs. Philadelphia, 1947
Fewest Yards Gained, Game
−10   NFC: Green Bay vs. Cleveland, 1965
−9   NFC: Dallas vs. Green Bay, 1966
      AFC: Kansas City vs. Oakland, 1968
−7   NFC-D: San Francisco vs. Atlanta, 1998
Most Yards Gained, Both Teams, Game
166   NFC-D: Dallas (155) vs. Cleveland (11), 1967
      AFC-D: Baltimore (99) vs. Pittsburgh (67), 2001
160   NFC: Chi. Cardinals (150) vs. Philadelphia (10), 1947
152   NFC-D: Atlanta (152) vs. St. Louis (0), 2004
Fewest Yards Gained, Both Teams, Game
−9   NFC: Dallas (−9) vs. Green Bay (0), 1966
−6   AFC-D: Miami (−5) vs. Oakland (−1), 1970
−3   NFC-D: San Francisco (−5) vs. Dallas (2), 1972

TOUCHDOWNS
Most Touchdowns, Game
1   By 21 teams

KICKOFF RETURNS

Most Kickoff Returns, Game

- 10 NFC-D: L.A. Rams vs. Washington, 1983
  - NFC-FR: Detroit vs. Philadelphia, 1995
- 9 NFC: Chi. Bears vs. N.Y. Giants, 1956
  - AFC: Boston vs. San Diego, 1963
  - AFC: Houston vs. Oakland, 1967
  - SB: Denver vs. San Francisco, 1989
  - AFC-D: Miami vs. Buffalo, 1990
  - AFC: L.A. Raiders vs. Buffalo, 1990
  - AFC-D: Miami vs. Jacksonville, 1999
  - SB: Oakland vs. Tampa Bay, 2002
- 8 By many teams

Most Kickoff Returns, Both Teams, Game

- 15 AFC-D: Miami (9) vs. Buffalo (6), 1990
- 14 NFC-FR: Detroit (10) vs. Philadelphia (4), 1995
- 13 NFC-D: Green Bay (7) vs. Dallas (6), 1982
  - NFC-FR: Green Bay (7) vs. San Francisco (6), 1998
  - AFC-FR: N.Y. Jets (8) vs. Oakland (5), 2001
  - NFC-FR: San Francisco (7) vs. N.Y. Giants (6), 2002
  - AFC-D: Tennessee (7) vs. Pittsburgh (6), 2002
  - SB: Oakland (9) vs. Tampa Bay (4), 2002
  - NFC-FR: Seattle (7) vs. Green Bay (6), 2003 (ot)
  - AFC-D: Kansas City (7) vs. Indianapolis (6), 2003
  - AFC: Pittsburgh (8) vs. New England (5), 2004
  - AFC: New England (8) vs. Indianapolis (5), 2006

Fewest Kickoff Returns, Both Teams, Game

- 1 NFC: Green Bay (0) vs. Boston (1), 1936
  - AFC-FR: San Diego (0) vs. Kansas City (1), 1992
  - AFC-FR: Houston (0) vs. Cincinnati (1), 2011
  - AFC-FR: Pittsburgh (0) vs. Denver (1), 2011 (ot)
- 2 NFC-D: Los Angeles (0) vs. Chi. Bears (2), 1950
  - AFC: Houston (0) vs. San Diego (2), 1961
  - AFC-D: Oakland (1) vs. Pittsburgh (1), 1972
  - AFC-D: N.Y. Jets (0) vs. L.A. Raiders (2), 1982
  - AFC: Miami (1) vs. N.Y. Jets (1), 1982
  - NFC: N.Y. Giants (0) vs. Washington (2), 1986
  - AFC-FR: Indianapolis (0) vs. Baltimore (2), 2012
- 3 In many games

YARDS GAINED

Most Yards Gained, Game

- 244 SB: San Diego vs. San Francisco, 1994
- 232 NFC-D: Atlanta vs. Green Bay, 2010
- 231 AFC: New England vs. Indianapolis, 2006

Most Yards Gained, Both Teams, Game

- 379 AFC-D: Baltimore (193) vs. Oakland (186), 1977 (ot)
- 348 NFC-D: Minnesota (174) vs. St. Louis (174), 1999
- 323 AFC-D: New England (231) vs. Indianapolis (92), 2006

Fewest Yards Gained, Both Teams, Game

- 5 AFC-FR: San Diego (0) vs. Kansas City (5), 1992
- 15 NFC: N.Y. Giants (0) vs. Washington (15), 1986
- 19 AFC-FR: Pittsburgh (0) vs. Denver (19), 2011 (ot)

TOUCHDOWNS

Most Touchdowns, Game

- 1 NFC-D: San Francisco vs. Dallas, 1972
  - AFC-D: Miami vs. Oakland, 1974
  - AFC-D: Baltimore vs. Oakland, 1977 (ot)
  - SB: Miami vs. Washington, 1982
  - SB: Cincinnati vs. San Francisco, 1988
  - AFC-D: Cleveland vs. Buffalo, 1989
  - SB: San Diego vs. San Francisco, 1994
  - SB: Green Bay vs. New England, 1996
  - NFC: San Francisco vs. Green Bay, 1997
  - SB: Atlanta vs. Denver, 1998
  - AFC-FR: Tennessee vs. Buffalo, 1999
  - AFC-FR: Seattle vs. Miami, 1999
  - NFC-D: Washington vs. Tampa Bay, 1999
  - NFC-D: St. Louis vs. Minnesota, 1999
  - AFC: Tennessee vs. Jacksonville, 1999
  - NFC-D: N.Y. Giants vs. Philadelphia, 2000

- SB: Baltimore vs. N.Y. Giants, 2000
- SB: N.Y. Giants vs. Baltimore, 2000
- AFC-D: Kansas City vs. Indianapolis, 2003
- NFC-FR: Dallas vs. Seattle, 2006
- SB: Chicago vs. Indianapolis, 2006
- NFC-FR: Dallas vs. Seattle, 2006
- NFC-D: Atlanta vs. Green Bay, 2010
- AFC-D: Denver vs. Baltimore, 2012 (2 ot)
- SB: Baltimore vs. San Francisco, 2012

Most Touchdowns, Both Teams, Game

- 2 SB: Baltimore (1) vs. N.Y. Giants (1), 2000

PENALTIES

Most Penalties, Game

- 17 AFC-FR: L.A. Raiders vs. Denver, 1993
- 14 AFC-FR: Oakland vs. Houston, 1980
  - NFC-D: San Francisco vs. N.Y. Giants, 1981
  - AFC: Oakland vs. Tennessee, 2002
  - NFC-FR: Dallas vs. Philadelphia, 2009
- 13 AFC-FR: Houston vs. Cleveland, 1988
  - AFC-D: Houston vs. Denver, 1991
  - NFC-D: Arizona vs. Minnesota, 1998
  - NFC-D: Carolina vs. St. Louis, 2003 (2 ot)

Fewest Penalties, Game

- 0 NFC: Philadelphia vs. Green Bay, 1960
  - NFC-D: Detroit vs. Dallas, 1970
  - AFC-D: Miami vs. Oakland, 1970
  - SB: Miami vs. Dallas, 1971
  - NFC-D: Washington vs. Minnesota, 1973
  - SB: Pittsburgh vs. Dallas, 1975
  - NFC: San Francisco vs. Chicago, 1988
  - SB: Denver vs. San Francisco, 1989
  - AFC-D: L.A. Raiders vs. Cincinnati, 1990
  - AFC-D: Miami vs. San Diego, 1992
  - SB: Atlanta vs. Denver, 1998
  - AFC-FR: N.Y. Jets vs. Oakland, 2001
  - NFC-FR: Carolina vs. Dallas, 2003
  - NFC-D: New Orleans vs. San Francisco, 2011
  - AFC-D: Baltimore vs. Houston, 2011
- 1 By many teams

Most Penalties, Both Teams, Game

- 27 AFC-FR: L.A. Raiders (17) vs. Denver (10), 1993
- 23 NFC-FR: Dallas (14) vs. Philadelphia (9), 2009
- 22 AFC-FR: Oakland (14) vs. Houston (8), 1980
  - NFC-D: San Francisco (14) vs. N.Y. Giants (8), 1981
  - AFC-FR: Houston (13) vs. Cleveland (9), 1988
  - NFC-D: Arizona (13) vs. Minnesota (9), 1998

Fewest Penalties, Both Teams, Game

- 1 AFC-D: L.A. Raiders (0) vs. Cincinnati (1), 1990
- 2 NFC: Washington (1) vs. Chi. Bears (1), 1937
  - NFC-D: Washington (0) vs. Minnesota (2), 1973
  - SB: Pittsburgh (0) vs. Dallas (2), 1975
  - NFC-FR: Carolina (0) vs. Dallas (2), 2003
- 3 AFC: Miami (1) vs. Baltimore (2), 1971
  - NFC: San Francisco (1) vs. Dallas (2), 1971
  - SB: Miami (0) vs. Dallas (3), 1971
  - AFC-D: Pittsburgh (1) vs. Oakland (2), 1972
  - AFC-D: Miami (1) vs. Cincinnati (2), 1973
  - SB: Miami (1) vs. San Francisco (2), 1984
  - NFC: San Francisco (0) vs. Chicago (3), 1988
  - AFC: New England (1) vs. Pittsburgh (2), 2004
  - AFC: San Diego (1) vs. New England (2), 2007
  - NFC-D: New Orleans (0) vs. San Francisco (3), 2011
  - AFC-D: Baltimore (0) vs. Houston (3), 2011

YARDS PENALIZED

Most Yards Penalized, Game

- 145 NFC-D: San Francisco vs. N.Y. Giants, 1981
- 133 SB: Dallas vs. Baltimore, 1970
- 130 AFC-FR: L.A. Raiders vs. Denver, 1993

Fewest Yards Penalized, Game

- 0 By many teams

Most Yards Penalized, Both Teams, Game
- 228 NFC-FR: Philadelphia (116) vs. Dallas (112), 2009
- 227 AFC-FR: L.A. Raiders (130) vs. Denver (97), 1993
- 206 NFC-D: San Francisco (145) vs. N.Y. Giants (61), 1981

Fewest Yards Penalized, Both Teams, Game
- 5 AFC-D: L.A. Raiders (0) vs. Cincinnati (5), 1990
- 9 NFC-D: Washington (0) vs. Minnesota (9), 1973
- 11 NFC-FR: Carolina (0) vs. Dallas (11), 2003

FUMBLES

Most Fumbles, Game
- 8 SB: Buffalo vs. Dallas, 1992
- 7 AFC-D: Houston vs. Kansas City, 1993
- 6 By 13 teams

Most Fumbles, Both Teams, Game
- 12 AFC: Houston (6) vs. Pittsburgh (6), 1978
  SB: Buffalo (8) vs. Dallas (4), 1992
- 10 NFC: Chi. Bears (5) vs. N.Y. Giants (5), 1934
  SB: Dallas (6) vs. Denver (4), 1977
  AFC: Jacksonville (5) vs. Tennessee (5), 1999
- 9 NFC-D: San Francisco (6) vs. Detroit (3), 1957
  NFC-D: San Francisco (5) vs. Dallas (4), 1972
  NFC: Dallas (5) vs. Philadelphia (4), 1980
  NFC: Minnesota (6) vs. New Orleans (3), 2009 (OT)

Most Fumbles Lost, Game
- 5 SB: Buffalo vs. Dallas, 1992
  AFC-D: Miami vs. Jacksonville, 1999
- 4 NFC: N.Y. Giants vs. Baltimore, 1958 (ot)
  AFC: Kansas City vs. Oakland, 1969
  SB: Baltimore vs. Dallas, 1970
  AFC: Pittsburgh vs. Oakland, 1975
  SB: Denver vs. Dallas, 1977
  AFC: Houston vs. Pittsburgh, 1978
  AFC: Miami vs. New England, 1985
  SB: New England vs. Chicago, 1985
  NFC-FR: L.A. Rams vs. Washington, 1986
  NFC-FR: Minnesota vs. Dallas, 1996
  AFC-FR: Buffalo vs. Miami, 1998
  AFC: N.Y. Jets vs. Denver, 1998
  AFC: Jacksonville vs. Tennessee, 1999
- 3 By many teams

Fewest Fumbles, Both Teams, Game
- 0 NFC: Green Bay vs. Cleveland, 1965
  AFC-D: Houston vs. San Diego, 1979
  NFC-D: Dallas vs. Los Angeles, 1979
  SB: Los Angeles vs. Pittsburgh, 1979
  AFC-D: Buffalo vs. Cincinnati, 1981
  NFC: Minnesota vs. Washington, 1987
  NFC-D: San Francisco vs. Washington, 1990
  NFC: Dallas vs. Green Bay, 1995
  AFC-D: New England vs. Pittsburgh, 1996
  SB: Green Bay vs. New England, 1996
  AFC-FR: Miami vs. Seattle, 1999
  AFC-FR: Miami vs. Indianapolis, 2000 (ot)
  AFC-D: Baltimore vs. Tennessee, 2000
  SB: Pittsburgh vs. Seattle, 2005
  SB: Indianapolis vs. New Orleans, 2009
  NFC-FR: N.Y. Giants vs. Atlanta, 2011
- 1 In many games

RECOVERIES

Most Total Fumbles Recovered, Game
- 8 SB: Dallas vs. Denver, 1977 (4 own, 4 opp)
- 7 NFC: Chi. Bears vs. N.Y. Giants, 1934 (5 own, 2 opp)
  NFC-D: San Francisco vs. Detroit, 1957 (4 own, 3 opp)
  NFC-D: San Francisco vs. Dallas, 1972 (4 own, 3 opp)
  AFC: Pittsburgh vs. Houston, 1978 (3 own, 4 opp)
- 6 AFC: Houston vs. San Diego, 1961 (4 own, 2 opp)
  AFC-D: Cleveland vs. Baltimore, 1971 (4 own, 2 opp)
  AFC-D: Cleveland vs. Oakland, 1980 (5 own, 1 opp)
  NFC: Philadelphia vs. Dallas, 1980 (3 own, 3 opp)
  SB: Dallas vs. Buffalo, 1992 (1 own, 5 opp)

NFC-D: Green Bay vs. San Francisco, 1996 (4 own, 2 opp)
  AFC: Denver vs. N.Y. Jets, 1998 (2 own, 4 opp)
  AFC: Tennessee vs. Jacksonville, 1999 (2 own, 4 opp)

Most Own Fumbles Recovered, Game
- 5 NFC: Chi. Bears vs. N.Y. Giants, 1934
  AFC-D: Cleveland vs. Oakland, 1980
- 4 By many teams

TOUCHDOWNS

Most Touchdowns, Game
- 2 SB: Dallas vs. Buffalo, 1992

TURNOVERS

Numbers of times losing the ball on interceptions and fumbles.

Most Turnovers, Game
- 9 NFC: Washington vs. Chi. Bears, 1940
  NFC: Detroit vs. Cleveland, 1954
  AFC: Houston vs. Pittsburgh, 1978
  SB: Buffalo vs. Dallas, 1992
- 8 NFC: N.Y. Giants vs. Chi. Bears, 1946
  NFC: Los Angeles vs. Cleveland, 1955
  NFC: Cleveland vs. Detroit, 1957
  SB: Denver vs. Dallas, 1977
  NFC-D: Minnesota vs. Philadelphia, 1980
  NFC-D: Green Bay vs. St. Louis, 2001
- 7 In many games

Fewest Turnovers, Game
- 0 By many teams

Most Turnovers, Both Teams, Game
- 14 AFC: Houston (9) vs. Pittsburgh (5), 1978
- 13 NFC: Detroit (9) vs. Cleveland (4), 1954
  AFC: Houston (7) vs. San Diego (6), 1961
- 12 AFC: Pittsburgh (7) vs. Oakland (5), 1975

Fewest Turnovers, Both Teams, Game
- 0 SB: Buffalo vs. N.Y. Giants, 1990
  AFC-FR: Kansas City vs. Pittsburgh, 1993 (ot)
  NFC-FR: Detroit vs. Green Bay, 1994
  AFC-FR: Denver vs. Jacksonville, 1996
  SB: St. Louis vs. Tennessee, 1999
  NFC-FR: N.Y. Giants vs. Atlanta, 2011
- 1 AFC-D: Baltimore (0) vs. Cincinnati (1), 1970
  AFC-D: Pittsburgh (0) vs. Buffalo (1), 1974
  AFC: Oakland (0) vs. Pittsburgh (1), 1976
  NFC-D: Minnesota (0) vs. Washington (1), 1982
  NFC-D: Chicago (0) vs. N.Y. Giants (1), 1985
  SB: N.Y. Giants (0) vs. Denver (1), 1986
  NFC: Washington (0) vs. Minnesota (1), 1987
  AFC-D: Cincinnati (0) vs. L.A. Raiders (1), 1990
  NFC: N.Y. Giants (0) vs. San Francisco (1), 1990
  NFC-FR: N.Y. Giants (0) vs. Minnesota (1), 1993
  AFC-FR: L.A. Raiders (0) vs. Denver (1), 1993
  NFC: Dallas (0) vs. San Francisco (1), 1993
  AFC: Indianapolis (0) vs. Pittsburgh (1), 1995
  NFC-D: San Francisco (0) vs. Minnesota (1), 1997
  AFC-D: Indianapolis (0) vs. Tennessee (1), 1999
  AFC-FR: Baltimore (0) vs. Denver (1), 2000
  AFC-D: Baltimore (0) vs. Tennessee (1), 2000
  AFC-D: Oakland (0) vs. New England (1), 2001
  NFC-FR: Green Bay (0) vs. Seattle (1), 2003 (ot)
  AFC-D: Indianapolis (0) vs. Kansas City (1), 2003
  AFC-FR: N.Y. Jets (0) vs. San Diego (1), 2004 (ot)
  NFC: Philadelphia (0) vs. Atlanta (1), 2004
  NFC-FR: Philadelphia (0) vs. N.Y. Giants (1), 2006
  NFC-D: Philadelphia (0) vs. New Orleans (1), 2006
  NFC-D: N.Y. Giants (0) vs. Dallas (1), 2007
  SB: New Orleans (0) vs. Indianapolis (1), 2009
  AFC-FR: Indianapolis (0) vs. N.Y. Jets (1), 2010
  NFC-D: Seattle (0) vs. Chicago (1), 2010
  AFC-D: N.Y. Jets (0) vs. New England (1), 2010
  SB: N.Y. Giants (0) vs. New England (1), 2011
  AFC-D: New England (0) vs. Houston (1), 2012
- 2 In many games

Rules

2013 NFL ROSTER OF OFFICIALS AS OF MAY 2013

Dean Blandino, Vice President of Officiating
Alberto Riveron, Senior Director of Officiating
David Coleman, Director of Officiating
Ed Coukart, Supervisor of Officials

Neely Dunn, Supervisor of Officials
Johnny Grier, Supervisor of Officials
Gary Slaughter, Supervisor of Officials

No.	Name	Position	College	No.	Name	Position	College
20	Anderson, Barry	Field Judge	North Carolina State	77	McAulay, Terry	Referee	Louisiana State
66	Anderson, Walt	Referee	Texas	5	McGrath, John	Head Linesman	Kentucky
108	Arthur, Gary	Line Judge	Wright State	8	McKenzie, Dana	Head Linesman	Toledo
26	Baltz, Mark	Head Linesman	Ohio	110	McKinnely, Phil	Head Linesman	UCLA
72	Banks, Michael	Side Judge	Illinois State	48	Mello, Jim	Head Linesman	Northeastern
56	Baynes, Allen	Side Judge	Auburn	118	Meslow, David	Field Judge	Augsburg College
59	Baynes, Rusty	Line Judge	Auburn-Montgomery	78	Meyer, Greg	Side Judge	Texas Christian
32	Bergman, Jeff	Line Judge	Robert Morris	115	Michalek, Tony	Umpire	Indiana
91	Bergman, Jerry	Head Linesman	Robert Morris	111	Miles, Terrence	Back Judge	Arizona State
34	Blakeman, Clete	Referee	Nebraska	135	Morelli, Pete	Referee	St. Mary's
23	Boger, Jerome	Referee	Morehouse College	124	Paganelli, Carl	Umpire	Michigan State
18	Boston, Byron	Line Judge	Austin	105	Paganelli, Dino	Back Judge	Aquinas College
74	Bowers, Derick	Head Linesman	East Central	46	Paganelli, Perry	Back Judge	Hope College
98	Bradley, Greg	Head Linesman	Tennessee	87	Parham, Keith	Side Judge	Howard
31	Brown, Chad	Umpire	East Texas State	132	Parry, John	Referee	Purdue
43	Brown, Terry	Field Judge	Tennessee-Knoxville	15	Patterson, Rick	Side Judge	Wofford
11	Bryan, Fred	Umpire	Northern Iowa	79	Payne, Kent	Head Linesman	Nebraska Wesleyan
86	Buchanan, Jimmy	Field Judge	South Carolina State	9	Perlman, Mark	Line Judge	Salem
134	Camp, Ed	Head Linesman	William Paterson	47	Podraza, Tim	Line Judge	Nebraska
126	Carey, Don	Back Judge	California-Riverside	109	Prioleau, Dyrol	Field Judge	Johnson C. Smith
94	Carey, Mike	Referee	Santa Clara	30	Prukop, Todd	Back Judge	Cal State-Fullerton
60	Cavaletto, Gary	Field Judge	Hancock	63	Quirk, Jim	Back Judge	Middlebury
41	Cheek, Boris	Field Judge	Morgan State	44	Rice, Jeff	Umpire	Northwestern
51	Cheffers, Carl	Referee	California-Irvine	128	Rose, Larry	Side Judge	Florida
95	Coleman, James	Side Judge	Arkansas	67	Rosenbaum, Doug	Field Judge	Illinois Wesleyan
65	Coleman, Walt	Referee	Arkansas	129	Schuster, Bill	Umpire	Alfred
99	Corrente, Tony	Referee	Cal State-Fullerton	45	Seeman, Jeff	Line Judge	Minnesota
70	Dawson, Scott	Umpire	Virginia Tech	104	Shaw, Dale	Back Judge	Allegheny
58	DeBell, Jimmy	Side Judge	SUNY-Brockport	2	Smith, Billy	Back Judge	East Carolina
53	DeFelice, Garth	Umpire	San Diego State	90	Spanier, Mike	Line Judge	St. Cloud State
6	Dornan, Kirk	Back Judge	Central Washington	24	Stabile, Tom	Head Linesman	Slippery Rock
27	Dyer, Lee	Back Judge	Tennessee-Chattanooga	12	Steed, Greg	Back Judge	Howard
3	Edwards, Scott	Field Judge	Alabama	88	Steenson, Scott	Field Judge	North Texas
81	Ellison, Roy	Umpire	Savannah State	84	Steinkerchner, Mark	Line Judge	Akron
61	Ferguson, Keith	Back Judge	San Jose State	22	Stelljes, Steve	Head Linesman	Friends
64	Ferrell, Dan	Umpire	Cal State-Fullerton	68	Stephan, Tom	Line Judge	Pittsburg State
71	Fowler, Ruben	Umpire	Huston-Tillotson	114	Steratore, Gene	Referee	Kent State
133	Freeman, Steve	Back Judge	Mississippi State	112	Steratore, Tony	Back Judge	California
80	Gautreaux, Greg	Field Judge	S.W. Louisiana	102	Stritesky, Bruce	Umpire	Embry Riddle
19	Green, Scott	Referee	Delaware	100	Symonette, Tom	Line Judge	Florida
49	Hall, Rich	Umpire	Arizona	62	Torbert, Ronald	Side Judge	Michigan State
40	Hannah, Butch	Umpire	Middle Tennessee State	42	Triplette, Jeff	Referee	Wake Forest
125	Hayes, Laird	Side Judge	Princeton	75	Vernatchi, Rob	Side Judge	California-Riverside
54	Hayward, George	Head Linesman	Missouri Western	36	Veteri, Tony	Head Linesman	Manhattan College
93	Helverson, Scott	Back Judge	Iowa	52	Vinovich, Bill	Referee	San Diego
29	Hill, Adrian	Line Judge	Buffalo	25	Waggoner, Bob	Field Judge	Juniata College
97	Hill, Tom	Side Judge	Carson Newman	96	Wash, Undrey	Umpire	Texas-Arlington
28	Hittner, Mark	Head Linesman	Pittsburg State	7	Washington, Keith	Side Judge	Virginia Military Institute
85	Hochuli, Ed	Referee	Texas-El Paso	116	Weatherford, Mike	Side Judge	Oklahoma State
82	Horton, Buddy	Field Judge	Oregon State	50	Weir, Mike	Field Judge	Missouri
37	Howey, Jim	Field Judge	Erskine College	119	Wilson, Greg	Back Judge	USC
35	Hussey, John	Line Judge	Idaho State	14	Winter, Ron	Referee	Michigan State
76	Jenkins, Darrell	Umpire	San Jose State	4	Wrolstad, Craig	Field Judge	Washington
101	Johnson, Carl	Line Judge	Nicholls State	16	Wyant, David	Side Judge	Virginia
121	King, Paul	Umpire	Nicholls State	38	Yette, Greg	Back Judge	Howard
103	Lamberth, Jeff	Side Judge	Texas A&M	33	Zimmer, Steve	Field Judge	Hofstra
73	Larrew, Joe	Side Judge	St. Louis				
127	Leavy, Bill	Referee	San Jose State		*Roster as of May 2013*		
130	Lewis, Darryll	Line Judge	Dartmouth				
89	Lucivansky, Jon	Field Judge	Minnesota				
106	Mackie, Wayne	Head Linesman	Colgate				
10	Mapp, Julian	Head Linesman	Grambling State				
107	Marinucci, Ron	Line Judge	Glassboro State				

NUMERICAL ROSTER

No.	Name	Position
2	Billy Smith	BJ
3	Scott Edwards	FJ
4	Craig Wrolstad	FJ
5	John McGrath	HL
6	Kirk Dornan	BJ
7	Keith Washington	SJ
8	Dana McKenzie	HL
9	Mark Perlman	LJ
10	Julian Mapp	HL
11	Fred Bryan	U
12	Greg Steed	BJ
14	Ron Winter	R
15	Rick Patterson	SJ
16	David Wyant	SJ
18	Byron Boston	LJ
19	Scott Green	R
20	Barry Anderson	FJ
22	Steve Stelljes	HL
23	Jerome Boger	R
24	Tom Stabile	HL
25	Bob Waggoner	FJ
26	Mark Baltz	HL
27	Lee Dyer	BJ
28	Mark Hittner	HL
29	Adrian Hill	LJ
30	Todd Prukop	BJ
31	Chad Brown	U
32	Jeff Bergman	LJ
33	Steve Zimmer	FJ
34	Clete Blakeman	R
35	John Hussey	LJ
36	Tony Veteri	HL
37	Jim Howey	FJ
38	Greg Yette	BJ
40	Butch Hannah	U
41	Boris Cheek	FJ
42	Jeff Triplette	R
43	Terry Brown	FJ
44	Jeff Rice	U
45	Jeff Seeman	LJ
46	Perry Paganelli	BJ
47	Tim Podraza	LJ
48	Jim Mello	HL
49	Rich Hall	U
50	Mike Weir	FJ
51	Carl Cheffers	R
52	Bill Vinovich	R
53	Garth DeFelice	U
54	George Hayward	HL
56	Allen Baynes	SJ
58	Jimmy DeBell	SJ
59	Rusty Baynes	LJ
60	Gary Cavaletto	FJ
61	Keith Ferguson	BJ
62	Ronald Torbert	SJ
63	Jim Quirk	BJ
64	Dan Ferrell	U
65	Walt Coleman	R
66	Walt Anderson	R
67	Doug Rosenbaum	FJ
68	Tom Stephan	LJ
70	Scott Dawson	U
71	Ruben Fowler	U
72	Michael Banks	SJ
73	Joe Larrew	SJ
74	Derick Bowers	HL
75	Rob Vernatchi	SJ
76	Darrell Jenkins	U
77	Terry McAulay	R
78	Greg Meyer	SJ
79	Kent Payne	HL
80	Greg Gautreaux	FJ
81	Roy Ellison	U
82	Buddy Horton	FJ
84	Mark Steinkerchner	LJ
85	Ed Hochuli	R
86	Jimmy Buchanan	FJ
87	Keith Parham	SJ
88	Scott Steenson	FJ
89	Jon Lucivansky	FJ
90	Mike Spanier	LJ
91	Jerry Bergman	HL
93	Scott Helverson	BJ
94	Mike Carey	R
95	James Coleman	SJ
96	Undrey Wash	U
97	Tom Hill	SJ
98	Greg Bradley	HL
99	Tony Corrente	R
100	Tom Symonette	LJ
101	Carl Johnson	LJ
102	Bruce Stritesky	U
103	Jeff Lamberth	SJ
104	Dale Shaw	BJ
105	Dino Paganelli	BJ
106	Wayne Mackie	HL
107	Ron Marinucci	LJ
108	Gary Arthur	LJ
109	Dyrol Prioleau	FJ
110	Phil McKinnely	HL
111	Terrence Miles	BJ
112	Tony Steratore	BJ
114	Gene Steratore	R
115	Tony Michalek	U
116	Mike Weatherford	SJ
118	David Meslow	FJ
119	Greg Wilson	BJ
121	Paul King	U
124	Carl Paganelli	U
125	Laird Hayes	SJ
126	Don Carey	BJ
127	Bill Leavy	R
128	Larry Rose	SJ
129	Bill Schuster	U
130	Darryll Lewis	LJ
132	John Parry	R
133	Steve Freeman	BJ
134	Ed Camp	HL
135	Pete Morelli	R

Roster as of May 2013

2013 OFFICIALS AT A GLANCE
REFEREES
Walt Anderson, No. **66,** Texas, college officiating coordinator, retired dentist, 18th year.

Clete Blakeman, No. **34,** Nebraska, attorney, 6th year.

Jerome Boger, No. **23,** Morehouse College, commercial insurance underwriter, 10th year.

Mike Carey, No. **94,** Santa Clara, owner, skiing accessories, 24th year.

Carl Cheffers, No. **51,** California-Irvine, sales manager, 14th year.

Walt Coleman, No. **65,** Arkansas, manager dairy processor, 25th year.

Tony Corrente, No. **99,** Cal State-Fullerton, educator, 19th year.

Scott Green, No. **19,** Delaware, president, government support services, 23rd year.

Ed Hochuli, No. **85,** Texas-El Paso, attorney, 24th year.

Bill Leavy, No. **127,** San Jose State, retired firefighter, 19th year.

Terry McAulay, No. **77,** Louisiana State, college officiating coordinator, 16th year.

Pete Morelli, No. **135,** St. Mary's, high school principal, 17th year.

John Parry, No. **132,** Purdue, financial advisor, 14th year.

Gene Steratore, No. **114,** Kent State, co-owner, supply company, 11th year.

Jeff Triplette, No. **42,** Wake Forest, restructuring consultant, 18th year.

Bill Vinovich, No. **52,** San Diego, certified public accountant, 8th year.

Ron Winter, No. **14,** Michigan State, university professor, 19th year.

UMPIRES
Chad Brown, No. **31,** East Texas State, executive manager of facilities/student affairs administration, 22nd year.

Fred Bryan, No. **11,** Northern Iowa, superintendent, juvenile correctional facility, 5th year.

Scott Dawson, No. **70,** Virginia Tech, president/owner, commercial construction company, 19th year.

Garth DeFelice, No. **53,** San Diego State, distribution center manager, beverage company, 16th year.

Roy Ellison, No. **81,** Savannah State, technical staff member, 11th year.

Dan Ferrell, No. **64,** Cal State-Fullerton, director, parts logistics, 11th year.

Ruben Fowler, No. **71,** Huston-Tillotson, retired firefighter, 8th year.

Rich Hall, No. **49,** Arizona, custom cabinetry, 10th year.

Butch Hannah, No. **40,** Middle Tennessee State, retired federal probation officer, 15th year.

Darrell Jenkins, No. **76,** San Jose State, retired, 12th year.

Paul King, No. **121,** Nicholls State, teacher, 5th year.

Tony Michalek, No. **115,** Indiana, USA Football officiating director, 12th year.

Carl Paganelli, No. **124,** Michigan State, federal probation officer, 15th year.

Jeff Rice, No. **44,** Northwestern, attorney, 19th year.

Bill Schuster, No. **129,** Alfred, insurance broker, 14th year.

Bruce Stritesky, No. **102,** Embry Riddle, airline pilot, 8th year.

Undrey Wash, No. **96,** Texas-Arlington, claims controller, 14th year.

HEAD LINESMEN
Mark Baltz, No. **26,** Ohio, sales consultant, 25th year.

Jerry Bergman, No. **91,** Robert Morris, sales executive, 12th year.

Derick Bowers, No. **74,** East Central, sales representative, 11th year.

Greg Bradley, No. **98,** Tennessee, chemical engineer, 5th year.

Ed Camp, No. **134,** William Paterson, physical education teacher, 14th year.

George Hayward, No. **54,** Missouri Western, vice-president and manager, warehouse company, 23rd year.

Mark Hittner, No. **28,** Pittsburg State, investment broker, 17th year.

Wayne Mackie, No. **106,** Colgate, director of housing, 7th year.

Julian Mapp, No. **10,** Grambling State, project leader, 5th year.

John McGrath, No. **5,** Kentucky, vice president of sales, 12th year.

Dana McKenzie, No. **8,** Toledo, claims adjuster, 6th year.

Phil McKinnely, No. **110,** UCLA, inventory control, 11th year.

Jim Mello, No. **48,** Northeastern, facilities manager, 10th year.

Kent Payne, No. **79,** Nebraska Wesleyan, teacher, 10th year.

Tom Stabile, No. **24,** Slippery Rock, secondary educational administrator, 19th year.

Steve Stelljes, No. **22,** Friends, business planning manager, 12th year.

Tony Veteri, No. **36,** Manhattan College, physical education teacher, 22nd year.

LINE JUDGES
Gary Arthur, No. **108,** Wright State, president, commercial printing company, 17th year.

Rusty Baynes, No. **59,** Auburn-Montgomery, general manager, safety services, 4th year.

Jeff Bergman, No. **32,** Robert Morris, president and chief executive officer, medical services, 22nd year.

Byron Boston, No. **18,** Austin, tax consultant, 19th year.

Adrian Hill, No. **29,** Buffalo, software engineer, 4th year.

John Hussey, No. **35,** Idaho State, sales representative, retail logistics group, 12th year.

Carl Johnson, No. **101,** Nicholls State, full-time official, 10th year.

Darryll Lewis, No. **130,** Dartmouth, associate professor, 15th year.

Ron Marinucci, No. **107,** Glassboro State, vice president, novelty cone company, 17th year.

Mark Perlman, No. **9,** Salem, teacher, 13th year.

Tim Podraza, No. **47,** Nebraska, banker, 6th year.

Jeff Seeman, No. **45,** Minnesota, brokerage sales, 12th year.

Mike Spanier, No. **90,** St. Cloud State, middle school principal, 15th year.

Mark Steinkerchner, No. **84,** Akron, vice-president, 20th year.

Tom Stephan, No. **68,** Pittsburg State, president and CEO, 15th year.

Tom Symonette, No. **100,** Florida, certified public accountant, 10th year.

Roster as of May 2013

FIELD JUDGES

Barry Anderson, No. **20,** North Carolina State, builder/developer, 7th year.
Terry Brown, No. **43,** Tennessee, probation supervisor, 8th year.
Jimmy Buchanan, No. **86,** South Carolina State, insurance agent, 5th year.
Gary Cavaletto, No. **60,** Hancock, general manager, agricultural operations, 11th year.
Boris Cheek, No. **41,** Morgan State, director of operations and management, 18th year.
Scott Edwards, No. **3,** Alabama, environmental engineer, 15th year.
Greg Gautreaux, No. **80,** S.W. Louisiana, athletic programs manager, 12th year.
Buddy Horton, No. **82,** Oregon State, water service worker, 15th year.
Jim Howey, No. **37,** Erskine College, director of adult education, 15th year.
Jon Lucivansky, No. **89,** Minnesota, college educator, 5th year.
David Meslow, No. **118,** Augsburg College, marketing manager, 3rd year.
Dyrol Prioleau, No. **109,** Johnson C. Smith, manager, law firm, 7th year.
Doug Rosenbaum, No. **67,** Illinois Wesleyan, financial consultant, 13th year.
Scott Steenson, No. **88,** North Texas, commercial real estate broker, 23rd year.
Bob Waggoner, No. **25,** Juniata College, probation officer, 17th year.
Mike Weir, No. **50,** Missouri, owner, sporting goods store, 12th year.
Craig Wrolstad, No. **4,** Washington, athletic director, 4th year.
Steve Zimmer, No. **33,** Hofstra, attorney, 17th year.

SIDE JUDGES

Michael Banks, No. **72,** Illinois State, carpenter foreman, 12th year.
Allen Baynes, No. **56,** Auburn, realtor, 6th year.
James Coleman, No. **95,** Arkansas, electrical engineer, 9th year.
Jimmy DeBell, No. **58,** SUNY-Brockport, high school teacher, 5th year.
Laird Hayes, No. **125,** Princeton, professor, physical education & athletics, 19th year.
Tom Hill, No. **97,** Carson Newman, teacher, 15th year.
Jeff Lamberth, No. **103,** Texas A&M, attorney, 12th year.
Joe Larrew, No. **73,** St. Louis, attorney, 12th year.
Greg Meyer, No. **78,** Texas Christian, banker, 12th year.
Keith Parham, No. **87,** Howard, advertising operations manager, 3rd year.
Rick Patterson, No. **15,** Wofford, banker, 18th year.
Larry Rose, No. **128,** Florida, financial planner, 17th year.
Ronald Torbert, No. **62,** Michigan State, attorney, 4th year.
Rob Vernatchi, No. **75,** California-Riverside, enforcement investigator, 10th year.
Keith Washington, No. **7,** Virginia Military Institute, program financial analyst, 6th year.
Mike Weatherford, No. **116,** Oklahoma State, energy trader, 12th year.
David Wyant, No. **16,** Virginia, consulting engineer, 23rd year.

BACK JUDGES

Don Carey, No. **126,** California-Riverside, contract manager, 19th year.
Kirk Dornan, No. **6,** Central Washington, purchasing manager, 20th year.
Lee Dyer, No. **27,** Tennessee-Chattanooga, sales manager, 11th year.
Keith Ferguson, No. **61,** San Jose State, sales, 14th year.
Steve Freeman, No. **133,** Mississippi State, custom home builder, 13th year.
Scott Helverson, No. **93,** Iowa, sales, printing and promotions, 11th year.
Terrence Miles, No. **111,** Arizona State, quality control manager, 6th year.
Jim Quirk, No. **63,** Middlebury, financial advisor, 4th year.
Dino Paganelli, No. **105,** Aquinas College, educator, 8th year.
Perry Paganelli, No. **46,** Hope College, retired high school administrator, 16th year.
Todd Prukop, No. **30,** Cal State-Fullerton, medical sales representative, 5th year.
Dale Shaw, No. **104,** Allegheny, pharmaceutical sales, 1st year.
Billy Smith, No. **2,** East Carolina, retired federal government, 20th year.
Greg Steed, No. **12,** Howard, computer systems analyst, 11th year.
Tony Steratore, No. **112,** California, PA., co-owner, supply company, 14th year.
Greg Wilson, No. **119,** USC, law enforcement, 6th year.
Greg Yette, No. **38,** Howard, defense contractor, 4th year.

Roster as of May 2013

1

**TOUCHDOWN, FIELD GOAL,
or SUCCESSFUL TRY**
Both arms extended above head.

2

SAFETY
Palms together above head.

3

FIRST DOWN
Arm pointed toward defensive
team's goal.

4

**DEAD BALL or
NEUTRAL ZONE ESTABLISHED**
One arm above head
with an open hand.
With fist closed: **Fourth Down.**

5

**BALL ILLEGALLY
TOUCHED, KICKED,
or BATTED**
Fingertips tap both shoulders.

6

TIME OUT
Hands crisscrossed above head.
Same signal followed by placing one
hand on top of cap: **Referee's Time Out.**
Same signal followed by arm swung at
side: **Touchback.**

7

**NO TIME OUT or
TIME IN WITH WHISTLE**
Full arm circled to
simulate moving clock.

8

**DELAY OF GAME
or EXCESS TIME OUT**
Folded arms.

9

**FALSE START,
ILLEGAL FORMATION, or
KICKOFF or SAFETY KICK
OUT OF BOUNDS or
KICKING TEAM PLAYER
VOLUNTARILY OUT OF BOUNDS
DURING A PUNT**
Forearms rotated over and over
in front of body.

10

PERSONAL FOUL
One wrist striking the other above head.
Same signal followed by swinging leg:
Roughing the Kicker.
Same signal followed by raised arm
swinging forward:
Roughing the Passer.
Same signal followed by grasping
facemask: **Major Facemask.**

11

HOLDING
Grasping one wrist,
the fist clenched,
in front of chest.

12

**ILLEGAL USE OF HANDS,
ARMS, or BODY**
Grasping one wrist,
the hand open and facing
forward, in front of chest.

13

PENALTY REFUSED, INCOMPLETE PASS, PLAY OVER, or MISSED FIELD GOAL or EXTRA POINT
Hands shifted in horizontal plane.

14

PASS JUGGLED INBOUNDS AND CAUGHT OUT OF BOUNDS
Hands up and down in front of chest (following incomplete pass signal).

15

ILLEGAL FORWARD PASS
One hand waved behind back followed by loss of down signal (23), when appropriate.

16

INTENTIONAL GROUNDING OF PASS
Parallel arms waved in a diagonal plane across body. Followed by loss of down signal (23).

17

INTERFERENCE WITH FORWARD PASS or FAIR CATCH
Hands open and extended forward from shoulders with hands vertical.

18

INVALID FAIR-CATCH SIGNAL
One hand waved above head.

19

**INELIGIBLE RECEIVER
or INELIGIBLE
MEMBER OF KICKING TEAM
DOWNFIELD**
Right hand touching top of cap.

20

ILLEGAL CONTACT
One open hand extended forward.

21

**OFFSIDE, ENCROACHMENT, or
NEUTRAL ZONE INFRACTION**
Hands on hips.

22

ILLEGAL MOTION AT SNAP
Horizontal arc with one hand.

23

LOSS OF DOWN
Both hands held behind head.

24

**INTERLOCKING
INTERFERENCE, PUSHING, or
HELPING RUNNER**
Pushing movement of hands
to front with arms downward.

25

**TOUCHING A FORWARD
PASS or SCRIMMAGE KICK**
Diagonal motion of
one hand across another.

26

**UNSPORTSMANLIKE
CONDUCT**
Arms outstretched,
palms down.

27

ILLEGAL CUT
Hand striking front of thigh.
ILLEGAL BLOCK BELOW THE WAIST
One hand striking front of thigh
preceded by personal-foul signal (10).
CHOP BLOCK
Both hands striking side of thighs
preceded by personal-foul signal (10).
CLIPPING
One hand striking back of calf
preceded by personal-foul signal (10).

28

ILLEGAL CRACKBACK
Strike of an
open right hand
against the right mid-thigh
preceded by personal foul
signal (10).

29

PLAYER DISQUALIFIED
Ejection signal.

30

TRIPPING
Repeated action of right foot
in back of left heel.

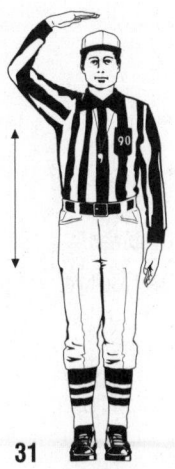

31

**UNCATCHABLE
FORWARD PASS**
Palm of right hand held
parallel to ground above head
and moved back and forth.

32

**TWELVE MEN IN OFFENSIVE HUDDLE
or TOO MANY MEN
ON THE FIELD**
Both hands on top of head.

33

FACEMASK
Grasping facemask with one
hand.

34

ILLEGAL SHIFT
Horizontal arcs with two hands.

35

**RESET PLAY CLOCK–
25 SECONDS**
Pump one arm vertically.

36

**RESET PLAY CLOCK–
40 SECONDS**
Pump two arms vertically.

345 Park Avenue, New York, New York 10154 (212) 450-2000

www.NFL.com

Commissioner: Roger Goodell

Executive Vice President/Football Operations: Ray Anderson

Executive Vice President of Media/
   President and Chief Executive Officer of NFL Network: Steve Bornstein

Executive Vice President of NFL Ventures and Business Operations: Eric Grubman

Executive Vice President of Human Resources/Chief Diversity Officer: Robert Gulliver

Executive Vice President of Communications and Public Affairs: Paul Hicks

Executive Vice President/General Counsel: Jeff Pash

Executive Vice President/Chief Financial Officer: Joe Siclare